THE
AFRICAN
AMERICAN
ALMANAC

SEVENTH EDITION

THE AFRICAN AMERICAN ALMANAC

SEVENTH EDITION

Formerly

The Negro

Almanac

L. Mpho Mabunda,
Editor

Foreword by
Chuck Stone
Walter Spearman Professor
School of Journalism and Mass Communication
University of North Carolina at Chapel Hill

GALE

DETROIT • NEW YORK • TORONTO • LONDON

Linda Hubbard, *Managing Editor*
L. Mpho Mabunda, *Editor*
David G. Oblender, *Associate Editor*
Beth Baker, Craig Barth, Dawn Berry, Gene Brady, Carol Brennan, Melissa Walsh Doig, DeWitt S. Dykes, Jr., Kimberly Burton
Faulkner, Simon Glickman, Joyce Harrison, Bob Jacobson, Carmen Johnson, Michael Knes, Jeffrey Lehman, Sipho C. Mabunda,
William J. Moses, Anna Sheets, David Sprinkle, Stephen Stratton, Chris Tower, Aaron Turley, *Contributing Editors*

George Hobart, *Photo Researcher*

Marlene Hurst, *Permissions Manager*
Margaret McAvoy-Amato, *Permissions Assistant*

Victoria B. Cariappa, *Research Manager*
Barbara McNeil, Andrew Guy Malonis, Gary J. Oudersluys, *Research Specialists*
Norma Sawaya, Cheryl L. Warnock, *Research Associates*
Laura C. Bissey, *Research Assistant*

Mary Beth Trimper, *Production Director*
Evi Seoud, *Assistant Production Manager*
Shanna Heilveil, *Production Assistant*

Cynthia Baldwin, *Art Director*
Barbara J. Yarrow, *Graphic Services Supervisor*
Mark C. Howell, *Cover Designer*
Arthur Chartow, *Page Designer*
C.J. Jonik, *Desktop Publisher*
Randy Bassett, *Image Database Supervisor*
Robert Duncan, Mikal Ansari, *Imaging Specialists*
Pamela Hayes, *Photographic Coordinator*

Benita L. Spight, *Data Entry Supervisor*
Gwendolyn S. Tucker, *Data Entry Group Leader*
Beverly Jendrowski, *Senior Data Entry Associate*

 The paper used in this publication meets the minimum requirements of American National Standard for Information Sciences—Permanence Paper for Printed Library Materials, ANSI Z 39.48-1984.

ISBN 0-8103-7867-1

Printed in the United States of America

Advisory Board

Contributors

Stephen W. Angell
Associate Professor of Religion, Florida A&M University

Robin Armstrong
Adjunct Lecturer, University of Michigan, Dearborn

Claudette Bennett
Bureau of the Census, United States Department of Commerce

Allen G. Harris
President, Air Force Association, General Daniel James Chapter

Hayward Derrick Horton
Assistant Professor of Sociology, Iowa State University

George Johnson
Professor of Law, Howard University School of Law

Faustine C. Jones-Wilson
Professor of Education, Howard University; Editor, *The Journal of Negro Education*

Donald Franklin Joyce
Director, Felix G. Woodward Library, Austin Peay State University

Mark Kram
Sportswriter, *Philadelphia Daily News*

Robyn M. Lupa
Assistant Branch Manager, Middle Village, Queens Borough Public Library

Doris H. Mabunda
Director of Youth Programs, YWCA-Grand Rapids, MI

Ionis Bracy Martin
Lecturer, Central Connecticut State University

Marilyn Hortense Mackel
Associate Professor, Western State University College of Law,
Judge Pro Tempore, Los Angeles County Superior Court, Juvenile Department

Dan Morgenstern
Director, Institute for Jazz Studies, Rutgers University

Wilson J. Moses
Professor of History, Pennsylvania State University

Richard Prince
National Association of Black Journalists

Floyd Thomas, Jr.
Curator of Fine Art and Military History, National Afro-American Museum and Cultural Center

Michael D. Woodard
Director, Los Angeles Institute for Multicultural Training;
Visiting Scholar, UCLA Center for Afro-American Studies

Contents

Foreword

History is a people's memory and without a memory, man is demoted to the level of the lowest animals.

—Malcolm X
New York City
Feb. 14, 1965

In this information age of the internet, online services, computer data-bases, and television images, *The African American Almanac (AAA)* still prevails as one of the most utilized written sources of knowledge. In its 19 years of publication (inlcuding its first incarnation as *The Negro Almanac*) the *AAA* has achieved national recognition as the ultimate one-stop, interdisciplinary authority on Americans in the African Diaspora.

Almanacs usually contain statistics, and tabular and general information. The *AAA* not only fulfills that lexicographical mandate but goes further. As a living record of the African American culture, it encompasses the arts, civil rights, education, government, history, literature, medicine, military, music (jazz, blues, popular, rock, and classical), politics, religion and sports.

If a brother or sister distinguished him- or herself, the *AAA* recorded it. But the *AAA* has not restricted itself to a prosaic litany of facts. "Facts are mere drosses of history," educator Nannie Burroughs wrote. "It is from the abstract truth which interpenetrates them and lies latent among men, like gold in the ore, that the mass drives its whole."

The *AAA*'s interpenetration does not succumb to value judgments. Instead, it records and contextualizes factually all of the public energies with which African Americans have empowered this nation—from poets, writers, ministers, editors, politicians and educators to the leaders of slave revolts, civil rights leaders, ghetto insurrectionists, inventors, labor leaders and businesspersons. That diversity has been the has been the unifying strength of African America's survival.

And yet, some African American amanuenses (i.e. transcribers) occasionally have been tempted to record only the trivia of "the first Negro" obsession. It typified writer Alice Walker's school days when the only black history she said she learned was "the once-a-year hanging up of the pictures of [educator] Booker [T.] Washington, [agriculturalist] George Washington Carver, and [educator] Mary McLeod Bethune.... We did not know know how much of the riches of America we had missed." She knew that catharsis of pride is a poor substitute for the majesty of knowledge.

The riches that Alice Walker—and all of us—have yearned for, comprise *The African American Almanac*, "not Negro history," as historian Carter G. Woodson explained, "but the Negro *in* history." (my emphasis).

That distinction is critical. The authentic African American maker of history is he or she whose decisions precipitated white America's responses with supporting or opposing agendas, whose actions helped configure the majority culture, whose political strategies changed the nation's economic course, and whose surgical genius still saves lives.

By studying *The African American Almanac*, teenagers can learn how African Americans influenced political events and social causes. Adults can become more knowledgeable about the historical complexity of black leadership. The researcher can glean from its statistics that the exuberant Gay Nineties were sorrowed by the lynchings of 1,111 African Americans. White Americans can become informed about the sociology of black-white discrepancies in employment, education, health, infant mortality and the criminal justice system. And only the *AAA* can teach stamp collectors of all races that 67 African Americans have been honored, as of September of 1996, by their depictions on a stamp.

This seventh edition of *The African American Almanac*, however, radiates a splendid uniqueness. By being published in 1996, the edition celebrates the 100th anniversary of five landmark events—the beginning of W. E. B. Du Bois's brilliant sociological study, *The Philadelphia Negro*; his publication of the *Suppression of the Slave Trade* (the first of 20 articles); *Plessy v. Ferguson*, which upheld the constitutionality of "separate but equal"; the founding of the National Association of Colored Women's Clubs; and the election of the last African American in the 19th century to Congress, North Carolina's George H. White, whose two terms would result in a lilywhite Congress for the next 28 years.

Plessy left an indelible segregationst mark on the escutcheon of American democracy for 58 years, until it was blotted out by *Brown v. Board of Education*. Du Bois's study of *The Philadelphia Negro*, one of the first studies in systematic sociology, anticipated by 25 years another epochal study, Thomas and Znaniecki's *The Polish Peasant in Europe and American*. Only 28 years old, Du Bois had authenticated with Thucydidean flair, Woodson's definition of the Negro in history.

Du Bois also proved that knowledge is indivisible. Any divisibility is more methodological than epistemological. "Knowledge is of two kinds," the lexicographer, Samuel Johnson, wrote. "We know a subject ourselves, or we know where we can find information about it." *The African American Almanac* is an audacious repository for the second half of that cognitive dichotomy.

In its pages, a symbiosis of black, white, Latino, and Asian readers, students, researchers, curiosty-seekers, intellectuals, journalists, and scholars will find almost all of the information they need about African Americans. As the researcher's resource, the *AAA* is *primus inter pares*. As the griot's written word, the *AAA* is African America's permanent memory for generations unborn.

Chuck Stone
Walter Spearman Professor
School of Journalism and Mass Communication
University of North Carolina at Chapel Hill

Introduction

Since the first edition of *The Negro Almanac* was published in 1967, the work has been hailed as the most comprehensive reference product of its kind. *The Almanac* has been named "Outstanding Reference Source" by the American Library Association/*Library Journal*. Now in its seventh edition and renamed *The African American Almanac*, it continues to provide students, teachers, researchers, and interested readers with insight into the history, growth, and achievements of black Americans.

New Features in This Edition

All material appearing in the sixth edition of *The Almanac* was extensively reviewed by the editor and a board of prominent advisors, and, where appropriate, updated and/or expanded for the seventh edition; in many instances, completely new topics were added to existing essays. Some chapters appearing in the sixth edition were totally rewritten to focus on issues facing contemporary African Americans. The most significant changes include the expansion of chapters three ("Significant Documents"), five ("Africa and the Black Diaspora"), 15 ("The Family"), and 19 ("Media"); and the revision of key essays within chapter ten ("Law"), chapter 11 ("Politics"), chapter 16 ("Education"), chapter 22 ("Blues and Jazz"), chapter 23 ("Popular Music"), chapter 24 ("Fine and Applied Arts"), chapter 25 ("Science and Medicine"); chapter 26 ("Sports"), and chapter 27 ("Military"). All 27 chapters were also made as current as possible, including chapter one ("Chronology") and chapter 2 ("African American Firsts").

Anyone familiar with the sixth edition will be excited to find such new features such as a chronology current to April of 1996; coverage of newly anointed African American pioneers from 1994 and 1995; inclusion of "The Million Man March Mission Statement;" more and more useful information regarding the black diaspora; more extensive information regarding the origins of those enslaved in America; an essay on the history of federal judges in the United States; a brief history of African American involvement in the political system along with a list of addresses for current Congressional Black Caucus members; more profiles of trailblazing entrepreneurs both current and historical; coverage of more topics related to health and increased discussion of such issues related to family as marriage; a complete listing of African American chaired professors and endowed university chairs; summarization of the rash of black church fires; an accounting of black involvement on the information superhighway, including a list of more than 30 World Wide Web sites of interest to African Americans; new information on African American craft art, the Black Arts movement, and the role of historically black learning institutions in the preservation and presentation of African American art; more about black contributions to science and technology; more dynamic discussion of African American military participation in the Revolutionary War as well as the wars in Vietnam and the Persian Gulf; and better coverage of the blues, popular music, and sports.

Content and Arrangement

Information in this edition of *The Almanac* appears in 27 subject chapters. Many chapters open with an essay focusing on historical developments or the contributions of African Americans to the subject area, followed by concise biographical profiles on selected individuals. Although the listees featured in *The Almanac* represent only a small portion of the African American community, they embody excellence and diversity in their respective fields of endeavor. Where an individual has made a significant contribution in more than one area, his or her biographical profile appears in the subject area for which he or she is best known.

In order to facilitate further research, a bibliography is provided at the end of *The Almanac*. The bibliography has been divided into two major divisions: "Africana" and "African Americana." Within these two divisions titles are arranged alphabetically by author under categories indicative of their subject matter.

More than five hundred maps and illustrations aid the reader in understanding the topics and people covered in the work. A name and keyword index provides access to the contents of *The Almanac*.

Acknowledgments

The editor wishes to acknowledge the contributions of the advisors, writers, and copyeditors who assisted in the compilation of *The Almanac*. In particular, the editor gratefully acknowledges Chuck Stone for his valuable collaboration; Sharon Malinowski for her skillful assistance in project development and management; Linda Hubbard for her generous support; Ken Estell, editor of the sixth edition—the seventh edition's foundation; Barbara McNeil for her research skills; David and Doris Mabunda their support and expertise regarding the African continent; and Jeffrey Muhr and Casey Roberts for adapting their technical prowess to the project's needs. In addition, special thanks are due to associate editor Dave Oblender, who held primary responsibility for improvements made to chapters one, two, four, eight, nine, 12, 13, 14, 16, 19, 20, 21, 24, and 27.

Comments Welcome

Although considerable effort was expended to ensure the accuracy and currency of the information present in the edition, omissions are inevitable. Therefore, the editor welcomes all comments and suggestions for future editions. Send comments and suggestions to:

The African American Almanac
Gale Research Inc.
835 Penobscot Bldg.
Detroit, MI 48226-4094

THE
AFRICAN
AMERICAN
ALMANAC

SEVENTH EDITION

1

Chronology

Chronology

1492 • Blacks are among the first explorers to the New World. Pedro Alonzo Niño, identified by some scholars as a black man, arrives with Christopher Columbus.

1501 • The Spanish throne officially approves the use of African slaves in the New World.

1502 • Portugal brings its first shipload of African slaves to the Western Hemisphere, selling them in what is now Latin America.

1513 • **Cuba**
Spain authorizes the use of African slaves in Cuba. Thirty black men accompany Balboa when he discovers the Pacific Ocean.

1526 • **South Carolina**
The first group of Africans to set foot on what is now the United States are brought by a Spanish explorer to South Carolina to erect a settlement. However, they soon flee to the interior and settle with Native Americans.

1538 • Estevanico, a black explorer, leads an expedition from Mexico into what is now Arizona and New Mexico.

1562 • Britain enters the slave trade when John Hawkins sells a large cargo of African slaves to Spanish planters.

1600 • Historical records indicate that by the year 1600, over 900,000 slaves have been brought to Latin America. In the next century, 2,750,000 are added to that total. Slave revolts in the sixteenth century are reported in Hispaniola, Puerto Rico, Panama, Cuba, and Mexico.

1618 • **Gambia**
The government grants monopolies to a group of companies established for the purpose of slave trading.

1619, August • **Jamestown, Virginia**
Twenty African indentured servants arrive aboard a Dutch vessel. Most indentured servants are released after serving one term, usually seven years in duration, and are allowed to own property and participate in political affairs. The arrival of these indentured servants is the precursor of active slave trade in the English colonies.

1624 • **West Indies**
The Dutch, who had entered the slave trade in 1621 with the formation of the Dutch West Indies Company, import Africans to serve on Hudson Valley farms.

1629 • **Connecticut**
African slaves are imported into Connecticut (1629), Maryland and Massachusetts (1634), and New Amsterdam (1637).

1630 • **Massachusetts**
A law protecting black slaves from abusive owners is enacted.

1639 • **Salem, Massachusetts**
New England enters the slave trade when Captain William Pierce sails to the West Indies and purchases a group of African slaves.

1640 • **West Indies**
The increasing use of sugar as a cash crop leads to a rapid rise in the African slave population in the West Indies. However, growth in mainland English colonies remains slow. The African slave population in Barbados, for example, grows from a few hundred in 1640 to 6,000 in 1645. In contrast, there are only 300 black slaves in Virginia in 1649 and only 2,000 by 1671.

1640 • **Connecticut**
Punitive fugitive laws applying to both indentured ser-

A new shipload of African slaves enroute to America.

vants and black slaves are enacted in Connecticut, Maryland, New Jersey, South Carolina, and Virginia. The Virginia law, passed in 1642, penalizes violators 20 pounds of tobacco for each night of refuge granted to a fugitive slave. Slaves are branded after a second escape attempt.

1641 • Massachusetts
Massachusetts becomes the first colony to legalize slavery, adding a modification that forbids capture by "unjust violence." This provision was subsequently adopted by all of the New England colonies.

1643 • The groundwork is laid for eighteenth and nineteenth century fugitive slave laws in the United States when an intercolonial agreement of the New England Confederation declares that mere certification by a magistrate is sufficient evidence to convict a runaway slave.

1651 • North Hampton, Virginia
Anthony Johnson, a black man, imports five servants and qualifies to receive a 200 acre land grant along the Puwgoteague River in Virginia. Others soon join Johnson and attempt to launch an independent African community. At its height, the settlement has 12 African homesteads with sizable holdings.

1662 • Virginia
The colony passes a law which provides that the status of children, slave or free, be determined by the lineage of the mother.

1663 • Maryland
Settlers pass a law stipulating that all imported Africans are to be given the status of slaves. Free white women who marry black slaves are also considered slaves during the lives of their spouses; children of such unions are also to be classified as slaves. In 1681, a law is passed which stipulates that children born from a union of a white servant woman and an African are free citizens.

1670 • Virginia
Voting rights are denied to recently freed slaves and indentured servants. All non-Christians imported to the territory, "by shipping," are to be slaves for life. However, slaves who enter Virginia by land route are to serve until the age of 30 if they are children and for 12 years if they are adults when their period of servitude commences.

African slaves arrive on the shores of America.

1672 • Virginia
A law is enacted providing for a bounty on the heads of Maroons—black fugitives who form communities in the mountains, swamps, and forests of southern colonies. Many members of Maroon communities attack towns and plantations.

1685 • French West Indies
The French Code Noir is enacted. The code requires religious instruction for African slaves, permits intermarriage, outlaws working of slaves on Sundays and holidays, but forbids emancipation of mulatto children who have reached the age of 21 if their mothers are still enslaved. However, the code is largely ignored by the French settlers.

1688 • Germantown, Pennsylvania
Mennonites sign an anti-slavery resolution, the first formal protest against slavery in the Western Hemisphere. In 1696, Quakers importing slaves are threatened with expulsion from the society.

1700 • The population of black slaves in the English Colonies is estimated at 28,000. 23,000 of these slaves reside in the South.

1704 • New York City, New York
Elias Neau, a French immigrant, opens a "Catechism School" for black slaves.

1705 • Virginia
The Virginia assembly declares that "no Negro, mulatto, or Indian shall presume to take upon him, act in or exercise any office, ecclesiastic, civil or military." Blacks are forbidden to serve as witnesses in court cases and are condemned to lifelong servitude, unless they have been either Christians in their native land or free men in a Christian country.

1711 • Pennsylvania
The colonial legislature, after receiving intense pressure from the Mennonite and Quaker communities, outlaws slavery in the Pennsylvania colony but is overruled by the British Crown.

1712, April 6 • New York City, New York
The Maiden Lane slave revolt claims the lives of nine whites and results in the execution of twenty-one black slaves. Six others commit suicide.

1723 • Virginia
The colony of Virginia enacts laws to limit the rights of freed blacks. Free blacks are denied the right to vote and forbidden to carry weapons of any sort.

1739 • South Carolina
Three black slave revolts occur, resulting in the deaths of fifty-one whites and many more slaves. One of the insurrections results in the death of thirty whites.

1740 • South Carolina
The South Carolina colony passes a slave code which forbids black slaves from raising livestock, provides that any animals owned by slaves be forfeited, and imposes severe penalties on slaves who make "false appeals" to the governor on the grounds that they have been placed in bondage illegally.

1744 • Virginia
The colony of Virginia amends its 1705 law declaring that blacks cannot serve as witnesses in court cases; it decides, instead, to admit "any free Negro, mulatto, or Indian being a Christian," as a witness in a criminal or civil suit involving another black, mulatto, or Indian.

1746 • Deerfield, Massachusetts
Slave poet Lucy Terry writes *Bars Fight*, a commemorative poem recreating the Deerfield Massacre. Terry, generally considered the first black poet in America, later tries unsuccessfully to convince the Board of Trustees at Williams College to admit her son to the school.

1747 • South Carolina
The South Carolina assembly commends black slaves for demonstrating "great faithfulness and courage in repelling attacks of His Majesty's enemies." It then makes provisions for the utilization of black recruits in the event of danger or emergency.

1749 • Georgia
Prohibitions on the importation of African slaves are approved in a law which also attempts to protect slaves from cruel treatment and from being hired out.

1750 • The black slave population in the English Colonies reaches 236,400, with over 206,000 of the total living south of Pennsylvania. Slaves comprise about 20 percent of the population in the colonies.

1752 • Mount Vernon, Virginia
George Washington acquires his estate at Mount Vernon. Prior to Washington's arrival, there are eighteen slaves at Mount Vernon. This number eventually swells to 200. Records indicate that while Washington was concerned

An advertisement for an African slave auction.

for the physical welfare of black slaves, he also utilized their services on many occasions and did not advocate their freedom from servitude.

1754 • Baltimore, Maryland
Benjamin Banneker, a 22-year-old free black man, becomes the first person in the North American colonies to construct a clock.

1754 • Philadelphia, Pennsylvania
A Quaker, John Woolman, publishes *Some Considerations On the Keeping Of Negroes*, an exhortation to fellow members of the Society of Friends to consider emancipating their slaves on grounds of morality. Three years later, some Quakers take legal action against members who ignore this plea.

1760 • New York City, New York
Jupiter Hammon, a black poet, publishes *Salvation By Christ With Penitential Cries*.

1767 • Boston, Massachusetts
Phillis Wheatley, a 14-year-old slave, authors *A Poem by Phillis, A Negro Girl, On the Death of Reverend Whitefield*. It is printed in 1770 by The University of Cambridge in New England.

1769 • Virginia
In the Virginia House of Burgesses, Thomas Jefferson unsuccessfully presses for a bill to emancipate African slaves.

African slaves being sold at an auction.

1770, March 5 • Boston, Massachusetts
Crispus Attucks is shot and killed during the Boston Massacre, becoming one of the first casualities of the American Revolution.

1770 • Philadelphia, Pennsylvania
Led by Anthony Benezet, the Quakers open a school for blacks.

1773 • Savannah, Georgia
George Liele and Andrew Bryan organize the first Baptist Church for blacks in the state.

1774 • The Continental Congress demands elimination of the trans-Atlantic slave trade and economic embargoes on all countries participating in it. Rhode Island enacts a law prohibiting slavery. However, this law does not apply to slaves brought into Rhode Island before 1774.

1775 • Bunker Hill, Massachusetts
Peter Salem, Salem Poor, and other blacks fight heroically during the Battle of Bunker Hill.

1775 • Germany
Johann Friedrich Blumenbach publishes the first article refuting the theory that blacks are racially inferior. In *On the Natural Variety of Mankind*, Blumenbach asserts that the skulls and brains of blacks are the same as those of Europeans. Blumenbach's paper serves as a counter to the views of Voltaire, Hume, and Linne that blacks are akin to apes.

1775 • Philadelphia, Pennsylvania
The Continental Congress bars blacks from serving in the army during the American Revolution.

1775 • Philadelphia, Pennsylvania
The first abolitionist society in the United States is organized.

1775 • Virginia
Lord Dunmore, British governor of Virginia, offers freedom to all male slaves who join the loyalist forces. General George Washington, originally opposed to the enlistment of blacks, is alarmed by the response to the Dunmore proclamation and orders recruiting officers to accept free blacks for service.

Typical slave life in early America.

1776 • Trenton, New Jersey
Two blacks, Prince Whipple and Oliver Cromwell, cross the Delaware with George Washington en route to an attack on the British and their Hessian mercenaries in Trenton, New Jersey.

1776 • Philadelphia, Pennsylvania
The amended form of the Declaration of Independence, which does not include Thomas Jefferson's proposal denouncing slavery, is adopted.

1776 • Long Island, New York
French general Marquis de Lafayette praises black soldiers for successfully assisting Washington's retreat to Long Island. Blacks also help assist Washington's retreat at Trenton and Princeton.

1778 • A black battalion consisting of 300 former slaves is formed. They are compensated on a par with their white comrades-in-arms and promised freedom after the war. The battalion kills 1,000 Hessians and takes part in a battle at Ponts Bridge in New York.

1779 • New York
Alexander Hamilton endorses the plan of South Carolina's Henry Laurens to use slaves as soldiers in the South. "I have not the least doubt that the Negroes will make very excellent soldiers," says Hamilton, "....for their natural faculties are as good as ours." Hamilton reminds the Continental Congress that the British will make use of blacks if the Americans do not. In Hamilton's words: "The best way to counteract the temptations they will hold out, will be to offer them ourselves."

1780 • Pennsylvania
The Pennsylvania assembly enacts a law providing for the gradual emancipation of slaves.

1782 • Virginia
Thomas Jefferson's *Notes on the State of Virginia* exhibits a curious mixture of perception and naivete with regard to blacks. On the one hand, Jefferson believes that "the whole commerce between master and slave is a perpetual exercise of the most boisterous passions," on the other, he invents the fantasy that black's "griefs are transient."

1783 • Massachusetts
Slavery in the Commonwealth is abolished by the Massachusetts Supreme Court; Blacks in taxable categories are granted suffrage.

1783 • At the end of the American Revolution, some 10,000 blacks have served in the continental armies—5,000 as regular soldiers.

1787 • New York City, New York
The African Free School is opened by the New York Manumission Society.

1787 • Congress passes the Northwest Ordinance which forbids the extension of slavery into this area.

1787 • Philadelphia, Pennsylvania
Black preachers Richard Allen and Absalom Jones organize the Free African Society.

1787 • The Constitution of the United States is adopted. In it, importation of slaves cannot be prohibited before 1808, and five slaves are considered the equivalent of three free men in congressional apportionment.

1790 • According to the first census, there are 757,000 blacks in the United States, comprising 19 percent of the total population. Nine percent of blacks are free.

1790 • Dominican Republic
Blacks comprise seven-eighths of the islands' 529,000 inhabitants. Less than 3 percent are free. Mulattoes in French Santo Domingo own 10 percent of the slaves and land.

1790 • Chicago, Illinois
Jean Baptiste Pointe du Sable, the son of a French mariner and African slave mother, establishes the first permanent settlement at what is to become the city of Chicago.

1791 • Washington, District of Columbia
On the recommendation of Thomas Jefferson, Benjamin Banneker—astronomer, inventor, mathematician and gazetteer—is appointed to serve as a member of the commission charged with laying out plans for the city of Washington.

1791 • Haiti
Toussaint L'Ouverture, a self-educated slave, leads an unsuccessful uprising.

1791 • Louisiana
Twenty-three slaves are hanged and three white sympathizers deported, following suppression of a black revolt.

1791 • Philadelphia, Pennsylvania
Congress excludes blacks and Indians from serving in peacetime militia.

1793 • Mulberry Grove, Georgia
Eli Whitney patents the cotton gin, which strengthens slavery by vastly increasing profits in cotton growing.

1793 • Philadelphia, Pennsylvania
Congress passes the Fugitive Slave Act, which makes it a criminal offense to harbor a slave or prevent his or her arrest.

1793 • Virginia
The state of Virginia passes a law which forbids free blacks from entering the state.

1794 • Philadelphia, Pennsylvania
The First African Church of St. Thomas, the first black Episcopal Congregation in the United States, is dedicated. This same year, Richard Allen organizes the Bethel Church, a black Methodist Episcopal Church.

1795 • Louisiana
Several slave uprisings are suppressed with some 50 blacks killed and executed.

1796 • Tennessee
Tennessee is admitted to the Union as a slave state. The

Marquis de Lafayette with a black orderly.

state's constitution, however, does not deny suffrage to free blacks.

1797 • North Carolina
Congress refuses to accept the first recorded anti-slavery petition seeking redress against a North Carolina law which requires that slaves, although freed by their Quaker masters, be returned to the state and to their former condition.

1798 • Washington, District of Columbia
Secretary of the Navy Stoddert forbids the deployment of black sailors on men-of-war, in violation of a nonracial enlistment policy which had been operative in the Navy for many years. Nevertheless, a few blacks slip past the ban, including William Brown, who serves as a "powder monkey" on the *Constellation* and George Diggs, quartermaster of the schooner *Experiment*.

1799 • Mount Vernon, Virginia
George Washington dies. His last will and testament

Thomas Jefferson

An overseer weighs cotton picked by slaves.

declares: "It is my will and desire that all the slaves which I hold in my right, shall receive their freedom."

1800 • Richmond, Virginia
Gabriel Prosser, a slave insurrectionist, plans to lead thousands of slaves in an attack on Richmond. The plan fails and Prosser and 15 of his followers are arrested, tried, and hanged.

1800 • Washington, District of Columbia
By a vote of 85 to 1, Congress rejects a petition by free blacks in Philadelphia to gradually end slavery in the United States.

1803 • South Carolina
The state legislature, which had been trying to limit importation of slaves, reopens the slave trade with Latin America and the West Indies.

1804 • New Jersey
New Jersey passes an emancipation law. All states north of the Mason-Dixon Line now have laws forbidding slavery or providing for its gradual elimination.

1804 • Ohio
The legislature enacts the first of a group of laws restricting the rights and movements of blacks. Other western states soon follow suit. Illinois, Indiana, and Oregon later have anti-immigration clauses in their state constitutions.

1807 • New Jersey
The state alters its 1776 constitution by limiting the vote to free white males.

1808, January 1 • Congress bars the importation of any new slaves into the territory of the United States (effective January 1, 1808). The law is widely ignored.

1808 • The 1807 ban on the importation of slaves is scheduled to take effect. There are one million slaves in the country.

1810 • Louisiana
Courts declare, in *Adelle v. Beauregard*, that a black is free unless it is otherwise proven.

1811 • Delaware
The state forbids the immigration of free blacks and declares that any native-born free black who has lived outside of Delaware for more than six months will be deemed a nonresident.

1811 • Louisiana
United States troops suppress a slave uprising in two

parishes (counties) of Louisiana, some 35 miles from New Orleans. The revolt is led by Charles Deslands. Some 100 slaves are killed or executed.

1811 • Westport, Connecticut
Paul Cuffe, son of black and Indian parents and later a wealthy shipbuilder, sails with a small group of blacks to Sierra Leone to underscore his advocacy of a black return to Africa.

1812 • Louisiana
Louisiana is admitted to the Union as a slave state. State law enables freed men to serve in the state militia.

1815 • Fort Blount, Florida
Blacks and Creek Indians capture Fort Blount from Seminoles and use it as a haven for escaped slaves and a base for attacks on slave owners. An American army detachment eventually recaptures the fort.

1816 • Baltimore, Maryland
Bethel Charity School is founded by Daniel Coker, a black man.

1816 • Louisiana
State laws are enacted which prohibit slaves from testifying against whites and free blacks, except in cases involving slave uprisings.

1816 • New Orleans, Louisiana
James P. Beckwourth, a black man and one of the great explorers of the nineteenth century, signs on as a scout for General William Henry Ashley's Rocky Mountain expedition.

1816 • Philadelphia, Pennsylvania
The African Methodist Episcopal Church is organized.

1816 • Virginia
A slave rebellion led by George Boxley, a white man, fails.

1816 • Washington, District of Columbia
The American Colonization Society, which seeks to transport free blacks to Africa, is organized. Protest meetings are subsequently held by many free blacks in opposition to the society's efforts.

1817 • Mississippi
Mississippi enters the union as a slave state. New York passes a gradual slavery abolition act.

1818 • Connecticut
Blacks are denied the right to vote in Connecticut.

1818 • Philadelphia, Pennsylvania
Free blacks form the Pennsylvania Augustine Society "for the education of people of colour."

1819 • Alabama
Alabama enters the Union as a slave state, although its constitution provides the legislature with the power to abolish slavery and compensate slave owners. Other measures include jury trials for slaves accused of crimes above petty larceny, and penalties for malicious killing of slaves.

1820 • Liberia
The *Mayflower of Liberia* sails for the west African nation of Sierra Leone with 86 blacks aboard.

1820, March 3 • The Missouri Compromise is enacted. It provides for Missouri's entry into the Union as a slave state and Maine's entry as a free state. There are thus 12 slave and 12 free states in the United States. All territory north of latitude 36 degrees 30′ is declared free; all territory south of that line is open to slavery.

1821 • New York City, New York
The African Methodist Episcopal Zion Church is founded, with James Varick as its first bishop.

1821 • New York
The state constitutional convention alters the voting requirements of 1777 by establishing higher property and longer residence requirements for blacks.

1822 • Charleston, South Carolina
The Denmark Vesey conspiracy, one of the most elaborate slave revolts on record, fails. Vesey, a sailor and carpenter, and 36 collaborators are hanged, an additional 130 blacks and four whites are arrested, and stricter controls are imposed on free blacks and slaves. Following this insurrection, slave states adopt laws to further restrict the mobility of blacks.

1822 • Rhode Island
Free blacks are denied the right to vote in Rhode Island.

1822 • Liberia
Liberia is founded by blacks with the aid of the American Colonization Society.

1823 • Mississippi
A law is enacted in Mississippi which prohibits the teaching of reading and writing to blacks and meetings of more than five slaves or free blacks.

1824 • As the United States moves toward universal male suffrage, more states in the North and West as well as the South move to deny the vote to blacks. Illinois, Indiana, Iowa, and Michigan require blacks to post bond in guarantee of good behavior.

1825 • Maryland
Josiah Henson leads a group of slaves to freedom in Kentucky. Henson later crosses the border into Ontario and becomes leader of a community of ex-slaves.

1826 • Virginia
Thomas Jefferson dies. His will stipulates that only five of his many slaves should be freed. The remainder are bequeathed to his heirs.

1827, March 16 • New York City, New York
Freedom's Journal, the first black newspaper, begins publication on March 16.

1827, July 04 • New York
Slavery is abolished in New York on July 4.

1828 • Bennington, Vermont
William Lloyd Garrison, a journalist and reformer, writes his first anti-slavery article in the *National Philanthropist*.

1829 • Boston, Massachusetts
David Walker, a free black, publishes the anti-slavery pamphlet *An Appeal to the Colored People of the World* which is distributed throughout the country and arouses a furor among slaveholders.

1829 • Cincinnati, Ohio
After a riot in which whites attack black residents in Cincinnati and loot and burn their homes, 1,200 blacks flee to Canada.

1830 • North Carolina
Slavemasters, in compliance with a state law, transfer control of more than 400 slaves to Quaker residents of North Carolina. The Quakers retain theoretical ownership, but allow slaves virtual freedom until they can afford to transport them to free states.

1830 • Philadelphia, Pennsylvania
The first National Negro Convention meets on September 20 at Philadelphia's Bethel Church. The four-day convention launches a church-affiliated program to improve the social status of the American Black.

1830 • In an attempt to counter the increasing strength of the abolitionist movement, a number of states pass laws restricting the education, legal safeguards, and citizenship rights of slaves and free blacks. Many states

William Lloyd Garrison

require the deportation of free blacks; slave codes are enforced more strictly and the number of slave emancipations decline.

1830 • The United States Census Bureau reports that 3,777 black heads of families own slaves, mostly in Louisiana, Maryland, Virginia, North Carolina, and South Carolina.

1831, January 1 • Boston, Massachusetts
The Liberator, an abolitionist newspaper, is founded by William Lloyd Garrison.

1831 • Philadelphia, Pennsylvania
The first Annual Convention of the People of Color meets at Wesleyan Church, where delegates from five states resolve to study black conditions, explore settlement possibilities in Canada, and raise money for an industrial college in New Haven. Delegates oppose the American Colonization Society and recommend annual meetings.

1831, August • Southampton County, Virginia
Nat Turner leads the greatest slave rebellion in history. Some 60 whites are killed and the entire South is thrown

into panic. Turner is captured on October 30 and hanged in Jerusalem, Virginia, twelve days later.

1831 • Virginia

Thomas Dew, a legislator, proudly refers to Virginia as a "Negro-raising state" for the nation. Between 1830 and 1860, Virginia exports some 300,000 slaves, and South Carolina exports 179,000. The price of slaves increases sharply due to expanding territory in which slaves are permitted and a booming economy in products harvested and processed by slave labor.

1832 • Boston, Massachusetts

The New England Anti-Slavery Society is established by twelve whites at the African Baptist Church on Boston's Beacon Hill.

1833 • Philadelphia, Pennsylvania

Black and white abolitionists organize the American Anti-Slavery Society.

1834 • South Carolina

South Carolina enacts a law prohibiting the teaching of black children, either free or slave.

1834 • Parliament abolishes slavery in the British Empire; 700,000 slaves are liberated at a cost of 20 million British pounds sterling.

1835 • North Carolina

North Carolina, the last southern state to deny suffrage to blacks, repeals a voting rights provision of the state constitution. The state also makes it illegal for whites to teach free blacks.

1835 • Washington, District of Columbia

President Andrew Jackson seeks to restrict the mailing of abolitionist literature to the South.

1836 • Washington, District of Columbia

The United States House of Representatives adopts the "gag rule" which prevents congressional action on anti-slavery resolutions or legislation.

1837 • Alton, Illinois

Elijah P. Lovejoy, an abolitionist, is murdered by a mob in Alton after refusing to stop publishing anti-slavery material.

1837 • Boston, Massachusetts

A series of abolitionist works are published, including Reverend Hosea Eaton's *A Treatise on the Intellectual Character and Political Condition of the Colored People of the United States.*

1837 • Canada

Blacks are given the right to vote in Canada.

1838 • Montauk, New York

The slaveship *Amistad* is brought into Montauk by a group of Africans who have revolted against their captors. The young African leader Joseph Cinque and his followers are defended before the United States Supreme Court by former President John Quincy Adams, and awarded their freedom.

1839 • Warsaw, New York

The first anti-slavery political organization, the Liberty Party, is founded. Black abolitionists Samuel R. Ward and Henry Highland Garnet are among its leading supporters. The party urges boycotts and exclusion of southern crops and products.

1839 • Washington, District of Columbia

The United States State Department rejects a black man's application for a passport on the grounds that blacks are not citizens.

1840 • Massachusetts

Massachusetts repeals a law forbidding intermarriage between whites and blacks, mulattoes, or Indians.

1840 • New York

These states institute a law advocating jury trials for fugitive slaves.

1840 • Pope Gregory XVI declares his opposition to slavery and the slave trade.

1841 • Massachusetts

Frederick Douglass begins his career as a lecturer with the Massachusetts Anti-Slavery Society.

1841 • Throughout the country, increasingly restrictive segregation statutes are enacted. The New York state legislature grants school districts the right to segregate their educational facilities. South Carolina forbids white and black mill hands from looking out the same window. Whites and blacks in Atlanta are required to swear on different Bibles in court.

1841 • Hampton, Virginia

Slaves aboard the vessel *Creole* revolt en route from Hampton, Virginia to New Orleans. The slaves overpower the crew and sail the ship to the Bahamas, where they are granted asylum and freedom.

1842 • Boston, Massachusetts

The capture of George Latimer, an escaped slave, precipitates the first of several famous fugitive slave cases straining North-South relations. Latimer is later purchased from his master by Boston abolitionists.

1842 • Rhode Island
Blacks are granted the right to vote in Rhode Island.

1842 • Washington, District of Columbia
In the case *Prigg v. Pennsylvania*, the United States Supreme Court finds a Pennsylvania anti-kidnapping law unconstitutional, claiming that the authority to regulate the recapture of fugitive slaves was an exclusive power of Congress. The case arises when Edward Prigg is convicted of kidnapping for his recapture of an escaped slave.

1843 • Buffalo, New York
Henry Highland Garnet calls for a slave revolt and general strike while addressing the National Convention of Colored Men. Garnet, Samuel R. Ward, and Charles Ray participate in the Liberty Party convention, becoming the first blacks to take part in a national political gathering.

1843 • Massachusetts
The Massachusetts and Vermont state legislatures defy the Fugitive Slave Act and forbid state officials from imprisoning or assisting federal authorities in the recapture of escaped slaves.

1843 • Washington, District of Columbia
The Webster-Ashburton Treaty, in which Britain and the United States agree to prevent slave ships from reaching the African coast in order to suppress the slave trade there, is approved. No agreement is reached, however, to restrict slave trade within the Western Hemisphere.

1845 • Washington, District of Columbia
The United States Congress overturns the gag rule of 1836. Texas is admitted to the Union as a slave state.

1847 • New York
The plan of abolitionist Gerritt Smith to parcel up thousands of acres of his land in New York fails to attract prospective black farmers. Lack of capital among blacks and the infertility of the land doom the project.

1847 • Rochester, New York
Frederick Douglass publishes the first issue of his abolitionist newspaper, *The North Star*.

1847 • St. Louis, Missouri
Dred Scott files suit for his freedom in the Circuit Court of St. Louis.

1848 • Buffalo, New York
The convention of the Free Soil Party is attended by a number of black abolitionists.

1848 • Virginia
Postmasters are forced to inform police of the arrival of pro-abolition literature and turn it over to authorities for burning.

1849 • Maryland
Harriet Tubman, soon to be a conductor on the Underground Railroad, escapes from slavery. Tubman later returns to the South no less than 19 times to help transport more than 300 slaves to freedom. In the same year, the Maryland legislature enacts laws to override restrictions on the importation of slaves.

1849 • Maryland
The Maryland Supreme Court establishes the "separate but equal" doctrine in response to a suit brought by Benjamin Roberts to have his daughter admitted to a white school.

1850 • New York
Samuel R. Ward becomes president of the American League of Colored Laborers, a union of skilled black workers who train black craftsmen and encourage black-owned business.

1850 • Washington, District of Columbia
The Compromise of 1850, also known as Clay's Compromise, is enacted, strengthening the 1793 Fugitive Slave Act. Federal officers are now offered a fee for the slaves they apprehend. California is admitted to the union as a free state.

1851 • Virginia
New laws require freed slaves to leave Virginia within a year or be enslaved again.

1852 • Akron, Ohio
Sojourner Truth addresses the National Women's Suffrage Convention.

1852 • Boston, Massachusetts
The first edition of Harriet Beecher Stowe's controversial *Uncle Tom's Cabin* is published.

1853 • London
William Wells Brown publishes *Clotel, or The President's Daughter: A Tale of the Southern States* the first published, African-American novel.

Photograph of a typical slave family.

1853 • Oxford, Pennsylvania
Lincoln University, the first black college, is founded as Ashmum Institute.

1854 • Boston, Massachusetts
Anthony Burns, a fugitive slave, is arrested and escorted through the streets of Boston by United States troops prior to being returned to his master. His master refuses an offer of $1,200 from Boston abolitionists attempting to purchase his freedom.

1854 • The New England Emigration Society is founded to help settle ex-slaves in Kansas.

1854 • Under the Kansas-Nebraska Act, the territories of Kansas and Nebraska are admitted to the Union without slavery restrictions, in direct contradiction to the provisions of the Missouri Compromise of 1820.

1855 • Maine
The slavery issue is further polarized by enactment, in these states, of laws forbidding state officials from

Dred Scott

aiding the federal government in enforcement of the fugitive slave laws. The Massachusetts legislature abolishes school segregation and integration proceeds without incident.

1855 • New York
The Liberty Party nominates Frederick Douglass for Secretary of State.

1856 • Kansas
Pro-slavery forces sack the town of Lawrence, noted for its abolitionist, free-soil sentiment.

1857 • Maine
These states, in defiance of the fugitive slave laws, grant freedom and citizenship to people of African descent.

1857, March 6 • Washington, District of Columbia
In the case of *Dred Scott v. Sandford* decision, the United States Supreme Court, by a 6 to 3 vote, opens federal territory to slavery, denies citizenship rights to blacks, and decrees that slaves do not become free when taken into free territory. The *Dred Scott* decision is followed by a ruling that blacks are not entitled to land grants.

1858 • Vicksburg, Mississippi
The Southern Commercial Convention calls for reestablishment of the slave trade, despite opposition from Tennessee and Florida delegations.

1859 • Baltimore, Maryland
Businessmen attending a slaveholders convention complain that free black laborers and entrepreneurs monopolize some service industries. However, a resolution to expel free blacks from the state fails.

1859, October 16 • Harpers Ferry, West Virginia
John Brown and his followers seize the U.S. Armory. Two blacks are killed, two are captured, one escapes. Brown is captured and hanged at Charles Town, West Virginia.

1859 • Washington, District of Columbia
In the case of *Ableman v. Booth,* the United States Supreme Court upholds the Fugitive Slave Act of 1850. The case arises when Sherman Booth rescues a fugitive slave from a Wisconsin jail and is charged by federal marshals with violating federal law.

1860 • As the Civil War approaches, the United States is sharply divided between pro- and anti-slavery forces. In Virginia, a law stipulates that free blacks can be sold into slavery for committing imprisonable offenses. Maryland forbids emancipation of slaves. President James Buchanan advocates a constitutional amendment confirming the fugitive slave acts. The Democratic party platform supports the *Dred Scott v. Sandford* decision. The Republican platform opposes the expansion of slavery into the western territories, and Abraham Lincoln, still a moderate on the subject of abolition, is elected president. On December 17, South Carolina secedes from the Union.

1861 • Fort Sumter, South Carolina
The Confederacy attack Fort Sumter, South Carolina, marking the beginning of Civil War. Jefferson Davis is elected president of the Confederate States of America and defends slavery as necessary to "self-preservation." The Confederates conscript slaves for military support jobs. Some Confederate states use free blacks in their armed forces.

1861 • Washington, District of Columbia
The Secretary of the Navy solicits enlistment of blacks into the Union Army, but most black offers to help militarily are rejected. Federal policy toward liberated slaves is erratic, depending mostly on the viewpoint of individual commanders. Lincoln moves warily, countermanding General Freemont's order that slaves of masters who fight against the Union are to be "declared free men."

1862 • New York
The National Freedmen's Relief Association, one of many groups dedicated to assist the black slave in

Harriet Tubman (far left) with a group of slaves she assisted through the Underground Railroad.

making the transition to freedom, is formed. Groups in Philadelphia, Cincinnati, and Chicago are eventually consolidated as the American Freedmen's Aid Commission.

1862 • Washington, District of Columbia
The United States Congress authorizes the enlistment of blacks for military service in the Union Army.

1862 • Washington, District of Columbia
President Abraham Lincoln proposes a plan for the gradual, compensated emancipation of slaves. Included is a provision to subsidize emigration to Haiti or Liberia. Lincoln's cautious policies are clarified in a letter to Horace Greeley in which he states his paramount objective as saving the Union "not either to save or destroy slavery." However, Lincoln does sign bills abolishing slavery in the territories and freeing slaves of masters disloyal to the United States. Military commanders are forbidden from returning fugitive slaves to owners and, in September, Lincoln issues an ultimatum giving hostile areas until January 1 to cease fighting or lose their slaves.

1863 • Cow Island, Haiti
Lincoln sends a ship to bring back 500 black settlers after a colonization attempt in Haiti fails.

1863 • New York
In anti-draft riots, 1,200 people, mostly blacks, are killed. The riot is spurred in part by the provision that exemption from military service can be bought for $300, a provision bitterly resented by poor white immigrants, who vent their frustrations on blacks.

1863, January 1 • Washington
Lincoln issues the Emancipation Proclamation, declaring freedom for all slaves in rebellious areas.

1864 • Louisiana
The Louisiana legislature, elected under auspices of occupying Union forces, votes to abolish slavery. However, it denies suffrage to blacks.

1864 • Virginia
Fourteen black soldiers are awarded the Medal of Honor by President Lincoln.

John Brown on his way to the gallows.

1865 • Montgomery, Alabama
Jefferson Davis authorizes the enlistment of blacks into the Confederate Army. However, Davis stipulates that the number of black troops cannot exceed twenty-five percent of the able-bodied slave population.

1865 • Appomattox, Virginia
The Confederacy surrenders. Of the 179,000 blacks who served in the Union army, 3,000 were killed in battle, 26,000 died from disease, and 14,700 deserted. Blacks represented nine to ten percent of the Union's armed forces.

1865 • Tennessee
The Ku Klux Klan is formed with the purpose of reasserting white supremacy in the South.

1865 • All-white legislatures in many states enact black codes. These codes impose heavy penalties for "vagrancy," "insulting gestures," "curfew violations," and "seditious speeches." South Carolina requires blacks enter-

President Abraham Lincoln meets with Union generals during the Civil War.

ing the state to post a $1,000 bond in guarantee of good behavior and entitles employers to whip black employees.

1865 • Wisconsin
Wisconsin, Connecticut, and Minnesota deny suffrage to blacks.

1865 • Washington, District of Columbia
Abraham Lincoln is assassinated. The new President, Andrew Johnson, calls for ratification of the Thirteenth Amendment, but opposes black suffrage. The Thirteenth Amendment, abolishing slavery and involuntary servitude in all of the United States, was ratified December 16, 1865.

1865, December 6 • Washington, District of Columbia
Congress establishes the Freedmen's Bureau and passes the Thirteenth Amendment to the Constitution, which abolishes slavery.

1866 • Memphis, Tennessee
In a race riot in Memphis, 48 blacks and two white sympathizers are killed. Also, 35 blacks are killed in a riot in New Orleans.

1866 • Washington, District of Columbia
Congress passes civil rights legislation despite President Johnson's veto. The act is intended to nullify the black codes. In the District of Columbia, a referendum is held on black suffrage. Over 6,500 vote against extension of the franchise to blacks; only 35 favor it. The Fourteenth Amendment passes the House and Senate despite opposition from Johnson.

1867 • Iowa
Iowa and the Dakota Territory grant suffrage to blacks.

1868 • Hampton, Virginia
Samuel Chapman Armstrong, an ex-Union officer, founds Hampton Institute.

1868 • Nine states grant suffrage to blacks, but two deny it. The Republican Party platform omits demand for black suffrage in northern states.

1868 • Many states are readmitted to the Union. The Alabama legislature votes to racially segregate all state schools.

A copy of the Emancipation Proclamation.

The Freedman's Bureau sought to keep peace between bands of white southerners and former slaves.

1868 • Louisiana
Oscar Dunn, an ex-slave and captain in the Union army, is elected lieutenant governor of Louisiana. Blacks outnumber whites 87 to 40 in the South Carolina legislature, but whites maintain a majority in the state Senate.

1868 • Washington, District of Columbia
The Fourteenth Amendment is ratified, establishing the concept of "equal protection" for all citizens under the United States Constitution. President Johnson's veto of the bill granting vote to blacks in the District of Columbia is overridden by Congress.

1869 • Washington, District of Columbia
The Colored National Labor Union is organized and advocates purchase and distribution of land.

1870 • Washington, District of Columbia
Recruitment of blacks for the United States Cavalry intensifies. By 1890, 14 black cavalrymen had received Medals of Honor for bravery in campaigns in the West.

1870 • Washington, District of Columbia
The Fifteenth Amendment to the Constitution, guaranteeing all citizens the right to vote, is ratified.

1871 • Washington, District of Columbia
Congress enacts the Ku Klux Klan Act to enforce the provisions of the Fourteenth Amendment.

1874 • Washington, District of Columbia
Reverend Patrick F. Healy is named president of Georgetown, the oldest Catholic University in the United States.

1875 • Kentucky
Oliver Lewis, a black jockey, rides the horse Aristides to victory in the first Kentucky Derby.

1875 • Washington, District of Columbia
Congress passes civil rights legislation prohibiting discrimination in such public accommodations as hotels, theaters, and amusement parks.

1876 • Hamburg, South Carolina
Federal troops are sent by President Ulysses S. Grant to restore order after five blacks are killed.

1876 • Washington, District of Columbia
In *United States v. Cruikshank*, the Supreme Court declares that the Fourteenth Amendment provides blacks with equal protection under the law but does not add

Freed slaves wait for work opportunities.

anything "to the rights which one citizen has under the Constitution against another." The Court rules that "the right of suffrage is not a necessary attribute of national citizenship."

1878 • Washington, District of Columbia
In the case, *Hall v. DeCuir*, the United States Supreme Court rules that states cannot prohibit segregation on public transportation.

1878 • Washington, District of Columbia
The United States attorney general reveals widespread intimidation of blacks attempting to vote and stuffing of ballot boxes in several southern states.

1879 • Frustrated by poverty and discrimination, large numbers of blacks start to emigrate north and west. A leader of the emigration movement is Benjamin Single-ton, an ex-slave who had earlier escaped to Canada and favors separate black communities. Emigration is vigorously opposed by many whites, some of whom prevent ships from transporting blacks on the Mississippi River.

1879 • Washington, District of Columbia
Upon hearing the case of *Strauder v. West Virginia*, the

United States Supreme Court rules that the Fourteenth Amendment insures blacks all rights that, under law, are enjoyed by whites. In a separate case, the Court ruled that one of the purposes of both the Thirteenth and Fourteenth Amendments was to raise the condition of blacks to one of perfect equality with whites.

1881 • Tennessee passes a "Jim Crow" railroad law which sets a trend soon taken up by Florida (1887), Mississippi (1888), Texas (1889), Louisiana (1890), and a host of other southern and border states.

1881 • Tuskegee, Alabama
Booker T. Washington opens Tuskegee Institute with a $2,000 appropriation from the Alabama legislature.

1883 • Washington, District of Columbia
Upon hearing a set of cases challenging the Civil Rights Act of 1875, the United States Supreme Court declares the act unconstitutional.

1884 • New York
The first issue of the *New York Age* is published by T. Thomas Fortune.

Jim Crow

1884 • Washington, District of Columbia
Former Reconstruction Representative John Roy Lynch is elected temporary chairman of the Republican convention—the first black to preside over a national political gathering.

1888 • Richmond, Virginia
Two black banks are founded—the Savings Bank of the Grand Fountain United Order of True Reformers in Virginia and the Capital Savings Bank in Washington.

1889 • Washington, District of Columbia
Frederick Douglass is appointed United States Minister to Haiti.

1890 • Mississippi
The Mississippi constitutional convention begins the systematic exclusion of blacks from the political arena by adopting literacy and other complex "understanding" tests as prerequisites to voting. Seven other southern states follow suit.

1890 • Washington, District of Columbia
In the *In re Green* decision, the United States Supreme Court sanctions control of elections by state officials, thus weakening federal protection for southern black voters. In the case *Louisville, New Orleans and Texas Railway v. Mississippi* the Court permits states to segregate public transportation facilities.

1891 • Baffin Bay, Greenland
Matthew Henson accompanies Admiral Peary in his exploration of the Arctic.

1891 • Chicago, Illinois
Dr. Daniel Hale Williams founds Provident Hospital, with the first training school for black nurses in the United States.

1895 • Atlanta, Georgia
Booker T. Washington delivers his famous "Atlanta Compromise" speech at the Cotton States International Exposition.

1896 • Cambridge, Massachusetts
W. E. B. Du Bois publishes *Suppression of the African Slave Trade*, the first of some 20 annual sociological studies of blacks in the United States.

1896 • Washington, District of Columbia
The National Association of Colored Women, a politically active self-help group, is formed.

1896 • Washington, District of Columbia
The United States Supreme Court in the *Plessy v. Ferguson* decision upholds the doctrine of "separate but equal," paving the way for segregation of blacks in all walks of life.

1898 • Louisiana
The addition of a "grandfather clause" to the state constitution enables poor whites to qualify for the franchise while curtailing black voter registration. In 1896, there were over 130,000 black voters on the Louisiana rolls. Four years later, that number has been reduced to roughly 5,000.

1898 • Santiago, Cuba
Four black regiments in the United States Army compile an outstanding combat record in and around Santiago during the Spanish-American War. Five blacks receive Medals of Honor. At the close of the war, over 100 blacks are promoted to officer status.

1900 • Boston, Massachusetts
Booker T. Washington organizes the National Negro Business League.

1900 • London, England
W. E. B. Du Bois attends the conference of the African

and New World Intellectuals, where he delivers an address incorporating his famous dictum: "The problem of the twentieth century is the problem of the color line." Du Bois also attends the first Pan-African Congress, an international body of concerned African nations protesting Western imperialism and promoting the concept of self-government among colonized peoples.

1902 • Richmond, Virginia
Virginia joins other southern states in adopting the "grandfather clause" as a means of denying African Americans access to the polls.

1903 • Georgia
Whites attack blacks in riots, which are spurred by charges that blacks have murdered whites.

1903 • Washington, District of Columbia
Upon hearing the case *Giles v. Harris*, the United States Supreme Court rules that it cannot remedy discrimination in voter registration.

1904 • Atlanta, Georgia
Financier Andrew Carnegie brings together a group of prominent black leaders, including Booker T. Washington and W. E. B. Du Bois, who discuss "the interests of the Negro race." The personal and ideological differences between Washington and DuBois are evident at the meeting, though there is agreement that the group should press for "absolute civil, political, and public equality." The group shows little fire in advancing familiar proposals for black self-help.

1905 • Fort Erie, New York
Twenty-nine militant black intellectuals from 14 states organize the Niagara Movement, a forerunner of the National Association for the Advancement of Colored People.

1906 • Atlanta, Georgia
An extended riot, in which respected black citizens are killed, brings the city to a stand-still for several days. After the riot, interracial groups are formed which attempt to improve conditions for blacks. Despite the efforts of these groups, many blacks decide to leave Georgia.

1906 • Brownsville, Texas
Several black soldiers of the 25th Infantry Division are involved in a riot with Brownsville police and merchants. Following the incident, President Theodore Roosevelt dishonorably discharges three companies of black troops. These dishonorable discharges are finally reversed by the United States Army in 1972. The lone

W. E. B. Du Bois

survivor from these companies is awarded $25,000 by the Army in 1973.

1907 • Washington, District of Columbia
The United States Supreme Court upholds the right of railroads to segregate passengers traveling between states, even when this runs counter to the laws of states in which the train is traveling.

1908 • Washington, District of Columbia
The United States Supreme Court, in the case *Berea College v. Kentucky* upholds a state statute requiring segregation in private institutions.

1909 • New York City, New York
The National Association for the Advancement of Colored People is founded in New York. The signers of the original charter of incorporation include Jane Addams, John Dewey, W. E. B. Du Bois, William Dean Howells, and Lincoln Steffens.

1909 • Matthew Henson places the flag of the United States at the North Pole. Henson, a black man, was part of the Admiral Robert E. Peary expedition.

1910 • On separate lecture tours of Great Britain, W. E. B. Du Bois and Booker T. Washington paint contrasting versions of the black condition in the United States. Washington tells the British that blacks are making progress; Du Bois underscores injustices and accuses Washington of acquiescing to powerful white interests.

1910 • New York City, New York
The first edition of *Crisis* magazine, edited by W. E. B. Du Bois, is published. Only 1,000 copies are in print, but before the end of the decade circulation of the magazine has increased one-hundred fold.

1910 • New York City, New York
The National Urban League is founded. The new organization stresses employment and industrial opportunities for blacks. Eugene Kinckle Jones serves as the first executive secretary.

1911 • Jamaica
Marcus Garvey forms the Universal Negro Improvement Association.

1912 • New York City, New York
James Weldon Johnson's *The Autobiography of an Ex-Colored Man* is published, spurring white recognition of black culture and the advent of the Harlem Renaissance.

1913 • Washington, District of Columbia
President Woodrow Wilson refuses to appoint a National Race Commission to study the social and economic status of blacks.

1915 • Spurred by boll weevil devastation of cotton crops, the great migration of blacks to the North begins. Dr. Carter G. Woodson establishes the Association for the Study of Negro Life and History.

1915 • Washington, District of Columbia
The United States Supreme Court, in *Guinn v. United States*, declares the "grandfather clause" in the Oklahoma constitution unconstitutional.

1917 • East St. Louis, Illinois
A riot erupts after blacks are hired at a local factory. Forty blacks are killed.

1917 • New York City, New York
Over 10,000 blacks parade down Fifth Avenue in New York, New York to protest lynchings and the East St. Louis riot. Marchers include W. E. B. Du Bois and James Weldon Johnson.

1917 • The United States enters World War I. Joel Spingarn presses the War Department to establish an officers' training camp for blacks. Spingarn's proposal alienates many of his National Association for the Advancement of Colored People colleagues who feel that such a camp would only perpetuate segregation and validate theories of black inferiority. Others concede that the move is prudent, since it is the only way for black officers to be trained. The NAACP ultimately approves of separate training camps. In October, over 600 blacks are commissioned officers, and 700,000 blacks register for the draft.

1917 • Washington, District of Columbia
In the case of *Buchanan v. Warley*, the United States Supreme Court declares that a Louisville "block" segregation ordinance is unconstitutional.

1918 • France
Two black infantry battalions are awarded the Croix de Guerre and two black officers win the French Legion of Honor. Blacks are in the forefront of fighting from 1917 until the defeat of Germany in 1918.

1919 • Membership in the National Association for the Advancement of Colored People approaches 100,000 despite attempts in some areas to make it illegal.

1919 • Washington, District of Columbia
The United States Supreme Court rules, in the case *Strauder v. West Virginia*, that blacks should be admitted to juries.

1920 • New York City, New York
James Weldon Johnson becomes the first black secretary of the National Association for the Advancement of Colored People and campaigns for the withdrawal of United States troops occupying Haiti.

1921 • Tulsa, Oklahoma
Twenty-one blacks and ten whites are killed in a riot.

1922 • Washington, District of Columbia
Republicans in the Senate vote to abandon the Dyer Anti-Lynching Bill, which imposed severe penalties and fines on "any state or municipal officer convicted of negligence in affording protection to individuals in custody who are attacked by a mob bent on lynching, torture, or physical intimidation." The bill, which was approved by the House of Representatives, had also provided for compensation to the families of victims.

1923 • New York City, New York
Marcus Garvey is sentenced to a five-year term for mail fraud.

Black soldiers leave by train to serve in the war.

1924 • Washington, District of Columbia
Congress passes the Immigration Act which excludes blacks of African descent from entering the country.

1924 • Washington, District of Columbia
New York Representative Emanuel Cellar introduces legislation to provide for the formation of a blue-ribbon panel to study racial issues. The idea is met with disdain from the black press, particularly the *Chicago Defender*, which editorializes: "We have been commissioned to death.... We have too many studies and reports already." *The Defender* asserts that blacks need only to look after their own interests through the creation of a strong party vehicle and potent political leadership in the halls of Congress.

1926 • New York City, New York
Controversy rages among the black intelligentsia after publication of *Nigger Heaven* by white writer Carl van Vechten. The book glamorizes the free wheeling style of Harlem life amid the general contention that blacks are less ashamed of sex and more morally honest than whites. W. E. B. Du Bois finds the assumptions deplorable; James Weldon Johnson, on the other hand, believes the book is neither scandalous nor insulting.

1926 • New York City, New York
Langston Hughes, writing in *The Nation* magazine, urges black artists to write from their experience and to stop imitating white writers.

1926 • A. Philip Randolph founds the Brotherhood of Sleeping Car Porters.

1926 • Washington, District of Columbia
Negro History Week is introduced by Dr. Carter G. Woodson and the Association for the Study of Negro Life and History.

1926 • Washington, District of Columbia
President Coolidge tells Congress that the country must provide "for the amelioration of race prejudice and the extension to all of the elements of equal opportunity and equal protection under the laws, which are guaranteed by the Constitution." Twenty-three blacks are reported lynched during 1926.

1927 • Atlanta, Georgia
Marcus Garvey is released from prison and deported to the British West Indies.

Blacks protest lynching in the South during the "Silent Protest Parade."

1927 • Chicago, Illinois
The National Urban League organizes a boycott of stores that don't hire blacks. In 1929, boycotts are started in several other Midwest cities.

1927 • Washington, District of Columbia
In the case of *Nixon v. Herndon* the United States Supreme Court strikes down a Texas law which bars blacks from voting in party primaries. Texas goes on to enact a law allowing local committees to determine voter qualifications.

1928 • Illinois
Oscar DePriest, a Republican, is elected as the first black Representative from a northern state.

1930 • Detroit, Michigan
W.D. Fard founds the Temple of Islam, later to become the Nation of Islam.

1930 • Washington, District of Columbia
A National Association for the Advancement of Colored People campaign helps prevent confirmation of United States Supreme Court nominee John H. Parker, a one-

time, self-admitted opponent of the franchise for blacks. The NAACP also helps unseat three of the senators who voted for him in later congressional elections.

1931 • Alabama
The first trial of the Scottsboro Boys results in a battle between the National Association for the Advancement of Colored People and the International Labor Defense, a Communist-controlled group, for the right to represent the young defendants who are charged with rape. The case, which becomes a worldwide *cause celebre* and important propaganda weapon for Communists, drags on for 20 years despite the recanting of a charge by one of the two plaintiffs and medical testimony that rape was not committed.

1932 • Washington, District of Columbia
Following the Supreme Court's 1927 ruling in *Nixon v. Herndon* the state of Texas passes a statute authorizing the state Democratic party to set up its own rules regarding primary elections. As a result, the state of Texas adopts a resolution that denies blacks the right to vote in Democratic Party primaries. However, the Supreme Court's ruling in rules that such legislation violates provisions of the Fourteenth Amendment.

A. Philip Randolph

The "Scottsboro Boys"

1934 • Chicago, Illinois
The headquarters of the Nation of Islam are established, with Elijah Muhammad as leader.

1934 • Washington, District of Columbia
A bill that prohibits lynching fails, as President Roosevelt refuses to support it.

1935 • New York City, New York
Mary McLeod Bethune founds the National Council of Negro Women.

1935 • St. Louis, Missouri
The National Association for the Advancement of Colored People bitterly criticizes President Franklin Delano Roosevelt for his failure to present or support civil rights legislation.

1935 • Washington, District of Columbia
In the case of *Grovey v. Townsend* the United States Supreme Court upholds a Texas law that prevents blacks from voting in the Texas Democratic primary. The decision is a setback to the National Association for the Advancement of Colored People, which has waged sev-

eral effective legal battles to equalize the ballot potential of the black voter.

1936 • Berlin/ Germany
Jesse Owens wins four gold medals in the 1936 Olympics, but is snubbed by the Chancellor of Germany, Adolf Hitler.

1936 • Washington, District of Columbia
In the case of *Gibbs v. Montgomery County* the United States Supreme Court requires Maryland University to admit a black student, Donald Murray, to its graduate law school.

1937 • New York City, New York
Richard Wright becomes editor of *Challenge*, changes the title to *New Challenge*, and urges blacks to write with greater "social realism."

1937 • Pennsylvania
A new Pennsylvania state law denies many state services to unions discriminating against blacks.

1937 • Spain
Between 60 to 80 of the 3200 Americans who fight for

the Republican side in the Spanish Civil War are black. Oliver Law, a black man from Chicago, commands the Lincoln Battalion.

1937 • The Virgin Islands
Adam Clayton Powell, Jr. and other black leaders convince white merchants in Harlem to hire blacks and to promise equal promotion opportunities.

1938 • New York City, New York
Adam Clayton Powell, Jr. and other black leaders convince white merchants in Harlem to hire blacks and to promise equal promotion opportunities.

1938 • Pennsylvania
Crystal Bird Fauset of Philadelphia, the first black woman state legislator, is elected to the Pennsylvania House of Representatives.

1939 • Miami, Florida
Intimidation and cross-burning by the Ku Klux Klan in the black ghetto of Miami fail to discourage over 1,000 of the city's registered blacks from appearing at the polls. The Klan parades with effigies of blacks who will allegedly be slain for daring to vote.

1939 • New York City, New York
Jane Bolin is appointed Judge of the Court of Domestic Relations in New York, New York, by Mayor Fiorello LaGuardia, becoming the first female black judge in the United States.

1939 • Washington, District of Columbia
Marian Anderson, denied the use of Constitution Hall by the Daughters of the American Revolution, sings on Easter Sunday before 75,000 people assembled at the Lincoln Memorial.

1940 • New York
In a mass meeting of West Indians, they oppose the transfer of West Indian islands to the United States.

1940 • Eighty thousand blacks vote in eight southern states. Five percent of voting age blacks are registered.

1940 • The 1940 census places life expectancy for blacks at 51 years, compared with 62 years for whites. Nearly one-fourth of blacks live in the North and West.

1940 • Virginia
The Virginia legislature chooses "Carry Me Back to Ole Virginia," written by black composer James A. Bland, as the official state song.

1940 • Washington, District of Columbia
Benjamin O. Davis, Sr. is appointed as the first black general in the history of the United States armed forces. Responding to National Association for the Advancement of Colored People pressure, President Franklin Roosevelt announces that black strength in the Armed Forces will be proportionate to black population totals. Several branches of the military service and several occupational specialties are to be opened to blacks. However, Roosevelt rules out troop integration because it will be "destructive to morale and detrimental to ... preparation for national defense." At the start of Selective Service, less than 5000 of 230,000 men in the Army are black and there are only two black combat officers. Approximately 888,000 black men and 4,000 black women are to serve in the armed forces during World War II. Blacks are mostly confined to service units.

1940 • Washington, District of Columbia
The United States Supreme Court rules that black teachers cannot be denied wage parity with white teachers.

1941, December 07 • Pearl Harbor, Hawaii
Dorie Miller, messman aboard the *USS Arizona*, mans a machine gun during the Pearl Harbor attack, downs four enemy planes and is awarded the Navy Cross.

1941 • Washington, District of Columbia
Dr. Charles R. Drew, a black physician, sets up the first blood bank.

1941 • Washington, District of Columbia
Dr. Robert Weaver is appointed director of the government office charged with integrating blacks into the national defense program.

1941 • Washington, District of Columbia
The threat by blacks to stage a massive protest march on the nation's capital results in the issuance of Executive Order No. 8802, prohibiting discrimination in the defense establishment.

1941 • Washington, District of Columbia
The United States Supreme Court, in the case of *Mitchell v. United States* rules that separate facilities in railroad travel must be substantially equal. The case is brought before the Supreme Court by black congressman Arthur Mitchell.

1942 • Chicago, Illinois
The Congress of Racial Equality (CORE), a civil rights group dedicated to a direct-action, nonviolent program, is founded. In 1943, CORE stages its first "sit-in" in a Chicago restaurant.

The Ku Klux Klan marches down Pennsylvania Avenue in Washington, DC.

1942 • Washington, District of Columbia
The Justice Department threatens to file suit against a number of black newspapers which it believes are guilty of sedition because of their strong criticism of the government's racial policies in the armed services. The National Association for the Advancement of Colored People steps in to suggest guidelines which will satisfy the Justice Department. The clear alternative is suppression of the black press, should it remain unruly.

1944 • The National Association for the Advancement of

Colored People secures the release of servicemen detained for protests of discrimination in the armed forces.

1944 • The European Theater of War
The black 99th Pursuit Squadron flies its 500th mission in the Mediterranean Theater. Another black unit, the 92nd Division, enters combat in Italy. On June 6, 500 blacks land on Omaha Beach as part of the D-Day invasion of northern France. Among them is the 761st Tank Battalion which spends 183 days in action and is cited for conspicuous courage. Also cited in January

Marian Anderson

1945 is the 969th Field Artillery Battalion for their support in the defense of Bastogne.

1944 • The restriction of black seamen to shore duty is ended, as is the exclusion of blacks from the Coast Guard and Marine Corps. The War Department officially ends segregation in all Army posts, but the order is widely ignored.

1944 • Washington, District of Columbia
In the case of *Smith v. Allwright*, the United States Supreme Court rules that "white primaries" violate the provisions of the Fifteenth Amendment.

1945 • Italy
Black troops are in the forefront of victorious assaults in Germany and northern Italy. However, the use of black troops in World War II is more limited than in World War I or the Spanish-American War. Despite efforts by some enlightened naval officers, over 90 percent of blacks in the Navy are still messmen when the war ends.

1945 • New York
The first state Fair Employment Practices Commission

is established in New York as a result of the Ives-Quinn Bill.

1945 • Washington, District of Columbia
Congress denies funds to the federal Fair Employment Practices Commission, which was established during the war to enforce fair employment policies.

1946 • Washington, District of Columbia
The United States Supreme Court rules, in *Morgan v. Virginia*, that segregation on interstate buses is unconstitutional.

1947 • Atlanta, Georgia
The Southern Regional Council releases figures which demonstrate that only 12 percent of the blacks in the Deep South (nearly 600,000) meet voting qualifications. In the states of Louisiana, Alabama, and Mississippi, the figure is approximately 3 percent. In Tennessee, more than 25 percent of adult blacks meet the state voting requirements.

1947 • CORE's first "freedom ride" travels through southern states to press for the integration of transportation facilities.

1947 • Tuskegee, Alabama
Statistics indicate that 3,426 blacks have been lynched in the United States in the period 1882-1947. Of these, 1,217 were lynched in the decade 1890-1900. From 1947 to 1962, 12 blacks are lynched.

1947 • Washington, District of Columbia
The Truman Committee on Civil Rights formally condemns racial injustice in America in the widely quoted report, *To Secure These Rights*.

1948 • California
The California Supreme Court declares the state statute banning racial intermarriage unconstitutional.

1948 • New York City, New York
Ralph Bunche is confirmed by the United Nations Security Council as acting U.N. mediator in Palestine.

1948 • Washington, District of Columbia
The United States Supreme Court in *Shelley v. Kraemer* rules that federal and state courts may not enforce restrictive covenants. However, the Court does not declare such covenants illegal. In a separate case, *Sipuel v. University of Oklahoma*, the Court holds that states are required to provide blacks with the same educational opportunities as whites. President Truman issues Executive Order No. 9981 directing "equality of treatment and opportunity" in the armed forces and creates

The Greyhound Bus Station in Memphis, Tennessee, with its "white waiting room," sign is indicative of the South's segregated transportation facilities.

the Fair Practices Board of the Civil Service Commission to deal with complaints of discrimination in government employment.

1949 • Connecticut
Connecticut becomes the first state in the Union to extend the jurisdiction of the Civil Rights Commission into the domain of public housing.

1949 • Washington, District of Columbia
Representative William L. Dawson becomes the first

black to head a Congressional committee when he is named chairman of the House Committee on Government Operations.

1950 • Yech'on, Republic of Korea
The black 24th Infantry Regiment recaptures the city of Yech'on, the first American victory in the Korean War.

1950 • New York City, New York
Edith Sampson is appointed an alternate delegate to the United Nations.

The victim of a lynching in the Deep South.

1950 • Oslo, Norway
Ralph Bunche wins the Nobel Peace Prize.

1950 • The 1950 census places the net 10-year black emigration from the South at 1.6 million.

1950 • Washington, District of Columbia
Several United States Supreme Court decisions open university facilities to blacks. In the case of *Henderson v. United States*, the Court rules that segregated tables on dining cars violate the provisions of the Interstate Commerce Act. A special committee reports to President Truman that black servicemen are still barred from many military specialties and training programs, but that the armed forces has largely been desegregated.

1952 • In a series of legal maneuvers, the National Association for the Advancement of Colored People and other black groups succeed in desegregating a number of colleges and high schools in southern and border areas. In addition, public housing projects are opened to blacks in some northern and western cities and desegregation is achieved in several businesses and unions. A public swimming pool is integrated in Kansas City, a golf course in Louisville, and Ford's Theater in Baltimore.

1952 • Tuskegee, Alabama
A Tuskegee report indicates that, for the first time in its 71 years of tabulation, no lynchings have occurred in the United States.

1953 • Washington, District of Columbia
District of Columbia Commissioners order the abolition of segregation in several district agencies. The fire department is among those which escape the mandate. The Defense Department orders an end to segregation in schools on military bases and in veterans hospitals.

1953 • New York City, New York
Hulan Jack is sworn in as Borough President of Manhattan.

1953 • Washington, District of Columbia
The United States Supreme Court asks to re-hear five school segregation cases first argued in 1942. Sensing a major opportunity, the National Association for the Advancement of Colored People puts 100 lawyers, scholars, and researchers to work in preparation. The NAACP also files a complaint with the Interstate Commerce Commission to execute earlier Supreme Court desegregation orders in transportation facilities.

1956 • Washington, District of Columbia
The United States Supreme Court, in the case of *Flemming v. South Carolina Electric*, strikes down a state statute requiring segregation on public transportation.

1954, March 4 • Washington, District of Columbia
President Eisenhower appoints a black, J. Ernest Wilkins, as Undersecretary of Labor.

1954, May 17 • Washington, District of Columbia
By a unanimous vote, the United States Supreme Court, in the case of *Brown v. Board of Education of Topeka, Kansas*, declares that "separate but equal" educational facilities are "inherently unequal" and that segregation is therefore unconstitutional. The decision overturns the "separate but equal" doctrine that has legalized segregation since 1896. In the case of *Hawkins v. Board of Control*, the Court rules that the University of Florida must admit blacks regardless of any "public mischief" it might cause.

1954, September • In the autumn following the *Brown* decision, 150 formerly segregated school districts in eight states and the District of Columbia integrate. However, a number of groups opposing integration emerge in the South. Most prominent among these are White Citizens Councils, which soon claim 80,000 members and propose constitutional amendments reinstating segregation.

1954, October 1 • Baltimore, Maryland
White parents and students protest the admission of black students to Baltimore's Southern High School. Anti-desegregation demonstrations are also staged in nearby Washington, D.C.

1954, October 1 • Florida
State Attorney General Richard Ervin files a brief with the United States Supreme Court warning that violent resistance would result from any effort to force desegregation in Florida schools.

1954, October 30 • Washington, District of Columbia
The Department of Defense reports the end of "all-Negro" units in the Army. However, some bases still refuse to integrate. The Veteran's Administration announces their hospitals have been desegregated, but the Department of Health, Education and Welfare declares it will continue to give funds to segregated hospitals.

1954, November 13 • Boca Raton, Florida
Governors attending the Southern Governors Conference pledge to uphold state control over schools and warn that forced school desegregation will create unrest which they claim does not currently exist in their states.

1955, May 31 • Washington, District of Columbia
The United States Supreme Court orders school boards to draw up desegregation procedures. The Court asserts that school authorities have the responsibility of assessing and solving desegregation problems and must do so "with all deliberate speed." The decision reenforces the Court's ruling in *Brown v. Board of Education*. Reactions to this ruling in the South are mixed. Kansas, Missouri, Oklahoma, and Texas desegregate their school systems with minimal disruption. Georgia's Board of Education adopts a resolution revoking the license of any teacher who teaches integrated classes. Mississippi repeals its compulsory school attendance law and establishes a branch of government for the sole purpose of maintaining segregation. White Citizens Councils in Mississippi initiate economic pressures against blacks who try to register to vote, while more extreme groups resort to direct terror.

1955, July 14 • Richmond, Virginia
The United States Circuit Court of Appeals rules that segregation on city buses is illegal. The Court claims that the same principle which outlawed segregation in public schools should be applied.

1955, August 31 • Greenwood, Mississippi
Two white men are arrested in Greenwood on charges of kidnapping, beating, and shooting 15-year-old Emmitt Till. Till, who allegedly whistled at and insulted a white woman, was found dead in the Tallahatchie River. Jurors acquit the defendants on grounds that the body could not be positively identified.

1955, November 25 • Washington, District of Columbia
In accordance with United States Supreme Court edicts, the Interstate Commerce Commission outlaws segregated buses and waiting rooms for interstate passengers. However, many communities ignore the order.

1955, December 1 • Montgomery, Alabama
Rosa Parks takes a seat in the front of a city bus, refuses to surrender it to a white man, and is arrested. Four days later, the Reverend Martin Luther King, Jr. urges the city's black community to boycott the buses. This marks the beginning of the Montgomery bus boycott, which leads to the desegregation of Montgomery's city bus system the following year.

1956, February 3 • Tuscaloosa, Alabama
Autherine Lucy is admitted to the University of Alabama by court order, but riots ensue and she is expelled on a technicality.

1956, March 11 • Washington, District of Columbia
Southern members of the Senate, led by Harry Byrd of Virginia, launch a fight against school integration. Byrd obtains the signatures of 100 congressmen on a "Southern Manifesto", attacking the rulings of the United States Supreme Court.

1956, July 13 • Washington, District of Columbia
Southern members of the House of Representatives unite in opposition to an Eisenhower administration sponsored civil rights bill. The bill would provide for the investigation of civil rights complaints and permit action by the Attorney General in federal courts.

1956, September • By September 1956, approximately 800 school districts containing 320,000 black children are desegregated in compliance with the United States Supreme Court's 1954 decision. However, nearly 2.5 million black children remain in segregated schools and there are still no desegregated districts in Virginia, North and South Carolina, Georgia, Florida, Mississippi, Alabama, and Louisiana.

1956, November 13 • Washington, District of Columbia
The United States Supreme Court rules that the segregation of city buses is unconstitutional.

1957, February 14 • New Orleans, Louisiana
The Southern Christian Leadership Conference is formed by Martin Luther King, Jr., and others to coordinate the

Rosa Parks is arrested and fingerprinted by Deputy Sheriff D. H. Lackey following her refusal to move to the back of a segregated bus.

activities of nonviolent groups devoted to integration and citizenship for blacks.

1957, February 26 • Little Rock, Arkansas
Governor Orval Faubus signs four segregation bills enabling parents to refuse to send their children to desegregated schools, authorizing the use of school district funds to pay legal expenses incurred in integration suits, creating a committee to make anti-integration studies, and requiring organizations such as the National Association for the Advancement of Colored People to publish membership rosters.

1957, April 9 • Madison, Wisconsin
The state Supreme Court rules that blacks can be refused membership in trade unions, since such organizations are voluntary associations.

1957, September 9 • Washington, District of Columbia
President Eisenhower signs a civil rights bill. The bill provides for the creation of a commission on civil rights to investigate allegations of civil rights and voting rights violations.

1957, September 4 • Little Rock, Arkansas
Nine black students are turned away from Central High School by a white mob and the Arkansas National Guard when they arrive for classes on September 4. The National Guard, which was called to Little Rock by Governor Orval Faubus, is forced by court order to withdraw on September 20. As mobs of angry whites assemble outside of the school and the threat of mob violence escalates, President Dwight Eisenhower issues a proclamation on September 23 ordering an end to any obstruction to court-ordered integration. On September 24, the President issues Executive Order No. 10730 authorizing the use of federal troops to assist in the integration of Central High School.

1958, February 19 • New Orleans, Louisiana
The United States Court of Appeals rules that segregation on buses and streetcars in New Orleans is illegal. The Louisiana state assembly later passes a bill which stipulates that the first person seated in a bus's double seat can decide whether a rider of a different race may sit in the adjoining seat. The bill is vetoed by Governor Earl Long, because it would require a white rider to request permission to sit next to a black rider.

Governor Orval Faubus argues for the continued segregation of Arkansas public schools.

1958, April 14 • Jackson, Mississippi
Governor J. P. Coleman asserts that blacks in Mississippi are not ready to vote and vetoes a bill which would have given control of voter registration to a court appointed registrar.

1958, July 16 • Baton Rouge, Louisiana
Governor Earl Long signs a bill requiring that blood plasma be labeled according to the race of donor.

1960, February 1 • Greensboro, North Carolina
Four black students refuse to leave a segregated lunch counter, marking the beginning of "sit-in" protests throughout the South.

1960, April • Atlanta, Georgia
The Student Non-Violent Coordinating Committee is formed to organize student protest activities. Church "kneel-ins" and beach "wade-ins" soon join lunch counter and bus station "sit-ins" as effective means of protesting segregation.

1960, April 24 • Biloxi, Mississippi
Rioting erupts when a group of blacks attempt to swim at the city's 26-mile whites-only beach. A curfew is ordered by the mayor and riot police patrol the city. On April 27, the state legislature passes a law authorizing prison terms for anyone convicted of inciting a riot.

1960, May 6 • Washington, District of Columbia
President Eisenhower signs the Civil Rights Act of 1960. This act authorizes judges to appoint referees who can help blacks register to vote in federal elections. The act also prohibits intimidation of black voters through bombing and mob violence.

1960, July 31 • New York City, New York
Black Muslim leader, Elijah Muhammad, calls for the creation of a black state, either in America or in Africa.

1960, August • As of August 1, "sit-ins" have led to the successful desegregation of lunch counters in 15 American cities.

1960, September 8 • New York City, New York
New York Governor Nelson Rockefeller, in an address at the National Urban League Conference, declares that the "sit-ins" are "an inspiration to the nation."

1960, October 3 • The Southern Christian Leadership Conference organizes voter "stand-ins" in several American cities to protest against the remaining barriers to black voter registration.

1960, November 10 • New Orleans, Louisiana
The city approves a plan to admit black students to an all-white school. Meeting in a special session, the state legislature votes to take control of the city's school system and to have the schools closed on the day the black students are scheduled to arrive. On November 14, United States marshals escort four black students to the selected schools. On November 15, 11 whites are arrested in disturbances; on November 17 the city experiences severe rioting.

1960, November 14 • Washington, District of Columbia
The United States Supreme Court, in the case of *Gomillion v. Lightfoot*, rules that a law designed to redraw the city boundaries of Tuskegee, Alabama is unconstitutional. The case was brought before the Court after the city of Tuskegee redrew its borders, which excluded all but four or five of the city's 400 black residents. The Court asserted that such legislation was in violation of the Fifteenth Amendment.

1960, November 23 • Baton Rouge, Louisiana
At its annual convention, the Louisiana Teachers Association vows to resist all attempts to integrate the state's public schools.

1961, May 4 • Washington, District of Columbia
Several busloads of "freedom riders," organized by the Congress of Racial Equality (CORE), embark on a journey through the South to test the compliance of bus

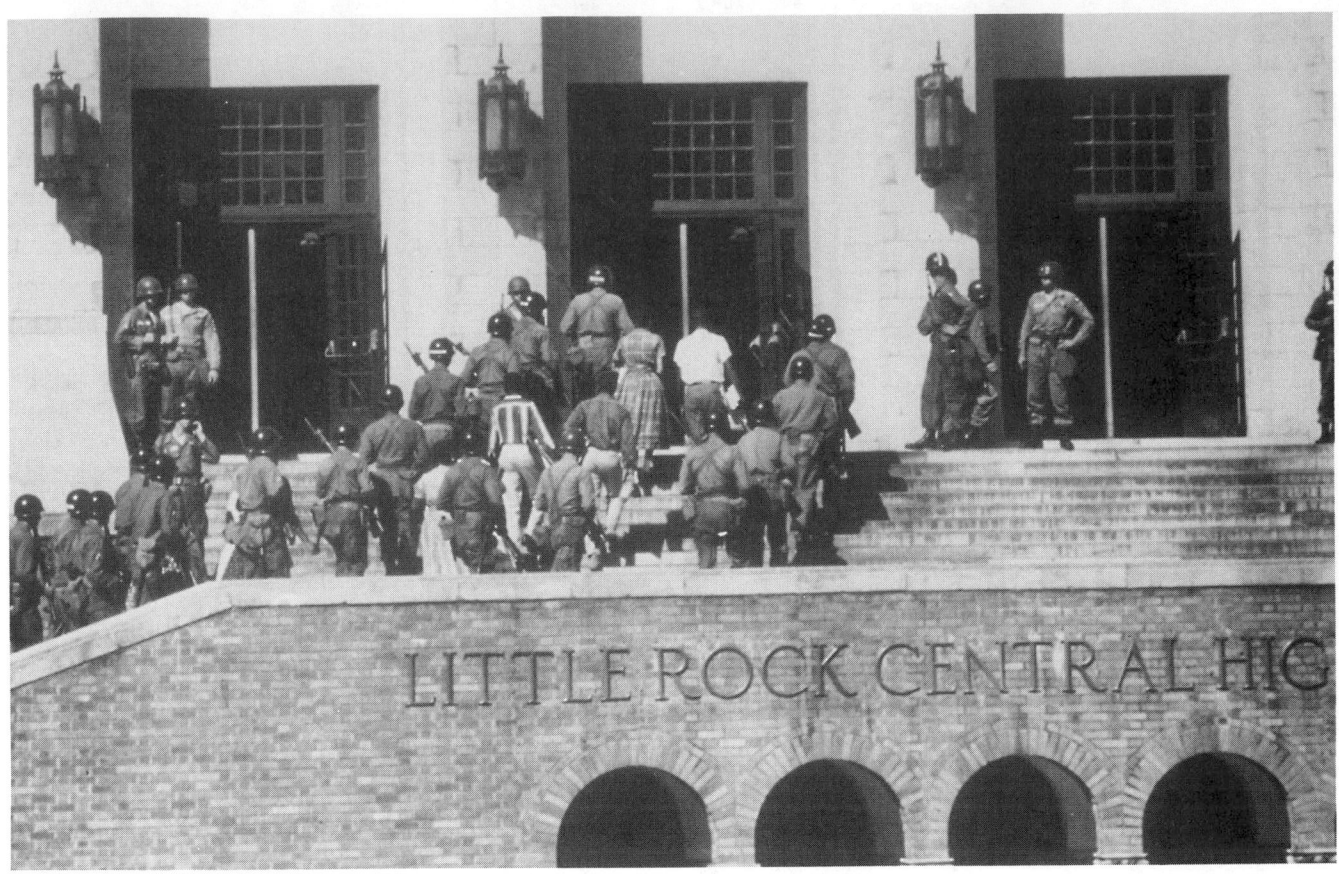

Federal troops escort nine black students into Little Rock Central High School following violent disturbances by white demonstrators.

stations with the Interstate Commerce Commission's desegregation order. Many of the "freedom riders" are arrested or encounter angry mobs as they travel throughout the South.

1961, May 20 • Montgomery, Alabama
A bus carrying "freedom riders" is attacked by a mob and set on fire. Attorney General Robert Kennedy orders federal marshals into Montgomery to maintain order. On May 21, a mob forms outside of the First Baptist Church, where Dr. Martin Luther King, Jr. and Ralph Abernathy, pastor of the church, are conducting a meeting. The situation in Montgomery becomes so volatile that Governor John Patterson is forced to deploy the Alabama National Guard and declares martial law in the city.

1961, May 22 • Washington, District of Columbia
Upon hearing the case *Louisiana ex rel. Gremillion v. NAACP* the United States Supreme Court unanimously rules that two Louisiana laws designed to harass the National Association for the Advancement of Colored People are unconstitutional. The laws required that

organizations disclose members' names and attest that its officers are not affiliated with subversive activities.

1961, June 2 • Montgomery, Alabama
Federal Judge Frank Johnson, Jr. issues a restraining order to prevent "freedom riders" from traveling through the state.

1961, September 29 • Atlanta, Georgia
The Southern Regional Council reports that business establishments in more than 100 cities have been desegregated as a result of "sit-ins."

1961, December 11 • Washington, District of Columbia
Ruling on its first cases pertaining to student "sit-ins", the United States Supreme Court decides unanimously to reverse the conviction of 16 black students. The cases, *Briscoe v. Louisiana*, *Garner v. Louisiana*, and *Hoston v. Louisiana* result from a Baton Rouge lunch counter "sit-in" staged in March 1960. The students, who had not been asked to leave by the proprietor, had refused a police order to leave and were charged with "disturbing the peace."

Students "sit-in" at Woolworth's segregated lunch counter in Atlanta.

1962, February 26 • Washington, District of Columbia
The United States Supreme Court rules on a suit challenging Mississippi laws that require segregation in intrastate transportation. The case *Bailey v. Patterson* is remanded to district court, since, as the Court contends, the issue is no longer litigable; no state may require racial segregation in either inter- or intrastate transportation.

1962, March 24 • Columbia, South Carolina
The National Association for the Advancement of Colored People files suit in district court to prohibit the Orangeburg Regional Hospital from operating segregated facilities.

1962, May 2 • Biloxi, Mississippi
A United States District Court finds nine Mississippi laws requiring segregated travel accommodations unconstitutional.

1962, September 30 • Jackson, Mississippi
Riots erupt on the campus of the University of Mississippi when James Meredith, a 29-year-old black veteran, is admitted to the university by court order. Federal troops are sent to restore order.

1962, November 20 • Washington, District of Columbia
The Kennedy administration issues orders banning segregation in federally financed housing.

1963, April 3 • Birmingham, Alabama
Dr. Martin Luther King, Jr. targets Birmingham for a drive against discrimination. The protesters are driven back by police armed with water hoses and attack dogs. The confrontation, which has been captured on film, awakens public opinion across the country.

1963, June 12 • Jackson, Mississippi
Civil rights leader Medgar Evers is assassinated in the doorway of his home on June 12. Thousands attend a march mourning the death of Evers on June 15.

1963, August 28 • Washington, District of Columbia
Some 250,000 people gather at the Lincoln Memorial to demonstrate on behalf of the civil rights bill pending in Congress. The march has been organized by several civil rights organizations, including the National Association for the Advancement of Colored People, the Southern Christian Leadership Conference, the Council on Racial Equality, the Urban League, and the Negro American Labor Council. Dr. Martin Luther King, Jr., one of many

"Freedom riders" march through Granada, Mississippi in support of civil rights.

scheduled speakers, gives what will become his most famous oration—" I Have a Dream."

1963, September • The South
Less than 10 percent of black public school students attend integrated classes in the fall term. Governor George Wallace of Alabama declares: "I draw the line in the dust and toss the gauntlet before the feet of tyranny and I say "segregation now, segregation tomorrow, segregation forever."

1963, September 15 • Birmingham, Alabama
Four black children are killed in the bombing of the 16th Street Baptist Church.

1963, November 22 • Dallas, Texas
President John F. Kennedy, a major advocate of civil rights, is assassinated in Dallas, Texas. Kennedy's successor, Vice President Lyndon B. Johnson, promises to continue support for civil rights legislation.

1964, January 23 • The Twenty-fourth Amendment to the Constitution is ratified prohibiting the use of poll taxes in federal elections.

1964, March 8 • New York City, New York
Malcolm X leaves the Black Muslim organization, Nation of Islam, to form the Organization for Afro-American Unity—an organization emphasizing black nationalism and social action.

1964, June 2 • Washington, District of Columbia
A major civil rights bill, forbidding discrimination in public accommodations and employment, is signed into law by President Johnson.

1964, June 25 • St. Augustine, Florida
A mob attacks marchers protesting the city's pro-segregation policies. State police watch as some 50 blacks are prevented from using the city beach.

1964, July-August • New York and New Jersey
On July 18 riots erupt in the Harlem section of New York, New York. One person is killed, 140 injured, and 500 arrested. This is considered the first of many large riots that were to strike urban black neighborhoods during the sixties. Shortly after the Harlem disturbances, riots erupt in Brooklyn, New York; Rochester, New York; Jersey City, New Jersey; and Paterson, New Jersey.

Betty Shabazz leaves the morgue at Bellevue Hospital in New York after identifying the body of her husband, Malcolm X.

Governor George Wallace presents his segregationist views to the Senate Commerce Committee in 1963.

1964, August 4 • Philadelphia, Mississippi

Three young civil rights volunteers, James Chaney, Michael Schwerner, and Andrew Goodman, are murdered. A number of arrests on federal charges, less severe than murder, follow. Among the 19 suspects are the sheriff and a deputy sheriff of Neshoba County. But no convictions are obtained and charges are dismissed in December.

1964, December 10 • Oslo, Norway

Dr. Martin Luther King, Jr. is awarded the Nobel Prize for Peace.

1965, January 2 • Selma, Alabama

On January 2 Reverend Martin Luther King, Jr. announces his intention to call for demonstrations if Alabama blacks are not permitted to register to vote in appropriate numbers. Twelve blacks, including Dr. King himself, book rooms on January 18 at Selma's Hotel Albert, becoming the first blacks accepted at this formerly all-white hotel. While signing the guest register, Dr. King is accosted by a white segregationist who is later fined $100 and given a 60-day jail sentence. On January 19, Sheriff James G. Clark arrests sixty-two

blacks in Selma after they refuse to enter the Dallas County court-house through an alley door. Clark and his deputies arrest 150 other black voter-registration applicants the next day. A federal district court order issued on January 23 bars law enforcement officials from interfering with voter registration and warns that violence against black voters will not be tolerated.

1965, January 15 • Philadelphia, Mississippi

A federal grand jury hands down indictments for the June 1964 slaying of three civil rights workers—James Chaney, Andrew Goodman, and Michael Schwerner in Philadelphia, Mississippi. The following day eighteen men, including two law enforcement officers, are arrested. On February 25, United States District Court Judge W. Harold Cox dismisses a federal indictment against seventeen of the accused.

1965, January 18 • Washington, District of Columbia

Ruling on the case *Cox v. Louisiana* the United States Supreme Court reverses the conviction of protesters charged with disturbing the peace.

1965, February 1 • Selma, Alabama

Reverend Martin Luther King, Jr. and some 770 blacks are arrested during protest demonstrations. Dr. King remains in jail for four days before posting bond. During this time, more than 3,000 persons are arrested. On February 4, a federal district court bars the county board of registrars from administering a literacy test to

Nearly 250,000 people from across the nation gather near the Washington Monument to protest for civil rights.

voter applicants or from rejecting their application on petty technicalities.

1965, February 21 • New York City, New York
Malcolm X, a 39-year-old black nationalist leader and former member of the Black Muslim sect, is shot to death in the Audubon Ballroom as he is about to deliver an address before a rally of several hundred followers. Following the murder, Black Muslim headquarters in New York and San Francisco are burned, and most Muslim leaders are placed under heavy police guard.

Three blacks—Talmadge Hayer, Norman 3X Butler, and Thomas 15X Johnson—are later taken into custody, and charged with first-degree murder. The trio is convicted and sentenced to life imprisonment on March 10, 1966.

1965, March 26 • Washington, District of Columbia
President Lyndon Johnson announces the arrest of four Ku Klux Klan members in connection with the murder of Viola Gregg Liuzzo. Liuzzo, a 39-year-old white civil rights worker from Detroit, was slain on a Lowndes County highway during the Selma-to-Montgomery

Malcolm X addresses a Harlem rally in support of integration efforts in Birmingham, Alabama.

Freedom March. The President declares war on the Klan, calling it a "hooded society of bigots." Robert M. Shelton Jr., Imperial Wizard of the United Klans of America, Inc., answers the President's charges by branding him "a damn liar." On March 30, the House Un-American Activities Committee votes to open a full investigation of the activities of the Klan. The Committee chairman, a Louisiana Democrat, asserts that the Klan is committing "shocking crimes."

1965, July 13 • Washington, District of Columbia
Thurgood Marshall is nominated as Solicitor General of the United States, the first black person to hold this office.

1965, August 6 • Washington, District of Columbia
President Johnson signs the 1965 Voting Rights Act, providing for the registration by federal examiners of those black voters turned away by state officials.

1965, August 11 • Los Angeles, California
The arrest and alleged mistreatment of a black youth by white policemen sparks an orgy of looting, burning, and rioting in the predominantly black section of Watts. Thousands of National Guardsmen and state police are rushed in to quell the violence. The rioting, which lasts six days, claims the lives of thirty-five people and causes nearly 46 million dollars in property damage. On August 20, President Johnson denounces the Los Angeles rioters, comparing them to Ku Klux Klan extremists. He declares that the existence of legitimate grievances in Watts is no justification for lawlessness. "We cannot ... in one breath demand laws to protect the rights of all our citizens, and then turn our back ... and ... allow laws to be broken that protect the safety of our citizens."

1966, January 13 • Washington, District of Columbia
President Lyndon B. Johnson names Robert Weaver as head of the Department of Housing and Urban Development. Weaver is the first black appointed to serve in a presidential cabinet in United States history. Lisle Carter, also black, is named as an assistant secretary in the Department of Health, Education and Welfare. Constance Baker Motley, former NAACP lawyer and Borough President of Manhattan, becomes the first black woman to be named to a federal judgeship.

1966, February 7 • Lowndes County, Alabama
A federal court finds Lowndes County, Alabama guilty of "gross, systematic exclusion of members of the black

Dr. Martin Luther King, Jr. (front center) and his wife Coretta Scott King lead marchers from Selma to Montgomery, Alabama in support of civil rights.

race from jury duty." County officials are ordered to prepare a new jury list. Lowndes County is also ordered to desegregate its school system within two years, to close twenty-four "blacks only" schools, and to introduce remedial programs designed to close the educational gap between white and black students.

1966, February 23 • Washington, District of Columbia
The United States Supreme Court, in the case of *Brown v. Louisiana* reverses the convictions of five blacks charged with disturbing the peace when they refused to leave a whites-only reading room in a public library.

1966, March 25 • Washington, District of Columbia
The United States Supreme Court, in the case of *Harper v. Virginia State Board of Elections*, outlaws the use of poll taxes in state elections. The ruling upholds the Twenty-Fourth Amendment, which bars the use of such taxes in federal elections.

1966, June 6 • Tennessee
James Meredith is shot shortly after beginning a 220-mile voting rights pilgrimage from Memphis, Tennessee to Jackson, Mississippi. Aubrey James Norvell, 40, is

arrested at the scene and taken to jail where, according to authorities, he admits to the shooting. Meredith suffers multiple injuries, but recovers.

1966, June 26 • Jackson, Mississippi
The march begun by James Meredith ends with a rally in front of the state capitol in Jackson. Addresses are delivered by Meredith, Martin Luther King, Jr., and Stokely Carmichael, who urges the 15,000 blacks in attendance to "build a power base ... so strong that we will bring them [whites] to their knees every time they mess with us." The march results in the registration of about 4,000 black voters.

1966, July 10 • Chicago, Illinois
Martin Luther King, Jr. addresses a predominantly black crowd of 30,000 to 45,000 at Soldier Field and launches a drive to make Chicago an "open city." The rally is sponsored by the Coordinating Council of Committee Organizations, a coalition consisting of some forty-five local civil rights groups. From July 12-15, violence erupts on Chicago's west side in protest of a decision by Chicago police to shut off a fire hydrant which had been opened illegally to give black children relief from the

Thurgood Marshall (left) pictured with Senator Robert Kennedy.

stifling heat. Two blacks are killed, scores of police and civilians wounded, and 372 persons are arrested.

1966, July 18 • Cleveland, Ohio
Shootings, fire-bombings, and looting spread throughout Cleveland's east side. Four people are killed and fifty are injured. Most of the 164 persons arrested are charged with looting. The riot results in widespread property damage.

1967, January • Washington, District of Columbia
Representative Adam Clayton Powell, Jr. of New York is stripped of his chairmanship of the House Committee on Education and Labor, and barred from assuming his seat in the 90th Congress. A congressional committee investigating the case later proposes public censure, loss of seniority, and a $40,000 fine. Powell and his lawyers indicate their intention to challenge the constitutionality of this decision in federal court.

1967, February 15 • Washington, District of Columbia
President Johnson asks Congress to pass new civil rights legislation pertaining to the sale and rental of housing. In a special address to Congress, Johnson outlines the scope of the proposed bill. The bill, Johnson

states, is designed to end discrimination in jury selection, permit the Equal Employment Opportunity Commission to issue cease-and-desist orders, extend the life of the Commission on Civil Rights, and authorize 2.7 million dollars in appropriations for the Community Relations Service. The bill would enable individuals to file damage suits in housing discrimination cases. Violators of the bill would be subject to court orders and fines issued by the Secretary of Housing and Urban Development.

1967, March 1 • Washington, District of Columbia
By a vote of 307-116, the United States House of Representatives bars Adam Clayton Powell, Jr. from the 90th Congress. Powell immediately files suit in United States District Court to combat his ouster, asserting that he has met all citizenship, age, and residency requirements for House membership. The congressman also charges that his constituency is left without representation and, therefore, vulnerable to discrimination.

1967, March 29 • The Fifth Circuit Court of Appeals upholds the legality of revised federal school desegregation guidelines. The Court, in an 8-4 ruling, calls for the desegregation of all students, teachers, school transportation facilities, and school-related activities in six

An aerial view of the Watts area during the six days of rioting in 1965.

Southern states. The guidelines establish rough percentage goals to be used in determining compliance with the Civil Rights Act of 1964.

1967, May 3 • Montgomery, Alabama

A federal district court overturns an Alabama statute designed to prevent school desegregation. The court rules that no state may nullify the action of "a federal department or agency without initiating Court action" which only the United States Supreme Court can review.

1967, May 10 • Jackson, Mississippi

A black delivery man, Benjamin Brown, is shot and killed during riots on the campus of Jackson State College. Within full view of police, Brown is left at the scene unattended until he is taken to the University Hospital by black bystanders. The police, unable to contain the demonstrators, are reinforced by more than 1,000 National Guardsmen.

1967, June 2 • Boston, Massachusetts

Rioting erupts in Boston's predominantly black section

of Roxbury. The disturbance occurs in the wake of an attempt by welfare mothers to barricade themselves inside a building as a protest against police brutality. The rioting results in the arrest of nearly 100 people, while scores of others are severely injured.

1967, June 13 • Washington, District of Columbia
Thurgood Marshall is appointed an associate justice of the United States Supreme Court, the first black so designated.

1967, June 12 • Newark, New Jersey
The "long hot summer" begins in earnest in Newark, New Jersey, scene of the most devastating riot to sweep an urban center since the 1965 Watts uprising.

1967, June 19 • Washington, District of Columbia
United States District Court Judge J. Skelly Wright rules that *de facto* segregation of blacks in the District of Columbia is unconstitutional and orders the complete desegregation of the district's schools by the fall.

1967, June 27 • Buffalo, New York
Three days of rioting result in more than 85 injuries, 205 arrests, and property damage estimated at $100,000.

1967, July 19 • Washington, District of Columbia
The United States House of Representatives passes legislation which states that it is a federal crime to cross state lines or to use interstate facilities for the purpose of inciting a riot. The bill is aimed at alleged professional agitators who travel from city to city to inflame the people. New York's Emanuel Celler finds the bill "neither preventive nor curative," and fears it will only arouse black hostility even further.

1967, July 20 • Newark, New Jersey
Despite objections by New Jersey Governor Hughes, a four-day conclave of black leaders, many of them Black Power advocates, convenes in Newark. Militancy and a call for separate nationhood dominates the meeting. One participant at the conference, Alfred Black of the Newark Human Relations Commission, states that "the black today is either a radical or an Uncle Tom. There is no middle ground."

1967, July 22 • Detroit, Michigan
Rioting erupts in the morning hours of July 22. By July 29, over 7,000 persons are arrested and 43 persons killed.

1967, July 27 • Washington, District of Columbia
President Johnson appoints a blue-ribbon panel to "investigate the origins of the recent disorders in our cities." The President instructs the commission to set

aside political considerations and concern itself solely with the health and safety of American society and its citizens. On August 10, the National Advisory Commission on Civil Disorders urges President Johnson to increase the number of blacks in the Army and Air National Guard. The panel also recommends increased riot-control training for the Guard, as well as a review of promotion procedures. The recommendations, delivered in a letter to President Johnson, are forwarded to Defense Secretary Robert McNamara.

1967, August 14 • Dorchester County, Maryland
H. Rap Brown is indicted *in absentia* by a grand jury on charges of inciting to riot, arson, and other related actions which threaten the public peace. Brown is arrested in New York on August 19 and charged with carrying a gun across state lines while under indictment. After strenuous objections are voiced by his white lawyer, William Kunstler, Brown's bail is reduced to $15,000. On August 22, he is released from jail in time to address a crowd of 100 blacks on the steps of the Foley Square courthouse. Pointing to whites nearby, Brown says: "That's your enemy out there. And you better not forget, because I ain't going to."

1967, August 19 • New Haven, Connecticut
Nearly 450 persons are arrested during five days of looting, arson, and vandalism. No serious injuries are reported, and no shots are fired by police despite frequent curfew violations.

1967, October 20 • Philadelphia, Mississippi
An all-white federal jury of five men and seven women returns a guilty verdict in a retrial for the 1964 murder of three civil rights workers near Philadelphia, Mississippi. Seven men are convicted of conspiracy. However, eight defendants are acquitted, and three are declared victims of a mis-trial. Among the guilty are Chief Deputy Sheriff Cecil Price and Sam Bowers, Imperial Wizard of the Ku Klux Klan.

1968, February 5 • Orangeburg, South Carolina
Three black youths are shot to death and more than 30 people are wounded in a racial outburst involving police and students at South Carolina State College. The violence is the culmination of student protests against the segregation of a local bowling alley. On February 7, the campus is sealed off and classes are suspended in the wake of rock and bottle-throwing incidents. On February 8, three students are fired on by police who mistakenly believe one of their troopers has been shot. In reality, the trooper was knocked down by a piece of lumber thrown by a demonstrator. On February 9, Governor McNair orders a curfew and attributes the violence to "Black Power" advocates. On February 11,

Police and National Guardsmen arrest rioters in Newark.

local blacks call for the removal of the National Guard and announce plans for a boycott of white businesses. The city leaders counter by establishing a Human Relations Commission which resolves to prevent further outbreaks of violence. On February 24, the Southern Regional Council issues a report analyzing the Orangeburg upheaval. The report blames the outbreak of violence on the emotional appeal of black power to young blacks, overreaction by white citizens and police, feelings of hopelessness among blacks, and the expectations by whites that police power and military force must be utilized to cope with all forms of public demonstrations.

1968, February 29 • Washington, District of Columbia
President Johnson's National Advisory Commission on Civil Disorders issues an exhaustive report on the causes of the civil disorders that disrupted the nation in 1967. The commission identifies the major cause of the rioting as the existence of two separate bodies in America—"one black, one white, separate and unequal." It charges that white racism, more than anything else, was the chief catalyst in the already explosive mixture of discrimination, poverty, and frustration that ignited so many urban ghettos in the tragic summer of 1967. It reminds white America how deeply it is implicated in

the existence of the ghetto. "White institutions created it, white institutions maintain it, and white society condones it." To overcome this terrible and crushing legacy, the commission implores the nation to initiate a massive and sustained commitment to action and reform, and appeals for unprecedented levels of "funding and performance" in housing, education, employment, welfare, law enforcement, and the mass media.

1968, March 11 • Washington, District of Columbia
The United States Senate passes the Civil Rights Bill of 1968. Among its major provisions are sweeping housing and anti-riot measures which go far beyond the federal protection offered to civil rights workers in the 1967 House version of the bill.

1968, March 29 • Memphis, Tennessee
A teen-aged black youth is slain in Memphis after a protest march led by Dr. Martin Luther King, Jr. deteriorates into violence and looting. The march marks the culmination of six weeks of labor strike activity involving the sanitation workers of the city—90 percent of whom are black. Civil rights leaders and black ministers call for a boycott of downtown businesses and urge massive civil disobedience to express support for the

Numerous arson fires are evident in this photograph of the Detroit riot of 1967.

strikers. Such action broadens the thrust of the strike and transforms it into a general civil rights action. On the day of the march, disturbances begin almost immediately. Some black students who have been refused the right to leave school and participate in the march begin pelting police with bricks; others smash department store windows along Beale Street. However, most of the 6,000 to 20,000 marchers demonstrate peacefully. City and county police join the National Guard in quelling the disturbances. After Dr. King is spirited away to safety at the nearby Lorraine Motel, tear gas is fired at the crowds. More than 150 people are arrested, 40 of them on looting charges.

1968, April 4 • Memphis, Tennessee
The world is shocked by the assassination of Dr. Martin Luther King, Jr. Felled by a single bullet, Dr. King is pronounced dead at St. Joseph's Hospital at 7:05 P.M. CST, barely one hour after the shooting. Attorney General Ramsey Clark, on hand to conduct the preliminary investigation in person, declares that the early evidence points to the crime as being the work of a single assassin. Witnesses report seeing a white man running from the doorway of a rooming house at 420 South Main Street minutes after the shooting. The killing triggers a

wave of violence in over 100 cities, including such urban centers as Baltimore, Chicago, Kansas City, Missouri, and Washington, DC. Some 70,000 federal troops and National Guardsmen are dispatched to restore order. Official figures report 46 dead: 41 blacks, five whites. Thousands are injured and arrested. On April 5, Reverend Ralph Abernathy is named to succeed King and discloses that Southern Christian Leadership Conference's first public gesture will be to lead the march King himself was planning. Three days later, Coretta Scott King takes her place in the front ranks of the marchers, locking arms with two of the 42,000 people on hand for the demonstration. King's body is put on public view at Ebenezer Baptist Church on April 6. He is buried at South View Cemetery on April 9 after funeral services are held at the church and a general memorial service is conducted at Morehouse College, his alma mater.

1968, April 10 • Washington, District of Columbia
The assassination of Dr. Martin Luther King, Jr. moves the United States House of Representatives to submit to President Johnson a Senate-passed civil rights bill prohibiting racial discrimination in the sale or rental of 80 percent of the nation's housing. Johnson signs the measure on April 11 and counsels the nation to stay on

President Lyndon Johnson signs a new civil rights bill in 1968.

the road to progress by recognizing "the process of law."

1968, May 11 • Washington, District of Columbia

On May 11, caravans of people representing the Poor People's Campaign begin arriving in Washington, DC. The Defense Department alerts "selected troop units" to help DC police in the event of violence. On Mother's Day, May 12, Coretta Scott King leads a march of welfare mothers from 20 cities and declares at a subsequent rally that she will try to enlist the support of all the nation's women "in a campaign of conscience." The next day, Ralph Abernathy, clad in blue denim and using carpenter's tools, presides at the christening of Resurrection City, the plywood shanty town erected within walking distance of the White House and the Capitol. Abernathy is able to report, as the campaign draws to a close, that certain gains have been recorded. The Department of Agriculture, for instance, agrees to "provide food to the neediest counties in this country." The United States Senate approves a bill to increase low-income housing construction and the OEO allocates 25 million dollars for expanded programs, including one encouraging participation from poor people.

1968, June 5 • Los Angeles, California

Senator Robert Kennedy, a champion of civil rights, is shot and killed moments after leaving a rally celebrating his victory over Eugene McCarthy in the California Democratic primary.

1968, June 8 • London

James Earl Ray, alleged assassin of Dr. Martin Luther King, Jr. is arrested.

1968, July 23 • Cleveland, Ohio

Racial violence erupts in Cleveland's Glenville district, resulting in the deaths of eleven persons, eight of them black, and three white policemen. Mayor Carl Stokes helps to restore order after a night of burning and looting which results in over a million dollars worth of property damage. Over 3,000 National Guardsmen are on the scene, but they are not widely utilized. Ahmed (Fred) Evans, a 37-year-old anti-poverty worker and head of the Black Nationalists of New Libya, is blamed for starting the disturbances. On June 26, Ahmed Evans is arraigned on three charges of first degree murder.

1968, July 27 • Washington, District of Columbia

The Kerner Commission releases preliminary findings

Coretta Scott King and her children lead the funeral procession for Dr. Martin Luther King, Jr.

that indicate a sharp rise in the number of blacks who accept urban riots as a justifiable or inevitable response to conditions prevailing in the nation's ghettos.

1968, August 7 • Miami, Florida
Two days of looting, fire bombing, and shooting in the black section of Miami culminate in Florida Governor Claude Kirk's decision to summon the National Guard to quell the disorders. Despite Ralph Abernathy's plea for an end to the violence, crowds of blacks battle police over an eight-block area. On August 8, three blacks are killed in gun battles with law enforcement officials. Although Dade County Mayor Chuck Hall accuses outsiders of instigating the trouble, the ten percent unemployment rate among blacks in the 16-22 age bracket is cited as a major factor contributing to the violence.

1968, September 8 • California
Black Panther Huey P. Newton is tried and convicted of manslaughter in the October 28, 1967, shooting death of a white policeman. Nearly three weeks later, Newton is sentenced to 2-15 years imprisonment. The trial and the conviction introduce the nation at large to a new and formidable Black Panthers.

1968, October 8 • Washington, District of Columbia
Some 250 blacks protest the fatal shooting of a black pedestrian by a policeman. Demonstrators set fires and block traffic until police reinforcements disperse them with tear gas. The policeman is eventually exonerated of all charges by a federal grand jury.

1968, December 1 • New Jersey
Three members of the Black Panthers are arrested on charges of carrying out a machine gun attack on a Jersey City police station on November 29. A Black Panther spokesman claims that a December 1 bombing of party headquarters in Newark is in response to the Jersey City attack. A police sergeant cites the arrest of seven Newark Panthers on November 28 as the cause of the precinct attack.

1969, January 3 • Washington, District of Columbia
After a long and bitter debate concerning his qualifications and conduct, the House of Representatives votes to seat Adam Clayton Powell, Jr. However, it fines him $25,000 for alleged misuse of payroll funds and travel allowances, and demotes him to freshman status by stripping him of his seniority rank.

Resurrection City.

1969, February 6 • Washington, District of Columbia
President Nixon appoints James Farmer as an assistant secretary of Health, Education and Welfare; Arthur Fletcher as an assistant secretary of Labor, and William Brown III, as chairman of the Equal Employment Opportunity Commission.

1969, June 6 • Houston, Texas
Testimony released in a federal court indicates that the telephones of Martin Luther King, Jr. and Elijah Muhammad were tapped by the FBI, despite the fact that President Johnson had ordered a halt to all wiretaps in 1965.

1969, June 16 • Washington, District of Columbia
The United States Supreme Court rules that the suspension of Representative Adam Clayton Powell, Jr., by the House of Representatives is unconstitutional.

1969, July 6 • New York City, New York
James Forman of the National Black Economic Development Conference receives a check for $15,000 from the Washington Square United Methodist Church. The church is the first predominantly white organization to support Forman's demand that American churches pay $500 million in reparations for helping to perpetuate slavery.

1969, August 1 • Washington, District of Columbia
The United States Justice Department files suit against the state of Georgia to end segregation in its schools. Governor Lester G. Maddox condemns the action as criminal and declares the state will "win the war against these tyrants."

1969, August 19 • California
Black Panther leader Bobby Seale is arrested for the May 19 murder of alleged Panther informer Alex Rackley in New Haven, Connecticut. Bobby Seale's defense attorney accuses the Justice Department of initiating a national campaign to intimidate and harass the Black Panther Party. Seale is later extradited to Connecticut.

1969, August 25 • Pittsburgh, Pennsylvania
Five construction sites are closed by several hundred black construction workers and members of the Black Construction Coalition to protest "discriminatory hiring practices." Four hundred angry white workers stage counter demonstrations on August 28 and 29 to protest the work stoppage.

1969, September 2 • Hartford, Connecticut
After a relatively quiet summer, the nation is stunned when Hartford becomes the scene of widespread civil disorders including fire bombings and sniping. Scores of people are placed under arrest, and a dusk-to-dawn curfew is imposed.

1969, September 23 • Washington, District of Columbia
Secretary of Labor George P. Schultz orders federally assisted construction projects in Philadelphia to follow the guidelines for minority hiring suggested in the so-called "Philadelphia Plan."

1969, October 29 • Washington, District of Columbia
Ruling in the case of *Alexander v. Holmes Board of Education*, the United States Supreme Court orders an end to all school segregation. The decision replaces the Warren Court's doctrine of "all deliberate speed," and is regarded as a setback for the Nixon administration.

1970, January 2 • Washington, District of Columbia
FBI director J. Edgar Hoover claims that, in 1969, there were over 100 attacks on police by "hate-type" black groups such as Black Panthers.

1970, January 03 • Mississippi
Governor John Bell Williams announces his intention to submit to the state legislature a proposal to authorize income tax credits of up to $500 a year for contributors to "private" educational institutions. The plan is designed to create a "workable alternative" to school desegregation. That same day, the Department of Health, Education, and Welfare reports that a comprehensive survey indicates that 61 percent of the nation's black students and 65.6 percent of its white students attended segregated schools in 1968. On January 5, black children are enrolled in three formerly all-white Mississippi districts under the watchful eyes of federal marshals and Justice Department officials. Scores of white parents picket the schools, while others keep their children home or send them to private schools.

1970, January 10 • Georgia
Four southern governors, Maddox of Georgia, Brewer of Alabama, McKeithen of Louisiana, and Kirk of Florida, promise to reject all busing plans designed for their states by the federal government or the courts. Maddox asks the state legislature to abolish compulsory attendance; McKeithen reveals no plan, but describes himself as "drawing the line in the dust;" Brewer denies that the courts have the constitutional authority to order busing as a device to achieve racial balance and promises to use his full executive powers to prevent it; Kirk vows to issue an executive order to block further desegregation of Florida schools.

1970, January 12 • Washington, District of Columbia
The United States Supreme Court refuses to review the ruling of an Ohio state court which upholds an equal

employment plan comparable to the Nixon administration's "Philadelphia Plan." The plan requires state contractors to give assurances that they will employ a specified number of black workers in projects constructed with federal funds or sponsored completely by the federal government. The Ohio contractor who brought suit in the case had refused to provide such assurances.

1970, January 15 • Though it is not yet a national holiday, the birthday of Martin Luther King, Jr. is celebrated with impressive ceremonies, eulogies, and church services in many parts of the country. Public schools are closed in many cities; in others, they are kept open for formal study of Dr. King's life and work. In Atlanta, Coretta Scott King dedicates the Martin Luther King, Jr. Memorial Center, which includes his home, the Ebenezer Baptist Church, and the crypt housing his remains.

1970, January 19 • Washington, District of Columbia
G. Harrold Carswell's nomination to the United States Supreme Court draws the immediate fire of civil rights advocates. On January 21, the National Association for the Advancement of Colored People condemns Carswell's "pro-segregation record." Two days later, the Southern Christian Leadership Conference's Ralph Abernathy sends a telegram to Senate leaders pleading for "reassurance to the black community that there is... understanding and support... for our needs." AFL-CIO President George Meany calls the appointment "a slap in the face to the nation's black citizens." Testifying before the Senate Judiciary Committee on January 27, Carswell states: "I am not a racist. I have no notions, secretive or otherwise, of racial superiority." This statement contrasts sharply with a 1948 remark that Carswell would yield to no man "in the firm, vigorous belief in the principles of white supremacy."

1970, February 6 • Denver, Colorado
Approximately one-third of Denver school buses are destroyed by bombs in an attempt by segregationists to disrupt the city's school integration plans.

1970, February 16 • Washington, District of Columbia
President Nixon establishes a cabinet-level task force to assist and counsel local school districts which have been ordered to desegregate their schools immediately. The objective is to spare the public school system undue disruption while, at the same time, insuring compliance with the law. On February 18 the Senate passes, by a 56-36 vote, an amendment to deny federal funds to school districts whose racial imbalance is the result of residential segregation. On February 19, southerners in the House and Senate incorporate, into two appropriation bills, riders designed to restore "freedom-of-choice" school plans and to prevent the federal government

from resorting to busing as a vehicle to promote racial balance.

1970, February 21 • Texas
Texas Governor Preston Smith recommends a statewide referendum to give voters the opportunity to approve or reject integrated public school busing. Governors Maddox of Georgia and McKeithen of Louisiana sign bills prohibiting busing and student/teacher transfers to achieve racial balance. Governor Brewer calls a special session of the legislature to sponsor a similar bill for Alabama.

1970, February 28 • Washington, District of Columbia
A memo written by Daniel Patrick Moynihan to President Nixon is revealed. In the memo, Moynihan, domestic advisor to the President, counseled him that "the time may have come when the issue of race could benefit from a period of benign neglect." Moynihan later claims that the memo was intended to suggest ways that the "extraordinary black progress" in the last decade could be "consolidated." However, black leaders including Bayard Rustin and Representative John Conyers, charge that the memo is "symptomatic of a calculated, aggressive, systematic effort of the Nixon administration to wipe out civil rights progress of the past twenty years."

1970, March 6 • Mississippi
The state Senate approves a tax relief bill designed to grant financial support to white parents who intend to enroll their children in private academies.

1970, March 9 • Washington, District of Columbia
The United States Supreme Court orders the Memphis school system to end racial segregation and remands the case to a lower court where it issues instructions to develop an effective desegregation plan.

1970, April 7 • Detroit, Michigan
The school board approves a busing plan for some 3,000 high school students and announces the initiation of a decentralization plan aimed at dispersing white students among the city's secondary schools. In Detroit, 63 percent of the system's 294,000 students are nonwhite, as are 42 percent of the teachers.

1970, May 12 • Augusta, Georgia
Six blacks are shot and twenty other people are wounded during a night of violence punctuated by looting, burning, and sniper activity. The immediate cause of the violence is said to be the killing of a black youth in a county jail a few days earlier. Autopsies of blacks slain during the protests indicate that they were shot in the

Protesters against forced busing.

back. The *New York Times* later reports that at least three of the dead were unarmed bystanders.

1970, May 14 • Jackson, Mississippi

Two black students are shot and killed after a night of violence outside a women's dormitory at Jackson State College. Witnesses charge that police simply moved in and indiscriminately blasted the residence hall with shotguns. President Nixon dispatches Justice Department officials to search out the facts, but contradictory explanations make it impossible to assemble a wholly coherent story. On May 17, the Mississippi United Front vows to provide students and other groups with independent protection.

1970, May 23 • Atlanta, Georgia

A five-day, 100-mile march against repression ends in downtown Atlanta with a rally by the Southern Christian Leadership Conference and the National Association for the Advancement of Colored People. Speakers at the rally include Ralph Abernathy, Coretta Scott King, and Senator George McGovern. The speakers condemn racism, the Vietnam War, student killings at Kent State and Jackson State, and alleged police brutality in Augusta.

1970, July 10 • Washington, District of Columbia

The Internal Revenue Service announces its intention to tax private academies practicing racial discrimination in their admissions policies. The greatest impact of the policy is expected to be felt in the South. The new policy promises these schools sufficient flexibility to avoid immediate revocation of their tax-exempt status.

1970, August 7 • San Rafael, California

A dramatic shootout results in the death of Superior Court Judge Harold Haley and three blacks on trial. Later investigation traces the sale of the weapons used in the shootout to Angela Davis, controversial UCLA professor and self-admitted Communist. Davis flees the state following the trial and is placed on the FBI's 10 most-wanted list.

1970, September • Some 300,000 black children are

integrated in over 200 southern school districts. However, parental boycotts and delaying tactics by states and cities slow the pace of desegregation. Whites who are opposed to desegregation are encouraged by the Nixon administration's "southern policy" which has delayed enforcement of integration orders. Nevertheless, the Internal Revenue Service continues to revoke the tax exempt status of all-white private academies that refuse to admit black students.

1970, October 13 • New York City, New York

Angela Davis is arrested and arraigned in federal court on charges of unlawful flight to avoid prosecution for her alleged role in the August 7th killing of Superior Court Judge Harold Haley.

1970, November 5 • Henderson, North Carolina

Violence erupts when blacks protest the reopening of a segregated school. The National Guard is called out to restore order and over 100 arrests are made.

1970, December 30 • Philadelphia, Pennsylvania

The United States Court of Appeals for the Third Circuit

rules that the Department of Housing and Urban Development must promote fair housing when it considers applications for mortgage insurance and rent supplements.

1971, February 4 • Washington, District of Columbia
Eight black federal employees file suit in federal court claiming that the Federal Service Entrance Examination, the principal test for qualifying college graduates for civil service posts is "culturally and racially discriminatory."

1971, March 8 • Media, Pennsylvania
Files stolen from a Federal Bureau of Investigation (FBI) office and released to the press reveal that in November 1970, J. Edgar Hoover ordered an investigation of all groups "organized to project the demands of black [college] students, because they posed a threat to the nation's stability and security."

1971, March 29 • Washington, District of Columbia
President Nixon meets with the Congressional Black Caucus, which had been trying to schedule a meeting with him for several months. The black members of Congress request increased attention to welfare services, desegregation, housing, and social justice programs. President Nixon reportedly promises stronger enforcement of civil rights laws.

1971, May 5 • Brooklyn, New York
A riot erupts in the Brooklyn's Brownsville section after thousands of residents take to the streets to protest cuts in state welfare, Medicaid, food stamps, and educational programs. One policeman is shot, 12 are injured.

1971, May 17 • Washington, District of Columbia
Senator McGovern of South Dakota urges the government to divert $31 billion of current federal spending in an effort to end racial discrimination by the end of the century. Dr. Milton Eisenhower, former chairman of President Johnson's Commission on Causes and Preventions of Violence, warns that the United States faces a racial war if it does not remedy the social injustice, inequitable law enforcement, and the availability of firearms in American society.

1971, June 1 • Washington, District of Columbia
By a vote of 5 to 4, the United States Supreme Court declares unconstitutional a Cincinnati city ordinance making it unlawful for small groups of people to loiter in an annoying manner in public places. Many blacks claimed that such ordinances had been used by police to harass them.

1971, June 04 • Washington, District of Columbia
The Department of Labor announces that it is removing

support from the voluntary "Chicago Plan," which was to hire 4,000 blacks and Spanish-speaking Americans for construction jobs on federal projects. After 18 months, less than 900 blacks had been accepted in training programs and only a few had been admitted to Chicago construction unions.

1971, June 28 • Washington, District of Columbia
By an 8 to 0 vote, with Justice Thurgood Marshall abstaining, the United States Supreme Court overturns draft evasion charges against Muhammad Ali. In its decision, the Court agreed that Ali, a Muslim, was objecting to military service on religious grounds, rather than on a political basis, as the Department of Justice had charged.

1971, July 24 • Columbus, Georgia
Fifteen blacks are arrested and several hospitalized during racial disturbances following the dismissal of eight black policemen. Fire bombings and sniping are reported. State troopers are summoned to maintain order.

1971, August 07 • Georgia
State Representative Julian Bond tours the state to spark the political interests of blacks who remain unregistered six years after the passage of the Voting Rights Act. Bond notes that due to a blend of apathy and activism, many blacks do not perceive the ballot as an effective political weapon that can be used to bring a change in their lives. Bond cites as an example the failure of blacks in 1970 to elect black officials in a district where they represented a majority of the registered voters. Nevertheless, leaders of the Southern Christian Leadership Conference announce that their goal of electing a southern black to Congress is feasible in view of the redistricting in a number of southern states.

1971, August 18 • Jackson, Mississippi
Eleven members of the Republic of New Africa, a black separatist organization, are charged with murder and assault of federal officers after the death of Lieutenant I. Skinner, a Mississippi policeman. Skinner was shot when police and FBI agents raided the organization's headquarters in order to serve fugitive warrants on three members. The county district attorney requests that a special grand jury charge the separatists with treason and that the Justice Department allow these charges to take precedence over any federal prosecution.

1971, August 21 • San Quentin, California
George Jackson, author of *Soledad Brothers* and a folk hero to many black and white radicals, is killed during a prison break. Some supporters of Jackson claim he was

"set-up" for assassination, while others feel the official version of Jackson's death is essentially correct.

1971, October • Chicago, Illinois
"Black Expo," a four-day cultural and business exposition, attracts some 800,000 people. The exposition is conducted by Jesse Jackson and a number of black businessmen.

1972, January 10 • Richmond, Virginia
A federal judge orders the consolidation of Richmond's predominantly black school system with two all-white suburban systems. Judge Robert Mehirge bases his decision on the failure of state officials to take positive action to reverse *de facto* segregation.

1972, January 10 • Baton Rouge, Louisiana
Two Black Muslims and two white police officers are killed in a shootout. Disturbances following the shootings injure thirty-one people and the National Guard is called in to restore order.

1972, March • Gary, Indiana
Some 8,000 blacks, representing a wide spectrum of political views, attend the first National Black Political Convention. The convention is chaired by Imamu Amiri Baraka, with Mayor Richard Hatcher of Gary, Indiana as the keynote speaker. The group approves a political platform, the "Black Agenda," which demands reparations, proportional congressional representation for blacks, an increase in federal spending to combat crime and drug trafficking, reduction of the military budget, and a guaranteed annual income of $6,500 for a family of four.

1972, March 16 • Washington, District of Columbia
President Nixon proposes a moratorium on all court-ordered busing until July 1973. Black members of Congress charge that the President is suggesting a return to "separate but equal" schools.

1972, June 4 • San Jose, California
After 13 hours of deliberation, a jury of 11 whites and one Mexican-American acquits Angela Davis of murder and other charges in connection with a 1970 courthouse shootout in San Rafael, California.

1972, June 6 • Richmond, Virginia
A United States Appeals Court, by a 5 to 1 vote, overturns a plan which would have required the busing of school children between Richmond and two nearly all-white suburbs.

1972, July 12 • Miami Beach, Florida
Senator George McGovern of South Dakota wins the

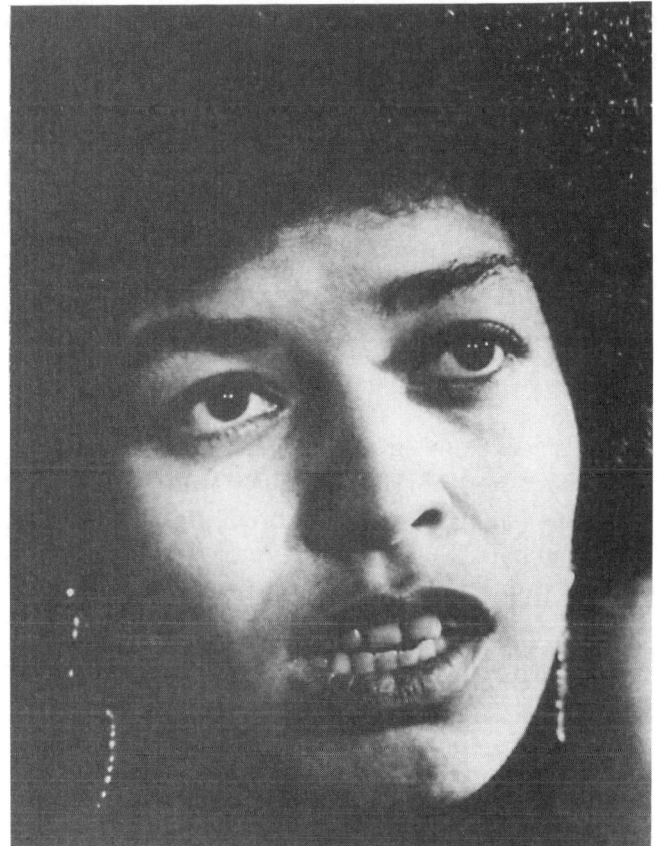

Angela Davis

presidential nomination at the Democratic Party's national convention. Black delegates make-up approximately 15 percent of the total delegates in attendance. New York Representative Shirley Chisholm, the first black woman to seek a presidential nomination, receives 151 votes.

1972, August • Washington, District of Columbia
Attorney General Richard Kleindienst files suit against the cities of Los Angeles, California and Montgomery, Alabama for discrimination in hiring for public service jobs.

1972, November • Cincinnati, Ohio
The Association for the Study of Black Life History, meeting for its fifty-seventh annual convention, changes its name to the Association for the Study of African American History. The change is based on a mail ballot of the Association's membership, some two-thirds of whom opt to substitute "African-American" for "black" in the title. Prominent speakers at the convention include: Andrew F. Brimmer, a governor of the Federal Reserve Board; Representative Louis Stokes of Cleveland; Dr. John Hope Franklin, professor of history at

Duke University; and Dr. Rayford W. Logan, professor of history at Howard University.

1972, November • Richard Nixon is reelected president in a landslide victory over Senator George McGovern, despite the fact that some 86 percent of the black vote went to McGovern. However, blacks achieve a number of electoral successes—the number of blacks in Congress increases from 12 to 15; Barbara Jordan of Houston, Texas and Andrew Young of Atlanta become the first Southern blacks elected to Congress since Reconstruction. Senator Edward Brooke, a black Republican from Massachusetts, wins reelection and black representation in state legislatures increases dramatically.

1972, November 16 • Baton Rouge, Louisiana
Two young black men, Denver A. Smith and Leonard Douglas Brown, are killed on the campus of Southern University during a confrontation between students and police. The students had been pressing for the resignation of the university's president, Dr. G. Leon Netterville, whom they charged with arbitrarily dismissing teachers he regarded as militant, and for being unreceptive to student demands for better living and academic facilities. Following the shootings, Louisiana Governor Edwin W. Edwards closes the school and sends the National Guard to the Baton Rouge campus.

1972, December 14 • Washington, District of Columbia
The United States Supreme Court, in the case of *Banks v. Perks*, rules unanimously that residents of racially segregated housing projects can sue to have them integrated. In its opinion, the Court states that white residents living in segregated housing projects suffer the same social and economic injuries as those denied access to these facilities.

1973, April 28 • Washington, District of Columbia
A government panel releases its final report determining whether the Tuskegee Syphilis Study, conducted between 1932 and 1972 by the Public Health Service, was justified. The study involved observing the effects of untreated syphilis on 430 black men living in rural Macon County, Alabama. The panel found no evidence that participants in the study had been given any type of informed consent. The panel concluded that the study was unjustified on both scientific and humanitarian grounds and that all policies regarding research on humans be reformed.

1973, May 29 • Los Angeles, California
Thomas Bradley is elected mayor of Los Angeles after defeating the incumbent Sam Yorty by 100,000 votes. Yorty had defeated Bradley in the 1969 mayoral election.

Shirley Chisholm

1973, June • Washington, District of Columbia
The Joint Center for Political Studies reports that as of April 1973, 2,621 blacks held elective offices in the United States at every level from school boards to the Congress. When the first list was compiled, in 1969, the total was only 1,185.

1974, March • Washington, District of Columbia
The Department of Justice releases memos revealing that in the 1960s and early 1970s, the Federal Bureau of Investigation had waged a campaign designed to disrupt, discredit, and neutralize black nationalist groups, including the Black Panther Party. A major objective of the effort, according to the memo, was to prevent the emergence of a black leader capable of uniting disparate factions and inspiring violence. Reverend Jesse Jackson remarks that the documents implicate the FBI in the deaths of the Reverend Dr. Martin Luther King, Jr., Malcolm X, and Fred Hampton.

1974, March 15 • Little Rock, Arkansas
The second Black National Political Convention is held. Mayor Richard B. Hatcher of Gary, Indiana and Imamu Amiri Baraka are among the speakers. Delegates to the convention approve several resolutions including the establishment of a fund to provide money for civil rights causes and a resolution voicing support for African liberation movements.

1974, June • Washington, District of Columbia
A draft report from the Senate committee investigating

the "Watergate" scandal indicates that the Nixon administration tried to gain the support or neutrality of prominent blacks during the 1972 presidential campaign by withholding federal funds for government programs. Among those contacted by the Nixon administration were Reverend Jesse Jackson, head of Operation PUSH, and James Farmer, an administration official during Nixon's first term.

1974, July 25 • Washington, District of Columbia
The United States Supreme Court, in the case of *Milliken v. Bradley*, nullifies an attempt to implement the "metropolitan integration" of predominantly black schools in Detroit with those of nearby white suburbs. Chief Justice Warren Burger, writing for the majority, declares that segregation in a city's schools does not justify its combination with schools in its suburbs. Justice Thurgood Marshall calls the Court's decision "an emasculation of the constitutional guarantee of equal opportunity."

1974, November • The number of black elected officials increases at the federal, state, and local levels. Black members of Congress are reelected and one new member, Harold Ford of Memphis, Tennessee is added. Blacks are also elected to the post of lieutenant governor in California and Colorado.

1974, December 11 • Boston, Massachusetts
Violence erupts between supporters and opponents of public school integration.

1975, January 16 • Washington, District of Columbia
William T. Coleman is named Secretary of Transportation by President Ford, becoming the second black in the nation's history to hold a cabinet post.

1975, January 25 • The *New York Times* reports that the Federal Bureau of Investigation had wiretapped conversations of civil rights leaders, including Dr. Martin Luther King, Jr.

1975, May 3 • Department of Labor figures report the national unemployment rate at 9 percent, the black rate at fifteen percent. Vernon L. Jordan, Jr. of the National Urban League reports that the black rate is actually 26 percent.

1975, August 18 • Washington, District of Columbia
District of Columbia Appellate Court Judge Julia Cooper is confirmed by the Senate, becoming the highest ranking black woman in the federal courts.

1975, August 20 • Washington, District of Columbia
Senator Edward Brooke calls for a $10 billion federal employment program to end the economic "depression" in black America by creating one million public service jobs.

1975, August 29 • Washington, District of Columbia
General Daniel James, Jr., becomes commander-in-chief of the North American Air Defense Command (NORAD). On the same day, he is promoted and becomes the first black four-star general in United States history.

1975, September 27 • Washington, District of Columbia
The Congressional Black Caucus holds its fifth annual dinner. The major theme of the affair is "From Changing Structures to Using Structure—1879-1976." Panelists recommend the federal takeover of the welfare system and poverty assistance, that the states assume more fiscal responsibility for education, and that Caucus-directed programs develop a national black position on matters of policy.

1975, December • Washington, District of Columbia
United States Attorney General Edward Levy opens an official review of the Martin Luther King, Jr. assassination. Although James Earl Ray was convicted of the crime, many facts point to a conspiracy and suggest that those really responsible for the murder are still at large.

1976, April 26 • New York City, New York
The Metropolitan Applied Research Center, a major black research organization founded to serve as an advocate for the urban poor, announces that it must close due to declining funds.

1976, August 31 • Mississippi
A chancellery court orders the National Association for the Advancement of Colored People to pay the sum of $1,250,058 to twelve white Port Gibson merchants. The money is compensation for the financial hardships inflicted on the merchants due to the NAACP's successful boycott of white businesses in 1966.

1976, November 2 • Black voters play a vital role in Jimmy Carter's victory over President Gerald Ford in the presidential election. Carter received about 94 percent of some 6.6 million black votes.

1976, November 14 • Plains, Georgia
The congregation of President-elect Jimmy Carter's Baptist church votes to drop its eleven-year ban on attendance by blacks.

1976, December 16 • Washington, District of Columbia
President-elect Jimmy Carter appoints Andrew Young as chief delegate to the United Nations and Patricia

Roberts Harris as Secretary of the Department of Housing and Urban Development.

1977, January 20 • Washington, District of Columbia
Clifford Alexander, Jr. is sworn in as the first black Secretary of the Army. President Carter appoints nineteen blacks to his cabinet, while thirty-seven other blacks obtain executive positions within the Carter administration.

1977, April 19 • New York City, New York
Author Alex Haley receives a Pulitzer Prize for his book *Roots.*

1977, July 29 • St. Louis, Missouri
Roy Wilkins, a 42-year veteran of the National Association for the Advancement of Colored People, announces his retirement during the organization's sixty-eighth annual convention.

1977, September 4 • New York City, New York
At a meeting of the National Urban League, fifteen black members agree to form a loose coalition of members who will work to combat perceived anti-black sentiment within the nation and seek greater job opportunities for blacks.

1978, January 17 • Major Guion S. Bluford, Jr., Major Frederick D. Gregory, and Dr. Ronald E. McNair join the space program and begin training as astronauts for future space missions.

1978, May 29 • Washington, District of Columbia
Files made public by the FBI reveal that an unidentified black leader worked with the agency during the 1960s in an effort to remove Dr. Martin Luther King, Jr. from national prominence in the civil rights movement. The information released is from the files of the late J. Edgar Hoover.

1978, June 28 • Washington, District of Columbia
Hearing the case *University of California v. Bakke*, the United States Supreme Court, in a 5 to 4 decision, orders that white student Allan P. Bakke be admitted to the medical school at The University of California, Davis. The Court rules that the refusal to admit Bakke is tantamount to reverse discrimination and that the use of racial or ethnic quotas is an improper means of achieving racial balance. The Court also holds that the college's affirmative action program is invalid since it had the effect of discriminating against qualified white applicants, although the Court perceived the goal of attaining a diverse student body constitutional and permissible.

1978, December 3 • The United States Census Bureau

reports that from 1960 to 1977, the number of blacks living in suburban areas increased from 2.4 million to 4.6 million, and that 55 percent of the 24.5 million blacks in the United States live in central cities, indicating a decline from the 1970 figure of 59 percent.

1979, February 27 • Washington, District of Columbia
The Department of Housing and Urban Development announces that it will foreclose on the financially troubled Soul City, a new town in rural North Carolina that was to have been controlled by blacks but open to members of all races. Since 1969, when Floyd B. McKissick announced the idea for the city, $27 million had been spent by federal, state, and local sources. McKissick vows to continue efforts to keep the project alive.

1979, May 2 • Washington, District of Columbia
The Congressional Black Caucus and delegates from eleven southern states set up an "action alert communications network." This network is designed to exert pressure on at least 100 white congressional representatives from predominantly black districts to vote with the Caucus on important issues.

1979, June 19 • The United States Census Bureau announces a study indicating that although black Americans have made enormous advances in employment, income, health, housing, political power, and other measures of social well-being, they remain far behind white Americans.

1979, June 25 • Washington, District of Columbia
Amalya L. Kearse becomes the first woman to receive an appointment to the United States Court of Appeals.

1979, June 29 • Washington, District of Columbia
The United States Supreme Court, in the case of *United States Steel v. Brian Weber*, rules that private employers can legally give special preference to black workers to eliminate "manifest racial imbalance" in traditionally white jobs.

1979, August 1 • Washington, District of Columbia
The United States House of Representatives votes 408 to 1 to place a bust of the late Dr. Martin Luther King, Jr. in the Capitol. The bust is the first work of art in the Capitol honoring a black American.

1979, August 16 • New York City, New York
Andrew Young resigns as the chief United States delegate to the United Nations after being publicly criticized for conducting unauthorized talks with the Palestine Liberation Organization in New York. The resignation

Demonstrators protest the Supreme Court's decision in the case of *University of California v. Bakke.*

sets off a storm of controversy and animosity between segments of the Jewish and black communities.

1979, December 22 • Washington, District of Columbia
The Joint Center for Political Studies reveals that between 1978 and 1979, the number of blacks elected to public office increased by 104. This two percent increase is considered meager, especially because such officials were elected in states with substantial black populations.

1980, February 6 • Washington, District of Columbia
The Congressional Black Caucus criticizes President Carter's fiscal 1981 budget proposals because they increase the amount of military spending while reducing the funding for social programs. Caucus members promise to initiate legislation to reduce military spending increases and pronounce the budget "an unmitigated disaster for the poor, the unemployed and minorities."

1980, April 22 • Washington, District of Columbia
Hearing the case *City of Mobile v. Bolden*, the United States Supreme Court, in a 6 to 3 decision, overturns a lower court ruling that an at-large city electoral system is unconstitutional because it dilutes the voting strength of blacks.

1980, May 11 • Washington, District of Columbia
Early primary results reveal that the black community is supporting President Carter's second-term bid despite criticism of his record by national black leaders, according to reports. The "resounding" victories won by Carter in the southern primaries are interpreted as blacks lacking faith in their ability to enact a "Great Society-style social renewal" agenda as proposed by Senator Edward M. Kennedy.

1980, May 14 • Birmingham, Alabama
J.B. Stoner, a white supremacist, is convicted for the 1958 bombing of a black church in Birmingham, Alabama.

1980, May 18 • Miami, Florida
The black Liberty City area and predominantly black Coconut Grove section of Miami erupt into riotous violence, ending with 9 dead and 163 injured, following the acquittal of four white Dade County police officers in the beating death of a black man. In the night-long unrest, stores are looted, property burned, and whites fatally beaten. During the violence, blacks are heard

screaming the name "McDuffie" (Arthur), the black insurance executive beaten to death following a high-speed chase with Dade County police officers for a traffic violation. Dade County officials impose an 8 p.m. to 6 a.m. curfew; 350 National Guard troops set up headquarters in an armory with 450 more enroute from Orlando.

1980, May 29 • Fort Wayne, Indiana
Vernon E. Jordan Jr., president of the National Urban League, is shot and seriously wounded by an unknown assailant. Stating that the shooting evidenced "an element of premeditation," William H. Webster, director of the Federal Bureau of Investigation, says, "the shooting was not accidental, and was in furtherance of an apparent conspiracy to deprive Vernon Jordan of his civil rights." The shooting occurred just outside Jordan's motel room.

1980, July 3 • Washington, District of Columbia
A ruling authorizing Congress to impose racial quotas to remedy past discrimination against minority contractors in federal jobs programs is upheld by the Supreme Court in 6 to 3 vote. It validates the 10 percent minority set-aside of federal public works contracts, challenged by white contractors in *Fullilove V. Klutznick*.

1980, July 3 • Cincinnati, Ohio
In a consent decree with the Justice Department, the city of Cincinnati agrees to hire and promote more blacks and women within the police department. The decree permanently enjoins the city from engaging in any employment discrimination. Over a five year period, 34 percent of new police officer vacancies will be filled by blacks and 23 percent by women. The Fire Department of the City of Chicago, in a similar action (April 2, 1980), was permanently prohibited from discrimination against any candidate for promotion on the basis of race or national origin. The settlement of this discrimination action was filed in federal district court and resulted from a suit charging violations of the Civil Rights Act of 1964 and the Federal Sharing Act of 1972. In New York, New York, the United States Court of Appeals (August 1, 1980) overturned a lower court ruling that 50 percent of all new police officer hirings be black and Hispanic. The Appeals Court, however, ruled that the written test used for hiring had "significant disparate racial impact" in violation of the Civil Rights Act of 1964. It concluded that until a new test was implemented, one-third of all newly hired police must be black or Hispanic.

1980, September 3 • St. Louis, Missouri
St. Louis schools are desegregated peacefully after eight years of struggle. Over 16,000 students are bused on the first day of classes under court ordered power. No violence is reported.

1980, September 26 • Detroit, Michigan
Federal district judge Horace W. Gilmore invalidates the 1980 census on the ground that it undercounts blacks and Hispanics, thus violating the one-person, one-vote principle. The action was precipitated by a suit initiated by the city of Detroit with support from dozens of other cities. The census was later upheld in higher courts.

1980, September 26 • Washington, District of Columbia
The Congressional Black Caucus marks its tenth anniversary with its annual legislative weekend. The group of bipartisan representatives cite as their major achievements the Humphrey-Hawkins Full Employment Bill and the 10 percent "minority-set-aside," law established to ensure minority firms a nearly representative share of federal contracts. The caucus identifies its current concern as the potential reapportionment of congressional districts affected by the outcome of the 1980 census.

1980, September 29 • New York City, New York
The Schomburg Center for Research in Black Culture opens a new $3.8 million building in Harlem.

1980, September 30 • Washington, District of Columbia
The first annual Black College Day is attended by 18,000 black students. Speeches on the preservation of black colleges and universities are given by black officials and student leaders. The march is organized by black journalist Tony Brown in an effort to draw public attention to the impact of integration and merging of black private and public colleges and universities. Brown contends seven out of ten blacks attending predominantly white colleges do not graduate.

1980, November 23 • Philadelphia, Pennsylvania
About 1,000 people from 25 states attend a convention and form the National Black Independent Party. The idea grows out of a National Black Political Assembly in Gary, Indiana in 1972.

1980, December 12 • Washington, District of Columbia
Black leaders of the nation's major civil rights organizations meet with President-elect Ronald Reagan, who says he will defend the civil rights of minorities. The leaders urge him to appoint a black to a cabinet position in his administration. Present at the meeting are Vernon E. Jordan, Jr., president of the National Urban League, Benjamin Hooks, executive director, National Association for the Advancement of Colored People, and Dorothy I. Height, president of the National Council of Negro Women.

Members of the Congressional Black Caucus, William Gray, Charles Rangel, Cardiss Collins, Walter Fauntroy, and Bennett Stewart, outside the United States Capitol, 1980.

1980, December 18 • San Antonio, Texas
A federal grand jury acquits Charles Veverka, thirty, of four counts of violating the civil rights of Arthur McDuffie, a black who was beaten to death while in police custody. The jury deliberates for 16 hours, finally breaking an 11 to 1 deadlock that threatened a mistrial. Veverka was indicted following violent riots in Miami resulting from the acquittal of four white police officers accused of executing the fatal beating.

1980, December 23 • Washington, District of Columbia
Samuel R. Pierce, Jr. is named by President-elect Ronald Reagan to the Cabinet post of Secretary of the Department of Housing and Urban Development. As such, Pierce is the highest ranking black appointee of the new administration. According to reports, Pierce is a life-long Republican, widely respected in legal, financial, and civil rights circles.

1981, February 7 • Miami, Florida
Three Miami youths are convicted of murder in connection with the beating deaths of three whites during the Liberty City riots in May 1980. A fourth youth, who was tried with the others, is acquitted. Attorneys for the defendants announce plans to appeal the verdicts.

1981, May 7 • Washington, District of Columbia
Representative Robert S. Walker, a Republican from Pennsylvania, introduces a bill which prohibits the use of numerical quotas devised to increase the hiring or school enrollment of minorities and women. Entitled the "Equal Employment Opportunity Act," it seeks to amend the Civil Rights Act of 1964 and prevents the federal government from imposing rules on employers or schools to hire workers or to admit students on the basis of race, sex, or national origin. In effect, the proposal no longer requires companies and educational institutions to make up for past discrimination by taking on a set number of minorities and women within a specified time frame.

1981, May 13 • Washington, District of Columbia
The Labor Department proposes revisions of Executive Order No. 11246 (prohibiting employment discrimination by federal contractors based on race, sex, color, national origin, or religion) in its continuing effort to ease job-discrimination rules for federal contractors.

Samuel R. Pierce

The contents of an internal memorandum reveal the effort seems targeted toward reducing the record-keeping and affirmative action requirements for small contractors and eliminating "unnecessary confrontations" with all contractors. Timothy Ryan, Labor Department solicitor, says that the revisions make the program more manageable and cut the number of companies covered by two-thirds for certain requirements. Secretary Raymond Donovan maintains that a final decision on revisions within the Office of Federal Contracts Compliance Programs has not been made. Administration officials plan to alter the proposal before its effective date of June 29.

1981, May 23 • Washington, District of Columbia
Calling them "ineffective" and unfair remedies to discrimination, Attorney General William French Smith announces that the Justice Department will no longer continue its vigorous pursuit of mandatory busing and the use of racial quotas in employment discrimination cases. It also considers amendments which would make "reverse discrimination" illegal under the Civil Rights Act of 1964.

1981, June 10 • Washington, District of Columbia
The House once again approves an anti-busing provision by a vote of 265 to 122, forbidding the Justice Department from taking any direct or indirect action to require the busing of students to schools other than those closest to where they live, with the exception of cases involving special education needs. The provision is known as an "anti-busing rider" because of its attachment to the Department's $2.3 billion authorized bill.

1981, June 16 • Washington, District of Columbia
The Reagan administration, in a letter to Attorney General William French Smith, requires the Justice Department to determine whether the political rights of minority Americans are best served by the Voting Rights Act of 1965. Stating that the act marks the nation's commitment to full equality for all Americans, the administration says that what must be answered is whether the Act continues to be the most appropriate means of guaranteeing their rights. The completed report is due October 1.

1981, September 9 • New York City, New York
Roy Wilkins, former head of the National Association for the Advancement of Colored People and one of the key players in the civil rights movement of the 1960s, dies at New York University Medical Center at the age of eighty.

1981, September 10 • New York City, New York
Vernon Jordan announces his plans to resign as executive director of the National Urban League and join the Dallas-based law firm of Akin, Grump, Hauer and Field. Jordan's office will be in Washington, DC.

1981, October 7 • Washington, District of Columbia
A House vote, 389 to 24, in favor of extending the Voting Rights Act of 1965, seems to ensure the likelihood of an equally strong measure in the Senate, according to Capitol Hill analysts. The House version makes the preclearance provisions of the act permanent (requiring six southern states and Alaska to submit proposed changes in election laws to the Justice Department before implementation), but also features the so-called bailout provision that exempts jurisdiction from the requirement if they can prove a clean 10-year voting rights record and efforts to encourage minority voting.

1981, November 28 • Washington, District of Columbia
The nomination of Clarence M. Pendleton, president of the Urban League of San Diego, to head the United States Commission on Civil Rights, results in divided opinion over his suitability for the post. Pendleton's selection is controversial because of his promotion of

private industry as a cure-all for black economic problems and because of his opposition to other positions taken traditionally by the civil rights movement on issues such as busing and affirmative action.

1981, December 8 • Washington, District of Columbia
William Bradford Reynolds, Assistant Attorney General of the Justice Department's civil rights division, announces plans to seek a ruling by the Supreme Court which would find it unconstitutional to give minorities and women preference in hiring and promotion. Reynolds wants a reversal of the high court's decision in *Weber v. Kaiser Aluminum and Chemical Corp.*, which upheld the legality of affirmative action hiring and promotion practices negotiated by the company and the United Steel Workers of America. Reynolds contends the *Weber* decision was "wrongly decided" and that different sets of rules for the public sector and the private sector should not exist. Under his direction, the Justice Department has ceased such hiring preferences; the action sought by Reynolds would prohibit individuals, the Labor Department, or the Equal Employment Opportunity Commission from seeking such preferences.

1982, January 2 • Los Angeles, California
Los Angeles Mayor Tom Bradley opens his campaign to become the first black governor of California. The sixty-four-year-old former policeman has been elected to the mayoralty three times.

1982, January 20 • Alabama
Two black civil rights workers, Julia Wilder and Maggie Bozeman, are charged with vote fraud.

1982, February 1 • New York City, New York
Representative Shirley Chisholm, a Democrat from New York and the first black woman to win a seat in Congress, announces that she will not seek another term. She has served the Brooklyn communities of Bedford-Stuyvesant and Bushwick since 1968.

1982, February 1 • Washington, District of Columbia
The Justice Department proposes that the City of Chicago be allowed to try to desegregate its schools following a plan that would rely mainly on voluntary student transfers rather than mandatory busing.

1982, February 6 • Alabama
A small band of southern civil rights workers, followed by 300 sympathizers, start a 140-mile march in support of the Federal Voting Rights Act and in protest against the vote fraud conviction of two black political activists. The marchers travel from Carrollton, Alabama through Selma to the state capitol, Montgomery, a route made famous in early civil rights marches.

1982, February 14 • Alabama
Hundreds of voting rights marchers going from Carrollton to Montgomery march peacefully across the Edmund Pettis Bridge.

1982, April 4 • Washington, District of Columbia
The Bureau of Census reports that the 1980 census missed counting 1.3 million blacks and that the undercount represented 4.8 percent of the nation's 28 million blacks. The Bureau says that in 1970 the census missed 1.9 million out of 24.4 million blacks.

1983, January 12 • Washington, District of Columbia
A majority of the United States Civil Rights Commission charges that the Reagan administration's Justice Department has been moving in the direction of getting judicial approval to end affirmative action. The two-and-a-half-page text issued by the majority asserts that cases in several cities, given the current position of the Justice Department, could result in continued discrimination. The committee's assertion is opposed by the chairman of the committee, Clarence Pendleton, a black Reagan appointee.

1983 • Washington, District of Columbia
A test case of the Justice Department to eliminate court-ordered busing to desegregate public schools is turned down by the United States Supreme Court. It was the contention of the Justice Department that a desegregation plan in Nashville, Tennessee was contributing to "white flight" from the city.

1983, April 13 • Chicago, Illinois
Harold Washington becomes the first black mayor of Chicago. Washington received 656,727 votes (51 percent), while his opponent, Bernard Epton received 617,159 votes (48 percent). The voting followed racial lines with 90 percent of the votes in black areas going to Washington, as well as some 44 percent of the vote in the city's white liberal areas.

1983, April 22 • Greensboro, North Carolina
After 29 months of investigation, a federal grand jury indicts six Ku Klux Klansmen and three members of the American Nazi Party in the deaths of five members of the Communist Workers Party who participated in a "Death-to-the-Klan" rally in Greensboro, North Carolina in 1979.

1983, May 18 • New York City, New York
Benjamin L. Hooks, executive director of the National Association for the Advancement of Colored People, is suspended indefinitely by the association's chairman, Margaret Bush Wilson. The controversy was said to

Harold Washington

have begun with Wilson's criticism of some internal aspects as to how well the organization was doing.

1983, May 25 • Washington, District of Columbia
In an 8 to 1 decision the Supreme Court rules that private schools which discriminate on the basis of race are not eligible for tax exemptions. The ruling in *Bob Jones University v. IRS*, rejects the Reagan administration's contention that because there is nothing in the Internal Revenue Service code banning such exemptions, they are permissible. The opinion, rendered by Chief Justice Warren E. Burger, stated that racial discrimination in education violates deeply and widely accepted views of elementary justice, and "that to grant tax exempt status to racially discriminatory educational entities would be incompatible with the concepts of tax exemption."

1983, May 26 • Washington, District of Columbia
President Ronald Reagan presents three nominees to replace three current members of the United States Commission on Civil Rights. If confirmed, the administration would have a majority of its appointees on the six-member commission. A storm of protest and controversy arises from civil rights groups and members of Congress accusing the President of efforts to pack the Commission. The three nominees are John H. Bunzel, Morris B. Abram, and Robert A. Destro. The commissioners to be replaced are Mary Frances Berry, Rabbi Murray Saltzman, and Blandina Cardenas Ramirez. However, lawyers from various private and governmental agencies indicated that the President probably does not have the legal authority to dismiss personnel who in effect are members of an independent bipartisan deliberative body with no powers. Jack Greenberg of the NAACP Legal Defense and Educational Fund stated that it was illegal for the President to do what he proposes and that the Fund would represent the Commissioners if they decided to mount a challenge.

1983, May 28 • New York City, New York
The National Association for the Advancement of Colored People's executive director Benjamin L. Hooks is reinstated to his post after an eight-day suspension by board chairman Margaret Bush Wilson. Wilson states that the objective of the action has been achieved and its continuance no longer serves a useful purpose.

1983, August • Washington, District of Columbia
Surveys in the state of Mississippi indicate a probability that enforcement of the Voting Rights Act will be extremely difficult in many counties. As a result, Assistant Attorney General William Bradford Reynolds announces that he will send 300 federal observers into the state to see that the Act is enforced. Many civil rights leaders believe the response to be totally inadequate and the Reverend Jesse Jackson believes that the planned observers are untrained and will be unable to see or understand many violations.

1983, October 20 • Washington, District of Columbia
By a vote of 78 to 22, action is completed in the Senate and the President signs into law a bill making the third Monday of each January a day honoring the memory of slain civil rights leader Dr. Martin Luther King, Jr. Initially opposed by President Ronald Reagan, many prominent Republican senators urged and got the President's support of the bill, thus insuring passage in the Senate. The bill had previously passed in the house by a margin of 338 to 90. Senator Jesse Helms (Republican, North Carolina) leads an effort to defeat the bill. Helms accuses King of "Marxist" ways. Helms also attempts to have controversial FBI tapes on Dr. King opened and made public in the hope that such disclosure would create public scandal. Senator Edward Kennedy (Democrat, Massachusetts) is outraged by Helms and asks for a renunciation of the Senator in the nation and in his home state.

1983, October 25 • Washington, District of Columbia
In a surprise move President Ronald Reagan fires three members from the United States Commission on Civil Rights because their views are critical of many aspects of the administration's policies in this area. Those fired were Mary Frances Berry, a professor of history and law at Howard University, Blandina Cardenas Ramirez of

Benjamin Hooks

Margaret Bush Wilson

San Antonio, and Rabbi Murray Saltzman of Baltimore; all highly regarded as effective spokespersons for minorities.

1983, November 10 • In general elections throughout the nation, blacks make some significant gains. Wilson Goode is elected mayor of Philadelphia, becoming that city's first black to serve in such capacity and making his city the fourth of the nation's six largest cities to have a black as chief executive. Other black winners are Democrat Harvey Gantt, who becomes the first black elected mayor of Charlotte, North Carolina; James A. Sharp, Jr., the first elected black mayor of Flint, Michigan; Thirman Milner wins a second term in Hartford, Connecticut; and Richard Hatcher wins a fifth term in Gary, Indiana.

1983, December 1 • Washington, District of Columbia In a supposed compromise bill President Ronald Reagan signs into law a newly reorganized United States Commission on Civil Rights comprised of four presidential and four congressional appointees. As the first of his appointments Reagan reappoints Clarence M. Pendleton, Jr. as chairman of the new commission.

1984, June 6 • Washington, District of Columbia Margaret Bush Wilson, former chairperson of the National Association for the Advancement of Colored People, loses the battle to get herself reinstated as a member of the association's governing board. Wilson was the first woman chairperson of the NAACP and had been a member of the national board of directors since 1963.

1984, June 13 • Washington, District of Columbia In a 6-3 decision the United States Supreme Court invalidated a United States District Court decision that allowed the layoff of three white firefighters who had seniority over three black firefighters. The Supreme Court decided that affirmative action employment gains are not preferential when jobs must be decreased and that "legitimate" seniority systems are protected from court intervention. However, a dissenting opinion by justices Blackmun, Brennan, and Marshall argued that under Title 7 of the Civil Rights Act of 1964, race related preferential practice was an acceptable application. As a result of the Court's decision, the Justice Department announces that it will reexamine all federal anti-discrimination settlements and will advise government agencies to not continue the practice of using racial employment quotas when negotiating affirmative action plans.

1984, July 6 • Washington, District of Columbia

Secret tapes of President John F. Kennedy are made public and demonstrate a sincere effort by Kennedy to get mayors, governors and congressmen to accept integration and support his civil rights programs. The recordings made during the Kennedy presidency also reveal a dramatic conversation with Dr. Martin Luther King, Jr. in which Dr. King, after a bombing in Birmingham, Alabama in which four children at a black church are killed, calls upon the President to send Federal troops into the city to help protect the black community and to prevent riots. In a conversation with mayor Allen Thompson of Jackson, Mississippi, the President urges him to hire black police officers. After the mayor assures the President that he will hire blacks, he said to Kennedy "don't get your feelings hurt" about public statements he may have to make about the President, to which Kennedy replies "well, listen I give you full permission to denounce me in public as long as you don't do it in private."

1984, November 14 • Washington, District of Columbia

The Supreme Court rules that redistricting plans and election laws that have discriminatory results are affirmed to be illegal under a provision of the 1982 Voting Rights Act. The ruling came as a result of a Mississippi redistricting plan.

1984, November 12 • Atlanta, Georgia

The Reverend Martin Luther King, Sr. dies of a heart ailment at the age of eighty-two. For forty-four years he had been pastor of the Ebenezer Baptist Church and was one of the South's most influential black clergymen.

1985, January 5 • South Africa

Senator Edward Kennedy visits South Africa at the invitation of Nobel Peace Prize recipient Bishop Desmond Tutu. Kennedy also visits Winnie Mandela, the wife of jailed black nationalist Nelson Mandela, but his request to meet with the imprisoned leader is refused by the government.

1985, February 21 • New York City, New York

As a cost-savings measure the National Association for the Advancement of Colored People will move from its headquarters in New York, New York to Baltimore, Maryland by 1986. The association is negotiating the purchase of a suitable building for $2 million in Baltimore after being unable to find a suitable and economically sound location in New York, New York that is not in conflict with their budget.

1985, February 26 • Washington, District of Columbia

The United States Commission on Civil Rights gives enthusiastic support to a Supreme Court decision giving existing seniority systems preference over affirmative action programs even though the blacks were hired to remedy previously contended discriminatory hiring practices. United States Civil Rights Commissioners Mary Frances Berry and Blandina Cardenas Ramirez, in heated disagreement with the Supreme Court and the Civil Rights Commission's report, state that civil rights laws are designed to protect blacks, minorities, and women, not white men. The statement creates new controversy as to the meaning of the existence of the Civil Rights Commission.

1985, March 7 • Washington, District of Columbia

Charging that the United States Commission on Civil Rights had already decided to oppose such measures as timetables and quotas, national civil rights groups boycott hearings on the use of such goals to achieve racial balance or to remedy discriminatory hiring practices.

1985, March 13 • Washington, District of Columbia

Clarence Pendleton, chairman of the United States Commission on Civil Rights, estimates that after the issue of preferential treatment is settled, the Civil Rights Commission should be abolished. Responsibility for civil rights, says Pendelton, should be in the hands of the Justice Department and the Equal Employment Opportunity Commission.

1985, May 1 • Washington, District of Columbia

A statue of Martin Luther King, Jr. is dedicated at the Washington Cathedral (Washington, DC) as a memorial to his comprehensive contributions and celebrated leadership in the struggle for civil rights.

1985, May 6 • Washington, District of Columbia

The federal government and the state of Maryland reach tentative agreement on a plan to desegregate the state's public colleges and universities. White enrollment at traditionally black colleges will be increased to 19 percent and black enrollment at predominantly white schools will reach 15 percent from 11 percent. The implementation of this plan is to take five years.

1985, August 2 • Washington, District of Columbia

Because of the policy of apartheid in South Africa, the U.S. House of Representatives gives final approval to a bill imposing economic sanctions against the South African government by a vote of 380 to 48. The Reagan administration remains opposed to the legislation.

1985, December 6 • Yonkers, New York

Stating that "discriminatory housing practices" on the

part of Yonkers, New York, were responsible for the segregation of blacks from whites in the city's schools, United States District Court Judge Leonard B. Sand indicated for the first time in school desegregation cases that a city's housing policies are inextricably linked to school segregation. Judge Sand held that since 1949 Yonkers public housing had been deliberately built in low income neighborhoods which had the effect of confining students to "inferior and racially unmixed schools." The Justice Department in 1980 charged the city of Yonkers with bias in housing and schools, and received from the city a tentative plan in 1984 to build public housing in predominantly white East Yonkers. The case could have landmark implications since busing had been the primary means for cities to comply with desegregation rulings.

1985, December 23 • Birmingham, Alabama
Federal District Judge Sam Pointer, Jr. dismisses a reverse discrimination suit instituted on behalf of 14 white firefighters in Birmingham, Alabama. It was claimed that the 14 whites were denied advancement because of a city hiring and promotion plan favoring less qualified blacks. Judge Pointer ruled that the city accepted the consent decree along with the Justice Department in 1981, and therefore the decree is valid; he also ruled that the firefighters failed to prove that the plan violated that agreement.

1986, January 11 • Richmond, Virginia
L. Douglas Wilder becomes the first black lieutenant governor of the state of Virginia. Wilder, the grandson of a slave, was a Bronze Star recipient in the Korean War and a former member of the state senate.

1986, January 20 • Dr. Martin Luther King, Jr.'s birthday, as a federal holiday, is observed for the first time.

1986, March 19 • Washington, District of Columbia
The Supreme Court in *Wygant v. Jackson Board of Education*, the first of three major affirmative action decisions, rules 5 to 4 that broad affirmative action plans including hiring goals are permissible if they are carefully tailored to remedy past discrimination. In a ruling involving teachers laid off in Jackson, Michigan, the court sends a mixed signal by deciding that public employers cannot give affirmative action plans as a substitute for seniority when reducing their work forces.

1986, June 16 • Norfolk, Virginia
The United States Supreme Court denies an injunction sought by black parents that would prevent the Norfolk, Virginia, school board from ending school busing to stem "white flight" from the city's public schools. Ac-

cording to the petition, the change would result in "a general resegregation of the public schools of the South."

1986, July 2 • Cleveland, Ohio
The United States Supreme Court ruling on an action regarding Cleveland printers and New York sheet-metal workers upholds the use of affirmative action plans designed to remedy past discrimination. The decision, *Sheet Metal Workers International v. EEOC*, rejects the Reagan administration's argument that only specific victims of discrimination are entitled to such relief.

1986, August 5 • Washington, District of Columbia
Black leaders representing major black organizations meet to urge the passage of legislation that would impose more stringent economic sanctions on South Africa.

1986, September 11 • South Africa
Coretta Scott King visits South Africa, meets with Archbishop Desmond Tutu, cancels a meeting with the prime minister, and later visits Winnie Mandela, wife of the imprisoned South African anti-apartheid leader.

1986, October 3 • Washington, District of Columbia
In an effort to win Senate support for his veto of a sanctions bill against South Africa for their apartheid policies, Ronald Reagan appoints a black career diplomat, Edward J. Perkins, to be the new American ambassador to that country. The bill had been overridden by a wide majority (313 to 83) in the House. The Senate, despite the appointment, votes with the House by a vote of 78 to 21 to override the veto.

1986, October 7 • Washington, District of Columbia
The thirty-two-year-old case of *Brown v. Board of Education of Topeka, Kansas* is reopened by the original plaintiff and others who maintain that the school district has failed to integrate fully its schools or to eradicate the remaining elements that permitted racial separation in the past. Richard Jones, the lawyer for the plaintiffs, says he will show that the school board approved boundaries that perpetuate racially separate schools and have allowed white parents to avoid compliance with desegregation efforts by offering school attendance alternatives.

1986, October 20 • Baltimore, Maryland
Four days of dedication ceremonies commence as the National Association for the Advancement of Colored People opens its new headquarters. The NAACP was founded in New York in 1909 and maintained its headquarters there until this move. There is official indication that the organization will begin new and diverse programs, including business development, in addition

Leon Sullivan, Coretta Scott King, Randall Robinson, Representatives Walter Fauntroy and William Gray meet to push for South African sanctions legislation.

to its more fundamental activities such as voter registration and protest demonstrations in its general goal of social and economic justice.

1986, November 4 • Norfolk, Virginia
The Supreme Court declines to review two school desegregation cases, one which allows the city of Norfolk to end its busing plan, and another that attempts to sanction the authority of the Oklahoma City School Board to end busing for students in grades one through four. It is speculated that some high court justices want to leave the lower courts with the means of interpreting law on a local and regional basis. In the Norfolk case, black parents had claimed that the lower court ruling ending busing would have the effect of reinstating school segregation.

1986, December 2 • Birmingham, Alabama
A federal district judge rejects the reverse discrimination suit of 14 white firefighters and another municipal employee of the city of Birmingham who allege they have been denied promotions in favor of blacks whom they consider less qualified. The judge rules that the plaintiffs have failed to show the city to be in violation of a 1981 consent decree signed with the Justice Department designed to encourage the hiring and promotion of blacks and minorities.

1986, December 21 • Queens, New York
Michael Griffith, a 23-year-old black man, is struck by an auto and killed while seeking safety from a white mob beating him with bats and fists. The incident occurred in the white community of Howard Beach, Queens. The whites were reported shouting, "Niggers, you don't belong here!" The black youths were in the neighborhood looking for a tow for their disabled car.

1987, January 7 • Washington, District of Columbia
New regulations are issued to strengthen the federal government's authority to reject changes in local election laws that have a discriminatory result. No longer does the legal process have to prove that the intent of the local law was to discriminate, it need only demonstrate that it could have a discriminatory result.

1987, February 11 • Queens, New York
In Howard Beach, three white teenagers who participated in a racial attack against three black youths are

charged with murder as a result of the death of one of the black youths who was killed by an auto along an adjacent parkway as he attempted to escape from his white attackers.

1987, April 5 • Washington, District of Columbia
Representative Charles Rangel (Democrat, New York) introduces two measures in Congress to have the late revolutionary civil rights leader Marcus Garvey exonerated of mail fraud charges of which he was convicted in 1924. The move by Rangel came after Robert Hill, editor of the Marcus Garvey papers project at the University of California at Los Angeles, discovered new evidence which could indicate that Garvey's conviction may have been politically motivated. In 1927 Garvey's sentence was commuted by President Calvin Coolidge after which he was deported to Jamaica, his place of birth.

1987, April 7 • Chicago, Illinois
Mayor Harold Washington wins re-election to a second four-year term and his supporters win control of the city council for the first time. Voting was along strong racial lines with Washington receiving 97 percent of the black vote cast, and his white opponent Edward R. Vrdolyak receiving 74 percent of the white vote. Hispanics cast 57 percent of their vote for Washington.

1987, April 18 • Los Angeles, California
Al Campanis, vice president of personnel for the Los Angeles Dodgers, is pressured to resign from his job after stating that blacks might not be qualified to be managers or hold executive positions in baseball. The remarks were made by Campanis on the ABC News program *Nightline*.

1987, April 25 • Fort Smith, Arkansas
A federal grand jury indicts ten white supremacists on charges of conspiring to assassinate federal officials including a judge, and to kill members of ethnic groups through bombings. Richard Girnt Butler, the leader of the Aryan Nations Church, was named in the indictment, along with nine others affiliated with the church and other white supremacist groups such as the Order and the Ku Klux Klan.

1987, May 3 • Washington, District of Columbia
Japanese Prime Minister Yasuhiro Nakasone meets with the Congressional Black Caucus and other black leaders after being accused of making racial slurs in a speech angering blacks and other ethnic groups. Following the meeting Nakasone agreed to pursue Japanese investments in minority-owned American banks, to exchange programs between Japanese colleges and black American colleges, and to locate Japanese companies in predominantly black areas.

1987, July 1 • Phoenix, Arizona
As a result of his decision to rescind state observance of Dr. Martin Luther King, Jr.'s birthday, Governor Evan Mecham (Republican) faces a citizens' effort to recall him as the governor of the state. The plan has strong state support from both parties and many Republicans wear "Recall Mecham" buttons.

1987, July 28 • Montgomery, Alabama
After 15 years a tentative settlement is reached between the Alabama State Police Department and the Justice Department. Accordingly there will be an increase in the number of blacks at various ranks on the force to as high as 25 percent over a three-year period. The department will promote 15 blacks to the rank of corporal in a month, and will eventually have blacks comprise 20 percent of its sergeants, 15 percent of its lieutenants, and 10 percent of its captains. Federal District Judge Myron Thompson, who originally ordered the police department to hire one black officer for every white officer hired, has to approve the suggested settlement.

1988, August 15 • Dallas, Texas
The predominantly black Bishop College, at one time the largest black college in the west, closes its doors, unable to pay creditors $20 million. Founded in 1881 in Marshall, Texas, Bishop moved to Dallas in 1961. In 1967 Bishop had an enrollment of 1,500; in 1987 its enrollment had dwindled to 300.

1988, August 26 • Boston, Massachusetts
In an effort to prevent a housing settlement between the city of Boston and the United States Department of Housing from being implemented, the National Association for the Advancement of Colored People files suit to have the agreement blocked, stating that a housing settlement, among other things, should include monetary compensation for people previously denied public housing because of their race and therefore forced to pay higher rentals. The Housing Authority of the City of Boston was the largest housing authority in the country to enter into a fair housing voluntary compliance agreement with the Federal Government.

1988, October 4 • Washington, District of Columbia
The General Accounting Office of the federal government makes public a report charging that the Equal Employment Opportunity Commission failed to properly investigate as many as 82 percent of the claims made regarding job discrimination filed with the Commission during a three-month period.

1988, November 26 • Chicago, Illinois
As tensions increase between Jews and blacks, the Reverend Jesse Jackson meets with Jewish leaders in an

Jesse Jackson greets voters during the 1988 presidential campaign.

effort to reduce the anger and heal the wounds. The Congregation Hakafa turns out to overflow capacity to hear Reverend Jackson deliver the evening sermon and say, "The sons and daughters of the Holocaust, and the sons and daughters of slavery, must find common ground again." The tension between Jews and blacks reached a zenith in May when Mayor Sawyer of Chicago was severely criticized for taking a week to condemn the anti-Jewish remarks made by Steve Cokley, an aide to the mayor. Underlying the problem is the political struggle for power in Chicago. In 1983, Jews gave Harold Washington almost 50 percent of their votes and helped give Chicago its first black mayor; in that race Washington defeated the white Republican candidate, Bernard Epton, who was Jewish.

1988, December 1 • Washington, District of Columbia Lieutenant General Colin Powell, President Reagan's national security advisor and the top black official in the administration, is nominated to become one of 10 four-star generals in the United States Army. Along with the rank goes the assignment to command all United States troops in the continental borders of the country and to be responsible for mainland defense. The new rank also puts General Powell in a strong position to become Chief of Staff as early as 1991 when the post becomes vacant with the retirement of General Carl E. Vuono. General Powell is credited with helping President Reagan's summit meetings in Moscow and Washington to become diplomatic successes.

1989, January 16 • Miami, Florida
Rioting erupts on the evening of January 16 in the predominantly black neighborhood of Overtown, following the killing of Anthony Lloyd, a 23-year-old black, by an Hispanic police officer. On January 18, Miami Mayor Xavier Suarez announces that an independent panel would be appointed to investigate the killing.

1989, January 23 • Decatur, Alabama
Six members of the Ku Klux Klan receive jail sentences and fines for their part in harassing blacks in a civil rights march conducted ten years earlier in Decatur, Alabama. The May 1979 march had been to protest the jailing of Tommy Lee Hines, a retarded black man convicted of raping three white women. Hines' 30-year jail sentence was overturned in 1980 and he was committed to a Montgomery mental hospital.

1989, January 23 • Washington, District of Columbia
Hearing the case *City of Richmond v. J.A. Croson Co.*, the Supreme Court strikes down a law in Richmond, Virginia which required 30 percent of public works funds to be channeled to minority-owned construction companies. The landmark decision was decried by minority leaders, hailed by anti-quota officials, and predicted to have national impact on affirmative action and set-aside programs. The "Richmond decision," which was written by Associate Justice Sandra Day O'Connor and carried by a 6 to 3 majority, said set-aside programs were only justified if they redressed "identified discrimination." O'Connor specifically suggested that "rigid numerical quotas" be avoided, in order to avoid racially motivated hirings of any kind. The ruling only pertains to the disposition of federal, state and local government contracts and does not affect affirmative action programs in private industry.

1989, January 26 • Richmond, Virginia
Lieutenant Governor L. Douglas Wilder announces his candidacy for governor of Virginia. If successful, he would become the nation's first black elected to a governorship.

1989, February 7 • The American Council on Education reports that the number of black men attending college is declining. In 1976, 470,000 black males were

enrolled in college. Ten years later, that number dropped to 436,000. Meanwhile the number of black female students grew during the same period, from 563,000 in 1976 to 645,000 in 1986. Reasons for the decline of black male collegians were military enrollment, prohibitive college costs, "school phobia" and the seduction of crime or drugs.

1989, February 10 • Washington, District of Columbia
Washington lawyer Ronald H. Brown, who held high-level positions in the presidential campaigns of Senator Ted Kennedy and Reverend Jesse Jackson, is elected chairman of the Democratic National Committee. The election of Brown marks the first time a black has been chosen to lead a major American political party.

1989, February 10 • Washington, District of Columbia
FBI Director William Sessions orders sweeping changes in the Bureau's affirmative action program after finding that the bureau had discriminated against minority employees. Black and Hispanic agents were immediately placed on lists for promotions. Sessions then ordered that FBI employees receive training in racial sensitivity, and that the equal employment office budget be increased. Ironically, the FBI is the agency charged with enforcing the nation's civil rights laws.

1989, February 10 • Washington, District of Columbia
Dr. Louis W. Sullivan, on sabbatical leave as president of Morehouse School of Medicine in Georgia, becomes Secretary of the Department of Health and Human Services. He is the only black selected in the first round of Cabinet posts in the Bush administration.

1989, March • Washington, District of Columbia
Statistics show that the nation's capital has already taken the lead for having the highest homicide rate in the country. Local police figures show the homicide rate as 55.1 percent higher than the same time in 1988. Figures from the District of Columbia Office of Criminal Justice said 80 percent of the time, the motive for the murders was related to drug activity.

1989, April • Los Angeles, California
Mayor Tom Bradley wins re-election to a fifth term by a total of 157,000 votes.

1989, April 21 • New Orleans, Louisiana
The nation's first nonpartisan African American summit convenes April 21-23. Its purpose is to discuss "an African American agenda for the next four years and onto the year 2000," said general chairman and Democratic party leader Richard Hatcher. More than 4,000 delegates from the United States, the District of Columbia and the Virgin Islands were invited.

1989, March 6 • Washington, District of Columbia
The United States Supreme Court declares a second affirmative action plan unconstitutional in the case *Milliken v. Michigan Road Builders Association*. The Michigan law required that seven percent of state contracts be awarded to minority-owned businesses.

1989, March 7 • Washington, District of Columbia
A student "sit-in" at Howard University results in the resignation of Republican National Committee Chairman Lee Atwater from the university's board of trustees four days following his appointment. The students claim that Atwater's stand on civil rights is the cause for the protest.

1989, June 5, 12 • Washington, District of Columbia
In the case *Wards Cove Packing Company v. Antonio*, the United States Supreme Court toughens the requirements for proof of discriminatory impact in job discrimination suits. The Court also declared that in such cases, an employer might justify policies which have a discriminatory impact by providing a reasonable business explanation. In a second case, *Martin v. Wilks*, the Supreme Court rules by a 5 to 4 majority that white workers claiming unfair treatment due to affirmative action settlements can seek compensation under civil rights legislation. The case involved white fire fighters in Birmingham, Alabama who claimed that affirmative action had deprived them of promotions. Civil rights leaders call the decisions a civil rights setback.

1989, July 2 • Washington, District of Columbia
The Reverend George A. Stallings, Jr. conducts the first Mass since the founding of the Imani Temple African American Catholic Congregation

1989, August 6 • Washington, District of Columbia
The National Urban League holds its annual conference. Addressing the conference, President George Bush remarks that he will not strive for stronger affirmative action legislation. He claims that the 1990s will see a surplus of available jobs and a shrinking worker pool.

1989, August 23 • Brooklyn, New York
Yusuf K. Hawkins, a black youth, is fatally shot by five white youths in Brooklyn's predominantly white Bensonhurst section igniting racial tension throughout the New York City area. The attack is regarded as the most serious racial incident in the city since 1986. On August 31, marches are held protesting the killing. On September 2, blacks protesting in Bensonhurst are confronted by white residents. Of the five youths charged with the killing of Hawkins, only one is convicted.

1989, October 12 • The publication of Reverend Ralph

Abernathy's book *And the Walls Came Tumbling Down* is greeted with outrage. The book claims that Dr. Martin Luther King, Jr. spent the night before his murder with two women. Twenty-seven black leaders issue a statement denouncing Abernathy's book.

1989, November 5 • Montgomery, Alabama
The first memorial dedicated to the civil rights movement is unveiled. The memorial is commissioned by the Southern Poverty Law Center and designed by Maya Lin, who also created the Vietnam War Memorial in Washington, DC.

1989, November 7 • New York City, New York
Black candidates do well in elections. In Virginia, L. Douglas Wilder becomes the first elected black governor in United States history. In New York, New York, David N. Dinkins is elected the city's first black mayor. Coleman A. Young, in Detroit, is reelected to a fifth consecutive term as mayor. Michael R. White is elected as mayor of Cleveland. Black mayors are also elected in Seattle, Washington; New Haven, Connecticut; and Durham, North Carolina for the first time in history.

1990, January 9 • The United States
The Quality Education for Minorities Project releases its report and recommendations aimed at making schools more responsive to the needs of minority students. The project concludes that minority students are taught in "separate and decidedly unequal" schools resulting in a "gap between minority and non-minority educational achievements."

1990, January 18 • Washington, District of Columbia
Mayor Marion S. Barry, Jr. is arrested after being videotaped purchasing and smoking crack cocaine. Following a split verdict, Barry is sentenced to six months in prison. The arrest generates speculation that the Reverend Jesse Jackson will enter the 1990 Washington, DC mayoral race.

1990, February 8 • Selma, Alabama
Black students stage a "sit-in" following the firing of the city's first black school superintendent, Norward Roussell, on February 5. The firing is viewed as a battle to control the city's school board—white school board members outnumber black members six to five, while 70 percent of Selma's student population is black. The conflict ends after six days of protest. The board amends its position to permit Roussell to stay on as superintendent until the end of his contract.

1990, February 23 • Dallas, Texas
Bishop College, founded in 1881 by a group of freed

Virginia governor L. Douglas Wilder.

slaves and once the largest black college in the western United States, is sold at a bankruptcy auction.

1990, March 6 • Washington, District of Columbia
Clarence Thomas, chairman of the Equal Employment Opportunity Commission, is appointed judge on the United States Circuit Court of Appeals for the District of Columbia.

1990, April 18 • Washington, District of Columbia
By a 5 to 4 majority, the United States Supreme Court upholds the authority of federal judges to order local governments to increase taxes to finance school desegregation in the case *Missouri v. Jenkins*. The cases arose when United States District Court Judge Russell G. Clark adopted a desegregation plan which would create magnet schools to lure whites back into the inner city. To support this plan, Clark ordered that 75 percent of the costs be paid by the state and 25 percent by the district.

1990, June 27 • Washington, District of Columbia
The United States Supreme Court, by a 5 to 4 majority, upholds federal affirmative action policies created to increase the number of broadcast licenses held by

minorities and women in the case *Metro Broadcasting v. FCC*.

1990, August 9 • Georgia
The state's runoff primary system is challenged by the Justice Department. The Justice Department claims that the system is biased against black candidates who often win a plurality of the vote in multicandidate primaries, but lose when matched with a single white candidate in a runoff election. While seven Southern states have similar primary systems, Georgia is targeted in the lawsuit because, statistically, blacks make up 26 percent of the population but hold only 10 percent of all elected positions.

1990, August 11 • Chicago, Illinois
Operation PUSH calls for a boycott of Nike products. The organization reveals that black consumers purchase approximately 30 percent of all Nike products, but are not represented on Nike's board of directors or in upper management. Nike is one of the country's largest manufacturers of athletic gear.

1990, August 21 • Washington, District of Columbia
Paul R. Philip, the FBI's highest ranking black agent, is

chosen to investigate racial discrimination within the Bureau. The investigation centers around charges made by a black agent against several white agents in the Chicago and Omaha offices.

1990, September 26 • The United States Census Bureau releases its annual report on household income. The bureau reports that the average household income of blacks is $18,083; Hispanics, $21,921; whites, $30,406; and Asians, $36,102. Ten percent of whites live in poverty, while 26.2 percent of Hispanics and 30.7 percent of blacks live in poverty. Fifty percent of black children below age 6 are classified as poor.

1990, September 27 • Washington, District of Columbia
At its annual conference, members of the Congressional Black Caucus charge law enforcement officials with targeting black politicians for harassment and investigation. The prosecution of Washington, DC mayor Marion Berry is cited as an example.

1990, October 12 • Cook County, Illinois
The Illinois Supreme Court validates a lower court decision to bar the Harold Washington Party from the ballot. The court cited an inadequate number of nominating signatures as the reason for its decision. The party, a mostly black third party slate of candidates, is named for the late mayor of Chicago. Cook County Democrats had expressed concern that the Harold Washington Party would take votes from their candidates and guarantee the election of Republicans.

1990, October 22 • Washington, District of Columbia
President George Bush vetoes the Civil Rights Act of 1990. On October 16, the Senate passed the bill by a vote of 62 to 34; the House of Representatives passed the bill on October 17, by a 273 to 154 vote. The legislation was designed to reverse the Court's 1989 decision in the case *Wards Cove Packing Co. v. Antonio*, which made it more difficult for minorities and women to prove job discrimination. Bush cites his fear of the introduction of quotas in the workplace as his reason for rejecting the act. On October 24, an attempt to override the veto in the Senate falls one vote short of the two-thirds majority needed.

1990, November 6 • Arizona
Voters in Arizona defeat two initiatives to reestablish a Dr. Martin Luther King, Jr. holiday. The holiday had been a source of conflict since the Democratic governor, Bruce Babbitt, marked the day in 1986 by an executive order only to see it rescinded in 1987 by his successor, Republican Evan Mecham.

1984 • The Center for Disease Control releases figures on the homicide rate for young black males. Between 1984 and 1988, the homicide rate among black males ages 15 to 24 had risen 68 percent.

1990, December 12 • The Department of Education announces that it will bar colleges and universities that receive federal funds from awarding minority scholarships. The department claims that race-specific scholarships are discriminatory and violate federal civil rights laws. On December 18, the department revises the policy, allowing schools that receive federal funds to award minority scholarships if the money comes from private sources or federal programs designed to aid minority students. On March 20, 1991, the policy is reversed completely.

1990, December 18 • Mississippi
Byron de la Beckwith is charged for the third time with the 1963 murder of civil rights leader Medgar Evers. Beckwith was tried twice in 1964 with both trials ending in a deadlock.

1991, January 8 • Results from a nationwide survey sponsored by the National Science Foundation reveals that white Americans continue to hold negative stereotypes of blacks and Hispanics. Three-quarters of the whites surveyed felt that blacks and Hispanics are more likely to prefer welfare to work. A Census Bureau report shows the household worth of whites with families to average eight times that of Hispanic households and ten times that of black households.

1991, January 15 • Washington, District of Columbia
In a 5 to 3 decision, the United States Supreme Court puts an end to court ordered busing in the Oklahoma City school district. Ruling in the case *Oklahoma City v. Dowell*, the Court declares that the reemergence of single-race schools, resulting from shifting housing patterns, does justify continued court ordered busing. The decision overturns an appeals court ruling refusing to turn the once segregated school district over to local control.

1991, January 20 • A *New York Times*/CBS poll of public support for military action in the Persian Gulf reveals that only 47 percent of blacks polled compared to 80 percent of whites favored intervention. One theory on the difference in support points to the disproportionate number of blacks to whites serving in the armed forces. While accounting for only 12 percent of the total United States population, blacks represent 24.6 percent of the United States troops in the Gulf. Many blacks point to the problems of drugs and crime as good places to direct government resources.

1991, February 26 • Detroit, Michigan
By a 9 to 1 majority, the Detroit Board of Education approves the creation of an all-male school for kindergarten through grade eight. The school's goal would be to provide black male students with an improved learning environment by focusing on the unique problems facing the black male. Critics of the school label the program discriminatory. The American Civil Liberties Union and the National Organization for Women Legal Defense Fund both file suit in federal district court. On August 15, the court rules that such a school must also be open to girls.

1991, March 3 • Los Angeles, California
Black motorist Rodney King is severely beaten by several white police officers after being stopped for a speeding violation. The incident is videotaped by a witness, watching from his apartment balcony.

1991, May 6 • Washington, District of Columbia
Washington, DC The creation of a National African American Museum within the Smithsonian Institution is approved by the institution's board of regents. The museum will include print and broadcast images of African Americans, along with black art and artifacts.

1991, May 12 • Hampton, Virginia
Students at Hampton University hold a silent protest while President George Bush gives the commencement address. The students point to the administration's policies regarding civil rights as a reason for the demonstration.

1991, May 14 • The Washington-based Urban Institute releases its study on job discrimination. The study, conducted in Washington, DC and Chicago, Illinois, reveals that whites seeking entry-level positions were three times more likely to receive favorable treatment than equally qualified blacks.

1991, June 3 • Washington, District of Columbia
The United States Supreme Court, in the case of *Edmonson v. Leesville Concrete Co.*, rules that potential jurors can not be excluded from civil cases on the basis of race. The Court had, in two earlier cases, ruled that jurors could not be excluded because of race in criminal cases.

1991, June 4 • Washington, District of Columbia
After defeating two other civil rights bills, the United States House of Representatives, by a vote of 273 to 158, passes a civil rights bill. The bill is an effort by Congress to reverse the Supreme Court's 1989 ruling in *Wards Cove Packing Co. v. Antonio* and make it easier for victims of job discrimination to sue for damages. President Bush opposes such legislation, claiming that it will force employers to set quotas for hiring minorities, in order to protect themselves from possible discrimination suits.

1991, June 20 • Washington, District of Columbia
The United States Supreme Court, hearing in two separate cases, *Chison v. Roemer* and *Houston Lawyers v. Texas*, rules that the Voting Rights Act of 1965 is applicable to judicial elections. The cases arose from lower court rulings in Louisiana and Texas, which claimed that judges were not representatives, and therefore the election of such was not covered by the act.

1991, June 27 • Washington, District of Columbia
United States Supreme Court Justice Thurgood Marshall, citing his poor health and advancing age, announces his plans to retire from the bench. Marshall, appointed to the Court by President Lyndon B. Johnson in 1967, was the first African American to serve on the nation's highest court.

1991, July • Washington, District of Columbia
President George Bush nominates black Court of Appeals Judge Clarence Thomas to replace the retiring Justice Thurgood Marshall. Thomas, a conservative and former chairman of the Equal Employment Opportunity Commission, was appointed by Bush in 1990 to the federal appeals court. Stating that while chairman of the EEOC, Thomas failed to display sensitivity regarding affirmative action, major national organizations, including the National Association for the Advancement of Colored People, the NAACP Legal Defense Fund, the Leadership Conference on Civil Rights, and the Congressional Black Caucus, voice opposition to the Thomas nomination.

1991, July 4 • Memphis, Tennessee
The National Civil Rights Museum, housed in the former Lorraine Motel, is dedicated. It was at the Lorraine Motel that the Reverend Dr. Martin Luther King, Jr. was shot on April 4, 1968.

1991, August 19 • Brooklyn, New York
Tensions between blacks and Jews in Brooklyn's Crown Heights section increase, when seven-year-old Gavin Cato is struck and killed by a car driven by a Jewish driver. Rioting erupts, and a Jewish rabbinical student is stabbed to death.

1991, September 13 • Richmond, Virginia
Governor L. Douglas Wilder announces his plans to run for the 1992 Democratic presidential nomination. However, by January 1992, Wilder withdraws from the race. In 1989, Wilder became the first black elected governor in United States history.

General Colin Powell visits American troops in Saudi Arabia during the Persian Gulf War.

1991, September 29 • The Department of Justice releases its report on death-row inmates. The report reveals that 40 percent of the inmates awaiting execution in the United States are African-American, whereas blacks constitute only 12.1 percent of the general population.

1991, October 11 • Los Angeles, California
Korean grocer Soon Ja Du is convicted of voluntary manslaughter for the death of Latasha Harlins. The shooting exacerbates racial tension between blacks and Koreans.

1991, October 30 • Washington, District of Columbia
The United States Senate approves a new civil rights bill.

1991, November 1 • Washington, District of Columbia
In a public ceremony, Judge Clarence Thomas is formally seated as the 106th associate justice of the United States Supreme Court.

1991, November 2 • Washington, District of Columbia
Rev. Jesse L. Jackson announces he will not seek the 1992 Democratic presidential nomination.

1991, November 5 • Washington, District of Columbia
In the case *Hafer v. Melo* the United States Supreme Court votes unanimously and rules that state officials can be sued as individuals acting in an official status and be held personally liable in civil rights suits.

1991, November 7 • Washington, District of Columbia
The House of Representatives passes Senate Bill 1745, which was passed by the Senate on October 30. President Bush signs the bill into law on November 21. However, the signing ceremony for the long-anticipated law is dominated by controversy over a proposed presidential directive that tried to impose a conservative interpretation on the new legislation. Immediately after circulation of the draft, civil rights leaders, senators and cabinet members condemn it as an attack on all civil rights progress.

1991, December 30 • Alabama
United States District Court Judge Harold L. Murphy orders the Alabama state university system to rectify racial discrimination in its hiring, admissions and financing practices. It is ruled that Alabama's higher-education system, divided into predominantly white and predominantly black schools, fosters inferior fund-

ing for the predominantly black universities. Judge Murphy states he will retain jurisdiction over the case for ten years to ensure his orders are carried out.

1992, January 2 • Washington, District of Columbia
A lawsuit filed by the National Treasury Employees Union challenges the Equal Employment Opportunity Commission's policy which states that the 1991 Civil Rights Act does not apply to job discrimination lawsuits filed prior to the law's enactment in November, 1991.

1992, January 17 • Atlanta, Georgia
President George Bush visits the Martin Luther King, Jr. Center for Nonviolent Social Change to sign a proclamation officially declaring January 20, Martin Luther King, Jr.'s birthday, as a holiday.

1992, January 19 • The American Council on Education releases their 10th annual report confirming the number of minority students attending college increased during the 1980s. The report shows 33 percent of black, 29 percent of Hispanic and 39.4 percent of white high-school graduates were attending college in 1990, up respectively from 21.6 percent, 26.1 percent and 34.4 percent in 1985.

1992, January 20 • Denver, Colorado
The seventh commemoration of Martin Luther King, Jr.'s birthday as a national holiday triggers violence in Denver between civil-rights supporters and members of the Ku Klux Klan following a Klan rally. Civil-rights supporters throw bricks and bottles at a bus carrying Klan members away from the rally.

1992, February 10 • Seattle, Washington
Alex Haley, the Pulitzer Prize-winning author of *Roots* and *The Autobiography of Malcolm X*, dies of heart failure.

1992, February 15 • Baltimore, Maryland
The National Association for the Advancement of Colored People's Benjamin L. Hooks announces his plans to resign from his position as the organization's director. The announcement is made after Hazel Dukes, the national president, and several other prominent board members are denied reelection.

1992, March 31 • Washington, District of Columbia
In the case of *Freeman v. Pitts*, the United States Supreme Court rules unanimously that school districts operating under court-supervised desegregation orders can slowly be released from court supervision to local control as they achieve racial equality. Reaction to the ruling by educators and civil-rights experts is mixed, with general uncertainty as to how the decision will be applied by district courts reviewing individual desegregation orders.

1992, April 29 • Los Angeles, California
Riots erupt in Los Angeles following the acquittal of four white police officers in the beating of black motorist Rodney King. The suburban Simi Valley jury that acquitted the police officers had no black members. The videotaped beating was broadcast around the world and provoked outrage condemning police brutality. With the announcement of the verdict, looting and violence break out across the South Central section of Los Angeles. By the end of the first day, 12 people are killed and more than 100 arson fires engulf the area. Mayor Tom Bradley declares a local state of emergency and Governor Pete Wilson orders the National Guard to assist local police in controlling the increasing violence. President George Bush orders the deployment of 1,500 Marines and 3,000 Army troops to Los Angeles. Many of the shops targeted for looting are those owned by Korean immigrants. Tension between Los Angeles blacks and Koreans had been rising since the 1991 fatal shooting of a young black girl, Latasha Harlins, by a Korean grocer. The Bush administration blames the riots on urban decay, crime and welfare dependency which it claims grew out of the social-welfare programs passed by Congress in the 1960s and 1970s.

1992, June 13 • Washington, District of Columbia
Governor Bill Clinton speaks at the Rainbow Coalition convention and criticizes questionable statements made by rap singer Sister Souljah (Lisa Williamson) in reference to the Los Angeles riots. The Reverend Jesse Jackson, founder of the Rainbow Coalition, says he thinks Clinton's comments were intended to embarrass and provoke him.

1992, June 26 • Washington, District of Columbia
In the case of *United States v. Fordice*, the United States Supreme Court rules 8-1 that the state of Mississippi has not sufficiently desegregated its public universities. Despite "race-neutral" admissions standards, certain policies are targeted as causing informal segregation. Examples include wording of mission statements and higher admissions standards at the predominantly white colleges.

1992, July 23 • Washington, District of Columbia
The 1990 United States Census shows black median household incomes at $19,758 compared to $31,435 for whites and $30,056 for the national median average. The statistics show that blacks earn 63 percent of the median white income, only slightly better than the 62 percent earned by blacks ten years prior.

A California National guardsman stands watch in front of a graffiti covered wall in Los Angeles.

1992, August 29 • Washington, District of Columbia
The FBI's Uniform Crime Reports gives the rate of violent offenses by juveniles (ages 10 to 17) as 430 out of 100,000 in 1990. Black arrests are 1,429 out of 100,000, five times the amount of whites arrested.

1992, September 3 • Washington, District of Columbia
A 1991 United States Census Bureau report finds that the number of Americans below the poverty level is the highest number since 1964. 14.2 percent of Americans were in poverty in 1991 compared to 13.5 percent in 1990. 32.7 percent of black Americans were in poverty in 1991 compared to 31.9 percent in 1990.

1992, September 16 • Washington, District of Columbia
The United States Department of Education's report on high school dropout rates shows a 13.6 percent dropout of black students (ages 16 to 24) in 1991 compared to 21.3 percent in 1972. The dropout rate of Hispanics rose from 34.3 percent to 35.3 percent, whereas the rate for whites dropped from 12.3 percent to 8.9 percent.

1992, September 28 • Berkeley, California
The University of California at Berkeley Law School is found in violation of federal civil rights laws by the United States Department of Education Office for Civil Rights. It is discovered that minority applicants to the school receive preferential treatment over other candidates. As a result of this ruling, the school's admission policies are revised.

1992, October 8 • Boston, Massachusetts
A study conducted by the Federal Reserve's regional bank shows evidence of bank discrimination against minorities applying for mortgages. The study measures black, Hispanic, and white rejection rates when all applicants had similar application criteria. The findings show 17 percent rejection of minorities compared to 11 percent rejection of whites. This study is the first to investigate loan application criteria.

1992, November 3 • The Presidential election brings 16 new black members to Congress for a total of 38. Senator Earl F. Hilliard is the first black Alabaman elected to Congress. The District of Columbia's Marion Barry wins a seat on Washington's city council. Florida's first three blacks benefit from court-ordered redistricting. They include Representative Corrine Brown, Representative Carrie Meek, and Representative Alcee Hastings. In Georgia, three blacks join Congress, including

Senator Nathan Deal, Representative Jackie Barrett, and Representative Cynthia McKinney. McKinney is the first black woman voted into the Georgia House of Representatives.

1992, November • Detroit, Michigan
Two Detroit policemen are charged with murder and two policemen are charged with lesser criminal charges in the beating death of black motorist Malice Green. Larry Nevers and Walter Budzyn, two white police officers, pulled Green out of his car and beat him on the head with metal flashlights. Sgt. Freddie Douglas, a black policeman, is charged with failing to stop the beating. White policeman Robert Lessnau is charged with participating in the beating and aggravated assault. Innocent pleas are entered for all four officers.

1992, November 6 • Washington, District of Columbia
United States Labor Department figures show a decrease in unemployment rates from 7.5 percent in September to 7.4 percent in October. In September, jobless rates drop from 6.7 percent to 6.5 percent for whites, from 11.9 percent to 11.8 percent for Hispanics, and rose to 13.9 percent from 13.7 percent for blacks.

1992, November 7 • An outline for one of Martin Luther King, Jr.'s speeches is purchased at an auction for $35,000 by New Jersey Group, Kaller and Associates. The King estate filed a lawsuit requesting the return of the document plus $5 million in punitive damages from the dealer, Superior Galleries. King rarely made outlines or notes for his speeches, which explains the inflated worth.

1992, November 18 • *Malcolm X*, Spike Lee's motion picture based on Alex Haley's biography of the slain civil rights leader, opens in theaters nationwide.

1992, December 12 • Washington, District of Columbia
President Bill Clinton's Cabinet and White House appointments include five black men and one black woman. They are Clifton R. Wharton, Jr. as Deputy Secretary of State; Hazel R. O'Leary as Secretary of Energy; Mike Espy as head of the Agriculture Department; Ron Brown, the former Democratic National Committee Chairman, as Secretary of Commerce; Jesse Brown as Veterans Affairs Secretary; and a woman, Dr. Joycelyn Elders, as Surgeon General.

1993, January 5 • Washington, District of Columbia
The House of Representatives passes, by twenty-two votes, a rules change which will allow an increase in voting rights to delegates from Washington, DC and the United States territories of American Samoa, Guam, Puerto Rico, and the United States Virgin Islands. (The

Commerce Secretary Ron Brown with President Bill Clinton.

District of Columbia and the Virgin Islands have large African-American populations.) In the past, the delegates took part in committee actions and votes, but not votes on the House floor, which were restricted to representatives from "the states" because the Constitution stipulated that only "the states" should have legislative authority. Delegates may now participate in all but the final votes affecting legislation.

1993, January 7 • Washington, District of Columbia
Senator Carol Moseley Braun is one of two women elected to the Senate Judiciary Committee. Braun claimed she was inspired to run partly as a result of angry feelings over the Anita Hill-Clarence Thomas hearings in 1991. The all-male Judiciary Committee had been admonished by the public for its role in the handling of the hearings.

1993, January 8 • Washington, District of Columbia
The unemployment rate for December 1992 reaches 7.3 percent, according to United States Labor Department figures.

1993, January 24 • Bethesda, Maryland
Thurgood Marshall, the first black Supreme Court Jus-

Veteran Affairs Secretary Jesse Brown with President Bill Clinton.

tice and lifelong supporter of civil rights, dies of heart failure.

1993, January 18 • New Hampshire renames its January holiday from Civil Rights Day to King Day. This is the first time all 50 states have a holiday for Martin Luther King, Jr.

1993, March 2 • Washington, District of Columbia
The United States Supreme Court, in the case of *Voinovich v. Quilter*, rules that the authority to create voting districts dominated by ethnic minorities is held by individual states. The issue was brought before the Court because of concern over the reorganization practices of Ohio's state legislative voting districts in 1990.

1993, April 9 • Baltimore, Maryland
Civil rights champion Benjamin F. Chavis, Jr. is elected as leader of the National Association for the Advancement of Colored People.

1993, April 17 • Los Angeles, California
In a civil suit, two of the four Los Angeles police officers charged in the beating of black motorist Rodney King

are convicted, while the other two are acquitted. Officer Lawrence M. Powell is convicted of violating King's rights to an arrest without "unreasonable force." Powell delivered the majority of hits to King with his baton. Sgt. Stacey C. Koon is convicted of allowing the violation by Powell to occur. Officers Theodore J. Briseno and Timothy E. Wind are found not guilty on all charges. As a result of the riots in 1991, the people of Los Angeles were on edge awaiting the new verdict. Riot training for 7,000 Los Angeles police officers and advance notice of the verdict to the police prepared them for the possibility of future rioting.

1993, May 17 • Washington, District of Columbia
The United States Supreme Court sends the case of *American Family Mutual Insurance Co. v. National Association for the Advancement of Colored People* back to the lower courts. Until decisions by the lower courts, the federal Fair Housing Act may be interpreted to extend coverage toward homeowner's insurance. The NAACP charged that the insurance company refused to sell to blacks or charged them exorbitant fees. The practice is also known as "redlining."

1993, May 23 • Washington, District of Columbia
The Washington Post begins publishing portions of the late Supreme Court Justice Thurgood Marshall's papers. Immediately following Marshall's death, his papers are made available for use by "researchers or scholars engaged in serious research." These conditions were requested by Marshall when he turned his papers over to the Library of Congress after his retirement. Supreme Court Chief Justice Rehnquist wrote Librarian of Congress James H. Billington a letter admonishing him for lack of judgment in releasing the papers so soon. Marshall's friends, family, and colleagues displayed similar feelings of anger at the papers' speedy release.

1993, June 3 • Washington, District of Columbia
President Bill Clinton retracts his nomination of Lani Guinier for the position of head of the civil-rights division in the Justice Department. Guinier, a black law professor, had expressed some controversial ideas relating to race and voting rights in some previous professional writings. Clinton justifies his decision by explaining that the views expressed in the writings clashed with his own opinions on the same topics.

1993, June 7 • Pop star Prince changes his name to a symbol that combines the signs for male and female.

1993, June 26 • Woodland Hills, California
Hall of Fame catcher Roy Campanella, one of the first African Americans to play in the major leagues, dies of a heart attack.

1993, July 23 • Fayetteville, North Carolina
James Jordan, father of Chicago Bulls star Michael Jordan, is shot and killed during a robbery attempt.

1993, July 27 • Waltham, Massachusetts
Boston Celtics guard Reggie Lewis collapses and dies at Brandeis University during a practice.

1993, August 4 • Los Angeles, California
A federal judge sentences Sgt. Stacy Koon and Officer Laurnece Powell to two and a half years in prison for violating the civil rights of motorist Rodney King during a 1991 beating.

1993, August 4 • New York City, New York
Leonard Jeffries Jr. is reinstated as chairman of City College's black studies department. A judge rules that the decision by college administrators to remove Jeffries following a controversial 1991 speech violated his constitutional right to free speech.

1993, August 23 • Detroit, Michigan
Two white officers, Larry Nevers and Walter Budzyn, are convicted of second-degree murder in the beating death of motorist Malice Green.

1993, September 7 • West Palm Beach, Florida
Two white men are convicted of kidnapping and setting afire an African American tourist on January 1, 1993. The men are also convicted of attempted murder and armed robbery. They are sentenced to life imprisonment on October 22.

1993, September 8 • Washington, District of Columbia
Dr. Joycelyn Elders is sworn in as U.S. Surgeon General.

1993, September 14 • Philadelphia, Pennsylvania
The University of Pennsylvania decides not to suspend a group of black students who seized 14,000 copies of the student newspaper *Daily Pennsylvanian*. The students took the newspapers to protest what they viewed as the *Daily Pennsylvanian*'s conservative and racially biased views.

1993, September 30 • Fort Myer, Virginia
Colin L. Powell retires as chairman of the Joint Chiefs of Staff.

1993, October 6 • Chicago, Illinois
Chicago Bulls star Michael Jordan announces his retirement from the NBA.

1993, October 8 • New York City, New York
Actor Ted Danson is chastised for appearing onstage in blackface and telling several racist and sexist jokes during a Friars Club roast for actress Whoopi Goldberg.

1993, October 18 • Los Angeles, California
Two African American men are acquitted of attempted murder in the beating of truck driver Reginald Denny during the 1992 riot.

1993, October 20 • Don Cornelius steps down as host of the syndicated dance show "Soul Train" after 22 years.

1993, November 2 • New York City, New York
Mayor David Dinkins is defeated in a mayoral election by former U.S. attorney Rudolph Giuliani.

1993, November 2 • Detroit, Michigan
Dennis Archer defeats Sharon McPhail to become mayor of Detroit, succeeding Coleman Young.

1994, February 3 • Washington, District of Columbia
Nation of Islam leader Louis Farrakhan censures aide Khalid Abdul Muhammad for anti-Semitic remarks made in a November, 1993 speech.

1994, February 5 • Jackson, Mississippi
Byron de la Beckwith, a white supremacist, is convicted of the 1963 murder of civil rights leader Medgar Evers. Beckwith is sentenced to life in prison.

1994, March 1 • Berkeley, California
Former Black Panther leader Eldridge Cleaver is hospitalized after suffering a brain hemorrhage.

1994, March 23 • Los Angeles, California
Magic Johnson is named coach of the Los Angeles Lakers

1994, April 12 • Washington, District of Columbia
Randall Robinson, executive director of TransAfrica, a lobbying group for African and Caribbean issues, begins a liquid-fast diet to protest the U.S. government's "discriminatory policy" on Haiti.

1994, April 22 • Washington, District of Columbia
Franklyn Jenifer, president of Howard University, resigns after being named the president of the University of Texas at Dallas.

1994, May 24 • Santa Ana, California
Denny's Restaurants agree to pay $54 million to settle lawsuits by African Americans who claim they were discriminated against by the restaurant chain.

1994, May 26 • Dominican Republic
Pop star Michael Jackson and Lisa Marie Presley, daughter of Elvis Presley, are married.

1994, June 20 • Los Angeles, California
Ex-football star O.J. Simpson is arrested and charged with the murder of his wife, Nicole Brown Simpson, and her friend, Ron Goldman.

1994, August 20 • Chicago, Illinois
Benjamin F. Chavis is ousted as executive director of the NAACP by the civil rights organization's board of directors. Earl T. Shinhoster is named interim director.

1994, August 30 • Detroit, Michigan
Civil rights activist Rosa Parks is beaten and robbed in her home.

1994, October 3 • Washington, District of Columbia
Mike Espy, secretary of the U.S. Department of Agriculture, resigns following a federal ethics investigation in which Espy is accused of receiving gifts from businesses regulated by the U.S. Department of Agriculture.

1994, October 21 • Atlanta, Georgia
Dexter Scott King, the youngest son of the late Rev. Martin Luther King, Jr. is named chief executive and chairman of the Martin Luther King Jr. Center for Nonviolent Social Change.

1994, December 9 • Washington, District of Columbia
Dr. Joycelyn Elders resigns as U.S. Surgeon General after making controversial statements regarding drug use and sex education.

1994, December 10 • New York City, New York
University of Colorado running back Rashaan Salaam wins the Heisman Trophy.

1994, December 14 • Washington, District of Columbia
Rep. Donald M. Payne, a Democrat from New Jersey, is elected to a two-year term as chairman of the Congressional Black Caucus.

1995, January 12 • Minneapolis, Minnesota
Qubilah Bahiyah Shabazz, daughter of the late black nationalist leader Malcolm X, is arrested and charged with plotting to kill Nation of Islam leader Louis Farrakhan.

1995, March 18 • Chicago, Illinois
Chicago Bulls star Michael Jordan announces his return to the NBA after retiring in 1993.

1995, March 25 • Plainfield, Indiana
Boxer Mike Tyson is released from prison after serving three years for a 1992 rape conviction.

1995, April 21 • Washington, District of Columbia
H. Patrick Swygert is named president of Howard University, replacing Franklyn G. Jenifer.

1995, June 21 • Washington, District of Columbia
The Senate rejects Dr. Henry Foster Jr.'s bid to become U.S. Surgeon General. Foster, a gynecologist and obstetrician, is rejected due to pressure from anti-abortion groups and Senate Republicans.

1995, June 29 • Washington, District of Columbia
The Supreme Court, by a 5-4 vote, rules that electoral districts drawn to ensure fair political representation of African Americans and other minorities are unconstitutional if race is used as the predominant factor in drawing district boundaries.

1995, July 20 • Davis, California
The University of California votes to eliminate affirmative action policies in the admission of students.

1995, October 3 • Los Angeles, California
O.J. Simpson is acquitted of the murder of his ex-wife Nicole Brown Simpson and her friend, Ron Goldman. The O.J. Simpson trial was televised daily throughout the United States and fueled extensive debate regarding race relations in America.

1995, October 16 • Washington, District of Columbia
The Million Man March, organized by Nation of Islam leader Louis Farrakhan, draws African American men to the nation's capital. The purpose of the march is to offer African American men an opportunity to meet for a day of atonement and to pledge their commitment to themselves, their families, and their communities.

1995, November 8 • Alexandria, Virginia
Former Chairman of the Joint Chiefs of Staff, Colin L. Powell, ends months of speculation by announcing that he will not run for the U.S. presidency in 1996.

1995, December 9 • Chicago, Illinois
Kweisi Mfume is unanimously elected as president and chief executive officer of the NAACP.

1995, December 12 • Washington, District of Columbia
Jesse Jackson Jr., son of civil rights activist Rev. Jesse

Jackson, is elected as the representative of Illinois's 2nd Congressional District. He replaced Rep. Mel Reynolds who resigned from Congress after being sentenced to five years in prison for sexual misconduct.

1996, January 15 • Five of the largest African American congregations in the United States announce the formulation of Revelation Corporation of America, a for-profit company designed to improve the buying power of African American consumers.

1996, January 18 • **Los Angeles, California**
Lisa Marie Presley files for divorce from her husband, pop singer Michael Jackson.

1996, January 30 • **Los Angeles, California**
Los Angeles Lakers star Earvin (Magic) Johnson announces his return to the NBA after retiring in 1991.

1996, February 20 • **Washington, District of Columbia**
Kweisi Mfume is sworn in as the top executive of the NAACP.

1996, April 3 • **Dubrovnik, Croatia**
Commerce Secretary Ronald H. Brown and distinguished American business leaders are killed in a plane crash.

2

African American Firsts

2

African American Firsts

While not comprehensive, the following list of firsts covers a wide spectrum of pioneering events and people in history. Many of the individuals and events described hold considerable intrinsic significance—such as the first publication of a novel by an African American author in 1853—while other events listed are merely interesting. Nevertheless, all are trendsetters in African American history.

1619 • First Africans arrive.

1623 • The first African American in the colonies to be baptized a Christian is a child named , son of Isabel and William, who becomes a member of the Anglican Church in Jamestown.

1624 • Jamestown, Virginia
William Tucker, who is believed to have been the first African American child born in the American colonies, is born in Jamestown, Virginia.

1758 • Born in 1702 to free parents in Jamaica, Frances Williams graduates from Cambridge University and becomes the first black college graduate in the western hemisphere.

1783 • James Derham, born a slave in Philadelphia in 1762, becomes the first African-American physician in the United States. Having served as an assistant to his master (a doctor by profession), Derham purchases his freedom in 1783, and goes on to develop a thriving practice with both black and white clientele.

1785, May 15 • New York
The first African American missionary minister to work with Native Americans is John Morront of New York. He was ordained a Methodist minister on May 15 in London, England. Among his converts to the Christian faith are a Cherokee chieftain and his daughter.

1786 • Lemuel Haynes, who served during the American Revolution as a Minuteman in Connecticut, becomes the first African American minister with a white congregation.

1787 • Prince Hall organizes the first African American Masonic Lodge in America.

1829 • The first African American congregation of Catholic nuns, the Oblate Sisters of Providence, is founded in the United States by Mary Rosine Boegues, Mary Frances Balas, Mary Theresa Duchemin, and Elizabeth Lange.

1834 • Greenross, Maryland
The first African American believed to have been granted a patent from the United States Patent Office is Henry Blair of Greenross, Maryland.

1845 • Worcester, Massachusetts
Macon B. Allen becomes the first African American lawyer formally admitted to the bar after he passes the state bar examination in Worcester, Massachusetts.

1847 • David John Peck graduates from Rush Medical College, becoming the first African American to graduate from an American school of medicine.

1853 • The first novel written and published by an African American is a work by William Wells Brown, entitled *Clotel, A Tale of the Southern States.*

1854 • Brownhelm, Ohio
John Mercer Langston, who is believed to have been the first African American elected to public office, is elected clerk of Brownhelm, Ohio.

1860 • The first African-American baseball team to tour various parts of the country is called the Brooklyn Excelsiors.

John Mercer Langston

Henry McNeal Turner

1861 • Nicholas Biddle becomes one of the first African Americans wounded during the Civil War. An escaped slave, Biddle attaches himself to a troop unit heading for the defense of Washington, but is stoned by an angry mob in Baltimore. He manages to escape death only with the aid of his white comrades-in-arms.

1861 • Boston, Massachusetts
In Boston, Massachusetts, William C. Nell is appointed postal clerk, becoming the first African American to hold a federal civilian post.

1862 • Oberlin, Ohio
Mary Patterson becomes the first African American woman in the United States to earn a Master of Arts degree, awarded by Oberlin College.

1863 • The first African American appointed a chaplain in the United States Army is Henry McNeal Turner.

1864 • Rebecca Lee Crumpler, believed to be the first African American woman physician, graduates from New England Female Medical College.

1865 • Martin R. Delany becomes the first African

American to attain the rank of major in the United States Army. A graduate of Howard University Medical School, Delany served in the Medical Corps. He was also a writer.

1865 • John Rock becomes the first African American lawyer admitted to practice before the United States Supreme Court. His admittance is moved by Senator Charles Sumner of Massachusetts. Chief Justice Salmon P. Chase presides.

1865 • Augusta, Georgia
The first African American newspaper in the South— *The Colored American*—is published in Augusta, Georgia, and edited by J. T. Shutten.

1866 • Massachusetts
Edward G. Walker and Charles L. Mitchell are elected to the Massachusetts House of Representatives, becoming the first African Americans to serve in a legislative assembly.

1867 • Cambridge, Massachusetts
Robert Tanner Freeman becomes the first African Ameri-

can to graduate from Harvard University's School of Dentistry.

1869 • Ebenezer Don Carlos Bassett, believed to be the first African American to receive an appointment in the diplomatic service, becomes United States Minister to Haiti.

1870 • Cambridge, Massachusetts
Richard Greener becomes the first African American to receive a degree from Harvard. Active as a teacher and editor, Greener is admitted to the South Carolina bar in 1876 and becomes Dean of Howard University Law School in 1879.

1870 • Mississippi
Hiram R. Revel, of Mississippi, becomes the first African American elected to the United States Senate. Joseph H. Rainey, of South Carolina, and Jefferson F. Long, of Georgia, are the first black elected members of the House of Representatives.

1872 • The first African American midshipman to attend the United States Naval Academy is James Henry Conyers of South Carolina. Conyers did not graduate, however, and left the academy on November 11, 1873.

1872 • Louisiana Lieutenant Governor Pinckney Benton Stewart Pinchback, becomes the first African American governor upon impeachment of the incumbent.

1872 • Washington, District of Columbia
The first African American woman lawyer, Charlotte E. Roy, receives her degree from Howard University School of Law in Washington, DC.

1872 • Philadelphia, Pennsylvania
The first African American delegates to the presidential nominating convention of a major party appear at the Republican Convention in Philadelphia.

1873 • Little Rock, Arkansas
The first African American municipal judge, M. W. Gibbs, is elected in Little Rock, Arkansas.

1873 • Susan McKinney, believed to be the first African American woman to formally enter the medical profession, is certified as a physician. (Records at the medical college of the New York Infirmary indicate that Rebecca Cole was the first African American woman physician in the United States, having practiced from 1872 to 1881.)

1875 • Reverend James Augustine Healy becomes the first African American Roman Catholic bishop in the United States.

1875 • Oscar Lewis, an African American riding in the first Kentucky Derby, becomes the race's first winner

1876 • New Haven, Connecticut
Graduating from Yale University, Edward A. Bouchet becomes the first African American to earn a Ph.D. from an American university. Bouchet is also the first African American Phi Beta Kappa.

1877 • Henry O. Flipper becomes the first African American to graduate from the United States Military Academy at West Point.

1879 • Boston, Massachusetts
In Boston, Mary E. Mattoney becomes the first African American woman to receive a diploma in nursing from New England Hospital for Women and Children.

1882 • Illinois
The first daily newspaper owned by an African American, *The Cairo Illinois Gazette*, is published by W. S. Scott.

1884 • John Roy Lynch becomes the first African American to preside over a national political convention, when he is nominated temporary chairman of the Republican Party's national convention.

1884 • Toledo, Ohio
Moses Fleetwood Walker becomes the first African American major league baseball player when he plays for Toledo in the American Association.

1885 • The first African American state legislator elected to represent a majority white constituency is Bishop Benjamin William Arnett of the African Methodist Episcopal Church.

1885 • New York City, New York
The first African American professional baseball team, The Cuban Giants, is formed in New York City by Frank Thompson from a group of waiters at a Long Island hotel.

1885 • The first African American Protestant Episcopal bishop in the United States, the Reverend Samuel David Ferguson, is elected to the House of Bishops.

1885 • Jonathan Jasper Wright becomes the first African American elected to the State Supreme Court of South Carolina. He is also the first African American to be admitted to the bar in Pennsylvania.

1890 • Louisiana
Thomy Gafon, a real estate speculator and money-

lender in Louisiana, is believed to have been the first African American millionaire in the United States.

1890 • London/ England
George Dixon of Halifax, Nova Scotia, becomes the first black to win a world boxing title when he beats Nunc Wallace in eighteen rounds in London.

1892 •
The first African American college football game is played between Biddle College (now Johnson C. Smith University) and Livingstone College. Biddle wins 4 to 0.

1893 •
Dr. Daniel Hale Williams becomes the first surgeon to successfully enter the chest cavity and suture the heart of a living patient.

1894 • Massachusetts
William Edward Burghardt Du Bois becomes the first African American to be awarded a Ph.D. by Harvard University.

1902 • Paris, France
Off Bloomingdale Asylum, a satirical comedy, is the first film to use African American actors. The film is made in Paris, France.

1903 • Richmond, Virginia
Maggie Walker becomes the first African American woman bank president when she founds the Saint Luke Penny Thrift Savings Bank in Richmond, Virginia.

1904 • Ithaca, New York
The first African American fraternity, Alpha Phi Alpha, is organized at Cornell University.

1907 •
Alain Leroy Locke becomes the first African American awarded a coveted Rhodes Scholarship.

1908 • Washington, District of Columbia
The first African American sorority, Alpha Kappa Alpha, is founded at Howard University in Washington, DC.

1908 •
Jack Johnson wins a bout with Tommy Burns to become the first African American heavyweight champion.

1918 •
Hugh N. Mulzac becomes the first African American in the United States to earn a shipmaster's license and have the right to take command of a ship. Mulzac, however, is not able to find employment as a shipmaster and instead must take jobs at sea as a cook and steward

for the next twenty-four years. He finally takes command of a ship in 1942, a Liberty cargo vessel transporting troops and supplies into the war zones.

1919 •
Fritz Pollard becomes the first African American to play professional football for a major team, the Akron Indians. In 1916, Pollard had been the first African American to play in the Rose Bowl, for Brown University.

1923 •
The first African American basketball team, known as the Renaissance, is organized.

1926 •
Violette Anderson becomes the first African American woman lawyer to practice before the United States Supreme Court.

1931 • Columbia, New York
Estele Massey Osborne becomes the first African American recipient in the United States of a master's degree in nursing education when she graduates from Columbia Teachers College.

1933 •
The first transcontinental flight by African Ameri-

Fritz Pollard

can civilian pilots is made by Charles Alfred Anderson of Bryn Mawr, Pennsylvania and Albert Ernest Forsythe of Atlantic City, New Jersey.

1937 • Virgin Islands of the United States

William H. Hastie is the first African American appointed to the federal district court.

1938 •

Crystal Bird Fauset becomes the first African American woman elected to a state legislature in the United States, acquiring this distinction when she was named to the Pennsylvania House of Representatives on November 8, 1938.

1939 •

The first African American woman judge, Jane Matilda Bolin, is appointed to the bench of the Court of Domestic Relations by Mayor Fiorello LaGuardia of New York City.

1940 •

Benjamin O. Davis, Sr., is promoted to the rank of brigadier general, becoming the first African American to hold this post in the United States Army.

1940 •

For her role as supporting actress in the movie *Gone with the Wind*, Hattie McDaniel becomes the first African American to win an Oscar from the Academy of Motion Picture Arts and Sciences.

1940 • Tuskegee, Alabama

The first postage stamp honoring an African American, the ten-cent Booker T. Washington stamp, goes on sale at Tuskegee Institute. The stamp, which is a part of the Famous American Series, is the culmination of a seven-year campaign sponsored by Major R. R. Wright, president of the Citizens and Southern Bank and Trust Company of Philadelphia. (Seven years later, a three-cent postage stamp honoring George Washington Carver is issued on the fourth anniversary of the renowned scientist's death.)

1942 •

Bernard W. Robinson, a medical student at Harvard, becomes the first African American commissioned an officer in the United States Naval Reserve.

1943 • New Jersey

The first Liberty ship named for an African American, the *George Washington Carver*, is launched from a New Jersey shipyard to begin its career of carrying war cargo to Europe during World War II. The *USS Harmon* becomes the first fighting ship to be named for an African American. Leonard Roy Harmon won the Navy Cross for his heroism aboard the *USS San Francisco* in a battle with the Japanese near the Solomon Islands. Harmon died of wounds suffered during the engagement.

1943 •

Dr. William Edward Burghardt Du Bois becomes the first African American admitted to the National Institute of Arts and Letters. At the time of his admittance, Dr. Du Bois is head of the Department of Sociology at Atlanta University.

1944 •

Harry McAlpin of Atlanta's *Daily World* becomes the first accredited African American White House news correspondent.

1945 • New York City, New York

Phyllis Mae Daley becomes the first African American nurse commissioned in the Navy Reserve Corps. Daley, a registered nurse from New York City, is sworn in as an ensign.

1945 •

Irving Charles Mollison becomes the first African American appointed judge of the United States Customs Court.

1946 • Nashua, New Hampshire

Roy Campanella, a catcher for a Nashua, New Hampshire, team, becomes the first African American to manage an organized baseball team on the field when the regular manager Walt Alston is ejected from the field by the umpire. Nashua wins the game when an African American pitcher, Don Newcombe, hits a pinch hit home run.

1946 •

The first coin honoring African Americans is issued. The coin is a fifty-cent piece bearing a relief bust of Booker T. Washington, the founder of Tuskegee Institute.

1947 • Brooklyn, New York

Dan Bankhead of the National League's Brooklyn Dodgers becomes the first African American pitcher in the major leagues. The first African American pitcher in the American League, Leroy Satchel Paige, follows in 1948.

1947 •

Louis Lautier, Washington Bureau Chief of the Negro Newspaper Publishers Association, becomes the first African American issued credentials for both the Senate and the House press galleries. Lautier is admitted to the galleries after a Senate Rules Committee overrides the refusal of the Standing Committee of Newspaper Correspondents to grant him the necessary credentials.

1947 • Indianapolis, Indiana

John Lee of Indianapolis, Indiana, becomes the first African American commissioned officer in the United States Navy. His first assignment upon being commissioned is on the *USS Kearsage*.

General O. Davis (left) with General George Patton.

1948 • Washington, District of Columbia
William Thaddeus Coleman, Jr., becomes the first appointed African American clerk of the United States Supreme Court, when he is named to the post by Supreme Court Justice Felix Frankfurter.

1948 • John Earl Rudder becomes the first African American commissioned officer in the United States Marine Corps.

1949 • Jesse Leroy Brown becomes the first African American pilot in United States Naval Reserve. On December 4, 1950, at Changjin Reservoir in Korea, Brown is the first African American naval pilot killed in action.

1949 • Annapolis, Maryland
Wesley A. Brown becomes the first African American to graduate from the Naval Academy at Annapolis.

1949 • William H. Hastie becomes the first African American judge appointed to the United States Circuit Court of Appeals. Hastie is also the first African Ameri-

The *USS Harmon* named in honor of Roy Harmon.

Roy Campanella

can appointed governor of the United States Virgin Islands.

1949 • Jackie Robinson becomes the first African American baseball player to win his league's "Most Valuable Player" award. The first African American to win the award three times is Roy Campanella, who is awarded the title in 1951, 1953, and 1955.

1950 • Gwendolyn Brooks is awarded the Pulitzer Prize for her volume of poetry titled *Annie Allen*. She is the

first African American woman to win the award and also the first African American woman elected to the National Institute of Arts and Letters.

1950 • United Nations Undersecretary Ralph Bunche becomes the first African American to receive a Nobel Peace Prize.

1950 • **Atlantic City, New Jersey**
Arthur Dorrington becomes the first African American

Coin and stamps depicting George Washington Carver and Booker T. Washington.

professional hockey player when he plays the 1950-1951 season with the Atlantic City Sea Gulls.

1950 • Juanita Hall becomes the first African American to win a Tony Award for her supporting role in the musical *South Pacific*.

1951 • New York City, New York
Janet Collins becomes the first African American to dance for the Metropolitan Opera in New York. Collins, signed by an agent of the company, makes her debut in *Aida*.

1951 • New York City, New York
William L. Rowe becomes the first African American deputy police commissioner. He is appointed to this position in New York by Mayor Vincent Impellitieri.

1952 • Frank E. Petersen, Jr. becomes the first African American United States Marine pilot.

1953 • Ralph Ellison, author of *The Invisible Man*, becomes the first African American to receive the National Book Award.

1954 • Charles H. Mahoney becomes the first African American appointed a permanent delegate to the United Nations.

1954 • New York City, New York
Dr. James Joshua Thomas becomes the first African American pastor of the Reformed Dutch Church. He is installed as minister of the Mott Haven Reformed Church in the Bronx, New York City.

1954 • New York
The first African American radio network, the National Negro Network, begins programming. The New York outlet is station WOV. The first program of the network, a soap opera titled *The Story of Ruby Valentine*, stars Juanita Hall and is carried on forty stations. The program, sponsored by Phillip Morris and Pet Milk, runs five days a week.

1956 • Compton, California
Charles Dumas, a freshman at Compton College, Compton, California, becomes the first athlete to high jump over seven feet.

1957 • Althea Gibson becomes the first African American tennis player to win at Wimbledon.

1958 • New York City, New York
Gloria Davy sings *Aida* at New York's Metropolitan Opera and becomes the first African American to appear in song at this celebrated palace of music.

1958 • Ruth Carol Taylor becomes the first African American airline stewardess when she is hired to work for Mohawk Airlines.

1959 • Lorraine Hansberry's play *A Raisin in the Sun* is the first play by an African American to receive the New York Drama Critics' Circle Award for Best American Play.

1959 • Cleveland, Ohio
John McLendon becomes the first African American to coach an integrated professional basketball team, the Cleveland Pipers of the National Industrial Basketball League.

1962 • Mal Goode becomes the first African American television news correspondent.

1962 • Lieutenant Commander Samuel L. Gravely, Jr. becomes the first African American to command a United States warship when he assumes command of the *USS Falgout*, a destroyer escort.

Judge William H. Hastie being sworn in by Chief Judge John Biggs, Jr.

1966 • Emmett Ashford, the first African American umpire in the major leagues, makes his debut in the American League inaugural between the Cleveland Indians and the Washington Senators. Ashford umpired in the Southwestern International League in 1952 and in the Pacific Coast League where he was Umpire-in-Chief in 1965.

1966 • Constance Baker Motley becomes the first African American to serve as a federal judge.

1966 • Boston, Massachusetts
Bill Russell, star center of the world-champion Boston Celtics, becomes the first African American to direct a major league sports team when he is named to succeed Red Auerbach as coach of the Boston basketball franchise.

1966 • Washington, District of Columbia
Robert C. Weaver is named as secretary of the newly created Department of Housing and Urban Development, becoming the first African American appointed to serve in a presidential cabinet.

1967 • Thurgood Marshall is appointed an associate justice of the United States Supreme Court, becoming the first African American to serve on the nation's highest court.

1967 • Washington, District of Columbia
Walter E. Washington is appointed to head the newly reorganized municipal government of Washington, DC. Washington is the first African American to govern a major American city.

1968 • Arthur Ashe becomes the first African American to win the American Singles Tennis Championship. In 1963 Ashe was the first African American to play on the United States Davis Cup team.

1968 • Martin Briscoe becomes the first African American quarterback in professional football.

1968 • New York
Shirley Chisholm of New York is elected to the United States House of Representatives. Chisholm is the first African American woman to serve in Congress.

1968 • Newark, New Jersey
Henry Lewis is the first African American director of an

Gwendolyn Brooks

American orchestra—the Newark-based New Jersey Symphony.

1969 • Federal Judge A. Leon Higginbotham, Jr. is elected a trustee of Yale University, the first African American to be so honored.

1969 • Parks Sausage Company becomes the first African American-owned company to become a publicly traded company, having its stock traded on the National Association of Securities Dealers Automated Quotation (NASDAQ) exchange.

1969 • Joseph L. Searles III becomes the first African American proposed for a seat on the New York Stock Exchange. Searles, former aide in the administration of New York City Mayor John Lindsay, resigned to become one of the three floor traders, as well as a general partner, for Newburger, Loeb and Co.

1970 • Chris Dickerson becomes the first African American to win the title "Mr. America," one of fifteen body building titles Dickerson will earn during his career. One of a set of triplets born in Montgomery, Alabama on August 25, 1939, Dickerson proves to be an outstanding athlete throughout his school years. An early interest in a singing career and the desire to improve his voice quality and breath control led him into bodybuilding in the mid-1960s.

1970 • Philadelphia, Pennsylvania
Renard Edwards becomes the first African American musician to play for the Philadelphia Orchestra when he is hired as a violist for the 1970-71 season. Edwards was formerly with the Symphony of the New World, an integrated orchestra, one-third to one-half of whose members are African Americans.

1971 • Samuel L. Gravely, Jr. becomes the first African American admiral in the history of the United States Navy.

1973, May 29 • Los Angeles, California
Thomas Bradley, of Los Angeles, becomes the first African American elected mayor of a city with population exceeding one million. He defeated the incumbent Sam Yorty by 100,000 votes. Yorty had defeated Bradley in the 1969 mayoral election.

1974 • Washington, District of Columbia
Barbara Hancock becomes the first African American woman White House Fellow.

1975 • The United States Navy commissions Dr. Donna P. Davis as a lieutenant in the Navy's medical corps, making Davis the first African American woman physician in the corps history.

1975 • General Daniel James, Jr., becomes commander-in-chief of the North American Air Defense Command (NORAD). On the same day, he is promoted and becomes the first African American four-star general in United States history.

1975 • Cleveland, Ohio
Frank Robinson becomes the first African American to manage a major league baseball team and leads his Cleveland Indians to an opening-day victory over the New York Yankees, hitting a home run himself.

1975 • Detroit, Michigan
WGPR-TV, in Detroit, goes on the air, becoming the first African American-owned and operated television station in the United States.

1977 • Clifford Alexander, Jr. becomes the first African American to be appointed Secretary of the Army.

1977 • Milwaukee, Wisconsin
Former basketball player Wayne Embry becomes the

Judge Constance Baker Motley with President Lyndon B. Johnson.

first African American general manager of an NBA team—the Milwaukee Bucks.

1977 • Washington, District of Columbia
Karen Farmer becomes the first African American member of the Daughters of the American Revolution. It was the DAR that refused to allow Marian Anderson to perform in concert in Washington, DC in 1939.

1977 • Patricia Roberts Harris is appointed Secretary of the Department of Housing and Urban Development, becoming the first African American woman to serve in a Cabinet-level position.

1978 • New York City, New York
Reverend Emerson Moore, Jr. is named the first African American monsignor of the Catholic Church in the United States. Monsignor Moore is pastor of St. Charles Borromeo Church in New York City.

1979 • United States Army Second Lieutenant Marcella A. Hayes, a graduate of the University of Wisconsin and the Army ROTC program, earns her aviator wings and becomes the first African American woman pilot in United States armed services history.

1979 • New Jersey
Audrey Neal becomes the first African American woman (or woman of any ethnic group), longshoreperson. Neal is employed at the Bayonne Military Ocean Terminal in New Jersey.

1980 • Dr. Levi Watkins, Jr., an African American, performs the first surgical implantation of the automatic implantable defibrillator in the human heart. The device corrects an ailment known as ventricular fibrillator, or arrhythmia, which prevents the heart from pumping blood.

1981 • Ithaca, New York
Pamela Johnson is named publisher of the *Ithaca Journal* and becomes the first African American woman to hold such a position with a major newspaper in the United States.

1981 • Chicago, Illinois
Dr. Ruth Love becomes the first African American to serve as superintendent of the Chicago school system. Prior to her appointment to this top post, Love held a similar position in Oakland, California.

Newly sworn-in Associate Justice Thurgood Marshall with wife Cecilia.

1983 • Guion Bluford becomes the first African American to travel in space when he serves as a crew member on the Space Shuttle Challenger.

1983 • Atlantic City, New Jersey
Representing New York, Vanessa Williams becomes the first African American Miss America in the 62-year history of the Atlantic City pageant. The first runner-up is Suzette Charles representing New Jersey, who, coincidentally, is also African American and also the first African American Miss New Jersey. When Williams is forced to surrender her title, Charles is crowned Miss America.

1984 • Methodist Reverend Leontine Turpeau Current Kelly becomes the first African American woman bishop of a major religious denomination.

1984 • Philadelphia, Pennsylvania
W. Wilson Goode takes the oath of office as the first African American mayor of Philadelphia.

Clifford Alexander, Jr.

1986 • Lieutenant Commander Donnie Cochran becomes the first African American pilot in the United States Navy to fly with the Navy's elite special flying squadron, the Blue Angels. The precision flight team was formed in the 1940s and has performed its highly sophisticated aerobatics in air shows in the United States and Europe ever since.

1988 • Atlanta, Georgia
Eugene Antonio Marino becomes the first African American Roman Catholic archbishop in the United States as he is named archbishop of the Atlanta archdiocese. Marino was one of three auxiliary bishops in Washington, D.C.

1989 • Washington, D.C., lawyer Ronald H. Brown is elected chairman of the Democratic Party's national committee. Brown is the first African American to head a major American political party.

1989 • Episcopal Reverend Barbara C. Harris, an African American, becomes the first female bishop in the worldwide Anglican communion. The Episcopal Church decided in 1976 that women could be ordained priests.

1989 • Vermont
Rodney S. Patterson, an ordained Baptist minister, starts the first African American congregation in Vermont, which a magazine has dubbed "the whitest state in America" because of its small African American population. Patterson, who moved to Burlington to join the staff at the University of Vermont, names the church the New Alpha Missionary Baptist Church.

Patricia Harris

Bishop Barbara Harris

1989 • Army General Colin L. Powell becomes the first African American to serve as chairman of the Joint Chiefs of Staff and principal military advisor to the President of the United States, the Secretary of Defense, and the National Security Council.

1989 • Former St. Louis Cardinal first baseman Bill White assumes office as president of the National League, becoming the first African American to head a professional sports league.

1990 • New York City, New York
David Dinkins becomes the first African American mayor of New York City.

1990 • Michigan
Carole Gist of Michigan becomes the first African American Miss USA.

1990 • Virginia
In Virginia, L. Douglas Wilder becomes the first African American elected governor of a state.

1991 • Corporal Freddie Stowers is posthumously awarded the Medal of Honor for serving in France during World War I. Stowers is the first African American to receive the medal for service in either world war. In 1988, the Secretary of the Army directed the army to conduct a study to determine whether African-American soldiers had been overlooked in the recognition process. Research found that Stowers had been recommended for the medal, but for reasons unknown, the recommendation had not been processed.

1991 • Former Roman Catholic nun Rose Vernell is ordained a priest of the Imani Temple African American Catholic Congregation by Bishop George A. Stallings, Jr. Vernell is the first female priest in the church. The congregation was founded in 1989 when Stallings broke with the church; this was the first split from the Roman Catholic Church in the United States since 1904.

1992 • Illinois
Carol Moseley Braun of Illinois is elected to the United States Senate, becoming the first African American female senator.

1992 • Mae C. Jemison, 35, a physician and chemical engineer, is the first African American woman in space on the United States space shuttle *Endeavor* mission. The crew studies the behavior of living organisms in a weightless atmosphere and looks for ways to cure space sickness.

1993 • Washington, District of Columbia
Dr. Joycelyn Elders, Arkansas health director, is named

David Dinkins

L. Douglas Wilder

Carol Mosely Braun

surgeon general of the United States. Elders is the first African American and the second woman to hold this position. She is sworn into office as U.S. surgeon general in a private ceremony. Elders, 59, is the former head of the Arkansas Health Department.

1993 • Eleanor Holmes Norton becomes the first voting delegate in the United States House of Representatives for Washington, DC. Previously, delegates representing the District of Columbia and the United States Trust Territory were not allowed to vote on the House floor because the Constitution of the United States specifically restricts legislative authority to state representatives.

1993 • Toni Morrison becomes the first African American woman to recieve the Nobel Prize for literature.

1993 • African American candidates in Selma, Alabama, win a majority of seats on the city council for the first time, despite efforts by white council members to maintain a majority.

1993 • South Carolina's Kimberly Clarice Aiken is crowned Miss America, becoming the first African American woman from the South to win the pageant.

1993 • Sharon Sayles Belton becomes the first woman and first African American mayor of Minneapolis, Minnesota.

1994 • Eighteen year-old Eldrick (Tiger) Woods becomes the youngest player and the first African American to win the U.S. Amateur Golf Championship.

1995 • Ronald Kirk is elected Dallas's first African American mayor and is the first African American to lead a major Texas city.

1995 • Willie L. Brown, Jr. defeats incumbent Frank Jordan to become San Francisco's first African American mayor.

3

Significant Documents in African American History

3

Significant Documents in African American History

◆ The Germantown Mennonite Resolution Against Slavery
◆ The Declaration of Independence
◆ The Omitted Anti-Slavery Clause to the Declaration of Independence
◆ The Constitution of the United States ◆ The Bill of Rights ◆ Fugitive Slave Act (1793)
◆ Benjamin Franklin's Address to the Public ◆ George Washington's Last Will and Testament
◆ Act to Prohibit the Importation of Slaves ◆ Editorial from the First Edition of *Freedom's Journal*
◆ Editorial from the First Edition of *The Liberator*
◆ Excerpt from the American Anti-Slavery Society's *American Slavery As It is*
◆ Editorial from the First Edition of *The North Star* ◆ Fugitive Slave Act (1850)
◆ Act to Suppress the Slave Trade in the District of Columbia
◆ Frederick Douglass's Independence Day Address ◆ *Dred Scott v. Sandford*
◆ The Emancipation Proclamation ◆ Freedman's Bureau Act
◆ Amendment Thirteen to the United States Constitution ◆ Black Codes of Mississippi
◆ Civil Rights Act (1866) ◆ Amendment Fourteen to the United States Constitution
◆ Amendment Fifteen to the United States Constitution
◆ Ku Klux Klan Act ◆ Civil Rights Act (1875)
◆ Booker T. Washington's "Atlanta Compromise" Speech ◆ Plessy v. Fergusson
◆ "Lift Every Voice and Sing" ◆ Marcus Garvey's Speech at Liberty Hall, New York City
◆ Executive Order No. 8802 ◆ Executive Order No. 9981 ◆ *Brown v. Board of Education of Topeka*
◆ Civil Rights Act of 1957 ◆ Executive Order No. 10730 ◆ Civil Rights Act of 1960
◆ Executive Order No. 11053 ◆ The Birmingham Manifesto
◆ Dr. Martin Luther King's Speech at the Lincoln Memorial
◆ Amendment Twenty-Four to the United States Constitution ◆ Civil Rights Act of 1964
◆ Executive Order No. 11246 ◆ Voting Rights Act of 1965 ◆ The Black Panther Manifesto
◆ Civil Rights Act of 1968
◆ President George Bush's Message to the Senate Returning without Approval
the Civil Rights Act of 1990
◆ Civil Rights Act of 1991
◆ The Challenge to Ourselves
(An Excerpt from the Mission Statement for the Million Man March, 1995)

The text of proclamations and orders, legislative enactments, speeches, letters, and even poems and songs representing the course of American and African American history. display the presence of African Americans in the yesterday of this country and provide a picture of the changing place blacks have held in the national consciousness. The documents collected here separately capture for a moment in time the African American's role in American society. However, together these documents bare witness to the black experience.

◆ THE GERMANTOWN MENNONITE RESOLUTION AGAINST SLAVERY (1688)

The Mennonites, a group of Protestant Christians who settled mainly in Pennsylvania and the Northwest Territory, rejected the use of violence, refused to bear arms or take oaths, and advocated the separation of church and state and the separation of their community from society. The Germantown Mennonite resolution against slavery represents one of the earliest protests against slavery in colonial America. It was passed sixty-nine years after the introduction of the first African slaves in America—at a time when the number of slaves in the colonies was comparatively small. It was not until 1775, however, that the Quakers, a religious group similarly opposed to the institution, formed the first antislavery society in the colonies.

This is to the monthly meeting held at Richard Worrell's:

These are the reasons why we are against the traffic of men-body, as followeth: Is there any that would be done or handled at this manner? viz., to be sold or made a slave for all the time of his life? How fearful and faint-hearted are many at sea, when they see a strange vessel, being afraid it should be a Turk, and they should be taken, and sold for slaves into Turkey. Now, what is *this* better done, than Turks do? Yea, rather it is worse for them, which say they are Christians; for we hear that the most part of such negers are brought hither against their will and consent, and that many of them are stolen. Now, though they are black, we cannot conceive there is more liberty to have them slaves, as it is to have other white ones. There is a saying, that we should do to all men like as we will be done ourselves; making no difference of what generation, descent, or colour they are. And those who steal or rob men, and those who buy or purchase them, are they not all alike? Here is liberty of conscience, which is right and reasonable; here ought to be likewise liberty of the body, except of evil-doers, which is another case. But to bring men hither, or to rob and sell them against their will, we stand against. In Europe there are many oppressed for conscience-sake; and here there are those oppressed which are of a black colour. And we who know that men must not commit adultery—some do commit adultery *in* others, separating wives from their husbands, and giving them to others: and some sell the children of these poor creatures to other men. Ah! do consider well this thing, you

who do it, if you would be done at this manner—and if it is done according to Christianity! You surpass Holland and Germany in this thing. This makes an ill report in all those countries of Europe, where they hear of (it), that the Quakers do here handel men as they handel there the cattle. And for that reason some have no mind or inclination to come hither. And who shall maintain this your cause, or plead for it? Truly, we cannot do so, except you shall inform us better hereof, viz.: that Christians have liberty to practice these things. Pray, what thing in the world can be done worse towards us, than if men should rob or steal us away, and sell us for slaves to strange countries; separating husbands from their wives and children. Being now this is not done in the manner we would be done at; therefore, we contradict, and are against this traffic of men-body. And we who profess that it is not lawful to steal, must, likewise, avoid to purchase such things as are stolen, but rather help to stop this robbing and stealing, if possible. And such men ought to be delivered out of the hands of the robbers, and set free as in Europe. Then is Pennsylvania to have a good report, instead, it hath now a bad one, for this sake, in other countries; especially whereas the Europeans are desirous to know in what manner *the Quaker* do rule in *their* province; and most of them do look upon us with an envious eye. But if this is done well, what shall we say is done evil?

If once these slaves (which they say are so wicked and stubborn men) should join themselves—fight for their freedom, and handel their masters and mistresses, as they did handel them before; will these masters and mistresses take the sword at hand and war against these poor slaves, like, as we are able to believe, some will not refuse to do? Or, have these poor negers not as much right to fight for their freedom, as you have to keep them slaves?

Now consider well this thing, if it is good or bad. And in case you find it to be good to handel these black in that manner, we desired and require you hereby lovingly, that you may inform us herein, which at this time never was done, viz., that Christians have such a liberty to do so. To the end we shall be satisfied on this point, and satisfy likewise our good friends and acquaintances in our native country, to whom it is a terror, or fearful thing, that men should be handled so in Pennsylvania.

This is from our meeting at Germantown, held ye 18th of the 2nd month, 1688, to be delivered to the monthly meeting at Richard Worrell's.

Garret Henderich,

Derick op de Graeff,

Francis Daniel Pastorius,

Abram op de Graeff.

◆ THE DECLARATION OF INDEPENDENCE

A concept of particular interest of eighteenth-century men and women was the theory of natural rights, the idea that all individuals possess certain fundamental rights which no government can deny. Using this argument as a justification for revolt, the American colonists, on July 4, 1776, formally announced their intention to separate from Great Britain in a Declaration of Independence.

The responsibility of writing this document was given to Thomas Jefferson. In his original draft, Jefferson included among the colonists' grievances the denial of the "most sacred rights of life and liberty" to African slaves. However, the draft was revised, and the final version of the declaration was accepted by Congress without Jefferson's indictment against slavery.

When in the Course of human events, it becomes necessary for one people to dissolve the political bands which have connected them with another, and to assume among the Powers of the earth, the separate and equal station to which the Laws of Nature and of Nature's God entitle them, a decent respect to the opinions of mankind requires that they should declare the causes which impel them to the separation.

We hold these truths to be self-evident, that all men are created equal, that they are endowed by their Creator with certain unalienable Rights, that among these are Life, Liberty and the pursuit of Happiness. That to secure these rights, Governments are instituted among Men, deriving their just powers from the consent of the governed, That whenever any Form of Government becomes destructive of these ends, it is the Right of the People to alter or to abolish it, and to institute new Government, laying its foundation on such principles and organizing its powers in such form, as to them shall seem most likely to effect their Safety and Happiness. Prudence, indeed, will dictate that Governments long established should not be changed for light and transient causes; and accordingly all experience hath shown, that mankind are more disposed to suffer, while evils are sufferable, than to right themselves by abolishing the forms to which they are accustomed. But when a long train of abuses and usurpations, pursuing invariably the same Object evinces a design to reduce them under absolute Despotism, it is their right, it is their duty, to throw off such Government, and to provide new Guards for their future security.—Such has been the patient sufferance of these Colonies; and such is now the necessity which constrains them to alter their former Systems of Government. The history of the present King of Great Britain is a history of repeated injuries and usurpations, all having in direct object the establish-

ment of an absolute Tyranny over these States. To prove this, let Facts be submitted to a candid world.

He has refused his Assent to Laws, the most wholesome and necessary for the public good.

He has forbidden his Governors to pass Laws of immediate and pressing importance, unless suspended in their operation till his Assent should be obtained; and when so suspended, he has utterly neglected to attend to them.

He has refused to pass other Laws for the accommodation of people, unless those people would relinquish the right of Representation in the Legislature, a right inestimable to them and formidable to tyrants only.

He has called together Legislative bodies at places unusual, uncomfortable, and distant from the depository of their Public Records, for the sole purpose of Fatiguing them into compliance with his measures.

He has dissolved Representative Houses repeatedly, for opposing with manly firmness his invasions on the rights of the people.

He has refused for a long time, after such dissolutions, to cause others to be elected; whereby the Legislative Powers, incapable of Annihilation, have returned to the People at large for their exercise; the state remaining in the meantime exposed to all the dangers of invasion from without, and convulsions within.

He has endeavoured to prevent the Population of these States; for that purpose obstructing the Laws of Naturalization of Foreigners; refusing to pass others to encourage their migration hither, and raising the conditions of new Appropriations of Lands.

He has obstructed the Administration of Justice, by refusing his Assent to Laws for establishing Judiciary Powers.

He has made Judges dependent on his Will alone, for the tenure of their offices, and the amount and payment of their salaries.

He has erected a multitude of New Offices, and sent hither swarms of Officers to harass our People, and eat out their substance.

He has kept among us, in times of peace, Standing Armies without the Consent of our legislature.

He has affected to render the Military independent of and superior to the Civil Power.

He has combined with others to subject us to a jurisdiction foreign to our constitution, and unacknowledged by our laws; giving his Assent to their acts of pretended legislation:

For quartering large bodies of armed troops among us:

For protecting them, by a mock Trial, from Punishment for any Murders which they should commit on the Inhabitants of these States:

For cutting off our Trade with all parts of the world:

For imposing taxes on us without our Consent:

For depriving us in many cases, of the benefits of Trial by Jury:

For transporting us beyond Seas to be tried for pretended offenses:

For abolishing the free System of English Laws in a neighboring Province, establishing therein in an Arbitrary government, and enlarging its Boundaries so as to render it at once an example and fit instrument for introducing the same absolute rule into these Colonies:

For taking away our Charters, abolishing our most valuable Laws, and altering fundamentally the Forms of our Governments:

For suspending our own Legislature, and declaring themselves invested with Power to legislate for us in all cases whatsoever.

He has abdicated Government here, by declaring us out of his Protection and waging War against us.

He has plundered our seas, ravaged our Coasts, burnt our towns, and destroyed the lives of our people.

He is at this time transporting large armies of foreign mercenaries to complete the works of death, desolation and tyranny, already begun with circumstances of Cruelty and perfidy scarcely paralleled in the most barbarous ages, and totally unworthy the Head of a civilized nation.

He has constrained our fellow Citizens taken Captive on the high Seas to bear Arms against their Country, to become the executioners of their friends and Brethren, or to fall themselves by their Hands.

He has excited domestic insurrections amongst us, and has endeavoured to bring on the inhabitants of our frontiers, the merciless Indian Savages, whose known rule of warfare, is an undistinguished destruction of all ages, sexes and conditions.

In every stage of these Oppressions We have Petitioned for Redress in the most humble terms: Our repeated Petitions have been answered only by repeated injury. A Prince, whose character is thus marked by every act which may define a Tyrant, is unfit to be the ruler of a free People.

Nor We have been wanting in attention to our British brethren. We have warned them from time to time of attempts by their legislature to extend an unwarrantable jurisdiction over us. We have reminded them of the circumstances of our emigration and settlement here.

We have appealed to their native justice and magnanimity, and we have conjured them by the ties of our common kindred to disavow these usurpations, which would inevitably interrupt our connections and correspondence. They too have been deaf to the voice of justice and of consanguinity. We must, therefore, acquiesce in the necessity, which denounces our Separation, and hold them, as we hold the rest of mankind, Enemies in War, in Peace, Friends.

We, therefore, the Representatives of the United States of America, in General Congress, Assembled, appealing to the Supreme Judge of the world for the rectitude of our intentions, do, in the Name, and by Authority of the good People of these Colonies, solemnly publish and declare, That these United Colonies are, and of Right ought to be Free and Independent States; that they are Absolved from all Allegiance to the British Crown, and that all political connection between them and the State of Great Britain, is and ought to be totally dissolved; and that as Free and Independent States, they have full Power to levy War, conclude Peace, contract Alliances, establish Commerce, and to do all other Acts and Things which Independent States may of right do. And for the support of this Declaration, with a firm reliance on the Protection of Divine Providence, we mutually pledge to each other our Lives, our Fortunes and our sacred Honor.

◆ THE OMITTED ANTI-SLAVERY CLAUSE TO THE DECLARATION OF INDEPENDENCE (1776)

Thomas Jefferson's attitudes regarding African slaves wavered during the course of his life. In his early years, Jefferson thought Africans to be biologically inferior. Later, spurred by his conviction that natural rights accrued to all men, he decided that slavery had a destructive conditioning effect which stamped Africans with "odious peculiarities."

When Jefferson was assigned the task of drafting a declaration calling for separation from Great Britain, he included a short, passionate attack on King George III's indulgence of the slave traffic. However, at the request of delegates from South Carolina and Georgia and of northern delegates whose ports sheltered and profited from slave ships, the clause was omitted from the final version. Many historians and critics have since argued that the elimination of this passage offers adequate proof that Africans in America were never meant to share in the fruits of independence and equally in their adopted homeland.

He [King George III] has waged cruel war against human nature itself, violating its most sacred rights of life and liberty in the persons of a distant people who never offended him, captivating and carrying them into slavery in another hemisphere, or to incur miserable death in their transportation thither. This piratical warfare, the opprobium of *infidel* powers, is the warfare of the *Christian* king of Great Britain. Determined to keep open a market where MEN should be bought and sold, he has prostituted his negative for suppressing every legislative attempt to prohibit or restrain this execrable commerce.

◆ THE CONSTITUTION OF THE UNITED STATES, ART. 1, SECTIONS 2 AND 9, ART. 4, SECTION 2 (1787)

Drawn up in 1787 and ratified a year later, the Constitution of the United States outlines the fundamental principles upon which the American republic is built. In a historical context, the Constitution and its amendments are a manifestation of the issues which have faced Americans and their attempts at resolving these issues.

Among the concepts important to Americans living during the eighteenth century were the ideas that all people were created equal and were endowed with certain unalienable rights and that a government derives its power from the consent of those it governs. However, despite the fact that almost twenty percent of the population was bound in slavery, the economic and social arguments of the time regarding the status of African slaves overrode the tenets of natural rights. In 1857, Chief Justice Roger Brook Tangy, delivering the Court's opinion in the case Dred Scott v. Sandford, summarized the attitude of the writers of the Constitution toward African slaves.

...They are not included, and were not intended to be included, under the word "citizens" in the constitution, and can therefore claim none of the rights and privileges which that instrument provides and secures....On the contrary, they were at that time considered as a subordinate and inferior class of beings....

Specifically, it is Article I, Sections 2 and 9, and Article IV, Section 2 of the Constitution, which deal directly with the status of Africans in America.

Preamble

We the People of the United States, in order to form a more perfect Union, establish Justice, insure domestic Tranquility, provide for the common defense, promote the general Welfare, and secure the Blessings of Liberty to ourselves and our Posterity, do ordain and establish this Constitution for the United States of America.

Article I

Section 2. ...Representatives and direct Taxes shall be apportioned among the several States which may be included within this Union, according to their respective Numbers, which shall be determined by adding to the whole Number of free Persons, including those bound to Service for a Term of Years, and excluding Indians not taxed, three-fifths of all other Persons. The actual Enumeration shall be made within three Years after the first Meeting of the Congress of the United States, and within every subsequent Term of Ten Years, in such manner as they shall by Law direct....

Section 9. The Migration or Importation of such Persons as any of the States now existing shall think proper to admit, shall not be prohibited by the Congress prior to the Year one thousand eight hundred and eight, but a Tax or duty may be imposed on such Importation, not exceeding ten dollars for each Person....

Article IV

Section 2. The Citizens of each State shall be entitled to all privileges and Immunities of Citizens in the several States.

A Person charged in any State with Treason, Felony, or other Crime, who shall flee from Justice, and be found in another State, shall on Demand of the executive authority of the State from which he fled, be delivered up, to be removed to the State having Jurisdiction of the Crime.

No Person held to Service or Labour in one State, under the Laws thereof, escaping into another, shall, in Consequence of any Law or Regulation therein, be discharged from such Service or Labour, but shall be delivered up on Claim of the Party to whom such Service or Labour may be due.

◆ THE BILL OF RIGHTS (1791)

Ratified in 1791, the first ten amendments to the Constitution of the United States, commonly referred to as the Bill of Rights, further outline the fundamental rights and freedoms of citizens of the United States. This set of additions to the Constitution was a crucial part of the constitutional ratification process (several states had only ratified the Constitution on the condition that a bill of rights would be added), since eighteenth-century Americans held dearly to the concept of personal freedom. Despite these beliefs, it was not until after ratification of the Fourteenth Amendment to the Constitution and several civil rights laws that the freedoms protected in the Bill of Rights were extended to all United States citizens.

Delegates meet to draft a national constitution.

Amendment 1

Congress shall make no law respecting an establishment of religion, or prohibiting the free exercise thereof; or abridging the freedom of speech, or of the press; or the right of the people peaceably to assemble, and to petition the government for a redress of grievances.

Amendment 2

A well regulated Militia, being necessary to the security of a free State, the right of the people to keep and bear Arms, shall not be infringed.

Amendment 3

No Soldier, shall, in time of peace be quartered in any house, without the consent of the Owner, nor in time of war, but in a manner to be prescribed by law.

Amendment 4

The right of the people to be secure in their persons, houses, papers and effects, against unreasonable searches and seizures, shall not be violated and no Warrants shall issue, but upon probable cause, supported by Oath or affirmation, and particularly describing the place to be searched, and the persons or things to be seized.

Amendment 5

No person shall be held to answer for a capital, or otherwise infamous crime, unless on a presentment or indictment of a Grand Jury, except in cases arising in the land or naval forces, or in the Militia, when in actual service in time of War or public danger; nor shall any person be subject for the same offense to be twice put in jeopardy of life or limb; nor shall be compelled in any criminal case to be a witness against himself, nor be deprived of life, liberty, or property, without due process of law; nor shall private property be taken for public use, without just compensation.

Amendment 6

In all criminal prosecutions, the accused shall enjoy the right to a speedy and public trial, by an impartial jury of the State and district wherein the crime shall have been committed, which district shall have been previously ascertained by law, and to be informed of the nature and cause of the accusation; to be confronted with witnesses against him; to have compulsory process for obtaining witnesses in his favor, and to have the Assistance of Counsel for his defence.

Amendment 7

In Suits at common law, where the value in controversy shall exceed twenty dollars, the right of trial by jury shall be preserved, and no fact tried by a jury, shall be otherwise re-examined in any Court of the United States, than according to the rules of the common law.

Amendment 8

Excessive bail shall not be required, nor excessive fines imposed, nor cruel and unusual punishments inflicted.

Amendment 9

The enumeration in the Constitution, of certain rights, shall not be construed to deny or disparage others retained by the people.

Amendment 10

The powers not delegated to the United States by the Constitution, nor prohibited by it to the States, are reserved to the States respectively, or to the people.

◆ FUGITIVE SLAVE ACT CH. 7, 1 STAT. 302 (1793)

The Fugitive Slave Act of 1793 was designed to enforce Article IV, Section 2 of the Constitution and incur penalties against those who aided or abetted attempts of slaves to escape bondage.

Section 1. *Be it enacted by the Senate and House of Representatives of the United States of America in Congress assembled,* That whenever the executive authority of any state in the Union, or of either of the territories northwest or south of the river Ohio, shall demand any person as a fugitive from justice, of the executive authority of any such state or territory to which such person shall have fled, and shall moreover produce the copy of an indictment found, or an affidavit made before a magistrate of any state or territory as aforesaid, charging the person so demanded, with having committed treason, felony or other crime, certified as authentic by the governor or chief magistrate of the state or territory from whence the person so charged fled, it shall be the duty of the executive authority of the state or territory to which such person shall have fled, to cause him or her to be arrested and secured, and notice of the arrest to be given to the executive authority making such demand, or to the agent of such authority

appointed to receive the fugitive, and to cause the fugitive to be delivered to such agent when he shall appear: But if no such agent shall appear within six months from the time of the arrest, the prisoner may be discharged. And all costs or expenses incurred to the state or territory making such demand, shall be paid by such state or territory.

Section 2. *And be it further enacted,* That any agent, appointed as aforesaid, who shall receive the fugitive into his custody, shall be empowered to transport him or her to the state or territory from which he or she shall have fled. And if any person or persons shall by force set at liberty, or rescue the fugitive from such agent while transporting, as aforesaid, the person or persons so offending shall, on conviction, be fined not exceeding five hundred dollars, and be imprisoned not exceeding one year.

Section 3. *And be it also enacted,* That when a person held to labour in any of the United States, or in either of the territories on the northwest or south of the river Ohio, under the laws thereof, shall escape into any other of the said states or territory, the person to whom such labour or service may be due, his agent or attorney, is hereby empowered to seize or arrest such fugitive from labour, and to take him or her before any judge of the circuit or district courts of the United States, residing or being within the state, or before any magistrate of a county, city or town corporate, wherein such seizure or arrest shall be made, and upon proof to the satisfaction of such judge or magistrate, either by oral testimony or affidavit taken before and certified by a magistrate of any such state or territory, that the person so seized or arrested, doth, under the laws of the state or territory from which he or she fled, owe service or labour to the person claiming him or her, it shall be the duty of such judge or magistrate to give a certificate thereof to such claimant, his agent or attorney, which shall be sufficient warrant for removing the said fugitive from labour, to the state or territory from which he or she fled.

Section 4. *And be it further enacted,* That any person who shall knowingly and willing obstruct or hinder such claimant, his agent or attorney in so seizing or arresting such fugitive from labour, or shall rescue such fugitive from such claimant, his agent or attorney when so arrested pursuant to the authority herein given or declared; or shall harbor or conceal such person after notice that he or she was a fugitive from labour, as aforesaid shall, for either of the said offenses, forfeit and pay the sum of five hundred dollars. Which penalty may be recovered by and for the benefit of such claimant, by action of debt, in any court proper to try the same; saving moreover to the person claiming such labour or service, his right of action for or on account of the said injuries or either of them.

◆ BENJAMIN FRANKLIN'S ADDRESS TO THE PUBLIC (1798)

Despite the frames of the Constitution's handling of the slavery issue, influential opponents to slavery attempted to exert pressure on the Congress to enact an antislavery amendment to the Constitution. Among such groups was the Pennsylvania Society for Promoting the Abolition of Slavery and the Relief of Free Negroes Unlawfully Held in Bondage. Over the signature of the president of the Society, Benjamin Franklin, the following "Address to the Public," urged abolition.

It is with peculiar satisfaction we assure the friends of humanity that, in prosecuting the design of our association, our endeavors have proved successful, far beyond our most sanguine expectations.

Encouraged by this success, and by the daily progress of that luminous and benign spirit of liberty which is diffusing itself throughout the world, and humbly hoping for the continuance of the divine blessing on our labors, we have ventured to make an important addition to our original plan; and do therefore earnestly solicit the support and assistance of all who can feel the tender emotions of sympathy and compassion, or relish the exalted pleasure of beneficence.

Slavery is such an atrocious debasement of human nature, that its very extirpation, if not performed with solicitous care, may sometimes open a source of serious evils.

The unhappy man, who has long been treated as a brute animal, too frequently sinks beneath the common standard of the human species. The galling chains that bind his body do also fetter his intellectual faculties, and impair the social affections of his heart. Accustomed to move like a mere machine, by the will of a master, reflection is suspended; he has not the power of choice; and reason and conscience have but little influence over his conduct, because he is chiefly governed by the passion of fear. He is poor and friendless; perhaps worn out by extreme labor, age, and disease.

Under such circumstances, freedom may often prove a misfortune to himself, and prejudicial to society.

Attention to emancipated black people, it is therefore to be hoped, will become a branch of our national police; but, as far as we contribute to promote this emancipation, so far that attention is evidently a serious duty incumbent on us, and which we mean to discharge to the best of our judgment and abilities.

To instruct, to advise, to qualify those who have been restored to freedom, for the exercise and enjoyment of civil liberty; to promote in them habits of industry; to furnish them with employments suited to their age, sex, talents, and other circumstances; and to procure their

Benjamin Franklin

children an education calculated for their future situation in life,—these are the great outlines of the annexed plan, which we have adopted, and which we conceive will essentially promote the public good, and the happiness of these our hitherto too much neglected fellow-creatures.

A plan so extensive cannot be carried into execution without considerable pecuniary resources, beyond the present ordinary funds of the Society. We hope much from the generosity of enlightened and benevolent freemen, and will gratefully receive any donations of subscriptions for this purpose which may be made to our Treasurer, James Starr, or to James Pemberton, Chairman of our Committee of Correspondence.

Signed by order of the Society,

B. FRANKLIN, President

Philadelphia, 9th of November, 1789

◆ GEORGE WASHINGTON'S LAST WILL AND TESTAMENT (1799)

By the eighteenth century, the slavery of Africans had become a firmly entrenched institution of American life, particularly in the South where it was justified as an economic necessity. This argument notwithstanding, it was Washington's decision, at the writing of his last will and testament in 1799, to free all those slaves which he held in his "own right."

In the Name of God Amen

I, George Washington of Mount Vernon—a citizen of the United States,—and lately President of the same, do make, ordain and declare this Instrument; which is written with my own hand and every page thereof subscribed with my name, to be my last Will and Testament, revoking all other....Upon the deceased of my wife, it is my Will and desire that all the Slaves which I hold in my *own right*, shall receive their freedom....And whereas among those who will receive freedom according to this devise, there may be some, who from old age or bodily infirmities, and others who on account of their infancy, that will be unable to support themselves; it is my Will and desire that all who come under the first and second description shall be comfortably clothed and fed by my heirs while they live;—and that such of the latter description as have no parents living, or if living are unable, or unwilling to provide for them, shall be bound by the Court until they shall arrive at the age of twenty-five year;—and in cases where no record can be produced, whereby their ages can be ascertained, the judgment of the Court upon its own view of the subject, shall be adequate and final.—The Negros thus bound, are (by their Masters or Mistresses) to be taught to read and write; and to be brought up to some useful occupation, agreeably to the Laws of the Commonwealth of Virginia, providing for the support of Orphan and other poor Children.—And I do hereby expressly forbid the Sale, or transportation out of the said Commonwealth of any Slave I may die possessed of, under any pretence whatsoever.—And I do moreover most pointedly, and most solemnly enjoin it upon my Executors hereafter named, or the Survivors of them, to see that this clause respecting Slaves, and every part thereof be religiously fulfilled at the Epoch at which it is directed to take place; without evasion, neglect or delay, after the Crops which may then be on the ground are harvested, particularly as it respects the aged and infirm;—Seeing that a regular and permanent fund be established for their Support so long as there are subjects requiring it; not trusting to the uncertain provision to be made by individuals.—And to my Mulatto man William (calling himself William Lee) I give immediate freedom; or if he should prefer it (on account of the accidents which have befallen him, and which have rendered him incapable of walking or of any active employment) to remain in the situation he now is, it shall be optional in him to do so: In either case however, I allow him an annuity of thirty dollars during his natural life, which shall be independent of the vict-

uals and cloaths he has been accustomed to receive, if he chooses the last alternative; but in full, with his freedom, if he prefers the first;— and this I give him as a testimony of my sense of his attachment to me, and for his faithful services during the Revolutionary War.

◆ ACT TO PROHIBIT THE IMPORTATION OF SLAVES CH.22, 2 STAT. 426 (1807)

In adherence with the provisions of Article I, Section 9 of the Constitution, Congress passed and President Thomas Jefferson signed into law an act to end the slave trade. The act, however, which went into effect January 1, 1808, was not rigidly enforced. Evidence of this can be found in the fact that, between 1808 and 1860, some 250,000 slaves were illegally imported into the United States.

An Act to prohibit the importation of Slaves into any port or place within the jurisdiction of the United States, from and after the first day of January, in the year of our Lord one thousand eight hundred and eight.

Be it enacted, that from and after the first day of January, one thousand eight hundred and eight, it shall not be lawful to import or bring into the United States or the territories thereof from any foreign kingdom, place, or country, any negro, mulatto, or person of colour, as a slave, or to be held to service or labour.

Section 2. That no citizen of the United States, or any other person, shall, from and after the first day of January, in the year of our Lord one thousand eight hundred and eight, for himself, or themselves, or any other person whatsoever, either as master, factor, or owner, build, fit, equip, load or to otherwise prepare any ship or vessel, in any port or place within the jurisdiction of the United States, nor shall cause any ship or vessel to sail from any port or place within the same, for the purpose of procuring any negro, mulatto, or person of colour, from any foreign kingdom, place, or country, to be transported to any port or place whatsoever within the jurisdiction of the United States, to be held, sold, or disposed of as slaves, or to be held to service or labour: and if any ship or vessel shall be so fitted out for the purpose aforesaid, or shall be caused to sail so as aforesaid, every such ship or vessel, her tackle, apparel, and furniture, shall be forfeited to the United States, and shall be liable to be seized, prosecuted, and condemned in any of the circuit courts or district courts, for the district where the said ship or vessel may be found or seized....

Section 4. If any citizen or citizens of the United States, or any person resident within the jurisdiction of the same, shall, from after the first day of January, one thousand eight hundred and eight, take on board, re-

A cell used to hold newly arrived African slaves.

ceive or transport from any of the coasts or kingdoms of Africa, or from any other foreign kingdom, place, or country, any negro, mulatto, or person of colour in any ship or vessel, for the purpose of selling them in any port or place within the jurisdiction of the United States as slaves, or be to held to service or labour, or shall be in any ways aiding or abetting therein, such citizen or citizens, or person, shall severally forfeit and pay five thousand dollars, one moiety thereof to the use of any person or persons who shall sue for and prosecute the same to effect....

Section 6. That if any person or persons whatsoever, shall, from and after the first day of January, one thousand eight hundred and eight, purchase or sell any negro, mulatto, or person, of colour, for a slave, or to be held to service or labour, who shall have been imported, or brought from any foreign kingdom, place, or country, or from the dominions of any foreign state, immediately adjoining to the United States, after the last day of December, one thousand eight hundred and seven, knowing at the time of such purchase or sale, such negro, mulatto, or person of colour, was so brought within the jurisdiction of the United States, as aforesaid, such purchaser and seller shall severally forfeit and pay for every negro, mulatto, or person of colour, so purchased, or sold as aforesaid, eight hundred dollars....

Section 7. That if any ship or vessel shall be found, from and after the first day of January, one thousand eight hundred and eight, in any river, port, bay, or harbor, or on the high seas, within the jurisdictional limits of the United States, or hovering on the coast thereof, having on board any negro, mulatto, or person of colour, for the purpose of selling them as slaves, or with intent to land the same, in any port or place within the jurisdiction of the United States, contrary to the prohibition of the act, every such ship or vessel, together with her tackle, apparel, and furniture, and the goods or effects which shall be found on board the same, shall be forfeited to the use of the United States, and may be seized, prosecuted, and condemned, in any court of the United States, having jurisdiction thereof. And it shall be lawful for the President of the United States, and he is hereby authorized, should he deem it expedient, to cause any of the armed vessels of the United States to be manned and employed to cruise on any part of the coast of the United States, or territories thereof, where he may judge attempts will be made to violate the provisions of this act, and to instruct and direct the commanders of armed vessels of the United States, to seize, take, and bring into any port of the United States all such ships or vessels, and moreover to seize, take, or bring into any port of the U.S. all ships or vessels of the U.S. wheresoever found on the high seas, contravening the provisions of this act, to be proceeded against according to law....

◆ EDITORIAL FROM THE FIRST EDITION OF *FREEDOM'S JOURNAL* (1827)

Freedom's Journal, published by Samuel Cornish and John B. Russwurm, was the first African American owned and edited newspaper to be published in the United States. This editorial, printed here in its entirety, illustrates the *Journal*'s aim at bringing an end to slavery and discrimination.

To Our Patrons

In presenting our first number to our Patrons, we feel all the diffidence of persons entering upon a new and untried line of business. But a moment's reflection upon the noble objects, which we have in view by the publication of this Journal; the expediency of its appearance at this time, when so many schemes are in action concerning our people—encourage us to come boldly before an enlightened public. For we believe, that a paper devoted to the dissemination of useful knowledge among our brethren, and to their moral and religious improvement, must meet with the cordial approbation of every friend to humanity.

The peculiarities of this Journal, renders it important that we should advertise to the world our motives by which we are actuated, and the objects which we contemplate.

We wish to plead our own cause. Too long have others spoken for us. Too long has the public been deceived by misrepresentations, in things which concern us dearly, though in the estimation of some mere trifles; for though there are many in society who exercise towards us benevolent feelings; still (with sorrow we confess it) there are others who make it their business to enlarge upon the least trifle, which tends to the discredit of any person of colour; and pronounce anathemas and denounce our whole body for the misconduct of this guilty one. We are aware that there are many instances of vice among us, but we avow that it is because no one has taught its subjects to be virtuous; many instances of poverty, because no sufficient efforts accommodated to minds contracted by slavery, and deprived of early education have been made, to teach them how to husband their hard earnings, and to secure to themselves comfort.

Education being an object of the highest importance to the welfare of society, we shall endeavor to present just and adequate views of it, and to urge upon our brethren the necessity and expediency of training their children, while young, to habits of industry, and thus forming them for becoming useful members of society. It is surely time that we should awake from this lethargy of years, and make a concentrated effort for the education of our youth. We form a spoke in the human wheel, and it is necessary that we should understand our pendency on the different parts, and theirs on us, in order to perform our part with propriety.

Though not desiring of dictating, we shall feel it our incumbent duty to dwell occasionally upon the general principles and rules of economy. The world has grown too enlightened, to estimate any man's character by his personal appearance. Though all men acknowledge the excellency of Franklin's maxims, yet comparatively few practice upon them. We may deplore when it is too late, the neglect of these self-evident truths, but it avails little to mourn. Ours will be the task of admonishing our brethren on these points.

The civil rights of a people being of the greatest value, it shall ever be our duty to vindicate our brethren, when oppressed; and to lay the case before the public. We shall also urge upon our brethren, (who are qualified by the laws of the different states) the expediency of using their elective franchise; and of making an independent use of the same. We wish them not to become the tools of party.

And as much time is frequently lost, and wrong principles instilled, by the perusal of works of trivial importance, we shall consider it a part of our duty to recommend to our young readers, such authors as will not only enlarge their stock of useful knowledge, but such as will also serve to stimulate them to higher attainments in science.

WE trust also, that through the columns of the FREEDOM'S JOURNAL, many practical pieces, having for their bases, the improvement of our brethren, will be presented to them, from the pens of many of our respected friends, who have kindly promised their assistance.

It is our earnest wish to make our Journal a medium of intercourse between our brethren in the different states of this great confederacy: that through its columns an expression of our sentiments, on many interesting subjects which concern us, may be offered to the public: that plans which apparently are beneficial may be candidly discussed and properly weighed; if worth, receive our cordial approbation; if not, our marked disapprobation.

Useful knowledge of every kind, and everything that relates to Africa, shall find a ready admission into our columns; and as that vast continent becomes daily more known, we trust that many things will come to light, proving that the natives of it are neither so ignorant nor stupid as they have generally been supposed to be.

And while these important subjects shall occupy the columns of the FREEDOM'S JOURNAL, we would not be unmindful of our brethren who are still in the iron fetters of bondage. They are our kindred by all the ties of nature; and though but little can be effected to us, still let our sympathies be poured forth and our prayers in their behalf, ascend to Him who is able to succor them.

From the press and the pulpit we have suffered much by being incorrectly represented. Men whom we equally love and admire have not hesitated to represent us disadvantageously, without becoming personally acquainted with the true state of things, nor discerning between virtue and vice among us. The virtuous part of our people feel themselves sorely aggrieved under the existing state of things—they are not appreciated.

Our vices and our degradation are ever arrayed against us, but our virtues are passed by unnoticed. And what is still more lamentable, our friends, to whom we concede all the principles of humanity and religion, from these very causes seem to have fallen into the current of popular feeling and are imperceptibly floating on the stream—actually living in the practice of prejudice, while they abjure it in theory, and feel it not in their hearts. Is it not very desirable that such should know more of our actual condition; and of our efforts and feelings, that in forming or advocating plans for our amelioration, they may do it more understanding? In the spirit of candor and humility we intend by a simple representation of facts to lay our case before the public, with a view to arrest the progress of prejudice, and to shield ourselves against the consequent evils. We wish to conciliate all and to irritate none, yet we must be firm and unwavering in our principles, and persevering in our efforts.

If ignorance, poverty and degradation have hitherto been our unhappy lot; has the Eternal decree gone forth, that our race alone are to remain in this state, while knowledge and civilization are shedding their enlivening rays over the rest of the human family? The recent travels of Denham and Clapperton in the interior of Africa, and the interesting narrative which they have published; the establishment of the republic of Haiti after years of sanguinary warfare; its subsequent progress in all the arts of civilization; and the advancement of liberal ideas in South America, where despotism has given place to free governments, and where many of our brethren now fill important civil and military stations, prove the contrary.

The interesting fact that there are FIVE HUNDRED THOUSAND free persons of color, one half of whom might peruse, and the whole be benefitted by the publication of the Journal; that no publication, as yet, has been devoted exclusively to their improvement—that many selections from approved standard authors, which are within the reach of few, may occasionally be made—and more important still, that this large body of our citizens have no public channel—all serve to prove the real necessity, at present, for the appearance of the FREEDOM'S JOURNAL.

It shall ever be our desire so to conduct the editorial department of our paper as to give offence to none of our patrons; as nothing is farther from us than to make it the advocate of any partial views, either in politics or religion. What few days we can number, have been devoted to the improvement of our brethren; and it is our earnest wish that the remainder may be spent in the same delightful service.

In conclusion, whatever concerns us as a people, will ever find a ready admission into the FREEDOM'S JOURNAL, interwoven with all the principal news of the day.

And while every thing in our power shall be performed to support the character of our Journal, we would respectfully invite our numerous friends to assist by their communications, and our coloured brethren to strengthen our hands by their subscriptions, as our labour is one of common cause, and worthy of their consideration and support. And we most earnestly solicit the latter, that if at any time we should seem to be zealous, or too pointed in the inculcation of any important lesson, they will remember, that they are equally interested in the cause in which we are engaged, and attribute our zeal to the peculiarities of our situation; and our earnest engagedness in their well-being.

◆ EDITORIAL FROM THE FIRST EDITION OF *THE LIBERATOR* (1831)

The Liberator, one of the most well known abolitionist newspapers in the nineteenth century, was published weekly out of Boston, Massachusetts between 1831 and 1865. The paper's founder, William Lloyd Garrison, who was also the founder of the American Anti-Slavery Society, was white. However, most of *The Liberator*'s subscribers were black. During its thirty-four years of publication, Garrison worked at shifting the sentiment of the nation away from the notion of gradual emancipation toward that of total abolition—as illustrated in this except from the paper's first editorial.

...During my recent tour for the purpose of exciting the minds of the people by a series of discourses on the subject of slavery, every place that I visited gave fresh evidence of the fact, that a greater revolution in public sentiment was to be effected in the free states—and particularly in New England—than at the south. I found contempt more bitter, opposition more active, detraction more relentless, prejudice more stubborn, and apathy more frozen, than among slave owners themselves. Of course, there were individual exceptions to the contrary. This state of things afflicted, but did not dishearten me. I determined, at every hazard, to lift up the standard of emancipation in the eyes of the nation, within sight of Bunker Hill and in the birth place of liberty. That standard is now unfurled; and long may it float, unhurt by the spoliations of time or the missiles of a desperate foe—yea, till every chain be broken, and every bondman set free! Let Southern oppressors tremble—let their secret abettors tremble—let their Northern apologists tremble—let all the enemies of the persecuted blacks tremble.

I am aware that many object to the severity of my language; but is there not cause for severity? I will be as harsh as truth, and as uncompromising as justice. On this subject, I do not wish to think, or speak, or write, with moderation. No! No! Tell a man whose house is on fire to give a moderate alarm; tell the mother to gradually extricate her babe from the fire into which it has fallen;—but urge me not to use moderation in a cause like the present. I am in earnest—I will not equivocate—I will not excuse—I will not retreat a single inch—AND I WILL BE HEARD....

William Lloyd Garrison

◆ EXCERPT FROM THE AMERICAN ANTI-SLAVERY SOCIETY'S *AMERICAN SLAVERY AS IT IS* (1839)

In 1839, The American Anti-Slavery Society compiled a massive portfolio of testimonies, entitled *American Slavery As It Is*, which sought to document the inhumanities of slavery. The introduction, by Theodore D. Weld of New York, written in the style of a prosecutor addressing a court, stirred abolitionist sentiments in the North and was attacked by proslavery forces in the South.

READER, YOU are empaneled as a juror to try a plain case and bring in an honest verdict. The question at issue is not one of law, but of act—"What is the actual condition of slaves in the United States?"

A plainer case never went to jury. Look at it. TWENTY SEVEN HUNDRED THOUSAND PERSONS in this country, men, women, and children, are in SLAVERY. Is slavery, as a condition for human beings, good, bad, or indifferent?

We submit the question without argument. You have common sense, and conscience, and a human heart—pronounce upon it. You have a wife, or a husband, a child, a father, a mother, a brother or a sister—make the case your own, make it theirs, and bring in your verdict.

The case of Human Rights against Slavery has been adjudicated in the court of conscience times innumerable. The same verdict has always been rendered—"Guilty;" the same sentence has always been pronounced "Let it be accursed;" and human nature, with her million echoes, has rung it round the world in every language under heaven. "Let it be accursed...."

As slaveholders and their apologists are volunteer witnesses in their own cause, and are flooding the world with testimony that their slaves are kindly treated; that they are well fed, well clothed, well housed, well lodged, moderately worked, and bountifully provided with all things needful for their comfort, we propose—first, to disprove their assertions by the testimony of a multitude of impartial witnesses, and then to put slaveholders themselves through a course of cross-questioning which will draw their condemnation out of their own mouths.

We will prove that the slaves in the United States are treated with barbarous inhumanity; that they are overworked, underfed, wretchedly clad and lodged, and have insufficient sleep; that they are often made to wear round their necks iron collars armed with prongs, to drag heavy chains and weights at their feet while working in the field, and to wear yokes and bells, and iron horns; that they are often kept confined in the stocks day and night for weeks together, made to wear gags in their mouths for hours or days, have some of their front

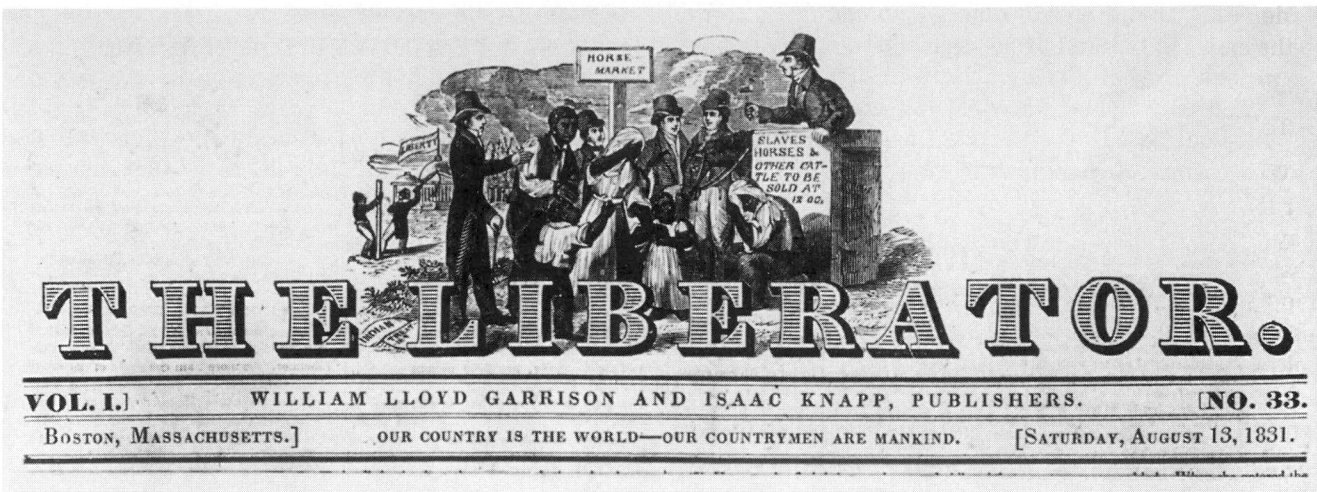

Masthead from William Lloyd Garrison's newspaper, *The Liberator.*

teeth torn out or broken off, that they may be easily detected when they run away; that they are frequently flogged with terrible severity, have red pepper rubbed into their lacerated flesh, and hot brine, spirits of turpentine etc., poured over the gashes to increase the torture; that they are often stripped naked, their backs and limbs cut with knives, bruised and mangled by scores and hundreds of blows with the paddle, and terribly torn by the claws of cats, drawn over them by their tormentors; that they are often hunted with bloodhounds and shot down like beasts, or torn in pieces by dogs; that they are often suspended by the arms and whipped and beaten till they faint, and when revived by restoratives, beaten again till they faint, and sometimes till they die; that their ears are often cut off, their eyes knocked out, their bones broken, their flesh branded with red hot irons; that they are maimed, mutilated and burned to death, over slow fires. All these things, and more, and worse, we shall *prove*....

We shall show, not merely that such deeds are committed, but that they are frequent; not done in corners, but before the sun; not in one of the slave states, but in all of them; not perpetrated by brutal overseers and drivers merely, but by magistrates, by legislators, by professors of religion, by preachers of the gospel, by governors of states, by "gentlemen of property and standing," and by delicate females moving in the "highest circles of society."

We know, full well, the outcry that will be made by multitudes, at these declarations; the multiform cavils, the flat denials, the charges of "exaggeration" and "falsehood" so often bandied, the sneers of affected contempt at the credulity that can believe such things, and the rage and imprecations against those who give them currency. We know, too, the threadbare sophistries by which slaveholders and their apologists seek to evade such testimony. If they admit that such deeds are committed, they tell us that they are exceedingly rare, and therefore furnish no grounds for judging of the general treatment of slaves; that occasionally a brutal wretch in the *free* states barbarously butchers his wife, but that no one thinks of inferring from that, the general treatment of wives at the North and West.

They tell us, also, that the slaveholders of the South are proverbially hospitable, kind, and generous, and it is incredible that they can perpetrate such enormities upon human beings; further, that it is absurd to suppose that they would thus injure their own property, that self-interest would prompt them to treat their slaves with kindness, as none but fools and madmen wantonly destroy their own property; further, that Northern visitors at the South come back testifying to the kind treatment of the slaves, and that slaves themselves corroborate such representations. All these pleas, and scores of others, are build in every corner of the free States; and who that hath eyes to see, has not sickened at the blindness that saw not, at the palsy of heart that felt not, or at the cowardice and sycophancy that dared not expose such shallow fallacies. We are not to be turned from our purpose by such vapid babblings. In their appropriate places, we proposed to consider these objections and various others, and to show their emptiness and folly.

◆ EDITORIAL FROM THE FIRST EDITION OF *THE NORTH STAR* (1847)

The first edition of Frederick Douglass's newspaper, *The North Star* was published on December 3, 1847, in Rochester, New York. Douglass, an escaped slave and leader in the abolitionist movement, dedicated his paper to the cause of blacks in America—as displayed in this, the paper's first editorial.

To Our Oppressed Countrymen

We solemnly dedicate the *North Star* to your cause, our long oppressed and plundered fellow countrymen. May God bless the offering to your good! It shall fearlessly assert your rights, faithfully proclaim your wrongs, and earnestly demand for you instant and even-handed justice. Giving no quarter to slavery at the South, it will hold no truce with oppressors at the North. While it shall boldly advocate emancipation for our enslaved brethren, it will omit no opportunity to gain for the nominally free, complete enfranchisement. Every effort to injure or degrade you or your cause—originating wheresoever, or with whomsoever—shall find in it a constant, unswerving and inflexible foe.

We shall energetically assail the ramparts of Slavery and Prejudice, be they composed of church or state, and seek the destruction of every refuge of lies, under which tyranny may aim to conceal and protect itself....

While our paper shall be mainly Anti-Slavery, its columns shall be freely opened to the candid and decorous discussions of all measures and topics of a moral and humane character, which may serve to enlighten, improve, and elevate mankind. Temperance, Peace, Capital Punishment, Education,—all subjects claiming the attention of the public mind may be freely and fully discussed here.

While advocating your rights, the *North Star* will strive to throw light on your duties: while it will not fail to make known your virtues, it will not shun to discover your faults. To be faithful to our foes it must be faithful to ourselves, in all things.

Remember that we are one, that our cause is one, and that we must help each other, if we would succeed. We have drunk to the dregs the bitter cup of slavery; we have worn the heavy yoke; we have sighed beneath our bonds, and writhed beneath the bloody lash;—cruel mementoes of our oneness are indelibly marked in our living flesh. We are one with you under the ban of prejudice and proscription—one with you under the slander of inferior—one with you in social and political disfranchisement. What you suffer, we suffer; what you endure, we endure. We are indissolubly united, and must fall or flourish together....

We shall be the advocates of learning, from the very want of it, and shall most readily yield the deference due to men of education among us; but shall always bear in mind to accord most merit to those who have labored hardest, and overcome most, in the praiseworthy pursuit of knowledge, remembering "that the whole need not a physician, but they that are sick," and that "the strong ought to bear the infirmities of the weak."

Brethren, the first number of the paper is before you. It is dedicated to your cause. Through the kindness of our friends in England, we are in possession of an excellent printing press, types, and all other materials necessary for printing a paper. Shall this gift be blest to our good, or shall it result in our injury? It is for you to say. With your aid, cooperation and assistance, our enterprise will be entirely successful. We pledge ourselves that no effort on our part shall be wanting, and that no subscriber shall lose his subscription—"*The North Star* Shall live."

◆ FUGITIVE SLAVE ACT CH. 60, 9 STAT. 462 (1850)

For almost fifteen years the provisions of the Missouri Compromise had quieted the debate over the expansion of slavery in the United States. However, following the annexation of Texas in 1845 and the ending of the war with Mexico in 1848, the question of expansion reignited tensions between proslavery forces and opponents to the institution.

With Southern members of Congress threatening to withdraw, a compromise was reached in 1850 between advocates of expression and their rivals. The compromise, a package of five statute s, attempted to address the major points of the sectional conflict. One of the provisions of the compromise, which was supported by many Southerners, was a strengthening of the existing federal fugitive slave law. On September 18, 1850, an act amending the 1793 fugitive slave statute was signed into law. Both the 1850 and the 1793 acts were finally repealed on June 28, 1864.

Section 5. That it shall be the duty of all marshals and deputy marshals to obey and execute all warrants and precepts issued under the provisions of this act, when to them directed; and should any marshal or deputy marshal refuse to receive such warrant, or other process, when tendered, or to use all proper means diligently to execute the same, he shall, on conviction thereof, be fined in the sum of one thousand dollars, to the use of such claimant,... and after arrest of such fugitive, by such marshal or his deputy, or whilst at any time in his custody under the provisions of this act, should such fugitive escape, whether with or without the assent of such marshal or his deputy, such marshal shall be liable, on his official bond, to be prosecuted for the benefit of such claimant, for the full value of the service or labor of said fugitive in the State, Territory, or District whence he escaped: and the better to enable the said commissioners, when thus appointed, to execute their duties faithfully and efficiently, in conformity with the requirements of the Constitution of the United States and of this act, they are hereby authorized and empowered, within their counties respectively, to appoint,...any one or more suitable persons, from time to time, to execute all such warrants and other processes as may be issued by them in the lawful performance of their respective duties....

Section 6. That when a person held to service or labor in any State or Territory of the United States, has heretofore or shall hereafter escape into another State or Territory of the United States, the person or persons to whom such service or labor may be due,...may pursue and reclaim such fugitive person, either by procuring a warrant from some one of the courts, judges, or commissioners aforesaid, of the proper circuit, district, or county, for the apprehension of such fugitive from service or labor, or by seizing and arresting such fugitive, where the same can be done without process, and by taking, or causing such person to be taken, forthwith before such court, judge, or commissioner, whose duty it shall be to hear and determine the case of such claimant in a summary manner; and upon satisfactory proof being made, by deposition of affidavit, in writing, to be taken and certified by such court, judge, or commissioner, or by other satisfactory testimony, duly taken and certified by some court,...and with proof, also by affidavit, of the identity of the person whose service or labor is claimed to be due as aforesaid, that the person so arrested does in fact owe service or labor to the person or persons claiming him or her, in the State or Territory from which such fugitive may have escaped as

aforesaid, and that said person escaped, to make out and deliver to such claimant, his or her agent or attorney, a certificate setting forth the substantial facts as to the service or labor due from such fugitive to the claimant, and of his or her escape from the State or Territory in which he or she was arrested, with authority to such claimant,...to use such reasonable force and restraint as may be necessary, under the circumstances of the case, to take and remove such fugitive person back to the State or Territory whence he or she may have escaped as aforesaid.

Section 7. That any persons who shall knowingly and willingly obstruct, hinder, or prevent such claimant, his agent or attorney, or any person or persons lawfully assisting him, her, or them, from arresting such a fugitive from service or labor, either with or without process as aforesaid, or shall rescue, or attempt to rescue, such fugitive from service or labor, from the custody of such claimant,... or other person or persons lawfully assisting as aforesaid, when so arrested,... or shall aid, abet, or assist such person so owing service or labor as aforesaid, directly or indirectly, to escape from such claimant,... or shall harbor or conceal such fugitive, so as to prevent the discovery and arrest of such person, after notice or knowledge of the fact that such person was a fugitive from service or labor... shall, for either of said offenses, be subject to a fine not exceeding one thousand dollars, and imprisonment not exceeding six months...; and shall moreover forfeit and pay, by way of civil damages to the party injured by such illegal conduct, the sum of one thousand dollars, for each fugitive so lost as aforesaid....

Section 9. That, upon affidavit made by the claimant of such fugitive... that he has reason to apprehend that such fugitive will be rescued by force from his or their possession before he can be taken beyond the limits of the State in which the arrest is made, it shall be the duty of the officer making the arrest to retain such fugitive in his custody, and to remove him to the State whence he fled, and there to deliver him to said claimant, his agent, or attorney. And to this end, the officer aforesaid is hereby authorized and required to employ so many persons as he may deem necessary to overcome such force, and to retain them in his service so long as circumstances may require.

Drawing depicting an escaped slave being returned.

◆ ACT TO SUPPRESS THE SLAVE TRADE IN THE DISTRICT OF COLUMBIA CH. 63, 9 STAT. 467 (1850)

Although the importation of new slaves from Africa had been outlawed in 1808, the breeding and trading of slaves was still a big business; the Washington, Mary-

land, and Virginia area served as headquarters to some of the nation's largest traders.

The renewed debate in Congress over the expansion of slavery during the late 1840s led to what has been referred to as the Compromise of 1850—a package of five resolutions, one of which was the 1850 Fugitive Slave Act. Another of the provisions, a concession to the anti-slavery forces, was an act abolishing the slave trade in the District of Columbia.

Be it enacted,... That from and after January 1, 1851, it shall not be lawful to bring into the District of Columbia any slave whatsoever, for the purpose of being sold, or for the purpose of being placed in depot, to be subsequently transferred to any other State or place to be sold as merchandise. And if any slave shall be brought into the said District by its owner, or by the authority or consent of its owner, contrary to the provisions of this act, such slave shall thereupon become liberated and free.

◆ FREDERICK DOUGLASS'S INDEPENDENCE DAY ADDRESS (1852)

In 1852, over three million blacks were being held as slaves in the United States. Knowing this and understanding the irony implicit in the notion of a holiday commemorating the coming of independence to the United States, Frederick Douglass lost little time in laying bare the contradiction inherent in allowing slavery to exist within a society professedly dedicated to individual freedom.

Fellow Citizens

Pardon me, and allow me to ask, why am I called upon to speak here today? What have I or those I represent to do with your national independence? Are the great principles of political freedom and of natural justice, embodied in that Declaration of Independence, extended to us? And am I, therefore, called upon to bring our humble offering to the national altar, and to confess the benefits, and express devout gratitude for the blessings resulting from your independence to us?

Would to God, both for your sakes and ours, that an affirmative answer could be truthfully returned to these questions. Then would my task be light, and my burden easy and delightful. For who is there so cold that a nation's sympathy could not warm him? Who so obdurate and dead to the claims of gratitude, that would not thankfully acknowledge such priceless benefits? Who so stolid and selfish that would not give his voice to swell the hallelujahs of a nation's jubilee, when the chains of servitude had been torn from his limbs? I am not that man...

I am not included within the pale of this glorious anniversary! Your high independence only reveals the immeasurable distance between us. The blessings in which you this day rejoice are not enjoyed in common. The rich inheritance of justice, liberty, prosperity, and independence bequeathed by your fathers is shared by you, not by me. The sunlight that brought life and healing to you has brought stripes and death to me. This Fourth of July is *yours*, not *mine*. You may rejoice, I must mourn. To drag a man in fetters into the grand illuminated temple of liberty, and call upon him to join you in joyous anthems, were inhuman mockery and sacrilegious irony. Do you mean, citizens, to mock me, by asking me to speak today?...

Fellow citizens, above your national, tumultuous joy, I hear the mournful wail of millions, whose chains, heavy and grievous yesterday, are today rendered more intolerable by the jubilant shouts that reach them. If I do forget, if I do not remember those bleeding children of sorrow this day, "may my right hand forget her cunning, and may my tongue cleave to the roof of my mouth!" To forget them, to pass lightly over their wrongs, and to chime in with the popular theme, would be treason most scandalous and shocking, and would make me a reproach before God and the world. My subject, then, fellow citizens, is "American Slavery." I shall see this day and its popular characteristics from the slave's point of view. Standing here, identified with the American bondman, making his wrongs mine, I do not hesitate to declare, with all my soul, that the character and conduct of this nation never looked blacker to me than on this Fourth of July. Whether we turn to the declarations of the past, or to the professions of the present, the conduct of the nation seems equally hideous and revolting. America is false to the past, false to the present, and solemnly binds herself to be false to the future. Standing with God and the crushed and bleeding slave on this occasion, I will, in the name of humanity, which is outraged, in the name of Liberty, which is fettered, in the name of the Constitution and the Bible, which are disregarded and trampled upon, dare to call in question and to denounce, with all the emphasis I can command, everything that serves to perpetuate slavery—the great sin and shame of America! "I will not equivocate; I will not excuse"; I will use the severest language I can command, and yet not one word shall escape me that any man, whose judgment is not blinded by prejudice, or who is not at heart a slave-holder, shall not confess to be right and just.

But I fancy I hear some of my audience say it is just in this circumstances that you and your brother Abolitionists fail to make a favorable impression on the public mind. Would you argue more and denounce less, would

Engraving showing a slave auction.

you persuade more and rebuke less, your cause would be much more likely to succeed. But, I submit, where all is plain there is nothing to be argued. What point in the anti-slavery creed would you have me argue? On what branch of the subject do the people of this country need light? Must I undertake to prove that the slave is a man? That point is conceded already. Nobody doubts it. The slave-holders themselves acknowledge it in the enactment of laws for their government. They acknowledge it when they punish disobedience on the part of the slave. There are seventy-two crimes in the State of Virginia, which, if committed by a black man (no matter how ignorant he be), subject him to the punishment of death, while only two of these same crimes will subject a white man to like punishment. What is this but the acknowledgment that the slave is a moral, intellectual, and responsible being? The manhood of the slave is conceded. It is admitted in the fact that the Southern statute-books are covered with enactments, forbidding, under severe fines and penalties, the teaching of the slave to read and write. When you can point to any such laws in reference to the beasts of the field, then I may consent to argue the manhood of the slave. When the dogs in your streets, when the fowls of the air, when the cattle on your hills, when the fish of the sea, and the reptiles that

crawl, shall be unable to distinguish the slave from a brute, then I will argue with you that the slave is a man!

For the present it is enough to affirm the equal manhood of the Negro race. Is it not astonishing that, while we are plowing, planting, and reaping, using all kinds of mechanical tools, erecting houses, constructing bridges, building ships, working in metals of brass, iron, copper, silver, and gold; that while we are reading, writing, and ciphering, acting as clerks, merchants, and secretaries, having among us lawyers, doctors, ministers, poets, authors, editors, orators, and teachers; that while we are engaged in all the enterprises common to other men—digging gold in California, capturing the whale in the Pacific, feeding sheep and cattle on the hillside, living, moving, acting, thinking, planning, living in families as husbands, wives, and children, and above all, confessing and worshipping the Christian God, and looking hopefully for life and immortality beyond the grave—we are called upon to prove that we are men?

Would you have me argue that man is entitled to liberty? That he is the rightful owner of his own body? You have already declared it. Must I argue the wrongfulness of slavery? Is that a question for republicans? Is it to be settled by the rules of logic and argumentation, as a

Frederick Douglass

matter beset with great difficulty, involving a doubtful application of the principle of justice, hard to understand? How should I look today in the presence of Americans, dividing and subdividing a discourse, to show that men have a natural right to freedom, speaking of it relatively and positively, negatively and affirmatively? To do so would be to make myself ridiculous, and to offer an insult to your understanding. There is not a man beneath the canopy of heaven who does not know that slavery is wrong *for him.*

What! Am I to argue that it is wrong to make men brutes, to rob them of their liberty, to work them without wages, to keep them ignorant of their relations to their fellow men, to beat them with sticks, to flay their flesh with the lash, to load their limbs with irons, to hunt them with dogs, to sell them at auction, to sunder their families, to knock out their teeth, to burn their flesh, to starve them into obedience and submission to their masters? Must I argue that a system thus marked with blood and stained with pollution is wrong? No; I will not. I have better employment for my time and strength than such arguments would imply.

What, then, remains to be argued? Is it that slavery is not divine; that God did not establish it; that our doctors

of divinity are mistaken? There is blasphemy in the thought. That which is inhuman cannot be divine. Who can reason on such a proposition? They that can, may; I cannot. The time for such argument is past.

At a time like this, scorching irony, not convincing argument, is needed. Oh! had I the ability, and could I reach the nation's ear, I would today pour out a fiery stream of biting ridicule, blasting reproach, withering sarcasm, and stern rebuke. For it is not light that is needed, but fire; it is not the gentle shower, but thunder. We need the storm, the whirlwind, and the earthquake. The feeling of the nation must be quickened; the conscience of the nation must be startled; the hypocrisy of the nation must be exposed; and its crimes against God and man must be denounced.

What to the American slave is your Fourth of July? I answer, a day that reveals to him more than all other days of the year, the gross injustice and cruelty to which he is the constant victim. To him your celebration is a sham; your boasted liberty an unholy license; your national greatness, swelling vanity; your sounds of rejoicing are empty and heartless; your denunciation of tyrants, brass-fronted impudence; your shouts of liberty and equality, hollow mockery; your prayers and hymns, your sermons and thanksgivings, with all your religious parade and solemnity, are to him mere bombast, fraud, deception, impiety, and hypocrisy—a thin veil to cover up crimes which would disgrace a nation of savages. There is not a nation of the earth guilty of practices more shocking and bloody than are the people of these United States at this very hour.

Go where you may, search where you will, roam through all the monarchies and despotisms of the Old World, travel through South America, search out every abuse and when you have found the last, lay your facts by the side of the every-day practices of this nation, and you will say with me that, for revolting barbarity and shameless hypocrisy, America reigns without a rival.

◆ *DRED SCOTT V. SANDFORD* 19 HOWARD 393 (1857)

In 1835, Dred Scott, born a slave in Virginia, became the property of John Emerson, an Army doctor, in the slave state of Missouri. From there, he was taken into the free state of Illinois and later to the free territory of Minnesota. In 1847, Scott instituted suit in the circuit court of the St. Louis County, Missouri, arguing that he should be given his freedom by virtue of his having resided on free soil. After nine years, his case was certified to the United States Supreme Court, where five of the nine justices, were Southerners.

In delivering his opinion, Chief Justice Roger Brooke Taney declared that, by virtue of both the Declaration of

Independence and the Constitution, African Americans could not be regarded as citizens of the United States. Moreover, the Court could not deprive slaveholders of their right to take slaves into any part of the Union, North or South. In effect, therefore, the Missouri Compromise, as well as other antislavery legislation, was declared to be unconstitutional.

Under the terms of the Missouri Compromise, Missouri was allowed to join the Union with a slave population of almost 10,000; Maine was admitted as a free state. However, the compromise also prohibited the expansion of slavery into any part of the Louisiana Territory north of Latitude 36 degrees 30'N. It was here, into Illinois and the territory of Wisconsin, that Dred Scott's master brought him, and in 1846 Scott sued his master for his freedom.

After numerous delays, trials, and retrials, the case reached the United States Supreme Court in 1856. Hearing this case, the Court was not only faced with the question as to whether Scott was a free man, as a result of his sojourn in a free territory, but it also had to consider whether Congress had the authority under the Constitution to outlaw slavery in the territories. Although, each of the nine justices delivered a separate opinion, the opinion of Chief Justice Roger Brook Tangy has been generally accepted as the Court's ruling on the matter.

The question is simply this: Can a negro, whose ancestors were imported into this country and sold as slaves, become a member of the political community formed and brought into existence by the constitution of the United States, and as such become entitled to all the rights, and privileges, and immunities, guaranteed by that instrument to the citizen?....

The words "people of the United States" and "citizens" are synonymous terms, and mean the same thing. They both describe the political body who, according to our republican institutions, form the sovereignty, and who hold the power and conduct the government through their representatives. They are what we familiarly call the "sovereign people," and every citizen is one of this people, and a constituent member of this sovereignty. The question before us is, whether the class of persons described in the plea in abatement compose a portion of this people, and are constituent members of this sovereignty? We think they are not, and that they are not included, and were not intended to be included, under the word "citizens" in the constitution, and can therefore claim none of the rights and privileges which that instrument provides for and secures to citizens of the United States. On the contrary, they were at that time considered as a subordinate and inferior class of beings, who had been subjugated by the dominant race, and, whether emancipated or not, yet remained subject to their authority, and had no rights or privileges....

It is not the province of the court to decide upon the justice or injustice, the policy or impolicy, of these laws. The decision of that question belonged to the political or law-making power; to those who formed the sovereignty and framed the constitution. The duty of the court is, to interpret the instrument they have framed, with the best lights we can obtain on the subject, and to administer it as we find it, according to its true intent and meaning when it was adopted.

In discussing this question, we must not confound the rights of citizenship which a State may confer within its own limits, and the rights of citizenship as member of the Union. It does not by any means follow, because he has all the rights and privileges of a citizen of a State, that he must be a citizen of the United States. He may have all of the rights and privileges of the citizen of a State, and yet not be entitled to the rights and privileges of a citizen in any other State. For, previous to the adoption of the constitution of the United States, every State had the undoubted right to confer on whomsoever it pleased the character of citizen, and to endow him with all its rights. But this character of course was confined to the boundaries of the State, and gave him no rights or privileges in other States beyond those secured to him by the laws of nations and the comity of States. Nor have the several States surrendered the power of conferring these rights and privileges by adopting the constitution of United States....

It is very clear, therefore, that no State can, by any act or law of its own, passed since the adoption of the constitution, introduce a new member into the political community created by the constitution of the United States. It cannot make him a member of this community by making him a member of its own. And for the same reason it cannot introduce any person, or description of persons, who were not intended to be embraced in this new political family, which the constitution brought into existence, but were intended to be excluded from it.

The question then arises, whether the provisions of the constitution, in relation to the personal rights and privileges to which the citizen of a State should be entitled, embraced the negro African race, at that time in this country, or who might afterwards be imported, who had then or should afterwards be made free in any State; and to put it in the power of a single State to make him a citizen of the United States, and endue him with the full rights of citizenship in every other State without consent? Does the constitution of the United States act upon him whenever he shall be made free under the laws of a State, and raised there to the rank of a citizen, and immediately clothe him with all the privileges of a citizen in every other State, and in its own courts?

The court thinks the affirmative of these propositions cannot be maintained. And if it cannot, the plaintiff in error could not be a citizen of the State of Missouri, within the meaning of the constitution of the United States, and, consequently, was not entitled to sue in its courts.

It is true, every person, and every class and description of persons, who were at the time of the adoption of the constitution recognized as citizens in the several States, became also citizens of this new political body; but none other; it was formed by them, and for them and their posterity, but for no one else. And the personal rights and privileges guaranteed to citizens of this new sovereignty were intended to embrace those only who were then members of the several State communities, or who should afterwards by birthright or otherwise become members, according to the provisions of the constitution and the principles on which it was founded....

In the opinion of the court, the legislation and histories of the times, and the language used in the declaration of independence, show, that neither the class of persons who had been imported as slaves, nor their descendants, whether they had become free or not, were then acknowledged as a part of the people, nor intended to be included in the general words used in that memorable instrument....

... The government of the United States had no right to interfere for any other purpose but that protecting the rights of the owner, leaving it altogether with the several States to deal with this race, whether emancipated or not, as each State may think justice, humanity, and the interests and safety of society, require....

The act of Congress, upon which the plaintiff relies, declares that slavery and involuntary servitude, except as a punishment for crime, shall be forever prohibited in all that part of the territory ceded by France, under the name of Louisiana, which lies north of thirty-six degrees thirty minutes north latitude and not included within the limits of Missouri. And the difficulty which meets us at the threshold of this part of the inquiry is whether Congress was authorized to pass this law under any of the powers granted to it by the Constitution; for, if the authority is not given by that instrument, it is the duty of this Court to declare it void and inoperative and incapable of conferring freedom upon anyone who is held as a slave under the laws of any one of the states....

We do not mean ... to question the power of Congress in this respect. The power to expand the territory of the United States by the admission of new states is plainly given; and in the construction of this power by all the departments of the government, it has been held to authorize the acquisition of territory, not fit for admission at the time, but to be admitted as soon as its population and situation would entitle it to admission. It is acquired to become a state and not to be held as a colony and governed by Congress with absolute Authority; and, as the propriety of admitting a new state is committed to the sound discretion of Congress, the power to acquire territory for that purpose, to be held by the United States until it is in a suitable condition to become a state upon an equal footing with the other states, must rest upon the same discretional....

But the power of Congress over the person or property of a citizen can never be a mere discretionary power under our Constitution and form of government. The powers of the government and the rights and privileges of the citizen are regulated and plainly defined by the Constitution itself....

These powers, and others, in relation to rights of person, which it is not necessary here to enumerate, are, in express and positive terms, denied to the general government; and the rights of private property have been guarded with equal care. Thus the rights of property are united with the rights of person and placed on the same ground by the Fifth Amendment to the Constitution, which provides that no person shall be deprived of life, liberty, and property without due process of law. And an act of Congress which deprives a citizen of the United States of his liberty of property, without due process of law, merely because he came himself or brought his property into a particular territory of the United States, and who had committed no offense against the law, could hardly be dignified with the name of due process of law....

It seems, however, to be supposed that there is a difference between property in a slave and other property and that different rules may be applied to it in expounding Constitution of the United States. And the laws and usages of nations, and the writings of eminent jurists upon the relation of master and slave and their mutual rights and duties, and the powers which governments may exercise over it, have been dwelt upon in the argument.

But, in considering the question before us, it must be borne in mind that there is no law of nations standing between the people of the United States and their government and interfering with their relation to each other. The powers of the government and the rights of the citizen under it are positive and practical regulations plainly written down. The people of the United States have delegated to it certain enumerated powers and forbidden it to exercise others. It has no power over the person of property of a citizen but what the citizens of the United States have granted. And no laws or usages of other nations, or reasoning of statesmen of jurists upon the relations of master and slave, can enlarge the powers of the government or take from the citizens the rights they have reserved. And if the Constitution recognizes the right of property of the master in a slave, and makes no distinction between that description of property and other property owned by a citizen, no tribunal, acting under the authority of the United States, whether it be legislative, executive, or judicial, has a right to draw such a distinction or deny to it the benefit of the provisions and guaranties which have been provided for the protection of private property against the encroachments of the government.

Now, as we have already said in an earlier part of this opinion, upon a different point, the right of property in a slave is distinctly and expressly affirmed in the Constitution. The right to traffic in it, like an ordinary article of merchandise and property, was guaranteed to the citizens of the United States, in every state that might desire it, for twenty years. And the government in express terms is pledged to protect it in all future time if the slave escapes from his owner. That is done in plain words—too plain to be misunderstood. And no word can be found in the Constitution which gives Congress a greater power over slave property or which entitles property of that kind to less protection than property of any other description. The only power conferred is the power coupled with the duty of guarding and protecting the owner in his rights.

Upon these considerations it is the opinion of the court that the act of Congress which prohibited a citizen from holding and owning property of this kind in the territory of the United States north of the line therein mentioned is not warranted by the Constitution and is therefore void; and that neither Dred Scott himself, nor any of his family, were made free by being carried into this territory; even if they had been carried there by the owner with the intention of becoming a permanent resident....

◆ THE EMANCIPATION PROCLAMATION NO. 17, 12 STAT. 1268 (1863)

In an attempt to bring an end to the Civil War, President Abraham Lincoln, acting on his authority as commander-in-chief, on September 22, 1862 issued a warning that slavery would be abolished in any state that continued to rebel. With the war still raging, Lincoln issued the Emancipation Proclamation on January 1, 1863, freeing slaves in those states that had seceded from the Union. The proclamation did not apply, however, to those areas occupied by Union forces—there remained some 800,000 slaves unaffected by the provisions of the document.

By the President of the United States of America: A Proclamation

Whereas on the 22d day of September, A.D. 1862, a proclamation was issued by the President of the United States, containing, among other things, the following, to wit:

"That on the 1st day of January, A.D. 1863, all persons held as slaves within any State or designated part of a State the people whereof shall then be in rebellion against the United States shall be then, henceforward, and forever free; and the executive government of the United States, including the military and naval authority thereof, will recognize and maintain the freedom of such persons and will do no act or acts to repress such persons, or any of them, in any efforts thcy may make for their actual freedom."

"That the executive will on the 1st day of January aforesaid, by proclamation, designated the States and parts of States, if any, which the people thereof, respectively, shall then be in rebellion against the United States; and the fact that any State or the people thereof shall on that day be in good faith represented in the Congress of the United States by members chosen thereto at elections wherein a majority of the qualified voters of such States shall have participated shall, in the absence of strong countervailing testimony, be deemed conclusive evidence that such State and the people thereof are not then in rebellion against the United States.":

Now, therefore, I, Abraham Lincoln, President of the United States, by virtue of the power in me vested as Commander-in-Chief, of the Army and Navy of the United States in time of actual armed rebellion against the authority and government of the United States, and as a fit and necessary war measure for suppressing said rebellion, do, on this 1st day of January, A.D. 1863, and in accordance with my purpose so to do, publicly proclaimed for the full period of one hundred days from the first day above mentioned, order and designate as the States and parts of States wherein the people thereof, respectively, are this day in rebellion against the United States the following, to wit:

Arkansas, Texas, Louisiana (except the parishes of St. Bernard, Plaquemines, Jefferson, St. John, St. Charles, St. James, Ascension, Assumption, Terrebonne, Lafourche, St. Mary, St. Marti, and Orleans, including the city of New Orleans), Mississippi, Alabama, Florida, Georgia, South Carolina, North Carolina, and Virginia (except the forty-eight counties designated as West Virginia, and also the counties of Berkeley, Accomac, Northampton, Elizabeth City, York, Princess Anne, and Northfolk, including the cities of Norfolk and Portsmouth), and which excepted parts are for the present left precisely as if this proclamation were not issued.

And by virtue of the power and for the purpose aforesaid, I do order and declare that all persons held as slaves within said designated States and parts of States are, and henceforward shall be, free; and that the Executive Government of the United States, including the military and naval authorities thereof, will recognize and maintain the freedom of said persons.

And I hereby enjoin upon the people so declared to be free to abstain from all violence, unless in necessary self-defense; and I recommend to them that, in all cases when allowed, they labor faithfully for reasonable wages.

And I further declare and make known that such persons of suitable condition will be received into the armed service of the United States to garrison forts, positions, stations, and other places, and to man vessels of all sorts in said service.

And upon this act, sincerely believed to be an act of justice, warranted by the Constitution upon military necessity, I invoke the considerate judgment of mankind and the gracious favor of Almighty God.

◆ FREEDMEN'S BUREAU ACT CH. 90, 13 STAT. 507 (1865)

On March 3, 1865, Congress passed legislation designed to provide basic health and educational services to former slaves and to administer abandoned land in the South. Under the act, the Bureau of Refugees, Freedman and Abandoned Lands, commonly referred to as the Freedmen's Bureau, was created.

An Act to Establish a Bureau for the Relief of Freedmen and Refugees

Be it enacted, That there is hereby established in the War Department, to continue during the present war of rebellion, and for one year thereafter, a bureau of refugees, freedmen, and abandoned lands, to which shall be committed, as hereinafter provided, the supervision and management of all abandoned lands and the control of all subjects relating to refugees and freedmen from rebel states, or from any district of country within the territory embraced in the operations of the army, under such rules and regulations as may be prescribed by the head of the bureau and approved by the President. The said bureau shall be under the management and control of a commissioner to be appointed by the President, by and with the advice and consent of the Senate.

Section 2. That the Secretary of War may direct such issue of provisions, clothing, and fuel, as he may deem needful for the immediate and temporary shelter and supply of destitute and suffering refugees and freedmen and their wives and children, under such rules and regulations as he may direct.

Section 3. That the President may, by and with the advice and consent of the Senate, appoint an assistant commissioner for each of the states declared to be in insurrection, not exceeding ten in number, who shall, under the direction of the commissioner, aid in the execution of the provisions of this act.... And any military officer may be detailed and assigned to duty under this act without increase of pay of allowances.....

Section 4. That the commissioner, under the direction of the President, shall have authority to set apart, for the use of loyal refugees and freedmen, such tracts of land within the insurrectionary states as shall have been abandoned, or to which the United States shall have acquired title by confiscation or sale, or otherwise, and to every male citizen, whether refugee or freedman, as aforesaid, there shall be assigned not more than forty acres of such land, and the person to whom it was so assigned shall be protected in the use and enjoyment of the land for the term of three years at an annual rent not exceeding six per centum upon the value of such land, as it was appraised by the state authorities in the year eighteen hundred and sixty, for the purpose of taxation, and in case no such appraisal can be found, then the rental shall be based upon the estimated value of the land in said year, to be ascertained in such manner as the commissioner may by regulation prescribe. At the end of said term, or at any time during said term, the occupants of any parcels so assigned may purchase the land and receive such title thereto as the United States can convey, upon paying therefor the value of the land, as ascertained and fixed for the purpose of determining the annual rent aforesaid....

◆ AMENDMENT THIRTEEN TO THE UNITED STATES CONSTITUTION (1865)

Ratified December 18, 1865, the Thirteenth Amendment formally abolishes slavery within the United States.

Section 1. Neither slavery nor involuntary servitude, except as a punishment for crime whereof the party shall have been duly convicted, shall exist within the United States, or any place subject to their jurisdiction.

Section 2. Congress shall have power to enforce this article by appropriate legislation.

◆ BLACK CODES OF MISSISSIPPI (1865)

Following emancipation many states sought to impose restrictions on African Americans to prevent them from enjoying equal social status with whites. These restrictions were designed to not only hold blacks in a subordinate condition, but to impose restrictions upon

President Abraham Lincoln at the first reading of the Emancipation Proclamation.

them not unlike those which prevailed before the Civil War. Black codes imposed heavy penalties of "vagrancy", "insulting gestures", curfew violations, and "seditious speeches." In November 1865, Mississippi was the first state to enact such laws.

An Act to Confer Civil Rights on Freedmen, and for other Purposes

Section 1. All freedmen, free negroes and mulatto es may sue and be sued, implead and be impleaded, in all the courts of law and equity of this State, and may acquire personal property, and choses in action, by descent or purchase, and may dispose of the same in the same manner and to the same extent that white persons may: Provided, That the provisions of this section shall not be so construed as to allow any freedman, free negro or mulatto to rent or lease any lands or tenements except in incorporated cities or towns, in which places the corporate authorities shall control the same.

Section 2. All freedmen, free negroes and mulattoes may intermarry with each other, in the same manner and under the same regulations that are provided by law for white persons: Provided, that the clerk of probate shall keep separate records of the same.

Section 3. All freedmen, free negroes or mullatoes who do now and have herebefore lived and cohabited together as husband and wife shall be taken and held in law as legally married, and the issue shall be taken and held as legitimate for all purposes; and it shall not be lawful for any freedman, free negro or mulatto to intermarry with any white person; nor for any person to intermarry with any freedman, free negro or mulatto; and any person who shall so intermarry shall be deemed guilty of felony, and on conviction thereof shall be confined in the State penitentiary for life; and those shall be deemed freedmen, free negroes and mulattoes who are of pure negro blood, and those descended from a negro to the third generation, inclusive, though one ancestor in each generation may have been a white person.

Section 4. In addition to cases in which freedmen, free negroes and mulattoes are now by law competent witnesses, freedmen, free negroes or mulattoes shall be competent in civil cases, when a party or parties to the suit, either plaintiff or plaintiffs, defendant or defendants; also in cases where freedmen, free negroes and mulattoes is or are either plaintiff or plaintiffs, defendant or defendants. They shall also be competent witnesses in all criminal prosecutions where the crime charged is alleged to have been committed by a white person upon or against the person or property of a freedman, free negro or mulatto: Provided, that in all cases said witnesses shall be examined in open court, on the stand; except, however, they may be examined before the grand jury, and shall in all cases be subject to the rules and tests of the common law as to competency and credibility.

Section 5. Every freedman, free negro and mulatto shall, on the second Monday of January, one thousand eight hundred and sixty-six, and annually thereafter, have a lawful home or employment, and shall have written evidence thereof as follows, to wit: if living in any incorporated city, town, or village, a license from the mayor thereof; and if living outside of an incorporated city, town, or village, from the member of the board of police of his beat, authorizing him or her to do irregular and job work; or a written contract, as provided in Section 6 in this act; which license may be revoked for cause at any time by the authority granting the same.

Section 6. All contracts for labor made with freedmen, free negroes and mulattoes for a longer period than one month shall be in writing, and a duplicate, attested and read to said freedman, free negro or mulatto by a beat, city or county officer, or two disinterested white persons of the county in which the labor is to be performed, of which each party shall have one: and said contracts shall be taken and held as entire contracts, and if the laborer shall quit the service of the employer before the expiration of his term of service, without good cause, he shall forfeit his wages for that year up to the time of quitting.

Section 7. Every civil officer shall, and every person may, arrest and carry back to his or her legal employer any freedman, free negro, or mulatto who shall have quit the service of his or her employer before the expiration of his or her term of service without good cause; and said officer and person shall be entitled to receive for arresting and carrying back every deserting employee aforesaid the sum of five dollars, and ten cents per mile from the place of arrest to the place of delivery; and the same shall be paid by the employer, and held as a set off for so much against the wages of said deserting employee: Provided, that said arrested party, after being so returned, may appeal to the justice of the peace or member of the board of police of the county, who, on notice to the alleged employer, shall try summarily whether said appellant is legally employed by the alleged employer, and has good cause to quit said employer. Either party shall have the right of appeal to the county court, pending which the alleged deserter shall be remanded to the alleged employer or otherwise disposed of, as shall be right and just; and the decision of the county court shall be final.

Section 8. Upon affidavit made by the employer of any freedman, free negro or mulatto, or other credible person, before any justice of the peace or member of the board of police, that any freedman, free negro or mulatto legally employed by said employer has illegally deserted said employment, such justice of the peace or member of the board of police issue his warrant or warrants, returnable before himself or other such officer, to any sheriff, constable or special deputy, commanding him to arrest said deserter, and return him or her to said employer, and the like proceedings shall be had as provided in the preceding section; and it shall be lawful for any officer to whom such warrant shall be directed to execute said warrant in any county in this State; and that said warrant may be transmitted without endorsement to any like officer of another county, to be executed and returned as aforesaid; and the said employer shall pay the costs of said warrants and arrest and return, which shall be set off for so much against the wages of said deserter.

Section 9. If any person shall persuade or attempt to persuade, entice, or cause any freedman, free negro or mulatto to desert from the legal employment of any person before the expiration of his or her term of service, or shall knowingly employ any such deserting freedman, free negro or mulatto, or shall knowingly give or sell to any such deserting freedman, free negro or mulatto, any food, raiment, or other thing, he or she shall be guilty of a misdemeanor, and, upon conviction, shall be fined not less than twenty-five dollars and not more than two hundred dollars and costs; and if the said fine and costs shall not be immediately paid, the court shall sentence said convict to not exceeding two months imprisonment in the county jail, and he or she shall moreover be liable to the party injured in damages: Provided, if any person shall, or shall attempt to, persuade, entice, or cause any freedman, free negro or mulatto to desert from any legal employment of any person, with the view to employ said freedman, free negro or mullato without the limits of this State, such costs; and if said fine and costs shall not be immediately paid, the court shall sentence said convict to not exceeding six months imprisonment in the county jail.

Section 10. It shall be lawful for any freedman, free negro, or mulatto, to charge any white person, freedman, free negro or mulatto by affidavit, with any criminal offense against his or her person or property, and upon such affidavit the proper process shall be issued and executed as if said affidavit was made by a white person, and it shall be lawful for any freedman, free negro, or mulatto, in any action, suit or controversy pending, or about to be instituted in any court of law equity in this State, to make all needful and lawful affidavits as shall be necessary for the institution, prosecution or defense of such suit or controversy.

Section 11. The penal laws of this state, in all cases not otherwise specially provided for, shall apply and extend to all freedman, free negroes and mulattoes.....

An Act to Regulate the Relation of Master and Apprentice, as Relates to Freedmen, Free Negroes, and Mulattoes

Section 1. It shall be the duty of all sheriffs, justices of the peace, and other civil officers of the several counties in this State, to report to the probate courts of their respective counties semiannually, at the January and July terms of said courts, all freedmen, free negroes, and mulattoes, under the age of eighteen, in their respective counties, beats, or districts, who are orphans, or whose parent or parents have not the means or who refuse to provide for and support said minors; and thereupon it shall be the duty of said probate court to order the clerk of said court to apprentice said minors to some competent and suitable person on such terms as the court may direct, having a particular care to the interest of said minor: Provided, that the former owner of said minors shall have the preference when, in the opinion of the court, he or she shall be a suitable person for that purpose.

Section 2. The said court shall be fully satisfied that the person or persons to whom said minor shall be apprenticed shall be a suitable person to have the charge and care of said minor, and fully to protect the interest of said minor. The said court shall require the said master or mistress to execute bond and security, payable to the State of Mississippi, conditioned that he or she shall furnish said minor with sufficient food and clothing; to treat said minor humanely; furnish medical attention in case of sickness; teach, or cause to be taught, him or her to read and write, if under fifteen years old, and will conform to any law that may be hereafter passed for the regulation of the duties and relation of master and apprentice: Provided, that said apprentice shall be bound by indenture, in case of males, until they are twenty-one years old, and in case of females until they are eighteen years old.

Section 3. In the management and control of said apprentices, said master or mistress shall have the power to inflict such moderate corporeal chastisement as a father or guardian is allowed to infliction on his or her child or ward at common law: Provided, that in no case shall cruel or inhuman punishment be inflicted.

Section 4. If any apprentice shall leave the employment of his or her master or mistress, without his or her consent, said master or mistress may pursue and recapture said apprentice, and bring him or her before any justice of the peace of the county, whose duty it shall be to remand said apprentice to the service of his or her master or mistress; and in the event of a refusal on the part of said apprentice so to return, then said justice shall commit said apprentice to the jail of said county, on failure to give bond, to the next term of the county court; and it shall be the duty of said court at the first term thereafter to investigate said case, and if the court shall be of opinion that said apprentice left the employment of his or her master or mistress without good cause, to order him or her to be punished, as provided for the punishment of hired freedmen, as may be from time to time provided for by law for desertion, until he or she shall agree to return to the service of his or her master or mistress: Provided, that the court may grant continuances as in other cases: And provided further, that if the court shall believe that said apprentice had good cause to quit his said master or mistress, the court shall discharge said apprentice from said indenture, and also enter a judgment against the master or mistress for not more than one hundred dollars, for the use and benefit of said apprentice, to be collected on execution as in other cases.

Section 5. If any person entice away any apprentice from his or her master or mistress, or shall knowingly employ an apprentice, or furnish him or her food or clothing without the written consent of his or her master or mistress, or shall sell or give said apprentice spirits without such consent, said person so offending shall be guilty of a misdemeanor, and shall, upon conviction there of before the county court, be punished as provided for the punishment of persons enticing from their employer hired freedmen, free negroes or mulattoes.

Section 6. It shall be the duty of all civil officers of their respective counties to report any minors within their respective counties to said probate court who are subject to be apprenticed under the provisions of this act, from time to time as the facts may come to their knowledge, and it shall be the duty of said court from time to time as said minors shall be reported to them, or otherwise come to their knowledge, to apprentice said minors as hereinbefore provided.

Section 9. It shall be lawful for any freedman, free negro, or mulatto, having a minor child or children, to apprentice the said minor child or children, as provided for by this act.

Section 10. In all cases where the age of the freedman, free negro, or mulatto cannot be ascertained by record testimony, the judge of the county court shall fix the age.....

An Act to Amend the Vagrant Laws of the State

Section 1. All rogues and vagabonds, idle and dissipated persons, beggars, jugglers, or persons practicing unlawful games or plays, runaways, common drunkards, common night-walkers, pilferers, lewd, wanton, or lascivious persons, in speech or behavior, common railers and brawlers, persons who neglect their calling or employment, misspend what they earn, or do not provide for the support of themselves or their families, or dependents, and all other idle and disorderly persons, including all who neglect all lawful business, habitually misspend their time by frequenting houses of ill-fame, gaming-houses, or tippling shops, shall be deemed and considered vagrants, under the provisions of this act, and upon conviction thereof shall be fined not exceeding one hundred dollars, with all accruing costs, and be imprisoned, at the discretion of the court, not exceeding ten days.

Section 2. All freedmen, free negroes and mulattoes in this State, over the age of eighteen years, found on the second Monday in January, 1866, or thereafter, with no lawful employment or business, or found unlawfully assembling themselves together, either in the day or night time, and all white persons assembling themselves with freedmen, free negroes or mulattoes, or usually associating with freedmen, free negroes or mulattoes, on terms of equality, or living in adultery or fornication with a freed woman, freed negro or mulatto, shall be deemed vagrants, and on conviction thereof shall be fined in a sum not exceeding, in the case of a freedman, free negro or mulatto, fifty dollars, and a white man two hundred dollars, and imprisonment at the discretion of the court, the free negro not exceeding ten days, and the white man not exceeding six months.

Section 3. All justices of the peace, mayors, and aldermen of incorporated towns, counties, and cities of the several counties in this State shall have jurisdiction to try all questions of vagrancy in their respective towns, counties, and cities, and it is hereby made their duty, whenever they shall ascertain that any person or persons in their respective towns, and counties and cities are violating any of the provisions of this act, to have said party or parties arrested, and brought before them, and immediately investigate said charge, and, on conviction, punish said party or parties, as provided for herein. And it is hereby made the duty of all sheriffs, constables, town constables, and all such like officers, and city marshals, to report to some officer having jurisdiction all violations of any of the provisions of this act, and in case any officer shall fail or neglect any duty herein it shall be the duty of the county court to fine said officer, upon conviction, not exceeding one hundred dollars, to be paid into the county treasury for county purposes.

Section 4. Keepers of gaming houses, houses of prostitution, prostitutes, public or private, and all persons who derive their chief support in the employments that militate against good morals, or against law, shall be deemed and held to be vagrants.

Section 5. All fines and forfeitures collected by the provisions of this act shall be paid into the county treasury for general county purposes, and in case of any freedman, free negro or mulatto shall fail for five days after the imposition of any or forfeiture upon him or her for violation of any of the provisions of this act to pay the same, that it shall be, and is hereby, made the duty of the sheriff of the proper county to hire out said freedman, free negro or mulatto, to any person who will, for the shortest period of service, pay said fine and forfeiture and all costs: Provided, a preference shall be given to the employer, if there be one, in which case the employer shall be entitled to deduct and retain the amount so paid from the wages of such freedman, free negro or mulatto, then due or to become due; and in case freedman, free negro or mulatto cannot hire out, he or she may be dealt with as a pauper.

Section 6. The same duties and liabilities existing among white persons of this State shall attach to freedmen, free negroes or mulattoes, to support their indigent families and all colored paupers; and that in order to secure a support for such indigent freedmen, free negroes, or mulattoes, it shall be lawful, and is hereby made the duty of the county police of each county in this State, to levy a poll or capitation tax on each and every freedman, free negro, or mulatto, between the ages of eighteen and sixty years, not to exceed the sum of one dollar annually to each person so taxed, which tax, when collected, shall be paid into the county treasurer's hands, and constitute a fund to be called the Freedman's Pauper Fund, which shall be applied by the commissioners of the poor for the maintenance of the poor of the freedmen, free negroes and mulattoes of this State, under such regulations as may be established by the boards of county police in the respective counties of this State.

Section 7. If any freedman, free negro, or mulatto shall fail or refuse to pay any tax levied according to the provisions of the sixth section of this act, it shall be *prima facie* evidence of vagrancy, and it shall be the duty of the sheriff to arrest such freedman, free negro, or mulatto, or such person refusing or neglecting to pay such tax, and proceed at once to hire for the shortest time such delinquent taxpayer to any one who will pay the said tax, with accruing costs, giving preference to the employer, if there be one.

Section 8. Any person feeling himself or herself aggrieved by judgment of any justice of the peace, mayor, or alderman in cases arising under this act, may within five days appeal to the next term of the county court of the proper county, upon giving bond and security in a sum not less than twenty-five dollars nor more than one hundred and fifty dollars, conditioned to appear and prosecute said appeal, and abide by the judgment of the county court; and said appeal shall be tried *de novo* in the county court, and the decision of the said court shall be final.....

◆ CIVIL RIGHTS ACT CH. 31, 14 STAT. 27 (1866)

This act, enacted April 9, 1866, was designed to protect recently freed African Americans from black codes and other repressive state and local legislation. It was intended to provide all citizens with basic civil rights, including the right to make and enforce contracts, to bring suits in court, to purchase and sell real and personal property, and to enjoy security of person and property.

An Act to protect all Persons in the United States in their Civil Rights, and furnish the Means of their Vindication

*Be it enacted...*That all persons born in the United States and not subject to any foreign power, excluding Indians not taxed, are hereby declared to be citizens of the United States; and such citizens, of every race and color, without regard to any previous condition of slavery or involuntary servitude, except as a punishment for crime whereof the party shall have been duly convicted, shall have the same right in every State and Territory in the United States, to make and enforce contracts, to sue, be parties, and give evidence, to inherit, purchase, lease, sell, hold, and convey real and personal property, and to full and equal benefit of all laws and proceedings for the security of person and property, as is enjoyed by white citizens, and shall be subject to like punishment, pains, and penalties, and to none other, any law, statute, ordinance, regulation, or custom, to the contrary notwithstanding.

Section 2. *And be it further enacted,* That any person who, under color or any law, statute, ordinance, regulation, or custom, shall subject, or cause to be subjected, any inhabitant of any State or Territory to the deprivation of any right secured or protected by this act, or to different punishment, pains, or penalties on account of such person having at any time been held in a condition of slavery or involuntary servitude, except as a punishment for crime whereof the party shall have been duly convicted, or by reason of his color or race, than is prescribed for the punishment of white persons, shall be deemed guilty of a misdemeanor, and, on conviction, shall be punished by fine not exceeding one thousand

dollars, or imprisonment not exceeding one year, or both, in the discretion of the court....

◆ AMENDMENT FOURTEEN TO THE UNITED STATES CONSTITUTION (1868)

This amendment, ratified July 23, 1868, provided a definition of both national and state citizenship. When the Supreme Court heard the case Dred Scott v. Sandford in 1857, it ruled that Africans imported into this county as slaves, and their descendants, where not and could never become citizens of the United States. The passage of the Fourteenth Amendment resolved the question of African-American citizenship.

The amendment also reversed what had been the traditional federal-state relationship in the area of citizen's rights. The Fourteenth Amendment provides for the protection of the privileges of national citizenship, and basic civil rights, and guarantees for all citizens equal protection under the law. It also provides the federal government with authority to intervene in cases where state governments have been accused of violating the constitutional rights of individuals.

Section 1. All persons born or naturalized in the United States, and subject to the jurisdiction thereof, are citizens of the United States and of the State wherein they reside. No state shall make or enforce any law which shall abridge the privileges or immunities of citizens of the United States; nor shall any State deprive any person of life, liberty, or property, without due process of law; nor deny to any person within its jurisdiction the equal protection of the laws.

Section 2. Representatives shall be apportioned among the several States according to their respective numbers, counting the whole number of persons in each State, excluding Indians not taxed. But when the right to vote at any election for the choice of electors for President and Vice President of the United States, Representatives in Congress, the Executive and Judicial officers of a State, or the members of the Legislature thereof, is denied to any of the male inhabitants of such State, being twenty-one years of age, and citizens of the United States, or in any way abridged, except for participation in rebellion, or other crime, the basis of representation therein shall be reduced in the proportion which the number of such male citizens shall bear to the whole number of male citizens twenty-one years of age in such State.

Section 3. No person shall be a Senator or Representative in Congress, or elector of President and Vice

President, or hold any office, civil or military, under the United States, or under any State, who, having previously taken an oath, as a member of Congress, or as an office of the United States, or as a member of any State legislature, or as an executive or judicial officer of any State, to support the Constitution of the United States, shall have engaged in insurrection or rebellion against the same, or given aid or comfort to the enemies thereof. But Congress may by a vote of two-thirds of each House, remove such disability.

Section 4. The validity of the public debt of the United States, authorized by law, including debts incurred for payment of pensions and bounties for services in suppressing insurrection or rebellion shall not be questioned. But neither the United States nor any State shall assume or pay any debt or obligation incurred in aid of insurrection or rebellion against the United States, or any claim for the loss or emancipation of any slave; but all such debts, obligations and claims shall be held illegal and void.

Section 5. The Congress shall have power to enforce, by appropriate legislation, the provisions of this article.

◆ AMENDMENT FIFTEEN TO THE UNITED STATES CONSTITUTION (1870)

The Fifteenth Amendment, ratified March 30, 1870, was intended to protect the right of all citizens to vote. However, the amendment was not successful in bringing about a complete end to techniques designed to prevent blacks from voting; many state and local governments continued to employ such tactics as the use of grandfather clauses, literacy tests, "white primaries," and poll taxes as prerequisites to, or deterrents to voting.

Section 1. The right of citizens of the United States to vote shall not be denied or abridged by the United States or by any State on account of race, color, or previous conditions of servitude.

Section 2. The Congress shall have power to enforce this article by appropriate legislation.

◆ KU KLUX KLAN ACT CH. 22, 17 STAT. 13 (1871)

Following the Civil War, white terrorist groups began to spring up throughout the South. These early organizations, consisting mainly of Confederate veterans

still obsessed with the goals and aspirations of their Southern heritage, terrorized blacks who sought increased participation in their communities and whites who aided them. Known as the Knights of the White Camelia, the Jayhawkers, or the Ku Klux Klan, by 1871 these groups had become well organized. The Ku Klux Klan Act of 1871 was an attempt by Congress to end intimidation and violence by such organizations. The law, however, failed to exterminate the Klan or to eliminate the continued use of terrorist tactics against blacks and those whites who gave support to black concerns.

Be it enacted,...that any person who, under color of any law, statute, ordinance, regulation, custom, or usage of any State, shall subject, or cause to be subjected, any person within the jurisdiction of the United States to the deprivation of any rights, privileges, or immunities secured by the Constitution of the United States; shall any such law, statute, ordinance, regulation, custom, or usage of the state to the contrary notwithstanding, be liable to the party injured in any action at law, suite in equity, or other proper proceeding for redress; such proceeding to be prosecuted in the several district or circuit courts of the United States, with and subject to the same rights of appeal, review upon error, and other remedies provided in like cases in such courts, under the provisions of the [Civil Rights Act of April 9, 1866]... and the other remedial laws of the United States which are in their nature applicable in such cases.

Section 2. That if two or more persons within any State or Territory of the United States shall conspire together to overthrow, or to put down, or to destroy by force the government of the United States, or to levy war against the United States or to oppose by force the authority of the government of the United States, or by force, intimidation, or threat to prevent... any person from accepting or holding any office or trust or place of confidence under the United States, or from discharging the duties thereof... or to injure him in his person or property on account of his lawful discharge of the duties of his office, or to injure his person while engaged in the lawful discharge of the duties of his office, or... to deter any party or witness in any court of the United States from attending such court, or from testifying in any matter pending in such court fully, freely, and truthfully, or to injure any party or witness in his person or property on account of his having so attended or testified, or by force, intimidation, or threat to influence the verdict, presentment, or indictment, of any juror or grand juror in any court of the United States, or to injure such juror in his person or property on account of any verdict, presentment, or indictment lawfully assented to by him, or on account of his being or having been such

A Klan cross burning near Edinburg, Mississippi.

juror, or shall conspire together, or go in disguise upon the public highway or upon the premises of another for the purpose, either directly or indirectly, of depriving any person or any class of persons of the equal protection of the laws, or of equal privileges or immunities under the laws, or for the purpose of preventing or hindering the constituted authorities of any State from giving or securing to all persons within such State the equal protection of the laws, or shall conspire together for the purpose of in any manner impeding, hindering, obstructing, or defeating the due course of justice in any State or Territory, with the intent to deny to any citizen of the United States the due and equal protection of the laws, or to injure any person in his person or in his property for lawfully enforcing the right of any person or class of persons to the equal protection of the laws, or by force, intimidation, or threat to prevent any citizen of the United States lawfully entitled to vote from giving his support or advocacy in a lawful manner... or to injure any such citizen in his person or property on account of such support or advocacy, each and every person so offending shall be deemed guilty of a high crime.....

Section 3. That in all cases where insurrection, domestic violence, unlawful combinations, or conspiracies in any State shall so obstruct or hinder the execution of the laws thereof, and of the United States, as to deprive any portion or class of the people of such State of any of the rights, privileges, or immunities, or protection, named in the Constitution and secured by this act, and the constituted authorities of such State shall either be unable to protect, or shall from any cause fail in or refuse protection of the people in such rights, such facts will be deemed a denial by such State of the equal protection of the laws to which they are entitled under the Constitution of the United States; and in all such cases, or whenever any such insurrection, violence, unlawful combination, or conspiracy shall oppose or obstruct the laws of the United States or the due execution thereof, or impede or obstruct the due course of justice under the same, it shall be lawful for the President, and it shall be his duty to take such measures, by the employment of the militia or the land and naval forces of the United States, or either, or by other means, as he may deem necessary for the suppression of such insurrection, domestic violence, or combinations; and any person who shall be arrested under the provisions of this and the preceding section shall be delivered to the marshal of the proper district, to be dealt with according to law.

Section 4. That whenever in any State or part of a State the unlawful combinations named in the preceding section of this act shall be organized and armed, and so numerous and powerful as to be able, by violence, to either overthrow or set at defiance the constituted authorities of such State, and of the United States within such State, or when the constituted authorities are in complicity with, or shall connive at the unlawful purpose of, such powerful and armed combinations; and whenever, by reason of either or all of the causes aforesaid, the conviction of such offender and the preservation of the public safety shall become in such district impracticable, in every such case such combinations shall be deemed a rebellion, against the government of the United States, and during the continuation of such rebellion, and within the limits of the district which shall be so under the sway thereof, such limits to be prescribed by proclamation, it shall be lawful for the President of the United States, when in his judgment the public safety shall require it, to suspend the privileges of the writ of habeas corpus, to the end that such rebellion may be overthrown.....

Section 6. That any person, or persons, having knowledge that any of the wrongs conspired to be done and mentioned in the second section of this act are about to be committed, and having power to prevent or aid in preventing the same, shall neglect or refuse so to do, and

such wrongful act shall be committed, such person or persons shall be liable to the person injured, or his legal representatives, for all damages caused by any such wrongful act which such first-named person or persons by reasonable diligence could have prevented; and such damages may be recovered in an action on the case in the proper circuit court of the United States, and any number of persons guilty of such wrongful neglect or refusal may be joined as defendants in such action....

◆ CIVIL RIGHTS ACT OF 1875 CH. 114, 18 STAT. 335 (1875)

The Civil Rights Act of 1875 concerned itself primarily with the prohibition of racial discrimination in places of public accommodation. Eight years later, however, the United States Supreme Court addressed the issue. Ruling in a set of disputes, which came to be known as the Civil Rights Cases, the Court declared the law unconstitutional, stating that Congress did not have the authority to regulate the prevalent social mores of any state.

An Act to Protect All Citizens in Their Civil and Legal Rights.

Whereas it is essential to just governments we recognize the equality of all men before the law, and hold that it is the duty of government in its dealings with the people to mete out equal and exact justice to all, of whatever nativity, race, color, or persuasion, religious or political; and it being the appropriate object of legislation to enact great fundamental principles into law: Therefore, *Be it enacted*, That all persons within the jurisdiction of the United States shall be entitled to the full and equal enjoyment of the accommodations, advantages, facilities, and privileges of inns, public conveyances on land or water, theaters, and other places of public amusement; subject only to the conditions and limitations established by law, and applicable alike to citizens of every race and color, regardless of any previous condition of servitude.

Section 2. That any person who shall violate the foregoing section by denying to any citizen, except for reasons by law applicable to citizens of every race and color, and regardless of any previous condition of servitude, the full enjoyment of any of the accommodations, advantages, facilities, or privileges in said section enumerated, or by aiding or inciting such denial, shall for, every such offense, forfeit and pay the sum of five hundred dollars to the person aggrieved thereby ... and shall also, for every such offense, be deemed guilty of a misdemeanor, and upon conviction thereof, shall be fined not less than five hundred nor more than one thousand dollars, or shall be imprisoned not less than thirty days nor more than one year.....

Section 4. That no citizen possessing all other qualifications which are or may be prescribed by law shall be disqualified for service as grand or petit juror in any court of the United States, or of any State, on account of race, color, or previous condition of servitude; and any officer or other person charged with any duty in the selection or summoning of jurors who shall exclude or fail to summon any citizen for the cause aforesaid shall, on conviction thereof, be deemed guilty of a misdemeanor, and be fined not more than five thousand dollars.

Section 5. That all cases arising under the provisions of this act... shall be renewable by the Supreme Court of the U.S., without regard to the sum in controversy....

◆ BOOKER T. WASHINGTON'S "ATLANTA COMPROMISE" SPEECH (1895)

Booker T. Washington, a major voice in the movement for the advancement of African Americans, was often criticized for encouraging blacks to cultivate peaceful coexistence with whites. Washington advocated the use of technical and industrial self-help programs—even if such programs tended to discount the importance of the cultivation of intellectual and aesthetic values. In address to the 1895 Atlanta Exposition, Washington outlined his philosophy.

Mr. President and Gentlemen of the Board of Directors and Citizens:

One-third of the population of the South is of the Negro race. No enterprise seeking the material, civil, or moral welfare of this section can disregard this element of our population and reach the highest success. I but convey to you, Mr. President and Directors, the sentiment of the masses of my race when I say that in no way have the value and manhood of the American Negro been more fittingly and generously recognized than by the managers of this magnificent Exposition at every stage of its progress. It is a recognition that will do more to cement the friendship of the two races than any occurrence since the dawn of our freedom.

Not only this, but the opportunity here afforded will awaken among us a new era of industrial progress. Ignorant and inexperienced, it is not strange that in the first years of our new life we began at the top instead of at the bottom; that a seat in Congress or the State Legislature was more sought than real estate or industrial skill; that the political convention or stump speaking had more attractions than starting a dairy farm or truck garden.

A ship lost at sea for many days suddenly sighted a friendly vessel. From the mast of the unfortunate vessel was seen a signal: "Water, water; we die of thirst!" The answer from the friendly vessel at once came back: "Cast down your bucket where you are." A second time the signal, "Water, water; send us water!" ran up from the distressed vessel, and was answered: "Cast down your bucket where you are." And a third and fourth signal for water was answered: "Cast down your bucket where you are." The captain of the distressed vessel, at last heeding the injunction, cast down his bucket, and it came up full of fresh, sparkling water from the mouth of the Amazon River. To those of my race who depend on bettering their condition in a foreign land, or who underestimate the importance of cultivating friendly relations with the Southern white man, who is their next door neighbor, I would say: "Cast down your bucket where you are"—cast it down in making friends in every manly way of the people of all races by whom we are surrounded.

Cast it down in agriculture, mechanics, in commerce, in domestic service, and in the professions. And in this connection it is well to bear in mind that whatever other sins the South may be called to bear, when it comes to business, pure and simple, it is in the South that the Negro is given a man's chance in the commercial world, and in nothing is this Exposition more eloquent than in

Booker T. Washington

emphasizing this chance. Our greatest danger is, that in the great leap from slavery to freedom we may overlook the fact that the masses of us are to live by the productions of our hands, and fail to keep in mind that we shall prosper in proportion as we learn to dignify and glorify common labor, and put brains and skill into the common occupations of life; shall prosper in proportion as we learn to draw the line between the superficial and the substantial, the ornamental gewgaws of life and the useful. No race can prosper till it learns that there is as much dignity in tilling a field as in writing a poem. It is at the bottom of life we must begin, and not at the top. Nor should we permit our grievances to overshadow our opportunities.

To those of the white race who look to the incoming of those of foreign birth and strange tongue and habits for the prosperity of the South, were I permitted, I would repeat what I say to my own race, "Cast down your bucket where you are." Cast it down among the 8,000,000 Negroes whose habits you know, whose fidelity and love you have tested in days when to have proved treacherous meant the ruin of your firesides. Cast down your bucket among those people who have, without strikes and labor wars, tilled your fields, cleared your forests, builded your railroads and cities, and brought forth treasures from the bowels of the earth, and helped make possible this magnificent representation of the progress of the South. Casting down your bucket among my people, helping and encouraging them as you are doing on these grounds, and, with education of head, hand and heart, you will find that they will buy your surplus land, make blossom the waste place in your fields, and run your factories. While doing this, you can be sure in the future, as in the past, that you and your families will be surrounded by the most patient, faithful, law-abiding, and unresentful people that the world has seen. As we have proved our loyalty to you in the past, in nursing your children, watching by the sick bed of your mothers and fathers, and often following them with tear-dimmed eyes to their graves, so in the future, in our humble way, we shall stand by you with a devotion that no foreigner can approach, ready to lay down our lives, if need be, in defense of yours, interlacing our industrial, commercial, civil, and religious life with yours in a way that shall make the interests of both races one. In all things that are purely social we can be as separate as the fingers, yet one as the hand in all things essential to mutual progress.

There is no defense or security for any of us except in the highest intelligence and development of all. If anywhere there are efforts tending to curtail the fullest growth of the Negro, let these efforts be turned into stimulating, encouraging, and making him the most useful and intelligent citizen. Effort or means so invested will pay a thousand percent interest. These efforts will be twice blessed—"blessing him that gives and him that takes."

There is no escape through law of man or God from the inevitable:

The laws of changeless justice bind
Oppressor with oppressed;
And close as sin and suffering joined
We march to fate abreast.

Nearly sixteen millions of hands will aid you in pulling the load upwards, or they will pull against you the load downwards. We shall constitute one-third and more of the ignorance and crime of the South, or one-third its intelligence and progress; we shall contribute one-third to the business and industrial prosperity of the South, or we shall prove a veritable body of death, stagnating, depressing, retarding every effort to advance the body politic.

Gentlemen of the Exposition, as we present to you humble effort at an exhibition of our progress, you must not expect over much. Starting thirty years ago with ownership here and there in a few quilts and pumpkins and chickens (gathered from miscellaneous sources), remember the path that has led from these to the invention and production of agricultural implements, buggies, steam engines, newspapers, books, statuary, carving, paintings, the management of drug stores and banks, has not been trodden without contact with thorns and thistles. While we take pride in what we exhibit as a result of our independent efforts, we do not for a moment forget that our part in this exhibition would fall far short of your expectations but for the constant help that has come to our educational life, not only from the Southern States, but especially from Northern philanthropists, who have made their gifts a constant stream of blessing and encouragement.

The wisest among my race understand that the agitation of questions of social equality is the extremist folly, and that progress in the enjoyment of all the privileges that will come to us must be the result of severe and constant struggle rather than of artificial forcing. No race that has anything to contribute to the markets of the world is long in any degree ostracized. It is important and right that all privileges of the law be ours, but it is vastly more important that we be prepared for the exercise of those privileges. The opportunity to earn a dollar in a factory just now is worth infinitely more than the opportunity to spend a dollar in an opera house.

In conclusion, may I repeat that nothing in thirty years has given us more hope and encouragement, and drawn us so near to you of the white race, as this opportunity offered by the Exposition; and here bending, as it were, over the altar that represents the results of the struggle of your race and mine, both starting practically empty-handed three decades ago, I pledge that, in your effort to work out the great and intricate problem which God has laid at the doors of the South, you shall have at all time the patient, sympathetic help of my race; only let this be constantly in mind that, while from representations in these buildings of the product of field, of forest, of mine, of factory, letters, and art, much good will come, yet far above and beyond material benefits will be that higher good, that let us pray God will come, in a blotting out of sectional differences and racial animosities and suspicions, in a determination to administer absolute justice, in a willing obedience among all classes to the mandates of law. This, coupled with our material prosperity, will bring into our beloved South a new heaven and a new earth.

◆ *PLESSY V. FERGUSON 163 US 537 (1896)*

On February 23, 1869, the Louisiana state legislature enacted a law prohibiting segregation on public transportation. In 1878, ruling in the case Hall v. DeCuir, *the United States Supreme Court declared that state governments could not prohibit segregation on common carriers. Twelve years later, the Court hearing the case* Louisville, New Orleans and Texas Railway v. Mississippi *approved a state statute requiring segregation on intrastate carriers.*

In 1896, the Court once again faced the issue of segregation on public transportation. Homer Adolph Plessy, a black traveling by train from New Orleans to Covington, Louisiana, was arrested when he refused to ride in the "colored" railway coach; Louisiana state law required that "separate but equal" accommodations be maintained in public facilities for blacks and whites. In its majority opinion, the Court declared that "separate but equal" accommodations constituted a "reasonable" use of state police power and that the Fourteenth Amendment "could not have been intended to abolish distinctions based on color, or to enforce social... equality, or a commmingling of the two races upon terms unsatisfactory to either."

In effect, the Court's ruling had significantly reduced the authoritativeness of the Fourteenth Amendment and Fifteenth Amendment to the Constitution, which were designed to provide blacks specific rights and protections; The "separate but equal" doctrine paved the way for segregation of blacks in all walks of life. The "separate but equal" doctrine stood until the Brown v. Board of Education of Topeka *decision of 1954.*

Justice Brown delivered the opinion of the Court.

This case turns upon the constitutionality of an act of the General Assembly of the state of Louisiana, passed in 1890, providing for separate railway carriages for the white and colored races.....

The constitutionality of this act is attacked upon the ground that it conflicts both with the Thirteenth Amendment of the Constitution, abolishing slavery, and the Fourteenth Amendment, which prohibits certain restrictive legislation on the part of the states.

1. That it does not conflict with the Thirteenth Amendment, which abolished slavery and involuntary servitude, except as a punishment for crime, is too clear for argument. Slavery implies involuntary servitude—a state of bondage; the ownership of mankind as a chattel, or at least the control of the labor and services of one man for the benefit of another, and absence of a legal right to the disposal of his own person, property, and services.....

A statute which implies merely a legal distinction between the white and colored races—a distinction which is founded in the color of the two races, and which must always exist so long as white men are distinguished from the other race by color—has no tendency to destroy the legal equality of the two races, or reestablish a state of involuntary servitude. Indeed, we do not understand that the Thirteenth Amendment is strenuously relied upon by the plaintiff in error in this connection.

2. By the Fourteenth Amendment, all persons born or naturalized in the United States, and subject to the jurisdiction thereof, are made citizens of the United States and of the state wherein they reside; and the states are forbidden from making or enforcing any law which shall abridge the privileges or immunities of citizens of the United States, or shall deprive any person of life, liberty, or property without due process of law, or deny to any person within their jurisdiction the equal protection of the laws.....

The object of the amendment was undoubtedly to enforce the absolute equality of the two races before the law, but in the nature of things it could not have been intended to abolish distinctions based upon color, or to enforce social, as distinguished from political, equality, or a commingling of the two races upon terms unsatisfactory to either. Laws permitting, and even requiring, their separation in places where they are liable to be brought into contact do not necessarily imply the inferiority of either race to the other, and have been generally, if not universally, recognized as within the competency of the state legislatures in the exercise of their police power. The most common instance of this is connected with the establishment of separate schools for white and colored children, which has been held to be a valid

The "separate but equal" doctrine paved the way for segregation of blacks in all walks of life.

exercise of the legislative power even by courts of states where the political rights of the colored race have been longest and most earnestly enforced.....

So far, then, as a conflict with the Fourteenth Amendment is concerned, the case reduces itself to the question whether the statute of Louisiana is a reasonable regulation, and with respect to this there must necessarily be a large discretion on the part of the legislature. In determining the question of reasonableness it is at liberty to act with reference to the established usages, customs, and traditions of the people, and with a view to the promotion of their comfort, and the preservation of the public peace and good order. Gauged by this standard, we cannot say that a law which authorizes or even requires the separation of the two races in public conveyances is unreasonable or more obnoxious to the Fourteenth Amendment than the acts of Congress requiring separate schools for colored children in the District of Columbia, the constitutionality of which does not seem to have been questioned, or the corresponding acts of state legislatures.

We consider the underlying fallacy of the plaintiff's argument to consist in the assumption that the enforced separation of the two races stamps the colored race with a badge of inferiority. If this be so, it is not by reason of anything found in the act, but solely the colored race chooses to put that construction upon it. The argument necessarily assumes that if, as has been more than once the case, and is not unlikely to be so again, the colored race should become the dominant power in the state legislature, and should enact a law in precisely similar terms, it would thereby relegate the white race to an inferior position. We imagine that the white race, at least, would not acquiesce in this assumption. The argument also assumes that social prejudices may be overcome by legislation and that equal rights cannot be secured to the Negro except by an enforced commingling of the two races. We cannot accept this proposition. If the two races are to meet upon terms of social equality, it must be the result of natural affinities, a mutual appreciation of each other's merits, and a voluntary consent of individuals..... Legislation is powerless to eradicate racial instincts or to abolish distinctions based upon physical differences, and the attempt to do so can only result in accentuating the difficulties of the present situation. If the civil and political rights of both races be equal, one cannot be inferior to the other civilly or politically. If one race be inferior to the other socially, the Constitution of the United States cannot put them upon the same plane.

It is true that the question of the proportion of colored blood necessary to constitute a colored person, as distinguished from a white person, is one upon with there is a difference of opinion in the different states, some holding that any visible admixture of black blood stamps the person as belonging to the colored race... others that it depends upon the preponderance of blood... and still others that the pre-dominance of white blood must only be in the proportion of three-fourths.... But these are questions to be determined under the laws of each state and are not properly put in issue in this case. Under the allegations of his petition it may undoubtedly become a question of importance whether, under the laws of Louisiana, the petitioner belongs to the white or colored race.

The judgment of the court below is therefore, *Affirmed.*

Justice Harlan Dissenting

In respect of civil rights, common to all citizens, the Constitution of the United Stats does not, I think, permit any public authority to know the race of those entitled to be protected in the enjoyment of such rights. Every true man has pride of race, and under appropriate circumstances with the rights of others, his equals before the law, are not to be affected, it is his privilege to express such pride and to take such action based upon it as to him seems proper. But I deny that any legislative body or judicial tribunal may have regard to the race of citizens when the civil rights of those citizens are involved. Indeed, such legislation, as that here in question, is inconsistent not only with that equality of rights which pertains to citizenship, national and state, but with the personal liberty enjoyed by everyone within the United States.

The Thirteenth Amendment does not permit the withholding or the deprivation of any right necessarily inhering in freedom. It not only struck down the institution of slavery as previously existing in the United States, but it prevents the imposition of any burdens or disabilities that constitute badges of slavery or servitude. It decreed universal civil freedom in this country. This Court has so adjudged. But that amendment having been found inadequate to the protection of the rights of those who had been in slavery, it was followed by the Fourteenth Amendment, which added greatly to the dignity and glory of the American citizenship, and to the security of personal liberty, by declaring that "all persons born or naturalized in the United States, and subject to the jurisdiction thereof, are citizens of the United States and of the state wherein they reside," and that "no state shall make or enforce any law which shall abridge the privileges or immunities of citizens of the United States; nor shall any state deprive any person of life, liberty, or property without due process of law, nor deny to any person within its jurisdiction the equal protection of the laws." These two amendments, if enforced according to their true intent and meaning, will protect all the civil rights that pertains to freedom and citizenship. Finally, and to the end that no citizen should be denied, on account of his race, the privilege of participating in the political control of his country, it was declared by the Fifteenth Amendment that "the right of citizens of the United States to vote shall not be denied or abridged by the United States or by any state on account of race, color, or previous condition of servitude."

These notable additions to the fundamental law were welcomed by the friends of liberty throughout the world. They removed the race line from our governmental systems.

It was said in argument that the statute of Louisiana does not discriminate against either race but prescribes a rule applicable alike to white and colored citizens. But this argument does not meet the difficulty. Everyone knows that the statute in question had its origin in the purpose, not so much to exclude white persons from railroad cars occupied by blacks, as to exclude colored people from coaches occupied by or assigned to white persons. Railroad corporations of Louisiana did not make discrimination among whites in the matter of accommodation for travelers. The thing to accomplish was, under the guise of giving equal accommodation for whites and blacks, to compel the latter to keep to themselves while traveling in railroad passenger coaches. No one would be wanting in candor as to assert the contrary. The fundamental objections, therefore, to the statute is that it interferes with the personal freedom of citizens. If a white man and a black man choose to occupy the same public conveyance on a public highway, it is their right to do so, and no government, proceeding alone on grounds of race, can prevent it without infringing the personal liberty of each.

It is one thing for railroad carriers to furnish, or to be required by law to furnish, equal accommodations for all whom they are under a legal duty to carry. It is quite another thing for government to forbid citizens of the white and black races from traveling in the same public conveyance, and to punish officers of railroad companies for permitting persons of the two races to occupy the same passenger coach. If a state can prescribe, as a rule of civil conduct, that whites and blacks shall not travel as passengers in the same railroad coach, why may it not so regulate the use of the streets of its cities and towns as to compel white citizens to keep on one side of a street and black citizens to keep on the other? Why may it not, upon like grounds, punish whites and blacks who ride together in streetcars or in open vehicles on a public road or street? Why may it not require sheriffs to assign whites to one side of a courtroom and blacks to other? And why may it not also prohibit the commingling of the two races in the galleries of legislative halls or in public assemblages convened for the consideration of the political questions of the day? Further, if this statute of Louisiana is consistent with the personal liberty of citizens, why may not the state require the separation in railroad coaches of native and naturalized citizens of the United States, or of Protestants and Roman Catholics?

The answer given as the argument to these questions was that regulations of the kind they suggest would be unreasonable and could not, therefore, stand before the law. Is it meant that the determination of questions of legislative power depends upon the inquiry whether the statute whose validity is questioned is, in the judgment of the courts, a reasonable one, taking all the circumstances into consideration? A statute may be unreasonable merely because a sound public forbade its enactment. But I do not understand that the courts have anything to do with the policy or expediency of legislation. The white race deems itself to be the dominant race in this country. And so it is, in prestige, in achievements, in education, in wealth, and in power. So, I doubt not, it will continue to be for all time, if it remains true to its great heritage and holds fast to the principles of constitutional liberty. But in view of the Constitution, in the eye of the law, there is in this country no superior, dominant, ruling class of citizens. There is no caste here. Our Constitution is color-blind and neither knows nor tolerates classes among citizens. In respect of civil rights all citizens are equal before the law. The humblest is the peer of the most powerful. The law regards man as a man and takes no account of his surroundings or of his color when his civil rights, as guaranteed by the supreme law of the land, are involved. It is, therefore, to be regretted that this high tribunal, the final expositor of the fundamental law of the land, has reached the conclusion that it is competent for a state to regulate the enjoyment by citizens of their civil rights solely upon the basis of race.....

The sure guarantee of the peace and security of each is the clear, distinct, unconditional recognition by our governments, national and state, of every right that inheres in civil freedom, and of the equality before the law of all citizens of the United States without regard to race. State enactments, regulating the enjoyment of civil rights, upon the basis of race, and cunningly devised legitimate results of the war, under the pretense of recognizing equality of rights, can have no other result than to render permanent peace impossible, and to keep alive a conflict of races, the continuance of which must do harm to all concerned.....

The arbitrary separation of citizens, on the basis of race, while they are on a public highway, is a badge of servitude wholly inconsistent with the civil freedom and the equality before he law established by the Constitution. It cannot be justified upon any legal grounds.

If evils will result from the commingling of the two races upon public highways established for the benefit of all, they will be infinitely less than those that will surely come from state legislation regulating the enjoyment of civil rights upon the basis of race. We boast of the freedom enjoyed by our people above all other peoples. But it is difficult to reconcile that boast with a state of the law which, practically, puts the brand of servitude and degradation upon a large class of our fellow-citizens, our equals before the law. The thin disguise of "equal" accommodations for passengers in railroad coaches will not mislead anyone, nor atone of the wrong this day done.....

I am of opinion that the statute of Louisiana is inconsistent with the personal liberty of citizens, white and black, in that state, and hostile to both the spirit and letter of the Constitution of the United States. If laws of like character should be enacted in the several states of the Union, the effect would be in the highest degree mischievous. Slavery, as an institution tolerated by law, would, it is true, have disappeared from our country, but there would remain a power in the states, by sinister legislation, to interfere with the full enjoyment of the blessings of freedom; to regulate civil rights, common to all citizens, upon the basis of race, and to place in a condition of legal inferiority a large body of American citizens, now constituting a part of the political community called the People of the United States, for whom, and by whom through representatives, our government is administered. Such a system is inconsistent with the guarantee given by the Constitution to each state of a republican form of government, and may be stricken down by congressional action, constitutional or laws of any state to the contrary notwithstanding.

For the reasons stated, I am constrained to withhold my assent from the opinion and judgment of the majority.....

◆ "LIFT EVERY VOICE AND SING" (1901)

Originally intended for use in a program given by a group of Jacksonville, Florida school children to celebrate Lincoln's birthday, "Lift Every Voice and Sing" has become known as the black "national anthem." The song's words, written by poet and civil rights leader James Weldon Johnson, serve as a tribute to African American heritage. The song's music was composed by Johnson's brother and songwriting partner, J. Rosamond Johnson.

> Lift every voice and sing
> Till earth and heaven ring,
> Ring with the harmonies of Liberty;
> Let our rejoicing rise
> High as the listening skies,
> Let it resound loud as the rolling sea.
> Sing a song full of the faith that the dark past has taught us,
> Sing a song full of the hope that the present has brought us,
> Facing the rising sun of our new day begun
> Let us march on till victory is won
>
> Stony the road we trod,
> Bitter the chastening rod,
> Felt in the days when hope unborn had died;
> Yet with a steady beat,
> Have not our weary feet
> Come to the place for which our fathers sighed?
> We have come over a way that with tears have been
> watered,
> We have come, treading our path through the blood
> of the slaughtered
> Out from the gloomy past,
> Till now we stand at last
> Where the white gleam of our bright star is cast.

> God of our weary years,
> God of our silent tears,
> Thou who has brought us thus far on the way;
> Thou who has by Thy might
> Led us into the light,
> Keep us forever in the path, we pray.
> Lest our feet stray from the places, Our God,
> where
> We met Thee,
> Lest, our heart's drunk with the wine of the world,
> We forget Thee;
> Shadowed beneath Thy hand,
> May we forever stand.
> True to our God,
> True to our native land.

◆ MARCUS GARVEY'S SPEECH AT LIBERTY HALL, NEW YORK CITY (1922)

Marcus Garvey, black nationalist and founder of the Universal Negro Improvement Association, dedicated his life to uplifting Africans throughout the world. In this 1922 address, Garvey outlined the goals of the Universal Negro Improvement Association.

Over five years ago the Universal Negro Improvement Association placed itself before the world as the movement through which the new and rising Negro would give expression of his feelings. This Association adopts an attitude not of hostility to other races and peoples of the world, but an attitude of self-respect

...Wheresoever human rights are denied to any group, wheresoever justice is denied to any group, there the U.N.I.A. finds a cause. And at this time among all the peoples of the world, the group that suffers most from injustice, the group that is denied most of those rights that belong to all humanity, is the black group... even so under the leadership of the U.N.I.A., we are marshalling the 400,000,000 Negroes of the world to fight for the emancipation of the race and of the redemption of the country of our fathers.

We represent a new line of thought among Negroes. Whether you call it advanced thought or reactionary thought, I do not care. If it is reactionary for people to seek independence in government, then we are reactionary. If it is advanced thought for people to seek liberty and freedom, then we represent the advanced school of thought among the Negroes of this country. We of the U.N.I.A. believe that what is good for the other folks is good for us. If government is something that is worth while; if government is something that is appreciable and helpful and protective to others, then we also want to experiment in government. We do not mean a government that will make us citizens without rights or subject without consideration. We mean a kind of gov-

Marcus Garvey

ernment that will place our race in control, even as other races are in control of their own government.

... The U.N.I.A. is not advocating the cause of church building, because we have a sufficiently large number of churches among us to minister to the spiritual needs of the people, and we are not going to compete with those who are engaged in so splendid a work; we are not engaged in building any new social institutions,... because there are enough social workers engaged in those praiseworthy efforts. We are not engaged in politics because we have enough local politicians,... and the political situation is well taken care of. We are not engaged in domestic politics, in church building or in social uplift work, but we are engaged in nation building.

In advocating the principles of this Association we find we have been very much misunderstood and very much misrepresented by men from within our own race, as well as others from without. Any reform movement that seeks to bring about changes for the benefit of humanity is bound to be misrepresented by those who have always taken it upon themselves to administer to, and lead the unfortunate.....

... The Universal Negro Improvement Association stands for the Bigger Brotherhood; the Universal Negro

Improvement Association stands for human rights, not only for Negroes, but for all races. The Universal Negro Improvement Association believes in the rights of not only the black race, the white race, the yellow race and the brown race. The Universal Negro Improvement Association believes that the white man has as much right to be considered, the yellow man has as much right to be considered, the brown man has as much right to be considered as the black man of Africa. In view of the fact that the black man of Africa has contributed as much to the world as the white man of Europe, and the brown man and yellow man of Asia, we of the Universal Negro Improvement Association demand that the white, yellow and brown races give to the black man his place in the civilization of the world. We ask for nothing more than the rights of 400,000,000 Negroes. We are not seeking, as I said before, to destroy or disrupt the society or the government of other races, but we are determined that 400,000,000 of us shall unite ourselves to free our motherland from the grasp of the invader.....

The Universal Negro Improvement Association is not seeking to build up another government within the bounds or borders of the United States of America. The Universal Negro Improvement Association is not seeking to disrupt any organized system of government, but the Association is determined to bring Negroes together for the building up of a nation of their own. And why? Because we have been forced to it. We have been forced to it throughout the world; not only in America, not only in Europe, not only in the British Empire, but wheresoever the black man happens to find himself, he has been forced to do for himself.

To talk about Government is a little more than some of our people can appreciate..... The average man ...seems to say, "why should there be need for any other government?" We are French, English or American. But we of the U.N.I.A. have studied seriously this question of nationality among Negroes—this American nationality, this British nationality, this French, Italian or Spanish nationality, and have discovered that it counts for nought when that nationality comes in conflict with the racial idealism of the group that rules. When our interests clash with those of the ruling faction, then we find that we have absolutely no rights. In times of peace, when everything is all right, Negroes have a hard time, wherever we go, wheresoever we find ourselves, getting those rights that belong to us in common with others whom we claim as fellow citizens; getting that consideration that should be ours by right of the constitution, by right of the law, but in the time of trouble they make us all partners in the cause, as happened in the last war.....

We have saved many nations in this manner, and we have lost our lives doing that before. Hundreds of thousands—nay, millions of black men, lie buried under the ground due to that old-time camouflage of saving the nation. We saved the British Empire; we saved the French Empire; we saved this glorious country more than once; and all that we have received for our sacrifices, all that we have received for what we have done, even in giving up our lives, is just what you are receiving now, just what I am receiving now.

You and I fare no better in America, in the British Empire, or any other part of the white world; we fare no better than any black man wheresoever he shows his head.....

The U.N.I.A. is reversing the old-time order of things. We refuse to be followers anymore. We are leading ourselves. That means, if any saving is to be done,... we are going to seek a method of saving Africa first. Why? And why Africa? Because Africa has become the grand prize of the nations. Africa has become the big game of the nation hunters. Today Africa looms as the greatest commercial, industrial and political prize in the world.

The difference between the Universal Negro Improvement Association and the other movements of this country, and probably the world, is that the Universal Negro Improvement Association seeks independence of government while the other organizations seek to make the Negro a secondary part of existing governments. We differ from the organizations in America because they seek to subordinate the Negro as a secondary consideration in a great civilization, knowing that in America the Negro will never reach his highest ambition, knowing that the Negro in America will never get his constitutional rights. All other organizations which are fostering the improvement of Negroes in the British Empire know that the Negro in the British Empire will never reach the height of his constitutional rights. What do I mean by constitutional rights in America? If the black man is to reach the height of his ambition in this country—if the black man is to get all of his constitutional rights in America—then the black man should have the same chance in the nation as any other man to become president of the nation, or a street cleaner in New York. If the black man in the British Empire is to have all his constitutional rights it means that the Negro in the British Empire should have at least the same right to become premier of Great Britain as he has to become a street cleaner in the city of London. Are they prepared to give us such political equality? You and I can live in the United States of America for 100 more years, and our generations may live for 200 years or for 5000 more years, and so long as there is a black and white population, when the majority is on the side of the white race, you and I will never get political justice or get political equality in this country. Then why should a black man with rising ambition, after preparing himself in every possible way to give expression to that highest ambition, allow himself to be kept down by racial prejudice within a country? If I am as educated as the next man, if I am as prepared as the next man, if I have passed through the best schools and colleges and universities as the other fellow, why should I not have a fair chance to compete with the other fellow for the biggest position in the nation?...

We are not preaching a propaganda of hate against anybody. We love the white man; we love all humanity..... The white man is as necessary to the existence of the Negro as the Negro is necessary to his existence. There is a common relationship that we cannot escape. Africa has certain things that Europe wants, and Europe has certain things that Africa wants,... it is impossible for us to escape it. Africa has oil, diamonds, copper, gold and rubber and all the minerals that Europe wants, and there must be some kind of relationship between Africa and Europe for a fair exchange, so we cannot afford to hate anybody.

The question often asked is what does it require to redeem a race and free a country? If it takes man power, if it takes scientific intelligence, if it takes education of any kind, or if it takes blood, then the 400,000,000 Negroes of the world have it.

It took the combined power of the Allies to put down the mad determination of the Kaiser to impose German will upon humanity. Among those who suppressed his mad ambition were two million Negroes who have not yet forgotten how to drive men across the firing line... when so many white men refused to answer to the call and dodged behind all kinds of excuses, 400,000 black men were ready without a question. It was because we were told it was a war of democracy; it was a war for the liberation of the weaker peoples of the world. We heard the cry of Woodrow Wilson, not because we liked him so, but because the things he said were of such a nature that they appealed to us as men. Wheresoever the cause of humanity stands in need of assistance, there you will find the Negro ever ready to serve.

He has done it from the time of Christ up to now. When the whole world turned its back upon the Christ, the man who was said to be the Son of God, when the world cried out "Crucify Him," when the world spurned Him and spat upon Him, it was a black man, Simon, the Cyrenian, who took up the cross. Why? Because the cause of humanity appealed to him. When the black man saw the suffering Jew, struggling under the heavy cross, he was willing to go to His assistance, and he bore that cross up to the heights of Calvary. In the spirit of Simon, the Cyrenian, 1900 years ago, we answered the call of Woodrow Wilson, the call to a larger humanity, and it was for that we willingly rushed into the war.....

We shall march out, yes, as black American citizens, as black British subjects, as black French citizens, as black Italians or as black Spaniards, but we shall march out with a greater loyalty, the loyalty of race. We shall march out in answer to the cry of our fathers, who cry out to us for the redemption of our own country, our motherland, Africa.

We shall march out, not forgetting the blessings of America. We shall march out, not forgetting the blessings of civilization. We shall march out with a history of peace before and behind us, and surety that history shall be our breast-plate, for how can a man fight better than knowing that the cause for which he fights is righteous?... Glorious shall be the battle when the time comes to fight for our people and our race.

We should say to the millions who are in Africa to hold the fort, for we are coming 400,000,000 strong.

◆ EXECUTIVE ORDER NO. 8802, 3 C.F.R., 1938-1943 COMP. P. 957 (1941)

Issued by President Franklin D. Roosevelt on June 25, 1941, Executive Order 8802 was intended to eliminate discriminatory practices in the defense industry during World War II (1941-1945).

Whereas it is the policy of the United States to encourage full participation in the national defense program by all citizens of the United States, regardless of race, creed, color, or national origin, in the firm belief that the democratic way of life within the Nation can be defended successfully only with the help and support of all groups within its borders, and

Whereas there is evidence that available and needed workers have been barred from employment in industries engaged in defense production solely because of considerations of race, creed, color, or national origin, to the detriment of workers' morale and of national unity:

Now, Therefore, by virtue of the authority vested in me by the Constitution and the statues, and as a prerequisite to the successful conduct of our national defense production effort, I do hereby reaffirm the policy of the United States that there shall be no discrimination in the employment of workers in defense industries or Government because of race, creed, color, or national origin, and I do hereby declare that it is the duty of employers and of labor organizations, in furtherance of said policy and of this order, to provide for the full and equitable participation of all workers in defense industries, without discrimination because of race, creed, color, or national origin;

And it is hereby ordered as follows:

1. All departments and agencies of the Government of the United States concerned with vocational and training programs for defense production shall take special measures appropriate to assure that such programs are administered without discrimination because of race, creed, color, or national origin;

2. All contracting agencies of the Government of the United States shall include in all defense contracts hereafter negotiated by them a provision obligating the contractor not to discriminate against any worker because of race, creed, color, or national origin;

3. There is established in the Office of Production Management a Committee on Fair Employment Practice, which shall consist of a chairman and four other members to be appointed by the President. The Chairman and members of the Committee shall serve as such without compensation but shall be entitled to actual and necessary transportation, subsistence and other expenses incidental to performance of their duties. The Committee shall receive and investigate complaints of discrimination in violation of the provisions of this order and shall take appropriate steps to redress grievances which it finds to be valid. The Committee shall also recommend to the several departments and agencies of the Government of the United States and to the President all measures which may be deemed by it necessary or proper to effectuate the provisions of this order.

◆ EXECUTIVE ORDER NO. 9981, 3 C.F.R. 1943-1948 COMP. P.720 (1948)

Signed by President Harry S. Truman on July 26, 1948, Executive Order 9981 ended segregation in the Armed Forces of the United States.

Whereas it is essential that there be maintained in the armed services of the United States the highest standards of democracy, with equality of treatment and opportunity for all those who serve in our country's defense:

Now, therefore, by virtue of the authority vested in me as President of the United States, by the Constitution and the statutes of the United States, and as Commander-in-Chief of the armed services, it is hereby ordered as follows:

1. It is hereby declared to be the policy of the President that there shall be equality of treatment and opportunity for all persons in the armed services without regard to race, color, religion or national origin. This policy shall be put into effect as rapidly as possible, having due regard to the time required to effectuate any necessary changes without impairing efficiency or morals.

2. There shall be created in the National Military Establishment an advisory committee to be known as the President's Committee on Equality of Treatment and Opportunity in the Armed Services, which shall be composed of seven members to be designated by the President.

3. The Committee is authorized on behalf of the President to examine into the rules, procedures and practices of the armed services in order to determine in what respect such rules, procedure and practices may be altered or improved with a view to carrying out the policy of this order. The Committee shall confer and advise with the Secretary of the Army, the Secretary of the Air Force, and shall make such recommendations to the President and to said Secretaries as in the judgment of the Committee will effectuate the policy hereof.

4. All executive departments and agencies of the Federal Government are authorized and directed to cooperate with the Committee in its work, and to furnish the Committee such information or the services of such persons as the Committee may require in the performance of its duties.

5. When requested by the Committee to do so, persons in the armed services or in any of the executive departments and agencies of the Federal Government shall testify before the Committee and shall make available for the use of the Committee such documents and other information as the Committee may require.

6. The Committee shall continue to exist until such time as the President shall terminate its existence by Executive order.

◆ BROWN V. BOARD OF EDUCATION OF TOPEKA 347 U.S. 483 (1945)

Beginning in the late 1930s, the United States Supreme Court began to review numerous cases dealing with segregation in public education; by the 1950s it had become evident that segregated educational facilities were not equal.

In 1938, ruling in the case Missouri ex rel. Gaines v. Canada, *the Court ruled that states were required to provide equal educational facilities for blacks within its boundaries. (The state of Missouri at that time had maintained a practice of providing funds for blacks to attend graduate and professional schools outside of the state, rather than provide facilities itself.) Taking an even greater step, in 1950 the Court in* Sweatt v. Painter *ruled that a separate law school for blacks provided by the state of Texas violated the equal protection clause of the Fourteenth Amendment.*

In 1952, five different cases, all dealing with segregation in public schools but with different facts and from different places, reached the United States Supreme Court. Four of the cases, Brown v. Board of Education of Topeka *(out of Kansas),* Briggs v. Elliott *(out of South Carolina),* Davis v. Prince Edward County School Board *(out of Virginia), and* Gebhart v. Belton *(out of Delaware) were considered together; the fifth case,* Bolling v. Sharpe, *coming out of the District of Columbia, was considered separately (since the district is not a state).*

After hearing initial arguments, the Court found itself unable to reach an agreement. In 1953, the Court heard reargument. Thurgood Marshall, legal consul for the National Association for the Advancement of Colored People Legal Defense and Education Fund, presented arguments on behalf of the black students. On May 17, 1954, the Court unanimously ruled that segregation in all public education deprived minority children of equal protection under the Fourteenth Amendment. (In the Bolling *case, the Court determined that segregation violated provisions of the Fifth Amendment, since the Fourteenth Amendment is expressly directed to the states.)*

Chief Justice Warren delivered the opinion of the Court.

These cases come to us from the States of Kansas, South Carolina, Virginia and Delaware. They are premised on different facts and different local conditions, but a common legal question justifies their consideration together in this consolidated opinion.

In each of these cases, minors of the Negro race, through their legal representatives, seek the aid of the courts in obtaining admission to the public schools of their community on a nonsegregated basis. In each instance, they had been denied admission to schools attended by white children under laws requiring or permitting segregation according to race. This segregation was alleged to deprive the plaintiffs of the equal

Prior to the *Brown* decision, black children were often subjected to inferior educational facilities.

protection of the laws under the Fourteenth Amendment. In each of the cases other than the Delaware case, a three-judge federal district court denied relief to the plaintiffs on the so-called "separate but equal" doctrine announced by this Court in this Court in *Plessy v. Ferguson....*

Under that doctrine, equality of treatment is accorded when the races are provided substantially equal facilities, even though these facilities be separate. In the Delaware case, the Supreme Court of Delaware adhered to that doctrine, but ordered that the plaintiffs be admitted to the white schools because of their superiority to the Negro schools.

The plaintiffs contend that segregated school public schools are not "equal" and cannot be made "equal," and that hence they are deprived of the equal protection of the laws. Because of the obvious importance of the question presented, the Court took jurisdiction. Argument was heard in the 1952 Term, and reargument was heard this Term on certain questions propounded by the Court.

Reargument was largely devoted to the circumstances surrounding the adoption of the Fourteenth Amendment in 1868. It covered exhaustively consideration of the Amendment in Congress, ratification by the states, then existing practices in racial segregation, and the views of proponents and opponents of the Amendment. This discussion and our own investigation convince us that, although these sources cast some light, it is not enough to resolve the problem with which we are faced. At best, they are inconclusive. The most avid proponents of the post-War Amendments undoubtedly intended them to remove all legal distinctive among "all persons born or naturalized in the United States." Their opponents, just as certainly, were antagonistic to both the letter and the spirit of the Amendments and wished them to have the most limited effect. What others in Congress and the state legislatures had in mind cannot be determined with any degree of certainty.

An additional reason for the inconclusive nature of the Amendment's history, with respect to segregated schools, is the status of public education at that time. In the South, the movement toward free common schools, supported by general taxation, had not yet taken hold. Education of white children was largely in the hands of private groups. Education of Negroes was almost nonexistent, and practically all of the race were illiterate. In fact, any education of Negroes was forbidden by law in some states. Today, in contrast, many Negroes have achieved outstanding success in the arts and sciences as well as in the business and professional world. It is true that public school education at the time of the Amend-

ment had advanced further in the North, but the effect of the Amendment on Northern States was generally ignored the congressional debates. Even in the North, the conditions of public education did not approximate those existing today. The curriculum was usually rudimentary; ungraded schools were common in rural areas; the school term was but three months a year in many states; and compulsory school attendance was virtually unknown. As a consequence, it is not surprising that there should be so little in the history of the Fourteenth Amendment relating to its intended effect on public education.

In the first cases in this Court construing the Fourteenth Amendment, decided shortly after its adoption, the Court interpreted it as proscribing all state imposed discriminations against the Negro race. The doctrine of "separate but equal" did not make its appearance in this Court until 1896 in the case of *Plessy v. Ferguson...,* involving not education but transportation. American courts have since labored with the doctrine for over half a century. In this Court, there have been six cases involving the "separate but equal" doctrine in the field of public education. In *Cumming v. County Board of Education...* and *Gong Lum v. Rice...,* the validity of the doctrine itself was not challenged. In more recent cases, all on the graduate school level, inequality was found in that specific benefits enjoyed by white students were denied to Negro students of the same educational qualifications. In none of these cases [*Missouri ex rel. Gaines v. Canada, Sipuel v. University of Oklahoma, Sweatt v. Painter* and *McLaurin v. Oklahoma State Regents*] was it necessary to reexamine the doctrine to grant relief to the Negro plaintiff. And in *Sweatt v. Painter...,* the Court expressly reserved decision on the question whether *Plessy v. Ferguson* should be held inapplicable to public education.

In the instant cases, that question is directly presented. Here, unlike *Sweatt v. Painter,* there are findings below that the Negro and white schools involved have been equalized, or are being equalized, with respect to buildings, curricula, qualifications and salaries of teacher, and other "tangible" factors. Our decision, therefore, cannot turn on merely a comparison of these tangible factors in the Negro and white schools involved in each of the cases. We must look instead to the effect of segregation itself on public education.

In approaching this problem, we cannot turn the clock back to 1868 when the Amendment was adopted, or even to 1896 when *Plessy v. Ferguson* was written. We must consider public education in the light of its full development and its present place in American life throughout the Nation. Only in this way can it be determined if segregation in public schools deprives these plaintiffs of the equal protection of the laws.

Today, education is perhaps the most important function of state and local governments. Compulsory school attendance laws and the great expenditures for education both demonstrate our recognition of the importance of education to our democratic society. It is required in the performance of our most basic public responsibilities, even service in the armed forces. It is the very foundation of good citizenship. Today it is a principal instrument in awakening the child to cultural values, in preparing him for later professional training, and in helping him to adjust normally to his environment. In these days, it is doubtful that any child may reasonably be expected to succeed in life if he is denied the opportunity of an education. Such an opportunity, where the state has undertaken to provide it, is a right which must be made available to all on equal terms.

We come then to the question presented: Does segregation of children in public schools solely on the basis of race, even though the physical facilities and other "tangible" factors may be equal, deprive the children of the minority group of equal educational opportunities? We believe that it does.

In *Sweatt v. Painter* in finding that a segregated law school for Negroes could not provide them equal educational opportunities, this Court relied in large part on "those qualities which are incapable of objective measurement but which make for greatness in the law school." In *McLaurin v. Oklahoma State Regents*... the Court, in requiring that a Negro admitted to a white graduate school be treated like all other students, again resorted to intangible considerations: "...his ability to study, to engage in discussions and exchange views with other students, and, in general, to learn his profession." Such considerations apply with added force to children in grade and high schools. To separate them from others of similar age and qualifications solely because of their race generates a feeling of inferiority as to their status in the community that may affect their hearts and minds in a way unlikely ever to be undone. The effect of this separation on their educational opportunities was well stated by a finding in the Kansas case by a court which nevertheless felt compelled to rule against the Negro plaintiffs:

"Segregation of white and colored children in public school has a detrimental effect upon the colored children. The impact is greater when it has the sanction of the law; for the policy of separating the races is usually interpreted as denoting the inferiority of the negro group. A sense of inferiority affects the motivation of a child to learn. Segregation with the sanction of law, therefore, has a tendency to [retard] the educational and mental development of Negro children and to deprive

them of some of the benefits they would receive in a racial[ly] integrated school systems."

Whatever may have been the extent of psychological knowledge at the time of *Plesssy v. Ferguson*, this finding is amply supported by modern authority. Any languages in *Plessy v. Ferguson* contrary to this finding is rejected.

We conclude that in the field of public education the doctrine of "separate but equal" has no place. Separate educational facilities are inherently unequal. Therefore, we hold that the plaintiffs and other similarly situated for whom the actions have brought are, by reason of the segregation complained of, deprived of the equal protection of the laws guaranteed by the Fourteenth Amendment. This disposition makes unnecessary any discussion whether such segregation also violates the Due Process Clause of the Fourteenth Amendment.

Because these are class actions, because of the wide applicability of this decision, and because of the great variety of local conditions, the formulation of decrees in these presents problems of considerable complexity. On reargument, the consideration of appropriate relief was necessarily subordinated to the primary question—the constitutionality of segregation in public education. We have now announced that such segregation is a denial of the equal protection of the laws. In order that we may have the full assistance of the parties in formulating decrees, the cases will be restored to the docket, and the parties are requested to present further argument on Questions 4 and 5 previously propounded by the Court for the reargument this Term. The Attorney General of the United States is again invited to participate. The Attorneys General of the states requiring or permitting segregation in public education will also be permitted to appear as amici curiae upon request to do so by September 15, 1954, and submission of briefs by October 1, 1954.

It is so ordered.

◆ CIVIL RIGHTS ACT OF 1957, PUB.L. NO. 85-315, 71 STAT. 634 (1957)

This act, signed by President Eisenhower on September 9, 1957, was the first piece of compressive legislation in the area of civil rights since the Civil Rights Act of 1875, which the Supreme Court in 1883 declared unconstitutional. The new act provided for the creation of a Commission on Civil Rights, extended the jurisdiction of the federal district courts to include civil action arising out of the act, and empowered the United States Attorney General to take action in cases where rights secured by the act were believed to have been violated.

An Act to provide means of further securing and protecting the civil rights of persons within the jurisdiction of the United States.

Part I—Establishment of the Commission on Civil Rights

Sec. 101. (a) There is created in the executive branch of the Government a Commission on Civil Rights (hereinafter called the "Commission").

(b)The Commission shall be composed of six members who shall be appointed by the President by and with the advice and consent of the Senate. Not more than three of the members shall at any one time be of the same political party.

(c) The President shall designate one of the members of the Commission as Chairman and one as Vice Chairman. The Vice Chairman shall act as Chairman in the absence or disability of the Chairman, or in the event of a vacancy in that office.

(d) Any vacancy in the Commission shall not affect its powers and shall be filled in the same manner, and subject to the same limitation with respect to party affiliations as the original appointment was made.....

Part IV—To Provide Means of Further Securing and Protecting the Right to Vote

Sec. 131. Section 2004 of the Revised Statutes (42 U.S.C. 1971), is amended as follows:

...No person, whether acting under cover of law or otherwise, shall intimidate, threaten, coerce, or attempt to intimidate, or coerce any other person for the purpose of interfering with the right of such other person to vote as he may choose, or of causing such other person to vote, for, or to vote as he may choose, or of causing such other person to vote for, or not to vote for, any candidate for the office of President, Vice President, presidential elector, Member of the Senate, or Member of the House of Representatives, Delegates or Commissioners from the Territories or possessions, at any general, special, or primary election held solely or in part for the purpose of selecting or electing any such candidate.

...Whenever any person has engaged or there are reasonable grounds to believe that any person is about to engage in any act or practice which would deprive any right or privilege secured by subsection (a) or (b), the Attorney General may institute for the United States, or in the name of the United States, a civil action or other proper proceeding for preventive relief, including an application for a permanent or temporary injunction, restraining order, or other order. In any proceeding hereunder the United States shall be liable for costs the same as a private person....

◆ EXECUTIVE ORDER NO. 10730, 3 C.F.R. 1954-1958 COMP. P. 388 (1957)

In September 1957, Arkansas Governor Orval Faubus mobilized the Arkansas National Guard in an effort to prevent black students from entering Little Rock's Central High School. As a result, on September 24, President Dwight D. Eisenhower issued an executive order authorizing the use of the National Guard and the Air National Guard of the United States to assist in desegregation in Little Rock.

Whereas on September 23, 1957, I issued Proclamation No. 3204 reading in part as follows:

Whereas certain persons in the State of Arkansas, individually and in unlawful assemblages, combinations, and conspiracies, have wilfully obstructed the enforcement of orders of the United States District Court for the Eastern District of Arkansas with respect to matters relating to enrollment and attendance at public schools, particularly at Central High School, located in Little Rock School District, Little Rock, Arkansas; and

Whereas such wilful obstruction of justice hinders the execution of the laws of that State and of the United States, and makes it impracticable to enforce such laws by the ordinary course of judicial proceedings; and

Whereas such obstruction of justice constitutes a denial of the equal protection of the laws secured by the Constitution of the United States and impedes the course of justice under those laws;

Now, therefore, I, Dwight D. Eisenhower, President of the United States, under and by virtue of the authority vested in me by the Constitution and Statutes of the United States, including Chapter 15 of Title 10 of the United States Code, particularly sections 332, 333 and 334 thereof, do command all persons engaged in such obstruction of justice to cease and desist therefrom, and to disperse forthwith, and

Whereas the command contained in that Proclamation has not been obeyed and wilful obstruction of enforcement of said court orders still exists and threatens to continue:

Now, therefore, by virtue of the authority vested in me by the Constitution and Statutes of the United

Federal troops escorting black students to class at Little Rock's Central High School.

States, including Chapter 15 of Title 10, particularly sections 332, 333 and 334 thereof, and section 301 of Title 3 of the United States Code, it is hereby ordered as follows:

Section 1. I hereby authorize and direct the Secretary of Defense to order into the active military service of the United States as he may deem appropriate to carry out the purposes of this Order, any or all of the units of the National Guard of the United States and of the Air National Guard of the United States within the State of Arkansas to serve in the active military service of the United States for an indefinite period and until relieved by appropriate orders.

Section 2. The Secretary of Defense is authorized and directed to take all appropriate steps to enforce any orders of the United States District Court for the Eastern District of Arkansas for the removal of obstruction of justice in the State of Arkansas with respect to matters relating to enrollment and attendance at public schools in the Little Rock School District, Little Rock, Arkansas. In carrying out the provisions of this section, the Secretary of Defense is authorized to use the units, and members thereof, ordered into the active military

service of the United States pursuant to Section 1 of this Order.

Section 3. In furtherance of the enforcement of the aforementioned orders of the United States District Court for the Eastern District of Arkansas, the Secretary of Defense is authorized to use such of the armed forces of the United States as he may deem necessary.

Section 4. The Secretary of Defense is authorized to delegate to the Secretary of the Army or the Secretary of the Air Force, or both, any of the authority conferred upon him by this Order.

◆ CIVIL RIGHTS ACT OF 1960, PUB.L. NO. 86-449, 74 STAT. 86 (1960)

This act, signed by President Eisenhower on May 6, 1960, further defined civil rights violations and outlined penalties connected with such violations. It guaranteed the provision of criminal penalties in the event a suspect crosses state lines to avoid legal process for the actual or attempted bombing or burning of any vehicle or building, and provided penalties for persons

President Dwight Eisenhower meets with black leaders Martin Luther King, Jr. (left) and A. Phillip Randolph (right) at the White House.

who obstructed or interfered with any order of a federal court.

An Act to enforce constitutional rights, and for other purposes.

Title II

Sec. 201. Chapter 49 of title 18, United States Code, is amended by adding at the end thereof a new section as follows:

Section 1074. Flight to avoid prosecution for damaging or destroying any building or other real or personal property.

...Whoever moves or travels in interstate or foreign commerce with intent either (1) to avoid prosecution, or custody, or confinement after conviction, under the laws of the place from which he flees, for willfully attempting to or damaging or destroying by fire or explosive any building, structure, facility, vehicle, dwelling house, synagogue, church, religious center or educational institution, public or private, or (2) to avoid giving

testimony in any criminal proceeding relating to any such offense shall be fined not more than $5,000 or imprisoned not more than five years, or both.

...Violations of this section may be prosecuted in the Federal judicial district in which the original crime was alleged to have been committed or in which the person was held in custody or confinement.....

Sec. 203. Chapter 39 of title 18 of the United States Code is amended by adding at the end thereof the following new section:

Section 837. Explosives; illegal use or possession; and, threats or false information concerning attempts to damage or destroy real or personal property by fire or explosives.

...Whoever transports or aids and abets another in transporting in interstate or foreign commerce any explosive, with the knowledge or intent that it will be used to damage or destroy any building or other real or personal property for the purpose of interfering with its use for educational, religious, charitable, residential, business, or civic objectives or of intimidating any person pursuing such objectives, shall be subject to imprisonment for not more than one year, or a fine of not more than $1,000 or both; and if personal injury results shall be subject to imprisonment for not more than ten years or a fine of not more than $10,000, or both; and if death results shall be subject to imprisonment for any term of years or for life, but the court may impose the death penalty if the jury so recommends.

...The possession of an explosive in such a manner as to evince an intent to use, or the use of, such explosive, to damage or destroy any building or other real or personal property used for educational, religious, charitable, residential, business, or civic objectives or to intimidate any person pursuing such objectives, creates rebuttable presumptions that the explosive was transported in interstate or foreign commerce or caused to be transported in interstate or foreign commerce by the person so possessing or using it, or by a person aiding or abetting the person so possessing or using it: Provided, however, that no person may be convicted under this section unless there is evidence independent of the presumptions that this section has been violated.

...Whoever, through the use of the mail, telephone, telegraph, or other instrument of commerce, willfully imparts or conveys, or causes to be imparted or conveyed, any threat, or false information knowing the same to be false, concerning an attempt or alleged attempt being made, or to be made, to damage or destroy any building or other real or personal property for the purpose of interfering with its use for educational, religious, charitable, residential, business, or civic objectives, or of intimidating any person pursuing such objectives, shall be subject to imprisonment for not more than one year or a fine of not more than $1,000, or both.

◆ EXECUTIVE ORDER NO. 11053, 3 C.F.R. 1959-1963 COMP P.645 (1962)

On September 30, 1962, riots erupted on the campus of the University of Mississippi when governor Ross Barnett attempted to block the court ordered admission of black student James H. Meredith. President John F. Kennedy quickly responded by authorizing the use of federal troops to restore order.

Whereas on September 30, 1962, I issued Proclamation No. 3497 reading in part as follows:

Whereas the Governor of the State of Mississippi and certain law enforcement officers and other officials of that State, and other persons, individually and in unlawful opposing and obstructing the enforcement of orders entered by the United States District Court for the Southern District of Mississippi and the United States Court of Appeals for the Fifth Circuit; and

Whereas such unlawful assemblies, combinations, and conspiracies oppose and obstruct the execution of the laws of the United States, impede the course of justice under those laws and make it impracticable to enforce those laws in the State of Mississippi by the ordinary course of judicial proceedings; and

Whereas I have expressly called the attention of the Governor of Mississippi to the perilous situation that exists and to his duties in the premises, and have requested but have not received from him adequate assurances that the orders of the courts of the United States will be obeyed and that law and order will be maintained:

Now, therefore, I, John F. Kennedy, President of the United States, under and by virtue of the authority vested in me by the Constitution and laws of the United States, including Chapter 15 of Title 10 of the United States Code, particularly sections 332, 333 and 334 thereof, do command all persons engaged in such obstructions of justice to cease and desist therefrom to disperse and retire peaceably forth-with; and

Whereas the commands contained in that proclamation have not been obeyed and obstruction of enforcement of those court orders still exists and threatens to continue:

Now, therefore, by virtue of the authority vested in me by the Constitution and laws of the United States, including Chapter 15 of Title 10, particularly Sections 332, 333 and 334 thereof, and Section 301 of Title 3 of the United States Code, it is hereby ordered as follows:

Section 1. The Secretary of Defense is authorized and directed to take all appropriate steps to enforce all orders of the United States District Court for the Southern District of Mississippi and the United States Court of Appeals for the Fifth Circuit and to remove all obstructions of justice in the State of Mississippi.

Section 2. In furtherance of the enforcement of the aforementioned orders of the United States District Court for the Southern District of Mississippi and the United States Court of Appeals for the Fifth Circuit, the Secretary of Defense is authorized to use such of the armed forces of the United States as he may deem necessary.

Section 3. I hereby authorize the Secretary of Defense to call into the active military service of the United States, as he may deem appropriate to carry out the purposes of this order, any or all of the units of the Army National Guard and of the Air National Guard of the State of Mississippi to serve in the active military service of the United States for an indefinite period and until relieved by appropriate orders. In carrying out the provisions of Section 1, the Secretary of Defense is authorized to use the units, and members thereof, ordered into the active military service of the United States pursuant to this section.

Section 4. The Secretary of Defense is authorized to delegate to the Secretary of the Army or the Secretary of the Air Force, or both, any of the authority conferred upon him by this order.

◆ THE BIRMINGHAM MANIFESTO (1963)

In 1963, a series of events in Birmingham, Alabama made known the plight of African Americans to the nation at large. Black citizens were arrested en masse during peaceful demonstrations—demonstrations which were crushed by police dogs and firehoses. The Manifesto, dated April 3, 1963, embodied the hope of the African-American community in Birmingham that law, order, and peace would somehow prevail.

The patience of an oppressed people cannot endure forever. The Negro citizens of Birmingham for the last several years have hoped in vain for some evidence... [of the] ...resolution of our just grievances.

Birmingham is part of the United States and we are bona fide citizens. Yet the history of Birmingham reveals that very little of the democratic process touches the life of the Negro in Birmingham. We have been segregated racially, exploited economically, and dominated politically. Under the leadership of the Alabama Christian Movement for Human Rights, we sought relief by petition for the repeal of city ordinances requiring segregation and the institution of a merit hiring policy in city employment. We were rebuffed. We then turned to the system of the courts. We weathered set-back after set-back, with all of its costliness, finally winning the terminal, bus, parks and airport cases. The bus decision has been implemented begrudging and the parks decision prompted the closing of all municipally-owned recreational facilities with the exception of the zoo and Legion Field.....

We have always been a peaceful people, bearing our oppression with superhuman effort. Yet we have been the victims of repeated violence, not only that inflicted by the hoodlum element but also that inflicted by the blatant misuse of police power..... For years, while our homes and churches were being bombed, we heard nothing but the rantings and ravings of racist city officials.

The Negro protest for equality and justice has been a voice crying in the wilderness. Most of Birmingham has remained silent, probably out of fear. In the meanwhile, our city has acquired the dubious reputation of being the worst big city in race relations in the United States. Last fall, for a flickering moment, it appeared that sincere community leaders from religion, business and industry discerned the inevitable confrontation in race relations approaching. Their concern for the city's image and commonwealth of all its citizens did not run deep enough. Solemn promises were made, pending a postponement of direct action, that we would be joined in a suit seeking the relief of segregation ordinances. Some merchants agreed to desegregate their restrooms as a good faith start, some actually complying, only to retreat shortly thereafter. We hold in our hands now, broken faith and broken promises. We believe in the American Dream of democracy, in the Jeffersonian doctrine that "all men are created equal and are endowed by their Creator with certain inalienable rights, among these being life, liberty and the pursuit of happiness."

Twice since September we have deferred our direct action thrust in order that a change in city government would not be made in the hysteria of a community crisis. We act today in full concert with our Hebraic-Christian traditions, the law of morality and the Constitution of our nation. The absence of justice and progress in Birmingham demands that we make a moral witness to give our community a chance to survive. We demonstrate our faith that we believe that the beloved community can come to Birmingham. We appeal to the citizenry of Birmingham, Negro and white, to join us in this witness for decency, morality, self-respect and human dignity. Your individual and corporate support can hasten the day of "liberty and justice for all." This is Birmingham's moment of truth in which every citizen can play his part in her larger destiny.....

◆ MARTIN LUTHER KING'S SPEECH AT THE LINCOLN MEMORIAL, WASHINGTON, DC (1963)

On August 28, 1963, some 250,000 people gathered at the Lincoln Memorial in Washington, DC in order to raise the nation's consciousness and to demonstrate on behalf of the civil legislation being debated in Congress. It was during this demonstration that Dr. Martin Luther King, Jr. gave the "I Have a Dream" speech.

I am happy to join with you today in what will go down in history as the greatest demonstration for freedom in the history of our nation.

Five score years ago, a great American, in whose symbolic shadow we stand today, signed the Emancipation Proclamation. This momentous decree came as a great beacon of light of hope to millions of Negro slaves who had been seared in the flames of withering injustice. It came as a joyous daybreak to end the long night of their captivity.

250,000 gather in Washington, DC for the largest protest demonstration in history.

But one hundred years later, the Negro is still not free. One hundred years later, the life of the Negro is still sadly crippled by the manacles of segregation and the chains of discrimination. One hundred years later, the Negro lives on a lonely island of poverty in the midst of a vast ocean of material prosperity. One hundred years later, the Negro is still languished in the corners of American society and finds himself an exile in his own land. So we have come here today to dramatize a shameful condition.

In a sense we have come to our nation's capitol to cash a check. When the architects of our republic wrote the magnificent words of the Constitution and the Declaration of Independence, they were signing a promissory note to which every American was to fall heir. This note was a promise that all men, yes black men as well as white men, would be guaranteed the unalienable rights of life, liberty, and the pursuit of happiness. It is obvious today that America has defaulted on this promissory note insofar as her citizens of color are concerned. Instead of honoring this sacred obligation, America has given the Negro people a bad check: a check which has come back marked "insufficient funds." But we refuse to believe that the bank of justice is bankrupt. We refuse to believe that there are insufficient funds in the great vaults of opportunity of this nation. So we have come to cash this check—a check that will give us upon demand the riches of freedom and the security of justice.

We have also come to this hallowed spot to remind America of the fierce urgency of now. This is not the time to engage in the luxury of cooling off or to take the tranquilizing drug of gradualism. Now is the time to make real the promises of democracy. Now is the time to rise from the dark and desolate valley of segregation to the sunlit path of racial justice. Now is the time to lift our nation from the quicksands of racial injustice to the solid rock of brotherhood. Now is the time to make justice a reality for all of God's children.

It would be fatal for the nation to overlook the urgency of the moment and to underestimate the determination of the Negro. This sweltering summer of the Negro's legitimate discontent will not pass until there is an invigorating autumn of freedom and equality. Nineteen-hundred and sixty-three is not an end, but a beginning. Those who hope that the Negro needed to blow off steam, and will now be content will have a rude awakening if the Nation returns to business as usual. There will neither be rest nor tranquility in America until the Negro is granted his citizenship rights. The whirlwinds of revolt will continue to shake the foundations of our Nation until the bright day of justice emerges.

But there is something that I must say to my people who stand on the warm threshold which leads into the palace of justice. In the process of gaining our rightful place we must not be guilty of wrongful deeds. Let us not seek to satisfy our thirst for freedom by drinking from the cup of bitterness and hatred.

We must forever conduct our struggle on the high plane of dignity and discipline. We must not allow our creative protest to degenerate into physical violence. Again and again we must rise to the majestic heights of meeting physical force with soul force. The marvelous new militancy which has engulfed the Negro community must not lead us to a distrust of all white people, for many of our white brothers, as evidenced by their presence here today, have come to realize that their destiny is tied up with our destiny and their freedom is inextricably bound to our freedom. We cannot walk alone.

And as we walk, we must make the pledge that we shall always march ahead. We cannot turn back. There are those who are asking the devotees of civil rights, "when will you be satisfied?" We can never be satisfied as long as the Negro is the victim of the unspeakable horrors of police brutality. We can never be satisfied as long as our bodies, heavy with the fatigue of travel, cannot gain lodging in the motels of the highways and the hotels of the cities. We cannot be satisfied as long as the Negro's basic mobility is from a smaller ghetto to a larger one. We can never be satisfied as long as our children are stripped of their self-hood and robbed of their dignity by signs reading "For Whites Only." We can never be satisfied as long as a Negro in Mississippi cannot vote and a Negro in New York believes he has nothing for which to vote. No. No we are not satisfied, and we will not be satisfied until justice rolls down like waters, and righteousness like a mighty stream.

I am not unmindful that some of you have come here out of great trials and tribulations. Some of you have come fresh from narrow jail cells. Some of you have come from areas where your quest for freedom left you battered by the storms of persecution and staggered by the winds of police brutality. You have been the victims of creative suffering. Continue to work with the faith that unearned suffering is redemptive.

Go back to Mississippi, go back to Alabama, go back to South Carolina, go back to Georgia, go back to Louisiana, go back to the slums and ghettos of our northern cities, knowing that somehow this situation can and will be changed. Let us not wallow in the valley of despair.

I say to you today, my friends, that in spite of the difficulties and frustrations of the moment, I still have a dream. It is a dream deeply rooted in the American dream. I have a dream that one day this nation will rise up and live out the true meaning of its creed: "We hold these truths to be self-evident—that all men are created equal."

I have a dream that one day on the red hills of Georgia the sons of former slaves and the sons of former slaveowners will be able to sit down together at the table of brotherhood. I have a dream that one day even the state of Mississippi, a desert state sweltering with the heat of injustice and oppression, will be transformed into an oasis of freedom and justice.

I have a dream that my four little children will one day live in a nation where they will not be judged by the color of their skin but by the content of their character.

I have a dream today.

I have a dream that one day the state of Alabama, whose governor's lips are presently dripping with the words of interposition and nullification, will be transformed into a situation where little black boys and black girls will be able to join hands with little white boys and white girls and walk together as sisters and brothers.

I have a dream today.

I have a dream that one day every valley shall be exalted, every hill and mountain shall be made low, the rough places will be made plain, and the crooked places will be made straight, and the glory of the Lord shall be revealed, and all flesh shall see it together.

This is our hope. This is the faith with which I return to the South. With this faith we will be able to transform the jangling discords of our nation into a beautiful symphony of brotherhood. With this faith we will be able to work together, to pray together, to struggle together, to go to jail together, to stand up for freedom together, knowing that we will be free one day.

This will be the day when all of God's children will be able to sing the new meaning "My country 'tis of thee, sweet land of liberty, of thee I sing. Land where my fathers died, land of the pilgrim's pride, from every mountainside, let freedom ring."

And if America is to be a great nation this must become true. So let freedom ring from the prodigious hilltops of New Hampshire! Let freedom ring from the mighty mountains of New York! Let freedom ring from the heightening Alleghenies of Pennsylvania!

Let freedom ring from the snowcapped Rockies of Colorado!

Let freedom ring from the curvaceous peaks of California!

But not only that; let freedom ring from Stone Mountain of Georgia!

Let freedom ring from Lookout Mountain of Tennesse.

Let freedom ring from every hill and mole hill of Mississippi. From every mountainside, let freedom ring.

When we let freedom ring, when we let it ring from every village and every hamlet, from every state and every city, we will be able to speed up that day when all God's children—black men and white men, Jews and Gentiles, Protestants and Catholics—will be able to join hands and sing in the words of that old Negro spiritual, Free at last! Free at last! Thank God almighty, we are free at last!

◆ AMENDMENT TWENTY-FOUR TO THE UNITED STATES CONSTITUTION (1964)

By 1964, when the Twenty-Fourth Amendment was ratified, most states had already discontinued the use of the poll tax, which had proved to be one of the most effective means of keeping blacks from the polls—only the states of Alabama, Arkansas, Mississippi, Texas, and Virginia still implemented such a tax. The amendment, proposed in 1962, banned the use of poll taxes as a prerequisite to participating in federal elections; ruling in the case Harper v. Virginia Board of Elections, the United States Supreme Court banned the use of poll taxes in state elections.

Section 1. The right of citizens of the United States to vote in any primary or other election for President or Vice President, for electors for President or Vice President, or for Senator or Representative in Congress, shall not be denied or abridged by the United States or any State by reason of failure to pay any poll tax or other tax.

Section 2. The congress shall have power to enforce this article by appropriate legislation.

◆ CIVIL RIGHTS ACT OF 1964, PUB. L. NO. 88-352, 78 STAT. 241 (1964)

This civil rights act was signed by President Lyndon B. Johnson on July 2, 1964, although it had been initiated by President John F. Kennedy in June 1963. More comprehensive than previous acts, the 1964 act contained eleven titles covering the areas of voting rights, access to public facilities, federal aid to schools engaged in the process of desegregation, discrimination in federally funded programs, and discrimination in employment. The act also strengthened earlier voter registration protection; made racial discrimination in restaurants, hotels, and motels illegal; provided for equal access to public parks, pools, and other facilities; outlined unlawful employment practice; and mandat-

ed the creation of a federal Equal Employment Opportunity Commission.

An act to enforce the constitutional right to vote, to confer jurisdiction upon the district courts of the United States to provide injunctive relief against discrimination in public accommodations, to authorize the Attorney General to institute suits to protect constitutional rights in public facilities and public education, to extend the Commission on Civil Rights, to prevent discrimination in federally assisted programs, to establish a Commission on Equal Employment Opportunity, and for other purposes.

Title I—Voting Rights

Sec. 101. Section 2004 of the Revised Statutes (42 U.S.C. 1971)...is further amended as follows:....

..."No Person acting under color of law shall—"

"(A) In determining whether any individual is qualified under State law or laws to vote in any Federal election, apply any standard, practice, or procedure different from the standards, practices, or procedures applied under such law or laws to other individuals within the same county, parish, or similar political subdivision who have been found by State officials to be qualified to vote;"

"(B) deny the right of any individual to vote in any Federal election because of an error or omission on any record or paper relating to any application, registration, or other act requisite to voting, if such error or omission is not material in determining whether such individual is qualified under State law to vote in such election; or"

"(C) employ any literacy test as a qualification for voting in any Federal election unless (i) such test is administered to each individual and is conducted wholly in writing, and (ii) a certified copy of the test and of the answers given by the individual is furnished to him within twenty-five days of the submission of his request made within the period of time during which records and papers are required to be retained and preserved pursuant to title III of the Civil Rights Act of 1960 (42 U.S.C. 1974-74e; 74 Stat. 88)...."

Sec. 201. (a) All persons shall be entitled to the full and equal enjoyment of the goods, services, facilities, privileges, advantages, and accommodations of any place of public accommodation, as defined in this section, without discrimination or segregation on the ground of race, color, religion, or national origin.

(b) Each of the following establishments which serves the public is a place of public accommodation within the meaning of this title if its operations affect commerce, or if discrimination or segregation by it is supported by State action:

(1) any inn, hotel, motel, or other establishment which provides lodging to transient guests, other than an establishment located within a building which contains not more than five rooms for rent or hire and which is actually occupied by the proprietor of such establishment as his residence;

(2) any restaurant, cafeteria, lunchroom, lunch counter, soda fountain, or other facility principally engaged in selling food for consumption on the premises, including, but not limited to, any such facility located on the premises of any retail establishment; or any gasoline station;

(3) any motion picture house, theater, concert hall, sports arena, stadium or other place of exhibition or entertainment; and

(4) any establishment (A)(i) which is physically located within the premises of any establishment otherwise covered by this subsection, or (ii) within the premises of which is physically located any such covered establishment, and (B) which holds itself out as serving patrons of such covered establishment.....

(e) The provisions of this title shall not apply to a private club or other establishment not in fact open to the public, except to the extent that the facilities of such establishment are made available to the customers or patrons of an establishment within the scope of subsection (b).

Sec. 206. (a) Whenever the Attorney General has reasonable cause to believe that any person or group of persons is engaged in a pattern or practice of resistance to the full enjoyment of any of the rights secured by this title, and that the pattern or practice is of such a nature and is intended to deny the full exercise of the rights herein described, the Attorney General may bring a civil action in the appropriate district court of the United States.....

Title IV—Desegregation of Public Education

Sec. 407. (a) Whenever the Attorney General receives a complaint in writing—

(1) signed by a parent or group of parents to the effect that his or their minor children, as members of a class of persons similarly situated, are being deprived by a school board of the equal protection of the laws, or

(2) signed by an individual, or his parent, to the effect that he has been denied admission to or not permitted to continue in attendance at a public college by reason of race, color, religion, or national origin and the Attorney

President Lyndon B. Johnson signs the Civil Rights Bill. In attendance are (left) Edward Brooke, (right) Walter Mondale, and Thurgood Marshall.

General believes the complaint is meritorious and certifies that the signer or signers of such complaint are unable, in his judgment, to initiate and maintain appropriate legal proceedings for relief and that the institution of an action will materially further the orderly achievement of desegregation in public education, the Attorney General is authorized, after giving notice of such complaint to the appropriate school board or college authority and after certifying that he is satisfied that such board or authority has had a reasonable time to adjust the conditions alleged in such complaint, to institute for or in the name of the United States a civil action in any appropriate district court of the United States against such parties and for such relief as may be appropriate.....

Title VI—Nondiscrimination In Federally-Assisted Programs

Sec. 601. No person in the United States shall, on the ground of race, color, or national origin, be excluded from participation in, be denied the benefits of, or be subjected to discrimination under any program or activity receiving Federal financial assistance....

Title VII—Equal Employment Opportunity

Sec. 703. (a) It shall be an unlawful employment practice for an employer—

(1) to fail or refuse to hire or to discharge any individual, or otherwise to discriminate against any individual with respect to his compensation, terms, conditions, or privileges of employment, because of such individual's race, color, religion, sex, or national origin; or

(2) to limit, segregate, or classify his employees in any way which would deprive or tend to deprive any individual of employment opportunities or otherwise adversely affect his status as an employee, because of such individual's race, color, religion, sex, or national origin.

(b) It shall be an unlawful employment practice for an employment agency to fail or refuse to refer for employment, or otherwise to discriminate against, any individual because of his race, color, religion, sex, or national origin, or to classify or refer for employment any individual on the basis of his race, color, religion, sex, or national origin.

(c) It shall be an unlawful employment practice for a labor organization—

(1) to exclude or to expel from its membership, or otherwise to discriminate against, any individual because of his race, color, religion, sex, or national origin;

(2) to limit, segregate, or classify its membership, or to classify or fail or refuse to refer for employment any individual, in any way which would deprive or tend to deprive any individual of employment opportunities, or would limit such employment opportunities or otherwise adversely affect his status as an employee or as an applicant for employment, because of such individual's race, color, religion, sex, or national origin; or

(3) to cause or attempt to cause 'an employer to discriminate against an individual in violation of this section.

(d) It shall be an unlawful employment practice for any employer, labor organization, or joint labor-management committee controlling apprenticeship or other training or retraining, including on-the-job training programs to discriminate against any individual because of his race, color, religion, sex, or national origin in admission to, or employment in, any program established to provide apprenticeship or other training.

(e) Notwithstanding any other provision of this title, (1) it shall not be an unlawful employment practice for an employer to hire and employ employees, for an employment agency to classify, or refer for employment any individual, for a labor organization to classify its membership or to classify or refer for employment any individual, or for an employer, labor organization, or joint labor-management committee controlling apprenticeship or other training or retraining programs to admit or employ any individual in any such program, on the basis of his religion, sex, or national origin in those certain instances where religion, sex, or national origin is a bona fide occupational qualification reasonably necessary to the normal operation of that particular business or enterprise.....

Sec. 705. (1) There is hereby created a Commission to be known as the Equal Employment Opportunity Commission, which shall be composed of five members, not more than three of whom shall be members of the same political party, who shall be appointed by the President by and with the advice and consent of the Senate....

◆ EXECUTIVE ORDER NO. 11246, 3 C.F.R., 1964-1965 COMP. P.339-348 (1965)

On September 24, 1965, President Lyndon B. Johnson issued the following executive order, prohibiting discrimination in government employment and government contracting.

Under and by virtue of the authority vested in me as President of the United States by the Constitution and statutes of the United States, it is ordered as follows:

Part I—Nondiscrimination in Government Employment

Section 101. It is the policy of the Government of the United States to provide equal opportunity in Federal employment for all qualified persons, to prohibit discrimination in employment because of race, creed, color, or national origin, and to promote the full realization of equal employment opportunity through a positive, continuing program in each executive department and agency. The policy of equal opportunity applies to every aspect of Federal employment policy and practice.

Section 102. The head of each executive department and agency shall establish and maintain a positive program of equal employment opportunity for all civilian employees and applicants for employment within his jurisdiction in accordance with the policy set forth in Section 101.

Section 103. The Civil Service Commission shall supervise and provide leadership and guidance in the conduct of equal employment opportunity programs for the civilian employees of and applications for employment within the executive departments and agencies and shall review agency program accomplishments periodically. In order to facilitate the achievement of a model program for equal employment opportunity in the Federal service, the Commission may consult from time to time with such individuals, groups, or organizations as may be of assistance in improving the Federal program and realizing the objectives of this part.

Section 104. The Civil Service Commission shall provide for the prompt, fair, and impartial consideration of all complaints of discrimination in Federal employment on the basis of race, creed, color, or national origin. Procedures for the consideration complaints shall include at least one impartial review within the executive department or agency and shall provide for appeal to the Civil Service Commission.

Section 105. The Civil Service Commission shall issue such regulations, orders, and instructions as it deems necessary and appropriate to carry out its responsibilities under this Part, and the head of each executive department and agency shall comply with the regulations, orders, and instructions issued by the Commission under this Part.

Part II—Nondiscrimination In Employment By Government Contractors And Subcontractors

Section 201. The Secretary of Labor shall be responsible for the administration of Parts II and III of this Order and shall adopt such rules and regulations and issue such orders as he deems necessary and appropriate to achieve the purposes thereof.

Section 202. Except in contracts exempted in accordance with Section 204 of this Order, all Government contracting agencies shall include in every Government contract hereafter entered into the following provisions:

"(1) The contractor will not discriminate against any employee or applicant for employment because of race, creed, color, or national origin. The contractor will take affirmative action to ensure that applicants are employed, and that employees are treated during employment, without regard to their race, creed, color, or national origin. Such action shall include, but not be limited to the following: employment, upgrading, demotion, or transfer; recruitment or recruitment advertising; layoff or termination; rates of pay or other forms of compensation; and selection for training, including apprenticeship. The contractor agrees to post in conspicuous places, available to employees and applicants for employment, notices to be provided by the contracting officer setting forth the provisions of this nondiscrimination clause."

"(2) The contractor will, in all solicitations or advertisements for employees placed by or on behalf of the contractor, state that all qualified applicants will receive consideration for employment without regard to race, creed, color, or national origin....."

Part III—Nondiscrimination Provisions In Federally Assisted Construction Contracts

Section 301. Each executive department and agency which administers a program involving Federal financial assistance shall require as a condition for approval of any grant, contract, loan, insurance, or guarantee thereunder, which may involve a construction contract, that the applicant for Federal assistance undertake and agree to incorporate, or cause to be incorporated, into all construction contracts paid for in whole or in part with funds obtained from the Federal Government or borrowed on the credit of the Federal Government pursuant to such grant, contract, loan, insurance, or guarantee, or undertaken pursuant to any Federal program involving such grant, contract, loan, insurance, or guarantee, the provisions prescribed for Government contracts by Section 202 of this Order or such modification thereof, preserving in substance the contractor's obligations thereunder, as may be approved by the Secretary of Labor, together with such additional provisions as the Secretary deems appropriate to establish and protect the interest of the United States in the enforcement of those obligations.....

◆ VOTING RIGHTS ACT OF 1965 PUB.L. NO. 89-110, 79 STAT. 437 (1965)

Signed by President Lyndon B. Johnson on August 6, 1965, the Voting Rights Act was an outgrowth of the protest demonstrations organized by blacks to draw attention to discriminatory voter-registration practices in several Southern states. The 1965 law abolished literacy, knowledge, and character tests as qualifications for voting; empowered federal registrars to register potential voters in any county where, in the judgments of the Attorney General of the United States, registrars were indeed necessary to enforce the Fifteenth Amendment; and gave the Attorney General of the United States the right to take whatever legal action he deemed necessary to eliminate any equivalent of the poll tax.

Although the single aim of the Voting Rights Act of 1965 was African American enfranchisement in the South, obstacles to registration and voting faced by all minorities were affected. Its potential as a tool for Hispanic Americans, however, was not fully realized for nearly a decade.

An Act to enforce the Fifteenth Amendment to the Constitution of the United States, and for other purposes.

Section 2. No voting qualification or prerequisite to voting, or standard, practice, or procedure shall be imposed or applied by any State or political subdivision to deny or abridge the right of any citizen of the United States to vote on account of race or color.

Section 4. (a) To assure that the right of citizens of the United States to vote is not denied or abridged on account of race or color, no citizen shall be denied the right to vote in any Federal, State, or local election because of his failure to comply with any test or device in any State with respect to which the determinations have been made under subsection (b) or in any political subdivision with respect to which such determinations have been made as a separate unit, unless the United States District Court for the District of Columbia in an action for a declaratory judgment brought by such State or subdivision against the United States has determined that no such test or device has been used during the five years preceding the filing of the action for the purpose or with the effect of denying or abridging the right to vote on account of race or color: *Provided,* That no such declaratory judgment shall issue with respect to any plaintiff for a period of five years after the entry of a final judgment of any court of the United States, other than the denial of a declaratory judgment under this section, whether entered prior to or after the enactment of this Act, determining that denials or abridgments of the right to vote on account of race or color through the use of such tests or devices have occurred anywhere in the territory of such plaintiff.....

(d) For purposes of this section no State or political subdivision shall be determined to have engaged in the use of tests or devices for the purpose or with the effect of denying or abridging the right to vote on account of race or color if (1) incidents of such use have been few in number and have been promptly and effectively corrected by State or local action, (2) the continuing effect of such incidents has been eliminated, and (3) there is no reasonable probability of their recurrence in the future.....

Section 10. (a) The Congress finds that the requirement of the payment of a poll tax as a precondition to voting (i) precludes persons of limited means from voting or imposes unreasonable financial hardship upon such persons as a precondition to their exercise of the franchise, (ii) does not bear a reasonable relationship to any legitimate State interest in the conduct of elections, and (iii) in some areas has the purpose or effect of denying persons the right to vote because of race or color. Upon the basis of these findings, Congress declares that the constitutional right of citizens to vote is denied or abridged in some areas by the requirement of the payment of a poll tax as a precondition to voting.....

Section 11. (a) No person acting under color of law shall fail or refuse to permit any person to vote who is entitled to vote under any provision of this Act or is otherwise qualified to vote, or willfully fail or refuse to tabulate, count, and report such person's vote.

(b) No person, whether acting under color of law or otherwise, shall intimidate, threaten, or coerce, or attempt to intimidate, threaten or coerce any person for voting or attempting to vote, or intimidate, threaten, or coerce, or attempt to intimidate, threaten, or coerce any person for urging or aiding any person to vote or attempt to vote, or intimidate, threaten, or coerce any person for exercising any powers or duties under section 3 (a), 6, 8, 9, 10, or 12 (e).....

Section 14. (c) (1) The terms "vote" or "voting" shall include all action necessary to make a vote effective in any primary, special, or general election, including, but not limited to, registration, listing pursuant to this Act, or other action required by law prerequisite to voting, casting a ballot, and having such ballot counted properly and included in the appropriate totals of votes cast with respect to candidates for public or party office and propositions for which votes are received in an election.....

Sec. 17. Nothing in this Act shall be construed to deny, impair, or otherwise adversely affect the right to vote of any person registered to vote under the law of any state or political subdivision.....

◆ THE BLACK PANTHER MANIFESTO (1966)

The Black Panther Party relied on a strict and uncompromising regimen to mold its members into a unified and cohesive revolutionary force. Like the Muslims, the party denounced all intoxicants, drugs, and artificial stimulants "while doing party work." The intellectual fare of every party member was the ten-point program, which every member was obliged to know, understand, and even to commit to memory.

1. We want FREEDOM. We want power to determine the destiny of our Black Community.

We believe that black people will not be free until we are able to determine our destiny.

2. We want full employment for our people.

We believe that the federal government is responsible and obligated to give every man employment or a guaranteed income. We believe that if the white American businessman will not give full employment, then the means of production should be taken from the businessmen and placed in the community so that the people of the community can organize and employ all of its people and give a high standard of living.

3. We want an end to the robbery by the CAPITALIST of our Black Community.

We believe that this racist government has robbed us and now we are demanding the overdue debt of forty acres and two mules. Forty acres and two mules was promised 100 years ago as restitution for slave labor and mass murder of black people. We will accept the payment in currency which will be distributed to our many communities. The Germans are now aiding the Jews in Israel for the genocide of the Jewish people. The Germans murdered six million Jews. The American racist has taken part in the slaughter or over fifty million black people, therefore, we feel that this is a modest demand that we make.

4. We want decent housing, fit for shelter of human beings.

We believe that if the white landlords will not give decent housing to our black community, then the housing and the land should be made into cooperatives so that our community, with government aid, can build and make decent housing for its people.

5. We want education for our people that exposes the true nature of this decadent American society. We want education that teaches us our true history and our role in the present-day society.

Black Panthers demonstrating outside a Manhattan, New York courthouse.

We believe in an educational system that will give to our people a knowledge of self. If a man does not have knowledge of himself and his position in society and the world, then he has little chance to relate to anything else.

6. We want all black men to be exempt from military service.

We believe that Black people should not be forced to fight in the military service to defend a racist government that does not protect us. We will not fight and kill other people of color in the world who, like black people, are being victimized by the white racist government of America. We will protect ourselves from the force and violence of the racist police and the racist military, by whatever means necessary,

7. We want an immediate end to POLICE BRUTALITY and MURDER of black people.

We believe we can end police brutality in our black community by organizing black self-defense groups that are dedicated to defending our black community from racist police oppression and brutality. The Second Amendment to the Constitution of the United States gives a right to bear arms. We therefore believe that all black people should arm themselves for self-defense.

8. We want freedom for all black men held in federal, state, county and city prisons and jails.

We believe that all black people should be released from the many jails and prisons because they have not received a fair and impartial trial.

9. We want all black people when brought to trial to be tried in court by a jury of their peer group or people from their black communities, as defined by the constitution of the United States.

We believe that the courts should follow the United States Constitution so that black people will receive fair trials. The 14th Amendment of the U.S. Constitution gives a man a right to be tried by his peer group. A peer is a person from a similar economic, social, religious, geographical, environmental, historical and racial background. To do this the court will be forced to select a jury from the black community from which the black defendant came. We have been, and are being tried by all-white juries that have no understanding of the "average reasoning man" of the black community.

10. We want land, bread, housing, education, clothing, justice and peace. And as our major political objective, a United Nations-supervised plebiscite to be held throughout the black colony in which only black colonial subjects will be allowed to participate, for the purpose of determining the will of black people as to their national destiny.

When, in the course of human events, it becomes necessary for one people to dissolve the political bands which have connected them with another, and to assume, among the powers of the earth, the separate and equal station to which the laws of nature and nature's God entitle them, a decent respect to the opinions of mankind requires that they should declare the causes which impel them to the separation.

We hold these truths to be self-evident, that all men are created equal; that they are endowed by their Creator with certain inalienable rights; that among these are life, liberty, and the pursuit of happiness.

That, to secure these rights, governments are instituted among them, deriving their just powers from the consent of the governed; that, whenever any form of government becomes destructive of these ends, it is the right of the people to alter or to abolish it, and to institute a new government, laying its foundation on such principles, and organizing its powers in such form, as to them shall seem most likely to effect their safety and happiness.

Prudence, indeed, will dictate that governments long established should not be changed for light and transient causes; and, accordingly, all experience hath shown, that mankind are more disposed to suffer, while evils are sufferable, than to right themselves by abolishing the forms to which they are accustomed. But, when a long train of abuses and usurpations, pursuing invariably the same object, evinces a design to reduce them under absolute despotism, it is their right, it is their duty, to throw off such government, and to provide new guards for their future security.

◆ CIVIL RIGHTS ACT OF 1968 PUB.L. NO. 90-284, TITLES VIII & IX, 82 STAT. 284 (1968)

Title VIII of Public Law 90-284, the Civil Rights Act of 1968, is better known as the Fair Housing Act. It was signed by President Lyndon B. Johnson on April 11, 1968 and created a national housing policy. The act made discrimination in the sale or rental or financing of housing illegal, and empowered the United States Attorney General to take action in such cases.

Title VIII—Fair Housing

Sec. 801. It is the policy of the United States to provide, within constitutional limitations, for fair housing throughout the United States.

Section 804. As made applicable by section 803 and except as exempted by sections 803(b) and 807, it shall be unlawful—

(a) to refuse to sell or rent after the making of a bona fide offer, or to refuse to negotiate for the sale or rental of, or otherwise make unavailable or deny, a dwelling to any person because of race, color, religion, or national origin.

(b) to discriminate against any person in the terms, conditions, or privileges of sale or rental of a dwelling, or in the provision of services or facilities in connection there-with, because of race, color, religion, or national origin.

(c) to make, print, or publish or cause to be made, printed, or published any notice, statement, or advertisement, with respect to the sale or rental of a dwelling that indicates any preference, limitation, or discrimination based on race, color, religion, or national origin, or an intention to make any such preference, limitation, or discrimination.

(d) to represent to any person because of race, color, religion, or national origin that any dwelling is not available for inspection, sale, or rental when such dwelling is in fact so available.

(e) for profit, to induce or attempt to induce any person to sell or rent any dwelling by representations regarding the entry or prospective entry into the neighborhood of a person or persons of a particular race, color, religion, or national origin.

Sec. 805. After December 31, 1968, it shall be unlawful for any bank, building and loan association, insurance company or other corporation, association, firm or enterprise whose business consists in whole or in part in the making of commercial real estate loans, to deny a loan or other financial assistance to a person applying therefor for the purpose of purchasing, constructing, improving, repairing, or maintaining a dwelling, or to discriminate against him in the fixing of the amount, interest rate, duration, or other terms or conditions of such loan or other financial assistance, because of the race, color, religion, or national origin of such person or of any person associated with him in connection with such loan or other financial assistance or the purposes of such loan or other financial assistance, or of the present or prospective owners, leases, tenants, or occupants of the dwelling or dwellings in relation to which such loan or other financial assistance is to be made or given....

Title IX—Prevention of Intimidation in Fair Housing Cases

Section 901. Whoever, whether or not acting under color of law, by force or threat of force willfully injures, intimidates or interferes with, or attempts to injure, intimidate or interfere with—

(a) any person because of his race, color, religion or national origin and because he is or has been selling, purchasing, renting, financing, occupying, or contracting or negotiating for the sale, purchase, rental, financing or occupation of any dwelling, or applying for or participating in any service, organization, or facility relating to the business of selling or renting dwellings; or

(b) any person because he is or has been, or in order to intimidate such person or any other person or any class of persons from—

(1) participating, without discrimination on account of race, color, religion or national origin, in any of the activities, services, organizations or facilities described in subsection 901(a)....

◆ PRESIDENT GEORGE BUSH'S MESSAGE TO THE SENATE RETURNING WITHOUT APPROVAL THE CIVIL RIGHTS ACT OF 1990 26 WEEKLY COMP. PRES.DOC. 1632-34 (OCT. 22, 1990)

In June 1989, the United States Supreme Court delivered opinions in several cases dealing with seniority systems and racial discrimination in employment. Ruling in the cases Lorance v. ATT Technologies Inc., Martin v. Wilks, Patterson v. McLean Credit Union, *and* Wards Cove Packing Co. v. Antonio, *the Court appeared to reverse earlier civil rights rulings. Civil rights organizations were quick to protest the rulings; opponents of the ruling, including the NAACP Legal Defense and Educational Fund, the Leadership Conference on Civil Rights, the American Civil Liberties Union, and the National Organization of Women, argued that the Court had undermined the protection granted by federal civil rights and equal employment legislation.*

On October 16 and 17, 1990 both houses of Congress approved a bill designed to reverse the Court's ruling. On October 22, President Bush vetoed the bill, claiming that the bill's provisions would encourage employers to establish hiring quotas.

To the Senate of the United States.

I am today returning without my approval [Senate Bill] 2104, the "Civil Rights Act of 1990." I deeply regret having to take this action with respect to a bill bearing such a title, especially since it contains certain provisions that I strongly endorse.

Discrimination, whether on the basis of race, national origin, sex, religion, or disability, is worse than wrong. It is a fundamental evil that tears at the fabric of our society, and one that all Americans should and must oppose. That requires rigorous enforcement of existing antidiscrimination laws....

...Despite the use of the term "civil rights" in the title of S. 2104, the bill actually employs a maze of highly legalistic language to introduce the destructive force of quotas into our Nation's employment system. Primarily through provisions governing cases in which employment practices are alleged to have unintentionally caused the disproportionate exclusion of members of certain groups, S. 2104 creates powerful incentives for employers to adopt hiring and promotion quotas. These incentives are created by the bill's new and very technical rules of litigation, which will make it difficult for employers to defend legitimate employment practices. In many cases, a defense against unfounded allegations will be impossible. Among other problems, the plaintiff often need not even show that any of the employer's

President George Bush meeting with civil rights leaders. Dr. Dorothy Height and Dr. Benjamin Hooks pictured.

practices caused a significant statistical disparity. In other cases, the employer's defense is confined to an unduly narrow definition of "business necessity" that is significantly more restrictive than that established by the Supreme Court in *Griggs v. Duke Power Co.* and in two decades of subsequent decisions. Thus, unable to defend legitimate practices in court, employers will be driven to adopt quotas in order to avoid liability.

Proponents of S. 2104 assert that it is needed to overturn the Supreme Court's *Wards Cove Packing Co. v. Antonio* decision and restore the law that had existed since the Griggs case in 1971. S. 2104, however, does not in fact codify Griggs or the Court's subsequent decisions prior to Ward Cove. Instead, S. 2104 engages in a sweeping rewrite of two decades of Supreme Court jurisprudence, using language that appears in no decision of the Court and that is contrary to principles acknowledged even by the Justice Stevens' dissent in Wards Cove: "The opinion in Griggs made it clear that a neutral practice that operates to exclude minorities is nevertheless lawful if it serves a valid business purpose."

I am aware of the dispute among lawyers about the proper interpretation of certain critical language used in this portion of S. 2104. The very fact of this dispute

suggests that the bill is not codifying the law developed by the Supreme Court in Griggs and subsequent cases. This debate, moreover, is a sure sign that S. 2104 will lead to years—perhaps decades—of uncertainty and expensive litigation. It is neither fair nor sensible to give the employers of our country a difficult choice between using quotas and seeking a clarification of the law through costly and very risky litigation.

D. 3205 contains several other unacceptable provisions as well. One section unfairly closes the courts, in many instances, to individuals victimized by agreements, to which they were not a party, involving the use of quotas. Another section radically alters the remedial provisions in Title VII of the Civil Rights Act of 1964, replacing measures designed to foster conciliation and settlement with a new scheme modeled on a tort system widely acknowledged to be in a state of crisis. The bill also contains a number of provisions that will create unnecessary and inappropriate incentives for litigation. These include unfair retroactivity rules; attorneys fee provisions that will discourage settlements; unreasonable new statutes of limitation; and a "rule of construction" that will make it extremely difficult to know how courts can be expected to apply the law. In order to assist the Congress regarding legislation in this area, I enclose herewith a memorandum from the Attorney General explaining in detail the defects that make S. 2104 unacceptable.

Our goal and our promise has been equal opportunity and equal protection under the law. That is a bedrock principle from which we cannot retreat. The temptation to support a bill—any bill—simply because its title includes the words "civil rights" is very strong. This impulse is not entirely bad. Presumptions have too often run the other way, and our Nation's history on racial questions cautions against complacency. But when our efforts, however well intentioned, result in quotas, equal opportunity is not advanced but thwarted. The very commitment to justice and equality that is offered as the reason why this bill should be signed requires me to veto it.....

George Bush

The White House,

October 22, 1990.

◆ CIVIL RIGHTS ACT OF 1991 PUB.L. NO. 102-166, 105 STAT 1071 (1991)

After vetoing Congress' 1990 civil rights legislation, the Bush administration joined both houses of Congress in working on alternative bills. Following months of negotiation, the Senate passed Senate Bill 1745 on October 30; the House passed the bill on November 7. On November 21, President George Bush signed the Civil Rights Act of 1991.

This act is designed to provide additional remedies to deter harassment and intentional discrimination in the workplace, to provide guidelines for the adjudication of cases arising under Title VII ... and to expand the scope of civil rights legislation weakened by Supreme Court decisions, particularly the Court's ruling in *Wards Cove Packing Co. v. Antonio*, 490 US 642 (1989).

Sec. 2. Findings

The Congress finds that—

(1) additional remedies under Federal law are needed to deter unlawful harassment and intentional discrimination in the workplace;

(2) the decision of the Supreme Court in *Wards Cove Packing Co. v. Antonio*, 490 U.S. 642 (1989) has weakened the scope and effectiveness of Federal civil rights protections; and

(3) legislation is necessary to provide additional protections against unlawful discrimination in employment.

Sec. 3. Purposes.

The purposes of this Act are—

(1) to provide appropriate remedies for intentional discrimination and unlawful harassment in the workplace;

(2) to codify the concepts of "business necessity" and "job related" enunciated by the Supreme Court in *Griggs v. Duke Power Co.*, 401 U.S. 424 (1971), and in the other Supreme Court decisions prior to *Wards Cove Packing Co. v. Antonio*, 490 U.S. 642 (1989);

(3) to confirm statutory authority and provide statutory guidelines for the adjudication of disparate impact suits under title VII of the Civil Rights Act of 1964 (42 U.S.C. 2000e et seq.); and

(4) to respond to recent decisions of the Supreme Court by expanding the scope of relevant civil rights statutes in order to provide adequate protection to victims of discrimination.

Title I—Federal Civil Rights Remedies

Sec. 105. Burden of Proof in Disparate Impact Cases.

(a) Section 703 of the Civil Rights Act of 1964 (42 U.S.C. 2000e-2) is amended by adding at the end the following new subsection:

... An unlawful employment practice based on disparate impact is established under this title only if—

... A complaining party demonstrates that a respondent used a particular employment practice that causes a disparate impact on the basis of race, color, religion, sex, or national origin and the respondent fails to demonstrate that the challenged practice is job related for the position in question and consistent with business necessity....

... With respect to demonstrating that a particular employment practice causes a disparate impact as described in subparagraph

(A)(i), the complaining party shall demonstrate that each particular challenged employment practice causes a disparate impact, except that if the complaining party can demonstrate to the court that the elements of a respondent's decisionmaking process are not capable of separation for analysis, the decisionmaking process may be analyzed as one employment practice.

... If the respondent demonstrates that a specific employment practice does not cause the disparate impact, the respondent shall not be required to demonstrate that such practice is required by business necessity....

Sec. 106. Prohibition Against Discriminatory Use of Test Scores.

Section 703 of the Civil Rights Act of 1964 (42 U.S.C. 2000e-2) (as amended by section 105) is further amended by adding at the end of the following new subsection:

... It shall be an unlawful employment practice for a respondent, in connection with the selection or referral of applicants or candidates for employment or promotion, to adjust the scores of, use different cutoff scores for, or otherwise alter the results of, employment related tests on the basis of race, color, religion, sex, or national origin....

Title II—Glass Ceiling

Sec. 202 Findings and Purpose.

(a) Findings—Congress finds that—

(1) despite a dramatically growing presence in the workplace, women and minorities remain underrepresented in management and decision-making positions in business;

(2) artificial barriers exist to the advancement of women and minorities in the workplace;

(3) United States corporations are increasingly relying on women and minorities to meet employment requirements and are increasingly aware of the advantages derived from a diverse work force;

(4) the "Glass Ceiling Initiative" undertaken by the Department of Labor, including the release of the report entitled "Report on the Glass Ceiling Initiative," has been instrumental in raising public awareness of—

(A) the underrepresentation of women and minorities at the management and decision-making levels in the United States work force;

(B) the underrepresentation of women and minorities in line functions in the United States work force;

(C) the lack of access for qualified women and minorities to credential-building developmental opportunities; and

(D) the desirability of eliminating artificial barriers to the advancement of women and minorities to such levels;

(f) the establishment of a commission to examine issues raised by the Glass Ceiling Initiative would help—

(A) focus greater attention on the importance of eliminating artificial barriers to the advancement of women and minorities to management and decision-making positions in business; and

(B) promote work force diversity....

◆ THE MILLION MAN MARCH/DAY OF ABSENCE MISSION STATEMENT

(by Dr. Maulana Karenga; an excerpt)

I. Introduction

The Black men and women, the organizations and persons, participating in this historic Million Man March and Day of Absence held in Washington, D.C., on October 16, 1995, on the eve of the 21st century, and supported by parallel activities in cities and towns throughout the country: *conscious* of the critical juncture of history in which we live and the challenges it poses for us; *concerned* about increasing racism and the continuing commitment to white supremacy in this country; deteriorating social conditions, degradation of the environment and the impact of these on our community, the larger society and the world; *committed* to the ongoing struggle for a free and empowered community, a just society and a better world; *recognizing* that the country and government have made a dangerous and regressive turn to the right and are producing policies with negative impact on people of color, the poor and the vulnerable; *realizing* that every man and woman and our community have both the right and responsibility to resist evil and contribute meaningfully to the creation of a just and good society; *reaffirming* the best values of our social justice tradition which require respect for the dignity and rights of the human person, economic justice, meaningful political participation, shared power, cultural integrity, mutual respect for all peoples, and uncompromising resistance to social forces and structures which deny or limit these; *declare* our commitment to assume a new and expanded responsibility in the struggle to build and sustain a free and empowered community, a just society and a better world. We are aware that we make this commitment in an era in which this is needed as never before and in which we cannot morally choose otherwise.

In doing this, we self-consciously emphasize the priority need of Black men to stand up and assume this new and expanded responsibility without denying or minimizing the equal rights, role and responsibility of Black women in the life and struggle of our people.

Our priority call to Black men to stand up and assume this new and expanded sense of responsibility is based on the realization that the strength and resourcefulness of the family and the liberation of the people require it;

that some of the most acute problems facing the Black community within are those posed by Black males who have not stood up; that the caring and responsible father in the home; the responsible and future-focused male youth; security in and of the community; the quality of male/female relations, and the family's capacity to avoid poverty and push the lives of its members forward all depend on Black men's standing up;

that in the context of a real and principled brotherhood, those of us who have stood up, must challenge others to stand also; and that unless and until Black men stand up, Black men and women cannot stand together and accomplish the awesome tasks before us.

II. The Historical Significance of the Project

This Million Man March, forming a joint project with its companion activity, The Day of Absence, speaks to who we are, where we stand and what we are compelled to do in this hour of meeting and posing challenges. Its significance lies in the fact that:

1. It is a timely and necessary state of challenge both to ourselves and the country in a time of increasing racism, attacks on hard won gains, and continually deteriorating conditions for the poor and vulnerable and thus an urgent time for transformative and progressive leadership;

2. It is a declaration of the resolve of Black men, in particular and the Black community in general, to mobilize and struggle to maintain hard won gains, resist evil and wrong wherever we find it and to continue to push our lives and history forward;

3. It is a reaffirmation of our self-understanding as a people that we are our own liberators, that no matter how numerous or sincere our allies are, the greatest burdens to be borne and the most severe sacrifices to be made for liberation are essentially our own;

4. It is an effective way to refocus and expand discussion on critical issues confronting our people, this country and the world and put forth our positions on them;

5. It is both an example and encouragement of operational unity; unity in diversity, unity without uniformity and unity on principle and in practice for the greater good;

6. It is a galvanizing and mobilizing process to raise consciousness, cultivate commitment and lay the groundwork for increased positive social, political and economic activity;

7. And finally, it is a necessary continuation of our ancient and living moral tradition of speaking truth to power and seeking power for the vulnerable, justice for the injured, right for the wronged and liberation for the oppressed...

VII. Continuing Practice and Projects

38. The Million Man March and Day of Absence can only have lasting value if we continue to work and struggle beyond this day. Thus, our challenge is to take the spirit of this day, the process of mobilization and the possibilities of organization and turn them into ongoing structures and practices directed toward our liberation and flourishing as a people.

39. Central to sustaining and institutionalizing this process is:

a. the follow-up development of an expanded Black political agenda and the holding of a Black Political Convention to forge this agenda for progressive political change;

b. a massive and ongoing voter registration of Black people as independents; using our vote to insist and insure that candidates address the Black agenda; and creating and sustaining a progressive independent political movement;

c. the building and strengthening of Black united fronts and collective leadership structures like the National African American Leadership Summit to practice and benefit from operational unity in our addressing local, national and international issues;

d. the establishment of a Black Economic Development Fund to enhance economic development, cultivate economic discipline and cooperative practices and achieve economic self-determination;

e. the reaffirmation and strengthening of family through quality male/female relations based on principles of equality, complementarity, mutual respect and shared responsibility in love, life and struggle; and through loving and responsible parenthood that insists on discipline and achievement, provides spiritual, moral and cultural grounding and through expanding rites of passage programs, mentorships and increasing adoptions;

f. the ongoing struggle for reparations in the fullest sense, that is to say: public admission, apology and recognition of the Holocaust of African Enslavement and appropriate compensation by the government; and support for the Conyers Reparations Bill on the Holocaust;

g. the continuing struggle against police abuse, government suppression, violations of civil and human rights and the industrialization of prisons; and in support of the freedom of all political prisoners, prisoners' rights and their efforts to transform themselves into worthy members of the community;

h. the critical task of organizing the community as a solid wall in the struggle against drugs, crime and violence in the community which we see as interrelated and which must be joined with the struggle to reduce and end poverty, increase employment, strengthen fatherhood, motherhood and family, support parents, provide education and prevention programs; and expose and reject those who deal in death for the community.

None of this denies external sources of drugs nor stops us from demanding uniform sentencing and penalties for those involved in the drug trade on the local, national and international level, but it compels us to stand up and take responsibility for the life we must live in spite of external impositions;

i. continuing and expanding our support for African-centered independent schools through joining their boards, enrolling our children, being concerned and active parents, donating time, services and monies to them and working in various other ways to insure that they provide the highest level of culturally-rooted education; and intensifying and broadening the struggle for quality public education through heightened parental concern and involvement and social activism which insist on a responsible administration, professional and committed teachers, continuing faculty and staff development; safe pleasant, encouraging and fully-equipped campuses and an inclusive and culture-respecting curriculum which stresses mastery of knowledge as well as critical thinking, academic excellence, social responsibility and an expanded sense of human possibility;

j. continuing and reinforced efforts to reduce and eliminate negative media approaches to and portrayals of Black life and culture; to organize a sustained and effective support for positive models, messages and works; to achieve adequate and dignified representation of Blacks in various media and in various positions in these media; to expand support for and development of independent Black media; and to challenge success

ful and notable African Americans in various media to support all these efforts;

k. strengthening and supporting organizations and institutions of the Black community concerned with the uplifting and liberation of our people by joining as families and persons, volunteering service, giving donations and providing and insisting on the best leadership possible;

l. building appropriate alliances with other peoples of color, supporting their liberation struggles and just demands and engaging in mutually supportive and mutually beneficial activities to create and sustain a just and good society;

m. standing in solidarity with other African peoples and other Third World peoples in their struggles to free themselves, harness their human and material resources and live full and meaningful lives;

n. reaffirming in the most positive ways the value and indispensability of the spiritual and ethical grounding of our people in accomplishing the historical tasks confronting us by freeing and renewing our minds and reaffirming our commitment to the good, the proper and the beneficial, by joining as families and persons the faith communities of our choice, supporting them, living the best of our traditions ourselves and challenging other members and the leadership to do likewise and constantly insisting that our faith communities give the best of what we have to offer to build the moral community and just society we struggle for as a people;

o. and finally, embracing and practicing a common set of principles that reaffirm and strengthen family, community and culture, The Nguzo Saba (The Seven Principles); Umoja (Unity); Kujichagulia (Self-Determination); Ujima (Collective Work and Responsibility); Ujamaa (Cooperative Economics); Nia (Purpose); Kuumba (Creativity) and Imani (Faith).

For full text of the Mission Statement, contact University of Sankore Press, 2560 W. 54th St., Los Angeles, CA 9004; phone (800)997-2656; fax (213)299-0261.

4

African American Landmarks

As far back as the establishment of the first permanent European settlement in America, African Americans have made significant contributions to the social, economic, scientific, and cultural development of this country. The American landscape is covered with sites commemorating this African American experience. From the war for independence, through the conflicts fought on the western frontier, and on to more recent battles, sites have been established to commemorate black participation in the defense of this nation. The African American quest for knowledge has been embodied at the first institutions organized to educate blacks in this country. The trail from slavery to freedom can be retraced by way of the many markers noting stations along the Underground Railroad. Other sites commemorate the achievements of blacks in the sciences and the arts or in pursuit of equal rights. Landmarks, unlike most textual documents, stand through time as public testaments to the strength and courage of African Americans.

◆ ALABAMA

Florence

William Christopher Handy Birthplace

W. C. Handy, composer of "St. Louis Blues," was born in 1873. The cabin in which he was born was moved from its original site to its current location in Florence, Alabama. The restored cabin contains his piano, trumpet, and other mementoes.

Montgomery

Civil Rights Memorial
Washington St.

Inscribed with the names of 40 civil rights martyrs and the words of Dr. Martin Luther King, Jr., "Until justice rolls down like waters and righteousness like a mighty stream," this memorial was commissioned by the Southern Poverty Law Center and dedicated in 1989.

Dexter Avenue Baptist Church
454 Dexter Avenue

The Dexter Avenue Baptist Church was the church where Dr. Martin Luther King, Jr. organized the 1955 boycott of Montgomery's segregated bus system. It was this boycott that brought Dr. King into national prominence as a civil rights leader.

Dr. King pastored the church from 1954 to 1959. In the church is housed a mural depicting scenes of the civil rights movement, as well as a library containing personal mementoes of Dr. King and his family. The church, which has been in existence since 1878, was declared a National Historic Landmark in 1974.

Selma

Edmund Pettis Bridge

On Sunday, March 7, 1965, civil rights leaders started out from Selma, Alabama, on what was to be a 55-mile march to Montgomery, Alabama, protesting the denial of voting rights to blacks who had attempted to register in Selma. Reaching the Edmund Pettis Bridge, the marchers were met by state troopers—the orders to deploy the troopers had been issued by Governor George Wallace to enforce his executive order forbidding such demonstrations. The unarmed marchers were turned back by tear gas and night sticks; numerous injuries resulted.

On March 21, a second march started out, organized by the Reverend Dr. Martin Luther King, Jr.; this march concluded five days later on the steps of the state capitol building in Montgomery.

Talladega

Talladega College and Swayne Hall

The first college for blacks in Alabama, Talladega College, was founded by the American Missionary Association as a primary school in 1867. The school pursued a liberal arts program at a time when vocational education dominated black institutions. Its Slavery Library houses three fresco panels (the celebrated Amistad Murals) by Hale Woodruff, who studied in France under the renowned Henry Ossawa Tanner.

Swayne Hall, built in 1857, is the oldest building on the campus of Talladega College. The building was constructed by slave labor before the school was established. It was declared a National Historic Landmark on December 2, 1974.

Tuskegee

Tuskegee Institute

Tuskegee Institute, a world-renowned center for agricultural research and extension work, first opened on July 4, 1881, with a $2,000 appropriation from the Alabama state legislature. It consisted of a single shanty, a student body of 30, and one teacher—Booker T. Washington. Tuskegee functioned originally as a normal school for the training of black teachers, the first of its kind established in the United States. Eventually it came to specialize in agricultural and manual training, areas which were to make both the school and Booker T. Washington famous.

In 1882, Washington moved the school to a 100-acre plantation and began a self-help program that enabled students to finance their education. Most of the early buildings were built with the aid of student labor.

Next to Washington, the most notable person to be associated with the institute was George Washington Carver, who became its director of agricultural research in 1896. Carver persuaded many Southern farmers to cultivate peanuts, sweet potatoes, and other crops instead of cotton, which was rapidly depleting the soil. Ultimately, Carver's research programs helped develop 300 derivative products from peanuts and 118 from sweet potatoes. At one point, he even succeeded in making synthetic marble from wood pulp.

Today, Tuskegee covers nearly 5,000 acres and has more than 150 buildings. Places to visit include the Founder's Marker (the site of Washington's original shanty), the Oaks (Washington's home), the Booker T. Washington Monument, and the George Washington Carver Museum (operated by the National Parks Serv-

ice), which houses the scientist's plant, mineral, and bird collections, and exhibits of various products he developed. Tuskegee is also home to the George Washington Carver Foundation, a research center founded by Carver in 1940.

◆ ALASKA

Fairbanks

Mattie Crosby's Home

One of the few black pioneers of Alaska, Mattie Crosby first came to the territory in 1900 with a Maine family that adopted her. Some blacks came into the territory during the era of the Gold Rush, and others were occasionally seen on board ships that brought in supplies. However, for nearly 17 years, Mattie Crosby lived in Fairbanks, Alaska, without meeting another black.

◆ ARIZONA

Tombstone

John Swain Grave Site
Boot Hill Cemetery

Born a slave in 1845, John Swain went to Tombstone, Arizona, in 1879 as a cowhand in the employ of John Slaughter. Swain was an expert rider and only one of several blacks to work for Slaughter.

In 1884, Swain is said to have fought and lost a one-round boxing match with John L. Sullivan, then heavyweight champion of the world. He died just three months short of his one hundredth birthday and was buried with honors by the citizens of Tombstone. A special tablet stands on the grave site, commemorating the close ties between Swain and Slaughter.

◆ ARKANSAS

Little Rock

Central High School
14th and Park Streets

In the fall of 1957, the first major confrontation over implementation of the Supreme Court's 1954 ruling in outlawing racial segregation in public schools took place at Central High School in Little Rock, Arkansas.

Upon their arrival for classes on September 23, 1957, black students were turned away by the Arkansas National Guard on the order of Arkansas Governor Orval Faubus. President Dwight D. Eisenhower responded to the crisis, issuing an executive order on September 24,

The chapel at Tuskegee Institute

which called for the use of federal troops to enforce the Court's order to desegregate public schools.

Philander-Smith College
812 West 13th Street

In 1877 this institution was opened under the sponsorship of the African Methodist Episcopal church as Walder College in Little Rock, Arkansas. After receiving a large donation that enabled the school to construct a permanent brick edifice, the college was renamed.

◆ CALIFORNIA

Allensworth

Allensworth Colony

Established as an all black community, the town of Allensworth was founded by Allen Allensworth in 1910. Now a state park, this landmark serves as a memorial to its founder.

Allen Allensworth, as a slave just prior to the Civil War, was a well-known racing jockey in Louisville,

Kentucky. With the beginning of the Civil War, Allensworth was allowed to enter the Navy, where he advanced to rank of chief petty officer. Following the war, Allensworth studied for the ministry and returned to the military service as chaplain of the famed 24th U.S. Infantry. Around 1900 he migrated to California, where he dedicated himself to improving the status of African Americans.

Arcadia

Santa Anita Race Track

Santa Anita Race Track is located in Arcadia, California, on the former site of the E. J. "Lucky" Baldwin Ranch, at which John Fisher, a former slave, was a prominent breeder and trainer. Fisher, a native of St. Louis, was at first reluctant to follow Baldwin to California out of fear of American Indians, but was eventually persuaded to join him. He later became a foreman on the ranch.

Beckwourth

Beckwourth Pass

Beckwourth Pass, which runs through the Sierra Nevadas in Beckwourth, California, was discovered by

Central High School, Little Rock, Arkansas.

Jim Beckwourth, one of a number of black traders and trappers dubbed "Mountain Men" by chroniclers of American history.

Hornitos

Gold Mining Camp

This was the home of Moses Rodgers, a successful and affluent black mine-owner who was one of the finest engineers and metallurgists in the state. Rodgers was only one of several black miners who struck it rich in gold and quartz.

Red Bluff

Oak Hill Cemetery

Located in Red Bluff, California, this is the burial place of Aaron Coffey, the only black member of the Society of California Pioneers. Coffey, descendant of an officer who fought under Jackson at New Orleans, came to California as a slave in 1849. By day, he worked for his master; by night, as a cobbler, he accumulated money toward his $1,000 emancipation fee. Betrayed by his owner, he was forced to return to Missouri, where he was again sold. Coffey pleaded with his new master to allow him to return to California and earn the necessary money to free himself and his family, which he had left behind as collateral. That mission accomplished, Coffey returned to Red Bluff, took up farming and settled down to a contented family life.

Sacramento

St. Andrew's African Methodist Episcopal Church
2131 Eighth Street

St. Andrew's was the first African Methodist Episcopal congregation in California. Organized in a private residence in 1850, within four years the congregation had founded a school for African, Asian, and Native American children in the church's basement.

San Francisco

Leidesdorff Street

This street in San Francisco, California, is named for William Alexander Leidesdorff, a wealthy and influential California pioneer of black and Danish ancestry and a native of the Danish West Indies. A merchant, Leidesdorff operated the first steamer to pass through the Golden Gate strait. Leidesdorff was later appointed U.S. vice-consul and ultimately became a civic and educational leader in San Francisco.

◆ COLORADO

Central City

"Aunt Clara" Brown's Chair
Central City Opera House
Eureka Street

"Aunt Clara" Brown, believed to have been the first black resident of the Colorado Territory, was born a slave in Virginia. Brown moved to Missouri, where her husband and children were sold before she herself gained freedom through her master's last will and testament. From Missouri, she headed for Kansas and then for the gold fields of Colorado, where she opened the territory's first laundry. She soon began putting aside money from her earnings for the purchase of her family's freedom.

Even when the Emancipation Proclamation set her immediate family free, she nonetheless returned to Missouri and brought back to Central City a group of 38 relatives. She remained in the mining community for the rest of her life, nursing the sick and performing other charitable works.

Brown died in 1877 and was buried with honors by the Colorado Pioneers Association, of which she was a member. The Central City Opera House Association dedicated a chair to her in 1932.

Denver

Inter-Ocean Hotel
16th and Market Streets

Built by Barney Ford, the Inter-Ocean Hotel in Denver, Colorado, was once a showplace for millionaires and presidents. Ford, a black entrepreneur active during the gold rush days, joined the fight over the organization of the Colorado territory and the question of statehood. Originally allowed to vote, Ford saw this privilege abrogated by the territorial constitution, and as a result, sought to delay statehood for the territory until black voting rights were reinstated. Enlisting the aid of the famed Massachusetts abolitionist Senator Charles Sumner, Ford urged President Andrew Johnson to veto the bill for statehood.

The Inter-Ocean Hotel.

After Ford retired, he spent the remainder of his life in Denver, where he died in 1902. He is buried alongside his wife Julia in Denver's Riverside Cemetery.

Pueblo

El Pueblo Museum
905 South Prairie Avenue

The El Pueblo museum houses a replica of the Gantt-Blackwell Fort, which Jim Beckwourth, black explorer, scout, and trader, claimed to have founded in 1842. The validity of the claim has not been established, as Beckwourth had something of a reputation as a teller of tall tales.

◆ CONNECTICUT

Canterbury

Prince Goodin Homestead

This parcel of land in Canterbury was once the home of Prince Goodin, a free African American who fought with the British against the French in the French and Indian War. Goodin enlisted in 1757, after hearing a fiery speech by Canterbury's Reverend James Cogswell that stressed the danger of encroachment against "properties, liberties, religion and our lives." While serving at Fort William Henry, he was captured during a French attack upon the fort and taken to Montreal, where he was sold into slavery. After three years of captivity, Goodin was freed when the British took the city in 1760.

Enfield

Paul Robeson Residence
1221 Enfield St.

Purchased by Paul Robeson and his wife in 1940, this residence served as their home until 1953. Robeson, a singer, actor, and civil rights activist, is best known for his roles in the film *The Emperor Jones* and the musical and film version of *Show Boat*.

Farmington

First Church of Christ
75 Main Street

When in 1839, the mutinied Cuban slave ship *Amistad* landed off the coast of Connecticut, abolitionists in the area demanded protection for the Africans. The First Church of Christ in Farmington, Connecticut, served as the center of community life for the *Amistad* insurrectionists while they awaited trial. The church was designated a National Historic Landmark on December 8, 1976.

Washington

Jeff Liberty Grave Site
Judea Cemetery

Here lies the grave site of Jeff Liberty, a black soldier in the Continental Army during the Revolution. His grave marker, erected by the Sons of the American Revolution, states simply "in remembrance of Jeff Liberty and his colored patriots." Liberty, a slave at the time of the rebellion, asked his owner to be allowed to serve in the struggle for independence. His request granted, he fought throughout the Revolution with an all-black regiment and was granted freedman status at the end of the war.

◆ DELAWARE

Wilmington

Asbury Methodist Episcopal Church
Third and Walnut Streets

The Asbury Methodist Episcopal Church was dedicated in 1789 by the distinguished orator Bishop Francis Asbury. Tradition has it that on one occasion a number of the town's leading citizens, many of whom were eager to hear Asbury preach but considered Methodism socially beneath them, stayed outside within hearing distance of the sermon but refused to enter the church. The listeners were impressed by the eloquence of the man

Jeff Liberty grave marker.

they heard—but, as it turned out, the voice they heard was not that of the bishop, but of his black servant Harry, whose compelling testimony reached their ears and inspired their admiration. In its early years, the church welcomed black members. However, by 1805 blacks had left this church, driven out by the decision of white worshippers to confine black members to the gallery.

◆ DISTRICT OF COLUMBIA

Mary McLeod Bethune Memorial
Lincoln Park

The Mary McLeod Bethune Memorial, unveiled in 1974, is the first monument to a black or a woman to be erected on public land in the nation's capital. Bethune, an educator, was concerned about the children of the laborers working on the Florida East Coast Railroad. Thus, in 1904, she established the Daytona Normal and Industrial Institute for black girls. In 1926, she merged the institute with the Cookman Institute of Jacksonville to form the Bethune-Cookman College.

The monument, located in Lincoln Park, District of Columbia, is inscribed with the following words:

The Mary McLeod Bethune Memorial, Washington, DC.

I leave you love, I leave you hope. I leave you the challenge of developing confidence in one another. I leave you a thirst for education. I leave you respect for the use of power. I leave you faith. I leave you racial dignity.

Bethune Museum and Archives
1318 Vermont Avenue, NW

Named for Mary McLeod Bethune, the Bethune Museum and Archives was opened in November 1979 and was granted national historic-site status in April 1982. The Bethune Museum and Archives is a fully independent nonprofit organization that works to document the contributions made by black women to society and to enrich the lives of America's children through educational material programs and other services.

Blanche K. Bruce House
909 M Street, NW

Blanche K. Bruce, from Mississippi, was the first African American to serve a full term in the U.S. Senate. Born in Farmville, Virginia, Bruce learned the printer's trade in Missouri. In 1861, prior to the Civil War, he escaped to Hannibal, Missouri, and set up a school for blacks. He studied at Oberlin College in Ohio and, after moving to Mississippi, became a wealthy planter. A Republican, Bruce was elected by the Mississippi state legislature to the U.S. Senate in 1874. The Blanche K. Bruce House was designated a National Historic Landmark on May 15, 1975.

Mary Ann Shadd Cary House
1421 W Street, NW

Between 1881 and 1886, this house, located in Washington, DC, served as the residence of Mary Ann Shadd Cary, the first black newspaperwoman in America. Cary, a lecturer, writer, educator, lawyer, and abolitionist, appeared before audiences throughout the country, usually speaking on the topics of slavery and women's suffrage. The house was designated a National Historic Landmark on December 8, 1976.

Frederick Douglass House
1411 W Street, SE

Cedar Hill, the 20-room colonial mansion in which Frederick Douglass lived for the last 13 years of his life, has been preserved as a monument to the great nineteenth-century abolitionist. In 1964, it was declared a National Historic Landmark. Credit for the restoration and preservation of the home belongs largely to the National Association of Colored Women's Clubs, which worked hand-in-hand with the Douglass Association.

Edward Kennedy "Duke" Ellington Birthplace
1212 T Street, NW

Born April 29, 1899, Duke Ellington was one of the world's great jazz composer/bandleaders.

Emancipation Statue
Lincoln Park
East Capitol Street

Former slaves were responsible for financing and erecting the oldest memorial to Abraham Lincoln in the Washington, D.C., area. Following Lincoln's assassination in 1865, the first five dollars for the statue were donated by a Mrs. Charlotte Scott of Marietta, Ohio. Contributions were soon pouring in, whereupon Congress finally set aside grounds for Thomas Bell's statue depicting Lincoln breaking slavery's chains. The memorial was dedicated on April 14, 1876—the eleventh anniversary of Lincoln's assassination.

Charlotte Forten Grimké House
1608 R Street, NW

Charlotte Forten Grimké, born of wealthy free black parents in Philadelphia, was among the first wave of Northerners engaged in educating slaves in the occupied Union territories of the South. Her activities as an

The Frederick Douglass House.

activist, writer, poet, and educator forged a path for other black women. The house was designated a National Historic Landmark on May 11, 1976.

General Oliver Otis Howard House
Howard University

This house, on what is now the campus of Howard University, was the residence of the Union Civil War General who became head of the Freedmen's Bureau. Howard University is named in honor of General Howard, and his residence is the only one of four original university buildings still standing at this distinguished institution.

Howard University

Howard University, founded in 1867, is the largest institution of higher learning established for African Americans immediately following the Civil War.

Covering more than 50 acres, the campus is situated on one of the highest elevations in the District of Columbia. Of particular interest is the university's famed Founders Library, which contains more than 300,000 volumes and includes the Moorland-Spingarn Collec-

tion, one of the finest collections on African American life and history in the United States.

Lincoln Memorial

The Lincoln Memorial has been the site of several important events underscoring African Americans' quest for dignity and struggle for equal opportunity. In 1939, when singer Marian Anderson was refused permission to appear at Constitution Hall by the Daughters of the American Revolution, she performed an Easter Sunday concert on the steps of the Lincoln Memorial before a crowd of 75,000. Her rendition of "Nobody Knows the Trouble I've Seen" prompted NAACP Executive Secretary Walter White to foresee the advent of "a new affirmation of democracy." Another such pivotal event involved the 1963 March on Washington, which was climaxed by the Reverend Martin Luther King, Jr.'s "I Have A Dream" speech.

National Museum of African Art
950 Independence Avenue, SW

A part of the Smithsonian Institution, the National Museum of African Art maintains exhibitions, research

Emancipation Statue.

components, and public programs on the art and culture of sub-Saharan Africa. The museum was established in 1964 and incorporated as a bureau of the Smithsonian in 1979.

Mary Church Terrell House
326 T Street, NW

This house served as the residence of the civil rights activist Mary Church Terrell, who achieved national prominence as the first president of the National Association of Colored Women.

St. Luke's Episcopal Church
15th and Church Streets, NW

From 1879 until 1934, the pulpit of St. Luke's Episcopal Church was filled by Alexander Crummell, a black scholar who became a leading spokesman for African and African American liberation. He was the founder of the American Negro Academy, established with the intention of forming a cadre of black intellectuals and scholars. The church, located in Washington, D.C., was designated a National Historic Landmark on May 11, 1976.

Tidal Basin Bridge

Designed and constructed by black engineer Archie Alphonso Alexander, the Tidal Basin Bridge is one of Washington's major tourist attractions. Alexander, born in Ottumwa, Iowa, in 1888, later became the first Republican governor of the U.S. Virgin Islands in 1954.

Carter G. Woodson House and the Association for the Study of Negro Life and History
1538 Ninth Street, NW

Founded in 1915, the Association for the Study of Negro Life and History was formed to study and preserve the historical record of African American culture. The pioneer behind the association was Carter G. Woodson, who operated the organization out of his home until his death in 1950.

A scholar and lecturer, Woodson began publication of the *Journal of Negro History* in 1916. Ten years later, Woodson initiated the observance of "Negro History Week," to be celebrated in February as close as possible to the birthdays of both Frederick Douglass and Abraham Lincoln, during which African American leaders would be appropriately honored. Negro History Week has grown into what is now Black History Month.

The Woodson house was designated a National Historic Landmark on May 11, 1976. Today, the organization is headquartered at 1401 14th Street, NW, and is known as the Association for the Study of Afro-American Life and History.

◆ FLORIDA

Daytona Beach

Bethune-Cookman College
640 Second Avenue

One of the leading institutions in the South for the training of black teachers, Bethune-Cookman College, located in Daytona Beach, Florida, was founded in 1904 by Mary McLeod Bethune on "faith and a dollar-and-a-half."

Bethune served as advisor to Presidents Franklin D. Roosevelt and Harry S. Truman and was one of the most influential women in the United States.

Mary McLeod Bethune House
Bethune-Cookman College

The two-story frame house belonging to the black activist and educator Mary McLeod Bethune was built in 1920 on the campus of the school she established in 1904. The house was proclaimed a National Historic Landmark on December 2, 1974.

Key West

Dry Tortugas

Black artisans and laborers worked in the construction of Dry Tortugas, a fort in Key West, Florida, which helped control the Florida straits. The largest all-masonry fortification in the western world, it served as a prison until 1873. Among the prisoners was Doctor Samuel A. Mudd, who had set John Wilkes Boothe's broken leg after the assassination of Abraham Lincoln.

Fort George Island

Kingsley Plantation

Zephaniah Kingsley traded extensively in slaves, and the headquarters for his operation was on this plantation on Fort George Island. The oldest known plantation in Florida, the Kingsley Plantation was established in 1763. The plantation, which has been restored as a museum, displays exhibits and furnishings that depict the plantation and island life during the period from 1763 to 1783.

Franklin County

Fort Gadsen

In 1814, the British built the fort as a base for recruiting Seminole Indians and runaway slaves during the War of 1812. The British abandoned it to their allies in 1815, along with its artillery and military supplies. It became known as the Negro Fort and served as a beacon for rebellious slaves and a threat to supply vessels on the river. On May 15, 1975, the British fort was named a National Historic Landmark.

◆ GEORGIA

Andersonville

Andersonville Prison

Andersonville, the infamous Confederate prison in Andersonville, Georgia where thousands of Union soldiers perished as a result of the brutal manner in which they were confined, is now a national monument. Corporal Henry Gooding of the black 54th Massachusetts regiment was imprisoned here, where he died on July 19, 1864. It was Corporal Gooding who had started a protest regarding the pay of black soldiers, going over the heads of military brass to write President Lincoln. At that time the pay of blacks was a flat $7 per month. For whites, it ranged from $9 to $30. Encouraged by Colonel Robert Shaw, the black soldiers of the 54th refused to accept any remuneration unless it were equal to that of white comrades. This financial inequity was subsequently rectified, but Corporal Gooding died at Andersonville without ever having drawn a day's pay.

Atlanta

Clark Atlanta University

Atlanta University was founded in 1865, holding its first classes for freed slaves in abandoned railway cars. Clark College was founded four years later. The two schools were incorporated in 1988. Today the campus of the Clark Atlanta University System, centered in Atlanta, Georgia, is one of the most beautiful in the nation, housing not only Clark Atlanta University, but also Morris Brown, Morehouse, and Spelman colleges.

Stone Hall, built in 1882, is oldest building in the complex. It was named a National Historic Landmark on December 2, 1974.

Ebenezer Baptist Church
407 Auburn Avenue

Built in 1922, Ebenezer Baptist Church had as its associate pastor the Reverend Martin Luther King, Jr. It was from this church that Dr. King's movement radiated outward to the rest of the South, organizing chapters of the Southern Christian Leadership Conference (SCLC), the civil rights coalition of which he served as president.

When Dr. King was assassinated on April 4, 1968, funeral services were held in this church. As millions watched on television, mourners lined up for miles behind the mule drawn wagon that carried Dr. King from Ebenezer to Morehouse College, his alma mater. There, the eulogies were delivered, and more than 150,000 mourners paid their last respects.

Martin Luther King Jr. Historic District
Auburn Avenue

The district, which consists of several blocks of Atlanta's Auburn Avenue and Boulevard, includes Dr. Martin Luther King, Jr.'s birthplace and grave site, and the church where King served as assistant pastor. The environs of his childhood are largely intact. Private efforts to create a living monument to Dr. King and his beliefs have been carried on primarily through the Martin Luther King, Jr. Center for Non-Violent Social Change, Inc. The Martin Luther King Historic District was designated a National Historic Landmark on May 5, 1977.

South View Cemetery

Dr. Martin Luther King, Jr., was laid to rest in South View Cemetery, where a marble crypt was inscribed with the words he used to conclude his famous speech

Ebenezer Baptist Church.

The birthplace of Dr. Martin Luther King, Jr.

delivered on the occasion of the 1963 march on Washington—"Free at last, free at last, thank God Almighty I'm free at last."

South View cemetery was founded in 1886 by blacks who balked at a prevailing policy requiring that they be buried in the rear of the municipal cemetery.

Sweet Auburn Historic District
Auburn Avenue

Although only a remnant of its original one-mile expanse has survived, the Sweet Auburn district typified the rapid growth of black enterprise in the post-Civil War period. Forced to adjust to segregated residential and commercial patterns, wealthy blacks settled in the area. Auburn Avenue was once known as the "richest Negro street in the world." The district was designated a National Historic Landmark on December 8, 1976.

Columbus

"Blind Tom" Marker
U.S. Route 27A

This marks the grave site of the famous black pianist, "Blind Tom" Bethune. Born Thomas Green Bethune,

son of a slave, he was a prodigy whose astonishing talent brought him into the salons of Europe, where royalty marveled at his virtuoso performances.

Bragg Smith Grave Site and Memorial
Columbus Colored Cemetery
Fourth Street and Seventh Avenue

This memorial, located in the Columbus Colored Cemetery, was built in memory of Bragg Smith, who was killed while attempting to rescue a city engineer trapped in a cave-in. The marble memorial is believed to have been the first civic memorial in the country dedicated to an African American.

Savannah

Reverend George Liele Memorial
First Bryan Baptist Church
559 West Bryan Street

Inside the First Bryan Baptist Church is a memorial dedicated to the Reverend George Liele, the first black Baptist missionary. Following Lisle's death, his work was continued by his assistant, Andrew Bryan, after whom the church is named.

◆ ILLINOIS

Chicago

Robert S. Abbott House
4742 Martin Luther King Drive

This house was occupied by Robert Stengstacke Abbott from 1926 until his death in 1940. Under Abbott, the *Chicago Defender*, a newspaper targeted to black readers, encouraged Southern blacks to migrate northward, particularly to Chicago. Probably more than any other publication, the *Defender* was responsible for the large northward migration of blacks during the first half of the twentieth century. The house was named a National Historic Landmark on December 8, 1976.

Oscar Stanton DePriest House
45336-4538 Dr. Martin Luther King, Jr. Drive

This house served as the residence of the first black American elected to the House of Representatives from a northern state. Oscar DePriest was born in Florence, Alabama, but moved with his family to Kansas and later to Chicago. While in Chicago, he worked as a real estate broker; in 1928, he was elected to the U.S. House of Representatives, where he served three terms. Following his tenure, he returned to the real estate business, but remained politically active in Chicago—including serving as vice-chairman of the Cook County Republican Committee. The DePriest house was designated a National Historic Landmark on May 15, 1975.

Milton L. Olive Park
Lake Shore Drive

Milton L. Olive Park was dedicated by Chicago Mayor Richard Daley in honor of the first black soldier to be awarded a Congressional Medal of Honor during the Vietnam War. Olive died in action after exhibiting extraordinary heroism, which saved the lives of several other soldiers exposed to a live grenade.

Jean Baptiste Point Du Sable Homesite
401 North Michigan Avenue

Jean Baptiste Point Du Sable, born in Haiti to a French mariner father and a black mother, immigrated to French Louisiana and became a fur trapper. He established trading posts on the sites of the present cities of Michigan City, Indiana; Peoria, Illinois; and Port Huron, Michigan—but the most important post was on the site of Chicago, Illinois. This site, where he constructed a log home for his wife and family, is recognized as the first settlement in the Chicago area. In 1796, Du Sable sold his Chicago home and went to live with his son in St. Charles, where he died in 1814.

The homesite was designated a National Historic Landmark on May 11, 1976. The site of Du Sable's home is marked by a plaque on the northeast approach to the Michigan Avenue Bridge. Two other plaques recognizing Du Sable exist—one in the Chicago Historical Society, the other in the lobby of Du Sable High School, at 49th and State Streets.

Provident Hospital and Training School
500 East 51st Street and Vincennes Avenue

The original Provident Hospital and Training School was established as the first training school for black nurses in the United States. It was founded by Dr. Daniel Hale Williams, the renowned surgeon who performed one of the first successful operations on the human heart in 1893. The current hospital was opened in 1933.

Underground Railroad Marker
9955 South Beverly Avenue

This marks one of many transit points used by slaves escaping from the South to Canada.

Victory Monument
35th Street and South Parkway

Sculpted by Leonard Crunelle, Victory Monument honors the black soldiers of Illinois, who served in World War I. The monument and tomb of Stephen A. Douglas, once the owner of much of the land in the area, is also located near 35th Street

Ida B. Wells Barnett House
3624 South Dr. Martin Luther King, Jr. Drive

This house was the home of the 1890s civil rights advocate and crusader for black women, Ida Wells Barnett. The Wells house was designated a National Historic Landmark on May 30, 1974.

Daniel Hale Williams House
445 East 42nd Street

This house was the home of one of America's first black surgeons, whose accomplishments include performing one of the first successful heart operations in 1893 and establishing quality medical facilities for blacks. Daniel Hale Williams was born in Hollidaysburg, Pennsylvania. He had managed a barber shop prior to apprenticing under Dr. Henry Palmer, who was surgeon-general of Wisconsin. Williams received his medical degree from Chicago Medical College in 1883 and later opened an office in Chicago; he was the first black to win a fellowship from the American College of Surgeons. The Williams house was designated a National Historic Landmark on May 15, 1975.

Quincy

Father Augustine Tolton Grave Site
St. Peter's Cemetery
Broadway and 32nd Street

The Father Augustine Tolton grave site marks the resting place of the first black American to be ordained as a Roman Catholic priest. Ordained in 1886, Father Tolton opened a school for black children, was pastor at St. Joseph's Church in Quincy, and later served as pastor at St. Monica's Church in Chicago. He died in 1897.

◆ INDIANA

Bloomingdale

Underground Railroad Marker
U.S. Route 41

This marks one of several points once used to assist fugitive slaves seeking freedom and safety in Canada. One such slave, William Trail, liked Indiana so much he decided to stay and go into farming. His efforts were successful, and he became one of many prosperous farmers active in Union County, Indiana.

Fountain City

Levi Coffin House
North Main Street

Born in North Carolina in 1798, Levi Coffin, a Quaker abolitionist who was also known as "The President of the Underground Railroad," used his own home in Fountain City as a way station for runaway slaves. Between 1827 and 1847, Coffin hid more than 300 slaves heading for Illinois, Michigan, or Canada.

Coffin left Fountain City for Ohio, where he continued his activities, eventually helping over 3,000 slaves escape from the South—he was still engaged in the resettlement of former slaves long after the Civil War had ended. Coffin died in Avondale, Ohio in 1877.

◆ IOWA

Clinton

Underground Railroad Marker
Sixth and South Second Streets

Before the Lafayette Hotel was built, the small house that once stood at this location had been a point of shelter and sustenance for fugitive slaves escaping from Missouri (Iowa was a free territory by virtue of both the Northwest Ordinance of 1787 and the Missouri Compromise of 1820). Many Quakers, who had come to the state before the Civil War, took great pains to maintain an efficient and effective Underground Railroad network.

Des Moines

Fort Des Moines Provisional Army Officer Training School
Southwest Ninth Street

Fort Des Moines Provisional Army Officer Camp was opened on June 15, 1917, for the purpose of training talented black soldiers for officer's rank. On October 14, 1917, 639 black soldiers were commissioned as second lieutenants and assigned to the American Expeditionary Forces being sent to France to fight in World War I. Black units led by men trained at the school were assembled in France as the 92nd Division. The camp was abandoned at the end of the war, and the site was designated a National Historic Landmark on May 30, 1974.

Sioux City

Pearl Street

Sioux City was a refuge for many slaves escaping from Missouri. Pearl Street, once the city's main thoroughfare, was named for a black pioneer who had arrived in the town by boat more than a century earlier and achieved widespread popularity as a cook.

◆ KANSAS

Beeler

George Washington Carver Homestead

Along Route K-96 in Ness County lies the plot of land once homesteaded by George Washington Carver, the famed black agricultural scientist. He spent two years here before attending college in Iowa.

Nicodemus

Nicodemus Colony

Located along U.S. Route 24, two miles west of the Rooks-Graham county line, the Nicodemus Colony is the last of three now virtually deserted colonies that were founded by the Exodusters—a group of black homesteaders who migrated to Kansas during the 1870s. The name "Nicodemus" was derived from a slave who, according to legend, foretold the coming of the Civil War.

Arriving in 1877, the first settlers lived in dugouts and burrows during the cold weather. From the outset, they were plagued by crop failures. Although never more than 500 in number, they managed nonetheless to establish a community—with teachers, ministers, and civil servants. The state of Kansas has commemorated this site with a historical marker located in a roadside park in Nicodemus.

Osawatomie

John Brown Memorial State Park
Tenth and Main Streets

This state park, named in honor of insurrectionist John Brown, contains the cabin in which he lived during his brief sojourn in Kansas.

Topeka

Sumner Elementary School
330 Western Avenue

In 1951, Linda Brown was refused enrollment in Sumner Elementary School because she was black. What followed was the landmark case *Brown v. Board of Education of Topeka.* Upon hearing the case, the U.S. Supreme Court concluded that "separate education facilities are inherently unequal," striking down all legal basis for segregation in public schools.

◆ KENTUCKY

Berea

Lincoln Hall
Berea College

Opened in 1855, Berea College was the first college established in the United States for the specific purpose of educating blacks and whites together. The school's Lincoln Hall, built in 1887, was designated as a National Historic Landmark on December 2, 1974.

Lincoln Ridge

Whitney M. Young Jr. Birthplace

Lincoln Ridge, Kentucky was the birthplace and boyhood home of Whitney M. Young, Jr. Young served as executive director of the National Urban League from 1961 to 1971.

◆ LOUISIANA

New Orleans

James H. Dillard House
571 Audubon Street

This house served as the home of James Dillard from 1894 to 1913. Dillard played an important role in black education in the nineteenth century, strengthening vocational and teacher-training programs. Dillard's home was designated a National Historic Landmark on De-

cember 2, 1975. Dillard University, founded in 1869, was named for this educator.

Louisiana State Museum

The Louisiana State Museum contains a tablet inscribed in the memory of Norbert Rillieux, inventor of the sugar evaporating pan that revolutionized the sugar refining industry.

Melrose

Yucca Plantation
Route 119

The Yucca Plantation in Melrose, Louisiana was established in the eighteenth century by a former slave and wealthy business woman. The African House located on the plantation, a unique structure with an umbrella-like roof, is believed to be of direct African derivation. The site was declared a National Historic Landmark on May 30, 1974.

◆ MARYLAND

Annapolis

Banneker-Douglass Museum
84 Franklin Street

This museum, located in the city's historic district, is dedicated to the black surveyor and inventor Benjamin Banneker and the abolitionist Frederick Douglass, both born in Maryland.

Matthew Henson Plaque
Maryland State House

The Matthew Henson Plaque honors the memory of the only man to accompany Admiral Robert E. Peary on all of his polar expeditions. On April 6, 1909, Henson became the first man actually to reach the North Pole. Peary himself, barely able to walk, arrived there after Henson had taken a reading of his position and proudly planted the U.S. flag.

Baltimore

Benjamin Banneker Marker
Westchester Avenue at Westchester School

This marker in Baltimore, Maryland is a tribute to Benjamin Banneker, the black mathematician, astronomer, and inventor who, in 1792, produced an almanac regarded as among the most reliable. His scientific knowledge led to his assignment as a member of the surveying and planning team that helped lay out the nation's capital.

Beulah M. Davis Collection
Soper Library
Morgan State University

Morgan State University houses an interesting collection of artifacts on Benjamin Banneker, noted astronomer, compiler of almanacs, and—together with Pierre-Charles L'Enfant—surveyor of the District of Columbia. It also houses a number of artifacts on Frederick Douglass and Matthew Henson.

Frederick Douglass Monument
Morgan State University

On the campus of Morgan State University is the Frederick Douglass memorial statue created by the noted black sculptor James Lewis. The work, completed in 1956, stands 12 feet tall with pedestal. Its simple inscription reads "Frederick Douglass 1817–1895 Humanitarian, Statesman."

Rockville

Uncle Tom's Cabin

This is site of the log cabin believed to have been the birthplace of Josiah Henson, the escaped slave immortalized as Uncle Tom in Harriet Beecher Stowe's famous abolitionist study.

Born in 1789, Henson was sold at auction at an early age and transferred among many masters until he managed to escape in 1830. After setting up a community for fugitive slaves in Dawn, Canada, Henson frequently returned to the South to liberate others. Meeting with Stowe, Henson outlined his slave experiences, which later formed the bases for her celebrated story—in the introduction to Henson's autobiography, published some years later, she acknowledged his story as the source of her own tale.

◆ MASSACHUSETTS

Boston

Abiel Smith School and Museum of Afro-American History
46 Joy Street

Now housing the Museum of Afro-American History, this building, built in 1834, was the site of the city's first school for black children.

African American National Historic Site

This area contains the largest concentration of pre-Civil War black history sites anywhere in the United States. Among them are the African Meeting House and the Abiel Smith School.

African Meeting House
8 Smiths Court

This is the site of the first black church in Boston and oldest surviving black church building in the United States. It was designated a National Historic Site on May 30, 1974, and is a part of the Boston African American National Historic Site.

Bunker Hill Monument

Standing in the Charlestown district of Boston, Massachusetts, the Bunker Hill Monument commemorates the famous Revolutionary War battle which—contrary to popular belief—was actually fought on Breed's Hill on June 17, 1775. A number of blacks fought alongside the colonists during the battle, including Peter Salem, Salem Poor, Titus Coburn, Cato Howe, Alexander Ames, Seymour Burr, Pomp Fiske, and Prince Hall, founder of the Negro Masonic order.

Crispus Attucks Monument

The Crispus Attucks Monument, located in the Boston Common, was dedicated in 1888 to the five victims of the Boston Massacre—Crispus Attucks, Samuel Maverick, James Caldwell, Samuel Gray, and Patrick Carr. The site of the Massacre is marked by a plaque on State Street, near the Old State House.

Attucks is believed by many historians to have been the same man who in 1750 was advertised as a runaway black slave from Framingham, Massachusetts. Although a stranger to Boston, he led a group that converged on a British garrison which was quartered in King Street to help enforce the Townshend Acts. One of the soldiers of the garrison panicked and fired, and Attucks was the first to fall. Gray and Caldwell were also killed on the same spot; Maverick and Carr died later of wounds sustained during the clash. The British soldiers were later tried for murder but acquitted. The five men are buried a few blocks away in Granary Burying Ground, together with such famous Revolutionary figures as John Adams and John Hancock, as well as Governor William Bradford of Plymouth Colony.

William C. Nell House
3 Smith Court

From the 1830s to the end of the Civil War, William C. Nell was one of the leading black abolitionists. Born in

Crispus Attucks Monument.

Boston, he studied law in the office of William I. Bowditch. Nell refused to take an oath to be admitted to the bar because he did not want to support the Constitution of the United States, which compromised on the issue of slavery. He then began organizing meetings and lecturing in support of the antislavery movement. The Nell house was designated a National Historic Landmark on May 11, 1976.

Colonel Robert Gould Shaw Monument
Beacon and Park Streets

Executed by the famed sculptor Augustus Saint-Gaudens, the Shaw monument depicts Colonel Robert Gould Shaw and the 54th Massachusetts Volunteers, a black regiment that served in the Union Army during the Civil War. The regiment particularly distinguished itself in the battle for Fort Wagner, during which Colonel Shaw was killed. Sergeant William H. Carney's valiant exploits during this battle later earned him the Medal of Honor.

Cambridge

Maria Baldwin House
196 Prospect and H Streets

This house was the permanent address of Maria Baldwin from 1892 until her death in 1922. Baldwin served as principal and later as "master" of the Agassiz School in Cambridge, as a leader in organizations such as the League for Community Service, as a gifted and popular speaker on the lecture circuit, and as a sponsor of charitable activities such as establishing the first kindergarten in Atlanta, Georgia. Baldwin exemplified the achievements that were attainable by an African American in a predominantly white society. The house was designated as a National Historic Landmark on May 11, 1976.

Phillis Wheatley Folio
Harvard University

During her celebrated trip to England in 1773, Phillis Wheatley was presented with a folio edition of John Milton's *Paradise Lost*, which now is housed in the library of Harvard University in Cambridge, Massachusetts.

Wheatley, who came to America in 1761 as a child aged seven or eight, made rapid strides in mastering the English language, and by the time she was 14, had already completed her first poem. Always in delicate health, she died in Boston on December 5, 1784.

Central Village

Paul Cuffe Memorial

Paul Cuffe, son of a freedman, was born in 1759 and became a prosperous merchant seaman. Cuffe resolved to use his wealth and position to campaign for the extension of civil rights to blacks. On one occasion, he refused to pay his personal property tax on the grounds that he was being denied full citizenship rights; a court of law eventually upheld his action, whereupon he was granted the same privileges and immunities enjoyed by white citizens of the state. In 1815, Cuffe transported 38 blacks to Sierra Leone in what was intended to launch a systematic attempt to repatriate the black inhabitants of the United States. However, with the growth of abolitionist sentiment, the repatriation movement lost favor.

Plaque honoring Colonel Shaw and the 25th Infantry.

Great Barrington

W. E. B. Du Bois Homesite
Route 23

This location served as the boyhood home of William Edward Burghardt Du Bois from 1868 to 1873. Du Bois, the prominent black sociologist and writer, was a major figure in the civil rights movement during the first half of the twentieth century. Du Bois fought discrimination against blacks through his writing, as a college professor, and as a lecturer. The Du Bois homesite was designated on May 11, 1976 as a National Historic Landmark.

Lynn

Jan Ernst Matzeliger Statue

The Matzeliger Statue is one of the few extant memorials to this black inventor, whose shoe-lace machine revolutionized the industry and made mass-produced shoes a reality in the United States. A native of Dutch Guiana, Matzeliger came to the United States in 1876, learned the cobbler's trade, and set out to design a machine that would simplify shoe manufacturing. Always sickly, he died at an early age, unable to capitalize on his successful patent, which was purchased by the United Shoe Machinery Company of Boston. After his death, Matzeliger was awarded a gold medal at the 1901 Pan-American Exposition.

New Bedford

New Bedford Whaling Museum

The museum maintains a treasury of whaling artifacts and information, including the names and histories of blacks who participated in the whaling industry. The museum also houses versions of the toggle harpoon—invented by Lewis Temple, a black metalsmith—which revolutionized the whaling industry.

Suffolk County

William Monroe Trotter House
97 Sawyer Avenue

This house in Suffolk County, Massachusetts served as the home of William Monroe Trotter, noted black journalist and civil rights activist. Trotter, the first black member of Phi Beta Kappa, worked as an insurance and mortgage broker in Boston from 1897 to 1906. In 1901, he became publisher and editor of *The Guardian*, a crusading newspaper, until his death in 1934. The Sawyer Avenue house was designated a National Historic Landmark on May 11, 1976.

Westport

Paul Cuffe Farm and Memorial
1504 Drift Road

Paul Cuffe was a self-educated black man who became a prosperous merchant. He was a pioneer in the struggle for minority rights in the eighteenth and early nineteenth centuries, and was active in the movement for black resettlement in Africa. The Paul Cuffe Farm was designated a National Historic Landmark on May 30, 1974.

◆ MICHIGAN

Battle Creek

Sojourner Truth Grave Site
Oakhill Cemetery

This site in the Oakhill Cemetery marks the resting place of one of the most powerful abolitionist and lecturers of the nineteenth century, Sojourner Truth. Sojourner settled in Battle Creek after the Civil War, but continued to travel on lecture tours until a few years before her death on November 26, 1883.

Cassopolis

Underground Railroad Marker
Route M-60

This marks one of many as rest places used by slaves escaping from the South to Canada. The marker is located approximately two miles east of Cassopolis.

Detroit

Douglass-Brown Marker
William Webb House
East Congress Street

The Douglass-Brown Marker in Detroit, Michigan indicates the site of the William Webb House, where fellow abolitionists Frederick Douglass and John Brown met in March of 1859 to map out the strategy for the raid on the federal armory at Harpers Ferry, West Virginia. Douglass was strongly opposed to this course of action.

Sojourner Truth's grave site.

Nevertheless, on October 16, 1959, Brown's forces seized the fort, only to be overtaken by federal troops two days later.

Ralph Bunche Birthplace
5685 West Fort Street

A plaque marks the site of the birthplace of the undersecretary-general of the United Nations and Nobel Peace Prize winner, Ralph Bunche, who was born in 1927. Bunche, the first African American to receive this honor, was awarded the prize in 1950 for his work as a United Nations mediator following the Arab-Israeli war of 1948.

Elmwood Cemetery
1200 Elmwood

Elmwood Cemetery contains the grave sites of 14 members of the 102nd U.S. Colored Regiment.

Elijah McCoy Home Site
5730 Lincoln

A plaque marks the site of one of Elijah McCoy's residences. McCoy, born in Ontario, Canada, settled in the Detroit area, opening a manufacturing company in 1870. McCoy is best known for his lubricating device.

Motown Museum
2648 West Grand Boulevard

This location served as the early headquarters of Motown Records, founded in 1958 by songwriter and independent record producer, Berry Gordy, Jr. Performers including the Four Tops, Marvin Gaye, the Jackson Five, Martha and the Vandellas, Smokey Robinson, the Supremes, the Temptations, Mary Wells, and Stevie Wonder, all played an important part in the early success of Motown. In 1972, the company moved its headquarters from Detroit to Los Angeles, California, but a museum containing restored sound studios and memen toes is maintained at this site.

National Museum of the Tuskegee Airmen
Historic Fort Wayne

The museum houses memorabilia of the Tuskegee Airmen, an all black unit of fighter pilots active during World War II. The airmen, who were trained at Alabama's Tuskegee Institute, played an important role in the combat against racial discrimination in the armed forces.

Underground Railroad Marker
Second Baptist Church
441 Monroe

One of many stops along the Underground Railroad, the basement of the Second Baptist Church was used to hide runaway slaves. The church, founded in 1836, is one of the oldest African American congregations in the Midwest.

Second Baptist Church, 1922.

Marshall

Crosswhite Boulder
Michigan Avenue and Mansion Street

The Crosswhite Boulder in Marshall, Michigan marks the site of two confrontations that occurred in 1846 in defense of Adam Crosswhite, a fugitive slave who had fled from Kentucky. The Crosswhite case is said to have been instrumental in the enactment of the Fugitive Slave Law of 1850.

◆ MINNESOTA

Minneapolis-St. Paul

Fort Snelling State Park

Fort Snelling was the outpost in the Wisconsin Territory to which the slave later to become known as Dred Scott was transported from Illinois in 1836. Scott met and married his wife Harriet at the fort and saw his first child born there. Later taken to Missouri by his master, he filed suit for his freedom and became a national figure as his case was tried, from 1847 to 1857, before numerous tribunals en route to the U.S. Supreme Court.

Scott argued that he should be considered free by virtue of his having previously resided in Illinois and at Fort Snelling.

◆ MISSISSIPPI

Alcorn

Oakland Memorial Chapel, Alcorn State University

Alcorn State University, founded in 1871, is the oldest black land grant college in the United States. The chapel on the Alcorn University campus was built in 1838. The chapel was designated a National Historic Landmark on May 11, 1976.

Mound Bayou

Isiah Thornton Montgomery House
West Main Street

This location served as the home of Isiah Thornton Montgomery, who in 1887 founded the town of Mound Bayou—a place where black Americans could obtain social, political, and economic rights in a white supremacist South. The house was declared a National Historic Landmark on May 11, 1976.

Natchez

Natchez National Cemetery

This cemetery is the final resting place of many black war dead, including landsman Wilson Brown, a Medal of Honor recipient during the Civil War. Brown and seaman John Lawson received their medals for courage in action while serving aboard the U.S.S. *Hartford* in its Mobile Bay engagement of August 5, 1864.

◆ MISSOURI

Diamond

George Washington Carver Birthplace and National Monument
U.S. Route 71

Located in a park in Diamond, Missouri, Carver National Monument commemorates the place where the great black scientist George Washington Carver was born and spent his early childhood.

Kidnapped when he was just six weeks old, Carver was eventually ransomed for a horse valued at $300.

Raised in Missouri by the family of Moses Carver, his owner, he made his way through Minnesota, Kansas, and Iowa before being "discovered" by Booker T. Washington in 1896. That same year, Carver joined the faculty of Tuskegee Institute, where he conducted most of the research for which he is now famous.

The monument, one of the first created in honor of an African American, consists of a statue of Carver as a boy, and encloses several trails leading to places of which he was particularly fond. The park also houses a visitors' center and a museum displaying many of his discoveries and personal belongings.

Jefferson City

Lincoln University

The more than $6,000 raised by the 62nd and 65th U.S. Colored infantries constituted the initial endowment for a 22-square-foot room in which classes were held in 1866 at what is now Lincoln University. Known then as the Lincoln Institute, the school began receiving state aid to expand its teacher-training program in 1870. It became a state institution nine years later, and instituted college-level courses in 1887. It has been known as Lincoln University since 1921, and has offered graduate programs since 1940.

Kansas City

Mutual Musicians Association Building
1823 Highland Avenue

This building served as the home of the American Federation of Musicians Local 627 from the 1920s to the 1940s. Its members created the Kansas City style of jazz and included such jazz greats as Count Basie, Hershel Evens, Lester Young, and Charlie Parker.

St. Louis

Old Courthouse
Jefferson National Expansion Memorial
11 North Fourth Street

It was in the Old Courthouse in 1847 that Dred Scott first filed suit to gain his freedom; for the next ten years, the Dred Scott case was a burning political and social issue throughout America. In 1857, the case reached the Supreme Court, where Chief Justice Roger Taney handed down the decision that slaves could not become free by escaping or by being taken into free territory, nor could they be considered American citizens. Ironically, a few weeks after the decision was rendered, Scott was set free by his new owner. He died a year later.

Houston Hall, Lincoln University.

Scott Joplin House
2685-A Delmar Avenue

Known as "king of ragtime," Scott Joplin was born in Texarkana, Texas but he left home to earn a living when he was 14 years of age. Joplin played piano in the St. Louis and Sedalia, Missouri area, and this house built in the 1890s is the last surviving residence of Joplin. The house was declared a National Historic Landmark on December 8, 1976.

◆ MONTANA

Big Horn Station

Fort Manuel Marker

Captain William Clark and his party, which included a slave named York, camped at this site on July 26, 1806, a year before Manuel Lisa established Montana's first trading post. This site also was chosen by Major Andrew Henry as the Rocky Mountain Fur Company's first trading post; the leader of that expedition was Edward Rose, another of the famed black mountain men and explorers active in the territory.

◆ NEVADA

Reno

Beckwourth Trail

In the early days of pioneer settlement, the barren stretch of trail between Reno and the California line was the last obstacle before passing through to the West Coast. The original trail was laid out by a black explorer, Jim Beckwourth, one of the legendary mountain men.

◆ NEW HAMPSHIRE

Jaffrey

Amos Fortune Grave Site

This grave site marks the resting place of the eighteenth-century African slave, Amos Fortune, who purchased his freedom in 1770 at the age of 60 and went on to become one of the leading citizens of Jaffrey, his adopted hometown. Nine years after purchasing his freedom, Fortune was able to buy freedom for his wife, Violet Baldwin, and his adopted daughter, Celyndia. In 1781, he moved to Jaffrey and set himself up as a tanner, employing both black and white apprentices. In 1795, six years before his death, Fortune founded the Jaffrey Social Library, and in his will directed that money be left to the church and to the local school district. (The school fund begun by Fortune is still in existence.)

The Fortune house and barn still stand intact, and both Fortune and his wife lie in the meeting house burial ground. Fortune's freedom papers and several receipt slips for the sale of his leather are on file at the Jaffrey Public Library.

◆ NEW JERSEY

Lawnside

Site of Free Haven

Located just east of the city of Camden, New Jersey, is the town of Lawnside, originally known as Free Haven. The town served as a major stop on the Underground Railroad, and following the Civil War attracted a large population of freed slaves from the South.

Red Bank

T. Thomas Fortune House
94 West Bergen Place

From 1901 to 1915, this location was the home of black journalist T. Thomas Fortune. Born a slave in Marianna, Florida, Fortune was freed by the Emancipation Proclamation in 1863. He received training as a printer and founded the *New York Age* newspaper. The Fortune House was designated a National Historic Landmark on December 8, 1976.

◆ NEW MEXICO

Lincoln

Old Court House

During the Lincoln County Cattle War of 1877–1878, Billy the Kid, the notorious outlaw, was held in custody at the Old Court House in Lincoln, New Mexico, now a frontier museum. Black cowhands were involved on both sides of this struggle and, on one occasion, a group of black cavalry men is said to have surrounded Billy the Kid during a particularly bloody battle.

Zuni

Zuni Pueblo

Zuni Pueblo was discovered in 1539 by Estevanico, a Moorish slave, who was one of the original party of Spanish explorers to land in Tampa Bay in 1528.

Having heard of the legend of the Seven Cities of Gold, reputed to be located in the Southwest, Estevanico signed on as an advance scout for an expedition led by a Father Marco. Often traveling ahead of the main party, Estevanico sent most of his messages back via friendly Indians. His last message—a giant cross emblematic of a major discovery—led the expedition to the Zuni Pueblo, which Estevanico apparently thought formed part of the legendary Seven Cities. By the time the expedition arrived, however, the suspicious Zuni had already put Estevanico to death. Today, Estevanico is credited with the European discovery of the territory comprising the states of Arizona and New Mexico.

◆ NEW YORK

Albany

Emancipation Proclamation
New York State Library

The New York State Library houses President Abraham Lincoln's original draft of the Emancipation Proclamation, which was issued in September 1862. The draft was purchased by Gerritt Smith, a wealthy abolitionist and patron of the famed revolutionary John Brown. The January 1, 1863 version of the proclamation resides in the National Archives of Washington, D.C.

Auburn

Harriet Tubman House
180 South Street

Born a slave in Maryland, Harriet Tubman escaped from slavery at the age of 25, only to return to the South at least 19 times to lead others to freedom. Rewards of up to $40,000 were offered for her capture, but she was never arrested, nor did she ever lose one of her "passengers" in transit.

During the Civil War, she served as a spy for Union forces. At the close of the war, Tubman settled in this house in Red Bank, New Jersey years after it had outlived its original function as a major way station on the north-bound freedom route of fugitive slaves. In 1953, the house was restored at a cost of $21,000. The house now stands as a monument to the woman believed to have led some 300 slaves to freedom via the Underground Railroad.

Greater New York City

Abyssinian Baptist Church
132 West 138th Street

The Abyssinian Baptist Church is one of the oldest and largest black Baptist congregations in the United States. The church building was completed in 1923, under the leadership of the Reverend Adam Clayton Powell, Sr. In 1937, Powell retired and was succeeded by his son Adam Clayton Powell, Jr., who was elected to the U.S. Congress in 1960.

Amsterdam News Founding Place
2293 Seventh Avenue

The *Amsterdam News* was founded on December 4, 1909 in the home of James H. Anderson on 132 West 65th Street in New York City. At that time one of only 50 black "news sheets" in the country, the *Amsterdam News* had a staff of ten, consisted of six printed pages, and sold for two cents a copy. Since then, the paper has been printed at several Harlem addresses. This building was designated a National Historic Landmark on May 11, 1976.

Apollo Theater
West 125th Street

The Apollo Theater in Harlem, once an entertainment mecca for all races, is one of the last great vaudeville houses in the United States.

Louis Armstrong House
3456 107th Street, Corona, Queens

For years this was the home of Louis Armstrong, the famous jazz musician whose talents entertained millions throughout the world. Whenever Armstrong was at his Corona home in Queens, New York on a break from his concert dates, he was a favorite with neighborhood youngsters; he would often entertain them in his home and on the street. The house was designated a National Historic Landmark on May 11, 1976.

Ralph Bunche House
115-125 Grosvenor Road, Kew Gardens, Queens

The house served as the home of Ralph Bunche, the distinguished black diplomat and undersecretary to the United Nations. In 1950 Bunche was awarded the Nobel Peace Prize for his contribution to peace in the Middle East. The house was designated a National Historic Landmark on May 11, 1976.

Will Marion Cook Residence
221 West 138th Street

This residence in New York City served as the home of the early-twentieth century black composer Will Marion Cook, whom Duke Ellington called "the master of all masters of our people." Cook was born in Washington, DC. He began studying violin at 13 years of age, and at 15 he won a scholarship to study with Joseph Joachim at the Berlin Conservatory. Syncopated ragtime music was introduced to theatergoers in New York City for the first time with Cook's operetta *Clorinda*. The residence was designated a National Historic Landmark on May 11, 1976.

Edward Kennedy "Duke" Ellington Residence
935 St. Nicholas Avenue, Apt. 4A

When Duke Ellington recorded "Take the A Train" to Harlem, he meant just that, because the A train express stops on St. Nicholas Avenue and was the quickest and fastest way for Ellington to get home. This St. Nicholas Avenue address was the long-term residence of Ellington, who has been regarded by critics as the most creative black composer of the twentieth century. The residence was designated a National Historic Landmark on May 11, 1976.

Fraunces Tavern
Broad and Pearl Streets

One of the most famous landmarks in New York City, Fraunces Tavern was bought in 1762 from a wealthy Huguenot by Samuel Fraunces, a West Indian of black and French extraction. Known as the Queen's Head Tavern, it served as a meeting place for numerous patriots.

On April 24, 1774, the Sons of Liberty and the Vigilance Committee met at the tavern to map out much of the strategy later used during the war. George Washington himself was a frequenter of the tavern, as were many of his senior officers. Washington's association with Fraunces continued for a number of years, with Fraunces eventually coming to be known as Washington's "Steward of the Household" in New York City. It was at Fraunces Tavern, in fact, that Washington took leave of his trusted officers in 1783 before retiring to Mount Vernon.

Much of the tavern's original furnishings and decor are still intact. The third floor, now a museum, contains several Revolutionary War artifacts, while the fourth floor holds a historical library featuring paintings by John Ward Dunsmore. A restaurant is maintained on the ground floor.

Abyssinian Baptist Church

Freedom National Bank
275 West 125th Street

Freedom National Bank, Harlem's first black-chartered and black-run commercial bank, was founded in 1965.

Matthew Henson Residence
Dunbar Apartments, 246 West 150th Street

This residence served as the home of Matthew Henson, the black explorer who was an assistant to Robert E. Peary. Henson's best known achievement came in 1909, when he became the first man to reach the North Pole. The residence was designated a National Historic Landmark on May 15, 1975.

Hotel Theresa
2090 Seventh Avenue at 125th Street

Built in 1913, the Hotel Theresa was once a luxury hotel serving white clientele from lower Manhattan and accommodating "white only" dinner patrons in its luxu-

The Apollo Theater.

Fraunces Tavern

rious Skyline Room. In 1936, a corporation headed by Love B. Woods tried to take over the hotel and transform it into a black business establishment. This move failed when Seidenberg Estates, the realtor, set a price beyond the reach of the group. Woods, however, was eventually able purchase the hotel, which now serves as an office building.

James Weldon Johnson Residence
187 West 135th Street

From 1925 to 1938, this residence in New York City was the home of James Weldon Johnson, the versatile black composer of popular songs as well as poet, writer, general secretary of the NAACP and civil rights activist. Johnson is best known for composing the song "Lift Every Voice and Sing," which has been called the black national anthem. Johnson was born in Jacksonville, Florida and did graduate work at Columbia University. The residence was named a National Historic Landmark on May 11, 1976.

Maiden Lane-The First Slave Revolt in New York

In 1712, on Maiden Lane and William Street, the first organized slave revolt in New York City occurred. Approximately 30 slaves joined and attempted to fight their way to freedom. Many people were injured in the melée that ensued as the slaves escaped to the woods with the militia close behind. Surrounded in the woods, several slaves committed suicide. The rest were captured and subsequently executed.

Malcolm X Residence
23-11 97th Street, East Elmhurst, Queens

Black Muslim leader Malcolm X resided at this location with his family from 1954 until his death in 1965. The house, which was owned by the Nation of Islam while he and his family lived there, was the scene of a fire-bombing on February 13, 1965. Fortunately, Malcolm and his family escaped without injury.

Claude McKay Residence
180 West 135th Street

From 1941 to 1946, this residence in New York City was the home of the black poet and writer Claude McKay, who has often been called the father of the Harlem Renaissance. McKay was born in Jamaica, British West Indies and was in Kingston's constabulary prior to coming to the United States. His residence was named a National Historic Landmark on December 8, 1976.

Florence Mills Residence
220 West 135th Street

This residence was the home of the popular black singer who in the 1920s achieved stardom both on Broadway and in Europe. The Florence Mills' residence was designated a National Historic Landmark on December 8, 1976.

Paul Robeson Residence
555 Edgecomb Avenue

This residence in New York City was the home of the famous black actor and singer, Paul Robeson. In the 1940s and the 1950s, Robeson suffered public condemnation for his socialist political sympathies even while he was widely acclaimed for his artistic talents. The residence was named a National Historic Landmark on December 8, 1976.

John Roosevelt "Jackie" Robinson House
5224 Tilden Street, Brooklyn

This house served as the home of Jackie Robinson, the baseball player who in 1947 became the first black to play in the major leagues. His baseball contract broke down the color barrier to black participation in professional sports. While a Brooklyn Dodger, Robinson lived for many years in the same borough of New York City where he played baseball. The residence was designated a National Historic Landmark on May 11, 1976.

St. George's Episcopal Church
Third Avenue and First Street

Located in New York City, this was the church home of Harry Thacker Burleigh, the black composer, arranger, and singer who helped establish the Negro spiritual as an integral part of American culture. The church was designated a National Historical Landmark on December 8, 1976.

Schomburg Center for Research in Black Culture
515 Malcolm X Boulevard

Part of the New York Public Library System, the Schomburg Center for Research in Black Culture is devoted to documenting black experience around the world. The collection is built around the private library of Arthur A. Schomburg, a Puerto Rican of African descent. It contains books, pamphlets, manuscripts, photographs, art objects, and recordings that cover virtually every aspect of black life—from ancient Africa to present-day black America. Material in the Schomburg is not circulated but can be used or viewed in the library.

Sugar Hill, Harlem

Sugar Hill is a handsome residential section in uptown Harlem, New York. It is bordered on the west by Amsterdam Avenue, on the north by 160th Street, on the east by Colonial Park, and on the south by 145th Street. An area of tall apartment buildings and private homes, it is peopled largely by middle-class blacks, sometimes referred to as the *black bourgeoisie*. Its only counterparts in the area of central Harlem are Riverton and Lenox Terrace.

Booker T. Washington Plaque
New York University

Booker T. Washington, educator and founder of Tuskegee Institute, is the only black honored by a plaque in the Hall of Fame at New York University.

Roy Wilkins House
147-15 Village Road, Jamaica, Queens

This location served as the home of civil rights leader and former NAACP executive secretary Roy Wilkins from 1952 until his death in 1981. Wilkins had served as executive secretary of the NAACP for 22 years before retiring in 1977.

Greenburgh

Villa Lewaro

Designed by the noted black architect Vertner Woodson Tandy for Madame C. J. Walker, the successful cosmetics manufacturer, Villa Lewaro, located in Greenburgh, New York, illustrates the achievements of blacks in both architecture and business. The Villa Lewaro was declared a National Historic Landmark on May 11, 1976.

Lake Placid

John Brown House and Grave Site

Just six miles south of Lake Placid on Route 86A is the farm Brown purchased after he had left Ohio, now the location of his grave. The farm was part of 100,000 acres set aside for both freedmen and slaves by Gerritt Smith, a wealthy abolitionist. Smith hoped to build an independent community peopled by former slaves who had learned farming and other trades. Brown joined Smith in the venture, but the idea failed to take hold and was eventually abandoned. Brown lived there until he joined the free-soil fight in Kansas.

Rochester

Frederick Douglass Monument
Central Avenue and Paul Street

New York Governor Theodore Roosevelt dedicated the Frederick Douglass Monument in 1899, four years after Douglass' death. In Rochester, Douglass edited his newspaper, *The North Star;* Douglass was buried in Mount Hope Cemetery, not far from the memorial.

South Granville

Lemuel Haynes House
Route 149

This house, located in South Granville, Washington County, New York, was built in 1793. It served as the home of Lemuel Haynes, the first black ordained minister in the United States. Haynes was also the first black to minister to a white congregation. The South Granville home site was declared a National Historic Landmark on May 15, 1975.

◆ NORTH CAROLINA

Durham

North Carolina Mutual Life Insurance Company
114-116 West Parish Street

This Parish Street address is the home office of North Carolina Mutual Life Insurance Company, a black-managed enterprise that was founded in 1898 and achieved financial success in an age of Jim Crow. The site was declared a National Historic Landmark on May 15, 1975.

Milton

The Yellow Tavern

For more than 30 years, the Yellow Tavern (also known as Union Tavern) was the workshop of Tom Day, one of the great black artisans and furniture makers of the Deep South prior to the Civil War. Day began making hand-wrought mahogany furniture in 1818, and within five years accumulated enough money to convert the old Yellow Tavern into a miniature factory. Both white apprentices and black slaves were taught this skilled trade under his coveted tutelage. Day's artistry was so revered by the citizens of Milton that they went to great pains to secure a special dispensation from a North Carolina law that made it illegal for any free black or mulatto to migrate into the state. The Yellow Tavern was declared a National Historic Landmark by the Department of the Interior on May 15, 1975. Examples of Day's furniture can be seen in the North Carolina State Museum.

Raleigh

John Chavis Memorial Park
East Lenoir and Worth Streets

This park in Raleigh, North Carolina is named after John Chavis, a black educator and preacher who founded an interracial school in Raleigh, which later numbered among its graduates several important public figures including senators, congressmen, and governors. As a result of the abortive Nat Turner slave rebellion in 1831, however, blacks were barred from preaching in North Carolina, obliging Chavis to retire from the pulpit. He died in 1838.

◆ OHIO

Akron

John Brown Monument

The John Brown Monument was built in honor of the abolitionist whose ill-fated Harpers Ferry revolt led to his conviction for treason and execution by hanging in 1859.

Cincinnati

Harriet Beecher Stowe House
2950 Gilbert Avenue

The Harriet Beecher Stowe House has been preserved as a memorial to the internationally known author of *Uncle Tom's Cabin*. The house served as the Beecher family residence from 1832 to 1836.

Dayton

Paul Laurence Dunbar House
219 North Summit Street

Paul Laurence Dunbar, the first black poet after Phillis Wheatley to gain anything approaching a national reputation in the United States, was also the first to concentrate on dialect poetry and exclusively black themes. His first collection of poetry, *Oak and Ivy*, was published before he was 20. By 1896, his book *Majors and Minors* had won critical favor in a *Harper's Weekly* review. Dunbar contracted tuberculosis in 1899 and was in failing health until his death on February 9, 1906.

Oberlin

John Mercer Langston House
207 East College Street

Elected township clerk in 1855, John Mercer Langston is believed to have been the first black American to be elected to public office. Langston later served for the Freedman's Bureau, became the first dean of the Howard University Law School, and served as a U.S. Minister Resident to Haiti. The Langston House was designated a National Historic Landmark on May 15, 1975.

Oberlin College

Before the Civil War, Oberlin was one of the centers of underground abolitionist planning. The college was one of the first institutions to graduate blacks and women; three of John Brown's raiding party at Harpers Ferry were identified as blacks from Oberlin.

After the war, Oberlin was able to devote more time to its stated mission: providing quality education to all regardless of race. Among the distinguished alumni of Oberlin was Blanche K. Bruce, who served a full term in the U.S. Senate (1875–1881).

Ripley

John Rankin House and Museum

An Underground Railroad station prior to the Civil War, the John Rankin House in Ripley, Ohio, is believed to have been the haven of the fugitive slave on whose story the novelist Harriet Beecher Stowe based the flight incident in *Uncle Tom's Cabin*.

Wilberforce

Colonel Charles Young House
Route 42 between Cliffton and Stevenson Roads

This address was the residence of the highest ranking black officer in World War I and the first black military attache. Colonel Charles Young was the son of former slaves and was born in Mays Lick, Kentucky. The Army had declared Young unfit physically because of high blood pressure; to prove that he was physically fit, he rode horseback 500 miles from Wilberforce to Washington, DC, in 16 days. The Army, however, still stuck by its ruling. The house was declared a National Historic Landmark on May 30, 1974.

Wilberforce University

Established by the Methodist Church in 1856, Wilberforce University is named for William Wilberforce, an English abolitionist. In 1863 the school was purchased by the African Methodist Episcopal Church; in 1981 the institution was sold to the state of Ohio. Wilberforce is the site of the National Afro-American Museum.

◆ OKLAHOMA

Boley

Boley Historic District

This is the largest of the black towns established in Oklahoma to provide African Americans with the opportunity for self-government in an era of white supremacy and segregation. The Boley Historic District was designated a National Historic Landmark on May 15, 1975.

Ponca City

101 Ranch

During the latter part of the nineteenth century, the 101 Ranch was one of the largest and most famous in the West. The ranch was established in 1879, and in its prime it employed several black cowhands, the most celebrated of whom was Bill Pickett.

The originator of the art of bulldogging or steer wrestling, Pickett also perfected a unique style unlike any used by contemporary rodeo participants. In March 1932, though then in his seventies, Pickett was still active—the last of the original 101 hands. He died on April 21, 1932, after being kicked by a horse, and was buried on a knoll near the White Eagle Monument. The ranch was declared a National Historic Landmark on May 15, 1975.

◆ PENNSYLVANIA

Erie

Harry T. Burleigh Birthplace

A friend of famed Czech composer Antonin Dvorak and a composer/arranger in his own right, Harry T. Burleigh was born in 1866 in Erie, Pennsylvania. Burleigh set to music many of the stirring poems of Walt Whitman and arranged such unforgettable spirituals as *Deep River*. He died in 1949.

Lancaster

Thaddeus Stevens Grave Site
Schreiner's Cemetery
Chestnut and Mulberry Street

Senator Thaddeus Stevens of Pennsylvania, a white abolitionist and civil rights activist, was one of the chief architects of the Fourteenth Amendment to the Constitution. Upon his death in 1868, five black and three white pallbearers escorted the body to Washington, D.C. Stevens' body lay in state on the same catafalque that had borne the body of Lincoln, and was guarded by black soldiers of the 54th Massachusetts Regiment. Two days later the body was returned to Lancaster, where over 10,000 blacks attended the funeral. Stevens was buried in Schreiner's Cemetery, a cemetery for blacks— in his will, he had rejected burial in a white cemetery because of segregationist policy.

Montgomery County

James A. Bland Grave Site
Merion Cemetery

In Merion Cemetery in Montgomery County, Pennsylvania lies the grave of black composer James A. Bland, who wrote *Carry Me Back to Old Virginny*, now the state song of Virginia. Bland was one of the most popular black minstrels of the nineteenth century.

Philadelphia

Frances Ellen Watkins Harper House
1006 Bainbridge Street

This was the home of the black writer and social activist Frances Ellen Watkins Harper, who participated in the nineteenth-century abolition, woman's suffrage, and temperance movements. The house was named a National Historic Landmark on December 8, 1976.

Mother Bethel African Methodist Episcopal Church
419 South Sixth Street

The current building, located in Philadelphia, Pennsylvania and built in 1859, is the fourth church to be erected on the site where Richard Allen and Absalom Jones founded the Free African Society in 1787. This organization later grew into the African Methodist Episcopal Church, one of the largest black religious denominations in the United States.

Allen, the first black bishop, was born a slave and became a minister and circuit rider after winning his freedom. In 1814, he and James Forten organized a force of 2,500 free blacks to defend Philadelphia against the British. Allen organized the first black convention in Philadelphia 16 years later, and was instrumental in getting the group to adopt a strong platform denouncing slavery and encouraging abolitionist activities. Allen died in 1831 and was buried in the church crypt.

As for Forten, he had been born free in 1766, and despite his youth, served aboard a Philadelphia privateer during the Revolutionary War. In 1800, he was one of the signers of a petition requesting Congress to alter the Fugitive Slave Act of 1793. Opposed to the idea of resettling slaves in Africa, Forten chaired an 1817 meeting held at Bethel to protest existing colonization schemes. In 1833, he put up the funds that William Lloyd Garrison needed to found *The Liberator*. After his death, Forten's work was continued by his successors, who remained active in the abolitionist cause throughout the Civil War and fought for black rights during Reconstruction. The Forten home served as a meeting place for many of the leading figures in the movement. The church was named a National Historic Landmark on May 30, 1974.

Negro Soldiers Monument
West Fairmount Park
Lansdowne Drive

The Negro Soldiers Monument was erected by the state of Pennsylvania in 1934 to pay tribute to its fallen black soldiers.

Henry O. Tanner House
2903 West Diamond Street

Born in Pittsburgh in 1859, Henry Ossawa Tanner was the first black to be elected to the National Academy of Design. The Diamond Street residence was the artist's boyhood home. The house was designated a historical landmark on May 11, 1976.

Bessie Smith Residence
7003 South Twelfth Street

This location served as home to blues singer Bessie Smith from about 1926 until her death in 1937.

◆ SOUTH CAROLINA

Beaufort

Robert Smalls House
511 Prince Street

Robert Smalls, a former slave, served in both the state legislature and the U.S. Congress. While in office, Smalls was an advocate for the rights of African Americans. He had lived in Beaufort, South Carolina both as a slave and as a free man. The Smalls house was designated a National Historic Landmark on May 30, 1973.

Charleston

Dubose Hayward House
76 Church Street

Dubose Hayward, the author of *Porgy*, the book upon which George Gershwin's opera *Porgy and Bess* was based, lived here from 1919 to 1924. It was designated a National Historic Landmark on November 11, 1971.

Denmark Vesey House
56 Bull Street

This was the residence of Denmark Vesey, the free black Charleston carpenter whose 1822 plans to organize a slave insurrection were discovered. The Denmark Vesey House, located in Charleston, South Carolina, was declared a National Historic Landmark on May 11, 1976.

Rantowles

Stono River Slave Rebellion Historic Site

This was the site of a 1739 slave insurrection, during which some 100 slaves escaped. The .site, located in Rantowles, South Carolina, was named a National Historic Landmark on July 4, 1974.

Columbia

Chapelle Administration Building
1530 Harden Street

This building is one of the finest works of John Anderson Lankfor, a pioneer black architect who helped gain recognition for African American architects among the architectural community. The building was named a National Historic Landmark on December 8, 1976.

Frogmore

Penn School Historic District
Lands End Road

Organized by Quaker missionaries from the North, the Penn School, located in Frogmore, South Carolina, was one of the first southern schools for blacks in Frogmore. On December 2, 1974, the district was named a National Historic Landmark.

Georgetown

Joseph H. Rainey House
909 Prince Street

Joseph Hayne Rainey(1832–1887), a former slave, was the first black to serve in the U.S. House of Representatives. His election, along with the election of Hiram R. Rebels, the first black citizen to be elected to the U.S. Senate in 1870, marked the beginning of black participation in the federal legislative process. The house was designated a National Historic Landmark on April 20, 1984.

◆ SOUTH DAKOTA

Deadwood

Adams Memorial Museum

Only one of the legendary claimants to the title of

Nat Love

"Deadwood Dick" is black, but he can back his assertion with a colorful autobiography that takes the reader through his childhood in slavery, his early bronco-busting efforts, and his fabled life as a range rider and Indian fighter in the old West. Nat Love claimed he won the title during a public competition held in Deadwood on the Fourth of July in 1876. The presence of other black cowboys, gambling house operators, and escort soldiers in the area during these years, as well as the convincing style of Love's narrative, lend a high degree of credibility to his adventurous tales—although, like Jim Beckwourth, he was probably given to moments of wanton exaggeration.

◆ TENNESSEE

Henning

Alex Haley House
Haley Avenue at South Church Street

Best known for the television adaptation of his Pulit-zer Prize-winning book, *Roots,* author Alex Haley has

awakened both black and white Americans to the rich-ness of African and African American history and cul-ture. The house, built in 1918 by Haley's grandfather, served as his home from 1921 to 1929, and was where he heard many of the stories that inspired him to write *Roots.* Today the house serves as a museum.

Jackson

Casey Jones Railroad Museum

On Chester Street in Jackson, Tennessee is found the Casey Jones Railroad Museum, filled with memorabilia of a bygone era. Jones was immortalized through the song about Casey Jones' legendary train ride. The song, which became popularized in vaudeville and music halls, was written by Wallace Saunders, a black fireman aboard Jones' locomotive. The Railroad Museum serves to remind us of the enormous unsung contributions of blacks to the railroad industry in the United States.

Memphis

Beale Street Historic District
Beale Street from Main to Fourth Streets

The "blues," a unique black contribution to American music, was born on a Beale Street lined with saloons, gambling halls, and theaters. The street was immortal-ized by William Christopher Handy, who composed "Beale Street Blues." Beale Street, located in Memphis, Tennessee, was designated a National Historic Land-mark on May 23, 1966.

William Christopher Handy Park

The city of Memphis, Tennessee pays tribute to famed blues composer William Christopher Handy in the form of a park and a heroic bronze statue overlooking the very same Beale Street that he immortalized in the tune "Beale Street Blues." The statue, showing Handy stand-ing with horn poised, was executed by Leone Tomassi of Italy and was dedicated in 1960, at the close of a memorial campaign instituted by the city shortly after Handy's death in 1958.

Tom Lee Memorial
Beale Street

The 30-foot-high Tom Lee granite memorial, located in Memphis, Tennessee, was erected in 1954 to honor a black who, on May 8, 1925, saved the lives of 32 passen-gers aboard the *M. E. Norman,* an excursion boat that had capsized some 20 miles below Memphis near Cow Island. Alerted to the disaster, Lee pulled 32 people from the water onto his skiff. He was honored for his feat by

Alex Haley (right) and Samba Fye at Haley's boyhood home.

the Memphis Engineers Club, which provided him with money for the duration of his life. A fund was also raised to purchase him a home. After his death in 1952, a committee raised the money needed to erect the memorial.

Lorraine Hotel
406 Mulberry Street

It was on the balcony of the Lorraine Hotel in Memphis, Tennessee that Martin Luther King, Jr. was assassinated while emerging from a second-floor room, in the presence of a pair of his trusted advisers, Ralph Abernathy and Jesse Jackson. King died in the emergency room of St. Joseph's Hospital on April 4, 1968. The Lorraine closed for business in 1988. It is now operated as the National Civil Rights Museum.

Nashville

Fisk University

Opened in 1866, Fisk University was founded in Nashville, Tennessee following the Civil War by the American Missionary Association to provide a liberal arts education for blacks. Fisk first began operation as the Fisk Free School.

Jubilee Hall, a Victorian Gothic structure, is the oldest building on the Fisk University campus. The hall was named a National Historic Landmark on December 2, 1974.

James Weldon Johnson House
911 18th Avenue

Writer and civil rights leader James Weldon Johnson resided at this location in Nashville, Tennessee from about 1930 until his death in 1938, teaching literature and writing at Fisk University. Johnson was born in 1871 in Jacksonville, Florida. Johnson, in collaboration with his brother J. Rosamond Johnson, was responsible for creating the song "Lift Every Voice and Sing."

◆ TEXAS

Amarillo

First Black School

Matthew Bones Hooks was born in central Texas in 1867. The story goes that he rode wild horses at the age of eight, had his first paid job as a cowhand at the age of

Hampton University.

ten, and later herded cattle for Colonel Charles Goodnight, moving them from Texas to Dodge City, Kansas. Hooks homesteaded in New Mexico, rode broncos in Romfa, Texas in 1910, and then moved to Amarillo, Texas, where he established the first school for blacks in that city. The school was in the North Heights section, an all-black community. He also founded the Dogie Club, an organization for underprivileged boys, in cooperation with the Boy Scouts. He was the only black member of the old Settlers Association of Amarillo and the first black of Amarillo to serve on a grand jury.

◆ VIRGINIA

Alexandria

Franklin and Armfield Office
1315 Duke Street

The office of the Franklin and Armfield slave-trading company in Alexandria, Virginia, was from 1828 to 1836 the South's largest slave-trading firm. (During the company's operation, Alexandria was part of the District of

Booker T. Washington's boyhood home.

Columbia.) The building was designated a National Historic Landmark on June 2, 1978.

Colonial National Historic Park

Jamestown Island is where the first black slaves arrived in the English colonies in 1619. At the battle of Yorktown in 1781, three blacks served in patriot militia units and also worked for the Hessian forces as musicians and servants.

Arlington

Benjamin Banneker Boundary Stone
18th and Van Buren Streets

The boundary stone in Arlington, Virginia commemorates the accomplishments of Benjamin Banneker, who helped survey the city of Washington, D.C., and who was perhaps the most well-known black man in Colonial America. Banneker, a mathematician and scientist, was born in Ellicott Mills, Maryland and received his early schooling with the aid of a Quaker family. Banneker was a national hero for black people and many schools have been named after him. The boundary stone was declared a National Historic Landmark on May 11, 1976.

Charles Richard Drew House
2505 First Street, South

Located in Arlington, Virginia, this house served as the home of Charles Richard Drew from 1920 to 1939. Drew, a noted black physician and teacher, is best remembered for his pioneer work in discovering means to preserve blood plasma. The house was named a National Historic Landmark on May 11, 1976.

Chatham

Pittsylvania County Courthouse
U.S. Business Route 29

The Pittsylvania County Courthouse in Chatham, Virginia was closely associated with the 1878 case *Ex parte Virginia*. This case, over the issue of black participation on juries, stemmed from a clear attempt by a state official to deny citizens the equal protection of law guaranteed by the Fourteenth Amendment to the Constitution. The courthouse was designated a National Historic Landmark on May 4, 1987.

Capahosic

Holley Knoll House

From 1935 to 1959, this house served as the retirement home of Robert R. Moton. Moton, who succeeded Booker T. Washington as head of Tuskegee Institute in 1915, guided the school's growth until 1930. He was an influential educator and active in many African American causes.

Glen Allen

Virginia Randolph Cottage
2200 Mountain Road

As the first supervisor of the Jeanes Fund, set up by a wealthy Philadelphia Quaker to aid black education, Virginia Randolph worked to upgrade black vocational training. The cottage in Glen Allen, Virginia was named a National Historic Landmark on December 2, 1974.

Hampton

Hampton University

Founded in 1868 as Hampton Institute, this was one of the earliest institutions of higher learning for blacks in the United States. Hampton Institute was attended by the great Booker T. Washington before he went to Tuskegee. Washington also taught for a time at Hampton.

Norfolk

Black Civil War Veterans' Memorial
Elmwood Cemetery
Princess Anne Road

In a section of Norfolk's Elmwood Cemetery marked by a granite monument lie the grave sites of several black soldiers who served during the Civil War.

Richmond

Jackson Ward Historic District

Bounded by Fourth, Marshall, and Smith Streets and the Richmond-Petersburg Turnpike, this was the foremost black community of the nineteenth and early twentieth centuries and an early center for ethnic social

Harpers Ferry National Historic Park.

organizations and protective banking institutions. The district was named a National Historic Landmark on June 2, 1978.

Maggie Lena Walker House
110-A East Leigh Street

In 1903, Maggie Lena Walker, a black woman, founded the successful Saint Luke Penny Savings Bank and became the first woman to establish and head a bank. In addition to being the first woman president of a bank, she was editor of a newspaper considered to be one of the best journals of its class in America and a concerned community leader. The house is located in the Jackson Ward Historic District of Richmond; it was declared a National Historic Landmark May 15, 1975.

Rocky Mount

Booker T. Washington National Monument

The Burroughs plantation, on which educator and scholar Booker T. Washington was born, can be found in a 200-acre park located 22 miles southeast of Roanoke, Virginia. Born a slave, Washington lived here until the end of the Civil War, when he and his mother moved to Malden, West Virginia.

◆ WASHINGTON

Centralia

George Washington Park

This park is named after a liberated slave who escaped from slavery in Virginia when he was adopted by a white couple and taken to Missouri. He then left Missouri with a wagon train heading for the Pacific Northwest, settling on a homestead along the Chehalis River. Once the location was reached by the Northern Pacific Railroad, Washington laid out a town, setting aside acreage for parks, a cemetery, and churches. Soon over 2,000 lots were in the hands of a thriving population that formed the nucleus of Centerville.

◆ WEST VIRGINIA

Harpers Ferry

Harpers Ferry National Historic Park

Harpers Ferry derives its historical fame from the

much-publicized anti-slavery raid conducted by John Brown and a party of eighteen men, including five blacks, from October 16 to 18, 1859. Brown hoped to set up a fortress and refuge for slaves that he could transform into an important way station for black fugitives en route to Pennsylvania.

Brown lost two of his sons in the battle and was himself seriously wounded. Later tried and convicted of treason, he was hanged at Charles Town on December 2, 1859.

Malden

Booker T. Washington Monument
U.S. Route 60

This monument, erected in 1963, marks the site where Booker T. Washington labored for several years in the salt works. At the time, Washington credited his employer, Mrs. Violla Ruffner, with having encouraged him to pursue a higher education at Hampton Institute.

◆ WISCONSIN

Milton

Milton House and Museum
18 South Jamesville Street

The Milton House, the first structure made of poured concrete in the United States, was once used as a hideaway for fugitive slaves escaping by means of the Underground Railroad.

Portage

Ansel Clark Grave Site
Silver Lake Cemetery

Ansel Clark, "born a slave, died a respected citizen," settled in Wisconsin after the Civil War, in which he served as an impressed laborer in the Confederate cause before escaping. Brought to Portage by a man he had tended in a Union hospital, Clark served as town constable and deputy sheriff. For 30 years he worked in law enforcement, standing up to the town's rough characters and keeping them in line with his "firmness and dignity."

5

Africa and the Black Diaspora

5

Africa and the Black Diaspora

◆ A Brief History of Africa ◆ The Modern Day People of Africa ◆ Blacks in the Western Hemisphere
◆ Country Profiles

by Kenneth Estell, Doris H. Mabunda, and Lorna M. Mabunda

According to renowned Kenyan scholar Dr. Ali Mazrui, modern Africa has been heavily influenced by three main forces—indigenous traditions, the tenants of Islam, and Western culture, including Christianity—with both positive and negative results. Among the benefits are a strong sense of continuity and regard for heritage, moral order, and membership in the global village. However, the mingling of such dynamic and divergent threads has caused a clash of cultures, with an aftermath of "inefficiency, mismanagement, corruption, and decay of the infrastructure." (Ali Mazrui, The Africans: A Triple Heritage, 1986, p. 12.)

◆ A BRIEF HISTORY OF AFRICA

Archeologists have come to believe that early humans, *Hominidea*, originated in Africa some two to three million years and migrated to other continents. By the Middle Stone Age, three distinct groups had evolved—Bushmanoid, Pygmoid, and Negroid. Only a few Bushmen, and related Hottentot people, are still found in parts of the south-west portion of the continent, while a few isloated Pygmy groups have survived, mainly in the Congo forests. However, it was the Negroid group which became dominant on the continent.

Sophisticated societies developed in early Africa, among them the Kush, between 700 B.C. and A.D. 200 and the ancient Ghana, Kanen, Mali Songhai, and the Haissa states. In the Congo, the Kingdoms of Lunda, Lula, Bushong, and Kongo were founded, probably between the sixteenth and eighteenth centuries. On the Guinea Coast, the city states of Benin, Ite, Oyo, Ashanti, and Yoruba date back to the fifteenth century. These states traded extensively in gold, ivory, salt, and livestock.

Trade with Europe began around the fifteenth century, with the slave trade an important part; an estimated ten to 30 million people were sold into slavery by the mid-nineteenth century. The interior of Africa was first exposed to Europeans in the eighteenth century by missionaries, traders, and adventurers. Reports of the continent's resources eventually spurred European conquest and direct control of virtually all of Africa. By 1900 only Ethiopia and Liberia, remained free of European control.

In 1910 the British granted dominion status to the Union of South Africa. However, independence for the black-dominated regions of Africa, did not come until some 40 years later. In 1957, independence movements started with a rush in Kenya, Ghana, and Guinea. By the late 1960s most of Africa had achieved independence.

◆ THE MODERN DAY PEOPLE OF AFRICA

Geography

The second largest continent on the globe, Africa is bisected by the equator and bordered to the west by the Atlantic Ocean and to the east by the Indian Ocean. Roughly the shape of an inverted triangle—with a large bulge on its northwestern end and a small horn on its eastern tip—it contains 52 countries and six islands that, together, make up about 20 percent of the world's land mass, or 11.5 million square miles.

Africa is essentially a huge plateau divided naturally into two sections. Northern Africa, a culturally and historically Mediterranean region, includes the Sahara desert—the world's largest expanse of desert, coming close to the size of the United States. Sub-Saharan, or so-called "Black Africa," also contains some desert

Cyrille Adoula, Jomo Kenyatta, and other members of the Pan-African Movement for East and Central Africa meet, 1962.

land, but is mainly tropical, with rain forests clustered around the equator; vast savanna grasslands covering more than 30 percent of continent and surrounding the rain forests on the north, east, and south; some mountainous regions; and rivers and lakes that formed from the natural uplifting of the plateau's surface.

Notable geographical marvels in Africa include Mts. Kenya and Kilamanjaro (the latter of whose highest peak is one of the tallest in the world); the rivers Niger, Senegal, Congo, Zambezi (home of the mile-wide Victoria Falls, one of the world's seven natural wonders), Orange, Limpopo, Malawi, and Nile (the longest river in the world); Tanganyika, Albert, Rudolf, and Victoria (the second largest freshwater body in the world) lakes; and the Libyan, Nubian, and Kalahari deserts.

Economics/Natural Resources

A mineral rich continent, Africa is the pristine source of copper, diamonds, gold, manganese, oil, uranium, zinc, and several other deposits. The equatorial forests produce ebony, teak, and rosewood, while cash crops like bananas, cocoa, coffee, cloves, cotton, sisal, sugar cane, tobacco, yams, and all kinds of nuts, including

cashews and groundnuts. In fact, agriculture has formed the basis of most African economies for centuries. Despite such a wealth of resources, many African nations rank amongst the poorest in the world. Tribal and political wars, illiteracy, droughts, lack of technological prowess, and the commonality of corruption among government officials all contribute to the weak economy encountered in much of the continent.

Though Africa does have booming urban and industrial centers—for example, Johannesburg, South Africa; Lagos, Nigeria; Dakar, Senegal; Harare, Zimbabwe— the continent is better known to visitors for the national parks and reserves of East and Southern Africa. Wildlife concentrations in these locations vary but include antelope, impala, Thompson's gazelles, and wildebeests; buffalo, hippos, and rhinos; elephants; giraffes; zebras; crocodiles; a variety of bird species; hyenas, jackels, and wild dogs; and "big cats," i.e. cheetahs, jaguars, leopards, lions, and tigers.

Kenya, located in East Africa, is one of the oldest and most popular game-viewing destinations for safari-seeking tourists. The Samburu National Reserve, Lake Nakuru (also known as the "pink lake" because of an abundance of flamingos), Masai Mara National Re-

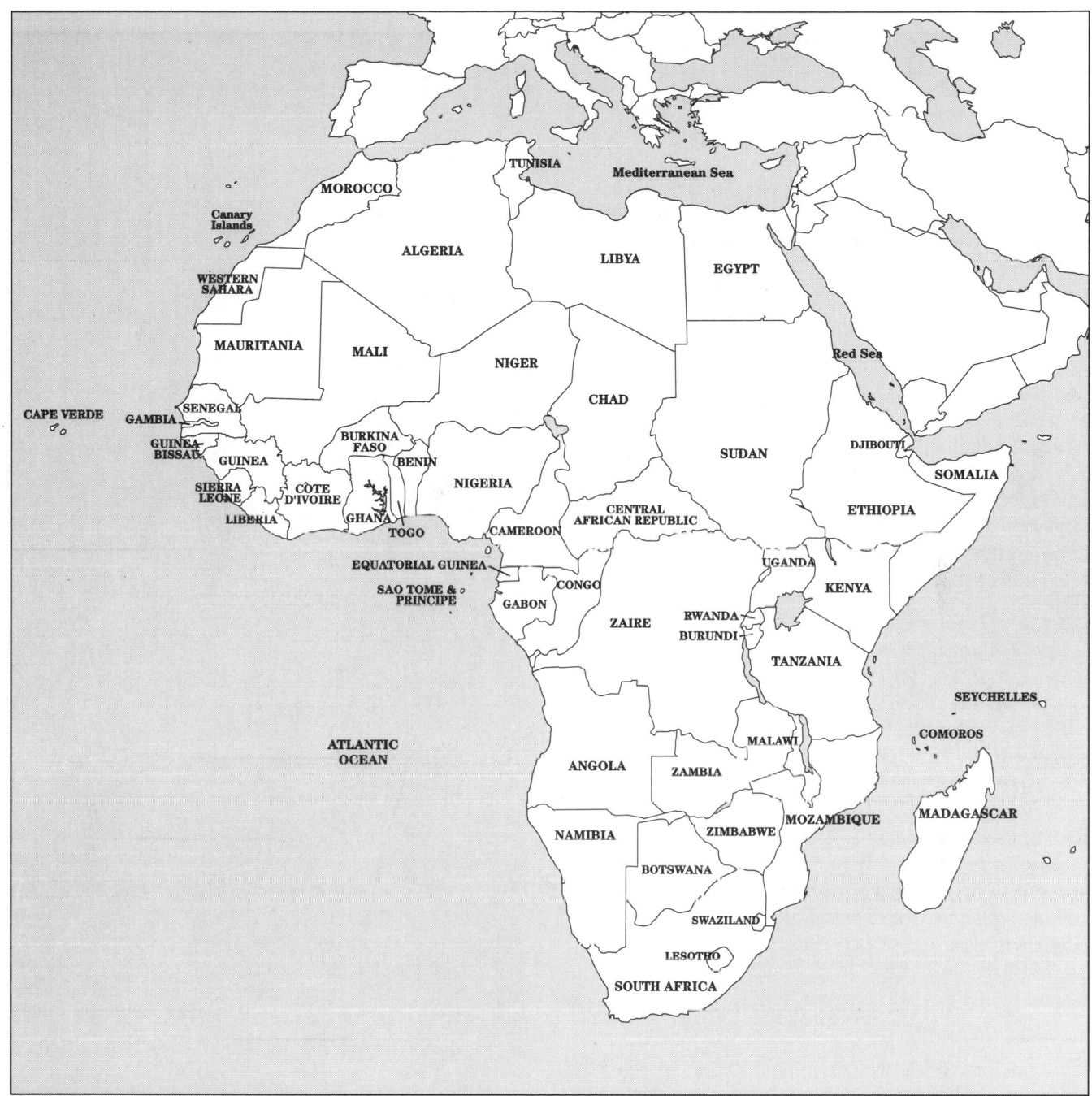

Africa.

serve, and Amboseli, are all favored spots. Nearby, Tanzania offers Lake Manyara National Park, Serengeti National Park, and Ngorongoro Crater (a natural amphitheatre that formed by the collapse of a volcano). Uganda features Bwindi Forest, home of the Buhoma Gorilla Camp. In the southern region of Africa, South Africa contains ostrich farms; Kruger National Park, one of the continent's largest reserves; Cango Caves; and Kirstenbosch Botanical Gardens. Zimbabwe contributes man-made Lake Kariba, a permanent water source for monkeys, warthogs, waterbuck, and other species, including birds; Hwange, a game reserve filled with more than 107 species; and the Zambezi Nature Sanctuary and Crocodile Farm.

Population

The African population is most heavily concentrated in Nigeria, southern Ghana, along the Gulf of Guinea, Benin and Togo, the Nile Valley, in northern Sudan, the East Africa highlands of Ethiopia, Kenya, and Tanzania, eastern Zaire, the eastern and southern coasts, and the inland High Veld of South Africa. The desert and mountain regions are largely uninhabited.

In recent years the population of Africa has grown rapidly. In 1950 the total population was estimated at 281 million; by 1990 the population had reached 817 million, making it the third most populous continent on the planet. No African nation has developed an effective population control program, and such practices as having multiple wives and early marriages continue. By the year 2020, the population of Sub-Sharan Africa alone is expected to reach 1.2 billion.

Until recently, almost 90 percent of Africa's population lived in rural areas. African cities with populations exceeding one million include Accra, Ghana; Addis Ababa, Ethiopia; Cape Town and Johannesburg, South Africa; Cairo, Egypt; Maputo, Mozambique; Ibadan and Lagos, Nigeria; and Kinshasa, Zaire. In addition to indigenous Africans, about 5 million people are of predominantly European descent, and 1 million are of Asian descent.

During a 1959 archaeological expedition in Olduvai Gorge, Tanzania, Kenyan-born anthropologist L. S. B. Leakey and his wife Mary discovered a skull of a species thought to date back more than 2 million years called Australopithecus boisei, Zinjanthropus, *or "Nutcracker Man" in popular vernacular. Within the next ten years they unearthed* Homo habilis, *also estimated to date between 1.5 to 2 million years ago, and* Kenyapithecus africanus. *Fossils of early hominoids resembling man have been found in Ethiopia, Kenya, and South Africa by other scientists. The remains are believed to be predecessors of our own human species,* Homo sapiens.

Language

The diversity of Africa's people is underscored by the existence of more than 2,000 languages and dialects, including africanized forms of English, French, and Portugues. Some 50 major languages are spoken by groups of one million or more people. The major language groups include Arabic (spoken mainly in north Africa), Fula, Hausa, Lingala, Malinke, Nguni (which includes SiNdebele, Xhosa, and Zulu), SeTwana-SeSotho, Swahili, and Yoruba.

"African-language" names are often derived from the names of the ethnic tribes that speak them. For example, Zulu is spoken primarily by Zulus and Kibondi is the language of the Bondi tribe. Swahili, the most widely spoken language on the continent, is the only one that breaks the pattern. A commercial language originally

A Malian woman pounding grain.

used among traders and business people, it evolved from Portuguese, Arabic, and Bantu.

As many languages were never translated into written form, Africa acquired a very long and rich oral tradition—in many cases, the only method of passing literature and history from generation to generation in ancient times. After the fourteenth century, the use of Arabic by educated Muslim blacks was extensive, and some oral literature was subsequently reduced to a more permanent written form. But, in spite of the Arab influence, the oral heritage of Africans remained strong, serving not only as an educational device, but as a guide for the administration of government and the conduct of religious ceremonies.

A wealth of proverbs from African culture have survived through the generations. Some of the more popular ones are: If you want to know the end, look at the beginning; When one door closes, another one opens; If we stand tall it is because we stand on the backs of those who came before us; Two men in a burning house must not stop to argue; Where you sit when you are old shows where you stood in youth; You must live within your sacred truth; The one who asks questions doesn't lose his way; If you plant turnips you will not harvest grapes; God makes three requests of his children: Do the best you can, where you are, with what you have now; You must act as if it impossible to fail; Some would be great drinkers but they haven't got the wine; some great eaters but they haven't got the food.

Some of Africa's best known authors include Cameroon's Mongo Beti; Ghana's Ayi Kwei Armah and J. E. Casely-Hayford; Kenya's Ngugi wa Thiong'o; Lesoto's Thomas Mofolo; Nigeria's Chinua Achebe, Wole Soyinka, Amos Tutuola, and Ken Saro-Wiwa; Senegal's Sembène Ousmane and Léopold Sédar Senghor; Somali's Nuruddin Farah; South Africa's Bessie Head, Ezekiel Mphahlele, and Lewis Nkosi; Uganda's Okot p'Bitek; and Zimbabwe's Dennis Brutus.

Unfortunately for prose writers, freedom of the press is a scarce commodity in much of Africa, with many of those who dare to report the truth about government corruption or abuse of human rights being forced into exile or constantly threatened and harrassed if they stay. For that reason, many Africans learn more about their neighbors—both locally and continentally— through Western media. But among Africa's most courageous and well-respected journalists are Liberia's Kenneth Y. Best and Issac Bantu, Ghana's Ben Ephson, and South Africa's Percy Qoboza.

Music

Despite the Western stereotype that associates the beating of tribal drums with the whole of "traditional" music, African music is incredibly diverse and reflective of the vast array of peoples, cultures, and traditions. Confined to localities, some of the world's greatest and most unheralded musicians—many self-taught—play to crowds in Africa. In the past few decades, "cross-over" artists have breached the boundaries of their homeland to win acclaim and fans in the United States and Europe. The irony is that these so-called "African superstars" may not even be stars in their own countries, let alone on the rest of the continent.

Nonetheless, many contemporary American forms such as blues and jazz have been heavily influenced by African styles and polyrhythms carried over by slaves. In fact the African lute evolved into the modern day guitar. Guitars form the basis of *benga* music (popular in Kenya); *juju* (a Nigerian music replete with talking drums and vocal call and response); palm wine music (an acoustic form popular in regions of West Africa, where palm wine is a favorite elixir); highlife (a jazzy, complex West African dance music punctuated by horns); and *soukous* (derived by the French word for "shake," a peppy dance form originating mainly in Zaire and the Congo). Percussion-based music includes *apala* (a street-form emergent from Islamic music); *mbalax* (a modern dance style popularized in Senegal); and *jit* (a Zimbabwean hybrid of traditional *chimurenga* guitar, disco-style drum beats, highlife, and *soukous*). *Kora* features a 21-string harp, *kwela* incorporates a penny whistle, and *mbira* got its moniker from the Zimbabwean name for a finger piano. Cameroonians may jive to *makossa* while those in Sierre Leone pop their fingers to milo jazz and Cape Verdeans release their troubles with the deep blues of *morna*. South Africans may party to *mbaquanga* on one night and get spiritual with the choral vocals of *mbube* the next. Permutations of once solely African music include *salsa* (Spanish folk music combined with African drums and Cuban rhythms), *soca* (African music with a heady dose of English and Latin folk music), and *zouk* (a mix of French, African, and Guadeloupian music).

Some of Africa's biggest artists, "cross-over" or otherwise include Angola's Kuenda Bonga (a political-minded singer-songwriter); Burkina Faso's Farafina (a group led by balafon virtuoso Mahama Konaté); Cape Verde's Cesaria Evora ("The Barefoot Diva"); Gabon's Pierre Akendengue (a blind singer, guitarist, poet, and playwright); Guinea's Bembeya Jazz National (featuring Sekou "Diamond Fingers" Diabate); Mali's Toumani Diabate (considered the world's greatest kora player), Oumou Sangare (the country's favorite female "praise singer") and Ali Farka Toure ("The Bluesman of Mali"); Nigeria's King Sunny Ade ("The King of Juju") and Fela Anikulapo Kuti (an outspoken social critic, pianist, saxophonist, and singer), Sierre Leone's Abdul Tee-Jay (a London-based studio guitarist adept at several forms, including highlife, soukous, makossa, and soca); South Africa's Ladysmith Black Mambazo (an a capella group led by tenor vocalist Joseph Shabalala), Mahlathini (legendary, deep voiced "King of the Groaners"), the Mahotella Queens (mbaqanga mavens), Miriam Makeba ("The Empress of African Song"), Hugh Masekela (trumpet– and flugelhorn–playing jazz legend), West Nkosi (multi-talented musician, arranger, producer, and bandleader), and The

Soul Brothers (one of the nation's biggest selling groups); Tanzania's Zuhura Swaleh (a female taarab singer); Zaire/Congo's 4 Etoiles (featuring soukous guitarist Syran Mbenza), Les Bantous (a rhumba band), Mbilia Bel (one of Africa's most successful female singers), Tshala Muana ("Queen of Mutuashi," a dance form), Tabu Ley (a soukous master), Papa Wemba (one of the world's greatest singers), and Zap Mama (an all-female group led by poet Marie Daulne); and Zimbabwe's Thomas Mapfumo (credited with having created chimurenga, or liberation music) and Stella Chiweshe ("The Queen of Mbira").

Family

Family is the social backbone of Africa. Within most African cultures, family impacts all realms of day to day living, both politically and economically. Familial obligations are not restricted just to immediate family; tribal conflict notwithstanding, in Africa each individual is regarded as a dear cousin. In fact, the Western method of breaking familial relationships down to degree's—e.g. first cousin, second aunt, great-great grandfather twice removed—is virtually nonexistent. Either two people are related or not—and more often then not, without even looking, those individuals will find ties. This unique kinship is inclusive of ancestors. The dead are forever remembered among the living, and the elderly are held with a special regard. Rather than being hidden away or considered burdens, older Africans are viewed as storehouses of wisdom and are a welcome part of society. Women, too, are highly-esteemed in much of African tradition, particularly in the agri-based cultures. Often women, not men, are heads of households.

Among Africans, marriage represents a union of two families, not just a bride and groom. Parents and extended family members offer emotional support to a couple throughout their marriage. The bonding of families begins when a man obtains formal permission to marry a prospective bride. In true oral tradition, Africans often deliver the news of their upcoming nuptials by word of mouth. Any offspring are extremely valued. Additions to the family are cause for celebration.

In some cultures bride prices or dowries are still negotiated as are pre-arranged marriages.

Health

Diseases that have been successfully monitored and controlled in Western nations—diphtheria, measles, pertussis, poliomyelitis, tetanus, and tuberculosis—con-tinue to be a problem in many parts of Africa. Diarrhea and tuberculosis account for one-half of all deaths in children. The emergence of Acquired Immune Deficiency Syndrome (AIDS) has had a devastating effect on the continent. In 1990, an estimated 1.2 million AIDS cases surfaced, including some 400,000 cases in children under the age of five.

In the mid-1990s, Ebola outbreaks have wreaked havoc in Zaire, Liberia, Gabon, and the Ivory Coast. Spread through contact with bodily fluids, the virus is hardy and can survive on moist surfaces such as bodies or food for long periods. The deadly Ebola virus disinigrates the mebranous linings of blood vessels and organs, usually leading to heart and other organ failure. Each erruption of the modern day plague has warranted strict quarantines. One of most contagious and lethal viruses known to mankind, the international scientific community has come together in trying to locate the sources of contamination, in hopes of bringing an end to a virus whose newer strains have increased the fatality rate of the afflicated from 80 percent to 97 percent since earlier Sudanese and Zairean outbreaks in the mid-to-late 1970s.

Food shortages caused by drought and civil conflicts continue to cause mass starvation and malnutrition in Ethiopia, Somalia, and Mozambique, as well as in parts of Western Africa. In the late 1980s and into the 1990s, the international community has joined forces to try to alleviate the situation by sending food and aid to the needy and even resorting to peace-keeping military personnel in situations caused by on-going civil disturbances.

The practice of female circumcision or genital mutilation—one of many varying rites of passage performed in parts of Africa—has been denounced by Western society as the harbinger of medical problems for women later in life, including the inability to walk, chronic infections, and difficult childbirth. While an African and Western effort to stamp out the sometimes fatal ritual is growing, many others decry what they deem to be cultural interference. Tradition holds that the surgery preserves the chastity of those upon whom it is performed.

Medicine and medical advice are often dispensed by traditional healers in Africa, often referred to as "witch doctors" by skeptical Westerners. Diviners and healers treat mental disorders as well as physical ones. They also provide advice for resolving social disputes.

Senegalese microbiologist Soulyemane Mboup and other African researchers have made significant contributions to the fight against AIDS. While Mboup is credited as one of the discoverers of the HIV-2 virus, other African scientists seem to have developed a method of using interferon, an immune system-enhancing protein, to alleviate the symptoms of both Ebola and AIDS. In some cases researchers have claimed to completely eradicate the presence of these diseases in affected patients.

Cuisine

Food plays a large role in African traditions, customs, and beliefs. Africans make liberal use of fresh, locally grown foods in their cooking. Papayas, coconuts, avocados, mangos, guavas, and other "exotic" fruits are abundant and along with other fruits and vegetables are eaten much more liberally than in the United States; many such as yams and cassava root are used as staples. For example maize, cassava, and plaintains are often dried and ground into flour. Legumes are also prevalent in African meals. Particularly in the coastal nations, seafood and fish, including shark, is frequently eaten fresh, dried, or smoked. Bat, beef, chicken, goat, monkey, pigeons, and pork are just some of the meats that can be found in different regions. Most Africans enjoy very spicy-hot food. An African pepper that goes by many names—*pilli-pilli*, *piri-piri*, *beri-beri*—is frequently used. Much hotter than cayenne pepper, *pilli-pilli* does more than increase the palatability of meal. Like garlic, pepper is thought to enhance the body's immune system. Coconut flesh is incorporated into many dishes as is coconut milk, which is also imbibed as a refreshing beverage. African beer, wine, and liquor—both homemade and commercial—also provide good libations.

In many African cultures, food is served in one large common bowl; diners then eat with their hands, thus re-enforcing the idea of community.

◆ BLACKS IN THE WESTERN HEMISPHERE

The black population of the Caribbean and much of South America, like that in North America, is decended from African slaves who were transported to the New World to work on European settlements. On many islands of the Caribbean persons of African descent make up the majority of the population; on Barbados and Jamaica, blacks are the overwhelming majority. In other areas, notably on the continental mainland from Mexico south to Argentina, Africans have been largely absorbed into the mainstream of the population. In South America, the black population consists of a mix-

ture of Africans and Indians, known as Zambos. Those who are primarily a mixture of Caucasian and American Indian are known as mestizos, and those who are a mixture of Caucasian and black are, as in the United States, referred to as mulattoes.

In recent years, the Caribbean basin has been a source of black immigration, with immigrants primarily from Jamaica and Haiti entering the United States in search of work. In 1980, the *Mariel* boatlift was successful in bring Cuban refugees to the United States. More recently, thousands of Haitians have attempted, with little success, to emigrate to the United States, since the September of 1991 coup that ousted President Jean-Bertrand Aristide, later reinstated with the aid of the U.S. government.

◆ COUNTRY PROFILES

Africa

Algeria
Official name: Democratic and Popular Republic of Algeria
Independence: July 5, 1962
Capital: Algiers
Currency: Dinar
Income: (per capita US$) 2,060 (1991)
Area: 918,497 sq. mi.
Population: (1991 estimate) 23 million
Illiteracy: 42.5% (1991)
Ethnic divisions: Arab and Berber
Religious groups: Sunni Islam
Languages spoken: Arabic (official), Berber dialects, French
International relations: UN, OAU, Arab League

Since the fifth century BC, the area that makes up what is now Algeria has been populated by indigenous tribes who have been progressively pushed back from the coast by invaders. As a result, the country boundaries have shifted during various stages of the conquests. Nearly all Algerians are Muslim, of Arab, Berber, or mixed Arab-Berber stock.

French colonization began in 1830 and continued until 1954, when the indigenous population staged a revolt on November 1. The revolution was launched by a small group of nationalists who called themselves the National Liberation Front. Negotiations led to a cease-fire signed by France and the National Liberation Front on March 18, 1962; France declared Algeria independent on July 3.

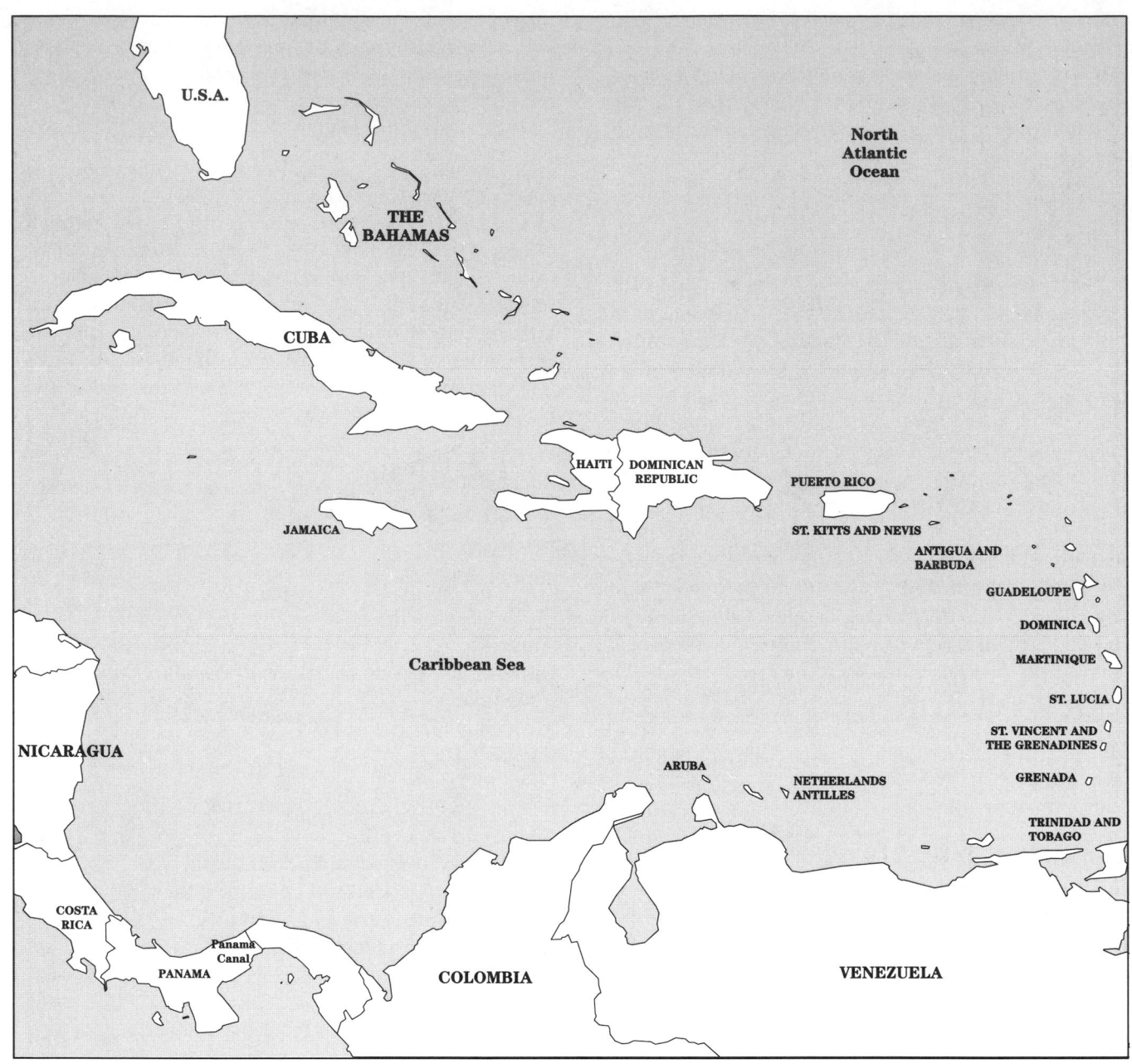

The Caribbean

Mohammed Ben Bella became Algeria's first post-independence president only to be ousted three years later. In 1965, Col. Boume'dienne lead a successful *coup de' etat.* After he died, Chadi Benjadid became the head of state. In 1991, Algeria held its first free election after 30 years of a one-party system, and the National Liberation Front was defeated by the Islamic Salvation Front.

Angola
Official name: People's Republic of Angola

Independence: November 11, 1975
Capital: Luanda
Currency: Kwanza
Income (per capita US$) 750 (1990)
Area: 481,351 sq. mi.
Population: (1991 estimate) 8.6 million
Illiteracy: 72% (1991)
Ethnic divisions: Ovimbundu 37%, Kimbundu 25%, Bakongo 15%, Lunda-Chokwe 8%, Nganguela 6%, Haneca and Humbe 3%, Ovambo 2%, mestico and European 2%, other 2%

South America

Religious groups: Roman Catholic, Protestant, traditional belief

Languages spoken: Portuguese (official), tribal languages and dialects

International relations: UN, OAU, EC

Form of Government: Multi-party

Exports: Crude oil, petroleum-based products, coffee, diamonds

Angola's boundaries were formally established by the Berlin West Africa Congress of 1884 to 1885. Following World War II, Portuguese interest in colonizing Angola increased. Here, the Portuguese established a slave trade and a strict and harsh colonial rule.

Discontent over Portuguese unwillingness to concede eventual independence led to the formation of the Popular Movement for the Liberation of Angola (MPLA), the National Front for the Liberation of Angola (FNLA) and the National Union for the Total Independence of Angola (UNITA). In January 1975, the Portuguese and the three liberation movements worked out a complicated agreement—the Alvor Accord—which provided for a transitional government composed of all three groups and for elections in preparation for independence in November of 1975. Since 1976, Angola has been politically unstable because of civil war and repeated incursions by South African forces operating from Namibia. The United States does not maintain diplomatic relations with Angola, but since 1978 the two countries have had frequent contacts to discuss regional and bilateral matters.

The MPLA party's Augustinho became the first president of the newly independent People's Republic of Angola. Upon his death in 1979, José Eduardo Dos Santos became the head of state. UNITA, led by Jonas Savimbi and supported by South Africa, continued to wage a war against MPLA, which was back by Cuba. An agreement withdrawing foreign troops was signed in 1988. Following a cease fire, a national election was scheduled to be held under the watching eyes of the United Nations.

Angolans are almost entirely Bantu of various ethnic subgroupings. The Ovimbundu, in central and southeastern Angola are the largest group, consisting of about 37 percent of the population. The Bakongo, concentrated in the northwest but also living in areas adjacent to the Congo and Zaire as well as Cabinda, constitute about 15 percent. The Kimbundu, about 25 percent of the population, are concentrated in the area around Luanda and out toward the east.

Benin
Official name: People's Republic of Benin
Independence: August 1, 1960
Capital: Cotonou

Angolans celebrating independence from Portugal.

Currency: CFA franc

Income (per capita US$) 421 (1990)

Area: 43,483 sq. mi.

Population: (1991 estimate) 4.8 million

Illiteracy: 73% (1991)

Ethnic divisions: Fon, Adja, Bariba, Yoruba

Religious groups: traditional belief 61%, Christian 17%, Muslim 12%

Languages spoken: French (official)

International relations: UN, OAU, EC

Form of government: Multi-party

Exports: Coffee, cocoa beans, cotton, palm products

During the precolonial era, Benin was a collection of small principalities, the most powerful of which was the Fon Kingdom of Dahomey. By the seventeenth and eighteenth centuries, first the Portuguese and later other Europeans established trading posts along the coast. From there thousands of slaves were shipped to the New World, primarily to Brazil and the Caribbean—this part of West Africa became known as the Slave Coast.

In 1892, the King of Dahomey was subjugated and the country organized as the French protectorate of Dahomey. It remained a French colony until independence in 1960, when the name was changed to the Republic of Dahomey,

The Bakongo people of Angola are concentrated in the northwest part of the country, adjacent to the Congo and Zaire.

and Hubert Maga became president. Three years later, he was overthrown by military commanders. Mathieu Ke're'kou took over the military regime in 1972. In 1975, the name was finally changed to the People's Republic of Benin. When the government reverted to civilian control in 1980, Ke're'kou was re-elected president of the republic.

The population of Benin comprises about 20 socio-cultural groups. Four groups—the Fon, Aja (who are related), Bariba, and Yoruba—account for more than half of the population.

Botswana
Official name: Republic of Botswana
Independence: September 30, 1966
Capital: Gaberoni
Currency: Pula
Income (per capita US$) 2,200 (1990)
Area: 224,710 sq. mi.
Population: (1991 estimate) 1.3 million
Illiteracy: 29.2% (1991)
Ethnic divisions: Tswana 55%-60%, Kalanga 25%-20%, Kgalagadi, Yei, Herero, Mbukushu, Basarwa (Bushmen), Khoi (Hottentots), whites about 1%
Religious groups: Traditional belief 50%, Christianity 50%
Languages spoken: English (official), SeTswana
International relations: UN, OAC, Commonwealth, EC
Form of government: Multi-party
Exports: Meat, diamonds, copper, nickel

Europeans made first contact with the area in the early ninteenth century. In the last quarter of the century, hostilities broke out between the Botswana and the Afrikaners from South Africa (Transvaal). Following appeals by the Botswana for assistance, the British government in 1885 proclaimed "Bechuanaland" to be under British protection. In 1909, despite South African pressure, inhabitants of Bechuanaland, Basutoland (now Lesotho), and Swaziland demanded and received British agreement that they not be included in the proposed Union of South Africa.

In June 1964, the British government accepted proposals for a form of self-government for Botswana that would lead to independence. Botswana became independent on September 30, 1966, and Seretse Khama was installed as the prime minister after the Bechuanaland Democratic Party won majority votes. The country was later named Botswana, and upon Khama's death in 1980, Quett Masire became the president.

In 1977, the Botswana Defense Force was formed, largely in response to the Rhodesian conflict, which was affecting Botswana. Facing a threat of overt or covert military raids from South Africa directed against believed African National Congress targets, Botswana has embarked on modernization and expansion of the BDF. The nation remains opposed to South Africa's policy of apartheid and maintains no formal diplomatic relations with that country. In part because of its geographic location and reliance on South African transportation systems and goods, Botswana, nevertheless, maintains a pragmatic working relationship and close economic ties with South Africa. Large deposits of diamonds have been discovered in Botswana in recent years, making the country one of the world's major producers of the valuable gemstone.

Some 50 to 60 percent of the country's population is made up of the Tswana tribe (Botswana), which is divided into eight subgroups: Bamangwate, Bakwena, Batawana, Bangwaketse, Bakgatla, Bamalete, Barolong, and Batlokwa. The Kalanga, Herero, Bushmen (Basarwa), Yei, and Kgalagadi are minorities.

Burkina Faso (formerly Upper Volta)
Independence: August 5, 1960
Capital: Ouagadougou
Currency: CFA franc

The Fon constitute one of the largest groups in Benin.

Income (per capita US$): 370 (1990)
Area: 106,000 sq. mi.
Population: (1991 estimate) 9.3 million
Illiteracy: 81.8% (1991)
Ethnic divisions: Mossi, Bobo, Mande, Fulani
Religious groups: Traditional belief 45%, Muslim 40%, Christian 15%
Languages spoken: French (official), More, other tribal languages
International relations: UN, OAU, EC
Form of government: M.ulti-party
Exports: Cotton, petroleum, live animals

Until the end of the ninteenth century, the history of Burkina Faso was dominated by the Mossi, who are believed to have come from central or eastern Africa in the eleventh century. When the French arrived and claimed the area in 1896, the Mossi resisted but were defeated when their capital at Ouagadougou was captured. After World War II, the Mossi renewed their pressure for separate territorial status; Upper Volta became an autonomous republic in the French Community on December 11, 1958, and achieved independence on August 5, 1960. The country became known as Burkino Faso in 1984.

The majority of the population belong to two major West African cultural groups, the Voltaic and the Mande. The Voltaic are far more numerous and include the Mossi, which make up about one-half of the population. The Mossi are still bound by the traditions of the emperor, the Mogho Naba, who holds court in Ouagadougou. One of the poorest nation's in the world, most inhabitants subsist on agriculture and animal husbandry.

Burundi
Official name: Republic of Burundi
Independence: July 1, 1962
Capital: Bujumbura
Currency: Burundi franc
Income (per capita US$) 210 (1990)
Area: 10,747 sq. mi.
Population: (1991 estimate) 5.8 million
Illiteracy: 50% (1991)
Ethnic divisions: Hutu 85%, Utusi 14%, Twa 1%
Religious groups: Roman Catholic 62%, traditional belief 32%, Protestant 5%, Muslim 1%
Languages spoken: Kirundi and French (both official), Swahili
International relations: UN, OAU, EC

Form of government: Military
Exports: Coffee, cotton, animal hides

Prior to the arrival of Europeans, Burundi was a kingdom with a highly stratified, feudal social structure. Rulers were drawn from princely dynastic families *(ganwa)*, from whom a king or *mwami* was chosen. A *mwami* continued to rule even after independence was granted.

European explorers and missionaries began making brief visits to the area as early as 1858; however, Burundi did not come under European administration until the 1890s, when it became part of German East Africa. In 1916 Belgian troops occupied the country; the League of Nations mandated it to Belgium in 1923 as part of the Territory of Ruanda-Urundi, now the nations of Rwanda and Burundi. Burundi became independent on July 1, 1962.

Burundi's population is made up of three ethnic groups—Hutu, Tutsi, and Twa. Hutus, who make up 85 percent of the population, are primarily farmers whose Bantu-speaking ancestors migrated into Burundi 800 to 1,000 years ago. The Tutsi, who make up 14 percent of the population, are a pastoral people who apparently migrated from Ethiopia several hundred years later. Years of dispute with neighboring Rwanda has continued into the 1990s. Ethnic conflict between the Hutus and Tutsis has led to many attrocities.

Cameroon

Official name: Republic of Cameroon
Independence: January 1, 1960
Capital: Yaoundé
Currency: CFA franc
Income (per capita US$): 1090 (1990)
Area: 183,568 sq. mi.
Illiteracy: 43% (1991)
Population: (1991 estimate) 11.7 million
Ethnic divisions: More than 200 groups
Religious groups: Christian, Muslim, traditional belief
Languages spoken: English and French (official), more than 200 tribal languages
International Relations: EC, OAU, UN
Form of government: Multi-party
Exports: Bananas, cocoa, coffee, cotton

The earliest inhabitants of Cameroon were probably Pygmies, who still inhabit the southern forests. However, Bantu-speaking people were among the first to invade Cameroon from equatorial Africa, settling in the south and later in the west. The Muslim Fulani from the Niger basin arrived in the eleventh and nineteenth centuries and settled in the north.

Europeans first made contact with the area in the 1500s. For the next three centuries, Spanish, Dutch, and British traders visited the area.

In July of 1884, Germany, the United Kingdom, and France each attempted to annex the area. A 1919 declaration divided Cameroon between the United Kingdom and France, with the larger, eastern area under France. In December of 1958, the French trusteeship was ended; French Cameroon became the Republic of Cameroon on January 1, 1960.

The Republic of Cameroon is made up of a federal system integrating the French controlled south and the British controlled north under the leadership of president Ahmadou Ahidjo. The country heavily depends on foreign capital and has been faced with internal problems both ethnic and social under the leadership of Ahidjo's successor, Paul Biya.

Cameroon has about 200 tribal groups and clans, speaking at least as many languages and dialects.

Cape Verde

Official name: Republic of Cape Verde
Independence: July 5, 1975
Capital: Praia
Currency: Escudo
Income (per capita US$): 890 (1990)
Area: 1,557 sq. mi.
Population: (1991 estimate) 386,000
Illiteracy: 53% (1991)
Ethnic divisions: Creole (mixed African and Portuguese), African, European
Religious groups: Roman Catholic, Protestant
Languages spoken: Portuguese (official), Crioulo (national)
Form of government: Multi-party
Exports: Animal products, vegetable products

Located in the north Atlantic Ocean, the Cape Verde archipelago remained uninhabited until the Portuguese visited it in 1456, and African slaves were brought to the islands to work on Portuguese plantations. As a result, Cape Verdeans have mixed African and Portuguese origins.

In 1951, Portugal changed Cape Verde's status from a colony to an overseas province. In 1956, the African Party for the Independence of Guinea-Bissau and Cape Verde (PAIGC) was organized to bring about improvement in economic, social, and political conditions in Cape Verde and Portuguese Guinea. The PAIGC began an armed rebellion against Portugal in 1961. Acts of sabotage eventually grew into a war in Portuguese Guinea that pitted 10,000 Soviet bloc-supported PAIGC soldiers against 35,000 Portuguese and African troops.

In December of 1974, the PAIGC and Portugal signed an agreement providing for a transitional government

Cameroonian women husking corn.

composed of Portuguese and Cape Verdeans. On June 30, 1975, Cape Verdeans elected a National Assembly, which received the instruments of independence from Portugal on July 5, 1975. After winning independence, the country voted for a union with Guinea-Bissau. In 1980, the link ended when Joao Vieira seized power in Guinea-Bissau. The PAIGC was dissolved and replaced by PAICV (African Party for the Independence of Cape Verde). Aristides Pereira was elected head of state in 1986.

The official language is Portuguese. However, most Cape Verdeans speak a Creole dialect, Crioulo, which consists of archaic Portuguese modified through contact with African and other European languages.

Central African Republic
Independence: August 13, 1960
Area: 242,000 sq. mi.
Capital: Bangui
Currency: CFA franc
Income: (per capita US$) 440 (1990)
Population: (1991 estimate) 2.9 million
Illiteracy: 62% (1991)
Ethnic divisions: More than 80 groupos, including Baya 34%, Banda 28%, Sara 10%, Mandja 9%, Mboum 9%, M'Baka 7%
Religious groups: Traditional belief 35%, Protestant 25%, Roman Catholic 25%, Muslim 15%
Languages spoken: French (official), Sangho (national)
International relations: EC, OAU, UN
Form of government: One-party system (1996)
Exports: Coffee, cotton, diamonds

The first Europeans to settle in the area that is now the Central African Republic were the French. In 1889, the French established an outpost at Bangu. United with Chad in 1906, the outpost formed the Oubangui-Chari-Chad colony.

In 1910, it became one of the four territories of the Federation of French Equatorial Africa, along with Chad, Congo (Brazzaville), and Gabon. However, a constitutional referendum of September 1958 dissolved the federation. The nation became an autonomous republic within the newly established French Community on December 1, 1958, and acceded to complete independence as the Central African Republic on August 13, 1960. The first president, revered as the founder of the Central African Republic, was Bathelemy Boganda.

Boganda's successor, David Dacko, was overthrown in 1966 by Gen. Jean-Badel Bokassa, who embarked on a reign of terror, proclaiming himself "emperor." A 1981 *coup d'e'tat* put Dacko back in power. Gen. André Kolingba succeeded Dacko and a multi-party state was established in 1991.

Central African woman preparing a meal.

The Central African Republic is made up of more than 80 ethnic groups, each with its own language. About 70 percent of the population comprises Baya-Mandjia and Banda, with approxiamtely seven percent M'Baka. Sangho, the language of a small group along the Oubangui River, is the national language spoken by the majority of Central Africans. The country is one of the poorest nations in Afrcia, with a high mortality rate and widespread malnutrition and illiteracy.

Chad
Official name: Republic of Chad
Independence: August 11, 1960
Capital: N'Djamena.
Currency: CFA franc
Income: (per capita US$) 207 (1990)
Area: 496,000 sq. mi.
Population: (1991 estimate) 5.8 million
Illiteracy: 82.% (1991)
Ethnic divisions: More than 200 groups including, Toubou (Gourane), Arabs, Fulbe, Kotoko, Hausa, Kanembou, Bagirmi, Boulala, Zaghawa, Hadjerai, and Maba; about 2,500 French citizens live in Chad
Religious groups: Muslim, Christian, traditional beliefs
Languages spoken: French and Arabic (official); 200 tribal languages
International relations: EC, OAU, UN
Form of government: One-party
Exports: Cotton, diamonds, petroleum products, wood

The region that is now Chad was known to Middle Eastern traders and geographers as far back the late

Middle Ages. Since then, Chad has served as a cross-roads for the Muslim peoples of the desert and savanna regions and the animist Bantu tribes of the tropical forests.

The Sao people populated the Chari River basin for thousands of years, but their relatively weak chiefdoms were overtaken by the powerful chiefs of what were to become the Kanem-Bornu and Baguirmi kingdoms. At their peak, these two kingdoms and the kingdom of Ouaddai controlled a good part of what is now Chad, as well as parts of Nigeria and Sudan.

The French first made contact with the region in 1891. The first major colonial battle for Chad was fought in 1900 between the French major Lamy and the African leader Rabah. Although the French won that battle, they did not declare the territory until 1911; armed clashes between colonial troops and local bands continued for many years thereafter. Although Chad joined the French colonies of Gabon, Oubangui-Charo, and Moyen Congo to form the Federation of French Equatorial Africa in 1910, Chad did not have colonial status until 1920.

In 1959, the territory of French Equatorial Africa was dissolved, and four states—Gabon, the Central African Republic, Congo (Brazzaville), and Chad—became autonomous members of the French Community. In 1960, Chad became an independent nation under its first president, Francois Tombalbaye. He was faced with the pressure of resolving the on-going conflict between the Muslim north and the black south and responded by instituting authoritarian rule. Backed by Libya, FRONAT (Front de Libération Nationale) guerillas of the north gained power, naming Goukouni Oueddei as head of state. In 1982, he was succeeded by Hisséne Habré, but civil war broke out one year later. In the 1990s, Chad remains impoverished, having faced long periods of drought and civil strife.

Chad is made up of more than 200 ethnic groups. Those in the north and east are generally Muslim; most southerners are animists and Christians.

Comoros

Official name: Comoros Federal Islamic Republic
Independence: July 6, 1975
Capital: Moroni
Currency: CFA franc
Income: (per capita US$) 480 (1990)
Area: 838 sq. mi.
Population: (1991 estimate): 476,000
Illiteracy: 46% (1991)
Ethnic divisions: Antalote, Cafre, Makoa, Oimatsaha, Sakalava
Religious groups: Sunni Muslim 98%, Roman Catholic 2%

Rural farmers in Chad.

Languages spoken: Shikomoro (a Swahili-Arab dialect), Malagasy, French
International relations: EC, OAU, UN
Form of government: One-party
Exports: Cloves, vanilla, ylang ylang

Located off the northwestern coast of Madagascar, Portuguese explorers visited the archipelago in 1505. In 1843, the sultan of Mayotte was persuaded to relinquish the island of Mayotte to the French. By 1912, France had established colonial rule over the islands of Grande Comore, Anjouan, and Hoheli and placed the islands under the administration of the governor general of Madagascar. After World War II, the islands became a French overseas territory and were represented in France's National Assembly. On July 6, 1975, the Comorian Parliament passed a resolution declaring unilateral independence. However, the deputies of Mayotte abstained; as a result, the Comorian government has effective control over only Grande Comore, Anjouan, and Moheli—Mayotte remains under French administration. After gaining independence, the country faced an enormous economical crisis.

The Comorians inhabiting the islands of Grande Comore, Anjouan, and Moheli (about 86 percent of the population) share African-Arab origins. Islam is the dominant religion, but a substantial minority of the citizens of Mayotte (the Mahorais) are Catholic and have been influenced strongly by French culture. The most common language is Shikomoro, a Swahili dialect. French and Malagasy are also spoken.

Congo

Official name: People's Republic of the Congo
Independence: August 15, 1960
Capital: Brazzaville
Currency: CFA franc
Income: (per capita US$) 1010 (1991)
Area: 132,000 sq. mi.

Children studying at a Koranic school in Chad.

Population: (1991) 2.4 million
Illiteracy: 43.% (1991)
Ethnic divisions: 15 main groups, 75 subgroups; largest
   groups are Bacongo, Bateke, M'Bochi, Sangha
Religious groups: Traditional belief 48%, Christian 47%,
   Muslim 2%
Languages spoken: French (official), Lingala, Kikongo
International relation: Member EC, OAU, UN
Form of government: Multi-party
Exports: Crude petroleum, diamonds, wood

The early history of the Congo is believed to have focused on three tribal kingdoms—the Kongo, the Loango, and the Teke. Established in the fourth century AD, the Kongo was a highly centralized kingdom that later developed a close commercial relationship with the Portuguese, the first Europeans to explore the area.

With the development of the slave trade, the Portuguese turned their attention from the Kongo Kingdom to the Loango. By the time the slave trade was abolished in the 1800s, the Loango Kingdom had been reduced to many small, independent groups. The Teke Kingdom of the interior, which had sold slaves to the Loango Kingdom, ended its independence in 1883, when the Teke king concluded a treaty with Pierre Savorgnan de Brazza,

placing Teke lands and people under French protection. Under the French, the area became known as Middle Congo.

In 1910, Middle Congo became part of French Equatorial Africa, which also included Gabon, the Central African Republic, and Chad.

A constitutional referendum in September 1958 replaced the Federation of French Equatorial Africa with the French Community. Middle Congo, under the name Republic of the Congo, and the three other territories of French Equatorial Africa became fully autonomous members within the French Community. On April 15, 1960, it became an independent nation but retained close, formal bonds with the community. President Fulbert Youlou instituted a dictatorship for the first three years following independence,then was succeeded by a revolutionary government headed by Alphonse Massamba Debat. The military imposed themselves as head of the nation under Gen. Marien Ngouabi, who declared the Congo a republic to be governed under a one-party system.

Cote d' Ivoire (Ivory Coast)
Independence: August 7, 1960
Capital: Abidjan
Currency: CFA franc
Income: (per capita US$) 730 (1990)
Area: 124,500 sq. mi.
Population: (1991 estimate): 12.9 million
Illiteracy: 46% (1991)
Ethnic divisions: More than 60 groups
Religious groups: Muslim 55%, Traditional belief 25%, Christian 20%
Languages spoken: French (official), tribal dialects
International relations: EC, OAU, UN
Form of government: Multi-party
Exports: Cocoa, cocoa butter, coffee, petroleum products, wood

The first Europeans, the French, made its initial contact with Cote d'Ivoire in 1637, when missionaries landed at Assinie near the Gold Coast (now Ghana) border. However, these early contacts were limited. In 1843 and 1844, France signed treaties with the kings of the Grand Bassam and Assinie regions, placing their territories under a French protectorate. French explorers, missionaries, trading companies, and soldiers gradually extended the area under French control, until 1893 when Cote d'Ivoire was officially made a French colony.

In December of 1958, Cote d'Ivoire became an autonomous republic within the French community. Cote d'Ivoire became independent on August 7, 1960. Felix Houphouët-Boigny led the country under a one-party system. He maintained ties with Europe, which helped bring about rapid development and economic stability.

Cote d'Ivoire's more than 60 ethnic groups usually are classified into seven principal divisions—Akan, Krou, Lagoon, Nuclear Mande, Peripheral Mande, Senoufo, and Lobi. The Baoule, in the Akan division, is probably the largest single subgroup, with perhaps 20 percent of the overall population. The Bete, in the Krou division, and the Senoufo in the north are the second and third largest groups, with roughly 18 and 15 percent of the national population, respectively.

Djibouti
Official name: Republic of Djibouti
Independence: June 27, 1977
Capital: Djibouti
Currency: Djibouti franc
Income: (per capita US$) 1250 (1990)
Area: 9,000 sq. mi.
Population: (1991 estimate) 541,000
Illiteracy: 41% (1987)
Ethnic divisions: Somalis (Issas), Afars, French, Arab, Ethiopian, Italian
Religious groups: Muslim 94%, Christian 6%
Languages spoken: French (official) Somali, Afar, Arabic
International relations: Arab League, EC, OAU, UN
Form of government: One-party.
Exports: Cereals, coffee, leather and skins, tea

The region, which now makes up the Republic of Djibouti, was first settled by the French in 1862, as a result of growing French interest in British activity in Egypt. In 1884, France expanded its protectorate to include the shores of the Gulf of Tadjourah and the hinterland, designating the area French Somaliland. The boundaries of the protectorate, marked out in 1897 by France and Emperor Manelik II of Ethiopia, were affirmed further by agreements with Emperor Haile Selassie I in 1945 and 1954.

A July of 1967 directive from Paris formally changed the name of the territory to the French Territory of Afars and Issas. In 1975, the French Government began to accommodate increasingly insistent demands for independence. In June of 1976, the territory's citizenship law, which had favored the Afar minority, was revised to reflect more closely the weight of the Issa Somali. In a May of 1977 referendum, the electorate voted for independence, and the Republic of Djibouti was inaugurated on June 27, 1977. Independence was followed by a republican form of government.

The indigenous population of the Republic of Djibouti is divided between the majority Somalis (predominantly of the Issa tribe with minority Ishaak and Gadaboursi representation) and the Afars and Danakils.

Egypt
Official name: Republic of Egypt
Independence: February 28, 1922
Capital: Cairo
Currency: Egyptian pound
Income: (per capita US$) 600 (1990)
Area: 386,650 sq. mi
Population: (1991 estimate) 54.8 million
Illiteracy: 52% (1991)
Ethnic divisions: Egyptian, Bedouin Arab, Nubian
Religious groups: Sunni Muslim 90%, Coptic Christian
Languages spoken: Arabic (official), English
International relations: Arab League, OAU, UN
Form of government: Presidential republic

Egypt has endured as a unified state for more than 5,000 years, and archeological evidence indicates that a developed Egyptian society has existed much longer. In about 3100 BC, Egypt was united under a ruler known as Mena, or Menes, who inaugurated the thirty pharaonic dynasties into which Egypt's ancient history is divided— the Old and Middle Kingdoms and the New Empire.

In 525 BC, Persians dethroned the last pharaoh of the 26th dynasty. The country remained a Persian province until the conquest of Alexander the Great in 332 BC. After Alexander's death in 323 BC, the Macedonian commander, Ptolemy, established personal control over Egypt, assuming the title of pharaoh in 304 BC. The Ptolemaic line ended in 30 BC with the suicide of Queen Cleopatra. The Emperor Augustus then established direct Roman control over Egypt, initiating almost seven centuries of Roman and Byzantine rule.

Egypt was invaded and conquered by Arab forces in AD 642; a process of Arabization and Islamization ensued. The French arrived in Egypt in 1798. An Anglo-Ottoman invasion force drove out the French in 1801, and following a period of chaos, the Albanian Muhammad Ali obtained control of the country.

In 1882, the British occupies Egypt and declared a formal protectorate over Egypt on December 18, 1914. In deference to growing nationalist feelings, Britain unilaterally declared Egyptian independence on February 28, 1922. King Faud I ruled after independence until 1952, when he was overthrown and Gamal Abdel Nasser was elected president of the republic a few years later. Upon his death, Anwar el-Sadat took over the leadership until he was brutally assassinated in 1981 and succeeded by Hosni Mubarak.

The Egyptian population is fairly homogenous—Mediterranean and Arab influences appear in the north, as well as some mixing in the south with the Nubians of northern Sudan. Ethnic minorities include a small number of Bedouin Arab nomads dispersed in the eastern and western deserts and in the Sinai, as well as some 50,000 to 200,000 Nubians clustered along the Nile in Upper Egypt.

Eritrea

Official name: Eritrea
Independence: May 25, 1993
Capital: Asmara
Currency: Ethiopian birr
Area: 46,761 sq. mi.
Population: (1996 estimate) 3.1 million
Religious groups: Muslim 50%, Monophysite Christian 35%, Animist 15%

Eritrea was an integral part of the kingdom of Aksum and has shared its destiny with Ethiopia. Islamic colonists became established in the coastal area. Consequently, the Arab domination of the region lasted until the later half of the nineteenth century, when Egyptians settled in the area. Founded in 1890 by the Italians, the colony of Eritrea was annexed by Ethiopia after World War II. For years the Eritrian People's Liberation Forum waged a struggle for independence that was eventually won on May 25, 1993.

Once a marvel, Asmara, the capital city was built by Italians in the 1920s. During conflicts between Soviet-backed Ethiopian troops and Eritrean rebels, Asmara's railway system was destroyed. Upon gaining independence, the former rebels, along with hundreds of other local workers, discovered all the missing parts in order to reassemble the crucial rail link and repair the vintage steam locomotives. The system was to by readied by 1997. Meanwhile, hundreds of exiles returned, bringing with them necessary capital and technological expertise. The ruling party, People's Front for Democracy and Justice and the country's president, Isais Afewerki, have promoted privitization and encouraged foreign investors to do business in Eritrea. These events have led many to consider the new nation one of Africa's greatest successes.

Equatorial Guinea

Official name: Republic of Equatorial Guinea
Independence: October 12, 1968
Capital: Malabo
Currency: CFA franc
Income: (per capita US$) 310 (1990)
Area: 10,820 sq. mi.
Population: (1991 estimate) 360,000
Illiteracy: 69% (1991)
Ethnic divisions: Fang 80%, Bubi 15%, other 5%
Religious groups: Roman Catholic 83%, Protestant, traditional belief
Languages spoken: Spanish (official), Fang, Bubi, pidgin, English, French, other tribal languages
International relations: EC, OAU, UN
Form of government: One-party

state. A military coup occurred in 1979, deposing Nguema, who was put to death for "crimes against humanity."

The majority of the Equatoguinean people are of Bantu origin. The largest tribe, the Fang, constitute 80 percent of the population and are divided into about 67 clans. Those to the north of Rio Benito on Rio Muni speak Fang-Ntumu, and those to the south speak Fang-Okak, two mutually intelligible dialects. The Bubi, who form 15 percent of the population, are indigenous to Bioko Island. In addition, several coastal tribes exist, who are sometimes referred to as "Playeros," and include the Ndowes, Bujebas, Balengues, and Bengas on the mainland and small islands, and Fernandinos, a Creole community, on Bioko. These groups comprise five percent of the population.

Ethiopia

Official name: People's Democratic Republic of Ethiopia
Capital: Addis Ababa
Income: (per capita US$) 120 (1990)
Area: 472,000 sq. mi.
Population: (1990 estimate) 51.3 million
Illiteracy: 95% (1991)
Ethnic divisions: Oromo 40%, Amhara 25%, Tigre 12%, Sidama 9%
Religious groups: Muslim 40%-45%, Ethiopian Orthodox Christian 35%-40%, traditional beliefs 15%-25%
Languages spoken: Amharic (official), Tigrinya, Orominga, Arabic, English
International relations: EC, OAU, UN
Form of government: Multi-party
Exports: Coffee, hides and skins, live animals

Ethiopia is the oldest independent country in Africa and one of the oldest in the world. Herodotus, the Greek historian of the fifth century BC, describes ancient Ethiopia in his writings; the Old Testament of the Bible records the Queen of Sheba's visit to Jerusalem. Missionaries from Egypt and Syria introduced Christianity in the fourth century AD. The Portuguese established contact with Ethiopia in 1493.

In 1930 Haile Selassie, was crowned emperor. His reign was interrupted in 1936 when Italian fascist forces invaded and occupied Ethiopia. The emperor was eventually forced into exile in England despite his plea to the League of Nations for intervention. Five years later, the Italians were defeated by British and Ethiopian forces, and the emperor returned to the throne. After a period of civil unrest, which began in February 1974, the aging Haile Selassie I was deposed on September 13, 1974. After deposing Selasie, the military, led by Col. Mariam Haile Mengistu, took over the government and nationalized nearly all the country's economic institutions.

Equatoguinean children.

Exports: Cocoa, coffee

The first inhabitants of the region that is now Equatorial Guinea are believed to have been Pygmies, of whom only isolated pockets remain in northern Rio Muni. Bantu migrations between the seventeenth and ninteenth centuries brought the coastal tribes and later the Fang people to the area.

The Portuguese, seeking a route to India, landed on the island of Bioko in 1471. The Portuguese retained control until 1778, when the island and adjacent islets, were ceded to Spain. From 1827 to 1843, Britain established a base on the island to combat the slave trade. Conflicting claims to the mainland were settled in 1900 by the Treaty of Paris.

In 1959, the Spanish territory of the Gulf of Guinea was established. In 1963, the name of the country was changed to Equatorial Guinea. In March 1968, under pressure from Equatoguinean nationalists and the United Nations, Spain announced that it would grant independence to Equatorial Guinea. In September 1968, Francisco Macias Nguema was elected first president of Equatorial Guinea, and independence was granted in October with Francisco Macias Nguema as the head of

Haile Selassie

Discontent had been spreading throughout Ethiopian urban elites, and an escalating series of mutinies in the armed forced, demonstrations, and strikes led to the seizure of state power by the armed forces coordinating committee, which later became the Provisional Military Administrative Council (PMAC). The PMAC formally declared its intent to remake Ethiopia into a socialist state. It finally destroyed its opposition in a program of mass arrests and executions known as the "red terror," which lasted from November of 1977 to March of 1978. An estimated 10,000 people, mostly in Addis Ababa, were killed by government forces. Mengistu's failure to respond to growing national problems—compounded by droughts, an armed struggle by Eritre and Tigre, and declining Soviet aid—brought him down. Early in 1991, he was forced into exile in Zimbabwe.

Ethiopia's population is highly diverse. Most of its people speak a Semitic or Cushitic language. The Amhara, Tigreans, and Oromo make up more than three-fourths of the population, but there are more than 40 different ethnic groups within Ethiopia.

Gabon
Official name: Gabonese Republic
Independence: August 17, 1960
Capital: Libreville
Currency: CFA franc
Income: (per capita US$) 3450 (1990)
Area: 102,317 sq. mi.
Population: (1990 estimate): 1.2 million

Illiteracy: 39% (1991)
Ethnic divisions: Fang, Myene, Bapounou, Eschira, Bandjabi, Beteke/Obamba
Religious groups: Christian, Muslim, traditional belief
Languages spoken: French (official), Fang, Myene, Bateke, Bapounou/Eschira, Bandjabi
International relations: EC, OAU, UN
Form of government: Multi-party
Exports: Crude petroleum, manganese, uranium

Gabon's first European visitors were Portuguese traders who arrived in the 15th century. The coast became a center of the slave trade. Dutch, British, and French traders came in the 16th century. France assumed the status of protector by signing treaties with Gabonese coastal chiefs in 1839 and 1841. In 1910, Gabon became one of the four territories of French Equatorial Africa, a federation that survived until 1959. The territories became independent in 1960 as the Central African Republic, Chad, Congo (Brazzaville), and Gabon, which, Léon M'ba led the government after independence. Upon his death in 1967, Albert Bongo took over has head of state.

Almost all Gabonese are of Bantu origin. Gabon has at least forty tribal groups, with separate languages and cultures; the largest group is the Fang. Other tribes include the Myene, Bandjabi, Eshira, Bapounou, Bateke/Obamba, and Okande.

Gambia
Official name: Republic of The Gambia
Independence: February 18, 1965
Capital: Danjul
Currency: Dalasi
Income: (per capita US$) 260 (1990)
Area; 4,361 sq. mi.
Population: (1991 estimate) 874,000
Illiteracy: 73% (1991)
Ethnic divisions: Mandinka 36.1%, Fula 16.8%, Wolof 13.4%, Jola 9.2%, Serahuli 7.3%, other 1.4%
Religious groups: Muslim 95%, Christian traditional belief
Languages spoken: English (official), Mandinka, Wolof, Fula, other traibal languages
International relations: Commonwealth, EC, OAU, UN
Form of government: Multi-party
Exports: Groundnuts

Gambia was once part of the Empire of Ghana and the Kingdom of Songhai. When the Portuguese visited in the fifteenth century, it was part of the Kingdom of Mali.

By the sixteenth century, Portuguese slave traders and gold seekers had settled. In 1588, the Portuguese sold exclusive trade rights on the Gambia River to English merchants. During the late seventeenth century

An Ethiopian market

and throughout the eighteenth, England and France struggled continuously for political and commercial supremacy in the regions of the Senegal and Gambia Rivers.

In 1807, slave trading was abolished throughout the British Empire, and the British tried unsuccessfully to end the slave traffic in Gambia. An 1889 agreement with France established the present boundaries, and Gambia became a British Crown Colony. Gambia achieved independence on February 18, 1965, as a constitutional monarchy within the British Commonwealth. In 1970, Gambia became a republic. Several attempts were made to establish a post-independence union with Senegal. A contingent of Senegalese soldiers were stationed in Gambia, but the arrangement soured. Coupled with mounting economic problems, the confederation ended.

Ghana
Official name: Republic of Ghana
Independence: March 6, 1957

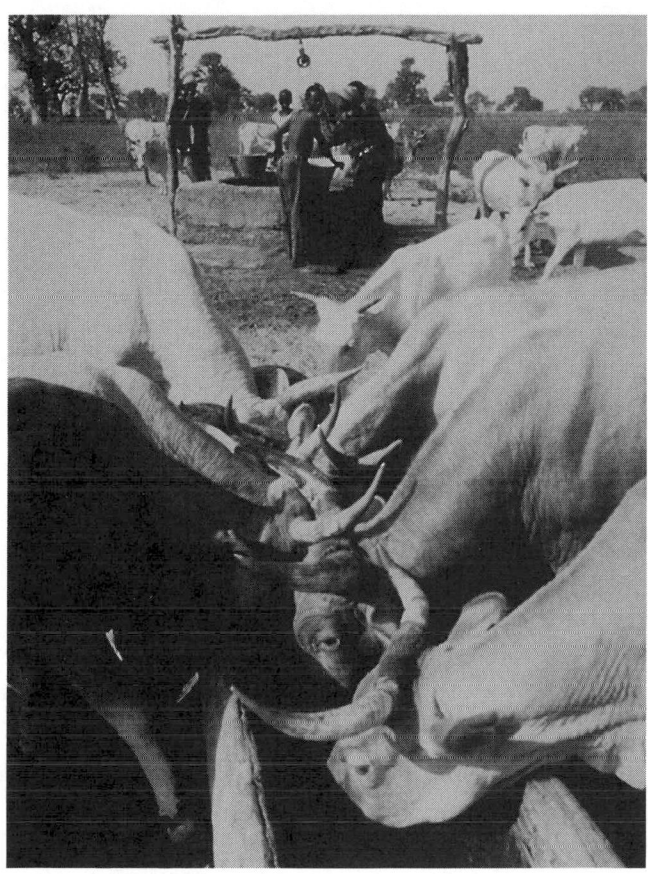
Cattleherders in rural Gambia.

Capital: Accra
Currency: Cedi
Income: (per capita US$) 390 (1990)
Area: 92,100 sq. mi.
Population: (1991 estimate): 15,6 million
Illiteracy: 40% (1991)
Ethnic divisions: Akan, Ewe, Ga
Religious groups: Christian 42%, traditional belief 38%, Muslim 12%, other 7%
Languages spoken: English (official), Akan 44%, Mole-Dagbani 16%, Ewe 13%, Ga-Adangbe 8%
International relations: Commonwealth, EC, OAU, UN
Form of government: Provisions for multi-party has been set
Exports: Cocoa, diamonds, gold, manganese ore, wood

The first contact between Europe and the Gold Coast dates from 1470, when a party of Portuguese landed. For the next three centuries, the English, Danes, Dutch, Germans, and Portuguese controlled various parts of the coastal areas. In 1821, the British government took control of the British trading forts on the Gold Coast. In 1844, Fanti chiefs in the area signed an agreement with the British. Between 1826 and 1900, the British fought a series of campaigns against the Ashantis, whose king-dom was located inland. By 1902, the British had suc-ceeded in colonizing the Ashanti region.

On March 6, 1957, the United Kingdom relinquished its control over the Colony of the Gold Coast and Ashanti, the Northern Territories Protectorate, and Brit-ish Togoland. The Gold Coast and the former British Togoland merged to form what is now Ghana. Focusing on anti-imperialism and pan-Africanism, Ghana be-came a model for the whole continent. Though he had idolized throughout the diaspora, Nkruma was over-thrown in 1966, subjecting the nation to military and dictatorial regimes. When Jerry Rawlings, who had masterminded two successfuly coups in 1979 and 1981, became head of state in 1982, he promised to return the country to pluralism. In 1992, he was elected to the presidency in a multi-party election.

Most Ghanaians descended from migrating tribes that probably came down the Volta River valley in the thirteenth century. Ethnically, Ghana is divided into small groups speaking more than 50 languages and dialects. Among the more important linguistic groups are the Akans, which include the Fantis along the coast and the Ashantis in the forest region north of the coast; the Guans, on the plains of the Volta River; the Ga- and Ewe-speaking peoples of the south and southeast; and the Moshi-Dagomba-speaking tribes of the northern and upper regions.

Guinea

Official name: Republic of Guinea
Independence: October 2, 1958
Capital: Conakry
Currency: Guinea franc
Income: (per capita US$) 480 (1990)
Area: 95,000 sq. mi.
Population: (1991 estimate) 7.4 million
Illiteracy: 72% (1991)
Ethnic divisions: Foulah, Malinke, Soussou, 15 smaller groups
Religious groups: Muslim 85%, Christian 10%, traditional belief 5%
Languages spoken: French (official), tribal languages
International relations: EC, OAU, UN
Form of government: Military
Exports: Agricultural products, minerals

The empires of Ghana, Mali, and Songhai spanned the period from about the tenth to the fifteenth centuries. French military penetration into the area began in the mid-nineteenth century. By signing treaties with the French in the 1880s, Guinea's Malinke leader, Samory Toure, secured a free hand to expand eastward. In 1890, he allied himself with the Toucouleur Empire and King-dom of Sikasso and tried to expel the French from the area. However, he was defeated in 1898, and France

Gambian President, Dauda Jawara addresses local authorities.

gained control of Guinea and the Ivory Coast (now Cote d'Ivoire).

Guinea became an independent republic in 1958, and voted against entering the French community. Se'kou Touré was the first president until his death in 1984. The country then heavily relied upon aid from the Soviet bloc and attempts were made to insitute socialism. A military committee for national redressment (CMRN) lead a coup and later dissolved the one-party system with promises to restore democracy.

Guinea consists of four main ethnic groups—Peuls (Foulah or Foulani), who inhabit the mountainous Fouta Djallon; Malinkes (or Mandingos), in the savannah regions; Soussous in the coastal areas; and Forestal tribes in the forest regions.

Guinea-Bissau

Official name: Republic of Guinea-Bissau
Independence: September 24, 1973
Capital: Bissau
Currency: Guinea peso
Income: (per capita US$) 155 (1990)
Area: 14,000 sq. mi.
Population: (1991 estimate) 1 million

Illiteracy: 64% (1991)
Ethnic divisions: Balanta 27%, Fula 23%, Mandinka 12%, Manjaco 11%, Papel 10%, Biafada 3%, Mancanha 3%, Bijagos 3%
Religious groups: Traditional belief 65%, Muslim 30%, Christian 5%
Languages spoken: Portuguese (official); Criolo, tribal languages
International relations: EC, OAU, UN
Form of government: Pluralism
Exports: Coconuts, fish, groundnuts

The rivers of Guinea and the islands of Cape Verde were one of the first areas in Africa explored by the Portuguese in the fifteenth century. Portugal claimed Portuguese Guinea in 1446. In 1630, a "captaincy-general" of Portuguese Guinea was established to administer the territory. With the assistance of local tribes, the Portuguese entered the slave trade, exporting large numbers of Africans to the New World via Cape Verde. The slave trade declined in the ninteenth century and Bissau, originally founded as a fort in 1765, became the major commercial center.

In 1956, the African Party for the Independence of Guinea and Cape Verde (PAIGC) was organized by

Amilcar Cabral and Raphael Barbosa. Despite the presence of more than 30,000 Portuguese troops, the PAIGC exercised influence over much of the country; the Portuguese were increasingly confined to their garrisons and larger towns. The PAIGC National Assembly declared the independence of Guinea-Bissau on December 24, 1973, the same year that PAIGC leader Amilcar Cabral was assassinated by the Portuguese secret police; Portugal granted *de jure* independence on September 19, 1974, when the United States recognized the new nation. Luis Cabral, Amilcar's brother, became president of Guinea-Bissau and Cape Verde. In 1980 Cape Verde established its independence from Guinea-Bissau and its leader, Joao Bernado Vieira.

The population of Guinea-Bissau comprises several diverse tribal groups, each with its own language, customs, and social organization. The Fula and Mandinka tribes, in the north and northeast of the country, are mostly Muslim. Other important tribal groups are the Balanta and Papel, living in the southern coastal regions, and the Manjaco and Mancanha, occupying the central and northern coastal areas.

Kenya

Official name: Republic of Kenya
Independence: December 12, 1963
Capital: Nairobi
Currency: Kenyan shilling
Income:(per capita 370 (1990)
Area: 224,960 sq. mi.
Population: (1991 estimate) 25.2 million
Illiteracy: 41% (1991)
Ethnic divisions: Kikuyu 21%, Luhya 14%, Luo 13%, Kalenjin 11%, Kamba 11%, Kisii 6%, Meru 5%. Non-Africans 1%
Religious groups: Traditional belief 26%, Protestant 38%, Roman Catholic 28%, Muslim 6%
Languages spoken: Swahili (official), English, tribal languages
International relations: Commonwealth, EC, OAU, UN
Form of government: Multi-party
Exports: Coffee, hides and skins, petroleum products, soda ash, tea

The Cushitic-speaking people, who occupied the area that is now Kenya around 1000 BC, were known to have maintained contact with Arab traders during the first century AD; Arab and Persian settlements were founded along the coast as early as the eighth century AD. By then, Bantu and Nilotic peoples also had moved into the area. The Arabs were followed by the Portuguese in 1498, by Islamic control under the Imam of Oman in the 1600s, and by British influence in the

Nairobi, Kenya.

ninteenth century. In 1885, European powers first partitioned east Africa into spheres of influence. In 1895, the British government established the East African Protectorate.

From October 1952 to December 1959, Kenya was under a state of emergency, arising from the Mau Mau rebellion against British colonial rule. The first direct elections for Africans to the legislative council took place in 1957. Kenya became fully independent on December 12, 1963. Jomo Kenyatta, a member of the predominant Kikuyu tribe and head of the Kenya African National Union, became Kenya's first president. He adopted a moderate, pro-Western policy and persued capitalism internally, allowing Kenya to achieve a higher level of economic prosperity than its neighbors. Kenyatta died in 1978, and was succeeded by Daniel Arap Moi, who insisted on persuing a one-party system until recently.

Lesotho

Official name: Kingdom of Lesotho
Independence: October 4, 1966
Capital: Maseru
Currency: Loti

A Masai tribesman.

Income: (per capita US$) 485 (1990)
Area: 11,718 sq. mi.
Population: (1991): 1.8 million
Illiteracy: 26% (1991)
Ethnic divisions: Basotho
Religious groups: Roman Catholic, Lesotho Evangelical,
    Anglican
Languages spoken: English, Sesotho
International relations: Commonwealth, EC, OAU, UN
Form of government: Constitutional monarchy
Exports: Diamonds, live animals, mohair, wool

Until the end of the sixteenth century, Basutoland, now Lesotho, was sparsely populated by bushmen (Qhuaique). Between the sixteenth and ninteenth centuries, refugees from surrounding areas gradually formed the Basotho ethnic group. In 1818, Moshoeshoe I, consolidated various Basotho groupings and became king. During his reign from 1823 to 1870, a series of wars with South Africa resulted in the loss of extensive lands, now known as the "Lost Territory." Moshoeshoe appealed to Queen Victoria for assistance, and in 1868 the country was placed under British protection.

In 1955, the Basutoland Council asked that it be empowered to legislate on internal affairs, and in 1959 a new constitution gave Basutoland its first elected legislature. On October 4, 1966, the new Kingdom of Lesotho attained full independence. Three years later, Leabua Jonathan became the head of state and embarked on repressing internal opposition. Years later, when he appeared to be losing the presidential elections, he seized pwoer in order to retain his leadership. Soon after, he was overthrown by the military.

Liberia

Official name: Republic of Liberia
Capital: Monrovia
Currency: Liberian dollar
Income: (per capita US$) 250 (1990)
Area: 43,000 sq. mi.
Population: (1991 estimate) 2.7 million
Illiteracy: 78% (1991)
Ethnic divisions: 5% descendants of freed American slaves, 95% indigenous tribes (the largest of which are Kpélle, Bassa, Gio, Kru, Grebo, Mano, Krahn, Gola, Gbandi, Loma, Kissi, Vai, Mandingo, and Belle)
Religious groups: Traditional belief 65%, Muslim 20%, Christian 15%
Languages spoken: English (official), more than 20 tribal languages of the Niger-Congo language group
International relations: EC, OAU, UN
Exports: Cocoa, coffee, diamonds, iron ore, rubber, wood

It is believed that the forebears of many present-day Liberians migrated into the area from the north and east between the twelefth and seventeenth centuries. Portuguese explorers visited Liberia's coast in 1461, and during the next 300 years, European merchants and coastal Africans engaged in trade.

The history of modern Liberia dates from 1816, when the American Colonization Society, a private organization, was given a charter by the United States Congress to send freed slaves to the west coast of Africa. The United States government, under President James Monroe, provided funds and assisted in negotiations with native chiefs for the ceding of land for this purpose. The first settlers landed at the site of Monrovia in 1822. In 1838, the settlers united to form the Commonwealth of Liberia, under a governor appointed by the American Colonization Society.

In 1847, Liberia became Africa's first independent republic. The republic's first 100 years have been described as a "century of survival" due to attempts by neighboring colonial powers (France and Britain) to encroach on Liberia. Independence gave power to the black elite of American origin and technically excluded the indigenous population, creating social tension. In

1980, Sargent Samuel Doe and his Council of Popular Redemption came to power in a bloody coup. Doe leaned on the Soviet Union and established himself as a dictator. He was killed, however, during an insurrection led by the National Patriotic Front. The nation continues to be in turmoil.

Libya

Official name: Socialist People's Libyan Arab Jamahiriya
Independence: December 24, 1951
Capital: Tripoli
Currency: Dinar
Income: (per capita US$) 6,060 (1990)
Area: 679,536 sq.mi.
Population: (1991 estimate) 4.3 million
Illiteracy: 36% (1991)
Ethnic divisions: Arab and Arab/Berber 80%, Berber 15%, Touareg and Tebous Arab
Religious groups: Sunni Muslim 97%
Languages spoken: Arabic
International relations: Arab League, OAU, UN
Form of government: Military

In the seventh century AD, Arabs conquered the area that is now Libya. In the following centuries, most of the inhabitants adopted Islam and the Arabic language and culture. The Ottoman Turks conquered the country in the sixteenth century. Libya remained part of their empire—although at times virtually autonomous—until Italy invaded in 1911 and, after years of resistance, incorporated Libya as its colony.

King Idris I, Emir of Cyrenaica, led a Libyan resistance to Italian occupation between the two World Wars. Under the terms of the 1947 peace treaty with the allies, Italy relinquished all claims to Libya. On November 21, 1949, the United Nations General Assembly passed a resolution stating that Libya should become independent before January 1, 1952. Libya declared its independence on December 24, 1951.

In a military coup of 1969, King Idris was overthrown by Muammar al-Qaddafi, who, nationalized all the petroleum resources and embarked on supporting international terrorism against the Western countries Some of Qaddafi's activities have also created friction with some of the neighboring countries, and, in 1986, the United States bombed Tripoli and Benghazi.

Madagascar

Official name: Democratic Republic of Madagascar
Independence: June 26, 1960
Capital: Antananarivo
Currency: Malagasy franc
Income:(per capita US$) 230 (1990)
Area: 228,880 sq. mi.
Population (1991 estimate) 12.1 million

Illiteracy: 20% (1991)
Ethnic divisions: 18 Malagasy tribes, small groups of Comorians, French, Indians, and Chinese
Religious groups: Traditional belief 55%, Christian 40%, Muslim 5%
Languages spoken: Malagasy (official), French
International relations: EC, OAU, UN
Form of government: Multiparty
Exports: Coffee, cloves, crude petroleum, sugar, vanilla

Located east of the African mainland in the Indian Ocean, Madagascar is home to people who arrived from Africa and Asia during the first five centuries AD. Three major kingdoms ruled the island—Betsimisaraka, Merina, and Sakalava. In the seventh century AD, Arabs established trading posts in the coastal areas of what is now Madagascar. Portuguese sighted the island in the sixteenth century, and in the late seventeenth century, the French established trading posts along the east coast.

In the 1790s, the Merina rulers succeeded in establishing hegemony over the major part of the island including the coast. The Merina ruler and the British governor of Mauritius concluded a treaty abolishing the slave trade, which had been important in Madagascar's economy, and in return the island received British military assistance. British influence remained strong for several decades. The British accepted the imposition of a French protectorate over Madagascar in 1885. France established control by military force in 1895, and the Merina monarchy was abolished. The Malagasy Republic was proclaimed on October 14, 1958, as an autonomous state within the French community. A period of provisional government ended with the adoption of a constitution in 1959 and full independence in 1960.

Madagascar persued a moderate policy after independence and collaboration with France continued until 1972 when a military coup took over and launched a socialist policy aligning itself with the eastern block. Malagasy as the country is know today, has suffered a severe economic crisis after having nationalized all the French property and having very little foreign investment.

Madagascar's population is predominantly of mixed Asian and African origin. The largest groups are the Betsimisaraka (one million), the Tsimihety (500,000), and the Sakalava (500,000).

Malawi
Official name: Republic of Malawi
Independence: July 6, 1964
Capital: Lilongwe
Currency: Kwacha
Income: (per capita US$) 212 (1990)
Area: 45,747 sq. mi.
Population: (1991 estimate) 9.4 million

Illiteracy: 59% (1991)
Ethnic divisions: Chewa, Nyanja, Tumbuka, Yao, Lomwe, Sena, Tonga, Ngoni Asians
Religious groups: Protestant 55%, Roman Catholic 20%, Muslim 20%, traditional belief
Languages spoken: Chicewa and English (official), tribal languages
International relations: EC, OAU, UN
Form of government: Multi-party
Exports: Cotton, groundnuts, sugar, tea, tobacco

Hominid remains and stone implements, dating back more than 1 million years, have been identified in Malawi; early humans are belived to have inhabited the area surrounding Lake Malawi 50,000 to 60,000 years ago.

Malawi derives its name from the Maravi, a Bantu people who came from the southern Congo about six hundred years ago. By the sixteenth century, the two divisions of the tribe had established a kingdom stretching from north of today's Nkhotakota to the Zambezi River in the south and from Lake Malawi in the east to the Luangwa River in Zambia in the west.

The Portuguese first reached the area in the sixteenth century. David Livingston reached the shore of Lake Malawi in 1859. By 1878 a number of traders, mostly from Scotland, formed the African Lakes Company to supply goods and services to the missionaries. In 1891, the British established the Nyasaland Protectorate. Nyasaland joined with Northern and Southern Rhodesia in 1953 to form the Federation of Rhodesia and Nyasaland.

Throughout the 1950s, pressures were exerted within Nykasaland for independence. In July 1958, Dr. H. Kamazu Banda returned to the country after a long stay in the United States (where he had obtained his medical degree at Meharry Medical College in 1937), the United Kingdom, and Ghana. He assumed leadership of the Nyasaland African Congress, which later became the Malawi Congress Party (MCP). In 1959, Banda was sent to Gwele Prison for his political activities but was released in 1960.

On April 15, 1961, the MCP won an overwhelming victory in elections for a new Legislative Council. In a second constitutional conference in London in November of 1962, the British government agreed to give Nyasaland self-governing status the following year. Dr. Banda became prime minister on February 1, 1963, although the British still controlled Malawi's financial security and judicial systems. The Federation of Rhodesia and Nyasaland was dissolved on December 31, 1963, and Malawi became fully independent on July 6, 1964. Two years later, Malawi adopted a new constitution and became a republic with Dr. Banda as its first president. In 1996, Bakili Mluzi, a woman, was elected to the presidency.

The Chewas constitute 90 percent of the population of the central region; the Nyanja tribe predominates in the south and the Tumbuka in the north. In addition, significant numbers of the Tongas live in the north; Ngonis—an offshoot of the Zulus who came from South Africa in the early 1800s—live in the lower northern and lower central regions; and the Yao, who are mostly Muslim, live along the southeastern border with Mozambique.

Mali

Official name: Republic of Mali
Independence: September 22, 1960
Capital: Bamako
Currency: CFA franc
Area: 474,764 sq. mi.
Population: (1991 estimate) 8.3 million
Illiteracy: 90% (1991)
Ethnic divisions: Mande (Bambara or Bamana, Malinke, Sarakole) 50%, Peul 17% Voltaic 12%, Songhai 6%, Tuareg and Moor 5%
Religious groups: Islam 90%, traditional belief 9%, Christian 1%
Languages spoken: French (official) and Bambara (spoken by about 80% of the population)
International relations: EC, OAU, UN
Exports: Cotton, groundnuts, live animals

Mali is the cultural heir to the succession of ancient African empires—Ghana, Malinke, and Songhai—that occupied the West African savanna. The Ghana empire, dominated by the Soninke people and centered in the area along the Malian-Mauritanian frontier, was a powerful trading state from about 700 to 1075 AD. The Malinke kingdom of Mali, from which the republic takes its name, had its origins on the upper Niger River in the eleventh century. Expanding rapidly in the thirteenth century under the leadership of Soundiata Keita, it reached its height about 1325, when it conquered Timbuktu and Gao. The Songhai empire expanded its power from its center in Gao during the period 1465 to 1530. At its peak under Askia Mohammad I, it encompassed the Hausa states as far as Kano (in present-day Nigeria) and much of the territory that had belonged to the Mali Empire in the west. It was destroyed by a Moroccan invasion in 1591.

French military penetration of the area began around 1880. A French civilian governor of Soudan (the French name for the area) was appointed in 1893, but resistance to French control was not abrogated until 1898 when the Malinke warrior, Samory Toure, was defeated after seven years of war. In January 1959, Soudan joined Senegal to form the Mali Federation, which became fully independent within the French Community on June 20, 1960. The federation collapsed on August 20, 1960, when Senegal seceded. On September 22, Soudan proclaimed itself the Republic of Mali and withdrew from the French Community.

The first head of state—Modibo Keita followed a socialist orientation but gradually increased his authoritarian leadership. In 1968, Military Committee of National Liberation coup overthrew Keita's government. Mali remains a poor country, compounded by the fact that more than half of its territory is a desert.

Mali's population consists of diverse sub-Saharan ethnic groups, sharing similar historic, cultural, and religious traditions. Exceptions are the Tuaregs and Moors, desert nomads, who are related to the North African Berbers.

Mauritania

Official name: Islamic Republic of Mauritania
Independence: November 28, 1960
Capital: Nouakchott
Currency: Ouguiya
Income (per capita US$) 500 (1990)
Area: 419,229 sq. mi.
Population: (1991 estimate) 1.9 million
Illiteracy: 72% (1991)
Ethnic divisions: Arab-Berber, Arab-Berber-Negroid, Negroid
Religious groups: Moslem
Languages spoken: Hassaniya Arabic (national), French (official), Pular, Wolof, and Soninke
International relations: Arab League, EC, OAU, UN
Form of government: Military
Exports: Fish, gypsum, iron ore

Archeological evidence suggests that Berber and Negroid Mauritanians lived beside one another before the spread of the desert drove them southward. Migration of these people increased during the third and fourth centuries AD, when Berber groups arrived seeking pasture for their herds and safety from political unrest and war in the north. The Berbers established a loose confederation, called the Sanhadja. Trading towns were established to facilitate the trade of gold, ivory, and slaves.

In the tenth century, conquests by warriors of the Soudanese Kingdom of Ghana broke up the Berber confederation. In the eleventh century, the conquest of the Western Sahara regions by a Berber tribe, decimated the Ghanaian kingdom and firmly established Islam throughout Mauritania. However, these people were defeated by Arab invaders in the sixteenth century.

French military penetration of Mauritania began early in the twentieth century. However, the area come

Malian men on camels.

under French control until about 1934. Until independence, the French governed the country largely by relying on the authority of the tribal chiefs, some of whom, such as the Emirs of Trarza and Adrar, had considerable authority. Under French occupation, slavery was legally abolished.

Mauritania became a French colony in 1920. The Islamic Republic of Mauritania was proclaimed in November 1958. Mauritania became independent on November 28, 1960 and withdrew from the French Community in 1966.

Mokhtar Ould Daddah, leader of the Mauritian People's Party was the first head of state, but a series of coups took place: the first, in 1978, replaced Daddah with Col. Moustabpha Ould Mohammed Salek, who was then replaced by Prime Minister Mohammed Khouma Ould Haidalla. In 1984, another coup, this one led by Maawiya Ould Sid'Ahmed Taya took place.

Moors, heterogeneous groups of Arab-Berber people who speak Hassaniya dialects, make up an estimated three-quarters of the population and are traditionally nomadic pastoralists. The country's black population—the Toucouleur, Soninke, Bambara, and Wolof—are mainly cultivators and are concentrated along the Senegal River.

Mauritius

Independence: March 12, 1968
Capital: Port Louis
Currency: Rupee
Income: (per capita US$) 2300 (1990)
Area: 720 sq. mi.
Population: (1991 estimate) 1 million
Illiteracy: 17% (1991)
Ethnic divisions: Indo-Mauritians 68%, Creoles 27%, Sino-Mauritians 3%, Franco-Mauritians 2%
Religious groups: Hindo, Muslim, Roman Catholic
Languages spoken: English (official), Creole, French, Hindi, Urdu, Hakka, Bhojpuri
International relations: Commonwealth, EC, OAU, UN
Form of government: Multi-party
Exports: Garments, molasses, sugar, tea, textiles

Portuguese sailors first visited Mauritius in the early sixteenth century, although the island has been known to Arabs and Malays much earlier. Dutch sailors, who named the island in honor of Prince Maurice of Nassau, established a small colony in 1638, but abandoned it in

A Bamana artistian.

1710. The French claimed Mauritius in 1715, renaming it Ile de France. In 1810, Mauritius was captured by the British, whose possession of the island was confirmed four years later by the Treaty of Paris. After slavery was abolished in 1835, indentured laborers from India brought an additional cultural influence to the island. Mauritius achieved independence on March 12, 1968. After independence Mauritius continued to face not only severe economic problems but also ethnic diversity crisis between the French cultural influence and English.

27 percent of Mauritians are of mixed European and African descent, tracing their origins to the plantation owners and slaves who were the first to exploit the island's potential for growing sugar. Descendants of the Indian immigrants constitute 68 percent of the population and are the principal laborers in the sugar industry.

Mayotte (Mahoré)
Independence: n/a (overseas territory of France)
Capital: Dziaodzi
Area: 375 sq.km.
Population: (1992 estimate) 86,628
Religious groups: Muslim 99%; remainder Christian (mostly Roman Catholic)

Languages spoken: Mahorian (a Swahili dialect), French
Exports: Coconut, sugar cane, vanilla, ylang-ylang

Part of the Comoros archipelago, Mayotte shares its history with the Comoros Federal Islamic Republic. When Comoros declared independence in 1975, Mayotte voted to remain an overseas territory of France. Although Comoros has since claimed Mayotte, the French have promised the islanders that they may remain French citizens for as long as they wish.

Morocco
Official name: Kingdom of Morocco
Independence: March 2, 1956
Capital: Rabat
Currency: Dirham
Income: (per capita US$) 950 (1990)
Area: 173,413 sq. mi.
Population (1991 estimate) 26.1 million
Ethnic divisions: Arab-Berber
Religious groups: Sunni Muslim
Languages spoken: Arabic (official), French, Berber dialects
International relations: Arab League, UN
Form of government: Mornachy

Arab forces began occupying Morocco in the seventh century AD, bringing with them Arab civilization and Islam. Morocco's location and resources led to early competition among Europeans in Africa, beginning with successful Portuguese efforts to control the Atlantic coast in the fifteenth century. France showed a strong interest in Morocco as early as 1830. The Treaty of Fez (1912) made Morocco a protectorate of France. By the same treaty, Spain assumed the role of protecting power over the northern and southern (Saharan) zones. The Kingdom of Morocco recovered its political independence from France on March 2, 1956. By agreements with Spain in 1956 and 1958.

From 1904 until 1975, Spain occupied the entire territory, which is divided into a northern portion, the Saguia el Hamra, and the southern two-thirds, known as Rio de Oro. Calls for the decolonization of these territories began in the 1960s, first from the surrounding nations and then from the United Nations.

Morocco's claim to sovereignty over the Western Sahara is based largely on the historical argument of traditional loyalty of the Saharan tribal leaders to the Moroccan sultan as spiritual leader and ruler. The International Court of Justice, to which the issue was referred, delivered its opinion in 1975 that while historical ties exist between the inhabitants of the Western Sahara and Morocco, they are insufficient to establish Moroccan sovereignty.

Dancers from Morocco.

The monarchy has been under King Hassan II since the death of Mohammed V who tends to be authoritarian. Moroccan economy has had a boost from the discovery of phosphate and increased tourism, but the gross domestic product is low and the populations subsist on farming and livestock.

Mozambique

Official name: People's Republic of Mozambique
Independence: June 25, 1975
Capital: Maputo
Currency: Metical
Income: (per capita US$) 85 (1990)
Area: 303,769 sq. mi.
Population (1991) 15.1 million
Illiteracy: 83% (1991)
Ethnic divisions: Makua, Tsonga, Makonde, and other tribal groups
Religious groups: Traditional belief 50%, Muslim 30% Christian 15%
Languages spoken: Portuguese (official), tribal languages
International relations: EC, OAU, UN
Form of government: Multi-party
Exports: Cotton, molasses, nuts, sugar, tea

Mozambique's first inhabitants were Bushmanoid hunters and gatherers, ancestors of the Khoisani peoples. During the first four centuries AD, waves of Bantu-speaking peoples migrated from the north through the Zambezi River Valley and then gradually into the plateau and coastal areas. When Portuguese explorers reached Mozambique in 1498, Arab trading settlements had existed along the coast for several centuries. Later, traders and prospectors penetrated the hinterland seeking gold and slaves.

After World War II, while many European nations were granting independence to their colonies, Portugal clung to the concept that Mozambique and other Portuguese possessions were "overseas provinces." In 1962, several Mozambican anti-Portuguese political groups formed the Front for Liberation of Mozambique (FRELIMO) which in September 1964 initiated and armed campaign against Portuguese colonial rule. After ten years of sporadic warfare and major political changes in Portugal, Mozambique became independent on June 25, 1975.

Samora Machel led Frelimo to independence in 1975, and immediately faced civil war with RENAMO (Mozambique National Resistance). More than 600,000 were killed; farms, roads, railways were destroyed; and half of the population was dislocated. After Samora was killed in air crash, Joaquim Chissano became head of state. A cease fire was entered with RENAMO in 1992, and multi-party elections were scheduled.

The ten major ethnic groups living in Mozambique are divided into subgroups with diverse languages, dialects, cultures, and history; the largest are the Majua and Tsonga.

Namibia (Formerly South West Africa)

Official name: Republic of Namibia
Capital: Windhoek
Currency: South African rand
Income: per capita 1342 (1990)
Area: 320,827 sq. mi.
Population (1991 estimate) 1.5 million
Illiteracy: 28% (1991)
Ethnic divisions: Black 87%; White 6%; mixed race 7%
Religious groups: Predominantly Christian, traditional belief
Languages spoken: English (official), Afrikaans, German, tribal languages
International relations: OAU, UN
Form of government: Multi-party

In 1878, the United Kingdom annexed Walvis Bay on behalf of Cape Colony, and the area was incorporated into the Cape of Good Hope in 1884. In 1883, a German trader, Adolf Luderitz, claimed the remainder of the coastal region after negotiations with a local chief. German administration ended during World War I, when the territory was occupied by South African forces in 1915.

On December 17, 1920, South Africa undertook the administration of South West Africa under the terms of Article 22 of the Covenant of the League of Nations and a mandate agreement confirmed by the League Council. The mandate agreement gave South Africa full power of administration and legislation over the territory as an integral part of South Africa. During the 1960s, as other Afican nations gained independence, pressure mounted on South Africa to do so in South West Africa.

In 1966, the United Nations General Assembly revoked South Africa's mandate. Also in 1966, the South

West Africa People's Organization (SWAPO) began guerrilla attacks on Namibia, infiltrating the territory from bases in Zambia. In a 1971 advisory opinion, the International Court of Justice upheld United Nation authority over Namibia, determining that the South African presence in Namibia was illegal and that South Africa therefore was obligated to withdraw its administration from Namibia immediately. In 1977, the United Nations approved as Security Council Resolution 435, calling for, among other things, the holding of elections in Namibia under United Nations supervision and control the cessation of hostile acts by all parties. South Africa agreed to cooperate in achieving implementation of Resolution 435. Nevertheless, in December 1978, in defiance of the United Nations proposal, it unilaterally held elections in Namibia which were boycotted by SWAPO and other political parties.

Intense discussions between the concerned parties continued during the 1978–1988 period. In May 1988, an American mediation team brought negotiators from Angola, Cuba, and South Africa and observers from the Soviet Union together in London. On April 1, the Republic of South Africa agreed to withdraw its troops. Implementation of Resolution 435 officially began on April 1, 1989. The elections held November 7–11, 1989, were certified as free and fair by the special representative, with SWAPO taking 57 percent of the vote; the Democratic Turnhalle Alliance, the principal opposition party, received 29 percent of the vote. By February 9, 1990, the constituent assembly had drafted and adopted a constitution. March 21 was set as the date for independence. SWAPO's Sam Nujoma won elections, and he became the first head of state in 1990.

Namibia is one of the least populated country in Africa. Namibia's indigenous Africans are of diverse linguistic and ethnic origins. The principal groups are the Ovambo, Kavango, Herero/Himba, Damara, mixed race ("Colored" and Rehoboth Baster), white (Afrikaner, German and Portuguese), Nama, Caprivian (Lozi), Bushman, and Tswana. The minority white population is primarily of South African, British, and German descent. Approximately 60 percent of the white population speaks Afrikaans (a variation of Dutch), 30 percent German, and ten percent English.

Niger
Official name: Republic of Niger
Independence: August 3, 1960
Capital: Niamey
Currency: CFA franc
Income: (per capita US$) 300 (1990)
Area: 490,000 sq. mi.
Population (1991) 8.1 million
Illiteracy: 86% (1991)

Ethnic divisions: Hausa 56%, Djerma 22%, Fulani 8.5% Tuareg 8%, Beri Beri (Kanouri) 4.3% Arab, Toubou, and Gourmantche 1.2%
Religious groups: Muslim, traditional belief, and Christians
Languages spoken: French (official), Hausa, Djerma
International relations: Ec, OAU, UN
Form of government: Multi-party
Exports: Crude materials, live animals, uranium

Considerable evidence indicates that about 600,000 years ago, humans inhabited what has since become the desolate Sahara of northern Niger. Niger was an important economic crossroads, and the empires of Songhei, Mali, Gao, Kanem, and Bornu, as well as a number of Hausa states, claimed control over portions of the area.

During recent centuries, the nomadic Taureg formed large confederations, pushed southward, and siding with various Hausa states, clashed with the Fulani empire of Sokoto, which had gained control of much of the Hausa territory in the late eighteenth century. In the ninteenth century, the first European explorers reached the area searching for the mouth of the Niger River.

Although French efforts at colonization began before 1900, dissident ethnic groups, especially the desert Taureg, were not defeated until 1922. On December 4, 1958, after the establishment of the Fifth French Republic, Niger became an autonomous state within the French Community. Following full independence on August 3, 1960, however, membership was allowed to lapse. Hamani Diori was overthrown in a military coup and replaced by Col. Seyni Kountche as president. 13 years later Ali Saibou succeeded him.

The two largest ethnic groups in Niger are the Hausa, who also constitute the major ethnic group in northern Nigeria, and the Djerma-Songhai. Both groups are farmers who live in the arable, southern tier. The rest of the population consists of nomadic or seminomadic livestock-raising peoples, which include the Fulani, Tuareg, Kanouri, and Toubou.

Nigeria
Official name: Federal Republic of Nigeria
Independence: October 1, 1960
Capital: Abuja
Currency: Naira
Income (per capita US$) 270 (1990)
Area: 356,700 sq. mi.
Population (1991): 88.5 million
Illiteracy: 58% (1991)
Ethnic divisions: 250 tribal groups, the largest are Hausa-Fulani, Ibo, and Yoruba
Religious groups: Muslim, Christian, traditional belief
Languages spoken: English (official), Hausa, Ibo, Yoruba
International relations: Commonwealth, EC, OAU, UN

Hausa men on horseback.

Form of government: Military

Evidence shows that more than 2,000 years ago, the Nok people who lived in what is now the Plateau state worked iron and produced sophisticated terra cotta sculpture. In the centuries that followed, the Hausa kingdom and the Bornu empire, near Lake Chad, prospered as important terminals of north-south trade between North African Berbers and forest people who exchanged slaves, ivory, and kola nuts for salt, glass beads, coral, cloth, weapons, brass rods, and cowrie shells used a currency. In the southwest, the Uoruba kingdom of Oyo, which was founded about 1400 and reached its height between the seventeenth and nineteenth centuries, attained a high level of political organization and extended as far as modern Togo. In the south-central part of present-day Nigeria, as early as the fifteenth century, the kingdom of Benin had developed an efficient army, an elaborate ceremonial court, and artisans whose works in ivory, wood, bronze, and brass are prized throughout the world today.

Between the seventeenth and ninteenth centuries, European traders established coastal ports for the increasing traffic in slaves destined for the Americas. In 1855, British claims to a sphere of influence in that area received international recognition, and, in the following year, the Royal Niger Company was chartered. In 1900, the company's territory came under the control of the British government. In 1914, the area was formally united as the "Colony and Protectorate of Nigeria." Nigeria was granted full independence on October 1, 1960, as a federation of three regions.

Since independence, Nigeria has faced numerous coups. The Ibos tried to cesede and tension between various ethnic groups increased, while the country began a rapid economic development based on oil production. Yakubu Gowon who had managed to stay in power was overthrown in 1976 by Mohammed Murtala, followed by Ge. Olusegun Obasanjo. A return to civilian rule came in 1979, under Shehu Shagari, however the military returned in 1984 under Mohammed Buhari and then again under Maj. Gen. Ibrahim Babangida. Sani Abacha ascended to power on November 17, 1993. His government has been internationally announced for hurman rights abuses, including executions.

The most populous country in Africa, Nigeria accounts for one quarter of Sub-Saharan Africa's people. The dominant ethnic group in the northern two-thirds of the country is the Hausa-Fulani, most of whom are

A minaret in Agadez, Niger.

Tomi of Ede John Adetoyese with a boy drummer.

Muslims. Other major ethnic groups of the north are the Nupe, Tiv, and Kanuri. The Yoruba people are predominant in the southwest. About half of the Yorubas are Christian and half Muslim. The predominately Catholic Ibos are the largest ethnic group in the southeast, with the Efik, Ibibio, and Ijaw comprising a substantial segment of the population in that area as well.

Réunion

Independence: n/a (overseas department of France)
Area: 2,510 sq. km.
Population: (1992 estimate) 626,414
Ethnic divisions: Intermixed African, French, Malagasy, Chinese, Pakistani, and Indian ancestry
Religious groups: Roman Catholic 94%
Languages spoken: French (official), Creole

The island of Réunion, located in the Indian Ocean, remained uninhabited until 1654, when the French East India Company established bases and brought in slaves from Africa and Madagascar. France governed the island as a colony until 1946, when it was granted department status.

The population of Réunion is of mixed African, French, Indian, and Chinese origin.

Rwanda

Official name: Republic of Rwanda
Independence: July 1, 1962
Capital: Kigali
Currency: Rwandan franc
Income (per capita US$) 310 (1990)
Area: 10,169 sq. mi.
Population: (1991 estimate): 7.9 million
Ethnic divisions: Hutu 85%, Tutsi 14%, Twa 1%
Religious groups: Christian 74%, traditional belief 25%, Muslim 1%
Languages spoken: French, Kinyarwanda
Exports: Coffee, tea, tin

For centuries Hutu farmers farmed the area that is now Rwanda; in the fifteenth century Tutsi herders settled in the area. In 1899, the court of Mwami submitted to a German protectorate with resistance. Belgian troops from Zaire occupied Rwanda in 1916; after World War I, the League of National mandated Rwanda and its southern neighbor, Burundi, to Belgium as the Territory of Ruanda-Urundi. Following World War II, Ruanda-Urundi became a United Nations trust territory with Belgium as the administering authority. The Party of the Hutu Emancipation Movement (PARMEHUTU) won an overwhelming victory in a United Nations-supervised referendum.

The PARMEHUTU government, formed as a result of the September 1961 election, was granted internal autonomony by Belgium on January 1, 1962. A June of 1962 United Nations General Assembly resolution terminated the Belgian trusteeship and granted full independence to Rwanda (and Burundi) effective July 1, 1962. Gregiore Kayibanda, leader of the PARMEHUTU Party, became Rwanda's first elected president.

Ethnic clashes continued with neighboring Burundi. Gen. Juve'nal Habyarimana, who had been a military head of state, returned to power in the presidential elections of 1978 and 1983 (both having been the only candidate). In 1990 the BaTutsi launched an armed struggle. The ethnic crisis was still continuing in the mid-1990s.

The indigenous population consists of three ethnic groups. The Tutsi (14 percent) are a pastoral people of Nilotic origin. The Hutus, who comprise the majority of the population (85 percent), are farmers of Bantu origin. The Twa pygmies (1 percent) are thought to be the remnants of the earliest settlers of the region.

Saint Helena

Independence: n/a (dependent territory of the United Kingdom)
Area: 410 sq. km.
Population: (1992 estimate) 6,698
Religious groups: Anglican majority, Baptist, Seventh-Day Adventist, and Roman Catholic
Languages spoken: English
Exports: Fish, livestock

The islands of Saint Helena, Ascension, and Tristan da Cunha lie about one-thirds of the way between Africa and South America in the South Atlantic Ocean. The islands remained uninhabited, until they were visited by the Portuguese in 1502. In 1659, the British East India Company established a settlement on Saint Helena and in 1673 was granted a charter to govern the island. These islands represent the last of what was once the British Empire.

Sao Tome and Principe

Official name: Democratic Republic of Sao Tome and Principe
Independence: July 12, 1975
Capital: Sao Tomé
Currency: Dobra
Income: (per capita US$) 380 (1990)
Area: 372 sq. mi.
Population: (1991 estimate) 128,000
Ethnic divisions: Mixed African, Portuguese-African
Religious groups: Christian 80%

Languages spoken: Portuguese
International relations: EC, OAU, UN
Form of government: Multi-party
Exports: Cocoa, coffee, cinchona bark, copra, palm kernels

These uninhabited islands were first visited by Portuguese navigators between 1469 and 1472. The first successful settlement of Sao Tome was established in 1493. Principe was settled in 1500. By the mid-1500s, with the help of slave labor, the Portuguese settlers had turned the islands into Africa's foremost exporter of sugar. Sao Tome and Principe were taken over and administered by the Portuguese crown in 1522 and 1573 respectively. By 1908, Sao Tome had become the world's largest producer of cocoa, still the country's most important crop.

The rocas system, which gave the plantation managers a high degree of authority, led to abuses against the African farm workers. Although Portugal officially abolished slavery in 1876, the practice of forced paid labor continued. Sporadic labor unrest and dissatisfaction continued well into the twentieth century, culminating in an outbreak of riots in 1953 in which several hundred African laborers were killed.

By the late 1950s, a small group of Sao Tomeans had formed the Movement for the Liberation of Sao Tome and Principe (MLSTP). In 1974, Portuguese representatives met with the MLSTP in Algiers and worked out an agreement for the transfer of sovereignty. After a period of transition, Sao Tome and Principe achieved independence on July 12, 1975, choosing as its first president the MLSTP Secretary General Manuel Pinto da Costa. Four years after independence, da Costa consolidated his power by eliminating the position of prime minister and assuming those duties himself.

Sao Tome and Principe's population, consists of people descended from groups that have migrated to the islands since 1485. Six groups are identifiable: Mestico, of mixed-blood, descendants of African slaves brought to the islands during the early years of settlement from Benin, Gabon, Congo, and Angola. Anglares, reputedly descendants of Angolan slaves who survived on a 1540 shipwreck and now earn their livelihood fishing; Forros, descendants of freed slaves; Servicais, contract laborers from Angola, Mozambique, and Cape Verde, living temporarily on the islands; Tongas, children of servicais born on the islands; and Europeans, primarily Portuguese.

Senegal

Official name: Republic of Senegal
Independence: April 4, 1960
Capital: Dakar
Currency: CFA franc
Income: (per capita US$) 658 (1988)

Area: 76,000 sq. mi.
Population: (1991 estimate): 7.9 million
Illiteracy: 62% (1990)
Ethnic divisions: Wolof 43%, Fulani (Peulh) and Toucouleur 23%, Serer 15%, Diola, Mandingo, others 22%
Religious groups: Muslim 94%, Christian 5%, traditional belief 1%
Languages spoken: French (official), Solof, Pulaar, Diola, Mandingo
International relations: EC, OAU, UN
Form of government: Multi-party
Exports: Fish, groundnuts, petroleum, phosphates

Archaeological findings throughout the area indicate that Senegal was inhabited in prehistoric times. Islam established itself in the Senegal River valley during the eleventh century. In the thirteenth and fourteenth centuries, the area came under the influence of the great Mandingo empires to the east, during which the Jolof empire of Senegal was founded. The empire comprised the states of Cayor, Baol, Oualo, Sine, and Soloum until the sixteenth century, when they revolted for independence.

The Portuguese were the first Europeans to trade in Senegal, arriving in the fiteenth century. They were soon followed by the Dutch and French. During the ninteenth century, the French gradually established control over the interior regions and administered them as a protectorate until 1920, and as a colony thereafter.

In January of 1959, Senegal and the French Soudan merged to form the Mali Federation, which became fully independent on June 20, 1960. Due to internal political difficulties, the federation broke up on August 20, 1960; Senegal and Soudan (renamed the Republic of Mali) each proclaimed separate independence. Leopold Sedar Senghor, internationally renowned poet, politician, and statesman, was elected Senegal's first president in August of 1960. Senghor guided the nation and instituted a multi-party state by 1978. He resigned three years later (an unheard of action in Africa) and Abdou Dious became the head of state. In the summer of 1995, Dakar hosted the African–African American Summit.

Seychelles

Official name: Republic of Seychelles
Independence: June 29, 1976
Capital: Victoria
Currency: Rupee
Income: (per capita US$) 4670 (1990)
Area: 171 sq. mi.
Population (1991 estimate): 68,000
Illiteracy: 43% (1991)
Ethnic divisions: Creole (mixture of Asians, Africans, and Europeans)

Religious groups: Roman Catholic 90%, Anglican 8%, other 2%
Languages spoken: Creole, English, and French
International relations: Commonwealth, EC, OAU, UN
Form of government: One-party
Exports: Cinnamon bark, copra, fish

In 1742, the French governor of Mauritius, sent an expedition to the islands. A second expedition in 1756 reasserted formal possession by France. The Seychelles islands were captured and freed several times during the French Revolution and the Napoleonic wars, then passed officially to the British under the Treaty of Paris in 1814. Negotiations with the British resulted in an agreement by which Seychelles became a sovereign republic on June 29, 1976. After independence Seychelles had a multi-party government but one year later Albert René instituted his People's Progressive Front as the only party. He was overthrown in a coup in 1981.

Most Seychellois are descendants of early French settlers and the African slaves brought to the Seychelles in the nineteenth century by the British, who freed them from slave ships on the East African coast. Indians and Chinese (1.1 percent of the population) account for the other permanent inhabitants.

Sierra Leone

Official name: Republic of Sierra Leone
Independence: April 27, 1961
Capital: Freetown
Currency: Leone
Income (per capita US$) 160 (1990)
Area: 27,925 sq. mi.
Population: (1991 estimate) 4.2 million
Illiteracy: 79% (1991)
Ethnic divisions: Temne 30%, Mende 29%, Creole 2%
Religious groups: Muslim 60%, Animist 30%, Christian 10%
Languages spoken: English (official), Krio (lingua franca), Temne, Mende, other tribal languages
International relations: Commonwealth, EC, OAU, UN
Exports: Bauxite, cocoa, coffee, diamonds, rutile

Sierra Leone was one of the first West African British colonies. Foreign settlement did not occur for another two centuries, when the British laid plans for a refuge within the British Empire for freed slaves. In 1787, the site of Freetown received the first four-hundred freedmen from Great Britain. Disease and hostility from the indigenous people almost eliminated this first group. Five years later, however, another group of settlers, 1,000 freed slaves who had fled from the United States to Nova Scotia during the American Revolution, arrived under the auspices of the newly formed British Sierra

Leone Company. In 1800, about 550 blacks arrived from Jamaica via Nova Scotia; these were the Maroons, escaped slaves who maintained their independence in the mountains of Jamaica.

The 1951 constitution provided the framework for decolonization. Independence came in April 1961, and Sierra Leone became a parliamentary system within the British Commonwealth. In April 1971, it adopted a republican constitution, cutting the link to the British monarchy but remaining with the Commonwealth. Siaka Steven who fought for government control of the country's major resources, namely—iron and diamonds—eventually held the power. In 1984 countrywide disturbances spread and several attempted coups have took place.

18 ethnic groups make up the indigenous population of Sierra Leone. The Temne in the north and the Mende in the south are the largest. About 60,000 are Creoles, descendants of black settlers from Great Britain or North America.

Somalia

Official name: Somalia Democratic Republic
Independence: July 1, 1960
Capital: Mogadoshu
Currency: Somalian shilling
Income:(per capita US$) 150 (1990)
Area: 246,000 sq. mi.
Population: (1991 esttimate): 6.7 million
Illiteracy: 45% (1991)
Ethnic divisions: Somali 98.8%, Arab and Asian 1.2%
Religious groups: Muslim
Languages spoken: Somali
Exports: Bananas, fish, hides, live animals

The British East India Company's desire for unrestricted harbor facilities led to the conclusion of treaties with the sultan of Tajura as early as 1840. It was not until 1886, however, that the British gained control over northern Somalia through treaties with various Somali chiefs. The boundary between Ethiopia and British Somaliland was established in 1897 through treaty negotiations between British negotiators and King Menellik.

In 1855, Italy obtained commercial advantages in the area from the sultan of Zanzibar and in 1889 concluded agreements with the sultans of Obbia and Caluula, who placed their territories under Italy's protection. Between 1897 and 1908, Italy made agreements with the Ethiopians and the British that marked out the boundaries of Italian Somaliland. In June 1940, Italian troops overran British Somaliland and drove out the British garrison. In 1941, British forces began operations against the Italian East African Empire and quickly brought the greater part of the Italian Somaliland under British control.

From 1941 to 1950, while Somalia was under British military administration, transition toward self-government had begun. Elections for the Legislative Assembly were held in February 1960. The protectorate became independent on June 26, 1960; five days later, on July 1, it joined Italian Somaliland to form the Somali Republic. Gen. Mohammed Siad Barre led a military coup in 1969, and established a Marxist political system. Years later Barre concentrated power in his own family and clan. In 1991, he was toppled, but opposing factions have continued fighting for power. After years of civil war, and severe drought, the United States and the international community gave aid to starving Somalians. It was not clear whether any true government existed.

The Somali people are herders and farmers. The largest group in the country is the Somali, who are nomadic or seminomadic herders. The remaining population consists of Jiiddu, Tunni, and Maay.

South Africa

Official name: Republic of South Africa
Capital: Pretoria
Currency: Rand
Income: (per capita US$) 2680 (1990)
Area: 472,359 sq. mi.
Population: (1991 estimate) 40.6 million
Illiteracy: 21% (1991)
Ethnic divisions: Black 75%; white 14%; "colored" (mixed-race) 8%; Asian (Indian) 3%.
Religious groups: Christian, traditional belief, Hindu, Muslim, Jewish
Languages spoken: English and Afrikaans (official), Zulu, Xhosa, Luvenda, North and South SeSotho, SeTswana, other tribal languages.
Form of government: Multi-party
Exports: Diamonds, gold

Of the present inhabitants of South Africa, the earliest are Bushmen and Hottentots—members of the Khoisan language group, of whom only a few survive. The Portuguese were, in 1988, the first Europeans to reach the Cape of Good Hope. Permanent white settlement began when the Dutch East India Company established a provisioning station there in 1652. In subsequent decades, French Huguenot refugees, Dutch, and Germans settled in the Cape area to form the Afrikaner segment of the modern population.

Britain seized the Cape of Good Hope at the end of the eighteenth century. Partly to escape British political rule and cultural hegemony, many Afrikaner farmers (Boers) undertook a northern migration (the "Great Trek") beginning in 1836. This movement brought them into contact with several African groups, the most formidable of which were the Zulu. Under their powerful leader, Shaka (1787–1828), the Zulu conquered most of

Two black South African youth.

the territory between the Drakensberg Mountains and the sea (now Natal). The Zulu were defeated at the Battle of Blood River in 1838.

The independent Boer republics of the Transvaal (the South African Republic) and the Orange Free State were created in 1852 and 1854. Following the two Boer wars from 1880 to 1881 and 1899 to 1902, British forces conquered the Boer republics and incorporated them into the British Empire. A strong resurgence of Afrikaner nationalism in the 1940s and 1950s led to a decision, through a 1960 referendum among whites, to give up dominion status and establish a republic. The republic was established on May 31, 1961.

South African laws are based on the doctrine of apartheid, which prescribes basic rights and obligations according to racial or ethnic origin. The country's black majority continues to suffer from pervasive, legally sanctioned discrimination based on race in political, economic, and social aspects of life. The "colored" and Asian minorities also suffer from discrimination, although to a somewhat lesser degree than blacks. Political rights of the black majority are confined to participation in tightly controlled urban councils in the country's black residential areas (townships) and in the ten so-

called homelands. The National Party extended racial segregation through passage of a number of legislative acts.

In 1950, the white parliament passed the Group Areas Act, which established residential and business sections in urban areas for each race and strengthened existing "pass laws," which require blacks to carry documents authorizing their presence in restricted areas. In the 1960s and the 1970s, other laws were passed to restrict every black African, irrespective of actual residence. Other laws were enacted to forbid most social contacts between the races, mandate segregated public facilities, establish separate educational standards, restrict each race to certain kinds of jobs, curtail black labor unions, and abolish nonwhite participation (through white representatives) in the national government.

The African National Congress (ANC), a predominantly black South African political and paramilitary organization founded in 1912, is the oldest organization opposing legalized racism and white rule in South Africa. It was banned by the South African government from 1960 to 1990, operating underground and in exile. The ANC was founded with the objectives of eliminating all restrictions based on color and obtaining black representation in Parliament. The long-term aims of the ANC were set forth in the "Freedom Charter," which was adopted in 1955. This document states that the ANC's ultimate goal is a liberated, nonracial South Africa in which individual rights would be guaranteed and nationalization of certain industries would occur within a basically mixed economy.

The government released two elderly long-term prisoners in 1988, Zeph Mothopeng, President of the Pan African Congress, and Henry Gwala, an ANC leader. In December 1988, under great international pressure, the government commuted the death sentences of the Sharpeville Six, who were convicted of murder for their presence in a crowd that killed a black township official. President F. W. DeKlerk took several steps in 1989 and 1990 to demonstrate his commitment to ending apartheid, including the release of ANC leader Nelson Mandela, imprisoned in 1962 and sentenced to life in 1964 for treason and sabotage, and other political prisoners and detainees; and unbanning the ANC and 32 other antiaparthied organizations. The tide of social and political changes instigated by De Klerk led to a new constitution and eventually a multi-party election that put Mandela in power as the first black African president of the nation. With Mandela's rise has come a new middle class among blacks, comprising nearly eight percent of the economically active citizenship.

South African law divides the population into four major racial categories—Africans (blacks), whites, "coloreds," and Asians. The Africans, who comprise 72

South African children behind a fence that separates them from a white community near Johannesburg.

percent of the population, are mainly descendants of the Sotho and Nguni peoples, who migrated southward centuries ago. The largest African ethnic groups are the Zulu (nearly six million) and Xhosa (nearly 5.8 million).

Africans are officially subdivided into ten groups corresponding to the ten ethnically based, government-created "homelands"—Bophuthatswana, Ciskei, Lebowa, Gazankulu, KaNgwane, KwaNdebele, KwaZaulu, Qwaqwa, Transkei, and Venda. The so-called homelands have been granted various degrees of automony (four have

been granted independence) but none have been recognized by any other government. The four independent homelands are: Bophuthatswana, which is made-up of mostly SeTswana-speaking people; Ciskei and Transkei, which consists of mainly Xhosa; and Venda, which is composed largely of Luvenda-speaking peoples.

The white population consists primarily of descendants of Dutch, French, English, and German settlers, with smaller admixtures of other European peoples, and constitutes about 14 percent of the total population.

Johannesburg, South Africa.

"Coloreds" are mostly descendants of indigenous peoples and the earliest European and Malay settlers in the area. "Coloreds" comprise nine percent of the population and live primarily in Cape Province. Asians, mainly descendants of the Indian workers brought to South Africa in the mid-nineteenth century to work as indentured laborers on sugar estates in Natal, constitute about three percent of the population.

Sudan

Official name: Republic of the Sudan
Independence: January 1, 1956
Capital: Khartoum
Currency: Sudanese pound
Income(per capita US$) 150 (1990)
Area: 967,500 sq. mi.
Population (1991 estimate): 27.2 million
Illiteracy: 78% (1991)
Ethnic divisions: Arab, black
Religious groups: Islam, traditional belief (southern Sudan), Christian
Languages spoken: Arabic (official), English, tribal languages
International relations: Arab Leageu, EC, OAU, UN

Form of government: Military
Exports: Cotton, groundnuts, sorghum

From the beginning of the Christian era until 1820, Sudan existed as a collection of small, independent states. In 1881, a religious leader named Mohammed Ahmed Ibn Abdalla proclaimed himself the Mahdi, or "expected one," and began to unify tribes in western and central Sudan. The Mahdi led a nationalist revolt culminating in the fall of Khartoum in 1855. He died shortly thereafter, but his state survived until overwhelmed by Anglo-Egyptian forces in 1898; in 1899, Sudan was proclaimed a condominium under British-Egyptian administration. In February 1953, the United Kingdom and Egypt concluded an agreement providing for Sudanese self-government. Col. Nimeiry reintroduced the law of Koran in 1983. Another military coup led by Omar Hasan el-Bashir seized power in 1989. Sudan achieved independence on January 1, 1956. Clashes have continued for years between the Arab north and black south made up of non-Muslims.

Swaziland

Official name: Kingdom of Swaziland

The Black South African village of Cross Roads.

Independence: September 6, 1968
Capital: Mbabane
Currency: Lilangeni
Income: (per capita US$) 789(1990)
Area: 6,704 sq. mi.
Population (1991 estimate): 859,000
Illiteracy: 32% (1991)
Ethnic divisions: Swazi, some Zulu
Religious groups: Christian and indigenous belief
Languages spoken: English, SiSwazi (both official)
International relations: Commonwealth, EC, OAU, UN
Form of government: Monarchy
Exports: Asbestos, citrus, sugar, wood pulp

The people of the present Swazi nation migrated south sometime before the sixteenth century to what is now Mozambique. After a series of conflicts with people living in the area that is now Maputo, the Swazi settled in northern Zululand in about 1750. Unable to match the growing Zulu strength there, the Swazis moved gradually northward in the early 1800s and established themselves in the area of modern Swaziland. The Swazi consolidated their hold in this area under several able leaders. The most important of these was Mswati, from whom the Swazi derive their name. Under his leadership

in the 1840s, the Swazi expanded their territory to the northwest and stabilized the southern frontier with the Zulus.

The first Swazi contact with the British came early in Mswati's reign when he asked the British agent general in South Africa for assistance against Zulu raids into Swaziland. Agreements made between the British and the Transvaal (South Africa) governments in 1881 and 1884 provided that Swaziland should be independent. In 1903, Britain formally took over the administration of Swaziland.

Sobhuza II became head of the Swazi Nation in 1921. By the 1960s, political activity intensified, partly in response to events elsewhere in Africa. Several political parties were formed that agitated for independence. The traditional Swazi leaders, including King Sobhuza and his council, formed the Imbokodvo National Movement. In 1966, the British agreed to hold talks on a new constitution. The constitutional committee, consisting of representatives of the king and of the Swazi National Council, other political parties, and the British government agreed on a constitutional monarchy for Swaziland, with self-government to follow parliamentary elections in 1967. Swaziland became independent on September

6, 1968. In 1973, Sobhuza II repealed the constitution and dissolved the political parties and assumed full power and died in 1982. Mswati III became king in 1986.

Tanzania

Official name: United Republic of Tanzania
Independence: December 9, 1961
Capital: Dodoma
Currency: Tanzanian shilling
Income:(per capita US$) 120 (1991)
Area: 363,950 sq. mi.
Population: (1991 estimate) 26.8 million
Illiteracy: 15% (1991)
Ethnic divisions: More than 130 groups
Religious groups: Muslim 35%, traditional belief 35%, Christian 30%
Languages spoken: Swahili (official), English
International relations: Commonwealth, EC, OAU, UN
Form of government: Multi-party
Exports: Cashews, coffee, cloves, cotton, diamonds, sisal, tea

The area, that is now Tanzania, is believed to have been inhabited originally by ethnic groups using a click-tongue language similar to that of southern Africa's Bushmen and Hottentots. Although remnants of these early tribes still exist, most were gradually displaced by Bantu farmers migrating form the west and south and by Nilotes and related northern peoples.

The coastal area first felt the impact of foreign influence as early as the eighth century. By the twelfth century, traders and immigrants came from as far away as Persia (now Iran) and India. The Portuguese navigator, Vasco da Gama, first visted the East African coast in 1498 on his voyage to India; by 1506, the Portuguese claimed control over the entire coast. This control was nominal, however, for the Portuguese did not attempt to colonize the area or explore the interior. By the early eighteenth century, Arabs from Oman had assisted the indigenous coastal dwellers in driving out the Portuguese from the area north of the Ruvuma River. They established their own garrisons at Zanzibar, Pemba, and Kilwa and carried on a lucrative trade in slaves and ivory.

German colonial interests were first advanced in 1884. Karl Peters, who formed the Society for German Colonization, concluded a series of treaties by which tribal chiefs in the interior accepted German protection. In 1886 and 1890, Anglo-German agreements were negotiated that delineated the British and German spheres of influence in the interior of East Africa. In 1891, the German government took over direct administration of the territory from the German East Africa Company and appointed a governor with headquarters at Dar es Sa-

A Swazis woman.

laam. German colonial administration provided African resistance, culminating in the Maji Maji rebellion of 1905 to 1907. German colonial domination of Tanganyika ended with World War I. Control of most of the territory passed to the United Kingdom under a League of Nations mandate.

In the following years, Tanganyika moved gradually toward self-government and independence. In 1954, Julius K. Nyerere, a schoolteacher educated abroad, organized the Tanganyika African Union (UANU). In May 1961, Tanganyika became autonomous, and Nyerere became prime minister under a new constitution. Full independence was achieved on December 9, 1961. On April 26, 1964, Tanganyika united with Zanzibar to form the United Republic of Tanganyika and Zanzibar, renamed the United Republic of Tanzania on October 29, 1964. Julius Nyerere became one of the few leaders on the continent to retire peacefully. Multi-parties were allowed to organize and participate in a national election in 1995. Chama cha Mapinduzi (Revolutionary Party) won the last election, and Ben Mkapa became the new head of state.

Tanzania's population consists of more than 130 ethnic groups, of which only the Sukuma has more than

Tanga, Tanzania

one million members. The majority of Tanzanians, including such large tribes as the Sukuma and the Nyamwezi, are of Bantu stock. Groups of Nilotic or related origin include the nomadic Masai and the Luo, both of which are found in greater numbers in neighboring Kenya. Two small groups speak languages of the Khoisan family peculiar to the Bushman and Hottentot peoples. Cushitic-speaking peoples, originally from the Ethiopian highlands, reside in a few areas of Tanzania.

Togo

Official name: Republic of Togo
Independence: April 27, 1960
Capital: Lomé
Currency: CFA franc
Income:(per capita US$) 390 (1989)
Area: 21,853 sq. mi.
Population: (1991 estimate) 3.8 million
Illiteracy: 57% (1991)
Ethnic divisions: Ewe, Mina, Kabye, Cotocoli, Moba
Religious groups: Animist 50%, Christian 30%, Muslim 20%
Languages spoken: French (official), Ewe, Mina, Kabye
International relations: EC, OAU, UN
Exports: Cocoa, coffee, phosphates

The Ewe people first moved into the area that is now Togo from the Niger River Valley, sometime between the twelfth and fourteenth centuries. During the fifteenth and sixteenth centuries, Portuguese explorers and traders visited the coast. For the next two hundred years, the coastal region was a major raiding center for Europeans in search of slaves, earning Togo and the surrounding region the name "the Slave Coast."

In a 1884 treaty signed at Togoville, Germany declared a protectorate over the area. In 1914, Togoland was invaded by French and British forces and fell after a brief resistance. Following the war, Togoland became a

League of Nations mandate divided for administrative purposes between France and the United Kingdom. By statute in 1955, French Togo became an autonomous republic within the French Union. In 1957, the residents of British Togoland voted to join the Gold Coast as part of the new independent nation of Ghana. On April 27, 1960, Togo severed its juridical ties with France, shed its United Nations trusteeship status, and became fully independent. The first president— Sylvanus Olympia was overthrown three years after independence in 1963. Nicholas Grunitzky headed the government for short period; in 1976 Col. Gnassingbé Eyadema sized power and instituted a one- party state He was elected president in 1979 and 1986 and was deposed in 1991. Since then, a multi-party system has existed.

Togo's population is composed of about 21 ethnic groups. The two major ones are the Ewe in the south and the Kabye in the north.

Tunisia

Official name: Republic of Tunisia
Capital: Tunis
Currency: Dinar
Income: (per capita US$) 1560 (1991)
Area: 63,378 sq. mi.
Population (1991 estimate) 8.2 million
Illiteracy: 35% (1991)
Ethnic divisions: Arab 98%, Berber 1%, European 1%
Religious groups: Muslim 99%, Christian and Jewish less than 1%
Languages spoken: Arabic (official), French

Tunisians are descended mainly from indigenous Berber tribes and from Arab tribes which migrated to North Africa during the seventh century AD. Recorded history in Tunisia begins with the arrival of Phoenicians, who founded Carthage and other North African settlements. In the seventh century, the Muslim conquest transformed North Africa, and Tunisia became a center of Arab culture until its assimilation in the Turkish Ottoman Empire in the sixteenth century. In 1881, France established a protectorate there, only to see a rise of nationalism lead to Tunisia's independence in 1956.

One year after independence, Habib Bourguiba deposed the president and instituted a socialist system, later declaring himself president for life. He was later removed and his position was assumed by Gen. Al Ben Ali, who promoted democratization.

Uganda

Official name: Republic of Uganda
Independence: October 9, 1962
Capital: Kampala

Magila Mission, Tanzania

Currency: Ugandan shilling
Income: (per capita US$) 220 (1000)
Area: 93,354 sq. mi.
Population: (1991 estimate) 18.6 million
Illiteracy: 52% (1991)
Ethnic divisions: Baganda, Iteso, Basoga, Banyaruanda, Bakiga, Bagisu
Religious groups: Christian (majority), Muslim, traditional belief
Languages spoken: English (official), Luganda, Swahili, other Bantu and Nilotic languages
International relations: Commonwealth, EC, OAU, UN
Exports: Coffee, copper, cotton, tea

Arab traders moving inland from Indian Ocean coastal enclaves reached the interior of Uganda in the 1830s and found several African kingdoms, one of which was the Buganda kingdom, that had well-developed political institutions dating back several centuries.

In 1888, control of the emerging British sphere of interest in East Africa was assigned by royal charter to the Imperial British East Africa Company, an arrangement strengthened in 1890 by an Anglo-German agreement confirming British dominance over Kenya and Uganda. In 1894, the Kingdom of Uganda was placed under a formal British protectorate. The British protectorate period began to change formally in 1955, when constitutional changes leading to Uganda's independence were adopted. The first general elections in Uganda were held in 1961, and the British government granted internal self-government to Uganda on March 1, 1962, with Benedicto Kiwanuka as the first prime minister.

In February of 1966, Prime Minister Milton Obote suspended the constitution, assumed all government powers, and removed the president and vice president. On January 25, 1971, Obote's government was ousted in a military coup led by armed forces commander Idi Amin Dada. Amin declared himself president, dissolved the parliament, and amended the constitution to give himself absolute power. Idi Amin's eight-year rule produced economic decline, social disintegration, and massive human rights violations. In 1978, Tanzanian forces pushed back an incursion by Amin's troops. Backed by Ugandan exiles, Tanzanian forces waged a war of liberation against Amin. On April 11, 1979, the Ugandan capital was captured, and Amin and his remaining forces fled.

Milton Obote, the first president, was overthrown in 1971 by Gen. Idi Amin who led the country through a

A Togolese woman making pottery.

reign of terror and violence. In 1973, Amin was toppled and during that year with the aide of neighboring country Tanzania. A chaotic year followed when three presidents attempted to lead the government and failed. Eventually Yuveri Museveni assumed power, bringing some stability to the country.

Bantu, Nilotic, and Nilo-Hamitic peoples constitute most of Uganda's population. The Bantu are the most numerous and include the Baganda, with more than one million members. The Nilo-Hamitic Iteso is the second largest group, followed by the Banyankole and Basoga, both of Bantu extraction.

Zaire
Official name: Republic of Zaire
Independence: June 30, 1960
Capital: Kinshasa
Currency: Zaire
Income (per capita US$) 230 (1990)
Area: 905,063 sq. mi.
Population: (1991 estimate) 37.8 million
Illiteracy: 39% (1991)
Ethnic divisions: 250 tribal groups
Religious groups: Roman Catholic 50%, Protestant 20%, Muslim 10%, Kimbanguist 10%, other syncretic sects and traditional belief 10%
Languages spoken: French, Lingala, Swahili, Kingwana (a variant), Kikongo, Tshiluba

The area that is now Zaire is believed to have been populated as early as 10,000 years ago. An influx of peoples occurred in the seventh and eighth centuries AD, when Bantu people from present-day Nigeria settled, bringing with them knowledge of the manufacture and use of metals. In 1482, the Portuguese arrived at the mouth of the Congo River. They found an organized society—the Bakongo Kingdom—which included parts of present-day Congo, Zaire, and Angola. The Portuguese named the area Congo. At the Berlin Conference of 1885, King Leopold's claim to the greater part of the Zaire River basin was recognized. The Congo Free State remained his personal possession until he ceded it to the Belgian State in 1907, when it was renamed the Belgian Congo.

Following riots in Leopoldville in 1958, Belgian King Bedouin announced that the colony could look forward to independence. Roundtable conferences were convened at Brussels in January 1960, and Belgium granted independence on June 30, 1960. Parliamentary elections

Tutsi dancers form Zaire.

were held in April of 1960. The Congolese National Movement (MNC) obtained a majority of the seats, and Patrice Lumumba was named prime minister. After much maneuvering, the leader of the Alliance of the Bakongo (ABAKO) Party, Joseph Kasavubu, was named president.

Chaos started right after independence. Moise Tshombe declared Katanga (a copper-rich province) independent. Belgian military intervened and soon after UN troops arrived to help normalize the situation. Meanwhile, Lumumba got assassinated. Tshombe served as prime minister until 1965, when Joseph Désiré Mobutu organized a coup. Still at the helm in the early 1990s, opposition to his regime and attempts are regular. The country has been rumored to be on the verge of bankruptcy while Mobutu has amassed huge fortunes abroad.

As many as 250 ethnic groups in Zaire have been distinguished and named. The largest group, the Kongo, may include as many as 2.5 million persons. Other socially and numerically important groups are the Luba, Lunda, Bashi, and Mongo. Some groups, including the aboriginal Pygmies, occupy isolated ecological niches and number only a few thousand.

Approximately 700 local languages and dialects are spoken; four serve as official languages. Lingala developed along the Congo River in the 1880s in response to the need for a common commercial language. Swahili, introduced into the country by Arabs and especially the Zanzibari Swahilis during the nineteenth century slaving operations, is spoken extensively in the eastern half of the country. Kikongo is used primarily in the area between Kinshasa and the Atlantic Ocean, as well as in parts of Congo and Angola. Tshiluba is spoken primarily by the tribal groups of south-central Zaire.

Zambia

Official name: Republic of Zambia
Independence: October 24, 1964
Area: 290,585 sq. mi.
Population: (1991 estimate) 8.4 million
Ethnic divisions: More than 70 tribal groups
Religious groups: Christian, indigenous belief
Languages spoken: English (official), about 70 local languages and dialects, including Bemba, Tonga, Nyanja, Lozi, Luvale, Ndembu (Lundu), and Kaonde

About 2,000 years ago, the indigenous hunter-gatherer occupants of Zambia began to be displaced or absorbed by more advanced migrating tribes. By the fifteenth century, the major waves of Bantu speaking immigrants began, with the greatest influx occuring between the late seventeenth and early nineteenthth centuries. These groups came primarily from the Luba and Lunda tribes of southern Zaire and northern Angola but were joined in the nineteenth century by Ngoni peoples from the south. By the latter part of that century, the various peoples of Zambia were largely established in the areas they currently occupy.

Except for an occasional Portuguese explorer, the area lay untouched by Europeans for centuries, until the mid-nineteenth century, when it was penetrated by European explorers, missionaries, and traders. In 1888, Northern and Southern Rhodesia (now Zambia and Zimbabwe) were proclaimed a British sphere of influence. In 1953, both Rhodesias were joined with Nyasaland (now Malawi) to form the Federation of Rhodesia and Nyasaland.

Northern Rhodesia was the center of much of the turmoil and crises that characterized the federation in its last years. At the core of the controversy were insistent African demands for greater participation in government and the Europeans' fear. A two-stage election held in October and December 1962 resulted in an African majority in the Legislative Council. The council passed resolutions calling for Northern Rhodesia's secession from the federation and demanding full internal self-government. On December 31, 1963, the federation was dissolved, and Northern Rhodesia became the Republic of Zambia on October 24, 1964. Robert Mugabe continues to serve as the head of state since independence, and has managed-to get himself re-elected several times. The government is multi-party, including ZAPU officials. A cautious land reform has been institut-

Mbuti people of the Ituri forest in Zaire.

ed giving land to black farmers. Frederick Chiluba was ruler of the nation in 1996.

Zambia's population comprises more than 70 Bantu-speaking tribes. Some tribes are small, and only two have enough people to constitute at least ten percent of the population.

Zimbabwe

Independence: April 18, 1980
Area: 151,000 sq. mi.
Population: (1991 estimate)
Ethnic divisions: Shona 80%, Ndebele 19%
Religious groups: 50% syncretic (part Christian, part traditional belief), Christian 25%, traditional beliefs 24%, Hindu and Muslim less than 1%
Languages spoken: English (official), Shona, SiNdebele

Archaeologists have found Stone Age implements and pebble tools in several areas of Zimbabwe, suggesting human habitation for many centuries, and the ruins of stone buildings provide evidence of early civilization.

In the sixteenth century, the Portuguese were the first Europeans to attempt colonization of south-central Africa, but the hinterland lay virtually untouched by Europeans until the arrival of explorers, missionaries, and traders some three hundred years later. In 1888, the area that became Southern and Northern Rhodesia was proclaimed a British sphere of influence. The British South Africa Company was chartered in 1889, and the settlement of Salisbury (now Harare, the capital) was established in 1890.

In 1895, the territory was formally named Rhodesia. In 1923, Southern Rhodesia's white settlers were given the choice of being incorporated into the Union of South Africa or becoming a separate entity within the British Empire. The settlers rejected incorporation, and Southern Rhodesia was formally annexed by the United Kingdom. In September 1953, Southern Rhodesia was joined with the British protectorates of Northern Rhodesia and Nyasaland. The federation was dissolved at the end of 1963 after much crisis and turmoil, and Northern Rhodesia and Nyasaland became the independent states of Zambia and Malawi in 1964.

Although prepared to grant independence to Rhodesia, the United Kingdom insisted that the authorities at Salisbury first demonstrate their intention to move toward eventual majority rule. Desiring to keep their dominant position, the white Rhodesians refused to give such assurance. On November 11, 1965, after lengthy and unsuccessful negotiations with the British government, Prime Minister Ian Smith issued a Unilateral Declaration of Independence (UDI) from the United Kingdom. The British government considered the UDI unconstitutional and illegal but made clear that it would not use force to end the rebellion. The British government imposed unilateral economic sanctions on Rhodesia and requested other nations to do the same. On December 16, 1966, the United Nations Security Council, for the first time in its history, imposed mandatory economic sanctions on a state.

In the early 1970s, informal attempts at settlement were renewed between the United Kingdom and the Rhodesia administration. In 1974, the major African nationalist groups—the Zimbabwe African People's Union (ZAPU) and the Zimbabwe African National Union (ZANU), which split away from ZAPU in 1963—were united into the "Patriotic Front" and combined their military forces. In 1976, the Smith government agreed in principle to majority rule and to a meeting in Geneva with black nationalist leaders. Blacks represented at the Geneva meeting included ZAPU leader Joshua Nkomo, ZANU leader Robert Mugabe, UANC chairman Bishop Abel Muzorewa, and former ZANU leader, the Reverend Ndabaningi Sithole. The meeting failed.

On March 3, 1978, the Smith administration signed the "internal settlement" agreement in Salisbury with Bishop Muzorewa, Reverend Sithole, and Chief Jeremiah Chirau. The agreement provided for qualified majority rule and elections with universal suffrage. Following elections in April 1979, in which his UANC part won a majority, Bishop Muzorewa assumed office on June 1, becoming Zimbabwe's first black prime minister. However, the installation of the new black majority government did not end the guerrilla conflict that had claimed more than 20,000 lives.

The British and the African parties began deliberations on a Rhodesian settlement in London on September 10, 1979. On December 21, the parties signed an agreement calling for a cease-fire, new elections, a transition period under British rule, and a new constitution implementing majority rule while protecting minority rights. The elections were supervised by the British government and monitored. Robert Mugabe's ZANU Party won an absolute majority and was asked to form Zimbabwe's first government. The British government formally granted independence to Zimbabwe on April 18, 1980. Most nations recognized Zimbabwe following independence. The 6th annual All Africa Games were held in Harawe in September of 1995. Athletes from more than 30 nations participated.

Zimbabwe's population is divided into two major language groups, which are subdivided into several tribal groups. The Mashona (Shona speakers), who constitute about eighty percent of the population, have lived in the area the longest and are the majority language groups. The Matabele (Sindebele speakers), representing about nineteen percent of the population and centered in the southwest near Bulawayo, arrived within the last 150 years. An offshoot of the South African Zulu group, they had maintained control over the Mashona until the white occupation of Rhodesia.

Western Hemisphere

Anguilla

Independence: n/a (dependent territory of the United Kingdom)
Area: 91 sq. km.
Population: (1992 estimate) 6,963
Ethnic divisions: Black Africans
Religious groups: Anglican 40%, Methodist 33%, Seventh-Day Adventist 7%, Baptist 5%, Roman Catholic 3%, other 12%
Languages spoken: English
Exports: Fish, lobster

Beginning in 1816, the islands of Anguilla, the (British) Virgin Islands, Saint Christopher (Saint Kitts) and Nevis were governered by the British as a single colony. However, when Saint Christopher was granted statehood in 1967, Anguilla unilaterally declared independence from Saint Christopher. Anguilla has remained an economically dependent territory of the United Kingdom.

Antigua and Barbuda

Independence: November 1, 1981
Capital: St. John's
Currency: East Caribbean dollar
Income (per capita US$): 4600 (1990)
Area: 108 sq. mi.
Population: (1991 estimate) 64,400
Illiteracy: 10% (1991)
Ethnic divisions: Black Africans, some British and Portuguese
Religious groups: Principally Anglican, with evangelical Protestant and Roman Catholic minorities.
Languages spoken: English (official), regional dialects

Christopher Columbus first visited the islands of Antigua and Barbuda in 1493. Missionaries attempted to settle on the island but were hindered by the Carib Indians, who inhabited the islands, and the absence of natural freshwater springs. In 1632, the British successfully established a colony; Sir Christopher Codrington established the first large sugar estate in Antigua in 1674, bringing slaves from Africa's west coast to work the plantations. Although Antiguan slaves were emancipated in 1834, they remained bound to their plantation owners. Economic opportunities for the new freemen

A Zimbabwean man with ox-drawn cart.

were limited by a lack of surplus farming land, no access to credit, and an economy built on agriculture rather than manufacturing. The Labor Party retained power after the 1989 elections.

Argentina
Official Name: Republic of Argentina
Capital: Buenos Aires
Currency: Austral
Income (per capita US$) 2370 (1990)
Area: 1,072,156 sq. mi.
Population: (1980 estimate) 27,947,446
Illiteracy: 5% (1991)
Form of government: Presidential republic
Exports: Iron ore, livestock, petroleum

Blacks consistute a very small percentage of the population of Argentina.

Aruba
Independence: (Autonomous part of the Kingdom of the
  Netherlands)
Population: 60,000
Ethnic divisions: Mixed European and Carib Indian 85%,
  black Africans

Religious groups: Roman Catholic, Protestant, Jewish
Languages spoken: Papiamento, English, Dutch, Spanish

The Spanish landed in Curacao (now the Netherlands Antilles) in 1499 and in 1527 took possession of Curacao, Bonaire, and Aruba. In 1634, the three islands passed to the Netherlands, where they have remained, except for two short periods of British rule during the Napoleonic Wars. Before the war, the Dutch Caribbean islands were administered as Dutch colonies; afterward, negotiations to confer a greater measure of self-government began. On December 15, 1954, the Netherlands Antilles became an autonomous part of the kingdom. In 1983, Aruba sought autonomy from the Netherlands Antilles; on January 1, 1986, it achieved separate status equal to that of the Antilles and is slated to become fully independent in 1996.

Some 40 nationalities are represented in the Netherlands Antilles and Aruba; Arubans mostly are a mixture of European and Caribbean Indian.

Bahamas
Official Name: Commonwealth of The Bahamas
Independence: July 10, 1973
Capital: Nassau

Currency: Bahamian dollar
Income (per capita US$) 11,400 (1990)
Area: 5,380 sq. mi
Population: (1991 estimate) 251,000
Illiteracy: 5% (1991)
Ethnic divisions: Black African 85%, European 15%
Religious groups: Baptist, Anglican, Roman Catholic, Methodist
Languages spoken: English, Creole
International relations: CARICOM, EC, OAS, UN
Exports: Shellfish, sugar, timber, turtles

Christopher Columbus first visited the islands of the Bahamas in 1492, when he first landed in the Western Hemisphere, either on Samana Cay or San Salvador Island. In 1647, the first permanent European settlement was founded. In 1717, the islands became a British crown colony. The Bahamas were granted self-government through a series of constitutional and political steps, culminating in independence on July 10, 1973. The Progressive Liberal Party led the Bahamas to independence and remain in power in the 1990s.

85 percent of Bahamians are of African descent. Many of their ancestors arrived in the Bahamas when it was a staging area for the slave trade, or were brought there by the thousands of British loyalists who fled the American colonies during the Revolutionary War.

Barbados
Independence: November 30, 1966
Capital: Bridgetown
Currency: Barbados dollar
Income (per capita US$) 6,745 (1990)
Area: 166 sq. mi.
Population: (1991 estimate) 254,000
Illiteracy: 2% (1991)
Ethnic divisions: African 80%, mixed 16%, European 4%
Religious groups: Anglican 70%, Roman Catholic, Methodist, Baptist and Moravian
Languages spoken: English
International relations: CARICOM, EC, OAS, UN
Form of government: Independenct state under British sovereignty
Exports: Fish, sugar

From the arrival of the first British settlers in 1627 until independence in 1966, Barbados had been under uninterrupted British control. As the sugar industry developed into the main commercial enterprise, Barbados was divided into large plantation estates. Slaves were brought from Africa to work on these plantations until slavery was abolished throughout the British Empire in 1834. From 1958 to 1962, Barbados was one of ten members of the West Indies Federation. Barbados negotiated its own independence at a constitutional confer-

Nassau Police Band.

ence with the United Kingdom in June 1966. The country attained self-rule on November 30, 1966.

Ethnically, the population of Barbados is 80 percent African, 16 percent mixed, and four percent European.

Belize
Independence: September 21, 1981
Capital: Belmopan
Currency: Belize dollar
Income (per capita US$) 1,975 (1990)
Area: 8,866 sq. mi.
Population: (1991 estimate): 228,000
Illiteracy: 7% (1991)
Ethnic divisions: Creole, African, mestizo, Amerindian
Religious groups: Roman Catholic, Anglican, Methodist, Muslim, Buddhist
Languages spoken: English (official), Spanish, Mayan
International relations: CARICOM, EC, UN
Exports: Bananas, citrus fruit, sugar, wood

The Mayan civilization spread into the area of Belize between 1500 BC and AD 300 and flourished until about AD 1000. European contact began in 1502 when Columbus sailed along the coast; the first recorded European settlement was 1638. During the next 105 years, more English settlements were established. Belize was named the Colony of British Honduras in 1840; it became a crown colony in 1862. Self-government was granted in January 1964. The official name of the territory was changed from British Honduras to Belize in June of 1973, and full independence was granted on September 21, 1981, with George C. Price of the People's United Party installed as the head of government.

Most Belizeans are of multiracial descent. Nearly 40 to 45 percent of the population is of African ancestry; more than 25 percent is of mixed local Indian and European descent (mestizo). Another one-fifth of the population is composed of Carib, Mayan, or other Amerindian ethnic groups.

Bermuda

Independence: n/a (parliamentary British colony with internal government since 1620)
Capital: Hamilton
Income (per capita US$) 17,000 (1987)
Area: 20.6 sq. mi.
Population (1987 est.): 57,619
Ethnic divisions: Black Africans 61%, white and others 39%
Religious groups: Anglican 37%, Protestant 21%, Roman Catholic 14%, other 28%
Languages spoken: English
Form of government: Semi-autonomous British colony
Exports: Bananas, coffee, cotton, tobacco

Located in the Atlantic Ocean about 650 miles east of North Carolina, Bermuda is relatively isolated.

The first Europeans to visit Bermuda were Spanish explorers in 1503. In 1609, a group of British explorers became stranded on the islands, and their reports aroused great interest about the islands in England. In 1612, British colonists arrived and founded the town of Saint George, the oldest, continuously inhabited English-speaking settlement in the Western Hemisphere.

Slaves from Africa were brought to Bermuda soon after the colony began. When the slave trade was outlawed in Bermuda in 1807, all slaves were freed in 1834. Although Bermuda is a British colony, it has a great degree of internal autonomy, based on the June 8, 1968 constitution.

Nearly two-thirds of the Bermudians are of African descent. An estimated 7,000 U.S. citizens live on the island; approximately 2,800 of them are military personnel and their dependents.

Bolivia

Official Name: Republic of Bolivia
Capital: La Paz
Currency: Boliviano
Income (per capita US$) 590 (1990)
Area: 424,162 sq. mi.
Population: 4,613,486 (c.1976)
Illiteracy: 22% (1990)
International relations: LAIA, OAS, UN
Form of government: Presidential republic
Exports: Copper, gold, zinc

Military regimes and authoritarian governments ruled Bolivia for years, until 1989, when Jaime Paz Zamora, representing Movimiento de la Izquierda Revolucionaria (MIR) was elected president. Blacks comprise a very small percentage of Bolivia's population.

Brazil

Official Name: Federative Republic of Brazil
Independence: September 7, 1822
Capital: Brasilia
Currency: Cruzado
Income (per capita US$: 2680 (1990)
Area: 3,290,000 sq. mi.
Population: (1991 estimate) 150.1 million
Illiteracy: 19% (1991)
Ethnic divisions: Portuguese, black Africans, Indians (principally Tupi and Guarani linguistic stock), Italian, German, Japanese
Religious groups: Roman Catholic 89%
Form of government: Presidential republic
Exports: Coffee, iron ore, soybean, steel, sugar

Brazil was formally claimed in 1500 by the Portuguese and was ruled from Lisbon as a colony until 1808. Brazil successfully declared independence on September 7, 1922. Four major groups make up the Brazilian population: indigenous Indians of Tupi and Guarani language stock; the Portuguese; Africans brought to Brazil as slaves; and various European and Asian immigrant groups that have settled in Brazil since the mid-ninteenth century.

Slavery was introduced into Brazil in the 1530s, expanded greatly after 1540, when sugar became important, and grew most rapidly between 1580 and 1640, when Spain controlled the country. Estimates of the total number of slaves brought to Brazil varies from six to 20 million. Slavery did not finally end in Brazil until 1888. Though slavery in Brazil was often extremely brutal, and the death rate of blacks on sugar, coffee and cotton plantations was enormous, large numbers of Africans achieved freedom. About 25 percent of Brazil's blacks were free during slavery.

During the nineteenth century, free blacks intermarried so rapidly their numbers fell from about 400,000 in 1800 to 20,000 by 1888 when slavery was finally abolished. Free blacks enjoyed full legal equality during both the period of slavery and after it was abolished.

In Brazil, slaves who served masters in cities were often allowed to seek part-time and temporary employment elsewhere. They were able to read and write and develop employable skills. Blacks became important to the development and economy of the country and some became prominent in public life. Black Brazilian Nilo Pecanha served as vice-president and briefly as president of Brazil in the first decade of this century. Blacks also achieved fame in Brazil's intellectual and artistic life.

After the oppressive military regimes of the 1960s, José Sarney was elected in 1985.

Canada

Capital: Ottawa

Currency: Canadian dollar
Income (per capita US$) 22,040 (1990)
Illiteracy: 4% (1991)
International relations: Commonwealth, NATO, OECD, UN
Form of government: Independent state with British sovereignty
Exports: manufactured goods, minerals

Blacks comprise a very small portion of Canada's population—less than 25,000, or 0.1 percent of the total population. Canada's major race problem reflects in its treatment of the Indians and Eskimos, who total about 200,000.

Blacks were prominent in the early seventeenth-century explorations and development of Canada by French explorers and Jesuit missionaries. The first black slave is believed to have been a native of Madagascar (Malagasy) and to have been sold to a French resident of Quebec in 1628. As French Canada expanded, slaves were purchased in the United States.

In 1749, the British brought slaves to Halifax, and slavery was legalized in British Canada in 1762. Slavery increased shortly thereafter, when the British took all of Canada in the French and Indian Wars. Many British fleeing from the revolutionary colonies to the south after 1775 brought slaves with them.

British slave codes were more severe than the French, under whom slaves could marry, own property, and maintain parental rights. However, the British were not to sustain slavery for long. London had divided Canada into two governments, Upper Canada and Lower Canada. The governor of Upper Canada, Colonel James Simcoe, an ardent abolitionist, induced the area's legislature to pass laws forbidding importation of slaves and freeing every slave born in the area by the age of 25. As a result, slavery in Upper Canada soon collapsed.

Similar legislation was not enacted in Lower Canada. However, by 1800 the courts, through complex legal decisions, established the principle that a slave could leave his master whenever he wished. In the Maritime Provinces, courts also acted so as to eliminate slavery in fact if not in theory. Slavery was formally abolished in Canada in 1833.

Meanwhile, starting slowly in the eighteenth century, Canada was becoming a haven for slaves fleeing across her southern borders. Slaves who had served with the British in the American War for Independence came to Halifax from New York in large numbers in 1782 and 1783. Though many were to migrate to Freetown on the West Coast of Africa, others stayed. In 1826, Canada defied the United States and formally refused to return fugitive slaves. In 1829, the legislature of Lower Canada announced that every slave that entered the Province was immediately free, a declaration that gave impetus to the underground railroad and stimulated moves for resettlement by blacks in Canada.

The passage of the Fugitive Slave Act in 1850 meant that any escaped slave who remained in the United States was to be returned to his owner. Within a year after passage of the law, some ten thousand slaves arrived in Canada, welcomed by a majority of Canadians who provided communities and services for them.

African Americans were accepted into the mainstream of Canadian life, were allowed to choose separate or integrated schools, were elected to local office and served as officers in the Canadian Army. Black laborers contributed substantially to the expansion of the Canadian Pacific Railroad, as immigrants from Eastern and Southern Europe were to contribute to the development of railroads in the United States. Black skilled laborers were much in demand. By 1861, at the outbreak of the Civil War in the United States, there were 50,000 blacks in Canada. However, after the Civil War, feelings of fear among white Canadians led to discrimination in employment and schools. Many African Americans re-emigrate to the United States, feeling that, with slavery outlawed there, a bright future awaited them. By 1871, the black population of Canada dipped to about 20,000.

Canada, the most sparsely populated country in the world with 1.5 persons per square mile, has become a haven for so many refugees that it has earned awards for outstanding achievement from human rights organizations. In fact, so many immigrants from Asia, Africa, the Caribbean and elsewhere have moved to Canada, that the established British-Caucasian population has expressed fears it will become extinct (assimilated) within 100 years. Toronto alone has become one of the world's most cosmopolitan cities with more than 100 cultural or ethnic groups. Canada maintains close ties with both the United Kingdom and the United States, and plays a major role in world peace and aid to poor nations. The movement of independence of Quebec Province continues to grow.

Cayman Islands

Independence: n/a (dependent territory of the United Kingdom)
Capital: Georgetown
Currency: Dollar
Income (per capita US$) 11,000
Area: 260 sq. km.
Population: (1992 estimate) 29,139
Ethnic divisions: 40% mixed, 20% white, 20% black
Religious groups: United Church (Presbyterian and Congregational), Anglican, Baptist, Roman Catholic, Church of God, other Protestant denominations

Languages spoken: English
Form of government: British colony
Exports: Farm products, wood

Chile

Capital: Santiago
Currency: Peso
Income (per capita US$) 2010 (1990)
Area: 292,257 sq. mi.
Population: 11, 568,000 (1982)
International relations: LAIA, OAS, UN
Form of government: Presidential republic
Exports: Almonds, copper, gold, grapes, nitrate, silver, sulfur

Blacks comprise a very small percentage of Chile's population. After the coalition government of president Salvador Allende ended in a coup of 1973, Gen. Augusto Pinichet Ugarte became a dictator for 14 years. A civilian government was established in 1990, when the Christian Democrat Patricio Aylwin was elected president.

Colombia

Official Name: Republic of Colombia
Independence: July 20, 1810
Capital: Bogota
Currency: Columbian peso
Income (per capita US$) 1200 (1990)
Area: 440,000 sq. mi.
Population: (1991 estimate) 33.7 million
Illiteracy: 14% (1990)
Ethnic divisions: Mestizo 589%, white 20%, Mulatto 14%, black 4%, mixed black-Indian 3%, Indian 1%
Religious groups: Roman Catholic 95%
Languages spoken: Spanish
International relations: LAIA, OAS, UN
Form of government: Presidential republic
Exports: Coffee, emeralds, petroleum, silver

The diversity of ethnic origins results from the intermixture of indigenous Indians, Spanish colonists, and African slaves. In 1549, the area was established as a Spanish colony with the capital at Bogota. In 1717, Bogota became the capital of the viceroyalty of New Granada, which included what is now Venezuela, Ecuador, and Panama. On July 20, 1810, the citizens of Bogota created the first representative council to defy Spanish authority. Total independence was proclaimed in 1813, and in 1819 the Republic of Greater Colombia was formed.

Blacks comprise a small part of Colombia's population. Pledad Corboda de Castro became the first black woman to be elected to the Senate in the 1990s. In 1993, she wrote a law instituting equal rights for black Colombians.

Costa Rica

Official Name: Republic of Costa Rica
Independence: September 15, 1821
Capital: San José
Currency: Colon
Income (per capita US$: 1759 (1990)
Area 51,032 sq. km.
Population: (1991 estimate) 3.1 million
Illiteracy: 7% (1991)
Ethnic divisions: European (including a few mestizos), 96%, black 3%, indigenous 1%
Languages spoken: Spanish, Jamaican dialect of English spoken around Puerto Limon
International relations: CACMO, OAS, UN
Form of government: Presidential republic
Exports: Bananas, cocoa, sugar, timber

In 1502, on his fourth and last voyage to the New World, Christopher Columbus made the first European landfall in the area. Settlement of Costa Rica began in 1522. In 1821, Costa Rica joined other Central American provinces in a joint declaration of independence from Spain. Unlike most of their Central American neighbors, Costa Ricans are largely of European rather than mestizo descent, and Spain is the primary country of origin. The indigenous population today numbers no more than 25,000. Blacks, descendants of nineteenth-century Jamaican immigrant workers, constitute a significant English-speaking minority of about 30,000, concentrated around the Caribbean port city of Limon.

Cuba

Official name: Republic of Cuba
Independence: May 20, 1902
Capital: Havana
Currency: Cuban peso
Income (per capita US$): 1000 (1990)
Area: 44,200 sq. mi.
Population: (1991 estimate) 10.7 million
Illiteracy: 6% (1991)
Ethnic divisions: Spanish-African mixture
Languages spoken: Spanish
International relations: CELA, UN
Form of government: Socialist Military
Exports: Chromium, nickel, sugar

Cuba is a multi-racial society with a population of mainly Spanish and African origins. Before the arrival of Columbus in 1492, Cuba was inhabited by three groups—Cyboneys, Guanahabibes, and Tainos. As Spain developed its colonial empire in the Western Hemisphere, Havana became an important commercial seaport. Settlers eventually moved inland, devoting themselves mainly to sugarcane and tobacco farming. As the native Indian population died out, African slaves were imported to work on the plantations. A 1774 census counted 96,000 whites, 31,000 free blacks, and 44,000 slaves in Cuba. Slavery was abolished in 1886.

Fidel Casro, who seized power in 1959, transformed Cuba into a socialist nation with the aid of the Soviet Union. Castro became a champion of anti-colonialism, which made him popular in "third world" countries struggling for independence. Soviet ties have created difficulties in Cuba, and many Cubas are still trying to leave the island.

Dominica
Official name: Commonwealth of Dominica
Independence: November 3, 1978
Capital: Roseau
Currency: Eastern Caribbean Dollar
Income (per capita US$: 1940 (1990)
Area: 290 sq. mi.
Population: (1991 estimate) 86,000
Illiteracy: 6% (1991)
Ethnic divisions: Black African, Carib Indians
Religious groups: Roman Catholic 80%, Church of England, other Protestant denominations
Languages spoken: English (official), a French patois is widely spoken
International relations: CARICOM, Commonwealth, OAS, UN
Form of government: Parliamentary republic
Exports: Citrus fruit, cocoa, coconuts

Dominica was first visited by Europeans on Columbus's second voyage in 1493. Spanish ships frequently landed on Dominica during the sixteenth century, but toiled at establishing settlements. In 1635, France claimed Dominica. As part of the 1763 Treaty of Paris that ended the Seven Years' War being fought in Europe, North America, and India, the island became a British possession.

In 1763, the British established a legislative assembly, representing only the white population. In 1831, reflecting a liberalization of official British racial attitudes, the "Brown Privelege Bill" conferred political and social rights on nonwhites. Three blacks were elected to the Legislative Assembly the following year, and by 1838 the recently enfranchised blacks dominated that body. Most black legislators were smallholders or merchants, who held economic and social views diametrically opposed to the interests of the small, wealthy English planter class. Reacting to a perceived threat, the planters lobbied for more direct British rule. In 1865, after much agitation and tension, the colonial office replaced the elective assembly with one of half of the members appointed.

The power of the black population progressively eroded until all political rights for the vast majority of the population were effectively curtailed. On November 3, 1978, the Commonwealth of Dominica was granted independence by the United Kingdom. Almost all 81,000 Dominicans are descendants of African slaves imported by planters in the eighteenth century.

In 1980, Mary Eugenia Charles became the first woman to come to power in the Carribbean as well as the only black woman to lead an independent nation. Her longevity and determination earned her the nickname "The Iron Lady of the Caribbean." Trained as a lawyer, Charles rose through the ranks of government, spending most of her career in politics. She was elected to the prime ministership for three terms; in 1996, she was thinking of retiring.

Dominican Republic
Independence: February 27, 1844
Capital: Santo Domingo
Currency: Dominican peso
Income (per capita US$: 820 (1990)
Area: 18,704 sq. mi.
Population: (1991 estimate) 7.3 million
Illiteracy: 18% (1991)
Ethnic divisions: Mixed 73%, black African 11%
Religious groups: Roman Catholic 95%
Languages spoken: Spanish
International relations: OAS, UN
Form of govt: Presidential republic
Exports: Gold, silver, sugar cane

The island of Hispaniola, of which the Dominican Republic forms the eastern two-thirds and Haiti the remainder, was originally occupied by members of the Taino tribe when Columbus and his companions landed there in 1492. Brutal colonial conditions reduced the Taino population from an estimated one million to about five hundred in only fifty years. To assure adequate labor for plantations, the Spanish began bringing African slaves to the island in 1503.

In the next century, French settlers occupied the western end of the island, which Spain ceded to France in 1697. In 1804, this became the Republic of Haiti. The Haitians conquered the whole island in 1822 and held it until 1844, when forces led by Juan Pablo Duarte, the hero of Dominican independence, drove the Haitians out and established the Dominican Republic as an independent state. In 1861, the Dominicans voluntarily returned to the Spanish Empire; in 1865, independence was restored.

After Rafael Trujillo's dictatorship ended in a 1961 assassination, Joaquín Balaguer became president and instituted a police state. He was however reelected

Improvised housing in Santo Domingo, Dominican Republic.

between 1966 and 1990. Pro- Cuban groups have been active in the nation.

Ecuador

Official name: Republic of Ecuador
Capital: Quito
Currency: Sucre
Income (per capita US$): 940 (1990)
Area: 109,483 sq. mi.
Population (1974 estimate) 6,521,710
Illiteracy: 14% (1991)
International relations: LAIA, OAS, UN
Form of government: Presidential republic
Exports: Coffee, cocoa, gold, petroleum

Blacks comprise a very small percentage of Ecuador's population.

El Salvador

Official name: Republic of El Salvador
Capital: San Salvador
Currency: Colon
Income (per capita US$): 1040 (1990)

Area: 8260 sq. mi.
Population (1980 estimate) 4,748,000
Illiteracy: 30 (1991)
International relations: CACM, OAS, UN
Form of government: Presidential republic
Exports: Coffee

Blacks comprises a very small percentage of El Salvador's population. After a long period of military dictatorships and conservative regimes, Napoléon Duarte of the Christian Democratic Party became president in 1980. In 1989, he was succeeded by Alfredo Cristiani leader of ARENA party.

French Guiana

Capital: Cayenne
Area: 43,740 sq. mi.
Population: (1988 estimate) 90,240
Ethnic divisions: African and Afro-European 66%, European 18%, East Asian, Chinese, Amerindian, Brazilian 16%
Religious groups: Roman Catholic, Protestant sects, Hindu, traditional African belief
Languages spoken: French

Stevedores transferring bananas in the Caribbean.

Exports: Cocoa, coffee, gold, sugar cane

The first French settlement in French Guiana was established in 1604. The first permanent settlement began in 1634, and in 1664, the town of Cayenne was established. Following the abolition of slavery in 1848, the fragile plantation economy declined precipitously. French Guiana as an overseas department of France since 1946, is an integral part of the French Republic. About two-thirds of the population of French Guiana are Afro-European Creoles or Guianese. The remainder include French serving in military or administrative positions.

Grenada
Independence: February 7, 1974
Capital: Saint George
Currency: East Caribbean dollar
Income (per capita US$): 2120 (1990)
Area: 133 sq. mi.
Population (1991 estimate) 84,000

Illiteracy: 15% (1991)
Ethnic divisions: Black African descent, some East Indian, European, Arawak/Carib Indian
Religious groups: Roman Catholic 63%, Church of England, other Protestant denominations
Languages spoken: English (official), some vestigial French patois
International relations: CARICOM, EC, OAS, UN
Form of government: Independent within British sovereignty
Exports: Banana, cocoa, coffee, coconuts

Like the rest of the West Indies, Grenada was originally settled to cultivate sugar, which was grown on estates using slave labor. Most of Grenada's population is of African descent; little trace of the early Arawak and Carib Indians remains.

Columbus first visited Grenada in 1498. Grenada remained uncolonized for more than one hundred years after the first visit by Europeans; British efforts to settle the island were unsuccessful. In 1650, a French company purchased Grenada from the British and established a small settlement. The island remained under French control until captured by the British a century later during the Seven Year's War. Slavery was outlawed in 1833, the same year Grenada was made part of the British Windward Islands Administration. In 1958, the Windward Islands Administration dissolved. Grenada became an associated state on March 3, 1967, but sought full independence, which the British government granted on February 7, 1974.

The New Jewel Movement led by Maurice Bishop assumed power in 1979. He was overthrown and killed in 1983 when Bernard Coard took over. The United States, along with forces from the other Caribbean countries intervened.

Guadeloupe

Independence: n/a (overseas department of France)
Capital: Point-à-Pitre
Area: 660 sq. mi.
Population: (1988 estimate) 337,524
Ethnic divisions: Afro-European, European, Afro-East Asian, East Asian
Religious groups: Roman Catholic, Hindu, and traditional African belief
Languages spoken: French, creole
Exports: Bananas, rum, sugar cane

Columbus sighted Guadeloupe in 1493. The area was permanently settled by the French in the seventeenth century. The first slaves were brought from Africa to work the plantations around 1650, and the first slave rebellion occurred in 1656. Guadeloupe was poorly administered in its early days and was a dependency of Martinique until 1775.

An open-air market in Guadeloupe.

Most Guadeloupeans are of mixed Afro-European and Afro-Indian ancestry (descendants of laborers brought over from India during the ninteenth century). Several thousand metropolitan French reside there; most are civil servants, business people, and their dependents.

Guatemala

Capital: Guatemala City
Currency: Quetzal
Income (per capita US$) 900 (1990)
Area: 42,042 sq. mi.
Population: (1981 estimate) 6,043,559
Illiteracy: 53% (1991)
International relations: CACM, OAS, UN
Form of government: Presidential republic

Blacks comprise a very small percentage of Guatemala's population.

Guyana

Official name: Co-operative Republic of Guyana
Independence: May 26, 1966
Capital: Georgetown
Currency: Guyana dollar
Income (per capita US$): 370 (1990)
Illiteracy: 4% (1991)
Area: 83,000 sq. mi.
Population (1991 estimate): 748,000
International relations: CARICOM, Commonwealth, EC, UN

Ethnic divisions: East Indian 49.6%, African 30.4%, mixed 14.1%, European and Chinese 0.5%
Religious groups: Christian 46%, Hindu 37%, Muslim 9%, other 8%
Languages spoken: English, Guyanese Creole, Amerindian dialects
Form of government: Multi-party
Exports: Bauxite, gold, sugar

Guiana was the name given the area sighted by Columbus in 1498, comprising modern Guyana, Suriname, French Guiana, and parts of Brazil and Venezuela. The Dutch settled in Guyana in the late sixteenth century. Dutch control ended when the British became the de facto rulers in 1796. In 1815, the colonies of Essequibo, Demerara, and Berbice were officially ceded to the British by the Congress of Vienna and, in 1831, were consolidated as British Guiana.

Slave revolts, such as the one in 1763 led by Guyana's national hero, Cuffy, stressed the desire to obtain basic rights and were underscored by a willingness to compromise. Following the abolition of slavery in 1834, indentured workers were brought primarily from India but also from Portugal and China. A scheme in 1862 to bring black workers from the United States was unsuccessful.

Independence was achieved in 1966, and Guyana became a republic on February 23, 1970, the anniversary of the Cuffy slave rebellion. Between 1968 and 1972 Guyana was ruled by the PNC party. In 1975, Guyana gained unfortuante international recognition after a religious cult in Jonestown was led into mass suicide by its leader, Jim Jones.

Political conflict with opposing parties resulted in the assassination of the nations leader, Dr. Walter Roberts, in 1980. Human rights were continually being violated under the Forbes Burnham government (1980-85). Upon his death he was succeeded by Desmond Hoyte. Cheddi Jagan who had been a prominent political figure of Peoples's Progressive Party many years ago was elected president in 1992.

Haiti

Official name: Republic of Haiti
Independence: 1804
Capital: Port-au-Prince
International relations: EC, OAS, UN
Currency: Gourde
Income (per capita US$): 400 (1989)
Area: 10,714 sq. mi.
Population: (1991 estimate): 6.2 million
Illiteracy: 53% (1991)
Ethnic Group: Black African 95%, mulatto and European 5%

Religious groups: Roman Catholic 80%, Protestant 10%, traditional (voodoo) practices 10%
Languages spoken: French (official), Creole
Form of government: Multi-party
Exports: Coffee, cotton, sugar

Columbus first visited the Island of Hispaniola in 1492. In 1697, Spain ceded the western third of Hispaniola to France. During this period, slaves were brought from Africa to work the sugarcane and coffee plantations. In 1791, the slave population, led by Toussaint L'Ouverture, Jean Jacques Dessalines, and Henri Christophe, revolted and gained control of the northern part of Saint-Domingue. The French were unable to regain control. In 1804, the slaves established an independent nation, renaming the area Haiti.

Haiti is the world's oldest black republic and the second oldest republic in the Western Hemisphere, after the United States. In September 1991, the newly elected President Jean-Bertrand Aristide was ousted in a coup leading by Brigadier General Raoul Cedras. Since Aristide's ouster, thousands of Haitians have attempted to immigrate to the United States, with no success. In 1994, U.S. forces took control and Aristide was returned to power, only to lose in the following years elections. The U.S. government has also forcibly returned Haitian refugees illegally attempting to emigrate, maintaining that the majority have been economic, and not political, refugees.

Almost 95 percent of the Haitians are of black African descent; the rest of the population are mostly of mixed African-Caucasian ancestry (mulattoes).

Honduras

Official name: Republic of Honduras

Blacks comprise a very small percentage of Honduras' population.

Jamaica

Independence: August 6, 1962
Capital: Kingston
Currency: Jamaican dollar
Income (per capita US$): 1510 (1990)
Area: 4,244 sq.mi.
Population: (1991 estimate) 2.4 million.
Illiteracy: 18% (1990)
Ethnic divisions: African 76.3%, Afro-European 15.1%, Chinese and Afro-Chinese 1.2%, East Indian and Afro-East Indian 3.4%, European 3.2%
Religious groups: Anglican, Baptist and other Protestant denominations, Roman Catholic
Languages spoken: English, Creole
International relations: CAROCOM, EC, OAS, UN
Form of government: Independent under British sovereignty
Exports: Bauxite

Workers on a banana plantation in Central America.

Jamaica was first visited in 1494 by Christopher Columbus and settled by the Spanish during the early sixteenth century. In 1655, British forces seized the island, and in 1670 gained formal possession through the Treaty of Madrid.

In 1958, Jamaica joined nine other British territories in the West Indies Federation but withdrew when, in a 1961 referendum, Jamaican voters rejected membership. Jamaica gained independence from the United Kingdom in 1962 but has remained a member of the Commonwealth. Sugar and slavery, were important elements in Jamaica's history and development. With the abolition of slavery in 1834, the settlers were forced to recruit other sources of cheap labor, resorting to the importation of East Indian and Chinese farm hands. As a result, Jamaica is a multi-racial society.

Extreme povery is a distinguishing factor of all the lesser developed nations, and Jamaica is no exception. A new phenomenon has became particularly apparent in Jamaica, a country that has lost nearly 30 percent of its population to the United States. Though prevalent in all countries that experience heavy emigration, tens of thousands of Jamaican parents have gone abroad, leaving behind children whom they hope to one day be able to summon. The youngsters have acquired the nickname "barrel children" from the barrels filled with goodies—food, clothing, photographs—the parents send back whenever possible. Though these children have not actually been abandoned, they are often passed from relative to relative or to friends or strangers. Highly at risk, the children are often susceptible to abuse from their supposed benfactors, many drop out of school, some get into trouble with the law.

After years under the Jamaican Labor party, the 1972 elections put Michael Norman Manley in power and reelected in 1989. His regime ended when Perciaval Patter was elected in 1992.

Martinique
Independence: n/a (overseas region of France)
Capital: Fort-de-France
Area: 425 sq. mi.
Population: (1988 estimate): 351,105
Ethnic divisions: Afro-European, Afro-Indian, European
Religious groups: Roman Catholic 95%, Baptist, Seventh-day Adventist, Jehovah Witness, Pentecostal, Hindu, traditional African belief 5%
Languages spoken: French

Linstead market, Jamaica.

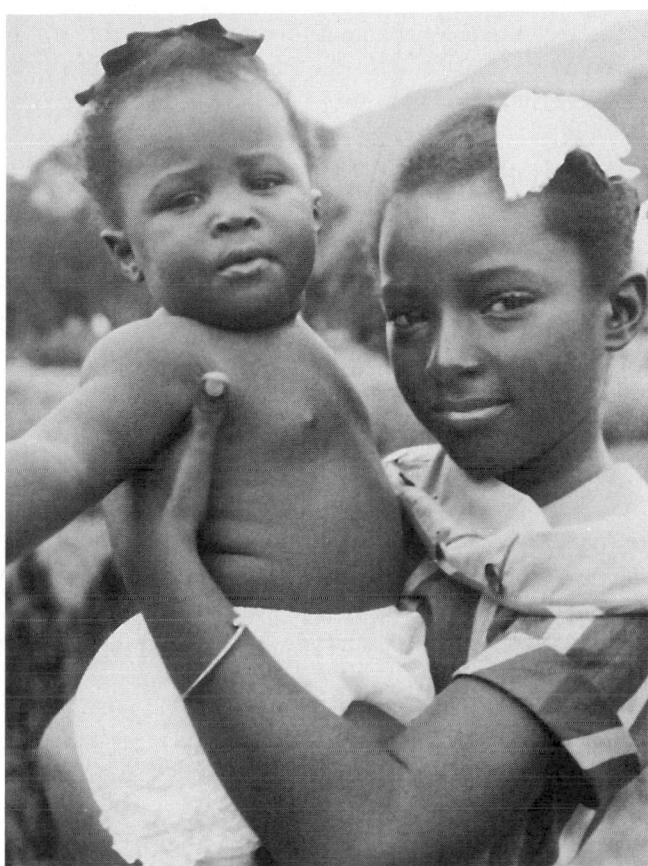

Two Jamaican children.

Exports: Bananas, pineapples, sugar cane

Columbus sighted Martinique in 1493 or 1502. The area was permanently settled by the French in the seventeenth century. Except for three short periods of British occupation, Martinique has been a French possession since 1635.

About 95 percent of the people of Martinique are of Afro-European or Afro-European-Indian descent. The rest are traditional white planter families, commonly referred to as bekes or creoles, and a sizable number of metropolitan French work in administration and business.

Mexico
Official name: The United Mexican States
Capital: Mexico City
Currency: Mexican peso
Income (per capita US$: 2604 (1992)
International relations: LAIA, SELA, UN
Form of government: Federal republic
Exports: Coffee, copper, cotton, petroleum, silver, sugar, sulfur

Blacks accompanied the Spanish as conquerors to Mexico in the sixteenth century, and later were brought in large numbers as slaves. It is estimated that there were 150,000 black slaves in Mexico in the sixteenth century. One of the earlier slaves, Estevanico, is credited with opening up the northern interior lands of what is now New Mexico and Arizona, to Spanish conquest.

The use of slavery dropped sharply in the eighteenth and early nineteenth centuries. In 1829, Mexico abolished slavery in all its states except Texas, allowing it to remain there to pacify the United States. As slavery in the United States moved westward into Texas, Mexico became a haven for escaped slaves who slipped into the heart of the country and blended with the population.

Since the sixteenth century, Mexico's blacks have intermarried with Indians and whites so that their African heritage is no longer clearly identifiable. Some 100,000 blacks, about 0.5 percent of the population, do live in Mexico, mostly in the port cities of Vera Cruz and Acapulco. Blacks in lesser density live in Mexico City and in border cities across the Rio Grande River from Texas.

In 1988, a 39-year-old economist, Carlos Salinas de Gortari was elected to the presidency. The North American Free Trade Agreement (NAFTA) was concluded in

1992, and Mexico became a member of this fair trade agreement. 1994 brought an uprising by the Zapatista Army of National Liberation.

Montserrat

Independence: n/a (dependent territory of the United Kingdom)
Capital: Plymouth
Population: (1992 estimate) 12,617
Ethnic divisions: Black African, European
Religious groups: Anglican, Methodist, Roman Catholic, Pentecostal, Seventh-Day Adventist, other Christian denominations
Languages spoken: English

When the Leeward Islands (Antigua, Anguilla, Barbuda, Montsarrat, Nevis, and Saint Kitts) were first visited by Christopher Columbus in 1493, they were inhabited by Carib Indians. Montserrat was first colonized in 1632. The French captured some of the islands in 1666 and again in 1782, but the islands were returned to the British under the Treaty of Versailles in 1783. Most of the population is an intermixture of European settlers and the descendants of West African slaves.

Netherlands Antilles

Independence: n/a (Autonomous part of the Kingdom of the Netherlands)
Currency: Guilder or florin
Area: 324 sq. mi.
Population: 187,500
Ethnic divisions: Black African 85%, European, Carib Indian
Religious groups: Roman Catholic, Protestant
Languages spoken: Papiamento, English, Dutch, Spanish
Form of government: Dutch colony

The Spanish first landed in Curacao in 1499, and in 1527 they took possession of Curacao, Bonaire, and Aruba. In 1634, the three islands were passed to the Netherlands, where they have remained except for two short periods of British rule during the Napoleonic Wars.

Curacao was the center of the Caribbean slave trade until emancipation in 1863. Before the war, the Dutch Caribbean islands were administered as Dutch colonies; afterward, negotiations to confer a greater measure of self-government began. On December 15, 1954, the Netherlands Antilles became an autonomous part of the kingdom.

Some 40 nationalities are represented in the Netherlands Antilles and Aruba. The people of the Netherlands Antilles primarily are of African or mixed African and European descent.

Nicaragua

Official name: Republic of Nicaragua
Independence: 1821
Capital: Managua
Currency: Cordoba
Income (per capita US$): 434 (1991)
Area: 57,000 sq. mi.
Population: 3.3 million
Illiteracy: 13% (1991)
Ethnic divisions: Mestizo (mixed) 69%, white 17%, black African 9%, Indian 5%
Religious groups: Roman Catholic 85%
Languages spoken: Spanish
International relations: CACM, OAS, UN
Form of government: Presidential republic
Exports: Bananas, coffee, gold

Columbus sailed along the Nicaraguan coast on his last voyage in 1502. Wars between the Spanish on the Pacific and Indians and British on the Caribbean (the British presence did not end until 1905) marked the colonial period. Guatemala declared its independence from Spain in 1821, but Nicaragua did not become an independent republic until 1838.

In 1974, Anastasio Somoza Garcia won elections and immediately faced opposition by the Sandinist National Liberation front. After 13 politicians were kidnaped, martial law was instituted which eventually led Somoza to lose all support. He left the country in 1980, and was later assassinated. More than 30,000 people lost their lives during that time. A peace accord was finally reached between the Sandinistas and the Contras (anti-Sandinistas). Leading a 10-party alliance, Violetta Chamorro was elected president in 1990.

Most Nicaraguans are a mix of European and Indian. Only the Indians of the Caribbean coast remain ethnically distinct and retain tribal customs and dialects. A large black minority (of Jamaican origin) is concentrated on the Caribbean coast.

Panama

Official name: Republic of Panama
Independence: November 3, 1903
Capital: Panama City
Currency: Balboa
Income (per capita US$): 1790 (1990)
Area: 29,762 sq. mi.
Population: (1991 estimate) 2.4 million
Illiteracy: 12% (1991)
Ethnic divisions: Mestizo 70%, West Indian 14%, white 10%, Indian 6%
Religious groups: Roman Catholic 93%, Protestant (Evangelical) 6%

A market at Managua, Nicaragua.

A Panamanian craftsman.

Languages spoken: Spanish (official), English, Indian languages

International relations: OAU, UN

Form of government: Presidential republic

Exports: Cocoa, coffee

Prior to the arrival of Europeans, Panama was inhabited by Amerindian groups. By 1519 the Spanish had established settlements, killing or enslaving much of the indigenous Indian population. Africans were brought in to replace the Indian slave population. Today, most Panamanians are of mixed parentage—Spanish, Indian, or black.

The most importance source of income is the operation of the Panama Canal, which the United States, under the Carter administration agreed to return to the Panamian sovereignty by 1999. During the 1980s, the political scene was dominated by Gen. Manuel Antonio Noriega, who was accused of trafficking drugs. A U.S. military attack forced him to surrender his leadership in 1989, after he was incarcerated in a U.S. jail.

Paraguay

Official name: Republic of Paraguay

Blacks comprise a very small percentage of Paraguay's population.

Peru

Official name: Republic of Peru

Blacks comprise a small percentage of Peru's population.

Puerto Rico

Independence: n/a (commonwealth associated with the United States)

Capital: San Juan

Income (per capita US$): 5,000

Area: 9,104 sq. km.

Population: (1992 estimate) 3,776,654

Illiteracy: 10%

Ethnic division: Mixed, black, indian, whites

Religious groups: Roman Catholic 85%, Protestant denominations and other 15%

Languages spoken: Spanish (official), English

First visited by Columbus in 1493 on his second voyage to the New World, Puerto Rico was soon conquered by the Spaniard Ponce de Leon, who was appointed governor of the island in 1509. The indigenous Carib Indians, almost all of whom were utilized by the Spaniards as plantation laborers, were eventually wiped out to be replaced in 1513 by African slaves. Puerto Rico was held by the English in 1598 and San Juan was besieged by the Dutch in 1625. Otherwise, Spanish control remained unchallenged until the Spanish-American War.

The island was captured by United States forces during this conflict and ceded outright to the United States under the Treaty of Paris (1898). In 1900, Congress established a local administration, with a governor appointed by the American president, an executive council, and an elected house of delegates. Puerto Ricans were granted United States citizenship in 1917. After World War II, Congress provided that the governor of the island be an elected official. In 1950, a further act of Congress enabled Puerto Rico to draft its own constitution and, in three years, it became a U.S. Commonwealth; Puerto Ricans are considered U.S. citizens, but they do not have the right to vote. Unemployment has been on the rise precipitating two thirds of families to depend of government aid.

Many Puerto Ricans today are of mixed black and Spanish ancestry. Africans were slaves in Puerto Rico until 1873, when slavery was abolished. The United States acquired the island in 1898, and Puerto Ricans have been U.S. citizens since the 1917 passage of the Jones Act. Sexual relations between the descendants of the African slaves and the Spanish colonizers resulted in a multiracial population. For the most part, the original Indian inhabitants of the island were exterminated in the sixteenth century.

Saint Kitts and Nevis

Official name: Federation of Saint Kitts and Nevis
Independence: September 19, 1983
Captial: Basseterre
Currency: Eastern Caribbean dollar
Income (per capita US$): 1610 (1990)
Form of govt: Independent within British Commonwealth
Area: Saint Kitts, (68 sq. mi.); Nevis, (36 sq. mi.)
Population: (1991 estimate) 40,293
Illiteracy: 15% (1989)
Ethnic divisions: Black Africans, some British
Religious groups: Principally Anglican, with evangelical Protestant and Roman Catholic minorities
Languages spoken: English
International relations: EC, OAS, UN
Exports: Sugar cane

Christopher Columbus first visited the islands in 1493 on his second voyage to the area, naming the larger Saint Christopher, after his patron saint. In 1624, Saint Christopher became the first English settlement in the West Indies, and it was from here that colonists spread to other islands in the region. In 1624, the French colonized part of the island. However, it was ceded entirely to Britain by the Treaty of Utrecht in 1713. The Federation of Saint Kitts and Nevis attained full independence on September 19, 1983.

Saint Lucia

Independence: February 22, 1979
Capital: Castries
Currency: East Caribbean dollar
Income (per capita US$): 1950 (1990)
Area: 238 sq. mi.
Population: (1991 estimate) 163,075.
Illiteracy: 10% (1991)
Ethnic divisions: Black African 90.3%, mixed 5.5%, East Indian 3.2%, Caucasian 0.8%
Religious groups: Roman Catholic 90%, Church of England 3%
Languages spoken: English (official), French patois
International relations: CARICOM, EC, OAS, UN
Form of government: Independent state within British Commonwealth

Exports: Bananas, coconuts

Europeans first visited the island in either 1492 or 1502. In the seventeenth century, the Dutch, English, and French all tried to establish trading outposts on Saint Lucia but faced opposition from Carib Indians, who inhabited the island. The French, who had claimed the island, established a successful settlement in 1651 as an offshoot of the colony in neighboring Martinique; for the next century and a half, ownership was disputed hotly between France and England.

The English, with their headquarters in Barbados, and the French, centered on Martinique, found Saint Lucia even more attractive when the sugar industry developed in 1765. By 1780, nearly 50 sugarcane estates had been established on the island; heavy labor needs of the estates led to large scale importation of slaves from West Africa.

A 1924 constitution gave the island its first form of representative government. As an associated state of the United Kingdom from 1967 to 1979, Saint Lucia had full responsibility for internal self-government, but left its external affairs and defense responsibilities to Great Britain. This interim arrangement ended on February 22, 1979, when Saint Lucia achieved full independence. John Compton, leader of the United Workers' Party, became the prime minister at independence. In the 1992 elections the UWP won again.

Saint Lucia is now inhabited mainly by people of African and mixed African-European descent, with small Caucasian and East Indian minorities.

Saint Vincent and the Grenadines

Independence: October 27, 1979
Capital: Kingstown
Currency: East Caribbean dollar
Income (per capita US$): 1610 (1990)
Population: (1992 estimate) 115,339
Illiteracy: 15% (1989)
Ethnic division: Black African, white, East Indian, Carib Indian
Religious groups: Anglican, Methodist, Roman Catholic, Seventh-Day Adventist
Languages spoken: English, French patois
International relations: CARICOM, EC, OAS, UN
Form of government: Independent within British Commonwealth
Exports: Bananas, coconuts, cotton

Saint Vincent and the Grenadine islands began as a British territory during the eighteenth century. The islands were granted full autonomy in 1969 and attained full independence in 1979. Following independence, St.

Vincent was faced with a rebellion when the Union Island attempted to secede. The New Democratic Party led by James FitzAllen Mitchel won at the 1989 elections.

Suriname
Official name: Republic of Suriname
Independence: November 25, 1975
Capital: Paramaribo
Currency: Surinam guilder
Income (per capita US$): 3050 (1990)
Area: 63,037 sq. mi.
Population: (1991 estimate) 402,000
Illiteracy: 5% (1990)
Ethnic divisions: Hindustani (East Indian) 37%, Creole 31%, Javanese 15%, Bush Negro 10%, Amerindians 3%, Chinese 1.7%
Religious groups: Hindu, Muslim, Roman Catholic, Dutch Reformed, Moravian and several other Christian groups
Languages spoken: Dutch (official) English, Sranang Tongo (a Creole language), Hindustani, Javanese
International relations: EC, OAS, UN
Form of government: Constitutional republic
Exports: Bananas, bauxite, citrus, coffee, cocoa, sugar cane

Columbus first sighted the Suriname coast in 1498; Spain claimed the area in 1593. Suriname became a Dutch colony in 1667. However, the new colony, Dutch Guiana did not thrive. The colony experienced frequent uprisings by the slave population, which was often treated with extraordinary cruelty. Many of the slaves fled to the interior, where they resumed a West African culture and established the five major Bush Negro tribes in existence today: the Djuka, Saramaccaner, Matuwari, Paramaccaner, and Quinti.

Beginning in 1951, Suriname began to acquire an increasing measure of autonomy from the Netherlands. On December 15, 1954, Suriname became an autonomous part of the Kingdom of the Netherlands and gained independence on November 25, 1975. Désiré Bourtese led a military coup in 1980, and instituted a socialist state. Political upheaval continued in spite of the elections held in 1987. International pressure prevailed and the military relinquished. Ronald Venetiaan was elected in 1991.

Trinidad and Tobago
Official name: Republic of Trinidad and Tobago
Independence: August 31, 1962.
Capital: Port of Spain
Currency: Trinidad/Tobago dollar
Income (per capita US$): 3470 (1990)

A statue of former Surinamese President John Adolf Pengel.

Area: 1,980 sq. mi.
Population: (1988) 1,279,920
Ethnic divisions: (1988): African 43%, East Indian 40%, mixed 14%
Religious groups: Roman Catholic 32,9%, Hindu 25.0%, Anglican 14.7%, other Christian denominations 14.3%, Muslim 5.9%
Languages spoken: English
International relations: CARICOM, Commonwealth, EC, OAS, UN
Form of government: Constitutional republic
Exports: Natural asphault, petroleum

The island of Trinidad was first visited by Columbus in 1498 on his third voyage to the Western Hemisphere. The Spanish made the first successful attempt to colonize Trinidad in 1592. Trinidad continued under Spanish rule until it was captured by the British in 1797. Africans were brought to the islands during the eighteenth century to provide labor on the sugar cane plantations. Following the abolition of slavery, Indian and Chinese labour was brought in.

Trinidad was ceded formally to the United Kingdom in 1802; the island of Tobago was ceded to the United Kingdom in 1814. In 1888, Trinidad and Tobago merged to form a single colony. In 1958, the United Kingdom established the autonomous Federation of the West Indies. Jamaica withdrew in 1961, and when Trinidad and Tobago followed, the federation collapsed. Trinidad and Tobago obtained full independence and joined the Commonwealth in 1962.

Eric Williams became prime minister a independence and held that position until he died in 1981. During the 1991 elections Patric Augustus Mervyn Manning was elected prime minister. Black-led since 1956, the two-island nation elected its first Indian prime minister, Basdeo Panday, in 1996.

Turks and Caicos Islands

Independence: n/a (dependent territory of the United Kingdom)
Capital: Grand Turk
Currency: US dollar
Area: 430 sq. km.
Population: (1992 estimate) 12,697
Ethnic divisions: Black African
Religious groups: Baptist 41.2%, Methodist 18.9%, Anglican 18.3%, Seventh-Day Adventist 1.7%
Languages spoken: English (official)
Exports: Conch, lobster

Between 1874 and 1959, the Turks and Caicos islands were administered as a dependency of Jamaica. In 1962, the islands became a separate colony. In 1985, Norman B. Saunders, the chief minister and two other ministers caused a scandal when they were arrested in Florida on drug charges and later charged, convicted, and jailed. One year later the ministerial government ended when other ministers were found guilty of "unconstitutional behavior." The islands remain a crown colony.

Venezuela

Official name: Republic of Venezuela
Independence: July 5, 1821
Capital: Caracas
Currency: Bolivar
Income (per capita US$) 2560 (1990)
Area: 352,143 sq. mi.
Population: (1991 estimate) 20.1 million.
Illiteracy: 12%
Ethnic divisions: Spanish, Italian, Portuguese, Amerindian, black African
Religious groups: Roman Catholic 96%
Languages spoken: Spanish (official), Indian dialects
International relations: LAIA, OAS, UN
Form of government: Presidential republic
Exports: Coffee, cocoa, cotton, sugar cane, tobacco

About 900,000 of Venezuela's 17 million people are black and another 500,000 are Zambos. In the sixteenth and seventeenth centuries, Caracas was a major center for the import of slaves. In the early nineteenth century, blacks and mulattoes comprised more than half of the population of The Captaincy General of Caracas, as Venezuela was known then. Blacks remain a significant part of the country because of its proximity to the Caribbean and employment opportunities that have been available in this oil-rich nation.

Carlos Andrés Pérez, who had been president 15 years earlier was elected again in 1988. He immediately imposed austerity measures, removing governemnt subsidies on consumer goods. This resulted in mass riots that had to be quelled by the military. In 1992, two coups were unsuccessful. Pérez was eventually suspended from office for allegations of embezzlement and theft. In the 1993 elections, Rafael Caldera became the head of state.

Uruguay

Official name: Oriental Republic of Uruguay

Blacks comprise a very small percentage of Uruguay's population.

Virgin Islands, British

Independence: n/a (dependent territory of United Kingdom)
Capital: Road Town
Area: 150 sq. km.
Population: (1992 estimate) 12,555
Ethnic divisions: Black African 90%, remainder white and Asian
Religious groups: Protestant 86% Methodist 45%, Anglican 21%, Church of God 7%, Roman Catholic 6%, Seventh-Day Adventist 5%, Baptist 4%, Jehovah's Witnesses 2%, other 6%
Languages spoken: English (official)
Exports: Bananas, citrus fruit, coconut, sugar

First visited by Christopher Columbus in 1493, the Virgin Islands (an archipelago of 74 islands) is now divided into two distinct clusters—the British Virgin Islands (six main islands, nearly forty islets) and the U.S. Virgin Islands (three main islands, 65 islets). Great Britain obtained title to the islands and islets in 1666 and, until 1960, administered them as part of the Leeward Islands. At present, the government is headed by a Crown-appointed administrator who is assisted by both executive and legislative councils. Almost the entire population is of African descent. Recreational boating accounts for nearly 55 percent of the nation's gross national product and employs one third of the population.

Virgin Islands, United States

Independence: n/a (territory of the United States)
Area: 352 sq. km.

Population: (1992 estimate) 98,942

Ethnic divisions: Black African

Religious groups: Baptist, 42%, Roman Catholic 34%, Episcopalian 17%, other 7%

Languages spoken: English (official), Spanish, Creole

The U.S. Virgin Islands—the largest of which are the islands of Saint Croix, Saint John, and Saint Thomas—were originally settled by the Danish West India Company. Saint Thomas was the first to be colonized in 1672; in 1683 Saint John was colonized; and by 1733, Saint Croix had been acquired from France. Some twenty years later, the holdings of this company were taken over by the Danish crown, which then reconstituted them as the Danish West Indies.

The United States bought the territory from Denmark in 1917 for some $25 million and granted citizenship to its inhabitants ten years later. In 1931, its administration was transferred from the United States Navy to the Department of the Interior. The first black governor, William H. Hastie, was appointed in 1946.

Under the terms of the constitution, the United States retains the authority to introduce and enact legislation to govern the territory. The courts are also controlled by the United States, with an American district judge serving as the territory's highest judicial officer. Pursuant to a bill passed by Congress in 1968, the governor of the island is elected, rather than appointed. In 1972, the Virgin Islands were granted the right to send one nonvoting delegate to the House of Representatives. Island residents enjoy the same rights as mainlanders with the exception that they may not vote in a presidential election.

6

Africans in America: 1600 to 1900

6

Africans in America: 1600 to 1900

◆ Exploration and the First Settlements in the Americas ◆ Slavery in Colonial America: 1619-1787
◆ African American Status in the New Republic ◆ Expansion of Slavery ◆ Anti-Slavery Movements
◆ The Compromise of 1850 ◆ Civil War ◆ Reconstruction
◆ African American Status after Reconstruction ◆ Early African American Gatekeepers

◆ EXPLORATION AND THE FIRST SETTLEMENTS IN THE AMERICAS

The presence of the first African Americans in the Americas is a point of contention among historians. Some scholars assert that Africans established contact with the Americas prior to the Europeans, arguing from archeological, anthropological, botanical, and linguistic evidence that Africans were present in pre-Columbian America; the work of Ivan Van Sertima is notable in this regard. Others mark the advent of the African presence as coinciding with the presence of the Europeans. Pedro Alonzo Nino, an explorer and companion to Christopher Columbus on his exploratory journey of 1492, appears to have been African; and it is known that an African named Estevanico accompanied the Spanish explorers Panfilo de Narvaez and Alvar Nuñez Cabeza de Vaca on trips throughout the American southwest during the 1500s. Several other European explorers, including Vasco Nuñez de Balboa and Hernán Cortés, also had African members in their parties.

In 1496 Santo Domingo was established as the first permanent European settlement in the Americas. Indigenous Carib Indians were at first used as laborers; however, they were ill suited to the rigors of the European system of slavery and died in large numbers from either disease or the constant pressure of forced labor. Portuguese explorers first visited the west coast of Africa in the fifteenth century and found that slave trading was an established institution. West Africans had for some time sold each other to Arabic traders from North Africa. By the early sixteenth century the Portuguese and Spanish were supplying newly established colonies in the Americas with African slave labor, and by the seventeenth century several other European nations had entered the trade. African slaves proved to be a relatively cheap and inexhaustible source of labor, and from about 1501 they were increasingly used as slaves, replacing the dwindling Native American labor pool.

Clearly, relations between African Americans and Native Americans were extensive. Occasionally, African Americans made slaves of Native Americans—sometimes with the same harshness that whites showed black slaves—but most scenarios involved African American slaves running away, finding sanctuary with Native American tribes, and eventually being assimilating into the tribe. Most notable were African American contacts with the Seminoles in Florida, and the Cherokee, Creeks, Choctaws, Chickasaws, and others in North Carolina, Tennessee, Georgia, Alabama, Mississippi, and Oklahoma. (The most extensive data available to trace and document family ties of African Americans and Native Americans was collected by the U.S. government, starting in the late nineteenth century, to determine all individuals who were tribal members and thus eligible for benefits from the federal government.)

◆ SLAVERY IN COLONIAL AMERICA: 1619-1787

The Emergence of Slave Status

Twenty Africans accompanied the Europeans who landed at Jamestown, Virginia, in 1619. These people were not slaves but indentured servants, and upon completing their contracts they were free to enjoy the liberties and privileges of the "free laboring class." By 1650 there were about three hundred Africans in the American colonies, most of whom were indentured servants and some of whom eventually became property holders and active citizens. The first African American born in the colonies, William Tucker, shared with the other settlers the common birthright of freedom. The slave Anthony Johnson apparently became free about 1622 and had by 1651 amassed enough wealth to import five servants of his own, for which he obtained two hundred and fifty acres from the colonial government. The African American carpenter Richard Johnson imported two white servants in 1654 and received one hundred acres.

It is unclear when the first African slaves arrived in the North American colonies. From the 1640s Africans were increasingly regarded as chattel (or persons regarded as fixed items of personal property). In 1641 Massachusetts became the first state to make perpetual bondage legal, and the institution gradually spread among the original thirteen colonies. Rhode Island had an anti-slavery ordinance, but this was openly violated, and only Pennsylvania maintained a sustained opposition to slavery. By the 1650s Africans were commonly sold for life, and in 1661 the Virginia House of Burgesses formally recognized the institution of black slavery. The erosion of African indentured servitude in Maryland was finalized with the slave law of 1663, which stated specifically that "All negroes or other slaves within the province, [and] all negroes to be hereafter imported, shall serve *durante vita.*"

As white indentured servitude gradually disappeared from the colonial labor market, the flow of African labor into the colonies was accelerated, and planters rigidly institutionalized the perpetual servitude of Africans. One practical reason for this system was that slaves of African origin could be more easily detected than whites should they escape. And among the common rationalizations for the enslavement of Africans was reference to their non-Christian status; it was asserted that Africans were primitive and savage, and fit for nothing better than a life of unbroken labor. Even after African Americans became Christianized, their slave status was not altered; in 1667 the Virginia legislature enacted a statute which proclaimed that "baptism doth not alter the condition of the person as to his bondage or freedom."

The Trans-Atlantic Slave Trade

The Dutch West Indies Company began to provide slave labor to the American colonies in 1621. By the late seventeenth century the Royal African Company, an English company whose most profitable commodity was slaves, began to exert powerful influence within the English court and parliament. The British government in turn exerted great pressure upon the American colonies to develop attitudes and laws which would support a slave economy. The influence of the Royal African Company contributed to William Penn's decision to overrule the objections of fellow Quakers and permit slavery in Pennsylvania. The company also drew the shipping industry of New England into the slave trade. By the time the Royal African Company lost its monopoly on the West African slave trade in 1696, the sea captains of New England were participating in the massive slave incursions into Africa.

According to Donald Wright in *African Americans in the Colonial Era*, most slaves brought to the North American English colonies by English and colonial American traders came from a 3,500-mile area of west and west-central Africa, stretching from "the mouth of the Senegal River to Benguela on the Angola coast" (p. 25). Most of these slaves came from the following areas: Congo-Angola (25 percent, including the Mbundu peoples), an area within 500 miles north or south of the Zaire (formerly the Congo) River; the coast of Nigeria (25 percent, including the Ibo and Ibibio), known in slave trade times as the "Bight of Benin" and the "Bight of Biafra"; Senegambia (15 percent, including the Mandinka, Fulbe, Serer, Wolof, Bambara, and Jola tribes), from the land between and around the Senegal and Gambia rivers; the Gold Coast (15 percent, including the Ashanti, Fanti, and Akan), present-day Togo, Benin, and Ghana; the Sierre Leone-Ivory Coast area (15 percent, including the Vai, Mende, Kpelle, and Kru peoples); and the Malagasy Republic (formerly Madagascar) and coast of Mozambique (1.6 percent). The number of Africans who reached the Americas is estimated at between ten and twenty million. About six hundred thousand Africans were brought during the sixteenth century, two million in the seventeenth century, five million in the eighteenth century; and three million in the nineteenth century. In addition to those who reached the Americas must be added the enormous number who died in passage. It is estimated that 15 percent of those who were shipped to the Americas died of disease on the overcrowded boats of the "Middle Passage," and that another 30 percent died during the brutal training period faced in the West Indies before shipment to the American mainland.

Slavery Expansion in Colonial America

The colonies of New England played a principal role in the slave trade, despite their having little local need for slave labor. By 1700 African Americans of New England numbered only one thousand among a population of ninety thousand. In the mid-Atlantic colonies the

Early map of Virginia.

population comprised a larger percentage, as small slaveholdings employed slaves as farm laborers, domestics, and craftsmen. In New York slaves comprised 12 percent of the population during the mid-eighteenth century. The Quakers of Pennsylvania protested that slavery violated the principles of Christianity and the rights of man, and passed laws prohibiting the slave trade in 1688, 1693, and 1696, but the British parliament overruled these statutes in 1712. Most slaves lived in the South. The southern colonies were divided between the tobacco producing provinces of Virginia, Maryland, and North Carolina, and the huge rice and indigo plantations now comprising Carolina and Georgia. Tobacco tended to be grown on family farms around the Chesapeake Bay area, and because of this the slave population was not as concentrated as it was on the plantations further to the south.

The growth of a plantation economy and the concentration of a large number of African Americans in the southern states led first Virginia (1636) and then the other states to form all white militias. The terror of slave uprisings led the slaveholders to institute ever harsher slave codes. Ultimately, a slave could not own anything, carry a weapon, or even leave his plantation without a written pass. Murder, rape, arson, and even lesser offenses were punishable by death; small offenses were commonly punished by whipping, maiming, and branding. In the area where 90 percent of colonial African Americans lived, a slave had no rights to defend himself against a white, and as far north as Virginia it was impossible for a white to be convicted for the murder of a slave.

The Maiden Lane slave revolt in New York City in 1712 and the public paranoia over the alleged slave conspiracy of 1741 led to the development of slave codes which were in some cases as severe as those in the South, but in general the North was a relatively less oppressive environment. In Pennsylvania the Quakers allowed African Americans a relative degree of freedom, and in New England the slave codes tended to reflect Old Testament law, maintaining the legal status of slaves as persons with certain limited rights.

Military Service before and during the Revolutionary War

Records of King William's War (1689-1697) relate that the first to fall in Massachusetts was "an Naygro of Colo. Tyng," slain at Falmouth. During Queen Anne's

A group of African slaves disembark in America.

War (1702-1713), African Americans were drafted and sent to fight the French and the Indians when white colonists failed to provide the number of requisitioned men. Many armed African Americans fought at Fort William Henry in New York. Slaves sought freedom as their payment for fighting, and those who were already free sought the wider benefits of land and cash payments. The colony of Virginia ended its policy of excluding African Americans from the militia by 1723, and in 1747 the South Carolina Company made slaves eligible for enlistment in the territorial militia according to a quota system in which a 3:1 ratio was maintained between whites and blacks, thus abating the white's fears of insurrection. African Americans also fought for the British in the French and Indian War.

African American Patriots

In the years leading up to the Revolutionary War it became apparent that, despite the growth of slavery, at least some African Americans were willing to fight alongside white Americans. On March 5, 1770, an African American named Crispus Attucks was one of the first men killed in the Revolutionary War, when British troops fired on a crowd of protesters in the Boston Massacre. Many African-American Minutemen fought at the defense of Concord Bridge: among them were Lemuel Haynes, a gifted speaker and later a prominent Congregationalist minister; and Peter Salem, who had received his freedom to enlist. Other figures of the Revolutionary War include Pomp Blackman, Caesar Ferrit and his son John, Prince Estabrook (who was wounded at Lexington), Samuel Craft, and Primas Black and Epheram Blackman (who were members of Ethan Allen's Green Mountain Boys).

The Move to Disarm African Americans

A major issue during the Revolutionary War was whether African-American slaves, and even freemen, should be permitted to bear arms. On May 29, 1775, the Massachusetts Committee of Safety, in a move which reflected their desire to strengthen ties with southern states, proclaimed that the enlistment of slaves "was inconsistent with the principles that are to be supported, and reflect[ed] dishonor on the colony." On July 9, 1775, Horatio Gates, the adjutant general of the Continental Army, issued from General Washington's headquarters the order that recruiting officers should not accept "any stroller, Negro, or vagabond."

The enormous slave populations of certain southern states meant that many whites lived in perpetual fear of slave uprisings. In South Carolina slaves outnumbered whites, and in Georgia the population was above 40 percent slaves. To minimize the risk of slaves arming themselves, Edward Rutledge of South Carolina introduced a measure in Congress to discharge all African Americans (whether free or enslaved) from the Continental Army. Although the proposal was rejected, General George Washington's own council of war decided to terminate all African-American enlistment two weeks later, and on October 13, 1775, Congress passed the law. Colonial generals like John Thomas argued that African Americans soldiered as well as whites and had already "proved themselves brave" in action, but their protests went unheeded. At the close of 1775 it was extremely difficult for African Americans to join the revolutionary forces at any level.

As the leaders of the Revolution realized that there were inadequate numbers of white troops, they brought an end to their racially exclusionary policy. Local militias which were unable to fill their muster rolls won the quiet agreement of recruiting boards and the reluctant acceptance of slave owners as slaves were substituted for those white men who bought their way out of service. As the war progressed slaveowners were compensated for the enlistment of slaves who were then made free. During the course of the Revolution many colonies granted freedom to slaves in return for military service. Rhode Island passed the first slave enlistment act on

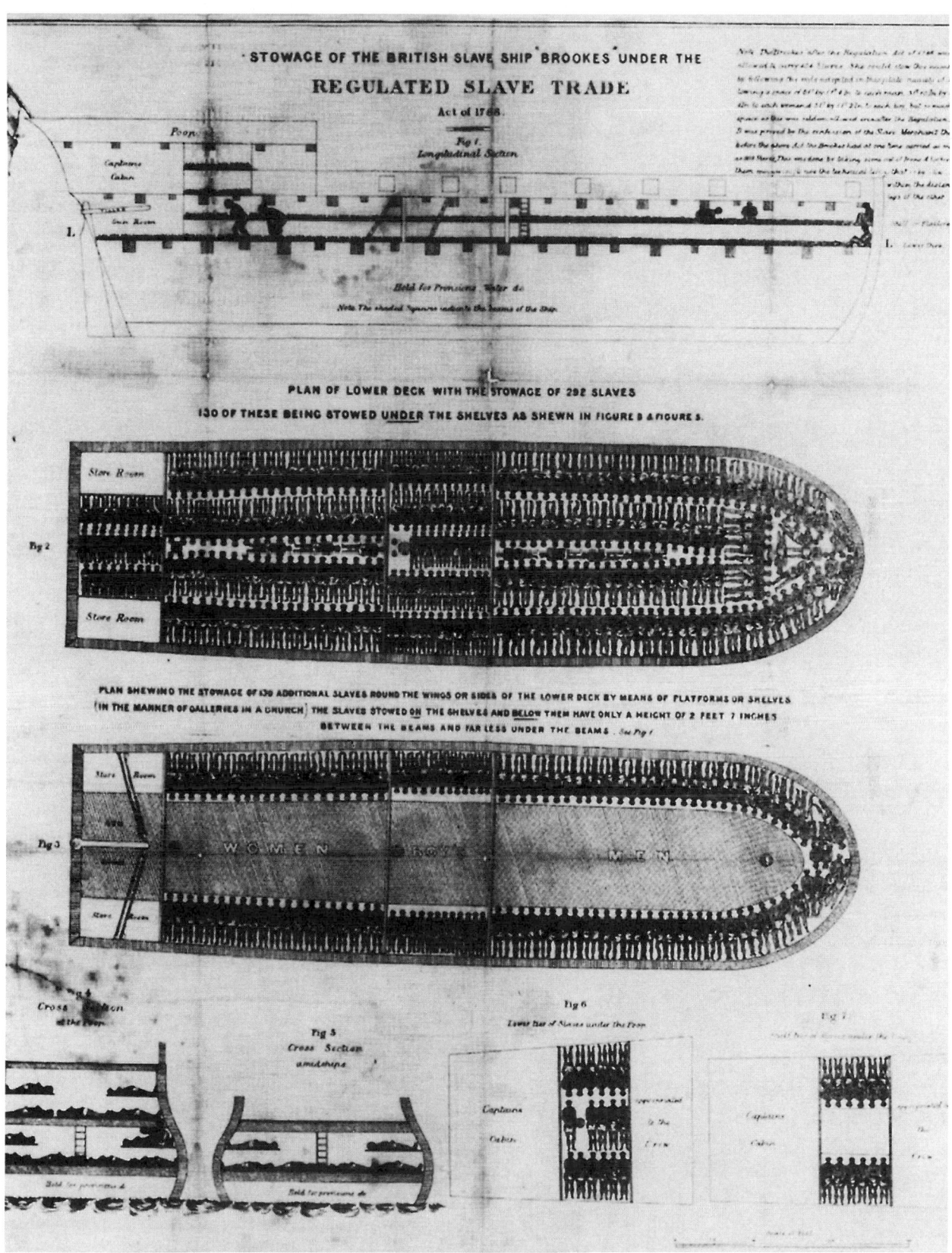

Diagram illustrating the layout of a slave ship.

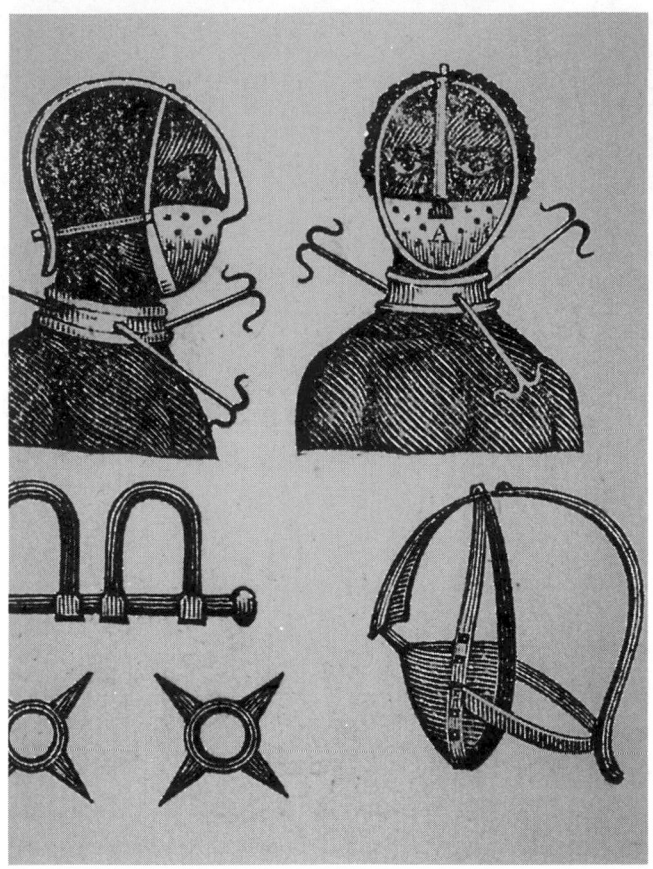

Slave catching and trading apparatuses.

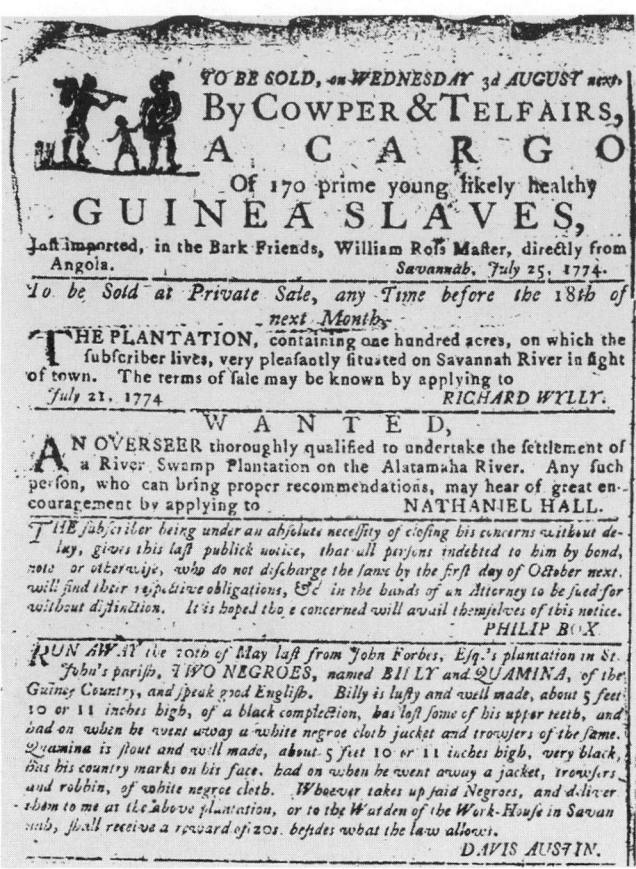

Poster advertising a slave sale.

February 2, 1778, raising a regiment that participated gallantly in many important battles. In 1780 Maryland became the only southern state to enroll slave troops, while South Carolina and Georgia refused altogether to even arm their slaves. While slave conscripts were at first assigned to combat support, in the heat of battle they were often armed. African Americans were often enlisted for longer terms than whites, and by the latter years of the war many of the most seasoned veterans were African American troops.

◆ AFRICAN AMERICAN STATUS IN THE NEW REPUBLIC

Slaves and Freemen after the Revolution

At the end of the war about five thousand African Americans had been emancipated through military service. In the following years the northern states abolished slavery: Vermont in 1777, Massachusetts in 1783, Connecticut and Rhode Island in 1784, New York in 1785,

New Jersey in 1786, and Pennsylvania in 1789. In the mid-Atlantic state of Virginia, Thomas Jefferson convinced the state legislature to allow slaveowners to manumit their slaves in 1783. In 1790 there were 757,208 African Americans comprising 19 percent of the population of the United States: 697,681 were slave, and 59,527 were free. During this time the free population faced many of the same restrictions as the slave population: they could not walk on the streets after dark, travel between towns without a pass, or own weapons. There was also the danger of being captured and enslaved, whether one was free or not.

The United States Constitution

The U.S. Constitution, drafted in 1787 and ratified in 1788, provided fundamental political principles for the nation. Key among these principles were the belief that all people share a fundamental equality, that they possess certain unalienable rights, and that government derives its power from the people. But African Americans were not afforded the rights and privileges of the Constitution. At the time, it was generally believed by

Crispus Attucks

whites that people of African descent were racially inferior and incapable of being assimilated into society. It was also widely believed that they were not citizens of the new republic. Article I, Section 2 of the Constitution specifies that all persons who are not free shall be counted as three-fifths a person for the sake of tax purposes, and Article I, Section 9 authorizes the continued importation of slaves until 1808.

Slavery in the New Nation

In 1793 Eli Whitney invented the cotton gin, which separated cotton from cotton fiber, led to a subsequent increase in the consumption of cotton, and heightened the demand for slaves in the cotton-producing states. In 1800 there were more than 893,600 African slaves in the United States; by 1810 there were 1,191,300. Although the slave trade was technically discontinued in 1808, it is estimated that from that date until 1860 more than 250,000 slaves were illegally imported; furthermore, nothing prohibited slaves from being bartered, and the breeding of slaves for sale became a specialized business. Some of the largest slave trading firms in the

nation were located in Maryland, Virginia, and the District of Columbia. Such was the expansion of slavery that, between 1800 and 1859, the population of Mississippi grew from 3489 slaves and 5179 whites to 309,878 slaves and 295,718 whites.

By the mid-eighteenth century, three-fourths of the cotton produced in the world came from the United States, and profits from cotton were so great that vast plantations were hacked from the wilderness, allowing armies of slaves to work the fields. By mid-century the states of Georgia, Alabama, Mississippi, and Louisiana annually produced 1,726,349 bales of cotton, forty-eight million pounds of rice, and 226,098,000 pounds of sugar. With the outbreak of the Civil War there were nearly four million slaves in the United States, and nearly three-fourths of them worked in cotton agriculture.

Slave Life

Slavery was by its very nature a brutal and exploitative business, and the average slave lived a terribly grim life. The more fortunate slaves tended to work on family sized farms or had positions as house servants. Whatever one's surroundings, much of one's fortune depended on the kindness of the master. On the larger plantations slaves were divided between house and field hands. The former group was charged with such assorted tasks as caring for the grounds and garden of the house, maintenance of the rigs and appliances, house cleaning, and caring for the master's children. House servants were frequently allowed to practice trades such as smithery, masonry, and tailoring; some even became skilled musicians and doctors. Body slaves served their masters as valets and personal messengers, and from this intimacy real friendships sometimes developed.

But house servants were in a sense aristocrats among slaves. Their daily lives had little in common with those of the faceless masses of field hands who confronted the brutal monotony of sowing and reaping without respite or prospect of change. On larger plantations with 25 or more slaves, the only contact between field hands and whites occurred through the overseer, who often employed cruel and vicious brutality to maintain control. Many planters felt that the largest profits were made by working a slave to death in eight or ten years and then buying a new one. Even tenderhearted masters often had little contact with their field workers, and so long as the overseer returned a profit no questions were asked. In many places slaves were given no free time at all, but were forced to work fourteen or fifteen hours a day. Louisiana was the only state with a law regarding

Engraving depicting slaves cultivating cotton.

the amount of work that could be demanded of a slave; the law permitted a slave to be worked 21 hours every day.

Most slaves could only expect to live with the bare necessities of shelter, clothing, and food. Shelter often consisted of a cramped, windowless, mud-floored shack in which a large family was expected to live; clothing was basic in design and made of course materials; and food was often limited to a bucket of rice or corn per week with no meat. The only break in the routine occurred on holidays such as Christmas, though in some cases slaves were able to hunt, fish, or garden in the hours after work.

Slave Naming Practices

Slaves had purposeful naming practices that were distinctively different from those of their masters. Most slaves were able to choose the names of their children, usually naming sons after fathers and daughters after female relatives other than the mother, in order to help identify kin relationships and keep track of which cousins one should not marry. (Slaves following marriage rules that prohibited marrying one's cousin, even though many planters and free blacks did.)

Generally, many slaves used English or European names for themselves and their children to satisfy the preferences of masters. Yet many Africans kept alive their sense of cultural independence and roots by choosing English equivalents of African names or English names that sounded similar to African names. Still, some African slaves used African names all their lives.

In addition to given or first names, slaves could also have surnames distinctive from those of their owners, although owners were usually unaware of the surnames.

Normally, slaves chose a surname that represented or identified the first slave owner of the earliest born-in-Africa ancestor who came to North America as a slave. The surname would then be handed down over the generations to help track relations and lineage. Though many slaves had their own surnames, or "titles" many did not. After the end of slavery, those who already possessed surnames revealed them, while others chose one for the first time. During and immediately after the Civil War, government agencies often insisted that slaves have surnames to enroll in their programs or receive government benefits. Those whose family had been owned by members of the same family for several generations might have the same last name as the last owner although the name was originally chosen to identify a more distant owner within the same family. Those who were aware of a slave family surname extending over two or more generations were likely to keep it in order to feel connected with ancestors even if the name was one associated with a disliked master. Some persons changed names several times to avoid the possibility of re-enslavement. Even after a name was chosen, it was often recorded differently at various times due to the low level of literacy and variations in spelling.

The Denmark Vesey Conspiracy

The mistreatment of slaves in the years after the Revolution led to an atmosphere of suspicion and terror. Masters lived in constant fear of uprisings, and much time was given over to surveillance. Although organized rebellions were rare, there were many instances of angry slaves burning dwellings and murdering their masters. Slave codes became increasingly strict, but no amount of regulation could dissipate the anger of the slaves, nor the guilt and unease which many slave owners experienced.

In 1800 an African American named Denmark Vesey purchased his freedom and from about 1817 planned a slave revolt in Charleston, South Carolina. The revolt was scheduled to begin on July 14, 1822. With the help of five other African Americans as many as nine thousand slaves were recruited before their plans were uncovered. As word of the revolt began to leak out, Vesey was forced to move the date forward to June 16; again word was leaked. The state militia was mustered, and an intense investigation of the plot was begun. 135 slaves were arrested during the course of the investigation; 97 were bound over for trial; 45 were transported out of the country; and Vesey and 34 others were hanged. As news of the conspiracy spread, southern states further tightened their slave codes.

Slaves outside their quarters.

◆ EXPANSION OF SLAVERY

Slavery in the Northwest Territory

In the early seventeenth century the French began to settle in what comprises present-day Illinois, Indiana, Michigan, Ohio, and Wisconsin, and part of Minnesota. The British began to settle in the area during the mid-eighteenth century; and, in July of 1787, Congress passed the Northwest Ordinance, which established a govern-

ment for the Northwest Territory and provided terms under which states could be formed for entrance into the Union. The ordinance also contained controversial provisions: one prohibited slavery and involuntary servitude in the territory, and the other provided for the return of fugitive slaves to the states from which they had escaped. The European farmers who had brought slaves into the territory were angered by the clause prohibiting slavery and Congress was petitioned for its repeal. The prohibition against slavery was practically circumvented when the Illinois and Indiana territories

Fieldworkers returning from the fields.

Slaves working on a cotton plantation.

established a system of indentured servitude under which any person owning slaves could bring them into the region and place them under lifetime indenture. The restrictions placed on these servants were much like the slave codes of the southern colonies—indentured servants could not travel alone without a pass or attend public gatherings independently.

The Missouri Compromise

In April of 1803 the United States paid $15 million for the Louisiana Territory, an area comprising the entire Mississippi drainage basin, which had been settled by the French in the late seventeenth century. Many southerners hoped to extend slavery into the vast new territory, and it was widely expected that Missouri would be admitted to the Union as a slave state. A series of heated debates erupted over the extension of slavery in the region, and in 1819 the House of Representatives introduced legislation authorizing statehood for Missouri while prohibiting the further introduction of slavery into the new state. This drew angry protest from proslavery supporters. The controversy was further escalated by two events: Alabama was admitted to the Union as a slave state in 1819, making the total number of slave and free states equal, and Maine applied for statehood in 1820. In 1820-1821 the Missouri Compromise was reached, admitting Missouri to the Union as a slave state with a slave population of almost 10,000, and Maine as a free state, with the understanding that the future expansion of slavery would be prohibited above the latitude of 36 degrees 33'N.

Texas and the Mexican-American War

The territory comprising Texas was part of the Louisiana Territory when the United States purchased it in 1803, but, by 1819, it had become part of Mexico. Mexico provided land grants to American settlers (many of whom brought their slaves with them), and soon Americans outnumbered the Mexicans of the region. In 1836, Texas declared its independence from Mexico and requested annexation to the United States. The possibility of another slave state entering the Union stirred fresh debate. On March 1, 1845, President John Tyler signed the joint resolution of Congress to admit Texas as a slave state; the voters of Texas supported the action, and Texas became a slave state on December 29, 1845. In 1846, Mexican and American troops clashed in Texas, and the United States declared war on the Republic of Mexico. The war ended in 1848 with the Treaty of Guadalupe Hidalgo, whereby Mexico relinquished its claims to Texas and the United States acquired all of the land extending to the Pacific Ocean.

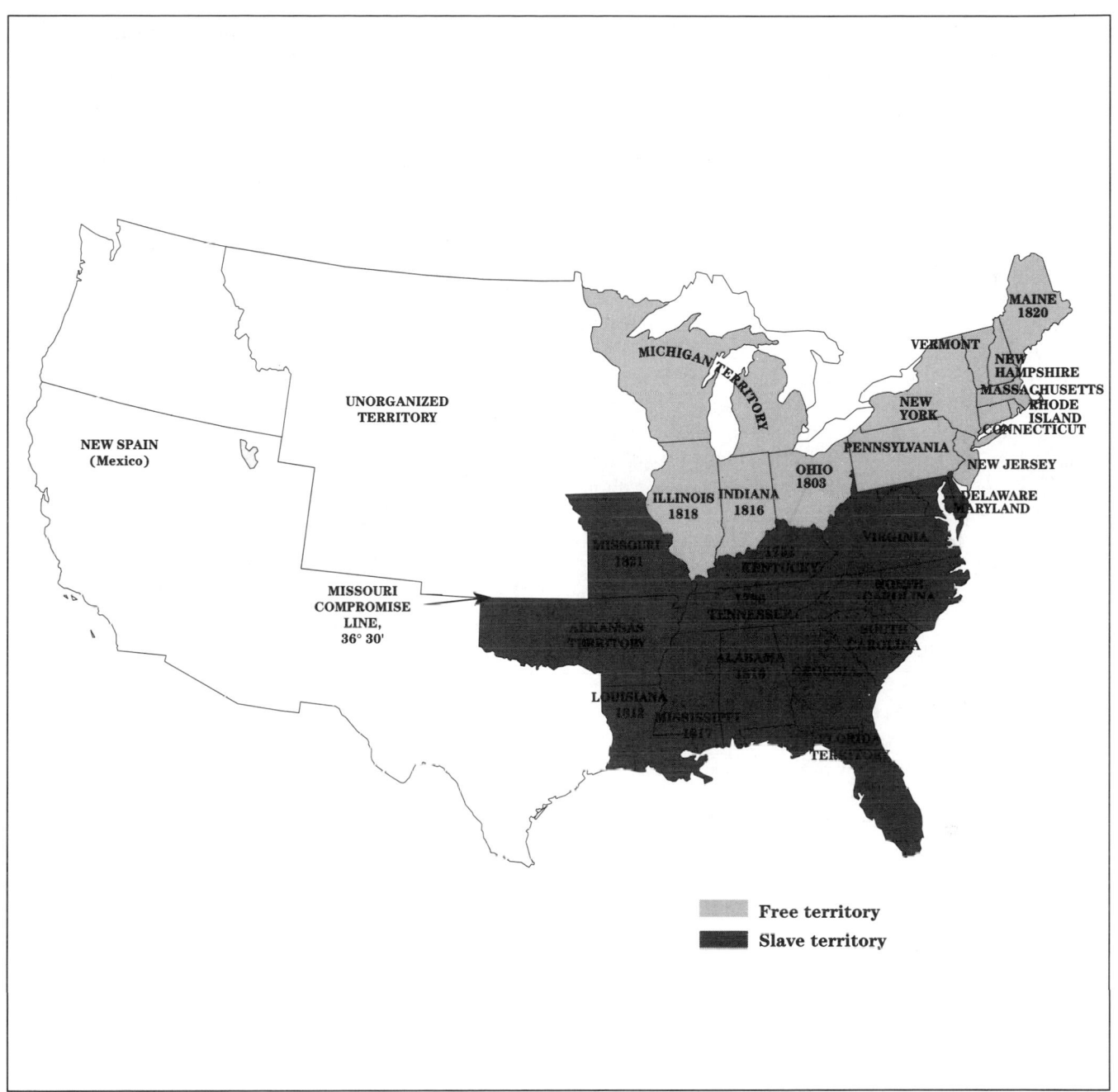

The United States c. 1821.

The Wilmot Proviso

In 1846 David Wilmot, a Democrat from Pennsylvania, introduced an amendment to a bill appropriating $2 million for President James Polk to use in negotiating a territorial settlement with Mexico; the amendment stipulated that none of the newly acquired land would be open to slavery. Although the amendment received strong support from northern Democrats and was passed by the House of Representatives, the Senate adjourned without voting on it. During the next session of Con-

gress a new bill providing $3 million for territorial settlement was introduced. Wilmot again proposed an amendment prohibiting the expansion of slavery into the newly acquired territory. The bill was passed by the House of Representatives, but the Senate drew up a new bill excluding the Wilmot Proviso.

Fugitive Slave Laws

Tensions between northern and southern politicians continued to mount over the issue of fugitive slaves.

Article IV, Section 2 of the Constitution authorized the return of fugitive slaves and provided procedures for recovery, and in 1793 the Fugitive Slave Act was passed. In northern states that strongly opposed slavery, "personal liberty" laws were passed in order to undermine federal law; liberty laws placed the burden of proof on masters in cases concerning alleged fugitive slaves. Such a law was enacted in Pennsylvania in 1826, requiring state certification before alleged fugitives could be returned. When Edward Prigg, a professional slave catcher, attempted to capture a fugitive slave residing in the state, he was arrested on kidnapping charges for failing to acquire necessary certification. The Supreme Court ruled in *Prigg v. Pennsylvania* (1842) that the state's law could not interfere with federal action regarding fugitives and the right of slaveholders to recover property; it also found that states would not be obligated to enforce federal fugitive slave statutes. This led abolitionists to seize upon the idea of not enforcing federal statutes. Following the court's decision several northern states enacted even more radical personal liberty laws prohibiting the enforcement of the Fugitive Slave Act.

◆ ANTI-SLAVERY MOVEMENTS

Quakers and Mennonites

The early opposition to slavery was generally based on religious beliefs; Christian ethics were seen as incompatible with slavery. Quakers (or the Society of Friends) and Mennonites were two of first groups to oppose the practice in the United States. Quakers and Mennonites settled mainly in Pennsylvania, though also in the South, and advocated simple living, modest dress, and nonviolence. In 1652 the Quakers passed a resolution against lifetime indenture, and in 1688 the Mennonites did the same. With the continued rise of slavery in the South, many Quakers protested and moved north into Indiana and Ohio.

The Free African Society

In 1787 the Free African Society was organized in Philadelphia by two African Americans, the Reverend Richard Allen and Absalom Jones; Adams later founded the Bethel African Methodist Church, and Jones became the rector of a Protestant Episcopal Church. The society was an important model for political consciousness and economic organization for African Americans throughout the country. It provided economic and medical aid, advocated abolition, and maintained channels of communication with African Americans in the South. Like

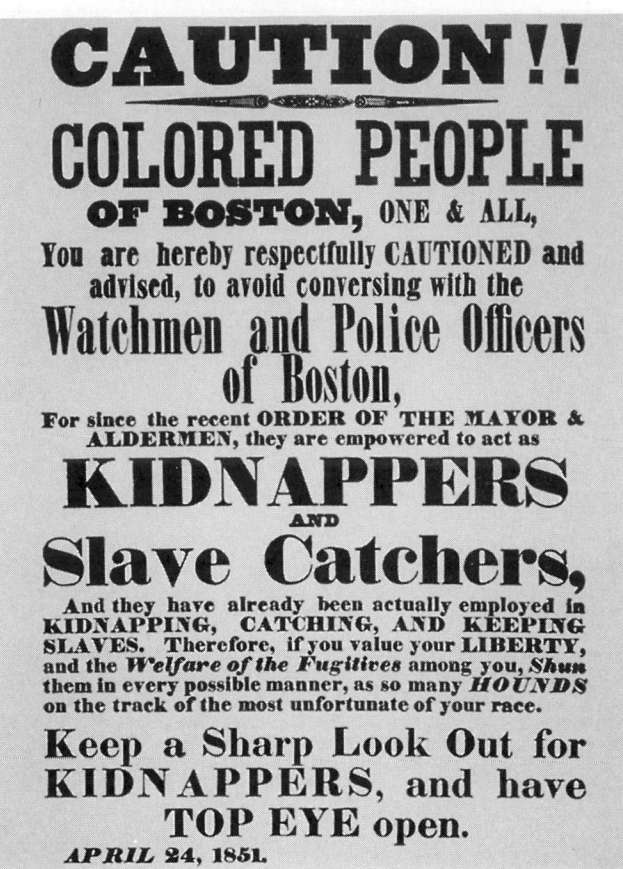

Poster warning blacks of the ever present danger of slave catchers.

the many other African American organizations that followed, the society was rooted in religious principles. Throughout the nineteenth century a number of mutual aid societies also sprung up in African American communities of the eastern seaboard, providing loans, insurance, and various other economic and social services to their members and the larger community.

American Colonization Society

In 1816 the American Colonization Society was organized in Washington, DC, with the objective of encouraging the repatriation of African Americans to Africa. While the idea of returning free African Americans was motivated in part by humanitarian intent, the society was rather moderate in its opposition to slavery. Support for the society came in part from those who feared the possibility of a large free African American population in the United States.

Congress issued a charter to the society for the transportation of freed slaves to the west coast of Africa, provided funds, and assisted in negotiations with African chiefs who ceded the land that comprised what

A photograph of the Pennsylvania Abolition Society.

became Liberia. While northerners contributed support and donations to the society, southern patrols threatened freedmen into emigrating. In 1822 the first settlers landed at the site on the western coast of Africa which was later named Monrovia after President James Monroe. In 1838 the Commonwealth of Liberia was formed and placed under the administration of a governor appointed by the society.

Abolition Societies Formed in Philadelphia and New York

The earliest abolition societies were the Pennsylvania Society for Promoting the Abolition of Slavery, formed in Philadelphia in 1775, and the New York Manumission Society, formed in the city in 1785. Prior to the 1830s a number of anti-slavery societies arose in both the North and the South, and during the 1830s and 1840s numerous abolitionist organizations arose alongside the women's rights organizations as part of the general social reform movement. The American Anti-Slavery Society was formed in Philadelphia in 1833, and after attending one of its meetings, the Quaker abolitionist Lucretia Coffin Mott formed the Philadelphia

Female Anti-Slavery Society with the assistance of Elizabeth Cady Stanton. Mott and her husband, James, were active in the underground railroad and various other anti-slavery activities, and James served as a delegate to the World Anti-Slavery Convention.

The press served as the primary tool of the anti-slavery movement. In 1827, the journalists Samuel Cornish and John Russwurm launched *Freedom's Journal*, the first African American owned and edited newspaper; in 1831, William Lloyd Garrison published the first issue of *Liberator;* and other anti-slavery papers followed, including *Anti-Slavery Record;* the *Emancipator; Human Rights;* and the *North Star*, launched by Frederick Douglass.

While many of the anti-slavery organizations were dominated by whites, African American leaders played an important role in the abolition movement. Some of the most notable leaders were Alexander Crummell, Frederick Douglass, Sarah Mapp Douglass, Charlotte Forten, Henry Highland Garnet, Sojourner Truth, and David Walker. Most of these leaders were committed to cooperative relations with whites and opposed separatist doctrines, while some of the more militant abolition-

A page from the *American Anti-Slavery Almanac,* 1840.

Nat Turner

In February of 1831, Nat Turner, a slave in Southampton County, Virginia, began to plan a slave revolt, and on August 22, Turner and his co-conspirators killed Turner's master and family. Within 24 hours about 60 whites in the county had been killed. Turner was captured on October 30 and hung on November 11. The incident contributed to the increasing paranoia of southern society.

Free Labor and Free Soil Movements

Radical Democrats and members of the Whig party who opposed slavery united to form a new political party in Buffalo, New York, in 1848. The party adopted a platform supporting free labor and free soil in response to feelings among northerners that slavery restricted the freedom of northern workers to contract for work and should therefore be excluded from the developing regions of the West. Southerners wanted the freedom to expand westward and take their slaves with them. Senator John C. Calhoun of South Carolina and other southern delegates maintained that both Congress and the territorial legislatures lacked the authority to restrict the expansion of slavery into the territories. The control of northern states over the national government led these men to consider secession from the Union.

ists (like Garnet and Walker) stressed the conditional necessity of violence in the struggle against slavery.

In the South the activities of the abolition movement only hardened the resolve of the slaveholding class to maintain the system of slavery. Depending on the circumstances, southern justification of slavery continued along several lines: it was an economic necessity, a means of converting African pagans to Christianity, and a means of controlling an inferior race.

The Underground Railroad Transports Slaves to Freedom

A vast network of individuals and groups developed throughout the country to assist African Americans in escaping from slavery, reaching their height between 1835 and 1865. Abolitionists provided "stations," food, shelter, and financial assistance, while experienced "conductors," who were often themselves runaway slaves, led thousands of "passengers" to freedom in the North, Canada, and the Caribbean. Most of the movement occurred at night, with passengers hiding in the barns and homes of sympathetic whites and African Americans during the day. Two of the most famous conductors were Josiah Henson and Harriet Tubman.

◆ THE COMPROMISE OF 1850

As the debate over the admission of new western states continued, southerners argued that the South should be given guarantees of equal positioning in the territories. In 1850 Senator Henry Clay proposed a compromise in which California would be admitted as a free state, the new territories of New Mexico and Utah would be organized, slavery would be abolished in the District of Columbia, more forceful fugitive slave legislation would be enacted, and the Texas war debt would be resolved. At the time the compromise was hailed by many as the solution to the debate over slavery.

Dred Scott v. Sandford

The slavery debate presented supporters and opponents of the institution with two very important questions: how should fugitives from slavery be treated in jurisdictions where slavery was illegal, and should a slave brought into a free state by his master be viewed as free? The first question was partially addressed by Article IV, Section 2 of the Constitution and by the Fugitive Slave Acts of 1793 and 1850; however the second question had not as yet been addressed. During

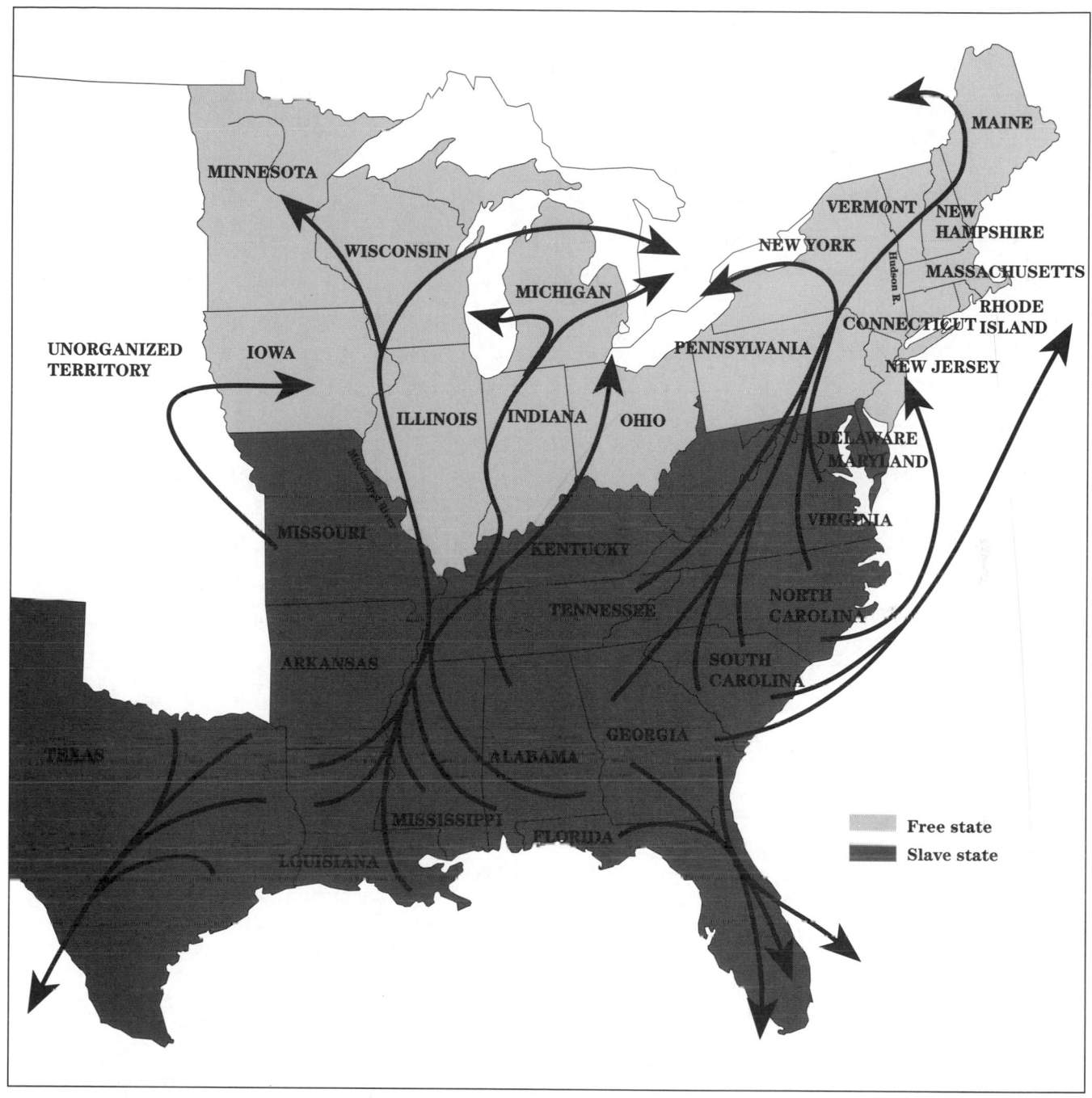

Underground Railroad Routes.

the 1830s and 1840s a slave by the name of Dred Scott accompanied his master, a surgeon in the U.S. Army on numerous trips to military posts around the country, including the free states of Illinois and the territory of Wisconsin. In 1846 Scott sued his master for his freedom, asserting that his sojourns in free jurisdictions made him free. After numerous delays, trials, and retrials, the case reached the Supreme Court in 1856. The court responded with nine separate opinions, and Chief Justice Roger Brook Taney delivered the deciding opinion. The ruling was both complex and controversial: the

Missouri Compromise of 1820 was ruled unconstitutional on the grounds that Congress did not have authority to limit the expansion of slavery; slavery was found to be legal in the territories until the citizens voted for or against it; and Africans and their descendants were found to be ineligible for citizenship in the United States as the framers of the Constitution had not viewed Africans as citizens. Since African Americans were not viewed by the court as citizens, they could not file suit. Despite the finality of the court's decision, the issue of slavery remained unresolved.

Slaves believed to have used the Underground Railroad to escape the South.

John Brown and Harpers Ferry

On October 16, 1859, a white, visionary abolitionist named John Brown led a band of 21 men (five of whom were African Americans) in the seizure of the federal arsenal at Harpers Ferry. After holding the site for several hours, Brown and his followers were captured by federal troops under the command of Robert E. Lee. Southerners were outraged by Brown's actions, interpreting them as symptomatic of a willingness among northerners to attempt the forcible overthrow of slavery. In December of 1859, Brown was hanged alongside Dangerfield Newby, a runaway slave; John A. Copeland of Carolina; Sheridan Leary, a harness maker and freedman; and Shields Gree, a sailor from South Carolina.

election southerners became even more fearful of an ideological assault on state's rights and the abolition of slavery nationwide. In 1860 a delegation from South Carolina voted unanimously for the repeal of the state's 1788 ratification of the Constitution and the severing of all relations with the Union; Georgia, Florida, Alabama, Mississippi, Louisiana, and Texas soon followed. In February of 1861, the seven states drew up a constitution and elected Jefferson Davis as president of the Confederate States of America. As northern leaders sought a means of preserving the nation, southern troops seized federal installations, post offices, and customs houses, and in April of 1861 Confederate forces took one of the last Union holds in the south, Fort Sumter in Charleston Harbor, South Carolina. Lincoln was forced to retaliate.

◆ CIVIL WAR

In 1860 Abraham Lincoln, a northern Republican, was elected president amid continuing polarization over the issue of slavery. Lincoln had voiced opposition to the expansion of slavery in the past, and with his

African American Soldiers in the Civil War

From the beginning of the war African Americans engaged in the fighting, although Lincoln at first refused to officially employ them in the Union army. By 1862 Lincoln concluded that the use of African American

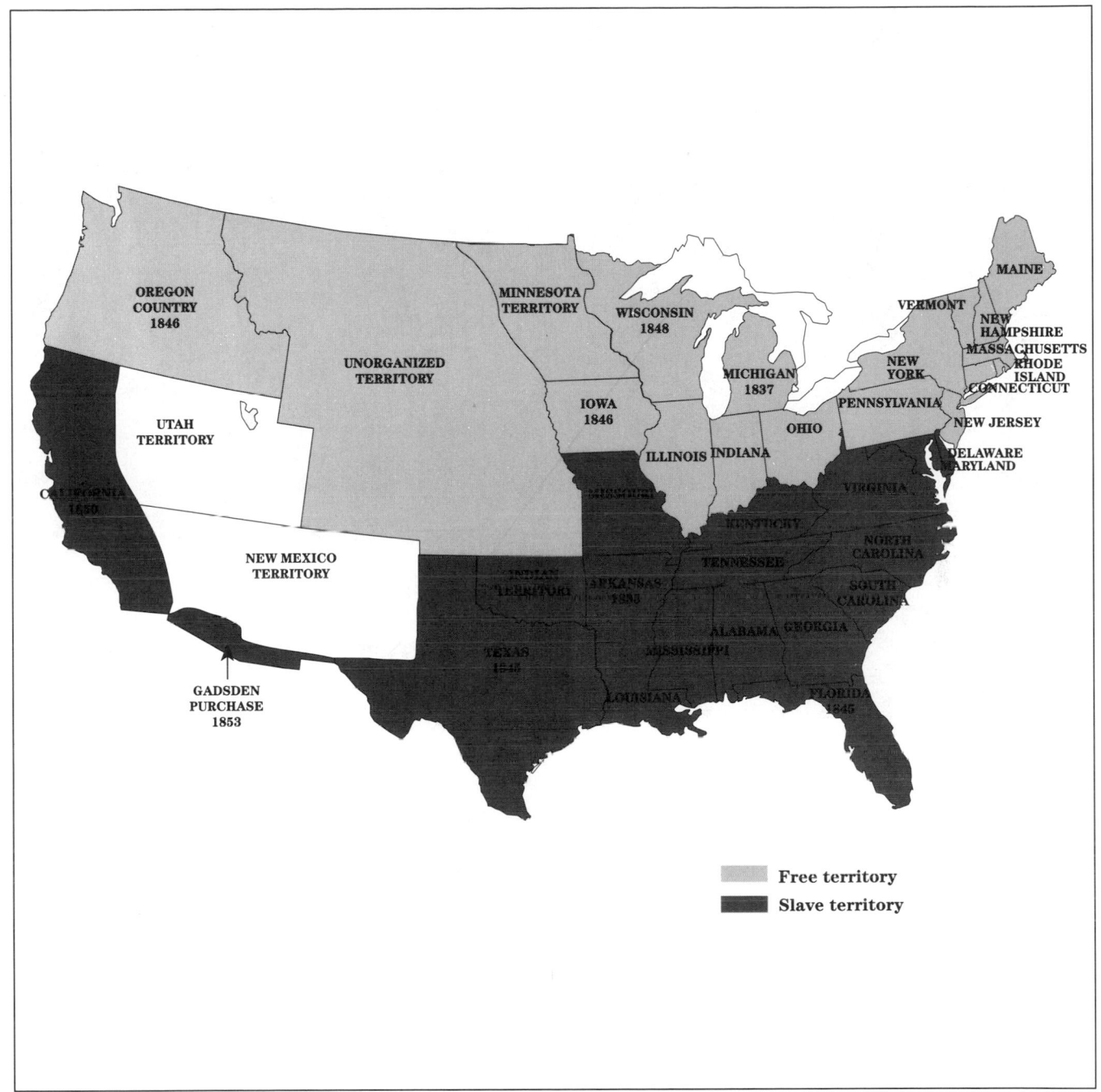

The United States c. 1850.

soldiers was a necessity. An estimated 180,000 black soldiers served in the Union army and another 20,000 served in its navy; however, not all of those African Americans who participated in the war fought on the Union side. There are no accurate records of how many black soldiers fought for the south, but their numbers grew as white southerners became more desperate.

Lincoln faced a dilemma in that if he issued an order of universal emancipation, as the abolitionists encouraged him to do, he risked alienating the border states

that remained supportive of the Union: these were Delaware, Maryland, Kentucky, and Missouri. In a letter to Horace Greeley, Lincoln stated:

> "If I could save the Union without freeing any slave, I would do it; if I could save it by freeing all the slaves, I would do it; and if I could save it by freeing some and leaving others alone, I would also do that. What I do about slavery and the colored race, I do because I believe it helps save the Union...."

Abraham Lincoln

Freed black migrants leaving the South.

During the summer of 1862, Lincoln began to feel that the emancipation of the slaves would be necessary to realizing victory over the South, and on January 1, 1863, he issued the Emancipation Proclamation, freeing slaves in those states that had seceded from the Union. Because the proclamation did not apply to the areas under occupation by Union forces, 800,000 slaves remained unaffected by its provisions. He dared not alienate the slave owning states on the Union side, especially in light of the growing antipathy toward African Americans in many northern cities. In the Draft Riots of July 13-16, 1863, huge mobs of whites in New York City (angry over the provisions of the Conscription Act) attacked blacks and abolitionists, destroying property and viciously beating many to death.

The Civil War lasted from April 1861 to April 1865, and at the end more than 360,000 Union soldiers and 258,000 Confederate solders were dead. By the end of the war twenty-one African Americans had received the Medal of Honor, and indeterminate numbers of others had made sacrifices for the cause. On December 18, 1865, the Thirteenth Amendment of the Constitution was ratified, formally abolishing slavery in the United States.

◆ RECONSTRUCTION

Civil Rights and Reconstruction Acts

On March 3, 1865, Congress enacted the first of several acts, which set up and empowered the Bureau of Refugees, Freedmen and Abandoned Lands (or the Freedmen's Bureau). The organization provided former slaves with basic health and educational services, and administered land that had been abandoned during the war. In 1866 Congress passed the Civil Rights Act, in which a number of personal liberties were outlined, including the right to make contracts, sue or be sued, own and sell property, and receive the equal benefit of the law. The Reconstruction Act of March 2, 1867, outlined the terms under which the southern states might re-enter the Union; one of these terms required the drafting of a new state constitution with the guarantee of voting rights for all races. President Andrew Johnson vetoed this bill, but radical Republicans in Congress were able to muster the necessary two-thirds majority needed to override the veto.

◆ AFRICAN AMERICAN STATUS AFTER RECONSTRUCTION

The Fourteenth and Fifteenth Amendments

On July 23, 1868, the Fourteenth Amendment was ratified, providing definitions of national and state citizenship, effectively overriding the Supreme Court's de-

Engraving depicting freed blacks in North Carolina.

cision in Dred Scott v. Sandford, and providing for equal privileges of citizenship and protection of the law. On March 30, 1870, the Fifteenth Amendment was ratified to ensure the right to vote. But the amendment proved unsuccessful in its aims, as many state and local governments created voting regulations that ensured African Americans would not vote; these included grandfather clauses, requiring that one's grandfather had voted; literacy tests; poll taxes; and "white primaries," which were held prior to general elections and permitted only whites to vote. In addition, southern states enacted many laws (known as black codes) that curbed the new rights of the freed slaves: South Carolina made it illegal for African Americans to possess firearms, and other states restricted their right to make and enforce contracts; to marry and intermarry; and even to assemble, "wander," or be "idle."

The Civil Rights Act of 1875

In 1875, Congress attempted to establish a semblance of racial equality by enacting a law that made it illegal to deprive another person of the "full and equal enjoyment of the accommodations, advantages, facilities, and privileges of inns, public conveyance, ... and other places of

public amusement" on account of race. In a number of cases (known as the Civil Rights Cases) the Supreme Court ruled that the Fourteenth Amendment did not authorize Congress to legislate against discriminatory state action, while disregarding discrimination by private individuals, including the owners of hotels, theaters, and restaurants. This point led to an end of federal efforts to protect the civil rights of African Americans until the mid-twentieth century.

Plessy v. Ferguson

In *Hall v. DeCuir* (1878) the Supreme Court decided that states could not outlaw segregation on common carriers such as streetcars and railroads, and in 1896 the Court again faced the issue of segregation on public transportation in the case of *Plessy v. Ferguson*. The case concerned Homer Adolph Plessy, an African American who was arrested for refusing to ride in the "colored" railway coach while traveling by train from New Orleans to Covington, Louisiana. The law in Louisiana required that "equal but separate" accommodations for blacks and whites be maintained in public facilities, but Plessy challenged this. Justice Billings Brown delivered the majority opinion that separate but equal accommo-

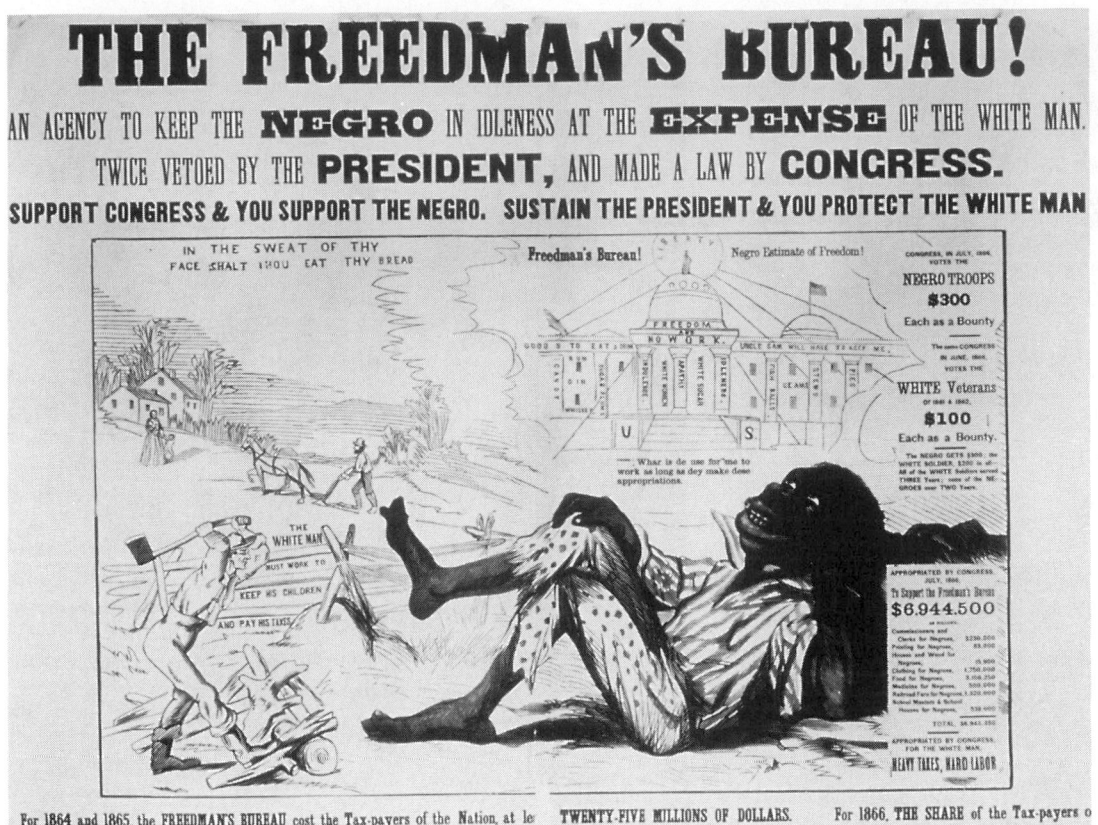

Poster mocking the Freedman's Bureau.

dations constituted a reasonable use of state police power and that the Fourteenth Amendment could not have been an effort to abolish social or racial distinctions or to force a co-mingling of the races. In his dissenting opinion, Justice John Marshall Harlen remarked that, "The judgement this day rendered will, in time, prove to be quite as pernicious as the decision made by this tribunal in the *Dred Scott v. Sandford* case. The thin disguise of equal accommodation for passengers in railroad coaches will not mislead anyone nor atone for the wrong this day done."

The ruling paved the way for the doctrine of separate but equal in all walks of life, and not until the case of *Brown v. Board of Education of Topeka* (1954) would the constitutionality of segregation be seriously challenged.

◆ EARLY AFRICAN AMERICAN GATEKEEPERS

Crispus Attucks 1723?-1770
Revolutionary Patriot

A runaway slave who lived in Boston, he was the first of five men killed on March 5, 1770, when British troops fired on a crowd of colonial protesters in the Boston Massacre. The most widely accepted account of the incident is that of John Adams, who said at the subsequent trial of the British soldiers that Attucks undertook "to be the hero of the night; and to lead this army with banners, to form them in the first place in Dock Square, and march them up to King Street with their clubs." When the crowd reached the soldiers it was Attucks who "had hardiness enough to fall in upon them, and with one hand took hold of a bayonet, and with the other knocked the man down." At that point the panicked soldiers fired, and in the echoes of their volley, five men lay dying; the seeds of the Revolution were sown. Attucks is remembered as "the first to defy, the first to die."

Joseph Cinque 1811-1912
Insurrectionist

Born in 1811 and purchased by Spaniards in Havana, Cuba, in 1838, Cinque was placed aboard the *Amistad* bound for Puerto Principe. When the crew became exhausted from battling a storm, Cinque led the slaves in seizing the ship and killing all but two of the crew, who were kept alive to navigate a course back to Africa. The captive pilots headed north, against the slaves'

A typical rural residence.

knowledge, and when the ship was sighted off the coast of Long Island the slaves were taken to Connecticut and placed in prison. Abolitionists took up the cause of the men and enabled Cinque to raise funds for judicial appeals by speaking on their lecture circuit; his words were translated from Mendi, and he became known as an excellent speaker. In 1841, John Quincy Adams won the slaves' case, and they were released.

Frederick Douglass 1817-1895
Lecturer, Abolitionist, Editor, Diplomat, Federal Government Official, Federal Legislator, Municipal Government Official, Marshall

Born in Talbot County, Maryland, on February 14, 1817, Frederick Douglass was sent to Baltimore as a house servant at the age of eight, where his mistress taught him to read and write. Upon the death of his master, he was sent to the country to work as a field hand. During his time in the South, he was severely flogged for his resistance to slavery. In his early teens he began to teach in a Sunday school which was later forcibly shut down by hostile whites. After an unsuccessful attempt to escape from slavery, he succeeded in making his way to New York disguised as a sailor in 1838. He found work as a day laborer in New Bedford, Massachusetts, and after an extemporaneous speech before the Massachusetts Anti-Slavery Society, he became one of its agents.

Douglass quickly became a nationally recognized figure among abolitionists. In 1845 he bravely published his *Narrative of the Life of Frederick Douglass*, which related his experiences as a slave, revealed his fugitive status, and further exposed him to the danger of reenslavement. In the same year, he went to England and Ireland, where he remained until 1847, speaking on slavery and women's rights, and ultimately raising sufficient funds to purchase his freedom. Upon returning to the United States, he founded the *North Star*. In the tense years before the Civil War he was forced to flee to Canada when the governor of Virginia swore out a warrant for his arrest.

Douglass returned to the United States before the beginning of the Civil War and, after meeting with President Abraham Lincoln, he assisted in the formation of the 54th and 55th Negro regiments of Massachusetts. During Reconstruction, he became deeply involved in

Joseph Cinque

Frederick Douglass

the civil rights movement, and, in 1871, he was appointed to the territorial legislature of the District of Columbia. He served as one of the presidential electors-at-large for New York in 1872 and, shortly thereafter, became the secretary of the Santo Domingo Commission. After serving for a short time as the police commissioner of the District of Columbia, he was appointed marshall in 1871, and held the post until he was appointed the recorder of deeds in 1881. In 1890, his support of the presidential campaign of Benjamin Harrison won him his most important federal post: he became minister resident and consul general to the Republic of Haiti and, later, the charge d'affaires of Santo Domingo. In 1891, he resigned the position in protest of the unscrupulous business practices of American businessmen. Douglass died at home in Washington, DC, on February 20, 1895.

Lemuel Haynes 1753-1833
Religious Leader

The son of a black father and white mother, and born in 1753, he was deserted and brought up by Deacon David Rose of Granville, Massachusetts. He was a precocious child and began writing mature sermons while still a boy. His preparation for the ministry was interrupted by the American Revolution. On April 19, 1775, he fought in the first battle of the war at Lexington, Massachusetts; he then joined the regular forces and served with Ethan Allen's Green Mountain Boys at the capture of Fort Ticonderoga.

Josiah Henson 1789-1883
Educational Administrator, Abolitionist, Religious Leader

Born a slave in a log cabin in Charles County (near Rockville), Maryland, on June 15, 1789, Josiah Henson grew up with the experience of his family being cruelly treated by his master. By the time he was 18, Henson was supervising the master's farm. In 1825 he and his wife and children were moved to Kentucky, where conditions were greatly improved, and in 1828 he became a preacher in a Methodist Episcopal Church. Under the threat of being sold, he and his family escaped to Ohio in 1830, and in the following year entered Canada by way of Buffalo, New York. In Canada he learned to read and write from one of his sons, and he soon began preaching in Dresden, Ontario.

While in Canada he became active in the underground railroad, helping nearly two hundred slaves to escape to freedom. In 1842 he and several others attempted to start the British-American Manual Labor Institute, but the industrial school proved unsuccessful. Henson related his story to Harriet Beecher Stowe (the author of Uncle Tom's Cabin), and it has been disputed whether or not her story is based in part on aspects of

Lemuel Haynes

his life. He traveled to England three times, where he met distinguished people, was honored for his abolitionist activities and personal escape from slavery, and was offered a number of positions which he turned down in order to return to Canada. He published his autobiography in 1849 and rewrote and reissued it in 1858 and 1879. Henson died in Ontario.

James Armistead Lafayette 17??-?
Spy

Born a slave, he risked his life behind enemy lines collecting information for the Continental Army. He furnished valuable information to the Marquis de Lafayette and enabled the French commander to check the troop advances of British General Cornwallis; this set the stage for General George Washington's victory at Yorktown in 1781 and for the end of the Revolutionary War. In recognition of his services, he was granted his freedom by the Virginia legislature in 1786, although it was not until 1819 that Virginia awarded him a pension of $40 a year and a grant of $100. He adopted the surname "Lafayette" in honor of his former commander, who visited him during a trip to the United States in 1824.

Toussaint L'Ouverture 1743-1803
Insurrectionist

Born Francois Dominique Toussaint L'Ouverture, a slave on the island of Hispaniola (now Haiti and the Dominican Republic) in 1743, he learned to read and write under a benevolent master. When he was 50 a violent revolt erupted on the island. White French planters, African slaves, and free mulattoes (some of whom owned slaves) clashed over issues of rights, land, and labor, as the forces of France, Britain, and Spain manipulated the conflict. At first the slaves and mulattoes shared the goals of the French revolution in opposition to the royalist French planters, but with time a coalition of planters and mulattoes arose in opposition to the slaves.

L'Ouverture became the leader of the revolutionary slave forces, which by 1794 consisted of a disciplined group of four thousand mostly ex-slaves. He successfully waged various campaigns first against the British, and was at the height of his power and influence, when, in 1796, General Rigaud (who led the mulatto forces) sought to re-impose slavery on the black islanders. He quickly achieved victory, captured Santo Domingo, and by 1801 had virtual control of the Spanish part of the island. In 1802, a French expeditionary force was sent to re-establish French control of the island. L'Ouverture was tricked, captured, and sent to France where he died on April 7, 1803, under inhumane conditions.

Gabriel Prosser 1775-1800
Insurrectionist

Gabriel Prosser was born around 1775. He became the coachman of Thomas Prosser of Henrico County, Virginia, and planned a large, highly organized revolt to take place on the last night of August of 1800 around Richmond, Virginia. About 32,000 slaves and only eight thousand whites were in the area, and it was his intention to kill all of the whites except for the French, Quakers, elderly women, and children. The ultimate goal was that the remaining 300,000 slaves in the state would follow his lead and seize the entire state. The revolt was set to coincide with the harvest so that his followers would be spared any shortage of food, and it was decided that the conspirators would meet at the Old Brook Swamp outside of Richmond and marshal forces to attack the city.

The insurrection fell apart when a severe rainstorm made it impossible for many of the slaves to assemble and a pair of house slaves who did not wish their master killed revealed the plot. Panic swept through the city, martial law was declared, and those suspected of involvement were rounded up and hanged; when it became clear that the slave population would be decimated if all of those implicated were dealt with in like fashion, the courts began to mete out less severe sen-

James Armistead Lafayette

tences. Prosser was apprehended in the hold of a schooner that docked in Norfolk, Virginia. Brought back in chains, he was interrogated by the governor. When he refused to divulge details of the conspiracy, he was hanged.

Dred Scott 1795-1858
Negotiator

Born in Southhampton, Virginia, in 1795, his first name was simply "Sam." He worked as a farmhand, handyman, and stevedore, and moved with his master to Huntsville, Alabama, and later to St. Louis, Missouri. In 1831 his owner, Peter Blow, died, and he was bought by John Emerson, a surgeon in the U.S. Army. Sam accompanied his new master to Illinois (a free state) and Wisconsin (a territory). Sometime after 1836 he received permission to marry, and by 1848 he had changed his name to Dred Scott. At various times he attempted to buy his freedom or escape but was unsuccessful. In 1843, Emerson died and left his estate to his widow Irene Emerson, who also refused Scott his freedom. He then obtained the assistance of two attorneys who helped him to sue for his freedom in county court.

Scott lost this case, but the verdict was set aside, and in 1847 he won a second trial on the grounds that his slave status had been nullified upon entering into a free state. Scott received financial backing and legal representation through the sons of Peter Blow, Irene Emerson's brother John Sanford, and her second husband Dr. C. C. Chaffee, all of whom apparently saw the case as an important challenge to slavery. In 1857, the U.S. Supreme Court ruled against Scott, stating that slaves were not legally citizens of the United States and therefore had no standing in the courts. Shortly after the decision was handed down, Mrs. Emerson freed Scott. The case led to the nullification of the Missouri Compromise of 1820, allowing the expansion of slavery into formerly free territories, and strengthening the abolition movement.

Sojourner Truth 1797-1883
Lecturer, Abolitionist

Born Isabella Baumfree in Ulster County, New York, around 1797, she was freed by the New York State Emancipation Act of 1827 and lived in New York City for a time. After taking the name Sojourner Truth, which she felt God had given her, she assumed the "mission" of spreading "the Truth" across the country. She became famous as an itinerant preacher, drawing huge crowds with her oratory (and some said "mystical gifts") wherever she appeared. She became one of an active group of black women abolitionists, lectured before numerous abolitionist audiences, and was friends with such leading white abolitionists as James and Lucretia Mott and Harriet Beecher Stowe. With the outbreak of the Civil War she raised money to purchase gifts for the soldiers, distributing them herself in the camps. She also helped African Americans who had escaped to the North to find habitation and shelter. Age and ill health caused her to retire from the lecture circuit, and she spent her last days in a sanatorium in Battle Creek, Michigan.

Harriet (Ross) Tubman 1826-1913
Lecturer, Abolitionist, Nurse

Born in 1826 in Dorchester County, Maryland, she had the hard childhood of a slave: much work, little schooling, and severe punishment. In 1848 she escaped, leaving behind her husband John Tubman, who threatened to report her to their master. As a free woman, she began to devise practical ways of helping other slaves escape. Over the following ten years she made about twenty trips from the North into the South and rescued more than three hundred slaves. Her reputation spread

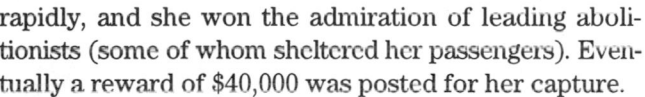

Sojourner Truth

Harriet Tubman

rapidly, and she won the admiration of leading abolitionists (some of whom sheltered her passengers). Eventually a reward of $40,000 was posted for her capture.

Tubman met and aided John Brown in recruiting soldiers for his raid on Harpers Ferry—Brown referred to her as "General Tubman." One of her major disappointments was the failure of the raid, and she is said to have regarded Brown as the true emancipator of her people, not Lincoln. In 1860 she began to canvass the nation, appearing at anti-slavery meetings and speaking on women's rights. Shortly before the outbreak of the Civil War she was forced to leave for Canada, but she returned to the United States and served the Union as a nurse, soldier, and spy; she was particularly valuable to the army as a scout because of the knowledge of the terrain she had gained as a conductor on the Underground Railroad.

Tubman's biography (from which she received the proceeds) was written by Sarah Bradford in 1868. Tubman's husband, John, died two years after the end of the war, and in 1869 she married the war veteran Nelson Davis. Despite receiving many honors and tributes (including a medal from Queen Victoria), she spent her last

days in poverty, not receiving a pension until thirty years after the Civil War. With the $20 dollars a month that she finally received, she helped to found a home for the aged and needy, which was later renamed the Harriet Tubman Home. She died in Auburn, New York.

Nat Turner 1800-1831
Insurrectionist

Born a slave in Southampton County, Virginia, on October 2, 1800, he was an avid reader of the Bible who prayed, fasted, and experienced "voices," ultimately becoming a visionary mystic with a belief that God had given him the special destiny of conquering Southampton County. After recruiting a handful of conspirators, he struck at isolated homes in his immediate area, and within 48 hours the band of insurrectionists had reached 60 armed men. They killed 55 whites before deciding to attack the county seat in Jerusalem, but while en route they were overtaken by a posse and dispersed. Turner took refuge in the Dismal Swamp and remained there for six weeks before he was captured, brought to trial, and hanged along with 16 other African Americans.

Denmark Vesey 1767-1822
Religious Leader

Born in 1767, Vesey was sold by his master at an early age and later bought back because of epilepsy. He sailed with his master, Captain Vesey, to the Virgin Islands and Haiti for twenty years. He enjoyed a considerable degree of mobility in his home port of Charleston, South Carolina, and eventually purchased his freedom from his master for $600—he had won $1500 in a lottery. He became a Methodist minister and used his church as a base to recruit supporters to take over Charleston. The revolt was planned for the second Sunday in July of 1822.

Vesey's plans were betrayed when a slave alerted the white authorities of the city. Hundreds of African Americans were rounded up, though some of Vesey's collaborators most likely escaped to the Carolinas where they fought as maroons. After a twenty-two day search, Vesey was apprehended and stood trial. During the trial he adeptly cross–examined witnesses, but ultimately could not deny his intention to overthrow the city, and he was hanged along with several collaborators.

The Slave Population: 1630 to 1780

Year	Total	North	South
1630	60	10	50
1640	597	427	170
1650	1,600	880	720
1660	2,920	1,162	1,758
1670	4,535	1,125	3,410
1680	6,971	1,895	5,076
1690	16,729	3,340	13,389
1700	27,817	5,206	22,611
1710	44,866	8,303	36,563
1720	68,839	14,091	54,748
1730	91,021	17,323	73,698
1740	150,024	23,958	126,066
1750	236,420	30,222	206,198
1760	325,806	40,033	285,773
1770	459,822	48,460	411,362
1780	575,420	56,796	518,624

7

Civil Rights

7

Civil Rights

◆ Early Rights Movements ◆ Civil Rights at the End of the Civil War
◆ Civil Rights in the Twentieth Century ◆ Civil Rights Gatekeepers
◆ Federal and State Civil Rights Agencies

Throughout the history of the United States, African Americans have struggled to obtain basic civil rights. It is a stuggle that has spanned several centuries—from the mutinies by Africans during the Atlantic crossing, to the insurrections organized by slaves in the New World, to the founding of such organizations as the Free African Society, the abolition movement, and to the civil rights marches and demonstrations of the twentieth century.

◆ EARLY RIGHTS MOVEMENTS

The Free African Society

In 1787, as a result of segregation and discriminatory practices within the Methodist church, the Reverends Richard Allen and Absalom Jones formed the Free African Society in Philadelphia. Adams later founded the Bethel African Methodist Church, and Jones became the rector of a Protestant Episcopal Church. The society was an important model for political consciousness and economic organization for African Americans throughout the country. It provided spiritual guidance and religious instruction; economic aid, burial assistance, and relief to widows; and medical and financial assistance to orphans. The society also advocated abolition and maintained channels of communication with African Americans in the South. Like the many other African American organizations that followed, the society was rooted in religious principles. Throughout the nineteenth century a number of mutual aid societies sprung up in African American communities in eastern cities such as New York, Newport, and Boston, providing loans, insurance, and various other economic and social services to their members and the larger community.

The society also helped to faciliate communications between free blacks throughout the country.

The Abolition Movement

The press and the pulpit served as important tools in the anti-slavery movement. In 1827 in New York, Samuel Cornish and John Russwurm founded Freedom's Journal, the first black owned and operated newspaper in the United States. *Freedom's Journal*, which ceased publication after only three years, was concerned not only with eradicating slavery but also with the growing discrimination and cruelty against free blacks in both the South and North.

In 1847 abolitionist Frederick Douglass published the first edition of the *North Star*, which eventually became one of the most successful black newspapers in America prior to the outbreak of the Civil War. Douglass, an escaped slave from Maryland, became one of the best known black abolitionists in the country. He lectured extensively throughout the United States and England. In 1845 he published his autobiography, *Narrative of the Life of Frederick Douglass*.

Although the abolition movement was dominated by whites, numerous black leaders played a major role in the movement, including such figures as Henry Highland Garnet, Harriet Tubman, and Sojourner Truth.

◆ CIVIL RIGHTS AT THE END OF THE CIVIL WAR

Following the war, Republicans, who controlled the U.S. Congress, took up the cause of the newly freed

Richard Allen

Frederick Douglass

African Americans. Between 1865 and 1875, three amendments to the Constitution and a string of civil rights and Reconstruction legislation was passed by Congress. The Thirteenth Amendment, ratified December 18, 1865, abolished slavery and involuntary servitude. The Fourteenth Amendment, ratified July 28, 1868, guaranteed citizenship and provided equal protection under the laws. Ratified March 30, 1870, the Fifteenth Amendment was designed to protect the right of all citizens to vote. In 1866, 1870, 1871, and 1875 Congress passed civil rights legislation outlining and protecting basic rights, including the right to purchase and sell property and access to public accommodations. The Reconstruction acts, passed between 1867 and 1869, called for new state constitutional conventions in those states that had seceded from the Union prior to the Civil War.

Reconstruction eventually produced a wave of anti-African sentiment. White organizations, like the Ku Klux Klan, aimed at intimidating blacks and preventing them from taking their place in society, sprang up throughout the North and the South. In 1871 Congress enacted the Ku Klux Klan Act as an effort to end intimidation and violence directed at blacks. However the act failed to exterminate the Klan and other terrorist organizations.

The civil rights and Reconstruction legislation were difficult for many whites to accept and did little to change their attitudes. The last of the civil rights acts, passed by Congress in 1875, prohibited discrimination in public accommodations. However, by the 1880s the debate as to the constitutionality of such legislation had reached the U.S. Supreme Court. Ruling in a group of five cases in 1883, which became known as the *Civil Rights Cases*, the U.S. Supreme Court concluded that the 1875 Civil Rights Act was unconstitutional on the grounds that the Fourteenth Amendment authorized Congress to legislate only against discriminatory state action, and not discrimination by private individuals. The Court's ruling brought about an end to federal efforts to protect the civil rights of African Americans until the mid-twentieth century.

Anti-lynching Efforts

By the late nineteenth and early twentieth century, lynching had become a weapon used by whites against blacks throughout the country. Between 1882 and 1990, approximately 1,750 African Americans were lynched in the United States. Victims, who included women, had been accused of a variety of "offenses" ranging from testifying in court against a white man to failing to use the word "mister" when addressing a white person. Ida B. Wells Barnett, a journalist and social activist, became one of the leading voices in the anti-lynching crusade by writing and lecturing throughout the United States against the practice of lynching.

Institutionalized Segregation

In 1896, the U.S. Supreme Court was faced with the issue of segregation on public transportation. At the time, as was the case in many parts of the South, a Louisiana state law was enacted requiring that "equal but separate" accommodations for blacks and whites be maintained in all public facilities. When Homer Adolph Plessy, a black man traveling by train from New Orleans to Covington, Louisiana, refused to ride in the "colored" railway coach, he was arrested.

Prior to the case of *Plessy v. Ferguson*, the court had started to build a platform upon which the doctrine of separate but equal would be based. In 1878, ruling in the case *Hall v. DeCuir* the court declared that states could not outlaw segregation on common carriers, such as streetcars and railroads. Segregation laws sprung up throughout the South.

With Justice Billings Brown delivering the majority opinion in the *Plessy* case, the Court declared that "separate but equal" accommodations constituted a reasonable use of state police power and that the Fourteenth Amendment of the Constitution could not be used to abolish social or racial distinctions or to force a co-mingling of the two races. The Supreme Court had effectively reduced the significance of the Fourteenth Amendment, which was designed to give blacks specific rights and protections. The ruling, in the *Plessy* case, which was termed the "separate but equal" doctrine, paved the way for the segregation of African Americans in all walks of life.

◆ CIVIL RIGHTS IN THE TWENTIETH CENTURY

Booker T. Washington and W. E. B. Du Bois

During the late nineteenth and early twentieth centuries, two figures— Booker T. Washington and William Edward Burghardt Du Bois—emerged as leaders in the struggle for black political and civil rights. Washington,

Ida B. Wells Barnett

an educator and founder of the Tuskegee Normal and Industrial Institute, was a strong advocate of practical, utilitarian education and manual training as a means for developing African Americans. Tuskegee Normal and Industrial Institute, which was founded in 1881 and based on a program at Hampton Institute, provided vocational training and prepared its students to survive economically in a segregated society. In Washington's opinion, education was to provide African Americans with the means to become economically self-supporting. Speaking at the Cotton States International Exposition in Atlanta in 1895, Washington outlined his philosophy of self-help and cooperation between blacks and whites:

> "To those of my race who depend on bettering their condition in a foreign land, or who underestimate the importance of cultivating friendly relations with the Southern white man, who is their next door neighbor, I would say: 'Cast down your bucket where you are'—cast it down in making friends in every manly way of the people of all races by whom we are surrounded."

W. E. B. Du Bois, a young historian and Harvard graduate, challenged Washington's passive policies in a

A Colored drinking fountain in North Carolina.

series of stinging essays and speeches. Du Bois advocated the uplifting of African Americans through an educated black elite, which he referred to as the "Talented Tenth", or roughly a tenth of the African American population. He believed that these African Americans must become proficient in education and culture, which would eventually benefit all. In 1905 Du Bois, along with a group of other black intellectuals, formed the Niagara Movement. The group drew up a platform which called for full citizenship rights for blacks and public recognition of their contributions to America's stability and progress. The movement eventually evolved into what became known as the National Association for the Advancement of Colored People (NAACP).

Civil Rights in the Mid-to Late-Twentleth Century

The civil rights movement suffered many defeats in the first half of the twentieth century. Repeated efforts to obtain passage of federal anti- lynching bills failed.

Booker T. Washington

W. E. B. Du Bois

The all-white primary system, which effectively disenfranchised southern blacks, resisted numerous court challenges. The Depression worsened conditions on farms and in ghettos. On the positive side, the growing political power of blacks in northern cities and an increasing liberal trend in the Supreme Court portended the legal and legislative victories of the 1950s and 1960s.

Brown v. Board of Education of Topeka

A great deal of the civil rights struggle throughout this period was carried on by the NAACP, which had begun chipping away at the roots of legalized segregation in a series of successful lawsuits. A major breakthrough for the NAACP came in 1954, when the U.S. Supreme Court ruled in *Brown v. Board of Education of Topeka* that discrimination in education was unconstitutional. This decision was as momentous as the Supreme Court's ruling in *Plessy v. Ferguson* in 1896, which legalized the doctrine of "separate but equal" treatment for blacks.

The *Brown* case involved the practice of denying black children equal access to state public schools due to state laws requiring or permitting racial segregation. The U.S. Supreme Court unanimously held that segregation deprived the children of equal protection under the Fourteenth Amendment to the U.S. Constitution, overturning the "separate but equal" doctrine established in *Plessy*.

A. Philip Randolph

In 1941, A. Philip Randolph, organizer of an employment bureau for untrained blacks and founder the Brotherhood of Sleeping Car Porters, came up with the idea of leading a protest march of blacks in Washington, DC to protest discrimination. On July 25, less than a week before the scheduled demonstration, President Franklin D. Roosevelt issued Executive Order No. 8802, which banned discrimination in the defense industry and led to the creation of the Fair Employment Practices Committee.

Civil Rights in the 1960s

Rosa Parks was one of the major catalysts of the 1960s civil rights movement. When on December 1,

Police officers using police dogs to break up a demonstration in Birmingham, Alabama, 1963.

1955, Parks refused to give up her seat on a Montgomery bus to a white man, as the law required, she was arrested and sent to jail. As a result of Parks' arrest, blacks throughout Montgomery refused to ride city buses. The Montgomery Bus Boycott led by Martin Luther King, Jr. was highly successful and ultimately led to the integration of all Montgomery city buses.

The eventual success of the Montgomery Bus Boycott encouraged a wave of massive demonstrations that swept across the South. In 1960 a group of students denied service at a Greensboro, North Carolina lunch counter started the sit-in movement. That same year, the Student Non-Violent Coordinating Committee was created and would include among its members Julian Bond, H. Rap Brown, Stokely Carmichael, and John Lewis.

The civil rights movement of the 1960s galvanized blacks and sympathetic whites as nothing had ever done before, but was not without cost. Thousands of people were jailed because they defied Jim Crow laws. Others were murdered and homes and churches were bombed. People lost their jobs and their homes because they supported the movement.

On August 28, 1963, nearly 250,000 people marched in Washington, DC to awaken the nation's consciousness regarding civil rights and to encourage the passage of civil rights legislation pending in Congress. The march was a cooperative effort of several civil rights organizations, including the Southern Christian Leadership Conference, the Congress of Racial Equality, the National Association for the Advancement of Colored People, the Negro American Labor Council, and the National Urban League. It was during this demonstration that Dr. Martin Luther King, Jr., in the shadow of the Lincoln Memorial, gave his "I Have a Dream" speech.

At its zenith, the civil rights movement was the most important event taking place in America. Through demonstrations, "sit-ins," marches, and soaring rhetoric, the movement aroused widespread public indignation, thus creating an atmosphere in which it was possible to make positive changes in American society.

Civil Rights Legislation in the 1990s

Although the civil rights movement of the 1950s and 1960s produced significant gains for African Americans, progress continues today. This progress is evident in the passage of the most recent civil rights legislation. In June of 1989, the U.S. Supreme Court delivered opinions in several cases dealing with seniority systems and racial discrimination in employment. Ruling in the cases *Lorance v. AT&T Technologies Inc.*, *Martin v. Wilks*, *Patterson v. McLean Credit Union*, and *Wards Cove Packing Co. v. Antonio* the Court appeared to reverse earlier civil rights rulings.

Prior to the Court's ruling in *Wards Cove*, the burden of proof in job discrimination suits had been placed on employers, requiring businesses to prove that there was a legitimate business reason for alleged discriminatory practices. With the *Wards Cove* decision, the Court made it more difficult for groups to win such suits by requiring workers to prove that no clear business reason existed for an employer's use of practices that result in discrimination. Civil rights organizations were quick to protest the rulings; opponents of the ruling, including the NAACP Legal Defense and Educational Fund and the Leadership Conference on Civil Rights argued that the Court had undermined the protection granted by federal civil rights and equal employment legislation.

On October 16 and 17, 1990, both houses of Congress approved a bill designed to reverse the Court's ruling. The proposed legislation, not only reversed the Court's ruling in *Wards Cove*, but strengthened provisions of the 1964 Civil Rights Act. On October 22, President George

Bayard Rustin (left) and A. Philip Randolph at a news conference, 1963

Bush vetoed the bill, claiming that the bill's provisions would encourage employers to establish hiring quotas.

This was not the first time that Congress moved to reverse a Court action in the area of civil rights—in 1987 Congress passed the Civil Rights Restoration Act of 1988 which reversed the Court's ruling in *Grove City College v. Bell* (1984). In the *Grove City College* case, the U.S. Supreme Court ruled that not all programs and activities of an institution were covered by Title IX of the Education Amendments of 1972 (Public Law 89-10, 79 Stat. 27), prohibiting discrimination in educational programs receiving federal financial assistance.

After vetoing Congress' 1990 civil rights legislation, the Bush administration joined both houses of Congress in working on alternative bills. On October 30, following months of negotiation, the Senate passed a bill, designed to provide additional remedies to deter harassment and intentional discrimination in the workplace, provide guidelines for the adjudication of cases arising under Title VII of the Civil Rights Act of 1964, and expand the scope of civil rights legislation weakened by Supreme Court decisions 1745. The House of Representatives passed the bill on November 7, and on No-

vember 21, President George Bush signed the Civil Rights Act of 1991

◆ CIVIL RIGHTS GATEKEEPERS

Ralph D. Abernathy 1926-1990
religious leader, Civil Rights/Human Rights Activist, Organization Executive/Founder

Born March 11, 1926, in Linden, Alabama, the Reverend Ralph David Abernathy was ordained a minister in 1948. He received his bachelor's degree from Alabama State College (now Alabama State University) in 1950 and his master's degree from Atlanta University in 1951. The alliance between Abernathy and Martin Luther King, Jr. stretched back to the mid-1950s. While attending Atlanta University, Abernathy had the opportunity to hear King preach at Ebenezer Baptist Church.

After obtaining his master's degree, Abernathy returned to Alabama to serve as a part-time minister at the Eastern Star Baptist Church in Demoplis. In 1951 Abernathy moved to First Baptist Church in Montgomery. Around this time King accepted a position at Montgomery's Dexter Avenue Baptist Church; Abernathy and King became close friends. In 1955, the two organized

High pressure hoses are turned on demonstrators in Birmingham, Alabama, 1963.

the Montgomery Improvement Association to coordinate a citywide bus boycott. The success of the Montgomery Bus Boycott led to the creation of the Southern Negro Leaders Conference; the organization's name was later changed to the Southern Leadership Conference and finally the Southern Christian Leadership Conference (SCLC). In January of 1957, Dr. King was elected the organization's first president.

From the time of Martin Luther King's death in 1968 until 1977, Abernathy served as president of the Southern Christian Leadership Conference. Abernathy continued as a leading figure in the movement until his resignation in 1977, when he made an unsuccessful bid for a U.S. Congressional seat. In 1989, he published his autobiography, *And The Walls Came Tumbling Down*, which was criticized by some black leaders for Abernathy's inclusion of details regarding King's extramarital affairs. Abernathy died of cardiac arrest on April 17, 1990.

Ella Josephine Baker 1903-1986

Community Activist, Civil Rights/Human Rights Activist, Executive/General Manager

In 1903, Ella Baker was in Norfolk, Virginia, to Blake and Georgiana Ross Baker, both educated people who worked hard to educate their children. The family and community in which she grew up instilled in her a sense of sharing and community cooperation; neighbors shared food from their gardens and gave a helping hand when needed. Her family instilled in her a sense of racial pride and resistance to any form of oppression. Her grandfather, a minister and community leader, was an ardent proponent of civil rights and universal suffrage, and passed his beliefs on to her.

When she was 15, Baker was sent to the Shaw Boarding School in Raleigh. The Shaw school was both a high school and college, and she graduated with a bachelor's degree as valedictorian in 1927. After graduation, she moved to New York City. She quickly became involved in progressive politics and attended as many meetings and discussions as she could find. During the Depression, she was outraged at the poverty she saw in the black areas of the city. Believing in the power of community and group action, she became involved with the Young Negroes Cooperative League, a buying cooperative that bought food in bulk to distribute at low prices to members; in 1931, she became the national director of the League. When President Franklin Roosevelt's Works Progress Administration started, she be-

Nearly 250,000 gather in Washington, DC, August 1963.

came involved with their literacy program. Throughout these years she worked closely with other politically aware and motivated people, discussing and evolving a political philosophy of cooperation, equality, and justice.

In the 1940s, Baker began to work for the NAACP. Between 1940 and 1943, she was a field secretary, traveling all over the country setting up branch offices and teaching people to fight for their own rights; her traveling gave her the opportunity to develop a vast network of contacts in the south that she later relied on

when working for the Student Non-Violent Coordinating Committee and Southern Christian Leadership Conference. In 1943, she became the director of branches for the NAACP. During the 1950s, she started fund raising activities in New York for the civil-rights struggles in the south, and in 1958, moved to Atlanta to work with the SCLC.

Working for the Southern Christian Leadership Conference, Baker became disillusioned with the top-heavy, male-dominated organizational structure of the group.

Ralph Abernathy

In 1960 she quit the SCLC and took a job with the Young Women's Christian Association instead. When students began leading sit-ins, she shifted her focus to the development of the Student Non-Violent Coordinating Committee. She acted as an unofficial advisor for the group, counseling them to set up their own student-run organization rather than be subsumed under the SCLC or the NAACP. She helped launch the Mississippi Freedom Democratic Party that challenged the all-white Democratic delegation at the 1964 presidential convention. She also acted as staff consultant for the interracial SCLC educational fund.

Baker returned to New York City in 1965, but kept working with national and international civil rights organizations. Among her other activities, she raised money to send to the freedom fighters in Rhodesia and South Africa. She remained an active organizer and speaker as long as her health allowed. Baker's belief in the power of communal action and reliance on the workers rather than the leaders had an enormous impact. She worked for all of the major civil-rights organizations at their time of greatest need. By the time the SCLC and the SNCC were formed, she had almost 30 years of civil-rights and community organizing experi-

ence to offer. She continually strove to keep the movement people oriented, and she succeeded in helping the SNCC remain a student group. Through her philosophy and actions, she motivated hundreds to act, to help themselves, and their neighbors as she had learned to do as a child.

Daisy Lee Gatson Bates 1920-
Publisher, Civil Rights/Human Rights Activist, Executive/General Manager

After attending segregated schools where all of the new equipment and up-to-date texts were reserved for whites only, Daisy Bates spent much of her energy as an adult successfully integrating the schools of Little Rock, Arkansas.

Shortly after their marriage in 1941, Daisy and her husband Lucius Christopher Bates, a journalist, started to publish a newspaper, the Arkansas *State Press*. They made it a point in their paper to keep track and report incidents of police brutality and other racially-motivated violence; their paper became known throughout the state for its campaign to improve the social and economic circumstances of African Americans. Because of their work, the city of Little Rock began to hire black police officers, and the number of racial incidents lessened.

In 1952, Daisy Bates became the Arkansas president of the NAACP; after the 1954 court decision in the *Brown v. Board of Education* case, she became very active in school desegregation. She began taking black children to white schools to be registered. If the school refused to register the children, she would report it in her paper. In 1957, the superintendent of schools in Little Rock decided to try to integrate the schools and chose nine students, now called the Little Rock Nine, to be the first black children to attend Central High, a white school. Most white citizens of Little Rock objected. Bates organized the Little Rock Nine, accompanied them to Central High, and stood with them against the state troopers that Governor Orval Faubus had sent in to prevent the integration. For days she escorted the children to school, only to be turned away by an angry mob. On September 25, 1957, Daisy Bates entered Central High in Little Rock with the nine children, escorted by 1000 paratroopers President Dwight Eisenhower had sent in; the first steps towards integration were successful. For the rest of their years at Central High, Bates kept track of the students and acted as their advocate when problems arose, frequently accompanying them and their parents to meetings with school officials.

Ralph Abernathy (left) and Martin Luther King, Jr. (rear) were active in the boycott of segregated buses in Montgomery, Alabama.

In October of 1957, one month after she marched into Central High, Daisy Bates was arrested on charges of failing to provide membership information on the NAACP to city officials. The charges were later overturned. Two years later, the Arkansas *State Press* folded, but Bates kept active in the civil-rights fight, touring and speaking, and working with the Student Non-Violent Coordinating Committee to register voters. In 1985, the *State Press* began to publish again, and it has continued to serve the needs of the African-American community in Little Rock.

Stokely Carmichael (Kwame Toure) 1941-
Civil Rights/Human Rights Activist, Nationalist/ Repatriationist, Executive/General Manager

If, during the 1960s, one individual stood at the forefront of the Black Power movement, Stokely Carmichael was that person. He soared to fame as popularizer of the dynamic phrase "Black Power" and as one of the most powerful and influential leaders of the Student Non-Violent Coordinating Committee (SNCC).

Daisy Bates leaving Little Rock Police headquarters, 1957.

Stokely Carmichael

Carmichael was born in Trinidad, on June 29, 1941, and moved to the United States with his family when he was 11. As a teenager, Carmichael was jolted by ghetto life in which "black" and "impotent" seemed to be synonymous terms. He was not reassured later when he was admitted to the Bronx High School of Science, encountered white liberals, and felt he had been adopted by them as a mascot. Although he was offered good scholarships to white universities, Carmichael opted to attend Howard University. During his first year there, 1960, he joined the Congress of Racial Equality (CORE) in its efforts to integrate public accommodations in the South. After graduation in 1964, he rejected scholarship opportunities for graduate school, and went south to join the SNCC. As one of their finest organizers, he worked ceaselessly, registering and educating voters in the south. In 1966, he was elected chairman of the SNCC, but as the youngest chair the group had, his views were considered too radical by some members.

Carmichael's cry for "black power" thrilled many disenfranchised young African Americans, but troubled others, who thought it sounded too violent. He was labeled as potentially violent by the media and the legal authorities. Disagreement with SNCC members arose over the issues of self-defense versus nonviolence, and the participation of whites in black grass-roots organizations. In 1967, he resigned as chairperson, and was later expelled from the SNCC.

Carmichael spent much of 1968 traveling around the world, speaking to many organizations, including some in communist countries. His travels included Ghana, where he joined the Pan-African movement. After returning to the United States, he went to work for the Black Panther party. In this country, however, he was subject to almost constant harassment from the FBI because of his connection with the Panthers, and because he had visited communist countries while traveling. In 1969, he resigned from the Black Panthers, and moved to Guinea, where he had been offered political asylum.

In Guinea, Carmichael turned his efforts to supporting Pan-Africanism; he has organized many local chapters through the world of the All African Peoples Revolutionary Party. In 1978, to honor the two men who most influenced his Pan-African philosophical education, SeKou Toure and Kwame Nkrumah, he changed his name to Kwame Toure. Toure continues to live in

Guinea and travel throughout the world, working toward a united African people.

Mandy Carter 1946-
Civil Rights/Human Rights Activist

Carter was born in Albany, New York, in the late 1940s and spent her childhood in orphanages. She attended community college for a time in Troy, New York—and lived at the downtown YWCA—but moved to New York City in 1967 with a savings of $100. There she slept in Central Park before taking a job at drug guru Timothy Leary's League for Spiritual Discovery; she moved to San Francisco later that year and soon became active in protests against the war in Vietnam. For several years Carter was involved with the War Resister's League, and it was to her colleagues there that she first admitted her sexual orientation. She worked for the group's San Francisco offices for a number of years, and it was during this time, the late 1970s, that she first became active in gay and lesbian politics.

In 1982, Carter moved to North Carolina, where she continued her work with the War Resister's League, and also became involved on a national level with gay and lesbian organizations; one of her accomplishments was helping coordinate the 1987 lesbian and gay march on the nation's capital, a role she reprised in 1993. In addition to co-producing an annual festival of women's music and art, Carter has also been instrumental (but ultimately unsuccessful) in campaigns to unseat North Carolina's right-wing Republican senator Jesse Helms. She has also worked to combat the Christian Right's attempts to infiltrate African American churches in efforts to stymie support of gay and lesbian rights among the congregations; she has done this work in her role as liaison of the Human Rights Campaign Fund to the National Black and Gay Lesbian Leadership Forum. Carter has spoken of her political activism in the 1994 volume *Uncommon Heroes: A Celebration of Heroes and Role Models for Gay and Lesbian Americans.*

Angela Yvonne Davis 1944-
Women's Rights Activist, Civil Rights/Human Rights Activist, Professor, Lecturer, Author/Poet

Angela Davis was born on January 26, 1944, in Birmingham, Alabama, to middle class parents who stressed both academic excellence and political awareness and activism. Her mother, Sallye E. Davis, had been politically active since her college days, and Angela participated in demonstrations with her mother from the time she was in elementary school. To insure her a better education than she would be able to receive in the segregated schools of the south, her parents sent her to

Angela Davis

Elizabeth Irwin High School, a private progressive school in New York. The school had many radical teachers and students, and Angela soon joined a Marxist study group.

After graduation, Davis continued to seek high quality education. She majored in French at Brandeis College, studying at the Sorbonne in Paris her junior year. She then pursued graduate studies in philosophy at the Goethe University in Frankfurt, and in 1967 she returned to the United States to study with the well known philosopher, Herbert Marcuse, at the University of California at San Diego. When she was almost done with her degree, she took a teaching job at the University of California at Los Angeles.

In 1969, Davis joined the communist party; the regents of UCLA tried to fire her, but she fought them in court. The following year she became involved with the Black Panther Party. Guns she had bought for self defense were used by a member of the Black Panthers in a courtroom shooting. Believing she was involved, the Federal Bureau of Investigation (FBI) sought her arrest, so she went underground to avoid them. She was put on the FBI's ten most wanted list, and later arrested. In 1972, she was acquitted of all charges, but was not hired back by the university. Then-California governor Ronald Reagan and the Regents of the University decreed that she would never teach in California again.

Following her trial, Davis founded the National Alliance against Racism and Political Repression, a legal group providing defense of minority prisoners. In 1980 and 1984, she ran for vice president of the United States on the Communist Party ticket. A writer and philosopher, Davis has written several books, including *If They Come in the Morning* (1971), *Women, Race and Class* (1983), *Angela Davis: An Autobiography* (1988), and *Women, Culture and Politics* (1989).

In the 1990s, politically active Davis has remained a popular yet controversial figure. Davis's 1995 appointment as presidential chair in charge of developing new ethnic studies courses at University of California-Santa Cruz was heavily opposed by state Republican legislators concerned with her Communist Party affiliation. A much sought after though often protested against Davis has lectured around the country about "envisioning a new movement" set apart from the radicalism of the 1960s. Meanwhile, Davis continues to write and to support such causes as women's rights, workers' rights, health care, and nuclear disarmament.

William Edward Burghardt Du Bois 1868-1963

Organization Executive/Founder, Civil Rights/Human Rights Activist, Professor, Lecturer, Author/Poet, Editor, Critic, Women's Rights Activist, Sociologist, Executive Director, Political Scientist, Correspondent/Reporter

An outstanding critic, editor, scholar, author, and civil rights leader, W. E. B. Du Bois is certainly among the most influential blacks of the twentieth century. Born in Great Barrington, Massachusetts on February 23, 1868, Du Bois received a bachelors degree from Fisk University and went on to win a second bachelors, as well as a Ph.D., from Harvard. He was for a time professor of Latin and Greek at Wilberforce and the University of Pennsylvania, and also served as a professor of economics and history at Atlanta University.

One of the founders of the National Association for the Advancement of Colored People (NAACP) in 1909, Du Bois served as that organization's director of publications and editor of *Crisis* magazine until 1934. In 1944, he returned from Atlanta University to become head of the NAACP's special research department, a post he held until 1948. Dr. Du Bois emigrated to Africa in 1961, and became editor-in-chief of the *Encyclopedia Africana,* an enormous publishing venture which

W. E. B. Du Bois

had been planned by Kwame Nkrumah, since then deposed as president of Ghana. Du Bois died in Ghana on August 27, 1963, at the age of 95.

Du Bois's numerous books include *The Suppression of the Slave Trade* (1896), *The Philadelphia Negro* (1899), *The Souls of Black Folk* (1903), *John Brown* (1909), *Quest of the Silver Fleece* (1911), *The Negro* (1915), *Darkwater* (1920), *The Gift of Black Folk* (1924), *Dark Princess* (1928), *Black Folk: Then and Now* (1939), *Dusk of Dawn* (1940), *Color and Democracy* (1945), *The World and Africa* (1947), *In Battle for Peace* (1952), and a trilogy, *Black Flame* (1957-1961). It is this enormous literary output on such a wide variety of themes which offers the most convincing testimony to Du Bois's lifetime position that it was vital for blacks to cultivate their own aesthetic and cultural values even as they made valuable strides toward social emancipation. In this he was opposed by Booker T. Washington, who felt that the black should concentrate on developing technical and mechanical skills before all else.

Du Bois was one of the first male civil rights leaders to recognize the problems of gender discrimination. He was among the first men to understand the unique problems of black women, and to value their contributions. He supported the women's suffrage movement and strove to integrate this mostly white struggle. He encouraged many black female writers, artists, poets, and novelists, featuring their works in *Crisis* and sometimes providing personal financial assistance to them. Several of his novels feature women as prominently as men, an unusual approach for any author of his day. Du Bois spent his life working not just for the equality of all men, but for the equality of all people.

Medgar Evers 1925-1963
Civil Rights/Human Rights Activist

Medgar Evers was one of the first martyrs of the civil-rights movement. He was born in 1925 in Decatur, Mississippi to James and Jessie Evers. After a short stint in the army, he enrolled in Alcorn A&M College, graduating in 1952. His first job out of college was traveling around rural Mississippi selling insurance. He soon grew enraged at the despicable conditions of poor black families in his state, and joined the NAACP. In 1954, he was appointed Mississippi's first field secretary.

Evers was outspoken, and his demands were radical for his rigidly segregated state. He fought for the enforcement of the 1954 court decision of *Brown v. Board of Education of Topeka* which outlawed school segregation; he fought for the right to vote, and he advocated boycotting merchants who discriminated. He worked unceasingly despite the threats of violence that his speeches engendered. He gave much of himself to this struggle, and in 1963, he gave his life. On June 13, 1963, he drove home from a meeting, stepped out of his car, and was shot in the back.

Immediately after Evers's death, the shotgun that was used to kill him was found in bushes nearby, with the owner's fingerprints still fresh. Byron de la Beckwith, a vocal member of a local white-supremacist group, was arrested. Despite the evidence against him, which included an earlier statement that he wanted to kill Evers, two trials with all-white juries ended in deadlock decisions, and Beckwith walked free. 20 years later, in 1989, information surfaced that suggested the jury in both trials had been tampered with. The assistant District Attorney, with the help of Evers's widow, began putting together a new case. In 1990, Beckwith was arrested one more time; on February 5, 1994, Beckwith was convicted of murder and sentenced to life in prison.

While knowing that Evers did not die in vain is small comfort, it is nevertheless true. His death changed the tenor of the civil-rights struggle. Anger replaced fear in

Medgar Evers

the south, as hundreds of demonstrators marched in protest. His death prompted President John Kennedy to ask Congress for a comprehensive civil-rights bill, which President Lyndon Johnson signed into law the following year. Evers death, as his life had, contributed much to the struggle for equality.

Fannie Lou Townsend Hamer 1917-1977
Lecturer, Civil Rights/Human Rights Activist, Organization Executive/Founder

As a poor sharecropper she had only an elementary education, yet Fannie Lou Hamer was one of the most eloquent speakers for the civil rights movement in the south. She worked for political, social and economic equality for herself and all African Americans; she fought to integrate the national Democratic party, and became one of its first black delegates to a presidential convention.

The youngest of 20 siblings, Hamer was born in 1917 to Jim and Ella Townsend in Montgomery County, Mississippi. She began picking cotton at the age of six; she attended school until she had to drop out in the sixth grade to work full time. She worked first as a share-

Fannie Lou Hamer

cropper and then as a time keeper on the same plantation in Mississippi for almost forty years. In 1962, because she tried to exercise her right to vote, she lost her job and, frightened by threats of violent reprisals, was forced to move away from her home and her family. Angered into action, she went to work for the Student Non-Violent Coordinating Committee (SNCC), helping many blacks register to vote.

Because the Democratic party refused to send blacks as delegates to the national presidential convention, in 1964, Hamer and others formed the Mississippi Freedom Democratic party to send black delegates to the convention. They challenged the Democratic delegates from Mississippi for their seats at the convention, arguing that the all-white delegation could not adequately represent their state which had a large black population. Hamer's own speech on their behalf frightened the incumbent President Lyndon Johnson so much so that he tried to block the televised coverage of her. The MFDP lost its bid that year, but their actions did result in a pledge from the national party not to seat delegations excluding blacks in the 1968 convention. In 1968, Fannie Lou Hamer was among the first black delegates to the Democratic National Convention.

For the next decade, Hamer remained active in the struggle for civil and economic rights. In 1969, she founded the Freedom Farms Corporation to help needy families raise food and livestock. They also provided basic social services, scholarships and grants for education, and helped fund minority business opportunities.

She became a sought-after speaker, and in the 1970s, even as her health was failing from cancer, she still toured the country speaking about civil rights for all.

Jesse Jackson 1941-
Religious Leader, Civil Rights/Human Rights Activist, and *Organization Executive/Founder*

Jesse Louis Jackson was born October 8, 1941, in Greenville, South Carolina. In 1959 Jackson left South Carolina to attend the University of Illinois. Dissatisfied with his treatment on campus, he decided to transfer to North Carolina Agricultural and Technical College. After receiving his B.A. in sociology, Jackson attended the Chicago Theological Seminary. He was ordained a Baptist minister in 1968.

Jackson joined the Southern Christian Leadership Conference (SCLC) in 1965. In 1966 Jackson became involved with the SCLC's Operation Breadbasket, and from 1967 to 1971, he served as the program's executive director. Jackson resigned from the SCLC in 1971 to found his own organization, Operation PUSH (People United to Save Humanity). Through PUSH Jackson continued to pursue the economic objectives of Operation Breadbasket and expanded into areas of social and political development.

Jackson soon became the most visible and sought-after civil rights leader in the country. His magnetic personality came across as appealing on television, and while he described himself as "a country preacher," his command of issues and his ability to reach the heart of matters marked him as an individual of intellectual depth. Of all the civil rights leaders, Jackson was the one who could relate best to the young. He was possessed with a gift of being able to summon out the best in them, in a phrase that became his trademark, "I am somebody."

Out of this came Jackson's program, PUSH-EXCEL, which sought to motivate young school children to do better academically. In 1981, *Newsweek* magazine credited Jackson with building a struggling community improvement organization into a nationwide campaign to revive pride, discipline, and the work ethic in inner-city schools. With funding from the Carter administration, the PUSH-EXCEL program was placed in five other cities.

The Jesse Jackson of the 1980s will be best remembered for his two runs for the Democratic nomination for President of the United States. In 1983, many, but not all, black political leaders endorsed the idea of a black presidential candidate to create a "people's" platform, increase voter registration and have a power base from which there could be greater input into the political process. His 1984 campaign was launched under the aegis of the National Rainbow Coalition, Inc., an umbrella organization of minority groups. Black support was divided, however, between Jackson and former Vice President Walter Mondale. During this campaign, Jackson attracted considerable media coverage with controversial remarks and actions, demonstrating a lack of familiarity with national politics.

The 1988 campaign of Jackson showed enormous personal and political growth; his candidacy was no longer a symbolic gesture but was a real and compelling demonstration of his effectiveness as a candidate. By the time the Democratic convention rolled around, media pundits were seriously discussing the likelihood of Jackson's nomination as the Democratic presidential candidate, and "what to do about Jesse" became the focus of the entire Democratic leadership. At the end of the primary campaign, Jackson had finished a strong second to Massachusetts Governor Michael Dukakis, and changed forever the notion that a black President in America was inconceivable. Jackson took his defeat in stride and continued to campaign for the Democratic ticket until the November election.

Since the 1988 election, Jackson has worked less publicly, but no less energetically. In 1989 he moved with his Rainbow Coalition from Chicago to Washington, DC; he believed that the coalition could be more effective in the nation's capital. Jackson continues to write, speak, and lead protests for social change. His primary concerns include crime, violence, drug use, and teenage pregnancy in inner-city neighborhoods; voter registration; health care; affirmative action; and baseball hiring practices. In 1993 Jackson was awarded the Martin Luther King, Jr. Nonviolent Peace Prize.

Jackson has been active in foreign affairs as well. In 1991, he traveled to Iraq, and convinced Saddam Hussein to begin releasing Americans held hostage after Hussein's invasion of Kuwait. In 1994, Jackson met with Fidel Castro in Cuba and, later that year, President Clinton sent him on a peace mission to Nigeria. Although many expected him to run for president again in 1992 or 1996, Jackson decided against it, saying that he was too tired, and the strain on his family too severe. He did support his son, Jesse Jackson, Jr., who was elected to the House of Representatives (Chicago's 2nd Congressional District) on December 12, 1995.

Coretta Scott King 1927-

Organization Executive/Founder, Civil Rights/Human Rights Activist, Women's Rights Activist, Lecturer, National/International Diplomat, Educator, Community Activist

As the wife of civil-rights leader Martin Luther King, Jr., Coretta Scott King was ready to continue his work and perpetuate his ideals after his 1968 assassination. While her primary role in the early years of marriage was to raise her four children, she became increasingly involved in the struggle for civil rights through her husband's activities. After his death, she quickly became a dynamic activist and peace crusader.

Born one of three children on April 27, 1927, King is a native of Heilberger, Alabama. During the Depression she was forced to contribute to the family income by hoeing and picking cotton, but she resolved early to overcome adversity, seek treatment as an equal, and struggle to achieve a sound education. After graduating from the private Lincoln High School in 1945, she entered Antioch College in Yellow Springs, Ohio, on a scholarship, majoring in education and music. A teaching career appealed to her, but she became badly disillusioned when she was not allowed to do her practice teaching in the public schools of the town. No black had ever taught there, and she was not destined to be the first to break the tradition.

Musical training in voice and piano absorbed much of her time, with the result that, upon graduation, she decided to continue her studies at the New England Conservatory of Music in Boston, attending on a modest fellowship which covered tuition but made part-time work a necessity. Her meeting with Martin Luther King thrust her into a whirlwind romance, and also presented her with the opportunity to marry an exceptional young minister whose intense convictions and concern for humanity brought her a measure of rare self-realization early in life. Sensing his incredible dynamism, she suffered no regrets at the prospect of relinquishing her own possible career.

Completing her studies in 1954, King moved back south with her husband, who became pastor of Dexter Avenue Baptist Church in Montgomery, Alabama. Within a year, King had led the Montgomery bus boycott, and given birth to a new era of civil rights agitation. Two years later, he was the head of the Southern Christian Leadership Conference (SCLC).

Over the years King gradually became more involved in her husband's work. She would occasionally perform at his lectures, raising her voice in song as he did in speech. She became involved in separate activities as well. In 1962, she served as a Woman's Strike for Peace delegate to the 17-nation Disarmament Conference in Geneva, Switzerland. In the mid 1960s, she sang in the multi-arts Freedom Concerts that raised money for the SCLC. As demands on Martin became too much, she began to fill the speaking engagements he could not. After his assassination, she filled many of the commitments his death left empty, but soon became sought-after in her own right.

King's speech on Solidarity Day, June 19, 1968, is often identified as a prime example of her emergence

Coretta Scott King

from the shadow of her husband's memory. In it, she called upon American women to "unite and form a solid block of women power" to fight the three great evils of racism, poverty, and war. Much of her subsequent activity revolved around building plans for the creation of a Martin Luther King, Jr. Memorial in Atlanta, which she began to work on in 1969, and which was established under the care of the National Park Service in 1980. She also published *My Life with Martin Luther King, Jr.*, a book of reminiscences.

King's activism has extended beyond U.S. borders. For example, in the mid-1980s, she and two of her children were arrested for demonstrating against apartheid outside of the South African embassy in Washington, DC. The following year, in 1986, she visited South Africa for eight days, meeting with businessmen and anti-apartheid leaders. King has also decried the human rights violations of the Haitian military regime against Haitian citizens. In 1993, she implored the United Nations to reimpose an embargo against the nation.

Meanwhile, the well-respected Martin Luther King Jr. Center for Non-Violent Social Change became involved in an ugly scuffle with the National Park Service over the issue of how best to utilize some of the historic Atlanta district in which the King memorial are located. As CEO, King was forced to mediate between the family's desire for an interactive museum with exhibitions and programs for youngsters and the National Park Service's plan for a visitor's center on the same site. The dispute was not resolved until April of 1995, a few

months after King had officially stepped down, handing the reigns over to her son Dexter, who was unanimously voted the center's director and CEO.

Controversy continued brewing. In 1964, Martin Luther King, Jr. had given nearly 83,000 documents, including correspondence and other manuscripts to Boston University. Mrs. King had hoped to regain control of that legacy, but in April of 1995, the Massachusetts Supreme Judicial Court ruled in favor of the university, leaving King, and many other Atlantans displeased.

On a brighter note, King remains an eloquent and respected spokesperson on behalf of black causes and nonviolent philosophy. She is often recognized for keeping her husband's dream alive. In September of 1995, King, along with two other famous civil rights widows—Myrlie Evers-Williams and Betty Shabazz—were honored for their influence by the National Political Congress of Black Women.

Martin Luther King Jr. 1929-1968.
Religious Leader, Civil Rights/Human Rights Activist, Author/Poet, Labor Activist, Organization Executive/Founder, Minister, Antiwar Activist

Any number of historic moments in the civil rights struggle have been used to identify Martin Luther King Jr.—prime mover of the Montgomery bus boycott (1956), keynote speaker at the March on Washington (1963), youngest Nobel Peace Prize laureate (1964). But in retrospect, single events are less important than the fact that King, and his policy of nonviolent protest, was the dominant force in the civil rights movement during its decade of greatest achievement, from 1957 to 1968.

King was born Michael Luther King in Atlanta on January 15, 1929—one of the three children of Martin Luther King, Sr., pastor of Ebenezer Baptist Church, and Alberta (Williams) King, a former schoolteacher. (He did not receive the name of "Martin" until he was about six years of age.) After attending grammar and high schools locally, King enrolled in Morehouse College (also in Atlanta) in 1944. At this time he was not inclined to enter the ministry, but while there he came under the influence of Dr. Benjamin Mays, a scholar whose manner and bearing convinced him that a religious career could have its intellectual satisfactions as well. After receiving his B.A. in 1948, King attended Crozer Theological Seminary in Chester, Pennsylvania, winning the Plafker Award as the outstanding student of the graduating class, and the J. Lewis Crozer Fellowship as well. King completed the course work for his doctorate in 1953, and was granted the degree two years later upon completion of his dissertation.

Married by then, King returned South, accepting the pastorate of the Dexter Avenue Baptist Church in Mont-

Coretta Scott King (left), Dr. Martin Luther King, Jr. (center) and Floyd McKissick attend a rally in Chicago, 1966.

gomery, Alabama. It was here that he made his first mark on the civil rights movement, by mobilizing the black community during a 382-day boycott of the city's bus lines. Working through the Montgomery Improvement Association, King overcame arrest and other violent harassment, including the bombing of his home. Ultimately, the U.S. Supreme Court declared the Alabama laws requiring bus segregation unconstitutional, with the result that blacks were allowed to ride Montgomery buses on equal footing with whites.

A national hero and a civil rights figure of growing importance, King summoned together a number of black leaders in 1957 and laid the groundwork for the organization now known as the Southern Christian Leadership Conference (SCLC). Elected its president, he soon sought to assist other communities in the organization of protest campaigns against discrimination, and in voter-registration activities as well.

After completing his first book and making a trip to India, King returned to the United States in 1960 to become co-pastor, with his father, of Ebenezer Baptist Church. Three years later, in 1963, King's nonviolent tactics were put to their most severe test in Birmingham, Alabama during a mass protest for fair hiring

practices, the establishment of a biracial committee, and the desegregation of department-store facilities. Police brutality used against the marchers dramatized the plight of blacks to the nation at large with enormous impact. King was arrested, but his voice was not silenced as he issued his classic "Letter from a Birmingham Jail" to refute his critics.

Later that year King was a principal speaker at the historic March on Washington, where he delivered one of the most passionate addresses of his career. At the beginning of the next year *Time* magazine designated him as its Man of the Year for 1963. A few months later he was named recipient of the 1964 Nobel Peace Prize. Upon his return from Oslo, where he had gone to accept the award, King entered a new battle, in Selma, Alabama, where he led a voter-registration campaign which culminated in the Selma-to-Montgomery Freedom March. King next brought his crusade to Chicago where he launched a slum-rehabilitation and open-housing program.

In the North, however, King soon discovered that young and angry blacks cared little for his pulpit oratory and even less for his solemn pleas for peaceful protest. Their disenchantment was clearly one of the factors

Dr. King joins other civil rights leaders at a rally in Selma, Alabama, 1965.

influencing his decision to rally behind a new cause and stake out a fresh battleground: the war in Vietnam. Although his aim was to fuse a new coalition of dissent based on equal support for the peace crusade and the civil rights movement, King antagonized many civil rights leaders by declaring the United States to be "the greatest purveyor of violence in the world."

The rift was immediate. The National Association for the Advancement of Colored People (NAACP) saw King's shift of emphasis as "a serious tactical mistake"; the Urban League warned that the "limited resources" of the civil rights movement would be spread too thin; Bayard Rustin claimed black support of the peace movement would be negligible; Ralph Bunche felt King was undertaking an impossible mission in trying to bring the campaign for peace in step with the goals of the civil rights movement.

From the vantage point of history, King's timing could only be regarded as superb. In announcing his opposition to the war, and in characterizing it as a "tragic adventure" which was playing "havoc with the destiny of the entire world," King again forced the white middle class to concede that no movement could dra-

matically affect the course of government in the United States unless it involved deliberate and restrained aggressiveness, persistent dissent, and even militant confrontation. These were precisely the ingredients of the civil rights struggle in the South in the early 1960s.

As students, professors, intellectuals, clergymen and reformers of every stripe rushed into the movement (in a sense forcing fiery black militants like Stokely Carmichael and Floyd McKissick to surrender their control over antiwar polemics), King turned his attention to the domestic issue which, in his view, was directly related to the Vietnam struggle: the War on Poverty. At one point, he called for a guaranteed family income, he threatened national boycotts, and spoke of disrupting entire cities by nonviolent "camp-ins." With this in mind, he began to draw up plans for a massive march of the poor on Washington, DC itself, envisioning a popular demonstration of unsurpassed intensity and magnitude designed to force Congress and the political parties to recognize and deal with the unseen and ignored masses of desperate and downtrodden Americans.

King's decision to interrupt these plans to lend his support to the Memphis sanitation men's strike was and with the surrounding buildings is a national historic landmark under the administration of the National Park Service. His birthday, January 15, is a national holiday, celebrated each year with educational programs, artistic displays, and concerts throughout the United States. The Lorraine Hotel where he was shot is now the National Civil Rights Museum.

Rosa Louise McCauley Parks 1913-
Aide, Civil Rights/Human Rights Activist

Rosa Parks has been called the spark that lit the fire, and the mother of the movement. Her courage to defy custom and law to uphold her personal rights and dignity inspired the African Americans in Montgomery, Alabama, to fight for their rights by staging one of the longest boycotts in history.

Born Rosa Louise McCauley on February 4, 1913, in Tuskegee, Alabama, she was raised by her mother and grandparents in Tuskegee and Montgomery. After attending segregated schools, she went to the all-black Alabama State College. In 1932, she married Raymond Parks, a barber. Both of them worked for the local National Association for the Advancement of Colored People (NAACP) chapter, and Rosa became local NAACP secretary in the 1950s.

On December 1, 1955, as Parks was riding home from work, she was ordered by the bus driver to give up her seat so that a white man might sit. She refused. She was arrested and fined $14. Her case was the last straw for the blacks of Montgomery, as tired of being underclass citizens as Parks was. A city-wide boycott was organized to force the city to desegregate public transportation. A young, unknown minister by the name of Martin Luther King, Jr. became involved, and lectured the nation on the injustice of it all. Blacks, and a few whites, organized peacefully together to transport boycotters to and from work, and they continued, despite opposition from the city and state governments, for 382 days.

When the boycott ended on December 21, 1956, both Parks and King were national heroes, and the Supreme Court had ruled that segregation on city buses was unconstitutional. The mass movement of non-violent social change that was started would last over a decade, and would culminate in the Civil Rights Act of 1964 and the Voting Rights Act of 1965. Because of the harassment Rosa Parks and her family received during and after the boycott, they moved to Detroit, Michigan, in 1957. She found a job with Congressman John Conyers, but continued to be involved in the civil rights struggle. She gave speeches and attended marches and demonstrations. She marched on Washington in 1963, and into

Dr. Martin Luther King, Jr.

based in part on his desire to discourage violence, as well as to focus national attention on the plight of the poor, unorganized workers of the city. The men were bargaining for little else beyond basic union representation and long-overdue salary considerations. Though he was unable to eliminate the violence which had resulted in the summoning and subsequent departure of the National Guard, King stayed on in Memphis and was in the process of planning for a march which he vowed to carry out in defiance of a federal court injunction if necessary.

Death came for King on the balcony of the black-owned Lorraine Hotel just off Beale Street on the evening of April 4. While standing outside with Jesse Jackson and Ralph Abernathy, a shot rang out. King fell over, struck in the neck by a rifle bullet which left him moribund. At 7:05 P.M. he was pronounced dead at St. Joseph's Hospital. His death caused a wave of violence in major cities across the country. However, King's legacy has lasted much longer than the memories of those post-assassination riots. In 1969, his widow, Coretta Scott King, organized the Martin Luther King Jr. Center for Non-Violent Social Change. Today it stands next to his beloved Ebenezer Baptist Church in Atlanta,

Dr. King addressing a crowd of protestors.

Montgomery in 1965. Even as her life has quieted down, she has received tributes for her dedication and inspiration; in 1980, she received the Martin Luther King, Jr. Nonviolent Peace Prize. As she headed towards retirement from John Conyers office in 1988, she became involved in other activities, like the Rosa and Raymond Parks Institute of Self Development in Detroit, founded in 1987.

Al Sharpton 1954-

Religious Leader, Community Activist, Sports Manager, Marketing, Advertising, Public Relations Manager, Organization Executive/Founder

While being shunned by many middle class African Americans, Al Sharpton draws support from the ranks of the youth and the disenfranchised. Sharpton was born in 1954 in Brooklyn, New York. He went to public schools, graduated from Tilden High School and briefly attended Brooklyn College. At the early age of four, Sharpton began delivering sermons and at the age of 13 he was ordained a Pentecostal minister. During and after high school Sharpton preached in neighborhood churches and went on national religious tours, often

with prominent entertainers. Sharpton was soon befriended by a number of well known and influential African Americans including Congressman Adam Clayton Powell, Jr., Jesse Jackson, and singer James Brown.

In 1969, Jackson appointed Sharpton youth director of Operation Breadbasket. Around this same time James Brown made Sharpton one of his bodyguards and soon he was doing promotions for the singer. In 1983, Sharpton married singer Kathy Jordan and soon became involved with fight promoter Don King. Even though Sharpton was promoting boxers and entertainers he had long before put himself in the public spotlight in the role of social activist. In 1971 he founded the National Youth Movement (later called the United African Movement) ostensibly to combat drug use. The movement however soon became a vehicle for Sharpton to draw attention to himself. He urged children to forsake Christmas in favor of a Kwanza celebration and the elderly to protest New York City police tactics.

Sharpton made himself part of the publicity surrounding the Bernard Goetz murder trial (1984), the Howard Beach racial killing (1986), the Twana Brawley debacle (1987) and the Yusef Hawkins-Bensonhurst

Outside of Ebenezer Baptist Church in Atlanta, while King's body had been lying in state.

killing (1989). In 1988, Sharpton was accused of being an FBI informant and passing on information about Don King, reputed organized crime figures and various African American leaders. In 1989 and 1990, he was acquitted on charges of income tax evasion and embezzling National Youth Movement funds. In 1991, Sharpton was briefly hospitalized after being stabbed by a man wielding a pocket knife.

On August 2, 1994, Sharpton announced the formation of a new political party. He aimed at countering the Liberal Party and at reaching black voters that traditional, mainstream parties have ignored. Sharpton unsuccessfully ran for the U.S. Senate as a candidate of his own Freedom Party, even participating in that year's New York Democratic primary.

Leon Howard Sullivan 1922-
Civil Rights/Human Rights Activist

Sullivan was born October 16, 1922, in Charlestown, West Virginia. After being ordained a Baptist minister at the age of 17, Sullivan earned a B.A. from West Virginia State College (1943) and an M.A. from Columbia University (1947). Sullivan also attended the Union Theological Seminary (1945) and earned a D.D. from Virginia Union University.

From 1950 to 1988 Sullivan was the pastor of the Zion Baptist Church in Philadelphia. While there he entered into a lifelong crusade to provide better and expanding job opportunities for African Americans. Sullivan fought racist hiring practices by protest and economic boycott. He provided job training through the Opportunities Industrialization Center. Opening in 1964 with money from a Ford Foundation grant, the Center offered training in electronics, cooking, power-sewing and drafting. Sullivan also founded Zion Investment Associates, which makes available seed money for new African American business ventures. Sullivan has also been associated with Progress Aerospace Inc., General Motors, Mellon Bank, and he is a cofounder of Self-Help.

Sullivan is a recipient of the Russwurm Award (National Publisher's Association, 1963), American Exemplar Medal (1969), Philadelphia Book Award (1966), Philadelphia Fellowship Community Award (1964) and the Franklin D. Roosevelt Four Freedoms Medal (1987).

Al Sharpton (center) leads a demonstration in New York City, 1992.

Upon retiring from the Zion Baptist Church in 1988, Sullivan was made Pastor Emeritus.

William Monroe Trotter 1872-1934

Organization Executive/Founder, Civil Rights/Human Rights Activist

Born in 1872, Trotter became an honor student and Phi Beta Kappa at Harvard and founded the militant newspaper, *Boston Guardian*, in 1901, for the purpose of "propaganda against discrimination." In 1905, Trotter joined W. E. B. Du Bois in founding the Niagara Movement but refused to move with him into the National Association for the Advancement of Colored People because he felt it would be too moderate. Instead, Trotter formed the National Equal Rights League. In 1919 Trotter appeared at the Paris Peace Conference in an unsuccessful effort to have it outlaw racial discrimination. The State Department had denied him a passport to attend, but he had reached Paris nonetheless, by having himself hired as a cook on a ship.

Because of his strident unwillingness to work with established groups, the civil rights movement has been slow to recognize Trotter. But many of his methods were to be adopted in the 1950s, notably his use of nonviolent protest. In 1903, Trotter deliberately disrupted a meeting in Boston at which Booker T. Washington was preaching support of segregation; Trotter's purpose was to be arrested to gain publicity for his militant position. Trotter also led demonstrations against plays and films that glorified the Ku Klux Klan.

Booker Taliafero Washington 1856-1915

Lecturer, Civil Rights/Human Rights Activist, Educational Administrator, Professor, Organization Executive/Founder, Author/Poet

Booker T. Washington was born a slave in Hale's Ford, Virginia, reportedly on April 5, 1856. After emancipation, his family was so poverty stricken that he worked in salt furnaces and coal mines from age nine. Always an intelligent and curious child, he yearned for an education and was frustrated when he could not receive good schooling locally. When he was 16 his parents allowed him to quit work to go to school. They had no money to help him, so he walked 200 miles to attend the Hampton Institute in Virginia and paid his tuition and board there by working as the janitor.

Booker T. Washington

Dedicating himself to the idea that education would raise his people to equality in this country, Washington became a teacher. He first taught in his home town, then at the Hampton Institute, and then in 1881, he founded the Tuskegee Normal and Industrial Institute in Tuskegee, Alabama. As head of the Institute, he traveled the country unceasingly to raise funds from blacks and whites both; soon he became a well-known speaker.

In 1895, Washington was asked to speak at the opening of the Cotton States Exposition, an unprecedented honor for a black man. His Atlanta Compromise speech explained his major thesis, that blacks could secure their constitutional rights through their own economic and moral advancement rather than through legal and political changes. Although his conciliatory stand angered some blacks who feared it would encourage the foes of equal rights, whites approved of his views. Thus his major achievement was to win over diverse elements among southern whites, without whose support the programs he envisioned and brought into being would have been impossible.

In addition to Tuskegee Institute, which still educates many today, Washington instituted a variety of programs for rural extension work, and helped to establish the National Negro Business League. Shortly after the election of President William McKinley in 1896, a movement was set in motion that Washington be named to a cabinet post, but he withdrew his name from consideration, preferring to work outside the political arena. He died on November 14, 1915.

◆ FEDERAL AND STATE CIVIL RIGHTS AGENCIES

Equal Employment Opportunity Commission
1801 L St., NW
Washington, DC 20507
(202)663-4900

United States Commission on Civil Rights
1121 Vermont Ave. NW
Washington, DC 20425
(800)552-6843

Alabama Attorney General's Office
State House
Montgomery, AL 36130
(205)242-7300)

Alaska Human Rights Commission
800 A St., Ste. 202
Anchorage, AK 99501-3669
(907)276-7474

Arizona Attorney General's Office
1275 W. Washington
Phoenix, AZ 85007
(602)542-5025

Arkansas Attorney General's Office
200 Tower Bldg.
323 Center St.
Little Rock, AR 72201-2610
(501)682-2007

California Attorney General
Public Rights Div.
1515 K. Street Suite 511
PO Box 944255
(916)445-9555

California Fair Employment and Housing Department
2014 T. St., Ste. 210
Sacramento, CA 95814-6835
(916)739-4600

Colorado Attorney General's Office
1525 Sherman St., 5th Fl.
Denver, CO 80203
(303)866-3611

Connecticut Attorney General's Office
55 Elm St.
Hartford, CT 06106
(203)566-2026

Delaware Attorney General's Office
Carvel State Office Bldg.
820 N. French St.
Wilmington, DE 19801
(302)577-3047

Florida Attorney General's Office, Legal Affairs Dept.
The Capitol
Tallahassee, FL 32399-1050
(904)488-2526

Georgia Equal Opportunity Commission
710 Cain Tower, Peachtree Ctr.
229 Peachtree St. NE
Atlanta, GA 30303
(404)656-1736

Hawaii Attorney General's Office
425 Queen St.
Honolulu, HI 96813
(808)586-1500

Idaho Human Rights Commission
450 W. State St.
1st Fl. West
Boise, ID 83720
(208)334-2873

Illinois Human Rights Department
100 W. Randolph St.
Ste. 10-100
Chicago, IL 60601
(312)814-6200

Indiana Civil Rights Commission
Indiana Government Ctr. North
100 N. Senate Ave., Rm. N-103
Indianapolis, IN 46204
(317)232-2600

Iowa Human Rights Department
Lucas Bldg
Des Moines, IA 50319
(515)281-5960

Kansas Human Rights Commission
851-S. Landon State Office Bldg.
900 SW Jackson St.
Topeka, KS 66612-1252
(913)296-3206

Kentucky Human Rights Commission
The Heyburn Bldg., 7th Fl.
PO Box 69
Louisville, KY 40202-0069
(502)588-4024

Louisiana Attorney General's Office
Justice Dept.
PO Box 94005
(504)342-7013

Maine Human Rights Commission
State House Sta. 51
Augusta, ME 04333-0051
(207)624-6050

Maryland Human Relations Commission
20 E. Franklin St.
Baltimore, MD 21202-2274
(410)333-1700

Massachusetts Attorney General's Office
1 Ashburton Pl., Rm. 2010
Boston, MA 02108
(617)727-2200

Michigan Attorney General's Office
Law Bldg.
PO Box 30212
Lansing, MI 48909
(517)373-1100

Michigan Civil Rights Department
303 W. Kalamazoo, 4th Fl.
Lansing, MI 48913
(517)335-3165

Minnesota Human Rights Department
500 Bremer Tower
St. Paul, MN 55101
(612)296-5663

Missouri Human Rights Commission
3315 W. Truman Blvd.
PO Box 504
Jefferson City, MO 65102
(314)751-3325

Montana Attorney General's Office
Justice Bldg.
215 N. Sanders
Helena, MT 59620
(406)444-2026

Nebraska Equal Opportunity Commission
PO Box 94934
Lincoln, NE 68509-4934
(402)471-2024

Nevada Equal Rights Commission
1515 E. Tropicana Ave., Ste. 590
Las Vegas, NV 89158
(702)486-7161

New Hampshire Human Rights Commission
163 Loudon Rd.
Concord, NH 03301
(603)271-2767

New Jersey Attorney General's Office
Civil Rights Division
383 W. State St.
CN 089
Trenton, NJ 08625
(609)984-3100

New Mexico Labor Department
Human Rights Division
Aspen Plaza
1596 Pacheco St.
Santa Fe, NM 87502
(505)827-6838

New York Human Rights Division
55 W. 125th St.
New York, NY 10027
(212)870-8400

North Carolina Human Relations Commission
Elks Bldg.
121 W. Jones St.
Raleigh, NC 27603-1368
(919)733-7996

North Dakota Attorney General's Office
State Capitol, 1st Fl.
600 E. Boulevard Ave.
Bismarck, ND 58505
(701)224-2210

Ohio Civil Rights Commission
220 Parsons Ave.
Columbus, OH 43266-0543
(614)466-2785

Oklahoma Human Rights Commission
2101 N. Lincoln Blvd., Rm. 480
Oklahoma City, OK 73105
(405)521-3441

Oregon Attorney General's Office
Justice Department
100 Justice Bldg.
Salem, OR 97310
(503)378-4400

Pennsylvania Human Relations Commission
101 2nd St., Ste. 300
Box 3145
Harrisburg, PA 17015-3145
(717)787-4410

Rhode Island Human Rights Commission
10 Abbott Park Pl.
Providence, RI 02903-3768
(401)277-2661

South Carolina Human Affairs Commission
PO Box 4490
Columbia, SC 29240
(803)253-6336

South Dakota Attorney General's Office
State Capitol
500 E. Capitol Ave.
Pierre, SD 57501-5070
(605)773-3215

Tennessee Human Rights Commission
400 Cornerstone Square Bldg.
530 Church St.
Nashville, TN 37243-0745
(615)7411-5825

Texas Attorney General's Office
Price Daniel, Sr. Bldg.
PO Box 12548
Austin, TX 78711-2548
(512)463-2100

Utah Attorney General's Office
236 State Capitol
Salt Lake City, UT 84114
(801)538-1015

Vermont Attorney General's Office
Pavilion Office Bldg.
109 State St.
Montpelier, VT 05609-1001
(802)828-3171

Virginia Human Rights Council
PO Box 717
Richmond, VA 23206
(804)225-2292

Washington Human Rights Commission
711 S. Capitol Way, Ste. 402
PO Box 42490
Olympia, WA 98504-2490
(206)753-4840

West Virginia Human Rights Commission
1321 Plaza East
Charleston, WV 25301
(304)558-2616

Wisconsin Attorney General's Office
PO Box 7857
Madison, WI 53707-7857
(608)266-1221

Wyoming Attorney General's Office
123 State Capitol
Cheyenne, WY 82002
(307)777-7841

8

Black Nationalism

8

Black Nationalism

◆ The Ideology of Black Nationalism ◆ Early Black Nationalism in the United States
◆ Black Nationalism in the Twentieth Century ◆ Black Nationalist and Pan-African Gatekeepers

by William Jeremiah Moses

Black nationalism, in its classic nineteenth-century form, consisted of efforts by African-American groups and individuals to create a sovereign nation-state. The quest for a national homeland expressed a perceived need to demonstrate the capacity of black people for self-government. In its more inclusive form, black nationalism has been indistinguishable from such movements as African Civilizationism, Pan-Negro Nationalism, and Pan-Africanism. Sometimes it has advocated a "back-to-Africa movement," but often it has simply implied moral support for decolonizing Africa and advancing the material and spiritual interests of African peoples everywhere.

◆ THE IDEOLOGY OF BLACK NATIONALISM

The back-to-Africa movement went through several phases of rise and decline, from its resurgence in the 1850s to its apex in the Garvey movement, to its denouement thereafter. The major proponents of classical black nationalism invariably placed religious historicism and teleology at the center of their ideological conceptions or utopian visions. While their goals were political and economic, they usually included a cultural agenda as well—though the cultural concerns of nineteenth-century nationalists were often Eurocentric and are not to be confused with the Negritude movement or the cultural nationalism of the late twentieth century. Black nationalism met the psychological need for a response to the slavery, colonialism, and racism imposed by Europeans and white Americans. In the minds of its adherents, it was the only sensible reaction to the almost universal military, technological, and economic domination of blacks by whites.

Documents expressing the ideology of black nationalism began to appear during the late eighteenth century. As Elie Kedourie has argued, nationalism, the idea that peoples are naturally divided into nations, is European in its origins. The American and French revolutions, and conceptions of the nation-state arising with them, came to dominate political thought, not only in the North Atlantic but also among African and Asian peoples. The 1804 slave revolt and seizure of the state in Haiti, as W. E. B. Du Bois and Eugene Genovese have argued, was both a cause and an effect of rising conceptions of nationalism and manifest destiny in the United States. It was also an inspiration to black nationalism among both the slaves and the free African Americans of the black population in the United States. Literary documents of black nationalism in England and the United States coincided with the revolutions in France or Haiti. Immanuel Geiss has referred to these expressions, typified by *The Interesting Narrative of the Life of Olaudah Equiano or Gustavus Vassa, the African, Written by Himself* (1787), as "proto Pan-Africanism." (For a time Gustavus Vassa believed that the African condition could be improved by repatriating Afro-Europeans in Africa. Although he was to abandon that plan, he remained committed to the destruction of African slavery through the agencies of Christian missionary activity and free trade.)

◆ EARLY BLACK NATIONALISM IN THE UNITED STATES

Early black nationalism in the United States is associated with the activities of two enterprising capitalists in the maritime industries, Paul Cuffe, a New Bedford sea captain, and James Forten, a Philadelphia sail-maker. These two figures combined a bourgeois economic nationalism with a Christian thrust, and hoped to develop Christianity, commerce, and civilization in Africa while providing a homeland for African Americans. Their repatriationist activities were brought to a halt in 1817, when Henry Clay, Andrew Jackson, and other white Americans formed the American Society for Colonizing the Free People of Color in the United States, usually called the American Colonization Society. The American Colonization Society had other prominent slave holders among its leadership, and expressly denied any sympathy for abolition; large numbers of blacks reacted by demonstrating a marked hostility to the society and its aims. Cuffe died shortly after the society's founding, and Forten felt constrained to silence, although he continued to believe that black Americans would "never become a people until they come out from amongst the white people." Those who continued to support repatriation, or who migrated under the auspices of the American Colonization Society, became the objects of extreme vituperation.

Black nationalism and repatriationism were not the same thing, however, and hostility to the American Colonization Society did not always lead to the abandonment of nationalist rhetoric. Maria Stewart referred

Early black nationalism in the United States has been associated with Paul Cuffe.

to herself as an African, but was hostile to the colonization movement. She insisted on her rights as an American, but at the same time denounced the United States with strident jeremiadic rhetoric. Stewart clearly viewed black America as a captive nation, existing in a type of Babylonian captivity, and conceived of African Americans as a people with a national destiny without advocating political separatism or the desire to form a nation-state. In a similar vein, David Walker denounced colonization and emigration with the religious fervor of an Old Testament prophet. Curiously, he insisted on the separate mission and destiny of African Americans as colored citizens of the world, while simultaneously maintaining that black and white Americans could be "a united and happy people."

Black nationalist motivations have been attributed to the major slave conspiracies of Gabriel Prosser and Denmark Vesey, who were inspired by the Haitian revolt, and both seem to have had as their goal the creation of a black nation with ties to the Caribbean. For the most part, however, evidence of black nationalism in the United States is found among the free black population of the North. It was in the so-called Free African Societies, which sprang up in the black communities of New York, Boston, and Philadelphia, that a conception of black historical identity and destiny was strongest. During the 1830s and 1840s, black nationalist thinking was associated with religious leadership such as that provided by the bishop of the African Methodist Episcopal Church, Richard Allen, who believed in a special God-given mission for black Americans as a people, but steadfastly opposed the American Colonization Society. Peter Williams, leader of the Afro-American Group of the Episcopal Church in New York, took a more tolerant view of colonization. He eulogized Paul Cuffe and remained friendly with John Russwurm, even after the latter emigrated to Liberia and was burned in effigy by anti-colonization activists.

The flourishing of black nationalism occurred during the 1850s and 1860s. To some degree, the movement owed its rebirth to the passage of the Fugitive Slave Act (1850) and the *Dred Scott v. Sandford* decision (1858). Emigration sentiment, which had been quiescent since the death of Cuffe, experienced a resurgence marked by the calling of several colonization conventions. The leaders of the movement were Henry Highland Garnet and Martin R. Delany, who founded the African Civilization Society in 1858. Edward Wilmot Blyden, the principal nineteenth-century Pan-African theorist, migrated to Liberia in 1850. Alexander Crummell emigrated to Liberia under the auspices of the Domestic and Foreign Missionary Society of the Protestant Episcopal Church in 1853, but eventually became involved with the American Colonization Society. During the early years of the

Civil War, *The Weekly Anglo-African* became the principal journal of the emigration movement.

Emigrationism died out during the peak years of Reconstruction that followed the Civil War, as the black American population strove to take advantage of opportunities presented by emancipation. During the years from 1876 to 1914, a number of back-to-Africa movements were organized. Most prominent among these were the movements under the leadership of Rev. Henry McNeal Turner, an AME Bishop, Rev. Orishatukeh Faduma, a Yoruba man from Barbados, and Chief Alfred C. Sam, a Twi speaker from the Gold Coast. Some scholars have detected black nationalist elements in the Kansas Exodus of the 1870s and the Oklahoma movement that established all-black towns during the 1890s. Fadumah had been a missionary in Oklahoma, which proved an important recruiting ground for Alfred C. Sam.

◆ BLACK NATIONALISM IN THE TWENTIETH CENTURY

Marcus Garvey's revitalization of the emigration movement came at an opportune moment. He arrived in the

Martin R. Delany

United States in 1916, shortly after Alfred C. Sam's voyage to the Gold Coast and a few months after the death of Bishop Henry McNeal Turner. His Universal Negro Improvement Association was, according to some speculations, the largest mass movement ever to occur among black Americans. Although Garvey was less successful as a repatriationist than some of his predecessors, he enjoyed tremendous success as a journalist and community organizer. His reputation became a source of great inspiration to many black leaders, and spread among the masses of people in Africa and the Americas.

Cultural nationalism, the exaltation of the "African personality" and the celebration of the contributions of black people to world history, made its appearance in the mid-nineteenth century. Cultural nationalist rhetoric occasionally has been adopted even by persons who have strongly opposed political nationalism. Frederick Douglass shared with Edward Wilmot Blyden an admiration for the ancient Egyptians, whom he believed to be of exactly the same racial type as African Americans. Towards the end of the century, younger scholars, such as W. E. B. Du Bois, were to make much of Egypt, Ethiopia, and Meroe as black contributors to world civilization. Writers such as William H. Ferris and John E. Bruce, who, like Du Bois, were proteges of Alexander Crummell, sought to vindicate the black race and to popularize the notion that black peoples of the upper Nile were the progenitors of civilization. The height of the vindicationist school was reached in the writings of Joel Augustus Rogers, sometime contributor to Marcus Garvey's paper, the *Negro World*.

During the 1930s, new versions of cultural nationalism began to focus on the importance of West Africa, in addition to that of ancient Egypt. This development was partially due to the Negritude movement among Francophone intellectuals, but also due to the "Jazz Age" interest in Africa among white artists and social scientists. The researches of Leo Frobenius, the German scholar, kindled the interest of Du Bois, Aime Cesaire, and Leopold Senghor in the cultures of "tribal" Africa. The growing interest of European artists such as Picasso and Modigliani in primitivism and African cultural expression led black Americans to a revaluation of their folk heritage and its African roots. The new-found respectability of jazz after its acceptance in continental Europe was another factor in the rise of black cultural nationalism. The ideology of scientific relativism in the writings of Franz Boas and Melville Herskovits, which stressed cultural relativism and a respect for "primitive" cultures also helped to make an interest in sub-Saharan Africa fashionable.

After the deportation of Marcus Garvey in 1925, black nationalism went into decline, as John Henrik Clarke

Although Garvey was less successful as a repatriationist than some of his predecessors, he enjoyed tremendous success as a journalist and community organizer.

and other scholars have noted. The search for a black nationality was kept alive by such religious groups as the Black Jews of Harlem, the Moorish Science Temple, and the Nation of Islam, which was under the leadership of the Honorable Elijah Muhammad. The rise of Malcolm X, a follower of Elijah Muhammad, did much to popularize black nationalism with young radical intellectuals during the early 1960s. After his split with Elijah Muhammad, Malcolm X seemed to abandon traditional black nationalist separatism as well, embracing social-

ism and, at the same time, his white Muslim brethren. Black nationalist attitudes persisted in some radical groups during the late 1960s, but seldom showed any relationship to or awareness of the black nationalist traditions of the nineteenth century. In recent years, cultural black nationalists such as Molefi K. Asante have shown a renewed interest in black nationalist intellectual history, especially as it relates to figures like Edward Wilmot Blyden and Marcus Garvey.

In the twentieth century, the search for a black nationality was kept alive by such religious groups as the Nation of Islam.

◆ BLACK NATIONALIST AND PAN-AFRICAN GATEKEEPERS

Edward Wilmot Blyden (1832-1912)
Black Nationalist, Repatriationist

Although he was not an American, Edward Blyden had a great influence on American Pan-African philosophy. As a scholar he wrote at great length about blacks in Africa and America, and about Christianity and Islam. He also held many different political and diplomatic offices in Liberia where he tried to put his beliefs into action.

Blyden was born in St. Thomas in the West Indies in 1832. When he was twelve, a white pastor undertook his education, encouraging him to become a minister. When he was eighteen he went to America, but was unable to find a seminary that would accept a black student. Instead, under the sponsorship of the New York Colonization Society, he went to Liberia to study at the new Alexander High School in Monrovia. Seven years later, he became the principal of the school.

Throughout his adult life, Blyden had two concurrent careers. He was a teacher and scholar. As a writer and editor, he constantly defended his race, championed the achievements of other blacks, attacked slavery, and advocated the repatriation of blacks in Africa. As a teacher, he held many prominent posts, including professor of classics (1862-1871) and president of Liberia College (1880-1884). At the same time, Blyden was also a politician and diplomat in Liberia, holding many different offices. He was secretary of state from 1864 to 1866, minister of the interior from 1880 to 1882, minister to Britain from 1877 to 1878 and again in 1892, and minister plenipotentiary to London and Paris in 1905.

Blyden traveled to America eight times. In 1861, he was commissioned by the Liberian government to interest Americans in a Liberian education. He returned again the following year to recruit African-American immigrants to Africa. His last visit in 1895 was in hopes of furthering racial accommodation in the south so that racial problems in America would not travel to Africa with new emigrants.

Because of his own religious training, Blyden was interested in Islam as a religion for Africans. Between 1901 and 1906, he was director of education in Sierra Leone. He studied both Christianity and Islam extensively, and summed up his views in an influential book,

Elijah Muhammad being interviewed by Buzz Anderson.

Christianity, Islam and the Negro Race. After his death in 1912, his funeral was attended by large numbers of both Christians and Muslims.

Elaine Brown (1943-)
Political Activist, Author

When Huey Newton, the founder of the Black Panther Party, fled the country in 1974 on a murder charge, he appointed Brown as his successor. In the mid-1960s, Brown became involved with the Black Congress, a group of African American organizations in the Los Angeles area that served the needs of black people. By 1967, Brown had become acquainted with the Black Panther Party, and in 1968, joined the Southern California chapter, agreeing to live by the strict Black Panther code.

The Black Panther program combined revolutionary rhetoric, violent actions in the name of self-defense and a strong commitment to building and strengthening black communities. The last tenet particularly appealed to Brown, who saw the party as a way of unifying the African American community. But the support of violent actions drew the attention of the FBI.

By the early 1970s, much of the party leadership had been killed or jailed in police battles. In 1974, with the expulsion of cofounder Bobby Seale, Brown became chairperson of the Black Panther Party. Later that same year, she was appointed the minister of defense by Huey Newton after he fled to Cuba to escape criminal prosecution.

During Brown's tenure as head of the party, she sought legitimate channels of power. She guided the Black Panther Party's efforts to electing an African American mayor in the city of Oakland, California. The party registered 90,000 black Democrats and secured the endorsement of California Governor Jerry Brown for Black Panther candidate Lionel Wilson. Wilson won, becoming the first black mayor of Oakland in 1976.

With Wilson in as mayor, Newton, who was acquitted of his crime, was allowed to come home. All the progress Brown had made, in the area of women's rights in the Black Panther Party and in the political arena, had become inconsequential as Newton focused on supporting the brothers in the party. The brothers quickly withdrew their support of Brown, ending their years of frustration at having been led by a progressive woman. For her safety, and the safety of her daughter, Brown

Black Muslim rally, 1961.

Edward Wilmont Blyden

left Oakland and immigrated to France in 1977, where she now lives just outside of Paris. In 1992 she penned the autobiography, *A Taste of Power: A Black Woman's Story*.

Alexander Crummell (1819-1898)
Black Nationalist, Repatriationist, Minister

Crummell was born in New York City on March 3, 1819. He was descended from African royalty, as his paternal grandfather was the son of a West African ruler. Crummell began his schooling at the Mulberry Street School in New York City. In 1831 he began attending high school but in 1835 transferred to a school founded by abolitionists in Canaan, New Hampshire. The school however was destroyed by a mob of angry townspeople and Crummell began attending the Oneida Institute in Whitesboro, New York, where he stayed for three years. He later studied in Boston and was ordained into the Episcopal Church in 1844. In 1847 he went to England and studied at Queens College, Cambridge, from 1851 to 1853 where he was awarded an A.B. degree.

Crummell then spent twenty years in Liberia and Sierra Leone where he served as professor of Mental

and Moral Science at the College of Liberia. In 1873 he returned to St. Mary's Mission in Washington, DC and soon founded St. Luke's Protestant Episcopal Church where he spent his last twenty-two years. In 1897 he was instrumental in the founding of the American Negro Academy.

Crummell published many collections of his essays and sermons including *Future of Africa* (1862), *Greatness of Christ* (1882), and *Africa and America* (1892). Crummell died on September 10, 1898, at Point Pleasant, New York.

Paul Cuffe (1759-1817)
Black Nationalist, Repatriationist, Entrepreneur

Cuffe was born January 17, 1759, on Cuttyhunk Island near New Bedford, Massachusetts. He was the son of Cuffe Slocum, a freed slave and Ruth Moses, a Wampanoag Indian.

By the time Cuffe was sixteen he was earning a living as a sailor on a whaling vessel. After making numerous voyages he was captured by the British but later released. He studied arithmetic and navigation but soon returned to the sea. In 1795 he had his own ship, *Ranger*, and in eleven years he had become a landholder and owner of numerous other sailing vessels.

Besides being a merchant seaman, Cuffe was also a civil rights activist. He discarded his father's slave surname and took his father's Christian first name in its place. He filed suffrage complaints in the Massachusetts' court and although unsuccessful, his court actions laid the groundwork for later civil rights legislation.

Cuffe was also a believer in free blacks voluntarily returning to Africa. In 1811 aboard his ship *Traveller* he sailed to Sierra Leone where he founded the Friendly Society which helped blacks return to Africa. In 1815 he sailed with thirty-eight colonists for Africa. It was to be his last voyage however, for he died September 9, 1817.

Martin Robins Delany (1812-1885)
Black Nationalist, Repatriationist

Born in Charles Town, West Virginia, in 1812, editor, author, physician, abolitionist and black nationalist Martin Delany received his first education from a book peddler who also served as an itinerant teacher. Since blacks in the south were forbidden to learn to read, when others found out he could read, the family was forced to flee north to Pennsylvania so that their children could continue to study. At the age of nineteen, he left home to seek further education. He studied with a young divinity student and a white doctor for a time.

As an adult, he became involved in anti-slavery reform, and the literacy movement. He began to publish *The Mystery*, a weekly newspaper devoted to news of the anti-slavery movement. When it folded after only a year of publication, Delany became co-editor of the *North Star*, a newspaper started by Frederick Douglass.

In 1848, Delany quit the *North Star* to pursue his medical studies. After being rejected on account of his race from several prominent Pennsylvania medical schools, he was able to attend the Harvard Medical School for a year before he was expelled from there due to his race. While he did not receive his degree, he did learn enough to practice medicine the rest of his life. In the 1850s, he became something of a local legend when he saved many lives during a fierce cholera epidemic in Pittsburgh.

The years following medical school were a grave disappointment to Delany, for blacks in America continued to be treated inhumanely no matter how hard he worked against slavery. He became an ardent black nationalist and recommended emigration to establish an independent colony for African Americans in South America or Africa. He wrote prolifically on the subject, held several national conventions, and set out on an exploratory expedition to Africa.

After the Emancipation Proclamation of 1863, Delany met with President Abraham Lincoln to discuss the establishment of black regiments in the army. Lincoln commissioned him as the first black major in the United States Army.

After the Civil War, Delany continued to work with reconstructionists trying to get fair treatment for newly freed slaves, still advocating emigration. He continued to pursue his scholarship, and in 1879 published his *Principal of Ethnology: The Origin of Races and Color* in which he discussed the role of black people in the world's civilization. He died in 1885, before he was able to actually move to Africa himself.

Louis Farrakhan (1933-)
Black Nationalist, Nation of Islam National Minister

Born in New York City in 1933, Louis Farrakhan (then known as Louis Eugene Walcott) was an outstanding student at Boston English High School and then attended (but did not earn a degree at) Winston-Salem Teacher's College. Farrakhan was an excellent musician; he played the violin and was a calypso singer. It was as a singer that he earned his livelihood prior to converting to Elijah Muhammad's Nation of Islam in the 1950s. He quickly worked his way up to a leadership position, becoming the minister of the Boston mosque. He loudly denounced Malcolm X after the latter split with Elijah Muhammad in 1963. He soon assumed leadership of the Harlem mosque which Malcolm had previously led. After Elijah Muhammad's death in 1975, he briefly supported Muhammad's son and designated successor, Warith Muhammad, as leader of the Nation of Islam. Shortly after Warith Muhammad began accepting whites as members within the Nation of Islam, now renamed the World Community of Al-Islam in the West, Farrakhan split from him and established a rival organization with about 10,000 members.

Farrakhan's vigorous support for Jesse Jackson's presidential candidacy in 1984 quickly became an issue after Farrakhan made several controversial statements, most notably calling Judaism a "gutter religion." Overshadowed in the controversy was the involvement of Nation of Islam leaders in American electoral politics for the first time. Previously, Black Muslims had generally followed Elijah Muhammad's counsel not to vote or to take part in political campaigns.

In January 1995 Qubilah Bahiyah Shabazz, daughter of slain black nationalist leader Malcolm X, was arrested and charged with trying to hire an FBI informant to kill Farrakhan, who some believe was involved in the 1965 assassination of her father. Farrakhan publicly defended Shabazz, claiming that the charges were an

Louis Farrakhan

FBI attempt to entrap her. On May 1, 1995, Shabazz avoided a trial and possible prison sentence by accepting responsibility for the plot. The court ordered her to seek psychiatric counseling, enter a drug and alcohol treatment program, and to obtain a steady job.

On October 16, 1995, African American men from across the United States convened in Washington D.C. for the Million Man March, which was organized by Farrakhan. Billed as a "holy day of atonement and reconciliation," marchers were urged to make a commitment to improve themselves, their families, and their communities. Those who could not attend the march were urged to stay home from work and avoid spending money at businesses as a show of solidarity with the marchers. Farrakhan closed the march with a two-hour speech in which he condemned the doctrine of white supremacy and claimed that there are still "two Americas, one black, one white, separate and unequal." He also challenged the marchers to return home and work to make their communities "safe and decent places to live."

Farrakhan embarked on a controversial 18-nation tour of Africa and the Middle East in early 1996. During the tour, he visited Iran and Libya, nations which the

United States government believes support international terrorism. Although he claimed that the trip was designed to promote peace and reconciliation, Farrakhan was widely criticized by U.S. officials for several anti-American statements he made while overseas.

James Forten (1766-1842)
Black Nationalist, Entrepreneur

Forten was born of free African-American parents in Philadelphia on September 2, 1766. He studied at a Quaker school, but at the age of fifteen, he quit to serve as a powder boy aboard the privateer *Royal Louis* during the American Revolution. He was captured by the British and held prisoner for seven months. He eventually spent a year in England where he was introduced to abolitionist philosophy.

Upon returning to America he was apprenticed to a sailmaker, but by 1786 he was foreman, and, in 1798, he became owner of the company. The business prospered and in 1832 employed forty white and African American workers.

By the 1830s Forten had become active in the abolitionist movement and was a strong opponent of African colonization. He became a noted pamphleteer, a nineteenth century form of social activism and was an early fund-raiser for William Lloyd Garrison's *The Liberator*.

Forten was president and founder of the American Moral Reform Society and was active in the American Anti-Slavery Society. He was a vigorous opponent of northern implementation of the Fugitive Slave Act of 1793. Forten died in Philadelphia on March 4, 1842.

Marcus Garvey (1887-1940)
Black Nationalist, Pan-African Theorist

Born in St. Ann's Bay, Jamaica, on August 17, 1887, Garvey was the youngest of eleven children. Garvey moved to Kingston at the age of fourteen, found work in a printshop, and became acquainted with the abysmal living conditions of the laboring class. He quickly involved himself in social reform, participating in the first Printers' Union strike in Jamaica in 1907 and in setting up the newspaper *The Watchman*. Leaving the island to earn money to finance his projects, he visited Central and South America, amassing evidence that black people everywhere were victims of discrimination.

Garvey returned to Jamaica in 1911 and began to lay the groundwork of the Universal Negro Improvement Association, to which he was to devote his life. Undaunted by lack of enthusiasm for his plans, Garvey left for England in 1912 in search of additional financial backing. While there, he met a Sudanese-Egyptian journalist, Duse Mohammed Ali. While working for Ali's publication *African Times and Oriental Review*, Garvey began to study the history of Africa—particularly, the exploitation of black peoples by colonial powers. He read Booker T. Washington's *Up From Slavery*, which advocated black self-help.

In 1914 Garvey organized the Universal Negro Improvement Association and its coordinating body, the African Communities League. In 1920 the organization held its first convention in New York. The convention opened with a parade down Harlem's Lenox Avenue. That evening, before a crowd of 25,000, Garvey outlined his plan to build an African nation-state. In New York City his ideas attracted popular support, and thousands enrolled in the UNIA. He began publishing the newspaper *The Negro World* and toured the United States preaching black nationalism to popular audiences. In a matter of months, he had founded over thirty UNIA branches and launched some ambitious business ventures, notably the Black Star Shipping Line.

In the years following the organization's first convention, the UNIA began to decline in popularity. With the Black Star Line in serious financial difficulties, Garvey promoted two new business organizations—the African Communities League and the Negro Factories Corporation. He also tried to salvage his colonization scheme by sending a delegation to appeal to the League of Nations for transfer to the UNIA of the African colonies taken from Germany during World War I.

Financial betrayal by trusted aides and a host of legal entanglements (based on charges that he had used the U.S. mail to defraud prospective investors) eventually led to Garvey's imprisonment in Atlanta Federal Penitentiary for a five-year term. In 1927 his half-served sentence was commuted, and he was deported to Jamaica by order of President Calvin Coolidge.

Garvey then turned his energies to Jamaican politics, campaigning on a platform of self-government, minimum wage laws, and land and judicial reform. He was soundly defeated at the polls, however, because most of his followers did not have the necessary voting qualifications.

In 1935 Garvey left for England where, in near obscurity, he died on June 10, 1940, in a cottage in West Kensington.

Malcolm X (El-Hajj Malik El-Shabazz) (1925-1965)
Black Nationalist

Malcolm X was one of the most fiery and controversial blacks of the twentieth century.

Born Malcolm Little in Omaha, Nebraska on May 19, 1925, Malcolm was the son of a Baptist minister, who was an avid supporter of Marcus Garvey's Universal Negro Improvement Association. While living in Omaha, the family was often harassed—at one point the family's house was set afire. In 1929 the family moved to Lansing, Michigan. While in Michigan, Malcolm's father was killed; his body severed in two by a streetcar and his head smashed. In his autobiography, written with Alex Haley, Malcolm asserted that his father may have been killed by members of the Ku Klux Klan. His mother, stricken by the death of her husband and the demands of providing for the family, was committed to a mental institution.

Leaving school after the eighth grade, Malcolm made his way to New York, working for a time as a waiter at Smalls Paradise in Harlem. Malcolm began selling and using drugs, turned to burglary, and, in 1946, was sentenced to a ten-year prison term on burglary charges.

While in prison Malcolm became acquainted with the Black Muslim sect, headed by Elijah Muhammad, and was quickly converted. Following his parole in 1952, he soon became an outspoken defender of black Muslim doctrines, accepting the basic argument that evil was an inherent characteristic of the "white man's Christian world."

Unlike Muhammad, Malcolm sought publicity, making provocative and inflammatory statements to predominantly white civic groups and college campus audiences. Branding white people "devils," he spoke bitterly of a philosophy of vengeance and "an eye for an eye." When, in 1963, he characterized the Kennedy assassination as a case of "chickens coming home to roost," he was suspended from the Black Muslim movement by Elijah Muhammad.

Disillusioned with Elijah Muhammad's teachings, Malcolm formed his own organizations, the Organization of Afro-American Unity and the Muslim Mosque Inc. In 1964 he made a pilgrimage to Islam's holy city, Mecca, and adopted the name El-Hajj Malik El Shabazz. He also adopted views that were not popular with other black nationalists, including the idea that not all whites were evil and that blacks could make gains by working through established channels.

As a result of Malcolm's new views, he became the victim of death threats. On February 14, 1965, his home was firebombed; his wife and children escaped unharmed.

Malcolm X

A week later, on the 21st, Malcolm was shot and killed at the Audubon Ballroom in Harlem, while preparing to speak. Three of the men arrested were later identified as members of the Nation of Islam.

Malcolm X had a profound influence on both blacks and whites. Many blacks responded to a feeling that he was a man of the people, experienced in the ways of the street rather than the pulpit or the college campus, which traditionally had provided the preponderance of black leaders. Many young whites responded to Malcolm's blunt, colorful language and unwillingness to retreat in the face of hostility.

The memory and image of Malcolm X has changed as much after his death as his own philosophies changed during his life. At first thought to be a violent fanatic, he is now understood as an advocate of self-help, self-defense, and education; as a philosopher and pedagogue, he succeeded in integrating history, religion, and mythology to establish a framework for his ultimate belief in world brotherhood and in human justice. Faith, in his view, was a prelude to action; ideas were feckless without policy. At least three books published since his death effectively present his most enduring thoughts. In 1992, a monumental film by Spike Lee, based on Malcolm's autobiography, renewed interest and understanding in the meaning of the life and death of Malcolm X.

Elijah Muhammad (1897-1975)
Black Nationalist, Nation of Islam Spiritual Leader

Elijah Muhammad was born Elijah Poole in Sandersville, Georgia, on October 10, 1897. His father, a Baptist preacher, had been a slave.

As a boy, Elijah worked at various jobs involving manual labor. At the age of twenty-six, he moved with his wife and two children (he was to have eight children in all) to Detroit. There in 1930, Poole met Fard Muhammad, also known as W.D. Fard, who had founded the Lost-Found Nation of Islam. Poole soon became Fard's chief assistant and in 1932 went to Chicago where he established the Nation of Islam's Temple, Number Two, which soon became the largest. In 1934, he returned to Detroit. When Fard disappeared in that year, political and theological rivals accused Poole of foul play. He returned to Chicago where he organized his own movement, in which Fard was deified as Allah and Elijah (Poole) Muhammad became known as Allah's Messenger. This movement soon became known as the Black Muslims.

During World War II, Elijah Muhammad expressed support for Japan, on the basis of its being a nonwhite

Elijah Muhammad

country, and was jailed for sedition. The time Muhammad served in prison was probably significant in his later, successful attempts to convert large numbers of black prison inmates, including Malcolm X, to the Nation of Islam. During the 1950s and 1960s, the Nation grew under Muhammad's leadership. Internal differences between Muhammad and Malcolm X, followed by the break between the two men and Malcolm's assassination, for which three Black Muslim gunmen were convicted, provided a great deal of unfavorable media coverage, but this did not slow the growth of the movement. In the late 1960s and early 1970s, Elijah Muhammad moderated the Nation's criticism of whites without compromising its message of black integrity. When Muhammad died on February 25, 1975, the Nation was an important religious, political, and economic force among America's blacks, especially in this country's major cities.

Elijah Muhammad was not original in his rejection of Christianity as the religion of the oppressor. Noble Drew Ali and the Black Jews had arrived at this conclusion well before him. But Muhammad was the most successful salesman for this brand of African American religion. Thus he was able to build the first strong black religious group in the United States that appealed primarily to the unemployed and underemployed city dweller, and ultimately to some in the black middle class. In addition, his message on the virtues of being black was explicit and uncompromising, and he sought with at least a little success to bolster the economic independence of African Americans by establishing schools and businesses under the auspices of the Nation of Islam.

Khalid Abdul Muhammad (1951?-)
Nation of Islam Spokesperson

Muhammad was born Harold Moore Vann in Houston, Texas, in the early 1950s. Raised by an aunt, he excelled in academics and athletics as a youth and graduated from high school in 1966. He spent then four years at Dillard University, where his attendance at a speech given by Nation of Islam figure Louis Farrakhan in 1967 changed his life. He became one of Farrakhan's original security personnel and soon changed his name to Khalid Abdul Muhammad as he immersed himself in the tenets of the faith.

After the death of longtime Nation of Islam leader Elijah Muhammad, the organization fell into disarray and Khalid Muhammad relocated to Uganda to work with black nationalist leader Idi Amin. He returned to the United States upon learning that Farrakhan was reviving the Nation of Islam, and by the late 1970s was a minister of the group's Los Angeles mosque. He later headed congregations in New York City and Atlanta, while continuing to play an important role in the Fruit of Islam, the security team assigned to protect the outspoken Farrakhan. In 1988 Muhammad was charged with the fraudulent use of a Social Security number to obtain a mortgage and spent nine months in prison, despite Farrakhan's appeal to the judicial authorities for leniency.

After his release, Muhammad became supreme captain of the Fruits of Islam and in 1991 became Farrakhan's national assistant, a position of public prominence once held by Farrakhan himself as well as Malcolm X. Muhammad's speeches soon attracted renewed interest in the Nation of Islam, especially from among prominent figures in rap music. His discourses often promote an independent nation for people of African descent, one free from what he sees as dead-end dreams of integration with the white community; he also points out that millions of blacks have died over the centuries at the hands of white oppression, a trend which continues to modern times in the worst sectors of urban America. A 1993 oration given in Union, New Jersey, however, landed Muhammad in trouble with the Nation of Islam for his fiery pronouncements on black-white relations and what Jewish leaders later denounced as anti-Semitic remarks. Muhammad was demoted shortly after by

Farrakhan, but still continues his work as a lecturer and activist.

Henry McNeal Turner (1834-1915)
Black Nationalist, Repatriationist, Minister

Henry McNeal Turner was born on February 1, 1834, near Abbeville, South Carolina, of free parents. He was ordained a minister in the African Methodist Episcopal Church in 1853 and bishop in 1880. In 1863 Turner became the first African-American Army chaplain. He was also president of Morris Brown College for twelve years.

Turner was a leading advocate of repatriation. In 1876 he was elected vice president of the American Colonization Society. He made several trips to Africa and lectured throughout world.

Turner was convinced that blacks had no future in America. Instead, he felt that God had brought blacks to the New World as a means of spreading Christianity and preparing them to redeem Africa. Turner edited and published several papers, including *Voice of Missions* and *Voice of the People*, in which he advocated black colonization of Africa. Turner died on May 8, 1915.

Robert F. Williams (1925–)
Civil Rights and Political Activist

When Robert F. Williams was ten years old, he saw a grinning policeman drag a black woman by her heels down the street, her dress over her hips, her back scraping the pavement. The impression this must have made on the young boy stayed with him into his adult years, adding fuel to his lifelong political activism.

In 1956, in Williams's hometown of Monroe, North Carolina, he was elected president of the Monroe NAACP. The organization's membership had dwindled to six. Williams went out and recruited working class people and the unemployed to become members, as opposed to the NAACP's practice of appealing to middle and upper-class professionals. The membership grew to become more militant than past groups had been.

Williams then targeted institutions in Monroe for desegregation, first being the County Library. It was desegregated without protest. Williams then tried to desegregate Monroe's municipal swimming pool, which didn't happen. In response, Williams led groups of black youths on sit-ins and other organized protests.

The Ku Klux Klan retaliated against Williams and the activities of Monroe's NAACP by holding rallies attended by several thousand members. When Monroe's police refused to quell the sometimes violent rallies, Williams encouraged a program of armed self-defense by Monroe's black community, which proved effective in reducing the number of midnight rides by the Klan.

In 1959, responding to the unjust acquittal in Monroe of the attempted rape by a white man on a pregnant black woman, Williams exhorted the black men and women on the courthouse steps with his legendary statement: "Since the federal government will not bring a halt to lynching in the South, and since the so-called courts lynch our people legally, if it's necessary to stop lynching with lynching, then we must be willing to resort to that method. We must meet violence with violence." The next day the national office of the NAACP suspended Williams from office for six months. Later in 1959, through a grave misunderstanding, Williams was indicted for kidnapping. He became a fugitive by the FBI, fleeing to Cuba with his family.

Bringing the Monroe chapter into the center of a national controversy did not hurt Williams's local popularity in the African American community, as he was reelected president of Monroe's NAACP chapter in 1960. From Cuba, Williams produced a revolutionary radio program, *Radio Free Dixie*, and produced a Cuba edition of the *Crusader*. In 1966, Williams sought refuge in the People's Republic of China. In 1968, Williams published a pamphlet, "Listen Brother!" hoping to dissuade African American servicemen to stop fighting against their Asiatic "dark-skinned brothers."

In 1968, a group of African Americans, dedicated to establishing a separate black nation within the United States, formed the revolutionary Marxist–Leninist Re-

Henry McNeal Turner

public of New Africa (RNA). The RNA elected Williams as its president in exile. In 1969, the U.S. embassy granted Williams a passport to return to the United States, which he did later that year. Disillusioned with the RNA's prevalent internal struggles, he resigned as its president in December of 1969.

9

National Organizations

9

National Organizations

◆ A Brief History ◆ Organization Leaders ◆ National Organizations

In a dispute between the National Association for the Advancement of Colored People and the state of Alabama, Justice Harlen of the United States Supreme Court, pointed out the significance of association membership, claiming that it is through associations that individuals have sought "to make more effective the expression of their own views." Associations are one of the largest and most influential forces in the United States and have played an important part in the economic, social, and educational development of African Americans; organizations have been crucial in developing and disseminating information, ensuring representation for private interests, and promoting social and policy objectives.

◆ A BRIEF HISTORY

Early Black Organizations

Due to restrictive ordinances and limited tolerance by whites, prior to the eighteenth century only the most informal and limited assembling of blacks was permitted. Most often meeting as religious assemblies, African Americans were forced to meet secretly, in small numbers. Thus the very first black organizations to exist in the United States cannot definitively be identified.

The Free African Society , organized in Philadelphia in 1787, has been generally accepted as the first African American organization in the United States. Founded by Methodist ministers Richard Allen and Absalom Jones, the Free African Society served as an important source of political consciousness and welfare for blacks throughout the country, combining economic and medical aid for poor blacks with support of abolition and sub rosa communication with blacks in the South.

The abolitionist movement of the nineteenth century, produced numerous organizations concerned with issues of importance to African Americans, including the American Colonization Society (founded in 1816), the New England Anti-Slavery Society (founded in 1832), and the American Anti-Slavery Society (founded in 1833). Although most of these organizations were dominated by whites, black leaders, including Paul Cuffe and Frederick Douglass played an active role in the movement and in anti-slavery organizations of the time.

During the late nineteenth and early twentieth centuries a great many black organizations came into existence; the thrust of most of these groups was toward education, betterment, and religious training. In 1895 the National Medical Association was founded to further the interests of black physicians, pharmacists, and nurses; Mary McLeod Bethune organized the National Association of Colored Women in 1896; and in 1900 the National Negro Business League was formed to promote commercial development.

The Niagara Movement

The Niagara Movement of 1905, marked a turning point in African American history. This new organization, founded by a group of black intellectuals—headed by W. E. B. Du Bois.

The Niagara Movement, however, suffered from weak finances and a policy which restricted membership to black intellectuals. In 1909 the Niagara Movement was succeeded by a new organization—one which would later become the National Association for the Advancement of Colored People.

National Association for the Advancement of Colored People

The new organization was largely the brainchild of three people: William English Walling, a white Southerner who feared that racists would soon carry "the race war to the North"; Mary White Ovington, a wealthy young white woman who had attended the 1905 meeting

W. E. B. Dubois

of the Niagara group as a reporter for the *New York Evening Post* and had experience with conditions in the black ghettos of New York City; and Dr. Henry Moskowitz, a New York social worker. The trio proposed that a conference be called "for the discussion of present evils, the voicing of protests, and the renewal of the struggle for civil and political liberty." The three-day conference, held May 30 through June 1, was followed by four meetings, the results of which were an increase in membership and the selection of an official name—the National Negro Committee. In 1910 the organization adopted its present name and was incorporated in New York state; by 1914 the association had established some 50 branches throughout the country.

Over the years, the organization has attempted to better the condition of African Americans through litigation, legislation, and education; *Crisis* magazine, edited by W. E. B. Du Bois, became its chief vehicle for the dissemination of information. Perhaps its most significant victory was won in 1954 when the historic *Brown v. Board of Education of Topeka* case threw out the "separate but equal" doctrine established by the Supreme Court in *Plessy v. Ferguson* in 1896 and eliminated segregation in public education.

NAACP Legal Defense and Educational Fund, Inc.

Established in 1939 by the National Association for the Advancement of Colored People, the NAACP Legal Defense and Educational Fund maintained its own board, program, staff, office, and budget for some 20 years. It has served in the forefront of legal assaults against discrimination and segregation and has an outstanding record of victories. In addition to its litigation, the Legal Defense Fund provides scholarships and training for young lawyers, advises lawyers on legal trends and decisions, and monitors federal programs.

Originally for tax purposes, the NAACP Legal Defense Fund had been maintained as a separate arm of the NAACP, until it officially was divorced from its parent organization in 1959. Following the separation of the organizations, a dispute over identity and the use of the parent organization's name erupted. The National Association for the Advancement of Colored People sued the NAACP Legal Defense Fund for name infringement. However, after several months of legal wrangling, a federal court ruled that the LDF could keep NAACP in its name, since the NAACP was its parent organization.

Organizations Concerned with Urban Problems

During the early part of the twentieth century several organizations concerned with the plight of urban blacks emerged. In 1906, at the urging of William H. Baldwin, president of the Long Island Railroad, a group of blacks and whites met for the purpose of studying the employment needs of African Americans. This group, known as the Committee for the Improvement of Industrial Conditions Among Negroes in New York, studied the racial aspects of the labor market (particularly the attitudes and policies of employers and unions) and sought to find openings for qualified African Americans.

At the same time, the League for the Protection of Colored Women was established to provide similar services for black women in New York and Philadelphia arriving from various parts of the South. These women, who often had no friends or relatives in the North, often fell prey to unscrupulous employment agencies which led them into low wage jobs.

A third organization, the Committee on Urban Conditions Among Negroes, appeared in 1910. It was organized by Ruth Standish Baldwin, widow of the former Long Island Railroad president, and Dr. George Edmond Haynes, one of only three trained black social workers in the country and the first black person to receive a doctorate from Columbia University. Haynes was named as the first executive secretary of the new agency. A year later the organization merged with the Committee for the Improvement of Industrial Conditions Among

An early NAACP office.

Negroes in New York and the National League for the Protection of Colored Women to form the National League on Urban Conditions Among Negroes. That name was later shortened to the now-familiar National Urban League.

From the outset, the organization focused on the social and economic needs of blacks, seeking training, improved housing, health, recreation, and job assistance for blacks. The organizational model that the League had established in New York City attracted attention and soon affiliates were formed in various cities across the country.

A major goal of the National Urban League and its affiliates was to broaden economic opportunities for African Americans. It was not until the 1960s when Whitney M. Young, Jr. became its new leader that the League began to emerge as a force in the civil rights struggle.

Leadership Conference on Civil Rights

The Leadership Conference on Civil Rights was organized in 1950 by A. Philip Randolph, Roy Wilkins, and Arnold Aronson to implement the historic report of President Harry S. Truman's Committee on Civil Rights, *"To Secure These Rights."* Beginning with only 30 organizations, the conference has grown in numbers, scope, and effectiveness, and has been responsible for coordinating the campaigns that have resulted in the passage of the civil rights legislation of the 1950s and 1960s, including the Civil Rights Act of 1957, the Civil Rights Act of 1960, and the Civil Rights Act of 1964, the Voting Rights Act of 1965, and the Fair Housing Act of 1968 (also known as the Civil Rights Act of 1968).

The Leadership Conference on Civil Rights currently consists of approximately 157 national organizations representing minorities, women, major religious groups, the handicapped, the aged, labor, and minority businesses and professions. These organizations speak for a substantial portion of the population and together comprise one of the most broad based coalition in the nation.

Southern Christian Leadership Conference

Following the arrest of Rosa Parks, who had refused to give up her seat on a public bus, the Reverends Dr. Martin Luther King, Jr. and Ralph Abernathy organized the Montgomery Improvement Association in 1955 to

Black women looking for work in Northern cities often fell prey to unscrupulous employment practices and to low wage jobs.

coordinate a citywide bus boycott. The success of the boycott led to the creation of a new organization.

This new organization, consisting mainly of black ministers, met at the Ebenezer Baptist Church in January 1957 and elected Dr. King as its first president. Initially called the Southern Negro Leaders Conference, and later the Southern Leadership Conference, the Southern Christian Leadership Conference grew to become one of the most influential and effective of all the civil rights organizations.

Organizations and the Court

Although public and private associations of all kinds have traditionally flourished in this country, it has not always been an easy road for organizations for blacks and other minorities. The freedom of association—the freedom to assemble, immunity from state scrutiny—like the First Amendment freedoms of speech and press, has from time to time been questioned and challenged.

Since the founding of the National Association for the Advancement of Colored People and similar organizations, state and local governments have attempted to prevent the operation of such groups. During the late

1950s the state of Alabama set out to ban the NAACP from conducting activities with the state, claiming that the association had failed to comply with statutes governing corporations operating within the state. The dispute, *NAACP v. Alabama*, was finally resolved by the United States Supreme Court in 1958 in favor of the association. However, the association was met with other interferences—some of the most notable disputes include, *Bates v. Little Rock* (1960), Louisiana ex rel. Gremillion v. NAACP (1961), and *Gibson v. Florida Legislative Investigating Committee* (1963).

Congress of Racial Equality

The Congress of Racial Equality (CORE), an interracial organization organized to confront racism and discrimination, was founded in 1942 by James Farmer, as the result of a campaign protesting discrimination at a Chicago restaurant. From Chicago, the organization spread to other cities and other causes, organizing sit-ins and Freedom Rides throughout the South.

By the mid-1960s, CORE had changed directions, and Farmer turned leadership of the organization over to Floyd McKissick, a North Carolina lawyer. With McKissick

A. Philip Randolph

Dr. Martin Luther King, Jr.

as national director, the organization moved toward an all black membership and staff. (In 1967 CORE, at its convention, eliminated the word "multiracial" from its constitution). McKissick left the organization in 1968 and was replaced by the present national director, Roy Innis, former chairman of the Harlem chapter.

Student Non-Violent Coordinating Committee

In 1960 a group of black college students founded the Student Non-Violent Coordinating Committee (SNCC) to coordinate the activities of students engaged in direct action protest. SNCC achieved enormous results in the desegregation of public facilities and earned respect from the country for its determination to act peacefully, no matter how violent or demeaning the provocation.

However, by 1964 the organization's leader, Stokely Carmichael, had become convinced that the American system could not be turned around without the threat of wholesale violence. In 1967 Carmichael left the organization to join the more militant Black Panther Party. H. Rap Brown, the former minister of justice in the old organization, took over leadership, renaming the organization the Student National Coordinating Committee and promoting violent retaliation when situations so

demanded. The organization gradually declined in membership and is now essentially defunct.

Black Panther Party

From its founding by Huey P. Newton and Bobby Seale in 1966, the Black Panther Party departed from the platform and tactics of other civil rights organizations. It rejected the institutional structure which, in its view, made American society corrupt; it rejected established channels of authority which oppressed the black community; it rejected middle-class values, which it felt contributed to indifference toward, and contempt for, the disinherited black urban youth.

The party imposed strict discipline on its members, denouncing the use of intoxicants, drugs, and artificial stimulants "while doing party work." The intellectual fare of every party member is the ten-point program (supplemented by daily reading of political developments), which every member is obliged to know and understand, presumably even to commit to memory.

However, by 1970 most of the organization's leadership was either jailed, in exile, or dead—Newton was

Benjamin Chavis speaks at a commission meeting in Los Angeles, 1993.

jailed in 1968 on manslaughter changes; Seale had been jailed on charges stemming from the 1968 Chicago convention riot; minister of information, Eldridge Cleaver, in 1969 fled to Algeria to avoid a prison sentence; in 1970 Mark Clark and Fred Hampton were killed during a police raid.

Organizations Providing Community Support

In 1967 the National Urban Coalition was founded to improve the quality of life for the disadvantaged in urban areas through the combined efforts of business, labor, government, and community leaders. Another organization, the National Black United Fund, which provides financial and technical support to projects serving the critical needs of black communities nationwide, was founded in 1972.

The Reverend Jesse Jackson, in 1971, organized Operation PUSH (People United to Save Humanity). The organization has pursued its economic objectives through its Operation Breadbasket program. It also has worked to motivate young people through its PUSH-EXCEL program, which is designed to instill pride and build confidence in young people. Jackson left Operation

PUSH to organize another group, the National Rainbow Coalition, Inc., in 1984.

Organizations Responding to Africa and the Caribbean

During the nineteenth and early part of the twentieth century, a number of individuals and organizations arose to unite Africans throughout the world. Most notable was Marcus Garvey, black nationalist and advocate of repatriation of blacks to Africa, who founded the Universal Negro Improvement Association in 1914. Garvey's organization, whose goal was to instill pride, gain economic and political power for blacks in the United States, and to establish an independent black colony in Africa, and to promote unity between African throughout the world, attracted millions worldwide. On February 19 1918, under the leadership of W. E. B. Du Bois, the first Pan-African Congress was held in Paris. The meeting was attending by blacks from around the world and focused on the problems facing Africans worldwide.

More recently new organizations have formed to address the concerns of Africans around the world. Founded in 1977 by Randall Robinson, TransAfrica has

Stokely Carmichael at a rally at the University of California, 1966.

worked to influence American foreign policy regarding political and human rights in African and the Caribbean by informing the public of violations of social, political, and civil rights. Responding to the policy of apartheid in South Africa, TransAfrica supported sanctions against South Africa and organized demonstrations in front of the South African embassy in Washington, D.C. During one such demonstration, Robinson and numerous others were arrested. Other organizations have also taken a stand on policies affecting Africans around the world. In 1986 leaders representing major black organizations united to press for passage of the more stringent legislation regarding sanctions against South Africa.

◆ ORGANIZATION LEADERS

H(ubert) Rap Brown (Jamil Abdullah Al-Amin) (1943-)
Student National Coordinating Committee Chairman

H. Rap Brown was born on October 4, 1943, in Baton Rouge, Louisiana. In 1967 he took over leadership of the Student Non-Violent Coordinating Committee renaming the organization the Student National Coordinating Com-

mittee. During his leadership of the Student National Coordinating Committee, Brown was an advocate of violence against the white establishment and used fiery rhetoric in many of his speeches, often saying that "violence is as American as cherry pie." Since the late 1960s the organization has gradually declined in membership and is now essentially defunct.

In 1968 Brown was charged with inciting a riot in Cambridge, Maryland, and was convicted in New Orleans on a federal charge of carrying a gun between states. In 1969 Brown published the book *Die Nigger Die.* Brown disappeared in 1970, after being slated for trial in Maryland, and in 1972 he was shot, arrested, and eventually convicted for a bar holdup in New York City.

While in prison, Brown converted to the Islamic faith and took the name of Jamil Abdullah Al-Amin. On his release, he founded a community grocery store in Atlanta. He is currently leader of the Community Mosque in Atlanta.

In August 1994, Al-Amin was arraigned on weapons possession and assault charges stemming from a shooting in an Atlanta city park. Al-Amin claimed that the charges were the result of harrassment by federal agents

Bobby Seale (left) and Huey Newton, 1969.

who targeted him because of his radical past and Muslim beliefs.

Benjamin Franklin Chavis, Jr. (1948-)
Former National Association for the Advancement of Colored People Executive Director

Benjamin Chavis was born on January 22, 1948 in Oxford, North Carolina. He received a B.A. from the University of North Carolina in 1969. Chavis went on to earn an M.A. from the Duke University Divinity School

and a Ph.D. in theology from Howard University in Washington D.C.

He came to national attention in 1971, when as a civil rights organizer for the United Church of Christ he was indicted along with nine other people for the fire-bombing of a grocery store in Wilmington, Delaware, during a period of racial unrest. In the controversial trial that followed all of the "Wilmington 10" were found guilty. Chavis was sentenced to a prison term of 29 to 34 years. Chavis was granted parole and in 1980 his conviction

Randall Robinson meets with African National Congress President, Nelson Mandela, 1991.

was reversed amidst conflicting testimony by various witnesses.

Prior to becoming active in the civil rights movement, Chavis taught chemistry at the high school level. He also worked as an AFSCME labor organizer (1969), a civil rights organizer for the Southern Christian Leadership Council (1967–1969), as a minister for the United Church of Christ, and as director of their Commission for Racial Justice in Washington, D.C. (1972). In 1985 he was appointed executive director of the Commission for Racial Justice. Chavis has also served as co-chairman of the National Alliance Against Racism and Political Repression (1977) and as co-chairman of the Organizing Committee for Economic and Social Justice.

In 1977 Chavis wrote *Let My People Go: Psalms From Prison*. He also received the George Collins Service Award (1977), given by the Congressional Black Caucus, the William L. Patterson award given by the Patterson Foundation, and the Shalom award presented by the Eden Theological Seminary. He is also a recipient of the Gertrude E. Rush Distinguished Service Award, J. E. Walker Humanitarian Award, and the Martin Luther King Jr. Freedom Award. Chavis has since become active in the South African civil rights struggle and continues his position with the United Church of Christ.

On April 9, 1993, the NAACP board of directors elected Chavis to succeed retiring executive director, Benjamin Hooks. Chavis assumed leadership of the NAACP with an agenda designed to increase the mem-

H. Rap Brown

bership of young African Americans and revitalize an organization that some people viewed as stagnant. However, Chavis's early initiatives, which included defending "gangsta rap" music, meetings with street gang leaders, and seeking closer ties with controversial Nation of Islam leader Louis Farrakhan, angered many of the NAACP's more traditional members. By the time the NAACP met for its 85th annual convention in July 1994, the NAACP had been split into two factions, one supporting Chavis and the other which believed the organization was being overrun by radical and extremist elements.

In August 1994, it was disclosed that Chavis committed hundreds of thousands of dollars of NAACP money in November 1993 to settle a sexual harassment suit against him. On the weekend of August 20, 1994, the NAACP board of directors met and voted to oust Chavis as executive director. Chavis sued the NAACP, claiming that he had been wrongfully terminated. The NAACP settled out of court with Chavis, but he was not reinstated as executive director.

Following his dismissal from the NAACP, Chavis formed a new civil rights organization, the National

Benjamin Chavis

African American Leadership Summit. He continued his close association with Louis Farrakhan and together they organized the Million Man March, which convened on October 16, 1995 in Washington D.C. Chavis also serves as a talk show host on Washington D.C.'s WOL-AM.

Ramona Hoage Edelin (1945-)
National Urban Coalition President and Chief Executive

Born in Los Angeles, California, on September 4, 1945, Ramona Hoage Edelin received her B.A. (magna cum laude) from Fisk University, her M.A. from the University of East Anglia, in Norwich, England, and her Ph.D. from Boston University. She has been a lecturer at the University of Maryland and a visiting professor at Brandeis University; she has also served as chair of Afro-American studies at Emerson College.

In 1977 Edelin joined the National Urban Coalition as an executive assistant to the president. The National Urban Coalition, an organization to improve the quality of life for the disadvantaged in urban areas, has been active in advocating initiatives designed to encourage youth and promote leadership. Between 1979 and 1982 she moved from director of operations, to vice president of operations, then to senior vice president of program and policy, during which time she directed programs in housing, health, education, and advocacy. In 1982 Edelin became the organization's chief executive.

Marian Wright Edelman (1939-)
Children's Defense Fund President

Born in Bennettsville, South Carolina, on June 6, 1939, Marian Wright Edelman received her undergraduate degree from Spelman College and her law degree from Yale. In 1963 she joined the NAACP Legal Defense and Education Fund as staff attorney. A year later she organized the Jackson, Mississippi, branch of the NAACP Legal Defense and Education Fund, serving as its director until 1968. In 1968 she founded the Washington Research Project of the Southern Center for Public Policy which later developed into the Children's Defense Fund.

Wright has served as director of the Harvard University Center for Law and Education, chairman of the Spelman College board of trustees, a member of the Yale University Corporation, the National Commission on Children, and on the boards of the Center on Budget and Policy Priorities, the US Committee for UNICEF, and the Joint Center for Political and Economic Studies.

As Children's Defense Fund president, Edelman has become the nation's most effective lobbyist on behalf of children. Even while social spending was being cut, she has managed to score some victories. In 1986, nine federal programs known as "the Children's Initiative" received a $500 million increase in their $36 billion budget for families and children's health care, nutrition, and early education.

The most visible focus of CDF is its teen pregnancy prevention program. Through Edelman's efforts, Medicaid coverage for expectant mothers and children was boosted in 1984. In 1985, Edelman began holding an annual Pregnancy Prevention Conference, bringing thousands of religious leaders, social and health workers and community organizations to Washington to discuss ways of dealing with the problem. In 1996, Edelman and the CDF staged the well-attended "Stand for Children" rally in Washington, DC.

In her 1987 book, *Families in Peril: An Agenda for Social Change*, Edelman wrote, "As adults, we are responsible for meeting the needs of children. It is our moral obligation. We brought about their births and their lives, and they cannot fend for themselves." Her other books include, *Children Out of School in America, School Suspensions: Are They Helping Children?, Portrait of Inequality: Black and White Children in America, Families in Peril: An Agenda for Social Change, The Measure of Our Success: A Letter to My Children*, and *Guide My Feet: Prayers and Meditations on Loving and Working for Children.*

James Farmer (1920-)
Congress of Racial Equality Founder and Former National Director

Born in Marshall, Texas, on January 12, 1920, Farmer attended public schools throughout the South. He earned his B.S. degree in chemistry from Wiley College in 1938 and his B.D. degree from Howard University in 1941. Active in the Christian Youth Movement, and once vice-chairman of the National Council of Methodist Youth and the Christian Youth Council of America, Farmer refused ordination when confronted with the realization that he would have to practice in a segregated ministry.

In 1941 Farmer accepted a post as race relations secretary for the Fellowship of Reconciliation. The following year he and a group of University of Chicago students organized the Congress of Racial Equality (CORE), the first protest organization in the United States to utilize the techniques of nonviolence and passive resistance advocated by the Indian nationalist Mohandas Karamchand Gandhi.

In June 1943 CORE staged the first successful sit-in demonstration at a restaurant in the Chicago Loop. The organization soon supplemented this maneuver with what came to be known as the standing-line, which involved the persistent waiting in line by CORE members at places of public accommodation where blacks had been denied admission.

In 1961 CORE introduced the Freedom Ride into the vocabulary and methodology of civil rights protest, dispatching bus riders throughout the South for the purpose of testing the desegregation of terminal facilities. Attacked in Alabama and later arrested in Mississippi, the Freedom Riders eventually succeeded in securing the court ordered desegregation of bus terminals, with the United States Supreme Court decision of 1960 which outlawed segregation in interstate transportation.

Farmer left the organization in 1966. In 1969, President Richard Nixon appointed Farmer to the post of assistant secretary of Health, Education and Welfare. The appointment created a furor in some black circles, where it was felt that it was inappropriate for a former civil rights leader to serve in such an administration; in other circles, the appointment was praised by those who thought it necessary for African Americans to be represented in all areas. However, Farmer found that there was little of substance in the position and resigned.

Farmer began to give lectures, and for a while headed a think tank at Howard University. In 1976 he broke all ties with CORE, criticizing its leader, Roy Innis, for such things as attempting to recruit black Vietnam veterans as mercenaries in Angola's civil war. Disturbed over the course that the organization had taken, Farmer and a score of former CORE members attempted to create a

James Farmer, 1965.

new racially mixed civil rights organization in 1980. Farmer, along with Floyd McKissick, attempted to meet with Innis to reach an agreement on the future of the organization, but nothing developed.

Farmer has written several books, including *Freedom When?* and *Lay Bare the Heart*.

Prince Hall (1735?-1807)
Founder of Black Freemasonry in the United States

Prince Hall is believed to have been born in Bridge Town, Barbados, around 1735. Historians contend that he migrated to the United States in 1765; others claim that during the late 1740s he had been a slave to William Hall of Boston, Massachusetts, and freed by William Hall on April 9, 1770.

In March 1775 Hall along with 15 other blacks were initiated into a lodge of British army Freemasons stationed in Boston. The group of black masons was issued a permit to meet at a lodge on March 17, 1775, and on July 3, 1775, they organized the African Lodge No. 1, with Hall as master of the lodge. The lodge received official recognition from England as a regular Lodge of Free and Accepted Masons in 1784 and was designated the African Lodge 459.

Hall, in addition to leading the organization of black Freemasonry, was active as an abolitionist. In January 1777, he was the prime force behind a black petition sent to the Massachusetts state legislature requesting the abolition of slavery in the state. Another important petition, drawn up under his leadership in 1788, called

Grand Lodge No. 1, Greensville, Mississippi, 1887.

for an end to the kidnapping and sale of free blacks into slavery. He also actively lobbied for the organization of schools for black children in Boston. Prince Hall died on December 4, 1807, in Boston.

Dorothy I. Height (1912–)
National Council of Negro Women President

Born in 1912 in Richmond, Virginia, Dorothy Height holds a masters degree from New York University and has studied at the New York School of Social Work. In the fall of 1952, she served as a visiting professor at the Delhi School of Social Work in New Delhi, India. Six years later, she was appointed to the Social Welfare Board of New York by Governor Averell Harriman, and was reappointed by Governor Nelson Rockefeller in 1961. Since 1957 she has been president of the National Council of Negro Women, an organization founded by Mary McLeod Bethune in 1935.

Before becoming the fourth president of the National Council of Negro Women, Height had served on the organization's board of directors. She has also served as associate director for leadership training services for the Young Women's Christian Association, as a member of the Defense Advisory Committee on Women in the

Services, as president of Delta Sigma Theta sorority, as vice president of the National Council of Women, as president of Women in Community Services, Inc., as well as in numerous other organizations. Height is also the founder of the Black Family Reunion, which she created in the 1980s to combat negative media stereotypes of African Americans.

In 1994, President Bill Clinton presented Height and nine other distinguished Americans with the Medal of Freedom, America's highest civilian honor. She was also awarded the Salute to Greatness Award.

Benjamin L. Hooks (1925–)
Former National Association for the Advancement of Colored People Former Executive Director

Hooks was born in Memphis, Tennessee, on January 31, 1925, and attended LeMoyne College and Howard University. He received his J.D. degree from DePaul University College of Law in 1948. During World War II he served in the 92nd Infantry Division in Italy. From 1949 to 1965, and again from 1968 to 1972, Hooks worked as a lawyer in Memphis. In 1966 Hooks became the first black judge to serve in the Shelby County

Dorothy Height

Benjamin Hooks

(Tennessee) criminal court. As an ordained minister, he preached at Middle Baptist Church in Memphis and the Greater New Mount Moriah Baptist Church in Detroit. As a prominent local businessman, he was the cofounder and vice president of the Mutual Federal Savings and Loan Association in Memphis.

On January 10, 1977, Hooks was unanimously elected executive director of the National Association for the Advancement of Colored People by the NAACP board of directors, succeeding the retiring Roy Wilkins.

Under his progressive leadership, the association took an aggressive posture on United States policy toward African nations. Among his many battles on Capitol Hill, Hooks led the historical prayer vigil in Washington, D.C., in 1979 against the Mott anti-busing amendment, which was eventually defeated in Congress; led in the fight for passage of the District of Columbia Home Rule bill; and was instrumental in gathering important Senate and House votes on the Humphrey-Hawkins Full Employment Bill.

At the NAACP's national convention in 1986, Hooks was awarded the association's highest honor, the Spingarn Medal. In March 1993, Hooks retired as executive director of the NAACP and was replaced by Benjamin Chavis.

Following his retirement, Hooks became senior vice president of Chapman Co., a minority brokerage firm. He was also installed as professor of social justice at Fisk University.

Roy Emile Alfredo Innis (1934–)
Congress of Racial Equality National Chairman

Born June 6, 1934, in St. Croix, Virgin Islands, Roy Emile Alfredo Innis has lived in the United States since the age of twelve. He attended Stuyvesant High School in New York City and majored in chemistry at City College of New York.

In 1963 Innis joined the Congress of Racial Equality (CORE). In 1965 Innis was elected chairman of the Harlem branch and went on to become associate national director three years later. In 1968 Innis became national director of the organization. Innis founded the Harlem Commonwealth Council, an agency designed to promote the development of black-owned businesses and economic institutions in Harlem. He also took a plunge into journalism, serving with William Haddad as

Roy Innus, 1976.

co-editor of the *Manhattan Tribune*, a weekly featuring news from Harlem and the upper West Side.

Innis' leadership of CORE, however, has been marked with controversy. Numerous members have left the organization, charging that Innis has run the organization as a one-man show. CORE was also the target of a three-year investigation by the New York state attorney general's office into allegations that it had misused charitable contributions. (An agreement was reached in 1981 that did not require CORE to admit to any wrong doing in its handling of funds, but stipulated that Innis would have to contribute $35,000 to the organization over the next three years.) Innis was challenged by a group of former CORE members, headed by James Farmer, the founder and former chairman of organization; the effort was unsuccessful and Innis continued as head of the organization. In 1981 Innis became national chairman of the organization.

While remaining president of the largely inactive CORE, Innis has sought to build a political base in Brooklyn. He has run for public office on several occasions. In 1986, Innis was a Republican candidate for Brooklyn's twelfth Congressional district, but lost the election. He also ran unsuccessfully for the Democratic

mayoral nomination in New York City in 1993 against David Dinkins. In 1994, Innis unsuccessfully challenged Mario Cuomo for the governorship of New York.

John Edward Jacob (1934-)
Former National Urban League President

Born in Trout, Louisiana, on December 16, 1934, John Edward Jacob grew up in Houston, Texas. He received his bachelor's and master's degrees in social work from Howard University. During the early 1960s Jacob worked for the Baltimore Department of Public Welfare, first as a caseworker, then later as a child welfare supervisor. In 1965 he joined the Washington Urban League as director of education and youth incentives.

During his early career with the organization he held a number of increasingly important positions, serving as director of its Northern Virginia Branch in 1966, associate director for administration of the affiliate in 1967, and as its acting executive director from 1968 until 1970. He also spent several months as director of community organization training in the Eastern Regional Office of the NUL.

Jacob left the Washington Urban League in 1970 to serve as executive director for the San Diego Urban League, a post he held until his return to the Washington Urban League in 1975. In 1982 Jacob replaced Vernon E. Jordan, Jr. as the organization's president, when Jordan retired after ten years as Urban League president.

Jacob has also served on the Howard University board of trustees, the Board of the Local Initiatives Support Corporation, the board of A Better Chance, Inc., the community Advisory Board of New York Hospital, and the National Advertising Review Board, among others.

In 1994, Jacob retired as president of the National Urban League and was succeeded by Hugh P. Price. Jacob is currently an executive vice president for Anheuser-Busch Inc.

Vernon Eulion Jordan, Jr. (1935-)
Former National Urban League President

Vernon Eulion Jordan, Jr. was born in Atlanta on August 15, 1935. After graduating from DePauw University in 1957 and from Howard Law School in 1960, he returned to Georgia.

From 1962 to 1964 Jordan served as field secretary for the Georgia branch of the NAACP. Between 1964 and 1968 Jordan served as director of the Voter Education Project of the Southern Regional Council and led its successful drives that registered nearly two million blacks in the South. In 1970 Jordan moved to New York to become executive director of the United Negro College Fund, helping to raise record sums for its member

John Jacob

colleges, until he was tapped by the Urban League to become the successor to the late Whitney Young.

Taking over as National Urban League executive director in January 1972, Jordan moved the organization into new areas, including voter registration in northern and western cities, while continuing and strengthening the League's traditional social service programs. An outspoken advocate of the cause of the black and the poor, Jordan has taken strong stands in favor of busing, an income maintenance system that ends poverty, scatter-site housing, and a federally financed and administered national health system. Maintaining that the "issues have changed," since the 1960s, Jordan has called for "equal access and employment up to and including top policy-making jobs."

The nation was stunned on May 29, 1980 when Jordan, who had just delivered an address to the Fort Wayne Urban League, was shot by a sniper as he returned to his motel; Jordan was confined to the hospital, first in Fort Wayne and later in New York City, for 90 days.

On September 9, 1981, Jordan announced his retirement, after ten years as head of the National Urban League. During Jordan's tenure, the League increased its number of affiliates from 99 to 118, its staff from 2,100 to 4,200, and its overall budget, from $40 million annually to $150 million.

In January 1993, Jordan served as a member of President Bill Clinton's transition team. President Clinton appointed Jordan to his Foreign Intelligence Advisory Board in April 1993. He is also senior partner at the Washington D.C. law firm of Akin, Gump, Strauss, Hauer & Feld.

Joseph E. Lowery (1924-)
Southern Christian Leadership Conference President

The Reverend Joseph E. Lowery was born in Huntsville, Alabama, on October 6, 1924. He holds a doctor of divinity degree, among others, and has attended numerous educational institutions, including Clark College, the Chicago Ecumenical Institute, Garrett Theological Seminary, Payne College and Theological Seminary, and Morehouse University. Reverend Lowery's ministry began in 1952 at the Warren Street Church in Birmingham, where he served until 1961. From there he moved on to become pastor of St. Paul Church from 1964 to 1968.

Vernon Jordan

Since 1986, Lowery has served as pastor of the Cascade United Methodist Church in Atlanta, Georgia.

Lowery was one of the co-founders of the Southern Negro Leaders Conference (which later became the Southern Christian Leadership Conference); the Reverend Dr. Martin Luther King, Jr. served as the organizations' first president, with Lowery serving as vice-president.

In 1977, Lowery succeeded Reverend Ralph David Abernathy, as president of the SCLC. Under his leadership, SCLC has broadened its activities to include the reinstitution of its Operation Breadbasket to encourage businesses that earn substantial profits in the black community to reinvest equitably and employ blacks in equitable numbers; involvement in the plight of Haitian refugees jailed by the American government; and a march from Selma to Washington, D.C., in connection with the renewal of the Voting Rights Act of 1982.

Jewell Jackson McCabe (1945-)
Chairperson of the National Coalition of 100 Black Women

Jewell Jackson was born in Washington D.C. on August 2, 1945. She later kept her married name from her second marriage becoming Jewell Jackson McCabe. McCabe studied at New York City's High School for the Performing Arts as a teen, and after graduating, she studied dance at Bard College from 1963 to 1966. She married Frederick Ward, who worked in advertising, while at Bard, whom she later divorced. Her marriage to Eugene McCabe, president of North General Hospital in New York City, also ended in divorce, but McCabe chose to keep his name.

After studying at Bard, it was a few years before McCabe took a job as director of public affairs for the New York Urban Coalition in 1970, and concurrently, she joined an organization called the New York Coalition of 100 Black Women, founded by her mother, business woman Julia Jackson. At that time, the group was about 75 women shy of the 100 mark. The group reached this goal by the mid-1970s. During this time, McCabe tried to find her niche. She left the Urban Coalition in 1973 to become the public relations officer for Special Services for Children in New York City. In 1975, she took a post as associate director of public information in the Women's Division of the Office of the Governor in New York City and from there to become director of government and community affairs at WNET-TV in 1977.

From 1975 to 1977, she published *Women In New York* through the state office as well as donating her time to the United Way, the NAACP, the United Hospital Fund, and the Association for the Betterment of New York. In 1977, because of her good work, she was named president of the, soon to be, National Coalition of 100 Black Women, a post she held until 1991, when she became chair of the board of directors. By 1981, McCabe had established the organization nationally with chapters in 22 states, attracting the most well-known black women in the country.

Within two years, McCabe received several prestigious awards, including an Eastern Region Urban League Guild Award in 1979 and a Seagrams Civic Award, a Links Civic Award, and an outstanding community leadership award from Malcolm/King College all in 1980. Also, in 1980, she served as deputy grand marshal of the annual Martin Luther King Jr. parade in New York City. In addition to her chairman of the board duties for the Coalition, McCabe is president of her own Jewell Jackson McCabe Associates, a firm that does consulting work on government relations, marketing, and events dealing with minority issues.

Floyd Bixler McKissick (1922-1981)
Congress of Racial Equality Former National Director

Born in Asheville, North Carolina on March 9, 1922, Floyd Bixler McKissick did his undergraduate work at Morehouse and North Carolina colleges. Having determined that he wanted to become a lawyer, McKissick

Reverend Joseph Lowery, 1988.

applied to the University of North Carolina at Chapel Hill Law School. Since the school was not integrated at that time, he was denied admission. With the help of NAACP lawyer Thurgood Marshall, McKissick sued the university and became the first African American to earn an LL.B. degree there.

While still in school, McKissick had become an active member of the Congress of Racial Equality (CORE). When McKissick replaced James Farmer as head of CORE on January 3, 1966, he quickly made a name for himself. Under McKissick's direction, the organization moved more firmly into the Black Power movement, refusing to support Martin Luther King's call for massive nonviolent civil disobedience in northern cities, concentrating instead on programs aimed at increasing the political power and improving the economic position of African Americans. In 1967 the organization moved to eliminate the word "multiracial" from its constitution.

McKissick resigned as national director of CORE in 1968. After leaving CORE, he launched a plan to establish a new community, Soul City, in Warren County, North Carolina. McKissick saw Soul City as community with sufficient industry to support a population of 50,000.

For his venture, he received a $14 million bond issue guarantee from the Department of Housing and Urban Development and a loan of $500,000 from the First Pennsylvania Bank.

Soul City, however, ran into difficulties and despite the best efforts of McKissick, the project never developed as planned. In June 1980 the Soul City Corporation and the federal government reached an agreement that would allow the government to assume control of the project. Under the agreement, the company retained 88 acres of the project, including the site of a mobile home park and a 60,000 square foot building that had served as the project's headquarters.

McKissick died on April 28, 1991, of lung cancer and was buried at Soul City.

Huey P. Newton (1942-1989)
Black Panther Party Cofounder

The youngest of seven children, Huey Newton was born in Monroe, Louisiana on February 17, 1942. He attended Oakland City College, where he founded the Afro-American Society, and later studied at San Francisco Law School. In 1966, Newton joined forces with Bobby Seale and established the Black Panther Party for Self-Defense.

Newton and his partner almost immediately became targets of sharp police resentment and uneasiness. The hostility came to a climax in 1967, when Newton allegedly killed an Oakland police officer. His eight-week trial was a cause celebre in which more than 2,500 demonstrators surrounded the courthouse chanting Panther slogans and demanding his release. Newton was convicted of voluntary manslaughter and sent to the California Men's Colony. His conviction was later overturned by the California court of appeals.

By the 1970s the Black Panther Party became a potent political force in California. Co-leader Bobby Seale made an almost-successful bid for the mayorship of Oakland in 1973. In 1977, the Panthers helped to elect the city's first black mayor, Lionel Wilson. Meanwhile, Newton continued to have problems with the law. He was charged with shooting a prostitute, but after two hung juries, the charges were dropped. He was retried and convicted for the 1969 death of the police officer; however, the conviction was reversed.

In 1980, he earned his Ph.D. in philosophy from the University of California; his doctoral thesis was "War Against the Panthers: Study of Repression in America." However, this achievement was followed by further problems. He was charged with embezzling state and federal funds from an educational and nutritional program he headed in 1985 and in 1987, he was convicted of illegal possession of guns. In 1989, he was fatally shot by a small-time drug dealer.

Hugh B. Price (1941-)
National Urban League President and CEO

When Hugh Price was named president and CEO of the National Urban League in 1994, he inherited an organization with financial problems and a lack of visibility. But he was just the person to address and eradicate those problems. Price graduated from Amherst in 1963, then received his law degree from Yale in 1966. Immediately going to work in the inner city, Price worked first as an attorney for the New Haven Legal Assistance Association, than as executive director of the Black Coalition of New Haven.

Price continued his focus on the inner city by joining, in 1970, the urban affairs consulting firm of Cogen, Holt & Associates in New Haven, specializing in the analysis of municipal government. After serving as Human Resources Administration director for the city of New

Huey Newton

Haven, Price was offered the opportunity to express his opinions to a much larger audience: he was named to the editorial board of the *New York Times*. Price primarily concentrated on writing about domestic policy issues.

After spending six years working at WNET-TV, New York City's public television station, Price became vice president of the Rockefeller Foundation, helping minorities get more opportunities in groups served by the organization. With his background of serving the inner city community, speaking out on urban concerns, supervising large programs and being able to get funding for them, Price caught the attention of the people responsible for choosing a new president in 1994 for the National Urban League.

Price continued to focus on poor schools, inner city youngsters with time on their hands, and high unemployment. But he vowed that the Urban League would not be race–specific in its help—it would be need–specific. Price felt that a better approach the Urban League could take would be to focus on helping entire urban neighborhoods, instead of singling out a particular race in that neighborhood. This approach has gained Hugh Price the deserved attention in the media for his worthwhile efforts.

Asa Philip Randolph (1889-1979)
Brotherhood of Sleeping Car Porters and A. Philip Randolph Institute Founder

Asa Philip Randolph was born in Crescent City, Florida on April 15, 1889. He attended Cookman Insti-

A. Philip Randolph Institute, Cincinnati, Ohio.

tute in Jacksonville, Florida, before moving to New York City.

In New York Randolph worked as a porter, railroad waiter, and an elevator operator. While attending the College of the City of New York, he was exposed to the socialist movement, and in 1917 he organized *The Messenger*, a socialist newspaper. In 1925 Randolph founded the Brotherhood of Sleeping Car Porters to help black railway car attendants working for the Pullman Palace Car Company. After a ten year struggle, in 1935, Randolph and the union negotiated a contract with Pullman.

Randolph served as a member of New York City's Commission on Race and as president of the National Negro Congress. In 1941 Randolph organized a march on Washington, D.C., to bring attention to discrimination in employment. In 1942 he was appointed to the New York Housing Authority and in 1955 was appointed to the AFL-CIO executive council.

In 1960 Randolph organized the Negro American Labor Council. He was also one of the organizers of the 1963 march on Washington. In 1964 he founded the A. Philip Randolph Institute in New York City to eradicate

discrimination and to defend human and civil rights. He died on May 16, 1979.

Randall S. Robinson (1942-)
TransAfrica Founder and Director

Randall Robinson, brother to the late news anchor Max Robinson, was born in Richmond, Virginia, in the early 1940s and is a graduate of Virginia Union University and Harvard Law School. In 1977 Robinson founded TransAfrica to lobby Congress and the White House on foreign policy matters involving Africa and the Caribbean. Since its creation, the organization has grown from two to over 15,000 members.

In 1984 and 1985, in protest to the policy of apartheid in South Africa, TransAfrica organized demonstrations in front of the South African embassy in Washington, D.C.; Robinson along with other protesters, including singer Stevie Wonder, were arrested. In addition to its opposition to apartheid, the organization was active in the Free South Africa Movement and is an advocate for the cessation of aid to countries with human rights problems. In 1981 TransAfrica Forum, an educational and research arm of TransAfrica, was organized to

Randall Robinson

collect and disseminate information on foreign policy affecting Africa and the Caribbean and to encourage public participation in policy debates.

In 1994, the United States was beseiged by scores of refugees seeking to escape Haiti's brutal military dictatorship. Many of these refugees, upon reaching the United States or the American military base in Guantanamo, Cuba, were often sent back to Haiti without receiving asylum hearings. On April 12, 1994, Robinson began a liquid-fast diet in an attempt to increase awareness of the plight of Haitian refugees and to pressure the Clinton administration to change its refugee policy. On May 8, Robinson ended his fast after the Clinton administration announced that it would grant Haitian refugees asylum hearings.

On March 16, 1995, Robinson announced that TransAfrica would lead a group of prominent African Americans to pressure Nigeria's brutal military leaders to step down from power. Along with other demonstrators, Robinson was arrested during protests in front of the Nigerian Embassy in Washington D.C. on April 21, 1995 and Aug. 31, 1995. On November 10, 1995, Robinson, along with notable South African Archbishop Desmond Tutu, announced that they would seek eco-

nomic sanctions or an oil embargo against Nigeria after its military regime executed a prominent Nigerian writer and eight other minority rights activists.

Bayard Rustin (1910-1987)
A. Philip Randolph Institute Former Executive Director

Bayard Rustin was born in West Chester, Pennsylvania, on March 17, 1910. While in school, he was an honor student and star athlete, experiencing his first act of discrimination when he was refused restaurant service in Pennsylvania while on tour with the football team. He attended Wilberforce University, Cheyney State Normal School (now Cheyney State College) and the City College of New York.

Rustin was active in various peace organizations, efforts to restrict nuclear armaments, and movements toward African independence. Between 1936 and 1941, Rustin worked as an organizer of the Young Communist League. In 1941 he joined the Fellowship of Reconciliation, a nonviolent antiwar group, and later served as its director of race relations. In 1942 Rustin, along with James Farmer, became active in the Chicago Committee of Racial Equality, out of which the Congress of Racial Equality grew.

Rustin was one of the founding members of the Southern Christian Leadership Conference (SCLC). In 1963 he was named chief logistics expert and organizational coordinator of the March on Washington. From 1964 to 1979, Rustin served as executive director of the A. Philip Randolph Institute in New York City. In 1975 he founded the Organization for Black Americans to Support Israel.

Throughout the 1960s Rustin was hard pressed to maintain support for the nonviolent philosophy to which he had dedicated his life. Nonviolence, he argued, was not outdated; it was a necessary and inexorable plan called for by the black's condition in the United States. Guerrilla warfare and armed insurrection, Rustin explained, required friendly border sanctuaries, a steady source of arms and equipment, and the support of the majority of a country's inhabitants. Rustin continued to be active in the civil rights movement until his death on August 24, 1987, at the age of 77.

Bobby Seale (1936-)
Black Panther Party Co-Founder

Born Robert George Seale in Dallas, Texas on October 20, 1936, Bobby Seale, along with Huey P. Newton and Bobby Hutton, was one of the founding members of the Black Panther Party for Self-Defense. His family, poverty-stricken, moved from Dallas to Port Arthur, Texas, before settling in Oakland, California.

Seale joined the United States Air Force and trained as a sheet-metal mechanic, after leaving high school. However, he was discharged for disobeying an officer. Returning home, he found sporadic work as a sheet-metal mechanic. In 1959 Seale enrolled at Merritt College in engineering drafting. While attending Merritt, Seale joined the Afro-American Association, a campus organization that stressed black separatism and self-improvement. It was through this organization that Seale met Panther co-founder Huey Newton.

Seale and Newton soon became disenchanted with the association. In 1966 Seale and Newton formed the Black Panther Party for Self-Defense. One of their objectives was to form armed patrols to protect citizens from what they considered racist police abuse.

In March of 1971, Seale was charged with kidnapping and killing Panther Alex Rackley, a suspected police informant. However, a mistrial was declared, and the charges dismissed. Seale began to steer the Panthers away from its revolutionary agenda and toward one of creating community action programs. In 1974 Seale left the party to form Advocates Scene, an organization aimed at helping the underprivileged from grass-root political coalitions.

More recently Seale has served as a community liaison for Temple University's African American Studies department. He has lectured throughout the country and has written several books—*Seize the Time: The Story of the Black Panther Party* (1970), *A Lonely Rage: The Autobiography of Bobby Seale* (1978), and *Barbeque'n with Bobby Seale* (1987).

Roy Wilkins (1901-1981)
National Association for the Advancement of Colored People Former Executive Director

Born in St. Louis, Missouri on August 30, 1901, Wilkins was reared in St. Paul, Minnesota. He attended the University of Minnesota, where he majored in sociology and minored in journalism. He served as night editor of the *Minnesota Daily* (the school paper) and edited a black weekly, the St. Paul *Appeal*. After receiving his B.A. in 1923, he joined the staff of the Kansas City *Call*, a leading black weekly.

In 1931 Wilkins left the *Call* to serve under Walter White as assistant executive secretary of the NAACP. In 1934 he succeeded W. E. B. Du Bois as editor of *Crisis* magazine. Wilkins was named acting executive secre-

Bobby Seale

tary of the NAACP in 1949, when White took a year's leave of absence from the organization. Wilkins assumed the position as executive secretary of the NAACP in 1955. He quickly established himself as one of the most articulate spokesmen in the civil rights movement. He testified before innumerable Congressional hearings, conferred with United States Presidents, and wrote extensively.

For several years, Wilkins served as chairman of the Leadership Conference on Civil Rights, an organization of more than 100 national civic, labor, fraternal, and religious organizations. He was a trustee of the Eleanor Roosevelt Foundation, the Kennedy Memorial Library Foundation, and the Estes Kefauver Memorial Foundation. He was also a member of the Board of Directors of the Riverdale Children's Association, the John LaFarge Institute, and the Stockbridge School, as well as the international organization Peace with Freedom. Wilkins died on September 8, 1981.

Whitney Moore Young, Jr. (1922-1971)
National Urban League Former Director

Whitney Moore Young, Jr., was born in Lincoln Ridge, Kentucky, on July 31, 1922. He received his B.A. degree

Roy Wilkins

Whitney Young, Jr.

from Kentucky State College in 1941. He went on to attend the Massachusetts Institute of Technology, and in 1947 he earned an M.A. degree in social work from the University of Minnesota.

In 1947 Young was made director of industrial relations and vocational guidance for the St. Paul, Minnesota, Urban League. In 1950 he moved on to become executive secretary at the St. Paul chapter. Between 1954 and 1961 Young served as dean of the Atlanta University School of Social Work. He also served as a visiting scholar at Harvard University under a Rockefeller Foundation grant.

In 1961 the National Urban League's board of directors elected Young as president of the organization. Young instituted new programs like the National Skills Bank, the Broadcast Skills Bank, the Secretarial Training Project and an on-the-job training program with the United States Department of Labor. Between 1961 and 1971, the organization grew from 63 to 98 affiliates.

In addition to his work with the National Urban League, Young served as president of the National Association of Social Workers and the National Conference on Social Welfare, and on the boards and advisory committees of the Rockefeller Foundation, Urban Coalition, and Urban Institute, and on seven presidential commissions. In 1969 Young was selected by President Johnson to receive the Medal of Freedom, the nation's highest civilian award. Young authored two books, *To Be Equal* (1964) and *Beyond Racism: Building an Open Society* (1969), and coauthored *A Second Look* (1958).

Young died on March 11, 1971, while attending a conference in Africa.

◆ NATIONAL ORGANIZATIONS

A. Philip Randolph Educational Fund
1444 I Street, NW, No. 300
Washington, DC 20005
(202) 289-2774

Founded in 1964. Seeks to eliminate prejudice and discrimination from all areas of life; educate individuals and groups on their rights and responsibilities; defend human and civil rights; assist in the employment and education of the underprivileged; combat community deterioration, delinquency, and crime.

Africa Faith and Justice Network

401 Michigan Ave
PO Box 29378
Washington, DC 20017
(202) 832-3412

Founded in 1983. Purpose is to examine the role the network believes Europe, America, and other northern countries play in causing injustices in Africa. Challenges national policies found to be detrimental to the interest of African peoples. Gathers information on issues and policies that adversely affect Africa, analyzes the data, and makes recommendations for advocacy or action. Consults with churches of Africa, field missionaries, and other African individuals and groups.

The Africa Fund

17 John St
New York, NY 10038
(212) 962-1210

Founded in 1966. Established by the American Committee on Africa. Works to: defend human and civil rights of needy Africans by providing or financing legal assistance; provide medical relief to Africans, particularly refugees; render aid to indigent Africans in the United States, Africa, or elsewhere who are suffering economic, legal, or social injustices; provide educational aid or grants to Africans, particularly refugees; inform the American public about the needs of Africans; engage in study, research, and analysis of questions relating to Africa. Encourages divestment by U.S. corporations in South Africa; seeks to increase public support for U.S. economic sanctions against South Africa; has supported legislation which prevents U.S. corporations operating in South Africa from claiming U.S. tax credits for taxes paid to the South African government. Operates Unlock Apartheid's Jails Project, which seeks to inform the U.S. public about the plight of political prisoners in South Africa; disseminates information on the activities of South African puppet forces, including those in other areas of southern Africa.

Africa News Service

PO Box 3851
Durham, NC 27702
(919) 286-0747

Founded in 1973. News agency whose purpose is to supply material on Africa for broadcast and print media. Covers African politics, economy and culture, and U.S. policy and international issues affecting Africa. Obtains news by monitoring African radio stations on short-wave equipment, by subscribing to African publications, and through a network of reporters based in Africa. Also produces investigative stories on U.S. policy and its implications. Provides audio news and programming for radio, articles and graphics for newspapers and magazines, and prints for libraries and institutions. Carries out research for feature articles, news programs, and individuals.

Africa Travel Association

347 Fifth Avenue, Suite 610
New York, NY 10016
(212) 447-1926

Founded in 1975. Conducts regional seminars and trade show exhibitions. Sponsors Africa Guild (see separate entry) to help develop a general interest in Africa.

Africa Watch

485 Fifth Avenue
New York, NY 10017
(212) 972-8400

Founded in 1988. Monitors and promotes internationally recognized human rights in Africa.

Africa World Press

PO Box 1892
Trenton, NJ 08607
(609) 771-1666

Founded in 1979. Scholar activists and members of the African intellectual community. Promotes and maintains the development of an independent, democratic, and critical thinking African intellectual community. Utilizes the scientific knowledge and skills of the community to give service to African peoples and social movements. Conducts seminars on subjects such as the energy crisis, human rights, political repression, and food.

African-American Institute

833 United Nations Plaza
New York, NY 10017
(212) 949-5666

Founded in 1953. Works to further development in Africa, improve African American understanding, and inform Americans about Africa. Engages in training, development assistance, and informational activities. Sponsors African American conferences, media and congressional workshops, and regional seminars.

African-American Labor Center

1925 K Street, NW, Suite 300
Washington, DC 20006
(202) 778-4600

Founded in 1964. Assists, strengthens, and encourages free and democratic trade unions in Africa. Has undertaken projects in 43 countries in partnership with African trade unions. Programs are developed upon request and advice of African unions with knowledge of host government. Projects are geared to eventual assumption of complete managerial and financial responsibility by African labor movements. Objective is to help build sound national labor organizations that will be of lasting value to workers and the community, institutions that contribute to the economic and social development of their countries and to Africa's total political and economic independence. Major areas of activity are workers' education and leadership training, vocational training, cooperatives and credit unions, union medical and social service programs, administrative support for unions, and communication and information. Sponsors study tours and visitor programs to permit African and American trade unionists to become familiar with each other's politics, economies, and trade union movements; Africans are exposed to technical training not available in their homeland.

Africare
440 R Street, NW
Washington, DC 20001
(202) 462-3614

Founded in 1971. Seeks to improve the quality of life in rural Africa. Provides health and environmental protection services in rural areas of Africa; works to improve African water and agricultural resources; conducts public education programs in the United States on African development.

Alcoholism in the Black Community
ABC Addiction Services
East Orange General Hospital
East Orange, NJ 07019

All-African People's Revolutionary Party
1738 A Street, SE
Washington, DC 20003

Founded in 1971. Africans and persons of African descent who support Pan-Africanism, "the total liberation and unification of Africa under an all-African socialist government."

Alliance of Minority Women for Business and Political Development
PO Box 13858
Silver Spring, MD 20911-3858
(301) 230-5583

Founded in 1982. Objectives are to unite Minority women entrepreneurs and to encourage joint ventures and information exchange.

Alliance to End Repression
523 South Plymouth Ct., Suite 800
Chicago, IL 60605
(312) 427-4064

Founded in 1970. Religious, community, and human relations organizations united to safeguard the Bill of Rights and constitutional freedoms and to ensure the just application of state and local laws. Has initiated and developed three organizations: Citizens Alert (deals with police and community problems); Illinois Gay and Lesbian Task Force; and Illinois Prisons and Jails Project (monitoring county and state prisons). Other areas of activity include media accountability, cable television license ordinances, rights of minors, juvenile justice, national and state legislation, and rights of immigrants.

Alpha Kappa Alpha
5656 South Stony Island Avenue
Chicago, IL 60637
(317) 684-1282

Founded in 1908. Social and service sorority.

Alpha Phi Alpha
2313 St. Paul Street
Baltimore, MD 21218
(410) 554-0040

Founded in 1906. Service fraternity.

Alpha Pi Chi
PO Box 255
Kensington, MD 20895
(301) 559-4330

Founded in 1963. Service sorority.

American-African Affairs Association
1001 Connecticut Avenue, NW, Suite 1135
Washington, DC 20036
(202) 223-5110

Founded in 1965. Educational organization designed to circulate information about African countries to the people of the United States, especially with respect to "the cause of freedom in its struggle against world Communism and the best interests of the United States of America." Distributes literature to opinion molders, political leaders, university personnel, and business leaders, both here and in other countries.

American Association of Blacks in Energy
927 15th Street, NW, Suite 200
Washington, DC 20005
(202) 371-9530

Founded in 1977. Blacks in energy-related professions, including engineers, scientists, consultants, academicians, and entrepreneurs; government officials and public policymakers; interested students. Represents blacks and other minorities in matters involving energy use and research, the formulation of energy policy, the ownership of energy resources, and the development of energy technologies. Seeks to increase the knowledge, understanding, and awareness of the minority community in energy issues by serving as an energy information source for policymakers, recommending blacks and other minorities to appropriate energy officials and executives, encouraging students to pursue professional careers in the energy industry, and advocating the participation of blacks and other minorities in energy programs and policymaking activities. Updates members on key legislation and regulations being developed by the Department of Energy, the Department of Interior, the Department of Commerce, the Small Business Administration, and other federal and state agencies.

American Baptist Black Caucus
Beth Eden Baptist Church
Tenth and Adeline Streets
Oakland, CA 94607
(510) 444-1625

Founded in 1968. Concerned with reforming the American Baptist Convention in terms of bridging the gap between whites and minority members. Seeks to develop convention support for: scholarship aid for disadvantaged students; resources for business and religious projects in the inner city; adequate representation of minorities in the convention structure; support for black colleges and universities; open hiring policies on local, state, and national levels.

American Black Book Writers Association
PO Box 10548
Marina Del Rey, CA 90295
(213) 822-5195

Founded in 1980. Represents African Americans in the United States publishing industry. Encourages development of black authors; works to preserve and advance black literature. Promotes and gives market support to members' works; holds mutual promotions and tours; sponsors cooperative advertising in black-oriented media. Conducts research on problems affecting black authors and their works in the United States.

American Black Chiropractors Association
1918 East Grand Boulevard
St. Louis, MO 63107
(314) 531-0615

Founded in 1980. Objectives are to: educate the public, health care institutions, and health care providers about chiropractic and promote black chiropractic in the community; develop career orientation programs for high school and college students and sponsor schol-

arship funds; study history of chiropractic; sponsor publicity programs, public forums, counseling services, research, and establishment of free chiropractic clinics; provide for exchange of information, techniques, and reports of researchers and clinicians.

American Committee on Africa
198 Broadway
New York, NY 10038
(212) 962-1210

Founded in 1953. Devoted to supporting African people in their struggle for freedom and independence. Focuses on southern Africa and the Western Sahara and support for African liberation movements. Works with legislators, churches, trade unions, and interested students to help stop what the group feels is U.S. collaboration with racism in South Africa. Arranges speaking tours for African leaders; publicizes conditions and developments in Africa; sponsors research, rallies, and demonstrations.

Anti-Repression Resource Team
PO Box 8040
State College, PA 16803-8040
(814) 237-3095

Founded in 1979. Combats all forms of political repression including: police violence and misconduct; Ku Klux Klan and Nazi terrorism; spying and covert action by secret police and intelligence agencies. Focuses on research, writing, lecturing, organizing, and publishing. Conducts training workshops for church, labor, and community organizations.

Association of African American People's Legal Council
c/o William Bert Johnson
13902 Robson Street
Detroit, MI 48227
(313) 837-0627

Founded in 1959. Seeks to achieve equal justice under the law for African Americans and to provide free legal counsel to people of African American descent. Compiles statistics and reports on cases of international inequality. Obtains research from public systems on education and its effect on discrimination.

Association of Black Admissions and Financial Aid Officers of the Ivy League and Sister Schools
Admissions Office
PO Box 208234
Yale University
New Haven, CT 06520-8234
(203) 432-9316

Founded in 1970. Present and former minority admissions and financial aid officers employed at Ivy League or sister schools. These schools include: Brown, Columbia, Cornell, Dartmouth, Harvard/Radcliffe, Massachusetts Institute of Technology, University of Pennsylvania, Princeton, Yale, Barnard, Bryn Mawr, Mount Holyoke, Smith, and Wellesley. Aids minority students who wish to pursue a college education. Seeks to improve methods of recruitment, admittance, and financial services that support the growth and maintenance of the minority student population at these institutions. Encourages Ivy League and sister schools to respond to the needs of minority students and admissions and financial aid officers.

Association of Black Anthropologists

4350 North Fairfax Drive, Suite 640
Arlington, VA 22203
(703) 528-1902

Founded in 1970. Works to: formulate conceptual and methodological frameworks to advance understanding of all forms of human diversity and commonality; advance theoretical efforts to explain the conditions that produce social inequalities based on race, ethnicity, class, or gender; develop research methods that involve the peoples studied and local scholars in all stages of investigation and dissemination of findings.

Association of Black Cardiologists

13404 Southwest 128th Street, No. A
Miami, FL 33186-5800
(305) 641-2224

Founded in 1974. Seeks to improve prevention and treatment of cardiovascular diseases.

Association of Black Foundation Executives

1828 L Street, NW
Washington, DC 20036
(202) 466-6512

Founded in 1971. Encourages increased recognition of economic, educational, and social issues facing blacks in the grantmaking field. Promotes support of blacks and their status as grantmaking professionals. Seeks an increase in the number of blacks entering the grantmaking field; helps members improve their job effectiveness. Though involved with grantmaking organizations, the ABFE itself does not award grants.

Association of Black Nursing Faculty

5823 Queens Cove
Lisle, IL 60532
(708) 969-3809

Founded in 1987. Works to promote health-related issues and educational concerns of interest to the black community and ABNF. Serves as a forum for communication and the exchange of information among members; develops strategies for expressing concerns to other individuals, institutions, and communities. Assists members in professional development; develops and sponsors continuing education activities; fosters networking and guidance in employment and recruitment activities. Promotes health-related issues of legislation, government programs, and community activities.

Association of Black Psychologists

PO Box 55999
Washington, DC 20040-5999
(202) 722-0808

Founded in 1968. Aims to: enhance the psychological well-being of black people in America; define mental health in consonance with newly established psychological concepts and standards; develop policies for local, state, and national decision-making which have impact on the mental health of the black community; support established black sister organizations and aid in the development of new, independent black institutions to enhance the psychological, educational, cultural, and economic situation.

Association of Black Sociologists

Dept. of Sociology
Central Michigan University
Mt. Pleasant, MI 48859
(517) 774-3160

Founded in 1968. Purposes are to: promote the professional interests of black sociologists; promote an increase in the number of professionally trained sociologists; help stimulate and improve the quality of research and the teaching of sociology; provide perspectives regarding black experiences as well as expertise for understanding and dealing with problems confronting black people; protect professional rights and safeguard the civil rights stemming from executing the above objectives.

Association of Black Women in Higher Education

234 Hudson Avenue
Albany, NY 12210
(516) 572-7141

Founded in 1979. Objectives are to nurture the role of black women in higher education, and to provide support for the professional development goals of black women.

Association of Concerned African Scholars

PO Box 11694
Berkeley, CA 94701-2694

Founded in 1977. Facilitates scholarly analysis and opinion in order to impact U.S. policy toward Africa; formulates alternative government policy toward Africa and disseminates it to the public; works to develop a communication and action network among African scholars. Mobilizes support on current issues; participates in local public education programs; stimulates research on policy-oriented issues and disseminates findings; informs and updates members on international policy developments.

A Better Chance
419 Boylston Street
Boston, MA 02116
(617) 421-0950

Founded in 1963. Identifies, recruits, and places academically talented and motivated minority students into leading independent and selected public secondary schools. Prepares students to attend selective colleges and universities and encourages their aspirations to assume positions of responsibility and leadership in American society.

Big Eight Council on Black Student Government
Minority Student Services
Hester Hall, Room 213
731 Elm Avenue
University of Oklahoma
Norman, OK 73019

Founded in 1978. Black student unions and other groups at Big Eight Athletic Conference universities. Seeks to represent the concerns of black collegians at universities where the majority of students are white. Encourages the genesis of all black student organizations and lends support to them. Seeks to effect changes in curricula and to help legitimize and develop black studies departments as accredited degree programs. Functions as a communications medium among member schools and assists in efforts to reduce the attrition rate of black students. Promotes the placement of students and the hiring of black faculty and staff.

Black Affairs Center for Training and Organizational Development
c/o Margaret V. Wright
10918 Jarboe Court
Silver Spring, MD 20901
(301) 681-9827

Founded in 1970. Multidisciplinary management research organization which promotes social change, educational improvement, organization renewal and goal achievement, systematic problem solving, and multicultural skills development through custom-designed training programs and consultation services. Individuals, groups, educational systems, and governmental and community

agencies use programs such as Equal Employment Opportunity Training; Employee Motivation, Productivity and Improvement Training; Career Education and Development Training. Programs are continually being developed in areas including women's concerns, single parents, youth and sex, drugs and alcoholism, the aging, day-care, sexual harassment, and stress management.

Black American Cinema Society
3617 Monclair Street
Los Angeles, CA 90018
(213) 737-3292

Founded in 1975. Works to bring about an awareness of the contributions made by blacks to the motion picture industry in silent films, early talkies, and short and feature films. Feels that by viewing these films black children can see the sacrifice and humiliation endured by black actors and actresses, directors, film writers, and producers while making films. Maintains collection of early black films owned by the Western States Black Research Center. Conducts research projects, film shows, and Black History Month seminars. Provides financial support to independent black filmmakers.

Black American Response to the African Community
127 North Madison Avenue, Suite 400
Pasadena, CA 91101
(818) 584-0303

Founded in 1984. A grass roots organization of entertainers, journalists, clergy, and business, health, and community leaders working to assist the victims of drought and famine in Africa. Focuses on emergency efforts involving medical needs, water irrigation, housing, and food supplies. Provides relief for orphans through its Family Network Program. Disseminates current information on drought-stricken areas in Africa; assists in the development of regeneration projects in affected areas. Maintains the National Education Task Force to educate Americans on the African crisis; sponsors media updates.

Black Americans for Life
419 Seventh Street, NW, Suite 500
Washington, DC 20004
(202) 626-8800

Promotes alternatives to abortion for women with crisis pregnancies; strives to be a visible presence defending the rights of the unborn in the black community. Asserts that black women are twice as likely as white women to have abortions; believes that abortions are counterproductive to advances made through civil rights efforts.

Black and Indian Mission Office

2021 H Street, NW
Washington, DC 20006
(202) 331-8542

Founded in 1884. Coordinates the distribution of funds from the annual Black and Indian Mission Collection in Catholic churches across the United States; these funds go to support priests, nuns, and other religious workers at black and Indian missions and schools.

Black Awareness in Television

13217 Livernois
Detroit, MI 48238-3162
(313) 931-3427

Founded in 1970. Produces black media programs for television, video, radio, film, and theater. Trains individuals in the media and conducts research projects including surveys. Produces public affairs, cultural arts, soap opera, and exercise programs; sponsors theater companies. Seeks television exposure for black-produced products and black performing artists. Promotes "September is Black Reading Month" program.

Black Business Alliance

PO Box 26443
Baltimore, MD 21207
(410) 467-7427

Founded in 1979. Acts as a national and international support system for black businesses, providing assistance in organizational management and resource development. Provides children's services; sponsors fundraising events; offers placement services.

Black Caucus of Health Workers

353 Lewis
Carbondale, IL 62901

Black Caucus of the American Library Association

Newark Public Library
5 Washington Street
Newark, NJ 07101
(718) 522-4827

Founded in 1970. Promotes librarianship; encourages active participation of blacks in library associations and boards and all levels of the profession. Monitors activities of the American Library Association with regard to its policies and programs and how they affect black librarians and library users. Reviews, analyzes, evaluates, and recommends to the ALA actions that influence the recruitment, development, advancement, and general working conditions of black librarians.

Facilitates library services that meet the informational needs of black people including increased availability of materials related to social and economic concerns. Encourages development of authoritative information resources concerning black people and dissemination of this information to the public.

Black Citizens for a Fair Media

156-20 Riverside Drive, No. 13L
New York, NY 10032
(212) 568-3168

Founded in 1971. Community organizations concerned with employment practices in the television industry, images of black people projected by television, and how those images affect viewers. Works to improve programming, employment practices, and training of blacks; evaluates compliance with the Federal Communication Commission's equal opportunity rules for the electronic media. Believes that the airways belong to the people and seeks to prevent any change in that ownership.

Black Coaches Association

PO Box J
Des Moines, IA 50311
(515) 271-3010

Founded in 1986. Promotes the creation of a positive environment in which issues such as stereotyping, lack of significant media coverage, and discrimination can be exposed, discussed, and resolved. Provides member services. Petitions the NCAA legislative bodies to design, enact, and enforce diligent guidelines and policies to improve professional mobility for minorities.

Black Data Processing Associates

PO Box 7466
Philadelphia, PA 19101
(215) 843-9120

Founded in 1975. Seeks to accumulate and share information processing knowledge and business expertise in order to increase the career and business potential of minorities in the information processing field.

Black Entertainment and Sports Lawyers Association

3432 West Vollmer Road, Suite 314
Olympia Fields, IL 60461
(708) 798-3798

Founded in 1979. Purpose is to provide more efficient and effective legal representation to African American entertainers and athletes. Offers referral system for legal representation and a resource bank for providing information to students, groups, and nonprofit and civic organizations involved in the entertainment industry; and serves as an industry watchdog in protecting the rights of blacks within the entertainment community.

Black Filmmaker Foundation

Tribeca Film Center
375 Greenwich, Suite 600
New York, NY 10013
(212) 941-3944
Susan Christian, Exec. Dir.

Founded in 1978. Fosters audience development by programming local, national, and international film festivals. Maintains video library. Conducts seminars and workshops.

Black Filmmakers Hall of Fame, Inc.

405 14th Street, Suite 515
Oakland, CA 94612
(510) 465-0804

Founded in 1973. Seeks to study, teach, and preserve the contributions of black filmmakers to American cinema. Fosters cultural awareness through educational, research, and public service programs in the film arts. Holds film-lecture series, Black Filmworks Festival, and annual International Film Competition.

Black Health Research Foundation

14 East 60th Street, Suite 307
New York, NY 10022
(212) 408-3485

Founded in 1988. Voluntary health agency devoted to reducing preventable causes of premature death among African Americans. Funds scientific research in areas including AIDS, alcoholism, infant mortality, sickle cell disease, substance abuse, and other diseases that have a disproportionate impact on African Americans. Seeks recognition as the foremost authority on health and science regarding African Americans. Promotes professional and community education; recruits and trains volunteers. Seeks to influence public policy on crucial issues.

Black Methodists for Church Renewal

601 West Riverview Avenue
Dayton, OH 45406
(513) 227-9460

Founded in 1968. Serves as platform from which blacks can express concerns to the general church on issues such as: revival and survival of the black church; involvement of blacks within the structure of the church; the conduct of the church as it relates to investment policies and social issues; economic support in the black community; and the support of the 12 black colleges. Encourages black Methodists to work for economic and social justice. Works to expose racism in agencies and institutions of the United Methodist church. Seeks improvement of educational opportunities for blacks, the strengthening of black churches, and an increase in the number of black persons in Christian-related vocations. Advocates liberation, peace, justice, and freedom for all people. Supports programs that alleviate suffering in third world countries.

Black Military History Institute of America

PO Box 1134
Fort Meade, MD 20755
(410) 757-4250

Founded in 1987. Seeks to: provide archival facilities to collect, preserve, and exhibit materials pertaining to military history; motivate and support underprivileged youths by using military role models as a source of inspiration; foster a spirit of camaraderie and goodwill among all persons sharing an interest in community involvement programs for the underprivileged.

Black Psychiatrists of America

c/o Dr. Isaac Slaughter
2730 Adeline Street Oakland, CA 94607
(510) 465-1800

Founded in 1968. Black psychiatrists, either in practice or training, united to promote black behavioral science and foster high quality psychiatric care for blacks and minority group members. Sponsors public information service.

Black Resources Information Coordinating Services

614 Howard Avenue
Tallahassee, FL 32304
(904) 576-7522

Founded in 1972. Designed to solidify the various sources of information and research by and about minority groups in America and convert them into a coordinated information system by using bibliographic control, storage, retrieval, transfer, and dissemination. Focuses on information by and about African Americans, but also includes other minorities. Acts as referral and consulting service; aids in genealogical research and archival management and organization. Offers bibliographic services and lecture demonstrations on African American culture. Sponsors seminars, workshops, and institutes.

Black Revolutionary War Patriots Foundation

1612 K Street, NW, Suite 1104
Washington, DC 20006
(202) 452-1776

Founded in 1985. Raises private funds for the establishment of a memorial, in Washington, DC, to commemorate black patriots of the American Revolutionary War.

Black Rock Coalition
PO Box 1054, Cooper Station
New York, NY 10276
(212) 713-5097

Founded in 1985. Promotes, produces, and distributes alternative/black music and provides information, technical expertise, and performance and recording opportunities for "musically and politically progressive musicians." Also works to increase the visibility of black rock artists in music media and on college radio stations.

Black Silent Majority Committee of the U.S.A.
Box 5519
San Antonio, TX 78201
(210) 340-2424

Founded in 1970. Seeks to show the people of America and the world that there is a black majority in the United States which is patriotic and believes in saluting the flag, going to church, and paying taxes. Organizes Americans who do not want to be identified with black "radicals" and emphasizes the positive gains that blacks have made. Works throughout the United States and the world for better race relations. Opposes forced busing and supports prayer in public schools.

Black Student Leadership Network
25 East Street, N.W.
Washington, DC 20001
(202) 662-3515

Black Stuntmen's Association
8949 West 24th Street
Los Angeles, CA 90034
(213) 870-9020

Founded in 1966. Serves as an agency for stuntpeople in motion pictures and television. Plans to operate school for black stuntpeople.

Black Tennis and Sports Foundation
1893 Amsterdam Avenue
New York, NY 10032

Founded in 1977. Participants include members of the business community involved in sports who are dedicated to helping black and minority inner-city youths and developing athletes interested in tennis or other individual sports such as skating and gymnastics. Acts as a source of support and resources for black and minority youth. Organizes tennis teams and sponsors these teams and their coaches on trips and games overseas. Sponsors the Annual Arthur Ashe/Althea Gibson Tennis Classic in New York City.

Black Veterans for Social Justice
686 Fulton Street
Brooklyn, NY 11217
(718) 935-1116

Founded in 1979. Seeks to aid black veterans in obtaining information concerning their rights, ways to upgrade a less-than-honorable discharge, and Veterans Administration benefits due them and their families. Seeks to prohibit discrimination against black veterans. Provides educational programs; facilitates veterans' sharing of skills acquired while in service. Services include counseling and community workshops on veteran issues and a program to provide services to veterans in local prisons. Assists veterans who have suffered from the effects of Agent Orange, an herbicide containing dioxin, used as a defoliant in Vietnam until 1969.

Black Women in Church and Society
c/o Interdenominational Theological Center
671 Beckwith Street, SW
Atlanta, GA 30314
(404) 527-7740

Founded in 1982. Seeks to provide: structured activities and support systems for black women whose goals include participating in leadership roles in church and society; a platform for communication between laywomen and clergywomen. Conducts research into questions and issues pivotal to black women in church and society. Maintains a research/resource center and a library with subject matter pertaining to liberation and black theology, feminism, and womanist movements.

Black Women in Publishing
10 East 87th Street
New York, NY 10128
(212) 427-8100

Founded in 1979. A networking and support group whose purpose is to encourage minorities interested in all sectors of the print industry, including book, newspaper, and magazine publishing. Promotes the image of minorities working in all phases of the book, newspaper, and magazine industries; recognizes achievements of minorities in the media. Works for a free and responsible press. Facilitates the exchange of ideas and information among members, especially regarding career planning and job security. Keeps members informed about the publishing industry and their impact on it. Encourages and works to maintain high professional standards in publishing. Collaborates with other organizations in striving to improve the status of women and minorities.

Black Women Organized for Educational Development
518 17th Street, Suite 202
Oakland, CA 94612
(510) 763-9501

Founded in 1984. Fosters self-sufficiency in and encourages empowerment of low-income and socially disadvantaged women by establishing and maintaining programs that improve their social and economic well-being. Sponsors mentor program for junior high-aged young women in low-income urban areas; offers support groups, workshops, and seminars. Maintains Black Women's Resource Center, an information and referral service for African American women and youth.

Black Women's Agenda
208 Auburn Avenue, NE
Atlanta, GA 30303
(404) 524-8279

Founded in 1977. Works to educate the public about the economic, social, and political issues relevant to African American women. Recommends public policy that will benefit women and their families. Conducts workshops.

Black Women's Educational Alliance
6625 Greene Street
Philadelphia, PA 19119

Founded in 1976. Active and retired women in the field of education. Seeks a strong union among members in order to foster their intellectual and professional growth. Conducts public awareness programs to improve educational standards and delivery of educational services; works for equal opportunities for women.

Black Women's Network
PO Box 12072
Milwaukee, WI 53212
(414) 562-4500

Founded in 1979. Black professional women organized to improve the political, economic, and educational conditions of minority women. Offers support services and networking opportunities to address issues affecting African American women.

Black Women's Roundtable on Voter Participation
1629 K Street, NW, Suite 801
Washington, DC 20006
(202) 659-4929

Founded in 1983. A program of the National Coalition on Black Voter Participation (see separate entry). Black women's organizations committed to social justice and economic equity through increased participation in the political process. Organizes voter registration, education, and empowerment programs in the black community; emphasizes the importance of the women's vote. Seeks to: develop women's leadership skills through nonpartisan political participation; encourage black women's involvement in discussions concerning the influence of the women's vote in elections. Supports volunteer coalitions that work on voter registration, voter education, and get-out-the-vote efforts.

Black World Foundation
PO Box 2869
Oakland, CA 94609
(510) 547-6633

Founded in 1969. Black persons united to develop and distribute black educational materials and to develop black cultural and political thought. Offers books in the areas of black literature, history, fiction, essays, political analysis, social science, poetry, and art. Maintains library.

Blacks in Government
1820 Eleventh Street, NW
Washington, DC 20001-5015
(202) 667-3280

Founded in 1975. Federal, state, or local government employees or retirees concerned with the present and future status of blacks in government. Develops training and other programs to enhance the liberty and sense of well-being of blacks in government.

Blacks in Law Enforcement
256 East McLemore Avenue
Memphis, TN 38106
(901) 774-1118

Founded in 1986. Seeks to educate the public concerning the contributions made by blacks in the field of law enforcement. Documents the lives and achievements of the first blacks to participate in law enforcement in the United States. Develops programs to improve the public image of law enforcement officers; has established a short-term training program for law enforcement officers.

Catholic Interracial Council of New York
899 Tenth Avenue
New York, NY 10019
(212) 237-8255

Founded in 1934. Works in cooperation with local parishes and governmental and voluntary groups to combat bigotry and discrimination and to promote social justice for all racial, religious, and ethnic groups.

Sponsors research, educational forums, workshops, and community action programs. Presents annual John LaFarge Memorial Award for Interracial Justice to community leaders and annual Hoey Award to community leaders who have worked to promote objectives of the council.

Center for Constitutional Rights
666 Broadway, Seventh Floor
New York, NY 10012
(212) 614-6464

Founded in 1966. Works in areas such as abuse of the grand jury process, women's rights, civil rights, freedom of the press, racism, electronic surveillance, criminal trials, and affirmative action. Conducts the Ella Baker Student Program, the Movement Support Network, and in Mississippi, The Voting Rights Project.

Center for Third World Organizing
1218 East 21st Street
Oakland, CA 94606-3132
(510) 533-7583

Founded in 1980. Provides training, issue analyses, and research to low-income minority organizations including welfare, immigrant, and Native American rights groups. Monitors and reports on incidents of discrimination against people of color. Sponsors Minority Activist Apprenticeship Program, which works to develop minority organizers and leaders for minority communities.

Center for Urban Black Studies
Graduate Theological Union
2465 LeConte Avenue
Berkeley, CA 94709
(415) 841-8401

Founded in 1969. Provides seminarians and laypersons with resources "to respond to life in the urban community and to represent its oppressed minority people." Develops and offers courses, seminars, and other training programs dealing with issues of race, social justice, urban life, and the black religious experience. Initiates new ministries; develops and implements community service programs; counsels and assists black seminarians in placement and in obtaining and developing employment. Conducts workshops and seminars addressing racial justice, church and race, and urban ministry.

Chi Eta Phi
3029 13th Street, NW
Washington, DC 20009
(202) 232-3858

Founded in 1932. Registered and student nurses. Objectives are to: encourage continuing education; stimulate friendship among members; develop working relationships with other professional groups for the improvement and delivery of health care services. Sponsors leadership training seminars. Offers educational programs for entrance into nursing and allied health fields. Presents scholarships and other financial awards to assist students. Sponsors recruitment and retention programs for minority students. Operates speakers' bureau on health education and biographical archives on African American nurses.

Christians Concerned for Racial Equality
PO Box 1643
Oroville, WA 98844
(604) 498-3895

Citizens for a Better America
PO Box 356
Halifax, VA 24558
(804) 476-7757

Founded in 1975. Churches and individuals united to create a better America by strengthening individual rights in the United States. Serves as a public advocacy organization that lobbies for civil rights and environmental legislation. Conducts legal research in civil rights cases; provides research services to communities investigating issues such as fair housing and toxic waste disposal.

Coalition of Black Trade Unionists
PO Box 66268
Washington, DC 20035
(202) 429-1203

Founded in 1972. Members of 76 labor unions united to maximize the strength and influence of black and minority workers in organized labor. Activities include voter registration and education, improvement of economic development, and employment opportunities for minority and poor workers. Sponsors regional seminars.

Co-ette Club
2020 West Chicago Boulevard
Detroit, MI 48206
(313) 867-0880

Founded in 1941. Teenage high school girls "outstanding in one or all of the following categories—Academic Scholarship, School and Community, Extra-Curricular, Community Volunteer Service, and Leadership." Helps members channel interests and become leaders in educational, cultural, and artistic activities on local and national levels. Raises funds for the United Negro College Fund and contributes to local charity and social service groups in each community.

Commission for Racial Justice
475 Riverside Drive, 16th Floor
New York, NY 10115
(212) 870-2077

Founded in 1963. A racial justice agency representing the 1.7 million members of the United Church of Christ. Promotes human rights programs and strategies to foster racial justice in black, Third World, and other minority communities.

Community Access Producers and Viewers Association
PO Box 68002
Jackson, MS 39286-8002
(601) 352-3398

Founded in 1965. Researches activities of workers, blacks, and grass roots organizations through the FIS Deep South People's History Project. Maintains extensive Mississippi-centered library and archives. Distributes press releases on current southern news; reprints items on women's liberation and political education.

Conference of Minority Public Administrators
1120 G Street, NW, Suite 700
Washington, DC 20005
(202) 393-7878

Founded in 1971. Members of the American Society of Public Administration who belong to a minority group or are interested in the promotion of minorities within public administration.

Conference of Prince Hall Grand Masters
Fourth and State Streets
Pine Bluff, AR 71601

Congress of National Black Churches
1225 I Street, NW, Suite 750
Washington, DC 20005-3914
(202) 371-1091

Founded in 1978. Seeks to find answers to problems that confront blacks in the United States and Africa, including economic development, family and social support, housing, unemployment, education, and foreign relations. Focus is on religious education and evangelism.

Congressional Black Associates
1504 Longworth
Washington, DC 20515
(202) 225-5865

Founded in 1979. Provides information on the operations of the federal government to members and the black community; fosters contacts among members and the community. Works to enhance the social, political, and economic status of all people, but concentrates on the black experience in America.

Congressional Black Caucus
2244 Rayburn
Washington, DC 20515
(202) 225-3121

Founded in 1971. Black members of the U.S. House of Representatives. Seeks to address the legislative concerns of black and other underrepresented citizens and to formalize and strengthen the efforts of its members. Establishes a yearly legislative agenda setting forth the key issues which it supports: full employment, national health care, education, minority business assistance, urban revitalization, rural development, welfare reform, and international affairs. Works to implement these objectives through personal contact with other House members, through the dissemination of information to individual black constituents, and by working closely with black elected officials in other levels of government. Operates the Congressional Black Caucus Foundation.

Delta Sigma Theta
1707 New Hampshire Avenue, NW
Washington, DC 20009
(202) 986-2400

Founded in 1913. Service sorority.

Educational Equity Concepts
114 East 32nd Street, Suite 701
New York, NY 10016
(212) 725-1803

Founded in 1982. Organized to create educational programs and materials that are free of sex, race, and disability bias. Offers training programs for parents, teachers, and students; conducts seminars, symposia, and workshops. Provides conference planning, consulting, and materials development services. Conducts Women and Disability Awareness Project, which discusses and writes on matters concerning disabled women, feminism, and the links between the disability rights and women's movements.

Episcopal Commission for Black Ministries
815 Second Avenue
New York, NY 10017
(212) 867-8400

Founded in 1973. Works to strengthen the witness of black Episcopalians in the church through programs that include parish and clergy development, scholarships and grants, and international relations. Provides financial assistance and consultations to parishes and church organizations.

Eta Phi Beta
c/o Elizabeth Anderson
1724 Mohawk Boulevard
Tulsa, OK 74110
(918) 425-8612

Founded in 1942. Professional business sorority.

Institute for the Advanced Study of Black Family Life and Culture
175 Filbert Street, Suite 202
Oakland, CA 94607
(510) 836-3245

Seeks to reunify African American families and to revitalize the black community. Advocates the reclamation of what the group considers traditional African American culture. Conducts research on issues impacting the black community such as teenage pregnancy, child-rearing practices, mental health support systems, and the effects of alcohol and drugs. Maintains HAWK Federation (High Achievement, Wisdom, and Knowledge Federation), a training program employed in school systems to aid in the character development of young black males. Sponsors in-service training for agencies, school systems, and the juvenile justice system. Develops training curricula for teen parents.

International Association of African and American Black Business People
18900 Schoolcraft
Detroit, MI 48223

Founded in 1965. Establishes, operates, and fosters business education and related activities among African American and African members of the business community worldwide.

International Association of Black Professional Fire Fighters
8700 Central Avenue, Suite 206
Landover, MD 20785
(301) 808-0804

Founded in 1970. Strives to: promote interracial communication and understanding; recruit blacks for the fire services; improve working conditions for blacks in the fire services; assist blacks in career advancement; promote professionalism; represent black fire fighters before the community.

International Black Toy Manufacturers Association
PO Box 348
Springfield Gardens, NY 11413

Founded in 1987. Works to provide shelf space and distribution opportunities commensurate with the spending power of the black community. Promotes black toy manufacturers.

International Black Women's Congress
1081 Bergen Street
Newark, NJ 07112
(201) 926-0570

Founded in 1983. Objective is to unite members for mutual support and socioeconomic development through: annual networking tours to Africa; establishing support groups; assisting women in starting their own businesses; assisting members in developing resumes and other educational needs; offering to answer or discuss individual questions and concerns.

International Black Writers
PO Box 1030
Chicago, IL 60690
(708) 331-6421

Founded in 1970. Seeks to discover and support new black writers. Conducts research and monthly seminars in poetry, fiction, nonfiction, music, and jazz. Operates library of 500 volumes on black history. Provides writing services and children's services. Plans to establish hall of fame, biographical archives, and museum.

International Black Writers and Artists
PO Box 43576
Los Angeles, CA 90043
(213) 964-3721

Founded in 1974. Black writers and artists in the United States and West Indies. Provides encouragement and support to members.

International Committee Against Racism
231 West 29th Street
Brooklyn, NY 10001
(212) 629-0003

Founded in 1973. Is dedicated to fighting all forms of racism and to building a multi-racial society. Opposes racism in all its economic, social, institutional, and cultural forms. Believes racism destroys not only those minorities that are its victims, but all people.

International Council of African Women
PO Box 91812
Washington, DC 20090
(202) 546-8459

Founded in 1982. Promotes worldwide networking between African American women. Addresses such issues as: employment, poverty and welfare, health, child care, housing. Disseminates information to disadvantaged women on developments and events of interest to women. Conducts self-help programs.

Iota Phi Lamba

503 Patterson Street
Tuskegee, AL 36088
(205) 727-5210

Founded in 1929. Business and professional civic sorority. Seeks to develop leadership expertise among business and professional women. Promotes increased interest in business education among high school and college women through planned programs and scholarships.

John Brown Anti-Klan Committee

PO Box 14422
San Francisco, CA 94114
(415) 567-9699

Activists fighting racism and sexism; advocates of freedom for political prisoners. (Abolitionist John Brown is best known for his command of the "raiders", a group of men who burned a U.S. armory at Harpers Ferry in 1859 in order to further the fight against slavery.) Offers educational programs. Disseminates information.

Kappa Alpha Psi

2322-24 North Broad Street
Philadelphia, PA 19132
(215) 228-7184

Founded in 1911. Social fraternity.

Leadership Conference on Civil Rights

1629 K Street, NW, Suite 1010
Washington, DC 20006
(202) 466-3311

Founded in 1950. Coalition of national organizations working to promote passage of civil rights, social and economic legislation, and enforcement of laws already on the books. Has released studies examining former President Ronald Reagan's tax and budget programs in areas including housing, elementary and secondary education, social welfare, Indian affairs, and tax cuts. Has evaluated the enforcement of activities in civil rights by the U.S. Department of Justice; has also reviewed civil rights activities of the U.S. Department of Education.

Minorities in Media

PO Box 9198
Petersburg, VA 23806
(804) 524-5902

Founded in 1975. Works to facilitate communication and convey ideas in the area of educational communications and technology.

Minority Business Enterprise Legal Defense and Education Fund

900 Second Street, Suite 8
Washington, DC 20002
(202) 289-1700

Founded in 1980. Serves as an advocate and legal representative for the minority business community.

Most Worshipful National Grand Lodge Free and Accepted Ancient York Masons

PO Box 2789
Orangeburg, SC 29116-2789
(803) 531-1985

Founded in 1847. Also known as the Most Worshipful National Grand Lodge Free and Accepted Ancient York Masons Prince Hall Origin National Compact U.S.A.

NAACP Legal Defense and Educational Fund

99 Hudson Street, 16th Floor
New York, NY 10013
(212) 219-1900

Founded in 1940. Legal arm of the civil rights movement, functioning independently of the National Association for the Advancement of Colored People since the mid-1950s. Works to provide and support litigation in behalf of blacks, other racial minorities, and women defending their legal and constitutional rights against discrimination in employment, education, housing, and other areas. Represents civil rights groups as well as individual citizens who have bona fide civil rights claims. Contributed funds are used to finance court actions for equality in schools, jobs, voting, housing, municipal services, land use, and delivery of health care services. Has organized litigation campaign for prison reform and the abolition of capital punishment. Hosts annual institute to develop public awareness of new problems being faced by minorities. Maintains Herbert Lehman Education Fund, through which scholarships are awarded to black students attending state universities; sponsors Earl Warren Legal Training Program, which provides scholarships to black law students.

National Action Council for Minorities in Engineering

3 West 35th Street
New York, NY 10001
(212) 279-2626

Founded in 1980. Seeks to increase the number of minority students enrolled in and graduating from engineering schools. Works with support organizations to motivate and encourage pre-college students to engage in engineering careers. Operates project to assist engineering schools in improving the retention and graduation rates of minority students.

National Alliance Against Racist and Political Repression
11 John Street, Room 702
New York, NY 10038
(212) 406-3330

Founded in 1973. Coalition of political, labor, church, civic, student, and community organizations; individuals dedicated to protecting people's right to organize. Seeks to mobilize millions of people to unite in word and action against many forms of repression of human rights in the United States including: persecution and jailing of political activists; attempts to suppress prisoners' rights movements and use of behavior control against prisoners and the poor; assaults on labor's right to organize, strike, and act effectively; police crimes against the people, especially nonwhites; legislation and court decisions repressing basic rights; the death penalty.

National Alliance of Black Interpreters
PO Box 70322
New Orleans, LA 70172-0322
(504) 943-6597

National Alliance of Black Organizations
3724 Airport Boulevard
Austin, TX 78722
(512) 478-9802

Founded in 1976. Presidents of black organizations and associations. Coordinates and encourages voter registration efforts among member organizations. Serves as a forum for the exchange of ideas and experiences.

National Alliance of Black School Educators
2816 Georgia Avenue, NW
Washington, DC 20001
(202) 483-1549

Founded in 1970. Purpose is to promote awareness, professional expertise, and commitment among black educators. Goals are to: eliminate and rectify the results of racism in education; work with state, local, and national leaders to raise the academic achievement level of all black students; increase members' involvement in legislative activities; facilitate the introduction of a curriculum that more completely embraces black America; improve the ability of black educators to promote problem resolution; create a meaningful and effective network of strength, talent, and professional support. Plans to establish a National Black Educators Data Bank and offer placement service.

National Alumni Council of the United Negro College Fund
8260 Willow Oaks Corporate Drive
PO Box 10444
Fairfax, VA 22031
(703) 205-3463

Founded in 1946. Provides a structure for cooperation among black college alumni groups and friends of black colleges. Works to acquaint the public with the value of black colleges and black higher education. Informs students and the public about contributions of black college alumni to civic betterment and community progress. Recruits students for United Negro College Fund member colleges.

National Association for Black Veterans
PO Box 11432
Milwaukee, WI 53211
(414) 265-8940

Founded in 1970. Represents the interests of minority veterans before the Veterans Administration. Operates Metropolitan Veterans Service to obtain honorable discharges for minority and low-income veterans who in the organization's opinion unjustly received a less than honorable discharge. Defends incarcerated veterans through its Readjustment Counseling Program; operates job creation program; offers services to geriatric and homeless veterans.

National Association for Equal Educational Opportunities
2181 Brigden Road
Pasadena, CA 91104
(714) 856-6362

Founded in 1975. College and university professionals concerned with the development and operation of secondary school and collegiate programs to serve the needs of low-income and disadvantaged students.

National Association for the Advancement of Black Americans in Vocational Education
PO Box 04437
Detroit, MI 48204
(313) 494-1660

Founded in 1977. Goal is to generate national leadership and increase the impact of blacks in the field of vocational/technical education by: assuring opportunities and promoting recruitment and the retention of black Americans in all areas and levels; utilizing research discoveries as a basis for influencing key funding sources at the national, state, and local levels; providing a career information exchange system. Develops training models for marketable skills; links black talent with vocational/technical employment opportunities in the public and private sectors at the federal, state, and local levels; identifies, assesses, and evaluates critical issues that affect the extent of participation of blacks and offers recommendations for improvement.

National Association for the Advancement of Colored People
4805 Mt. Hope Drive
Baltimore, MD 21215
(410) 358-8900

Founded in 1909. Persons "of all races and religions" who believe in the objectives and methods of the NAACP. To achieve equal rights through the democratic process and eliminate racial prejudice by removing racial discrimination in housing, employment, voting, schools, the courts, transportation, recreation, prisons, and business enterprises. Offers referral services, tutorials, job referrals, and day care. Sponsors seminars; maintains law library. Awards Spingarn Medal annually to a black American for distinguished achievement. Sponsors the NAACP National Housing Corporation to assist in the development of low and moderate income housing for families.

National Association of Black Accountants
7249A Hanover Parkway
Greenbelt, MD 20770
(301) 474-6222

Founded in 1969. Works to unite accountants and accounting students who have similar interests and ideals, who are committed to professional and academic excellence, who possess a sense of professional and civic responsibility, and who are concerned with enhancing opportunities for minorities in the accounting profession.

National Association of Black and White Men Together
1747 Connecticut Ave. NW
Washington, DC 20009-1108
(800) NA4-BWMT, (202) 462-3599
Fax: (202) 462-3690

National Association of Black Catholic Administrators
1531 West Ninth Street
Los Angeles, CA 90015-1194
(213) 251-3435

Founded in 1976. Assists the church in its role of evangelization and in defining its mission to the black community. Seeks to provide an inner resource for the social and spiritual needs and concerns of Catholics of African ancestry.

National Association of Black Consulting Engineers
1979 Beaumont Drive
Baton Rouge, LA 70806
(504) 927-7240

Founded in 1975. Purpose is to gain recognition and increase professional opportunities for black consulting engineers. Lobbies the federal government.

National Black Deaf Advocates
c/o Arkansas Rehabilitation Services
PO Box 3781
1616 Brookwood
Little Rock, AR 72203
(501) 296-1635
TDD: (501) 296-1670
Fax: (501) 296-1675

National Association of Black Geologists and Geophysicists
PO Box 720157
Houston, TX 77272

Founded in 1981. Assists minority geologists and geophysicists in establishing professional and business relationships. Informs minority students of career opportunities in geology and geophysics. Seeks to motivate minority students to utilize existing programs, grants, and loans. Provides scholarships and oversees the educational careers of scholarship recipients.

National Association of Black Hospitality Professionals
PO Box 8132
Columbus, GA 31908-8132
(706) 569-6105

Founded in 1985. Works to develop global educational and economic opportunities for the hospitality industry through the expansion and diversification of minority involvement in the industry. Encourages professional development and opportunity in the industry through the design and implementation of workshops and seminars. Seeks to increase the number, size, and capability of minority-owned businesses within the hospitality and tourism industries.

National Association of Black Journalists
PO Box 17212
Washington, DC 20041
(703) 648-1270

Founded in 1975. Aims are to: strengthen the ties between blacks in the black media and blacks in the white media; sensitize the white media to the "institutional racism in its coverage"; expand the white media's coverage and "balanced reporting" of the black community; become an exemplary group of professionals that honors excellence and outstanding achievement among black journalists. Works with high schools to identify potential journalists; awards scholarships to journalism programs that especially support minorities.

National Association of Black Owned Broadcasters
1333 New Hampshire Avenue, NW, Suite 1000
Washington, DC 20036
(202) 463-8970

Founded in 1976. Represents the interests of existing and potential black radio and television stations. Is currently working with the Office of Federal Procurement Policy to determine which government contracting major advertisers and advertising agencies are complying with government initiatives to increase the amount of advertising dollars received by minority-owned firms. Conducts lobbying activities; provides legal representation for the protection of minority ownership policies.

National Association of Black Professors
PO Box 526
Crisfield, MD 21817
(410) 968-2393

Founded in 1974. Goals are to: provide a forum for the exchange of information among college professors; enhance education for black people and enrich the educational process in general; support and promote intellectual interests of black students.

National Association of Black Real Estate Professionals
PO Box 21421
Alexandria, VA 22320
(703) 920-7661

Founded in 1984. Provides a forum for the discussion of information related to the industry. Offers career development and networking opportunities.

National Association of Black Social Workers
271 West 125th, Room 317
New York, NY 10027
(212) 348-0035

Founded in 1968. Seeks to support, develop, and sponsor community welfare projects and programs which will serve the interest of the black community and aid it in controlling its social institutions. Assists with adoption referrals.

National Association of Black Storytellers
PO Box 67722
Baltimore, MD 21215
(410) 947-1117

Founded in 1984. Seeks to establish a forum to promote the black oral tradition and to attract an audience. Works for the reissue of out-of-print story collections.

National Association of Black Women Attorneys
724 Ninth Street, NW, Suite 206
Washington, DC 20001
(202) 637-3570

Founded in 1972. Seeks to: advance jurisprudence and the administration of justice by increasing the opportunities of black and non-black women at all levels; aid in protecting the civil and human rights of all citizens and residents of the United States; expand opportunities for women lawyers through education; promote fellowship among women lawyers.

National Association of Black Women Entrepreneurs
PO Box 1375
Detroit, MI 48231
(313) 559-9255

Founded in 1979. Black women who own and operate their own businesses; black women interested in starting businesses; organizations and companies desiring mailing lists. Acts as a national support system for black businesswomen in the United States and focuses on the unique problems they face. Objective is to enhance business, professional, and technical development of both present and future black businesswomen.

National Association of Blacks in Criminal Justice
Criminal Justice Building, Room 106
PO Box 19788
Durham, NC 27707
(919) 683-1801

Founded in 1972. Criminal justice professionals concerned with the impact of criminal justice policies and practices on the minority community. Advocates with local, state, and federal criminal justice agencies for the improvement of minority recruitment practices and for the advancement of minority career mobility within those agencies. Sponsors regional conferences, career development seminars, and annual training institutes; maintains speakers' bureau. Provides financial and in-kind services to community groups.

National Association of Blacks Within Government
1820 Eleventh Street, NW
Washington, DC 20001-5015
(202) 667-3280

Founded in 1982. Purpose is to enhance and increase the employability of black officials within government and to prepare black youths for government and private sector careers. Sponsors yearly seminar to help young people develop management, learning, interpersonal, and specialized skills.

National Association of Colored Women's Clubs
5808 16th Street, NW
Washington, DC 20011
(202) 726-2044

Founded in 1896. Federation of black women's clubs. Carries on civic service, education, social service, and philanthropy programs.

National Association of Investment Companies
1111 14th Street, NW, Suite 700
Washington, DC 20005
(202) 289-4336

Founded in 1971. Represents the minority small business investment company industry. Monitors regulatory action. Collects and disseminates trade and business information.

National Association of Minority Automobile Dealers
1250 Connecticut Avenue, NW
Washington, DC 20036
(202) 637-9095

Founded in 1980. Serves as a liaison between automobile dealers, the government, the community, and industry representatives.

National Association of Minority Contractors
1333 F Street, NW, Suite 500
Washington, DC 20004
(202) 347-8259

Founded in 1969. Minority construction contractors and companies interested in doing business with minority contractors. Identifies procurement opportunities. Provides specialized training. Serves as a national advocate for minority construction contractors.

National Association of Minority Political Women
6120 Oregon Avenue, NW
Washington, DC 20015
(202) 686-1216

Founded in 1983. Professional women interested in the American political process. Conducts research and educational programs.

National Association of Minority Women in Business
906 Grand Avenue, Suite 200
Kansas City, MO 64106
(816) 421-3335

Founded in 1972. Serves as a network for the exchange of ideas and information on business opportunities for minority women.

National Association of Negro Business and Professional Women's Clubs
1806 New Hampshire Avenue, NW
Washington, DC 20009
(202) 483-4206

Founded in 1935. Women actively engaged in a business or a profession and who are committed to rendering service through club programs and activities.

National Association of Negro Musicians
11551 South Laflin Street
Chicago, IL 60643
(312) 568-3818

Founded in 1919. Promotes the advancement of all types of music, especially among young black musicians. Sponsors annual competitions in which winners compete for scholarships.

National Association of Urban Bankers
1010 Wayne Avenue, Suite 1210
Silver Spring, MD 20910
(301) 589-2141

Founded in 1975. Minority professionals in the financial services industry.

National Bankers Association
1802 T. Street, NW
Washington, DC 20009
(202) 588-5432

Founded in 1927. Minority banking institutions. Serves as an advocate for the minority banking industry.

National Bar Association
1225 Eleventh Street, NW
Washington, DC 20001
(202) 842-3900

Founded in 1925. Minority attorneys, members of the judiciary, law students, and law faculty. Sponsors educational and research programs.

National Black Alcoholism Council

1629 K Street, NW, Suite 802
Washington, DC 20006
(202) 296-2696

Founded in 1978. Works to support and initiate activities that will improve alcoholism treatment services and lead to the prevention of alcoholism in the black community. Provides training on how to treat black alcoholics from a cultural perspective. Compiles statistics concerning alcoholism among blacks.

National Black Catholic Clergy Caucus

343 North Walnut Street
PO Box 1088
Opelousas, LA 70571
(318) 942-2392

Founded in 1968. Black priests, brothers, seminarians, and deacons. Purpose is to support the spiritual, theological, educational, and ministerial growth of the black Catholic community within the church. Serves as a vehicle to bring contributions of the black community to the church. Advances the fight against racism within the Catholic church and society.

National Black Catholic Seminarians Association

780 Porter Street
Beaumont, TX 77701

Founded in 1969. Black Catholic seminarians united for the growth and development of each member as a person, Christian, and potential priest or religious brother. "Attempts to reflect both the heritage of the church and black people in terms of the richness of their spirituality." Stresses the importance of individual contribution and total involvement of each black seminarian to the organization.

National Black Caucus of Local Elected Officials

1301 Pennsylvania Avenue, NW, Suite 600
Washington, DC 20004
(202) 626-3000

Founded in 1970. Elected black municipal and county officials united to recognize and deal with problems of members. Attempts to provide the organizational structure required to better present and respond to issues affecting constituents. Seeks to influence the National League of Cities in the development of policies affecting black Americans; promotes legislative and economic development initiatives directed toward the needs of the black community.

National Black Caucus of State Legislators

Hall of States
444 North Capitol Street, NW, Suite 622
Washington, DC 20001
(202) 624-5457

Founded in 1977. Organized to provide more political networking to black legislators from the federal and state levels. Goals are to: provide a network through which state legislators can exchange information and ideas on state and national legislation; provide a unified front or platform; serve as a focal point for involvement of black legislators in the "new federalism." Activities include arranging meetings between all governmental groups representing black elected officials and analyzing and forming a position on the "new federalism." Conducts seminars. Maintains speakers' bureau and biographical archives; compiles statistics.

National Black Chamber of Commerce

117 Broadway
Oakland, CA 94609-1709
(510) 215-5410

Founded in 1983. Black chambers of commerce organized to create a strategy for members of local chambers to share in the collective buying power of black minority communities. Primary focus is on the tourism industry, because, according to the association, blacks spend approximately $25 billion in the tourism market each year, but black-owned businesses net very little from this industry. Conducts training sessions to acquaint black businesspeople with the tourism market and marketing strategies.

National Black Child Development Institute

1023 15th Street, NW, Suite 600
Washington, DC 20005
(202) 387-1281

Founded in 1970. Conducts direct services and advocacy campaigns aimed at both national and local public policies focusing on issues of health, child welfare, education, and child care. Organizes and trains network of members in a volunteer grassroots affiliate system to voice concerns regarding policies that affect black children and their families. Stimulates communication between black community groups, through conferences and seminars, to discuss and make recommendations that will be advantageous to the development of black children. Analyzes selected policy decisions and legislative and administrative regulations to determine their impact on black children and youth. Informs national policymakers of issues critical to black children.

National Black Coalition of Federal Aviation Employees

Washington Headquarters
PO Box 44392
Washington, DC 20026-4392
(202) 267-7911

Founded in 1976. Purposes are to: promote professionalism and equal opportunity in the workplace; locate and train qualified minorities for FAA positions; help the FAA meet its affirmative action goals; monitor black, female, and minority trainees; educate members and the public about their rights and FAA personnel and promotion qualifications; develop a voice for black, female, and minority FAA employees.

National Black Gay and Lesbian Leadership Forum (BGLLF)

1219 S. La Brea Ave.
Los Angeles, CA 90019
(213) 964-7820
Fax: (213) 964-7830

The nation's leading organization addressing the leadership and skill development needs of the black lesbian and gay communities relative to social, legal, economic, and health issues. BGLLF maintains the AIDS Prevention Team, an innovative national AIDS education and prevention model. Other major BGLLF programming includes the Womyns Caucus and sponsorship of the 1995 "Black Lesbian and Gay Leadership Summit: Our Families, Our Communities, Our Lives." Held in Los Angeles, sessions included symposiums, on AIDS/health care and public policy; workshops on community organizing and outreach; and an awards ceremony.

National Black Law Student Association

1225 Eleventh Street, NW
Washington, DC 20001

Founded in 1967. Black law students united to meet the needs of black people within the legal profession and to work for the benefit of the black community. Objectives are to: articulate and promote professional competence, needs, and goals of black law students; focus on the relationship between black students and attorneys and the American legal system; instill in black law students and attorneys a greater commitment to the black community; encourage the legal community to bring about change to meet the needs of the black community.

National Black Leadership Roundtable

1424 Longworth House Building
Washington, DC 20515

Founded in 1983. Goals are to: provide a forum for leaders of national black organizations to discuss and exchange ideas on issues critical to black Americans; aid in the development of political, economic, and networking strategies that are advantageous to the needs of the black community; ensure that elected and appointed officials represent and are accountable to the black community.

National Black MBA Association

180 North Michigan Avenue, Suite 1515
Chicago, IL 60601
(312) 236-2622

Founded in 1971. Business professionals, lawyers, accountants, and engineers concerned with the role of blacks who hold Master of Business Administration degrees. Encourages blacks to pursue continuing business education; assists students preparing to enter the business world. Provides programs for minority youths, students, and professionals, including workshops, panel discussions, and Destination MBA seminar. Works with graduate schools; grants scholarships to graduate business students.

National Black McDonald's Operators Association

6363 West Sunset Boulevard, Suite 809
PO Box 8204
Los Angeles, CA 90008
(213) 296-5495

Founded in 1972. Provides a forum for the exchange of ideas on the improvement of community relations and on the operation and management of restaurants. Seeks to build and improve the McDonald's restaurant image throughout the community. Sponsors training seminars on marketing, better sales practices, labor relations, and profit sharing.

National Black Media Coalition

38 New York Avenue, NE
Washington, DC 20002
(202) 387-8155

Founded in 1973. Black media advocacy group seeking to maximize media access for blacks and other minorities in the communications industry through employment, ownership, and programming. Has been recognized by the FCC, Congress, and trade organizations concerned with blacks and other minorities in the media. Past activities include participating in FCC rulemaking proceedings, speaking before university and professional audiences, conducting classes, and negotiating affirmative action plans with large media corporations.

National Black Music Caucus of the Music Educators National Conference

University of Michigan School of Music
Ann Arbor, MI 48109
(313) 764-0586

Founded in 1972. Purpose is to foster the creation, study, and promotion of black-derived music in education. Seeks to heighten public awareness of the problems faced by black music educators and students and to increase public understanding of those problems. Provides a forum for the discussion of concerns. Coordinates and disseminates materials concerning black-derived music in order to assist music teachers in teaching black music and students. Encourages blacks to aspire to leadership positions and to demand inclusion in the development and presentation of Music Educators National Conference activities, including participation in MENC's regional conferences.

National Black Nurses Association

1511 K Street, NW., Suite 415
Washington, DC 20005
(202) 393-6870

Founded in 1971. Functions as a professional support group and as an advocacy group for the black community and their health care. Recruits and assists blacks interested in pursuing nursing as a career.

National Black on Black Love Campaign

1000 East 87th Street
Chicago, IL 60619
(312) 978-0868

Founded in 1983. Individuals and businesses united to promote the motto, "Replace Black on Black crime with Black on Black love" and foster love and respect in all communities where people are, the group believes, inordinately affected by crime. Organizes No Crime Day in various communities and Adopt A Building Program for businesses. Sponsors youth organizations and seminars in schools and communities to educate the public in ways of dealing with crime.

National Black Police Association

3251 Mt. Pleasant Street, NW
Washington, DC 20010-2103
(202) 986-2070

Founded in 1972. Seeks to: improve relationships between police departments and the black community; recruit minority police officers on a national scale; eliminate police corruption, brutality, and racial discrimination.

National Black Programming Consortium

929 Harrison Avenue, Suite 101
Columbus, OH 43215
(614) 299-5355

Founded in 1979. Objectives are to: assist the public broadcasting system in supplying programming that serves the needs of all population segments of the United States; serve as a collection, distribution, and archival center for black-oriented television programming; coproduce black programming; serve as a liaison between the black community and telecommunications systems with regard to black programming; provide funds for and encourage more and better black productions. Participates in the acquisition and distribution of programs for the cable and international markets.

National Black Republican Council

375 South End Avenue, Plaza 400-84
New York, NY 10280
(212) 662-1335

Founded in 1972. Black Republicans in the United States. Works to elect more black Republicans to national, state, and local offices. Maintains speakers' bureau.

National Black Sisters' Conference

3027 Fourth Street, NE
Washington, DC 20017
(202) 529-9250

Founded in 1968. Seeks to develop the personal resources of black women; challenges society, especially the church, to address issues of racism in the U.S. Activities include: retreats; consulting, leadership, and cultural understanding; formation workshops for personnel. Maintains educational programs for facilitating change and community involvement in inner-city parochial schools and parishes. Operates Sojourner House to provide spiritual affirmation for black religious and laywomen.

National Black Survival Fund

PO Box 3885
Lafayette, LA 70502-3885
(318) 232-7672

Founded in 1982. A project of the Southern Development Foundation. Objective is to improve the ability of black and other minority poor to achieve economic progress through their own effort and initiative. Believes that the economic, cultural, and physical survival of the nation's black community is endangered due to the recession, discrimination, and government cutbacks in social assistance programs. Seeks to maintain and increase support for programs that can avert the economic and human catastrophe the fund says will result if the opportunities offered to blacks are undermined by current assistance cutbacks. Maintains: Food for Survival Program in which landowners and sharecroppers in Mississippi volunteer land, equipment, and labor to provide food and employment for needy families; Health Care for Survival Program, a cooperative low-cost health center in Mississippi; Jobs for Survival Program, which has assisted in providing jobs for black workers in Alabama in construction, farming, and community service.

National Black United Front
PO Box 470665
Brooklyn, NY 11247

Founded in 1980. Purpose is to unite black people of diverse political ideologies, age groups, socioeconomic backgrounds, and religious beliefs in order to build "a viable force for social transformation." Goals are: the elimination of racism, sexism, bigotry, and racial violence; redistribution of the resources and wealth of the nation to provide abundantly for all citizens; elimination of the "genocidal mis-education system," police brutality, and denial of human rights nationally and internationally. Believes that current conditions in the United States threaten the survival of black people as a whole, and urges blacks to overlook individual differences by working together for common goals. Addresses such issues as unemployment, police brutality, budget cuts harmful to black communities, and the resurgence of the Ku Klux Klan. Conducts seminars and forums; maintains speakers' bureau; offers charitable program; sponsors competitions. Plans to organize boycotts, hold demonstrations, engage in electoral politics, and seek new vehicles for change.

National Black United Fund
50 Park Pl., Suite 1538
Newark, NJ 07102
(201) 643-5122

Founded in 1972. Provides financial and technical support to projects serving the critical needs of black communities nationwide. Local affiliates solicit funds through payroll deduction to support projects in the areas of education, health and human services, economic development, social justice, arts and culture, and emergency needs. Programs supported by NBUF emphasize self-help, volunteerism, and mutual aid. Maintains Walter Bremond Memorial Fund campaign.

National Black Women's Consciousness Raising Association
1906 North Charles Street
Baltimore, MD 21218
(410) 727-8900

Founded in 1975. Acts as a support group for women. Provides educational and informational workshops and seminars on subjects of concern to black women and women in general.

National Black Women's Health Project
1237 Ralph David Abernathy Boulevard, SW
Atlanta, GA 30310
(404) 758-9590

Founded in 1981. Encourages mutual and self-help advocacy among women to bring about a reduction in health care problems prevalent among black women. Urges women to communicate with health care providers, seek out available health care resources, become aware of self-help approaches, and communicate with other black women to minimize feelings of powerlessness and isolation, and thus realize they have some control over their physical and mental health. Points out the higher incidence of high blood pressure, obesity, breast and cervical cancers, diabetes, kidney disease, arteriosclerosis, and teenage pregnancy among black women than among other racial or socioeconomic groups. Also notes that black infant mortality is twice that of whites and that black women are often victims of family violence. Offers seminars outlining demographic information, chronic conditions, the need for health information and access to services, and possible methods of improving the health status of black women. Sponsors Center for Black Women's Wellness.

National Black Women's Political Leadership Caucus
3005 Bladensburg Road, NE, No. 217
Washington, DC 20018
(202) 529-2806

Founded in 1971. Women interested in understanding their political role and the need for females to work toward equality; auxiliary membership includes men, senior citizens, and youths. Works to educate and incorporate all black women and youth in the political and economic process through participation. Encourages women to familiarize themselves with the role of city, state, and federal governments. Presents awards for humanitarianism; trains speakers and conducts research on the black family and on topics concerning politics and economics; compiles statistics.

National Black Youth Leadership Council

250 West 54th Street, Suite 800
New York, NY 10019
(212) 541-7600

Founded in 1983. Conducts workshops for groups involved with black youth and minority student academic and leadership development; works to reduce the number of minority students that do not finish high school. Provides resources, information, skills, and strategies for fostering such development. Advises educators and parents on their role and responsibility to display leadership and success skills to youths they come in contact with; makes available to educational institutions training and expertise on cultural diversity, multiculturalism, and problems of bigotry and racism. Sponsors drug abuse awareness programs.

National Brotherhood of Black Skiers

National Headquarters
1525 East 53rd Street, Ste. 408
Chicago, IL 60615
(312) 955-4100

Founded in 1975. Bringing together African American ski clubs throughout the United States. A primary focus of the group is sponsoring black youth in hopes of placing an African American on the U.S. Ski Team and eventually getting a black skier into the Olympics.

National Business League

1511 K. Street, NW, Suite 432
Washington, DC 20005
(202) 737-4430

Founded in 1900. Encourages minority ownership and management of small businesses and supports full minority participation in the free enterprise system.

National Catholic Conference for Interracial Justice

3033 Fourth Street, NE
Washington, DC 20017-1102
(202) 529-6480

Founded in 1959. Catholic organization working for interracial justice and social concerns in America. Initiates programs within and outside the Catholic church to end discrimination in community development, education, and employment.

National Caucus and Center on Black Aged

1424 K Street, NW, Suite 500
Washington, DC 20005
(202) 637-8400

Founded in 1970. Seeks to improve living conditions for low-income elderly Americans, particularly blacks. Advocates changes in federal and state laws in improving the economic, health, and social status of low-income senior citizens. Promotes community awareness of problems and issues effecting low-income aging population. Operates an employment program involving 2000 older persons in 14 states. Sponsors, owns, and manages rental housing for the elderly. Conducts training and intern programs in nursing home administration, long-term care, housing management, and commercial property maintenance.

National Center for the Advancement of Blacks in the Health Professions

PO Box 21121
Detroit, MI 48221
(313) 345-4480

Founded in 1988. Participants belong to organizations including the American Public Health Association, National Urban League, National Black Nurses Association, and the American Hospital Association. Promotes the advancement of blacks in the health professions. Publicizes the disparity between the health of black and white Americans and its relationship to the underrepresentation of blacks in the health professions. (According to the National Center for Health Statistics, blacks have a higher death rate from cancer, heart disease, stroke, and diabetes than whites; blacks also have a higher infant mortality rate.) Acts as clearinghouse.

National Coalition for Quality Integrated Education

1201 16th Street, NW
Washington, DC 20036
(202) 822-7708

Founded in 1975. National organizations committed to desegregating and improving the quality of elementary and secondary schools in the United States. Serves as a forum for issues and developments pertaining to quality integrated education; encourages and coordinates citizen involvement in legislative developments.

National Coalition of Black Lesbians and Gays

New York, NY
(718) 622-3576

National Coalition of Black Meeting Planners

8630 Fenton Street, Suite 328
Silver Spring, MD 20910
(202) 628-3952

Founded in 1983. Purposes are to: act as liaison with hotels, airlines, convention centers, and bureaus in an effort to assess the impact of minorities in these fields; assess the needs of the convention industry and how best to meet these needs; enhance members' sophistication in planning meetings; maximize employment of minorities in the convention industry.

National Coalition of 100 Black Women
38 West 32nd Street, 16th Floor
New York, NY 10001-3816
(212) 974-6140

Founded in 1981. African American women actively involved with issues such as economic development, health, employment, education, voting, housing, criminal justice, the status of black families, and the arts. Seeks to provide networking and career opportunities for African American women in the process of establishing links between the organization and the corporate and political arenas. Encourages leadership development; sponsors role-model and mentor programs to provide guidance to teenage mothers and young women in high school or who have graduated from college and are striving for career advancement.

National Coalition on Black Voter Participation
1629 K Street, NW, Suite 801
Washington, DC 20006
(202) 659-4929

Founded in 1976. Seeks to: increase black voter registration and participation in electoral voting; develop and fund local independent coalitions that will conduct campaigns to increase nonpartisan voter participation and citizenship empowerment programs. Conducts training programs. Collects and analyzes data; disseminates information on voter education including data on the black voting age population. Sponsors Operation Big Vote and Black Women's Roundtable on Voter Participation.

National Conference of Black Lawyers
2 West 125th Street
New York, NY 10027
(212) 864-4000

Founded in 1968. Maintains projects in legal services to community organizations, voting rights, and international affairs; provides public education on legal issues affecting blacks and poor people. Researches racism in law schools and bar admissions. Conducts programs of continuing legal education for member attorneys. Maintains general law library. Compiles statistics; maintains lawyer referral and placement services.

National Conference of Black Mayors
1422 West Peachtree Street, NW, Suite 800
Atlanta, GA 30309
(404) 892-0127

Founded in 1974. Objectives are to: improve the executive management capacity and efficiency of member municipalities in the delivery of municipal services; create viable communities within which normal government functions can be performed efficiently; provide the basis upon which new social overhead investments in the infrastructure of municipalities can utilize federal, state, local, and private resources to encourage new industry and increase employment; assist municipalities in stabilizing their population through improvements of the quality of life for residents and, concurrently, create alternatives to outward migration. Facilitates small town growth and development through energy conservation.

National Conference of Black Political Scientists
c/o Franklin D. Jones
Dept. of Public Affairs
Texas Southern University
Houston, TX 77045
(404) 656-0763

Founded in 1969. Political and social science faculty, lawyers, and related professionals interested in black politics and related fields. Seeks to encourage research, publication, and scholarship by black Americans in political science; and to improve the political life of black Americans.

National Conference of Black Student Retention
PO Box 10121
Tallahassee, FL 32302-2121
(904) 599-3466

Founded in 1985. Members share programs, research, and strategies to reduce the dropout rate of minority students in colleges and universities.

National Consortium for Black Professional Development
PO Box 18308
Louisville, KY 40218-0308
(502) 896-2838

Founded in 1974. Goal is to increase substantially, by the year 2000, the number of black professionals in business administration, communications, applied and natural sciences, engineering, and law. Sponsors a science and engineering competition for black students and Ph.D. programs in the agricultural sciences and business administration. Maintains clearinghouse and placement bureau for black professionals seeking employment. Provides recruitment service for universities seeking qualified black faculty and students.

National Consortium of Arts and Letters for Historically Black Colleges and Universities

c/o Dr. Walter Anderson
The Westbridge, Suite 818
2555 Pennsylvania Avenue, NW
Washington, DC 20037
(202) 833-1327

Founded in 1984. Encourages academic excellence with an emphasis on cultural growth. Promotes study of African American history and culture in the context of the scholarly study of world cultures. Offers no grants, but helps sponsor programs through fundraising efforts.

National Council for Black Studies

Ohio State University
208 Mount Hall
1050 Carmack Road
Columbus, OH 43210
(614) 292-1035

Founded in 1975. Faculty members, students, and institutions united to promote and strengthen academic and community programs in black and/or African American studies. Bestows awards for scholarly contributions; sponsors undergraduate and graduate student essay contests. Offers professional opportunities referral service; compiles statistics on black studies activities including information on students, faculty, research, and curricula.

National Council of Negro Women

1001 G Street, NW, Suite 800
Washington, DC 20006
(202) 628-0015

Founded in 1935 by Mary McLeod Bethune. Assists in the development and utilization of the leadership of women in community, national, and international life. Maintains the Women's Center for Education and Career Advancement, which offers programs designed to aid minority women in pursuing nontraditional careers; also maintains the Bethune Museum and Archives for Black Women's History.

National Council on Black Aging

Box 51275
Durham, NC 27717
(919) 493-4858

Founded in 1975. Persons interested in research and policies affecting older blacks and other minorities and

in the dissemination of research findings. Maintains speakers' bureau. Conducts lectures on minority aging.

National Emergency Civil Liberties Committee

175 Fifth Avenue, Room 814
New York, NY 10010
(212) 673-2040

Founded in 1951. To reestablish in full the traditional freedoms guaranteed under the Constitution and Bill of Rights. Committee "stands uncompromisingly for civil liberties for everyone and every variety of dissent." Legal staff handles test cases in the courts, without charge to the clients. Also functions as information service.

National Forum for Black Public Administrators

777 North Capitol Street, NE, Suite 807
Washington, DC 20002
(202) 408-9300

Founded in 1983. Works to promote, strengthen, and expand the role of blacks in public administration. Seeks to focus the influence of black administrators toward building and maintaining viable communities. Develops specialized training programs for managers and executives. Provides national public administrative leadership resource and skills bank. Works to further communication among black public, private, and academic institutions. Addresses issues that affect the administrative capacity of black managers. Maintains Executive Leadership Institute which grooms mid-level executives for higher positions in government, the Mentor Program which matches aspiring black managers with seasoned executives over an 8-month period, and the Leadership Institute for Small Municipalities, which provides intensive training for elected and appointed officials from small communities. Offers training programs for black South Africans intent on achieving public administrative positions in the post-apartheid era. Sponsors the National Minority Business Development Forum to increase the participation of small and minority businesses in local government procurement and contracting programs.

National Hook-Up of Black Women

c/o Wynetta Frazier
5117 South University Avenue
Chicago, IL 60615
(312) 643-5866

Founded in 1975. Purpose is to provide a communications network in support of black women who serve in organizational leadership positions, especially those elected or appointed to office and those wishing to elevate their status through educational and career ventures. Works to form and implement a Black Women's Agenda that would provide representation for women, families, and communities and that would help surmount economic, educational, and social barriers. Supports efforts of the Congressional Black Caucus in utilizing the legislative process to work toward total equality of opportunity in society. Seeks to highlight the achievements and contributions of black women.

National Institute Against Prejudice and Violence
Towson State University
Stephens Hall Annex
Towson, MD 21204-7097
(410) 830-2435

Founded in 1984. Purpose is to study and respond to the problem of violence and intimidation motivated by racial, religious, ethnic, or anti-gay prejudice. Collects, analyzes, produces, and disseminates information and materials on programs of prevention and response. Conducts research on the causes and prevalence of prejudice and violence and their effects on victims and society; provides technical assistance to public agencies, voluntary organizations, schools, and communities in conflict; analyzes and drafts model legislation; conducts educational and training programs; sponsors conferences, symposia, and other forums for information exchange among experts.

National Minority AIDS Council
300 I St. NE, #400
Washington, DC 20012
(202) 544-1076

National Minority Health Association
PO Box 11876
Harrisburg, PA 17108
(717) 763-1323

Founded in 1987. Health care providers and associations, consumers, executives and administrators, educators, pharmaceutical and health insurance companies, and other organizations with an interest in health. Seeks to focus attention on the health needs of minorities.

National Office for Black Catholics
3025 Fourth Street, NE
Washington, DC 20017
(202) 635-1778

Founded in 1970. Participating organizations include National Black Sisters' Conference; National Black Catholic Clergy Caucus. Serves as a "foundation for the renewal of the credibility of the church in the black community." Works to coordinate actions designed "to liberate black people and to serve as a unifying strength." Plans to: have specialists and technicians working within the black community to coordinate community or-

ganization and development; provide leadership training for youth; attack problems of poverty and deprivation; sensitize blacks to their heritage through historical, cultural, and liturgical experience. Seeks cooperation with groups working toward black liberation. Concerns include: training black and white clergy and religious, Catholic, and non-Catholic laity; influencing decisions involving race and the church; monitoring, in order to prevent, manifestations of racism. Sponsors Pastoral Ministry Institute and Afro-American Culture and Worship Workshop; provides workshops and leadership training for parish councils and parochial schools.

National Organization for the Professional Advancement of Black Chemists and Chemical Engineers
525 College Street, NW
Washington, DC 20059
(202) 667-1699

Founded in 1972. Seeks to aid black scientists and chemists in reaching their full professional potential; encourages black students to pursue scientific studies and employment; promotes participation of blacks in scientific research. Provides volunteers to teach science courses in selected elementary schools; sponsors scientific field trips for students; maintains speakers' bureau for schools; provides summer school for students of the U.S. Naval Academy. Conducts technical seminars in Africa.

National Organization of Black College Alumni
PO Box 729
Bluefield, WV 24701
(304) 325-6869

Founded in 1982. Works to ensure the survival of black colleges by addressing their concerns and needs and providing resources to meet these needs. Coordinates and focuses alumni support for black colleges; strengthens existing alumni associations; urges black youth to obtain a college education.

National Organization of Black County Officials
440 First Street, NW, Suite 500
Washington, DC 20001
(202) 347-6953

Founded in 1982. Black county officials organized to provide program planning and management assistance to selected counties in the United States. Acts as a technical information exchange to develop resolutions to problems on the local and national levels. Promotes the sharing of knowledge and methods of improving resource utilization and government operations. Conducts seminars and training sessions. Plans to maintain resource file on the achievements and history of black county officials.

National Organization of Black Law Enforcement Executives
4609 Pinecrest Office Park Drive, Suite 2-F
Alexandria, VA 22312
(703) 658-1529

Founded in 1976. Goals are: to provide a platform from which the concerns and opinions of minority law enforcement executives and command-level officers can be expressed; to facilitate the exchange of programmatic information among minority law enforcement executives; to increase minority participation at all levels of law enforcement; to eliminate racism in the field of criminal justice; to secure increased cooperation from criminal justice agencies; to reduce urban crime and violence. Seeks to develop and maintain channels of communication between law enforcement agencies and the community; encourages coordinated community efforts to prevent and abate crime and its causes.

National Rainbow Coalition, Inc.
1700 K Street, NW, Suite 800
Washington, DC 20006
(202) 728-1192

Founded in 1984 by the Reverend Jesse L. Jackson. Works to build a consensus in the area of civil rights, government, politics, labor, education, and business. Provides a platform for debate; encourages the development of a new political leadership committed to progressive domestic and international policies and programs.

National Society of Black Engineers
1454 Duke Street
Alexandria, VA 22313-5588
(703) 549-2207

Founded in 1975. Seeks to increase the number of minority graduates in engineering and technology.

National Society of Black Physicists
1601 East Market Street
101 Martena Hall
Greensboro, NC 27411
(919) 334-7646

Addresses the needs of black physicists; works to create opportunities for minorities in the field. Sponsors mentor program and lectures on research findings.

National Urban Coalition
8601 Georgia Avenue, Suite 500
Silver Spring, MD 20910
(301) 495-4999

Founded in 1967. The National Urban Coalition seeks to improve the quality of life for the disadvantaged in urban areas through the combined efforts of business, labor, government, and community leaders. Operates programs which work to increase the participation by minority students in science, math, and computer education; operates the Say Yes to a Younger's Future program.

National Urban League
500 East 62nd Street
New York, NY 10021
(212) 310-9000

Founded in 1910. Aims to eliminate racial segregation and discrimination in the United States and to achieve parity for blacks and other minorities in every phase of American life. Works to eliminate institutional racism and to provide direct service to minorities in the areas of employment, housing, education, social welfare, health, family planning, mental retardation, law and consumer affairs, youth and student affairs, labor affairs, veterans' affairs, and community and minority business development.

Negro Airmen International
PO Box 1340
Tuskegee, AL 36087
(205) 727-0721

Founded in 1967. Seeks greater participation of blacks in the field of aviation through the encouragement of broader job opportunities. Encourages black youth to remain in school and enter the field. Maintains a Summer Flight Academy for teenagers at Tuskegee Institute in Alabama.

Office for Advancement of Public Black Colleges of the National Association of State Universities and Land Grant Colleges
1 Dupont Circle NW, Suite 710
Washington, DC 20036-1191
(202) 778-0818

Founded in 1968. Collects, organizes, interprets, and disseminates data on 35 predominantly black public colleges. The colleges, located in 18 states, enroll over 135,000 students.

Omega Psi Phi
2714 Georgia Avenue, NW
Washington, DC 20001
(202) 667-7158

Founded in 1911. Social fraternity.

Operation Crossroads Africa

475 Riverside Drive, Room 830
New York, NY 10115
(212) 870-2106

Founded in 1958. Students and professionals, mostly from the United States, who live and work with African counterparts during July and August on self-help community development projects in Africa. Opportunities are provided for interaction with village elders, educators, and political and other community leaders. Emphasizes community growth from within a "Third World" structure. Before departure, participants make an intensive study of Africa; after their return, they give speeches about their experiences. Participants pay part of the cost of the project. Organizes workcamp projects for U.S. high school students in the Caribbean and programs the visits of African and Caribbean leaders to the United States. Sponsors training and exchange programs.

Operation PUSH (People United to Save Humanity)

930 East 50th Street
Chicago, IL 60615
(312) 373-3366

Founded in 1971 by the Reverend Jesse Jackson. National and international human rights organization directed toward education and economic equity and parity for all, particularly black, Hispanic, and poor people. Seeks to create an ethical atmosphere; encourages self and community motivation and social responsibility. Sponsors PUSH for Education Program to aid the nation's public schools and restore academic excellence and discipline.

Organization of Black Airline Pilots

PO Box 5793
Englewood, NJ 07631
(201) 568-8145

Founded in 1976. Seeks to enhance minority participation in the aerospace industry. Maintains liaison with airline presidents and minority and pilot associations. Conducts lobbying efforts, including congressional examinations into airline recruitment practices. Provides scholarships; cosponsors Summer Flight Academy for Youth at Tuskegee Institute in Alabama.

Phi Beta Sigma

145 Kennedy Street, NW
Washington, DC 20011-5294
(202) 726-5424

Founded in 1914. Service fraternity. Sponsors the Sigma Beta Club for high school aged males.

Phylaxis Society

PO Box 75680
Washington, DC 20013

Founded in 1973. Prince Hall Masonic writers and editors of Masonic publications.

Planning and the Black Community

Department of the Army
PO Box C-3755
Seattle, WA 98124-2255
(206) 764-3614

Founded in 1980. Members of the American Planning Association interested in issues related to planning in the black community. Objectives are to: formulate and articulate positions on national, regional, and statewide policy issues related to blacks for presentation to the APA and the public; provide a forum for exchange of practical experience and knowledge among black planners; establish and strengthen liaison with black professionals and groups such as social workers, economists, lawyers, public administrators, International City Management Association, National Association for the Advancement of Colored People, and National League of Cities.

Project Equality

1020 East 63rd Street, Suite 102
Kansas City, MO 64110
(816) 361-9222

Founded in 1965. A nationwide interfaith program enabling religious organizations, institutions, and others to support equal opportunity employers with their purchasing power. Services include: validation of hotels for conventions and meetings of organizations, validations of suppliers to member organizations and institutions, and consultant and educational services to assist employers in affirmative action and equal employment opportunity programs.

Quality Education for Minorities Network

1818 N Street, NW, Suite 350
Washington, DC 20036
(202) 659-1818

Founded in 1987. Created to implement the plan developed by the Quality Education for Minorities Project. Believes that minorities are underserved by the educational system and thus disproportionately lack the skill needed to participate effectively in a society increasingly based on high technology. Plans to work with school systems, communities, universities, and public and private sector institutions to ensure that minority students have equal access to educational opportunities.

Sigma Pi Phi

920 Broadway, Suite 703
New York, NY 10010
(212) 477-5550

Founded in 1904. Social fraternity. Maintains the Boule Foundation. Sigma Pi Phi is the oldest black Greek letter society in the United States.

Southern Christian Leadership Conference

334 Auburn Avenue, NE
Atlanta, GA 30303
(404) 522-1420

Founded in 1957. Nonsectarian coordinating and service agency for local organizations seeking full citizenship rights, equality, and the integration of African Americans in all aspects of life in the United States and subscribing to the Ghandian philosophy of nonviolence. Works primarily in 16 southern and border states to improve civic, religious, economic, and cultural conditions. Fosters nonviolent resistance to all forms of racial injustice, including state and local laws and practices. Conducts leadership training program embracing such subjects as registration and voting, social protest, use of the boycott, picketing, nature of prejudice, and understanding politics. Sponsors citizenship education schools to teach reading and writing, help persons pass literacy tests for voting, and provide information about income tax forms, tax-supported resources, aid to handicapped children, public health facilities, how government is run, and social security. Conducts Crusade for the Ballot, which aims to double the black vote in the South through increased voter registrations.

Southern Coalition for Educational Equity

PO Box 22904
Jackson, MS 39225-2904
(601) 362-6774

Founded in 1978. Coalition of parents, students, teachers, and administrators that operates in Alabama, Georgia, Louisiana, Mississippi, and North Carolina, with plans to include eight additional states. Works toward developing more efficient educational programs and eliminating racism and sexism within southern schools. Has organized projects including: Arkansas Career Resources Project, which provides minorities and single heads of households with marketable skills and jobs; New Orleans Effective Schools Project, which attempts to increase school effectiveness through high expectations, stressing academic achievement, and quality instruction; Project MiCRO, which seeks to provide computer access for, and sharpen analytical skills of, minority students; Summer Program, which focuses on students' reading comprehension skills.

Southern Poverty Law Center

PO Box 2087
Montgomery, AL 36102
(205) 264-0286

Founded in 1971. Seeks to protect and advance the legal and civil rights of poor people, regardless of race, through education and litigation. Does not accept fees from clients. The center is currently involved in several lawsuits representing individuals injured or threatened by activities of the Ku Klux Klan and related groups. Attempts to develop techniques and strategies that can be used by private attorneys. Operates Klanwatch.

Southern Regional Council

1900 Rhodes Haverty Building
134 Peachtree Street, NW
Atlanta, GA 30303-1825
(404) 522-8764

Founded in 1944. Leaders in education, religion, business, labor, the community, and the professions interested in improving race relations and combatting poverty in the South. Comprises an interracial research and technical assistance center that addresses issues of social justice and political and economic democracy. Seeks to engage public policy as well as personal conscience in pursuit of equality. Develops educational programs; provides community relations consultation and field services when requested by official and private agencies. Distributes pamphlets pertaining to desegregation of various public facilities and fosters elimination of barriers to black voting registration. Acts as official sponsor of overseas government officials, leaders, and other visitors who wish to view race relations in the South.

Special Committee on the Situation With Regard to the Implementation of the Declaration on the Granting of Independence to Colonies

United Nations, Room S-3341
New York, NY 10017
(212) 963-5515

Founded in 1961. United Nations committee comprising representatives of 25 nations concerned with the progress of people under colonial rule toward self-determination and independence. Considers situations in 18 territories based on information received from administering powers or local governments, nongovernmental organizations, published sources, and observations of the committee's visiting missions. Reviews military activities and activities of foreign economic interests in colonial territories; enlists support of United Nations specialized agencies and international institutions to assist decolonization efforts, especially through aid to colonial people; seeks to mobilize public opinion in support of decolonization by disseminating information.

369th Veteran's Association
369th Regiment Armory
1 369th Plaza
New York, NY 10037
(212) 281-3308

Founded in 1953. Seeks to support all patriotic endeavors of the United States, and to assist members and their families through charitable programs and community activities. Donates funds, equipment, and other supplies to children's camps, needy families, religious institutions, Veterans Administration Hospitals, and community and senior citizen centers. Conducts seminar and counseling sessions to assist unemployed veterans, and offers study classes to adults for preparation in Civil Service examinations.

Trade Union Leadership Council
8670 Grand River Avenue
Detroit, MI 48204
(313) 894-0303

Founded in 1957. Seeks to eradicate injustices perpetrated upon people because of race, religion, sex, or national origin. Seeks increased leadership and job opportunities for blacks.

TransAfrica
1744 R Street, NW
Washington, DC 20009
(202) 797-2301

Founded in 1977. Concerned with the political and human rights of people in Africa and the Caribbean, and those of African descent throughout the world. Attempts to influence U.S. foreign policy in these areas by informing the public of violations of social, political, and civil rights, and by advocating a more progressive attitude in the U.S. policy stance. Supports the work of the United Nations in Africa. Sponsors TransAfrica Action Alert to mobilize black opinion nationally on foreign policy issues by contacting influential policymakers.

TransAfrica Forum
1744 R Street, NW
Washington, DC 20009
(202) 797-2301

Founded in 1981. Research and education arm of TransAfrica. Seeks to provide an independent review of differing perspectives on political, economic, and cultural issues affecting black communities globally through its publications. Conducts seminars with scholars and government officials.

Try Us Resources
2105 Central Avenue, NE
Minneapolis, MN 55418
(612) 781-6819

Founded in 1968. Compiles and publishes minority business directories. Sponsors minority purchasing seminars.

Tuskegee Airmen, Inc.
2643 Jackson Street
Denver, CO 80205
(313) 965-8858

Founded in 1972. Former airmen who flew in the segregated U.S. Army Air Corps during World War II, men and women involved in military aviation, service academies, and ROTC units. Seeks to maintain a relationship among those who fought and served in World War II. Provides information about the contributions black Americans have made to aviation history. Operates a museum at Historic Fort Wayne in Detroit, MI.

Unitarian Universalist Association Black Concerns Working Group
25 Beacon Street
Boston, MA 02108
(617) 742-2100

Founded in 1985. Attempts to raise denominational public awareness of racism as a current justice issue. Works to implement recommendations regarding racial justice that were adopted by the Unitarian Universalist General Assembly in 1985. Conducts local and regional workshops in an effort to coordinate racial justice work among Unitarian Universalist congregations.

United Black Christians
1380 East Hyde Park Boulevard, No. 815
Chicago, IL 60615

Founded in 1970. Seeks to increase the relevance of United Church of Christ in the struggle for liberation and justice.

United Black Church Appeal
c/o Christ Church
860 Forest Avenue
Bronx, NY 10456
(718) 665-6688

Founded in 1980. Objective is to awaken the power of the black clergy and the black church to provide leadership for the liberation of the black community. Is concerned with black economic development and political power, and the strengthening of black families and churches. Believes pastors in black churches should reestablish legitimate leadership roles within the black community. Works with troubled black youths in the community; rallies against drugs in urban areas. Supports community betterment projects including surplus food programs and distribution of food to needy families.

United Black Fund of America
1101 14th Street, NW, Suite 601
Washington, DC 20005
(202) 783-0430

Founded in 1969. Nonprofit agencies that provide human care services to low-income or disabled blacks and other minorities. Assists disadvantaged blacks and other minorities in becoming self-sufficient by providing funding to member agencies for the establishment of health and welfare programs.

United Church of Christ Commission for Racial Justice
c/o United Church of Christ
700 Prospect Avenue, East
Cleveland, OH 44115-1110
(216) 736-2161

Founded in 1965. Works to ensure racial justice and social equality for ethnic and racial minorities worldwide. Maintains higher education program to provide scholarships to minority college students.

United Negro College Fund
8260 Willow Oak Corporation Drive
Fairfax, VA 22031
(703) 205-3432

Founded in 1944. Fundraising agency for historically black colleges and universities which are private and fully accredited. Provides information on educational programs. Sponsors college fairs for high school and community college students. Administers scholarship awards and corporate and foundation programs.

Universal Masonic Brotherhood
PO Box 1067
South Orange, NJ 07079
(201) 763-1780

Universal Masonic Order of the Eastern Star
PO Box 1067
South Orange, NJ 07079
(201) 763-1780

Universal Negro Improvement Association and African Communities League of the World
1611 West Columbia Avenue
Philadelphia, PA 19151
(215) 236-6063

Washington Office on Africa
110 Maryland Avenue, NE, Suite 112
Washington, DC 20002
(202) 546-7961

Founded in 1972. Established to monitor and analyze developments in U.S. policy toward southern Africa and work with national and local groups which support the attainment of majority rule. Lobbies on congressional legislation affecting southern Africa.

World Africa Chamber of Commerce
PO Box 33144
Washington, DC 20033

Founded in 1973. Sponsors trade missions to Africa and seminars to assist members with personal contacts and in gaining knowledge in the market and the needs of the countries they service. Conducts research and development studies on the changing economic developments and attitudes in specific countries and on the continent as a whole. Provides professional consulting in areas including market development, export promotion, joint venture projects, trade finance counseling, and market research studies. Operates trade center to provide facilities for exhibits, meetings, and other activities. Additional services include: assistance with visas and business trip planning; job referrals; clearinghouse on business, political, and cultural information; office and secretarial aid for businessmen and dignitaries traveling abroad. Maintains the Continental Africa Chamber Foundation.

Young Black Programmers Coalition
PO Box 1051
Vicksburg, MS 39181
(601) 631-7191

Founded in 1976. Provides professional training and offers technical assistance to black entrepreneurs in the broadcast and music industries. Conducts lobbying activities pertaining to legislation affecting the music industry. Provides scholarships to attend black colleges and universities.

Zeta Phi Beta
1734 New Hampshire Avenue, NW
Washington, DC 20009
(202) 387-3103

Founded in 1920. Service and social sorority. Maintains the Zeta Phi Beta Sorority Educational Foundation.

10

Law

Law

◆ The Legal Status of African Americans: 1790-1883
◆ African Americans and the Criminal Justice System
◆ African Americans in the Federal Courts ◆ African Americans on the U.S. Supreme Court
◆ Major Federal Legislation ◆ Major U.S. Supreme Court Decisions ◆ Legal Gatekeepers

by George R. Johnson, Jr., Marilyn Hortense Mackel, and Lorna M. Mabunda

◆ THE LEGAL STATUS OF AFRICAN AMERICANS: 1790-1883

by George R. Johnson, Jr.

The legal treatment of African Americans during the period 1790 to 1883, like their treatment in most other periods in American history, was one of decided ambivalence. Consequently, no useful discussion of the Supreme Court's treatment of African Americans can begin in 1790. An understanding of the period must begin with 1787 and the adoption of the American Constitution. Moreover, the Supreme Court's treatment of African Americans during this period in the nation's history must be viewed in context—in the context of the history and of the events which gave shape to the period.

In 1776, the nation began with a declaration of universal equality. But that promise ended at the color line. The ringing testimony to equality in the Declaration of Independence had its limits: it did not include the African American. In short, America began with a contradiction that centered on race. The constitutional debates of the 1780s highlight the nation's contradictory, confusing positions on race questions: this was a nation founded on the principle of individual liberty, but that liberty did not extend to the African slaves and their progeny. In the 1790s, as in the 1990s, the ambivalence persisted: Should the slaves be counted for purposes of representation? Should Congress be empowered to prohibit slavery and the slave trade? Should an escaped slave be "free" to live among the rest of us? These were some of the issues that dominated much of the discussion among the framers of the new constitution.

Perhaps one should not be surprised by this ambivalence on matters of race and equality in this country. It always has been present. The history of Constitution and the Supreme Court reveals dramatic instances of the nation's tortuous history on matters of racial equality. The "race" problem has a long history in the United States, a history as long as the history of the nation itself. This country's inability squarely to face the "race" question can trace its origins to the institution of African slavery. That blot on the national history still clouds the country's ability to discuss issues of race with candor. It cannot be surprising: slavery itself was never discussed with candor, either in the Constitution or in the country. As far as the Constitution was concerned, slavery was the shame "that dare not speak its name."

At the outset, the United States was mired in a debate over the question of slavery. While the debates about the composition of the national legislature were openly about the number of representatives to be accorded each state, the institution of human slavery and what to do about it clearly were major subtexts. Underneath those lofty discussions, however, lay the real issue: how to count the black slaves, who were to be found largely in the planting regions of the South? The problem of race predated the Constitution, and it would persist into the 1790s and beyond.

Even though the institution of human slavery vexed members of the constitutional convention, not once was the word itself used in the document that they submitted to the convention for ratification. Perhaps in their own minds they recognized that their championing of equality was vitiated and debased by the specter of slavery that they silently tolerated. Even though their document alluded to slavery's existence, it failed to acknowledge its presence.

In setting forth the number of representatives to be accorded each state in the lower house of Congress, the Constitution originally counted the African slaves as "three-fifths of all other persons." The "three-fifths" clause augured the history of the African American in the United States: the black American would share less in the promise of the new nation. That clause, though no longer effective, proved to be prophetic.

The original Constitution also forbade the new federal government from abolishing the slave trade or otherwise affecting matters of race before the year 1808. Again, however, the language is so abstract: "The Migration or Importation of such Persons as any of the States now existing shall think proper to admit, shall not be prohibited by the Congress prior to the Year one thousand eight hundred and eight..." (Art. 1, section 9, part. 1).

Runaway slaves were referred to as "person[s] held to service or labour in one state...escaping into another...." This fugitive-slave clause sought to ensure that the slaveowners' "escaped" property, when found, would be returned to him. Despite these deliberately neutral and innocuous-sounding provisions, there was no mistaking their purpose: to enshrine and ensure by law the political superiority of white Americans over the African slaves and their progeny. At the time of the Constitution's framing, one thing was certain: the African slaves and their descendants would be politically inferior to white people.

Even though the framers of the Constitution recognized the peculiar dilemma of racial discrimination as it then existed, they nonetheless decided that they could postpone a decision on the "race question," that its resolution could wait. So may have developed the recurrent American idea that matters of racial justice and racial equality can always be put off, postponed, to be decided at some other time. With such constitutional antecedents, it is not surprising that the Supreme Court has been enormously conflicted on matters of race. The Court takes its cases as it finds them, and cases on race have never been easily or calmly settled in this country. They are not now. They were not in the period 1790-1883.

The Early Days: *Prigg v. Pennsylvania*

Before the 1800s the Court had very few opportunities to render a decision directly on the question of slavery, so accepted was the institution as a feature of American life. Not that it was universally supported, but the law clearly recognized slaves as species of property and therefore subject to regulation as other real property might be. This regulation was often justified by citing the fugitive-slave clause of the Constitution (Art. 4, section 2). One of the few pre-Civil War cases to address the slavery question and state regulatory powers in any degree was *Prigg v. Pennsylvania* (41 US [16 Peters] 539, 1842).

Pennsylvania had enacted a statute prohibiting any person from removing blacks from the state by force or violence with the intention of detaining them as slaves. The Court explained that the fugitive-slave clause "contemplates the existence of a positive, unqualified right on the part of the owner of the slave, which no state law or regulation can in any way qualify, regulate, control, or restrain." The statute was declared invalid with respect to an escaped slave because, in the words of the Court, "any state law which interrupts, limits, delays, or postpones the right of the owner to the immediate possession of the slave, and the immediate command of his service and labor, operates pro tanto, a discharge of the slave therefrom." The Court further held that the clause implicitly vested Congress with the power to assist owners in securing the return of escaped slaves, that Congress had exercised that power by enacting the Fugitive Slave Act of 1793, that this national power was exclusive, and that any state laws regulating the means by which slaves were to be delivered up were unconstitutional.

Prigg announced no landmark policy in 1842. It simply affirmed the social and political realities of its time. However, during the period 1790 to 1883, two major cases involving African Americans and the issues of race did reach the Supreme Court. These two cases—*Dred Scott v. Sandford* (60 US [19 Howard] 393, 1856), *The Civil Rights Cases* (109 US 18, 1883), and the relatively minor case *Strauder v. West Virginia* (100 US 303, 1880) reveal the abiding ambivalence that consistently has characterized American racial relations.

Dred Scott v. Sandford

The 1800s were consumed with sectional strife, primarily strife about race. And that period gave the nation *Dred Scott* and an irreversible impetus toward civil war. No other case in judicial American history has achieved as much notoriety as has *Dred Scott*. The case continues to symbolize the marginal status in which African Americans often have been held in the nation's social and political order.

Dred Scott declared that no African American, whether free or slave, could claim U.S. citizenship. It also held that Congress could not prohibit slavery in the U.S.

territories. In addition, the decision also includes what is undoubtedly the most infamous line in American constitutional history. In his opinion, Chief Justice Roger Brook Taney wrote that African Americans had "no rights which any white man was bound to respect."

This decision—only the second in the nation's history in which the Supreme Court declared an act of Congress unconstitutional—was a clear victory for the political interests that supported slavery, particularly the South. Southerners long had argued that neither Congress nor the territorial legislature had the power to exclude slavery from a territory. Only a state could exclude slavery, they maintained.

Of course, the ruling in *Dred Scott* aroused angry resentment in the North and other parts of the country and launched the nation further along the course to civil war. It also influenced the introduction and the adoption of the Fourteenth Amendment to the Constitution after the Civil War. The 1868 Amendment, which explicitly overruled *Dred Scott*, extended citizenship to former slaves and sought to give them full civil rights.

Dred Scott was the slave of a U.S. Army surgeon, John Emerson of Missouri, a state that permitted slavery. In 1834, Scott traveled with Emerson to live in

Dred Scott

Illinois, where slavery was prohibited. They later lived in the Wisconsin Territory, where slavery was prohibited by the Missouri Compromise. In 1838, Scott returned to Missouri with Emerson. Emerson later died there in 1843, and three years later Scott sued Emerson's widow for his freedom.

Scott's claim was based on the argument that his former residence in a free state and a free territory—Illinois and Wisconsin, respectively—made him a free man. A Missouri state circuit court ruled in Scott's favor, but the Missouri Supreme Court later reversed that decision. Meanwhile, Scott had become legally regarded as the property of John F.A. Sanford of New York. Because Sanford did not live in Missouri, Scott's lawyers were able invoke the diversity of citizenship jurisdiction to transfer the case to a federal court. The lower federal court ruled against Scott, and his lawyers appealed to the Supreme Court of the United States. By a vote of seven to two, the Supreme Court ruled that Scott could not bring a suit in federal court. The decision was announced on March 6, 1857, two days after the inauguration of President James Buchanan.

Each justice in the majority wrote a separate opinion. However, Chief Justice Taney's opinion is most often cited because of its far-reaching implications for sectional crisis and for the monumentally horrible view of the rights of African Americans that it announced. Speaking for the majority, Chief Justice Taney declared that Scott was not entitled to rights such as the right to vote or to sue in a federal court, because, as an African American, he was not a citizen of the United States (60 US 393, 1856).

The Court did not dismiss the case after ruling on Scott's citizenship, as it could easily have done. Because there was a growing national desire for a ruling on the constitutionality of such laws as the Missouri Compromise of 1820, the Taney court seized the opportunity to express its views on both congressional power and the legal status of African Americans (Catton. p. 86).

The Missouri Compromise had forbidden slavery in that part of the Louisiana Territory north of the latitude 36 degrees 30', except for Missouri. Instead of dismissing the suit, the Court discussed this issue as a part of its decision in *Dred Scott*. By the same seven to two margin, it ruled that the Missouri Compromise, which had been repealed in 1854, was unconstitutional. Taney argued that because slaves were property, Congress could not forbid slavery in territories without violating a slaveowner's right to own property under the fifth Amendment. As for Scott's temporary residence in the free state of Illinois, the majority ruled that Scott then had still been subject to Missouri law. Dred Scott was sold shortly afterward, and his new owner gave him his freedom two months after the decision.

The *Dred Scott* decision could have been a mortal blow to the newly created Republican Party, which had been formed to curb the expansion of slavery into the western territories. The decision forced Stephen A. Douglas, an advocate of popular sovereignty to devise a system that would enable settlers to ban slavery in their jurisdictions. President Buchanan, the South, and a majority of the Supreme Court had hoped that the decision would end the antislavery agitation that consumed the country. Instead, the decision increased antislavery sentiment in the North, strengthened the Republican Party, and fed the sectional antagonisms that finally exploded into war in 1861.

Strauder v. West Virginia and the *Civil Rights Cases*

Between the time of the Civil War and the *Civil Rights Cases*, one exception to the otherwise bleak and ambivalent record of the U.S. Supreme Court existed in the civil-rights area. That was in the case of *Stauder v. West Virginia* (100 US 303, 1880). The state of West Virginia permitted only "white male persons who are 21 years of age" to serve on juries in the state. This, of course, meant that it was impossible for African Americans brought before West Virginia courts ever to have another African American serve on a jury deliberating in their cases. The Supreme Court invalidated this provision as a violation of the Fourteenth Amendment's guarantee of equal protection.

Ironically, the Civil War, caused in part by Justice Taney's dictum in *Dred Scott* that Congress could not bar slavery in the territories, actually resulted in the destruction of slavery. Moreover, the war also resulted in a completely new balance of power between the national and the state governments. Federalism, unlike it had been understood prior to the Civil War, now would function with a totally new calculus, a calculus in which the federal government was the defining constant.

The years following the war produced the Civil War amendments—the Thirteenth Amendment, the Fourteenth Amendment, and the Fifteenth Amendment to the Constitution—with their concerted purpose completely to emancipate and empower the former slaves. These three amendments are compelling evidence of the new calculus that operated on federalism. In fact, the text of the Fourteenth Amendment, overturning *Dred Scott*, emphasized the significance of this new relationship and the new power realignments that now obtained: "All persons born or naturalized in the United States and subject to the jurisdiction thereof are citizens of the United States and of the state wherein they reside..." (United States Constitution, Amendment 14, section 1).

Now no dispute that citizenship in the United States was defined and protected by the national constitution and that state citizenship derived from national citizenship and was not independent of it could be had. Augmented by Congress' enforcement powers, these amendments were the constitutional foundations that supported reconstruction, where the recently freed slaves were affirmatively supported and protected by the federal government. A principal legislative result of this period was the passage of the Civil Rights Act of 1875 (18 Stat. 335). According to the statute, its purpose was "to protect all citizens in their civil and legal rights." Even though couched in disarmingly general terms, it was clear that the statute was designed with particular solicitude for the recently emancipated slaves, whose fate otherwise might largely have remained in the hands of people who generally were not favorably disposed to them and their new status.

The 1870s became unique years for testing race relations in the United States. Interestingly, during this period, no state had laws requiring the separation of the races in places of public accommodation. Whatever the practice in a particular establishment or a particular jurisdiction, it was a matter of local custom, individual choice, or personal preference. An earlier statute, the Civil Rights Act of 1866, and the ratification of the Fourteenth Amendment in 1868 had spawned several test suits throughout the country—among them suits for denying sleeper accommodations to African Americans on a Washington-to-New York train, for refusing to sell theater tickets to blacks in Boston, for restricting blacks to front platforms in Baltimore streetcars, and for barring African-American women from the waiting rooms and parlor cars of railroads in Virginia, Illinois, and California. There also had been massive resistance on the part of whites to the social integration of the races.

Faced with these challenges, Congress, controlled by the republicans, enacted a new civil-rights act in 1875. The 1875 statute sought to invalidate all racially motivated interference by individuals with other individuals' exercise of the right to make use of "the accommodations, advantages, facilities, and privileges of inns, public conveyances and theatres..." (109 US 9-10). In short, the statute sought to provide legislative specificity to the constitutional norms embodied in the Thirteenth and Fourteenth amendments.

The *Civil Rights Cases* (109 US 3, 1883) were actually six different cases: *United States v. Singleton, United States v. Stanley, United States v. Nichols, United States v. Ryan, United States v. Hamilton,* and *Robinson v. Memphis & Charleston Railroad.* Five of these cases were criminal prosecutions, which directly challenged the constitutionality of the 1875 statute. The first of these cases, *United States v. Singleton*, involved the refusal of Samuel Singleton, doorkeeper of New York's Grand Opera House to honor the tickets of William R. Davis, Jr. and his fiance.

On November 22, 1879, the pair had attempted to see a matinee performance of Victor Hugo's *Ruy Blas*, starring Edwin Boothe. Davis, business agent of the African American newspaper, *The Progressive-American*, was obviously black. However, Davis's fiance, who without incident, had purchased the tickets earlier that day was described as "a bright octoroon, almost white" (Allan F. Westin. 1964. "The Case of the Prejudiced Doorkeeper," p. 129). When the couple returned for the performance, they were told by Singleton that "these tickets are no good."

Stanley presented the refusal of hotelier, Murray Stanley, to serve a meal to Bird Gee, an African American, in Murray's Topeka, Kansas, hotel. *Nichols* involved the refusal of owner of Nichols House in Jefferson City, Missouri, to accept an African American as a guest. In *Ryan*, the doorkeeper at Maguire's Theater in San Francisco denied a black man named George M. Tyler entry to the dress circle at Maguire's. In *Hamilton*, the conductor of the Nashville Chattanooga & St. Louis Railroad denied an African American woman with a first-class ticket access to the ladies' car. Instead, she was relegated to "a dirty, disagreeable coach known as a smoking car."

The sixth of these cases, *Robinson v. Memphis & Charleston Railroad*, was different. This case involved travel on the Memphis & Charleston Railroad by a young African American woman, Mrs. Sallie Robinson, and her nephew, Joseph C. Robinson. Mr. Robinson was described as a young African American "of light complexion, light hair, and light blue eyes." The train's conductor attempted forcibly to refuse the two passengers entry to the first-class parlor car for which they had purchased tickets. The conductor mistook the pair for a white man and his paramour, whose association he had thought to be for "illicit purposes." In fact, he testified at trial that these couples usually "talked, drank, smoked and acted disorderly, and were objectionable to the other passengers" in the first-class section."

The railroad conceded the constitutionality of the 1875 statute, but argued that it did not apply to the conductor's actions. The trial judge ruled that motive was dispositive under the act. So, if the conductor believed Mrs. Robinson to be a prostitute, whether reasonable or not in that assumption, the exclusion was not based on race and, therefore, the railroad was not liable. The jury found for the railroad and the Robinsons appealed.

The United States, represented before the Supreme Court by Solicitor General Samuel F. Phillips, argued strongly that the act should be upheld in all these cases. In addition, the government's brief discussed the history of the American race relations and the genesis of the Civil War amendments and their statutory descendants. The government stressed particularly the importance of equal access to public accommodations. The Solicitor General emphasized that this act was one of several enacted by "a Congress led by men who had fought in the Civil War and had framed the war amendments." Implicit in the Solicitor General's position was the idea that Congress understood, as clearly as anyone could, that it was not sufficient to outlaw slavery and to declare equal protection to be the law of the land. More was needed: specific statutory protection was necessary to ensure that every vestige of slavery and every reminder of its stigma were eliminated from public life.

The government's arguments, however, did not persuade the high court. The Court announced its decision on October 15, 1883. The Court ruled against the United States, dashing the hopes of these African American petitioners and other citizens who believed the Civil War had eliminated racial discrimination in the United States. The vote in the *Civil Rights Cases* was eight to one. The majority included Chief Justice Waite and Associate Justices Blatchford, Bradley, Fields, Gray, Matthews, Miller, and Woods. Justice Bradley wrote the opinion of the court, which asserted two simplistically devastating conclusions: (1) the Fourteenth Amendment is prohibitory upon the states only (101 US at 11), and (2) the Thirteenth Amendment relates only to slavery and involuntary servitude (101 US at 21).

Bradley and his colleagues maintained that the Fourteenth Amendment operated only as a prohibition and restriction against the states. Because the Civil Rights Act of 1875 sought to outlaw acts of private individuals, shopkeepers, and other businesses, it violated the constitution. This "state action" doctrine holds that, because the government was not the actor in these cases, the Fourteenth Amendment did not empower Congress to outlaw these practices. Also, Bradley's opinion held that, while Congress was empowered by the Thirteenth Amendment to eliminate slavery and all its vestiges, the denial of access to accommodations in commercial establishments, public conveyances, and public amusements was not a "badge or incident of slavery" (109 US at 21). Bradley's opinion effectively halted the progress of civil rights and limited the ability of the federal government, acting through its legislature, to eliminate and eradicate racial discrimination in this country for almost 90 years.

A single justice on the Court dissented—John Marshall Harlan. At the time, Harlan was the court's only southerner and a former slaveholder himself. Ironically, he had also been a bitter critic of the civil war amendments during the 1860s. Between that time and the time of the decision in the case, Harlan had undergone a radical transformation. (His transformation was to achieve its fullest development 13 years later, when he dissented again in another famous civil-rights case, *Plessy v. Ferguson).*

Justice Harlan's dissent was not announced on the day of the majority's decision. In fact, the dissent probably was not written until early November of 1883. His dissent proceeds directly to attack the central failing of the majority's assertions: the grounds for the decision were "too narrow and artificial" (109 US at 26). According to Harlan, the majority have refused to embrace both "the substance and the spirit" of the Civil Rights Act. "It is not the words of the law but the internal sense of it that makes the law. The letter of the law is the body; the sense and reason of the law is the soul." And, in Justice Harlan's view, the purpose of the act "was to prevent *race* [emphasis in original] discrimination." The majority, as Harlan develops the dissent, betrayed this purpose "by a subtle and ingenious verbal criticism."

Justice Harlan's voice was eloquent, but it was a lone one, crying in the wilderness. Neither the majority of the Supreme Court nor the nation it represented cared to do much else to promote the civil rights of its new black citizens. Harlan's dissent in the *Civil Rights Cases* forecasted his more famous one in *Plessy v. Ferguson* (163 US 537, 1896), because the decision in the *Civil Rights Cases* led inexorably to the black codes, Jim Crow, and other examples of *de jure* segregation that came to define race relations in the United States.

The *Civil Rights Cases* starkly revealed the nation's ambivalence on the questions of race. On the one hand, Congress had sought to guarantee the rights of the recently freed slaves by proposing constitutional amendments that were ultimately ratified, even if some coercion was necessary. Congress went further and augmented the constitutional guarantees with additional legislative protections and safeguards. The Supreme Court, however, frustrated these constitutional and legislative initiatives with a cold and constricted reading of the Thirteenth and the Fourteenth amendments. An ancient pattern had reasserted itself.

◆ AFRICAN AMERICANS AND THE CRIMINAL JUSTICE SYSTEM

by Marilyn Hortense Mackel

Criminal justice in the United States consists of three major components, law enforcement, judicial and legal services, and corrections. In the past 25 years, African Americans have assumed significant leadership roles in both law enforcement and correctional services as evidenced by the rising number of African American judges, prosecutors, and defense attorneys. However, since 1970, employment of African Americans as judges and prosecutors has not increased at the rate necessary to give a formidable presence blacks working in the system. As a result, courts in large metropolitan areas have begun a critical examination of the impact of low numbers of African American judges on the perpetuation of racism in the court system—particularly on the disproportionate arrest rate, and the harsher sentences imposed on African Americans.

The Creation of Twentieth Century Slave Ships

Criminal justice statistics published by the U.S. Department of Justice provide documentation of the widespread perpetuation of discrimination in America. It is indeed not difficult to argue that the American system of criminal justice is giving birth to "Twentieth Century Slave Ships." Little Rock, Arkansas artist, Alice Ayers, provides, in her work entitled "20th Century Slave Ship" perceptual impetus of the phrase. The incarceration rate of African American males is alarming—such that a common expression in the African American community is that on any given day, more African American males of college age are in prisons and jails than in colleges or universities. Black males generally have been sentenced to long mandatory minimum sentences, including life without parole, for such offenses as drug possession, while white importers of drugs are seldom arrested or are able to negotiate a lessor charge and plea bargain a for lighter sentence.

Law Enforcement

The largest, and to some extent, the most imposing arm of the criminal justice system, police are the most visible criminal justice servants. As the first point of contact for persons entering the system, officers make discretionary, often quasi–judicial decisions to whether to arrest when an offense is alleged to have occurred. As implementors of local and national legal and political policy, police officers are agents of interest groups with power to effectuate their interest in our politically organized society. Law enforcers are organized and empowered to support the interest of those with means to shape law, a factor that may have significant bearing on why African Americans have had a particularly duplicitous relationship with the police.

Just like any other community, African Americans look to law enforcement for protection from an criminal elements present in their midst; the irony for most African Americans lies in the fact that those sworn to

Thurgood Marshall, 1958

protect have historically had little regard for the humanity of blacks, and have, in the exercise of their discretionary authority failed to enforce the law or to respond, when protection is sought by blacks. African Americans have for some time been perceived and treated as a race of people whose very existence threatens the dominant social group—the fact that the African American community has this duplicitous relationship with law enforcement is consistent with the purpose of law and law enforcement.

One way of mending the fences between law enforcement and minorities is to include them within the higher ranks of the organizations. In 1996, law enforcement executives included such big city police chiefs as Atlanta's Beverly Harvard, one of the first three women of any race and the first African American woman to head a major police force; Los Angeles's Willie L. Williams, that city's first black police chief; and Detroit's Isaiah "Ike" McKinnon.

Judicial and Legal Services and the Correctional System

Prosecutors have sole discretionary authority over the charges (if any) that are filed against offenders.

Discrimination in charging occurs when African American offenders are subjected to multiple charges, including all possible lessor offenses, for one act, while an white offender is charged with lessor one offense for a similar criminal act. Plea bargaining, a process also coordinated by prosecutors, can be a source of discrimination as well.

The oppressive reality is that, like freed slaves, offenders released from prison, and or parole or probation, often are unable to pursue meaningful careers—rewarding work, and even menial work, is forever closed to them despite any possible genuine efforts to reform and to conform to the expectations of law abiding citizenship. To examine the statistical data demonstrating the likelihood that the criminal justice system is fostering twentieth century slave ships in the African American community, one need only examine the numerous statistical bases annually distributed by the U.S. Department of Justice. When viewing these statistics, it is important that the reader keep in mind that African Americans comprise 12 percent of the population of this country, approximately 30 million people.

In 1990, 3,224,060 African Americans were arrested compared to 7,712,339 whites (U.S. Department of Justice, Office of Justice Programs, Bureau of Justice Statistics. 1992. *Sourcebook of Criminal Justice Statistics—1991*, Washington, DC: U.S. Government Printing Office. p. 444). An examination of selected juvenile justice data shows that in 1990, whites and Hispanics under the age of 18 constituted 71.3 percent of the arrests made, while African Americans constituted 26.2 percent. Of adult offenders (those age eighteen and older), whites constitute 68.8 percent of persons arrested, while African Americans constitute only 29.4 percent (*Sourcebook of Justice Statistics—1991*).

African American youth between the ages of 14 and 18, are being removed from the juvenile courts where rehabilitation and treatment is available, at least theoretically, and subjected at a young age to the harsh world of adult corrections. In 1989, 7,500 whites and Hispanics were transferred from the juvenile court to be tried as adults, while 8,500 African Americans were similarly transferred. In 1990, the number of whites and Hispanics in the system decreased to 7,400, while the number of African Americans increased to 9,200 (National Center for Juvenile Justice, National Institute of Justice, Juvenile Justice Clearing House). In addition, increased numbers of juvenile offenders are being subjected to life sentences without possibility of parole, and to the death penalty.

African Americans do not commit crimes in larger numbers. However, African Americans are treated more harshly by the criminal justice system. An examination of persons under correctional supervision is equally revealing. At public juvenile facilities in 1989, whites comprise 40 percent of the population, African Americans 42 percent, and Hispanics 16 percent (*Sourcebook of Criminal Justice Statistics*). African Americans, in 1991 made up 43.4 percent of the jail population, whites 41.1 percent. In 1988, African Americans constituted 46.9 percent of the state prison population, whites 49.7 percent. In 1988 African Americans constituted 22.7 percent of the federal prison population, while whites constituted 75.2 percent. Significant is the fact that 53.8 percent of the African American male population and 68.4 percent of the female population of the federal prisons are incarcerated for drug offenses.

Because of the ravages of slavery, African Americans have long been placed "well outside of the pale" of American life (Arthur M. Schlesinger, Jr. 1992. *The Disuniting of America: Reflections on a Multicultural Society*, New York: W.W Norton & Company. p. 14). During slavery, and thereafter, African Americans were hung, castrated, raped, and otherwise physically and mentally devastated. Today, the same psychological and physical ravagement occurs at the hands of the criminal justice system, which affords them little or no protection from crime and removes them in large numbers from their communities to be barred upon return from reasonable opportunities in American life.

The "Trial of the Century"

On June 12, 1994, a brutal, double-murder led to one of the most pivotal criminal trials of the twentieth century. Nicole Brown Simpson, former wife of African American football legend O. J. Simpson, was brutally slain outside of her house; also killed was her friend Ron Goldman. Almost immediately, evidence pointed to O. J. Simpson as the primary suspect. The subsequent, year-long trial was aired on television, allowing viewers to witness the entire spectacle almost as if it were a soap opera. Many decried the circus atmosphere promoted by the entire media industry, not just television.

In one corner was the State of California, represented by prosecutors Marcia Clark and Christopher Darden, an African American. They portrayed Simpson as a jealous husband who had for years been locked in a pattern of domestic abuse. The murders would, therefore, be a case of spousal abuse taken to the extreme, the built-up result of the couple's breakup. In the other corner, Simpson's so-called "Dream Team" of defense attorneys focused on an alleged police-conspiracy theory based on race.

Simpson was found not guilty via jury verdict in October of 1995, a finding that divided the nation along color, class, and gender lines. *Broadcasting & Cable* reported that "the verdict ... broke all previous TV viewing records, with over 150 million people tuning in to watch the jury's decision."

Ultimately, the case had little to do with the actual murders. Rather than addressing the heinous crime that took place, the proceedings brought the ugly under belly of the country's prejudices, fears, and values to light. Polls showed that most whites thought Simpson was guilty, while most blacks thought him innocent. Many African Americans viewed Simpson as another black man caught trapped in a judicial system operated by bigots—a victim of racist law enforcement officials. Others lamented the black community's loss of a hero and accused the "white establishment" of systematic destruction of African American role models. Many sided against Simpson on the basis of his wealth, perceiving him as a rich man able to literally get away with murder because he could buy high-powered attorneys. Some women, certain that the murders were an extension of the physical abuse he had heaped on his wife, used the case as a way to turn public attention to the prevalence of domestic violence. Many black women were angry with Simpson for having divorced his first wife, a black woman, to marry a white woman, and determined him guilty in their own minds for that reason alone. Some of the public followed the case merely because it was one of the most prominent to rely on new forensic methodolgies, namely DNA testing. Whatever the attraction, most of those who believed in Simpson's innocence before the trial still believed he was innocent. Those who thought he was guilty remained against him. Following the verdict, the Brown and Goldman families filed a wrongful death civil suit against Simpson.

The Case of Mumia Abu-Jamal

Though not as big a newsmaker as "The Trial of the Century," the case of outspoken journalist and former Black Panther Mumia Abu-Jamal caused quite a ripple in the legal system during the mid-1990s. During an altercation between a Philadelphia police officer and Jamal's brother, Jamal claims to have entered the fracas in order to keep his brother from being beaten. Though details are sketchy and contested, the aftermath of the fray left Jamal wounded by a gunshot from the officer's gun and the officer dead. Arrested and convicted, Jamal received the death sentence in 1982 for that death.

Since then, a group of national and international supporters have advocated for Jamal's release, alleging that aspects of Jamal's case were improperly handled in regards to the U.S. Constitution and to correct legal procedure. Many believe Jamal was framed by the Philadelphia police who wanted to keep the blunt and forthright reporter from exposing evidence of corruption within the law enforcement agency.

On August 7, 1995, ten days before his execution was scheduled, Jamal was granted a one-year stay of execution, given the extension in order to complete his state court appeals. In July of 1996, that issue was still pending. Meanwhile, Jamal filed a suit against National Public Radio (NPR), who had hired him in 1994 as a news commentator. Jamal's commentaries about life on death row did not bode well in the conservative sector, however. In Jamal's suit, he claims that NPR gave in to pressure from U.S. Senator Bob Dole and others and refused to air his segments. Jamal hoped the court would force NPR to broadcast his prison recordings and then return them to him.

◆ AFRICAN AMERICANS IN THE FEDERAL COURTS

by Lorna M. Mabunda

When one considers that more than three-quarters of a century have passed since the first presidential appointment to a any judgeship—Theodore Roosevelt appointed Robert H. Terrell to a municipal jurisdiction in 1901—the specter of less than four percent of all

judges being African American is daunting. Nonetheless, the amazing fact is that despite African Americans' complete lack of legal rights in the previous century—while in the midst of slavery—slaves, ironically, made the first in-roads into the courts. In separate incidents, escaped slave Elizabeth Freeman (c. 1775), New England slave Lucy Prince (1775), and Southern slave Dred Scott (1846) all blasted through racial barriers with unheralded courage and dignity.

Blacks did not enter the courts just as parties to actions; they also participated in the system in professional capacities. In 1844, Macon Allen became the first black admitted to a state bar; Charlotte Ray became the first black woman to gain the same distinction. Other pioneering woman followed, including Ellen Craft, Francis Watkins Harper, Laetitia Rowley, Maria Stewart, Mary Church Terrell, and Ida B. Wells. John S. Rock became the first African American lawyer to argue a case before the Supreme Court in 1865. In 1873, Mifflin Gibbs became the first black municipal judge. Though he only served a single term, his reputation for fairness was legendary, and he was named U.S. consul to Madagascar in 1897. Jonathan Jasper White was elected to the South Carolina State Supreme Court in 1870. In 1937, President Franklin D. Roosevelt appointed William H. Hastie to the Territorial Court of the Virgin Islands, making him the first black federal trial court judge. Hastie was succeeded by a black man, Herman E. Moore, in 1939, the same year Jane Matilda Bolin became the first black female judge, appointed by New York City Mayor Fiorello LaGuardia. In 1945, President Harry S. Truman appointed Irwin C. Mollison to what was then known as the U.S. Customs Court and is now the U.S. Court of International Trade, thus making him the first black lifetime appointee to a federal court. The 1996 swearing in of Joyce London Alexander as chief U.S. Magistrate judge for the District Court of Massachusetts made her the first African American female chief judge in the state and the first black chief U.S. magistrate judge in the United States.

The Federal System

The federal system is empowered to hear cases that present federal questions, i.e. questions about the Constitution or U.S. laws or treaties; actions involving more that $50,000; cases involving diverse citizenship, either between two or more states, between the United States and a state, by a state and citizens of other nations, or controversies involving ambassadors or other representatives of foreign states. As dictated by Article III, Section I of the U.S. Constitution, the Judicial Code statute outlines the specificities of a tiered federal court system, each level with its own exclusive legislative rights.

Each of the 94 districts, as drawn by Congress, has a U.S. District Court with original jurisdiction over matters under $10,000, landlord/tenant disputes, small claims, traffic matters, and arraignments/exams for certain felonies. 12 regional circuit courts and one "federal" circuit court possess original jurisdiction over matters greater than $10,000, divorces, and felony criminal trials. Furthermore, probate matters are handled by probate courts, which are a division of the circuit court system—literally a court system within a court system. The circuit courts also hear appeals from the district courts. Courts of Appeals hear appeals from the lower courts. The highest court in the land, the U.S. Supreme Court, examines case law and state laws/statutes. The Supreme Court also deals with appeals from circuit and appeals courts.

Nominated by the U.S. president and confirmed through Senate hearings, federal judgeships are lifetime appointments, usually crowning a distinguished legal career. Of the less than 1,000 active federal judges, in 1995, a scant 71 were African American, including 16 women. Still, blacks have steadily received appointments since the early 1960s, beginning with James B. Parsons, who was nominated by President John F. Kennedy to sit on the bench of the U.S. District Court for the Northern District of Illinois in 1961. At that time, the lack of federal black judges was glaring. Kennedy made great strides, successfully appointing Wade Hampton McCree, Jr., to the U.S. District Court for the Eastern Districts of Michigan in 1961, and Thurgood Marshall to the Second Circuit Court of Appeals in 1962. In five years, Marshall would go on to become the first African American appointed to the Supreme Court of the United States.

President Lyndon B. Johnson followed Kennedy's suit, nominating 11 blacks to federal benches. Among them were A. Leon Higginbotham, Jr.—Johnson's first appointee—and Constance Baker Motley. As a member of the U.S. District Court for the Southern District of New York, she became the first African American woman to hold a federal judgeship in 1966. The next female appointee did not come for 12 years, until Mary Johnson Lowe was seated in the same district court venue in 1978, by President Jimmy Carter. Carter also chose Amalya Lyle Kearse, who, in 1979, became the first black woman on the U.S. Court of Appeals. She was seated in the same venue in which Thurgood Marshall had started, the Second Circuit.

Interestingly, Republican presidents have had the poorest record of nominating blacks to the federal courts. For example, presidents Richard Nixon and Gerald R. Ford together only nominated 11 African American judges over an eight-year period. Democrat Lyndon Johnson nominated the same number in half the time, though it should be mentioned that Ford placed four black judges during his shortened, two-year term. Also of note is Nixon's appointment of Robert M. Duncan to the U.S. Court of Military Appeals in 1971, another notable black first. Republicans Ronald Reagan and George Bush had poor track records, particularly when compared with Democrat Bill Clinton. By 1995, Clinton had appointed 30 black federal judges, more than any other president with the exception of Carter.

◆ AFRICAN AMERICANS ON THE U.S. SUPREME COURT

Thurgood Marshall, a graduate of Lincoln University and Howard University Law School, was admitted to the Maryland Bar in 1933. He joined the National Association for the Advancement of Colored People staff as assistant to special counsel Charles Hamilton Houston. In 1938 Marshall succeeded Houston as special council, and in 1950 he became director of the NAACP Legal Defense and Education Fund. While working the NAACP and the NAACP Legal Defense and Education Fund, Marshall played a major role in some of the Supreme Court history's most important cases, including *Smith v. Allwright* (1944), *Morgan v. Virginia* (1946), *Shelley v. Kraemer* (1948), *Sweatt v. Painter* (1950), and *Brown v. Board of Education of Topeka*. Between 1938 and 1961, Marshall argued 32 cases before the U.S. Supreme Court, winning 29.

In 1961, Marshall became the second African American to serve on the U.S. Circuit Court of Appeal, when President John F. Kennedy named Marshall to fill a vacancy. In 1965, President Lnydon B. Johnson appointed Marshall to the post of U.S. Solicitor General. With the retirement of Associate Justice Tom Campbell Clark in 1967, Marshall was nominated to fill the vacancy. Marshall's nomination was met with objections from Southern Senators. Nevertheless, he was confirmed, becoming the first African American justice in Unites States history. While on the Court, Marshall served as a supporter of affirmative action, free speech, and the rights of workers. He wrote few famous decisions, but his dissenting opinions in such cases as *Milliken v. Bradley* (1974) and *Regents of the University v. Bakke* (1978).

On June 27, 1991, Justice Marshall announced his plan to retire, due to advancing age and poor health, after some 24 years on the nation's highest court. On July 1 President George Bush announced that he had chosen Clarence Thomas, a black, conservative appeals court judge, as his choice to fill the vacancy created by Marshall. In 1981, President Ronald Reagan appointed Clarence Thomas, a graduate of a Holy Cross College and Yale University Law School, to head the civil rights division of the Department of Education. A year later, Thomas was appointed to head the Equal Employment Opportunity Commission. In 1990 Thomas was appointed by President Bush to fill a vacancy on the U.S. Court of Appeals for the District of Columbia.

In a flurry of controversy, Clarence Thomas was appointed an associate justice of the U.S. Supreme Court in 1991, after being nominated by President George Bush. Besides Thomas's relative youth and judicial inexperience, his nomination hearings were marred by the accusations from Anita Hill that she had suffered from sexual harassment while under his employ at the Equal Employment Opportunity Commission (EEOC). The nomination committee chose to approve Thomas's nomination despite the serious accusations from Hill.

Anita Hill, a relatively unknown law professor at the University of Oklahoma, became a household name when she came forward with charges of sexual harassment against Judge Thomas, purportedly committed when both had worked for the EEOC. Hill claimed that Thomas repeatedly pressured her to date him, told her plots of pornographic movies, and bragged about his sexual exploits. When asked why she didn't quit her job or report Thomas when the incidents occurred during the early 1980s, Hill answered that she feared she would not be able to get another job.

The nation, as well as the Senate, seemed divided by the shocking testimony. Thomas denied the allegations and had many of his former coworkers testify for him. The case became highly politicized as conservatives and liberals fought for ground. Thomas, who was nominated by President George Bush, was supported by the conservatives in the Republican party because his appointment would mean an African American on the court who would uphold conservative policies. Therefore, Hill's case was taken up by many Democrats.

After the confirmation votes were counted, Thomas was nominated by the narrow margin of 52 to 48—one of the closest margins in Supreme Court history. Apparently, the American public mirrored the pro–Thomas view. In a poll taken soon after the hearings, 60 percent sided with Thomas and only 20 percent with Hill. One year later, however, only 38 percent of those Americans polled agreed with Thomas, while an equal number supported Hill's version.

◆ MAJOR FEDERAL LEGISLATION

Emancipation Act (April 1862)

ch.54, 12 state. 376

This act, abolishing slavery in the District of Columbia, was enacted April 16, 1862.

Clarence Thomas

Emancipation Act (June 1862)

ch. 111, 12 Stat. 432

This act, abolishing slavery in all other territories of the United States, was enacted June 19, 1862.

Amendment Thirteen to the U.S. Constitution (1865)

This Amendment, abolishing slavery and involuntary servitude in all of the United States, was ratified December 16, 1865.

Civil Rights Act (1866)

ch. 31, 14 Stat. 27

This act was enacted April 9, 1866, to provide all citizens, especially recently freed slaves, with basic civil rights, including the right to make and enforce contracts, to bring suits in court, to purchase and sell real and personal property, and to enjoy security of person and property.

Amendment Fourteen to the United States Constitution (1868)

This Amendment defined United States and state citizenship, and provided all citizens with the privileges and immunities of citizenship, the right to life, liberty and property, and equal protection under the law. It was ratified July 20, 1868.

Anita Hill testifies before the Senate Judiciary Committee.

Amendment Fifteen to the United States Constitution (1870)

This Amendment was designed to protect the right of all citizens to vote. It was ratified March 30, 1870.

Civil Rights Act (1870)
ch. 114, 16 Stat. 140

This act was enacted May 31, 1870, to carry–out the provision of the Fifteenth Amendment. It established penalties for violations of the provisions of the Amendment.

Civil Rights Act (1871)
ch. 99, 16 Stat. 433

This act was enacted February 28, 1871, to further define the protections established in the Fifteenth Amendment.

Civil Rights Act (April 1871)
ch. 22, 17 Stat. 13

This act was enacted April 20, 1871 to further outline the protections provided for by the Fourteenth Amendment. It provides for the vindication of crimes committed under the act in federal court.

Civil Rights Act (1875)
ch. 114, 18 Stat. 335

This act was designed to provide all citizens with equal access to public places. Ruling in 1883 in a set of cases, known as the *Civil Rights Cases*, the U.S. Supreme court invalidated the act.

Civil Rights Act of 1957
Pub.L. No. 85–315, 71 Stat. 634

This act created the Commission on Civil Rights and empowered it to investigate allegations of deprivation of a United States citizen's right to vote, and to appraise laws and policies of the federal government with respect to equal protection of the law, and to submit a report to the President and to the Congress within two years.

Civil Rights Act of 1960
Pub.L. No. 86–449, 74 Stat. 86

Guaranteed the provision of criminal penalties in the event a suspect crosses state lines to avoid legal process

Engraving depicting blacks celebrating the abolition of slavery in the District of Columbia.

for the actual or attempted bombing or burning of any vehicle or building, and provided penalties for persons who obstructed or interfered with any order of a federal court.

Civil Rights Act of 1964
Pub.L. No. 88–352, 78 Stat. 241

This act prohibited discrimination in the use of public accommodations whose operations involve interstate commerce, and provided enforcement measures to ensure equal access to public facilities. Also the Civil Rights Act of 1964 prohibited racial discrimination in any program receiving federal aid and prohibited discrimination in most areas of employment.

Voting Rights Act of 1965
Pub.L. No. 89–110, 79 Stat. 437

The Voting Rights Act of 1965 struck down requirements such as literacy and knowledge tests and poll tax payments which had been used to restrict black participation in voting, and provided for federal registrars to register voters should state registrars refuse to do so. It further stipulated that registered voters cannot be prohibited from voting.

Civil Rights Act of 1968
Pub.L. No. 90–284, 82 Stat. 73

This act provided for open housing by prohibiting discrimination based on race, color, religion, or national origin.

Equal Employment Opportunity Act of 1972
Pub.L. No. 92–261, 86 Stat. 103

This act provided the Equal Employment Opportunity Commission (which was established by the Civil Rights Act of 1964) with the authority to issue judicially enforceable cease and desist orders in cases involving discriminatory employment practices.

Public Works Employment Act of 1977
Pub.L. No. 95–28, 91 Stat. 116, Title I

The Public Works Employment Act of 1977 provided that ten percent of funds expended as a result of federal

Engraving depicting the trial of a freedman, Florida, 1867.

grants be earmarked for and paid to minority business enterprises.

Voting Rights Act of 1965 Amendment
Pub.L. No. 97–205, 96 Stat. 131 (1982)

This Amendment was a congressional response to the Supreme Court's ruling in *City of Mobile v. Bolden* that required proof of discriminatory intent in voting rights cases. Section 2 of the voting rights Act prohibits any voting practice or procedure "imposed or applied by any state or political subdivision in a manner which results in a denial or abridgement of the right of any citizen of the United States to vote on account of race or color"

Civil Rights Commission Act of 1983
Pub.L. No. 98–183, 87 Stat. 1301

This act created an eight–member bipartisan commission with four members appointed by the president, and two by the Senate and House, respectively. The Commissioners are appointed to four or six year terms and can be fired only for neglect of duty or malfeasance in office. The statute was enacted after President Reagan attempted to fire Commissioners who did not express his views on civil rights. The Act extended the life of the Civil Rights Commission Authorization Act of 1978, which was scheduled to expire in 1983.

Civil Rights Restoration Act of 1988
Pub.L. No. 100–259, 102 Stat. 31

Ruling in 1984 in the case *Grove City College v. Bell*, the U.S. Supreme Court ruled that not all programs and activities of an institution were covered by Title IX of the Education amendments of 1972 (Public Law 89–10, 79 Stat. 27) and that discrimination can be barred only in programs that directly receive federal funds. Section 6 of Public Law 100–259 amended portions of the Civil Rights Act of 1964, refined the definition of programs and activities which are covered by the Civil Rights Act and other legislation. Specifically the Amendment addressed Title IX of the Education amendments of 1972, which prohibits discrimination in educational programs receiving federal financial assistance.

Fair Housing amendments Act of 1988
Pub.L. No. 100–430, 102 Stat 1619

The Fair Housing amendments Act of 1988 strengthens laws that resulted from passage of the Fair Housing act of 1968. The Act of 1988 gives the Department of Housing and Urban Development (HUD) the authority to issue discrimination charges, allows administrative law justices the ability to review housing discrimination cases, and removed the $1000 limit on punitive damages that a victim of discrimination may receive.

Civil Rights Act of 1991
Pub.L. 102–166, 105 Stat. 1071

This act is designed to provide additional remedies to deter harassment and intentional discrimination in the workplace, to provide guidelines for the adjudication of cases arising under Title VII of the Civil Rights Act of 1964, and to expand the scope of civil rights legislation weakened by Supreme Court decisions, particularly the Court's ruling in *Wards Cove Packing Co. v. Antonio*, 490 US 642 (1989).

Glass Ceiling Act of 1991
Pub.L. 102–166, 105 Stat. 1081

Title II of the Civil Rights Act of 1991, designed to establish a means for studying and addressing the underrepresentation of women and minorities at management and decision making levels in the workforce.

◆ MAJOR U.S. SUPREME COURT DECISIONS

Access to the Polls

United States v. Reese
92 US 214 (1876)

Prior to the Fifteenth Amendment, states regulated all details of state and local elections; states prescribed the qualifications of voters, and the manner in which those desiring to vote at an election should make their qualifications known to the election officers. Thus, the Fifteenth Amendment interferes with the past sovereignly

Entrance to a segregated waiting room in Jackson, Mississippi.

practice and provides rules not prescribed by state law. However, this court restricted the scope of the Fifteenth Amendment and the ability of Congress to enforce it by not punishing election officials who unlawfully interfere and prevent the free exercise of the elective franchise.

The federal government indicted two Kentucky election inspectors for refusing to receive and count the vote of a black citizen. The Supreme Court held, that Congress had not yet provided "appropriate legislation'" for the punishment of the offense charged under any sections of the Fifteenth Amendment.

Guinn v. United States
238 US 347 (1915)

In 1910, an amendment to the constitution of Oklahoma, restricted the franchise according to a "grandfather clause" that provided that no illiterate person could be registered to vote. The clause, however, granted an exemption for persons who resided in a foreign country prior to January 1, 1866, and had been eligible to register prior to that date or had a lineal ancestor who was eligible to vote at that time. Since no blacks were eligible to vote in Oklahoma prior to 1866, the law disenfranchised all blacks.

The U.S. Supreme Court in *Guinn v. United States* ruled that the grandfather clause was invalid in Oklahoma or in any other state.

Nixon v. Herndon
273 US 536 (1927)

Dr. L. A. Nixon, an African American, was refused the right to vote in a primary election because of a state statute that prohibited blacks from participating in Democratic Party elections in Texas. Nixon filed suit against the election officials and his case ultimately reached the U.S. Supreme Court. In his opinion, on *Nixon v. Herndon* Justice Oliver Wendell Holmes wrote: "It is too clear for extended argument that color cannot be made the basis of a statutory classification affecting the right set up in this case." As a result of *Nixon v. Herndon* the Texas statute was declared unconstitutional.

Nixon v. Condon
286 US 73 (1932)

As a result of the U.S. Supreme Court ruling in *Nixon v. Herndon*, the Texas legislature passed a new statute. This statute empowered the state Democratic executive committee to set up its own rules regarding primary

President Lyndon B. Johnson

electors. As a result, nonwhites were unable to participate in a Democratic party primary. In *Grovey v. Townsend* (295 U.S. Supreme Court Reports 45), the Supreme Court had upheld this limitation because it was made by the party in convention, not by a party executive committee. In *Smith v. Allwright*, the Supreme Court overruled *Grovey*, stating, "The United States is a constitutional democracy. Its organic law grants to all citizens a right to participate in the choice of elected officials without restriction by any state because of race." The Court noted that political party makes its selection of candidates as an agency of the state and, therefore, cannot exclude participation based on race and remain consistent with the Fifteenth Amendment.

elections. The party promptly adopted a resolution stipulating that only white Democrats be allowed to participate in primaries. Dr. Nixon again filed suit, and his right to vote was again upheld by the U.S. Supreme Court.

Lane v. Wilson
307 US 268 (1939)

In an attempt to restrict voter registration, the Oklahoma legislature stated that all Oklahomans who were already registered would remain qualified voters, but that all others would have to register within 12 days (from April 30 to May 11, 1916) or be forever barred from the polls. In 1934, I. W. Lane, an African American, was refused registration on the basis of this statute. The U.S. Supreme Court declared that the statute was in conflict with the Fifteenth Amendment to the U.S. Constitution, and, therefore was unconstitutional.

Smith v. Allwright
321 US 649 (1944)

The Texas State Democratic party, during its convention in 1932, limited the right of membership to white

Newspaper illustration depicting white opposition to black suffrage.

Gomillion v. Lightfoot
364 US 339

In this case African American citizens challenged an Alabama statute that redefined the boundaries of the City of Tuskegee. The statute altered the shape of Tuskegee and placed all but four of Tuskegee's 400 African American voters outside of the city limits, while not displacing a single white voter.

Baker v. Carr
369 US 186 (1962)

Baker v. Carr was brought to the Supreme Court by electors in several counties of Tennessee, who asserted that the 1901 legislative reapportionment statute was unconstitutional because the numbers of voters in the various districts had changed substantially since 1901. The plaintiffs requested that the Supreme Court either direct a reapportionment by mathematical application of the Tennessee constitutional formula to the 1960 Census, or instruct the state to hold direct at-large elections. The state district court had dismissed the case on the grounds that it was a political question and, as such, did not fall within the protection of the Fourteenth Amendment. The U.S. Supreme Court ruled that the case involved a basic constitutional right and thereby was within court jurisdiction, and remanded the case to the state district court.

South Carolina v. Kalzenback
383 US 301 (1966)

The Voting Rights Act of 1965 was designed to eliminate racial discrimination in voting, which had influenced the electoral process for nearly a century. The act abolished literacy tests, waived accumulated poll taxes, and alloted the U.S. Attorney General vast discretionary powers over regions suspect of discriminatory legislation and practices against black voters.

The Supreme Court dismissed South Carolina's petition asserting that the act violated the U.S. Constitution because it encroached on state sovereignty. The Constitution holds true under Section 1 of the Fifteenth Amendment, "... [t]he right of citizens of the United States to vote shall not be denied or abridged by the United States or by any state on account of race, color, or previous condition of servitude."

Allen v. State Board of Elections
393 US 110 (1969)

In *Allen v. State Board of Education,* the Supreme Court emphasized that subtle, as well as obvious state regulations, "which have the effect of denying citizens their right to vote because of their race" are prohibited. The court confirmed that Section 5 of the Voting Rights Act covered a variety of practices other than voter registration.

Georgia v. United States
411 US 526 (1973)

This case confirmed the propriety of the Voting Rights Act of 1965, which forbids states with a history of racial discrimination (Alabama, Georgia, Louisiana, Mississippi, North Carolina, South Carolina and Virginia) from implementing any change in voting practices and procedures without first submitting the proposed plan to the U.S. Attorney General for approval.

White v. Regester
412 US 755 (1973)

The Supreme Court in *White v. Regester,* struck down a Texas multi-member districting scheme that was used to prevent blacks from being elected to public office. The court upheld a finding that even though there was no evidence that blacks faced official obstacles to registration, voting or running for office, they had been excluded from effective participation in the political process in violation of the Equal Protection Clause of the Constitution.

City of Mobile, Alabama v. Wiley L. Bolden
446 US 55 (1980)

A class action suit was filed in the U.S. District Court for the Southern District of Alabama on behalf of black citizens in Mobile. The suit alleged that the city's practice of electing commissioners at large by a majority vote unfairly diluted the voting strength of blacks in violation of the Fourteenth Amendment and the Fifteenth Amendment. The District Court, ruled that the constitutional rights of Mobile's black citizens had been violated and entered a judgment in their favor. The court also ruled that Mobile's city commissioners be replaced by a municipal government consisting of a mayor and a city council composed of persons selected from single member districts.

Thornburg v. Gingles
478 US 30 (1986)

Thornburg v. Gingles was the Supreme Court's first decision interpreting the provisions of Section two of the Voting Rights Act, as amended in 1982. The amendments which prohibit voting schemes that result in a denial or abridgement of the right to vote due to race or color. In this landmark decision, the Court ruled that the redistricting plan adopted by the North Carolina legislature, which led to racially polarized voting by whites and diluted black voting strength is in violation of the Voting Rights Act. The Voting Rights Act prohibits voting requirements that have a discriminatory effect, as well as those that are intentionally discriminatory.

Martin v. Wilks
490 US 755 (1989)

In an attempt to remedy past racial discrimination in hiring and promotion practices, the City of Birmingham and its fire department consented to hiring blacks as firefighters as part of a settlement. White firefighters subsequently challenged the city, alleging that because of their race they were denied promotions in favor of less qualified blacks in violation of Title VII. Promotion decisions were made on the basis of race in reliance on the consent decree. The court held that a voluntary settlement between one group of employees and their employer cannot possibly settle voluntarily or otherwise, the conflicting claims of another group of employees who do not join in the agreement, on the basis that you can not deprive a person of legal rights in a proceeding to which he is not a party.

Education

Missouri ex rel. Lloyd Gaines v. Canada
305 US 339 (1938)

Gaines v. Canada was brought before the Supreme Court by Lloyd Lionel Gaines, an African American who had been refused admission to the School of Law of the State University of Missouri. Gaines contended that the University of Missouri's actions were a violation of his rights under the Fourteenth Amendment of the U.S. Constitution.

The University of Missouri defended its action by maintaining that Lincoln University, a predominantly black institution, would eventually establish its own law school. The Supreme Court of Missouri dismissed Gaines' petition and upheld the university's decision to reject his application. The U.S. Supreme Court, however, reversed this decision, maintaining that the State of Mis-

Lloyd Gaines

souri was obliged to provide equal facilities for blacks or, in the absence of such facilities, to admit them to the existing facility.

Sipuel v. Board of Regents of the University of Oklahoma
332 US 631 (1948)

Ada Lois Sipuel, an African American, was denied admission to the law school of the University of Oklahoma in 1948, Sipuel requested legal assistance from the National Association for the Advancement of Colored People (NAACP), which filed a petition in the Oklahoma courts requesting an order directing her admission. The petition was denied on the grounds that the *Gaines* decision did not require a state with segregation laws to admit a black student to its white schools. In addition, the Oklahoma court maintained that the state itself was not obligated to set up a separate school unless first requested to do so by blacks desiring a legal education. The Oklahoma court's decision was affirmed by the Supreme Court of Oklahoma. The U.S. Supreme Court, however, reversed this decision, and held that the state was required to provide African Americans with equal educational opportunities.

Sweatt v. Painter
339 US 629 (1950)

Herman Marion Sweatt, the African American petitioner in this case, was refused admission to the University of Texas Law School on the grounds that substan-

tially equivalent facilities were already available in another Texas State law school open only to black students. The U.S. Supreme Court ruled that Sweatt be admitted to the University of Texas Law School. Chief Justice Fred M. Vinson wrote that "in terms of number of the faculty, variety of courses and opportunity for specialization, size of the student body, scope of the library, availability of law review and similar activities, the University of Texas Law School is superior" to those in the state law school for blacks. Therefore, the refusal to admit Sweatt to the University of Texas Law School was unconstitutional.

McLaurin v. Oklahoma State Regents for Higher Education
339 US 637 (1950)

After having been admitted to the University of Oklahoma, G. W. McLaurin, an African American, was required by school officials to occupy a special seat in each classroom and a segregated table in both the library and the cafeteria because of his race. The U.S. Supreme Court declared unanimously that the black student must receive the same treatment at the hands of the state as other students and could not be segregated.

Gray v. University of Tennessee
342 US 517 (1952)

This case resulted from the refusal of a U.S. District Court to force the University of Tennessee to admit black students. The lone judge to whom the matter was then referred ruled that the black students were entitled to admission, but did not order the university to enforce this ruling. The Supreme Court was asked to refer the case back to the District Court for further proceedings. Pending this appeal, however, one of the students seeking admission was enrolled at the University of Tennessee. Since the court found no suggestion that persons "similarly situated would not be afforded similar treatment," the case was dismissed as moot.

Brown v. Board of Education of Topeka
347 US 483 (1954)

This case involved the practice of denying black children equal access to state public schools due to state laws requiring or permitting racial segregation. The U.S. Supreme Court unanimously held that segregation deprived the children of equal protection under the Fourteenth Amendment to the U.S. Constitution. The "separate but equal" doctrine of *Plessy v. Ferguson* was overturned. After reargument a year later, the case was remanded (along with its four companion cases) to the

A black schoolroom in Missouri, c. 1930.

District Court, which was instructed to enter such orders as were necessary to ensure the admission of all parties to public schools on a racially nondiscriminatory basis.

Hawkins v. Board of Control
347 US 971 (1954)

This case resulted from a ruling of the Florida Supreme Court which denied an African American the right to enter the University of Florida Law School on the grounds that he had failed to show that a separate law school for blacks was not substantively equal to the University of Florida Law School. The U.S. Supreme Court vacated the judgment and remanded the case to the Florida Supreme Court for a decision in light of the ruling in *Brown* which overruled the separate but equal doctrine.

After two years, the Florida Supreme Court continued to deny Hawkins the right to enter the University of Florida. Also, it had appointed a commissioner to determine when in the future Hawkins could be admitted "without causing public mischief." However, the U.S. Supreme Court ruled that Hawkins should be admitted to the school promptly, since there was no palpable reason for further delay.

Turead v. Board of Supervisors
347 US 971 (1954)

This case was the result of a provisional injunction requiring the admittance of blacks to Louisiana State University. The state court of appeals reversed this action, declaring that it required the decision of a district court of three judges. The U.S. Supreme Court vacated this judgment and remanded the case for consideration, in light of *Brown v. Board of Education of Topeka.*

Frazier v. University of North Carolina
350 US 979 (1956)

The U.S. Supreme Court affirmed a District Court judgment that blacks may not be excluded from institutions of higher learning because of their race or color.

Cooper v. Aaron
358 US 1 (1958)

The impact of *Brown v. Board of Education of Topeka* was very slight until the Justice Department began to initiate its own desegregation lawsuits. Arkansas state officials passed state laws contrary to the Fourteenth Amendment holdings in *Brown I* and *Brown II* forbidding states to use their governmental powers to bar children on racial grounds from attending schools where there is state participation through any arrangement, management, funds or property; and to cease and desist from desegregation practices immediately.

In *Cooper,* the Attorney General of the United States filed a petition on behalf of the U.S. government to enjoin the governor of Arkansas and officers of the National Guard from preventing the admittance of nine black children into Central High School September 1957 in Little Rock. A law was passed relieving school children from compulsory attendance at racially mixed schools. The Supreme Court declared that the Fourteenth Amendment outlined in the *Brown* case is the supreme law of the land and cannot be nullified by state legislators, executive or judicial officers or evasive schemes for segregation.

Lee v. Macon County Board of Education
389 US 25 (1967)

The U.S. Supreme Court in *Lee v. Macon County Board of Education,* affirmed a lower court decision ordering the desegregation of Alabama's school dis-

tricts and declared state school grants to white students attending segregated private schools unconstitutional.

Alexander v. Holmes County Board of Education
396 US 19 (1969)

The U.S. Supreme Court, in *Alexander v. Holmes County Board of Education,* ordered all thirty-three school districts in Mississippi to desegregate. The Department of Health, Education and Welfare (HEW) had asked that the districts be granted more time to desegregate. This was the first time HEW had sought a delay in integration, but the Court ordered that integration proceed immediately.

North Carolina State Board of Education v. Swann
402 US 43 (1971)

&

Swann v. Charlotte Mecklenburg Board of Education
402 US 1 (1971)

In these two cases the U.S. Supreme Court affirmed the use of busing and faculty transfers to overcome the effects of dual school systems-segregated school systems resulting from residential patterns. Writing the decision, Chief Justice Warren E. Burger noted that "bus transportation has long been a part of all public educational systems and it is unlikely that a truly effective remedy could be devised without continued reliance upon it." The court declared that segregation resulted from past misconduct and affirmed the lower court's order that the school board bus students to

Black students being bused.

achieve a racial mix at each school. The ruling, however, left local district judges the authority to decide whether a desegregation plan was constitutionally adequate.

Wright v. City of Emporia
402 US 43 (1971)

&

Cotton v. Scotland Neck Board of Education
407 US 485 (1972)

The Supreme Court held that two towns with heavy concentrations of white students could not secede from a largely black county school system and form its own school district in an attempt to frustrate integration.

Richmond, Virginia School Board v. State Board of Education
412 US 92 (1973)

By a four to four vote, the U.S. Supreme Court declined to order the integration of the predominantly black schools in Richmond with those of two white suburbs. Though the Court wrote no decision, integrationists expressed concern that permitting de facto segregation to stand in this manner would hinder corrective action in other metropolitan areas, perpetuate "neighborhood" one-race schools, and lessen the extent of integration in unitary school systems.

Runyon v. McCrary
427 US 160 (1976)

In an unanimous decision, it was held that the Constitution places no value on discrimination, and while invidious, private discrimination may be characterized as a form of exercising the freedom of association protected by the First Amendment. In the 1976 decision, two black children were denied admission to private schools in Virginia. The Civil Rights Act of 1866 prohibits racial discrimination in the making and enforcing of contracts. The children's parents sought to enter into a contractual relationship with the private schools on an equal basis to white and nonwhite students.

Regents of University of California v. Allan Bakke
438 US 265 (1978)

Allan Bakke, a white male who had been denied admission to the University of California Medical School at Davis for two consecutive years, charged that the university's minority quota system—under which only disadvantaged members of certain minority races were considered for 16 of the 100 places in each year's class—denied him equal protection.

The trial court declared that the school could not take race into account in making the admissions decision and held that the challenged admissions program violated the federal and state constitutions and Title VI of the 1964 Civil Rights Act. The university appealed. Upon hearing the case, the U.S. Supreme Court ruled that Bakke had been illegally discriminated against and that numerical quotas based on race were unconstitutional.

Bob Jones University v. IRS
461 US 574 (1983)

Contrary to long-standing IRS policy, the Reagan administration sought to extend tax-exempt status to schools that discriminate on the basis of race. The U.S. Supreme Court recognized the inability of the Justice Department to argue the case fairly, and requested former Secretary of Transportation William T. Coleman to present the argument. The Supreme Court rebuffed the Justice Department's arguments and unanimously agreed with Coleman's position that the denial of tax-exempt status to racially discriminatory schools is unconstitutional.

Allen v. Wright
488 US 737 (1084)

Parents of African American children instituted a nationwide lawsuit claiming that the Internal Revenue Service's failure to deny tax-exempt status to racially discriminating private schools constituted federal financial aid to racially segregated institutions and diminished the ability of their children to receive a racially an adequate education. The U.S. Supreme Court refused to hear the case on the grounds that the plaintiffs did not have "standing" because they failed to show that the injury suffered was "fairly traceable" or caused by the conduct of the IRS. In addition the Court maintained that the remedy was "speculative" since there was no evidence that the withdrawal of tax-exempt status would cause schools to end their racially discriminatory practices. The court's imposition of such an artificial and stringent standing requirement, which had not been used in other cases involving school desegregation, effectively denied the African American parents their day in court.

Employment

Griggs v. Duke Power Co.
401 US 424 (1971)

Black employees challenged their employer's requirement of a high school diploma or passing of intelligence tests as a condition of employment or transfer to jobs at the plant that were previously held solely by whites prior to the enactment of Title VII of the Civil Rights Act of 1964. Blacks were employed only in the Labor Department where the highest paying jobs paid less than the lowest jobs in the other departments. When the company abandoned its policy restricting blacks to Labor in 1965, completion of high school and median scores on two aptitude tests were required to transfer from Labor to another department.

The Supreme Court found the objective of Congress in Title III was to achieve equality of employment opportunities and remove barriers that have operated in the past to favor an identifiable group of whites over other employees. Under the Act, practices, procedures, or tests neutral on their face and even neutral in their intent cannot be maintained if they operate to "freeze" the status quo of prior discrimination. The employment practice must be related to job performance.

It was determined that neither the high school diploma nor the intelligence tests were shown to bear a demonstrable relationship to successful job performance. Good intent or absence of discriminatory intent does not redeem employment procedures and practices. The employment policies had a discriminatory effect toward black employees.

Albemarle Paper Co. v. Moody
422 US 405 (1975)

African American employees of a paper mill in Roanoke Rapids, North Carolina successfully challenged the company's use of written tests which allegedly measured numerical and verbal intelligence. Based upon the standards enunciated in *Griggs v. Duke Power Co.*, the U.S. Supreme Court determined that the tests were discriminatory because they were not job-related and did not predict success on the job. More importantly, the Supreme Court held that the plaintiffs were entitled to "complete justice" and necessary relief that would "make them whole." The court awarded the African American employees back pay and made it clear that back pay should rarely be denied once there has been a showing of discrimination. The court also stated that back pay cannot be denied simply because the employer acted in good faith or did not intend to discriminate.

Hazelwood School District v. United States
433 US 299 (1977)

In this case, several African American teachers seeking jobs in suburban St. Louis, Missouri offered statistical data indicating they had been denied employment opportunities. The plaintiffs attempted to prove their case by showing that the percentage of black students was greater than the percentage of black teachers in the school district.

Although the U.S. Supreme Court affirmed that "statistics can be an important source of proof in employment discrimination cases," it rejected the plaintiffs'

statistical evidence calling it irrelevant. The court concluded that relevant statistical data would be the percentage of qualified black teachers in the relevant geographical area compared with the percentage of blacks in Hazelwood's teaching staff.

Teamsters v. United States
431 US 324 (1977)

In enforcing the Civil Rights Act of 1964, the U.S. Supreme Court held that victims of past union discrimination were entitled to retroactive seniority benefits. However, the Supreme Court required proof of "intent to discriminate," in order to establish that a given seniority system is illegal. Subsequent cases in lower federal courts during the late 1970s entitled discrimination victims to retroactive back pay in addition to retroactive seniority benefits.

Louis Swint and Willie Johnson v. Pullman Standard and the United Steelworkers of America
72 L.Ed 66 (1982)

African American employees of Pullman Standard brought a lawsuit into federal district court against Pullman Standard and the United Steelworkers of America. The lawsuit alleged that Title VII of the Civil Rights Act of 1964 was violated by a seniority system. In its decision, the District Court ruled "that the difference in terms, conditions or privileges of employment resulting from the seniority system are not the result of an intention to discriminate because of race or color" and held, therefore, that the system satisfied the requirements of Section 703(h) of the Civil Rights Act. This decision was later reversed by the Court of Appeals for the Fifth Circuit which stated that, "because we find the differences in the terms, conditions and standards of employment for black workers and white workers at Pullman Standard resulted from an intent to discriminate because of race, we hold that the system is not legally valid under Section 703(h) of Title VII U.S.C. 2000e-2(h)."

Meritor Savings Bank, FSB v. Vinson
106 S.Ct. 2399 (1985)

Michelle Vinson, an African American woman employed as a teller at a bank in Washington, DC, claimed that she had been sexually harassed for more than two months by her supervisor, Sidney Taylor, a white male. Vinson alleged that employment benefits were granted or denied based upon her performance of sexual favors.

In this first U.S. Supreme Court ruling on sexual harassment, the Court firmly condemned sexual harassment that creates an intimidating, hostile, and offensive working environment even when the harassment does not have economic ramifications. The unanimous ruling made it clear that Title VII of the Civil Rights Act prohibits sexual harassment that involves economic reprisals or harassment that creates a hostile, sexually charged atmosphere in the workplace.

Watson v. Fort Worth Bank and Trust
108 US 2777 (1987)

In the case of *Watson v. Fort Worth Bank and Trust* Clara Watson, an African American woman, alleged that she was repeatedly denied promotion to supervisory positions which were awarded to white employees with equivalent or lesser experience. The bank contended that its promotion decisions were based on various subjective criteria including experience, previous supervisory experience, and the ability to get along with others.

The U.S. Supreme Court held that Watson did not have to prove intentional discrimination. The court concluded that subjective facially neutral selection devices which disadvantage blacks in much the same way as objective criteria written tests are unlawful.

Lorance v. AT&T Technologies
490 US 900 (1989)

This case was brought by three women employed by ATT. A new seniority system was adopted and under the change the women were promoted from laborers to testers but lost some seniority in the process. The loss was intended to be temporary with full seniority restored in five years, but before that occurred the women were demoted. The women allege that their employer violated Title VII of the Civil Rights Act of 1964 by adopting the new seniority system with the purpose and effect of protecting incumbent testers—jobs traditionally dominated by men—from female employees who had greater plantwide seniority and who were becoming testers in increasing numbers. Unfortunately, the claims were brought too late. The court held that the charges had not been filed within the required period after the alleged unlawful employment practice occurred and therefore were thwarted.

Patterson v. McLean Credit Union
491 US 164 (1989)

A black female was employed as a teller and file coordinator for ten years until she was laid-off. She alleged that she had been harassed, denied promotion to accounting clerk, and later discharged because of her race. Petitioner filed suit asserting violations of Section 1981 of the Civil Rights Act.

Racial harassment relating to conditions of employment are not actionable under Section 1981 which provides, "... [a]ll persons ... shall have the same right to make and enforce contracts ... as any white citizen," because that provision does not apply to conduct which occurs after the formation of a contract including the breach of the contracts terms and enforcement thereof. Rather, the harassment asserted by the petitioner is past formation conduct of the employer which is actionable only under Title VII of the Civil Rights Act of 1964.

Wards Cove Packing Co. Inc. v. Antonio
490 US 642 (1989)

This case was brought by a class of nonwhite salmon cannery workers alleging that the employer's hiring and promotion practices were responsible for the workforces racial stratification and had denied them employment opportunities as noncannery workers on the basis of race. There were two types of jobs: unskilled cannery jobs, which were filled predominately by nonwhites; and noncannery jobs, mostly classified as skilled positions held by whites and virtually all paid more. Statistics were used to show a high percentage of nonwhites in cannery jobs and a low percentage in noncannery positions, in order to show a disparate impact caused by specific identifiable employment practices.

The U.S. Supreme Court found that the cannery workforce did not reflect the pool of qualified job applicants or the qualified labor force population. An employer's selection methods or employment practices cannot be said to have a disparate impact on nonwhites if the absence of minorities holding such skilled jobs reflects a dearth of qualified nonwhite applicants. A mere showing that nonwhites are underrepresented in the noncannery jobs will not suffice for a Title VII violation.

Jury Selection and Service

Neal v. Delaware
103 US 370 (1880)

The jury commissioner's conduct was found in violation of the U.S. Constitution where a black criminal defendant asserted that blacks were excluded from the jury based on their race. Every citizen is afforded the right to equal protection of the laws including that the selection of jurors to pass upon his life, liberty or property shall not be hindered by the exclusion of his race based on race.

Strauder v. West Virginia
100 US 303 (1880)

In this case, the Supreme Court granted immunity to a black criminal defendant from discrimination against him in the selection process of jurors based on their race. West Virginia's state law prohibited black men from eligibility to serve as a member of a grand jury or a petit jury in the state. Thereby, denying the equal protection of the laws to a citizen based solely on their race.

Virginia v. Rives
100 US 313 (1880)

The petitioners in *Rives* asserted that blacks had never been allowed to serve as jurors in their county in any case where a black man was interested. Virginia had no formalized or specific statute restricting black jurors from certain trials. It was held, that a mixed jury in a particular case is not essential to the equal protection of the laws, and that the right is not given by any state or federal statute.

Hollins v. Oklahoma
295 US 394 (1935)

The defendant in this case, an African American, was charged with rape and convicted on December 29, 1931 at a trial held in the basement of the jail in Sapula, Oklahoma. Three days before the scheduled execution, the National Association for the Advancement of Colored People secured a stay, and later, a reversal of his conviction by the Supreme Court of Oklahoma.

The U.S. Supreme Court—in a memorandum opinion—affirmed the principle that the conviction of an African American by a jury from which all blacks had been excluded was a denial of the equal protection clause of the Fourteenth Amendment to the U.S. Constitution.

Hale v. Commonwealth of Kentucky
303 US 613 (1938)

In 1936 Joe Hale, an African American, was charged with murder in McCracken County, Kentucky. Hale moved to set aside the indictment on the grounds that the jury commissioners had systematically excluded blacks from jury lists. Hale established that one out of every six residents of the county was black, and that at least 70 blacks out of a total of 6,700 persons qualified for jury duty. Still, there had not been a black on jury duty between 1906 and 1936. Hale's conviction and death sentence were upheld by the court of appeals of Kentucky, but both were struck down by the U.S. Supreme Court on the grounds that he had been denied equal protection of the law.

Patton v. Mississippi
332 US 463 (1947)

This case involved Eddie Patton, an African American who was indicted, tried, and convicted of the murder of a white man in Mississippi. At his trial and as part of his appeal, Patton alleged that all qualified blacks had been systematically excluded from jury service solely because of race. The state maintained that, since jury service was limited by statute to qualified voters and since few blacks were qualified to vote, such a procedure was valid in the eyes of the law. The U.S. Supreme Court, however, reversed Patton's conviction on the grounds that such a jury plan, resulting in the almost automatic elimination of blacks from jury service, constituted an infringement of Patton's rights under the Fourteenth Amendment.

Shepherd v. Florida
341 US 50 (1951)

The U.S. Supreme Court reversed the convictions of a Florida state court involving black defendants solely on the grounds that the method of selecting the grand jury discriminated against blacks.

Turner v. Fouche
396 US 346 (1970)

The U.S. Supreme Court, in *Turner v. Fouche*, affirmed the right of defendants to bring an action in federal court to end discrimination in jury selection.

Castanda v. Partida
430 US 482 (1977)

The U.S. Supreme Court in *Castanda v. Partida*, upheld the use of statistical evidence demonstrating that Mexican-Americans had been systematically excluded from jury selection, and that such discrimination on the basis of race or color violated the equal protection clause of the Constitution. The principle established in this case, that statistical evidence can be used to prove intentional discrimination, has been used in later cases involving employment, housing, voting and education.

Batson v. Kentucky
476 US 79 (1986)

In the U.S. Supreme Court ruling on *Batson v. Kentucky*, Justice Lewis F. Powell writing for the majority, held that the prosecution in a criminal case may not use its "preemptory challenge," those challenges to an individual juror for which no cause need be stated, to exclude black jurors in a case involving a black defendant.

Turner v. Murray
106 US 1683 (1986)

The U.S. Supreme Court in *Turner v. Murray*, expanded the right of black defendants in capital cases to question potential white jurors to uncover their racial prejudices and biases.

Public Accomodations

Hall v. DeCuir
95 US 485 (1878)

This case involved an unsuccessful attempt of the Louisiana legislature to prohibit racial desegregation in any form of transportation in the state. The statute was attacked as an interference with interstate commerce because it imposed a direct burden and control over common carriers when entering the state. The statute was declared unconstitutional and void because it required those engaged in the transportation of passengers among the states to carry black passengers in Louisiana in the same cabin with white passengers.

The congressional legislature will have to cure the defects in the existing laws, by refraining from action, Congress, in effect adopts the common or civil law; although, the State of Louisiana may see the need for adoption of new regulations for the public good concerning desegregation the enactments can only come from Congress where it effects interstate trade and influences business prospects.

Plessy v. Ferguson
163 US 537 (1896)

The *Plessy* case was a test of the constitutionality of an 1890 Louisiana statute providing for "separate but equal" railway carriages for whites and blacks. The information filed in the criminal District Court charged in substance that Homer Plessy, being a passenger between two stations within the state of Louisiana, was assigned by officers of the company to the coach used by the race to which he did not belong.

In the majority opinion of the U.S. Supreme Court, "separate but equal" accommodations for blacks constituted a "reasonable" use of state police power. Furthermore, it was said that the Fourteenth Amendment "could not have been intended to abolish distinctions based on color, or to enforce social ... equality or a co-mingling of the two races upon terms unsatisfactory to either."

Civil Rights Cases
332 US 46, 332 US 784, 333 US 831, 334 US 834, 378 US 226 (1883)

This group of civil rights cases was heard before the U.S. Supreme Court in an effort to determine the constitutionality of the Civil Rights Act of 1875, the first piece of national legislation which attempted to guarantee people of all races "full and equal enjoyment" of all public accommodations, including inns, public conveyances, theaters, and other places of amusement.

The court ruled, however, that the 1875 Civil Rights Act was unconstitutional inasmuch as it did not spring directly from the Thirteenth and Fourteenth Amendment s to the Constitution. In the view of the Court, the Thirteenth Amendment was concerned exclusively with the narrow confines of slavery and involuntary servitude. The Fourteenth Amendment, by a comparable yardstick of interpretation, did not empower Congress to enact direct legislation to counteract the effect of state laws or policies. The effect of this ruling was to deprive blacks of the very protections which the three postwar Freedom amendments were designed to provide.

Morgan v. Commonwealth of Virginia
328 US 373 (1946)

Irene Morgan, an African American, refused to move to the rear seat of a Greyhound bus which was traveling from Virginia to Washington, D.C., and was subsequently convicted in the lower Virginia courts for violating a state statute requiring segregation of the races on all public vehicles.

National Association for the Advancement of Colored People (NAACP) attorneys then carried the case through the Virginia courts and on to the U.S. Supreme Court, where it was decided that the Virginia statute could not apply to interstate passengers or motor vehicles engaged in such traffic.

Bob-Lo v. Michigan
333 US 28 (1948)

In this case, the operator of a line of passenger ships used to transport patrons from Detroit to an island amusement park was convicted of violating the Michigan Civil Rights Act for refusing passage to an African American. The U.S. Supreme Court upheld the application of the Michigan Civil Rights Act.

Rice v. Arnold
340 US 848 (1950)

This case involved the successful attempt to abolish segregation on a Miami, Florida golf course owned and operated by the city. The U.S. Supreme Court granted a writ of certiorari and overturned the judgment of the Florida Supreme Court which authorized the segregated use of the course.

District of Columbia v. John R. Thompson
346 US 100 (1952)

The Supreme Court unanimously held that a restaurant owner had violated federal law by discriminating

Lunchcounter sit-in protesters.

against and refusing service to patrons on the basis of race.

Muir v. Louisville Park Theatrical Association
347 US 971 (1954)

In 1954, several African Americans were refused admission to an amphitheater located in a Louisville city park, leased and operated by a privately owned group not affiliated in any way with the city. The Kentucky court of appeals found no evidence of unlawful discrimination, but the U.S. Supreme Court overturned this judgment and remanded the case for consideration in the light of the prevailing legal climate as articulated in Brown v. Board of Education.

Mayor and City Council of Baltimore v. Dawson
350 US 377 (1955)

The U.S. Supreme Court affirmed a judgment that the enforcement of racial segregation in public beaches and bathhouses maintained by public authorities is unconstitutional.

Holmes v. Atlanta
350 US 859 (1955)

This case involved a suit brought by African Americans to integrate a city-owned and city-operated golf course in Atlanta, Georgia. The segregated arrangements were ordered sustained by a lower court, but that order was overturned by the U.S. Supreme Court and the case remanded to the District Court with directions to enter a decree for plaintiffs in conformity with Mayor and City Council of Baltimore v. Dawson.

Flemming v. South Carolina Electric
351 US 901 (1956)

This case involved a suit brought by an African-American passenger against a bus company for damages due to the bus driver's having required her to change seats in accordance with South Carolina's segregation law. The trial judge dismissed the case on the grounds that the statute in question was valid, but the court of appeals reversed this decision, holding that the "separate but equal" doctrine was no longer valid. The U.S. Supreme Court upheld the court of appeals.

A segregated bus station in Durham, North Carolina.

Black bus riders in Montgomery, Alabama.

Gayle v. Browder
352 US 114 (1956)

This case challenged the constitutionality of state statutes and ordinances in effect in the city of Montgomery, Alabama, which required the segregation of whites and blacks on public buses. These statutes were first declared unconstitutional by the decision of a three-judge federal district court. The U.S. Supreme Court then affirmed this judgment.

Katzenbach v. McClung
379 US 802 (1964)

&

Heart of Atlanta v. United States
379 US 803 (1964)

In the *Katzenbach* case, the Attorney General of the United States sued Ollie's Barbecue Restaurant in Birmingham, Alabama for its refusal to serve blacks in its dining accommodations, a direct violation of the anti-discriminatory public accommodations clause of the 1964 Civil Rights Act. The U.S. District Court, Northern District of Alabama, held that the Civil Rights Act could not be applied under the Fourteenth Amendment to the U.S. Constitution, inasmuch as there was no "demonstrable connection" between food purchased in interstate commerce and sold in a restaurant that would affect commerce. The U.S. Supreme Court, however,

held that "the Civil Rights Act of 1964, as here applied, [is] plainly appropriate in the resolution of what. [Congress has]. found to be a national commercial problem of the first magnitude."

The *Heart of Atlanta* case dealt with a Georgia motel which solicited patronage in national advertising and had several out-of-state residents as guests from time to time. The motel had already instituted the practice of refusing to rent rooms to African Americans prior to the passage of the 1964 Civil Rights Act, and stated thereafter that it intended to continue this practice. The motel owner filed suit, maintaining that the 1964 Civil Rights Act violated both the Fifth Amendment and the Thirteenth Amendment. The United States countered with the argument that the refusal to accept blacks interfered with interstate travel, and that the Congress in voting to apply nondiscriminatory standards to interstate commerce was not violating either Amendment. The U.S. Supreme Court upheld the right of congressional regulation, stating that the power of Congress was not confined to the regulation of commerce among the states. "It extends to those activities intrastate which so affect interstate commerce, or the exercise of the power of Congress over it, as to make regulation of them appropriate means to the attainment of a legitimate end."

Bell v. Maryland
378 US 226 (1964)

The U.S. Supreme Court ordered a Maryland district court to reconsider its affirmation of a state court

Lunch counter protesters in Raleigh, North Carolina, 1960.

conviction of twelve African Americans for trespassing, when they refused to leave a restaurant that refused to serve them entirely on the basis of their color.

Evans v. Newton
382 US 296 (1966)

The U.S. Supreme Court ruled that transfer of a city park from municipal ownership to a board of private trustees does not remove its obligations under the Fourteenth Amendment.

Shuttlesworth v. Birmingham
394 US 147 (1969)

The U.S. Supreme Court invalidated Birmingham's Parade-Permit law which had been used in 1963 to harass participants in an Easter March organized by Dr. Martin Luther King, Jr. *New York State Club Association v. City of New York*

108 S.Ct. 2225 (1988)

In a unanimous decision, the U.S. Supreme Court upheld the constitutionality of a New York City ordinance that forbids so-called private clubs from discriminating against women and minorities.

Interacial Marriage

Loving v. Virginia
388 US 1 (1967)

This case virtually nullified the anti-miscegenation laws, many of which remain in southern state constitutions and legal codes. It concerned a white man and black woman, residents of Virginia, who married in Washington, D.C. The state of Virginia indicted and convicted them of violating its laws against racial intermarriage when the couple returned to Virginia and attempted to reside there, but released them when the couple agreed not to reside in the state for 25 years. The Lovings, however, decided to challenge the agreement and the law. Their appeal was rejected by the Virginia courts but upheld by the U.S. Supreme Court, which ruled the Virginia law unconstitutional. Soon thereafter, federal district courts in other states which forbade intermarriage were ordering local officials to issue marriage licenses to interracial couples applying for them.

Requirements for Legislative Membership

Powell v. McCormack
395 US 486 (1969)

According to the Constitution, only three basic factors govern eligibility to serve as a legislator in the U.S. House of Representatives: a minimum age requirement, the possession of U.S. citizenship, and the fulfillment of the state's residency requirement. When U.S. Representative Adam Clayton Powell, Jr. was excluded from the 90th Congress on the grounds that he had misused public funds and defied the courts of his home state, he filed suit in federal court in an attempt to force the House to review only the necessary credentials for membership.

The district court dismissed the first petition on the grounds that it lacked jurisdiction. By the time the case was finally heard before the U.S. Supreme Court, the

Plaintiffs Woodrow Lewis, Albert Dunn, and George Willis meet with attorneys William Alexander and D.L. Hollowell in a suit against an Atlanta restauranteur, 1965.

90th Congress had adjourned. Powell, however, was reelected and finally seated in the 91st Congress, a gesture which in the view of the court did not settle the case. The legal point on which the case hinged involved the distinction between "expulsion" and "exclusion." Despite the more than two-thirds majority required for expulsion, the Court ruled that the intent of the House was to "exclude," not to "expel." The court summation stated flatly that "the House was without power to exclude him from its membership."

Right of Sale and Restrictive Covenants

Buchanan v. Warley
245 US 60 (1917)

The plaintiff, Buchanan, brought an action in this case for the performance of a sale of certain real estate in Louisville, Kentucky. The purchaser, Warley an African American, maintained that he would be unable to occupy the land since it was located within what was defined by a Louisville ordinance as a white block. (The ordinance prohibited whites from living in black districts, and vice versa.) Buchanan alleged that the ordinance was in conflict with the Fourteenth Amendment

to the U.S. Constitution. The U.S. Supreme Court maintained that the ordinance was unconstitutional.

Shelley v. Kraemer
334 US 1 (1948)

&

Hurd v. Hodge
334 US 26 (1948)

On August 11, 1945, an African American family, the Shelleys, received a warranty deed to a parcel of land which, unknown to them, was subject to a restrictive covenant barring its sale to blacks. A lawsuit was subsequently brought in the Circuit Court of St. Louis seeking to divest the Shelleys of the title to the land. The Supreme Court of Missouri directed the trial court to strip the petitioners of their warranty deed.

The U.S. Supreme Court reversed this decision, maintaining that restrictive covenants, though valid contracts, could not be enforced by state courts. In the *Hurd v. Hodge* case, involving a similar set of circumstances, federal courts were similarly prohibited from enforcing such restrictive covenants.

Adam Clayton Powell leaves the Capitol after the House voted to take away his Education and Labor Committee chairmanship.

Reitman v. Mulkey
387 US 369 (1967)

In 1964, the California electorate voted in favor of a referendum granting "absolute discretion" to real estate owners in the sale and rental of real property, in effect voiding the state's fair housing laws. Lincoln Mulkey filed suit against property owners in Orange County to challenge the validity of the referendum. Mulkey's position failed in the lower courts but was sustained five to two by the California Supreme Court on the grounds that the California referendum violated the Fourteenth Amendment of the U.S. Constitution. The U.S. Supreme Court upheld the decision.

Jones v. Alfred H. Mayer, Co.
392 US 409 (1968)

Joseph Lee Jones alleged that the sole reason a realtor refused to sell him a home was because he was black. The U.S. Supreme Court held that 42 U.S.C. 1982, a federal statute created during the Reconstruction era to eliminate the vestiges of slavery, prohibits all racial discrimination, public and private in the sale or rental of property.

Trafficante v. Metropolitan Life Insurance
409 US 205 (1972)

The U.S. Supreme Court ruled that a complaint of racial discrimination in housing may be brought by parties who have not themselves been refused accommodation but who, as members of the same housing unit, allege injury by discriminatory housing practices. The suit had been filed by a black and a white resident of a housing development in San Francisco, who contended that the owner of the development, in maintaining a "white ghetto," was depriving plaintiffs of the right to live in a racially integrated community.

Sentencing and Incarceration

McKlesky v. Kemp
481 US 279 (1987)

In April of 1987, the U.S. Supreme Court decided one of the most significant cases involving the imposition of the death penalty in America. Warren McKlesky, a 38-year-old African-American man accused of killing a police officer while robbing a furniture store, was sentenced to death by the State of Georgia. In support of his claim that the sentence violated his constitutional rights, McKlesky introduced a sophisticated statistical study that analyzed more than 2,000 murder cases in Georgia. The study demonstrated that there is a disparity in the imposition of the capital sentence based on the race of the victim, as well as the race of the defendant.

Defendants charged with killing white persons received the death penalty in eleven percent of the cases, but defendants charged with killing blacks received the death penalty in only one percent of the cases. The study further showed that prosecutors asked for the death penalty in seventy percent of the cases involving black defendants and white victims, and only nineteen percent of the cases involving white defendants and black victims. In sum, the analysis revealed that African Americans who kill whites are 4.3 times more likely to receive the death sentence.

In the five to four opinion, written by Justice Lewis F. Powell, the U.S. Supreme Court acknowledged that it had accepted statistics as proof of intent to discriminate in employment, housing and voting cases. However, despite the compelling statistical evidence the Court rejected McKlesky's claim that the death penalty in Georgia is applied in a racially discriminatory manner. The court's reasoning was that although McKlesky showed the existence of racial discrimination in sentencing, he failed to prove that "racial considerations played a part in his sentence." Finally, Justice Powell expressed concern that acceptance of McKlesky's argument would open the floodgates of litigation by black defendants seeking to introduce statistical evidence to demonstrate that race affected the outcome of their case.

Slavery

Prigg v. Pennsylvania
16 Peters 539

In violation of a 1826 Pennsylvania anti-kidnapping statute, Edward Prigg, a professional slave catcher, Maryland, took captive Margaret Morgan, a fugitive slave residing in Pennsylvania, and was tried and convicted for kidnapping. Hearing the case, the U.S. Supreme Court ruled that the Pennsylvania law was unconstitutional, on the grounds that the statute was an interference with Congress' power under Article 4, Section 2 of the Constitution.

Strader v. Graham
10 Howard 82 (1850)

In 1841, three slaves owned by Christopher Graham of Kentucky, boarded a steamboat owned by Jacob Strader and traveled to Cincinnati, from where they ultimately escaped to freedom in Canada. Graham sued Strader for the value of the slaves and the expenses incurred while trying to recover them. Graham won the case. However, Strader appealed, claiming that the slaves had become free under Ohio law and provisions of the Northwest Ordinance. The U.S. Supreme Court ruled unanimously that each state had the right to determine the status of slaves within its jurisdiction, that the status of these slaves was to be determined by the state of Kentucky, and that the Northwest Ordinance was no longer in force, since those territories had become states.

Dred Scott v. Sandford
19 Howard 393 (1857)

In 1835, Dred Scott, born a slave in Virginia, became the property of John Emerson, an Army doctor, in the slave state of Missouri. From there, he was taken into the free state of Illinois and later to the free territory of Minnesota.

In 1847, Scott instituted suit in the circuit court of the St. Louis County, Missouri, arguing that he should be given his freedom by virtue of his having resided on free soil. After nine years, his case was certified to the U.S. Supreme Court, where five of the nine justices, were Southerners.

In delivering his opinion, Chief Justice Roger Brooke Taney declared that, by virtue of both the Declaration of Independence and the Constitution, African Americans could not be regarded as citizens of the United States. Moreover, the Court could not deprive slaveholders of their right to take slaves into any part of the Union,

A newspaper depiction of a fugitive slave, 1837.

North or South. In effect, therefore, the Missouri Compromise, as well as other antislavery legislation, was declared to be unconstitutional.

Ableman v. Booth
21 Howard 506 (1859)

The U.S. Supreme Court upheld Congress' fugitive slave law and all its provisions; but, more importantly upheld the supremacy of federal law over state law. Booth was held in a state jail for violating the federal fugitive slave laws. Booth secured a writ of habeas corpus from a state judge who declared the federal laws unconstitutional and the Wisconsin Supreme Court affirmed. The state court had stepped beyond its sphere of authority. The federal court held Booth guilty, although the State of Wisconsin is a sovereign within its territorial limits, it is limited and restricted by the U.S. Constitution.

State and Local Affirmative Action Requirements

United States Steelworkers of America v. Brian Weber
433 US 193 (1979)

The United Steelworkers of America and Kaiser Aluminum Company entered into a collective bargaining

Poster advertising a public hearing on the *Dred Scott v. Sanford case.*

agreement including a voluntary affirmative action plan designed to eliminate conspicuous racial imbalances in Kaiser's almost exclusively white skilled workforce. The plant in Gramercy, Louisiana agreed to reserve 50 percent of the openings in the skilled job training programs for blacks until the percentage of African-American skilled workers was equal to the percentage of blacks in the local labor force. Brian Weber, a white production worker, who was turned down for the training program although he had more seniority than many accepted blacks, sued the United Steelworkers of America, claiming that the affirmative action program discriminated against whites.

The U.S. Supreme Court limited the issue to the narrow question of whether Title VII prohibited private employers and unions from establishing voluntary affirmative action plans. In a five to two decision, the Court upheld the affirmative action plan and established three factors to determine the validity of racial preference. The court approved the plan because it was designed to break down Kaiser's historic patterns of racial segregation; did not unnecessarily diminish the rights of white employees since it did not require the firing of white employees; and was a temporary meas-

ure not intended to maintain racial balance but simply to eliminate an imbalance. *Fullilove v. Klutznik*

448 US 448 (1980)

The U.S. Supreme Court upheld a provision of the Public Works Employment Act of 1977 that required a ten percent set-aside of federal funds for minority business enterprises on local public work projects. The provision had been challenged as violation of the equal protection clause of the Fifth Amendment.

Firefighters Local Union No. 1784 v. Stotts
467 US 561 (1984)

In May of 1981, for the first time in its history, the City of Memphis announced layoffs of city employees, due to a projected budget deficit. The layoffs, which included the fire department, were to be made on a "last hired, first fired" city-wide seniority system that had been adopted in 1973. Carl Stotts, an African American firefighter, sued to stop the layoffs, claiming that since African Americans had been hired pursuant to the affirmative action provisions of a 1980 court decree, they would be laid off in far greater numbers than their white coworkers. In a six to three decision the U.S. Supreme

Court held that since the 1980 court decree did not say that African Americans had special protection during a layoff, the layoffs had to be made according to the 1973 seniority system.

Wygant v. Jackson Board of Education
476 US 267 (1986)

The U.S. Supreme Court dealt a tremendous blow to affirmative action in this case involving a public school system's affirmative action plan. The record reflected that the first African American school teacher was not hired in Jackson, Michigan until 1953. By 1969, only 3.9 percent of the teachers were African American although 15.2 percent of the students were African American. In response, the school board developed an affirmative action plan that protected African American faculty members during layoffs.

Although the U.S. Supreme Court had approved affirmative action plans in prior cases, it rejected the Jackson plan. The court found that the goal of the plan, to remedy societal discrimination and afford positive role models to black students, was nebulous and not sufficiently compelling.

Local No. 93, International Association of Firefighters v. City of Cleveland
106 S.Ct. 3063 (1986)

The city of Cleveland, which had a long history of racial discrimination, negotiated a consent decree with African American firefighters who had filed a lawsuit alleging that they had been unlawfully denied jobs and promotions. The decree included an affirmative action plan with numerical goals for promotion of African Americans to the position of supervisor.

In response to the union's challenge on behalf of white firefighters, the U.S. Supreme Court ruled that the lower courts had broad discretion to approve decrees in which employers settle discrimination suits by agreeing to preferential promotions of African Americans, in spite of the objections of white employees.

Local 28, Sheet Metal Workers International Association v. EEOC
106 S.Ct. 3019 (1986)

After finding that the all-white union had discriminated against African Americans and Hispanics seeking to enter the sheet metal trades for more than a decade, the trial court ordered the union to establish a 29

African Americans are now represented on most city fire and police forces.

percent non-white membership goal. The court also ruled that the union would have to pay substantial fines if the union failed to meet the goals. After the union failed to reach the goal, the court found the union in contempt and established a new goal of 29.3 percent. The union challenged the court's order.

In a complex opinion, the U.S. Supreme Court upheld the affirmative action goal in light of the union's "persistent or egregious discrimination" and to eliminate "lingering effects of pervasive discrimination." This was the first time the Court expressly approved the use of race conscious relief to blacks and Hispanics who were not identified victims of discrimination.

United States v. Paradise
480 US 149 (1987)

This case originated in 1972 when the NAACP sued the Alabama Department of Highways because of its long-standing history of racially discriminating employment practices. More than 11 years later, after the Department had failed to hire or promote blacks, the trial court ordered the promotion of one black trooper for every white. The U.S. Attorney General challenged the constitutionality of the plan. The U.S. Supreme Court upheld the use of strict racial quotas and found that the plan was "narrowly tailored to serve a compelling government interest"—remedying "egregious" past discrimination against blacks.

Johnson v. Transportation Agency, Santa Clara County, California
480 US 616 (1987)

The U.S. Supreme Court held that the state transportation agency's voluntary affirmative action plan, under which a female had been promoted to the position of road dispatcher over a male whose score was slightly higher, was consistent with Title VII of the Civil Rights Act of 1964. The court held that an employer does not have to admit or prove that it has discriminated in order to justify efforts designed to achieve a more racially balanced workforce. The employer only needs to demonstrate that there is a "conspicuous ... imbalance in traditionally segregated job categories."

City of Richmond v. J. A. Croson Co.
109 S.Ct. 706 (1989)

Richmond adopted a Minority Business Utilization Plan that was not sufficiently narrowly tailored to remedy past discrimination in the construction industry. The Plan allowed minorities a fixed 30 percent quota of the public contracts based solely on their race. The policy provided no guidance for the city's legislating body to determine the precise scope of the injury it sought to remedy except racial balancing.

◆ LEGAL GATEKEEPERS

Clifford L. Jr. Alexander 1933-
Attorney, Federal Government Official

Born in New York City, September 21, 1933, Clifford Alexander went to Harvard and earned a bachelor's degree *cum laude* in 1955, and attended Yale Law School afterwards, earning a LL.B. in 1958. After attending these prestigious universities, he went on to become the assistant district attorney of New York County, working there from 1959 to 1961. Positions as the executive director of the Hamilton Grange Neighborhood Conservation district in Manhattanville from 1961 to 1962, and as executive program director of HARYOU from 1962 to 1963, followed. In 1963, he became a member of the National Security Council.

Alexander was hired by President Lyndon Johnson as his deputy special assistant in 1964, and quickly rose to become the President's deputy special counsel in 1967. He became chairman of the Equal Employment Opportunity Commission in 1967, where he was under constant pressure from Republican Senators like Everett Dirksen, who accused him of bullying reluctant employers into complying with federal guidelines for minority employment. He left that position in 1969.

In the years between 1969 and 1976, Alexander worked for several different law offices in private practice. He

also became a Harvard overseer. At Harvard, he was involved in working out details with craft unions which were obliged to offer and implement concrete proposals for improving minority employment opportunities.

President Jimmy Carter appointed Alexander as the secretary of the Department of the Army, the first African American to serve in that position. Alexander won the Outstanding Civilian Service Award from the Department of the Army in 1980, after he finished his 1977–80 appointment to that position. Since 1981, Alexander has been president of Alexander Associates, Inc., and served as a consultant to Major League Baseball, working to improve minority hiring practices. In the early 1990s, Alexander served as Washington, DC's chief negotiator in hammering out a deal to build a new stadium for the National Football League's Washington Redskins.

In addition, Alexander has had his own television program, "Black on White," has been director of several Dreyfus money funds, has served on the board of directors for the Mexican–American Legal Defense and Education Fund, and has taught as a professor at Howard University.

Violette Anderson 1882-19??
Judge/Magistrate, Attorney

Violette Anderson was born July 16, 1882, in London, England, the daughter of Richard E. and Marie (Jordi) Neatley. When she was young, the family moved to the United States, where she attended North Division High School in Chicago, Illinois from 1895 to 1899; Chicago Athenaeum, 1903; the Chicago Seminar of Sciences from 1912 to 1915, and Chicago Law School from 1917 to 1920, earning her LL.B. in 1920. Soon after, she was wed to Albert E. Johnson. Anderson was a Republican and her church affiliation was Episcopalian.

Anderson worked as a court reporter from 1905 to 1920, a job which sparked her interest in law. She began a private practice in 1920, becoming the first African-American woman to practice law in the U.S. District Court Eastern Division. From 1922 to 1923, she served as the first female city prosecutor in Chicago.

After five years of practice before the high court of Illinois, by application of Judge James A. Cobb of Washington, DC, Anderson was admitted to practice for the Supreme Court of the United States, becoming the first African American woman to obtain this post. Her admission became a precedent that allowed other African American women to do the same.

Anderson also belonged to the Federal Colored Women's Clubs, was president of Friendly Big Sisters League of Chicago, First Vice-President of Cook County Bar

Association, and secretary of Idlewild Lot Owners Association. In addition, she was the member of the executive board of Chicago Council of Social Agencies.

Deborah A. Batts 1946?-
Judge/Magistrate

The first openly lesbian federal judge, Batts was confirmed to a Manhattan bench in 1994. A graduate of Radcliffe and Harvard Law School, Batts earned her credentials through hard work. A native Philadelphian, Batts clerked for a federal judge before joining Cravath, Swaine & Moore, where she worked as a litigator for six years. Next she served as assistant U.S. attorney in New York for five years before accepting a teaching post at Fordham University in 1994. There she taught property and family law.

A supporter of equal rights for gays and lesbians, Batts is known to be a an independent thinker unafraid to speak her mind. She was drawn to the legal field after experiencing the political turmoil of the 1960s, in particular, the bitter assassinations of Martin Luther King, Jr. and Bobby Kennedy. She was initially recommended for a federal judgeship during the Bush administration but did not receive a nomination. U.S. Senator Daniel Moynihan recommended her a second time when President Clinton assumed office. Clinton's nomination of Batts was confirmed by the Senate with no challenges.

Derrick Albert Bell 1930-
Attorney, Educator

Derrick Albert Bell, Jr. was born in Pittsburgh, Pennsylvania, November 6, 1930, the son of Derrick and Ada Bell. He attended Duquesne University and received his LL.B. from the University of Pittsburgh Law School. He married Jewel A. Hairston and the couple has three children. Bell is a member of the bar in Washington, DC, Pennsylvania, New York, California; the U.S. Supreme Court; the U.S. Courts of Appeals for fourth, fifth, sixth, eighth, and tenth circuits; and several federal district courts. Since 1969 he has been teaching law at Harvard Law School. Bell has written several important books on the law, including *Race, Racism and American Law*, second edition, 1980, and *And We Are Not Saved, The Elusive Quest for Racial Justice*, 1987. Bell also served as editor of *Desegregation Dialogue, Searching for Remedies Under Brown*.

After graduating from law school, Bell worked for the U.S. Department of Justice from 1957 to 1959, at the Pittsburgh Branch of the NAACP as executive secretary from 1959 to 1960, and for the NAACP Legal Defense and Education Fund as staff attorney from 1960 to 1966. In 1966 he was made deputy assistant to the secretary for civil rights for the Department of Health, Education and Welfare. He also served for a year as the director of the Western Center on Law and Poverty.

Bell began as a lecturer on law at Harvard Law School in 1969, became a professor in 1971, and left in 1980 to be dean of the University of Oregon Law School for five years. After spending one year teaching at Stanford University, he returned to Harvard Law School in 1986. Four years later, Bell took an unpaid extended leave from his teaching duties at Harvard in protest over the institution's lack of a tenured black woman professor. Student support for Bell's actions was immense, but Bell was formally removed from his position in 1992. Nonplussed, Bell went on to write two well-received books—1992's

Faces at the Bottom of the Well: The Permanence of Racism and 1994's *Confronting Authority: Reflections of an Ardent Protester.*

Jane Matilda Bolin 1908-
Judge/Magistrate, Attorney

At the relatively young age of 31, Jane Matilda Bolin was honored by being chosen to be the first African American woman judge in the United States. She presided over the Domestic Relations Court of the City of New York (subsequently called the Family Court of the State of New York) for forty years. Her first ten-year appointment came from Mayor Fiorello La Guardia in 1939. She was appointed to three more successive ten-year terms by mayors William O'Dwyer, John Lindsay, and Robert F. Wagner, Jr. After forty years of service, Bolin reached the mandatory retirement age and had to step down, but not before she became well known over the country for her work. Bolin was also known for her striking beauty. John Powers, head of a world-renowned modeling agency, named her one of the "Powers Girls" of 1949.

Born April 11, 1908 in Poughkeepsie, New York, her father was the first African American graduate of Williams College. Bolin attended Wellesley College and Yale University School of Law, where she received her LL.B. in 1931. She worked with her father, who was also a lawyer, until she passed the New York State Bar examination; she then practiced in Poughkeepsie before moving to New York City to practice law with her husband, Ralph E. Mizelle.

In 1937, Bolin was appointed assistant corporation counsel for New York City, a post which she held until she received her appointment to the Domestic Relations Court. Outside of her career, Bolin has taken an active role in the Wiltwyck School for Boys, the Child Welfare League of America, the Neighborhood Children's Center, and the local and national NAACP. She has also travelled extensively and met several heads of state in Africa. She counted among her friends Eleanor Roosevelt, educator Mary McLeod Bethune and Judge Waties Waring, who ruled in the first public school desegregation case. Bolin has received honorary degrees from Morgan State University, Western College for Women, Tuskegee Institute, Hampton University and Williams College.

After her retirement, Bolin became a volunteer reading teacher for the New York City public schools for a few years. She received an appointment to the Regents Review Committee of the New York State Board of Regents, which holds hearings involving professional discipline of more than 32 professions. Bolin was honored for her distinguished service by the corporation counsel's office on May 17, 1993.

Johnnie L. Cochran, Jr. 1937-
Attorney

Though he was born in Shreveport, Louisiana on October 2, 1937, Johnnie L. Cochran, Jr. grew up in Los Angeles. He received a bachelor's degree from the University of California in 1959. After finishing his law studies at the Loyola Marymount University School of Law, he passed the California bar exam in 1963. Cochran began his law career as prosecutor in the criminal division of the deputy city attorney's office in Los Angeles. In 1965, he left that post to join criminal lawyer Gerald Lenoir in private practice. Shortly thereafter, he created Cochran, Atkins & Evans, a three-partner law firm.

During his first stint in private practice, Cochran established himself with defending high-profile African American clients, such as Leonard Deadwyler's family, a young man shot to death by police while driving his pregnant wife to the hospital, and Geronimo Pratt, a former Black Panther charged with murder. Cochran lost both cases, but he demonstrated how such cases could garner media attention and foment the African American community into action.

Cochran returned to the Los Angeles County district attorney's office in 1978, in order to better his image as one of the best lawyers on the west coast. After five years as a prosecutor, he once again returned to private practice in 1983. Shortly thereafter, Cochran won a settlement for the family of Ron Settles, who had been strangled by police officers, though his death was originally identified as a suicide.

Cochran's victories increased from hundreds of thousands in settlements to millions, and he began representing celebrities such as pop-singer Michael Jackson actor Todd Bridges. Starting in the summer of 1994 and continuing through the summer of 1995, Cochran served as one of the team of defense lawyers for O. J. Simpson, accused of murdering his ex-wife Nicole Brown Simpson

and her friend Ronald Goldman. Cochran wore down the prosecution by challenging evidence and concentrating on racially prejudiced officers. Cochran's closing arguments charged the jury to stop racism such as the kind that, as he claimed, framed O. J. Simpson for murder. In response, the jury acquitted Simpson on all counts.

Following the Simpson case—described in the media as "The Trial of the Century," Cochran became one of the best known lawyers in the country and was offered a million-dollar advance for his memoirs. Cochran has served as an adjunct professor at both the Los Angeles School of Law and the Loyola University School of Law. He served as chairman of the Rules Committee of the Democratic National Convention in 1984. In 1995, he was awarded the Trumpet Award by the Turner Broadcasting System.

George Crockett, Jr. 1909-
Attorney, Judge/Magistrate, Legislator, Civil Rights/ Human Rights Activist

Born in Jacksonville, Florida, on August 10, 1909, Crockett began working when he was only 12 and later graduated from Morehouse College. Traveling north to Michigan to pursue a law degree, Crockett then returned to his hometown and opened a law practice. In 1939, his accomplishments as a lawyer and community activist led him to be chosen as the first African American attorney in the U.S. Department of Justice.

While in Washington, DC, Crockett distinguished himself as counsel for cases that came before the Fair Labor Standards Act, and, in 1943, his work led to his appointment by President Franklin D. Roosevelt as an examiner with the Fair Employment Practices Committee. That same year, he was hired by the United Auto Workers headquarters in Detroit, to serve as director of their Fair Employment Practices office during a time of increased racial tensions in the city. In 1946, he went into private practice in Detroit with three other attorneys and for many years their firm took on significant civil rights cases. The passion with which Crockett once argued a case on behalf of accused Communists in a contentious courtroom battle landed him in prison for four months for a contempt of court violation.

Crockett became intensely involved in the civil rights struggle in the South during the 1960s, leaving Michigan for a time to direct the National Lawyers Guild civil rights efforts through an effort known as Project Mississippi. In 1966, he was elected to Detroit Recorder's Court, a bench that handled the city's criminal docket. During a 1969, incident in which members of a leftist group who were meeting at an African American church were brought en masse into police custody after a shooting outside the church, Crockett went down to the station in the middle of the night and set up his own impromptu court, letting most of the charged free on the basis of constitutional law. He was vilified by Detroit's white establishment for his application of the Bill of Rights in the fracas.

In 1980, two years after he had left the Recorder's Court bench, Crockett was elected as a Democratic Congressional representative for a Michigan district that included part of Detroit. He served in Washington for the next decade, continuing to distinguish himself by speaking out on civil rights issues and even serving another—albeit one-night—stint in jail for participating in a demonstration against apartheid in South Africa. The legislator was also a vocal opponent of Reagan Administration policies in Central America, especially during his tenure as chair of the Foreign Affairs Subcommittee on the Western Hemisphere. After his retirement from politics in 1990, Crockett, founder of the National Bar Association Judicial Council, continued to live in the Washington, DC area.

Drew S. Days III 1941-
Attorney, Educator

Days was born in Atlanta, Georgia on August 29, 1941. He received a bachelor's degree from Hamilton College in 1963 and continued his studies at the Yale Law School. During his free summer months, Days returned to Georgia to champion civil rights causes and represent the poor as an intern in a one-lawyer office. After graduating from law school near the top of his class in 1966, Days moved to Chicago to represent minorities in cases of housing discrimination in the city. Later Days quit practicing law to work in Honduras for the U.S. Peace Corps.

Upon his return to the United States one year later, Days worked in the Legal Defense and Educational Fund for the National Association for the Advancement of Colored People (NAACP). While working for NAACP, he served as an associate professor at Temple University in Philadelphia. In 1977, Days accepted a post as the first African American as the head of the civil rights division of the U.S. Department of Justice. In 1980, when the power in Washington shifted from Carter to Reagan, Days left the government to teach at Yale University.

In 1992, President Bill Clinton nominated Days to the position of solicitor general of the United States, the second leading position at the Justice Department. In this position, Days has criticized poorly conceived or poorly managed minority-assistance programs, and in 1995, he argued before the Supreme Court to keep in place "minority voting districts" in the Deep South. Early in 1996, Days resigned his position at the Justice Department to return to teaching law at Yale University.

Jerome Farris 1930-
Attorney, Judge/Magistrate

Jerome Farris was elected circuit judge of the U.S. Court of Appeals Ninth Circuit in 1979, and continues to serve in that capacity. Judge Farris was born on March 4, 1930, in Birmingham, Alabama. Willie Joe and Elizabeth Farris were his parents. He earned his B.S. degree from Morehouse College in 1951. In 1952, he joined the U.S. Army Signal Corps. He received a M.S.W. from Atlanta University in 1955, and received his J.D. from the University of Washington in 1958. Farris is married to Jean Shy and has two children.

Farris started out in private practice with Weyer, Schroeter and Sterne in 1958, becoming a partner in 1959. He stayed in private practice until he became a Washington State court of appeals judge in 1969. He was the chairman of the State Federal Judicial Council of Washington from 1983 to 1987. In addition, he has served as president on the Washington State Jr. Chamber of Commerce from 1965 to 1966; a trustee with the Pacific Northwest Ballet from 1978 to 1983; and as a regent of the University of Washington since 1985.

Farris has been honored with the Clayton Frost Award from the Jaycees in 1966, received an honorary LL.D. from Morehouse College in 1978, and the Order of the Coif from the University of Washington Law School.

Archibald H. Grimké 1849-1930
Attorney, Writer, Activist, Diplomat

Archibald Grimké was born on a plantation near Charleston, South Carolina, in 1849. His father was a successful lawyer who had given up his profession to become a planter. His mother had been a family slave and served as the nurse for Henry Grimké's first wife, Selena. Archibald was considered a slave due to South Carolina law at the time. He, along with his mother and siblings, were passed on to relatives after his father's death. Grimké attended a special school during his youth. He later fled his home. Grimké enrolled in a school directed by Frances Pillsbury and impressed the instructors there with his superior academic abilities. He completed undergraduate studies in only three years and obtained his master's degree from Lincoln University two years following that, in 1872.

Grimké moved to Boston and practiced law there from 1875 to 1883. Beginning in 1885, he presided over the Women's Suffrage Association of Massachusets. In the early 1890's, Grimké wrote for Boston-area publications, before being appointed the American consul for Santo Domingo (now the Dominican Republic) for four years. He then assumed the presidential role for the Washington chapter of the NAACP while writing, lecturing, and presiding over the American Negro Academy.

Grimké write several books, including biographies of William Lloyd Garrison in 1891 and Charles Sumner in 1892, and numerous essays and speeches.

William H. Hastie 1904-1976
Attorney, Judge/Magistrate, State Government Official/Executive

From 1949 to 1971, William H. Hastie served as a U.S. Court of Appeals Judge of the Third Circuit, the first African American man to hold a federal appeals judicial position. Hastie was born in Knoxville, Tennessee, November 17, 1904. He was the son of William Henry and Roberta Child Hastie. He received his A.B. from Amherst College in 1925, an LL.B. from Harvard University in 1930 and a S.J.D. from the same institution in 1933. He received honorary LL.D.s from many institutions, including Rutgers University, Howard University and Temple University. In 1943, he married Beryl Lockhart. The couple had three children.

Hastie was admitted to the bar in 1930 and was in private practice from 1930 to 1933. In 1933, he became assistant solicitor of the Department of the Interior, where he served until 1937. In 1937, he became a judge of the District Court of the Virgin Islands, leaving in 1939 to become dean of the Howard University School of Law. In 1942, he was the first civilian aide to the secretary of war. He was governor of the Virgin Islands between 1946 and 1949, before his subsequent position as U.S. Circuit Court of Appeals judge. Hastie was also a Trustee of the Amherst College and a Fellow of the American Academy of Arts and Sciences. Hastie died April 14, 1976, in Philadelphia, Pennsylvania.

Joseph W. Hatchett 1932-
Attorney, Judge/Magistrate, Author/Poet

Judge Joseph W. Hatchett was appointed a U.S. Circuit Judge of the U.S. Court of Appeals on October 1, 1981, and he currently retains that position. Judge Hatchett was the first black to be appointed to the highest court of a state since reconstruction, the first black to be elected to public office in a statewide election in the South, and first black to serve on a federal appellate court in the South.

Born in Clearwater, Florida, September 17, 1932, Hatchett received his A.B. from Florida A&M University in 1954 and his J.D. from Howard University in 1959. He also has certification in his specialties—a Naval Justice School Certificate in 1973, an Appellate Judge Course in 1977, and an American Academy of Judicial Education Appellate Judge Course in 1978.

Hatchett was in private practice in Florida from 1959 to 1966, and served as the contract consultant for the City of Daytona Beach for three years. He became an

assistant U.S. attorney in Jacksonville, Florida in 1966, then served as the first assistant of the U.S. Attorney for the Middle District of Florida. In 1971, he became the U.S. magistrate for the Middle District of Florida, and was a Supreme Court justice for the state of Florida from 1975 to 1979. He was a U.S. Circuit judge for the U.S. Court of Appeals, Fifth Circuit from 1979 to 1981, before advancing to his current position.

Hatchett was honored with a Howard University Post Graduation Achievement Award in 1977, named Most Outstanding Citizen from the Broward County National Bar Association in 1976 received a Medallion for Human Relations from Bethune-Cookman in 1975, and has been awarded several honorary doctorates. He is the author of several publications in the field of law.

A. Leon Higginbotham, Jr. 1928-
Judge/Magistrate, Author

Leon Higginbotham, Jr. was appointed on October 13, 1977 by President Jimmy Carter to the U.S. Circuit Judge's position. Just prior to this appointment, he had served on the Federal Trade Commission—the first black and the youngest person ever to hold the post of commissioner. Born in Trenton, New Jersey, on February 25, 1928, Higginbotham began as an engineering student at Purdue University, but later went to Antioch College to study liberal arts. He received his LL.B. in 1952 from Yale School of Law. This was quite a step for a man who started out as a shoe store porter.

After graduation, he became an assistant district attorney in Philadelphia, and later moved into private practice. He was sought out by Pennsylvania Governor David Lawrence to become a member of the Pennsylvania Human Rights Commission. Elected president of the Philadelphia chapter of NAACP, Higginbotham later earned the honor of "One of the 10 Outstanding Young Men in America" by the U.S. Junior Chamber of Commerce. He was made district judge in 1964, where he served until his appointment as a federal appellate judge in 1977. Higginbotham was also a lecturer at Harvard Law School and an adjunct professor at the University of Pennsylvania. In 1993, he was nominated for a position on the New York Times Co. board of directors.

In 1995, a retired Higginbotham levied criticism at Supreme Court Justice Clarence Thomas, whose judicial philosophy differs greatly from his own. While Higginbotham advocated social engineering through legislation, Thomas vigorously held that law should be colorblind. Higginbotham was, in turn, criticized for what some saw as an unprovoked attack on a colleague.

Higginbotham is well known for his prolific writing. He has authored more than 100 articles as well as an acclaimed book, *In the Matter of Color: Race and the*

William Hastie, 1949

American Legal Process: The Colonial Period. He has also been praised for his unusual competency in logic and language; in his esteemed career, he has won more than 40 honorary degrees. Higginbotham was awarded the nation's highest medal in 1995, when the Presidential Medal of Freedom was bestowed upon him by President Clinton.

Anita Hill 1956-
Educator, Author, Lecturer

Born on July 30, 1956, in Morns, Oklahoma, Anita Hill was a relatively unknown law professor at the University of Oklahoma when her name became a household word virtually overnight. It was during the Senate confirmation hearings in October 1991, for U.S. Supreme Court Justice Clarence Thomas that Hill became famous. She came forward with sexual harassment charges against Judge Thomas that shocked the nation, and many watched as she poured out painful details of Thomas's alleged sexual harassment, purportedly committed when both had worked for the Equal Employment Opportunities Commission. Hill claimed that Thomas repeatedly pressured her to date him, told her plots of pornographic movies, and bragged about his sexual

exploits. When asked why she didn't quit her job or report Thomas when the incidents occurred during the early 1980s, Hill answered that she feared she would not be able to get another job.

Following the hearings, Hill continued to be hounded by the press. Several books were written and a 76-minute documentary composed of testimony clips entitled *Sex and Justice: The Highlights of the Anita Hill/ Clarence Thomas Hearings* was released. Her experience with the hearings had changed her life, as well as her career direction. She had been a professor of commercial law. She decided to take a year–long sabbatical in order to look at the possibility of founding an institute with the purpose of researching racism and sexism. Hill also made many speeches around the country about her experience.

Controversy did not escape her on campus, either. Several lawmakers made news when they requested that Hill be fired. However, the University of Oklahoma dean and other members of the faculty supported her. In 1993, a university professorship to be established in Hill's name was proposed; though the suggestion met much opposition, the endowed chair was approved two years later.(The Anita Faye Hill Professorship provides

A. Leon Higginbotham, Jr., 1969

a salary and money for research and travel expenses incurred in the study of women's rights in the workplace.)

On March 9, 1995, Hill cited no reasons as she announced her resignation from the university, but after taking an unpaid leave during which she presumably intended to write, she resumed her teaching post in September of the same year. *Race, Gender, and Power in America,* co-edited by Hill and Emma Coleman Jordan, was published in 1995.

Charles Hamilton Houston 1895-1950
Attorney, Educational Administrator

Charles Hamilton Houston was born in Washington, DC, on September 3, 1895. Finishing high school at the young age of fifteen, he went on to attend Amherst College and earned his A.B. from that institution in 1915, one of six valedictorians. He taught English briefly, then enlisted in the U.S. Army in 1917, and served in France and Germany until 1919. He attended Harvard Law School and became the first African American editor of the *Harvard Law Review*. He received his LL.B. in 1922, and was at the top five percent of his class. He also became the first African American to receive a S.J.D. from Harvard University in 1923. In 1923, he received a Sheldon Fellowship and studied civil law at the University of Madrid. He was admitted to the Washington, DC, bar in 1924.

Houston was in private practice with his father from 1924 to 1950. Between 1929 and 1935, he was vice dean of the school of law at Howard University. He was

Anita Hill

special counsel to the NAACP from 1935 to 1940, and a member of the national legal aid committee from 1940 to 1950. He served as the vice president for the American Council on Race Relations from 1944 to 1950, and was a member of the President's Commission on Fair Employment Practice in 1944.

While with the NAACP, Houston teamed with the American Fund for Public Service to direct a program of legal action and education aimed at the elimination of segregation. Former student Thurgood Marshall served under Houston for several years. While in this position, Houston argued several cases before the U.S. Supreme Court, including *Missouri ex rel. Gaines v. Canada.* The court ruled that Missouri could not keep an African American from attending the white state law school because no such school existed for African Americans. This ruling was a major blow to the separate but equal rule.

Historically, Houston's major impact was in his strengthening of Howard University's Law School, as well as his work in civil rights litigation. Much of the cases he argued were instrumental in setting precedents that were to be used in the historic *Brown v. Board of Education* and *Boling v. Sharpe* cases that were to outlaw racial segregation. In addition, he was a columnist for *The Afro-American*.

Houston died April 22, 1950, of a heart ailment and was buried in Lincoln Memorial Cemetery. Five Supreme Court justices attended his funeral. He received a great deal of recognition after his death, including the Springarn Medal, awarded by the NAACP.

Elaine R. Jones 1944-
Attorney, Organization Executive, Civil Rights/Human Rights Activist

Elaine Jones has maintained a very steady high profile throughout her career, holding the distinction of being "the first" in many of her life's experiences. Born on March 2, 1944, in Norfolk, Virginia, Jones always wanted to be a lawyer. Earning a bachelor's degree with honors in 1965 from Howard University, she became the first black female law student admitted to the University of Virginia School of Law.

Receiving her law degree in 1970, Jones was offered a job with a prestigious Wall Street firm. She eventually turned down the job on Wall Street and went to work instead for the NAACP Legal Defense and Educational Fund (LDF), following her conscience instead of her bank account. The LDF had argued more cases before the Supreme Court than any other organization except the U.S. Department of Justice.

In 1973, Jones became the managing attorney in the LDF's New York City office, the organization's largest. In the late 1970s, she helped set up and run the LDF's new Washington, DC, office. In 1988, Jones was promoted to deputy director-counsel of the LDF, making her second-in-command to the director, Julius Chambers. Jones used this higher profile position to challenge the administrations of Reagan and Bush on their federal judicial appointments. She was an outspoken opponent of both Robert Bork in 1987 and Clarence Thomas in 1991.

Julius Chambers resigned from the LDF directorship in 1993, and the organization's board unanimously chose Jones to succeed Chambers. As director, Jones has broadened the organization's agenda to include more cases of environmental and health care discrimination. In addition to litigation, she is concerned with the group's fundraising efforts.

Nathaniel R. Jones 1926-
Judge/Magistrate, Civil Rights/Human Rights Activist

Born in 1926, Nathaniel R. Jones is a distinguished judge, attorney and administrator. President Jimmy Carter appointed him to the Sixth Circuit Court of Appeals in Cincinnati, Ohio on October 15, 1979; Jones retired from the bench in 1995. Prior to that, he was general counsel for the NAACP from 1969 to 1979, executive director of the Fair Employment Practices Commission of the City of Youngstown, Ohio from 1966 to 1969, in private practice, and a U.S. Attorney for the Northern District of Ohio.

While with the NAACP, Judge Jones organized the attack against northern school segregation and also argued in the Supreme Court's Detroit school case *Bradley v. Milliken*. The Dayton and Columbus, Ohio school desegregation cases heard before the Supreme Court were also organized by Jones. He has headed a three-man team that investigated grievances of black servicemen in Germany and responded to the attacks against affirmative action. He was also a national liaison for the famous "Kalamazoo Case." He was made deputy general counsel to the President's Commission on Civil Disorders in 1967 and co-chairman of the Civilian Military Task Force on Military Justice in 1972.

Jones received a B.A. degree from Youngstown University in 1951, and his LL.B. in 1956. He has honorary degrees from Youngstown University and Syracuse University.

Star Jones 1962?-
Attorney

Star Jones was born Starlet Marie Jones in the early 1960s, and grew up in Trenton, New Jersey, the daughter of two city executives. Shortening her unusual moniker in 1979, upon entering American University, Jones took an active role in college and even served as a national officer of Alpha Kappa Alpha, the sorority to which she belonged. After earning a law degree from the University of Houston, Jones went to work for the Kings County District Attorney's office, whose jurisdiction included the crime-plagued New York City borough of Brooklyn. She served as a member of its prosecuting staff from 1986, until her promotion to senior assistant district attorney in 1991.

The year 1991 also landed Jones an invitation to appear on Court TV, a cable television network that broadcasts high-profile trials interjected with commentary from experts on the judicial system. The channel soon hired her to appear regularly in conjunction with the William Kennedy Smith rape trial in Florida, and Jones's eloquence before the camera and projection of intelligence and warmth soon had a major network knocking at her door.

NBC lured her away from her tough job at the Brooklyn D.A.'s office by offering her its legal correspondent slot. During the two years she appeared on the network, several notable trials attracted the attention of the

Nathaniel Jones, 1985

American viewing public, and Jones was there to provide commentary as well as explanation of some of the more complex legal points involved on both the *Today* show and *NBC Nightly News*. Those cases included the criminal trial of the Los Angeles police officers charged with beating motorist Rodney King and the rape trial of boxer Mike Tyson.

In 1994, Group W Communications offered Jones her own syndicated television show. Debuting that fall, *Jones & Jury* gave plaintiffs and defendants who had lawsuits pending in California's equivalent of small claims court a chance to resolve their disputes on television before a studio audience, who would then render the verdict. Jones was the moderator, an in-charge role that also showcased her deft explanations of the complexities of law. Unfortunately, the competitive world of syndicated television spelled cancellation for the show by the end of 1995.

Amalya Lyle Kearse 1937-
Judge/Magistrate

Judge Amalya Lyle Kearse was born June 11, 1937, in Vauxhall, New Jersey. She attended Wellesley College for her B.A. in 1959, and went to the University of

Michigan for her J.D. in 1962. Kearse was in private practice from 1962 to 1969, also working as an adjunct lecturer for the New York University Law School from 1968 to 1969. She was then made U.S. Court of Appeals Circuit Judge.

Kearse has won the Jason L. Honigman Award for Outstanding Contribution to the Law Review Editorial Board. She has also served on the board of directors for the NAACP Legal Defense and Education Fund, as well as the National Urban League. She was appointed to the President's Commission for the Selection of Judges and served between 1977 and 1978. She served on the executive committee for Civil Rights Under Law for nine years, has been a member of the American Law Institute since 1977 and a fellow in the American College of Trial Lawyers since 1979.

Damon J. Keith 1922-
Judge/Magistrate, Attorney

Damon J. Keith was appointed to the U.S. District Court by President Lyndon Johnson and served there from 1967 to 1977. From 1977 to 1995, he served as judge for the U.S. Court of Appeals, Sixth Circuit Court in Cincinnati, Ohio. Born July 4, 1922 in Detroit, Keith attended West Virginia State College, where he received his A.B. in 1943. Following graduation, he served in the army for three years. He returned to school to earn his LL.B. from Howard University in 1949. In 1951 Keith took a job as an attorney for the Office of the Friend of the Court in Detroit, and held that position from 1951 to 1955. He received an LL.M. from Wayne State University in 1956.

Keith worked for the Wayne County Board of Supervisors from 1958 to 1963, then went into private practice from 1964 to 1967 before being appointed a judge. He has been active in the Michigan Civil Rights Commission, a trustee in the Medical Corporation of Detroit, a member of the Citizen's Advisory Committee on Equal Educational Opportunity, first vice president emeritus of the Detroit Chapter of the NAACP, a member of the management committee of the Detroit YMCA, a member of the Detroit Council of the Boy Scouts of America, a member of the Detroit Arts Commission, and vice president of the United Negro College Fund of Detroit. Keith is also a trustee of Interlochen Arts Academy and the Cranbrook School.

Judge Keith has been honored with many accolades, including being named one of one hundred Most Influential Black Americans by *Ebony* magazine, in 1971 and 1977; he received a citizen award from Michigan State University and became a Springarn Medalist in 1974. He has received honorary degrees from the University of

Damon Keith

Michigan, Howard University, Wayne State University, Michigan State University, and New York Law School.

Willie Lipscomb, Jr. 1944?-
Judge

Willie Lipscomb, Jr. grew up in Flint, Michigan with the intention of becoming a bus driver. He rose to higher aspirations, however, and after attending Wayne State University, he graduated with a law degree from the University of Notre Dame Law School in the early 1980s. For nearly 12 years he served as a prosecutor for Wayne County, Michigan, before being elected to serve as a jurist in the 36th District Court.

More than a judge, Lipscomb has differentiated himself through his community mentorship. He initiated an anti-gun violence seminar as part of the three-hour-long Handgun Intervention Program, mandatory for anyone arraigned in Detroit for a crime involving a gun. The Saturday morning seminar, a graphic slide presentation of gunshot victims from the morgue, is further punctuated by Lipscomb's vocal commentary, including snippets of civil rights history and personal anecdotes such as his struggle to give up sugar after he was

diagnosed with diabetes. Part teacher and part preacher, Lipscomb tries to make his "students" realize that each person has choices in life. The program, one that Lipscomb runs on his own time, has been so successful that other cities have employed similar tactics. For his role, Lipscomb was named a Michiganian of the year in 1995.

Wade Hampton McCree, Jr. 1920-1987
Judge/Magistrate, Attorney

Wade Hampton McCree, Jr. was appointed to the post of solicitor general by President Jimmy Carter, where he served from 1977 to 1981. McCree had already led a distinguished career as a judge and lawyer by the time he reached that position. He died August 30, 1987. McCree was born in Des Moines, Iowa, on July 3, 1920. He attended Fisk University to earn his A.B. in 1941, and received his LL.B. from Harvard University in 1944. In 1948, he was admitted to the bar in Michigan.

McCree had a private law practice from 1948 to 1952. From 1952 to 1954 he was commissioner of the Michigan Workmen's Compensation Commission. He became a circuit judge for Wayne County, Michigan, in 1954 until 1961, then a judge for the U.S. District Court Eastern District in Michigan from 1961 to 1966. McCree had the honor of being the first African American judge in the state of Michigan. From 1966 to 1967 he presided over the U.S. Court of Appeals Sixth Circuit. From 1981 until his death in 1987, he was a member of the faculty at the University of Michigan Law School. Three years later, the Wade H. McCree, Jr. Professorship was established at the University of Michigan Law School, making it the first endowed chair at a major American law school to be named after an African American. McCree was honored with more than 30 honorary degrees in his lifetime, including LL.D. degrees from Howard University, Harvard University, Boston University, Brandeis University and Tuskegee Institute.

Theodore McMillian 1919-
Judge/Magistrate, Educator

Born January 28, 1919 in St. Louis, Missouri, Theodore McMillian attended Lincoln University, receiving his B.S. degree in 1941 and earned his LL.B. degree from St. Louis University Law School in 1949. He served in the Signal Corps from 1942 to 1946.

McMillian has been a lecturer at St. Louis University Law School as well as a faculty member of Webster College. He became a circuit judge for the state of Missouri and served as an assistant circuit attorney for the City of St. Louis from 1953 to 1956. From 1972 to

Wade McCree, Jr.

1978, he was a judge with the Missouri court of appeals. He became a U.S. Circuit Court of Appeals circuit judge for the eighth circuit in 1978. He continues to serve that capacity.

Judge McMillian has been a member of the board of trustees for Blue Cross, and a member of the Danforth Foundation Advisory Council. He served on the Presidential Council of St. Louis University, and as a board chairman for Human Development Corporation between 1964 and 1977. He has also been a member of the National Legal Aid Advisory Board. He has been honored with an Alumni Merit Award from St. Louis University, an Award of Honor from the Lawyers Association in 1970, and a Man of the Year Award in 1970.

Carmel Carrington Marr 1921-
Attorney, Diplomat, State Government Official/Executive

Carmel Carrington Marr was born in Brooklyn, New York, in 1921 and attended Hunter College for her B.A. (cum laude) in 1945, continuing education to earn her J.D. from Columbia University Law School in 1948. As an experienced lawyer in international law, she was appointed by President Harry Truman to the position of legal advisor to the U.S. Mission to the United Nations in 1953. She served that position until 1967, keeping in constant contact with missions from other parts of the world, and serving on a number of key committees of the United Nations General Assembly.

Marr began her career in private practice from 1949 to 1953. After her position as legal advisor to the United Nations, she became the senior legal officer of the United Nations Secretariat from 1967-68, and then left to become a member of the New York State Human Rights Appeal Board from 1968 to 1971. Between 1971 and 1986 she served as commissioner of the New York State Public Service Commission. She retired from that position, becoming an energy consultant from 1987 until 1990.

Marr was also the chairperson of the advisory council of the Gas Research Institute between 1979 and 1986, the chairperson of the U.S. Department of Transportation Technology Pipeline Safety Standards Commission from 1979 to 1985, and the chairperson of the National Association of Regulatory Utility Commissioners Gas Commission from 1984 to 1986. She became president of NARUC's Great Lakes Conference of Public Utility Commission, and was on the board of the National Arts Stabilization Fund.

Marr has been honored as an Outstanding Community Service by the Brooklyn Urban League, and has been honored by Gas Research Institute, NYS Public Service Commission, American Red Cross, National Council of Churches, and *Mademoiselle* magazine.

Thurgood Marshall 1908-1993
Judge/Magistrate, Federal Government Official, Attorney, Civil Rights/Human Rights Activist

Thurgood Marshall's long and illustrious career was capped by his 1967 nomination to the highest court in the land—the U.S. Supreme Court—where he became the first African-American to hold the coveted position of Supreme Court Justice. At fifty-nine, the son of a sleeping-car porter and the great-grandson of a slave became a sign of progress for many. He was viewed with the utmost respect for all of his years on the bench, retiring June 27, 1991. Marshall died at the age of eighty-four in 1993. He was laid in state in the Great Hall of the Supreme Court of the United States on the same bier where Abraham Lincoln once rested. More than 20,000 mourners paid their last respects to Justice Marshall.

Born in Baltimore, Maryland, on July 2, 1908, Marshall earned a B.A. degree from Lincoln University, hoping to become a dentist. He changed his mind, and instead went to Howard University's law school, gradu-

Carmel Carrington Marr, 1968

Thurgood Marshall

ating in 1933 at the top of his class. He immediately went into private practice in Baltimore, where he remained for five years. In 1936, Marshall entered into what was going to be a long and illustrious career with the NAACP, starting as an assistant special counsel, and eventually becoming director-counsel of the Legal Defense and Educational fund, a position he left in 1961. In 1938, as a national special counsel, he handled all cases involving the constitutional rights of African Americans. Then, in 1950, he was named director-counsel of the organization's 11-year-old Legal Defense and Education Fund.

In 1954, as part of an imposing team of lawyers, Marshall played a key role in the now-historic Supreme Court decision on school desegregation, *Brown v. Board of Education*, which overruled the "separate but equal" doctrine in public education. He also figured prominently in such important cases as *Sweatt v. Painter* (requiring the admission of a qualified black student to the law school of Texas University) and *Smith v. Allwright* (establishing the right of Texas blacks to vote in Democratic primaries). Of the 32 cases that he argued before the Supreme Court, Marshall won 29.

Marshall was also known for his lifelong support of rights for women. Constance Baker Motley commented

that Marshall hired her for a NAACP counsel position when virtually every other employer had turned her down. He also encouraged her when he argued cases before the Supreme Court, and made certain he pointed out other African-American women role models.

In 1961, Marshall became a federal circuit judge for the second circuit. In 1946, he was awarded the prestigious Springarn Medal for his many achievements. He had over twenty honorary degrees to his credit, including LL.D. honors from the University of Liberia in 1960, the University of Michigan in 1964, and University of Otago, in Dunedin, New Zealand, in 1968. Marshall was also the representative for the White House Conference on Youth and Children, and a member of the National Bar Association. He was once sent by President John F. Kennedy to be a personal representative to the independence ceremonies of Sierra Leone.

Constance Baker Motley 1921-
Federal Government Official, Judge/Magistrate, Civil Rights/Human Rights Activist, Attorney

Born September 14, 1921, in New Haven, Connecticut, Constance Baker Motley became the first African American woman to become a federal judge. Born of West Indian parents, she was appointed in 1966 by President Johnson to the U.S. District Court for Southern New York. The appointment marked the high point of her long career in politics and civic affairs.

While still a law student at Columbia University, Motley began working with the NAACP Legal Defense

Constance Baker Motley

and Educational Fund, beginning an association that was to make her famous as a defender of civil rights. In 1946, she was awarded her LL.B., and began to work full–time with the NAACP, eventually becoming an associate counsel. During her 20–year career with the organization, Motley had argued nine successful NAACP cases before the U.S. Supreme Court, and had participated in almost every important civil rights case that had passed through the courts since 1954—from Autherine Lucy in Alabama to James Meredith in Mississippi.

In 1964, Motley decided to make a run for the New York State Senate, and was successful. She became the first African American woman to hold that position. After only a year in the Senate, Motley ran for the position of Manhattan Borough President, emerging the victor by the unanimous final vote of the city council. She thus became the first woman to serve as a city borough president, and, therefore, also the first woman on the Board of Estimate.

Motley was appointed to the U.S. District Court in 1966. In 1982, she was named chief judge of the federal district court that covers Manhattan, the Bronx, and six counties north of New York City. In 1986 she was named senior U.S. district judge.

During her career, Motley has received several awards for her contributions to the legal profession and for her role in the advancement of civil rights. She holds more than 20 honorary degrees from prestigious universities, including Princeton and Howard universities. In 1993,

Motley was inducted into the National Women's Hall of Fame.

George Ruffin 1834-1886
Judge/Magistrate, Attorney, Civil Rights/Human Rights Activist

George Ruffin was born in Richmond, Virginia, in 1834, the first son of free African Americans. In 1853, the family moved to Boston and Ruffin graduated from Chapman Hall school and joined with the Republican party. He moved for a short while to Liverpool, England after becoming disillusioned by the *Dred Scott* decision. Returning to Boston, Ruffin worked as a barber. But he was busy with other works, writing a review for the *Anglo-African* in 1863, and attending the National Negro Convention in 1864.

As he continued his profession, Ruffin also began to read law with a local law firm. He was admitted to the Harvard Law School, which at that time did not require a bachelor's degree, and graduated in 1869. He became the first African American to earn the LL.B. from Harvard, and perhaps the first to graduate from a university law school in the United States He joined the firm of Harvey Jewell, and then won a seat on the Massachusetts legislature in 1869, becoming the second African American to serve in that body.

Ruffin became known as an exceptional speaker and debater as he focused his attention to the problems in the South. In 1876 and 1877, he won election to the Boston Common Council. He had the honor of presiding over the Negro convention of New Orleans in 1872. His law practice was also prospering at this time. Frederick Douglass was a friend of Ruffin's, and Ruffin was asked to contribute to the introduction to the 1881 revision of *The Life and Times of Frederick Douglass*. Ruffin was appointed in November of 1883 as judge of a municipal court in Charlestown. He became the first African American judge in Massachusetts, continuing his work on equality. He supported racial amalgamation, congratulating Douglass on his marriage to Helen Pitts, a white woman, despite the stormy controversy. In 1883, he was also made consul resident for the Dominican Republic in Boston. Ruffin's other activities included president of the Wendell Phillips Club of Boston, member and president of the Banneker Literary Club of Boston, and superintendent and officer of the Twelfth Baptist Church of Boston. Ruffin died of Bright's disease on November 20, 1886. Because of his generous giving to charities, he died a relatively poor man.

Clarence Thomas 1948-
Attorney, Judge/Magistrate

Thomas was born June 23, 1948, in Pin Point, Georgia. His parents were poor; when he was young, Thomas's father left the family. At the age of seven, the family's house burned down and his mother could no longer hold the family together. With his brother, Thomas went to live with his maternal grandparents in Savannah. While his grandfather had little education, he was determined that Thomas would go to school and make something of himself. Thomas's early atmosphere was one of strict discipline. He attended various all–black and mixed–race Catholic schools. He intended to enter the priesthood, but left when he encountered a racist seminarian.

Thomas transferred to Holy Cross College and earned his B.A. He was accepted into Yale Law School in 1971, after Yale had adopted an affirmative action program. Thomas was never certain whether he was admitted for his credentials or because of his race. This is perhaps one of the reasons he has remained staunchly against affirmative action. He earned his J.D. in 1974. After graduating, Thomas became an assistant attorney general for the state of Missouri, working there from 1974 to 1977. Thomas then worked briefly at Monsanto Company in St. Louis as an attorney, specializing in pesticide, fungicide, and rodenticide law. He also worked as a legal assistant for Senator John C. Danforth.

From 1981 to 1982, Thomas was an assistant secretary for civil rights with the Department of Education, then moved on to chair for the Equal Employment Opportunity Commission (EEOC), a position he held from until 1990. His time there was controversial, as he was not allied with either liberals or civil rights leaders, and he didn't feel comfortable with the white conservative hierarchy. It has been debated whether the status of African Americans was helped or hurt by the policies he set at the EEOC.

After Robert H. Bork resigned his Circuit Court position because he had been rejected for a place on the U.S. Supreme Court, Thomas was appointed to the post. He served there until he was made a justice on the Supreme Court in 1991, nominated by then-President George Bush. In flurry of controversy, Thomas's nomination hearings were marred by accusations of sexual harassment levied against him by former EEOC employee Anita Hill.

Then a relatively unknown law professor, Hill became a household name when she came forward with her allegations. The Senate was divided by Hill's shocking testimony. Though Thomas denied the charges and many of his former coworkers testified for him, the case became highly politicized as the nation's conservatives and liberals fought for ground. Thomas was nominated by a vote of 52 to 48, one of the closest margins in Supreme Court history. Results of a poll taken soon after the hearings suggested that the American public mirrored the pro-Thomas view, citing 60 percent buying

Clarence Thomas

with his account. However, one year later only 38 percent of those Americans polled believed Thomas, while the number of those supporting Hill's version of events rose by 18 percent to 38 percent.

Despite the "high-tech lynching," as Thomas has referred to the proceedings with Hill, Thomas has gone one to carve out a prominent role as one of the most conservative justices on the court. Together with Justice Scalia, a staunch conservative, Thomas forms the right-wing backbone of the court. In his tenure, Thomas has presented strong opinions against affirmative action and desegregation. He also supports limiting the fundamental powers of the federal government. In 1992, Thomas was one of ten people to receive the Horatio Alger Award.

Robert H. Terrell 1857-1915
Educator, Judge/Magistrate, Attorney

Robert H. Terrell was born in Charlottesville, Virginia, on November 27, 1857. He worked in a dining hall to pay for his classes at Harvard College, where he graduated in 1884, *magna cum laude*, the first African American to do so. He went to work in the Washington, DC public schools, and also attended Howard University Law School, earning his LL.B. in 1889 and his LL.M. in 1893. In 1889, he went to work as the chief clerk in the office of the auditor of the U.S. Treasury Department.

Terrell was involved in the private practice of law from 1892 to 1898, leaving to become a teacher again, and later became principal of the M Street High School. He was also elected to the Board of Trade in the 1890s. In 1901, he was appointed as a justice of the peace in Washington, DC, partially due to the influence of the conservative Booker T. Washington. Like many African Americans of his day, Terrell was torn between his strongly held civil rights beliefs and Washington's conservative ideas. Again, through Washington's influence, Terrell was nominated by President Taft for the position of judge of the Municipal Court of the District of Columbia in 1910. Despite racial protests in the Senate, Terrell signed the appointment, and held the position until his death on December 20, 1915. His tenure on the court was filled with Republican presidents. Terrell suffered from a stroke in 1911, and a second a year later. His health was also complicated with asthma.

Terrell taught at the Howard University Law School from 1910 to 1925. He was grand master of the Grand United Order of Odd Fellows of the District of Columbia. There was a Robert H. Terrell Law School in Washington, DC from August 12, 1931, to 1950, and an elementary school named after him.

Evelyn Williams 1922?-
Attorney

Born in the early 1920s, Williams grew up in Queens, New York, in a close-knit family. After graduating from Brooklyn College, she became a social worker for New York City, but was shaken by the poverty she encountered; hoping to take a more active role in helping her community, Williams became a juvenile probation officer, but that too offered little satisfaction.

In the late 1950s, Williams graduated from law school as one of two African Americans in her class. By 1960, she was active in defending those accused of crimes who had little means for expensive legal representation. She also helped raise her niece, who when grown became involved with the Black Liberation Army in the early 1970s. Williams's niece, Assata Shakur, was arrested in 1973, following a shoot-out with law enforcement officials.

For the next several years Williams—then working with the New York University Urban Affairs and Poverty Law Program—served as the attorney for Shakur and her co-defendants against a series of legal charges that seemed to demonstrate the zeal with which federal and state authorities were determined to obliterate the militant BLA. Often this zeal manifested itself in the suspension of the defendants' constitutional rights to a fair trial, but in several incidents Williams successfully battled and won small victories for Shakur and the others. The time-consuming case—which included the mysterious death of one of Williams's fellow attorneys—was chronicled in her 1993 autobiography *Inadmissable Evidence: The Story of the African-American Trial Lawyer Who Defended the Black Liberation Army*.

Williams's high-profile defense of Shakur—who escaped from federal prison in a surprising 1979 break and surfaced in Cuba a few years later—would cost her in more ways than she had imagined. During the 1980s, Williams again entered private practice, but became the target of an FBI sting operation whose ultimate aim was to disbar and discredit her, both of which proved unsuccessful. By 1989, she had joined the firm of Stevens, Hind and White in New York City, where she continued to work for social change.

African American Federal Judges

PRESIDENT FRANKLIN D. ROOSEVELT

| 1937 | William H. Hastie* | District Court, Virgin Islands |
| 1939 | Harnian E. Moore* | District Court, Virgin Islands |

PRESIDENT HARRY S. TRUMAN

1945	Irvin C. Mollison*	United States Customs Court
1949	William H. Hastie*	Court of Appeals, 3rd Circuit
1949	Hernian E. Moore (a)*	District Court, Virgin Islands

PRESIDENT DWIGHT D. EISENHOWER

| 1957 | Scovel Richardson* | United States Customs Court |
| 1958 | Walter Gordon* | District Court, Virgin Islands |

PRESIDENT JOHN F. KENNEDY

1961	James B. Parsons	Senior Judge, District Court, Illinois
1961	Wade M. McCree**	District Court, Michigan
1961	Thurgood Marshall**	Court of Appeals, 2nd Circuit

PRESIDENT LYDNON B. JOHNSON

1964	Spottswood Robinson**	District Court, District of Columbia
1964**	A. Leon Higginbotham	District Court, Pennsylvania
1965	William B. Bryant	Senior Judge, District Court, District of Columbia
1966	Wade H. McCree**/*	Court of Appeals, 6th Circuit
1966	James L. Watson	United States Customs Court
1966	Constance B. Motley	Senior Judge, District Court, New York
1966	Spottswood Robinson	Senior Judge, Court of Appeals for the Federal Circuit
1966	Aubrey E. Robinson	Chief Judge, District Court, District of Columbia
1967	Damon Keith	District Court, Michigan
1967	Thurgood Marshall	Associate Justice, Supreme Court
1967	Joseph C. Waddy*	District Court, District of Columbia

PRESIDENT RICHARD M. NIXON

1969	Almeric Christian**	District Court, Virgin Islands
1969	David W. Williams	Senior Judge, District Court, California
1969	Barrington D. Parker	Senior Judge, District Court, District of Columbia
1971	Lawrende W. Pierce**	District Court, New York
1971	Clifford Scott Green	District Court, Pennsylvania
1972	Robert L. Carter	Senior Judge, District Court, New York
1972	Rovert M. Duncan**	Military Court of Appeals
1974	Robert M. Duncan	District Court, Ohio

PRESIDENT GERALD R. FORD

1974	Henry Bramwell	Senior Judge, District Court, New York
1976	George N. Leighton	Senior Judge, District Court, Illinois
1976	Matthew Perry**	Military Court of Appeals
1976	Cecil F. Poole**	District Court, California

PRESIDENT JIMMY CARTER

1978	Almeric Christian (a)	Chief Judge, District Court, Virgin Islands
1979	U. W. Clemon	District Court, Alabama
1978	Robert F. Collins	District Court, Louisiana
1978	Julian A. Cook, Jr.	District Court, Michigan
1978	Damon J. Keith	Court of Appeals, 6th Circuit
1978	A. Leon Higginbotham	Court of Appeals, 3rd Circuit
1978	Mary Johnson Lowe	District Court, New York
1978	Theodore McMillian	Court of Appeals, 8th Circuit
1978	David S. Nelson	District Court, Massachusetts
1978	Paul A. Simmons	District Court, Pennsylvania
1978	Jack E. Tanner	District Court, Washington
1979	Harry T. Edwards	Court of Appeals for the Federal Circuit
1979	J. Jerome Farris	Court of Appeals, 9th Circuit
1979	Joseph W. Hatchett	Court of Appeals, 11th Circuit
1979	Terry J. Hatter	District Court, California
1979	Joseph C. Howard	District Court, Maryland
1979	Benjamin T. Gibson	District Court, Michigan
1979	James T. Giles	District Court, Pennsylvania
1979	Nathaniel R. Jones	Court of Appeals, 6th Circuit
1979	Amalya L. Kearse	Court of Appeals, 2nd Circuit
1979	Gabrielle Kirk McDonald**	District Court, Texas
1979	John Garrett Penn	District Court, District of Columbia
1979	Cecil F. Poole	Court of Appeals, 9th Circuit
1979	Matthew J. Perry	District Court, South Carolina
1979	Myron H. Thompson	District Court, Alabama
1979	Anne E. Thompson	District Court, New Jersey
1979	Odwll Horton	District Court, Tennessee
1979	Anna Digs Taylor	District Court, Michigan
1979	Horace T. Ward	District Court, Georgia
1979	Alcee L. Hastings****	District Court, Florida
1980	Clyde S. Cahill, Jr.	District Court, Missouri
1980	Richard C. Erwin	District Court, North Carolina
1980	Thelton E. Henderson	District Court, California
1980	George Howard, Jr.	District Court, Arkansas
1980	Earl B. Gilliam	District Court, California
1980	Norma Holloway Johnson	District Court, District of Columbia
1980	Consuela B. Marshall	District Court, California
1980	George White	District Court, Ohio

PRESIDENT RONALD REAGAN

1981	Lawrence W. Pierce	Court of Appeals, 2nd Circuit
1982	Reginald Gibson	United States Court of Claims
1984	John R. Hargrove	District Court, Maryland
1984	Henry Wingate	District Court, Mississippi
1985	Ann Williams	District Court, Illinois
1986	James Spencer	District Court, Virginia
1987	Kenneth Hoyt	District Court, Texas
1988	Herbert Hutton	District Court, Pennsylvania

PRESIDENT GEORGE BUSH

1990	Clarence Thomas	Court of Appeals for the Ferderal District
1990	James Ware	District Court, California
1991	Saundra Brown Armstrong	District Court, California
1991	Fernando J. Giatan	District Court, Missouri
1991	Donald L. Graham	District Court, Florida
1991	Sterling Johnson	District Court, New York
1991	J. Curtis Joyner	District Court, Pennsylvania
1991	Timothy K. Lewis	District Court, Pennsylvania
1991	Joe B. McDade	District Court, Illinois
1991	Clarence Thoma	Associate Justice, Supreme Court
1992	Garland E. Burrell, Jr.	District Court, California
1992	Carol Jackson	District Court, Missouri
1992	Timothy K. Lewis	Court of Appeals, 3rd Circuit

PRESIDENT BILL CLINTON

1993	Henry Lee Adams	District Court, Florida
1993	Wilkie Ferguson	District Court, Florida
1993	Raymond Jackson	District Court, Virginia
1993	Gary Lancaster	District Court, Pennsylvania
1993	Reginald Lindsay	District Court, Massachusetts
1993	Charles Shaw	District Court, Missouri
1994	Deborah Batts	District Court, New York
1994	Franklin Burgess	District Court, Washington
1994	James Beaty, Jr.	District Court, North Carolina
1994	David Coar	District Court, Illinois
1994	Audrey Collins	District Court, California
1994	Clarence Cooper	District Court, Georgia
1994	Michael Davis	District Court, Minnesota
1994	Raymond Finch	District Court, Virgin Islands
1994	Vanessa Gilmore	District Court, Texas
1994	A. Haggerty	District Court, Oregon
1994	Denise Page Hood	District Court, Michigan
1994	Napoleon Jones	District Court, California
1994	Blance Manning	District Court, Illinois
1994	Theodore McKee	Circuit Court, 3rd Circuit
1994	Vicki Miles-LaGrange	District Court, Oklahoma
1994	Solomon Oliver, Jr.	District Court, Ohio
1994	Barrington Parker, Jr.	District Court, New York
1994	Judith Rogers	Circuit Court, District of Columbia
1994	W. Louis Sands	District Court, Georgia
1994	Carl Stewart	Circuit Court, 5th Circuit
1994	Emmet Sullivan	Circuit Court, District of Columbia
1994	William Walls	District Court, New Jersey
1994	Alexander Williams	District Court, Maryland
1995	R. Guy Cole	Circuit Court, 6th Circuit
1995	Curtis Collier	District Court, Tennessee
1995	Wiley Daniel	District Court, Colorado
1995	Andre Davis	District Court, Maryland
1995	Bernice B. Donald	District Court, Tennessee

(a) Reappointment
  * Deceased
 ** Resigned
 *** Retired
**** Impeached

11

Politics

11

Politics

◆ Race, Politics, and Government
◆ Congressional Black Caucus Members (104th U.S. Congress) ◆ Political Gatekeepers

by Barbara C. Bigelow and Lorna M. Mabunda

◆ RACE, POLITICS, AND GOVERNMENT

African Americans have had a hand in American politics since the colonial days. In the seventeenth century, a small number of free blacks existed. Though the institution of slavery began taking root in the middle of the century, free black men did have property ownership, voting, and governmental representation rights. As slavery spread, those entitlements drastically diminished. Virginia was the first colony to pass an act that stripped away suffrage from African American men. The rest of the colonies did the same, thus closing blacks from a key form of political expression, although African Americans circumvented this exclusion by petitioning for their concerns. In the eighteenth and nineteenth centuries, a return to Africa was a frequent request. The American Colonization Society, founded by blacks in 1816, promoted this cause and eventually led to the genesis of the west African nation of Liberia, or "and of freedom." Meanwhile, others hoped to emigrate to other parts of the black diaspora, including Canada, Central and South America, and the island nations, such as Haiti.

For some years, blacks argued amongst themselves about whether or not to stay in the United States. Some free blacks in Philadelphia initiated the National Negro Convention movement, which gained momentum in 1830, and held annual meetings for five consecutive years. Their counterpart, the American Society of Free Persons of Colour, supported both emigration for those who wanted to leave and calls for freedom and equity for those choosing to remain in the United States. The more militant participants became extremely vocal over the ensuing years.

The abolitionist movement of the 1830s joined a multiracial coalition in the quest for black emancipation and equality. In addition to agitating for civil rights through traditional legal means, the abolitionists took a daring step by operating the legendary Underground Railroad system, a covert network of safe havens that assisted fugitive slaves in their flight to freedom in the North. Approximately 50,000 slaves are believed to have escaped to the northern United States and Canada through the Underground Railroad prior to the Civil War.

The Fugitive Slave Act was passed in 1850, fueling the position of such individuals as separatist Martin Delany. He would push for separatism into his old age, later joining forces with Henry McNeal Turner, an African Methodist Episcopal bishop in the 1880s. Spokesperson for those opposed to such a move, Frederick Douglass pushed for blacks to seek rights through assimilation. The ultimate compromise between the two factions was proposed in 1853, when the Colored National Convention in Rochester, New York, advanced the idea of a separate black society on American soil.

The Union victory in the Civil War and the abolition of slavery under President Abraham Lincoln consolidated black political support in the Republican party. This affiliation lasted throughout the end of the nineteenth century and into the early decades of the twentieth century—even after the Republicans began to loosen the reins on the Democratic South following the removal of the last federal troops from the area in 1876.

Early in the post-Civil War Reconstruction era, African Americans seemingly made significant legislative gains. Both the Civil Rights Act of 1866 and the Fourteenth Amendment to the Constitution were intended to provide full citizenship—with all its rights and privileges—to all blacks. The Fifteenth Amendment, ratified in 1870, granted black American men the right to vote. But

Representatives Maxine Waters (center), Eleanor Holmes Norton (far left), and Charles Hayes (right), 1991.

the voting rights amendment failed in its attempts to guarantee blacks the freedom to choose at the ballot box. Poll taxes, literacy tests, and grandfather clauses were established by some state and local governments to deny blacks their right to vote. (The poll tax would not be declared unconstitutional until 1964, with the passage of the Twenty-fourth Amendment.)

These legalized forms of oppression presented seemingly insurmountable obstacles to black advancement in the United States, but many gains were made in representation. In 1869, Ebenezer Don Carlos Bassett became the first black diplomat, when he was appointed consul general to Haiti. The Reconstruction period also saw 14 African Americans elected to the U.S. House of Representatives and two to the U.S. Senate. While Hiram R. Revels was the first black senator—in 1870, he finished former confederate president Jefferson Davis's last year of term—Blanche K. Bruce became the first African American elected to the Senate for a full term five years later. Of note, P. B. S. Pinchback had won a Senate seat in 1873, but a vote of the other Senators rejected him in 1876. The same thing had happened one year earlier, when, in 1875, Pinchback was ejected from a House seat he had been elected to in 1872.

A flashy, colorful individual, Pinchback had made enemies through his gambling and because he was never afraid to voice his opinions regarding equal rights for blacks. Nonetheless, for 43 days, Pinchback was the nation's first black governor. Named lieutenant governor of Louisiana in 1871, Pinchback superseded that position after getting Governor Warmouth impeached on bribery charges. Warmouth's term was almost over; when the new election was held, Pinchback lost, but another African American had made an in-road.

During the 1870s other forms of white supremacist sentiment came to the fore. The so-called "Jim Crow" laws of segregation—allowing for legal, systematic discrimination on the basis of race—were accepted throughout the nation. Voting rights abuses persisted. Violence became another common tool of oppression: between 1889 and 1922, nearly 3,500 lynchings took place, mainly in the southern states of Alabama, Georgia, Louisiana, and Mississippi, but also in some northern cities.

During the nineteenth century most blacks were Republican Party supporters, but as the century drew to a close, a backlash occurred. In the 1890s, a group of white Republicans calling themselves the "Lily Whites" were heavily opposed to rights for blacks and thus resented the presence of the so-called "Black and Tan Republicans" in their party. But blacks would remain locked into a pattern of almost automatic support of Republicans until the late 1920s.

By the turn of the twentieth century, Booker T. Washington had gained prominence as the chief spokesperson on the state of black America and the issue of racial reconciliation. Recognized throughout the United States as an outstanding black leader and mediator, he advocated accommodationism as the preferred method of attaining black rights. His leading opponents included journalist Thomas T. Fortune, a close friend, and black historian, militant, and author W. E. B. Du Bois.

Fortune, who had founded the paper the *New York Freeman* in 1884, attempted to create a national political organization for blacks. His short-lived, Chicago-based National Afro-American League was aimed at remedying the disenfranchisement of blacks. Du Bois, on the other hand, felt it was necessary to take more aggressive measures in the fight for equality. Besides participating in the first Pan-African Conference (London) in 1900, he spearheaded the Niagara Movement, a radical black intellectual forum, in 1905. Members of the group merged with white progressives four or five years later to form the National Association for the Advancement of Colored People (NAACP). After Washington's death in 1915, the NAACP became a greater force in the struggle for racial reform.

Women played a significant role at the turn of the century as well, coming together as the National Association of Colored Women in 1896. Extremely active, the female activists met with much success in their agitation for rights. Standouts included founder Mary Church Terrell and presidents Ida B. Wells and Mary McLeod Bethune. Chief among their causes were speaking out against lynching and the promotion of women's rights.

A massive black migration to the North in the 1920s showed that racial tension was no longer just a rural, southern issue. In 1928, Oscar DePriest became the first African American elected to Congress in the twentieth century. His career began in 1915, when he was elected to the Chicago City Council, a feat that could not have happened without the influx of Southern blacks.

Anti-black attitudes, combined with the desperate economic pressures of the Great Depression, exerted a profound effect on politics nationwide. Democrat Franklin Delano Roosevelt attracted black voters with his "New Deal" relief and recovery programs in the 1930s. For 70 years blacks had been faithful to the Republican Party, but their belief in Roosevelt led many to switch party allegiance. Housing and employment opportunities began opening up, and blacks gained seats in various state legislatures in the 1930s and 1940s.

The Communist Party of the U.S.A. offered an alternative for African Americans alienated by the G.O.P. and the Democrats. White Communists actively solicited blacks for their ranks, supporting civil rights through demonstrations and boycotts. They even selected an African American, James Ford, as their vice presidential candidate during the U.S. presidential campaigns of 1932, 1936, and 1940.

World War II ushered in an era of unswerving commitment to the fight for civil rights. As blacks migrated to the North in search of jobs, several urban entities gained new concentrations of African American. In cities such as Detroit, New York, Philadelphia, and Cleveland, blacks had such a presence that the course of local politics were often swayed by the influence of their vote. At times the black vote affected the balance of power on the national front as well.

The election of Adam Clayton Powell, Jr., to the New York City Council in 1941—the first black to hold that position—was the start of an impressive career. By 1944, the flamboyant Powell had gotten himself elected to the U.S. House of Representatives; there, he turned the white Congress on its ear. From integrating the congressional gymnasium and challenging a white racist representative who refused to sit next to him to initiating legislation against lynching, poll taxes, and discriminatory job hiring practices, Powell was powerful. The so-called "Powell Amendment" referred to his attempts to tack antidiscriminatory measures onto each and every measure that came before the House.

Progress was being made in all areas—national associations, political organizations, unions, the federal branch of the U.S. government, and the nation's court system. President Harry S. Truman, who assumed office on the death of Roosevelt in 1945, contributed to black advancement by desegregating the military, establishing fair employment practices in the federal service, and beginning the trend toward integration in public accommodations and housing. In 1949, Rep. William L. Dawson became the first black to head a standing committee of Congress when he was elected chairman of House Expenditures. Meanwhile, Truman's civil rights proposals of the late 1940s came to fruition a decade later during President Eisenhower's administration. Eisenhower's administrative aide, E. Frederic Morrow, was the first black granted an executive position amongst White House staff.

The Civil Rights Act of 1957, also known as the Voting Rights Act of 1957, was the first major piece of civil rights legislation passed by Congress in more than eight decades. It expanded the role of the federal government in civil rights matters and established the U.S. Commission on Civil Rights to monitor the protection of black rights. But the commission soon determined that unfair voting practices persisted in the South; blacks were still being denied the right to vote in certain southern districts. Because of these abuses, a second act was passed in 1960, that offered extra protection to blacks at the polls. In 1965, yet another Voting Rights Act was passed to eliminate literacy tests and safeguard black rights during the voter registration process.

The postwar agitation for black rights had yielded slow but significant advances in school desegregation and suffrage though met with bold opposition from some whites. By the mid- to late-1950s, as the black fight for progress gained ground, white resistance continued mounting. The Reverend Martin Luther King, Jr., took the helm of the fledgling Civil Rights movement—a multiracial effort to eliminate segregation and achieve equality for blacks through nonviolent resistance. The movement began with the boycott of city buses in Montgomery, Alabama, and, by 1960, had broadened in scope, becoming a national crusade for black rights. During the course of the next decade, civil rights agitators—black and white—organized economic boycotts of racist businesses and attracted front-page news coverage with black voter registration drives and anti-segregationist demonstrations, marches, and sit-ins. Bolstered by the new era of independence that was simultaneously sweeping through sub-Saharan Africa, the movement for African American equality gained international attention.

Around the same time, racial tensions—especially in the South—reached violent levels with the emergence of new white supremacist organizations and an increase in Ku Klux Klan activity. Racially-motivated discrimination in all arenas—from housing to employment—rose as Southern resistance to the civil rights movement intensified. By the late 1950s, racist hatred had once again degenerated into brutality and bloodshed: blacks were being murdered for the cause, and their white killers were escaping punishment.

In the midst of America's growing racial tragedy, Democrat John F. Kennedy gained the black vote in the 1960 presidential elections. His domestic agenda centered on the expansion of federal action in civil rights cases—especially through the empowerment of the U.S. Department of Justice on voting rights issues and the establishment of the Committee on Equal Employment Opportunity. Civil rights organizations continued their peaceful assaults against barriers to integration, but black resistance to racial injustice was escalating. The protest movement heated up in 1961, when groups like the Congress of Racial Equality (CORE), the Student Nonviolent Coordinating Committee (SNCC), and the Southern Christian Leadership Conference (SCLC) organized "freedom rides" that defied segregationist policies on public transportation systems.

Major demonstrations were staged that April, most notably in Birmingham, Alabama, under the leadership of King. Cries for equality met with harsh police action against the black crowds. Two months later, Mississippi's NAACP leader, Medgar Evers, was assassinated. Soon demonstrations were springing up throughout the nation, and Kennedy was contemplating his next move in the fight for black rights. Meanwhile, on August 28, 1963, more than 200,000 black and white demonstrators converged at the Lincoln Memorial to push for the passage of a new civil rights bill. This historic "March on Washington," highlighted by King's legendary "I Have a Dream" speech, brought the promise of stronger legislation from the president.

After Kennedy's assassination that November, President Johnson continued his predecessor's civil rights program. The passage of the Civil Rights Act of 1964 sparked violence throughout the country, including turmoil in cities in New York, New Jersey, Pennsylvania, and Illinois. The Ku Klux Klan stepped up its practice of black intimidation with venomous racial slurs, cross burnings, firebombings—even acts of murder.

The call for racial reform in the South became louder early in 1965. King, who had been honored with the Nobel Peace Prize for his commitment to race relations, commanded the spotlight for his key role in the 1965 Freedom March from Selma to Montgomery, Alabama. But African Americans were disheartened by the lack of *true* progress in securing black rights. Despite the legislative gains made over two decades, economic prospects for blacks were bleak.

Black discontent over economic, employment, and housing discrimination reached frightening proportions in the summer of 1965, with rioting in the Watts section of Los Angeles. This event marked a major change in the temper of the civil rights movement. Nearly one decade of nonviolent resistance had failed to remedy the racial crisis in the United States; consequently, a more militant reformist element began to emerge. "Black Power" became the rallying cry of the middle and late 1960s, and more and more civil rights groups adopted all-black leadership. Despite such gains as the election of Carl Stokes (1967) and Richard Hatcher (1972) as the first black mayors of major municipalities—Cleveland and Gary, Indiana, respectively—King's assassination in 1968, only compounded the nation's explosive racial situation. The Black Revolution had finally crystallized, and with it came a grave sense of loss and despair in the black community.

The new generation of black leaders seemed to champion independence and separatism for blacks rather than integration into white American society. Shirley Chisholm was elected to the U.S. House of Representatives in 1968, making her the first black woman to serve in Congress and paving the way for other women to come. The next year, Charles Diggs, Jr., a member of the U.S. House of Representatives, founded the Democratic Select Committee, a group comprised of the eight other African American members of Congress. Two years later and four members stronger, they renamed themselves the Congressional Black Caucus (CBC).

The 1970 creation of the Joint Center for Political Studies, geared towards monitoring political developments in the black community, has probably been the CBC's most important political contribution. The CBC also laid the groundwork for TransAfrica, a 40,000 strong organization dedicated to black foreign affairs. Founded by Randall Robinson in 1977, TransAfrica came about after the CBC protested against pat U.S. governmental policy towards minority white rule in such African nations as Rhodesia. Meeting with 130 leaders in September of 1976, the CBC planted the seed and helped Robinson's initiative gain credibility. In the 1990s, the CBC has produced such leaders as Kweisi Mfume, who would later head the NAACP. 41-members strong in 1995, the CBC played a significant role in guiding U.S. Policy toward Haiti.

In the late 1970s, President Jimmy Carter fully supported African Americans. During his tenure he appointed blacks to key Cabinet positions. For example, Andrew Young was named a United Nations ambassador and Patricia Roberts Harris was first the secretary of Housing and Urban Development and then of Health, Education, and Welfare. Fear of black advancement led many whites to shift their allegiance to the Republican party in the late 1960s. With the exception of Carter's term in office from 1977 to 1981, Republicans remained in the White House for the rest of the 1970s and 1980s. The rise of conserva-

tism gave birth to such important figures as black conservatives Thomas Sowell, Anne Wortham, and Shelby Steele, but a new era of black liberal activity sprung with the institution of Rev. Jesse Jackson's Rainbow Coalition. Despite two unsuccessful campaigns for the presidency in the 1980s, Jackson helped swing the pendulum back in favor of liberalism. The tides of change eventually led to the election of Democratic president Bill Clinton in 1992.

After a dozen years of conservatism under Presidents Reagan and Bush, Clinton was seen as a champion of "the people"—all people. Demonstrating a commitment to policies that would cut across the lines of gender, race, and economics, he offered a vision of social reform, urban renewal, and domestic harmony for the United States. Once in office, Clinton appointed African Americans to key posts in his cabinet, and the black population began wielding unprecedented influence in government. For example, the 102nd Congress included 25 African American representatives; the elections in 1993 brought black representation in the 103rd Congress up to 38.

In the 1990s, black participation in government and politics has been significant, including roughly 340 black mayors. In 1990, Gary Franks became the only black Republican in Congress when he earned a seat in the U.S. House; he was joined four years later by J. C. Watts, Jr., who was elected to the House by a 90 percent white, Democratic constituency. An ordained Baptist minister, Watts left the Democratic party in 1989. As Watts has declined membership in the CBC, Elijah Cummings election to the House in 1996 made him the only other Republican CBC member, along with Franks.

1992 saw the election of the first black woman, Carol Mosley Braun, to the U.S. Senate. She shocked political observers by scoring a stunning upset over incumbent Senator Alan Dixon in the Democratic primary on March 17, 1992. In the November 1992 election, she easily defeated her Republican challenger, Richard Williamson, by a wide margin. Braun, whose term in the Senate expires in 1998, is only the fifth African American to serve in the Senate and only the second since Reconstruction.

Elected on November 3, 1992, President Bill Clinton assembled a cabinet that included a record number of African Americans. Jesse Brown became the first black to head the Veterans Affairs Department; Lee P. Brown was selected as head of the Office of National Drug Control Policy; Ron Brown was chosen as Secretary of Commerce; Dr. Jocelyn Elders was named U.S. Surgeon General; Michael Espy was awarded the position of Secretary of Agriculture; Hazel O'Leary was chosen as Secretary of Energy; Rodney Slater was appointed Secretary of Transportation; and Clifton Wharton, Jr., became the deputy Secretary of State. Clinton also nominated a number of blacks to major positions in federal government agencies, including Jacqueline L. Williams-Bridgers to the State Department as Inspector General and Shirley A. Jackson to the Nuclear Regulatory Commission as chairperson. As director of the White House Office of Public Liaison, African American Alexis Herman has been one of the president's most trusted advisors. And during Clinton's regime, the Justice department's civil rights division has been headed by Deval Patrick, an African American.

As the 1996 presidential election approached, many African Americans hoped that Colin Powell, a 4-star general and former chairperson of the Joint Chiefs of Staff, would run for office. Also popular with much of white America, Powell was probably the first truly viable black candidate since Rev. Jesse Jackson. Though other blacks had pursued the same aspirations—most notably National Alliance Party founder Lenora Fulani, who ran in 1988 and 1992—Republican Powell appealed to more moderately conservative factions. Powell eventually decided not to enter the race, but another black man did. U.S. State Department foreign officer Alan Keyes entered the 1996 election race. His extreme conservatism may have been a voter turn-off, however, and he was eventually forced to drop out of the race after doing poorly in the Republican primaries.

◆ CONGRESSIONAL BLACK CAUCUS MEMBERS (104TH U.S. CONGRESS)

Sandford D. Bishop, Jr.
Democrat: Georgia, 2nd District
1632 Longworth H.O.B.
Washington, DC 20515
(202) 225-3631

Carol Mosely-Braun
Democrat: Illinois, Senator
320 Hart H.O.B.
Washington, DC 20510
(202) 224-2854

Corinne Brown
Democrat: Florida, 3rd District
1610 Longworth H.O.B.
Washington, DC 20515
(202) 225-0123

William Clay
Democrat: Missouri, 1st District
2306 Rayburn H.O.B.
Washington, DC 20515
(202) 225-2406

Eva M. Clayton
Democrat: North Carolina, 1st District
222 Cannon H.O.B.
Washington, DC 20515
(202) 225-3101

James E. Clyburn
Democrat: South Carolina, 6th District
319 Cannon H.O.B.
Washington, DC 20515
(202) 225-3315

Barbara-Rose Collins
First Vice Chairperson
Democrat: Michigan, 15th District
101 Cannon H.O.B.
Washington, DC 20515
(202) 225-2261

Cardiss Collins
Democrat: Illinois, 7th District
2308 Rayburn H.O.B.
Washington, DC 20515
(202) 225-5006

John Conyers, Jr.
Democrat: Michigan, 14th District
2426 Rayburn H.O.B.
Washington, DC 20515
(202) 225-5126

Elijah E. Cummings
Republican: Maryland, 7th District
2419 Rayburn H.O.B.
Washington, DC 20515
(202) 225-4741

Ronald V. Dellums
Democrat: California, 9th District
2108 Rayburn H.O.B.
Washington, DC 20515
(202) 225-2661

Julian C. Dixon
Democrat: California, 32nd District
2252 Rayburn H.O.B.
Washington, DC 20515
(202) 225-7084

Chaka Fattah
Whip
Democrat: Pennsylvania, 2nd District
1205 Longworth H.O.B.
Washington, DC 20515
(202) 225-4001

Cleo Fields
Democrat: Louisiana, 4th District
218 Cannon H.O.B.
Washington, DC 20515
(202) 225-8490

Floyd H. Flake
Democrat: New York, 6th District
1035 Longworth H.O.B.
Washington, DC 20515
(202) 225-3461

Harold E. Ford
Democrat: Tennessee, 9th District
2111 Rayburn H.O.B.
Washington, DC 20515
(202) 225-3265

Gary A. Franks
Republican: Connecticut, 5th District
133 Cannon H.O.B.
Washington, DC 20515
(202) 225-3822

Victor O. Frazer
Independent: Virgin Islands, Delegate
1711 Longworth H.O.B.
Washington, DC 20515
(202) 225-1790

Alcee L. Hastings
Democrat: Florida, 23rd District
1039 Longworth H.O.B.
Washington, DC 20515
(202) 225-1313

Earl F. Hilliard
Democrat: Alabama, 7th District
1007 Longworth H.O.B.
Washington, DC 20515
(202) 225-2665

Jesse Jackson, Jr.
Democrat: Illinois, 2nd District
312 Cannon H.O.B.
Washington, DC 20515
(202)225-0773

Sheila Jackson-Lee
Democrat: Texas, 18th District
1520 Longworth H.O.B.
Washington, DC 20515
(202) 225-3816

William J. Jefferson
Treasurer
Democrat: Louisiana, 2nd District
240 Cannon H.O.B.
Washington, DC 20515
(202) 225-6636

Eddie Bernice Johnson
Secretary
Democrat: Texas, 30th District
1123 Longworth H.O.B.
Washington, DC 20515
(202) 225-8885

John Lewish
Democrat: Georgia, 5th District
229 Cannon H.O.B.
Washington, DC 20515
(202) 225-3801

Cynthia A. McKinney
Democrat: Georgia, 11th Distict
124 Cannon H.O.B.
Washington, DC 20515
(202) 225-1605

Carrie P. Meek
Democrat: Florida, 17th District
404 Cannon II.O.B.
Washington, DC 20515
(202) 225-4506

Eleanor Holmes Norton
Democrat: District of Columbia, Delgate
1424 Longworth H.O.B.
Washington, DC 20515
(202) 225-8050

Juanita Millender-McDonald
Democrat: California, 37th District
419 Cannon H.O.B.
Washington, DC 20515
(202) 225-7924

Major R. Owens
Democrat: New York, 11th District
2305 Rayburn H.O.B.
Washington, DC 20515
(202) 225-6231

Donald M. Payne
Chairperson
Democrat: New Jersey, 10th District
2244 Rayburn H.O.B.
Washington, DC 20515
(202) 225-3436

Charles B. Rangel
Democrat: New York, 15th District
2354 Rayburn H.O.B.
Washington, DC 20515
(202) 225-4365

Bobby L. Rush
Democrat: Illinois, 1st District
131 Cannon H.O.B.
Washington, DC 20515
(202) 225-4372

Robert C. Scott
Democrat: Virginia, 3rd District
501 Cannon H.O.B.
Washington, DC 20515
(202) 225-8351

Louis Stokes
Democrat: Ohio, 11th District
2365 Rayburn H.O.B.
Washington, DC 20515
(202) 225-7032

Bennie G. Thompson
Democrat: Mississippi, 2nd District
1408 Longworth H.O.B.
Washington, DC 20515
(202) 225-5876

Edolphus Towns
Democrat: New York, 10th District
2232 Rayburn H.O.B.
Washington, DC 20515
(202) 225-5936

Maxine Waters
Democrat: California, 35th District
330 Cannon H.O.B.
Washington, DC 20515
(202) 225-2201

Melvin L. Watt
Democrat: North Carolina, 12th District
1230 Longworth H.O.B.
Washington, DC 20515
(202) 225-1510

Albert Russell Wynn
Democrat: Maryland, 4th District
418 Cannon H.O.B.
Washington, DC 20515
(202) 225-8699

◆ POLITCAL GATEKEEPERS

Dennis Archer 1942-
Municipal Government Official, Attorney

Prominent attorney and former Michigan State Supreme Court justice, Dennis Archer became mayor of Detroit on January 3, 1994. During his campaign he promised better city services, a tougher stance on crime, and increased incentives for business choosing to locate in the city. Coming on the heels of Coleman Young's 20-year reign, Archer represented a new generation.

Archer was born on January 1, 1942, in Detroit, to a day laborer and his wife. The family moved to Cassopolis, Michigan, a farming community, when he was still an infant. Though they lived in extreme poverty, Archer's parents had high hopes for their son, to whom they emphasized the importance of an education. After graduating from Cassopolis High School in 1959, he worked his way through college, washing dishes. Following studies at Wayne State University (1959-61) and the Detroit Institute of Technology (1961-63), Archer received his bachelor's degree from Western Michigan University in 1965.

For a time Archer worked with emotionally impaired children. While teaching he met Trudy DunCombe, who became his wife in 1967; she persuaded him to pursue a law degree. Taking night course, Archer was able to earn a J.D. from the Detroit College of Law in 1970. He practiced law for several years—as a partner with Hall, Stone, Allen, Archer & Glenn and then with Charfoos, Christensen & Archer—until he was appointed to the Michigan Supreme Court by then-Governor James Blanchard.

Meanwhile, Archer had been active in Democratic politics in the late 1970s and early 1980s, directing campaigns for mayor Coleman Young and congressman George Crocket, Jr. Though his legal career was skyrocketing, Archer, yearned for an opportunity to address the difficulties faced by his declining city. His wife, who had also gone through law school and had become a district court judge, fully supported her husband's decision to run for mayor. Facing Coleman Young, a city fixture, was a daunting proposition, even for one with the impressive political ties Archer had garnered over the years. Archer's tough decision to face such a formidable opponent became a moot point, when Young, citing poor health, decided not run for a sixth term. He did, however, back Archer's rival, Sharon McPhail, thus reinforcing the notion of a new blood versus old, staid ways.

The race became a vicious battle as McPhail suggested that Archer, who many considered to be a mild-mannered, upper-class elitist, would kowtow to whites. Archer balanced these assessments by recalling the hard times of his early life as well as by going on record in support of the city's disenfranchised, including children and the homeless. Trumpeting the battle cry, "Detroit for All, All for Detroit," Archer went on to win the election with 57 percent of the vote compared to McPhail's 43 percent, although she had also won 52 percent of the black vote.

One of Archer's first aims was to heal the racial breaches in the community by bringing his constituents together with common goals. In his first term, Archer made tremendous strides in bringing the city forward. Perhaps most importantly, Archer used his influence with the Clinton administration to capture a chunk for federal monies to be used for creating empowerment zones throughout the city. The high profile 1994 G-7 Jobs Conference was held in Detroit, creating the first positive media buzzes about the city in years. Unafraid of a fight, he challenged Governor Engler's veto of a decision by Detroit voters to build a casino downtown. He also managed to hammer out a deal with the Major League baseball's Detroit Tigers, who had threatened to leave the city if a compromise could not be reached in regards to building a new stadium in the city. Archer seemed to be the answer to Detroit's woes.

Marion Barry 1936-
Municipal Government Official

Born Marion Shepilov Barry in Itta Bena, Mississippi on March 6, 1936, Barry and his seven younger siblings grew up in Memphis, Tennessee. He earned both bachelors and masters degrees in chemistry by 1960, and it was while a graduate student at Fisk University that he became active in NAACP politics and the burgeoning Civil Rights movement. He eventually cofounded the famous Student Nonviolent Coordinating Committee (SNCC) with the support of the Reverend Martin Luther King, Jr., a civil-rights protest group that made significant gains in erasing the last institutional vestiges of racism in the South; Barry was the SNCC's first national chairperson.

Moving to Washington, DC in the mid-1960s, Barry became active in local politics through efforts to move the capital city toward self-government free from Congressional interference—an issue that had wide support among members of the African American community. Among other achievements, he was instrumental in obtaining federal funding for a citywide youth employment and community service program and was elected to the local school board in 1970. When the "Free D.C." political movement succeeded in loosening Congressional rule over the city, Barry ran for a seat on its first council, which he held for three years.

In 1977, Barry was wounded in an altercation involving the seizure of Washington's District Building by radical Muslims but survived the gunshot wound. Elected mayor in 1978, over the next few years his administration was marked by both controversy and achievement. His wife was charged with embezzling federal monies, but he also initiated community-improvement programs in efforts to better employment opportunities and housing conditions for Washington's more disadvantaged neighborhoods. He was reelected in 1982 and again in 1986, but near the end of his third term was indicted by a federal grand jury for drug possession. He was convicted of misdemeanor for usage—showing up what his supporters said were the trumped-up charges of the law-enforcement community's campaign against him—and served the maximum six months.

Despite the setback, Barry's support among his Washington, DC constituency seemed to have lessened little. In 1992, he again won a city council seat, and in 1994, ran successfully for mayor in a campaign his detractors said would never succeed. He was sworn in for his fourth term in January of 1995. Later that year Barry was diagnosed with prostate cancer but was expected to make a full recovery.

Thomas Bradley 1917-
Civil Rights/Human Rights Activist, Municipal Government Official/Executive, Organization Executive/Founder, City Council/Board Member, Attorney

Bradley was born December 29, 1917 in Calvert, Texas. In 1924 he moved with his family to Los Angeles. Bradley graduated from Polytechnic High School in 1937 and attended the University of California, Los Angeles, on an athletic scholarship. He excelled at track before quitting college in 1940 and joining the Los Angeles Police Department. While a member of the police force Bradley worked as a detective, community relations officer and in the departments juvenile division. In the early 1950s Bradley began studying law at two Los Angeles colleges, Loyola University and later at Southwestern University. He was awarded an LL.B. from Southwestern University in 1956. Bradley stayed with the LAPD until 1961 when he entered private law practice.

In 1963, Bradley became the first African American elected to the Los Angeles City Council. He was reelected in 1967 and 1971. In a hotly contested 1973 election Bradley became mayor of Los Angeles winning 56 percent of the vote. In his 20–year stint, Bradley compiled a bittersweet record and was both lauded and

Tom Bradley

criticized. While his defenders have credited Bradley with turning Los Angeles into a modern metropolis, his detractors accused him of not keeping up with the city's problems.

Certainly one of the toughest situations Bradley faced was the occurrence of the 1992 riots that followed the announcement of not guilty verdicts for Los Angeles Police Department (LAPD) officers who were charged with beating black motorist Rodney King. Bradley was vilified for what some considered to be his lack of response to the incident. Many demanded the firing of Police Chief Daryl Gates, whose LAPD was known for extreme and often unprovoked brutality. Under the limits of the law, however, Bradley could do no more than ask Gates to resign. Though Gates eventually did leave his most, many considered the situation a serious challenge to Bradley's authority.

Bradley did attempt to heal the community in other ways. Even before the rioting had ended, he set up the nonprofit Rebuild LA. That organization was criticized for creating unreal expectations, but Bradley's Neighbor to Neighbor was viewed as a real salve. Comprised of nearly 800 volunteers, the outreach group regularly canvassed neighborhoods to give residents an outlet for discussing problems and to help citizens organize themselves in order to solve their own difficulties. In a second trial, two of four LAPD officers charged with violating King's civil rights were found guilty.

One of Bradley's final acts as a city official was to sign a bill that banned smoking in all restaurants. He was

honored for his years of service by the US Conference of Mayors in June of 1993. He officially left the mayoral post on July 1, 1993, effectively ending a 30-year public career. Following his retirement, Bradley was involved in more than one imbroglio. The biggest came when he was ensnared in a political finance scandal that also caught other California lawmakers, including Governor Pete Wilson and Senator Dianne Feinstein. Laundered campaign funds were traced to Evergreen America Corp., the world's largest container shipping company. Los Angeles' Ethics Commission ordered Bradley and others to repay a total of $15,000, but Bradley refused, claiming he did not know the money had been improperly donated.

Bradley has served as president of the National League of Cities and the Southern California Association of Governments. He belongs to the Urban League of Los Angeles and is a founding member of the NAACP's Black Achievers Committee. On the National level he has served on President Gerald Ford's National Committee on Productivity & Work Quality and on the National Energy Advisory Council. Bradley has won numerous awards and honors including the University of California's Alumnus of the Year (1974), the Thurgood Marshall Award (1974), Award of Merit given by the National Council of Negro Women (1978) and the NAACP's Springarn Medal (1985). His legacy has helped pave the way for other blacks to hold public office.

Carol Moseley-Braun 1947-
Attorney, Federal Legislator, Civil Rights/Human Rights Activist

Born Carol Moseley in Chicago on August 16, 1947, Moseley-Braun received her B.A. from the University of Illinois in 1969 and her J.D. from the University of Chicago Law School in 1972. While attending law school, Moseley-Braun worked as a legal intern and an associate attorney for a number of private law firms. After graduating from law school Moseley-Braun was an assistant U.S. attorney for the northern district of Illinois from 1973 until 1977. In 1979, Moseley-Braun was elected an Illinois state representative from the 25th district, where she became known as an ardent supporter of civil rights legislation. After a bid for the lieutenant governorship was thwarted, Moseley-Braun was elected Cook County recorder of deeds in 1986.

In 1992 Moseley-Braun became the nation's first African American woman elected to the U.S. Senate, effectively making her an icon of the so-called Year of the Woman. The following year, Moseley-Braun, along with Senator Dianne Feinstein, was selected for the formerly all-male Senate Judiciary Committee. Moseley-Braun also got a set on the Banking Committee. Her first major legislative proposal—an amendment to an omni-

Carol Moseley Braun, the first black woman elected to the United States Senate.

bus crime bill that would try young offenders implicated in serious crime from the age of 13 and up as adults—was overwhelmingly approved by the Senate.

A recipient of many honors, Moseley-Braun won the Best Legislation Award presented by the Independent Voters of Illinois two years in a row, 1981 and 1982. She has also won the National Association of Negro Business & Professional Women's Clubs' Community Recognition Award (1981), the Chicago Alliance of Black School Educators' Recognition of Excellence in Education Award (1981), the Afro-American Voters Alliance Community Recognition Award (1982), and an Essence Award for black women of achievement (1993). In 1993 she was chosen as the keynote speaker for the annual, prestigious National Urban League dinner. Moseley-Braun belongs to the League of Black Women, Operation PUSH, Federal, Illinois and Chicago Bar Association and the Women's Political Caucus.

Sidney John Barthelemy 1942-
Sociologist, Municipal government official/executive, State Legislator

Barthelemy was born in New Orleans on March 17, 1942. He attended Epiphany Apostolic Junior College

from 1960 to 1963 and received a B.A. from the St. Joseph Seminary in 1967. Two years later he earned a Masters in Social Work from Tulane University. After graduation Barthelemy worked in administrative and professional positions at a wide variety of organizations including Total Community Action (1967-69), Adult Basic Education Program (1968-69), Parent-Child Center, Family Health Inc. (1969-71), Urban League of New Orleans (1969-72), and the Parent-Child Development Center (1971-72). From 1972 to 1974, Barthelemy was the director of the Welfare Department of the City of New Orleans. In 1974 he was elected to the Louisiana State Senate. In 1978 Barthelemy left the state legislature after winning a seat on the New Orleans City Council, where he stayed until his election as mayor of the city in 1986.

Barthelemy has taught at Xavier University as an associate professor of sociology (1974-86), and at Tulane University and the University of New Orleans. He has been the vice chairman for voter registration for the Democratic National Party (1988-89), second vice president for the National League of Cities (1988), and president of the Louisiana Conference of Mayors (1989). Barthelemy belongs to the NAACP, National Association of Black Mayors, Democratic National Committee, National Institute of Education, National League of Cities, and the New Orleans Association of Black Social Workers. He has won numerous awards including Outstanding Alumnus of Tulane University, and the Louisiana Chapter of the National Association of Social Workers' Social Worker of the Year Award (1987). He has also won the American Freedom Award presented by the Third Baptist Church of Chicago (1987), the American Spirit Award given by the U.S. Air Force Recruiting Service (1989), and the NAACP's New Orleans Chapter Daniel E. Byrd Award (1990).

Mary Frances Berry 1938-
Educator, Federal Government Official, Civil Rights/ Human Rights Activist, Attorney

Mary Frances Berry was born in 1938 and received her B.A. degree from Howard University in 1961 and her masters degree in 1962. In 1966, she received a Ph.D. from the University of Michigan and her J.D. from its law school in 1970. Berry worked several years as a professor of history and law at several universities throughout the United States. She was appointed Assistant Secretary of Education, U.S. Department of Health, Education and Welfare by President Jimmy Carter in 1977, and became commissioner and vice chairman of the U.S. Commission on Civil Rights in 1980. She was "fired" from the Civil Rights Commission by President Ronald Reagan in 1983. In a compromise with Congress, Berry was reinstated. She currently is a Geraldine R. Segal professor of American Social Thought at the University of Pennsylvania.

Julian Bond 1940-
State Representative, Lecturer, Civil Rights/Human Rights Activist, Organization executive/founder, State Senator, Educator, Television/Radio Anchor/Host, Communications/Media Executive

Throughout his successful career and personal and political adversity, Julian Bond has been labeled everything from a national hero to a national traitor. He has faced violent segregationists and his own political failures and scandals. In spite of everything, he has kept his head above water and has remained an influential voice in politics, education, and the media.

Bond was born on January 14, 1940 to well-educated parents in Nashville. His father, an eminent scholar and president of Lincoln University in Pennsylvania, wanted Julian to follow his footsteps into the world of academics. Although Julian attended fine private schools, he showed little desire for educational pursuits. In 1960, Bond attended Morehouse College in Atlanta where he was a mediocre student. While at Morehouse, however, Bond developed an interest in civil rights activism. He

Sidney Barthelemy campaigning for reelection in 1990.

and several other students formed the Atlanta Committee on Appeal for Human Rights (COHAR). Along with other members, Bond participated in several sit-ins at segregated lunch counters in downtown Atlanta. The activities of Bond and his cohorts attracted the attention of Dr. Martin Luther King and the Southern Christian Leadership Conference (SCLC). King invited Bond and other COHAR members to Shaw University in North Carolina to help devise new civil rights strategies. At this conference, the Student Nonviolent Coordinating Committee (SNCC) was created. The SNCC eventually absorbed COHAR and Bond accepted a position as the SNCC director of communications. By 1966, Bond had grown tired of the SNCC and decided to embark on a new career in politics.

In 1966, Bond campaigned for a seat in the Georgia House of Representatives. He won the election and prepared to take his seat in the Georgia legislature. However, Bond was soon embroiled in a bitter controversy when he publicly announced that he opposed U.S. involvement in Vietnam and supported students who burned their draft cards to protest against the Vietnam War. These statements outraged many conservative members of the Georgia House of Representatives and, on January 10, 1966, they voted to prevent Bond's admission to the legislature. Bond sought legal recourse to overturn this vote and the case eventually went to the U.S. Supreme Court. On December 5, 1966, the Court ruled that the Georgia vote was a violation of Bond's First Amendment right of free speech and ordered that he be admitted to the legislature. The members of the

Mary Frances Berry (middle) speaks at a news conferece in 1984.

Georgia House of Representatives reluctantly allowed Bond to take his seat, but treated him as an outcast.

Bond's battle with the Georgia House of Representatives would not be his last experience as the center of controversy. In 1968, Bond and several other members of the Georgia Democratic Party Forum protested Governor Lester Maddox's decision to send only six African American delegates out of 107 to the Democratic National Convention. Bond and his supporters arrived at the convention and set up a rival delegation. After several bitter arguments with Georgia's official delegation, Bond's delegation had captured nearly half of Georgia's delegate votes. Bond's actions made him a national hero to many African Americans. He became the Democratic Party's first black candidate for the U.S. vice presidency, a position he declined.

From 1974 to 1989, Bond was president of the Atlanta branch of the NAACP. He was elected to the Georgia Senate in 1975 and remained a member until 1987. In 1976, he refused a cabinet position in the Carter administration. Bond ran for a seat in the U.S. Congress in 1986, but lost the election. In 1989, he divorced his wife after twenty-eight years of marriage. Shortly thereafter, he became embroiled in a paternity suit. He initially

denied the allegations, but admitted in May of 1990 to fathering the child and was ordered to pay child support. (Bond remarried in March of 1990.)

Bond has served as a visiting professor at Drexel University, Harvard University, the University of Virginia, and American University. He is a popular lecturer and writer and is often called upon to comment on political and social issues. Bond has hosted a popular television program *America's Black Forum* and narrated the highly acclaimed public television series *Eyes on the Prize*. In 1994 he became involved in a power struggle with NAACP Board Chairman William Gibson, which cost Bond his position on the Board.

Edward W. Brooke 1919-
Attorney, Federal Legislator

Edward W. Brooke was born on October 26, 1919, in Washington, D.C. During his two terms in the U.S. Senate, Brooke—the first black to be elected to that body since 1881—defied conventional political wisdom. In a state that was overwhelmingly Democratic and in which blacks constituted only three percent of the population, he was one of its most popular political figures and a Republican. He first achieved statewide

Julian Bond

office in 1962 when he defeated Elliot Richardson to become Attorney General. He established an outstanding record in that post and in 1966 was elected to the Senate over former Massachusetts governor Endicott Peabody.

Born into a middle-class environment, Brooke attended public schools locally and went on to graduate from Howard. Inducted into an all-black infantry unit during World War II, Brooke rose to the rank of captain and was ultimately given a Bronze Star for his work in intelligence. Returning to Massachusetts after the war, Brooke attended the Boston University Law School, compiling an outstanding academic record and editing the *Law Review* in the process. After law school, he established himself as an attorney and also served as chairman of the Boston Finance Commission.

Brooke was later nominated for the attorney general's office, encountering stiff opposition within his own party. He eventually won both the Republican primary and the general election against his Democratic opponent. Upon entering the national political scene, Brooke espoused the notion that the Great Society could not become a reality until it was preceded by the "Responsible Society." He called this a society in which "it's more profitable to work than not to work. You don't help a man by constantly giving him more handouts."

When first elected, Brooke strongly supported United States participation in the Vietnam War, though most black leaders were increasingly opposing it. However, in 1971, Brooke supported the McGovern-Hatfield Amendment which called for withdrawal of the United States from Vietnam. As might be expected, matters of race rather than foreign affairs were to become Brooke's area of expertise. Reluctant and subdued, Brooke proceeded carefully at first, waiting to be consulted by President Nixon and loyally accepting the latter's apparent indifference to his views. However, as pressure mounted from the established civil rights groups and impatient black militants he decided to attack the Nixon policies. Brooke was roused into a more active role by the administration's vacillating school desegregation guidelines, its "firing" of HEW official Leon Panetta, and the nominations to the Supreme Court of judicial conservatives Clement Haynsworth and G. Harrold Carswell.

In 1972, Brooke was reelected to the Senate overwhelmingly, even though Massachusetts was the only state not carried by his party in the presidential election. While Brooke seconded the nomination of President

Edward Brooke, 1966.

Ron Brown

Nixon at the 1972 Republican Convention, he became increasingly critical of the Nixon administration. He also began to appear publicly at meetings of the Congressional Black Caucus, a group he had tended to avoid in the past. Brooke was considered a member of the moderate-to-liberal wing of the Republican Party. In 1978, Brooke's bid for a third term in the Senate was defeated by Democrat Paul Tsongas and he returned to his private law practice.

Ronald H. Brown 1941-1996
Attorney, Federal Government Official, Organization Executive/Founder

Born in Washington, DC, on August 1, 1941, Brown was raised in Harlem and attended White Plains High School and Rhodes and Walden Preparatory Schools in New York. He graduated from Middlebury College in Middlebury, Vermont with a B.A. in political science in 1962. Upon graduating he enlisted in the army where he achieved the rank of captain while serving in West Germany and Korea. Brown graduated from New York City's St. John's University Law School in 1970.

While attending law school, Brown began working for the National Urban League's job training center in the Bronx, New York, in 1968. He continued with them until 1979, working as general counsel, Washington spokesperson, deputy executive director, and vice president of Washington operations. In 1980 he resigned to become chief counsel of the U.S. Senate Judiciary Committee and in 1981, the general counsel and staff coordi-

nator for Senator Edward Kennedy. In that year he also became a partner in the Washington law firm of Patton, Boggs & Blow. In 1989 Brown was appointed Chairman of the Democratic National Committee, making him the first African American to head a major American political party. He has since been credited as the primary force behind President Bill Clinton's 1992 election. In 1993 President Clinton appointed Brown Commerce Secretary, but his cabinet position was marred somewhat by charges of financial impropriety. Brown died in a plane crash on April 3, 1996, near the Croatian coast while on a commercial mission in the war-torn Balkans.

Blanche K. Bruce 1841-1898
Federal Government Official, Civil Rights/Human Rights Activist, Federal Legislator

Blanche Kelso Bruce was born a slave in Farmville, Prince Edward County, Virginia on March 1, 1841. He received his early formal education in Missouri, where his parents had moved while he was still quite young, and later studied at Oberlin College in Ohio. In 1868, Bruce settled in Floreyville, Mississippi. He worked as a planter and eventually built up a considerable fortune in property.

Ron Brown opening the 1992 Democratic National Convention.

Blanche K. Bruce

In 1870, Bruce entered politics and was elected ser-geant-at-arms of the Mississippi Senate. A year later he was named assessor of taxes in Bolivar County. In 1872 he served as sheriff of that county and as a member of the Board of Levee Commissioners of Mississippi. Bruce was nominated for the U.S. Senate from Mississippi in February of 1874. He was elected, becoming the first black person to serve a full term in the Senate. Bruce became an outspoken defender of the rights of minority groups, including the Chinese and Indians. He also investigated alleged bank and election frauds and worked for the improvement of navigation on the Mississippi in the hope of increasing interstate and foreign commerce. Bruce also supported legislation aimed at eliminating reprisals against those who had opposed Negro emancipation.

After Bruce completed his term in the Senate, he was named Register of the U.S. Treasury Department by President James A. Garfield. Bruce held this position until 1885. In 1889, President Benjamin Harrison ap-pointed him recorder of deeds for the District of Colum-bia. Bruce served as recorder of deeds until 1893, when he became a trustee for the District of Columbia public schools. In 1897, President William McKinley reappointed

him to his former post as register of the treasurer. Bruce died on March 17, 1898.

Ralph J. Bunche 1904-1971
Federal Government Official, Diplomat, Educator

The first American black to win the Nobel Peace Prize, Ralph Bunche was an internationally acclaimed statesman whose record of achievement places him among the most significant American diplomats of the twentieth century. Bunche received the coveted award in 1950 for his role in effecting a cease fire in the Arab-Israeli dispute which threatened to engulf the entire Middle East in armed conflict.

Born in Detroit on August 7, 1904, Bunche graduated from UCLA in 1927 summa cum laude and with Phi Beta Kappa honors. A year later he received his M.A. in government from Harvard. Soon thereafter he was named head of the Department of Political Science at Howard University, remaining there until 1932 at which time he was able to resume work toward his doctorate from Harvard. (He later studied at Northwestern University, the London School of Economics, and Capetown Uni-versity.) Before World War II broke out in 1939, Bunche did field work with the Swedish sociologist Gunnar

Myrdal, author of the widely acclaimed *An American Dilemma*. During the war, he served initially as Senior Social Analyst for the Office of the Coordinator of Information in African and Far Eastern Affairs, and was then reassigned to the African section of the Office of Strategic Services. In 1942, he helped draw up the territories and trusteeship sections ultimately earmarked for inclusion in the United Nations charter.

The single event that brought the name of Ralph Bunche into the international spotlight occurred soon after his appointment in 1948 as chief assistant to Count Folke Bernadotte, U.N. mediator in the Palestine crisis. With the latter's assassination, Bunche was faced with the great challenge of somehow continuing ceasefire talks between Egypt and Israel. After six weeks of intensive negotiations, Bunche worked out the now-famous "Four Armistice Agreements," which brokered an immediate cessation of the hostilities between the two combatants. Once the actual ceasefire was signed, Bunche received numerous congratulatory letters and telegrams from many heads of state and was given a hero's welcome upon his return to the United States.

Bunche served as undersecretary of Special Political Affairs from 1957 to 1967. By 1968, Bunche had attained the rank of undersecretary general, the highest position ever held by an American at the United Nations. Bunche retired in October 1971 and died on December 9, 1971.

Yvonne Braithwaite Burke 1932-
Attorney, State Legislator

Attorney and former California State Assembly Woman Yvonne Braithwaite Burke became the first black woman from California ever to be elected to the House of Representatives in November of 1972. More than 20 years later, she became the first woman and African American to chair the Los Angeles County Board of Supervisors. Prior to her governmental career, Burke was a practicing attorney, during which time she served as a Deputy Corporation Commissioner, a hearing officer for the Los Angeles Police Commissioner, and an attorney for the McCone Commission, which investigated the Watts riots.

Born on October 5, 1932, in Los Angeles, Congresswoman Burke served in the State Assembly for six years prior to her election to Congress. During her final two years there, she was chairperson of the Committee on Urban Development and Housing and a member of the Health, Finance and Insurance committees. As a state legislator, Burke was responsible for the enactment of bills providing for needy children, relocation of tenants and owners of homes taken by governmental action, and one which required major medical insurance programs to grant immediate coverage to newborn infants of the insured.

Burke's district, created in 1971 by the California legislature, contained low-and middle-income black and integrated neighborhoods plus some white suburban tracts and beach communities, including Venice, noted for its "counterculture" scene. About 50 percent of the district's population is black, while another 10 percent is of Hispanic and Asian origin. In 1972, the district gave 64 percent of its vote to Burke. During Burke's first term in the Senate, she proved to be an ardent spokesperson for the downtrodden. She became a member of the Committee on Appropriations in December 1974 and used her position on this committee to advocate an increase in funding for senior citizen services and community nutrition and food programs. Although her proposal for increased spending was defeated by the House of Representatives, Burke's efforts earned the respect of the African American community. In January of 1977, Burke worked diligently for the passage of the Displaced Homemakers Act, which proposed the creation of counseling programs and job training centers for women entering the work force for the first time.

In 1978, Burke resigned to run for Attorney General in California. She lost that race but, in 1979, she was appointed to the five-member Los Angeles County Board of Supervisors. She resigned from the board in December 1980 and returned to her private law practice. Burke remained a prominent figure in California politics, taking on a number of civic responsibilities including serving as a member of the University of California Board of Regents. In 1992 Burke ran for and was elected as chairperson of her old stomping ground, the Los Angeles County Board of Supervisors.

Bill Campbell 1954-
Municipal Government Official

Bill Campbell ended up running for mayor of Atlanta in 1992, just four years before it hosted the 1996 Olympics. Born in 1954 in Raleigh, North Carolina, Campbell became mayor at the young age of 40, signaling a new generation of leadership for the people of Atlanta. A lawyer and long-time city council member, he was well qualified for the job.

In 1974, Campbell graduated *cum laude* from Vanderbilt University, completing a triple major (history, political science, and sociology) in just three years. He graduated from Duke University's law school in 1977, and went to work for an Atlanta law firm. Campbell then worked from 1980 to 1981 at the U.S. Justice Department's Atlanta office.

Campbell began his political in 1981, serving on the Atlanta City Council. He served three consecutive terms through 1993, cosponsoring more than 300 pieces of legislation. By 1993, he had become a partner in an

Yvonne Braithwaite Burke at a Washington news conference in 1976.

Atlanta law firm, along with serving as floor leader of the city council under Atlanta Mayor Maynard Jackson. When Jackson's health began to wane, Campbell was mentioned as a mayoral candidate. The importance of who would be the new mayor was heightened by the city's preparation for the 1996 Olympics.

The election for mayor included other city council members, former mayoral candidates, and 12 nonpartisan candidates. Campbell won 49 percent of the vote, shy of the 50 percent needed to win the office outright. The outcome of a runoff election between Campbell and his closest competitor, had Campbell winning by a landslide with 73 percent of the vote. The city believed in his pragmatic, businesslike style of approaching city problems with a business management viewpoint.

Taking office in 1994, Campbell appointed the first female police chief of a major American city. He installed mini-police precincts in Atlanta's housing projects, planned alliances between the city and historically black colleges, and encouraged young people to become active in community services. In 1996, Campbell hosted many dignitaries, including President Bill Clinton, in celebration of the 10th official holiday celebration of Martin Luther King, Jr. Day. In regards to the

Olympics, Campbell proposed a $150 million plan to repair Atlanta's infrastructure before the big event, seeing the Olympics as an opportunity to commit money to help his town. The highly touted event was one in which both the mayor and his city were able to shine.

Shirley Chisholm 1924-
Educator, Federal Legislator, Organization Executive/ Founder, Civil Rights/Human Rights Activist

Shirley Chisholm was born November 30, 1924, in New York City. She graduated *cum laude* from Brooklyn College in 1946 with a B.A. in sociology and an M.A. in elementary education from Columbia University in 1952. She had an early career in child care and preschool education culminating in her directorship of the Hamilton-Madison Child Care Center in New York. Leaving that position in 1959, she served until 1964 as a consultant to the Day Care Division of New York City's Bureau of Child Welfare.

In 1964, Chisholm was elected New York State Assemblywoman representing the 55th district in New York City. In 1968 she was elected to the U.S. House of Representatives 12th district until her retirement in 1982. A staunch Democrat, Chisholm served as a delegate to the Democratic National Mid-Term Conference in 1974 and as a Democratic National Committee-woman. After retiring from politics Chisholm taught political science at Mount Holyoke College.In 1984, Chisholm cofounded the National Political Congress of Black Women. She spent the next year as a visiting scholar at Spelman College. In 1993, U.S. president Bill Clinton hoped to appoint her as ambassador to Jamaica, but Chisholm declined the invitation.

An author of two books—*Unbossed & Unbought* (1970) and *The Good Fight* (1973)—Chisholm is a member of the NAACP, the National Association of Colored Women, and the League of Women Voters. She has won numerous awards, including the Woman of Achievement Award presented to her in 1965 by Key Women Inc. and the Sojourner Truth Award given to her by the Association for the Study of Negro Life and History in 1969.

William Clay 1931-
Civil Rights/Human Rights Activist, Federal Legislator

William Clay, the first black man to represent the state of Missouri in the U.S. Congress, was born on April 30, 1931, in the lower end of what is now St. Louis' 1st District. Clay was educated locally and later took a degree in political science at St. Louis University, where he was one of four blacks in a class of 1,100. After serving in the U.S. Army until 1955, Clay became active in a host of civil rights organizations, including the NAACP Youth Council and CORE. During this time he worked as a cardiographic aide, bus driver, and insurance agent, but his heart had already surrendered to politics, at least judging from the number of demonstrations and picket lines he had joined.

In 1959, and again in 1963, Clay was elected alderman of the predominantly black 26th Ward. During his first term, he served nearly four months of a nine-month jail sentence for demonstrations at a local bank. Meanwhile, on the outside, the number of white-collar jobs held by blacks in St. Louis banks began a steady ascent from a low of 16 to a high of 700. In 1964, Clay stepped down from his alderman's post to run for Ward Committeeman, winning handily and being reelected in 1968.

Clay's election platform in 1969 included a number of progressive, even radical, ideas. He advocated that all penal institutions make provisions for the creation of facilities in which married prisoners could set up house with their spouses for the duration of their sentences. He branded most testing procedures and diploma requirements, as well as references to arrest records and periods of unemployment, unnecessary obstacles complicating the path of a prospective employee. In his view, a demonstrated willingness to work and an acceptance of responsibility should be the criteria determining one's selection for a job.

Clay's last job before his election to Congress was as race relations coordinator for Steamfitters Union Local 562. Subjected to considerable criticism from other St. Louis blacks who labeled the union racist, Clay pointed out that dramatic changes in the hiring practices of the union since he had joined it in 1966 were responsible for the employment of 30 black steamfitters in St. Louis—30 more than the union had previously put to work. Still, Clay conceded that the high-paying job had led him to reduce his active involvement with the civil rights struggle to some degree.

As a member of the U.S. House of Representatives, Clay has proven himself a capable legislator. He has sponsored many pieces of legislation, including the Hatch Act Reform Bill, the City Earnings Tax Bill, and the IRS Reform Bill. Clay has served as chairman of the Subcommittee on Postal Operations and Civil Service, the House Education and Labor Committee, and the House Administration Committee. He has also been a member of the board of directors for Benedict College, Tougaloo College, and the Congressional Black Caucus Foundation. In 1993, Clay published *Just Permanent Interests: Black Americans in Congress, 1870-1991*.

Cardiss Collins 1931-
Accountant/Auditor, Federal Legislator, Civil Rights/Human Rights Activist

Collins was born Cardiss Robertson September 24, 1931, in St. Louis, Missouri and by the time she was ten years old her family had moved to Detroit. After graduating from Detroit's Commerce High School, Collins moved to Chicago where she worked as a secretary for the state's Department of Revenue. She began studying accounting at Northwestern University and was promoted to accountant and then auditor.

In 1973, Collins was elected U.S. Representative from Illinois's 7th district. She was elected to fill the seat vacated by her husband George Collins who was killed in an airplane crash. She soon became the first African American and the first woman to hold the position of Democratic whip-at-large. Collins served on congressional subcommittees dealing with consumer protection, national security, hazardous materials, narcotic abuse and control, and energy concerns. At various points, she also served as active secretary, vice chair,

Shirley Chisolm on the steps of the U.S. Capitol in 1969.

and chair of the CBC. Collins has been a proponent of civil rights, pro-busing, and anti-apartheid legislation.

In 1994, the CBC Foundation elected her the group's chair. Early in 1995, Collins became the top Democrat on the Government Reform and Oversight Committee. On November 8, 1995, Collins announced her decision to retire after 23 years in the House; her 12 terms made her the longest-serving black female member of Congress. Collins belongs to the NAACP, Chicago Urban League, Northern Virginia Urban League, National Wom-

en's Political Caucus, Alpha Kappa Alpha, Congressional Women's Caucus, Alpha Kappa Psi, Black Women's Agenda, and the National Council of Negro Women. Besides the degree she obtained from Northwestern in 1967, she has honorary degrees from Barber-Scotia College, Winston-Salem State University, and Spelman College. The Black Coaches Association (BCA) named Collins Sportsperson of the Year in 1994, after she supported the group's contention that standardized college entrance examinations are racially and culturally biased, and, therefore, should not be used by the National Collegiate Athletic Association (NCAA) to establish athletic eligibility.

John Conyers 1929-
Attorney, Federal Legislator, Federal Government Official, Civil Rights/Human Rights Activist, Organization Executive/Founder

Conyers was born in Detroit on May 16, 1929. In 1950, three years after graduating from high school, he enlisted in the U.S. Army as a private and served in Korea before being honorably discharged as a second lieutenant in 1957. He then attended Wayne State University in Detroit, and, after studying in a dual program, he received a B.A. in 1957 and a law degree in 1958.

Conyers served as a legislative assistant to Congressman John Dingell, Jr. from 1958 to 1961 and was a senior partner in the law firm of Conyers, Bell & Townsend from 1959 to 1961. In that year he took a referee position with the Michigan Workman's Compensation Department and stayed until 1963. In 1964 he won election as a Democrat to the U.S. House of Representatives. Conyers had long been active in the Democratic Party, belonging to the Young Democrats, University Democrats, and serving as a precinct delegate to the Democratic Party.

Cardiss Collins

After his election Conyers was assigned to the powerful House Judiciary Committee. From that position he worked for legislation dealing with civil rights, medicare, immigration reform, and truth-in-packaging laws. He was an early opponent of U.S. involvement in Vietnam and an early proponent on the Voting Rights Act of 1965.

In 1994, Conyers—the most senior African American member of Congress—supported a grass roots movement comprised of nearly 1,000 individuals seeking reparations from the federal government on behalf of their slave ancestors. The participants held their fifth annual Conference on Reparations in Conyers's hometown, Detroit. Other prominent blacks lending support included Rev. Jesse Jackson.

Conyers has been vice-chairman of the National Board of Americans for Democratic Action and the American Civil Liberties Union (ACLU). He is on the executive board of the Detroit Chapter of the NAACP and belongs to the Wolverine Bar Association. He is the recipient of the Rosa Parks Award (1967) and an honorary law degree from Wilberforce University (1969).

Ronald V. Dellums 1935-
Counselor/Social Worker, Federal Legislator, Organization Executive/Founder, Lecturer

A savvy and congenial political figure, Ronald Dellums was born in Oakland, California on November 24, 1935. After attending McClymonds and Oakland Technical

William Clay

John Conyers

Ron Dellums

High Schools Dellums joined the U.S. Marine Corps in 1954 and was discharged after two years of service. He returned to school, receiving an associate of arts degree from Oakland City College in 1958, a B.A. from San Francisco State College in 1960, and a masters degree in social work from the University of California at Berkeley in 1962.

For the next eight years, Dellums engaged in a variety of social work. He was a psychiatric social worker with the Berkeley Department of Mental Hygiene starting in 1962, then two years later he became the Bayview Community Center's program director. Following a one year stint there, Dellums spent one year as director of the Hunters Point Youth Opportunity Center and one as consultant to the Bay Area Social Planning Council. In 1967 Dellums worked as a program director for the San Francisco Economic Opportunity Council. Then from 1968 to 1970, Dellums lectured at San Francisco State College and the University of California's School of Social Work. He also served as a consultant to Social Dynamics Inc.

Dellums was elected to the Berkeley City Council in 1967, and served until his election as a Democrat to the

U.S. House of Representatives in 1971. As a representative he chaired the House Committee on the District of Columbia and served on the House Armed Services Sub-committee on Military Facilities and Installations as well as the Sub-committee on Military Research and Development. Dellums authored *Defense Sense: The Search for a Rational Military Policy* in 1983.

Dellums, who has chaired the Defense Policy Panel, became the first black to head the House Armed Services Committee on January 27, 1993. Once a militant pacifist, he is recognized as one of the most highly regarded members of Congress to extensively work towards U.S. demilitarization. Also considered a prominent leftist Congressional presence, Dellums chastised U.S. president Bill Clinton for giving into fear and ignorance, when the president did not follow through on his promise to lift the ban on homosexuals in the military.

Along with Colin Powell, Dellums is deemed one of the country's top African American military experts. Though he favors a radical stance, he is respected for the consistency of his record and his expertise in foreign policy matters. Dellums is a former chairman of the Congressional Black Caucus.

Oscar Stanton De Priest 1871-1951
County Commissioner , Federal Legislator

Oscar De Priest was the first black to win a seat in the U.S. House of Representatives in the twentieth century, and the first to be elected from a northern state. Born in Florence, Alabama, in 1871, De Priest moved to Kansas with his family at the age of six. His formal education there consisted of business and bookkeeping classes which he completed before running away to Dayton, Ohio with two white friends. By 1889, he had reached Chicago and become a painter and master decorator.

In Chicago, De Priest amassed a fortune in real estate and the stock market and in 1904 entered politics successfully when he was elected Cook County Commissioner. In 1908, he was appointed an alternate delegate to the Republican National Convention and in 1915 became Chicago's first black alderman. He served on the Chicago City Council from 1915 to 1917 and became Third Ward Committeeman in 1924. In 1928, De Priest became the Republican nominee for the Congressional seat vacated by fellow Republican Martin Madden. De Priest won the November election over his Democratic rival and an independent candidate to become the first black from outside the South to be elected to Congress.

Following his election to Congress, De Priest became the unofficial spokesman for the 11 million blacks in the United States during the 1920s and 1930s. He proposed that states that discriminated against black Americans should receive fewer Congressional seats. Also, he proposed that a monthly pension be given to ex-slaves over the age of seventy-five. During the early 1930s, with the United States mired in the Depression, De Priest was faced with a difficult dilemma. Although he empathized with the plight of poor black and white Americans, he did not support the emergency federal relief programs proposed by President Franklin Roosevelt. Rather, De Priest and his fellow Republicans believed that aid programs should be created and implemented by individual states or local communities. De Priest's stance on the issue of federal relief programs dismayed many of his constituents. In 1934, he was defeated by Arthur Mitchell, the first black Democrat elected to serve in Congress.

De Priest remained active in public life, serving from 1943 to 1947 as alderman of the Third Ward in Chicago. His final withdrawal from politics came about after a sharp dispute with his own party. De Priest returned to his real estate business, and he died on May 12, 1951.

David Dinkins 1927–
Attorney, Municipal Government Official/Executive, State Legislator

In September of 1989, David Dinkins surprised political observers by defeating incumbent Mayor Edward I. Koch in New York City's Democratic mayoral primary. Two months later, in the November election, he defeated Republican contender Rudolph Giuliani, a popular district attorney. Dinkins's victory marked the first time an African American was elected as mayor of New York. Dinkins thus faced the difficult task of leading a racially polarized and financially troubled city with mixed results. While many supporters cited Dinkins's calm, professional demeanor as having a soothing effect upon New York's festering racial problems, others chided him for not responding forcefully enough to the many fiscal and social challenges facing the city.

David Dinkins was born in Trenton, New Jersey in 1927. His parents separated when he was quite young and he moved to Harlem with his mother and sister. He returned to Trenton to attend high school. He was a fine student and well-liked by his peers. Following a stint in the Marines during World War II, he attended Howard University in Washington, DC and graduated with a bachelor of science degree in 1950. In 1953, Dinkins enrolled at Brooklyn Law School and graduated in 1956. He became an attorney, and, eventually, a partner in the law firm of Dyett, Alexander, Dinkins, Patterson, Michael, Dinkins, and Jones.

Dinkins's first foray into the world of politics occurred in 1965, when he won an election to the New York State Assembly. He served until 1967, but did not seek reelection after his district was redrawn. In 1972, Dinkins was appointed as president of elections for the City of New York and served for one year. Two years later, in 1975, he was appointed as city clerk and served until 1985. Dinkins ran for the office of Manhattan borough president in 1977 and 1981. He lost both elections by a wide margin. Dinkins ran again in 1985 and was elected. As Manhattan borough president, he was viewed as a mediator who tried to address a myriad of community concerns such as school decentralization, AIDS treatment and prevention services, and pedestrian safety.

As mayor, Dinkins remained true to the issues he had monitored in Manhattan. Other causes he championed included tolerance and acceptance of gays and lesbians, economic parity for women and minorities, and affirmative action. For example, Dinkins set up a program to provide government contracts to businesses owned by women and minorities. Though the program was blemished by faulty bookkeeping and by the complexity of determining which companies were truly eligible, Dinkins's successor kept it in place.

Poor management became an Achilles heel of the Dinkins administration. For example, in 1994, the New

Ron Dellums and other members of the Congressional Black Caucus meet with former President George Bush, 1989.

York Court of Appeals fined the city more than $3.5 million to compensate 5,000 homeless families forced to live in inadequate shelters. Race relations have always been in the fore of dilemmas for New York City, however. 1991 proved a watershed year for the city, when riots erupted between blacks and Jews in the Crown Heights neighborhood. Dinkins entreated both sides to think about their actions and possible consequences rather than react to the emotional volatility surrounding an incident in which a Jewish man's automobile accidentally struck and killed a black youth. When riots seized Los Angeles in 1992—after police officers from that city were initially found not guilty of using excessive force in a well-publicized incident involving black motorist Rodney King—most of the nation feared that the violence would spread to other large urban areas with mixed or predominately black populations. But Dinkins was able to assuage his constituents and prevent the terror and destruction that incapacitated Los Angeles.

In November of 1993, Dinkins's bid for reelection fell short when he was narrowly defeated by Rudolph W. Giuliani in a hotly contested mayoral race. Dinkins left office on December 31, 1993, but maintained a place in his beloved city, most notably hosting a radio talk show

twice each week on WLIB-AM, beginning in February of 1994. Later in the year, he became a member of AMREP Corp. board of directors and began teaching at Columbia University. Dinkins successfully underwent triple bypass heart surgery in 1995.

Julian C. Dixon 1934-
Attorney, Federal Legislator, Women's Rights Activist

Julian C. Dixon was born August 8, 1934, in Washington, DC. He received a B.S. in political science from California State University and in 1967, an LL.B. from Southwestern University Law School. In 1972, Dixon was elected on the democratic ticket to the California State Assembly. Staying in that position until 1978 Dixon wrote legislation dealing with criminal justice, education and fair employment. In 1978, he was elected to the U.S. House of Representatives.

While in the House of Representatives Dixon has served on the House Committee on Standards of Official Conduct, West Point Board of Supervisors, the Appropriations Sub-Committee on Foreign Operations and he chaired the Appropriations Sub-Committee on the Dis-

David Dinkins speaking at the Democratic National Convention, July 13, 1992.

Julian Dixon

trict of Columbia. This latter appointment made Dixon the first African American to chair an appropriations sub-committee. Dixon was an original co-sponsor of the Equal Rights Amendment and is active in the Congressional Black Caucus. Dixon also served in the U.S. Army from 1957 to 1960.

Sharon Pratt Dixon 1944-
Attorney, Municipal Government Official/Executive, Communications/Media Executive, Educator

Dixon was born Sharon Pratt in Washington, DC on January 30, 1944. She graduated from Howard University with a B.A. in political science in 1965 and a J.D. from their law school in 1968. (While in law school she married Arrington Dixon from whom she was divorced in 1982. In 1991 Dixon married James Kelly III.) She edited the Howard University Law School Journal in 1967.

From 1970 thru 1971 Dixon was the house counsel for the Joint Center for Political Studies in Washington, D.C. Between 1971 and 1976 she was an associate in the

law firm of Pratt and Queen. During this time she also taught at Antioch Law School. In 1976 Dixon began a 14 year association with the Potomac Electric Power Company. While there she held increasingly responsible positions including associate general counsel (1976-1979), director of consumer affairs (1979-1983), and vice president of public policy (1986-1990).

In 1990, Dixon left the private sector to win the office of mayor of Washington, DC. In doing so she became the first African American woman to be mayor of a major American city. Dixon has long been active in the Democratic Party. In 1976 and 1977 she was general counsel to the Washington D.C. Democratic Committee. Between 1985 and 1989 she was treasurer of the Democratic Party and has also sat as a national committeewoman on the Washington D.C. Democratic State Committee.

Dixon belongs to the American Bar Association and the Washington D.C. Women's Bar Association. She is affiliated with the Legal Aid Society, the American Civil Liberties Union and the United Negro College Fund. Dixon was a Falk Fellow at Howard University (1962-1965) and has received numerous awards including the NAACP's Presidential Award (1983), the United Negro

College Fund's Distinguished Leadership Award (1985) and the Distinguished Service Award presented by the Federation of Women's Clubs (1986).

Michael Espy 1953-
Federal Legislator, Federal Government Official, Attorney

Espy was born November 30, 1953. He received a B.A. from Howard University in 1975, and a J.D. from the Santa Clara School of Law in 1978. After graduating, Espy practiced law in Yazoo City, Mississippi and managed Central Mississippi Legal Services from 1978 to 1980. For the next four years, Espy worked for the State of Mississippi as assistant secretary of state for public lands, and from 1984 to 1985, as assistant attorney general for consumer protection.

Espy was elected to the U.S. House of Representatives in 1986, where he served on numerous committees including the House Budget Committee, House Agricultural Committee, Select Committee on Hunger, Sub-Committee on Cotton, Rice & Sugar, Sub-Committee on Conservation, Credit and Rural Development, Consumer Relations & Nutrition Committee; in addition, he chaired the Domestic Task Force on Hunger. In 1993, Espy was appointed Secretary of Agriculture by President Bill Clinton, the first African American to hold this post. However, Espy quickly became the subject of a federal ethics investigation into charges that he accepted gifts from companies that were regulated by the agency he headed, the U.S. Department of Agriculture. Although he denied any wrongdoing, Espy resigned his post on December 31, 1994. Nearly one year later, charges developed that Espy, while still a cabinet member—had improperly approached an agribusiness lobbyist for money, asking him to help pay off a debt incurred by his brother, who had unsuccessfully run for a House seat.

In 1977, Espy won the Law School Community Service Award. He is affiliated with the American Bar Association, Mississippi Trial Lawyers Association, National Conference of Black Leaders and is on the board of directors of the Jackson Urban League.

Chaka Fattah 1956-
State Legislator, Civil Rights/Human Rights Activist

Born as Arthur Davenport in Philadelphia, Pennsylvania, on November 21, 1956, Fattah was renamed after the legendary Zulu warrior Chaka by his mother, who with her husband, took new Swahili root names to represent their African heritage. Fattah's mother, Falaka Fattah started the nationally-known youth program House of Umoja as a means of combating and controlling gangs. At the age of 14 in an effort to assist his mother, Fattah received 20 or more abandoned houses in the neighborhood after giving a slide presentation

Sharon Pratt Dixon

and written proposal to the First Pennsylvania Bank. Falaka Fattah expanded the growing House of Umoja youth program with the buildings.

Fattah continued to help with the youth program while in high school. With the help of congressman Bill Gray, Fattah won a federal grant to renovate the houses. Meanwhile at Overbrook High School, Fattah organized the Youth Movement to Clean Up Politics. After attending the Community College of Philadelphia and the University of Pennsylvania, and Wharton Community Education Program, Fattah worked as a special assistant to the managing director of the Office of Housing and Community Development in Philadelphia for two years.

Then in 1982, Fattah decided to run for the Pennsylvania House of Representatives and won, becoming the youngest ever elected to the Pennsylvania General Assembly at the age of 25. While serving as a representative, Fattah earned a master's degree in government administration from Fels School for State and Local Government at the University of Pennsylvania. In 1988, Fattah won an election for state senator in the Seventh District. As a state senator, Fattah raised money for struggling city of Philadelphia and pioneered programs to rebuild 100 of the country's deteriorating cities. In 1994, Fattah won a seat in the U.S. House of Representatives. He has won an "outstanding contribution award" from the Pennsylvania House of Representatives and the Simpson Fletcher Award for religion and race.

Walter E. Fauntroy 1933-
Federal Legislator, Religious Leader, Civil Rights/Human Rights Activist

Born February 6, 1933, Walter E. Fauntroy represented the District of Columbia in the House of Representatives from 1971 until 1990. He was Washington, DC, coordinator for the March on Washington for Jobs and Freedom in 1963, coordinator for theSelma to Montgomery march in 1965, and national coordinator for the Poor People's Campaign in 1969. Fauntroy served as chairman of the Caucus task force for the 1972 Democratic National Committee and of the platform committee of the National Black Political Convention. He was the chief architect of legislation in 1973 that permitted the District of Columbia to elect its own mayor and city council and engineered the passage by both the House and Senate of a constitutional amendment calling for full Congressional representation for District of Columbia residents in the U.S. Congress. He had strong support from the city's overwhelmingly black population, especially the large population of black civil servants.

During his tenure in the House of Representatives, Fauntroy continued to build a record of achievement by playing key roles in the mobilization of black political power from the National Black Political Convention in 1972 to the presidential elections of 1972 and 1976. For 15 years, Fauntroy chaired a bipartisan congressional task force on Haiti. In November of 1984, Fauntroy and two prominent national leaders launched the "Free South Africa Movement" (FSAM) with their arrest at the South African embassy. He served as co-chair of the steering committee of the FSAM. He was a member of the House Select Committee on Narcotics Abuse and Control and co-sponsored the 1988 $2.7 billion anti-drug bill.

In the 95th Congress Fauntroy was a member of the House Select Committee on Assassinations and chairman of its Subcommittee on the Assassination of Martin Luther King Jr. He was a ranking member of the House Banking, Finance, and Urban Affairs Committee and chairman of its Subcommittee on Government Affairs and Budget. He was also the first ranking member of the House District Committee.

Fauntroy was the recipient of several awards during his political career. In 1984, he was presented with the Hubert H. Humphrey Humanitarian Award by the National Urban Coalition. He also received honorary degrees from Georgetown University Law School, Yale University, and Virginia Union University. After leaving public service, Fauntroy founded Project We Care, a social service located in the DC area. The project is comprised of teams of ministers and church members who canvass neighborhoods in order to serve as conduits between residents and the city. Fauntroy also began his own company, Walter E. Fauntroy & Associates.

Fauntroy encountered some difficulty in the early to mid-1990s. First, he contracted tuberculosis. Through a diligent regimen, however, he remained healthy and actually became an unofficial spokesperson for the disease, urging the public to get tested. Then a discovery was made that he was incorrectly listed a church donation on a disclosure form presented to the Congress. In 1995, Fauntroy was sentenced to a two-year probation, $1,000 fine, and 300 hours of community service after pleading guilty to a misdemeanor charge of falsifying a financial report to Congress. The incident did little to tarnish Fauntroy's reputation; many averred that Fauntroy's mistake was both victimless and free of wrongdoing in the sense that his action was committed without criminal intent.

Gary A. Franks 1953-
Federal Legislator, Organization Executive/Founder

A staunch conservative, Gary Franks was born February 9, 1953, in Waterbury, Connecticut. He received a B.A. from Yale University in 1975. Before being elected to the U.S. House of Representatives, Franks was active in local politics and business. He was president of GAF Realty in Waterbury. Franks was also on the Board of Alderman (1086 00), vice chairman of the Zoning Board (1986-87), a member of the Environmental Control Commission (1988-90), director of the Naugatuck, Connecticut chapter of the American Red Cross (1984 87), president of the Greater Waterbury Chamber of Commerce (1987-90), and a member of the Waterbury Foundation (1989-90).

In 1991, Franks was elected to the U.S. House of Representatives, thus becoming the only African American Republican in the House until J. C. Watts was elected in 1995. Franks has served on the Armed Services Committee, Small Business Committee, and the Select Committee on Aging. In 1993, he was appointed to the highly prized House Energy and Commerce Committee.

Franks has fulfilled a controversial role, that of an African American opposed to affirmative action and other programs based on preference for women and minorities. With such views, Franks has had his share of Congressional ruckuses. Formerly the only Republican member of the Congressional Black Caucus, he was actually voted out of the organization in 1993, by members who did not consider Franks a legitimate black spokesperson. (That vote was later reversed). In 1994,

Michael Epsy

Franks testified in support of a lawsuit to dismantle the majority-black 11th Congressional District of Cynthia McKinney, a black Democrat from Georgia. Franks and those like-minded felt that the district had been improperly designed to increase black voting strength in the area at the expense of the white electorate. Franks stance led to altercations with those who felt he was letting blacks down.

Despite having alienated many, Franks is known as one of the Republican party's most prominent black lawmakers. He entered the political landscape at a time when black Republicans were nonexistent as members of the Senate and at municipal and state levels as mayors of major American cities or governors of any states. Franks has been named Outstanding Young Man by the Boy's Club and Man of the Year by the Negro Professional Women's Club (1980).

Lenora Fulani 1950-
Political Party Leader, Psychologist, Social Therapist

Born Lenora Branch on April 25, 1950, in Chester, Pennsylvania, near Philadelphia, she changed her name to Lenora Branch Fulani in 1973. She received a bache-

lor's from Hofstra University. She furthered her education in social therapy with a master's from Columbia University Teachers College and a PH.D. from the New York Institute for Social Therapy and Research. Affiliated with the Institute, Fulani opened her own therapy practice in Harlem in the 1970s, the Eastside Center for Short Term Psychotherapy. Concurrently, she founded the National Alliance Party (NAP), a political party for social change.

As a politician, Fulani bid for election as lieutenant governor of New York in 1982 and governor in 1986 and 1990. She also campaigned for election as mayor of New York City in 1985. In between, she campaigned for election as president of the United States in 1988 and 1992. Fulani was the first African American woman to be included on the presidential ballot in all 50 states. In 1992, she became the first woman to qualify for federal primary matching funds to run her campaign. In 1994, she made a run again for governor of New York, garnering 21 percent of the votes in the primary. Following her gubernatorial defeat, Fulani contributed to the formation of the Patriot Party into which her NAP has merged. The Patriot Party planed to gain wide-range support by voters independent of the main two parties in the 1996 elections. The formation of this party was followed by Fulani's creation of the Committee for a Unified Party.

Fulani has written widely on the subject of politics, including in the 1990 book *Independent Black Leadership in America* and 1992's *The Making of a Fringe Candidate*. In the mid-1990s, her newspaper column, "This Way for Black Empowerment" was carried in more than 140 newspapers nationwide. She founded the All-Stars Talent Show Network, and she hosted her own *Fulani!*, a cable television program aired in more 20 cities nationwide each week.

W. Wilson Goode 1938-
Municipal Government Official/Executive

W. Wilson Goode was born on August 19, 1938, in Seaboard, North Carolina. He received a B.A. from Morgan State University in 1961. Goode served in the U.S. Army from 1961 to 1963, where he earned a commendation medal for meritorious service and the rank of captain with the military police. In 1968, he earned a master's degree in public administration from the University of Pennsylvania's Wharton School.

Between 1966 and 1978 Goode held a wide variety of positions including probation officer, building maintenance supervisor, insurance claims adjuster and president of the Philadelphia Council for Community Advancement. From 1978 until 1980, Goode was chairman of the Pennsylvania Public Utilities Commission, and from 1980 until 1982 he was managing director of the City of Philadelphia. In 1983, Goode was elected the first African American mayor of Philadelphia.

Goode's tenure as mayor of Philadelphia was marred by charges that he was a weak and ineffective leader who was unable to handle the traditionally rough and tumble politics of Philadelphia city government. This charge seemed to be borne out in May of 1985 during a violent confrontation between the city of Philadelphia and members of MOVE, a radical "back-to-nature" cult that took over a row house in West Philadelphia. When Goode ordered police to drop a bomb on the roof of the house to evict MOVE–members, a massive explosion and fire resulted that killed 11 people, destroyed 61 homes, and caused $8 million dollars in damage. Goode's political career was irreparably damaged.

Goode barely won reelection in 1987, and was faced with mounting problems. Decades of corruption, racial tension, and urban decay had dampened Philadelphia's civic spirit and created a sense of apathy. Acute tensions between Goode and the city council resulted in a huge budget deficit. In September of 1990, Goode announced that the city was on the verge of bankruptcy. Although a consortium of banks helped to avert disaster, Philadel-

W. Wilson Goode

phia reported a massive $200 million deficit in June of 1991.

Barred by law from seeking a third term, Goode was succeeded as mayor by Edward Rendell in January of 1992. That same year, he wrote his autobiography *In Goode Faith*. After leaving office, Goode started his own company, Goode Group.

Patricia Roberts Harris 1924-1985
Organization Executive/Founder, Diplomat, Civil Rights/Human Rights Activist, Federal Government Official, Attorney, Educator

As ambassador to Luxembourg, Patricia Harris was the first black woman to hold this diplomatic rank in United States history. Until President Ronald Reagan took office in 1980, Harris served as Secretary of the Department of Health and Human Services and also Secretary of Housing and Urban Development under President Jimmy Carter. She served in these positions from 1977 to 1981.

Born in Mattoon, Illinois, on May 31, 1924, Harris attended elementary school in Chicago, and received her undergraduate degree from Howard University in 1945. While at Howard, Harris also served as vice-chairman of a student branch of the National Association for the Advancement of Colored People (NAACP) and was involved in early nonviolent demonstrations against racial discrimination. Harris worked for the YWCA in Chicago (1946-49) and served as executive director of Delta Sigma Theta, a black sorority, from 1953 to 1959. After completing post-graduate work at the University of Chicago and at American University, she earned her doctorate in jurisprudence from George Washington University Law School in 1960.

An attorney and professor before she entered politics, Harris was appointed as co-chairman of the National Women's Committee on Civil Rights by President John F. Kennedy and was later named to the Commission on the Status of Puerto Rico. In 1965, Harris was chosen by President Lyndon Johnson to become US ambassador to Luxembourg, the first black woman ever to be named an American envoy.

In 1977, Harris was chosen by President Jimmy Carter to serve as Secretary of Housing and Urban Development. She was also selected as secretary of the Department of Health and Human Services in 1979. Harris remained in these positions until the inauguration of President Ronald Reagan in 1981. Harris ran an unsuccessful campaign for mayor of Washington, DC in 1982. She became a law professor at George Washington University in 1983 and remained there until her death from cancer on March 23, 1985.

Maynard Jackson 1938-
Attorney, Municipal Government Official/Executive, Organization Executive/Founder

Jackson was born on March 23, 1938, in Dallas, Texas. At the age of 14 he was admitted to Morehouse College as a Ford Foundation Early Admissions Scholar. He graduated with a B.A. in 1956, with a concentration in history and political science. After graduation, he worked for the Ohio State Bureau of Unemployment Compensation as claims examiner from 1957 to 1958 and as a sales manager and associate district sales manager for P.F. Collier Inc. from 1958 to 1961.

In 1964, Jackson received a J.D. from the North Carolina Central University School of Law and then worked as a lawyer for the National Labor Relations Board. In 1968 and 1969 Jackson was named the managing attorney and director of community relations for the Emory Community Legal Service Center in Atlanta and from 1970 to 1973 he was a senior partner in the law firm of Jackson, Patterson & Parks.

Jackson had been active in Democratic politics and, from 1970 to 1974, he was the vice mayor of Atlanta. In 1974, he was elected mayor. At the time of his election to Atlanta's highest office, Jackson was the youngest mayor of a major U.S. city. He remained mayor of Atlanta until 1982. Jackson returned to private life and worked as a bond lawyer before being re-elected mayor of Atlanta in 1989. The selection of Atlanta as host of the 1994 Super Bowl and the site of the 1996 Summer Olympic Games were two of the greatest achievements of Jackson's second term. He left office in 1993, with a mixed record.

For example, in 1993, Jackson vetoed domestic partnership legislation claiming that the City Council did not provide details on funding benefits for partners of city employees. The response of the gay and lesbian community was surprisingly fervent, as leaders of 40 Atlanta-based lesbian and gay organizations coordinated a barrage of protest actions during that year's Fourth of July holiday. In another incident, Jackson was deluged with complaints from angry city taxpayers who felt that Jackson's decision to order more than $45,000 worth of furniture for the mayor's office was government waste in action. Jackson admitted that city purchasing guidelines had not been followed.

Even after leaving office, Jackson has fallen into controversy. Accusations were levied against him that while he was in office, Jackson improperly influenced the manner in which a $1.3 billion financial portfolio was invested; a city audit unveiled the fact that nearly 80 percent of the city's 1993 investments were turned over to a firm whose principal was Jackson's 1989 campaign treasurer. Jackson emphatically denied the allegations that he swayed any investment decisions.

Despite the alleged improprieties, Jackson earned a repuation as an agressive and outspoken mayor. He had the difficult task of leading Atlanta through the difficult transition years from predominantly white leadership to a more equitable power balance. Under Jackson's leadership Atlanta made serious gains as a financial center and distribution hub. Expanded international convention facilities turned Atlanta into a major convention center. In 1981, the prestigious *Almanac of Places Rated* named Atlanta the best major city in which to live and work. Jackson had taken advantage of affirmative action programs to improve city housing and social conditions. He also transformed the mass transit system into one of the most modern in the country.

Shortly after his last term, Jackson became chairman of the board and a majority stockholder in Jackson Securities Inc, a banking firm. He also holds interest in Jackmont Hospitality, a group of real estate company that hoped to stimulate the economy of some of Atlanta's depressed areas. In 1995, Jackson became the principal owner of a joint venture to operate a TGI Friday's restaurant at the city's Hartfield International Airport. Many complained that Jackson's use of Atlanta's affirmative action program to land the premier location was an abuse of a system designed to aid the disadvantaged.

Jackson has served as vice chairman of the White House Committee on Balanced Growth & Economic Development and the White House Committee on the Windfall Profits Tax. He is also the founding chairman of the Atlanta Economic Development Corporation and the chairman of the Atlanta Urban Residential Finance Authority. Jackson belongs to the Georgia and New York Bar Associations, the National League of Cities and the National Black Caucus of Local Elected Officials.

In 1975, Jackson was named to *Time* magazine's list of 200 young American leaders and *Ebony* magazine's list of 100 Most Influential Black Americans in 1976. In 1994, Jackson and six other Morehouse graduates were honored at the college's sixth annual Candle in the Dark awards dinner.

Barbara Jordan 1936-1996
Educator, Federal Legislator, Civil Rights/Human Rights Activist, State Legislator, Attorney

An eloquent orator, Barbara Jordan was born on February 21, 1936, in Houston, Texas. Afflicted with multiple sclerosis, she died of viral pneumonia, a complication of leukemia, on January 17, 1996. The 59-year-old was beloved in the nation for her visions of virtue and convictions.

Jordan attended Phyliss Wheately High School, where she graduated a member of the Honor Society in 1952. In 1956, Jordan an received a B.A. from Texas Southern University in history and political science. She went on to Boston University, where she earned a J.D. in 1959. After teaching at Tuskegee Institute for one year, Jordan returned to Houston, where she practiced law and was appointed administrative assistant to a Harris County judge. In 1966, Jordan was elected to the Texas Senate. She was the first African American to serve as president *pro tem* of that body and to chair the important Labor and Management Relations Committee. In 1972, Jordan was elected to the U.S. House of Representatives where she stayed until 1978. While a representative Jordan served on the House Judiciary and Government Operations committees. During her terms in both the Texas Senate and U.S. House, Jordan was known as a champion of civil rights, minorities, and the poor and for her integrity.

From 1979 to 1982 Jordan taught at the Lyndon Baines Johnson School of Public Affairs at the Austin campus of the University of Texas. In 1982, she was made holder of the Lyndon Baines Johnson Centennial Chair of National Policy. After 15 years out of politics, Jordan was appointed as chair of the U.S. Commission on Immigration Reform by U.S. president Bill Clinton in 1993. Jordan strongly felt that the stereotype of immi-

Barbara Jordan

grants taking lower-paying jobs out of the hands of U.S. citizens is erroneous. Jordan was credited for her efforts to address the burgeoning U.S. hostility towards immigrants.

Jordan co-authored two books, *Barbara Jordan: A Self-Portrait* (1979) and *The Great Society: A Twenty Year Critique* (1986). She also served on the Democratic Caucus Steering and Policy Committee, and in 1976 and 1992, she was the keynote speaker at the Democratic National Convention.

Jordan belonged to the American Bar Association as well as the Texas, Massachusetts, and District of Columbia bars. She was a member of the Character Counts Coalition, a group whose aim is to address the values of American society, particularly emphasizing youth. She had been on the board of directors of the Mead Corporation and the Henry J. Kaiser Family Foundation. Jordan is the recipient of a long list of awards and honors including the Eleanor Roosevelt Humanities Award (1984), Texas Women's Hall of Fame (public service category 1984), Ladies Home Journal "100 Most Influential Women in America", and *Time* magazine's "Ten Women of the Year" list (1976). She was bestowed the nation's highest civilian honor in 1994, when President

Clinton gave her the Presidential Medal of Freedom for her distinguised career in public service. Jordan had also received 27 honorary doctorate degrees.

Alan L. Keyes 1950-
Federal Government Official, Lecturer, Author

Alan Lee Keyes was born on August 7, 1950 in New York City. Keyes lived throughout the United States and Italy during his childhood. He began his political career early, serving as president of his high school's student council and president of the American Legion Boys Nation at the age of 16, the first African American so elected. Keyes earned a bachelor's from Harvard in 1972, after starting his education at Cornell, which was interrupted by a year of living in Paris. He received his Ph.D. in political science from Harvard in 1979.

Following his graduate work, Keyes took a position at the U.S. State Department in 1978. He won Jeane Kilpatrick as a mentor by defending her from verbal attack while serving as U.S. vice consul in India. At the State Department, Keyes served in the South African Affairs division, on the Policy Planning Council, in UNESCO (the United Nations Educational, Scientific, and Cultural Organization), and as an assistant secretary of state for International Organizational Affairs. Though Keyes was the African American of highest station at the State Department in 1987, he resigned over a dispute over allocation of U.S. funds to the United Nations.

In 1988 and 1992, Keyes lost a senatorial elections in Maryland. In between, he served as president of the Washington, DC organization, Citizens Against Government Waste from 1989 to 1991 as well as touring as a public speaker. He also served as interim president in 1991 for Alabama A&M University. In 1992, following his second defeat, Keyes started his own talk radio show in Baltimore, *America's Wake-Up Call: The Alan Keyes Show*. Bolstered by the response to his radio show, Keyes announced his candidacy for the U.S. presidency on March 26, 1995. In so doing, he became the first Republican African American in the twentieth century to run for president.

Ron Kirk 1954-
Attorney, Municipal Government Official

Ron Kirk was born on June 27, 1954, in Austin, Texas. He received a bachelor's degree in political science and sociology from Austin College in 1976, during which time he served as a legislative aide to the Texas Constitutional Convention in 1974. This experience prompted an interest in politics and drove him to complete his law degree at the University of Texas School of Law in 1979. After two years, Kirk was unsatisfied as a private prac-

tice attorney, he moved to Washington, DC, to work for U.S. Senator Lloyd Bentsen from 1981 to 1983. He returned to Dallas in 1983 to work for the Dallas City Attorney's office soon becoming chief lobbyist of Dallas until 1989, when he switched to private practice again, working for the firm of Johnson & Gibbs and volunteering his time for Big Brothers/Big Sisters of America, Dallas Zoological Society, Dallas Helps, and North Texas Food Bank among other organizations. In 1994, Kirk took over the Secretary of State position as appointed by Governor Ann Richards to replace John Hannah, who left for a federal judgeship. Kirk vaulted from that role to campaign for and win the election for mayor of Dallas in 1995 with 62 percent of the vote.

Though Kirk maintains his role as a partner in the law firm of Gardere & Wynn, he manages his city efficiently developing new economic opportunities in Dallas. Kirk's good service has been recognized many times. He was honored in 1992 with a Volunteer of the Year award from Big Brothers/Big Sisters and a Distinguished Alumni Award from the Austin College Alumni Association. He was named Citizen of the Year by Omega Psi Phi in 1994, the same year, he won the C.B. Bunkley Community Service Award from the Turner Legal Association.

John Mercer Langston 1829-1897
Educational Administrator, Federal Legislator, Diplomat, Attorney, Lecturer

Congressman John Mercer Langston was born in Virginia in 1829. Upon the death of his father, Ralph Quarles, an estate owner, young Langston was emancipated and sent to Ohio, where he was given over to the care of a friend of his father. Langston spent his childhood there, attending private school in Cincinnati before graduating from Oberlin College in 1849. Four years later, after getting his degree from the theological department of Oberlin, he studied law and was admitted to the Ohio bar in 1854.

Langston began his practice in Brownhelm, Ohio. He was chosen in 1855 to serve as clerk of this township by the Liberty Party. During the Civil War, he was a recruiting agent for Negro servicemen, helping to organize such famed regiments as the 54th and 55th Massachusetts, and the 5th Ohio. In 1867, Langston served as inspector-general of the Freedmen's Bureau and as dean and vice president of Howard University from 1868 to 1875. In 1877 he was named minister resident to Haiti and chargé d'affaires to Santo Domingo, remaining in diplomatic service until 1885.

Soon after returning to his law practice in the United States, Langston was named president of the Virginia Normal and Collegiate Institute. In 1888, he was elected to Congress from Virginia, but was not seated for two years until vote-counting irregularities had been investigated. He was defeated in his bid for a second term. In 1894 Langston wrote an autobiography, *From the Virginia Plantation to the National Capital.* (Eleven years earlier, he had published a volume of his speeches, *Freedom and Citizenship.*) Langston died in 1897.

George Thomas "Mickey" Leland 1944-1989
Civil Rights/Human Rights Activist, Federal Legislator, Educator

Leland was born on November 27, 1944 in Lubbock, Texas. He graduated from Texas Southern University in 1970 with a B.S. in pharmacy and taught clinical pharmacy there for a short time. Leland had been active in the civil rights movement during his student years and in an effort to affect social change he ran for and was elected to the Texas state legislature in 1973. In 1978 he was elected to the U.S. House of Representatives filling Barbara Jordan's vacated seat. While a representative Leland served on various committees including Interstate and Foreign Commerce, Post Office and Civil Service and the committee on the District of Columbia.

In spite of serving on these committees, Leland was devoted to easing the hunger of starving persons in the United States and in other countries, especially African countries. To this end he chaired the House Select Committee on World Hunger and visited starving peoples throughout Africa. In 1989, while traveling to a United Nations refugee camp in Ethiopia the plane Leland was flying on crashed near Gambela, Ethiopia, killing all on board.

John Robert Lewis 1940-
Civil Rights/Human Rights Activist, Federal Legislator, Organization Executive/Founder

Committed to nonviolence and the advancement of blacks, John Lewis was born in Troy, Alabama on February 21, 1940. He received a B.S. in 1961, from the American Baptist Theological Seminary and in 1967, another B.A. from Fisk University. Before entering politics Lewis was associated with numerous social activist organizations including the Student Non-violent Coordinating Committee (1963-66), associate director of the Field Foundation (1966-67), project director of the Southern Regional Council (1967-70) and executive director of the Voter Education Project Inc. beginning in 1970.

In 1982, Lewis was elected Atlanta City Councilman-at-Large, and in 1986, voters sent him to the U.S. House of Representatives as a Democrat. While in the House, Lewis has served on the Public Works, Interior and Insular Affairs committees as well as the powerful House Ways and Means Committee. He has also been a

Mickey Leland

member of the Select Committee on Aging. Lewis's pet project over the years has been the encouragement of a museum bill that would allow for a museum of black history at the Smithsonian Institution in Washington, DC.

A man of convictions, Lewis denounced the rhetoric of his homophobic colleagues during a House debate that ultimately led to the adoption of legislation to discourage homosexual enlistment in the military. He considered the so-called Republican "Contract With America," as the genesis of a wave of intolerance in American society in the early to mid-1990s. In 1995, Lewis headed a group of nearly 100 trade unionists who interrupted a speech on proposed Medicare changes by House Speaker Newt Gingrich during a conference sponsored by the Congressional Institute; the demonstrators felt that the plan would covertly finance tax cuts for the rich. Many of Lewis's critics suggested that the demonstration did little but gain media attention, but Lewis countered that saving Medicare benefits for the elderly was his priority, and he was willing to seize any opportunity to stir up a public debate.

In the 1960s, Lewis was known for his involvement with the U.S. civil rights movement. A strict follower of nonviolent social protest, Lewis was a relentless organizer and participant in numerous sit-ins, freedom rides, and protest marches throughout the South. He abstained from the 1995 Million Man March because he felt that he could not, in good conscience, participate in an effort led by Louis Farrakhan, whom many regard to be racist, misogynistic, and anti-Semitic. Lewis worked steadfastly in the mid-1990s to help produce a spirit of racial harmony and team spirit in Atlanta, as the city prepared for the 1996 Olympics.

Lewis is a recipient of the Martin Luther King Jr. Non-Violent Peace Prize and has been named to Ebony's "One of the Nation's Most Influential Blacks" list (1991-92) and Time magazine's "One of America's Rising Leaders" list (1974). He belongs to the Martin Luther King Jr. Center for Social Change, the National Democratic Institute for International Affairs, Friends of Vista, and the African-American Institute. He was elected president of Americans for Democratic Action, a part-time position, in 1993.

Kweisi Mfume 1948-
Federal Legislator, Educator, Civil Rights/Human Rights Activist, Organization Executive

Kweisi Mfume was born Fizzell Gray in Baltimore on October 24, 1948. A remarkable figure, Mfume once ran the streets, fathering five children out of wedlock, but he remade himself into a respected leader, viewed by the Democratic establishment as a rising star and by many blacks as a beacon of hope. He received a B.S. from Morgan State University in 1976, and an M.A. from Johns Hopkins University in 1984.

In 1978, Mfume was elected to the Baltimore City Council, where he became especially interested in health issues. A member of the Maryland Democratic State Central Committee and a delegate to the Democratic National Convention in 1980, 1984, and 1988, Mfume was elected to the U.S. House of Representatives in 1987. During his tenure, he served on the Banking, Finance & Urban Affairs Committee, the Small Business Committee, the Education & Labor Committee, and the Narcotics Abuse & Control subcommittee. He also served as vice chair, and later as chairperson, of the Congressional Black Caucus. Mfume was also a member of the Caucus for Women's Issues, the Congressional Arts Caucus and the Federal Government Service Task Force.

Near the end of 1995, Mfumi decided that he could be more effective outside of the Capitol and accepted his selection as the president and CEO of the NAACP. He aimed to restore the faith of the seminal organization's members by gaining the confidence of the private sector

John Lewis

to gain funding. Within weeks of Mfume's appointment, Nissan Motor Corp USA donated $100,000 to the NAACP, indicating that Mfume was perhaps the symbol of integrity needed to help the troubled civil rights organization regain the right footing.

Mfume is a trustee of the Baltimore Museum of Art and the Morgan State University Board of Regents, where he previously taught political science and communications.

Arthur W. Mitchell 1883-1968
Civil Rights/Human Rights Activist, Federal Legislator, Lecturer, Attorney, Organization Executive/Founder

Born to slave parents in 1883 in Chambers County, Alabama, Mitchell was educated at Tuskegee Institute and at Columbia and Harvard universities. By 1929, he had founded Armstrong Agricultural School in West Butler, Alabama, and become a wealthy landowner and a lawyer with a thriving practice in Washington, DC When he left the nation's capital that year, it was with the avowed purpose of entering politics and becoming a representative from Illinois.

President Bill Clinton meets with Kweisi Mfume and Senator Carol Moseley Braun.

Mitchell won Democratic approval only after Harry Baker (who had defeated him in the primary) died suddenly, leaving the nomination vacant. Aided by the overwhelming national sentiment for the Democratic party during this period, he unseated Oscar De Priest by the slender margin of 3,000 votes. Mitchell's most significant victory on behalf of civil rights came, not in the legislative chamber, but in the courts. In 1937, Mitchell brought suit against the Chicago and Rock Island Railroad after having been forced to leave his first class accommodations en route to Hot Springs, Arkansas, and sit in a "Jim Crow" car. He argued his own case before the Supreme Court in 1941, and won a decision which declared "Jim Crow" practices illegal.

Mitchell used his influence in Congress to improve the lot of African Americans. He proposed that states that discriminated against black Americans should receive fewer Congressional seats and advocated strong sanctions against states that practiced lynching. Also, he worked for the elimination of poll taxes to make it easier for black persons to vote. Following the end of World War II, Mitchell held that because blacks fought bravely for the United States, they should be able to vote for their government representatives.

In 1942, Mitchell retired from Congress and continued to pursue his civil rights agenda as a private citizen. He also lectured occasionally and pursued farming on his estate near Petersburg, Virginia, where he died in 1968 at the age of 85.

Eleanor Holmes Norton 1938-
Attorney, Federal Legislator, Civil Rights/Human Rights Activist, Organization Executive/Founder, Educator

Eleanor Norton was born Eleanor Holmes on April 8, 1938, in Washington, DC. She attended Antioch College in Ohio but transferred to Yale University and received an M.A. in American Studies in 1963 and a J.D. from Yale's law school in 1964. After graduating from law school, Norton clerked for a federal judge in Philadelphia before joining the American Civil Liberties Union in 1965, as a litigator specializing in free speech issues. She stayed with the ACLU until 1970, reaching the position of assistant legal director and successfully arguing a first amendment case before the U.S. Supreme Court. In 1970, she became chairwoman of the New York City Commission on Human Rights, a post she held

Arthur Mitchell, 1934.

until 1977, when she headed the Equal Employment Opportunity Commission. In 1981, she was a senior fellow at the Urban Institute, and, in 1982, she accepted the position of professor of Law at Georgetown University. Norton had previously taught black history at Pratt Institute in Brooklyn, New York, and law at New York City University Law School.

In 1990, Norton was elected congressional delegate to the U.S. House of Representatives for the District of Columbia, a non-voting position. In 1993—the same year she sponsored legislation that would make Washington, DC the 51st state—she was allowed to cast a vote in the full house, thus becoming the first resident of the District to vote on the floor of Congress. In 1995, however, the House voted to strip Washington, DC of it's floor voting right. Norton protested that she was elected by federal tax-paying citizens who are entitled to full representation. A bipartisan alliance was formed between Norton, Republican House Speaker Newt Gingrich, and Democratic Washington, DC Mayor Marion Barry in an effort to save home rule for the District.

Norton has been named to the *Ladies Home Journal* "One Hundred Most Important Women" list (1988) and

the "One Hundred Most Powerful Women in Washington" list by *Washington Magazine* (1989). Norton is also a recipient of the Distinguished Public Service Award presented by the Center for National Policy (1985).

Hazel O'Leary 1937-
Attorney, Federal Government Official, Financial Planner

Hazel O'Leary was born Hazel Reid on May 17, 1937, in Newport News, Virginia. She received a B.A. from Fisk College in 1959, and a J.D. from Rutgers University School of Law in 1966. O'Leary was a utilities regulator under U.S. presidents Ford and Carter and an executive vice-president of the Northern States Power Co., where she functioned as a Washington lobbyist. A proponent of energy conservation and alternative energy sources, U.S. president Bill Clinton appointed her to his cabinet as Secretary of Energy in 1993.

In addition to formulating energy policy, Energy Secretary O'Leary has been instrumental in dismantling the nation's nuclear weaponry complex and in helping energy producers finance nuclear-waste storage programs. Reorganizing the Department of Energy to reflect the end of the Cold War was one of the first accountabilities assigned to O'Leary. One means to doing so was O'Leary's campaign to unveil the expansive network of secret atomic laboratories and weapons plants harbored in the nation. Results of Cold War nuclear test, radiation releases, and experiments on civilians were also revealed. As a cabinet member, O'Leary has also encouraged domestic resource development.

In the mid-1990s, O'Leary came under heavy scrutiny. First she was criticized for having spent thousands of government dollars on hiring a consultant firm to rank a number of reporters to find out which had given her the most favorable coverage. Then a disclosure was made that she had spent much more than other Cabinet members on overseas travel and had done so in particularly lavish manner. U.S. vice president Al Gore came to O'Leary's defense by noting that her trips had helped create new job opportunities in the United States. For example, O'Leary led a delegation of nearly 100 aides, energy experts, and business leaders to South Africa to uncover possibilities in the newly democratic country. This explanation did not satisfy some Republican members of government who called for the elimination of the Department of Energy altogether.

O'Leary is a certified financial planner, a member of the New Jersey and Washington bars, and has been vice president and general counsel of O'Leary Associates in

Washington, DC. In 1993, the Congressional Black Caucus honored O'Leary for her achievements.

Clarence McClane Pendleton, Jr. 1930-1988
Federal Government Official, Organization Executive/Founder

Clarence Pendleton, Jr. was born in Louisville, Kentucky on November 10, 1930. Raised in Washington, DC, he attended Dunbar High School and received a B.S. from Howard University in 1954. Pendleton served three years in the U.S. Army where he was assigned to a medical unit. After his discharge in 1957 Pendleton returned to Howard University where he received a masters degree in 1961 and coached swimming, football, rowing and baseball.

In 1968, Pendleton became the recreation coordinator of the Baltimore Model Cities Program and in 1970 the director of the Urban Affairs Department of the National Recreation and Parks Association. Pendleton soon began attracting national attention and in 1972 he headed San Diego's Model Cities Program and in 1975 he became the director of the San Diego Urban League.

By 1980, however, a change had taken place in Pendleton's political philosophy. He began to feel that African Americans' reliance on government programs were trapping them in a cycle of dependence and welfare handouts. Pendleton believed that it was in the best interest of African Americans to build strong ties with a strong, expanding private sector and eschew the more traditional ties with liberal bureaucrats and liberal philosophies.

To this end he supported the election of Ronald Reagan to the presidency and in 1981 Pendleton was appointed chairman of the Civil Rights Commission by President Reagan. Pendleton's chairmanship was controversial mostly because of his opposition to affirmative action and forced bussing as a means of de-segregating schools. Pendleton retained a more liberal philosophy on other matters however by supporting the Equal Rights Amendment and the Voting Rights Act. Pendleton died unexpectedly of an apparent heart attack on June 5, 1988 in San Diego.

Pinckney Benton Stewart Pinchback 1837-1921
Attorney, Federal Legislator, State Government Official, Municipal Government Official

Pinchback was born in Macon, Georgia on May 10, 1837. Although his mother had been a slave, by the time Pinchback was born she had been emancipated by

Clarence M. Pendleton, Jr.

Pinchback's father. Moving to Ohio with his mother, Pinchback attended high school in Cincinnati in 1847 but, in 1848, he began working on riverboats, first as a cabin boy and then as a steward.

At the outbreak of the Civil War, Pinchback went to Louisiana and in 1862 he enlisted in the Union Army. He soon began recruiting soldiers for an African-American troop variously known as the Louisiana Native Guards and the Corps d'Afrique. Racial problems soon arose with the military hierarchy and Pinchback resigned his commission in protest. After the war Pinchback became active in Louisiana politics. He organized a Republican Club in 1867 and in 1868 was a delegate to a state constitutional convention. In that year he was also elected to the state senate and in 1871 he became president pro-tem of that body. He soon became lieutenant governor of Louisiana through the line of succession. For five weeks in late 1872 and early 1873 Pinchback was governor of Louisiana while the elected official underwent impeachment proceedings. In 1872 and 1873 Pinchback was elected to the U.S. Senate and the U.S. House of Representatives. He was refused seating both times when the elections were contested and ruled in favor of his Democratic opponent. He did however receive what would have been his salary as an elected official.

In 1877, Pinchback switched his allegiance to the Democratic Party and in 1882 was appointed surveyor of customs for New Orleans. In 1887, he began attending law school at Straight University in New Orleans and was later admitted to the bar. In 1890, Pinchback moved to Washington, DC, where he died December 21, 1921.

Adam Clayton Jr. Powell 1908-1972
Federal Legislator

Born on November 29, 1908, in New Haven, Connecticut, to Mattie Fletcher and Adam Clayton Powell Sr., Adam Jr. was raised in New York City, attended high school there, and then went to Colgate University where he earned a bachelors degree in 1930. In 1931, Powell graduated from Columbia University with a masters degree in religious education. The young Powell launched his career as a crusader for reform during the Depression. He forced several large corporations to drop their unofficial bans on employing blacks and directed a kitchen and relief operation which fed, clothed, and provided fuel for thousands of Harlem's needy and destitute. He was instrumental in persuading officials of Harlem Hospital to integrate their medical and nursing staffs, helped many blacks find employment along Harlem's "main stem," 125th Street, and campaigned against the city's bus lines, which were discriminating against Negro drivers and mechanics.

When Powell Sr. retired from Abyssinian Baptist Church in 1936, his son, who had already served as manager and assistant pastor there, was named his successor. In 1939, Powell served as chairman of the Coordinating Committee on Employment, which organized a picket line before the executive offices of the World's Fair in the Empire State Building and eventually succeeded in getting employment at the fair for hundreds of blacks.

Powell won a seat on the New York City Council in 1941 with the third highest number of votes ever cast for a candidate in municipal elections. In 1942, he turned to journalism for a second time (he had already been on the staff of the New York *Evening Post* in 1934), and published and edited the weekly *The People's Voice*, which he called "the largest Negro tabloid in the world." He became a member of the New York State Office of Price Administration in 1942 and served until 1944.

In 1944, Powell was elected to Congress and represented a constituency of 300,000, 89% of whom were black. Identified at once as "Mr. Civil Rights," he en-

countered a host of discriminatory procedures upon his arrival in the nation's capital. He could not rent a room or attend a movie in downtown Washington. Within Congress itself, he was not allowed to use such communal facilities as dining rooms, steam baths, showers, and barber shops. Powell met these rebuffs head on by making use of all such facilities and insisting that his entire staff follow his lead.

As a freshman legislator, Powell engaged in fiery debates with segregationists, fought for the abolition of discriminatory practices at U.S. military installations, and sought—through the controversial Powell amendment—to deny federal funds to any project where discrimination existed. This amendment eventually became part of the Flanagan School Lunch Bill, making Powell the first black Congressman since Reconstruction to have legislation passed by both houses.

Powell also sponsored legislation advocating federal aid to education, a minimum-wage scale, and greater benefits for the chronically unemployed. He also drew attention to certain discriminatory practices on Capitol Hill and worked toward their elimination. It was Powell who first demanded that a Negro journalist be allowed to sit in the Senate and House press galleries, introduced the first Jim Crow transportation legislation, and the first bill to prohibit segregation in the Armed Forces. At one point in his career, the *Congressional Record* reported that the House Committee on Education and Labor had processed more important legislation than any other major committee. In 1960, Powell, as senior member of this committee, became its chairman. He had a hand in the development and passage of such significant legislation as the Minimum Wage Bill of 1961, the Manpower Development and Training Act, the Anti-Poverty Bill, the Juvenile Delinquency Act, the Vocational Educational Act, and the National Defense Education Act. In all, the Powell committee helped pass forty-eight laws involving a total outlay of fourteen billion dollars. The flamboyant congressman, however, was accused of putting an excessive number of friends on the congressional payroll, of a high rate of absenteeism from congressional votes, and of excessive zeal for the "playboy's" life.

In 1967, the controversies and irregularities surrounding him led to censure in the House and a vote to exclude him from his seat in the 90th Congress. The House based its decision on the allegation that he had misused public funds and was in contempt of the New York courts due to a lengthy and involved defamation case which had resulted in a trial for civil and criminal contempt. Despite his exclusion, Powell was readmitted to the 91st Congress in 1968. In mid-1969, the Supreme Court ruled

Adam Clayton Powell

that the House had violated the Constitution by excluding him from membership, but left open the questions of his loss of twenty-two years seniority and the chairmanship of the Education and Labor Committee. Also unresolved were the $25,000 fine levied against him and the matter of back pay.

However, rather than return to Congress, Powell spent most of his time on the West Indian island of Bimini, where process servers could not reach him. But photographers did and the ensuing photos of Powell vacationing on his boat while crucial votes were taken in Congress began to affect Powell in his home district. In 1970, he lost the Democratic Congressional primary to Charles Rangel by 150 votes. Powell retired from public office and worked as a minister at the Abyssinian Baptist Church. On April 4, 1972, Powell died in Miami.

Joseph H. Rainey 1832-1887
Civil Rights/Human Rights Activist, Federal Legislator, Federal Government Official

Joseph H. Rainey, the first black member of the House of Representatives, was born on June 21, 1832, in Georgetown, South Carolina. Rainey's father purchased his family's freedom and moved them to Charleston in 1846. During the Civil War, Rainey was drafted to work on Confederate fortifications in Charleston harbor and serve passengers on a Confederate ship. However, Rainey escaped with his wife to the West Indies and remained there until the end of the Civil War in 1865.

Rainey and his wife returned to South Carolina in 1866. In 1868, Rainey was elected as a delegate to the state constitutional convention and was elected to the State Senate in 1870. A year later, he was elected to the House of Representatives. As a member of Congress, Rainey presented some 10 petitions for a civil rights bill which would have guaranteed blacks full constitutional rights and equal access to public accommodations. On one occasion, Rainey dramatized the latter issue by refusing to leave the dining room of a hotel in Suffolk, Virginia. He was forcibly ejected from the premises. Rainey was a staunch supporter of legislation that prevented racial discrimination in schools, on public transportation, and in the composition of juries. He supported legislation that protected the civil rights of the Chinese minority in California, and advocated the use of federal troops to protect black voters from intimidation by the

Adam Clayton Powell giving a speech to civil rights demonstrators in 1963.

Ku Klux Klan. Rainey was reelected in 1872 and, during a debate on Indian rights in 1874, became the first black representative to preside over a session of Congress. Rainey gained reelection to Congress in 1874 and 1876.

Rainey retired from Congress in 1879. He was appointed as a special agent for the U.S. Treasury Department in Washington, DC. He served until 1881, after which he worked for a banking and brokerage firm. Unfortunately, the firm failed and Rainey took a job at a wood and coal factory. In 1886, he returned to Georgetown, where he died on August 2, 1887.

Charles Rangel 1930-
Federal Legislator

Harlem-born Charles Rangel vaulted into the national spotlight in 1970, when he defeated Adam Clayton Powell for the Democratic nomination in New York's 18th Congressional District. Rangel's upset victory stirred hopes among black leaders that a grassroots political movement generated from within Harlem, rather than stemming from beyond the community, might result in the grooming of an energetic, capable, and untainted successor to the volatile and unpredictable Powell.

Born June 11, 1930, Rangel attended Harlem elementary and secondary schools before volunteering to serve in the U.S. Army during the Korean War. While stationed in Korea with the 2nd Infantry, he saw heavy combat and received the Purple Heart and the Bronze Star

Medal for Valor, as well as U.S. and Korean Presidential citations. Discharged honorably as a staff sergeant, Rangel returned to finish high school and to study at New York University's School of Commerce, from which he graduated in 1957. The recipient of a scholarship, Rangel then attended St. John's Law School, graduating in 1960.

After being admitted to the bar, Rangel earned a key appointment as assistant U.S. Attorney in the Southern District of New York in 1961. For the next five years, he acquired legal experience as legal counsel to the New York City Housing and Redevelopment Board, as legal assistant to Judge James L. Watson, as associate counsel to the speaker of the N.Y. State Assembly, and as general counsel to the National Advisory Commission on Selective Service. In 1966, Rangel was chosen to represent the 72nd District, Central Harlem, in the State Assembly. Since then, he has served as a member of, and secretary to, the New York State Commission on Revision of the Penal Law and Criminal Code.

In 1972, Rangel easily defeated Livingston Wingate in the Democratic primary and went on to an overwhelming victory in November. In 1974, he was elected chairperson of the Congressional Black Caucus. In his first term, he was appointed to the Select Committee on Crime and was influential in passing the 1971 amendment to the drug laws that authorized the president to cut off all military and economic aid to any country that refused to cooperate with the United States in stopping the international traffic in drugs. In 1976, Rangel, a leading Congressional expert on the subject, was appointed to the Select Committee on Narcotics Abuse and Control.

Rangel served as chairperson of the Congressional Black Caucus in 1974 to 1975 and was a member of the Judiciary Committee when it voted to impeach U.S. president Nixon. In 1975, he moved to the Ways and Means Committee, becoming the first black to serve on the powerful committee. Two years later, his colleagues in the New York Congressional delegation voted him the majority whip for New York State. Rangel, who has served as deputy whip for the House Democratic Leadership, was a speaker at the 1995 Million Man March.

Kenneth Reeves 1951?-
Municipal Government Official, Attorney

Born of the pragmatism he fine-tuned as a lawyer, Reeves is committed to future. The first openly gay mayor in the state of Massachusetts, Reeves was popular enough to be elected to a second term in 1994, running on the same platform: He promised to break down the barriers between city government and local political groups. One such is the Cambridge Civic Association (CCA), a progressive group/political party, to which Reeves belonged before his second term began. Criticized for jumping the CCA ship, Reeves defended his action by noting that his primary concerns lie with jobs and the protection of children, whereas his former CCA colleagues were more concerned with the issue of rent control.

Born to Jamaican parents, Reeves grew up in a middle-class Detroit neighborhood. After high school, he attended Harvard and fell in love with Cambridge. In college, he was active in community service, working at a housing development in Dorchester, Massachusetts. With his undergraduate degree in hand, Reeves traveled to the African nation of Benin, studying there for one year before returning to the United States. He graduated from the University of Michigan Law School in 1976. Seeking a position in Cambridge, he was hired by the National Consumer Law Center. Hoping to get back in direct contact with the community, he ran for public office in a grass-root effort. Losing, he opted to run for city council a second time and was elected in 1989. During that time he also founded the W. E. B. Du Bois Academy, a mentor program pairing established black professional men with young black males for intense tutoring sessions. Following his mayoral victories in the 1990s, Reeves planned to run for a congressional seat.

Hiram Rhodes Revels 1827-1901
Federal Legislator

Hiram Rhodes Revels, a native of North Carolina, was the first black to serve in the U.S. Senate. Revels was elected from his adopted state of Mississippi, and served for approximately one year, from February of 1870 to March of 1871.

Born in 1827, in Fayetteville, North Carolina, Revels was educated in Indiana and attended Knox College in Illinois. Ordained a minister in the African Methodist Church, he worked among black settlers in Kansas, Maryland, Illinois, Indiana, Tennessee, Kentucky, and Missouri before settling in Baltimore in 1860. There he served as a church pastor and school principal.

During the Civil War, Revels helped organize a pair of Negro regiments in Maryland, and in 1863 he went to St. Louis to establish a freedmen school and to carry on his work as a recruiter. For a year he served as chaplain of a Mississippi regiment before becoming provost marshal of Vicksburg. Revels settled in Natchez, Mississippi, in 1866 and was appointed alderman by the Union military governor of the state. In 1870, Revels was elected to the U.S. Senate to replace Jefferson Davis, the former president of the Confederacy. Revels' appointment caused a storm of protest from white Southerners. However, Revels was allowed to take his seat in the Senate.

As a U.S. Senator, Revels quickly won the respect of many of his constituents for his alert grasp of important state issues and for his courageous support of legislation which would have restored voting and office-holding privileges to disenfranchised Southerners. He believed that the best way for blacks to gain their rightful place in American society was not through violent means, but by obtaining an education and leading an exemplary life of courage and moral fortitude. He spoke out against the segregation of Washington DC's public school system and defended the rights of black men who were denied work at the Washington Navy Yard because of their race.

Revels left the Senate in 1871 after serving one full term. He was named president of Alcorn University near Lorman, Mississippi. He left Alcorn in 1873 to serve as Mississippi's secretary of state on an interim basis. He returned to Alcorn in 1876. That year, he became editor of the *South-Western Christian Advocate*, a religious journal. He retired from Alcorn University in 1882. Revels lived in Holly Springs, Mississippi, during his later years and taught theology at Shaw University. He died on January 16, 1901.

Norm Rice 1943-
Municipal Government Official

Although "fair politician" may be a contradiction in terms, Norm Rice has received kudos from both critics and allies alike for his work as mayor of Seattle, Washington. Known by the nickname "Mr. Nice," Rice has promoted Seattle as a top city in the nation for business and industry.

Born on May 4, 1943, in Denver, Colorado, Rice went to high school there, then attended the University of Colorado. He was disappointed by the segregated housing and work load, and dropped out in his second year. Moving to Seattle in 1969, Rice went back to college in the Economic Opportunity Program at the University of Washington, earning a bachelor's degree in communications and a master's degree in public administration in 1974.

Rice became firmly ensconced in his new city, becoming committed to helping the urban community. At the age of 35, he ran for City Council in 1978 and beat the incumbent. In 1983, Rice was named president of the council, and was encouraged to run for mayor. He did and lost in 1985, regrouped and ran again in 1989, winning by a large margin. He became the first African American to become mayor of Seattle. As mayor, he held an education summit to include all those interested in discussing ways to improve Seattle's public schools.

Hiram Rhodes Revels

With only ten percent of Seattle's population being black, Rice forged a consensus and ran for reelection in 1993. He was overwhelmingly voted in for a second term, and continued his leadership role to bring Seattle together as a vital, progressive city. Along with his many duties as mayor of Seattle, Rice is also president of the Conference of Mayors. In March of 1996, Rice announced that he was running for governor. If elected, he would be the first African American to be governor of Washington and the second elected African American governor in the United States.

Edith Sampson 1901-1979
Attorney, Diplomat, Judge/Magistrate, Lecturer

Sampson was born on October 13, 1901, in Pittsburgh, Pennsylvania. The first black woman to be named an official representative to the United Nations, Sampson served in this body from 1950 until 1953, first as an appointee of President Harry S. Truman and later during a portion of the Eisenhower administration. A native of Pittsburgh, Sampson acquired a Bachelor of Laws degree from the John Marshall Law School in Chicago in 1925, and two years later became the first woman to receive a Master of Laws from Loyola University.

A member of the Illinois bar since 1927, one of Sampson's cases took her all the way to the Supreme Court in 1934. During the 1930s, she maintained her own private practice, specializing particularly in domestic relations and in criminal law. After her U.N. appointment, Sampson traveled around the world, often as a lecturer under State Department auspices. She was elected Associate Judge of the Municipal Court of Chicago in 1962, becoming the first black woman ever to sit as a circuit court judge. Sampson presided over divorce courts, traffic courts, and landlord-tenant relations courts. She gained acclaim for her superior mediating powers, her heartfelt sincerity, and her humanistic approach to rendering judgments. In 1978, she retired from Cook County Circuit Court. Sampson died on October 7, 1979, at Northwestern Hospital in Chicago, Illinois.

Kurt L. Schmoke 1949-
Attorney, Municipal Government Official/Executive, Federal Government Official

Born on December 1, 1949, Kurt L. Schmoke was inaugurated as the first black mayor of Baltimore, his hometown, on December 8, 1987. Schmoke had grown up and attended public school there, graduating with honors from Baltimore City College high school. In 1967, he won the award as the top scholar-athlete in the City. Schmoke went on to receive his Bachelor of Arts degree from Yale University in 1971, studied at Oxford University as a Rhodes Scholar, and in 1978 earned his law degree from Harvard University.

After graduating from Harvard, Schmoke began his law practice with the prestigious Baltimore firm of Piper & Marbury, and shortly thereafter was appointed by U.S. president Carter as a member of the White House Domestic Policy staff. Schmoke returned to Baltimore as an assistant U.S. Attorney, where he prosecuted narcotics and white collar crime cases, among others. He then returned to private practice and immersed himself in assorted civic activities.

In November of 1982, Schmoke was elected State's Attorney for Baltimore, the chief prosecuting office of the city. In that role, he created a full time Narcotics Unit to prosecute all drug cases and underscored the criminal nature of domestic violence and child abuse by setting up separate units to handle those cases. Also, Schmoke hired a community liaison officer to make sure that his office was being responsive to neighborhood questions and concerns.

In his inaugural address, Schmoke set the tone and future direction for his administration when he said that he wanted Baltimore to reduce its large high school dropout and teenage pregnancy rates and combat illiteracy. He has overseen the passage of the largest ever

Edith Sampson (1951)

increase in the city's education budget, and in partnership with Baltimore businesses and community based organizations, Schmoke developed the Commonwealth Agreement and the College Bound Foundation with the goal of guaranteeing opportunities for jobs or college-entrance to qualifying high school graduates. Since taking office, Schmoke has also begun major initiatives in housing, economic development, public safety, and has proposed educational programs to prepare Baltimore's citizens for high-tech jobs.

Despite being considered the leading contender for the role of Maryland Governor, Schmoke decided to run for a third term as Baltimore mayor. Interested in drug reform, Schmoke ran on the platform of decriminalizing drugs to stop related crime. An unexpectedly high turn-out of close to 52 percent of registered Democrats gave Schmoke a racially polarized election win in 1995.

Throughout his career, Schmoke has been active in the civic and cultural life of the Baltimore community by serving as a member of numerous boards of trustees. In recognition of his commitment to excellence in education and his service to the community, Schmoke has received honorary degrees from several colleges and universities.

Robert Smalls 1839-1915
Federal Legislator

Robert Smalls of South Carolina served a longer period in Congress than any other black Reconstruction congressman. Born a slave in Beaufort, South Carolina in 1839, Smalls received a limited education before moving to Charleston with the family of his owner. While in Charleston, Smalls worked at a number of odd jobs and eventually became adept at piloting boats along the Georgia and South Carolina coasts.

At the outbreak of the Civil War, Smalls was forced to become a crew member on the Confederate ship *Planter*, a transport steamer. On the morning of May 13, 1862, Smalls smuggled his wife and three children on board, assumed command of the vessel, and sailed it into the hands of the Union squadron blockading Charleston harbor. Single-handedly, he was thus responsible for the freedom of his own family and for that of the 12 black crewmen. His daring exploit led President Lincoln to name him a pilot in the Union Navy. He was also awarded a large sum of money for what constituted the delivery of war booty. In December 1863, during the siege of Charleston, Smalls again took command of the *Planter* and sailed it to safety—a feat for which he was

Kurt L. Schmoke

Robert Smalls

promoted to captain, the only black to hold such a rank during the Civil War.

After the war, Smalls was elected to the South Carolina House of Representatives, serving there from 1868 to 1870. In 1870, Smalls became a member of South Carolina's State Senate and served there until 1874. Smalls campaigned for a U.S. Congressional seat in 1874 against an independent candidate and won the election. He took his seat in Congress on March 4, 1875. During his tenure in Congress, Smalls consistently supported a wide variety of progressive legislation, including a bill to provide equal accomodations for blacks in interstate travel and an amendment designed to safeguard the rights of children born of interracial marriages. He also sought to protect the rights of black Americans serving in the armed forces.

Smalls won reelection in 1876, an election that was bitterly contested by Smalls' Democratic challenger, George Tillman. Tillman tried unsuccessfully to have Smalls' election to Congress overturned. However, Tillman's supporters were undeterred. In 1877, Smalls was accused of taking a $5,000 bribe while serving as a senator. Although Smalls was exonerated by Governor William D. Simpson, his popularity plummeted. Smalls

lost his reelection bid in 1878. Although Smalls was defeated, he did not fade from the political scene. In 1880, Smalls ran again for Congress. He lost the election, but maintained that the results were invalid due to vote-counting irregularities. Smalls' charges were substantiated and he was allowed to take his seat in Congress in July 1882. Two months later, another Congressional election was held and Smalls lost his seat to fellow Republican Edward W.M. Mackey. However, Mackey died in January 1884 and Smalls was allowed to serve the remainder of Mackey's term. In 1886, Smalls' career in Congress was ended when he lost an election to Democratic challenger William Elliott. though Smalls was no longer a Congressman, he remained involved in political activities. From 1889 to 1913, Smalls served as collector of the port of Beaufort. He died on February 22, 1915.

Louis Stokes 1925-
Civil Rights/Human Rights Activist, Federal Legislator, Attorney

Stokes was born in Cleveland, Ohio, on February 23, 1925. He was in the U.S. Army from 1943 until 1946. After leaving the service he attended Case Western Reserve University from 1946 to 1948 and in 1953 was awarded a J.D. from Cleveland Marshall Law School. After 14 years in private practice with the law firm of Stokes, Character, Terry and Perry he was elected as a democrat to the U.S. House of Representatives in 1969.

As Ohio's first African American representative Stokes has served on a number of committees including Education and Labor, House Internal Security, Appropriations and he has chaired the House Ethics Committee. As part of the House Assassination Committee Stokes has investigated the deaths of Martin Luther King, Jr. and President John F. Kennedy. In 1972 and 1973 Stokes chaired the Congressional Black Caucus and in 1972, 1976 and 1980 he was a delegate to the Democratic National Convention.

Stokes belongs to the Urban League, the American Civil Liberties Union, the American Legion and the African American Institute. He is on the board of trustees of the Martin Luther King Jr. Center for Social Change and in 1965 and 1966 he was vice-president of the Cleveland chapter of the NAACP. He is a recipient of the Distinguished Service Award, the William C. Dawson Award and a Certificate of Appreciation from the U.S. Commission on Civil Rights of which he was vice-chairman of the Cleveland subcommittee in 1966.

Louis Sullivan

Louis W. Sullivan 1933-
Educational Administrator, Federal Government Official

Louis W. Sullivan was born on November 3, 1933, in Atlanta, Georgia. On March 1, 1989, the U.S. Senate confirmed Dr. Sullivan as Secretary of Health and Human Services by a vote of 98 to 1, making him the first African American appointed to a cabinet position in the administration of U.S. President George Bush.

Instrumental in the development of the Morehouse School of Medicine, which he founded in 1975 as a separate entity from Morehouse College, Sullivan served as professor of biology and medicine and as director and founder of the medical education program at Morehouse College. In 1981, he became Morehouse School of Medicine's first dean and president.

Sullivan graduated from Morehouse College *magna cum laude* with a bachelor's of science degree in 1954, and went on to medical school at Boston University, graduating *cum laude* in 1958. He completed his internship at New York Hospital Cornell Medical Center and his medical and general pathology residencies at Cornell Medical Center and Massachusetts General Hospital. He then fulfilled two fellowships and served in a variety of positions with Harvard Medical School, Boston City Hospital, New Jersey College of Medicine, Boston University Medical Center, the Boston Sickle Cell Center, and others.

Sullivan has led an academic and professional life of excellence. He has been involved in numerous educational, medical, scientific, professional, and civic organizations, advisory, consulting, research and academic positions, and has received many professional and public service awards. Sullivan's research and activities focus on hematology, a branch of biology that deals with the formation of blood and blood-forming organs, and he has authored and coauthored more than 60 publications on this and other subjects. He is also the founding president of the Association of Minority Health Professions.

On January 20, 1989, Sullivan was nominated by President George Bush for the position of Secretary of Health and Human Services. He was sworn in on March 10, 1989. As Secretary of Health and Human Services, Sullivan was responsible for ensuring the safety of food, drugs, and medical research, and promoting health education. Upon the expiration of his term in January of 1993, he returned to Atlanta to resume his presidency of

Harold Washington after his victory in Chicago's 1983 mayoral race.

the Morehouse School of Medicine. In that position he was able to pursue his lifelong dream of training doctors to serve in poor communities by raising funds through his corporate connections on behalf of the school.

Harold Washington 1922-1987
Federal Legislator, Municipal Government Official, Attorney

Washington was born in Chicago on April 15, 1922. After serving with the Army Air Corp. in the Pacific theatre during World War II he received a B.A. from Roosevelt University in 1949 where he studied political science and economics. Washington then received a J.D. from Northwestern University Law School in 1952. After graduation Washington worked as an assistant city prosecutor in Chicago from 1954 to 1958 and while establishing a private law practice he was an arbitrator with the Illinois Industrial Commission from 1960 to 1964.

Running on the democratic ticket Washington was elected to the Illinois State House of Representatives (1965-76) and the Illinois State Senate (1977-80). While a legislator he helped establish Illinois' Fair Employment Practices Commission and the naming of Martin Luther King, Jr.'s birthday as a state holiday. Washington was also concerned with consumer protection legislation and the Illinois Legislative Black Caucus. In 1980 Washington was elected to the U.S. House of Representatives and in 1983 after a tightly contested primary and subsequent election Washington became Chicago's first African American mayor.

Although Washington's mayoralty was marked by political infighting he did manage to institute some reforms including increased city hiring of minorities, deficit reduction, the appointment of an African American police commissioner and reduction of patronage influence. Washington died while in office on November 25, 1987.

Maxine Waters 1938-
Federal Legislator, Diplomat, State Representative

Waters was born in St. Louis on August 15, 1938. After graduating from high school she moved to Los Angeles where she worked at a garment factory and for a telephone company. She eventually attended college and received a B.A. in sociology from California State University. She became interested in politics after teaching in a Head Start program and serving as a delegate to the Democratic National Convention in 1972 (she would also attend in the same capacity in 1976, 1980, 1984, and 1988).

In 1976, Waters was elected to the California State Assembly, where she served on numerous committees including the Ways and Means Subcommittee on State Administration, Joint Committee of Public Pension Fund Investments, Joint Legislative Budget Committee, Judiciary Committee, Joint Committee on Legislative Ethics, Select Committee on Assistance to Victims of Sexual Assault, California Committee on the Status of Women, Natural Resources Committee and the Elections, Reapportionment and Constitutional Amendment Committee.

In 1990, Waters was elected to the U.S. House of Representatives. She has served there on the Banking, Finance and Urban Affairs Committee and the Veterans Affairs Committee, and is a vociferous spokesperson for the poor and minorities. She has fought for legislation promoting aid to poor and minority neighborhoods in American cities and combating apartheid in South Africa. Waters is on the board of directors of *Essence* magazine and is involved with the National Woman's Political Caucus, the National Steering Committee on Education of Black Youth and the national Steering Committee of the Center for Study of Youth Policy. Waters won a 1996 Essence Award.

J. C. Watts, Jr. 1957-
Federal Legislator, Religious Leader

Born on November 18, 1957, in Eufaula, Oklahoma, Julius Caesar Watts, Jr. comes from a long line of socially conscious individuals: his father is a minister and Eufaula City councilman and his uncle once headed Oklahoma's NAACP chapter. Educated at the University of Oklahoma, Watts was a star quarterback and was named Most Valuable Player of two successive Orange Bowls in 1980 and 1981. That year he graduated with a journalism degree but chose to continue in athletics, joining the Canadian Football League's Ottawa Rough Riders. While spending five years with that team and the 1986 season with the Toronto Argonauts, Watts's interest in social issues and politics never abated. An ordained minster and sometime motivational speaker for youth and church groups, Watts served as youth director at the Sunnylane Baptist Church at Del City, Oklahoma, starting in 1987, while he presided over the Watts Energy Corp.

Though he had long considered himself a Democrat, Watts became disenchanted with the direction the party was taking and decided to go Republican in 1989. The following year he was elected chairperson of Oklahoma's Corporation Commission. The win made him the first black Oklahoman to win a statewide election.

Maxine Waters

Strongly in favor of welfare reform, defense spending cuts, and a balanced budget, the charismatic Watts built a rapport with his home state that led to his 1994 election victory of the Democratic incumbent to the U.S. House of Representatives. In doing so, Watts became the first black Republican from a Southern state to win a seat in Congress since the Reconstruction. Along with Gary Franks, he is one of the most successful African American Republicans.

Robert C. Weaver 1907-
Lecturer, Federal Government Official, Educator

Robert Weaver became the first black appointed to a presidential cabinet when Lyndon B. Johnson named him to head the newly created Department of Housing and Urban Development (HUD) on January 13, 1966. Previously, Weaver had served as head of the Housing and Home Finance Agency (HHFA) from 1961 to 1966.

Robert Weaver was born on December 29, 1907, in Washington, DC, where he attended Dunbar High School and worked during his teens as an electrician. Encountering discrimination when he attempted to join a union, he decided instead to concentrate on economics, and eventually received his Ph.D. in that field from Harvard

University. Weaver's grandfather, Dr. Robert Tanner Freeman, was the first black American to earn a doctorate in dentistry at Harvard.

During the 1940s and 1950s, Weaver concentrated his energies on the field of education. He had already been a professor of economics at the Agricultural and Technical College of North Carolina in Greensboro from 1931 to 1932. In 1947, he became a lecturer at Northwestern University and then became a visiting professor at Teachers College, Columbia University and at the New York University School of Education. During this period, he was also a professor of economics at the New School for Social Research. From 1949 to 1955 he was director of the Opportunity Fellowships Program of the John Hay Whitney Foundation. Weaver also served as a member of the National Selection Committee for Fulbright Fellowships (1952-1954), chairman of the Fellowship Committee of the Julius Rosenwald Fund, and a consultant to the Ford Foundation (1959-60).

In 1955, Weaver was named Deputy State Rent Commissioner by New York's Governor Averell Harriman. By the end of the year, he had become State Rent Commissioner and the first black to hold state cabinet rank in New York. From 1960 to 1961, he served as vice chairman of the New York City Housing and Redevelopment Board, a three-man body which supervised New York's urban renewal and middle-income housing programs. Weaver headed the Department of Housing and Urban Development until 1968. From 1969 to 1970, he served as president of Baruch College. Weaver accepted a teaching position at the Department of Urban Affairs at Hunter College in New York in 1971. He retired from Hunter College in 1978.

Wellington Webb 1941-
Municipal Government Official

Born February 17, 1941, Webb had to leave his South Side Chicago home to live with his grandmother in Denver, Colorado when his asthma became too severe for the urban setting. After graduating from Colorado State College in 1964 with a bachelor's degree in education, Webb worked in various public service-sector jobs, including welfare caseworker and special education teacher, while obtaining a master's degree.

In 1972, Webb was elected to the Colorado state legislature as a representative from the northeast section of Denver. There he served four years, and rose to prominence within the Democratic Party during that time; in 1976 Democratic presidential hopeful Jimmy Carter chose Webb to head the state's national election committee. Upon Carter's election success, Webb was named a regional director of the U.S. Department of Health, Education, and Welfare, a post he held until 1980. He then became executive director of the Colo-

rado's Department of Regulatory Agencies, and during his tenure in the early 1980s was the only African American in the state cabinet.

Webb ran for mayor of Denver first in 1983, but lost; in 1987, he ran successfully for the city auditor post. In 1991, he faced his city hall colleague, a popular African American district attorney, in another mayoral race; Webb won with 58 percent of the vote, despite being at a severe disadvantage in comparison to his well-financed opponent. He was re-elected for a second term in 1995, but has said that two stints as mayor of the state's capital would be enough for him, and he probably would not run for a third.

Michael R. White 1951-
Municipal Government Official

Born and raised on the east side of Cleveland, Ohio, Michael White pursued and accomplished a 24-year-old goal, when he was elected mayor of Cleveland in 1989. At the time, 40 percent of the city's population was at or below the poverty line. White symbolized the renewed potential to turn this situation around.

An alumnus of Ohio State University, White received a B.A. in education and a year later a master's degree in public administration. His political career started in 1974, when he became a special assistant for the mayor's office in Columbus, Ohio. In 1978, White began six years on Cleveland's city council, followed by four years in Columbus as a state senator. In 1989, White entered Cleveland's mayoral race, running against three white candidates and the City Council's president, George Forbes. Forbes was supported by the African American community, but had alienated the white community. This was not a shrewd political strategy, with Cleveland's population fairly even balanced between African Americans and whites. West won the election with a combination of voter support for him and voter animosity towards Forbes.

The central issue for White's administration was the future of Cleveland's young people. Two focal points White worked towards was an upgrade of public education and the development of new jobs programs. White also fought against a two level community— the low level of the inner city set against Cleveland's high level, the prosperous downtown area. To address this disparity, White has supported the development of the Lake Erie waterfront and the completion of the Rock and Roll Hall of Fame.

When Bill Clinton became president in 1982, White was invigorated by the potential changes with government's relationship to the cities. He was an outspoken supporter of Clinton's plans to get rid of the old welfare system. In 1995, White met with the National Football

League Commissioner Paul Tagliabue to try and keep the Browns from moving to Baltimore. He was unsuccessful in his quest, which pitted White's social factors against the NFL's financial factors. The checkbook won. Meanwhile, White views himself as a "pragmatic idealist" when it comes to change, committed to the job of redirecting long held ways of running government.

Lawrence Douglas Wilder 1931-
Attorney, State Government Official

Wilder was born on January 17, 1931, in Richmond, Virginia. He graduated from Virginia Union University in 1951 with a B.S. in chemistry. After graduation he was drafted into the U.S. Army and assigned to a combat infantry unit in Korea. During the Korean War he was awarded a Bronze Star for bravery and valor in combat. After being discharged from the army in 1953 Wilder worked as a chemist in the Virginia State Medical Examiner's Office. In 1959 Wilder graduated with a J.D. from Howard University Law School.

Wilder practiced law in Richmond until he became the first African American elected to the Virginia State Senate since Reconstruction. While there Wilder chaired the important Privileges and Elections committee and worked on legislation supporting fair-housing, union rights for public employees, minority hiring and voted against capital punishment (a position he has since rescinded.) In 1985 Wilder was elected lieutenant-governor and in 1989 he became Virginia's first African American governor, winning the election by a razor thin one third of one per cent of the vote.

In 1979, Wilder won the Distinguished Alumni Award presented by Virginia Union University. In succeeding years he was a recipient of the President's Citation (Norfolk State University 1982), Alumnus of the Year (Howard Law School Alumni Association (1983) and the Distinguished Postgraduate Achievement in Law and Politics Award (Howard University 1985). Wilder belongs to the Richmond Urban League, Richmond Bar Association, American Judicature Society, American Trial Lawyers Association, Virginia Trial Lawyers Association, National Association of Criminal Defense Lawyers, NAACP and he is vice-president of the Virginia Human Relations Council.

Andrew Young 1932-
Diplomat, Municipal Government Official/Executive, Federal Legislator, Civil Rights/Human Rights Activist

Andrew Young came into national prominence nearly three decades ago and has become a figure of international prominence and stature. He was born in New Orleans, on March 12, 1932, and received a B.S. degree from Howard University and a Bachelor of Divinity degree from Hartford Theological Seminary in 1955. He was ordained a minister in the United Church of Christ and then served in churches in Alabama and Georgia before joining the National Council of Churches in 1957.

The turning point of Young's life came in 1961, when he joined Reverend Martin Luther King, Jr. and became a trusted aide and close confidante. He did much of the negotiating for the Southern Christian Leadership Conference (SCLC) and was respected for his coolness and rationality. He became executive vice president of SCLC in 1967, and remained with King, until the latter's murder in 1968. During those years with SCLC, Young also developed several programs including antiwar protests, voter registration projects and other major civil rights drives.

In 1970 Young lost a bid for the U.S. House of Representatives. In the aftermath of the election, Young was appointed chair of the Community Relations Committee (CRC). Though the CRC was an advisory group with no enforcement powers, Young took an activist role, pressing the city government on many issues, from sanitation and open housing to mass transit, consumer affairs, and Atlanta's drug problem. Young's leadership in the CRC led to a higher public profile and answered critics charges that he was inexperienced in government.

Young launched another bid for a congressional seat in 1972. The campaign was difficult for Young. Blacks comprised only 44 percent of the voters in Young's congressional district and his Republican opponent, Rodney Cook, was a more appealing candidate than Fletcher Thompson had been in 1970. However, Young captured 23 percent of the white vote and 54 percent of the total vote to win by a margin of 8,000 votes. Young was the first black representative to be elected from Georgia since Jefferson Long in 1870. Thereafter, Young was reelected with ease every two years.

Young was one of the most vocal supporters of his fellow Georgian Jimmy Carter's campaign for the U.S. presidency in 1976. Following President Carter's inauguration, Young left Congress in 1977, to become America's ambassador to the United Nations (UN). Young's tenure there was marked by controversy—his outspoken manner sometimes ruffled diplomatic feathers—as well as solid achievement—represented primarily in the tremendous improvement he fostered in relations between the United States and lesser developed countries.

Young's career as a diplomat came to an end in 1979, when he met secretly with a representative of the Palestine Liberation Organization (PLO) to discuss an upcoming vote in the UN. America had a policy that none of its representatives would meet with the PLO as long as it refused to recognize the right of Israel to exist

Robert Weaver

as a state. When the news of Young's meeting leaked out, an uproar immediately followed. Young had originally told the State Department that the meeting was by chance, but later he admitted that it had been planned.

Though the meeting had secured a vote in the UN that the United States wanted, the pressure mounted and Young tendered his resignation, which President Carter accepted. The incident badly strained black-Jewish relations as blacks felt Jewish leaders were instrumental in Young's removal. Young became a private citizen, but not for long.

When Maynard Jackson was prevented by law from running for his third term of office as mayor of Atlanta in 1981, Young entered the race. Race entered the campaign when the outgoing mayor, himself a black, charged blacks who supported the white candidate, State Legislator Sidney Marcus, with "selling out" the civil rights movement. Jackson's remarks were widely criticized, and it was feared that they would create a backlash against Young, too. However, Young ended up with 55 percent of the total vote. He had won 10.6 percent of the white vote, compared to the 12 percent he had won in the primary, and 88.4 percent of the black vote, up from 61 percent earlier.

Young took office at a time when Atlanta was going through several economic and social problems, including a shrinking population and a stagnating tax base. In addition, almost a quarter of the city's residents were below the poverty line, and the city was still shaken by the recent murders of 28 black youths and the disappearance of another—even though a suspect had already been convicted of several of the murders. Some critics doubted Young's ability to deal with Atlanta's problems. He was seen as antibusiness and a weak administrator. But by 1984, the city had become so successful at attracting new businesses that it was experiencing a major growth spurt. In addition, the crime rate dropped sharply and racial harmony seemed an established fact. Young was reelected decisively in 1985.

Limited by law to two terms as mayor, Young ran unsuccessfully for governor of Georgia in 1990. His wife died of cancer four years later. The grief-stricken man who had had a tumultuous public career, turned his attention other matters, such as writing his autobiography, *A Way Out of No Way: The Spiritual Memoirs of Andrew Young*, which was published in 1994. He was kept busy as co-chair of the Atlanta Committee for the

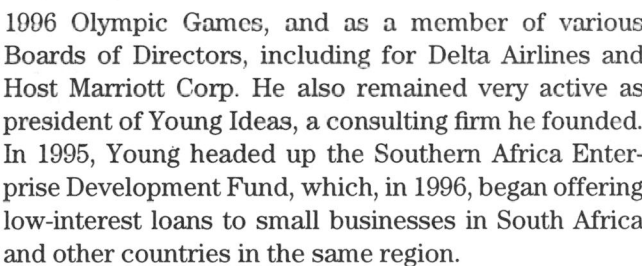

L. Douglas Wilder announcing his candidacy for the Democratic presidential nomination in 1991.

Andrew Young announces former President Jimmy Carter at the Democratic National Convention in 1992.

1996 Olympic Games, and as a member of various Boards of Directors, including for Delta Airlines and Host Marriott Corp. He also remained very active as president of Young Ideas, a consulting firm he founded. In 1995, Young headed up the Southern Africa Enterprise Development Fund, which, in 1996, began offering low-interest loans to small businesses in South Africa and other countries in the same region.

Coleman A. Young 1918-
Municipal Government Official/Executive

Long-time Detroit icon Coleman Young announced on June 22, 1993, that he would not seek reelection for the mayorship of the city that fall. Thus ended a 20-year reign for a community hero who had had his shares of ups and downs. Young had won each of his mayoral elections by a wide margin. The only mayor in the history of Detroit to serve five consecutive terms led the media to dub him "mayor for life." Once recognized as an urban savior, Detroit's highly publicized problems—crime, declining population, and poor economic standing—had finally instilled doubts in the votership regarding Young's abilities.

Young was born in Tuscaloosa, Alabama, on May 24, 1918. His family moved to Detroit's east side in 1926, after the Ku Klux Klan ransacked a neighborhood in Huntsville, where his father was learning to be a tailor. In Detroit, Young attended Catholic Central and then Eastern High School, graduating from the latter with honors. He had to reject a scholarship to the University of Michigan when the Eastern High School Alumni Association, in contrast to policies followed with poor white students, declined to assist him with costs other than tuition.

Young entered an electrician's apprentice school at the Ford Motor Company. He finished first in the program but was passed over for the only available electrician job in favor of a white candidate. Working on the assembly line, he soon became engaged in underground union activities. Attacked by a company man one day, Young defended himself by hitting his assailant on the head with a steel bar. The incident led to Young's being fired.

During World War II, Young was a navigator in the U.S. Army Air Force and was commissioned a second lieutenant. Stationed at Freeman Field, Indiana, he dem-

Coleman A. Young (1981)

onstrated against the exclusion of blacks from segregated officers' clubs and was arrested along with 100 other black airmen, among them the late Thurgood Marshall, and Percy Sutton, former president of New York's Borough of Manhattan. Young spent three days in jail. Shortly thereafter, the clubs were opened to black officers.

After the war, Young returned to his union organizing activities and in 1947, was named director of organization for the Wayne County AFL-CIO. However, the union fired him in 1948, when he supported Henry Wallace, candidate of the Progressive Party, in the presidential election. The union regarded Wallace as an agent of the Communist Party and supported Harry Truman. Young managed a dry cleaning plant for a few years, then founded and directed the National Negro Labor Council in 1951. The council successfully prevailed on Sears Roebuck & Co. and the San Francisco Transit System to hire blacks. However, they also aroused the interest of the House Un-American Activities Committee, which was in the midst of hunting for alleged Communists. Their method was to holding hearings at which defendants were required to produce names of people purportedly associated with the party. When

brought before the committee, Young, who denies he was ever a Communist, refused to name anyone. Though he emerged from the battle with his self-respect intact, his Labor Council was placed on the Attorney General's subversive list. In 1956, the Labor Council was disbanded, and charges of Young's Communist involvement were used against him, albeit unsuccessfully, during his first mayoral campaign.

After working at a variety of jobs, Young won a seat on the Michigan Constitutional Convention in 1961. The following year he lost a race for state representative but became director of campaign organization for the Democratic gubernatorial candidate in Wayne County (Detroit). He sold life insurance until 1964, when, with union support, he was elected to the State Senate. In the Senate, he was a leader of the civil rights forces fighting for low-income housing for people dislocated by urban renewal and for bars to discrimination in the hiring practices of the Detroit Police Force.

Young declared his candidacy for mayor of Detroit in 1973, and mounted a vigorous campaign for the office. He won the office after a racially divisive campaign. Among his early successes in office were the integration of the Detroit Police Department and promotion of black officers into administrative positions. The new mayor also created a coalition of business and labor to preserve the industries remaining in Detroit and attract new ones. Young's outspoken and opinionated nature—and a fondness for using explicatives—earned him both passionate supporters and bitter enemies, in the city and nation-at-large. A Democrat, and one of the first big-city mayors to support Jimmy Carter's presidential campaign in 1976, Young had a very close relationship with the Carter administration. He turned down a federal cabinet position offered to him by Carter, but his relationship with the president proved helpful in securing funds for Detroit.

In the 1980s, Young was intensely critical of the Reagan and Bush administrations, with their massive cutbacks in federal aid to urban areas. The federal government seized serval opportunities to scrutinize Young as well. Over the years, Young's administration was investigated on more than six different charges, including improprieties in the awarding of city contracts and illegal personal use of city funds by the police department; however, Young himself was never personally implicated in the scandals.

Young's popularity was bolstered by a number of citywide improvements credited to him such as the expansion of riverfront attractions, which brought increased convention and tourist traffic to the city and favorable tax abatements that attracted new businesses, including two major automobile plants. Still, a number of daunting problems remained for Detroit, chief among them its dwindling population. Middle-class and white flight to the suburbs that had begun at the end of the 1960s, continued robbing the city's coffers of essential tax revenue. Some critics argued that Young's attitude toward suburbanites—whom he viewed as hostile or indifferent to the city—contributed to the phenomenon. Near the end of his tenure, Young endured a barrage of disapproval for autocratic style and his emphasis on cosmetic improvements rather than focusing on true remedies for the decay of the city.

In 1989, Coleman Young won his fifth term as Motor City mayor. Despite a high unemployment rate, a shortage of cash, and a high crime rate, the voters returned Young to office—a testament to his popularity. During 1990, both Detroit and its mayor were targets of highly critical feature stories in the *New York Times* and on CBS. Commentary revolved around Detroit's sagging economy, brutal crime statistics, racial stratification, and a supposed general air of despair. Young countered that under his administration, the city managed to balance its budget despite a dramatic cutback in federal and state aid, many neighborhoods had undergone extensive renovation, a new automobile manufacturing plant had opened within the city limits.

In 1993, when Young felt that he no longer had the necessary vitality to run a big city, a major chapter in Detroit politics came to a close. Young turned his attentions towards writing, with Lonnie Wheeler, *Hard Stuff: The Autobiography of Coleman Young* and became a faculty member of Detroit's Wayne State University, where he continued to raise dialogue about race and class issues.

12

Population

12

Population

◆ The Size of the African American Population ◆ Regional Distribution
◆ Contemporary Demographic Characteristics
◆ Population Projections

by Claudette E. Bennett and Kenneth Estell

In 1995, according to the United States Bureau of the Census, the African American population of 33.0 million constituted 13.0 percent of the nation's total resident population. Approximately 193.3 million people, roughly 74.0 percent of the population considered themselves non-Hispanic white. 26.8 million people, or 10.0 percent of the population, were of Hispanic heritage. Asians and Pacific Islanders numbered 9.2 million, or 4.0 percent of the population.

◆ THE SIZE OF THE AFRICAN AMERICAN POPULATION

1619 to 1790

The beginning of America's black population is usually dated to the year 1619, when a small number of colonists and indentured servants landed in Jamestown, Virginia. Historians are uncertain as to the exact number, but between 14 and 20 black indentured servants were evidently part of this first settlement; within a short time the practice of enslaving newly arrived Africans developed and spread throughout the colonies. By 1630, there were some 60 slaves in the American colonies; by 1660, the number had increased to 2,920.

Within two decades, the colonies were beginning to flourish. The emerging agrarian society demanded a larger labor force, and this labor was supplied by additional slaves. By 1690, 70 years after the first importation of Africans, the total slave population in the American colonies had grown to 16,729. By 1740, the slave population reached 150,000, and 575,000 by 1780. Although a free black population did exist, it grew at a slower rate than the slave population; in 1780, only one free black existed for every nine slaves.

1790 to 1900

In the first official census of the United States, taken in 1790, some 757,208 blacks were counted. At that time, blacks constituted 19.3 percent of the nation's population, of which nine percent, or some 59,527, were free blacks. (By 1790, Pennsylvania, Massachusetts, Connecticut, Rhode Island, New York, New Jersey, and the Northwest Territory had enacted legislation providing for the gradual emancipation of slaves.) By 1860, there were almost 4,000,000 blacks in the United States, over 90 percent of them in the South; the freed population, most of whom were in the North, numbered under 500,000.

Population Growth since 1900

During the late nineteenth and early twentieth centuries, the white population grew faster than the black population. The primary reasons were the increased European immigration into the United States and the decline and eventual cessation of the slave trade. In 1900, there were 8.8 million blacks in the United States, representing 11.6 percent of the total population. Between 1910 and 1930, the percentage of black population declined, reaching a low point in 1930, when blacks constituted only 9.7 percent of the total United States population. Since 1930, however, the African American population has grown at a rate faster than the national

According to the 1990 census, the black population constituted 12.1 percent of the population.

average. According to the 1990 census, the black population constituted 12.1 percent of the population, up from 11.7 percent in 1980. By 1995, the black population in the United States had grown to roughly 33 million.

The growth of the black population since the 1980 census is largely due to natural increase and net immigration. Natural increase has been the major source of growth. This increase in the number of births over deaths was due mainly to two factors: (1) a young age structure, placing a large percentage of African Americans in the childbearing ages and a smaller percentage in the ages of high mortality risk, and (2) a high age-specific fertility rate for black women under 25 years of age.

The African American population has also grown through immigration—legal as well as illegal. While streams of Asian and Hispanic migrants to the United States have been more highly publicized, black immigration has also increased. The Caribbean basin is one source of black immigration, with immigrants primarily from Jamaica and Haiti entering the United States to look for work. The Mariel boatlift in 1980 also brought some blacks from Cuba. Political and economic condi-

tions in Africa, in addition, have provided many people with incentive to emigrate to the United States. African students overstaying their student visas and working in the United States have contributed to immigration rates. Estimations of the size and effects of these sources of new population growth are speculative.

The increase in the African American population can also be attributed to higher than average fertility rates. As a result, the black population is somewhat younger than the white population, and contains a slightly larger proportion of persons in the prime reproductive ages. A second reason is that blacks have higher age-adjusted fertility rates than whites (i.e. higher fertility even when differences in age composition are taken into account).

Census Bureau reports from 1995 show that the black population is roughly 33,000,000, or approximately 13.0 percent of the American population. This figure is higher than the total populations for many nations. The black population in the United States, for example, is slightly larger than the entire population of Canada. The only African nations with populations larger than the African American population are Nigeria (101 million), Ethiopia (56 million), Zaire (44 million), and South

By the year 2010, the median age for blacks in the United States is expected to rise approximately 30 years.

Africa (45 million). Population figures for these African countries are 1995 estimates.

◆ REGIONAL DISTRIBUTION

1790 to 1900

From 1790 until 1900, 90 percent or more of the African American population resided in the South, mostly in rural areas. Even the abolition of slavery following the Civil War had only a minimal short-term impact on the southern, rural character of the black population.

Early Migration

Episodic migration from the South, nonetheless, did occur during this period. One early exodus occurred in the period 1879 to 1881, when some 60,000 blacks moved into Kansas. The impetus behind this initial migration was the need for social and economic free-

Three men, c. 1910.

A black family living in rural Georgia.

was minor; when the Emancipation Proclamation was signed, under eight percent of all blacks lived in the Northeast or Midwest. After the Civil War, the percentage of the nation's black population living in the Northeast fell slightly, while the percentage rose in the Midwest. By 1900, only 10 percent of all blacks lived in these two northern regions.

dom. The immigration to Kansas strained the resources of the state and several cities became black refugee camps. One of the towns created by this exodus was Nicodemus, Kansas, which still exists as a small, all-black community.

Although other migrations by Southern blacks to the Midwest or Northeast have been chronicled, the effect on the regional distribution of the total black population

Early settlers of Nicodemus, Kansas.

Harlem in the early 1930s.

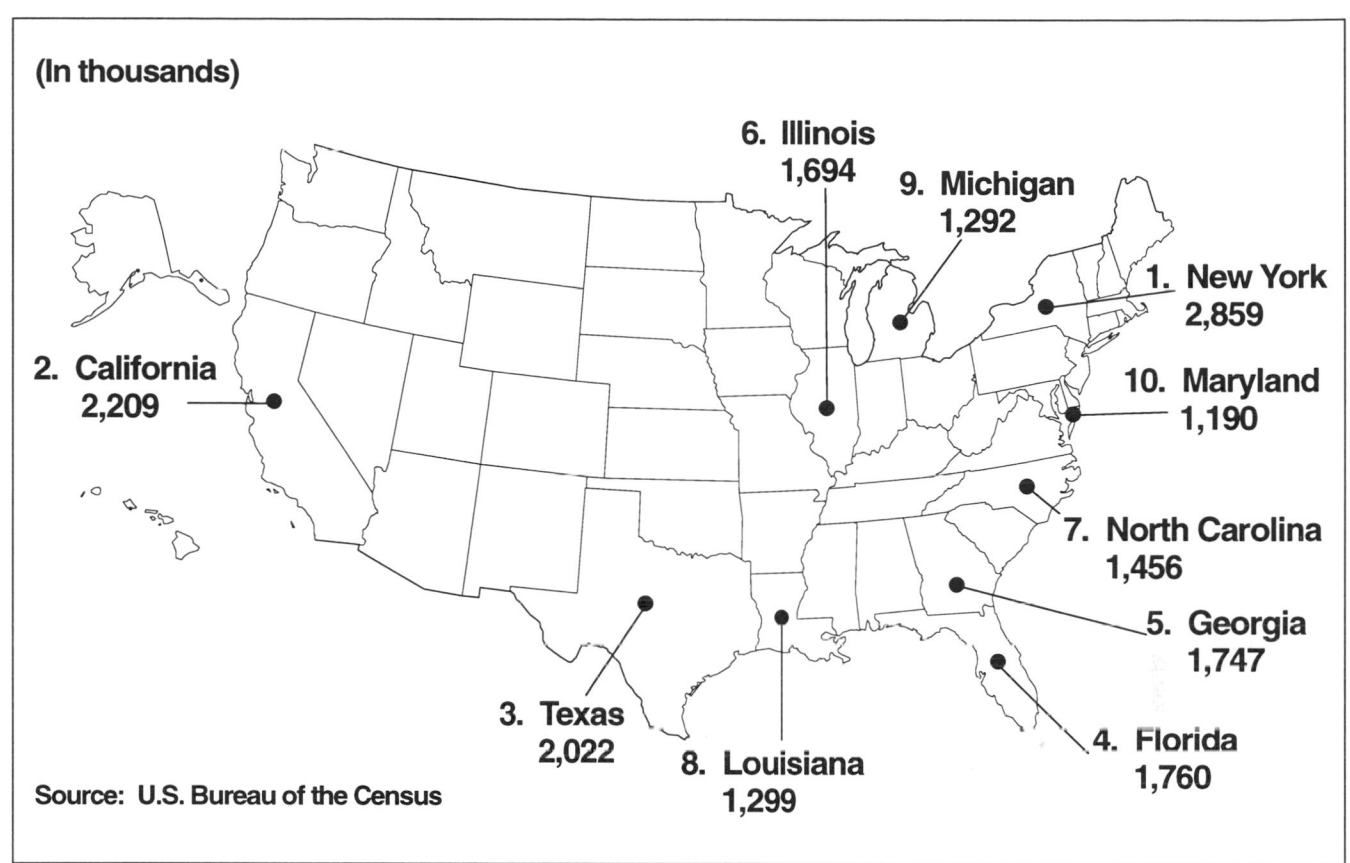

(In thousands)

6. **Illinois**
1,694

9. **Michigan**
1,292

1. **New York**
2,859

2. **California**
2,209

10. **Maryland**
1,190

7. **North Carolina**
1,456

5. **Georgia**
1,747

3. **Texas**
2,022

8. **Louisiana**
1,299

4. **Florida**
1,760

Source: U.S. Bureau of the Census

Ten States with the Largest Black Population, 1990.

1900 to 1970

In 1900, almost 90 percent of African Americans still lived in the South. Between 1910 and 1920, however, the percentage of blacks living in the South began to fall. By 1930, more than 21.2 percent of blacks resided outside of the South.

For the next four decades, the percentage of African Americans living in the South steadily fell. In 1970, about 39 percent of blacks were Northerners, 53 percent were Southerners, and about 7.5 percent lived in the West.

The Great Migration

Historians and social scientists have long debated why blacks failed to leave the South in larger numbers at the end of the Civil War. Virtually every migration stream is the product of both push and pull factors—prejudice, discrimination, and a poor economic opportunities in the South obviously provided the strong push factors needed to generate out-migration, while a somewhat more open society and the presence of jobs in the industrializing North should have provided the pull to

establish a strong south to north migration stream. Some blacks did leave the South during the last decades of the nineteenth century, typically following transportation routes directly northward. However, the number of blacks moving North has always seemed smaller than what might be expected given the combined push and pull forces.

European immigration may be one explanation for the relatively slow start of the southern exodus by blacks. As the North industrialized in the late nineteenth and early twentieth centuries, it generated a huge demand for labor, which was met in large part by massive immigration of Europeans. Many of the urban factory jobs were filled first by Irish and German laborers, and later by immigrants from southern and eastern Europe, particularly Italy. If northern industries not been able to meet their labor needs through immigration, they might have relied more on domestic sources, including Southern blacks.

As immigration to the United States was curtailed by World War I and restrictive legislation passed in the 1920s, blacks began to leave the South in larger numbers. As a consequence, the proportion of the nation's

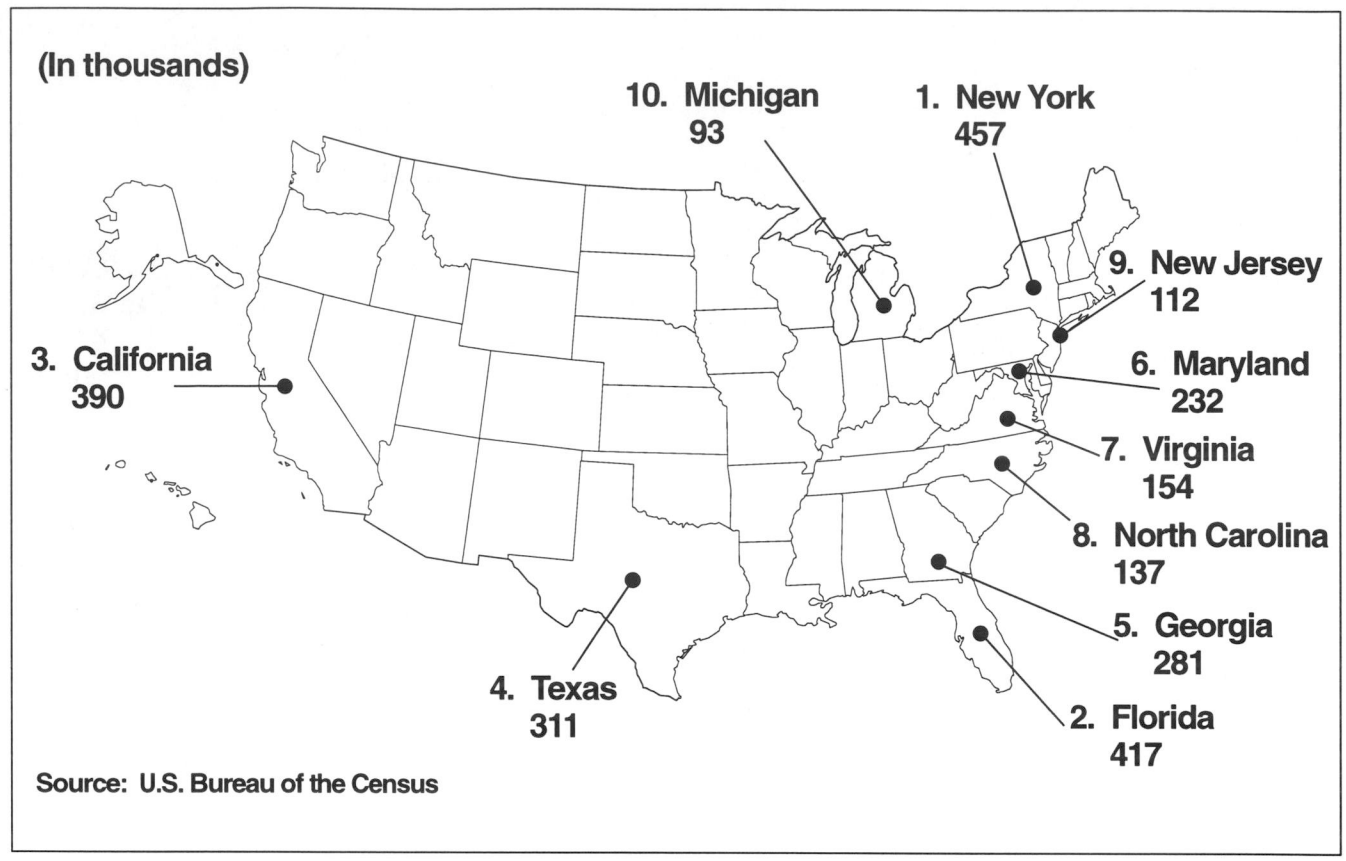

(In thousands)

10. Michigan
93

1. New York
457

9. New Jersey
112

6. Maryland
232

7. Virginia
154

8. North Carolina
137

5. Georgia
281

2. Florida
417

4. Texas
311

3. California
390

Source: U.S. Bureau of the Census

Ten States with the Largest Increases in Black Population, 1980 to 1990.

black population living in the South fell more rapidly between 1910 and 1920 than during the entire period since emancipation.

Although black migration from the South was reduced somewhat during the Great Depression of the 1930s, the proportion of blacks living in the South continued to decrease. The greatest volume of migration of Southern blacks occurred in the decade between 1940 and 1950. This migration was precipitated partly by mobilization for World War II. Therefore, both World War I and World War II provided a powerful impetus for blacks to leave the South.

During the 1940s, 1950s, and 1960s, the net migration of blacks from the South totaled about 4.3 million persons. Mechanization of Southern agriculture after World War II decreased the demand for low-wage labor and gave blacks further incentive to leave agricultural areas. The continued exodus of rural blacks decreased the supply of farm labor and encouraged Southern farmers to adopt labor-saving methods.

The exodus of blacks from the South, during the thirty years between 1940 and 1970 is one of the major migrations in American history. In volume, it equals the total Italian immigration to the United States during its peak, the 30-year period from the mid-1890s to the mid-1920s. For most blacks, this journey out of the South meant exchanging a rural, agricultural existence for an urban life based on factory jobs.

Migration since 1970

By the 1970s, the black migration from the South had slowed dramatically. Although blacks continued to leave the South, many returned; a few northern-born blacks, the children of earlier migrants, moved to the South in response to the availability of jobs and a change in the political and social climate. In the early 1970s, as many blacks were moving to the region as were leaving it. By the mid-1980s, due to reduced economic growth in some areas of the South, particularly in those areas where economies had been built around the oil and gas industries, black migration to the South had leveled off. The percentage of African Americans living in the western United States has increased from 0.5 percent in 1910 to 9.4 percent in 1990. In the year 2000, about 37 percent of blacks are likely to live in the North, 53 percent in the South, and 10 percent in the West.

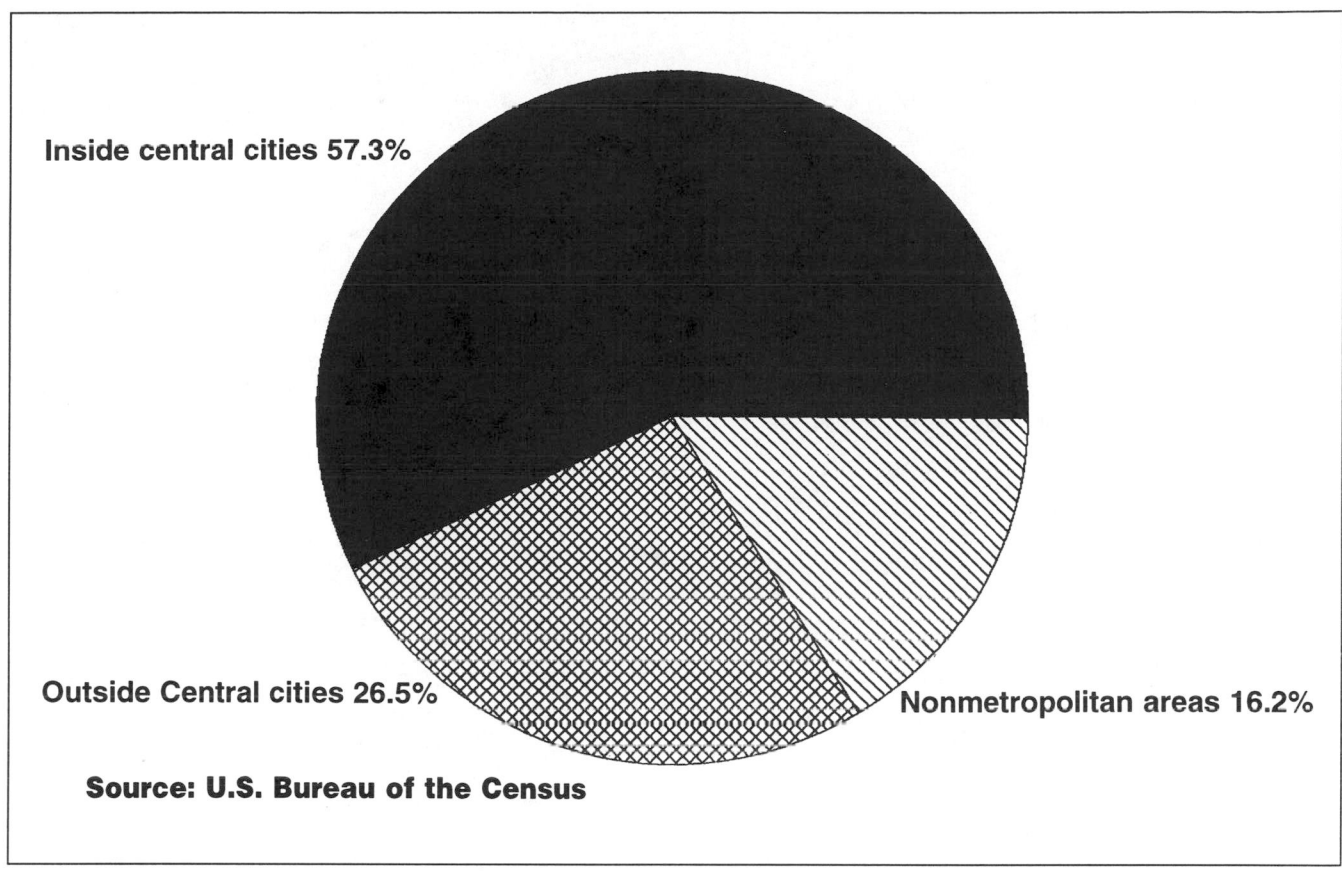

Inside central cities 57.3%

Outside Central cities 26.5%

Nonmetropolitan areas 16.2%

Source: U.S. Bureau of the Census

Distribution of the Black Population by Metropolitan and Nonmetropolitan Residence, 1990.

◆ CONTEMPORARY DEMOGRAPHIC CHARACTERISTICS

The Black Population by State

Blacks are most populous in the South, which contains 53 percent of the nation's total black population. In 1990, of the ten states with the largest black populations (New York, California, Texas, Florida, Georgia, Illinois, North Carolina, Louisiana, Michigan, and Maryland), six were in the South. 58 percent of the black population resided in these states. Six other states had black populations of 1 million or more in 1990: Virginia (1,163,000), Ohio (1,155,000), Pennsylvania (1,090,000), South Carolina (1,040,000), New Jersey (1,037,000), and Alabama (1,021,000).

The Black Urban Population

In 1960, 64.7 percent of the black population resided in metropolitan areas in the United States, 51.4 percent

of whom resided in central cities, as opposed to suburban areas and rural areas outside the city. In 1970, 74.3 percent of the black population resided in metropolitan areas, with 58.2 percent living in central cities. By 1990, 83.8 percent of the black population resided in metropolitan areas, while the proportion residing in central cities declined slightly to 57.3 percent.

In 1960, blacks constituted 16.7 percent of all central city residents; by 1970, blacks constituted 20.6 percent. One reason for this increase has been the continued growth (although at a slower rate than in earlier decades) of the black population. A second reason for this change has been the migration of whites out of the central cities to suburban and rural areas.

In 1980, African Americans made up 22.5 percent of the total central city population. However, by 1990 this number fell to 22.1 percent. Like the white population, though in smaller numbers, the black population was migrating out of central cities to suburban and rural areas.

The city of New York, the most populous city in the United States, also has the largest black population in

Throughout most of the twentieth century, the African American population has remained younger than the white population.

the nation; in 1990, more than 2.1 million African Americans resided in Greater New York City. Chicago, Detroit, Philadelphia, and Los Angeles follow, in that order, as cities with the largest black populations.

Among the fifteen cities with the largest black concentrations, Washington, DC and Atlanta had black majorities by 1970. By 1990, four additional cities (Detroit, Baltimore, Memphis, and New Orleans) had black majorities, and five of the eleven largest cities in the nation were more than 50 percent black.

The Black Suburban and Nonmetropolitan Populations

The 1970s marked a turning point in the percentage of African Americans outside of central cities. Between 1980 and 1990, the black population living in suburbs grew faster than did the white suburban population. The white suburban population grew by 9.1 percent, whereas the black suburban population increased by 9.9 percent. In 1980, African Americans constituted 6.1 percent of the suburban population; by 1990, blacks constituted

Compared with the white population, a greater percentage of the African American population is under 18 years of age.

6.9 percent. In 1960, only 13.3 percent of African Americans residing in metropolitan areas lived in suburban areas. By 1970 this number increased to 16.1 percent, by 1980 to 23.3 percent. In 1990, 26.6 percent of the black metropolitan population resided in suburban areas.

This is an important development since it signifies that for the first time, the number of blacks moving to suburban areas has become large enough to significantly affect the overall distribution of the black population. The access by African Americans to suburban residenc-

es is important for many reasons. One reason is that black suburbanization may further such ideals as an open housing market, freedom of movement, and the ability to choose a neighborhood that balances a family's income and its preferences and needs, such as the availability of quality public schools for children.

Black suburbanization may be beneficial in other ways as well. Since many jobs have moved from cities to the suburbs, a greater share of blacks living in suburbs might have long-term consequences for improving employment opportunities and occupational mobility. Finally, for many Americans, a move to the suburbs has meant owning a home, a major form of wealth accumulation for middle-class families. African Americans have been less likely to own their own home than whites, even when income and other socioeconomic characteristics are taken into account. A trend toward suburbanization might offer more blacks the opportunity to build equity in a home and thus help to secure middle-class status and the transmission of that status across generations.

The reasons for the increased movement of blacks to suburbs are doubtlessly heterogeneous. On the one hand, open housing legislation and changing attitudes have contributed to breaking down the barriers to black access to the suburbs. On the other hand, there has been an increase in the number of middle-income black families. Many of these black families rely on dual incomes, allowing them to afford the safety, good schools, acreage, and other amenities often cited by those who have chosen to move from the city to the suburbs.

Although the number of African Americans residing in suburban areas has increased, the numbers are still far below those of the white population. According to the Bureau of the Census, in 1991 only 26.7 percent of the African-American population resided in suburbs, compared to 50.7 percent of the white population.

Median Age

Although both the black and white populations have aged, the African-American population has remained younger than the white population throughout most of the twentieth century. In 1980, the black population had a median age of 24.8 years, the white population a median age of 30.8 years. In 1991, the black population's median age rose to 27.9 years, while the median age for the white population rose to 33.7 years.

The aging of the "Baby Boomers" (persons born between the years 1946 and 1964) was the primary reason for the rise in median ages for both the black and white populations. One reason for the difference between the black and white median ages is the differing age structures of the two populations. Compared with the white population, a greater percentage of the African American population is under 18 years of age, while a smaller percentage of the population is over 65 years. In 1991, 33 percent of the African American population was under the age of 18, and 8 percent over the age of 65 years. Only 25 percent of the white population was under the age of 18 in this same year, while 13 percent of the population was over the age of 65. By the year 2010, the median age for blacks in the United States is expected to rise to approximately 30 years, and that of whites to 39 years.

◆ POPULATION PROJECTIONS

The African American population is projected to be one of the fastest growing population groups in the United States during the next sixty years. The black population is projected to increase by over 4 million by 2000, almost 9 million by 2010, and over 19 million by 2030. Overall, during the next sixty years, the black population is projected to grow by almost 100 percent, to 62 million. The black share of the total national population is expected to increase from 12 percent in 1992 to 13 percent in 2000, 14 percent in 2010, 15 percent in 2030, and 16 percent in 2050.

Black Population by State, 1790

State	Slaves	Free
Connecticut	2,759	2,801
Delaware	8,887	3,899
Georgia	29,264	398
Kentucky	11,830	114
Maryland	103,036	8,043
New Hampshire	158	630
New Jersey	11,423	2,762
New York	21,324	4,654
North Carolina	100,572	4,975
Pennsylvania	3,737	6,537
Rhode Island	952	3,469
South Carolina	107,094	1,801
Vermont	17	255
Virginia	293,437	12,766
Ohio Territory	3,417	5,463
Maine	None	538

Black Population Growth

Year	Total	Slave
1790	757,208	697,681
1800	1,002,037	893,602
1810	1,377,808	1,191,362
1820	1,771,656	1,538,022
1830	2,328,642	2,009,043
1840	2,873,648	2,487,355
1850	3,638,808	3,204,313
1860	4,441,830	3,953,760

Resident Population By Race, 1970, 1980, 1990

United States	Number			Percent Distribution		
	1990	1980	1970	1990	1980	1970
Total	248,709,873	226,545,805	203,211,926	100.0	100.0	100.0
White	199,686,070	188,371,622	177,748,975	80.3	83.1	87.5
Black	29,986,060	26,495,025	22,580,289	12.1	11.7	11.1
American Indian, Eskimo and Aleut	1,959,234	1,420,400	827,268[2]	0.8	0.6	0.4
Asian and Pacific Islander[1]	7,273,662	3,500,439	1,538,721[3]	2.9	1.5	0.8
Other	9,804,847	6,758,319	516,673	3.9	3.0	0.3
Persons of Hispanic Origin	22,354,059	14,608,673	9,072,602[4]	9.0	6.4	4.5
Persons Not of Hispanic Origin	226,355,814	211,937,132	194,139,324	91.0	93.6	95.5

Source: U.S. Bureau of the Census

[1] In 1970 and 1980 Asian and Pacific Islander groups such as Cambodian, Laotian, and Thai were included in the "other" race category. In sample tabulations, these groups were included in the Asian and Pacific Islander category.

[2] Excludes Aleuts and Eskimos in Alaska only.

[3] Excludes Koreans and Hawaiians in Alaska.

[4] Based on sample.

Regional Distribution of the Black Population, 1850 to 1990

Year	Northeast	Percentage of Blacks Living in: North Central	South	West
1850	4.1	3.7	92.1	<0.1
1860	3.5	4.1	92.2	0.1
1870	3.7	5.6	90.6	0.1
1880	3.5	5.9	90.5	0.2
1890	3.6	5.8	90.3	0.4
1900	4.4	5.6	89.7	0.3
1910	4.9	5.5	89.0	0.5
1920	6.5	7.6	85.2	0.8
1930	9.6	10.6	78.7	1.0
1940	10.6	11.0	77.0	1.3
1950	13.4	14.8	68.0	3.8
1960	16.0	18.3	59.9	5.8
1970	19.2	20.2	53.0	7.5
1980	18.3	20.1	53.0	8.5
1990	18.7	19.1	52.8	9.4

Percentage of Population Living in Urban Territory, 1880 to 1990

Year	Total Population	Blacks	Whites
1880[1]	26.3	12.9	28.3
1890[1]	32.9	17.6	35.1
1900[1]	37.3	20.5	39.7
1910	46.3	27.4	48.7
1920	51.4	34.0	53.4
1930	56.2	43.7	57.6
1940	56.5	48.6	57.5
1950	64.0	62.4	64.3
1960*	69.9	73.2	69.5
1970	73.5	81.3	72.4
1980	73.7	85.3	71.3
1990	75.2	87.2	71.9

* Denotes first year for which figures include Alaska and Hawaii.

[1] Definition modified to exclude population in incorporated places and New England towns in the 2,500-3,999 size range.

Population Totals

Year	Total Population	Black Population	Percentage
1790	3,929,214	757,208	19.3
1800	5,308,483	1,002,037	18.9
1810	7,239,881	1,377,808	19.0
1820	9,638,453	1,771,656	18.4
1830	12,866,020	2,328,642	18.1
1840	17,069,453	2,873,648	16.8
1850	23,191,876	3,638,808	15.7
1860	31,443,321	4,441,830	14.1
1870[1]	39,818,449	5,392,172	13.5
1880	50,155,783	6,580,793	13.1
1890	62,947,714	7,488,676	11.9
1900	75,994,575	8,833,994	11.6
1910	91,972,266	9,827,763	10.7
1920	105,710,620	10,463,131	9.9
1930	122,775,046	11,891,143	9.7
1940	131,669,275	12,865,518	9.8
1950	151,325,798	15,044,937	9.9
1960[2]	179,323,175	18,871,831	10.5
1970	203,211,926	22,580,289	11.1
1980	226,545,805	26,495,025	11.7
1990	248,709,873	29,986,060	12.1

[1] Revised to include adjustments for underenumeration in the Southern states.
[2] Denotes first year for which figures include Alaska and Hawaii.

Black Population Change in 14 Central Cities, 1970 to 1990

Area	Black Population			Percent Change in Black Population			Percent Black		
	1990	1980	1970	80 to 90	70 to 80	70 to 90	1990	1980	1970
Central Cities									
New York City	2,102,512	1,784,337	1,668,115	17.8	7.0	26.0	28.7	25.2	21.2
Chicago City	1,087,711	1,197,000	1,102,602	-9.1	8.6	-1.4	39.1	39.8	32.7
Detroit City	777,916	758,939	660,428	2.5	14.9	17.8	75.7	63.1	43.7
Philadelphia City	631,936	638,878	653,791	-1.1	-2.3	-3.3	39.9	37.8	33.6
Los Angeles City	487,674	505,210	503,606	-3.5	0.3	-3.2	14.0	17.0	17.9
Houston City	457,990	440,346	316,551	4.0	39.1	44.7	28.1	27.6	25.7
Baltimore City	435,768	431,151	420,210	1.1	2.6	3.7	59.2	54.8	46.4
Washington, D.C.	399,604	448,906	537,712	-11.0	-16.5	-25.7	65.8	70.3	71.1
Memphis City	334,737	307,702	242,513	8.8	26.9	38.0	54.8	47.6	38.9
New Orleans City	307,728	308,149	267,308	-0.1	15.3	15.1	61.9	55.3	45.0
Dallas City	296,994	265,594	210,238	11.8	26.3	41.3	29.5	29.4	24.9
Atlanta City	264,262	282,911	255,051	-6.6	10.9	3.6	67.1	66.6	51.3
Cleveland City	235,405	251,347	287,841	-6.3	-12.7	-18.2	46.6	43.8	38.3
Milwaukee City	191,255	146,940	105,088	30.2	39.8	82.0	30.5	23.1	14.7
St. Louis City	188,408	206,386	254,191	-8.7	-18.8	-25.9	47.5	45.6	40.9

Age of the Resident Population by Race and Hispanic Origin, 1990

Age	Total	White	Black	American Indian, Eskimo, and Aleut	Asian and Pacific Islander	Other	Persons of Hispanic Origin
All ages	248,709,873	199,686,070	29,986,060	1,959,234	7,273,662	9,804,847	22,354,059
Under 5 years	18,354,443	13,649,490	2,785,902	201,950	589,845	1,127,256	2,387,524
5 to 9 years	18,099,179	13,616,268	2,671,109	199,446	596,133	1,016,223	2,193,852
10 to 14 years	17,114,249	12,853,558	2,601,590	188,000	551,552	919,549	2,001,617
15 to 19 years	17,754,015	13,342,703	2,658,493	180,516	603,761	968,542	2,053,957
20 to 24 years	19,020,312	14,523,912	2,578,953	165,549	632,258	1,119,640	2,304,441
25 to 34 years	43,175,932	33,990,057	5,389,489	346,245	1,417,252	2,032,889	4,403,542
35 to 44 years	37,578,903	30,587,996	4,212,828	276,336	1,242,012	1,259,731	2,944,994
45 to 54 years	25,223,086	21,090,574	2,584,777	173,531	717,241	656,963	1,709,899
55 to 64 years	21,147,923	18,179,539	1,994,368	113,208	469,150	391,658	1,192,950
65 to 74 years	18,106,558	16,026,201	1,503,460	71,980	300,731	204,186	723,029
75 to 84 years	10,055,108	9,037,720	774,908	33,268	123,989	85,223	343,690
85 years and over	3,080,165	2,788,052	230,183	9,205	29,738	22,987	94,564
Median age (years)	32.9	34.4	28.1	26.2	29.8	23.9	25.5

Percent Distribution

Age	Total	White	Black	American Indian, Eskimo, and Aleut	Asian and Pacific Islander	Other	Persons of Hispanic Origin
All ages	100.0	100.0	100.0	100.0	100.0	100.0	100.0
Under 5 years	7.4	6.8	9.3	10.3	8.1	11.5	10.7
5 to 9 years	7.3	6.8	8.9	10.2	8.2	10.4	9.8
10 to 14 years	6.9	6.4	8.7	9.6	7.6	9.4	9.0
15 to 19 years	7.1	6.7	8.9	9.2	8.3	9.9	9.2
20 to 24 years	7.6	7.3	8.6	8.4	8.7	11.4	10.3
25 to 34 years	17.4	17.0	18.0	17.7	19.5	20.7	19.7
35 to 44 years	15.1	15.3	14.0	14.1	17.1	12.8	13.2
45 to 54 years	10.1	10.6	8.6	8.9	9.9	6.7	7.6
55 to 64 years	8.5	9.1	6.7	5.8	6.4	4.0	5.3
65 to 74 years	7.3	8.0	5.0	3.7	4.1	2.1	3.2
75 to 84 years	4.0	4.5	2.6	1.7	1.7	0.9	1.5
85 years and over	1.2	1.4	0.8	0.5	0.4	0.2	0.4

13

Employment and Income

13

Employment and Income

◆ Employment Trends ◆ Factors in Employment and Unemployment Levels ◆ Income and Poverty ◆ Status of African Americans

by Hayward Derrick Horton

The changing social and economic status of blacks continues to be a major issue in contemporary America. Many point to the increase in the number of blacks in high-status occupations as proof that discrimination is no longer a dominant force in the lives of African Americans.

◆ EMPLOYMENT TRENDS

In the United States government, African Americans are well represented in the Clinton administration, as well as the House of Representatives and the Senate. In the past, blacks in the entertainment world were primarily singers and dancers. Today, many of the biggest stars in the music, television and film industries are black. In addition, blacks are increasingly making strides as producers, directors and screenwriters. Similar success has been experienced by blacks in professional sports. To say that the conditions have not changed in the United States for African Americans is certainly inconsistent with the facts.

Yet, despite the increase in opportunities for the black upper and middle class, blacks as a whole trail whites in every measure of socioeconomic standing. Blacks continue to be disproportionately employed in lower-paying, blue-collar jobs. Unemployment for blacks has consistently been twice that for whites for at least two decades. Black personal and family income continues to be a fraction of that for whites. The poverty rate for African Americans has been three times as high as that for whites for more than thirty years. Perhaps the most troubling aspect of these trends is the lack of indication that these measures will improve in the foreseeable future.

In a sense, the story of African Americans has two very different chapters. The first is one of the growing black middle class that is experiencing a greater range of occupational and economic opportunities than ever before. The second part of the story is more somber. It tells of an increasing number of blacks who are disadvantaged and, for all intents and purposes, locked out of the mainstream of American life. This growing schism in the social and economic conditions among blacks has serious implications for the future of the African American community.

◆ FACTORS IN EMPLOYMENT AND UNEMPLOYMENT LEVELS

Unemployment is a major problem in the African American community. Historically, the levels of unemployment among blacks and their patterns of employment are rooted in the discrimination that they experience in the job market (John Hope Franklin and Alfred A. Moss, Jr., *From Slavery to Freedom: A History of Negro Americans*, 1988). High levels of unemployment among blacks have persisted for several decades. Recent data from the United States Bureau of the Census show that this pattern continues into the 1990s. For example, in 1980 the unemployment rate for blacks was 14.3 percent. The rate among whites for that year was 6.3 percent. In other words, the rate for blacks was 2.3 times as high as that for whites. Over the decade of the 1980s and into the 1990s, the unemployment rate fluctuated for both blacks and whites. However, in no year did the unemployment rate for blacks drop below 11 percent. Throughout the 1980 to 1991 period, unemployment rates for blacks were two and one-half times as great as those for whites.

Blacks continue to be disproportionately employed in blue-collar jobs.

The Effects of Occupational Discrimination

Much of the variance in unemployment rates between blacks and whites is a direct result of discrimination, past and present, in the job market and other spheres of economic opportunity. In fact, until relatively recently, there were many occupations that blacks were not allowed to enter—irrespective of their levels of education (John Sibley Butler, *Entrepreneurship and Self-Help among Black Americans*, 1991.) This has resulted in an occupational structure for blacks that is substantially different from that for whites. These differences remain despite advances due to Civil Rights legislation. Data from the United States Census reveal that, in 1991, 18 percent of all employed blacks held managerial and professional positions, compared to 31 percent of whites. 22 percent of blacks, as compared to 13.2 percent of whites, were employed in the operators, fabricators and labor category.

However, this data becomes more revealing when the occupational categories are subdivided by gender for both groups. This shows that black males are more likely than any other group to be in the most vulnerable occupational category—operators, fabricators and labor. In 1991, 32 percent of all employed black males held these types of jobs. For white males, black females and white females the percentages were 17.7, 12.6, and 7.6, respectively. Also, only 15.3 percent of employed black males held managerial and professional jobs. For white males, this figure was 30.5 percent, representing the largest single category for this group.

Approximately 21 percent of employed black females held professional and managerial jobs. The corresponding figure for employed white females was 31 percent, indicating a level of professional and managerial employment comparable to that of white males. The highest category of employment for both black and white females was the technical/sales and administrative area. 36 percent of black females and 43.2 percent of white females held these types of jobs.

Public Policy on Discrimination in Employment

Data shows that African Americans experience disadvantage in the labor force. Despite gains by the black upper and middle class, blacks in general have higher levels of unemployment and hold disproportionately more blue-collar jobs.

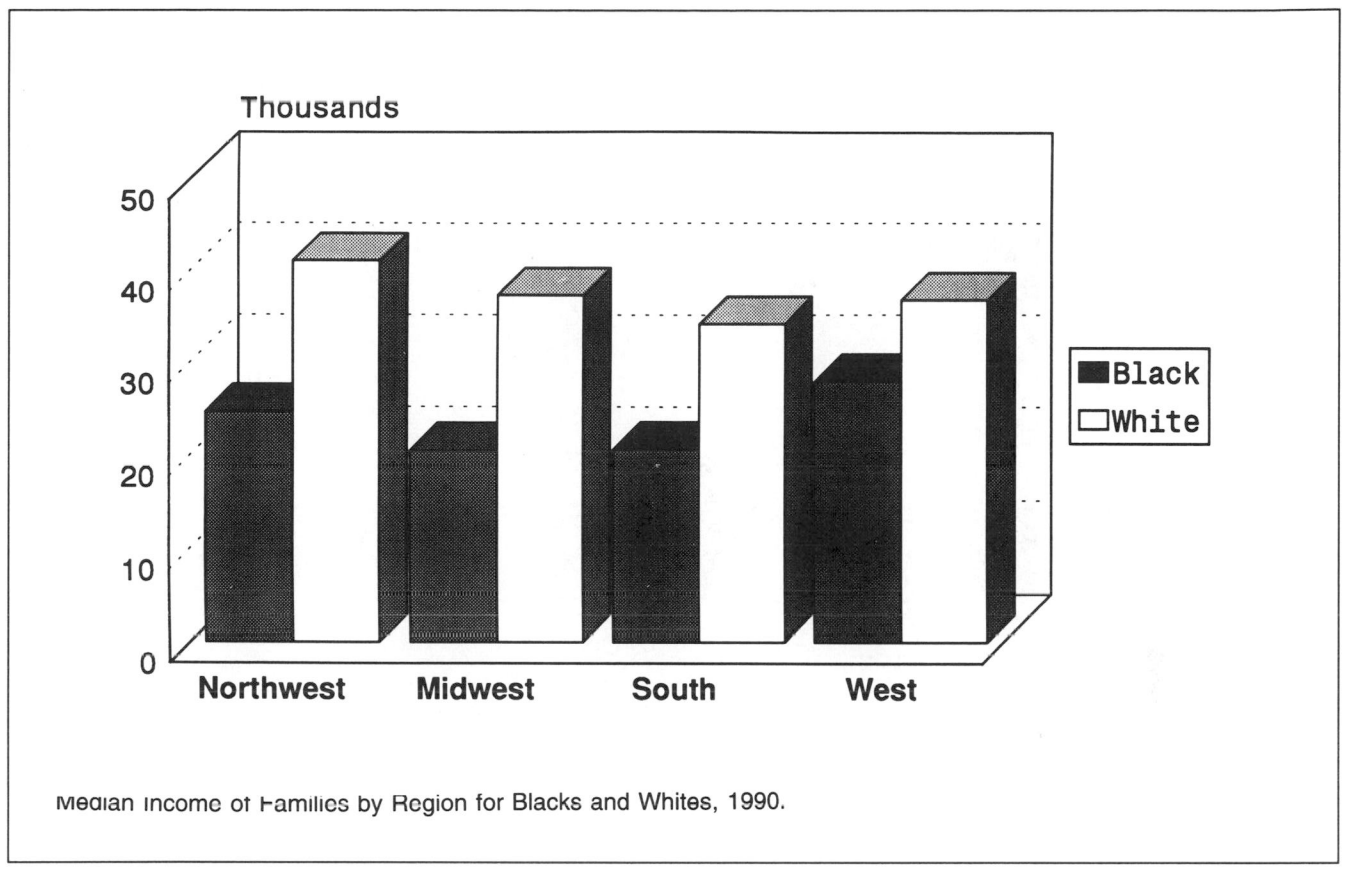

Median Income of Families by Region for Blacks and Whites, 1990.

Source: Statistical Abstract of the United States, U.S. Bureau of the Census, 1992, p. 383.

The Civil Rights Act of 1964 prohibits discrimination on the basis of race, color, gender or national origin. This law formed part of an array of public programs that comprised the "Great Society" legislation of the Kennedy-Johnson administrations. Among these measures was the Economic Recovery Act of 1964, which included the Job Corps, the Manpower Training Programs and many other social interventions. It is generally acknowledged that these programs were important to improving the employment prospects of African Americans.

However, according to many policy experts, the Reagan administrations of the 1980s "turned back the clock" to a time of overt and blatant discrimination toward blacks (James E. Blackwell, *The Black Community: Diversity and Unity*, 1991.) They argue that Reagan attacked many of the social programs that protected the rights of minorities and used the United States Civil Rights Commission to advance his conservative agenda. Indirect support to their claim is the fact that only 4.1 percent of Reagan's appointments were black, as compared to 21 percent for Carter, the previous president. Moreover, experts claim that Reagan's record of recruitment and hiring of blacks was worse than those the previous administrations of Johnson, Nixon and Ford as well. In the estimation of many analysts, the Bush administration extended the damaging trends of the Reagan years.

◆ INCOME AND POVERTY

Despite gains in occupational status over the last two decades, African American households have yet to gain equality in income with whites. Recent sociological studies have found that blacks of comparable levels of education, occupation, and experience tend to earn less than their white counterparts (Melvin E. Thomas and Hayward D. Horton, "Race, Class, and Family Structure: The Case of Family Income," *Sociological Perspectives*, 1992, 35:433-50). Data on household income from the United States Department of Commerce confirm those findings. In 1988, the median income for black families was $19,823, compared to $34,222 for whites. In other words, black families had a median income that was approximately 58 percent of that for whites. In 1989, the essential disparity between black and whites in median family income—$20,911 compared to $36,325—remained unchanged. By 1990, median family income for

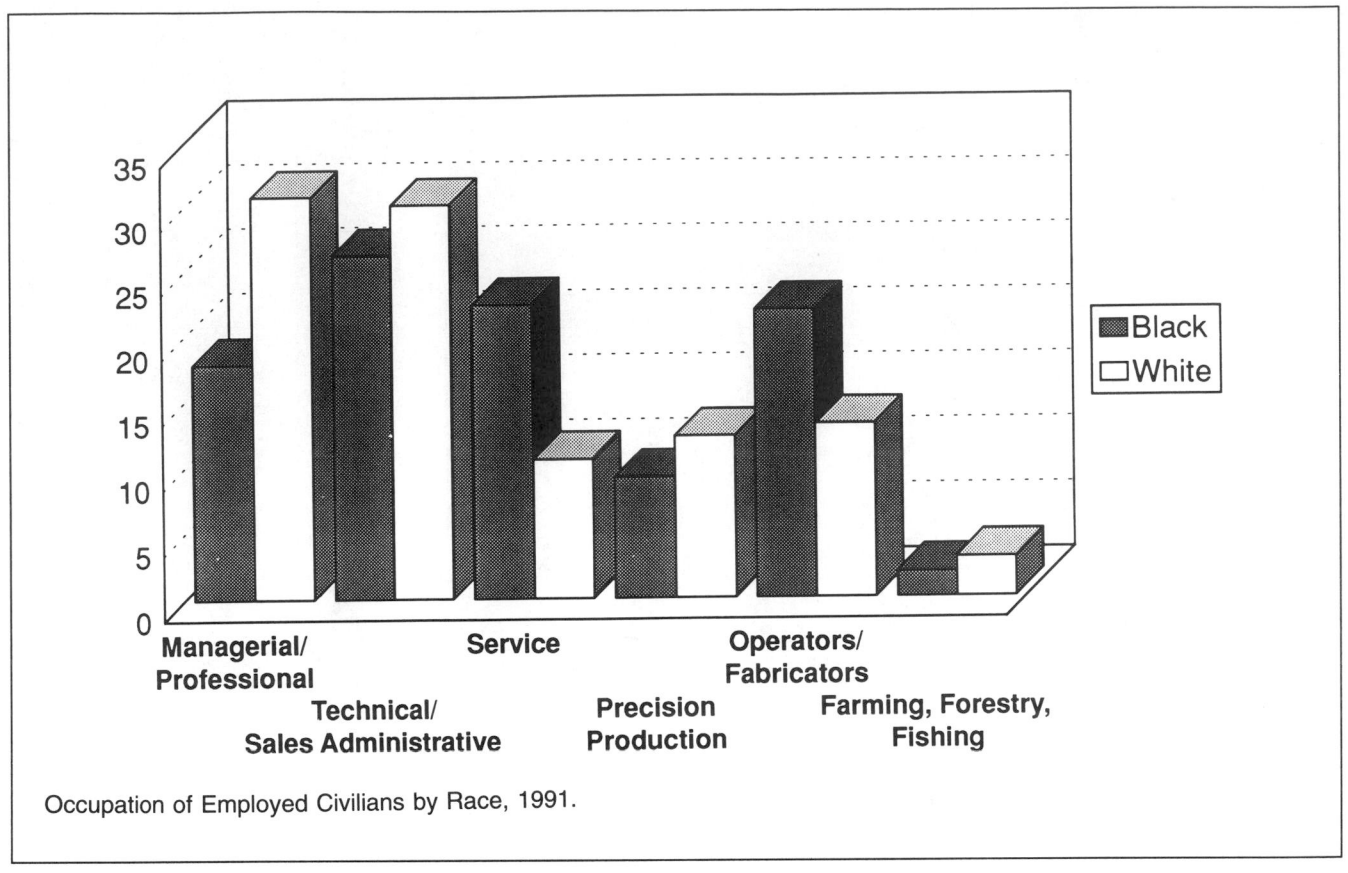

Occupation of Employed Civilians by Race, 1991.

Source: Statistical Abstract of the United States, U.S. Dept. of Commerce, 1992, p. 396.

blacks was still only 59 percent of that for whites, despite an increase in income for black families over the three years. The corresponding increase for white families offset any gains made by blacks during the period.

The Impact of Family Structure on the Income of Black Families

Family structure has a bearing on the incomes of African American families and how they compare to white families. For instance, black married-couple households had a median income in 1988 of $30,424. This represents 82 percent of the $36,883 median income reported for white married-couple families that year. This figure declined to 78 percent in 1989, but rose again to 84 percent in 1990.

It is important to note that the ratio of black/white income in this category is the highest among the various family types. Single black male householders made only 64 percent as much as single white male householders in 1988; this figure fluctuated to 62 percent in 1989 and 73 percent in 1990. Among racial comparisons based on family-structure types, black single female household-

ers fared the worst. Single black female householders made only 59 percent as much as single white female householders in 1988, and only 60 percent as much in 1990.

The Distribution of Black Family Income

Another perspective on African American economic life can be gained by examining the income distribution of this group. In 1990, 14.1 percent of all black households had income of less than $15,000. Only 5.2 percent of whites were found in this category. Approximately 52 percent of all black households had income that was less than $20,000. Slightly more than 68 percent of blacks, compared to 50 percent of whites, had less than $30,000 in income in 1990. 88 percent of all black households had less than $50,000 in income, compared to 75.4 percent of white households. In short, black and white income distributions continue to be disparate in contemporary America. Blacks are still more likely than whites to have households at the lower ends of the income distribution. This trend is consistent with the gap persisting over the years in overall family income for blacks and whites.

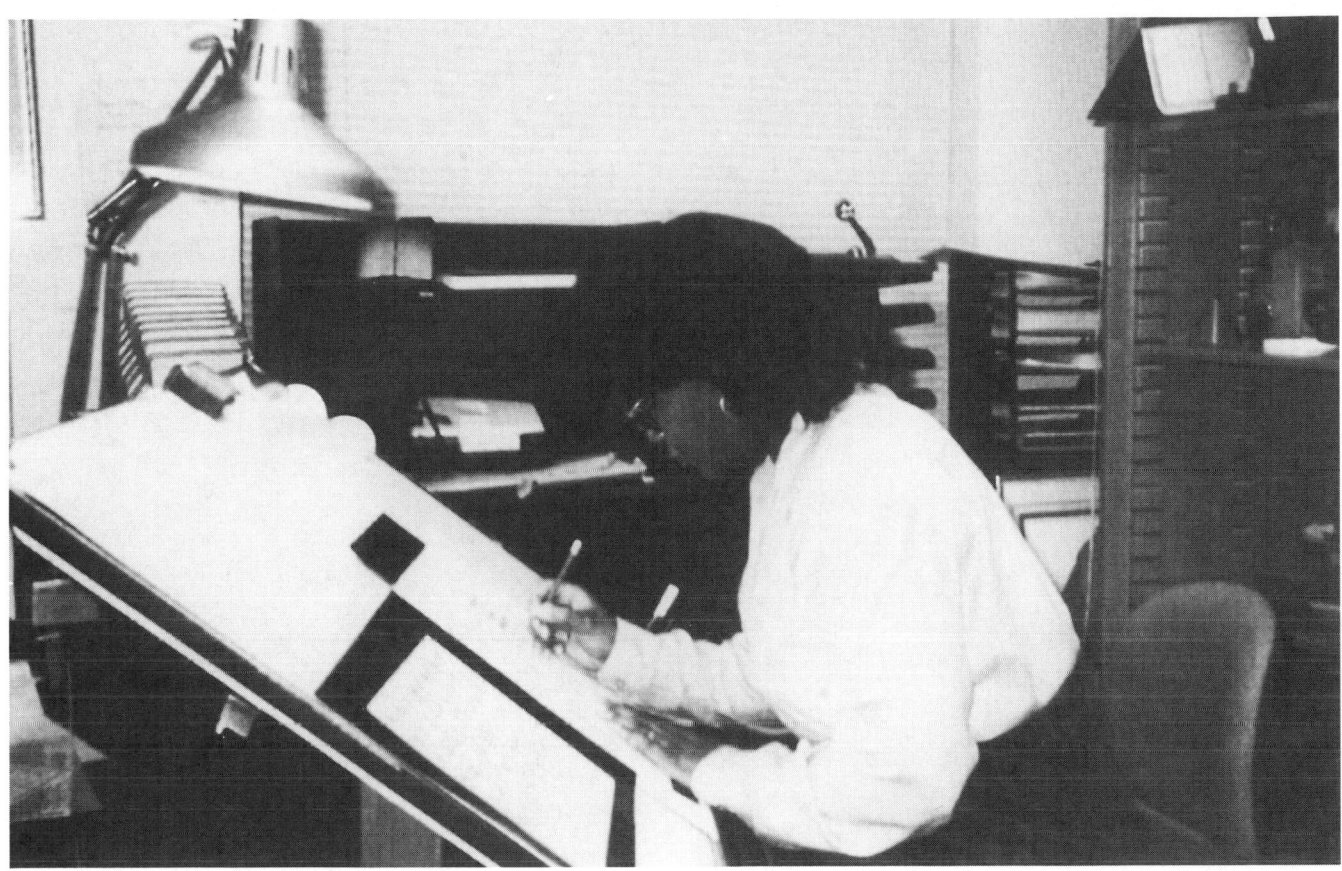

Approximately 21 percent of employed black females held professional and managerial jobs.

Household Size and Black Family Income

Factoring in household size is another way of assessing the degree of economic progress that blacks have made in recent years. Data from the Department of Commerce show that these income differences remain across household size categories. For one-person households, the black median income is $10,156. For four-person households, the black median income is $25,683. For white four-person households, the figure is $43,363. In no household size category does the black median income equal that of whites. Black median income across household sizes ranges from 55 to 66 percent of white median income. A similar pattern is observed when comparing mean incomes across household sizes for blacks and whites.

Regional Differences in Black Family Income

Income for African American families is likely to vary among different regions of the country. Data from 1990 show that the median family income for blacks was highest in the West, at $27,947, and lowest in the midwest, at $20,512. These two regions also reported the highest and lowest percentages of black-to-white

median family income. These differences reflect the variations in regional economies and occupational opportunities for blacks and whites.

Age of Householder and Black Family Income

Age is one of the most important factors to consider when assessing income within the African-American community as it is a reasonably accurate measure of work experience. One fact that is often overlooked when considering black-white income differences is the significant variation in the age distributions of two groups—variation in itself reflecting sociological factors. In other words, it is necessary to compare blacks and whites in the same age categories to obtain a complete picture of the African American income situation. Family income data for 1990 from the United States Department of Commerce confirm the relationship between income and age. Generally speaking, family income increases for African Americans as the age of the householder increases. Black householders in the 15 to 24 years category had a median family income of $7,218. For those in the 25 to 34 age category, the median family income was $17,130. Family income gradually rises for blacks until it peaks in the 45 to 54 years category at

Family structure has a bearing on the incomes of African American families and how they compare to white families.

$30,847. Beyond that age, a gradual and expected decline in income is evident as householders withdraw from the labor force. Nonetheless, in no age category do blacks equal whites in median family income. The figures range from 40 percent in the 15 to 24 age group to 72 percent in the 65 to 74 age group. Overall, black householders under age 65 earn only 59 percent as much as their white counterparts.

Poverty and the African American Community

Employment, unemployment and income all have an impact on the level of poverty that exists in the African American community. Government statistics on poverty show that, in total numbers, there were nearly as many blacks in poverty in 1990 as there were thirty years before. In 1959, 9.9 million blacks were living below the poverty line. In 1990 that figure was 9.8 million. The major difference is between the poverty rates in the two periods. In 1959 the poverty rate was 55.2 percent compared to the 1990 rate of 31.9 percent. One trend that has not changed is the ratio of black to white poverty over a 30–year span. In 1959, the rate of poverty for blacks was three times as great as the rate for whites. In 1990, that ratio was unchanged.

2.2 million African American families were living in poverty in 1990. This represented a poverty rate of 29.3 percent. However, important differences in rates of poverty across family types existed. For instance, black married-couple families had the lowest level of poverty. Black married-couple families without children had a poverty rate of 12.6 percent; those with children had a poverty rate of 14.3 percent. The highest rates were those for female-headed householders. Female-headed householders without children had a poverty rate of 48.1 percent. For those with children, the poverty rate was 56.1 percent. Comparing the poverty rates racially shows that, in every category, black family poverty exceeded that for whites. Black families overall had a poverty rate that was nearly four times the rate for whites. Even in the category that was lowest for blacks, married-couple families without children, the rate of poverty was two and one-half times that for white families of this type.

Poverty and Black Teenage Pregnancy

One problem associated with poverty in the African American community is that of teenage pregnancy. However, black teenage pregnancy is part of a larger

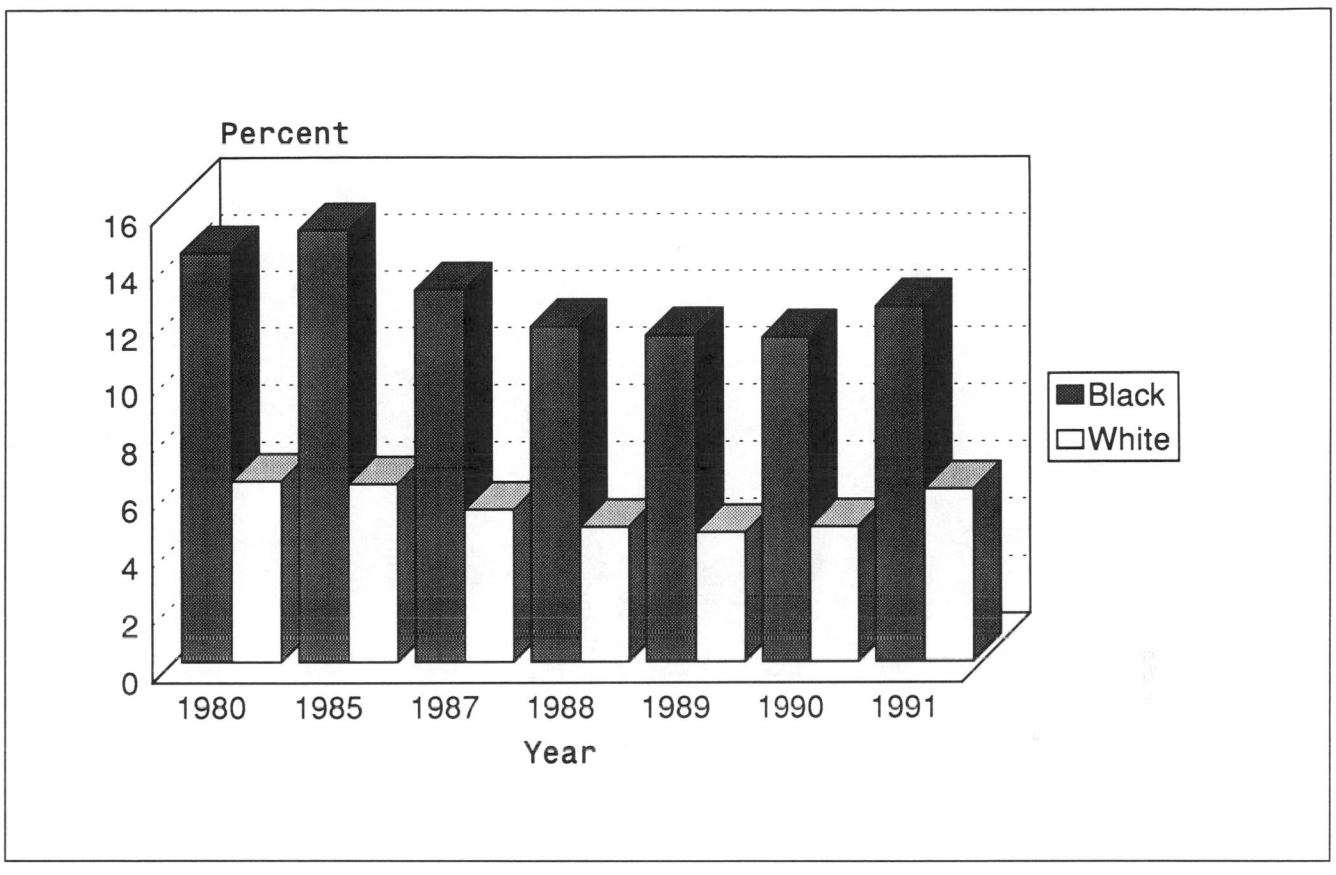

Unemployment for Blacks and Whites, 1980–1991. Source: Statistical Abstract of the United States, U.S. Bureau of the Census, 1992, p. 383.

problem of nonmarital births. Rates of pregnancy and nonmarital childbirth are higher for black teenagers than whites, though the gap is closing. Studies indicate that the differences between the two groups can be explained by differences in (1) sexual activity; (2) rates of abortion; (3) the use of contraceptives; and (4) rates of marriage before the child's birth (James E. Blackwell, *The Black Community: Diversity and Unity*, 1991).

Irrespective of the causes of black teenage pregnancy, the consequences are dramatic for the African American community. Generally speaking, teenage mothers are more likely to be poor and are less likely to finish high school. In more cases than not, the fathers are absent or nonsupportive. Thus, it is not unusual for teenage mothers to be dependent on public assistance as a means of support. Teenage mothers tend to be unprepared for the adult responsibilities of parenting. Their children are more likely to be the victims of child abuse and to suffer physical, emotional, and educational problems later on in life.

African American community organizations have attempted to tackle the problem of teenage pregnancy. Groups such as the Children's Defense Fund, the National Urban League, Delta Sigma Theta and a host of others have developed teenage pregnancy prevention programs. Often these efforts focus on teenage males as well as females.

Public Programs to Address Poverty and Employment Discrimination

The issue of black teenage pregnancy is only one dimension of the overall problem of poverty within the African American community. Many of the programs that address the needs of the poor were developed during the Great Society era of the 1960s. Headstart, Medicaid and Medicare, the Food Stamp Program and several other forms of assistance were part of a comprehensive effort referred to as the "War on Poverty." Critics of the Great Society programs argue that these programs were expensive, wasteful, and ineffective. Supporters claim that the programs have not failed, but America's determination to secure a Great Society has.

Certainly, the sentiment toward programs that address poverty and employment discrimination has changed. The most controversial program to date is affirmative action. Affirmative action was initiated during the late 1960s by the Nixon administration rather

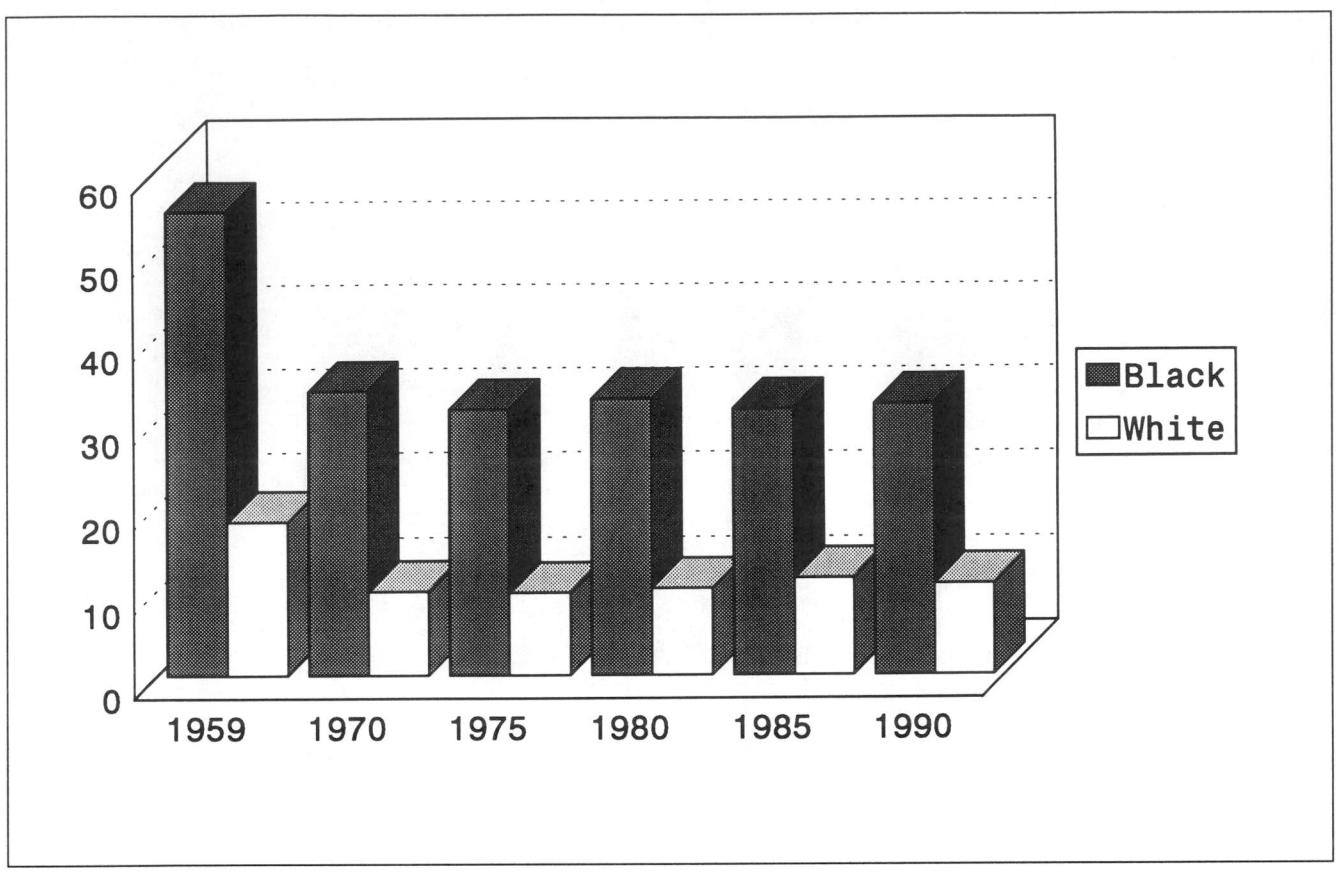

Poverty Status of Blacks and Whites, 1959–1990. Source: Current Population Reports, 1991.

than during the Great Society era of Kennedy and Johnson. Affirmative action programs call for guidelines and goals in the hiring of underutilized groups: racial/ethnic minorities, the handicapped and women. They also require documentation of a good faith effort to hire persons from these groups. Affirmative action programs have been effective in promoting change in hiring practices because they have the weight of the federal government behind them. As a direct result, a broader range of opportunities have become available for African Americans in government, the corporate world, and colleges and universities.

Affirmative action programs have their critics and have been under particularly heavy attack in the mid-1990s, with several programs being restricted or dismantled altogether. One major criticism is that affirmative action programs do not promote occupational opportunities in general. Studies have documented that while whites support the general principle of equality for all, most do not support the idea of programs and social intervention specifically designed to improve the conditions of blacks and other minorities (Herbert J. Gans, *Middle American Individualism*, 1988). Also, an increasing number of white Americans are of the opin-

ion that social and economic differences between blacks and whites are due to individual factors rather than racial discrimination (James R. Kluegel, "Trends in White's Explanation of the Black-White Gap in Socioeconomic Status, 1977-1989. *American Sociological Review*, 1991, 56:101-16). This backlash is a direct result of the large-scale restructuring of America's economy and the resulting unemployment and underemployment for many white Americans—both working and middle class.

However, affirmative action programs have their share of black critics as well. Many black conservatives argue that affirmative action programs do not help the black disadvantaged. They claim that these programs primarily benefit the black middle class—a group that needs no assistance in achieving its economic goals. In addition, critics of affirmative action argue that it unfairly stigmatizes all blacks. Therefore, the success of African Americans in any field is often dismissed as being due to affirmative action. Whites can also perceive the need for affirmative action as confirming their belief in the inferiority of blacks. (Hayward D. Horton, "Population Change and the Employment Status of College-Educated Blacks," *Research in Race and Ethnic Relations*; Thomas Sowell, *Civil Rights: Rhetoric or Reality*).

Affirmative action programs call for guidelines and goals in the hiring of under-utilized groups.

◆ STATUS OF AFRICAN AMERICANS

The issue of the social and economic status of African Americans is complex. It is clear that major changes have occurred within the black community as a result of the civil rights movement, civil rights legislation, and affirmative action policies. Many blacks are holding more higher-status jobs and earning higher incomes than ever before. Yet, the number of African Americans who are impoverished remains extremely high. In other words, when one speaks of the conditions or the future of the African American community, one has to be clear that it is a community that consists of many segments. The lifestyles and opportunities for African Americans in one segment may be vastly different than the conditions experienced by African Americans in another segment.

Despite the dramatic changes that have occurred within the African American community as a whole, one thing has remained the same: blacks have yet to achieve equality with whites on any measure of social and economic standing. Blacks have consistently had rates of unemployment that were at least twice as high as

Blacks who are employed are more likely than whites to hold blue collar jobs.

those for whites. Blacks who are employed are more likely than whites to hold blue collar jobs—the type of jobs that are most likely to be eliminated during the restructuring of the American economy.

The gap between blacks and whites persists in family income as well. Black families still have only a fraction of the income of white families. Neither family size, family structure, age of householder, presence of children, marital status nor regional location fully explains the black-white difference in family income. The gap that remains demonstrates that racial discrimination is still pervasive within American society. This persisting inequality explains many of the problems that are associated with poverty, such as teenage pregnancy and financially unstable female-headed households.

Many of the programs developed to address poverty and racial discrimination in employment were initiated during the 1960s. Generally speaking, these programs have been instrumental in providing opportunities to African Americans that had been denied long after the end of slavery. However, in recent years, whites have increasingly come to resist and resent programs that secure such opportunities for blacks and other racial/ethnic minorities. As opportunities decline for whites, the competition for good jobs in this country is expected to increase. Blacks and other minority populations are growing at rates that far exceed that of whites. As these populations become better educated, the struggle for desirable jobs is expected to intensify.

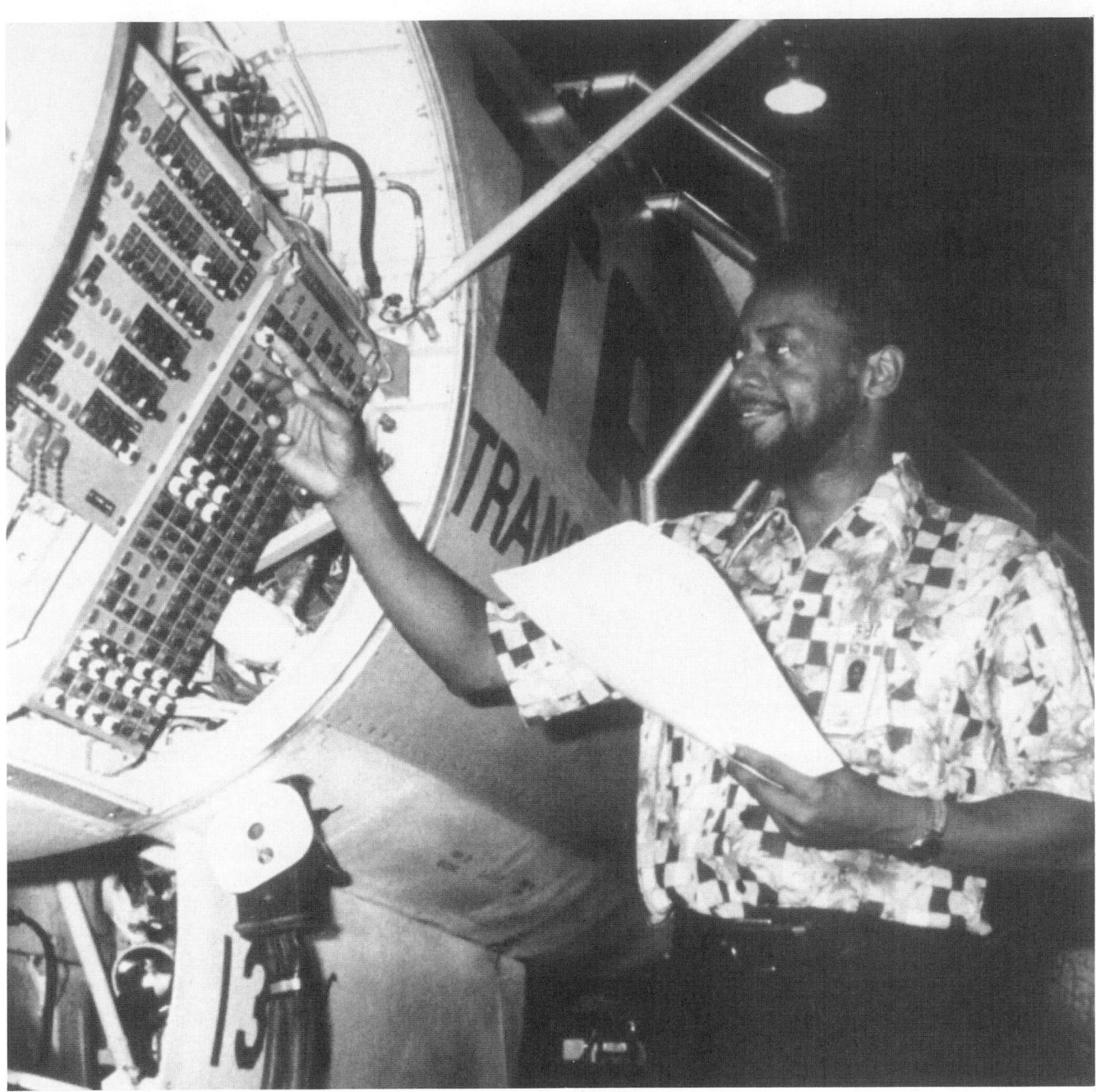

Blacks are holding more higher status jobs and earning higher incomes than ever.

Major social programs are not likely to be initiated by the federal government within the near future. Because of the changing social and political climate in the United States, many African Americans are advocating a greater emphasis on self-help and internal community development. One sociological model of black community development is the Black Organizational Autonomy (BOA) Model (Hayward D. Horton, "A Sociological Approach to Black Community Development," *Journal of the Community Development Society*, 1992, 25:1-19). This model maintains that viable black communities are those that possess community-based organizations with five basic components: (1) economic autonomy; (2) internally developed and controlled data sources; (3) programs to develop and promote black female leadership; (4) programs that emphasize black history and culture; and (5) programs that are socially inclusive in leadership. The model proved successful in a case study in Little Rock, Arkansas of a church-based black community organization and has considerable potential for meeting the present and future needs of the African American community.

The highest category of employment for both black and white females was the technical/sales and administrative area.

The African American community is undergoing fundamental change. Some of these changes are internal, as blacks with different levels of education and experience are differentially able to take advantage of once-denied opportunities. Some of these changes are external, as the competition for existing jobs increases at a time when government and industry are downsizing their respective labor forces. Clearly, the present and future will continue to be filled with obstacles. However, as American history has shown, African Americans are equal to the challenge.

Unemployment for Blacks and Whites, 1980-1991

(in thousands)

Year	Black Number	%	White Number	%	B/W Ratio
1980	1,553	14.3	5,884	6.3	2.3
1985	1,864	15.1	6,191	6.2	2.4
1987	1,684	13.0	5,501	5.3	2.5
1988	1,547	11.7	4,944	4.7	2.5
1989	1,544	11.4	4,770	4.5	2.5
1990	1,527	11.3	5,091	4.7	2.4
1991	1,679	12.4	6,447	6.0	2.1

Source: Statistical Abstract of the United States, U.S. Bureau of the Census, 1992, page 383.

Median Income of Families by Age of Householders, 1990

Age of Householder	Black	White	B/W
Under 65 years	$22,221	$37,661	.59
15 to 24 years	7,218	18,234	.40
25 to 34 years	17,130	33,457	.51
35 to 44 years	27,025	42,632	.63
45 to 54 years	30,847	49,249	.62
55 to 64 years	25,442	40,416	.63
65 years and over	16,585	25,864	.64
65 to 74 years	20,158	28,027	.72
75 years and over	12,574	21,549	.58

Source:"Money Income of Households, Families and Persons in the United States, 1990," Current Population Reports: Consumer Income, series P-60, No. 174, Table 13, pp. 53-54, U.S. Dept. of Commerce, August 1991.

Poverty Status for Black and Whites, 1959-1990

Year	Black Number*	%	White Number	%	B/W Ratio
1959	9,927	55.1	28,484	18.1	3.0
1970	7,548	33.5	17,484	9.9	3.4
1975	7,545	31.3	17,770	9.7	3.2
1980	8,579	32.5	19,669	10.2	3.2
1985	8,926	31.3	22,860	11.4	2.8
1990	9,837	31.9	22,326	10.7	3.0

* number in thousands

Source: "Poverty in the United States, 1990," Current Population Reports: Consumer Income, Series P-60, No. 175, Table 2, pp. 16-17, U.S. Dept of Commerce, August 1991

Occupation of Employed Civilians by Race, 1991

(in thousands)

Occupation	Black		White	
	Number	**Percent**	**Number**	**Percent**
Managerial/Professional	1,819	18.0	26,263	31.0
Technical/Sales Administrative	2,664	26.4	25,880	30.3
Service	2,263	22.5	9,040	10.6
Precision Production	929	9.2	10,494	12.3
Operators/Fabricators	2,213	22.0	11,305	13.2
Farming, Forestry, Fishing	190	1.9	2,556	3.0
Total	10,078	100.0	85,538	100.4*

*Number exceeds one hundred due to rounding.

Source: Statistical Abstract of the United States, U.S. Dept. of Commerce, 1992, page 396.

Occupation Distribution by Sex, 1991

(in thousands)

	Black				White			
	Male		Female		Male		Female	
Occupation	Number	%	Number	%	Number	%	Number	%
Managerial/Professional	758	15.3	1,061	20.7	14,464	30.5	11,799	31.0
Technical/Sales, Admin.	819	16.5	1,845	36.0	9,425	19.8	16,455	43.2
Service	832	16.7	1,431	27.9	3,449	7.3	5,591	14.7
Precision Production	810	16.3	199	2.3	9,640	20.3	854	2.2
Operators/Fabricators	1,566	32.0	647	12.6	8,396	17.7	2,909	7.6
Farming, Forestry, Fishing	173	3.5	17	.0**	2,109	4.4	447	1.2
Total	4,957	100.3*	5,121	99.5*	47,483	100.0	38,055	99.9*

* Number does not equal one hundred percent due to rounding.

** Number less than .1 percent.

Source: Statistical Abstract of the United States, U.S. Dept. of Commerce, 1992, page 396.

Median Income of Households by Race, 1988-1990

	1988 Black	White	B/W	1989 Black	White	B/W	1990 Black	White	B/W
All Households	$16,407	$28,781	.57	$18,083	$30,406	.59	$18,676	$31,231	.60
Family Households	$19,823	$34,222	.58	$20,911	$36,325	.58	$21,899	$37,219	.59
Married Couple families	$30,424	$36,883	.82	$30,833	$39,328	.78	$33,893	$40,433	.84
Male Householder, no wife present	$19,501	$30,689	.64	$20,044	$32,218	.62	$24,048	$32,869	.73
Female Householder, no husband present	$10,995	$18,685	59	$12,170	$20,164	.60	$12,537	$20,867	.60
Total Number of Households	10,561	79,734	—	10,486	80,163	—	10,671	80,968	—

Source: "Money Income of Households, Families and Persons in the United States, 1990," Current Population Reports: Consumer Income, Series P-60, pp. 174. Table 5, pp. 21-22, U.S. Department of Commerce.

Income Distribution for Black and White Households, 1990

Total Money Income	Number (in thousands)	Black Percent	Cumulative Percent	Number	White Percent	Cumulative Percent
Less than $5,000	1,500	14.1	14.1	4,901	5.2	5.2
$5,000 to $9,999	1,786	16.7	30.8	9,184	9.7	14.9
$12,000 to $14,999	1,240	11.6	42.4	8,925	9.5	24.4
$15,000 to $19,999	1,050	9.8	52.2	8,296	8.8	33.2
$20,000 to $24,999	988	9.3	61.5	8,427	8.9	42.1
$25,000 to$29,999	741	6.9	68.4	7,501	8.0	50.1
$30,000 to $34,999	695	6.5	74.9	7,363	7.8	57.9
$35,000 to $39,999	613	5.7	80.6	6,395	6.8	64.7
$40,000 to $44,999	412	3.9	84.5	5,372	5.7	70.4
$45,000 to $49,999	378	3.5	88.0	4,702	5.0	75.4
$50,000 to $54,999	293	2.8	90.8	4,088	4.3	79.7
$55,000 to $59,999	197	1.9	92.7	3,227	3.4	83.1
$60,000 to $64,999	128	1.2	93.9	2,767	2.9	86.0
$65,000 to $69,999	132	1.2	95.1	2,170	2.3	88.3
$70,000 to $74,999	113	1.1	96.2	1,809	1.9	90.2
$75,000 to $79,999	96	.9	97.1	1,555	1.7	91.9
$80,000 to $84,999	69	.7	97.8	1,204	1.3	93.2
$85,000 to $89,999	51	.5	98.3	982	1.0	94.2
$90,000 to $94,999	44	.4	98.7	769	.8	95.0
$95,000 to $99,999	23	.2	98.9	590	.6	95.6
$1000,000 and over	122	1.1	100.0	4,085	4.3	99.9*
Total Number of Households	10,671			94,312		
Median Income		$18,676			$29,943	
Mean Income		$24.814			$91,403	

Source: "Money Income of Households, Families and Persons in the United States: 1990," Current Population Reports: Consumer Income, Series P-60, No. 174, Table 5, pp. 21-22, U.S. Department of Commerce.

Total Money Income by Household Size for Blacks and Whites, 1990

	One	**Two**	**Three**	**Four**	**Five**	**Six**	**Seven**
			Number of Persons in Household				
*Black							
Median	$10,156	$20,122	$21,474	$25,683	$24,342	$26,742	$22,361
Mean	15,193	25,061	27,820	30,573	31,598	33,395	29,790
Income per household member	15,193	11,786	8,933	7,441	6,330	5,479	3,746
White							
Median	15,981	32,561	38,930	43,363	40,715	40,420	40,822
Mean	21,314	40,726	45,837	50,342	48,802	47,331	47,351
Income per household member	21,314	20,107	15,063	12,616	9,786	7,873	6,804
B/W Ratio							
Median	.64	.62	.55	.59	.60	.66	.55
Mean	.71	.62	.61	.61	.64	.71	.63
Income per household member	.71	.59	.59	.59	.65	.70	.62

Source: "Money Income of Households, Families and Persons in the United States, 1990," Current Population
Reports: Consumer Income, Series P-60, No. 174, Table 9, Page 40, U.S. Department of Commerce, August 1991

Poverty Status of Families by Type of Family, 1990

Family Type	Black Number*	Black Percent	White Number	White Percent	B/W
With & Without Children Under 18 Years					
All Families	2,193	29.3	4,622	8.1	3.6
Married Couple Families	448	12.6	2,286	5.1	2.5
Male Householder, no wife present	97	20.6	226	9.9	2.1
Female Householder, no husband present	1,648	48.1	2,010	26.8	1.8
With Children Under 18 Years of Age					
All Families	1,887	37.2	3,553	12.6	3.0
Married Couple Families	301	14.3	1,572	7.1	2.0
Male Householder, no wife present	73	27.3	167	16.0	1.7
Female Householder, no husband present	1,513	56.1	1,814	37.9	1.5

* Number in thousands.

Source: "Poverty in the United States, 1990," Current Population Reports: Consumer Income, Series P-60, No. 175, Table 4, pp. 21-22, U.S. Dept. of Commerce, August 1991.

14

Entrepreneurship

⑭

Entrepreneurship

◆ Pre-Civil War Entrepreneurship in the Black Community
◆ Post-Civil War Entrepreneurship in the Black Community
◆ Black Entrepreneurs in the Post-Civil Rights Era ◆ Recent Trends ◆ Entrepreneurial Gatekeepers

by Michael D. Woodard

African Americans have a long and rich history of entrepreneurship in America; blacks have been in business since before the Civil War and continue their entrepreneurial tradition today. Segments of the African American population have exhibited the same entrepreneurial spirit as segments of other ethnic groups who have migrated to this country. Very often, however, the history of black entrepreneurship has been either overlooked or misconstrued.

◆ PRE-CIVIL WAR ENTREPRENEURSHIP IN THE BLACK COMMUNITY

As the United States began to take shape, a number of people of African origin were successful in their attempt to carve out an economic stake for themselves. Anthony Johnson, who accumulated substantial property in Jamestown, Virginia, is believed to be the first person of African descent to have become an entrepreneur in America. Jean Baptist DuSable, a wholesaler and merchant who established the first settlement in Chicago in the early 1770s, was another pre-Civil War era entrepreneur.

Prior to the Civil War, nonetheless slavery defined the existence of most African Americans. Thus, two categories of business persons were able to develop and sustain business enterprises. The first group was composed of free African Americans, numbering approximately 60,000, who could accumulate the capital to generate business activity. They developed enterprises in almost every area of the business community, including merchandising, real estate, manufacturing, construction, transportation, and extractive industries.

The second group consisted of slaves who—as a result of thrift, ingenuity, industry, and/or the liberal paternalism of their masters—were able to engage in business activity. Although the constraints of slavery were such that even highly skilled slaves could not become entrepreneurs in the true sense of the word, slaves did, during their limited free time, sell their labor and create products to sell.

The fact that African American entrepreneurship existed at all during the era of slavery is testimony to an entrepreneurial spirit and the determination of a people to achieve economic freedom even under the harshest conditions.

If it was all but impossible for slaves to engage in private enterprise, it was also hazardous for "free" blacks to do so, since they were effectively only half free. Free blacks lived under a constant fear of being labeled as "run-away" slaves and being sold into slavery. In addition, in areas where free blacks lived, laws were passed to restrict their movement and thus their economic freedom. This was one intention, for example, of the laws Virginia, Maryland, and North Carolina had passed by 1835 forbidding free blacks to carry arms without a license. The right of assembly was also denied blacks throughout the South—leaving it illegal for black civic, business, or benevolent organizations to convene. In addition to reflecting white slaveowners' fears of an African American uprising, such legal restriction had the purpose and effect of making it difficult for free blacks to earn a living.

However, the Southern economic exploitation of blacks indirectly had a positive impact on black entrepreneurship: the development of business enterprise by African Americans in the North. In 1838, for example the *Register of Trades of Colored People* in the city of Philadelphia listed eight bakers, 25 blacksmiths,

During their limited free time, slaves did sell their labor and self-created products.

three brass founders, 15 cabinet makers and carpenters, five confectioners, two caulkers, two chair bottomers, 15 tailoring enterprises, 31 tanners, five weavers, and six wheelwrights.

The Philadelphia business register also listed businesses run by African American women. Among these were 81 dressmakers and tailors, four dyers and scourers, two fullers, and two glass and paper makers. The 98 hairdressers registered, comprising the largest trade group, operated some of the most lucrative enterprises.

Another profitable business controlled by African Americans in Philadelphia during the 1820s and 1830s was sail-making. In 1838, 19 sail-makers were recorded in the business register for that year. James Forster, who lived between 1766 and 1841, ran a major manufacturing firm that made sails; in 1829, Forster employed 40 workers, black and white.

Although several individuals succeeded in the manufacturing trades, the business enterprise that brought prosperity to the largest number of African Americans in Philadelphia was catering. Robert Boyle, a black waiter, is believed to have developed the idea of contracting to provide formal dinners to serve in domestic entertaining. Catering quickly spread across the developing country, but it was in Philadelphia, the city of its birth, that catering was king.

Significantly, most of the businesses discussed thus far involved the craft or service trades. These were small enterprises that required only a modest capital investment and allowed African Americans to develop a niche without threatening larger white-owned businesses.

◆ POST-CIVIL WAR ENTREPRENEURSHIP IN THE BLACK COMMUNITY

The promise of freedom and political enfranchisement held out by Lincoln's Emancipation Proclamation of 1863 was soon undermined by racist judicial rulings. In 1878, in *Hall v. DeCuir*, the U.S. Supreme Court ruled that a state could not prohibit segregation on a common carrier. In 1896, with the Plessy v. Ferguson ruling, "separate but equal" became the law of the land. Following these decisions, a pattern of rigid segregation of the races was established that remained the norm until the advent of the civil rights movement in the 1960s.

Freedom National Bank, Harlem's first black commercial bank, was founded in 1965.

Nevertheless, even within the context of disenfranchisement and segregation, Booker T. Washington saw the possibility of securing African American economic stability through business development. In 1900, Washington spearheaded the development of the National Negro Business League to encourage black enterprise. During the organization's first meeting, the delegates concluded that:

> a useless class is a menace and a danger to any community, and ... when an individual produces what the world wants, whether it is a product of the hand, heart, or head, the world does not long stop to inquire what is the color of the skin of the producer. ...[I]f every member of the race should strive to make himself the most indispensable man in his community, and to be successful in business, however humble that business might be, he would contribute much toward soothing the pathway of his own and future generations. (John Sibly Butler. 1991. *Entrepreneurship and Self-Help Among Black Americans*. New York: State University of New York Press, pp. 67–68.)

During the early 1900s, although services continued to be the cornerstone of the black business community,

blacks found it easier to raise capital and ventured into more entrepreneurial endeavors.

In 1905, for example, Madame C. J. Walker developed a hair care system that gave dry hair a soft texture; millions of women, both black and white, became customers for Madame Walker's products. Before her death in 1919, Madame Walker had more than 2000 agents marketing her ever expanding line of products, which made her America's first black female millionaire.

Durham, North Carolina: A Special Case

Turn of the century Durham, North Carolina represented a special case of enterprise and economic resilience. In publications of the time, Durham was referred to as "The Wall Street of Negro America." By the late 1940s, more than 150 businesses owned by African Americans flourished in Durham. Among these businesses were traditional service providers, such as cafes, movie-houses, barber shops, boarding houses, pressing shops, grocery stores, and funeral parlors. What distinguished Durham, however, was the presence of large black businesses.

Booker T. Washington

One of the largest and most successful black businesses in the nation was the North Carolina Mutual Life Insurance Company. Surrounding the North Carolina Mutual Life Insurance Company were the Banker's Fire Insurance Company, the Mutual Building and Loan Association, the Union Insurance and Realty Company, the Durham Realty and Insurance Company, the People's Building and Loan Association, the Royal Knights Savings and Loan Association, T. P. Parham and Associates (a brokerage corporation), and the Mortgage Company of Durham (Butler, *Entrepreneurship and Self-Help*

Among Black Americans, p. 175). Such businesses established a "city of enterprise" for African Americans.

Although Durham was a success, external economic pressure and racial hostility made it impossible for blacks, on a large scale, to develop stores that could compete in the larger economy. As a result of Jim Crow laws and segregation, most black-owned businesses were forced to limit their market to their own community. A partial exception was the Durham textile mill, at the time the only hosiery mill in the world owned and

Madame C. J. Walker

operated by African Americans. It operated 18 knitting machines and did business in the open market; their salesman, who traveled mostly in North Carolina, Indiana, Georgia, South Carolina and Alabama, were white. This manufacturing firm was exceptional in the sense that it was perhaps the first large-scale black-owned enterprise to hire whites.

Nevertheless, race relations in Durham during this time were such that the most successful retail and service businesses tended to generate a white clientele. For example, in 1940 Smith's Fish Market, established by the former postal clerk Freeman M. Smith, supplied Durham's largest white-operated hotel, the Washington Duke. Smith was also the major supplier for smaller white and black-owned businesses. In 1940, Smith grossed more than $90,000 and opened four other outlets throughout the city. Similarly, Rowland and Mitchell established a tailor shop in 1930 where they did work for "exclusive whites and department stores." It was estimated that 80 percent of their customers were white. Among other successful businesses was Thomas Baily & Sons, a meat and grocery store that opened in 1919 and grossed $80,000 a year by 1940. The Home Modernization and Supply Company, founded in 1938 by the brothers U. M. and R. S. George, grossed more than $100,000 in constructing 500 homes in the Durham area and employed 35 people by 1948.

Many people came to Durham to learn the beautician trade by attending the commercial hair care school established by Jacqueline DeShazor. Beginning in three rooms, she expanded in 1945 to 36 rooms in a three-story building, which she purchased for $42,500.

African American businesses were so stable and looked so promising for the future that, in 1924, Durham was chosen as the location for the headquarters of the National Negro Finance Corporation, which was capitalized at $1 million. The organization was started to provide working capital to individuals, firms, and corporations in all parts of the country. Durham, from the turn of the century until the 1950s, remained unrivaled as the black business capital of America.

Present-Day Durham

Today, 150 or so black entrepreneurs and professionals are still held together by the Durham Business and Professional Chain, an organization founded more than 50 years ago. It would be difficult, however, to replicate the entrepreneurial excitement that existed in Durham between 1900 and 1950. Indeed, scholars have noted that grass roots entrepreneurship tends to develop quickly by groups who newly enter the economy of a country, as did African Americans after the abolition of slavery. However, from generation to generation, there is typically a decrease in the number or rate of entrepreneurs. In the case of African Americans, a full blown civil rights movement was required to create another surge in the entrepreneurial spirit.

◆ BLACK ENTREPRENEURS IN THE POST-CIVIL RIGHTS ERA

The civil rights movement prompted the development of legislation and a number of government agencies to ensure the social, political, and economic rights of African Americans. Perhaps the greatest boost to black entrepreneurship came in 1967 with the establishment of the Small Business Administration (SBA) Section 8 (a) program. Under Section 8 (a) of the Small Business Act Amendments (Pub.L. 90-104), the SBA is authorized to enter into contract with federal agencies on behalf of small and disadvantaged businesses. Entry into the 8 (a) program is contingent upon SBA approval of the business plan prepared by prospective firms. The total dollar value of contracts processed through Section 8 (a) has grown from $8.9 million in 1969 to $2.7 billion in 1985. Through the program, many small and black-owned businesses have been able to stabilize and grow.

Another product of the civil rights movement has been the 1977 Public Works Employment Act (Pub.L. 95-28). Supplementing the SBA 8 (a) Program, the Public Works Act requires that all general contractors bidding for public works projects allocate at least 10 percent of their contracts to minority sub-contractors.

During the early 1980s, the SBA Section 8 (a) program was criticized because less than 5 percent of the firms have achieved open-market competitiveness, which implies that the program is in effect assisting the marginal entrepreneur, as opposed to the promising self-employed minority businessperson.

The fundamental concept of set-aside minority assistance programs was called into question during the height of the Reagan-Bush era. In 1989, the landmark U.S. Supreme Court ruling in *City of Richmond v. Croson* struck down as unconstitutional under the Fourteenth Amendment a city ordinance of Richmond, Virginia requiring that 30 percent of each public construction contract to be set aside for minority businesses. The Supreme Court did make a distinction between local/state and federally enacted business development programs, holding that the U.S. Congress has far more authority than the states in formulating remedial legislation.

The *Croson* decision has had a devastating impact on minority businesses. In Richmond, during the month of July 1987 when a lower court first ruled against the city's set-aside program, 40 percent of the city's total construction dollars were allocated for products and services provided by minority-owned construction firms. Immediately following the court's decision, the minority businesses' share of contracts fell to 15 percent, dropping to less than 3 percent by the end of 1988. In Tampa, Florida the number of contracts awarded to black-owned companies decreased 99 percent, and contracts with Latino-owned firms fell 50 percent, after *Croson*. Such dramatic decreases in contracts awarded to minority businesses occurred throughout the country. More than 33 states and political subdivisions have taken steps to dismantle their racial/ethnic set-aside programs; more than 70 jurisdictions are conducting studies and/or holding hearings to review and evaluate their programs in light of *Croson*.

Growth Industries

Historically, African American businesses have been restricted to the narrow range of service enterprises. They have tended to establish businesses that require relatively limited capital and technical expertise—personal services, and small-scale retailing. These firms have had to rely heavily on the African American community as their market for goods and services.

Recent business initiation trends indicate increasing diversity among black businesses. An examination of the nation's largest black owned corporations reveals considerable diversity.

The location of corporate headquarters in urban areas has provided increased business opportunity for black business service enterprises. Large cities have become areas where administrative and service functions are the dominant economic activities. The growth in corporate and government administration in central city business districts has created a need for complementary advertising, accounting, computer, legal, temporary secretarial, and maintenance business services. Employment in such business firms owned by African Americans grew by 224 percent between 1972 and 1987; the number of firms increased nearly five times, and gross receipts grew by 700 percent.

◆ RECENT TRENDS

Since 1962, the Bureau of the Census has published a survey of minority-owned businesses every five years. The most recent survey, from 1987, indicates that African Americans owned 424,165 businesses, a 37.6 percent increase from 308,260 in 1982, and nearly an 85 percent increase from the 1977 total of 231,203. The 37.6 percent increase between 1982 and 1987 is greater than the 26.2 percent increase for all U.S. forms for this time period. These numbers indicate that African Americans are starting business enterprises at a greater rate than Americans in general.

Gross Receipts and Legal Organization

According to the Bureau of the Census, the overwhelming majority of black-owned firms, 94.4 percent or 400,339 firms, operated as sole proprietorships in 1987; this is consistent with 1982 and 1977 statistics in which 95 percent and 94.3 percent of black-owned firms were sole proprietorships. Partnerships represented 2.7 percent or 11,261 firms in 1987, and 3.3 percent in 1982. Subchapter S corporations (corporations with fewer than 35 stockholders, which are not taxed as regular corporations, but provide legal liability protection to shareholders) accounted for 3 percent of the total number of black-owned firms in 1987.

By 1987, the total gross receipts (the total amount of money received before deductions for expenses and taxes) for African American businesses also increased. From 1982 to 1987, receipts increased by 105 percent, from $9.6 billion to $19.8 billion. However, gross receipts were unevenly distributed among firms in 1987. Only 0.5 percent of the total number of black-owned firms grossed $1 million or more; these firms accounted for 37 percent of the total gross receipts. Slightly more than a third (35 percent) of the firms had gross receipts of less than $5,000; the average annual gross receipt for a black-owned business was approximately $47,000.

There is a direct correlation between the organizational structure of black businesses and receipts. Sole proprietorships earned relatively less money. Sole proprietorship accounted for 50.9 percent of gross receipts

Historically, black-owned firms have been concentrated in a narrow range of service business, including small restaurants.

in 1987, compared to 68.4 percent in 1982 and 55.7 percent in 1977. Partnerships accounted for 10 percent of the gross receipts in 1987, down from 13.7 percent in 1982.

In contrast, while Subchapter S corporations accounted for only 3 percent of the total number of firms, such corporations accounted for 39.2 percent of the gross receipts. This is up from 1.7 percent of the firms and 17.2 percent of the gross receipts in 1982. Thus, the real increase in gross receipts among black-owned businesses has occurred among subchapter S corporations.

Geographic Distribution of Black Businesses

The geographic concentration of black firms coincides with the African American population concentration. California had the greatest number of black-owned firms in 1987, with 47,728. California firms' gross receipts were $2.4 billion. New York was second with 36,289 firms and $1.9 billion in gross receipts. Slightly less than 44 percent of black-owned firms and 44.7 percent of gross receipts (185,563 firms and $8.8 billion in gross receipts) were concentrated in California, New York, Texas, Florida, Georgia, and Illinois.

The next tier of states includes Michigan with 13,708 firms that grossed $701.3 million; Maryland, with 21,678 businesses and nearly $720 million in receipts; and Pennsylvania, with 11,728 businesses that grossed $747.5 million.

The District of Columbia had the greatest share of firms owned by African Americans, with 28.3 percent of the firms and 6.3 percent of the gross receipts in that city. Black-owned firms had the smallest share of business in Montana, with 0.1 percent of the firms and gross receipts.

Size of Firm and Industry Characteristics

Only a modest portion of firms owned by African Americans have paid employees; in 1987, 83.3 percent of black-owned firms had no paid employees. The 16.7 percent of black-owned firms with paid employees, however, accounted for 71.5 percent of the gross receipts. There were 189 firms with 100 or more employees, which accounted for $2 billion in gross receipts, or 14.2 percent of the total receipts of black-owned employer firms.

Historically, black-owned firms have been concentrated in a narrow range of service businesses including small restaurants, cleaning establishments, funeral parlors, shoe shops, hair salons, and gas stations. The trend, by and large, continued throughout the late 1980s. Service industries accounted for 49 percent of all black-owned firms, and 31 percent of the gross receipts. Retail trade comprised the next greatest concentration of black-owned firms, with 15.6 percent of the firms and 29.8 percent of the gross receipts. The industry that grossed the greatest total receipts in 1987 was automobile dealers and service stations, with nearly $2.2 billion in earnings.

◆ ENTREPRENEURIAL GATEKEEPERS

Wally Amos (1936-)
Entrepreneur

Wallace Amos, Jr. was born in Tallahassee, Florida on July 1, 1937 and grew up there until his parents divorced when he was 12. Following his parents divorce, he went to New York City to live with his Aunt Della. She loved to cook and often made Amos her special chocolate chip cookies. After spending several years in New York City, he dropped out of high school to join the U.S. Air Force, where he earned his high school equivalency degree.

Upon discharge from the Air Force, Amos achieved success as the first African American talent agent for the William Morris Agency. Starting there as a mail clerk, he quickly worked his way up to executive vice

The growth in corporate and government administration has created a need for complementary advertising, accounting, computer, legal, and temporary secretarial services.

president. While there he "discovered" Simon & Garfunkel for the agency and has been the agent for such well known acts and entertainers as the Supremes, the Temptations, Marvin Gaye, Dionne Warwick, and Patti Labelle.

In 1975 Amos founded Famous Amos Chocolate Chip Cookies. Based on his Aunt Della's recipe, the cookies became a nationwide success as they spread across the country from his original store on Sunset Boulevard in Los Angeles. By 1980 Amos was selling 5 million dollars worth of cookies each year and his operation had expanded to include a large production facility in Nutley, New Jersey. Amos's success and expansion was enhanced by the backing of such well known entertainers as Bill Cosby and Helen Reddy. In 1985 Amos became vice-chairman of the company and served in that capacity until 1989. Amos left the Famous Amos Cookie Corporation in 1989 following a dispute with a group of investors and financial difficulties. He began a new business, Wally Amos Presents ... Chip & Cookie, in 1990. In 1993, Amos started yet another company, Uncle Noname Cookie Company, and serves as its president. Uncle Noname Cookie Company, based in Honolulu, Hawaii, specializes in five varieties of gourmet cookies.

Proceeds from the sale of Uncle Noname cookies are donated to the support of Cities in Schools, a national dropout-prevention program of which he is a member of the board of directors.

Amos has donated personal items to the Business Americana Collection at the Smithsonian's Collection of Advertising History and received the Presidential Award for Entrepreneurial Excellence Award from President Ronald Reagan in 1986. In 1987, he received a citation from the Horatio Alger Association. Amos serves as a national spokesperson for Literacy Volunteers of America.

James Pierson Beckwourth (1798-1866)
Author, Trapper, Entrepreneur

Jim Beckwourth was born on April 26, 1798, near Fredericksburg, Virginia. His father was a landowner and member of a prominent Virginia family; his mother was an African American woman, possibly a slave. The family moved to a farm near St. Charles, Missouri in 1806 and Jim attended school in St. Louis from 1810 to 1814. He was apprenticed to a St. Louis blacksmith but soon found himself heading west. Like many other events in Beckwourth's life there are conflicting stories

Wally Amos

James Beckwourth

concerning the dissolution of the apprenticeship. Evidently at this time Beckwourth also changed the spelling of his last name.

In 1824, Beckwourth joined a westward bound fur trapping and trading expedition under the leadership of William Henry Ashley. Beckwourth soon became known as a man of many adventures and exploits. Although the basis of these stories are factual many, with Beckwourth's approval, have been greatly exaggerated. Nevertheless he undoubtedly embodied the spirit of the legendary mountain men of the American west. In 1827, while still engaged in the fur trade he married a Blackfoot Indian woman. In 1829, he took refuge from a debt collector by hiding with the Crow Indians where he married again. It must be remembered that marriage on the frontier was a much less formal arrangement than it is today. Beckwourth claims he was made a Crow chief in recognition of his fighting prowess against the Blackfeet.

By 1837, Beckwourth was with the U.S. Army in Florida serving as a scout during the Seminole wars. He soon returned to the Rocky Mountains, married a woman in New Mexico, and, in 1842, opened a trading post near what is now Pueblo, Colorado. Between 1844 and 1850, he fought in the California uprising against Mexico

and the Mexican-American War. In 1850, Beckwourth joined the California gold rush and while in the Sierra Nevadas discovered a mountain pass that bears his name today. He made the gap more passable, opened an inn, and, by 1851, was guiding wagon trains through the pass.

Beckwourth's memoirs, entitled *Life and Adventures of James P. Beckwourth, Mountaineer, Scout and Pioneer*, were in part ghost written by T.D. Bonner and published in 1856. Beckwourth traveled to St. Louis and Kansas City where the popularity of his book enhanced his reputation and he was regarded as somewhat of a celebrity. Beckwourth returned to Denver, married again, opened a trading post, and was acquitted on a charge of manslaughter. Tiring of city life he signed on with the Army as a scout and fought the Cheyenne Indians. Beckwourth probably died of food poisoning on or around September 25, 1866 while riding to a Crow encampment. Accounts of his purposely being poisoned by Crows are largely discounted today.

Dave Bing (1943-)
Business Executive, Former Professional Basketball Player

Dave Bing

Bing was born November 29, 1943, in Washington, D.C., where he played basketball at Springarn High School. He was named to play on a national All-Star team and was voted most valuable player on the tour. Bing attended Syracuse University on a basketball scholarship graduating in 1966 with a B.A. in economics. He was the second overall pick in the 1966 National Basketball Association draft and was chosen by the Detroit Pistons.

During his first season he was the league's top rookie and the league's high scorer his second year. In the 1974-1975 season Bing played for the Washington, D.C., Bullets and in the 1977-1978 season he was with the Boston Celtics. Bing was voted the league's Most Valuable Player in 1976 and played in seven NBA All-Star games. The Professional Basketball Writer's Association of America gave him their Citizenship Award in 1977. Bing was named National Minority Small Businessperson of the Year in 1984. In 1990 he was elected to the Naismith Memorial Basketball Hall of Fame.

After being associated with management programs at the National Bank of Detroit, Chrysler Corporation, and Paragon Steel, Bing formed Bing Steel Inc. in Detroit, a very successful steel supplier to the automobile industry.

Bing has served on the board of directors of Children's Hospital of Detroit, Michigan Association of Retarded Children and Adults, Black United Fund, Detroit Urban League, and the March of Dimes.

Marie Dutton Brown (1940-)
Entrepreneur

Marie Brown's career is a picture book example of the kind of tenacious nature entrepreneurs need to have, and how to expand on opportunities when they present themselves. She received a degree in psychology in 1962, from Penn State University, where she was part of the one percent of the student body's African American population. She went to work as a social studies teacher in the Philadelphia public school system. Two years later, when a salesperson from a publishing firm in New York came to sell her some of his company's titles for the school, the meeting turned into a job offer to work for Doubleday.

Brown stayed at Doubleday for two years, then moved to Los Angeles with her new husband. She moved back to New York in 1972 and returned to Doubleday as an associate editor. During the 1970s, as an interest in African American literary titles grew, so grew Brown's position, as she brought many ethnic titles to print.

In 1980, Brown quit Doubleday to become founding editor of *Elan* magazine, which focused on the cultural life of the international black community. After only three issues were launched, Brown's financial backers pulled out, leaving Brown jobless. She went to work at a bookstore, giving her first-hand retail experience.

In the fall of 1984, Brown started her own business, Marie Brown Associates, a literary agency that was run from Brown's Harlem apartment. Although, like any new business venture, times were lean for several years, things started to turn around as Brown began signing more and more writers through her agency. As the 1990s began, the larger publishing houses began courting African American writers, but Brown was far ahead of them, as one of only five African American literary agents in the country. Brown still contributes her time to the community, sitting on several boards, including the Studio Museum of Harlem.

Malcolm CasSelle (1970-)
Computer Entrepreneur

Born on March 22, 1970, in Allentown, Pennsylvania, CasSelle has accomplished a great deal at a young age. Growing up in Allentown, Pennsylvania, CasSelle developed a passion for writing computer programs in high school. CasSelle attended and graduated from Massachusetts Institute of Technology (MIT).

CasSelle left for Japan three days after finishing his undergraduate work in order to enter MIT's Japan program. While overseas, he worked for Shroders Securities and NTT Software Labs. Upon his return to the United States he took a job with Apple Computers. After earning his master's at Stanford, he occupied the position of director of digital publishing and marketing for Blast Publishing. CasSelle would later introduce E. David Ellington, his partner, to the wonders of cyberspace.

Along with Ellington, CasSelle cofounded NetNoir Inc., an African American-oriented online site. Based in San Francisco and available through America Online, NetNoir explores a wide range of news and information. *Vibe* magazine, along with Motown Records and the clothing company Blue Marlin all channel their through services or goods through CasSelle's cybersite.

Comer Cottrell (1931-)
Entrepreneur

Cottrell was born in Mobile, Alabama, on December 7, 1931. He began his sales career at the age of eight, joining his father for visits to clients selling insurance. Cottrell continued his sales career at Sears Roebuck after graduating from the University of Detroit in 1952. Years later, while managing a post exchange at a military base, Cottrell observed that there were no hair products for black people. Cottrell decided to form a company that would sell products specifically for hair styles worn by African Americans.

In 1970, Cottrell began his company with an empty Los Angeles warehouse, $600, and a typewriter. He started out marketing hair spray to black beauticians and barbers. With the moderate success of this product, the Proline company was born. Five years later, Proline opened a distribution center in Birmingham, Alabama. By 1980, Proline had outgrown Los Angeles and moved to Dallas, coinciding with the release of the Curly Kit Home Permanent product. Soon Proline enjoyed sales figures in excess of $11 million dollars and began to expand into overseas markets. By 1989, Proline was ranked nineteenth on *Black Enterprise*'s list of top 100 black businesses with sales of $36 million annually.

In 1989, Cottrell became—as a member of a 14-owner consortium of investors that purchased the Texas Rangers—the first African American to own a Major League Baseball franchise. Cottrell used his position to speak out about affirmative action in professional sports. In 1990, he continued his philanthropy by purchasing the bankrupt Bishop College, a Dallas school founded by free slaves and Baptist missionaries, and he convinced Paul Quinn College to relocate from Waco, Texas, to the Bishop College grounds. In 1994, Cottrell visited South Africa as part of an envoy of black businessmen sponsored by Langston University's National Institute for the Study of Minority Enterprise to establish links with black-owned businesses there.

E. David Ellington (1960-)
Computer Entrepreneur

Ellington was born in New York, New York on July 10, 1960. Growing up in Harlem, he was raised primarily by his mother. While earning his undergraduate degree at Adelphi University, which he received in 1981, Ellington worked in the office of a U.S. congressman. In 1983, he received his master's from Howard University, then spent a great deal of his time travelling in places like Europe, Japan, China, and India. Later, he earned his law degree from Georgetown University. He founded the Law Offices of E. David Ellington and chaired for the International Law Section of the Beverly Hills Bar Association.

In 1995, Ellington and computer entrepreneur, Malcolm CasSelle, cofounded NetNoir Online, a black-oriented site on the Internet. Billing itself as "The Cybergateway to Afrocentric Culture," NetNoir explores a wide range of news and information. Participants include journalist Charlayne Hunter-Gault and athlete Carl Lewis. Extremely innovative, NetNoir was named one of the "25 Cool Companies of the Year" by *Fortune* magazine. With minority investors, NetNoir News Media Services planned to venture into CD-ROMs and the designing of web sites in 1996.

Ann Marie Fudge (1951-)
Corporate Executive

Ann Marie Fudge was born in Washington, D.C., in 1951. She received a bachelor's of arts with honors from Simmons College in 1973 and an Master's of Business Administration from Harvard Business School in 1977. She began her business career at General Electric in 1973 as a manpower specialist, where she worked until 1975, when she received a job at General Mills in Minneapolis. There she began as a marketing assistant until she was promoted to assistant product manager in 1977, product manager in 1980, and marketing director in 1983. She remained in that position until she joined Kraft General Foods in 1986.

At Kraft, Fudge started out as the associate director of strategic planning, but by 1989, her worth to the company earned her a vice-presidency in charge of marketing and development of the Dinners and Enhancers Division working on products, such as Log Cabin Syrup, Minute Rice, and Stove Top Stuffing. She managed to reposition the products in the overburdened food market and increased sales. She moved up to general manager of that division in 1991, and executive vice president in 1994. That year Fudge took over as president of Kraft's struggling Maxwell House Coffee division.

Fudge has served as president and vice president of the Executive Leadership Council and holds memberships with the National Black MBA Association and the Junior League. She serves on the board of directors for Allied Signal Inc., Liz Clairborne Inc., Simmons College, Harvard Business School, and the Catalyst Advisory Board. She was a COGME Fellow in 1975 and won a Leadership Award from the Young Women's Christian Association in 1979.

Arthur G. Gaston (1892-1996)
Entrepreneur

Arthur G. Gaston was the living embodiment of what makes up an entrepreneur. He had stated many times in interviews, that one of his primary rules for business success is "Find a need and fill it." Gaston's business accomplishments are a testimony to the man's lifelong adherence to this rule. He started his business career in 1923 by founding the Booker T. Washington Burial Society, guaranteeing African Americans a decent burial. In 1932 it had grown large enough to be incorporated. In 1930, Smith and Gaston Funeral Directors was formed to complement the services of the burial society. The "Smith" was A. L. Smith, Gaston's father-in-law, who helped him financially get started in business.

Finding it hard to staff his growing company with skilled clerical employees, Gaston started the Booker T. Washington Business College in 1939. The college provided a place where African American students could learn proficiency in working on business machines. (The school continues to this day.)

In 1946, Gaston started the Brown Belle Bottling Company, offering Joe Louis Punch. Next came a cemetery in 1947, a motel in 1954, an investment firm in 1955, a savings and loan association in 1957, a senior citizens home in 1963, two radio stations in 1975. In 1986, at the hearty age of 94, Gaston opened the A. G. Gaston Construction Company. From the original burial society in 1923 to his sprawling empire seven decades later, bringing in more than $24 million in revenues in 1991, Arthur Gaston was the quintessential self-made man. Gaston died in his hometown of Birmingham, Alabama, at the age of 103.

Archibald H. Grimké (1849-1930)
Lawyer, Writer, Activist, Diplomat

Archibald Grimké was born on a plantation near Charleston, South Carolina, in 1849. His father was a successful lawyer who had given up his profession to become a planter. His mother had been a family slave and served as the nurse for Henry Grimké's first wife, Selena. Archibald was considered a slave due to South Carolina law at the time. He, along with his mother and siblings, were passed on to relatives after his father's death. Grimké attended a special school during his youth. He later fled his home. Grimké enrolled in a school directed by Frances Pillsbury and impressed the instructors there with his superior academic abilities. He completed undergraduate studies in only three years and obtained his master's degree from Lincoln University two years following that, in 1872.

Grimké moved to Boston and practiced law there from 1875 to 1883. Beginning in 1885, he presided over the Women's Suffrage Association of Massachusets. In the early 1890's, Grimké wrote for Boston-area publications, before being appointed the American consul for Santo Domingo (now the Dominican Republic) for four years. He then assumed the presidential role for the Washington chapter of the NAACP while writing, lecturing, and presiding over the American Negro Academy. Grimké write several books, including biographies of William Lloyd Garrison in 1891 and Charles Sumner in 1892, and numerous essays and speeches.

Robert Holland, Jr. (1940-)
Business Executive

Robert Holland, Jr. was born in April of 1940, in Albion, Michigan. Holland earned a bachelor's of science in mechanical engineering from Union College in Schenectady, New York in 1961, and in 1963, he completed a master's of business administration in international marketing at Bernard Baruch Graduate School of Manhattan. In 1968, Holland moved from his job at the Mobil Oil Co. as an engineer and sales manager to join the McKinsey & Co. consulting firm, where he worked as an associate and eventually a partner until 1981. During that time, he worked abroad in the Netherlands, England, Mexico, and Brazil. He returned to Michigan in 1981 as CEO of City Marketing, a beverage distributor. In 1987, he switched companies again, accepting the chair position for Gilreath Manufacturing, Inc. in Howell, Michigan, a manufacturer of plastic injection molds.

In 1991, Holland started Rohker-J Inc. in White Plains, New York, a company of his own that bought struggling companies, turning them around, and selling them. In 1994, Holland's business savvy and his whimsy with poetic verse won him a position as president and CEO of Ben & Jerry's Homemade Ice Cream, Inc. In addition to his work for Ben & Jerry's, Holland sits on the board of directors for the Harlem Junior Tennis

Program, UNC Ventures, and Atlanta University Center. He's chairman of the board at Spelman College.

George E. Johnson (1927-)
Business Executive

Johnson was born in Richton, Mississippi on June 16, 1927. He attended Wendell Phillips High School in Chicago then went to work as a production chemist for a firm that produced cosmetic products for African Americans. While there, he developed a hair straightener for men and began marketing it himself in 1954. By 1957 he had formed Johnson Products and was selling products under the Ultra-Sheen label. The company prospered and by 1971 its stock was being traded on the American Stock Exchange. Johnson Products was the first African American owned company to trade on a major stock exchange. In June, 1993 Joan B. Johnson, chair and CEO of Johnson Products, announced the sale of the company to Ivax Corp., a white-owned pharmaceutical firm. Johnson Products was officially sold to Ivax in August, 1993.

Johnson has served as a director of the Independence Bank of Chicago, the U.S. Postal Service and the Commonwealth Edison Co. Johnson also is responsible for

George E. Johnson

the George E. Johnson Foundation which funds charitable and educational programs for African Americans.

Johnson has received the Abraham Lincoln Center's Humanitarian Service Award (1972), *Ebony* magazine's Black Achievement Award (1978) and the public service award presented by the Harvard Club of Chicago. He has also been awarded the Horatio Alger Award (1980) and the Babson Medal (1983).

Johnson has received honorary degrees from many institutions of learning including Chicago State University (1977), Fisk University (1977) and the Tuskegee Institute (1978).

Dennis Kimbro (1950-)
Author, Educator, Motivational Speaker

Dennis Paul Kimbro was born on December 29, 1950, in Jersey City, New Jersey. He graduated from Oklahoma University with a bachelor's in 1972 and later from Northwestern University with a Ph.D. in political economy in 1984, while working as a salesperson at Smithkline Beckman pharmaceutical corporation. In 1987, he left Smithkline to work at ABC Management Consultants Inc. until 1991. Meanwhile, Kimbro worked at revising a manuscript left to publisher W. Clement Stone written by the late Napoleon Hill, the author of *Think and Grow Rich*. Hill had been working on a version for a black audience when he died. Stone gave the manuscript to Kimbro. Kimbro interviewed many successful black Americans to chart how they managed to maximize potential and channel positive thinking to build their success.

In 1991, Kimbro's book—co-authored originally by Hill—*Think and Grow Rich: A Black's Choice* was published by Ballantine Books and became the first ever major release black self-help book. In the next two years, the book sold more than 250,000 copies and was a best seller among black audiences, earning Kimbro an Award of Excellence from the Texas Association of Black Personnel in Higher Education in 1992. Kimbro already held a Dale Carnegie Personal Achievement award from 1988. In 1992, Kimbro accepted a post as associate professor and director of the Center for Entrepreneurship at Clark Atlanta University School of Business and Administration. *Daily Motivations for African-American Success*, Kimbro's second book, was published by Ballantine in 1993.

Reginald F. Lewis (1942-1993)
Business Executive

Lewis was born December 7, 1942, in Baltimore, Maryland. He received an A.B. from Virginia State Col-

Reginald Lewis

lege in 1965 and a law degree from Harvard Law School in 1968. He first worked with the firm of Paul, Weiss, Rifkind, Wharton & Garrison until 1970. He was a partner in Murphy, Thorpe & Lewis, the first African American law firm on Wall Street until 1973. Between 1973 and 1989 Lewis was in private practice as a corporate lawyer. In 1989 he became president and CEO of TLC Beatrice International Holdings Inc. With TLC's leveraged acquisition of the Beatrice International Food Co. Lewis became the head of the largest African American owned business in the United States. TLC Beatrice had revenues of $1.54 billion in 1992.

Lewis was a member of the American and National Bar Associations and the National Conference of Black Lawyers. He was on the board of directors of the New York City Off-Track Betting Corp., the Central Park Conservance, the NAACP Legal Defense Fund and WNET-Channel 13, the public television station in New York. He was the recipient of the Distinguished Service Award presented by the American Association of MESBIC (1974) and the Black Enterprise Achievement Award for the Professions.

Lewis died unexpectedly January 19, 1993 in New York.

James B. Llewellyn (1927-)
Business Executive

James Llewellyn was born July 16, 1927, in New York City and earned a B.S. from City College of New York. He attended Columbia University's Graduate School of Business and New York University's School of Public Administration before receiving a degree from New York Law School.

Before attending law school Llewellyn was the proprietor of a retail liquor store. While attending law school he was a student assistant in the District Attorney's Office for New York County from 1958 to 1960. After graduating he practiced law as part of Evans, Berger and Llewellyn. Between 1964 and 1969 he worked in a variety of professional positions for various governmental agencies including the Housing Division of the Housing and Re-Development Board (1964-1965), Small Business Development Corporation (1965) and the Small Business Administration (1965-1969).

In 1969, as part of a syndicate buy-out, he became president of Fedco Food Stores of New York. By 1975 the company had grown from 11 to 14 stores and had annual revenues of $30 million and 450 employees.

James B. Llewellyn

Llewellyn has served on the boards of the City College of New York and its Graduate Center, American Can Co., American Capital Management Research and the Freedom National Bank. He has belonged to the Harlem Lawyers Association, the New York Interracial Council for Business Opportunity and the New York Urban Coalition and its Venture Capital Corporation.

Llewellyn has honorary doctorates from Wagner College, City University of New York and Atlanta University. He spent four years in the U.S. Army Corps of Engineers from 1944 to 1948. He is currently CEO of Queen City Broadcasting Inc.

Rose Meta Morgan (1912?-)
Entrepreneur

Rose Meta Morgan was born c. 1912 in Shelby, Mississippi, but spent most of her growing years in Chicago. She started her own business at the early age of ten, making and selling artificial flowers door-to-door with the assistance of other neighborhood children. By the age of 14, she was earning money styling hair. Morgan claims she was a high school drop out even though she may have actually finished. Either way, she attended Morris School of Beauty, and after graduating, she rented space in a salon and began styling, grooming, and cutting hair full time. It was during this time that Morgan met Ethel Waters, a famous actress/singer, during a run of performances in Chicago in 1938. Waters invited Morgan to New York because of the stylist's prowess in hair design.

Within six months of moving to New York, Morgan opened her own beauty shop. Later, running out of room, she signed a ten-year lease for an old dilapidated mansion and began to renovate it. Three years later, Morgan's salon—the Rose Meta Morgan House of Beauty—was the most prestigious, most successful African American beauty salon in the world. By 1946, she drew 1,000 customers a week and increased her staff to 29 people, including a nurse and masseurs. Morgan began producing and selling a line of cosmetics and hosting fashion shows that matured into major social events at the Renaissance Casino and Rockford Plaza in Harlem. Soon she was considered one of the richest businesswomen in New York. Customers came from all over the country to visit the House of Beauty, and Morgan travelled abroad with her cosmetics, fashion designs, and ideas about beauty and women of color.

In the mid-1950s, Morgan bought and refurbished a new building for the House of Beauty. Thousands of people attended the grand opening and the building was dedicated by the New York City Mayor's wife. The new salon offered more features, such as a dressmaking department, a charm school, and a fitness department and later a wig salon to cash in on the renewed popularity in hair pieces. In 1965, Morgan created the Freedom National Bank, New York's only commercial bank run by and for black people. In 1972, Morgan created the Trim-Away Figure Contouring business, and shortly thereafter, in the 1980s, she retired with a salon and a set of businesses as a legacy that are the only ones of their kind in the world.

Morgan's marriages were less successful than her businesses. In 1955, she married Joe Louis, the heavyweight boxing champion of the world. But in 1957, they separated and their marriage was annulled in 1958. Later, Morgan married lawyer Louis Saunders, and though they separated in the early 1960s, Saunders died before they were divorced.

Henry G. Parks (1916-)
Entrepreneur, Business Executive

Parks was born September 20, 1916, in Atlanta, Georgia. He received a B.S. from Ohio State University and did graduate work there in marketing.

After graduating Parks worked at the Resident War Production Training Center in Wilberforce, Ohio, where he was associated with Dr. Mary McLeod Bethune. In 1939 he was a national sales representative for the Pabst Brewing Co. In addition he has been involved in a variety of enterprises including theatrical bookings in New York City, a failed attempt at marketing a beverage with Joe Louis, the former heavyweight boxing champion (now deceased), real estate, drug store operations and cement block production, mostly in Baltimore, Maryland.

Parks ultimately bought into Crayton's Southern Sausage Company of Cleveland, Ohio. After becoming familiar with the meat packing industry he sold his interest in the company for a profit. In 1951 he started H. G. Parks Inc., a sausage packer and distributor with the aid of a group of investors. By 1971 the company had annual revenues of $10.4 million dollars and was distributing its products to over 12,000 east coast stores.

Parks has also been vice-president of the Chamber of Commerce of Metropolitan Baltimore, served on the board of directors of Magnavox, held a seat on the Baltimore City Council and has an interest in Tuesday Publications.

Richard Dean Parsons (1948-)
Corporate Executive

Born in the Bedford-Stuyvesant neighborhood of Brooklyn, New York on April 4, 1948, Richard Dean Parsons grew up in the borough of Queens, New York. He graduated from high school at the age of 16 and attended the University of Hawaii, where he played varsity basketball. He earned a bachelor's from the university in 1968, and continued his education at the Union University of the University of Albany Law School. He graduated at the top of his class and received the highest score on the state bar exam in 1971.

Parsons started his career as a member of New York governor Nelson Rockefeller's legal staff, where he served when Rockefeller became vice president of the United States under Gerald Ford in 1974. He continued in this capacity, also providing legal counsel for President Ford as deputy counsel and then as associate director of the domestic council. He left government service in 1977, to join the New York City law firm, Patterson, Belknap, Webb & Tyler, where he became a partner in 1979. He defended clients, such as Happy Rockefeller and Estee Lauder.

Parsons was appointed chief operating officer of the Dime Savings Bank of New York in 1988, becoming the first black man to manage a financial institution of Dime's size. Parsons lead the bank to a comeback from severe debt. In 1993, because of Parsons's remarkable leadership skills, newly-elected Mayor Rudolph Giuliani chose Parsons to head his transition council and later to be the Deputy Mayor for Economic Development. Parsons instead chose to act as chairman of the Economic Development Corporation for the city. Parsons, no stranger to sitting on boards of directors, has served on boards for Time Warner Inc., Philip Morris, Tristar Pictures, Howard University, and the Metropolitan Museum of Art. Due to these ties, Parsons took an offered position as president of Time Warner Inc. in January of 1995. Parsons has also served as a member of the presidential Drug Task Force, as chairperson of Wildcat Service Organization, and as a member of the board of the New York Zoological Society.

Naomi R. Sims (1949-)
Business Executive, Model

Sims was born March 30, 1949, in Oxford, Mississippi. She attended New York University, where she studied psychology, and the Fashion Institute of Technology, where she graduated in 1967

Sims was a fashion model with the Ford Agency in New York from 1970 to 1973. She was the first African American woman to be a high fashion model and the first to appear in a television commercial. She also appeared on the cover of *Life* Magazine.

In 1970 Sims also started lecturing and writing fashion and beauty articles on a free-lance basis. In 1973 she co-developed a new fiber for her line of wigs and founded the Naomi Sims Collection which by 1977 had annual revenues of $4 million. Sims has also written a number of books including, *All About Health and Beauty for the Black Woman* (1975), *How to Be a Top Model*

Naomi Sims

(1979), *All About Hair Care for the Black Woman* (1982), and *All About Success for the Black Woman.*

In 1969 and 1970 Sims was voted Model of the Year by International Mannequins and won the *Ladies Home Journal* Women of Achievement Award. For her work with underprivileged children in Bedford-Stuyvesant, she also won an award from the New York City Board of Education. In 1977 Sims was voted into the Modeling Hall of Fame by International Mannequins and made the International Best Dressed List 1971-73, 1976-77. Sims has also received recognition for her fund raising efforts for sickle cell anemia and cancer research. She belongs to the NAACP and works closely with drug rehabilitation programs.

She is currently with Naomi Sims Beauty Products Limited in New York City.

Percy E. Sutton (1920-)
Business Executive, Attorney

Sutton was born November 24, 1920 in San Antonio, Texas. He graduated from the Phillis Wheatley High School and attended a number of colleges including Prairie View College, Tuskegee Institute and the Hamp-

Percy Sutton

ton Institute. His education was interrupted by World War II when Sutton enlisted in the U.S. Army Air Corps. He was promoted to captain and served as a combat intelligence officer in the Italian and Mediterranean theaters. He was decorated with Combat Stars for his service.

After his discharge Sutton, attended law school on the G.I. Bill, first at Columbia University in New York, and then Brooklyn Law School where he received an LL.B. in 1950. During the Korean conflict Sutton re-enlisted in the USAF and served as an intelligence officer and a trial judge advocate.

Returning to civilian life, he opened a law office in Harlem with his brother and another attorney. In 1964, he was elected to the New York State Assembly, where he served until 1966. In 1966, he was appointed and later elected to the office of president of the Borough of Manhattan, a post he held until 1977.

Sutton then founded the Inner-City Broadcasting Corporation, from which he retired in 1990.

Sutton has been a civil rights advocate both as an attorney and a politician. He was a national director of the Urban League and a past president of the New York

branch of the NAACP. He was voted Assemblyman of the Year by the Intercollegiate Legislative Assembly in 1966. Sutton has also served as a director of the Museum of the City of New York and the American Museum of Natural History.

Madame C. J. Walker (1867-1919)
Entrepreneur

Walker was born Sarah Breedlove near Delta, Louisiana, in 1867. She was orphaned as a child, raised by a sister in Vicksburg, Mississippi, married at the age of 14, and widowed in 1887 at the age of 20.

Walker moved with her daughter to St. Louis where she earned a living by taking in laundry and sewing. By 1905 she had become interested in hair care products for African American women and began working on a hot comb and her "Wonderful Hair Grower." In 1906 she moved to Denver and, with $1.50 in her pocket, started a hair preparations company. She soon married C. J. Walker, a newspaperman who taught her the fundamentals of advertising and mail order promotion. In 1908 she moved with her daughter to Pittsburgh where she founded a beauty school which trained cosmetologists in the use of her products.

In 1910, with a more central location in mind, she moved to Indianapolis, Indiana where she established a laboratory and factory and developed a nationwide network of 5000 sales agents, mostly African American women.

Her business prospered and Walker became very wealthy. She had a townhouse in Harlem and a custom built mansion on the Hudson River near Irvington, New York. She died in New York on May 25, 1919.

Walker was a strong believer in self-reliance and education. She was proud of her accomplishments, especially of providing employment for thousands of African Americans who might otherwise have had less meaningful jobs. Walker was also a genius at marketing, promotion, and mail order sales. Beneficiaries of her estate included Mary McLeod Bethune's school in Daytona, Florida and other African American schools, the NAACP and the Frederick Douglass home restoration project in Florida.

Maggie Lena Walker (1867-1934)
Banker

Walker was born on or around July 15, 1867 in Richmond, Virginia. She was the daughter of Elizabeth Draper, a former slave, and Eccles Cuthbert, a New York journalist of Irish extraction.

Walker attended Richmond public schools including Armstrong Normal School which functioned as a high

Maggie L. Walker

school. After graduating in 1883 she taught in the Richmond schools for three years before marrying building contractor Armstead Walker in 1886.

While she had been in school, Walker joined the Grand United Order of Saint Luke, a mutual aid society that served as an insurance underwriter for African Americans. Walker became active in the organization and held a number of lesser positions before becoming the Right Worthy Grand Secretary in 1899. She soon changed the name of the organization to the Independent Order of Saint Luke and moved its headquarters to Richmond.

In 1903 she became the head of the Saint Luke Penny Bank and the first woman in the United States to hold such a position. Although legally separate, the bank had a close financial association with the Independent Order of Saint Luke. The bank later became the Saint Luke Bank and Trust Company and finally the Consolidated Bank and Trust Company.

By 1924 under Walker's guidance, the Order had a membership of 100,000, a new headquarters building, over 200 employees and its own newspaper—the *Saint Luke Herald.*

Walker was active in many other organizations including the National Association of Colored Women, the Virginia Federation of Colored Women's Clubs and its Industrial School for Colored Girls. In 1912 she founded the Richmond Council of Colored Women and was a founding member of the Negro Organization Society, a blanket association for African American clubs and organizations.

She was a board member of the NAACP from 1923 to 1934 and the recipient of an honorary degree from Virginia Union University. In 1927 she received the Harmon Award for Distinguished Achievement. Walker died December 15, 1934.

15

The Family

15

The Family

◆ Family Structure and Stability ◆ Marriage ◆ Homosexuality/Bisexuality ◆ Fertility and Births
◆ Children ◆ Health ◆ Life Expectancy ◆ Exercise and Fitness
◆ Assessment ◆ Social Gatekeepers

by Faustine C. Jones-Wilson and Lorna M. Mabunda

The family, as defined by the U.S. Bureau of the Census, is a group of two or more persons (one of whom is the householder) who are related by birth, marriage, or adoption, and who reside together. In everyday social usage, this definition is usually refined to include diverse family pattern variations; however, the American value system has traditionally embraced the concept of lifetime monogamous marriage and prized the "nuclear" family pattern of husband and wife living with their own children in the same household. Yet, with divorce rates currently hovering at about 50 percent, the prevalence of this prized pattern has diminished. Fewer than 50 percent of existing American families conform to this "norm." Remarriages have created increasing numbers of "blended" families comprised of various configurations of stepparents and stepchildren. Formal adoptions of stepchildren and increasing adoptions of children from other countries are also more common today than in the past. The growth in the numbers of single-parent families headed by women has been called "one of the most startling social developments of the past quarter century."

◆ FAMILY STRUCTURE AND STABILITY

The black family's structure and status have changed dramatically over the last 40 years, and its configuration, while following the majority population's general post-World War II trends, reflects historical inequities between the races that make the African American family's security especially tenuous as the nation prepares to enter the twenty-first century. The same forces that have molded the United States into what it is today have been at work on all facets of African American family life and culture. In that sense, the fortunes of

African Americans ebb and flow with the tide of the general economic and social conditions of the nation. The African American family also faces dilemmas that emanate from its unique position and identity within American society. African Americans experience problems related to their general minority group status as well as to their unique historical experiences of slavery, oppression, second-class citizenship, and the continuing stigma related thereto.

Census data reveal that since the late 1960s the black unemployment rate has been twice as high as the white unemployment rate—no matter what the economic condition of the country. The 1970s and 1980s, however, were periods of severe economic instability and recession in the United States. African American males were particularly hard-hit by joblessness and/or underemployment during these decades due to the decline of the manufacturing industries in which many African American males were employed (the automobile and steel industries, for example). This combination of double-digit inflation and high levels of unemployment over the past two decades—"stagflation"—disproportionately eroded the purchasing power of African American families. (Robert Hill. "Critical Issues for Black Families by the Year 2000." *The State of Black America 1990.* 1989).

Income is not the only area in which African Americans lag behind whites. According to figures published in the *Dollars & Sense* (February 1996), four of every 10 black households have less than $1,000 in net worth and nearly 41 percent of black households are worth less $11,612 versus 16 percent of white houeholds. Most whites fall into the $25,000 to $49,999 net worth range. The discrepancy is partially attributed to the fact that blacks tend not to have accumulated assets to pass on

Photograph of a black family taken around the turn of the century.

the next generation through inheritance—one of the most significant ways in which people amass wealth.

While disproportionate segments of the black family are poor, significant growth in the number of middle-class and affluent African American families at the upper end of the family spectrum has occurred, particularly of younger, college-educated, dual-income, married-couple families. This growth has occurred since the opening of the opportunity structure in the mid-1960s with the passage of the Civil Rights Act of 1964 and the Voting Rights Act of 1965. Less research has been focused on these upper-strata families than on low-income black families; as a result, less is known about African American families that are prospering in the current economic climate, though they are one of the largest and fastest growing segments of the nation's consumer population.

In Feburary of 1996, Stephen Garnett of *Dollars & Sense* noted that "blacks represent less than 13 percent of the American population but exercise a purchasing power that equals the gross national product of the ninth largest country in the world." In 1994, African Americans spent $304 billion—much of it on leisure-oriented goods and services, reflecting a more sophisticated consumer. In the recent past, blacks tended to spend more on cars, furniture, and home appliances and to devoutly express brand loyalty. In the 1990s, African Americans are more apt to seek superior quality and value rather than blindly purchasing products based on established shopping habits. Support of black-owned businesses remains an issue, however.

African American families in the lower economic strata are plagued by the proliferation of their numbers headed by poor, single, never-married black females; teenage pregnancies;the shortage of marriageable, employed black males; disparities between African-American and white earning power; inadequate housing and

social services; chronic unemployment and underemployment; and rising welfare dependency. Some of the social and psychological costs of these phenomena are the crime, violence, drug abuse, and despair that are frequently endemic in many low-income communities, along with the disproportionate levels of imprisonment of black males from those communities. Also, unprecedented levels of crime and gang violence have also destabilized African-American families. With drug trafficking rampant in most inner-city areas, drug-related homicides among African Americans have reached record levels. These activities continue to have very negative impacts on black families and communities.

Some analysts place the primary blame for the deterioration of inner-city black families on public policies that are inimical to these families, or on the absence of public policies that provide corrective measures (incentives) that could empower them to help themselves. Representative of those analysts is Robert B. Hill, who in his article "Economic Forces, Structural Discrimination, and Black Family Instability" (1990), contends that "the key economic policies that undermined black family stability have been anti-inflation fiscal and monetary policies, trade policies, plant closings, social welfare, block grants, and federal per capita formulas for allocating funds to states and local areas that have not been corrected for the census undercount."

Particularly crippling in Hill's view is the absence of policy to provide affordable housing for moderate and low-income families, an absence that has a greater impact on African American families because of their unique employment and income problems. One consequence of this shortage is a return to traditional black extended or augmented family arrangements as dispossessed family members seek temporary housing with relatives and as friends share their abodes with the less-fortunate. Another consequence is that increasing numbers of black families are homeless. Hill estimated the number of homeless individuals and families in 1989 at two to three million (Hill, "Critical Issues for Black Families by the Year 2000." 1989). Many of these families, but not all, were single-parent families headed by women.

K. Sue Jewell maintains that "policies, procedures, and assumptions underlying social and economic programs in the 1960s and 1970s, the "Great Society" years, contributed to the disintegration of black two-parent and extended families and to an increase in black families headed by women." Jewel asserts that "social and economic programs and civil rights legislation could not effectively remove social barriers, which prevent black families from participating fully in mainstream American society." In her view, the liberal social policy of the Great Society era resulted in modest, not substan-

In recent years there has been significant growth in the number of middle-class and affluent African American families.

tial, gains for middle-class African-American families (K. Sue Jewell, *Survival of the Black Family: The Institutional Impact of U.S. Social Policy*, 1988).

Other scholars, many of them neoconservative or conservative in their sociopolitical orientation, continue to attribute the marked erosion in the social and economic stability of African-American families to internal factors within the families themselves, to the welfare system, and to the "Great Society" programs. For example, Irving Kristol ("Family Values: Not a Political Issues." *On the Issue* No. 55. 1992) notes that, while illegitimate births have increased startlingly since World War II, among blacks the rate had risen to 66 percent in 1992. Kristol decries the decline in "family values" among these "single moms" who, after having one illegitimate child, opt for and remain on public welfare support as they continue to produce additional children. Daniel Patrick Moynihan ("How the Great Society Destroyed the American Family." *The Public Interest* 108 (1992): 53-64) alleges that "Great Society" programs destroyed the inner-city black family structure, largely through welfare policies, and argues that social scientists still do not know what public policies will reverse the downward spiral of life conditions of inner-city black families. Moynihan enjoys reminding his readers that he had forecast the crisis in the social structure of inner-city black families in March of 1965 in his U.S. Department of Labor paper entitled "The Negro Family: The Case for National Action." Central to Moynihan's analysis and that of his neoconservative successors who have sought to understand changes in African-American community and family relations are the relationships between black family stability and male employment, unemployment, and labor force nonparticipation rates. In 1965, Moynihan and his staff reported strong indicators of change in behaviors of the black urban poor, including a rise in Aid to Families with Dependent Children (AFDC) even as the black unemployment rate declined, and an increase in the percentage of non-white married women separated from their husbands. As a result of these factors, Moynihan argued, the black community had become immersed in "a tangle of pathology" that included family breakdown. Many prominent African Americans disputed Moynihan's conclusions and accused him of "blaming the victims" of social conditions rather than looking at the causes of their problems (i.e., racism, segregation, economic inequities).

Extended families have long been a strong support system within the African American community.

Family Structures—Extended and Augmented

One family pattern, that has historically been common among African Americans, is that of the "extended" family. This family grouping includes other relatives such as grandparents, aunts, uncles, cousins, nieces, nephews, or other relatives, formally or informally adopted, who share the household temporarily or for a longer time period with a nuclear family. Extended families have long been a strong support system within the African American community. Today, members of extended families may not all live in the same household, because of the migratory patterns of family members, but they nonetheless function as a supportive intergenerational kinship unit.

Andrew Billingsley, in his now-classic work, *Black Families in White America* (1968), identifies an additional category of families called "augmented" families, which include unrelated persons. In a more recent publication, "Understanding African American Family Diversity," Billingsley describes these supportive, dependable, family-like networks of relationships. Another classification, "fictive kin" (as Carol Stack calls them), includes "play" mothers, brothers, sisters, and so on, who usually do not live together. In some communities,

these friendship networks resemble and substitute for extended family networks that may no longer exist. Foster families are also a growing phenomenon in the African American community, and the increase in single-female headed households is more characteristic of the black population than of any other American racial or ethnic grouping today.

As Billingsley contends, diversity is and always has been characteristic of African American family life. African American households presently fall into the following categories: (1) married couples with children, (2) married couples without children, (3) extended families (usually those including grandparents), (4) blended families, (5) single-parent families (usually but not always headed by women), (6) cohabitating adults (with or without children), (7) single-person households (predominantly female).

Number and Size of Families

According to Census reports, there were 10.7 million African-American households in the United States in 1991, up from 4.8 million in 1960. However, the average size of black households declined to 2.9 persons in 1991, compared to 2.6 persons for whites and 3.5 persons for

Hispanics. The period from 1980 to 1991 experienced the greatest growth (44 percent) in the number of black households. This growth is attributable to the increase in the number of never-married, separated, and divorced black householders, particularly in the proportion of never-married black female householders (not all of whom have borne children), which jumped from 9 percent in 1950 to 41 percent in 1991. Sixteen percent of these female householders were separated, 23 percent were divorced, and 17 percent were widowed. Male-headed households with no spouse present represented a mere 6 percent of black families in 1991.

In 1991, the number of African American families increased to 7.5 million, up from 3.4 million in 1950. This increase was most evident in the number of married-couple families and female-headed families with no husband present. In 1991, married-couple families comprised only 48 percent of all African American families, contrasted with 1950 when they comprised 78 percent. 46 percent of African American families in 1991 were headed by a female householder with no husband present, quite an increase from the 1950 proportion of 18 percent. This proportion is moving swiftly toward being equal with the percentage of married-couple families. The increase in black female-headed families can be attributed to a multiplicity of factors: the shortage of eligible black males, the shorter life expectancy of black males, increasing separation and divorce rates among African Americans, the rising rate of out-of-wedlock parenthood, increasing societal permissiveness regarding sexuality, and the wider availability of welfare assistance to aid father-absent families with dependent children.

Families in Poverty

Proportionally many more black than white families were in poverty in 1990, 29.3 percent, compared with 8.1 percent of white families. African-American families were more than 3-1/2 times more likely to be poor than were white families, a situation which has not changed measurably since 1967 (U.S. Bureau of the Census). Of 7,471,000 black families in 1990, 2,193,000 were below poverty level, whereas only 4,622,000 of 56,803,000 white families were in similar circumstances. In absolute numbers, more white families than black ones were poor, but the proportions of poor families was racially lopsided.

75 percent of the African American families in poverty in 1990 were maintained by women alone, 20 percent were maintained by married couples, and the remainder by men alone. For the past 23 years, the poverty rate for female-headed black families has been consistently higher than the rate for other African American family types.

37 percent of all black families with related children under eighteen years old were poor in 1990. This was not statistically different from the 1967 level of 39 percent or the 1982 level of 41 percent (United States Bureau of the Census). 56 percent of black families maintained by women with children under 18 years old were poor in 1990, less than the 64 percent in 1982 at the end of the 1981-82 recession (U.S. Bureau of the Census).

In 1990, 34 percent of elderly black individuals (65 years old and over) were poor. While this marks an improvement over the 1967 figure of 53 percent, proportionally more elderly blacks than whites were poor in both comparison years—10 percent of elderly whites were poor in 1990 and 28 percent in 1967 (U.S. Bureau of the Census). Despite the presence of policies such as Social Security, Medicare, and Supplemental Security Income (SSI), designed to help all elderly Americans, elderly African Americans were twice as likely as elderly whites to be poor in 1967, and, in 1990, they were three times more likely to be poor (U.S. Bureau of the Census).

The Rural Underclass

The findings of O'Hare and Curry-White's (1992) study of rural, inner-city, and suburban underclass populations reveals that approximately 3 million underclass adults in were in these areas in 1990. Using 1990 Current Population Survey (CPS) data on adults aged 19 to 64, they reported that underclass characteristics were much more prevalent in central cities and rural areas than in the suburbs, noting that 2.4 percent of the underclass lived in rural areas and 3.4 percent lived in central cities, yet only 1.1 percent lived in suburban areas. Approximately 32 percent (almost a third) of the rural underclass was found to be black in 1990, compared to 49 percent (almost half) of the inner-city underclass. The rate of black underclass membership was also higher in rural areas—9.1 percent—compared to 7.5 percent in central cities. A sizable body of impoverished rural African Americans lived in the South. Blacks in the rural South have higher underclass rates (about 1 in 10) than do blacks in large northern cities.

◆ MARRIAGE

In 1990, only 40.2 percent of African American women, 15 years of age and over, were married, compared to 60.3 percent in 1960. The corresponding percentages for African American men were 45.1 percent in 1990 and 63.3 percent in 1960. More research must be done to reveal the causes for this very drastic change in marriage patterns among African Americans in the last 30 years. For females some non-male-related causative factors may be: increased earnings of women in the labor market, increased opportunity to be employed, heightened desire to work, and the increased availability of government welfare payments for female householders.

The Unavailability of Black Men

The population of black males aged 15 years old and over in 1990 stood at 10,074,000, compared to 12,124,000 black females in the same age grouping. The resulting ratio of approximately 83 males to every 100 females makes the matching of every black female with a same-race male for the traditionally valued lifetime monogamous marriage a numerical impossibility—there simply are not enough African American men alive. When one also removes from consideration those males who are gay, the proportion of eligible black men for black women dwindles even more. Further, when one counts the number of black males who are poorly educated and therefore educationally mismatched for marriage to their relatively more highly educated black female counterparts, the pool of eligible men shrinks even lower. High black male unemployment rates further compound the problem. These factors also help to explain the increasing numbers of never-married black females.

Incarcerated single black men are unavailable as marriage partners, and black men in prison who are married are unavailable to be at home with their families and/or provide for them. Data provide only partial figures on incarcerated black men because federal prisoners are often not itemized by race or sex. According to *Statistical Abstracts,* among inmates of state prisons there were 211,021 black men in 1986, or 46.9 percent of the total state prison population. In 1990, there were 174,335 black male prison inmates (not including those in federal and state prisons or juvenile institutions). A somewhat lower figure was reported for 1986 in the *Sourcebook of Criminal Justice Statistics—1990.* The

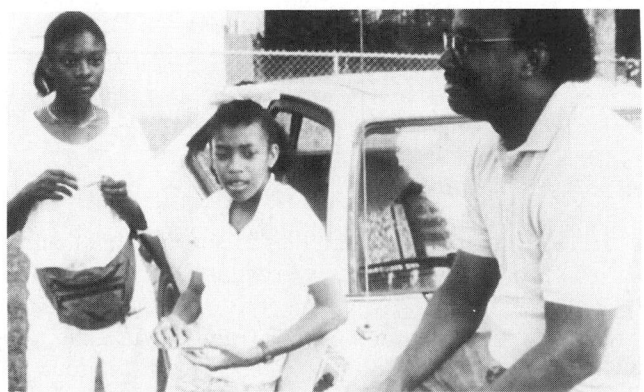

Male-headed households with no spouse present represented a mere six percent of black families in 1991.

latter source placed the percentage of black male jail inmates at 37.0 in 1986.

Reportedly, many of today's young black men delay marriage or never marry because of their unemployment or underemployment status, the rationale being that lack of a job or small earnings will not enable them to support families. However, well-educated black men who are employed at good salaries are also less likely to be married than their white counterparts (David T. Ellwood & Johnathan Crane. 1990.) Documentation of their reasons for not marrying is lacking; additional research is needed. Marriage outside the race further reduces the number of black men available for marriage to black women. In 1991, there were 156,000 marriages of black men to white women, compared to 75,000 marriages of white men to black women. This represented the "loss" of another 81,000 marriageable black men.

Interracial Marriage

In the three decades between 1960 and 1990, interracial marriages more than quadrupled in the United States, but the number remains small. By 1992 less than one percent of all marriages united blacks with people of another racial heritage (U.S. Bureau of the Census, 1993). As late as 1967, antimiscegenation laws prohibiting the marriage of whites to members of another race were still on the books in 17 states; that year, the U.S. Supreme Court finally declared such laws unconstitutional. Surveys indicate that young Americans approaching adulthood at the dawn of the 21st century are much more open to the idea of interracial unions than earlier generations. A decline in social bias has led experts to predict an increase in cross-cultural marriages throughout the 1990s.

Still, according to the 1994 National Health and Social Life Survey, 97 percent of black women are likely to choose a partner of the same race. Conflict in the United States over black-white relationships stems from the nation's brutal history of slavery, when white men held all the power in society. More than a century after the abolition of slavery, America's shameful legacy of racism remains. According to some observers, high rates of abortion, drug abuse, illness, and poverty among African Americans seemed to spark a movement of black solidarity in the early 1990s. Many black women—"the culture bearers"—oppose the idea of interracial marriage, opting instead for racial strength and unity through the stabilization of the black family.

◆ HOMOSEXUALITY/BISEXUALITY

African American gays, lesbians, and bisexuals have made great strides in the 1990s, in terms of allowing their presence to be known and in terms of the increasing levels of acceptance with which they have been met by mainstream society. Certainly most would agree that true equality and acceptance have hardly been achieved, but a course has been set for those looking to break the same chains of oppression with which all African Americans, gay or straight, are familiar. In the mainstream, the gay/les/bi community has had the most success in the field of entertainment, including often being the fodder of talk shows such as *Oprah*. Historically, from Bruce Nugent, "The Bohemian of the Harlem Renaissance," and the first black writer to deal openly with homosexuality to James Baldwin and Audre Lorde, literature has had its share of gay/les/bi icons. In the 1980s and 1990s the mantle has been passed to Samuel R. Delany, E. Lynn Harris, and Alice Walker's *The Color Purple*. In music and fashion, supermodel/house music maven/actor RuPaul had an impact on the American psyche as has bassist and songwriter Me'Shell NdegeOcello. In Hollywood, Wesley Snipes was unafraid to play a drag queen in *To Woo Fong, Thanks For Everything! Julie Newmar* while Denzel Washington played an extremely homophobic lawyer who has a change of heart after working with a gay client dying of AIDS in *Philadelphia*. The poignant documentary *Paris Is Burning*, a depiction of several cross-dressers and drag queens in New York City, was well-received by audiences and critics alike. Another penetrating documentary, gay African American filmmaker Marlon Riggs's *Black Is . . . Black Ain't* attempted to peel away the levels of meaning attached to black skin and the impact of those meanings on gay and straight members of the African American community. Black actresses, meanwhile, had prominent roles in the lesbian-focused commercial releases *Go Fish, The Incredibly True Adventures of Two Girls in Love,* and *Bar Girls*.

Outside of the mainstream, the black gay/les/bi community is replete with heros and heroines unknown to the rest of society. Rights activists include Gregory Adams, Bayard Rustin Alliance founder and executive director; Derek Charles Livingston, North Carolina Pride PAC (Political Action Committee) executive director; Gilberto Gerald, African American Gay and Lesbian Studies Center founder and director; Cary Allen Johnson, International Lesbian and Gay Human Rights Commission board member; Ron Simmons, Us Helping Us, People Into Living, Inc. executive director; Paul Davis, Minority AIDS Project of Los Angeles director of education; Nadine Smith, Human Rights Task Force of Florida executive director; Cornelius Baker, National Association of People With AIDS president; Charles W. B. Tarver, IV, the first black male lobbyist for the Human Rights Campaign Fund (HRCF); and Keith Boykin, National Black Gay and Lesbian Leadership Forum executive director.

Peter Gomes, Harvard University chaplain; Willa Taylor, the education program coordinator for the Lincoln Center Theater; Sabrina Sojourner, legislative aide for California Congresswoman Maxine Waters; Wynn P. Thomas, production and set designer for director Spike Lee's film production company; H. Alexander Robinson, legal representative for both the American Civil Liberties Union AIDS Project and the Lesbian and Gay Civil Rights Project; Darlene Garner, the first African American Elder in the Metropolitan Community Church, a universal fellowship created in 1968 by and for gay Christians; Sherry Harris, Seattle City Council member; Evelyn C. White, *San Francisco Chronicle* reporter and editor of *Black Women's Health Book: Speaking for Ourselves*; Bill E. Jones, president of New York City's Health and Hospitals Corporation, the largest public health network in the United States; Pat Norman, San Francisco Institute for Community Health Outreach executive director and Stonewall 25 Organizing Committee member; Suzanne Shende, director of the Center for Constitutional Rights' Anti-Bias Violence Project; Sandra Robinson, president and CEO of Samaritan College, the international school of ministry for the Universal Fellowship of Metropolitan Community Churhes; Keith St. John, the first black, openly gay elected official in the United States (Second Ward Alderman, Albany, New York)—are examples of nonheterosexual individuals who contribute much to society at large. They are joined in every field and industry and in every region of the country by a host of peers who face challenges because of their sexual orientation, but who do not allow intolerance to hold them back.

◆ FERTILITY AND BIRTHS

Fertility Rates

1989 saw 90.4 live births per 1,000 black women aged 15 to 44 years of age, and 64.7 such live births to comparable white women. The 673,124 live births by black females that year accounted fro approximately 17 percent of all births nationwide. Black women have had higher fertility rates than white women for the past two centuries; however, birth rates are similar for black and white women with the same level of educational attainment (William P. O'Hare, et al. 1991. "African Americans in the 1990s." *Population Bulletin* 46(1)).

Teenage Pregnancy

For a number of years Marian Wright Edelman of the Children's Defense Fund has stressed that teenage pregnancy is a special problem among poor and minority groups who usually have limited opportunities to offer their offspring ("Address to the National Conference on Educating Black Children." *Education Black Children: America's Challenge.* 1987). Joyce Ladner has explained that the causes of teenage pregnancy range from attempts to find emotional fulfillment and the desire to achieve "womanhood" to ignorance of contraceptives (1987. "Black Teenage Pregnancy: A Challenge for Educators." *The Journal of Negro Education* 56(1): 53-63). Political conservatives and neoconservatives maintain that poor teenagers view welfare programs such as Aid to Families with Dependent Children (AFDC) as a viable source of economic support and consequently perceive pregnancy as a means of tapping into the welfare system at an early age (Irving Kristol, 1992).

Teenage pregnancy is both a national problem and a African American problem. Data from the National Center for Health Statistics reveal that in 1989 the birth rate for all teenagers aged 15 to 17 years old was 36.5 live births per 1,000. African American girls in that age group were almost 3 times more likely than white girls to give birth (80.0 compared with 28.3 per 1,000). Among girls younger than 15 years old, the birth rate was seven times higher among blacks than whites. Further, in 1989, African American girls in the fifteen to 17 year-old age group were almost five times more likely to have a second baby and seven times more likely to have a third baby as white girls in this age group. This state of affairs and its moral, economic and political ramifications cause great consternation in the African American community as well as in the larger society. Teenage childbearing exacerbates such social problems as high infant mortality, maintaining good physical and mental health, educational insufficiencies, long-term welfare dependency, and poverty. Many teenage mothers do not complete high school, the basic educational expectation in this country; as a result, they are often seriously undereducated and lack marketable skills. Others do not know how or know enough to care adequately for their children. By and large, their children will not have the same opportunities and life-chances as their more advantaged counterparts in any race or ethnic group.

Various efforts have been aimed at stemming the tide of teenage pregnancy. At the bureaucratic level, some states have decreed punitive measures such as sterilization and/or reduced welfare payments for girls and women on public assistance who have more than one out-of-wedlock birth. Black sororities, fraternities, churches, and civil groups have initiated programs to work directly with African American teenagers. The Children's Defense Fund continues to enlighten the public via a multimedia campaign that urges black males as well as females to be more responsible for their sexual behavior.

Births of Mixed Racial Parentage

According to the Population Reference Bureau's December of 1992 report, the proportion of mixed-race births for which the race of both parents was known increased from 1 percent to 3.4 percent between 1968 and 1989; births of children with a black and a white parent increased from 8,700 in 1968 to 45,000 in 1989. This increase was described as "a striking sign of social change" with respect to attitudes about interracial marriage (Susan Krafft. 1991. "Black Death: The Demographic Difference." *American Demographics* 13(12):12-13).

Attitudes towards persons with "bi- or multi-racial" identities have remained volitile in the 1990s, but those with mixed heritages who refuse to be reduced to "black" or "white" have become more vocal. A key issue has been the manner in which the federal government catergorized people. In 1977, guidelines for creating race and ethnicity on all federal forms were established with four major groups identified: American Indian/ Alaskan Native, Asian/Pacific Islander, black, and white. Specification of a less broad ethnicity would have to fall into one of the "big four." In 1995, however, the federal Office of Management and Budget was considering making changes to the existing policy in response to a deluge of complaints from people of all walks of life, including European Americans who want to recognized as more than just white. To address such issues, the government proposed a "multi-racial" category.

The Association of Multi Ethnic Americans (AMEA), a national "confederation" of support groups for multiracial individuals, and the Atlanta-based Project RACE (Reclassify All Children Equally) were the two main groups spearheading the census movement. While they and other like-minded coalitions sought to increase the self-esteem of multiracial individuals by helping them to embrace their heritage(s), opponents believed that the creation of a "new" minority could lead to the denial of the heritages already accorded them and by default would distance the newly categorized from the struggles of such groups as African Americans have long endured. For example, persons who are designated as Hispanic or African American under the current system might "flee" to the new category thus instilling a hidden caste-system such as the one already in existence between lighter and darker skinned blacks. Political implications would rise in such a scenario as shrinking racial minorities would also lose political power and undermine civil rights gains. Opponents also felt that the new categoy would validate the concept of racial categories instead of championing one human race. In July of 1996 supporters of the new census category staged the Multiracial Solidarity March in Washington, DC. Interestingly, *Newsweek* reported in 1996 that 49 percent of blacks favored the new category versus 36 percent of the whites polled.

◆ CHILDREN

Living Arrangements of Children

In 1991, only 36 percent of African American children lived with both parents, compared to 67 percent in 1960 and 58.5 percent in 1970. This dramatic decline roughly parallels the changes in living arrangements of African American adults resulting from increased divorce and separation rates as well as increases in births to never-married females. By contrast, 78.5 percent of white children were living with both their parents in 1991, down from 90.9 percent in 1960 and 89.5 percent in 1970. In 1990, 12 percent of black children lived with their grandparents, compared to 4 percent of whites and 6 percent of Hispanics (William P. O'Hare, et. al. 1991). Comparable figures were released for the previous year, 1990 (*The State of Black America*, 1992). Black grandparents, particularly grandmothers, are more likely to care for their grandchildren than are whites or Hispanics. Also in 1990, 6.5 percent of black children lived with other relatives, and 1 percent lived with non-relatives. According to the National Adoption Center, nearly 60,000 black children were awaiting adoption in the early to mid-1990s.

In 1991, 67 percent of black female-headed families had one or more children under eighteen years old present in the household; 56 percent had two or more. These families were more likely to be poor than were married-couple families. They were also more likely to live in inner cities; about 30 percent lived in public housing. Many economic analysts maintain that there is a very strong probability that children from such households will grow up poor and on welfare, be environmentally disadvantaged compared to their middle class counterparts, may drop out of school, have one or more out-of-wedlock births themselves, and be unemployed or unemployable in their adult lives (David T. Ellwood & Johnathan Crane. 1990).

Child Support

In years past, when parents have been unable to support their children, extended family members were expected to assist in the process. In today's dismal economic climate, many more mothers than in the past are working in the paid labor force and contributing a larger share of their earned income to their families. Grandparents continue to do and provide what they can, including providing child care while the parent or par-

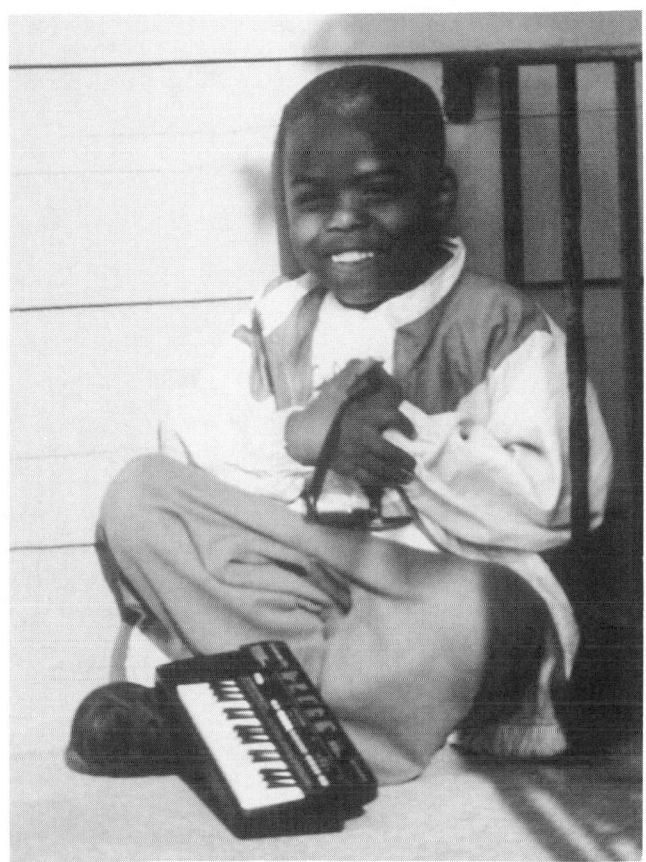

In 1991, only 36 percent of African American children lived with both parents.

ents work. Poor families are supported by the welfare system. Many families have been forced to accept unemployment compensation as their support base when one or more member loses a job.

When African American parents divorce or are separated, how many former wives receive child support from their estranged mates? In 1989 there were 2,770,000 ever-divorced and currently separated black women. Child support payments were court-awarded to only 955,000 (35 percent) of these women. Of the 791,000 who were supposed to receive child support, only 70 percent actually received payment. The mean child support amount received was $2,263.00, or 16 percent of total household income. As these figures reveal, in the event of divorce or separation, African American women were primarily responsible for the support of their children. In terms of dollars received, African American women with incomes below the poverty level fared worse than the average in 1989. Of 325,000 such women who were supposed to receive child support, 70 percent actually received payment. Their mean child support sum, a mere $1,674.00, nevertheless amounted to 32 percent of their total household income.

In 1991, 67 percent of black female-headed families had one or more children under eighteen years old present in the household.

◆ HEALTH

For African Americans, the incidence of heart disease, high blood pressure, diabetes, obesity, cancer, asthma, and several other conditions is higher than the national average. Blacks are more likely to incur early tooth loss, greater tooth decay, and higher incidence of periodontal disease. Another area in which African Americans lag is donorship. In 1995, nearly 20,000 minorities were in need of an organ transplant according to statistics from the Center for Organ Recovery and

Education. That year *CQ Researcher* projected that by 2010, one out of every 20 people will need an organ, tissue, or corneal transplant at some point in their lives. While medical advances have improved survival rates, the best chances for a successful transplant—particularly with bone marrow transplants and skin grafts—are when an organ comes from someone of the same race. Unfortunately, not nearly enough African Americans choose to donate. The lack of available organ donors ultimately means long waits for a compatible organ, death for those who do not receive one, higher costs due to low supply and high demand, and lack of coverage by insurance carriers because of the expense.

Medicaid

Many American families receive health care through the federally funded Medicaid program. Disproportionately high percentages of these families are black. The total number of Medicaid recipients in the United States increased from 17.6 million in 1972 to 25.3 million in 1990. In 1990, 44.4 percent of the recipients were children in AFDC families, for whom health care vendors received an average payment of $811.00 each. That same year, 23.8 percent of Medicaid recipients were adults in AFDC families; vendors received $1,429 each for serving them (United States Department of Health and Human Services, 1992). In 1990, 7,809,000 black persons were covered by Medicaid; 5,686,000 of these had incomes below the poverty line and 2,123,000 had incomes above it.

Child Health

Thousands of children are not being immunized, although our society knows that the spread of communicable diseases can be prevented thereby. In 1990, only about half of inner-city young children had been immunized against measles, mumps, and rubella (National Commission on Children, 1991). The government suspended data collection on polio and whooping cough in 1985, so data on those communicable diseases are not available. Measles outbreaks have erupted in many American cities in the 1990s; most were among poor, inner-city children. Nearly 100 deaths from measles were reported in 1990 (National Commission on Children, 1991).

A new and growing population of children are born of mothers who used drugs (including alcohol) during their pregnancies. Many of these children experience after-birth withdrawal problems from drugs that affected them *in utero*; they are later more prone to physical and mental disabilities, followed by behavioral problems and learning impairments when they arrive in the nation's schools. Infants whose mothers drink alcoholic beverages during pregnancy are at risk of Fetal Alcohol Syndrome. Each year, Acquired Immune Deficiency Syndrome (AIDS) afflicts a growing number of children, who usually contract the disease from their mothers before or at birth. Urban children who live in old and/or poor housing also remain at risk of being exposed to high levels of lead. It has been estimated that 12 million American children, primarily those who are poor, are at risk of lead poisoning and potentially will have their intellectual growth stunted because of exposure to lead (National Commission on Children, 1991). Like black adults, and perhaps due to their affiliation with them,

black children are also at greater risk of accidents, physical abuse, and other violence that may result in disability or death.

AIDS

African Americans suffer disproportionately from Acquired Immune Deficiency Syndrome (AIDS), the final stage of a disease caused by the Human Immunodeficiency Virus (HIV). The HIV virus severely weakens the body's immune system, leaving HIV-infected people vulnerable to other infections of various kinds. At this writing, there is no cure for AIDS—although the life expectancy of its victims varies, it is 100 percent fatal. Though African Americans represent only 12 percent of the United States population, 31 percent of all new AIDS cases in 1989 were black. This figure was up from 27 percent in 1988. A new report, "The Challenge of HIV/AIDS in Communities of Color," stated that blacks and Hispanics, representing 21 percent of the population, accounted for 46 percent of all AIDS cases in September 1992 ("AIDS and Race," *Washington Post*, January 25, 1993). Unknown is the number of such persons infected with HIV who have not as yet experienced symptoms of the disease.

Data from the U.S. Department of Health and Human Services show that in 1989 the age-adjusted HIV death rate for African American men was three times higher than that for white men (40.3 and 13.1 deaths per 100,000). The death rate for African American women was nine times that for white women (8.1 and 0.9 deaths per 100,000). The Population Reference Bureau's analysis shows that, between 1987 and 1989, the number of black AIDS cases escalated 59 percent, compared to a 38 percent increase in its incidence among white gay or bisexual men. The U.S. Centers for Disease Control have also kept updated statistics concerning reported cases of AIDS, deaths caused by the disease with breakdowns for various age groups, and various data on the occurrence of AIDS across ethnicities.

AIDS is spread by viral passage during unprotected sexual intercourse, intravenous drug use, or blood transfusions; it can also be transmitted from mother to child *in utero* or during birth. It is estimated that 52 percent of the AIDS cases among African Americans in 1989 resulted from intravenous drug use. While AIDS is fatal, it is preventable if sexually active adults and teenagers engage in "safe sex" practices such as using condoms and avoid behaviors that put them at risk of AIDS infection such as promiscuity, having multiple sex partners, using drugs, and exchanging drug paraphernalia. The African-American community and the larger society are saturating the public with information about AIDS in the hope that education will cause people to behave differently and thereby slow the progress of the disease.

Lupus

Lupus is a chronic, autoimmune disorder in which the body's immune system loses the ability to differentiate between itself and foreign substances and forms antibodies that attack healthy tissues and organs. Inflammation of the skin, joints, and kidneys are the most common result, although other areas of the body are subject to swelling as well. The medical community has not yet discovered why the disease overwhelmingly tends to affect women more than men. In fact, 9 of every 10 sufferers are women. Lupus seemingly targets women of childbearing age, i.e. between the ages of 15 and 40 and is three times more common in African American women than caucasian women.

An incurable, excruciating, and often debilitating condition, lupus can present itself in many different forms, making the initial diagnosis difficult. A range of mild to severe symptoms gradually develop, including hair and/or weight loss, fatigue, photosensitivity, loss of appetite, fever, nausea, abdominal pain, and pain in any inflamed areas. Once identified, treatment varies according to the manner in which the disease has manifested itself. With improvements in early diagnosis and better treatments, lupus is no longer considered fatal. Most patients are able to continue with their lives and lifestyles. The American Lupus Society (1-800-331-1802) and the Lupus Foundation of America (1-800-558-0121) can both offer more information.

Diabetes

Persons with diabetes are unable to convert food sugar, or glucose into energy that is used by the body's cells or stored for later use. The hormone insulin, produced by the pancreas, plays a crucial role in the conversion. Diabetics either do not produce enough insulin, or any at all, or may produce ineffective insulin. Regardless, the unused glucose collects in the blood and urine and can damage organs such as the kidneys and eyes. The onset of insulin-dependent, or type I diabetes, which usually affects children and young adults, can be very rapid. Symptoms can include frequent urination, excessive thirst, extreme hunger, weight loss, irritability, weakness and fatigue, nausea, and vomiting. 90 percent of diabetes is noninsulin-dependent. Known as type II diabetes, the illness most often occurs in adults over the age of 40 and particularly in obese individuals. Symptoms are similar to those associated with the type I form, however, type II is also characterized by the chronic presence of wounds that will not heal, stubborn infections, blurred vision, tingling or numbness in the extremities, and burning or itching sensations.

Like lupus, diabetes is noncontagious, incurable, potentially debilitating, and disproportionately strikes Af-

rican Americans. Figures from the American Diabetes Association estimate that blacks are 1.6 times more likely than whites to contract the condition and in the mid-1990s, afflicted nearly 2 million African Americans. Blacks also experience higher rates of serious complications from the disease, including blindness, kidney failure, and the need for amputations of the legs or feet. Unfortunately, nearly half of those African Americans affected are unaware of their illness, a dangerous statistic because immediate, appropriate medical attention is crucial.

Once informed of their condition, diabetics can maintain relative good health by eating low fat, high carbohydrate meals with a moderate amount of protein; through physical activity that stimulates the body's cells into utilizing glucose; and by tracking their glucose levels. Low blood sugar, or hypoglycemia is just as much a danger as is the presence of a high glucose level. Overweight individuals are very much encouraged to lose excess weight in order to increase the body's ability to use insulin. Physicians can prescribe medication, including insulin shots to help a patient maintain a normal glucose level.

In an effort to reach the black community, the American Diabetes Association launched the African American Program in 1994. They educate the public through media campaigns and community-based forums such as local churches. For more information contact the American Diabetes Association, 1680 Duke St., Alexandria, VA 22314 or call 1-800-DIABETES.

Cigarette, Alcohol, and Drug Use

The use and abuse of cigarettes, alcohol, marijuana, and cocaine (including addiction thereto) is a serious social problem in contemporary American society. The National Center for Health Statistics reports that, in a given month in 1991, four percent of black youth 12 to 17 years old smoked cigarettes, compared with 13 percent of whites and nine percent of Hispanics of the same age. Cigarette smoking has been identified as a major risk factor in lung cancer, cardiovascular disease, and chronic obstructive lung disease. 20 percent of blacks, 20 percent of whites and 23 percent of Hispanics in this same age group had used alcohol; five percent of African Americans and Hispanics but four percent of whites had used marijuana; and 0.5 percent of blacks, 0.3 percent of whites, and 1.3 percent of Hispanic youths had used cocaine. In the 18 to 25 year-old group in the given month, 22 percent of blacks had smoked cigarettes, compared to 36 percent of whites and 25 percent of Hispanics; and 56 percent of blacks had used alcohol, compared to 67 percent of whites and 53 percent of Hispanics. 15 percent of blacks, compared to 14 percent of whites and nine percent of Hispanics had used marijuana; and 3.1 percent of blacks had used cocaine, compared to 1.7 percent of whites and 2.7 percent of Hispanics. It is clear that youth are using these substances as early as age twelve and that usage increases through the young adult period. These percentages represent large numbers of young people. In regard to all age groups, a higher percentage of whites, 60 percent, reported alcohol use compared to 42 percent of blacks. According to the same poll, 58 percent of blacks considered themselves total abstainers from alcohol, compared to 40 percent of whites (Gallup, 1990). This trend is supported by updated statistics provided by the Department of Justice in 1992.

Sickle Cell Anemia

Sickle Cell Anemia (SCA) is a chronic inherited affliction caused by a defect in the hemoglobin component of the blood. It occurs as a result of the mating of two people, each of whom carries the gene for the defective trait, which is passed on to their children. The presence of this abnormal hemoglobin trait can cause distortion (sickling) of the red blood cells and a decrease in their number. The source of SCA seems to be malarious countries; people with sickle cell disease are almost always immune to malaria, so it appears that the sickle cell is a defense mechanism against malaria.

Sickled red blood cells have been found in 1 of every 12 American blacks; but the active disease occurs about once in every 600 American blacks and once in every 1,200 American whites. It is estimated that about 50,000 persons in the United States suffer from the disease. Persons of other races and nationalities are affected by the trait and the anemia including people from Southern India, Greece, Italy, Syria, Caribbean Islands, South and Central America, Turkey, and other countries.

The disease is diagnosed through microscopic and electrophoretic analysis of the blood. The first symptoms of SCA usually appear in children with the disease at about six months of age. Because SCA is a chronic disease, medical management is directed toward both the quiescent and active periods (called "crises") of the malady. Good medical and home care may make it possible for persons with SCA to lead reasonably normal lives. When crises occur, they experience fever, pain, loss of appetite, paleness of the skin, generalized weakness, and sometimes a striking decrease in the number of red blood corpuscles. Complications and infections from these crises can be controlled with antibiotic drugs. A new drug, hydroxyurea, has been developed to stimulate fetal hemoglobin to produce more red blood cells and thereby ameliorate SCA crises. However, hydroxyurea is very toxic, and thus far has only been tested on adults with SCA. In other efforts, a female SCA sufferer, also stricken with leukemia, re-

cently received a radical bone-marrow transplant from her brother. Since the transplant, she has been free of symptoms from both diseases. This case, the first of its kind, is being closely monitored to determine the mechanisms by which the patient's remission occurred and to see if the results of this procedure can be duplicated with other persons with SCA.

African American people who intend to have children are advised to undergo blood tests to determine whether they are carriers of the sickle cell gene. Two such carriers should agree not to produce children, since half the children will have the trait and one in four the anemia. There is only one chance in four that their child will be free of the disease. Some jurisdictions (Washington, DC, for example) have enacted laws mandating that newborns be screened for sickle cell anemia, along with other diseases. As a result of such legislation, newborns found to be afflicted with SCA can be cared for from birth.

Breast Cancer

In 1993, the National Cancer Institute estimated that one in eight women in the United States will develop breast cancer during her life, the risk increasing as age does. Breast cancer is the leading cause of cancer death among African American women. Although African American women develop breast cancer at slightly lower rates than white women, blacks are twice as likely to die from the disease and at a younger age. Though more research needs to be done, some reasons for the discrepancy include the facts that black women are often in poorer general health than whites; are often less likely to seek out preventive medical care and when they do are less likely to receive adequate medical care; are more likely to have worse prognoses for tumors that do not respond to treatment; and are often pessimistic about their own outlooks. (Studies have shown that maintaining a positive attitude can have an impact on just about any illness.)

Black women must focus on early detection. Approximately 90 percent of breast cancers are found via self-examination. Besides self-examinations—which should be conducted monthly, one week after one's menstrual period—the importance of mammograms should not be overlooked. In 1987, the U.S. Department of Health and Human Services determined that nearly three out of four African American women over the age of 40 had never had a mammogram, though all women regularly should once reaching 40. Many women do not follow early detection guidelines because they can not afford health care, because they have had no prior incidence in their family history, or because they do not display any symptoms, failing to acknowledge that treatment prior to symptoms is more effective. Once discovered, breast lumps may be diagnosed as premenstrual lumpiness or fluid retention caused by hormonal changes; cysts; benign tumors; or cancers.

Treatment programs are determined on a case by case basis. In the mid-1990s, the experimental drug tamoxifen was being introduced to breast cancer patients. The Cancer Information Service Center can provide more information at 1-800-4-CANCER as can the Washington, DC-based Breast Cancer Resource Committee (1765 N Street, N.W., Ste. 100; Washington, DC 20036-2802; telephone: 1-202-463-8040), founded by Zora Brown, an African American.

Prostate Cancer

The most common cancer for men, prostate cancer afflicts African American men more often than whites; in fact, blacks are more than twice likely to get the disease and are three-times as likely to die of the disease. Particularly at risk are those living in rural areas; possibly these men are less likely to regularly visit a physician. As with other forms of cancer, early detection plays a role in treatment and in deterring the likelihood of dying from the disease. Diet is a factor as well; high-fat, low-fiber diets increase the risk of developing cancer. Genetics and personal history are a third factor. In 1996, a new type of radiation treatment option, offering a 20 percent more effective than conventional radiation, was being used on patients with early cancer. Called neutron therapy, Seattle's University of Washington and Detroit's Karmanos Cancer Institute were the first two facilities to make the innovative technique available.

Medical Research

With the ominous exception of such heinous incidents as the Tuskegee Syphilis Study, minorities have traditionally been excluded in the area of medical research. In 1993, the National Institutes of Health (NIH) Revitalization Act was implemented in hopes of including women and minorities in NIH-funded or regulated clinical studies. The importance of bringing the ethnic component into play can not be overlooked, particularly when one considers that blacks suffer disproportionally from so many diseases.

◆ LIFE EXPECTANCY

Life expectancy at birth increased substantially during the first ninety years of this century, from 33 years for African Americans of both sexes in 1900 to 70.3 years in 1990. Corresponding figures for both sexes of all races are 47.3 years in 1900 and 75.4 years in 1990. Provisional data of the National Vital Statistics System project a life expectancy of 66 years for black males

born in 1990 and 74.5 years for black females born that year, an average of 70.3 years for both sexes. Corresponding life expectancy projections for white males and females born in 1990 are 72.6 and 79.3 years, averaged at 76.0 years. That black babies born in one of the most affluent countries in the world in this last decade of the twentieth century should have a lower life expectancy at birth than their white counterparts is an ignominious social problem. At the other end of the age continuum, black males aged 65 years old in 1990 are projected to live 14.2 more years, and black females 17.6 additional years, averaged for both sexes at 16.1 years. This compares with 15.3 more years for white males, and 19 additional years for white females, averaged for both sexes at 17.3 years. Thus the same pattern holds: white people in the United States continue to have longer life expectancy than African Americans.

These black/white differences can be attributed to a number of factors. African Americans have higher death rates due to the following major causes: accidents, homicides, suicides, heart disease, strokes, liver disease, cancer, diabetes, and AIDS. It is also true that whites, more than blacks, have health insurance coverage of some kind and sufficient personal income to partake of higher-quality health care, both preventive and curative. Whites' higher education and income levels also assure them the greater likelihood of eating nutritionally balanced, healthy meals. Dietary patterns and food choices of low-income blacks include too many fats and sweets, factors that contribute to obesity and high blood pressure, which carry their own sets of health risks.

Homicide and Death by Accident

Homicide among African American men is a primary cause for the drop in their life expectancy. In 1989, 61.1 percent of all black male deaths and 12.9 percent of all black female deaths from accidents and violence were due to homicide. Some social theorists claim that the increasing numbers of African Americans who are poor and hopeless, added to those who are involved in drugs or other substance abuses, account for the homicide rates among African Americans. Motor vehicle deaths and other accidents also accounted for many deaths among black males since 1970.

Suicide

Suicide rates are lower among African Americans than whites, but black suicide rates are on the rise, a most undesirable form of parity. In 1985, the suicide rate for white males exceeded that for black males by 70 percent; by 1989, the difference had narrowed to 40 percent. Data from the National Center for Health Statistics show that more than 30,000 lives are lost through suicide annually. Among all Americans, the age-adjusted death rate by suicide in 1989 was 11.3 deaths per 100,000. For black males, the rate was 12.5 per 100,000, and for black females, it was 2.4 per 100,000. Among black adolescents and young adults aged 15 to 24 years old, the suicide rate for males was 16.7 per 100,000, and 2.8 per 100,000 for black females, increases of 49 percent (from 1984 to 1989) and 40 percent (from 1986 to 1989), respectively.

Infant Mortality

Infant mortality rates for African Americans remain more than double that of whites. In 1989, 17.7 deaths per 1,000 live births were reported for black infants, compared to 8.2 deaths per 1,000 live births for whites. The black/white infant death ratios have not changed appreciably since 1950, when the black infant mortality rate was 43.9 deaths per 1,000 live births, and the white rate was 26.8 deaths per 1,000. Some progress has been made since 1950, however, as the infant mortality statistics have improved for both races. Nonetheless, the infant mortality rate in the United States is higher than those of twenty-one other industrialized countries.

African American women are more likely than whites to give birth to low-weight babies, many of whom fall victim to serious health problems or die during their first year. These babies are particularly susceptible to Sudden Infant Death Syndrome (SIDS), respiratory distress syndrome, infections, and injuries. This phenomenon occurs because disproportionate numbers of babies are born to low-income, less-educated, and/or teenage mothers who have inadequate prenatal care and poor nutrition, and who smoke, use drugs, or otherwise fail to take care of themselves properly during their pregnancies.

◆ EXERCISE AND FITNESS

Making physical fitness a part of one's daily routine is one of the best methods of maintaining good health. Coupled with proper dieting and adequate amounts of sleep, exercise can change one's life. The key is finding or developing the proper program in terms of one's interests as well as one's goals. From getting involved with team sports to working out at home in front of a VCR, a wide range of possibilities exists.

Aerobic exercise strengthens the heart, builds stamina, burns calories, and improves one's overall level of fitness. A typical aerobic workout combines fast-paced motions in a manner that increases one's metabolism, meaning that even after the workout is completed, one's body will continue to burn fat for as much as several hours. Aerobic workouts can lead to muscle toning by the introduction of light weights to a routine. In addition to traditional low and high impact floor routines, "step aerobics" has become an extremely popular exercise option in the 1990s. Such routines involve the use of a two- to ten-inch platform upon which one steps in varying ways. Stepping provides cardiovascular benefits while toning the lower half of the body. Slide aerobics, performed on a flat, slippery sheet, provides lateral fitness. Indoors, other cardiovascular equipment includes treadmills, stair-stepping machines, rowing machines, stationary bikes and cross-country skiing machines. Indoors or out, swimming and walking are still considered the best overall fitness activities. Outdoors, biking and in-line skating have both experienced an explosion of participants in the mid-1990s.

Muscle-toning and -building exercises increase strength and improve muscle definition; routines can be modified to target designated areas. Whereas using lighter weights and a high number of repetitions increases one's endurance, the use of heavier weights and a lower number of repetitions is necessary to truly build muscle. Those with casual goals of "looking fit" will usually combine light weight and heavy weight routines. Resistance can be provided in a home gym by dumbbells and barbells, rubber tubing, latex sheets, or more complex home gyms as sold by such companies as Nordic and Soloflex. a greater array of equipment can obviously be accessed through membership in a health club gym.

The importance of stretching can not be overemphasized. When done properly, stretching can prevent injury by increasing flexibility and lengthening muscles. By diminishing muscle tension, stretching can also reduce one's stress level. Many exercisers have difficulty squeezing any sort of routine into the day and will skip stretching in order to shorten a workout. Although it's best to stretch both before and after a vigorous routine, it's probably more beneficial to stretch afterwards. Many will find it relaxing. Tai Chi, the 2,000-year old Chinese art of meditation and physical movement; yoga, which concentrates on breathing and mental focus; and the common athletic stretches can all generate the same balance between one's mental and physical selves.

Many African Americans have broken into the business of physical fitness instruction, including Hollywood trainer Kacy Duke, also a creative consultant at the New York City-based Equinox Fitness Clubs. As aforementioned, the use of exercise videos has increased significantly since Jane Fonda's first foray into the medium and blacks have made contributions as well. Those who are already fairly active may like to try the following sampling of exercise videos featuring African Americans:

- Alexander, Karen, *Karen Alexander's Workout*, (muscle toning), 1995.

- Belafonte, Shari, *Massage for Health*, (instructional stress release), 1988.

- Berg, Maria, *Aerobics with Soul—Serengetti*, *(floor aerobics)*; *Aerobics with Soul—Kilimanjaro*, (floor aerobics), 1995.

- Gray, David, *Dance Fever*, (floor aerobics w/ toning), 1995.

- Hogan, Kendall, *ESPN BodyShaping Step Aerobics*, (step aerobics), 1995.

- Jackson, LaToya, *Step-Up Workout*, (step aerobics).

- Johnson, Victoria, *Cardio Soul*, (floor aerobics), 1993; *Dance Step Formula,*; *Hip Hop Solution,*; *Power Shaping II*, (floor aerobics w/ toning), 1993; *Step Training with Power*, (step aerobics w/ toning), 1995; *Step with Style,*, (step aerobics), 1993; *TechniFunk 2000*, (floor aerobics), 1991; *Trim and Tone* (muscle toning).

- Joyce, Barry, *Sleek Physique with Barry Joyce*, (floor aerobics w/ toning), 1994; *Three Times the Funk*, (aerobics).

- Joyner, Florence Griffith *The Flo-Jo Workout: Mind, Body & Spirit*, (floor aerobics w/ toning), 1995.

- Lavell, Milo, *Hip Hop Body Shop*, (floor aerobics), 1994.

- Leonard, Sugar Ray, *BoxOut*, (floor aerobics), 1993.

- Olajide, Michael, *Kathy Smith's AeroBox*, (boxing-oriented floor aerobics), 1994.

- Richardson, Donna, *Back to Basics,*, (floor and step aerobics), 1994; *Donna-Mite*, (floor aerobics), 1995; *4-Day Rotation*, (muscle toning), 1995; *Perfect Balance Attitude Aerobics,*; *Step and Awesome Abs*, 1994.

- Soremenkun, Kai, *The Firm, Vol. IV*, (step aerobics w/ toning), 1990.

- Watley, Jody, *Dance to Fitness*, (floor aerobics).

- Williams, Charlotte, *Funk It Up*, (floor aerobics), 1991; *Love Your Body*, (floor aerobics w/ toning), 1995; *Power Dance Mix* (aerobics).

Keep in mind that each of these tapes appeal to a different fitness level and may required additional equipment. Beginners who are overweight or have not exercised for more than six months should seek the advice of a medical doctor before beginning any training routine. Some videos feature basic or moderate choreography and others are more complex or dance-oriented and may range from low impact—reducing stress to vulnerable joints such as knees and ankles—to higher or mixed impact. To avoid the guess work, try contacting Collage Video Specialties, Inc., 5390 Main Street, N.E., Minneapolis, MN 55421; telephone: 1-800-433-6769. They have the largest selection of videos in the United States, all ranked according to a number of criteria.

◆ ASSESSMENT

Families in the African American Community

In the mid-1990s, a growing economic differentiation among America's black families has been evident; approximately one-third are prospering. Indeed, some African American families—primarily married-couple families headed by highly educated spouses with two or more fully employed year-round earners—are becoming more affluent. These families, who tend to live in suburban areas, are primarily nuclear families, though some are blended units. They may also be part of supportive friendship networks.

Affluent black families have benefitted from the abolition of segregation and other legal barriers to blacks' social, educational, occupational, and residential access and equity. Many of them are headed by persons who are second-, third-, and even fourth-generation college graduates, the beneficiaries of a heritage of education, motivation, and hard work. Nonetheless, such affluent African Americans continue to face "glass ceilings" and attitude-related barriers in many places of employment as they seek to move upward in corporate or government hierarchies.

Another third of black families, the working (middle) class, is comprised of families that are struggling to maintain themselves and provide support systems for their young in the face of reductions in force (RIFs), layoffs, or terminations as the corporations upon which they depend for their livelihood have downsized, moved to different regions of this country, gone out of business, or exported jobs to other countries. The extended or augmented family structure is visible in many of these homes. "Fictive kin" often are part of these family relationships.

The final third includes the nation's poorer black families. This grouping includes (1) former working-class families who have fallen on hard times; (2) the "working poor," who are employed daily but at minimum wages that do not permit secure or dependable livelihoods; and (3) families of the "underclass," poorest of the poor, most of which are headed by females alone. Many of this latter group have been supported by the welfare system for one or more generations.

In 1990, married-couple families were only 50.2 percent of all African-American families. 44 percent of African American families were headed by a female householder with no husband present. Overwhelmingly, the nation's poor black families fell into this latter category. Like other American families, they need federal, state, and local policies that are designed to strengthen all families regardless of race, class, or composition. Gun-control laws could solve some of the problems related to family violence and homicides (most of which involve family members or other closely related persons). Law enforcement related to drugs and alcohol is an urgent priority, too. In fact, since the 1980s, African American women have been the fastest growing group in the U.S. prison system. Drug offenses are partially responsible for the rise, which does not bode well for black families.

Blacks and other Americans also need universal health care policies, jobs that pay cost-of-living wages, and affordable housing in safer neighborhoods. Education of quality and substance is critically needed by the children and adults in many of these families. Recreational and other leisure-time outlets must also be made available to the youth and children in cities. Middle- and upper-income black families would benefit from an end to discriminatory employment and promotion policies designed to limit their upward mobility.

Within the African American community itself, certain attitudinal and behavioral changes are essential. For example, more highly educated young black men must decide to marry and to produce and maintain families. Family planning information, including sex education and intervention programs, must be disseminated among teenage males and females, so that the out-of-wedlock birth rate can be dramatically reduced. Substance abuse must be curtailed; people who have hope for the future and who feel that they have some power and control over their lives are less likely to "escape" through drugs or alcohol. Children and youth need more adult interaction and supervision in their lives, whether it comes from family members or "significant others" such as mentors provided by organizations like Concerned Black Men, Inc., or other community service-minded groups.

So many of the problems faced by African American and other low-to-moderate-income families are systemic and interlocking. Action on only one problem will not solve the network of family woes that our society has allowed to accumulate. Once again, the National Urban League has called for a "Marshall Plan for the Cities" to address the totality of current problems (Tidwell, 1992). If our society wants to save its cities and a significant portion of its human capital—of which these families comprise a significant part—it must give serious consideration to the formation and implementation of such a plan in both the cities and the rural areas. By so doing, the nation can help all its citizens become productive workers, consistent taxpayers, meritorious parents, and contributing members of stable families.

The Million Man March

On October 16, 1995, The Million Man March, a rally masterminded by Nation of Islam Minister Louis Farrakhan, was held 21 blocks from the steps of the U.S. Capitol Building in Washington, DC. Intended as "a national day of atonement," the 1.18 million attendees (according to a U.S. Navy Intelligence Satellite laser count), pledged their commitments to family and community. The gathering had spiritual, economic, and political implications for nonmarchers as well, including women and children; they were asked to stay home from work/school and spend the day praying and fasting.

The march was organized by the Nation of Islam and promoted by the National African American Leadership Summit. Women, excluded from the actual demonstration, were welcome in the nearly 120 local organizing committees scattered about the country. A grass-roots affair, expenses were covered mostly by donations. Linda Green, appointed as national director of fundraising, also found sources of income for the march.

Other forms of support came from a wide range of camps—political, religious, and business-oriented— including civil rights heroine Rosa Parks; former NAACP head Rev. Ben Chavis; Rainbow Coalition leader Rev. Jesse Jackson; Georgia Congresswoman Cynthia McKinney; Southern Christian Leadership Conference (SCLC) executive director E. Randel Osburn; and Melvin Foote and Ambassador Andrew Young, Constituency for Africa's executive director and chairperson, respectively. Black colleges scheduled bus trips to the march and the NAACP Youth Councils also encouraged participation from the younger generation. Nonetheless, many African Americans who upheld the tenants of the march, distanced themselves from the socio-political action because of Farrakhan and his anti-Semitic, misogynistic, anti-gay, anti-Catholic, and generally inflammatory stance.

Still, the march was deemed a success on many levels and did much to help shake the myth of all black men as convicts, hustlers, and pimps and replaced that image with one of responsible, self-confident, culturally aware

In 1991, married-couple families were only 48 percent of all African American families.

men. A highlight of the march was the speech delivered by 13-year-old Ayinde Jean-Baptiste. Appealing to black fathers, the young scholar's powers of oration led to many comparisons with leaders of other generations, from Frederick Douglass to Malcolm X to Martin Luther King, Jr. Political America was also served notice as for the first time in their live, a number of men registered to vote and a national database of black male voters was established. The march spawned a number of spin-offs, including the cross-theological gathering, "The New Revival in America: The Emerging Black Male as Man,

Husband, Father, and Leader," which took place November 16-18, 1995.

◆ SOCIAL GATEKEEPERS

Paula Giddings 1947–
Editor, Educator, Journalist, Social Historian

Paula Giddings has followed a definite focus in her life's work, that of giving a voice to generations of American black women. Through her writings, many

Recreational and other leisure-time outlets must be made available to the youth and children in cities.

issues previously not talked about were brought to the forefront of discussion. Those topics include, race, gender, and discrimination. Beginning at a young age, Giddings knew she wanted to write. She attended Howard University in Washington, DC, became editor of the literary magazine *Afro–American Review*, and began moving away from creative writing and toward journalism and social history. Giddings received an undergraduate degree in English in 1969.

After graduating, Giddings worked as a Random House copy editor during a very exciting time—some of the authors there included the political activists Stokely Carmichael and Angela Davis. A fellow editor was the soon to be famous author Toni Morrison. In 1984, after five years of extensive research, and with the help of a Ford Foundation Grant, Giddings's first book was published, *When and Where I Enter: The Impact of Black Women on Race and Sex in America*. Some of the themes covered in the book include the relationship between sexism and racism, the effect of "double discrimination" on the basis of gender and race on black women, and the relevance of historical issues to contemporary life.

In 1988, Giddings came out with a second book called *In Search of Sisterhood: Delta Sigma Theta and the Challenge of the Black Sorority Movement*. Giddings has been lauded for her accomplishments by many groups, such as the New York Urban League, the National Coalition of 100 Black Women, and Bennett College in North Carolina awarded her an honorary doctorate in human letters in 1990. In 1992, she was a visiting professor at Princeton University, earned several fellowships during the next few years, and spent an academic years as a visiting scholar with Phi Betta Kappa in 1995 and 1996.

Lorraine Hale 1926?-
Humanitarian, Educator, Hale House Cofounder

Hale was born in Philadelphia in the mid-1920s but came with her family to New York City shortly afterward. Her father owned his own business, but died when Hale was six; their mother took both day and evening work as a cleaning person to support the family, but was dismayed about leaving her daughter and two sons in child care facilities of the era. Eventually the elder Hale began taking in children in her own home, and by 1940 was a foster parent whose modest Harlem apartment often included her own three offspring and seven or eight foster children as well.

Growing up in such an atmosphere, Hale was determined to make a difference in her community, earning a B.A. from Long Island University in 1960 and then becoming a public school teacher in New York City. She also pursued her master's degree in special education, and worked variously as a guidance counselor, school psychologist, and special education teacher until 1969.

One spring night that year, Hale was driving home from a visit with her mother, who had recently retired as a foster parent; she saw a young woman in obvious distress on a street corner, and felt sympathy for both the woman and the baby she had with her. She gave the woman her mother's address, and within a few months the elder Hale's apartment was again home to several children—but this time babies born addicted to drugs. For the next year and a half, Hale and her two brothers worked overtime to financially support what would come to be known as Hale House, a pioneering facility in the treatment of babies born to substance-abuser mothers. Their organization received a city grant in 1971 and a federal one four years later that helped it move into its own five-story Harlem facilities. Hale served as its executive director from 1969 to 1989, and then assumed the post of chief executive officer and president.

Hale House has become renowned for its innovative treatment and research into mother-infant addictions, and boasts a tremendous success rate in helping the women overcome their abuse patterns to reunite with their children. Hale chronicled this work in her 1992 book *Hale House: Alive With Love*. The elder Hale—known affectionately as "Mother" Clara Hale, passed away in 1987, but her daughter has continued the work her mother began, expanding the foundation's services to assist mothers and children afflicted with AIDS; she is also working toward establishing a hospice retreat for such needs in a rural setting. In 1994 Hale traveled to Zaire under the auspices of the relief organization AmeriCares to provide aid for children in refugee camps.

Charleszetta (Mother) Waddles 1912-
Community Activist, Spiritual leader

Waddles was born in St. Louis in 1912, the oldest of seven children of a successful barber. When her father, an upstanding member of his local church, was ostracized when his business failed, his daughter vowed to repudiate the hypocrisy she witnessed in organized religion by instead promoting truly Christian principles. As a young girl Waddles worked as a domestic and married at the age of 14. Widowed before she was 20, she married again and eventually had ten children. She left her second husband due to his lack of ambition after they had relocated to Detroit. In 1946, Waddles learned that her neighbor, a single mother of two, was about to be evicted; Waddles collected food from neighboring businesses so to enable the woman to feed her children while making immediate payments to keep her home. Soon afterward, Waddles entered a bible study course and eventually became an ordained Pentecostal minister. Her religious work soon turned into charitable work, however, and in 1950 she opened her Helping Hand restaurant in a rough area of Detroit, where the indigent could get a sit-down, home-cooked meal for 35 cents. The meals, of course, were cooked by Waddles. Her third husband, Payton Waddles, provided much support for his wife's work during these years.

In 1956, Waddles expanded her the aims of restaurant when she founded the Perpetual Mission for Saving Souls of All Nations, which later became simply the Mother Waddles Perpetual Mission. The center is home to numerous community-outreach programs, including a medical clinic, a job-placement service, and a tutoring program. Staffed entirely by volunteers—that sometimes number up to 200—and financed solely through the donations Waddles extracts from a supportive local business community, the Mission is famous in Detroit for its decades of service. Still actively involved even though well into her eighties, Waddles sees her work as evidence of Christian principles in action. She has won numerous awards, including several presidential commendations and the National Urban League's 1988 Humanitarian Award.

Phill Wilson (1956-)
Activist and educator

Wilson was born into a close-knit Chicago family in 1956, and during his formative years became an active participant in local African American issues-raising organizations such as Operation PUSH. He graduated from Illinois Wesleyan University with a dual degree in Spanish and theater, but forsook law school for marriage and career with AT&T. Both choices left Wilson with a troubling feeling that there was something lacking, and he ventured into Chicago's gay community in the late 1970s. He met his partner, Chris Brownlie, in 1979, and two years later they relocated to the Los Angeles area where they began an African American-centered giftware company.

The specter of AIDS changed Wilson's life in several ways. He and Brownlie first became politically active in 1986 when they campaigned to win voter rejection of Proposition 64, a ballot referendum that called for the quarantine of all AIDS patients in California. It was also during this time that Brownlie was diagnosed with AIDS himself, and before he died in 1989 he and Wilson had founded the AIDS Health Care Foundation and the National Black Gay and Lesbian Conference and Leadership Forum. Wilson has also been involved as Stop AIDS Los Angeles's director of community outreach and has served as the national director of training for the National Task Force on AIDS Prevention. Of especial import to the activist is the building of recognition and support between the African American community and the gay community, and he was a significant force behind the 1990 "Summit on Homosexuality in the Black Community" symposium at Atlanta's Martin Luther King, Jr. Center. Since 1992 Wilson has been the director of public policy for AIDS Project Los Angeles, and as a spokesperson for gay issues met with Bill Clinton shortly after his election in 1992.

Children under 18 Years Living with Both Parents

Living arrangement	1960	1970	1980	1990	1991
Black					
Total, children under 18	8,650	9,422	9,375	10,018	10,209
Percent living with both parents	67.0	58.5	42.2	37.7	35.9
White					
Total, children under 18	55,077	58,790	52,242	51,390	51,918
Percent living with both parents	90.9	89.5	82.7	79.0	78.51

Percent Distribution of Families by Type, Region, and Race, 1950 to 1991

Year and race	Black All families (thous.)	Black Percent of all families Total	Black Married couple	Black Male house-holder, no spouse present	Black Female house-holder, no spouse present	White All families (thous.)	White Percent of all families Total	White Married couple	White Male house-holder, no spouse present	White Female house-holder, no spouse present
United States										
1950[1]	3,432	100.0	77.7	4.7	17.6	35,021	100.0	88.0	3.5	8.5
1960	3,950	100.0	74.1	4.1	21.7	40,873	100.0	89.2	2.7	8.1
1970	4,856	100.0	68.3	3.7	28.0	46,166	100.0	88.9	2.2	8.9
1980	6,184	100.0	55.5	4.1	40.3	52,243	100.0	85.7	2.8	11.6
1990	7,470	100.0	50.2	6.0	43.8	56,590	100.0	83.0	4.1	12.9
1991	7,471	100.0	47.8	6.3	45.9	56,803	100.0	82.8	4.0	13.2
South										
1950[1]	2,205	100.0	77.9	4.6	17.5	9,348	100.0	88.7	3.0	8.3
1960	2,290	100.0	74.1	4.3	21.6	11,189	100.0	89.4	2.3	8.3
1970	2,533	100.0	69.4	4.0	26.6	13,571	100.0	89.4	1.9	8.7
1980	3,202	100.0	57.9	3.9	38.2	16,773	100.0	87.2	2.5	10.4
1990	4,147	100.0	52.3	5.5	42.2	18,746	100.0	84.5	3.6	11.9
1991	4,169	100.0	50.6	6.5	43.0	18,764	100.0	83.8	3.4	12.7
North and West										
1950[1]	1,227	100.0	77.3	4.9	17.8	25,674	100.0	87.8	3.7	8.5
1960	1,660	100.0	74.2	4.0	21.8	29,683	100.0	89.1	2.9	8.0
1970	2,323	100.0	67.1	3.4	29.4	32,595	100.0	88.7	2.4	8.9
1980	2,982	100.0	53.0	4.4	42.7	35,470	100.0	85.0	3.7	12.2
1990	3,323	100.0	47.5	6.5	45.9	37,845	100.0	82.3	4.3	13.4
1991	3,301	100.0	44.2	6.1	49.6	38,038	100.0	82.2	4.3	13.5

Note: 1950 and 1960 data are from the decennial censuses.

[1]Data include families of "Other races" for Black.

Source: U.S. Bureau of the Census, Current Population Reports, The Black Population in the United States: March 1991, Washington, DC, 1992,. p.8.

Selected Characteristics of Families Maintained by Women with no Spouse Present, 1950 to 1991

(Numbers in thousands)

Characteristic	Black 1950[1]	1960[1]	1970	1980	1990	1991	White 1950[1]	1960[1]	1970	1980	1990	1991
AGE												
Female householder, no spouse present	605	843	1,382	2,495	3,275	3,430	2,966	3,297	4,165	6,052	7,306	7,512
Percent	100.0	100.0	100.0	100.0	100.0	100.0	100.0	100.0	100.0	100.0	100.0	100.0
15 to 34 years	26.0	29.0	35.2	44.0	42.3	39.6	12.0	15.0	20.8	30.8	30.3	31.0
35 to 64 years	59.0	58.0	53.0	46.4	48.6	51.2	61.0	59.0	56.2	52.6	54.1	53.9
65 years and over	15.0	13.0	11.9	9.6	9.2	9.2	27.0	26.0	23.0	16.7	15.6	15.1
PRESENCE OF OWN CHILDREN UNDER 18 YEARS												
Female householder, no spouse present	605	890	1,382	2,495	3,275	3,430	2,966	3,306	4,165	6,052	7,306	7,512
Percent	100.0	100.0	100.0	100.0	100.0	100.0	100.0	100.0	100.0	100.0	100.0	100.0
With own children	47.0	56.0	66.0	71.9	68.2	66.9	33.0	42.0	47.9	58.8	57.5	57.7
With 2 or more own children	59.0	70.0	71.4	63.4	56.0	56.1	50.0	54.0	60.9	52.2	48.1	48.7
With no own children	53.0	44.0	34.0	28.1	31.8	33.1	67.0	58.0	52.1	41.2	42.5	42.3
MARTIAL STATUS												
Female householder, no spouse present	612	843	1,382	2,495	3,275	3,430	2,960	3,297	4,165	6,052	7,306	7,512
Percent	100.0	100.0	100.0	100.0	100.0	100.0	100.0	100.0	100.0	100.0	100.0	100.0
Seperated or divorced	35.0	40.0	48.0	48.7	42.0	39.2	21.0	28.0	36.6	53.7	56.2	56.3
Seperated	27.0	29.0	33.9	26.8	18.9	16.4	8.0	10.0	11.3	13.9	13.6	14.2
Divorced	8.0	11.0	14.2	21.9	23.1	22.9	13.0	18.0	25.3	39.8	42.6	42.1
Other	65.0	60.0	51.8	51.3	58.0	60.7	79.0	72.0	63.4	46.3	43.8	43.8
Single (never married)	9.0	12.0	16.0	27.3	39.4	41.0	12.0	11.0	9.2	10.6	15.0	16.5
Widowed	51.0	42.0	30.2	22.2	16.6	16.9	61.0	53.0	47.1	32.7	26.1	23.6
Husband temporarily absent	5.0	6.0	5.6	1.8	2.0	2.9	5.0	8.0	7.2	3.0	2.8	3.7

Note: Totals for female family heads 1950 and 1960 may not agree in some cases because data are from different tabulations.

[1] Data for 1950 and 1960 are from previously published tables where percents were rounded to the nearest whole number (1950 and 1960 data are from the decennial censuses.)

Source: U.S. Bureau of the Census, Current Population Reports, The Black Population in the United States: March 1991, Washinton, DC, 1992. p. 9.

Selected Characteristics of Families Below the Poverty Level

Characteristic	1967 Black	1967 White	1971 Black	1971 White	1976 Black	1976 White	1981 Black	1981 White
Type of Family								
All families	4,589	44,813	5,157	47,641	5,804	50,083	6,413	53,269
Number below poverty level	1,555	4,056	1,484	3,751	1,617	3,560	1,972	4,670
Percent below poverty level	33.9	9.1	28.8	7.9	27.9	7.1	30.8	8.8
Married-couple families	3,118	39,821	3,289	42,039	3,406	43,397	3,535	45,007
Number below poverty level	(NA)	(NA)	(NA)	(NA)	450	2,071	543	2,712
Percent below poverty level	(NA)	(NA)	(NA)	(NA)	13.2	4.8	15.4	6.0
Female householder, no husband present	1,272	4,008	1,642	4,489	2,151	5,467	2,605	6,620
Number below poverty level	716	1,037	879	1,191	1,122	1,379	1,377	1,814
Percent below poverty level	56.3	25.9	53.5	26.5	52.2	25.2	52.9	27.4
Male householder, no wife present	199	984	226	1,113	247	1,219	273	1,642
Number below poverty level	(NA)	(NA)	(NA)	(NA)	45	110	52	145
Percent below poverty level	(NA)	(NA)	(NA)	(NA)	18.2	9.0	19.1	8.8
Families with related children under 18 years	3,200	25,531	3,660	26,745	4,047	26,812	4,455	27,223
Number below poverty level	1,261	2,276	1,261	2,372	1,382	2,566	1,652	3,362
Percent below poverty level	39.4	8.9	34.5	8.9	34.2	9.6	37.1	12.4
Married-couple families	(NA)	(NA)	(NA)	(NA)	2,146	22,872	2,202	22,334
Number below poverty level	(NA)	(NA)	(NA)	(NA)	311	1,242	357	1,723
Percent below poverty level	(NA)	(NA)	(NA)	(NA)	14.5	5.4	16.2	7.7
Female household, no husband present	(NA)	(NA)	1,369	2,664	1,781	3,456	2,118	4,237
Number below poverty level	(NA)	(NA)	821	982	1,043	1,260	1,261	1,564
Percent below poverty level	(NA)	(NA)	60.0	36.9	58.6	36.4	59.5	36.9
Male householder, no wife present	(NA)	(NA)	(NA)	(NA)	120	484	135	652
Number below poverty level	(NA)	748	(NA)	(NA)	28	64	34	75
Percent below poverty level	(NA)	34.9	(NA)	(NA)	23.3	13.2	25.0	11.6
Householder 65 years old and over	(NA)	(NA)	632	6,794	695	7,362	763	8,511
Number below poverty level	265	1,246	211	842	191	515	227	611
Percent below poverty level	48.4	19.2	33.4	12.4	27.4	7.0	29.7	7.2

Characteristic	1982 Black	1982 White	1986 Black	1986 White	1989 Black	1989 White	1990 Black	1990 White
Type of Family								
All families	6,530	53,407	7,096	55,676	7,470	56,590	7,471	56,803
Number below poverty level	2,158	5,118	1,987	4,811	2,077	4,409	2,193	4,622
Percent below poverty level	33.0	9.6	28.0	8.6	27.8	7.8	29.3	8.1
Married-couple families	3,486	45,252	3,742	46,410	3,750	46,981	3,569	47,014
Number below poverty level	543	3,104	403	2,591	443	2,329	448	2,386
Percent below poverty level	15.6	6.9	10.8	5.6	11.8	5.0	12.6	5.1
Female householder, no husband present	2,734	6,507	2,967	7,227	3,275	7,306	3,430	5,512
Number below poverty level	1,535	1,813	1,488	2,041	1,524	1,858	1,648	2,010
Percent below poverty level	56.2	27.9	50.1	28.2	46.5	25.4	48.1	26.8
Male householder, no wife present	309	1,648	388	2,038	446	2,303	472	2,277
Number below poverty level	79	201	96	179	110	223	97	226
Percent below poverty level	25.6	12.2	24.9	8.8	24.7	9.7	20.6	9.9
Families with related children under 18 years	4,470	27,118	4,806	27,929	5,031	27,977	5,069	28,117
Number below poverty level	1,819	3,709	1,699	3,637	1,783	3,290	1,887	3,553
Percent below poverty level	40.7	13.7	35.4	13.0	35.4	11.8	37.2	12.6
Married-couple families	2,093	22,390	2,236	22,466	2,179	22,271	2,104	22,289
Number below poverty level	360	2,005	257	1,692	291	1,457	301	1,572
Percent below poverty level	17.2	9.0	11.5	7.5	13.3	6.5	14.3	7.1
Female householder, no husband present	2,199	4,037	2,386	4,522	2,624	4,627	2,698	4,786
Number below poverty level	1,401	1,584	1,384	1,812	1,415	1,671	1,513	1,814
Percent below poverty level	63.7	39.3	58.0	39.8	53.9	36.1	56.1	37.9
Male householder, no wife present	178	692	185	911	228	1,079	267	1,042
Number below poverty level	58	120	58	132	77	162	73	167
Percent below poverty level	32.7	17.4	31.5	14.5	33.8	15.0	27.3	16.0
Householder 65 years old and over	813	8,635	886	9,201	880	9,643	923	9,797
Number below poverty level	239	632	196	498	173	510	224	443
Percent below poverty level	29.4	7.3	22.1	5.4	19.6	5.3	24.2	4.5

Source: U.S. Bureau of the Census, Current Population Reports, The Black Population in the United States: March 1991, Washington, DC, 1992. p. 26.

Marital Status of the Population 15 Years Old and Over

Marital status, sex, and race	1960[1]	1970	1980	1990	1991
BLACK					
Men					
Total, 15 years and over	5,713	6,936	8,292	9,948	10,074
Percent	100.0	100.0	100.0	100.0	100.0
Never married	29.6	35.6	41.1	43.4	44.8
Married	63.3	56.9	48.9	45.1	43.1
Widowed	4.6	4.4	3.7	3.4	3.3
Divorced	2.4	3.1	6.3	8.1	8.8
Women					
Total, 15 years and over	6,375	8,108	10,108	11,966	12,124
Percent	100.0	100.0	100.0	100.0	100.0
Never married	21.7	27.7	33.7	36.9	38.7
Married	60.3	54.0	44.6	40.2	38.4
Widowed	14.3	13.8	13.0	11.6	11.9
Divorced	3.7	4.4	8.7	11.2	11.0
WHITE					
Men					
Total, 15 years and over	55,080	62,868	71,887	78,908	79,555
Percent	100.0	100.0	100.0	100.0	100.0
Never married	24.4	27.2	28.1	28.0	28.0
Married	70.3	68.0	65.0	62.7	62.4
Widowed	3.3	2.7	2.3	2.4	2.5
Divorced	2.1	2.1	4.7	6.8	7.1
WOMEN					
Total, 15 years and over	58,040	68,888	77,882	84,508	85,012
Percent	100.0	100.0	100.0	100.0	100.0
Never married	18.6	21.3	21.0	20.6	20.8
Married	66.7	62.8	60.7	59.2	59.0
Widowed	11.9	12.4	11.9	11.6	11.2
Divorced	2.8	3.4	6.4	8.6	8.9

Note: 1960 and 1970 data are from the decennial censuses.

[1]Data for 1960 are for persons 14 years old and over.

Source: U.S. Bureau of the Census, Current Population Reports, The Black Population in the United States: March 1991, Washington, DC, 1992, p. 5

Black-White Married Couples, 1980 to 1991

Item	Number (in thousands)			Percent		
	1980	1990	1991	1980	1990	1991
Total married couples	49,714	53,256	53,227	100.0	100.0	100.0
Black-White married couples, total	167	211	231	0.3	0.4	0.4
Husband Black, wife White	122	150	156	0.2	0.3	0.3
Wife Black, husband White	45	61	75	0.1	0.1	0.1

Source: U.S. Bureau of the Census, Statistical Abstract of the United States: 1992 (112th edition), Washington DC, 1992, p. 45.

Selected Characteristics of Persons Covered by Medicaid, 1980 to 1990

POVERTY STATUS	1980	1985	1988	1990 Total[1]	White	Black	Hispanic[2]	Under 18 years old	18-44 years old	45-64 years old	65 years and over
Persons covered, total	18,966	19,204	21,185	24,261	15,078	7,809	3,912	12,094	7,284	2,302	2,582
Below poverty level	11,113	12,652	13,325	15,175	8,758	5,686	2,686	8,313	4,490	1,261	1,112
Above poverty level	7,854	6,552	7,860	9,086	6,320	2,123	1,226	3,781	2,794	1,041	1,470
Percent of total population	8.4	8.1	8.6	9.7	7.2	25.3	18.3	18.5	6.8	4.9	8.6
Below poverty level	39.1	39.7	42.3	45.2	39.2	57.8	44.7	61.9	36.1	31.0	30.4
Above poverty level	4.0	3.2	3.7	4.2	3.4	10.2	7.9	7.3	3.0	2.4	5.6

[1]Includes other races not shown separately. [2]Persons of Hispanic origin may be of any race.
Source: U.S. Bureau of the Census, Statistical Absrtact of the United States: 1992 (112th edition) Washington dc, 1992. p.103

16

Education

16

Education

◆ The Origins of Black Educational Institutions ◆ Afrocentrism
◆ Educational Gatekeepers ◆ Historically and Predominantly Black Colleges and Universities
◆ Research Institutions ◆ African American Chaired Professors (1996)
◆ African Americans Holding Endowed University Chairs (1996)

by Kenneth Estell and David G. Oblender

In 1995, nearly $47 billion in college funding was available, from federal, state, private, and corporate sponsors, including loans, grants, and scholarships. High grades and/or entrance exam test scores have ceased to be the only consideration in awarding scholarships. The key to tapping into monies, many of which remain unclaimed year after year, is defining a financial plan as early as during a high school student's freshman year. The U.S. government offers a Free Application for Federal Student Aid (FAFSA) in order to help families determine how much they can contribute to the cost of a member's education. Local libraries, school libraries, or school counselors can help uncover sources.

◆ THE ORIGINS OF BLACK EDUCATIONAL INSTITUTIONS

Since the first arrival of Africans in America, the African American community has worked to sustain a system for educating its youth. In addition to the efforts of individuals, churches and charitable organizations have also played an important role in the creation of educational institutions for blacks in this country.

Early Christian Missionary Endeavors

Early attempts at educating blacks in America can be traced back to efforts by Christian churches. Although the primary goal of these missionaries was to convert Africans to Christianity, the process often involved general education.

French Catholics in Louisiana were probably the earliest group to begin providing instruction to black laborers in the early 1600s. The French code noir, a system of laws, made it incumbent upon masters to educate slaves.

Pennsylvania Quakers, who were in opposition to the institution of slavery, during the early 1700s organized monthly educational meetings for blacks, so they might have the opportunity for improvement. One such Quaker, Anthony Benezet, in 1750 established an evening school in his home which remained successful until 1760. In 1774 Quakers in Philadelphia joined together to open a school for blacks.

The Society for the Propagation of the Gospel in Foreign Parts, organized by the Church of England in 1701 for the purpose of converting African slaves to Christianity, was another organization which provided educational opportunities to blacks. In 1751 the Society sent Joseph Ottolenghi to convert and educate blacks in Georgia. Ottolenghi "promised to spare no pains to improve the young children."

African Free Schools in New York and Philadelphia

Like the Church, the anti-slavery movement played an important part in the creation of schools. In 1787 the Manumission Society founded the New York African Free School; by 1820 more than 500 black children were enrolled. Support increased as other African Free Schools were established in New York, until 1834 when the New York Common Council took over control of the schools.

In 1804, African Episcopalians in Philadelphia organized a school for black children. In 1848 a black industrial training school opened in Philadelphia at the House of Industry. Other schools in operation in Philadelphia included the Corn Street Unclassified School (1849), the Holmesburg Unclassified School (1854), and the Home for Colored Children (1859). By the mid-1860s there were 1,031 pupils in the black public schools of Philadelphia; 748 in the charity schools; 211 in the benevolent schools, and 331 in private schools.

Freedmen's Organizations and Agencies

At the close of the Civil War hundreds of thousands of free blacks were left without homes and adequate resources. As a means for providing temporary assistance to the newly freed slaves, numerous organizations were formed.

The New England Freedmen's Aid Society, organized in Boston on February 7, 1862, was founded to promote education among free African-Americans. Supporters of the organization included Edward Everett Hale, Samuel Cabot, Charles Bernard, William Lloyd Garrison, and William Cullen Bryant. In New York a similar organization was founded, the National Freedmens Relief Association on February 20, 1862. This was followed by the Port Royal Relief Committee, later known as the Pennsylvania Freedmens Relief Association, founded in Philadelphia on March 3, 1862. In 1863 several of these organizations merged to form the United States Commission for the Relief of the National Freedmen, which, in 1865, became the American Freedman's Aid Union.

During the 1860s Congress passed several Freedman's Bureau Acts, creating and financing an agency designed to provide temporary assistance to newly freed slaves. Under the acts, the bureau's chief functions were to provide food, clothing, and medical supplies. Working in conjunction with various benevolent organizations, bureau Commissioner General Oliver Otis Howard established and maintained schools, and managed to provide provisions for teachers. By 1870 the bureau operated over 2,600 schools in the South with 3,300 teachers educating 150,000 students; almost 4,000 schools were in operation prior to the abolition of the agency.

Independent Schools in the Late Nineteenth Century

The education of African Americans has been largely a function of independent schools, private institutions founded to meet the educational and employment needs of African Americans.

One of the earliest surviving black independent schools, Tuskegee Normal and Industrial Institute (now Tuskegee Institute) was established in 1881 by an act of the Alabama general assembly. Booker T. Washington, the school's organizer and first principal, established at the school a curriculum which was to provide black students with the means to become economically self-supporting.

Similarly other independent schools developed around the country. In a lecture room at the Christ Presbyterian Church, Lucy Laney in 1883 opened what would become the Haines Normal and Industrial Institute in Savannah, Georgia. In 1901 Nannie Helen Burroughs founded the National Training School for Women and Girls in Washington, DC. By the end of the first year the school had enrolled thirty-one students; twenty-five years later more than 2,000 women had trained at the school. In Sedalia, North Carolina in 1901, Charlotte Hawkins Brown founded the Palmer Memorial Institute.

With only $1.50 and five students, in 1904 Mary McLeod Bethune founded Daytona Normal and Industrial Institute for Girls (now Bethune-Cookman College) in Daytona Beach, Florida. Nineteen years later, the institute merged with the Cookman Institute of Jacksonville, Florida, founded in 1872 by D.S.B. Darnell. Some 2,000 students now study at Bethune-Cookman College.

Early Black Institutions of Higher Education

One of the oldest of the historically black institutions of higher education, named for the English abolitionist William Wilberforce, Wilberforce College (now Wilberforce University) was founded in 1856 by the African Methodist Episcopal Church. The school awarded its first degree in 1857. The oldest institution in operation today, Cheyney State in Pennsylvania, was founded in 1837.

Between 1865-1871 several predominantly black institutions of higher learning were founded, including Atlanta University (now Clark-Atlanta University), Shaw University and Virginia Union University (1865); Fisk University and Lincoln Institute (now Lincoln University) (1866); Talladega College, Augusta Institute (now Morehouse College), Biddle University (now Johnson C. Smith University), Howard University and Scotia Seminary (now Barber-Scotia College) (1867); Tougaloo College (1869); and Alcorn College (now Alcorn State University) and Benedict College (1871). Religious organizations were instrumental in the founding and support of these early black institutions. Atlanta, Fisk, Talladega, and Tougaloo were founded by the American Missionary Association; Benedict, Shaw, and Virginia Union were founded and supported by the American Baptist Home Mission Society.

Alcorn College, founded in 1871, was the first black land grant college. This was made possible under the

An engraving depicting an early black schoolroom.

Morrill Act of 1862, which provided federal land grant funds for higher education. In 1890 Congress passed the second Morrill Act, also known as the Land Grant Act of 1890. The second act stipulated that no federal aid was to be provided for the creation or maintenance of any white agricultural and mechanical school unless that state also provided for a similar school for blacks. As a result a system of separate, black land grant institutions developed, and became the basis of black higher education in the South.

By 1900 there were some thirty-four black institutions in the United States for higher education and more than 2,000 blacks with earned degrees. (John Hope Franklin. 1988. *From Slavery to Freedom, A History of Negro Americans*, 6th ed., New York: McGraw-Hill. p. 243.)

Early Promoters of African American Studies

From its beginnings, the purpose of African American studies has been to disseminate knowledge about the social, cultural, political, and historical experiences of Africans (see Darlene Clark Hine. 1992. "The Black Studies Movement: Afrocentric-Traditionalist—Feminist Paradigms for the Next Stage," *The Black Scholar* 22-3:11-18).

One of the forerunners in the field of black studies, theologian and educator Reverend Alexander Crummell, along with a group of black intellectuals, in 1897 founded the American Negro Academy in Washington, DC. The purpose of the organization was to foster scholarship and promote literature, science, and art among African Americans. The organization's members hoped that through the academy, an educated black elite, which would shape and direct society, would be born. Crummell first conceived the idea of an American Negro Academy while a student at Cambridge University, England. The organization's founding members included Paul Laurence Dunbar, William Sanders Scarborough, and W.E.B. DuBois, among other noted educators. Following Crummell's death in 1908, DuBois was elected president of the academy.

In September 1915 Carter G. Woodson, a Harvard Ph.D. graduate, organized the Association for the Study of Negro Life and History (now the Association for the Study of Afro-American Life and History). The associa-

New York's African Free School No. 2

tion's primary purpose was to promote research, encourage the study of African American history, and to publish material on black history. In 1916 the organization began publishing the *Journal of Negro History*, for which Woodson served as editor until his death in 1950.

Other early scholars of African American studies include sociologist E. Franklin Frazier (1894-1963), historian George Washington Williams (1849-1991), John Edward Bruce (1856-1924) and Arthur Schomburg, founders of the Negro Society for Historical Research

(1911), and Alain Locke, founder of the Associates in Negro Folk Education (1934).

The End of Segregation in Public Education

In the years that followed the United States Supreme Court's 1896 ruling in the case *Plessy v. Ferguson*, segregation in public education became general practice. Prior to the Court's decision in *Brown v. Board of Education*, black children were often subjected to infe-

School-aged children in the rural South, c. 1865.

rior educational facilities. However, by the 1930s a string of school desegregation cases reached the Court.

When Lloyd Lionel Gaines, an African American, had been refused admission to the law school of the State University of Missouri, he applied to state courts for an order to compel admission on the grounds that refusal constituted a denial of his rights under the Fourteenth Amendment of the U.S. Constitution. At that time, the state of Missouri maintained a practice of providing funds for blacks to attend graduate and professional schools outside of the state, rather than provide facilities itself. The university defended its action by maintaining that Lincoln University, a predominantly black institution, would eventually establish its own law school, which Gaines could then attend. Until then the state would allow him to exercise the option of pursuing his studies outside the state on a scholarship. Ruling in the case Missouri ex rel. *Gaines v. Canada* in 1938, the United States Supreme Court ruled that states were required to provide equal educational facilities for blacks within its borders.

A freedman's school in Beaufort, South Carolina, 1862.

Taking an even greater step, in 1950 the United States Supreme Court ruled that a separate law school for blacks provided by the state of Texas violated the equal protection clause of the Fourteenth Amendment, when Herman Marion Sweat, was refused admission to the law school of the University of Texas on the grounds that substantially equivalent facilities were already available in another Texas school open to blacks only. Ruling in the case *Sweatt v. Painter*, the Court ruled that the petitioner be admitted to the University of Texas Law School, since "in terms of number of the faculty, variety of courses and opportunity for specialization, size of the student body, scope of the library, availability of law review and similar activities, the University of Texas Law School is superior."

In 1952, five different cases, all dealing with segregation in public schools but with different facts and from different places, reached the United States Supreme Court. Four of the cases, *Brown v. Board of Education* (out of Kansas), *Briggs v. Elliott* (out of South Carolina), *Davis v. Prince Edward County School Board* (out of Virginia), and *Gebhart v. Belton* (out of Delaware) were considered together; the fifth case, *Bolling v. Sharpe*, coming out of the District of Columbia, was considered separately (since the district is not a state).

After hearing initial arguments, the Court found itself unable to reach an agreement. In 1953, the Court heard reargument. Thurgood Marshall, legal consul for the NAACP Legal Defense and Education Fund, presented arguments on behalf of the black students. On May 17,

1954, the Court unanimously ruled that segregation in all public education deprived minority children of equal protection under the Fourteenth Amendment. (In the *Bolling* case, the Court determined that segregation violated provisions of the Fifth Amendment, since the Fourteenth Amendment is expressly directed to the states.)

In 1996, the 5th U.S. Circuit Court of Appeals made a strong ruling against affirmative action in education. The court deemed that the University of Texas at Austin law school could not use different admissions standards for minority students than it does for white applicants—a direct blow aimed at the 1978 *Bakke* decision that prohibited quotas but still allowed schools to consider race as a factor for admissions. The court's declaration also affected state schools in Louisiana and Mississippi and private institutions that were recipients of federal funding.

Black Colleges in the Twentieth Century

Predominantly black colleges and universities continue to account for the majority of black graduates. This is especially true in the areas of science, mathematics, and engineering. In 1964, over 51 percent of all blacks in college were still enrolled in the historically black colleges and universities. By 1970 the proportion was 28 percent, and by fall 1978, 16.5 percent. As recently as 1977, 38 percent of all blacks receiving baccalaureate degrees earned their degrees at black institutions. In 1980 some 190,989 African Americans were enrolled at historically black institutions. By 1988 the total black enrollment at these institutions reached 217,462.

Independent Schools in the Late Twentieth Century

For years independent schools have been founded in order to exert greater control, ensure quality in education and to meet the needs of African American children.

In 1932, in order to promote religious growth in the Muslim community, the Nation of Islam founded the University of Islam, an elementary and secondary school to educate black Muslim children in Detroit. Clara Muhammad, wife of Elijah Muhammad served as the school's first instructor. In 1934 a second school was opened in Chicago; by 1965 schools were operating in Atlanta and Washington, DC. The current system of black Muslim schools, named for Clara Muhammad, is an outgrowth of the earlier University of Islam. There are currently thirty-eight Sister Clara Muhammad schools in the United States (Hakim M. Rashid and Zakiyyah Muhammad. 1992 "The Sister Clara Muhammad Schools," *The Journal of Negro Education*, 61:178-185).

Students at Snow Hill Institute, 1902.

Gertrude Wilks and other black community leaders in East Palo Alto, California in 1966 organized the Nairobi Day School, a Saturday school. In 1969 the school became a full-time school. It closed in 1984.

Also founded as a Saturday school program in 1972, the New Concept Development Center in Chicago set out to create an educational institution which promoted self-respect, cooperation, and an awareness of African-American history and culture. In 1975 public school teacher and nurse, Marva Collins founded the Westside Preparatory School in Chicago.

In recent years, the educational and social needs of urban youth, particularly African American males, have been given increased attention. Studies show that nearly forty percent of adult black males are functionally illiterate, and that the number of African-American males incarcerated far outnumbers the number of black males in college (Donald O. Leake and Brenda L. Leake. 1992. "Islands of Hope: Milwaukee's African American Immersion Schools," *The Journal of Negro Education*. 61:24-29). Addressing these issues, large urban school systems, including Baltimore, Detroit, and Milwaukee, have attempted to create programs which focus on the needs of African American males.

Although African American students have shown improved performance on achievement tests, gaps between black students and white still exist. Although progress has been made in the quality of education for black children, inadequacies remain in the provision of resources for the education of blacks. In recent years, efforts at creating alternative schools designed to meet the needs of African-American children and to reflect the culture and social experiences of blacks have received increased attention. In 1991 the Institute for Independent Education, an organization providing technical assistance to independent neighborhood schools, reported an estimated 300 such schools serving children of color in the United States (Gail Foster. 1992 "New York City's Wealth of Historically Black Independent Schools," *The Journal of Negro Education* 61:186-200).

◆ AFROCENTRISM

by David G. Oblender

An educational methodology that has sparked both widespread praise and criticism is Afrocentrism. Afrocentrism is based, in part, on the belief that the

An early schoolroom.

ancient Greeks stole most of their great philosophical and mathematical thought from the Egyptians, an African people, that the Greek philosopher Aristotle gleaned much of his philosophy from books plundered from the Egyptian city of Alexandria, and that the notable Greek philosopher Socrates was black. Afrocentrists claim that the current educational system in America is deeply flawed and promotes white supremacy. It teaches history, arts, science, and other disciplines from a purely traditional European point of view, while African contributions to these fields of endeavor are ignored entirely or given inadequate consideration. Proponents of Afrocentrism theorize that teaching African American children from an African-centered perspective through the championing of black culture, history, and achievement will increase their feelings of self-worth and give them a greater sense of identity and ethnic pride.

The doctrine of Afrocentrism is not a new phenomenon. Notable early 20th century African Americans such as activist Marcus Garvey and scholar Carter G. Woodson were among its most ardent supporters. Today, Afrocentrism is championed by African American scholars such as Dr. Leonard Jeffries, Dr. Molefi Asante, Dr. Asa Hillard, and Dr. John Henrik-Clark. Some public school systems with predominantly African American enrollment, such as Atlanta, New Orleans, Cleveland, Indianapolis, New York, Oakland, and Philadelphia have introduced African-centered principles to their curriculums.

Afrocentrism is not without its critics, however. Among them is Mary Lefkowitz, a professor of humanities at Wellesley College. In her book *Not Out of Africa: How Afrocentrism Became an Excuse to Teach Myth as History*, Lefkowitz disagrees with the assertions of Afrocentrists that the Greeks stole their philosophical and mathematical thought from the Egyptians or that Socrates was black. She argues that Afrocentrist beliefs are based on myth and conjecture, not historical fact and are designed to promote a political agenda. This

Booker T. Washington

criticism is echoed by Arthur Schlesinger, author of *The Disuniting of America*. Schlesinger remarks that African-centered education is divisive, un-American, and promotes the teaching of inaccuracy and distorted history.

Whether one is a supporter or critic, it is clear that Afrocentrism will continue to inspire heated debate for many years to come.

◆ EDUCATIONAL GATEKEEPERS

Molefi Kete Asante (1942-)
Scholar

Asante was born Arthur Lee Smith, Jr. on August 14, 1942 in Valdosta, Georgia. His name was legally changed to Molefi Kete Asante in 1973. In 1962, Asante graduated with an associate's degree from Southwestern Christian College. He graduated cum laude with a B.A. from Oklahoma Christian College in 1964, received an M.A. from Pepperdine University in 1965 and a Ph.D. from UCLA in 1968.

Asante has taught speech and communications at many universities in the United States. He was an in-

First site of Atlanta University.

structor at California State Polytechnic University at Pomona (1966-1967) and California State University at Northridge (1967). In 1968 he accepted an assistant professorship at Purdue University in Lafayette, Indiana where he remained until 1969 when he began teaching at UCLA where he advanced from assistant to associate professor of speech. While at UCLA he also served as the director of the Center for Afro-American Studies (1970-1973). In 1973 he accepted the position of professor of communications at the State University of New York. He soon became department chairman, a position he held until 1979 when he became a visiting professor at Howard University in Washington, DC (1979-1980). In 1981 and 1982, he was a Fullbright Professor at the Zimbabwe Institute of Mass Communications. Since 1980, he has been a professor at Temple University in Philadelphia in the Department of African American Studies.

Asante is a prolific author with over thirty-three books dealing with both communication theory and the African-American experience. Some of his most recent titles include *Afrocentricity: The Theory of Social Change* (1980), *African Culture: The Rhythms of Unity* (1985), *The Afrocentric Idea* (1987), *Afrocentricity* (1987),

Kemet, Afrocentricity and Knowledge (1990), *The Historical and Cultural Atlas of African-Americans* (1991) and *Fury in the Wilderness* (1993).

Asante is also a founding editor of the *Journal of Black Studies* and has been a member of the advisory board of the *Black Law Journal* (1971-1973) and *Race Relations Abstract* (1973-1977).

Asante has served as the vice president for the National Council of Black Studies and the African Heritage Studies Association.

Mary McLeod Bethune (1875-1955)
Educator, Bethune-Cookman College Founder

Born on July 10, 1875 in Mayesville, South Carolina, Mary McLeod received a sporadic education in local schoools. She eventually received a scholarship and studied for seven years at the Scotia Seminary in Concord, North Carolina. In 1893 she went on to study at the Moody Bible Institute in Chicago in lieu of a missionary position in Africa. In 1895 she began teaching at the Haines Institute in Augusta, Georgia. Between 1900 and 1904 she taught in Sumter, Georgia and Palatka, Florida.

Students at Tuskegee Institute, 1902.

In 1904 she founded her own school in Daytona Beach, Florida—the Daytona Educational and Industrial School for Negro Girls. John D. Rockefeller became an early admirer and supporter of the school after hearing a performance by its choir. Bethune went on to found the Tomoka Missions and in 1911 the McLeod Hospital. In 1922 her school merged with the Cookman Institute to become Bethune-Cookman College.

Bethune's work received national attention and she served on two conferences under President Herbert Hoover. In 1936 President Franklin Roosevelt appointed her director of the Division of Negro Affairs of the National Youth Administration. During World War II she served as special assistant to the Secretary of War, responsible for selecting Negro WAC officer candidates.

Bethune also served on the executive board of the National Urban League and was a vice-president of the NAACP. She received the Spingarn Award in 1935, the Frances A. Drexel Award in 1936 and the Thomas Jefferson Medal in 1942. Bethune was also instrumental in the founding of the National Council of Negro Women. She retired from public life in 1950 on her seventy-fifth birthday and died five years later on May 18, 1955.

Much of Bethune's philosophy had to do with ennobling labor and empowering African Americans to achieve economic independence. Although a tireless fighter for equality, she eschewed rhetorical militancy in favor of a docrine of universal love.

Nannie Helen Burroughs (1879-1961)
Educator

Born in Orange Springs, Virginia, Nannie Helen Burroughs was one of the most significant Baptist lay leaders of the twentieth century, a lifelong booster of women's education, and a tireless civic organizer. She addressed the National Baptist Convention in Virginia in 1900 on the subject, "How the Sisters are Hindered from Helping," and from that time until her death more than sixty years later she exercised pivotal leadership.She was elected corresponding secretary for the Woman's Convention, Auxiliary to the National Baptist Convention, U.S.A., Inc., and in 1948 she became President of the Women's Convention.

In 1901 Burroughs founded and presided over the National Training School for Women and Girls, which emphasized industrial arts and proficiency in African-American history. After only one year, she had recruited

Fisk University, c. 1868.

31 students. In honor of her efforts, the school's curriculum was changed to accomodate elementary education and its name was changed to Nannie Hellen Burroughs School.

Burroughs was active in the anti-lynching campaign and a life member of the Association for the Study of Negro Life and History. She helped organize the Women's Industrial Club of Louisville and was responsible for organizing Washington, DC's first black self-help program. She also edited such periodicals as the *Christian Banner*, and was the author of *Roll Call of Bible Women*.

Fanny Coppin (1873-1913)
Educator

Fanny Coppin was born in 1873 into slavery but rose to prominence in the field of education. After her aunt purchased her freedom, Coppin went on to become the second African-American woman to receive a degree from Oberlin College.

Coppin was appointed principal of the women's department of the Institute for Colored Youth, a high school established by Quakers in 1837, and later principal of the entire school. In 1894 Coppin founded the Women's Exchange and Girls' Home. She served as president of the local Women's Mite Missionary Society and the Women's Home and Foreign Missionary Society, and as a vice president of the National Association of Colored Women.

Coppin, an active member of the African Methodist Episcopal Church, served as president of the AME Home Missionary Society and accompanied her husband, Levi J. Coppin, on a missionary venture to South Africa.

Before her death in 1913 Coppin began writing an autobiography, *Reminiscences of School Life, and Hints on Teaching*.

Joe Clark (1939-)
Former Educator

Best known as the feisty, dedicated, baseball-bat-wielding school principal portrayed by actor Morgan Freeman in the film *Lean on Me*, Clark has served as an exemplar of school discipline and boasts a distinguished record of achievements and laurels. A fourteen-year member of the New Jersey Board of Education and an elementary and secondary-school principal until 1990, he has been honored by the White House, the NAACP, his alma mater Seton Hall University, and various newspapers and magazines.

Born in Rochelle, Georgia, Clark served in the United States Army Reserve from 1958-1966. He received a B.A. from New Jersey's William Paterson College in 1960 and his master's degree from Seton Hall in 1974. From 1960-1974, Clark served on the Board of Education in Paterson, New Jersey. He was a coordinator of language arts from 1976 until 1979. Clark became a school principal for the first time in 1979 and quickly earned the admiration and respect of educators for his somewhat controversial, non-nonsense managerial style. In 1983, Clark received the NAACP Community Service Award and was named New Jerseyan of the Year by the Newark *Star Ledger*. The following year, *New Jersey Monthly* honored Clark as Outstanding Educator. In 1985, Clark appeared in Washington, D.C., to receive honors at a presidential conference on academic and disciplinary excellence, and also gained awards from Seton Hall and Farleigh Dickinson University. The National School Safety Center gave Clark the Principal of Leadership award in 1986 and the National Black Policemen's Association bestowed their Humanitarian Award upon him in 1988.

In 1990, Clark ended his tenure as principal of Eastside High School in Paterson, New Jersey and traveled the country as a lecturer. He accepted a job as the director of the Essex County, New Jersey, Youth House, a juvenile detention center in Newark, in August, 1995.

Septima Clark (1898-1987)
Educator, Civil Rights Activist

In her nonassuming, workmanlike way, Septima Clark made a major impact on the voting bloc of thousands of African American southerners, though many Americans have never heard of her. Clark dedicated her life to education, and drove home through her actions a simple concept in which she believed, namely that before one

Arthur Schomburg, founder of the Negro Society for Historical Research, with staff.

could get people to register and vote, one had to teach them to read and write. Born on May 3, 1898, in Charleston, South Carolina, Clark was a schoolteacher for most of her life. She dedicated her entire career to educating her community.

In 1937 Clark studied under W. E. B. Du Bois at Atlanta University. She later went on to receive her B.A. at Benedict College in 1942, and her M.A. from Hampton Institute four years later. After teaching for nearly ten years in the Charleston school system, Clark began the "citizenship schools" program, through her position at Tennessee's Highlander Folk School, a center for civil organizing and dialogue in 1956. These citizenship schools taught people to write their names, balance check books, fill out a voting ballot, and understand their rights and duties as U.S. citizens. The schools were a success, and, by 1961, had grown too big for Highlander to handle. The Southern Christian Leadership Conference (SCLC) expressed an interest in taking over, so Clark went to work for the SCLC as director of education.

After retiring from the SCLC in 1970, Clark stayed active in civil rights struggles. In 1974, at the age of 76, Clark was elected to serve on the Charleston school

board-the same school board that had fired her 20 years earlier for her active involvement with the NAACP.

Johnnetta B. Cole (1936-)
Spelman College President

A distinguished scholar, Johnnetta Cole has served on the faculties of Washington State University, University of Massachusetts-Amherst, Hunter College, and Spelman College, the historically black women's institution in Atlanta. Born in Jacksonville, Florida, on October 19, 1936, Cole attended Oberlin College, which awarded her a BA in 1957. She went on to earn her master's and doctorate degrees at Northwestern in 1959 and 1967, respectively.

In 1967, Cole began her first teaching assignment at Washington State University, where she taught anthropology and served as director of black studies. The university honored her as Outstanding Faculty Member of the Year for 1969-70. From 1970 until 1983, Cole was professor of anthropology and African American Studies at the University of Massachusetts-Amherst. She left the University of Massachusetts-Amherst in 1983 for a position as professor of anthropology at Hunter College

Daisy Bates with four black students, who will attend formerly all-white high schools in Little Rock, Arkansas, 1959.

of the City of New York. Cole also served as director of Latin American and Caribbean Studies at Hunter College from 1984 until 1987. In 1987, Cole was named president of Spelman College, a position she currently retains.

As an anthropologist, Cole has done field work in Liberia, Cuba, and in the African-American community. A prolific writer, she has published in many mainstream periodicals as well as scholarly journals. Since 1979 she has been a contributor and advising editor to *The Black Scholar.* Her most recent book, *Conversations: Straight Talk with America's Sister President,* was published in 1993. She is a member of the National Council of Negro Women and a fellow of the American Anthropological Assocation.

Cole has received numerous awards and honorary degrees. She was presented with the Elizabeth Boyer Award in 1988 and the Essence Award in Education in 1989. In 1990, Cole won the American Women Award, the Jessie Bernard Wise Woman Award, and was inducted into the Working Woman Hall of Fame. In 1994, she received the Jewish National Fund's highest honor, the Tree of Life Award, which is named for the efforts of the

Jewish National Fund to reclaim and develop barren land in Israel.

Marva Delores Nettles Collins (1936-)
Educator

Marva Delores Nettles Collins was born in Monroeville, Alabama on August 31, 1936. She received a bachelor's degree from Clark College in 1957 and pursued graduate studies at Chicago Teachers College and Columbia University from 1965 until 1967.

Collins' teaching career began at the Monroe County Training School in her hometown in 1958. She taught at Chicago's Delano Elementary School from 1960 until 1975. In 1975, Collins founded the Westside Preparatory School in Chicago and currently serves as its director.

Collins has conducted educational workshops throughout the United States and Europe and has appeared on several television programs, including *60 Minutes, Good Morning America,* and *The Phil Donahue Show.* She has served as director of the Right to Read Foundation and has been a member of the President's Commission on White House Fellowships since 1981. Collins has also been a consultant to the National Department of Child-

Predominantly black colleges and universities continue to account for the majority of black graduates.

ren, Youth, and Family Services and a council member of the National Institute of Health.

A number of organizations have honored Collins for her distinguished career, including the NAACP, the Reading Reform Foundation, the Fred Hampton Foundation, the Chicago Urban League, the United Negro College Fund, Phi Delta Kappa, and the American Institute for Public Service. Among the institutions that have given her honorary degrees are Washington University, Amherst College, Dartmouth University, Chicago State University, Howard University and Central State University.

Delores E. Cross (1938-)
Educational Administrator

Born on August 29, 1938, in Newark, New Jersey, Delores Cross grew up to become the first black female president of a State of Illinois university, when she named appointed the position at Chicago State University. A 20-year education veteran, Cross pursued her own education at three prestigious institutions: Seton Hall University, from where she received a B.A. in elementary education in 1963; Hofstra University, from where she earned a master's degree in 1968; and the University of Michigan, from where she garnered a

doctorate in 1971. Contact with a fourth well-reputed institution came in 1970, when she began a four-year stint as an assistant professor at Northwestern University.

In 1974, Cross joined the Claremont Graduate School as director of teacher education. After three years, moved New York City, where she served as vice chancellor for student affairs and special programs at City University of New York, then spent most of the 1980s as president of the New York State Higher Education Service Corporation. From 1988 to 1990, she was associate provost and associate vice president for academic affairs at the University of Minnesota. Then, in 1990, she was called to the predominantly black Chicago State University, (CSU) with a dropout rate of 81 percent amongst enrolled freshman student.

Faced with such a daunting statistic—particularly since nearly one-third of all black students in Illinois' public institutions attend CSU—Cross embarked on an ambitious program to turn the situation around. She created a model for success for the students, with one of the main tenants being the maintenance of pre-college initiatives going all the way back to elementary school-level children. Meanwhile, improvements to the actual facilities have included first time plans for residence

Students being bused in Woodville, Mississippi.

Marva Collins with her class at the Westside Preparatory School, Chicago.

halls and the addition of a $30 million science center. The latter is of grave importance since, in 1993, CSU boasted a nearly 100 percent pass rate for nursing school graduates and the same percentage acceptance rate amongst graduate entrants to medical schools. Meanwhile, enrollment has increased 58 percent during Cross's tenure, making CSU the only public university in the state to have significant growth.

Throughout her career, Cross has been the recipient of several awards, including honorary doctorates from Marymount Manhattan (1984) and Skidmore College (1988), the NAACP's Muriel Siverberg Award (1987), and the New York State Commission of Independent Colleges and Universities' John Jay Award (1989).

Howard Dodson, Jr. (1939-)
Historian, Educator, Curator

Born in Chester, Pennsylvania, on June 1, 1939, Howard Dodson, Jr. was always at or near the top of his class throughout junior high and high school. Out of 89 students at Chester High School, Dodson was one of nine who graduated from college. In 1961, he received a bachelor's of science from West Chester State College, and in 1964, he received a master's degree in history and

political science from Villanova University. In 1964, driven by an interested in African people transplanted in the Western Hemisphere, Dodson worked in Ecuador as a member of the U.S. Peace Corps.

In 1969, Dodson entered the doctoral program in Black History and Race Relations at the University of California at Berkeley after spending one year in Puerto Rico following the assassination of Martin Luther King, Jr. During that time Dodson studied the socio-political factors behind the civil rights and Black Power movements of the time. As part of his doctoral studies, Dodson earned a position at the Institute of the Black World, a research branch of the Martin Luther King, Jr. Center for Nonviolent Social Change in Atlanta. Dodson served as director of the Institute from 1974 to 1979.

Dodson's doctoral dissertation, "The Political Economy in South Carolina: 1780-1830," demonstrates that black slave workers were not victims of their circumstances but rather contributors to a complex socio-economic system. In addition to his dissertation, Dodson has written widely on the subject of African American history. He served as editor-in-chief of *Black World View* magazine in 1977, and he has published books, including *Thinking and Rethinking U.S. History* (1988),

Principal Dr. Clifford Watson with students of the Malcolm X Academy, Detroit, Michigan.

a book for children written with Madelon Bedell, and *Black Photographers Bear Witness: 100 Years of Social Protest* (1989), a book published by Williams College Museum of Art on which he collaborated Deborah Willis.

In 1984, Dodson took a post as the head of the Schomburg Center for Research in Black Culture at the New York Public Library. In 1991, due to his ministrations and fund-raising, the Schomburg Center opened an expanded complex. Dodson has served as consultant to the National Endowment for the Humanities, the African American Museums Association, the Library of Congress, the U.S. Department of Education, the Congressional Black Caucus, and the National Council of Churches. He won the Association for the Study of Afro-American Life and History Service Award in 1976 and a Governor's Award for African Americans of Distinction in 1982.

Sarah Mapp Douglass (1806-1882)
Educator

The free-born Sarah Mapp Douglass was an outspoken antislavery activist and accomplished educator. She attended the Ladies Institute of the Pennsylvania Medical University. In the 1820s she organized a school for black children in Philadelphia.

Douglass was an active member of the Philadelphia Female Anti-Slavery Society, which also provided support to Douglass's school. Moreover, she served as vice chairman of the Freedman's Aid Society and was a member of the New York Anti-Slavery Women.

In 1853 Douglass was appointed head of the girls' department at the Institute of Colored Youth (forerunner of Cheney State College). She remained there until her retirement in 1877. Douglass died in Philadelphia on September 8, 1882.

Michael Eric Dyson (1958-)
Educator and Writer

Michael Eric Dyson was born into a middle-class family in Detroit, Michigan, in 1958. He was ordained as a Baptist minister and attended divinity school at Tennessee's Knoxville College, ultimately earning a bachelor's degree in 1982 from Carson-Newman College. Three years later he accepted a graduate fellowship at Princeton University, obtaining his master's and doctor-

In an African-centered environment, the classroom is transformed into a holistic learning environment, in which the student is the center.

Molefi Kete Asante

ate degree by 1993. Dyson went on to become an assistant professor at Brown University. A non-traditional scholar, he chose to target his interests to a popular audience. Dyson reviewed books and films for newspapers, contributed record reviews to *Rolling Stone,*, and became a columnist for *Christian Century* and *The Nation. Reflecting Black: African-American Cultural Criticism,* Dyson's first book-length collection of essays, addressed black pop-culture icons.

In 1994 Dyson published *Making Malcolm: The Myth and Meaning of Malcolm X.* The book was written in response to a confrontation with some of Dyson's black male students at Brown University who objected to the presence of whites in his course on the radical Muslim leader. True to his goal of reaching beyond the scholarly community, Dyson's book was deliberately marketed to a wide, youthful readership. In his third book, *Between God and Gangsta Rap.* Dyson attempted to put gangsta rap in its cultural and social perspective and established himself as an authority. As a result, he was asked to testify on the genre before a congressional subcommittee, gained popularity as a lecturer, and became a

sought-after guest on talk shows. Dyson has been considered one of a group of "new intellectuals." In 1996, he was heading the Institute of African American Research at the University of North Carolina in Chapel Hill and continued to address issues of race and culture in both scholarly and popular publications.

John Hope Franklin (1915-)
Scholar

Franklin's long and distinguished career has included the publication of numerous books of history and biography, numerous awards and honorary degrees and a position of great stature in the scholarly community.

Franklin was born in Rentiesville, Oklahoma, in 1915. He received his bachelor's degree from Fisk University in 1935 and then began graduate work at Harvard, which awarded him a master's in 1936 and a Ph.D. in 1941. He taught history at Fisk and St. Augustine's College while working on his doctorate, later moving on to North Carolina College at Durham, Howard University, Brooklyn College (where he chaired the history department), Cambridge University, the University of Chicago, and Duke University.

Mary McLeod Bethune

Joe Clark

Among his many publications are such books as *From Slavery to Freedom, A History of Negro Americans, Militant South, Reconstruction After the Civil War, The Emancipation Proclamation, A Southern Odyssey, Race and History: Selected Essay* and *The Color Line: Legacy for the Twenty-First Century.*

Twice a Guggenheim Fellow, Franklin received honors from the Fellowship of Southern Writers, Encyclopedia Britannica and many other organizations, was made professor emeritus of history at Duke and earned the Publications Prize of the American Studies Association established in his name in 1986. Franklin was also granted the Britannica Award in 1990 and has been the recipient of over 90 honorary degrees. In 1995, President Clinton awarded Franklin the Presidential Medal of Freedom, America's highest civilian honor.

Henry Louis Gates, Jr. (1950-)
Literary Scholar, Professor, Critic

Henry Louis Gates, Jr. was born on September 16, 1950, in Keyser, West Virginia. He was *summa cum laude* in 1973 at Yale University, where he earned a bachelor's in history. He went on to receive a master's in 1974 and in 1979 a Ph.D., from the Clare College of England's Cambridge University. He served as a staff correspondent for *Time* magazine in London until 1975. There he studied with Nobel laureate playwright Wole Soyinka of Nigeria. His post-graduate studies examined African American literature as it has derived from the traditions of Africa and the Caribbean. He returned to the states as a guest lecturer for Yale periodically from 1976 to 1979.

In 1979, Gates accepted an assistant professorship in the English Department at Yale, where he served as director of the department of undergraduate Afro-American studies until 1985. In 1981, the MacArthur Foundation awarded him $150,000 for his critical essays about black literature. And in 1983, when he republished Harriet E. Wilson's *Our Nig*, he vaulted to the top of the world of black scholarship. He has also been a Rockefeller Foundation fellow and has enjoyed grants from the National Endowment for the Humanities. During this time, he also created the PBS television series *The Image of the Black in the Western Imagination,* which aired in 1982. From 1985 to 1990, he served as a professor of English and African Studies at Cornell University and as a W. E. B. Du Bois Professor of Literature at Duke University from 1988 to 1990. He continued his DuBois

Johnetta Cole

professorship at Harvard in 1990, where he became chair of the department of African-American Studies in 1991.

In 1989, Gates won the American Book Award for *The Signifying Monkey* and an Ainsfield-Wolfe Book Award the same year for *Towards a Theory of Afro-American Literary Criticism*. In 1994, Gates's memoir, *Colored People*, was published; the work encompasses his experiences growing up in rural West Virginia. In 1996, Gates earned prestige for his African American Studies de-

partment by attracting some of the country's leading scholars to Harvard. In addition, that year he and Kwame Anthony Appiah collaborated on *The Dictionary of Global Culture*, a guide highlighting the achievements of the non-Western world.

William H. Gray III (1941-)
United Negro College Fund President

Born to a minister and a high school teacher in Baton Rouge, Louisiana, on August 20, 1941, William H. Gray

Marva Collins

John Hope Franklin

III earned a bachelor's degree from Franklin and Marshall College in 1963, serving during his senior year as an intern for Pennsylvania congressman Robert N.C. Nix. He received a Master's of Divinity from Drew Theological School in 1966 and a Master of Theology degree from Princeton Theological Seminary in 1970. He also attended the University of Pennsylvania, Temple University and Oxford University.

Gray served as assistant pastor at Union Baptist Church in Montclair, New Jersey from 1964 until 1966. He was promoted to senior pastor in 1966 and served in this capacity until 1972. Gray moved to Philadelphia in 1972 to become pastor of Bright Hope Baptist Church.

In 1976, Gray decided to become involved in politics, challenging Robert N.C. Nix for his congressional seat. His first attempt to unseat Nix was unsuccessful. However, in 1978, Gray defeated Nix and was elected to Congress. He became a vocal and influential member of the House, challenging the administration of Ronald Reagan on such issues as social spending and U.S. support for the government of South Africa. He served on the House Budget Committee, becoming chair in 1985 and earned the admiration and respect of even his most implacable political foes. Gray was a member of

the House Foreign Affairs Committee for twelve years. For ten of those twelve years, he served on the Appropriations Subcommittee on Foreign Operations. He was also vice-chair of the Congressional Black Caucus. Gray left the House of Representatives in 1991 to head the United Negro College Fund.

On May 8, 1994, President Bill Clinton appointed Gray as his special envoy to Haiti. In this capacity, Gray played an instrumental role in the eventual removal of Haiti's brutal military government in October 1994.

William Leo Hansberry (1894-1965)
Historian, Educator

William Leo Hansberry was born on February 25, 1894 in Gloster, Mississippi. He earned a bachelor's in anthropology in 1921. Determined to eliminate American ethnocentrism regarding Africa, he issued a missive to black schools and colleges called "Announcing an Effort to Promote the Study and Facilitate the Teaching of the Fundamentals of Negro Life and History." The flier brought Hansberry three job offers from schools, and he accepted a post at Howard University in Washington, DC. Beginning in 1922, he began designing courses on Negro and African history.

William Gray

Despite Hansberry's ability to prove the material taught in his courses, the board of Howard University pulled his financial backing after spurious accusations by colleagues but agreed to keep the African Studies program in place. Still, the scuffle cost him much in funds and promotions. Nevertheless, in 1932, Hansberry returned to Harvard to complete his master's in anthropology and history continuing his studies in the mid-1930s at the University of Chicago's Oriental Institute. His studies won him a Rockefeller Foundation grant that allowed him to study at Oxford University in England from 1937 to 1938, when Howard University finally recognized his achievements with an assistant professorship. But entrenched racial prejudice kept Hansberry from earning more grants and fellowships to continue his work.

Howard University made little effort to compensate him and after over 20 years of service, he remained only an associate professor in 1945. But then the university climate changed and Hansberry was appointed advisor to African students in 1946; in 1950, he was made Emergency Aid to the African Students' Committee at Howard University in addition to his teaching load. Due to increased interest in African studies, Hansberry won

a Fullbright Scholarship to lecture at Cairo University and to study in Egypt, Ethiopia, and the Sudan in 1953. He also visited Kenya, Uganda, and Zimbabwe.

bell hooks (1952-)
Social Activist, Feminist Theorist, Educator, Writer

Feminst educator bell hooks has done her most important work as a teacher in programs that allow a critique of racism that was absent during her own undergraduate years. She contributes essays to a variety of scholarly journals and also publishes fiction and poetry. hooks has gained notoriety as a writer of critical essays on systems of domination, making herself a vital name in feminist debate. Her titles include *Talking Back: Thinking Feminist, Thinking Black* (1989) *Black Looks: Race and Representation*, (1992) and *Killing Rage: Ending Racism*, (1995) *Black Is a Woman's Color* (1996).

Born Gloria Jean Watkins in 1952, hooks grew up with five siblings in Hopkinsville, a small town in rural Kentucky. Despite her family's poverty and hardship, hooks reveled in lessons of diligence and community. She attended segregated public schools, where her role models were single black female teachers. Verbally and through written poetry, hooks began defiantly resisting the sexism she perceived within her neighborhood. Rejecting her expected role as an obedient southern girl, the writer eventually adopted a pseudonym to represent a new sense of self—a woman who spoke her mind and was not afraid to talk back.

When she won a scholarship to Stanford University, hooks sought out intellectual and political affirmation from the campus feminist movement. Disillusioned and alienated by the absence of material by or discussion about black women, hooks began criticizing the persistent racism within feminism. Having gained her bachelor's degree in 1973, hooks faced obstacles at the University of Wisconsin and the University of California at Santa Cruz, where male faculty members were determined to prevent her from becoming a university professor. In 1981, hooks published *Ain't I a Woman: Black Women and Feminism*, which was sharply criticized for its defiance of academic convention. Nonetheless, the work became central to discussions of racism and sexism. hooks persisted with her studies, earned a Ph.D. in 1983, and went on to teach African American and Women's studies at Yale University, Oberlin College, and City College of New York.

John Hope (1868-1936)
Educator, Activist

The progress made in higher education for African American students has been strongly helped by the efforts of John Hope. His life was committed to improving the school system of his time to afford more access to minorities. Hope was one of the most influential leaders of his time in the field of higher education.

In 1894, Hope graduated from Brown University in Worcester, Massachusetts, elected class orator for the commencement service. In later years, Hope would receive an honorary master of arts and law degree from Brown, along with being admitted into the Phi Beta Kappa Society. Upon graduating, Hope accepted a teaching job at Roger Williams University in Nashville, Tennessee. Four years later he accepted a teaching position at Atlanta Baptist College, located in Georgia, the state of his birth. At the college Hope began a long-time friendship with the educator W. E. B. DuBois. They both attended the 1895 Macon Convention which turned into the Georgia Equal Rights Convention.

In 1906, John Hope became acting president of Atlanta Baptist College, and the next year he was named president. He was the first African American to be appointed president at a Baptist school. As president, Hope expanded the college with funds donated by John T. Rockefeller and Andrew Carnegie. In 1913, the school was renamed Morehouse College, and was very progressive in its stressing of the dignity of its African American students. During the 1920's the college continued to expand, as Hope developed the Atlanta School of Social Work.

In 1929, Hope fulfilled his lifelong ambition of affiliating Atlanta's African American schools by having the Atlanta University Affiliation signed by the presidents of Atlanta University, Spelman, and Morehouse College. Hope was appointed president of Atlanta University while continuing as president of Morehouse College. For his efforts in education, Hope received the Harmon Award in 1930, for distinguished achievement in education.

Franklin G. Jenifer (1939-)
University of Texas at Dallas President

A distinguished scholar, Franklin Jenifer, born in 1939 in Washington, D.C., was trained as a biologist and taught in the biology departments of such institutions as Livingston College at Rutgers University, where he chaired the biology department from 1974-77. He obtained his doctorate from the University of Maryland, but it was to his alma mater, Howard University—where he received his bachelor's and master's degrees—that he would return to take up his most visible position: university president. He became Howard's president in 1990 after a series of assignments ranging from vice chancellor of the New Jersey Department of Higher Education to chancellor of the Massachusetts Board of Regents. On April 22, 1994, Jenifer resigned as president of Howard University to assume leadership of the University of Texas at Dallas.

A native of Washington, DC, Jenifer is chairman of the AAAS National Council for Science & Technology Education and a board member of the American Council on Education and the Council for Aid to Education. He holds honorary doctorates from Babson College, Boston College, Mount Holyoke College, the University of Medicine and Dentistry of New Jersey, and Wheelock College.

Charles S. Johnson (1893-1956)
Scholar, Former Fisk University President

Charles Spurgeon Johnson was born in Bristol, Virginia, in 1893. He earned a B.A. degree from Virginia Union University and in a Ph.D. from the University of Chicago.

Johnson occupied a number of diverse positions, from editor to administrator. He served as the assistant executive secretary of the Chicago Commission on Race Relations and as research director of the National Urban League, where he founded the organization's journal, *Opportunity*.

In 1928 Johnson was made chairman of Fisk University's department of social sciences. While at Fisk he established the Fisk Institute of Race Relations. In 1933 he was appointed director of Swarthmore College's Institute of Race Relations. In 1946 Johnson was appointed president of Fisk University—the first black to hold the position.

Johnson wrote several books before his death in 1956, including *The Negro in American Civilization* (1930), *The Economic Status of the Negro* (1933), *The Negro College Graduate* (1936), and *Educational and Cultural Crisis* (1951).

E. J. Josey (1924-)
Librarian, Activist, Author

E. J. Josey was born in Norfolk, Virginia on January 20, 1924. He studied music and played a church organ until 1943, when he was drafted into the U.S. Army for three years. Josey went on to complete his education at Howard University's School of Music, later moving on to Columbia University's master's program in history, and the State University of New York's Library School. In 1953, Josey began his career in libraries and rapidly became a leader in confronting segregation within them.

After his initial struggle against the Georgia Library Association when they denied him membership in 1960, Josey persevered within a diverse public and academic library career and gained a reputation as a wise, impassioned speaker on social issues. His publication, *The*

Black Librarian in America was a pioneering look into conditions for African Americans within librarianship. Its 1994 sequel, *The Black Librarian in America Revisited* was an appraisal of any real changes that had been made in intervening years. Josey helped organize the Black Caucus of the American Library Association, which combated institutional racism and widespread discrimination both within the profession and in conjunction with library services.

As president of the American Library Association from 1984 to 1985, Josey fostered awareness of the value of libraries as an integral part of the nation's infrastructure. Fighting against severe budget cuts imposed by the Reagan administration, Josey rallied library advocates in Washington, DC to march with him in protest. Josey has, in addition to his professional achievements, led community advocacy for civil and human rights as a leading member of the NAACP, was a contributor to intellectual development in emerging African countries, and was awarded four honorary doctorates. In the late 1980s until his retirement in 1995, Josey joined the faculty of the School of Library and Information Science at the University of Pittsburgh and devoted himself to achieving a racial balance in library education.

Maulana Karenga (1941-)
Activist-scholar, Educator, Ethicist

Dr. Maulana Karenga is professor and chair of the Department of Black Studies at California State University, Long Beach, where he also chairs the President's Task Force on Multicultural Education and Campus Diversity. He holds Ph.D. degrees in political science from United States International University and in social ethics with a focus on the classical African ethics of ancient Egypt from the University of Southern California.

Karenga came to prominence in the 1960s as founder of The Organization Us, a cultural and social change group whose name he explains, "simply means us Black people and stresses the communitarian focus of the organization and its philosophy, *Kawaida*, which is an ongoing synthesis of the best of African thought and practice in constant exchange with the world." Karenga and Us have greatly influenced the development of the discipline of Black Studies, the Black Arts and Black Student movements, Afrocentricity, and ancient Egyptian studies. They have also advanced the independent school and rites of passage movements through the *Nguzo Saba* (The Seven Principles of Kawaida).

Moreover, Karenga and Us played important roles in the founding of the initial Black Power Conferences in the 1960s and the National Black United Front in the 1980s. More recently they were in the forefront of organizing the National African American Leadership Summit and the Million Man March/Day of Absence. Karenga was a member of the executive council for the landmark 1995 gathering in Washington and authored its Mission Statement, co-editing the subsequent volume, *The Million Man March/Day of Absence: A Commemorative Anthology*. Having celebrated its thirtieth anniversary in 1995, The Organization Us continues its declared commitment to "Struggle, service, and institution-building."

An internationally recognized activist-scholar, Karenga has published numerous scholarly articles and books, among them the widely used *Introduction to Black Studies*; his retranslation and commentary on ancient Egyptian texts, *Selections from the Husia: Sacred Wisdom of Ancient Egypt*; and the influential *The African American Holiday of Kwanzaa*. In fact, he created the Kwanzaa celebration now observed throughout the world African community. He has lectured throughout the United States and the world and earned numerous scholarship, leadership, and community service awards.

Sara Lawrence-Lightfoot (1944-)
Educator, Sociologist, Writer

Sara Lawrence-Lightfoot's sociological writing has been an attempt to create a clearer picture of the kind of lives African Americans really live. She has felt much of what has been written is a distorted view of who African Americans really are.

Lawrence-Lightfoot's 1994 book, *I've Known Rivers: Lives of Loss and Liberation*, details life in the African American middle class through interviews with six African American professionals. It was chosen as a Book-of-the-Month Club main choice. In 1978, her book *Worlds Apart* promoted cooperation between parents and teachers for the education of children. Her third book, *The Good High School: Portraits of Character and Culture*, chronicles the positive methods of six schools in the United States, offering the book as a catalyst for institutional change.

Lawrence-Lightfoot departed from her sociological writings to write a personal account of her mother's life in her 1988 book, *Balm in Gilead: Journey of a Healer*. She received a MacArthur Award to fund the writing of the book. Along with writing her books, teaching at Harvard University as a professor of education, and doing her research, Lawrence-Lightfoot gives lectures and serves on numerous committees and national boards, among them the National Academy of Education, the *Boston Globe*, and the John D. and Catherine T. MacArthur Foundation.

David Levering Lewis (1936-)
Educator and Writer

David Levering Lewis was born May 25, 1936 in Little Rock, Arkansas. He earned a bachelor's in history from Fisk University in 1956 and continued his studies at Columbia University, where he earned a master's in 1958 and later a Ph.D. at the London School of Economics and Political Science in 1962. He published his first paper as an undergraduate, called "History of the Negro Upper Class In Atlanta, Georgia 1890-1958."

Lewis eventually found himself studying African American history after years as a scholar of French history, teaching widely at places, such as the University of Ghana, Notre Dame University, and Howard University. In the late 1960s, he undertook to write a scholarly biography of Martin Luther King, Jr. published in 1971 as *Martin Luther King: A Critical Biography*. Lewis followed this work with one on anti-Semitism called *Prisoners of Honor: The Dreyfus Affair* in 1973 at which time he accepted a teaching post at Federal City College in Washington D.C. In 1974, he became a full professor of history at the University of the District of Columbia.

Throughout the 1970s, he studied the Harlem Renaissance of the 1920s and 1930s, writing a work of definitive scholarship on the subject, published in 1981, as *When Harlem Was In Vogue: The Politics of the Arts in the Twenties and Thirties*. Next, Lewis tackled W. E. B. Du Bois, the great scholar and writer. His biography of Du Bois, *W. E. B. Du Bois: Biography of a Race, 1868-1919* won Lewis a Pulitzer Prize for biography in 1994 and a National Book Award the same year. By the time his Du Bois biography was published in 1993, Lewis had taken a position as the chair of the history department of Rutgers University to which he commuted by train from his home on Capitol Hill in Washington, DC. Lewis contributes regularly to scholarly journals and the *Washington Post*.

Alain Locke (1886-1954)
Scholar

Born on September 3, 1886 in Philadelphia, Locke graduated Phi Beta Kappa with a B.A. degree from Harvard University in 1907. He was then awarded a Rhodes Scholarship for two years of study at Oxford University in England and did further graduate study at the University of Berlin (1910-1911). Upon returning to the United States, Locke took an assistant professorship in English and philosophy at Howard University in Washington, DC. He received his Ph.D. from Harvard in 1918 and the same year was made chairman of the philosophy department at Howard where he stayed until his retirement in 1953.

In 1934 Locke founded the Associates in Negro Folk Education. In 1942 he was named to the Honor Role of Race Relations. A prolific author, Locke's first book was entitled *Race Contacts and Inter-Racial Relations* (1916). His best known works include, *The New Negro: An Interpretation* (1925), a book that introduced America to the Harlem Renaissance, and *The Negro in Art: A Pictorial Record of the Negro Artist and of the Negro Theme in Art* (1940). Locke died in New York City on June 9, 1954.

Benjamin E. Mays (1894-1984)
Former Morehouse College President

In addition to occupying the president's office at Morehouse, Benjamin Mays wrote, taught mathematics, worked for the federal Office of Education, served as chairman of the Atlanta Board of Education, preached in a Baptist church, acted as an advisor to the Southern Christian Leadership Council, and was a church historian.

Born in Epworth, South Carolina, in 1894, Dr. Mays attended Bates College and later received his master's and Ph.D. from the University of Chicago. He served as a pastor at Georgia's Shiloh Baptist Church from 1921-24, and later taught at Morehouse College and South Carolina's State College at Orangeburg. After a stint at the Tampa Urban League, he worked for the YMCA as National Student Secretary and then directed a study of black churches for the Institute of Social and Religious Research. From 1934-40 he acted as dean of Howard University's School of Religion, before taking up the presidency of Morehouse from 1940-67. He served in several other distinguished posts, including the Atlanta Board of Education chairmanship and positions at HEW and the Ford Foundation. Awards earned by Dr. Mays include 43 honorary degrees, the Dorie Miller Medal of Honor, and the 1971 Outstanding Older Citizen award. He died in 1984.

Jesse Edward Moorland (1863-1940)
Archivist, Clergyman

Jesse Moorland was born on September 10, 1863 in Coldwater, Ohio. Following the untimely death of his parents, Moorland was reared by his grandparents. His early education consisted of sporadic attendance at a small rural schoolhouse and being read to by his grandfather. Moorland eventually attended Normal University in Ada, Ohio, married and taught school in Urbana, Ohio. He went on to Howard University in Washington and graduated with a degree in theology in 1891.

Moorland was ordained a congregational minister and between 1891 and 1896 he served at churches in South Boston, Virginia, Nashville and Cleveland. In 1891

Alain Locke

he also became active in the YMCA, an association he would maintain for much of his life.

In 1909 Moorland's well known essay "Demand and the Supply of Increased Efficiency in the Negro Ministry" was published by the American Negro Academy. In it Moorland called for a more pragmatic ministry, both in terms of the education of its members and its approach to dealing with social issues.

By 1910 Moorland had become quite active in the YMCA and was appointed secretary of the Colored Men's Department. In this position Moorland raised millions of dollars for the YMCA's construction and building fund.

Having reached the mandatory retirement age in 1923, Moorland resigned from the YMCA and began devoting his time and considerable energy to other pursuits. Moorland was active with the Association for the Study of Negro Life and History, the National Health Circle for Colored People, and the Frederick Douglass Home Association.

From 1907 on Moorland served as a trustee of Howard University. In 1914 he donated his private library of

African-American history to the university. Out of this gift grew the Moorland Foundation. The collection was renamed the Moorland-Spingarn Collection and later renamed the Moorland-Spingarn Research Center. This collection of documents on black history and culture was the first African-American research collection in a major American university. Moorland died in New York on April 30, 1940.

Frederick Douglass Patterson (1901-1988)
United Negro College Fund President

Frederick Douglass Patterson was born in Washington, D.C., on October 10, 1901. He received a D.V.M. degree in 1923 and a M.S. degree in 1927 from Iowa State University. In 1932 he received a Ph.D. from Cornell University.

Patterson joined the faculty of Tuskegee Institute in 1928, st as an instructor of veterinary science, later as director of the school of agriculture, and finally as president. He also chaired the R.R. Moton Memorial Institute and served as director of education for the Phelps-Stokes Fund.

In 1944 Patterson organized the United Negro College Fund, a cooperative fund-raising organization to provide financial assistance to predominantly black colleges and universities.

Benjamin F. Payton (1932-)
Tuskegee University President

Born in Orangeburg, South Carolina, in 1932, Benjamin Franklin Payton took a bachelor's degree with honors from South Carolina State College in 1955. He earned a B.D. from Howard University in 1958, a master's degree from Columbia University in 1960, and a Ph.D. from Yale University in 1963. He took a position as assistant professor at Howard University before working for the National Council of Churches as the Commission on Religion and Race's executive director of social justice, a position which he retained even as he took over the presidency of Benedict College in 1967. He left Benedict in 1972 for a position at the Ford Foundation, where he remained until he became Tuskegee's president in 1981.

Payton holds honorary degrees from Eastern Michigan University, Morris Brown, Benedict, and Morgan State. A recipient of the Napoleon Hill Foundation Gold Medal Award and the Benjamin E. Mays Award, he served as educational advisor to Vice President George Bush on Bush's seven nation tour of Africa in 1982. Payton has also served as a member of several organiza-

Benjamin Mays and others meet with President John F. Kennedy.

tions, including the National Association for Equal Opportunity in High Education, the Alabama Industrial Relations Council, the National Association of Independent Colleges and Universities, the Executive Board of the National Consortium for Educational Access.

Arthur A. Schomburg (1874-1938)
Archivist, American Negro Academy President

Born in Puerto Rico in 1874, Arturo Schomburg led a richly varied public life. He worked as a law clerk and was a businessman, journalist, editor, lecturer, New York Public Library curator, and teacher of Spanish.

In 1911 Schomburg co-founded the Negro Society for Historical Research. He was also a lecturer for the United Negro Improvement Association. Schomburg was a member of the New York Puerto Rico Revolutionary Party and served as secretary of the Cuban Revolutionary Party. In 1922 he headed the American Negro Academy, an organization founded by Alexander Crummell in 1879 to promote black art, literature, and science.

Schomburg, who died in 1938, collected thousands of works on black culture over his life time. In 1926

Schomburg's personal collection was purchased by the Carnegie Corporation and given to the New York Public Library. In 1973 the collection became known as the Schomburg Collection of Negro Literature and History, the name was later changed to the Schomburg Center for Research in Black Culture.

Shelby Steele (1946-)
Scholar

Steele was born January 1, 1946 in Chicago but grew up in Phoenix, Illinois, a blue collar suburb of Chicago. He attended high school in Harvey, Illinois, where he was student council president his senior year prior to graduating in 1964. Steele then attended Coe College in Cedar Rapids, Iowa where he was active in SCOPE—an organization associated with Martin Luther King's Southern Christian Leadership Council. He graduated in 1968 and in 1971 received an M.S. in sociology from Southern Illinois University. He went on to receive a Ph.D. in English literature from the University of Utah in 1974. While at Southern Illinois University he taught African-American literature to impoverished children in East Saint Louis. Steele is currently a professor of English literature at San Jose State University.

Arthur Schomburg

Shelby Steele

In 1990 Steele published *The Content of Our Character: A New Vision of Race in America*, which won the National Book Critics Circle Award. In this controversial book Steele argued that African-American self-doubt and it's exploitation by the white and black liberal establishment is as great a cause of problems for African Americans as more traditional forms of racism. Steele has also written articles on this theme for such respected publications as *Harper's*, *New Republic*, *American Scholar*, and *Commentary*.

Because of his beliefs Steele has been identified as part of an emerging black neo-conservative movement, but in an interview with *Time* magazine (August 12, 1991) he categorized himself as a classical liberal focusing on the freedom and sacredness of the individual.

Clifton R. Wharton, Jr. (1926-)
Former University President

Clifton R. Wharton, born on September 13, 1926, was the first African American to head the largest university system in the United States—the State University of New York. He was also president of Michigan State University and served as chairman and CEO of the

Teachers Insurance and Annuity Association and College Retirement Equities Fund.

A native Bostonian, Wharton took a bachelor's degree cum laude from Harvard in 1947. He received a master's at Johns Hopkins the following year, as the first African American admitted into the university's School for Advanced International Studies. In 1956 he took a second M.A. from the University of Chicago, which awarded him a Ph.D. in 1958. Between master's degrees he worked as a research associate for the University of Chicago. He then proceeded to the Agricultural Development Council, Inc., where he worked for twelve years. He also held a post as visiting professor at the University of Malaya and served as director and eventually vice president of the American Universities Research Program. Wharton took over the presidency of Michigan State in 1970 and stayed there for eight years; he moved on to the SUNY system from 1978 to 1987. He then worked for the Teachers Insurance and Annuity Association and has since become the first African American to chair the Rockefeller Foundation.

Wharton won the President's Award on World Hunger in 1983 and has earned honorary degrees from more than 45 colleges and universities.

Clifton Wharton

Carter G. Woodson

Carter Godwin Woodson (1875-1950)
Scholar

Carter Godwin Woodson was born December 9, 1875, in New Canton, Virginia. He received a B.Litt. degree from Berea College in 1903, a B.A. and an M.A. in 1907 and 1908 from the University of Chicago, and a Ph.D. from Harvard University in 1912.

Known as the "Father of Modern Black History," Woodson was a passionate exponent of African-American economic self-sufficiency. In 1915 Woodson founded the Association for the Study of Negro Life and History (now the Association for the Study of Afro-American Life and History). One year later, the organization began publishing the *Journal of Negro History*. In 1920 he founded Associated Publishers Inc. and in 1921 he founded the *Negro History Bulletin*. In 1926 Woodson launched Negro History Week (now Black History Month) to promote the study of African-American history.

An historian, author, editor, and teacher, Woodson served as dean of the Howard University School of Liberal Arts and of the West Virginia Institute, and was a Spingarn Medalist. His works include *The Education of*

the *Negro Prior to 1861* (1915), *A Century of Negro Migration* (1918), *The Negro in Our History* (1922), and *The Miseducation of the Negro* (1933).

Ivan Van Sertima (1935-)
Scholar

Born in British Guyana in 1935, anthropologist, linguist, and literary critic Ivan Van Sertima is currently professor of African studies at Rutgers University.

In 1977 Van Sertima published *They Came Before Columbus: The African Presence in Ancient America*. Drawing from various disciplines, Van Sertima, presents evidence of pre-Columbian contact with the New World by Africans.

In 1979 Van Sertima founded *The Journal of African Civilizations*, which presents a revisionist approach to world history. He is also the author of *Caribbean Writers*, a collection of essays.

◆ HISTORICALLY AND PREDOMINANTLY BLACK COLLEGES AND UNIVERSITIES

Alabama A and M University
PO Box 908
Normal, AL 35762
(205) 851-5245

Alabama State University
915 S. Jackson St.
Montgomery, AL 36101-0271
(205) 293-4291

Albany State College
504 College Dr.
Albany, GA 31705-2797
(912) 430-4646

Alcorn State University
PO Box 300
Lorman, MS 39096
(601) 877-6147

Allen University
1530 Harden St.
Columbia, SC 29204
(803) 376-5716

Arkansas Baptist College
1600 Bishop St.
Little Rock, AR 72202
(501) 574-7856

Atlanta Metropolitan College
1630 Stewart Ave. SW
Atlanta, GA 30310
(404) 756-4441

Barber-Scotia College
145 Cabarrus Ave.
Concord, NC 28025
(704) 786-5171

Benedict College
Harden and Blanding Sts.
Columbia, SC 29294
(803) 253-5143

Bennett College
900 E. Washington St.
Greensboro, NC 27401-3239
(919) 370-8624

Bethune-Cookman College
640 2nd Ave.
Daytona Beach, FL 32115
(904) 255-1402

Bishop State Community College
351 N. Broad St.
Mobile, AL 36603-5898
(205) 690-6800

Bluefield State College
219 Rock St.
Bluefield, WV 24701
(304) 327-4065

Bowie State College
1400 Jericho Park Rd.
Bowie, MD 20715
(301) 464-6563

Central State University
Wilberforce, OH 45384
(513) 376-6478

Charles R. Drew University of Medicine and Science
1621 E. 120th St.
Los Angeles, CA 90059
(213) 563-4960

Cheyney University of Pennsylvania
Cheyney, PA 19319
(215) 399-2275

Chicago State University
95th St. at King Dr.
Chicago, IL 60628
(312) 995-2513

Claflin College
College Ave. NE
Orangeburg, SC 29115
(803) 534-2710

Clark Atlanta University
James P. Brawley Dr. at Fair St., SW
Atlanta, GA 30314-4389
(404) 880-8017

Clinton Junior College
PO Box 968
Rock Hill, SC 29731
(803) 327-5587

Coahoma Community College
Rt. 1, Box 616
3240 Friars Point Rd.
Clarksdale, MS 38614-9799
(601) 627-2571

Compton Community College
1111 Last Artesia Blvd.
Compton, CA 90221-5393
(310) 637-2660

Concordia College
1804 Green St.
Selma, AL 36701
(205) 847-5736

Coppin State College
2500 W. North Ave.
Baltimore, MD 21216
(410) 383-5990

Cuyahoga Community College
Metropolitan College Campus
2900 Community College Ave.
Cleveland, OH 44115
(216) 987-4000

Delaware State College
Dover, DE 19901
(302) 736-4917

Denmark Technical College
Solomon Blatt Blvd.
PO Box 327
Denmark, SC 29042-0327
(803) 793-3301

Dillard University
2601 Gentilly Blvd.
New Orleans, LA 70122
(504) 286-4670

Edward Waters College
1658 Kings Rd.
Jacksonville, FL 32209
(904) 366-2528

Elizabeth City State University
Campus Box 901
Elizabeth City, NC 27909
(919) 355-3305

Fayetteville State University
1200 Murchison Rd.
Newbold Station
Fayetteville, NC 28301-4298
(919) 486-1371

Fisk University
1000 17th Ave. N
Nashville, TN 37208
(615) 329-8665

Florida A and M University
1500 Wahnish Way
Tallahassee, FL 32307
(904) 599-3796

Florida Memorial College
15800 NW 42nd Ave.
Miami, FL 33054
(305) 623-4141

Fort Valley State College
805 State College Dr.
Fort Valley, GA 31030
(912) 825-6307

Grambling State University
PO Box 864
Grambling, LA 71245
(318) 274-2435

Hampton University
Hampton, VA 23668
(804) 727-5328

Harris-Stowe State University
3026 LaClede Ave.
St. Louis, MO 63103
(314) 340-3300

Hinds Community College
Raymond, MS 39154-9799
(601) 857-3212

Howard University
2400 6th St. NW
Washington, DC 20059
(202) 806-2752

Howard University School of Law
2900 Van Ness St., NW
Washington, DC 20008
(202) 806-8008

Huston-Tillotson College
1820 E. 8th St.
Austin, TX 78702
(512) 505-3027

Interdenominational Theological Center
671 Beckwith St. SW
Atlanta, GA 30314
(404) 527-7709

J.F. Drake State Technical College
3421 Meridian St. N.
Huntsville, AL 35811
(205) 539-8161

Jackson State University
1400 John R. Lynch St.
Jackson, MS 39217
(601) 968-2100

Jarvis Christian College
PO Drawer G
Hawkins, TX 75765
(214) 769-2174

Johnson C. Smith University
100 Beatties Ford Rd.
Charlotte, NC 28216
(704) 378-1010

Kennedy-King College
6800 S. Wentworth Ave.
Chicago, IL 60621-3798
(312) 602-5049

Kentucky State University
E. Main St.
Box PG-92
Frankfort, KY 40601
(502) 227-6813

Knoxville College
901 College St. NW
Knoxville, TN 36921
(615) 524-6525

LaGuardia Community College
31-10 Thompson Ave.
Long Island City, NY 11101
(718) 482-7206

Lane College
545 Lane Ave.
Jackson, TN 38301
(901) 424-4600

Langston University
PO Box 728
Langston, OK 73050
(405) 466-3428

Lawson State Community College
3060 Wilson Rd. SW
Birmingham, AL 35221
(205) 925-2515

LeMoyne-Owen College
807 Walker Ave.
Memphis, TN 38126
(901) 942-7302

Lewis College of Business
17370 Meyers Rd.
Detroit, MI 48235
(313) 862-6300

Lincoln University (Missouri)
820 Chestnut St.
Jefferson City, MO 65101-9880
(314) 681-5599

Lincoln University of Pennsylvania
Lincoln University, PA 19352
(215) 932-8300

Livingstone College
701 W. Monroe St.
Salisbury, NC 28144
(704) 638-5505

Lomax-Hannon Junior College
PO Box 779
Greenville, AL 36037
(205) 382-2115

Mary Holmes College
Hwy. 50 W
PO Drawer 1257
West Point, MS 39773
(601) 494-6820

Medgar Evers College of City University of New York
1150 Carroll St.
Brooklyn, NY 11225
(718) 735-1948

Meharry Medical College
1005 D.B. Todd Blvd.
Nashville, TN 37208
(615) 327-6223

Miles College
PO Box 3800
Birmingham, AL 35208
(205) 923-2771

Mississippi Valley State University
Highway 82 West
Itta Bena, MS 38941
(601) 254-9041

Morehouse College
830 Westview Dr. SW
Atlanta, GA 30314
(404) 215-2632

Morehouse School of Medicine
720 Westview Dr., SW
Atlanta, GA 30310-1495
(405) 752-1652

Morgan State University
Cold Spring Ln. and Hillen Rd.
Baltimore, MD 21239
(301) 444-3000

Morris Brown College
643 Martin Luther King Jr. Dr. NW
Atlanta, GA 30314
(404) 220-0152

Morris College
100 W. College St.
Sumter, SC 29150-3599
(803) 775-9371

New York City Technical College
300 Jay St.
Brooklyn, NY 11201
(718) 260-5510

Norfolk State University
2401 Corprew Ave.
Norfolk, VA 23504
(804) 683-8396

North Carolina A and T State University
1601 E. Market St.
Greensboro, NC 27411
(919) 334-7946

North Carolina Central University
PO Box 19717
Durham, NC 27707
(919) 560-6066

Oakwood College
Oakwood Rd. NW
Huntsville, AL 35896
(205) 726-7000

Paine College
1235 15th St.
Augusta, GA 30910
(706) 821-8320

Paul Quinn College
3837 Simpson Stuart Rd.
Dallas, TX 75241
(241) 376-1000

Philander-Smith College
812 W. 13th St.
Little Rock, AR 72202
(501) 370-5217

Prairie View A and M University
PO Box 2610
Prairie View, TX 77446-2610
(409) 857-2626

Roxbury Community College
1234 Columbus Ave.
Roxbury Crossing, MA 02120
(617) 427-0060

Rust College
150 Rust Ave.
Holly Spring, MS 38635-2330
(601) 252-4461

Saint Augustine's College
1315 Oakwood Ave.
Raleigh, NC 27610
(919) 828-4451

Saint Paul's College
406 Windsor Ave.
Lawrenceville, VA 23868-9988
(804) 848-3111

Savannah State College
PO Box 20499
Savannah, GA 31404
(912) 356-2181

Selma University
1501 Lapsley St.
Selma, AL 36701
(205) 872-2533

Shaw University
118 E. South St.
Raleigh, NC 27611
(919) 546-8275

Shorter College
604 Locust St.
North Little Rock, AR 72114
(501) 374-6305

Simmons University Bible College
1811 Dumesnil St.
Louisville, KY 40210
(502) 776-1443

Sojourner-Douglass College
500 N. Caroline St.
Baltimore, MD 21205
(410)276-0306

South Carolina State University
PO Box 1568
Orangeburg, SC 29117
(803) 536-7185

Southern University and A&M University-Baton Rouge
PO Box 9901
Baton Rouge, LA 70813
(504) 771-2011

Southern University at New Orleans
6400 Press Dr.
New Orleans, LA 70126
(504) 286-5314

Southern University at Shreveport
Martin Luther King Jr. Dr.
Shreveport, LA 71107
(318) 674-3342

Southwestern Christian College
PO Box 10
Terrell, TX 75160
(214) 524-3341

Spelman College
350 Spelman Lane SW
Box 277
Atlanta, GA 30314-9811
(404) 681-3643

Stillman College
PO Box 1430
Tuscaloosa, AL 35403
(205) 349-4250

Talladega College
627 W. Battle St.
Talladega, AL 35160
(205) 362-0206

Tennessee State University
3500 John Merritt Blvd.
Nashville, TN 37209-1561
(615) 320-3420

Texas College
2404 N. Grand Ave.
Tyler, TX 75702-2404
(903) 593-8311

Texas Southern University
3100 Cleburne Ave.
Houston, TX 77004
(713) 527-7070

Tougaloo College
300 E. County Line Rd.
Tougaloo, MS 39174
(601) 977-7770

Trenholm State Technical College
1225 Air Base Blvd.
Montgomery, AL 36108
(205) 832-9000

Tuskegee University
Tuskegee, AL 36088
(205) 727-8500

University of Arkansas, Pine Bluff
N. Cedar St.
Pine Bluff, AR 71601
(501) 543-8493

University of Maryland, Eastern Shore
Princess Anne, MD 21853
(410) 651-2200

University of the District of Columbia
4200 Connecticut Ave. NW
Washington, DC 20008
(202) 274-5010

Virginia Seminary and College
2058 Garfield Ave.
Lynchburg, VA 24501
(804) 524-5070

Virginia State University
PO Box 18
Petersburg, VA 23803
(804) 524-5902

Virginia Union University
1500 N. Lombardy St.
Richmond, VA 23220
(804) 257-5855

Voorhees College
1411 Voorhees Rd.
Denmark, SC 29042
(803) 793-3351

Wayne County Community College
100 W. Fort
Detroit, MI 48225-9975
(313) 496-2500

Wilberforce University
1055 N. Bickett Rd.
Wilberforce, OH 45384
(513) 376-2911

Wiley College
71 Rosborough Springs Rd.
Marshall, TX 75670
(214) 927-3311

Winston-Salem State University
601 Martin Luther King Blvd.
Winston-Salem, NC 27110
(919) 750-2070

Xavier University of Louisiana
7325 Palmetto St.
New Orleans, LA 70125
(504) 486-7411

◆ RESEARCH INSTITUTIONS

African American Studies Center
Boston University
138 Mountfort St.
Brookline, MA 02146
(617) 353-2795
Fax: (617)353-2053

African American Studies Program
University of Houston
College of Humanities and Fine Arts
Agnes Arnold Hall
Houston, TX 77204-3783
(713) 743-2811
Fax: (713) 743-2818

African and Afro-American Studies Center
University of Texas at Austin
Jester Center, Rm. A232A
Austin, TX 78705
(512) 471-1784
Fax: (512) 471-1798

African Studies Program
University of Wisconsin, Madison
1454 Van Hise Hall
1220 Linden Dr.
Madison, WI 53706
(608) 262-2380

Africana Research Center
Brooklyn College of City University of New York
2900 Bedford Ave.
Brooklyn, NY 11210
(718) 951-5000
Fax: (718) 951-4707

Africana Studies and Research Center
Cornell University
310 Triphammer Rd.
Ithaca, NY 14850
(607) 255-5218
Fax: (607) 255-0784

African Studies and Research Institute
Queens College of City University of New York
65-30 Kissena Blvd.
Flushing, NY 11367
(718) 520-7545
Fax: (718) 520-7241

Afro-American Arts Institute
Indiana University Bloomington
109 N. Jordan Ave.
Bloomington, IN 47405
(812) 855-9501

Afro-American Studies and Research Program
606 S. Gregory
Urbana, IL 61801
(217) 333-7781
Fax: (217) 244-4809

Afro-American Studies Center
Purdue University
1367 LAEB
West Lafayette, IN 47907
(317) 494-5680
Fax: (317) 496-1521

Afro-American Studies Program
Princeton University
112 Dickinson Hall
Princeton, NJ 08544-1017
(609) 258-4270
Fax: (609) 258-5095

Afro-American Studies Program
Brown University
Box 1904
Providence, RI 02912
(401) 863-3137
Fax: (401) 863-3559

Amistad Research Center
Tulane University
6823 St. Charles Ave.
New Orleans, LA 70118
(504) 865-5535
Fax: (401) 863-3559

Association for Study of Afro-American Life and History, Inc.
1407 14th St. NW
Washington, DC 20005
(202) 667-2822
Fax: (202) 387-9802

Black Abolitionist Papers Project
Florida State University
Department of History
Tallahassee, FL 32306
(904) 644-4527

Black Americana Studies
Western Michigan University
814 Sprau Tower
Kalamazoo, MI 49008
(616) 387-2661
Fax: (616) 387-3999

Black Periodical Literature Project, 1827-1940
Harvard University
77 Dunster St.
Cambridge, MA 02138
(617) 496-7404
Fax: (617) 496-8547

Bureau of Educational Research
Howard University
School of Education
2441 14th St. NW
Washington, DC 20059
(202) 806-8120
Fax: (202) 806-8130

Carter G. Woodson Institute for Afro-American and African Studies
University of Virginia
1512 Jefferson Park Ave.
Charlottesville, VA 22903
(804) 924-3109

Center for African-American History and Culture
Temple University
Weiss Hall, Ste. B18
13th and Cecil B. Moore Ave.
Philadelphia, PA 19122
(215) 204-4851
Fax: (215) 204-3794

Center for Afro American Studies
University of California, Los Angeles
160 Haines Hall
405 Hilgard Ave.
Los Angeles, CA 90024-1545
(310) 825-7403
Fax: (310) 206-3421

Center for Afro American Studies
Ohio University
300 Lindley Hall
Athens, OH 45701
(614) 593-4546

Center for African American Studies
Wesleyan University
Middleton, CT 06457
(203) 344-7943

Center for Afro-American and African Studies
University of Michigan
W. Engineering Bldg., Rm. 200
550 E. University
Ann Arbor, MI 48109-1092
(313) 764-5513
Fax: (313) 764-0543

Center for Black Music Research
Columbia College Chicago
600 S. Michigan Ave.
Chicago, IL 60605-1996
(312) 663-1600
Fax: (312) 663-9019

Center for Black Studies
University of California, Santa Barbara
South Hall 4603
Santa Barbara, CA 93106-3140
(805) 893-3914
Fax: (805) 893-7243

Center for Black Studies
Northern Illinois University
DeKalb, IL 60115
(815) 753-1709

Center for Research on Multi-Ethnic Education
University of Oklahoma
455 Lindsey St., Rm. 804
Norman, OK 73019-0535
(405) 325-4529
Fax: (405) 325-4991

Center for Southern History and Culture
University of Alabama
PO Box 870342
University, AL 35487-0342
(205) 348-7467

Center for Studies of Ethnicity and Race in America
University of Colorado at Boulder
Ketchum 30
CB 339
Boulder, CO 80309-0339
(303) 492-8852
Fax: (303) 492-7799

Center for the Study and Stabilization of the Black Family
Niagara University
PO Box 367
Niagara University, NY 14109
(716) 285-1212

Center for the Study of Southern Culture
University of Mississippi
Barnard Observatory
University, MS 38677
(601) 232-5993
Fax: (601) 232-5814

Center for the Study of Black Literature and Culture
University of Pennsylvania
3808 Walnut St.
Philadelphia, PA 19104-6136
(215) 898-5141
Fax: (215) 898-0764

Center for the Study of Civil Rights
University of Virginia
1512 Jefferson Park Ave.
Charlottesville, VA 22903
(804) 924-3109

Center for the Study of Race and Ethnicity in America
Brown University
Box 1886
Providence, RI 02912
(401) 863-3080
Fax: (401) 863-7589

Committee on African and African-American Studies
University of Chicago
5828 S. University Ave.
Chicago, IL 60637
(312) 702-8344
Fax: (312) 702-2587

Frederick Douglass Institute for African and African-American Studies
University of Rochester
302 Morey Hall
Rochester, NY 14627-1205
(716) 275-7235
Fax: (716) 256-2594

Institute for African American Affairs
Kent State University
Department of African Studies
18 Ritchie Hall
Kent, OH 44242
(216) 672-2300
Fax: (216) 672-4837

Institute for African American Studies
College of Staten Island of City University of New York
130 Stuyvesant Pl., 8th Fl.
Staten Island
New York, NY 10301
(718) 390-7990
Fax: (718) 272-0533

Institute for African-American Studies
University of Connecticut
241 Glenbrook Rd., U-162
Storrs, CT 06269-2162
(203) 486-3630
Fax: (203) 486-3083

Institute for Black Leadership Development and Research
University of Kansas
1028 Dole
Lawrence, KS 66045-0048
(913) 864-3990
Fax: (913) 864-5323

Institute for the Preservation and Study of African-American Writing
PO Box 50172
Washington, DC 20004
(202) 727-4047

Institute of Afro American Affairs
New York University
269 Mercer St., Ste. 601
New York, NY 10003
(212) 998-2130
Fax: (212) 995-4040

Institute of Jazz Studies
Rutgers University
135 Bradley Hall
Newark, NJ 07102
(201) 648-5595
Fax: (201) 648-5944

Joint Center for Political and Economic Studies
1090 Vermont Ave. NW, Ste. 1100
Washington, DC 20005-4961
(202) 789-3500

Martin Luther King Jr. Center for Nonviolent Social Change, Inc.
449 Auburn Ave. NE
Atlanta, GA 30312
(404) 524-1956
Fax: (404) 522-6932

Moorland-Spingarn Research Center
Howard University
500 Howard Pl. NW
Washington, DC 20059
(202) 806-7239
Fax: (202) 806-6405

Morehouse Research Institute
Morehouse College
830 Westview Dr.
Atlanta, GA 30314
(404) 215-2676
Fax: (404) 222-0422

National Afro-American Museum and Cultural Center
Box 758
Wilberforce, OH 45384
(513) 376-4944
Fax: (513) 376-2007

National Black Child Development Institute
1023 15th St. NW, Ste. 600
Washington, DC 20005
(202) 387-1281
Fax: (202) 234-1738

National Study of Black College Students
University of California, Los Angeles
Department of Sociology
405 Hilgard Ave.
Los Angeles, CA 90024-1551
(310) 206-7107
FAx: (310) 206-9838

New York African American Research Foundation
State University of New York
State University Plaza
Central Administration Bldg.
Albany, NY 12246
(518) 443-5798
Fax: (518) 443-5803

Program for Research on Black Americans
University of Michigan
5118 Institute for Social Research
426 Thompson St.
PO Box 1248
Ann Arbor, MI 48106-1248
(313) 763-0045
Fax: (313) 763-0044

Race Relations Institute
Wayne State University
College of Urban, Labor and Metropolitan Affairs
656 W. Kirby, Rm. 3198 FAB
Detroit, MI 48202
(313) 577-5071
Fax: (313) 577-8800

Rites and Reason
Brown University
Box 1148
Providence, RI 02912
(401) 863-3558
Fax: (401) 863-3700

Schomburg Center for Research in Black Culture
515 Malcolm X Blvd.
New York, NY 10037-1801
(212) 491-2200
(212) 491-6760

W. E. B. Du Bois Institute for Afro-American Research

Harvard University
44 Brattle St.
Cambridge, MA 02138
(617) 495-4192
Fax: (617) 496-8547

William Monroe Trotter Institute for the Study of Black Culture

University of Massachusetts at Boston
Harbor Campus
Boston, MA 02125-3393
(617) 287-5880

Women's Research and Resource Center

Spelman College
Box 115
Atlanta, GA 30314
(404) 223-7528
Fax: (404) 753-8383

◆ AFRICAN AMERICAN CHAIRED PROFESSORS (1996)

- Wanda Coleman, Fletcher Jones Professor of Literature and Writing, Loyola Marymount University, Los Angeles.

- Donna Franklin, John Milner Professor of Child Welfare, School of Social Work, University of Southern California.

- LaSalle D. Leffall, Jr., Charles R. Drew Professor and chairperson, Department of Surgery, Howard University.

- John McFadden, Benjamin Elijah Mays Professor, College of Education, University of Southern Carolina.

- Donald E. McHenry, University Research Professor of Diplomacy, Georgetown University.

- Orlando Patterson, John Cowles Professor of Sociology, Department of Sociology, Harvard University.

- Gayle Pemerton, William Rand Kenan Professor of the Humanities, Wesleyan University.

- William Raspberry, Knight Professor in Communication and Journalism.

- Charlotte H. Scott, University Professor of Commerce and Education at the University of Virginia.

- Hereket H. Selassie, William E. Leuchtenburg Professor of African and Afro-American Studies, University of North Carolina at Chapel Hill.

- Jessie Carney Smith, William and Camille Cosby Professor of the Humanities and University Librarian, Fisk University.

- Jon Michael Spencer, Tyler and Alice Haynes Professor of American Studies, University of Richmond.

- Chuck Stone, Walter Spearman Professor, School of Journalism and Mass Communication, University of North Carolina at Chapel Hill.

- Gerald E. Thomson, Samuel Lambert Professor of Medicine at Columbia University.

- Mary McKelvey Welch, Albert Werthan Professor of Biology, Fisk University.

- May L. Wykle, Florence Cellar Professor of Gerontological Nursing, Frances Payne Bolton School of Nursing at Case Western Reserve University.

◆ AFRICAN AMERICANS HOLDING ENDOWED UNIVERSITY CHAIRS (1996)

Endowed university chairs are an honor—both for the person for whom the chair is named as well as for the person who is named to the chair. Endowments are bestowed upon academian's of great talent who have distinguished themselves in their careers. Usually an organization separate from a collegiate institution will approach a university in hopes of setting up a chair and endowment fund. Ten such chairs have been endowed and named for African Americans, including Hannah Diggs Atkins, Constance E. Clayton, Bille and Camille Cosby, W. E. B. Du Bois, Martin Luther King, Jr. (three), Wade H. McCree, Jr., Paul Robeson, and Roy Wilkins.

In 1996, 101 African American professors held endowed chairs, including eight of those named for African Americans. 14 others have either retired from endowed chairs, are professors emeriti, or are deceased, including T. J. Anderson (Tufts University); John Hope Franklin (three: Cambridge University, Duke University, and University of Chicago); James Lowell Gibbs, Jr. (Stanford University); Edmund Gordon (Columbia Teachers College); Harry E. Groves (University of North Carolina, Chapel Hill); James E. Jones, Jr. (University of Wisconsin); Barbara C. Jordan (the University of Texas at Austin); C. Eric Lincoln (Duke University and Clark University); Bertha Maxwell-Roddy (University of North Carolina, Charlotte); Samuel DeWitt Proctor (Rutgers University); William H. Peterson (Campbell University); Nathan A. Scott (University of Virginia); John B. Turner (University of North Carolina, Chapel Hill); and Marilyn V. Yarborough (University of North Carolina, Chapel Hill).

- Delores P. Aldridge, Grace Towns Hamilton Professor of Sociology and African-American Studies, Emory University.

- Jacqul Alexander, Irwin Visiting Chair in Women's Studies, Hamilton College.

- Gloria Long Anderson, Fuller E. Callaway Professor of Chemistry, Morris Brown College.

- Maya Angelou, Reynolds Professor of American Studies, Wake Forest University.

- Hannah Diggs Atkin, Hannah Diggs Atkins Professor of Public Service, Oklahoma State University.

- Mario J. Azevedo, Frank Porter Graham Professor, University of North Carolina, Charlotte.

- Houston A. Baker, Jr., Albert M. Greenfield Professor of Human Relations, University of Pennsylvania.

- Lucius Barker, Professor of Political Science, William Bennett Monroe Professor in Political Science, Stanford University.

- Mary Frances Berry, Geraldine R. Segal Professor of American Social Thought and professor of history, University of Pennsylvania.

- Bernard Boxhill, Pardue Professor, Department of Philosophy, University of North Carolina at Chapel Hill.

- Joanne Braxton, Francis L. and Edwin L. Cummings Professor of American Studies and professor of English, College of William and Mary.

- Frank Brown, Cary C. Boshumer Professor, School of Education, University of North Carolina.

- Herrington Bryce, Life of Virginia Professor of Business Administration, College of William and Mary.

- Roy S. Bryce-Laporte, MacArthur Professor of Sociology and director, Africana and Latin American Studies Program, Colgate University.

- John S. Butler, Dallas TACA Centennial Professor in the Liberal Arts and Arthur James Douglass Centennial Professor in Entrepreneurship and Small Business, The University of Texas at Austin.

- Stephen L. Carter, William Nelson Cromwell Professor of Law, Yale University Law School.

- John Cartwright, Martin Luther King, Jr. Professor of Social Ethics, Boston University.

- Michelle Cliff, Allan K. Smith Professor of English Language and Literature, Trinity College.

- James P. Comer, Maurice K. Falk Professor of Child Psychiatry, Yale University, Child Center.

- William W. Cook, Israel Evans Professor of Oratory and Belles Lettres, Dartmouth College.

- Jean D'Costa, Leavenworth Professor of English, Hamilton College.

- Willaim Darlty, Jr., Cary C. Boshamer Professor, Department of Economics, University of North Carolina at Chapel Hill.

- Charles Edward Daye, Henry P. Brandis Professor of Law, School of Law, University of North Carolina at Chapel Hill.

- Dennis C. Dickerson, Stanfield Professor of History, Williams College.

- Rita Dove, Commonwealth Professor of English, University of Virginia.

- Edgar G. Epps, Marshall Field Professor of Education, Department of Education, University of Chicago.

- Slayton A. Evans, Jr., Kenan Professor, Department of Chemistry, University of North Carolina at Chapel Hill.

- Etta Faloner, Calloway Professor of Mathematics, Associate Provost for Science, Spelman College.

- Bertram O. Fraser-Reid, James B. Duke Professor, Department of Chemistry, Duke University.

- Lawrence E. Gary, Samuel S. Wurtzel Chair for Eminent Scholars, School of Social Work, Virginia Commonwealth University.

- Fannie Gaston-Johansson, Lawler Professor, School of Nursing, Johns Hopkins University.

- Henry Louis Gates, Jr., W. E. B. Du Bois Professor of African-American Studies, Harvard University.

- Jewelle Taylor Gibbs, The Zellerbach Family Fund Chair in Social Policy, Community Change and Practice, University of California, Berkeley.

- Cheryl Townsend Gilkes, MacArthur Associate Professor of Sociology and African-American Studies, Colby College.

- Richard A. Goldsby, John Woodruff Simpson Lecturer and professor of biology, Amherst College.

- Peter J. Gomes, Plummer Professor of Christian Morals and chaplain, Harvard University.

- William B. Gould, IV, Charles A. Beardsley Professor of Law, Stanford University.

- J. Lee Greene, Bowman and Gordon Gray Professor of English, University of North Carolina at Chapel Hill.

- Pamela Gunter-Smith, Porter Professor of Physiology, Spelman College.

- Beverly Guy-Sheftall, Anna Julia Cooper Professor and director of women's studies, Spelman College.

- Charles V. Hamilton, Wallace S. Sayre, Professor of Government, Columbia University.

- Michael S. Harper, University Professor, I. J. Kapstein Professor of English, Brown University.

- Trudler Harris, Augustus Baldwin Longstreet Professor of American Literature, Emory University.

- John W. Hatch, William Rand Kenan, Jr., Professor, Health, Behavior, and Health Education, University of North Carolina, Chapel Hill.

- J. K. Haynes, D. Packard Professor of Biology, Morehouse College.

- Asa Grant Hilliard, III, Fuller E. Callaway Professor of Urban Education, Georgia State University.

- Darlene Clark Hine, John A. Hannu Professor of History, Michigan State University.

- Matthew Holden, Jr., The Henry L. and Grace M. Doherty Professor of Government and Foreign Affairs, University of Virginia.

- Thomas Holt, James Westfall Thompson Professor, Department of History, The University of Chicago.

- Alton Hornsby, Jr., Fuller E. Callaway Professor of Urban Education, Emory University.

- Jacqueline Irvine, Charles Howard Candler Professor of Urband Education, Emory University.

- Alex M. Johnson, Jr., Harrison Foundation Research Professor of Law, University of Virginia.

- James H. Johnson, Jr., E. Maynard Adams Professor, Department of Geography, University of North Carolina at Chapel Hill.

- Richard A. Joseph, Asa G. Chandler Professor of Politcal Science, Emory University.

- Martin Luther Kilson, Jr., Frank G. Thomson Professor of Government, Harvard University.

- Franklin W. Knight, Leonard and Helen R. Stulman Professor, Department of History, Johns Hopkins University.

- George M. Langford, Ernest Everett Just 1907 Professorship, professor of biological sciences, Dartmouth College.

- David Levering Lewis, Martin Luther King, Jr. Professor, Department of History, Rutgers University.

- Richard A. Long, Atticus Haygood Professor, Graduate Institute of Liberal Arts, Emory University.

- Kenneth R. Manning, Thomas Meloy Professor of Rhetoric and History of Science, Massachusetts Institute of Technology.

- Ali Mazuri, Albert Schweitzer Professor of Political Science, SUNY, Binghamton.

- Reuben R. McDaniel, Jr., Charles and Elizabeth Prothro Regents Chair in Health Care Management, the University of Texas at Austin.

- John S. McNell, Louis and Ann Wolens Centennial Chair in Gerontology, School of Social Work, the University of Texas at Austin.

- Ruth G. McRoy, Ruby Lee Piester Centennial Professor in Services to Children and Families, School of Social Work, the University of Texas at Austin.

- William Moore, Jr., A. M. Alkin Regents Chair in Junior and Community College Education Leadership, the University of Texas at Austin.

- Toni Morrison, Robert Goheen Professor in the Humanities Council, Princeton University.

- John Howard Morrow, Jr., Franklin Professor and chairperson of the History Department, University of Georgia.

- Valentin Mudimbe, Ruth F. Devarney Professor of Romance Studies and profesor of cultural anthropology, Duke University.

- Samuel L. Myers, Jr., Roy Wilkins Professor, Hubert H. Humphrey Institute of Public Affairs, University of Minnesota.

- Robert G. O'Meally, Zora Neale Hurston Professor of English, Columbia University.

- Lucius Outlaw, T. Wistar Brown Professor of Philosophy, Haverford College.

- Nell I. Painter, Edwards Professor of American History, Princeton University.

- Collin A. Palmer, William Rand Kenan, Jr., Professor of History, University of North Carolina at Chapel Hill.

- Albert Jordy Raboteau, Henry W. Putnam Professor of Religion, Princeton University.

- Arnold Rampersad, Woodrow Wilson Professor of Literature and professor of English, Princeton University.

- Robert L. Reddick, Kenneth Brinkhous Distinguished Professor, Department of Pathology, School of Medicine, University of North Carolina at Chapel Hill.

- Joe Ritchie, Knight Professor of Journalism, School of Journalism, Media and Graphic Arts, Florida A&M University.

- Sophia B. Sanchez, Laura H. Carnull Professor of English, Temple University.

- Lemma W. Senbet, William E. Mayor Professor of Finance, Univeristy of Maryland at College Park.

- Willis B. Sheftall, Jr., Merrill Professor of Economics and Business, Morehouse College.

- George Shirley, Joseph Edgar Maddy Distinguished University Professor of Music, School of Music, University of Michigan.

- Elliot P. Skinner, Franz Boas Professor of Anthropology, Columbia University.

- John Stanfield, III, Cummings Professor of American Studies and professor of sociology, College of William and Mary.

- Claude M. Steele, Martin Luther King, Jr., Centennial Professor, Stanford University.

- Chuck Stone, Walter Spearman Professor of Journalism and Mass Communication, School of Journalism and Mass Communication, University of North Carolina at Chapel Hill.

- Dorothy S. Strickland, State of New Jersey Professor of Education, Rutgers University; former Arthur I. Gates Professor, Columbia Teachers College.

- Ora L. Strickland, Independence Foundation Professor of Nursing, Emory University.

- Michel Rolph Troulliot, Krieger/Eisenhower Professor, Department of Anthropology, Johns Hopkins University.

- Lonnie H. Wagstaff, M. K. Hage Centennial Professor in Education, College of Education, the University of Texas at Austin.

- Sheila S. Walker, Annabel Irion Worsham Centennial Professor and director, Center for African and Afro-American Studies, Department of Anthropology, the University of Texas at Austin.

- Jerry W. Ward, Jr., Lawrence Durgin Professor of English, Tougaloo College.

- Isiah M. Warner, Philip W. West Professor of Analytical and Environmental Chemistry, Department of Chemistry, Louisiana State University.

- Roger W. Wilkins, Clarence J. Robinson Professor of History and American Culture, George Mason University.

- James H. Williams, Jr., School Engineering Professor in Teaching Excellence Professor of Engineering, Massachusetts Institute of Technology.

- John A. Williams, Paul Robeson Professor of English, Rutgers University.

- Preston Noah Williams, Houghton Professor of Theology and Contemporary Change, Harvard University.

- Walter A. Williams, John M. Olin Professor of Economics, George Mason University.

- Jan Willis, Walter A. Crowell University Professor of Social Sciences, Religion Department, Wesleyan University.

- William Julius Wilson, Lucy Flower University Professor of Sociology, University of Chicago.

- Herbert Graves Winful, The Arthur F. Turneau Professor of Electrical Engineering and Computer Science, University of Michigan.

Enrollment at Historically Black Colleges and Universities, 1980 and 1988

	Total	Public		Private	
		4-year	2-year	4-year	2-year
Number of institutions, fall 1989	106	40	11	49	6
Total enrollment, fall 1980	233,557	155,085	13,132	62,924	2,416
Men, total	106,387	70,236	6,758	28,352	1,041
Men, black	81,818	53,654	2,781	24,412	971
Women, total	127,170	84,849	6,374	34,572	1,375
Women, black	109,171	70,582	4,644	32,589	1,356
Total enrollment, fall 1988	239,755	158,606	15,066	64,644	1,439
Men, total	100,561	66,097	6,772	27,219	473
Men, black	78,268	50,545	3,192	24,081	450
Women, total	139,194	92,509	8,294	37,425	966
Women, black	115,883	73,893	5,894	35,145	951

Source: *Digest of Education Statistics 1991*, November 1991, p. 215. Primary source: Department of Education, National Center for Education Statistics.

Educational Attainment for Blacks Age 25 and Older

	Both sexes	1990 Male	Female	Both Sexes	1990 Male	Female
Total, 25 years old and over	16,751	7,471	9,280	16,395	7,315	9,080
Percent	100.0	100.0	100.0	100.0	100.0	100.0
Elementary	16.1	17.1	15.3	17.3	18.6	16.3
High School	55.0	53.9	55.8	54.6	53.5	55.4
College	28.9	29.0	28.8	28.1	27.9	28.3
Percent for 4 years of high school or more	66.2	65.8	66.5	54.6	64.2	65.0

Source: *Black Population in the United States: March 1990 and 1989, 1991*, pp. 31-32. Primary source: U.S. Bureau of the Census, Current Population Reports.

College Enrollment Projections, 1995-2000

In thousands

Year	Total	White Men	Women	Total	Black Men	Women
1995	11,020	4,885	6,135	1,339	568	771
1996	11,019	4,878	6,140	1,431	604	827
1997	11,259	4,967	6,292	1,376	573	802
1998	11,310	4,965	6,345	1,478	615	862
1999	11,476	5,019	6,457	1,499	622	877
2000	11,637	5,069	6,568	1,521	627	895

Source: *Black Issues in Higher Education, Vol. 8*, No. 24, January 30, 1992, p. 40. Primary source: U.S. Bureau of Census, Current Population Reports.

17

Religion

Religion

◆ The Origins and History of African American Religious Traditions
◆ African American Female Religious Leadership ◆ African American Churches During Reconstruction
◆ African American Churches in the Twentieth-Century ◆ African American Denominations
◆ Religious Gatekeepers

by Stephen W. Angel

The first Africans who arrived on North American shores (an event traditionally dated to 1619) brought their own religious world views with them. While a minority had been Muslims or Christians prior to their kidnapping by slave traders, most adhered to their native African religions. Hundreds of these religions developed, but, in general, the Africans believed that the world had been created by a high god who removed himself from direct intervention in worldly affairs after the act of creation.

◆ THE ORIGINS AND HISTORY OF AFRICAN AMERICAN RELIGIOUS TRADITIONS

Early African American Belief Systems

In Africa, worshipers directed their prayers to intermediary spirits, chief among whom were their ancestors, or the "living dead." If proper offering was made to an ancestor, the individual would be blessed with great prosperity, but if the ancestor was slighted, misfortune would result. In addition, the Yorubas worshiped a variety of nature spirits (or orishas). These spirits often possessed their devotees, who then became mediums of their gods. This kind of spirit-possession is a prominent feature of some modern African American religions such as santería, which recently has spread in large urban areas, including Miami and New York. Also a part of the African world view, especially among the Bakongo, was the practice of magic, variously known in the New World as obeah, vaudou (voodoo), or conjure. This magic, designed to help friends (myalism) or to hurt

enemies (obeah), at one time was widely practiced by Africans throughout the Western Hemisphere.

The type of African spirituality that took root in North America merged elements from many African cultures. Since slave masters intentionally mixed Africans from many tribal backgrounds, no "pure" African religion preserving one tradition emerged. Nevertheless, the longstanding scholarly controversy over the extent to which African traditions have been retained in African-based religions is gradually being resolved in favor of those who see extensive survivals. Scholars generally concede that African influences are prevalent in the church music and preaching styles of African Americans and likely in the funeral practices and methods of church organization as well.

Missionary Efforts by Christians

The first sustained effort at converting African Americans to Christianity was made by the Anglican Society for the Propagation of the Gospel in Foreign Parts, which sent missionaries to North America in 1701. These missionaries had little success among the Africans; many mocked those who imitated the whites too closely, and thus resisted the missionaries. In addition, white slave masters often resented losing slaves' time to church services and feared that slaves would lay a claim to freedom through conversion. The numerous colonial laws, starting with Virginia in 1669, proclaiming that conversion failed to entitle slaves to freedom did not comfort some slave masters, who suspected that Christianity would undermine slave discipline—indeed, some remained unconvinced of the advisability of missionary efforts up until emancipation occurred. On the other hand, some slave masters believed the Christianization of Africans to be justification for enslaving them.

Subsequent efforts to convert African Americans to Christianity were more successful. In his seven missionary tours throughout North America between 1742 and 1770, the spellbinding orator George Whitefield effected the conversions of large numbers of both black and white Americans. The ministry of Methodist circuit riders, such as Francis Asbury, was also well received by African Americans at the end of the eighteenth century. Baptist and Methodist churches were the most successful in attracting black members. Since these churches did not require their ministers to be well educated, doors were opened for aspiring African American ministers, many of whom lived in states where teaching African Americans to read and write was forbidden by law. Furthermore, the Baptists and Methodists were not as hostile to the emotionalism of black preachers and congregations as were more staid denominations such as the Episcopalians. Finally, the antislavery stance of notable Methodist and Baptist leaders, such as John Wesley, Francis Asbury, and John Leland, and the greater degree of equality nurtured within many Baptist and Methodist congregations were attractive to African Americans.

Early Christian Congregations

Probably the first organizing effort by African Americans to bear fruit in an independent black congregation was the Silver Bluff Baptist Church in South Carolina, which came into existence between 1773 and 1775. David George, an African American, and seven other men and women formed its organizing nucleus. George Liele, one of George's associates, often preached at the Silver Bluff Church before emigrating to Jamaica in 1782. Andrew Bryan, one of Liele's converts, founded the First African Baptist Church in Savannah, Georgia, in 1788.

Bryan's life well represented the complex predicament faced by African American religious leaders in the antebellum South. In the early years of his ministry, Bryan was whipped and twice imprisoned by whites who feared him. But he bought his freedom, prospered, and eventually came to own much property, including eight black slaves; his death in 1812 was mourned by blacks and whites alike. While many black churches continued to be served by white ministers until 1865, black pastors, licensed ministers, and exhorters ministering to black Baptist and Methodist congregations were not at all unusual at this time, either in the South or the North.

Black Catholics

Before the Civil War, black Catholics were confined largely to Maryland and Louisiana. However, Catholics made greater efforts to convert African Americans after the Civil War. By the end of the nineteenth century, nearly 200,000 black Catholics were worshiping in the United States, but more Protestant black ministers existed than did black priests in the Catholic churches.

Discrimination in White Churches

While white preachers urged black Americans to convert and many predominantly white congregations welcomed them into membership, racial prejudice was never absent from the religious scene. Although the level of discrimination varied from region to region, and congregation to congregation, some factors were relatively constant.

One such factor was the relative paucity of ordained African American clergy. To take the Methodists as an example, some African American ministers were ordained as deacons within the Methodist Episcopal Church prior to 1820, but none in the four decades thereafter. No African American Methodist minister was ordained by the Methodist Episcopal Church to the higher office of elder or consecrated as a bishop prior to the Civil War, unless he was willing to emigrate to Liberia.

Other discriminatory practices also formed part of the religious landscape. The Methodists, and many other denominations, tried to reserve the administration of sacraments as the exclusive province of white clergy. Segregated seating in churches was pervasive in both the North and the South. Church discipline was often unevenly applied. Of course, racial discrimination in the churches was only a small part of the much larger political and moral controversy over slavery.

Resistance to discrimination took many forms. In the North, Peter Spencer in Wilmington, Delaware, Richard Allen in Philadelphia, and James Varick in New York, led their black followers out of white Methodist churches and set up independent black congregations. In Allen's case, his departure was preceded by a dramatic confrontation over segregated seating in Philadelphia's white Methodist church. Each of these men then used his congregation as the nucleus of a new black Methodist denomination—Spencer formed the African Union Church in 1807, Allen the African Methodist Episcopal Church (AME) in 1816, and Varick a denomination eventually called the African Methodist Episcopal Zion Church (AME Zion) in 1821.

Meanwhile, in Charleston, South Carolina, a more explosive situation was taking shape. Morris Brown, a black Methodist minister from Charleston, who had

First African Baptist Church, Savannah, Georgia.

helped Richard Allen organize the African Methodist Episcopal Church, organized an independent black Methodist church in his home city. The authorities harassed Brown's church and sometimes arrested its leaders. Nevertheless, within a year, more than three-quarters of Charleston's black Methodists had united with him. The oppression of African Americans in Charleston was so severe that many members of Brown's congregation, including prominent lay leaders, joined the insurrection planned by Denmark Vesey to take over the Charleston armory and, eventually, the whole environs of Charleston. The conspirators, apprehended before they could carry out their plans, testified that Brown had not known of their scheme, and the minister was allowed to move to Philadelphia, where Richard Allen made him the second bishop of the African Methodist Episcopal Church.

A few African Americans became acquiescent as a result of Christianity. One such example was Pierre Toussaint, a black Haitian slave who fled in 1787 to New York with his white owners, the Berards, just prior to the Haitian Revolution. In 1811, Mrs. Berard manumitted Toussaint on her death bed. Over the next forty years, Toussaint became a notable philanthropist, con-tributing funds to the building of St. Patrick's Cathedral. However, when the cathedral opened, Toussaint did not protest when a white usher refused to seat him for services. Some American Catholics recently revived the controversy over Toussaint, by campaigning for his canonization. Many black Catholics have strongly objected, seeing Toussaint as passive and servile and thus a poor candidate for sainthood.

Emancipation Efforts of Black Church Leaders

The mid-nineteenth century saw increased anti-slavery activity among many black church leaders and members. Some gave qualified support to the gradual emancipation program sponsored by the American Colonization Society, which sought to encourage free African Americans to emigrate to Africa to westernize and Christianize the Africans. Virginia Baptist pastor Lott Cary and Maryland Methodist minister Daniel Coker were the two most prominent African American religious leaders to emigrate to Africa in the 1820s. By the 1850s, enough black Methodists were in Liberia for the Methodist Episcopal Church to consecrate a black bishop, Francis Burns, to serve the Liberian churches. While some black Americans were emigrating to Africa, others

Reverend Richard Allen

emigrated to the West Indies—Episcopalian Bishop James T. Holly, for example, settled in Haiti to undertake missionary work.

Because of the extreme repression in the slave states, Southern blacks were unable to express openly their views on political issues. They were, however, often able to make their views clear; for example, a white minister who dwelled too long on the Biblical text that servants should obey their masters was apt to find his African American listeners deserting him. In addition, black Christians often held secret meetings in "brush arbors" (rude structures made of pine boughs) or in the middle of the woods. There they could sing spirituals and pray openly for the quick advent of freedom. Slave revolts provided a violent outbreak of dissent much feared by whites. The 1831 revolt of Nat Turner, a Baptist preacher, in Northampton County, Virginia, was suppressed only after tremendous bloodshed had been visited upon both blacks and whites. Frightened whites in the South intensified their surveillance of black churches in the aftermath of the Turner revolt. Even conservative black preachers such as Presbyterian John Chavis in North Carolina and the Baptist "Uncle Jack" in Virginia were prohibited from preaching.

Northern African American leaders could afford to be more open and forthright in their political stance. Most rejected outright the views of the American Colonization Society in favor of the immediate abolition of slavery. Presbyterian minister Henry Highland Garnet was a prominent abolitionist, urging African American slaves in 1843 to "let your motto be RESISTANCE! RESISTANCE! RESISTANCE!" African Methodist Episcopal Bishop Daniel Payne and African Methodist Episcopal Zion Bishop Christopher Rush, both emigrants from the Carolinas to the North, were outspoken abolitionists who, after the mid-1840s, became the most prominent leaders in their respective churches. Frederick Douglass was one of the few leading black abolitionists who did not pursue a ministerial career, and even he had briefly served as an African Methodist Episcopal Zion preacher in New Bedford, Massachusetts. Black clergy were extraordinarily active in recruiting black men to join the Union armies during the Civil War, after the Emancipation Proclamation opened up the possibility of military service to them. During the Civil War nearly a dozen black ministers, including the African Methodist Episcopal Church's Henry McNeal Turner, served as chaplains to black army regiments.

◆ AFRICAN AMERICAN FEMALE RELIGIOUS LEADERSHIP

Early black women ministers sometimes served as travelling evangelists, especially within the black denominations. While Sojourner Truth's oratory has become appropriately famous, Maria Stewart, Jarena Lee, Zilpha Elaw and other early nineteenth-century women also spoke eloquently and, in Lee's and Elaw's cases, travelled widely and labored diligently. None of these women were ordained, but Elizabeth (no last name known), a former slave from Maryland whose ministry began in 1796, spoke for many female preachers when she was accused of preaching without a license: "If the Lord has ordained me, I need nothing better." Rebecca Cox Jackson left the African Methodist Episcopal Church in the 1830s, when she felt that men denied her the chance to exercise her ministry, and she eventually became head eldress of a predominantly black Shaker community in Philadelphia.

During the postbellum years, some black women sought and obtained formal ordination from their denominations. Sarah Ann Hughes, a successful North Carolina evangelist and pastor, was ordained by Bishop Henry McNeal Turner in 1885, but complaints from male pastors caused her ordination to be revoked two years later. Two women were ordained by African Methodist Episcopal Zion bishops not long thereafter—Mary J. Small in 1895 as a deacon and 1898 as an elder, and Julia

A baptism on the Potomac River.

A. J. Foote in 1894 and 1900. Many women exercised their ministry through para-ecclesiastical structures, such as women's temperance and missionary societies, while others, such as Anna Cooper and the African Methodist Episcopal Church's Frances Jackson Coppin, became renowned educators.

◆ AFRICAN AMERICAN CHURCHES DURING RECONSTRUCTION

Black church membership grew explosively after the Civil War, especially in the South, where the black clergy played a prominent part in the Reconstruction governments. African Methodist Episcopal minister Hiram Revels became the first African American to serve as a United States Senator, when the Mississippi legislature sent him to Washington, DC, in 1870. However, Revels, was only the ground breaker; many black ministers went on to serve in the Congress or in their state governments. African American participation in Reconstruction politics was effective in large part because ministers in the AME and AME Zion Churches, and many black Baptist ministers, carefully and patiently educated their congregation members on every civic

and political issue (although the newly established black denomination, the Colored Methodist Episcopal Church, largely stayed away from politics during Reconstruction).

Even though African Americans were largely expelled from southern state governments after the end of political Reconstruction in the 1870s, many black ministers and laity continued to play an active political role on such issues as temperance, often campaigning on behalf of prohibition referenda. The southern white campaign of terror, lynching, and disfranchisement steadily reduced black political power and participation, however, until the onset of mid-twentieth century civil rights movements.

The Black Church's Response to Segregation

As the system of racial segregation imposed in the 1880s and 1890s took hold, black ministers coordinated a manifold response. First, they forthrightly challenged new segregation laws, engaging in civil disobedience and boycotts. For example, when the city of Nashville, Tennessee, segregated its street cars in 1906, influential Baptist minister R. H. Boyd led a black boycott of the streetcars, even operating his own streetcar line for a time. No defeat was ever seen as final.

An African Methodist Episcopal congregation, 1898.

Second, black ministers helped to nurture a separate set of black institutions to serve African Americans excluded from white establishments. The Congregationalists, Baptists, and Northern Methodists established schools in the South for African Americans during Reconstruction, but the African Methodist Episcopal, African Methodist Episcopal Zion, and Christian Methodist Episcopal bishops forged ahead with the establishment of their own network of schools. The black denominations also built up their publishing houses, and the books and periodicals that they published were vital to the black community. Virtually every institution with ties to African-American communities received some support from black churches.

Third, some black ministers believed that the civil rights retreats of the late nineteenth century should spur African Americans to leave the United States for a destination where their full civil rights would be respected. A "Back to Africa" movement grew to enable African Americans to find a home where they could run governments, banks, and businesses without interference from whites. Thus, Bishop Turner helped to organize a steamship line to carry black Americans back to Africa, and two shiploads of black emigrants sailed to

Liberia in 1895 and 1896 as a result of his efforts. Some black church leaders, such as Christian Methodist Episcopal Bishop Lucius Holsey and AME Bishop Richard Cain, held views similar to those advocated by Turner, but many more church leaders opposed Turner's emigrationism vigorously. Simultaneously, African American missionary work continued to occupy the attention of African Americans at the end of the nineteenth century. Under the guidance of Bishops Payne and Turner, for example, the African Methodist Episcopal Church had a vigorous missionary presence in Sierra Leone, Liberia, and South Africa.

◆ AFRICAN AMERICAN CHURCHES IN THE TWENTIETH-CENTURY

In the twentieth century, black religious life has become characterized by a far greater degree of diversity and pluralism. At the same time, traditional African-American concerns, including the continuing quest for freedom and justice, have been not only maintained but strengthened. Pentecostalism, which burst on the American scene in 1906, has become a major religious force within the black community. The Church of God in

Christ, a Pentecostal denomination, has become the second largest black denomination in the United States. Meanwhile, the charismatic or Neo-Pentecostal movement has revitalized many congregations within mainline black denominations. The black nationalism of Bishop Turner came to full flower in the work of such men as Marcus Garvey (and his chaplain general, George A. McGuire), Elijah Muhammad, and Malcolm X. A spectacular rise of storefront churches has occurred, some of which were led by flamboyant showmen such as Father Divine and "Sweet Daddy" Grace. Each of these trends has been significantly aided by the black migrations from the South to the North, which greatly strengthened Northern black communities.

Many black ministers became advocates of a "Social Gospel." One of the most famous was Reverend Ransom of the African Methodist Episcopal Church, who came into prominence between 1901 and 1904 as pastor of an Institutional Church in Chicago. ("Institutional churches" provided a whole panoply of social services to needy members and neighbors, in addition to regular worship.) Social Gospellers highlighted the reality of collective, societal sin such as the starvation of children and the denial of human rights, and maintained that Christian repentance of these sins must be followed by concrete actions to rectify injustice and to assist the poor. The Reverend Dr. Martin Luther King, Jr., was profoundly influenced by this Social Gospel movement.

It is worth recalling that many black religious leaders in the 1960s thought that King's brand of social activism was too radical. One of King's most determined critics during the 1960s was the theologically conservative president of the National Baptist Convention of the U.S.A., Inc., Joseph H. Jackson. The attempt by King's ministerial allies to unseat Jackson as president of the Convention in 1960 and 1961 led to a schism, with King and his supporters forming a new denomination, the Progressive National Baptist Convention. King came under further criticism when, in 1967 and 1968, he made it clear that his advocacy of pacifism extended to opposition to American military involvement in Vietnam.

The "Black Theology" movement, which grew rapidly after King's assassination, attempted to fashion a critique of the prevalent Christian theology out of the materials that King and Malcolm X provided. One such theologian, Albert Cleage, pastor of the Shrine of the Black Madonna in Detroit, argued that Jesus is a black messiah and that his congregation should follow the teachings of Jehovah, a black god. "Almost everything you have heard about Christianity is essentially a lie," he stated. Cleage was representative of black theologians in arguing that black liberation should be seen as situated at the core of the Christian gospels. In the 1980s, black women such as Jacquellyn Grant, Delores Wil-liams, and Katie Cannon have formulated "womanist" theologies that seek to combat the triple oppression of race, class, and gender suffered by most black women.

Current Trends

African American churches remain strong, healthy institutions in the 1990s. Some denominations are growing substantially, and none is declining precipitously. While secularization has diminished its influence somewhat, the black church is still the central institution in the black community. Many black churches are vigorously confronting such problems as drug abuse and homelessness that are visible symptoms of the increasing desperation of the black underclass.

The largest denomination among the black churches remains the National Baptist Convention of the U.S.A., Inc. One of its more noted presidents, veteran civil rights activist Theodore J. Jemison, was first elected in 1982. Under Jemison's leadership, the denomination in 1989 completed a $10,000,000 world headquarters building in Nashville, Tennessee. More recently, Jemison came under criticism for his role in attempting to forestall Mike Tyson's 1992 trial (and eventual conviction) on rape charges.

Black churches continue to address a wide variety of social problems affecting the African American community. Perhaps most urgently, many churches have strong anti-drug programs. The First AME Church of Los Angeles sponsors a "Lock In" program, which on weekends presents anti-drug messages to youth. Similarly, many congregations have undertaken vigorous action against "crack" houses. Parochial schools, feeding centers, and housing for senior citizens are also part of the black church's outreach to the black community. Many black ministers have noted, however, the growing division of the African American community along lines of social class and have exhorted middle-class black Americans to give more generously to programs that aid the poor. James Cone, a leading black theologian, has stated that black churches need to devote less time and attention to institutional survival and more to finding ways to deal with such pressing issues as poverty, gang violence, and AIDS.

Towards this end, black churches participate in a wide variety of ecumenical projects among themselves and often additionally, in conjunction with white denominations. The Congress of National Black Churches, a consortium of six black churches, continues to sponsor a variety of projects to improve the economic and social situation of the African American community. Partners in Ecumenism, a project of the National Council of Churches, has challenged white denominations to

Pentecostalism, which burst on the American scene in 1906, has become a major religious force within the black community.

be more responsive to black concerns. At a grassroots level, African American churches are successfully joining forces to combat problems that are too large for any congregation to address alone. In Marks, Mississippi, for example, the Quitman County Development Organization has sponsored a Black Church Community and Economic Development Project. This organization has assisted church leaders in developing programs on teen pregnancy and parenting.

The spirit of cooperation has inspired individual denominations to explore merging or establishing close working relationships with other denominations with similar backgrounds and traditions. Three black Methodist churches, the African Methodist Episcopal Zion, Christian Methodist Episcopal, and United American Methodist Episcopal churches have been planning a merger that they hope to consummate in the near future. In the spring of 1991, bishops of the AME, AME Zion, Christian Methodist Episcopal, and United Methodist churches requested that their denominations approve a study commission to explore an even broader reunion of churches. The Progressive National Baptists have recently entered into a formal dialogue with the Southern Baptist Alliance, an organization of more than 72,000

mostly white Baptists who recently have distanced themselves from the Southern Baptist Convention.

Black churches also have found themselves compelled to address issues related to the multi-ethnic tensions of the 1990s. Leading black pastors in Los Angeles have deplored both the violence of police revealed in the Rodney King incident and the violence of inner city rioters, while advocating urgent attention to the problems of inner-city residents. For example, James Lawson of the Holman United Methodist Church stated that those who burned buildings during the 1992 Los Angeles riots were "responding to a society of violence, not simply a society of racism," and issued "a call to repent." In Queens, New York, a black Baptist congregation in 1991 warmly welcomed the opportunity to perform an ordination service for a Korean American minister, Chong S. Lee.

In a few recent cases, furthermore, tensions have surfaced between black pastors and predominantly white congregations. For example, after Joan Salmon Campbell resigned in 1992 as pastor of the Old Pine Presbyterian Church in Philadelphia, black ministers protested to the Philadelphia Presbyters that the differences over preaching style and theology that led to her resignation

Reverend Gardner Taylor, pastor of Concord Baptist Church in Brooklyn, addressing a protest rally, 1963.

had been caused by alleged racist attitudes in her former congregation.

While many black Methodist and Baptist denominations are showing only limited membership growth, other black denominations are showing marked membership increases. Foremost among these are the Pentecostalist churches, whose lively worship and extensive social ministries are attracting members from all classes within the black community. The largest of these denominations, the Church of God in Christ, is now estimated to have over three million members. Charismatic congregations (also known as neo-Pentecostalist) within mainline black churches such as the African Methodist Episcopal Church are also thriving, and for similar reasons.

Other groups that have made substantial membership gains among African Americans include Roman Catholicism and Islam. While estimates differ, apparently more than 1.5 million African Americans now belong to the Roman Catholic Church, which has worked hard

Members of the Ministers Coalition for Peace pray for an end to civil unrest in Los Angeles.

in recent years to be sensitive to their needs. In many inner cities, it has maintained churches and schools in predominantly African American neighborhoods, although closings, mostly for financial reasons, are increasing in such dioceses as Detroit. Moreover, the Roman Catholic Church has been receptive to some liturgical variation, allowing gospel choirs and African vestments for priests in black churches. Nevertheless, Roman Catholics confront some serious problems in serving black parishioners. Fewer than 300 of the 54,000 priests in the United States are black, meaning that some black congregations must be served by white priests. In 1989, George A. Stallings, Jr., a priest in Washington, DC, broke away from Catholicism, arguing that the Catholic Church was still racist and did not do enough for its African American members.

Mainstream Islam, despite raising its own complexities, has also made large gains in the United States. Of the six million Muslims in this country, one million are believed to be black. Most African American Muslims do not distinguish between people of different races and worship cordially side by side with recent Muslim immigrants from Asia and Africa. Louis Farrakhan's Nation

of Islam, however, which retains Elijah Muhammad's black separatist teachings, continues to maintain a devoted following. Due to its very conservative stance on gender issues, Islam has proven to be more popular among black men than among black women.

The cause of gender equality continues to progress slowly in black churches. While two predominantly white denominations, the United Methodist and Protestant Episcopal churches, have elevated black women to the episcopacy in the past decade, none of the largest historically black denominations have done so. Nevertheless, women in some black churches are achieving ever-more-prestigious ministerial assignments. Vashti McKenzie, a former model, disc jockey, and radio program director, has recently been appointed pastor of the Payne Memorial AME church, an "old-line" church in Baltimore. Her innovative ministry, she says, is designed to "provide a message of hope for a hurting community." Presently more than 600 female pastors are ensconced in the African Methodist Episcopal church.

Preaching the gospel in a faithful but relevant fashion remains the most important objective of black churches. In a recent survey, 22 percent of black clergy considered the most important problem of the black church to be "lack of evangelism in fulfilling its religious role." That was more than twice the figure for any other problem identified. Ministerial training and financial support is another area needing improvement in many black churches. Black churches are not in danger of losing sight of their many, vital and extremely significant functions, within both the black community and American society as a whole. It is safe to predict that the black churches will continue to sustain and develop their important and prophetic witness.

Confederate Fear and Hatred Revisited

Reminiscent of the church bombings of the 1960s, in 1990s America, black churches have been under fire—literally—in the South. Between 1989 and June of 1996 more than 32 arsons have erupted in Tennessee, Alabama, Louisiana, South Carolina, Virginia, North Carolina, and Kentucky. Most of the cases have gone unsolved; in one Alabama case, two more houses of worship were destroyed by fire after two white men were convicted, in January of 1996, of vandalizing three area black churches. In Tennessee that month, 18 molotov cocktails and nearly 75 gallons of flammable liquid were used to burn down a small, nondenominational church. Racial graffiti was still legible after the smoke had cleared.

Still, neither the Federal Bureau of Investigation (FBI) nor the Treasury Department's Bureau of Alcohol, Tobacco and Firearms (ATF)—which together have

President Bill Clinton visits an African American congregation.

more than 200 agents on the case—have been able to find a common link among these crimes. African Americans concerned that the conflagrations are related have taken steps towards fighting the terrorism; to that end the NAACP urged the Justice Department to investigate; in compliance, a full scale civil rights investigation was initiated. The House Judiciary Committee also got involved, conducting a probe hearing in June of 1996. The Southern Christian Leadership Conference (SCLC) instituted a fund for the affected congregations. Donations were being accepted at the SCLC National Headquarters, "Burned Churches," 334 Auburn Ave., N.E., Atlanta, Georgia 30312.

The Folk Art of Preaching

In most African American congregations, sermonizing is an interpersonal skill that blacks have elevated to the level of art with such notable elements as call and response, and repetition of phrases. The exuberance of all participants is highly dependent upon the tradition within which one worships. For example, in the highly liturgical traditions such as Roman Catholicism and Eastern Orthodoxy, sermons tend only to be instructional. By contrast, nonliturgical Protestant denomina-

tions, including Baptist and Pentecostal churches, tend to view sermons as verbal sacraments. In the 1990s, nondenominational churches have reached a new high in popularity, usually centered upon a solitary, charismatic figure. As the medium is the message, performance is as important as the words themselves. Among the most highly regarded "artists" are Gardner C. Taylor, pastor emeritus of Brooklyn, New York's Concord Baptist Church of Christ; Barbara King, founder and minister of Atlanta's nondenominational Hillside Chapel and Truth Center, Inc.; and James Forbes, senior minister of New York City's Riverside Church. They are just a few of those who have been earmarked as the great preachers of the late twentieth century. In 1996, both Forbes and Taylor were deemed two of the 12 most effective preachers by a Baylor University survey, and Taylor was named as one of President Bill Clinton's favorite evangelists.

◆ AFRICAN AMERICAN DENOMINATIONS

African Methodist Episcopal Church

The African Methodist Episcopal (AME) Church was founded in 1816 at a conference convened in Philadel-

Reverend George Clements giving communion. More than 1.5 million African Americans belong to the Roman Catholic Church.

phia by Richard Allen, who was elected as its first bishop. In the following years, it grew throughout the North and Midwest, and after the Civil War, it expanded quickly throughout the South and the West. In 1989, membership was 2.2 million, about 1 million of whom are found in churches in Africa and the Caribbean as a result of successful missionary efforts. It oversees about 5,000 churches, as well as six colleges and two seminaries. Payne Theological Seminary is located in Wilberforce, Ohio, at the site of the Church's oldest school, Wilberforce University, founded in 1856. Turner Theological Semi-

nary is one of six schools that have joined to form the Interdenominational Theological Center in Atlanta. The African Methodist Episcopal Church's chief governing bodies are the General Conference, the Council of Bishops, and the General Board. It publishes the following periodicals: the *Christian Record*; the *Voice of Missions*; and the *AME Church Review*.

African Methodist Episcopal Zion Church

Originally known as the African Methodist Episcopal Church, the African Methodist Episcopal Zion Church

African American churches remain strong, healthy institutions.

was founded in 1821 in New York City. James Varick was elected its first "superintendent"; the title of the presiding officer was later changed to bishop. In 1848, the word "Zion" was added to the name of this church in order to avoid confusion with that founded by Richard Allen. It grew slightly prior to 1860, but expanded quickly in such southern states as North Carolina and Alabama after the Civil War.

As of 1989, the African Methodist Episcopal Zion Church had 1.3 million members, 100,000 of whom lived in Africa or the Caribbean. It possesses 2,900 churches. The church supports three colleges (two of which are junior colleges) and one seminary. The four-year college and the seminary are Livingstone College and Hood Theological Seminary, both located in Salisbury, North Carolina. The denomination is governed by a General Conference, a Board of Bishops, and a Correctional Council. Its publications include the weekly *Star of Zion*, the *Quarterly Review*, the monthly *Missionary Seer*, and the quarterly *Church School Herald*.

African Orthodox Church

The African Orthodox Church was founded in 1921 by Archbishop George Alexander McGuire, once a priest in the Protestant Episcopal Church. McGuire was the chaplain for Marcus Garvey's United Negro Improvement Association, but Garvey soon disavowed his chaplain's efforts to found a new denomination. This church is today an autonomous and independent body adhering to an "orthodox" confession of faith. Its nearly 6,000 members worship in some 25 to 30 churches.

African Union First Colored Methodist Protestant Church, Inc.

This denomination was formed in 1866 by a merger of the African Union Church and the First Colored Methodist Protestant Church. The African Union Church traced its roots to a Union Church of Africans founded in 1813 by Peter Spencer in Wilmington, Delaware. Today, this denomination has more than 309 churches and a membership of about 8,000.

Apostolic Overcoming Holy Church of God

This Pentecostal denomination, originally known as the Ethiopian Overcoming Holy Church, was incorpo-

Black parishioners attending mass at the Church of the Transfiguration in Los Angeles.

rated in Alabama in 1919. Evangelistic in purpose, it emphasizes sanctification, holiness, and the power of divine healing. As of 1975, it claimed 350 churches and about 100,000 members.

Bible Way Churches of Our Lord Jesus Christ

Founded in 1957, this Pentecostal tradition had 300 churches and 250,000 members in 1994.

Black Jews

Nearly 100,000 African Americans consider themselves Jewish. Included among these are the Commandment Keepers, founded in Harlem in 1919 by a Nigerian-born man known as "Rabbi Matthew"; the Church of God and Saints in Christ, founded in 1896 in Lawrence, Kansas, by William Crowdy; and the Church of God founded in Philadelphia by Prophet F. S. Cherry. In terms of doctrine, these groups share little more than a dislike of Christianity and an affection for the Old Testament. Some black Jews claim descent from the Falasha Jews of Ethiopia, who now reside in Israel.

However, few black Jews are recognized as such by orthodox rabbis.

The Church of God and Saints of Christ is probably the largest of these groups, with more than 200 churches and a membership of 38,000. The World African Hebrew Israelite Community—a religious sect that believes blacks in the Western Hemisphere are the descendants of the originial Hebrews and as such are the rightful heirs of the Holy Land of Israel—has 25,000 members throughout the United States and an additional 1,500 living in Israel. Since the late 1960s, they have been led by spiritual leader Ben Ami Ben-Israel, formerly a Chicago bus driver named Ben Carter.

Christian Methodist Episcopal Church

The Christian Methodist Episcopal (CME) church, known until 1954 as the Colored Methodist Church, is the third largest black Methodist body in the United States. It was founded after the Civil War, when some black Methodist churches desiring to join neither the African Methodist Episcopal or African Methodist Episcopal Zion Churches successfully petitioned the Meth-

First African Methodist Episcopal Church, Los Angeles.

odist Episcopal Church, South, for the right to form their own denomination. The first CME General Conference was held at Jackson, Tennessee, in 1870. There the church's first two bishops, William H. Miles and Richard Vanderhorst, were elected.

In 1989, the Christian Methodist Episcopal church had about 900,000 members, of whom 75,000 were located overseas. It possesses about 3,000 churches and maintains five church-affiliated colleges, as well as the Phillips School of Theology, a seminary which is part of the consortium known as the Interdenominational Theological Center in Atlanta. Its periodicals include the bimonthly *Christian Index* and the monthly *Missionary Messenger*.

Church of Christ (Holiness) Inc.

This denomination was organized in 1907 by Bishop Charles Price Jones, a renowned and prolific gospel song and hymn writer. Some 160 churches and 9,300 members belong to this denomination, which upholds the possibility of sanctification and Christian perfection. The church operates Christ Missionary and Industrial College, in Jackson, Mississippi.

Church of God by Faith

This Pentecostal denomination was founded in 1919.

Church of God in Christ

The Church of God in Christ (COGIC) was organized in 1897 by two former Baptist preachers, Charles H. Mason and C. P. Jones and was initially strongest in Alabama, Mississippi, and Tennessee. Mason reorganized COGIC in 1907, when he and Jones parted on the issue of speaking in tongues. At that time, Mason was appointed "General Overseer and Chief Apostle" of the church, as well as its first bishop. It has subsequently expanded very rapidly throughout the United States, especially in black neighborhoods in the inner cities.

As of 1995, COGIC has about 8.5 million members, 57 of which are located in foreign countries, and about 10,000 churches. It possesses bible colleges and a junior college, with plans for a university (All Saints University in Memphis) some time in the future. Its Charles H. Mason Theological Seminary is part of the Interdenominational Theological Center in Atlanta. It is governed by

A black rabbi stands in front of his Bronx, New York synagogue.

a General Assembly, a General Council of Elders, the Board of Bishops, and the General Board composed of 12 bishops elected by the General Assembly to four-year terms. In 1995, Bishop Chandler David Owens was elected presiding Bishop over the organization, the fastest-growing Christian group in the United States.

Churches of God, Holiness

This denomination was organized by K. H. Burruss in Georgia in 1914. Membership in the group's 40-odd churches totals some 25,000.

Fire Baptized Holiness Church

This church was organized on an interracial basis as the Fire Baptized Holiness Association in Atlanta, Georgia, in 1898; its African American members formed the Fire Baptized Holiness Church in 1908. The church subscribes to standard Pentecostalist doctrines on divine healing, speaking in tongues, and sanctification. As of 1958, it had about 50 churches and a membership of about 1,000.

Imani Temple African-American Catholic Congregation

The Imani Temple was founded in Washington, DC, by George Augustus Stallings, Jr., a former Roman Catholic priest, in July of 1989. The schism occurred when Stallings performed a mass based on an experimental rite currently being used in Zaire, in defiance of the prohibition of his archbishop, James Hickey. This was the first schism from the Roman Catholic Church in the United States since 1904. Stallings also voiced a number of criticisms of the Roman Catholic Church at the time of the schism: "There are not enough black priests, not enough black church members, and some of the relatively few black churches that exist are being closed and consolidated. The black experience and black needs are addressed minimally in church services and life." He also asserted that "we could no longer afford to worship white gods in black houses." 13 black American Catholic bishops issued a statement denouncing Stallings and accused him of expressing "personal disappointment [and] individually felt frustration" under the cover of charges of racism.

Black Catholic reactions to these developments were mixed. Many expressed sympathy for Stallings's con-

Reverend George Stallings (right) with Reverend George Clements.

cerns but were unwilling to leave the Roman Catholic church. Stallings assumed the title of archbishop of Imani Temple in 1991, and at the same time ordained a woman to the priesthood of the African American Catholic Congregation. In forming his denomination, he has experienced some setbacks. Several formerly close associates split with Stallings in 1991, alleging a lack of fiscal accountability in the church and accusing him of taking his liturgical innovations too far. The denomination currently claims 3,500 members in six cities.

Nation of Islam

After the death of Elijah Muhammad in 1975, his son Warith D. Muhammad assumed leadership of the movement. Warith Muhammad shifted dramatically away from his father's teachings of black nationalism, stating that whites could become members. He sought to bring his movement in accord with Orthodox Islam, and he eventually succeeded, renaming the Nation of Islam as the World Community of Al-Islam in the West and then as the American Muslim Mission before the merger was accomplished. Three other splinter groups formed, the largest headed by Louis Farrakhan, who split from Muhammad to re-establish the Nation of Islam on the basis of Elijah Muhammad's original black separatist teachings. The remaining two traditions are led by John Farrakhan and Caliph Emmanuel A. Muhammad.

National Baptist Convention of America, Unincorporated

The National Baptist Convention of America was formed in 1915 as a result of a schism with the National Baptist Convention, USA, Inc., over the issue of control of the denominational publishing house. In 1989 it possessed 2.4 million members and 7,800 churches. It has missions in Jamaica, Panama, and Africa, and supports ten colleges.

National Baptist Convention of the USA, Inc.

The National Baptist Convention was formed in 1895, through the union of three smaller church organizations, the oldest of which had been founded only 15 years earlier: the Baptist Foreign Mission Convention of the U.S.A.; the American National Baptist Convention; and the National Baptist Educational Convention of the USA. The Convention incorporated itself after a dispute over the publishing house led to a schism in 1915.

Elijah Muhammad

The National Baptist Convention, Inc., as of 1989, had 7.5 million members, 100,000 of whom were in foreign countries. It possesses more than 30,000 local churches. The convention is governed by a 15-member board of directors and a nine-member executive board. It is a supporter of the American Baptist Theological Seminary in Nashville, Tennessee. Its publications include the semi-monthly *National Baptist Voice*. In 1995, Rev. Dr. Henry J. Lyons was elected president of the National Baptists, the largest black religious order in the United States.

National Missionary Baptist Convention

Founded in 1988, this group boasted 3,200,000 million members in 1995.

National Primitive Baptist Convention of America

Black and white Primitive Baptists separated after the Civil War. Although having long avowed opposition to church organization above the congregational level, it was not until 1907 that black Primitive Baptists formed the National Primitive Baptist Convention. Each con-gregation is independent, and a decision by officials of a local church is final. In 1975, they possessed a membership of 1,645,600 in 2,198 churches.

The Pentecostal Assemblies of the World, Inc.

1,000,000 members belong to the 1,700 churches of an organization founded in 1906.

Progressive National Baptist Convention, Inc.

The Progressive National Baptist Convention, Inc., was formed in 1961, as a result of a schism in the National Baptist Convention of the U.S.A., Inc. The schism resulted from a dispute over leadership occasioned by differences over tactical strategies in the struggle for civil rights. Those, including Martin Luther King, Jr., committed to such provocative tactics as nonviolent civil disobedience left to form the new denomination. The convention's motto is "Unity, Service, Fellowship, and Peace." The Convention has 2 million members and 1,000 churches, and is governed by a 60-member executive board headed by Rev. Bennett Smith, Sr. Although it has no publishing house of its own, it does publish a quarterly periodical, the *Baptist Progress*.

First Baptist Church, Washington, DC

Rastafarians

Members of this religion regard Ethiopian Emperor, who died in 1975, as God. Marcus Garvey, a Jamaican-born nationalist who advocated a back-to-Africa movement in the United States in the early 1920s, is also a central figure in the faith. Reggae musician Bob Marley, a Rastafarian, helped to increase the religion's popularity in the United States.

Today, Rastas differ on specific dogma, but they basically believe that they are descended from black Hebrews exiled in Babylon and therefore are true Israelites. They also believe that Haile Selassie (whose name before ascending the throne was Lij Ras Tafari Makonnen) is the direct descendent of Solomon and Sheba, and that God is black. Most white men, they believe, have been worshipping a dead god and have attempted to teach the blacks to do likewise. They hold that the Bible was distorted by King James and that the black race sinned and was punished by God with slavery. They view Ethiopia as Zion, the Western world as Babylon, and believe that one day they will return to Zion. They preach love, peace, and reconciliation between races but warn that Armageddon is imminent.

Rastas do not vote, tend to be vegetarians, abhor alcohol, and wear their hair in long, uncombed plaits called dreadlocks. The hair is never cut, since it is part of the spirit, nor is it ever combed. An estimated 50,000 Rastas reside in Britain and almost one million in the United States, approximately 80,000 of whom live in New York City, mainly in Brooklyn, where a high concentration of West Indians and Haitians exists.

◆ RELIGIOUS GATEKEEPERS

Jaramogi Abebe Agyeman 1911-
Shrine of the Black Madonna Founder

Jaramogi Abebe Agyeman was born Albert Cleage, Jr., in 1911, in Indianapolis, Indiana. His physician father relocated the family to Detroit a short time later, and Cleage undertook social work as a profession before earning a degree in divinity from Oberlin College in 1943. After his ordination, he headed Congregational churches in Kentucky and Massachusetts; Cleage's work at the latter was notable for the community outreach and economic programs he enacted. Returning to Detroit, the minister became head of a Presbyterian congregation that split off into its own church in 1953.

This fellowship, known as the Central United Church of Christ (CUCC), soon became a political powerhouse among Detroit's increasingly significant African American community during the 1950s. Cleage's growing interest in the Black Power movement of the 1960s—and especially the teachings of Nation of Islam leader Malcolm X—led the pastor to create a separate denomination from the CUCC in 1967, based on historical surmisings that Jesus was of African descent. The focal point of the church—and the symbolic gesture that attracted many to it—was a powerful 18-foot mural of the Black Madonna. This Black Christian Nationalist Movement and its cornerstone congregation, the Shrine of the Black Madonna, soon became an influential religious, social, political, and economic force in the city.

Basing the church's tenets on both teachings of visionaries such as Malcolm X, Elijah Muhammed, and Marcus Garvey, Cleage preached economic self-sufficiency to his flock and put the words into action by the creation of numerous social service programs, a community grocery outlet in answer to the inflated prices then common to white-owned stores in the African American neighborhoods, and a bookstore stocked with the significant African nationalist literature of the day. The Shrine of the Black Madonna expanded into other American cities over the next several years, but the imprint it left on Detroit was perhaps Cleage's most significant achievement. In the late 1960s and early 1970s, after contentious 1967 race riots forever put aside any hopes of smooth integration between a diminishing white population and an increasingly fed-up African American citizenry, Cleage and the church's active membership were credited with helping elect numerous African American political leaders, judges, and school board members who remain a vital force in the city well into the 1990s. Cleage authored two books, *The Black Messiah* and *Black Christian Nationalism*, before taking the name Jaramogi Abebe Agyeman.

Noble Drew Ali 1886-1929
Religious Leader

Noble Drew Ali, whose birth name was Timothy Drew, was born in North Carolina in 1886. He is principally important for his role in establishing the first North American religious movement combining black nationalist and Muslim themes with rejection of Christianity as the religion of whites. In 1913, he established the first Moorish Science Temple in Newark, New Jersey. He taught that black Americans were "Asiatics" who had originally lived in Morocco before enslavement. Every people, including black Americans, needed land for themselves, he proclaimed, and North America, which he termed an "extension" of the African continent, was the proper home for black Americans. The holy book for the Moorish Science Temple was a "Holy Koran" which was "divinely prepared by the Noble Prophet Drew Ali." (This book should not be confused with the Q'uran of Islam). Every member of the Temple carried a card stating that "we honor all the Divine Prophets, Jesus, Mohammed, Buddha and Confucius" and that "I AM A CITIZEN OF THE U.S.A."

In the 1920s, the Moorish Science Temple expanded to Pittsburgh, Detroit, and Chicago. Noble Drew Ali also started several small businesses, which he ran together with his followers. Drew Ali was stabbed to death in his Chicago offices in apparent strife over the leadership of the Temple. The Moorish Science Temple survived Drew Ali's death, but the Nation of Islam was able to attract some of its followers.

Richard Allen 1760-1831
Civil Rights/Human Rights Activist, Bishop, Exporter

Born a slave in Philadelphia on February 14, 1760, Allen converted to Christianity in 1777 and soon thereafter bought his freedom. He traveled widely through the Middle Atlantic States as an exporter. Francis Asbury, the first bishop of the Methodist Episcopal Church, asked Allen to join him as a travelling companion, stipulating that Allen would not be allowed to fraternize with slaves and would sometimes have to sleep in his carriage. Allen refused to accept such an offer, instead settling down in Philadelphia, where he helped to found the Free African Society, an African American society for religious fellowship and mutual aid. One day in the early 1790s, Allen was worshipping in Philadelphia's St. George's Methodist Church when he was pulled off his knees during prayer by white deacons who insisted that Allen was sitting outside the area reserved for African Americans. Allen left, establishing his own church for Philadelphia's African Americans in a converted blacksmith shop in 1794. White Methodists tried to exert their control over his church in various ways, and Allen resisted successfully. In 1816, after the Pennsylvania Supreme Court settled a suit over this church in Allen's favor, Allen called for a conference of black Methodists. The African Methodist Episcopal Church was founded at this conference, and Allen was consecrated as its first bishop. Allen remained both religiously and politically active in his later years, and he was especially active in opposing schemes to colonize free African Americans in Africa.

Carl Bean 1946?-
Clergyman

Since 1985, Bishop Carl Bean, D.M. has been running two projects: the Minority AIDS Project (MAP) and the Unity Fellowship Church for black gays and lesbians. Starting as a Bible-study group, the church quickly took root, with chapters spreading to New York City, Detroit, Washington, DC, Philadelphia, Dallas, and Seattle by 1996. Meanwhile, MAP has become the largest AIDS agency serving African Americans in the United States.

Born and raised in Baptist in Baltimore, Bean was an avid churchgoer in his youth. He grew up singing gospel, even participating in a Broadway gospel revue. Openly gay and HIV-negative, Bean wanted to help liberate ostracized people of color—gay or straight—because he himself had once felt shunned by the church. Reaching out to the disenfranchised, Bean's followers believe that "Love is for everyone."

In 1991, the fellowship embarked on a campaign to work with gangs. Often getting referrals from social workers, Bean's congregation has earned a reputation for doing whatever is required to get people's lives on track. From distributing cash grants for food and bills to paying for funerals, Unity Fellowship members give back to the community.

Sister Thea Bowman 1938-1990
Writer, Educator, Religious Leader

Born in Canton, Mississippi, in 1938, Thea Bowman, daughter of a medical doctor, joined the Roman Catholic Church at age 12 because of the Catholic education she had received. Three years later, she joined the Franciscan Sisters of Perpetual Adoration. She was extensively educated, earning a Ph.D. in literature and linguistics. Bowman was a distinguished teacher, who taught elementary and high school as well as college. She helped to found the Institute of Black Catholic Studies at Xavier University and was a distinguished scholar known for her writings on Thomas More. But it is probably for the spiritual inspiration that she provided in numerous lectures, workshops and concerts that she will be best remembered. She said that she brought to her church "myself, my black self, all that I am, all that I have, all that I hope to become, my history, my culture, my experience, my African American song and dance and gesture and movement and teaching and preaching and healing."

Nannie Helen Burroughs 1883-1961
Baptist Lay Leader, Educator

Born in Orange Springs, Virginia, Nannie Helen Burroughs became one of the most significant Baptist lay leaders of the twentieth century. She addressed the National Baptist Convention in Virginia in 1900 on the subject, "How the Sisters Are Hindered from Helping," and from that time until her death more than 60 years later she exercised pivotal leadership. She was elected corresponding secretary for the Woman's Convention, Auxiliary to the National Baptist Convention, U.S.A., Inc., and in 1948, she became President of the Women's Convention. She founded the National Training School for Women and Girls, emphasizing industrial arts and proficiency in African American history, in Washington, DC. She edited such periodicals as the *Christian Banner*, and was the author of such books as the *Roll Call of Bible Women*.

Calvin O. Butts, III 1949-
Religious Leader

Calvin Butts spent the first eight years of his life on the Lower East Side of New York City, where he was born in 1949. In 1957, the family moved to Queens, New York. During the summer breaks from school Butts's parents would send him down south to stay with his grandmothers who lived near another in rural Georgia. It was in these early formative years that Butts first became acquainted with the church.

After graduating from Flushing High School, where he was class president his senior year, Butts was accepted to Morehouse College. The year was 1967, an explosive time in the American civil rights struggle. Butts attended lectures, rallies, and speeches at Morehouse by Martin Luther King, Jr. and other black leaders. Following one of these very emotional events Butts found himself immersed in a riot and actually assisted in the firebombing of a local store. Shortly thereafter, he renounced his capitulation to violence.

Just before his graduation from college, Butts was approached by two young seminarians trying to recruit students for their school. Later, he would receive his Masters of Divinity from Union Theological Seminary. While attending the Seminary, Butts raised a few eyebrows through his controversial stance on homosexuality. He has since defended the social and civil rights of gays, which he had once denounced.

Butts was recruited as a junior minister in 1972, by William Epps. During this time his responsibilities included making hospital visits and conducting funeral services. From the very beginning, though, Butts realized the Abyssinian pulpit provided a great foundation from which to preach. For instance, he was quite vocal in his opposition to police brutality; along with any other form of violence.

Since assuming the pastoral role at Harlem's Abyssinian Baptist Church, which boasts more than 5,000 parishioners, Butts has also been involved the community. He has sat on the board of the Harlem Young Men's Christian Association (YMCA). Also, Butts has supported presidential hopefuls such as Ross Perot. He was the co-chair of Perot's New York campaign. The political arena is one in which Calvin Butts will continue to explore. In the 1990s, he showed interest in running for city mayor and for statewide office.

Katie Cannon 1950-
Presbyterian Minister, Educator, Feminist

Cannon was born January 3, 1950, in Kannopolis, North Carolina. As she approached adulthood, Cannon found that only two roads were available to most black women in her community—they could work in the local mill or become a school teacher. The teachers she knew played an important role in the early years of her life; she thrived in the supportive and protective environment of the academic environment, though the bite of racism was still all too real to her. Blacks were prohibited from public places such as the library and the local pool, and Cannon was determined to escape.

Cannon enrolled in Barber-Scotia College. She graduated with a B.S. in 1971, after rising to the top of her senior class, making the dean's list and being named Miss Barber-Scotia. The following fall, Cannon went on to study at Johnson C. Smith Seminary of the Interdenominational Theological Center (ITC) in Atlanta, Georgia—one of the two accredited black seminaries at the time. During her time there Cannon was exposed to every aspect of the ministry. Majoring in Old Testament studies, she was only one of four women in her class. Upon completion of her studies, Cannon received her master's degree in Divinity in 1974.

Cannon served as pastor at the Ascension Presbyterian Church in New York City for three years. Her work there was followed by an administrative position at the New York Theological Seminary, then, ready to resume her scholarly endeavors, Cannon decided to attend Union Theological Seminary, where she received her master's degree in Philosophy and her Ph.D. As of 1993, Cannon serves as the associate professor of Christian ethics at Philadelphia's Temple University. In 1995, a compilation of previously published essays was released as *Katie's Cannon: Womanism and the Soul of the Black Community.*

James Cone 1938-
Author, Theologian, Educator

Born in Fordyce, Arkansas, in 1938, James Cone received a B.A. from Philander Smith College, a B.D. from Garrett Evangelical Seminary, and an M.A. and Ph.D. from Northwestern University. After teaching at Philander Smith and Adrian Colleges, Cone moved to Union Theological Seminary in 1969. He is currently the Charles A. Briggs Professor of Systematic Theology. Cone is the author of numerous books, including *Black Theology and Black Power* (1969); *The Spirituals and the Blues* (1972); *For My People: Black Theology and the Black Church* (1984); and most recently, *Martin and Malcolm and America: A Dream or a Nightmare* (1991).

Perhaps more than any other black theologian, Cone has provided a systematic exposition of the argument that since God, according to the Bible, is on the side of the poor and oppressed, that in the American context, God is siding with the black liberation struggle. He has made this argument using a diverse set of sources, including the writings of modern European theologians such as Karl Barth, and the writings and speeches of Malcolm X and Martin Luther King, Jr. Cone has worked painstakingly in the past two decades to build ties between black, feminist, and third world liberation theologians.

Suzan Johnson Cook
Religious Leader, Author

Raised in the Bronx, New York, Rev. Suzan Johnson Cook was a communications student at Emerson College, when she went to Ghana as an exchange student.

There she entertained notions of joining the ministry. She would later enroll at the United Theological Seminary, where she pursued a doctorate. Just as her role model Presbyterian minister Katie Cannon had found earlier, entering into the pastorship was a task rote with difficulty for a woman, but Cook carved a niche and perservered. Eager to assist other women in pursuing the ministry, she later directed Black Women in the Ministry, sponsored by the New York City Mission Society.

In 1983, Cook began 11 years of preaching at Mariner's Temple, the oldest Baptist facility in Manhattan. Her rapport with the small congregation led her to become the first African American woman elected to senior pastor of a Baptist church in the United States. During her years with the church membership swelled from 60 to more than 1,000 members. Cook became the first woman to be appointed chaplain of the New York City Police Department in 1990, when then-Mayor David Dinkins selected her. Three years later, President Bill Clinton chose her for a White House Fellowship, the first female minister to be so recognized. Cook has authored two books, *Wise Women Bearing Gifts: Joys and Struggles of Their Faith* and *Preaching in Two Vocies: Sermons on the Women in Jesus's Life.*

Father Divine 1877–1965
Religious Leader, Organization Executive/Founder

Mystery shrouds the early identity and real name of Father Divine. He is thought to have been born George Baker in the late 1870s on Hutchinson's Island near Georgia. In 1907, he became a disciple of Sam Morris, a Pennsylvania black man who called himself Father Jehovia. Two years later he switched over to John Hickerson's "Lift Ever, Die Never" group before returning to Georgia, where he began his own campaign to promote himself as a "divine messenger."

Threatened by local authorities (he was once booked as "John Doe, alias God"), Father Divine left Georgia in 1914 and later settled in New York City, where he worked as an "employment agent" for the few followers still loyal to him. Calling his meeting place "Heaven," he soon attracted a larger following and moved to Sayville, Long Island, in 1919. It was at this time that Father Divine began to provide shelter and food to the poor and homeless. Spiritually, Father Divine fostered what amounted to a massive cooperative agency, based on the communal spirit of the Last Supper. His movement practiced complete racial equality. Services included songs and impromptu sermons and were conducted without Scripture readings and the use of clergy. Once he was sentenced to six months in jail as a public nuisance. Four days after his trial, the judge in his case died of a heart attack, whereupon Father Divine was quoted as having said: "I hated to do it." The ensuing publicity enhanced his popularity.

The Divine movement, a non-ritualistic cult whose followers worshipped their leader as God incarnate on earth, grew rapidly in the 1930s and 1940s, with "Father" speaking out across the country and publicizing his views in the *New Day*, a weekly magazine published by his organization. He set up "Peace Mission Kingdom" throughout the United States and the world. In 1946, he married his "Sweet Angel," a 21-year old Canadian stenographer known thereafter as Mother Divine. Father Divine died peacefully at Woodmont, an estate he had acquired in the Philadelphia suburbs, and his wife pledged to continue the work of the movement.

Elijah John Fisher 1858–1915
Community Activist, Minister

Elijah Fisher exemplifies the great charismatic black preachers of the nineteenth and early twentieth centuries who, with very little formal education, built large religious institutions, counseled racial pride, and expounded the cause of blacks as a people.

Born in La Grange, Georgia, in 1858, the youngest of eight boys in a family of 17 children, Fisher's father was an unordained preacher of a Baptist congregation that met in a white church. Fisher worked in a Baptist parsonage as a boy slave, and was taught to read by a former house slave and a white missionary. In his teens, he worked in mines in Alabama and then as a butler, all the while studying theology on his own time. Though he lost a leg in an accident, Fisher in his early twenties became pastor of several small country churches, and then in 1889, of the Mount Olive Baptist Church in Atlanta. In that year, when past the age of 30, he enrolled in the Atlanta Baptist Seminary, passed his examinations, went to preach in Nashville and then Chicago where he led the Olive Baptist Church from 1902 until his death.

Throughout his life, Fisher continued his studies, preached from coast to coast, and involved the churches in youth work, food programs for poor people, and black-run businesses. An active member of the Republican Party, Fisher strongly criticized blacks who advised their brethren to rely solely on the good will of whites and publicly criticized Booker T. Washington for not speaking out against lynching.

"Sweet Daddy" Grace 1881–1960
Religious Leader, Sales Agent

Born in 1881 in the Cape Verde Islands, "Sweet Daddy" Grace probably opened his first church in New

Father Divine

Bedford, Massachusetts, in 1921, but his first success occurred five years later when he opened a church in Charlotte. Grace's church, the United House of Prayer for All People, had an ecstatic worship style, where speaking in tongues was encouraged. Grace claimed great powers, including the power of faith healing, and he stated that "Grace has given God a vacation, and since God is on His vacation don't worry Him...If you sin against God, Grace can save you, but if you sin against Grace, God cannot save you." Even the numerous products that he sold, such as "Daddy Grace" coffee, tea,

soaps, and hand creams, were reputed to have healing powers. By the time of his death in 1960, the church had 375 branches and about 25,000 members nationwide.

Barbara C. Harris 1930-
Executive Director, Bishop, Deacon

Born in Philadelphia in 1930, Barbara Harris, a former public relations executive, was ordained a deacon in the Protestant Episcopal Church in 1979 and a priest one year later. She served as the priest-in-charge of an

Barbara Harris

Episcopalian Church in Norristown, Pennsylvania, the interim pastor of a church in Philadelphia, and the executive director of the publishing company associated with the Episcopal Church. In February of 1989, she was consecrated as suffragan (or assistant) bishop for the diocese of Massachusetts. She thus became the first woman bishop in the history of the Episcopal Church. She received considerable support despite the concerns of some that her views were too liberal. Her supporters said that despite the lack of a college degree or seminary training, she would broaden the outreach of her church.

James Augustine Healy 1830-1900
Educator, Religious Leader

James Augustine Healy was the first black Catholic bishop in the United States. (Healy's brother, Patrick Francis Healy, was a Jesuit priest who served as president of Georgetown University from 1873 to 1882.) For 25 years he presided over a diocese covering the states of Maine and New Hampshire. A native of Macon, Georgia, Healy received his education in the North, first at Franklin Park Quaker School in Burlington, New York, and later at Holy Cross in Worcester, Massachusetts. Healy graduated from the latter with first honors.

Healy continued his studies abroad, and was ordained in Paris at Notre Dame Cathedral in 1854. He then returned to the United States.

Pastor of a predominantly Irish congregation which was at first reluctant to accept him, Bishop Healy performed his priestly duties with devotion and eventually won the respect and admiration of his parishioners—particularly after performing his office during a typhoid epidemic. Thereafter, he was made an assistant to Bishop John Fitzpatrick of Boston, who appointed him chancellor and entrusted him with a wide variety of additional responsibilities. In 1875, he was named Bishop of Portland, Maine, and in this capacity, he founded sixty parishes, as well as 18 schools.

Joseph Henry Jackson 1904-1990
Organization Executive/Founder, Theologian, Civil Rights/Human Rights Activist

From 1953 to 1982, Joseph H. Jackson was the president of the National Baptist Convention, U.S.A., Inc., the third largest Protestant denomination in the United States and the largest of the predominantly black churches. Born in Rudyard, Mississippi, in 1904 Jackson held a

Bishop James A. Healy

Dr. Joseph Jackson

B.A. from Jackson College, a M.A. from Creighton University, and a B.D. from Rochester Colgate School of Divinity. After pastoring churches in Mississippi, Jackson accepted a call to pastor the historic Olivet Baptist Church in 1941. His role in the civil rights movement was a fairly conservative one. He was supportive of the efforts of Martin Luther King, Jr. during the Montgomery bus boycott of 1955, but criticized the massive nonviolent civil disobedience campaigns of the early 1960s. Jackson's main emphasis was on the need for African Americans to build a viable economic base. His favorite slogan was "From Protest to Production." He was supportive of Baptist missions in Africa and attempted to finance them by developing farmland in Liberia.

Leontine T. C. Kelly 1920-
Bishop

Leontine T. C. Kelly, the first black woman bishop in any large American denomination, was born in Washington, DC, in 1920. She received a M.Div. degree from Union Theological Seminary in Richmond, Virginia, in 1969. She served as a schoolteacher, pastor of Virginia churches, and a staff member of the Virginia Conference of Churches before being elected a bishop in the United Methodist Church in 1984. She currently presides over the California-Nevada conference of that denomination. She is married to James David Kelly and has four children.

Isaac Lane 1834-1937
Educational Administrator, Religious Leader

A great religious leader and educator whose life spanned more than a century, Isaac Lane was born a slave in Jackson, Tennessee, in 1834. Self-educated, in 1856 he was granted a license to exhort, a category assigned to blacks who were forbidden to preach, in the Methodist Episcopal Church South. Lane was ordained a minister in 1865 and in 1873 was made a bishop of the Colored Methodist Episcopal Church (now known as the Christian Methodist Episcopal Church) at a salary so low he had to raise cotton to supplement his income and support his family—which contained 11 children. His missionary work was instrumental in establishing the CME Church in Louisiana and Texas. In the 1880s, he established Lane College in Jackson with $9,000 he himself raised. He died in 1937.

Jarena Lee 1783-1849
Women's Rights Activist, Minister

Born in 1783, in Cape May, New Jersey, Lee worked as a servant for a family who lived near Philadelphia. She had a conversion experience in 1804, but was unable to find a church with which to unite until she heard Richard Allen, founder of the African Methodist Episcopal church, preach in Philadelphia. She experienced a call to preach about 1808, and sought permission from Richard Allen on two occasions. On her first attempt in 1809, Allen refused her request, but eight years later, he granted it and licensed her as a preacher. Subsequently, she traveled widely throughout the North and Midwest, and many of her listeners, especially women, were moved by her eloquent preaching. After Allen's death in 1831, male African Methodist Episcopal preachers in Philadelphia attempted to deny her permission to preach from their pulpits, but she continued her ministry despite such harassment. In 1848, she attempted to form a connection of female African Methodist Episcopal preachers for mutual support, but her organization soon fell apart. Many black women, especially within the African Methodist Episcopal Church, view Jarena Lee as a courageous foremother and a model for church activism.

George Liele 1750-1820
Educator, Religious Leader

Born a slave in Virginia around 1750, George Liele was sold while very young into Georgia. He experienced a Christian conversion after hearing a sermon by Matthew Moore, a white preacher, in 1773. Liele began conducting worship services on nearby plantations, and, with Moore's sponsorship, he soon became the first ordained black Baptist preacher in America. Liele's slave master, Henry Sharp, granted him his freedom before Sharp was killed in the American Revolution. Liele preached at the Silver Bluff Baptist Church in Silver Bluff, South Carolina, probably the first independent black congregation formed in North America, and at a location outside Savannah. One of his notable converts was Andrew Bryan, who founded the First African Baptist Church in Savannah. Some whites attempted to re-enslave Liele, but a British officer in Savannah ensured that he would maintain his freedom. Liele emigrated to Jamaica in 1784, and he started a school and preached to a small Baptist congregation in Kingston. Liele was married to a woman he converted in Savannah, and his four American-born children accompanied him to Jamaica.

Eugene A. Marino 1934-
Archbishop

Born May 29, 1934, in Biloxi, Mississippi, Eugene Marino received his training at Epiphany Apostolic

Archbishop Eugene Marino

College and St. Joseph Seminary. He was ordained to the priesthood in 1962. The next year Marino was made director of St. Joseph Seminary. He also continued his educational studies at Catholic University, Loyola University, and Fordham University, where he earned a master of arts degree in 1967.

In 1971, Marino was named vicar general of the Josephites and served as an auxiliary bishop in Washington, DC. after his ordination to the episcopate in 1974. Marino became the first black Roman Catholic archbishop in 1988, when he was made archbishop of the Atlanta Archdiocese. He retired in 1990, in the midst of sex scandal, when an affair he was having with a woman was exposed. In 1993, ex-bishop Marino and Vicki Long, the woman in question, reunited and were planning a life together.

Charles H. Mason 1866-1961
Religious Leader

Born to former slaves on a farm outside Memphis, Tennessee, in 1866, Charles Mason was converted at the age of 14, and he joined a Missionary Baptist Church. Mason obtained a preaching license from the Missionary Baptists in 1893, and, in the same year, he claimed to have the experience of entire sanctification, thus aligning himself with the Holiness Movement. He had little formal education beyond a brief period of study at the Arkansas Bible College. In 1895, the Baptists expelled him because of his beliefs on sanctification. Mason then held holiness revivals in Mississippi with the help of Charles Price Jones, a prolific writer of hymns and gospel songs, and others. In Lexington, Mississippi, his meetings were held in an abandoned cotton gin house. Despite an armed attack, probably by hostile African Americans, he achieved much success and many new converts with his revival preaching. In 1897, Mason and Jones founded a new Holiness Church and called it the Church of God in Christ; they worked together harmoniously over the next decade.

In 1907, Mason attended the Azusa Street Revival, conducted by William Seymour in Los Angeles, and he received the gift of speaking in tongues. He believed that the ability to speak in tongues was a necessary precondition for Baptism of the Spirit. He and Jones disagreed on this point and parted company. Mason reformed the Church of God in Christ along the lines of his new spiritual insights. Over the next four decades, Mason, as bishop, general overseer, and "chief apostle," shepherded his denomination through a period of tremendous growth. He traveled extensively, preaching at revivals throughout the United States and the world. He was imprisoned for making pacifist statements during World War I. He died in 1961.

William Henry Miles 1828-1892
Religious Leader

Born a slave in Kentucky in 1828, Miles was manumitted by his owner in her will. He joined the Methodist Episcopal Church, South, and soon perceived a call to preach. In 1859, he was ordained a deacon. Uncertain about church affiliation after the war, he investigated the possibility of joining the African Methodist Episcopal Zion Church, but soon thought better of it. Thus he remained a preacher in the Methodist Episcopal Church, South, until its African American members, those who had decided not to join the African Methodist Episcopal or African Methodist Episcopal Zion Churches, were allowed to form a separate denomination, the Colored Methodist Episcopal Church. At the first General Conference of the Colored Methodist Episcopal Church in 1870, Miles was elected one of the denomination's first two bishops. He was an active advocate of black colleges, especially those affiliated with the CME Church, such as Lane College in Jackson, Tennessee, and Paine Seminary in Atlanta, Georgia. He died in 1892.

Reverend Harold Perry

Harold Robert Perry 1916-1991
Educator, Religious Leader

Harold Robert Perry was consecrated a Bishop of New Orleans on January 6, 1966—and thus became the first Catholic bishop in the United States in the twentieth century. One of six children, Perry was born the son of a rice-mill worker and a domestic cook in Lake Charles, Louisiana, in 1916. He entered the Divine Word Seminary in Mississippi at the age of 13, was ordained a priest in 1944, and spent the next fourteen years in parish work. In 1958, he was appointed rector of the seminary. Louisiana has the largest concentration of black Catholics in the South, some 200,000 in all. In 1989, Perry was one of thirteen African American bishops serving Catholic parishes around the nation. He died on July 17, 1991.

Adam Clayton Sr. Powell 1865-1953
Religious Leader, Community Activist

Adam Clayton Powell, Sr., father of the late Harlem congressman, was largely responsible for building the Abyssinian Baptist Church into one of the most celebrated black congregations in the world. Born in the backwoods of Virginia in 1865, Powell attended school

Reverend Adam Clayton Powell, Sr.

locally, and between sessions, worked in the coal mines of West Virginia. After deciding to enter the ministry, he began his studies at Wayland Academy (now Virginia Union University), working his way through as a janitor and waiter. He later attended the Yale University School of Divinity and served as pastor of the Immanuel Baptist Church in New Haven.

Powell became pastor of Abyssinian in 1908 when it had a membership of only 1,600 and indebtedness of more than $100,000. By 1921, the church had not been made solvent but was able to move into a $350,000 Gothic structure at its present location on 138th Street in Harlem. During the Depression, Powell opened soup kitchens for Harlem residents and served thousands of meals. Later he and his son campaigned vigorously to expand job opportunities and city services in Harlem. Powell retired from Abyssinian in 1937 and died in 1953.

Joseph Charles Price 1854-1893
Civil Rights/Human Rights Activist, Minister, Prohibitionist

Born in Elizabeth City, North Carolina, in 1854, to a free mother, Price was educated in the school established for freed people, and later at Shaw and Lincoln

Universities, graduating from the latter in 1879. At age 21, he was licensed to preach in the African Methodist Episcopal Zion Church, and he received the ordination of elder six years later. Price was renowned for the eloquence of his public addresses. It was Price who was the most responsible for the African Methodist Episcopal Zion Church's success in establishing a church college—Livingstone College in North Carolina—after ministers in that denomination had failed in several previous attempts. As president of Livingstone College, he quickly gave his school a solid grounding both academically and financially. For example, he raised $10,000 for his school during a lecture tour of England. He was an active participant in politics, campaigned for civil rights and prohibition, and assumed such offices as chairman of the Citizens' Equal Rights Association of Washington, DC. He died a tragically early death from kidney failure in 1893.

William Joseph Seymour 1870-1922
Civil Rights/Human Rights Activist, Religious Leader

Born in Centerville, Louisiana, in 1870, to parents who had been slaves, Seymour taught himself to read and write. In 1900, Seymour encountered the prominent promoter of Holiness doctrine, Martin Knapp, and studied under him. He suffered a bout of smallpox which left him blind in one eye. He was ordained as an evangelist by the "Evening Light Saints," a group that eventually became known by the title Church of God (Anderson, Indiana). Moving to Houston, he sat immediately outside the door of white evangelist Charles Parham's segregated classroom, while Parham lectured on Christian doctrine and, especially, on the importance of speaking in tongues.

In 1906, Seymour moved to Los Angeles to pastor a small black Holiness church, but his congregation, opposed to Seymour's contention that speaking in tongues was a very important part of Christian experience, dismissed him after one week. Seymour continued to hold religious meetings, attracting an interracial audience. A widely publicized outburst of speaking in tongues brought him an ever-larger audience, so he moved his "Apostolic Faith Gospel Mission" to a former AME Church building on Azusa Street. The extremely successful meetings that he held before ecstatic, interracial throngs of listeners over the next three years have been universally acknowledged as the beginnings of modern Pentecostalism in the United States and around the world. Seymour was greatly saddened when the racial unity displayed in the early stages of Pentecostalism began to break apart under the pressures exerted by racial discrimination in the nation at large. He was holding services at the Azusa Street mission until his death in 1922.

Amanda Berry Smith 1837-1915
Organization Executive/Founder, Evangelist/Missionary

Born in Long Green, Maryland, in 1837, Smith was manumitted during her childhood after her father paid for her freedom. She had an spiritual conversion experience in 1856. She began attending religious meetings faithfully, and while she resisted identification with any single denomination, her religious practice was most strongly influenced by Quakers and Methodists. Attendance at the religious meetings of white evangelists Phoebe Palmer and John Inskip introduced her to Holiness doctrine, and she experienced entire sanctification in 1868. Her husband died the following year, and Smith soon became a full-time traveling evangelist. She never sought to breach the barriers against women's ordination erected by male preachers, stating that the calling she had received directly from God was justification enough for her ministry.

From 1878 to 1890, Smith worked as a missionary in England, Ireland, Scotland, India, and Liberia. A Methodist bishop who heard her preach in India stated that he "had never known any one who could draw and hold so large an audience as Mrs. Smith." On her return to the United States in 1890, she preached widely and wrote her autobiography in 1893, an extremely detailed work now regarded as a classic. Her last twenty years were devoted to the construction and management of the Amanda Smith Orphan's Home for Colored Children in Illinois. She died in 1915.

Stephen Gill Spottswood 1897-1974
Organization Executive/Founder, Religious Leader, Civil Rights/Human Rights Activist

Bishop of the African Methodist Episcopal Zion Church from 1952 to 1972 and board chairman of the National Association for the Advancement of Colored People from 1961 until his death in 1974, Bishop Spottswood embodied the religious faith and intellectual incisiveness that has produced so many effective black religious activists.

Spottswood was born in Boston on July 18, 1897, attended Albright College, Gordon Divinity School, and then received a Doctor of Divinity from Yale University. As a religious leader, Bishop Spottswood was president of the Ohio Council of Churches and served on the boards of numerous interfaith conferences as well as heading the African Methodist Episcopal Zion Church.

His activity with the NAACP started in 1919, when he joined the organization. He was appointed to the national board in 1955. In 1971, he became the center of a political storm when he chastised the Nixon administration for its policies toward blacks and refused, under strong pressure from the administration, to retract his comments. He died on December 1, 1974.

George Augustus Stallings, Jr. 1948-
Theologian

Born in New Bern, North Carolina, in 1948, Stallings received his bachelor of arts degree from St. Pius X Seminary in 1970. He received his bachelor of science degree in theology from the University of St. Thomas Aquinas in 1973 and his master of arts degree in pastoral theology the following year. In 1974 Stallings was ordained and in 1976 was named pastor of St. Teresa of Avila, located in one of Washington, DC's poor black neighborhoods. In 1975, he was granted a licentiate in sacred theology by the University of St. Thomas Aquinas.

While pastor at St. Teresa, Stallings stressed that the contributions of Africans and African Americans to Christianity should be recognized and that the needs of blacks must be addressed by the church. In an effort to confront what he considered the church's racial insensitivity, he made use of what is known as the Rite of Zaire, incorporated jazz and gospel music to the Mass, and added readings by celebrated African-American writers to the litgery. Stallings received much criticism and in 1988 was removed from St. Teresa and named head of evangelism for Washington, DC.

In 1989 Stallings, still convinced that the church was not meeting the cultural, spiritual, and social needs of African American Catholics, announced that he would leave the diocese to found a new congregation, the Imani Temple African-American Catholic Congregation. In 1991, Bishop Stallings ordained former Roman Catholic nun Rose Vernell a priest. The congregation's membership is currently estimated at 3,500 members.

Leon Howard Sullivan 1922-
Labor Activist, Civil Rights/Human Rights Activist, Vocational/Educational Counselor, Organization Executive/Founder

Sullivan was born October 16, 1922, in Charlestown, West Virginia. After being ordained a Baptist minister at the age of seventeen, Sullivan earned a B.A. from West Virginia State College (1943) and an M.A. from Columbia University (1947). Sullivan also attended the Union Theological Seminary (1945) and earned a D.Div. from Virginia Union University.

From 1950 to 1988, Sullivan was the pastor of the Zion Baptist Church in Philadelphia. Much of his efforts

Bishop Stephen Spottswood

during his ministry were directed toward improving employment prospects of African Americans. During the 1950s, he organized a selective patronage campaign, boycotting Philadelphia-area businesses which employed too few black employees. Sullivan's campaign experienced some success, but businesses requested black workers with technical skills that few possessed.

Accordingly, Sullivan founded the Opportunities Industrialization Center (O.I.C.) in 1964 in order to impart employment skills to inner city youths. With money from a Ford Foundation grant, the Center offered training in electronics, cooking, power-sewing, and drafting. By 1980, the O.I.C. operated programs in 160 cities. Sullivan was also a major force in many other economic development initiatives, such as the Philadelphia Community Investment Cooperative; Zion Investment Associates, which makes available seed money for new African American business ventures; and Self-Help. His acceptance within the American business community is well symbolized by his long-time membership on the boards of General Motors and Philadelphia's Girard

Reverend Howard Thurman (left) with O. D. Foster, 1952.

Bank as well as his association with Progress Aerospace Inc. and Mellon Bank.

Sullivan is also renowned for his leadership in addressing international issues as they affect the African American community, and in particular, for his intensive involvement in political and economic reform in South Africa. In the mid-1970s, he devised his "Sullivan Principles," which successfully encouraged American-owned companies to hire more black South African workers and to treat them equitably in relation to promotions and working conditions. Sullivan, however, parted company with President Reagan's "constructive engagement" policy toward South Africa, and endorsed a policy of South African divestment in 1987. In the same year, Sullivan received the Franklin D. Roosevelt Four Freedoms Medal. Upon retiring from the Zion Baptist Church in 1988, Sullivan was made Pastor Emeritus.

Gardner C. Taylor 1918-
Civil Rights/Human Rights Activist, Religious Leader, Community Activist

Reverend Taylor is widely regarded as the dean of the nation's black preachers. He received a B.A. degree from Leland College in 1937 and a B.D. degree from the Oberlin Graduate School of Theology in 1940. Taylor has long been a community activist. He demonstrated for civil rights and suffered arrest for civil disobedience with Martin Luther King, Jr., in the 1960s, and introduced Nelson Mandela to a New York audience in 1990. He is a trusted counselor to New York Mayor David Dinkins. Taylor served on the New York City Board of Education. He is the past president of the New York Council of Churches and the past vice president of the Urban League in New York, City. After 42 years as pastor of the Concord Baptist Church in Brooklyn, Taylor resigned his post in 1990.

Howard Thurman 1899-1981
Author, Theologian, Civil Rights/Human Rights Activist, Educator

Born in Daytona Beach, Florida, on November 18, 1899, Thurman studied at Morehouse College, Rochester Theological Center, and Haverford College. Thurman, named by *Life* magazine as one of the twelve great preachers of the twentieth century, served as a pastor to a Baptist church in Ohio and, from 1944 to 1953, an interracial and interdenominational Fellowship Church he founded in San Francisco. He also served as dean of the chapel at Howard University from 1932 to 1944, and Boston University from 1953 until his retirement. Thurman was one of the leading theologians of his time, writing *The Negro Spiritual Speaks of Life and Death* and his opposition to segregation and support of the civil rights movement in *This Luminous Darkness*. Altogether, he authored nineteen books, including an autobiography published in 1979. He died on April 10, 1981.

James Varick 1750-1827
Abolitionist, Bishop, Deacon

Born near Newburgh, New York, around 1750, to a slave mother, Varick was a leader in the movement among African-American Methodists in New York to set up a separate congregation. This was accomplished with the formation of the Zion Church in 1796. Varick was ordained a deacon by Bishop Francis Asbury ten years later. Varick sought to obtain full ordination (as elder) for himself and other African-American ministers, and would have preferred to have received such an ordination within the Methodist Episcopal Church, but this did not prove possible. He did not favor joining Richard Allen's African Methodist Episcopal Church, especially since Allen had been attempting to set up a New York congregation seen by Varick as in competition with the Zion Church. Eventually, Varick participated in setting up the African Methodist Episcopal Zion Church, and he was elected the first superintendent or bishop. He was also deeply involved in issues relating to freedom and human rights, preaching against the slave trade in 1808 and subscribing to the first newspaper in the country owned by African Americans, *Freedom's Journal*. He died in 1827.

Cornel West 1953-
Scholar, Educator, Social Critic, Author

The grandson of Rev. Clifton L. West, Sr., pastor of the Tulsa Metropolitan Baptist Church, Cornel West was born on June 2, 1953, in Tulsa, Oklahoma. West developed skills of critical thinking and political action almost from birth. By age 17, he was enrolled as an undergraduate student at Harvard. Taking eight courses per semester during his junior year, he was able to graduate *magna cum laude* one year early. He received an A.B. in Near Eastern languages and literature in 1973. Immediately afterward, he completed his master's (1975) and Ph.D. (1980) at Princeton University.

Professor of religion and director of Afro-American Studies at Princeton University since 1989, Cornel West's analytical speeches and writing on issues of morality, race relations, cultural diversity, and progressive politics have made him a keeper of the prophetic African American religious tradition. West has taught the philosophy of religion at both Union Theological Seminary (1977-83, 1988) and Yale Divinity School (1984-87). A complex individual, he juggles his theological concerns with his political convictions. West serves dual roles as prophet and intellectual within and beyond the black community. His writings combine a castigation for moral failure with an optimism that insists on the possibility—through struggle—of making a world of stricter morality real.

18

Literature

18

Literature

◆ African American Writers Before the Harlem Renaissance ◆ The Harlem Renaissance
◆ African American Writers After the Harlem Renaissance ◆ The Black Aesthetic Movement
◆ The Post Aesthetic Movement ◆ African American Novelists, Poets, Playwrights

by Nancy Rampson

African American literature in the United States reached an artistic pinnacle in the period between the two world wars with the Harlem Renaissance. Since then African American writing has reached a level of high visibility; the themes have varied from highly charged and political to private and introspective. The Black Aesthetic Movement of the 1960s and 1970s brought acclaim and prominence to many African American writers and fostered the growth of many black studies departments at universities around the country. In the 1980s and 1990s, African American writers were working in every genre—from scriptwriting to poetry—and the names of African American writers consistently were found on best-seller lists around the country.

◆ AFRICAN AMERICAN WRITERS BEFORE THE HARLEM RENAISSANCE

Perhaps the greatest satisfaction for black writers before the 1920s, or the Harlem Renaissance, was to have the freedom to write; in fact, knowing how to read and write was a tremendous accomplishment for many post- Reconstruction African Americans.

For Frederick Douglass, to write stirring diatribes against slavery powerful enough to shake the consciousness of a nation was more of a political than an artistic accomplishment. Likewise, when Jupiter Hammon, George Moses Horton, and Frances Harper prosaically wrote about the evils of slavery and racism, their verse seemed somewhat stilted; they followed the molds of Methodism, neoclassicism, and the Bible, traditions ill suited to their subject matter. However admirable their writing was, they never quite found a vehicle that fit their revolutionary thoughts.

As the bonds of slavery were loosened, black writers clamored to be heard, but the range of their work was limited. Since slavery and plantations were practically the only subjects in their repertoire, early African American works were often locked into these themes. In addition, being a black writer before 1920 was certainly a unique profession, almost an oddity. Many writers were essentially unknown during their lives. Still others, like Phillis Wheatley and George Moses Horton, gained a certain amount of acclaim. In fact, a number of blacks, including Paul Laurence Dunbar and Charles W. Chesnutt, became truly appreciated as writers.

White society, however, still controlled much of publishing in America; African American work was often filtered and distorted through this lens. As a result, much of the post-Reconstruction era work by African Americans was an attempt to prove that blacks could fit into middle-American society. In fact, much of the literature of this era was an attempt by blacks to appear happy with their assigned lot. Yet some writers, Dunbar and Chestnutt for example, tried to break the chains of this imposed expression. They attempted to present a view of black life as it really was, not as society wanted it to be.

Although the accomplishments of writers of this era were remarkable, existing conditions seemed to keep African American letters from truly flourishing. What these authors most notably did was to pave the way for the Harlem Renaissance and to provoke authors to think about and develop a truly African American culture.

◆ THE HARLEM RENAISSANCE

Resistant to the easy categorization of a timeline, the Harlem Renaissance began roughly around World War I

Phillis Wheatley's first poem was printed in 1770 under the title "A Poem by Phillis, A Negro Girl on the Death of Reverend George Whitefield."

and extended into the early 1930s. It began mostly as a movement of African American artists and writers into Harlem from practically every state in the country. At the same time, another hub of artistic activity was forming in Washington, DC. In fact, Harlem artists often journeyed to Washington for a break and a new perspective.

What was on the conscious agenda of these mostly young, African American artists was to define and celebrate black art and culture and to change the preconceived and erroneous notions most Americans had of black life.

As African American journals such as *Crisis* and *Opportunity* began to appear, it became much easier for black writers to publish in a style that suited their tastes. Also, African American writers were finding that some white patrons in the publishing fields were, in fact, interested in promoting their work. Bohemianism was flourishing, and many of the Harlem Renaissance artists fit this label. Being called "New Negroes," they sought to chisel out a unique, African-centered culture for blacks, and to improve race relations while maintaining a distinct cultural identity.

Important writers of this era include Langston Hughes, Countee Cullen, Claude McKay, Nella Larsen, and Zora Neale Hurston. These younger writers were encouraged by the older, established writers, critics and editors, including W. E. B. Du Bois, with his journal, *Crisis* and Charles S. Johnson, editor of *Opportunity*, a sponsor of many literary contests. In fact, Langston Hughes actual-

ly believed that the Renaissance was due to the nurturing of older writers, including Jessie Fauset and Alain Locke.

The Harlem Renaissance was marked by a shift away from the moralizing work, which had been characteristic of much post-reconstruction writing that decried racism. Even though much of this writing was excellently written and eloquently executed, people like Du Bois and Locke realized that it was doing very little to change the consciousness of the country. For this reason, they decided instead to challenge these new writers to produce works that came directly out of personal experience—to communicate the ills of the racist world with art rather than essay. In this way, readers were not struck so bluntly with the grim realities presented by African American writers. These issues could be experienced through the lives of characters and in verse, and the message delivered more subtly and effectively.

◆ AFRICAN AMERICAN WRITERS AFTER THE HARLEM RENAISSANCE

As the economic Depression deepened, the Harlem Renaissance slowly faded. Richard Wright's publication

Jessie Fauset, Langston Hughes, and Zora Neale Hurston.

in 1940 of *Native Son* marked a new era in African American literature. The years from 1940 to 1955 served as a transition period for black letters; they bridged the wildly creative period of the Renaissance with the more intense creativity and political activity that was to define the work produced during the civil rights movement.

With the publication of his classic novel, Wright maintained that the era of the Harlem Renaissance—with its motto of 'art for art's sake'—must die and be replaced instead with works directly intended to end racism. He believed that blacks were an essential part of American society. This seeming dichotomy was one of the foundations for the ideology of the civil rights movement.

During this time, other black writers, notably poets, were taking a different road in their quest to be heard. Poets such as Gwendolyn Brooks, Melvin B. Tolson and Robert Hayden were using classical and mythical themes in their works. Indeed, Brooks was to win a Pulitzer Prize in 1950 for her book *Annie Allen*. These poets used a blend of extreme eclecticism with realistic, African-American issues. The blend seemed to work, as their writing was met with acceptance in the university community and beyond.

Richard Wright

Ralph Ellison's *Invisible Man*, arguably one of the best novels published in America during this century, and James Baldwin's *Go Tell It on the Mountain* were two other books that brought serious African-American issues to mainstream culture. In addition, many African-American works were gaining acceptance with the literary establishment and being taught in English classes around the country.

◆ THE BLACK AESTHETIC MOVEMENT

The Black Aesthetic Movement, or the Black Arts Movement, has been the first major African-American artistic movement since the Harlem Renaissance. Beginning in the early 1960s and lasting through the mid-1970s, this movement was brought on not by white patrons (as the Renaissance had been in part). Rather, it was made possible by the anger of Richard Wright, Ralph Ellison, and other notable African American writers.

This artistic movement was closely paralleled by the civil rights marches and the call for independence being experienced in the African American community. As phrases like "Black is beautiful" were popularized, African American writers of the Aesthetic Movement consciously set out to define what it meant to be a black writer in a white culture. While writers of the Harlem Renaissance seemed to stumble upon their identity within, writers of the Aesthetic Movement were serious about defining themselves and their era before being defined by others.

For the most part, Black Aesthetics were supportive of separatist politics and a black nationalist ideology. Rebelling against the mainstream society by being essentially anti-white, anti-American and anti-middle class, these artists moved from the Renaissance view of art for art's sake into a philosophy of art for politics' sake.

The Black Aesthetic Movement attempted to produce works of art that would be meaningful to the black masses. Towards this end, popular black music of the day, including John Coltrane's jazz and James Brown's Rhythm and Blues, as well as street talk, were some of the inspirational forces for their art. In fact, much of the language used in these works was vulgar and shocking—this was often a conscious attempt to show the vitality and power of black activists. These writers tended to be revolutionaries rather than diplomats—Malcolm X was more of an idol than Martin Luther King, Jr. In addition, they believed that artists had more of a responsibility than just art: artists also had to be political activists in order to achieve nationalist goals.

Leading writers in this movement include Imamu Amiri Baraka (Leroi Jones), whose poetry was as well known as his political prowess; Haki R. Madhubuti (Don

L. Lee), a poet and essayist who was overwhelmingly popular—selling more than 100,000 copies of his books without a national distributor. Ishmael Reed, on the other hand, an early organizer of the Black Aesthetic Movement, later dissented with some of the movement's doctrines; he became inspired more and more by the black magic and spiritual practices of the West Indies (in what he called the "HooDoo Aesthetic").

Sonia Sanchez was another leading voice of the movement. She managed to combine feminism with her commitment to nurturing children and men in the fight for black nationalism. She joined up with the Nation of Islam from 1972 to 1975, and through her association with the Black Aesthetic Movement, managed to instill stronger support for the role of some in that religion.

◆ THE POST AESTHETIC MOVEMENT

Many black women wrote in response to the Black Aesthetic Movement, protesting the role which they felt women were placed into in the male-oriented black nationalist movement. Zora Neale Hurston's work was resurrected and used for inspiration and impetus in their work. These women were also supported by the women's liberation movement, allowing their works to reach a wider audience. In this way, the somewhat female-repressive politics of the Black Aesthetic Movement provoked women writers to express their own unique voice. Alice Walker, Gayl Jones, Toni Morrison, Terry McMillan, and Gloria Naylor are examples of successful women authors who have become prominent figures in the publishing world. In fact, during the 1980s, black women writers were at the leading edge of publishing—in quality as well as quantity of work.

Since the Black Aesthetic Movement, African American writing has become more legitimized in America, and black studies departments have emerged in many universities around the country. Variety was the key to African American writing after 1950, and barriers went down in various genres. For example, Octavia Butler and Samuel Delany broke into the world of science fiction. Donald Goines wrote detective fiction that rivaled his contemporaries. Novels of both folk history and the urban experience were equally well received, and many artists found that they could straddle more than one genre—Alice Walker and Gayl Jones being good examples—and delve into the worlds of fiction, poetry, essay, and children's books.

Imamu Amiri Baraka

Gloria Naylor

Alex Haley's *Roots* was perhaps one of the greatest African-American writing coups of the post 1950s era. With his book, as well as the highly popular television mini-series that followed, many blacks became interested in their African ancestors. Other books explored the history of blacks in other areas, namely the American West, the South, and the North.

Writers after the 1960s seem to have changed the tone a bit—no longer was there as much emphasis on the disparity between black and white in America. In the words of Toni Morrison, John Edgar Wideman, and Kristin Hunter, the themes of self-reflection and healing were evident. African Americans were portrayed as looking into their own inner worlds for answers, rather than letting themselves be defined by the outer world.

◆ AFRICAN AMERICAN NOVELISTS, POETS, PLAYWRIGHTS

Raymond Andrews (1934-)
Novelist

Born in 1934 in Madison, Georgia, Raymond Andrews left his sharecropper farm home at 15 to live, work, and attend high school at night in Atlanta. After graduation, he served in the U.S. Air Force (1952-1956) and attended Michigan State University before moving to New York City, where he worked in a variety of jobs: airline reservations clerk, hamburger cook, photo librarian, proofreader, inventory taker, mail room clerk, messenger, air courier dispatcher, and bookkeeper. During his spare time, Andrews perfected his literary skills.

Andrew's first novel, *Appalachee Red* (1978) set in the black neighborhood of a northern Georgia town called Appalachee, was widely acclaimed. In the view of the reviewer for the *St. Louis Globe Democrat*, it marked the literary debut of a significant modern American novelist of the stature of a Richard Wright or James Baldwin. The following year Raymond Andrews was the first recipient of the annual James Baldwin Prize presented by The Dial Press at a ceremony attended by Baldwin.

Andrews's second work, *Rosiebelle Lee Wildcat Tennessee: A Novel* (1980), chronicled the 40-year reign in Appalachee, beginning in 1906, of the spiritual and temporal leader of the black community there. And like his previous novel, it was illustrated by his brother Benny. Andrew's third novel titled *Baby Sweets* (1984) was also published by Dial Press and illustrated by his brother Benny. Baby Sweets is the name given to the brothel opened by the eccentric son of Appalachee's leading citizen to provide black prostitutes to the white population. This novel examines how the intermingling of the races affects an entire community.

Maya Angelou (1928-)
Novelist, Poet

Born Marguerite Johnson on April 4, 1928, writer, journalist poetess, actress, singer, dancer, playwright, director, and producer Maya Angelou spent her formative years shuttling between her native St. Louis, a tiny, totally segregated town in Arkansas, and San Francisco, where she realized her ambition of becoming that city's first black streetcar conductor. But her true mark came later in life as her words became a symbol of hope that touched the soul of America. Perhaps the ultimate recognition of her talent came when President-elect Bill Clinton asked the poet to compose and recite an inaugural poem for his swearing-in ceremony in 1993. Before reaching that point, however, Angelou experienced a great variety of life's offerings, inspired by her mother, grandmother, and other women role models in her life.

During the 1950s, Angelou studied dance with Pearl Primus in New York City, later appearing as a nightclub singer there and in San Francisco and Hawaii. She toured with the U.S. State Department's production of *Porgy and Bess* in the mid-1950s. She began the following decade with a stint as the northern coordinator of the Southern Christian Leadership Conference. Then she went abroad again, working as an editor for *The Arab Observer*, an English-language weekly published in Cairo; living in Accra, Ghana, where under the black nationalist regime of Kwame Nkrumah she taught music, drama, and wrote for the *Ghanian Times*; and studying cinematography in Sweden.

Angelou became a national celebrity in 1970, with the publication of *I Know Why the Caged Bird Sings*, the first volume of her autobiography, which detailed her encounters with southern racism and a pre-pubescent rape by her mother's lover. The work was nominated for that year's National Book Award. Three additional volumes of Angelou's autobiography were been published: *Gather Together in My Name* (1974); *Singin' and Swingin' and Gettin' Merry Like Christmas* (1976); and *The Heart of a Woman* (1981).

Angelou's published works also include 1971's *Just Give Me a Cool Drink of Water 'fore I Die: The Poetry of Maya Angelou*, 1975's *Oh Pray My Wings Are Gonna Fit Me Well*; 1979's *And Still I Rise*; 1983's, *Shaker Why Don't You Sing?*, 1986's *All God's Children Need Traveling Shoes*, and 1993's *Wouldn't Take Nothing for My Journey Now*. Angelou's other works include *Mrs. Flowers: A Moment of Friendship*, *Now Sheba Sings the Song*, and *Phenomenal Woman: Four Poems Celebrating Women*.

Not limited to writing, Angelou has dabbled both in front of and behind cameras. In 1977, she was nominated for an Emmy award for her portrayal of Nyo Boto in

Maya Angelou

the television adaptation of Alex Haley's best-selling novel *Roots*. The made-for-television movie *There Are No Children Here*, co-starred Angelou and Oprah Winfrey in 1993. That same year, Angelou wrote poetry for John Singleton's *Poetic Justice*, as well as playing a small role in the film. The following year, Angelou appeared in a television commercial, reading a version of her poem "Still I Rise," for the United Negro College Fund's 50th Anniversary. She co-starred with Winona Ryder, Anne Bancroft, and Ellen Burstyn in 1995's *How to Make an American Quilt*. Also active behind the scenes, Angelou became the first African American woman to have a movie produced, when 1972's *Georgia, Georgia*, based on one of her books, was released; she had directed the film *All Day Long* in 1974.

The 1990s held many highlights for the oft-sought-after poetess, who remained as active then as she had earlier in her career. On January 20, 1993, Angelou read her newly created "On the Pulse of Morning" during the inauguration of President Bill Clinton. Just a few days before, her play "And Still I Rise," one she had directed herself in 1976, was performed in Washington, DC. In 1994, Angelou narrated a World Choir '94 concert held at the Georgia Dome; the festival featured 10,000 singers

from 10 different countries. She also gave a reading at the National Black Arts Festival that year. In 1995, Angelou delivered "A Brave and Startling Truth" at a United Nation's 50th anniversary ceremony held in San Francisco, read Sterling Brown's "Strong Men" at the inauguration of Washington, DC Mayor Marion Barry, and was a keynote speaker, along with First Lady Hillary Rodham Clinton, at the 25th anniversary of the Joint Center for Political and Economic Studies.

Angelou has been the recipient of many awards, including a Golden Eagle Award for 1977 documentary *Afro-Americans in the Arts*, a Matrix Award from Women in Communications, Inc. in 1983, a North Carolina award in literature in 1987, a "best-mannered" citation from the National League of Junior Cotillions in 1993, a Medal of Distinction from the University of Hawaii's Board of Regents in 1994, and a Spingarn Medal from the NAACP that year as well. In 1981, Wake Forest University gave Angelou a lifetime appointment as Reynolds Professor of American Studies.

James Baldwin (1924-1987)
Novelist, Essayist, Playwright

Born in New York City on August 2, 1924, Baldwin turned to writing after an early career as a boy preacher in Harlem's storefront churches. He attended Frederick Douglass Junior High School in Harlem and later graduated from DeWitt Clinton High School, where he was editor of the school magazine. Three years later, he won a Eugene Saxton Fellowship, which enabled him to write full-time. After leaving the United States, Baldwin resided in France as well as in Turkey.

Baldwin's first novel, *Go Tell It on the Mountain*, was published in 1953, and received critical acclaim. Two years later, his first collection of essays, *Notes of a Native Son*, again won favorable critical acclaim. This was followed, in 1956, by the publication of his second novel, *Giovanni's Room*. His second collection of essays, *Nobody Knows My Name*, brought him into the literary spotlight and established him as a major voice in American literature.

In 1962, *Another Country*, Baldwin's third novel, was a critical and commercial success. A year later, he wrote *The Fire Next Time*, an immediate best-seller and regarded as one of the most brilliant essays written in the history of the black protest. Since then, two of Baldwin's plays, *Blues for Mister Charlie* and *The Amen Corner*, have been produced on the New York stage, where they achieved modest success. His novel *Tell Me How Long The Train's Been Gone* was published in 1968. Baldwin himself regards it as his first "grown-up novel," but it has generated little enthusiasm among critics.

Much to the distress of his public, Baldwin then entered an extended fallow period, and the question of whether he had stopped writing was widely debated. After a silence of several years, he published the 1974 novel *If Beale Street Could Talk*. In this work, the problems besetting a ghetto family, in which the younger generation is striving to build a life for itself, are portrayed with great sensitivity and humor. Baldwin's skill as a novelist is evident as he sets and solves the difficult problem of conveying his own sophisticated analyses through the mind of his protagonist, a young woman. To many critics, however, the novel lacks the undeniable relevance and fiery power of Baldwin's early polemical essays.

Baldwin's other works include *Going to Meet the Man* (short stories); *No Name in the Street*; *One Day When I Was Lost*, a scenario based on Alex Haley's *The Autobiography of Malcolm X*; *A Rap on Race* with Margaret Mead; and *A Dialogue* with Nikki Giovanni. He was one of the rare authors who worked well alone or in collaboration. Other books by Baldwin are *Nothing Personal* (1964) with photographs by Richard Avedon; *The Devil Finds Work* (1976), about the movies; his big sixth novel *Just Above My Head* (1979); and *Little Man, Little Man: A Story of Childhood* (1977), a book for children. He wrote 16 books including the book for children, and co-authored three others. There are six books about Baldwin's life and writings including a reference guide and bibliography.

Just Above My Head, published in 1979, dealt with the intertwined lives from childhood to adulthood of a gospel singer, his brother, and a young girl who is a child preacher. The next year Baldwin's publisher announced *Remember This House*, described as his "memoirs, history and biography of the civil rights movement" interwoven with the biographies of three assassinated leaders: Martin Luther King, Jr., Malcolm X, and Medgar Evers. Meanwhile, in his lectures Baldwin remained pessimistic about the future of race relations.

His last three books were *The Evidence of Things Not Seen* (1985) about the killing of 28 black youths in Atlanta, Georgia in the early 1980s; *The Price of the Ticket: Collected Non-fiction 1948-1985* (1985), and *Harlem Quartet* (1987). Baldwin spent most of the remainder of his life in France. In 1986, the French government made him a commander of the Legion of Honor, France's highest civilian award. He died at his home in France, on November 30, 1987, at the age of sixty-three.

Imamu Amiri Baraka (Leroi Jones) (1934-)
Poet, Playwright, Essayist

Baraka was born in Newark on October 7, 1934. He attended Rutgers University, in Newark, New Jersey,

and Howard University, in Washington, DC. In 1958 he founded *Yugen* magazine and Totem Press. From 1961 to 1964 Baraka worked as an instructor at New York's New School for Social Research. In 1964 he founded the Black Arts Repertory Theater. He has since taught at the State University of New York at Stony Brook, University of Buffalo, Columbia University, George Washington University, and San Francisco University, and has served as director of the community theater Spirit House, in Newark.

In 1961, Baraka published his first book of poetry, *Preface to a Twenty Volume Suicide Note*. His second book, *The Dead Lecturer* was published in 1964. However, he did not achieve fame until the publication of his play *Dutchman* in 1964, which received the Obie award for the best Off-Broadway play of the season. The shocking honesty of Baraka's treatment of racial conflict in this and later plays became the hallmark of his work.

During the late 1960s Baraka became a leading black power spokesman in Newark. He became head of the Temple of Kawaida, which Baraka describes as an "African religious institution—to increase black consciousness." The Temple and Baraka soon became a focal point of black political activism in the racially polarized city. In 1972 Baraka achieved prominence as a black leader as chairman of the National Black Political Convention.

In 1966, Baraka's play *The Slave* won second prize in the drama category at the First World Festival of Dramatic Arts in Dakar, Senegal. Baraka's other published plays include: *The Toilet* (1964); *The Baptism* (1966); *The System of Dante's Hell* (1965); *Four Black Revolutionary Plays* (1969); *J-E-L-L-O* (1970); and *The Motion of History and Other Plays* (1978). He has edited, with Larry Neal, *Black Fire: An Anthology of Afro-American Writing* (1968) and *Afrikan Congress: A Documentary of the First Modern Pan-African Congress* (1972). His works of fiction include *The System of Dante's Hell* (novel, 1965) and *Tales* (short stories, 1967). Baraka has also published *Black Music, Blues People: Negro Music in White America, Home: Social Essays, In Our Terribleness: Some Elements and Meanings in Black Style* with Billy Abernathy, *Raise Race Rays Raze: Essays Since 1965, It's Nation Time, Kawaida Studies: The New Nationalism, A Black Value System and Strategy and Tactics of a Pan Afrikan Nationalist Party*.

Arna Bontemps (1902-1973)
Poet, Novelist

Arna Bontemps was one of the most productive black writers of the twentieth century. Born in Alexandria,

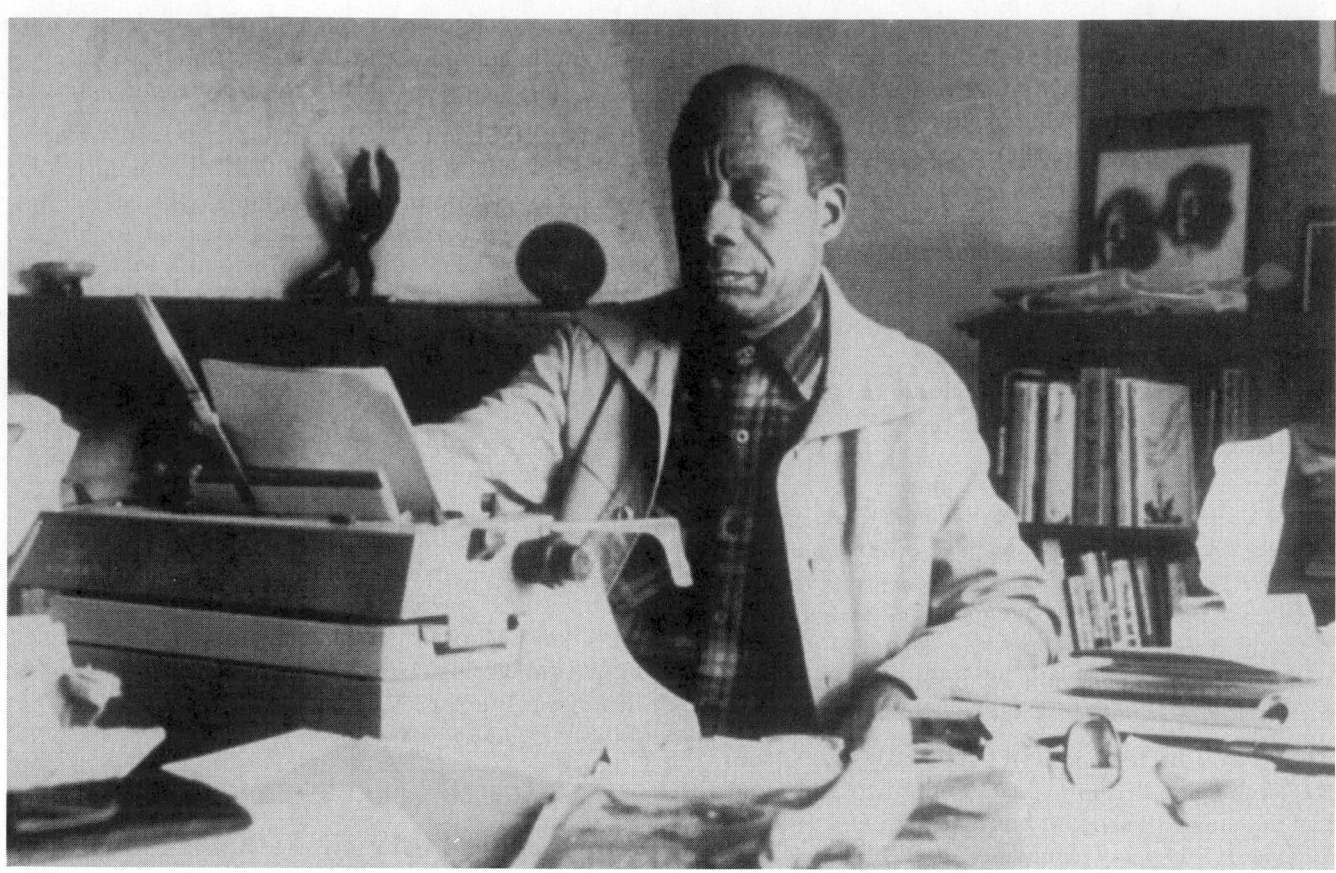

James Baldwin

Louisiana, on October 13, 1902, and raised in California, Bontemps received his B.A. degree from Pacific Union College in Angwin in 1923. The next year, his poetry first appeared in *Crisis* magazine, the NAACP periodical edited by Dr. W. E. B. Du Bois. Two years later, *Golgotha Is a Mountain* won the Alexander Pushkin Award, and in 1927, *Nocturne at Bethesda* achieved first honors in the *Crisis* poetry contest. *Personals*, Bontemps' collected poems, was published in 1963.

In the late 1920s, Bontemps decided to try his hand at prose, and over the next decade produced such novels as *God Sends Sunday* (1931); *Black Thunder* (1936); and *Drums at Dusk* (1939). His books for young people include *We Have Tomorrow* (1945); and *Story of the Negro* (1948). Likewise of literary merit are such children's books as *Sad-Faced Boy* (1937); and *Slappy Hooper* (1946). He edited *American Negro Poetry* and two anthologies, with Langston Hughes among others.

In 1968, Bontemps completed the editing of a volume of children's poetry. Other publications were *One Hundred Years of Negro Freedom* (1961); *Anyplace But Here* (published in 1966 in collaboration with Jack Convoy); *Black Thunder* (1968 reprint); *Great Slave Narratives* (1969); *The Harlem Renaissance Remem-*

bered: Essays (1972, 1984); and *The Old South*. He also edited several anthologies.

Gwendolyn Brooks (1917-)
Poet

Gwendolyn Brooks was the first black to win a Pulitzer Prize. Brooks received this prestigious award in 1950, for *Annie Allen*, a volume of her poetry that had been published one year earlier. Illinois state poet laureate, Brooks has been associated with the Black Consciousness movement of the late 1960s. Long a trailblazer, in 1985, she became the first black woman to be appointed poetry consultant by the Library of Congress.

Brooks was born on June 7, 1917, in Topeka, Kansas, moved to Chicago at an early age, and was educated there, graduating from Wilson Junior College in 1936. In 1945, she completed a book of poems, *A Street in Bronzeville* and was selected by *Mademoiselle* as one of the year's ten most outstanding American women. She was made a fellow of the American Academy of Arts and Letters in 1946, and received Guggenheim Fellowships for 1946 and 1947. In 1949, she won the Eunice Tietjen Prize for Poetry in the annual competition sponsored by *Poetry* magazine for the same work that won her that

Arna Bontemps

Gwendolyn Brooks

year's Pulitzer. She was named poet laureate of the state of Illinois in 1968.

Brooks's insights into the potential alienation of black life have been represented in her body of work, which includes a collection of children's poems, *Bronzeville Boys and Girls* (1956); a novel, *Maud Martha* (1953); and two books of poetry, *The Bean Eaters* (1960); and *Selected Poems* (1963). She has also written *In the Mecca*, winner of the 1968 Anisfield-Wolf Award; *Riot*; *The World of Gwendolyn Brooks*; *Report from Part One: The Autobiography of Gwendolyn Brooks*; *Family Pictures*; *Beckonings*; *Aloneness*; *Primer for Blacks*; and *To Disembark.*. Her poems and stories have also been published in magazines and two anthologies *Soon, One Morning*; and *Beyond the Angry Black*. The publication of *Selected Poems* in 1964, earned her the Robert F. Ferguson Memorial Award. She has edited *A Broadside Treasury* and *Jump Bad, A New Chicago Anthology*.

Among the other honors Brooks has received, Western Illinois University established The Gwendolyn Brooks Center for African American Literature in 1985. In 1988, she was inducted in the National Women's Hall of Fame. She won an *Essence* Award that year and a Frost Medal from the Poetry Society of America the next. In 1994,

Brooks was named the year's Jefferson Lecturer by the National Endowment for the Humanities, the highest honor for intellectual achievement bestowed by the U.S. government. The same year, Chicago's Harold Washington Library Center unveiled a bronze bust of Brooks prominently located in the facility and the National Book Foundation awarded her the Medal for Distinguished Contribution to American Letters and $10,000 for her lifetime of achievement. The next year, Brooks received the 1995 National Medal of Arts from U.S. president Bill Clinton.

Claude Brown (1937-)
Novelist

Claude Brown was born in 1937 in New York state. His claim to literary fame rests largely on his best-selling autobiography *Manchild in the Promised Land*, which was published in 1965, when its author was 28. The book is the story of Brown's life in Harlem and, in the process, becomes a highly realistic documentary of life in the ghetto. It tells of Brown's escapades with the Harlem Buccaneers, a "bopping gang," and of his later involvement with the Forty Thieves, an elite stealing division of this same gang.

After attending the Wiltwyck School for emotionally disturbed and deprived boys, Brown returned to New York, was later sent to Warwick Reform School three times, and eventually made his way downtown to a small loft apartment near Greenwich Village. Changing his style of life, Brown finished high school and went on to graduate from Howard University in 1965.

Brown began work on his book in 1963, submitting a manuscript of some 1,500 pages which was eventually cut and reworked into the finished product over a two-year period. Brown completed law school in the late 1960s and is now practicing in California. In 1976, he published *The Children of Ham* about a group of young blacks living as a family in a condemned Harlem tenement, begging, stealing, and doing whatever is necessary to survive.

William Wells Brown (1815-1884)
Novelist, Playwright

William Wells Brown was the first American black to publish a novel, the first to publish a drama, and the first to publish a travel book. Born a slave in Lexington, Kentucky, in 1815, and taken to St. Louis as a young boy, Brown worked for a time in the offices of the *St. Louis Times*, and then took a job on a riverboat in service on the Mississippi. In 1834, Brown fled to Canada, taking his name from a friendly Quaker whom he met there. While working as a steward on Lake Erie ships, he educated himself and became well known as a public speaker. In 1849, he went to England and Paris to attend the Peace Congress, remaining abroad for five years.

Brown's first published work, *The Narrative of William H. Brown*, went into three editions within eight months. A year later, a collection of his poems, *The Anti-Slavery Harp*, was published, and in 1852 his travel book *Three Years in Europe* appeared in London. Brown's *Clotel, or the President's Daughter*, a melodramatic novel about miscegenation, was first published in London in 1853. As the first novel by an American black (it subsequently went through two revisions), its historical importance transcends its aesthetic shortcomings.

Brown's other books include the first black drama *The Escape, or a Leap for Freedom* (1858); *The Black Man: His Antecedents, His Genius, and His Achievements* (1863); *The Negro in the American Rebellion: His Heroism and Fidelity* (1867); and *The Rising Son* (1874).

Ed Bullins (1935-)
Playwright, Essayist, Poet

Ed Bullins was born in Philadelphia in 1935 and grew up in Los Angeles. Bullins is a writer of drama, and one of the founders of the Black Arts/West in the Fillmore District of San Francisco. He patterned this experiment after the Black Arts Repertory Theater School in Harlem, which was founded and directed by Imamu Baraka. In 1977, when *Daddy*, the sixth play in his "Twentieth-Century Cycle" opened at the New Federal Theatre in New York's Henry Street Settlement, Bullins in an interview with the *New York Times* foresaw black theatrical producers taking plays to cities with large black populations and spreading out unless something happens to kill the economy. A leader of the black theater movement and creator of more than 50 plays, he has yet to have a play produced on Broadway.

Bullins's main themes are the violence and tragedy of drug abuse and the oppressive life style of the ghetto. He presents his material in a realistic and naturalistic style. Between 1965 and 1968 he wrote *The Rally*; *How Do You Do*; *Goin' a Buffalo*; *Clara's Old Man*; *The Electronic Nigger*; and *In The Wine Time*. He has also produced *The Fabulous Miss Marie*.

He has been a creative member of Black Arts Alliance, working with Baraka in producing films on the West Coast. Bullins has been connected with the New Lafayette Theater in Harlem where he was a resident playwright. His books include *Five Plays*; *New Plays from the Black Theatre* (editor); *The Reluctant Rapist*; *The New Lafayette Theatre Presents*; *The Theme Is Blackness*; *Four Dynamite Plays*; *The Duplex*; *The Hungered One: Early Writings*; and *How Do You Do: A Nonsense Drama*.

Octavia E. Butler (1947-)
Novelist

Born in Pasadena, California, in 1947, Octavia Butler is a graduate of Pasadena City College. She has attended science fiction workshops, including the Clarion Science Fiction Writers' Workshop, and is a member of Science Fiction Writers of America. Her writing has focused on the impact of race and gender on future society. In 1985, Butler won three of science fiction's highest honors for her novella *Bloodchild: Novellas and Stories*: the Nebula, Hugo, and Locus awards. She had also won a Hugo in 1984, for her short story "Speech Sounds." The 1987 novella *The Evening and the Morning and the Night* was nominated for a Nebula Award. In 1995, Butler won a MacArthur Foundation Fellowship.

Butler's other works include the Patternmaster series, consisting of the novels *Patternmaster* (1976), *Mind of My Mind* (1977), *Survivor* (1978), *Wild Seed* (1980), and *Clay's Ark* (1984); the historical fantasy *Kindred* (1979); the Xenogenesis Trilogy: *Dawn: Xenogenesis* (1987), *Adulthood Rites* (1988), and *Imago* (1989); and the dystopian *Parable of the Sower* (1993). She has also served as a contributor to such science

Ed Bullins

fiction publications as *Clarion, Future Life,* and *Isaac Asimov's Science Fiction Magazine.*

Charles Waddell Chesnutt (1858-1932)
Novelist

Born in Cleveland, Ohio, on June 20, 1858, Chesnutt moved to North Carolina with his family at the age of eight. Largely self-educated, he was admitted to the Ohio bar in 1887, the same year in which his first story, "The Gophered Grapevine," was published in the *Atlantic Monthly.* This was followed in 1899 by two collections of his stories, *The Conjure Woman* and *The Wife of His Youth.*

Chesnutt's first novel, *The House Behind the Cedars* (1900), dealt with a young girl's attempt to "pass" for white. A year later, *The Marrow of Tradition* examined the violence of the post-Reconstruction period. His final novel, *The Colonel's Dream,* was published in 1905 and typified Chesnutt's basically ingratiating approach to his art, one which the writers of the Harlem School were later to reject. Chesnutt also wrote a biography, *Frederick Douglass* (1899). He died on November 15, 1932.

Alice Childress (1920-1994)
Playwright, Novelist

Born in Charleston, South Carolina, in 1920, actress and author Alice Childress studied acting at the American Negro Theatre and attended Radcliffe Institute from 1966 to 1968, through a Harvard University appointment as a scholar-writer. Her plays are *Florence* (one-act play); *Gold Through the Trees; Just a Little Simple* (based on Langston Hughes's *Simple Speaks His Mind*); *Trouble in Mind; Wedding Band; Wine in the Wilderness;* and *When the Rattlesnake Sounds: A Play about Harriet Tubman.*

Childress also edited *Black Scenes* (1971), excerpts from plays in the Zenith series for children. Her other books include *Like One of the Family: Conversations from a Domestic's Life* (1956); *A Hero Ain't Nothing but a Sandwich* (1973) (novel); and *A Short Walk* (1979), *Rainbow Jordan* (1981), and *Many Closets* (1987). Childress's play *Trouble in Mind* won the Obie Award in 1956, as the best original off-Broadway production. Her book *Rainbow Jordan* for young people was published in 1982. She wrote, in the 1980s, a play based on the life of the black woman comedian Jackie (Moms) Mabley. The play was produced in New York City.

Childress's work was noted for its frank treatment of racial issues, its compassionate yet discerning characterizations, and its universal appeal. Her books and plays often dealt with such controversial subjects as miscegenation and teenage drug addiction. Childress died of cancer complications on August 14, 1994.

Countee Cullen (1903-1946)
Poet

Born Countee Porter on May 30, 1903 in Baltimore, he was orphaned at an early age and adopted by Reverend Frederick Cullen, pastor of New York's Salem Methodist Church. At New York University, Cullen won Phi Beta Kappa honors and was awarded the Witter Bynner Poetry Prize. In 1925, while still a student at New York University, Cullen completed *Color*, a volume of poetry which received the Harmon Foundation's first gold medal for literature two years later.

In 1926, Cullin earned his M.A. at Harvard and a year later finished both *The Ballad of the Brown Girl* and *Copper Sun*. This was followed in 1929 by *The Black Christ*, written during a two-year sojourn in France on a Guggenheim Fellowship. In 1927, he edited *Caroling Dusk: An Anthology of Verse by Negro Poets*. The book was reprinted in 1972.

Upon his return to New York City, Cullen began a teaching career in the public school system. During this period, he also produced a novel, *One Way to Heaven* (1932); *The Medea and Other Poems* (1935); *The Lost Zoo* (1940); and *My Lives and How I Lost Them* (1942, 1971). In 1947, a year after his death, Cullen's own selections of his best work were collected in a volume published under the title *On These I Stand*.

Samuel R. Delany (1942-)
Novelist

Born in Harlem on April 1, 1942, and a published writer at the age of 19, Delany has been a prolific writer of science fiction, novelettes and novels. His first book was *The Jewels of Aptor* (1962); followed by *Captives of the Flame* (1963); *The Towers of Toron* (1964); *City of a Thousand Suns* (1965); *The Ballad of Beta-2* (1965); *Babel-17* (1966); *Empire Star* (1966); *The Einstein Intersection* (1967); *Out of the Dead City* (1968); and *Nova* (1968). *Babel-17* and *The Einstein Intersection* both won Nebula Awards from the Science Fiction Writers of America, as have his short stories "Aye, and Gomorrah" and "Time Considered as a Helix of Semi-Precious Stones," that also won a Hugo Award at the World Science Fiction Convention at Heidelberg. Delany

Countee Cullen

co-edited the speculative fiction quarterly *Quark, Nos. 1, 2, 3, 4* with his former wife, National Book Award winning poet Marilyn Hacker. He also wrote, directed, and edited the half-hour film *The Orchid*. In 1975, Delany was Visiting Butler Chair Professor of English at the State University of New York at Buffalo.

Delany's other books include: *Distant Stars* (1981), *Stars in My Pocket Like Grains of Sand* (1984), *The Splendor and Misery of Bodies of Cities* (1985), *Flight from Neveryon* (1985), *Neveryona* (1986), and *The Bridge of Lost Desire* (1988). His non-fiction works includes: *The Jewel-Hinged Jaw*; *The American Shore*; *Starboard Wine*; *The Straits of Messina*; *The Motion of Light in Water* (autobiography; 1988); *The Mad Man* (1994); *They Fly at Ciron* (1995); *Atlantis: Three Tales*. (1995).

Rita Dove (1952-)
Poet, Educator

Rita Dove was born on August 28, 1952, in Akron, Ohio. She received a B.A. from Miami University in Oxford, Ohio, in 1973, and a Master of Fine Arts from the University of Iowa in 1977. Dove also attended the University of Tubingen in Germany in 1974 and 1975.

Dove began her teaching career at Arizona State University in 1981, as an assistant professor. She spent 1982 as a Writer in Residence at the Tuskegee Institute. By 1984, she was an associate professor and by 1987, a full professor. Dove, who has served on the editorial boards of the literary journals *Callaloo*, *Gettysburg Review*, and *TriQuarterly*, joined the University of Virginia's English department in 1989. She teaches creative writing.

Dove won the 1987 Pulitzer Prize for Poetry for a collection titled *Thomas & Beulah*. Her themes are universal, encompassing much of the human condition and occasionally commenting on racial issues. She has also published *Yellow House on the Corner* (1980), *Museum* (1983), *Fifth Sunday* (short stories, 1985), *Grace Notes* (1989), *Selected Poems* (1993), *Through the Ivory Gate* (novel, 1993), *Mother Love* (1995), and *The Darker Face of the Earth: A Verse Play in Fourteen Scenes* (1995).

In addition to the Pulitzer Prize, Dove has won many honors, including Presidential Scholar (1970); Fulbright Scholar (1974, 1975); a Literary Grant from the National Endowment for the Humanities (1978, 1989); Guggenheim Fellow (1983, 1984); General Electric Foundation Award for Younger Poets (1987); Ohio Governor's Award (1988); Andrew W. Mellon Fellowship (1988, 1989); University of Virginia Center For Advanced Studies Fellow (1989-1992); the Walt Whitman Award (1990); and the Kennedy Center Fund for New American Plays Award, for *The Darker Face of the Earth* (1995).

Dove was named U.S. Poet Laureate, a one-year Library of Congress post, in 1993. She was the first black and the youngest person ever to earn the appointment. On April 22, 1994, PBS aired a piece entitled "Poet Laureate Rita Dove" on *Bill Moyer's Journal*. She hoped to use the position to replenish public interest in serious literature.

Paul Laurence Dunbar (1872-1906)
Poet

The first black poet to gain a national reputation in the United States, Paul Laurence Dunbar was also the first to use black dialect within the formal structure of his work.

Born of former slaves in Dayton, Ohio, on June 27, 1872, Dunbar went to work as an elevator operator after graduating from high school. His first book of poetry, *Oak and Ivy*, was privately printed in 1893 and was followed by *Majors and Minors*, which appeared two years later. Neither book was an immediate sensation,

but there were enough favorable reviews in such magazines as *Harper's* to encourage Dunbar in the pursuit of a full-fledged literary career. In 1896, Dunbar completed *Lyrics of a Lowly Life*, the single work upon which his subsequent reputation was irrevocably established.

Before his untimely death in 1906, Dunbar had become the dominant presence in the world of American Negro poetry. His later works included *Lyrics of Sunshine and Shadow* (1905), *Li'l Gal* (1904), *Howdy, Honey, Howdy* (1905), *A Plantation Portrait* (1905), *Joggin'erlong* (1906), and *Complete Poems*, published posthumously in 1913. This last work contains not only the dialect poems which were his trademark, but many poems in conventional English as well. The book has enjoyed such enormous popularity that it has, to this day, never gone out of print. He also published four novels including *The Sport of Gods*, *The Love of Landry*, and *The Uncalled*, and four volumes of short stories.

Ralph Ellison (1914-1994)
Novelist, Essayist

Ralph Ellison's critical and artistic reputation rests largely on a single masterpiece, his first and only novel, *Invisible Man*. An instant classic, the novel was given the National Book Award for fiction in 1952. Years in the making, the novel's success heralded the emergence of a major writing talent. Ellison worked at a second novel for more than 40 years, but at the time of his death, the untitled work was still incomplete. He died of pancreatic cancer on April 16, 1994.

Ellison was born in Oklahoma City, Oklahoma, on March 1, 1914, and came to New York City in the late 1930s, after having studied music at Tuskegee Institute for three years. Initially interested in sculpture, he turned to writing after coming under the influence of T.S. Eliot's poetry, and as a direct consequence of his friendship with novelist Richard Wright. He worked for the Federal Writer's Project and wrote for a variety of publications during the late 1930s to early 1940s. In 1942, he became the managing editor of the *Negro Quarterly*. He began writing *Invisible Man* in 1945. During World War II, Ellison had worked as a cook in the U.S. Merchant Marines.

Three years after the publication of *Invisible Man*, the American Academy of Arts and Letters awarded Ellison the Prix de Rome, which enabled him to live and write in Italy until 1957. Back in the United States, Ellison began an academic career. He taught Russian and American literature courses at Bard College in Annadale-on-Hudson, New York, for three years and spent the early 1960s as a visiting professor at University

Ralph Ellison

of Chicago, Yale, and Rutgers, where he was a writer-in-residence. From 1970 to 1980, Ellison was the Albert Schweitzer Professor of Humanities at New York University.

Ellison's second work was a book of essays entitled *Shadow and Act*. Published in 1964, excerpts from the book have been published in several literary journals. A 1967 fire destroyed 350 pages of his unfinished second novel's manuscript. In 1986, a second collection of essays and talks was published as *Going to the Territory*. *The Collected Essays of Ralph Ellison*, edited by John F. Callahan, was published posthumously, in 1995.

In addition to the National Book Award, *Invisible Man* won the 1953 Russwurm Award. Ellison won a Rockefeller Foundation Award in 1954; was elected to the National Institute of Arts and Letters; received a Medal of Freedom from U.S. president Lyndon Johnson in 1969; named chevalier de l'Ordre des Arts et Lettres by France in 1969; and was given a National Medal of Arts in 1985. Ellison was the recipient of more than one dozen honorary degrees, including honorary Doctor of Letters degrees from Harvard University (1974) and Wesleyan University (1980). In 1982, the 30th anniversary edition of *Invisible Man* with a new introduction by Ellison was published.

Ralph Ellison died of pancreatic cancer in New York City on April 16, 1994. On May 26, 1994, a memorial tribute to Ellison was held at the American Academy of Arts and Letters in New York.

Mari Evans (1923-)
Poet

Born in Toledo, Ohio, in 1923, Evans studied at the University of Toledo. In 1963, her poetry was published in *Phylon*, *Negro Digest*, and *Dialog*. Two years later she was awarded a John Hay Whitney Fellowship. One of her better known works is *The Alarm Clock*, which deals with the rude awakening of the black American to the white "establishment." It captures and summarizes the scene of the 1960s in the United States.

Evans books include *I Am A Black Woman*; *Where Is All the Music?*; *Black Women Writers (1950-1980): A Critical Evaluation* (1984) edited by Evans, covering fifteen black women poets, novelists, and playwrights; *Nightstar: Poems From 1973-1978* (1982); *J. D.*; *I Look at Me*; *Singing Black*; *The Day They Made Benani*; and *Jim Flying High*.

Charles Fuller (1939-)
Playwright

Charles Fuller was born on March 5, 1939, in Philadelphia, Pennsylvania. He became "stagestruck" in his high-school days when he went to the Old Walnut Street Theater in his native Philadelphia, and saw a Yiddish play starring Molly Picon and Menasha Skulnik. He didn't understand a word of it, "but it was live theater, and I felt myself responding to it."

In 1959, Fuller entered the army and served in Japan and South Korea, after which he attended Villanova University and La Salle College. While Fuller was working as a housing inspector in Philadelphia, the McCarter Theater in Princeton, New Jersey produced his first play. The theme was intermarriage, and its creator is quick now to tag it "one of the world's worst interracial plays." However, during this time he met members of The Negro Ensemble Company, and in 1974 he wrote his first play for them, *In the Deepest Part of Sleep*. For NEC's tenth anniversary Fuller wrote *The Brownsville Raid* about the black soldiers who were dishonorably discharged on President Teddy Roosevelt's orders in 1906 after a shoot-out in Brownsville, Texas. The play was a hit and Fuller followed it a few seasons later with *Zooman and the Sign*, a melodrama that won two Obie awards.

A Soldier's Play, which won a Pulitzer Prize in 1982, is his fourth play for The Negro Ensemble Company. This

Charles Fuller

drama dealing with a murder set in a backwater New Orleans Army camp in 1944, opened NEC's fifteenth anniversary season in 1981 with a long run and was hailed by the *New York Times* as "tough, taut and fully realized." *A Soldier's Play* became *A Soldier's Story* when it was produced as a film in 1984 by Columbia Pictures. Fuller wrote the screenplay and black actor Howard E. Rollins, Jr. was the film's star.

The recipient of the Guggenheim Foundation Fellowship, the Rockefeller Foundation, and the National Endowment for the Arts and CAPS Fellowships in playwrighting, Fuller describes himself as a playwright who happens to be black, rather than a black playwright.

Ernest J. Gaines (1933-)
Novelist, Short Story Writer

Ernest Gaines was born on a plantation in Louisiana, on January 15, 1933. He moved to California in 1949, where he did his undergraduate study at San Francisco State College. In 1959, he received the Wallace Stegner Fellowship in creative writing. The following year he was awarded the Joseph Henry Jackson Literary Award.

Gaines first novel was *Catherine Carmier* (1964). Other followed, including: *Of Love and Dust* (1967);

Barren Summer (completed in 1963 but never published); *The Autobiography of Miss Jane Pittman* (1971); *A Warm Day in November* (for young people); and *In My Father's House* (1978). Ironically, the book *The Autobiography of Jane Pittman* was banned in a Conroe, Texas seventh grade racial tolerance course in 1995; the school censored the work, citing the liberal use of racial slurs. The 1974 television production of *The Autobiography of Miss Jane Pittman* starring Cicely Tyson boosted Gaines's reputation. Gaines's *A Gathering of Old Men*, published in 1983, was made into a movie, too. In 1994, Gaines's 1993 work, *A Lesson Before Dying*, won the National Book Critics Circle award for fiction.

Nikki Giovanni (1943-)
Poet

Nikki Giovanni was born in Knoxville, Tennessee, on June 7, 1943. She studied at the University of Cincinnati from 1961 to 1963 and later received her B.A. from Fisk University in 1967. She also attended the University of Pennsylvania School of Social Work for one year and Columbia University School of the Arts for one year in the late 1960s.

In 1969, Giovanni taught at Queens College (CUNY) and Rutgers University before founding a communications and publishing company called NikTom, Ltd. In the mid- to late 1980s, she resumed teaching, spending 1984 as a visiting professor at Ohio State University and the subsequent three years at Mount Joseph on the Ohio as a creative writing professor. Since 1987, Giovanni has taught at Virginia PolyTechnic Institute and State University, first as a visiting professor and then as a full professor of English beginning in 1989. That year, she also directed the Warm Hearth Writer's Workshop. From 1990 to 1993, Giovanni served on the Board of Directors for the Virginia Foundation for the Humanities and Public Policy.

Giovanni's first book of poetry, *Black Feeling, Black Talk*, published in the mid-1960s, was followed by *Black Judgment* in 1968. These two were combined as *Black Feeling, Black Talk, Black Judgment* in 1970. By 1974, Giovanni's poems were to be found in many black literature anthologies, and she had also become a media personality through her TV appearances, where she read her poetry. Many of her poems were put to soul or gospel music accompaniment. Such recordings include *Truth Is on Its Way*, winner of the National Association of Radio and Television Announcers Award in 1972, and *Spirit to Spirit*, a videocassette produced by PBS, winner of the Oakland Museum Film Festival Silver Apple Award in 1988.

A prolific author, Giovanni's other books include *Re: Creation* (poetry); *Spin a Soft Black Song: Poems for Children*; *Night Comes Softly: Anthology of Black Female Voices* (nonfiction); *My House* (poetry); Gemini: An Extended Autobiographical Statement (nonfiction); *Ego Tripping and Other Poems for Young People*; *A Dialogue: James Baldwin and Nikki Giovanni* (nonfiction, with James Baldwin); and *A Poetic Equation: Conversations Between Nikki Giovanni and Margaret Walker* (nonfiction). Her other works include: *The Women and the Men: Poems* (1975); *Cotton Candy on a Rainy Day* (poetry, 1978); *Vacation Time: Poems for Children* (1980), dedicated to her son, Tommy, and winner of the Children's Reading Roundtable of Chicago Award; *Those Who Ride the Night Winds* (poetry, 1984); *Sacred Cows ... and Other Edibles* (nonfiction, 1988), winner of the Ohioana Library Award in 1988; *Grand Mothers: Poems, Reminiscences, and Short Stories About the Keepers of Our Traditions* (1994), *Racism 101* (nonfiction), *Knoxville, Tennessee* (coauthored with Larry Johnson, 1994), and *The Selected Poems of Nikki Giovanni* (1995).

Giovanni has won several awards throughout her career, including the Highest Achievement Award in 1971, from *Mademoiselle*; life membership to the National Council of Negro Women in 1973; the Outstanding Woman of Tennessee in 1985; and the Cincinnati *Post* Post-Corbett Award in 1986. In addition, Giovanni has received honorary degrees from numerous institutions. Giovanni underwent a partial removal of her lung and ribs in 1995.

Eloise Greenfield (1929-)
Children's Author

Born Eloise Little on May 17, 1929, in Parmele, North Carolina, Greenfield moved to Washington, DC, as a baby and grew up happily in a close-knit, urban neighborhood. After attending Minor Teachers College, she was employed in various clerical and secretarial positions. By 1950, she had began experimenting with creative writing. After years of studying and persevering, Greenfield met fellow writers and made valuable contacts when she joined the District of Columbia Black Writers Workshop in the early 1970s. Soon thereafter, her picture book *Bubbles* was published.

With that initial success, Greenfield established her own niche within the arena of children's books and has published, on average, one book each year. Having a goal of encouraging children to develop positive attitudes toward themselves, Greenfield's stories capture both the unique and universal experiences of growing up as a black American. Much of her fiction, as in the novel *Sister*, is concerned with bonding within black families. Greenfield's biographies of distinguished African Americans and poetic picture books have appeared on "notable" book lists and have placed the author in demand as a speaker at writers' conferences and in classrooms of her young fans.

Alex Haley (1921-1992)
Journalist, Novelist

The author of the widely acclaimed novel *Roots* was born in Ithaca, New York on August 11, 1921, and reared in Henning, Tennessee. The oldest of three sons of a college professor father and a mother who taught grade school, Haley graduated from high school at fifteen and attended college for two years before enlisting in the United States Coast Guard as a messboy in 1939.

A voracious reader, Haley began writing short stories while working at sea, but it took eight years before small magazines began accepting some of his stories. By 1952, the Coast Guard had created a new rating for Haley, chief journalist, and he began handling United States Coast Guard public relations. In 1959, after 20 years of military service, he retired from the Coast Guard and launched a new career as a freelance writer. He eventually became an assignment writer for *Reader's Digest* and moved on to *Playboy* where he initiated the "Playboy Interviews" feature.

Alex Haley

One of the personalities Haley interviewed was Malcolm X—an interview that inspired Haley's first book, *The Autobiography of Malcolm X* (1965). Translated into eight languages, the book has sold more than 6 million copies. Pursuing the few slender clues of oral family history told him by his maternal grandmother in Tennessee, Haley spent the next 12 years traveling three continents tracking his maternal family back to a Mandingo youth, named Kunta Kinte, who was kidnaped into slavery from the small village of Juffure, in The Gambia, West Africa. During this period, he lec-

tured extensively in the United States and in Great Britain on his discoveries about his family in Africa, and wrote many magazine articles on his research in the 1960s and the 1970s. He received several honorary doctor of letters degrees for his work.

The book *Roots*, excerpted in *Reader's Digest* in 1974 and heralded for several years, was finally published in the fall of 1976 with very wide publicity and reviews. In January 1977, ABC-TV produced a 12-hour series based on the book, which set records for the number of viewers. With cover stories, book reviews, and interviews with Haley in scores of magazines and many newspaper articles, the book became the number one national best-seller, sold in the millions, and was published as a paperback in 1977. *Roots* became a phenomenon. It was serialized in the *New York Post* and the *Long Island Press*. Instructional packages, lesson plans based on *Roots* and other books about *Roots* for schools were published along with records and tapes by Haley.

Haley's book stimulated interest in Africa and in black genealogy. The United States Senate passed a resolution paying tribute to Haley and comparing *Roots* to *Uncle Tom's Cabin* by Harriet Beecher Stowe in the 1850s. The book received many awards, including the National Book Award for 1976 special citation of merit in history and a special Pulitzer Prize in 1976 for making an important contribution to the literature of slavery. *Roots* was not without its critics, however. A 1977 lawsuit brought by Margaret Walker charged that *Roots* plagiarized her novel *Jubilee*. Another author, Harold Courlander also filed a suit charging that *Roots* plagiarized his novel *The African*. Courlander received a settlement after several passages in *Roots* were found to be almost verbatim from *The African*. Haley claimed that researchers helping him had given him this material without citing the source.

Haley received the NAACP's Spingarn Medal in 1977. Four thousand deans and department heads of colleges and universities throughout the country in a survey conducted by *Scholastic Magazine* selected Haley as America's foremost achiever in the literature category. (Dr. Martin Luther King, Jr. was selected in the religious category). The ABC-TV network presented another series, *Roots: The Next Generation*, in February 1979 (also written by Haley). *Roots* had sold almost 5 million copies by December 1978 and had been reprinted in 23 languages.

In 1988, Haley conducted a promotional tour for a novella titled *A Different Kind of Christmas* about slave escapes in the 1850s. He also promoted a drama, *Roots: The Gift*, a 2-hour television program shown in December 1988. This story revolved around two principal characters from *Roots* who are involved in a slave break for freedom on Christmas Eve.

Haley died February 10, 1992, of a heart attack.

Virginia Hamilton (1936-)
Children's and Young Adult Author

Virginia Hamilton was born on March 12, 1936, into a large extended family in rural Yellow Springs, Ohio. Her career as an author was directly influenced by her parents, who were avid storytellers themselves. She attended nearby Antioch College from 1952 to 1955,

ultimately graduating from Ohio State University in 1958. Determined to be a writer, Hamilton settled in New York City and studied the craft at the New School for Social Research. She worked at a variety of jobs and moved back to Yellow Springs before publishing her first book, *Zeely*, in 1967. Issued during an era of racial strife, *Zeely* was one of the first books for young readers in which black characters were portrayed as people living with average, universal circumstances as opposed to constantly dealing with politically and racially related problems such as integration.

After her second novel, *The House of Dies Drear* received the 1968 Edgar Allen Poe Award for best juvenile mystery of the year, Hamilton went on to write and edit more than 30 children's and young adult books within various genres. Her canon includes well-researched historical fiction, contemporary urban novels about teenagers, science fiction and supernatural tales, biographies of the historical figures Paul Robeson and W. E. B. Du Bois, and collections of African American folklore and slavery-era "liberation" stories.

Hamilton has been repeatedly honored for her work, including winning the Hans Christian Andersen Medal, Newberry Honor Book Award, National Book Award, Coretta Scott King Award, and the MacArthur Foundation prize in 1995. Many of her works have appeared on notable "best books" lists, and she has inspired an Annual Virginia Hamilton Conference. Hamilton stands as one of the predominant creative forces behind multicultural works for young readers.

Jupiter Hammon (1720?-1800?)
Poet

Hammon was the first black poet to have his work published in America. *An Evening Thought, Salvation by Christ, with Penitential Cries* appeared in 1761, when Hammon was a slave belonging to a Mr. Lloyd of Long Island, New York. Due to his fondness for preaching, the major portion of Hammon's poetry is religious in tone, and is usually dismissed by critics as being of little aesthetic value because of its pious platitudes, faulty syntax, and forced rhymes. Hammon's best-known work is a prose piece, *An Address to the Negroes of the State of New York*, delivered before the African Society of New York City on September 24, 1786. This speech was published the following year and went into three editions.

Lorraine Hansberry (1930-1965)
Playwright

Born in Chicago on May 19, 1930, Hansberry studied art at Chicago's Art Institute, the University of Wisconsin, and, finally, in Guadalajara, Mexico. Hansberry wrote the award winning *A Raisin in the Sun* while living in New York's Greenwich Village, having conceived the play after reacting distastefully to what she called "a whole body of material about Negroes. Cardboard characters. Cute dialect bits. Or hip-swinging musicals from exotic scores." The play opened on Broadway on March 11, 1959, at a time when it was generally held that all plays dealing with blacks were "death" at the box-office. Produced, directed, and performed by blacks, it was later made into a successful movie starring Sidney Poitier. It was then adapted into *Raisin*, a musical that won a Tony Award in 1974.

Hansberry's second Broadway play, *The Sign in Sidney Brustein's Window*, dealt with "the western intellectual poised in hesitation before the flames of involvement." Shortly after its Broadway opening, Hansberry succumbed to cancer on January 12, 1965, in New York City.

Hansberry's books, in addition to the two published plays, include *To Be Young, Gifted and Black*; *The Movement: Documentary of a Struggle for Equality*; and *Les Blancs: The Collected Last Plays of Lorraine Hansberry*.

Lorraine Hansberry

Robert E. Hayden (1913-1980)
Poet

Robert E. Hayden was born on August 4, 1913, in Detroit, Michigan. A graduate of Detroit City College, now Wayne State University, Hayden was chief researcher on African-American history and folklore for the Federal Writers Project in 1936, and later went on to do advanced work in English, play production, and creative writing at the University of Michigan. While there, he won the Jule and Avery Hopwood Prize for poetry twice. Hayden also completed radio scripts and a finished version of a play about the Underground Railroad, *Go Down Moses*.

Hayden's first book of poems, *Heart-Shape in the Dust*, was published in 1940 shortly before he assumed the music and drama critic function for the *Michigan Chronicle*. He taught at Fisk University from 1946 to the early 1970s and later at the University of Michigan. His works include *The Lion and the Archer* (with Myron O'Higgins); *A Ballad of Remembrance*; *Selected Poems*; *Words in the Mourning Time*; and *The Night-Blooming Cereus*. He edited *Kaleidoscope: Poems by American Negro Poets*; and *Afro American Literature: An Introduction* (with David J. Burrows and Frederick R. Lapsides). His other books include *Figure of Time*; *Angle of Ascent: New and Selected Poems*; and *American Journal* (poems). In 1975, the Academy of American Poets elected him its Fellow of the Year, and in 1976, he was awarded the Grand Prize for Poetry at the First World Festival of Negro Arts in Dakar, Senegal. From 1976 to 1978, he served as Consultant in Poetry at the Library of Congress. He was a professor of English at the University of Michigan at the time of his death on February 25, 1980.

Essex Hemphill (1957-1995)
Poet, Essayist, Editor, Gay Rights Activist

Hemphill was born in 1957 in Chicago, but spent parts of his childhood in Indiana, South Carolina, and Washington, DC. After attending the University of Maryland and the University of the District of Columbia, Hemphill began to explore the inner conflicts he was experiencing as a gay African American male by writing poetry.

For several years Hemphill was a contributor of verse to journals such as *Essence*, *Black Scholar*, and *Obsidian*. In the late 1980s he became involved with a project begun by Joseph Beam, an anthology of gay African American poetry called *In the Life*. Hemphill was a contributor to the 1986 volume, and took up the editorship of its sequel after Beam died of AIDS-related illnesses in 1988. The work was published as *Brother to Brother: New Writings by Black Gay Men* in 1991.

Hemphill also became involved in several film projects around this time as well, nearly all of them controversial in some way—which coincided with his aim to make the two communities, the African American and the gay American, enter into a new, more contemporary dialogue with one another. He wrote verse for *Looking for Langston*, a British film which addressed the sexuality of Harlem Renaissance poet Langston Hughes and brought down the ire of the executor of the Hughes estate, and also contributed to and appeared in *Tongues Untied*. This last project, Marlon Riggs's celebratory look at gay African American male culture, was deemed too spicy even for public television at one point.

In 1992 Hemphill saw another book of his own verse published, *Ceremonies: Prose and Poetry*. During the early part of the decade, he became involved in a project interviewing elderly members of the African American gay community in order to provide a glimpse into a period before either gay or civil rights were spoken of. He also contributed to the book *Life Sentences: Writers, Artists, and AIDS*. Hemphill passed away on November 4, 1995 at the age of 38.

Chester Himes (1909-1984)
Novelist

Born in Jefferson City, Missouri, on June 29, 1909, Himes was educated at Ohio State University, and later lived in France and in Spain. In 1945, he completed his first novel *If He Hollers Let Him Go*, the story of a black working in a defense plant. His second book, *The Lonely Crusade* (1947), was set in similar surroundings. His other books include *The Third Generation, Cotton Comes to Harlem, Pinktoes, The Quality of Hurt: The Autobiography of Chester Himes*, and *Black on Black: Baby Sister and Selected Writings*.

Following a stroke, which had confined him to a wheelchair, Himes and his wife lived in Alicante, Spain. In 1977, they returned to New York City for the publication of the concluding volume of his autobiography *My Life of Absurdity*. Himes died in Spain on November 12, 1984, at the age of 75. A prolific author of almost twenty books, several of his popular novels are being reprinted posthumously in hard and paperback editions.

George Moses Horton (1797-1883)
Poet

George Moses Horton was the first black professional man of letters in America and one of the first professional writers of any race in the South. Horton was the first black southerner to have a volume of poetry published. Horton was born into slavery in North Carolina. While growing up on a farm, and between chores, Horton was able to cultivate a love of learning. With the aid of his mother and her Wesley hymnal, Horton learned

Chester Himes

to read. He did not learn to write until years later. While working as a janitor at the University of North Carolina, Horton wrote light verse for some students in exchange for spending money.

Some of Horton's early poems were printed in the newspapers of Raleigh and Boston. When Horton published his first book of poems in 1829, he entitled it *The Hope of Liberty* in the belief that profits from its sales would be sufficient to pay for his freedom. His hopes did not materialize, however, with the result that he remained a slave until the coming of Emancipation. This book was reprinted in 1837 under the title *Poems by a Slave*. In 1865, he published *Naked Genius*, a poem containing many bitter lines about his former condition which are in sharp contrast to the conformist verse of earlier black poets. Richard Walser's *The Black Poet* was written about Horton and published in 1967.

Langston Hughes (1902-1967)
Poet, Novelist, Playwright

Born in Joplin, Missouri, on February 1, 1902, Hughes moved to Cleveland at the age of fourteen, graduated from Central High School, and spent a year in Mexico before studying at Columbia University. After roaming the world as a seaman and writing some poetry as well, Hughes returned to the United States. While attending Lincoln University, he won the Witter Bynner Prize for undergraduate poetry. In 1930, he received the Harmon Award, and in 1935, with the help of a Guggenheim Fellowship, traveled to Russia and Spain.

The long and distinguished list of Hughes's prose works includes *Not Without Laughter* (1930), a novel; *The Big Sea* (1940); and *I Wonder as I Wander* (1956), his autobiography. To this must be added such collections of poetry as *The Weary Blues* (1926); *The Dream Keeper* (1932); *Shakespeare in Harlem* (1942); *Fields of Wonder* (1947); *One Way Ticket* (1947); *Selected Poems* (1959); and the posthumously published *The Panther and the Lash: Poems of Our Times* (1969).

Hughes was also an accomplished song lyricist, librettist, and newspaper columnist. Through his newspaper columns he created Jesse B. Semple, a Harlem character known as Simple. Simple is the quintessential "wise fool" whose experiences and insights capture the frustrations felt by black Americans. Hughes's Simple sketches have been collected in several volumes, and were adapted for the musical stage in *Simply Heavenly*.

Langston Hughes

Throughout the 1960s, Hughes edited several anthologies in an attempt to popularize black authors and their works. Some of these are *An African Treasury* (1960); *Poems from Black Africa* (1963); *New Negro Poets: U.S.A.* (1964); and *The Best Short Stories by Negro Writers* (1967). Published posthumously was *Good Morning Revolution: Uncollected Writings of Social Protest*. Hughes wrote many plays, including *Emperor of Haiti*, and *Five Plays by Langston Hughes*. *Mulatto* was produced on Broadway in the 1930s. He also wrote gospel music plays such as *Tambourines to Glory*; *Black Nativity*; and *Jericho—Jim Crow*. He died on May 22, 1967.

Zora Neale Hurston (1903-1960)
Novelist, Folklorist

Zora Neale Hurston was born on January 7, 1903, in Eatonville, Florida. After traveling north as a maid with a Gilbert and Sullivan company, Hurston acquired her education at Morgan State, Howard, and Columbia. While at Howard, under Alain Locke's influence, she became a figure in the Harlem Renaissance, publishing short stories in *Opportunity* and serving with Langston Hughes and Wallace Thurman on the editorial board of the magazine *Fire*.

In 1934, *Jonah's Gourd Vine* was published after her return to Florida. Her most important novel, *Their Eyes Were Watching God*, appeared three years later. *Moses, Man of the Mountain* (1939), was followed in 1948 by *Seraph on the Suwanee*. Her other three works are two books of folklore, *Mules and Men* (1935); *Tell My Horse* (1938); and *Dust Tracks on a Road* (1942), and her autobiography which was reprinted in 1985 with a new introduction and with several altered or expunged chapters restored.

Toward the end of her life, Hurston was a drama instructor at the North Carolina College for Negroes in Durham. She died in obscurity and poverty on January 28, 1960. Since then, six of her works have been reprinted with new introductions.

Georgia Douglas Johnson (1886-1966)
Poet

As one of the first modern black female poets to gain recognition, Georgia Douglas Johnson, whose collections of verse were published between 1918 and 1930, is an important link in the chain of American black female lyric poets. Johnson's life spanned most of the literary movements of this century, and her Washington, DC home was the popular gathering place of early Harlem Renaissance writers.

Zora Neale Hurston

Johnson was born in Atlanta, Georgia, on September 10, 1886. She was educated in the public schools of the city and at Atlanta University, and she went on to attend Howard University in Washington, DC, and Oberlin Conservatory of Music in Ohio.

Initially, she was interested in musical composition, but gradually she turned toward lyric poetry. After teaching school in Alabama, she moved to Washington, DC with her husband, who had been appointed as Recorder of Deeds by President William Howard Taft. While in the nation's capital, she too engaged in government work while completing such books as *The Heart of a Woman* (1918); *Bronze* (1922); *An Autumn Love Cycle* (1928); and *Share My World*, published in 1962.

Johnson was a prolific writer; over 200 of her poems were published in her four literary works; other poems and several dramas have appeared in journals and books primarily edited by blacks.

James Weldon Johnson (1871-1938)
Poet, Lyricist, Civil Rights Leader

Like W. E. B. Du Bois, black intellectual James Weldon Johnson played a vital role in the civil rights movement of the twentieth century—as poet, teacher, critic, diplomat, and NAACP official. Johnson is perhaps most often remembered as the lyricist for *Lift Every Voice and Sing*, the poem which is often referred to as the black national anthem.

Born on June 17, 1871, in Jacksonville, Florida, Johnson was educated at Atlanta and Columbia Universities. His career included service as a school principal, a lawyer, and a diplomat (United States Consul at Puerto Cabello, Venezuela, and later, in Nicaragua). From 1916 to 1930, he was a key policy maker of the NAACP, eventually serving as the organization's executive secretary.

In his early days, Johnson's fame rested largely on his lyrics for popular songs, but in 1917 he completed his first book of poetry, *Fifty Years and Other Poems*. Five years later, he followed this with *The Book of American Negro Poetry*, and in 1927, he established his literary reputation with *God's Trombones*, a collection of seven folk sermons in verse. Over the years, this work has been performed countless times on stage and television.

In 1930, Johnson finished *St. Peter Relates an Incident of the Resurrection*, and three years later, his lengthy autobiography *Along This Way*. Johnson died on June 26, 1938, following an automobile accident in Maine.

Gayl Jones (1949-)
Novelist, Poet, Short Story Writer

Born in Lexington, Kentucky, in 1949, Jones received a bachelor's degree in English from Connecticut College in 1971 and a master's degree in creative writing from Brown University in 1973. Jones' work includes two novels, *Corregidora* (1975) and *Eva's Man* (1976), short stories, and several collections of poetry, including *Song for Anninho* (1981), *The Hermit Woman* (1983), and *Xarque and Other Poems* (1985).

June Jordan (1936-)
Poet, Novelist

Born in Harlem, New York, on July 9, 1936, poet, novelist, essayist, educator, and activist, June Jordan attended Barnard College and the University of Chicago. Throughout the 1960s and 1970s, she taught Afro-American literature, English, and writing at several colleges and universities, including CUNY, Connecticut College, Sarah Lawrence College, Yale University, and State University of New York at Stoney Brook, where she spent most of her career. Director of the poetry center and creative writing program, she left State University in 1989, to teach Afro-American studies and women's studies at the University of California at

Berkeley. Jordan cofounded and codirected of The Voice of the Children, Inc., a creative workshop.

A prolific writer, Jordan's poems have been published in many magazines, newspapers, and anthologies, and she received a Rockefeller Grant in creative writing in 1969. Her poetry includes *Who Look at Me* (1969); *Some Changes* (1971); *New Days: Poems of Exile and Return* (1974); *Passion: New Poems, 1977-1980* (1980); *Living Room: New Poems* (1985); *Lyrical Campaigns: Selected Poems* (1989); and *Naming Our Destiny: New and Selected Poems* (1989). Jordan's books for children and young people include *His Own Where* (1971), nominated for the National Book Award; *Fannie Lou Hamer* (1972); *Dry Victories* (1972); and *Kimako's Story* (1981).

Author of two plays, Jordan has also published essays—including *Civil Wars* (1981); *On Call: Political Essays* (1985); *Moving Towards Home: Political Essays* (1989); and *Technical Difficulties: African American Notes on the State of the Union* (1992)—and edited several anthologies such as *Soulscript: Afro-American Poetry* (1970).

Adrienne Kennedy (1931-)
Writer, Playwright

Born in Pittsburgh, Pennsylvania, on September 13, 1931, Adrienne Lita Hawkins grew up in Cleveland, Ohio. She received a bachelor's in education from Ohio State in 1953, and married Joseph C. Kennedy one month later, taking his last name. In 1955, she and her husband moved to New York, and Kennedy studied writing at the American Theatre Wing and at Columbia University, completing her first play *Pale Blue Flowers*, which was never produced or published.

In 1960, Kennedy and her husband traveled to Europe and then Ghana on a grant from the Africa Research Foundation. Her writing became more focused, and she published a story in *Black Orpheus* magazine. At the age of 29, Kennedy wrote *Funnyhouse of a Negro*, a one-act play. Edward Albee selected the play for production in New York's Circle in the Square. Later, it ran from January 14 to February 9, 1964 at the East End Theatre in New York, codirected by Albee.

Kennedy's next play, *The Owl Answers*, produced in 1965, won her a second Stanley Award from Wagner College of Staten Island, New York. Since the mid-1960s, she has written many full-length and one-act plays, including *Sun: A Poem for Malcolm X Inspired by His Murder* (1969), *A Movie Star Has to Star in Black and White* (1976), *Black Children's Day* (1980), and *Diary of Lights* (1987). Later, University of Minnesota

Press published collections of her work, including *The Alexander Plays* (1992). In 1996, her latest plays *Sleep Deprivation Chamber* and *June and Jean in Concert* were produced at the Joseph Papp Public Theater and the Susan Stein Shiva Theater, respectively. Kennedy wrote an autobiography by Knopf published in 1987 called *People Who Led to My Plays*.

Kennedy's plays are hallmarks of the American experimental theater, avant-garde, and non-traditional in the extreme. She has won many awards for her bold and clear vision, including an Obie Award in 1964 and a Pierre Lecomte du Novy award from the Lincoln Center in 1994. In addition to winning many fellowships and grants, Kennedy has been a lecturer at Universities, like Yale, Princeton, Brown, Harvard, and at Berkeley of California. She has also served as an International Theatre Institute representative in Budapest in 1978.

Yusef Komunyakaa (1941-)
Poet, Educator

Yusef Komunyakaa was born James Willie Brown, Jr., in 1941, in the segregated, culturally desolate mill town of Bogalusa, Louisiana. He came to love reading and poetry as a child and at age 16 began pursuing his own talents. After high school graduation, Komunyakaa joined the U.S. Army and was sent to Vietnam to act as a reporter and editor for a military newspaper in 1969. Although he felt estranged from American society upon his return from Vietnam, Komunyakaa enrolled at the University of Colorado and later graduate school at Colorado State University and a second master's degree at the University of California at Irvine. A creative writing workshop proved inspirational and his first book of poetry, *Dedication and Other Darkhorses* was published in 1977. With the release of his second volume two years later, Komunyakaa accepted a series of fellowships and teaching positions, enabling him to pursue a career as a poet.

While working in New Orleans in 1983, Komunyakaa began to come to terms with his experiences in Vietnam through his writing. This challenge resulted in several sophisticated books filled with cultural influences that portray basic elements of humanity. In 1985, the poet left New Orleans to accept a position as a visiting professor at Indiana University in Bloomington. By 1987, having published two more books of poetry, Komunyakaa became an associate professor in the Afro-American and English studies departments at Bloomington. For personal and religious reasons, the poet changed his name from James Willie Brown, Jr. to Yusef Komunyakaa. With the publication of *Neon Vernacular*, he was awarded the 1994 Pulitzer Prize in poetry along with the $50,000 Kingsley Tufts Poetry Award given by the Claremont Graduate School. Komunyakaa's themes of memory and self-definition—as an African American man and a veteran of Vietnam—lend his works a sense of strength and spiritual tenacity.

Nella Larsen (1891-1964)
Novelist, Librarian, Nurse

Nella Larsen was born in 1891 in Chicago, Illinois, to a Danish mother and a West Indian father. She attended Fisk University's Normal (High) School, in Nashville, Tennessee, and from 1909 to 1912, the University of Copenhagen, in Denmark. Three years later, she graduated from the Lincoln School for Nurses in New York City. In addition to her writing, she worked alternately as a nurse and librarian, having attended the New York Public Library training school from 1921 to 1923. After one year as head nurse at the Tuskegee Institute (1915-16), she became supervising nurse at the Lincoln Hospital in New York City until 1918, when she joined the city's Department of Health. During the next 40 years, she would work as a children's librarian at the New York Public Library (1924-26), Gouverneur Hospital (1944-61), and the Metropolitan Hospital (1961-64), all in New York City. But writing is what made her famous.

In the 1920s, Larsen began contributing to children's magazines. At the same time she found herself immersed in the literay and political activities of the ongoing Harlem Renaissance.

Larsen's first novel, *Quicksand* (1928), received a bronze medal from the Harmon Foundation. The groundbreaking novel developed themes around black women's sexuality and about mixed racial identity. Her second major work, *Passing* (1929), led to her becoming the first black American woman to be awarded a Guggenheim Fellowship in creative writing (1930). More than 30 years after her death in 1964, Larsen's novels were reissued, and she finally achieved recognition as one of the most important wirters of the Harlem Renaissance.

Julius Lester (1939-)
Writer, Educator

Julius Lester was born in St. Louis, Missouri in 1939. He grew up in Kansas City, Kansas and Nashville, Tennessee, where his father led congregations as a Methodist minister. Lester spent the summers of his youth in rural Arkansas, experiencing racism and segregation firsthand. A gifted student, he was an avid musician and aspired to become a writer.

Lester obtained a bachelor's degree in English from Fisk University. He became politically active in the civil rights struggle as a folksinger and photographer of Southern rallies. As a member of the Student Non-Violent Coordinating Committee (SNCC) in the mid-1960s, Lester became head of its photo department and visited North Vietnam to document the effects of U.S. bombing missions. He began publishing ideological books that defended black militancy, including *The Angry Children of Malcolm X* and *Revolutionary Notes*. From 1966 to 1968 Lester served as director of the prestigious Newport Folk Festival and released two record albums himself.

Having achieved fame from his artistic pursuits, Lester was hired to host live radio shows at the public broadcasting station WBAI-FM in New York City. Around the same time, he published two books for children that saw immediate success. *Black Folktales* compiled African legends and slave narratives and *To Be a Slave*, a collection of stories based on oral history accounts, received a Newberry Honor Book citation. In 1971, Lester began hosting the New York public television program *Free Time*. His career as an award-winning academician began that same year, when he was hired as professor of Afro-American Studies at the University of Massachusetts—Amherst. He settled there in 1975, and became a full-time professor and author.

Lester flourished as an author by releasing novels and storybooks (with illustrator Jerry Pinkney) that reflected his interests in African American history, folklore, and politics. *Long Journey Home*, a finalist for the National Book Award, explores the everyday lives of African Americans during the Reconstruction period. Lester's *Tales of Uncle Remus: The Adventures of Brer Rabbit*, traditional stories retold in a contemporary southern black voice, were well-received by teachers and librarians who granted them the Coretta Scott King Award. His 1994 adult novel, *And All Our Wounds Forgiven*, tracks dramatic events within the 1960s. Lester's individualism and resistance to racial and religious categorization is evident in two autobiographies, *All Is Well* and *Lovesong: Becoming a Jew*.

When he converted to Judaism in mid-life, Lester was ousted from Amherst's renamed African American Studies Department in 1988. Persevering through yet another career change, he moved to the university's Near Eastern and Judaic Studies Department. Since that time he has also taught in the history and English departments. Lester's latest publication for young adults was his 1995 racially repositioned novelization of *Othello*.

Audre Lorde (1934-1993)
Poet

Audre Lorde was born in New York City; educated at Hunter College with a masters in library science from

Columbia University; was poet-in-residence at Tougaloo College; taught at Lehman College, Bronx; and taught at John Jay College, CCNY, during her career. She received a National Endowment for the Arts grant for poetry and a Cultural Council Foundation grant also for poetry.

Her books of poetry include: *Cables to Rage* (1970); *The First Cities* (1968); *From a Land Where Other People Live* (1973); *Coal* (1968); *The New York Head Shop and Museum* (1974); *Between Ourselves* (1976); *The Black Unicorn* (1978); *Chosen Poems-Old and New* (1982); *Zami: A New Spelling of My Name* (1982); *Sister/Outsider: Essays and Speeches* (1984); *Lesbian Poetry: An Anthology* (1982); and *Woman Poet—The East* (1984). Lorde's poetry has been published in many anthologies, magazines and lesbian books and periodicals.

Claude McKay (1890-1948)
Poet

Born the son of a farmer in Jamaica (then British West Indies) on September 15, 1890, McKay began writing early in life. Two books of his poems, *Songs of Jamaica* and *Constab Ballads*, were published just after he turned twenty. In both, he made extensive use of Jamaican dialect.

In 1913, McKay came to America to study agriculture at Tuskegee Institute and at Kansas State University, but his interest in poetry induced him to move to New York City, where he published his work in small literary magazines. McKay then made a trip abroad, visiting England. While there, he completed a collection of lyrics entitled *Spring in New Hampshire*. When he returned to the United States, he became associate editor of *The Liberator* under Max Eastman. In 1922, he completed *Harlem Shadows*, a landmark work of the Harlem Renaissance period.

McKay then turned to the writing of such novels as *Home to Harlem* (1928), *Banjo* (1929), and four other books including an autobiography and a study of Harlem. *The Passion of Claude McKay: Selected Prose and Poetry 1912-1948* edited by Wayne Cooper, was published in 1973. McKay traveled extensively abroad before returning to the United States, where he died. His final work, *Selected Poems*, was published posthumously—McKay died on May 22, 1948—in 1953.

During World War II, when Winston Churchill addressed a joint session of the United States Congress in an effort to enlist American aid in the battle against Nazism, the climax of his oration was his reading of the famous poem "If We Must Die," originally written by McKay to assail lynchings and mob violence in the South. McKay's *Trial by Lynching* (1967), edited and translated stories, and his *The Negroes in America*

(1979 or 1980), edited and translated from the Russian language, have also been published. Many of his books or works have been reprinted since his death: *Home to Harlem; Banana Bottom; Banjo* (1970); *A Long Way From Home* (1970); *Harlem: Negro Metropolis* (1972), and *Selected Poems of Claude McKay* (1971). *Songs of Jamaica* and *Constab Ballads* have been bound together as *The Dialect Poems of Claude McKay*. Wayne F. Cooper's *Claude McKay: Rebel Sojourner in the Harlem Renaissance* (1987) is an important book detailing McKay's life and work.

Terry McMillan (1951-)
Novelist

Terry McMillan was born on October 18, 1951, and raised in Port Huron, Michigan. She attended Los Angeles City College, but later transferred to Berkeley and then to Columbia University to study film. She later enrolled in a writing workshop at the Harlem Writers Guild and was accepted at the MacDowell Colony in 1983. She has taught at the University of Wyoming and the University of Arizona.

McMillan published her first short story when she was 25 years old. Her subsequent novels include *Mama (1987), Disappearing Acts* (1989), and *Waiting to Exhale* (1992). She also edited the anthology of contemporary African American fiction entitled *Breaking Ice: An Anthology of Contemporary African-American Fiction* (1992).

Waiting to Exhale hit the *New York Times'* best-seller list within one week of being in print, and remained there for several months. Hardcover publisher Viking, printed 700,000 copies and Pocket Books, who published the soft-cover version paid $2.64 million for the rights to the work. In 1995, the novel was adapted into one of the most highly touted films of the year. Directed by Forest Whitaker, the movie starred Angela Bassett, Whitney Houston, Lela Rochon, and Loretta Devine. Wesley Snipes and Gregory Hines had smaller roles.

In 1993, New York Women in Communication gave McMillan a Matrix Award. In 1994, the NAACP Legal Defense and Educational fund honored McMillan at a luncheon.

James Alan McPherson (1943-)
Short Story Writer

James McPherson, born in Savannah, Georgia, on October 16, 1943, received his B.A. degree in 1965 from Morris Brown College in Atlanta, a law degree from Harvard University in 1968, and an M.F.A. degree from the University of Iowa in 1969. He has taught writing at several universities, presently at the University of Iowa, and is a contributing editor of *Atlantic Monthly*. His short stories have appeared in several magazines. *Hue and Cry*, a collection of short stories published in 1969, was highly praised by Ralph Ellison. A Guggenheim Fellow in 1972-1973, McPherson's second book of short stories, *Elbow Room*, was published in 1977 and was given the Pulitzer Prize for fiction in 1978. He taught fiction writing for several years at the University of Virginia in Charlottesville. McPherson was one of the three black writers who in 1981, with Elma Lewis, were awarded five-year grants by the McArthur Foundation of Chicago for exceptional talent.

Loften Mitchell (1919-)
Playwright

Born on April 15, 1919, in Columbus, North Carolina, and raised in the Harlem of 1920s, Loften Mitchell first began to write as a child, creating scripts for backyard shows he and his brother put on. After completing junior high school, he decided to enroll at New York Textile High because he had been promised a job on the school newspaper there. But Mitchell soon realized that he needed the training of an academic high school, and with the help of one of his teachers, transferred to DeWitt Clinton.

Graduating with honors, Mitchell found a job as an elevator operator and a delivery boy to support himself while he studied play writing at night at the City College of New York. However, he met a professor from Talladega College in Alabama who helped him win a scholarship to study there. He graduated with honors in 1943, having won an award for the best play written by a student.

After two years of service in the Navy, Mitchell enrolled as a graduate student at Columbia University in New York. A year later, he accepted a job with the Department of Welfare as a social investigator and continued to go to school at night. During this time, he wrote one of his first successful plays, *Blood in the Night*, and in 1957 he wrote *A Land Beyond the River*, which had a long run at an off-Broadway theater and was published as a book.

The following year Mitchell won a Guggenheim award, which enabled him to return to Columbia and write for a year. Since then, he has written a new play, *Star of the Morning*, the story of Bert Williams, famous black entertainer.

In 1967 Mitchell published a study African-American theater entitled *Black Drama*. His other books include: *Tell Pharaoh*, a play; *The Stubborn Old Lady Who Resisted Change* (1973), a novel; and *Voices of the Black*

Theatre (1976). Mitchell also wrote the books for the Broadway musicals *Ballads for Bimshire* (1963); *Bubbling Brown Sugar* (1975); *Cartoons for a Lunch Hour* (1978); *A Gypsy Girl* (1982); *Miss Ethel Waters* (1983).

Toni Morrison (1931-)
Novelist, Editor

Born Chloe Anthony Wofford in Lorain, Ohio, on February 18, 1931, Toni Morrison received a B.A. degree from Howard University in 1953, and an M.A. from Cornell in 1955. After working as an instructor in English and the humanities at Texas Southern University and Howard University, Morrison eventually became a senior editor at Random House in New York City, where she was responsible for the publication of many books by blacks, including Middleton Harris's *The Black Book* (edited by Toni Morrison) and books by Toni Cade Bambara and others. From 1971 to 1972, Morrison was also an associate professor at the State University of New York at Purchase. Throughout the 1970s and 1980s, she wrote and published her novels, as well as holding visiting professorships at Yale University and Bard College. From 1984 to 1989, she served as Albert Schweitzer Professor of the Humanities at the State University of New York at Albany, after 20 years as a senior editor for Random House. In 1989, Morrison became the Robert F. Goheen Professor of the Humanities at Princeton University.

Morrison's first novel, *The Bluest Eye*, was published in 1969, followed by *Sula*, which won the 1975 Ohioana Book Award. Morrison's third novel, *Song of Solomon* (1977), received the 1977 National Book Critics Circle Award and the 1978 American Academy and Institute of Arts and Letters Award. 1981 saw the publication of *Tar Baby*, which was followed by the play *Dreaming Emmett*, first produced in Albany, New York, in 1986. *Beloved*, published in 1987, is regarded by some as her most significant work. The historical novel won both the Pulitzer Prize for fiction and the Robert F. Kennedy Award. *Beloved* was also a finalist for the 1988 National Book Critics Circle Award and was one of the three contenders for the Ritz Hemingway prize in Paris, from which no winner emerged. In addition, *Beloved* was a National Book Award finalist. In the 1990s, Morrison has written a collection of essays and *Jazz*, a novel.

Morrison was elected to the American Institute of Arts and Letters in 1981, and gave the keynote address at the American Writers' Congress in New York City in the fall of that year. She won the New York State Governor's Art Award in 1986. In 1993, the American Literature Association's Coalition of Author Societies founded The Toni Morrison Society, an education group, in Atlanta. Later in the year, Morrison received her highest honor

Toni Morrison

and made history when she became the first black recipient of the Nobel Prize in Literature, an award that included an $825,000 prize. In 1995, her *alma mater* Howard bestowed her with an honorary doctorate.

Walter Mosley (1952-)
Novelist

Walter Mosley achieved national publicity when, during the 1992 U.S. presidential campaign, Bill Clinton credited him as his favorite mystery writer. Born on January 12, 1952, and raised in the Watts and Pico-Fairfax districts of Los Angeles, Mosely's unique heritage is attributed to an African American father from the deep south and a white, Jewish mother whose family emigrated from Eastern Europe. After drifting among a variety of jobs, including potter, caterer, and computer programmer, he settled in New York City and attended the writing program at City College. By 1987 he had become a full-time writer. Although Mosley's first book, a short psychological novel entitled *Gone Fishin'* was turned down by numerous agents, he achieved rapid success in 1990, with *Devil in a Blue Dress*. In the next several years, *A Red Death*, *White Butterfly*, and *Black Betty* were also greeted with critical acclaim.

Mosley incorporates social and racial issues into gripping novels that authentically portray inner city life in the black neighborhoods of post-World War II Los Angeles. His creation of the recurring multidimensional character, private investigator Ezekiel ("Easy") Rawlins, was heavily influenced by the experiences of Mosley's own father as a black soldier in World War II and later a southern immigrant in California. With his black American viewpoint and confrontation of shifting societal and moral issues, Mosley has been praised for breaking new ground within the mystery and detective genre and inspiring a new brand of African American fiction. Mosley's success is destined to continue as he is planning nine or ten novels in all for the Rawlins series, bringing the protagonist into the early 1980s.

Mosley has been bestowed several honors, including the John Creasey Memorial Award and Shamus Award for outstanding mystery writing. In 1990, the Mystery Writers of America nominated *Devil in a Blue Dress* for an Edgar. The film version of *Devil in a Blue Dress*, with a screenplay penned by the author, was widely released in 1996. Directed by Carl Franklin, the film starred Denzel Washington as Rawlins. In 1995, Mosely published *R. L.'s Dream*, a fictional meditation on the blues.

Walter Dean Myers (1937-)
Young Adult Writer

Walter Dean Myers was born William Milton Myers in Martinsburg, West Virginia, in 1937. Upon the death of his mother at age three, he was raised by a foster couple, Herbert and Florence Dean, in Harlem. Myers began writing as a child and was praised in grade school for his academic achievements. Determined to further his education, he joined the U.S. Army at 17, enabling him to pay part of his college tuition with money from the G.I. Bill. In 1969, upon the publication of his first picture book for children, Myers was determined to become a professional writer. *Where Does the Day Go?* was honored by the Council on Interracial Books for Children and established Myers as an author who addressed the needs of minority children.

Myers worked as a senior editor for the Bobbs-Merrill publishing house, released more picture books, and began writing young adult stories in the 1970s. Since then he has published more than two dozen novels in which he tackles urban social issues such as teen pregnancy, crime, drug abuse, and gang violence. Myers's authentic dialogue and ability to capture the universal ties and strengthening powers of family and friendship within black communities prompted great response from teenage readers. Committed to producing quality literature for black children, he branched into fairy tales, ghost stories, science fiction, adventure sagas, and a popular biography entitled *Malcolm X: By Any*

Means Necessary. Myers has won a variety of awards, including the Coretta Scott King Award and the Newberry "honor book" citation for *Scorpions.* Myers's novels, particularly *Hoops, Fallen Angels,* and *Motown* and *Didi: A Love Story* are an enduring presence on "best books" and high school reading lists.

Gloria Naylor (1950-)
Novelist

Gloria Naylor was born in New York City on January 25, 1950, and still lives there. She received a B.A. in English from Brooklyn College in 1981 and a M.A. in Afro-American studies from Yale University in 1983. She has taught writing and literature at George Washington University, New York University, Brandeis University, Cornell University, and Boston University. In 1983, she won the American Book Award for first fiction for her novel *The Women of Brewster Place* which was produced for television in 1988. Her second novel was *Linden Hills* published in 1985. Her third novel, *Mama Day,* (1988) was written with the aid of a grant from the National Endowment for the Arts. In 1988, Naylor was awarded a Guggenheim Fellowship. In 1993, Naylor published a new novel, *Bailey's Cafe.*

Ann Lane Petry (1912-)
Novelist, Short Story Writer

Ann Petry was born in Old Saybrook, Connecticut, on October 12, 1912, where her father was a druggist. After graduating from the College of Pharmacy at the University of Connecticut, she went to New York where she found employment as a social worker and newspaper reporter, studying creative writing at night.

Her early short stories appeared in *Crisis* and *Pylon.* In 1946, after having received a Houghton Mifflin Fellowship, she completed and published her first novel, *The Street.* This was followed by *Country Place* (1947); *The Narrows* (1953); and *Miss Munel and Other Stories* (1971). Her works for children and young people include: *The Drugstore Cat; Harriet Tubman; Tituba of Salem Village; Legends of Saints*; and a fourth book for children and young people. Many of her earlier novels are being reprinted.

Ishmael Reed (1938-)
Novelist, Poet

Born in Chattanooga, Tennessee, on February 22, 1938, Ishmael Reed grew up in Buffalo, New York. He attended State University of New York at Buffalo from 1956 to 1960. He worked as a reporter and later as an editor for the *Newark Advance* in New Jersey before cofounding the *East Village Other* in 1965. Reed spent the next few years teaching prose and guest lecturing at

Ann Petry

different institutions, including the University of California at Berkeley. In 1971, he cofounded Yardbird Publishing Co., Inc. After four years as the editorial director, he cofounded Reed, Cannon & Johnson Communications Co., a publisher and producer of videos, and in 1976, the Before Columbus Foundation, which produced and distributed works by unestablished ethnic writers.

A controversial man, Reed has published poetry, novels, plays, and prose. Considered by some to be misogynistic and cynical, others find his work innovative. He is committed to creating an alternative black aesthetic, which he calls Neo-HooDooism. One hallmark of the movement is the reliance on satire and social criticism.

Reed's works of poetry include *catechism of d neoamerican hoodoo church* (1971); *Conjure* (1972), which was nominated for the National Book Award; *Chattanooga* (1973); *A Secretary to the Spirits* (1978); and *New and Collected Poetry* (1988). His poetry has also appeared in numerous anthologies and magazines, including *The Poetry of the Negro, The New Black Poetry, The Norton Anthology, Cricket,* and *Scholastic* magazine.

Ishmael Reed

Reed's novels include *The Free-lance Pallbearers* (1967); *Yellow Back Radio Broke Down* (1969); *Mumbo Jumbo*, which also received a National Book Award nomination; *The Last Days of Louisiana Red* (1974); *Flight to Canada* (1976); *The Terrible Twos* (1982); *Reckless Eyeballing* ; *The Terrible Threes* (1989); and *Japanese by Spring*. He authored three plays: *The Lost State of Franklin* (1976); *Savage Wilds*; and its sequel, *Savage Wilds II.*

Prose works by Reed include 1978's *Shrovetide in Old New Orleans*, 1982's *God Made Alaska for the Indians: Selected Essays*, and 1988's *Writin' Is Fightin': Thirty-seven Years of Boxing on Paper.*

Reed's career has been rich in recognition. In 1974, he won the John Simon Guggenheim Memorial Foundation Award for fiction. The next year he received a Rosenthal Foundation Award and an honor from the National Institute of Arts and Letters. In 1978, Reed earned the Lewis Michaux and American Civil Liberties awards. The following year he was given the Pushcart Prize. His fellowships include ones from the Wisconsin Board and Yale University's Calhoun College in 1982; grants have come from New York State, the National Endowment for the Arts, and the California Arts Council.

Sonia Sanchez (1934-)
Poet, Playwright

Sonia Sanchez was born on September 9, 1934, in Birmingham, Alabama. She studied at New York University and Hunter College in New York City. She is married to Etheridge Knight, a black writer of poetry and fiction. She has taught at San Francisco State College and is now teaching in the Black Studies Department of Temple University in Philadelphia. Her plays are published in the special black drama number of *The Drama Review* (Summer 1968), and in *New Plays from the Black Theatre* (1969) edited by Ed Bullins. Her poems have been published in many magazines and anthologies. Books written or edited by her include six volumes of poetry: *Homecoming* (1969); *We a Bad People* (1970); *It is a New Day* (1971); *A Blues Book for Blue Black Magical Women* (1973); *Love Poems* (1975); and *I've Been a Woman* (1978). Sanchez has edited two anthologies: *Three Hundred and Sixty Degrees of Blackness Comin at You, An Anthology of the Sonia Sanchez Writers Workshop at Countee Cullen Library in Harlem* (1971); and *We Be Word Sorcerers: Twenty-five Stories by Black Americans* (1973). She has also written *A Sound Investment* (1979), a collection of short stories; and *homegirls and handgrenades* (1984).

Ntozake Shange (1948-)
Playwright, Poet, Novelist

Born Paulette Linda Williams, in Trenton, New Jersey, on October 18, 1948. A playwright and poet, she changed her name to Ntozake Shange in 1971. She graduated from Barnard College and received her masters degree from the University of Southern California, where she also did some graduate work. She studied Afro-American dance in California and actually performed with the Third World Collective, Raymond Sawyer's Afro-American Dance Company, Sounds in Motion, and West Coast Dance Works.

Shange taught at Sonoma Mills College in California from 1972 to 1975. She went on to teach at CUNY and Douglas College to finish out the 1970s, before becoming the Mellon Distinguished Professor of Literature at Rice University in 1983. For three years she worked as an associate professor of drama at the University of Houston.

Shange's play *For Colored Girls Who Have Considered Suicide When the Rainbow is Enuf*, a choreopoem (poetry and dance), was first produced in California after her dance-drama *Sassafrass* was presented in 1976. Later *For Colored Girls* was produced in New York City, where it had a long run before going on to other cities. It earned Tony, Grammy, and Emmy award

Ntozake Shange

nominations in 1977. Among the works by Shange that have been produced on the stage are *Spell #7, A Photograph: Lovers in Motion* (1979), and *Boogie Woogie Landscapes* (1979). *For Colored Girls* has been published as a book and Shange's collection *Three Pieces* (1981) contains *Spell #7, A Photograph: Lovers in Motion*, and *Boogie Woogie Landscapes*.

Other books by Shange include: *Nappy Edges* (poetry, 1978); *Sassafrass, Cypress & Indigo* (novel, 1982); *A Daughter's Geography* (poetry, 1983) and *From Okra to Greens* (a play, 1984); *See No Evil: Prefaces & Accounts, 1976-1983* (1984); *Betsey Brown* (novel, 1985); *Liliane: Resurrection of the Daughter* (novel, 1994).

A version of *Betsey Brown* for the stage, with music by the jazz trumpeter and composer Baikida Carroll, opened the American Music Theater Festival in Philadelphia, March 25, 1989. Shange directed Ina Cesaire's *Fire's Daughters* in 1993. The Broadway version of *For Colored Girls/When the Rainbow Is Enuf* was revived in 1995.

Shange received an Obie Award in 1981 for *Mother Courage and Her Children* and a *Los Angeles Times* Book Prize for poetry that year for *Three Pieces*. A

Guggenheim fellow, Shange has been given awards by the Outer Critics Circle and the National Black Theater Festival (1993). She also won the Pushcart Prize.

Lucy Terry (1730-1821)
Poet

Lucy Terry is generally considered to be the first black poet in America. In a ballad which she called "Bars Fight," she recreated an Indian massacre which occurred in Deerfield, Massachusetts in 1746 during King George's War; "Bars Fight" has been hailed by some historians as the most authentic account of the massacre.

A semi-literate slave in the household of Ensign Ebenezer Wells, she won her freedom and was married to a freed man named Prince. The Prince house served as a center for young people who gathered to listen to their hostess's storytelling. Lucy Terry was a strong woman who argued eloquently for her family's rights in several cases.

Jean Toomer (1894-1967)
Novelist, Poet

Jean Toomer's *Cane*, published in 1923, has been called one of the three best novels ever written by an American black—the others being Richard Wright's *Native Son* and Ralph Ellison's *Invisible Man*. According to Columbia University critic Robert Bone, "*Cane* is by far the most impressive product of the Negro Renaissance."

A mixture of poems and sketches, *Cane* was written during that period in which most black writers were reacting against earlier "polite" forms by creating works marked by literary realism. Toomer even went beyond this realm to the threshold of symbol and myth, using a "mystical" approach which is much more akin to the contemporary mood than it was to the prevailing spirit of his own day. *Cane* sold only 500 copies on publication, and was still little known until it was reprinted recently with new introductions. A lot has been written about Toomer and *Cane* in recent years including a *Cane* casebook.

Born in Washington, DC in December of 1894, Toomer was educated in law at the University of Wisconsin and City College of New York before he turned to writing. The transcendental nature of his writings is said to have stemmed in part from his early study under Gurdjieff, the Russian mystic.

Toomer also published quite a bit of poetry. Darwin T. Turner edited *The Wayward and The Seeking: A Collection of Writings by Jean Toomer* (1980), a book of his poetry, short stories, dramas, and autobiography. Other books about Toomer and his writings are Therman O'Daniel (editor) *Jean Toomer: A Critical Evaluation* (1985), over 40 essays of the most thorough, up to date scholarship on Toomer; Robert B. Jones and Margery Toomer Latimer (editors) *The Collected Poems of Jean Toomer* (1988), 55 poems; and Nellie Y. McKay's *Jean Toomer, Artist: A Study of His Literary Life and Work, 1894-1936* (1984, 1987).

Gustavus Vassa (1745?-1801?)
Narrative Writer

Gustavus Vassa was born around 1745 in Southern Nigeria. At the age of eleven, he was kidnapped and shipped to the New World as a slave. His masters included a Virginia plantation owner, a British officer, and a Philadelphia merchant from whom he eventually purchased his freedom. Vassa then settled in England where he worked diligently for the elimination of slavery. He even went so far as to present a petition to Parliament calling for its abolition.

Vassa's autobiography, *The Interesting Narrative of the Life of Oloudah Equiano, or Gustavus Vassa*, was published in London in 1789 and went through five

Gustavus Vassa

editions in the next five years. It is regarded as a highly informative account of the evils of slavery as it affected both master and slave. Vassa died around 1801.

Alice Walker (1944-)
Poet, Novelist

Alice Walker was born in Eatonton, Georgia, on February 9, 1944. She was educated at Spelman College (1961-63) and Sarah Lawrence College, from which she received her B.A. in 1965. That year, she worked as a voter registrator in Georgia and she worked for the welfare department in New York City. In 1967, she moved to Mississippi, where she was a black literature consultant for Friends of the Children of Mississippi. From 1968 to 1971, she was a writer-in-residence at Jackson State and Tougaloo colleges. Moving to Boston, she lectured at Wellesley and the University of Massachussetts until 1973. While teaching in the early 1970s, she was a Radcliffe Institute fellow.

Walker's work began to be published in the late 1960s, starting with *Once: Poems* in 1968. Two years later she published the novel *The Third Life Grange Copeland*. These two works were quickly followed by a succession of works both creative and prose. Among them were 1973's *Revolutionary Petunias and Other Poems*, which earned a National Book Award nomination and the Lillian Smith Award; *In Love and Trouble: Stories of Black Women*, recipient of a Richard and Hinda Rosenthal Foundation Award from the American Academy and Institute of Arts and Letters; and *Langston Hughes: American Biography* (for children).

The novel *Meridian* (1976) was followed in 1979 by a book of poetry entitled *Goodnight, Willie Lee, I'll See You in the Morning* and a work Walker edited called *I Love Myself When I'm Laughing ... and Then Again When I Am Looking Mean and Impressive: A Zora Neale Hurston Reader*. The reader was particularly important because it brought about a resurgence of interest in a Harlem Renaissance writer who had been overshadowed by other, better known authors.

In the 1980s, Walker more formally resumed her teaching career, spending 1982 as the Fannie Hurst Professor of Literature at Brandeis Unversity, while also serving as a distinguished writer as the Unversity of California at Berekely. In 1984, she cofounded Wild Trees Press. That decade's works include the short story collection *You Can't Keep a Good Woman Down* (1981); two collections of essays and journal entries, *In Search of Our Mothers' Gardens: Womanist Prose* (1983) and *Living by the Word: Selected Writings, 1973-1987)*; a book of poetry entitled *Horses Make a Landscape Look More Beautiful* (1984); *To Hell With Dying* (juvenile story, 1988); and the novel *The Temple of My Familiar*

Alice Walker

(1989). In 1986, she was bestowed the O. Henry Award for her "Kindred Spirits."

Walker's most well received work, however, was the 1983 novel *The Color Purple*. Written in the form of a series of letters, the novel was nominated for the National Book Critics Circle Award and won the 1983 Pulizer Prize as well as an American Book Award. The best-selling book was adapted into an award-winning film featuring Whoopi Goldberg, Danny Glover, Oprah Winfrey, and Margaret Avery.

In the 1990s, Walker has continued writing. *Possessing the Secret of Joy*, loosely a sequel to *The Color Purple* was released in 1992. *The Same River Twice: Honoring the Difficult* came out four years later.

Holder of numerous honorary degrees, Walker has received the Merrill Fellowship for Writing, the National Endowment for the Arts Grant, the Radcliffe Institute Fellowship and other honors.

Margaret Abigail Walker (Margaret Walker Alexander) (1915-)
Poet, Novelist

Margaret Walker was born on July 7, 1915 in Birmingham, Alabama, and received her early education in

Alabama, Louisiana, and Mississippi. She earned her B.A. from Northwestern University and her M.A. from the University of Iowa (1940).

In 1942, Walker published *For My People* and two years later was awarded a Rosenwald Fellowship for creative writing. She has taught English and literature at Livingston College in North Carolina, at West Virginia State College, and at Jackson State College in Mississippi. Her novel appeared in 1965 and is entitled *Jubilee*. *For My People* was reprinted in 1969. Her other works are *Prophets for a New Day*, *How I Wrote Jubilee*, *October Journey*, and *A Poetic Equation: Conversations Between Nikki Giovanni and Margaret Walker*. June 17, 1976, was proclaimed Margaret Walker Alexander Day by the mayor of her native Birmingham.

Walker's other works include *Richard Wright: Daemonic Genius* (1988). A second edition of *A Poetic Equation: Conversations between Nikki Giovanni and Margaret Walker* was published in 1983.

Dorothy West (1907-)
Writer

Dorothy West is the last surviving member from the Harlem Renaissance, the period of the late 1920s and early 1930s when an outpouring of writing and poetry exuded from the pens and typewriters of African American writers based in Harlem. West was known as "the Kid" by such luminaries as poet Countee Cullen and Langston Hughes and novelists Richard Wright and Zora Neale Hurston. West wrote short stories for the New York *Daily News* in the 1930s, and twice, through the Great Depression, founded African American literary journals, most notably *New Challenge*.

Raised in Boston, West eventually left New York City to return home, moving into her family's summer home in Oak Bluffs, on Martha's Vineyard, in 1943. Five years later she wrote her first novel, *The Living Is Easy*, based on the affluent world of African American achievers. West continued to write short stories for the *Daily News* from her Oak Bluffs home for the next 25 years.

In the 1950s, West began a second novel, *The Wedding*, but could not find a publisher interested in handling it. With its theme of interracial marriage, it may have been too hot a topic with which to deal and was put aside by West unfinished. West had started contributing short pieces to the Vineyard's daily newspaper in the 1970s.

West once again enjoyed fame in the 1990s. In 1992, West's stories caught the eye of former First Lady Jacqueline Onassis, an editor at Doubleday and a summer resident of Martha's Vineyard. Onassis encouraged

Margaret Walker

West to finish *The Wedding*, and the two of them began meeting weekly. With Onassis acting as West's editor, the novel finally became published in 1995. West dedicated the novel to Onassis.

Phillis Wheatley (1753-1784)
Poet

Born in Senegal in 1753, Phillis Wheatley was brought to the United States as a slave and received her name from Mrs. Susannah Wheatley, the wife of the Boston tailor who had bought Phillis. Wheatley received her early education in the household of her master. Her interest in writing stemmed from her reading of the Bible and the classics under the guidance of the Wheatley's daughter, Mary.

In 1770, her first poem was printed under the title "A Poem by Phillis, A Negro Girl on the Death of Reverend George Whitefield." Her book *Poems on Various Subjects: Religious and Moral* was published in London in 1773. After a trip to England, for health reasons she later returned to the United States, and was married. She published the poem "Liberty and Peace" in 1784, shortly before her death. Most of the old books of her poems,

letters, and memories about her life were reprinted in the late 1960s and early 1970s. Two books about her are Julian D. Mason Jr.'s *The Poems of Phillis Wheatley* (1966); and William H. Robinson's *Phillis Wheatley, A Biography* (1981). Robinson also compiled and published *Phillis Wheatley: A Bio-Bibliography* (1981).

Although George Washington was among her admirers (she had once sent him a tributary poem, which he graciously acknowledged), her poetry is considered important today largely because of its historical role in the growth of American Negro literature. Wheatley's poetry reflects Anglo-Saxon models, rather than her African heritage. It is, nevertheless, a typical example of the verse manufactured in a territory—the British colonies—not yet divorced from its maternal origins. Wheatley died on December 5, 1784.

John Edgar Wideman (1941-)
Writer, Educator

Wideman has been one of the leading chroniclers of life in urban black America, depicting the widening chasm between the urban poor and the white power structure in the United States. He is known for intertwining ghetto experiences with experimental fiction techniques, personal history, and social events to highlight deep cultural conflicts. A prolific writer, Wideman is the only two-time winner of the prestigious PEN/Faulkner Award for literature, one for 1983's *Sent for You Yesterday* and once for 1990's *Philadelphia Fire*. In addition to novels, he has written short stories and nonfiction, including 1984's *Brothers and Keepers*, a juxtaposition of his life and that of his younger brother, incarcerated for taking part in a larceny/murder. The examination of the two brothers' different lives was nominated for the National Book Critic's Circle Award.

Born on June 14, 1941, in Washington, DC, Wideman was the first of five children. Growing up in Pittsburgh, where the family moved, Wideman attended the highly regarded Peabody High School. A top student, he was also class president and captain of the basketball team. Enrolling at the University of Pittsburgh on a scholarship, he earned a B.A. in 1963. During his undergraduate career, Wideman made the Big Five Basketball Hall of Fame as well as winning the university's creative writing prize and being elected Phi Beta Kappa. He received a Rhodes Scholarship to England's Oxford University, becoming the first African American to receive such recognition in more than 50 years. Armed with a bachelors of philosophy obtained from Oxford's New College in 1966, Wideman began writing and teaching at such institutions as the Universities of Pennsylvania, Wyoming, and, since 1986, Massachusetts at Amherst.

August Wilson (1945-)
Playwright

Playwright August Wilson was born in 1945, in Pittsburgh. After a brief stint in the U.S. Army in the early 1960s, Wilson cofounded Black Horizons on the Hill, a Pittsburgh-based theater company, in 1968. Wilson has also been variously employed as a sheet-metal worker, porter, gardener, and short-order cook.

Though Wilson's poetry was first published in the early 1970s in *Black World* and *Black Lines*, he established himself in the drama genre with a series of award-winning works. The first of Wilson's plays was *Ma Rainey's Black Bottom*. First produced at the Yale Repertory Theater and directed by Lloyd Richards in 1984, then produced on Broadway at the Cort Theatre later that year, the play was named best new play by the New York Drama Critics Circle. It was published in 1985. The following year, Wilson was one of ten writers to win a Whiting Writer's Awards, each carrying a monetary prize of $25,000. The awards were established in 1985 by the Whiting Foundation to reward "exceptionally promising, emerging talent."

Wilson's next play *Fences*, was first staged at the Yale Repertory Theater in 1985, before playing at the 46th Street Theatre on Broadway in 1987. Also named the best new play of the year by the New York Drama Critics Circle, *Fences* also received a Tony Award for best drama. Published in 1986, the work earned Wilson the 1987 Pulitzer Prize for best drama in 1987.

Joe Turner's Come and Gone, premiered at the Yale Repertory Theater in 1986 and was produced at the Barrymore Theatre on Broadway and published in 1988. The New York Drama Critics Circle gave Wilson yet another award for best new play. He also received an honorary degree from Yale University that year.

Published in 1990, Wilson's *The Piano Lesson* was awarded a Pulitzer Prize that year. The play followed the same pattern of playing on Broadway, this time at the Walter Kerr Theatre in 1990, after debuting at the Yale Repertory Theater in 1987. The work was filmed for television in 1995.

Other plays by Wilson include *Jitney* and *Fullerton Street*, first produced in Pittsburgh at the Allegheny Repertory Theatre, and *Two Trains Running*, which was produced at the Yale Repertory Theater in 1991 and published and produced at the Walter Kerr Theatre the

August Wilson

following year. After a three-year hiatus, Wilson returned to writing with *Seven Guitars,* which played at Chicago's Goodman Theater in 1995.

Richard Wright (1908-1960)
Novelist

Born on September 4, 1908, on a plantation near Natchez, Mississippi, Wright drew on his personal experience to dramatize racial injustice and its brutalizing effects. In 1938, under the auspices of the WPA Illinois Writers Project, Wright published *Uncle Tom's Children*, a collection of four novellas based on his Mississippi boyhood memories. The book won an award for the best work of fiction by a WPA writer, and Wright received a Guggenheim Fellowship.

Two years later, *Native Son,* a novel of Chicago's black ghetto, further enhanced Wright's reputation. A Book-of-the-Month Club choice, it was later a successful Broadway production under Orson Welles's direction and was filmed in South America with Wright himself in the role of Bigger Thomas. He published *Twelve Million Black Voices* in 1941.

In 1945, Wright's largely autobiographical *Black Boy* was selected by the Book-of-the-Month Club and went on to become his second best-seller. Wright later moved to Paris where he continued to write fiction and nonfiction including *The Outsider* (1953); *Black Power* (1954); *Savage Holiday* (1954, 1965); *The Color Curtain* (1956); *White Man Listen* (1957); *The Long Dream* (1958); *Lawd Today* (1963); *Eight Men* (1961); and *American Hunger* (1977), a continuation of Wright's autobiographical work *Black Boy*.

19

Media

19

Media

◆ Book Publishers ◆ Newspaper and Magazine Publishers
◆Broadcasting ◆ African Americans in Cyberspace ◆ Communications Gatekeepers
◆ Publishers, Newspapers, Magazines and Journals, Radio Networks,
Radio Stations, Cable Television Networks, and Television Stations

by Donald Franklin Joyce, Richard Prince, and Lorna M. Mabunda

◆ BOOK PUBLISHERS

by Donald Joyce and Lorna M. Mabunda

Since black book publishing began in the United States in 1817, three types of publishers have emerged in this sector of the American book publishing industry: religious publishers; institutional publishers; and trade book publishers.

Religious Publishers

Religious publishing enterprises were established by black religious denominations in order to publish books and other literature to assist clergy and laity in recording denominational history and provide religious instruction. Some black religious publishers also published books on secular subjects which were generally related to celebrating some aspect of black culture or documenting black history.

Prior to the Civil War, two black religious publishing enterprises existed. The African Methodist Episcopal Church organized the AME Book Concern in Philadelphia in 1817—the first black-owned book publishing enterprise in the United States. Publishing its first book in that same year, *The Book of Discipline*, the AME Book Concern published a host of classic religious and secular books until its operations were suspended in 1952 by the General Conference of the African Methodist Episcopal Church. In 1841 the African Methodist Episcopal Zion Church formed the AME Zion Book Concern in New York City. This firm, which only published religious works, was moved to its present location in Charlotte, North Carolina, in 1894, where it continues to be an active book publisher.

In Jackson, Tennessee, the Colored Methodist Episcopal Church (CME), presently known as the Christian Methodist Episcopal Church, started the CME Publishing House in 1870. The CME Publishing House, which only publishes books on religious subjects, is currently located in Memphis, Tennessee.

Another book publishing enterprise owned by black Methodists is the AME Sunday School Union and Publishing House, which was established in Bloomington, Illinois, in 1882, but moved to Nashville, Tennessee, in 1886. Publishing secular and religious books, the AME Sunday School Union and Publishing House remains today as the oldest publishing unit owned by the African Methodist Episcopal Church.

One of the most successful black religious publishers to come into existence during the nineteenth century was the National Baptist Publishing Board. Under the leadership of Dr. Richard Henry Boyd and the auspices of the National Baptist Convention, USA, the National Baptist Publishing Board was organized in Nashville in 1896. By 1913, this well-managed firm, publishing religious and secular books, grew to become one of the largest black-owned businesses in the United States. In 1915, however, a dispute arose between the National Baptist Convention, USA and Dr. Richard Henry Boyd over the ownership of the National Baptist Publishing Board. In a court suit, the Tennessee Supreme Court decided in favor of Dr. Boyd; today the National Publishing Board, owned by the Boyd family, is a thriving religious publishing enterprise.

In 1907 the Church of God in Christ established the Church of God in Christ Publishing House in Memphis. Restricting its publications to religious books and pamphlets, this publisher continues today to meet the ever expanding needs for religious literature for one of the fastest growing black religious denominations in the United States.

Faced with the loss of the National Baptist Publishing Board, the National Baptist Convention, USA, Inc. established in 1916 the Sunday School Publishing Board of the National Baptist Convention, USA, Inc., in Nashville. Over the years, this firm has developed into one of the largest black-owned publishing enterprises in the United States, publishing religious and secular books and pamphlets.

Like the Sunday School Publishing Board of the National Baptist Convention, USA, Inc., Muhammad's Temple No. 2, Publications Department, which was founded in 1956 by the Nation of Islam, published religious as well as secular books. Between 1956 and 1974, several books were issued by this firm. However, since 1974, Muhammad's Temple No. 2, Publications Department has become inactive.

Institutional Publishers

During the last decades of the nineteenth century and the early decades of the twentieth century, educational, cultural, social, and political institutions were established to meet the specific needs of black Americans. Many of these institutions developed publishing programs, which included book publishing.

Colleges and Universities

Hampton Institute became the first black educational institution to published books when the Hampton Institute Press was established in 1871. An active publisher until 1940, the Hampton Institute Press published travel books, poetry, textbooks, songbooks, conference proceedings, and *The Southern Workman*, one of the leading national African-American periodicals published between 1871 and its demise in 1939.

In 1896 the Atlanta University Press entered the book publishing market with the release of *Atlanta University Publication Series*, which were monographs reporting on the findings of studies conducted by the university's department of sociology under the direction of Dr. W.E.B. DuBois. These works represented some of the earliest studies in urban sociology conducted in the South. The Atlanta University Press remained in operation until 1936.

Industrial Work of Tuskegee Graduates and Former Students During the Year 1910, compiled by Monroe N. Work (1911), was the first book released by the Tuskegee Institute Press. With the publication of this book and other works by the press, Booker T. Washington sought to publicize the success of Tuskegee's program to white philanthropists in the North. The Tuskegee Institute Press, which was active until 1958, published several other important works, including John Kenny's *The Negroes in Medicine* (1912) and *Lynching by States, 1882-1958* (1958), by Jessie Parkhurst Guzman.

In 1910 another book publishing enterprise was launched on the campus of Tuskegee Institute—the Negro Yearbook Publishing Company. A partnership consisting of Robert E. Park, the famed white sociologist, Emmett J. Scott, secretary to Booker T. Washington, and Monroe N. Work, a sociology professor, this firm published the first edition of *The Negro Yearbook* in 1912. The most comprehensive reference book to appear to date on African Americans, *The Negro Yearbook* was highly regarded as the definitive work on statistics and facts on blacks worldwide. However, the Negro Yearbook Publishing Company fell into financial trouble in 1929, and was taken over by Tuskegee Institute, which financed its operation until 1952. Between 1912 and 1952, *The Negro Yearbook* remained a classic model for most general reference works on blacks.

John W. Work's *The Negro and His Song* (1915) was the first book issued under the Fisk University Press imprint. During the 1930s and 1940s, when Charles Spurgeon Johnson chaired the university's department of sociology, several important studies were issued by the Fisk University Press, including E. Franklin Frazier's *The Free Negro Family* (1932); *The Economic Status of the Negro*, by Charles Spurgeon Johnson (1933); and *People versus Property*, by Herman Long and Charles Spurgeon Johnson (1947). The last publication released by the Fisk University Press was *Build a Future: Addresses Marking the Inauguration of Charles Spurgeon Johnson* (1949).

Although the board of trustees of Howard University approved the establishment of a university press on February 17, 1919, no university press was organized at the university until 1974. Nonetheless, between 1919 and 1974, several books bearing the "Howard University Press" imprint were published, including *The Founding of the School of Medicine of Howard University, 1868-1873*, by Walter Dyson (1929); and *The Housing of Negroes in Washington, DC: A Study in Human Ecology*, by William H. Jones (1929). On April 8, 1974, the Howard University Press was officially organized as a separate administrative unit within the university with a staff of twelve professionals experienced in book publishing. The Howard University Press' inaugural list of thirteen books included such titles as *A Poetic Equation: Conversations Between Nikki Giovanni and Margaret Walker* (1974) and *Saw the House in Half, a Novel,* by Oliver Jackman (1974). The Howard University Press continues to flourish as one of the most viable university presses in the country.

Cultural and Professional Organizations and Institutions

Black cultural and professional organizations and institutions have also developed publishing programs which included book publishing. The books published by these organizations documented areas of black history and depicted various aspects of African American culture.

Founded in 1897 by the Reverend Alexander Crummell, nineteenth century black scholar, clergyman, and missionary, the American Negro Academy quickly organized a publishing program which embraced book publishing. The Academy, whose membership included many of the foremost black intellectuals of the day, released twenty-one occasional papers as pamphlets and monographs. The American Negro Academy went out of existence in 1928.

The Association for the Study of Negro Life and History (now the Association for the Study of Afro-American History and Literature) began its book publishing program in 1918. By 1940, the association had published twenty-eight books. After that year, the book publishing activities of the association declined until 1950, when its founder Carter G. Woodson died and provided in his will for the transfer of the Associated Publishers, Inc. to the association.

The Associates of Negro Folk Education, organized in Washington, D.C. by Howard University philosophy professor Alain Locke, with a grant from the American Adult Education Association, published a series of seven books, known as the Bronze Booklets, from 1935 to 1940. Written by black scholars on various aspects of black American life and edited by Dr. Locke, some of these titles included *A World View of Race*, by Ralph J. Bunche (1936), *The Negro and Economic Reconstruction*, by T. Arnold Hill (1937), and *Negro Poetry and Drama*, by Sterling Brown (1937).

Civil Rights, Social Welfare, and Political Organizations

In 1913, five years after its founding, the National Association for the Advancement of Colored People launched its book publishing program with the publication of three books: *A Child's Story of Dunbar*, by Julia L. Henderson (1919); *Norris Wright Cuney*, by Maude Cuney Hare (1913); and *Hazel*, by Mary White Ovington (1913). In 1914 George Williamson Crawford's *Prince Hall and His Followers* appeared and in 1919, *Thirty Years of Lynching in the United States, 1889-1918* was

released. After 1919 few books were published by the NAACP, with the organization limiting its publishing to *Crisis* magazine, pamphlets, and its annual reports.

In contrast, the National Urban League has been a very active book publisher. The League first embarked on book publishing in 1927 when it published *Ebony and Topaz*, an anthology of Harlem Renaissance writers, poets, and artists edited by Charles Spurgeon Johnson. Through the years numerous sociological and economic studies on the plight of black Americans have been published by the Urban League, including *Negro Membership in Labor Unions* (1930), *Race, Fear and Housing in a Typical American Community* (1946), and *Power of the Ballot: A Handbook for Black Political Participation* (1973). In addition to these monograph studies, the organization began publishing *The State of Black America* in 1976.

Although the publishing program of the Universal Negro Improvement Association and African Communities League focused on the publication of its newspaper, *The Negro World*, this political organization also published books. Two volumes of *The Philosophy and Opinions of Marcus Garvey*, compiled and edited by Amy Jacques-Garvey, were published under the imprint of the Press of the Universal Negro Improvement Association.

Commercial Publishers

Until the 1960s, most black commercial publishers engaged in book publishing enterprises were short-lived. However, in 1967 Haki Madhubuti founded Third World Press in Chicago. Third World Press is now the oldest continually operating black commercial book publisher in the United States.

Over the years, black publishers have come to find that a sizable black readship exists; since 1970 several major black publishers have emerged. In 1978 Black Classic Press was founded by librarian Paul Coates to publish obscure, but significant, works by and about people of African descent. In 1978 Dempsey Travis founded Urban Research Press. Open Hand Publishing Inc. was founded in 1981 by Anna Johnson.

In 1983 Kassahun Checole founded Africa World Press to publish material on the economic, political, and social development of Africa. Checole, a former African studies instructor at Rutgers University, found it difficult to attain books needed for his courses. Now African World Press publishes nearly sixty titles a year and its sister company, Red Sea Press, is now one of the largest distributors of material by and about Africans.

Just Us Books, Inc., founded by writer Wade Hudson and graphic artists Cheryl Willis Hudson, publishes books and educational material for children that focus

Haki Madhubuti

Headquarters for the *Baltimore Afro-American*, founded in 1892

on the African-American experience. The idea to start the children's book publisher first came to Cheryl in 1976, when she was unable to find black images to decorate her daughter's nursery. Just Us Books published its first book in 1988—an alphabet book featuring African-American children posed to create the letters. The company currently has sales of over $800,000.

Comic Book Publishers

In the 1990s, black comics have peaked in popularity. Once relegated to a form of children's entertainment, comic books have found an audience with young adults in their 20s to 30s. In fact, in 1990, Cable News Network noted that sales of multiracial comics had jumped nine perecent, thus accounting for ten percent of all comic book sales. One reason for the growth among the black adult readership is collectibility—since most African American series are shortlived, each issue has the potential to become a rarity. Another reason is the fact that nowadays, black comics better represent African Americans by addressing their cultural and artistic concerns.

Black characters of yore, often grotesquely drawn by whites, were either sidekicks or afterthoughts—never the stars. For example Ebony, a black character, pa-

raded around with white superhero The Spirit in the 1940s. Meanwhile, Captain America had his own version of the Lone Ranger's Native American sidekick Tonto in Falcon. Other black characters were protrayed as ignorant, uneducated, and inept at worst. Blatently stereotypical, most were created and drawn by white males who did not know much about the reality of blacks. Over the years the status of black comic book characters evolved in the same negative ways that whites' perceptions of blacks did. By the 1960s and 1970s, blacks were depicted either drug addicts or Uncle Toms.

True change did not occur until a few enterprising African Americas took matters into their own hands. By 1992, Africa Rising Comics, Afrocentric Books, Dark Zulu Lies, Omega7 Comics and UP Comics had created ANIA Comics under the leadership of Eric Griffin. Though the group disbanded within a short time, their existence highlighted the growing line of black and other culturally diverse superheros.

For example, in the mid-1990s, Big City Comics was producing *Brotherman*, revolving around a public defender who also fights crime as an alter-persona known as the "dictator of discipline." Omega7 introduced fans to *The Original Man*, champion of morality and supporter and protector of black women; *The Mighty Ace*, with an anti-drug, anti-gang, anti-violence message; and *DarkForce*, about a revolutionary black hero. UP Comics was offering *Purge*, detailing the trials and tribulations of a man whose sole goal is to rid his city of evil. Prophesy Comics' *Lionheart* also emphasized morality lessons. And in a unique twist, Castel Publications came up with *The Grammer Patrol*, multi-ethnic heros with a penchant for good grammer. Geared towards children, that comic showed that the medium can be used for more than entertainment purposes.

Most of these companies were black-owned and operated, with everyone from the artists to the story writers to the marketers being African American. But mainstream publishers entered the fray when industry giant DC Comics began distributing Milestone Comics in 1991 as part of their new imprint Milestone Media, formerly a black-owned, independent publisher run by Derek T. Dingle. With a broad, full-process color system and access to such expensive techniques as airbrushing at hand, the company made history as the first major publisher to back African American creators. Among their titles have been *Hardware*, *Blood Syndicate*, *Icon*, *Kobalt*, *Shadow Cabinet*, *Xombi*, and *Static*, the latter featuring a teen hero.

◆ NEWSPAPER AND MAGAZINE PUBLISHERS

Newspapers

The black press in the United States is heir to a great, largely unheralded tradition. It began with the first black newspaper, *Freedom's Journal*, edited and published by Samuel Cornish and John B. Russwurm, on March 16, 1827. *The North Star*, the newspaper of abolitionist Frederick Douglass, was first published on December 3, 1847.

In the 1880s, African Americans' ability to establish a substantial cultural environment in many cities of the North led to the creation of a new wave of publications, including the *Washington Bee*, the *Indianapolis World*, the *Philadelphia Tribune*, the *Cleveland Gazette*, *Baltimore Afro-American* and the *New York Age*. By 1900, daily papers appeared in Norfolk, Kansas City, and Washington, DC.

Among famous black newspaper editors were William Monroe Trotter, editor of the *Boston Guardian*, a self-styled "radical" paper that showed no sympathy for the conciliatory stance of Booker T. Washington; Robert S. Abbott, whose *Chicago Defender* pioneered the use of headlines; and T. Thomas Fortune of the *New York Age*, who championed free public schools in an age when many opposed the idea.

In 1940 there were over 200 black newspapers, mostly weeklies with local readerships, and about 120 black magazines in the country. The *Pittsburgh Courier*, a weekly, had the largest circulation, about 140,000 per issue.

The National Negro Newspaper Publishers Association

The National Negro Newspaper Publishers Association, was founded in 1940 to represent black newspaper publishers. The organization scheduled workshops and trips abroad to acquaint editors and reporters with important news centers and news sources. A result was a trend to more progressive and interpretive reporting. In 1956 the association changed its name to the National Newspaper Publishers Association. Today it represents 148 publishers.

The Amsterdam News

Founded in 1909 by James H. Anderson, the *Amsterdam News*, has become one of the most well-known black newspaper in the nation. It was first published on December 4, 1909 in Anderson's home on 132 W. 65th Street in New York City. At that time one of only fifty black "news sheets" in the country, the *Amsterdam News* had a staff of ten, consisted of six printed pages, and sold for 2 cents a copy. Since then, the paper has been printed at several Harlem addresses.

In 1935 the paper was sold to two black physicians, Clilan B. Powell and P.M.H. Savory. In 1971 the paper was again sold to a group of investors, headed by Clarence B. Jones and Percy E. Sutton.

Black Newspapers in the 1990s

A number of newspapers that began publishing in the 1960s, 1970s, and 1980s have gone out of business, mainly due to their inability to attract advertising, both locally and nationally, and because of general economic decline. Today there are a reported 214 black newspapers in the United States. Of these, the papers with the largest paid circulations include New York's *Black American*, the *Hartford Inquirer*, and the *Atlanta Voice*.

Magazines

As early as the 1830s, black magazines were being published in the United States. However, it was not until the 1900s that the first truly successful magazines appeared. In 1910 the National Association for the Advancement of Colored People began publishing Crisis. In November 1942 John H. Johnson launched the *Negro Digest* and in 1945 he published the first issue of *Ebony*. The idea for the new magazine came form two *Digest* writers, and the magazine's name was given to it by

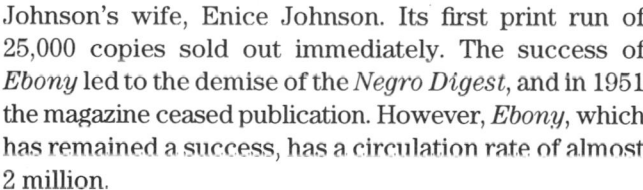

John Johnson with daughter, Linda Johnson.

Mal Goode

Johnson's wife, Enice Johnson. Its first print run of 25,000 copies sold out immediately. The success of *Ebony* led to the demise of the *Negro Digest*, and in 1951 the magazine ceased publication. However, *Ebony*, which has remained a success, has a circulation rate of almost 2 million.

In 1950 Johnson launched the magazine *Tan*, and in 1951 *Jet* magazine. Like *Ebony*, *Jet* was an instant success, selling over 300,000 copies in its first year. *Tan*, a woman's magazine, was later converted into a show business and personality monthly called *Black Stars*.

Since the founding of *Ebony*, several new and specialized black magazines have appeared. In 1967 *Black American Literature Review*, a journal presenting essays, interviews, poems, and book reviews, was founded. Also in 1967 Project Magazines, Inc. began publishing *Black Careers*. In 1969 the Black World Foundation published the first edition of *The Black Scholar*.

Earl G. Graves, a young businessman, in 1970 embarked on a concept to publish a monthly digest of news, commentary, and informative articles for blacks interested in business enterprise. Within a few short years his magazine, *Black Enterprise*, was accepted as

the authority on African Americans in business and as an important advocate for an active, socially responsive, black middle class. Today *Black Enterprise* has a subscription rate of over 251,000. A second magazine directed at black women founded in 1970, *Essence*, has steadily gained in its circulation since its inception. Featuring health and beauty, fashion, and contemporary living sections, *Essence* is considered one of the top women's magazines. Since 1981 Susan Taylor has been the magazine's editor-in-chief.

In 1980 *Black Family*, a magazine promoting positive lifestyles for African Americans, was founded. In 1986 *American Visions: The Magazine of Afro-American Culture*, the official magazine of the African American Museums Association was first published.

◆ BROADCASTING

by Richard Prince

There were black journalists before there was a broadcast industry, but in the Jim Crow America of the 1920s, there had to be black-oriented radio before there could be black broadcast journalists. That mission fell

Ed Bradley

to a vaudevillian jack-of-all trades from Cincinnati, Jack L. Cooper (1888-1970).

Radio

While early radio shows featured black singing groups, they featured no blacks talking. To Jack L. Cooper, this "was like taxation without representation," and so on Sunday, November 3, 1929, at 5 P.M., Chicago's white-owned WSBC premiered "The All-Negro Hour," starring Cooper and friends. Born was the concept of black radio, and Cooper went on to become the nation's first black radio station executive, the first black newscaster, the first black sportscaster, and the first to use radio as a service medium.

Cooper wore many hats. He played second base for a semi-pro baseball team; he had been a singer, a buck-and-wing dancer, and an end man in a minstrel show. He fought 160 amateur boxing bouts and he managed theaters. Between about 1910 and 1924, he worked as a journalist, writing for a number of black newspapers, including the *Freeman, Ledger* and *Recorder* in Indianapolis; and the *Bluff City News* and *Western World Reporter* in Memphis. In 1924, he became the assistant theatrical editor of the *Chicago Defender*.

"The All-Negro Hour" was like a vaudeville revue on the air, featuring music, comedy, and serials. While it ended its run in 1935, Cooper continued with WSBC, pioneering the black-radio format by producing several black-oriented shows. Crucial to that format was local news and public affairs of interest to African Americans.

The first example of public service programming aired December 9, 1938, when Cooper launched the "Search for Missing Persons" show. Aimed at reuniting people who had lost contact with friends and relatives through migration and over time, it reportedly had reunited 20,000 people by 1950. According to *Ebony* magazine, Cooper also remodeled a van into a mobile unit to relay "on-the-spot news events directly to four radio stations in the Chicago and suburban area," including news flashes from the *Pittsburgh Courier* and interviews of famous personalities who came to town, such as boxer Joe Louis. Cooper also did play-by-play sportscasts of black baseball games from the van.

"Listen Chicago," a news discussion show that ran from 1946 to 1952, provided African Americans with their first opportunity to use radio as a public forum. Following Cooper's lead, between 1946 and 1955 the number of black-oriented stations jumped from 24 to 600. News was a part of the explosion. "We have learned to do newscasts that answer the question, 'How is this news going to affect me as a Negro?,'" Leonard Walk of WHOD Pittsburgh said in 1954. "We have learned that church and social news deserves a unique place of importance in our daily Negro programming."

Yet by and large these broadcasters were not trained journalists. Black stations did not begin to broadcast news as we know it today until the 1960s.

In 1972, the Mutual Black Network was formed for news and sports syndication, under the auspices of the Mutual Broadcasting Network. By the end of the 1970s, the Mutual Black Network had just over 100 affiliates and 6.2 million listeners. The Sheridan Broadcasting Corporation, a black-owned broadcasting chain based in Pittsburgh, purchased the Mutual Black Network in the late 1970s, renaming it the Sheridan Broadcasting Network. A second African-American radio network, the National Black Network, was formed in 1973. Among its regular features was commentary by journalist Roy Wood, which he named "One Black Man's Opinion." In January 1992 the American Urban Radio Network was formed, and the National Black Network has since gone out of business.

The networks were a mixed blessing. They provided their affiliates with broadcast-quality programs produced from an African-American perspective. But this relatively inexpensive access to news, sports, and public affairs features discouraged the local stations that

Earl Graves

subscribed from producing their own shows. News and public affairs staffs at the black-oriented stations remained minimal. There were some notable exceptions. New York's WLIB-AM had a black format that included a highly acclaimed news and public affairs department. A series of shows produced by the station on disadvantaged youth in the city won two Peabody Awards in 1970. After the station was purchased in 1972 by African-American civic leader Percy Sutton, the station became "Your Total Black News and Information Station," offering more news and public affairs programming than any other black-formatted radio outlet in the country.

In Washington, DC, *The Washington Post* donated its commercial FM radio license to Howard University in 1971. The new station, WHUR-FM, inaugurated "The Daily Drum," a full hour-long evening newscast that featured special coverage of the local black community, as well as news from Africa and the diaspora.

Television

Until the late 1960s, most serious black journalists were in print journalism—chiefly the black press—not in broadcasting. An exception was Lionel Monagas, who

died at age seventy on April 5, 1992, and who worked in the early 1950s as a director of CBS-TV network programs such as "Person to Person" and "Face the Nation." He had started out as a traffic typist with the CBS affiliate in Washington, DC.

In 1956 Monagas became the first black professional at public station Channel 35 in Philadelphia, later known as WHYY-TV. He produced several children's programs there, including a ten-part series on "The History of the Negro," narrated by Ossie Davis.

Mal Goode became the first African American network TV reporter in 1962, at ABC-TV. Baseball great Jackie Robinson complained to James Hagerty, the former press secretary to President Eisenhower who was hired as an ABC vice president to set up a competitive news department. Robinson told Hagerty that the only two Negroes he had seen at ABC were "a lady with a white uniform in the lobby dusting and a Negro doorman. [Hagerty's] face got red, and he said we intend to do something about that," Goode said. Goode was a reporter at *The Pittsburgh Courier* at the time, but in 1949 Pittsburgh's KQV Radio had given the newspaper two 15-minute slots to fill on Tuesday and Wednesday nights. Goode read the news on the program. According

NBC "Today Show" host Bryant Gumbel interviews former President Richard Nixon, 1990.

to Goode, ABC chose him for the job after spending half a year interviewing thirty-eight black male candidates. One reason he was chosen, he said, was because he was considered dark enough so blacks would know he was black, but light enough so that whites wouldn't feel threatened. Goode went on to work for ABC for eleven years. He was its United Nations correspondent, and covered the Cuban missile crisis, the aftermath of Martin Luther King Jr.'s assassination and the Poor People's March on Washington.

Jobs like Goode's were hard to come by. In his memoir *Black Is the Color of My TV Tube*, Emmy-winner Gil Noble of New York's WABC-TV recalls being at WLIB-AM radio during this era. "We would sit in the newsroom and fantasize about earning $300 a week, but few of our number worked at that level. Pat Connell, a former disc jockey at Newark's WNJR, known as 'Pat the Cat,' was anchoring the CBS morning newscast. Mal Goode was reporting for ABC-TV news, as well as for the local station WABC. NBC didn't have any blacks at that time, as far as I can recall, and in the mid-'60s, WNEW-TV had none, nor did WPIX-TV or WOR-TV have any." When Noble went downtown to audition for a major radio station job, he recalled, he would intone in the ultimate radio voice—"a [Walter] Cronkite delivery that outdid the original"—only to get the familiar brushoff, "Thanks very much. You're fine, but we already have a Negro on staff."

However, a few blacks were allowed on the white-controlled airwaves. William C. Matney, Jr., who had been managing editor of the *Michigan Chronicle*, a black community paper, and a reporter for the *Detroit News*, in 1963 became a TV and radio reporter for WMAQ-TV, the NBC-owned station in Chicago. He joined NBC-TV news in 1966. Veteran Norma Quarles, now at CNN, was hired as a trainee at NBC News in 1966, moving a year later to the NBC station in Cleveland as a reporter and anchor. Lem Tucker, who died in March 1991, joined NBC News as a copy boy in 1965 and moved up to assistant bureau chief in Vietnam.

In 1967, a self-described "teacher moonlighting as a jazz disc jockey" who also called play-by-play for basketball games and read the news, applied for a job at soon-to-be all-news WCBS radio in New York. Ed Bradley, who would later co-host CBS-TV's most successful news show, "60 Minutes," impressed a news director by refusing to write some copy and record it because, he explained, "You won't learn enough about me that way." Instead, he borrowed a tape recorder, went out on the street, did an update of a story about an anti-poverty program, and got the job. But in Portsmouth, Virginia, an audacious twenty-five-year-old newscaster named Max Robinson was fired from a UHF station after he broke the rules by showing his face on camera.

It was 1964, and only the word "News" was to appear on the screen. White viewers were enraged to see that one of "those" people was allowed to work in the studio. According to his news director, James Snyder, in 1971 Robinson became the first black anchor in a major market, at WTOP-TV in Washington, DC. Later, at ABC-TV, Robinson would be the networks' first black regular co-anchor. But that wouldn't happen until 1978.

It took the riots of the 1960s and a stern warning from a federal commission for the broadcast industry to undertake any concentrated hiring of African Americans. When American cities began to burn, blacks held about 3.6 percent of TV news jobs. White news directors had to scramble to find black journalists to cover the story. In 1968, the National Advisory Commission on Civil Disorders, also known as the Kerner Commission, concluded that "the world that television and newspapers offer to their black audience is almost totally white, in both appearance and attitude." "Within a year," wrote Noble, "many of us found ourselves working downtown at major radio and TV stations."

In June 1969 the Federal Communications Commission adopted rules prohibiting discrimination in broadcast industry employment and required stations to file annual reports showing the racial makeup of their workforce by job category. Black public-affairs shows were aired, such as Noble's "Like It Is," public broadcasting's "Black Journal" hosted by Tony Brown, Philadelphia's "Black Perspectives on the News," in nearly every city with a substantial black population. Still, by the time Mal Goode retired in 1973, there were only seven black reporters at the three networks.

By the 1990s, African Americans were breaking into broadcast management and ownership, although the numbers were still small. TV general managers included Charlotte Moore English of KSHB-TV Kansas City; Marcellus Alexander of WJZ-TV in Baltimore; Eugene Lothery of WCAU-TV in Philadelphia; Clarence McKee, CEO and chairman of WTVT-TV in Tampa, Florida; and Dorothy Brunson, owner of a small UHF station, WGTW-TV, in Philadelphia.

Ronald Townsend, president of the Gannett Television Group, comprising ten stations, chaired the National Association of Broadcasters' TV board. Jonathan Rodgers became president of the CBS Television Stations Division in August 1990, making him network television's highest-ranking African-American news executive. Bryant Gumbel, co-host of the NBC-TV "Today" show, CBS News correspondent Ed Bradley, and talk-show host Oprah Winfrey became three of the highest paid and most-recognized faces on television, and Bradley among the most respected. ABC-TV's Carole Simpson became a substitute and weekend network TV anchor. African Americans were anchoring local newscasts in markets around the country.

Still, African Americans, while 12 percent of the population in the 1990 census, represented only 9.8 percent of the television news workforce and 5 percent of the radio workforce. They were four percent of the news directors at commercial TV stations and about five percent at commercial radio stations. Those heading news operations included Gary Wordlaw at WJLA-TV Washington, DC and Will Wright at WWOR-TV New York. And, according to an annual survey by the Center for Media and Public Affairs, most of the news on nightly network television shows continued to be presented by white males. Blacks accounted for only five percent of all field reports and anchor stories combined, its 1991 survey found. The most visible African American correspondent was George Strait, ABC-TV health reporter, who tied for fifty-seventh in the number of stories filed. Simpson was in sixth place, based on the number of brief news reports read.

Public Television

For most of its short history, public television, begun in the early 1950s, failed to realize the hopes of many African Americans. Tony Brown's "Black Journal," later "Tony Brown's Journal," was well-received by black viewers as the only national black public affairs series on television. It was constantly threatened with cancellation, however, after conservatives complained about its anti-administration attitude. The show was rescued after it secured underwriting from Pepsi Cola.

In 1975, the only black FCC commissioner, Benjamin Hooks, joined the critics, accusing public broadcasters of "arrogance" and of concentrating their efforts on the cultured, white cosmopolitans. A United States House of Representatives subcommittee held hearings. A 1975 review of public broadcasting stations' top three job categories (officials, managers, and professionals) showed that 59 percent (or 108) of the 184 public radio licensees and 33 percent (52) of the 160 public television licensees had no minority staff at these levels.   In the early 1990s, the highest-ranking African Americans in public television were Jennifer Lawson, who joined PBS in November 1989 as its first executive vice president for national programming and promotion services; Donald L. Marbury, director of the Television Program Fund of the Corporation for Public Broadcasting; and George L. Miles, Jr., executive vice president and chief operating officer of WNET-TV New York. Lawson was responsible for obtaining and commissioning the programs PBS provides to its member stations as well as the promotion of those programs. Marbury was charged

Tony Brown

with managing the $45 million television program fund, which provides funding support for major series in public television, such as "Frontline."

The most visible African American journalist on public television has been "MacNeil-Lehrer News Hour" correspondent Charlayne Hunter-Gault, a former *New York Times* reporter noted for her in-depth reporting. Other black journalists with the show include Kwame Holman, Washington correspondent, and producer Jackie Farmer. PBS' most acclaimed piece of African American journalism was "Eyes on the Prize," a history of the civil rights movement produced by Henry Hampton, which aired in 1987, with a sequel in 1990. Its most controversial was a one-hour film on black gay men, "Tongues Untied," by filmmaker Marlon Riggs in 1991.

In 1980, Howard University launched WHMM-TV, becoming the first licensee of a public TV station on a black campus and the only black-owned public television station in the nation. On August 31, 1991, San Francisco's Minority Television Project went on the air with KMTP-TV, which became the nation's second black-owned public television station. One of the principals was Adam Clayton Powell III, son of the late Harlem congressman, Adam Clayton Powell, Jr.

Public Radio

Before 1967, there were only two black educational outlets in the country; by 1990 there were 40 black public radio stations. Many of them were community radio stations, owned and operated by nonprofit foundations, controlled by a local board of directors, and relying on listener donations. Others were on college campuses. One of the most successful was WPFW-FM, a 50,000-watt outlet controlled by African Americans, launched in 1977 by the Pacifica Foundation.

Stations such as WCLK-FM at Clark College in Atlanta, WBVA-FM in Harrodsburg, Kentucky, and WVAS-FM at Alabama State University in Montgomery, tailored news and public affairs programming to their local, African-American audiences. WVAS was used as a broadcast journalism lab by students majoring in the field. On National Public Radio, African American journalists Phyllis Crockett, Vertamae Grosvenor, Cheryl Duvall, and Brenda Wilson have won awards for reports on South Africa and issues involving African Americans.

Cable Television

The 1980s saw the explosion of cable television and the decline of the television networks. Black Entertainment Television, founded by former congressional aide Robert L. Johnson, made its debut in 1980 and established a news division by the end of the decade. That division produced a weekly news show, "BET News" and "Lead Story," a talk show featuring black pundits.

The biggest development in cable journalism, however, was the spectacular growth of Ted Turner's Cable News Network, which went on line in June 1980. By the 1991 Persian Gulf war, CNN had established itself as the station to watch in a crisis. Transmitted across the globe, it became a medium for world leaders to communicate among one another.

Veteran journalist Bernard Shaw, principal Washington anchor, was one of three CNN reporters who captivated the world's audiences with their continuous coverage of the first night of bombing on Baghdad during Operation Desert Storm on January 16, 1991. Other African Americans at CNN include Jay Suber, vice president and executive producer, news features, CNN Newsroom; Graylian Young, Southeast bureau chief; CNN anchors Andrea Arceneaux, Leon Harris and Joe Oliver; Cassandra Henderson, anchor for CNN Newsroom, Lyn Vaughn and Gordon Graham, Headline News anchors; sports anchor Fred Hickman, and correspondent Norma Quarles.

Robert Johnson

◆ AFRICAN AMERICANS IN CYBERSPACE

by Lorna M. Mabunda

Despite the financial burden presented by computers and modems, African Americans were cruising the information superhighway—a vast electronic communications network comprised of telephones, computers, and televisions—in growing numbers during the mid-1990s. In fact, an African American was one of the key spokespeople for cyberspace-related equity issues. Branded "The Net's Conscience," Larry Irving was director of the National Telecommunications and Information Administration. But far from being the only person of color with clout on the net, Irving was one of many experts working in the burgeoning industry that links millions of people across the globe, providing access to a wide array of information for educational, business, and entertainment purposes. Other high-ranking African Americans included Andrew C. Barrett, the only black commissioner of the Federal Communications Commission (FCC); Ray Winbush, director of the Bishop Joseph Johnson Black Cultural Center at Vanderbilt University—a network linking black colleges, students, and professors; Jimmy Davies, who partnered with Apple Computer, Inc. to establish a national electronic bulletin board service for blacks called the African American Information Network; Sandra Hall, owner of Artronics, a website developer (including AFROAM Griot Online and Afrigeneas) and the WebDiva's InfoCenter caretaker; Eugene and Phyllis Tucker Vinson Jackson, founders of the World African Network, a 24-hour, pay cable television network for blacks; Cleo Manago, founder of the Black Men's Xchange (BMX), an Africentric national communications clearinghouse; and Omar Wasow, founder and president of New York Online, the largest black-owned "cyberservice" in the United States, with nearly 2,000 New York-area subscribers (40 percent black) in 1996.

The World Wide Web comprises a major component of the "highway." Many African American-oriented sites have developed, emphasizing business, art, religion, literature, history, and other cultural content areas. Among them are:

The African-American Mosaic: A Library of Congress Resource Guide for the Study of Black History and Culture
http://www.cweb.loc.gov/exhibits/African.American/intro.html

A guide to the institution's African American collections, including books, periodicals, prints, photographs, music, and film. Covers 500 years of history.

AfricaNews Online
http://www.nando.net/ans/africa.html

Reports from Africa's leading newspapers, magazines, and news agencies.

Africa Online
http://www.he.tdl.com/~africaol

An African and African American information magazine.

AfricaOnline's Women's Issues Forum
http://www.Africaonline.com/AfricaOnline/women.html

Centers on African and African American culture.

AfriNET
http://www.afrinet.net

An electronic community geared towards minority organizations and businesses.

Afro-Americ@
http://www.afroam.org

News from around the nation of interest to the African American community, including culture, history, and a kids' zone.

AFROAM-L Griot Online
http://www.afrinet.net/~griot

A discussion group for African historians, including research about African life, culture, and history in the diaspora.

Black Enterprise Magazine Online
http://206.20.2.64

Business news, strategies, information, and resources for African American entrepreneurs, corporate executives, managers, and other professionals.

Black Information Network
http://www.bin.com

Business-, education-, family-, and health-oriented associations and organizations.

BLK Homie Pages
http://www.blk.com/blk

News and information about the black lesbian and gay community.

Black on Black Communications
http://www.i-media.com/BOBC

An electronic newsletter covering issues of interest to African Americans via news stories and positive dialogue. Available only by subscription.

The Conduit: The Definitive Technological Guide for the African AMerican
http://www.imhotech.com

Advocates African American involvement in technology.

CPTime
http://www.home.earthlink.net/~afrolink

Conscious Peoples Time Online was conceived in 1988. CPTime Online was launched as a bulletin board service in 1990. An intuitive, interactive experience, including clip art, a world glossary, a directory of black bookstores, and an art guide.

The Drum
http://FAQ@drum.ncat.edu

A mailing list of more than 1,000 participants—from Canada, France, Great Britain, South Africa, and the United States—that allows one to post e-mail messages to subscribers. Also includes information regarding such diverse topics as African American universities, a holistic page, federal government internship opportunities, and a speeches page. Supports anti-censorship.

Gravity Discussion Zones

http://www.newsavanna.com

Discussion pages geared towards African Americans.

Isis Plus

http://www.netdiva.com/isisplus.html

Focuses upon the art, culture, and spirituality of women of the African diaspora.

MelaNet: The UnCut Black Experience

http://www.melanet.com

Building upon the legacy of our ancestors to provide a presence for African American businesses via an online marketplace, a year-round Kwanzaa Bazaar, an African Wedding Guide, the Ida Wells Media Center, and the UnCut Chat Series—dialogues with black newsmakers.

Minority Information

http://web.fie.com/htdoc/fie/any/any/any/search/any/allminor.htm

This is a U.S. government-sponsored site, including minority information on all federal agencies.

The Museum of Slavery in the Atlantic

http://squash.la.psu.edu/~plarson/smuseum/homepage.html

Designed to provide accurate, engaging, and provocative information regarding the history of slavery.

NETLiNKS

http://www.interlog.com/~csteele/afro.html

Celebrates Afrocentricity via a comprehensive guide to African American and African Canadian web links and resources.

NetNoir Online: The Soul of Cyberspace

http://www.netnoir.com/index.html

A gateway to everything Afrocentric—Afro-Latin, Afro-Carribbean, Afro-European, continental African, and African-American cultures, lifestyles, music, sports, businesses, and education.

The Network Journal

http://www.tnj.com

Professional and small business news, including columns on technology.

PanAfrican News

http:www.nando.net/ans/pana/FEED/PANAFEED.html

News stories and focused topics such as economics, the environment, science and health, sports, and the Africa Press Review.

Peeps Republic

http://www.peeps.com

Sponsored by BMG Entertainment. Focuses on black music and culture.

Rainbow's Black Stripe

http://abacus.oxy.edu/qrd/www/culture/black/blackstripe.html

Resources for lesbians, gay men, bisexuals, and transgendered people of African Descent.

Sistah-Net: A List for Lesbians & Bisexual Women of African Descent

http://www.sistah-request@igc.org

The Universal Black Pages

http://www.gatech.edu/bgsa/blackpages.html

Though not formally affiliated with the university, this information service originates from Georgia Institute of Technology.

Vibe Online

http://www.vibe.com

Features underground news and information, a gallery of hip hop computer art, and a bimonthly rap column.

Virtually Afrocentric

http://www.he.net/~awe/makheru.htm

This repository of afrocentric links is a centerpiece of The Aframian WebNet.

World African Network

http://www.worldafricannet.com

Centers around 24 basic "Life Interest" areas for the world African family, including art & culture, business, children, community, consumers, education, elders and ancestors, the environment, family, fashion, fitness and health, food, travel, history, lifestyles, entertainment, love, news, politics, religion, science and technology, sports, and preservation.

The Zone I Gallery: The Showcase for African American Photography

http://www.gate.net/~eak3

Founded in 1995 by E. A. Kennedy III, a *Palm Beach Post* photographer. The site supports the protest against censorship.

Also of note is 1996's *The East Village*, a "cybersoap" situated in Manhattan's Lower Eastside. African American "actress" Gloria Lynne Henry is one of the central characters—"Daphene Monique Butler, the Jamaican, Swedish, English, Ethiopian daughter of a geologist and a social worker." The serial can be located at http://www.theeastvillage.com.

◆ COMMUNICATIONS GATEKEEPERS

Robert S. Abbott (1870-1940)
Newspaper Publisher

A native of St. Simon Island, Georgia, Abbott studied at Beach Institute in Savannah, and later completed his undergraduate work at Claflin College in Orangeburg, South Carolina. Migrating to Chicago, he attended Kent Law School and took a job in a printing house until he completed his law studies in 1899.

Abbott returned to Chicago and published the first edition of the *Defender* on May 5, 1905, which he initially sold on a door-to-door basis. After Abbott's death the *Defender* was handed over to his nephew, John H. Sengstacke, who introduced a daily edition of the paper in 1956.

William Banks (1903-1985)
Broadcasting executive, attorney, and minister

Born in Geneva, Kentucky, in 1903, William Banks relocated to Detroit as a young man and earned a law degree there and later became a Baptist minister during his 40s. Long active in numerous African American community organizations in the city, Banks founded the International Free and Accepted Masons and Eastern Star in 1950, and under his guidance, the growing group soon became a financially sound and charity-driven fraternal organization. He continued to work as an attorney in private practice until well past the age of retirement.

In 1964, the Black Masons made their first venture into media ownership with a Detroit FM radio outlet that mixed R&B music and religious broadcasting. Banks's business savvy helped make the station a financial success in the same way that the Masons' other ventures—such as vocational training schools—also made the organization a thriving one. His ties to the Republican community eventually brought him to U.S. president Richard Nixon's White House as a guest in the early 1970s, and the chief executive helped him obtain the first television station license granted to an African American in the United States by the Federal Communications Commission.

The UHF television outlet that Banks and the Masons went on the Detroit airwaves with in 1975 was called WGPR, or "Where God's Presence Radiates." Its first years in operation were shaky, since many members of Banks's team—employees that included his wife, Ivy Bird, and daughter Tenicia Gregory—had little media experience. Within a few years, however, the station gained ratings and financial health. More importantly, WGPR-TV served as a training ground for a legion of African American on-air and behind-the-scenes technical personnel, a group of young people who would eventually go on to figure prominently in Detroit media. Banks died in 1985 at the age of 82. The Black Mason organization that Banks founded owned the station until 1994, when it was purchased by CBS as a local affiliate.

Don H. Barden (1943-)
Communications Executive

Born on December 20, 1943, Don Barden struggled in a number of low-wage jobs as an adult, dreaming of one day working for himself in some sort of entreprenurial venture. A nest egg of $500 helped him to open a record store, then launch a record label, then a public relations firm in Lorain, Ohio. The capital Barden accumulated through these ventures was later parlayed into real-estate deals. By the early 1970s, the executive had become a dynamic member of Lorain's business community, owning a newspaper, holding a seat on the city council, and hosting a talk show on Cleveland's NBC affiliate.

Barden's interest in and familiarity with cutting-edge media evolved into his most lucrative undertaking. Foreseeing the rise of the cable industry—and the lack of African American representation within it—Barden invested in Lorain's new cable television provider and used the remunerative rewards to begin his own cable company, Barden Cablevision. He researched and found African American communities entertaining franchise offers from giants in the industry and offered them a socially-conscious alternative. One of the first cities to award Barden's company a contract was Inkster, Michigan, a suburb of Detroit. His success in wiring the city for cable service and the obvious financial soundness of his company paid off when the city of Detroit awarded Barden Cablevision its much-coveted contract.

Barden launched cable television in Detroit with the help of Canadian financing and began wiring the city in 1986. Always looking into what was on the forefront of the communications industry, Barden's next venture was in the realm of Personal Communications Services, a new messaging technology that would allow small devices to transmit faxes, voice messages, and computer data. He planned to bid on several of the licenses when they were to be auctioned off for the first time by the Federal Communications Commission in 1994. That same year, he sold his interest in Barden Cablevision for a reported $100 million, reaping a dramatic profit from the company he had started with only a few thousand dollars. In early 1995, it was announced that Indiana authorities had granted Barden a riverboat casino operating license, one of two to be established in the city of Gary.

Ida Bell Wells Barnett (1864-1931)
Editor, Anti-lynching Crusader

Ida Bell Wells Barnett was born on July 16, 1862, in Mississippi and educated at Rusk University. She served as editor of the black newspaper, the *Memphis Free Speech*, and in 1892 became part-owner. Through the paper she engaged in a vigorous campaign against the practice of lynching. On May 27, 1882 the paper's offices were destroyed by a mob.

In 1895 she married *Chicago Conservator* editor Ferdinand Lee Barnett. That same year Barnett published her first pamphlet against lynching, *A Red Record*. Over the years Barnett wrote numerous other pamphlets and articles and conducted speaking tours throughout the United States and Europe.

Edward R. Bradley (1941-)
Television News Correspondent

Born on June 22, 1941, in Philadelphia, Pennsylvania, Edward R. Bradley received a B.S. degree in education from Cheyney State College in 1964. From 1963 to 1967 Bradley worked as a disc jockey and news reporter for WDAS radio in Philadelphia. From there he moved on to WCBS radio in New York. He joined CBS as a stringer in the Paris bureau in 1971. Within a few months he was transferred to the Saigon bureau, where he remained until he was assigned to the Washington bureau in June 1974. From 1974 until 1978, Bradley served as White House correspondent for CBS.

Bradley worked as an anchor for "CBS Sunday Night News" from 1976 until 1981 and as principal correspondent for "CBS Reports." In 1981, he replaced Dan Rather as a correspondent for the weekly news program, "60 Minutes." In 1992, Bradley was made host of the CBS news program, "Street Stories."

Bradley has won seven Emmy Awards for broadcast journalism, two Alfred I. duPont-Columbia University Awards for broadcast journalism, a George Foster Peabody Broadcasting Award, a George Polk Award, and an NCAA Anniversary Award. In 1992, he won an Emmy for his "60 Minutes" segment "Made in China." The National Press Foundation presented Bradley with the Sol Taischoff Award in 1993.

Ed Bradley

Tony Brown (1933-)
Commentator, Columnist, Producer

William Anthony Brown, born in Charleston, West Virginia, in 1933, is probably best known as the producer and host of the longest-running minority affairs program in history, "Tony Brown's Journal."

He received his bachelor of arts degree in 1959 and his master's degree in social work in 1961 from Wayne State University in Detroit. Brown took a job with the *Detroit Courier* as drama critic. It was during this time that he began to be active in the civil rights movement, helping to organize the 1963 "March to Freedom" with Dr. Martin Luther King in Detroit. After leaving the paper, where he had worked up to the position of city editor, Brown landed a job with the local PBS station, WTVS, where he became involved in television programming and production. At WTVS he produced the station's first series aimed at a black audience, "C.P.T." (Colored People's Time). He joined the New York staff of the PBS program "Black Journal" in 1970, as the show's executive producer and host—in 1977 the show's name was changed to "Tony Brown's Journal" and can still be seen on PBS.

In 1971 Brown founded and became the first dean of Howard University's School of Communications. He continued in that post until 1974.

Brown has been an advocate of community and self-help programs. In 1980 he organized a "Black College Day," designed to emphasize the importance of historically black colleges and universities. In 1985 Brown organized the Council for the Economic Development of Black Americans and launched the "Buy Freedom" campaign (now known as the "Buy Freedom Network"), which encourages black consumers nationwide to patronize black-owned businesses.

Brown has written, produced, and directed a film, *The White Girl*, and has appeared as a commentator for National Public Radio and has a syndicated newspaper columnist. He is a member of the National Association of Black Television and Film Producers, the National Association of Black Media Producers, the National Communications Council, and the National Black United Fund. Brown is the recipient of a Black Emmy Award and the NAACP Image Award. He is currently president of Tony Brown Productions in New York City.

Ron Buckmire (1968-)
Mathematician, Internet Directory Founder

Creator of the oldest and largest Internet online resource of information about gay, lesbian, bisexual, and transgenered people, Ron Buckmire spent nearly ten years in Barbados. While attending high school there, he was introduced to chess and became so skilled at the game that he was nationally ranked. In 1986, Buckmire relocated to Troy, New York, earning a B.A. (1989), a masters (1992), and a Ph.D. in applied mathematics (1994), all from Rensselaer Polytechnic Institute.

The Queer Resources Directory (QRD) initially started as an electronic archive for the radical group Queer Nation in 1991. Buckmire transformed the repository into a broader-based electronic library, featuring news clippings, political contact information, essays, images, and hyperlinks—all dedicated to sexual minorities that have traditionally beared the brunt of discrimination. Since 1993, the QRD has been one of the most frequently accessed libraries of its kind, operated entirely by volunteers working on donated equipment.

As executive director of the QRD, Buckmire is responsible for quality control and for auditing user services. Accessible via the World Wide Web—[http://www.qrd.org/qrd], one can also reach the directory through electronic mail and bulletin board services. Information can be accessed through keyword searching, through the browsing room, or by reading highlights of files—all for free.

Buckmire accepted a two-year, post-doctoral fellowship at Occidental College in 1995. In addition to his self-imposed QRD duties, he was teaching mathematical modeling and complex analysis there in 1996. Meanwhile, he hoped to later secure a new position in academia or industry.

Edward J. Castleberry (1928-)
Broadcast Journalist

Born July 28, 1928 in Birmingham, Alabama, Castleberry spent two years at Miles College in that city. His career has been in radio broadcasting at many stations in the United States. He started as a disc jockey at WEDR and WJLD in Birmingham, Alabama (1950-1955), and has worked in the various capacities of disc jockey, program director and newsman at WMBM in Miami, Florida (1955-1958), WCIN in Cincinnati, Ohio (1958-1961), WABQ in Cleveland, Ohio (1961-1964), WVKD in Columbus, Ohio (1964-1967), WHAT in Philadelphia, Pennsylvania (1967-1968) and WEBB in Baltimore, Maryland. He then became an anchorman and entertainment editor at the Mutual and National Black Networks.

Castleberry was named Newsman of the Year in 1980 by both the Coalition of Black Media Women and Jack the Rapper Family Affair and received the Outstanding Citizen Award from the Alabama House of Representatives in 1983. In 1985 he was honored by the Smithsonian Institution in Washington DC. Castleberry was awarded the World War II Victory Medal for his service in the United States Navy 1945-1947.

Spencer Christian (1947-)
Television Weatherperson

Born in Richmond, Virginia, in 1947, Spencer Christian received his B.A. degree in English from Hampton University in 1970. Upon graduation he went to work as a teacher in New York.

In 1971 Christian went to work for WWBT-TV in Richmond as a news reporter; from 1972 to 1975 he served as the station's weatherperson. In 1975 he moved to WBAL-TV in Baltimore and to New York's WABC-TV in 1977. Christian joined the "Good Morning America" team on ABC in 1986, where he is currently weatherperson and co-host. In 1993, Christian hosted the "Triple Threat" game show on Black Entertainment Television. He published *Spencer Christian's Weather Book*, with Tom Biracree in 1993.

Xernona Clayton (1930-)
Broadcast Executive

Clayton was born Xernona Brewster on August 30, 1930 in Muskogee, Oklahoma. She received a B.S. from Tennessee State University in 1952 and pursued gradu-

Spencer Christian

Xernona Clayton

ate studies at the University of Chicago. She also attended the Ru–Jac School of Modeling in Chicago.

Clayton was the first African American woman to have her own television show in the south when she became hostess of the "Xerona Clayton Show" at WAGA-TV in Atlanta. She has also been a newspaper columnist for the *Atlanta Voice*, taught public school in Chicago and Los Angeles and has dabbled in photography and fashion modeling.

Clayton has also been active in the civil rights movement. Her first husband, now deceased, was the public relations director for Martin Luther King. Clayton came to the attention of Atlanta officials and was appointed to the position of community relations director of the Model Cities Program. She has also raised funds for sickle cell anemia research and the Martin Luther King Jr. Birthplace Memorial Restoration Committee.

In 1968 Clayton won the Outstanding Leadership award given by the National Association of Market Developers and a year later the Bronze Woman of the Year in Human Relations award given by Phi Delta Kappa sorority. She is also the recipient of the Georgia Associated Press award for Superior Television Pro-

gramming 1969–1971. In 1987, Clayton won an Emmy Award for a documentary on juvenile justice. She was named Media Woman of the Year in 1989.

Clayton is the founder of the Atlanta chapter of the National Association of Media Women and a member of the National Academy of Television Arts and Sciences and the National Association of Press Women. She is also a member of the Urban League's board of directors. She has co–starred in a major motion picture, *House on Skull Mountain*. Clayton has re-married and is currently the corporate vice-president for urban affairs at the Turner Broadcasting System in Atlanta, Georgia.

David E. Driver (1955-)
Book publisher, Writer, Social activist, Investor

David E. Driver was born on October 17, 1955, and grew up on Chicago's west side. Because of his excellent grades, he attended Lindbolm High School, an exceptional public trade school. From there, he earned a bachelor's of arts from Bradley University in Peoria, Illinois, and after he passed the CPA exam, he joined Arthur Young & Company as a staff accountant. In 1978, Driver took a job at the International Hospital Supply Corporation. Until 1980, Driver worked as a finance manager, specializing in foreign currency markets. He moved on to Merrill Lynch Capital Markets where he was promoted to vice president in 1982. While working in stock and bond futures, he received his MBA from the University of Chicago in 1984.

In 1988 with $250,000 and one book that he had written himself—*The Good Heart Book: A Guide to Volunteering*—he found the Noble Press. Within three years, he had a staff of five, a renovated loft for office space, and books receiving critical attention. The book that earned the Noble Press its reputation was the 1993 release, *Volunteer Slavery: My Authentic Negro Experience* by Janet Nelson, that sold 40,000 hardcover copies. Driver sold the paperback rights to Penguin for whom it became a national best-seller and earned an American Book Award in 1994.

By 1993, Noble's annual sales reached the million mark and its distribution outlets grew to number 6,000. Driver founded the Black Literary Society, a book club that posts reading lists on the Internet. Driver also started Young Chicago Authors, a workshop program for aspiring teenage authors. In addition, Driver has written *Defending the Left: An Individual's Guide to Fighting for Social Justice, Individual Rights and the Environment*, published in 1992. He has served as secretary of the Society of Illinois Book Publishers and is a founding member of the National Association of Black Book Publishers.

Timothy Thomas Fortune (1856-1928)
Newspaper Publisher

Born on October 3, 1856, in Marianna, Florida, Timothy Thomas Fortune was one of the most prominent black journalists involved in the flourishing black press of the post-Civil War era.

Born in Florida, the son of a Reconstruction politician, Fortune was particularly productive before his thirtieth year, completing such works as *Black and White: Land, Labor and Politics in the South* and *The Negro in Politics* while in his twenties.

Fortune attended Howard University for two years, leaving to marry Carrie Smiley of Jacksonville, Florida. The couple went to New York in 1878, with Fortune taking a job as a printer for the *New York Sun*. In time, Fortune caught the attention of *Sun* editor Charles A. Dana, who eventually promoted him to the editorial staff of the paper.

Fortune also edited *The Globe*, a black daily, and was later chief editorial writer for *The Negro World*. In 1900 Fortune joined Booker T. Washington in helping to organize the successful National Negro Business League. His later activity with Washington gained him more notoriety than his earlier writing, although his written work is more vital in affording him an important niche in the history of black protest.

In 1883 Fortune founded the *New York Age*, the paper with which he sought to "champion the cause" of his race. In time, the *Age* became the leading black journal of opinion in the United States. One of Fortune's early crusades was against the practice of separate schools for the races in the New York educational system.

Fortune was later responsible for coining the term "Afro-American" as a substitute for Negro in New York newspapers. He also set up the Afro-American Council, an organization which he regarded as the precursor of the Niagara Movement. In 1907 Fortune sold the *Age*, although he remained active in journalism as an editorial writer for several black newspapers. He died on June 2, 1928.

Malvin Russell Goode (1908-1995)
Television News Correspondent

Malvin Russell Goode had been with the *Pittsburgh Courier* 14 years when in 1962 he joined ABC to cover the United Nations. His first test was the Cuban Missile Crisis, just two months later, during which Goode distinguished himself with incisive TV and radio reports during the long hours of UN debate.

Goode was born in White Plains, Virginia, in 1908; educated in the public schools of Homestead, Pennsylvania; and graduated from the University of Pittsburgh in 1931. He was employed for twelve years as a laborer in the steel mills while in high school and college and for five years after graduation. In 1936, he was appointed to a post in Juvenile Court and became boys work director of the Centre Avenue YMCA, where he led the fight to eliminate discrimination in Pittsburgh branches of the YMCA.

Goode served with the Pittsburgh Housing Authority for six years and in 1948 joined the *Pittsburgh Courier*. The following year he started a career in radio with station KQV, doing a 15–minute news show two nights each week. In 1950, he started a five minute daily news program on WHOD.

Goode was named news director at WHOD in 1952. He and his sister, the late Mary Dee, had the only brother–sister team in radio for six years. He was the first African American to hold membership in the National Association of Radio and TV News Directors and the first African American correspondent on TV network news.

For two months, in 1963, he joined with three colleagues to conduct courses in journalism for 104 African students in seminars at Lagos, Nigeria; Addis Ababa, Ethiopia; and Dar es Salaam, Tanzania.

On September 12, 1995, Goode died of a stroke in Pittsburgh, Pennsylvania.

Ed Gordon (1960-)
News Anchor

Born Edward Lansing Gordon III in Detroit, Michigan, the future journalist was inspired to achieve in part by his schoolteacher mother and Olympic gold medalist father, who unfortunately passed away when Gordon was eleven. After graduating with a degree in communications and political science from Western Michigan University in 1982, Gordon moved back to Detroit to launch his career in broadcasting.

Taking an unpaid internship with the city's public broadcasting affiliate in 1983 eventually landed him a job as host of its *Detroit Black Journal* a few years later. During that time he also began freelance reporting from his hometown for an upstart cable network called Black Entertainment Television. In 1988 the Washington, DC-based channel hired him to anchor their weekly news program *BET News*.

Since then Gordon has become an increasing presence on the well-regarded alternative to traditional network news, interviewing prominent African Americans on his *Conversations with Ed Gordon* show and hosting programs of special interest such as his "Black Men Speak Out: The Aftermath," which aired in the wake of the 1992 Los Angeles riots. Gordon has also interviewed the last two sitting presidents as well as more outspoken figures such as the Reverend Al Sharpton and Nation of Islam leader Louis Farrakhan, and also hosts the BET staple *Lead Story*. Though the demands of the job are sometimes arduous at the still-new network, Gordon derives a special satisfaction from his work in journalism when young African American males point out to him that they never were interested in news programs before his began airing.

Earl G. Graves (1935-)
Publisher and Media Executive

In the 1970s, Earl Graves emerged as one of America's leading publishers and exponents of black entrepreneurship. Within a few short years his magazine, *Black Enterprise*, was accepted as the authority on African Americans in business and as an important advocate for an active, socially responsive, black middle class.

Born in Brooklyn in 1935, Graves graduated from Morgan State College in 1958 with a bachelor's degree in economics. In 1965, he was hired to a position on the staff of Robert Kennedy, then senator from New York. In 1968, he organized Earl Graves Associates, a firm which serves as a consultant on urban affairs, black economic development and publishes *Black Enterprise*. Graves is also president and chief executive officer of Earl G. Graves Ltd., Earl G. Graves Publishing Co. Inc., Earl G. Graves Marketing and Research Co., and Earl G. Graves Development Co.

Graves also has interests in radio as president of EGG Dallas Broadcasting, Inc., which operates KNOK–AM and KNOK–FM in Fort Worth, Texas. Graves is also sole owner of Pepsi-Cola of Washington D.C.

Bryant Gumbel (1948-)
Television Anchor

Bryant Gumbel was born in New Orleans, Louisiana, on September 29, 1948. In January 1981 Bryant Gumbel was named co–anchor (with Jane Pauley) of the "Today" show on NBC. Prior to that time, Gumbel had made regular sports reports on "Today," although his primary responsibilities were with NBC Sports as host of pre–game programming during coverage of the National Football League, Major League Baseball, and other sports broadcasts.

He began his broadcasting career in October 1972 when he was named a weekend sportscaster for KNBC, the NBC station in Los Angeles. Within a year, he became weekday sportscaster and was appointed the station's sports director in 1976. He remained in that post until July 1980.

Before embarking on his career in television, Gumbel was a sports writer. After submitting his first piece to *Black Sports* magazine in 1971, he was given additional free–lance assignments and was soon hired as a staff writer. Within eight months he was elevated to editor–in–chief.

A native of New Orleans, Gumbel grew up in Chicago. He received a liberal arts degree from Bates College in Lewiston, Maine in 1970. Gumbel debuted as host of HBO's "Real Sports" program on April 2, 1995.

Ragan A. Henry (1934-)
Broadcast and Newspaper Executive

Ragan A. Henry is president of Broadcast Enterprises National Inc. and former publisher of *The National Leader*, a black national newspaper launched in May 1982, both headquartered in Philadelphia. Henry is also president of radio stations in several states and is a partner in the Philadelphia law firm of Wolf, Black, Schorr, and Solis-Cohen.

Henry was born in Sadiesville, Kentucky on February 2, 1934. He received his B.A. from Harvard College in 1956 and his L.L.B. from Harvard Law School in 1961. He also attended Temple University Graduate School in 1963. Prior to joining his current law firm, he had been a

Earl Graves

Bryant Gumbel

partner in the Philadelphia firm of Goodis, Greenfield, Henry, and Edelstein from 1964 to 1977.

Henry has been a visiting professor at Syracuse University's S.I. Newhouse School of Communications since 1979 and was a lecturer at LaSalle College from 1971 to 1973. He serves on the boards of directors of Continental Bank, Abt Associates, Inc., National Association of Black Owned Broadcasters (president of the board), LaSalle College, and the Hospital of the University of Pennsylvania. He has been chairman of the John McKee Scholarship Committee Fellowships of the Noyes and Whitney Foundation.

Cheryl Willis Hudson (1948-)
Publishing Executive

Cheryl Willis Hudson, publisher, and Wade Hudson, president and chief executive officer, founded Just Us Books, Inc. in 1988 to publish children's books and learning material that focus on the African–American experience.

A native of Portsmouth, Virginia, Cheryl Willis Hudson graduated (cum laude) from Oberlin College in 1970, and has studied at Northeastern University, the

Arts Students League and Parsons School of Design. Prior to founding Just Us Books, she worked as an art editor and designer for several publishers, including Houghton Mifflin, MacMillan Publishing, Arete Publishing, and Paperwing Press/Angel Entertainment.

Wade Hudson (1948-)
Publishing Executive

Wade Hudson is the president and chief executive officer of Just Us Books, Inc., a company he co-founded with Cheryl Willis Hudson in 1988 to publish children's books and learning material that focus on the African-American experience.

A native of Mansfield, Louisiana, he attended Southern University and has worked with numerous civil rights organizations, including CORE, the Southern Christian Leadership Conference, and the Society for Opportunity, Unity and Leadership, which he co-founded. He also has worked as a public relations specialist for Essex County and Kean colleges in New Jersey.

Eugene D. Jackson (1943-)
Broadcast Executive

Eugene D. Jackson is president of Unity Broadcasting Network in New York City, parent company of the

National Black Network, and of four radio stations of which Jackson is also president—WDAS-AM and -FM in Philadelphia and KATZ-AM and WZEN-FM in St. Louis.

Jackson was born in Wauhomis, Oklahoma on September 5, 1943. He received a B.S. degree from the University of Missouri at Rolla in 1967 and an M.S. from Columbia University in 1971.

Jackson serves on the boards of directors of the National Association of Broadcasters, the Council of Concerned Black Executives, Freedom National Bank, and Trans Africa (1977). He was a member of the Council on Foreign Relations in 1978 and on the board of governors of the International Radio and Television Society from 1974 to 1976.

From 1969 to 1971, Jackson directed major industry programs for the Interracial Council for Business Opportunity in New York City. He was a production and project engineer for the Black Economic Union in New York City from 1968 to 1969 and an industrial engineer for Colgate-Palmolive from 1967 to 1968.

John H. Johnson (1918-)
Publisher, Media Executive

One of America's foremost businessmen, John H. Johnson sits at the head of the most prosperous and powerful black publishing company in the United States. Beginning with *Negro Digest* in 1942, and following with *Ebony* in 1945, Johnson built a chain of journalistic successes that now also includes *Jet*, *Ebony Jr.*, and *EM: Ebony Man*.

Born in Arkansas City, Arkansas, on January 19, 1918, Johnson, at age six, lost his father, a mill worker, and was raised by his mother and stepfather. His segregated schooling was obtained locally until the family moved to Chicago. Johnson attended DuSable High School in Chicago, excelling academically and in extracurricular activities, writing for the yearbook and school paper.

After graduation, an insurance executive heard a speech delivered by Johnson, and was so impressed he offered him a partial scholarship at the University of Chicago. After two years, however, Johnson quit classes, although he entered the Northwestern School of Commerce in 1938, studying for an additional two years before joining the Supreme Liberty Life Insurance Company. While running the company's house organ, it occurred to Johnson that a digest of weekly or monthly gathered news items of special interest and importance to the black community might achieve a wide black

John H. Johnson

readership. The idea resulted in the creation of *Negro Digest*, a periodical containing both news reprints and feature articles. Of the latter, perhaps the most beneficial to circulation was Eleanor Roosevelt's contribution, "If I Were a Negro."

Buoyed by success, Johnson decided to approach the market with yet another offering, a pictorial magazine patterned after *Life*. The first issue of *Ebony* sold out its press run of 25,000 copies and soon became a permanent staple in the world of journalism as large companies began to advertise regularly in it.

In addition to serving as president and publisher of Johnson Publishing Company, Inc., Johnson is chairman and chief executive officer of Supreme Life Insurance Company, chairman of WJPC–AM in Chicago, and president of Fashion Fair Cosmetics. He has served on the boards of directors of the Greyhound Corporation, Verex Corporation, Marina Bank, Supreme Life Insurance Company, and Zenith Radio Corporation. Johnson also serves as a trustee for the Art Institute of Chicago and United Negro College Fund; on the advisory council of the Harvard Graduate School of Business; as a director for the Chamber of Commerce of the United States; on the advertising council of Junior Achievement, and Chicago USO. He has received honorary doctoral degrees from numerous colleges and universities, and many honors and awards from civil and professional organizations.

In 1993, Johnson wrote *Succeeding Against the Odds: The Autobiography of a Great American Business*.

Robert L. Johnson (1946-)
Cable Television Executive

Born on April 8, 1946, in Hickory, Illinois, Robert L. Johnson worked for the Washington, DC, Urban League, the Corporation for Public Broadcasting, and as a press secretary, before joining the National Cable Television Association in 1976. While serving as vice president of government relations for the association, Johnson came up with the idea of creating a cable channel aimed at black viewers. In 1979, he took out a $15,000 personal loan to start Black Entertainment Television (BET). BET has evolved into an extremely popular twenty-four hour cable station with shows that cater to the interests of African Americans. In 1994, in cooperation with Blockbuster Entertainment, Johnson announced the creation of two new film production ventures, BET Pictures and BET Films.

In addition to running BET, Johnson functions as the publisher of the magazines *Emerge* and *YSB: Young Sisters and Brothers* and operates a radio network. He serves as a board member of the Cable Television Advertising Bureau and has been awarded the Pioneer award by the Capitol Press Club (1984) and the Business of the Year award by the Washington, DC, Chamber of Commerce in 1985.

Clarence B. Jones (1931-)
Publishing Executive

Born in Philadelphia in 1931, Jones graduated from Columbia University and Boston University Law School and then practiced as an attorney, specializing in civil rights and copyright cases for a New York City law firm. During this period, he was counsel for Dr. Martin Luther King Jr. and the Southern Christian Leadership Conference. In 1968 and again in 1972, he served as a delegate from New York State to the Democratic Convention. Jones was also an observer at Attica prison during the uprising there in 1971.

In 1971, Jones, as head of Inner City Broadcasting, led a group of investors in the purchase of the New York *Amsterdam News*, the nation's largest black newspaper. Inner City Broadcasting also owned radio station WLIB and has full ownership of WBLS-FM.

Delano Lewis (1938-)
Business and Broadcasting Executive

Born in Arkansas City, Kansas on November 12, 1938, Delano Eugene Lewis grew up in Kansas City, Kansas. He received his bachelor's degree in political science and history from the University of Kansas in 1960 and a law degree from Washburn School of Law in 1963. Fresh out of law school, Lewis became one of only ten African American attorneys in the U.S. Department of Justice in

Washington, DC. After two years, he took a post with the Equal Employment Opportunity Commission (EEOC), and after only one year, in 1966, he volunteered for the Peace Corps and was sent to Nigeria and Uganda. Returning from Africa in 1969, Lewis worked as legislative assistant to various senators and congressmen and donated his time to advisory boards and community service organizations.

In 1973, Lewis left government and joined the private sector. He started as public affairs manager for Chesapeake and Potomac Telephone Company, where he became vice president in 1983 and later president in 1988 and CEO in 1990. He vaulted from the top of the telephone company to the role of president and CEO of National Public Radio (NPR) in 1994. Also in 1994, Lewis was named to the National Information Infrastructure (NII) to develop policies for America's Internet. On his way to his position at NPR, Lewis has served on many boards of directors, such as the Greater Washington Board of Trade, the Eugene and Agnes Meyer Foundation, Mainstream, Africare, Washington Performing Arts Society, and D.C. Vocational Education and Career Opportunities Commission. Lewis was named "Washingtonian of the Year" by *Washingtonian* magazine in 1978. He was named to the Sovereign Military Order of Malta in 1987 and was awarded the President's Medal from Catholic University in 1978.

Haki R. Madhubuti (1942-)
Publisher, Poet, Writer

Born Don Luther Lee in Little Rock, Arkansas, in 1942, Madhubuti has studied at Wilson Junior College, Roosevelt University, and the University of Illinois. He received an associate's degree from Chicago City College in 1966 and a master of fine arts degree from the University of Iowa in 1984. His published works include *Think Black*; *Black Pride*; *For Black People (and Negroes Too)*; *Don't Cry, Scream*; *We Walk the Way of the New World*; *Directionscore: Selected and New Poems*; *Book of Life*; *Enemies: The Clash of Races*; *Killing Memory: Seeking Ancestors*; and *Black Men: Obsolete, Single, Dangerous?*. He has taught and served as writer–in–residence at numerous universities, including Chicago State University, Cornell, Howard, Morgan State, and the University of Illinois.

Madhubuti was one of the founding members of the Organization of Black American Culture, Writers' Workshop, and has served as vice chairperson of the African Liberation Day Support Committee and on the executive council of the Congress of African People.

Currently, Madhubuti is director of the Institute of Positive Education in Chicago, publisher and editor of Third World Press, president of the African–American

Publishers and Booksellers, and Writers' Association, and the operator of a chain of book stores.

The Third World Press, founded by Madhubuti in 1967, has published numerous titles by African–American writers, including Frances Cress–Welsing's *The Isis Papers: The Keys to the Colors*, and Chancellor Williams' *The Destruction of Black Civilization*.

Madhubuti has won several awards, including the DuSable Museum Award for Excellence in Poetry, National Council of Teachers of English Award, the Sidney R. Yates Arts Advocate Award, and the African Heritage Studies Association citation.

John Henry Murphy (1840-1922)
Publisher

John Henry Murphy was born a slave in Baltimore, Maryland, in 1840. He became superintendent of Bethel African Methodist Episcopal Church and founded the Sunday school newspaper, the *Sunday School Helper*. In 1892 he purchased the *Baltimore Afro-American* for $200. By 1922 the *Afro-American* had reached a circulation of 14,000, becoming the largest black newspaper in the Northeast.

At first, Murphy set the paper's type himself, having acquired this skill during his forties. Throughout, he insisted that his paper maintain political and editorial independence. Murphy died April 5, 1922. The paper grew and is now under the helm of Murphy's great-nephew, John H. Murphy III.

Norma Quarles (1936-)
Television News Correspondent

Born in New York City in 1936, Norma Quarles is an alumnus of Hunter College and City College of New York. She first worked as a buyer for a New York specialty shop before moving to Chicago where she became a licensed real estate broker.

In 1965 she began her broadcast career in Chicago at WSDM Radio, working as a news reporter and disk jockey. She later returned to New York where she joined NBC in 1966 for a one-year training program. After three years with WKYC-TV in Cleveland, she was transferred to WNBC–TV in 1970. In 1978, Quarles moved to NBC News as a correspondent based in Chicago. She had been producing and reporting the "Urban Journal" series for WMAQ-TV for a year at that time. Before joining WMAQ, Quarles was an award-winning reporter for WNBC-TV in New York, where she also anchored the early local news broadcasts during the "Today" show. In 1988 Quarles left NBC, after twenty-one years, to join Cable News Network's New York bureau. Quarles served as a daytime anchor at CNN until 1990, when she became a correspondent.

John Henry Murphy

Quarles is a member of the National Academy of Television Arts and Sciences, National Association of Broadcast Journalists, Sigma Delta Chi, and a board member of the Governor's National Academy of Television Arts and Sciences. In 1990, Quarles was inducted into the National Association of Black Journalists Hall of Fame.

Dudley Randall (1914-)
Publisher, Poet, Librarian

Dudley Randall was born in Washington, DC, on January 14, 1914 and was living in Detroit by the time he was nine years old. An early harbinger of Randall's poetic talent was the appearance of one of his poems in the *Detroit Free Press* at the early age of thirteen. After serving in the United States Army Signal Corp. (1942-1946) Randall worked in the foundry at the Ford Motor Company and as a postal carrier and clerk while attending Wayne State University in Detroit. He received his B.A. in 1949 and a Master of Arts in Library Science from the University of Michigan in 1951. He has also done graduate work at the University of Ghana.

Randall worked in progressively responsible librarian positions at Lincoln University in Jefferson City, Missouri (from 1951 to 1954), Morgan State College in Baltimore, Maryland (from 1954 to 1956) and the Wayne County Federated Library System in Wayne, Michigan (1956 to 1969). From 1969 to 1975 he was a reference librarian and poet-in-residence at the University of Detroit. In 1969 he also served as a visiting lecturer at

Norma Quarles

1966. He continues writing today as a nationally syndicated columnist.

Raspberry has also appeared as a television panelist and commentator and in 1965 was named Journalist of the Year by the Capital Press Club for his coverage of the Los Angeles Watts riot. He is generally regarded as an independent thinker holding to no particular orthodoxy. His 1991 book *Looking Backward at Us*, like much of his other writings, deals with the African–American experience and social conditions and race relations in the United States.

Raspberry has taught journalism at Howard University and the University of Maryland School of Journalism. He is also a member of the Poynter Institute for Media Studies board of advisors and the Pulitzer Prize Board, Grid Iron Club, Capitol Press Club, Washington Association of Black Journalists, and Kappa Alpha Psi. Raspberry won the Pulitzer Prize in 1994.

Max Robinson (1939-1988)
Television News Correspondent

Born in Richmond, Virginia, on May 1, 1939, Max Robinson attended Oberlin College, Virginia Union University, and Indiana University. He began his career as a newsreader at WTOV-TV in Portsmouth, Virginia. In 1965 he worked as a studio floor director at WTOP-TV (now WUSA) in Washington, DC, before moving on to WRC-TV, to work as a news reporter, and to WTOP-TV, where he worked as anchor.

In 1978 Robinson joined ABC "World News Tonight," becoming the first black network anchor. Almost immediately, Robinson took it upon himself to fight racism at whatever cost necessary. ABC management became frustrated with Robinson and moved him to the post of weekend anchor. In 1983 Robinson left ABC for WMAQ-TV in Chicago, where he remained until 1985.

Robinson died of complications from acquired immune deficiency syndrome (AIDS) on December 20, 1988, in Washington, DC. He was the recipient of three Emmy awards, the Capital Press Club Journalist of the Year Award, and the Ohio State Award, as well as an award from the National Education Association. He also taught at Federal City College, in Washington, DC, and the College of William and Mary, in Williamsburg, Virginia.

Carl Thomas Rowan (1925-)
Commentator, Journalist

Carl Rowan was born August 11, 1925 in Ravenscroft, Tennessee. He attended Tennessee A&I (now Tennessee State University) in Nashville and Washburn University in Topeka, Kansas. He received his bachelor of arts degree from Oberlin College in 1947; in 1948 he received a master of arts degree from the University of Minnesota.

the University of Michigan. Randall's love of poetry led to his founding of the *Broadside Press* and in 1980 he founded the Broadside Poets Theater and the Broadside Poetry Workshop.

Randall has been active in many Detroit cultural organizations and institutions including the Detroit Council for the Arts and the International Afro-American Museum in Detroit. In 1981 Randall received the Creative Artist Award in Literature from the Michigan Council for the Arts and in 1986 he was named the first poet laureate of Detroit.

William J. Raspberry (1935-)
Commentator, Journalist

Born in Okolona, Mississippi on October 12, 1935, Raspberry received his B.S. degree in history from Indiana Central College in 1958. While a student there he worked at the *Indianapolis Recorder* as a reporter, photographer, and editorial writer from 1956 through 1960. In 1960 Raspberry was drafted by the Army and he served as a Public Information Officer until his discharge in 1962. He began working for the *Washington Post* as a teletypist but soon worked his way up to reporter, assistant city editor and finally a columnist in

William Raspberry

Max Robinson

In 1948 he was hired as a copywriter, then later as a staff writer, by the *Minneapolis Tribune*, where he worked until 1961. In 1961 he was hired by the United States Department of State as deputy assistant secretary for public affairs. After three years with the Department of State, Rowan was appointed United States ambassador to Finland by President Lyndon Johnson in 1963, and in 1964 he was appointed director of the United States Information Agency, which operates overseas educational and cultural programs, including the worldwide radio service "Voice of America." In 1965 Rowan resigned from the USIA to work as a columnist for the Chicago Sun Times.

He has authored several books, including *South of Freedom, Wait Till Next Year, Between Us Blacks, Dream Makers, Dream Breakers: The World of Justice Thurgood Marshall*, and a memoir entitled *Breaking Barriers*. He is a syndicated columnist, and his work appears in numerous newspapers across the country.

Rowan has served as a political commentator for the Post-Newsweek Broadcasting Company, and has been a frequent panelist on the NBC program "Meet the Press" and the syndicated programs "Agronsky & Co." and "Inside Washington."

Rowan is the founder of the Project Excellence program, a scholarship program for African American high school students. Scholarships are awarded to students who embrace academic achievement and resist negative peer pressure.

John B. Russwurm (1799-1851)
Newspaper Publisher

Born in Port Antonio, Jamaica, on October 1, 1799, Russwurm graduated from Bowdoin College in Brunswick, Maine in 1826. From Brunswick, Russwurm moved to New York, where on March 16, 1827, he and Samuel E. Cornish published the first edition of Freedom's Journal—the nation's first African-American newspaper.

In 1829 Russwurm decided to immigrate to Monrovia, Liberia. From 1830 to 1835 he published the *Liberia Herald*. Cornish, who had left the paper in late 1827, resumed his role as editor in 1830, publishing the paper under the name *Rights of All*.

Russwurm went on to serve as superintendent of education in Monrovia, and later as governor of a settlement. He died June 17, 1851.

Carl Rowan

John Herman Henry Sengstacke (1912-)
Publishing Executive

A nephew of the great publisher Robert Abbott, John Sengstacke was born in Savannah, Georgia, on November 25, 1912. He received a B.A. from Hampton Institute in 1933. Upon graduation, he went to work with Robert Abbott, attended school to learn printing, and wrote editorials and articles for three Abbott papers. In 1934, he became vice president and general manager of the company.

During World War II, Sengstacke was an advisor to the United States Office of War Information, during a period of severe tension between the government and black press. He also presided over the Chicago rationing board.

In 1940, after the death of his uncle, Sengstacke became president of the Robert S. Abbott Publishing Company. In 1956, Sengstacke founded the *Daily Defender*, one of only three black dailies in the country. In 1940 he founded the Negro Newspaper Publishers Association, now known as the National Newspaper Publishers Association, and served six terms as president. Today he is president of *Tri-State Defender*, Inc., *Florida Courier* Publishing Company, New *Pittsburgh Courier* Publishing Company, and Amalgamated Publishers, Inc., and chairman of *Michigan Chronicle* Publishing Company and Sengstacke Enterprises, Inc., and treasurer of Chicago Defender Charities, Inc.

Sengstacke has served in leadership positions with many professional, educational, and civic organizations, received a number of presidential appointments, and is the recipient of several academic awards. He has been trustee of Bethune-Cookman College, chairman of the board of Provident Hospital and Training School Association, member of the board of directors of the American Society of Newspaper Editors, on the advisory board of the Boy Scouts of America, and a principal in Chicago United.

Bernard Shaw (1940-)
Television News Anchor

Bernard Shaw was born on May 22, 1940, in Chicago. He is the Washington anchor for the Cable News Network (CNN). He was on board as anchor from the Washington desk at CNN when that cable network went on the air on June 1, 1980. Shaw has often reported first-hand on major international news stories. He was present when the Chinese government's tanks rolled into Tiananmen Square in May 1989, crushing the student-led pro-democracy movement. In January of 1991, Shaw, along with two other colleagues from CNN, were stranded in Baghdad when allied bombing attacks launched Operation Desert Storm. From their hotel room, Shaw and the others provided first-hand accounts of the bombing raid on the city.

Shaw's first job as a television journalist came in 1971 with CBS News at their Washington bureau where he conducted an exclusive interview with Attorney General John Mitchell at the height of the Watergate scandal. In 1977 he left CBS to join ABC News as Miami bureau chief and Latin American correspondent. Shaw was one of the first reporters to file from location on the Jonestown massacre story in Guyana and he and his team provided the only aerial photos of the mass suicide-murder site. ABC sent Shaw to Iran to report on the 1979 hostage crisis in at the American Embassy in Teheran. He then returned to Washington as ABC's senior Capitol Hill correspondent.

Prior to joining CBS News, Shaw was a reporter for Group W, Westinghouse Broadcasting Company, based first in Chicago and then in Washington (1966-1971). Shaw served as Group W's White House correspondent during the last year of the Johnson Administration (1968). His other assignments included local and national urban affairs, the struggles of the Mexican Americans and Puerto Ricans, and the plight of the American Indians in Billings, Montana. In 1968, he reported on the aftermath of the assassination of Dr. Martin Luther King Jr. in Memphis and his funeral in Atlanta.

Carole Simpson (1940-)
Television News Anchor

Born in Chicago on December 7, 1940, Carole Simpson graduated from the University of Michigan with a bache-

Bernard Shaw

lor of arts degree in journalism and did graduate work in journalism at the University of Iowa. She first entered broadcasting in 1965 as a reporter for a local radio station, WCFL, in Morris, Illinois. In 1968 she moved to radio station WBBM in Chicago and in 1970 she went to work as a reporter for the Chicago television station WMAQ.

Simpson made her first network appearance as a substitute anchor for NBC "Nightly News" in 1974 and as anchor on NBC's "Newsbreak" on weekends. In 1982 Simpson joined ABC in Washington as a general assignment correspondent. She is currently an ABC News correspondent and weekend anchor.

Simpson has served as president of the Radio and Television Correspondents Association, as chairperson of the ABC Women's Advisory Board, as a member of the board of directors of the Washington Chapter of the Society of Professional Journalists, and is a member of Theta Sigma Phi, the Radio Televison News Directors Association, and the National Association of Black Journalists. She has been awarded the Media Journalism Award, the Milestone Award in Broadcast Journalism from the National Commission of Working Women, and the Silver Bell Award from the Ad Council. In 1992,

Simpson was named Journalist of the Year by the National Association of Black Journalists.

Barbara Smith (1946-)
Publisher, Editor, Writer

Barbara Smith was born on November 16, 1946 in Cleveland, Ohio. She earned a bachelor's degree from Mount Holyoke College in 1968 and a master's degree from the University of Pittsburgh in 1971. She served as an instructor at the University of Massachusetts from 1976 until 1981, Barnard College in 1983, and New York University in 1985. Together with Myrna Bain, Cherrie Moraga,and Mariana Romo–Carmona, Smith operates Kitchen Table: Women of Color Press, the first publisher in the United States committed to publishing and distributing the work of third world women.

Smith has co–authored and co–edited numerous books, including *Yours in Struggle, Three Feminist Perspectives on Anti–Semitism and Racism, Home Girls, A Black Feminist Anthology, But Some of Us Are Brave*, and *Black Women's Studies*.

Chuck Stone (1924-)
Journalist, Educator

Chuck Stone was born in 1924 into a family that initially lived in luxury surroundings due to his father's executive position with a hair-care company; however, alcoholism resulted in divorce and Stone's mother moved him and his three younger sisters to Connecticut. After high school, he enrolled in the famed Tuskegee training program for African American bomber pilots during World War II and became a navigator with the U.S. Air Corps. After the war's end, Stone earned degrees from Wesleyan University and the University of Chicago, and for a time worked with an international development agency in Africa.

In 1959 Stone entered the profession of journalism with his hire at the *New York Age*, a Harlem paper. Within a short time he had become its editor as well as launched a career noted for outspoken opinions. During the early 1960s he became the White House correspondent for the *Washington Afro-American*, for which he often wrote critically of the Kennedy Administration's lack of progress on civil rights issues. Stone later spent time at the *Chicago Daily Defender*, a stint also notable for his signing on with a local television station in 1964, which made him the first African American to provide on-air news commentary in the country.

In 1965 Stone joined the staff of Adam Clayton Powell, Jr., the controversial Harlem activist who was then serving as a member of the U.S. House of Representatives. When Powell's political career ended amid charges of misuse of public funds two years later, Stone chan-

Carole Simpson

neled his feelings of anger toward the white political establishment in the fictional chronicle of Powell, *King Strut*. It would be Stone's third book, after the 1968 collection of his newspaper columns, *Tell It Like It Is*, and 1970's *Black Power in America*.

Stone became a regular columnist for the *Philadelphia Daily News* in 1972, and spent the next several years lambasting the city's corrupt political machinery and heavy-handed police force. Equal in his criticisms unleashed first at the administration of former cop Frank Rizzo, and later at the city's first African American mayor, Wilson Goode, Stone's columns—which continued on after he was made senior editor in 1979—made him both a revered and feared civic personage. In an unusual development, his condemnations of police brutality toward Philadelphia's African American citizenry often prompted suspects to turn themselves in at the columnist's home or office first and wait for authorities to arrest them there.

After nearly two decades Stone resigned from the *Philadelphia Daily News* to pursue his career in academia further, in 1991 becoming the Walter Spearman Professor at the University of North Carolina at Chapel Hill's School of Journalism and Mass Communication.

His column continues to live on, syndicated nationally to over a hundred newspapers, and in the spring of 1996 Stone honored with the Missouri Honor Medal for Distinguished Service in Journalism from the University of Missouri; he joined an impressive roster of past recipients that included Walter Kronkite and Charlayne Hunter-Gault. Stone was also selected to be a torch carrier for the Olympic flame that journied across the nation before the opening of the 1996 Summer Games in Atlanta, Georgia.

Pierre Montea Sutton (1947-)
Broadcast Executive

Pierre Sutton is president of Inner City Broadcasting Corporation in New York City and president of its radio stations in New York and California. He is the son of Percy E. Sutton, chairman of the board of Inner City Broadcasting and former borough president of Manhattan.

Pierre Sutton was born in New York City on February 1, 1947. He received a B.A. degree from the University of Toledo in 1968 and attended New York University in 1972. He began his career in 1971 as vice president of Inner City Research and Analysis Corporation, was executive editor of the *New York Courier* newspaper in 1971-1972, served a public affairs director for WLIB radio from 1972 to 1975, was vice president of Inner City Broadcasting from 1975 to 1977, and became president in 1977. He has served as a board member of the Minority Investment Fund, first vice president of the National Association of Black Owned Broadcasters, chairman of the Harlem Boy Scouts, member of the board and executive committee of the New York City Marathon, trustee of the Alvin Ailey Dance Foundation, board member of the Better Business Bureau of Harlem, and member of the board of the Hayden Planetarium.

Susan L. Taylor (1946-)
Editor

Susan Taylor was born in New York City on January 23, 1946 in New York City and received a bachelor of arts degree from Fordham University. Since 1981, Susan Taylor has been editor–in–chief of *Essence*, a magazine established in 1970 for black women.

A former actress, cosmetologist, and founder of her own cosmetics company, Nequai Cosmetics, Taylor began her relationship with *Essence* magazine as a free–lance writer. In 1971 she became the magazine's beauty editor; from 1971 to 1980 she served as fashion and beauty editor. Taylor, as editor–in–chief, is also executive coordinator of Essence Communications.

Taylor is author of the "In the Spirit" column in *Essence* magazine. In 1993, she wrote a book entitled *In the Spirit: The Inspirational Writings of Susan Taylor*.

Lem Tucker (1938-1991)
Television News Correspondent

Born in 1938 in Saginaw, Michigan, Lemuel Tucker was a graduate of Central Michigan University. Tucker worked as a Washington bureau correspondent for CBS news from 1977 until 1988. Prior to that he was with ABC News as New York City correspondent, from 1972 until 1977. From 1965 through 1972, Tucker was with NBC News where he served for some of that time as assistant bureau chief in Vietnam. He was awarded an Emmy for his reporting on hunger in the United States, a series of seven reports broadcast during 1968 and 1969. He died in March of 1991 in Washington, DC.

◆ PUBLISHERS

Afram Press
PO Box 2262
Philadelphia, PA 19101
(609) 871-6992

Susan Taylor

Africa Fund
198 Broadway, 4th Fl.
New York, NY 10038
(212) 964-8570

Africa World Press, Inc.
PO Box 1892
Trenton, NJ 08607
(609) 771-1666
Fax:(609) 844-0198

African-American Institute
833 United Nations Plaza
New York, NY 10017
(212) 949-5666

African and Caribbean Imprint Library Services
236 Main St.
Falmouth, MA 02540
(508)540-5378
Fax:(508) 548-6801

Lem Tucker

African Studies Association Press
Credit Union Bldg.
Emory University
Atlanta, GA 30322
(404) 329-6410
Fax:(404) 329-6433

Africana Publishing Co.
160 Broadway, East Bldg.
New York, NY 10038
(212) 374-0100
Fax:(212) 374-1313

Afro-Am Publishing/Distributing Co., Inc.
1909 W. 95th St.
Chicago, IL 60643
(312)791-1611

Akili Books of America
PO Box 1291
South Gate, CA 90280
(213) 635-7191

Amen-Ra Publishing Co.
PO Box 328642
Columbus, OH 43232
(614)863-5189
Fax:(614) 445-8373

Ankh Enterprises
7850 Sunset Blvd., No. 105
Los Angeles, CA 90046
(213)850-7203

Arts and Communications Network Inc.
PO Box 435
Rosendale, NY 12472
(914) 687-0767
Fax:(914) 687-0267

Asante Publications
218 Main St., No. 425
Kirkland, WA 98033-6199
(619) 287-7926

Associated Publishers, Inc.
1407 14th St. NW
Washington, DC 20005-3704
(202) 265-1441
Fax:(202) 328-8677

Association of Caribbean Universities and Research Institutes
PO Box 11532
Caparra Heights Station
San Juan, Puerto Rico 00922
(809) 764-0000

Aye-Aye Press
31 Queen St.
PO Box 1122
Christiansted, VI 00821
(809) 778-8465
Fax:(809) 778-8465

Balamp Publishing
4205 Fullerton
Detroit, MI 48238
(313) 491-1950

Beckham House Publishers, Inc.
PO Box 8008
Silver Spring, MD 20907
(301) 384-7995
Fax:(301) 384-7995

Benin Press Ltd.
5225 S. Blackstone Ave.
Chicago, IL 60615
(312) 643-2363

Benin Publishing Co.
802 Columbus Dr.
Teaneck, NJ 07666
(201) 837-8641

Black Classic Press
PO Box 13414
Baltimore, MD 21203
(410) 358-0980
Fax:(410) 358-0987

Black Economic Research Team Inc.
PO Box 13513
Baltimore, MD 21203
(410) 366-7668

Black Entrepreneurs Press
4502 S. Congress Ave., Ste. 254
Austin, TX 78744
(512) 444-9962

Black Graphics International
PO Box 732, Linwood Station
Detroit, MI 48206
(313) 890-1128

Black Resource Guide, Inc.
501 Oneida Pl. NW
Washington, DC 20011
(202) 291-4373
Fax:(202) 291-4373

Blacklight Fellowship
128 S. Paulina St.
Chicago, IL 60612
(312) 563-0081
Fax:(312) 563-0086

Broadside Press
PO Box 04257
Detroit, MI 48204
(313) 934-1231
Fax:(313) 934-1231

Calaloux Publications
PO Box 812028
Wellesley, MA 02181-0012
(617) 237-2230

Carib House (USA)
11305 Goleta St.
Los Angeles, CA 91342
(818) 890-1056

Carver Publishing, Inc.
PO Box 9353
Hampton, VA 23670-0353
(804) 838-1244

Charill Publishers
4468 San Francisco Ave.
St. Louis, MO 63115
(314) 382-4998
Fax:(314) 531-2627

Communicators Press
3636 Georgia Ave., Ste. B2
Washington, DC 20011
(202) 726-8618
Fax:(202) 291-9149

Detroit Black Writers' Guild, Inc.
5601 W. Warren
Detroit, MI 48210
(313) 897-2551

Duncan and Duncan, Inc.
2809 Pulaski Hwy.
Edgewood, MD 21040
(410) 538-5579
Fax:(410) 538-5584

Essai Seay Publications
PO Box 55
East St. Louis, IL 62202-0055
(618) 271-7890

Famous Black Quotations
PO Box 64898
Chicago, IL 60664
(312) 667-2227

Freeland Publications
PO Box 18941
Philadelphia, PA 19119
(215) 226-2507

Gumbs and Thomas Publishers, Inc.
142 W. 72nd St., Ste. 9
New York, NY 10023
(212) 769-8022
Fax:(212) 348-5449

Heritage Press
PO Box 18625
Baltimore, MD 21216
(410) 728-8521

Holloway House Publishing Co.
8060 Melrose Ave.
Los Angeles, CA 90046
(213) 653-8060
Fax:(213) 655-9452

Institute for Southern Studies
2009 Chapel Hill Rd.
PO Box 531
Durham, NC 27702
(919) 419-8311
Fax:(919) 419-8315

Joint Center for Political and Economic Studies
1090 Vermont Ave. NW, Ste. 1100
Washington, DC 20005-4961
(202) 789-3500
Fax:(202) 789-6391

Just Us Books, Inc.
356 Gleenwood Ave., 3rd Fl.
East Orange, NJ 07017
(201) 672-7701
Fax:(201) 677-7570

Kitchen Table: Women of Color Press
PO Box 40-4920
Brooklyn, NY 12140
(718) 935-1082
Fax:(718) 935-1107

M.L. Williams Publishing Co., Inc.
PO Box 53552
1315 Walnut St., Ste. 1624
Philadelphia, PA 19105
(215) 735-1121
Fax:(215) 471-4550

Majority Press
PO Box 538
Dover, MA 02030
(508) 655-5636
Fax:(508) 655-1631

National Center for Urban Ethnic Affairs
PO Box 20
Washington, DC 20064
(202) 232-3600

New Day Press, Inc.
Karamu House
2355 E. 89th St.
Cleveland, OH 44106
(216) 795-7070

The Noble Press
213 W. Institute Pl., Ste. 508
Chicago, IL 60610
(312) 642-1168

Omenana
25 Huntington Ave., No. 302A
Boston, MA 02116
(617) 445-0161

Open Hand Publishing Inc.
PO Box 22048
Seattle, WA 98122
(206) 323-2187
Fax:(206) 323-2188

Path Press, Inc.
53 W. Jackson Blvd., Ste. 724
Chicago, IL 60604
(312) 663-0167
Fax:(312) 663-5318

Raw Ink Press
Southwest Sta., PO Box 70417
Washington, DC 20024-0417
(202) 686-4686

Red Sea Press, Inc.
15 Industry Ct.
Trenton, NJ 08638
(609) 771-1666
Fax:(609) 771-1616

Shamal Books, Inc.
GPO Box 16
New York, NY 10116

Third World Press
PO Box 19730
Chicago, IL 60619
(312) 651-0700
Fax:(312) 651-7286

Universal Black Writer Press
PO Box 5, Radio City Sta.
New York, NY 10101-0005

Urban Research Press, Inc.
840 E. 87th St.
Chicago, IL 60619
(312) 994-7200
Fax:(312) 994-5191

WREE (Women for Racial and Economic Equality)
198 Broadway, Rm. 606
New York, NY 10038
(212) 385-1103

◆ NEWSPAPERS

Alabama

Birmingham Times
The Birmingham Times Publishing Co.
115 3rd Ave. W
PO Box 10503
Birmingham, AL 35202
(205) 251-5158
Circulation: 10,350

Birmingham World
407 15th St. N
Birmingham, AL 35203-1877
(205) 251-6523
Fax:(205) 328-6729
Circulation: 12,600

Campus Digest
Tuskegee University
Tuskegee, AL 36083
(205) 727-8263

Greene County Democrat
Greene County Newspaper Co.
214 Boligee St.
PO Box 598
Eutaw, AL 35462
(205) 372-3373
Fax:(205) 372-2243
Circulation: 3,500

Inner City News
Inner City Enterprises, Inc.
PO Box 1545
Mobile, AL 36633-1545
(334) 452-9329
Fax:(334) 452-9330
Circulation: 8,000

Mobile Beacon
2311 Costarides St.
PO Box 1407
Mobile, AL 36633
(205) 479-0629
Circulation: 4,952

Montgomery-Tuskegee Times
880 S. Court St., Ste. A
Montgomery, AL 36104
(205) 262-5026
Circulation: 10,000

The New Times
The New Times Group, Inc.
156 S. Broad St.
Mobile, AL 36602-0356
(205) 432-0356
Fax:(205) 432 8320
Circulation: 5,150

Shoals News Leader
PO Box 427
Florence, AL 35631
(205) 766-5542
Circulation: 10,000

Speakin' Out News
2006 Poole Ave. NW, Ste. A
PO Box 2826
Huntsville, AL 35804
(205) 852-9449
Fax:(205) 852-9484
Circulation: 16,500

Arizona

Arizona Informant
1746 E. Madison, No. 2
Phoenix, AZ 85034
(602) 257-9300
Fax:(602) 257-0547
Circulation: 1,800

Arkansas

Arkansas State Press
PO Box 164037
Little Rock, AR 72216
(501) 371-9991
Circulation: 5,000

California

Bakersfield News Observer
1219 20th St.
Bakersfield, CA 93301
(805) 324-9466
Fax:(805) 324-9472

Alameda Publishing Corp., Berkeley Tri City Post
The Alameda Publishing Corp.
PO Box 1350
Oakland, CA 94604
(510) 763-1120
Fax:(510) 763-9670
Circulation: 20,000

Black Voice News
PO Box 1581
Riverside, CA 92502
(909) 682-6070
Fax:(909) 276-0877
Circulation: 7,500

California Advocate
452 Fresno St.
PO Box 11826
Fresno, CA 93775
(209) 268-0941
Fax:(209) 266-6947
Circulation: 22,500

California Voice
2956 Sacramento St., Ste. C
Berkeley, CA 94702
(510) 644-2446
Circulation: 37,325

Carson Bulletin
Rapid Publishing
349 W. Compton
PO Box 4248
Compton, CA 90224
(213) 774-0018
Circulation: 17,000

Central Star/Journal Wave
Central News-Wave Publications
2621 W. 54th St.
Los Angeles, CA 90043
(213) 290-3000
Fax:(213) 291-0219
Circulation: 35,292

Compton/Carson Wave
Central News-Wave Publications
2621 W. 54th St.
Los Angeles, CA 90043
(213) 290-3000
Fax:(213) 291-0219
Circulation: 40, 183

Compton Bulletin
Rapid Publishing
349 W. Compton
PO Box 4248
Compton, CA 90224
(213) 774-0018
Circulation: 22,000

Compton Metropolitan Gazette
First-Line Publishers
17939 Chatsworth St., Ste. 429
Granada Hills, CA 91344
(818) 782-8695
Fax:(818) 782-2924
Circulation: 60,000

Culver City Star
Central News-Wave Publications
2621 W. 54th St.
Los Angeles, CA 90043
(213) 290-3000
Fax:(213) 291-0219
Circulation: 25,827

Firestone Park News/Southeast News Press
PO Box 19027A
Los Angeles, CA 90019
(213) 291-9486
Fax:(213) 291-2123
Circulation: 24,000

Herald Dispatch
4053 Marlton Ave.
PO Box 19027A
Los Angeles, CA 90008
(213) 291-9486
Fax:(213) 291-2123
Circulation: 35,000

Inglewood/Hawthorne Wave
Central News-Wave Publications
2621 W. 54th St.
Los Angeles, CA 90043
(213) 290-3000
Fax:(213) 291-0219
Circulation: 45,332

Inglewood Tribune
Rapid Publishing
349 W. Compton
PO Box 4248
Compton, CA 90244
(213) 774-0018
Circulation: 10,000

L.A. Metropolitan Gazette
First-Line Publishers/L.A. Metro Group
14621 Titus St., Ste. 228
Van Nuys, CA 91402
(818) 782-8695
Circulation: 60,000

Long Beach Express
First-Line Publishers/L.A. Metro Group
17939 Chatsworth St., Ste. 249
Van Nuys, CA 91344
(818) 782-8695
Fax:(818) 782-2924
Circulation: 60,000

Los Angeles Sentinel
3800 S. Crenshaw
PO Box 11456
Los Angeles, CA 90008
(213) 299-3800
Fax:(213) 299-3890
Circulation: 28,000

Lynwood Journal
Rapid Publishing
349 W. Compton
PO Box 4248
Compton, CA 90224
(213) 774-0018

Lynwood Wave
Central News-Wave Publications
2621 W. 54th St.
Los Angeles, CA 90043
(213) 290-3000
Fax:(213) 291-0219
Circulation: 23,707

Mesa Tribune Wave
Central News-Wave Publications
2621 W. 54th St.
Los Angeles, CA 90043
(213) 290-3000
Circulation: 31,081

Metro Reporter
270 Francisco St.
San Francisco, CA 94133-2120
(415) 391-2030
Fax:(415) 391-2527
Circulation: 108,895

Metro Star
42353 47th St. W.
Quartz Hill, CA 93534

New Bayview
Double Rock Press
1624 Oakdale Ave.
PO Box 24477
San Francisco, CA 94124-0477
(310) 282-7894
Circulation: 12,000

Oakland Post
The Alameda Publishing Corp.
PO Box 1350
Oakland, CA 94604-1350
(510) 763-1120
Fax:(510) 763-9670
Circulation: 62,496

Pasadena Gazette
First-Line Publishers/L.A. Metro Group
14621 Titus St., Ste. 228
Van Nuys, CA 91402
(818) 782-8695
Fax:(818) 782-2924
Circulation: 60,000

Precinct Reporter
1677 W. Baseline St.
San Bernardino, CA 92411
(909) 889-0597
Fax:(909) 889-1706
Circulation: 55,000

Richmond Post, Alameda Publishing Corp.
The Alameda Publishing Corp.
PO Box 1350
Oakland, CA 94604-1350
(510) 763-1120
Fax:(510) 763-9670
Circulation: 21,900

Sacramento Observer
The Observer Newspapers
PO Box 817
San Leandro, CA 94577
(510) 483-7119
Circulation: 49,090

San Bernardino American News
1583 W. Baseline St.
San Bernardino, CA 92411-1756
(909) 889-7677
Fax:(909) 889-2882
Circulation: 5,000

San Diego Voice and Viewpoint
1729 N. Euclid Ave.
San Diego, CA 92105
(619) 266-2233
Fax:(619) 266-0533
Circulation: 13,000

San Fernando Gazette Express
First-Line Publishers/L.A. Metro Group
14621 Titus St., Ste. 228
Van Nuys, CA 91402
(818) 782-8695
Circulation: 60,000

San Francisco Post
The Alameda Publishing Corp.
PO Box 1350
Oakland, CA 94604-1350
(510) 763-1120
Fax:(510) 763-9670
Circulation: 18,289

Seaside Post News-Sentinel
The Alameda Publishing Corp.
1244A Broadway Ave.
PO Box 670
Seaside, CA 93955
(408) 394-6632
Circulation: 10,120

Southwest News Wave
Central News-Wave Publications
2621 W. 54th St.
Los Angeles, CA 90043
(213) 290-3000
Fax:(213) 291-0219
Circulation: 38,323

Southwest Topics/Sun Wave
Central News-Wave Publications
2621 W. 54th St.
Los Angeles, CA 90043
(213) 290-3000
Circulation: 30,000

Sun-Reporter
Reporter Publications
1366 Turk St.
San Francisco, CA 94115
(415) 931-5778
Circulation: 11,249

Watts Star Review
Firestone Park News/Southwest News Press
PO Box 19027A
Los Angeles, CA 90019
(213) 291-9486
Fax:(213) 291-2123
Circulation: 30,000

Wilmington Beacon
Rapid Publishing
349 W. Compton
PO Box 4248
Compton, CA 90224
(213) 774-0018

Colorado

Denver Weekly News
PO Box 38939
Denver, CO 80238-0939
(303) 839-5800
Circulation: 17,500

Hartford Inquirer
Inquiries Newspaper Group
PO Box 1260
Hartford, CT 06143
(203) 522-1462
Fax:(203) 522-3014
Circulation: 125,000

Inner-City
2 Eld St.
New Haven, CT 06511
(203) 773-0688
Circulation: 25,000

Delaware

The Defender
1702 Locust St.
Wilmington, DE 19802
(302) 656-3252
Fax:(302) 471-1130
Circulation: 15,300

District of Columbia

Metro Chronicle
529 14th St., Ste. 1143
Washington, DC 20045
(202) 347-1114

New Observer
811 Florida Ave. NW
Washington, DC 20001
(202) 232-3060
Fax:(202) 232-1711

Washington Capital Spotlight Newspaper
1264 National Press Bldg.
Washington, DC 20045
(202) 628-0700
Circulation: 60,000

Washington Informer
3117 Martin Luther King Jr.Ave. SE
Washington, DC 20032
(202) 561-4100
Fax:(202) 574-3785
Circulation: 27,000

Washington New Observer
811 Florida Ave. NW
Washington, DC 20001
(202) 232-3060
Fax:(202) 232-1711
Circulation: 20,000

Florida

Black Miami Weekly
PO Box F
Miami, FL 33147

The Bulletin
2490 Dr. M.L. King, Jr. Way
PO Box 2560
Sarasota, FL 34230-2560
(813) 953-3990
Circulation: 18,000

Capital Outlook
417 N. Duval St.
Tallahassee, FL 32301
(904) 681-1852
Fax:(904) 681-1093
Circulation: 11,333

Daytona Times
Daytona Times, Inc.
429 S. Dr. M.L. King Blvd.
PO Box 1110
Daytona Beach, FL 32115
(904) 253-0321
Fax:(904) 254-7510
Circulation: 20,150

Famuan
Florida A and M University
Tallahassee, FL 32307
(904) 599-3159
Fax:(904) 561-2570
Circulation: 5,000

Florida Sentinel-Bulletin
2207-21st Ave.
PO Box 3363
Tampa, FL 33601
(813) 248-1921
Fax:(813) 248-4507
Circulation: 23,345

Florida Star Times
PO Box 40629
Jacksonville, FL 32203
(904) 354-8880

Florida Sun Review
LMH Publications
1032 N. Pine Hills Rd.
Orlando, FL 32808
(407) 423-8146
Fax:(407) 849-1286
Circulation: 16,500

Ft. Pierce Chronicle
1527 Avenue D
Fort Pierce, FL 34950
(407) 461-7093
Circulation: 10,500

Miami Times
900 NW 54th St.
Miami, FL 33127
(305) 757-1147
Fax:(305) 757-5770
Circulation: 28,250

News Reporter
1610 N. Howard Ave.
Tampa, FL 33607
(813) 254-2608
Circulation: 9,694

Orlando Times
PO Box 555339
Orlando, FL 32855-5339
(407) 841-3710
Fax:(407) 849-0434
Circulation: 5,710

Pensacola Voice
213 E. Yonge St.
Pensacola, FL 32503
(904) 434-6963
Fax:(904) 469-8745
Circulation: 35,896

Voice of the Wildcats, Bethune-Cookman College
Bethune-Cookman College
640 2nd Ave.
Daytona Beach, FL 32115
(904) 255-1401
Fax:(904) 257-4832
Circulation: 3,000

Weekly Challenger
2500 9th St. S.
Saint Petersburg, FL 33705
(813) 896-2922
Circulation: 32,000

Westside Gazette
PO Box 5304
Fort Lauderdale, FL 33310
(305) 523-5115
Fax:(305) 522-2553
Circulation: 21,500

Georgia

Atlanta Daily World
145 Auburn Ave. NE
Atlanta, GA 30335-1201
(404) 659-1110
Circulation: 18,000

Fort Valley Herald
Atlantic Communications of Georgia, Inc.
315 N. Camellia Blvd.
PO Box 899
Fort Valley, GA 31030
(912) 822-9714
Fax:(912) 232-8666
Circulation: 6,000

Metro Courier
PO Box 2385
Augusta, GA 30903
(404)724-6556
Fax:(404) 722-7104
Circulation: 19,040

Southeastern News
PO Box 489
Cordele, GA 31015
(912) 273-6714

The Atlanta Inquirer
947 Martin Luther King Jr. Dr. NW
Atlanta, GA 30314
(404) 523-6086
Fax:(404) 523-6088
Circulation: 60,000

Atlanta Voice
633 Pryor St. SW
Atlanta, GA 30312
(404) 524-6426
Fax:(404) 523-7853
Circulation: 103,000

The Columbus Times
2230 Buena Vista Rd.
PO Box 2845
Columbus, GA 31993-2999
(706) 324-2404
Fax:(706) 596-0657
Circulation: 20,000

The Herald
PO Box 486
Savannah, GA 31402
(912) 232-4505
Circulation: 8,000

Savannah Tribune
Savannah Tribune, Inc.
916 Montgomery St.
PO Box 2066
Savannah, GA 31402
(912) 233-6128
Fax:(912) 232-8666
Circulation: 16,000

Illinois

Chatham-Southeast Citizen
Citizen Newspapers
412 E. 87th St.
Chicago, IL 60619
(312) 487-7700
Fax:(312) 487-7931
Circulation: 26,630

Chicago Crusader
Crusader Newspapers
6429 S. Martin Luther King Dr.
Chicago, IL 60637
(312) 752-2500
Fax:(312) 752-2817
Circulation: 57,000

Chicago South Shore Scene
7426 S. Constance
Chicago, IL 60649
(312) 363-0441
Circulation: 20,000

Chicago Citizen
Citizen Newspapers
412 E. 87th St.
Chicago, IL 60619
(312) 487-7700
Fax:(312) 487-7931

Chicago Independent Bulletin
2037 W. 95th St.
Chicago, IL 60643
(312) 783-1040
Circulation: 64,000

Chicago Metro News
3437 S. Indiana Ave.
Chicago, IL 60616-3840
(312) 842-5950
Circulation: 84,500

Chicago Shoreland News
AJA Enterprise
11740 S. Elizabeth
Chicago, IL 60643
(312) 568-7091
Fax:(312) 928-6056
Circulation: 38,000

Chicago Standard News
Standard Newspapers
615 S. Halsted
Chicago Heights, IL 60411
(708) 755-5021
Fax:(708) 755-5020
Circulation: 15,000

Chicago Weekend
Citizen Newspapers
412 E. 87th St.
Chicago, IL 60619
(312) 487-7700
Fax:(312) 487-7931
Circulation: 21,300

Decatur Voice
625 E. Wood St.
Decatur, IL 62523
(217) 423-2231
Fax:(217) 423-2231
Circulation: 19,000

East St. Louis
10th and State St.
East Saint Louis, IL 62205
(618) 271-2000

East St. Louis Monitor
East St. Louis Monitor Publishing, Inc.
1501 State St.
Box 2137
East Saint Louis, IL 62205
(618) 271-0468
Circulation: 22,500

Hyde Park Citizen
Citizen Newspapers
412 E. 87th St.
Chicago, IL 60619
(312) 487-7700
Fax:(312) 487-7931
Circulation: 15,000

Muslim Journal
Muslim Journal Enterprises, Inc.
910 W. Van Buren St., No. 100
Chicago, IL 60607-3523
(312) 243-7600
Fax:(312) 243-9778
Circulation: 16,000

Observer
6040 S. Harper St.
Chicago, IL 60637
(312) 288-5840
Circulation: 30,000

South End Citizen
Citizen Newspapers
412 E. 87th St.
Chicago, IL 60619
(312) 487-7700
Fax:(312) 487-7931
Circulation: 25,375

South Suburban Citizen
Citizen Newspapers
412 E. 87th St.
Chicago, IL 60619
(312) 487-7700
Fax:(312) 487-7931
Circulation: 18,500

South Suburban Standard
615 S. Halsted
Chicago Heights, IL 60411
(708) 755-5021
Fax:(708) 755-5020
Circulation: 25,000

The Final Call
734 W. 79th St.
Chicago, IL 60620
(312) 602-1230
Fax:(312) 602-1013
Circulation: 600,000

Mississippi Enterprise
540 1/2 N. Farish St.
PO Box 87236
Chicago, IL 60680-0236
Circulation: 2,800

Tri-City Journal
8 S. Michigan Ave., Ste. 1111
Chicago, IL 60603
(312) 346-8123
Fax:(312) 236-2221
Circulation: 50,000

Indiana

Frost Illustrated
Frost, Inc.
3121 S. Calhoun
Fort Wayne, IN 46807-1901
(219) 745-0552
Circulation: 1,375

Gary American
2268 Broadway
Gary, IN 46407
(219) 883-4903
Circulation: 11,000

Gary New Crusader
1549 Broadway
Gary, IN 46407
(219) 885-4357
Fax:(219) 885-4359
Circulation: 27,000

Info
Info Printing and Publishing, Inc.
PO Box M 587
Gary, IN 46401
(219) 882-5591
Fax:(219) 886-1090
Circulation: 21,055

Indianapolis Recorder
The George P. Stewart Printing, Inc.
2901 N. Tacoma Ave.
PO Box 18499
Indianapolis, IN 46218
(317) 924-5143
Fax:(317) 924-5148
Circulation: 10,281

Iowa

New Iowa Bystander
PO Box 762
Des Moines, IA 50303

Kansas

Kansas City Voice
2727 N. 13th St.
Kansas City, KS 66104
(913) 371-0303

Kentucky

Louisville Defender
PO Box 2557
Louisville, KY 40201
(502) 772-2591
Circulation: 2,270

Suspension Press
PO Box 2064
Covington, KY 41012
Circulation: 41,200

Louisiana

Baton Rouge Community Leader
1010 North Blvd.
Baton Rouge, LA 70802
(504) 343-0544
Circulation: 21,700

Community Leader
1210 North Blvd.
Baton Rouge, LA 70802

Louisiana Weekly
1001 Howard Ave., Ste. 2600
New Orleans, LA 70113
(504) 524-5563
Fax:(504) 527-5826
Circulation: 5,500

New Orleans Data News Weekly
Data Enterprises, Inc.
1001 Howard Ave., Ste. 2309
PO Box 51933
New Orleans, LA 70151
(504) 522-1418
Fax:(504) 523-7364
Circulation: 20,000

Alexandria News Weekly
1746 Mason
Alexandria, LA 71301
(318) 443-7664
Circulation: 13,750

Shreveport Sun
The Shreveport Sun, Inc.
PO Box 38357
Shreveport, LA 71133-8357
(318) 631-6222
Circulation: 5,000

Maryland

Baltimore Afro-American, Afro-American Co.
The Afro-American Co.
2519 N. Charles St.
Baltimore, MD 21218
(410) 554-8200
Fax:(410) 554-8213
Circulation: 12,490

Every Wednesday
The Afro-American Co.
2519 N. Charles St.
Baltimore, MD 21218
(410) 554-8200
Fax:(410) 554-8213
Circulation: 42,777

Washington Afro-American
The Afro-American Co.
628 N. Eutaw St.
Baltimore, MD 21201
(410) 728-8200
Circulation: 5,500

Massachusetts

Bay State Banner
925 Washington St.
Dorchester, MA 02124
(617) 288-4900
Circulation: 11,500

Boston Greater News
PO Box 497
Roxbury, MA 02119-0004
(617) 445-7063
Circulation: 12,300

Michigan

Ecorse Telegram
4122 10th St.
PO Box 4585
Ecorse, MI 48229
(313) 928-2955
Circulation: 12,000

Blazer News
PO Box 806
Jackson, MI 49204
(517) 787-0450
Fax:(517) 787-2907
Circulation: 6,100

Michigan Chronicle
Sengstacke Newspaper Corp.
479 Ledyard St.
Detroit, MI 48201
(313) 963-5522
Fax:(313) 963-8788
Circulation: 35,000

Michigan Citizen
New Day Publishing Enterprises
12541 2nd St.
Highland Park, MI 48203
(313) 869-0033
Circulation: 41,520

Detroit Times
B and Y Publications
11000 W. McNichols
Detroit, MI 48221
(313) 342-1717
Circulation: 20,000

The Grand Rapids Times
PO Box 7258
Grand Rapids, MI 49510
(616) 245-8737
Fax:(616) 245-1026

Michigan Sentinel
28440 Southfield Rd.
Lathrup Village, MI 48076
(313) 559-1010
Circulation: 18,000

Minnesota

Minneapolis Spokesman
3744 4th Ave. S.
Minneapolis, MN 55409
(612) 827-4021
Fax:(612) 827-0577
Circulation: 4,300

St. Paul Recorder
3744 4th Ave. S.
Minneapolis, MN 55409
(612) 827-4021

Twin Cities Courier
84 S. 6th St., Ste. 501
Minneapolis, MN 55402
(612) 332-3211

Mississippi

Jackson Advocate
Natchez Democratic Inc.
PO Box 3708
Jackson, MS 39207-3708
(601) 948-4122
Fax:(601) 948-4125
Circulation: 23,000

Mississippi Memo Digest
2511 5th St.
Box 5782
Meridian, MS 39301
(601) 693-2372
Circulation: 3,050

Missouri

Call
Kansas City Call Inc.
PO Box 410-477
Kansas City, MO 64141
(816) 842-3804
Fax:(816) 842-4420

Kansas City Globe
Jordan Communications Co., Inc.
615 E. 29th St.
PO Box 090410
Kansas City, MO 64109
(816) 531-5253
Fax:(816) 531-5256
Circulation: 30,000

Evening Whirl
Thomas Publication Co.
PO Box 5088 Nagel Sta.
Saint Louis, MO 63115
(314) 383-3875
Fax:(314) 383-7335
Circulation: 40,000

St. Louis American
American Publishing Co.
4144 Lindell Blvd., Ste. 13-5
Saint Louis, MO 63108-2927
(314) 533-8000
Fax:(314) 533-0038
Circulation: 1,442

St. Louis Argus
4595 Martin Luther King Dr.
Saint Louis, MO 63113
(314) 531-1323
Fax:(314) 361-6421
Circulation: 33,000

St. Louis Crusader
4371 Finney Ave.
Saint Louis, MO 63113
(314) 531-5860
Circulation: 9,150

St. Louis Sentinel Newspaper
Woods Publications
2900 N. Market
Saint Louis, MO 63106
(314) 531-2691
Fax:(314) 531-4442
Circulation: 23,200

Nevada

Las Vegas Sentinel-Voice
1201 S. Eastern Ave.
Las Vegas, NV 89104
(702) 383-3114
Circulation: 5,000

New Jersey

Afro-American
429 Central Ave.
East Orange, NJ 07108
(201) 672-9102

Black Voice/Carta Boricua
Rutgers University
Student Activities Center
Box 28
George St.
New Brunswick, NJ 08903
(908) 463-1626
Fax:(908) 463-1702
Circulation: 4,000

New Jersey Afro-American
PO Box 22162
Newark, NJ 07103
(201) 242-5364
Circulation: 20,000

New York

Afro-American Times
The Challenge Group
1360 Fulton St.
Brooklyn, NY 11216
(718) 636-9500
Fax:(718) 857-9115
Circulation: 55,000

Afro-Americans in New York Life and History
Afro-American Historical Association of the Niagara
    Frontier, Inc.
PO Box 63
Buffalo, NY 14207
(716) 878-4078
Circulation: 600

Amsterdam News
2340 Frederick Douglass Blvd.
New York, NY 10027
(212) 932-7400
Fax:(212) 222-3842
Circulation: 30,877

Big Red News
Smith Haj Enterprises
155 Water St., 4th Fl.
Brooklyn, NY 11201
(718) 852-6001
Circulation: 53,766

Black American
Cool Magazine, Inc.
310 Lenox Ave., No. 304
New York, NY 10027-4411
(212) 564-5110
Circulation: 352,640

Brooklyn New York Recorder
86 Bainbridge St.
Brooklyn, NY 11233
(718) 493-4616

Buffalo Criterion
623 William St.
Buffalo, NY 14206
(716) 882-9570

Buffalo Fine Print News
806 Fillmore Ave.
Buffalo, NY 14205
(716) 855-3810
Circulation: 10,000

Communicade
Okang Communications Corp.
104 Magnolia St.
PO Box 60739
Rochester, NY 14606
(716)235-6695
Circulation: 3,000

Daily Challenge
1360 Fulton St.
Brooklyn, NY 11216
(718) 636-9500
Fax:(718) 857-9115

Hudson Valley Black Press
PO Box 2160
Newburgh, NY 12550
(914) 562-1313
Circulation: 42,500

Jamaica Shopping and Entertainment Guide
North American Publications
164-11 89th Ave., Ste. 190
Jamaica, NY 11432
(718) 591-7777
Circulation: 30,000

NY Carib News
15 W. 39th St.
New York, NY 10018
(212) 944-1991
Fax:(212) 944-2089
Circulation: 71,500

The Challenger
1303 Fillmore Ave.
Buffalo, NY 14211
(716) 897-0442
Fax:(716) 897-3307
Circulation: 10,000

City Sun
The City Sun Publishing Co., Inc.
44 Court St., Ste. 307
GPO 560
Brooklyn, NY 11202
(718) 624-5959
Fax:(718) 596-7429
Circulation: 8,834

New York Voice-Harlem U.S.A.
75-43 Parsons Blvd.
Flushing, NY 11366
(718) 591-6600
Circulation: 1,624

Westchester County Press
PO Box 1631
White Plains, NY 10602
(914) 684-0006
Circulation: 20,000

Westchester Observer
542 E. 3rd St.
Mount Vernon, NY 10553

North Carolina

Carolina Peacemaker
400 Summit Ave.
Greensboro, NC 27405
(919) 274-6210
Fax:(919) 273-5103
Circulation: 5,490

Iredell County News
PO Box 407
Statesville, NC 28687
(704) 873-1054
Circulation: 5,000

Star of Zion
A.M.E. Zion Publishing House
PO Box 31005
Charlotte, NC 28231-1005
(704) 377-4329
Fax:(704) 333-1769
Circulation: 7,700

The 'M' Voice Newspaper
PO Box 8361
Greenville, NC 27834
(919) 757-0365

The Carolina Times
PO Box 3825
Durham, NC 27702
(919) 682-2913
Circulation: 5,300

The Carolinian
PO Box 25308
Raleigh, NC 27601
(919) 834-5558
Fax:(919) 832-3243
Circulation: 9,200

The Charlotte Post
1531 Camden Rd.
PO Box 30144
Charlotte, NC 28230
(704) 376-0496
Fax:(704) 342-2160
Circulation: 11,500

Fayetteville Black Times
The Black Press, Inc.
108 Webb St.
PO Box 863
Fayetteville, NC 28302

The Public Post
PO Box 1951
Laurinburg, NC 28352
(919) 875-8938

Wilmington Journal
412 S. 7th St.
PO Box 1618
Wilmington, NC 28401
(919) 762-5502
Fax:(919) 343-1334
Circulation: 8,600

Winston-Salem Chronicle
617 N. Liberty St.
PO Box 1636
Winston-Salem, NC 27102
(919) 722-8624
Fax:(919) 723-9173
Circulation: 10,000

Ohio

Call and Post
1949 E. 105 St.
Cleveland, OH 44106
(216) 791-7600
Fax:(216) 791-6568
Circulation: 43,283

Cincinnati Herald
Porter Publishing
836 Lincoln Ave.
Cincinnati, OH 45206
(513) 221-5440
Fax:(513) 221-2959
Circulation: 24,500

South East Times
3249 E. 137th St.
Cleveland, OH 44120
(216) 921-2788

Akron Reporter
1046 S. Arlington
PO Box 2042
Akron, OH 44309
(216) 773-4196
Fax:(216) 773-2992
Circulation: 17,000

Buckeye Review
William Publishing Co.
626 Belmont Ave.
Youngstown, OH 44502
(216) 743-2250
Circulation: 5,100

Toledo Journal
3021 Douglas Rd.
PO Box 2536
Toledo, OH 43606
(419) 472-4521
Fax:(419) 472-1604
Circulation: 19,000

Oklahoma

The Black Chronicle
PO Box 17498
Oklahoma City, OK 73136
(405) 424-4695
Fax:(405) 424-6708
Circulation: 28,927

Oklahoma Eagle
PO Box 3267
Tulsa, OK 74101
(918) 582-7124
Circulation: 12,800

Oregon

Portland Observer
PO Box 3137
Portland, OR 97211
(503) 288-0015
Circulation: 10,000

The Portland Skanner
Skanner Group Inc.
PO Box 5455
Portland, OR 97228-5455
(503) 287-3562
Fax:(503) 284-8200
Circulation: 20,000

Pennsylvania

New Pittsburgh Courier
Sengstac Newspapers
315 E. Carson St.
Pittsburgh, PA 15219
(412) 481-8302
Fax:(412) 481-1360
Circulation: 30,000

Philadelphia New Observer
1930 Chestnut St., Ste. 900
PO Box 30092
Philadelphia, PA 19103
(215) 665-8400
Circulation: 81,000

The Leader
The New Hope Gazette
2923 W. Cheltenham Ave.
Philadelphia, PA 19150
(215) 862-9435
Fax:(215) 968-3501
Circulation: 29,000

The Lincolnian
Lincoln University
English Dept
Lincoln University, PA 19352
(215) 932-8300
Circulation: 1,300

The Philadelphia Tribune
524-526 S. 16th St.
Philadelphia, PA 19146
(215) 893-4050
Fax:(215) 735-3612
Circulation: 33,890

Rhode Island

Ocean State Grapevine
PO Box 16333
Providence, RI 02916-0693

South Carolina

Charleston Black Times
South Carolina Black Media Group
1310 Harden
Columbia, SC 29204
(803) 799-5252
Fax:(803) 799-7709
Circulation: 6,883

Columbia Black News
South Carolina Black Media Group
PO Box 11128
Columbia, SC 29211
(803) 799-5252
Fax:(803) 799-7709
Circulation: 22,834

Florence Black Sun
1310 Harden
PO Box 11128
Columbia, SC 29204
(803) 799-5252
Fax:(803) 799-7709
Circulation: 5,734

Greenville Black Star
South Carolina Black Media Group
1310 Harden
Columbia, SC 29204
(803) 799-5252
Fax:(803) 799-7709
Circulation: 6,849

Orangeburg Black Voice
PO Box 11128
Columbia, SC 29211
(803) 799-5252
Fax:(803) 799-7709
Circulation: 5,365

Rock Kill Black View
South Carolina Black Media Group
1310 Harden
PO Box 11128
Columbia, SC 29204
(803) 799-5252
Fax:(803) 799-7709
Circulation: 5,164

Sumter Black Post
1310 Harden
Columbia, SC 29211
(803) 799-5252
Circulation: 5,355

Charleston Chronicle
Chronicle Communications Corp.
1109 King St.
PO Box 20548
Charleston, SC 29413-0548
(803) 723-2785
Fax:(803) 577-6099
Circulation: 6,000

The Coastal Times
701 E. Bay St.
BTC Box 1407
Charleston, SC 29403
(803) 723-5318
Circulation: 4,580

View South News
PO Box 1849
Orangeburg, SC 29116
(803) 531-1662
Fax:(803) 531-1662
Circulation: 5,000

Tennessee

The Catholic Mentor
Winston Derek Publishers, Inc.
PO Box 90883
Nashville, TN 37209
(615) 321-0535

Fisk News
Fisk University
1000 17th Ave. N.
Nashville, TN 37208
(615) 329-8710
Circulation: 1,000

Memphis Silver Star News
3144 Park Ave.
Memphis, TN 38111

Tri-State Defender
PO Box 2065
Memphis, TN 38101-2065
(901) 523-1818
Fax:(901) 523-1820
Circulation: 15,000

Texas

Dallas Examiner
424 Centre St.
Dallas, TX 75208
(214) 948-9175
Fax:(214) 948-9176
Circulation: 50,000

Dallas Post Tribune
2726 S. Beckley
Dallas, TX 75224
(214) 946-7678
Fax:(214) 946-6823
Circulation: 30,000

Houston Forward Times
Forward Times Publishing Co.
4411 Almeda Rd.
PO Box 8346
Houston, TX 77288-8346
(713) 526-4727
Fax:(713) 526-3170
Circulation: 52,260

Houston Informer
PO Box 3086
Houston, TX 77253
(713) 527-8261
Fax:(713) 524-7028
Circulation: 23,000

Houston Defender
PO Box 8005
Houston, TX 77288
(713) 663-7716
Fax:(713) 663-7116
Circulation: 15,000

Houston Sun
2322 Blodgett St.
PO Box 600603
Houston, TX 77260-5218
(713) 524-4474
Circulation: 80,000

Lubbock Southwest Digest
902 E. 28th St.
Lubbock, TX 79404
(806) 762-3612
Fax:(806) 762-0264
Circulation: 3,000

Dallas Weekly Newspaper
Ad-Mast Publishing, Inc.
Anthony T. Davis Bldg.
3101 Martin Luther King, Jr. Blvd.
Dallas, TX 75215
(214) 428-8958
Fax:(214) 428-2807
Circulation: 15,236

The Villager
1223-A Rosewood Ave.
Austin, TX 78702
(512) 476-0082
Fax:(512) 476-0179
Circulation: 6,000

Waco Messenger
Smith Printing Co.
PO Box 2087
Waco, TX 76703
(817) 799-6911
Circulation: 3,000

Virginia

Journal and Guide
362 Campostella Rd.
Norfolk, VA 23523-2204
(804) 625-3686
Circulation: 25,000

Richmond Afro-American
The Afro-American Co.
214 E. Clay St.
Richmond, VA 23219
(804) 649-8478
Fax:(804) 649-8477

Roanoke Tribune
PO Box 6021
Roanoke, VA 24017
(703) 343-0326
Fax:(703) 343-0326
Circulation: 5,200

Washington

Facts Newspaper
2765 E. Cherry St.
PO Box 22015
Seattle, WA 98122
(206) 324-0552
Fax:(206) 324-1007
Circulation: 42,650

Northwest Dispatch
PO Box 5637
Tacoma, WA 98405
(206) 272-7587
Circulation: 11,600

Seattle Medium
Piloven Publishing
2600 S. Jackson
Seattle, WA 98144
(206) 323-3070
Fax:(206) 322-6518
Circulation: 37,000

Tacoma True Citizen
Piloven Publishing
2600 S. Jackson St.
Seattle, WA 98144
(206) 323-3070
Fax:(206) 322-6518
Circulation: 13,500

West Virginia

West Virginia Beacon Digest
PO Box 981
Charleston, WV 25324
(304) 342-4600
Circulation: 35,861

Wisconsin

Milwaukee Community Journal
Community Journal, Inc.
3612 N. Martin Luther King Dr.
Milwaukee, WI 53212
(414) 265-5300
Fax:(414) 265-1536
Circulation: 39,960

Milwaukee Courier
2431 W. Hopkins St.
Milwaukee, WI 53206
(414) 449-4860
Fax:(414) 449-4872
Circulation: 15,000

Milwaukee Star
3815 N. Teutonia Ave.
Milwaukee, WI 53206
(414) 449-4870
Fax:(414) 449-4872
Circulation: 5,000

Milwaukee Times
2183 N. Sherman Blvd.
PO Box 16489
Milwaukee, WI 53216-0489
(414) 444-8611
Fax:(414) 871-7634

◆ MAGAZINES AND JOURNALS

A and T Register
North Carolina Agricultural and Technical University
Box E25
Greensboro, NC 27411
(919) 334-7700

About...Time
About...Time Magazine, Inc.
283 Genesee St.
Rochester, NY 14611
(716) 235-7150
Fax:(716) 235-7195
Circulation: 27,700

African American Review
Indiana State University
Dept. of English
Terre Haute, IN 47809
(812) 237-2968
Fax:(812) 237-4382
Circulation: 4,235

Alternative Press Index
PO Box 33109
Baltimore, MD 21218
(410) 243-2471
Fax:(410) 235-5325
Circulation: 650

American Visions: The Magazine of Afro-American Culture
Dialogue Diaspora, Inc.
2101 S St. NW
Washington, DC 20008-4090
(202) 462-1779
Fax:(202) 462-3997
Circulation: 125,000

Atlanta Tribune
L and L Communications, Inc.
875 Old Roswell Rd., Ste. C-100
Roswell, GA 30076
(404) 587-0501
Fax:(404) 642-6501
Circulation: 32,000

AUC Digest
Atlanta University Center
PO Box 3191
Atlanta, GA 30302
(404) 523-6136
Fax:(404) 523-5467
Circulation: 15,100

Black Careers
Project Magazine, Inc.
PO Box 8214
Philadelphia, PA 19101-8214
(215) 387-1600
Circulation: 400,000

Black College Sports Review
Winston-Salem Chronicle
617 N. Liberty St.
Winston-Salem, NC 27102
(919) 723-9026
Fax:(919) 723-9173

Black Collegian
Black Collegiate Services, Inc.
140 Carondelet St.
New Orleans, LA 70130-2526
(504) 523-0154
Fax:(504) 523-0271
Circulation: 108,184

Black Employment and Education Magazine
Hamdani Communications Inc.
2625 Piedmont Rd.
Bldg. 56, Ste. 282
Atlanta, GA 30324
(404) 469-5891
Circulation: 175,000

Black Enterprise
Earl Graves Publishing
130 5th Ave.
New York, NY 10011
(212) 242-8000
Fax:(212) 886-9610
Circulation: 288,303

Black Family
Kent Enterprises, Inc.
Box 1046
Herndon, VA 22070-1046
Circulation: 225,000

Black Health
Altier and Maynard Communications, Inc.
59 Oakwood Dr.
Madison, CT 06443-1823
(203) 421-3494
Circulation: 26,000

Black News Digest
U.S. Dept. of Labor
Office of Information and Public Affairs
200 Constitution Ave. NW
Washington, DC 20210
(202) 219-7316
Fax:(202) 219-8699

Black Scholar
Black World Foundation
PO Box 2869
Oakland, CA 94609
(510) 547-6633
Fax:(510) 547-6679
Circulation: 70,000

Black Tennis Magazine
PO Box 210767
Dallas, TX 75211
(214) 670-7618
Fax:(214) 330-1318
Circulation: 5,000

BLK Publishing Company
Box 83912
Los Angeles, CA 90083-0912
(310) 410-0808, (310) 410-9250
Circulation: 60,000

Callaloo
The Johns Hopkins University Press
University of Virginia
Dept. of English
Wilson Hall
Charlottesville, VA 22903
(804) 924-6616
Circulation: 1,740

Chocolate Singles
Chocolate Singles Enterprises, Inc.
PO Box 333
Jamaica, NY 11413
(718) 978-4800
Fax:(718) 978-4819

Christian Index
The Christian Methodist Episcopal Publishing House
PO Box 665
Memphis, TN 38101
(901) 345-1173
Fax:(901) 332-2269
Circulation: 6,000

Class Magazine
R.E. John-Sandy Communications Ltd.
900 Broadway
New York, NY 10003
(212) 677-3055
Fax:(212) 677-3341
Circulation: 204,845

Confrontation/Change Review
3955 Denlinger Rd.
Dayton, OH 45426
(513) 837-0498
Fax:(513) 837-5888
Circulation: 3,200

The Crisis
NAACP/Crisis Publishing
6565 Sunset Boulevard
Los Angeles, CA 90028-7206
(212) 481-4100
Fax:(212) 779-9277
Circulation: 350,000

Dollars and Sense Magazine
National Publications Sales Agency, Inc.
1610 E. 79th St.
Chicago, IL 60649
(312) 375-6800
Fax:(312) 375-6149
Circulation: 286,346

Ebony
Johnson Publishing Co., Inc.
820 S. Michigan Ave.
Chicago, IL 60605
(312) 322-9200
Fax:(312) 322-9375
Circulation: 1,937,095

EM: Ebony Man
Johnson Publishing Co.
820 S. Michigan Ave.
Chicago, IL 60605
(312) 322-9200
Fax:(312) 322-9375
Circulation: 200,000

Emerge
Emerge Communications Inc.
1700 N. Moore St., Ste. 2200
Arlington, VA 22209
(703) 875-0430
Fax:(703) 516-6406
Circulation: 150,000

Essence
Essence Communications, Inc.
1500 Broadway 6th Fl.
New York, NY 10036
(212) 642-0600
Fax:(212) 921-5173
Circulation: 950,634

Ivy Leaf
Alpha Kappa Alpha Sorority, Inc.
5656 S. Stony Island Ave.
Chicago, IL 60637
(312) 684-1282
Fax:(312) 288-8251
Circulation: 40,000

Jet
Johnson Publishing Co., Inc.
820 S. Michigan Ave.
Chicago, IL 60605
(312) 322-9200
Fax:(312) 322-9375
Circulation: 948,254

Journal of Black Studies
Sage Periodicals Press
2455 Teller Rd.
Thousand Oaks, CA 91360
(805) 499-0721
Fax:(805) 499-0871
Circulation: 1,735

Journal of Negro Education
Howard University
PO Box 311
Washington, DC 20059
(202) 806-8120
Fax:(202) 806-2130
Circulation: 2,200

Journal of Negro History
Association for the Study of Afro-American Life and
    History
Morehouse College
Box 20
Atlanta, GA 30314
(404) 681-2650
Fax:(404) 215-2715
Circulation: 4,000

Journal of the National Medical Association
Slack, Inc.
6900 Grove Rd.
Thorofare, NJ 08086-9447
(609) 848-1000
Fax:(609) 853-5991
Circulation: 24,500

Lincoln Review
The Lincoln Institute for Research and Education, Inc.
1001 Connecticut Ave. NW, Ste. 1135
Washington, DC 20036
(202) 223-5112
Circulation: 7,000

Living Blues
Center for the Study of Southern Culture
University of Mississippi
301 Hill Hall
University, MS 38677
(601) 232-5743
Fax:(601) 232-7842
Circulation: 18,000

Message Magazine
Review and Herald Publishing Assn.
55 W. Oak Ridge Dr.
Hagerstown, MD 21740
(301) 791-7000
Fax:(301) 680-6695
Circulation: 78,330

Minority Business Entrepreneur
3528 Torrance Blvd., Ste. 101
Torrance, CA 90503-4803
(310) 540-9398
Fax:(310) 792-8263
Circulation: 40,000

Minority Business Social and Cultural Directory
The Augusta Focus
PO Box 10112
Augusta, GA 30903
(706) 722-7327
Fax:(706) 724-6969
Circulation: 18,000

Negro History Bulletin
The Assn. for the Study of Afro-American Life and
    History, Inc.
1407 14th St. NW
Washington, DC 20005-3704
(202) 667-2822
Fax:(202) 387-9802
Circulation: 10,000

New Visions
16360 Broadway
Maple Heights, OII 44137
(216) 581-7070
Fax:(216) 581-7072

NSBE Magazine
NSBE Publications
1454 Duke St.
Alexandria, VA 22314
(703) 549-2207
Fax:(703) 683-2932
Circulation: 22,934

Players
Players International Publications
8060 Melrose Ave.
Los Angeles, CA 90046
(213) 653-8060
Fax:(213) 682-2932
Circulation: 175,000

Right On!
Sterling/Macfadden Partnership
233 Park Avenue South, 6th Floor
New York, NY 10003
(212) 979-4800
Fax:(212) 979-7342
Circulation: 350,000

SENGA
Megasin Publications
7501 Morrison Rd.
New Orleans, LA 70126
(504) 242-6022

Shooting Star Review
Shooting Star Productions Inc.
7123 Race St.
Pittsburgh, PA 15208-1424
(412) 731-7464

Sophisticate's Black Hairstyles and Care Guide
Associated Publications Inc.
875 N. Michigan Ave., Ste. 2434
Chicago, IL 60611-1901
(312) 266-8680
Circulation: 182,250

Upscale
Upscale Communications
594 Fielding Ln.
Atlanta, GA 30311
(404) 758-1467
Fax:(404) 758-2314
Circulation: 200,000

US Black Engineer
Career Communications Group, Inc.
729 E. Pratt St., Ste. 504
Baltimore, MD 21202
(410) 244-7101
Fax:(410) 752-1837
Circulation: 15,636

Voice of Missions
A.M.E. Sunday School Union
475 Riverside Dr., Rm. 1926
New York, NY 10115
(212) 870-2258
Fax:(212) 870-2242

Washington View
Viewcomm, Inc.
1101 14th St. NW
Washington, DC 20005
(202) 371-1313
Circulation: 40,000

The Western Journal of Black Studies
Cooper Publication
Pullman, WA 99164-5910
(509) 335-8681
Circulation: 430

Word Up!
Word Up! Publications, Inc.
63 Grand Ave.
River Edge, NJ 07661
(201) 487-6124

◆ RADIO NETWORKS

American-Urban Radio Network
463 7th Ave.
New York, NY 10018
(212) 714-1000

Black Radio Network
166 Madison Ave., 6th Fl.
New York, NY 10016
(212) 686-6850

Sheridan Broadcasting Network
411 7th Ave., Ste. 1500
Pittsburgh, PA 15219
(412) 456-4000

◆ RADIO STATIONS

Alabama

WBIL-FM
PO Box 666
Tuskegee, AL 36083
(205) 727-2100
Fax:(205) 727-2969

WBLX-AM
1204 Dauphin St.
Mobile, AL 36604
(205) 432-7609
Fax:(205) 432-2054

WBLX-FM
1204 Dauphin St.
Mobile, AL 36604
(205) 432-7609
Fax:(205) 432-2054

WENN-FM
424 16th St. N.
Birmingham, AL 35203
(205) 254-1820
Fax:(205) 254-1833

WGOK-AM
Box 1425
Mobile, AL 36633
(334) 432-8661
Fax:(334) 432-1921

WHBB-AM
505 Lauderdale St.
PO Box 1055
Selma, AL 36701
(334) 875-3350
Fax:(334) 875-4254

WJLD-AM
1449 Spaulding Ishkooda Rd.
Birmingham, AL 35211
(205) 942-1776
Fax:(205) 942-4814

WLAY-FM
620 E. 2nd St.
Muscle Shoals, AL 35661
(205) 383-2525
Fax:(205) 381-1450

WMML-FM
1050 Government St.
Mobile, AL 36604-2404
(205) 433-9577

WMMV-FM
PO Box 901
Spanish Fort, AL 36527-0901

WQGL-FM
PO Box 566
Butler, AL 36904
(205) 459-3222
Fax:(205) 459-4140

WRAG-AM
Hwy. 17 S.
PO Box 71
Carrollton, AL 35447
(205) 367-8136
Fax:(205) 367-8689

WSBM-AM
624 Sam Phillips St.
PO Box 932
Florence, AL 35631
(205) 764-8121
Fax:(205) 764-1869

WSLY-FM
11474 U.S. Hwy. 11
York, AL 36925
(205) 392-5234
Fax:(205) 392-5234

WTUG-FM
142 Skyland Blvd.
Tuscaloosa, AL 35405
(205) 345-7200
Fax:(205) 349-1715

WZMG-AM
915 Saugahatchee Lake Rd.
PO Box 2329
Opelika, AL 36803
(334) 745-4656
Fax:(334) 749-1520

WZZA-AM
1570 Woodmont Dr.
Tuscumbia, AL 35674
(205) 381-1862

Arkansas

KCAT-AM
PO Box 8808
Pine Bluff, AR 71611-8808
(501) 534-5001

KELD-AM
2525 Northwest Ave.
El Dorado, AR 71730
(501) 862-7777
Fax:(501) 863-4555

KXAR-FM
PO Box 320
Hope, AR 71801
(501) 777-3601
Fax:(501) 777-3535

California

KJLH-FM
161 N. LaBrea Ave.
Inglewood, CA 90301
(213) 330-5550
Fax:(213) 330-5555

KDIA-AM
384 Embarcadero W. 3rd
Oakland, CA 94607-3734
(510) 251-1400
Fax:(510) 251-2110

KBLA-AM
1700 N. Alvarado St.
Los Angeles, CA 90026
(213)665-1580

KFSR-FM
California State University Fresno
5201 N. Maple Ave.
Fresno, CA 93740-0046
(209) 278-2598
Fax:(209) 278-6985

KGFJ-AM
1100 S. LaBrea Ave.
Los Angeles, CA 90019
(213) 930-9090
Fax:(213) 930-9056

KKBT-FM
6735 Yucca St.
Los Angeles, CA 90028
(213) 466-9566
Fax:(213) 466-2592

KSRH-FM
185 Mission Ave.
San Rafael, CA 94901
(415) 457-5774

WILD-FM
55 Green St., Ste. 200
San Francisco, CA 94111
(415) 391-1077
Fax:(415) 616-5700

Colorado

KDKO-AM
2559 Welton St.
Denver, CO 80205
(303) 295-1255
Fax:(303) 295-1521

KEPC-FM
5675 S. Academy Blvd.
Colorado Springs, CO 80904
(719) 540-7489
Fax:(719) 540-7489

KKMG-FM
411 Lakewood Circle
Colorado Springs, CO 80910-2617
(719) 576-1100
Fax:(719) 576-2003

Connecticut

WKND-AM
544 Windsor Ave.
PO Box 1480
Windsor, CT 06095
(203) 688-6221
Fax:(203) 688-0711

WNHC-AM
112 Washington Ave.
North Haven, CT 06473
(203) 234-1340
Fax:(203) 239-6712

WQTQ-FM
Weaver High School
415 Granby St.
Hartford, CT 06112
(203) 722-8661
Fax:(203) 286-9909

WYBC-FM
165 Elm St.
PO Box WYBC
New Haven, CT 06520
(203) 432-4118
Fax:(203) 432-4117

District of Columbia

WHUR-FM
529 Bryant St.NW
Washington, DC 20059
(202) 806-3500
Fax:(202) 806-3522

WMMJ-FM
400 H St. NE
Washington, DC 20002
(202) 675-4800
Fax:(202) 675-4842

WOL-AM
400 H St. NE
Washington, DC 20002
(202) 675-4800
Fax:(202) 675-4800

Florida

WAMF-FM
Florida A and M University
314 Tucker Hall
Tallahassee, FL 32307
(904) 599-3083
Fax:(904) 561-2829

WANM-AM
PO Box 10174
Tallahassee, FL 32302-2174
(904) 222-1070
Fax:(904) 561-3645

WAVS-AM
6360 SW 41st Place
Davie, FL 33314
(305) 584-1170
Fax:(305) 581-6441

WEDR-FM
Box 551748
Opa-Locka, FL 33055
(305) 623-7711
Fax:(305) 624-2736

WEXY-AM
412 W. Oakland Park Blvd.
Fort Lauderdale, FL 33311-1712
(305) 561-1520
Fax:(305) 561-9830

WHJX-FM
10592 E. Balmoral Circle, Ste. 1
Jacksonville, FL 32218
(904) 696-1015
Fax:(904) 696-1011

WHQT-FM
1401 N. Bay Causeway
Miami, FL 33141
(305) 759-4311
Fax:(305) 757-7516

WPJS-AM
3033 Riviera Dr., No. 200
Naples, FL 33940-4134
(803) 248-9040

WMBM-AM
814 1st St.
Miami Beach, FL 33139
(305) 672-1100
Fax:(305) 673-1194

WPOM-AM
6667 42nd Terrace N.
West Palm Beach, FL 33407
(407) 844-6200
Fax:(407) 840-0061

WPUL-AM
PO Box 4010
South Daytona, FL 32121-4010
(904) 767-1131
Fax:(904) 254-7510

WRBD-AM
4431 Rock Island Rd.
Fort Lauderdale, FL 33319
(305) 731-4800
Fax:(305) 739-7917

WRTO-FM
2960 Coral Way
Miami, FL 33145
(305) 445-4040

WRXB-AM
1700 34th St. S.
Saint Petersburg, FL 33711
(813) 327-9792
Fax:(813) 321-3025

WSWN-AM
2001 State Road 715
PO Box 1505
Belle Glade, FL 33430
(407) 996-2063
Fax:(407) 996-1852

WTCL-AM
Box 157
Chattahoochee, FL 32324
(904) 663-2323

WTMP-AM
5207 Washington Blvd.
Tampa, FL 33619
(813) 620-1300
Fax:(813) 628-0713

WTOT-AM
140 W. Lafayette St., Ste. A
PO Box 569
Marianna, FL 32446
(904) 482-3046
Fax:(904) 482-3249

WWAB-AM
1203 W. Chase St.
Lakeland, FL 33802
(813) 682-2998

WYFX-AM
400 Gulfstream Blvd.
Delray Beach, FL 33444
(407) 737-1040
Fax:(407) 278-1040

WZAZ-AM
9454 Phillips Hwy, Ste. 1
Jacksonville, FL 32256
(904) 292-0811
Fax:(904) 292-0434

Georgia

WBKZ-AM
548 Hawthorne Ave.
PO Box 88
Athens, GA 30606
(706) 548-8800
Fax:(706) 549-8800

WIBB-FM
369 2nd St.
PO Box 4527
Macon, GA 31208
(912) 742-2505

WGOV-AM
Hwy. 84 W.
PO Box 1207
Valdosta, GA 31603
(912) 242-4513
Fax:(912) 247-7606

WHGH-AM
PO Box 2218
Thomasville, GA 31799
(912) 228-4124
Fax:(912) 225-9508

WJGA-FM
PO Box 3878
Jackson, GA 30233
(404) 775-3151
Fax:(404) 957-9915

WPGA-FM
PO Drawer 980
Perry, GA 31069
(912) 987-2980
Fax:(912) 987-7595

WQVE-FM
Box 434
Camilla, GA 31730
(912) 294-0010
Fax:(912) 294-0010

WRDW-AM
1480 Eisenhower Dr.
Augusta, GA 30904
(706) 667-8999
Fax:(706) 481-0092

WSNT-AM
PO Box 150
Sandersville, GA 31082
(912) 552-5182
Fax:(912) 552-5183

WSNT-FM
PO Box 150
Sandersville, GA 31082
(912) 552-5182
Fax:(912) 552-5183

WVEE-FM
120 Ralph McGill Blvd., Ste. 1000
Atlanta, GA 30365-6901
(404) 898-8900
Fax:(404) 898-8916

WVVS-FM
Box 142
Valdosta, GA 31698
(912) 333-5661

WXGC-FM
Box 3124
Milledgeville, GA 31061-1000
(912) 453-4102

WXRS-AM
Box 1590
Swainsboro, GA 30401
(912) 237-2534
Fax: (912) 237-3559

Illinois

WBCP-AM
PO Box 1023
Champaign, IL 61820
(217) 359-1580
Fax:(217) 359-1583

WCFJ-AM
1000 Lincoln Hwy.
Ford Heights, IL 60411
(708) 758-8600
Fax:(708) 758-8602

WGCI-FM
332 S. Michigan Ave., Ste. 600
Chicago, IL 60604
(312) 427-4700
Fax:(312) 427-7410

WKRO-AM
Rte, 1, US-51
Box 311
Cairo, IL 62914
(618) 734-1490
Fax:(618) 734-0884

WLUV-FM
2272 Elmwood
Rockford, IL 61103
(815) 877-9588
Fax:(815) 877-9649

WOUI-FM
3300 S. Federal St.
Chicago, IL 60616
(312) 567-3087
Fax:(312) 567-5180

Indiana

WSYW-AM
8203 Indy Ct.
Indianapolis, IN 46214-2300
(317) 271-9799
Fax:(317) 273-1507

WTLC-FM
2255 Hawthorne Lane
Indianapolis, IN 46218
(317) 351-1310
Fax:(317) 351-1307

WUEV-FM
1800 Lincoln Ave.
Evansville, IN 47722
(812) 479-2022
Fax:(812) 479-2320

Iowa

KALA-FM
518 W. Locust St.
Davenport, IA 52803-2898
(319) 383-8911
Fax:(319) 383-8909

KIGC-FM
William Penn College
201 Trueblood Ave.
Oskaloosa, IA 52577
(515) 673-1095

KRUI-FM
897 South Quad
Iowa City, IA 52242
(319) 335-9525
Fax:(319) 335-9526

KUNI-FM
University of Northern Iowa
Cedar Falls, IA 50614-0359
(319) 273-6400
Fax:(319) 273-2682

Kansas

KSWC-FM
Southwestern College
Winfield, KS 67156
(316) 221-1070

Kentucky

WLBN-AM
Box 680
Lebanon, KY 40033
(502) 692-3126
Fax:(502) 692-6003

WLOU-AM
2600 W. Broadway
Lyles Mall, Ste. 303
Louisville, KY 40211
(502) 778-3535
Fax:(502) 778-7394

WQKS-AM
905 S. Main St.
Hopkinsville, KY 42240
(502) 886-1480
Fax:(502) 886-6286

Louisiana

KBCE-FM
Box 69
Boyce, LA 71409
(318) 793-4003
Fax:(318) 793-8888

KFXZ-FM
3225 Ambassador Caffery Pkwy.
Lafayette, LA 70506-7214
(318) 898-1112
Fax:(318) 988-0443

KGRM-FM
Drawer K
Grambling, LA 71245
(318) 274-2345
Fax:(318) 274-3245

KJCB-AM
413 Jefferson St.
Lafayette, LA
(318) 233-4262

KNEK-FM
PO Box 598
Washington, LA 70589
(318) 826-3921
Fax:(318) 826-3206

KNWD-FM
Northwestern State University
PO Box 3038
Natchitoches, LA 71497
(318) 357-5693
Fax:(318) 357-6564

KRUS-AM
Box 430
500 N. Monroe St.
Ruston, LA 71270
(318) 255-2530
Fax:(318) 225-2100

KSCL-FM
2911 Centenary Blvd.
Shreveport, LA 71104
(318) 869-5296
Fax:(318) 869-5294

KTRY-AM
Box 1075
Bastrop, LA 71220
(318) 281-3656

KXZZ-AM
311 Alamo St.
Lake Charles, LA 70601
(318) 436-7277
Fax:(318) 436-7278

KYEA-FM
516 Martin St.
West Monroe, LA 71292
(318) 322-1491
Fax:(318) 325-7203

WABL-AM
Bankston Rd.
PO Box 787
Amite, LA 70422
(504) 748-8385
Fax:(504) 748-3918

WQUE-FM
2228 Gravier
New Orleans, LA 70119
(504) 827-6000
Fax:(504) 827-6047

WXOK-AM
7707 Waco Dr.
Baton Rouge, LA 70806
(504) 499-1460
Fax:(504) 928-1606

WYLD-AM
2228 Gravier
New Orleans, LA 70119
(504) 822-1945
Fax:(504) 821-3273

Maine

WMHB-FM
Colby College
Waterville, ME 04901
(207) 872-3686
Fax:(207) 872-3555

Maryland

WANN-AM
PO Box 631
Annapolis, MD 21404
(410) 269-0700
Fax:(410) 269-0830

WESM-FM
University of Maryland, Eastern Shore
Backbone Rd.
Princess Anne, MD 21853
(410) 651 2816
Fax:(410) 651-2819

WJDY-AM
1633 N. Division St.
Salisbury, MD 21801
(410) 742-5191

WPGC-FM
6301 Ivy Ln., Ste. 800
Greenbelt, MD 20770
(301) 441-3500
Fax:(301) 982-0981

WWIN-FM
100 St. Paul St.
Baltimore, MD 21202
(410) 332-8200
Fax:(410) 783-4791

WXYV-FM
1829 Reistertown Rd.
Baltimore, MD 21208
(410) 653-2200
Fax:(410) 486-8057

Massachusetts

WAIC-FM
1000 State St.
Springfield, MA 01109
(413) 736-7662
Fax:(413) 737-2803

WILD-AM
90 Warren St.
Boston, MA 02119
(617) 427-2222
Fax:(617) 427-2677

WJJW-FM
N. Adams State College
Merdock Hall
North Adams, MA 01247
(413) 662-5405

WKKL-FM
Cape Cod Community College
Rte. 132
West Barnstable, MA 02668
(508) 362-4941

Michigan

WDZZ-FM
120 E. 1st St., Ste. 1830
Flint, MI 48502
(810) 767-0130
Fax:(810) 238-7310

WGPR-FM
3146 E. Jefferson Ave.
Detroit, MI 48207
(313) 259-8862
Fax:(313) 259-6662

WILS-AM
PO Box 25008
Lansing, MI 48909-5008
(517) 393-1320
Fax:(517) 393-0882

WJLB-FM
645 Griswold St., Ste. 633
Detroit, MI 48226-4177
(313) 965-2000
Fax:(313) 965-1729

WKWM-AM
PO Box 828
Kentwood, MI 49518-0828
(616) 676-1237
Fax:(616) 676-2329

WXYT-FM
15600 W. 12 Mile Rd.
Southfield, MI 48076
(810) 569-8000
Fax:(810) 569-6400

WNMC-FM
1701 E. Front St.
Traverse City, MI 49684
(616) 922-1091

WQBH-AM
Penobscot Bldg.
Detroit, MI 48226
(313) 965-4500
Fax:(313) 965-4608

WTLZ-FM
126 N. Franklin St., Ste. 514
Saginaw, MI 48607
(517) 754-1071
Fax:(517) 754-4292

Minnesota

KMOJ-FM
501 Bryant Ave. N
Minneapolis, MN 55405
(612) 377-0594
Fax:(612) 377-6919

Mississippi

WACR-AM
1910 14th Ave. N
PO Box 1078
Columbus, MS 39703
(601) 328-1050
Fax:(601) 328-1054

WALT-AM
3436 Hwy. 45 N
PO Box 5797
Meridian, MS 39302
(601) 693-2661
Fax:(601) 483-0826

WBAD-FM
PO Box 4426
Greenville, MS 38704-4426
(601) 335-9265
Fax:(601) 335-5538

WCLD-FM
Drawer 780
Cleveland, MS 38732
(601) 843-4091
Fax:(601) 843-9805

WESY-AM
7 Oaks Rd.
PO Box 5804
Greenville, MS 38704-5804
(601) 378-9405
Fax:(601) 335-5538

WJMG-FM
1204 Gravel Line St.
Hattiesburg, MS 39401
(601) 544-1941

WKXG-AM
Browning Rd.
PO Box 1686
Greenwood, MS 38930
(601) 453-2174
Fax:(601) 455-5733

WMIS-AM
20 E. Franklin
Natchez, MS 39120
(601) 442-2522
Fax:(601) 446-9918

WMPG-AM
4307 Highway 39 N.
Meridian, MS 39301
(601) 693-2381
Fax:(601) 485-2972

WNBN-AM
1290 Hawkins Crossing Rd.
Meridian, MS 39301
(601) 483-7930

WORV-AM
1204 Graveline
Hattiesburg, MS 39401
(601) 544-1941
Fax:(601) 544-1947

WQFX-FM
Security Bldg., Penthouse Ste.
PO Box 789
Gulfport, MS 39502
(601) 374-4967

WQIS-AM
Rte. 2
Box 151
Laurel, MS 39441
(601) 425-1491
Fax:(601) 426-8255

WTYJ-FM
20 E. Franklin
Natchez, MS 39120
(601) 442-2522
Fax:(601) 446-9918

Missouri

KCOU-FM
University of Missouri
101-F Pershing Hall
Columbia, MO 65201
(314) 882-7820
Fax:(314) 882-6262

KCXL-AM
310 S. LaFrenz
Liberty, MO 64068

KIRL-AM
3713 Hwy. 94 N
St. Charles, MO 63301
(314) 946-6600
Fax:(314) 946-6662

KMJM-FM
PO Box 4888
St. Louis, MO 63108
(314) 361-1108
Fax:(314) 361-2276

KWUR-FM
Washington University
Box 1205
Saint Louis, MO 63130
(314) 935-5952
Fax:(314) 935-8597

Nebraska

KIOS-FM
3230 Burt St.
Omaha, NE 68131
(402) 554-6444

KZUM-FM
941 O St., Ste. 1025
Lincoln, NE 68508-3608
(402) 474-5086

Nevada

KCEP-FM
330 W. Washington St.
Las Vegas, NV 89106
(702) 648-4218
Fax:(702) 647-0803

New Hampshire

WPCR-FM
Plymouth State College
Plymouth, NY 03264
(603) 535-2242
Fax:(603) 535-2783

New Jersey

WRRC-FM
2083 Lawrenceville Rd.
Lawrenceville, NJ 08648
(609) 896-5211
Fax:(609) 896-8029

New York

WBLK-FM
712 Main St., Ste. 112
Buffalo, NY 14202
(716) 852-5955
Fax:(716) 852-6605

WBLS-FM
3 Park Avenue
New York, NY 10016
(212) 447-1000
Fax:(212) 447-5194

WDKX-FM
683 E. Main St.
Rochester, NY 14605
(716) 262-2050
Fax:(716) 262-2626

WHCR-FM
City College of New York
138th and Convent Ave.
New York, NY 10031
(212) 650-7481

WJPZ-FM
316 Waverly Ave.
PO Box 239
Syracuse, NY 13210
(315) 443-4689
Fax:(315) 443-4379

WOLF-AM
401 W. Fitzpatrick Ave.
Syracuse, NY 13204-1305
(315) 472-0222
Fax:(315) 472-0224

WRKS-FM
1440 Broadway
New York, NY 10018
(212) 642-4300
Fax:(212) 642-4336

WUFO-AM
89 LaSalle Ave.
Buffalo, NY 14214
(716) 834-1080
Fax:(716) 837-1438

North Carolina

WAAA-AM
4950 Indiana Ave.
Box 11197
Winston-Salem, NC 27106
(910) 767-0430
Fax:(910) 767-0433

WBCG-FM
PO Box 38
Murfreesboro, NC 27855
(919) 398-4111
Fax:(919) 332-8329

WBMS-AM
716 Princess St.
PO Box 2578
Wilmington, NC 28402
(910) 763-4633
Fax:(910) 251-0534

WIKS-FM
207 Glenburnie Dr.
PO Box 12684
New Bern, NC 28561
(919) 633-1500
Fax:(919) 633-0718

WJMH-FM
7819 National Service Rd., Bldg. 401
Greensboro, NC 27409
(910) 605-5200
Fax:(910) 855-5899

WLWL-AM
PO Box 1536
Rockingham, NC 28379
(910) 997-2526
Fax:(910) 997-2526

WNAA-FM
NC A and T State University
Price Hall, Ste. 200
Greensboro, NC 27411
(919) 334-7936

WPEG-FM
520 Hwy. 29 N
PO Box 128
Concord, NC 28025
(704) 786-9111
Fax:(704) 788-7628

WQOK-FM
8601 Six Forks Rd., Ste. 609
Raleigh, NC 27615
(919) 848-9736
Fax:(919) 848-4724

WRRZ-AM
701 Bus. S.
Clinton, NC 28328
(910) 592-2165
Fax:(910) 592-8556

WRVS-FM
PO Box 800
Elizabeth City, NC 27909
(919) 335-3517
Fax:(919) 335-3745

WSMY-AM
PO Box 910
Roanoke Rapids, NC 27870
(919) 536-3115
Fax:(919) 536-3045

WSNC-FM
Winston-Salem State University
601 MLK Junior Dr.
Winston-Salem, NC 27110
(910) 750-2320
Fax:(910) 750- 2459

WZFX-FM
106-108 Hay Street, Ste. 200
Fayetteville, NC 28301
(919) 486-4991
Fax:(919) 486-6720

Ohio

WCKX-FM
510 E. Mound St.
Columbus, OH 43215-5539
(614) 464-0020
Fax:(614) 464-2960

WIZF-FM
7030 Reading Rd., No. 316
Cincinnati, OH 45237
(513) 351-5900
Fax:(513) 351-0020

WJMO-AM
2510 St. Claire Ave.
Cleveland, OH 44114
(216) 621-9300
Fax:(216) 771-4164

WJTB-AM
105 Lake Ave.
Elyria, OH 44035
(216) 327-1844
Fax:(216) 322-8942

WVKO-AM
4401 Carriage Hill Ln.
Columbus, OH 43220
(614) 451-2191
Fax:(614) 451-1831

WZAK-FM
2510 St. Claire Ave.
Cleveland, OH 44114
(216) 621-9300
Fax:(216) 771-4164

WZIP-FM
1004 University of Akron
Akron, OH 44325-1004
(216) 972-7105
Fax:(216) 972-5521

Oklahoma

KHIB-FM
Southeastern State University
Box 4129, Sta. A
Durant, OK 74701
(405) 924-0121

KTLV-AM
3336 SE 67th St.
Oklahoma City, OK 73135
(405) 672-1220
Fax:(405) 672-5858

KTOW-FM
8886 W. 21st St.
Sand Springs, OK 74063
(918) 245-0254
Fax:(918) 245-0255

KWSH-AM
Old Hwy. 270
PO Box 1260
Wewoka, OK 74884
(405) 257-5441
Fax:(405) 257-5441

Pennsylvania

WAMO-FM
411 7th Ave., Ste. 1500
Pittsburgh, PA 15219
(412) 471-2181
Fax:(412) 391-3559

WCXJ-AM
7138 Kelly St.
Pittsburgh, PA 15208
(412) 243-3050
Fax:(412) 243-0644

WDAS-FM
Belmont Ave. at Edgely Rd.
Philadelphia, PA 19131
(215) 878-2000
Fax:(215) 878-3478

WDNR-FM
PO Box 1000
1 University
Chester, PA 19013
(610) 499-4439
Fax:(610) 876-9751

WHAT-AM
2471 N. 54th St.
Philadelphia, PA 19131
(215) 581-5161
Fax:(215) 581-5185

WIXQ-FM
Millersville University
SMC Basement
Millersville, PA 17551
(717) 872-3333
Fax:(717) 871-2321

WKDU-FM
3210 Chestnut St.
Philadelphia, PA 19104
(215) 895-5920
Fax:(215) 895-1414

WLIU-FM
Office of Student Activities
Lincoln University, PA 19352
(215) 932-8300
Fax:(215) 932-9105

WUSL-FM
440 Domino Ln.
Philadelphia, PA 19128
(215) 483-8900
Fax:(215) 483-5930

Rhode Island

WRBU-FM
88 Benevolent St.
Providence, RI 02906
(401) 272-9550
Fax:(401) 272-9728

South Carolina

WASC-AM
840 Wofford
PO Box 5686
Spartanburg, SC 29304
(803) 585-1530
Fax:(803) 573-7790

WCIG-FM
U.S. Hwy. 76
Mullins, SC 29574
(803) 423-1140

WDOG-FM
PO Box 442
Allendale, SC 29810
(803) 584-3500

WELP-AM
PO Box 19104
Greenville, SC 29602-9104
(803) 235-4600
Fax:(803) 859-4473

WFXA-FM
104 Bennett Ln.
North Augusta, SC 29841
(803) 279-2330
Fax:(803) 279-8149

WGCD-AM
PO Box 746
Chester, SC 29706
(803) 581-1490

WHYZ-AM
PO Box 4309
Greenville, SC 29608
(803) 246-1970
Fax:(803) 246-8121

WLBG-AM
Box 1289
Laurens, SC 29360
(803) 984-3544
Fax:(803) 984-3545

WLGI-FM
Rte. 2, PO Box 69
Hemingway, SC 29554
(803) 558-2977
Fax:(803) 558-2921

WMNY-FM
PO Box 459
Santee, SC 29648
(803) 854-2671

WMTY-AM
PO Box 459
Greenwood, SC 29648
(803) 223-4096

WMTY-FM
PO Box 459
Greenwood, SC 29648
(803) 223-4300
Fax:(803) 223-4096

WORG-AM
Rte. 1, Box 189
Santee, SC 29142-9718
(803) 854-2671

WQKI-AM
Riley Road
St. Matthews, SC 29135
(803) 874-2777

WUJM-AM
PO Box 1165
Goose Creek, SC 29445-1165
(919) 251-8881

WWWZ-FM
PO Box 30669
Charleston, SC 29417
(803) 556-9132
Fax:(803) 769-0876

WYNN-FM
170 E. Palmetto St.
PO Box 100531
Florence, SC 29501-0531
(803) 662-6364
Fax:(803) 669-2654

Tennessee

KJMS-FM
80 N. Tillman
Memphis, TN 38111
(901) 323-0101
Fax:(901) 320-1754

WABD-AM
150 State Line Rd.
Clarksville, TN 37042
(615) 431-5555
Fax:(615) 431-4986

WBOL-AM
PO Box 191
Bolivar, TN 38008
(901) 658-3690
Fax:(901) 658-3408

WFKX-FM
425 E. Chester
Jackson, TN 38301
(901) 427-9616

WHRK-FM
112 Union Ave.
Memphis, TN 38103
(901) 529-4300
Fax:(901) 529-9557

WJTT-FM
409 Chestnut St., Ste. A154
Chattanooga, TN 37402
(615) 265-9494
Fax:(615) 266-2335

WQQK-FM
1320 Brick Church Pike
PO Box 70085
Nashville, TN 37207
(615) 227-1470
Fax:(615) 227-2740

WQZZ-AM
609 W. 7th St.
Columbia, TN 38401
(615) 381-7100

WRVU-FM
PO Box 9100, Sta. B
Nashville, TN 37235
(615) 322-3691
Fax:(615) 343-2582

WVOL-AM
1320 Brick Church Pike
PO Box 70085
Nashville, TN 37207
(615) 227-1470
Fax:(615) 227-2740

Texas

KALO-AM
7700 Gulfway
Port Arthur, TX 77642
(409) 963-1276
Fax:(409) 963-1640

KBWC-FM
711 Wiley Ave.
Marshall, TX 75670
(903) 938-8341
Fax:(903) 938-8100

KCOH-AM
5011 Almeda
Houston, TX 77004
(713) 522-1001
Fax:(713) 521-0769

KGBC-AM
Pelican Island
Galveston, TX 77554
(409) 744-4567
Fax:(409) 740-0944

KIIZ-AM
Box 24699
Harker Heights, TX 76543
(817) 699-5000
Fax:(817) 628-8840

KJMZ-FM
545 E. John Carpenter Fwy., 17th Fl.
Irving, TX 75062
(214) 556-8100
Fax:(214) 988-1003

KKDA-FM
PO Box 530860
Grand Prairie, TX 75053
(214) 263-9911
Fax:(214) 554-0010

KMHT-FM
PO Box 330
Huntsville, TX 77342-0330
(214) 938-6789

KMJQ-FM
24 Greenway Plaza, No. 1508
Houston, TX 77046
(713) 623-0102
Fax:(713) 623-0106

KSFA-AM
PO Box 631508
Nacogdoches, TX 75963
(409) 560-6677
Fax:(409) 569-6677

KYOK-AM
6420 Richmond Ave., Ste. 600
Houston, TX 77057
(713) 780-0228
Fax:(713) 780-0211

KZEY-AM
PO Box 4248
Tyler, TX 75712
(903) 593-1744
Fax:(903) 593-2666

Utah

KWCR-FM
Weber State University
3750 Harrison Blvd., Ste. 1906
Ogden, UT 84408-1906
(801) 626-6000

Virginia

WARR-AM
553 Michigan Dr.
Hampton, VA 23669-3899
(804) 723-1270

WILA-AM
865 Industrial Ave.
PO Box 3444
Danville, VA 24543
(804) 792-2133
Fax:(804) 792-2134

WKBY-AM
Rte. 2, Box 105A
Chatham, VA 24531
(804) 432-8108
Fax:(804) 432-9529

WMYK-FM
645 Church St., Ste. 400
Norfolk, VA 23510
(804) 622-4600
Fax:(804) 624-6515

WOWI-FM
645 Church St., Ste. 201
Norfolk, VA 23510-2809
(804) 627-5800
Fax:(804) 627-4048

WPAK-AM
446 Old Plank Rd.
Farmville, VA 23901
(804) 392-8114
Fax:(804) 392-1080

WSVY-AM
645 Church St., Ste. 201
Norfolk, VA 23510-2809
(804) 627-5800
Fax:(804) 627-4048

WULR-AM
1105 Main St.
Madison Heights, VA 24572
(804) 847-1266
Fax:(804) 845-4385

WWHS-FM
Box 606
Hampden-Sydney College
Hampden-Sydney, VA 23943
(804) 223-6809

Washington

KASB-FM
10416 SE Kilmarnock
Bellevue, WA 98004-6698
(206) 455-6154

KKFX-AM
1509 Queen Anne Ave., N612
Seattle, WA 98109-5730
(206) 728-1250
Fax:(206) 728-1949

KRIZ-AM
2600 S. Jackson St.
Seattle, WA 98144
(206) 329-7880

KZIZ-AM
c/o KRIZ-AM
2600 S. Jackson St.
Seattle, WA 98144
(206) 627-1103
Fax:(206) 322-6518

Wisconsin

KUWS-FM
1800 Grand Ave.
Superior, WI 54880-2898
(715) 394-8530
Fax:(715) 394-8454

WBZN-AM
2400 S. 102nd St.
West Allis, WI 53227
(414) 321-1007
Fax:(414) 321-2231

WMVP-AM
4222 W. Capitol Dr., Ste. 1290
Milwaukee, WI 53216
(414) 444-1290
Fax:(414) 444-1409

◆ CABLE TELEVISION NETWORKS

BET (Black Entertainment Television)
1232 31st St. NW
Washington, DC 20007
(202) 337-5260

◆ TELEVISION STATIONS

California

KMTP-TV
211 Brannan
San Francisco, CA 94107
(415) 777-3232
Fax:(415) 512-4379

KNTV-TV
645 Park Ave.
San Jose, CA 95110
(408) 286-1111
Fax:(408) 286-1530

District of Columbia

WHMM-TV
2222 4th St. NW
Washington, DC 20059
(202) 806-3200
Fax:(202) 806-3300

WTVT-TV
3213 W. Kennedy Blvd.
Tampa, FL 33609
(813) 876-1313
Fax:(813) 875-8329

Florida

WGXA-TV
559 Broadway
Macon, GA 31497
(912) 745-2424
Fax:(912) 750-4347

WEEK-TV
2907 Springfield Rd.
Peoria, IL 61611
(309) 698-2525
Fax:(309) 698-9335

Indiana

WPTA-TV
3401 Butler Rd.
Box 2121
Ft. Wayne, IN 46801
(219) 483-0584
Fax:(219) 484-8240

WRTV-TV
1330 N. Meridian St.
Indianapolis, IN 46202
(317) 635-9788
Fax:(317) 269-1400

Louisiana

WNOL-TV
1661 Canal St.
New Orleans, LA 70112
(504) 525-3838
Fax:(504) 569-0908

Maine

WVII-TV
371 Target Industrial Circle
PO Box 1101
Bangor, ME 04401
(207) 945-6457
Fax:(207) 942-0511

Michigan

WGPR-TV
3140-3146 E. Jefferson, Ave.
Detroit, MI 48207
(313) 259-8862
Fax:(313) 259-6662

Minnesota

KBJR-TV
230 E. Superior St.
Duluth, MN 55802
(218) 727-8484
Fax:(218) 727-9688

Mississippi

WLBT-TV
715 S. Jefferson St.
Jackson, MS 39202
(601) 948-3333
Fax:(601) 960-4435

New York

WHEC-TV
191 East Ave.
Rochester, NY 14604
(716) 546-5670
Fax:(716) 454-7433

WKBW-TV
7 Broadcast Plaza
Buffalo, NY 14202
(716) 845-6100
Fax:(716) 842-1855

Oregon

KBSP-TV
4923 Indian School Rd. NE
Salem, OR 97305
(503) 390-2202
Fax:(503) 390-6829

Texas

KTXS-TV
U.S. Hwy. 83 Anson Bypass
PO Box 2997
Abilene, TX 79604
(915) 677-2281
Fax:(915) 676-9231

Virginia

WJCB-TV
910 W. Mercury Bldg., Ste. 2-C
Hampton, VA 23666
(804) 838-4949
Fax:(804) 838-4840

Wisconsin

WJFW-TV
S. Oneida Ave.
PO Box 858
Rhinelander, WI 54501
(715) 369-4700
Fax:(715) 369-1910

20

Performing Arts

⑳

Performing Arts

◆ The Origins of African American Performance Art ◆ Minstrelsy
◆ Reclaiming the Black Image: 1890 to 1920
◆ The African American Actor, Dancer, and Comedian, 1920 to 1950
◆ The African American Performance Artist since 1960 ◆ African American Performance Artists

by Donald Franklin Joyce

For more than 200 years, African American perform-ers have appeared on the American stage, often in the face of prejudice and bigotry. Showcasing their talents, they have made unique contributions to American performance art. The artistic heritage of today's Afri-can American actors, dancers and comedians can be traced back to the last decades of the eighteenth century.

◆ THE ORIGINS OF AFRICAN AMERICAN PERFORMANCE ART

The Earliest Plays with African American Actors

The first performances by African American actors on the American stage were in plays authored by white playwrights who portrayed blacks as buffoons or intel-lectually inept characters. In 1769, for example, Lewis Hallam's comedy *The Padlock* was staged with a West Indian slave character named Mongo, who was a clown to be played by a black. Other white-authored plays from the period that depicted blacks in demoralizing roles were *Robinson Crusoe, Harlequin* (1792), and *The Triumph of Love* (1795) by John Randolph, which in-cluded the native black character named Sambo). Thus, the earliest appearances of blacks on the American stage were as characters void of intellectual and moral sensibilities.

The African Grove Theatre

New York City's free African American community founded the first African American theater in 1821—the

African Grove Theatre, located at Mercer and Bleecker streets "in the rear of the one-mile stone on Broadway." A group of amateur African American actors organized by Henry Brown presented *Richard III* at the theater on October 1, 1821. The African Grove Theatre subsequent-ly produced *Othello, Hamlet,* and such lighter works as *Tom and Jerry* and *The Poor Soldier, Obi.*

One of the principal actors at the African Grove Theatre was James Hewlet, a West Indian-born black who distinguished himself in roles in *Othello* and *Rich-ard III.* Hewlet later toured England and billed himself as "The New York and London Colored Comedian." Ira Aldridge, who later distinguished himself as one of the great Shakespearean tragic actors, was also a member of the permanent group that performed at the African Grove Theatre. Aldridge was cast in comic and singing roles as well as in Shakespearean tragedies.

It was at the African Grove Theatre that the first play written and produced by an African American was performed on the American stage. The play was Henry Brown's *The Drama of King Shotaway,* which was presented in June 1823.

Because of disturbances created by whites in the audience, the local police raided the African Grove Theatre on several occasions. The theater evidently was wrecked by police and hoodlums during one of these raids, which forced its closing in late 1823. The group of black actors attached to the African Grove Theatre, determined to preserve their company, continued for several years to present plays at different rented loca-tions throughout New York City.

◆ MINSTRELSY

Talented slaves were among the earliest black entertainers in colonial and antebellum America. On plantations throughout the South, slave performers—using clappers, jawbones, and blacksmith rasps—danced, sang and told jokes for the entertainment of their fellow slaves as well as their masters, who often showcased their talents at local gatherings. Some masters hired out talented slaves to perform in traveling troupes.

During the late 1820s and early 1830s, white entertainers, observing the artistry of black performers, began to imitate blacks in their routines. Blackening their faces with cork, these white entertainers performed jigs, songs, and jokes with topical allusions to blacks in their lyrics. Thus, the art of minstrelsy as theatrical material was born.

White minstrel troupes in blackface became very popular on the American stage in the 1830s. Among some of the more famous white minstrel performers were Thomas Dartmouth Rice, "Daddy Rice," the original "Jim Crow," Edwin Forrest and Dan Emmett, and the Christy Minstrels.

Some traveling white minstrel troupes used African American performers to enhance the authenticity of their productions. One such troupe was the Ethiopian Minstrels, whose star performer was William Henry Lane, an African American dancer who used the stage name "Master Juba." Lane was one of the greatest dancers of his generation. Throughout the United States and England, "Master Juba" was enthusiastically praised by audiences and critics alike. One anonymous English critic, quoted by dance historian Marian Hannah Winter, wrote the following critique of one of Lane's performances:

> Juba exceeded anything ever witnessed in Europe. The style as well as the execution is unlike anything seen in this country. The manner in which he beats time with feet, and the extraordinary command he possesses over them, can only be believed by those who have been present at the exhibition. (1948. "Juba and American Minstrelsy." *Chronicles of the American Dance*, edited by Paul Magriel).

Although black minstrel troupes began to appear in the 1850s, it was not until after the Civil War that they became established on the American stage. Although black minstrels inherited the negative stereotypes of blacks that white minstrels had established, the African American performer won a permanent place on the American stage, providing a training ground for the many black dancers, comedians, singers and composers to come. Notable among these stage personalities were dancer-comedians Billy Kersands, Bert Williams, Bob Height, Dewey "Pigmeat" Martin, and Ernest Hogan; singers like Gertrude "Ma" Rainey and Bessie Smith; and composers James Bland and William Christopher Handy. To a great extent, black minstrelsy created a national appreciation for the talent of black stage entertainers, drawing audiences to black shows and other forms of black entertainment for generations to come.

◆ RECLAIMING THE BLACK IMAGE: 1890 TO 1920

By the 1890s, black producers, writers and stage performers sought to reform the demeaning images of blacks that were prevalent on the American stage. *The Creole Show*, cast by black producer Sam Jack, in 1891, was the first all-black musical to depart from minstrelsy. Featuring an all-black chorus line, *The Creole Show* premiered in Boston in 1891 and later played at the Chicago World's Fair for the entire season. In 1895 black producer John W. Ishaw presented *The Octoroon*, another all-black musical that moved away from the minstrel tradition. *Oriental America*, which Ishaw also produced, broke further from minstrel conventions by not closing with the traditional walkaround, but with an operatic medley.

Trip to Coontown, written and directed by Bob Cole in 1898, completely broke away from the minstrel tradition. The plot of this all-black musical was presented completely through music and dance. The first musical produced, written and performed by African Americans on Broadway, it ushered in a new era for blacks on the American stage.   Between 1898 and 1911, 13 all-black musicals opened on Broadway, showcasing the talents of black musicians, lyricists, directors, producers, and writers.

The highly popular *Clorinda: The Origin of the Cakewalk*, with music by composer Will Marion Cook and lyrics by poet Paul Laurence Dunbar, opened in 1898 at the Casino Roof Garden and featured comedian-singer Ernest Hogan. The comic-dance duo of Bert Williams and George Walker premiered their first Broadway musical, *The Policy Players*, in 1899. This success was followed by Williams and Walker's *Sons of Ham*, which played on Broadway for two seasons beginning in September 1900. Their *In Dahomey*, premiered on Broadway in 1903 and, after a long run, toured successfully in England. *The Southerners*, with music by Will Marion Cook, opened on Broadway in 1904 with an interracial cast starring Abbie Mitchell. The Williams and Walker team returned to Broadway in 1906 with a new musical, *Abyssinia*, which consistently played to a full house.

In the same year the versatile Ernest Hogan appeared on Broadway in *Rufus Rastus*, and in 1902 Hogan starred in *Oyster Man*, which enjoyed a successful run on Broadway. Bob Cole, J. Rosamond Johnson, and

Poster advertising a minstrel performance.

Bert Williams and George Walker

James Weldon Johnson wrote and performed in *The Shoo-Fly Regiment*, another musical that opened on Broadway in 1902. Williams and Walker appeared in their last Broadway production together, *Bandanna Land*, in 1908. George Walker fell into ill health after the show closed, and died in 1911. Bert Williams went on to appear in *Mr. Lord of Koal* on Broadway in 1909, and later was the star comedian performer in the *Ziegfield Follies*. The last black musical to open on Broadway before the 1920s was *His Honor the Barber* in 1911, with S. H. Dudley in the lead.

Black actors on the dramatic stage, like the performers in all-black musicals, struggled to shed the demeaning image of the African American projected by most white-produced minstrelsy and drama. The presentation of three plays—*The Rider of Dreams*, *Granny Maumee*, and *Simon the Cyrenian*—by white playwright Ridgely Torrence at the Garden Theatre in Madison Square Garden on April 5, 1917 was an exceptional and highly successful effort to objectively portray the African American on the dramatic stage.

◆ THE AFRICAN AMERICAN ACTOR, DANCER AND COMEDIAN, 1920 TO 1950

Black Musicals

On May 23, 1921, *Shuffle Along* opened on Broadway, signaling the return of black musicals to "The Great White Way" and the arrival of the Harlem Renaissance on the American stage. Featuring the talented singer-dancer Florence Mills, *Shuffle Along* was written by Noble Sissle, Eubie Blake, Flournoy Miller, and Aubrey Lyles. Florence Mills quickly became a sought-after performer, appearing in *The Plantation Revue*, which opened on Broadway on July 17, 1922, and touring England. In 1926, Mills returned to Harlem and played

the lead in *Black Birds* at the Alhambra Theatre, for a six-week run. Subsequently, Mills performed in Paris for six months.

Noble Sissle and Eubie Blake returned to Broadway on September 24, 1924, with their new musical *Chocolate Dandies*. Two years later, in 1926, Flournoy Miller and Aubrey Lyles opened on Broadway in *Runnin' Wild* which introduced the Charleston to the country. Bill "Bojangles" Robinson, starring in *Blackbirds of 1928*, dazzled Broadway audiences with his exciting tap dancing style. Several other black musicals opened on Broadway during the 1920s, including *Rang Tang* (1927), *Keep Shuffling* (1928), and *Hot Chocolates* (1929).

Porgy and Bess, opening on Broadway in 1935, became the major all-black musical production of the 1930s. With music by George Gershwin, this adaptation of the novel and play by DuBose and Dorothy Heyward was an immediate success as a folk opera. Todd Duncan was cast as Porgy, with Ann Brown as Bess, and comedian-dancer John Bubbles as the character Sportin' Life.

In the 1940s, black musicals were scarce on Broadway. *Cabin in the Sky*, starring Ethel Waters, Dooley Wilson, Todd Duncan, Rex Ingram, J. Rosamond Johnson, and Katherine Dunham and her dancers ran for 165 performances after it opened on October 25, 1940. *Carmen Jones*, perhaps the most successful all-black musical of the decade, opened in 1943 with Luther Saxon, Napoleon Reed, Carlotta Franzel and Cozy Cove; it had a run of 231 performances and was taken on tour. In 1946 *St. Louis Woman*, featuring Rex Ingram, Pearl Bailey, Juanita Hall and June Hawkins, played a short run to mixed reviews.

The Dramatic Theater

During the Harlem Renaissance years, the African American dramatic actor remained less active than the black performer in musicals, and the image of the African American projected by white playwrights was generally inadequate. For example, when Charles Gilpin starred in Eugene O'Neill's *Emperor Jones* at the Provincetown Theatre in 1920, critic Loften Mitchell noted that:

> This play, while offering one of the most magnificent roles for a Negro in the American theatre, is the first in a long line to deal with the Negro on this level. O'Neill obviously saw in the Negro rich subject matter, but he was either incapable or unwilling to deal directly with the matter. (1967, *Black Drama, the Story of the American Negro in the Theatre*).

Nonetheless, African American actors and actresses had to accept the roles in which they were cast by white

Bill "Bojangles" Robinson performing with Shirley Temple in the movie "The Little Colonel," 1935.

playwrights. In 1924, the O'Neill play *All God's Chillun' Got Wings* opened at the Provincetown Theatre, with Paul Robeson and Mary Blair to mixed reviews because of its interracial theme. Rose McClendon starred in Paul Green's Pulitzer Prize-winning *In Abraham's Bosom* in 1926, and was ably supported by Abbie Mitchell and Jules Bledsoe. Marc Connelly's *Green Pastures* opened on Broadway on February 26, 1930; with Richard B. Harrison playing "De Lawd" it ran for 557 performances and was taken on an extensive road tour.

Three plays by Langston Hughes that did treat the African American objectively were produced successfully on Broadway in the 1930s. *Mulatto*, which opened in 1935 and starred Rose McClendon and Morris McKenney, had the longest Broadway run of any play written by an African American in the history of the American theater, with 373 consecutive performances. It was followed by *Little Ham* (1935) and *Troubled Island* (1936).

The Federal Theater Project

In the mid-1930s the Works Progress Administration (WPA) sponsored one of the greatest organized efforts to assist and encourage American actors, especially African American actors. The Federal Theater Project employed a total of 851 black actors to work in 16 segregated units of the project in Chicago, New York, and other cities from 1935 until 1939, when Congress ended the project. While the project was in operation, black actors appeared in 75 plays, including classics, vaudeville contemporary comedy, children's shows, circuses, and "living newspaper" performances. Notable among the black actors who worked in the project, and later became stars on Broadway and in the film, were Butterfly McQueen, Canada Lee, Rex Ingram, Katherine Dunham, Edna Thomas, Thomas Anderson and Arthur Dooley Wilson.

In the wake of the Federal Theater Project, The American Negro Theater was established in Harlem by Abram Hill, Austin Briggs-Hall, Frederick O'Neal, and Hattie King-Reeves. Its objective was to authentically portray black life and to give black actors and playwrights a forum for their talents. Some of their productions eventually made it to Broadway. In 1944, the theater produced *Anna Lucasta* in the basement of the 135th Street Library in Harlem. It was successful enough to move to Broadway, and featured Hilda Simms, Frederick O'Neal, Alice Childress, Alvin Childress, Earle Hyman, and Herbert Henry. Abram Hill's *Walk Hard* opened in Harlem in 1946, and became a Broadway production with Maxwell Glanville in the lead. The American Negro Theater provided a training ground for many black actors who later became stars on Broadway and in Hollywood, including Ruby Dee, Ossie Davis, Harry Belafonte, and Sidney Poitier.

Dramatic Theater in the 1950s

The rise of television in the 1950s generally had an adverse affect on the American theater. Employment for all actors fell sharply, especially for black actors. Ethel Waters did, however, open on Broadway in 1950 as the lead in *Member of the Wedding*, which was well-received. Louis Peterson's *Take a Giant Step* opened on Broadway in September 1953 to critical praise; in the cast were Frederick O'Neal, Helen Martin, Maxwell Glanville, Pauline Myers, Estelle Evans, and Louis Gossett, Jr.

One of the most successful all-black plays to appear on Broadway opened in March 1959: Lorraine Hansberry's *Raisin in the Sun*, which won the New York Drama Critics Circle Award. Its cast included Sidney Poitier, Ruby Dee, Diana Sands, Claudia McNeil, Louis Gossett, Jr., Ivan Dixon, Lonnie Elder, III, and Douglas Turner Ward. *Raisin in the Sun* indicated the future of blacks in the American theater.

Black Dance

Black dance, like other forms of black entertainment, had its beginnings in Africa and on the plantations of early America, where slaves performed to entertain themselves and their masters. White minstrels in blackface incorporated many of these black dance inventions into their shows, while dancers in black minstrelsy, such as "Master Juba" (William Henry Lane) thrilled audiences with their artistry.

Many performers in the early black musicals that appeared on Broadway from 1898 and 1910 were expert show dancers, such as George Walker and Bert Williams. Similarly, in the all-black musicals of the 1920s, performers like Florence Mills and Bill "Bojangles" Robinson captivated audiences with their show dancing. The musical *Runnin' Wild* (1926) was responsible for creating the Charleston dance craze of the "Roaring Twenties."

By the early 1930s, black pioneers of modern dance were appearing on the dance stage. Four of these black innovators were Hemsley Winfield, Asadata Dafore, Katherine Dunham, and Pearl Primus.

Hemsley Winfield presented what was billed as "The First Negro Concert in America" in Manhattan's Chanin Building on April 31, 1931. Two suites on African themes were performed, along with solos by Edna Guy and Winfield himself. In 1933, Winfield became the first black to dance for the Metropolitan Opera, performing the role of the Witch Doctor in *Emperor Jones*.

Austin Asadata Dafore Horton, a native of Sierra Leone, electrified audiences in New York with his 1934 production of *Kykunkor*. Dance historian Lynne Fauley Emery concludes that *Kykunkor* "was the first performance by black dancers on the concert stage which was entirely successful. It revealed the potential of ethnic material to black dancers, and herein lay Dafore's value as a great influence on black concert dance" (1988, *Black Dance from 1619 to Today*).

Katherine Dunham had her first lead dance role in Ruth Page's West Indian ballet *La Guiablesse* in 1933. In 1936, Dunham received a master's degree in anthropology from the University of Chicago; her thesis was on *The Dances of Haiti*, the result of her on-site study of native dances in the West Indies. For the next 30 years, Dunham and her dance company toured the United States and Europe, dazzling audiences with her choreography. During the 1963-64 season, Dunham choreographed the Metropolitan Opera's production of *Aida*, becoming the first black American to do so.

Pearl Primus, like Katherine Dunham, was trained in anthropology. Her research in primitive African dance inspired her first composition performed as a profes-

Katherine Dunham, a pioneer of modern dance, 1992.

sional dancer, *African Ceremonial*, which she presented on February 14, 1943. On October 4, 1944, Primus made her Broadway debut at the Belasco Theater in New York. Her performance included dances of West Indian, African and African American origin; the concert was widely acclaimed and launched her career as a dancer. Primus has traveled to Africa many times to research African dances; in 1959 she was named director of Liberia's Performing Arts Center. She later opened the Primus-Borde School of Primal Dance with her husband, dancer Percival Borde, and is currently involved in Pearl Primus Dance Language Institute in New Rochelle, New York.

By late 1950s, several black dancers and dance companies were distinguishing themselves on the concert stage. Janet Collins was the "premiere danseuse" of the Metropolitan Opera Ballet from 1951 until 1954. Arthur Mitchell made his debut as a principal dancer with the New York City Ballet in 1955. Alvin Ailey established his company in 1958. And Geoffrey Holder, who made his Broadway debut in 1954 in *House of Flowers*, became a leading choreographer.

The Black Comedian

The earliest black comedian in America, like other early black entertainers, were slaves who in their free time entertained themselves and their masters. In the early minstrel shows, white comedians in blackface created comic caricatures of blacks, whom they referred to as "coons." When African Americans began appearing in minstrel shows shortly after the Civil War, they found themselves burdened with the "coon" comic caricatures created by white performers. The dance-comedy team of Bert Williams and George Walker were the most famous of the early black comedians, appearing in numerous black musicals between 1899 and 1909.

In the all-black musicals of the 1920s, a new comic movement emerged: the comedy of style, which emphasized such antics as rolling the eyes or shaking the hips. The venom and bite of black folk humor was replaced by a comedy of style that was more acceptable to the white audiences of these all-black musicals.

Real black folk humor, however, did survive and thrive in black nightclubs and black theaters such as the Apollo, in Harlem and the Regal in Chicago in the 1930s, 1940s, and 1950s. In these settings, known as the "Chitterling Circuit," such black comedians as Tim Moore, Dusty Fletcher, Butterbeans and Susie, Stepin Fetchit, Jackie "Moms" Mabley, Redd Foxx, and Slappy White performed without restrictions.

◆ THE AFRICAN AMERICAN PERFORMANCE ARTIST SINCE 1960

As the black civil rights movement challenged the national conscience in the 1960s, every facet of African American life changed, including black performing arts. More plays about African Americans by both black and white playwrights were produced, providing increased employment for black actors. On the dance stage, more opportunities were opened to blacks as composers, choreographers, and dancers. And many black comedians, by invitation, moved from the "Chittering Circuit" to posh white-clientele nightclubs, and in some instances to theaters.

The Dramatic Theater

Three events in the 1960s signaled trends that would affect African American dramatic actors for the next 30 years: the production of Jean Genet's play, *The Blacks;* the staging of the Leroi Jones' (Imamu Amiri Baraka) play, *The Dutchman;* and the founding of the Negro Ensemble Company.

On May 4, 1961 *The Blacks,* by French playwright/author Jean Genet, opened off-Broadway at the St. Mark's Theater. A play about African Americans written for white audiences, *The Blacks* provided employment for a host of black actors, including Roscoe Lee Browne, James Earl Jones, Louis Gossett, Jr., Helen Martin, Cicely Tyson, Godfrey Cambridge, Raymond St. Jacques, Maya Angelou, Charles Gordone and many others who appeared in its road tours. Subsequently, black dramatic actors appeared on and off-Broadway in

The Apollo Theater, a popular venue for black entertainment

several major plays by white playwrights. Notable among them were *In White America* by Judith Rutherford Marechal (1968), with Gloria Foster and Moses Gunn; *The Great White Hope* by William Sackler (1968), starring James Earl Jones; and *So Nice, They Named It Twice* by Neil Harris (1975), featuring Bill Jay and Veronica Redd.

On May 23, 1961, when the Leroi Jones play *The Dutchman* opened at the Cherry Lane Theatre, the black revolutionary play was introduced to theater audiences. Black actors were provided with the opportunity to perform in roles that not only affirmed blackness, but portrayed black political militancy. Several black revolutionary plays followed that afforded opportunities for black actors, including James Baldwin's *Blues for Mr. Charlie* (1964), with Al Freeman, Jr. and Diana Sands; and *The Toilet/The Slave,* (1964) by Leroi Jones, starring James Spruill, Walter Jones, Nan Martin, and Al Freeman, Jr. In 1991, black revolutionary plays such as *General Hag's Skeezag* continued to provide important roles for black actors.

Perhaps most beneficial to black actors was the founding of the Negro Ensemble Company in New York in 1967. This theatrical production company, initially

James Earl Jones performing in the play *Fences*, 1987.

financed by a three-year grant of $1,200,000 from the Ford Foundation, was the brainchild of playwright/actor Douglas Turner Ward. Housed originally at the St. Mark's Theater and currently at Theater Four, the Negro Ensemble is headed by actor Robert Hooks as executive director, Gerald Krone as administrative director, and Douglas Turner Ward as artistic director. The Negro Ensemble's objective is to develop African American managers, playwrights, actors, and technicians.

The Negro Ensemble has staged more than 100 productions, including the work of 40 black playwrights, and provided work for countless aspiring and seasoned black actors. Several plays produced by the Negro Ensemble have eventually gone to Broadway, including Douglas Turner Ward's *The River Niger* (1973), which won a Tony Award and an Obie Award, and Charles Fuller's Pulitzer Prize-winning *The Soldier's Play* (1981). A plethora of outstanding black actors and actresses have appeared in Ensemble productions, including Marshall Williams, Denise Nichols, Esther Rolle, Roxie Roker, Adolph Ceasar, Denzel Washington, Moses Gunn, and Barbara Montgomery.

Several black playwrights had plays successfully produced on Broadway independently of the Negro Ensem-

ble Company. Ntozake Shange's widely-acclaimed *For Colored Girls Who Have Considered Suicide/When the Rainbow Is Enuf* (1972) had a cast of seven black women actresses. August Wilson's *Fences*, which opened on March 26, 1987 and featured James Earl Jones, won the 1987 Pulitzer Prize in drama. Wilson's *Two Trains Running*, which opened April 13, 1992 and starred Roscoe Lee Browne and Laurence Fishburne, received the New York Drama Critic's Award for 1992.

Black Musicals

The years from 1961 to the mid-1980s constituted one of the most active periods for African American performers in musical theater. Many of the black musicals produced during these years, both on and off-Broadway, enjoyed substantial runs and extended road tours.

Langston Hughes' musical *Black Nativity* opened on Broadway on December 11, 1961. Directed by Vinette Carroll, the cast was headed by gospel singers Marion Williams and the Stars of Faith, and also featured Alex Bradford, Clive Thompson, Cleo Quitman, and Carl Ford. Although it ran for only 57 performances on

Broadway, it went on to tour extensively throughout the United States and abroad.

In 1964, Sammy Davis, Jr. dazzled Broadway in Clifford Odets' *Golden Boy*. Davis was supported by a brilliant cast which included Robert Guillaume, Louis Gossett, Jr., Lola Falana, and Billy Daniels. *Golden Boy* ran for 586 performances.

Leslie Uggams and Robert Hooks appeared in *Hallelujah Baby*, which opened in New York's Martin Beck Theater on April 26, 1967. *Hallelujah Baby*, a musical look at five decades of black history, received a Tony Award and ran for 293 performances.

Purlie, based on Ossie Davis' 1961 play *Purlie Victorious*, opened on May 9, 1970, with Melba Moore and Robert Guillaume in lead roles. *Purlie* received good reviews and enjoyed a run of 688 performances.

Micki Grant's *Don't Bother Me, I Can't Cope*, starring Micki Grant and Alex Bradford, opened on April 19, 1972 to rave reviews. For this musical, which ran for 1,065 performances, Micki Grant received a Drama Desk Award and an Obie award.

Virginia Capers, Joe Morton and Helen Martin opened *Raisin*, based on Lorraine Hansberry's play *Raisin in the Sun*, on October 13, 1973. *Raisin* received the Tony Award for the best musical in 1974 and had a run of 847 performances.

Despite initially poor reviews, *The Wiz*, a black musical version of *The Wizard of Oz*, became a highly successful show. Opening on Broadway on January 5, 1975, *The Wiz* featured an array of talented performers, including Stephanie Mills, Hinton Battle, Ted Ross, Andre De Shields, Dee Dee Bridgewater, and Mabel King. *The Wiz* swept the Tony Award ceremonies in 1975 and became the longest-running black musical in the history of Broadway, with 1,672 performances.

Ain't Misbehavin', another popular black musical of the 1970s, opened on May 8, 1978. Based on a cavalcade of songs composed by Thomas "Fats" Waller, *Ain't Misbehavin'* starred Nell Carter, Andre DeShields, Armelia McQueen, Ken Page, and Charlene Woodard. It played to Broadway audiences for 1,604 performances and Nell Carter received a Tony Award as "best featured actress."

Two spectacular black musicals premiered on Broadway in the 1980s. *Dream Girls*, which opened at the Imperial Theater on December 20, 1981, captivated Broadway audiences with a cast that included Jennifer Holiday, Cleavant Derricks, Loretta Devine and Cheryl Alexander. *Dream Girls* ran for 1,522 performances on Broadway and had an extensive road tour. Jennifer

Ossie Davis, with co-star Ruby Dee, in the play *Purlie Victorious*, 1961.

Holiday won a Tony Award for her role as Effie Melody White. On April 27, 1986, Debbie Allen opened in the lead role of *Sweet Charity*. Reviews were favorable and the musical enjoyed a run of 386 performances, establishing Debbie Allen as a musical theater actress.

A few new all-black musicals have opened in the early 1990s, including *Five Guys Name Moe*, a tribute to musician Louis Jordan with Clarke Peters and Charles Augin, and *Jelly's Last Jam*, featuring Gregory Hines.

Black Dance

Since the early 1960s, two of the leading dance companies in the United States have been headed by black males and composed largely of black dancers. They are the Alvin Ailey American Dance Theater and the Dance Theater of Harlem.

The Alvin Ailey American Dance Theater

The Alvin Ailey American Dance Theater, since its founding in 1958, has performed before more people throughout the world than any other American dance company. With a touring circuit that has included 48 states and 45 countries on all continents, the Alvin Ailey American Dance Theater has been seen by more than 15,000,000 people. Today, the Alvin Ailey organization consists of three components: the Alvin Ailey American Dance Theater, the Alvin Ailey Repertory Ensemble, and the Alvin Ailey American Dance Center.

Between 1958 and 1988, the Alvin Ailey Dance Theater performed 150 works by 45 choreographers, most of whom were black. Notable among these black choreographers have been Tally Beatty, Donald McKayle, Louis Johnson, Eleo Romare, Billy Wilson, George Faison, Pearl Primus, Judith Jamison, Katherine Dunham, Ulysses Dove, Milton Myers, Kelvin Rotardier, and Gary DeLoatch. More than 250 dancers, again mostly black, have performed with the dance theater. Among its star performers have been Judith Jamison, Clive Thompson, Dudley Wilson, Donna Wood, Gary DeLoatch, George Faison and Sara Yaraborough. A prolific choreographer, Alvin Ailey has created numerous works for his dance theater and other dance companies, including *Revelations* (1958); *Reflections in D*, with music by Duke Ellington (1962); *Quintet* (1968); *Cry* (1971); *Memoria* (1974); and *Three Black Kings* (1976). Alvin Ailey choreographed *Carmen* for the Metropolitan Opera in 1973 and *Precipice* for the Paris Opera in 1983.

The Alvin Ailey Repertory Ensemble was established in 1974 as a training and performing company. Many of its graduates advance to the dance theater or perform with other dance companies. In 1988, the AARE had more than 100 members.

The Alvin Ailey American Dance Center is the official school of the Ailey organization. It attracts students from across the United States and abroad and offers a certificate in dance. The center's curriculum includes training in ballet, the Dunham Technique, jazz, and modern dance.

The Dance Theater of Harlem

In 1969, Arthur Mitchell, who had established himself as one of the leading ballet dancers in the United States, and Karel Shook, a white ballet teacher, founded the Dance Theater of Harlem. The Dance Theater of Harlem made its formal debut in 1971 at the Guggenheim Museum in New York City. Three of Mitchell's works were premiered at this concert: *Rhythmetron*, *Tones*, and *Fete Noire*.

Today, the dance theater's repertory is wide-ranging. It includes works in the Balanchine tradition such as *Serenade*, as well as black-inspired works like *Dougla*. Among the most spectacular works performed by the

Alvin Ailey

theater are *Firebird*, *Giselle*, *Scheherazade*, and *Swan Lake*. Some of the dancers who have had long associations with the theater are Lowell Smith, Virginia Johnson, Shelia Rohan and Troy Game. Many of the theater's graduates have gone on to perform with other dance companies in the United States and Europe. The Dance Theater of Harlem's school currently has about 1,000 students.

Between 1960 and 1990, several other black dancers have led distinguished careers in concert dance and show dancing. Among them have been Eleo Pomare, Debbie Allen, Rod Rogers, Fred Benjamin, Pepsi Bethel, Eleanor Hampton, Charles Moore, Garth Fagan, Carmen de Lavallade, and Mary Hinkson. Foremost among black choreographers have been Geoffrey Holder, Louis Johnson, and Donald McKayle. Prominent among the black dancers who are reviving the tap dance tradition are Chuck Green, Buster Brown, Honi Coles, Hinton Battle, Gregory Hines, Lavaughn Robinson, and Nita Feldman.

The Black Comedian

Black comedians enjoyed greater exposure during the 1960s. No longer confined to the "Chitterling Cir-

Judith Jamison, a dancer in the Alvin Ailey Dance Theater, performing in 1977.

cuit," comedians such as Jackie "Moms" Mabley, Redd Foxx, and Slappy White began to perform to audiences in exclusive white clubs as well as to audiences within the black community. They used black folk humor to comment on politics, civil rights, work, sex, and a variety of other subjects. Jackie "Moms" Mabley made two popular recordings: *Moms Mabley at the UN* and *Moms Mabley at the Geneva Conference.* In January 1972, Redd Foxx premiered on television as Fred Sanford in "Sanford and Son," which remains one of the most popular syndicated shows.

Several younger black comedians came into prominence in the early 1960s. Dick Gregory used black folk humor to make political commentary. Bill Cosby specialized in amusing chronicles about boyhood in America. Godfrey Cambridge, although successful, did not rely on black folk humor. During the late 1960s and the early 1970s, Flip Wilson, who parodied historical and social experience by creating black characters who lived in a black world, became extremely popular on television. His cast of characters, which included "Freddy the Playboy," "Sammy the White House Janitor," and

Arthur Mitchell

"Geraldine," were the epitome of black folk humor as commentary on an array of issues.

Another pivotal black comedian who began his career in the 1960s was Richard Pryor. His well-timed, risque, sharp folk humor quickly won him a large group of faithful fans. Pryor, who has recorded extensively, has starred successfully in several films, including *Lady Sings the Blues*, *Car Wash*, and *Stir Crazy*.

During the 1980s and 1990s, numerous black comedians have become successful in the various entertain-ment media. Eddie Murphy made his first appearance on the television show "Saturday Night Live" on November 15, 1980. From television, Murphy went on to Hollywood, making his movie debut in the film *48 Hours* in 1982. Starring roles followed in such films as *Beverly Hills Cop*, which was the highest-grossing comedy film in history, and *Coming to America*. Murphy has established his own company, Eddie Murphy Productions, to create and produce television and film projects. Arsenio Hall came to prominence in 1987 as a successful interim guest host on the now defunct "The Late Show," which

Gregory Hines (right) dancing with his brother Maurice, 1982.

won him a lucrative movie contract with Paramount Pictures. In 1988, Hall was featured with Eddie Murphy in the film *Coming to America*. and hosted his own highly successful late-night talk show.

◆ AFRICAN AMERICAN PERFORMANCE ARTISTS

Alvin Ailey (1931-1989)
Dancer, Choreographer

Alvin Ailey was born in Rogers, Texas, on January 5, 1931. He was the founder of the Alvin Ailey American Dance Theatre and won international fame as both dancer and choreographer. Ailey studied dancing after graduating from high school, where he was a star athlete. After briefly attending college, Ailey joined the stage crew of the Lester Horton Theater in Los Angeles, for which Ailey eventually performed as a dancer. In 1953, after Horton's death, Ailey became the company choreographer. In 1954, Ailey performed on Broadway as the lead dancer in *House of Flowers*.

Ailey formed his own dance group in 1958 and began giving four performances annually. In 1962, the Ailey

troupe made an official State Department tour of Australia, receiving accolades throughout the country. One critic called Ailey's work "the most stark and devastating theatre ever presented in Australia."   After numerous appearances as a featured dancer with Harry Belafonte and others, Ailey performed in a straight dramatic role with Claudia McNeil in Broadway's *Tiger, Tiger Burning Bright*. Other Broadway appearances included *Ding Dong Bell*, *Dark of the Moon*, and *African Holiday*. Ailey also choreographed or staged several operas, including Barber's *Anthony and Cleopatra* (1966), Bernstein's *Mass* (1971), and Bizet's *Carmen*. In addition, Ailey created works for various international ballet stars and companies.

In 1965, Ailey took his group on one of the most successful European tours ever made by an American dance company. In London, it was held over six weeks to accommodate the demand for tickets, and in Hamburg it received an unprecedented 61 curtain calls. A German critic called this performance "a triumph of sweeping, violent beauty, a furious spectacle. The stage vibrates. One has never seen anything like it." In 1970, Ailey's company became the first American modern dance group to tour the Soviet Union.

Bill Cosby, 1992.

Eddie Murphy

During the mid-seventies Ailey, among his other professional commitments, devoted much time to creating special jazz dance sequences for America's Bicentennial celebration. Among numerous honors, including several honorary degrees, Ailey was awarded the NAACP's Spingarn Medal in 1976. Ailey died on December 1, 1989.

Ira Aldridge (1805-1867)
Actor

Born around 1805 in New York City, Ira Aldridge was one of the leading Shakespearean actors of the nineteenth century. Although he was denied the opportunity to perform before the American public in his prime, the fame that he won abroad established him as one of the prominent figures of international theater.

Aldridge's origins are obscure. Some accounts give his birthplace as Africa; others name Bel-Air, Maryland; still others list New York City. The year of his birth is also uncertain, reported dates range from 1804 to 1807. It seems clear that he attended the African Free School in New York until he was about 16 years old, at which time he left home.

Aldridge's early dramatic training centered around the African Grove Theatre in New York in 1821. His first

role was in *Pizarro,* and he subsequently played a variety of small roles in classical productions before accepting employment as a steward on a ship bound for England.

After studying briefly at the University of Glasgow in Scotland, Aldridge went to London in 1825 and appeared in the melodrama *Surinam, or a Slave's Revenge.* In 1833, he appeared in London's Theatre Royal in the title role of *Othello,* earning wide acclaim. For the next three decades, he toured the continent with great success, often appearing before European royalty.

Aldridge died in Lodz, Poland, in August, 1867. He is honored by a commemorative tablet in the New Memorial Theatre in Stratford-upon-Avon, England.

Debbie Allen (1950-)
Actress, Singer, Dancer, Director

Debbie Allen was born on January 16, 1950, in Houston, Texas. A cum laude graduate of Howard University, Allen began her career on the Broadway stage in the chorus line of the hit musical *Purlie* (1972). She then portrayed Beneatha in the Tony and Grammy award winning musical *Raisin* (1973). Other early stage roles were in the national touring company of *Guys and Dolls* and the drama *Anna Lucasta,* performed for the New Federal Theatre at the Henry Street Settlement in New York.

Allen was subsequently selected to star in an NBC pilot, *3 Girls 3,* and then appeared on other television

Debbie Allen

hits such as "Good Times" and "The Love Boat." At this time, her talent as a choreographer recognized, she worked on such television projects as "Midnight Special" as well as two films, *The Fish that Saved Pittsburgh* (1979) and *Under Fire* (1981).

The year of 1982 was pivotal for Allen. She appeared in the film *Ragtime* and the television series, "Fame" as well as the Joseph Papp television special, "Alice at the Palace." Allen also starred in a dance performance for the Academy Awards ceremonies.

Allen's career continued with roles in the television special, *Ben Vereen ... His Roots* and the miniseries "Roots: The Next Generation" (1979). She also appeared on stage again in *Ain't Misbehavin* (1979) and a revival of *West Side Story* (1980), which earned her a Tony Award nomination and a Drama Desk Award.

As each season passed on "Fame," Allen became more involved as choreographer and was soon regularly directing episodes of the series. In 1988, she was selected by the producers to become director of the television sitcom "A Different World." In another acknowledgment of her stature as a performer and creative talent, she starred in her own television special during the 1988-89 season.　In 1995, Allen appeared with LL Cool J in the TV show "In the House." She also worked as director of the TV program "Out of Sync."

Eddie "Rochester" Anderson (1905-1977)
Comedian

For many years, Eddie Anderson was the only black performing regularly on a network radio show. As the character Rochester on the Jack Benny program, he became one of the best-known black American entertainers.

Anderson was born in Oakland, California on September 18, 1905, the son of "Big Ed" Anderson, a minstrel performer, and Ella Mae, a tightwire walker. During the 1920s and early 1930s, Anderson traveled throughout the Middle and Far West singing, dancing, and performing as a clown in small clubs. On Easter Sunday 1937, he was featured on Jack Benny's radio show, in what was supposed to be a single appearance; Anderson was such a hit that he quickly became a regular on the program.

Anderson is best known for his work with Benny (in television as well as on radio), but he also appeared in a number of movies, including *What Price Hollywood?* (1932), *Cabin in the Sky* (1943), and *It's a Mad, Mad, Mad, Mad World* (1963).

Anderson died on February 28, 1977 at the age of 71.

Pearl Bailey (1918-1990)
Singer, Actress

Born March 29, 1918 in Newport News, Virginia, Pearl Bailey moved to Philadelphia with her family in 1933. She sang at small clubs in Scranton, Pennsylvania and in Washington, D.C., before becoming the vocalist for the band of Cootie Williams and later for Count Basie. In the early 1940s, Baily had her first successful New York engagements at the Village Vanguard and the Blue Angel. During World War II, she toured with the USO. Bailey made her New York stage debut in 1946 in *St. Louis Woman*, for which she won a Donaldson Award as the year's most promising new performer. She also appeared in the films *Variety Girl* (1947) and *Isn't it Romantic?* (1948).

During the 1950s Bailey appeared in the movies *Carmen Jones*, *That Certain Feeling*, and *Porgy and Bess*, and on Broadway in *House of Flowers*. In the 1950s and 1960s, she worked as a recording artist, nightclub headliner, and television performer. In 1967, she received a special Tony Award for her starring role on Broadway in *Hello, Dolly*. In 1969, she published an autobiography, *The Raw Pearl*. Her other books include

Eddie Anderson

Talking to Myself (1971), *Pearl's Kitchen* (1973), *Duey Tale* (1975), and *Hurry Up, America, and Spit* (1976).

In 1975, Bailey was named a special adviser to the United States Mission to the United Nations. In 1976, she appeared in the film *Norman, Is That You?* with Redd Foxx, and on stage in Washington, D.C., in *Something To Do*, a musical saluting the American worker. She also received an award in 1976 from the Screen Actors Guild for Outstanding Achievement in Fostering the Finest Ideals of the Acting Profession. Georgetown University made her an honorary doctor of Human Letters in 1977.

In January 1980, Bailey gave a one-night concert at Radio City Music Hall in New York. In 1981, she performed as the voice of the cartoon character "Owl" in the Disney movie *The Fox and the Hound*.

Bailey married the jazz drummer Louis Bellson in 1952. She died August 17, 1990, in Philadelphia.

Josephine Baker (1906-1975)
Dancer, Singer

Born in St. Louis on June 3, 1906, Josephine Baker received little formal education; she left school at the age of eight to supplement the family income by working as a kitchen helper and baby-sitter. While still in elementary school, she took a part-time job as a chorus girl. At 17, she performed as a chorus girl in Noble Sissle's musical comedy *Shuffle Along*, which played in Radio City Music Hall in 1923. Her next show was *Chocolate Dandies*, followed by a major dancing part in *La Revue Nègre*, an American production that introduced *le jazz hot* to Paris in 1925.

In Paris, Baker left the show to create her most sensational role, that of the "Dark Star" of the Folies Bergère. In her act, she appeared topless on a mirror, clad only in a protective waist shield of rubber bananas. The spectacular dance made her an overnight star and a public figure with a loyal following. In true "star" tradition, she catered to her fans by adopting such flamboyant eccentricities as walking pet leopards down the Champs-Elysèes.

In 1930, after completing a world tour, Baker made her debut as a singing and dancing comedienne at the Casino de Paris. Critics called her a "complete artist, the perfect master of her tools." In time, she ventured into films, starring alongside French idol Jean Gabin in *Zouzou* (1934), and into light opera, performing in *La Créole* (1934), an operetta about a Jamaican girl.

During World War II, Baker served first as a Red Cross volunteer, and later did underground intelligence work through an Italian Embassy attaché. After the war, the French government decorated her with the Legion of Honor. She returned to the entertainment world, regularly starring at the Folies Bergère, appearing on French television, and going on another extended international tour. In 1951, in the course of a successful American tour, Baker made headlines by speaking out against discrimination and refusing to perform in segregated venues.

Beginning in 1954, Baker earned another reputation—not as a lavish and provocative entertainer, but as a progressive humanitarian. She used her fortune to begin adopting and tutoring a group of orphaned babies of all races, retiring from the stage in 1956 to devote all her time to her "rainbow family." Within three years, however, her "experiment in brotherhood" had taken such a toll on her finances that she was forced to return to the stage, starring in *Paris, Mes Amours*, a musical based in part on her own fabled career.

Baker privately, and without voicing discouragement, survived numerous financial crises. Illness hardly managed to dampen her indomitable spirit. Through her long life, she retained her most noteworthy stage attributes—an intimate, subdued voice, coupled with an infectiously energetic and vivacious manner.

Josephine Baker

Baker died in Paris on April 12, 1975, after opening a gala to celebrate her fiftieth year in show business.

Angela Bassett (1959?-)
Actress

Born in St. Petersburg, Florida, in the late 1950s, Angela Bassett was one of two daughters of a single mother and grew up in public housing. Inspired to the acting craft after witnessing a stage performance by James Earl Jones when she was a teenager, Bassett earned top grades and enrolled in Yale University. After receiving a master's degree from its prestigious school of drama in the early 1980s, Bassett settled in New York City and began winning acting roles in an industry not particularly known for a wealth of interesting, non-stereotypical roles offered to African American women.

Bassett found work in television commercials, the CBS daytime television drama *The Guiding Light,* and debuted on Broadway in the acclaimed musical *Ma Rainey's Black Bottom.* Film roles were next on the horizon; in 1991, she appeared in two notable films, John Singleton's *Boyz N the Hood* —a casting that came with the good word of her friend, actor Larry Fishburne—and John Sayles' *City of Hope.* Her work attracted the

attention of filmmaker Spike Lee, who cast her as Betty Shabazz, wife of Malcolm X, in his 1992 film biography of the slain leader. Bassett's portrayal won high marks from critics for its intensity and sensitivity.

Once again voicing strong support for his acting colleague, Fishburne agreed to play the role of 1960s soul musician Ike Turner in a film on the condition that Bassett won its starring role based on Tina Turner's autobiography. The 1993 film *What's Love Got to Do With It* catapulted Bassett into major stardom and won her rave reviews from critics for the vivid depiction of some of the more harrowing years of the singer's life. She won Golden Globe for her efforts as well as two NAACP Image Awards. Late in 1995, Bassett appeared in a lead role in the cyberspace thriller *Strange Days* opposite Ralph Fiennes and in the Eddie Murphy comedy *Vampire in Brooklyn.* Later that same year the actress won further critical acclaim for her ensemble-cast part in 1995's *Waiting to Exhale,* the box-office hit based on novelist Terry McMillan's tale of a close-knit quartet of African American women.

Tyson Beckford (1970-)
Fashion Model

Born December 19, 1970, in the Bronx borough of New York City, Beckford spent part of his childhood in Jamaica but has lived in Harlem since the age of seven. His mother's own modeling career would later prove the catalyst—of sorts—for Beckford's career; she took him with her to runway shows, but more importantly raised him with a strong hand that helped him negotiate around much of the trouble that can tempt teens in some of the rougher areas of Harlem. Beckford did get involved in some reckless incidents, however, and even spent one night in jail once.

Beckford's entry into modeling came when New York City-based rap music/hip-hop culture magazine *The Source* liked his unusual features (Beckford's grandfather was of Asian descent) and asked him to pose for a layout, an offer he came close to refusing. That 1993 spread led him to Bethann Hardison, the premier agent for African African modeling talent who is also a vociferous proponent of the need to integrate the plethora of images in advertising that assault the public on a daily basis.

Beckford's entry into the high-stakes world of modeling happened quickly, and his projection of "street cred" looks instantly made him one of the hottest male models in an industry not particularly known for its celebration of the black male. Soon Beckford was appearing in *Gentleman's Quarterly* and the *New York Times,* and became the first African American male to wear Ralph Lauren clothing in the American designer's glossy spreads. When he signed a lucrative contract with Lauren, Beckford became the first male "supermodel," joining the ranks of such top-earning female talents as Christy Turlington and Naomi Campbell. Ironically, Lauren's high-priced duds have long been a status symbol among urban-dwelling African American males much like the pre-stardom Beckford and his friends, who live worlds apart from the multi-page posh-life ad spreads for which Lauren is best known.

Beckford continues to reside in Harlem and keeps company with the same set of friends he had before becoming famous. With Hardison helping him negotiate the somewhat shark-infested waters of the fashion industry, Beckford is poised to make serious inroads into projecting a distinctly more truer vision of the African American male to the world. In 1995, *People* named him one of the "50 Most Beautiful People," and he was dubbed Male Model of the Year at the 1995 VH1 Fashion and Video Awards ceremony.

Harry Belafonte (1927-)
Singer, Actor

Born on March 1, 1927, in New York City, Harry Belafonte moved to the West Indies at the age of eight. At 13, Belafonte returned to New York, where he attended high school. Belafonte joined the Navy in 1944; after his discharge, while working as a janitor in New York, he became interested in drama. He studied acting at Stanley Kubrick's Dramatic Workshop and with Erwin Piscator at the New School for Social Research, where his classmates included Marlon Brando and Walter Matthau. A successful singing engagement at The Royal Roost, a New York jazz club, led to other engagements around the country. But Belafonte, dissatisfied with the music he was performing, returned to New York, opened a restaurant in Greenwich Village, and studied folk singing. His first appearances as a folk singer in the 1950s "helped give folk music a period of mass appeal," according to John S. Wilson in a 1981 *New York Times* article. During his performances at the Palace Theater in New York, Belafonte had audiences calypsoing in the aisles.

Belafonte produced the first integrated musical shows on television, which both won him two Emmy awards and resulted in his being fired by the sponsor. The famous incident in which white British singer Petula Clark touched his arm while singing a song caused a national furor in pre-civil rights America. When Dr. Martin Luther King marched on Montgomery, Alabama, and Washington, D.C., Harry Belafonte joined him and brought along a large contingent of performers. Touring in the stage musical *Three for Tonight* in which he had appeared on Broadway in 1955, Belafonte was forced to flee in the middle of a performance in Spartanburg, South Carolina, and be rushed to the airport in the mayor's car. Word had come that the Ku Klux Klan was marching on the theater.

Belafonte also appeared on Broadway in John Murray Anderson's *Almanac* (1953), and his movies include *Carmen Jones* (1954), *Island in the Sun (1957)*, *The World, the Flesh, and the Devil* (1958), *Odds against Tomorrow* (1959), *The Angel Levine* (1969), *Buck and the Preacher* (1972), *Uptown Saturday Night* (1974), and *White Man's Burden* (1995). He also directed the film *Port Chicago* in 1994.

In the 1980s, Belafonte appeared in his first dramatic role on television in the NBC presentation of "Grambling's White Tiger," and in 1981, Columbia Records released his first album in seven years, *Loving You Is Where I Belong*, consisting of mostly ballads. He has received numerous awards and honors, including the 1982 Martin Luther King, Jr. Nonviolent Peace Prize and three honorary doctorates. Belafonte received the Thurgood Marshall Lifetime Achievement Award in 1993 and the National Medal of Arts in 1994.

James Hubert "Eubie" Blake (1883-1983)
Musician, Composer

Eubie Blake was born in Baltimore on February 7, 1883. The son of former slaves, Blake was the last of ten children and the only one to survive beyond two months. His mother worked as a laundress, his father as a stevedore.

At the age of six, Blake started taking piano lessons. He studied under the renowned teacher Margaret Marshall and subsequently was taught musical composition by Llewelyn Wilson, who at one time conducted an all-black symphony orchestra sponsored by the city of Baltimore. At the age of 17, Blake was playing for a Baltimore night club.

In 1915, Blake joined Noble Sissle. That year, Blake and Sissle sold their first song, "It's All Your Fault," to Sophie Tucker, and her introduction of the song started them on their way. Blake and Sissle moved to New York and, together with Flournoy Miller and Aubrey Lyles, created one of the pioneer black shows, *Shuffle Along*, in 1921; the show was produced again on Broadway in 1952. *Chocolate Dandies* and *Elsie* followed in 1924.

During the early 1930s, Blake collaborated with Andy Razaf and wrote the musical score for Lew Leslie's *Blackbirds*. Out of this association came the hit *Memories of You*. During World War II, Blake was appointed musical conductor for the United Services Organizations (USO) Hospital Unit. In 1946 he announced his retirement and enrolled in New York University.

For many years, Blake's most requested song was "Charleston Rag," which he composed in 1899 and which was written down by someone else because

Blake could not then read music. Among his most famous songs were "How Ya' Gonna Keep 'Em Down on the Farm," "Love Will Find a Way," and "You're Lucky to Me." Some of his other works include "I'm Just Wild About Harry," "Serenade Blues," "It's All Your Fault," and "Floradora Girls," with lyrics by Sissle.

Though known as the master of ragtime, Blake always most loved the music of the classical masters. In the intimacy of his Brooklyn studio, Blake rarely played the music for which the world reveres him. In 1978, Blake's life and career were celebrated in the Broadway musical *Eubie!*. Several thousand people attended concerts at the Shubert Theatre and St. Peters Lutheran Church celebrating Blake's 100th birthday on February 8, 1983. Blake also received honorary doctorates from numerous colleges and universities. He died on February 12, 1983.

John Bubbles (1902-1986)
Dancer, Singer

John Bubbles, inventor of rhythm tap dancing, was born John William Sublett in 1902 in Louisville, Kentucky. At the age of seven, he teamed with a fellow bowling-alley pinboy, Ford "Buck" Washington, to form what became one of the top vaudeville acts in show business. Throughout the 1920s and 1930s, Buck and Bubbles played the top theaters in the country at fees of up to $1,750 a week. The two appeared in several films, including *Cabin in the Sky* (1943). Bubbles captured additional fame as "Sportin' Life" in the 1935 version of *Porgy and Bess*. After Buck's death in 1955, Bubbles virtually disappeared from show business until 1964, when he teamed up with Anna Maria Alberghetti in a successful nightclub act.

In 1979, at the age of 77 and partially crippled from an earlier stroke, Bubbles recreated his characterization of "Sportin' Life" for a one-night show entitled *Black Broadway* at New York's Lincoln Center. The show was repeated in 1980 for a limited engagement at the Town Hall in New York. In the fall of 1980, Bubbles received a Lifetime Achievement Award from the American Guild of Variety Artists and a Certificate of Appreciation from the city of New York.

Bubbles died on May 19, 1986, at the age of 84.

Anita Bush (1883-1974)
Actress, Singer

Born in 1883, Anita Bush was involved with the theater from early childhood. Her father was the tailor for the Bijou, a large neighborhood theater in Brooklyn, and Anita would carry the costumes to the theater for him, giving her a backstage view of performers and productions. Her singing/acting career took off in her early twenties, when she was in the chorus of the Williams and Walker Company. With Williams and Walker, she performed in such Broadway hits as *Abyssinia* and *In Dahomey*, which also had a successful European tour. When the group split up in 1909, she went on to form the Anita Bush Stock Company, which included her own show of chorus girls and such greats as Charles Gilpin and Dooley Wilson, with whom she also founded the Lafayette Players.

Bush died on February 16, 1974.

Godfrey Cambridge (1933-1976)
Actor, Comedian

Born in New York on February 26, 1933, Godfrey Cambridge's parents had emigrated from British Guiana. He attended grammar school in Nova Scotia, while living with his grandparents. After finishing his schooling in New York at Flushing High School and Hofstra College, he went on to study acting.

Cambridge made his Broadway debut in *Nature's Way* (1956), and was featured in *Purlie Victorious* both on stage in 1961, and later on screen. He also appeared off-Broadway in *Lost in the Stars* (1958), *Take a Giant Step*, and *The Detective Story* (1960). Cambridge won the Obie award for the 1960-1961 season's most distinguished off-Broadway performance for his role in *The Blacks*. In 1965, he starred in a stock version of *A Funny Thing Happened on the Way to the Forum*.

As a comedian, Cambridge appeared on "The Tonight Show" and many other variety hours. His material, drawn from the contemporary racial situation, was often presented in the style associated with the contemporary wave of black comedians. One of Cambridge's most memorable roles was as the star of a seriocomic Hollywood film, *The Watermelon Man* (1970), in which the comedian played a white man who changes color overnight. Cambridge has also performed dramatic roles on many television series.   During the mid-seventies, Cambridge remained in semi-retirement, making few public appearances. Cambridge died at the age of 43 in California on November 29, 1976. His death occurred on a Warner Brothers set, where he was playing the role of Ugandan dictator Idi Amin for the television film "Victory at Entebbe."

Diahann Carroll (1935-)
Actress, Singer

Diahann Carroll was born in the Bronx on July 17, 1935, the daughter of a subway conductor and a nurse.

Godfrey Cambridge

As a child, she was a member of the Abyssinian Baptist Church choir; at the age of ten, Carroll won a Metropolitan Opera scholarship. Singing lessons held little appeal for her, however, so she continued her schooling at the High School of Music and Art. As a concession to her parents, Carroll enrolled at New York University, where she was to be a sociology student, but stage fever led her to an appearance on a television talent show, which netted her $1,000. A subsequent appearance at the Latin Quarter club launched her professional career.

In 1954, Carroll appeared in *House of Flowers*, winning favorable press notices. In that year, she also appeared in a film version of *Carmen Jones*, in the role of Myrt.

Movie and television appearances kept Carroll busy until 1958, the year she was slated to appear as an Asian in Richard Rodgers' *Flower Drum Song*. The part did not materialize. Three years later, Rodgers cast her in *No Strings* as a high-fashion model, a role for which she earned a Tony award in 1962.

In the late 1960s, Carroll was cast as lead in the television series "Julia," in which she played a nurse and war widow. She also appeared in the films *Porgy and*

Bess (1959); *Goodbye Again* (1961); *Paris Blues* (1961); *Claudine*, with James Earl Jones (1974); *Sister, Sister* (1982); and *The Five Heartbeats* (1991). She has been featured in the television series "Dynasty" and "A Different World" and has written an autobiography.

In 1995, Carroll appeared on stage in the Broadway musical *Sunset Boulevard*.

Bill Cosby (1937-)
Actor, Comedian

Born on July 12, 1937, Bill Cosby is one of the most successful performers and businessmen in the United States.

A native of Philadelphia, Cosby dropped out of high school to become a medic in the Navy, obtaining his diploma while in the service. On becoming a civilian, he entered Temple University, where he played football and worked evenings as a bartender.

While doing this work, Cosby began to entertain the customers with his comedy routines and, encouraged by his success, left Temple in 1962 to pursue a career in show business. He began by playing small clubs around Philadelphia and in New York's Greenwich Village. Within two years, he was playing the top nightclubs around the country and making television appearances on the Johnny Carson (also acting as guest host), Jack Paar, and Andy Williams shows. Cosby became the first black to star in a prime time television series. "I Spy" ran from 1965 to 1968 and won Cosby three Emmy Awards.

In the 1970s, Cosby appeared regularly in nightclubs in Las Vegas, Tahoe, and Reno, and did commercials for such sponsors as Jell-O, Del Monte and Ford. From 1969 until 1972, he had his own television series, *The Bill Cosby Show*. During the early 1970s he developed and contributed vocals to the Saturday morning children's show "Fat Albert and the Cosby Kids." He appeared in such films as *Uptown Saturday Night* (1974), *Let's Do It Again* (1975), *A Piece of the Action* (1977), and the award-winning television movie *To All My Friends on Shore*.

In 1975, Random House published his book, *Bill Cosby's Personal Guide to Tennis: or, Don't Lower the Lob, Raise the Net*. For several years, he was involved in educational television with the Children's Television Workshop. He returned to college, spending five years at the University of Massachusetts earning a master's degree and then in 1977, a doctorate in education.

He was star and creator of the consistently top-rated "The Cosby Show," from 1985 to 1992, author of two best-selling books, *Fatherhood* (1986) and *Time Flies*

Bill Cosby, with cast members of "The Cosby Show", 1987.

(1987), and a performer at the top venues in Las Vegas, where he earned $500,000 a week. He also won top fees as a commercial spokesman for Jell-O, Kodak, and Coca Cola. He has recorded more than 27 albums and has received five Grammy Awards. Cosby also hosted a new version of the old Groucho Marx game show, "You Bet Your Life." In 1994, Cosby reunited with Robert Culp, his co-star from the "I Spy" TV show, for a new TV movie *I Spy Returns*. He also starred in the TV series "The Cosby Mysteries," which was cancelled in 1995 after only one season.

Cosby and his wife, Camille, live in rural New England with their five children. The Cosbys made headlines when they donated $20 million to Spelman College in Atlanta.

Rupert Crosse (1928-1973)
Actor

Born in Nevis, British West Indies, on November 29, 1928, Rupert Crosse moved to Harlem at an early age. Crosse returned to Nevis at the age of seven, after the death of his father. Reared by his grandparents and strongly influenced by his grandfather, a schoolmaster,

Crosse received a solid education before returning to New York, where he attended Benjamin Franklin High School. Crosse also later worked at odd jobs before interrupting high school to spend two years in military service in Germany and Japan. Once out of service, Crosse finished high school and entered Bloomfield College and Seminary in New Jersey. Though he intended to become a minister, it was obvious from the jobs he had held—machinist, construction worker, and recreation counselor—that his career plans were not yet definite.

Crosse subsequently enrolled at the Daykarhanora School, studying acting and appearing in the Equity Library Theatre off-Broadway production *Climate of Eden*. He then transferred to John Cassavetes' workshop, where he helped to create *Shadows* (1961), winner of a Venice Film Festival Award. Crosse's first Hollywood role was in a Cassavetes movie, *Too Late Blues* (1962). His most important film role was as Ned McCaslin in the screen adaptation of William Faulkner's Pulitzer Prize-winning novel, *The Reivers* (1969). Crosse was nominated for an Academy Award as best supporting actor for this outstanding performance. His other film credits include *The Wild Seed* and *Ride in the Whirlwind*.

Crosse's stage credits are also numerous, including appearances in *Sweet Bird of Youth*, *The Blood Knot*, and *Hatful of Rain*. Television viewers saw Crosse in "Dr. Kildare," "I Spy," and "The Man from U.N.C.L.E.," as well as several other series.

Rupert Crosse died of cancer on March 5, 1973, at the age of 45 at his sister's home in Nevis.

Dorothy Dandridge (1922-1965)
Actress

Dorothy Dandridge was born on November 9, 1922, in Cleveland, Ohio; her mother was the actress Ruby Dandridge. As children, Dorothy and her sister, Vivian, performed as "The Wonder Kids," touring the United States. In 1934, they were joined by a third performer, Etta Jones, and the trio became the Dandridge Sisters. The Dandridge Sisters were a popular act, performing at the Cotton Club in Harlem and in the motion picture *A Day at the Races* (1937). By the 1940s, Dorothy Dandridge had struck out on her own, appearing in the "soundies" (musical shorts) *Easy Street*, *Yes, Indeed*, *Cow Cow Boogie*, *Jungle Jig*, *Paper Doll*, and *Sing for My Supper*.

Dandridge married Harold Nicholas (of the famed Nicholas Brothers dance team) in 1942, and had a daughter, Harolyn, in 1943. Harolyn was diagnosed as having a severe developmental disability, and was sent

Dorothy Dandridge, 1956.

to an institution; shortly thereafter, Dandridge divorced Nicholas. she carried on a fairly successful career as a nightclub singer during the 1940s and 1950s. Her greatest triumph, however, came as a film actress, particularly in the all-black musical *Carmen Jones* (1954), for which she received an Oscar nomination for Best Actress, becoming the first African American woman to receive this nomination. Another important role was in *Island in the Sun* (1957), where she was paired romantically with a white man, John Justin—a breakthrough in desegregating the screen. In 1959, Dandridge played Bess opposite Sidney Poitier's Porgy in the movie version of *Porgy and Bess*. Ultimately, she appeared in over 25 films.

Dandridge married the white Las Vegas restaurateur Jack Dennison in 1959, but three years later divorced and declared personal bankruptcy. She died of an overdose of a prescription antidepressant on September 8, 1965.

Ossie Davis (1917-)
Actor

Ossie Davis grew up in Waycross, Georgia, and attended Howard University in Washington, D.C., where Dr. Alain Locke suggested he pursue an acting career in New York. After completing service in the Army, Davis landed his first role in 1946 in the play *Jeb*, where he met Ruby Dee, whom he married two years later.

After appearing in the movie *No Way Out* (1950), Davis won Broadway roles in *No Time for Sergeants*, *Raisin in the Sun*, and *Jamaica*. In 1961, he and Dee starred in *Purlie Victorious*, which Davis himself had written. Two years later, they repeated their roles in the movie version, *Gone Are the Days*.

Davis' other movie credits from this period include *The Cardinal* (1963), *Shock Treatment* (1964), *The Hill* (1965), *A Man Called Adam* (1966), and *The Scalphunter* (1968).

Davis then directed such films as *Cotton Comes to Harlem* (1970) and *Black Girl* (1972). His play *Escape to Freedom: A Play about Young Frederick Douglass* had its debut at Town Hall in New York and later was published by Viking Junior Books. Davis has also been involved with television scripts and educational programming. "The Ruby Dee/Ossie Davis Story Hour" was produced for television in 1974. The arts education television series "With Ossie and Ruby" appeared in 1981. Davis and Ruby Dee also founded the Institute of New Cinema Artists and the Recording Industry Training Program.

Davis' continued movie appearances include roles in *Let's Do It Again* (1975), *Hot Stuff* (1979), and *Nothing Personal* (1979). Recent film credits include *Harry and Son* (1984) and Spike Lee's *School Daze* (1988) and *Do the Right Thing* (1989). In addition, Davis has appeared on such television series as "The Defenders," "The Nurses," "East Side, West Side," and "Evening Shade." In 1993, Davis starred in the TV miniseries "Queen," the sequel to the classic miniseries "Roots." He also appeared in the TV movie *The Android Affair* in 1995.

Davis is also the author of *Just Like Martin*, a novel for young adults.

Sammy Davis, Jr. (1925-1990)
Actor, Comedian, Dancer, Singer

Sammy Davis Jr. was often called "the world's greatest entertainer," a title that attested to his remarkable versatility as singer, dancer, actor, mimic, and musician.

Davis was born in New York City on December 8, 1925. Four years later he was appearing in vaudeville with his father and "uncle" in the Will Mastin Trio. In 1931, Davis made his movie debut with Ethel Waters in *Rufus Jones for President*; this was followed by an appearance in *Season's Greetings*.

Ossie Davis with Ruby Dee, 1987.

Throughout the 1930s, the Will Mastin Trio continued to play vaudeville, burlesque, and cabarets. In 1943, Davis entered the Army and served for two years by writing, directing, and producing camp shows. After his discharge, he rejoined the trio, which in 1946 cracked the major club circuit with a successful Hollywood engagement.

Davis recorded a string of hits ("Hey There," "Mr. Wonderful," "Too Close for Comfort") during his steady rise to the top of show business. In November 1954, he lost an eye in an automobile accident, which fortunately did not interfere with his career. He scored a hit in his first Broadway show *Mr. Wonderful* (1956), and later repeated this success in *Golden Boy* (1964).

In 1959, Davis played Sportin' Life in the movie version of *Porgy and Bess*. Other Davis movies from this period include *Oceans 11* (1960) and *Robin and the Seven Hoods* (1964). His 1966 autobiography *Yes, I Can* became a best seller, and he starred in his own network television series.

In 1968, the NAACP awarded Davis its Spingarn Medal. In the 1970s, Davis appeared in films, television, and nightclubs. In 1972, he was involved in a controversy over his support of Richard Nixon which was publi-cized by a famous photograph of Nixon hugging Davis at the 1972 Republican Convention. In 1974, Davis re-nounced his support of Nixon and Nixon's programs. In the same year, his television commercials for Japan's Suntory Whiskey won the grand prize at the Cannes Film Festival, and the National Academy of TV Arts and Sciences honored him for his unique contributions to television.

In 1975, Davis became host of an evening talk and entertainment show. In 1980, he marked his fiftieth anniversary as an entertainer and the Friars Club honored him with its Annual Life Achievement Award. In 1989, he appeared in the film *Tap* with Gregory Hines and Harold Nicholas.

Davis married three times. His first marriage was in 1959 to singer Loray White. He married his second wife, actress Mai Britt, in 1961; she is the mother of his three children. In 1970, he married dancer Altovise Gore.

Ruby Dee (1924-)
Actress

Ruby Dee was born in Cleveland on October 27, 1924, but grew up in Harlem, attending Hunter College in New York. In 1942, she appeared in *South Pacific* with

Sammy Davis Jr.

Canada Lee. Five years later, she met Ossie Davis while they were both playing in *Jeb*. They were married two years later.

Ruby Dee's movies roles from this period include parts in *No Way Out* (1950), *Edge of the City* (1957), *Raisin in the Sun* (1961), Genet's *The Balcony* (1963, and *Purlie Victorious* (1963), written by Davis. Since 1960, she has appeared often on network television.

In 1965, Ruby Dee became the first black actress to appear in major roles at the American Shakespeare Festival in Stratford, Connecticut. Appearances in movies including *The Incident* (1967), *Uptight* (1968), *Buck and the Preacher* (1972), *Black Girl* (directed by Davis) (1972), and *Countdown at Kusini* (1976) followed. Her musical satire *Take It from the Top*, in which she appeared with her husband in a showcase run at the Henry Street Settlement Theatre in New York premiered in 1979.

As a team, Ruby Dee and Ossie Davis have recorded several talking story albums for Caedmon. In 1974, they produced "The Ruby Dee/Ossie Davis Story Hour," which was sponsored by Kraft Foods and carried by more than 60 stations of the National Black Network. Together they founded the Institute of New Cinema

Artists to train young people for jobs in films and television, and then the Recording Industry Training Program to develop jobs in the music industry for disadvantaged youths. In 1981, Alcoa funded a television series on the Public Broadcasting System titled "With Ossie and Ruby," which used guests to provide an anthology of the arts. Recent film credits include *Cat People* (1982) and, with Ossie Davis, Spike Lee's *Do the Right Thing* (1989).

Katherine Dunham (1910-)
Choreographer, Dancer

Katherine Dunham has for many years been one of the leading exponents of primitive dance in the world of modern choreography.

Born in Joliet, Illinois on June 22, 1910, Dunham attended Joliet Township Junior College and the University of Chicago, where she majored in anthropology. With funding from a Rosenwald Fellowship, she was able to conduct anthropological studies in the Caribbean and Brazil. She later attended Northwestern University, where she earned her Ph.D., MacMurray College, where she received a L.H.D in 1972, and Atlanta University, where she received a Ph.D.L. in 1977.

In the 1930s, she founded the Dunham Dance Company whose repertory drew on techniques Dunham learned while studying in the Caribbean. She has used her training in anthropology and her study of primitive rituals from tropical cultures to create unique dance forms that blend primitive qualities with sophisticated Broadway stage settings. In 1940, she appeared in the musical *Cabin in the Sky*, which she had choreographed with George Balanchine. She later toured the United States with her dance group; after the war, she played to enthusiastic audiences in Europe.

Among Dunham's choreographic pieces are *Le Jazz Hot* (1938), *Bhahiana* (1939), *Plantation Dances* (1940), *Haitian Suite (II)* (1941), *Tropical Revue* (1943), *Havana 1910/1919* (1944), *Carib Song* (1945), *Bal Negre* (1946), *Rhumba Trio* (1947), *Macumba* (1948), *Adeus Terras* (1949), *Spirituals* (1951), *Afrique du Nord* (1953), *Jazz Finale* (1955), *Ti 'Cocomaque* (1957), and *Anabacoa* (1963). Under the pseudonym Kaye Dunn, Dunham has written several articles and books on primitive dance. She has been referred to as "the mother of Afro-American dance."

On January 15, 1979, at Carnegie Hall in New York, Dunham received the 1979 Albert Schweitzer Music Award, and selections from her dance repertory from 1938 to 1975 were staged.

Dunham has founded schools of dance in Chicago, New York, Haiti, Stockholm, and Paris. She has also lectured at colleges and universities across the country.

Stepin Fetchit (1902-1985)
Actor

Stepin Fetchit's place in movie history is a controversial one. Praised by some critics as an actor who opened doors for other African Americans in Hollywood, he has been berated by others for catering to racist stereotypes and doing little to raise the status of black actors. His characters—lazy, inarticulate, slow-witted, and always in the service of whites—have become so uncomfortable to watch that his scenes are sometimes cut when films in which he appeared are shown on television. Even at the height of his career, civil rights groups protested his roles, which they considered demeaning caricatures.

Born Lincoln Theodore Monroe Andrew Perry in Key West, Florida on May 30, 1902, Stepin Fetchit's early career was in the Royal American Shows plantation revues. He and his partner, Ed Lee, took the names "Step 'n' Fetchit: Two Dancing Fools from Dixie." When the duo broke up, Fetchit appropriated "Stepin Fetchit" for himself.

Fetchit appeared in numerous motion pictures in the 1920s and 1930s, including *In Old Kentucky* (1927), *Salute* (1929), *Hearts in Dixie* (1929), *Show Boat* (1929), *Swing High* (1930), *Stand Up and Cheer* (1934), *David Harum* (1934), *One More Spring* (1936), and *Zenobia* (1939). Fetchit earned a great deal of income from these films, and spent it wildly. His extravagant lifestyle ended when he filed for bankruptcy in the 1930s.

Fetchit made sporadic appearances in films later in his life, among them *Miracle in Harlem* (1949), *Bend of the River* (1952), *Amazing Grace* (1974), and *Won Ton Ton, The Dog Who Saved Hollywood* (1976).

Redd Foxx (1922-1991)
Actor, Comedian

Redd Foxx's most famous role was Fred Sanford, the junkman on the popular NBC series "Sanford and Son," which began in 1972. It was the second most popular role on television (after Archie Bunker in "All in the Family"). As a result, Foxx became one of the highest paid actors in show business. In 1976, it was reported that he was earning $25,000 per half-hour episode, plus 25 percent of the producer's net profit.

Sanford is actually Foxx's family name. He was born John Elroy Sanford in St. Louis on December 9, 1922, and both his father and his brother were named Fred. As a boy, he concocted a washtub band with two friends and played for tips on street corners, earning as much as $60 a night. At 14, Foxx and the band moved to Chicago; the group broke up during World War II.

Foxx then moved to New York, where he worked as a rack pusher in the garment district as he sought for work in night clubs and on the black vaudeville circuit. While in New York, he played pool with a hustler named Malcolm Little, who was to change his name to Malcolm X.

In the early 1950s, Foxx tried to find work in Hollywood. He had a brief stint with *The Dinah Washington Show*, but mostly survived by performing a vaudeville act and working as a sign painter. This comedy act was adult entertainment, which limited his bookings.

Foxx's first real success came in 1955, when he began to record party records. He ultimately made more than 50 records, which sold over 20 million copies. His television career was launched in the 1960s with guest appearances on "The Today Show," "The Tonight Show," and other variety programs. He also began to appear in Las Vegas nightclubs.

Throughout the long run of "Sanford and Son," Foxx disputed with his producers over money. Originally, he was not receiving a percentage of the show's profits, which led him to sit out several episodes; a breach of contract suit filed by the producers resulted. There were racial undertones to these disputes, with Foxx referring to himself as a "tuxedo slave" and pointing to white stars who owned a percentage of their shows. Eventually, Foxx broke with the show and with NBC.

Foxx then signed a multimillion dollar, multiyear contract with ABC, which resulted in a disastrous comedy variety hour that he quit on the air in October 1977. The ABC situation comedy "My Buddy," which he wrote, starred in, and produced followed. In 1978, however, ABC filed a breach of contract suit. In 1979, Foxx was back at NBC planning a sequel to "Sanford and Son." He also made a deal with CBS, which in 1981 was suing him for a second time, allegedly to recover advances not paid back.

In 1976, Foxx performed in the MGM movie *Norman, Is That You?* He continued his appearances in nightclubs in Las Vegas and New York. In 1979, the book *Redd Foxx, B.S.* was published, comprised of chapters written by his friends.

In 1973, Foxx received the Entertainer of the Year Award from the NAACP. In 1974, he was named police chief of Taft, Oklahoma, an all-black village of 600 people. He also ran a Los Angeles nightclub to showcase aspiring young comedians, both black and white. In addition, Foxx did numerous prison shows, probably more than any other famous entertainer, which he paid for out of his own pocket. Foxx died on October 11, 1991.

Redd Foxx, 1977.

Al Freeman, Jr. (1934-)
Actor

Al Freeman, Jr. has won recognition for his many roles in the theater and motion pictures. His title role in the television film *My Sweet Charlie* (1970) earned him an Emmy Award nomination.

Albert Cornelius Freeman, Jr. was born in San Antonio, Texas, on March 21, 1934, son of the pianist Al Freeman Sr. and Lottie Coleman Freeman. After attending schools in San Antonio and then Ohio, Freeman moved to the West Coast to study law at Los Angeles City College. Following a tour of duty with the Army in Germany, Freeman returned to college and decided to change his major to theater arts after being encouraged by fellow students to audition for a campus production.

Freeman did radio shows and appeared in little theater productions in the Los Angeles area before performing in his first Broadway play, *The Long Dream* (1960). Other Broadway credits include *Kicks and Company* (1961), *Tiger, Tiger Burning Bright* (1962), *Blues for Mr. Charley* (1964), *Conversations at Midnight* (1964), *The Dozens* (1969), *Look to the Lilies* (1970), and *Medea* (1973). Off-Broadway, Freeman worked in *The Living Premise* (1963), *Trumpets of the Lord* (1963), *The Slave* (1964) and *Great MacDaddy* (1974). He also appeared in *Troilus and Cressida* (1965) and *Measure for Measure* (1966) for the New York Shakespeare Festival. He has also done more than a dozen feature films, including *Dutchman* (1967), *Finian's Rainbow* (1968), *The Detective* (1968), *The Lost Man* (1969), *Castle Keep* (1969), *Malcolm X* (1992), and *Once Upon a Time When We Were Colored* (1995).

Freeman has appeared in such television series as "The Defenders," "The FBI," and "Naked City," and was featured as Lieutenant Ed Hall in ABC's daytime drama "One Life to Live." He also appeared on television in Norman Lear's "Hot l Baltimore" (1975).

Morgan Freeman (1937-)
Actor

Born in Memphis, Tennessee, on June 1, 1937, Morgan Freeman grew up in Greenwood, Mississippi. He joined the U.S. Air Force in 1955, but left a few years later to pursue an acting career in Hollywood, taking classes at Los Angeles City College. He moved to New York City in the 1960s.

Freeman's first important role was in the short-running off-Broadway play *The Nigger-Lovers* in 1967. Soon thereafter, he appeared in the all-black version of the musical *Hello, Dolly!*.

Americans who grew up in the 1970s remember Freeman fondly as a regular on the public television program "The Electric Company," in which he appeared from 1971-76; his most notable character was the hip Easy Reader. More theater roles followed in productions of *The Mighty Gents* (1978), *Othello* (1982), *The Gospel at Colonus* (1983), and *The Taming of the Shrew* (1990).

In 1987, Freeman was cast in the Broadway play *Driving Miss Daisy*. He won an Obie award for his portrayal of Hoke, the chauffeur for a wealthy white woman in the American south. Freeman recreated his Broadway role for the 1989 movie version of the play, receiving an Academy Award nomination for Best Actor. In the same year, Freedman appeared in the highly-successful movie *Glory*, about an all-black Union regiment in the Civil War. Other film credits include: *Clean and Sober* (1988), *Lean on Me* (1989), *Johnny Handsome* (1989), *Unforgiven* (1993), *The Shawshank Redemption* (1994), *Outbreak* (1995), and *Seven* (1995). Freeman also directed the 1993 film *Bopha!*. In 1995, Freeman was nominated again for an Academy Award for his role in *The Shawshank Redemption*.

Charles Gilpin (1878-1930)
Actor

Charles Gilpin was born in Richmond, Virginia, on November 20, 1878. After a brief period in school, he took up work as a printer's devil. In 1890, he began to travel intermittently with vaudeville troupes, a practice he continued for two decades, working as a printer, elevator operator, prizefight trainer, and porter during long interludes of theatrical unemployment.

Morgan Freeman, 1992

From 1911 to 1914, Gilpin toured with a group called the Pan-American Octette. In 1914 he had a bit part in a New York production, *Old Ann's Boy*. Two years later he founded the Lafayette Theatre Company, one of the earliest black stock companies in New York.

After Eugene O'Neill saw Gilpin in *Abraham Lincoln*, he was chosen to play the lead in *Emperor Jones*, the role in which he starred from 1920 to 1924. In 1921, Gilpin was awarded the NAACP Spingarn Award for his theatrical accomplishment.

Gilpin lost his voice in 1926 and was forced to earn his living once again as an elevator operator. He died on May 6, 1930.

Danny Glover (1947-)
Actor

Born on July 22, 1947, in San Francisco, California, Danny Glover attended San Francisco State University and trained at the Black Actors Workshop of the American Conservatory Theatre.

Glover went on to appear in many stage productions, including *Island, Macbeth, Sizwe Banzi is Dead*, and New York productions of *Suicide in B Flat, The Blood Knot*, and *Master Harold ... and the Boys*, which won him a Theatre World Award.

Glover's film credits include *Escape from Alcatraz* (1979), *Chu Chu and the Philly Flash* (1984), *Iceman* (1984), *Witness* (1985), *Places in the Heart* (1985), *The Color Purple* (1985), *Mandela* (1987), *Lethal Weapon* (1987) and its sequels, *Bat 21* (1988), *Predator 2* (1990), *To Sleep With Anger* (1990), *Flight of the Intruder* (1991), *A Rage in Harlem* (1991), *Pure Luck* (1991), *Grand Canyon* (1991), *Bopha!* (1993), *The Saint of Fort Washington* (1993), *Angels in the Outfield* (1994), and *Operation Dumbo Drop* (1995).

On television, Glover appeared in the hit series "Hill Street Blues," the miniseries "Chiefs," "Lonesome Dove," and other projects including "Many Mansions," "Face of Rage," "A Place at the Table," "Mandela," and "A Raisin in the Sun."

Whoopi Goldberg (1949-)
Actress, Comedienne

Born Caryn E. Johnson in Manhattan's Chelsea district on November 13, 1949, Whoopi Goldberg began performing at the age of eight at the children's program at Hudson Guild and Helen Rubeinstein Children's Theatre. After trying her hand at theater, improvisation and chorus parts on Broadway, she moved to San Diego in 1974 and appeared in repertory productions of *Mother Courage* and *Getting Out.*

Goldberg joined the Black St. Hawkeyes Theatre in Berkeley as a partner with David Schein, and then went solo to create *The Spook Show*, performing in San Francisco and later touring the United States and Europe.

In 1983, Goldberg's work caught the attention of Mike Nichols, who created and directed her Broadway show a year later. She made her film debut in *The Color Purple* (1985), winning an NAACP Image Award as well as a Golden Globe Award.

Goldberg's other film credits include *Jumpin' Jack Flash; Burglar; Fatal Beauty; The Telephone; Homer and Eddie; Clara's Heart; Beverly Hills Brats; Ghost*, for which she won an Academy Award as best supporting actress; *The Long Walk Home; Soapdish; Sister Act; The Player; Sarafina; Made in America; Sister Act 2: Back in the Habit; Naked in New York; Corrina, Corrina; Star Trek: Generations; Boys on the Side* and *Moonlight and Valentino*.

On television, she starred in "Whoopi Goldberg on Broadway," "Carol, Carl, Whoopi and Robin," "Funny, You Don't Look 200," and hosted "Comedy Tonight." She received an Emmy nomination in 1985 for her guest appearance on "Moonlighting," has had a recurring role on "Star Trek: The Next Generation," and was a founding member of the Comic Relief benefit shows.

Danny Glover, 1992.

In 1993, Goldberg received the Woman of the Year Award from Harvard University's Hasting Pudding Theatricals organization. She also won People's Choice Awards in 1993 and 1994.

Goldberg served as host of the Academy Awards in 1994 and 1996.

Louis Gossett, Jr. (1936-)
Actor

Born in Brooklyn on May 27, 1936, Louis Gossett began acting at the age of 17 when a leg injury prevented him from pursuing his first love—basketball. In 1953, he won out over 445 contenders for the role of a black youngster in *Take A Giant Step*, for which he received a Donaldson Award as Best Newcomer of the Year.

While performing in *The Desk Set* in 1958, Gossett was drafted by the professional basketball team the New York Knicks, but decided to remain in theater. Ultimately, he would appear in more than 60 stage productions, including such plays as *Lost in the Stars, A Raisin in the Sun, The Blacks* and *Murderous Angels*.

On television, Gossett played characters roles in such series as "The Nurses," "The Defenders" and "East Side, West Side." In 1977, he won an Emmy for his performance in the acclaimed mini-series, "Roots." He also starred in such films as *Skin Game* (1971), *The Deep* (1977), *Officer and a Gentleman* (1983), *Iron Eagle* (1986), *Iron Eagle II* (1988), and *Diggstown* (1993).

In 1989, Gossett starred in his own television series, "Gideon Oliver."

Gossett has also starred in television movies such as *Father and Son: Dangerous Relations* and *Ray Alexander: A Taste for Justice*.

Pam Grier (1949-)
Actress

Pamala Suzette Grier was born May 26, 1949, in Winston-Salem, North Carolina. Her father's military career kept the family moving. Grier spent her early years in Europe, until the age of 14, when her family returned to the United States. They settled in Denver, Colorado, where she would enroll in Metropolitan State College with aspirations of a future career in medicine.

In 1967, Grier entered the Miss Colorado Universe contest in hopes of winning prize money to battle the

Whoopi Goldberg

rising tuition costs. There she attracted the attention of an agent with her second place finish. David Baumgarten, who handled many great talents, invited her to Hollywood to begin a career in acting. Grier was disinclined to go, but she was encouraged by her mother to take the agent up on his offer.

After signing with the Agency of Performing Arts, Grier attended acting classes and worked the office switchboard. Acting roles did not come right away, but she eventually landed a small part in 1969's *The Bird Cage*. Throughout the 1970s, she was a box-office draw, often appearing in "blaxploitation" movies such as *Coffy* and *Foxy Brown*. Though she was usually cast as a strong, independent woman and enjoyed being one of the few actresses given the chance to create such portrayals, she felt hemmed in by the stereotypes these films encouraged. One of the few bankable female stars of the time, Grier unofficially retired. Then in 1981, she costared in *Fort Apache: The Bronx*.

A demanding film, Grier felt validated by the success of her difficult performance. Since then, Grier has appeared on stage, in films, and on television. She was recognized by the NAACP Image Awards as the best actress in 1986 for *Fool for Love*. In 1993, she received

Louis Gossett, Jr.

awards from the National Black Theatre Festival and the African American Film Society.

Moses Gunn (1929-1993)
Actor

Born in St. Louis, Moses Gunn showed dramatic promise at a prodigious age—reading monologues aloud when he was nine. Six scholarships from other schools were offered to Gunn before he chose to earn a degree in speech and drama from Tennessee State University. There he organized a student troupe called Footlights Across Tennessee, a group that toured the South and Midwest, staging shows written by little-known black playwrights. While completing some graduate work at the University of Kansas, Gunn played his first Othello.

With his eye on a career on the New York stage, Gunn raised money by teaching drama at Grambling College in the early 1960s. He served as an understudy for an off-Broadway production, later joining the regular cast. Once he had gained more experience, Gunn gained a reputation as a leading Shakespearian actor. He appeared regularly with the New York Shakespeare Festival and won off-Broadway's Obie Award for his portrayal of Aaron the Moor in a 1967 production of *Titus Andronicus*. During the same era, he became a founding member of the Negro Ensemble Company, whose production of *The First Breeze of Summer* led to the actor's second Obie in 1975.

By the 1970s, Gunn had become a favorite on the national and international scenes. As a maturing performer, he did not limit his appearances to stage. Moviegoers enjoyed his supporting performances in films ranging from *Shaft* to *The Great White Hope*.. As Booker T. Washington in *Ragtime*, Gunn earned an Image Award from the NAACP in 1981. Gunn was successfully on the little screen, too, appearing in the made-for- television epic *Roots;* he earned an Emmy nomination for his portrayal in *Roots* of Kintango, a 17th-century African secret sect leader. He also did sitcoms and cop shows.

From a sensual Othello to a fiery Booker T. Washington, actor Moses Gunn specialized in crafting strong, memorable characters. His career spanned more than three decades. Beyond his own career, Gunn worked tirelessly as an advocate for other African American actors during a time when the theatrical establishment seemed all too willing to limit their presence both onstage and behind the scenes. He died of asthma complications at the age of 64.

Arsenio Hall (1955-)
Actor, Comedian, Talk Show Host

Born on February 12, 1955, in Cleveland, Ohio, Arsenio Hall started his professional career as a standup comic, making the rounds of clubs and honing his presentation. Soon, he was appearing on television specials as well as touring with noted musical performers.

Hall was selected as a guest-host of Fox Television's "Joan Rivers Show" when Rivers left, and soon won over both studio and television audiences. When this show concluded, he went on to star with Eddie Murphy in the movie *Coming To America* (1988). Hall also appeared in the movies *Harlem Nights* (1989) and *Bopha!* (1993).

Paramount then hired Arsenio Hall to be the host of his own show. Within weeks after the show's premiere in 1989, Hall had again built a solid audience following, particularly with young viewers, and provided the most substantial competition established evening talk shows had ever faced. In 1994, due to declining ratings and competition from talk show rivals Jay Leno and David Letterman, "The Arsenio Hall Show" went off the air.

Juanita Hall (1902-1968)
Singer

Born on November 6, 1902 in Keyport, New Jersey, Hall studied at the Juilliard School of Music after singing in Catholic Church choirs as a child. Hall devoted her life to music as a singer in stage and movie productions and choirs.

Her first major stage appearance was in Ziegfield's *Showboat* in 1927. Her lengthy stage career culminated in her role as "Bloody Mary" in Rodgers and Hammerstein's *South Pacific* in 1949. Hall went on to appear in *Flower Drum Song* and the movie version of both shows. She served as a soloist and assistant director of the Hall Johnson Choir (1931-1936), conducted the Works Progress Administration chorus in New York City (1936-1941) and organized the Juanita Hall Choir in 1942.

Hall performed at the Palladium in London and was a guest on the Ed Sullivan and Perry Como television shows. She was the recipient of the Donaldson, Antoinette Perry and Bill Bojangles awards. Hall died February 28, 1968 in Bay Shore, New York.

Robin Harris (1953-1990)
Comedian, Actor

Robin Harris was born August 30, 1953, in Chicago, Illinois. He attended Ottawa University in Kansas, where he ran a 4:18 mile on the track team. After college, he pursued a career in comedy rather than athletics, doing stand-up comedy as much as possible while working at Hughes Aircraft and Security Pacific Bank to support himself. Harris' interest in 1970s comedians like Redd Foxx motivated to create his own act in a similar style. Finally in 1985, after years of hard work, he began to build a name for himself as the master of ceremonies at Comedy Act Theater in Los Angeles. Due primarily to Harris' influence, the Comedy Act Theater became a stopping spot for black celebrities, such the Los Angeles Lakers.

Spike Lee was the first in the film industry to recognize Harris' talent and cast him in his 1989 film *Do The Right Thing*, which Harris followed with roles in *I'm Gonna Git You Sucka* and *Harlem Nights*. In 1990, he continued his successfully growing film career playing "Pops" in *House Party*. His movie career vaulted him into a new level of stardom, and he started playing 2,000-seat auditoriums with his comedy act though continuing his much smaller and less profitable gigs at the Comedy Act Theater.

In 1990, Harris' life became very hectic between his comedy act gigs, an HBO special, his album and soon-to-be movie *Bebe's Kids*. The schedule proved too much for him, and he died on March 18, 1990, of heart failure in his hometown of Chicago. The animated film version of Harris' comedy album *Bebe's Kids* was released posthumously as was his HBO comedy special.

Richard B. Harrison (1864-1935)
Actor

Richard B. Harrison was one of the few actors to gain national prominence on the basis of one role, his characterization of "De Lawd" in *Green Pastures*.

Harrison was born in Canada in 1864, and moved to Detroit as a young boy. There he worked as a waiter, porter, and handyman, saving whatever money he could to attend the theatrical offerings playing in town. After studying drama in Detroit, he made his professional debut in Canada in a program of readings and recitations.

For three decades, Harrison entertained black audiences with one-man performances of *Macbeth*, *Julius Caesar*, and *Damon and Pythias*, as well as with poems by Shakespeare, Poe, Kipling, and Paul Laurence Dunbar.

Arsenio Hall, on the set of his talk show "The Arsenio Hall Show", 1990.

In 1929, while serving on the faculty of North Carolina A and T as drama instructor, he was chosen for the part in *Green Pastures*.

When he died in 1935, Harrison had performed as "De Lawd" 1,656 times. His work earned him the 1930 Spingarn Medal and numerous honorary degrees.

Gregory Hines (1946-)
Actor, Dancer

After a distinguished career as a tap dancer, Gregory Hines made an unusual transition to dramatic actor.

Born in New York City on Valentine's Day, 1946, Hines began dancing with his brother Maurice under the instruction of tap dancer Henry LeTang. When Gregory was five, the brothers began performing professionally as the Hines Kids. Appearing in nightclubs and theaters around the country, they were able to benefit from contact with dance legends such as "Honi" Coles, Sandman Sims, the Nicholas Brothers and Teddy Hale.

As teenagers, the two performed as the Hines Brothers. When Gregory reached age 18, the two were joined by their father, Maurice Sr., on drums, and the trio became known as Hines, Hines and Dad. They performed internationally and appeared on "The Tonight Show." Eventually, Gregory tired of the touring and settled in California, where he formed the jazz-rock band Severance.

Gregory Hines subsequently moved back to New York and landed a role in *The Minstrel Show* (1978). He would later appear in such Broadway musicals as *Eubie!* (1978), *Sophisticated Ladies* (1981), and *Comin' Uptown* (1990) as well as feature films including *The Cotton Club* (1985), *White Nights* (1985), *Running Scared* (1985), and *Off Limits* (1988). Hines starred in the 1989 Tri-Star film *Tap* with Sammy Davis Jr., not only acting and dancing, but singing as well. Hines has also appeared in the films *White Man's Burden* (1994), *Renaissance Man* (1995), *Dead Air* (1995) and *Waiting to Exhale* (1995).

On television, Hines appeared in the series "Amazing Stories" and the special "Motown Returns to the Apollo," which earned him an Emmy nomination. When not appearing in films or television, he toured internationally with a solo club act. *Gregory Hines*, his first solo album, was released by CBS/Epic in 1988. The album was produced by Luther Vandross, who teamed with Gregory for a single, *There's Nothing Better Than Love*, which reached number one on the R&B charts in 1987.

Hines has received numerous awards, including the Dance Educators Award and the Theater World Award. Hines has been nominated for several Tony awards, and in 1992 received the award for best actor in a musical for his role in *Jelly's Last Jam*.

Gregory Hines, 1988.

Geoffrey Holder (1930-)
Actor, Dancer, Choreographer, Costume Designer, Director

Geoffrey Holder has succeeded as an artist in many areas. Holder was born on August 1, 1930, in Port-of-Spain, Trinidad. At an early age, he left school to become the costume designer for his brother's dance troupe, which he took over in 1948. Holder led the dancers, singers, and steel band musicians through a series of successful small revues to the Caribbean Festival in Puerto Rico, where they represented Trinidad and Tobago. His appearances with his troupe in the mid-1950s were so popular that he is credited with launching the calypso vogue.

Early in his career, Holder he appeared in New York as a featured dancer in *House of Flowers* (1954). He later performed with the Metropolitan Opera and as a guest star on many television shows. Film credits include *Live and Let Die* (1973), the James Bond adventure, and *Dr. Doolittle* (1967), the children's classic starring Rex Harrison.

Holder received two Tony Awards in 1976, as director and costume designer for the Broadway show *The Wiz*, the all-black adaptation of *The Wizard of Oz*. In

1978, he directed and choreographed the successful Broadway musical *Timbuktu*. In 1982, Holder appeared in the film *Annie* based on the hit Broadway musical, playing Punjab, a character from the original comic strip.

Holder received a Guggenheim Fellowship to pursue his painting, and his impressionist paintings have been shown in galleries such as the Corcoran in Washington, D.C. In 1995, an exhibition of Holder's paintings was held at the State University of New York in Albany. Holder also has written two books. *Black Gods, Green Islands* is a retelling of West Indian legends; his *Caribbean Cookbook* is a collection of recipes that Holder also illustrated.

Holder is married to the ballet dancer Carmen de Lavallade.

Lena Horne (1917-)
Actress, Singer

Lena Horne has been called the most beautiful woman in the world, and her beauty has been no small factor in the continued success of her stage, screen, and nightclub career.

Horne was born on June 30, 1917, in Brooklyn, New York. She joined the chorus line at the Cotton Club in 1933, and then left to tour as a dancer with Noble Sissle's orchestra. She was given a leading role in *Blackbirds of 1939*, but the show folded quickly, whereupon she left to join Charlie Barnett's band as a singer. She made her first records (including the popular "Haunted Town") with Barnett. In the early 1940s she also worked at New York's Cafe Society Downtown.

Horne then went to Hollywood, where she became the first black woman to sign a term contract with a film studio. Her films included *Panama Hattie* (1942), *Cabin in the Sky* (1943), *Stormy Weather* (1943), and *Meet Me in Las Vegas* (1956). In 1957, she took a break from her film and nightclub schedule to star in her first Broadway musical, *Jamaica*. Her popular recordings included "Stormy Weather," "Blues in the Night," "The Lady Is a Tramp," and "Mad about the Boy."

Throughout the 1960s and 1970s, Horne appeared in nightclubs and concerts. Her greatest recent success, however, was on Broadway. On May 12, 1981 she opened a one-woman show called *Lena Horne: The Lady and Her Music* to critical and box-office success. Although it opened too late to qualify for the Tony Award nominations, the show was awarded a special Tony at the June ceremonies. In December of that year, she received New York City's highest cultural award, the Handel Medallion.

Horne was married for 23 years to Lennie Hayton, a white composer, arranger, and conductor who died

Lena Horne

April 24, 1971. She had been married previously to Louis Jones. A generous and gracious woman, Horne has quietly devoted much time to humane causes.

In 1994, Horne released her first recording in a decade entitled *We'll Be Together Again*. This album was followed by *An Evening with Lena Horne* (1995) and *Lena Horne at Metro-Goldwyn-Mayer* (1996).

Eddie Hunter (1888-1974)
Comedian

Eddie Hunter got his start when working as an elevator operator in a building frequented by the great tenor Enrico Caruso. Hunter had been writing vaudeville comedy parts on the side, and Caruso encouraged and helped him. In 1923, Hunter's show *How Come?*, a musical revue, reached Broadway.

Hunter performed in his own persona in the majority of the shows he wrote. *Going to the Races*, produced at the Lafayette Theatre in Harlem, had Hunter and his partner live on stage, interacting with a movie of themselves playing on the screen. Hunter considered this show one of his best. As one of the principal performers in *Blackbirds*, he toured Europe during the late twenties. His show *Good Gracious* also toured Europe.

Depicting himself as "the fighting comedian," Hunter developed a reputation for speaking out against racial discrimination in the performing arts. He frequently told of his experience in Phoenix, Arizona, where the male members of the show were forced to sleep in the theater where they were performing; accommodations for blacks simply did not exist at the time. Hunter characterized his European reception as being relatively free of prejudice and felt that he only received the respect and recognition due to him when abroad.

By 1923, Hunter had a full recording contract with Victor Records. His recordings included "It's Human Nature to Complain," "I Got," and "My Wife Mamie." Shortly thereafter, he suspended his singing career to begin traveling with a new show he had developed. But when "talking" movies came into being, vaudeville fell out of favor. Eddie Hunter thus retired from show business and entered the real estate business in the 1930s.

Earle Hyman (1926-)
Actor

Earle Hyman was born in Rocky Mount, North Carolina on October 11, 1926. He began his acting career with the American Negro Theatre in New York City.

In 1963, Hyman made his foreign-language acting debut in Eugene O'Neill's *Emperor Jones* in Oslo, Norway, becoming the first American to perform a title role in a Scandinavian language. Hyman had originally become acquainted with Norway during a European trip made in 1957. He had planned to spend only two weeks in the Scandinavian country, but found himself so enchanted with Norway that he all but forgot the rest of Europe. When Hyman returned to New York, he resolved at once to learn Norwegian, and for practice, began to study the role of Othello (which he was performing for the Great Lakes Shakespeare Festival of 1962) in that language. By sheer coincidence, the director of *Den Nationale Scene* of Bergen, Norway, invited him to play Othello there in the spring of the following year, a performance which marked Hyman's first success in the Norwegian theater.

In 1965, Hyman returned to Norway to play *Emperor Jones* for a different theater company, and received high critical acclaim for his portrayal: Hyman remained in Norway, intermittently, for six years. Due to the interest in his life, Hyman has been the subject of several Norwegian radio broadcasts and television interviews. He still spends six months each year in Scandinavia playing "Othello" and other classical roles. A bronze bust of the actor as Othello has been erected in the Norwegian theater where Hyman performed, and he has also been presented with an honorary membership in the Norwegian Society of Artists, the third foreigner and first American to be so honored.

Hyman's many on and off-Broadway credits include *No Time for Sergeants* (1955), *St. Joan* (with Diana Sands at Lincoln Center) (1956), *Mister Johnson* (1956), *Waiting for Godot* (1957), Lorraine Hansberry's *Les Blancs* (1970), Edward Albee's *Lady from Dubuque*, the black version of Eugene O'Neill's *Long Day's Journey into Night* (at the Public Theatre) (1981), and *East Texas Hot Links* (1994). Among other film and television work, Hyman has appeared on the daytime drama "Love of Life" and "The Cosby Show."

Rex Ingram (1895-1969)
Actor

A major movie and radio personality during the 1930s and 1940s, Rex Ingram was born on October 20, 1895, in Cairo, Illinois, aboard the *Robert E. Lee*, a Mississippi riverboat on which his father was a stoker.

Ingram attended military schools, where he displayed an interest in acting. After working briefly as a cook for the Union Pacific Railroad and as head of his own small window-washing business, Ingram gravitated to Hollywood, where in 1919 he appeared in the original Tarzan film. Roles in such classics as *Lord Jim*, *Beau Geste* (1926), *King Kong* (1933), *The Green Pastures* (1936), and *Huckleberry Finn* (1939) followed. During the late 1920s and early 1930s, Ingram also appeared prominently in theater in San Francisco. During the late 1930s, he starred in daytime radio soap operas and in Works Progress Administration theater projects.

Ingram continued with a distinguished career on the New York stage, and in film and television. In 1957, he played Pozzo in *Waiting for Godot*. Later film credits include *Elmer Gantry* (1960), *Your Cheating Heart* (1964), *Hurry Sundown* (1967), and *Journey to Shiloh* (1968). He died on September 19, 1969.

Samuel L. Jackson (1949?-)
Actor

Samuel Jackson was born in Chattanooga, Tennessee in c. 1949. As a child, Jackson active imagination had him recreating scenes from his favorite movies. He also acted in various school plays. His first serious involvement in acting came as a student at Morehouse College in Atlanta. After deciding on drama as a major, Jackson began to enroll in theater classes at Morehouse's sister school Spellman College.

After receiving his Dramatic Arts degree, Jackson and his wife-to-be, La Tanya Richardson, moved to New

Earle Hyman, performing with Frances Sternhagen in *Driving Miss Daisy*.

York City. Jackson performed in various shows and films between the years of 1976 and 1981. As a cast member of Charles Burnett's *A Soldier's Play*, Jackson began to make connections. Morgan Freeman and Spike Lee both encouraged Jackson to keep pursuing his goals. Several years later, Jackson and Lee collaborated on the first of many films the two would film together.

School Daze and *Do the Right Thing* set the stage for the film that would create Jackson's reputation. *Jungle Fever*, also directed by Lee, displayed Jackson's versatility as he portrayed a crack addict. The role won Jackson various awards, including the Cannes Film Festival's Best Supporting Actor award. Lead rolls in major Hollywood productions continued to propel Jackson's career forward. In the 1990s, appearances in *Jurassic Park*, *Patriot Games*, and the Hughes brothers' *Menace II Society* all brought the actor praise. The height of all of Jackson's success came in his role in the 1994 blockbuster *Pulp Fiction*.

Despite the accolades and success his films produced, Jackson desired to work on-stage again. His wish came true as he was cast lead male in the play *Distant Fires*. Demand for Jackson's work has kept him busy. Movies such as *Die Hard with a Vengeance* and *The Great White Hype* have kept the actor busy in the mid-1990s.

Judith Jamison (1944-)
Choreographer

Born in Philadelphia on May 10, c. 1944, Judith Jamison started to study dance at the age of six. She was discovered in her early twenties by the choreographer Agnes De Mille, who admired her spontaneous style.

From 1965 to 1980, Jamison was a principal dancer for Alvin Ailey's American Dance Theater, performing a wide gamut of black roles, especially choreographed for her by Ailey. She has made guest appearances with many other dance companies, including the American Ballet Theatre, and with such opera companies as the Vienna State Opera and the Munich State Opera. In the 1980s, Jamison scored a great success on Broadway in *Sophisticated Ladies*, a musical featuring the music of Duke Ellington. In 1988, she formed the Jamison Project. Since 1989, Jamison has served as artistic director of the Alvin Ailey Dance Theatre. Among her latest dance works are "Hymn" (1993) and "Riverside" (1995).

In 1993, Jamison wrote the book *Dancing Spirit: An Autobiography*.

Bill T. Jones (1952-)
Dancer, Choreographer

Jones was born into a family of 12 children in Florida in the early 1950s; eventually his migrant worker parents moved north to New York, where Jones excelled in high school athletics. Enrolling in the State University of New York at Binghampton in the early 1970s—he was already an accomplished actor and wished to pursue a career in theater—Jones realized there that he was gay and entered into a relationship with his longtime partner, Arnie Zane; eventually he transferred into the university's dance department.

Jones and Zane left Binghampton for the wider pastures of Amsterdam for several years; when they returned to New York City they founded the American Dance Asylum, whose early mid-1970s performances caused a stir for the dancers' on-stage nudity. Next, Jones and Zane formed a more accessible dance company in 1982 they named after themselves, and one of their first performances that year occurred to great acclaim at the Brooklyn Academy of Music's innovative Next Wave Festival.

The Bill T. Jones/Arnie Zane dance company continued to thrive until Zane fell ill with AIDS; the principle's

Judith Jamison, 1989.

Rex Ingram, 1939.

inability to tour almost ended the troupe's existence financially, and his death in 1988 added greatly to Jones' burden. However, the dancer was able to use the grief to create a dance opus paying homage to his longtime partner, and the 1989 debut of *Absence* received laudatory reviews. The death of another member of the company resulted in another work that addresses issue of loss due to AIDS among the artistic community, *D-Man in the Waters*.

Jones has also addressed issues of the African American cultural experience, especially as experienced by those of alternative sexual orientation, as in the production of *Last Supper at Uncle Tom's Cabin*, and he has been candid about his own status as an HIV-positive person. In 1994 he was awarded a MacArthur Foundation fellowship; the following year saw the premier of *Still/Here* at the Brooklyn Academy of Music. Jones co-authored a book, 1995's *Last Night on Earth*, and collaborated with jazz drummer Max Roach and novelist Toni Morrison on a dance piece entitled *Degga* performed at Lincoln Center that same year as well. Later, *Still/Here* became the subject of media sniping between Jones and *New Yorker* writer Arlene Croce, who termed it "victim art" in early 1996. Jones asserted that the New York media is biased in favor of Jewish matters.

James Earl Jones (1931-)
Actor

Jones (whose father Robert Earl Jones was featured in the movie *One Potato, Two Potato*) was born in Tate County, Mississippi, on January 17, 1931, and raised by his grandparents on a farm near Jackson, Michigan. He turned to acting after a brief period as a premedical student at the University of Michigan (from which he graduated cum laude in 1953) and upon completion of military service with the Army's Cold Weather Mountain Training Command in Colorado.

After moving to New York, Jones studied at the American Theatre Wing, making his off-Broadway debut in 1957 in *Wedding in Japan*. Since then, he has appeared in numerous plays, on and off-Broadway, including *Sunrise at Campobello* (1958), *The Cool World* (1960), *The Blacks* (1961), *The Blood Knot* (1964), and *Anyone, Anyone*.

Jones' career as an actor progressed slowly until he portrayed Jack Jefferson in the Broadway smash hit *The Great White Hope*. The play was based on the life of

James Earl Jones

Jack Johnson, the first black heavyweight champion. For this performance, Jones received the 1969 Tony Award for the best dramatic actor in a Broadway play, and a Drama Desk Award for one of the best performances of the 1968-1969 New York season.

By the 1970s, Jones was appearing in roles traditionally performed by white actors, including the title role in *King Lear* and an award-winning performance as Lenny in Steinbeck's *Of Mice and Men*.

In 1978, Jones appeared in the highly controversial *Paul Robeson*, a one-man show on Broadway. Many leading blacks advocated a boycott of the show because they felt it did not measure up to the man himself. However, many critics gave the show high praise.

In 1980, Jones starred in Athol Fugard's *A Lesson from Aloes*, a top contender for a Tony Award that year. He also appeared in the Yale Repertory Theater Production of *Hedda Gabler*. In the spring of 1982, he co-starred with Christopher Plummer on Broadway in *Othello*, a production acclaimed as among the best ever done. In 1987, Jones received a Tony award for his performance in August Wilson's Pulitzer Prize-winning play, *Fences*.

Jones' early film credits include *Dr. Strangelove* (1964), *River Niger* (1976) and *The Greatest* (1977). He was the screen voice of Darth Vader in *Star Wars* (1977) and its sequels *The Empire Strikes Back* (1980) and *The Return of Jedi* (1983). Jones has also appeared in the movies: *Conan the Barbarian* (1982), *Allan Quartermain and the Lost City of Gold* (1986), *Soul Man* (1986), *Matewan* (1987), *Coming to America* (1988), *Field of Dreams* (1989), *Three Fugitives* (1989), *The Hunt for Red October* (1990), *Patriot Games* (1992), *Sommersby* (1993), *The Sandlot* (1993), *Excessive Force* (1993), *The Meteor Man* (1993), *Clean Slate* (1994), *Clear and Present Danger* (1994), *Jefferson in Paris* (1995), *Cry, the Beloved Country* (1995), and *A Family Thing* (1996).

Among numerous television appearances, Jones portrayed author Alex Haley in "Roots: The Next Generation" (1979) and has narrated documentaries for the Public Broadcasting System. During the early 1990s, Jones appeared in the television series "Gabriel's Fire" and the television movies *Percy and Thunder* and *The Vernon Johns Story*. He starred in the CBS series "Under One Roof" in 1995.

In 1976, Jones was elected to the Board of Governors of the Academy of Motion Picture Arts and Sciences. In 1979, New York City presented him with the "Mayor's Award of Honor for Arts and Culture." He received an honorary Doctorate of Humane Letters from the University of Michigan in 1971 and the New York Man of the Year Award in 1976. In 1985, he was inducted into the Theater Hall of Fame.

Canada Lee (1907-1952)
Actor

Canada Lee was born Leonard Corneliou Canagata in Manhattan on May 3, 1907. After studying violin as a young boy, he ran off to Saratoga to become a jockey. Failing in this, he returned to New York and began a boxing career. In 1926, after winning 90 out of 100 fights, including the national amateur lightweight title, he turned professional. Over the next few years, he won 175 out of some 200 fights against such top opponents as Jack Britton and Vince Dundee. In 1933, a detached retina brought an end to his ring career. He had acquired the name Canada Lee when a ring announcer could not pronounce his real name.

In 1934, Lee successfully auditioned at the Harlem YMCA for his first acting role which was in a Works Progress Administration production of *Brother Moses*. In 1941, Orson Welles, who had met Lee in the Federal Theatre's all-black production of *Macbeth*, chose him to play Bigger Thomas in the stage version of Richard Wright's famed novel, *Native Son*.

In 1944, Lee served as narrator of a radio series called "New World Comin'"— the first such series devoted to racial issues. That same year, he also appeared in Alfred Hitchcock's film *Lifeboat*, and in the Broadway play *Anna Lucasta*.

Spike Lee (1957-)
Filmmaker

Lee was born March 20, 1957 in Atlanta, Georgia. His family moved briefly to Chicago before settling in New York in 1959. Lee received a B.A. in mass communication in 1979 from Morehouse College. After a summer internship at Columbia Pictures in Burbank, California, Lee enrolled in New York University's prestigious Institute of Film and Television. He received an M.A. in filmmaking in 1983. While at New York University he wrote and directed *Joe's Bed-Sty Barbershop: We Cut Heads* for which he won the 1982 Student Academy award given by the Academy of Motion Picture Arts and Sciences. The movie was later shown on public television's Independent Focus Series.

Notable films by Lee include *She's Gotta Have It* (1986), *School Daze* (1988), *Do The Right Thing* (1989), *Mo' Better Blues* (1990), *Jungle Fever* (1991), *Malcolm X* (1992), *Crooklyn* (1994), *Clockers* (1995), and *Girl 6* (1996). *She's Gotta Have It* won the Los Angeles Film Critics New Generation award and the Prix de Juenesse at the Cannes Film Festival.

Lee has also written two books: *Spike Lee's Gotta Have It: Inside Guerilla Filmmaking* (1987) and *Uplift the Race* (1988). He has established a fellowship for minority filmmakers at New York University and is a

Canada Lee, 1951.

trustee of Morehouse College. Lee's production company, Forty Acres and a Mule Filmworks is located in Brooklyn, New York.

Jackie "Moms" Mabley (1894-1975)
Comedienne

Mabley was born Loretta Mary Aiken in Brevard, North Carolina, on March 19, 1894, and entered show business as a teenager when the team of Buck and Bubbles gave her a bit part in a vaudeville skit called "Rich Aunt from Utah."

With the help of comedienne Bonnie Bell Drew, Mabley developed a monologue, and was soon being booked on the black vaudeville circuit. Influenced by such acts as Butterbeans and Susie, she developed her own comic character, a world-weary old woman in a funny hat and droopy stockings, delivering her gags with a mixture of sassy folk wisdom and sly insights.

Her first big success came in 1923 at Connie's Inn in New York. Engagements at the Cotton Club in Harlem and Club Harlem in Atlantic City followed.

Moms Mabley was discovered by white audiences in the early 1960s. Her record album *Moms Mabley at the*

Spike Lee

U.N. became a commercial success, and was followed by *Moms Mabley at the Geneva Conference.* In 1962, she made her Carnegie Hall debut on a program with Cannonball Adderley and Nancy Wilson. Her subsequent Broadway, film, television, and record successes made her the favorite of a new generation.

Moms Mabley died on May 23, 1975 at the age of 78 in a White Plains, New York hospital.

Hattie McDaniel (1898-1952)
Actress

Hattie McDaniel was born on June 10, 1898 in Wichita, Kansas, and moved to Denver, Colorado as a child. After a period of singing for Denver radio as an amateur, she entered vaudeville professionally, and by 1924 was a headliner on the Pantages circuit.

By 1931, McDaniel had made her way to Hollywood. After a slow start, during which she supported herself as a maid and washer woman, she gradually began to get more movie roles. Her early film credits included *Judge Priest* (1934), *The Little Colonel* (1935), *Showboat* (1936), *Saratoga* (1937) and *Nothing Sacred.* Her portrayal of a "mammy" figure in *Gone with the Wind,* a role for which she received an Oscar award in 1940 as best supporting actress, is still regarded as a definitive interpretation. McDaniel was the first African American to receive an Oscar award.

McDaniel subsequently appeared in films such as *The Great Lie* (1941), *In This Our Life* (1942), *Johnny Come Lately* (1943), *Since You Went Away* (1944), *Margie*

(1946), *Never Say Goodbye* (1946), *Song of the South* (1946), *Mr. Blandings Builds His Dream House* (1948), *Family Honeymoon* (1948), and *The Big Wheel* (1949).

In addition to her movie roles, McDaniel enjoyed success in radio, in the 1930s, as Hi-Hat Hattie and in the 1940s in the title role of the very successful "Beulah" series.

McDaniel died on October 26, 1952.

Butterfly McQueen (1911-1995)
Actress

Butterfly McQueen's portrayal of Prissy in *Gone with the Wind* (1939) rivals Hattie McDaniel's Oscar-winning role as the "mammy," and is certainly as popular with audiences as Vivien Leigh's Scarlett O'Hara or Clark Gable's Rhett Butler.

Born Thelma McQueen on January 8, 1911 in Tampa, Florida, McQueen began her career in the 1930s performing as a radio actress in "The Goldbergs," "The Danny Kaye Show," "The Jack Benny Show," and "The Beulah Show." She also appeared on stage in *Brown Sugar* (1937), *Brother Rat* (1937), and *What a Life* (1938).

After her role in *Gone with the Wind* in 1939, McQueen was cast in other motion pictures such as *I Dood It* (1943), *Cabin in the Sky* (1943), *Mildred Pierce* (1945), and *Duel in the Sun* (1947). She appeared as Oriole on the television series "Beulah" from 1950 to 1952.

Given her outspokenness against racism and discrimination and her refusal to play stereotyped servant roles, McQueen's appearances after this period were sporadic. In 1968, she won accolades for her performance in the off-Broadway play, *Curley McDimple.* She was cast in the television program "The Seven Wishes of Joanna Peabody" in 1978, and the film *Mosquito Coast* in 1986. McQueen received a B.A. in Spanish from New York City College in 1975.

On December 22, 1995, McQueen died after being critically burned when a kerosine heater in her cottage caught fire.

Oscar Deveraux Micheaux (1884-1951)
Filmmaker, Author

Micheaux was born in 1884 in Metropolis, Illinois. Little is known about his early years other than he left home at 17 and worked briefly as a pullman porter. In 1904 he began homesteading in Gregory County, South Dakota.

Micheaux was a hard working farmer who loved to read and had a flair for writing. In 1913 he wrote, published and promoted *The Conquest: Story of a Negro Pioneer.* This novel was followed by *Forged Note: Ro-*

Spike Lee (center) in a scene from the movie *She's Gotta Have It,* 1986.

mance of the Darker Races in 1915 and *The Homesteader* in 1917. Much of his writing was melodramatic and probably autobiographical.

In 1918 the Lincoln Picture Company, an independent African American film production company, tried to buy the film rights to *The Homesteader*. When Micheaux insisted that he direct the planned movie, the deal fell through. Micheaux went to New York where he formed the Oscar Micheaux Corp. Between 1919 and 1937 Micheaux made about 30 films, including *Body and Soul*, a 1924 movie in which Paul Robeson made his first cinematic appearance.

Although Micheaux was an excellent self-promoter of his books and films, his company went into bankruptcy in 1928. By 1931 however, Micheaux was back in the film business producing and directing *The Exile* (1931), and *Veiled Aristocrats* (1932). Between 1941 and 1943 he wrote four more books, *Wind From Nowhere, Case of Mrs. Wingate, Masquerade* and *Story of Dorothy Stansfield*. In 1948 he made his last film *The Betrayal*. While none of Micheaux's films achieved critical acclaim, they were quite popular with African American audiences and attracted a limited white following. While his characters broke with the black stereotypes of the day, the themes of his movies ignored racial injustice and the day-to-day problems of African Americans.

Micheaux was known as a hard worker and a natty dresser who consumed neither alcohol or tobacco. Although he made a great deal of money, all of it was squandered away. Micheaux died penniless in Charlotte, North Carolina. Conflicting dates are given for his death—March 26, 1951 and April 1, 1951.

Florence Mills (1895-1927)
Singer, Dancer

Florence Mills was born in Washington, D.C., on January 25, 1895. She made her debut there at the age of five in *Sons of Ham*. In 1903, the family moved to Harlem, and in 1910 she joined her sisters in an act called the Mills Trio. She later appeared with a group called the Panama Four, which included Ada "Bricktop" Smith.

In 1921, Mills appeared in *Shuffle Along*, a prototype for African American musicals, and her success led to a long engagement at the Plantation, a New York night spot. After a successful appearance in London, she returned to the United States in 1924 to star in *From Dixie to Broadway*, in which she performed her trademark song, "I'm Just a Little Blackbird Lookin' for a Bluebird." Later, her own *Blackbirds* revue was a great success in London and Paris.

Mills returned to the United States in 1927. Exhausted by her work abroad, she entered the hospital on October 25 for a routine appendectomy, and died suddenly a few days later.

Abbie Mitchell (1884-1960)
Singer, Actress

Most celebrated as a concert artist, Abbie Mitchell (1884-1960) also performed on the stage and in light musical comedy. At the age of 13, she came to New York City from Baltimore, joining Will Marion Cook's Clorindy Company, and later achieving her first real success with the Williams and Walker Company.

By 1923, having performed in almost every European country, Mitchell returned home to give the first of her many voice concerts in the United States. Mitchell also performed with many opera companies and acted in several plays, including *Coquette* (with Helen Hayes) (1927), *Stevedore* (1934) and Langston Hughes' *Mulatto* (1937). She also headed the voice department at Tuskegee Institute for three years.

Hattie McDaniel

Butterfly McQueen

Arthur Mitchell (1934-)
Dancer, Choreographer

Mitchell was born in Harlem on March 27, 1934, and attended New York's famed High School of the Performing Arts. Mitchell was the first African American male to receive the high school's dance award in 1951.

Upon graduation in 1952, Mitchell enrolled on a scholarship in the School of American Ballet, run by the eminent choreographer George Balanchine, who also directed the New York City Ballet. In 1955, Mitchell was invited by Balanchine to join the New York City Ballet. Before long, he was a principal dancer in the company, performing in such works as *Agon* and *A Midsummer Night's Dream*.

Mitchell left the New York City Ballet in 1969 to establish the Dance Theater of Harlem, which he founded to give young African Americans an opportunity to get out of the ghetto through the arts. Mitchell and the studio have received numerous awards and citations, including the Changers award given by *Mademoiselle* magazine in 1970 and the Capezio Dance Award in 1971. Surviving a financial crisis in 1990, the school and

A poster from Oscar Micheaux's film *Within Our Gates*, 1920.

company are now back on their feet, though treading carefully due to the precarious state of the arts in the United States.

In 1993, New York City Mayor David Dinkins presented Mitchell with the Handel Medallion, the city's highest cultural honor. He was also one of the winners of the Kennedy Center Honors and the National Medal of Arts in 1993. The School of American Ballet presented Mitchell with a lifetime achievement award at its annual dinner on February 6, 1995.

Eddie Murphy (1961-)
Actor, Comedian

Eddie Murphy was born on April 3, 1961 in the Bushwick section of Brooklyn, the son of a New York City policeman and amateur comedian. As a youngster, he did imitations of cartoon characters and, as he grew older, began preparing comic routines with impressions of Elvis Presley, Jackie Wilson, Al Green and the Beatles.

Murphy attended Roosevelt Junior-Senior High School on Long Island and hosted a talent show at the Roosevelt Youth Center before beginning to call local talent agents to secure bookings at Long Island nightclubs. He was a little-known stand-up comedian when he made his first appearance on the late-night television show "Saturday Night Live" in 1980. He made a memorable impression, and within three years was hailed as a major new star based on his work in the hit films *48 Hours* (1982) and *Trading Places* (1983).

After his success with the first two Paramount films, Murphy starred in *Beverly Hills Cop* (1985) and its sequel *Beverly Hills Cop II* (1987), which were two of the major box office hits of the decade. The concert film *Raw* followed, as well as an effort at light-hearted fantasy, *The Golden Child*. Murphy's more recent film appearances include *Coming to America, Harlem Nights, Another 48 HoursBoomerang, The Distinguished Gentleman, Beverly Hills Cop III*, and *Vampire in Brooklyn*.

In 1993, Murphy married model Nicole Mitchell.

Clarence Muse (1889-1979)
Actor, Director

Born on October 14, 1889, Clarence Muse was perhaps best known for his film acting, He was, however, also successful as a director, playwright, and actor on the stage.

The Baltimore native's parents came from Virginia and North Carolina, and his grandfather from Martinique. After studying law at Dickinson University in Pennsylvania, Muse sang as part of a hotel quartet in Palm Beach, Florida. A subsequent job with a stock company took him on tour through the South with his wife and son. Coming to New York, he barely scraped a living together, mostly performing as a vaudevillian.

After several plays with the now-famous Lincoln Theatre group and the Lafayette Players in Harlem, and a Broadway stint in *Dr. Jekyll and Mr. Hyde*, where having white roles played by blacks in white-face created quite a controversy, Muse had established himself as an actor and singer.

Muse's first movie role was in *Hearts in Dixie* (1929), produced at the William Fox Studio, in which Muse played a 90-year-old man. Later, he returned to the stage for the role of a butler in the show that was to be called *Under the Virgin Moon*. After Muse wrote the theme song, the title was changed to his *When It's Sleepy Time Down South*. Both the song and the show were hits.

When the Federal Theatre Project in Los Angeles presented Hall Johnson's *Run Little Chillun*, Muse directed the show. After its successful two-year run, Muse made the screen adaption *Way Down South* (1939).

During Muse's career, he appeared in 219 films, and was at one time one of the highest paid black actors, often portraying faithful servant "Uncle Tom" characters. His movie credits include *Huckleberry Finn* (1931), *Cabin in the Cotton* (1932), *Count of Monte Cristo* (1934), *So Red the Rose* (1935), *Showboat* (1936), *The Toy Wife* (1938), *The Flame of New Orleans* (1941), *Tales of Manhattan* (1942), *Heaven Can Wait* (1943), *Night and Day* (1946), *An Act of Murder* (1948), *Porgy and Bess* (1959), *Buck and the Preacher* (1971), and *Car Wash* (1976). His last film was *Black Stallion* in 1979. He also appeared over the years in concerts and on radio.

Muse died October 13, 1979, the day before his ninetieth birthday. He had lived in Perris, California on his Muse-a-While Ranch.

Fayard Nicholas (1917-)
Harold Nicholas (1924-)
Dancers

The Nicholas Brothers were one of the great tap dance teams of the first half of the 20th century, whose acrobatics and precision were admired by the likes of Fred Astaire and George Balanchine, and whose appearances in motion pictures provide a record of their astounding abilities.

Fayard Nicholas was born in 1917; Harold in 1924. Their professional debut was, ironically, on the radio program "The Horn and Hardart Kiddie Hour" in 1931. In 1932, they became a featured act at Harlem's Cotton Club. They made their first Broadway appearance in the *Ziegfeld Follies* of 1936; this was followed by *Babes in Arms* in 1937.

The Nicholas Brothers' film debut was in *Pie Pie Blackbird* in 1932, and they appeared in several other movies in the 1930s and 1940s, including *The Big Broadcast of 1936* (1936), *The Great American Broadcast* (1941), *Sun Valley Serenade* (1941), *Stormy Weather* (1943), and *The Pirate* (1948). The latter is particularly memorable for the sequence in which they are featured.

Harold Nicholas married actress Dorothy Dandridge in 1942, but the couple later divorced. The two brothers continue to be active in the world of dance: Harold co-starred with Gregory Hines in the movie *Tap* in 1989, and Fayard won a Tony Award for Best Choreographer for the Broadway musical *Black and Blue* in the same year. In 1992, the Nicholas Brothers were honored by the Kennedy Center. They received awards from Dance Magazine in 1995.

Frederick O'Neal (1905-1992)
Actor

Frederick O'Neal was the first black person to hold the position of president of Actor's Equity, a fitting tribute to his long years of service to the American theater as both actor and teacher.

O'Neal was born August 27, 1905 in Brookville, Mississippi. After his father's death in 1919, he moved with his family to St. Louis, finishing high school there and appearing in several Urban League dramatic productions.

In 1927, with the help of some friends in St. Louis, O'Neal founded the Ira Aldridge Players, the second African American acting troupe in America. For the next ten years, he played in 30 of its productions. In 1937, he came to New York, and three years later helped found the American Negro Theater. Today, its alumni include such established stars as Sidney Poitier, Earle Hyman, Harry Belafonte, Ruby Dee, Ossie Davis, and Hilda Simms.

O'Neal himself starred in *Anna Lucasta* (1944), for which he won the Clarence Derwent Award and the Drama Critics Award for the best supporting performance by an actor on Broadway. He was later featured in *Take a Giant Step*, *The Winner*, and several other stage productions. His films include *Pinky* (1949) and *The Man with the Golden Arm* (1956). He also appeared on several televised dramatic and comedy shows.

In 1964, O'Neal became the first black president of Actor's Equity. After devoting himself full-time to Actor's Equity, O'Neal was in 1970 elected international president of the Associated Actors and Artists of America, the parent union of all show business performers' unions. He became president and chairman of the board of the Schomburg Center for Research in Black Culture, a position which included such responsibilities as raising money to conserve and preserve materials in the center, soliciting resources for the institution, and lobbying for the construction of a new building. He was a member of the New York State Council on the Arts, President of the Catholic Interracial Council, chairman of the AFL-CIO Civil Rights Committee, and vice president of the A. Philip Randolph Institute. In 1980, he received the National Urban Coalition's Distinguished

Trade Unionist Award. In 1990, he received a special tribute from the Black Filmmakers Hall of Fame. O'Neal died on April 27, 1992.

Sidney Poitier (1927-)
Actor

Sidney Poitier was born on February 20, 1927 in Miami, but moved to the Bahamas with his family at a very early age. At age 15, he returned to Miami; he later rode freight trains to New York City, where he found employment as a dishwasher. After the attack on Pearl Harbor, he enlisted in the Army and served on active duty for four years.

Back in New York, Poitier auditioned for the American Negro Theater, but was turned down by director Frederick O'Neal. After working diligently to improve his diction, Poitier was accepted in the theater group, receiving acting lessons in exchange for doing backstage chores.

In 1950, Poitier made his Hollywood debut in *No Way Out*, followed by successful appearances in *Cry the Beloved Country* (1952), *Red Ball Express* (1952), *Go, Man, Go* (1954), *Blackboard Jungle* (1956), *Goodbye,*

Sidney Poitier

My Lady (1956), *Edge of the City* (1957), *Band of Angels* (1957), *Something of Value* (1957), and *Porgy and Bess* (1959), among others. Poitier starred on Broadway in 1959 in Lorraine Hansberry's award-winning *Raisin in the Sun*, and repeated this success in the movie version of the play in 1961.

In 1965, Poitier became the first black to win an Oscar for a starring role, receiving this award for his performance in *Lilies of the Field*. Seven years earlier, Poitier had been the first black actor nominated for the award for his portrayal of an escaped convict in *The Defiant Ones*.

Subsequent notable film appearances include performances in *To Sir with Love* (1967), *Heat of the Night* (1967), *Guess Who's Coming to Dinner* (with Spencer Tracy and Katharine Hepburn) (1968), *Buck and the Preacher* (1972) and *A Warm December* (1973), in both of which he acted and directed, *Uptown Saturday Night* (1974), and *A Piece of the Action* (1977). After years of inactivity, Poitier performed in two additional films, *Little Nikita* and *Shoot To Kill*, both released in 1988. His directing ventures include *Stir Crazy* (with Richard Pryor and Gene Wilder) (1980), *Hanky Panky* (with Gilda Radner) (1982), and the musical *Fast Forward* (1985).

Poitier spent two years writing his memoirs, *This Life*, published by Knopf in 1980. In 1981, Citadel Press published *The Films of Sidney Poitier*, by Alvin H. Marill.

In 1993, Poitier won the Thurgood Marshall Lifetime Achievement Award and the Living Legend Award from the National Black Theater Festival. On December 3, 1995, he was presented with one of the Kennedy Center Honors.

Pearl Primus (1919-1994)
Dancer, Choreographer

Pearl Primus' anthropological approach to dance made her one of the most purposeful figures in that medium: for her, dance was education, not merely entertainment. Her aim was to show audiences and dancers alike the African roots of dance and to bring the African American experience alive.

Primus was born in Trinidad on November 29, 1919. Originally intending to pursue a career in medicine, she received a bachelor of arts degree in pre-medical sciences and biology from Hunter College, with graduate work in medical education and psychology. But 1940s America did not welcome blacks or women in medicine, and after seeking employment in vain, Primus sought assistance from the government's National Youth Administration. She was put into a youth administration dance group, and by 1941 was accepted into New York

City's New Dance Group. Her professional debut was at the Young Men's Hebrew Association in New York City on February 14, 1943. In April of that year, she began appearing at Café Society Downtown, the famed New York City nightclub, but left after ten months for an appearance on Broadway at the Belasco Theater. By this time she had her own dance company, Pearl Primus, Percival Borde, and Company. She toured Africa and the southern United States, and incorporated what she learned into her choreography.

Primus is best known for the dances *African Ceremonial* and *Strange Fruit*, which were incorporated into her *Solos for Performance at the Café Society* (ca. 1944), and *Hard Times Blues* (1945).

Primus died on October 29, 1994.

Richard Pryor (1940-)
Comedian, Actor

Comedian Richard Pryor has had great success as a stand-up comedian, writer, actor, and recording star. He has often used elements of his unconventional upbringing and adult life as material in his comedy routines.

Born Richard Franklin Lennox Thomas Pryor III on December 1, 1940, in New York City, he was raised by his grandmother in the Peoria, Illinois, brothel she ran. His mother worked there as a prostitute. His parents married when he was three years old, but the union did not last. His grandmother was a strict disciplinarian and young Richard was often beaten.

In school Pryor was often in trouble with the authorities. Pryor was expelled from high school for striking a teacher. In 1958 he joined the army and spent two years in Germany. He returned to Peoria after his military service and during the early 1960s began his work as a stand-up comic on a local circuit. He moved to New York City's Greenwich Village in 1963 where he honed his stand-up routine. A 1964 appearance on "The Ed Sullivan Show" led to his first movie role in *The Busy Body* (1966), followed by bit parts in *The Green Berets* and *Wild in the Streets*. During this time Pryor continued to play to live audiences.

In 1972, Pryor played Piano Man in *Lady Sings the Blues* and earned an Academy Award nomination for his performance. Throughout the 1970s, Pryor continued his work as a stand-up comic and also contributed his writing talents to television's "The Flip Wilson Show" and "Sanford and Son," Mel Brooks' film *Blazing Saddles*, and Lily Tomlin's television special, "Lily," for which he won an Emmy Award. He won two of his five Grammy Awards for his comedy albums *That Nigger's Crazy* (1974) and *Bicentennial Nigger* (1976).

Pryor wrote and starred in *Bingo Long and the Traveling All Stars and Motor Kings* (1976) and re-

Richard Pryor

ceived raves for his work in *Silver Streak* (also 1976). In 1979, the comedian's film *Richard Pryor Live in Concert* brought his stand-up act to millions.

In 1978, Pryor suffered a major heart attack, and in 1980, while freebasing cocaine, he set himself ablaze and suffered severe injuries. He addresses these incidents in his second concert movie, *Live on Sunset Strip* (1982). In 1985 Pryor co-wrote, directed and starred in *Jo Jo Dancer, Your Life Is Calling*, a semi-autobiographical tale of a comedian who relives his life immediately following a near fatal accident. Pryor's later films include *The Toy*, *Some Kind of Hero*, *Brewster's Millions*, *Critical Condition*, *Stir Crazy*, *Bustin' Loose*, *Moving*, and *See No Evil, Hear No Evil*. In 1989 Pryor co-starred with Eddie Murphy in *Harlem Nights*. He teamed with Gene Wilder in the 1991 film *Another You*.

Pryor has been in failing health in recent years. He was diagnosed with multiple sclerosis in 1986 and has had triple bypass heart surgery. He is reportedly often wheelchair bound and lives a reclusive life in his Bel Air, California, home. In 1993, Pryor was awarded with a star on the Hollywood Walk of Fame.

In 1995, Pryor's collection of memoirs *Pryor Convictions—and Other Life Sentences* was published, detailing his difficult childhood, his failed marriages, and his battles with cocaine addiction and multiple scerlosis.

Phylicia Rashad (1948-)
Actress

Known to millions as Claire Huxtable from "The Cosby Show," Phylicia Rashad has led a distinguished acting career on television and the stage. She was born on June 19, 1948, in Houston, Texas, and until 1985 was known as Phylicia Ayers-Allen. Her sister is the famous Debbie Allen; both sisters received early instruction in music, acting, and dance. Phylicia graduated magna cum laude from Howard University in 1970 with a B.F.A. in theater.

Early in her career, Rashad played the character Courtney Wright in the soap opera "One Life to Live." Her big break came with "The Cosby Show," in which she and Bill Cosby presided over the Huxtable family for seven years, from 1985 to 1992. Rashad has also appeared in Broadway and off-Broadway productions of *The Cherry Orchard*, *The Wiz*, *Zora*, *Dreamgirls*, *A Raisin in the Sun*, and *Into the Woods*.

Rashad has received two honorary doctorates, one from Providence College in Rhode Island and one from Barber-Scotia College in North Carolina. In 1995, Rashad was named spokesperson for the American Diabetes Association. She and her husband Ahmad Rashad, a sportscaster for NBC, live in Westchester County, New York.

Bill "Bojangles" Robinson (1878-1949)
Dancer

Bill Robinson was born on May 25, 1878 in Richmond, Virginia. Having been orphaned early, he was raised by his grandmother, a former slave. By the time he was eight, he was earning his own way by dancing in the street for pennies and working as a stable boy.

In 1887, Robinson toured the South in a show called *The South Before the War*. The following year, he moved to Washington, D.C., where he again worked as a stable boy. By 1896, he had teamed up with George Cooper. This act was successful on the Keith circuit until the slump of 1907 caused it to fold. Robinson returned to Richmond and worked as a waiter until a year later when he was taken up by a theatrical manager and became a cabaret and vaudeville headliner.

In 1927, Robinson starred on Broadway in *Blackbirds*, and in 1932 he had top billing in *Harlem's Heaven*, the first all-black motion picture with sound. Later, he scored a Hollywood success by teaching his famous stair dance to Shirley Temple in *The Little Colonel*

(1936). Robinson made 14 movies, including *The Littlest Rebel* (1935), *In Old Kentucky* (1936), *Rebecca of Sunnybrook Farm* (1938), *Stormy Weather* (1943), and *One Mile from Heaven* (1938).

Throughout his long career on stage and in movies, Robinson was known as the "King of Tap Dancers." Robinson died on November 25, 1949.

Richard Roundtree (1942-)
Actor

Richard Roundtree is best known as John Shaft, the tough, renegade detective from the movie *Shaft* (1971). Born in New Rochelle, New York, on July 9, 1942, Roundtree graduated from New Rochelle High School, and attended Southern Illinois University on a football scholarship. After brief stints as a suit salesman and a model, he began a stage career with the Negro Ensemble Company. With *Shaft* (1971) and its sequels *Shaft's Big Score* (1972) and *Shaft in Africa* (1973), Roundtree reached the peak of his career and became a pop icon.

Roundtree's subsequently appeared in the films *Embassy* (1972), *Charley One Eye* (1973), *Earthquake* (1974), *Diamonds* (1975), and *Man Friday* (1976). He appeared in the television miniseries "Roots" (1977), and continues to be cast in various television programs and motion pictures.

In 1995, Roundtree appeared in the films *Seven* and *When We Were Colored*. He has also served as host of the TV show "Cop Files."

Richard Roundtree

Sinbad (1956-)
Comedian, Actor

The 6-foot, 5-inch, red-haired Sinbad has delighted audiences with his comedy, which combines street parlance—noticeably free of obscenities—with tales of American life. Born David Adkins on November 10, 1956 in Benton Harbor, Michigan, Sinbad aspired to be a basketball star, winning a basketball scholarship to the University of Denver. A serious knee injury caused him to give up basketball, and he left college in 1978. Shortly thereafter, he renamed himself Sinbad, after the heroic character in *The Arabian Nights*, to boost his spirits. He spent three and a half years in the U.S. Air Force, hating every minute until his 1983 discharge.

By that time, Sinbad had decided to try his hand at stand-up comedy. A series of low-paying engagements throughout the United States followed, and his break came when he appeared on the television talent contest "Star Search" seven times in the mid-1980s. He later worked as a warm-up comedian for "The Cosby Show," and in 1989 was cast as dorm director Walter Oakes on "A Different World"—a role that was broadened in 1991 when Oakes became a counselor. In 1993, Sinbad starred in his own situation comedy, "The Sinbad Show," about a single foster parent. The show only lasted one season. He appeared in the movie *Houseguest* in 1995.

John Singleton (1968-)
Filmmaker

Singleton was born in Los Angeles in 1968. After graduating from high school in 1986 he enrolled in the University of Southern California's prestigious Film Writing Program which is part of their School of Cinema-Television. While there he formed an African American Film Association and did a six month director's internship for the "Arsenio Hall Show." He twice won the school's Jack Nicholson Award for Best Feature Length Screenplays. Before graduating in 1990, he signed with the well known Creative Artists Agency.

Singleton was soon approached by Columbia Pictures to sell the film rights to *Boyz N the Hood* his original screenplay and college thesis. Singleton agreed, but only if he would be the movie's director. The movie was released in July of 1991 to mixed critical reviews. Although its first showings were marred by moviehouse violence it garnered Singleton an Academy Award nomination for best director. He became the first African American and the youngest person to be so honored.

Since *Boyz N the Hood* Singleton has done a short cable television film for Michael Jackson entitled *Remember the Time*. His second film, *Poetic Justice*, was

John Singleton

released in the summer of 1993. His third film, *Higher Learning*, was released in 1995.

Noble Sissle (1889-1975)
Lyricist, Singer

Noble Sissle was born in Indianapolis, Indiana, on July 10, 1889. He reaped his early successes teamed up with the great Eubie Blake. Sissle wrote the lyrics and sang them in performance; Blake composed and played the music. Together the two created such songs as "I'm Just Wild about Harry," "It's All Your Fault," "Serenade Blues," and "Love Will Find a Way."

The 1921 *Shuffle Along*, the first black musical with a love theme, made Sissle and Blake famous. Joining forces with the writing and comedy team of Flournoy Miller and Aubrey Lyles, Sissle and Blake wrote the words and music to over a dozen songs for the show. *Shuffle Along* became a huge success in the United States and Europe, where it had a prolonged tour. As with most black performers in the early 1900s, Sissle and his troupe would have to travel as far as 20 or 30 miles out of their way to find a place to eat and sleep, since blacks were not welcome in the white hotels of the towns where they played.

Other Sissle and Blake shows included *Chocolate Dandies* (1924) and *Keep Shufflin* (1928). Noble Sissle died December 17, 1975 at his home in Tampa, Florida.

Wesley Snipes (1962-)
Actor

Born in Orlando, Florida, on July 31, 1962, Wesley Snipes spent his childhood in the Bronx, New York. At the age of 12, he appeared in his first off-Broadway production, a minor role in the play *The Me Nobody Knows*. His interest in dance led him to enroll in New York's High School for the Performing Arts. However, before completing the curriculum, his mother sent him back to Orlando to finish school, where he continued to study drama.

Upon high school graduation, Snipes was awarded a scholarship to study theater at the State University of New York at Purchase. Snipes subsequently appeared in on and off-Broadway productions, including Wole Soyinka's *Death and the King's Horsemen*, Emily Mann's *Execution of Justice*, and John Pielmeier's *The Boys of Winter*. He has also appeared in Michael Jackson's video "Bad" and in the HBO production *Vietnam War Story*, for which he received cable television's best actor award.

Snipes' film appearances include roles in *Wildcats* (1986), *Streets of Gold* (1986), *Major League* (1989), and *King of New York* (1990). In 1990 Snipes appeared in Spike Lee's *Mo' Better Blues*, with Denzel Washington. This was followed by a role in Mario Van Peebles' *New

Jack City (1991) and in Spike Lee's *Jungle Fever* (1991). His most recent films include *White Men Can't Jump*, *Passenger 57*, *Rising Sun* and *Sugar Hill*.

Billie "Buckwheat" Thomas (1931-1980)
Actor

Familiar to generations of Americans, Billie "Buckwheat" Thomas, better known simply as "Buckwheat," was one of the principal characters in the "Our Gang" film shorts of the 1930s and 1940s. Buckwheat succeeded the character Farina, and like Farina, his gender was ambiguous: he was in most respects a boy, but wore dress-like gingham smocks, and in some episodes sported pigtails.

Billie Thomas was born on March 12, 1931, in Los Angeles, California, and joined the "Our Gang" cast in 1934, appearing in 93 episodes, the last in 1944. The film historian David Bogle described the character of Buckwheat as "a quiet, odd-ball type, the perfect little dum-dum tag-along." The comedian Eddie Murphy's parodies of Buckwheat in the 1980s were enormously popular; Buckwheat's generally unintelligible speech, blank expression, and untidy hair provided a wealth of material for Murphy's routine.

Billie Thomas himself had an uneventful life after the "Our Gang" series ended. He died in 1980 at the age of 49.

Cicely Tyson (1939-)
Actress

During the early 1970s, Cicely Tyson emerged as America's leading black dramatic star. She achieved this through two sterling performances—as Rebecca, the wife of a southern sharecropper in the film *Sounder*, and as the lead in a television special, "The Autobiography of Miss Jane Pittman," the story of an ex-slave who, past her one hundredth year, challenges racist authority by deliberately drinking from a "white only" water fountain as a white deputy sheriff looks on.

Cicely Tyson was born in New York City on December 19, 1939, and raised by a very religious, strict mother, who associated movies with sin and forbade Cicely to go to movie theaters. Blessed with poise and natural grace, Tyson became a model, and appeared on the cover of America's two foremost fashion magazines, *Vogue* and *Harper's Bazaar*, in 1956. Interested in acting, she began to study drama, and in 1959 appeared on a CBS culture series, "Camera Three," with what is believed to be the first natural African hair style worn on television.

Tyson won a role in an off-Broadway production of Jean Genet's *The Blacks* (1961), for which she received the 1962 Vernon Rice Award. She then played a lead part

Wesley Snipes

in the CBS series "East Side, West Side." Tyson subsequently moved into film parts, appearing in *The Comedians* (1967) and *The Heart Is a Lonely Hunter* (1968). Critical acclaim led to her role as Rebecca in *Sounder* (1972), for which she was nominated for an Academy award and named best actress by the National Society of Film Critics. She won an Emmy television acting trophy for "Jane Pittman" (1974).

Tyson's other film appearances include *The Blue Bird* (1976) and *The River Niger* (1976). On television, she has appeared in "Roots" (1977), "King" (1978), and "Wilma" (1978). She portrayed Harriet Tubman in "A Woman Called Moses," and Chicago schoolteacher Marva Collins in a made-for-television movie in 1981. Recent television appearances include "Cry Freedom" (1987) and "The Women of Brewster Place" (1989). In 1995, Tyson starred in the television series "Sweet Justice."

In 1979, Marymount College presented Tyson with an honorary Doctor of Fine Arts. Tyson owns a house on Malibu Beach in California. In November 1981, she married jazz trumpeter Miles Davis but the couple divorced before Davis' death.

Leslie Uggams (1943-)
Singer, Actress

Born in the Washington Heights section of New York City on May 25, 1943, Leslie Uggams enjoyed a comfortable childhood. She made her singing debut at the age of six, performing with the choir of St. James Presbyterian Church in New York, and followed shortly thereafter with her acting debut in the television series "Beulah." Uggams developed her poise and stage presence early in life, attending the Professional Children's School, where she was chosen student body president in her senior year.

Uggams subsequently won $25,000 on the popular television quiz show, "Name That Tune," which renewed her interest in a singing career. In 1961, Uggams became a regular on "The Mitch Miller Show," a variety show featuring old favorites. She was at the time the only black performer appearing regularly on network television.

Throughout the 1960s, Uggams appeared in numerous nightclubs and had several supper club and television engagements. Her big break came when she was signed as a replacement for Lena Horne in *Hallelujah Baby*, a show that presented a musical chronicle of the civil rights movement. Uggams won instant stardom and received a Tony award for her performance.

In 1977, Uggams appeared as Kizzy in the television adaption of Alex Haley's novel, *Roots*. In May 1982, she performed in a new Broadway show, *Blues in the Night*, at the Rialto Theater in New York City. She has also

Leslie Uggams

appeared on television in "Backstairs at the White House," a miniseries, and "The Book of Lists," in the film *Skyjacked*, and in the musicals *Jerry's Girls*, *The Great Gershwin*, and *Anything Goes*.

Melvin Van Peebles (1932-)
Filmmaker, Actor, Writer

Melvin Van Peebles was born on August 21, 1932, in Chicago, Illinois. As a child, Van Peebles's family moved to Phoenix, Illinois, where he graduated from high school. Studied English literature, Van Peebles received his Bachelor in Arts from Wesleyan University in 1953. After spending three and a half years as a flight navigator for the U.S. Air Force, Van Peebles settled in San Francisco.

While in San Francisco, Van Peebles began to dabble in film making. *Three Pickup Men for Herrick*, completed in 1958, is the best known of his early work, but with success in his sight, Van Peebles took his films to Hollywood. Several rejections frustrated Van Peebles, prompting a move to Holland. There Van Peebles's luck changed for a short while. He acted with the Dutch National Theater while studying astronomy at the University of Amsterdam, but troubles with his wife forced

Van Peebles to move again. He found a home in Paris, where wrote several novels in self-taught French.

Experiences in France led to Van Peebles first international film success. *Three Day Pass* received generally positive criticism as it premiered at the San Francisco International Film Festival. This led to Van Peebles directing a string of films, including *Watermelon Man* and *Sweet Sweetback's Baadasssss Song*, which he wrote, directed, and produced. A smash, the film grossed nearly $14 million dollars.

In 1971, Van Peebles turned his attention toward Broadway. His productions of *Ain't Supposed to Die a Natural Death* and *Don't Play Us Cheap* received mixed reviews. Despite the lack of critical enthusiasm for his work, *Ain't Supposed to Die a Natural Death* closed as the fifth-longest running show on Broadway and *Don't Play* received first prize during a Belgian Festival. Throughout the 1970s, Van Peebles continued to write and direct for films, plays, and television. In 1987, his teleplay *The Day They Came to Arrest the Book* received an Emmy Award.

After a hiatus, Van Peebles returned to directing, for the film *Identity Crisis*, featuring his son Mario, who also penned the film. In 1993, the father-son team reversed roles in the film *Posse*, which Mario directed and in which Melvin acted. In the mid-1990s, they continued to develop a variety of projects together, including *Panther*, a fictionalized motion picture of the history of The Black Panthers.

Ben Augustus Vereen (1946-)
Dancer, Actor

Ben Vereen was born October 10, 1946, in the Bedford-Stuyvesant section of Brooklyn, New York and attended the High School of Performing Arts in Manhattan. His dancing ability had been discovered almost accidentally after he had been sent to dance school by his mother. Vereen has since been called America's premier song and dance man.

Ben Vereen made his stage debut in 1965 in *The Prodigal Son*. He went on to appear in *Sweet Charity* (1966), *Golden Boy* (1968), *Hair* (1968), and *No Place to Be Somebody* (1970). Vereen is best known for his Broadway role in *Pippin* (1972), which won him a Tony Award. He was also nominated for a Tony for his co-starring role in *Jesus Christ Superstar* (1971). His film appearances include roles in *Funny Lady* (1975), *All That Jazz* (1979), and *The Zoo Gang*.

Vereen has starred in the ABC comedy series "Tenspeed and Brown Shoe" and is known for his television specials; the highly-acclaimed "Ben Vereen—His Roots" (1978) won seven Emmy awards. He also portrayed

Louis "Satchmo" Armstrong and received wide acclaim for his role of Chicken George in television's adaption of Alex Haley's *Roots* (1977) and for his performance in *Jubilee*.

In 1994, Vereen announced plans to start the Ben Vereen School of the Performing Arts in Chicago. The school is designed to help students improve their artistic talents and provide positive alternatives to gangs and drugs.

Denzel Washington (1954-)
Actor

Born on December 28, 1954, in Mt. Vernon, New York, Denzel Washington attended an upstate private high school, the Oakland Academy, and then entered Fordham University as a pre-med major. Washington did not originally intend to become an actor, but when he auditioned for the lead role in a student production of Eugene O'Neill's *The Emperor Jones*, he won the part over theater majors. His performance in that play, and later in a production of *Othello*, led his drama instructor to encourage Washington to pursue an acting career.

Washington's first major role was in the off-Broadway drama *A Soldier's Story*; Washington re-created his

Denzel Washington

role when the play was adapted into a motion picture in 1984. He played Dr. Phillip Chandler on the television series "St. Elsewhere," and appeared in a string of films, including *Carbon Copy* (1980), *Cry Freedom* (in which he portrayed South African activist Steven Biko) (1987), *The Mighty Quinn* (1989), *Glory* (which won him an Academy Award for Best Supporting Actor) (1989), *Mo' Better Blues* (1990), *Mississippi Masala* (1992), and *Malcolm X* (1992). Washington also starred in *Philadelphia* (1993), playing an attorney for an HIV-positive lawyer played by Oscar winner Tom Hanks. In 1995, he starred in *Crimson Tide, Devil in a Blue Dress* and *Virtuosity.*

In addition to winning an Oscar, Washington won the Silver Beard Award at the Berlin International Film Festival in 1993.

Washington is married to the actress Pauletta Pearson.

Fredi Washington (1903-1994)
Actress, Dancer, Civil Rights Activist

Born Fredericka Carolyn Washington in Savannah, Georgia, in 1903, Washington and her younger sister were sent to a convent after the death of their mother and subsequent remarriage of their father. As a teenager, she left this sheltered world to live with relatives in New York City in order to pursue a career in the performing arts.

One of Washington's first big breaks came in 1919 when she was cast as a member of the Happy Honeysuckles, the back-up troupe for Josephine Baker. Two years later she began earning a good salary in the stage production of an all-black musical called *Shuffle Along.* Washington was next discovered by Broadway impresario Lee Shubert, who urged her to audition for a play called *Black Boy.* In the 1926 production, she starred—under the stage name Edith Warren—opposite Paul Robeson, but unfortunately much press and attendee attention at its debut was focused on Washington's light complexion. Indeed, she was often able to pass as white, especially when traveling in the segregated areas of the South with her first husband, a member of Duke Ellington's orchestra.

During the 1920s Washington continued to appear in stage roles and toured Europe for a time; she also appeared in the 1930 production of *Sweet Chariot.* Moving on to film, Washington again teamed with Robeson when she appeared in the 1933 drama *The Emperor Jones*—but Hollywood censors insisted she wear make-up to darken her complexion during her love scenes with him. The following year Washington appeared in her most acclaimed role in the film *Imitation of Life,* portraying a young woman who forsakes her heritage in order to pass as white.

Unfortunately Washington found her acting career stymied by a lack of roles for African American women in general, and especially for ones with light complexions; she fought for many decades to reverse such attitudes in the film industry in Hollywood. In 1937 she founded the Negro Actors Guild of America, and wrote extensively on the subject for the New York City-based paper *The People's Voice,* for which she served as theater critic and columnist. During the 1940s and '50s she worked as a cast consultant on numerous African American-themed films in Hollywood and continued to appear in stage productions. She died in June of 1994 in Stamford, Connecticut.

Ethel Waters (1900-1977)
Actress, Singer

The distinguished career of Ethel Waters spanned half a century, and made its mark in virtually every entertainment medium—stage, screen, television, and recordings.

Ethel Waters was born on October 31, 1900, and spent most of her childhood in her hometown of Chester, Pennsylvania. By the age of 17, she was singing professionally at the Lincoln Theatre in Baltimore. During this early phase of her career, she became the first woman to perform W. C. Handy's "St. Louis Blues" on stage.

After several years in nightclubs and vaudeville, Waters made her Broadway debut in the 1927 review *Africana.* In 1930, she appeared in *Blackbirds,* and in 1931 and 1932 she starred in *Rhapsody in Black.* The following year she was featured with Clifton Webb and Marilyn Miller in Irving Berlin's *As Thousands Cheer.* In 1935, she co-starred with Bea Lillie in *At Home Abroad,* and three years later she played the lead in *Mamba's Daughters.*

In 1940, Waters appeared in the stage version of *Cabin in the Sky,* a triumph which she repeated in the 1943 movie version. Her other film appearances include *Rufus Jones for President* (1931), *Tales of Manhattan* (1941), *Cairo* (1942), *Stage Door Canteen* (1943), and *Pinky* (1949).

Her autobiography, *His Eye Is on the Sparrow,* was a 1951 Book-of-the-Month Club selection. The title is taken from a song that she sang in her 1950 stage success, *Member of the Wedding.*

Keenen Ivory Wayans (1958-)
Comedian

Keenen Ivory Wayans was born in New York City on June 8, 1958. He began his career as a stand-up comic at

Denzel Washington as Malcolm X in Spike Lee's film *Malcolm X*.

the Improv clubs in New York City and Los Angeles. After appearances on such television series as "Benson," "Cheers," "Chips," and in the movies *Star 80* (1983) and *Hollywood Shuffle* (1987), Wayans struck fame with *I'm Gonna Git You, Sucka* (1989)—a hilarious sendup of 1970s "blaxploitation" films—which he wrote and produced. His greatest success has been the hit television series "In Living Color," a lively and irreverent show in which celebrities are often outrageously parodied. "In Living Color" won an Emmy award in 1990.

Wayans is the oldest of a family of ten; three of his siblings—Damon, Shawn, and Kim—are regulars on "In Living Color."

Veronica Webb (1965-)
Model, Journalist, Actress

Webb was born in Detroit, Michigan during the middle of a 1965 blizzard; her father was an electrician and her mother a public health nurse. Webb graduated from a private school (but would often cut classes to attend foreign films shown at the local art museum in the afternoons) and moved to New York City to study animation at the Parsons School of Design. She also

worked in a Soho housewares shop, where some fashion industry people encountered her and urged her to try modeling instead.

In 1984, Webb signed on with the Click Agency, known for its promotion of a less rigid, non-stereotypical standard of beauty. She did a few assignments, then decided to try her luck in Paris, taking only a $100 with her. Within a short time she was winning assignments for top European magazines and clothing designers, but she returned to New York in 1986, missing the energy and verve sometimes lacking in the more relaxed and rarefied European fashion scene. Signing on with the Ford Agency, Webb continued to earn top dollar in both print and runway work; she also began writing for a downtown New York magazine called *Paper*, and became a regular columnist for it in 1990.

It was also in the early 1990s that Webb won her first film role in the Spike Lee-directed *Jungle Fever*, in which she played a supporting role alongside Lee. The director also cast her in his epic 1992 biography *Malcolm X*. In 1992 Webb won a coveted contract with cosmetics giant Revlon, and the lucrative agreement launched Webb's face as the virtual symbol for its ColorStyle line in Revlon ads and made her one of only a few African American modeling professionals with such a high-profile deal. Webb handled much of the contract negotiations herself, and continues to write articles for magazines, including *Elle* and *Interview*. She is also involved in breast-cancer awareness and prevention efforts.

Bert Williams (1874-1922)
Comedian, Dancer

The legendary Bert Williams is considered by many to be the greatest black vaudeville performer in the history of the American stage.

Born on November 12, 1874 on New Providence Island in the Bahamas, Williams moved to New York with his family, and then on to California, where he graduated from high school. After studying civil engineering for a time, he decided to try his hand at show business.

In 1895, Williams teamed with George Walker to form a successful vaudeville team. Five years later, they opened in New York in *The Sons of Ham* and were acclaimed for the characterizations that became their stock-in-trade—Walker as a dandy, and Williams in

Keenan Ivory Wayans

blackface, complete with outlandish costumes and black dialect. The show ran for two years.

In 1902, their show *In Dahomey* was so popular that they took it to England, where it met with equal success. The partners continued to produce such shows as *The Policy Players*, *Bandanna Land*, and *Abyssinia* until Walker's death in 1909.

Thereafter, Williams worked as a featured solo performer in the *Ziegfeld Follies*, touring America for ten years in several versions of the show. His most famous songs were "Woodman, Spare That Tree"; "O, Death, Where is Thy Sting"; and "Nobody," his own composition and trademark.

Williams died of pneumonia on March 4, 1922.

Billy Dee Williams (1937-)
Actor

A screen, television and stage actor with impressive credits, Billy Dee Williams has starred in some of the most commercially popular films ever released.

Born William December Williams in Harlem on April 6, 1937, Williams was a withdrawn, overweight youngster who initially planned to become a fashion illustrator. While studying on scholarship at the School of Fine Arts in the National Academy of Design, a CBS casting director helped him secure bit parts in several television shows, including "Lamp Unto My Feet" and "Look Up And Live."

Williams then began to study acting under Sidney Poitier and Paul Mann at the Actors Workshop in Harlem. He made his film debut in *The Last Angry Man* (1959), and then appeared on stage in *The Cool World* (1960), *A Taste of Honey* (1960), and *The Blacks* (1962). He later appeared briefly on Broadway in *Hallelujah Baby* (1967) and in several off-Broadway shows, including *Ceremonies in Dark Old Men* (1970).

Williams' next major role was in the acclaimed television movie, *Brian's Song* (1970), a performance for which he received an Emmy nomination. Motown's Berry Gordy then signed Williams to a seven-year contract after which he starred in *Lady Sings the Blues* (1972) and *Mahogany* (1976) with Diana Ross. His last movie for Gordy was *The Bingo Long Traveling All-Stars and Motor King* (1976).

In the early 1980s, Williams appeared in two of George Lucas' *Star Wars* adventures, *The Empire Strikes Back* and *Return of the Jedi*. He has appeared in numerous television movies, including *Scott Joplin*, *Christmas Lilies of the Field*, and the miniseries "Chiefs." When he was cast opposite Diahann Carroll in the prime time drama "Dynasty," his reputation as a romantic lead was secured. At the end of the decade, he starred in

Bert Williams

Billy Dee Williams

action films such as *Oceans of Fire* and *Number One With a Bullet.*

In 1995, Williams played a detective in the TV murder mystery "Falling for You." He also hosted the Black Theatre Festival in Winston-Salem, North Carolina and the Infiniti Sports Festival. Some of Williams's paintings were featured in a computer screen-saver program, "Art in the Dark: Extraordinary Works by African American Artists."

Flip Wilson (1933-)
Comedian, Actor

Flip Wilson reached the pinnacle of the entertainment world with a series of original routines and ethnic characters rivaled only by those of Bill Cosby. Wilson's hilarious monologues, seen on a number of network television shows, made him the most visible black comedian of the early 1970s.   Born Clerow Wilson on December 8, 1933, Wilson was the tenth in a family of 24 children, 18 of whom survived. The family was destitute, and Wilson was a troublesome child during his youth in his hometown of Jersey City; he ran away from reform school several times, and was ultimately raised in foster homes.

Wilson's comic talents first surfaced while he was serving in the Air Force. Sent overseas to the Pacific, Wilson entertained his buddies with preposterous routines. Back in civilian life, he worked as a bellhop and part-time showman. Opportunity struck in 1959 when a Miami businessman sponsored him for one year at $50 a week, thus enabling Wilson to concentrate on the evolution of his routine. For the next five years or so, Wilson appeared regularly at the Apollo Theatre in Harlem. In 1965, he began a series of nationwide appearances on "The Tonight Show." Long-term contracts and several hit records followed in quick sequence, and Wilson became firmly established as one of the truly innovative talents in the comedy profession.

With "The Flip Wilson Show" in the early 1970s, Wilson became the first black to have a weekly prime time television show under his own name. He became famous for his original character creations such as "Geraldine." On January 31, 1972 he appeared on the cover of *Time* magazine. In 1976, he made his dramatic debut on television in the ABC series "The Six Million Dollar Man."

During the early 1980s, Wilson appeared in numerous nightclubs and television specials. He starred in the television series "People Are Funny" in 1984 and "Charlie & Co." in 1985. He has also made comedy albums, including *The Devil Made Me Buy This Dress*, for which he received a Grammy award.

Paul Winfield (1941-)
Actor

Born in Los Angeles on May 22, 1941, Paul Winfield grew up in a poor family. Excelling in school, he attended a number of colleges—the University of Portland, Stanford University, Los Angeles City College, and the University of California at Los Angeles—but left UCLA before graduation to pursue his acting career.

Winfield appeared on television shows in the late 1960s and early 1970s—most notably as one of Diahann Carroll's boyfriends in the series "Julia." His great success in that period was in the film *Sounder* (1972), in which he played a sharecropper father in the nineteenth-century American South. For this role, he received an Academy Award nomination for best actor.

Winfield subsequently appeared in the motion pictures *Gordon's War* (1973), *Conrack* (1974), *Huckleberry Finn* (1974), and *A Hero Ain't Nothing But a Sandwich* (1978). He received accolades for his portrayal of

Flip Wilson

Dr. Martin Luther King, Jr. in the NBC movie *King* (1978), for which he received an Emmy nomination. His second Emmy nomination came with his role in the television miniseries "Roots: The Next Generation" (1979).

In the 1980s, Winfield kept busy with appearances on television in "The Charmings," "The Women of Brewster Place," "Wiseguy," and "227"; on film in *Star Trek II: The Wrath of Khan* (1982), *Damnation Alley* (1983), and *The Terminator* (1984); and on the stage in *A Midsummer Night's Dream*, *Othello*, and *The Seagull*. In 1990, he played the sarcastic Judge Larren Lyttle in the movie *Presumed Innocent*, and in 1992 appeared on Broadway in the cast of *A Few Good Men*.

Winfield has won several major awards, including an NAACP Image Award and election to the Black Filmmakers Hall of Fame. In 1995, Winfield won an Emmy for best guest actor on a drama series for his work in "Picket Fences: Enemy Lines."

Oprah Winfrey (1954-)
Talk Show Host, Actress, Broadcasting Executive

Oprah Winfrey's rise to fame is a tale at once tragic and inspiring. She was born on January 29, 1954, in Kosciusko, Mississippi. Her name was supposed to have been "Orpah," after a biblical figure in the book of Ruth; sources vary as to the origin of the misspelling.

Winfrey was a precocious child who asked her kindergarten teacher to advance her to the first grade; Winfrey also skipped the second grade. Her parents, who were not married, separated when she was very young and sent her to live with her grandparents. At the age of six, Winfrey moved to Milwaukee to live with her mother. From the time she was nine, she was abused sexually by male family members and acquaintances; these events, which she did not discuss publicly until the 1980s, have had a profound effect on her life.

When she was 14, Winfrey went to live with her father in Nashville, Tennessee, and it was there that her life was put back on track. Her father insisted on hard work and discipline as a means of self-improvement, and Winfrey complied, winning a college scholarship that allowed her to attend Tennessee State University. In 1971, she began working part-time as a radio announcer for WVOL in Nashville. Two years later, after receiving a B.A. from Tennessee State, she became a reporter at WTVF-TV in Nashville. From 1976 to 1983, she lived in Baltimore, working for the ABC affiliate WJZ-TV, progressing from news anchor to cohost of the popular show, "People Are Talking." In 1984, she moved to

Chicago and took over the ailing morning show, "A.M. Chicago." By September of the next year, the show was so successful that it was expanded to an hour format and renamed "The Oprah Winfrey Show." Now in syndication across the country, "The Oprah Winfrey Show" is one of the most popular television programs in history. In 1986, Winfrey founded Harpo, Inc., her own production company ("Harpo" is "Oprah" spelled backwards).

A talented actress, Winfrey has appeared in the motion picture *The Color Purple* (1985), and in the television movie *The Women of Brewster Place* (1989).

In 1994, President Clinton signed the "Oprah Bill," a law designed to protect children from abuse.

Winfrey has won numerous awards for her work in television and film. She won the Horatio Alger Award in 1993 and was inducted into the TV Hall of Fame in 1994. At the 1995 Daytime Emmy Awards, the "Oprah Winfrey Show" won its seventh Emmy Award for best talk show and Winfrey won an Emmy as best daytime TV host.

George C. Wolfe (1954-)
Playwright, Stage Director, Producer

Wolfe was born September 23, 1954, into a Frankfort, Kentucky household; his father worked for the state and his mother was an educator and later school principal. Wolfe grew up in an insular African American community that stressed self-sufficiency and achievement, and a visit to New York City as a teenager helped instill a desire for a career in the theater. By 1976 he had earned a degree in theater from Pomona College.

After working for a few years in the Los Angeles theater scene, Wolfe moved to New York City in 1979. After earning a master's degree in musical theater from New York University, he had his first minor recognition with the 1985 off-off Broadway production of his play *Paradise*. Wolfe's 1986 satire on African American cultural icons, *The Colored Museum*, won rave reviews from critics but also weathered criticism as well; eventually the play was staged at New York's Joseph Papp Public Theater and broadcast on PBS. Wolfe became intently involved in the esteemed Public Theater, which stages the annual New York Shakespeare Festival, and directed several works for it beginning in 1990, including *Spunk* and *The Caucasian Chalk Circle*. With the 1992 Broadway debut of *Jelly's Last Jam*—a musical

Oprah Winfrey

about the life of 1920s jazz musician Jelly Roll Morton that Wolfe wrote and directed—he rose in prominence in New York's theater community; in 1993 he directed parts one and two of the Pulitzer-Prize-winning trilogy by playwright Tony Kushner, *Angels in America*. For his direction of first segment of the drama, "Millennium Approaches," Wolfe won a Tony Award.

Another honor was accorded Wolfe in 1993 when he was named director of the Joseph Papp Public Theater/ New York Shakespeare Festival; since then he has been praised for giving venerable institution a more multicultural focus. Recent works under his directorial aegis include a revival of *The Tempest* and the musical *Bring in 'Da Noise, Bring in 'Da Funk*, the latter receiving a 1995 Tony Award nomination.

21

Classical Music

㉑

Classical Music

◆ Black Musicians in Early America ◆ Classical Music in the Twentieth Century
◆ The Future for the Black Classical Musician ◆ Classical Gatekeepers

by Robin Armstrong

When the first Africans arrived in 1619 on the eastern coast of what is now the United States, they brought with them a rich musical heritage. In the culture from which these slaves were torn, music and dance accompanied almost every public activity. Each community had professional musicians, and everyone, from the youngest to the oldest, played, sang, and danced. Because theirs was an oral tradition, they did not need sheet music to bring their songs and dances with them—they carried it all in their heads. They brought to the new world not only their songs and dances, but their love of, and need for music as an integral part of daily life, and they participated in the music of their new world from the very beginning.

◆ BLACK MUSICIANS IN EARLY AMERICA

Slave Music

As slaves, the Africans assumed the lives and culture of their owners; they learned the Europeans' language, religion, and music. They sang English psalms and hymns in church as they converted to Christianity. They heard folk and popular tunes in the taverns and homes. Some slaves in the South studied with itinerant music teachers. The most talented musicians gained professional-level skills which were quickly put to use by the whites. Both bonded servants and slave musicians, playing instruments such as the violin, flute, and piano, provided much of the recreational music for their masters. They accompanied dance balls and played at dancing schools. On the self-sufficient plantation in the south, the most musical of the domestic slaves provided evening "entertainments." Once public concerts be-

came possible and popular in the new world, a few talented slaves publicly concertized. The pianist Thomas "Blind Tom" Green Bethune (1849-1909) began public concertizing while still a slave, and continued to perform after emancipation.

Art Music in the Nineteenth Century

As a free, black middle class arose in the nineteenth century and the popularity of public concerts increased, black musicians began to provide "art music" for both black and white audiences. As in white middle-and upper-class communities, genteel songs and piano pieces

Matilda Sisieretta Jones

863

could be heard in the parlors of the comfortable and well-off members of the black communities; music also accompanied most public celebrations and ceremonies. As these communities grew, they could support more professional musicians and music educators. Singing schools and private lessons on instruments were available to anyone interested. During much of the nineteenth century, the best black artists toured throughout the United States and Europe, performing for black and white audiences alike.

In the nineteenth century, a typical "art music" concert showcased a variety of musical pieces. Songs, arias, and ensemble vocal pieces were performed in the same show as chamber, band, and orchestral numbers. The most popular singers tended to be women such as Elizabeth Taylor Greenfield (c. 1824-1876), called the "Black Swan," and Matilda Sisieretta Jones (1869-1933), also known as the "Black Patti" after the contemporary reigning white diva, Adelina Patti. African-American singers Anna Madah Hyers (1853-1920), Emma Louise Hyers (1855-1890), Sidney Woodward (1860-1924), Nellie Brown Mitchell (1845-1924), Marie Selida (1849-1937), Flora Baston Bergon (1864-1906), Rachel Walker (1873-1940), Thomas Bowers (1823-1885) all graced the concert stage during the nineteenth century.

Men tended to dominate the realm of instrumental music. Pianists included John William Boone (1864-1927), and Samuel Jamieson (1855-1930) in addition to Blind Tom. John Thomas Douglas (1847-1886), Walter F. Craig (1854-1920), and Edmond Dede (1877-1903) played the violin. Morris Brown, Jr. (1812-1890), Robert Jones, Jacob Stans, William Appo, James Hermenway (1800-1849), Francis Johnson (1792-1844), and Aaron J.R. Connor conducted all-Black orchestras, bands, and choruses. Most composed music as well. The Original Colored American Opera Troupe of Washington, DC, and the Theodore Drury Colored Opera Company, both established in the second half of the nineteenth century, were the earliest long-lasting black opera companies.

◆ CLASSICAL MUSIC IN THE TWENTIETH CENTURY

Racism and Sexism in Performance Organizations

During most of the nineteenth century, African-American musicians performed for both black and white audiences. Towards the end of the century, however, white audiences began to favor European performers over any American performer, and white musicians over black. Despite their obvious success in classical music, by the beginning of the twentieth century, African Ameri-

Poster advertising the Jubilee Singers.

cans were not considered suitable as classical musicians, and white audiences accepted them only on the vaudeville and minstrel stage. Whites considered blacks to be unable to contribute to art music as either performer or composer. For example, in response to composer Scott Joplin's attempt to produce his opera *Treemonisha* in New York, the *New York Age* stated on March 5, 1908, "Since ragtime has been in vogue, many Negro writers have gained considerable fame as composers of that style of music. From the white man's standpoint of view . . . after writing ragtime, the Negro does not figure." This was the prevailing attitude for some time.

Flutist Dorothy Antoinette Handy (b. 1930) wrote in the preface of her book *Black Women in American Bands and Orchestras* that her book "originated in the mind of a fourteen-year-old black American female who decided that she wanted to be a symphonic orchestral flutist. She went to a New Orleans Philharmonic concert, and shortly before the end proceeded backstage from the reserved for colored section to the orchestra's first flutist. She asked, "Are you accepting any pupils?" and the flutist's response was, "Do you mean that you, a Negro, want to study flute?" Unfortunately, this attitude has continued to reign in the second half of the century as well. In 1975, San Francisco Symphony Orchestra timpanist Elayne Jones, the only black "first chair" player in a major American orchestra, filed a suit claiming contract violation on grounds of racism and sexism because she was denied tenure. She lost her case.

Despite this opposition, African Americans have never been absent from the world of classical music. While the merits of compositions by African-American composers have been undeniable, they have been ignored. Although for much of this century they have been denied entrance to this country's major metropolitan (white) symphonies they have constantly worked towards inclusion. William Grant Still's *Afro-American Symphony* was the first symphonic work written by a black composer to be performed by a major symphony orchestra when in 1931 it was performed by the Rochester Philharmonic Symphony. In 1933, Florence Price became the first black female to have a symphony played by a major orchestra, when the Chicago Symphony Orchestra performed her Symphony in E Minor at the Chicago World's Fair. In 1934, Price conducted her Concerto in F Minor in Chicago. William Grant Still became the first African American to conduct a major orchestra in the deep south when in 1955, he conducted the New Orleans Symphony Orchestra.

The Musical Styles of Black Classical Composers

Black symphonic music falls into two categories: black-stream music, synonymous with Gunther Schuller's *Third Stream*, which is serious music influenced by the ethnic background of the composer; and traditional European music created by black composers. At the end of the nineteenth century, black composers became the first group of American composers to write nationalistic pieces by incorporating black traditional folk idioms into their vocal and instrumental pieces.

Until a few years ago, compositions of either style were largely unknown, but the public relations efforts and researches of Paul Freeman, Domique de Lerma, C. Edward Thomas, and Eileen Southern have brought to light a great many first-rate symphonic compositions both old and new. Among the best black-stream pieces are Florence Price's Symphony in E Minor (1933), William Grant Still's *Afro-American Symphony* (1931), Margaret Bond's *Credo*, and Ornette Coleman's *Skies of America*. Examples of black symphonic music in which there is no obvious contribution from the black heritage include Chevalier de Saint-Georges's *Symphonic Concertante* (1782), Julia Perry's *Stabat Mater* (1951), and Ulysses Kay's *Markings* (1966).

Research and Recording of Music by Classical Composers

After years of neglect, the role of the African American in the history of music is finally being given serious attention. Rediscoveries of excellent classical pieces by African American composers, both contemporary and older, have begun to ventilate the stereotype of black music as a limited program of spirituals, jazz, and the blues. Studies of comprehensive musicology (the study of music in relation to the culture and society in which it exists) are beginning to focus on the unique, non-European nature of African American music.

Several new organizations have devoted time, energy and finances to promoting African American creations and performances in the arts. The now-defunct Afro-American Music Opportunities Association (AAMOA), in existence since 1969, was formed out of the need for more acknowledgment of black music and musicians. Since its formation, C. Edward Thomas has developed the organization's concepts into viable and dynamic programs which have already substantially changed American musical sociology. The AAMOA has put out its own record label for nonsymphonic repertoires with the release of David Baker's Sonata for Piano and String Quartet in a performance which features Brazilian virtuoso Helena Freire. On March 18, 1974, the first four records of the Black Composers Series were formally released by Columbia Records. These discs featured works by Chevalier de Saint-Georges, Samuel Coleridge-Taylor, William Grant Still, George Walker, Ulysses Kay, and Roque Cordero under the artistic direction of Paul Freeman. This Black Composer's Series grew out of an agreement between CBS and the AAMOA for at least twelve recordings of some twenty black composers. As of 1994, nine albums had been completed.

The Center for Black Music Research, established in 1982 at Chicago's Columbia College, has actively contributed to the research publications and performances of contemporary and historic compositions that they have sponsored. They have an ever-growing library and computer database of resources used by scholars all over the country. African American classical and popular music has received more and more attention in the mainstream academic world as musicologists and ethnomusicologists have begun to focus more attention in that direction.

Black and Integrated Performance Organizations

The Symphony of the New World (1965-1976) was established by timpanist Elayne Jones and conductor Benjamin Steinberg as the first racially integrated orchestra in the country. Other founding members include the cellist Kermit Moore and the bassist Lucille Dixon.

Conductor James DePriest rehearses with the New Philharmonic Orchestra, 1984.

This orchestra served as a stepping stone for many musicians, and many of the leading black artists in the nation have performed with them. The group has premiered many works by black composers.

In the 1970s two national black opera companies were formed. Opera/South was founded in 1970 by Sister Elise of the Catholic order of the Sisters of the Blessed Sacrament and members of the Mississippi Inter-Collegiate Opera Guild (Jackson State University, Utica Junior College, and Tougaloo College). In addition to staging grand opera, the company performed operas by black composers including *Highway No. 1 USA* and *A Bayou Legend*, both by William Grant Still, and *Jubilee* and *The Juggler of Our Lady* both by Ulysses Kay. In 1973, Sister Elise with Margaret Harris, Benjamin Matthews, and Wayne Sanders, organized Opera Ebony. Performers with these two companies have included conductors Leonard de Paur, Margaret Harris, and Everett Lee; pianist Way Sanders; and singers Donnie Ray Albert, William Brown, Alpha Floyed, Ester Hinds, Robert Mosely, Wilma Shakesnider, and Walter Turnbull. These companies, as well as the production by the Houston Opera Company in 1975 of Scott Joplin's *Treemonisha*, have served as a showcase for black

talent, and have sent some of the singers to major opera companies.

Black Representation in Major American Orchestras and Opera Companies

As in other areas of American life, the civil rights struggle continues. Programs begun as a response to the civil rights movements in the 1960s to support young black artists died as a result of the economic recession of the 1970s. A 1981 survey by the National Urban League disclosed that of the nearly 5,000 musicians playing regularly in fifty-six leading orchestras, only seventy were black. Only six of the 538 members of the "Big Five" orchestras—New York, Boston, Chicago, Cleveland, and Philadelphia—were black. Few employ black conductors. The American Symphony Orchestra League published a report in 1992 with similar findings. The 146 orchestras that participated in the survey reported that of a total 8326 positions, only 133 were filled by black musicians.

In the early 1980s, The Metropolitan Opera had fifteen black artists on its roster, and the New York City Opera had eleven singers in principal roles with two conductors and one stage director. Prior to World War

Composer Margaret Bonds

II, there were no black singers in any opera house in the United States, but now they are accepted almost anywhere.

◆ THE FUTURE FOR THE BLACK CLASSICAL MUSICIAN

It is impossible to know what lies in the future for African American classical composers, conductors, and other performing artists. Gains made by blacks in orchestras during the 1970s were lost in the 1980s; the conservative court and political systems of this country in the late 1980s and the 1990s has led to a feeling of backlash. Yet as the music of African Americans has been increasingly accepted and celebrated by both the musical and academic worlds, formation of the companies mentioned above have provided an avenue for blacks to accept classical music and be accepted into it. Optimistically, the black musician of the 1990s will be appreciated more as an integral part of the long and varied musical heritage of America.

◆ CLASSICAL GATEKEEPERS

Adele Addison (1925-)
Singer

Born on July 24, 1925, in New York City, Adele Addison received her musical training at Westminster Choir College in 1946 and the University of Massachusetts in 1963. After making her recital debut at Town Hall, New York City, in 1952, she went on to perform recital tours throughout the United States and Canada. In 1963, she made a tour of the Soviet Union under the cultural exchange program.

Addison has appeared with the New England, New York City, and Washington opera companies. Her premiere performances included John La Montaine's *Fragments from the Song of Songs* with the New Haven Symphony (1959) and Poulenc's *Gloria* with the Boston Symphony (1961). She performed the soloist opening concert at Philharmonic Hall, Lincoln Center in 1962.

Roberta Alexander (1949-)
Singer

Opera magazine said of Roberta Alexander "a soprano who, with a range of over two octaves, rich low notes and crystalline, brilliant top notes, excellent diction and clear execution of coloratura passages, should make a name for herself;" and so she has.

She was born in 1949 in Lynchburg, Virginia, grew up in Yellow Springs, Ohio and currently makes her home in Amsterdam, the Netherlands. She has a B.S. degree in music education from Central State University in Ohio and a master's degree in voice from the University of Michigan at Ann Arbor.

Her premier with the Metropolitan Opera came in 1983's fall season as Zerlina in *Don Giovanni*. Other Met successes were as Bess in *Porgy and Bess* and in the title role of *Jenufa*.

In the summer of 1984, she made her debut at the Aix-en Provence Festival in France in Mozart's *La Finta Giardiniera*, and in 1985, in Vienna she performed as Cleopatra in Handel's *Giulio Cesare*. She has also performed as Ilia in *Idomeneo* and in *La Boheme* in Berlin. She has also performed extensively at the Netherlands Opera, the London Opera, and in America at the Santa Fe Opera in New Mexico and at the Houston Grand Opera in Texas. In 1987, she returned to the Met where she once again performed the role of Mimi in *La Boheme*.

Betty Lou Allen (1930-)
Educator, Singer

Born on March 17, 1930, in Campbell, Ohio, Betty Lou Allen studied at Wilberforce University and toured with Leontyne Price as the Wilberforce Sisters. She continued her musical studies at the Hartford School of Music (1950) and the Berkshire Music Center (1951), and studied voice with Sarah Peck Moore, Paul Ulanowsky, and Zinka Milanov.

Allen's New York debut was in Virgil Thompson's *Four Saints in Three Acts* with the New York City Opera Company (1953) and her formal opera debut was at the

Director Walter Trumbull rehearses with the Boys Choir of Harlem.

Teatro Colon, Buenos Aires (1964). She has appeared as a soloist with leading orchestras and conductors, including Bernstein, Dorate, and Maazel.

Allen has served as a faculty member of such schools as the North Carolina School of the Arts, The Curtis Institute of Music in Philadelphia, and The Manhattan School of Music in New York City. She is currently the executive director and chair of the voice department at the Harlem School of the Arts in New York.

Marian Anderson (1902-1993)
Singer

At the peak of her career, Marian Anderson was regarded as the world's greatest contralto. When she made her Town Hall debut in New York on December 31, 1935, Howard Taubman, the *New York Times* reviewer, described it as "music-making that probed too deep for words."

Marian Anderson was born on February 27, 1902, in Philadelphia. As a young choir girl, she demonstrated her vocal talents by singing parts from soprano, alto, tenor and bass. At the age of nineteen she began studying with Giuseppe Boghetti, and four years later she appeared as soloist with the New York Philharmonic.

After a short engagement with the Philadelphia Symphony Orchestra, she traveled to Europe on a scholarship granted by the National Association of Negro Musicians.

On Easter Sunday in 1939 Anderson gave what is perhaps her most memorable concert—singing on the steps of the Lincoln Memorial after having been barred from making an appearance at Constitution Hall by the Daughters of the American Revolution.

In 1955, after years of successful concert work, she made her Metropolitan Opera debut in Verdi's *Un Ballo in Maschera*. Two years later, a State Department tour took her around the world. In September of 1958, she was named to the United States delegation to the United Nations.

In 1982, when Marian Anderson celebrated her eightieth birthday, Grace Bumbry and Shirley Verrett sang at New York City's Carnegie Hall in tribute to Anderson.

Thomas Jefferson Anderson (1928-)
Composer, Educator

Thomas Jefferson Anderson was born in 1928 in Coatesville, Pennsylvania. His mother was a musician, and as a teenager he toured with a jazz orchestra. He

Roberta Alexander

role of *Aida* and has since sung engagements with opera houses in Vienna, Berlin, Buenos Aires, London, and Hamburg. In addition to operatic appearances, she has also been a frequent guest soloist with many of the world's major orchestras.

In addition to *Aida*, Arroyo's Metropolitan repertoire includes Donna Anna in *Don Giovanni*, Liu in *Turandot*, Leonora in *Il Trovatore*, Elsa in *Lohengrin*, and the title role of *Madame Butterfly*. These performances have developed since 1958, the year she made her debut in Carnegie Hall in the American premiere of Pizzetti's *Murder in the Cathedral*. That same year she made her Metropolitan debut as the celestial voice in *Don Carlo*.

Arroyo sang at the White House in 1977, sharing the stage with Andre Previn and Isaac Stern at a dinner for twenty-six heads of state marking the signing of the Panama Canal treaty. In April 1987, she was guest artist for the New Mexico Symphony Orchestra, where she sang the overture of Verdi's *La Forza del Destino* as well as several other pieces. In 1988, she performed once again with New York's Met production of *Turandot*, *Cavalleria Rusticana* and *Aida*.

Over the past several years, Arroyo has taught as well as performed in various summer song festivals.

received a bachelor's in music from West Virginia State College in 1950 and a master's degree in education from Pennsylvania State University in 1951. Anderson went on to study at the Aspen School of Music, and in 1958 received a Ph.D. from the University of Iowa.

Anderson was composer-in-residence with the Atlanta Symphony Orchestra on a grant from the Rockefeller Foundation during the 1969-1971 seasons. His most widely performed works have been *Chamber Symphony* (1968); *Squares* (1965), an essay for orchestra; and *Personals* (1966), a cantata for narrator, chorus, and brass ensemble. He has also written music for bands *(In Memoriam Zach Walker)*, works for piano *(Watermelon)* and various compositions for solo voice and for chorus.

Dr. Anderson has taught music in public school and served as a faculty member at West Virginia State College, Langston University in Oklahoma, Tennessee State University in Maine.

Martina Arroyo (1939-)
Singer

Martina Arroyo, a New York native, made her debut at the Metropolitan Opera in February 1965 in the title

Marian Anderson

David Nathaniel Baker, Jr. (1931-)
Composer, Educator

David Nathaniel Baker Jr. was born in 1931 in Indianapolis and obtained his bachelor's and master's in music education from Indiana University. He taught music in the public schools of Indianapolis, and Indiana Central College and Lincoln University (Missouri) before returning to his alma mater as a faculty member. Baker has logged considerable experience with both jazz bands and college and municipal symphony orchestras. He was a member of Quincy Jones' All-Star Jazz Orchestra,

Grace Bumbry in Verdi's *Don Carlos.*

which toured Europe in 1961, and has performed with Stan Kenton, Lionel Hampton, and Wes Montgomery.

Baker is currently chairman of the jazz department at the Indiana University School of Music.

Kathleen Battle (1948-)
Singer

Soprano Kathleen Battle was born on August 13, 1948, in Portsmouth, Ohio, and is a graduate of the University of Cincinnati's College of Conservatory of Music, having received both a bachelor's and master's degree in music.

Battle made her Met debut in 1977 as the Shepherd in *Tannhauser* and has also been heard there as Sophie in *Werther* and Blondchen in *The Abduction from the Seraglio.* The 1980–1981 season included performances in *The Italian Girl in Algiers,* as well as debuts with the Zurich Opera and the Lyric Opera of Chicago. In 1982, she received critical praise for her Rosina in the Met's *Barber of Seville.*

In the 1987–1988 season, Battle returned to the Metropolitan Opera to sing the role of Zerbinetta in Strauss' *Ariadne auf Naxos.* She has since sung in major music festivals and with major orchestras, including the New York Philharmonic, Cleveland Orchestra, and Los Angeles Philharmonic.

In recent years, Battle has recorded such works as *Ariadne auf Naxos* and Mahler's Symphony No. 4. She has also recorded various Schubert Lieder and Handel Arias. Battle recently joined trumpeter Wynton Marsalis in a recording of baroque arias.

In 1994, Battle was dismissed from the Metropolitan Opera production of Donizetti's *Fille du Regiment* following a well-publicized dispute with management. She released several recordings that year, including "Kathleen Battle and Jean-Pierre Rampal in Concert" and "Bel Canto Arias." Battle made a successful move from opera to popular music in 1995 with the recordings, "So Many Stars" and "Honey and Rue."

Thomas Green Bethune (1849-1909)
Pianist

Thomas "Blind Tom" Bethune was born blind and born a slave in Columbus, Georgia, in 1849. He was also born a musical prodigy. His owner, James Bethune, allowed him access to his family's piano and realizing at once his musical and financial possibilities, arranged for his informal musical training. Young Tom quickly developed such skills that he could play whatever he heard; his training consisted mainly of having him listen to works to increase his repertoire.

Kathleen Battle

"Blind Tom" began performing for the profit of his owner while still a slave and a child, and continued to tour the North and South during the Civil War. After the war, the Bethune family retained financial control over his performances through contracts. Tom performed in this country and in Europe. His repertoire consisted of the usual concert fair of serious classics by composers like Bach, Beethoven, and Chopin, fancy virtuosic pieces by composers such as Goltschalk and Liszt, improvised variations on contemporary popular ballads and arias, and his own light compositions, few of which survive today. He was said to have been able to play any one of seven thousand pieces on command. Tom retired in 1898 and died in 1909.

Margaret Allison Bonds (1913-1972)
Composer, Pianist

Margaret Bonds (1913-1972) grew up in an artistically and creatively active family in Chicago. Her mother, Estelle C. Bonds, an accomplished musician herself, invited many of the prominent musicians and artists of the time into her home. Margaret Bonds became good friends with the likes of composer Florence Price, poet Langston Hughes, singer Abbie Mitchell, and sculptor

Richmond Barthe. She received her early piano lessons from her mother and composition lessons from Florence Price. While still in high school, she joined the National Association of Negro Musicians. She worked closely with such musicians as Price and Mitchell and played for dance rehearsals for Muriel Abbot.

Bonds continued her musical studies at Northwestern University in Evanston, Illinois, completing both a bachelor's and master's degree by age twenty-one. During the 1930s, she opened her own school for dance, music, and art in Chicago and frequently performed in solo recitals and with symphony orchestras. She moved to New York in 1989 to pursue her career and study further at the Juilliard School of Music. In the 1940s and 1950s, she performed as part of a piano duo with Gerald Cook. She soon left New York for Los Angeles where she taught piano, directed the Inner City Repertory Theatre, and wrote arrangements for the Los Angeles Jubilee Singers. Bonds' many compositions include songs, symphonies, musicals, ballets, a cantata and piano works.

Gwendolyn Bradley (1952-)
Singer

Soprano Gwendolyn Bradley was born in New York City in 1952 but grew up in Bishopville, South Carolina. She was a finalist in the 1977 Metropolitan Opera National Council auditions and a graduate of the North Carolina School of the Arts. She has also attended both the Curtis Institute of Music and the Academy of Vocal Arts in Philadelphia and has studied with Margaret Harshaw and Seth McCoy.

Bradley made her Metropolitan Opera debut as the Nightingale in the Met premiere of Raval's "L'Enfant et les Sortileges" in February 1981. Since making her professional operatic debut in 1976 with the Lake George Opera Festival as Nanetta in *Falstaff*, she has been heard as Titania in *A Midsummer Night's Dream* with the Central City Opera, Lakme with Opera/South, and Aurelia in *Rumpelstiltskin* with the Opera Company of Philadelphia. Bradley has sung with the Philadelphia Orchestra, the Kansas City Philharmonic, and the Charleston Symphony. From 1980 to 1981 she appeared with the Los Angeles Philharmonic at the Hollywood Bowl and with the Seattle Symphony. In addition to the Metropolitan Opera she has performed with the opera companies of Philadelphia, Cleveland and Michigan.

Grace Ann Bumbry (1937-)
Singer

Mezzo–soprano Grace Bumbry is the first black performer to have sung at the Wagner Festival in Bayreuth, Germany, and one of the few singers who can boast of having been called to play a command performance at the White House. Bumbry sang at a formal state dinner opening Washington's official social season in 1962 as a guest of the Kennedys and the nation.

A native of St. Louis, Missouri, Bumbry, like many black singers, had her first exposure to music in a church choir, singing with her brothers and her parents at the Union Memorial Methodist Church in St. Louis. After studying voice locally, she won a nationwide talent contest in 1954 and went on, with scholarship aid, to study successively at Boston and Northwestern universities. At the latter school, she attended master classes in opera and lieder given by the famed singer and teacher Lotte Lehmann.

In 1959, Bumbry traveled to various European countries, performing in the operatic capitals of the world. On July 23, 1961, Wieland Wagner, grandson of Richard Wagner, shocked many traditionalists by selecting Bumbry to sing the role of Venus in *Tannhauser*, a role which conventionally calls for a figure of so-called Nordic beauty, usually a tall and voluptuous blond. Bumbry proceeded to give a performance which won acclamation from both the harshest and the kindest of critics, all of whom praised her both for her physical radiance and her brilliant singing.

In 1974, Bumbry performed with the Met in *Cavalleria Rusticana*. She has since appeared successfully with various opera companies as Dalilah, Lady Macbeth, Medea, and other great dramatic roles, which have become her specialty.

On December 6, 1981, Bumbry participated in a benefit concert at Carnegie Hall for Artists to End Hunger; and January 31, 1982, she shared the stage with Shirley Verrett at Carnegie Hall to pay tribute to Marian Anderson on her eightieth birthday.

In the 1987–1988 season Grace Bumbry returned to the San Francisco Opera as Abigaille in *Nabucco* and starred as Lady Macbeth in a new production of *Macbeth* in Los Angeles. She celebrated her twenty–fifth anniversary at the Royal Opera, Covent Garden with a series of performances of *Tosca* and appeared at the Vienna State Opera in the same role. Bumbry returned to Barcelona for La Gioconda and was also heard in *Cavalleria Rusticana* and *Don Carlos* at the Hamburg State Opera. She has also appeared as Amneris in *Aida* at the Arena di Verona. In 1995, Bumbry played the role of Herodias in a performance of Massenet's opera *Herodiade* at New York's Carnegie Hall.

Henry Thacker "Harry" Burleigh (1866-1949)
Arranger, Composer, Singer

Harry Burleigh was born with talent, but was also born into poverty. He was unable to receive any formal

musical training until he was an adult. At the age of twenty-six, he moved from his home in Erie, Pennsylvania to New York City, where he won a scholarship to the National Conservatory of Music. After graduation, he pursued a very successful singing career that included concertizing throughout the United States and Europe. He was soloist at St. George's Protestant Episcopal Church in New York for fifty-three years, and at Temple Emanu-El for twenty-five.

As a composer and arranger, Burleigh was the first to arrange spirituals in the style of art songs, and was the first African American composer to receive critical acclaim for his art songs. As a performer, he established the tradition of concluding recitals with a group of spirituals. His art song compositions also included settings of poetry by Robert Burns and Langston Hughes, and he composed several pieces for violin and piano. He was a member of the American Society of Composers, Authors, and Publishers (ASCAP), and sat on its Board of Directors. He received an honorary master's degree from Atlanta University in 1918, and an honorary doctorate in 1920 from Howard University.

Frances Elaine Cole (1937-1983)
Violinist, Harpsichordist, Music Critic

Frances Cole began her musical life as a violinist. She studied at the Cleveland Institute of Music and at Miami University of Ohio, where she was concert master of the orchestra. She studied further in New York City privately and at Columbia University Teacher's College, receiving her doctorate in 1966. During these years she played violin for the National Orchestral Association.

In the mid-1960s, as she was finishing her doctorate at Columbia, she discovered her interest in the harpsichord; she began studying the instrument at the Landowska Center in Connecticut. In 1967, she became resident harpsichordist with the Gallery Players in Provincetown, Massachusetts, started appearing on national television shows, and began appearing publicly in concerts and recitals throughout the United States and Europe.

While Cole concertized as a serious classical artist, she did not limit herself by any means. She was as well known for her humor and innovation as for her elegant musical interpretations. In 1976, for example, at an outdoor concert at Lincoln Center, she arrived dressed as Anna Magalena Bach in a horse drawn carriage. She also played jazz with a bassist and percussionist, and sang in lounges and supper clubs under the name of Elaine Frances. In 1979, she began appearing on CBS's "Sunday Morning" as performer and music critic. Cole also served as assistant professor of music at Queens College and the Westminister Choir College, and gave workshops at many colleges and universities.

Samuel Coleridge-Taylor

Samuel Coleridge-Taylor (1875-1912)
Composer

Coleridge-Taylor was one of England's most celebrated composers at the turn of the century.

Born to a doctor from Sierra Leone and a British mother in 1875, he showed musical gifts at age five and ten years later entered the Royal College of Music in London. There he studied with Sir Charles Wood and Sir Charles Villiers Stanford. He achieved fame with the premiere of *Hiawatha's Wedding Feast.*

Coleridge-Taylor was very warmly received in this country. James Weldon Johnson and Booker T. Washington were among his friends, and he was President Theodore Roosevelt's guest at the White House. In 1901, the Coleridge-Taylor Society was organized in Washington, DC specifically to study and perform his music.

Will Marion Cook (1869-1944)
Violinist, Composer, Conductor

Will Marion Cook wrote and directed in both popular and classical venues. He was well educated in classical genres—he entered Oberlin Conservatory when he was fifteen to study violin, studied further in Berlin, Germa-

ny between 1887 and 1889, and attended the National Conservatory of Music in New York.

In 1890, he shifted his energies from performing to conducting. He directed an orchestra in Washington, DC in 1890, and performed at the Chicago World's Fair in 1893. In 1898, he became active in writing and directing black musical comedies in New York, producing the first such show to play in a major theater for a wide audience. He organized choral societies and promoted all-black concerts. He directed the New York Syncopated Orchestra, which traveled Europe, and taught and sponsored many young and talented black musicians. In addition to his musicals, he wrote art songs, choral works, instrumental pieces, and operas.

Roque Cordero (1917-)
Composer, Educator

Roque Cordero is respected as one of Latin America's most creative talents because of his abilities as a violinist, a conductor, and a composer who incorporates popular Panamanian forms into concert music.

Born in Panama in 1917, his interests developed from popular songwriting to classical music at the age of seventeen. Four years later he was appointed director of the Orquesta Sinfonica de la Union Musical in Panama, and he later joined the Orquesta Sinfonica de Panama as violist. In 1943, he began studying abroad. He was engaged by the University of Minnesota as Artistic Director of the Institute of Latin-American Studies, and after completing his course of study, was awarded a Guggenheim Fellowship. Dr. Cordero is presently music editor for the publishing company of Peer International Corporation and is professor of music at Illinois State University.

Philip Creech (1950-)
Singer

Philip Creech is a native of Hempstead, New York and a graduate of Northwestern University. Creech performed with Margaret Hillis' Chicago Symphony Chorus from 1973 to 1975 and frequently appeared as tenor soloist. Since 1976 he has sung with the Chicago Symphony, the Boston Symphony, the New York Philharmonic, and the Cincinnati Symphony. Creech made his debut at the Salzburg Festival in 1979 singing in the Berlioz *Requiem*. He made his Metropolitan Opera debut in September 1979 as Beppe in the season's premiere of Leoncavallo's *Pagliacci,* and was heard later that season as Edmondo in the premiere and subsequent live overseas telecast of the new production of Puccini's *Manon Lescaut.* Creech has also appeared at the Met as Tonio in *Pagliacci.*

Creech made his recording debut in Stravinsky's *Les Noces*, with the Chicago Symphony on RCA Red Seal's *Music from Raviniar* series. He has recently recorded *Carmina Burana* with James Levine and the Chicago Symphony, which was released on the DGG label and became a best-seller and a Grammy Award winner. Creech is also recognized as an accomplished recitalist and has sung well over one-hundred recitals throughout the United States.

James Anderson DePreist (1936-)
Conductor

Born in Philadelphia on November 21, 1936, James Anderson DePreist studied piano and percussion from the age of ten, but did not decide on a musical career until he reached his early twenties. After graduating from high school, he entered the Wharton School of the University of Pennsylvania as a prelaw student, receiving a bachelor of science in 1958 and a master of arts degree in 1961. DePreist also studied music history, the theory of harmony, and orchestration at the Philadelphia Conservatory of Music, and composition with the distinguished American composer Vincent Persichetti.

In 1962, the United States State Department sponsored a cultural exchange tour of the Near and the Far East, engaging DePreist as an American specialist in music. During this tour, DePreist was stricken with polio, paralyzed in both legs, and flown home for intensive therapy. Within six months he had fought his way back to the point where he could walk with the aid of crutches and braces. Courage, determination, and talent carried him to the semifinals of the 1963 Dmitri Mitropoulos International Music Competition for Conductors.

After another overseas tour as conductor in residence in Thailand, DePreist returned to the United States, appearing with the Minneapolis International Symphony Orchestra, the New York Philharmonic, and the Philadelphia Orchestra.

In 1964, he recorded what is perhaps his most satisfying triumph, capturing first prize in the Mitropoulos International Competition. Another highlight of his career occurred on June 28, 1965 when he conducted Marian Anderson's farewell concert at Philadelphia's Robin Hood Dell.

Currently DePriest is the music director of the Oregon Symphony. He is one of a select and talented circle of American-born and trained conductors who have appeared with the nation's five premier orchestras— New York, Boston, Philadelphia, Cleveland, and Chicago. He has also been guest conductor in most of the capitals of Europe and the United States.

Chevalier de Saint-Georges (1739-1799)
Composer

Chevalier de Saint-Georges is considered to be the first man of African ancestry to have made a major impression on European music.

Born on the Caribbean island of Guadeloupe to an African slave mother and a French father in 1739, he displayed early talent on the violin. He studied with Francois Gossec, whom he succeeded as concertmaster of the celebrated Concert des Amateurs in 1769. His musical output was enormous, including several operas, symphonies concertantes, a dozen string quartets, violin concertos, and other instrumental and vocal works. He died in 1799.

Dean Dixon (1915-1976)
Conductor

Dixon was born in Manhattan on January 10, 1915, and graduated from DeWitt Clinton High School in 1932. Exposed to classical music by his parents, (as a small boy he was regularly taken to Carnegie Hall) Dixon formed his own amateur orchestra at the Harlem YMCA while he was still in high school. On the basis of a successful violin audition, he was admitted to the Juilliard School where he received his bachelor's degree in 1936; three years later he acquired his master's from Columbia.

The Dean Dixon Symphony Society, which he had formed in 1932, began to receive financial support from the Harlem community in 1937, and in 1941 at the request of Eleanor Roosevelt, Dixon gave a concert at the Heckscher Theater. He was later signed by the musical director of NBC radio to conduct the network's summer symphony in two concerts. Two months after the NBC concerts, he made his debut with the New York Philharmonic. Dean Dixon was the first black and, at twenty-six, the youngest musician ever to conduct the New York Philharmonic Orchestra.

Lucille Dixon (Robertson) (1923-)
Bassist

Lucille Dixon began playing bass in high school and was soon studying with the New York Philharmonic's principal bassist, Fred Zimmermen. After high school, she was the second of two black women to play in the WPA-sponsored National Youth Administration Orchestra. While this group normally served as a hiring house for major United States orchestras, Dixon realized she, a black female, would not be hired by a symphony orchestra.

When the NYA orchestra folded, she turned to jazz for a living. She played for two years with the Earl Hines Band, and in 1946, formed a band of her own. However, she continued her classical pursuits. Dixon's affiliations

James DePriest

Dean Dixon

include National Symphony of Panama, Westchester Philharmonic, Ridgefield Symphony, and Scranton Symphony, and the Symphony of the New World, for which she served as manager from 1972 to 1976.

Carl Rossini Ditton (1886-1962)
Pianist, Singer, Composer

Carl Ditton received his first piano lesson from his father, who was a professional musician. He continued study at the University of Pennsylvania, receiving a bachelor's degree in 1909. Following graduation, he went on to become the first black pianist to make a cross-country concert tour. With the aid of an E. Azalia Hackley Scholarship, he furthered his piano studies in Munich.

During the 1920s, he began to study voice, and made his concert debut in Philadelphia in 1926. He later studied voice at Juilliard, where he received an artists diploma in 1930. That year he also received the Harmon

Award for composition; his compositions include primarily art songs and arrangements of spirituals.

Mattiwilda Dobbs (1925-)
Singer

One of the world's most gifted coloratura sopranos is Mattiwilda Dobbs. Now residing in Sweden, where she is a national favorite, Miss Dobbs has gained international fame.

Born in Atlanta, Georgia on July 11, 1925, Mattiwilda Dobbs graduated from Spelman College in 1946 as class valedictorian, having majored in voice training. After studying Spanish at Columbia, where she received her master's degree, she went on to Paris for two years on a Whitney Fellowship.

In October 1950, competing against hundreds of singers from four continents, she won the International Music Competition held at Geneva. She made her professional debut in Paris in 1953, and then became the first black to sing a principal role at La Scala in Milan. On March 8, 1954, she made her Town Hall debut in New York in the one-act opera *Ariadne auf Naxos* and received a rousing ovation. One year later she repeated the success with her first concert recital on the same stage.

Considered one of the world's most gifted coloratura sopranos, Dobbs has made numerous recordings, including *The Pearl Fishers* and *Zaidde* and has toured the world with great success.

Rudolph Dunbar (1917-1988)
Composer, Clarinetist

Born in British Guiana in 1917, Rudolph Dunbar received his musical education at the Institute of Musical Art in New York, as well as in Paris and Leipzig. He made his debut with the NBC Symphony Orchestra in New York City and conducted in Great Britain and throughout the United States. In addition to being a musical conductor, Dunbar was also a clarinetist. He is the author of *A Treatise on Clarinet Playing* and is known best for the composition *Dance of the 20th Century*.

Robert Todd Duncan (1903-)
Singer, Actor

Although thinking of himself primarily as a teacher, Todd Duncan has made notable contributions to the world of theater and concert.

Duncan was born into a well-to-do family in Danville, Kentucky on February 12, 1903. He graduated from Butler University in Indianapolis in 1925 and began a teaching career—first at a junior high school, and then in Louisville at the Municipal College for Negroes.

In 1934, he appeared in New York in a single performance of an all-black version of the opera *Cavalleria Rusticana*. On the strength of this alone, he was auditioned less than a year later by George Gershwin and received the role of Porgy in *Porgy and Bess*. He was such a success that he repeated his performance in the role in the 1938 and 1942 revivals of the play.

In 1940, he was a featured performer on Broadway in *Cabin in the Sky*. When the play closed, he headed for Hollywood to appear in the movie *Syncopation*.

His concert repertoire includes German lieder and French and Italian songs. Duncan retired in 1965 after singing at President Lyndon B. Johnson's inauguration. Only once has he come out of retirement, and that was in 1972 to sing the title role of *Job* at Washington's Kennedy Center. Duncan currently teaches voice in his home in Washington, DC.

Simon Lamont Estes (1938-)
Singer

Bass–baritone Simon Lamont Estes was the first black man to sing at the Bayreuth Festival, appearing in the title role of a new production of *Der Fliegende Hollander*, a portrayal he repeated there in three subsequent seasons. A native of Centerville, Iowa, Estes attended the University of Iowa and received a full scholarship to Juilliard, studying under Sergius Kagan and Christopher West. He won the Munich International Vocal Competition in 1965 and was the silver medalist in the Tchaikovsky Competition in 1966.

Estes made his operatic debut as Ramfis in *Aida* at the Deutsche Oper Berlin and since then has appeared in most of the world's major opera houses, including La Scala, the Hamburg State Opera, the Bavarian State Opera of Munich, the Vienna State Opera, the Lyric Opera of Chicago, the San Francisco Opera, and the Zurich Opera. He made his debut at the Metropolitan Opera in 1982, foregoing the honor of singing the national anthem on baseball's opening day—the day of his Met debut. Estes participated in the Metropolitan Opera's first production of *Porgy and Bess*.

Estes has appeared as soloist with most of the world's leading symphony orchestras. He has also performed recitals and orchestral engagements in numerous European cities, including Paris, Zurich, Brussels, Munich, Bonn, Madrid, and Bordeaux. His North American highlights include appearances with the Chicago Symphony Orchestra conducted by Sir George Solti, and the Montreal Symphony conducted by Charles Dutoit.

In addition to having recorded *Der Fliegende Hollander* Estes has recorded Handel's *Messiah*, the Faure

Requiem, Beethoven's Symphony No. 9, numerous spirituals, and highlights from *Porgy and Bess*.

Louis Moreau Gottschalk (1829-1869)
Composer, Pianist

Born in New Orleans in 1829, Louis Gottschalk was a violin prodigy at six years of age and later became a brilliant concert pianist. He was already something of a European matinee idol when he first appeared in New York, on February 10, 1853 and his romantic compositions enjoyed a wide vogue.

Although Gottschalk went to Paris when he was thirteen to study with Halle, Stamaty, and Maleden, much of his music reflected the Creole environment of his early childhood. One of his best-known compositions, *La Bambould*, is based on the sights and sounds of New Orleans' Congo Square. His autobiographical book, *Notes of a Pianist*, provides an interesting description of his background and method of composition. Louis Moreau Gottschalk was, perhaps, the first black composer born in the United States to achieve international renown. Chopin praised his debut at the Salle Pleyel in April 1844, and Berlioz, with whom he studied, applauded his "sovereign power."

Reri Grist (1932-)
Singer

Born in New York City in 1932, soprano Reri Grist, received her bachelor's degree in music in 1954 from Queens College. Grist first came to national attention when she performed the role of Consuela in Leonard Bernstein's *West Side Story*. This success was followed by a performance with the New York Philharmonic in Mahler's Symphony No. 4.

Considered one of America's best coloratura sopranos, Grist has sung at most of the world's great opera houses, including La Scala, Vienna State, Britain's Royal Opera, and the Metropolitan Opera.

When Dr. Herbert Graf, the former stage director of the Met, left in 1960 to become director of the Zurich Opera, he persuaded many operatic talents, including Grist, to accompany him there. While in Europe, Grist was asked by Stravinsky to sing under his direction in *Le Rossignol*.

In addition to a career in performance, Grist has taught voice at Indiana University and the Hochschule fur Musik in Germany.

In 1995, Grist performed on two new recordings of Mozart's *Die Zauberflote* and *Die Entfuhrung aus dem Serail*.

Louis Moreau Gottschalk

Emma Azalia Hackley (1867-1922)
Singer, Educator, Choral Director

Emma Azalia Hackley did as much to promote African American musicians as she did their traditional music. She received her own musical training while growing up in Detroit, Michigan, where she studied voice and piano and began giving local recitals at an early age. She attended the University of Denver, where she received her bachelor's degree in music in 1900. In 1905, she traveled to Paris where she continued her studies.

Hackley concertized extensively during the early years of the new century, but gradually turned to developing and supporting the careers of other talented young black artists. Through recitals, concerts, lecture/demonstrations, she raised funds for scholarships; in 1908 she established an ongoing scholarship to promote and fund study abroad. She sponsored debut recitals for young performers and helped many find good college-level teaching positions—many of the artists she supported and promoted went on to become successful musical leaders in their own right.

Hackley founded and directed the Vocal Normal Institute in Chicago between 1912 and 1916. In the last

Reri Grist

compositions. In 1918, she toured Europe entertaining World War I service men; in 1919, she became the first black musician to teach in Chicago's downtown district; and in 1921, she became the first black pianist to give a solo recital in a major New York concert Hall when she performed at Town Hall. During the 1930s she taught at Tennessee State A and M College and served as dean of music at Bishop College in Marshal, Texas. In 1935, she established the Helen Hagen Music Studio in New York City.

Dorothy Antoinette Handy (Miller) (1930-)
Flutist

Dorothy Antoinette Handy began to study music as a young child under the direction of her mother, who taught her violin and piano. She went on to study at Spelman College in Atlanta, at the New England Conservatory of Music (B.M. 1952), at Northwestern University in Illinois (M.M. 1953), and the National Conservatory in Paris (Artist's Diploma 1955).

Handy has worked with many orchestras, including the Chicago Civic Orchestra (1952-1953), the International Orchestra of Paris (1954-1955), Musica Viva Orchestra of Geneva (1955), Symphony of the Air on NBC (1956), The Orchestra of America in New York (1960-1962), the Symphony of the New World (1968-1971), and the Richmond (Virginia) Symphony (1966-1976). She is a founding member of the Trio Pro Viva which, among other activities, commissions and performs works by African American composers.

Handy also toured widely as a concert artist, played for films and television, and has been a lecturer, consultant, project director, and radio commentator. She has taught at Florida A and M University, Tuskegee Institute, Jackson State College, and Virginia State College. She has written numerous articles for professional journals, and three books: *Black Music: Opinions and Reviews* (1974), *Black Women in American Bands and Orchestras* (1981), and *The International Sweethearts of Rhythm* (1983).

Margaret Rosezarion Harris (1943-)
Pianist, Conductor, Composer

Margaret Harris began life as a child prodigy—she gave her first concert at age three, began touring nationally when she was four, and played with the Chicago Symphony when she was ten. She studied piano and conducting at the Curtis Institute and the Juilliard School of Music, receiving her bachelor's degree in 1964 and her master's in 1965.

Harris's conducting career has encompassed both symphony orchestras and Broadway shows. Her Broadway credits include *Hair* (1970–1972), *Two Gentlemen*

years of her life, she organized large community concerts promoting the importance of black folk music, raising the level of public interest and pride in African-American musical heritage. So much was her contribution that twenty years after her death, the National Association of Negro Musicians established the Hackley Collection of the Detroit Public Library for the preservation of materials relating to black musicians.

Helen Eugenia Hagen (1891-1964)
Pianist, Composer

Helen Hagen was born into a musical family—her mother played piano, and her father sang baritone. After receiving her initial musical education from her mother and the public school system in New Haven, Connecticut, in 1912 she became the first black pianist to earn a bachelor's of music degree from Yale University. She was also the first African American to win Yale's Sanford Fellowship, which permitted her to study in Europe. She earned a diploma in 1914 from the Schola Cantorum, and later received a master's degree from Columbia University Teacher's College in New York.

Between 1914 and 1918, Hagen toured in the United States; her repertoire included many of her own piano of *Verona* (1972–1974), *Raisin* (1974–1976), *Guys and Dolls* (1980), and *Amen Corner* (1983–1984). She has conducted major symphony orchestras in Chicago, Minneapolis, Detroit, San Diego, St. Louis, and Los Angeles—often in these concerts she both performed and conducted her own piano concertos. She was a founding member of Opera Ebony and has served as its music director. Her compositions include two piano concerti, four musical production scores, two ballets, themes for television shows, as well as choral and instrumental works.

When she is not performing, Harris serves as a visiting professor at the University of West Florida and as an adjunct professor at City University of New York, Bronx Community College. She is a member of the National Association of Negro Musicians and the Mu Phi Epsilon Professional Music Sorority.

In 1994, Harris performed on a concert tour throughout Germany. She also participated in a performance of *Porgy and Bess* in Russia in 1995.

Hazel Harrison (1883-1969)
Pianist

Hazel Harrison was one of the leading pianists of her day. As a child she studied with Victor Heinz, who arranged for her to study in Berlin for several years beginning in 1904. She studied with Ferruccio Busoni, gave recitals, and performed with the Berlin Philharmonic. Upon returning to the United States, she won an award that allowed her to return to Berlin between 1910 and 1914.

When she returned again to the States, she taught in Chicago and toured throughout the United States. In 1931 Harrison began teaching college—she taught at the Tuskegee Institute in Alabama (1931-1943), Howard University in Washington DC (1934-1959), and Alabama State A and M College at Montgomery (1959-1964). She continued to concertize frequently until retirement.

Roland Hayes (1887-1976)
Singer

Roland Hayes was born to former slave parents in Curryville, Georgia on June 3, 1887. His father, a tenant-farmer, died when Hayes was twelve. Determined that her seven children would not share her illiteracy, Hayes' mother sent them to Chattanooga, Tennessee, where they set up a rotating system whereby one brother worked while the others attended school. Hayes was employed in a machine shop, but when his turn came to go to school he passed it up, continuing to supply the family income while he studied at night.

In 1917, Hayes became the first black to give a recital in Boston's Symphony Hall. Three years later he traveled to London and gave a royal command performance, followed by other successes throughout Europe. His tenor voice was used to good advantage in programs blended from Negro spirituals, folk songs, operatic arias, and German lieder.

Hayes gave a well-received farewell concert at Carnegie Hall in New York on his seventy-fifth birthday in 1962. During his career, Hayes received many awards and citations including eight honorary degrees and the NAACP's Spingarn Medal for the most outstanding achievement among blacks. Hayes died in Boston on January 1, 1977 at the age of eighty-nine. The success of Roland Hayes in the concert field played a great part in broadening the opportunities later afforded to such singers as Paul Robeson and Marian Anderson.

Barbara Hendricks (1948-)
Singer

Barbara Hendricks was born in Stephens, Arkansas, in 1948. She graduated from the University of Nebraska with a bachelor of science degree in chemistry and mathematics, then attended the Juilliard School of music and received a bachelor of music degree in voice. Hendricks made her debut in 1974 with the San Francisco Spring Opera. She has since performed with major opera companies and festivals throughout the United States and Europe, including the Boston Opera, New York Metropolitan Opera, St. Paul Opera, Santa Fe Opera, Houston Opera, the Deutsche Opera in Berlin, the Nederlandse Operastichting and at the Aix Provence Festival and the Glyndebourne Festival Opera. She has performed with numerous symphony orchestras, and has appeared in a film version of *La Boheme*.

Hendricks has received numerous awards, including a French Grammy for best French performer of classical music in 1986, an honorary doctor of music from Nebraska Wesleyan University in 1988, and an honorable membership from the Institute of Humanitarian Law in 1990.

Hendricks is also a human rights activist. Since 1987, she has served as a goodwill ambassador for the United Nations High Commission for Refugees.

Gail Hightower (1946-)
Bassoonist

Gail Hightower displayed great musical promise as a child. She attended the High School of Performing Arts in New York City. Scholarships from the New Amsterdam Musical Association and the Rockefeller Foundation, and grants from the National Endowment for the Arts allowed her to attend the Manhattan School of Music from which she reveived her bachelor's degree in music and her master's in 1969.

She made her debut as a recitalist at Carnegie Hall in 1979, and in 1980, she was named the NAACP Outstanding Woman in the Arts. Hightower has performed with many symphony orchestras including the Symphony of the New World (1968-1978) and the Brooklyn Philharmonic (1979-1981; 1985). Her professional affiliations have included the Great Neck Symphony, Festival Orchestra in Siena, Italy, North Carolina School of the Arts Festival Orchestra, Urban Philharmonic (New York City and Washington DC) Harlem Philharmonic, and the instrumental ensemble of the Dance Theater of Harlem. She currently teaches at the Aaron Copland School of Music at the Queens College of City University of New York.

Ann Stevens Hobson (1943-)
Harpist

Ann Hobson, one of the first African-American women to hold a permanent position in a major national symphony orchestra, began studying piano with her mother at an early age. She took up the harp in high school so she would be playing an instrument on which her mother could not tell what she was doing wrong. Early in high school she tried to attend a summer program at the Maine Harp Colony, but was rejected on the basis of her race. Several years later she tried again and was accepted. While at the colony, she met harpist Alice Chalifoux of the Cleveland Symphony Orchestra and transferred from the Philadelphia Musical Academy to the Cleveland Institute of Music to study with Chalifoux.

In 1966, the first harpist of the National Symphony Orchestra broke a finger; the orchestra's manager called Chalifoux, who recommended Hobson. Hobson played with the group for three seasons, before joining the Boston Symphony Orchestra, with whom she has played ever since. Hobson's other activities have included performing with the Boston Symphony chamber players, the New England Harp Trio, and solo appearances with orchestras throughout the country. She has taught at the Philadelphia Musical Academy and the New England Conservatory and has conducted many clinics and workshops, always encouraging other young harpists.

Ben Holt (1956-)
Singer

Born in Washington, DC, in 1956, baritone Ben Holt attended the Oberlin Conservatory of Music and was a scholarship student at the Juilliard School of Music, where he worked with Sixten Ehrling, Tito Gobbi, and Manuel Rosenthal. He studied in Luciano Pavarotti's master classes and coached extensively with renowned pianist and coach Martin Isepp. While at the San Francisco Opera's Merola Program in master classes of Elisabeth Schwarzkopf, he was honored with an invitation to study privately at her studio in Zurich.

Holt made his Metropolitan Opera debut during the 1985-1986 season and in 1988 made his debut with the New York City Opera in the title role of *Malcolm X* by Anthony Davis. In addition, he sang *Porgy and Bess* with the Calgary Opera in Canada, and starred in *Le Nozze di Figaro* with the Cincinnati Opera. Holt was the winner of many competitions and awards, including the Joy of Singing Competition, Oratorio Society of New York, Independent Black Opera Singers, Washington International and D'Angelo Young Artists Competition.

Isaiah Jackson (1945-)
Orchestral conductor

Isaiah Jackson was born on January 22, 1945, in Richmond, Virginia. He started piano lessons at the age of four, was sent to a private boarding school in Vermont when he was fourteen years old, and traveled with his high school class to the former Soviet Union.

Although he wanted to be a musician as an adolescent, Jackson knew that his parents prefer he join the diplomatic corps. He eventually enrolled at Harvard University, where he graduated *cum laude* in 1966 with a degree in Russian history and literature. Upon graduation, Jackson decided to pursue studies in music at Stanford University, where he earned a master of arts degree in 1967. He then attended New York City's prestigious Julliard School of Music, completing an M.S. in 1969 and a D.M.A. in 1973.

While a student at Julliard, Jackson served briefly as assistant conductor to the renowned Leopold Stokowski at the American Symphony Orchestra. Established in his career shortly after graduation, he directed major American orchestras, including the New York Philharmonic, the Boston Pops, and the Los Angeles Philharmonic. In Europe, Jackson conducted the Vienna Symphony and performed with the Dance Theater of Harlem at the Spoleto Festival in Italy.

Traversing the United States, Jackson retained concurrent positions with several highly respected regional orchestras, including a fourteen-year appointment as associate director of the Rochester Philharmonic. While conducting for the Dance Theater of Harlem, Jackson was observed by management of London's Royal Opera House. In 1985, he appeared as guest conductor with the orchestra of the Royal Ballet. He advanced quickly from his post of principal conductor to become music director of the organization in 1987, becoming the first African American to occupy a chief position with the Royal Ballet. That same year, he became the first African American director of the Dayton Philharmonic Orchestra.

In recent years, Jackson has served as guest conductor with the San Francisco Symphony, Toronto Symphony, the Berlin Symphony, the Dallas Symphony, Detroit Symphony, and the Royal Liverpool Philharmonic. Since 1993, he has been principal guest conductor of the Queensland Symphony Orchestra.

Eva Jessye (1895-1992)
Choral Conductor, Composer

Eva Jessye, noted by *Ebony* magazine to be the "first black woman to receive international distinction as a choral director," was also the first black woman to succeed as a professional choral conductor. She began her formal training at Western University in Kansas and Langston University in Oklahoma. She taught in public schools in Oklahoma, at Morgan State College in Baltimore, Maryland, and Claflin College in Orangeburg, South Carolina.

In the 1920s Jessye went to New York City. She sang with musical shows and began organizing choirs. By 1926 she had established the Eva Jessye Choir as a successful professional venture. The group toured widely in this country and in Europe and performed with conductors such as Eugene Ormandy, Leopold Stokowski, and Dimitri Mitropoulous. In 1934, she directed the choir for Virgil Thompson and Gertrude Stein's opera *Four Saints in Three Acts;* in 1935 she served as choral director for Gershwin's *Porgy and Bess.* As a composer, Jessye chose to work mainly in the spiritual tradition and produced many choral arrangements. Her works include the oratorios *Paradise Lost and Regained, The Life of Christ in Negro Spirituals*, and *The Chronicle of Job.*

John Rosamond Johnson (1873-1954)
Composer

J. Rosamond Johnson, brother to writer and lyricist James Weldon Johnson, was born in Jacksonville, Florida, in 1873. He received his musical training at the New England Conservatory and, for a time, studied under composer Samuel Coleridge-Taylor.

In 1899, Johnson, eager to pursue a career in show business, teamed up with lyricist and vaudeville entertainer Bob Cole. Together, with lyrics supplied by his brother James, Johnson and Cole wrote numerous songs, including "Under the Bamboo Tree," "Congo Love Songs," "My Castle on the Nile," and "Lift Every Voice and Sing".

Johnson and Cole also wrote, directed, and produced several musicals, including *The Shoo-fly Regiment* in 1907 and *The Red Moon* in 1910.

In addition to songwriting, Johnson edited several collections of Negro spirituals.

Elayne Jones (1928-)
Timpanist

Elayne Jones began studying piano with her mother when she was six years old. When she enrolled in New York City's High School of the Performing Arts, she found all the piano positions in the orchestra taken so she was forced to switch to a new instrument. She told *The New York Times*, "I was small and the only thing I could handle were the drums, which were small. I took a liking to them."

Jones has played with the orchestras of the New York City Opera (1949-1961), the New York City Ballet (1949-1952), the Brooklyn Philharmonic (1969-1972), the Westchester Philharmonic (1969-1972), and the American Symphony Orchestra (1962-1972). In 1972, conductor Seiji Ozawa invited her to join the San Francisco Symphony, and she became the first black female to hold a principal chair in a major symphony orchestra. When she was refused tenure in 1974, and again in 1975, she filed a suit that lasted over a year. Despite her exemplary professional record, and despite the support of friends, colleagues, and the San Francisco public, she lost her battle.

In 1965, Jones provided the impetus for the founding of the Symphony of the New World. As she explained to *The New York Times* (5-2-65), when the conductor Benjamin Steinberg had money for one concert, "I suggest that he should make it have more purpose than playing one concert. He agreed that we would try to organize an orchestra of some caliber, mostly of Negroes with some white musicians." The orchestra played for eleven years, and during part of that time she also served as its president.

In addition to her symphonic work, Jones holds an extensive resume of free lance work that includes Broadway shows, films, and television. She has taught at the Metropolitan Music School, the Bronx Community College of the City University of New York, the Westchester Conservatory, and the San Francisco Conservatory. She has also traveled widely giving lecture demonstration.

Scott Joplin (1868-1917)
Pianist, Composer

Scott Joplin was born on November 24, 1868, in Texarkana, Texas. Coming from a musical family, Scott Joplin received much encouragement to study music. His father bought him a piano, and Joplin studied classical piano with a local German music teacher. When he left home, however, he could only find musical work in bars, brothels, and the like. In 1894, he settled in Sedalia, Missouri to teach piano and study theory and composition at George R. Smith College for Negroes. In 1899 he published "The Maple Leaf Rag" which was enormously successful; his piano rags appealed greatly to the public, and within a few years he had achieved great financial success with his ragtime compositions.

Joplin also composed larger works in the same style. He completed a ballet in 1899, his first opera in 1908 (the score of which is now lost), and his second opera, *Treemonisha*. He was determined to produce this opera and see it performed, but had no luck. He personally financed the publication of the vocal score and produced a non-staged version of the opera for critics, but New York audiences were not ready for an opera about blacks by a black composer, and no one would back a full production. After the "Ragtime Renaissance" of the early 1970s, Joplin's opera was given a world premiere in Atlanta, Georgia, and has been performed elsewhere many times including a masterful performance, video, and audio recording by the Houston Grand Opera Company.

Ulysses Kay (1917-1995)
Composer, Educator

Ulysses Kay was born in Tucson, Arizona, in 1917. He attended the University of Arizona, where he received a bachelor's degree in music. He later went on to attend

Ulysses Kay

the Eastman School of Music at the University of Rochester, where he received a master's degree in music. Kay also studied with Paul Hindemith at Yale and Otto Luening at Columbia. He spent the years between 1942 and 1945 in the Navy, playing in bands, and from 1949 to 1952 in Rome, studying music as a Fulbright fellow. Kay has taught at Boston University, the University of California, Los Angeles, and is currently professor of Music at Lehman College in New York.

Although his uncle was Joseph "King" Oliver, the legendary cornet player, Kay believes that jazz is a much more limited medium than symphonic music. His works for voice, chamber groups, and orchestra include *Choral Triptych*, *Six Dances* (for string orchestra), *Fantasy Variations* (for orchestra), *Sinfonia in E*, and *The Boor* (an opera). He has performed and recorded throughout the United States and Europe.

Kay was a member of the National Institute of Arts and Letters, American Music Center, and the American Composers Alliance. He also received honorary degrees from several colleges and universities.

On May 20, 1995, Ulysses Kay died from Parkinson's disease in Englewood, New Jersey.

Scott Joplin

Tania Justina León (1943-)
Composer, Conductor

Born on May 14, 1943, in Havana, Cuba, Tania León studied piano and composition at the Carlos Alfredo Peyrellado Conservatory, receiving a bachelor's degree in 1963, and a master's in 1964. She won the Young Composer's Prize from the National Council of Arts in Havana in 1966. She moved to the United States in 1967, and in 1968, she joined the Dance Theatre of Harlem as its music director and resident composer. She went on to receive a B.S. in music education from New York University in 1973, and an M.A. degree in music composition from New York University in 1975. León has studied conducting under such teachers and coaches as Laszlo Halasz, Leonard Bernstein, and Seiji Ozawa. She has maintained a busy schedule as a composer, recording artist, and as a guest conductor at most of the important symphonies throughout the United States and Puerto Rico, as well as in Paris, London, Spoleto, Berlin, and Munich. From 1977 to 1988, she was the director of the Family Concert Series for the Brooklyn Philharmonic Community. In 1985, León joined the faculty of Brooklyn College as an associate professor, teaching both composition and conducting, and became a full professor in 1993. Leon also serves as a visiting professor at Yale University and Harvard University. She has also served as music director for Broadway musicals, such as *The Wiz*. León is just one of a handful of women to have made a successful career as a conductor. Her honors include the Dean Dixon Achievement Award in 1985, the ASCAP Composer's Award from 1987 to 1989, the National Council of Women Achievement Award in 1980, the 1991 Academy-Institute Award in Music of the American Academy and Institute of Arts and Letters, and many others. In 1994, Leon was granted the Distinguished Alumni Award from New York University and the BMW Music Theater Prize for best composition from the Munich Biennale.

Leon received her introduction to conducting when the Dance Theatre attended the Spoletto Festival in the late 1960s; the director of the Dance Theatre, Arthur Mitchel, and the director of the festival, Gian–Carlo Menotti, encouraged her to conduct the festival orchestra instead of using recorded music for the dancers. When she returned to the States, she studied conducting at the Juilliard School of Music, the Berkshire Music Center at Tanglewood, and New York University. She has conducted such orchestras as Genoa Symphony Orchestra, the BBC Symphony Orchestra, and the Halle Orchestra; in 1978 she was appointed Music Director and Conductor of the Brooklyn Philharmonic.

Leon's compositions bring together the rich and varied elements of her cultural heritage as an African, Cuban, and American. She has written many ballets,

orchestra works, chamber pieces, and vocal works. She has taught composition at Brooklyn College, has served as the resident composer for the Lincoln Center Institute, and was the artistic director of the Composer's Forum in New York.

Henry Lewis (1932-1996)
Conductor, Bassist

Henry Jay Lewis was born in Los Angeles, California, on October 16, 1932, and attended the University of Southern California. He was only sixteen when he joined the Los Angeles Philharmonic Orchestra in 1948 as a double bassist, becoming the first African American instrumentalist with a major American orchestra. Lewis remained with the Los Angeles Philharmonic until 1954, when he was drafted into the United States Army.

Between 1955 and 1957, Lewis, while stationed in Germany, directed the Seventh Army Symphony Orchestra. Following his discharge from the Army, he returned to the Los Angeles Philharmonic as assistant conductor. In 1958, Lewis founded the Los Angeles Chamber Orchestra and served as guest conductor with orchestras throughout the United States. From 1965 until 1968, he served as musical director of the Los Angeles Opera Company. Lewis was selected as conductor and music director of the New Jersey Symphony Orchestra in 1968, becoming the first African American to lead a major American orchestra. He made his debut as a conductor in 1972 with the New York Philharmonic and became the first African American to conduct the Metropolitan Opera Orchestra. In 1976, Lewis resigned as conductor of the New Jersey Symphony. He remained active by conducting orchestras throughout the United States and Europe and making recordings with the Scottish Opera and the Radio Symphony Orchestra in the Netherlands. In 1991, Lewis was musical director of the London production of *Carmen Jones*. He was also music director of the Opera-Music Theater Institute of New Jersey.

Lewis was founder of the Black Academy of Arts & Letters and a member of the California Arts Commission and the Young Musicians Foundation.

On January 26, 1996, Lewis died of a heart attack at his home in New York.

Dorothy Leigh Maynor (1910-)
Singer

Born in Norfolk, Virginia, on September 3, 1910, Dorothy Leigh Mayner (she changed the spelling of her last name when she became a singer) was raised in an atmosphere of music and singing. She originally intended to become a home economics teacher and, with this in mind, entered Hampton Institute at the age of four-teen. She received her bachelor's degree in 1933. She was heard by the director of the Westminster Choir, who made it possible for her to receive a scholarship at Westminster Choir College in Princeton, New Jersey.

In 1935, she received her bachelor's degree in music and left for New York to study voice. Singing at the Berkshire Music Festival in 1939, she was heard by Boston Symphony Orchestra conductor, Serge Koussevitzky. Maynor was acclaimed by critics as one of America's leading singers. She has since performed with the country's major orchestras, including the New York Orchestra, and the Los Angeles Symphony Orchestra.

In 1965, Maynor organized the Harlem School of the Arts in the St. James Presbyterian Church, which was pastored by her husband, the Reverend Shelby A. Rooks. In 1971, Maynor received a doctor of humane letters from Oberlin. She was elected to the Metropolitan Opera's board of directors in 1975, becoming the first black to serve on the organization's board.

Bobby McFerrin (1950-)
Singer, Songwriter, Conductor

Bobby McFerrin was born on March 11, 1950 in New York City, the son of opera singers Robert and Sara McFerrin. In 1958, his family moved to Los Angeles. McFerrin attended Sacramento State University and Cerritos College, but dropped out to play piano for the Ice Follies. Over the next few years, he played keyboard with lounge acts and for dance troupes. McFerrin decided, in 1977, to become a singer. He sang with various bands and was eventually discovered by singer Jon Hendricks. While on tour with Hendricks, McFerrin's musical talents caught the attention of comedian Bill Cosby.

Through the efforts of Cosby, McFerrin was booked in Las Vegas and at the Playboy Jazz Festival in Los Angeles. He later performed at New York's Kool Jazz Festival and began touring or recording with such jazz greats as George Benson and Herbie Hancock. In 1982, he released his first album, *Bobby McFerrin*. This album was followed by *The Voice, Spontaneous Inventions, Simple Pleasures, Play, Medicine Music, Hush, Paper Music*, and *Bang! Zoom*. McFerrin is probably best known for his song "Don't Worry, Be Happy," which topped the popular-music charts in 1989.

McFerrin is the winner of ten Grammy Awards. He also recorded the theme for "The Cosby Show" and the soundtrack for "Just So," an animated series of specials that aired on cable television. He has appeared on "The Tonight Show" and "Sesame Street," and he provided vocals for Levi's commercials. He has also toured extensively.

In 1994, McFerrin made the transition from jazz to classical music when he was appointed conductor of the St. Paul Chamber Orchestra. As conductor and creative chair, McFerrin has infused some jazz sensibilities to the orchestra's performances and also performs as a solo vocalist.

In addition to his duties with the St. Paul Chamber Orchestra, McFerrin has also served as a guest conductor with several orchestras, including the Los Angeles Philharmonic, the Boston Pops, the Chicago Symphony Orchestra, the New Jersey Symphony Orchestra, the New York Philharmonic, and the Ravinia Festival Orchestra.

Robert McFerrin (1921-)
Singer, Educator

Born in Marianna, Arkansas, in 1921, baritone Robert McFerrin received his musical training at the Chicago Musical College, obtaining a bachelor's degree. He sang the title role in *Rigoletto* with the New England Opera Company in 1950 and was a baritone soloist in the Lewisohn Stadium Summer Concert Series in 1954. McFerrin made his Metropolitan Opera debut with the role of Amonasro in *Aida* in 1955. He became the first African American to perform regularly with the Metropolitan Opera.

McFerrin has served as a guest professor of voice at Sibelius Academy, Finland, and Roosevelt University in Chicago. He has also served as a member of the voice faculty at Nelson School of Fine Arts in Nelson, British Columbia, Canada. McFerrin has performed in Canada, Latin America, Germany, Belgium, England, Italy, and Greece. He received honorary doctorates from Stowe Teacher's College in St. Louis in 1987 and the University of Missouri in 1989.

Lena Johnson McLin (1928-)
Composer, Conductor, Educator

Lena Johnson McLin was born on September 5, 1928, in Atlanta, Georgia. Her musical life began in the Greater Mt. Calvary Baptist Church in Atlanta, where her father was minister, and her mother was music director. She received her first training in classical music from her mother, and learned traditional spirituals from her grandmother. She received a bachelor's degree from Spelman College in 1951 and an M.A. from the American Conservatory in 1954. She has also studied at Roosevelt University in Chicago State College. She taught high school music and director church choirs in Chicago for several decades, and helped to establish new music programs in the curriculum. She has conducted many workshops and clinics at colleges and university around the country; in 1972, she won the Teacher of the Year award in Chicago. In the early 1960s, she started the McLin Opera

Company to give promising young artists a performing venue.

McLin's compositions are primarily sacred pieces which combine spiritual traditions with classical musical styles. As a choir director, she wrote much music for her Sunday services. Her music also incorporates popular and rock idioms, and she served as the advisor on Rock Music for the Music Educators National Conference. Her compositions include cantatas, masses, spiritual arrangements, operas, works for piano, orchestras, and electronic music.

McLin is a member of the National Association of Negro Musicians and the Institute of Black American Music.

Leona Mitchell (1949-)
Singer

Soprano Leona Mitchell was born on October 13, 1949, in Enid, Oklahoma, and a 1971 graduate of Oklahoma University. Mitchell has been heard with the San Francisco Opera, the Washington Opera Society, the Houston Opera, and at the Gran Teatro del Liceo in Barcelona. Her orchestral appearances have included concerts with the Cleveland Orchestra, the London Symphony, and the New Jersey Symphony.

During the summer of 1980 she sang Bess in the Cleveland Orchestra Blossom Festival production of *Porgy and Bess* and performed the same role in their subsequent recording of the work. Mitchell made her Metropolitan Opera debut as Micaela in *Carmen* in 1975 and since has been heard there as Lauretta in *Gianni Schicci*, Pamina in *The Magic Flute*, and Madame Lidoine in *Dialogues of the Carmelites*.

Mitchell is a member of the American Guild Musicians Association, Sigma Alpha Iota, and Alpha Kappa Alpha. In 1983, she was inducted into the Oklahoma Hall of Fame.

Dorothy Rudd Moore (1940-)
Composer, Singer

Dorothy Rudd Moore studied music theory and composition at Howard University, graduating magna cum laude in 1963. She studied with Nadia Boulenger at the Conservatoire de Musique in France and at Columbia University in New York. She has taught at the Harlem School of Arts, New York University, and Bronx Community College, and has taught piano and voice privately. Her compositions have been performed throughout the United States, including at such eminent places as Carnegie Hall, Town Hall, Tuly Hall, and Philharmonic Hall. She has written symphonies, songs, chamber pieces, and an opera. The *New York Times* has called her "a

Leona Mitchell

gifted and creative mind at work." *Opera News* reported that in her opera *Frederick Douglass* "Moore displays rare ability to wed musical and dramatic motion, graceful lyric inventiveness, (and) a full command of the orchestral palette."

Kermit Moore (1929-)
Cellist, Composer, Conductor

Kermit Moore's original musical identity was as a cellist. He studied cello at the Cleveland Institute of Music (B.M. 1951), at New York University (M.A. 1952), and at the Paris Conservatory (Artists Diploma, 1956). He has performed with orchestras throughout the world, including the Orchestra de la Suisse Romande, the Concertgebouw of Amersterdam, the National Radio Symphony of Paris, and the Belgian National Orchestra. He played his debut recital at the New York Town Hall in 1949, and has since given recitals in almost every major city in the world, including Paris, Brussels, Vienna, Cologne, Hamburg, Munich, Geneva, Basel, Amersterdam, Tokyo, Seoul, New York, Boston, Chicago, and San Francisco.

In 1965, Moore co-founded the Symphony of the New World in New York; he not only performed as cellist with the group, but conducted occasionally as well. He has also served as guest conductor with, among other groups, the Detroit Symphony Orchestra, the Brooklyn Philharmonic, the Festival Orchestra at the United Nations, the Berkeley (California) Symphony, the Dance Theatre of Harlem, and Opera Ebony. Moore is a member of ASCAP, and was co-founder of the Society of Black Composers. His works include solo music for cello, a cello concerto, a timpani concerto, songs, arias, and various pieces for chamber ensemble.

Undine Smith Moore (1904-1989)
Composer, Educator

Undine Smith Moore was one of the most influential music educators of the twentieth century, as is evident by her numerous awards and honors. She received honorary doctorates from Virginia State University in 1972, and from Indiana University in 1976. The Mayor of New York City, John Lindsay, presented her with a Certificate of Appreciation, she received the Seventh Annual Humanitarian Award from Fisk University in 1973, she won the National Association of Negro Musicians Award in 1975, and in that same year Mayor Remmis Arnold of Petersburg, Virginia, proclaimed April 13th as Undine Moore Day.

Moore received her B.A. and B.M. degrees from Fisk University in Nashville, and an M.A. and professional diploma from Columbia University's Teachers College in New York. She also studied at the Juilliard School of Music, the Manhattan School of Music, and the Eastman School of Music in Rochester, New York. She taught at Virginia State College in Petersburg from 1927-1972, where she co-founded and directed the Black Music Center. She also served as visiting professor at numerous other schools, including Carleton College in Northfield, Minnesota; St. Benedict College in St. Joseph, Minnesota, St. Johns University in Collegeville, Minnesota, and Virginia Union University in Richmond.

As a composer, Moore wrote works for a variety of ensembles. Many of her works are for chorus, and she has also written for solo voice, piano, organ, flute, and clarinet. Her works have received much recognition, and her *Afro-American Suite*, commissioned by Antoinette Handy's Trio Pro Viva, has been performed widely. Her cantata *Scenes from the Life of a Martyr: To the Memory of Martin Luther King* received a nomination for a Pulitzer Prize.

Michael Morgan (1957-)
Conductor

Born in Washington DC, in 1957, Michael Morgan attended the Oberlin College Conservatory of Music. He pursued additional studies at the Vienna master classes of Witold Rowicki and the Berkshire Music Center at Tanglewood, where he was a conducting fellow and student of Seiji Ozawa and Gunther Schuller. Michael Morgan appeared with the New York Philharmonic in September of 1986 in the Leonard Bernstein Young American Conductors concerts. From 1980 to 1987, he was Exxon/Arts Endowment assistant conductor of the Chicago Symphony Orchestra, later becoming affiliate artist conductor. Previously, he was apprentice conductor of the Buffalo Philharmonic under music director Julius Rudel. In 1993, Morgan left his position as staff conductor with the Chicago Symphony for a job with the Oakland Symphony. Morgan has appeared as a guest conductor with many of our nation's major orchestras. He made his New York City Opera debut conducting multiple performances of *La Traviata* in New York, Wolftrap, and Taiwan. In Europe, Morgan has led performances of the Vienna State Opera, the Deutsche Staatsoper in East Berlin, the Vienna Symphony Orchestra, Warsaw Philharmonic Orchestra, and Danish Radio Orchestra.

The many awards Morgan has earned include first prizes in the 1980 Hans Swarowsky International Conductors Competition (Vienna), the Gino Marrinuzzi International Conductors Competition (San Remo, Italy) and the Baltimore Symphony Young Conductors Competition.

Jessye Norman (1945-)
Singer

Soprano Jessye Norman was born in Augusta, Georgia, in 1945, to a musical family. Her mother, a school teacher and amateur pianist, provided the family with piano lessons. At the age of sixteen, Norman went to Philadelphia to compete for the Marian Anderson Scholarship, but failed to win. However, once the director of the music department at Howard University heard her sing, she was granted a full four-year scholarship.

Norman graduated with honors from Howard in 1967 and went on to study at the Peabody Conservatory in Baltimore, Maryland and the University of Michigan, where she received a master's degree in 1968.

In 1968, Norman entered the Bavarian Radio Corporation's International Music Competition, receiving first prize. In 1969, she made her debut with the Deutsch Opera in Berlin as Elisabeth in Wagner's *Tannhauser*, and in 1970 she made her Italian opera debut. Appearing at La Scala in Milan, Wolf Trap in Virginia, the Tanglewood Music Festival, and at the Royal Opera House in Covent Garden, England, Norman has performed with some of the world's leading orchestras.

Following a temporary leave from opera in the mid-1970s, Norman returned to the stage in 1980 in Strauss's

Jessye Norman

Ariadne auf Naxos. She has since made numerous concert appearances, has made several recordings, including Berg's *Lulu Suite*, Berliozs' *Les nuits d'ete* and *Romeo and Juliette*, Bizet's *Carmen*, Mahler's *Kindertotenlieder*, and *Lucky To Be Me.* In 1994, Norman sang the title role on an album of the opera *Salome.*

Norman has received numerous awards for her work, including several Grammy awards, an Outstanding Musician of the Year Award, and several honorary degrees from American universities. In 1992, the Council of Fashion Designers of America presented Norman with its Woman of the Arts Award. She is also a member of the Royal Academy of Music, Gamma Sigma Sigma, Sigma Alpha Iota, and Pi Kappa Lambda.

Coleridge-Taylor Perkinson (1932-)
Composer

Coleridge-Taylor Perkinson has been a figure in explorative musical movements in both Hollywood and New York.

Born in New York in 1932, Perkinson took graduate and postgraduate degrees from the Manhattan School of Music (1953, 1954), before going on to study at the Berkshire Music Center, the Mozarteum, and the Netherland Radio Union Hilversum. Becoming first composer-in-residence for the Negro Ensemble Company, he wrote the music for many plays, including Peter Weiss's *Song of the Lusitanian Bogey*, Ray McIver's *God Is a (Guess What?)*, and Errol Hill's *Man Better Man.* In 1965, when the Symphony of the New World was organized in New York, Perkinson was named associate conductor. His concert pieces include *Concerto for Violin and Orchestra* (1954) and *Attitudes* (1964), written for black opera star George Shirley. Perkinson has also composed music for television and radio programs, the documentary film *Cross-roads Africa*, and ballet ensembles.

Julia Perry (1924-1979)
Composer, Conductor

Julia Perry was born in Lexington, Kentucky, in 1924, and raised in Akron, Ohio. She studied violin, piano, and voice as a child. In 1942, she enrolled at the Westminister Choir College in Princeton, New Jersey, studying violin, piano, voice, conducting, and composition. Even before graduating, she began publishing her compositions—*Carillon Heigh-Ho* was published in 1947. After receiving her master's from Westminister in 1948, she went on to attend Juilliard School of Music. In 1950, her cantata *Ruth* was premiered in New York.

Between 1951 and 1959 she lived in Europe. After studying with composer Luigi Dallapiccola at the Berkshire Music Center, she won a Guggenheim Fellowship to continue study with him in Florence and to study with Nadia Boulanger in Paris. Throughout the United States and Europe her work received acclaim. In 1954, her one act opera *The Cask of Amontillado* was produced at Columbia University.

After her return to the States in 1959, she continued to compose. She taught at a number of universities, including Florida A and M University in Tallahassee and the Atlanta Colleges Center. In 1955, she received the Boulanger Grand Prix Award, and in 1964 she won the American Academy and National Institute of Arts and Letters Award. In 1969, she received Honorable Mention in the ASCAP Awards. Perry's compositions include *Stabat Mater* for contralto and strings (1951), *Pastoral* for flute and strings (1959), *Homunchulus* for soprano and percussion (1960), and the operas *The Bottle*, *The Cask of Amontillado*, and *The Selfish Giant*.

Evelyn La Rue Pittman (1910-)
Choral Director Composer

While a senior at Spelman College in Atlanta studying African-American history, Evelyn Pittman committed herself to teaching black history through music. Her first work, a musical play, was produced at Spelman in 1933. During the years she taught in the public schools in Oklahoma City (1935 to 1956), she also conducted weekly broadcasts on a local radio station with her own professional group, The Evelyn Pittman Choir; she directed a 350-voice choir sponsored by the YWCA, and directed orchestras, choirs, and operettas in the schools. She also began composing songs about black leaders, and published a collection of songs, *Rich Heritage*, in 1944.

In 1948, she went to Juilliard to study composition, and then earned a master's degree from Oklahoma University in 1954. Between 1956 and 1958, she studied composition with Nadia Boulanger in Paris, and completed her first opera, *Cousin Esther*. It received its first performance in Paris in 1957 and in the next few years was performed in Europe and in the United States with rave reviews. She returned to public-school teaching in 1958 in New York State and continued to compose. After the assassination of Martin Luther King, Jr. in 1968, she wrote the opera *Freedom Child* in his memory and honor; when she retired, she dedicated herself to directing a touring company of *Freedom Child*. Her other compositions include choral arrangements of spirituals, and a stage work titled *Jim Noble*.

Karl Hampton Porter (1939-)
Bassoonist, Conductor, Educator

Karl Hampton Porter was born in Pittsburgh, Pennsylvania, in 1939. While in high school, he learned to play bassoon and saxophone. He received his musical training at Carnegie-Mellon University, the Peabody Conservatory and the Juilliard School of Music where he studied bassoon and conducting.

Porter has organized several musical groups throughout the New York area including the Harlem Youth Symphony, the Harlem Philharmonic Orchestra, the New Breed Brass Ensemble, the Harlem String Quartet, and the Harlem Woodwind Quintet. He has served as conductor of the Baltimore Symphony, the Massapequa Symphony, the Park West Symphony, and has served as musical director of numerous productions. Porter has taught at New York City Technical College, and has served as chairman of the Fine Arts Lecture Series at the College.

Florence Price (1888-1953)
Composer, Pianist

Florence Price was born in Little Rock, Arkansas, in 1888. She studied music first with her mother, a talented soprano and concert pianist. In 1902 she enrolled in the New England Conservatory of Music in Boston, majoring in piano and organ. After graduating in 1907, she returned to Little Rock as a music educator, performer, and composer. Her works, especially her songs, began to receive some notice. In 1927, due to racial tensions, she moved to Chicago and pursued further musical education. In the early 1920s Price's composition began to receive notice. She won the Rodman Wanamaker Foundation Award for a piano sonata and her *Symphony in E Minor*; the Chicago Symphony Orchestra premiered this work in 1933 at the Chicago World's Fair. She also presented a program of her pieces at the fair, and the Women's Symphony orchestra of Chicago also performed some of her works. In 1934, she appeared as soloist in her *Concerto in D Minor* in the Chicago Musical College and in Pittsburgh. That same year, she conducted a performance of her *Concerto in F Minor* with pianist/composer Margaret Bonds as the soloist.

Her fame grew steadily. In 1940, she performed her *Concerto in One Movement* with the WPA Symphony Orchestra in Detroit, which played her *Symphony No. 3 in C Minor* in the same program. Faculty members of the Music School of the University of Illinois, and the Forum String Quartet of Chicago, performed some of her chamber music. The British Conductor Sir John Barbirolli commissioned her to write a suite for strings, which he presented in Manchester, England. Marian Anderson sang her *Songs to the Dark Virgin* in her second American concert tour to rave reviews. In addi-

Leontyne Price

tion to her larger orchestral and chamber works, she wrote many art songs, spiritual arrangements, choral pieces, and piano, organ, and violin works.

Leontyne Price (1927-)
Singer

Born Mary Violet Leontyne Price in 1927, in Laurel, Mississippi, Price was encouraged by her parents, who were amateur musicians, to sing and play the piano at an early age. In 1949, she received her bachelor's degree from the College of Education and Industrial Arts (now Central State College) in Wilberforce, Ohio, where she had studied music education in hopes of becoming a music teacher.

Price received a scholarship to study at the Julliard School of Music in New York City. While appearing in a student production of Verdi's *Falstaff*, she was noticed by the composer and music critic, Virgil Thomson, and cast in her first professional role in a revival of his opera *Four Saints In Three Acts*.

Between 1952 and 1954, Price performed the role of Bess in a revival of Gershwin's *Porgy and Bess*. It was during this production that she met and married her co-

star, baritone William C. Warfield. The two, however, divorced in 1973, following years of separation.

In 1954, Price made her debut at New York's Town Hall. From there she went on to appear in Puccini's *Tosca*, in 1955, Mozart's *The Magic Flute*, in 1956, and Poulenc's *Dialogues of the Carmelites*. Between 1958 and 1960, she appeared at Verona, Vienna, Covent Gardens, and La Scala. Price had become one of the world's leading sopranos.

On January 27, 1961, Price made her debut with the Metropolitan Opera in Verdi's *Il Trovatore*, where she received a standing ovation. She has since appeared in numerous Met productions, including Puccini's *The Girl of the Golden West*, and the world premiere of Samuel Barber's *Antony and Cleopatra*, in 1966.

Price has made numerous appearances at the White House, and has performed at two presidential inaugurations.

On April 20, 1982, Price opened the convention of the Daughters of the American Revolution in Constitution Hall with a concert honoring Marian Anderson. It was in 1939 that Anderson was barred from appearing in Constitution Hall by the DAR, prompting Eleanor Roosevelt to resign in anger from the organization. In September

1981, Price opened the 1981-1982 concert series at Rutgers University in New Brunswick, New Jersey, which marked her first New Jersey appearance after fifteen years. In 1977, she was awarded the San Francisco Opera medal in honor of the twentieth anniversary of her debut with the company.

Price has received over twenty Grammy Awards and many honorary doctorates. In 1985, she won Kennedy Center Honors for lifetime achievement in the arts, the National Medal of Arts, and New York City's Handel Medallion. She has also received the Associated Black Charities Grammy Lifetime Achievement Award. She has also performed at two presidential inaugurations.

Kay George Roberts (1950-)
Violinist, Conductor

Kay Roberts was born on September 16, 1950 in Nashville, Tennessee and began her professional musical career as a violinist when she joined the Nashville Symphony during her last year in high school; she continued to play with the group until she graduated from Fisk University in 1972. In 1971, she represented the Nashville Symphony in Arthur Fiedler's World Symphony Orchestra. She received her M.M. in 1975, M.M.A. in 1976, and her D.M.A. in 1986 from Yale University. She has guest conducted for many orchestras, including the Bangkok Symphony in Thailand, the Nashville Symphony Orchestra, Cleveland Orchestra, Indianapolis Symphony, Chicago Symphony, Des Moines Symphony, New Haven Symphony, Chattanooga Symphony, the Mystic Valley Chamber Orchestra, and the Greater Dallas Symphony Orchestra. She became the music director of the New Hampshire Philharmonic in 1982, and the Music Director of the Cape Ann Symphony Orchestra in 1986. She has been teaching at the College of Music at the University of Lowell since 1978.

Roberts has received numerous awards throughout her career. The League of Black Women presented her with its Outstanding Achievement in the Performing Arts award in 1991. She also received the Distinguished Alumni of the Year Award from the National Association for Equal Opportunity in Higher Education in 1987. In 1993, the National Black Music Caucus presented Roberts with its National Achievement Award.

Paul Robeson (1898-1976)
Singer, Actor

Born in Princeton, New Jersey on April 9, 1898, Paul Robeson was the son of a runaway slave who put himself through Lincoln University and later became a Presbyterian minister. Robeson entered Rutgers College (now Rutgers University) on a scholarship, and won a total of twelve letters in track, football, baseball, and basketball. In addition to his athletic exploits, his

Paul Robeson

academic ability gained him Phi Beta Kappa honors in his junior year.

In 1923, Robeson received a law degree from Columbia University, financing his schooling by playing professional football. While at Columbia, Robeson was seen by Eugene O'Neill in an amateur play. After making his professional debut in *Taboo* (1922), Robeson appeared in O'Neill's *All God's Chillun Got Wings* and *Emperor Jones*. Called upon to whistle in the latter play, Robeson sang instead, and his voice met with instant acclaim. In 1925, he made his concert debut with a highly successful program of all-African American music. He went on to such stage successes as *Show Boat*, *Porgy*, and *Othello*.

A world traveler in the Soviet Union, Asia, and Europe, Robeson spoke several languages, including Chinese, Russian, Gaelic, and Spanish. Robeson's political affiliations at times tended to attract even more publicity than his artistic career. In 1950, for instance, his passport was revoked after refusing to sign an affidavit as to whether or not he had ever belonged to the Communist Party. Eight years later, the United States Supreme Court ruled that the refusal to sign such an affidavit was not valid grounds for denial of a passport.

Robeson subsequently settled in London, making a number of trips to the continent (and to the Soviet Union as well) before returning to the United States in 1963.

Robeson played an active role in civil and human rights issues. He was a co-founder of the Council on African Affairs, and a member of the Joint Anti-Fascist Refugee Committee, and the Committee to Aid China. Robeson died January 23, 1976 in Philadelphia, Pennsylvania.

Philippa (Duke) Schuyler (1932-1969)
Composer, Pianist

Born on August 21, 1932 in New York City, Philippa Schuyler was already playing the piano at the age of two and began composing a year later. By the time she was eight, she had some fifty compositions to her credit. Her published works include *Six Little Pieces* and *Eight Little Pieces*.

At the age of twelve, her first symphonic composition, *Manhattan Nocturne*, was performed at Carnegie Hall, and the following year her scherzo, *Rumpelstiltskin*, was performed by the Dean Dixon Youth Orchestra, the Boston Pops, the New Haven Symphony Orchestra, and the New York Philharmonic.

Philippa Schuyler, c. 1966.

Philippa Schuyler at age eight.

In 1953, Schuyler made her debut at Town Hall in New York as a pianist. She went on to travel to some fifty countries on good will concert tours sponsored by the United States State Department.

Philippa Schuyler was considered to be one of America's most outstanding musical prodigies. Remembered as a mature concert pianist, she died tragically at the height of her career.

George Shirley (1934-)
Singer

George Shirley was born April 18, 1934 in Indianapolis, and moved to Detroit in 1940. There he began giving vocal recitals in churches and decided on a musical career after playing baritone horn in a community band. In 1955, he graduated from Wayne State University in Detroit with a bachelor's degree in musical education.

After his discharge from the Army in 1959, he began serious vocal studies with Themy S. Georgi. In June of that year he made his operatic debut as Eisenstein in Strauss's *Die Fledermaus*, performing with the Turnau Players at Woodstock. A year later he won the American Opera Auditions, whereupon he journeyed to Milan,

Italy, making his opera debut there in Puccini's *La Boheme*.

In 1961, his career was given tremendous impetus by his victory in the Metropolitan Opera auditions. In 1963, he made his debut at Carnegie Hall with the Friends of French Opera, singing opposite Rita Gorr in Massenet's *La Navarraise*.

Since then, he has sung with several of the Met's leading divas, including Renata Tebaldi in *Simon Boccanegra* and Birgit Nilsson in *Salome*. In 1974, he sang the title role in Mozart's *Idomeneo* at the Glyndebourne Festival, and he has remained a favorite at the Met over the years.

William Grant Still (1895-1978)
Composer, Conductor

William Grant Still was born in Woodville, Mississippi, in 1895. Since both of his parents were musicians and his father was the town's bandmaster, he received his early musical training at home.

Intending to study medicine, Still enrolled at Wilberforce College, but left before graduating. Still began to seriously consider a career in music. After working with various jazz musicians, including W. C. Handy and Paul Whiteman, Still enrolled at Oberlin College Conservatory of Music.

Still became the first African American composer to have a large-scale work performed by a major American orchestra, when the Rochester Philharmonic Orchestra performed his *Afro-American Symphony*, in 1931. In 1936 Still became the first African American to conduct a major American orchestra, when he conducted the Los Angeles Philharmonic in a program of his work. He was also the first African American composer to have an opera performed by a major opera company, when the New York City Opera performed his *Troubled Island* in 1949.

Still was awarded the Harmon Award in 1928 for his contribution to black culture. He was the winner of two Guggenheim Fellowships—one in 1944 and the other in 1961. In 1961, the National Federation of Music Clubs awarded him $1,500 for his composition *The Peaceful Land*. His major works include his composition *Song of A New Race*, the symphonic poem *Darker America*, the suites *Pages from Negro History* and *The American Scene*, and numerous songs and arrangements of spirituals.

Howard Swanson (1909-1978)
Composer

Howard Swanson was born in Atlanta in 1909 and raised in Cleveland, where he studied at the Institute of

William Grant Still

Music. He was taught composition by Herbert Elwell. In 1938, he won a Rosenwald Fellowship to study with Nadia Boulanger in Paris. Returning to the United States, he devoted himself to composition, and in 1950, won wide acclaim, as well as serious attention, as an American composer when his *Short Symphony*, written in 1948, was performed by the New York Philharmonic with Dmitri Mitropoulos conducting. In 1952, this symphony won the New York Critics' Award. One of Swanson's well-known works is the song "The Negro Speaks of Rivers," based on a poem by Langston Hughes, which Marian Anderson has sung in recital.

Swanson died in 1978. In 1979, at the St. James Presbyterian Church in New York City a concert was given by the Triad Chorale as a memorial to him and the composer William Grant Still.

Shirley Verrett (1933-)
Singer

Born to musical family in New Orleans in 1933, Shirley Verrett moved to California at the age of five, but had no formal voice training during her childhood—largely because her father felt singing would involve his daughter in too precarious a career. Still, he offered his daughter the opportunity to sing in church choirs under his direction. She attended Ventura College, where she majored in business administration. By 1954, she was a prosperous real estate agent, but her longing for an artistic career had become so acute that she decided to take voice lessons in Los Angeles and train her sights on the concert stage anyway.

After winning a television talent show in 1955, she enrolled at the Juilliard School on a scholarship, earning her diploma in voice some six years later. Her debut at New York's Town Hall in 1958 was not a sensational one. However, by 1962, at Spoleto, Italy she delivered an excellent *Carmen* and a year later, she performed at Lincoln Center in New York, where her recital was said to be "simply without flaws, simply a great event in the annals of American music-making."

By 1964, her *Carmen* had improved so dramatically that the New York *Herald Tribune* critic was able to claim it as "the finest" performance "seen or heard in New York" for the past generation. Other performances in such roles as Orfeo in Gluck's *Orfeo ed Euridice*, Ulrica in Verdi's *Un Ballo de Maschera*, and Leonora in Beethoven's *Fidelio* have been met with comparable acclaim.

Shirley Verrett

In 1982, Verrett appeared with Grace Bumbry in a concert honoring Marian Anderson on her eightieth birthday. Her yearly recital tours take her to the major music centers throughout the country. During the 1986-1987 season the successes for Verrett included a series of operas staged especially for her by the Paris Opera; Rossini's *Mose*, Cherubini's *Medee*, and Gluck's *Iphigenie en Tauride* and *Alceste*. She made a triumphant return to the Metropolitan Opera in 1986 as Eboli in *Don Carlo* and also starred that year in a new production of *Macbeth* with the San Francisco Opera. In the 1987-1988 season, Verrett made her long awaited Chicago Lyric Opera debut as Lucena in *Il Trovatore*.

George Walker (1922-)
Pianist, Educator

Born in Washington, DC, in 1922, George Walker studied at Oberlin, the Curtis Institute of Music, and at the Eastman School, where he completed his doctorate. His teachers included Rudolf Serkin, Giancarlo Menotti, and Robert Casadesus. Following his well-received Town Hall piano debut in 1945, Walker gained twenty seasons of experience touring the United States, Canada, and Europe.

Walker has served on the faculty of Smith College, Northhampton, Massachusetts, University of Colorado, University of Delaware, and the Peabody Institute of Johns Hopkins University, Baltimore, Maryland. He is currently professor emeritus of Music at Rutgers University.

Walker has won several awards during his career. He was presented with the American Academy and Institute of Arts and Letters Award in 1981. In 1988, Walker was presented with the Guggenheim Fellow and the Koussevitsky Prize.

William C. Warfield (1920-)
Singer

Baritone William Warfield was born in West Helena, Arkansas, in 1920, and later moved with his family to Rochester, New York, where he attended school. The son of a Baptist minister, he received early training in voice, organ, and piano and, in 1938, while a student at Washington Junior High School, won the vocal competition at the Music Educators National Convention in St. Louis.

He studied at the Eastman School of Music and the University of Rochester, receiving his bachelor's degree in 1942. He received a doctorate in laws from the University of Arkansas in 1972. In 1976, Warfield received a doctorate of music from the University of Boston and a doctorate in music from Milliken University in 1981.

William Warfield

Andre Watts

Warfield made his debut at New York's Town Hall on March 19, 1950. After his resounding New York debut in 1950, he made an unprecedented tour of Australia under the auspices of the Australian Broadcasting Commission. A year later he made his movie debut in *Show Boat*.

Warfield has appeared on several major television shows and starred in the NBC television version of *Green Pastures*. Between 1952 and 1959 he made five international tours under the auspices of the United States State Department. In 1966, he appeared in a revival of the Jerome Kern–Edna Ferber classic *Showboat*. His performances as Porgy in the various revivals of *Porgy and Bess* have made him the best-known singer in this role. He was married to Leontyne Price, the brilliant opera star whom he met during a *Porgy and Bess* production.

Andre Watts (1946-)
Pianist

One of America's most gifted young pianists, Andre Watts achieved a substantial degree of fame while playing under the baton of Leonard Bernstein of the New York Philharmonic. He is the first African American concert pianist to achieve international stardom.

Born in Nuremberg, Germany, in 1946, of a Hungarian mother and an American G.I. father, Andre Watts spent the first eight years of his life on Army posts in Europe before moving to Philadelphia. By the time he was nine, he was already performing as a soloist with the Philadelphia Orchestra.

At the age of seventeen, Watts appeared on television in one of Leonard Bernstein's Young People's Concerts and was a huge success. After graduating from Lincoln Preparatory School in Philadelphia, he enrolled at Baltimore's Peabody Conservatory of Music.

On one occasion, when Glenn Gould became ill just prior to a performance with the New York Philharmonic, Bernstein chose Watts as a last-minute replacement. At the conclusion of the concerto, Watts received a standing ovation not only from the audience but from the orchestra as well.

In June 1966, Watts made his debut in London, and a month later was the soloist for the two-day Philharmonic Stravinsky Festival at Lincoln Center.

In the 1970s, Watts gave a concert in Teheran as part of the coronation festivities for the then Shah of Iran, and later, at a state dinner for Congo's President Mobutu, he was presented with the African republic's highest honor, the Order of the Zaire Congo. Watts other rewards include the Lincoln Center Medallion in 1971 and the National Society of Arts and Letters Gold Medal in 1982. He has also received numerous honorary doctorates.

Watts performs frequently and schedules annual appearances with the Philadelphia Orchestra, Chicago Symphony, Boston Symphony, Cleveland Orchestra, and several European orchestras.

Felix Fowler Weir (1884-1978)
Violinist

Felix Weir began studying violin when an uncle recognized his talent and encouraged him; he played his first public concert at age eleven. He attended the Chicago Musical College and the Conservatory in Leipzig, Germany. Between 1907 and 1914, he taught in public schools in Washington DC. In 1914, he began to perform again; he moved to New York, joined the New Amsterdam Musical Association, and played with the Clef-Club Orchestra. He formed a duo with cellist Leonard Jeter, and later a trio with pianist Olyve Jeter. In 1914, he formed the American String Quartet with cellist Jeter, violinist Joseph Lymos, and violinist Hall Johnson. In the 1920s, he formed another quartet with violinist Johnson, cellist Marion Cumbo, and violinist Arthur Boyd. During the 1920s and 1930s, he also played in the orchestras for Broadway musicals, and taught privately. In the 1930s, he returned to public school teaching in Washington, DC.

Clarence Cameron White (1880-1960)
Violinist, Composer

Clarence Cameron White (1880-1960) achieved success as both a violinist and composer early in life. When he was only fifteen, he performed one of his own compositions in a recital he gave in Washington, DC, and when he was seventeen, he played some of his works in recital in Chicago. White studied violin and composition at Howard University in Washington, DC, the Oberlin Conservatory of Music in Ohio, and in London, Paris, and at Juilliard. Between 1900 and 1910, White taught in the public schools in Washington, and headed the string program at the newly established Washington Conservatory of Music (1903-1907). Between 1912 and 1923, he lived and taught in Boston and concertized widely. In the 1920s and early 1930s, he curtailed his touring and concentrated on teaching at the college level and composing. In 1931, he completed his opera, *Ouanga*. He returned to the concert circuit in the late 1930s. He composed a variety of works for violin, piano, voice, chorus, orchestra, organ, and chamber ensembles.

Olly W. Wilson (1937-)
Composer, Educator

Olly Wilson was born in St. Louis, Missouri, in 1937. While in high school, his clarinet playing earned him a scholarship to his hometown's Washington University. In 1960, Wilson received a master of music degree, with honors, from the University of Illinois, and in 1964 he received a Ph.D. from the University of Iowa.

Wilson began his career at the University of California, Berkeley as a professor of music. He also played music with local jazz groups in St. Louis and played bass violin with the St. Louis Philharmonic Orchestra. Wilson also taught music at Florida A&M University and the Oberlin Conservatory of Music at the University of California at Berkeley. He has also served as assistant chancellor of international affairs at the University of California, Berkeley.

22

Blues and Jazz

Blues and Jazz

◆ The Blues Tradition ◆ The Jazz Tradition ◆ Women in Jazz and Blues
◆ Blues and Jazz Gatekeepers

by Dan Morgenstern and Bob Jacobson

In a time span of less than a century, the remarkable native American music called jazz has risen from obscure origins to become the most original form of musical expression of our times—loved, admired and played throughout the globe. Jazz has a long and rich ancestry. Its roots go back to the arrival of the first Africans on American soil and the encounter between native African and European musical traditions. Black music in America took many forms, including work songs, gospel and spirituals, and many and varied kinds of music for dancing.

◆ THE BLUES TRADITION

Ragtime and Blues

By the late nineteenth century, a dance music called ragtime became very popular. Its heavily syncopated rhythms and sprightly melodies had a distinctly Afro-American flavor. Its greatest exponent was Scott Joplin (1868-1917) whose music was rediscovered in the 1970s. About the same time, a form of black American folk music called the blues coalesced into a 12-bar pattern that made it adaptable to popular song writing. The blues has a unique harmonic quality derived from a "flattening" of the third and seventh notes of the tempered scale, and while seemingly simple, lends itself to infinite variation. The blues had an impact not only on jazz, but later on such styles as rock and soul music, both of which would be unthinkable without the blues element.

Blues History and Styles

The true origins of the blues as a musical style remain somewhat murky, seeming to have sprung up simultane-ously in a few places across the South around the turn of the century. From there, the blues more or less accompanied Southern blacks to wherever they migrated, evolving and incorporating whatever musical influences were encountered along the way. While the music clearly came from the country, blues became blues in the city of New Orleans.

W. C. Handy, a black New Orleans bandleader often credited with "inventing" jazz, did not invent blues, but he may have been the first individual to achieve commercial success playing it. Although the word "blues" was already being widely used to describe an assortment of work songs, field hollers, and folk tunes by around 1910, it was Handy's publication of "Memphis Blues" in 1912 that established the genre as a readily identifiable musical style. Handy's "discovery" of the blues aside, it was three rural areas—the Mississippi Delta; Texas; and Georgia and the Carolinas—that were the most important developing grounds for the blues.

Mississippi Delta Blues

It was at a train station in a sleepy Delta town that Handy claimed to have discovered the blues. The style that emerged in Mississippi has also been the one most instrumental in shaping the blues sound over the decades. Mississippi Delta blues consisted primarily of a singer accompanying himself on a guitar. The vocal style of the early Delta bluesmen was the most speech-like, as well as the most passionate, of the early regional styles. Slides or bottlenecks were frequently used as a guitar effect, one that Handy connected with Hawaiian guitar-playing.

Charley Patton was probably the most influential of the early Mississippi blues practitioners. His growling vocal style was emulated by countless other blues singers over the years. Among the performers whose work was shaped by Patton were Willie Brown, Eddie "Son" House, Johnny Shines, and Robert Johnson. Johnson, perhaps the biggest name to come out of the Delta blues tradition, in turn went on inspire yet another generation of blues artists, which included Chicago bluesmen Muddy Waters and Howlin' Wolf.

Texas Blues

Meanwhile in Texas, Blind Lemon Jefferson was the undisputed king of the blues. The blues style that developed in Texas, with Jefferson as its main proponent, contrasted with the Delta style in a number of ways. The guitar accompaniment was less percussive and made more frequent use of melodic lines and embellishments. Texas blues singers tended to enunciate their lyrics more clearly than their Mississippi counterparts, often in a high-pitched voice.

The Texas blues bloodline that begins with Jefferson can be traced through such well-known names as Lightnin' Hopkins, Clarence "Gatemouth" Brown, and T-Bone Walker, all the way to such modern blues stars as B. B. King. From Texas blues, the contemporary genre inherited much of its improvisational element. Jazzy electric guitar soloists owe much to the Texas line of blues heredity.

Classic Female Blues and Early Recordings

While most of the singers and musicians playing the blues on the rural porches and in the taverns of the South were men, women were fulfilling a large role in blues history through other channels. In fact, the first big recording stars of blues were women, performing a style that eventually came to be known as "classic blues." The first record made by a blues singer was *That Thing Called Love*, recorded in 1920, by Mamie Smith for Okeh Records. Another pioneering woman blues singer was Gertrude "Ma" Rainey, a blues belter from Georgia.

Perhaps the greatest of the classic blues singers was Bessie Smith, whose popularity stretched from the rural South all the way to the booming metropolises of the North. By the mid-1920s, several record companies, such as Columbia (Smith's label) and Paramount (Ma Rainey's) had caught on to the sales potential of so-called "Race" records. Other classic blues singers included Ida Cox and Victoria Spivey. Before achieving widespread fame, all of these women got their starts in the tent shows of the South. During the heyday of classic blues from the mid-1920s to the early 1930s, the singers were usually backed by big jazz combos, and the style maintained a much closer connection to mainstream pop music than to anything that could be called blues up to that time.

The commercial success of the women eventually led the record companies to begin recording some of the male artists, who until that time had been completely ignored by the industry. In 1924, Okeh made what may have been the first record by a male country blues singer, a performer named Ed Andrews. The first male blues recording star, however, was Papa Charlie Jackson, a talented banjo player who performed some of the earliest recorded versions of many country blues standards. Over the next several years, a number of record companies produced field recordings, so named because they were recorded not in Northern studios, but on location in the rural South with portable equipment.

Country Blues

Country blues is a catch-all term that refers to the sum total of the various regional blues styles that bloomed and comingled as the music spread across the country. During the Great Depression of the 1930s, millions of African Americans left the rural South for the cities of the North, and the blues traveled with them. The majority of the bluesmen who made the trek were of the younger generation. These performers adapted their traditional music to their new surroundings, incorporating the concerns of urban life into their lyrics. Blues scenes began to emerge in Chicago, St. Louis, Detroit, and elsewhere.

Older musicians, on the other hand, tended to stay put in the South. Skip James and Mississippi John Hurt were among the many bluesmen who did not migrate until later, if ever, and whose sounds remained countrified. Even today, blues can still be heard in the Delta that sounds much more like Charlie Patton's brand than like Buddy Guy's. In Memphis, the Beale Street jug band style emerged, played on home-made instruments by the likes of Furry Lewis, Memphis Minnie, and Bukka White.

The blues players of each region tended to relocate to a particular area as they fled the South. Musicians in the Piedmont region of North Carolina—whose style was most famously represented by Blind Boy Fuller—drifted toward New York. Heirs to Fuller's tradition who made this trip included Brownie McGhee and Sonny Terry.

Many of the Texans meanwhile headed westward to California. T-Bone Walker was one of the most important representatives of this migration, which led to the development of the West Coast blues sound through a lineage that included a number of important piano bluesmen as well as guitarist B. B. King.

Chicago Blues

Blues artists in the Mississippi Delta and other parts of the Deep South headed to several Northern cities, the most important of which was Chicago. In fact, the evolution of Chicago blues can reasonably be described as the amplifcation and small-band arrangement of traditional solo Delta blues. Taking their cue from the work of such Mississippi legends as Robert Johnson and Lonnie Johnson, arrivals from the South had established a blues scene in Chicago even before the onset of the Depression.

Popular Chicago blues performers during the 1920s and 1930s included Memphis Minnie, Tampa Red, Big Bill Broonzy, and Sonny Boy Williamson. A new wave of blues musicians after World War II solidified Chicago's position as the center of the blues universe. This generation of artists included Howlin' Wolf, Little Walter, and Muddy Waters.

Eventually, Chicago blues began to incorporate elements of blues styles from other areas. The most obvious input came from the Texas/West Coast guitar soloist line, following in the T-Bone Walker vein. This new emphasis on electric lead guitar improvisation was demonstrated in the work of such modern blues stars as Otis Rush, Magic Sam, and Buddy Guy.

The Varied Sounds of Blues

Like jazz, blues is a label that covers an incredibly diverse body of music. It defies convenient classification systems. Nevertheless, a number of recognizable styles and movements have emerged within the blues idiom over the years. Some of them are associated with the geographical areas in which they blossomed, while others transcend the boundaries of time and location.

Jump blues developed during the 1940s and 1950s, primarily in California. Jump was a jazzier, horn-driven style that relied less on guitar than many other blues forms. Its proponents have included Amos Milburn, Johnny Otis, and Big Joe Turner. In Louisiana, a laid-back "swamp" style was championed by Lightnin' Slim, Slim Harpo, and Lazy Lester. Louisiana also produced the blues offshoot called "zydeco," whose main proponents have included Clifton Chenier, Boozoo Chavis, and Rockin' Dopsie. The folk-flavored blues of the Carolina Piedmont region spawned the highly underrated Brownie Mc Ghee, who influenced rockers, folk musicians, and bluesmen alike. The term "piano blues" captures a wide variety of music spanning most of a continent and century, including the entire progression from barrelhouse to boogie-woogie to hard-rocking Chicago blues. Important piano bluesmen include Big Maceo Merriweather, Sunnyland Slim, Albert Ammons, and Otis Spann.

Two paths that blues has taken in recent years include modern acoustic blues and modern electric blues. Modern acoustic blues is essentially a movement for the revival of the older country blues sounds. Taj Mahal is one of its major proponents. Modern electric blues simply refers to the most contemporary trappings placed on urban blues. Robert Cray has been its most commercially successful practitioner.

◆ THE JAZZ TRADITION

New Orleans Jazz

It was when ragtime (primarily an instrumental music) and blues (at first primarily a vocal style) came together that jazz was born, and though this process was taking place in many parts of America, it was in New Orleans that the basic language of jazz was first spoken.

This was due not only to the rich musical tradition of this port city (with its international climate), but also because social conditions in New Orleans, while certainly not free from racist elements, were less restrictive and more open than in other large American cities of the time. Thus, there was much contact between musicians of varied ethnic background. Many histories of jazz mistakenly overemphasize the importance of the New Orleans red light district (called Storyville). While early jazz certainly was performed there, many other outlets for music-making existed. These included dances, parades, carnivals, and the traditional New Orleans funerals, for which a band would accompany the casket from church to cemetery with mournful strains, and then lead the march back to town with lively, peppy music including ragtime and early jazz.

Chicago Jazz

Musicians from New Orleans began to tour the United States from about 1907 on, and had a big influence wherever they went. However, their intricate style of collective improvisation, in which each instrument in the band had its own specific role, was not so easily absorbed. It is another myth of jazz history that most of these early jazz players were a special breed of self-taught "naturals;" in fact, almost all of them had good basic musical training, and many could read music well.

Ironically, the first New Orleans jazz to be recorded was performed by a white group, the Original Dixieland Jazz Band in 1917. By then, black musicians had already made records, but they were not in a jazz idiom. It would take some five more years before the best black New Orleans players got to make records. In the meantime, however, some of them had already visited Europe, notably the great clarinetist and soprano saxophonist

Louis Armstrong in Germany, 1952.

Sidney Bechet (1897-1959), who has been called the first great jazz soloist. But it was a somewhat younger New Orleanian, Louis Armstrong (1901-1971), who would have the biggest impact on the future of jazz.

Armstrong, who was brought to Chicago (by then the center of jazz activity) in 1922 by his mentor and fellow trumpeter Joe "King" Oliver (1885-1938) and made his first records there, came to New York two years later to join the band of Fletcher Henderson (1897-1952). This was the first musically significant big band in jazz.

Early African American Jazz Recordings

Jazz developed almost simultaneously with the phonograph, and without dissemination on records, it is unlikely that jazz would have spread as quickly as it did. By studying recorded performances, musicians anywhere could learn at least the rudiments of jazz, a spontaneous music in which improvisation played a considerable role. "Improvisation" is a much misunderstood concept. It does not mean inventing music on the spot, without guidelines. It does mean adding one's own personal ideas to a common musical text, and taking liberties as long as they fit within a shared framework. In addition, a jazz musician's personal style will be based on tonal qualities, a distinctive approach to rhythm and phrasing, and a vocabulary of melodic and thematic characteristics. Taken together, these ingredients are what makes it possible for a seasoned listener to almost immediately identify who is playing in a jazz performance, provided that the musician has developed his own personal style.

The Swing Era

While most New Orleans jazz bands used an instrumentation of trumpet, trombone, clarinet, piano, guitar (or banjo), bass (string or brass) and drums, the early big bands used three trumpets, one or two trombones, three reeds (saxophonists doubling clarinet), and the same rhythm section instruments. They employed written scores (called arrangements), but gave the soloists freedom to "improvise" their contributions.

Louis Armstrong's arrival was a revelation to New York's Henderson band. His first solos on its records stand out like diamonds in a tin setting. What Louis brought to jazz was, first of all, his superior sense of rhythm that made other players sound stiff and clumsy in comparison. He discovered the rhythmic element called "swing" that sets jazz apart from other musics; a

Fletcher Henderson

kind of rhythmic thrust that seems to float and soar. In addition, his sound on the trumpet was the biggest and most musically appealing yet heard, and he had exceptional range and powers of execution. Further, his gifts of melodic invention were so great that he can well be said to have laid the foundation for jazz as a medium for personal expression by an instrumental soloist.

One of his first Henderson colleagues to get the message was tenor saxophonist Coleman Hawkins (1904-1969), who soon created the first influential jazz style on his instrument. Also greatly affected was the band's chief arranger, Don Redman (1900-1964), who was the first to translate Armstrong's discoveries to big-band arranging. Many others followed suit, especially after Louis, now back in Chicago, began to make records with his own studio groups, the Hot Fives and Hot Sevens.

By the late 1920s, jazz had become a mainstay of American popular dance music and had spread to Europe as well. Black American musicians were touring world-wide, even in such exotic places as China and India, and wherever they went, their music left an imprint. Yet there was still quite a gap between jazz at its best and the more commercially acceptable versions of it. Not until the advent of the so-called "Swing Era" did

unadulterated jazz reach a level of popular acceptance which, thus far, remains unmatched.

This acceptance was due primarily to the big bands, which had reached a new height of artistic maturity. Duke Ellington (1899-1974), rightly called the greatest American composer, was partly responsible for this success. His unique band, for which he gradually created a perfect balance between written and improvised elements, not least due to such great soloists as Johnny Hodges (alto sax), Harry Carney (baritone sax), Barney Bigard (clarinet), Cootie Williams and Rex Stewart (trumpets), began a most important engagement at Harlem's famous Cotton Club in late 1927. Via appearances there, regular network radio broadcasts, and many recordings, Ellington's music was widely disseminated. His band visited Europe for the first time in 1933.

Other important work was done by Redman and by Benny Carter (b.1907), a brilliant multi-instrumentalist and arranger-composer. Fletcher Henderson himself had not previously arranged for his band, but began to do so in the early 1930s and soon became one of the best. Such efforts laid the foundation for the success of Benny Goodman (1909-1987), a white clarinetist and band leader, who commissioned the best black arrangers and also was the first white band leader to hire black musicians (pianist Teddy Wilson in early 1936 and vibraphonist Lionel Hampton later that year).

By 1936, the Swing Era was under way. Black dance styles set at such places as Harlem's Savoy Ballroom swept the nation, and young people jitterbugged to the sounds of an astonishing number of excellent bands. Those led by Jimmy Lunceford (1902-1947) and Count Basie (1905-1985) stood out among the many. The big bands spawned a host of gifted young players and also brought into the limelight many giants with established jazz reputations, such as Armstrong, who led his own big bands from 1929 to 1947.

World War II brought economic and social changes that affected the big bands. Gasoline rationing impaired the constant touring that was one of their mainstays. The singers, whose popularity was first established through their work with the bands, became stars in their own right. After the war, the advent of television wrought fundamental changes in the ways people entertained themselves. Among the chief victims of the new stay-at-home trend was ballroom dancing. The big bands went into rapid decline, and only a handful maintained themselves, among them Ellington and Basie.

Meanwhile, the music itself had also undergone fundamental changes. The new generation of players who had come to maturity by way of big-band experiences were eager to express themselves at greater length than most big-band work permitted, and they were also

Jazz greats Ella Fitzgerald, Oscar Peterson (piano), Roy Eldridge (trumpet), and Max Roach (drums) 1952.

coming up with new and potentially radical musical ideas.

The most advanced soloists of the Swing Era, such as Roy Eldridge (trumpet), Lester Young (tenor sax), Art Tatum(piano) and Sid Catlett (drums) had been extending the rhythmic, harmonic and technical resources of their instruments. Two young geniuses, both doomed to early death by tuberculosis, guitarist Charlie Christian (1916-1942), featured with Benny Goodman, and bassist Jimmy Blanton (1918-1942), featured with Duke Ellington, revolutionized the language of their respective instruments.

Christian was among the many notable players who participated in jam sessions (informal musical get-together) at Minton's Playhouse, a night club in Harlem, in the early 1940s. Here, where pianist Thelonious Monk and drummer Kenny Clarke were in the regular house band, experimentation took place that fed into the new jazz mainstream and led to the advent of modern jazz in 1944-45.

Bebop Gives Jazz a New Voice

The chief creators of this new jazz language were trumpeter (and band leader-composer) Dizzy Gillespie and alto saxophonist-composer Charlie Parker, both of whom had put in time with leading big bands. While working together in the band of pianist Earl Hines (the father of modern jazz piano style) in 1943, they began to solidify their mutually compatible ideas. When they joined forces in a small group in 1945, on records and in person, bebop (as the new jazz style soon was called) came into first flowering.

Though bebop was solidly grounded in earlier jazz styles, it did not seem that way to the public, which often was unable to follow the intricate rhythmic and harmonic elaborations of the boppers. Furthermore, the bop musicians, unlike most of the jazz players who preceded them, were not interested in pleasing the public, but more concerned with creating music that fulfilled their own artistic ambitions. (Gillespie himself, however, was something of an exception, perhaps because his irrepressible sense of humor made him a natural entertainer).

A New Audience

In any case, the advent of bop which had its beginnings in the Swing Era, went hand in hand with a change in the audience for jazz. By the mid-1930s, small clubs catering to jazz connoisseurs had begun to spring up in most larger urban areas. The biggest and most famous concentration was in New York, in two blocks on West 52nd Street, which soon became known as "Swing Street". In such clubs, musicians could perform for knowledgeable listeners without making musical compromises; most of them were too small for dancing, so people came strictly to listen. By this time, also, many people all over the world had become seriously interested in jazz. Some studied and documented its origins and history, others collected, researched and classified jazz records. Publications like *Downbeat* and *Metronome*, which catered to musicians and serious fans, sprang up. These magazines conducted polls and presented awards, as was also done, by 1944, by the prestigious *Esquire* magazine, which presented these awards at a huge all-star jazz concert on the stage of the Metropolitan Opera House in New York.

Jazz concerts had been a rarity in the 1920s. Then in 1938, Goodman staged one at Carnegie Hall, and from 1943, Duke Ellington gave an annual concert there. By the late 1940s, jazz concerts were regular events, among them the famous "Jazz at the Philharmonic" all-star tours. Thus, in many ways the stage was set for the acceptance, albeit in a limited way, of jazz as a music that no longer could be considered mere entertainment, or music primarily meant for dancing, but music having parity with "classical" music in its claim to serious artistic consideration.

Ornette Coleman

(In this way, the foundation was laid for the advent of rock music, which filled the need for young people to have their own music to dance to at a time when jazz had largely abandoned them. Nevertheless, rock was resented by many jazz musicians and fans. Eventually, of course, rock itself spawned its own constituency of "serious" performers, commentators, and magazines).

Bebop was in turn succeeded by more radical new forms of jazz, though it has shown considerable staying power. In 1959, a young Texas-born alto saxophonist, Ornette Coleman, brought his adventurous quartet to New York, setting off a huge controversy with music that seemed to have abandoned most of the harmonic and structural principles of jazz as it had hitherto been known. In fact, Coleman's music was deeply rooted in the blues and in well-established improvisational jazz procedures and in time his music was accepted as part of the jazz tradition.

Cool Jazz Is Developed

Toward the end of the 1940s, a reaction against the nervous energy of bop began to take form. This movement, spearheaded by trumpeter Miles Davis, came to be known as cool jazz. In contrast with the frenzied pace of bop solos, improvisors in the "cool" camp sought a more relaxed sound. The energy was sensual rather than frenetic.

While cool jazz began to take root primarily on the West Coast, largely among white musicians, African American musicians back East in the 1950s were pioneering the "hard-bop" style. Hard bop built on the harmonies and the fiery approach of bop, while adding a bluesy, hard-edged element. Tenor saxophonist Sonny Rollins, trumpet player Donald Byrd, and drummer Art Blakey were among the major shapers of hard-bop in the second half of the 1950s.

Avant garde jazz was very much evidence, in many and varied forms. By the 1960s, many people viewed the history of jazz as a linear progression toward maximum freedom for the player. Just as bop had opened new windows of creative opportunity to soloists, each new emerging style that followed stripped away additional layers of constraint. Some saw this trend as a return in African American music to the complete freedom of the field holler from the rhythmic and harmonic limitations that had been imported from the classical music of white Europe.

The trumpeter Miles Davis, who had worked with Charlie Parker and also led his own very influential groups, hired a then little-known tenor saxophonist, John Coltrane, in 1956. With Coltrane, who also worked with Thelonious Monk, Davis introduced a modal approach (based on scales rather than harmonies) to jazz

improvisation in 1958. Sometimes called simply "modal jazz," this new style came to be known most frequently as "post-bop." It was practiced by many of the same musicians who had been hard-boppers a few years earlier, including Byrd and drummer Max Roach, as well as younger performers such as Wayne Shorter and McCoy Tyner.

Coltrane soon formed his own group, which took modality much further and extended improvisation, both in length and intensity, to a point of near-ecstasy. The pianist Cecil Taylor, a virtuoso of the keyboard, further stretched the boundaries of jazz. Davis himself experimented with electronics and rock and soul rhythms. The bassist and composer Charles Mingus, deeply influenced by Ellington and Parker, found new and imaginative ways of combining written and improvised jazz. Tenor saxophonist Sonny Rollins, while remaining rooted in traditional harmonic ground, expanded solo improvisation dramatically. And by the end of the 1960s, Albert Ayler, a tenor saxophonist with roots in rhythm-and-blues music, brought another new and intensely personal voice to jazz.

Over the course of the decade, many others contributed to the dismantling of the melodic rulebook. Pharoah Sanders, Archie Shepp, and Sonny Sharrock were among those who learned their art at Coltrane's side. Ornette Coleman spawned a line of jazz innovators that has included trumpeter Don Cherry, bassist Jamaaledeen Tacuma, and guitarist James "Blood" Ulmer. Don Pullen, Sun Ra, and Anthony Braxton are also among the countless notable proponents of free jazz and its various offshoots.

Era of Rapid Changes Ends

When John Coltrane died suddenly in 1967, jazz was at the height of its experimental, expansionist stage, much of it inspired by the social and political upheavals of the time. By then, the term "free jazz" had begun to replace "avant garde," and many young musicians were following in the footsteps of Coltrane and other standard-bearers of innovation. But within a few years of Coltrane's passing, the storm quieted. There was some more experimentation, which was still going on within jazz in the late 1980s. Yet, by the early 1970s, it had become clear that the period of rapid and sometimes almost overpowering changes in jazz had come to an end.

Fusion was the most notable development in jazz in the 1970s. The groundwork had been laid one decade earlier by Miles Davis. Fusion was essentially a marriage between the rhythms of rock and the virtuosity of the jazz soloist. Other champions of fusion included Wayne Shorter (founder of the group Weather Report), drum-

John Coltrane

mer Jack DeJohnette, and keyboardist Herbie Hancock. Another type of fusion that gained popularity in the 1970s was world fusion, which incorporated rhythmic and melodic elements from a variety of international styles. Advocates have included Yusef Lateef, Don Cherry, and Ronald Shannon Jackson.

Of the many paths jazz took during the 1980s, free funk and neoclassicism are among the most important. Building on the rock/fusion model, free funk incorporates the rhythms and sounds of urban funk into a horn-driven, free improvisational framework. Ronald Shannon Jackson, James "Blood" Ulmer, and Jamaaledeen Tacuma—all one-time Ornette Coleman disciples—have been among its best practitioners.

In the 1990s, a goodly number of young musicians have turned to the rich tradition of jazz for inspiration, among them the gifted trumpeter Wynton Marsalis(also an expert classical player) and several other remarkable musicians from New Orleans, among them Wynton's slightly older brother Branford Marsalis (tenor and soprano saxophones), trumpeter Terence Blanshard, and alto saxophonist Donald Harrison. These young players reject both "fusion" with electronics and rock and the practices of "free jazz," and look to the bebop

tradition and even to Louis Armstrong and Duke Ellington for inspiration.

The so-called "young lions" of jazz persisted in this vein during the first half of the 1990s, with Wynton Marsalis serving as a sort of godfather figure to the group. The most commercially successful young star has been tenor saxophonist Joshua Redman, son of well-known saxman Dewey Redman. The younger Redman brought hard-bop to its largest audience ever—an audience that worships him like a rock star. Other successful lion cubs include trumpeter Roy Hargrove; alto saxophonist Antonio Hart; the drum and trumpet playing brothers, Winard and Phillip Harper; bassist Christian McBride, guitarist Mark Whitfield, saxophonist James Carter, and pianist Marcus Roberts. Although these performers have brought jazz to the attention of its broadist audience in decades—in fact, the resurgence of the traditional form led to the first-ever, all-jazz music cable channel, BET Jazz, in 1996— some older jazz artists worry that the reluctance of the younger generation to innovate or challenge the musical status quo does more harm than good to the genre. At the same time, many of these older musicians are seeing their careers revitalized, largely thanks to those same up-and-comers they criticize.

Emergence of Repertory Jazz Style

A direct way of dealing with the jazz tradition is the emergence in the late 1980s of the so-called "repertory jazz." This refers to the performance of big band compositions and arrangements. The most notable of these ensembles is the Lincoln Center Jazz Orchestra, with Wynton Marsalis as artistic director, which specializes in the music of Ellington, and the Smithsonian Jazz Masterpiece Ensemble, jointly directed by David Baker and Gunther Schuller, two master musicians with classical as well as jazz training.

The many gifted players who emerged from Chicago's 1960s Association for the Advancement of Creative Music (AACM) pursued their various approaches with stirring results, in such groups as the Art Ensemble of Chicago, the World Saxophone Quartet, and Lester Bowie's Brass Fantasy.

Musicians from the AACM school continued to refine their take on free jazz through the 1970s and 1980s, eventually creating a style often called neoclassicism. Neoclassicism applied the freedoms gained through the free jazz movement to more structured compositions. Important neoclassicists have included David Murray, Don Pullen, and Henry Threadgill. The AACM scene has remained vital into the 1990s, led by, among others, composer and saxophonist Edward Wilkerson.

◆ WOMEN IN BLUES AND JAZZ

Although the music industry, like most others, has historically been dominated by men, women have played a crucial role in the development of blues and jazz. As mentioned earlier, the first blues recording stars were women. While these singers were pioneering classic blues in the 1920s, many other women, including Edythe Turnham and Lil Hardin Armstrong, were already leading their own jazz bands. Trumpeters Ernestine "Tiny" Davis in the 1930s and Clora Byrant in the 1940s and 1950s were among the many women instrumentalists who enjoyed long and successful careers in jazz. In the 1990s, a highly respected, Detroit-based, all-female group emerged under the name Straight Ahead. In addition to pianist Eileen Orr, the former quintet originally featured four African Americans—singer Cynthia Dewberry, bassist Marion F. Hayden-Banfield, drummer Gayelynn McKinney, and violinist Regina Carter. When Carter left Straight Ahead after their first two recordings, the foursome continued recording and touring without her.

Among women in blues and jazz, however, it has always been the vocalists who have left the most lasting marks. The 1930s produced such giants as Billie Holiday and Ella Fitzgerald. The crop of female vocal stars that followed as beebop took over included Sarah Vaughn, Carmen McRae, Nancy Wilson, and Betty Carter. Dee Dee Bridgewater was one of the few jazz singers to break out of obscurity in the 1970s. In the 1980s, however, jazz vocals made a bit of a comeback, bringing the emergence of Diane Schuur and Dianne Reeves. Cassandra Wilson, Neenah Freelon, Shirley Horn, and Rachelle Farrelle have been among the leading jazz vocalists of the 1990s.

Vocal Stylists

The line of female blues vocalists has overlapped quite a bit with the jazz line from the start. Alberta Hunter, the last of the great classic blues singers, performed with Louis Armstrong and Fletcher Henderson in the 1920s. Dinah Washington was often called the "Queen of the Blues," and Betty Carter was seen by many as her successor. Etta James and Koko Taylor are among the prominent blues vocalists of the last few decades. As the blues sound percolated into other forms of pop music, its traces could be heard in the gospel-inspired voices of such soul and rock artists as Chaka Khan, Tina Turner, and most notably, Aretha Franklin.

The men have also created a strong vocal jazz tradition. Bandleaders Louis Armstrong and Billy Eckstine were both crooners. Joe Williams, a true vocal giant, got his start in the 1930s. He later worked with greats Coleman Hawkins, Lionel Hampton, Count Basie, Henry

"Sweets" Edison, and Cannonball Adderley, among others, before going on to lead his own groups since the 1960s. In the 1980s, Bobby McFerrin blasted on to the scene. His 1984 release *The Voice* made history as the first major label jazz album recorded entirely without accompaniment or overdubbing. A vocal improviser in the truest sense of the word, McFerrin recorded a number of classical works as well. Will Downing, Jon Lucien, and Kevin Mahogany picked up the slack in the 1990s, with Mahogany being touted as the leading figure among them. Vocal sextet Take 6, known for mixing elements of jazz, gospel, and pop, were also quite popular.

The Future of Jazz

No one can predict where jazz will go next. One interesting development of the 1990s has been the introduction of jazz sounds and instrumentation into hip hop and other urban dance genres. After a long and remarkable period of intense innovation, the music seems to have reached a point where it is taking stock of its past while looking to the future. Whatever that future may bring, one thing is certain: the story of jazz is one of the most remarkable chapters in the history of the twentieth century artistic creativity, and names like Armstrong, Ellington, and Parker are bound to loom large when that history is finally written.

Born in the crucible of slavery, jazz has become the universal song of freedom. (It's no coincidence that neither Hitler nor Stalin had any use for jazz and tried, unsuccessfully, to banish it.) Perhaps, Thelonious Monk put it best when he said that "jazz and freedom go hand in hand."

◆ BLUES AND JAZZ GATEKEEPERS

Muhal Richard Abrams (1930-)
Pianist, composer, Bandleader

Born in Chicago, Abrams began his professional career in 1948, playing with many of the city's best musicians and bands. In 1961, he formed the Experimental Band, which soon became an informal academy for Chicago's most venturesome players. Under Abram's quiet but firm guidance, this grew into the Association for the Advancement of Creative Music (AACM). The AACM helped young musicians perform and promote their own music, which could not be presented through established venues.

The AACM attracted such musicians as Roscoe Mitchell, Joseph Jarman, Lester Bowie, Malachi Favors, and Don Moye, who would later achieve world-wide prominence as the Art Ensemble of Chicago, as well as other future leaders of avant garde jazz. Though he never so appointed himself, Abrams was the recognized

Wycliffe Lincoln, Wynton Marsalis, and Wes Anderson at the JVC Jazz Festival, 1991.

leader and moral and spiritual force behind the AACM. In 1976, when his brood had come of age and flown the coop, Abrams moved to New York and finally began to get some of the national and international recognition he had so long deserved. In 1990, he was the first recipient of the prestigious Danish "Jazzpar" Award. His work as a pianist and composer spans the entire range of the black musical tradition. In 1995, Abrams and his Experimental Big Band performed at the Chicago Jazz Festival.

Lilian "Lil" Hardin Armstrong (1898-1971)
Pianist, Singer, Composer

Lil Armstrong was born in Memphis in 1898. Lil was a classically trained musician who received her music education at Fisk University. Her family moved from Memphis to Chicago somewhere around 1914 or 1915. One of her first jobs was selling sheet music in Jones music store in Chicago. It is said that she met Jelly Roll Morton while working there and it was Morton who influenced her style of hitting the notes "real heavy". She worked with the New Orleans Creole Jazz Band, The New Orleans Rhythm Kings, and King Oliver's Creole Jazz Band, where she met her husband Louis

Armstrong. Lil and Louie were married in 1924. She played and wrote music for many of Armstrong's Hot Five and Hot Seven concerts and recordings and helped Louie polish his raw brilliant talent. The Armstrongs were divorced in 1938. She also played in various bands and some combos of her own. Two of her songs "Bad Boy" and "Just For a Thrill" became big hits in the 1960s. While playing at a tribute to Louis Armstrong at Chicago's Civic Center Plaza, Lilian Armstrong collapsed and died of a heart attack on July 7, 1971.

Louis Armstrong (1901-1971)
Trumpeter, Singer

Born in New Orleans, Louis Armstrong was one of the most influential and durable of all jazz artists, and quite simply, one of the most famous people in the entire world.

On New Year's Eve in 1914, Armstrong was arrested in New Orleans for firing a pistol and sent to the Colored Waifs Home. It was there that he first learned to play the cornet. His skill increased with the experience he gained from playing in the Home's band. When he was finally released from the institution, he was already proficient enough with the instrument to begin playing for money.

Befriended by his idol, King Oliver, Armstrong quickly began to develop the jazz skills which he had, until then, been able to admire only from a distance. When Oliver left for Chicago in 1919, a place opened for Armstrong as a member of the Kid Ory band in New Orleans.

In 1922, Oliver asked Armstrong to join him in Chicago as second cornet with his Creole Jazz Band. The duets between "Dippermouth" (as Armstrong was called) and "Papa Joe" (Oliver's nickname) soon became the talk of the Chicago music world.

Two years later Armstrong joined the Fletcher Henderson band at the Roseland Ballroom in New York City. In 1925, he returned to Chicago to play with Erskine Tate, switching from cornet to trumpet, the instrument he played from then on. During the next four years he made a series of recordings which profoundly influenced the course of jazz.

In 1929, Armstrong returned to New York and there, in the revue "Hot Chocolates," scored his first triumph with a popular song (Fats Waller's "Ain't Misbehavin'"). This success was a turning point in his career. He now began to front big bands, playing and singing popular songs rather than blues or original instrumentals.

In 1932, Armstrong headlined the show at the London Palladium, where he acquired the nickname "Satchmo." From 1933 to 1935 he toured Europe, returning to the United States to film *Pennies from Heaven* with Bing Crosby. He continued to evolve from the status of musician to that of entertainer, and his singing soon became as important as his playing. In 1947, he formed a small group, which was an immediate success. He continued to work in this context, touring throughout the world.

Armstrong scored a tremendous success in 1964 with his recording of "Hello Dolly," which bounced the Beatles from the top spot on the Top 40 list, a great feat in the age of rock. Though his health began to decline, he kept up his heavy schedule of international touring, and when he died in his sleep at home in Corona, Queens, two days after his seventieth birthday, he had been preparing to resume work in spite of a serious heart attack suffered some three months before. "The music—it's my living and my life" was his motto.

Louis Armstrong's fame as an entertainer in the later stages of his extraordinary career sometimes made people forget that he remained a great musician to the end. More than any other artist, Louis Armstrong symbolized the magic of jazz, a music unimaginable without his contribution. "You can't play a note on the horn that Louis hasn't already played," said Miles Davis. "I mean even modern." And contemporary musicians like Wynton Marsalis echo that opinion.

In 1988, on the strength of its use in the film *Good Morning Vietnam*, Armstrong's recording of "What A Wonderful World" became a surprise hit, climbing to number eleven on the Billboard chart. In 1992, a Louis Armstrong Archive was established at Queens College in New York. It contains his personal papers, private recordings, memorabilia, instruments, etc.

William "Count" Basie (1904-1984)
Pianist, Bandleader

Count Basie is generally regarded as the leader of the best jazz band in the United States, and consequently, one of the major influences on jazz as a whole.

His musical career ranges from a boyhood spent watching the pit band at the local movie theater (he later learned the organ techniques of Fats Waller by crouching beside him in the Lincoln Theater in Harlem) to his dual triumphs in 1957 when his became the first American band to play a royal command performance for the Queen of England, and the first black jazz band ever to play at the Waldorf Astoria Hotel in New York City.

During the early 1920s, Basie toured in vaudeville. Stranded in Kansas City, he joined Walter Page's Blue Devils. (Jimmy Rushing was the singer.) After this band broke up, Basie joined Benny Moten, and in 1935 formed his own band at the Reno Club in Kansas City, where a local radio announcer soon dubbed him "Count."

At the urging of critic John Hammond, Basie brought his group to New York City in 1936. Within a year he had cut his first record and was well on his way to becoming an established presence in the jazz world.

The Basie trademark was his rhythm section, which featured Basie's own clean, spare piano style and outstanding soloists like Lester Young and Sweets Edison in the early years, and Lucky Thompson, J. J. Johnson, Clark Terry, and Benny Powell in the later period.

Except for the years 1950 and 1951 when he had a small group, Basie led a big band for almost 40 years. Immune to changing fashion, the Basie band completed numerous global tours and successful recording engagements without ever suffering an appreciable decline in its popularity. In 1974, on his seventieth birthday, the Count was honored at a "Royal Salute" party by virtually every big name in jazz.

Count Basie was again honored at Radio City Music Hall in New York City in 1982. Among those honoring The Count were Dionne Warwick and Lena Horne.

Sidney Bechet (1897-1959)
Saxophonist, Clarinetist

Sidney Bechet was the first jazzman to achieve recognition on the soprano saxophone, and also one of the

Count Basie

first to win acceptance in classical circles as a serious musician.

In 1919, Bechet played in England and on the Continent with Will Marion Cook's Southern Syncopated Orchestra. Even before this, his clarinet and soprano sax had been heard in the bands of King Oliver and Freddie Keppard in his native New Orleans.

During the early 1920s Bechet made a series of records with Clarence Williams' Blue Five, worked briefly with Duke Ellington (one of his great admirers), and then returned to Europe. He came back to the United States with Noble Sissle and expanded his career, making many records. In 1949, he moved to France where he enjoyed the greatest success of his career. He died there in 1959. After his death, a statue of Bechet was erected in Antibes.

Art Blakey (1919-1990)
Drummer, Bandleader

One of the greatest drummers in jazz, Art Blakey was also one of the music's foremost talent spotters. After early experience with Fletcher Henderson and Mary Lou Williams, he joined Billy Eckstine's band in 1944

and took part in the birth of bebop. After working with many of the greatest modern jazz musicians, he formed his own Jazz Messengers in 1954 with immediate success.

From then on until his death, Blakey hired and helped to stardom a vast number of gifted players, among them Horace Silver, Lee Morgan, Freddie Hubbard, Benny Golson, Woody Shaw, Wayne Shorter and Wynton Marsalis, to name but a very few. Blakey had one of the most powerful beats in jazz and took part in some of the finest recordings of his time.

Jimmy Blanton (1918-1942)
Bassist

During his brief life, Jimmy Blanton changed the course of jazz history by originating a new way of playing the string bass. Playing the instrument as if it were a horn, he lifted it from rhythmic back-up to melodic focal point.

Born in St. Louis, Missouri, in 1918, he played with Jeter Pillars and Fate Marable before joining Duke Ellington in 1939. Until this time the string bass rarely played anything but quarter notes in ensemble or solos, but Blanton began sliding into eighth- and sixteenth-note runs, introducing melodic and harmonic ideas that were totally new to the instrument. His skill put him in a different class from his predecessors; it made him the first true master of the bass and demonstrated the instrument's unsuspected potential as a solo vehicle.

Blanton died of tuberculosis in 1942.

Blind Lemon Jefferson (1897-1929)
Guitarist, Singer

Blind Lemon Jefferson was one of the pioneers of Texas blues. Born poor, back, and blind, music was one of the few career options open to Lemon—which was his given name, not a nickname. Jefferson's performing career began when he was 14. He would make a daily trek on foot into the nearest town, Wortham, where he would sit in front of some store and begin to play for tips. He eventually acquired a sizable local following, and was invited to play at country picnics and other such events. At 20, Jefferson moved to Dallas, where he made good money playing in brothels and taverns. Among the local boys he hired as guides during this period were the young Lightnin' Hopkins and T-Bone Walker.

In 1925 and 1926, Jefferson made a series of recording trips to Chicago, home of the Paramount record label. His records sold well to black audiences, and he became possibly the very first country blues recording star. He made a total of about 80 records over the next couple of years. Too many budding bluesmen to mention learned their first licks from these early Jefferson recordings.

In 1929, the heavy-drinking Jefferson got lost in a blizzard after leaving a party in Chicago and froze to death. Long a favorite of American folk fans, Jefferson's songs have since been covered by countless folksingers and rockers over the years, and he was honored in the naming of the rock group Jefferson Airplane.

Buddy Bolden (1868-1931)
Cornetist

Buddy Bolden, a plasterer by trade, formed what may have been the first real jazz band in the 1890s in New Orleans. By the turn of the century, his cornet was so popular that he was often called upon to sit in with several bands on a single evening. His cornet style was the starting point for a chain of musicians from King Oliver to Louis Armstrong to Dizzy Gillespie; put another way, from New Orleans to Chicago to New York. Because his career predates the recording of jazz, the only lasting memorial to his talent lies in the oral tradition which carries on his legend, and in the known successes of his descendants. Bolden was committed to East Louisiana State Hospital in 1907, suffering from schizophrenia, and remained there until his death, never playing another note.

Clarence "Gatemouth" Brown (1924-)
Guitarist, Singer

Clarence "Gatemouth" Brown may have gotten his nickname because of his big voice, but it is his guitar wizardry that has earned him a place in the blues pantheon. The son of a Cajun singer who could also play accordion, banjo, fiddle, and mandolin, Brown himself became a multi-instrumentalist at an early age. As a youth, he hated blues music, preferring both his father's lively Cajun tunes and the jazz being produced by the likes of Count Basie and Louis Jordan. His attitude changed when he was introduced to the jazz-inspired blues of guitar pioneer T-Bone Walker.

Brown's first big break came in 1947, when he was called in as a last-minute replacement for the ailing Walker at a prominent Houston nightclub. The club's owner immediately offered Brown a long-term contract to record for his newly-formed label, Peacock Records. Brown recorded more than 50 sides of music for Peacock by 1960. In 1964 Brown went to Europe, where he toured and recorded widely and attained a sizable following. He returned to the United States when blues began to show signs of a resurgence. Despite winning a

Grammy in 1981 for *Alright Again*, he has never quite become a household name in this country.

Clifford Brown (1930-1956)
Trumpeter, Composer, Bandleader

Clifford Brown's death at twenty-five in a car crash was one of jazz's great tragedies. Acclaimed as the greatest trumpet talent of his generation, Brown was on the brink of stardom as co-leader of the successful Clifford Brown- Max Roach Quintet (recently joined by Sonny Rollins); recording artist in his own right (his album with strings was very popular); and as a role model for aspiring jazz musicians (Brown had no vices, was raising a happy family, and was loved by all who knew him, not just for his music but also for his warm and gentle personality).

He studied music at the University of Maryland, but at twenty-one was injured, ironically, in a car accident that left him inactive for months. In 1952, he joined Chris Powell's R and B band (with which he made his first records), worked with the great composer-arranger Tadd Dameron, and toured Europe with Lionel Hampton's band. A year later, he teamed up with Max Roach and all seemed "go" until death struck, shocking the brilliant young trumpeter's friends and fans world-wide. Brown was also a gifted composer; tunes like "Joy Spring" and "Dahoud" are classics, as are Brown's recordings, which still influence young musicians more than thirty-seven years after his death.

Ray Brown (Raymond Matthews) (1926-)
Bassist

Producer and personal manager Ray Brown is perhaps the most versatile bass player in jazz today and is in demand around the world. He was born in Pittsburgh in 1926. In 1951, after having worked with Dizzy Gillespie and Charlie Parker, he joined Oscar Peterson's Trio—an association that lasted 15 years. During this time, he and Peterson produced award-winning records, and were in constant demand for concerts. Since leaving Peterson in 1966, Brown has joined forces with many famous artists in both live and recorded performances. Brown received a National Endowment for the Arts American Jazz Master Fellowship in 1995.

Cab Calloway (1908-1994)
Singer, Dancer, Bandleader, Author

Born Cabell Calloway, III, on December 25, 1908, in Rochester, New York, Cab Calloway was not only a beloved entertainer but the widely acknowledged father of scat singing and "jive" talk. He prowled countless nightclub stages with exuberance and catlike grace, predominately clad in his signature white tux and tails. A giant of the music industry from his days at Harlem's Cotton Club in the 1920s to his 1980 film performance in the *Blues Brothers*. Mentor to many of the twentieth century's best singers and musicians, the years never slowed down the energetic performer.

Earlier, in his youth, the living for which Calloway seemed destined was the law. The second of six children born to a Rochester, New York, attorney and his teacher-wife, Calloway, who grew up in Baltimore, actually did enroll in pre-law at Crane College in Chicago. But he was wooed away by the jazz world his older sister Blanche had already joined in the Windy City. Cab also had the bug: already skilled on the drums as a young man, he found a job at the Sunset Cafe; within six months he was up front on stage, leading his first group, the Alabamians. He also made a new friend in those days—a fellow musician named Louis Armstrong. Though the Alabamians's first New York booking, at the Savoy Ballroom, failed and the band broke up, Calloway stayed in the city. He landed a role in the all-black revue "Connie's Hot Chocolates," where he caught the attention of Broadway bigwig Irving Mills.

In 1929, Calloway took over as leader of another band, the Missourians, renamed Cab Calloway and His Orchestra. After the group replaced Duke Ellington's band at the glittery, famous Cotton Club, Calloway was performing there one night—plugged into a radio broadcast—and swung into a new song he had recently written called *Minnie the Moocher*. Suddenly, he realized he had forgotten the lyrics and filled in the blanks by scat-singing the first thing that came into his mind: "Hi-de-hi-de-hi-de-ho. Ho-de-ho-de-ho-de-hee." The band played along; the audience hollered back raucously. And Calloway had a hit: *Minnie the Moocher* in 1931 gave his band an identity; the Cotton Club gave Calloway's popular swing band a job, for nine consecutive years.

Those years, however, had their down side. The Cotton Club—decorated like an antebellum plantation, its black waiters dressed as Old South butlers, its audience virtually restricted to whites—smacked of blatant racism. Calloway did everything he could to protect his musicians from racism. Though prone to big gambling debts in those days, he still managed to make payroll and to rent separate railroad sleeping and dining cars for the comfort of the band members and to shelter them from having to deal with prejudice on the trains.

Calloway himself survived by developing his talents and venues. Already an excellent jazz saxophonist and

band leader, he immersed himself in movie musicals, appearing in such films as *Stormy Weather* in 1932 and *The Singing Kid*. Then, in 1952, came his biggest break yet: the role of Sportin' Life in the Broadway revival of *Porgy and Bess*. Some sources say that George Gershwin created the character of the unctuous drug dealer with Calloway in mind. The performer went on to star with Pearl Bailey in all-black production of *Hello Dolly* and movie roles in the *Cincinnati Kid* and the *Blues Brothers*.

Through the years, Calloway helped along such singers as Pearl Bailey and Lena Horne and musicians Dizzy Gillespie, Ben Webster, Doc Cheatham, Jonah Jones and Milt Hinton. He also found time to compile a guide to the language of Harlem, *The Hepster's Dictionary*. En route, many of his hits, including *Minnie* and *Reefer Man*, dealt with drug use, though Calloway himself said he did not condone drug use.

Information about Calloway's family life varies: some sources say he married twice, others say three times, and he fathered between four and six daughters. At the time of his death he was survived by his wife, Nuffie, whom he married in 1953. Calloway's autobiography, *Of Minnie the Moocher and Me*, was published in 1976. He died on November 18, 1994, in Hockessin, Delaware, following a stroke in June of 1994. His honors included a National Medal of Arts, presented by President Clinton at the White House.

Benny Carter (1907-)
Saxophonist, Trumpeter, Composer, Bandleader

Bennett Lester Carter, born August 8, 1907, in New York City, made his professional debut in 1923, and seventy years later still ranks at the top of jazz as an instrumentalist, composer-arranger and leader. In 1988, he toured Europe, visited Japan with his own band, performed in Brazil for the first time in his career, and recorded three albums. He continued at the same pace in 1993.

Admired and respected by generations of musicians, many of whom "went to school" in his bands (Sid Catlett, Miles Davis, J.J. Johnson, Max Roach and Teddy Wilson among them), Carter helped shape the language of big-band jazz. His scoring for saxophone sections was especially influential. On the alto saxophone, he and Johnny Hodges were the pacesetters before Charlie Parker and the heyday of bebop. He has few peers as a trumpeter and has composed many standards.

Carter was the first black composer to break the color barrier in the Hollywood film studios. He scored many major films and television shows, including "M-Squad." The subject of one of the best biographies of a jazz artist (*Benny Carter: A Life in American Music*), Carter received an honorary doctorate in music from Princeton University, where he taught, in 1974.

Ray Charles (1932-)
Singer, Pianist, Bandleader

Ray Charles was born on September 23, 1932, in Atlanta, Georgia. Blinded at the age of six, Charles received his first musical training at a school for the blind in St. Augustine, Florida. Originally from Georgia, he left school at the age of 15 to play local engagements. Two years later, he formed a trio which had some success in the Northwest. In 1954, he organized a seven-piece rhythm and blues group.

In 1957, Charles's first LP was released, consisting of a potpourri of instrumentals drawn from pop, gospel music, and modern jazz sources. His singing and piano playing found particular favor with a number of jazz artists who were drawing away from what they felt was a growing tendency for jazz to become overscored and underfelt. In Charles, they saw an artist who had restored both a sense of "soul" and instrumental "funkiness" to the jazz idiom.

By the end of the 1960s, Charles had become one of the world's most popular performers—evidenced by his late 1980s-early 1990s stint as a spokesperson for Pepsi-Cola Co.—and remains a star in the 1990s. He headlined the Boston Globe Jazz Festival and performed on NBC-TV's *Apollo Theatre Hall of Fame* special in 1993, the same year in which U.S. president Bill Clinton bestowed a National Medal of Arts upon him. Ever aware of current musical trends, Charles's 1993 recording, *My World*, exhibited snippets of hip-hop sensibilities. In 1995, Charles took part in the JVC Newport Jazz Festival.

Recipient of more than 10 Grammy awards, Charles has was inducted into the Rock and Roll Hall of Fame in 1986. The honorary life chairman of the Rhhythm-and-Blues Hall of Fame, Charles is also an inductee of the Playboy Jazz and Pop Hall of Fame and the Songwriters Hall of Fame.

Clifton Chenier (1925-1987)
Singer, Accordionist

Clifton Chenier is generally regarded as the "King of Zydeco," the dance music that evolved from blues among Louisiana's black French-speaking Creoles. The son of an accordionist, Chenier took up the instrument at an early age and moved with his brother Cleveland, who played the rub board, to Port Arthur, where work in the oil industry was available.

Performing nights for other refinery workers, Chenier was eventually discovered by a talent scout and signed to the Elko record label in 1954. After cutting two singles, he moved to the Specialty Records label a year later. His first big hit was "Ay, 'Tit Fille," which sold well throughout the South. Chenier quickly became a big attraction in the Gulf Coast region, but remained relatively unknown elsewhere. As zydeco started to become passé, he began including more conventional R&B in his sets.

Chenier moved to Houston in the early 1960s, where he was "rediscovered," this time by Chris Strachwitz of Arhoolie Records. He released his first album, *Louisiana Blues and Zydeco*, on Arhoolie in 1964. In the 1970s and 1980s, zydeco suddenly experienced something of a renaissance, and Chenier was its point man. He became a fixture on college campuses across the United States and eventually toured Europe as well. Although his health began failing—he had diabetes and kidney disease—in the 1980s, Chenier continued to work right up until his death in 1987.

Charlie Christian (1916-1942)
Electric Guitarist

Charlie Christian did for the electric guitar what Jimmy Blanton did for the bass. Christian joined Benny Goodman in 1939, and after only two years with the Goodman Sextet, achieved great fame as the first electric guitarist to play single-string solos. In his after-hour activities at such Harlem clubs as Minton's, he was an early contributor to the jazz revolution which would one day come to be called "Bop". In 1941, he was hospitalized with tuberculosis, and died the following year. His recordings are still an inspiration to young guitarists.

Kenny Clarke (Liaqa Ali Salaam) (1914-1985)
Drummer

Kenny Clarke was one of the "founding fathers" of the Bop movement. Along with Dizzy Gillespie, and Thelonious Monk, Clarke made Minton's in Harlem the late-hour haunt for musicians in the 1940s. A pioneer in the use of drums as a solo instrument and not just a background presence, he was one of the first musicians to move away from emphasis on the bass drum to a more flexible style in which he maintained a steady rhythm on the top cymbal while "dropping bombs" with surprise bass-drum punctuations. From a musically-inclined Pittsburgh family, Clarke studied vibes, piano, and trombone as well as musical theory. His early professional experience was gained with Roy Eldridge and Edgar Hayes. (He traveled to Finland and Sweden with Hayes in 1937.)

In the early 1940s, Clarke played with Teddy Hill and then moved into Minton's. Later he worked with Dizzy Gillespie, Coleman Hawkins, Tadd Dameron, and many others. In 1951, he toured with Billy Eckstine, and in the following year he helped organize the Modern Jazz Quartet, where he remained for the next three years. He moved to France in 1956 where he continued to work with a long list of visiting American talents, and co-led a fine "big band" with Belgian pianist and arranger Frency Boland from 1961 to 1972.

Ornette Coleman (1930-)
Saxophonist, Trumpeter, Violinist, Composer

Born on March 19, 1930, in Fort Worth, Texas, Ornette Coleman began his musical career in carnival and rhythm-and-blues bands. Fired by guitarist-singer Pee Wee Crayton for his unconventional style of playing, Coleman settled in Los Angeles, making his living as an elevator operator while studying music on his own. He began to compose and sat in at jam sessions, and made his first album in 1958. Encouraged by John Lewis, who recommended him for a scholarship to Gunther Schuller's Lennox School of Jazz in the summer of 1959, Coleman and his quartet (Don Cherry, pocket cornet; Charlie Haden, bass; Billy Higgins, drums) opened at the Five Spot in Manhattan, stirring up great debates among jazz musicians, critics and fans.

Coleman's music, while abandoning traditional rules of harmony and tonality, obviously wasn't the senseless noise that some heard it as. In fact, the music of the first Coleman quartet, which made many recordings, was very melodic, had a strong blues feeling, and sounds not at all startling. Eventually, Coleman was accepted by many of his peers. He continued to go his own way in music, creating a system he called "harmolodic," teaching himself to play trumpet and violin (the latter left-handed and amplified). In the seventies, he composed and performed a long work for symphony orchestra and alto sax, "The Skies of America," and in the 1980s, he formed Prime Time, a kind of jazz-fusion band with two electric guitars and two drummers. The original quartet was triumphantly reunited at the 1989 JVC Jazz Festival and also recorded again that year.

Though Coleman has influenced some players, (most notably Dewey Redman, Steve Coleman), his music remains a very personal means of expression; as such, it has much beauty and feeling to offer the open-minded listener. In 1993, a box set of Coleman's works entitled *Beauty Is a Rare Thing* was issued. The following year, Coleman, the father of free jazz, received a prestigious MacArthur fellowship. In previous years he had been made a Guggenheim fellow (1967).

John Coltrane (1926-1967)
Saxophonist, Bandleader

John Coltrane was the last great innovator in jazz to profoundly influence the course of the music. He played first clarinet, then alto saxophone in high school in his native North Carolina. After graduating, he moved to Philadelphia and continued to study music, winning several scholarships. After playing in a Navy band in Hawaii, he started his professional career with rhythm-and-blues bands, joining Dizzy Gillespie's big band (on alto) in 1949. When Dizzy broke up the band in 1951 and scaled down to a sextet, he had Coltrane switch to tenor sax and kept him with him. After stints with two great but very different alto saxophonists, Earl Bostic and Johnny Hodges, Coltrane was hired by Miles Davis in 1955. At first, some musicians and listeners didn't care for what they felt was Coltrane's "harsh" sound, but as the Davis Quintet became the most popular jazz group of its day, Coltrane was not only accepted but began to influence younger players. He briefly left Davis in 1957 to work with Thelonious Monk, an important relationship in developing what already was a highly original style. Back with Miles, he participated in the great *Kind Of Blue* record dates, and Miles' experiments with modal improvising set the stage for Coltrane's work as a leader.

In 1959, while still with Miles, he composed and recorded "Giant Steps," a piece so harmonically intricate and fast that it staggered most of his fellow saxophonists. With his own group, now including pianist McCoy Tyner, bassist Jimmy Garrison and drummer Elvin Jones, he recorded the song "My Favorite Things" from the musical and film *The Sound of Music*, in a performance that featured his soprano sax and lasted more than fifteen minutes, in 1960. This became such a hit with the jazz audience that it sustained Coltrane's popularity even when he began to experiment with very demanding music. The quartet became one of the most tightly knit groups in jazz history; the empathy between Coltrane and Elvin Jones was astonishing, and in their live performances, the four musicians would sometimes play for more than an hour, creating music so intense that some listeners likened it to a religious experience.

Coltrane was himself a deeply spiritual man. One of his masterpieces, the suite "A Love Supreme," was his

John Coltrane

offering to the Lord, and he wrote a poem to accompany the music. The quartet's live recordings at the Village Vanguard and Birdland also became instant classics, and Coltrane was regarded as the leading figure of the 1960s jazz avant garde, a position he himself did not seek, and which caused him (he was a very kind man who found it hard to say "no") to be surrounded, in the final stages of his life, by players who looked for exposure on his coat tails. The quartet broke up in 1966, and Coltrane searched for new roads of expression, never satisfied with his work at any given time in his career. His death at forty-one, of liver cancer, came as a shock to the jazz world. Since then, no comparably influential figure has come along, and Coltrane (or just "Trane," as he was known to many) has become a legend whose influence continues, though few have attempted to follow him into the uncharted realms of his final years, when he stretched both the physical and mental limits of what it was possible to do on a horn.

Miles Davis (1926-1991)
Trumpeter, Bandleader

Miles Davis played a major role in the transition from the hard, aggressive stance of Bop to the softer, more subtle side of jazz. As a teenage musician in St. Louis in the early 1940s, Davis sat in with his idols Charlie Parker and Dizzy Gillespie when they passed through town with the Billy Eckstine Band. In 1945, his well-to-do dentist father sent Davis to the Juilliard School of Music in New York. Within a short time, Davis was working the 52nd Street clubs with Parker and Coleman Hawkins, and touring with the bands of Billy Eckstine and Benny Carter.

In 1949, Davis formed a nine-piece band, including Lee Konitz, Gerry Mulligan, John Lewis, and Max Roach. The group was short lived, but its recordings had great impact on musicians and defined "cool" jazz. Success came in 1956, the year after Davis had formed a quintet with John Coltrane featured on tenor sax, and the year in which he made his first record with arranger Gil Evans, "Miles Ahead." This was followed by two other collaborations with Evans, "Porgy and Bess" and "Sketches Of Spain," both landmarks in jazz. In 1958, came *Kind Of Blue*, an album by a new sextet, still with Coltrane, but with Cannonball Adderley added on alto sax and Bill Evans on piano. This album established modal improvisation in jazz and set the stage for Coltrane's explorations on his own.

Davis continued to introduce new ideas and give exposure to new talent. By 1964, he had Wayne Shorter on saxophones, Herbie Hancock on piano, Ron Carter on bass and the sensational 18-year-old Tony Williams on drums. This was a group that introduced new ideas, mostly in the realm of rhythmic and harmonic freedom. However, in 1968 Davis got restless again, attracted by the possibilities of electronic instruments. Hancock, Chick Corea, Joe Zawinul and Keith Jarrett were among the keyboard players who contributed to the new stage of Miles, starting with the album *Bitches Brew*.

Some of his many fans, and quite a few musicians, did not care for this new Miles, but characteristically, he couldn't have cared less. Going his own way, he gradually moved further away from jazz into contemporary black pop music, or rather, an unclassifiable and frequently changing music that appealed to a young audience not much interested in jazz. In the late 1970s, Miles became a cult figure, and his famous reserve (he had long been known for not acknowledging applause, walking off the stand when he wasn't playing, and being a difficult interview subject) was replaced by a new open manner that included smiling, waving to the audience and even shaking hands with those nearest the stage, and giving frequent and amiable interviews.

But those who saw Miles as a jazz star lost to pop didn't listen to his trumpet. No matter what the setting, it always spoke the language of jazz, creating beautiful sounds and melodies.

Miles Davis

Eric Dolphy (1928-1964)
Alto Saxophonist, Clarinetist, Flutist

Eric Dolphy is greatly admired by musicians. Although his linear derivations were from Charlie Parker, his attack on alto sax and bass clarinet had a fierce bite that sprang from earlier jazz. His mastery of the bass clarinet has never been equaled.

Born in Los Angeles in 1928, his first recognition came with the Chico Hamilton quintet of 1958 to 1959. In 1960, he joined Charles Mingus in New York, and in 1961

he played many club dates with trumpeter Booker Little before joining John Coltrane for some historic tours, concerts, and recordings. Dolphy also played in a group with trumpeter Freddie Hubbard and recorded with Ornette Coleman. In 1964, while on tour again with Mingus, he decided to stay in Europe, where he recorded with Dutch, Scandinavian, and German rhythm sections. He died suddenly in Berlin of a heart attack possibly brought on by diabetes.

Dolphy was the winner of *Down Beat* magazine's

New Star award for alto, flute, and miscellaneous instruments in 1961, and was elected to that magazine's Hall of Fame in 1965. His legacy includes many recordings for Prestige, Blue Note, Impulse, and smaller companies, both as leader and sideman. Charles Mingus said of Dolphy that he had the "great capacity to talk in his music ... he knew the level of language which very few musicians get down to."

Roy "Little Jazz" Eldridge (1911-1989)
Drummer, Trumpeter, Singer

Born in Pittsburgh in 1911, Roy Eldridge played his first "job" at the age of seven on drums. When he was fifteen and had switched to trumpet, he ran away from home with a carnival band. After playing with some of the best bands in the Midwest, he arrived in New York in 1931, impressing the locals with his speed and range and finding jobs with good bands. But it wasn't until 1935 with Teddy Hill, that he could be heard on records. By the next year, he was the star of Fletcher Henderson's band, and in 1937, he put together his own group and made some records that stood other trumpeters on their ears. One of them was young Dizzy Gillespie, who had been listening to Roy on the radio since 1935 and tried his best to copy him. By 1938, Roy was setting the pace for swing trumpeters, playing higher and faster than even Louis Armstrong had dared anyone to do, and making musical sense as well. The fact that he was also a good singer didn't hurt.

In 1941, Roy, now known in the world of music as "Little Jazz," took up an offer from drummer Gene Krupa to join his big band, thus becoming the first black musician to be featured in a white band not just as a special attraction (like Teddy Wilson and Lionel Hampton with the Benny Goodman Quartet, though Hamp sometimes took over the drum chair in the Goodman band as well) but as a member of the band's section. Duetting with girl singer Anita O'Day, Roy scored a smash hit for Krupa with "Let Me Off Uptown," while his instrumental feature "Rockin' Chair" was hailed as a jazz classic. Roy led his own big band for a while, but joined Artie Shaw, another white band, in 1944. A brief stint with his own big band followed, but small groups proved more viable. By 1949, Roy was a star of "Jazz At The Philharmonic," a touring concert group of famous players including, at that time, Charlie Parker, Lester Young and Buddy Rich. An offer to tour with a Benny Goodman small group brought him to Paris, where he stayed for a year and regained his confidence, a bit shaken by the advent of bebop and the trumpet innovations of his former disciple Gillespie. (Rivalry aside, the two always remained good friends and often recorded together.)

The 1950s and 1960s saw a long association with Coleman Hawkins; the two went together like ham and eggs. During this time Roy also backed Ella Fitzgerald and toured with JATP. A full decade, from 1970 on, found Little Jazz leading the house band at Jimmy Ryan's club in New York City, but a heart attack in 1980 put an end to his trumpet playing, though he still worked occasionally as a singer and gave lectures and workshops on jazz. He died in 1989. Roy Eldridge comprised, in his music and personality, the essence of jazz as a music that comes straight from, and goes straight to, the heart and soul.

Edward Kennedy "Duke" Ellington (1899-1975)
Bandleader, Composer, Pianist

Edward Kennedy Ellington, nicknamed Duke in his teens for his dapper dress style and courtly manners, was born into a middle-class family in Washington, DC, on April 29, 1899. After graduating from high school, he was offered an art scholarship at Pratt Institute in New York, but he already had a taste of bandleading and preferred to stay with music. He had some success in his hometown, mainly because he had the biggest band advertisement in the telephone book, but by 1923 he felt the urge to go to New York—where careers were made. He didn't succeed at first (he later said that he and his friends were so broke they had to split a hot dog three ways), but by 1924 he was leading his Washingtonians at a Broadway nightclub and making his first records. That early band was only five pieces, but it had grown to ten by the time the young pianist-composer opened at the Cotton Club, the most famous Harlem night spot.

Here the unique Ellington style evolved during a five-year stay. Unlike most other bands, Duke's played almost only his own music, though a few pop tunes were occasionally thrown into their sets, and also unlike most other bands, Duke kept the same players with him once he'd decided that he liked what they could do. He had a great sense for their potential—almost like a great coach knows how to develop an athlete's skills—and some of Duke's bandsmen stayed with him for decades (none longer than baritone saxophonist Harry Carney, in the band from 1927 until the end). Many became stars in their own right (Johnny Hodges, alto sax; Cootie Williams, trumpet; Barney Bigard, clarinet) but somehow they always sounded better with Ellington, who knew just what to write for what he called their "tonal personalities." Ellington's scoring for the band was also strictly his own, and other arrangers found it hard to copy him.

By 1933, Ellington was ready for his first European tour; performing in London and Paris, the band, whose many recordings had prepared the way, was enthusiastically received. Back home, the band had already appeared in films and soon made more; they had long been well-exposed on radio and on records (Ellington was among the first musicians to truly understand the importance of records, and the fact that making good ones required something different than playing in public). In 1935, deeply touched by the death of his mother, Ellington composed "Reminiscing in Tempo," his longest work to date, but most of his output was tailored to the time limit of a little over three minutes imposed by the 78 rpm technology.

The band reached a first peak in 1940, when almost all of the musicians had been aboard for many years, though the two exceptions, tenor Ben Webster and bassist Jimmy Blanton, who both joined in 1939, were of key importance to the music. So was a third newcomer, who didn't play in the band but quickly became essential to Ellington as an associate composer-arranger; this was Billy Strayhorn (1915-1967), who would spend the rest of his life with Duke and his men. A second peak was reached in 1956, when the band gave a tremendous performance at the Newport Jazz Festival, which fortunately was recorded; the album, highlighted by "Crescendo and Diminuendo In Blue," featuring twenty-seven choruses by tenorman Paul Gonsalves, became the best-selling Ellington record of all (and Duke made more records than any other jazz artist). It was Duke's success as a composer of popular songs that allowed him to keep the big band going through five decades; among them are "Solitude," "Mood Indigo," "Sophisticated Lady," "Satin Doll," and "Don't Get Around Much Any More." All began as instrumentals. Ellington's major longer works include "Black, Brown and Beige," "Harlem," "Such Sweet Thunder," and "Far East Suite," the last two in collaboration with Strayhorn.

Ellington and his astonishing creations have been an inspiration to generations of musicians, most recently to Wynton Marsalis, who both in his own composing and in his efforts to get Ellington's music performed live (as with the Lincoln Center Jazz Ensemble) has done much to keep the Elllington legacy in the forefront of American music. There can be no doubt that Duke Ellington (who was also a brilliant pianist) will stand as one of the greatest composers of the 20th century. He died on May 24, 1975.

James Reese Europe (1881-1919)
Bandleader

James Resse Europe was born in Mobile, Alabama in 1881, but later moved to New York. In 1906 he organized the New Amersterdam Musical Association and in 1910 formed the Clef Club orchestra. During World War I, Europe directed the 369th Infantry Regimental Band,

which performed throughout France and was a major force in the development of jazz in that country. Following his return to the United States, Europe toured the country with his band. In 1919 he was stabbed to death by a member of his band while on tour.

Ella Fitzgerald (1918-1996)
Singer

Born in 1918, Ella Fitzgerald has emerged as the top female vocalist in virtually every poll conducted among jazz musicians and singers. No other vocalist has been so unanimously acclaimed. Fondly known as "The First Lady of Song," she has been the leading jazz interpreter of popular song for more than 50 years.

Discovered in 1934 by drummer-band leader Chick Webb at an amateur contest at Harlem's Apollo Theater in New York City, she cut her first side with Webb a year later. In 1938, she recorded "A Tisket, A Tasket," a novelty number that brought her commercial success and made her name widely known among the general public. Among musicians, however, her reputation rests on her singular ability to use her voice like an instrument, improvising effortlessly in a style filled with rhythmic subtleties. The entertainer also appeared in several

James Reese Europe

Ella Fitzgerald

films in her career, including *Ride 'Em Cowboy* 1940, *Pete Kelly's Blues* (1955), *St. Louis Blues* (1958), and *Let No Man Write My Epitaph* (1960).

In the 1990s, Fitzgerald remained beloved by her fans. Much of her work was reissued or commemorated in the boxed sets *75th Birthday Celebration: The Original Decca Recordings* and *The Complete Ella Fitzgerald Song Books*. In 1995, Fitzgerald was inducted into the National Women's Hall of Fame.

Other honors Fitzgerald has garnered throughout her career include 14 Grammys, Kennedy Center Honors (1979), Whitney Young Award (1984), National Medal of Arts (1987), Commander of Arts and Letters (France, 1990), Cole Porter Centennial Award (1991), Medal of Freedom (1992), and several honorary degrees from such institutions as Dartmouth, Harvard, Princeton, and Yale universities. In 1974, the University of Maryland named its performing arts school after her.

Since the 1970s she had been in steadily declining health and had been hospitalized for various ailments. In 1933, her legs were amputated below the knees as the result of complications from diabetes. Ella Fitzgerald died on June 15, 1996.

Tommy Flanagan (1930 -)
Pianist

Born in Detroit in 1930, Tommy Flanagan came to New York in the mid-1950s as part of the "Motor City" invasion of gifted jazzmen (fellow pianist Barry Harris; trumpeters Thad Jones and Donald Byrd; guitarist Kenny Burrell, etc.) and soon was much in demand for recordings and "live" dates with all the great names in modern jazz. A long stint as Ella Fitzgerald's accompanist and musical director (a role he also filled, much more briefly, with Tony Bennett) kept Flanagan out of the limelight, but since the mid-1970s, as leader of his own fine trios and recording prolifically in the United States, Europe and Japan, he has assumed his rightful place as one of the greatest living masters of jazz piano, his touch alone a thing of beauty.

Erroll Garner (1921-1977)
Pianist, Composer

A keyboard artist who played and composed by ear in the tradition of the founding fathers of jazz, Erroll Garner won the international acclaim of jazz lovers, music critics, and the general public. Strong and bouncy left-hand rhythms and beautiful melodies are the trademarks of his extremely enjoyable music. He was the best-selling jazz pianist in the world.

Born in Pittsburgh in 1921, Garner grew up in a musical family and began picking out piano melodies before he was three years old. He started taking piano lessons at six, but his first and only piano teacher gave up on him when she realized he was playing all his assignments by ear instead of learning to read notes. At seven, he began playing regularly on Pittsburgh radio station KDKA. He dropped out of high school to play with a dance band and first came to New York in 1939 as an accompanist for nightclub singer Ann Lewis. In 1946, he recorded "Laura," which sold a half million copies, and his fame began to grow. On March 27, 1950 he gave a solo recital at Cleveland's Music Hall, and in December a concert at New York's Town Hall. Gradually recitals and recording sessions took precedence over nightclub performances.

Garner's most famous composition, "Misty" was a big hit for Johnny Mathis and Sarah Vaughan. His unique piano style has often been copied but never equaled.

Dizzy Gillespie (1917-1993)
Trumpeter, Bandleader

Dizzy Gillespie and Charlie Parker were the co-founders of the most revolutionary movement in jazz during

Dizzy Gillespie

the 1940s—the phenomenon known as Bop. The role which each played in this revolution has been a subject of considerable debate. Billy Eckstine, whose band at one time included both Gillespie and Parker, defined Parker's role more as instrumentalist, and Gillespie's more as writer and arranger. Whatever their particular contributions were, however, it cannot be disputed that the sum total of their ideas brought about a change in jazz which continues to the present time.

Gillespie received his early musical training in his native South Carolina, and after moving to Philadelphia in 1935 and gaining more professional experience there, joined the Teddy Hill band where he replaced his early idol Roy Eldridge.

Gillespie toured Europe with Hill in 1939, and when he returned to New York to play with Cab Calloway, his bop experimentation was already beginning to develop and his career as arranger began. After working with Ella Fitzgerald, Benny Carter, Charlie Barnet, Earl Hines, and others, he joined Eckstine's band in 1944 and started his own jazz band the next year. Gillespie toured Europe, the Middle East, and Latin America with big bands and quintets, subsidized by the United States

State Department. He became a revered elder statesman of jazz.

Dexter Gordon (1923-1989)
Saxaphonist, Bandleader

Born in Los Angeles on February 27, 1923, the son of a prominent physician whose patients included famous jazz musicians, Dexter Gordon joined Lionel Hampton's newly formed big band in 1940. He was with Louis Armstrong in 1944, and later that year joined the Billy Eckstine Band. After freelancing in New York, he returned home and in 1946 recorded a "tenor battle," "The Chase," with Wardell Gray, which became one of the biggest modern jazz hits. He then teamed up with Gray on and off until 1952, after which he temporarily disappeared from the jazz spotlight.

Gordon made a major comeback in the early 1960s with a series of much-acclaimed recordings. In 1962, he settled in Copenhagen, and the Danish capital became his headquarters for the next fourteen years, though he made brief playing visits to his homeland. In 1977, he came home for good, forming his own group and winning many new fans. In 1986, he starred in the French feature film *Round Midnight*, in which his portrayal of a

Dexter Gordon

character based on Lester Young and Bud Powell won him an Oscar nomination as best actor. In 1988, he began work on an autobiography.

Dexter Gordon was the premier tenor saxophone stylist of bebop, but his strong, swinging music transcends categories. He greatly influenced the young John Coltrane.

Johnny Griffin (1928-)
Saxophonist

Johnny Griffin was born in Chicago in 1928 and played with most of the prominent jazz personalities over the years. Among them have been Lionel Hampton, Art Blakey, Thelonious Monk, and Eddie Lockjaw Davis. Griffin, like many Chicago musicians, preferred to stay and play in the Windy City, and much of his early development took place there. In December 1962, he moved to Europe and played all over the continent. He lived in Paris in the late 1960s and later moved to the Netherlands, where he owned a farm. In the late 1970s, Griffin moved back to the United States, celebrating the occasion with outstanding concerts and recordings with his friend Dexter Gordon.

Buddy Guy (1936-)
Guitarist

For the generation of British rock guitarists—Eric Clapton, Jeff Beck, Keith Richards, et. al.—who learned

their licks listening to blues in the early 1960s, Buddy Guy was the real thing. Although it was not until the 1990s that his playing was adequately captured on tape, Guy represents a direct link between the earlier generation of Chicago bluesman that included his mentor, Muddy Waters, and the crop of blues and rock guitarists, black and white, that dominates the genre to this day.

Born in Lettsworth, Louisiana, Guy began banging on acoustic guitars as a teenager, emulating the work of southern bluesmen Lightnin' Slim and Guitar Slim. He left the South for Chicago in 1957, and quickly made his mark on the local club scene. Before Guy's arrival, blues guitarists usually played sitting down. Guy would not only play standing, but would throw chairs off the stage, abuse his guitar, and wander outside with the aid of a 150-foot cord. Guy was quickly picked up as a sideman by Waters. Other blues legends he backed included Howlin' Wolf, Sonny Boy Williamson, and Little Walter.

Guy made his first album, *A Man & the Blues*, in 1968, but the recording failed to capture the excitement of his live performances. He recorded sparingly for the next 20 years. As a live act, however, he became a legend, both in the clubs of Chicago and at festivals around the world. In the 1970s Guy began his long and successful collaboration with harmonica player Junior Wells.

In 1983 Guy opened his own blues club, the Checkerboard Lounge, on Chicago's South Side. He sold the Checkerboard in 1985, then opened another club called Buddy Guy's Legends in 1989. In 1986 Eric Clapton stated that "Buddy Guy is by far and without a doubt the best guitar player alive." Apparently a lot of people believed him, because Guy's 1991 CD *Damn Right I've Got the Blues* sold some 600,000 copies and won a Grammy. His next album, *Feels Like Rain*, won a Grammy as well. By the mid-1990s, Guy could longer realistically be called the world's greatest *unknown* guitarist.

Lionel Hampton (1909-)
Vibraphonist, Pianist, Bandleader

Born on April 12, 1912 in Louisville, Kentucky, Lionel Hampton was the first jazz musician to feature the vibes, an instrument which has since come to play a vital role in jazz. His first recorded effort on the instrument was in 1930, on "Memories of You," which featured Louis Armstrong, then fronting the Les Hite band in California. Hampton later left Hite's band to form his own Los Angeles group. When Benny Goodman heard him in 1936, he used him on a record date with Teddy Wilson and Gene Krupa, and then persuaded him to join on a permanent basis.

Lionel Hampton and his orchestra.

Hampton played with the Goodman Quartet until 1940, the year he formed his own big orchestra. The following year, it scored its first big hit: "Flyin' Home." Hampton has enjoyed great success since then. In 1981, he became a professor of music at Howard University, but he continued to tour the world even after passing his 80th birthday in 1989. Dozens of musicians who later became famous started in his band. In 1995, many of them came together to perform a tribute to the former United Nations ambassador of music at the Kennedy Center Concert Hall.

Herbie Hancock (1940-)
Keyboardist, Composer, Bandleader

Herbie Hancock was born in Chicago on April 12, 1940, and has notably been associated with the piano, although he has also turned to electronics as a vehicle of communication in his music: electric guitar, electric bass, electric piano, echoplex, phase shifter, and synthesizer. From 1963 to 1968, he traveled and played with Miles Davis, establishing himself as a composer and instrumentalist of the first rank. While with Davis, Han-

cock recorded with numerous other groups and became firmly established as a major jazz figure.

In the 1990s, has remained in the spotlight. He briefly reunited with bassist Ron Carter, drummer Tony Williams, and saxophonist Wayne Shorter—the line up on Davis's 1965 *E.S.P.* recording—to release *A Tribute to Miles* and tour. He also lent a hand to the 1994 AIDS benefit album, *Stolen Moments: Red, Hot + Cool.* Earlier in the year he headlined the New Orleans Jazz and Heritage Festival and cohosted the PBS *Great Performances* installment "Carnegie Hall Salutes the Jazz Masters."

Hancock has won Grammys both for jazz composition and rhythm and blues performance. He also picked up a handful of MTV Video Music Awards for the video tied to his 1984 hit "Rockit." Hancock received an Academy Award for best original score in 1986 for his work on the film *'Round Midnight.*

William Christopher Handy (1873-1958)
Trumpeter, Composer, Bandleader

Although he began as a cornetist and bandleader in the 1890s, W.C. Handy's fame as the "Father of the

Herbie Hancock

Blues" rests almost entirely on his work as a composer. Handy was born on November 16, 1873, in Florence, Alabama. After studying at Kentucky Musical College, Handy toured with an assortment of musical groups, becoming the bandmaster of the Mahara Minstrels in 1896.

In 1909, during a political campaign in Memphis, Handy wrote "Mr. Crump," a campaign song for E.H. "Boss" Crump. Three years later, the song was published as the "Memphis Blues."

In 1914, Handy published his most famous song, "St. Louis Blues," and that same year, also wrote "Yellow Dog Blues." Others which have become perennial favorites are "Joe Turner Blues" (1915), "Beale Street Blues" (1916); "Careless Love" (1921); and "Aunt Hagar's Blues" (1922).

In the 1920s, Handy became a music publisher in New York. Despite his failing sight, he remained active until his death on March 29, 1958. His songs extended beyond the world of jazz to find their way into the general field of popular music in many forms. Their popularity continues unabated today.

Coleman Hawkins (1904–1969)
Saxophonist

With the position occupied by the tenor saxophone in jazz today, it is difficult to imagine that until Coleman "Bean" Hawkins came along, this instrument was not seriously considered as a suitable jazz vehicle. The full, rich tone which Hawkins brought to the tenor has helped make it one of the most vital instruments in the contemporary jazz ensemble.

Hawkins was born on November 21, 1904, in St. Joseph, Missouri. When Hawkins took up the tenor at the age of nine, he had already had four years of training on piano and cello. He continued his studies at Washburn College in Topeka, Kansas and in 1922 toured with Mamie Smith's Jazz Hounds. In 1924, he began a ten-year stint with Fletcher Henderson's band.

Hawkins left Henderson in 1934 to tour England and the continent, recording with Django Reinhardt, Benny Carter, and others. When he returned to the United States in 1939, he recorded his biggest hit, "Body and Soul," with his own band.

William Christopher Handy

Unlike many of his contemporaries, Hawkins was open to the experimentation of the young musicians of the 1940s. In 1944, for example, he formed an all-star band for the first Bop record session, and he gave help and encouragement to Dizzy Gillespie, Charlie Parker, Thelonious Monk and others he admired. Hawkins died on May 19, 1969.

With the advent of the "cool school," Hawkins lapsed into temporary decline, but the power of his style was recognized anew and he became a revered elder statesman of jazz.

Roy Haynes (1925–)
Drummer, Bandleader

Boston-born Roy Haynes (b. 1925) is one of the originators and greatest exponents of modern jazz drumming. Turning pro in his late teens, he went on the road with Luis Russell's big band, then joined Lester Young's sextet, with which he established his reputation. Settling in New York, he worked with Charlie Parker and Dizzy Gillespie, then toured for several years in Sarah Vaughan's trio.

Other important associations include Stan Getz, Gary Burton, Thelonious Monk and John Coltrane, for whom he was first choice when Elvin Jones was unavailable. Haynes recorded prolifically with these and many others, also as leader of his own groups, known from the 1980s on as the "Hip Ensemble." Haynes is both a fantastic soloist and a great, creative ensemble drummer. His foot is arguably the fastest ever, and his playing has an elegance that is reflected in his stylish appearance—he was once chosen by *Esquire* magazine as one of America's 10 best-dressed men. Never out of date, Haynes in his sixties teamed up with such modernists as Pat Metheny and Chick Corea, and always picks young players for his group.

Fletcher Henderson (1897–1952)
Bandleader, Arranger, Piano

Born in Cuthbert, Georgia, on December 18, 1897, Fletcher Henderson came to New York in 1920 to study chemistry, but took a job to earn some extra money as house pianist and musical director for Black Swan, the first black-owned and operated record company. Chemistry soon took a back seat, and in 1924 he was persuaded by some of his recording studio colleagues to audition with a band for a new club. They got the job, and soon graduated to the Roseland Ballroom on Broadway, where they resided for eight years, also touring and making hundreds of records.

The Henderson band was the first big band to play interesting jazz, and it became an incubator for some of the greatest stars of the day, among them Louis Arm-

The Fletcher Henderson Orchestra, 1927.

strong, Coleman Hawkins and Benny Carter. It was the arranger and saxophonist Don Redman who shaped the band's early style. When he left in 1928, Carter and others, including Fletcher's younger brother Horace, also a pianist and arranger, took over. It was not until 1933 that Fletcher himself began to write full-time for his band, but he had such a talent for arranging that he soon became one of the architects of swing. Ironically, just as he hit his stride as a writer, his band fell on hard days, and for a brief while he gave it up and became a freelance arranger, contributing mightily to the library of the newly formed Benny Goodman Band.

Though Henderson took up leading again soon and had such greats as Ben Webster and Roy Eldridge in his bands, he never again achieved the success of the 1920s. He died on December 29, 1952.

Joe Henderson (1937-)
Saxophonist, Composer

Born in 1937, one of the foremost tenor stylists of the post-Coltrane era, Joe Henderson studied music at Wayne State University in Detroit, where he played with visiting stars like Sonny Stitt and had his own first group in 1960. After military service, he came to New York

where he co-led a band with trumpeter Kenny Dorham, then joined Horace Silver in 1964, and Herbie Hancock in 1969. Since the 1970s, he has led his own groups and continued to develop an original and ultimately influential solo style.

Winner of a Grand Prix du Disque in 1981, Henderson won a Grammy Award in 1992 for his fine album of Billy Strayhorn compositions called *Lush Life.* and another for 1993's *So Near, So Far*. The latter was also deemed jazz record of the year by *Village Voice* and *Billboard*. *Billboard* considered Henderson the jazz artist of the year. In 1994 *Joe Henderson: The Milestone Years*, an eight-CD boxed set was released. He went on to open the 1995 JVC Jazz Festival.

Earl "Fatha" Hines (1903-1983)
Pianist, Bandleader

Except for increased technical proficiency, the piano style of Earl "Fatha" Hines has barely changed from what it was in the late 1920s.

Born on December 28, 1903 in Duquesne, Pennsylvania, and hailing from a Pittsburgh background musically rounded out by his trumpeter father and organist mother, Hines originally planned a concert career, but was soon caught up in the world of jazz. Forming his own trio while still in high school. he began to play in local clubs before moving on to Chicago in 1925.

While there, he made a brilliant series of records with Louis Armstrong's Hot Five, and soon became known as "the trumpet-style pianist." The intricacy of his style was well beyond that of his contemporaries, but served as a touchstone for a successive generation of pianists.

In 1928, Hines formed his own band at the Grand Terrace in Chicago. For the next twenty years, this band served as a proving ground for many great instrumentalists and innovators of the period (from Bud Johnson and Trummy Young in the early era to Dizzy Gillespie and Charlie Parker in the later years).

From 1948 to 1951, Hines worked again with Armstrong, then played a long engagement in San Francisco. In 1963, a New York recital revitalized his career, and he enjoyed great success in Europe, Japan, and at home until his death on July 22, 1983.

Milton J. "Milt" Hinton (1910-)
Bass

Milt Hinton was born in Vicksburg, Mississippi, in 1910, and is considered one of the greatest of bass players. He has played with many top jazz artists, including Cab Calloway, Count Basie, Louis Armstrong, Teddy Wilson, and Benny Goodman. Hinton has appeared in concerts throughout the world and on numerous television shows, and has made more records than any other jazz musician. He is also an accomplished photographer and writer, whose autobiography, *Bass Lines*, appeared in 1988. *Over Time: The Jazz Photographs of Milt Hinton* was published in 1992. In 1995, Hinton received two tributes, one from the New School for Social Research and the other from the 177-year-old collective, the Atlanta Jazz Party.

Billie Holiday (1915-1959)
Singer

Born in Baltimore, Maryland, on April 7, 1915, Billie Holiday, dubbed "Lady Day" by Lester Young, was one of the greatest jazz singers of all time.

While still a young girl, she moved to New York City, and in 1931 began her singing career in an assortment of Harlem night spots. In 1933, she cut her first sides with Benny Goodman, and from 1935 to 1939, established her reputation with a series of records made with Teddy Wilson. She also sang with the bands of Count Basie and Artie Shaw.

In such classic records as "Strange Fruit" and her own "God Bless the Child," she departed from popular material to score her greatest artistic triumphs, depicting the harsh reality of Southern lynchings and the personal alienation she had experienced.

Once addicted to drugs and alcohol, she had written in her 1956 autobiography, *Lady Sings the Blues*, "All dope can do for you is kill you—and kill you the long, slow, hard way." The subject of a feature film, several books, and videos, Billie Holiday is still a powerful force in music decades after her untimely death on July 17, 1959.

John Lee Hooker (1917-)
Blues Singer, Guitarist

John Lee Hooker was born in Clarksdale, Mississippi, on August 22, 1917. He first learned his "Delta licks" from his stepfather and his colleagues James Smith and Coot Harris. He travelled to Memphis, Cincinnati, and Detroit, where, in the mid-1940s, he cut a demo for distributor Bernie Besman.

"Boogie Chillen" and "Sally Mae," were on the first single he recorded for the Sensation label. It became a hit on the blues chart in 1949. He followed this record with "In the Mood for Love" and "Crawling King Snake" for Modern. During the folk movement of the later 1950s and early 1960s, Hooker's music flourished, and he was a favorite on the coffeehouse circuit. Hooker recorded for Vee Jay records from 1955 to 1964, under a number of pseudonyms, including Delta John, Johnny Lee, and Birmingham Sam and his Magic Guitar.

In the 1970s and 1980s, Hooker collaborated with other popular performers such as Canned Heat, Bonnie Raitt, and Van Morrison. He also appeared in the film *The Blue Brothers* starring Jim Belushi and Dan Ackroyd in 1980. Long recognized as one of the primary contributors to the blues genre, the prolific Hooker has made more than forty albums, many of which Chess Records has re-issued in the 1990s. Rhino released *The Ultimate Collection (1948-90)* in 1991. Hooker has received a wide range of recognition throughout his career, from the French Academie du Jazz Record Prix for Best Urban Blues Artist of 1968 to a Grammy in 1996 *Chill Out*, the best traditional blues recording of the previous year.

Howlin' Wolf (1910-1976)
Singer, Harmonica Player

Bluessinger and harmonica player Howlin' Wolf was born Chester Arthur Burnett in West Point, Mississippi, on June 10, 1910. He learned to play the harmonica from blues musician Sonny Boy Williamson and made his first recording in 1950; his baying style of singing won him the name Howlin' Wolf. His best known recordings

Billie Holiday

include, "Moanin' at Midnight," "Poor Boy," and "My Country Sugar Mama."

Jean-Baptiste "Illinois" Jacquet (1933-)
Saxophonist, Bandleader

Jean-Baptiste Jacquet was born in Broussard, Louisiana, on October 31, 1933, and raised in Texas. He began his career as an altoist but went on to contribute to making the tenor sax the most popular jazz horn; it was Lionel Hampton who made him switch to tenor when he joined the vibist's new big band in 1942. Soon thereafter, Jacquet recorded his famous solo on "Flyin' Home" and made both his own and the Hampton band's name.

After stints with Cab Calloway and Count Basie, Jacquet joined the Jazz at the Philharmonic touring group in which he starred in tenor "battles" with Flip Phillips and others. He soon formed his own swinging little band, and became a mainstay in the international jazz circuit, a position he still occupied in the early 1990s. He formed a fine big band in the 1980s which has toured Europe and recorded; the European tour and other incidents in Jacquet's life as a musician are part of the documentary film *Texas Tenor*, premiered at the 1992 JVC Jazz Festival.

Jacquet was one of the first to "overblow" the tenor sax, reaching high harmonics that were dismissed by some as a circus stunt but really got to audiences; eventually, of course, such overblowing became part and parcel of the instrument's vocabulary, as in the later work of John Coltrane and the style of David Murray. But Jacquet is also a warm ballad player, and first of all, one of the swingingest of tenormen.

Etta James (1938-)
Singer

Etta James was a child prodigy, singing gospel music on the radio in Los Angeles by the time she was five. As a teenager in the 1950s, she formed a singing group called The Creolettes with two friends. The trio was discovered by R&B star Johnny Otis in 1954. Otis changed the group's name to The Peaches, and took the girls on the road with him. The Peaches recorded their first song, "Roll with Me, Henry," the same year.

James scored her first hit, "Good Rocking Daddy," in 1955. The success of that record led to a tour with rock star Little Richard, and studio backup vocal jobs with the likes of Marvin Gaye, Minnie Riperton, and Chuck Berry. In the late 1950s, James signed with Chess, and cranked out ten chart-making hits between 1960 and 1963. In 1967 she switched to Alabama's Fame label, for which she recorded many of her biggest hits, including "I'd Rather Go Blind" and "Tell Mama."

Although successful on the R&B charts, James did not manage to catch on with white audiences in the 1960s. Back with Chess during the 1970s, James continued to record with moderate success in the gray region between blues, soul, R&B, and rock. After a recording lapse lasting for much of the 1980s, she recorded the album *The Seven Year Itch* for Island Records in 1988. Despite her inability to establish herself as a mainstream superstar, James was a major influence on many singers who did attain that status, including Diana Ross and Janis Joplin.

Skip James (1902-1969)
Singer, Guitarist, Songwriter

Although Skip James became much more popular during the blues revival of the mid-1960s than he had ever been before, it makes little sense to speak of his "rediscovery." The fact is, he had barely been discovered in the first place. Nehemiah "Skip" James was born in 1902 in Bentonia, Mississippi, home to a thriving Delta blues tradition. His father, a Baptist minister, was competent on both organ and guitar. When James became interested in blues—an interest sparked primarily by local player Henry Stuckey—at about age seven, his father was happy to become his first guitar teacher.

In his teens, James moved to Memphis to play dance hall and barrelhouse music. He returned to Mississippi, settling in Jackson, in the 1920s. There his unique falsetto vocal stylings and from-the-heart presentation earned him regional fame. In 1931 James was brought North to record 26 songs for Paramount Records. Only a handful of the songs were ever released, and James gradually withdrew from performing.

By the 1940s, James was out of the music business. In addition to becoming an ordained minister, he worked at a variety of nonmusic jobs during the next couple of decades. He was "rediscovered" from out of nowhere by blues revivalists John Fahey and Bill Barth in 1964, and by the following year he was earning standing ovations at blues festivals from audiences larger than just about any he had played to in his prime. James' highly personal style had an air of untarnished authenticity, completely devoid of commercial awareness, that sat well with the folk purists who made up his new generation of fans.

J. J. Johnson (1924-)
Trombonist, Bandleader

Born in 1924, J. J. Johnson is the unchallenged master of the modern jazz trombone. He is the first musician to have adapted this instrument to the demanding techniques called for by the advent of Bop. Early in his career, Johnson displayed such skill in performing high-speed and intricate solos that those who knew him only from records found it hard to believe that he was actually using a slide—and not a valve—trombone.

Johnson spent the 1940s with the bands of Benny Carter, Count Basie, and Dizzy Gillespie. During the those years, his trombone was as widely imitated as the trumpet and alto of Gillespie and Parker. In the 1950s, Johnson retired for a time, only to return as partner of fellow trombonist Kai Winding's in the popular Jay and Kai Quintet.

Johnson's ability as a composer has been widely praised. In 1959, he performed several of his works with the Monterey Festival Orchestra. He has also composed for films and TV and has been active as a teacher. In 1995, *Down Beat* readers and critics alike voted him into the magazine's hall of fame.

James P. Johnson (1894-1955)
Pianist, Composer

James P. Johnson is less known than his most famous protege, Fats Waller, but he made a substantial contribution to the fields of jazz piano and popular show music. Johnson was born on February 1, 1891, in New Brunswick, New Jersey.

Johnson was the master of the "stride piano," an instrumental style which derives its name from the strong, striding, left hand of the player. "Stride piano" came into its own during the 1920s, particularly in conjunction with the phenomenon known as the "rent party." Such a party was held for the purpose of raising rent money, and involved the payment of an admission fee which entitled a patron to food, drink, conviviality, and a stride piano session. Duke Ellington and Count Basie were among the many who sharpened their skills in the rent party training ground.

Johnson was also an early bridge between the worlds of jazz and Broadway. Numbered among his song hits are "If I Could Be With You," "Charleston," and "Runnin' Wild." Johnson died on November 17, 1955.

Lonnie Johnson (1894-1970)
Guitarist, Singer

It would not be unreasonable to say that Lonnie Johnson was the single most influential guitar player in the history of blues. Johnson not only invented the guitar solo; he invented just about everything else a guitar does in blues. He also invented a fair amount of what the instrument does in jazz, country, and rock as well. B. B. King, Robert Johnson, Skip James, Charlie

Christian, and T-Bone Walker are but a few of the giants in their own right who have tipped their hats to Johnson.

Johnson was born in New Orleans, somewhere around 1894. By 1912 he was playing on the streets behind his father, a violinist. He began developing his unique jazzy style almost from the start. During World War I, Johnson played with a theater troupe that entertained Allied soldiers. In 1920, after 13 members of his family had died in an influenza epidemic, he moved to St. Louis, where he played in theaters and on riverboats. Johnson signed a recording contract with OKeh Records in 1925 after winning a blues contest, and quickly attained a sizable following among black buyers of OKeh's "race" records.

In addition to his blues work, Johnson played with a number of top jazz artists in the 1920s, including Louis Armstrong, Duke Ellington, and Eddie Lang. He also played behind several of the classic female blues singers over the next several years. Altogether, Johnson made about 130 recordings between 1925 and 1932. He moved around quite a bit, eventually settling in Chicago, where he began working the bustling nightclub scene in about 1937. During the 1940s and early 1950s, Johnson toured endlessly, both in the U.S. and abroad, and recorded regularly. A string of hits after World War II brought him a certain amount of fame.

In spite of his tremendous activity, however, Johnson never achieved major stardom. By the early 1950s, his career was going nowhere, and he took job at a Philadelphia hotel. He was rediscovered in 1960 by jazz scholar Chris Albertson, who arranged a new recording contract with the Prestige label. Although Johnson became quite popular with young white audiences in the United States and Europe during the blues revival of the 1960s, these listeners preferred the raw country blues of Skip James, Son House, et. al., and again major stardom eluded him. In 1969, Johnson was hit by a car, then suffered a stroke. He died the following year, not exactly in obscurity, but with little notice for someone with so great an impact on popular music.

Elvin Jones (1927-)
Drummer, Bandleader

The youngest of the remarkable Jones Brothers (see Hank Jones and Thad Jones) broke in with jazz bands in Detroit (near his native Pontiac, Michigan), came to New York in the 1950s, and worked with such notables as J. J. Johnson, Sonny Rollins, and Donald Byrd before joining John Coltrane's quartet in 1960.

With this group—the most influential of its time—Elvin Jones astonished musicians and listeners with his awesome independence of limbs (he can keep four rhythms going at once), amazing drive (nothing seemed able to tire him out, no matter how fierce the tempo), and ability to respond within mini-seconds to Coltrane's furious flow of ideas.

Elvin Jones left Coltrane when the saxophonist added another drummer to his group (no doubt influenced by his new wife, the pianist Alice McLeod) and soon led his own groups, which almost always have featured fine saxophonists; in 1992, Coltrane's son Ravi joined him. One of jazz's master drummers, Elvin Jones integrated the drums with the front-line (melody) players to a further extent than anyone had done before, always maintaining the pulse.

Hank Jones (1918-)
Pianist

The eldest of the three extraordinary Jones brothers (see Elvin Jones and Thad Jones) Hank was born in 1918, and raised near Detroit, where he began his professional career as a jazz musician. He came to New York City in 1944, and worked and recorded with the great trumpeter and singer Hot Lips Page. His brilliant keyboard technique and skill as both soloist and accompanist soon found him in the company of such giants as Coleman Hawkins and Charlie Parker. He toured with Jazz at the Philharmonic and became Ella Fitzgerald's accompanist.

Settling into studio work in New York, Hank Jones became one of the most-recorded jazz musicians—he is to piano what Milt Hinton and George Duvivier were to the bass—in all sorts of contexts. From the 1970s on, happily, Hank Jones began to do more work in clubs and on tour and to record more as a soloist and trio leader, often billed as "The Great Jazz Trio," with various star bassists and drummers. In the 1990s, Jones remained at the head of the pack when it comes to great jazz piano.

Thad Jones (1923-1986)
Cornetist, Composer, Arranger, Bandleader

The middle brother of the gifted Jones family (see Elvin Jones and Hank Jones), in his early teens Thad (1923-1986) played in a band led by brother Hank and in the early 1950s was in a band that included Elvin. Coming to New York in 1954, he was quickly discovered by Charles Mingus, who recorded him for his Debut label and hailed him as the greatest jazz trumpeter (but Thad always preferred the cornet) since Dizzy Gillespsie. Thad joined Count Basie's band that same year, staying for almost a decade. During this time he honed his writing skills, but wasn't heard as much in solo as Joe

Newman and other section-mates whose styles were not as harmonically advanced as Thad's. However, he did solo on Basie's biggest instrumental hit, "April In Paris."

In New York in 1963, Thad Jones joined forces with the great drummer Mel Lewis to co-lead what began as a rehearsal band but soon became the most talked-about new big band in jazz. As the Thad Jones-Mel Lewis Jazz Orchestra, it gave new life to the language of big-band jazz as Thad Jones blossomed as a composer and arranger of music that was swinging but fresh. Perhaps his best-known composition, however, is the beautiful ballad "A Child Is Born." The band held together until 1979, when Thad Jones moved to Denmark and Mel took over, keeping much of Thad's "book" alive. Thad led his own bands in Scandinavia, then came home briefly in 1985 to take on leadership of the Count Basie Band, returning to Denmark in ill health six months prior to his death in August 1986.

B. B. King (1925-)
Singer, Guitarist, Bandleader

B. B. King is one of the most successful artists in the history of the blues. Riley B. King was born in 1925 in Indianola, Mississippi. He was first exposed to the blues through an aunt who owned a phonograph. While a teenager, King purchased his first guitar for eight dollars-money he earned working in the cotton fields. At nineteen he hitchhiked to Memphis where a relative found him work performing at the 16th Street Grill. King was paid twelve dollars a night. He then found a spot on a newly opened radio station in Memphis called WDIA where he played for ten minutes each afternoon and later became a disc jockey. The station named him "The Boy from Beale Street" and thereafter he was known as B. B. King.

King's first record was made in 1949 for RPM. After the release of his 1969 single "The Thrill Is Gone," which received the first of King's nine Grammys, King won international success, influencing such artists as the Rolling Stones. In addition to an average of 250 performances around the world each year, King has opened two jazz clubs-one in Memphis and one in Universal City, California-and co-founded the Foundation for the Advancement of Inmate Recreation and Rehabilitation with lawyer F. Lee Bailey. King's many prestigious honors include an honorary doctorate from Yale University (1977), induction into the Rock & Roll Hall of Fame (1987), the Lifetime Achievement Award from the National Academy of Recording Arts and Sciences (1987), and the Presidential Medal of the Arts (1990). In 1995 King was one of the recipients of the Kennedy Center Honors.

B. B. King

Rahsaan Roland Kirk (1936-1977)
Composer, Flutist, Saxophonist

At first called "gimmicky" by critics, Roland Kirk proved to be one of the most exciting jazz instrumentalists. His variety of instruments was matched only by the range of his improvisational styles, often switching in the middle of a number from a dissonant exploration to a tonal solo based on a conventional melody.

Born in Columbus, Ohio, in 1936, Kirk was technically blind, having been able to see nothing but light from infancy. Educated at the Ohio State School for the Blind, he began picking up horns at the age of nine. At nineteen, while touring with Boyd Moore, he started experimenting with playing more than one instrument at a time. Finding obscure horns like the stritch and the manzello, he worked out a technique for playing three-part harmony through the use of false fingering.

In 1960, Ramsey Lewis helped Kirk get his first important recording date (with Argo Records). In 1961, he played with Charles Mingus' group, and later that year he went on the international circuit.

Among his many compositions are "Three for Dizzy"; "Hip Chops"; "The Business Ain't Nothin' but the Blues";

"From Bechet, Byas, and Fats"; and "Mystical Dreams". Kirk died in 1977.

John Lewis (1920-)
Pianist, Composer, Bandleader

John Lewis has become an international force in the world of jazz as an arranger, conductor, composer, and instrumentalist.

Raised in a middle-class environment in Albuquerque, New Mexico, Lewis studied music and anthropology at the University of New Mexico until 1942. After three years in the Army, he went to New York City and soon became pianist and arranger with Dizzy Gillespie's band. Two years later at Carnegie Hall, Gillespie's band performed Lewis' first major work, "Toccata for Trumpet and Orchestra."

After a European tour with Gillespie, Lewis returned to the United States to play with Lester Young and Charlie Parker, and to arrange for Miles Davis. In 1952, after having finished his studies at the Manhattan School of Music, Lewis founded the group upon which a major part of his reputation rested: The Modern Jazz Quartet (MJQ). Though it briefly disbanded in 1974, the MJQ was still together in 1993.

Lewis has never confined his creativity to the MJQ but has assumed a variety of roles, ranging from conducting in Europe and Japan to serving as music director of the highly acclaimed Monterey Jazz Festival.

Lightnin' Hopkins (1912-1982)
Singer, Guitarist

Sam "Lightnin" Hopkins was one of the most prolific blues artist of all time, both in the recording studio and on the stage. Inspired by Texas predecessor Blind Lemon Jefferson, Hopkins built his first guitar out of a cigar box and chicken wire at the age of eight. While still very young, he left home for a life on the road, singing and playing for change throughout Texas. After a time, he hooked up with Jefferson once again, serving for a spell as his guide and learning his musical licks.

During the late 1920s and much of the 1930s, Hopkins played the Houston bar circuit as a duo with his cousin, legendary Texas bluesman Texas Alexander. After working as a sharecropper near Dallas for a few years, he returned to Houston in 1946 and resumed his beer hall career with Alexander. He was soon discovered by a scout from Aladdin Records and teamed with Wilson "Thunder" Smith to create the duo "Thunder and Lightnin'." Hopkins went on to record more than 40 sides for Aladdin.

Although he made the R&B charts a few times in the early 1950s, Hopkins' popularity declined over the course of the decade. In 1959, however, he was rediscovered by folklorist Mack McCormick. Introduced to a new audience consisting largely of educated, liberal, white people, Hopkins was reinvented as a "blues legend," and he quickly attained a level of acclaim that had previously eluded him. Hopkins recorded and toured constantly across the U.S., Canada, and Europe throughout the 1960s and 1970s, and was featured in a number of books and film documentaries. He died of throat cancer in 1982.

Abbey Lincoln (1940-)
Singer

Born Anna Marie Wooldridge in Chicago, Lincoln graduated from Kalamazoo Central High School in Kalamazoo, Michigan, and later studied music for a number of years in Hollywood under several prominent vocal and dramatic coaches. She began her professional career in Jackson, Michigan, in 1950, after winning an amateur singing contest. After performing in nightclubs, she began recording in 1956. She performed variously as Anna Marie, Gabby Lee, and Aminata Moseka. Throughout the 1950s to 1960s, she sang in a group led by drummer Max Roach, whom she married in 1962; the couple divorced in 1970. Their *Freedom Suite* mingled social and political theory with jazz and entered strongly into the collective mindset of the civil rights motivated 1960s.

As a soloist, Lincoln toured in Africa, Asia, Europe, and the Far East, before becoming an assistant professor of African-American Theater and Pan-African Studies at California State University. Lincoln made several film appearances, including *The Girl Can't Help It* (1956), *Nothing But a Man* (1964), *For the Love of Ivy* (1968), *A Short Walk to Daylight* (1972), and director Spike Lee's *Mo' Better Blues* (1990). In 1975, she produced her own play, *A Pig in a Poke*. The "black Marilyn Monroe" was awarded by the Federation of Italian Filmmakers and the First World Festival of Negro Arts for her work in *Nothing But a Man*, and the All American Press Association called her the most prominent screen person of the year after her role in *For the Love of Ivy*. Lincoln was inducted into the Black Filmmakers Hall of Fame in 1975.

Just as imporantly, however, Lincoln has been hailed by many outstanding black jazz performers, including Coleman Hawkins, Benny Carter, and Charles Mingus, as a singer to be classed with the likes of Billie Holiday. Fairly inactive in the 1980s, Lincoln regained her prominence in the 1990s. In 1993, a television documentary entitled *You Gotta Pay the Band: The Words, the Music, and the Life of Abbey Lincoln* aired on PBS.

Melba Liston (1926-)
Arranger, Trombonist

Melba Liston, who has played with the greatest names in jazz, is one of the very few female trombonists. Liston was born in Kansas City, Missouri, in 1926, but her family later moved to California. Her musical history began in 1937, in a youth band under the tutelage of Alma Hightower. Ms. Liston continued her trombone studies, in addition to music composition, throughout high school. She got work with the Los Angeles Lincoln Theater upon graduation. She met band leader Gerald Wilson on the night club circuit, and he introduced her to Dizzy Gillespie, Count Basie, Duke Ellington, Charlie Parker, and many others. By the late 1940s, she was playing alongside John Coltrane and John Lewis in Dizzy's band, and later toured with Billie Holiday as her assistant musical director and arranger. When the Big Band era waned, Liston jumped off the music circuit and returned to California, where she passed a Board of Education examination and taught for four years. She was coaxed back into performing by Dizzy, and during the next twenty years, led an all-female jazz group, toured Europe with Quincy Jones, and did arrangements for Ellington, Basie, Dizzy and Diana Ross. In 1974, she went to Jamaica to explore reggae. When she returned to the United States in 1979, she formed Melba Liston and Company, in which she revived swing, bebop, and contemporary compositions, many of which were her own. She is regarded as a brilliant and creative arranger and an exceptional trombonist by her peers.

Jimmy Lunceford (1902-1947)
Bandleader

"The Lunceford style"—although its originator himself never played an instrument while recording with his band (except flute in his recording of "Liza")—was one which influenced many band leaders and arrangers up to the 1950s. The Lunceford band reigned with those of Duke Ellington, Count Basie, and Benny Goodman as the leading and most influential of the big jazz orchestras in the 1930s.

Born on June 6, 1902, in Fulton, Missouri, Lunceford received his B.A. at Fisk University and later studied at City College in New York. After having become proficient on all reed instruments, Lunceford began his career as a leader in Memphis in 1927. By 1934, he was an established presence in the field of jazz. During the next decade, the Lunceford band was known as the best-disciplined and most showmanly black jazz ensemble in the nation and featured a host of brilliant instrumentalists.

The Lunceford vogue faded after 1943, by which time the band was already experiencing charges in personnel. Lunceford died of a heart attack on July 13, 1947, while the band was on tour.

Branford Marsalis (1960-)
Saxophonist, Bandleader

14 months older than his brother Wynton, Branford has gained equal fame, not least due to his wide exposure as band leader for the *Tonight* show from 1992 to 1995. Branford was also been seen beyond the jazz arena during his mid-1980s touring stint with pop artist Sting. Marsalis's forays into acting have included parts in several feature films such as 1987's *Throw Momma From the Train,* and director Spike Lee's 1988 motion picture *School Daze.* Marsalis's quartet provided the music for Lee's *Mo' Better Blues* in 1990.

Branford Marsalis was born on August 26, 1960, in New Orleans. A very gifted player, he got his start as a member of Art Blakey's Jazz Messengers in 1980. From 1982 to 1985, he played in his brother Wynton's quartet. He has since performed with a multitude of artists, from Mile Davis and Dizzy Gillespie to Tina Turner and Public Enemy. An inventive soloist and an imaginative leader-organizer, Marsalis formed the group Buckshot LeFonque after leaving late night television. Marsalis won a Grammy in 1993, and has hosted *JazzSet* on National Public Radio.

Wynton Marsalis (1961-)
Trumpeter, Bandleader

Born on October 18, 1961, into a musical family in New Orleans— his father, Ellis Marsalis, is a prominent pianist and teacher and brothers Branford and Delfeayo are both musicians in their own right—Wynton Marsalis was well-schooled in both the jazz and classical traditions. At 17, he won an award at the prestigious Berkshire Music Center for his classical prowess; one year later, he left the Juilliard School of Music to join Art Blakey's Jazz Messengers.

After touring and recording in Japan and the United States with Herbie Hancock, he made his first LP in 1981, formed his own group and toured extensively on his own. Soon he made a classical album, and, in 1984, became the first instrumentalist to win simultaneous Grammy awards as best jazz and classical soloist, with many other awards, including more Grammys, to follow. He also received a great deal of media coverage-more than any other serious young musician in recent memory, helping to bring jazz back to prominence. He has composed music for films and ballet and cofounded the Lincoln Center Jazz Ensemble.

A brilliant virtuoso of the trumpet with total command of any musical situation he chooses to place himself in, Marsalis has also made himself a potent

Wynton Marsalis

spokesman for the highest musical standards in jazz, to which he is firmly and proudly committed. He has urged young musicians to acquaint themselves with the rich tradition of jazz and to avoid the pitfalls of "crossing over" to pop, fusion, and rock. His own adherence to these principles and his stature as a player has made his words effective. In 1994, the same year his septet disbanded, Marsalis published *Sweet Swing Blues on the Road*, a collection of essays about the jazz life. Not content with simply playing, Marsalis also teaches. He has instructed through the educational outreach program Project Discovery and at such places as the New England Conservatory of Music.

Carmen McRae (1922-1994)
Singer, Pianist

Born in Brooklyn on April 8, 1922, Carmen McRae's natural talent on the keyboards won her numerous music scholarships. During her teen years, she carefully studied the vocal style of Billie Holiday and incorporated it into her own style. An early highlight came when Holiday recorded "Dream of Life," one of McRae's compositions. After finishing her education, McRae moved to Washington, DC, and worked as a government clerk by day and a nightclub pianist/singer by night. In the early 1940s, she moved to Chicago to work with Benny Carter, Mercer Ellington and Count Basie. She recorded her first solo record in 1953. By 1954, she had gained enough attention through her jazz and pop recordings to be dubbed a "new star" by *Down Beat* magazine.

In 1967, McRae appeared in the film *Hotel*, thus beginning a string of periodic television and film appearances that extended into the 1980s, when she had a part in the 1986 film *Jo Jo Dancer, Your Life Is Calling*. McRae had a flurry of activity in the 1990s, recording six albums between 1990 and 1991 alone. *Carmen Sings Monk* was nominated for a Grammy Award. Several months before her death in 1994, McRae was honored with a National Endowment for the Arts American Jazz Masters Award, which bore a $20,000 prize. Later in the year, the acclaimed singer suffered a stroke that eventually led to her death on November 10.

Charles Mingus (1922-1979)
Bassist, Composer, Bandleader

Born on April 22, 1922, in Nogales, Arizona, Mingus grew up in the Watts area of Los Angeles. Starting on

Charles Mingus

trombone and cello, he settled on the bass and studied with Red Callender, a noted jazz player, and Herman Rheinschagen, a classical musician. He also studied composition with Lloyd Reese. Early in his professional career he worked with Barney Bigard in a band that included the veteran New Orleans trombonist Kid Ory, and toured briefly in Louis Armstrong's big band; he also led his own groups and recorded with them locally. After a stint in Lionel Hampton's band, which recorded his interesting composition "Mingus Fingus," he joined Red Norvo's trio, with which he came to New York in 1951.

Settling there, he worked with many leading players, including Dizzy Gillespie and Charlie Parker, and with Max Roach, he founded his own record label, Debut. He also formed his first of many so-called jazz workshops, in which new music, mostly written by himself, was rehearsed and performed. Mingus believed in spontaneity as well as discipline, and often interrupted public performances by his band if the playing didn't measure up. Some musicians refused to work with him after such public humiliations, but there were some who thought so well of what he was trying to do that they stayed with him for years. Drummer Dannie Richmond was with

Mingus from 1956 to 1970 and again from 1974 until the end; other longtime Mingusians include trombonist Kimmy Knepper, pianist Jaki Byard, and the saxophonists Eric Dolphy, Booker Ervin and John Handy in the earlier years; saxophonist Bobby Jones and trumpeter Jack Walrath, later on.

Mingus' music was as volatile as his temper, filled with ever-changing melodic ideas and textures and shifting, often accelerating, rhythmic patterns. He was influenced by Duke Elllington, Art Tatum and Charlie Parker, and his music often reflected psychological states and social issues—Mingus was a staunch fighter for civil rights, and wrote such protest pieces as "Fables of Faubus," "Meditations On Integration" and "Eat That Chicken." He was also steeped in the music of the Holiness Church ("Better Git It In Your Soul," "Wednesday Night Prayer Meeting") and in the whole range of the jazz tradition ("My Jelly Roll Soul," "Theme For Lester Young," "Gunslinging Bird," "Open Letter To Duke").

Himself a virtuoso bassist, he drove his sidemen to their utmost, often with vocal exhortations that became part of a Mingus performance. He composed for films and ballet and experimented with larger forms; his most ambitious work, an orchestral suite called "Epitaph," lasts more than two hours and was not performed in full until years after his death from amiotrophic lateral sclerosis, a disease with which he struggled valliantly—composing and directing (from a wheelchair) until almost the end. Though he was often in financial trouble and once was evicted from his home, he also received a Guggenheim fellowship in composition and was honored by President Carter at a White House jazz event in 1978.

At its best, Mingus' music—angry, humorous, always passionate—ranks with the greatest in jazz. He also wrote a strange but interesting autobiography, *Beneath the Underdog* (1971). A group, Mingus Dynasty, continued to perform his music into the 1990s, and in 1992, a Mingus Big Band performed weekly in New York City.

Thelonious Monk (1917-1982)
Pianist, Composer

A native of Rocky Mount, North Carolina, Thelonious Monk was born on October 10, 1917. Along with Charlie Parker and Dizzy Gillespie, Thelonious Monk was a vital member of the jazz revolution which took place in the early 1940s. Some musicians (among them Art Blakey) have said that Monk actually predated his more renowned contemporaries. Monk's unique piano style and his talent as a composer made him a leader in the development of modern jazz.

Thelonious Monk

Jelly Roll Morton

Aside from brief work with the Lucky Millender Band, Coleman Hawkins, and Dizzy Gillespie, Monk generally was leader of his own small groups. He has been called the most important jazz composer since Duke Ellington. Many of his compositions ("Round About Midnight", "Ruby My Dear") have become jazz standards.

Monk was unique as both an instrumentalist and composer, maintaining his own musical integrity and his melodic originality.

Thelonious Monk died in Englewood, New Jersey, on February 17, 1982.

Ferdinand "Jelly Roll" Morton (1890-1941)
Composer, Pianist, Bandleader

New Orleans-born, Morton (1890-1941) claimed (in 1938) that he had "invented" jazz in 1902. That was at the height of the Swing Era, and the few who remembered Morton paid little attention to his boast. However, it did sufficiently intrigue Alan Lomax, a folklorist at the Library of Congress, to lead to Morton's recording his life story, interspersed with fine piano playing, for Loma's archives. Morton was then living in Washington, D.C.,

managing an obscure night club. He had made his last commercial records in 1930.

But in the mid-1920s, Morton had made some wonderful records for Victor, the leading label of that day, under the name of Jelly Roll Morton and his Red Hot Peppers. Most were his own compositions, all were his arrangements, and they showed that he was a major talent, quite possibly the first real composer in jazz, if not the inventor of the music. The 1920s were the peak decade in Morton's up-and-down career. He was a much-in-demand pianist in his hometown while still in his teens, working in the Storyville "houses." Restless and ambitious, he hit the road, working in vaudeville, hustling pool, running gambling halls, occasionally playing piano, and traveling as far as Alaska and Mexico. He finally settled in Chicago in 1923, made his first records, worked for a music publisher, and let everybody know that he was the greatest.

In 1927 he moved to New York, still with a Victor contract but no longer doing as well, and when big band swing came to the fore, Jelly's career took a dive. But after the Library of Congress sessions, Victor was persuaded to record him again, and he was briefly back in the spotlight. Failing health and restlessness led him to drive to California, where he had a lady friend. But the trip made him ill, and he died in his 50th year, just before the revival of interest in traditional jazz, which would have given him the break he needed, got under way.

In 1992, a musical, *Jelly's Last Jam*, opened with great success on Broadway. It was loosely based on Morton's life and featured new arrangements of his music. If nothing else, it rekindled interest in that music, which, in the original recordings, still sounds almost as great as Jelly thought he was.

Theodore "Fats" Navarro (1923-1950)
Trumpeter

Fats Navarro was born in Key West, Florida, in 1923. He started on trumpet at age thirteen, and also played tenor sax. Navarro was first heard nationally as a member of Andy Kirk's band from 1943 to 1944 when Dizzy Gillespie recommended him to Billy Eckstine, with whom he played for eighteen months. From 1947 to 1948 Fats played with Illinois Jacquet, Lionel Hampton, and Coleman Hawkins. He also worked with Tadd Dameron in 1948 to 1949. Navarro, a victim of drug addiction, was ranked with Dizzy Gillespie and Miles Davis as one of the greatest modern jazz trumpeters. He died in 1950.

Joseph "King" Oliver (1885-1938)
Cornetist

Joe Oliver (1885-1938) first earned the sobriquet "King" in 1917 after establishing himself as the best performer against the likes of Freddie Keppard, Manuel Perez, and a host of other cornetists who filled the nights with the first sounds of New Orleans jazz. Oliver soon teamed up with Kid Ory and organized what was to become the leading jazz band in New Orleans.

During the Storyville era, Oliver met and befriended Louis Armstrong. Lacking a son of his own, he became Armstrong's "unofficial father," sharing with him the musical knowledge which he had acquired over the years. In return, Armstrong treated him with great respect, referring to him as "Papa Joe."

With the closing of Storyville, Oliver left and Armstrong replaced him in Ory's band. By 1922, however, Oliver was in a position to summon Armstrong to Chicago to play in his Creole Jazz Band as second cornetist. In 1923, the Creole Jazz Band made the first important recordings by a black jazz group.

The work of Oliver and Armstrong put Chicago on the jazz map of the United States. However, changing tastes caused Oliver's music to decline in popularity and by the time he moved to New York in 1928, his best years were behind him.

From 1932, Oliver toured mainly in the South before ill health forced him to give up music. He died in Savannah, Georgia, where he worked in a poolroom from 1936 until his death in 1938.

Edward "Kid" Ory (1886-1973)
Trombonist, Bandleader

Kid Ory's musical career is in many ways emblematic of the story of jazz itself. They both reached a high point in New Orleans during the first two decades of this century. They both moved north during the 1920s, only to lapse into obscurity in the 1930s before being revived in the next two decades.

Ory was born on Christmas Day, 1886, in La Place, Louisiana. He was the best known of the so-called tailgate trombonists. He led his own bands in New Orleans and Los Angeles until 1924, when he moved to Chicago to play with King Oliver, Jelly Roll Morton and others. In 1926, with Louis Armstrong, he recorded his famous composition "Muskrat Ramble."

He returned to the West Coast in 1929, and after playing for a time with local bands, retired to run a successful chicken ranch from 1930 to 1939. In the 1940s, he gradually returned to music with Barney Bigard, Bunk Johnson, and other New Orleans notables.

He toured Europe successfully in 1956 and again in 1959, and spent his final years comfortably in Hawaii before his death on January 23, 1973.

Charlie "Bird" Parker (1920-1955)
Saxophonist

Charlie "Bird" Parker was born in Kansas City, Kansas, on August 29, 1920. His influence on the development of jazz has been felt not only in the realm of the alto saxophone, which he dominated, but on the whole spectrum of jazz ideas. The astounding innovations which he introduced melodically, harmonically, tonally, and rhythmically made it impossible for any jazz musician from the mid-1940s to the present time to develop without reflecting some of Parker's influence, with or without acknowledgment.

Parker left school at sixteen to become a professional musician in Kansas City, his hometown. Parker visited New York in 1939. Back in Kansas City, he joined pianist Jay McShann with whom he recorded his first sides. At this time Parker met Dizzy Gillespie, who was developing parallel ideas and who would become known as co-founder with Parker of the bop movement some four years later.

In the early 1940s, Parker played with the bands of Earl Hines, Cootie Williams and Andy Kirk, as well as the original Billy Eckstine band—the first big band formed expressly to feature the new jazz style in both solos and arrangements.

In 1945, Parker cut a series of remarkable sides with Gillespie that put Bebop on the map. Although Parker was revered by a host of younger musicians, his innovations, at first, met with a great deal of opposition from traditionalist jazz musicians and critics.

In 1946, Parker, addicted to heroin, suffered a breakdown and was confined to a state hospital in California. Six months later he was back recording with Erroll Garner. From this point until his death from a heart attack on March 12, 1955, he confined most of his activity to working with a quintet, but also recorded and toured with a string section, and visited Europe in 1949 and 1950. He made his final appearance in 1955 at Birdland, the club which had been named in his honor.

Charlie Patton (1887-1934)
Singer, Guitarist

Charley Patton was one of the very earliest practitioners of the Delta blues style. As such, he profoundly influenced succeeding generations of blues artist, as the Delta sound evolved and percolated into the genre's modern recognizable form. Born and reared in Edwards, Mississippi, Patton received his musical education from members of the Chatmon family, some of whom went on to forge their own recording careers in the 1920s and 1930s.

In about 1897, Patton moved to the plantation of Will Dockery, where music was a constant part of the sharecropper lifestyle. At local juke joints, Patton became one the earliest composers of songs in the 12-bar pattern that came to be recognized as the standard blues form.

For the next 30 years or so, Patton played wherever he could, at picnics, on the street, or at other plantations. He gradually developed a sophisticated guitar style that helped lay the groundwork for what eventually coalesced into the Delta style. Although his musical skills were polished, his performance style was not what one would call refined. On the stage, Patton was a clown, performing guitar tricks, singing unintelligibly at times, and improvising at will. He was almost as well-known for his hard-drinking ways and constant womanizing as he was for his raw baritone singing voice.

In 1929 Patton was brought North to record for the Paramount label. He recorded a handful of sides for both Paramount and Vocalion over the next few years, before his death in 1934 of heart disease.

Oscar Pettiford (1922-1960)
Bassist

Born on September 30, 1922, in Okmulgee, Oklahoma, Oscar Pettiford was the leading bassist in the modern era of jazz. Building his own style on the foundation established by Jimmy Blanton, Pettiford achieved renown as the most technically capable and melodically inventive bassist in the jazz world of the late 1940s.

Pettiford was born on an American Indian reservation and raised in Minneapolis. Until he was nineteen, he toured with the family band (father and eleven children), and was well known in the Midwest. In 1943, Charlie Barnet heard him in Minneapolis and hired him to team up with bassist Chubby Jackson.

Pettiford left Barnet later that year, and led his own group on 52nd Street and also played with Coleman Hawkins, Duke Ellington, and Woody Herman.

Pettiford's fame grew during the 1950s through his recordings and his tours of Europe and the Orient. In 1958, he settled permanently in Europe, where he continued to work until his death in Copenhagen in 1960.

Bud Powell (1924-1966)
Pianist, Composer

Along with Charlie Parker and Dizzy Gillespie, with whom he often worked, and Thelonious Monk, an early supporter, Earl "Bud" Powell (1924-1966) was one of the founding fathers of modern jazz. A piano prodigy, he had his first big-time job with trumpeter Cootie Williams' big band in 1943, and became involved in the "birth of bebop" at Minton's Playhouse in Harlem and on 52nd Street.

The first to transfer the melodic, harmonic and rhythmic innovations of bop to the piano keyboard, he set the style for modern jazz piano, though he was greatly influenced by Art Tatum as well. Although he suffered recurrently from mental instability from his early twenties until the end of his life, Powell was capable of long stretches of musical brilliance. He lived in Paris from 1959 to 1964, frequently working with his old friend Kenny Clarke. More than 5,000 people attended his funeral in Harlem. One of Powell's finest compositions and performances is the ironically titled "Un Poco Loco," but there was nothing crazy about his hugely influential playing.

Ma Rainey (1886-1939)
Singer

Ma Rainey, the "Mother of the Blues," who enveloped the 1920s with her powerful, message-oriented blues songs, is remembered as a genuine jazz pioneer. Born Gertrude Pridgett in Columbus, Georgia, on April 26, 1886, Rainey gave her first public performance as a 12-year-old at the local Springer Opera House. At age 18,

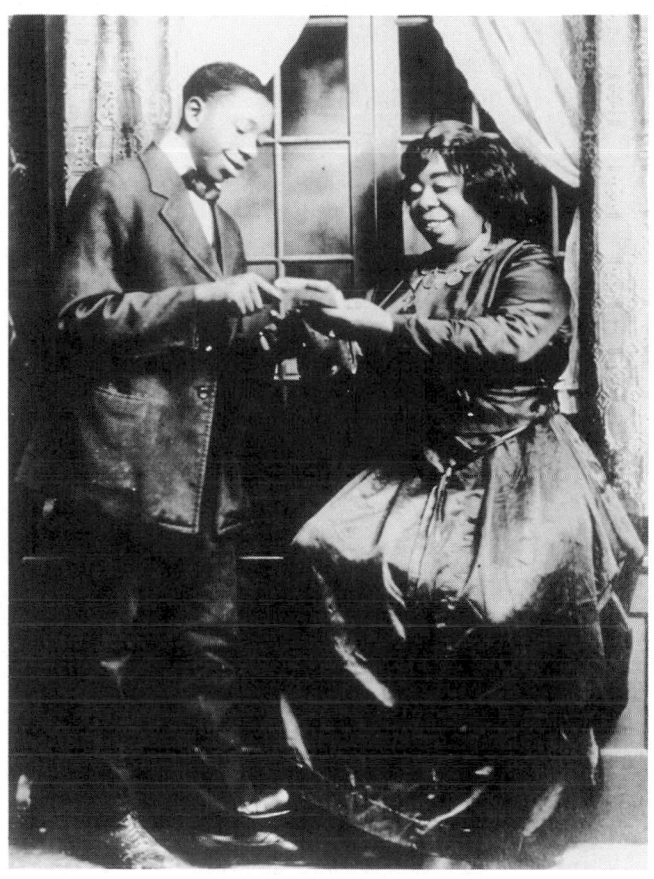

Ma Rainey

she married singer/dancer William "Pa" Rainey and the duo embarked on a long entertainment career. Around 1912, Rainey introduced a teen-aged Bessie Smith into her act, a move which was later seen as having a major impact on the blues/jazz singing styles. Ten years later, Rainey was recording with Fletcher Henderson, Louis Armstrong, and Coleman Hawkins and racking up the biggest record sales at the time for Paramount Records. She stopped recording in 1928, but continued to tour the South for a few more years. She retired in 1935, and until her death on December 22, 1939, managed the two theaters she owned in Georgia. Her eloquent and communicative voice lives on in the more than 100 recordings she made in her lifetime, singing of the many facets of black experience.

Dewey Redman (1931-)
Saxophonist

Dewey Redman has spent most of his life in search of a greater knowledge of his instrument, the tenor saxophone, constantly reevaluating his relationship to his music. Born in Ft. Worth, Texas, in 1931, he started playing the clarinet when he was 12, taking private lessons briefly for six months before he turned to self-

instruction. At 15, he got a job with an eight-piece band that performed in church as the minister passed the collection plate. At Prairie View A and M College, Dewey teamed up with a piano and bass player to work in local clubs, found a spot in the Prairie View "swing" band, and graduated in 1953 with a degree in industrial arts and a grasp on a new instrument he had worked on in college, the saxophone. After a stint in the Army, Dewey obtained a masters degree in Education at North Texas State University and taught school and directed school bands in west and south Texas.

In 1959, Redman moved to Los Angeles, where he found the music scene to be very cliquish, and then to San Francisco, where he remained for seven years, studying music, working out his own theories on chord progressions, improvisation and technique. In 1967, Dewey went to New York City, and fell in with Ornette Coleman, who brought him into his group with Dave Izenson on bass and Denardo Coleman on drums.

By 1973, Dewey was dividing his playing time between solo efforts, gigs with Ornette Coleman and Keith Jarrett, and the composition of *Peace Suite*, dedicated to the late Ralph Bunche. Later he co-founded the group Old and New Dreams. His son, Joshua, emerged as one of the finest young tenor saxophonists of the early 1990s.

Don Redman (1900-1964)
Saxophonist, Composer

The first composer-arranger of consequence in the history of jazz, Don Redman was known in the 1920s as a brilliant instrumentalist on several kinds of saxophones. He also made many records with Bessie Smith, Louis Armstrong, and other top-ranking jazz artists.

Born in Piedmont, West Virginia, on July 29, 1900, Redman was a child prodigy who played trumpet at the age of three, joined a band at six, and later studied harmony, theory, and composition at the Boston and Detroit conservatories. In 1924, he joined Fletcher Henderson's band as lead saxophonist and staff arranger, and in 1928 became leader of McKinney's Cotton Pickers.

During most of the 1930s, Redman led his own band, regarded as one of the leading black orchestras of the day, and the first to play a sponsored radio series. He also wrote for many other prominent bands, black and white.

In 1951, Redman became musical director for Pearl Bailey. From 1954 to 1955, he appeared in a small acting role in *House of Flowers* on Broadway. He continued to arrange and record until his death on November 30, 1964.

Maxwell "Max" Roach (1925-)
Percussionist, Composer

Born on January 10, 1925, in Brooklyn, New York, Max Roach was one of the key figures in the development of modern jazz. He was in the first group to play bebop on 52nd Street in New York, led by Dizzy Gillespie from 1943 to 1944, and later worked with Charlie Parker's finest group from 1947 to 1948. In 1954, he joined the brilliant young trumpeter Clifford Brown as co-leader of the Clifford Brown-Max Roach Quintet. After Brown's untimely death in a car crash, Roach began to lead his own groups of various sizes and instrumentation (including interesting work with solo and choral voices, an all percussion band, and a jazz quartet combined with a string quartet). His many compositions include *We Insist-Freedom Now*—a suite written with his wife at the time, singer Abbey Lincoln—was one of the first jazz works with a strong and direct political and social thrust.

A phenomenally gifted musician with a matchless percussion technique, Roach developed the drum solo to new heights of structural refinement; he has been an influence on every drummer to come along since the 1940s. A professor of music at the University of Massachusetts since 1972, Roach in 1988 became the first jazz artist to receive a MacArthur Fellowship, the most prestigious (and lucrative) award in the world of arts and letters. His daughter, Maxine, is a violinist, and they have worked and recorded together.

Sonny Rollins (1929-)
Saxophonist, Bandleader

Born on September 7, 1929, in New York City, Theodore Walter Rollins made his recording debut at 19, in such fast company as trombonist J. J. Johnson and pianist Bud Powell. Distinctively personal from the start, his style developed through work with pianist Thelonious Monk, Powell, drummer Art Blakey and trumpeter Miles Davis. In 1955, he joined the Clifford Brown- Max Roach Quintet. In 1959, he took two years off from active playing, studying and practicing. When he reappeared at the helm of his own quartet in 1961, he surprised even those who already knew the quality of his work with the power and conviction of his playing. He was named a Guggenheim fellow in 1972.

Since then, though briefly overshadowed by saxophonist John Coltrane, Rollins has been the unchallenged master of modern jazz tenor saxophone, with a sound and style totally his own. He often draws on his West Indian heritage for melodic and rhythmic inspiration and is one of the undisputed masters of extended improvisation, often playing all by himself as his group

Sonny Rollins

"lays out" in amazement—a feeling shared by his listeners. Still active in the 1990s, Rollins played at the New Orleans Jazz and Heritage Festival in 1993.

Otis Rush (1934-)
Guitarist, Singer

Otis Rush has been a mainstay of the Chicago blues scene for more than 40 years. A pioneer of the "West-Side" style of blues guitar work, Rush put together a sound that combined the best elements of the South-Side, delta-influenced approach with the smoother, modern, urban stylings that B. B. King and T-Bone Walker brought to the blues.

One of seven children, Rush was born in 1934 in Philadelphia, Mississippi. Although he was attracted to the country blues guitar of Lightnin' Hopkins and others, Rush started out as a harmonica player. In 1948 he moved to Chicago, where he continued to develop his harmonica skills while working a day job in the stockyards. He did not begin studying guitar until 1953. Initially, his guitar role model was Muddy Waters, but he gradually began to infuse the more modern phrasing and jazzier feel of Walker and King into the deep Mississippi foundation he had inherited from Waters.

Rush was noticed playing in the clubs by bassist Willie Dixon, who got him a contract with the newly-established Cobra label. His first record for Cobra, "I Can't Quit You," became a hit in 1956, and his work over the next few years was generally well-received. In 1959, Rush signed with Chess Records and recorded the successful single "So Many Roads, So Many Trains." He was unable to sell consistently for Chess, however, and his career slumped badly in the first half of the 1960s. He signed with the Houston-based Duke Records in 1962, but saw only one single released by that company. Meanwhile, he continued to perform regularly on the Chicago club circuit and occasionally in other cities.

Rush's appearance on the 1966 compilation album *Chicago: The Blues Today* revived his flagging career. It gained him a new generation of fans, including a number of white rock musicians, and he was much in demand for blues festival gigs. Nevertheless, large scale stardom continued to elude Rush, with the exception of a wildly enthusiastic reception in Japan in 1975. Discouraged, Rush stopped performing for a short spell in the early 1980s. By the middle of the decade, however, blues was enjoying another revival, and a revitalized Rush finally managed to establish himself as a true giant of the modern blues scene.

Jimmy Rushing (1903-1972)
Singer

The song "Mister Five by Five," written in tribute to him, is an apt physical description of Jimmy Rushing, who was one of the greatest male jazz and blues singers.

Born on August 12, 1903, in Oklahoma City, Oklahoma, Rushing played piano and violin as a boy, but entered music professionally as a singer in the after-hours world of California in 1925. After that, Rushing was linked with leading bands and musicians: Walter Page from 1927 to 1928; Benny Moten in 1929; and from 1936 to 1949 as a mainstay of the famed Count Basie Band.

Rushing formed his own small group when he left Basie and in the ensuing years worked most often as a "single." Following the rediscovery of the blues in the mid-1950s, Rushing regained widespread popularity.

His nightclub and festival engagements were always successful, and his world tours, on his own and also with Benny Goodman, earned him critical acclaim and commercial success. His style has endured across four decades of jazz largely due to its great warmth, a sure, firm melodic line, and a swinging use of rhythm. Late in life, he appeared in a featured acting role in Gordon Parks' film *The Learning Tree*. He died on June 12, 1972.

Bessie Smith

Bessie Smith (1894-1937)
Singer

Bessie Smith was born on April 15, 1894, in Chattanooga, Tennessee. They called her "The Empress of the Blues," and she had no peers. Her magnificent voice, sense of the dramatic, clarity of diction (you never missed a word of what she sang) and incomparable time and phrasing set her apart from the competition and made her appeal as much to jazz lovers as to lovers of the blues. Her first record, "Down Hearted Blues," sold more than a million copies, in 1923, when only Caruso and Paul Whiteman were racking up those kinds of figures.

By then, Bessie Smith had been singing professionally for some fifteen years, but records by black singers had only been made since 1920, and only by much less earthy voices. She already had a big following and had appeared in big shows, so the timing was right—not least for Columbia Records, whom she pulled out of the red. Before long, she was backed by the best jazz players, including Louis Armstrong, and by 1925 starred in her own touring show, which traveled in its own private Pullman car. By 1927, she was the highest paid black artist in the world, and in 1929 she made a short film, *St. Louis Blues*, that captures for posterity some of her magnetism as a stage performer. But tastes in music were changing rapidly, and though Bessie Smith added popular songs to her repertory (she'd always done some of those) and moved with the times, the Depression nearly killed the business for jazz and blues records, and in 1931, Columbia dropped her and she was soon touring as a "single."

John Hammond brought her back to the studios in 1933. Her records were wonderful, her singing as powerful and swinging as ever, but they didn't sell and turned out to be her last. She still found plenty of work on the traveling circuit, but the money was not what it used to be. On the road early one morning in Mississippi, she was fatally injured in a collision. For years, it was held as a fact that she died because a white hospital refused to treat her, but this wasn't so. The hospital in which her nearly severed right arm was amputated was black, but she had lost too much blood to survive. She was only forty-two. Had she lived, it is probable that her star would have risen once more. She died on September 26, 1937.

In 1968, Columbia reissued all of her records and did so again on CD in the 1990s. She would have been pleased with the response.

Billy Strayhorn (1915-1967)
Composer, Arranger, Pianist

Born in Dayton on November 29, 1915, and raised in Pittsburgh, Strayhorn early on showed an unusually sophisticated gift for songwriting (music and lyrics); while still in his teens, he wrote "Lushlife," and this was one of the songs he showed Duke Ellington in 1938, backstage during a visit by the band. A year or so later, the young man, who also was a gifted pianist, joined the Ellington entourage in New York. Duke first thought of him as a lyricist (something he was always looking for) but soon found out that Strayhorn had a knack for arranging.

Before long the two had established a working relationship that remains unique in the history of music—a collaboration so close that they were often themselves unsure of who had written what of a given composition. However, each man did also continue to work on his own, and among the many Strayhorn-signed contributions to Ellingtonia are such standouts as "Take the A Train," "Passion Flower," "Chelsea Bridge," "Rain Check," and "Blood Count,"— the latter written in the hospital as Strayhorn was dying of cancer.

Self-effacing and modest to a fault, Strayhorn stayed out of the limelight. But musicians and serious Ellington fans knew just how much he contributed to the band's

work during his lifetime within its ranks. He died on May 31, 1967.

Art Tatum (1910-1956)
Pianist

Born on October 13, 1910 in Toledo, Ohio, Art Tatum was a wizard of the keyboard. Nobody, not even the greatest classical virtuosi, surpassed his technique, but what made Tatum, nearly blind from birth, so very special was the musical imagination brought to life by his exceptional facility. Harmonically, he matched the boppers in sophistication—young Charlie Parker took a job as dishwasher in a club where Tatum worked so he could hear him every night. Rhythmically, he also anticipated modern jazz developments and could play rings around anyone, regardless of their instrument.

Though he enjoyed a full career, mostly as a soloist but also as leader of a trio (with electric guitar and bass, patterned on Nat King Cole's), and recorded quite prolifically, Tatum was born and died a bit too soon to benefit from the acceptance that came to jazz as a concert hall music. The concert hall, in which he rarely had the chance to perform, was Tatum's ideal medium. As it was, what he loved best was to play "after hours" for the edification of fellow musicians and perhaps in a challenge to some newcomer on the piano, whom he would cut down to size. When there were no rivals around, Tatum would challenge himself, setting seemingly impossible tempos or picking tunes with the toughest "changes."

There was no one like Art Tatum, and there never will be. Since his death on November 4, 1956, his records remain to keep generations of piano players from gaining too high an opinion of their own skills.

Billy Taylor (1921-)
Pianist, Composer, Educator

Born in Greenville, North Carolina, on July 24, 1921, few musicians have done more for the cause of jazz than Dr. Billy Taylor, who has been credited with obtaining proper respect and recognition for African American music since the 1950s by working in the media. Taylor's career started in the 1940s, shortly after graduating from Virginia State College with a B.A. in music in 1942. He established himself as a pianist on the New York scene, becoming a regular on "Swing Street" by playing with a quartet that featured Ben Webster. After a long stint as house pianist for the famed Birdland club, Taylor founded his own trio in 1952.

Taylor embarked on a campaign to educate the public through radio, television, and print. In 1958, he hosted *The Subject Is Jazz* on the Educational Television network. He also hosted radio programs on two

New York City stations, and garnered a Peabody Award for his work. In the 1960s, Taylor served as musical director for Tony Brown's *Black Journal Tonight* and in 1965, founded Jazzmobile as part of the Harlem Cultural Council's summer programs. Starting out as an idea for a parade float, Jazzmobile eventually developed into a service that seasonally brought major jazz artists out to poor urban areas for free performances.

From 1968 to 1972, Taylor led an 11-piece band for television's *David Frost Show*. He returned to school, earning a doctorate in music education from the University of Massachusetts in 1975; his dissertation was later published as "Jazz Piano: History and Development" and became the text for a course offered on National Public Radio (NPR). Taylor directed *Jazz Alive!* for NPR in the late 1970s to early 1980s. He also became a regular on *CBS Sunday Morning*, serving as the program's jazz correspondent since 1980, and earning an Emmy in 1983, for a segment on Quincy Jones. Taylor has served on numerous boards and panels, including a position with the prestigious National Council on the Arts. In 1994, he was named the Kennedy Center artistic advisor.

Taylor was won several honors in his career. Among them have been recognition for lifetime achievement (1984) from *Down Beat* and induction into the magazine's Hall of Fame; a Jazz Masters Fellowship from the National Endowment for the Arts (1988); induction into the International Association of Jazz Educators Hall of Fame (1991); a Tiffany Award from the International Society of Performing Arts Administrators (1991); a National Medal of the Arts (1992); and Man of the Year from the National Association of Jazz Educators. Taylor has also received several honorary degrees.

Cecil Taylor (1929-)
Pianist, Composer

Cecil Taylor, Ornette Coleman and John Coltrane—each completely different from the other—are the leading figures of avant garde jazz (later known as "free jazz," a perhaps more fitting term). Of these, Taylor is the farthest removed from the blues and swing roots of the music called jazz. He is a music unto himself—a fantastic virtuoso of the piano, with staggering energy and endurance and astonishing improvisatory abilities.

He attended New England Conservatory but says he learned more from listening to Ellington; another early influence was Bud Powell. He made his first recording (with Steve Lacy on soprano sax) in 1956; the following year he appeared at the Newport Jazz Festival and was also recorded there. Settling in New York City (he was born on Long Island on March 15, 1933) Taylor often

struggled with lack of work and acceptance but continued to go his own musical way, and making interesting if infrequent recordings. In the mid-1960s, he experimented with larger frameworks for his playing, recording with the Jazz Composers Orchestra and in the early 1970s, he briefly taught at various universities. Meanwhile, he had gained a following in Europe and Japan, and in the 1980s there was more frequent work and a spate of recordings, including some brilliant solo efforts. He also teamed for concerts with Mary Lou Williams and with Max Roach. In 1988, he was featured in a month-long festival of concerts and workshops in Berlin; some of the results were issued in a lavish eleven-CD boxed set. In that decade, Taylor, always fascinated by dance (which he sometimes included in his performances), teamed with the famous ballet star Mikhail Baryshnikov in concert. In 1992, Taylor received a MacArthur Fellowship—one of the greatest awards an artist can receive.

Koko Taylor (1935-)
Singer, Songwriter

As the reigning "Queen of the Blues," Koko Taylor has become one of the few women to achieve legendary status in a genre dominated by men wielding electric guitars. Taylor's vocal style is a throwback to the early Delta blues tradition, and she has credited her success to her refusal to dilute her singing to conform to modern fads.

Taylor was born Cora Walton on a farm near Memphis. After her mother died in 1939, she was raised, along with her five older siblings, by her sharecropper father. Working in the cotton fields, the entire family would sing the blues, influenced most strongly by the classic songs played by B. B. King on his radio show. At about the age of 18, she met and married Robert "Pops" Taylor, and moved with him to Chicago, where he had landed a job in a slaughterhouse.

In Chicago, Taylor worked cleaning suburban houses during the day and haunted South Side blues clubs by night. She frequently sat in with such legendary Chicago bluesmen as Howlin' Wolf, Buddy Guy, and Junior Wells. Taylor was soon "discovered" by blues star Willie Dixon, who hooked her up with Chess Records and wrote three songs for her. One of them, "Wang Dang Doodle," released in 1964, became a huge hit, selling a million copies.

Taylor quickly became a prominent member of the Chicago blues community. After Chess folded, she signed with Alligator Records, playing a large role in that label's transformation into a major blues outfit. Taylor continued to maintain a hectic tour schedule into the 1990s, and her albums have been regularly nominated for Grammy Awards.

McCoy Tyner (1938-)
Pianist, Composer, Bandleader

Philadelphia-born, pianist McCoy Tyner came to fame when he joined John Coltrane's quartet in 1960. Prior to that, his most important job was with the Art Farmer-Benny Golson Jazztet after having attended Granoff School of Music. During his five years with Coltrane, Tyner developed a unique two-handed, densely harmonic style and became one of the most widely admired and imitated pianists in jazz.

As leader of his own groups of various sizes—from trios to a unique big band—Tyner has continued to develop as a musician of great originality and integrity. Undergoing a resurgence of popularity in the 1990s, Tyner's band was named Jazz Big Band of the Year by *Down Beat* readers in 1994. Their recording *Journey* featured such players as vocalist Diane Reeves and trombonist Slide Hampton.

Sarah Vaughan (1924-1990)
Singer

Her voice was of such beauty, range and power, her ear so sure, her musicality so rare that Sarah Vaughan could have become an operatic star. Fortunately, she went the way of jazz and brought joy to the world since starting to sing professionally in 1943.

Vaughan was born on March 27, 1924. She sang in church in her native Newark and accompanied the choir on the piano (she played it well, one reason why she was so surefooted harmonically) and tried a few pop songs at high school parties when, on a dare, she entered the Wednesday night amateur contest at Harlem's famed Apollo Theater. As in a fairy tale, Billy Eckstine happened to be backstage. He ran out front as soon as he heard her voice, and recommended the young woman to his boss, band leader Earl Hines, who came, heard, and hired—of course she won the contest, which meant a week's work at the Apollo. In the Hines band of the time were Charlie Parker and Dizzy Gillespie. They and Sarah all left Hines when Eckstine decided to start his own band. By 1945, she'd made her first records under her own name. She also was the only singer to record with Bird and Dizzy together.

A year later, she started her solo career. Though she had some big pop hits during her long and rich career, she never strayed from jazz for long. Incredibly, as she got older, she got better, losing none of her amazing top range and adding to the bottom while her mastery of interpretation also grew. Her fans called her "the Divine One." She died in 1990.

Thomas "Fats" Waller

Thomas "Fats" Waller (1904-1943)
Composer, Pianist, Singer, Bandleader

Weighing in at over three hundred pounds and standing more than six feet tall, Tom Waller, a preacher's son (born in Greenwich Village in New York City on May 21, 1904), came by his nickname naturally. Big as he was, he was, as one of his many good friends said, "all music." His father wanted him to follow in his footsteps, but Fats liked the good times that came with playing the piano well, which he did almost from the start. At fifteen, he turned pro, backing singers in Harlem clubs and playing piano for silent movies. Wherever he went, people loved him, and he loved to spread joy. Few pianists, then or now, can match his terrific beat. He was also a master of the stride piano style. He also loved to play Bach, especially on the organ, which he was the first to make into a jazz instrument. In Paris in 1932, the world-famous Marcel Dupre invited Fats to play the organ at Notre Dame.

A talent for writing songs soon became evident. His first and biggest hit was "Ain't Misbehavin," from 1929; others include "Honeysuckle Rose," "Blue Turning Gray Over You," and "The Jitterbug Waltz." He also wrote "London Suite" for solo piano.

Fats was great on that new medium of the 1920s—the radio. He had an instant line of patter to go along with his great piano and carefree singing. He also made it to Hollywood. But his true medium was records. With his fine little group and occasional big band, he cut more than five hundred sides between 1934 and his untimely death at thirty-nine in 1943. He came across on records, and no matter how trite the tune, he turned it into a jazz gem. What killed Fats in his prime was his huge appetite (he was capable of consuming two whole chickens at one sitting, or polishing off two fullsize steak dinners) and drinking. Ironically, his first complete Broadway musical (he'd written songs for many others) was becoming a hit as he started off for home from California, where he had just finished filming *Stormy Weather*. He never arrived because pneumonia took him on December 15, just as the Superchief pulled into Kansas City.

T-Bone Walker (1910-1975)
Guitarist, Songwriter

The electric guitar is now the predominant solo instrument in American pop music largely thanks to T-Bone Walker. Walker was the first blues artist to use amplification as a music-making tool, and his playing represents a bridge between early jazz and modern, guitar-driven rock. He is cited as an important influence by countless subsequent guitar heroes, bluesmen and rockers alike.

Aaron Thibeaux Walker was born in 1910 in Linden, Texas, and grew up in Dallas. Both of his parents were working musicians, and Walker was exposed to many different instruments as a youth. He settled on guitar at the age of 13. As a boy, Walker worked for a time as Blind Lemon Jefferson's guide, escorting the legendary guitarist around town. By the time he was 16, T-Bone (a corruption of his middle name) was himself a working professional.

Recording as Oak Cliff T-Bone, Walker released two singles for Columbia Records in 1929. In 1934 he relocated to Los Angeles, leaving his steady guitar gig to his soon-to-be-famous pal Charlie Christian. In Los Angeles, Walker played in small combos at jazz clubs, before joining Les Hite's Cotton Club Orchestra as a singer, guitarist, and composer in 1939. With Hite, Walker established himself as one the pioneers of the electric guitar, which he used to successfully compete on equal terms with the band's horn section.

Having established his own reputation, Walker went solo in 1940. In 1947, he recorded his most famous hit, "Stormy Monday," which quickly became a blues standard of the highest order. After sticking close to home for most of the 1950s, Walker toured tirelessly during the 1960s, living the rugged, hard-drinking lifestyle that often goes with touring. He died of pneumonia in 1975.

An incurable showman, Walker dazzled audiences with an arsenal tricks—behind-the-back playing, splits, etc.—that may have influenced later rockers of the Jimi Hendrix ilk. More importantly, his innovative technique and jazz background helped to establish blues as a genre to be taken seriously.

Dinah Washington (1924-1963)
Singer

Dinah Washington's style defies categorization, but is seen as laying the groundwork for numerous rhythm and blues and jazz artists. Like many black singers, Washington, who was born on August 29, 1924, in Tuscaloosa, Alabama, got her start singing gospel music; in her case, at St. Luke's Baptist Church on Chicago's South Side. She toured churches with her mother, playing the piano and singing solos, until another opportunity beckoned, an amateur talent contest at Chicago's Regal Theater. Her triumphant performance there led to performances at local nightclubs, and in 1943, the nineteen year-old singer successfully auditioned for a slot in Lionel Hampton's band. She was soon discovered by composer and critic, Leonard Feather, and together Ms. Washington and Mr. Feather created several chart toppers, including "Baby Get Lost," "Salty Papa Blues," "Evil Gal Blues," and "Homeward Bound." She gained legendary status with "What A Difference A Day Makes" and "Unforgettable." Washington proved to be such a versatile artist that she was acclaimed—and mourned when she died at age thirty-nine—by blues, jazz, gospel, pop, and rhythm and blues audiences alike. Aretha Franklin dedicated one of her early albums to Ms. Washington, labelling it simply "Unforgettable." Washington died on December 14, 1963.

Muddy Waters (1915-1983)
Guitarist, Singer

Blues singer, guitarist, and harmonica player Muddy Waters was born Morganfield McKinley in Rolling Fork, Mississippi, on April 4, 1915. He began playing guitar at the age of 17, performing at parties and fish fries. After running a juke house in the early 1940s, Waters moved to Chicago in 1943, he played in clubs during the evenings and worked as a laborer during the days.

In 1946, he signed with Chess Records. Leading his own band in the 1950s, Waters produced such masterpieces "I'm Your Hoochie Coochie Man," "Got My Mojo Working," "Tiger in Your Tank," and "Manish Boy." Popularized by white British youth, Muddy Waters eventually played on stage with many of them, including Eric Clapton and Mike Bloomfield, both of whom considered Waters a guitar hero and living legend.

In the late 1960s and into the 1970s, Waters began receiving the kind of widespread recognition he deserved, including winning three Grammy awards, a Trendsetter Award, and getting inducted into the *Ebony* Readers' Poll Black Hall of Fame. The "Father of Electric Blues" died on April 30, 1983.

Ben Webster (1909-1973)
Saxophonist

Born in Kansas City in 1909, Ben Webster was at first a pianist, but switched to saxophone in his late teens. He worked with the family band led by Lester Young's father and with many other midwestern bands, and came to New York in 1931 with Benny Moten (whose pianist was Count Basie). After gaining a name among musicians as one of the most gifted disciples of Coleman Hawkins, he made many records and toured with many prominent bands (Fletcher Henderson, Cab Calloway, Teddy Wilson).

But it was when he joined Duke Ellington in 1939 that Webster really blossomed and soon became an influence in his own right. When he left Duke in 1943, he mainly led his own small groups, recorded prolifically, and also became one of the first black musicians to join a network radio musical staff. In 1964, he left on what had been planned as his first brief visit to Europe, but he never returned home. Settling in Copenhagen, he spent the final decade of his life as a revered and beloved elder statesman of jazz. During this period, his always masterful ballad playing ripened to full maturity, and his sound, ranging from a whisper to a gruff roar, became one of the unsurpassed landmarks of classic jazz. He died in 1973.

Mary Lou Williams (1910-1981)
Pianist, Composer, Arranger

Most women who have achieved fame in jazz have been singers, from Bessie Smith to Betty Carter. An exception to this rule was Mary Lou Williams, dubbed the "First Lady of Jazz."

Born in Atlanta on May 8, 1910, and brought up in Pittsburgh, Mary Elfrieda Scruggs had already performed in public at the age of six and was a pro by thirteen. Three years later she married saxophonist John Williams, with whom she made her record debut. When he joined Andy Kirk's band she took over the group. Soon, however, she was writing arrangements for Kirk, and in 1931, she became the band's pianist and musical director.

Though she also wrote for Benny Goodman and other bands, she stayed with Kirk until 1942, helping to make the band one of the swing era's best. Settling in New York, she led her own groups (sometimes all female) and began to compose longer works, including the "Zodiac Suite," performed at Town Hall in 1946. A champion of modern jazz, she gave advice and counsel to such rising stars as Dizzy Gillespie and Thelonious Monk. Miss Williams lived in England and France from 1952 to 1954. Back at home, she retired from music for some three years, but was coaxed out by Gillespie. Resuming her career, she toured widely, wrote several religious works including a Jazz Mass performed at St. Patrick's Cathedral, and in 1977 became artist-in-residence and teacher of jazz history and performance at Duke University, a position she held until her death. As pianist, composer and arranger, Mary Lou Williams ranks with the very best. She died on May 28, 1981.

Teddy Wilson (1912-1986)
Pianist, Bandleader

Theodore Wilson's father taught English and his mother was head librarian at Tuskegee Institute. Born on November 24, 1912, in Austin, Texas, he turned to music as a career while studying printing in Detroit in 1928, was befriended by the great Art Tatum, played in Louis Armstrong's big band, and was brought to New York by Benny Carter in 1933.

Two years later, Wilson (1912-1986) began to make a series of records—which became classics—often with Billie Holiday and always with the greatest musicians of the time. Meanwhile, he was becoming famous as the first black jazzman to be featured with a white band, playing with the Benny Goodman Trio and Quartet. His marvelously clear, harmonically impeccable piano style was a big influence on the pianists of the swing era. His own big band, formed in 1939 was excellent but not a commercial success. From 1940 on, he mostly led small groups or appeared as a soloist, touring world-wide and making hundreds of records. Though seriously ill, he continued to perform until a week before his death on July 31, 1986. Two of his three sons are professional musicians.

Lester "Prez" Young (1909-1959)
Saxophonist

It was Lester Young who gave Billie Holiday the name "Lady Day" when both were with Count Basie, and it was Lady Day in turn who christened Lester Young "President" (later shortened to "Prez").Young spent his youth on the carnival circuit in the Midwest with his musical family, choosing to concentrate on the tenor saxophone, only one of the many instruments he was able to play.

When Young took over Coleman Hawkin's chair in Fletcher Henderson's orchestra, he was criticized for not having the same style as his predecessor. As a result of this, he returned to Kansas City to play with Andy Kirk, and then with Count Basie from 1936 to 1940. During the Basie years, Young surpassed Hawkins as the vital influences on the tenor. Hardly a tenor man from the middle 1940s through the 1950s achieved prominence without building on the foundations laid by Lester Young. Young suffered a complete breakdown in 1955 but made a comeback the next year. He died within hours of returning from a long engagement in Paris.

23

Popular Music

Popular Music

◆ Gospel: The Root of Popular Music ◆ The Rise of Rhythm and Blues
◆ Sweet Soul Music and Social Revolution ◆ From Psychedelic Soul to Disco
◆ Rap: A Voice from the Subculture ◆ Popular Music Gatekeepers

by John Cohassey and Simon Glickman

Since the turn of the twentieth century, black music—whether gospel, rhythm and blues, soul, funk, or rap—has shaped American popular music. More recently, its impact can be heard in the emergence of world music coming out of Africa, South America, and the Caribbean Islands. From the church to the concert stage, thousands of gifted African American singers and musicians have bestowed upon America and the world a gift of unbounded spirit.

◆ GOSPEL: THE ROOT OF POPULAR MUSIC

The foundation of twentieth-century black popular music is rooted in the sounds of several folk styles including black minstrel and vaudeville tunes, blues, and ragtime. However, the music of the African American church has played one of the most significant roles in the evolution of black popular music.

Inextricably bound to the spirituals sung by slaves, the gospel style came to dominate the black religious experience in America. By the turn of the century, gospel music had reached popularity as black religious songwriters began to publish their own compositions. One of the earliest and most influential of these writers was Charles Albert Tindley, a Maryland-born Methodist preacher, who was responsible for writing several gospel music classics. His song "I'll Overcome Someday" resurfaced more than a half decade later as "We Shall Overcome," the anthem of the 1960s civil rights movement. Tindley's 1905 composition "Stand By Me" became a major hit for singer Ben E. King during the 1960s.

Tindley's music subsequently influenced Thomas A. Dorsey, whose talents as a religious songwriter, accom-

panist, and choir director earned him the title "the father of gospel music." Before dedicating his life to the Baptist church, Dorsey spent his youth as an itinerant blues pianist, performing under the name Georgia Tom. Like other bluesmen/preachers such as Reverend Gary Davis, Blind Willie McTell, and Gatemouth Moore, Dorsey performed both secular and religious music. In 1928, for example, he not only co-wrote the blues hit "Tight Like That" with guitarist Hudson "Tampa Red" Whitaker, but also composed his first gospel song "If You See My Savior Tell Him You Saw Me."

Four years later, Dorsey abandoned his career as a blues and jazz pianist to devote himself to a form of religious music that historian Michael W. Harris describes as gospel-blues style melding black religious and popular music into a unique and passionate form of gospel. During the Great Depression, Dorsey's new style of gospel served as an uplifting spiritual release from the pervasive poverty experienced in the black community. The performance of two of Dorsey's songs at the 1930 National Baptist Convention created a wave of enthusiasm for gospel across the nation. In the following year, Dorsey organized the world's first gospel choir. In 1932, he began a 40-year career as choir director at Chicago's Pilgrim Baptist Church. During his stay at Pilgrim Baptist, he launched the golden age of gospel music (c. 1945–1960), training and accompanying singers from Sallie Martin to Mahalia Jackson.

Gospel and the Recording Industry

The advent of the phonograph around the turn of the century helped to heighten the popularity of gospel music. The distribution of records helped break down the musical isolation imposed upon blacks since slav-

Thomas Dorsey with his group the Wandering Syncopators, 1923.

ery, allowing them to reach audiences outside their own communities. Recorded by the Victor label in 1902, the Jubilee and camp meeting shouts of the Dwinddie Colored Quartet appeared as one of the first black recordings. In the 1920s, black religious music became popular with the race record (a title designating the segregated sale of African American recordings). By 1924, Paramount Records sponsored its own Jubilee singers, and within three years Columbia Records began to send engineers into the field to record the richly complex harmonies of gospel quartets. Also popular were recorded sermons backed by occasional musical instruments, and evangelistic guitars, known commonly as "jack legs," which brought street singing gospel blues to a wider audience.

After a decline in recordings by evangelists during the 1930s and early 1940s, gospel music experienced an immense rise in popularity as hundreds of independent recording labels appeared after World War II. During the 1940s, numerous gospel quartets went on the road as full-time professionals, while thousands more sought work on weekends. Dressed in flowing robes and fashionably designed dress suits, quartets incorporated dance routines and expressive shouts into their performances.

Throughout the postwar period male gospel groups like the Five Blind Boys from Mississippi, the Mighty Clouds of Joy from Los Angeles, and the Sensational Nightingales from Memphis sang a capella (without instruments) on numerous recordings.

◆ THE RISE OF RHYTHM AND BLUES

As black veterans returned home from the Second World War, they found not only a new gospel sound, but an exciting blues style being played by small combos: jump blues. With its roots in boogie-woogie and the blues-swing arrangements of artists like Count Basie, Cab Calloway, Louis Jordan, and Lucky Millinder, this new blues style acquired an enormous following in black urban communities across the country. Unlike the swing-era big bands, jump blues groups featured fewer horns and a heavy rhythmic approach marked by a walking boogie bass line, honking saxophone solos, and a two-four drum pattern. Among the greatest exponents of postwar jump blues were guitarist T-Bone Walker, saxophonist Eddie "Cleanhead" Vinson, and blues shouter Big Joe Turner.

popularize rhythm and blues, but set the trend for modern pop radio.

R&B and the Black Church

In the early 1950s, numerous gospel quartets and street corner singing groups set out to establish careers in the black popular music scene. Influenced by gospel music and the secular singing of groups like the Inkspots, vocal groups appeared that performed complex harmonies in *a capella* style. As they would for rap artists in decades to come, street corners in urban neighborhoods became training grounds for thousands of young aspiring African American artists. This music, known as doo-wop, first arrived on the scene with the formation of the Ravens in 1945. Not long afterward, there followed a great succession of doo-wop "bird groups" including the Orioles who, in 1953, scored a nationwide hit with "Crying in the Chapel"—a song which, for the first time in black popular music, walked an almost indistinguishable line between gospel and mainstream pop music. In the same year, Billy Ward formed the Dominoes, featuring lead singer Clyde McPhatter, the son of a Baptist minister.

In the wake of the success of these vocal groups, numerous gospel singers left the church to become pop music stars. In 1952, for example, the Royal Sons became the Five Royales, the Gospel Starlighters (with James Brown), and finally the Blue Flames. Five years later, a young gospel singer named Sam Cooke landed a number-one pop hit with "You Send Me," a song which achieved popularity among both black and white audiences.

The strong relationship between gospel and rhythm and blues was evident in the music of more hard-edged R&B groups like Hank Ballard and the Midnighters. Maintaining a driving blues-based sound, Ballard's music, while featuring gospel-based harmonies, retained secular themes, as evidenced in his 1954 hit "Work With Me Annie." However, the capstone of gospel R&B appeared in the talents of Georgia-born pianist and singer Ray Charles, who in 1954 hit the charts with "I Got a Woman," which was based upon the gospel song "My Jesus Is All the World to Me." Charles' 1958 recording "What I'd Say" is famed for its call-and-response pattern which directly resembled the music sung in Holiness churches.

Rock and Roll

The rise of white rock and roll around 1955 served to open the floodgates for thousands of black R&B artists longing for a nationwide audience. A term applied to black R&B and its white equivalents during the mid-1950s, rock and roll represented a label given to a music form by the white media and marketplace in order to

Louis Jordan had a profound impact on the emergence of rhythm and blues.

Soon many jump blues ensembles began to feature singers versed in a smooth gospel-influenced vocal style. In 1949, the popularity of this style led *Billboard Magazine* to change its black pop chart title to rhythm and blues, thus coining the name of this new music. Just as blues, religious spirituals, and hymns formed gospel, rhythm and blues drew upon gospel, electric urban blues, and swing jazz to create a vibrantly modern sound appealing to the younger generation of postwar blacks. Some of the early recordings exemplifying the gospel influence on rhythm and blues were Cecil Grant's 1945 hit "I Wonder," Roy Brown's 1947 classic "Good Rocking Tonight," and Wynonie Harris's 1949 disc "All She Wants To Do Is Rock."

It was not long before this kind of raw-edged rhythm and blues emerged from hundreds of independent recording labels that appeared across the country in the postwar era. With the increased availability of rhythm and blues recordings, a handful of black radio disc jockeys became locally famous as the first promoters and salesmen of this music. Bringing their colorful street language to the airwaves, pioneer black DJs such as Al Benson and Vernon Winslow not only helped to

Chuck Berry revolutionized rhythm and blues.

attract a mass multiracial audience. As black music writer Nelson George explained, naming this music rock and roll, "dulled down the racial identification and made young white consumers of Cold War America feel more comfortable." Taken from a term common among the Delta and electric blues cultures, rock and roll was actually rhythm and blues rechristened with a more "socially acceptable" title. Of course, the term "rock and roll" had sexual connotations as well; this, along with its roots in black culture, allowed white cultural conservatives of the time to demonize the form.

Thus, the majority of R&B performers never made the distinction between rhythm and blues and rock and roll. Ike Turner, a talent scout for the pioneering Sun Studios record label, was a formidable bandleader and guitarist; his 1951 cut "Rocket 88" has been considered by some to be the very first rock and roll record. The song's distorted guitar tone was achieved by accident—coming from a broken amplifier speaker—but would later influence the gritty sound of many subsequent rock and blues guitarists. Turner achieved mainstream success in collaboration with his wife, singer Tina Turner, who would later eclipse him in fame. One R&B artist who established a prosperous career in rock and roll was New Orleans-born pianist Antoine "Fats" Domino. Although he had produced a great amount of strong R&B material before his career in rock and roll, Domino did not hit the charts until 1955 with "Ain't That A Shame," followed by the classics "Blueberry Hill," "I'm Walkin," and "Whole Lotta Loving." Another R&B pianist/singer to enter the rock and roll field was Little Richard Penniman, a former Pentecostal gospel singer whose career in pop music began in 1956 with the hit "Tutti Frutti." Before entering a Seventh Day Adventist seminary in 1959, Little Richard produced a string of hits: "Long Tall Sally," "Rip It Up," "The Girl Can't Help It," and "Good Golly Miss Molly."

In 1955, as Fats Domino's New Orleans style R&B tunes climbed the charts, a young guitarist from St. Louis named Chuck Berry achieved nationwide fame when his country-influenced song "Maybelleine" reached number five on the charts. Backed by bluesman Muddy Water's rhythm section, "Maybelleine" offered a unique form of R&B, combining white hillbilly, or rockabilly, with jump blues; Berry revolutionized R&B by featuring the guitar as a lead, rather than a rhythm instrument. Modeled after his blues-guitar mentor T-Bone Walker, Berry's double string guitar bends and syncopated up-stroke rhythm created a driving backdrop for his color-fully poetic tales of teenage life. A very eclectic and creative musician, Berry incorporated the sounds of urban blues, country, calypso, Latin, and even Hawaiian music into his unique brand of R&B. His classic "Johnny B. Goode," recorded in 1958, became a standard in

almost every rock and roll band's repertoire, including 1960s rock guitar hero Jimi Hendrix.

Poly Styrene, a black woman, emerged in the 1970s as the leader of the punk group X-Ray Spec. Folk and soft rock maven Tracy Chapman became the Ritchie Havens of the late 1980s. In that decade and in the 1990s, black rock groups such as the Bus Boys, Living Colour, and Body Count had varying degrees of success. Blacks were also prominent in such musically hybrid groups as Bad Brains, Fishbone, and Skunk Anasie.

Blacks and Country Music

Berry was not the only African American to take an interest in country music. Ray Charles' crossover into country music in the early 1960s caused controversy in many circles. In 1959, Charles recorded "I'm Moving On," a country tune by Hank Snow. Despite opposition, Charles went on to record a fine collection of songs in 1962 entitled *Modern Sounds in Country Music*. Filled with soulful ballads and backed by colorful string sections, the session produced two classic numbers "You Don't Know Me" and "I Can't Stop Loving You." Its popularity spawned a 1963 sequel *Modern Sounds in Country Music Volume 2*, producing several more hits including Hank Williams' "Your Cheating Heart" and "Take These Chains From My Heart."

Unlike other mainstream black country artists, Charles' renditions remained immersed in his unique gospel-blues sound. Before Charles' entrance into the country music field there had been many African American country artists like Dedford Bailey, a partially disabled harmonica player who became a regularly featured performer on the Grand Ole Opry from 1925 to 1941. However, it was not until 1965, when Charley Pride arrived on the country music scene with his RCA recordings "Snakes Crawl at Night" and "Atlantic Coastal Line," that a black artist emerged as a superstar in the country tradition. Pride's songs were so steeped in the country tradition that many radio listeners were astounded when they found out his racial identity. With the arrival of Pride, there appeared other black country artists like Linda Martel from South Carolina, O. B. McClinton from Mississippi, and Oklahoma-born Big Al Downing and Stoney Edwards. The most noted of these artists, Edwards recorded two nationwide hits in 1968 with Jesse Winchester's "You're On My Mind" and Leonard Cohen's "Bird on a Wire."

◆ SWEET SOUL MUSIC AND SOCIAL REVOLUTION

The tremendous social upheavals of the 1960s—including but not limited to the Civil Rights, Black Power, and women's movements and the coalescence

Ray Charles, one of the world's most popular musicians.

of a youth-based counterculture—were paralleled by numerous new musical forms. Perhaps no single genre of popular song encapsulated the highs and lows of this period more than soul music. Born in the black church, where testifying preachers and harmonizing choirs shepherded their congregations to weekly ecstasy, the form was escorted into the secular world by a handful of artists schooled simultaneously in gospel, jazz, country blues, R&B, and rock and roll.

Singer-keyboardist Ray Charles has been credited as one of the founders of the soul genre. His earliest hits— notably "What'd I Say" and "I Got a Woman"—brought the emotional testifying and call-and-response arrangements associated with gospel music into a non-religious context. He added the earthy pull of the blues and a jazz-influenced harmonic complexity to his distinctive musical blend. This hybrid of blue groove and spirit was the secular gospel known as soul music. Such innovations were controversial, but the sounds of soul sweetened and enriched rhythm and blues music from then on. Charles ruffled more feathers by mixing soul and country music. Blind "Brother Ray" became a cultural icon in the ensuing decades.

While R&B had functioned for some time as gospel's sinful, worldly counterpart—focusing largely on the concerns of the body while church music addressed the spirit—soul refused to deny either side of human experience. Even so, the young genre's exuberance and ambition made it ideal for reflecting the growing aspirations of America's black population. Inspired by the teachings and nonviolent organizing of Dr. Martin Luther King, Jr. and other civil rights leaders, African Americans also responded to songs that trumpeted change. "People Get Ready" and "We're a Winner" by Curtis Mayfield and the Impressions were early anthems; as soul grew and diversified many more would come.

Singer-bandleader James Brown, meanwhile, combined uplift and hard groove, gradually moving from heady soul/R&B into a new territory called funk with hits like "I Got You (I Feel Good)" and "Cold Sweat." Brown ran one of the tightest ships around, alternately inspiring and browbeating his musicians; turnover was high, but the ensemble was always a well-oiled machine. Though he would refine the funk style—driving rhythms emphasizing the "one" or first beat of each measure; repetitive vocal phrases and improvised, "churchy" shouts; and minimal, almost dissonant, instrumental figures—during the early 1960s, its content remained largely sexual for some time. Brown's political message did not fully materialize until the end of the decade. By then, his funky sermons championed black economic independence and freedom from addiction. Brown had a seismic effect on pop; not only funk artists but also scores of rock and rap musicians took his work as a point of departure.

Following Brown's lead, Sly and the Family Stone—led by Sylvester "Sly Stone" Stewart, a Northern California DJ and producer—lent a psychedelic rock tinge and communal good vibes to the bedrock funk groove. Featuring musicians black and white, male and female, the group offered one of the most inclusive visions in pop history. While "Dance to the Music" mapped out their utopia in musical terms, they trumpeted tolerance and equality in happy hits like "Everyday People," "Everybody Is a Star," and "You Can Make It If You Try." Stone's vision would darken substantially later on, however.

The syncopated rhythms of New Orleans were also fundamental to the development of modern funk. The Meters began as an instrumental foursome and eventually backed up acts as diverse as singer Lee Dorsey, vocal group The Pointer Sisters, and British popster Robert Palmer. During the 1960s they scored some instrumental hits—notably "Cissy Strut"—before adding vocals in the 1970s. Though they eventually flew apart and were partly subsumed by soul survivors the Neville Brothers, the Meters were profoundly influential.

Soul North and South: Stax/Volt, Atlantic, and Motown

Soul music's increasing hold on the public imagination during the 1960s had a great deal to do with two record companies, the Atlantic Records subsidiary Stax/Volt in the South and Motown in the North. Stax/Volt was a Memphis-based label that introduced the world to the rough-hewn "funky" sound of southern soul and R&B. The company's greatest successes came during the 1960s, thanks to a roster of powerful artists, gifted songwriters, and one of the greatest "house bands" in music history. The band in question, led by keyboardist Booker T. Jones, was a formidable mixed-race groove machine that not only backed the whole Stax roster and numerous acts on its parent label, Atlantic, but also achieved success as an instrumental recording act, Booker T. and the MG's. Their smoldering workouts "Green Onions" and "Hip Hug-Her" became signature themes of the era.

Stax's roster included vocal duo Sam and Dave, Rufus and Carla Thomas, Eddie Floyd, and Otis Redding. House songwriters Isaac Hayes and David Porter wrote hits like "Soul Man" and "Hold On, I'm Coming" for Sam and Dave; Hayes himself would later become a pop/soul superstar. Redding was both an extraordinary singer and a gifted tunesmith; he penned the luminous "Dock of the Bay" and the righteous "Respect." The latter song was transformed into an anthem of nascent feminism and black dignity thanks to the alchemy of Atlantic Records' Aretha Franklin, a gospel-bred singer turned pop maven; Franklin would become the "Queen of Soul" and one of the most enduring figures in popular music. While Franklin made "Respect" and other celebrated recordings—tracks like "Chain of Fools," the incandescent "(You Make Me Feel Like a) Natural Woman," and "I Never Loved a Man"—at the Fame studios in Muscle Shoals, Alabama, other Atlantic soul stars came to Memphis to make their hit records. The Stax crew collaborated with Wilson Pickett on hugely successful singles like "In the Midnight Hour" and "Land of 1000 Dances." Ultimately, however, Stax lost its commercial momentum; and by the 1970s was struggling to compete with a panoply of rivals.

As soul music gained a mass following in the black community, a black-owned and family-run Detroit record company emerged as one of the largest and most successful African American business enterprises in the United States. In 1959, Berry Gordy, a Detroit entrepreneur, songwriter, and modern jazz enthusiast, established the Motown Record Corporation.

James Brown, the "Godfather of Soul."

With its headquarters located in a modest two-story home, the company proudly displayed a sign on its exterior reading Hitsville USA. Taking advantage of the diversity of local talent, Gordy employed Detroit-based contract teams, writers, producers, and engineers. Motown's studio became a great laboratory for technological innovations, advancing the use of echo, multi-tracking, and over-dubbing. In the studio, Gordy employed the city's finest jazz and classical musicians to accompany the young singing talent signed to the company.

Unlike the soul music emerging in studios like Stax and Muscle Shoals, Motown's music was also marketed at the white middle class; Gordy called his music "The Sound of Young America," and sought to produce glamorous and well-groomed acts. "Blues and R&B always had a funky look to it back in those days," explained Motown producer Mickey Stevenson. "We felt that we should have a look that the mothers and fathers would want their children to follow."

Thus, Motown set out to produce a sound which it considered more refined and less "off-key" than the music played by mainstream soul and blues artists. In its early years of operation, Motown retained a R&B influ-

ence as evidenced in songs like the Marvelettes' "Please Mister Postman" (1961), Mary Wells' "You Beat Me to the Punch" (1962), and Marvin Gaye's "Pride and Joy" (1963).

One of the main forces responsible for the emergence of a unique "Motown sound" appeared in the production team of Brian and Eddie Holland, and Lamont Dozier, or H-D-H, as they came to be known. Utilizing the recording techniques of Phil Spector's "wall of sound," the H-D-H team brought fame to many of Motown's "girl-groups" such as Martha and the Vandellas, and the Supremes, featuring Diana Ross.

During 1966 and 1967, H-D-H began to use more complex string arrangements based upon minor chord structures. This gave rise to what has been referred to as their "classical period." As a result, many Motown songs reflected the darker side of lost love and the conditions of ghetto life. This mood was captured in such songs by the Four Tops as "Reach Out, I'll Be There," "Bernadette," and "Seven Rooms of Gloom."

After the Holland-Dozier-Holland team left Motown in 1968, the company, faced with numerous artistic and economic problems, fell into a state of decline. A year later, Gordy signed the Jackson Five, the last major act to join the label before its demise. The Jacksons landed 13 consecutive hit singles including "ABC" and "I'll Be There." In 1971, Gordy moved the Motown Record Corporation to Los Angeles, where the company directed its efforts toward film making. Through the late 1970s and early 1980s, Motown continued to sign such acts as the Commodores, Lionel Richie, and DeBarge. But in 1984, Gordy entered into a distribution agreement with MCA records and eventually sold Motown to an entertainment conglomerate.

◆ FROM PSYCHEDELIC SOUL TO DISCO

Disillusionment after the deaths of Dr. King and black power advocate Malcolm X, along with the lingering trauma of the Vietnam War and the worsening plight of America's inner cities, had a marked influence on soul's direction. Curtis Mayfield projected a vision of wary hope in his early 1970s work. His landmark soundtrack for the "Blaxploitation" film *Superfly* reflected the new soul paradigm: at once gritty and symphonic, encompassing soul's far-reaching ambition and funk's uncompromising, earthy realism. Isaac Hayes's theme from *Shaft*, another urban action film, earned an Academy Award. Much of the funk and soul of this period drew not only on the percolating rhythms developed by Brown but also on the trailblazing guitar work of Jimi Hendrix.

Hailed by many as the greatest electric guitarist of all time, Hendrix had toiled as a sideman for numerous R&B acts but emerged as a rocker of the first order during the mid-1960s. By the time of his death in 1970, he had revolutionized lead guitar playing forever; his use of the wah-wah pedal, an effect that lent a powerful percussive dimension to the instrument, became a staple of funk. His melding of psychedelic rock, hard blues, and soul tropes, meanwhile, influenced the "psychedelic soul" that emerged in his wake.

Commercial soul addressed the tenor of the times. Trailblazers Sly and the Family Stone focused less on the rainbow-colored sentiments of the preceding era and more on urban turmoil with their landmark album *There's a Riot Going On*, as did Marvin Gaye with hits like "Trouble Man" and "What's Goin' On." The O'Jays enjoyed chart success with such anxious singles as "Backstabbers" and "For the Love of Money," and the Temptations wrapped their prodigious vocal chops around inner-city woes on "Papa Was a Rolling Stone," among other smashes.

The 1970s did not lack for more traditionally romantic performers, however. Apart from Marvin Gaye, the period's most seductive male vocalists were arguably Al Green and Barry White. Green's rich falsetto and inti-

Jimi Hendrix redefined the sound of the electric guitar.

mate phrasing on hits like "Let's Stay Together" and "Love and Happiness" quickly established him as a visionary in the genre; though he left pop music to sing gospel music and preach, he remained a beloved figure in the soul world and returned to the fold for a 1995 album. White's bedroom soundtracks, meanwhile, kept lovers in thrall with an intoxicating blend of his baritone vocals and symphonic arrangements.

During the mid-1970s, club dance-floors were increasingly dominated by the pulsating sounds of disco. With its thumping beat and lush arrangements, the music was viewed by many as a saccharine and escapist form that betrayed the mission of funk and soul. While a number of powerful performers emerged from the disco scene, few could approach the star power of diva Donna Summer, who enjoyed a wave of hits before a religious conversion moved her into gospel. Though disco's "crossover" success meant that a number of artists who scored in that format were white, several all-black acts, notably Chic, Kool and the Gang, and LaBelle, flourished during this period.

These commercial laments were outstripped in daring—though not in sales—by the work of Detroit's Funkadelic. Fronted by singer and hairstylist George

Clinton, who led a doo-wop group called The Parliaments in the 1950s, Funkadelic mixed acid rock's cosmic guitar excursions with funk's relentless grooves; a danger existed in their work that limited its commercial appeal, but profoundly influenced rock and rap.

Eventually, Clinton established another group, Parliament, which focused on horn-driven funk and elaborate, fantasy-oriented concept albums. Funkadelic and Parliament, though manifestly different at first, gradually moved into similar territory as "P. Funk"; the "P" meaning "pure." Soon P. Funk was the umbrella term for a family of bands that included Bootsy's Rubber Band, The Brides of Funkenstein, and Parlet. Clinton scored in the 1980s as a solo artist, most notably with the mega-hit "Atomic Dog." P. Funk was so influential that for a time Parliament found itself competing with acts that appropriated its sound and themes, including hitmakers like the Ohio Players, Rick James, George Duke, and Earth, Wind and Fire. Though funk declined during the 1980s, artists like Prince took it in a new, eclectic direction.

◆ RAP: A VOICE FROM THE SUBCULTURE

While funk sold millions of records and received extensive radio airplay in the mid-1970s, rap music emerged within a small circle of New York artists and entertainers. In neighborhoods in Upper Manhattan and the South Bronx, disc jockeys at private parties discovered how to use "little raps" between songs to keep dancers on their feet. From behind the microphone, DJs created a call and response pattern with the audience. Taking advantage of their master of ceremonies status, they often boasted of their intellectual or sexual prowess. "Soon a division of labor emerged," explained Jefferson Morley. "DJs concentrated on perfecting the techniques of manipulating the turntables, while master of ceremonies (MCs or rappers) concentrated on rapping in rhymes." Through the use of a special stylus, rappers moved records back and forth on the turntable in order to create a unique rhythmic sound, known within the rap culture as needle rocking and later as "scratching."

Long before the modern rap, or hip-hop, culture appeared, however, African American artists existed who performed in a rap-style idiom. In 1929, for instance, New York singer-comedian Pigmeat Markham gave performances representative of an early rap-style.

Rap music is also rooted in the talking jazz style of a group of ex-convicts called the Last Poets. During the 1960s, this ensemble of black intellectuals rapped in complex rhythms over music played by jazz accompa-

nists. Last Poet member Jalal Uridin, recording under the name Lightning Rod, released an album entitled *Hustler's Convention.* Backed by the funk band Kool and the Gang, Uridin's recording became very influential to the early New York rappers.

Among one of the first New York rap artists of the early 1970s was Jamaican-born Clive Campbell, aka Kool Herc. A street DJ, Herc developed the art of sampling, the method of playing a section of a recording over and over in order to create a unique dance mix. Others to join the New York scene were black nationalist DJ Africa Bambaataa from the southeast Bronx and Joseph Saddler, known as Grandmaster Flash, from the central Bronx. Flash formed the group Grandmaster Flash and The Three MCs (Cowboy, Kid Creole, and Melle Mel). Later he added Kurtis Blow and Duke Bootee who founded the Furious Five.

However, rap music did not reach a broad audience until 1980, when the Sugar Hill Gang's song "Rapper's Delight" received widespread radio airplay. Small record companies began to affect the development of pop for the first time in years. Def Jam spearheaded the rise of influential rappers LL Cool J, Run-DMC, and Public Enemy, while Tommy Boy Records contributed to the rise of electro-funk. As rap groups assembled during the decade, they began to use their art to describe the harsh realities of inner city life. Unlike early rap music which was generally upbeat and exuberant in tone, the rap style of the 1980s exhibited a strong sense of racial and political consciousness. Grandmaster Flash's "The Message" was the first blatantly political rap hit; its yearning and desperation recalled the angst-ridden soul records of the preceding decade and hinted as rap's potential. Toward the end of the decade, rap came to express an increasing sense of racial militancy. Inspired by the Nation of Islam and the teachings of martyred race leader Malcolm X, rap groups like Public Enemy turned their music into voice supporting black power. Public Enemy's second LP *It Takes A Nation of Millions to Hold Us Back* sold more than one million copies. Their song "Fight the Power" appeared in director Spike Lee's film *Do the Right Thing.* The group's third album *Fear of a Black Planet* was released in 1990. While it is a statement against "western cultural supremacy," explained group member Chuck D., it is also "about the coming together of all races" in a "racial rebirth." Rapper KRS-One of Boogie Down Productions provided eloquent, barbed political commentary as well.

Women have also played a role in the shaping of rap music. Rap artists such as Queen Latifah, MC Lyte, and the group Salt-N-Pepa represent a growing number of female rappers who speak for the advancement of black women in American society. Queen Latifah has emerged as critic of male dominance in the music industry and the sexist image of women presented by some male rap artists.

The late 1980s also saw the birth of the "Native Tongues" school of rap, the graduates of which employed an eclectic array of samples and more heavily relied on humor and baroque rhymes than did their hardcore and political brethren. The best-known groups of this school were De La Soul, A Tribe Called Quest, and The Pharcyde; Digital Underground, meanwhile, openly aspired to be "Sons of the P." and wove elaborate Parliament-esque concepts. Artists with a more bohemian bent began to rely heavily on jazz; some, like Digable Planets and US3, sold briskly. A few, like Arrested Development and Spearhead, stayed close to their soul and funk roots.

The biggest story in rap during the 1990s was the rise of "Gangsta" rap, which utilized old-school funk beats and dwelt on hustling and violence—usually without soul's veneer of guarded optimism. The group N.W.A. (Niggaz With Attitude) upset social conservatives with their megahit "F— Tha Police," and its alumni Dr. Dre, Ice Cube, and Eazy-E would all become major solo artists. Ice-T put a slightly more deliberative spin on his gangster tales, but it was Dre's protege Snoop Doggy Dogg and former Digital Underground member Tupac Shakur who would become the biggest crossover acts of all. Snoop's laid-back style in particular earned him pop status with cuts like "Gin and Juice," "Murder Was the Case," and "Doggy Dogg World." The crossover success of these recordings was so worrisome to aforementioned conservatives that gangsta rap lyrics became a staple in political speeches, and politicians and activist groups threatened to take action against record companies that released such material.

Some pop rappers, like MC Hammer (who eventually dropped the "MC") and DJ Jazzy Jeff and the Fresh Prince, enjoyed periodic success and then faded from the charts. Those who retained a bit more street-level credibility, on the other hand, such as Naughty By Nature, who had a mega-smash with "O.P.P." and Coolio, who ruled the charts and scored a Grammy Award for his "Gangster's Paradise," enjoyed a longer reign.

In the mid-1990s, creative rhyme styles and techniques were perpetuated by Das Efx, Fu-Schnickens, Mystikal, Bone Thugs-N-Harmony, and Busta Rhymez, among others. With its array of styles and points of view, rap has emerged as a primary cultural form for young African Americans. Like the music of its predecessors, rap is filled with artistic energy and descriptions of the human experience. No longer considered a fad, rap has become a subculture.

Soul's New Directions

Perhaps in part to counter the increasing dominance of hardcore hip-hop in the marketplace, R&B and Soul moved in a softer direction during the 1980s; as bands were replaced by sequenced keyboards and drum machines, recordings in this genre were increasingly dominated by producers and vocalists. Even longtime soul legends like Aretha Franklin and Chaka Khan moved in a glossier direction. This period saw the rise of a handful of phenomenally successful singers, notably Whitney Houston, whose mother Cissy had sung with Franklin and many others. Following a monster debut, Houston collected a string of hits and awards; her apotheosis came with the gargantuan sales of the soundtrack to the film *The Bodyguard*, in which she also had a starring role. Houston's athletic vocal chops paved the way for a number of other new soul divas, including Toni Braxton, Mariah Carey, and Mary J. Blige. Producers L. A. Reid and Babyface were among the preeminent hitmakers of this era; like Babyface, R. Kelley was successful both as producer and recording artist.

While the soft-edged trend continued through the 1990s, some artists within the fold, like the smash groups TLC and En Vogue, flirted with old-school soul. Meanwhile, "alternative" soul emerged at the margins, thanks to artists like bassist/singer-songwriter Me'Shell Ndegeocello, Arrested Development refugee Dionne Farris, and Marvin Gaye-disciple D'Angelo.

According to the Recording Industry Association of America (RIAA)—the bestower of gold, platinum, and multi-platinum plaques—among the top black record sellers with units including CDs, cassettes, albums, and singles as tallied between 1985 and 1996 were Michael Jackson, Whitney Houston, Mariah Carey, Prince, Janet Jackson, Boyz II Men, Hammer, TLC, Luther Vandross, Lionel Richie, and Nigerian-born British singer Sade.

◆ POPULAR MUSIC GATEKEEPERS

Nicholas Ashford (1943–)
Valerie Simpson (1948–)
Singers, Songwriters

One of the most enduring songwriting teams to emerge from Motown has been Nicholas Ashford and Valerie Simpson. For over a quarter of a century, the team has written hit songs for artists from Ray Charles to Diana Ross.

Nicky Ashford was born in Fairfield, South Carolina, on May 14, 1943, and Valerie Simpson was born in the Bronx section of New York City on August 26, 1948. The two met in the early 1960s while singing in the same choir at Harlem's White Rock Baptist Church. With Ashford's gift for lyrics and Simpson's exceptional gospel piano and compositional skills, the two began to write for the staff of Scepter Records in 1964. Two years later, their song "Let's Go Get Stoned" became a hit for Ray Charles.

In 1962, Ashford and Simpson joined Motown's Jobete Music, where they wrote and produced hit songs for Marvin Gaye and Tammi Terrell, including "Ain't Nothing Like the Real Thing," "Good Loving Ain't Easy to Come By," and the "Onion Song." Next, they worked with Diana Ross who had just set out to establish a solo career producing such hits as "Remember Me," "Reach Out (and Touch Somebody's Hand)," and an updated version of "Ain't No Mountain High Enough."

Ashford and Simpson's success as songwriters led them to release their own solo recording *Exposed* in 1971. After signing with Warner Brothers in 1973, they recorded a number of hit LPs: *Is It Still Good To Ya* (1978), *Stay Free* (1979), *A Musical Affair* (1980), and their biggest seller *Solid* in 1985. More recently, the singing and songwriting duo have collaborated on projects with producer Quincy Jones and artists like Gladys Knight and Chaka Khan.

Anita Baker (1958–)
Singer

One of the most sophisticated soul divas to emerge in the 1980s, Baker considers herself "a balladeer" dedicated to singing music rooted in the tradition of gospel music and jazz. Inspired by her idols Mahalia Jackson, Sarah Vaughan,, and Nancy Wilson, Baker brings audiences a sincere vocal style which defies commercial trends and electronic overproduction.

Born on January 26, 1958, in Toledo, Ohio, Baker was raised in a single-parent middle class family in Detroit. She first sang in storefront churches, where it was common for the congregation to improvise on various gospel themes. After graduating from Central High School, Baker sang in the Detroit soul/funk group Chapter 8. Although Chapter 8 recorded the album *I Just Want To Be Your Girl* for the Ariola label, the group's lack of commercial success caused it to disband, and for the next three years, Baker worked as a receptionist in a law firm.

In 1982, Baker, after signing a contract with Beverly Glen, moved to Los Angeles, where she recorded the critically acclaimed solo album *Songstress*. Following a legal battle with Glen, Baker signed with Elektra and recorded her debut hit album *Rapture* in 1986. As the album's executive producer, Baker sought "a minimalist approach" featuring simple recording techniques which captured the natural sounds of her voice. The LP's single "Sweet Love" brought Baker immediate crossover success. Baker's follow-up effort, the multi-platinum

Anita Baker

selling *Giving You the Best I Got* is considered one of the finest pop music albums of the 1990s. Her third effort *Compositions*, recorded in 1990, featured a number of back-up musicians including Detroit jazz guitarist Earl Klugh.

After a nearly four-year hiatus, Baker released the double-platinum *Rhythm of Love* in 1994. Winner of five Grammys, two NAACP Image awards, two American Music awards, two Soul Train awards, and a star on Hollywood's Walk of Fame, Baker has brought her audiences music of eloquence and integrity that sets her apart from most of her contemporaries.

Chuck Berry (1926–)
Singer, Songwriter, Guitarist

The first guitar hero of rock and roll, Chuck Berry's 1950s jukebox hits remain some of the most imaginative poetic tales in the history of popular music. Influenced by bluesmen like Aron T-Bone Walker and the picking styles of rockabilly and country musicians, Berry's solo guitar work brought the guitar to the forefront of rhythm and blues. His driving ensemble sound paved the way for the emergence of bands from the Beach Boys to the Rolling Stones.

Born on October 18, 1926, in San Jose, California, Charles Edward Anderson Berry was raised in a middle class neighborhood on the outskirts of St. Louis. Berry first sang gospel music at home and at the Antioch Baptist Church. Although Berry was drawn to the sounds of bluesmen such as Tampa Red, Arthur Crudup, and

Muddy Waters, he did not become serious about music until he was given a guitar by local rhythm and blues musician Joe Sherman. Taken by the sounds of rhythm and blues, Berry formed a trio with Johnny Jones on piano and Ebby Harding on drums. Hired to play backyard barbecues, clubs, and house parties, the trio expanded their repertoire to include Nat "King" Cole ballads and country songs by Hank Williams.

By 1955, the 28-year-old Berry had become a formidable rhythm and blues guitarist and singer. While in Chicago, Berry visited a club to hear his idol, Muddy Waters, perform. At the suggestion of Waters, Berry visited Chess Studios where he eventually signed with the label. Berry's first hit for Chess was "Maybellene," a country song formally entitled "Ida May." In 1956 Berry continued on a path toward superstardom with the hits "Roll Over Beethoven," "Oh Baby Doll," followed by "Rock and Roll Music," and the guitar anthem "Johnny B. Goode."

Released from the Indiana Federal Prison in 1964 after serving a sentence for violating the Mann Act, Berry resumed his musical career, recording "Nadine" and "No Particular Place to Go." Since the 1970s, Berry has continued to record and tour. Berry's 1972 release of

Chuck Berry

the novelty tune "My-Ding-a-Ling" became his best-selling single. In 1988, Taylor Hackford paid tribute to the guitar legend in his film *Hail! Hail! Rock 'n Roll*. Berry was also a featured performer at the opening of Cleveland's Rock and Roll Hall of Fame and Museum in 1995.

Bobby Brown (1966–)
Singer

Savvy and street smart, singer Bobby Brown possesses a charismatic charm which has earned him numerous million-selling records. A founding member of the Boston-based group New Edition, Brown remained with the group from 1984 to 1987. His solo debut album *Kind of Strange* featured the single "Girlfriend." Brown's second release *Don't Be Cruel* produced the single "Don't Be Cruel" and the video hits "My Prerogative" and "Every Little Step."

In 1990, Brown embarked on a worldwide tour. After playing a small role in the box office smash film *Ghostbusters II*. In July of 1992 Brown married singer/actress Whitney Houston in a star-studded ceremony. Two years later, the two solo artists performed together for the first time on the televise 1994 Soul Train Music Awards program. Aside from maintaining a burgeoning music career, Brown is the owner of B. Brown Productions, as well as his own private recording studio. Brown's violent temper and brushes with the law have been the subject of much publicity in the 1990s, even eclipsing the release of his 1993 recording *Remixes in the Key of B*.

James Brown (1933–)
Singer, Bandleader

James Brown's impact on American and African popular music has been of seismic proportion. His explosive onstage energy and intense gospel music and R&B-based sound earned him numerous titles such as "The Godfather of Soul," "Mr. Dynamite," and "The Hardest Working Man in Show Business." During the 1960s and early 1970s, Brown's back–up group emerged as one of the greatest soul bands in the history of modern music, one that served as a major force in the development of funk and fusion jazz.

Born in Barnell, South Carolina on May 3, 1933, Brown moved to Augusta, Georgia at the age of four. Although he was raised by various relatives in conditions of economic deprivation, Brown possessed an undaunted determination to succeed at an early age. When not picking cotton, washing cars, or shining shoes, he earned extra money by dancing on the streets and at amateur contests. In the evening, Brown watched shows by such bandleaders as Louis Jordan and Lucky Millinder.

James Brown

At 15, Brown quit school to take up a full-time music career. In churches, Brown sang with the Swanee Quartet and the Gospel Starlighters, which soon afterward became the R&B group the Flames. During the same period he also sang and played drums with R&B bands. While with the Flames, Brown toured extensively, performing a wide range of popular material including the Five Royales' "Baby Don't Do It," the Clover's "One Mint Julep," and Hank Ballard and the Midnighters hit "Annie Had a Baby."

In 1956, Brown's talents caught the attention of Syd Nathan, founder of King Records. In the same year, after signing with the Federal label, a subsidiary of King, Brown recorded "Please Please Please." After the Flames disbanded in 1957, Brown formed a new Flames ensemble, featuring former members of Little Richard's band. Back in the studio the following year, Brown recorded "Try Me," which became a Top 50 pop hit. On the road, Brown polished his stage act and singing ability, producing what became known as the "James Brown Sound." His 1965 hit "Papa's Got a Brand New Bag" earned him a Grammy for best rhythm and blues recording, a feat he repeated in 1986 with "Living in America," a song that appeared on the soundtrack of the film *Rocky IV*.

After the release of "Out of Sight," Brown's music exhibited a more polyrhythmic sound as evidenced in staccato horn bursts and contrapuntal bass lines. Each successive release explored increasingly new avenues of popular music. Brown's 1967 hit "Cold Sweat" and the 1968 release "I Got the Feeling" not only sent shock waves through the music industry, they served as textbooks of rhythm for thousands of aspiring musicians. In 1970 Brown disbanded the Flames and formed the JBs, featuring Bootsy Collins. The group produced a string of hits like "Super Bad" and "Sex Machine." 1993's *Universal James* was Brown's 79th album.

Despite the negative publicity generated by the oft "in trouble" performer, Brown's career remained effervescent in the late 1980s to 1990s. Inducted into the Rock and Roll Hall of Fame in 1986, the ever-popular, Brown received the Ray Charles Lifetime Achievement Award from the Rhythm & Blues Foundation as part of the organization's Pioneer Awards program in 1993. Later that year, he awarded for his lifetime achievements at the Black Radio Exclusive awards banquet in Washington, DC. Steamboat Springs, Colorado voted to name a bridge after the soulster and Brown's hometown of Augusta, followed suit by naming a street after him. Perhaps the sweetest tribute paid to Brown has been the promotion of James Brown Cookeez by a Georgia-based cookie company. Many of his recordings were reissued in the 1990s.

Shirley Caesar (1938–)
Singer

The leading gospel music singer of her generation, Shirley Caesar was born in Durham, North Carolina, in 1938. One of 12 children born to gospel great "Big Jim" Caesar, Shirley sang in church choirs as a child. By age 14, Caesar went on the road as a professional gospel singer, touring the church circuit on weekends and during school vacations. Known as "Baby Shirley," Caesar joined the Caravans in 1958. Featured as an opening act in the show, Caesar worked the audience to a near fever pitch. When Inez Andrews left the Caravans in 1961, Caesar became the featured artist who provided crowds with powerful performances of such songs as "Comfort Me," "Running For Jesus," and "Sweeping Through the City."

After leaving the Caravans in 1966, Caesar formed her own group, the Shirley Caesar Singers. Her sheer energy and pugnacious spirit made her one of the reigning queens of modern gospel. Her first album *I'll Go* remains one of her most critically acclaimed. In 1969, she released a ten-minute sermonette with the St. Louis Choir that earned her a gold record. A six-time Grammy winner, Caesar conducts weekly sermons at the Mount

Calvary Holy Church in Raleigh, North Carolina, between performances and recording dates.

Reverend James Cleveland (1932–1991)
Singer, Pianist, Composer

Known by such titles as "King James" and the "Crown Prince," the Reverend James Cleveland emerged as a giant of the postwar gospel music scene. Likened to the vocal style of Louis Armstrong, Cleveland's raw bluesy growls and shouts appeared on more recordings than any other gospel singer of his generation.

Born on December 5, 1932, in Chicago, Illinois, James Cleveland first sang gospel under the direction of Thomas Dorsey at the Pilgrim Baptist Church. Inspired by the keyboard talents of gospel singer Roberta Martin, Cleveland later began to study piano. In 1951 Cleveland joined the Gospelaires, a trio which cut several sides for the Apollo label. With the Caravans, Cleveland arranged and performed on two hits "The Solid Rock" and an up-tempo reworking of the song "Old Time Religion."

By the mid-1950s, Cleveland's original compositions had found their way into the repertoires of numerous gospel groups, and he was performing with such artists as the Thorn Gospel Singers, Roberta Martin Singers,

Reverend James Cleveland

Mahalia Jackson, the Gospel Allstars, and the Meditation Singers. In 1960 Cleveland formed the Cleveland Singers featuring organist and accompanist Billy Preston. The smash hit "Love of God," recorded with the Detroit-based Voices of Tabernacle, won Cleveland nationwide fame within the gospel community. Signing with the Savoy label, Cleveland, along with keyboardist Billy Preston, released a long list of classic albums including *Christ Is the Answer*, and *Peace Be Still*. As a founder of the Gospel Workshop of America in 1968, Cleveland organized annual conventions which brought together thousands of gospel singers and songwriters. A year later, he helped found the Southern California Community Choir.

In 1972, Charles was reunited with former piano understudy Aretha Franklin, who featured Cleveland as a guest artist on the album *Amazing Grace*. Recipient of the NAACP Image Award, Cleveland also acquired a honorary degree from Temple Baptist College. Although the commercial gospel trends of the 1980s had caused a downturn in Cleveland's career, he continued to perform the gutsy blues-based sound which brought him recognition from listeners throughout the world. Cleveland died February 9, 1991, in Los Angeles, California.

George Clinton (1942–)
Singer, Songwriter, Bandleader, Producer

The father of "P. [i.e.'pure'] Funk," George Clinton spun the funk formula refined by James Brown into an institution. His groups Parliament and Funkadelic and a panoply of offshoots kept the rest of the R&B world straining to keep up during the 1970s; by the 1990s, the prodigious body of work recorded under the P. Funk moniker exercised a huge influence on rap, soul, and rock. Though he relied heavily on a group of talented musicians to bring his visions to life, Clinton was the visionary behind the legendary "Parliafunkadelicment Thang."

Born in North Carolina, Clinton moved with his family to New Jersey during his adolescence; there he helped form a doo-wop group called The Parliaments. After years of struggling and move to Detroit, the group managed to sell some songs to other artists, but never achieved success on its own. With the advent of psychedelic rock in the mid-1960s, The Parliaments began to change in form; they morphed into Funkadelic by 1968, adding hard rock guitar and spacy grooves. The early Funkadelic albums, notably *Maggot Brain*, became classics of untamed funk-rock.

Clinton deployed Parliament as a slightly more conventional funk vehicle in the early 1970s, emphasizing horns and more dance-oriented arrangements. By the middle of the decade, Parliament had become a major hitmaker with its fantasy-themed concept albums and its circus-like performances. Songs like "Flash Light," "Bop Gun (Endangered Species)," "Mothership Connection," and "Aqua Boogie" became funk staples.

Funkadelic began to take a more commercial turn, particularly after signing with Warner Bros. Records; its biggest hits came with the albums *One Nation Under a Groove* and *Uncle Jam Wants You.* Clinton helped his bassist Bootsy Collins become a funk legend in his own right, and oversaw albums by such P. Funk enterprises as The Brides of Funkenstein, Parlet, and the P. Funk All-Stars, among many others. He also released a slew of solo recordings; his biggest hit in this capacity was the boisterous "Atomic Dog." Though business declined for these acts during the 1980s, Clinton's influence were constant in black pop; by the 1990s, P. Funk recordings were among the most sampled in hip-hop. Clinton went so far as to set up an easy licensing system for rap artists who wanted to lift from his work. Thanks to the adoration of everyone from Dr. Dre to rockers like the Red Hot Chili Peppers, Clinton became a ubiquitous figure on the pop culture scene. He fronted the P. Funk All-Stars at the Lollapalooza rock festival, and appeared in numerous films and television commercials.

Nat "King" Cole

Nat "King" Cole (1919–1965)
Singer, Pianist

Nat Cole was born on March 17, 1919, in Montgomery, Alabama (the family name was Coles, but Cole dropped the "s" when he formed the King Cole Trio years later). When he was five, the family moved to Chicago, and he was soon playing piano and organ in the church where his father served as minister. While attending Phillips High School, Cole formed his own band, and also played with small combos, including one headed by his brother Edward, a bassist.

In 1936, Cole joined the touring company of *Shuffle Along.* After the show folded, he found work in small clubs in Los Angeles. In 1937, the King Cole Trio was formed when the drummer in his quartet failed to appear for a scheduled performance. That same year, Cole made his singing debut when a customer insisted he sing "Sweet Lorraine" (a number he later recorded with great success).

Cole's first record was made in 1943, "Straighten Up and Fly Right," which sold more than 500,000 copies. Over the years, one hit followed another in rapid succession—"Paper Moon," "Route 66," "I Love You for Sentimental Reasons," "Chestnuts Roasting on an Open Fire," "Nature Boy," "Mona Lisa," "Too Young," "Pretend," "Somewhere Along the Way," "Smile," and many others. Cole died of cancer in 1965.

Natalie Cole (1950–)
Singer

With five gold records and her star on Hollywood Boulevard, Natalie Cole has emerged since the 1980s as a major pop music star. Born on February 6, 1950, in Los Angeles, Natalie was the second daughter of jazz pianist and pop music legend Nat "King" Cole. During the early 1970s, Cole performed in nightclubs, while pursuing a degree in child psychology at the University of Massachusetts. In 1975, she recorded her first album *Insepa-rable* at Curtis Mayfield's Curtom Studios. Her other albums include *Thankful* (1978), *I'm ready* (1983), *Good to Be Back* (1989), *Take a Look* (1993), and *Holly and Ivy* (1994), which coincided with her PBS special *Natalie Cole's Untraditional Traditional Christmas.*

In 1991, Cole released a 22-song collection of her father's hits. The album, which contains a re-mixed version of the original title-track "Unforgettable," features a duet between Cole and her father and earned her "Record of the Year" and "Album of the Year" Grammys, complementing the Grammys she won in 1976 for best new artist and in 1976 and 1977 for best rhythm and blues female vocal performance. Cole also won two NAACP Image awards in the mid-1970s and an American Music Award in 1978.

Sean "Puffy" Combs (1971–)
Record Company Executive

Sean Combs was born in New York, New York in 1971. His ear for rap and hip hop combined with his production skills are a proven combination. He began to be noticed at the age of 19 in New York's hip-hop scene. As an intern at Uptown Records, Combs's talents earned him a permanent position. He headed up Uptown's Artist & Repertoire department where his primary responsibilities signing and developing new talents.

Luck took a turn for the worst as Combs was involved in an unfortunate event. In 1991, anxious fans for a charity basketball game rushed the entrance killing nine people. The event, staged by Combs, put a black mark on his young career. Media attacks and mayoral investigations pushed Combs into a depression. Unable to work, Combs confined himself to his Mt. Vernon, New York home. Within a year, Combs was fired from Uptown.

Frustration and rejection inspired Combs to pursue his life's dreams. Comb's talent had earned him a reputation prompting Arista Records to sign him to a deal. Combs called this division of Arista Records Bad Boy Entertainment. Success soon followed as Bad Boy released hits by rappers Craig Mack and the Notorious B.I.G., both of whom Combs is credited for discovering.

The ability to find such talent is what sets Combs apart from most other hip-hop producers. The success of Bad Boys hip-hop artists has lead to the development of new artists. Various projects, including the 1996 release of singer Faith Evans's debut keep Combs busy. Success and the drive instilled in Combs should keep Bad Boy on the rise.

Sam Cooke (1931-1964)
Singer, Songwriter

Sam Cooke's sophisticated vocal style and refined image made him one of the greatest pop music idols of the early 1960s. One of the first gospel music artists to crossover into popular music, Cooke produced songs of timeless quality, filled with human emotion and spiritual optimism.

Born in Clarksdale, Mississippi, on January 2, 1931, Sam Cooke grew up the son of a Baptist minister in Chicago, Illinois. At the age of nine, Cooke, along with two sisters and a brother, formed a gospel group called the Singing Children. While a teenager, he joined the gospel group the Highway QCs which performed on the same bill with nationally famous gospel acts.

By 1950, Cooke replaced tenor Rupert H. Harris as lead singer for the renowned gospel group the Soul Stirrers. Cooke's first recording with the Soul Stirrers, "Jesus Gave Me Water," was recorded for Art Rupe's Specialty label. Although the song revealed the inexperi-

Sam Cooke

ence of the 20–year–old Cooke, it exhibited a quality of immense passion and heightened feeling. Under the pseudonym Dale Cooke, Sam recorded the pop song "Loveable" in 1957. That same year, in a session for producer Bumps Blackwell on the Keen label, Cooke recorded "You Send Me" which climbed to number one on the rhythm and blues charts. On the Keen label, Cooke recorded eight more consecutive hits including "Everyone Likes to Cha Cha Cha," "Only Sixteen," and "Wonderful World," all of which were written or co-written by Cooke.

After his contract with the Keen label expired in 1960, Cooke signed with RCA, and was assigned to staff producers Hugo Peretti and Luigi Creatore. In August, Cooke's recording "Chain Gang" reached the number two spot on the pop charts. Under the lavish production of Hugo and Luigi, Cooke produced a string of hits such as "Cupid" in 1961, "Twistin' the Night Away," in 1962, and "Another Saturday Night" in 1963. Early in 1964, Cooke appeared on the "Tonight Show", debuting two songs from his upcoming LP which included the gospel-influenced composition "A Change Is Gonna Come." On December 11, Cooke checked into a three-dollar-a-night motel where he demanded entrance into the night manageress's room. After a brief physical struggle, the manageress fired three pistol shots which mortally wounded Cooke. Despite his tragic death, Cooke left behind a catalogue of classic recordings and over 100 original compositions including the hit "Shake" which was posthumously released in 1965.

Andrae Crouch (1942-)
Singer, Pianist

An exponent of a modern pop-based gospel style, Andrae Crouch became one of the leading gospel singers of the 1960s and 1970s. Born on July 1, 1942, in Los Angeles, Andrae Crouch grew up singing in his father's church. Along with his brother and sister, Crouch formed the Crouch Trio, which performed at their father's services as well as on live Sunday-night radio broadcasts. In the mid-1960s Crouch was "discovered" by white Pentecostal evangelists and subsequently signed a contract with Light, a white religious record label. Over the last three decades, Crouch has written numerous songs, many of which have become standards in the repertoire of modern gospel groups. Among his most famous songs are "I Don't Know Why Jesus Loved Me," "Through it All," and "The Blood Will Never Lose Its Power." In recognition for this work, Crouch received an ASCAP Special Songwriter Award.

During the late 1960s Crouch, inspired by the modern charismatic revival movement, began adopting street smart language and informal wardrobe. After forming the Disciples in 1968, Crouch recorded extensively and toured throughout the United States and Europe. His California style of gospel music combines rock, country music, and soul with traditional gospel forms. The Disciples won Grammys in 1975, for *Take Me Back* and in 1979, for *Live in London*, which also received a Dove Award. *This Is Another Day* garnered a Dove Award in 1976, as did Crouch's 1984 solo recording *No Time to Lose.*

Since the 1970s, Crouch's back–up groups have incorporated both electronic and acoustic instruments, including synthesizers. The new approach earned Grammys in 1980 and 1981. As the decade ensued, Crouch recorded as a solo artist and was bestowed the Gospel Music Excellence Award for best male vocalist in 1982, for *More of the Best.*

On September 23, 1995, Crouch assumed the pastorship of the Christ Memorial Church of God in Christ in Pacoima, California, the same pulpit once manned by his father. Nearly one year earlier, Crouch—a two-time NAACP Image Award recipient and one-time Golden Halo awardee-released *Mercy!*, his first album since 1984; others were reissued. His return was well-received.

Dr. Dre (1965?–)
Rap singer, Producer

From the time he was four years old, Dr. Dre, born Andre Ramelle Young, was playing DJ at his mother's parties. In 1981, he heard a song by Grandmaster Flash that inspired him to change his name in honor of basketball star Julius "Dr. J." Erving and become a DJ. Dr. Dre began spinning records at a Los Angeles nightclub, producing the dance tapes in the club's four-track studio. In addition to using the rap trademarks of sampling, scratching, and drum machines, he added keyboards and vocals.

In 1982, when Dre was 17 years old, he formed the World Class Wreckin' Cru with another DJ. Their first independently released single sold 50,000 copies. The following year, Dre graduated from Compton, California's Centennial High School and was offered a mechanical drafting position with an aircraft firm, he turned it down to devote himself to music. In 1985, Dr. Dre joined the newly formed group, N.W.A. (Niggaz with Attitude), along with Ice Cube, Eazy-E, Yella, M. C. Ren, and Arabian Prince. That year he also produced Eazy-E's first platinum album, *Eazy-Duz-It.*

N.W.A's successful yet controversial ouvre included the multi-platinum *Straight Outta Compton*, released in 1989 on Eazy-E and Dr. Dre's Ruthless Records. Dr. Dre produced the D.O.C., a rapper he had discovered in Texas. The result, *No One Can Do It Better*, went to Number One on Billboard's R&B album chart. Dre also produced a platinum album for Michel'le, another Number One recording.

In January of 1990, Ice Cube left N.W.A. over a financial dispute; N.W.A. recorded the last of their four recordings without him in 1991. Later that year, Dre left Ruthless to cofound Death Row Records with Suge Knight. Dre's first solo effort, *The Chronic* was released in 1993. The work, featuring such budding rap artists as Snoop Doggy Dogg, sold three million copies. He went on to produce Snoop's debut, *Doggystyle.*

In 1994, Dre received a Grammy Award for best rap solo performance. At the *Source* awards, he was named best producer, solo artist, and *The Chronic* was named best album. The following year he was named "One of the Top Ten Artists That Mattered Most, 1985-1995" by *Spin*. In 1996, Dre stunned the hip-hop community by announcing that he was leaving Death Row.

Fats Domino (1928-)
Singer

Antoine Domino was born on February 26, 1928, in New Orleans. As a teenager, Domino received piano lessons from Harrison Verret. In between playing night clubs, Domino worked at a factory and mowed lawns around New Orleans. At age 20, he took a job as a pianist with bassist Billy Diamond's combo at the Hideaway Club.

In 1949, while playing with Diamond's group, Domino was discovered by producer and arranger David Bartholomew, a talent scout, musician, and producer for the Imperial label. During the following year, Domino hit the charts with the autobiographical tune "Fat Man." After the release of "Fat Man," he played on tour backed by Bartholomew's band.

Although Domino released a number of sides during the early 1950s, it was not until 1955 that he gained national prominence with the hit "Ain't That A Shame." In the next six years, Domino scored 35 top hits with songs like "Blueberry Hill" (1956), "Blue Monday" (1957), "Whole Lotta Lovin" (1958), and "I'm Walkin" (1959). Domino's recording success led to his appearance in several films in the 1950s including *The Girl Can't Help It*, *Shake Rattle and Roll*, *Disc Jockey Jamboree*, and *The Big Beat*.

After Domino's contract with Imperial expired in 1963, he signed with ABC where he made a number of commercial recordings. In 1965 Domino moved to Mercury and then to Reprise in 1968. In the early 1970s, Domino began to tour with greater regularity than he had during the peak of his career. Today Domino continues to tour and make occasional television appearances.

Kenneth "Babyface" Edmonds (1958?–)
Songwriter, Producer

Edmonds was born in the late 1950s in Indianapolis, Indiana, and spent his high school years finagling interviews with pop star idols like the Jackson 5 and Stevie Wonder. After performing in a number of R&B bands, Edmonds began a collaboration with Antonio "L.A." Reid in 1981; they were then members of an act called the Deele, but soon gained acclaim writing and producing songs for other artists such as Shalamar and Bobby Brown.

In 1989, Edmonds and Reid formed their owned company, LaFace Records, backed by the Arista label. They continued their success in writing and producing pop, soul, and R&B hits for such artists as Paula Abdul and Whitney Houston, and Edmonds and Reid are also credited with giving considerable start to the careers of TLC and Toni Braxton. The duo has won numerous Grammy Awards, including one for producer of the year for the 1993 soundtrack to the Eddie Murphy film *Boomerang*, and have shared several songwriter of the year honors from Broadcast Music Inc. (BMI).

Edmonds is also a popular solo artist and performer in his own right, with three well-received releases to his name including the 1993 release *For the Cool in You*, a platinum-seller whose hit "When Can I See You" brought him the 1993 Grammy for best male R&B vocalist. For several months between 1994 and 1995 Edmonds was on the road, performing as an opening act for Boyz II Men, yet another one of the enormously successful groups he has written for and produced. In late 1995 he gained further accolades for producing for the soundtrack to the acclaimed film *Waiting to Exhale*. Edmonds won an Essence Award in 1996.

Roberta Flack (1939–)
Singer, Pianist

Born in Asheville, North Carolina, on February 10, 1939, Roberta Flack moved to Washington, DC with her parents at the age of nine. Three years later she studied classical piano with prominent African American concert musician Hazel Harrison. After winning several talent contests, Flack won a scholarship to Howard University, where she graduated with a bachelors degree in music education. During the early 1960s, Flack taught music in the Washington, DC public school system.

While playing a club date in 1968, Flack was discovered by Les McCann whose connections resulted in a contract with Atlantic Records. Flack's first album *First Take* appeared in 1970 and included the hit song "The First Time Ever I Saw Your Face." Throughout the 1970s, Flack landed several hits such as "Killing Me Softly With His Song" and "The Closer I Get to You," a duet with Donny Hathaway; both songs earned Grammys, and "Killing Me Softly" was remade in 1996, by the rappers The Fugees. In the early 1980s, Flack collaborated with Peabo Bryson to record the hit "Tonight I Celebrate My Love For You." More recently, Flack has been involved in educational projects, and in 1994, she recorded the album *Roberta*.

Aretha Franklin (1942–)
Singer, Pianist, Songwriter

During the 1960s, the collaboration of Aretha Franklin and Atlantic Records producer Jerry Wexler brought forth some of the deepest and most sincere popular music ever recorded. As "Queen of Soul," Franklin has reigned supreme for the last three decades. Her voice brings spiritual inspiration to her gender, race, and the world.

Daughter of the famous Reverend Charles L. Franklin, Aretha was born on March 25, 1942, in Memphis, Tennessee. Raised on Detroit's east side, Franklin sang at her father's New Bethel Baptist Church. Although she began to study piano at age eight, Franklin refused to learn what she considered juvenile and simple tunes. Thus, she learned piano by ear, occasionally receiving instruction from individuals like the Reverend James Cleveland. Franklin's singing skills were modeled after gospel music singers and family friends, including Clara Ward and R&B artists like Ruth Brown and Sam Cooke.

At 14, Franklin quit school to go on the road with her father's Franklin Gospel Caravan, an endless tour in which the family traveled thousands of miles by car. After four years on the road, Aretha traveled to New York City to establish her own career as a pop artist. In 1960, she signed with Columbia Records talent scout John Hammond. Her six year stay at Columbia, however, produced only a few hits and little material that suited Franklin's unique talents.

In 1966, Franklin signed with Atlantic Records, and, in the following year, recorded a session for Wexler that resulted in the hit "I Never Loved a Man (The Way That I Loved You)." That same year, Franklin's career received another boost when her reworking of the Otis Redding's song "Respect" hit the charts. Franklin's first LP *I Never Loved a Man* was followed by a succession of artistically and commercially successful albums: *Aretha Arrives*, *Lady Soul*, *Aretha Now!*, and *This Girl's In Love With You*. Her prominence grew so great that Franklin appeared on the cover of *Time* magazine in 1968. That year she performed at Martin Luther King, Jr.'s funeral and at the Democratic National Convention.

Aretha Franklin

During the 1970s, Franklin continued to tour and record. In 1971, she released the live LP *Aretha Live at the Fillmore West* backed by the horn and rhythm section of Tower of Power. Her next release, *Amazing Grace*, featured Reverend James Cleveland and the Southern California Community Choir. In 1977, she performed at U.S. president Jimmy Carter's inauguration, later doing the same for U.S. president Bill Clinton in 1993.

In 1980, Franklin appeared in the film *The Blues Brothers*. No stranger to television, she appeared in the specials *Aretha, Aretha Franklin: The Queen of Soul*, and *Duets*, in 1986, 1988, and 1993, respectively. The 1980s also saw Franklin score her first big commercial success in more than a decade with the album *Who's Zooming Who?*, featuring the single "Freeway of Love." In 1988, she released a double-live LP *One Lord, One Faith*—an effort dedicated to her father who passed away the previous year.

Franklin has won 15 Grammy awards in her career, including the lifetime achievement award, which was bestowed upon her in 1995. Other of her honors include an American Music Award and an *Ebony* magazine American Black Achievement Award, both in 1984; declaration as a "natural resource" of the State of Michigan in 1985; induction into the Rock and Roll Hall of Fame in 1987; an Essence Award in 1993; and a Kennedy Center Honors Award in 1994. Only Janet Jackson has matched Franklin's record of 14 gold singles, the most by a female solo artist.

Franklin stayed active in the 1990s, a decade in which many of her classic recordings were reissued. She was a headliner at the 1994 New Orleans Jazz and Heritage Festival and lent a track to the 1995 *Waiting to Exhale* soundtrack. Franklin also embarked on a new venture, launching her own label, World Class Records in 1995.

Marvin Gaye (1939–1984)
Singer, Songwriter

The son of a Pentecostal minister, Marvin Gay was born on April 29, 1939, in Washington, DC (the final "e" on his surname was not added until the early 1960s). Raised in a segregated slum-ridden section of Washington, D.C., Gaye experienced a strict religious upbringing. As Gaye later recalled: "Living with my father was like living with a king, a very peculiar, changeable, cruel, and all-powerful king." Thus Gaye looked to music for release. Around the age of three, he began singing in church. While attending Cardoza High School, Gaye studied drums, piano, and guitar. Uninspired by his formal studies, Gaye often cut classes to watch James Brown and Jackie Wilson perform at the Howard Theatre.

Marvin Gaye

Soon afterward, Gaye served a short time in the Air Force, until obtaining a honorable discharge in 1957. Returning to Washington, DC, Gaye joined the doo-wop group the Marquees. After recording for Columbia's subsidiary label, Okeh, the Marquees moved to the Chess/Checker label where they recorded with Bo Diddley. Although the Marquees performed their own compositions and toured regularly, they failed to gain popularity. It was not until they were introduced to Harvey Fuqua, who was in the process of reforming Moonglows, that the Marquees attracted notice in the pop music world. Impressed by their sound Fuqua hired the Marquees to form a group under the new name Harvey and the Moonglows. Still under contract at Chess, Fuqua brought the Moonglows to the company's studio in Chicago to record the 1959 hit the "Ten Commandments of Love."

In 1960, Fuqua and Gaye traveled to Detroit where Fuqua set up his own label and signed with Motown's subsidiary, Anna. After a stint as a back-up singer, studio musician, and drummer in Smokey Robinson's touring band, Gaye signed a contract with Motown as a solo artist. Released in 1962, Gaye's first album was a jazz-oriented effort entitled *The Soulful Moods of Marvin Gaye*. With his sights on a career modeled after the ballad singer Frank Sinatra, Gaye was not enthusiastic when Motown suggested he record a dance record of rhythm and blues material. Nevertheless, Gaye recorded the song "Stubborn Kind of Fellow" in 1962 which entered the top ten R and B charts. This was followed by a long succession of Motown hits, such as "Hitch Hike,"

"Pride and Joy," "Can I Get a Witness," and "Wonderful One."

Motown's next projects for Gaye included a number of vocal duets, the first of which appeared with singer Mary Wells on the 1964 album *Together*. In collaboration with singer Kim Weston, Gaye recorded the 1967 hit LP *It Takes Two*. His most successful partnership, however, was with Tammi Terrell. In their two year association, Gaye and Terrell recorded, under the writing and production team of Ashford and Simpson, such hits as "Ain't No Mountain High Enough" and "Your Precious Love" and "Ain't Nothing Like the Real Thing" in 1968.

Back in the studio as a solo act, Gaye recorded the hit "Heard It Through the Grapevine." With his growing success, Gaye achieved greater creative independence at Motown, which led him to co-produce the 1971 hit album *What's Going On,*,a session producing the best selling singles "What's Going On," "Mercy Mercy (the Ecology)," and "Inner City Blues (Make Me Wanna Holler)."

After his last LP for Motown, *In Our Lifetime*, Gaye signed with CBS Records in April 1981, and within the next year released the album *Midnight Lover*, featuring the Grammy award-winning hit "Sexual Healing." On Sunday, April 1, 1984 Gaye was shot dead by his father in Los Angeles, California. Despite his public image, Gaye had suffered from years of inner conflict and drug abuse. "This tragic ending can only be softened by the memory of a beautiful human being," described long-time friend Smokey Robinson. "He could be full of joy sometimes, but at others, full of woe, but in the end how compassionate, how wonderful, how exciting was Marvin Gaye and his music."

Berry Gordy, Jr. (1929–)
Songwriter, Producer

From assembly line worker to impresario of the Motown Record Corporation, Berry Gordy, Jr. emerged as the owner of one of the largest black-owned businesses in American history. A professional boxer, songwriter, producer, and businessman, Gordy, has been a self-made man. Through his determination and passion for music, the living legend helped to create one of the most celebrated sounds of modern music.

The seventh of eight children, Berry Gordy was born on November 28, 1929, in Detroit. Berry Gordy, Sr., the owner of a grocery store, a plastering company, and a printing shop, taught his children the value of hard work and family unity. Despite his dislike for manual labor, Berry possessed a strong desire to become commercially successful. After quitting high school to become a professional boxer, Berry won several contests before leaving the profession in 1950. A year later, Gordy was drafted into the U.S. Army, where he earned a high school equivalency diploma.

Upon returning from a military tour of Korea in 1953, Berry opened the 3-D Record Mart, a jazz-oriented retail store. Forced into bankruptcy, Berry closed the store in 1955, and subsequently took a job as an assembly line worker at the Ford Motor Company. His nightly visits to Detroit's thriving jazz and rhythm and blues scene inspired Gordy to take up songwriting. In 1957, one of Gordy's former boxing colleagues, Jackie Wilson, recorded the hit "Reet Petiti," a song written by Berry, his sister Gwen, and Billy Davis. Over the next four years, the Berry-Gwen-Davis writing team provided Wilson with four more hits, "To Be Loved," "Lonely Teardrops," "That's Why (I Love You So)," and "I'll Be Satisfied."

By 1959, Billy Davis and Gwen Gordy founded the Anna label, which distributed material through Chess Records in Chicago. Barret Strong's recording of "Money (That's What I Want)," written by Gordy and Janie Bradford, became the label's biggest selling single. With background as a writer and producer with the Anna label, Gordy decided to start his own company. In 1959, he formed Jobete Music Publishing, Berry Gordy, Jr. Enterprises, Hitsville USA, and the Motown Record Corporation. Employing a staff of local studio musicians, writers, and producers, Berry's label scored its first hit in 1961 with Smokey Robinson's "Shop Around." By the mid-1960s, Gordy assembled a wealth of talent including the Supremes, the Four Tops, the Marvelettes, Marvin Gaye, and Stevie Wonder.

In 1971, Gordy relocated the Motown Recording Corporation to Los Angeles. Although most of the original acts and staff members did not join the company's migration to the West Coast, Gordy's company became one of the country's top black-owned businesses. Throughout the 1970s and 1980s, Motown continued to produce artists like the Jackson Five, the Commodores, Lionel Richie, Rick James, and DeBarge. Gordy also tried his hand at producing feature films. *Lady Sings the Blues* (1972), *Mahogany* (1975), and *The Last Dragon* (1985) were not critical successes, but attracted the participation of such celebrities as Diana Ross, Billy Dee Williams, Richard Pryor, and Vanity. Faced with financial problems, Gordy signed a distribution agreement with MCA in 1982, and sold the label in entirety to the giant six years later.

Gordy's induction into the Hall of Fame in 1988, brought recognition to a giant of the recording industry who helped transform the sound of popular music. He was honored with a lifetime achievement award at the 1993 Black Radio Exclusive awards banquet ceremony. One of *Forbes* 400 richest Americans in the mid-1980s,

Gordy authored his autobiography, *To Be Loved: The Music, the Magic, the Memories of Motown* in 1994.

Al Green (1946–)
Singer, Songwriter, Preacher

Possessing one of the supplest voices in popular music, Al Green launched a series of hits up the soul charts during the 1970s. But the Arkansas native turned his back on pop later in that decade, singing gospel and preaching in a Memphis church. His influence on the development of soul was such, however, that he was tempted back to the secular realm for a 1996 album.

Green spent his early years singing gospel in the south, but switched to pop and scored a hit, "Back Up Train," in 1967. It wasn't until he hooked up with producer Willie Mitchell, however, that he found his niche. Recording for Mitchell's Hi Records in Memphis with an ace band, Green managed a remarkable synthesis of intimate, romantic pop and gritty soul. The fruits of this happy union included "Tired of Being Alone," "Love and Happiness," "Let's Stay Together," and "I'm Still in Love With You." His smoldering "Take Me to the River" was covered by numerous other artists.

Though he was "born again" into Christianity in 1973, Green continued to record largely secular music—albeit with a religious tinge—for several years. After founding his own church, the Full Gospel Tabernacle, in Memphis, he returned to gospel music. His recordings won regular honors in gospel circles and even a Grammy Award, but his presence continued to be felt in the soul/R&B world. Apart from the occasional duet, however, he steered clear of pop until his return in 1995 with *Your Heart's In Good Hands*.

Andre Harrell (1962?–)
Record Company Executive, Producer, Musician

Andre O'Neal Harrell was born in the Bronx, New York. While growing up with hard times in the housing projects there, young Harrell developed a desire to succeed. As a teenager, Harrell teamed up with Alonzo Brown to form the playful rap duo Dr. Jekyll (Harrell) and Mr. Hyde (Brown). Before long, they had three top 20 hits under their belts and were carving a niche for themselves in rap.

Despite the his early rap success, Harrell enrolled in classes at the Bronx's Lehman College. After three years of study in communications and business management, Harrell met Russell Simmons in 1983. Simmons lured Harrell to come work for him at Rush Management, a company that helped define the hip-hop of the day. Within two years, Harrell had worked his way up vice-president and general manager and was instrumental in building the career of such rap icons as LL Cool J, Run-DMC, and Whodini.

Success continued to follow Harrell wherever he went. He left Rush Management to begin his own record company, Uptown Records. In 1988, the achievements of Uptown Records prompted a $75,000 record deal from music mega-company MCA. Artists like Al B Sure!, Guy, and Heavy D all prospered under Harrell's direction. By 1992, Uptown and their artists had blazed a shiny trail of gold and platinum albums and had landed an unprecedented $50 million multimedia agreement with MCA. Soon projects like the television show *In Living Color* and a showcase of Uptown recording artists, including Mary J. Blige and Jodeci on MTV's *Unplugged* were in the works. In 1995, Harrell left the reigns of Uptown to became the new president of Motown Records.

Issac Hayes (1942–)
Singer, Pianist, Producer

Born on August 20, 1942, in Covington, Tennessee, Issac Hayes moved to Memphis at age seven, where he was introduced to the sounds of blues, country western, and the music of idol Sam Cooke. Through the connections of saxophonist Floyd Newman, Hayes began a career as a studio musician for Stax Records in 1964. After playing piano on a session for Otis Redding, Hayes formed a partnership with songwriter Dave Porter. Together they were responsible for supplying a number of hits to Carla Thomas, William Bell, and Eddie Floyd.

The first real break for the Hayes-Porter team came when they were recruited to produce the Miami-based soul duo Sam and Dave. In the span of four years, Hayes and Porter succeeded in making Sam and Dave Stax's hottest selling act, producing such hits as "Hold On I'm Coming," "Soul Man," and "I Thank You!" During this period Hayes and Porter continued to perform in a group that established them as an underground legend in the Memphis music scene.

In the late 1960s, Hayes's solo career emerged in an impromptu fashion, when a late night session with drummer Al Jackson and bassist Duck Dunn prompted Stax to release his next effort. Hot Buttered Soul went double platinum in 1969 Featuring a soul version of the country song, "By the Time I Get to Phoenix," Hayes's rendition set a trend for the disco/soul sound of the 1970s. Following the release of the albums *To Be Continued* and *Issac Hayes Movement*, Hayes recorded the soundtrack for the "blaxplotation" film *Shaft* and the album *Black Moses*. In 1971, "Theme from *Shaft*" won an Academy Award for best song in a motion picture and Grammy awards for best instrumental and best original score for a motion picture. *Black Moses* earned a Grammy, too, this one for best pop instrumental performance.

Hayes left the Stax label to join ABC in 1974. Hayes recorded a series of disco albums. In 1977, the commercial downturn in Hayes's career forced him to file bankruptcy. Though he composed Dionne Warwick's "Déjà Vu,"—nominated for a Grammy in 1978—his last gold record, "Don't Let Go," was released on the Polydor label in 1979. Hayes moved into the 1980s and 1990s appearing on television shows and in such films as the futuristic thriller *Escape From New York* (1981) and the comedy-spoof *Robin Hood: Men in Tights* (1993).

Winner of a 1994 Georgy Award, as bestowed by the Georgia Music Hall of Fame, Hayes has heavily influenced the music of the late 1980s and early 1990s; together with James Brown, Hayes has been one of the most-frequently sampled artists by purveyors of rap. Choosing not to jump ship, however, Hayes has stuck to his own brand of "hot buttered soul." In 1995, he issued his first new recordings in seven years—*Branded* and *Raw and Refined*—and contributed a track to the Hughes brothers' film *Dead Presidents.*

Jimi Hendrix (1942–1970)
Guitarist, Songwriter

When Jimi Hendrix arrived on the international rock music scene in 1967, he almost single-handedly redefined the sound of the electric guitar. Hendrix' extraordinary approach has shaped the course of music from jazz fusion to heavy metal.

On November 25, 1942, in Seattle, Washington, Johnny Allen Hendrix was born to an enlisted Army soldier and a teenage mother. Four years later, Johnny Allen was renamed James Marshall Hendrix. Because of his mother's fondness for night club life and his father's frequent absences, Hendrix was a lonely, yet creative, child. At school he won several contests for his science fiction-based poetry and visual art. At the age of eight, Hendrix, unable to afford a guitar, strummed out rhythms on a broom. Eventually, he graduated to a fabricated substitute made from a cigar box, followed by a ukelele, and finally an acoustic guitar that was purchased by his father.

By the late 1950s, Hendrix began to play in local bands in Seattle. While a teenager, he played along with recordings by blues artists like Elmore James and John Lee Hooker. After a 26-month stint (1961–1962) in the 101st Airborne Division, Hendrix played in the Nashville rhythm and blues scene with bassist Billy Cox. For the next three years, Hendrix performed under the name Jimi James, backing up acts such as Little Richard, Jackie Wilson, Ike and Tina Turner, and the Isley Brothers.

In 1964 Hendrix moved to New York City where he performed in various Greenwich Village clubs. While in New York he formed the group Jimi James and the Blue

Jimi Hendrix

Flames. After being discovered by producer and manager Chas Chandler, the former bassist with the Animals, Hendrix was urged to leave for England. Arriving in England in 1966, Hendrix, along with bassist Noel Redding and drummer Mitch Mitchell, formed the Jimi Hendrix Experience. In 1967, after touring Europe, the trio hit the charts with a cover version of the Leaves song "Hey Joe." In the same year, the group released the ground-breaking album *Are You Experienced?*.

In 1968 the Experience recorded *Axis Bold As Love* which led to extensive touring in the U.S. and Europe. On the Experience's next LP, *Electric Ladyland*, Hendrix sought to expand the group's trio-based sound. A double record effort, *Electric Ladyland* featured numerous guest artists such as keyboardists Steve Winwood and Al Kooper, saxophonist Freddie Smith, and conga player Larry Faucette. The record also contained "All Along the Watchtower," a song written by Hendrix's musical and poetic idol Bob Dylan.

After the Experience broke up in 1969, Hendrix played the Woodstock Music and Arts Festival with the Gypsy Sons and Rainbows, featuring bassist Billy Cox. Along with drummer Buddy Miles, Hendrix and Cox formed the Band of Gypsys, and in 1970 the group

released an album under the same title. Months later, Mitchell replaced Miles on drums. In August, the Mitchell-Cox line-up played behind Hendrix at his last major performance held at England's Isle of Wight Festival. On September 18, 1970, Hendrix died in a hotel room in England.

Whitney Houston (1963–)
Model, Singer, Actress

A multiple Grammy Award-winner whose face has graced the covers of magazines from *Glamour* to *Cosmopolitan*, Whitney Houston emerged as one of the most vibrant popular music talents during the 1980s. A talented singer, model, and actress, Houston dominated the pop charts into the 1990s. Her biggest successes were associated with two motion pictures in which she had major roles.

Born on August 9, 1963, Houston grew up in East Orange, New Jersey. As a member of the New Hope Baptist Choir, she made her singing debut at age 11. Later, Houston appeared as a back-up singer on numerous recordings, featuring her mother Cissy Houston and cousin Dionne Warwick. Despite her success as a fashion model, Houston found the profession "degrading," and, subsequently, quit in order to seek a career in music. She backed up the likes of Chaka Khan, Lou Rawls, and the Neville Brothers.

By age 19, Houston had received several recording contract offers. In 1985, she released her debut album on the Arista label entitled *Whitney Houston*, which produced four hits: "Saving All My Love for You," which won the Grammy for best female pop performance; "You Give Good Love"; "How Will I Know," which earned an MTV Video Music Award for best female video; and "The Greatest Love of All." The album won seven American Music awards, a feat she would duplicate in 1994. Houston's second LP, *Whitney*, appeared in 1987, and like her first effort, the work spawned a number of hits, including "I Wanna Dance With Somebody," "Didn't We Almost Have It All," "So Emotional," "Where Do Broken Hearts Go?," and "Love Will Save the Day." The album received four American Music awards. Following the success of her second record, Houston released *One Moment In Time* (1988) and the slickly produced *I'm Your Baby Tonight* (1990).

In 1992, Houston married singer Bobby Brown and made her acting debut in the film *The Bodyguard*, costarring Kevin Costner. The first single from the soundtrack, a remake of Dolly Parton's "I Will Always Love You," spent 14 weeks straight on the top of the pop singles chart; according to statistics from *Billboard* magazine, Houston set a record for the most time spent at the top of the charts, edging out Boyz II Men's "End of the Road" (13 weeks) and Elvis Presley's "Don't Be

Cruel" (11 weeks). Her vocal performance on the soundtrack won her seven American Music Awards, including the 1994 Award of Merit; four Grammy awards, including record of the year, album of the year, and best female pop performance; two Soul Train Music awards, including the Sammy Davis, Jr. Entertainer of the Year Award and the female R&B single award for "I Will Always Love You"; four NAACP Image awards; and the National Association of Black Owned Broadcasters' lifetime achievement award. Later in the year, AT&T signed Houston as the spokesperson for the corporation's "True Voice" campaign; Houston sang in two of the company's commercials.

Houston's next offering was not long in coming. With Angela Bassett, Lela Rochon, and Loretta Devine, Houston costarred in the 1995 film adaption of Terry McMillan's *Waiting to Exhale*. A box-office winner, the movie's soundtrack was written by producer Babyface and featured, in addition to Houston, such performers as Aretha Franklin and Toni Braxton. Houston sang the very successful first single, "Exhale (Shoop Shoop)."

Ice Cube (1969–)
Singer, Actor

Behind his oft misogynistic and racist gangster image, rapper Ice Cube is a serious artist. Dedicated to black pride, he is a staunch spokesperson for black nationalism. Ice Cube looks upon his music as a means of launching a "mental revolution" in order to awaken African American youth to the value of education and the creation of private black economic enterprises.

Born Oshea Jackson, Ice Cube grew up in the west side of South Central Los Angeles. While in the ninth grade Jackson wrote his first rhyme in typing class. Prompted by his parents to pursue an education after high school, he attended a one-year drafting course at the Phoenix Institute in 1988. In the following year, Ice Cube achieved great commercial success as a member of N.W.A. (Niggas With Attitude). One of the group's founding members, along with Dr. Dre and Eazy-E, Ice Cube wrote or cowrote most of the material for N.W.A.'s first two albums. *Boyz-n-the-Hood* was released in 1986. Ice Cube's authoritative baritone won him a legion of fans for his N.W.A. rap anthem "Gangsta Gangsta." He also scripted much of Eazy's first solo work, *Eazy-Duz-It*, followed by N.W.A.'s platinum *Straight Outta Compton*, which included the controversial single, "F— tha Police."

Though he still worked sporadically with Dr. Dre after leaving N.W.A., Ice Cube released his 1990 solo album *AmeriKKKa's Most Wanted*, produced with Public Enemy's Chuck D. and the Bomb Squad; the recording went gold within three months. He then formed Street Knowledge, a record production company and

produced female rapper Yo Yo's *Make Way for the Motherlode*. During the same year, Ice Cube also made his acting debut in director John Singleton's film *Boyz N' the Hood*. The rapper-actor went on to star in a number of films, including 1992's *Tresspass*, with Ice-T; *Higher Learning*, Singleton's vehicle of 1994; the 1995 comedy *Friday*, which he cowrote and co-produced; and Charles Burnett's 1995 work, *The Glass Shield*.

Having recorded his own *Kill at Will* and *Death Certificate* in 1991, Ice Cube remained active in Yo Yo's career, serving as executive producer of her *Black Pearl* in 1992, and worked with other artists, directing videos including one for blues-rock artist Ian Moore in 1993. Ice Cube stayed on top of his own music game as well, releasing *The Predator* in 1992; the recording debuted at number one on two *Billboard* charts—pop and R&B— at the same time, the first to do so since 1976 and Stevie Wonder's *Songs in the Key of Life*. In 1992, Ice Cube figured in the lineup of Lollapalooza II, an annual traveling rock festival. 1993's *Lethal Injection* featured the smash single "It Was a Good Day." Ice Cube also issued *Bootlegs & B-Sides*, and, in 1995, he contributed to the *Streetfigher* motion picture soundtrack. In 1996, he was working on a concept album with fellow rappers Mack 10 and WC.

Janet Jackson (1966–)
Singer

The youngest child of a family of talented children, Janet Jackson is a tremendously energetic performer, whose singing and dance styles have reached immense popularity around the world. She is one of the most successful of a family of highly successful performers, including her brother Michael, the so-called "King of Pop." In the 1990s, she has fully emerged from his shadow and has become a full-fledged sex symbol and role model.

Born on May 16, 1966, in Gary, Indiana, Janet Jackson began performing with her brothers at age six, doing impressions of famous stars like Mae West and Cher. She made her first professional singing debut at one of the Jackson Five's shows in the Grand Hotel in Las Vegas. Before she was ten years old, Jackson was spotted by television producer Norman Lear, resulting in her appearances on such television shows as *Good Times*, *Different Strokes*, and *Fame*.

In 1982, Jackson's debut album for the A&M label *Janet* contained only a few minor hits. Teamed with producers Jimmy Jam and Terry Lewis, Jackson released her more commercially successful LP *Dream Street*. Her 1986 release *Control* scored six hit singles, including "What Have You Done For Me Lately," "Nasty," "When I Think of You," "Control," "Let's Wait Awhile," and "Pleasure Principle." Under the direction of Jam and Lewis, Jackson released the dance-oriented album *Janet Jackson's Rhythm Nation 1814* in 1989, which went quadruple platinum. Among the record's numerous singles were "Miss You Much," "Come Back To Me," and "Black Cat."

After an extensive world tour in 1990, Jackson left the A&M label to sign a contract with Virgin Records in 1991. The four-album contract was worth an estimated $80 million with $50 million guaranteed up-front. Two years later, she starred alongside Tupac Shakur in John Singleton's *Poetic Justice*. Jackson played a soul-searching hairdresser prone to writing poetry; Maya Angelou, who was also featured in the film, provided the poems Jackson's character read. In 1994, Jackson released *janet.* Critically acclaimed, the album did well commercially, too. The single "Any Time, Any Place" earned Jackson her fourteenth gold single, the most by any female solo artist other than Aretha Franklin. The following year, Jackson collaborated with her brother Michael on a track entitled "Scream." The visually stunning video associated with the single was the most expensive ever made. Later in 1995, her *Design of a Decade: 1986–1996* made a splashy debut. She also contributed a song to the soundtrack for *Ready to Wear*.

Jackson has earned much recognition throughout her career. Between 1986 and 1992, she garnered four *Billboard* awards; seven American Music awards; two MTV Video Music awards; one Grammy Award; three Soul Train awards; a BMI Pop Award; and the 1992 Sammy Davis, Jr. Award or Entertainer of the Year. In 1990, she acquired a star on Hollywood "Walk of Fame," and, in 1992, the NAACP gave her its Chairman's Award. Three years later, she received an Essence Award.

Mahalia Jackson (1912–1972)
Gospel Singer

Hailed as the world's greatest gospel singer, Mahalia Jackson's rich contralto voice became a national institution. Through live performances, recordings, and television appearances, Jackson elevated gospel music to a level of popularity unprecedented in the history of African American religious music.

The third of six children, Jackson was born on October 26, 1912, in New Orleans, Louisiana. Growing in New Orleans, Jackson absorbed the sounds of parade music and brass bands. She later discovered the blues, a music labeled the "devil's music" by regular church-goers, and listened secretly to recordings of singers like Mamie Smith and Bessie Smith.

In 1927, at the age of 13, Jackson moved to Chicago where she joined the Greater Salem Baptist Church. Two years later, Jackson met the gospel musician and songwriter Thomas A. Dorsey who invited her to sing at

Mahalia Jackson

the Pilgrim Baptist Church. In 1937 Jackson recorded four sides for the Decca label including the song "God's Gonna Separate the Wheat From the Tares."

Jackson's big break did not come until 1947 when she released gospel music's first million-selling record "Move on Up a Little." In 1949 her song "Let the Holy Ghost Fall on Me" won the French Academy's Grand Prix du Disque. Soon afterward, she toured Europe and recorded the gospel hit "In the Upper Room." During the 1960s, Jackson became a musical ambassador. Not only did she perform at the White House and at London's Albert Hall, but she sang at Martin Luther King's 1963 March on Washington, as well as his funeral ceremony in 1968.

On January 27, 1972, Jackson died of a heart condition in Chicago. At her funeral at Great Salem Baptist, some 45,000 mourners gathered to pay their respects to a woman who brought gospel music into the hearts and homes of millions of listeners.

Michael Jackson (1958–)
Singer, Composer

From child singing star with the Jackson Five to his success as a solo performer in the 1980s, Michael Jackson has amassed the largest following of any African American singer in the history of popular music. Jackson has an audience that transcends the boundaries of nations and bridges the gaps brought about by generational differences. Despite some missteps in the early 1990s, the "King of Pop" reigns supreme.

The fifth of nine children, Michael Jackson was born on August 29, 1958, in Gary, Indiana. As a child, Michael, along with his brothers Tito, Jermaine, Jackie, and Marlon, comprised the Jackson Five. Under the tutelage of their father, Joe, the five boys learned to sing and dance. On weekends the family singing group traveled hundreds of miles to perform at amateur contests and benefit concerts.

After two years on the road, the group landed an audition with Motown records. Upon signing with the label in 1969, the Jackson Five hit the charts with the number one hit "I Want You Back," a song arranged and produced by Berry Gordy, Jr. On recordings and television shows, Michael's wholesome image and lead vocal style attracted fans from every racial and age group. During the group's six-year stay at Motown, the Jackson Five scored 13 consecutive top 20 singles such as "ABC," "The Love You Save," and "I'll Be There."

While lead vocalist for the Jackson Five, Michael had signed a separate contract with Motown in 1971, formalizing a solo career that produced the hits "Got to Be There" in 1971, "Ben" in 1972, and "Just a Little Bit of You" in 1975. When cast in the role of the scarecrow in the 1975 Motown film *The Wiz*, Jackson met producer Quincy Jones who later collaborated with him to record the 1979 hit LP *Off the Wall* on the Epic label. Two years later, Jackson, guided by the production skills of Jones, recorded the biggest selling album of all time, *Thriller*. The seven hit singles included "Beat It," "Billie Jean," "Wanna Be Startin' Something," and the title track, which featured a voice–over by horror-cult figure Vincent Price. The video for the song was almost a mini-movie staring Jackson as a dancing werewolf run amok, with special effects that rivaled any full-length feature film.

In 1985, Jackson cowrote the song "We Are the World" for the U.S.A. for Africa famine relief fund. After joining Jones to produce the *Bad* in 1987, Jackson led the most commercially successful tour in history. Four years later, Jackson released *Dangerous*, which includes the hit single "Black or White."

In 1993, Jackson announced that the progressive lightening of his skin has been the result of a skin disorder known as vitiligo and not from intentional bleaching. The public declaration was one of many Jackson would find himself making about various topics in the ensuing years. Scandal-ridden, Jackson hit a backslide in his career following allegations of child molestation—charges that were dropped—and the coming to light of a pain medication addiction brought about by poor health.

Coming on the heels of such devastating disclosures, 1995's *HIStory: Past, Present, and Future, Book I* featured hits from the past as well as new works. Compared to his previous recordings, sales were disappointing and the recording was not considered a commercial success. Fan loyalty to the gifted musician, however, drove some of the new songs into chart contention, including "The Earth Song," the controversial "They Don't Care About Us," and the lilting ballad "You Are Not Alone." The compilation also gave Jackson a chance to work with his sister Janet, when the two collaborated on the duet "Scream," the first single to be released. The ensuing video for "Scream" cost $7 million, making it

Michael Jackson

one of the most expensive, albeit eye-catching, videos ever produced.

Jackson had made headlines in 1994, when he announced his betrothal to Lisa Marie Presley, daughter of the late rock legend Elvis Presley. The marriage of Jackson and Presley was considered highly unusual, and many critics dismissed it as a publicity stunt. On June 14, 1995, Jackson and Presley were interviewed by Diane Sawyer on ABC's *Prime Time Live.* During the interview, the two insisted they were deeply in love and planned to eventually have children. However, in January of 1996, Lisa Presley announced that she was divorcing Jackson.

Jackson's business ventures have had more staying power. An astute business man, he entered into a $600 million joint publishing deal with Sony in 1995. The deal combined Sony's music publishing division with Jackson's ATV Music Catalog, which once owned the rights to the entire Beatles ouvre.

More importantly, Jackson continues to garner acclaim, despite his setbacks. In 1993, he received three American Music awards, including the first-ever International Artist Award and was recognized at the World Music Awards ceremony in Nonte Carlo, Monaco. In addition, he received special Grammy honors that year. Two years later, he won three MTV Video awards. While many argue that his work has been uneven, his contribution to modern pop has been enormous. Indeed, Jackson redefined stardom for the video era. Popular culture will never be the same.

Quincy Jones (1933–)
Trumpeter, Arranger, Producer

Winner of 20 Grammy Awards and the writer of more than 52 film scores, Quincy Jones is popular music's quintessential musician/producer. Aside from performing trumpet with the likes of jazzmen Lionel Hampton and Dizzy Gillespie, Jones has produced for artists from Frank Sinatra to Michael Jackson.

Quincy Jones was born on March 14, 1933, in Chicago, Illinois. At age ten, Jones moved to Bremerton, Washington. As a member of Bump Blackwell's Junior Orchestra, Jones performed at local Seattle social functions. In 1949, Jones played third trumpet in Lionel Hampton's band in the local Seattle club scene. After befriending jazz bassist Oscar Pettiford, Jones established himself as an able musician and arranger.

From 1950 to 1953, Jones became a regular member of Hampton's band, and, subsequently, toured the United States and Europe. During the mid-1950s, Jones began to record jazz records under his own name. In 1956, he toured the Middle East and South America with the U.S. State Department Band headed by Dizzy Gillespie.

Quincy Jones

In 1961, Jones was appointed musical director at Mercury Records. In search of new musical horizons, Jones began producing popular music, including Leslie Gore's 1963 hit "It's My Party." Jones's growing prestige at Mercury led to his promotion to vice president of the company, marking the first time an African American had been placed in an executive position at a major label. During this time, Jones also began to write and record film scores. In 1967, he produced the music score for the movie *In the Heat of the Night.* He also produced the music score for Alex Haley's television mini-series *Roots* and co-produced the film adaptation of Alice Walker's *The Color Purple* with Steven Spielberg.

After his production of the 1978 Motown-backed film *The Wiz,* Jones went on to produce the film's star, Michael Jackson, on such recordings as the 1979 release *Off the Wall* and the 1985 record-breaking hit *Thriller.* Jones's 1989 release *Back on the Block,* a Grammy winner, was praised by critics and was no doubt a sign of Jones's continuing role in the future development of African American popular music. Two years later, Jones sat down with his old buddy Miles Davis. The musical encounter was recorded and released in 1993 as *Miles & Quincy Live at Montreaux,* along with a video documentary of the same name. In 1995, Jones released his album *Q's Juke Joint,* featuring updated versions of tunes popularized in post-slavery roadhouses.

Jones is also influential in the media industry. He is chairman of Quest Broadcasting; in 1994, the group partnered with Chicago's Tribune Co. to buy television stations in Atlanta and New Orleans. His joint venture with Time Warner—*Vibe* magazine, which Jones founded—has been very successful. The publication covers urban music and culture and has a high readership among blacks and Latinos.

Louis Jordan (1908–1975)
Singer, Alto-Saxophonist, Bandleader

Louis Jordan led one of the most popular and influential bands of the 1940s. The shuffle boogie rhythm of his jump blues ensemble, the Tympany Five, had a profound impact on the emergence of rhythm and blues. As guitarist Chuck Berry admitted, "I identify myself with Louis Jordan more than any other artist." For it was Jordan's swinging rhythms, theatrical stage presence, and songs about everyday life that made him a favorite among musicians and listeners throughout the 1940s.

Born in Brinkley, Arkansas, July 8, 1908, Jordan was the son of a bandleader and music teacher. He received his music education in the Brinkley public schools and the Baptist College in Little Rock. Jordan's early music career as a clarinetist included stints with the Rabbit Foot Minstrels and Ruby Williams's orchestra. Soon after moving to Philadelphia in 1932, Jordan joined Charlie Gains' group; sometime around 1936, he joined drummer Chick Webb's band.

After Webb's death in 1938, Jordan started his own group. Because Jordan performed for both white and black audiences, he, to use his own words, learned to "straddle the fence" by playing music ranging from blues to formal dance music. Signing with Decca records during the same year, Jordan began a recording career which, by the early 1940s, produced a string of million selling recordings such as "Is You Is or Is You Ain't (My Baby)," "Choo Choo Ch'Boogie," "Saturday Night Fish Fry," and "Caledonia." Aside from working with artists like Louis Armstrong, Bing Crosby, and Ella Fitzgerald, Jordan appeared in several films such as the 1949 release *Shout Sister Shout.*

Although failing to achieve the success he experienced during the 1940s, Jordan fronted a big band in the early 1950s. During the 1960s and 1970s, he continued to tour the United States, Europe, and Asia. His career came to an end in 1975 when he suffered a fatal heart attack in Los Angeles.

Eddie Kendricks (1939–1992)
Singer

As a member of the Temptations in the 1960s, Eddie Kendricks' articulate soulful falsetto provided Motown with a number of pop music classics. Kendricks' gospel music background "enabled him to bring an unusual earnestness to the singing of love lyrics," wrote music historian David Morse. "He can be compared only with Ray Charles in his ability to take the most threadbare ballad and turn it into a dramatic and completely convincing statement."

Born on December 17, 1939, in Birmingham, Alabama, Kendricks grew up with close friend and Temptations' member Paul Williams. In 1956 Kendricks and Williams quit school and traveled northward to become singing stars in the tradition of their idols Clyde McPhatter and Little Willie John. In Detroit, Kendricks and Williams formed the doo-wop singing group the Primes which performed at talent contests and house parties. In 1961 the Primes recorded the songs "Mother of Mine" and the dance tune "Check Yourself" for Berry Gordy's short-lived Miracle label.

Upon the suggestion of Berry Gordy, the Primes changed their name to the Temptations and after adding David Ruffin as lead vocalist, they set out to become one of the most successful groups on the Motown label. Throughout the decade, Kendricks sang lead on several songs including the classics "My Girl" in 1965, "Get Ready" in 1966, and "Just My Imagination (Running Away With Me)" in 1972.

In June of 1971, Kendricks pursued a solo career and eventually recorded two disco-influenced hits "Keep on Truckin" in 1973, and "Boogie Down" in 1974. Kendricks' career soon fell into decline. Unable to find material to suit his unique artistic sensibility, Kendricks switched record labels several times before reuniting with the Temptations in 1982. After the reunion, Kendricks performed with the Temptations on the Live Aid broadcast and on the album *Live at the Apollo Theater with David Ruffin and Eddie Kendricks.* In 1987 Ruffin and Kendricks signed a contract with RCA and recorded the aptly titled LP *Ruffin and Kendricks.* Stricken by lung cancer, Kendricks died in October 1992.

Gladys Knight (1944–)
Singer

Born May 28, 1944, in Atlanta, Georgia, Gladys Knight was raised in a family which valued education and the sounds of gospel music. At age four, Knight began singing gospel music at the Mount Moriah Baptist Church. When she was eight, Knight won first prize on the television program "Ted Mack's Amateur Hour" for a rendition of the song "Too Young." Between the years 1950 to 1953, Knight toured with the Morris Brown Choir of Atlanta, Georgia. Around this same time, Knight joined her sister Brenda, brother Merald, and cousins William and Eleanor Guest to form a local church singing group. In 1957 the group took the name the Pips upon the suggestion of cousin and manager James "Pips" Woods.

Louis Jordan and the Tymphany Five, 1946.

Two years later Langston George and Edward Patten replaced Brenda Knight and Eleanor Guest. Though Gladys periodically left the group, she rejoined in 1964. After recording for several record labels, the Pips finally signed with Motown's subsidiary, Soul. Despite the lack of commercial success, the group released a number of fine recordings under the supervision of Motown's talented production staff including Norman Whitfield and Ashford and Simpson. In 1967 the group released the single "I Heard It Through the Grapevine" which reached number two on the Billboard charts. Following a long string of hits on Motown, the Pips signed with the Buddah label in 1973, releasing the album *Imagination* which provided the group with two gold singles, "Midnight Train to Georgia" and "I've Got to Use My Imagination."

By the late 1970s the group, faced with legal battles and contract disputes, began to fall out of popular vogue. For three years the group was barred from recording or performing together. As a result of an out-of-court settlement in 1980, the Pips signed a new contract with CBS, where they remained until 1985. Joined by Dionne Warwick and Elton John, Knight recorded the Grammy award winning gold single "That's

What Friends Are For" in 1986. Released in 1988, the title cut of the Pip's *Love Overboard* album became their biggest selling single in decades. That same year, Knight recorded the theme for the James Bond film *License To Kill*. Released on the MCA label, Knight's 1991 album *Good Women* features guest stars Patti Labelle and Dionne Warwick.

Suge Knight (1966–)
Record Company Executive

Born Marion Knight, Jr. in 1966, Knight grew up in the rough neighborhood of Compton, California. Despite being surrounded by violence, Knight picked up the nickname "Suge"—short for "Sugar"—because of his basic good-natured temperament. While in high school, Knight devoted his time to playing football with the hopes of gaining an athletic scholarship to college. Standing more than 6' tall and weighing nearly 300 pounds, Knight took his talents to the University of Nevada in Las Vegas. There he won several awards, including the Rookie of the Year on defense and a spot on the dean's list for academics. After college, Knight was drafted by the NFL's Los Angeles Rams but decide to pursue different avenues.

Gladys Knight and the Pips at the 1989 American Music Awards.

A string of run ins with the law almost put an end to any hopes Knight had. Between the years of 1987 and 1990, Knight was arrested for several crimes, including auto theft, battery, and attempted murder. His luck soon changed as he made a name for himself while working as a bodyguard for musicians. Eventually, Knight formed a publication company and made a significant amount of money from ownership rights to several of white rapper Vanilla Ice's songs.

Based on the success of his publishing company, Knight decided to venture into artist management. This led to Knight meeting Dr. Dre, formerly of N.W.A. At that time, Dre was managed by Ruthless Records, but Knight pulled some strings and signed Dre and two other Ruthless artists to new contracts. Controversy surrounded the transaction as Knight was accused of using force to finalize the deal. Together with Dr. Dre, Knight founded Death Row Records. Blistering success quickly followed as the label grossed more than $60 million in 1993. An already impressive artist roster, including Dr. Dre, Snoop Doggy Dogg, and Warren G. quickly improved with the signing of Mary J. Blige and Jodeci. With three multi-platinum albums under his belt, Knight

began to refer to Death Row Records as "the Motown of the 90s."

In luring top artists to Death Row, Knight often doubles their royalty rates, offers more creative control for the musician, and upgrades their contracts. In 1995, Knight even bailed jailed rapper Tupac Shakur out of prison in order to add more talent to the Death Row cluster. Despite the success Knight has enjoyed, many are skeptical of his tactics, but his peers simply view him as a master of the art of negotiation.

KRS-One (1965?–)
Rap singer

A self-described teacher whose Boogie Down Productions (BDP) was an important influence on hardcore rap, KRS-One survived street life, prision, homelessness, the murder of a close friend, and negative criticism to emerge as one of rap's most powerful figures. Born as Lawrence Parker c. 1965 in Brooklyn, New York, KRS-One (initially representative of "Kris, Number One," later an acronym for Knowledge Reigns Supreme Over Nearly Everyone") also went by Krishna Parker or Kris Parker. Leaving home at 13, he lived on the streets, taking odd jobs when available and hanging out in public libraries. Self-educated, he served a short stin in jail for selling marijuana. Upon his release, the 19-year-old met Scott Sterling, a social worker and DJ who worked under the name Scott LaRock. Together the two formed BDP.

BDP recored one album, *Criminal Minded* before LaRock was killed while trying to break up a fight. Perservering, KRS-One kept their music alive, recording several critically aclaimed works with the various musicians who comprised the BDP crew. In 1990, he created H.E.A.L., or Human Education Against Lies, an afro-centric, pro-educational organization. KRS-One also founded Edutainer Records that year. In 1991, he recorded *Live Hardcore Worldwide*, one of the first live rap albums ever and produced such artists as Queen Latifah and the Neville Brothers.

Little Richard (1932–)
Singer, Pianist

Flamboyantly dressed, with his hair piled high in a pompadour, Little Richard is a musical phenomenon, an entertainer hailed by pop superstar Paul McCartney as "one of the greatest kings of rock and roll." Richard's image, mannerisms, and musical talent set the trend for the emergence of modern popular music performers from Jimi Hendrix to Prince.

One of 12 children, Richard Wayne Penniman was born on December 5, 1932, in Macon, Georgia. As a child in Macon, Richard heard the sounds of gospel music groups, street musicians, and spiritual-based songs emanating from homes throughout his neighborhood. Nicknamed the "War Hawk" for his unrestrained hollers and shouts, Richard's voice projected with such intensity that he was once asked to stop singing in church. Richard's first song before an audience was with the Tiny Tots, a gospel group featuring his brothers Marquette and Walter. Later Richard sang with his family in a group called the Penniman Singers; they appeared at churches, camp meetings, and talent contests.

In high school, Richard played alto saxophone in the marching band. After school he took a part-time job at the Macon City Auditorium, where he watched the bands of Cab Calloway, Hot Lips Page, Lucky Millinder, and Sister Rosetta Thorpe. At age 14, Richard left home to become a performer in Doctor Hudson's Medicine Show. While on the road, he joined B. Brown's Orchestra as a ballad singer performing such compositions as "Good Night Irene" and "Mona Lisa." Not long afterward, he became a member of the traveling minstrel show of Sugarfoot Sam from Alabama.

Richard's first break came in 1951, when the RCA label recorded him live on the radio, producing the local hit "Every Hour." Traveling to New Orleans with his band the Tempo Toppers, Richard's group eventually played the Houston rhythm and blues scene, where he attracted the attention of Don Robey, president of Peacock Records. After cutting some sides for the Peacock label, Richard sent a demo tape to Art Rupe's Los Angeles-based Specialty label. Under the direction of Specialty's producer Bumps Blackwell, Richard recorded the 1956 hit "Tutti Frutti" at J&M Studios in New Orleans. Richard's subsequent sessions for Specialty yielded a long list of classic hits such as "Long Tall Sally," "Lucille," "Jenny, Jenny," and "Keep a Knocking." In 1957, Richard appeared in the films *Don't Knock Rock* with Billy Haley and *The Girl Can't Help It* starring Jane Mansfield.

In the following year, Richard quit his rock and roll career to enter the Oakland Theological College in Huntsville, Alabama. Between 1957 to 1959 Richard released several gospel recordings and toured with artists like Mahalia Jackson. In 1962, Richard embarked on a tour of Europe with Sam Cooke. One year later Richard hired an then-unknown guitarist, Jimi Hendrix, who went under the pseudonym of Maurice James. In Europe Richard played on the same bills as the Beatles and Rolling Stones.

By the 1970s, Richard pursued a career as a full-fledged evangelist and performer. In 1979, he set out on a nationwide evangelist tour. In the following decade, he appeared in the film *Down and Out in Beverly Hills* and recorded "Rock Island Line" on the tribute LP to Leadbelly and Woody Guthrie entitled *Folkways: A Vision Shared.*

Richard's continuing activity in show business represents the inexhaustible energy of a singer who had a profound impact on the careers of artists like Otis Redding, Eddie Cochran, Richie Valens, Paul McCartney, and Mitch Ryder. Having earned special Grammy honors in 1993, Richard was honored with a lifetime achievement award by the Rhythm & Blues Foundation the following year. Later that year, he headlined the 1994 New Orleans Jazz and Heritage Festival. He was called upon by the House of Blues Foundation to assist in the organizations Blues School House program in 1995.

Curtis Mayfield (1942–)
Singer, Songwriter, Producer

Born on June 3, 1942, in Chicago, Illinois, Curtis Mayfield learned to sing harmony as a member of the Northern Jubilee Singers and the Traveling Souls Spiritualist Church. In 1957, Mayfield joined the Roosters, a five-man doo wop singing group led by his close friend Jerry Butler. Renamed the Impressions, the group released the 1958 hit "Your Precious Love," featuring Butler's resonant baritone and Mayfield's wispy tenor. But in the following year, Butler left the group to pursue a solo career. In search of material, Butler collaborated with

Little Richard

Mayfield to write the hit songs "He Will Break Your Heart" and "I'm a-Telling You."

In 1960, Mayfield recruited Fred Cash to take Butler's place in the newly reformed Impressions. In the next year the Impressions hit the charts with the sensual soul tune "Gypsy Women." In collaboration with Butler, Mayfield also established the Curtom Publishing Company. With the loss of original members Richard Brooks and Arthur Brooks, the three remaining members of the Impressions, Mayfield, Cash, and Sam Goodman continued to perform as a trio. Under the direction of jazz musician/arranger Johnny Pate, the Impressions recorded "Sad Sad Girl" and the rhythmic gospel-based song "It's All Right" released in 1963.

During this time, Mayfield also wrote a number of songs for his Chicago contemporaries, including "Monkey Time" for Major Lance, "Just Be True" for Gene Chandler, and "It's All Over Now" for Walter Jackson. Writing for the Impressions, however, Mayfield turned to more socially conscious themes reflecting the current of the civil rights era. Mayfield's finest "sermon songs" were "People Get Ready" (1965), "We're a Winner" (1968), and "Choice of Colors" (1969).

After leaving the Impressions in 1970, Mayfield released his debut album *Curtis.* On his 1971 LP *Curtis Live!,* Mayfield was accompanied by a tight four-piece back-up group, which included guitar, bass, drums, and percussion. Mayfield composed the score for the 1972 hit film *Superfly.* The soundtrack became Mayfield's biggest commercial success, providing him two hits with the junkie epitaph "Freddie's Dead" and the wah-wah guitar funk classic "Superfly." Despite his commercial success, Mayfield spent the remainder of the decade in collaboration with other artists, working on such projects as the soundtrack for the film *Claudine,* featuring Gladys Knight and the Pips, and the production of Aretha Franklin's 1978 album *Sparkle.*

Throughout the next decade, Mayfield continued to record such albums as *Love Is the Place* in 1981, and *Honesty* in 1982. Joined by Jerry Butler and newcomers Nate Evans and Vandy Hampton, the Impressions reunited in 1983, for a 30-city anniversary tour. In 1983, Mayfield released the LP *Come in Peace With a Message of Love.* But in August of 1990, while performing at an outdoor concert in Brooklyn, New York, Mayfield received an injury that left him paralyzed from the neck down. In the following year, Mayfield's contributions to popular music were recognized when the Impressions were inducted into the Rock and Roll Hall of Fame. In 1994, Mayfield was presented with the Grammy Legend Award. Earlier that year a number of his peers, including Aretha Franklin, got together to record *All Men Are Brothers: A Tribute to Curtis Mayfield*.

Charley Pride (1939–)
Singer

The first African American superstar of country music, Charley Pride is a three-time Grammy Award winner whose supple baritone voice has won him international fame. He was the first black to perform at the Grand Ole Opry. A prolific artist, Pride has recorded more than 30 albums.

Born on March 18, 1939, in Slege, Mississippi, Charley Pride grew up listening to late night radio broadcasts of the Grand Ole Opry, country music's most famous showcase. Although he taught himself guitar at age 14, Pride soon turned his attention to a professional baseball career. At age 16, he left the cotton fields of Slege for a stint in the Negro American baseball league. During his baseball career, Pride sang on public address systems and in taverns. In 1963, country singer Red Sovine heard Pride and arranged for him to attend an audition in Nashville one year later. This led to a recording contract with the RCA label and produced the 1964 hit "Snakes Crawl at Night."

Throughout the 1960s, Pride toured incessantly, appearing at concert dates and state fairs, as well as on radio and television. In 1967, Pride debuted at the Grand Ole Opry and within the same year hit the charts with singles "Does My Ring Hurt Your Finger?" and "I Know One." With the release of 1969's *The Sensational Charley Pride* and the subsequent year's *Just Plain Charley*, Pride found himself entering the decade of his greatest recognition. By the time he received the Country Music Award for Entertainer of the Year in 1970, Pride had already achieved tremendous success as a major figure in the popular cultural scene of the United States. Other honors included *Billboard*'s Trendsetter Award and the Music Operators of America's Entertainer of the Year Award.

In the 1980s, Pride not only continued to find success as a music star, he became a successful entrepreneur. Making his home on a 240-acre estate in North Dallas, Texas, Pride emerged as a majority stockholder in the First Texas Bank and part owner of Cecca Productions. Pride made more history in the 1993, when he became the first black to join the cast of the Grand Ole Opry since DeFord Bailey's presence nearly 52 years earlier. The following year, Pride published his autobiography entitled *Pride: The Charley Pride Story*.

Charley Pride

Prince 1958-
Singer, Songwriter, Producer

Son of a jazz pianist, Prince Rogers Nelson was born on June 7, 1958, in Minneapolis, Minnesota. By age fourteen Prince taught himself to play piano, guitar and drums. His eclectic taste that led to Prince's creation of the Minneapolis sound. After forming the band Grand Central in high school in 1973, Prince renamed the group Champagne and eventually recruited the talents of Morris Day. In 1978 Prince signed with Warner Brothers and recorded his debut album *For You*. His follow–up album *Prince* featured the hit "I Wanna Be Your Lover." Rooted in the music of Sly and the Family Stone and Jimi Hendrix, Prince's third LP *Dirty Mind* was released in 1980.

Two years later, Prince achieved superstardom with his album *1999*, an effort that was followed by a spectacular tour comprised of Prince and the Revolution, the Time, and the bawdy girl trio Vanity 6. Prince's 1984 film soundtrack *Purple Rain*, which received rave reviews for Prince's portrayal of a struggling young musician, grossed sixty million dollars at the box office in the first two months of its release. Near the end of 1985 Prince established his own record label Paisley Park, the warehouse/studio located in the wooded terrain of Chanhassen, Minnesota. That same year, Prince released the album *Around the World in a Day* featuring the hit singles "Raspberry Beret," "Paisley Park," and "Pop Life."

Prince's next film project *Under the Cherry Moon*, filmed in France, was completed under his direction. The soundtrack *Parade Music from Under the Cherry Moon* produced a number of hit singles including "Kiss" and "Mountains." After re–forming the Revolution, Prince released *Sign of the Times* in 1987, which included a duet with Sheena Easton, "I Could Never Take the Place of Your Man." Following the LP *Lovesexy*, Prince recorded several songs which appeared on the soundtrack for the film *Batman*. This was followed by another film soundtrack *Graffiti Bridge* in 1990.

In September of 1992, Prince signed a six–album contract with Warner Brothers. Backed by his new first rate ensemble the New Power Generation, Prince embarked on a nationwide tour in April of 1993, which proved the most impressive since his commercial breakthrough in the early 1980s. Prince has not only become an owner of his own nightclub, the Grand Slam, he has contributed a set of original music to the Joffery Ballet's production of "Billboards," which opened in January of 1993 to rave reviews.

Prince

That year, the eccentric performer also changed his name to an unpronounceable symbol and announced the retirement of "Prince" from recording. In 1994, The Artist Formerly Known as Prince (TAFKAP) debuted interactive CD-ROM software and New Power Generation retail establishments. Two years later, the long-time bachelor married on Valentine's Day and commissioned a symphony from his band to commemorate the occasion.

Public Enemy
Rap group

As spokesmen of racial pride, and proponents of militant public activism, Public Enemy have redefined the sound and the lyrical message of rap music. The formation of Public Enemy centered around Adelphi University in Long Island, New York, where the group's founder Carlton Ridenhour a.k.a Chuck D., a graphic design major, joined fellow students Hank Shocklee and Bill Stephney at radio station WBAU. First appearing on Stephney's radio show, Ridenhour soon hosted his own three-hour program. Ridenhour's powerful rap voice attracted a number of loyal followers. Ridenhour soon recruited the talents of William Drayton a.k.a Flavor Flav, Norman Rodgers a.k.a Terminator X, and Richard Griffin a.k.a Professor Griff to form Public Enemy. Shocklee and his production-oriented peers in the group came to be known as the Bomb Squad and their talents were often sought by other artists.

In 1987, Public Enemy released the debut album *Yo! Bum Rush the Show*, which sold more than 400,000 copies. Two years later Professor Griff, the group's "minister of information," was fired by Chuck D. for making anti-Semitic comments. Under the leadership of Chuck D. the group went on to record the song "Fight the Power" for director Spike Lee's film *Do The Right Thing*. The group's second album *It Takes a Nation of Millions to Hold Us Back* became a million-seller.

Public Enemy's 1990 release *Fear of a Black Planet* featured themes regarding a world struggle for the advancement of the black race. The controversial "911 Is a Joke" led to widespread discourse over the song's allegations that emergency personnel respond slower, if at all, to calls originating from inner city or predominantly black areas. The follow-up, *Apocalypse '91: The Enemy Strikes Black*, was a startling statement of social and racial consciousness and featured a collaboration with the heavy metal band Anthrax on "Bring the Noise," a track that originally appeared on *It Takes a Nation*. Another single, "By the Time I Get to Arizona," sparked another nation-wide debate over the refusal of Arizona state officials to recognize Martin Luther King, Jr.'s birthday as a legal holiday.

Greatest Misses, a hits compilation released in 1992, seemed to single the end of an era for the Public Enemy camp. In a departure from their earlier work, 1994's *Muse Sick n Hour Mess Age* traded the sonic dissonances of the Bomb Squad for samples from classic soul recordings. Meanwhile, most of the members had established themselves as solo artists or developed other career directions in the early 1990s, but overall the group's popularity seemed to wane as "gansta" rap commandeered the airwaves.

Queen Latifah (1970–)
Singer, Actress

Born Dana Owens, rap artist Queen Latifah was raised in East Orange, New Jersey, and began performing in high school as the human beat box for the rap group Ladies Fresh. In 1989, she launched her solo recording career with the album *All Hail the Queen*, an afrocentric, pro-woman work. Her other recordings include 1991's *Nature of a Sista'*, featuring the single "Latifah Had It Up 2 Here, and 1993's *Black Reign*, which spawned the feminist anthem "U.N.I.T.Y."

Latifah manages the careers of other rap artists through her New Jersey-based Flavor Unit Records and Management Company, of which she is the CEO. In addition, she is a regular on the Fox network's *Living Single*, along with costars Kim Fields, Erika Alexander, and Kim Coles. She has also made appearances on *The Fresh Prince of Bel-Air* and in such films as the Hudlin Brothers' *House Party II*, Spike Lee's *Jungle Fever*, and Ernest Dickerson's *Juice*.

Otis Redding (1941–1967)
Singer, Songwriter

Born on September 9, 1941, in Dawson, Georgia, Otis Redding moved with his parents at age three to the Tindall Heights housing project in Macon. In grade school Redding played drums and sang in a church gospel group. A few years later he learned the vocals and piano style of his idol Little Richard. Quitting school in the tenth grade, Redding went on the road with Little Richard's former band, the Upsetters. But Redding's first professional break came when he joined Johnny Jenkins and the Pinetoppers. Redding's debut single was a Little Richard imitation tune "Shout Bamalama." Accompanying Jenkins to a Stax studio session in Memphis, Redding was afforded some remaining recording time. Backed by Jenkins on guitar, Steve Cropper on piano, Lewis Steinburg on bass, and Al Jackson on drums, Redding cut "Hey Hey Baby" and the hit "These Arms of Mine."

Signed to the Stax label, Redding released the 1963 album *Pain in My Heart*. Backed by members of Book-

Otis Redding

er T. and the MGs, Redding's follow-up LP *Otis Blue (Otis Redding Sings Soul)* featured the 1965 hit "Respect." In the next year, Redding broke attendance records at shows in Harlem and Watts. After releasing a cover version of the Rolling Stones' song "Satisfaction" in 1966, Redding embarked on a European tour which included his appearance on the British television show *"Ready Steady Go!"*

In August 1966, Redding established his own record company, Jotis, which was distributed through the Stax label. Following a few commercially unsuccessful ventures, Redding recorded singer Arthur Conley who provided the label with the million-selling single "Sweet Soul Music." Redding's recordings "Try a Little Tenderness," and the vocal duet "Tramp," featuring Carla Thomas, hit the charts in 1967. On June 16 Redding, backed by the MGs, performed a stunning high-paced set at the Monterey Pop Festival. On December 10, Redding's career came to an tragic end when the twin engine plane carrying him to a concert date in Wisconsin crashed in Lake Monona, just outside Madison. As if in tribute, Redding's song "Sitting on the Dock of the Bay," released a few weeks after his death, became his first gold record.

Lionel Brockman Richie (1949–)
Singer, Songwriter, Pianist

Lionel Brockman Richie was born on June 20, 1949, on the campus of Tuskegee Institute in Alabama. Richie's grandmother Adelaide Foster, a classical pianist, became his music instructor who introduced him to the works of Bach and Beethoven. While a freshman at the Tuskegee Institute, Richie formed the Mighty Mystics who, along with members of the Jays, became the Commodores. Combining gospel, classical, and country-western music, the Commodores emerged as a formidable live act throughout the 1960s and 1970s. After signing with the Motown label, the group landed its first hit in 1974 with the song "Machine Gun." In 1981 Richie recorded the hit theme song for Franco Zefferelli's film *Endless Love*.

A year later, Richie released his first solo album *Lionel Richie* which featured the hits "Truly," "You Are," and "My Love." His follow-up release *Can't Slow Down* produced five more hits: "All Night Long (All Night)," "Running with the Night," "Hello," "Stuck on You," and "Penny Lover." In collaboration with Michael Jackson, Richie co-wrote "We Are the World" for USA for Africa, the famine relief project organized and produced by Quincy Jones. In 1985 Richie received an Oscar nomination for "Best Original Song" for his composition "Say You, Say Me." A year later, Richie's third album *Dancing on the Ceiling* provided him with the hits "Dancing on the Ceiling," "Love Will Conquer All," "Ballerina Girl," and "Se La."

Smokey Robinson (1940–)
Singer, Songwriter, Producer

Proclaimed by Bob Dylan as one of America's greatest poets, Smokey Robinson is a pop music legend. He has risen to fame as a brilliant songwriter, producer, and singer. His instantly recognizable falsetto voice continues to bring Robinson gold records and a legion of loyal fans.

William Robinson, Jr. was born in Detroit, on February 19, 1940. After his mother died when he was ten years old, Robinson was raised by his sister. Nicknamed "Smokey" by his uncle, Robinson was a bright student who enjoyed reading books and poetry. A reluctant saxophone student, Robinson turned his creative energy to composing songs that he collected in a dime store writing tablet. While attending Detroit's Northern High School in 1954, Robinson formed the vocal group the Matadors, which performed at battle-of-the-band contests and at recreation centers.

Robinson's introduction to Berry Gordy in 1957, resulted in the Matadors' first record contract with George Goldner's End label. Upon joining the newly formed Motown label in 1960, the group changed their name, upon the suggestion of Gordy, to the Miracles. Although the Miracles' debut album failed to attract notice, they provided Motown with its first smash hit "Shop Around" in 1961, a song written and coproduced by Robinson.

In close collaboration with Gordy, Robinson spent the following decade as one of Motown's most integral singers and producers. With the Miracles he recorded such hits as "You Really Got a Hold On Me" in 1963, "Tracks of My Tears" in 1965, "I Second That Emotion" in 1967, and "Tears of a Clown" in 1970. As a writer he provided the label with hits like "My Guy" for Mary Wells, "I'll Be Doggone" for Marvin Gaye, and "My Girl" for the Temptations.

In 1972, Robinson left the Miracles to launch a solo career. Despite the moderate success of his records during the disco craze of the 1970s, Robinson continued to perform and record. In 1979, Robinson experienced a comeback with the critically acclaimed hit "Cruisin." Three years later, Robinson appeared on the NBC-TV special "*Motown 25: Yesterday, Today, and Tomorrow*." Between 1986 and 1991, Robinson released five more albums including *Smoke Signals*, *One Heartbeat*, and *Love, Smokey*. He was inducted into both the Rock and Roll Hall of Fame and the Songwriters Hall of Fame in 1986, and, in 1987, he won a Grammy for his vocal performance on "Just to See Her." In 1995, Robinson was signed by Music by Design, a U.K. company that solicits artists to create original music for television and radio commercials.

Diana Ross (1944–)
Singer, Actress

One of six children, Diane Ross was born in Detroit, on March 26, 1944. An extremely active child Ross swam, ran track, and sang in church. In 1959, she joined the Primetes, a group comprised of Mary Wilson, Florence Ballard, and Barbara Martin. After failing to attract notice on the Lupine label, the group auditioned for Berry Gordy, Jr. who signed them to Motown. Upon the suggestion of Berry, the group changed its name to the Supremes. Released in 1961, the group's song, "I Want a Guy," featuring Ross on lead vocals, failed to attract notice. Not long afterward, following Martin's departure, the trio continued to record with Ross on lead vocal.

The Supremes did not find commercial success on the Motown label until 1964, when they were placed under the guidance of the Holland-Dozier-Holland production team. In 1964, H-D-H turned out the Supreme's first smash hit "Where Did Our Love Go?" followed by numerous hits, such as "Baby Love" in 1964, "I Hear a Symphony" in 1965, "You Can't Hurry Love" in 1966, and "Reflections" in 1967. With preferential treat-

Diana Ross makes her last appearance with the Supremes: Cindy Birdsong (left) and Mary Wilson (center), 1970.

ment by Gordy, Ross became the dominant figure of the group. By the mid-1960s Ross's emerging talent prompted Gordy to bill the group as Diana Ross and the Supremes.

In 1970, Ross left the Supremes to launch her solo career. Her debut album *Diana Ross* featured the writing and production talents of Ashford & Simpson, an effort that included the hit "Reach Out and Touch (Somebody's Hand)." One year later she made her film debut in the Motown-sponsored movie *Lady Sings the Blues* in which she won an Oscar nomination for her biographical portrayal of jazz singer Billie Holiday. Her role in the 1975 Motown-backed film *Mahogany* brought her not only an Oscar nomination, but the number one selling single "Do You Know Where You're Going To." In 1978, Ross starred in the film version of *The Wiz*, the last full-scale motion picture to be backed by Motown.

After leaving Motown in 1981, Ross signed a $20-million contract with the RCA label. Her debut album *Why Do Fools Fall in Love?* went platinum. This was followed by four more LP's for RCA, including *Silk Electric* in 1982, *Swept Away* in 1984, *Eaten Alive* in 1985. Two years later, Ross left RCA to sign with the

London-based EMI label, which produced the albums *Red Hot Rhythm 'n Blues* in 1987, *Working Overtime* in 1987, and *Greatest Hits, Live* in 1990. Meanwhile, Ross had returned to Motown Records as a recording artist and partial owner in 1989, one year after being inducted into the Rock and Roll Hall of Fame.

In the 1990s, the Grammy and Tony award-winning Ross continued to enjoy popularity around the world; She achieved tremendous success as the owner of her own multi-million-dollar corporation Diana Ross Enterprises. Her autobiography, *Secrets of a Sparrow: Memoirs*, was published in 1993, and a compilation called *Diana Extended/The Remixes* hit the stores in 1994.

Russell Simmons (1957?–)
Record Company Executive, Producer, Music Promoter

Hollis, Queens, in New York City is the birth place of Russell Simmons. Although he grew up in a middle class neighborhood, Simmons got involved with gangs in his teens. The 1970s brought change to Simmons's life, however, as he enrolled in classes at the Harlem branch of City College of New York. While studying sociology, Simmons began noticing the influence rap music had on young inner-city blacks. The boasting and story telling skills of various rappers drew crowds on street corners and in neighborhood parks. Simmons found himself in the middle of a movement that would shape the sound of the music, particularly the rap genre.

Simmons left college to promote local rap artists. Hard work and perseverance led to the formation of Def Jam Records in 1984. Simmons and his partner, Rick Ruben, signed a deal with CBS Records to distribute their material. Simmons was primarily interested in promoting rap images that displayed the life and style of tough urban streets. Acts like the Beastie Boys, L.L. Cool J, and Run-DMC pushed Def Jam Records to early success. Other groups like Public Enemy enjoyed Simmons's input as their careers developed.

The music Simmons involved himself with not only revolutionized hip-hop but helped bring fashion to forefront as well. High top Addidas tennis shoes, black leather jackets, and t-shirts displaying the Def Jam Recording logo flooded the streets. These influences laid a foundation for Simmons's own line of clothing called Phat Pharm. Simmons furthered his own professional growth by getting involved in film production. He contributed to *Krush Groove* and *Tougher Than Leather* in the late 1980s. Simmons has moved into directing several music videos.

Donna Summer (1948–)
Singer

One of the biggest stars of the disco era, Donna Summer first gained notice with a pulsatingly erotic

Euro-hit, then moved on to mainstream popularity. She ruled the charts through the late 1970s, though the fading of disco left her with no choice but to streamline her style. Although her popularity declined in the ensuing years, she has become one of the few stars of the era to transcend the kitsch that surrounds it.

Born Donna Gaines in Boston, the singer got her first break when she was cast in a traveling production of a rock musical. While in Germany she met Helmut Sommer, whom she married; she later made the acquaintance of Italian producer Giorgio Moroder, who produced her first hit, the throbbingly sexual "Love to Love You Baby." Summers's moans and groans were her initial route to stardom. Through the late 1970s, however, she continually expanded her range. Her hits included a cover version of the pop standard "Macarthur Park," "On the Radio," "Bad Girls," "Hot Stuff," and "Last Dance."

Summer became a born-again Christian in the early 1980s, and gradually turned toward inspiration music. She earned Grammy awards for Best Inspirational Performance in 1984 and 1985, but she surfaced less and less frequently in the pop world. On dancefloors throughout the world, however, she is accorded the status of a deity.

Tina Turner (1939–)
Singer

With a music career spanning more than 30 years, Tina Turner has come to be known as the "hardest-working woman in show business." From soul music star to rock goddess, Turner's vocal style and energetic stage act remain a show-stopping phenomenon.

Born Annie Mae Bullock on November 25, 1939, in Brownsville, Tennessee, Turner moved to Knoxville with her parents at age three. Turner first sang in church choirs and at local talent contests. After moving with her mother to St. Louis at age 16, Turner met pianist Ike Turner, leader of the R and B group the Kings of Rhythm. Hired by the band to sing at weekend engagements, Annie Bullock married Ike Turner in 1958 and took the stage name Tina Turner. When the band's scheduled session singer failed to appear at a recording session in 1960, Tina stepped in to record the R and B song "Fool in Love" which became a million-seller.

With a major hit behind them, the Turners formed the Ike and Tina Turner Revue, complete with the Ikettes. Major international success came for the Turners in 1966, when producer Phil Spector combined his "wall of sound" approach with a R and B sound to record the hit "River Deep, Mountain High." Subjected to years of physical abuse by her husband, Turner divorced Ike in 1976 and set out on a solo career. That same year she co-

Tina Turner

starred in The Who's rock opera film *Tommy* as the Acid Queen.

In 1984 Turner's career skyrocketed with the commercial success of the album *Private Dancer* which featured the hit singles "What's Love Got to Do With It?" and "Better Be Good." Turner's sensuously vibrant image soon appeared on high budget videos, magazine covers, and in films such as the 1985 release *Mad Max 3: Beyond the Thunderdome* in which she played the tyrannical Aunty Entity. With the immense commercial success of her 1989 album *Foreign Affair*, Turner closed out the decade as one of the most popular singers on the international music scene. In 1995 she was even tapped to perform the title track of that year's James Bond flick, *Goldfinger*.

Luther Vandross (1951–)
Singer, Composer, Producer

One of the premier pop artists of the 1980s, Luther Vandross is responsible for the emergence of a new school of modern soul singers. Born in New York City on April 20, 1951, Vandross was the son of a gospel singer and a big band vocalist. Vandross received his musical education by listening to recordings of Aretha

Franklin and the Supremes. In high school Vandross formed numerous singing groups. Throughout the 1970s, he was great as a background singer, performing with such artists as David Bowie, Carly Simon, and Ringo Starr. He also sang advertising jingles like ATT's theme "Reach Out and Touch."

Following the release of his first album *Never Too Much* in 1981, Vandross was called upon to sing duets with a number of pop artists, including Aretha Franklin and Dionne Warwick. As a successful writer and producer, Vandross has released eight million-selling albums including the 1990 release *Best of Love*, which went multi-platinum.

Mary Wells (1943–1992)
Singer

Born in 1943 and raised in her hometown of Detroit, Michigan, Mary Wells started her music career as a featured soloist in her high school choir. After attracting the notice of Berry Gordy, Jr. at age 17, Wells signed a contract with Motown in 1959. With Smokey Robinson as her main producer and writer, Wells scored a number of hits such as "I Don't Want to Take a Chance," in 1961, "You Beat Me to the Punch" in 1962, and "My Guy" in 1964. In the same year, she recorded the album *Together* with Marvin Gaye, and toured England with the Beatles.

At the peak of her career, Wells left the Motown label to become an actress. After relocating in Los Angeles, she signed a contract with the Twentieth Century Fox records. Unfortunately, Wells could never find a producer who equaled Robinson's ability to record her material. Her debut single in 1965 "Use Your Head" achieved only modest commercial success. In the 1970s Wells left music to raise her children. For a brief period she was married to Cecil Womack, brother of the R&B great Bobby Womack.

During the 1980s, Wells returned to music performing on the oldies circuit. In 1985 she appeared in "Motown's 25th Anniversary" television special. Diagnosed as having cancer of the larynx in August 1990, Wells, without medical insurance to pay for treatment, lost her home. Not long afterward, the Rhythm and Blues Foundation raised over $50,000 for Wells' hospital costs. Funds were also sent by artists like Bruce Springsteen, Rod Stewart, and Diana Ross. Despite chemotherapy treatments, Wells died on July 30, 1992 and was buried at Forest Lawn Memorial Park in Los Angeles.

Jackie Wilson (1934–1984)
Singer

Between 1958 and 1963, Jackie Wilson reigned as one of the most popular R and B singers in America. Dressed in sharkskin suits and sporting a process hairstyle, Wilson exhibited a dynamic stage performance and a singing range which equaled his contemporaries James Brown and Sam Cooke.

Jack Leroy Wilson was born on June 9, 1934, in Detroit, Michigan. Wilson's mother sang spirituals and gospel songs at Mother Bradley's Church. As a youngster, he listened to the recordings of the Mills Brothers, Ink Spots, and Louis Jordan. In high school he became a boxer, and at age 16 he won the American Amateur Golden Gloves Welterweight title. But upon the insistence of his mother, Wilson quit boxing and pursued a career in music. While a teenager, Wilson sang with the Falcons in local clubs, and at talent contests held at the Paradise Theater. He also worked in a spiritual group with later members of Hank Ballard's Midnighters.

In 1953 Wilson replaced Clyde McPhatter as lead singer of the Dominoes. Wilson's only hit with the Dominoes was the reworking of the religious standard "St. Theresa of the Roses." Upon the success of the recording, Wilson signed a contract as a solo artist with the Brunswick label. Wilson's 1957 debut album *Rete Petite* featured the hit title track song which was written by songwriters Berry Gordy, Jr. and Billy Taylor. The

Jackie Wilson

songwriting team of Gordy and Taylor also provided Wilson with the subsequent hits "To Be Loved" in 1957, "Lonely Teardrops" in 1958, and "That's Why I Love You So," and "I'll Be Satisfied" in 1959.

During the early 1960s, Wilson performed and recorded numerous adaptations of classical music compositions in a crooning ballad style. This material, however, failed to bring out the powerful talent of Wilson's R and B vocal style. Although Wilson's repertoire contained mostly supper club standards, he did manage to produce the powerful pop classics "Dogging Around" in 1960 and "Baby Workout" in 1963. Teamed with writer/producer Carl Davis, Wilson also recorded the hit "Whispers" and the R and B masterpiece "Higher and Higher" in 1967.

Following Wilson's last major hit "I Get the Sweetest Feeling" in 1968, he performed on the oldies circuit and on Dick Clark's "Good Ol' Rock 'n' Roll Revue." In 1975 Wilson suffered a serious heart attack on stage at the Latin Casino in Cherry Hill, New Jersey. Forced into retirement, Wilson spent his last eight years in a nursing home until his death on January 21, 1984.

Mary Wilson (1944–)
Singer

As a member of the Motown supergroup the Supremes, Mary Wilson's musical career represents an American success story. Born on March 6, 1944, in Greenville, Mississippi, Wilson moved to Detroit at age 11. Raised in the Brewster-Douglas housing project on the city's east side, Wilson learned to sing by imitating the falsetto voice of Frank Lyman. Along with Barbara Martin and Betty Travis, Wilson formed the Primetes. Upon the departure of Travis, another neighborhood girl named Diana Ross joined the group. Appearing at talent shows and sock-hops, the Primetes went on to win first prize at the 1960 Detroit/Windsor Freedom Festival talent contest. Although the Primetes cut two singles on the Lupine label featuring Wilson on lead vocal, they failed to achieve commercial success.

On January 15, 1961, 16–year–old Wilson and Primete members Diana Ross, Florence Ballard and Barbara Martin signed with the Motown label as the Supremes. Wilson's effort to win the lead vocal spot, however, soon gave way to the dominance of Diana Ross. Released in 1964, the group's first gold single "Where Did Our Love Go?" made Wilson and the Supremes overnight celebrities. Between 1964 and 1968 Wilson sang background vocals on a number of hits, including "Baby Love," "You Can't Hurry Love," and "Reflections." Before leaving the group in 1976, Wilson also sang such recordings as "Love Child," "I'm Living in Shame," and "Someday We'll Be Together."

In 1983 Wilson was briefly reunited with the Supremes on "Motown's 25th Anniversary" television special. Making her home in Los Angeles, Wilson occasionally appears on the oldies circuit and at small Supremes revival shows.

Nancy Wilson (1937–)
Singer

Nancy Wilson was born in Chillicothe, Ohio, in 1937. Her musical talents were first noticed when, as a child, she performed for her family at various gatherings. The performances continued as Wilson became a member of her church choir. Influence from artists such as Billy Eckstine and Nat King Cole helped Wilson determine that singing would be her career. As a teen, Wilson and her family moved to Columbus, Ohio. Wilson soon became the host of her own radio show, Skyline Melody, during which she performed phoned in requests.

In 1955, Wilson enrolled in classes at Ohio's Central State College to pursue teaching credentials. Her stint in school was short lived, however, as Wilson dropped out to pursue her singing career. She spent the next three years touring the country as a member of Rusty Byrant's Carolyn Club Band. The experience Wilson gained while touring gave her the courage to go solo. New York City became Wilson's new home as her career began skyrocketing.

Shortly after her arrival in the Big Apple, Wilson obtained permanent work at a local night club. Word of her masterful performances soon spread all over the city prompting a recording session with Capitol records. 1960 marked the release of her debut album *Like in Love* and the recording of her first major hit, entitled "Save Your Love for Me." *How Glad I Am* won a Grammy in 1964, beginning a 30-year streak of acclaim.

Wilson's blend of rhythm and blues, jazz, and pop styles captivated thousands of fans around the world. Television executives began to take advantage of Wilson's talents as she was given her own weekly variety show. The Emmy Award-winning *The Nancy Wilson Show* was merely the beginning of Wilson's television appearances. Guest spots on *The Tonight Show*, *The Merv Griffin Show*, and *The Today Show* soon followed.

During the late 1970s and early 1980s, technology began to influence the fashion in which studio recordings were made. Wilson continued to record and tour despite differences with various recording companies issues of sound. Nonetheless, she was named Global Entertainer of the Year in 1986 by the World Conference of Mayors and the NAACP bestowed her with its Image Award that year as well.

Just as much heralded in the 1990s, Wilson's 54th full-length recording was completed in 1994. With a star on the Hollywood Walk of Fame, an Essence Award, a Martin Luther King Center for Social Change Award, and a Trumpet Award to her name, Wilson's bevy of honors is symbol of her timelessness and a testimony to the loyalty of her fans.

The Winans
Gospel singing group

Detroit's first family of gospel music, the Winans have won a number of Grammy awards for their infectious modern pop gospel sound. Known as funky gospel, the Winans's music features electric keyboards, guitar, and bass, as well as saxophone accompaniment. David Jr., Michael, and twins Marvin and Carvin, first sang at their great-grandfather's Zion Congregational Church of Christ on Detroit's east side; their father, a minister and singer, David Winan, Sr. first organized the quartet. While attending Mumford High School, the group attracted large crowds at school talent contests. Originally called the Testimonials, the quartet released two locally-produced albums *Love Covers* in 1977 and *Thy Will Be Done* in 1978.

Upon being discovered by gospel singer Andraé Crouch, the group released its first national debut album *Introducing the Winans* in 1981, which was nominated for a Grammy award. The follow-up 1983 LP *Long Time Coming* also received a Grammy nomination. 1985's *Tomorrow* won a Grammy as did *Let My People Go*, recorded on Quincy Jones's' Qwest label. Known to join secular pop artists in collaborative singing projects, the Winans featured Michael McDonald on their 1987 release *Decisions*. They also sang back-up on Anita Baker's Grammy-winning hit single "Ain't No Need To Worry" and provided vocal tracks for Michael Jackson's song "Man in the Mirror" featured on his *Bad*. *The Winans Live at Carnegie Hall* won a Grammy Award in 1988.

In 1992, the Winans appeared at "Culturefest 92" in West Africa. One year later they were invited to sing at U.S. president Bill Clinton's inauguration festivities. That year sisters Angie and Debbie became the newest additions to the family group, which has won Dove, Stellar, and Soul Train awards.

Stevie Wonder (1950–)
Singer, Pianist, Composer

Popular music's genius composer and singer Stevie Wonder has remained at the forefront of musical change. His colorful harmonic arrangements have drawn upon jazz, soul, pop, reggae, and rap-derived new jack rhythms. Wonder's gift to pop music is his ability to create serious music dealing with social and political issues while at the same time revealing the soulful and deeper mysterious nature of the human experience.

Steveland Morris Judkins was born on May 13, 1950, in Saginaw, Michigan. Raised in Detroit, Steveland Morris first sang in the church choir. But the music that attracted him most were the sounds of Johnny Ace and B. B. King that he heard on late night radio programs. By age eight Wonder learned to play piano, harmonica, and bongos. Through the connections of Miracles member Ronnie White, Wonder auditioned for Berry Gordy, Jr. who, immediately signing the 13-year-old prodigy, gave him the stage name of Little Stevie Wonder. After releasing his first singles "Thank You (For Loving Me All the Way)" and "Contract of Love," In 1963, "Fingertips, Pt. 2" became the first live performance of a song to reach the top of the pop charts. That year Wonder also became the first recording artist to hold number one slots on the *Billboard* Hot 100, R&B Singles, and album charts, simultaneously. In the following year, Wonder hit the charts with the song "Hey Harmonica Man."

With the success of his recording career, Wonder began touring more frequently. Motown assigned Wonder a tutor from the Michigan School for the Blind, allowing him to continue his education while on the road. In 1964, he performed in London with the Motown Revue, a package featuring Martha and the Vandellas, the Supremes, and the Temptations. Wonder's subsequent recording of the punchy R&B single "Uptight (Everything's Alright)" became a smash hit in 1966. Wonder's growing commercial success at Motown brought him greater artistic freedom in the studio. In collaboration with Clarence Paul, Wonder produced a long succession of hits including Bob Dylan's "Blowing in the Wind" in 1966, "I Was Made to Love Her" in 1967, and "For Once in My Life" in 1968. In 1969, U.S. president Richard Nixon gave Wonder a Distinguished Service Award from the President's Committee on Employment of Handicapped People. That year, *My Cherie Amour* generated a single of the same name.

After recording the 1970 album *Signed, Sealed & Delivered*, featuring the title-track, Wonder moved to New York City, where he founded Tarus Production Company and Black Bull Publishing Company, both of which were licensed under Motown. With complete control over his musical career, Wonder began to write lyrics addressing social and political issues. Through the technique of over-dubbing, he played most of the instruments on his recordings including the guitar, bass, horns, percussion, and brilliant chromatic harmonica solos. *Music From My Mind*, *Talking Book*, and *Inversions* all feature Wonder distinctive synthesizer accompaniment.

Released in 1979, Wonder's *Journey Through the Secret Life of Plants* was an exploratory musical soundtrack for a film documentary. In 1984, Wonder's soundtrack for the film *Woman in Red* won him an

Stevie Wonder

Academy Award for Best Song with "I Just Called To Say I Love You." One year later, Wonder participated in the recording of "We Are the World" for U.S.A for Africa, the famine relief project. He also teamed up with Paul McCartney for "Ebony and Ivory." Wonder's 1985 album *Square Circle* produced the hit singles "Part Time Lover" and "Overjoyed" and won a Grammy. After the 15-time Grammy Award winner was inducted into the Rock and Roll Hall of Fame in 1989, he composed material for the soundtrack to Spike Lee's film *Jungle Fever*. Eight years in the making, 1995's *Conversation Piece* hit fans the same year as did the double-live recording *Natural Wonder*. He also contributed to the tribute-recording *Inner City Blues: The Music of Marvin Gaye* and to Quincy Jones's *Q's Jook Joint*. He won an *Essence* Award that year.

24

The Visual and Applied Arts

The Visual and Applied Arts

◆ An Enduring African Legacy ◆ Black Artists in Europe ◆ Black Artists in Early America
◆ African American Artists Interpreting Euro-American Traditions
◆ African American Artists in the Harlem Renaissance ◆ African American Artists Since the Depression
◆ The Search for an African American Identity ◆ The HBCU Connection
◆ African American Exhibitions ◆ Architecture and the Applied Arts
◆ Visual and Applied Artists ◆ Museums and Galleries

by Ionis Bracy Martin and Floyd Thomas, Jr.

"The constructive lessons of African art are among the soundest and most needed of art creeds today. They offset with equal force the banalities of sterile, imitative classicism and the superficialities of literal realism. They emphasize intellectually significant form, abstractly balanced design, formal simplicity, restrained and unsentimental emotional appeal. Moreover, Africa's art creed is beauty in use, vitally rooted in the crafts, and uncontaminated with the blight of the machine. Surely the liberating example of such art will be marked as an influence in the contemporary work of Negro artists as it has been in that of the leading modernists: Picasso, Modigliani, Matisse, Epstein, Lipchitz, Brancusi and others too numerous to mention." (Alain Locke, Professor of Philosophy, Howard University, 1931).

This comment by one of America's foremost art critics over sixty-five years ago underscores the problems and the promise encountered by African Americans interested in expanding their artistic skills throughout their history in the United States.

The problems and obstacles encountered by black artists in America have been enumerated and discussed by scholars and critics alike. It has been argued that a multiplicity of factors have combined to impede or preclude the development of black artists and their art. According to this line of thought, black Americans were torn from their cultural roots in Africa, while enslaved they were prevented from practicing artistic traditions associated with "pagan" religious beliefs, and even as

citizens they were denied opportunities, training, and patronage others received for their artistic endeavors. Additionally, because of their comparative economic deprivation, African Americans were historically discouraged from pursuing careers in the visual arts. The cumulative effects of these obstacles, according to this theory, proved so devastating to African American creativity in the visual arts, that the promise seemingly implied in a great African artistic tradition could not be realized in America.

Unfortunately, these arguments have been repeated with such frequency and "authority" that they were accepted into the cannon of American art history. The omission of black artists from standard art history texts, classroom discussions and museum collections has been rationalized by the erroneous assumption that African Americans had simply not produced a significant body of work that merited serious consideration. In consequence, African American artists have long been denied their rightful place in the history of American art.

Despite the obstacles and difficulties unique to them, African Americans have produced a remarkable body of work clearly worthy of consideration. Black Americans have faced and overcome bewildering obstacles in every field of creative endeavor—in literature, music, dance, and the visual arts. While it is certainly true that the odds stacked against black visual artists overwhelmed many along the way, many persevered. Lynn Moody Igoe's massive annotated bibliography, *250 Years of Afro-American Art*, published in 1981, contains over

1,200 pages of information pertaining to the accomplishments of 3,900 black American visual artists. That so few black artists have been acknowledged by the "mainstream" art establishment is less a reflection on African American artistic ability than a failure of the art establishment to comprehend the reality that aesthetic values are not universal and that unique cultural experience manifests itself in unique artistic expressions.

◆ AN ENDURING AFRICAN LEGACY

A growing number of scholars are challenging the once widely embraced assumption that the period of enslavement totally obliterated the African heritage, leaving African Americans devoid of cultural roots and artistic creativity. Surviving African aesthetic influences have been discussed by Nkiru Nzegwu (crafts), John Michael Vlach (architecture), Floyd Willis Coleman and Bamidele Demerson (painting), Alan Lomax (music), Katrina Hazzard-Donald (dance), Reginia Perry (folk art), and Robert Farris Thompson (sculpture), to name a few.

The supposition that slavery reduced African Americans to "cultural zero" fails to consider not only residual African influences, but also the factor of re-discovery and renewal. This process was first espoused by Alain Locke, who urged black artists to re-Africanize by adopting and adapting their ancestral arts. Locke believed that the amalgam of African and American influences would surely result in a new and unique art, representative of a new philosophy and cultural identity. As Bamidele Demerson points out:

> There always have been some African Americans who, fearing their ethnic group had lost too much of its ancestral culture and consequently its identification with Africa, led a variety of revitalization movements. In a society that anathematized the African American, such movements were part of a repertoire of strategies that allowed members of the imprecated ethnic group to: pridefully assert a glorious past that spanned millennia; selectively reclaim and adapt some aspects of African beliefs and behavioral codes; and zealously rescue their dignity. The message imparted by these movements was, "Remember you are African!"

According to artist/educator Willis "Bing" Davis, "Because our forebears' culture, right down to their names, was suppressed when they came to America as slaves, we have had to dig to link our cultural roots with Africa." (Quoted in Susan MacDonald, "From US to Slave House," *West Africa* 17 June 1985; 1223.) Evidence of an interest in Africa as a source of inspiration can be found in the murals painted by Aaron Douglas during the 1930s and in the work of Bing Davis, whose travels to the land of his ancestors has inspired and given direction to his art, both in clay and on canvas. Though much of his work is viewed as abstract and non-representational, his *Spirit Dance* series captures the colors and movements he experienced while watching dancers in West Africa.

African aesthetic values, forms and techniques are well represented in African American craft art. Blended with influences derived from an African American experience, craft art forms a vital link between African and African American creative expression. While Mary Jackson has retained an ancient African basket making tradition that has endured through the ages in coastal Carolina, she pushes the boundaries to create beautiful sea grass baskets that are both functional and truly unique.

> "A medium of artistic expression, these coiled sweet grass forms were also memory vessels. The coiling, the twilled, twined, checkerboard, and fine-bias weaves draw from centuries-old geometric and skeuomorphic patterns of West Africa and give them an American feeling. In these utilitarian objects, African American modifications amounted to an artistic exploration of the tensile strength of weaves and of the plasticity and structural potential of the natural fibers." (Nkiru Nzegwu, "A Circle of Dibias: Making Vessels of Memory and Life," *Uncommon Beauty in Common Objects: The Legacy of African American Craft Art*, 1993:9).

Yvonne and Curtis Tucker and David MacDonald are among a number of late twentieth century ceramists who continue the legacy of work in clay passed down through "Dave the Potter" and a lineage of enslaved Africans and their descendants. While inspired by African cultural traditions, these artists shape their work to reflect a history that is both African and African American. This melding of African cultural tradition and African American craft can also be found in the work of enslaved blacksmiths who incorporated African symbolism in their ornamental ironwork. This tradition has continued in Charleston, South Carolina, through the skill and imagination of master craftsmen such as Philip Simmons, his mentor Peter Simmons, and generations of now unknown black blacksmiths who preceded them in practicing this ancient African art form.

Another ancient West African metalworking process, lost-wax bronze casting has been preserved in the work of John Beckley, who has invented a portable table-top furnace to produce his sculptures. Beckley's *Me Myself*, which represents the two halves of his identity joined together, is a graphic representation of the African and African American influences that guide his art and his life. Another contemporary artist who works in metals, Andrew F. Scott, has created a series of stools fabricated in steel and outdoor steel sculptures that mix the iconography of traditional African art forms with the formal structure of totems. These reflect the compelling strength of Africa's influence and aesthetic values on a contemporary African American sculptor implying a continuum with an age-old African craft skill. His *Nkonde Totem III* was the first artwork to be installed in the sculpture garden of the National Afro-American Museum and Cultural Center in Wilberforce, Ohio.

The African tradition of woodcraft can be found in the cabinetry and carpentry that was so integral to the development of the early American economy and the built environment, including public buildings and private homes, particularly in the South. Known for his finely crafted furniture and architectural pieces, Thomas Day (c. 1800-1860) achieved aesthetic beauty and financial success by blending Euro-American period styles with African American craftsmanship, at times incorporating design features that appear to be African in origin. Contemporary artist Manuel Gomez has honed his woodcraft skills in creating "Afro combs" that continue a Ghanaian Akan tradition. Carved from exotic woods, these utilitarian objects are endowed with aesthetic beauty that reflects both cultural pride and African American sensibilities. Another woodcarver, the late Elijah Pierce (1892-1982), is among the most widely acknowledged African American "folk" artists. Nkiru Nzegwu has called his narrative wood carvings "sermons in wood." Whether his subject is sacred or secular, Pierce takes on the role of a contemporary African American *griot*, a historian who documents history in the stories his woodcarvings tell.

Carolyn Mazloomi and Michael Cummings are *griots* who preserve history through another craft skill with traditional African precedents—quilting. Both Mazloomi and Cummings chronicle the history of the African diaspora in the Americas with equal emphasis in their art on craftsmanship and aesthetic considerations as on the subject portrayed. Cummings incorporates a collage style and shapes inspired by Abomey applique. Through this medium, Mazloomi "raises socio-political issues of cultural identity and marginalization, visually forcing her audience's attention to key events in American history." (Nkiru Nzegwu, *Uncommon Beauty in Common Objects: The Legacy of African American Craft Art*, 1993:74). Mazloomi, Cummings, Peggy Hartwell, Carole Harris, Sandra German, and Faith Ringgold are among a growing number of artists who are taking the quilt from the bed to the wall. Concerned that a traditional African American art form was dying out, Mazloomi formed the Women of Color Quilter's Network, which presently has 600 members.

The link to African aesthetic values and inspiration can take unusual forms in African American craft art, as evident in the stylized aluminum, wood and leather "Zebra Chair" that is Richard Bennett's tribute to "the motherland, the mother continent where all life began."

◆ BLACK ARTISTS IN EUROPE

Two artists who excelled in Europe in the seventeenth century have been documented. They are Juan de Pareja and Sebastian Gomez. Pareja was a slave, apprentice, and pupil of the great master Velasquez. Many of Pareja's works were of such a quality that they were mistakenly accepted as Velasquez's own and hung in the great museums and mansions of western Europe. Today, Pareja's paintings, properly credited to him, hang in the Dulwich Gallery in London, the Prado in Madrid, the Munich Gallery, and the Hermitage in Leningrad. Pareja's talent was recognized in his lifetime and in 1652 he was manumitted by King Philip IV.

Another well-known seventeenth-century black artist, Sebastian Gomez, a servant of Murillo, was discovered painting secretly at night in his master's studio after Murillo's pupils had departed. Murillo made Gomez his student, and eventually Gomez, known as The Mulatto of Murillo, became famous for paintings and murals in Seville.

Although Pareja and Gomez were black artists, their genius was nurtured in a European setting and tradition. Cut off from their African heritage, they naturally worked in the same style and format as their white contemporaries. Their paintings were devoted to the religious themes and aristocratic portraits desired by the art world of that historical era.

◆ BLACK ARTISTS IN EARLY AMERICA

The first known African-American artists were from the eighteenth century. African slaves had many skills: metal tooling and smithing, furniture making, masonry, weaving, woodcarving, pottery making, clay sculpting and metal casting. The most talented crafts people were among the first to gain their freedom before emancipation and, needless to say, were among the most successful during Reconstruction and the years to follow.

As we approach the twenty-first century, will artists of African descent continue following and developing their art from lessons learned and based upon "Africa's art creed . . . beauty in use, vitally rooted in the crafts, and uncontaminated with the blight of the machine"? Or will African-American artists, like the members of AFRI-COBRA (African Commune of Bad Relevant Artists), continue to establish their own aesthetics, while still others follow mainstream American tastes in their pursuit to be a part of the American fabric?

Newspaper Boy, Edward Mitchell Bannister, 1869.

◆ AFRICAN AMERICAN ARTISTS INTERPRETING EURO-AMERICAN TRADITIONS

The only eighteenth-century African American artist in Colonial America presently known to have left a historical record was Scipio Morehead. His artistic endeavors appear to have been aided by two prominent women who lived in Boston where he was a slave. One was the wife of his clergyman master, the Reverend John Morehead, who was a patron of the arts, and the other, poet Phillis Wheatley, who was herself a slave. Morehead's style has been reported to have been in keeping with the period—classically allegorical, resembling the work of Romney and Reynolds, British masters of the era. Although no major work is known to have survived, a small portrait of Phillis Wheatley is believed to be Morehead's work.

Certainly, there were other black artists and craftsmen in the eighteenth century about whom history has left little trace. Fortunately, as scholars have more of a desire to understand the nature and development of the American culture, a more multi-ethnic pattern is beginning to emerge with the basic foundation being Western European, African, and Native American. Records indicate that blacks skilled as painters, silversmiths, cabinet and coach makers, ornamentalists, and shipwrights, were among the most successful in buying their freedom. Eugene Warbourg, for example, a black sculptor from New Orleans, became well known for his ornamental gravestones and eventually went to study in Europe. Much colonial iron work and metal work on eighteenth century mansions, churches, and public buildings were created and executed by blacks and occasionally reached heights that can be classified as fine art.

Emerging African American artists in the eighteenth and nineteenth centuries found that to be successful they had to simulate European artistic styles. Many were trained by white artists and they traveled to Europe to study and receive validation. Their works received some degree of popular acceptance, but racism kept them out of the mainstream. Most continued to work in the United States in spite of their status. Some were able to overcome immense obstacles and win recognition for their art. Joshua Johnston (1765-1830) is believed to be the first black American to gain recognition as a portrait painter. Robert S. Duncanson (1821-1872), who captured the beauty and wonder of nature in romantic views of the land, won praise at home and abroad. He is recognized as among the greatest landscape artists in American history. Edward Mitchell Bannister (1828-1901) also excelled in romantic interpretations of nature. Edmonia Lewis (1843-1900?) was the first African American woman to receive recognition as

an artist in the United States and in Europe. The influence of Greco-Roman sculpture she studied in Rome can be seen in her later works that are strongly neoclassical. Meta Vaux Warrick (Fuller) (1877-1968) is best known for sculptures that express pathos in her interpretations of humanity.

Some African American artists attempted to escape the classical tradition into which they were confined and expressed themes closer to their heritage and existence. Some fine portraits of black freedmen were painted by talented but obscure black artists in the rural South during the period from 1870 through the early part of the twentieth century. Henry Ossawa Tanner's paintings in the 1880s of poor blacks, for example, stem from this unheralded school of African American art. But he gained his greatest recognition for paintings that reflected his father's strong religious influence. Tanner, who went to Paris to study art and decided to stay, won many prestigious honors, including membership in the National Academy of Design. In 1923, he was designated a chevalier of the French Legion of Honor.

Patrick Reason (1817-1850) was among the earliest African American artists whose work was directed toward social objectives. Though a free man, Reason was keenly aware of the injustice and inhumanity of slavery. He devoted his energies to the anti-slavery cause by employing his talents as a draftsman and printmaker. His "Kneeling Slave" and other engravings and lithographs were widely published in abolitionist literature.

The turn of the century brought few changes in the approach of most African American artists to their work. They continued to look toward Western Europe for their themes and development of expression, and there was little emphasis given to demonstrating an ethnic consciousness. Two important developments in art helped to push black artists towards cultural and social awareness and a visual aesthetic: the 1913 Armory Show of works by European cubist and modernist painters revealed an interest in, and influence from, African abstraction of form, and the mainstream American art world developed an interest in genre subjects. These movements toward social realism and abstract formalism in art opened the doors to new interpretations and values in artistic expression.

The period of transition, from 1900 to the 1920s showed a continued interest on the part of black artists, in expressing themselves in imitative styles. They felt that the interest in African American culture was sincere in Europe and many traveled there to study. New trends, showing expressions of personal dignity and ethnic awareness began. The artists of this period—Palmer Hayden, Archibald Motley, Malvin Gray John-

Hagar in the Wilderness, Edmonia Lewis.

son, William Edouard Scott, Meta Warrick Fuller, and Laura Wheeler Warring—were among the major contributors to this new awareness.

◆ AFRICAN AMERICAN ARTISTS IN THE HARLEM RENAISSANCE

This new respect for the African idiom and negritude that began to manifest itself after World War I can be attributed directly to cultural activities that developed in several important cities during the 1920s—Cleveland, Chicago, and New York being the major active centers.

From Karamu House, a center for cultural activities founded in 1915 in Cleveland, came such artists as Hughie Lee-Smith, Zell Ingrams, Charles Sallee, Elmer Brown, William E. Smith, and George Hulsinger. In 1924, the Spingarn Awards were established. Three years later, in 1927, the Harmon Foundation was established by philanthropist William E. Harmon to aid African-American artists. The foundation offered financial awards and exhibitions and encouraged the growth of art education programs in many black institutions throughout the country. The Harmon Foundation was to become one of the major organizations involved in the perpetuation and presentation of African-American art in the United States and continued to exist until the mid-1960s. A major exhibition on the Harmon Foundation and its pioneering support of African American artists was organized by Gary A. Reynolds with the assistance of Beryl J. Wright at The Newark Museum in 1989.

The 1930s brought the depression and the Works Project Administration. Black artists abandoned by the white philanthropists of the 1920s were rescued by the WPA. Aaron Douglas, Augusta Savage, Charles Alston, Hale Woodruff, and Charles White created murals and other works for public buildings under this program. In 1939, the Baltimore Museum Show, the first exhibition of African-American artists to be held in a southern region, presented the works of Richmond Barthe, Malvin Gray Johnson, Henry Bannarn, Florence Purviance, Hale Woodruff, Dox Thrash, Robert Blackburn, and Archibald Motley. The Harlem Art Center and the Chicago South Side Community Art Center also began with the WPA.

Representation of the African American through art became an important imperative in the first three decades of this century. At the urging of Alain Locke, W. E. B. Du Bois, and others, creative artists began collaborating in literature, music, theatre, and art to promote an important cultural heritage. Aaron Douglas was considered the leading painter of "The Negro Renaissance". Active in New York from 1923 to 1925, Douglas was the first to depict visual symbols, stylized African figures with overlays of geometric forms, that created movement and rhythm. The idea spread from Harlem's boundaries where many intellectuals and artists from the Caribbean and other parts of the United States had settled. This concept, while promoting ethnic awareness and pride, also counteracted the stereotypes and shallow interpretations prevalent in the popular culture.

◆ AFRICAN AMERICAN ARTISTS SINCE THE DEPRESSION

During this period, active artists continued to express the American social and political climate for

A mural by Hale Woodruff depicting the contribution of African Americans in the history of California.

African Americans. The Second World War seemed to bring a sense of urgency to the search for equality. When the armed services were integrated, a real sense of hope developed for equality in other areas of life. There was a great migration from the South to northern cities, documented by artists such as Romare Bearden, Beauford Delaney, Jacob Lawrence, and Hughie Lee-Smith. African Americans in search of self and a better life might be an appropriate interpretation of the 1940s and 1950s.

The influence of the previous decades shows in the continuation of muralist art. Samella Lewis in her book *Art: African American* (Handcraft Studios, Los Angeles, California) notes that African architectural traditions include exterior murals as an important aspect. Charles Alston, John Biggers, Jacob Lawrence, and Charles White became important muralists during this period. Inspired by Mexican mural artists (who advocated social change through their art), African American artists were especially drawn to the themes, bold forms, and bright colors of artists such as Diego Rivera, David Alfero Siqueiros, and Jose Clemente Orozco.

Conscious of the need to study the history, aesthetics, and formal qualities of art—like their successful white counterparts—African American artists contin-

ued to go abroad to Paris, Rome, and before the war, Germany. Most, however, stayed at home and attended classes at universities such as Columbia, Ohio State, and Pennsylvania State or some professional art schools such as the Art Institute of Chicago, the New York Art Students' League, and the Philadelphia Academy of Art. Black institutions such as Fisk, Hampton Institute, Howard, Morehouse, and Tuskegee emphasized art education as a means of survival, as well as the basis for continuing a future cultural aesthetic in the visual arts.

"Some historians and critics," Dr. Lewis notes, "have erroneously assumed that African American artists are unfamiliar with the formalized techniques of Western aesthetics." From the 1940s, more African Americans were being awarded degrees in art than ever before. Some turned to abstraction, non-objective art, and expressive forms as seen in many works by Norman Lewis who, for a time, was a part of the group known as the Action Painters. (Jackson Pollock, a European American artist, was an exponent of the Action Painters and listened to jazz as he worked). Romare Bearden studied Cubism, as did Aaron Douglas. Early on, they knew the African roots of this art form (long before American critics wrote about the significant influence of African

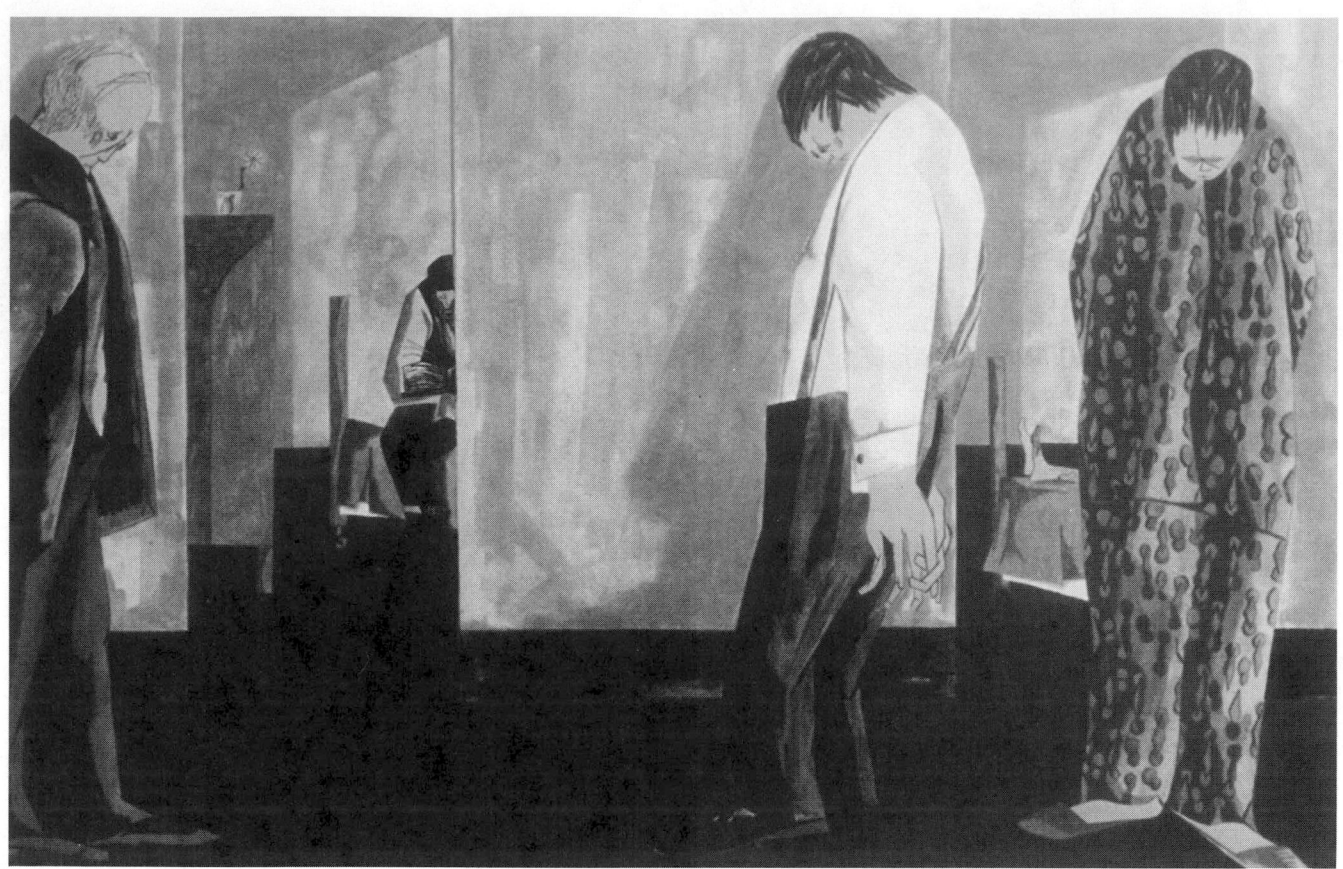

Depression, Jacob Lawrence, 1950.

art on the abstractionist painters of the twentieth century).

◆ THE SEARCH FOR AN AFRICAN AMERICAN IDENTITY

Following World War II, black soldiers came home to a land of greater opportunity by way of the G.I. Bill and employment possibilities previously denied to them. But victory abroad did not bring with it victory over racism and discrimination at home. This was a battle yet to be won. The civil rights movement employed legal challenges and civil disobedience to defeat segregation in the schools, at the lunch counter and on the bus. African American artists were there to document, to inspire, and to champion the "cause."

During the 1960s, many African American artists reassessed their role in and responsibility to the black community. Spiral Group was composed of New York artists who sought to reinforce the civil rights movement through their art. Reginald Gammon's *Freedom Now,* for example, incorporates an expressionistic technique to create a sense of unity and determination among marchers demanding their civil rights. Charles White challenged members of the newly formed National Conference of Artists (NCA) to create works that convey great ideas and great passions. Such groups profoundly affected many black artists, for they provided essential support, affirmation, and relief from creative isolation.

The transition from an emphasis on civil rights to the demand for "Black Power" and adherence to black aesthetic values is reflected in the development of AFRICOBRA (African Commune of Black Relevant Artists), and the rejection of art not directed toward the liberation of the black community. Jeff Donaldson, Wadsworth A. Jarrell, Nelson Stevens, Napoleon Jones Henderson, Murray N. DePillars and their fellow members of AFRICOBRA sought to create works "reflective of black visual ethos." (Robert L. Douglas, "Introduction," *Beyond 1984: Contemporary Perspectives on American Art,* Ohio University exhibition catalogue, 1985:n.p.). AFRICOBRA member Jeff Donaldson explained that AFRICOBRA members "strive for images inspired by African people/experience and images which African people can relate to directly without formal art training and/or experience." ("Ten in Search of a Na-

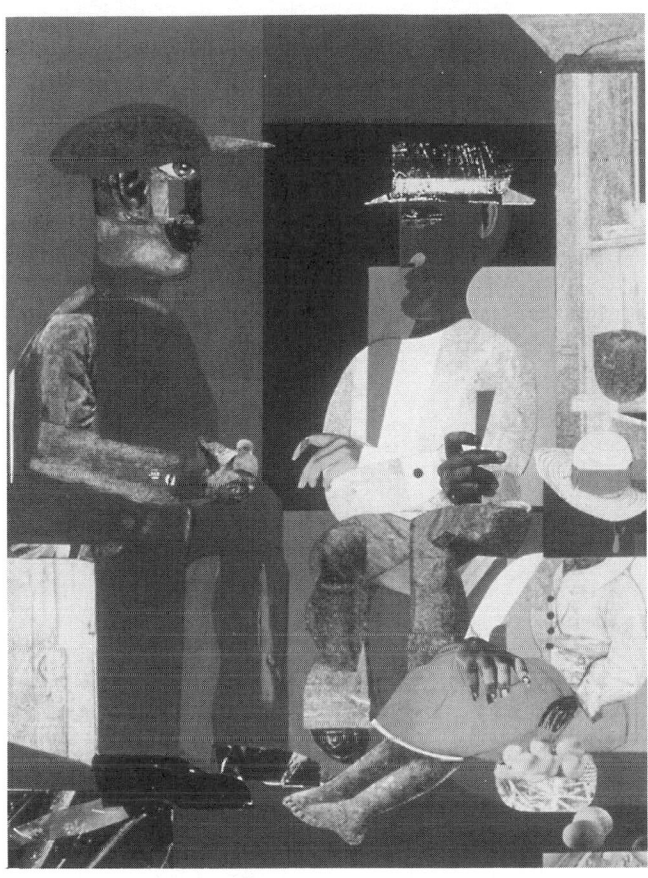

Eastern Barn, Romare Bearden, 1968.

tion," *Black World,* Oct. 1970:82). This philosophy was expressed earlier by members of OBAC (Organization of Black Artists in Chicago), who painted a huge mural depicting African American heroes on a building in the heart of Chicago's black community. Known as the *Wall of Respect,* the mural became a symbol of pride that was emulated by black artists who created murals in other major cities across the country.

Ron Karenga and others who espoused Black Cultural Nationalism, believed that "art must reflect and support the Black Revolution, and any art that does not discuss and contribute to the revolution is invalid." ("Ron Karenga and Black Cultural Nationalism," *Negro Digest,* Jan. 1968:18). Dana Chandler, an artist committed to the "Black Arts Movement," explained that he was not trying to be aesthetically pleasing; he was trying to be relevant. Widely acknowledged for his large murals painted on the exterior walls of buildings with the black neighborhoods of Boston, Chandler's concerns were "conceptual, didactic, and idealistic, not primarily aesthetic." He was not interested in pleasing the "art establishment." Rather, his objective was to inspire black unity, black dignity and respect "as the first steps in a long march toward social, economic and political goals." (Carroll Greene, Jr. "Perspective: The Black Artist in America," *The Art Gallery,* Apr. 1970:26).

Proponents of the Black Arts Movement believed that the purpose of their art was to liberate man, in keeping with their ancient traditions and their contemporary needs. The Black Power movement stimulated artists to convey pride in African American heroes and accomplishments by correcting the historical record. Betye Saar, Murray DePillars, and other black artists of the period confronted negative stereotypes and re-shaped them from a militant African American perspective. In a series entitled "Exploding the Myth," Betye Saar transformed derogatory images such as Uncle Tom and Aunt Jemima by recasting them as militants in the black liberation movement. In this series, "Jemimas," "Toms," and "Little Black Sambos" are shown armed with guns instead of hoes and pancake turners. With the establishment of the Black Emergency Cultural Coalition, African American artists challenged the society and cultural institutions to acknowledge their work and its meaning.

Not all African American artists during this period subscribed to the Black Arts Movement or considered themselves Black Nationalists whose primary objective in art was political. Norman Lewis undoubtedly spoke for many artists who believed that "political and social aspects should not be the primary concern: aesthetic ideas should have preference." (Jeanne Siegal, "Why Spiral?" *Art News* Sep. 1966:48). Philosophical questions regarding the nature of African American art and aesthetics were at the forefront during this period— debated among artists, inside the African American community, within institutions of cultural conservation, and through the art press. While some artists emphasized that they were African American artists, others thought of themselves as artists who happened to be black. Such philosophical differences are reflected in the broad range of creativity expressed through the visual arts of the period.

During this period, emotions could not always be contained on canvas, channeled into familiar forms, or exhibited in traditional settings. Art literally took to the streets of the ghetto to meet with, appeal to, and celebrate the people, as was richly illustrated in Chicago and Detroit murals.

In 1972, in New York City, African American and Hispanic teenagers combined the spray paint can and street pride into a colorful art form, "wall graffiti." The content of the wall graffiti has often been no more than the name of a street gang or the nickname of the individual painter and the name and number of the street on which he lives, or to which he gives loyalty. On the other hand, the paintings can be seen as extravagant as a scene with cartoon characters and lavishly flamboyant lettering. Towards the end of the 1970s and well into the 1980s, this graffiti style became so popular its value increased. Several of the young street artists were welcomed into the mainstream art world, making a few famous for a short period and promoting one young artist, Jean-Michael Basquiat, into a superstar.

There were also mainstream artists who took on the graffiti style and made it their own, such as artist Keith Haring, and galleries such as the Paula Cooper Gallery opened their doors to this new and defiant art. Choreographer Twyla Tharp choreographed a ballet for the Joffrey Company, "Deuce Coupe," showing dancers moving against a background provided by boys painting with spray cans on ceiling-hung sheets of paper.

Moving into the 1990s, multimedia art forms (developed in the 1960s and 1970s; expanded by video and computers in the 1980s) came to the forefront. Artists who were experimenting with combining traditional modes of artistic expression (painting, printmaking, sculpture) with dance, drama and other performance arts to emphasize the importance and place of process in the visual arts were finding alternative spaces as well, in the environment, factories and school buildings. Stones, hair, elephant dung, twigs, bricks, discards, and other objects often replace traditional materials. Words, symbols, and numbers of images have a new emphasis, along with the purely gestural marks of some artists.

Multicultural considerations (how groups of people see themselves and others) are dominant themes in the 1990s. Through an enormous range of Native, African, Asian, European, and Hispanic American intercultural sharing, and African American identity is still evolving.

◆ THE HBCU CONNECTION

Traditionally, black educational institutions have played a major role in the preservation and presentation of African American art. Many historically black colleges and universities were collecting art by African Americans when most museums and private collectors were not interested in their work. Hampton University, which has one of the strongest collections of African American art in existence, began collecting in 1892. Through the years these institutions have amassed over 5,000 works, constituting the largest body of art by African Americans in our nation. These collections contain work that was previously ignored, but is recognized today as being of great aesthetic and historic significance. To celebrate this art, Edmond Barry Gaither, Director and Curator of the Museum of the National Center of Afro-American Artists in Boston, organized an exhibit entitled *Our Commonwealth, Our Collections: Works from Traditionally Black Colleges and Universities*.

Historically black colleges and universities have played another crucial role in the history of African American art by establishing art programs and hiring faculty who were master artists and exceptional role models and mentors for their students. John Biggers, Claude Clark, Aaron Douglas, David Driskell, James V. Herring, Lois Mailou Jones, Jack Jordan, James Amos Porter, and Hale Woodruff are among the faculty members who have fit this mold. Their guidance and inspiration have stimulated the development of generations of young African American artists.

◆ AFRICAN AMERICAN EXHIBITIONS

During the late 1960s and early 1970s, leading mainstream museums began to respond to the demands being made by African American artists to open their doors and hire African American scholars as curators and administrators. At the time of the intensive demonstrations, Kynastan McShine, a young West Indian who had already established his reputation as a strong curator at the Jewish Museum, moved on to become the assistant curator of painting and sculpture at the Museum of Modern Art. Howardena Pindell had just begun her career at the Museum of Modern Art as the assistant curator of drawings and prints, would later move on to become the associate curator, and would in 1980 resign from that position to pursue her career as an artist. However, this progress was not satisfactory to the artists who demonstrated and wrote letters demanding that jobs be made available to black art historians.

In 1968, Gylbert Coker became the first African American to be hired at the Guggenheim Museum in an administrative trainee position. She later went on to work at the Museum of Modern Art as cataloguer in the museum's registration department. In 1976, she received the Rockefeller Fellowship in Museum Education and spent one year at the Metropolitan Museum of Art. The following year, she became curator of The Studio Museum in Harlem where she set up their registration department and organized such important exhibitions as The Bob Thompson Exhibition and the Hale Woodruff Retrospective, before leaving to pursue a career as a freelance critic and curator. In 1980 and again in 1982, Coker co-directed *Art Across the Park*, an outdoor exhibition created by the artist David Hammons. The project was so popular that several groups in New York tried to copy the concept. It was the first large-scale exhibit that openly encouraged all artists to take part, and it was in this exhibition that the term *multiethnic* was coined.

From the Whitney Museum's Museum Studies Program came Faith Weaver and Horace Brockington. Faith Weaver went on to teach American Art History at the School of Visual Arts. Brockington gained recognition for his exhibition *Another Generation* for The Studio Museum in Harlem in 1978, which set the stage for *African American Abstraction*, presented two years later at P.S. 1, an alternative art center.

Regina Perry was invited by the Metropolitan Museum of Art in 1976 to produce an exhibition called *Selections of Nineteenth-Century Afro-American Art.* It was an exhibition which highlighted, for the first time, many early African American portrait painters and landscape artists, and it even made attempts to document some important slave artifacts and put them into an aesthetic rather than sociological perspective. David C. Driskell's traveling exhibition *Two Centuries of Black American Art*, organized by the Los Angeles County Museum in 1976, brought national attention to the beauty and diversity of African American art. The exhibit included examples of craft art as well as paintings and sculpture and the exhibit catalogue is an excellent resource for the study of African American art. In 1987, Driskell and Mary Schmidt-Campbell curated *Harlem Renaissance: Art of Black America*, for the Studio Museum in New York. Also in 1976, Lowery Sims put together an exhibition of selected works by twentieth-century African American artists from the Metropolitan Museum of Art collection for the Bedford-Stuyvesant Restoration Corporation. Three years later, in 1979, Sims mounted another exhibition of African American paintings from the twentieth-century collection. This time, the exhibition was inside the Metropolitan Museum.

Against the Odds: African American Artists and the Harmon Foundation was another major exhibition organized by a "mainstream" institution, the Newark Museum, in 1989. The exhibit celebrated the art and artists represented in the historic Harmon Foundation exhibitions, and provided many of the artists and their work with broader exposure than they received in the original Harmon Foundation exhibitions. The Newark Museum held its first black exhibition in 1944. That exhibition included the works of Richmond Barthe, Romare Bearden, and William Edmonson. In 1974, the museum presented *Black Artists: Two Generations*, curated by Paul Waters.

Facing History: The Black Image in American Art 1710-1940 was a major exhibit curated by Guy C. McElroy, who also wrote a catalogue with an essay by Henry Louis Gates, Jr. This exhibit, organized by the Corcoran Gallery of Art in Washington, D.C., chronicled the way black people have been portrayed by American artists and perceived by American society. The Wadsworth Atheneum in Hartford, Connecticut, opened its first African American Gallery (believed to be the first in the country in a major "mainstream" museum, according to its curator) with an exhibit from the National Museum of American Art, *Free Within Ourselves: African American Art in the Collection of the National Museum of*

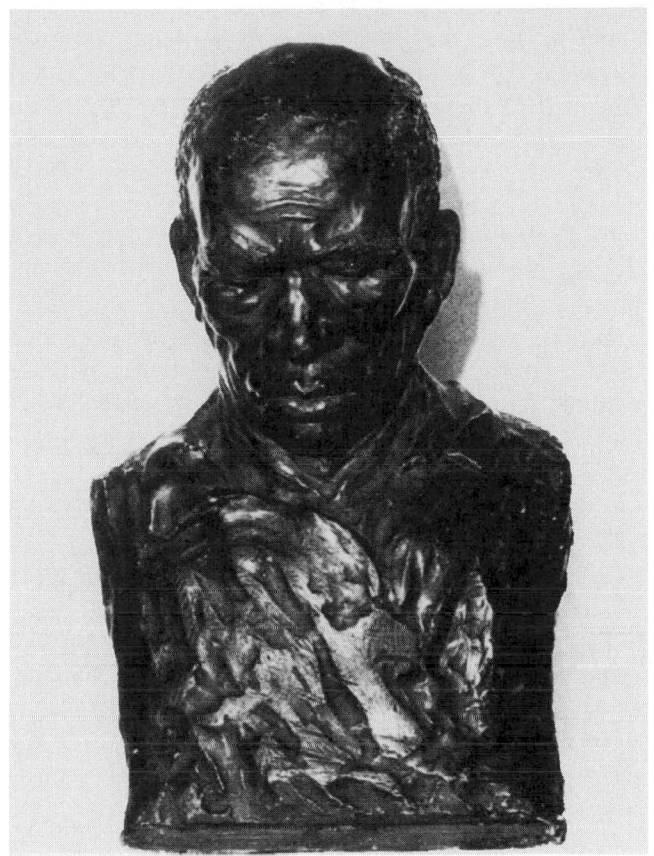

Bust by Richmond Barthe.

American Art, curated by Linda Roscoe Hartigan. The catalogue was written by Regenia Perry of the National Museum of Art, Smithsonian Institution.

In 1989, the Dallas Museum organized *Black Art: Ancestral Legacy* with an impressive exhibition staff that included Alia J. Wardlaw, chief curator; Regenia Perry and Edmund Barry Gaither, curators; David Boxer, David C. Driskell, William Ferris, and Robert Farris Thompson, advisers. The exhibit explored the impact of African culture on artists in the African diaspora, the Caribbean (Haiti, Jamaica, and the Bahamas), as well as the United States.

Black Folk Art in America: 1930-1980), organized by The Corcoran Gallery of Art in 1982, was a pioneering exhibition on a then neglected topic in African American art. Curated by Jane Livingston and John Beardsley, the exhibit featured many artists whose works are recognized today as national treasures. The catalogue, which includes an essay by Regenia Perry, features the work of twenty black "folk" artists.

The National Afro-American Museum and Cultural Center in Wilberforce, Ohio, organized *Uncommon Beauty in Common Objects: The Legacy of African American Craft Art*, in 1993. This exhibition, catalogue, and companion issue of the *International Review of African American Art* focused national attention on another important but little known aspect of African American creative genius. Created by Willis "Bing" Davis, the exhibit included the work of over one hundred contemporary African American craft artists, and traveled to major venues across the country. An earlier show, *The Afro-American Tradition in the Decorative Arts*, curated by John Michael Vlach and organized by The Cleveland Museum of Art, explored the "tradition" of African American craft, and included early examples of musical instruments as well as carved walking sticks, face jugs, ceramic jars, wrought iron work, etc. The McKissick Museum, University of South Carolina, organized *Row Upon Row: Sea Grass Baskets of the South Carolina Lowcountry*, curated by Catherine Wilson Horne, in 1986.

In terms of photographic exhibits, *Black Photographers Bear Witness: 100 Years of Social Protest*, is particularly noteworthy. It was curated by Deborah Willis and Howard Dodson, and organized by Williams College Museum of Art in 1989. *Songs of My People: African Americans: A Self Portrait*, is another major photographic exhibit, organized by the Smithsonian Institution in 1992.

The Seattle Museum launched a major retrospective in 1986 of the work of Jacob Lawrence—often referred to as the "Dean of the Black Painters." In 1991, the Philadelphia Museum of Art organized a retrospective of the works of its native son, Henry Ossawa Tanner. The Columbus (Ohio) Museum of Art honored a native son in 1992 with *Elijah Pierce: Woodcarver*.

By the 1990s, mainstream museums across the country, from Brooklyn, New York and Hartford, Connecticut in the East, to Detroit, Michigan, Atlanta, Georgia, and Dallas, Texas, and on to San Francisco, California, and Seattle, Washington in the West, were sponsoring major exhibits of African Americans and artifacts designed to appeal to black audiences.

Major funders of these exhibits included the National Endowment for the Arts, private charitable trusts and foundations, state and local arts commissions, universities, and private corporations such as IBM, Ford Motor Co., and Philip Morris Corp.

It is hoped that the audiences that have been introduced to museums through these exhibitions will support them through volunteerism, memberships, and gifts, and that members of the black community will be placed in positions of governance. More and more volunteers are working as docents, serving on committees and boards. If museums can come through this rite of passage, to become more inclusive and not just for the wealthy in our population, African American art will continue to enter the mainstream.

◆ ARCHITECTURE AND THE APPLIED ARTS

Architecture

Africans brought to America many skills in metalwork, woodcarving, masonry and toolmaking, to name a few. They built dwellings in Virginia and other parts of the Americas like rondavels found in Mali, Africa. These round brick slave quarters were topped with conical roofs and date from the eighteenth century. In the nineteenth century they built homes now called "shotgun houses," a part of the legacy from the Yoruba people of Western Africa. These came to Louisiana by way of Haiti. These mostly urban houses were narrow, frame dwellings 10' to 14' wide, with two or more rooms, varying in length from 22' to 65', and with ceilings from 6' to 12' in height. Slaves also built many mansions and public buildings. One built entirely by slaves was a courthouse in Vicksburg, Mississippi, which later became a museum.

Like other Africans, before and after emancipation, black craftsmen in the trades, interested in technology and art, sought to copy their European counterparts and were trained as slave labor or apprentices. They too, in time, began to do original works in wrought iron (later cast iron), wood and other metals.

The first African American to receive a degree from the Massachusetts Institute of Technology (in 1892) was Robert Taylor, who opened the first school of architecture in an African American school at Tuskegee Institute. In 1901, John A. Lankford built the Pythian Building, constructed entirely by African Americans. It was an office and social building designed by Lankford who was the first recorded African American architect with an office. The first African American to be accepted in the American Institute of Architects was Paul R. Williams (1926). The first African American woman to be elected was Norma Merrick Sklarek (1966).

Today, there are over eight hundred registered architects in the United States who are African American. The major schools of architecture in predominantly African American universities include: Florida A&M University, Tallahassee, Florida; Hampton University, Hampton, Virginia; Howard University, Washington, D.C.; Morgan State University, Baltimore, Maryland; Prairie View A&M University, Prairie View, Texas; Southern University, Baton Rouge, Louisiana; Tuskegee University, Tuskegee, Alabama; University of the District of Columbia, Washington, D.C.

In 1991, New York architect Jack Travis edited a book on thirty-three outstanding African American architects, which included a chronology of African Americans in architecture since 1868 by Vinson McKenzie of Auburn University, Auburn, Alabama. (*African American Architects in Current Practice*, Jack Travis, editor, Princeton Architectural Press.)

The Applied Arts: Crafts, Illustration, Fashion Design, and Automobile Design

The artistic heritage of African Americans includes dressmaking and tailoring, quilting, weaving, silversmithing, engraving, and ceramic production, as well as jewelrymaking, stitchery, stained-glass, blown glass, mosaics, and enameling. Many slaves learned their crafts in Africa. As these skills were discovered, the slave masters put these skilled workers to use and trained their slaves in new skills as needed.

The twentieth century saw a revival of functional art. There was a great crafts revival, and many artists began to employ traditional crafts methods and materials in their art. The line between art and craft has practically disappeared. Faith Ringgold and Michael Cummings are two artists/quilters, for example.

In illustration, the graphic artists Jerry Pinkney and Larry Johnson are examples of successful African Americans, among others, who have used their skills for designing postage stamps, children's books, editorial cartoons, and illustrations for other publications.

African American artists in fashion design include Stephen Burrows, Gordon Henderson, and Willi Smith. Historically, some household slaves were excellent dressmakers and tailors who turned these skills into self-supporting businesses after becoming free men and women.

In automobile design, Emeline King and Edward T. Welburn are successful artists. Careers in industrial design, unlike in the previous century, are filled by trained artists who combine engineering studies with art.

◆ VISUAL AND APPLIED ARTISTS

Charles Alston (1907-1972)
Painter, Sculptor, Muralist

It was the murals of painter Charles Alston that established his reputation and insured his fame as a black American artist of importance.

Born in Charlotte, North Carolina in 1907, Alston studied at Columbia University in New York, receiving

Stephen Burrows

B.A. and M.A. degrees. He was later awarded several fellowships and grants to launch his painting career.

Alston's paintings and sculpture are in such collections as those of IBM and the Detroit Institute of Arts. His murals depicting the history of medicine adorn the facade of Harlem Hospital in New York. Alston was a member of the National Society of Mural Painters. Notable works include *Exploration and Colonization* (1949); *Blues with Guitar and Bass* (1957); *Blues Song* (1958); *School Girl* (1958); *Nobody Knows* (1966); *Sons and Daughters* (1966); and *Frederick Douglass* (1968).

Benny Andrews (1930-)
Painter

Born in Madison, Georgia on November 13, 1930, Andrews studied at Fort Valley State College in Georgia and later at the University of Chicago. He was awarded a B.F.A. from the Art Institute of Chicago in 1958. During his career he has taught at the New York School of Social Research; New York City University; and Queens College in New York. His works have appeared in exhibitions around the country, including the Boston Museum of Fine Arts, The Martha Jackson Gallery in

New York City; and other museums and galleries too numerous to list.

Most notably, Andrews directed the Visual Arts Program for the National Endowment for the Arts, 1982-1984. He has directed the National Arts Program since 1985, offering children and adults an opportunity to exhibit and compete for prizes in many cities across the country.

Other honors include an Honorary Doctorate from the Atlanta School of Art, 1984; John Hay Whitney Fellowship, 1965–1967; New York Council on The Arts Grantee, 1971; NEA Fellowship, 1974; Bellagie Fellow, Rockefeller Foundation, 1987; National Endowment for the Arts Painting Fellowship, 1986. Notable works include *The Family; The Boxer; The Invisible Man; Womanhood; Flora;* and *Did the Bear.*

In late 1994, an exhibit of Andrews's work entitled "Benny Andrews: The America Series" appeared on display at the Wendell St. Gallery in Cambridge, Massachusetts.

Edward Mitchell Bannister (1828-1901)
Painter

Born in Nova Scotia in 1828, Bannister was the son of a West Indian father and African-American mother. Both parents died when he was very young. Bannister moved to Boston in the early 1850s, where he learned to make solar plates and worked as a photographer.

Influenced by the Barbizon style popular at the time, Bannister's paintings convey his own love of the quiet beauty of nature and his pleasure in picturesque scenes with cottages, cattle, dawns, sunsets and small bodies of water. In 1871, Bannister moved from Boston to Providence, Rhode Island, where he lived until his death in 1901. He was the only nineteenth-century African-American artist who did not travel to Europe to study art, believing that he was an American and that he wished to paint as an American. Bannister became one of the most outstanding artists in Providence in the 1870s and 1880s, and in 1880 was to become one of seven founders of the Providence Art Club, which later became known as the Rhode Island School of Design. Notable works include *After the Storm; Driving Home the Cows;* and *Narragansett Bay.*

Richmond Barthe (1901-1989)
Sculptor

Born on January 28, 1901, in Bay St. Louis, Mississippi, Barthe was educated at the Art Institute of Chicago from 1924 to 1928. He studied under Charles Schroeder and Albin Polasek. Barthe's first love was painting, but it

Richmond Barthe

was through his experiments with sculpture that he began initially to gain critical attention in 1927. His first commissions were busts of Henry Ossawa Tanner and Toussaint L'Ouverture. The acclaim resulting from them led to a one-man show in Chicago and a Rosenwald Fellowship for study in New York City.

Barthe's work has been exhibited at several major American museums. The Metropolitan Museum of Art in New York City purchased *The Boxer* in 1943. In 1946, he received the first commission given to a black for a bust of Booker T. Washington for New York University's Hall of Fame. A year later he was one of the committee of fifteen artists chosen to help modernize sculpture in the Catholic churches of the United States.

Barthe held membership in the National Academy of Arts and Letters. He died March 6, 1989, at his home in Pasadena, California at the age of eighty-eight. Notable works include *Singing Slave; Maurice Ens; Lot's Wife;* and *Henry O. Tanner.*

Jean-Michel Basquiat (1960-1988)
Painter

In a brief, tragic career, Jean-Michel Basquiat gained attention from wealthy collectors as a young artist discovered by Andy Warhol and promoted by other art consultants. He was raised in Brooklyn and attracted the New York art world with his trendy personal appearance (tangled dreadlocks) as a musician and artist at the age of eighteen. His works are autobiographical and deliberately "primitive" in style. In February 1985 he was a featured artist on the cover of the *New York Times Magazine*, shoeless in a suit, shirt and tie.

The Whitney Museum of American Art in New York City owns many of the six hundred works this artist produced, reportedly valued in the tens of millions of dollars, one might say symbolic of the excesses of the eighties. Jean-Michel Basquiat, was the example of a popular artist of the 1980s. The Whitney Museum mounted a retrospective exhibit of his work, October 23, 1992-February 14, 1993.

Basquiat began his career illegally painting images on buildings throughout the city. SAMO (slang for "same old s___") was his signature and trademark. He often used it in his paintings to preserve his reputation as a street artist. Basquiat was quoted as saying that his subject matter was, "Royalty, heroism and the streets."

He reportedly died of a drug overdose. Notable works include *Self Portrait as a Heel #3; Untitled (History of Black People); Hollywood Africans;* and *CPRKR* (in honor of Charlie Parker).

Romare Bearden (1914-1988)
Painter, Collagist

Romare Bearden was born on September 2, 1914, in Charlotte, North Carolina. His family moved to Pittsburgh and later to Harlem. Bearden studied with George Grosz at the Art Students League and later, on the G.I. Bill, went to Paris where he met Matisse, Joan Miro, and Carl Holty. A product of the new generation of Afro-Americans who had migrated from the rural areas of the South to the urban cities of the North, Bearden's work reflected the era of industrialization. His would become the visual images that would reflect the city life, the music jazz the city people. Bearden's earlier works belonged to the school of Social Realism, but after his return from Europe his images became more abstract.

In the 1960s, Bearden changed his approach to his picture-making and began to make collages, soon becoming one of the best known collagists in the world. His images are haunting montages of his memories of past experiences, of stories told to him by other people. They are for Bearden "an attempt to redefine the image of man in terms of the black experience." Notable works include *Street Corner; He Is Arisen; The Burial; Sheba;* and *The Prevalence of Ritual.*

John Biggers (1924-)
Painter

John Biggers has been a leading figure in Social Realism as a painter, sculptor, printmaker, and teacher, as well as an outstanding surrealistic muralist.

Born in Gastonia, North Carolina in 1924, Biggers has derived much of his subject matter from the contributions made by blacks to the development of the United States. While teaching at Texas Southern University, Biggers has become a significant influence on several young black painters.

Some of his most powerful pieces have been created as a result of his study trips to Africa: *The Time of Ede, Nigeria,* a series of works done in the 1960s are prime examples. Notable works include *Cradle; Mother and Child; The Contributions of Negro Women to American Life and Education;* and *Shotgun, Third Ward, #1.*

Camille Billops (1933-)
Sculptor, Photographer, Filmmaker

A sculptor of note in the art and retailing world, Camille Billops was born in California in 1933, graduated from California State College in 1960, and then studied sculpture on the west coast under a grant from the Huntington Hartford Foundation. In 1960, she had her first exhibition at the African Art Exhibition in Los Angeles, followed in 1963 by an exhibit at the Valley Cities Jewish Community Center in Los Angeles. In 1966, she participated in a group exhibition in Moscow. Since then, her multifaceted artistic talents, which include poetry, book illustration, and jewelry making, have earned the praise of critics throughout the world, particularly in Sri Lanka and Egypt, where she also has lived and worked.

Billops has also taught extensively. In 1975, she was active on the faculties of the City University of New York and Rutgers at Newark, New Jersey. In addition, she has conducted special art courses in the New York City jail (the Tombs) and in 1972 lectured in India for the United States Information Service on black American artists. She participated in an exhibit at the New York Cultural Center in 1973.

Billops is a printmaker, filmmaker, and photographer who has also been active in the mail–art movement which has made art more accessible to the public. She has written articles for the *New York Times, Amsterdam News* and *Newsweek.*

Her grants for film include the New York State Council on the Arts, 1987, 1988; NYSCA and New York Foundation for the Arts, 1989, Rockefeller Foundation, 1991, and National Endowment for the Arts, 1994.

Pepper Jelly Lady, Romare Bearden, 1980.

In 1992, Billops won the prestigious Grand Jury Prize for Best Documentary at the Sundance Film Festival, *Finding Christa*, an edited combination of interviews, home movies, still images and dramatic acting. Notable works include *Tenure; Black American; Portrait of an American Indian* (all three are ceramic sculptures); *Year after Year* (painting). *Older Women and Love* (film); *Suzanne, Suzanne* (film); *A String of Pearls* (film); and *The K.K.K. Boutique Ain't Just Rednecks* (film).

Billops is also the author of *The Harlem Book of the Dead*, with James Van der Zee and Owen Dodson.

Robert Blackburn (1921-)
Printmaker

Robert Blackburn was born in New York City in 1921. He studied at the Harlem Workshop, the Art Students League, and the Wallace Harrison School of Art. His exhibits include Art of the American Negro, 1940; Downtown Gallery, New York; Albany Museum; Contemporary Art of the American Negro, 1966; and numerous print shows in the United States and Europe. His work is represented in the Library of Congress, the Brooklyn and Baltimore museums, and the Atlanta University Collections. He is a member of the art faculty of Cooper Union.

Along with his other accomplishments, in 1949 he founded The Printmaking Workshop as an artist-run cooperative. In 1971, it was incorporated as a non-profit printmaking studio for work in lithography, etching, relief and photo-processes. The workshop, a magnet for third-world and minority artists that reflects Mr. Blackburn's warmth and encouraging personalty, remains a haven for artists "to turn out prints for the love of it" and to do anything from experimental hodgepodge to polished pieces. In 1988, Bob Blackburn and the Printmaking Workshop were given the Governor's Art Award for making "a significant contribution to the cultural life of New York State". Notable works include *Boy with Green Head* and *Negro Mother*.

Selma Burke (1900-1995)
Sculptor, Educator

Selma Burke was an artist whose career spanned more than sixty years. She was born in Mooresville, North Carolina on December 31, 1900. She received a bachelor of arts degree from Winston-Salem University, and RN degree from St. Augustine College in 1924, an MFA from Columbia University in 1941, and a PhD from Livingston College in 1970. Burke received her training as a sculptor at Columbia University in New York. She also studied with Maillol in Paris and in Vienna with Povoley.

Burke worked as an instructor in art & sculpture at Friends School/George's School/Forrest House in New York City from 1930 until 1949. From 1963 until 1976, she served as an instructor in art & sculpture at the Sidwell School, Haverford College, Livingston College, and Swarthmore College. The A.W. Mellon Foundation hired Burke as a consultant from 1967 until 1976. Burke founded New York City's Selma Burke School of Sculpture in 1940 and the Selma Burke Art Center in Pittsburgh in 1968, where she taught and supported many young artists.

In 1987, Burke received the Pearl S. Buck Foundation Women's Award. She also received honorary degrees from Livingston College, the University of North Carolina, and Moore College of Art.

Burke is best known for her relief sculpture rendering of Franklin Delano Roosevelt that was minted on the American dime. On August 29, 1995, she died of cancer.

The Pearl S. Buck Foundation Woman's Award was given to her in 1987 for her professional distinction and devotion to family and humanity. Notable works include *Falling Angel; Peace*; and *Jim*.

Stephen Burrows (1943-)
Fashion Designer

On September 15, 1943, in Newark, New Jersey, Stephen Burrows was born. He studied at his grandmother's knee as a boy and started making clothes at quite a young age. He later studied at the Philadelphia Museum College of Art and the Fashion Institute of Technology in New York City.

With a partner, he opened a boutique in 1968. He worked for Henri Bendel from 1969 to 1973 and returned to Bendel's in 1977. From 1974 to 1977 he tried, with a partner, to run a Seventh Avenue firm.

Known for his unique color combinations, he used patches of cloth for decorative motifs in the 1960s. Top-stitching of seams in contrasting threads, top stitched hems, known as "lettuce hems" because of their fluted effect, were widely copied. He preferred soft, clinging, easy-moving fabrics such as chiffon and matte jersey. He also liked asymmetry. His clothes were adopted readily by disco dancers, for whom he designed using natural fabrics with non-constricting, light and airy qualities. He won a Coty American Fashion Critics' Award in 1974 and a special Coty Award in 1977.

Robert Blackburn

Elizabeth Catlett (1919-)
Sculptor, Painter

Elizabeth Catlett was born on April 15, 1919. The granddaughter of North Carolina slaves, Catlett was raised in the northwest district of Washington, DC. As a young woman she attempted to gain admission into a then all-white art school, Carnegie Institute of Technology in Pittsburgh, Pennsylvania. She was refused entry and instead went to Howard University and graduated as an honor student in 1937. In 1940, she went on to study at the University of Iowa, where she became the first of their students to receive an M.F.A.

Her exhibition history dates back to 1937 and includes group and solo presentations at all the major American art museums as well as institutions in Mexico City, Moscow, Paris, Prague, Tokyo, Beijing, Berlin and Havana. Catlett's public sculpture can be found in Mexico City; Jackson, Mississippi; New Orleans; Washington, DC and New York. Her work is represented in the permanent collection of over twenty museums throughout the world. The artist resides in Cuernavaca, Mexico.

Catlett accepted teaching positions at various black colleges in order to earn a living, but by 1946 she had moved to Mexico, where she eventually settled. Always a promoter of human struggle—visually concerned with the recording of economic, social, and political themes-Catlett became involved with the Civil Rights Movement so deeply that it contributed greatly to her philosophy of life and art. Between 1941 and 1969, Catlett won eight prizes and honors, four in Mexico and four in America. Notable works include *Black Unity* (1968); *Target Practice* (1970); *Mother and Child* (1972); and *Woman Resting* (1981).

In 1993, Catlett worked with James Weldon Johnson on the book *Lift Every Voice and Sing*. An exhibition of her works entitled "Elizabeth Catlett: Works on Paper, 1944-1992" was on display at the Studio Museum in Harlem, New York in 1994.

Catlett was presented with an honorary doctorate of human letters from Morgan State University in 1993. In 1995, the New School for Social Research presented her with an honorary doctorate of fine arts.

Dana Chandler (1941-)
Painter

Dana Chandler is one of the most visible, outspoken, and provocative black painters on the American scene.

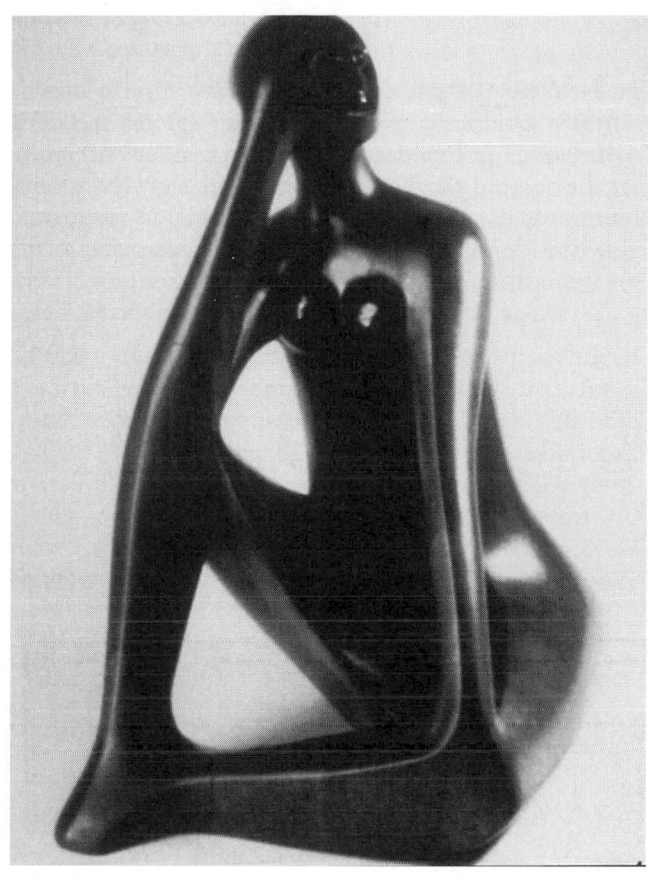

Woman Resting, Elizabeth Catlett.

Chandler's huge, colorful black power murals can be spotted throughout the ghetto area of Boston, a constant reminder of the resolve and determination displayed by the new breed of young black urban dwellers.

"All this stuff whites are buying," Chandler says, "tells the black man a lot about where the white community is at, namely, nowhere." Chandler's easel works are bold and simple. One, *The Golden Prison*, shows a black man with a yellow and red striped flag "because America has been yellow and cowardly in dealing with the black man." *Freddie Hampton's Door* shows a bullet-splintered door bearing a stamp of U.S. government approval.

Born in Lynn, Massachusetts, in 1941, Chandler received his B.S. from the Massachusetts College of Art in 1967. Chandler has worked as a critic of Afro American art for Simmons College in Boston, an assistant professor of art and art history at Bay State Banner, and an artist in residence at Northeastern University. Notable works include *Fred Hampton's Door; Martin Luther King, Jr. Assassinated; Death of Uncle Tom; Rebellion '68; Dynamite; Death of a Bigot;* and *The Golden Prison*.

Chandler is a member of the National Conference of Black Artists, Boston Black Artists Association, National Conference of Artists, Boston Union of Visual Artists, and the American Association of University Professors.

Robert Colescott (1925-)
Painter

Robert Colescott was born in California in 1925. He received his B.A. in 1949 from the University of California and later his M.A. in 1952, from the same university. In 1953, Colescott studied in Paris with Fernand Leger. His exhibitions include: The Whitney Museum of American Art 1983 Biennial; the Hirshorn Museum and Sculpture Garden, in Washington, DC, 1984; and the Institute of Contemporary Art at the University of Pennsylvania in 1985.

His works are in the Metropolitan Museum of Art, the Portland Art Museum, the Delaware Museum of Art, the Baltimore Museum of Art and the University of Massachusetts' fine art collection.

One of the most controversial artists, criticized by both African American groups and traditionalists, Colescott's work questions the "heroic" and "pushes the standards of taste." He has substituted black figures in place of white figures in famous European paintings as he explores racism and sex in his works, along with other taboos and stereotypes. Notable works include *Homage to Delacroix: Liberty Leading the People; Eat Dem Taters; Shirley Temple Black and Bill Robinson White;* and *The Power of Desire; The Desire for Power*.

Houston Conwill (1947-)
Performance Artist, Environment Artist

Born in Kentucky in 1947, Conwill spent three years studying for the priesthood. His strong Catholic upbringing and Catholic ritual play a part in his art that draws from both American and African myths and religions. In his explorations, he mostly uses non-traditional materials (he substitutes latex for canvas). The environments that he builds, paints, and fills with real chalices, candlesticks, carpets, or sand are works to which he adds his own personal iconography as well as some ancient symbols. Notable works include *The Cakewalk Manifesto; Passion of St. Matthew; East Shout; JuJu Funk*.

Aaron Douglas (1899-1988)
Muralist, Illustrator

Born in Topeka, Kansas in 1899, Aaron Douglas achieved considerable eminence as a muralist, illustrator, and academician. As a young man, Douglas studied at the University of Nebraska, Columbia University Teachers College, and l'Academie Scandinave in Paris. He had one-person exhibits at the universities of Kansas and Nebraska and also exhibited in New York at the Gallery of Modern Art. In 1939, Douglas was named to the faculty of Fisk and later became head of its Department of Art.

Douglas died on February 2, 1988. In 1992, Fisk opened a new gallery in his memory. Douglas is considered the most important painter and illustrator of the "Negro Renaissance" now known as the Harlem Renaissance. Notable works include murals at Fisk and in the Countee Cullen branch of the New York City Public Library; illustrations in books by Countee Cullen, James Weldon Johnson, Alain Locke, and Langston Hughes; Alexander Dumas, Marion Anderson, and Mary McLeod Bethune are among the many African Americans he painted or rendered in charcoal.

Emilio Cruz (1938-)
Painter

Emilio Cruz was born in New York City in 1938. His education includes work at the Art Students' League under Edwin Dickinson, George Grosz and Frank J. Reilly. Cruz has exhibited widely since 1959. Recent exhibits have included the Anita Shapolsky Gallery, 1986, 1991; The Studio Museum in Harlem, 1987; the Portland Museum of Art in 1987; and the Rhode Island School of Design, 1987; Gwenda Jay Gallery, Chicago, 1991; G.R. N'amdi Gallery, Birmingham, Michigan, 1991; and others.

An artist whose works are narrative and formalistic (emphasizing color and forms as the dominant elements), he combines these two theoretical approaches often with figurative subjects.

His awards include the Cintas Foundation Fellowship, 1965-66; John Hay Whitney Fellowship, 1964-65; Walter Gutman Foundation Award, 1962. Notable works include *Silver Umbrella; Figure Composition 6*; and *Striated Voodoo*.

Roy DeCarava (1919-)
Photographer

Roy DeCarava is an urban man. His existence in New York City prepared him for his destined work as a photographer. He began as a commercial artist in 1938 by studying painting at Cooper Union. This was followed by classes at the Harlem Art Center from 1940 to 1942, where he concentrated on painting and printmaking. By the mid–1940s, he began to use photography as a convenient method of recording ideas for his paintings. In 1958, DeCarava gave up his commercial work and became a full-time freelance photographer. Edward Steichen, a very important photographer at this time, began to study his work and suggested that he apply for a Guggenheim Fellowship. Winning the award allowed DeCarava the financial freedom to take his pictures and tell his story. One of DeCarava's photographs from this body of work appeared in Steichen's exhibition, "Family of Man", at the Museum of Modern Art. Later, Langston Hughes worked with DeCarava to create the book *Sweet Flypaper of Life*.

DeCarava has worked as a photographer for *Sports Illustrated* and taught photography at Hunter College, New York. His work can be found in many important collections throughout the country, among them: Andover Art Gallery, Andover–Phillips Academy, Massachusetts; Art Institute of Chicago, Chicago, Illinois; Atlanta University, Atlanta, Georgia; Belafonte Enterprises, Inc., New York; Center for Creative Photography, University of Arizona; the Corcoran Gallery of Art, Washington, DC; Harlem Art Collection, New York State Office Building, New York; Lee Witkin Gallery, New York; Menil Foundation, Inc., Houston, Texas; Metropolitan Museum of Fine Arts, Houston, Texas; The Museum of Fine Arts, Houston, Texas; Museum of Modern Art, New York; Olden Camera, New York; Joseph E. Seagram & Sons, Inc., New York; Sheldon Memorial Art Gallery, University of Nebraska, Nebraska.

DeCarava received a Distinguished Career in Photography Award in 1991 from the Friends of Photography. That same year, the American Society of Magazine Photographers presented him with a Special Citation for Photographic Journalism. DeCarava has also received honorary doctorates from The Maryland Institute, Rhode Island Institute of Fine Arts, and Wesleyan University.

Beauford Delaney (1910-1979)
Painter, Illustrator

Born in Knoxville, Tennessee, in 1910, Beauford Delaney was described by his elder brother Samuel as a "remarkably dutiful child." His father, the Reverend Samuel Delaney, and his mother, Delia Johnson Delaney, understood and recognized Beauford Delaney's artistic talent, as well as that of his brother Joseph, and when the time came they encouraged them in the development of their skills. For Beauford Delaney, recognition came by way of an elderly white artist of Knoxville, Lloyd Branson. Branson gave him lessons and after a time urged him to go to a city where he might study and come into contact with the art world.

In 1924, Beauford Delaney went to Boston to study at the Massachusetts Normal School, later studying at the Copley Society, where he took evening courses while working full-time at the South Boston School of Art. From Boston, Delaney moved on to New York and was swept up like many artists.

It was in New York that Delaney took on the life of a bohemian, living in the village in coldwater flats. Much of his time was spent painting the portraits of the personalities of the day, such as Louis Armstrong, Ethel

Roy DeCarava

Waters, and Duke Ellington. In 1938, Beauford Delaney gained national attention when *Life Magazine*, in an article on "negroes," featured a photograph of him surrounded by a group of his paintings at the annual outdoor exhibition in Washington Square in New York. In 1945, Henry Miller wrote the essay "The Amazing and Invariable Beauford Delaney," which was later reprinted in *Remember to Remember*. The essay describes Delaney's bohemian lifestyle in New York during the 1940s and 1950s.

In the 1950s, Delaney left New York with the intention of studying in Rome. Taking the *Ile de France*, he sailed to Paris, next visiting Greece, Turkey, Northern Italy—but he never got to Rome. Returning to Paris for one more visit, Delaney began to paint, make new friends, and create a new social life filled with the famous and the soon-to-be-famous, like James Baldwin, who at that time had not yet become a famous novelist. Paris was to become Beauford Delaney's permanent home.

By 1961, Delaney was producing paintings at such an intense rate that the pressure began to wear upon his strength, and he suffered his first mental collapse. He was confined to a clinic in Vincennes, and his dealer and

close friends began to organize his life, hoping to help relieve some of the pressure; but it was of little use. For the rest of his life, Delaney was to suffer repeated breakdowns and by 1971 was back in a sanitarium, where he was to remain until his death in 1979.

Beauford Delaney's numerous exhibitions took place in such venues as Artists Gallery, New York in 1948; Roko Gallery, New York, 1950-1953; Musée d'Art Moderne, Paris, 1963; American Negro Exposition, Chicago, 1940; and Newark Museum, 1971. His work can be found in the collections of the Whitney Museum of American Art, New York; the Newark Museum, New Jersey; and Morgan State College in Baltimore, Maryland. Notable works include *Greene Street; Yaddo; Head of a Poet;* and *Snow Scene.*

David Clyde Driskell (1931-)
Painter, Historian

Born in Eatonton, Georgia, in 1931, Driskell studied at Howard University and Catholic University of America (M.A., 1962). He also studied at the Skowhegan School of Painting and Sculpture and the Netherlands Institute for History of Art. He has taught at Talladega College, Fisk University, Institute for African Studies of the University of Ife in Nigeria, and the University of Maryland at College Park.

Immediately after the death of Alonzo Aden, Driskell was asked to direct the gallery housing the important Barnett-Aden collection of African-American Art. He has curated and mounted important exhibitions of African American Art, including the impressive *200 Years of African American Art*, shown at major museums to audiences across the country.

A recipient of many awards including the John Hope Award and prizes from the Danforth Foundation, American Federation of Arts, and Harmon Foundation, Driskell has exhibited at the Corcoran Art Gallery, National Museum, and Rhodes National Gallery in Salisbury, Rhodesia. Notable works include *Movement; The Mountain; Still Life With Gateleg Table*; and *Shango Gone*.

Robert Duncanson (1817-1872)
Painter

Robert Duncanson was the son of an African-American mother and a Scottish-Canadian father. Born in upstate New York in 1817, he was to spend much of his childhood in Canada. At some point in his youth, he and his mother moved to Mt. Healthy, Ohio, where in 1840 the Western Freedom's Aid Society, an anti-slavery group, raised funds to send him to Glasgow, Scotland, to study art. Returning to Cincinnati three years later, Duncanson turned to the local newspaper where he advertised as the proprietor of a daguerreotype studio. Even though he seemed to have been gaining a reputation as a painter, he continued to work at his daguerreotype until 1855, when he began to devote all of his time to his painting. Like many landscape artists of this time, Duncanson traveled around the United States drawing his compositions from the images of nature before him. In 1853, he made his second trip to Europe—this time to visit Italy, France and England.

Although Duncanson was active during and after the Civil War, with the exception of his painting of *Uncle Tom and Eva*, he made no attempts to present the turmoil that was taking place within America or the social pressures that he experienced. In September 1872, Duncanson, while at the height of his success, suffered a severe mental breakdown and ended his life on December 21 in the Michigan State Retreat in Detroit. Notable works include murals in the Taft Museum and *Bishop Payne*.

William Edmonson (1882-1951)
Sculptor

William Edmonson was a stonecutter and self-taught sculptor. Born in Nashville, Tennessee, in 1882, he supported himself, working as a hospital orderly at Baptist Hospital and other menial jobs. His work was discovered by Mrs. Meyer Dahl-Wolfe, who had an extensive private collection, and who brought him to the attention of the Museum of Modern Art. In an exhibition of self-taught artists, his work was received extremely well. In 1937 he was the first African American to have a one-person exhibit at the museum. Private collectors and museums have purchased his few sculptures, which are vigorously executed and original.

Inspired by biblical passages, Edmonson worked on tombstones and his sculpture, which he did in limestone, at the home he shared with his mother and sister until their deaths. He continued to live alone and work there until his own death in 1951. Notable works include *Choir Girls; Lion* and *Crucifixion*.

Elton Clay Fax (1909-1993)
Illustrator, Writer

Elton Fax was among America's leading fine artists and illustrators. He was also a noted essayist. Both his drawings and his writings reflect a proud interest in the African legacy of the American black.

Born in Baltimore in 1909, he graduated from Syracuse University (B.F.A., 1931). He taught at Claflin University from 1935 to 1936, and was an instructor at the Harlem Community Art Center from 1938 to 1939. His work has been exhibited at the Baltimore Art Museum, 1939; American Negro Exposition, 1940; the Metropolitan Museum of Art; and Visual Arts Gallery, New York, 1970. Examples of his work hang in some of the nation's best university collections, including Texas Southern, the University of Minnesota, and Virginia State University.

Publications by Fax are *Africa Vignettes; Garvey; Seventeen Black Artists;* and *Black Artists of the New Generation. The Portfolio Black and Beautiful* features his art work, and he has written *Hashar*, about the life of the peoples of Soviet Central Asia and Kazakhstan. Notable works include *Steelworker; Ethiopia Old and New; Contemporary Black Leaders;* and *Through Black Eyes*.

Tom Feelings (1933-)
Illustrator

Born in Brooklyn, New York, on May 19, 1933, Thomas Feelings grew up in the Bedford-Stuyvesant neighborhood of the city. Starting to draw cartoons at the age of four, his art work flourished under the guidance of teacher Thipadeux, a black artist, who encouraged Feelings to draw the people in his neighborhood. After high school, he attended the Cartoonists and Illustrators' School in New York City on a three-year scholarship. Feelings's art studies were interrupted by four years of

Elton Fax

service for the U.S. Air Force in England, but upon completion of his military service, he continued his art studies at the New York School of the Visual Arts.

While in art school, Feelings produced "Tommy Traveler in the World of Negro History," a comic strip published in *New York Age*, a Harlem newspaper. Completing art school in 1961, Feelings shopped around his sizable portfolio to earn freelance assignments, and he began to get work with magazines of primarily black readership. In 1964, Feelings traveled to Tema, a city in Ghana, with other African Americans enlisted by the Kwame Nkrumah, then head of Ghanian government, to help direct the newly-independent country toward the future. Africa changed Feelings's art on a spiritual and stylistic level. But in 1966, he was forced to leave when the Nkrumah government fell.

Feelings returned to a United States embroiled in a civil rights movement hungry for work by and depicting African Americans, especially children's books, Feelings's new specialty. In this new climate, Feelings illustrated such books as *To Be A Slave* (1968); and *Moja Means One: A Swahili Counting Book*, which won a Caldecott Honor Award in 1972. From 1971 to 1974, Feelings administered the Guyanese Ministry of Education's children's book project while living in Guyana. There he wrote his autobiography, *Black Pilgrimage*, published in 1972. After returning to the United States, Feelings illustrated more books spread over the next ten years, including *Now Sheba Sings the Song* (1987), a collaboration with the poet/writer Maya Angelou.

While serving as an artist in residence at the University of South Carolina, Feelings has completed illustrations for two books. In 1993, he finished illustrations for *Soul Looks Back In Wonder*, a book compiling the poems of many black authors. Two years later, he completed *The Middle Passage*, which portrays the passage of slave ships from Africa to the western hemisphere. Both books received Coretta Scott King awards from the American Library Association.

Feelings has earned many awards for his illustrations, including two Outstanding Achievement awards from the New York School of Visual Arts, Visual Artists Fellowship and National Endowment for the Arts grants, and Distinguished Service to Children Through Art Award from the University of South Carolina (1991). Feelings has earned three Coretta Scott King Awards.

Meta Vaux Warrick Fuller (1877-1968)
Sculptor

Meta Vaux Warrick Fuller was a part of the transitional period between the artists who chose to simulate Euro-American subjects and styles and the later periods to follow. Her subjects of *The Wretched*, exhibited at the Paris Salon, of African-American figures, shown in 1903 and 1904, did not suit popular tastes but they were sincere expressions of the talented artist.

Born in 1877, in Philadelphia and educated at the School of Industrial Art and the Pennsylvania Academy, Fuller's interest in sculpture led her to study with Charles Grafly and at the Academie Colarossi in Paris with Rodin. She was the first African-American woman to become a professional artist.

She married and settled in the Boston area where in 1910, most of her works were destroyed by fire. The Boston Art Club and the Harmon Foundation exhibited her works and today representative pieces of her sculpture can be found in the Cleveland Museum.

Sam Gilliam (1933-)
Painter

Born in Mississippi in 1933, Sam Gilliam produces hanging canvases which are laced with pure color pig-

ments rather than shades or tones. The artist bunches these pigments in weird configurations on drooping, drapelike canvases, giving the effect, in the words of *Time* Magazine, of "clothes drying on a line." His canvases are said to be "like nobody else's, black or white."

Gilliam received his M.A. from the University of Louisville, and was awarded National Endowment of Humanities and Arts grants. He has had one–man and group shows at the Washington Gallery of Modern Art; Jefferson Place Gallery; Adams–Morgan Gallery in Washington, DC; the Art Gallery of Washington University, St. Louis, Missouri; the Speed Museum, Louisville; the Philadelphia Museum of Art; the Museum of Modern Art; the Phillips Collection and Corcoran Gallery of Art, both in Washington, DC; the San Francisco Museum of Art; the Walker Art Center, Minneapolis, and the Whitney Museum of American Art. He is represented in the permanent collection of over forty-five American museums.

Gilliam has also been represented in several group exhibitions, including the First World Festival of Negro Arts in Dakar, Senegal (1966), "The Negro in American Art" at UCLA (1967), and the Whitney Museum's American Art Annual (1969).

In 1968, 1969 and 1970 his work was displayed in one-man shows at Washington, DC's Jefferson Place, and in 1971 he was featured in a one-man show at New York City's Museum of Modern Art.

In 1980, Sam Gilliam was commissioned, with thirteen other artists, to design an art piece for installation in the Atlanta, Georgia Airport Terminal, one of the largest terminals in the world and the first to install contemporary artwork on its walls for public viewing. Notable works include *Watercolor 4* (1969); *Herald* (1965); *Carousel Change* (1970); *Mazda* (1970); *Plantagenets Golden* (1984); and *Golden Element Inside Gold* (1994).

Gilliam's works have been on display at several exhibitions. In 1993, the Nancy Drysdale Gallery in Washington, D.C. hosted the exhibit "Sam Gilliam." The exhibition "Sam Gilliam: Bikers Move Like Swallows" was hosted by the Baumgartner Galleries in Washington, D.C. in 1994. Several works by Gilliam were included in the "Black Art" group exhibition at the Rockville Arts Place in Rockville, MD in 1995.

Tyree Guyton (1955-)
Multimedia Artist

Born in Detroit, on August 24, 1955, Tyree Guyton has transformed the blighted urban pocket in which he has spent much of his life into an enormous ongoing art project that utilizes the detritus of the abandoned cityscape. Interested in the arts from a young age, after graduating from high school Guyton served in the U.S. Army and then worked at Ford Motor Company for several years. He also began a family and in his spare time took art classes.

In 1984, Guyton left his firefighting job to become a full-time artist and set to work transforming the small city block in which he and wife Karen Smith and their several children lived. His grandfather, a former housepainter, was both a source of early inspiration and an integral contributor to Guyton's artistic project. Using ordinary housepaint, a wealth of old toys, bicycles, and other found objects they salvaged from the junk piles that plague the city, Guyton transformed Heidelberg Street into a dynamic and unique art installation. A crack house, one of the many abandoned residences on the street, was painted in wild colors that discouraged the drug sales that even the narcotics squad raids had not been able to stop. A tree was nailed several yards high with vintage bicycles. Polka dots decorated the street, Guyton's own home, and nearly every other available surface. The combination of dots, stripes, lively patterning, and re-invention of found objects had been inspired by the style in which Guyton's mother had beautified their home on a tight budget when he was growing up.

Long heralded by the international artistic community, Guyton's art has periodically come under fire, however. Other residents of the east-side Detroit neighborhood dismiss the out-of-town visitors and laudatory praise heaped on the Heidelberg Project by the art critics and harken for the days of a neatly manicured lawn and more placid environs. In the fall of 1991, city bulldozers demolished several of the houses that Guyton had transformed, one of which had been slated for inclusion on a tour of local artistic sites. Ironically, that year he was named the Michiganian of the Year and the following year earned the Governor's Arts Award. Guyton sued the city—with the support of prominent members of Detroit's artistic community—but the dropped the suit when a more sympathetic mayoral administration came into power in 1994.

Richard Hunt (1935-)
Painter, Sculptor

Richard Hunt was born in Chicago in 1935 and began his formal career after studying at the School of the Art Institute of Chicago, where he received a number of awards.

After graduating in 1957, Hunt was given the James Nelson Raymond Traveling Fellowship. He later taught at the School of the Art Institute of Chicago and at the University of Illinois. From 1962 to 1963, he pursued his craft while under a Guggenheim Fellowship.

Hunt's solo presentations have appeared at the Cleveland Museum of Art; Milwaukee Art Center; Museum of Modern Art; Art Institute of Chicago; Springfield Art Museum, Massachusetts; Indianapolis Museum of Art and a U.S.I.S.–sponsored show throughout Africa which was organized by the Los Angeles Museum of African American Art. Hunt sits on the board of governors at the School of the Art Institute of Chicago and the Skowhegan School of Painting and Sculpture; is a commissioner at the National Museum of American Art, Washington, DC; and serves on the advisory committee at the Getty Center for Education in the Arts, Malibu.

His works are in the Museum of Modern Art, New York; Cleveland Museum of Art, Ohio; Art Institute of Chicago; Milwaukee Art Center; Baltimore Museum of Art; Martin Gallery, Washington, DC; National Museum of American Art, Washington, DC; Hirshhorn Museum, Washington, DC; Museum of 20th Century Art, Vienna, Austria; the Albright Knox Gallery, Buffalo, New York; National Museum of Israel, Jerusalem; Terry Dintenfass Gallery, New York; Dorsky Gallery, New York; Whitney Museum of American Art, New York; and Howard University. He has had many other commissions. Notable works include *Man on a Vehicular Construct* (1956); *Linear Spatial Theme* (1962); *The Chase* (1965); and *Arching* (1986).

Some of Hunt's works appeared with those of Richmond Barthe at the "Richmond Barthe and Richard Hunt: Two Sculptors, Two Eras," exhibit at the Anacostia Museum in Washington, D.C. in 1993.

Larry Johnson (1949-)
Painter, Illustrator, Editorial Cartoonist

Born in Boston, Massachusetts, in 1949, Larry Johnsonattended Boston Schools and the School of the Boston Museum of Fine Arts. He became a staff illustrator at *The Boston Globe* in 1968, where he covered many assignments, including courtroom sketches, sports events, entertainment, editorial sports cartoons and drawings, and other features. Johnson is now nationally syndicated through Universal Press Syndicate.

Barry Gaither, director of the National Center of African–American artists in Boston, says, "Johnson's works can be divided horizontally between commercial illustration and fine art, and vertically between drawings and paintings in acrylics and watercolor." In addition to working for the *Globe*, Johnson worked for the now defunct *National Sports Daily* and has designed book jackets for Little Brown. Commissioned by Pepsi-Cola, the *Old Farmer's Almanac*, the National Football League, *Fortune*, and others, he has left the *Globe* to freelance and run his own company, Johnson Editions, producer of fine arts prints and other multiples, such as greeting cards. Johnson was awarded the Associated Press Editorial Cartoon Award in 1985. Notable works include *Island Chisel; Rainbow;* and *Promises.*

In 1995, several of Johnson's photographs were included in the six-artist exhibition entitled "New Testament", which was hosted by the Marc Foxx Gallery in Santa Monica, California. The Margo Leavin Gallery in Los Angeles also hosted an exhibition of Johnson's art work in 1995.

Lester L. Johnson (1937-)
Painter, Educator

Born in Detroit, Michigan, in 1937, Johnson attended the University of Michigan, where he received a B.F.A. in 1973, and an M.F.A. in 1974. He teaches at the Center for Creative Studies, College of Art and Design, in Detroit, Michigan.

His works are in many collections including: the Detroit Institute of Arts; Osaka University Arts, Japan; Johnson Publishers and The Masonite Corp., Chicago; Sonnenblick–Goldman Corp., New York; Taubman Co., Inc., Bloomfield Hills, Michigan; and St. Paul Co., St. Paul, Minnesota.

Commissions have included *Urban Wall Murals,* Detroit, 1974; New Detroit Receiving Hospital, 1980; and Martin Luther King Community Center. Johnson has exhibited at major institutions, including the Whitney Museum of American Art Biennial, 1973; National African–American Exhibit, Carnegie Institute, Pittsburgh, Pennsylvania; National Academy of Design, Henry Ward Ranger National Invitational, 1977.

Among his awards are the Andrew W. Mellon Foundation Grant, 1982 and 1984; and a Recognition Award, African–American Music Art Association.

In 1994, an exhibition of works by Lester Johnson was presented at the Edward Thorp Gallery in New York City.

Sargent Johnson (1888-1967)
Sculptor

Sargent Johnson, who three times won the Harmon Foundation's medal as the nation's outstanding black artist, worked in stylized idioms, heavily influenced by the art forms of Africa in sculpture, mural bas-reliefs, metal sculpture, and ceramics.

Born in Boston in 1888, he studied at the Worcester Art School and moved west to the San Francisco Bay area in 1915, where his teachers were Beniamino Bufano and Ralph Stackpole. He exhibited at the San Francisco

Artists Annual, 1925-1931; Harmon Foundation, 1928-1931, 1933; Art Institute of Chicago, 1930; Baltimore Museum, 1939; American Negro Exposition, Chicago, 1940. He was the recipient of numerous awards and prizes.

From the beginning of his career he spoke of his sculpture as an attempt to show the "natural beauty and dignity of the pure American Negro" and wished to present "that beauty not so much to the white man as to the Negro himself. Unless I can interest my race, I am sunk." Notable works include *Sammy; Esther; Golden Gate Exposition Aquatic Park murals;* and *Forever Free.* He died in 1967.

William Henry Johnson (1901-1970)
Painter

William H. Johnson was a pioneer black modernist whose ever-developing work went from abstract expressionist landscape and flower studies influenced by Vincent Van Gogh, to studies of black life in America, and finally to abstract figure studies in the manner of Rouault.

Born in Florence, South Carolina, on March 18, 1901, he studied at the National Academy of Design; Cape Cod School of Art, under Charles Hawthorne; in southern France, 1926-1929, and Denmark and Norway, 1930-1938. Exhibits include Harmon Foundation (Gold Medal in 1929); Aarlins, Denmark, 1935; Baltimore Museum, 1939; American Negro Exposition, Chicago, 1940. He produced one-person shows in Copenhagen in 1935, and at the Artists Gallery, New York, in 1938. Notable works include *Booker T. Washington; Young Man in Vest; Descent from the Cross;* and *On a John Brown Flight.* He died on April 13, 1970.

Joshua Johnston (1765-1830)
Painter

Active between 1789 and 1825, Joshua Johnston is the first known black portrait painter from the Baltimore area. At least two dozen paintings have been attributed to this artist who was listed as a "free householder of colour, portrait painter". He was listed in the Baltimore directories in various studio locations.

It is believed Johnston may have been a former slave of Charles Wilson Peale, the artist who is also known for having started a drawing school in Maryland in 1795; or Johnston may have simply known the artist and his works. In either case, the artist was most likely self-taught. A portraitist in the true style of the period, his work now seems quaint and sensitive. Only one black subject has been attributed to him, *Portrait of a Cleric.*

Going to Church, William H. Johnson, c. 1940.

Notable works include *Portrait of Adelia Ellender, Portrait of Mrs. Barbara Baker Murphy* and *Portrait of Sea Captain John Murphy.*

Ben Jones (1942-)
Painter, Sculptor

Ben Jones was born in Patterson, New Jersey, in 1942, and studied at the School of Visual Arts; New York University, where he received an M.A.; Pratt Institute; the University of Science and Technology, Ghana; and the New School of Social Research.

A professor of Fine Arts at Jersey City State College, Jones lives in New York. As a sculptor, his works (made during the height of the Black Art Movement in 1970) were cast in plaster from living models and painted in brightly colored patterns, as if inspired by traditional African symbols. Masks, arms and legs arranged in multiples or singly seem to have roots in African ceremony ritual and magic.

His pieces are in such collections as: the Newark Museum; Studio Museum in Harlem; Howard University; Johnson Publications, Chicago. His exhibits have included: The Museum of Modern Art; Studio Museum in Harlem; Black World Arts Festival, Lagos, Nigeria; Newark Museum; Fisk University, Nashville, Tennessee, and others.

Jones' awards have included grants from the National Endowment for the Arts; the New Jersey Arts Council; Delta Sigma Theta Sorority, and others. Notable works include *Five Black Face Images; High Priestess of Soul;* and *Untitled (6 Arms).*

Karl Kani (1968?-)
Fashion Designer

Born Carl Williams, Kani and his friends were preoccupied with style even when very young. His fashion sense first became noticed on the streets of Flatbush, a neighborhood of Brooklyn, New York. While his peers were buying the latest clothes, Williams was busy purchasing material he would later bring to various tailors, instructing them to make garments exactly how he wanted for a relatively small price. As time passed, people who had seen Williams in one of his "originals" wanted their own made-to-order duds. Williams began taking orders and supplying the demand.

When the death of a close friend prompted him to search of a "positive endevour," Williams headed for

California. While working at Seasons Sportswear in South-Central Los Angeles, Williams developed the name Kani, based on the question "Can I?" as in "Can I do it?" In 1989, Kani met Carl Jones, cofounder of Threads 4 Life. Jones, who had already proven his ability to sell clothes with his Cross Colours line, agreed to help Kani get his designs out to the public. By 1992, the Kani line of clothing had added roughly $35 million dollars to the Threads 4 Life profit margin. Despite the success, Kani was not happy. Disagreements with Threads 4 Life led to Kani to venture off on his own.

Kani began "Karl Kani Infinity" in 1994. The thrill of the risk-taking and the fact that Kani wanted to work for himself fed his desire to succeed. While competition for hip-hop clothing had become fierce, Kani saw potential in the previously ignored market. With a staff of 15, Kani took on all competitors. Rap stars like Tupac Shakur began wearing his designs, and the Kani name was now in the public eye. In 1995, his designs were sold in more than 300 hundred stores nationwide.

Emeline King
Automobile Designer

A native of Detroit, Michigan, Emeline King, the daughter of a Ford employee, acquired an ambition at an early age to design cars. King is a designer at the Ford Motor Company's Mustang studio.

King joined the company in 1983 after she graduated from Wayne State University where she majored in industrial design. She also studied in Detroit at the Center for Creative Studies. The Art Center College of Design in Pasadena, California awarded her a Bachelor of Science degree in transportation.

King was instrumental in the design of the 1994 Ford Mustang.

Jacob Lawrence (1917-)
Painter

Born on September 7, 1917, in Atlantic City, New Jersey, Jacob Lawrence received his early training at the Harlem Art School and the American Artist School. He honed his craft under the watchful eye of notable artists such as Charles Alston, Henry Bannarn, Anton Refregier, Sol Wilson, Philip Reisman, and Eugene Moreley. His rise to prominence was ushered in by his painting of several series of biographical panels commemorating important episodes in African-American history. A narrative painter, Lawrence creates the "philosophy of Impressionism" within his work. Capturing the essential meaning behind the natural appearance of a historical moment of personality, Lawrence creates a formal series of several dozen small paintings which relate to the course of a particular historic event in American

history, such as *The Migration Series* ("...and the Migrants keep coming"), which traces the migration of the African-American from the South to the North, or the discussion on the course of a man's life (e.g., Toussant L'Ouverture and John Brown).

Jacob Lawrence is a visual American historian. His paintings record the African American in trade, theater, mental hospitals, neighborhoods, or running in the Olympic races. Lawrence's works are found in such collections as the Metropolitan Museum of Art, Museum of Modern Art, Whitney Museum of American Art, the National Museum of American Art, and the Wadsworth Atheneum in Hartford, Connecticut.

Lawrence lives in Seattle, Washington. Notable works include *The Life of Toussaint L'Ouverture* (forty one panels-1937); *The Life of Harriet Tubman* (forty panels-1939); and *The Negro Migration Northward in World War* (sixty panels-1942). He has also produced commissioned book and magazine illustrations, murals, posters, drawings, and prints. Among these are a 1976 print for the United States Bicentennial, illustrations for a 1983 special edition of John Hersey's book *Hiroshima*, and a 1984 poster for the National Urban League.

In 1970, Lawrence was awarded the NAACP's Spingarn Medal. He also received an invitation to paint the 1977 presidential inauguration of Jimmy Carter. President George Bush bestowed on Lawrence the National Medal of Arts in 1990. He is also the recipient of numerous honorary degrees.

Lawrence wrote and illustrated the book "The Great Migration: An American Story" in 1993.

Hughie Lee-Smith (1915-)
Painter

Hughie Lee-Smith was born on September 20, 1915, in Eustis, Florida. He studied at the Cleveland Institute of Art and Wayne State University, where he received his B.S. in Art Education in 1953.

From childhood, Lee-Smith was encouraged to pursue his art and he has enjoyed a long and productive career. He worked for the Ohio Works Progress Administration and the Ford Factory at River Rouge during the 1930s and 1940s. He did a series of lithographic prints and painted murals at the Great Lakes Naval Station in Illinois. He taught art at Karamu House in Cleveland, the Grosse Pointe War Memorial in Michigan, Princeton Country Day School, Howard University, the Art Students League, and other institutions.

Lawrence's works can be seen in museums, schools, galleries, and collections across the United States, in-

Tombstones, Jacob Lawrence, 1942

Jacob Lawrence

cluding the American Negro Exposition, Chicago; Southside Community Art Center; Snowden Gallery; Detroit Artists Market; Cleveland Museum of Art; Whitney Museum of American Art; Museum of Modern Art; the June Kelly Gallery, New York City, and the Evans-Tibbs Collection, Washington, DC. His painted environments are often of decaying or ghetto environments in the state of revitalization peopled by a single or sometimes double-figured occupant. His subjects seem to suggest desolation or alienation, but waving banners or balloons in the scene counter the expression in their symbolism of hope and gaiety.

Lee-Smith's one-person shows and exhibitions are too numerous to list. He has received more than a dozen important prizes, including the Founders Prize of the Detroit Institute of Arts (1953), Emily Lowe Award (1957, 1985), Ralph Fabri Award, Audubon Artists, Inc. (1982), Binny and Smith Award (1983), and Len Everette Memorial Prize, Audubon Artists, Inc. (1986). He is a member of the Allied Artists of America, the Michigan Academy of the Arts, Sciences & Letters, and the Artists Equity Association. Notable works include *Portrait of a Sailor; Old Man and Youth; Waste Land; Little Diana;* and *Aftermath.*

In 1995, Bristol-Myers Squibb in Princeton, New Jersey featured the exhibit "Hughie Lee-Smith: An Overview, 1949-1995."

Edmonia Lewis (1845-1890)
Sculptor

Edmonia Lewis was America's first black woman artist and also the first of her race and sex to be recognized as a sculptor. Born on July 4, 1845 in Albany, New York, she was the daughter of a Chippewa Indian woman and a free black man. From 1859 to 1863, under the patronage of a number of abolitionists, she was educated at Oberlin College, the first American college to admit women on a nonsegregated basis.

After completing her schooling, Lewis moved to Boston, where she studied with Edmund Brackett and did a bust of Colonel Robert Gould Shaw, the commander of the first black regiment organized in the state of Massachusetts during the Civil War. In 1865, she moved to Rome, where she soon became a prominent artist. Returning to the United States in 1874, she fulfilled many commissions, including a bust of Henry Wadsworth Longfellow that was executed for the Harvard College Library.

Edmonia Lewis

Her works are fine examples of the neo-classical sculpture that was fashionable during her lifetime. It is believed that she died in Rome in 1890. Notable works include *Hagar in the Wilderness, Forever Free,* and *Hiawatha.*

Norman Lewis (1909-1979)
Painter

Norman Lewis was born in New York City in 1909. Lewis studied at Columbia University. He also studied under Augusta Savage, Raphael Soyer, Vaclav Vytacil, and Angela Streater. During the Great Depression he taught art through the Federal Art Project from 1936 to 1939 at the Harlem Art Center. He received a Carnegie International Award in Painting in 1956 and has had several one-person shows at the Willard Gallery in New York.

As one of the artists to develop the abstract movement in the United States, Lewis participated in many group shows in such institutions as the Whitney Museum of American Art, the Metropolitan Museum of Art, and the Art Institute of Chicago. Notable works include *Arrival and Departure* and *Heroic Evening.*

Ionis Bracy Martin (1936-)
Painter, Printmaker, Educator

Born on August 27, 1936, in Chicago, Illinois, Ionis Bracy Martin attended the Junior School of the Art Institute of Chicago before going to Fisk University, where she studied with Aaron Douglas and earned her B.S. in 1957. Martin received an M.Ed. degree from the University of Hartford (1969) and an M.F.A. from Pratt Institute, Brooklyn, New York (1987). She is a Trustee of the Wadsworth Atheneum, 1977, co-founder of the Artists Collective (with Jackie McLean, Dollie McLean, Paul Brown, and Cheryl Smith), 1972, co-trustee and chairperson of the Ella Burr McManus Trust for the Alfred E. Burr Sculpture Mall, 1985, and a member of the advisory board of the CRT Craftery Gallery, Hartford, 1973.

Exhibiting widely in the Hartford area, Martin has also exhibited in New York; Springfield, Boston, and Northampton, Massachusetts; Fisk University, Nashville, Tennessee; and the University of Vermont, Burlington, Vermont. Among her many prizes and honors are a grant from the Connecticut Commission on the Arts (1969); a graduate fellowship in Printmaking, Pratt Institute (1981); a Summer-Six Fellowship from Skidmore College (1987); and a fellowship with the WEB DuBois Institute, Harvard University (1994).

A teacher at Weaver and Bloomfield High Schools since 1961, and lecturer in African-American art at Central Connecticut State University since 1985, Martin also lectures on and demonstrates serigraphy. Notable works include *Mother and Child; Allyn's Garden; Gran' Daddy's Garden;* and *Little Women of the Amistad: Series.*

Geraldine McCullough (1928-)
Sculptor

Geraldine McCullough's steel and copper abstraction *Phoenix* won the George D. Widener Gold Medal at the 1964 exhibition of the Pennsylvania Academy of Fine Arts. In earning this award, she added her name to a roster of distinguished artists who have already won the same honor, including Jacques Lipchitz and Theodore Roszak. Of further note is the fact that this was her first showing in a major national exhibition.

A native of Arkansas, McCullough (b. 1928) has lived in Chicago since she was three and is a 1948 graduate of the Art Institute there. She also studied at the University of Chicago, DePaul University, Northwestern University, and the University of Illinois.

McCullough taught at Wendell Phillips High School (from 1950 to 1964) in Chicago and at Rosary College in River Forest, Illinois. Currently, she works and resides in Oak Park, Illinois. She has received many awards and commissions. Her works are represented in collections at Howard University; in Oak Park, Illinois; the Oakland, California museum, and many others. Notable works include *Bessie Smith; View from the Moon; Todd Hall Front; Atomic Rose; Phoenix*; and *Martin Luther King*.

Evangeline J. Montgomery (1933-)
Jeweler, Photographer, Sculptor

Evangeline Montgomery was born in New York City on May 2, 1933. She received an associate's degree from Los Angeles City College in 1958 and her B.F.A. from the California College of Arts and Crafts in 1969; she also studied at the University of California, Berkeley and California State University.

Montgomery has worked as a freelance artist, an art consultant to museums, community organizations, and colleges for EJ Associates, and program director for Arts America. Known primarily for her metal boxes, incense burners, and jewelry, Montgomery has also been awarded prizes for her photography. Her works are in collections at the Oakland Museum and the University of Southern Illinois.

Active with many organizations, Montgomery has served on the San Francisco Art Commission, the advisory board of Parting Ways Ethnohistory Museum, and the board of directors of the Museum of the National Center of Afro-American Artists. She is currently a member of the Michigan Chapter of the National Conference of Artists, the College Art Association, the American Museums Association, and the Women's Art Caucus. Montgomery is also on the board of directors of the DC Arts Center.

Her awards have included a Smithsonian Fellowship and a museum grant from the National Endowment for the Arts. In 1989, Montgomery was presented with a Special Achievement Award from Arts America. Notable works include *Ancestor Box 1* and *Justice for Angela Davis*.

Archibald Motley (1891-1980)
Painter

Archibald Motley touched on many topics and themes in his work but none was more gratifying to him than his candid depictions of black Americans.

Born in New Orleans in 1891, Motley's artistic talent was apparent by the time he attended high school. His father wanted him to become a doctor, but Archibald insisted on art and began formal education at the Art Institute of Chicago, earning his subsistence by working as a day laborer. During this time Motley came in contact with the drifters, scavengers, and hustlers of society, who are now immortalized in his street scenes. His genre scenes are highly stylized and colorful and are often associated with the *Ash-Can* school of art, which was popular in the 1920s.

In 1928, Motley had a one-person show at the new galleries in downtown New York and became the first artist, black or white, to make the front page of the *New York Times*. He was awarded a Guggenheim Fellowship in 1929 and studied in France. He was the recipient of a Harmon Foundation award for an earlier, more literal portrait. Notable works include: *The Jockey Club; The Plotters; Parisian Scene; Black Belt*; and *Old Snuff Dipper*. Motley died in 1980.

John Wilfred Outterbridge (1933-)
Sculptor

John Wilfred Outterbridge was born in Greenville, North Carolina, on March 12, 1933. He studied at Agricultural and Technical University, Greensboro, North Carolina; the Chicago Art Academy; the American Academy of Art, Chicago; and the Art Center School of Design, Los Angeles.

From 1964 until 1968, Outterbridge worked as an artist/designer for Traid Corporation. He worked as artistic director and co-founder of the Communicative Arts Academy from 1969 until 1975. He has also taught at California State University and Pasadena Art Museum. Outterbridge was director of the Watts Towers Art Center, Los Angeles, from 1976 until 1992.

Outterbridge's sculptures are assemblages constructed from discarded materials. Some of his works are tributes to African ancestors and their descendants in Los Angeles and in other communities. Outterbridge is known for making and helping others create "Street Art," a combination of painting, relief sculpture, and construction that incorporates words and symbols expressing community goals and social ideas.

Outterbridge was featured in *Black Artists on Art*, Volume I (Selma Lewis/Ruth Waddy, Los Angeles Contemporary Crafts, 1971, 1976). Notable works include *Shoeshine Box; Mood Ghetto*; and *Ethnic Heritage Group*.

In 1990, Outterbridge was presented with the Malcolm X Freedom Award by the New Afrikan People's Organization and the Lifetime Achievement Award from the 1st Annual King Blvd. Memorial Project. The National Endowment for the Arts awarded Outterbridge with its Visual Arts Fellowship in 1994. That same year, he was presented with an honorary doctorate of fine arts by the Otis College of Arts and Design and the J. Paul Getty Visual Arts Fellowship.

Gordon Parks (1912-)
Photographer, Composer, Writer, Director

Parks was born on November 30, 1912 in Fort Scott, Kansas. After the death of his mother, Parks went to St.

Archibald Motley with one of his paintings, 1932

Paul, Minnesota to live with relatives. While there he attended Central and Mechanical Arts high schools. Despite having fond childhood memories of his father on the family farm, Parks had a dysfunctional upbringing. Parks worked at a variety of jobs including janitor, busboy, and semi-pro basketball player. Always interested in the arts, Parks also tried sculpting, writing and touring with a band, but these artistic endeavors were largely without focus.

In 1933, Parks joined the Civilian Conservation Corps and in the late 1930s, while working as a railroad porter, he became interested in photography as a medium on which he could finally concentrate his considerable artistic talents. After purchasing a used camera, Parks worked as a freelance photographer and as a photojournalist. In 1942, he became a correspondent for the Farm Security Administration, and from 1943 to 1945 he was a correspondent for the Office of War Information. After the war he worked for Standard Oil Company of New Jersey, and in 1948 he became a staff photographer for *Life* magazine. He soon achieved national acclaim for his photographs and in the mid-1950s he began doing consulting work on Hollywood productions. In the 1960s Parks began doing television docu-

mentaries, and in 1966 he published his biography *A Choice of Weapons.*

Parks is also the author of *Flash Photography* (1947), *Camera Portraits: The Techniques and Principals of Documentary Portraiture* (1948), *The Learning Tree* (1963), *A Poet and His Camera* (1968), *Born Black* (1971), *Gordon Parks: Whispers of Intimate Things* (1971), *Moments without Proper Names* (1975), *Flavio* (1977), *To Smile in Autumn* (1979), *Shannon* (1981), *Voices in the Mirror* (1991), *Arias in Silence* (1994). In 1968 Parks produced, directed, and wrote the script and music for the movie production of *The Learning Tree.* Parks also directed and scored the movies *Shaft* (1971), *Shaft's Big Score* (1972), *The Super Cops* (1974), *Leadbelly* (1976), *Odyssey of Solomon Northrup* (1984) and *Moments Without Proper Names* (1986).

Parks is a recipient of the NAACP's Spingarn Award (1972), the Rhode Island School of Design's Presidents Fellow Award (1984), and Kansan of the Year (1986). In 1988 President Ronald Reagan presented him with the National Medal for the Arts. That same year, Parks won the World Press Photo Award. In 1989, he was awarded the Library of Congress National Film Registry Classics film honor for *The Learning Tree.* He was also present-

Gordon Parks

Marion Perkins

ed with the New York Mayor's Award and the Artist of Merit Josef Sudek Medal in 1989.

Parks is a member of the NAACP, Urban League, Newspaper Guild, Association of Composers and Directors, Writer's Guild, AFTRA, ASCAP, International Mark Twain Society, American Film Institute, Academy of Motion Pictures Arts and Sciences, and the American Society of Magazine Photographers.

On July 7, 1995, the Library of Congress announced that it had acquired the archives of Gordon Parks. The archives include roughly 15,000 manuscript pages of Parks's poems, novels and screenplays, as well as several thousand photographs and negatives.

Marion Perkins (1908-1961)
Sculptor

Born in Marche, Arkansas, in 1908, Perkins was largely a self-taught artist. His early works were composed while he tended a newspaper stand on Chicago's South Side. He later studied privately with Simon Gordon, and the two men became close friends.

Perkins's work has been exhibited at the Art Institute of Chicago, American Negro Exposition (1940), Xavier University, and Rockland College, Illinois (1965). As artist in residence at Jackson State College in Mississippi, where much of his sculpture is housed, Perkins founded a scholarship fund for art students. Perkins died in 1961.

Howardena Pindell (1943-)
Painter

Born in Philadelphia on April 14, 1943, Howardena Pindell received her education at Boston University (B.F.A., 1965) and Yale University (M.F.A., 1967). She first gained national recognition for her artistic skills in 1969 with the exhibition "American Drawing Biennial XXIII" at the Norfolk Museum of Arts and Sciences in Virginia. By the mid–1970s, Pindell's work began appearing in such exhibitions as "Eleven Americans in Paris," Gerald Piltzer Gallery, Paris, 1975; "Recent Acquisitions; Drawings," Museum of Modern Art, New York, 1976; and "Pindell: Video Drawings," Sonja Henie Onstad Foundation, Oslo, Norway, 1976.

Around this same time, Pindell began to travel around the world as a guest speaker. Some of her lectures included "Current American and Black American Art: A Historical Survey" at Madras College of Arts and Crafts,

Madras, India, 1975; and "Black Artists, U.S.A.," Academy of Art, Oslo, Norway, 1976. She is currently a professor of art at State University of New York at Stony Brook.

Her work is part of the permanent collection in over thirty museums including the Brooklyn Museum, High Museum in Atlanta, Newark Museum, Fogg Museum in Cambridge, Massachusetts, Whitney Museum of American Art, Museum of Modern Art, and the Metropolitan Museum of Art. Pindell has received two National Endowment for the Arts Fellowships and a Guggengeim Fellowship.

Pindell has received numerous awards throughout her career. In 1990, she won the College Art Association Award for Best Exhibitor. She received the Studio Museum in Harlem Award and Joan Mitchell Fellowship in 1994. In 1996, the Women Caucus for Art presented Pindell with its Distinguished Contribution to the Profession Award.

Jerry Pinkney (1939-)
Illustrator

Born in Philadelphia on December 22, 1939, Jerry Pinkney studied at the Philadelphia Museum College of Art. Pinkney has exhibited in illustrator shows throughout the country and is best known for his illustrations for children's books and text books.

From his studio in his home in Croton–on–Hudson, New York, Pinkney has been a major contributor to the United States Postal Service's stamps in the Black Heritage Series. Benjamin Banneker, Martin Luther King, Jr., Scott Joplin, Jackie Robinson, Sojourner Truth, Carter G. Woodson, Whitney Moore Young, Mary McLeod Bethune, and Harriet Tubman stamps were designed by this Citizens' Stamp Advisory Committee member.

A recipient of many honors, he has created illustrations in children's books that have been outstanding. For example, *The Talking Eggs*, written by Robert San Souci, was given a Caldecott Honor of Medal (Pinkney's second such honor) in 1989, received a Coretta Scott King Honor Book Award, was named an American Library Association Notable Book, and won the Irma Simonton Black Award from the Bank Street College of Education. In 1994, Pinkney won the Caldecott Medal for his illustrations in the book *John Henry*. That same year, he won two Parent's Choice Awards for the books *John Henry* and *The Sunday Outing*.

Pinkney has worked in Boston as a designer and illustrator. He is one of the founders of Kaleidoscope Studio in Boston, where he also worked for the National Center of Afro–American Art. For a while he was a Visiting Critic for the Rhode Island School of Design. He has taught at Pratt Institute, the University of Delaware

and in the Art Department at the State University of New York at Buffalo. Notable works include *The Tales of Uncle Remus*, published by Dial Brooks; *Call It Courage*, written by Armstrong Sperry and published by Aladdin Books; *Self Portrait*; and *Back Home*, written by his wife, Gloria Jean Pinkney.

Horace Pippin (1888-1946)
Painter

Horace Pippin has been ranked in the company of Henri Rousseau due to his accomplishment as a self-taught artist. Born on February 22, 1888, in West Chester, Pennsylvania, Pippin began painting in 1920, and continued until his death on July 6, 1946. Among his most vivid portrayals on canvas are the battle scenes that he remembered from his own experience in World War I, during which he was wounded and partially paralyzed.

Pippin's earliest works are designs burned into wood with a hot poker. He did not make his first oil painting until 1930—after working on it for three years. This task was complicated by his wartime injury; he had to guide his right arm with his left hand in order to paint. He painted family reunions, Biblical stories, and historical events. Notable works include *John Brown Goes to a Hanging; Flowers with Red Chair; The Den; The Milk Man of Goshen*; and *Dog Fight Over the Trenches*.

James A. Porter (1905-1971)
Art Historian, Painter

James A. Porter was a painter of considerable scholarship who also earned acclaim as a writer and educator. Born in Baltimore in 1905, he studied at Howard University (B.S., 1927), Art Students League, New York; Sorbonne; and New York University (M.A.). He was awarded numerous travel grants that enabled him to study African and European art firsthand.

Among his ten one-person shows are exhibits at Port-au-Prince, Haiti, 1946; Dupont Gallery, Washington, DC, 1949; and Howard University, 1965. His works are in the collections of Howard University; Lincoln University, Missouri; Harmon Foundation; IBM; and others. The first African-American art historian, he wrote the classic *Modern Negro Art* (1943) as well as numerous articles.

In 1953, he became chairman of the Department of Art and director of the Gallery of Art at Howard University, a position he held until his death. He was a delegate to the UNESCO Conference on Africa held in Boston in 1961, and to the International Congress of African Art and Culture in Salisbury, Southern Rhodesia, 1962. In 1965, at the twenty-fifth anniversary of the founding of the National Gallery of Art, he was named "one of

America's Most Outstanding Men of the Arts." His notable works include: *On a Cuban Bus*, *Portrait of F. A. as Harlequin*, *Dorothy Porter*, and *Nude.*.

Martin Puryear (1941-)
Sculptor

Martin Puryear was born in Washington, DC, in 1941. He attended Catholic University of America and received an M.F.A. from Yale University in 1971; he has studied in Sweden and worked in Sierra Leone with the Peace Corps from 1964 to 1966.

Representing the United States in the 1989 Sao Paulo Bienal in Brazil he received first prize. His work has been described as post-minimalist, but it really defies categorizing. Puryear executes his own large pieces in wood and metal.

Puryear was the only black artist in the contemporary section of the exhibit, "Primitivism in Twentieth-Century Art: Affinity of the Tribal and Modern", at the Museum of Modern Art 1984; his other exhibits include Brooklyn Museum, 1988-1989, the Whitney Biennal, 1989, and New York Galleries, since 1987.

Puryear studied in Japan in 1987 on a Guggenheim Fellowship. Notable works include *For Beckwith; Maroon Desire; Sentinel;* recent works (since 1985) have been untitled.

Faith Ringgold (1930-)
Painter, Fiber Artist

Committed to a revolutionary perspective both in politics and in aesthetics, Faith Ringgold is a symbolic expressionist whose stark paintings are acts of social reform directed toward educating the consciousness of her audience. Her most intense focus has been upon the problems of being black in America. Her works highlight the violent tensions which tear at American society, including the discrimination suffered by women. Ringgold is also known for her distinctive story quilts. These quilts feature paintings on canvas that are bordered with quilted textiles and handwritten strips of white fabric that contain fanciful stories.

Born in Harlem on October 8, 1934, she was raised by parents who made sure she would enjoy the benefits of a good education. She attended the City College of New York, receiving her B.S. in 1955 and her masters in Fine Arts in 1959. She is a professor of Art at the University of California at San Diego.

Ringgold's boldly political work has been well-received and widely shown. She has had several one-person shows, the first in 1968, and her paintings are included in the collections of the Chase Manhattan Bank, New York City; the Museum of Modern Art, the Bank Street College of Education, New York City; and the Solomon R. Guggenheim Museum.

In 1972, Ringgold became one of the founders of the Women Students and Artists for Black Liberation, an organization whose principal goal is to make sure that all exhibitions of black artists give equal space to paintings by men and women. In line with her interest in sexual parity, she has donated a large mural depicting the roles of woman in American Society to the Women's House of Detention in Manhattan.

Aesthetically, she believes that "black art must use its own color, black, to create its light, since that color is the most immediate black truth." Her most recent paintings have been an attempt to give pictorial realization to this vision.

Her first quilt, *Echoes of Harlem*, *Tar Beach* was completed in 1980. Other quilts produced by Ringgold include *The Sunflower Quilting Bee at Arles* and *Who's Afraid of Aunt Jemima*. In 1991, she illustrated and wrote a children's book, *Tar Beach* . This book was followed in 1992 by *Aunt Harriet's Underground Railroad in the Sky*. Notable artistic works include *The Flag Is Bleeding; Flag for the Moon; Die Nigger; Mommy & Daddy*; and *Soul Sister, Woman on a Bridge*.

Ringgold has received several awards for her work, including honorary doctorates from Moore College of Fine Art, Wooster College, Massachusetts College of Art, and City College of Art. In 1996, she received an award from the National Museum of Women in the Arts.

Betye Saar (1926-)
Painter, Sculptor

Betye Saar was born in California on July 30, 1926. She went to college, got married, and raised her children—all while creating artwork, images built upon discarded pieces of old dreams, postcards, photographs, flowers, buttons, fans, and ticket stubs. Her motifs range from the fetish to the everyday object. In 1978, Saar was one of a select group of American female artists to be discussed in a documentary film entitled *Spirit Catcher: The Art of Betye Saar*. It appeared on WNET-13 in New York as part of "The Originals: Women in Art" series. Her exhibitions include an installation piece especially designed for The Studio Museum in Harlem in 1980, and several one-person exhibitions at the Monique Knowlton Gallery in New York in 1981.

Saar studied at Pasadena City College, University of California (B.F.A. in 1949), Long Beach State College, University of Southern California, San Fernando State College, Valley State College, California, and the American Film Institute. She was a teacher in–residence at Hayward State College, California. She has exhibited throughout the United States. In 1994, Saar's works were displayed with over 200 other artists at Brazil's Bienal, a biannual art exhibition featuring the works of artists from over 71 countries. Notable works include *The Vision of El Cremo; Africa; The View from the Sorcerer's Window;* and *House of Gris Gris*, a mixed–media installation (with daughter Alison Saar).

Augusta Savage (1900-1962)
Sculptor

A leading sculptor who emerged during the Harlem Renaissance, Augusta Savage was one of the artists represented in the first all-black exhibition in America, sponsored by the Harmon Foundation at International House in New York City. In 1939, her symbolic group piece *Lift Every Voice and Sing* was shown at the New York World's Fair Community Arts Building.

Savage was born in Green Cove Springs, Florida, on February 29, 1900, studied at Tallahassee State Normal School, at Cooper Union in New York City, and in France as the recipient of Carnegie and Rosenwald fellowships. She was the first black to win acceptance in the National Association of Women Painters and Sculptors.

In the 1930s she taught in her own School of Arts and Crafts in Harlem and helped many of her students take advantage of Works Progress Administration projects for artists during the Depression. Notable works include: *Lift Every Voice and Sing; The Chase; Black Women; Lenore; Gamin; Marcus Garvey;* and *W.E.B. DuBois.*

Charles Searles (1937-)
Painter, Educator

Born in Philadelphia, Pennsylvania, in 1937, Searles studied at Fleicher Art Memorial, Penn Academy of Fine Arts (1968-1972). His works have been exhibited at the Dallas, the Brooklyn, Philadelphia, Reading, High, Milwaukee, Whitney, and Harlem Studio Museums; Columbia University; and many other galleries and museums.

Searles has traveled to Europe and Africa. He has taught at the Philadelphia College of Art, the Philadelphia Museum Art Studio Classes, University of the Arts, Brooklyn Museum Art School, Jersey State College, and Bloomfield College in New Jersey.

He was commissioned to execute several murals, including the U.S. General Service Administration interior; *Celebration* (1976) for Wm. J. Green Federal Building; *Play Time* (1976) for Malory Public Playground; Newark, New Jersey Amtrak Station wall sculpture (1985); Dempsy Service Center wall sculpture (1989).

His works are in the collections of the Smithsonian Institute, Washington, DC; New York State Office Building; Philadelphia Museum of Art; Federal Railroad Administration; Ciba-Gigy, Inc.; Dallas Museum of Art;

Gamin, Augusta Savage, 1930.

Montclair Art Museum; Phillip Morris, Inc.; and Howard University.

The human figure, color and rhythmic patterns dominate his paintings. Notable works include *Cultural Mix; Rhythmic Forms; Play Time;* and *Celebration.*

Lorna Simpson (1960-)
Photographer, Conceptual Artist

Simpson was born in Brooklyn, New York, on August 13, 1960, and attended the School of Visual Arts, where she earned her B.F.A. in 1982. She received her M.F.A. from the University of California, San Diego, in 1985. Her works are concerned with language and words, especially those with double and contradictory meanings, and stereotypes and cliches about gender and race.

Simpson is among the new young photographers who have broken into the mainstream of conceptual based art; her work has been shown at the Museum of Modern Art and the Wadsworth Atheneum. She is on the advisory board of the New Museum, New York City, and also on the board of Artists Space.

In 1990, Simpson became the first African American woman to have her work featured in the Venice Biennale, a prestigious international art exhibition. Her work has been shown in exhibitions thoroughout the United States, Europe, Latin America, and Japan. Several institutions have offered exhibitions of her work, among them the Ansel Adams Center in San Francisco, the Whitney Museum of American Art in New York City, and the Milwaukee Art Museum. Her works have also been exhibited in the Just Above Mid-Town Gallery, Mercer Union (Toronto), and the Wadsworth Atheneum Museum's Matrix Gallery. Notable works include *Outline; Guarded Conditions; Easy for Who to Say; Flipside; Bio; Untitled ("prefer/refuse/decide")*; and the interactive multimedia composition *Five Rooms*.

Norma Merrick Sklarek (1928-)
Architect

Sklarek was born on April 15, 1928 in New York City, and received a B.A. in architecture from the Barnard College of Columbia University in 1950. In 1954, she became the first African American woman to be licensed as an architect in the United States. In 1966, Sklarek became the first African American woman to be named a fellow of the American Institute of Architects.

Sklarek's career began at Skidmore, Owens, Merrill, where she worked as an architect from 1955 until 1960. She also served on the faculty of New York City College from 1957 until 1960. In 1960, she took a position with Gruen and Associates in Los Angeles, California, where she worked for the next twenty years. She also served as a faculty member at UCLA from 1972 until 1978. Sklarek became vice president of Welton Becket Associates in 1980 and worked there until 1985. From 1985 until 1989, Sklarek was a partner in the firm Siegel, Sklarek, and Diamond, the largest female-owned architectural firm in the United States. In 1989, she began working as a principal for The Jerde Partnership, retiring in 1992. Sklarek remains active by conducting classes and seminars.

Among the notable structures designed by Sklarek are the American Embassy in Tokyo; Courthouse Center, Columbus, Indiana; City Hall, San Bernardino, California; and Terminal One, Los Angeles International Airport.

Moneta Sleet, Jr. (1926-)
Photographer

Moneta Sleet was born on February 14, 1926, in Owensboro, Kentucky. He studied at Kentucky State College under Dr. John Williams, a family friend who was dean of the college and an accomplished photographer. In 1947, he received his bachelor's degree from Kentucky State College. He earned a master's degree from New York University in 1950.

Sleet taught photography at Maryland State College from 1948 until 1949. He moved to New York City in 1950 to work as a sportswriter for *Amsterdam News*. He also worked as a photographer for *Our World* from 1951 until 1955. Sleet moved to Chicago and took a job with the Johnson Publishing Company, where he has been staff photographer for *Ebony* and *Jet* magazines since 1955.

In 1969, Moneta Sleet became the first African American to win a Pulitzer Prize in Photography. Although employed by *Ebony*, he was eligible for the award because his photograph of Coretta Scott King at her husband's funeral was picked up by a wire service and published in daily newspapers throughout the country. He has also received awards from the Overseas Press Club of America, National Urban League, and the National Association of Black Journalists. In 1989, the University of Kentucky inducted Sleet into its Kentucky Journalism Hall of Fame.

His work has appeared in several group exhibitions at museums, including The Studio Museum in Harlem and Metropolitan Museum of Art. In 1970, solo exhibitions were held at the City Art Museum of St. Louis and at the Detroit Public Library. Other solo exhibitions of Sleet's work have been held at the New York Public Library, Newark Public Library, Chicago Public Library Cultural Center, Milwaukee Public Library, Martin Luther King Jr. Memorial Library, Albany Museum of Art, New York State Museum, and the Schomberg Center for Research in Black Culture.

Sleet is a member of the NAACP and the Black Academy of Arts and Letters.

Willi Smith (1948-1987)
Fashion Designer

Born on February 29, 1948, in Philadelphia, Pennsylvania, Willi Smith studied at the Parsons School of Design on a scholarship and became popular during the 1960s. He was known for his designer wear in natural fibers, that were fun, cross seasonal, and affordable. His clothes were sportswear pieces that mixed readily with Willi-wear from previous years as well as other clothes. Smith innovated in mixing and matching plaids, stripes, and vivid colors. He designed for both men and women. Smith had his clothes manufactured in India, traveling there several times a year to supervise the making of his functional and practical collections.

Willi Smith

In 1983 Willi Smith received the Coty American Fashion Critics Award for Women's Fashion. He died in 1987.

Nelson Stevens (1938-)
Muralist, Painter, Graphic Artist

Born in Brooklyn, New York, in 1938, Stevens studied at Ohio University (B.F.A. 1962) and Kent State University (M.F.A. 1969).

An active member of AFRICOBRA—a group exploring the aesthetics of African-American art which includes the use of the human figure, bright colors, African inspired patterns, text, letters and other symbols relating to the black experience—he is also a member of the National Conference of Artists.

Stevens is a professor of art at the University of Massachusetts in Amherst, Massachusetts. He has exhibited at the National Center of Afro-American Artists, Boston; The Studio Museum in Harlem; Howard University; Kent State University. Notable works include: *Madonna and Child*, for a 1993 calendar, *Art in the Service of the Lord*; *Malcolm—King of Jihad*; and *A Different Kind of Man*.

Henry Ossawa Tanner (1859-1937)
Painter

Alain Locke called Henry Ossawa Tanner the leading talent of the "journeyman period" of black American art. Born in Pittsburgh on June 21, 1859, Tanner chose painting rather than the ministry as a career, overcoming the strong objections of his father, an African Methodist Episcopal bishop. After attending the Pennsylvania Academy of Fine Arts, he taught at Clark University in Atlanta, supplementing his salary by working as a photographer. Some of Tanner's most compelling work—such as *The Banjo Lesson* (1890)—was produced during this period, with Tanner himself emerging as the most promising black artist of his day.

In 1891, however, Tanner abandoned black subject matter and left the United States for Paris, where he concentrated on religious themes. In 1896, his *Daniel in the Lion's Den*, a mixture of realism and mystical symbolism, won honorable mention at the Paris Salon. The following year, the French government purchased his *Resurrection of Lazarus*. In 1900, Tanner received the Medal of Honor at the Paris Exposition and the Lippincott Prize.

Tanner died in 1937. Notable works include *Flight into Egypt, The Annunciation, Thankful Poor* and *The Sabot Makers*.

Alma W. Thomas (1891-1978)
Painter

Born in Columbus, Georgia, in 1891, Alma Thomas moved to Washington, DC with her family when she was a teenager. She enrolled at Howard University and was the first graduate of its Art Department (1924). In 1934 she received her M.A. degree from Columbia University. She later studied at American University.

Retiring after a thirty-eight-year teaching career in public schools, Thomas concentrated solely on her painting. She is best known for her non-objective, mosaic-like works which emphasize color, pattern, and space. The optical relationships of her colors in flat shapes create three-dimensional forms, enlivening the painted surfaces with movement and pulsating rhythms. It is this later work that brought her many prizes and awards.

Her works are in the collections of the National Museum of American Art at the Smithsonian Institute, Howard University, Concord Gallery, Metropolitan Museum, La Jolla Museum, and private corporations. Notable works include *The Eclipse; Arboretum Presents White Dogwood; Elysian Fields; Red Sunset;* and *Old Pond Concerto*.

Abraham's Oak, Henry Ossawa Tanner, 1905.

Bob Thompson (1937-1966)
Painter

The death of Bob Thompson marked the loss of an outstanding African-American painter from the art world, a man who had studied extensively in the United States and traveled widely in Europe and North Africa, living in Paris (1961-1962), Ibiza (1962-1963), and Rome (1965-1966).

Born in Louisville, Kentucky, in 1937, Thompson studied at the Boston Museum School in 1955 and later spent three years at the University of Louisville. In 1960, Thompson participated in a two-person show at Zabriskie Gallery and two years later received a John Hay Whitney Fellowship. For the next several years, Thompson had several one-person exhibitions in New York and Chicago. His work was also seen in Spain. He died in Rome at the age of twenty-nine.

Thompson's work is in several permanent collections around the country, including the Chrysler Museum in Provincetown, Massachusetts. In 1970, Thompson's work was featured in the African-American Artist exhibition at the Boston Museum of Fine Arts. Notable works include *Ascension to the Heavens; Untitled Diptych; The Dentist* (1963); and *Expulsion and Nativity* (1964).

James VanDerZee (1886-1983)
Photographer

James VanDerZee was born on June 29, 1886, in Lenox, Massachusetts. His parents had moved there from New York in the early 1880s after serving as maid and butler to Ulysses S. Grant, who then resided on 34th Street in New York City. The second of six children, James grew up in a family filled with creative people. Everybody painted, drew, or played an instrument, so it was not considered out of the ordinary when, upon receiving a camera in 1900, VanDerZee became interested in photography.

By 1906 VanDerZee had moved to New York, married, and took odd jobs to support his growing family. In 1907, he moved to Phoetus, Virginia, where he worked in the dining room of the Hotel Chamberlin in Old Point Comfort, Virginia. During this time he also worked as a photographer on a part-time basis. In 1909, he returned to New York.

By 1915, VanDerZee had his first photography job as assistant in a small concession in the Gertz Department Store in Newark, New Jersey. With the money he saved from this job he was able to open his own studio in 1916, on 135th Street. World War I had begun and many young

James Van Der Zee

soldiers came to the studio to have their pictures taken. Over the course of a half-century, James VanDerZee would record the visual history of Harlem. His subjects included Marcus Garvey, Sweet Daddy Grace, Father Divine, Joe Louis, Madame Walker, and many other famous African Americans.

In 1969, the exhibition "Harlem On My Mind," produced by Thomas Hoving, then director of the Metropolitan Museum of Art, brought James VanDerZee international recognition. He died in 1983.

Laura Wheeler Waring (1887-1948)
Painter

Born in 1887 in Hartford, Connecticut, this portrait painter and illustrator received her first training at the Pennsylvania Academy of Fine Arts, where she studied for six years. In 1914, she won the Cresson Memorial Scholarship, which enabled her to continue her studies at the Academie de la Grande Chaumiere in Paris.

Waring returned to the United States as an art instructor at Cheyney State Teachers College in Pennsylvania, eventually becoming head of the art department there. Her work, particularly portraiture, has been exhibited at several leading American art galleries. In 1927,

she received the Harmon Award for achievement in fine art. With Betsy Graves Reyneau, Waring completed a set of twenty-four re-paintings of a variety of their works titled *Portraits of Outstanding Americans of Negro Origin* for the Harmon Foundation in the 1940s.

Waring was also the director in charge of the black art exhibits at the Philadelphia Exposition in 1926 and was a member of the national advisory board of Art Movements, Inc. She died in 1948. Notable works include: *Alonzo Aden; W.E. Burghardt DuBois; James Weldon Johnson;* and *Mother and Daughter*

Carrie Mae Weems (1953-)
Photographer, Conceptual Artist

Carrie Mae Weems was born in Portland, Oregon, in 1953, and went to California Institute of the Arts (B.F.A., 1981) and the University of California at San Diego (M.F.A., 1984). She received an M.A. in African-American Folklore from the University of Carlifornia at Berkeley.

A young artist who explores stereotypes, especially those of black women, Weems has exhibited widely in the last few years. Formerly a photo documentarian, Weems also teaches film-making and photography at Hampshire College in Amherst, Massachusetts. Her new works are "about race, gender, class and kinship."

She has exhibited at the Rhode Island School of Design, and Wadsworth Atheneum, Hartford, Connccticut. Notable works include *Mirror, Mirror; Black Woman With Chicken; High Yella Girl; Colored People; Family Pictures and Stories;* and *Ain't Jokin'.*

Edward T. Welburn (1950-)
Automobile Designer

Chief designer of automobiles at the Oldsmobile Studio for General Motors, Edward T. Welburn had one of the outstanding car designs on the market with the 1992 Achieva model. Welburn was born on December 14, 1950 and graduated with a bachelor of fine arts degree from Howard University in 1972. He is also a graduate of the Skip/Barber School for Auto Race Drivers.

Welburn began his career with the GM Design Staff as a creative designer in 1972, advancing to the positions of senior creative designer and assistant chief designer. While a member of the GM Design Staff, he designed the Cutlass Supreme, Cutlass Ciera, and the Oldsmobile Calais. In 1989, he moved to the Oldsmobile Studio as chief designer.

In 1985, the Indianapolis 500 pace car was designed by a team on which Welburn served. He was named Alumni of the Year in 1989 by the Howard University Student Association. Welburn won the Industrial De-

1993 Oldsmobile *Achieva SC,* Edward Welburn.

signers Society of America Award for Design Excellence for his part in the design for *Oldsmobile Aerotech* in 1992.

Welburn is a member of The Cabinet and the Founders Society of the Detroit Institute of Arts.

James Lesesne Wells (1902-1993)
Artist

Born on November 2, 1902, in Atlanta, James Lesesne Wells was a pioneer of modern American printmaking and the inspiration for a generation of black artists. After graduating from high school, Wells lived with relatives in New York City and worked for two years to earn money for college. Meanwhile, he studied drawing at the National Academy of Design for one term from 1918 to 1919. Wells spend one year at Lincoln University before transferring to Teachers College at Columbia University in 1923 and earning a B.S. in 1927. He received an MS from Columbia in 1938.

Immediately after earning his undergraduate degree, Wells created black print illustrations for magazines. He also made connections with art dealer and gallery-owner J. D. Neumann, who included Wells's work in a 1929 exhibition of "International Modernists." These projects captured the attention of Howard University's James V. Herring, who invited Wells to join the prestigious school's art faculty that year. Thus began a 39-year career at the university, during which Wells established a graphics arts department and taught several soon to be well-known artists, including Charles Alston and Jacob Lawrence. Wells taught clay modeling, ceramics, sculpture, metals, and block printing.

During the Great Depression, Wells devoted himself to printmaking; his prints from this period involved African American history and industrial themes. The art form began rising to the level of admiration later enjoyed by painting in the 1970s. Despite a lack of critical recognition, Wells's work won numerous art competitions throughout the 1930s, including the George E. Haynes Prize in 1933. At this time, he also served as the director of a summer art workshop that preceded the Harlem Community Art Center.

After World War II, Wells spent a sabbatical year working at Stanley Hayter's famous Atelier 17, then the most innovative center of etching and printmaking in the United States. Wells continued to teach and win awards for his artwork in the 1950s and 1960s. He moved the Washington, DC, and joined his brother-in-law Eugene Davidson, president of the local NAACP, in segregation protests. The harassment Wells suffered as a result of his outspokenness—a cross was burned in his yard in 1957—may have inspired the religious themes of much of his work from the era. He took first prize in a religious art exhibition sponsored by the Smithsonian in 1958.

After retiring from Howard in 1968, Wells continued to paint and make prints in the 1980s. In 1980, then-U.S. president Jimmy Carter bestowed Wells with a presidential citation for lifelong contributions to American art. Four years later, Washington, DC had a "James L. Wells Day." Designated a "Living Legend" by the National Black Arts Festival in 1991, Wells's work was featured in a retrospective exhibition by the Harmon Foundation, which had recognized him for his artwork as early as 1916, when he took a first prize in painting and second prize in woodworking. He died of congestive heart failure at the age of 90.

Charles White (1918-1979)
Painter

White was an eminent exponent of social art. The subject matter of his paintings were the notable achievements of famous American blacks, as well as the suffering of the lowly and anonymous.

White was born in 1918 in Chicago and was influenced as a young boy by Alain Locke's critical review of the Harlem Renaissance, *The New Negro*. At the age of twenty-three, White won a Rosenwald Fellowship which enabled him to work in the South for two years, during which time he painted a celebrated mural depicting the black's contribution to American democracy. It is now the property of the Hampton Institute in Virginia.

The bulk of White's work is done in black-and-white, a symbolic motif which he felt gave him the widest possible purview. Notable works include *Let's Walk Together; Frederick Douglass Lives Again; Women;* and *Gospel Singer.*

Paul Revere Williams (1894-1980)
Architect

Williams was born in Los Angeles, California, on February 18, 1894, and graduated from the University of California at Los Angeles. He later attended the Beaux Arts Institute of Design in Paris; he received honorary degrees from Howard, Lincoln, and Atlanta Universities as well as Hampton Institute.

Williams became a certified architect in 1915 and after working for Reginald Johnson and John Austin, distinguished designers and architects, he opened his own firm in 1923. Williams was known as America's "architect to the stars" (*African Architects in Current Practice*, edited by Jack Travis, 1991). Williams designed some four hundred homes and a total of 3,000 buildings including homes for Cary Grant, Barbara Stanwyk, William Holden, Frank Sinatra, Betty Grable, Bill "Bojangles" Robinson, and Bert Lahr.

In 1926 he was the first black to become a member of the American Institute of Architects. He served on the National Monument Commission, an appointee of President Calvin Coolidge. Notable works include *Los Angeles County Airport; Palm Springs Tennis Club*; and *Saks Fifth Avenue at Beverly Hills*. He died on January 23, 1980.

William T. Williams (1942-)
Painter

William T. Williams was born in Cross Creek, North Carolina, on July 17, 1942. He received his bachelor of fine arts degree from Pratt Institute in 1966 and his master of fine arts from Yale University in 1968.

In 1970, Williams taught painting classes at Pratt Institute and at the School of Fine Arts. Since 1971, he has been a professor of art at City University of New York, Brooklyn College. He also served as a visiting professor of art at Virginia Commonwealth University.

Critics have compared Williams' work more to Joseph Albers and the Bauhaus traditions from Europe than to his own statements about his work's relationships to the city, architecture, tension, things in flux, order from disorder, and to Africa and the United States.

Williams has been the recipient of several awards. In 1992, the Studio Museum in Harlem presented him with its Annual Award for Lifetime Achievement. He was also awarded the Mid-Atlantic Foundation Fellowship in 1994.

Exhibitions of Williams's work have been presented at, among others, The Studio Museum in Harlem, Wadsworth Atheneum, Art Institute of Chicago, and The Whitney Museum of American Art. Notable works include *Elbert Jackson L.A.M.F. Port II; Big Red for N.C.*; and *Buttermilk.*

John Wilson (1922-)
Painter, Printmaker

Born in Boston on April 14, 1922, John Wilson studied at the Boston Museum of Fine Arts; Fernand Leger School, Paris; The Institute Politecnico, Mexico City; and the Escuela de las Artes del Libro, Mexico City. In 1947, Wilson received a bachelor's degree from Tufts University. He has been a teacher at Boston Museum, Pratt Institute, and Boston University.

William T. Williams

His numerous exhibits include the Albany Institute; the Library of Congress National (and International) Print Exhibit(s); Smith College; Carnegie Institute; and the American International College, Springfield, Massachusetts. His work is represented in the collections of the Museum of Modern Art; Schomburg Collection; Department of Fine Arts, French Government; Atlanta University; and Bezalel Museum, Jerusalem. Notable works include *Roxbury Landscape* (oil, 1944); *Trabajador* (print, 1951); and *Child with Father* (graphic, 1969).

Wilson created the Dr. Martin Luther King Jr. Monument in Buffalo, New York in 1983 and the Dr. Martin Luther King Jr. Commemorative Statue at the U.S. Capitol in Washington, D.C. In 1987, he completed the monument "Eternal Presence," which resides at the Museum of the National Center of Afro-American Artists, Boston, Massachusetts.

Hale Woodruff (1900-1979)
Painter, Muralist

Hale Woodruff's paintings were largely modernist landscapes and formal abstractions, but he has also painted rural Georgia scenes evocative of the "red clay" country. Born in Cairo, Illinois, in 1900, he graduated from the John Herron Art Institute in Indianapolis. Encouraged by a bronze award in the 1926 Harmon Foundation competition, Woodruff went to Paris to study at both the Academie Scandinave and the Academie Moderne, as well as with Henry Ossawa Tanner.

In 1931, he became art instructor at Atlanta University and five years later accepted a similar post at New York University. In 1939, he was commissioned by Talladega College to do *The Amistad Murals*, an episodic depiction of a slave revolt.

In 1948, Woodruff teamed with Charles Alston to work on the Golden State Mutual Life Insurance Company Murals in California, which presented the contribution of African Americans to the history of the development of California. Woodruff's last mural assignment came in 1950 when he developed the series of mural panels for Atlanta University entitled "The Art of the Negro."

Hale Woodruff died in 1979 after creating a body of work with styles that moved from the figurative, to the Impressionistic period of his Paris experience, to a brief exploration of the cubist visual concepts, to moving comfortably into the abstract style. With all of these stylistic developments, Hale Woodruff also became one of America's strongest mural painters. Notable works include: *Ancestral Remedies; The Little Boy*; and *The Amistad Murals*.

Richard Yarde (1939-)
Painter

Richard Yarde was born in Boston, Massachusetts, on October 29, 1939. He studied at the School of the Museum of Fine Arts and at Boston University, where he received a B.F.A. in 1962 and an M.F.A. in 1964. He has taught at Boston University, Wellesley College, Amherst College, Massachusetts College of Art, Mount Holyoke College, and the University of Massachusetts.

Yarde has received numerous awards for his art, including Yaddo fellowships in 1964, 1966, and 1970, McDowell Colony awards in 1968 and 1970, and the Blanche E. Colman Award in 1970.

The Boston Museum of Fine Arts, Wadsworth Atheneum, Rose Art Museum, National Museum of African-American Artists, and Studio Museum in Harlem have all exhibited his works. He has held one-person shows at numerous galleries and universities. His works are in many collections, such as the Wadsworth Atheneum in Hartford, Connecticut. Notable works include *The Stoop, Passage Edgar and I, The Corner, Paul Robeson as Emperor Jones, Head and Hands 1, Josephine's Baffle Triptych*, and *Richard's Cards*.

◆ MUSEUMS AND GALLERIES

The 1960s was an era which saw a great many radical changes in both the social and the cultural aspects of the United States. African Americans throughout the country were demanding political, social, and cultural recognition. No longer satisfied with the limited support of such philanthropic organizations as the Harmon Foundation, these artists looked for alternative forms of exposure. The result of their demands was an outpouring of galleries, community art centers, and community art galleries.

In New York City, the Acts of Art Gallery was established in 1969 by Nigel Jackson, a former artist turned administrator, and provided exhibition space for contemporary artists. A non-profit organization, the gallery was dedicated to promoting these artists and providing them with the opportunity to attract collectors interested in their work. The gallery exhibitions included the works of such artists as James Denmark, Dinga McCannon, Frank Wimberly, Ann Tanksley, Don Robertson, Lloyd Toomes, Lois Mailou Jones, Jo Butler, Robert Threadgill, and Faith Ringgold. Largely because of the politically volatility of the period, but also because of the gallery's aggressive action policy, in 1971 the Acts of Art Gallery became the center for the controversial "Whitney Rebuttal Show."

The Studio Museum in Harlem began in 1969 under the direction of Edward Spriggs. Set up as a place for artists who needed working space, it eventually branched out into a cultural center where the artists could display their work, meet other artists and art supporters, and hold concerts, panel discussions, and other art related activities. The Studio Museum in Harlem had become by 1972, the cultural center of New York for the African-American community. Important retrospectives were presented including the works of Palmer Hayden, Hale Woodruff, Beauford Delaney, Bob Thompson, and James VanDerZee.

Also, the Lewis H. Michaux Book Fair took place for three years at the Studio Museum (1976-1979) under the direction of special program coordinator David Jackson. Lewis Michaux was a legend in the world of book selling, because he established a bookstore on 125th Street and Lenox Avenue which became a landmark for people from around the world who were interested in literature of or about African Americans, Africans, Caribbeans, and South Americans. The store opened in 1930 and continued to exist for the next forty-four years. It was called The National Memorial African Book Store.

While under the directorship of Edward Spriggs, the museum began the special holiday celebration Kwanzaa, a time during which the museum opened its doors to the entire neighborhood to share in dancing, singing, and eating with the artists. Dancer Chuck Davis would come to lead off the dancing, ending with the whole room filled with guests in the center of the floor dancing.

By 1980, the museum had grown out of its second floor loft space and moved into an old office building on 125th Street and 7th Avenue. The new space provided the museum with additional exhibition galleries, larger office areas, and space for its growing collection and the artist-in-residence program. In 1977, during this period of growth for the museum, a new director, Mary Campell Schmidt, took over the operations of the institution. In 1988, she was appointed commissioner of the Department of Cultural Affairs in New York. In January 1988, the Museum's deputy director Kinshasha Holman Conwill, wife of artist Houston Conwill, was named director. The Studio Museum has continued to expand its audience, exhibitions, and programs.

Just Above Midtown Gallery was the first organization to move into the gallery district in New York City. Established in 1976, it set up its operation base in a modest space on 57th Street in midtown Manhattan. Under the directorship of Linda Bryant, the organization

Two artists work with clay.

presented many of the leading contemporary artists of the 1970s including David Hammons, Senga Nengudi, Randy Williams, and Howardena Pindell. Placing the African American artists in direct competition with mainstream American artists was the objective of Bryant, her board, and her artists. No longer could art critics refuse to review these works because they could not get to Harlem, Queens, or Brooklyn. But the cost of running a gallery took its toll and in order to continue operations Bryant was forced to turn the gallery into a non-profit organization, adding educational programs for young artists, music concerts, performance programs, slide reviews and lectures.

By the end of 1979, Just Above Midtown moved from 57th Street to a larger space on Franklin Street in the Tribeca section of New York, changed its name to the Just Above Midtown/Downtown Alternative Art Center, and opened its doors to vanguard, new-wave artists.

The Schomburg Center for Research in Black Culture of the New York Public Library is one of the most widely used research facilities in the world and is devoted to the preservation of materials on black life. The Center's collections first won international acclaim in 1926 when the personal collection of the distinguished black scholar and bibliophile, Arthur A. Schomburg, was added to the Division of Negro Literature, History and Prints of the 135th Street Branch of the New York Public Library. Schomburg's collection included over 5,000 volumes, 3,000 manuscripts, 2,000 etchings and paintings, and several thousand pamphlets. He served as the curator in the Negro Division from 1932 until his death in 1938. Renamed in his honor in 1940, the collection grew steadily through the years. In 1972, it was designated as one of the Research Libraries of the New York Public Library and became The Schomburg Center for Research in Black Culture. Today, the Schomburg Center is the guardian of collections including over five million items, and provides services and programs for constituents from the United States and abroad.

The Cinque Gallery, another New York gallery, was the concept of three distinguished artists— Romare Bearden, Norman Lewis, and Ernest Crichlow. The gallery, which opened in 1969, was named after the famous African Joseph Cinque, who in 1839 led a successful revolt aboard the slave ship *Amistad*, won his freedom, and returned to Africa. It was the wish of Bearden, Crichlow, and Lewis to establish an exhibition space specifically for young African-American artists who needed to learn the process of being a professional artist. However, by the end of the 1970s it was decided that the gallery doors be opened to all new and emerging artists regardless of age.

The Weusi Ya Nambe Yasana Gallery, also in New York, was one of the few cooperative community galleries to come out of the late 1960s. Housed in a brownstone in Harlem, the gallery was established to present the art work of its members. Headed by Ademola Olagebefola, the other members included Otto Neals, Kay Brown, and Jean Taylor.

Genesis II was one of the alternative profit-making galleries that emerged out of the 1960s. Like many of its kind, the gallery functioned out of the dealer's apartment to cover the cost of overhead expenses. The dealer would invite his or her clients to come view the works in a living environment, so that they might better appreciate the art work. Also, at these gatherings, clients had the opportunity to meet other collectors as well as meet the artist and talk in detail about the work. The concept proved valuable for many African-American artists who needed to develop supporting collectors and to establish a real market for their work.

The New Muse Community Museum in Brooklyn began in the late 1960s, offering the African-American Brooklyn community the same kinds of art programs presented at the Studio Museum. In addition to the art programs, the New Muse also offered lessons in jazz with bassist Reggie Workman, who headed the program.

The Store Front Museum in Queens was established to satisfy the artistic needs of its community. Offering art classes in painting and drawing, its focus leaned more toward the performing arts—dancing and drama.

The Benin Gallery opened its doors in 1976. Director Edward Sherman operated the gallery as a non-profit, tax exempt corporation so that the public in Harlem would have a gallery to call its own. Located at 2366 Adam Clayton Powell, Jr., Boulevard in the St. Nicholas Historic District, the gallery focused on photography.

The Hatch-Billops Studio began in New York in 1968 as an organization designed to present multi-ethnic plays, performances and exhibitions. By 1973, the studio began collecting third world memorabilia. Based on the understanding that no one will protect your history or present your history the way you do, the collection became incorporated in 1975. Camille Billops and her husband Jim Hatch began taping the history of some black theater artists. Today the collection houses more than six hundred taped interviews and panel and media events about or by artists. There are well over 10,000 slides and 3,000 books, clippings, files, letters, memorabilia, programs, photographs, drawings, scrapbooks, and videotapes. This collection is one of the most complete reference centers focusing on African-American art—visual, literary, and theatrical. It is a collection available to artists, scholars, and students.

Meanwhile, galleries and museums for African-American artists were also developing in other parts of the country. In Los Angeles, Samella Lewis, a painter, art historian, and professor at Claremont College, founded the Contemporary Craft Center. Alonzo and Dale Davis established and directed the Brockman Galleries Productions, a nonprofit gallery showing contemporary African-American art and the work of other minority artists.

In Chicago, the Du Sable Museum was established in 1961 under the directorship of Margaret Burroughs to provide the South Side community with an art center. The museum grew out of an art center that was established under the Work-Progress Administration during the Depression. Some of the artists presented there include Charles White, Elizabeth Catlett, Gordon Parks, Rex Gorleigh, William McBride, Jr., and Eldzier Cortor.

In Boston, the museum of the National Center of Afro-American Artists, begun in 1969 under the curatorship of Edmond Barry Gaither, is a multi-media art center featuring dance, theater, visual arts, film, and educational programs.

In Washington, DC, the National Museum of African Art, formerly known as the Frederick Douglass Institute, was established in 1964 and until 1984 existed in a Victorian row house on Capitol Hill, nestled in the shadow of the United States Supreme Court. The house had belonged to Frederick Douglass, a former slave who became an advisor to President Lincoln. In 1984, the museum was moved to the Smithsonian Institute and the house was singularly devoted to early African-American art and memorabilia and continues to be known as the Frederick Douglass Institute. The museum was established to promote and familiarize Americans with the artistic heritage of Africa; today it includes a large and extensive collection devoted exclusively to African art and culture. One of the largest and most diverse of its kind in the United States, the collection consists of some 65,000 works including traditional carvings, musical instruments, and textiles with particular emphasis on works from Nigeria, Ghana, Liberia, the Ivory Coast, and Zaire. In the transition, the Smithsonian has also acquired the Eliot Elisofon Photographic Archives, which contains some 150,000 slides and motion pictures available to the public.

The Smith-Mason Gallery Museum located in Washington, DC is a four-story Victorian house established in 1968 to present its permanent collection, which features paintings, sculptures and graphics of African-American and Caribbean artists. The works remain on permanent display.

Alabama

George Washington Carver Museum
1212 Old Montgomery Rd.
PO Drawer 10
Tuskegee Institute, AL 36087-0010
(205) 727-6390
Fax:(205) 727-4597

California

San Francisco African American Historical Society
Fort Mason Center Bldg. C, No. 165
San Francisco, CA 94123
(415) 441-0640

Brockman Gallery
4334 Degnan Boulevard
Los Angeles, CA 90008
(213) 294-3766

California Afro-American Museum
600 State Drive; Exposition Park
Los Angeles, CA 90037
(213) 744-7432
Fax:(213)744-2050

Ebony Museum of Art
30 Jack Londo Boulevard, Ste. 209
Oakland, CA 94607
(415) 658-3158

Museum of African-American Art
4005 Crenshaw Boulevard, 3rd Floor
Los Angeles, CA 90008
(213) 294-7071

Colorado

Black American West Museum and Heritage Center
3091 California St.
Denver, CO 80207
(303) 292-2566

Connecticut

Amistad Foundation and Gallery of African-American Art, Wadsworth Atheneum
600 Main St.
Hartford, CT 06103
(203) 278-2670

Artists, Collective, Inc.
35 Clark St.
Hartford, CT 06120
(203) 527-3205

Connecticut Afro-American Historical Society
444 Orchard St.
New Haven, CT 06511

CRT's Craftery Gallery
1445 Main St.
Hartford, CT 06120
(203) 280-0170

Delaware

Afro-American Historical Society of Delaware
512 E. 4th St.
Wilmington, DE 19801
(302) 984-1421

District of Columbia

Anacostia Museum
1901 Fort Place SE
Washington, DC 20020
(202) 287-3306
Fax:(202) 287-3183

Bethune Museum-Archives, National Historic Society
1318 Vermont Ave. NW
Washington, DC 20005
(202) 332-1233
Fax:(202) 332-6319

Black Film Institute, University of the District of Columbia
Carnegie Building
8th St. and Mt. Vernon Pl. NW
Washington, DC 20001
(202) 727-2396

Evans-Tibbs Collection
1910 Vermont Ave., NW
Washington, DC 20001
(202) 234-8164

Howard University Gallery of Art
2455 6th St., NW
Washington, DC 20059
(202) 806-7070
Fax:(202) 806-6503

Sign of the Times Cultural Workshop and Gallery, Inc.
605 56th St., NE
Washington, DC 20019
(202) 399-3400

Smithsonian Institute, National Museum of African Art
950 Independence Ave., SW
Washington, DC 20560
(202) 357-4600
Fax:(202) 357-4879

Florida

Afro-Carib American Cultural Center
4511 N.W. 25th Pl.
Lauderhill, FL 33313
(305) 739-1015

Appleton Museum of Art/The Appleton Cultural Center
4333 E. Silver Springs Boulevard
Ocala, FL 32670

Black Archives Research Center and Museum, Florida A and M University
c/o Florida A and M University
PO Box 809
Tallahassee, FL 32307
(904) 599-3020

Black Heritage Museum
PO Box 570327
Miami, FL 33257-0327
(305) 252-3535

Gallery Antiqua
5138 Biscayne Boulevard
Miami, FL 33137
(305) 759-5355

Georgia

Apex Museum
135 Auburn Ave., NE
Atlanta, GA 30303
(404) 521-3739

Hammonds House Galleries
503 Peeples St., SW
Atlanta, GA 30310
(404) 752-8730

Herndon Home
587 University Pl. NW
Atlanta, GA 30314
(404) 581-9613

King-Tisdell Cottage of Black History Museum
502 E. Harris St.
Savannah, GA 31401
(912) 234-8000

Martin Luther King Jr. Center, Cultural Affairs Program
449 Auburn Ave., NE
Atlanta, GA 30312
(404) 524-1956

McIntosh Gallery
One Virginia Hill
587 Virginia Ave.
Atlanta, GA 30306
(404) 892-4023

National Black Arts Festival
70 Fairlie St., NW, Ste. 250
Atlanta, GA 30303
(404) 730-7315

Uncle Remus Museum
PO Box 184
Eatonton, GA 31024
(404) 485-6856

US National Park Service, Martin Luther King Jr. National Historic Site and Preservation District
522 Auburn Ave., NE
Atlanta, GA 30312
(404) 331-5190

Illinois

Afro-American Arts Alliance of Chicago
7558 S. Chicago Ave.
Chicago, IL 60619
(312) 288-5100

Afro-American Genealogical and Historical Society, Du Sable Museum of African American History
740 E. 56th Place
Chicago, IL 60637
(312) 947-0600

Isobel Neal Gallery Ltd.
200 W. Superior
Chicago, IL 60610
(312) 944-1570

Indiana

Indiana University Art Museum
Bloomington, IN 47405
(812) 855-5445
Fax:(812) 855-1023

Kansas

First National Black Historical Society of Kansas
601 N. Water
Wichita, KS 67201
(316) 262-7651

Maryland

Baltimore's Black American Museum
1765 Carswell St.
Baltimore, MD 21218
(301) 243-9600

Great Blacks in Wax Museum
1601-03 E. North Ave.
Baltimore, MD 21213
(410) 563-3404
Fax:(410) 675-5040

Maryland Museum of African Art
5430 Vantage Point Rd.
Columbia, MD 21044-0105
(410) 730-7105
Fax:(410) 715-3047

Massachusetts

Cousens-Rose Gallery
Circuit Ave.
Oak Bluffs, Martha's Vineyard, MA 02568

Liz Harris Gallery
711 Atlantic Ave.
Boston, MA 02111
(617) 338-1315

National Center of Afro-American Artists
300 Walnut Ave.
Boston, MA 02119
(617) 442-8614

Wendell Street Gallery
17 Wendel St.
Cambridge, MA 02138
(617) 864-9294

Michigan

Detroit Black Arts Alliance
13217 Livernois
Detroit, MI 48238-3162
(313) 931-3427

Museum of African-American History
301 Frederick Douglass St.
Detroit, MI 48202
(313) 833-9800
Fax:(313) 832-7933

G.R. N'namdi Gallery
161 Townsend
Birmingham, MI 48009
(313) 642-2700

Your Heritage House
110 E. Ferry
Detroit, MI 48202
(313) 871-1667

Minnesota

Pillsbury House/Cultural Arts
3501 Chicago Ave. S.
Minneapolis, MN 55407
(612) 824-0708

Mississippi

Smith Robertson Museum and Cultural Center
PO Box 3259
Jackson, MS 39207
(601) 960-2070

Missouri

Black Archives of Mid-America
2033 Vine St.
Kansas City, MO 64108
(816) 483-1300
Fax:(816) 483-1341

Vaughn Cultural Center
1408 N. Kings Highway, Ste. 205
St. Louis, MO 63113
(314) 361-0111

Nebraska

Great Plains Black Museum
2213 Lake St.
Omaha, NE 68110
(402) 345-2212

New Jersey

African Art Museum of the S.M.A. Fathers
23 Bliss Ave.
Tenafly, NJ 07670
(201) 567-0450

Merabash Museum
PO Box 752
Willingboro, NJ 08046

Newark Museum
49 Washington St.
Newark, NJ 07101-0540
(201) 596-6550
Fax:(201) 642-0459

New York

African-American Cultural Center of Buffalo
350 Masten Ave.
Buffalo, NY 14209
(716) 884-2013

African-American Culture and Arts Network
2090 Adam Clayton Powell, Jr. Boulevard
New York, NY 10027
(212) 749-4408

African-American Institute Museum
833 United Nations Plaza
New York, NY 10017
(212) 949-5666
Fax:(212) 682-6174

African American Museum of Nassau County
110 Franklin St.
Hempstead, NY 11550

Aunt Len's Doll and Toy House Inc.
6 Hamilton Terrace
New York, NY 10031
(212) 281-4143

Bedford-Stuyvesant Restoration Center for Arts and Culture
1368 Fulton, Ste. 4G
Brooklyn, NY 11216
(718) 636-6948

Black Fashion Museum
157 W. 126 St.
New York, NY 10027
(212) 666-1320

Black Filmmaker Foundation
Tribeca Film Center
375 Greenwich St., Ste. 600
New York, NY 10013
(212) 941-3944
Fax:(212) 941-3943

Black Spectrum Theater Co.
119 Roy Wilkens Park
Jamaica, NY 11434
(718) 723-1800

Center for African Art
52-54 E. 68th St.
New York, NY 10021
(212) 861-1200

Cinque Gallery
560 Broadway
New York, NY 10012
(212) 966-3464

Community Folk Art Gallery
2223 Genessee St.
Syracuse, NY 13210
(315) 424-8487

Genesis II Museum of International Black Culture
509 Cathedral Parkway
New York, NY 10025
(212) 666-7222

Grinnell Gallery
800 Riverside Dr.
New York, NY 10032
(212) 927-7941

Harlem Cultural Council
215 W. 125th St.
New York, NY 10027
(212) 316-6277

Harlem Institute of Fashion
157 W. 126th St.
New York, NY 10027
(212) 666-1320

Harlem School of the Arts
645 St. Nicholas Ave.
New York, NY 10030
(212) 926-4100

Hatch-Billops Collection, Inc.
491 Broadway
New York, NY 10012
(212) 966-3231

International Agency for Minority Artists Affairs Inc.
352 W. 71st St.
New York, NY 10023
(212) 873-5040

June Kelly Gallery
591 Broadway, 3rd Fl.
New York, NY 10012
(212) 226-1660

Museum of African and African-American Art and Antiquities
11 E. Utica St.
Buffalo, NY 14209
(716) 882-7676

New Muse Community Museum of Brooklyn
1530 Bedford Ave.
Brooklyn, NY 11216
(718) 774-2900

Studio Museum in Harlem
144 W. 125th St.
New York, NY 10027
(212) 864-4500
Fax:(212) 666-5753

"Where We At" Black Women Artists
1452 Bedford Ave.
Brooklyn, NY 11216
(718) 398-3871

North Carolina

African Heritage Center
North Carolina A and T State University
Greensboro, NC 27411
(919) 334-7874

African-American Atelier
Greensboro Cultural Center
200 N. Davie St.
Greensboro, NC 27401
(919) 333-6885

Afro-American Cultural Center
401 N. Meyers St.
Spirit Square
Charlotte, NC 28202

AM Studio
1610 E. 14th St.
Winston Salem, NC 27105
(919) 725-4959

Biggers Art Sales Traveling Gallery
1404 N. Oakwood St.
Gastonia, NC 28052
(704) 867-4525

Black Artists Guild
400 N. Queen St.
P.O. Box 2162
Kinston, NC 28501
(919) 523-0003

H C Taylor Gallery
North Carolina A and T State University
Greensboro, NC 27411
(919) 334-7784

Harambee Arts Festival
Lenoir Recreation Department
PO Box 958
c/o Viewmont Community Center
Lenoir, NC 28645
(704) 754-3278

Huff's Art Studio
2846 Patterson Ave.
Winston-Salem, NC 27105
(919) 724-7581

NCCU Art Museum
PO Box 19555
Durham, NC 27707
(919) 560-6211
Fax:(919) 560-5012

St. Augustine's College Art Gallery
Department of Art
Saint Augustine's College
Raleigh, NC 27611
(919) 828-4451

Selma Burke Gallery
Winston-Salem State University
Winston-Salem, NC 27110

Shaw University Art Gallery
Shaw University Dept. of Art
Raleigh, NC 27602
(919) 755-4845

Ubiquitous Gallery
PO Box 34606
Charlotte, NC 28234-4606
(704) 376-6944

Warehouse Arts
862 W. 4th St.
Winston-Salem, NC 27101-2516
(919) 723-4800

Winston-Salem State University Diggs
601 Martin Luther King, Jr. Dr.
Winston-Salem, NC 27110
(919) 750-2458

Young Men's Institute Cultural Center
PO Box 7301
Asheville, NC 28802
(704) 252-4614

Ohio

African American Museum
1765 Crawford Rd.
Cleveland, OH 44106
(216) 791-1700

Afro-American Cultural Center
Cleveland State University
Black Studies Program
2121 Euclid Ave., UC 103
Cleveland, OH 44115
(216) 687-3655

Art for Community Expressions
772 N. High St.
Columbus, OH 43215
(614) 252-3036

Black Historical Museum of Fashion Dolls, National Association of Fashion and Accessory Designers
2180 E. 93rd St.
Cleveland, OH 44106
(216) 231-0375

Cincinnati Art Museum
Eden Park
Cincinnati, OH 45202-1596
(513) 721-5204
Fax:(513) 721-0129

Karamu House
2355 E. 89th St.
Cleveland, OH 44106
(216) 795-7070

Malcolm Brown Gallery
20100 Chagrin Boulevard
Shaker Heights, Ohio 44122
(216) 751-2955

National Afro-American Museum and Cultural Center
1350 Brush Row Rd.
PO Box 578
Wilberforce, OH 45384
(513) 376-4944
Fax: (513) 376-2007

National Conference of Artists
1624 Grand Ave.
Dayton, OH 45407
(513) 278-6793

Resident Art and Humanities Consortium
1515 Linn St.
Cincinnati, OH 45214
(513) 381-0645

Watkins Academy Museum of Cultural Arts
724 Mineola Ave.
Akron, OH 44320
(216) 864-0673

Oklahoma

Kirkpatrick Center Museum Complex
2100 N.E. 52nd
Oklahoma City, OK 73111
(405) 427-5461

NTU Art Association
2100 N.E. 52nd St.
Oklahoma City, OK 73111
(405) 424-7760

Theater North
PO Box 6255
Tulsa, OK 74148
(918) 587-8937

Pennsylvania

Africamerica Festival
2247 N. Broad
Philadelphia, PA 19132
(215) 232-2900

African American Heritage, Inc.
4601 Market St.
Philadelphia, PA 19139
(215) 748-7817

African Cultural Art Forum
237 S. 60th Street
Philadelphia, PA 19139
(215) 476-0680

Afro-American Historical and Cultural Museum
701 Arch St.
Philadelphia, PA 19106
(215) 574-0380

Minority Arts Resource Council
1421 W. Girard Ave.
Philadelphia, PA 19130
(215) 236-2688

Rhode Island

Rhode Island Black Heritage Society
1 Hilton St.
Providence, RI 02905
(401) 751-3490

South Carolina

Avery Research Center for Afro-American History and Culture
125 Bull St.
College of Charleston
Charleston, SC 29424
(803) 792-5742

I.P. Stanback Museum and Planetarium
South Carolina State College
300 College St., NE
Orangeburg, SC 29117
(803) 536-7174

Mann-Simons Cottage: Museum of African-American Culture
1403 Richland St.
Columbia, SC 29201
(803) 252-1770

The Rice Museum
Intersection of Front and Screven Sts.
PO Box 902
Georgetown, SC 29442
(803) 546-7423
Fax:(803) 533-3624

South Dakota

Black History Museum
508 Cedar St.
Yankton, SD 57078

Tennessee

Black Cultural Exchange Center
1927 Dandridge Ave.
Knoxville, TN 37915
(615) 524-8461

Blues City Cultural Center
415 S. Main
Memphis, TN 38114
(901) 525-3031

Carl Van Vechten Gallery of Fine Arts
Fisk University
Dr D B Todd Boulevard and Jackson St. N.
Nashville, TN 37203
(615) 329-8543

Chattanooga African American Museum
200 E. Martin Luther King, Jr. Boulevard
Chattanooga, TN 37203
(615) 267-1076
Fax:(615)267-1076

Memphis Black Arts Alliance
985 S. Bellevue Boulevard
Memphis, TN 38174
(901) 948-9522

Tennessee State University Institute for African Affairs
Tennessee State University
PO Box 828
Nashville, TN 37209
(615) 320-3035

Texas

African American Cultural Heritage Center
Nolan Estes Educational Plaza
3434 S.R.L. Thornton Fairway
Dallas, TX 75224
(214) 375-7530

African American Museum
PO Box 150153
Dallas, TX 75315
(214) 565-9026
Fax:(214) 421-8204

Black Art Gallery
5408 Almeda Rd.
Houston, TX 77004
(713) 529-7900

Black Arts Alliance
1157 Navasota St.
Austin, TX 78702
(512) 477-9660

Utah

Utah Museum of Fine Arts
101 ACC
University of Utah
Salt Lake City, UT 84122
(801) 581-7332
Fax:(801) 585-5198

Virginia

Alexandria Black History Resource Center
20 N. Washington St.
Alexandria, VA 22314
(703) 838-4577

Black Historical Museum and Cultural Center
122 W. Leigh St.
Richmond, VA 23220
(804) 780-9093

Harrison Museum of African American Culture
523 Harrison Ave.
Roanoke, VA 24016
(703) 345-4818

Task Force of Historical Preservation and Minority Communities
500 N. 3rd St.
Richmond, VA 23219
(804) 788-1709

25

Science and Technology

25

Science and Technology

◆ Early African American Inventors ◆ Early African American Scientists
◆ African Americans in Medicine ◆ African Americans in Air and Space
◆ Modern Contributions to Science and Technology ◆ Discovery Gatekeepers

by Lorna M. Mabunda

America's earliest African American scientists and inventors are largely unknown—their contributions to America buried in anonymity. While Benjamin Banneker's eighteenth-century successes in timepieces and urban planning are known and applauded, numerous achievements of seventeenth- and eighteenth-century blacks in architecture, agriculture, and masonry can not be identified. While historians increasingly recognize that blacks had a significant impact on the design and construction of plantations and public building in the South and that rice farming in the Carolinas might not have been possible without blacks, the individuals who spearheaded these accomplishments remain unknown.

◆ EARLY AFRICAN AMERICAN INVENTORS

Perhaps in science more than in other areas, African Americans have been afforded few sanctioned opportunities to offer contributions. However, sheer will and exceeding intelligence helped a mass of individuals bring their ideas and dreams into the light, creating and perfecting them almost as if racial barriers did not exist. The industrial revolution swept blacks along just as dramatically as it did the white population. Though not all of them became household names, African Americans have made their mark in science and technology. For example, when Alexander Graham Bell invented the telephone, he chose Lewis Latimer, a black man, to draft the plans. Previously, Latimer had been a member of the Edison Pioneers, a group of inventors who worked for Thomas Edison from 1883 to the early 1900s.

One of the earliest stars of science was Benjamin Banneker, a free black who lived in the 1700s. Considered the first black scientist, Banneker's true forte lay in the areas of mathematics and astronomy, both of which he cultivated during his friendship with an influential white Quaker neighbor. In 1754, Banneker constructed what has been considered the first clock made in the United States. Later, Banneker and the Quaker's son were selected to survey the land that evolved into Washington, DC. Thus, not only was Bannker the first black to receive a presidential appointment, he was one of the first African American civil engineers. In the early 1790s, his almanac—a year-long calendar loaded with information such as the best planting times—was published with much success. New editions were issued for a succession of years.

In 1790, the U.S. government passed the U.S. Patent Act, legislation that extended patent rights to inventors, including free blacks. Slaves would not have this right until the passage of the 14th Amendment. In one of history's most absurd bureaucratic fiats, slaves could neither be granted patents nor could they assign patents to their masters. The underlying theory was that since slaves were not citizens they could not enter into contracts with their owners or the government. As a result, the efforts of slaves were dismissed, or when accepted, credited to their masters. One can only speculate on the extent to which slaves were active in invention. For example, Joe Anderson, a slave, was believed to have played a major role in the creation of a grain harvester his master Cyrus McCormick was credited with inventing, but available records are insufficient to determine the degree to which Anderson was involved. Similarly, Benjamin Montgomery, a slave belonging to Confederate President Jefferson Davis is thought to have concocted an improved boat propeller. Since the race of patent-seekers was rarely noted and other black inventions such as ice cream, created by Augustus Jackson of Philadelphia in 1832, were simply never patented, one cannot be sure how many inventions were made by free blacks either.

The first free blacks to have their inventions recorded were Thomas L. Jennings, whose dry-cleaning methodology received patent protection in 1821, and Henry Blair, who invented a seed planter in 1834. Free black Norbert Rillieux patented his sugar refining evaporator, thus revolutionizing the industry. The son of a French planter and a free black woman, Rillieux left his home in New Orleans to study engineering in Paris. After teaching mathematics there for a while, he created his vacuum pan evaporator. With his invention, a single person could do work that once required several people working at once. He returned to the United States and became wealthy as the device was implemented in sugar refineries in his home state and abroad in Cuba and Mexico.

In 1848, free black Lewis Temple invented the toggle-harpoon for killing whales, a major industry at the time. Temple's invention almost completely replaced the type of harpoon formerly used because it greatly diminished the mammal's ability to escape after being hooked. Prior to the Civil War, Henry Boyd created an improved bedframe, and James Foten, one of the few blacks that from era to gain extreme wealth from an invention, produced a device that helped guide ship sails. He used the money he earned in to build a sail factory.

The Reconstruction era unleashed a creativity that had been suppressed in blacks. Between 1870 and 1900, a time when nearly 80 percent of African American adults in the United States were illiterate, blacks were awarded several hundred patents. Many of the grantees were self-taught such as Elijah McCoy. Working as a locomotive fireman on a Michigan line, his job was to lubricate the hot steam engines during frequently scheduled train stops necessitated by the procedure. After years of work, in 1872, McCoy perfected and patented an automatic lubricator that regularly supplied oil, even as a train was in motion. The effect on the increasingly important railway system was profound as conductors were no longer forced to make oiling stops. McCoy adapted his invention for use on ships and in factories. When copycats tried to steal his thunder, the phrase "the real McCoy" came into vogue.

In 1884, Granville T. Woods invented a steam-boiler furnace in his Cincinnati electrical engineering shop. Three years later, Woods patented an "induction telegraphy" or synchronous multiplex railroad telegraph that allowed train personnel to communicate with workers on other trains while in motion. He was also responsible for what later became known as the trolley, when in 1888, he produced an overhead electrical power supply system for streetcars and trains. A prolific inventor, Woods, known as "The Black Edison," created more than 50 valuable inventions, including an airbrake, which he eventually sold to George Westinghouse, and an incubator.

Jan Matzeliger came to the United States from South America in 1877. Living in Lynn, Massachusetts, he obtained work in a shoe factory. There he witnessed the tedious process by which shoe soles were attached to shoe uppers by workers known as hand lasters. For six months he secretly labored at inventing a machine to automate the work. Unsatisfied with his original design, he spent several more years tweaking and perfecting his creation so that by the time he was granted a patent in 1883, the equipment was so successful that manufacturers the world over clamored for the gadgetry.

Progress has been a gift from women as well as men. For example, Sarah Goode is credited with creating a folding cabinet bed in 1996; Sarah Boone invented the ironing board in 1892; and photographer Claytonia Dorticus was granted several patents that were concerned with photographic equipment and developing solutions as well as a shoe dye. But Madame C. J. Walker, often regarded only as an entrepreneur, was one of the most successful female inventors. She developed an entire line of hair care products and cosmetics for blacks, claiming that her first idea had come to her in a dream.

During the next few years, Garret Morgan patented a succession of products, including a hair straightening solution that was still a best-seller in as late as the 1970s; a gas mask, or "breathing device" for firefighters, and an improved traffic signal. Morgan tried to pass himself off as Native American, but once his identity as a black man was discovered several of his purchase orders were canceled.

Nonetheless, the early inventors paved the way for future African Americans. All these men as well as the countless unknown ones were forced to endure the byproducts of racism. Whites were oftentimes hesitant to buy black inventions unless the smell of eventual monetary gains was too strong. McCoy, Woods, and several others died poor, although their creations sold like wildfire.

◆ EARLY AFRICAN AMERICAN SCIENTISTS

The contributions of African American scientists are better known than those of black inventors, partly

George Washington Carver

ever recipient of a Spingarn Medal in 1915, his first paper was published as "The Relation of First Cleavage Plane to the Entrance Point of the Sperm" in 1912. The work showed how the location of cell division in the marine worm *Nereis* is determined by the sperm's entry point on an egg. Teaching at Howard for several years, Just had a tenuous relationship with the school, paving the way for him to accept an offer to conduct research at the Kaiser Wilhelm Institute for Biology in Berlin, Germany. The first American to be invited to the internationally respected institution, he remained there from 1929 to 1933, at which point the Nazi regime was surging to power. Because he preferred working abroad to being shut out of the best laboratories in the United States on the basis of race, Just spent the rest of his career in France, Italy, Spain, and Portugal.

Blacks have had successes in the hard sciences, engineering, and mathematics as well. In 1876, Edward Bouchet became the first African American to earn a doctorate from a university in the United States, when he acquired a Ph.D in physics from Yale. In the twentieth century, Elmer Samuel Imes, husband of Harlem Renaissance writer Nella Larsen, received a doctorate in physics from the University of Michigan in 1918. In his dissertation, Imes took the works of white scientists Albert Einstein, Ernest Rutherford, and Niels Bohr, one step further, definitively establishing that quantum theory applied to the rotational states of molecules. His efforts would later play a role in space science, thus making Imes the first African American astro-industrial physicist.

Chemist Percy Julian carved a brilliant career for himself after obtaining a doctorate from Switzerland's University of Vienna in 1931. His specialty was creating synthetic versions of expensive drugs. Much of his work later in life was conducted at his Julian Research Institute in Franklin Park, Illinois. In the 1940s, another scientist, Benjamin Peery, switched his focus from aeronautical engineering to physics while still and undergraduate at the University of Minnesota. After garnering a Ph.D from the University of Michigan, Peery went on to a lengthy career teaching astronomy at Indiana University, the University of Illinois, and Howard University.

because of the recognition awarded to George Washington Carver, an agriculturalist, who, incidentally, refused to patent most of his inventions. Born into slavery in 1864, Carver was the first black to graduate from Iowa Agricultural State College, where he studied botany and agriculture. One year after earning a master's degree, Carver joined the Tuskegee Institute's agriculture department. In his role as department head, he engineered a number of experimental farming techniques that had practical applications for farmers in the area. His ideas, from crop rotation to replenish nutrient-starved soil to his advocacy of peanuts as a cash crop, Carver left an indelible mark in his field. An inventor at heart, he was behind the genesis of innumerable botanical products, by-products, and even recipes. Recognition of his efforts came in several forms, including induction into England's Royal Society of Arts and Manufacturing and Commerce in 1916. In 1923, he received an NAACP Spingarn Medal. Six years after his death, in 1949, Carver was the subject of a U.S. Postal Stamp.

Born approximately ten years before Carver earned his bachelor's degree, Ernest Everett Just was a pioneering marine biologist who had graduated *magna cum laude* from Dartmouth College in 1907. The first-

Between 1875 and 1943, only eight blacks were awarded doctorates in pure mathematics. One, David Blackwell, became the first black tenured professor at the University of California at Berkeley in 1955. An expert in statistics and probability, he has been a trailblazer despite a racially motivated setback he incurred soon after completing his doctoral work at the University of Illinois. Nominated for a Rosenwald fellowship from the Institute for Advanced Study at Princeton University, Blackwell was rejected because of his race. Undaunted, he went on to become the only African American mathe-

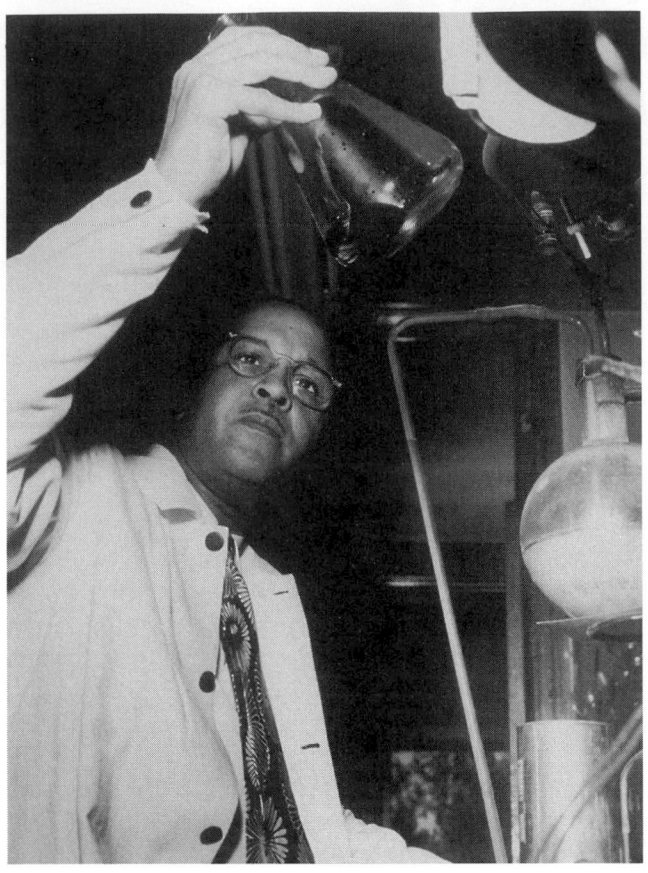

Dr. Percy Julian

matician to be elected into the National Academy of Sciences.

◆ AFRICAN AMERICANS IN MEDICINE

The medical profession has spawned a number of African Americans of high stature. As early as the 1860s, blacks had entered medical schools in the North and had gone on to practice as full-fledged physicians. In fact, during the Civil War, Dr. Alexander T. Augusta was named head of a Union army hospital and Rebecca Lee became the first female African American doctor by attending the New England Female Medical College in Boston. She was able to attend on a scholarship she received from Ohio Senator Benjamin Wade, an abolitionist. She used her schooling to provide health care to former slaves in the former confederate capital of Richmond, Virginia. Her 1883 *Book of Medical Discourses* taught women how to address their own health issues as well as those of their children.

Rebecca J. Cole was the second black woman to become a physician and the first African American graduate of the Woman's Medical College of Pennsylva-

nia. For the next 50 years she devoted her life to improving the lot of the poor. Her positions included performing a residency at the New York Infirmary for Women and Children and running Washington, DC's Government House for Children and Old Women and Philadelphia's Woman's Directory, a medical aid center.

In 1867, Susan McKinney Steward began studying at the New York Medical College for Women. Three years later she earned the distinction of being the third black female physician. Practicing in New York State, she specialized in homeopathic treatments and had black and white patients of both genders as clients. After opening a second office in New York City, she helped cofound the Brooklyn Woman's Homeopathic Hospital and Dispensary. She also served at the Brooklyn Home for Aged Colored People. A true humanitarian, Steward vigorously supported women's suffrage movement and conducted missionary work with her second husband, a chaplain for the Buffalo Soldier regiment. She ended her career by taking on the role of school doctor at Wilberforce University.

In 1868, Howard University opened its College of Medicine, the first black medical school in the country. The school nearly failed five years later when monetary problems arose and salaries for faculty were unavailable. Thanks to the efforts of Dr. Charles Parvis, who convinced the school to let him and his peers continue teaching on a nonpaid basis, the school survived the crisis. Parvis was later appointed chief surgeon of Washington, DC's Freedman's Hospital, a black institution, by U.S. president Chester Arthur. Parvis was thus the first African American to run a civilian hospital. He did so until 1894, when he began a private practice.

Meanwhile, Nashville's Meharry Medical College had emerged in 1876. Despite the decidedly low number of jobs for African American physicians who were routinely turned away from nearly every facility other than Freedman's Hospital, the school was a welcome addition to the slowly developing progress sought by black physicians, including Dr. Daniel Hale Williams, who replaced Parvis at Freedman's. Williams restored Freedman's to good health through internships, better nurses' training, and the addition of horse-drawn ambulances.

Williams had graduated from the Chicago Medical College in 1883 and entered into private practice almost immediately. Business was slow until 1890, when he met Emma Reynolds, an aspiring black nurse, whose skin color had kept her from gaining admission to any of the nursing schools in Chicago. Inspired by her unfortunate dilemma, Williams decided to operate his own hospital in hopes of initiating his own program for aspiring nurses. With 12 beds, Provident Hospital became the first black-operated facility in the United States, and Reynolds was the first to enroll in Williams's classes. Near the end of his career, Williams was appointed the first African American associate surgeon at Chicago's St. Luke Hospital and later was the only black charter member of the American College of Surgeons. During his career, Williams helped convince 40 hospitals to treat black patients.

Blacks in the South also received improved care in the late 1890s thanks to a dedicated black physician. In 1893, Alice Woodby McKane and her spouse, also a doctor, founded the first black-run health care center—a hospital, dispensary, and nursing school—in Savannah, Georgia. McKane had obtained her medical degree one-year earlier form the Woman's Medical College of Pennsylvania. Later the couple set up shop in Monrovia, Liberia, repeating their U.S. accomplishments.

Progress moved westward as another black woman used her training to benefit the region's black population though her patients transcended all racial barriers. From 1902 until nearly 50 years later, Denver's "Baby Doctor," Justina Ford, proudly served her community as the only black physician in Colorado. An obstetrician, she delivered more than 7,000 babies, making house calls whenever necessary.

Back East, Freedman's was the training ground for future head trauma authority Dr. Louis Wright, a Harvard Medical School graduate whose high academic standing meant nothing to Boston area hospitals that refused to hire blacks. When World War I erupted, Wright enlisted and found himself in charge of his unit's surgical ward. After the war, Wright, who had received a Purple Heart, became the first black physician to work in a New York City hospital when he was appointed to Harlem Hospital in 1919. Later he became directory of surgery, president of the medical board, and was admitted to the American College of Surgeons. Four years before his death in 1952, he founded the Cancer Research Foundation at Harlem Hospital. The son of two physicians, his father and his stepfather, the latter of whom was the first black graduate of Yale Medical School, Wright had two daughters who continued the family legacy by becoming doctors.

An almost legendary legacy was created by Dr. Charles R. Drew, a star high school athlete whose interest lay in medicine. A pathologist and expert on blood transfusions, Drew discovered that blood plasma was easier to store than whole blood. His experiments helped him become the first African American to receive a medical doctorate in 1940. During World War II, he helped Great Britain develop a national blood collection program and was later asked to do the same for the U.S. Armed

Forces. Unfortunately racism reared its ugly head again—black donors were first completely excluded from the program and later were only allowed to donate to other black servicemen. Frustrated, Drew withdrew from the program, briefly resuming his teaching career at Howard before joining the staff of Freedman's Hospital as medical director.

Howard continued developing new talents, however. Dr. Roland Scott, a physician at Howard University's College of Medicine, became a pioneer in the study and treatment of sickle cell anemia. His research was pivotal in drawing public attention to the disorder and prompting the U.S. government to devote money to more extensive study. Under the Sickle Cell Anemia Control Act passed in 1972, Congress forced the National Institutes of Health to set up treatment centers for patients. Scott was named director of the program that involved screening as well as treatment for those already afflicted.

◆ AFRICAN AMERICANS IN AIR AND SPACE

In 1920, Texan Bessie Coleman learned to fly at the École d'Aviation des Freres in France following a string of rejections from aviation schools in the United States. Having completed seven months of instruction and a rigorous qualifying exam, she earned her international aviator's license from the Federation Aeronautique Internationale the following year and went on to study further with aircraft designer Anthony H. G. Fokker. Known to an admiring public as "Queen Bess," Bessie Coleman was the first black woman ever to fly an airplane, the first African American to earn an international pilot's license, and the first black female stunt pilot. During her brief yet distinguished career as a performance flier, she appeared at air shows and exhibitions across the country, earning wide recognition for her aerial skill, dramatic flair, and tenacity. The tragic demise of the professional aviatrix occurred in 1926, when she was scheduled to parachute jump from a speeding plane at 2,500 feet. Ten minutes after take-off, however, the plane careened wildly out of control, flipping over and dropping Coleman, who plunged 500 feet to her death. Though he remained in the aircraft, the pilot, too, was instantly killed as the plane crashed to the ground. Later a service wrench mistakenly left behind in the engine was found to have been the cause of the accident.

Six years later, in 1932, pilot James Herman Banning and mechanic Thomas C. Allen flew from Los Angeles to New York City in 41 hours and 27 minutes. The transcontinental flight was followed by the first round-trip transcontinental flight the next year. That feat was accomplished by Albert Ernest Forsythe and Charles Alfred Anderson, who flew from Atlantic City to Los Angeles and back in 11 days, foreshadowing the advent of commericial flight.

Willa Brown-Chappell became the first black woman to hold a commercial pilot's license in the United States in 1934. Also the first African American woman to ascend to the rank of lieutenant, which she did as a member of the Civil Air Patrol Squadron; Brown-Chappell founded the National Airmen's Association of America, the first aviators group for blacks. With her husband, Cornelius R. Coffey, she established the first black-owned flying school—Coffey School of Aeronautics—and the first African American-owned school to receive certification from the Civil Aviation Authority. Brown-Chappell became the first African American member of the Federal Aviation Agency's Women's Advisory Council in 1972.

The second African American woman to earn a full commercial pilot's license was Janet Harmon Bragg, a Georgian nurse who took an interest in flying when she began dating Johnny Robinson, one of the first black aviation instructors. The first woman of any race to be admitted to Chicago's Curtiss Wright Aeronautical University, she was initially denied her commercial license despite having successfully fulfilled all preliminary requirements, including the airborne portion of the test. Her white instructor from the Federal Aviation Administration made it quite clear, however, that he would not grant a license to a black woman. Rather than give up, Bragg merely tested again with another instructor the same year and was granted her license in 1942. Along with a small group of black aviation devotees, she formed the Challengers Air Pilots Association (CAPA). Together, members of CAPA opened an airport in Robins, Illinois, the first owned and operated by African Americans.

Other black notables in the field of aviation include Perry H. Young, who, in 1957 became the first black pilot for a scheduled passenger commercial airline; New York Airways; Otis B. Young, Jr., who, in 1970, was the first African American pilot of a jumbo jet; and former naval pilot Jill Brown, who became the first black female to pilot for a major airline in 1987.

Military men were the first blacks to enter into the line of space exploration. In 1961, U.S. Air Force Captain Edward Dwight was invited by President John F. Kennedy to apply to test-pilot school. Two years later, Dwight was in the midst of spaceflight training when Kennedy was assassinated. Without the president's support, Dwight was pretty much ignored by National Aeronautics and Space Administration (NASA). Air Force Major Robert H. Lawrence thus became the first African American astronaut a few years later. A doctor of nuclear chemistry, Lawrence was killed in a plane crash in December of 1967, just six months after his selection by NASA. Blacks would not make in-roads in space until the genesis of the space shuttle program. Grounded African American scientists were prevalent, however.

For example, Katherine Johnson joined the National Advisory Committee on Aeronautics, the precursor to NASA, in 1953. Initially all she was asked to do was basic number crunching, but in a kind of fluke, she spent a short period filling in at the Flight Research Division. There her valued interpretation of data helped in the making of prototype spacecraft, and she soon developed into a sage aerospace technologist. She developed trajectories for the Apollo moon-landing project and devised emergency navigational methods for astronauts. She retired in 1986.

Emergencies of another sort have been tackled by air force flight surgeon Vance Marchbanks, whose research showed that adrenaline levels could affect the exhaustion level of flight crews. His work brought him to the attention of NASA, and he became a medical observer for NASA's Project Mercury. Along with several other personnel scattered about the globe, Marchbanks, stationed in Nigeria, was responsible for monitoring pioneering white astronaut John Glenn's vital signs as he orbited the earth in 1962. Later, Marchbanks received the civilian post of chief of environmental health services for United Aircraft Corporation, where he had a hand in designing the space suit and life-support systems used in the Apollo moon shot.

Also specializing in design, aeronautical test engineer Robert E. Shurney spent nearly his entire career, from 1968 to 1990, at the Marshall Space Flight Center, specializing in design utility. His products included refuse disposal units that stored solids in the bottom and liquid in tubes to prevent any materials from floating openly and contaminating an entire cabin. The units were used in the Apollo program, Skylab, and on the first space shuttle missions. He also crafted strong, yet lightweight aluminum tires for the lunar rover. Much of his experimentation was conducted on KC-135 test planes in order to achieve the condition of "weightlessness."

Assertiveness enabled O. S. Williams to bring forth his own achievements. In 1942, Williams talked his way into employment at Republic Aviation as part of the technical staff. Better known as "Ozzie," he took the experience he earned there to NASA contractor Grumman Corporation. The small rocket engines he codeveloped saved the lives of the Apollo 13 astronauts when the ship's main rocket exploded during flight in 1970.

Three missions later, George Carruthers, a Naval Research Laboratory astrophysicist designed the far-ultraviolet camera/spectograph for use on Apollo 16. The semiautomatic device was able to photograph deep space—regions too far to be captured by regular cameras—once set up on the surface of the moon. Carruthers, who earned a Ph.D in aeronautical and astronautical engineering from the University of Illinois in 1964, was granted his first patent in 1969, for an electromagnetic radiation image converter. He was only 25 years old.

With a 1965 doctorate in atomic and molecular physics from Howard University, Carruther's contemporary, George E. Alcorn, has been one of the most prominent people working with semiconductors and spectrometers. By the early 1990s, he had eight patents to his name, including secret projects concerning missile systems.

In a less clandestine fashion, aerospace engineer Christine Darden has been a leading NASA researcher in supersonic and hypersonic aircraft. Her main goal has been the reduction of sonic boom, a phenomenon that creates an explosive burst of sound that can traumatize those on the ground. Darden works at manipulating an aircraft's wing or the shape of its nose, to try to control the feedback produced by air waves resulting from a plane's flight.

Dealing with people rather than machinery, directory of psychophysiology at NASA's Ames Research Center, Patricia Cowlings credentials are impressive; her postdoctoral work has touched upon such fields as aerospace medicine and bioastronautics. Since the late 1970s, she has assisted astronauts by teaching them autogenic feedback—how to impose mind over matter when zero gravity wreaks havoc with one's system. By studying physical and emotional problems that arise in such a setting, she can seek the cause and prescribe a therapy to alleviate stress. She was also the first woman of any race in the United States to receive astronaut training.

These individuals are joined by numerous others in the field of aviation and space flight, including chemical engineer Henry Allen, Jr., a liquid and solid rocket fuel specialist; missle expert and inventor extraordinaire Otis Boykin; environmental health office Julian Earls; aerospace technologist Isabella J. Coles; astrodynamicist Robert A. Gordon; and operations officer Isaac Gillam, IV, to name a few. Once the space shuttle program began in earnest, however, African Americans also took to the skies.

Traveling in the space shuttle *Challenger*, U.S. Air Force Colonel Guion "Guy" Bluford was the first black to fly in space, where he coordinated experiments and was in charge of deploying satellites. After his first mission in 1983, Bluford participated in three more. The second African American in space, Ronald McNair, was aboard the tragic *Challenger* flight of 1986, his second trip on the shuttle. The vehicle exploded 73 seconds after liftoff, killing all seven crew members. Charles Bolden's first mission was aboard the 1986 flight of the shuttle *Columbia*. He has also flown on the *Discovery*. The first African American to pilot a space shuttle was Frederick Gregory, who did so in 1985, on his very first journey to outer space. A veteran pilot of both helicopters and airplanes, Gregory became an astronaut in 1978. Gregory also made history on his fourth flight, when he commanded the first mission comprised of Russians and Americans. Mae Jemison went into space as a science specialist in 1992's joint U.S.-Japanese Spacelab-J project on the shuttle *Endeavor*. The following year, Bernard Harris took off in the shuttle *Columbia*. He served as a mission specialist in Spacelab-D2 alongside Germans and Americans.

◆ MODERN CONTRIBUTIONS TO SCIENCE AND TECHNOLOGY

The achievements of black inventors and scientists of the mid- to late twentieth century have been obscured by reasons more complex than blatant racial prejudice, among them the advent of government and corporate research and development teams. Such work, whether contracted or direct, often precludes individual recognition, regardless of a person's race. Nonetheless, in the corporate world as well as in academia, African American scientists and engineers play a substantial role in the development of solid state devices, high-powered and ultra fast lasers, hypersonic flight—two to three thousand miles per hour—and elementary particle science. Black engineers employed by NASA in managerial and research positions have made and continue to make considerable contributions.

African American manufacturing and servicing firms in various computer and engineering areas are sprouting and blossoming rapidly. For example, black entrepreneur Marc Hannah has made a niche for himself in the field of computer graphics as confounder of Silicon Graphics Incorporated. Principal scientist and vice president of the innovative company, Hannah has adapted his electrical engineering and computer science knowhow to the medium of motion pictures since 1982. His computer-generated, 3-D special effects have been featured in such major films as *Terminator 2* (1991), *Aladdin* (1992), and *Jurassic Park* (1993).

Academia has more black science and technology faculty members, college presidents, and school of engineering deans than in the past. Many of these academics

Astronauts Guion Bluford, Ronald McNair, and Frederick Gregory, 1978.

are serving in the country's most prestigious institutions. As the United States faces the twenty-first century, a major challenge is being presented by European and Asian nations, with world leadership, maintenance of our position as a world super power, employment for our citizens, and our future standard of living at stake. A response has to come from America's young. In recent years, an increasing number of black students have demonstrated an interest in science. African American scientists and engineers already are an integral part of such institutions the National Aeronautics and Space Administration (NASA) and private research and development organizations such as Bell Laboratories. One area in which African Americans have been faltering, however, is medicine.

In the mid- to late 1990s, the number of black applicants to medical school was declining at an appalling rate. In a field thirsty for candidates, the search for African American physicians-to-be was nearing crisis-level status. The repercussions of this shortage includes difficulty for the poor and elderly in finding black attendants if they so desire. Primary care specialists—internists, pediatricians, obstetricians, gynecologists, etc.—were particularly in demand.

The health care profession began responding to this problem in 1991, when the Association of American Medical Colleges initiated Project 3000 by 2000—the primary aim being to graduate 3,000 minorities by the year 2000. As of 1996, the program was well on its way to success. In particular, Xavier University was the top school in the country for African American placement into medical school, gaining a reputation for placing an average of 70 percent of its premed seniors into medical schools each year. Meanwhile, black doctors already in practice were forming cooperatives amongst themselves in order to serve those African American patients who were discriminated against by Health Maintenance Organizations (HMOs) that considered them too poor or sick to be participants.

Similarly, the National Dental Association (NDA) launched the Networking Action Plan, an initiative aimed at addressing the dental needs of African Americans by emphasizing regular and routine dental care through the 6,000 dentists who are members. A second thrust involved recruiting partnerships with Howard University Dental School and Meharry Medical College in an effort to increase both students and faculty.

The situation is not nearly as dire in engineering, perhaps due in part to a mentoring program established in 1975, by the National Action Council for Minorities in Engineering (NACME). With industry backing, the council has focused on youngsters as early as at the fourth-grade level. More than 4,700 of their students have acquired engineering degrees and their graduates make up ten percent of all engineers from minority groups.

Still, the importance of role models with names and faces can not be overlooked. Some black scientists have entered into the public consciousness; for example, in 1973, Shirley Ann Jackson became the first black woman in the United States to earn a doctorate in theoretical particle physics as well as the first female African American to earn a Ph.D from the prestigious Massachusetts Institute of Technology (MIT). She has had a distinguished career, culminating with her appointment as chairwoman of the Nuclear Regulatory Commission by President Bill Clinton in 1995.

In 1996, Claude A. Verbal became the first African American president of the Society of Automotive Engineers (SAE) International. A General Motors (GM) Service Parts Operations plant manager, the business executive earned his engineering degree from North Carolina State University in 1964.

Another African American rose to the prominent rank of National Science Foundation (NSF) director,

the highest science-related administrative post in the United States. Holder of a physics doctorate from St. Louis' Washington University, Walter Massey was able to create a number of programs to provide science-oriented training to young blacks. During his two-year stint at the NSF, from 1991 to 1993, Massey repeated the kind of success he had had when he began the Inner City Teachers Science program while teaching at Brown University.

In the field of medical research, Charles Whitten founded the National Association for Sickle Cell Disease in 1971. His work has been complemented more recently by Griffin Rodgers, chief of the Molecular Hematology Unit at the National Institutes of Health. In the 1990s, Rodgers was working on an experimental anticancer drug that could possibly provide benefits for sickle cell anemia patients.

Patients with prostate cancer have been encouraged by the work of Detroit-based urologist and oncologist Isaac Powell. In 1995, the Centers for Disease Control and Prevention named his screening program as the outstanding community health project of the year. Powell has been pursuing the idea of advanced diagnostic testing for black men. Through a partnership with the Karmanos Cancer Institute and area churches, nurses, and hospitals, Powell has been able to educate the public about the importance of undergoing prostate cancer screening. Benefitting from a prostate-specific antigen test, patients have had their cancer caught early enough to undergo successful surgery. In 1996, Powell's program was being exported to other cities in the United States.

The cancer research of Jill Bargonetti, a young African American biologist has garnered much attention. She discovered a correlation between a specific gene's ability to bind with the genetic matter known as DNA and its ability to suppress tumors. In 1996, she received a $300,000, 3-year grant from the American Cancer Society and a $200,000, 4-year award from the Department of Defense to pursue her study of breast cancer.

In the early 1990s, Alabama-based rural health-care provider Dr. Regina Benjamin uncovered a 1977 health-clinic law that distributed additional federal monies for qualified practices. Since then, other towns have sought the M.B.A.-holder's advice on how to establish facilities in their own areas.

Outside of medical research, one-time Olympic athlete and physicist Meredith Gourdine earned a Ph.D from the California Institute of Technology in 1960. The Olympic medalist then formed Gourdine Systems, a research and development firm geared towards producing electricity—from chemical and thermal energy or from flowing gas. Though blinded by diabetes in 1973,

Gourdine went on to launch Energy Innovations the next year. An inventor at heart, he has more than 70 patents in his name and was inducted into the Black Inventors Hall of Fame.

The energy of earthquakes motivates geophysicist Waverly Person. His interest in seismology paid off when he was named director of the U.S. Geological Survey's National Earthquake Information Center in 1977. The first African American earthquake scientist, Person is also the first black in more than 30 years to hold such a prominent position in the U.S. Department of the Interior.

Similarly, meteorolgist and climatologist Warren Washington has been concerned with the earth's exterior. Since 1987, the "greenhouse effect" expert has been director of the Climate and Global Dynamics Division of the National Center for Atmospheric Research. After seven years there, he was elected to a one-year term as the first African American president of the American Meteorological Society. Finishing up there, Washington cofounded the Black Environmental Science Trust, introducing black children to the joys of science.

Along with hundreds of other notable blacks, African American scientists have been working towards restoring scientific education at all levels. Their presence, whether inside or outside of the public eye, is felt. Younger blacks who learn of their endeavors are thus encouraged to free their creative science minds.

◆ DISCOVERY GATEKEEPERS

Archie Alexander 1887-1958
Civil Engineer

Born in 1887, in Ottumwa, Iowa, Archie Alphonso Alexander graduated from the University of Iowa with a B.S. degree in civil engineering in 1912. During his collegiate years he was a star football player who earned the nickname "Alexander the Great" on the playing field. His first job was as a design engineer for the Marsh Engineering Company, which specialized in building bridges. Two years later, in 1914, Alexander formed his own company, A. A. Alexander, Inc. Most of the firm's contracts were for bridges and sewer systems. So successful was he that the NAACP awarded him its Spingarn Medal in 1928. The following year, he and formed Alexander and Repass with a former classmate. Alexander's new company was also responsible for building tunnels, railroad trestles, viaducts, and power plants. Some of Alexander's biggest accomplishments include the Tidal Basin Bridge and K Street Freeway in Washington, DC; a heating plant for his alma mater, the University of Iowa; a civilian airfield in Tuskegee, Alabama; and a sewage-disposal plant in Grand Rapids, Michigan.

A member of Kappa Alpha Psi, Alexander was awarded their "Laurel Wreath" for great accomplishment in 1925. Alexander received honorary civil engineering degrees from the University of Iowa in 1925 and Howard University in 1946. The following year, Alexander was named one of the University of Iowa's outstanding alumni and "one of the first hundred citizen of merit." Politically active, Alexander was appointed Governor of the Virgin Islands in 1954 by President Dwight Eisenhower though he was forced to resign one year later due to health problems. He died at his home in Des Moines, Iowa in 1958.

Benjamin Banneker 1731-1806
Mathematician/Statistician, Astronomer, Surveyor/ Explorer, Publisher

Benjamin Banneker was born on November 9, 1731 in Ellicott, Maryland. His mother was a free woman and his father was a slave, who ultimately purchased his own freedom. At the age of 21, Banneker constructed a clock based upon a pocket watch he had seen, calculating the ratio of the gears and wheels and carving them from wood. The clock operated for more than 40 years.

Banneker's aptitude for mathematics and knowledge of astronomy enabled him to predict the solar eclipse of 1789. Within a few years, he began publishing an almanac which contained tide tables, data on future eclipses, and a listing of useful medicinal products and formulas. The almanac, which was the first scientific book published by an African American, appeared annually for more than a decade.

Banneker served as a surveyor on the six-person team that helped lay out the base lines and initial boundaries for Washington, DC. When the chairman of the committee, Major Pierre Charles L'Enfant, abruptly resigned and returned to France with his plans, Banneker was able to reproduce the plans in their entirety. He died on October 9, 1806.

Andrew Jackson Beard 1850-1910
Railroad Porter, Inventor

While working in an Alabama railroad yard, Beard had seen men lose hands, even arms, in accidents occurring during the manual coupling of railroad cars. The system in use involved the dropping of a metal pin into place when two cars crashed together. Men were often caught between cars and crushed to death during this split-second operation. Beard's invention, the "Jenny Coupler" (patent 594,059), was an automatic device which secured two cars by merely bumping them together. In 1897 Beard received $50,000 for an invention which has since prevented the death or maiming of countless railroad men.

Henry Blair 1804-1860
Farmer, Inventor

Maryland native Henry Blair was one the first black inventors to receive a U.S. patent. He was granted a patent for a corn-planting machine in 1834, and two years later, a second patent for a similar device used in planting cotton. In the registry of the Patent Office, Blair was designated "a colored man" the only instance of identification by race in these early records. Since slaves could not legally obtain patents, Blair was evidently a free man.

Guion Stewart Bluford, Jr. 1942-
Space/Atmospheric Scientist, Aerospace Engineer, Air Force Officer, Airplane Pilot

Guy Bluford was born November 22, 1942, in Philadelphia. He graduated with a B.S. from Pennsylvania State University in 1964. He then enlisted in the U.S. Air Force and was assigned to pilot training at Williams Air Force Base in Arizona. Bluford served as a fighter pilot in Vietnam and flew 144 combat missions, 65 of them over North Vietnam. Attaining the rank of lieutenant colonel, Bluford received an M.S. from the Air Force Institute of Technology in 1974 and a Ph.D. in aeronautical engineering in 1978.

In 1979, Bluford was accepted in NASA's astronaut program as a mission specialist. On August 30, 1983, with the lift-off of the STS-8 Orbiter *Challenger* Bluford became the first African American in space. He flew two other space shuttle missions in 1985 and 1991 for a total of 314 hours in space. Bluford retired from NASA in 1993 to pursue a career in private industry.

Bluford has won numerous awards including the Distinguished National Science Award given by the National Society of Black Engineers (1979), NASA Group Achievement Award (1980, 1981), NASA Space Flight Medal (1983), and the NAACP Image Award in 1983. Some of his military honors include the National Defense Service Medal (1965), Vietnam Campaign Medal (1967), Air Force Commendation Medal (1972), Air Force Meritorious Service Award (1978), and the USAF Command Pilot Astronaut Wings (1983).

Charles Frank Bolden, Jr. 1946-
Airplane Pilot, Space/Atmospheric Scientist, Marine Officer, Operations and Systems Researcher/Analyst

A graduate of the U.S. Naval Academy and the University of Southern California, Charles Bolden, Jr., has a bachelor of science degree in electrical science and a master of science degree in systems management. Bolden began his career as a second lieutenant in the U.S. Marine Corps, becoming a naval aviator by 1970. In 1973, he flew more than 100 sorties while assigned in

Major Charles Bolden

Thailand. Upon return to the United States, Bolden began a tour as a Marine Corps selection and recruiting officer. In 1979, he graduated from the U.S. Naval Test Pilot School, and was assigned to the Naval Test Aircraft Directorates.

Bolden was selected as an astronaut candidate by NASA in May of 1980, and in July of 1981 completed the training and evaluation program—making him eligible for assignment as a pilot on space shuttle flight crews. Bolden has served as pilot for the Hubble Space Telescope mission and was commander of the first American-Russian space shuttle mission. In 1994, he accepted a position at the Naval Academy. Bolden has been awarded the Defense Superior Service Medal, the Defense Meritorious Service Medal, the Air Medal, and the Strike/Flight Medal.

Marjorie Lee Browne 1914-1979
Mathematician/Statistician, Educator

Browne was born September 9, 1914 in Memphis, Tennessee. She received a B.S. in mathematics from Howard University in 1935, an M.S. from the University of Michigan in 1939, and a Ph.D. in mathematics, again from the University of Michigan, in 1949. Browne taught at the University of Michigan in 1947 and 1948. She accepted the post of Professor of Mathematics at North Carolina Central University in 1949 and became department chairperson in 1951.

Browne's doctoral dissertation dealt with topological and matrix groups and she was published in the *American Mathematical Monthly*. She was a Fellow of the National Science Foundation in 1958-59 and again in 1965-66. Browne was a member of the American Mathematical Society, the Mathematical Association of America, and the Society for Industrial and Applied Mathematics. She died in 1979.

George E. Carruthers 1940-
Physicist

Dr. George Carruthers is one of the two naval research laboratory people responsible for the *Apollo* 16 lunar surface ultraviolet camera/spectrograph, which was placed on the lunar surface in April 1972. It was Carruthers who designed the instrument while William Conway adapted the camera for the lunar mission. The spectrographs, obtained from 11 targets, include the first photographs of the ultraviolet equatorial bands of atomic oxygen that girdle the earth.

Carruthers, born on Chicago's south side in 1940, built his first telescope at the age of ten. He received his Ph.D. in physics from the University of Illinois in 1964, the same year that he started employment with the Navy. Carruthers is the recipient of the NASA Exceptional Scientific Achievement medal for his work on the ultraviolet camera/spectrograph.

Ben Carson 1951-
Neurosurgeon

Born Benjamin Solomon Carson on September 18, 1951, in Detroit, Michigan, Dr. Carson has been recognized throughout the medical community for his prowess in performing complex neurosurgical procedures, particularly on children. Pediatric brain tumors have

been his main focus. Among his accomplishments are a number of faultless hemispherectomies, a process in which a portion of the brain of a critically ill seizure victim or other neurologically diseased patient is removed to restore normal functioning. Carson's most famous operation took place in 1987, earning him international acclaim. That year he successfully separated a pair of West German Siamese or conjoined twins, who had been attached at the backs of their heads. The landmark operation took 22 hours; Carson led a surgical team of 70 doctors, nurses, and technicians. Since then, he has saved thousands of childrens' lives worldwide.

Carson was raised in Detroit. A trouble-maker—he almost killed a peer during a knife fight when he was 14 years old—and a failing student, his mother imposed a reading program on him and limited his television viewing until his grades improved. In high school, he continued to excel and was accepted at Yale University in 1969, with a scholarship, when he had graduated. With a B.A. from that Ivy League institution, Carson entered the University of Michigan, where he obtained his M.D. in 1977. For one year he served as a surgical intern at the Johns Hopkins Hospital, later doing his residency there as well. From 1983 to 1984, Carson practiced at the Sir Charles Gairdner Hospital in Perth, Australia. In 1984, at 33 years of age, he became the youngest chief of pediatric neurosurgery in the United States. Then, in 1985, Johns Hopkins named him director of pediatric neurosurgery. In the mid-1990s, he was an associate professor neurosurgery, plastic surgery, and oncology at the Johns Hopkins School of Medicine in addition to his duties at the hospital. In 1996, Carson, who penned an autobiography called *Gifted Hands*, was in the midst of establishing a scholarship fund, USA Scholars Program, with the aid of his wife.

George Washington Carver 1864-1943
Educator, Agricultural/Food scientist, Farmer, Maid/ Housekeeper

George Washington Carver devoted his life to research projects connected primarily with southern agriculture. The products he derived from the peanut and the soybean revolutionized the economy of the South by liberating it from an excessive dependence on cotton.

Born a slave on January 5, 1864 in Diamond Grove, Missouri, Carver was only an infant when he and his mother were abducted from his owner's plantation by a band of slave raiders. His mother was sold and shipped away, but Carver was ransomed by his master in exchange for a race horse.

While working as a farm hand, Carver managed to obtain a high school education. He was admitted as the first black student of Simpson College, Indianola, Iowa.

George Washington Carver

He then attended Iowa Agricultural College (now Iowa State University) where, while working as the school janitor, he received a degree in agricultural science in 1894. Two years later he received a master's degree from the same school and became the first African American to serve on its faculty. Within a short time his fame spread, and Booker T. Washington offered him a post at Tuskegee.

Carver revolutionized the southern agricultural economy by showing that 300 products could be derived from the peanut. By 1938, peanuts had become a $200 million industry and a chief product of Alabama. Carver also demonstrated that 100 different products could be derived from the sweet potato.

Although he did hold three patents, Carver never patented most of the many discoveries he made while at Tuskegee, saying "God gave them to me, how can I sell them to someone else?" In 1938 he donated over $30,000 of his life's savings to the George Washington Carver Foundation and willed the rest of his estate to the organization so his work might be carried on after his death. He died on January 5, 1943.

W. Montague Cobb 1903-1990
Anthropologist, Organization Executive/Founder, Medical Researcher, Educator, Editor

W. Montague Cobb was born on October 12, 1903, in Washington, DC. For 51 years he was a member of the Howard University Medical School faculty, and thousands of medical and dental students studied under his

direction. At Howard, he built a collection of more than 600 documented skeletons and a comparative anatomy museum in the gross anatomy laboratory. In addition to a B.A. from Amherst College, an M.D. from Howard University, and a doctorate from Case Western Reserve, he received many honorary degrees. Cobb died on November 20, 1990, in Washington, DC.

As editor of the *Journal of the National Medical Association* for 28 years, Cobb developed a wide range of scholarly interests manifested by the nearly 700 published works under his name in the fields of medical education, anatomy, physical anthropology, public health and medical history. He was the first African American elected to the presidency of the American Association of Physical Anthropologists and served as the chairman of the anthropology section of the American Association for the Advancement of Science. Among his many scientific awards is the highest award given by the American Association of Anatomists. For 31 years was a member of the board of directors of the NAACP and served as the president of the board for many years.

Price M. Cobbs 1928-
Psychiatrist, Author, Management Consultant

Cobbs was born in Los Angeles, California, in 1928, and followed in his father's footsteps when he enrolled in medical school after earning a B.A. from the University of California at Berkeley. He graduated from Meharry Medical College in 1958 and within a few years had established his own San Francisco practice in psychiatry.

With his academic colleague at the University of California, William H. Grier, Cobbs authored the groundbreaking 1968 study *Black Rage*. In it, the authors argued that a pervasive social and economic racism had resulted in an endemic anger that stretched across all strata of African American society, from rich to poor; this anger was both apparent—and magnified by—the social unrest of the 1960s. Cobbs and Grier also co-authored a second book, *The Jesus Bag*, that discussed the role of organized religion in the African American community.

A seminar Cobbs held in 1967 with other mental health care professionals eventually led him to found his own diversity training company, Pacific Management Systems (PMS). Since its inception, the company has been instrumental in providing sensitivity training for Fortune 500 companies, community groups, law enforcement bodies, and social service agencies. A member of numerous African American professional and community organizations as well as an assistant clinical professor at the University of California at San Francisco, Cobbs continues to guide PMS well into its third decade, a firm that has pioneered the concept of ethnotherapy, which uses the principles of group therapy to help seminar participants rethink their attitudes toward members of other ethnic groups, the disabled, and those of alternative sexual orientations.

Elbert Frank Cox 1895-1969
Educator, Mathematician/Statistician

Cox was born in Evansville, Indiana on December 5, 1895. He received his B.A. from Indiana University in 1917 and his Ph.D. from Cornell University in 1925. His dissertation dealt with polynomial solutions and made Cox the first African American to be awarded a doctorate in pure mathematics. Cox was an instructor at Shaw University (1921-1923), a professor in physics and mathematics at West Virginia State College (1925-1929) and an associate professor of mathematics at Howard University from 1929 to 1947. In 1947, he was made full professor; he retired in 1966.

During his career, Cox speicalized in interpolation theory and differential equations.. Cox was a Brooks Fellow (1924, 1925) and an Erastus Brooks Fellow. He belonged to the Mathematical Society and the Physical Society. Cox died in 1969.

Ulysses Grant Dailey 1885-1961
Editor, Health Administrator, Organization Executive/Founder, Diplomat

From 1908 to 1912, Ulysses Grant Dailey served as surgical assistant to Dr. Daniel Hale Williams, founder of Provident Hospital and noted heart surgeon. Born in Donaldsonville, Louisiana, in 1885, Dailey graduated in 1906 from Northwestern University Medical School, where he was appointed a demonstrator in anatomy. He later studied in London, Paris, and Vienna and in 1926 set up his own hospital and sanitarium in Chicago. His name soon became associated with some of the outstanding achievements being made in anatomy and surgery.

An associate editor of the *Journal of the National Medical Association* for many years, Dailey traveled around the world in 1933 under the sponsorship of the International Collége of Surgeons, of which he was a founder fellow. In 1951, and again in 1953, the U.S. State Department sent him to Pakistan, India, Ceylon, and Africa. One year later he was named honorary consul to Haiti.

Charles Richard Drew 1904-1950
Educator, Medical Researcher, Health Administrator, Surgeon/Physician

Using techniques already developed for separating and preserving blood, Charles Drew pioneered further into the field of blood preservation and organized proce-

dures from research to a clinical level, leading to the founding of blood banks just prior to World War II. Born on June 3, 1904 in Washington, DC, Drew graduated from Amherst College in Massachusetts, where he received the Messman Trophy for having brought the most honor to the school during his four years there. He was not only an outstanding scholar but the captain of the track team and a star halfback on the football team.

After receiving his medical degree from McGill University in 1933, Drew returned to Washington, DC, to teach pathology at Howard. In 1940, while taking his D.Sc. degree at Columbia University, he wrote a dissertation on "banked blood" and soon became such an expert in this field that the British government called upon him to set up the first blood bank in England.

During World War II, Drew was appointed director of the American Red Cross blood donor project. Later, he served as chief surgeon at Freedmen's Hospital in Washington, DC as well as professor of surgery at Howard University Medical School from 1941-1950. He was killed in an automobile crash on April 1, 1950.

Joycelyn Elders 1933-
Physician, Endocrinologist, Former U.S. Surgeon General

Dr. Joycelyn Elders was born Joycelyn Minnie Jones, on August 13, 1933, in Schall, Arkansas. The first of eight children, she grew up working in cotton fields. An avid reader, Jones earned a scholarship to the all-black, Philander Smith College in Little Rock, after graduating from high school. Jones studied biology and chemistry in hopes of becoming a lab technician. She was inspired towards greater ambitions after meeting Edith Irby Jones (no relation), the first African American to study at the University of Arkansas School of Medicine. After obtaining her B.A., Jones served as a physical therapist in the U.S. Army in order to fund her post-graduate education. She was able to enroll in the University of Arkansas School of Medicine herself in 1956. However, as the only black woman and one of only three African American students, she and the other two blacks were forced to use a separate university dining facility—the one provided for the cleaning staff.

Having married Oliver B. Elders in 1960, the newly dubbed Joycelyn Elders fulfilled a pediatric internship at the University of Minnesota, then returned to Little Rock in 1961 for a residency at the University of Arkansas Medical Center. Her success in the position led her to be appointed chief pediatric resident, in charge of the all-white, all-male battery of residents and interns. During the next 20 years, Elders forged a successful clinical practice, specializing in pediatric endocrinology, the study of glands. She published more than 100 papers in that period and rose to professor of pediatrics, a position she maintained from 1976 until 1987, when she was named director of the Arkansas Department of Health.

Over the course of her career, Elders's focus shifted somewhat from diabetes in children to sexual behavior. At the Department of Health, Elders was able to pursue her public advocacy in regards to teenage pregnancy and sexually transmitted diseases. Under Elders, 18 school clinics were opened with the mission bringing sex education to the youth. In 1989, her lobbying efforts finally paid off, and the Arkansas State Legislature mandated a kindergarten to 12th grade course curriculum encompassing instruction in hygiene, substance-abuse prevention, elevation of self-esteem, and contraceptive responsibility for males as well as females.

In 1993, U.S. president Bill Clinton nominated Elders for the U.S. surgeon general post, making her the second African American and the fifth woman to hold the cabinet position. Though her confirmation was not un-challenged—many decried her liberal stance—she was formally voted into approval for the position by the Senate on September 7, 1993. Within six months, Elders's first annual Surgeon General's Report was issued under the title, "Preventing Tobacco Use Among Young People." The effort was historical in that it was the first to focus just on kids.

During her short-lived tenure, Elders would do just that, i.e. advocating for children as well as for the poor. She attacked Medicaid for failing to help poverty-stricken women prevent unwanted pregnancies and faulted pharmaceutical companies for overpricing contraceptives. Between 1993 and December of 1994, Elders spoke out in support of the medicinal use of marijuana, in favor of studying drug legalization, family planning and against toy guns for children. Many of her stances were deemed controversial by conservative factions, but the biggest flak occurred when Elders was reported to have recommended that masturbation be discussed in schools as part of human sexuality. She was forced to resignation by Clinton in December of 1994.

Elders returned to the University of Arkansas Medical School, though the state's General Assembly budget committee tried to block her return. There she resumed teaching. In 1995, she was hosting a daily talk show on AM stations KYSG in Little Rock and WERE in Cleveland.

Helene D. Gayle 1955-
Epidemiologist, AIDS Researcher

Helene Gayle was born in 1955 in Buffalo, New York, the third of five children of an entrepreneur father and social worker mother; her brother would also go on to become a doctor. After graduating from Barnard Col-

lege in 1976, she then won acceptance to the University of Pennsylvania's medical school.

Having heard a speech once on the cure of smallpox inspired Gayle to pursue public health medicine, and her direction would prove a significant one in the years to come as the plague of AIDS came to decimate communities across the globe. She received her medical school degree from University of Pennsylvania as well as an M.A. in public health from Johns Hopkins both in 1981. After a residency in pediatrics, she was selected to enter the epidemiology training program in 1984 at the Centers for Disease Control in Atlanta, Georgia, the nation's top research center for infectious diseases.

For much of the 1980s Gayle was intensely involved in the CDC's research into AIDS and HIV infection through her work first in the center's Epidemic Intelligence Service and later as a chief of international AIDS research, a capacity in which she oversaw the scientific investigations of over three hundred CDC researchers. The physician has been instrumental in raising public awareness about the disease, and is especially driven to point out how devastating AIDS has been to the black community. Sex education, better health care for the poor, and substance abuse prevention are some of the proposals Gayle has championed that she believes will help reduce deaths from AIDS.

In 1992 Gayle was hired as a medical epidemiologist and researcher for the AIDS division of the U.S. Agency for International Development, cementing the physician's reputation as one of the international community's top AIDS scientists.

Evelyn Boyd Glanville 1924-
Author, Educator, Lecturer

Born in 1924, Glanville attended Smith College from 1941 to 1946 and earned an A.B. and an M.A. in mathematics. She received a Ph.D. from Yale University in 1949. She was the first African American woman to be awarded a Ph.D. in pure mathematics. Glanville's first teaching position was as an instructor at New York University (1949-1950). She moved to Fisk University where she was an assistant professor (1950-1952) and then to the University of Southern California as a lecturer (1961-1973). Since then she has been an associate professor at California State University. Glanville is the author of *Theory of Applications of Math for Teachers*.

Frederick Drew Gregory 1941-
Airplane Pilot, Air Force Officer

Gregory was born January 7, 1941 in Washington, DC. He is the nephew of the late Dr. Charles Drew, noted African-American blood plasma specialist. Under the sponsorship of United States Representative Adam Clayton Powell, Gregory attended the U.S. Air Force Academy and graduated with a B.S. in 1964. In 1977, he received an M.S.A. from George Washington University.

Gregory was a helicopter and fighter pilot for the USAF from 1965 to 1970 and a research and test pilot for the USAF and National Aeronautics and Space Administration (NASA) in 1971. In 1978 he was accepted into NASA's astronaut program. In 1985 he went into space aboard the Spacelab 3 *Challenger* Space Shuttle as a pilot. Currently, Gregory is with NASA's astronaut program at the Johnson Space Center in Houston, Texas, and he is a colonel in the USAF.

Gregory belongs to the Society of Experimental Test Pilots, the Tuskegee Airmen, the American Helicopter Society, and the National Technical Association. He has won numerous medals and awards including the Meritorious Service Medal, the Air Force Commendation Medal, and two NASA Space Flight Medals. He has twice received the Distinguished Flying Cross and is also the recipient of George Washington University's Distinguished Alumni Award, NASA's Outstanding Leadership Award, and the National Society of Black Engineers' Distinguished National Scientist Award.

Lloyd Augustus Hall 1894-1974
Research Director, Chemist

Grandson of the first pastor of Quinn Chapel A.M.E. Church, the first African American church in Chicago, Lloyd Augustus Hall was born in Elgin, Illinois, on June 20, 1894. A top student and athlete at East High School in Aurora, Illinois, he graduated in the top ten of his class and was offered scholarships to four different colleges in Illinois. In 1916, Hall graduated from Northwestern University with a bachelor of science in chemistry. He continued his studies at the University of Chicago and the University of Illinois.

Hall served his country during World War I; as a lieutenant, his job was to inspect explosives at a Wisconsin plant. After the war, Hall joined the Chicago Department of Health Laboratories, where he quickly rose to senior chemist. In 1921, he took employment at Boyer Chemical Laboratory before becoming president and chemical director of the Chemical Products Corporation the following year. In 1924, he was offered a position with Griffith Laboratories. Within one year he was chief chemist and director of research.

There Hall entered the most unique and fruitful phase of his career. He discovered curing salts for the preserving and processing of meats, thus revolutionizing the meat-packing industry; discovered how to sterilize

spices; and researched the effects of antioxidants on fats. Along the way, he registered more than 100 patents for processes used in the manufacturing and packing of food, especially meat and bakery products.

In 1954, Hall became chairman of the Chicago chapter of the American Institute of Chemists. The following year, he was elected a member of the national board of directors, becoming the first African American man to hold that position in the institute's 32-year history. Upon his retirement from Griffith in 1959, Hall continued to serve as a consultant to various state and federal organizations. In 1961, he spent six months in Indonesia, advising the Food and Agricultural Organization of the United Nations. From 1962 to 1964, he was a member of the American Food for Peace Council, an appointment made by President John F. Kennedy.

Matthew Alexander Henson 1866-1955
Seaman, Explorer/Surveyor, Author

Mathew Henson was born August 8, 1866, in Charles County, Maryland near Washington, DC. He attended school in Washington for six years but at the age of thirteen signed on as a cabin boy on a ship headed for China. Henson worked his way up to seaman while he

Matthew Henson

sailed over many of the world's oceans. Tiring of life at sea, Henson took a job in a Washington, DC clothing store. While there he met Nicaragua-bound, U.S. Navy surveyor Robert Edward Peary. He was hired on the spot as Peary's valet. Henson was not pleased at being a personal servant but nonetheless felt his new position held future opportunities.

Peary eventually became obsessed with arctic exploration. After numerous trips to Greenland between 1893 and 1905, Peary became convinced that he could become the first man to stand at the North Pole. Henson accompanied Peary on these trips to Greenland and became an integral part of Peary's plans. In 1906, along with a number of Inuits, Peary and Henson set out from Greenland on their first attempt to reach the North Pole. They came within 160 miles of their goal but were forced to turn back because unseasonably warm weather had created open sheets of water that could not be traversed by dogsled.

Undaunted, Peary and Henson tried again in 1909. Although Peary was undoubtedly the driving force of these expeditions he was increasingly reliant on Henson. Henson's greatest asset was his knowledge of the Inuit language and his ability to readily adapt to their culture. He was also an excellent dog driver and possessed a physical stamina that Peary lacked due to leukemia. Henson felt that he was serving the black race by his example of loyalty, fortitude, and trustworthiness.

By the end of March of 1909, they were within 150 miles of their goal. Henson, because of his strength, would break trail and set up camp for the night, while Peary followed. On April 6th, Henson thought he had reached the Pole. When Peary arrived later he asserted that they were three miles short. After a brief rest they both set out together and stopped when they thought they were in the area of the North Pole. There have been conflicting theories ever since as to who was the first man to reach the top of the world.

In 1912, Henson wrote *A Negro at the North Pole* but the book aroused little interest. He took work first as a porter and then as a customs official in New York. By the 1930s, however, Henson began receiving recognition for his contributions to arctic exploration. In 1937 he was the first African American elected to the Explorers Club in New York. In 1945 he and other surviving members of the expedition received the Navy Medal. In the early 1950s Henson received public recognition for his deeds from President Eisenhower. Henson died in 1955 and was buried in New York. In 1988 his remains were exhumed and buried with full military honors at Arlington National Cemetery next to the grave of Robert Peary.

William Augustus Hinton 1883-1959
Lecturer, Medical Researcher, Educator

Long one of the world's authorities on venereal disease, Dr. William A. Hinton is responsible for the development of the Hinton test, a reliable method for detecting syphilis. He also collaborated with Dr. J. A. V. Davies on what is now called the Davies-Hinton test for the detection of this same disease.

Born in Chicago on December 15, 1883, Hinton graduated from Harvard in 1905. In 1912, he finished his medical studies in three years at Harvard Medical School. For three years after graduation, he was a voluntary assistant in the pathological laboratory at Massachusetts General Hospital. This was followed by eight years of laboratory practice at the Boston Dispensary and at the Massachusetts Department of Public Health. In 1919, Hinton was appointed lecturer in preventive medicine and hygiene at Harvard Medical School where he served for 34 years. In 1949, he was the first person of color to be granted a professorship there.

In 1931, at the Boston Dispensary, Hinton started a training school for poor girls so that they could become medical technicians. From these classes of volunteers grew one of the country's leading institutions for the training of technicians. Though he lost a leg in an automobile accident, Hinton remained active in teaching and at the Boston Dispensary Laboratory, which he directed from 1916 to 1952. He died in Canton, Massachusetts on August 8, 1959.

Shirley Ann Jackson 1946-
Lecturer, Physicist

Born in Washington, DC, in 1946, Shirley Ann Jackson graduated as valedictorian of her class from Roosevelt High School in 1964. In 1968, she received a bachelor of science degree from Massachusetts Institute of Technology. In 1973 she became the first African American woman in the United States to earn a Ph.D. in physics, which she also earned from Massachusetts Institute of Technology.

Jackson's first position—as a research associate at the Fermi National Accelerator Laboratory in Batavia, Illinois and where she studied large subatomic particles—reflected her interest in the study of particles found within atoms. Jackson has worked as a member of the technical staff on theoretical physics at AT&T Bell Laboratories, as a visiting scientist at the European Organization for Nuclear Research in Geneva, and as a visiting lecturer at the NATO International Advanced Study Institute in Belgium. In 1995, President Bill Clinton named Jackson as chairperson of the Nuclear Regulatory Commission.

Dr. Mae Jemison

Mae C. Jemison 1956-
Physician/Surgeon

Mae Jemison was born October 17, 1956, in Decatur, Alabama but her family moved to Chicago when she was three. She attended Stanford University on a National Achievement Scholarship and received a B.S. in chemical engineering and a B.A. in Afro–American studies in 1977. She then enrolled in Cornell University's medical school and graduated in 1981. Her medical internship was at the Los Angeles County/University of Southern California Medical Center in 1982. She was a general practitioner with the INA/Ross Loos Medical Group in Los Angeles until 1983, followed by two years as a Peace Corp medical officer in Sierra Leone and Liberia. Returning to the United States in 1985, she began working for CIGNA Health Plans, a health maintenance organization in Los Angeles.

In 1987, Jemison was accepted in NASA's astronaut program. Her first assignment was representing the astronaut office at the Kennedy Space Center in Cape Canaveral, Florida. On September 12, 1992, when the space shuttle *Endeavor* lifted off, Jemison was aboard and became the first African American woman in space. She served aboard the *Endeavor* as a science specialist.

Jemison resigned from NASA in 1993 to pursue personal goals related to science education and health care in West Africa. In 1994 Jemison founded the International Science Camp in Chicago to help young people become enthusiastic about science.

In 1988, Jemison won the Science and Technology Award given by *Essence* magazine and in 1990 she was Gamma Sigma Gamma's Woman of the Year. In 1991 she earned a Ph.D. from Lincoln University.

Frederick McKinley Jones 1892-1961
Mechanic

In 1935, Frederick McKinley Jones built the first automatic refrigeration system for long haul trucks. Later, the system was adapted to various other carriers including railway cars and ships. Previously, foods were packed in ice so slight delays led to spoilage. Jones' new method instigated a change in eating habits and patterns of the entire nation and allowed for the development of food production facilities in almost any geographic location.

Jones was born in Cincinnati in 1892. His mother died when he was a boy and he moved to Covington, Kentucky, where he was raised by a priest until he was sixteen. When he left the rectory, Jones worked as a pin boy, mechanic's assistant, and finally, as chief mechanic on a Minnesota farm. He served in World War I, and in the late 1920s, his mechanical fame spread when he developed a series of devices to adapt silent movie projectors into sound projectors.

Jones also developed an air conditioning unit for military field hospitals, a portable x-ray machine, and a refrigerator for military field kitchens. During his life, a total of 61 patents were issued in Jones's name. He died in 1961.

Percy Lavon Julian 1898-1975
Educator, Medical Researcher, Research Director

Born on April 11, 1898 in Montgomery, Alabama, Julian attended DePauw University in Greencastle, Indiana. He graduated Phi Beta Kappa and was valedictorian of his class after having lived during his college days in the attic of a fraternity house where he worked as a waiter. For several years, Julian taught at Fisk and Howard universities, as well as at West Virginia State College, before attending Harvard and the University of Vienna.

In 1935, Julian synthesized the drug physostigmine, which is used today in the treatment of glaucoma. He later headed the soybean research department of the Glidden Company and then formed Julian Laboratories in order to specialize in the production of sterols, which

Dr. Percy Julian

honors from Dartmouth and his Ph.D. in 1916 from the University of Chicago. His groundbreaking work on the embryology of marine invertebrates included research on fertilization—a process known as parthenogenesis—but his most important achievement was his discovery of the role protoplasm palys in the development of a cell.

A member of Phi Beta Kappa, Just received the Spingarn Medal in 1914 and served as associate editor of *Physiological Zoology, The Biological Bulletin,* and *The Journal of Morphology.* Between 1912 and 1937, he published more than 50 papers on fertilization, parthenogenesis, cell division, and mutation. In 1930 Just was one of 12 zoologists to address the International Congress of Zoologists and he was elected vice president of the American Society of Zoologists.

Samuel L. Kountz 1931-1981
Physician/Surgeon, Medical Researcher

Born in 1931 in Lexa, Arkansas, Samuel Kountz graduated third in his class at the Agricultural, Mechanical and Normal College of Arkansas in 1952. He pursued graduate studies at the University of Arkansas, earning a degree in chemistry. Senator J. W. Fulbright, whom he met while a graduate student, advised Kountz to apply for a scholarship to medical school. Kountz won the scholarship on a competitive basis and was the first black to enroll at the University of Arkansas Medical School in Little Rock. Kountz was responsible for finding out that large doses of the drug methylprednisolone could help reverse the acute rejection of a transplanted kidney. The drug was used for a number of years in the standard management of kidney transplant patients.

In 1964, working with Dr. Roy Cohn, one of the pioneers in the field of transplantation, Kountz made medical history by transplanting a kidney from a mother to a daughter—the first transplant between humans who were not identical twins. At the University of California in 1967, Dr. Kountz worked with other researchers to develop the prototype of a machine which is now able to preserve kidneys up to fifty hours from the time they are taken from the body of a donor. The machine, called the Belzer Kidney Perfusion Machine, was named for Dr. Folkert O. Belzer, who was Dr. Kountz's partner. Dr. Kountz died in 1981 after a long illness contracted on a trip to South Africa in 1977.

Theodore K. Lawless 1892-1971
Physician, Philanthropist

Theodore Kenneth Lawless was born on December 6, 1892, in Thibodeaux, Louisiana. He received his bachelor's from Talladega College in 1914 and continued to further his education through 1924 at Northwestern

he extracted from the oil of the soybean. The method perfected by Julian in 1950 eventually lowered the cost of sterols to less than 20 cents a gram, and ultimately enabled millions of people suffering from arthritis to obtain relief through the use of cortisone, a sterol derivative. Later, Julian developed methods for manufacturing sex hormones from soya bean sterols: progesterone was used to prevent miscarriages, while testosterone was used to treat older men for diminishing sex drive. Both hormones were important in the treatment of cancer.

In 1953, after serving as director of research for the Glidden Company, he founded his own company, the Julian Institute, in Franklin Park, Illinois and Mexico. Years later, the institute was sold to Smith, Klein and French. In 1947, Julian was awarded the Spingarn Medal, and in 1968 he was awarded the Chemical Pioneer Award by the American Institute of Chemists. He died on April 19, 1975.

Ernest Everett Just 1883-1941
Editor, Zoologist, Marine Biologist

Born in Charleston, South Carolina, on August 14, 1883, Ernest Just received his B.A. in 1907 with high

University, where he received his medical doctorate degree and on year of a master's in dermatology, which he finished at Columbia University from there he attended Harvard University, the University of Paris, the University of Freiburg, and the University of Vienna, where he continued his extensive work in dermatology.

Lawless started his own practice in the Chicago's predominantly black south side upon his return in 1924, which he continued until his death in 1971. He soon became one of the premier dermatologists in the country and earned great praise for researching treatments and cures for a variety of skin diseases, including syphilis, leprosy, and sporotrichosis. During the early years of his career, he taught dermatology at Northwestern University Medical School, where his research was instrumental in devising electropyrexia, a treatment for those suffering cases of syphilis in its early stages. Before he left his role at Northwestern in 1941, he aided in building the university's first medical laboratories.

After leaving Northwestern, Lawless entered the business world beginning as president of 4213 South Michigan Corporation, which sold low-cost real estate, and later as president of the Service Federal Savings and Loan Association. And by the 1960s, he was well-known as one of the 35 richest black men in the United States. During his lifetime, Lawless served on dozens of boards of directors and belonged to countless organizations. He served on the Chicago Board of Health, as senior attending physician at Provident hospital, as associate examiner in dermatology for the National Board of Medical Examiners as chairman of the Division of Higher Education, and as consultant to the Geneva Community Hospital in Switzerland. He was also recognized with many awards for his exemplary breakthroughs in medicine, public service, and philanthropy, including the Harmon Award in Medicine in 1929, the Churchman of the Year in 1952, the Springarn Medal from the NAACP in 1954, and the Daniel H. Burnham Award from Roosevelt University in 1963.He died in 1971.

Lewis Howard Latimer 1848-1928
Draftsperson, Electrical Engineer

Lewis Howard Latimer was employed by Alexander Graham Bell to make the patent drawings for the first telephone, and later went on to become chief draftsman for both the General Electric and Westinghouse companies. Born in Chelsea, Massachusetts, on September 4, 1848, Latimer enlisted in the Union Navy at the age of 15, and began studying drafting upon completion of his military service. In 1881, he invented a method of making carbon filaments for the Maxim electric incandescent lamp; he later patented this method. He also supervised the installation of electric light in New York, Philadelphia, Montreal, and London for the Maxim-Weston Electric Company. In 1884, he joined the Edison Company.

Robert H. Lawrence, Jr. 1935-1967
Astronaut, Airplane Pilot

Air Force Major Robert H. Lawrence, Jr. was the first African American astronaut to be appointed to the Manned Orbiting Laboratory. Lawrence was a native of Chicago, and while still in elementary school he became a model airplane hobbyist and a chess enthusiast. Lawrence became interested in biology during his time at Englewood High School in Chicago. As a student at Englewood, Lawrence excelled in chemistry and track, placing top in the 440 and 880. When he graduated, he placed in the top ten percent of the class.

Lawrence entered Bradley University, joining the Air Force Reserve Officer's Training Corps and attaining the rank of lieutenant colonel, the second highest ranking cadet at Bradley. Lawrence was commissioned a second lieutenant in the United States Air Force in 1956 and soon after received his bachelors degree in chemistry. Following a stint at an air base in Germany, Lawrence entered Ohio State University through the Air Force Institute of Technology as a doctoral candidate.

Major Robert H. Lawrence, Jr.

Lawrence's career came to an end in 1967 when his F-104D Starfighter jet crashed on a runway in a California desert.

Arthur C. Logan 1909-1973
Community Activist, Civil Rights/Human Rights Activist, Physician/Surgeon

Arthur Logan was born in Tuskegee, Alabama in 1909. When he was ten his family moved to New York City, where he received his middle school and high school education. After attending Williams College in Williamstown, Massachusetts, he went to medical school at Columbia University College of Physicians and Surgeons, graduating in 1934. Wishing to work among his people, Logan interned at Harlem Hospital and was affiliated with the hospital for the rest of his life.

In addition to his many years of medical service to Harlem residents and others, Logan also headed New York City's Council Against Poverty in 1965 at the request of Robert F. Wagner, then mayor of the city. Logan was a board member of New York City's Health and Hospital Corporation, as well as a longtime activist in the civil-rights movement, and a strong supporter of a wide range of community causes. He was active with the National Urban League and the NAACP Legal Defense Fund, and was an intimate friend of Martin Luther King, Jr., Whitney Young, and Roy Wilkins. His home in New York was often a meeting place for major figures in the civil-rights movement in the 1960s.

Miles Vandahurst Lynk 1871-1956
Publisher, Physician/Surgeon, Educational Administrator

Miles Vandahurst Lynk was born on June 3, 1871, near Brownsville, Tennessee. He was founder, editor, and publisher of the first black medical journal, the *Medical and Surgical Observer*, first published in December OF 1892. At the age of nineteen, Lynk received his M.D. degree from Meharry Medical College. Lynk was one of the organizers of the first black national medical association; the organization later became the National Medical Association. He also founded and was president of the School of Medicine at the University of West Tennessee.

Jan Matzeliger 1852-1889
Inventor, Shoemaker/Leather Worker

Born in 1852 in Paramaribo, Dutch Guiana, Matzeliger found employment in the government machine works at the age of 10. Eight years later, he immigrated to the United States, settling in Philadelphia, where he worked in a shoe factory. He later moved to New England, settling permanently in Lynn, Massachusetts. The Indus-

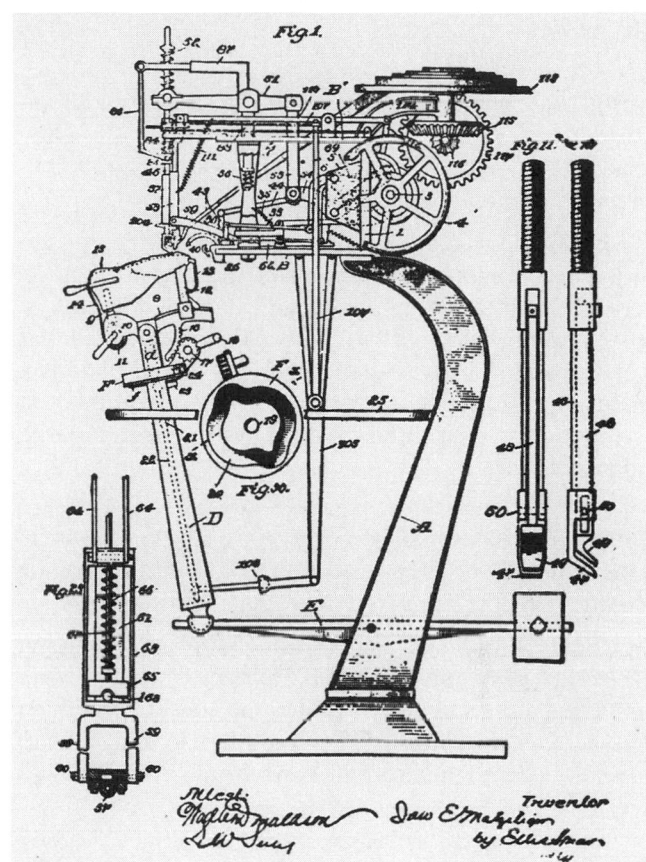

Drawings for Matzeliger's shoe lasting machine.

trial Revolution had by this time resulted in the invention of machines to cut, sew, and tack shoes, but none had been perfected to last a shoe. Seeing this, Matzeliger lost little time in designing and patenting just such a device, one which he refined over the years to a point where it could adjust a shoe, arrange the leather over the sole, drive in the nails, and deliver the finished product—all in one minute's time.

Matzeliger's patent was subsequently bought by Sydney W. Winslow, who established the United Shoe Machine Company. The continued success of this business brought about a 50 percent reduction in the price of shoes across the nation, doubled wages, and improved working conditions for millions of people dependent on the shoe industry for their livelihood. Between 1883 and 1891, Matzeliger received five patents on his inventions, all which contributed to the shoe making revolution. His last patent was issued in September 1891, two years posthumously.

Matzeliger died in 1889 at the age of 37, long before he had the chance to realize a share of the enormous profit derived from his invention. He never received any money. Instead, he was issued stock in the company which did not become valuable until after his death.

Elijah McCoy
Inventor, Machinist

Born in Canada, McCoy moved to Ypsilanti, Michigan, after the Civil War, and over the next 40 years, acquired some 57 patents for devices designed to streamline his automatic lubrication process.

Elijah McCoy's inventions were primarily connected with the automatic lubrication of moving machinery. Perhaps his most valuable design was the "drip cup," a tiny container filled with oil whose flow to the essential moving parts of heavy-duty machinery was regulated by means of a "stopcock." The drip cup was a key device in perfecting the overall lubrication system used in large industry today.

Ronald E. McNair 1950-1986
Astronaut

Ronald McNair was born on October 12, 1950, in Lake City, South Carolina. He was graduate of North Carolina A&T State University with a B.S. degree in physics. He also received a Doctor of Philosophy in Physics from Massachusetts Institute of Technology. He was presented an honorary Doctorate of Laws from North Carolina A&T in 1978.

McNair was working in optical physics when he was selected by NASA in 1978 to train as an astronaut. In August 1979, he completed a one-year training and evaluation period that made him eligible for assignment as mission specialist on space shuttle flight crews. He presented papers in the areas of lasers and molecular spectroscopy and gave many presentations in the United States and Europe. He was the second African American to orbit the earth on a NASA Mission.

Despite the rigorous training in the NASA program, he taught karate at a church, played the saxophone, and found time to talk to young people. McNair was aboard the flawed shuttle *Challenger* that exploded shortly after lift-off from Cape Kennedy and plunged into the waters off the Florida coast on January 28, 1986. The shuttle had a crew of seven persons, including two women, a mission specialist, and a teacher-in-space participant.

Garrett Augustus Morgan 1877-1963
Inventor

Born in Paris, Kentucky, in 1877, Morgan moved to Cleveland at an early age. His first invention was an improvement on the sewing machine which he sold for

Dr. Ronald McNair

Garret Morgan

$150. In 1923, having established his reputation with the gas inhalator, he was able to command a price of $40,000 from the General Electric Company for his automatic traffic signal.

The value of Garrett Morgan's "gas inhalator" was first acknowledged during a successful rescue operation of several men trapped by a tunnel explosion in the Cleveland Waterworks, some 200 feet below the surface of Lake Erie. During the emergency, Morgan, his brother, and two other volunteers—all wearing inhalators—were the only men able to descend into the smoky, gas-filled tunnel, and save several workers from asphyxiation.

Orders for the Morgan inhalator soon began to pour into Cleveland from fire companies all over the nation, but as soon as Morgan's racial identity became known, many of them were canceled. In the South, it was necessary for Morgan to utilize the services of a white man to demonstrate his invention. During World War I the Morgan inhalator was transformed into a gas mask used by combat troops. Morgan died in 1963 in Cleveland, the city which had awarded him a gold medal for his devotion to public safety.

Norbert Rillieux 1806-1894
Inventor, Mechanical Engineer

Norbert Rillieux's inventions were of great value to the sugar-refining industry. The method formerly used called for gangs of slaves to ladle boiling sugarcane juice from one kettle to another—a primitive process known as "the Jamaica Train." In 1845, Rillieux (1806-1894) invented a vacuum evaporating pan (a series of condensing coils in vacuum chambers) which reduced the industry's dependence on gang labor and helped manufacture a superior product at a greatly reduced cost. The first Rillieux evaporator was installed at Myrtle Grove Plantation, Louisiana, in 1845. In the following years, factories in Louisiana, Cuba, and Mexico converted to the Rillieux system.

A native of New Orleans, Rillieux was the son of Vincent Rillieux, a wealthy engineer, and Constance Vivant, a slave on his plantation. Young Rillieux's higher education was obtained in Paris, where his extraordinary aptitude for engineering led to his appointment at the age of twenty-four as an instructor of applied mechanics at L'Ecole Centrale. Rillieux returned to Paris permanently in 1854, securing a scholarship and working on the deciphering of hieroglyphics.

When his evaporator process was finally adopted in Europe, he returned to inventing with renewed interest—applying his process to the sugar beet. In so doing, he cut production and refining costs in half. Rillieux died in Paris on October 8, 1894, leaving behind a system which is in universal use throughout the sugar industry, as well as in the manufacture of soap, gelatin, glue, and many other products.

Mabel K. Staupers 1890-1989
Nursing Executive, Civil Rights/Human Rights Activist

Staupers was born in Barbados in 1890, and moved with her family to Harlem as a teenager. She graduated from Washington, DC's Freedmen's Hospital School of Nursing in 1917, returned to Harlem, and, by 1920, had cofounded a tuberculosis clinic for African American sufferers there. She served as the director of nursing at the clinic—named after Booker T. Washington—before deciding she could better serve in the profession as an educator.

The racism Staupers witnessed in a white hospital she became involved with—during her stint as superintendent of nursing at Mudget Hospital in Philadelphia—convinced her to work toward eradicating prejudice in the profession. Returning to New York, she served as executive secretary of the Harlem Committee of the New York Tuberculosis and Health Association from 1922 to 1934 before taking on a post of the same name at the National Association of Colored Graduate Nurses (NACGN), an organization that worked to improve working conditions for and erase racism toward African American nurses. With the outbreak of World War II, Staupers began enjoining the military branches to accept African American nurses into its medical Corps units.

The U.S. Army Nurse Corps was the first to integrate, but only grudgingly, with a quota system in place. Staupers fought—with the help of First Lady Eleanor Roosevelt—to end the quotas and win these African American nurses wishing to serve their country more equal assignments. By the war's end, the quota system had been eliminated and the Navy Nurse Corps had also been integrated. She dissolved the NACGN in 1951—shortly after serving as its president—because, as she said at the time, its aims had been accomplished. That same year Staupers was awarded the NAACP's distinguished Spingarn Medal. She recounted her life in the 1961 autobiography *No Time for Prejudice: A Story of the Integration of Negroes in Nursing in the United States.* Staupers died in 1989 a few months short of what would have been her one hundredth birthday.

Lewis Temple 1800-1854
Inventor

The toggle harpoon invented by Lewis Temple so improved the whaling methods of the nineteenth century that it more than doubled the catch for this leading New England industry. Little is known of Temple's early background, except that he was born in Richmond,

Virginia, in 1800 and had no formal education. As a young man he moved to New Bedford, Massachusetts, then a major whaling port. Finding work as a metal smith, Temple modified the design of the whaler's harpoon, and in the 1840s, manufactured a new version of the harpoon which allowed lines to be securely fastened to the whale. Using the "toggle harpoon," the whaling industry soon entered a period of unprecedented prosperity. Temple, who never patented his harpoon, died destitute.

Vivien Thomas 1910-1985
Surgical Research Technician

Born in Nashville, Tennessee, in 1910, Thomas had dreamed of a career as a physician since childhood. As a teenager, he worked as a carpenter and as an orderly to earn money for college, and enrolled in Tennessee Agricultural and Industrial College in 1929. Sadly, the stock market crash later that year eradicated Thomas's savings, and he was forced to quit school.

The following year, he was hired for a research assistant post at Vanderbilt University Medical School; he would be trauma researcher and surgeon Alfred Blalock's assistant. For the next decade, Thomas worked long hours in the lab, conducting medical experiments for Blalock that eventually led to lifesaving advances in medicine during World War II, especially in the use of blood transfusions.

When Blalock was hired by the prestigious medical school at Johns Hopkins University in 1940, he would accept the post only if they hired Thomas as well. Thomas then served as director of the medical school's Hunterian Surgical Research Laboratory, where he continued to test out the scientific theories Blalock presented. One of their most significant achievements together was a surgical procedure that restructured an infant's heart if the child was in danger of death due to poor circulation of blood into the lungs. Thomas virtually instructed the surgeon on some parts of the procedure he had already performed many times on dogs, and was present for the university's first 100 trials of the surgery.

Thomas became a well-known, and well-regarded figure on the campus of Johns Hopkins, and ironically became known as an unofficial expert in veterinary medicine because of his long research experience with lab dogs. He remained at the institution even after his mentor passed away in 1964, and in 1971 was honored by graduates of its medical school for his achievements. He became a medical school faculty member in 1977, but perhaps received more personal satisfaction from the honorary degree the university had awarded him. Thomas passed away in 1985, the same year a recounting of his life was published with *Pioneering Research*

in Surgical Shock and Cardiovascular Surgery: Vivien Thomas and His Work with Alfred Blalock.

Levi Watkins, Jr. 1945-
Surgeon, Educator

Watkins was born in Kansas in 1945 but grew up in Montgomery, Alabama, where through his involvement in local churches became acquainted with civil rights leaders Dr. Ralph David Abernathy and the Reverend Martin Luther King. Both were prominent members of the Montgomery community, as was Watkins's own father, a college professor. The teenager's participation in civil rights issues did not stop him from excelling academically, and he graduated as valedictorian of his high school class and went on to earn a 1966 honors degree from Tennessee State University.

Watkins's awareness of issues of racial inequality led him to apply to Vanderbilt University Medical School, and he first learned of his acceptance as its first African American student by reading the newspaper headline announcing the breakthrough. He graduated in 1970, and began his internship and surgical training at the prestigious medical school at Johns Hopkins University. Watkins also studied at Harvard University Medical School for a time, and there conducted research that led to the lifesaving practice of prescribing angiotensin blockers for patients susceptible to heart failure.

In 1978, Watkins became Johns Hopkins's first African American chief resident in cardiac surgery and became a faculty member that year as well. Two years later, he made medical history with the successful surgical implantation of an AID (Automatic Implantable Defibrillator) device, which has been credited with saving countless lives by its ability to keep the heart pumping blood at a normal rate. In 1991 he became a full professor of cardiac surgery at Johns Hopkins, another first for the institution. For several years, however, Watkins had been working to increase minority presence at this elite medical school, and he instituted a special minority recruiting drive when he was appointed to the medical school's admissions committee. Watkins was known for writing personal letters enjoining qualified minority applicants to apply to the school, and because of his work, minority enrollment increased 400 percent in four years. Such accomplishments lend an added import to the campus birthday celebration Watkins organizes annually on Martin Luther King, Jr. Day.

Daniel Hale Williams 1856-1931
Surgeon/Physician

A pioneer in open heart surgery, Daniel Hale Williams was born in Holidaysburg, Pennsylvania, on January 18, 1856. His father died when he was 11, and his mother

Dr. Daniel Hale Williams

deserted him after apprenticing him to a cobbler. He later worked as a roustabout on a lake steamer and as a barber before finishing his education at the Chicago Medical College in 1883.

Williams opened his office on Chicago's South Side at a time when Chicago hospitals did not allow African American doctors to use their facilities. In 1891 Dr. Williams founded Provident Hospital which was open to patients of all races. At Provident Hospital on July 10, 1893, Williams performed the operation upon which his later fame rests. A patient was admitted to the emergency ward with a knife wound in an artery lying a fraction of an inch from the heart. With the aid of six staff surgeons, Williams made an incision in the patient's chest and operated successfully on the artery.

For the next four days, the patient, James Cornish, lay near death, his temperature far above normal and his pulse dangerously uneven. An encouraging rally then brought him out of immediate danger, terminating the crisis period. Three weeks later, minor surgery was performed by Williams to remove fluid from Cornish's pleural cavity. After recuperating for still another month, Cornish fully recovered and was able to leave the hospital, scarred but cured.

Williams was instrumental in the forming of the Medico-Chirurgical Society and the National Medical Association. In 1913, he was inducted into the American Board of Surgery at its first convention. Williams died on August 4, 1931, after a lifetime devoted to his two main interests—the NAACP and the construction of hospitals and training schools for black doctors and nurses.

26

Sports

26

Sports

◆ Current Issues ◆ Baseball ◆ Football ◆ Boxing ◆ Basketball ◆ Other Sports
◆ Women in Sports ◆ Athletic Gatekeepers

by Mark Kram and Craig Barth

The image of the black athlete continues to develop a positive face on some fronts. Several athletes are actively and positively involved in the community. Football legend Jim Brown operates the Amer-I-Can program which teaches self-esteem to prison inmates with the hope that they will positively change their lives upon release. Many other current and former stars are presently taking advantage of their popularity by reaching out to a society in need of guidance and support. As an example, the NBA's Terrell Brandon of the Cleveland Cavaliers has generously donated funds to his hometown of Portland and is actively doing his part to help revitalize an inner city area there. This trend of "giving back" and remembering one's roots is both encouraging and significant.

◆ CURRENT ISSUES

Much rhetoric abounds about the representation of African Americans in the sports arena. In a broad sense, it is generally difficult to gauge the inroads or lack thereof that blacks are making. Northeastern University's Center for the Study of Sport in Society issues an annual Racial Report Card that assesses the competency of the NBA, National Football League (NFL) and Major League Baseball in relation to the racial composition of those sports. The center's 1995 report is noteworthy and revealing.

Overall, minority coaching positions manned by blacks in the above mentioned leagues declined despite the addition of several expansion teams. Administrative positions (i.e. business operations, community relations, marketing and public relations) have also taken a hit, most notably in the NBA and NFL. It is worth noting that playing great Isiah Thomas was recently appointed executive vice president of the NBA's expansion Toronto Raptors.

There is good news. African American assistant coaches employed by the National Basketball Association and Major League Baseball have reached an all-time high, with 40 and 18 percent representation, respectively. The center concludes its study by awarding final grades in the categories of front office and head-coach hiring practices. The NBA received Bs in top management and administrative positions and a B+ in coaching. The NFL received a C-, B-, and C+ respectively. Major League Baseball was granted a C in top management and B+ for managers.

The Sporting News annually ranks the 100 most powerful people in sports. The 1995 list includes nine African Americans, which is consistent with the prior year but does represent a 33 percent increase over 1992. The most recent tabulation includes Dr. Leroy Walker, president, United States Olympic Committee; Gene Upshaw, executive director, National Football League Players Association; Harold Henderson, executive vice president, National Football League; Bill Strickland, sports agent; and Rudy Washington, Head basketball coach at Drake University and the executive director of the Black Coaches Association, along with other figures. It is also worth noting that blacks are becoming increasingly prominent in broadcasting and as sports agents.

Other sports such as hockey, golf and horse racing continue to include only a smattering of African American participants. The reasons therefore are likely multifarious. One obvious cause is that these are traditionally "wealthy" sports. Many youths in American cities do not have the means to purchase equipment necessary to participate.

Basketball and football players continue to leave school early for the opulence of the NBA and NFL. Recently instituted rookie salary caps appear to be partially deterring early exits from college. However, the opportunity to receive more money than most young men have ever dreamed of is tempting. Some are now by-passing college entirely. This is not an entirely new trend, especially in the NBA. Historically, some have done so with great success (Moses Malone and Shawn Kemp). Others were somewhat less successful (Darryl Dawkins and Bill Willoughby). Minnesota Timberwolves' rookie Kevin Garnett was a Chicago high school senior in 1995 who has expressed some regret about his decision to forego a college education. Kobe Bryant, a prep phenom from Ardmore, Pennsylvania, announced his intention to enter the 1996 NBA draft. Other high school athletes are pondering a similar course of action.

Black attendance at sporting events continues to decline. In an ironic twist, the stratospheric salaries being paid to players such as Garnett have caused teams to raise ticket prices. This has made it virtually impossible for many inner city youths to attend games, reducing minority attendance. Another concern is the increasingly transient nature of sports franchises. Within the past year, four professional football teams have relocated, with several others considering similar moves. Often, ownership has to implement means beyond even lofty ticket prices, such as Personal Seat Licenses (PSL's), to raise funds to help defray the costs associated with these relocations. The upshot is to price less advantaged individuals and families almost entirely out of the market.

Drug abuse and more outwardly dangerous and degenerate behavior such as spousal abuse continue to pervade. These problems are obviously not limited to the African American community but are nonetheless a concern therein. Substance abuse policies exist in all major professional leagues, in varying degrees of severity. Unfortunately, reports of spousal abuse are prevalent. Recent incidents have involved athletes such as football's Warren Moon and Dan Wilkinson, baseball's Darryl Strawberry and basketball's Robert Parish and even a celebrated case involving University of Nebraska tailback Lawrence Phillips. The latter involved an abuse incident with a female student and stirred a maelstrom of controversy as Nebraska allowed Phillips to remain with the team. The fact that Nebraska won college football's 1995 national championship only served to fan the flames of the argument regarding the price of success and the exploitation of college athletes to reach that goal.

◆ BASEBALL

Long considered our "National Pastime," baseball was an incomplete entity prior to 1947. In an egregious miscarriage of justice that unfortunately was endemic of the era, African Americans were not permitted to participate in organized, professional baseball until 1945, when Jackie Roosevelt Robinson was signed to a minor league contract by the Brooklyn Dodgers organization and chief executive Branch Rickey, Sr., to play for the minor league Montreal Royals. Baseball's book on segregation in its Major Leagues finally began to close when Robinson took the field as a Dodger, at Ebbets Field, on April 15, 1947. Despite tremendous pressure and amid much hostility, Robinson persevered and was awarded baseball's rookie of the year award that season.

Unbeknownst to many, Robinson technically was not the first black to participate in professional baseball. Oberlin College's Moses Fleetwood Walker actually played with Toledo team of the American Association, then considered a major league, from 1884 until 1888, during which time baseball was actually integrated. However, a movement to purge blacks from baseball was initiated. Its leader was Adrian (Cap) Anson of the Chicago White Stockings, one of the great players of that era. His crusade gained momentum, and by the turn of the century, African Americans were essentially no longer represented in the Major Leagues.

Shortly after Robinson's arrival on the scene, also in 1947, Larry Doby became the first African American to appear in the American League, with the Cleveland Indians. Along with Robinson and Doby, other former Negro League stars, at various stages of their careers, had the opportunity to participate in the formerly all white Major Leagues, including Robinson's teammate Roy Campanella and Indians' pitcher Leroy (Satchel) Paige, long considered one of the sport's great characters.

Unfortunately, baseball's desegregation arrived too late for many. An all-time, all-star team of Negro Leaguers who, as victims of their birth dates, never appeared in the Major Leagues, could be assembled, which, arguably, would be comparable to any other. Catcher Josh Gibson; infielders Walter "Buck" Leonard, Judy Johnson and Ray Dandridge; outfielders James "Cool Papa" Bell and Oscar Charleston; and pitcher Andrew (Rube) Foster would have shone brightly in any era. Some baseball historians regard Gibson as the greatest baseball player of all-time, regardless of the league or era. Bell was perhaps the fastest player in history. It was said the he was so fast that "he could turn the switch off and be in bed before the room got dark." In all, 12 Negro Leaguers have been admitted to baseball's Hall of Fame on the basis of their careers in the Negro Leagues.

Josh Gibson was reputed to be the greatest hitter ever in the Negro baseball leagues of the 1930s.

After 1947, black baseball players began to make up for lost time as quickly as major league ownership would allow. By the 1970s, blacks dotted the rosters of every Major League team. Many have attained levels comparable to the greats of the early twentieth century and are now mentioned in the same breath with Babe Ruth, Ty Cobb, Lou Gehrig and other pre-1947 luminaries.

Remarkable achievements abound. Hank Aaron became baseball's all-time home run leader, considered the sport's most storied record, and has driven in more runs than anyone in history. Rickey Henderson is the stolen base king by a wide margin, with Lou Brock second. Lee Smith is the all-time leader in saves. Additionally, black players have been the recipients of the Most Valuable Player award in the American or National League over 35 percent of the time during the last half century. Center fielder Willie Mays is considered by many to be the greatest of all time at his position. Frank Robinson was the only player ever to win an MVP award in both the National and American League and was the first black named manager of a major league franchise. In 1996, Seattle's Ken Griffey Jr. became the highest paid player of all time, at over $8 million per year. Finally, many major leaguers, whose careers began after the desegregation of the sport, have found their rightful places in the Hall of Fame.

Curt Flood helped change the face of the game of baseball, but not because of his playing ability. In 1969, Flood decided to challenge his trade from the St. Louis Cardinals to the Philadelphia Phillies on the grounds that baseball's reserve clause—binding players to their existing teams—was in violation of Federal antitrust laws. A lawsuit brought by Flood was eventually heard by the U.S. Supreme Court, which decided that baseball could retain its posture as the only professional sport exempted from federal antitrust legislation. While Flood lost the case, he managed to open the door for the elimination of the reserve clause and the advent of free agency.

During the 1995 season, 19 percent of all players were African American, a decline from the peak seasons of the 1970s. One factor responsible for this change is the streamlining of inner city baseball programs and urban Little Leagues due to lack of financial support. The economic situation has become such in some American cities that even scholastic athletic programs are threatened with cutbacks or dissolution.

Baseball has made gradual, albeit modest, progress in the employment of blacks in top management positions. Although since deposed, Bill White was named president of the National League in 1988. The Colorado Rockies, San Francisco Giants and Toronto Blue Jays will begin the 1996 season with black field managers. Additionally, ten African Americans occupy top management positions.

The baseball landscape abounds with prominent black players. Aside from Griffey, current stars include Cincinnati's Barry Larkin, San Francisco's Barry Bonds, Cleveland's Albert Belle, Minnesota's Kirby Puckett, San Diego's Tony Gwynn, Boston's Mo Vaughn, Detroit's Cecil Fielder, and the Chicago White Sox' Frank Thomas. Cleveland's Eddie Murray and the recently retired Dave Winfield are likely to enter the Baseball Hall of Fame when eligible.

◆ FOOTBALL

Unlike the other major American sports, professional football was integrated from its inception. Beginning in 1919, with Fritz Pollard of the Akron Indians of the American Professional Football League as its first representative, African Americans participated until 1933. At that point, the National Football League initiated its eviction of blacks from professional football.

With the signing of Kenny Washington by the Los Angeles Rams in 1946, blacks began their re-emergence into professional football. The Cleveland Browns' fullback Marion Motley, who debuted that same year, was the earliest black superstar. Four years after the end of Motley's career, Syracuse University's Jim Brown began his career with the Browns and continued its legacy of great running backs. Considered by many observers to be the greatest at his position in the history of the NFL, he led the league in rushing for eight of his nine years and held the career mark for nineteen years after his retirement. Some consider Brown the greatest of all time, regardless of position.

By the end of Brown's career in the mid-1960s, several other black luminaries had emerged. New York Giants' safety Emlen Tunnel set the record for career interceptions while Chicago Bears running back Gale Sayers broke in as one of the league's most exciting and graceful players. Several other fine athletes were also dotting the NFL landscape.

African American stars continued to proliferate in the 1960s and 1970s. Charley Taylor was the first black to twice lead the league in receptions. Willie Wood was the first to lead the NFL in interceptions. In 1973, the Buffalo Bills' O.J. Simpson became the first player to rush for more than 2,000 yards in a single season. The visibility of blacks in the NFL became truly focalized with the popularity of certain teams' defensive lines and their familiar and catchy nicknames. The Minnesota Vikings offered the "Purple People Eaters", including Carl Eller, Alan Page and Jim Marshall. David "Deacon" Jones and Rosey Grier were mainstays on the Los Angeles Rams' "Fearsome Foursome". The great Pittsburgh Steeler defenses of the 1970s were fronted by the "Steel Curtain" which included "Mean" Joe Greene, among others.

During the 1980s, the Giants' Lawrence Taylor revolutionized the position of outside linebacker and made the quarterback sack popular lexicon for all football fans. In 1988, the Washington Redskins' Doug Williams became the first black to quarterback his team to a Super Bowl victory. During 1984, Walter Payton of the Bears eclipsed Jim Brown's record for career rushing yards and concluded his brilliant career in 1987 with more than 16,700 yards. Two current running backs, the Detroit Lions' dazzling Barry Sanders and the Dallas Cowboys' relentless Emmitt Smith have Payton's record in their sights. The San Francisco 49ers' record setting wide receiver Jerry Rice had scored an unparalleled 156 touchdowns at the conclusion of the 1995 season. Pittsburgh Steelers' cornerback Rod Woodson is an unquestioned superstar.

African Americans currently represent approximately 70 percent of those playing in the NFL. Minority representation in the NFL coaching fraternity as well as top management and administrative positions has re-mained somewhat constant in recent years. In the mid-1990s, the Philadelphia Eagles, Minnesota Vikings, and Tampa Bay Buccaneers employed black head coaches.

No discussion would be complete without mentioning the significant role played by predominantly black colleges in the development of football. Grambling's head coach Eddie Robinson continues to extend his record for victories by a head coach at any collegiate level and has now coached over 400 winners during his legendary career. Black colleges have also produced many all-time greats, including the above mentioned Payton, who starred at Jackson State. Currently, NFL teams feature several fine players from these schools.

◆ BOXING

Black athletes have been boxing professionally since colonial times. George "Little Chocolate" Dixon became the first African American to win a world boxing title, in 1886, and Jack Johnson became the first to win the heavyweight title, in 1908. In between, Joe Walcott captured the world lightweight and welterweight titles. Blacks have virtually dominated the sport since the 1930s, especially the most popular heavyweight division. Joe Louis held the world heavyweight title for a record 11 years and eight months in the 1930s and 1940s. Middleweight champion Sugar Ray Robinson is considered by many to be "pound for pound," the greatest boxer of all time. Henry Armstrong held three world titles at once-featherweight, lightweight, and welterweight-during the Great Depression.

Louis, Robinson and Armstrong were stars in what is considered the first Golden Age of blacks in boxing. A new Golden Age was ushered in on March 8, 1971, when Muhammad Ali and Joe Frazier drew the sport's first multimillion-dollar gate. Ali, a national figure since winning an Olympic gold medal in 1960, was one of the first athletes to exploit his position to comment on American political and social events. Almost single-handedly, he transformed boxing from a second-rank endeavor to a top drawing entertainment entity.

Other divisions too have featured stellar black fighters. During the 1970s and 1980s fans were thrilled by middle- and welterweight matchups featuring Sugar Ray Leonard, Marvin Hagler, and Thomas Hearns. When Ali was no longer able to defend his heavyweight crown, new challengers such as Larry Holmes and Leon Spinks ascended to the championship ranks.

As purses for major boxing events inched into the neighborhood of $100 million per match in the mid-

Eric Dickerson of the Los Angeles Raiders.

1980s, a new generation of fighters arose. "Iron" Mike Tyson, a tough youngster from Brooklyn, became the best known heavyweight champion since Ali and the wealthiest boxer of all time. His tumultuous reign ended with a knockout by James "Buster" Douglas, who in turn lost to Evander Holyfield. Holyfield was unseated in 1992 by Riddick Bowe, another product of the same Brooklyn projects in which Tyson had grown. Unlike the combative Tyson, Bowe earned a reputation for professionalism and social activism as he spoke against apartheid policies in South Africa and the need for more sports programs in the nation's ghettos. While other fighters, including Pernell Whitaker and Roy Jones Jr., have shone brightly in recent years, none have shone as brightly as Tyson, who regained the title in 1996, resoundingly defeating the Brit's Frank Bruno.

Top boxers can conceivably earn as much as $100 million for less than a dozen major ring events. The advent of pay-per-view television and cable network sponsorship has lead to soaring profits for the sport and its practitioners. Professional boxing features well-known black figures in all realms of the sport. Bowe, for instance, employs black trainers, including the well known Eddie Futch, and a black manager, Rock Newman.

Colorful entrepreneur Don King is both the most famous, wealthiest, and controverisal boxing promoter of the modern era. His powerful position in boxing's ranks, and his ability to ingratiate himself with champion after champion assure his continued success in the field.

The role of boxing's Golden Gloves Boxing Tournament cannot be overlooked in the development of the sport. Created in 1923 by *Chicago Tribune* sports editor Arch Ward, the Golden Gloves provided an organized forum for budding fighters to exhibit their skills. Integrated from the very beginning, the Golden Gloves served to bring the sport into the limelight as the boxers had a public platform to display their skills, in contrast to the dingy, shady clubs to which they were accustomed. For many, it became an avenue to great successes. To wit, future champions Joe Louis, Sugar Ray Robinson, Floyd Patterson, Muhammad Ali, and Sugar Ray Leonard all earned Golden Gloves titles.

Boxing is a brutal and dangerous sport, and it demands years of specialized training, rigorous conditioning, and singular dedication. The public appetite for major boxing events will continue to provide ample opportunities for talented athletes from all over the world.

Joe Frazier knocks down Jimmy Ellis, 1970.

◆ BASKETBALL

The integration of professional basketball saw its genesis in 1950, four years after the debut of the National Basketball Association. The initial African American representative in the league is arguable. Chuck Cooper, of Duquesne University, was the first to be drafted, by the Celtics, and owner Walter Brown. Nat "Sweetwater" Clifton was the first signed to a professional contract and is considered the most talented and colorful black player from that era. However, on October 31, 1950, when Earl Lloyd of the then Washington Capitols took the court, he became the first to actually participate in an NBA game.

Black presence in the game of basketball pre-dates those events. Until the NBA's formation, only loosely organized leagues existed, black or otherwise. The sport was more popular on the collegiate level. During 1916, educators, coaches, and faculty members from Hampton Institute, Shaw, Lincoln, Virginia Union, and Howard University formed the Central Interscholastic Ath-

Marvin Hagler

letic Association, the first black collegiate conference. Others soon followed, including the Southeastern Athletic Conference, Southwestern Athletic Conference and Southern Intercollegiate Athletic Conference.

Much of the legacy of black basketball history lies in its pioneers. Bob Douglas, who founded the Harlem Renaissance team during the 1920s, is considered the "Godfather of Black basketball." He was integral to the development of the game. His innovations included

Evander Holyfield

monthly player contracts; a custom designed team bus; and tours in the south, which was previously an untapped basketball bastion. John McLendon, legendary coach during the 1950s and 1960s is recognized as the strategic architect of the fast break and, furthermore, is the first African American to publish a book detailing his coaching philosophy. He is also the first to coach a national professional league team. Additionally, McLendon was a prominent advocate of the desegregation of intercollegiate athletics.

No discussion is complete without a mention of the world famous Harlem Globetrotters, basketball's "Ambassadors of Goodwill." From their inception in 1926, until the present, the Globetrotters have delighted basketball fans world-wide with their unique combination of skill and humor. Names such as "Meadowlark" Lemon, "Curly" Neal, "Goose" Tatum, and Marques Haynes are familiar to fans young and old.

A dazzling array of superstars has bridged the gap between the early years and today's NBA of Michael Jordan, Scottie Pippen, Shaquille O'Neal, Hakeem Olajuwon, David Robinson, Patrick Ewing, Karl Malone, Anfernee Hardaway, Charles Barkley, and others. Wilt Chamberlain once averaged more than 50 points per game in a single season and has more rebounds than any player in history. Bill Russell, considered the game's greatest defensive center, helped his Boston Celtics to an astounding 11 championships during the 1950s and 1960s. Kareem Abdul-Jabbar (formerly Lew Alcindor) holds the all-time record for points scored and games played in a career. Elgin Baylor and the remarkably versatile Oscar Robertson are considered among the best at their respective positions. Julius Erving revolutionized basketball with a rare combination of athleticism, style, and grace. All of these players have played roles in transforming the league into an exciting, fast paced affair that continues to gain in popularity globally.

African Americans now occupy more than 80 percent of the spots on NBA rosters, a figure that is increasing. Other areas indicate considerably less representation. Five teams began the 1996 season with black head coaches, although approximately 40 percent of NBA assistant coaches are African American. The Atlanta Hawks' Lenny Wilkens has won more games than any other coach in history, with more than 1,000 victories. Approximately 15 percent of top management and administrative positions are manned by blacks. It should be noted that in 1990, with the purchase of the Denver Nuggets, Bertram Lee and Peter C.B. Bynoe became the first African American owners of a professional sports franchise.

The NBA has received a spark from the recent comebacks of Magic Johnson, who retired in 1992, after testing positive for the HIV virus, and Michael Jordan,

Kareem Abdul-Jabbar

Michael Jordan following one of the Chicago Bulls NBA championship victories.

regarded by some as the greatest player in history. They have helped energize a sport that began to flourish in part with their original entry into the league. Their competitiveness and respect for the game is a welcome tonic for a league replete with precocious young stars and will only serve to enhance the sport.

◆ OTHER SPORTS

Black athletes have excelled in track and field, making an indelible mark at various Olympiads and other competitions. Their legacy began at the London Olympics of 1908, when John Baxtor Taylor became the first to capture a gold medal as part of the four by 400 meter relay team and was carried on via household names such as Jesse Owens, Bob Beamon, and Carl Lewis.

After lagging success during the decade of the 1920s, major strides were made in the following two decades. Prior to the 1930s, black colleges had been unable to offer quality track programs. Blacks therefore displayed their abilities at traditionally white colleges and in various clubs. During the 1930s and 1940s, African American track and field competitors ascended to the top of their sport, especially in the sprints and jumping events.

Jesse Owens was the beacon of the first half of the twentieth century. Owens is best known for his four gold medal performance at the "Hitler" Olympics in Berlin, Germany, in 1936, one of the most remarkable displays in Olympic history. However, it was on May 25, 1935, at Ann Arbor, Michigan, that Jesse Owens provided the greatest performance in track and field history at the Big Ten Championships as a member of Ohio State University. Owens began his day by equalling the world record in the 100-yard dash. He then proceeded to set the world records in the broad jump, 220-yard dash and 220-yard low hurdles, all in scarcely over one hour.

Others have left their imprints on the sport. At the Olympics of 1960, Ralph Boston broke Owen's long jump record, to win Olympic Gold. In so doing, he also became one of only two track stars to break a world record on six separate occasions. During the same games, Rafer Johnson set the standard for the decathlon. While Owens's day in 1935 is unmatched, Bob Beamon, at the 1968 Mexico City Games, provided the greatest singular achievement in track and field, and perhaps sports, history when he soared an astounding 29 feet, 2 1/2 inches to break his own world record in the long jump by approximately two feet. Beamon's record would stand for a quarter of a century, until finally topped by Mike Powell. In 1984, in Los Angeles, Carl Lewis, "the world's fastest human," became the first athlete since Owens in 1936 to win four gold medals. Edwin Moses, one of the sport's most respected athletes, became the greatest 400-meter hurdler in history, dominating his competition well into the 1980s. Of late, 1992 Olympic Gold medalist Michael Johnson has been one of the sport's most impressive athletes. Johnson, a specialist in both the 200 and 400-meters also captured gold at the World Track and Field championships in 1991, when he broke his own record in the 200 meters. He was named male athlete of the year for 1990 by *Track and Field News.*

One of the most noteworthy events in Olympic history occurred not in competition but during an awards ceremony. In 1968, after finishing first and third respectively, in the 200-meter dash, Tommie Smith and John Carlos, while on the victory stand, raised their arms in unison in what has become known as the "Black power salute". Their purpose was to focus the world's attention on the plight of blacks in society and was a reflection of the climate of the times. The upshot was to forever alter the image of the African American athlete.

Other sports bear the enduring imprint of black athletes. The professional tennis community was basically devoid of blacks through World War II, a time when African Americans were not welcome by the U.S. Lawn Tennis Association (USLTA). In a sport primarily associated with the upper class, their only avenues were universities and colleges, clubs (if admitted) and various minor tournaments. Shortly after the war, the USLTA loosened its discrimination policy and, in 1948, Oscar Johnson became the first black player to win a USLTA-sanctioned event. Players began to sprinkle onto the scene. None bore the impact of Arthur Ashe, however.

With Althea Gibson having paved the way in the 1950s, Ashe became her male counterpart of the following two decades. The classy and congenial champion won the Australian Open in 1970, and the Wimbledon title in 1975, along with several less celebrated tournaments during his career. He represented his country as a member of the U.S. Davis Cup team ten times and was its captain from 1981 to 1984. As is the case with Gibson, no black male player has even approached Ashe's accomplishments. Ashe may have been an even greater champion off the court. Beyond even his significant contributions as a human rights activist, Ashe retained a dignity and grace, before and during his battle with AIDS, that won him the respect and admiration of people the world over, spanning all races and walks of life. The current hope to carry Ashe's torch on the court

is the University of Michigan's Mali Vai Washington, a young, promising talent.

African Americans' attempts to break into golf prior to World War II paralleled those of their tennis counterparts to a certain degree. However, the Professional Golfers Association (PGA) did not rescind its white-only policy until 1959, when Charlie Sifford became the first black to be issued a PGA card as an "approved player"—in fact, no black woman was approved as an LPGA member until Renee Powell's admission in 1967. Sifford was the best known of the initial participants on the tour. He was the first to win a predominantly white event with his victory at the 1957 Long Beach Open. Others soon followed. The notables were Lee Elder during the 1960s and 1970s and Calvin Peete during the 1970s and 1980s. Recently, teenager Tiger Woods, in amateur competition, has shown potential for future greatness.

African American luminaries exist in other sports. By winning the Brunswick Memorial World Open, George Branam became the first African Americn bowler to win a Professional Bowling Association (PBA) title. Hockey goaltender Grant Fuhr won five Stanley Cup championships as a member of the Edmonton Oilers. The Boston

Arthur Ashe holds the Wimbledon trophy, 1975.

Bruins Willie O'Rhee became the first to perform in the NHL, during the 1958 season. The great weightlifter John Davis was the first athlete of any race to win eight consecutive World and Olympic Championships, during a remarkable career spanning three decades. Superlative bodybuilder Lee Haney reached the top of his field by winning eight consecutive Mr. Olympia titles (1984-1991). Chris Dickerson won the same award in 1982. At one point, at the turn of the nineteenth century, cyclist Marshall Taylor, was among the three most celebrated black athletes in the world. During the same era, jockey Isaac Murphy, viewed as the greatest in the world at his craft, was part of a triumphant half century of African American jockeys. Oliver Lewis was a part of this tradition, winning the inaugural Kentucky Derby aboard Aristedes, in 1875. Special mention should go to one of the generation's greatest athletes, two-sport star Bo Jackson. Injuries derailed what would have been, in all likelihood, stellar careers in professional football and/or baseball. Before settling on football, Deion Sanders also played both football and baseball.

◆ WOMEN IN SPORTS

The world of sports has been greatly enriched by the accomplishments of many woman who have, in often anonymous fashion, attained greatness. Their contributions span the athletic spectrum, ranging from tennis, to figure skating, to basketball. Many such exploits occurred during the Olympic Games.

Alice Coachman became the first African American woman to capture an Olympic Gold with her performance in the high jump in 1948 and thus became the forerunner for future hopefuls. The valiant Wilma Rudolph, a model in perseverance, overcame debilitating childhood illnesses to win three golds at the 1960 Olympiad in Rome. Her teammate, 15-year-old Barbara Jones, became the youngest female to win a Gold Medal in track and field. In the 1968 games, Wyomia Tyus became the second African American to win more than one Gold Medal in one Olympiad as well as the first to set world records in two different events. Debi Thomas became the first African American woman to win an Olympic medal in figure skating, in 1988. Two years earlier, she accomplished her goal of becoming the first American black woman to win an International Senior singles title. Florence Griffith Joyner, the world's fastest woman, in a performance similar in significance to Rudolph's, won four medals during the 1988 Olympiad, including three golds. Not to be overlooked is Jackie Joyner-Kersee, owner of two Olympic gold medals, or the courageous Gail Devers, who has overcome the effects of Graves' disease to achieve a level of excellence that included a gold medal at the 1992 Olympic Games.

Florence Griffith Joyner

African American women have reached the top of their fields in other endeavors as well. Ironically, the first female black athlete to dominate her sport was tennis' Althea Gibson who did so in a traditionally "non-black" sport. A superb, all-around athlete, Gibson was named 1957's female athlete of the year during which she captured the prestigious Wimbledon singles' title and U.S. Lawn Tennis Association championship. She won both titles again in 1958, and was the undisputed number one women's player in the world for those years. This trailblazer had become the first black woman to capture a Grand Slam event in 1956 with her singles and doubles championships at the French Open. To date, no other black women has come close to matching Gibson's accomplishments. Zina Garrison-Jackson has enjoyed quite a bit of success in the sport, including a one-time Top 10 world ranking. She was also named Female Athlete of the Year in 1981. More recent talents have included Venus Williams and Lori McNeil.

The sport of basketball has abounded with unmatched female players since the 1970s. Indiana Pacers' star Reggie Miller may not even be the best player in his family; his sister, Cheryl's exploits have become legend-

Althea Gibson

ary in basketball circles. She was named All-American at the conclusion of each of her four years at the University of Southern California, was national player of the year three times, and was inducted in the Basketball Hall of Fame in 1995. The decade of the 1970s featured the great center Lusia Harris, the first woman to be inducted into the Basketball Hall of Fame. Others who have left their marks in basketball annals include University of Kansas star Lynette Woodard, perhaps best known as the first female member of the Harlem Globetrotters, having joined them in 1985. Pam and Paula McGee, teammates of Miller at Southern California, are world class performers. Most recently, Texas Tech's dazzling Sheryl Swoopes vaulted to the top of the game of women's college basketball as well as becoming the first woman to have a line of shoes bearing her name.

Notables in other sports include but are certainly not limited to the late volleyballer Flo Hyman; bodybuilder Lenda Murray, who had won the Ms. Olympia title six times as of 1995; and standout gymnast Dominique Dawes. Playing second base for the Indianapolis Clowns and Kansas City Monarchs from 1953 to 1954, Marcenia Lyle Alberga, a.k.a. Toni Stone, was the first woman in

the Negro Leagues. She boasted a .243 batting average as well as a career highpoint of hitting a single off a Satchel Paige fastball in 1953. More than 20 years later, another black milestone was reached when Wendy Hilliard became the first African American member of the U.S. National Rhythmic Gymnastics Team. And in 1994, Fredia "The Cheetah" Gibbs became the first African American to hold the Women's World Super Light Weight Kickboxing Championship title.

Unfortunately, very few women have the opportunity to display their talents on a professional level. Traditionally, women's athletics have long been hamstrung by the dearth of non-amateur forums in which black female athletes could participate. For many, the Olympic Games or intercollegiate athletics have been the final step of their careers, with the exception of basketball. Many find different ways of expressing their athleticism. Hilliard, for example, went on to coach the National Rhythmic Gymnastics Team; then in 1996, she became president of the nonprofit Women's Sports Foundation, an organization dedicated to improving the emotional, mental, and physical well-being of young girls and women by encouraging participation in sports and fitness-related activities.

As aforementioned, women basketball players have had better luck in entering sustained professional competition. One reason is that basketball has long been the top participant choice among U.S. high school girls. Many continue into their adulthood. For example, the 1996 U.S. Women's Olympic Basketball team included eight African Americans on the 11-member roster. Among them were U.S. Army Reserves First Lieutenant Ruthie Bolton, the first American woman to play professionally in Hungary and Sweden; Teresa Edwards, a two-time University of Georgia All-American and the first American basketball player of either gender to compete in four Olympics, winning gold in 1984 and 1988 and bronze in 1992; runway model Lisa Leslie; Katrina McClain, the world's highest-paid female basketball player, earning a $250,000 salary while playing on a Japanese team; Nikki McCray; Carla McGhee; Dawn Staley, two-time college player of the year and a professional player in Brazil, France, Italy, and Spain; and Sheryl Swoopes. Though these stars were formerly forced to play abroad, the American Basketball League (ABL) was slated to debut in October of 1996 with teams in eight to 12 U.S. cities. Players' salaries were expected to average $70,000 per year.

Women's athletics received a boost with the enactment of Title IX of the Education Amendment Act of 1972, which stipulated that any university receiving federal funds was obligated to varsity sports for women who wanted them. As Cheryl Miller once noted, "Without Title IX, I wouldn't be here." Women may never gain acclaim similar to their male sporting counterparts. However, our history has already been enriched by their accomplishments. As attitudes evolve, it is hoped that their place in America's sporting landscape will become even more visible.

◆ ATHLETIC GATEKEEPERS

Hank Aaron (1934-)
Baseball Player

Born in Mobile, Alabama on February 5, 1934, Hank Aaron first played sandlot ball as a teenager. He later played for a team called the Black Bears, but soon thereafter signed a $200-per-month contract with the Indianapolis Clowns of the Negro American League.

In June of 1952, Aaron's contract was purchased by the Boston Braves. The following season, playing for their minor league team in Jacksonville, his .362 average led the South Atlantic League. This led, in 1954, to a promotion to the major league Braves, then based in Milwaukee, and the beginning of his brilliant career.

Aaron enjoyed perhaps his finest season in 1957, when he was named Most Valuable Player and led his team to a world championship. His stats that year included a .322 average, 44 homers, 132 RBIs, and 118 runs scored.

Aaron hit more home runs than anyone else in the history of major league baseball. He attained this plateau with his second home run of the 1974 season, a shot which marked his 715th career round-tripper and thus broke the previous record of 714 which had been held by Babe Ruth. Aaron finished that season with 20 homers and brought his career mark to a total of 733. He completed his career with a total of 755 home runs.

During his career, Aaron won a pair of batting titles and hit over .300 in 12 seasons. He won the home run and RBI crowns 4 times apiece, hit 40 or more homers 8 times, and hit at least 20 home runs for 20 consecutive years, a National League record. In addition, he was named to 20 consecutive all-star teams.

In January 1982, Aaron received 406 of 415 votes from the Baseball Writers Association, thereby being elected into the Baseball Hall of Fame. In the mid-1990s, he served as vice president/assistant to the president for the Braves.

Kareem Abdul-Jabbar (1947-)
Basketball Player

Jabbar was born Ferdinand Lewis Alcindor, Jr. on April 16, 1947, in New York City. In high school, at 7'1/2" tall, he was easily the most sought after basketball player, particularly after he established a New York City record of 2,067 points and 2,002 rebounds, leading

Hank Aaron, 1970.

Power Memorial High School to three straight championships. Power won 95 and lost only six games during Lew Alcindor's years with the team; 71 of these victories were consecutive.

Jabbar combined great height with catlike moves and a deft shooting touch to lead UCLA to three consecutive NCAA Championships. Twice, as a sophomore and a senior, he was chosen as the top collegiate player in the country. He finished his career at UCLA as the ninth all-time collegiate scorer, accumulating 2,325 points in 88 games for an average of 26.4 points per game. After leading UCLA to its third consecutive NCAA title, Jabbar signed a contract with the Milwaukee Bucks for $1.4 million.

In his rookie season, 1969-1970, he led the Bucks, a recently established expansion club, to a second place finish in the Eastern Division, only a few games behind the division winners—the New York Knickerbockers. Jabbar won personal acclaim for his outstanding play in the 1970 NBA All-Star game, combining with the Knicks' Willis Reed to lead the East to victory. After being voted Rookie of the Year, he went on to win the scoring championships in 1971 and 1972. He was one of the keys to the Bucks' world championship in 1971. In 1973, he finished second in scoring with a 30.2 point average, but he had become dissatisfied with life in Milwaukee. At the end of the 1974-1975 season he was traded to the L.A. Lakers. Jabbar enjoyed a very successful career with the Lakers, leading the team to NBA championships in 1980, 1982, 1985, 1987, and 1988.

A serious person both on and off the court, Abdul-Jabbar is a convert to the Hanafi Muslims. Greatly influenced by the life and struggles of Malcolm X, he believes that the Islamic religion (as distinct from the nationalistic Black Muslims) and determined effort have much to offer for a good life.

Abdul-Jabbar announced that his retirement after the 1988-89 season, one year after the Lakers had won back-to-back World Championships. He was inducted into the Baskeball Hall of Fame in 1995.

Muhammad Ali (1942-)
Boxer

Born Cassius Clay, in Louisville, Kentucky, on January 17, 1942, Ali started boxing because he thought it was "the quickest way for black people to make it." After winning the 1960 Olympic gold medal as light-heavyweight, Cassius Clay turned pro. In 1963 he converted to Islam, although the faith strongly disapproves of boxing, and changed his name to Muhammad Ali.. A year later, Ali won the world heavyweight championship by knocking out Sonny Liston.

Nine successful title defenses followed before Ali's famous war with the Army began. Refusing to serve in the armed forces during the Vietnam War, Ali maintained that it was contrary to Muslim tenets. Stripped of his title and banned from boxing in the United States, Ali faced prison, but he refused to back down and was finally vindicated by the United States Supreme Court in 1970.

Coming back to the ring after a 3 1/2 year layoff, he worked his way up for another title shot. His biggest

Kareem Abdul-Jabbar

matches along the way were Superfights I and II against Joe Frazier in which Ali suffered his first loss, and, in a return match, evened the score.

Few fans gave Ali a chance against heavyweight champion George Foreman when they met in Zaire on October 30, 1974. A 4-1 underdog at ring time, Ali amazed the boxing world, knocking out his stronger, younger opponent. After regaining the crown, Ali knocked-out Chuck Wepner and Ron Lyle, and decisioned Joe Bugner.

In December of 1981, Muhammad Ali entered the ring and lost a bout against Canadian heavyweight Trevor Berbick. It was a rare defeat and an inauspicious end to a career for a fighter who had won the heavyweight title three times.

As he gets older, Ali's personal dedication to helping black people everywhere becomes increasingly more generous, and he now places special emphasis on setting a good example for black youth.

Henry Armstrong (1912-1988)
Boxer

The only fighter ever to hold three titles at the same time is Henry Armstrong, who accomplished this feat on August 17, 1938, when he added the lightweight championship to the featherweight and welterweight titles which he had won earlier.

Armstrong was born on December 12, 1912 in St. Louis, Missouri. In 1929, while fighting under the name of Melody Jackson, he was knocked out in his professional debut in Pittsburgh. However, two weeks later he won his first fight. For the next eight years he traveled from coast to coast, fighting all comers until he was finally given a shot at the featherweight title on October 20, 1937, when he defeated Petey Sarron.

Less than a year later, on May 31, 1938, Armstrong picked up his second title with a decision over welterweight champion Barney Ross. Within three months he gained his own triple crown, winning a decision over lightweight champion Lou Ambers.

Armstrong was inducted into the Black Athletes Hall of Fame in 1975.

Arthur Ashe (1943-1993)
Tennis Player

Born in Richmond, Virginia, Ashe learned the game of tennis at the Richmond Racket Club, which had been formed by local black enthusiasts. Dr. R.W. Johnson, who had also served as an advisor and benefactor to Althea Gibson, sponsored Ashe's tennis career, spending thousands of dollars and a great deal of time with him.

Muhammad Ali

Henry Armstrong

By 1958, Ashe reached the semifinals in the under-15 division of the National Junior Championships. In 1960 and 1961, he won the Junior Indoors Singles title. He was ranked 28th in the country even before he finished high school he was ranked 28th in the country.

In 1961, Ashe entered UCLA on a tennis scholarship. Ashe was on his way to winning the United States Amateur Tennis Championship and the U.S. Open Tennis Championship, in addition to becoming the first black man ever named to a Davis Cup Team.

In 1975, Ashe was recognized as one of the world's greatest tennis players, having defeated Jimmy Connors at Wimbledon as well as taking the World Championship Tennis (WCT) singles title over Bjorn Borg.

In 1979, at the age of 35, Ashe suffered a heart attack. Following quadruple bypass heart surgery, Ashe retired from active tennis. He began writing a nationally syndicated column and contributed monthly articles to *Tennis Magazine*. He wrote a tennis diary, *Portrait in Motion* and his autobiography, *Off the Court* and the book *Advantage Ashe*. In addition, he compiled the historical work, *A Hard Road to Glory: A History of the African-American Athlete*.

Arthur Ashe was named captain of the U.S. Davis Cup team in 1981. He was a former president and active member of the board of directors of the Association of Tennis Professionals, and a co-founder of the National Junior Tennis League. Late in his career, he also served as a television sports commentator.

In April 1992, Ashe announced that he had contracted AIDS as the result of a tainted blood transfusion received during heart-bypass surgery. He died on February 6, 1993.

Ernie Banks (1931-)
Baseball Player

Nicknamed "Mr. Cub", Ernie Banks was a stellar shortstop and first baseman during his 19 year career, the entirety of which was spent with the Chicago Cubs. One of the most congenial and well-liked player the game has seen, Banks coined the now famous phrase "Let's play two"; an indication of his enthusiasm for the game.

Born in Dallas, Banks was slightly built at 6'1", 180 pounds but his powerful wrists help him produce a career total of 512 home runs. His 44 homers and five grand slams in 1955 were single season records for

Tennis great Arthur Ashe.

shortstops. His best season was 1958, during which he led the National League in at bats (617), home runs (47), runs batted in (129), and slugging percentage (.614). He was named the league's Most Valuable Player after the 1958 and 1959 seasons.

Banks, who was moved to first base during the 1961 season at the age of 31 was durable, a fact illustrated by his 717 consecutive games played streak. He may have the somewhat dubious distinction of being the greatest player to never play in a World Series, as his Cubs rarely produced winning ballclubs during his tenure.

Banks, along with second baseman Gene Baker, formed the majors' first all black double play combination. He was the second African American to play for the Cubs, after Baker. Banks was elected to the Baseball Hall of Fame in 1977, and is also a member of the Texas Sports Hall of Fame.

After his playing career, Banks became a bank executive with Seaway National Bank. He remained very visible on the community scene, becoming a board member of the Chicago Transit Authority, the Chicago Metropolitan YMCA and of the Los Angeles Urban League, Banks also served in the U.S. Army.

Elgin Baylor (1934-)
Basketball Player

Born on September 16, 1934, in Washington, DC, Elgin Baylor first became an all-American while attending Spingarn High School. While at Seattle University he was a college All-American. In 1959, Baylor made a sensational professional debut with the Minneapolis Lakers; he became the first rookie to be named Most Valuable Player in the All-Star Game. That same year, he was named to the All-League team, setting a scoring record of 64 points in a single game.

After five years as a superstar, Baylor injured his knee during a 1965 playoff game against the Bullets. Constant work brought him back to competitive form, but he never reached his former greatness. His career point total of 23,149 is fourth highest in NBA history, and his scoring average of 27.4 is second. His best year was 1961-62, when he averaged 38.2 points a game. When he retired in 1968, Baylor had made the All-Pro first team nine times and had played eight consecutive All-Star games.

Baylor was inducted into the Black Athletes Hall of Fame in 1975, and the Basketball Hall of Fame in 1976. He was head coach of the New Orleans Jazz in 1978-79. Since 1986, Baylor has been executive vice president-basketball operations for the Los Angeles Clippers.

Lou Brock (1939-)
Baseball Player

Born in El Dorado, Arkansas, Lou Brock is one of the greatest base stealers of all-time. He stole 938 bases during a 19-year career which began in 1961, and was spent predominantly with the St. Louis Cardinals. Brock became the standard bearer for stolen bases on August 29, 1977, when the 893rd steal of his career eclipsed the mark that had been held by Ty Cobb for 49 years. In 1974, at the age of 35, Brock's 114 steals broke Mary Wills' single season mark, still a National League record in 1996. 1974 was one of the eight seasons in which he led the National League in steals. Brock registered at least 50 steals in 12 consecutive seasons and at retirement was the only player to hold both the Major League single season and career record in any major statistical category (stolen bases).

In 1967, Brock led the league in at-bats, runs scored and steals. The following season he set the pace in triples and steals, leading the Cardinals to pennants both seasons. With Brock, St. Louis also claimed a National League pennant in 1964, and World Championships in 1964 and 1967, over the New York Yankees and Boston Red Sox, respectively.

On June 6, 1964, in one of the most lopsided trades in baseball history, Brock was traded from the Chicago

Cubs to the Cardinals primarily for pitcher Ernie Broglio, who would win only 14 more games in the big leagues. Brock who went on to become a coach and business executive was presented with the Jackie Robinson Award by *Ebony* magazine as well as the Roberto Clemente award, in 1975. He was also the recipient of the B'nai B'rith Brotherhood award and was voted Man of the Year by the St. Louis Jaycees. Brock was inducted into the Baseball Hall of Fame in 1985.

Jim Brown (1936-)
Football Player

James Nathaniel Brown was born February 17, 1936, on St. Simon Island, Georgia, but his family moved to Manhasset, Long Island, New York, when he was seven. While at Manhasset High School he became an outstanding competitor in baseball, football, track and field, basketball, and lacrosse; following graduation he had a choice of 42 college scholarships, as well as professional offers from both the New York Yankees and the Boston Braves. Brown chose Syracuse University, where he gained national recognition. An All-American performer in both football and lacrosse, he turned down the opportunity to compete in the decathlon at the 1956 Olympic games, since it would have conflicted with his football schedule. He also spurned a three-year $150,000 offer to become a professional fighter.

Brown's 1957 entry into professional football with the Cleveland Browns was emblematic of the manner in which he would dominate the game in the decade to come. He led the league in rushing; paced Cleveland to a division championship; and was unanimously named Rookie of the Year. Brown broke rushing and scoring records in both single season and lifetime totals, and he was All-League fullback virtually every season. His records include most yards gained, lifetime 12,312, and most touchdowns, lifetime 106. He was voted Football Back of the Decade for 1950-1960.

Brown announced his retirement in the summer of 1966, deciding to devote his time to a budding movie career, and to the improvement of black business. He has made several films, including *Rio Conchos*, *The Dirty Dozen*, and *100 Rifles*. In addition to his moviemaking activities., he is president and founder of Amer-I-can.

Roy Campanella (1921-1993)
Baseball Player

Born on November 19, 1921, in Philadelphia, Campanella began playing semi-professional baseball at the age of fifteen with the Bacharach Giants. In 1945, Campanella turned down the opportunity to become the first black in the major leagues, when he mistakenly understood Branch Rickey's offer to be a contract with a rumored black team in Brooklyn. A few days later, he learned from Jackie Robinson that the offer had involved the possibility of playing with the Brooklyn Dodgers of the National League.

In 1946, Campanella was signed by the Dodgers. However, before the year was out, Campanella was brought up to Brooklyn. Over the next eight years, the Dodger star played with five National League pennant winners, and one world championship team. He played on seven consecutive National League All-Star teams (1949-1955).

In January 1958, Campanella's career was ended by an automobile accident which left him paralyzed and confined to a wheelchair. In 1969, he was inducted into the Baseball Hall of Fame; he was inducted into the Black Athletes Hall of Fame in 1975.

Wilt Chamberlain (1936-)
Basketball Player

Wilt Chamberlain was born in Philadelphia on August 21, 1936. By the time he entered high school, he was already 6'11". When he graduated from high school, he had his choice of 77 major colleges, and 125 smaller schools. He chose Kansas University, but left after his junior year with two years of All-American honors behind him.

Before joining the NBA in 1959, Chamberlain played with the Harlem Globetrotters. Although dominating the sport with the Philadelphia 76ers (1959-1967) and with the Los Angeles Lakers (1968-1972), Chamberlain was a member of only two championship teams, Philadelphia (1961) and Los Angeles (1972). For his gargantuan effort in defeating the Knicks in the latter series, including playing the final game with both hands painfully injured, he was voted MVP. At the start of the 1974 season, he left the Lakers to become player-coach of the San Diego Conquistadors (ABA) for a reported $500,000 contract.

Wilt Chamberlain holds most major records for a single game, including most points (100); field goals made (36); free throws (28); and rebounds (55). His season records include highest scoring average (50.4); highest field goal percentage (.727); and most rebounds (23,924). He was inducted into the Basketball Hall of Fame in 1978.

Alice Coachman (1921-)
Track and Field

Alice Coachman, who attended both Tuskegee Institue and Albany State was the first African American to win an Olympic Gold medal and the only American woman to earn a gold medal at the 1948 Games, which she accomplished in the high jump. She was also an out-

Roy Campanella (right) with Sammy Hughes, 1942.

standing basketball player, earning All-American honors as a guard while at Tuskegee.

Hailing from Albany, Georgia, Coachman made a name for herself at a very early age, when, as a seventh grader, she high jumped 5'4 1/2", less than an inch from the world record. Very versatile, she won the Amateur Athletic Union (AAU) Outdoor 50-meter title four times; 100-meters three times; and the high jump ten times, dominating the latter event during her career. Indoors, Coachman won the 50-meter twice and the high jump on three occasions.

Coachman's ten victories without a loss, between 1939 and 1948, is an AAU record. She is a member of eight different Halls of Fame, including the National Track and Field Hall of Fame, the Black Athletes Hall of Fame, the Tuskegee Hall of Fame, and the Georgia State Hall of Fame.

Willie Davis (1934-)
Football Player

Born in Lisbon, Louisiana, Willie Davis's career got off to an inauspicious start. After playing collegiately at Grambling, he was signed by the Cleveland Browns,

where he was miscast as an offensive lineman during the first two years of his NFL career (1958-59). Moving to the Green Bay Packers in time for the 1960 season, Davis played for ten more seasons and enjoyed a magnificent decade on both a personal and team level.

Davis was an All-Pro during the 1962 and 1964 through 1967 seasons. He was an integral and inspirational cornerstone of a Packers dynasty, which included championships in 1961, 1962, 1965, 1966, and 1967 and did not miss a single game during his career with Green Bay. Following the conclusion of his illustrious career, Davis earned a master's degree in business administration from the University of Chicago—the impetus behind a very successful career in business and community relations.

Davis's off-field accomplishments rival those from the gridiron: He is president and owner of All-Pro Broadcasting, Inc. as well as serving on the Board of Directors of the Joseph Schlitz Brewing Company. Additionally, he is on the advisory board of the Black Peace Officers Association and president and director of the Los Angeles Urban League, among other endeavors. Davis speaks approximately once a week to a variety of civic and community groups.

Wilt Chamberlain

Lee Elder

Formerly a football analyst for NBC television, Davis has done public relations and promotional work for the Chrysler Corporation. He also toured Vietnam for the State Department in 1966, having previously served in the U.S. Army. He was named "Man of the Year" by the NAACP in 1978. Davis was elected to the Football Hall of Fame in 1981, and is also a member of the NAIA Hall of Fame.

Lee Elder (1934-)
Golfer

Born Robert Lee Elder in Washington, DC, on July 14, 1934, Elder first picked up golf as a caddie at the age of fifteen. After his father's death during World War II, Elder and his mother moved to Los Angeles, where he met the famed black golfer Ted Rhodes. He was later drafted by the United States Army, where he sharpened his skills as captain of the golf team.

Following his discharge from the Army, he began to teach golf. In 1962, he debuted as a professional, winning the United Golf Association (a black organization) national title. Elder had played seventeen years with the United Golf Association, prior to his participation in the PGA, participating in close to fifty tournaments. He

debuted with the PGA in November 1967, finishing one stroke out of the money. In thirty PGA tournaments, Elder earned $38,000; he was the first black professional golfer to reach $1 million in earnings.

George Foreman (1948-)
Boxer

Born in Marshall, Texas, George Foreman rose from a childhood of mischief and thievery to a championship career, eventually emerging as one of boxing's most endearing figures. During a turbulent childhood in Houston, Foreman was a truant, snatching purses and participating in petty larcenies. He claims to have been eventually saved by the Job Corps and football legend Jim Brown. His early success included a gold medal performance at the 1968 summer Olympic Games. Foreman was a physical presence in the ring, one of the fight game's most powerful punchers. His record featured 42 knockouts in his first 47 bouts.

Foreman captured the heavyweight title as a result of his victory over Joe Frazier, in Kingston, Jamaica, on January 22, 1973. Having twice defended his belt successfully, he prepared to face Muhammad Ali on October 30, 1974, in Kinshasa, Zaire, a fight that become known as the "Rumble in the Jungle." Despite being a three to one favorite, and considerably stronger than Ali, Foreman was out-strategized by the latter who used his "rope-a-dope" tactic to tire Foreman and victimize him in the eighth round. Ali spent much of the bout leaning against the ropes, protecting his head, and letting Foreman expend his energy. Ali took the crown.

Foreman eventually retired to become a minister and transformed his image into that of a congenial and very popular ex-champion. He initiated a comeback, which, after a series of tune-up bouts against overmatched opponents, resulted in a recapture of the heavyweight crown, when he defeated Michael Moorer on November 5, 1994.

Julius "Dr. J." Erving (1950-)
Basketball Player

Julius Erving was born in Hempstead, Long Island, on February 22, 1950. As a player at Roosevelt High School, Erving made the All-County and All-Long Island teams. He was awarded an athletic scholarship to the University of Massachusetts, but after completing his junior year, he left college, hired the services of a management firm, and signed a $500,000, four-year contract with the Virginia Squires of the ABA. Voted Rookie of the Year in 1972, he renegotiated his contract and eventually signed with the New Jersey Nets for $2.8 million over four years.

In his first season with the Nets (1973), Erving led the league in scoring for the second consecutive year and led his team to the ABA championship. After being traded to the 76ers, Erving became a favorite with Philadelphia fans, leading his team to the NBA championship in 1983. Between his combined seasons with the two teams, he became the 13th player to score 20,000 points. Erving retired following the 1986-87 season. In the 1990s, the articulate Erving remained in the midst of a successful broadcasting career. He was inducted into the Basketball Hall of Fame in 1993.

Althea Gibson (1927-)
Tennis Player

Althea Gibson was born on August 25, 1927, in Silver, South Carolina, but raised in Harlem, where she learned to play paddle tennis. After her paddle tennis days, she entered and won the Department of Parks Manhattan Girls' Tennis Championship. In 1942, she began to receive professional coaching at the interracial Cosmopolitan Tennis Club, and a year later, won the New York State Negro Girls Singles Title. In 1945 and 1946, she won the National Negro Girls Singles championship, and in 1948, began a decade of domination of the same title in the Women's Division.

A year later Gibson entered Florida A and M, where she played tennis and basketball for the next four years. In 1950, she was runner-up for the National Indoor Championship, and that same year became the first black to play at Forest Hills. The following year she became the first black to play at Wimbledon.

In 1957 Gibson won the Wimbledon singles crown, and teamed with Darlene Hard to win the doubles championship as well. In 1957 and 1958, Gibson won the U.S. Open Women's Singles title.

Gibson has served as a recreation manager, a member of the New Jersey State Athletic Control Board, the Governor's Council on Physical Fitness, and as a sports consultant. She is also the author of a book, *I Always Wanted to be Somebody.*

Bob Gibson (1935-)
Baseball Player

Bob Gibson was born in Omaha, Nebraska into abject poverty. Fatherless, he was one of seven children, and lived in a four room wooden shack. When able to sleep alone, he did so on an army cot. Denied a spot on Omaha Technical High School's baseball team because he was black, he was permitted to join the track and field and basketball teams; he became a star for each sport. During college at Creighton, he became the first black athlete there to play both basketball and baseball.

Gibson was proficient enough at basketball that he spent some time with the Harlem Globetrotters. While with them, he accepted an offer to join the St. Louis Cardinals minor league team at Omaha for a salary of $3,000 and a $1,000 bonus. Gibson debuted with the Cardinals in 1959, the start of a Hall of Fame career—he was inducted in 1981—that lasted 17 seasons and included five 20-victory seasons and 13 consecutive winning seasons. His highlights include a 1968 campaign in which he recorded a remarkable 13 shutouts, 22 victories, 268 strikeouts and an Earned Run Average of 1.12, still a National League record in 1996.

During his career, Gibson recorded 3,117 strikeouts, finishing with an ERA of 2.91. He was at his finest in the biggest games, winning seven and losing two games in three World Series appearances, with an ERA of 1.89. In Game 1 of the 1968 series he struck out 17 Detroit Tigers, though St. Louis eventually lost the series in seven games. Gibson did pitch the Cardinals to World Championships in 1964 and 1967.

Gibson, one of the most feared and intimidating pitchers of his era was considered sullen and difficult. Following his playing days, Gibson served as pitching coach with the New York Mets and Atlanta Braves. He currently is an announcer with the St. Louis Cardinals.

Althea Gibson, 1957.

Josh Gibson (1911-1947)
Baseball Player

Josh Gibson has been considered by some to be the greatest baseball player who ever lived, regardless of race. He was a catcher whose entire 16-year career was spent in the Negro League, beginning in 1929. With the exception of a stint with the Pittsburgh Crawfords, between 1934 and 1936, and one season in Mexico, in 1941, Gibson played for with the Homestead Grays.

Gibson was born in Buena Vista, Georgia, in 1911, and subsequently moved to Pittsburgh, where he left school at the age of 14, eventually finding work with Gimbels Department store. Gimbels had a baseball team, which is where Gibson first attracted attention. His first game with Homestead took place on July 25, 1929, when, as a spectator, he was called out of the stands where he was watching a game versus the Kansas City Monarchs, to replace an injured starter.

A great catcher, Gibson was better known for his legendary power. Playing at Yankee Stadium, he once hit a homerun over the left field bullpen and out of the stadium. An even greater feat was a ball Gibson powered out of the same ballpark, to the top of the bleach-

ers, an estimated 580 feet—the longest homerun ever seen to that date.

Gibson died in 1947, from a stroke thought to be brought on by his alcoholism. He was elected to the Hall of Fame in 1972.

Lusia Harris (1955-)
Basketball Player

Born in 1955, in Minter City, Mississippi, Lusia Harris is the greatest center in women's basketball history. The seventh of nine children, the 6'3" Harris participated on the silver medal- winning Olympic basketball team in 1976, when women's basketball made its debut at the games and scored the first two points in Olympic history. In addition to the Olympics, where she scored the most points, she was also the high scorer in the 1975 World University Games and Pan American Games. In college, she led Delta State University to three Association for Intercollegiate Athletics for Women titles from 1975 to 1977. She was named Mississippi's first amateur athlete of the year in 1976. An acknowledged leader on campus, Harris was selected as Delta State's homecoming queen, the first black so honored.

Harris, the dominant female player of her era, broke hundreds of records and won countless American and international awards. As a graduate student, she became assistant basketball coach and admissions counselor at Delta State. She played briefly with the Houston Angels of the new Women's Professional League in 1980.

In the 1990s, Harris has been coaching basketball and teaching physical education in Mississippi. In 1992, along with Nera White, Harris became the first woman inducted into the Basketball Hall of Fame. Additionally, she spends time addressing groups as a motivational speaker.

Larry Holmes (1949-)
Boxer

Larry Holmes was one of the most unheralded champions in boxing history. He lacked the flair of Muhammad Ali, the punching power of George Foreman, or the flamboyance of Sugar Ray Leonard. He was, however, one of the sport's most consistent and enduring champions.

Holmes was born in Cuthberth, Georgia, and turned professional at the age of 24. On June 9, 1978, he won the World Boxing Council heavyweight title from Ken Norton and defended it successfully seven times. On October 2, 1980, in Las Vegas, his conquest of Muhammad Ali by knockout unified the World title. The 38-year old Ali was no match for Holmes.

Holmes defended his title 12 times until losing to Michael Spinks on September 22, 1985, and again on

April 19, 1986, in 15-round decisions. In all, Holmes held the WBC/World heavyweight title for seven years, three months, and 13 days. A brief comeback attempt was stunted by a knockout at the hands of Mike Tyson on February 22, 1988. Holmes, who was voted one of the ten Most Outstanding Men in America by the Junior Chamber of Commerce, was currently in the throes of a second comeback attempt in the mid-1990s.

Reggie Jackson (1946-)
Baseball Player

Because of his outstanding performance in the early fall, Reggie Jackson became known as "Mr. October." During his years with the Oakland Athletics and New York Yankees, Jackson captured or tied 13 World Series records to become baseball's greatest record holder for the fall classic. Reggie Jackson ranks among baseball's crop of players with proven superstar ability. His temperament, long reported to be as explosive and dynamic as his skill with the bat, gave him the drive to reach the top.

Born in Wynecote, Pennsylvania, on May 18, 1946, he followed his father's encouragement to become an all-around athlete while at Cheltenham High School, where he ran track, starred at halfback, and batted .550. An outstanding football and baseball collegian at Arizona State University, he left after sophomore year to join the Athletics (then located in Kansas City).

In 1968, his first full season with the Athletics, Jackson hit 29 homers and batted in 74 runs, but made 18 errors and struck out 171 times, the second worst seasonal total in baseball history. After playing a season of winter ball, under Frank Robinson 's direction, Jackson was back on track. His performance continued to improve, and, in 1973, he batted .293, led the league in home runs (32), RBIs (117), and slugging average (.531), and was selected Most Valuable Player (MVP).

While with Oakland, Jackson helped the Athletics to three straight World Series championships, from 1972 to 1974. Later, with the New York Yankees, Jackson participated in the 1977, 1978, and 1981 World Series, with New York winning the first two. In 1977, he was named series MVP, after hitting five home runs, including three, on three consecutive pitches, in the sixth and deciding game.

The first of the big money free agents, Jackson hit 144 homers, drove in 461 runs, and boosted his total career home runs to 425 while with the Yankees. Jackson retired as an active player in 1987, and has occasionally served as a commentator during baseball broadcasts. He has also continued to devote more time to his collection of antique cars.

Earvin "Magic" Johnson, Jr. (1959-)
Basketball Player

Earvin Johnson, Jr. was born August 14, 1959 in Lansing, Michigan. He attended Everett High School, and, in 1974, made their varsity basketball team as a guard. While playing for Everett he picked up the nickname "Magic" because of his ball-handling abilities. While in high school, Johnson made the All-State Team and for three years was named the United Press International Prep-Player of the Year in Michigan.

In 1977, Johnson enrolled at Michigan State University and played college ball until 1979, when he was selected by the Los Angeles Lakers in the National Basketball Association draft. Johnson played with the Lakers until his forced retirement in 1991, when he tested positive for HIV, the virus that is closely associated with acquired immunodeficiency syndrome (AIDS).

Throughout his college and professional career, Johnson was an outstanding basketball player who brought much excitement, goodwill, and admiration to the game. He was the recipient of many awards and was chosen to play on many post-season all-star teams. He was All-Big Ten Team in 1977, and chosen as the NCAA Tournament-Most Valuable Player and consensus All-American (1979), NBA All-Rookie Team (1980), All-NBA Team (1982-89, 1991), NBA Finals Most Valuable Player (1987), and NBA All-Star Game Most Valuable Player (1990, 1992).

During his retirement, Johnson made appearances on the court, including playing on the U.S. Olympic Basketball Team in 1992, and the 1992 NBA All Star game, where he won another Most Valuable Player award. He also coached the Lakers briefly at the end of the 1994 season, became team vice president, and had an ownership stake in the Lakers, which he was forced to surrender upon his return as a player in 1996.

Jack Johnson (1878-1946)
Boxer

Jack Johnson, became the first black heavyweight champion, after winning the crown from Tommy Burns in Sydney, Australia on December 26, 1908.

Johnson was born in Galveston, Texas, on March 31, 1878, the son of a school janitor. He was so tiny as a boy that he was nicknamed "Li'l Arthur," a name that stuck with him throughout his career. As a young man, he "hoboed" around the country, making his way to Chicago, Boston, and New York, and learning the fighting trade by working out with veteran professionals whenever he could. When he finally got his chance at the title, he had already been fighting for nine years and had lost only three of approximately 100 bouts.

Reggie Jackson with the New York Yankees, 1977.

With his victory over Burns, Johnson became the center of a bitter racial controversy, as the American public clamored for the former white champion, Jim Jeffries, to come out of retirement and recapture the crown. When the two fought on July 4, 1910 in Reno, Nevada, Johnson knocked out Jeffries in the fourteenth round.

In 1913, Johnson left the United States because of legal entanglements. Two years later he defended his title against Jess Willard in Havana, Cuba and was knocked out in the twenty sixth round. His career record was 107 wins, 6 losses.

Johnson died on June 10, 1946, in an automobile crash in North Carolina. He was inducted into the Boxing Hall of Fame in 1954.

Michael Jordan (1963-)
Basketball Player

Michael Jordan was born in Brooklyn, New York, on February 17, 1963, and attended the University of North

Earvin "Magic" Johnson

Carolina. As a rookie with the Chicago Bulls in 1985, Jordan was named to the All-Star team. A skilled ball-handler and a slam-dunk artist, he became the second NBA player in history to score more than 3,000 points in a single season in 1986.

Jordan was the NBA's individual scoring champ from 1987 through 1993. He was also named the NBA's Most Valuable Player at the end of the 1987-88 season. In 1991, Jordan led the Chicago Bulls to their first NBA Championship and was the league's Most Valuable Player. Under Jordan's leadership, the Bulls experienced repeat NBA championships in 1992 and 1993. In 1992 Jordan played for the 1992 United States Olympic basketball team, which captured the gold medal in Barcelona, Spain.

In October of 1993, Jordan announced his retirement from basketball to pursue another lifelong dream—to become a professional baseball player. His decision was made in part because of the stresses related with his basketball superstardom but also because of the pain of coping with his father's untimely death. (James Jordan, his father, was murdered in North Carolina shortly before the season ended.)

Michael Jordan began his professional baseball career with the Chicago White Sox's Class AA team, the Birmingham Barons, in 1994. Despite having only a .202 batting average for the year, Jordan was voted the most popular man in baseball in a national poll and remained at the top of Forbes magazine's list of the world's top paid athletes for the third consecutive year.

In 1995, Jordan expected to move up to Class AAA ball, but on March 18, 1995, Michael Jordan released a two-word announcement to the Chicago Bulls organization and the media—"I'm back"—simultaneously announcing his retirement from baseball and his return to the NBA late in the 1994-95 season. He was named the 1996 All-Star game MVP during the next season. Entering the 1995-96 campaign, Jordan, considered by many to be the greatest player in history, held the mark for the highest career scoring average at 32.2. On June 16, 1996, Jordan led the Bulls to their fourth NBA championship.

Florence Griffith Joyner (1959-)
Track and Field Athlete

Born in Los Angeles on December 21, 1959, Florence Griffith started in track at an early age. She first attend-

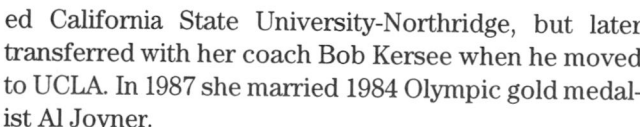

Michael Jordan

Florence Griffith Joyner

ed California State University-Northridge, but later transferred with her coach Bob Kersee when he moved to UCLA. In 1987 she married 1984 Olympic gold medalist Al Joyner.

At the 1984 Olympic games she won a silver medal. She returned to the Olympic games in 1988, winning a gold medal in the 100 meter, 200 meter, 400 meter relay, and 1600 meter relay races. She set the world record for the 100 meter and 200 meter races that year.

Jackie Joyner-Kersee (1962-)
Track and Field Athlete

Often touted as the world's greatest female athlete, Jackie Joyner-Kersee (b. 1962) won two gold medals at the 1988 Olympic games and a gold and a bronze medal at the 1992 games.

Born on March 3, 1962, in East St. Louis, Illinois, she studied previous outstanding woman athletes and soon teamed with her husband to pursue her dreams of success in the field of competition. Prior to winning the 1988 gold medal, she participated in the 1984 Olympics and came away with a silver medal for the heptathlon despite a torn hamstring muscle.

The only woman to gain more than 7,000 points in the heptathlon four times, she set a world record for the grueling two-day event with 7,215 points at the 1988 Olympic trials prior to the competition itself. Joyner-Kersee also earned another gold medal in the heptathlon and a bronze medal in the long jump at the 1992 Olympics in Barcelona, Spain.

Dick "Night Train" Lane (1928-)
Football Player

Born in Austin, Texas on April 16, 1928, Dick "Night Train" Lane became one of the NFL's best-ever free agent finds. After attending Scottsbluff Junior College, Lane's 14-year career spanned three teams, the Los Angeles Rams (1952-53), Chicago Cardinals (1954-59), and Detroit Lions (1960-65), during which he earned All-Pro honors six times.

A cornerback, Lane twice led the NFL in interceptions, including a record 14 as a rookie. His 68 career interceptions place him third on the all-time NFL list. Lane, who was chosen as an all-time NFL All-Pro in 1969, and was voted All-Time Player of the Century in 1968, was inducted into the Pro Football Hall of Fame in 1974, and the Black Athletes Hall of Fame in 1977 .

Jackie Joyner-Kersee

Lane coached at Southern University and Central University in the early to mid-1970s. He was also an assistant NFL coach. Lane became the Detroit Police Athletic League Athletic Director in 1975. He is the founder of the Michigan Youth Development Foundation and is Past-President of the Detroit Varsity Club. He has been involved with the Boy's Club of Metro Detroit as well as the Booker T. Washington Businessmen's Association. During his playing days, Lane had directed youth programs in Chicago and Detroit.

Carl Lewis (1961-)
Track and Field Athlete

Carl Lewis was born on July 1, 1961, in Birmingham, Alabama. In the 1984 Olympics in Los Angeles, Lewis became the first athlete, since Jesse Owens in 1936, to win four gold medals in Olympic competition.

An often controversial track and field performer, the New Jersey native went into the 1984 competition with the burden of tremendous expectations as the result of intense pre-Olympics publicity. He did not set any Olympic records, even as a gold medalist and found that his public image and statements were often the subject of public concern.

Lewis went to the 1988 Olympics in Seoul, South Korea, hoping to duplicate his four gold medal wins, and was the subject of widespread interest as he faced off against his arch-rival Canadian Ben Johnson.

Lewis won gold medals in the long jump and the 100-meter dash (but the latter prize came after Ben Johnson was disqualified following the race when he tested positive for steroid use) and a silver medal in the 200-meter dash. At the 1992 Olympics in Barcelona, Spain, Lewis won a gold medal for the long jump.

Joe Louis (1914-1981)
Boxer

Joe Louis held the heavyweight championship, for more than 11 years, longer than anyone else and defended the title more often than any other heavyweight champion. His 25 title fights were more than the combined total of the eight champions who preceded him.

Born on May 13, 1914, in a sharecropper's shack in Lexington, Alabama, Louis moved to Detroit as a small boy. Taking up boxing as an amateur, he won 50 out of 59 bouts (43 by knockout), before turning professional in 1934. He quickly gained a reputation in the Midwest.

Carl Lewis

Joe Louis, 1936.

In 1935 Lewis came East to meet Primo Carnera, former boxing champion who was then staging a comeback. Louis knocked out Carnera in six rounds, earning his nickname, "The Brown Bomber." After knocking out ex-champion Max Baer, Louis suffered his lone pre-championship defeat at the hands of Max Schmeling, the German title holder who knocked him out in the twelfth round. Less than a month later, Louis knocked out another former champion, Jack Sharkey, in three rounds. After defeating a number of other challengers, he was given a title fight with Jim Braddock on June 22, 1937. He stopped Braddock in the eighth round, and began the long championship reign that was to see him defending his crown as often as six times in six months.

One of Louis' greatest fights was his 1941 come-from-behind thirteenth-round-knockout of Billy Conn. After winning a disputed decision over Joe Walcott in 1947, Louis knocked out the Jersey challenger six months later, and then went into retirement. Joe Louis died April 12, 1981 at the age of 67.

Willie Mays (1931-)
Baseball Player

During his 21 seasons with the San Francisco Giants, Willie Mays hit more than 600 home runs. Besides being a solid hitter, Mays also has been called the game's finest defensive outfielder and perhaps its best baserunner as well.

Born in Fairfield, Alabama on May 6, 1931, Mays made his professional debut on July 4, 1948, with the Birmingham Black Barons. He was signed by the New York Giants in 1950 and reached the major leagues in 1951, in time to become the National League's Rookie of the Year with 20 home runs, 68 RBIs, and the sensational fielding which contributed to his team's pennant victory.

After two years in the Army, Mays returned to lead the Giants to the World Championship in 1954, gaining recognition as the league's Most Valuable Player for his 41 homers, 110 RBIs and .345 batting average.

When the Giants moved to San Francisco, Mays continued his phenomenal home run hitting, and led his team to a 1962 pennant. A year later, *Sport* magazine named him "the greatest player of the decade." He won the MVP award again in 1965, after hitting 52 home runs and batting .317.

Traded to the New York Mets before the 1972 season, he continued to play outfield and first base. At the end of the 1973 season, his records included 2,992 games (3rd on the all-time list), 3,283 hits (7th), and 660 home runs (3rd). Willie Mays is one of only seven ballplayers to have hit four home runs in one game. After acting as a coach for the Mets, Mays left baseball to pursue a business career. He was elected to the Baseball Hall of Fame in 1979.

Cheryl Miller (1964-)
Basketball Player

Cheryl Miller was born and raised in Riverside, California, and is thought by many as the greatest women's basketball player in history. She has occasionally been overshadowed by her brother, Reggie, a guard with the Indiana Pacers. Another brother, Darrell, played baseball professionally with the California Angels in the late 1980s.

The 6'3" Cheryl Miller began raising eyebrows at an early level, having once scored 105 points in a game while at Polytechnic High School. Miller was offered nearly 250 scholarships before deciding to enroll at the University of Southern California (USC). There she led the Trojans to two national titles, was All-American four times, and was named national player of the year three times.

Miller was a member of numerous national teams, including the U.S. Junior National Team in 1981, and the National Team the following year. She participated in the World Championships in 1983, the Pan American Games the same year, and, in 1984, was an integral component of the first American Olympic women's basketball team to claim a gold medal.

Since the end of her playing career, Miller has made numerous television appearances as a commentator. In 1993, she became the women's head basketball coach at her alma mater, USC, but announced her retirement in 1995, the same year she was voted into the Basketball Hall of Fame.

Edwin Moses (1955-)
Track and Field

Born in Dayton, Ohio, in 1955, Edwin Moses became the greatest hurdler in track and field history. Having attended Morehouse College, he was the top ranked intermediate hurdler in the world as early as 1976. That same year he earned a gold medal at the Olympic Games, a feat to be duplicated eight years later. Moses also won a bronze medal at the 1988 Games. A world record holder in the 400-meter hurdles, his greatest accomplishment is undoubtedly his remarkable streak of 122 consecutive victories in competition. *Sports Illustrated* presented Moses with its Athlete of the Year award in 1984, one year after he won the Sullivan award, given annually to the best amateur athlete, regardless of sport.

Moses is currently an MBA-candidate and a partner in the Platinum Group. He is the chairperson of the U.S. Olympic Committee Substance Abuse Center and serves on the International Olympic Committee Athletes Commission.

Jesse Owens (1913-1980)
Track and Field Athlete

The track and field records Jesse Owens set have all been eclipsed, but his reputation as one of the first great athletes with the combined talents of a sprinter, low hurdler, and broad jumper has hardly diminished with the passing of time.

Born James Cleveland Owens in Danville, Alabama, on September 12, 1913, Jesse and his family moved to Ohio when he was still young; the name "Jesse" derived from the way a teacher pronounced his initials, "J.C."

In 1932, while attending East Technical High School in Cleveland, Owens gained national fame with a 10.3 clocking in the 100-meter dash. Two years later, Owens entered Ohio State University, and for the next four years made track history, becoming universally known as "The Ebony Antelope." While competing in the Big Ten Championships at Ann Arbor, Michigan on May 25, 1935, Owens had what has been called "the greatest single day in the history of man's athletic achievements." In the space of about 70 minutes, he tied the world record for the 100-yard dash and surpassed the world record for five other events, including the broad jump, the 220-yard low hurdles, and the 220-yard dash.

In 1936, at the Berlin Olympics, Owens won four gold medals, at that time the most universally acclaimed feat in the history of the games. When Adolf Hitler refused to present him with the medals he had won in the various competitions, Owens' fame became even more widespread as a result of the publicity.

Willie Mays slides across home plate, 1956.

Leroy Robert "Satchel" Paige (1906-1982)
Baseball Player

Long before Jackie Robinson broke the color barrier of "organized baseball," Satchel Paige was a name well-known to the general sports public. As an outstanding performer in "Negro baseball," Paige had become a legendary figure whose encounters with major league players added considerable laurels to his athletic reputation.

Paige was born in Mobile, Alabama on July 7, 1906. He began playing semi-professional ball while working as an iceman and porter. In the mid-1920s, he became a professional player with the Birmingham Black Barons, and later, while playing at Chattanooga, acquired the nick-name "Satchel" because of his "Satchel-sized feet."

For the next two decades, Paige compiled a phenomenal record. In 1933, he won 31 games and lost four. Paige also dominated winter ball in Latin America during the 1930s. In 1942, Paige led the Kansas City Monarchs to victory in the Negro World Series, and four years later he helped them to the pennant by allowing only two runs in 93 innings, a performance which included a string of 64 straight scoreless innings.

In 1948, when he was brought up to the major leagues, Paige was well past his prime, but he still was able to contribute six victories in Cleveland's pennant drive. Four years' later, while pitching for the St. Louis Browns, he was named to the American League All-Star squad.

Until the 1969 baseball season, Paige was primarily active on the barnstorming circuit with the Harlem Globetrotters and a host of other exhibition teams. In 1969 the Atlanta Braves, in an attempt to make Paige eligible for baseball's pension plan, signed him to a one-year contract as coach. Paige died in June 1982.

Jim Parker (1934-)
Football Player

Born April 3, 1934 in Macon, Georgia, this guard from Ohio State University holds the distinction of being the first lineman ever inducted into the Pro Football Hall of Fame exclusively as an offensive player, an honor accorded him in 1973. He has also been elected to both the College and Georgia Halls of Fame.

While in college, Parker was the recipient of the Outland Trophy in 1956, awarded to the nation's outstanding lineman and was All-American in 1955 and 1966. A fine run-and-pass blocker, he provided protec-

Jesse Owens (left) with Ralph Metcalfe, 1936.

Jesse Owens (center) accepts the gold medal at the 1936 Olympic Games in Berlin, Germany.

tion for Hall of Fame teammate and quarterback Johnny Unitas during each of Parker's seasons in the NFL (1957-1967) and was named All-Pro eight consecutive years (1958-1965). The 6'3", 273 pound Parker was named to the first team Pro Football Hall of Fame Selection Committtte" All-NFL 1960-1984 All-Star Team."

Walter Payton (1954-)
Football Player

Walter Payton was born on July 25, 1954, in Columbia, Mississippi. When he retired as a running back for the Chicago Bears after the 1986 season, he was the National Football League's all-time leading rusher, breaking a record held for many years by Jim Brown.

A graduate of Jackson State University, Payton played his entire career in Chicago, receiving numerous awards and helping to lead the Bears to a victory in Super Bowl XX. Nicknamed "Sweetness," he broke O. J. Simpson's single game rushing record after gaining 275 yards during a game with the Minnesota Vikings in 1977. Seven years later, during a game agains the New Orleans Saints, he surpassed Jim Brown's career rushing record and concluded his career with a total of 16,726.

Following his retirement, Payton continued his pursuit of a career in the auto racing industry and also fronted a group of businessmen in an attempt to bring a professional football team to the city of St. Louis.

Calvin Peete (1943-)
Golfer

Born in Detroit, on July 18, 1943, Calvin Peete's ascendence to prominence is an unlikely story that finally landed him as the most accomplished African American golfer in history. During World War II, Peete moved with his family to Pahikee, Florida where he grew up. One of 19 children, he survived as a youth as a farm laborer and itinerant peddler, selling wares to farmers travelling up and down the east coast.

Constantly badgered by friends to take up golf, Peete's would respond "who wants to chase a little ball around under the hot sun." He finally relented, and at the age of 23, hit a golf ball for the first time, soon realizing that he possessed some aptitude for the sport. Unlike other black golfers of his era who were forced into caddying as a means of gaining entrance into the sport, Peete was able to move directly toward a professional career.

Walter Payton

Peete did, however, face the handicap of a left arm that he was unable to completely straighten; experts told him that he would never be successful.

After turning pro in 1971, Peete struggled. As late as 1978, he placed 108th in total money winnings on the PGA tour, but he soon made up for lost time. Peete's first tour victory came at the 1979 Greater Milwaukee Open, which he won again in 1982, along with the Anheuser-Busch Classic, BC Open, and the Pensacola Open. In 1981 and 1982, he finished first on the tour in the categories of driving accuracy and greens reached in regulation.

Despite his success, Peete was not considered fully accredited because the PGA does not recognize a golfer as such unless he has obtained a high school diploma. This was a requirement toward obtaining a spot on the prestigious Ryder Cup team. In 1982, with the assistance of his wife, a part-time teacher, Peete passed the Michigan General Equivalency examination 24 years after leaving high school. *Ebony* magazine rewarded him with a Black Achievement award, and, in 1983, Peete was presented with the Jackie Robinson award.

Peete captured two more PGA titles in 1983—the Georgia-Pacific Atlanta Classic and the Anheuser-Busch

Classic, for the third time. He was also asked to represent the U.S. as a member of the Ryder Cup team. That same year, he won the Ben Hogan award. The following year, Peete had the best scoring average on the PGA tour and was the most successful golfer of the decade to that point.

Willis Reed (1943-)
Basketball Player

Born in Bernice, Louisiana, on June 25, 1943, Willis Reed spent his boyhood picking cotton around his hometown. He attended Grambling College, where he was discovered by Red Holzman, the chief scout for the New York Knicks. Reed led the Knicks in scoring and rebounding on his way to becoming Rookie of the Year in 1965.

In 1970, when the Knicks won their first NBA Championship, Reed received three separate MVP awards—one for the regular season, one for the All-Star game, and one for the playoffs.

At 6'9" and 240 pounds, Reed was not big for a center. However, he was named to the All Star team his first seven seasons. In 1973 he led the Knicks to their second NBA title and was again named Most Valuable Player. Unfortunately, knee problems ended his career. In 1981 Reed was elected to the National Memorial Basketball Hall of Fame.

Jerry Rice (1962-)
Football Player

Born in Starkville, Mississippi, on October 13, 1962, San Francisco 49ers wide receiver Jerry Rice has been rewriting the NFL's record books at a dizzying pace. At a collegian at Mississippi Valley State, Rice set 18 Division II records. Drafted in the first round by the 49ers in 1985, the durable Rice, combined with quarterback Joe Montana to form the most elite pass-catching combination in pro football history.

Rice continues to add to his career record for touchdowns, regardless of position (156). His ten straight seasons with more than 1,000 receiving yards is also a league record. His best season was the strike-shortened 1987 campaign, during which he scored 22 touchdowns in only 12 regular season games. In that same year, Rice scored touchdowns in 13 straight games, including playoffs. In a 1990 contest with the Atlanta Falcons, Rice scored five touchdowns. He has been named to the Pro Bowl for ten straight seasons and was named the NFL's Player of the year by the *Sporting News* in 1987 and 1990. Rice was Most Valuable Player in the 49ers' Super Bowl XXIII victory over the Cincinnati Bengals.

Rice had helped lead the 49ers to Super Bowl victories after the 1988, 1989, and 1994 seasons and is known for his tireless work ethic. While on vacation, he has been known to travel with a parachute that he straps onto his back to add resistance while running on the beach. He traces the development of his superb hands to his childhood, during which his father would toss him bricks during construction work.

Eddie G. Robinson (1919-)
College Football Coach

Life for Eddie G. Robinson began on February 13, 1919, in Jackson, Louisiana. Even at an early age, Robinson's knack for coaching was noticeable. Once while in grade school, several high school football players visited Robinson's class. All of the younger children swarmed the teens except Robinson. He was busy hanging around the coach.

As a gifted athlete in high school, Robinson earned a scholarship to Leland College in Louisiana. A star quarterback, Robinson got involved in his first coaching clinic there. After obtaining his bachelor's degree, Robinson took his first college coaching job in 1941. Though only 22 years old at the time, Grambling State gave Robinson the opportunity to run both offense and defense as he saw fit. The early success of Grambling State's football team earned Robinson much respect. Segregation, oppression, and a world war could not impede him. As the years passed, the wins for his football teams kept coming. By 1985, Robinson had surpassed Bear Bryant, the "winningest" coach in college football history in career victories.

Frank Robinson (1935-)
Baseball Player

Born in Beaumont, Texas in 1936, Frank Robinson moved with his family to Oakland, California at the age of five. During his teens, he was a football and baseball star at McClymonds High School. After graduation in 1953, he signed with the Cincinnati Reds.

In 1956, Robinson made a smash debut in the major leagues, hitting 38 homers and winning Rookie of the Year honors. During the next eight years, he hit 259 homers and had 800 RBIs, an outstanding record, but one that was often underpublicized, because Robinson played in the shadow of such greats as Willie Mays and Hank Aaron.

In 1961, Robinson was named Most Valuable Player for leading Cincinnati to the National League pennant. Five years later, Robinson won the American League's Triple Crown and became the first player to win the MVP in both leagues. He retired as an active player after the 1976 season with a lifetime batting average of .294 in 2,808 games along with 2,943 hits, 1,829 runs, and 1,812 RBIs. His 586 home runs rank fourth all-time.

Frank Robinson was major league baseball's first black manager. Named to the head post of the Cleveland Indians in 1975, Robinson exhibited the same cool, confident demeanor that served him well during an 18-year career as a major league player.

Robinson left the Indians in 1977, and became the manager of the Rochester Red Wings, a minor league team, in 1978. In 1981, Robinson was hired by the San Francisco Giants, where he managed the team until 1984. He also managed the Baltimore Orioles during the late 1980s. He later became the assistant general manager of that team. Robinson was elected to the National Baseball Hall of Fame in 1982.

Jackie Robinson (1919-1972)
Baseball Player

Born in Cairo, Georgia, on January 31, 1919, Robinson was raised in Pasadena, California. At UCLA he gained all-American honorable mention as a halfback, but he left college in his junior year to play professional football for the Los Angeles Bulldogs. After serving as an Army lieutenant during World War II, Robinson returned to civilian life with the hope of becoming a physical education coach. To achieve this, he felt he had to make a name for himself, and for this reason decided to spend a few seasons in the Negro baseball league.

In 1945, while he was playing with the Kansas City Monarchs, Branch Rickey of the Brooklyn Dodgers assigned him to the Montreal Royals, the team's top farm club, where he was to be groomed for a career in the majors. On April 10, 1947, the Dodgers announced that they had purchased Robinson's contract and the following day he began his major league career. During a 10-year career, he hit .311 in 1,382 games with 1,518 hits, 947 runs, 273 doubles, and 734 RBIs. He stole home 19 times, once in World Series play. He won the National League's Most Valuable Player award in 1949, and played on six National League pennant winners, as well as one world championship team. Robinson was inducted into the National Baseball Hall of Fame in 1962.

After his retirement from baseball, Robinson became a bank official, president of a land development firm, and a director of programs to combat drug addiction. He died on October 24, 1972 in Stamford, Connecticut.

Oscar Robertson (1938-)
Basketball Player

Oscar Robertson was born in Charlotte, Tennessee in 1938, eventually moving to Indiana. As a teenager at Indianapolis' Crispus Attucks High School, he led his team to the prestigious Indiana state basketball title on two occasions and shortly thereafter became the first African American to play at the University of Cincinnati.

Brooklyn Dodger Jackie Robinson, 1949.

He helped Cincinnati reach the Final Four in 1959 and 1960, was named United Press International college player of the year for three consecutive seasons and set 14 major collegiate records. He is credited with attracting the recruits who led the school to two more Final Fours, including a championship in 1962. He also became the first to lead the NCAA in scoring for three consecutive seasons.

In 1960, and after participating on the U.S. gold medal winning Olympic basketball team as co-captain, Robertson signed a $100,000 contract with the Cincinnati Royals, earning Rookie of the Year honors during his initial season in the NBA. At 6'5", 210 pounds, he would become the NBA's first true "big guard". The multidimensional Robertson, known as the "Big O," was a textbook fundamental player and unyieldingly physical. During the 1962 season—only his second in the league—he led the NBA in assists, at 11.4 per game. His best season was the 1964 campaign in which he averaged 31.4 points per game, led once more in assists (868), shot free throws at a .853 clip and was named the league's Most Valuable Player.

Over the course of five separate seasons, Robertson, averaged more than 20 points and 10 assists per game,

something no other player in NBA history has accomplished. He was the Most Valuable Player of the 1961, 1964, and 1969 All-Star games. Robertson joined the Milwaukee Bucks in time to team with Kareem Abdul-Jabbar and lead the Milwaukee to their only NBA championship, in 1971.

Robertson became the President of the NBA Players Association. Under his leadership, the NBAPA established collective bargaining with the league's owners.

Florence Griffith Joyner and Wilma Rudolph, 1988.

Bill Russell

He was elected to the Basketball Hall of Fame in 1979, and was named to the NBA's 35th anniversary all-time team in 1980. Robertson was also elected to the Olympic Hall of Fame in 1984.

Robertson has remained extremely visible off the court, becoming a successful chemical company executive as President/CEO of ORCHEM, Inc. in 1981, and starting Oscar Robertson and Associates in 1983. He is a member of the NAACP Sports Board, a trustee of the Indiana High School and Basketball Halls of Fame, the National Director of the Pepsi-Cola Hot Shot Program and the President of the NBA Retired Players Association. Robertson was also the developer of affordable housing units in Cincinnati and Indianapolis. He served in the United States Army for eight years.

"Sugar Ray" Robinson (1920-1989)
Boxer

Born Walker Smith, in Detroit on May 3, 1920, he took the name Robinson from the certificate of an amateur boxer whose identity enabled him to meet the age requirements for getting a match in Michigan; the "Sug-

ar" came from his having been dubbed "the sweetest fighter."

As a 10-year-old boy, Robinson had watched a Detroit neighbor, Joe Louis, train for an amateur boxing career. When Robinson moved to New York two years later, he began to spend most of his time at local gyms in preparation for his own amateur career. After winning all 89 of his amateur bouts and the 1939 Golden Gloves featherweight championship, he turned professional in 1940 at Madison Square Garden, fighting for the first time on a card headlined by the Fritzie Zivic-Henry Armstrong fight.

After several years of being "the uncrowned king of the welterweights," Robinson beat Tommy Bell in an elimination title bout in December 1946. He successfully defended the title for five years, and on February 14, 1951, took the middleweight crown from Jake LaMotta.

In July 1951, he lost the title to Randy Turpin, only to win it back two months later. Retiring for a time, Robinson subsequently fought a series of exciting battles with Carl "Bobo" Olsen, Carmen Basilio, and Gene Fullmer before retiring permanently, on December 10, 1965, with six victories in title bouts to his credit—more than any other fighter in history.

O.J. Simpson

Suffering from diabetes, hypertension and Alzheimer's disease, one month shy of his 69th birthday, Robinson died of apparent natural causes at the Brotman Medical Center in Culver City, California on April 12, 1989. Over his career, he won 174 of 201 professional bouts, including titles in three weight classes.

Wilma Rudolph (1940-1994)
Track and Field Athlete

Wilma Rudolph was the only American woman runner ever to win three gold medals in the Olympic games. Her performance was all the more remarkable in light of the fact that she had double pneumonia and scarlet fever as a young child and could not walk without braces until age 11.

Rudolph was born on June 23, 1940, in St. Bethlehem, Tennessee, the 17th of 19 children, and soon moved with her family to Clarksville. At an early age, she survived polio and scarlet fever, only to be left with the use of one leg. Through daily leg massages administered in turn by different members of her family, she pro-

gressed to the point where she was able to walk only with the aid of a special shoe. Three years later, however, she discarded the shoe, and began joining her brother in backyard basketball games. At Burt High School in Clarksville, while a sophomore, Rudolph broke the state basketball record for girls. As a sprinter, she was undefeated in all her high school track meets.

In 1957, Rudolph enrolled at Tennessee State University and began setting her sights for the Olympic games in Rome. In the interim, she gained national recognition in collegiate meets, setting the world record for 200 meters in July of 1960. In the Olympics, she earned the title of the "World's Fastest Woman" by winning gold medals for the 100-meter dash, the 200-meter dash (Olympic record), and for anchoring the 400-meter relay (world record). She was named by the Associated Press as the U.S. Female Athlete of the Year for 1960, and also won United Press Athlete of the Year honors.

Rudolph served as a track coach, an athletic consultant, and assistant director of athletics for the Mayor's Youth Foundation in Chicago. She was also the founder of the Wilma Rudolph Foundation. Rudolph, a noted goodwill ambassador, was also a talk show hostess and

Bill White

active on the lecture circuit. On November 12, 1994, Wilma Rudolph died at her home in Brentwood, Tennessee of a malignant brain tumor.

Bill Russell (1934-)
Basketball Player

Bill Russell, who led the Boston Celtics to 11 titles, including eight in a row, is regarded as the finest defensive basketball player in the game's history. The 6'10'' star is also the first black to coach and play for a National Basketball Association team. His style of play is credited with revolutionizing basketball.

Russell was born on February 12, 1934, in Monroe, Louisiana. The family moved to Detroit when he was nine, but two years later the family continued on to Oakland, California. There, at McClyronds High School, Russell proved to be an awkward but determined basketball player who eventually received a scholarship to the nearby University of San Francisco.

In college, Russell came into his own, in his sophomore year becoming the most publicized athlete on the West Coast. Over the next two years, his fame spread across the nation as he led his team to 60 consecutive victories (a collegiate record) and two straight NCAA titles.

The Celtics had never won an NBA Championship before Russell's arrival in 1957. With the help of Russell's defensive capabilities, the Celtics became one of the most successful teams in the history of professional sports, winning the world championship eight years in a row. Russell himself was named Most Valuable Player on five separate occasions (1958, 1961-1963, 1965). In 1966, Russell became the Celtics player/coach.

After the 1968-1969 season, having led the Celtics to their eleventh NBA crown, Russell retired as both coach and player. He left the game as its all-time leader in minutes played (40,726), a record since surpassed by Kareem Abdul-Jabbar. In 1980, the Professional Basketball Writers Association of America selected Russell as the greatest player in NBA history.

After retirement, Russell was a color commentator on NBC-TV's NBA Game of the Week. In 1974, he accepted a lucrative contract to become head coach and

Willie Stargell

Michael Jordan

Charlie Joiner

general manager of the Seattle Supersonics. That year, he was inducted into the Basketball Hall of Fame. He remained at Seattle's helm through 1977 and returned to the coaching ranks ten years later for a one-year stint with the Sacramento Kings. He was named the team's director of player personnel in 1988.

Gale Sayers (1943-)
Football Player

Gale Sayers was born into an impoverished Wichita, Kansas household on May 30, 1943. He proceeded to star not only in football but also in track while in high school and decided to enroll at Kansas University. He signed with the Chicago Bears before graduating but returned to finish and eventually earn a master's degree.

Sayers quickly made his mark, garnering All-Pro honors in his rookie season of 1965 and three of the next four. His graceful, shifty running style soon became admired by anyone who had the opportunity to watch him perform. His ability to make defenders "miss" was uncanny. Sayers led the league in rushing in 1969, and was also its highest paid player. In a 1965 game against the San Francisco 49ers, he tied an NFL record by scoring six touchdowns.

Sayers's career was ended prematurely after the 1971 season due to a knee injury which robbed him of much of his trademark mobility. His final totals included 56 touchdowns; 39 scored rushing, 9 receiving, six via kickoff returns (including a 103 yarder in 1967), and two on punt returns. He was named to the "All-NFL 1960-1984 All-Star Team" as a kick returner. Despite his brief career, he was recognized by virtue of his induction into the Pro Football Hall of Fame in 1977.

Following his playing career, Sayers was named assistant to the athletic director at Kansas and in 1981, became the athletic director at Southern Illinois University. Very active in the community, Sayers has been the commissioner of the Chicago Park District; the co-chairperson of the legal defense fund for sports, NAACP

Jesse Owens, 1936.

Coordinator; and an honorary chairman of the American Cancer Society in addition to his involvement in the Reach Out Program. In 1984, Sayers founded his own company, "Computer Supplies by Sayers."

Charlie Sifford (1922-)
Golfer

The most famous African American golfer prior to 1970, Charlie Sifford, from Charlotte, North Carolina, was the first black to participate in a predominately white event, the 1957 Long Beach Open. Sifford's entry into golf began as a caddie at the age of nine. At 13, he won a caddie tournament shooting a 70. First prize consisted of $10 and a case of Pepsi-Cola. After moving to Philadelphia, Sifford worked as a teaching professional and chauffeur.

Sifford became the first African American to be awarded a PGA card as an approved player, in 1959, as the tour lifted its "Caucasian only" clause. He was also the first to win a major PGA event, the Los Angeles Open, in 1969. On the Seniors tour, Sifford triumphed at the PGA Seniors Open (1975), and the Suntree Seniors Open (1980). He also won the Negro National Title six times.

O. J. Simpson (1947-)
Football Player

Orenthal J. Simpson may have been the finest running back in pro football. Nicknamed "The Juice," he made his mark by becoming the first back to gain more than 2,000 rushing yards in a season, amassing a total of 2,003 in 1973.

Born in San Francisco on July 9, 1947, Simpson starred at the University of Southern California, winning the Heisman Trophy in 1968. One year prior to that, he was a member of the USC relay team that set a world record of 38.6 seconds in the 440-yard run. One year after graduation, ABC Sports voted him College Player of the Decade. He signed with the Buffalo Bills in 1969, and three years later achieved his first rushing title, gaining more than 1,200 yards.

Simpson enjoyed his finest season in 1973. On opening day, he rushed for 250 yards against the New England Patriots, breaking the record of 247 yards held by Willie Ellison. His astonishing yardage total for the entire season surpassed the previous mark of 1,863 held by Jim Brown. In addition, he scored 12 touchdowns, averaged six yards per carry, and had more rushing yardage than 15 other NFL clubs. He was named Player of the Year and won the Jim Thorpe Trophy.

Simpson retired from football in 1978. He has appeared in several feature films and worked as a sports commentator for ABC-TV and NBC-TV. In 1995, a jury found Simpson not guilty of charges that he had brutally slain his ex-wife and a male friend who had been found dead outside of her California home in the summer of 1994, a decision that divided the nation as the so-called "Trial of the Century" was completed.

Lawrence Taylor (1959-)
Football Player

Born in Williamsbug, Virginia, Lawrence Taylor is considered the best outside linebacker in professional football history and revolutionized the position. His style was so disruptive that opposing offenses occasionally would invariably design their game plans around stopping or at least slowing him down. His relentless forays to the quarterback popularized the term "quarterback sack," now an integral part of the football lexicon.

After an outstanding career at the University of North Carolina where he was named Atlantic Coast Conference Player of the Year in 1980, Taylor was taken by the New York Giants with the second pick of the 1981 draft, behind only running back George Rogers, chosen by the New Orleans Saints. Taylor amassed 132 1/2 career sacks, an NFL record that would eventually be broken by Reggie White, a defensive lineman. Taylor was an integral part of two Giants Super Bowl championships, following the 1986 and 1990 seasons. He was named to the NFL's All-Decade team for the 1980s.

Debi Thomas (1967-)
Figure Skater

Born in Poughkipsee, New York, Debi Thomas is the premier African American figure skater. The graceful and creative Thomas was the winner at the 1985 National Sports Festival in Baton Rouge. The following year she captured the U.S. and World figure skating titles, becoming the first African American to capture an international singles meet. Having attended Stanford and majored in pre-med, she was an Olympic bronze medalist at the 1988 Games. In 1985, Thomas had been the winner at the National Sports Festival in Baton Rouge.

Gene Upshaw (1945-)
Football Player

As a guard for Oakland/Los Angeles Raiders from 1967 to 1982, Gene Upshaw was an anchor on the Raiders offensive line. For 14 of those seasons, he teamed with future Raider coach Art Shell to form the greatest tandem guard/tackle in NFL history.

Born in Robstown, Texas, Upshaw attended Texas A&I University. He was named All-Pro or to the Pro-Bowl eight consecutive years, between 1967 and 1974, and received his induction to the Pro Football Hall of Fame in 1987.

Upshaw is currently the executive director of the National Football League Players Association, a post he has held since 1982. Under his leadership, the organization has expended considerable resources on education and rehabilitation for substance abuse. Upshaw is also the president of the Federation of Professional Athletes AFL-CIO as well as serving on the California Governor's Council on Wellness and Physical Fitness. He is the coordinator for voter registration and fundraising in Alameda, California county and served as the planning commissioner for that same county.

Upshaw was the recipient of the Byron (Whizzer) White Humanitarian award as voted by the NFL players in 1980. In 1982, he was presented with the A. Philip Randolph Award, by the A. Philip Randolph Institute. In a recent poll by the *Sporting News*, Upshaw was named the 45th most powerful figure in sports.

Marshall W. "Major" Taylor (1878-1932)
Cyclist

Marshall W. "Major" Taylor became America's first black U.S. National Champion in 1899. Born in Indianapolis in 1878, the son of a coachman, he worked at a bicycle store part-time as a teen. After attending his first race, his boss suggested that Major enter a couple of races. To their surprise, he won a 10-mile race and proceeded to compete as an amateur.

By the time he was 16, he went to work in a factory owned by a former champion, and with his new boss's encouragement, competed in races in Canada, Europe, Australia and New Zealand.

During nearly 16 years of competition, he won numerous championships and set several world records. Years after he retired, he met President Theodore Roosevelt, who told him that he had followed his career with admiration. Taylor was inducted into the Bicycle Hall of Fame. He died in 1932.

Bill White (1934-)
National League of Professional Baseball Clubs President

William DeKova White was born in Lakewood, Florida, on January 28, 1934. He began his major league career with the New York Giants in 1956 and spent thirteen years as a player with the San Francisco Giants, St. Louis Cardinals, and the Philadelphia Phillies. During his career, White was named to the National League All-Star team six times and won seven Gold Gloves. He retired form baseball in 1969, and in 1971 joined Phil Rizzuto as a television play-by-play announcer for the New York Yankees.

On April 1, 1989, Bill White became the first African American president of the National League.

African American Olympic Medalists

Place/Year	Athlete	Event	Place	Time or Distance
St. Louis, 1904	George C. Poag	200 m hurdles	3rd	
	George C. Poag	400 m hurdles	3rd	
London, 1908	J.B. Taylor	1600 m relay	1st	3:29.4
Paris, 1924	Dehart Hubbard	Long jump	1st	24'5.125"
	Edward Gourdin	Long jump	2nd	23'10"
Los Angeles, 1932	Eddie Tolan	100 m dash	1st	10.3
	Ralph Metcalfe	100 m dash	2nd	10.3
	Eddie Tolan	200 m dash	1st	21.2
	Ralph Metcalfe	200 m dash	3rd	21.5
	Edward Gordon	Long jump	1st	25' 0.75"
Berlin, 1936	Jesse Owens	100 m dash	1st	10.3
	Ralph Metcalfe	100 m dash	2nd	10.4
	Jesse Owens	200 m dash	1st	20.7
	Matthew Robinson	200 m dash	2nd	21.1
	Archie Williams	400 m run	1st	46.5
	James DuValle	400 m run	2nd	46.8
	John Woodruff	800 m run	1st	1:52.9
	Fritz Pollard, Jr.	110 m hurdles	3rd	14.4
	Cornelius Johnson	High jump	1st	6'8"
	Jesse Owens	Long jump	1st	26' 5.75"
	Jesse Owens	400 m relay	1st	39.8
	Ralph Metcalfe	400 m relay	1st	39.8
London, 1948	Harrison Dillard	100 m dash	1st	10.3
	Norwood Ewell	100 m dash	2nd	10.4
	Norwood Ewell	200 m dash	1st	21.1
	Mal Whitfield	400 m run	3rd	46.9
	Willie Steele	Long jump	1st	25' 8"
	Herbert Douglass	Long jump	3rd	25' 3"
	Lorenzo Wright	400 m relay	1st	40.6
	Harrison Dillard	1600 m relay	1st	3.10.4
	Norwood Ewell	1600 m relay	1st	3.10.4
	Mal Whitfield	1600 m relay	1st	3.10.4
	Audrey Patterson	200 m dash	3rd	25.2
	Alice Coachman	High jump	1st	5' 6.125"
Helsinki, 1952	Andrew Stanfield	200 m dash	1st	20.7
	Ollie Matson	400 m run	3rd	46.8
	Mal Whitfield	800 m run	1st	1:49.2
	Harrison Dillard	110 m hurdles	1st	13.7
	Jerome Biffle	Long jump	1st	24' 10"
	Meredith Gourdine	Long jump	2nd	24' 8.125"
	Harrison Dillard	400 m relay	1st	40.1
	Andrew Stanfield	400 m relay	1st	40.1
	Ollie Matson	400 m relay	1st	40.1
	Bill Miller	Javelin	2nd	237
	Milton Campbell	Decathlon	2nd	6,975 pts.
	Barbara Jones	400 m relay	1st	45.9
Melbourne, 1956	Andrew Stanfield	200 m dash	2nd	20.7
	Charles Jenkins	400 m run	1st	46.7
	Lee Calhoun	110 m hurdles	1st	13.5
	Charles Dumas	High jump	1st	6" 11.25"
	Gregory Bell	Long jump	1st	25' 8.25"
	Willye White	Long jump	2nd	19" 11.75"
	Ira Murchison	400 m relay	1st	39.5
	Leamon King	400 m relay	1st	39.5

Place/Year	Athlete	Event	Place	Time or Distance
	Charles Jenkins			
	Lou Jones	1600 m relay	1st	3:04.8
	Milton Campbell	Decathlon	1st	7,937 pts.
	Rafer Johnson	Decathlon	2nd	7,587 pts.
	Mildred McDaniel	High jump	1st	5' 9.25"
	Margret Matthews	400 m relay	3rd	44.9
	Isabelle Daniels	400 m relay	3rd	44.9
	Mae Faggs	400 m relay	3rd	44.9
	Wilma Rudolph	400 m relay	3rd	44.9
Rome, 1960	Les Carney	200 m dash	2nd	20.6
	Lee Calhoun	110 m hurdles	1st	13.8
	Willie May	100 m hurdles	2nd	13.8
	Hayes Jones	110 m hurdles	3rd	14
	Otis Davis	400 m run	1st	44.9
	John Thomas	High jump	3rd	7" 0.25"
	Ralph Boston	Long jump	1st	26' 7.75"
	Irvin Roberson	Long jump	2nd	26' 7.25"
	Otis Davis	1600 m relay	1st	3:02.2
	Rafer Johnson	Decathlon	1st	8,392 pts.
	Earlene Brown	Shot put	3rd	53' 10.25"
	Wilma Rudolph	100 m dash	1st	11
	Wilma Rudolph	200 m dash	1st	24
	Martha Judson	400 m relay	3rd	44.5
	Lucinda Williams	400 m relay	3rd	44.5
	Barbara Jones	400 m relay	3rd	44.5
	Wilma Rudolph	400 m relay	1st	44.5
Tokyo, 1964	Robert Hayes	200 m dash	1st	9.9
	Henry Carr	200 m dash	1st	20.3
	Paul Drayton	200 m dash	2nd	20.5
	Hayes Jones	110 m hurdles	1st	13.6
	Robert Hayes	400 m relay	1st	39.0
	Paul Drayton	400 m relay	1st	39.0
	Richard Stebbins	400 m relay	1st	39.0
	John Thomas	High jump	2nd	7' 1.75"
	John Rambo	High jump	3rd	7' 1"
	Ralph Boston	Long jump	2nd	26' 4"
	Wyomia Tyus	100 m dash	1st	11.4
	Edith McGuire	100 m dash	2nd	11.6
	Marilyn White	100 m dash	3rd	11.6
	Edith McGuire	200 m dash	1st	23
	Marilyn White	100 m dash	3rd	11.6
	Edith McGuire	200 m dash	1st	23
	Wyomia Tyus	400 m relay	2nd	43.9
	Edith Mcguire	400 m relay	2nd	43.9
	Willye White	400 m relay	2nd	43.9
	Marilyn White	400 m relay	2nd	43.9
Mexico City, 1968	Jim Hines	100 m dash	1st	43.9
	Charles Greene	100 m dash	3rd	10.0
	Tommie Smith	200 m dash	1st	19.8
	John Carlos	200 m dash	3rd	20.0
	Lee Evans	400 m run	1st	43.8
	Larry James	400 m run	2nd	43.9
	Ron Freeman	400 m run	3rd	44.4
	Willie Davenport	110 m hurdles	1st	13.3
	Ervin Hall	110 m hurdles	2nd	13.4
	Jim Hines	400 m relay	1st	38.2
	Charles Greene	400 m relay	1st	38.2
	Mel Pender	400 m relay	1st	38.2

Place/Year	Athlete	Event	Place	Time or Distance
	Ronnie Ray Smith	400 m relay	1st	38.2
	Wyomia Tyus	400 m relay	1st	42.8
	Barbara Ferrell	400 m relay	1st	42.8
	Margaret Bailes	400 m relay	1st	42.8
	Mildrette Netter	400 m relay	1st	42.8
	Lee Evans	1600 m relay	1st	2:56.1
	Vince Matthews	1600 m relay	1st	2:56.1
	Ron Freeman	1600 m relay	1st	2:56.1
	Larry James	1600 m relay	1st	2:56.1
	Edward Caruthers	High jump	2nd	7' 3.5"
	Bob Beamon	Long jump	1st	29' 2.5"
	Ralph Boston	Long jump	3rd	26' 9.25"
	Wyomia Tyus	100 m dash	1st	11.0
	Barbara Ferrell	100 m dash	2nd	11.1
	Madeline Manning	800 m run	1st	2:00.9
Munich, 1972	Robert Taylor	100 m dash	2nd	10.24
	Larry Black	200 m dash	2nd	20.19
	Vince Matthews	400 m run	1st	44.66
	Wayne Collett	400 m run	2nd	44.8
	Rod Milburn	100 m hurdles	1st	13.24
	Eddie Hart	400 m relay	1st	38.19
	Robert Taylor	400 m relay	1st	38.19
	Larry Black	400 m relay	1st	38.19
	gerald Tinker	400 m relay	1st	38.19
	Randy Williams	Long Jump	1st	27' 0.25"
	Arnie Robinson	Long jump	3rd	26' 4"
	Jeff Bennet	Decathlon	3rd	7,974 pts.
	Wayne Collett	400 m dash	2nd	44.80
	Cheryl Toussain	1600 m relay	2nd	3:25.2
	Mable Fergerson	1600 m relay	2nd	3:25.2
	Madeline Manning	1600 m relay	2nd	3:25.2
Montreal, 1976	Millard Hampton	200 m dash	2nd	20.29
	Dwayne Evans	200 m dash	3rd	20.43
	Fred Newhouse	400 m run	2nd	44.40
	Herman Frazier	400 m run	3rd	44.95
	Willie Davenport	110 m hurdles	3rd	13.38
	Edwin Moses	400 m hurdles	1st	47.64
	Millard Hampton	400 m relay	1st	38.83
	Steve Riddick	400 m relay	1st	38.83
	Harvey Glance	400 m relay	1st	38.83
	John Jones	400 m relay	1st	38.83
	Herman Frazier	1600 m relay	1st	2:58.7
	Benny Brown	1600 m relay	1st	2:58.7
	Maxie Parks	1600 m relay	1st	2:58.7
	Fred Newhouse	1600 m relay	1st	2:58.7
	Arnie Robinson	Long jump	1st	27' 4.75"
	Randy Williams	Long jump	2nd	26' 7.25"
	James Butts	Triple jump	2nd	56' 8.5"
	Rosalyn Bryant	1600 m relay	2nd	3:22.8
	Shelia Ingram	1600 m relay	2nd	3:22.8
	Pamela Jiles	1600 m relay	2nd	3:22.8
	Debra Sapenter	1600 m relay	2nd	3:22.8
Los Angeles, 1984	Carl Lewis	100 m dash	1st	9.9
	Sam Graddy	100 m dash	2nd	10.19
	Carl Lewis	200 m dash	1st	19.80
	Kirk Baptiste	200 m dash	2nd	19.96
	Alonzo Babers	400 m run	1st	44.27

Place/Year	Athlete	Event	Place	Time or Distance
	Antonio McKay	400 m run	3rd	44.71
	Earl Jones	800 m run	3rd	1:43.83
	Roger Kingdom	110 m hurdles	1st	13:20
	Greg Foster	110 m hurdles	2nd	13:23
	Edwin Moses	400 m hurdles	1st	47.75
	Danny Harris	400 m hurdles	2nd	48.13
	Sam Graddy	400 m relay	1st	37.83
	Ron Brown	400 m relay	1st	37.83
	Calvin Smith	400 m relay	1st	37.83
	Carl Lewis	400 m relay	1st	37.83
	Sunder Nix	1600 m relay	1st	2:57.91
	Roy Armstead	1600 m relay	1st	2:57.91
	Alonzo Babers	1600 m relay	1st	2:57.91
	Antonio McKay	1600 m relay	1st	2:57.91
	Michael Carter	shot put	1st	21.09m
	Carl Lewis	Long jump	1st	8.54m
	Al Joyner	Triple jump	1st	17.26m
	Mike Conley	Triple jump	2nd	17.18m
	Evelyn Ashford	100 m dash	1st	10.97
	Alice Brown	100 m dash	2nd	11.13
	Valerie Brisco-Hooks	200 m dash	1st	21.81
	Florence Griffith	200 m dash	2nd	22.04
	Valerie Brisco-Hooks	400 m run	1st	48.83
	Chandra Cheeseborough	400 m run	2nd	49.05
	Kim Gallagher	800 m run	2nd	1:58.63
	Benita Fitzgerald-Brown	100 m hurdles	1st	12.84
	Kim Turner	100 m hurdles	2nd	12.88
	Judi Brown	400 m hurdles	2nd	55.20
	Valerie Brisco-Hooks	1600 m relay	1st	3:18.29
	Chandra Cheeseborough	1600 m relay	1st	3:18.29
	Lillie Leatherwood	1600 m relay	1st	3:18.29
	Sherri Howard	1600 m relay	1st	3:18.29
	Jackie Joyner	Heptathlon	2nd	6,386pts.
	Patrick Ewing	Men's basketball	1st	
	Vern Fleming	Men's basketball	1st	
	Michael Jordan	Men's basketball	1st	
	Sam Perkins	Men's basketball	1st	
	Alvin Robertson	Men's basketball	1st	
	Wayman Tisdale	Men's basketball	1st	
	Leon Wood	Men's basketball	1st	
	Cathy Boswell	Women's basketball	1st	
	Teresa Edwards	Women's basketball	1st	
	Janice Lawrence	Women's basketball	1st	
	Pamela McGee	Women's basketball	1st	
	Cheryl Miller	Women's basketball	1st	
	Lynette Woodard	Women's basketball	1st	
Seoul, 1988	Carl Lewis	100 m dash	1st	9.92
	Calvin Smith	100 m dash	2nd	
	Joe DeLoach	200 m dash	1st	19.75
	Carl Lewis	200 m dash	2nd	
	Steve Lewis	400 m run	1st	43.87
	Butch Reynolds	400 m run	2nd	
	Danny Everett	400 m run	3rd	
	Roger Kingdom	110 m hurdles	1st	12.98
	Tonie Campbell	400 m hurdles	3rd	
	Andre Phillips	400 m hurdles	1st	47.19
	Edwin Moses	400 m hurdles	3rd	
	Butch Reynolds	1600 m relay	1st	2:56.16

Place/Year	Athlete	Event	Place	Time or Distance
	Steve Lewis	1600 m relay	1st	2:56.16
	Antonia McKay	1600 m relay	1st	2:56.16
	Danny Everett	1600 m relay	1st	2:56.16
	Carl Lewis	Long jump	1st	28'7.25"
	Mike Powell	Long jump	2nd	
	Larry Myricks	Long jump	3rd	
	Flo Griffith Joyner	100 m dash	1st	10.54
	Evelyn Ashford	100 m dash	2nd	
	Flo Griffith Joyner	200 m dash	1st	21.34
	Shelia Echols	400 m relay	1st	41.98
	Flo Griffith Joyner	400 m relay	1st	41.98
	Evelyn Ashford	400 m relay	1st	41.98
	Alice Brown	400 m relay	1st	41.98
	Jackie Joyner-Kersee	Long jump	1st	24'3.5"
	Jackie Joyner-Kersee	Heptathlon	1st	7,291 pts.
	Denean Howard-Hill	1600 m relay	2nd	3.15.51
	Valerie Brisco	1600 m relay	2nd	3.15.51
	Diane Dixon	1600 m relay	2nd	3.15.51
	Flo Griffith-Joyner	1600 m relay	2nd	3.15.51
	Kim Mitchell	800 m run	3rd	
	Andrew Maynard	Boxing- heavyweight	1st	
	Ray Mercer	Boxing- heavyweight	1st	
	Kennedy McKinney	Boxing-bantamweight	1st	
	Riddick Bowe	Boxing-super heavyweight	2nd	
	Roy Jones	Boxing-middleweight	2nd	
	Kenny Monday	Wrestling-freestyle	1st	
	Nate Carr	Wrestling-freestyle	3rd	
	Zina Garrison	Tennis-doubles	1st	
	Zina Garrison	Tennis-singles	3rd	
	Tom Goodwin	Baseball	1st	
	Ty Griffin	Baseball	1st	
	Cindy Brown	Women's basketball	3rd	
	Vicky Bullett	Women's basketball	3rd	
	Cynthia Cooper	Women's basketball	3rd	
	Teresa Edwards	Women's basketball	3rd	
	Jennifer Gillom	Women's basketball	3rd	
	Bridgette Gordon	Women's basketball	3rd	
	Katrina McClain	Women's basketball	3rd	
	Teresa Weatherspoon	Women's basketball	3rd	
	Willie Anderson	Men's basketball	3rd	
	Stacey Augmon	Men's basketball	3rd	
	Vernell Coles	Men's basketball	3rd	
	Jeff Grayer	Men's basketball	3rd	
	Hersey Hawkins	Men's basketball	3rd	
	Danny Manning	Men's basketball	3rd	
	J.R. Reid	Men's basketball	3rd	
	Mitch Redmond	Men's basketball	3rd	
	David Robinson	Men's basketball	3rd	
	Charles D. Smith	Men's basketball	3rd	
	Charles E. Smith	Men's basketball	3rd	
Barcelona, 1992	Dennis Mitchell	100 m dash	3rd	10.04
	Gail Devers	100 m dash	1st	10.82
	Mike Marsh	200 m dash	1st	20.01
	Michael Bates	200 m dash	3rd	20.38
	Gwen Torrence	200 m dash	1st	21.81
	Quincy Watts	400 m run	1st	43.50
	Steve Lewis	400 m run	2nd	44.21
	Johnny Gray	800 m run	3rd	1:43.97

Place/Year	Athlete	Event	Place	Time or Distance
	Mike Marsh	400 m relay	1st	37.40
	Leroy Burrell	400 m relay	1st	37.40
	Dennis Mitchell	400 m relay	1st	37.40
	Carl Lewis	400 m relay	1st	37.40
	Evelyn Ashford	400 m relay	1st	42.11
	Esther Jones	400 m relay	1st	42.11
	Carlette Guidry-White	400 m relay	1st	42.11
	Gwen Torrence	400 m relay	1st	42.11
	Tony Dees	110 m hurdles	2nd	13.24
	Kevin Young	400 m hurdles	1st	46.78
	Sandra Farmer	400 m hurdles	2nd	53.69
	Janeence Vickers	400 m hurdles	3rd	54.31
	Andrew Valmon	800 m relay	1st	2:55.74
	Quincy Watts	800 m relay	1st	2:55.74
	Michael Johnson	800 m relay	1st	2:55.74
	Steve Lewis	800 m relay	1st	2:55.74
	Natasha Kaiser	800 m relay	2nd	3:20.92
	Gwen Torrence	800 m relay	2nd	3:20.92
	Jearl Miles	800 m relay	2nd	3:20.92
	Rochelle Stevens	800 m relay	2nd	3:20.92
	Hollis Conway	High jump	3rd	7' 8"
	Carl Lewis	Long jump	1st	28' 5.5"
	Mike Powell	Long jump	2nd	28' 4.25"
	Joe Greene	Long jump	3rd	27' 4.5"
	Jackie Joyner-Dersee	Long jump	3rd	23' 2.5"
	Mike Conley	Triple jump	1st	59' 7.5"
	Charlie Simpkins	Triple jump	2nd	57'9"
	Jackie Joyner-Kersee	Heptathlon	1st	7,044 pts.
	Tim Austin	Boxing-flyweight	3rd	
	Chris Byrd	Boxing-middleweight	2nd	
	Kevin Jackson	Wrestling-middleweight	1st	
	Charles Barkley	Men's basketball	1st	
	Clyde Drexler	Men's basketball	1st	
	Patrick Ewing	Men's basketball	1st	
	Earvin Johnson	Men's basketball	1st	
	Michael Jordan	Men's basketball	1st	
	Karl Malone	Men's basketball	1st	
	Scottie Pippen	Men's basketball	1st	
	David Robinson	Men's basketball	1st	
	Vicky Bullett	Women's basketball	1st	
	Daedra Charles	Women's basketball	1st	
	Cynthia Cooper	Women's basketball	1st	
	Teresa Edward	Women's basketball	1sts	
	Carolyn Jones	Women's basketball	1st	
	Katrina McClai	Women's basketball	1stn	
	Vickie Orr	Women's basketball	1st	
	Teresa Weatherspoon	Women's basketball	1st	

Note: The United States did not attend 1980's Moscow games in protest of the Soviet Union's invasion of Afghanistan.

27

Military

Military

◆ The Colonial Period ◆ The Revolutionary War (1775-1783) ◆ The War of 1812 (1812-1815)
◆ The Civil War (1861-1865) ◆ The Indian Campaigns (1866-1890)
◆ The Spanish-American War (1898) ◆ World War I (1914-1918) ◆ The Interwar Years (1919-1940)
◆ World War II (1941-1945) ◆ The Korean War (1950-1953) ◆ The Vietnam War (1964-1973)
◆ Military Participation in the 1970s and 1980s ◆ The Persian Gulf War (1991)
◆ Outstanding Military Figures

by Allen G. Harris and Floyd Thomas, Jr.

As with other aspects of American society, the role of African American people in the nation's armed forces has been evolutionary. It was shaped by the white majority of an infant republic that embraced and then rejected slavery. Next was an adolescent "separate but equal" era of racial segregation. Finally, the United States has matured—as an increasingly multicultural society—in its understanding of race and racism.

Sadly, a nation's history is often shaped by its wars. Insofar as blacks and the American military are concerned, the historic linkage extends from before the Revolutionary War to the most recent military expeditions involving United States troops.

Based on European experiences, the early American colonists were wary of the military. Both the Declaration of Independence and the United States Constitution reflect the fear of a large and permanent military establishment. As a result, much of early American military history revolves around the locally recruited militia—now the National Guard of the states and territories.

◆ THE COLONIAL PERIOD

Fearful of Indian warfare and slave insurrection, colonial governments sought to reduce the risk of a confederation between Indians and slaves. Some colonial governments promised freedom and various other inducements to black slaves willing to help fight the Indian, and paid Indians to hunt down and return escaped slaves. As early as 1703, South Carolina authorities began to enlist slaves into its colonial militia. The

Massachusetts Bay government required that black men, free and slave alike, undergo militia training. Less concerned with an Indian attack than a slave uprising, Virginia forbid the arming of slaves. Though few in number, both enslaved and free blacks served in colonial militias and fought in the French and Indian War, 1754-1763.

As tensions mounted between England and the American colonies, confrontation led to bloodshed in the Boston Massacre, March 5, 1770. In protest against the manner of taxation and British authority, a crowd of angry Boston residents confronted a group of British soldiers charged with enforcing the laws of Great Britain. One of the soldiers fired on the crowd and an escaped slave leading the advance was struck. Crispus Attucks fell dead at the feet of the British soldiers, followed by four white citizens who with him became martyrs to the cause of American independence.

◆ THE REVOLUTIONARY WAR

In 1775, black men joined colonists in fighting the British during the battles of Lexington and Concord, the first battles of the Revolutionary War. A black man, Salem Poore, fought in the Battle of Bunker Hill. Credited with firing the shot that killed Major John Pitcairn, commander of the British force, Salem Poore received a commendation for gallantry. He would later serve with George Washington at Valley Forge.

Although a number of blacks were serving in New England units and proving themselves both capable and brave, Southern slave holders objected to their presence. In response to these critics, General Washington and his principal officers agreed to reject all slaves and bar free black veterans from reenlisting, a policy quickly ratified by the Continental Congress.

French and Spanish forces allied with the American colonists did not hesitate to enlist blacks into their ranks. The English also did not object to this valuable source of military manpower. When Lord Dunmore, the royal governor of Virginia, promised freedom to slaves who joined His Majesty's troops, he was able to organize an Ethiopian Regiment composed of approximately 300 men, "a mere fraction of those who gambled their lives on promises made by officers of King George III." (Nalty, p.18).

As it became increasingly difficult for the colonial militias and the Continental Army to meet recruiting needs, George Washington's initial belief that only whites should serve began to change. The success of the British in attracting black volunteers seeking to earn their freedom was a matter of concern. With troop strength dangerously low following the brutal winter at Valley Forge, Washington reversed his earlier policies and welcomed both free blacks and slaves into the Continental Army.

By 1778, the Continental Army was racially integrated. On average, each brigade contained 42 black soldiers. In the naval service, black sailors were engaged in nearly every phase of shipboard operations. In addition to cooking and cleaning, black seamen manned guns, joined boarding parties, and served as sharpshooters in Marine detachments. Ultimately, 5,000 blacks served in the war for American independence. Some won their freedom, others gained respect in their communities and a measure of economic security.

"The Revolutionary War thus lent credence to the belief, which later would become almost an article of faith among blacks, that military service in wartime represented a path toward freedom and greater postwar opportunity. Unfortunately, the conflict also set the pattern, followed for more than a century and a half, by which the American government used blacks in time of crisis and ignored them afterward. Only a handful of blacks succeeded in taking advantage of the mechanism the war provided for betterment. Despite the contributions of 5,000 blacks in the cause of liberty, their freedom was assured only in the handful of states that formally abolished slavery during the war or immediately afterward." (Nalty, p.18).

A memorial to the blacks who served the American cause during the Revolutionary War will be erected on the Mall in Washington, D.C. Ironically, that memorial honoring an eighteenth century contribution will be emplaced after similar recognition of the twentieth-century Tuskegee Airmen at the United States Air Force Academy, and the nineteenth-century "Buffalo Soldiers" at Fort Leavenworth, Kansas.

◆ THE WAR OF 1812 (1812-1815)

Following the Revolutionary War, the exclusion of blacks from military service was reinstituted. In 1792, Congress restricted military service to "free able-bodied white males." Six years later, the Secretary of War ordered the Commandment of the Marine Corps that "No Negro, mulatto or Indian is to be enlisted." However, when the need arose for recruits during the War of 1812, black sailors made up approximately twenty percent of Navy crews. Commodore Oliver Hazard Perry welcomed black sailors who served in his armada that defeated the British on Lake Erie.

While the Army and Marine Corps continued to exclude blacks, the Louisiana legislature authorized enlistments of free black land-owners. The combat bravery of these black troops was a key factor in the American victory at the Battle of New Orleans—though it was fought after the war had officially ended. Because blacks were not authorized to serve in the Army, their contributions went unrecognized by the United States Army.

◆ THE CIVIL WAR (1861-1865)

Only weeks after the Confederate assault on Fort Sumter in 1861 which initiated the Civil War, black men from Wilberforce College in Ohio answered Abraham Lincoln's call for volunteers to help subdue the Confederacy. Similar offers quickly came from Washington, D.C. and New York, where the governor was offered three black regiments to serve for the duration of the war, with their weapons, clothing, equipment, pay and provisions all to be provided by the black population of the state. These and other such requests to serve were spurned. Expecting a short war, Secretary of War Simon Cameron rebuffed the offers.

Although some Union leaders such as Major General John C. Fremont wanted to recruit blacks as soldiers, the Lincoln administration refused permission to proceed with the effort. Fearful that such action would antagonize slave-holding border states loyal to the Union, President Lincoln made it clear that this was a war to preserve the Union, not to free the slaves. Union General Benjamin Butler, who would later command black troops, offered Union soldiers to suppress a rumored slave uprising in Maryland. Meanwhile, the Confederacy enjoyed the fruits of slave labor in constructing fortifications and related combat service support roles.

As early as June 1861, some Southern states were recruiting free blacks for military service.

Though prohibited from enlisting blacks for military duty as troops, some Union generals began to use black fugitives from slave territory as teamsters, cooks, and laborers. Only after important military setbacks and considerable debate in the press and Congress did the legislature authorize the employment of black soldiers with the Militia Act of July 17, 1862. The War Department had not yet given permission to recruit black soldiers when General Jim Lane organized and trained the 1st Kansas Colored Volunteers and sent them into action against Confederate troops near Butler, Missouri in late October, 1862. The success of black troops in the first engagements in which they were permitted to fight for the Union, helped to reduce opposition to their recruitment.

United States Colored Troops (USCT)

Following the Emancipation Proclamation of September 1862, systematic recruitment of blacks began throughout the country. Massachusetts was permitted to organize the 54th and 55th Massachusetts Infantry regiments. Raised by Colonel Robert Gould Shaw, the 54th led the Union attack on Fort Wagner, July 18, 1863. This strategically located Confederate position on Morris Island dominated the shipping channel leading into the Charleston harbor, South Carolina. Although access to Fort Wagner was restricted to a narrow road and subject to fire from three Confederate forts and batteries nearby, Union General Truman Seymour boasted that he could take it in one night. A reporter for the New York *Tribune* quoted the general as saying that he would have General George C. Strong's brigade take the lead and ". . . put those damned niggers from Massachusetts in the advance; we might as well get rid of them one time as another."

Under intense fire, the 54th made their charge with Shaw urging his men over an earthwork and into the fort. The black soldiers and their white officers were met with a barrage of artillery and rifle fire and grenades. As he crossed the fort's parapet, Shaw was shot dead. Half of the officers and men of his regiment were killed, wounded, or captured in the battle. Although eventually driven from the fort, the 54th Massachusetts Infantry came to symbolize the courage and determination of black troops.

Despite repeated demonstrations of their ability and courage, skepticism regarding the usefulness of black soldiers remained. General Benjamin Butler was determined to prove the black troops under his command were fit to bear arms. On the dawn of September 29,

1864, Butler ordered his troops of the XVII Corps to storm a fortified Confederate position at New Market Heights, Virginia. "With the caps removed from the nipples of their guns so that there could be no confused or confusing firing during the advance, the Negro soldiers moved across a stream, up the slope, through two lines of obstructions, and into the fortifications. The garrison fled before the bayonet assault and the works were in Union hands—at a cost of 1,000 casualties." (Dudley Taylor Cornish, *The Sable Arm*, p. 280.) Butler recorded in his memoirs that "the capacity of the Negro race for soldiers had then and there been fully settled forever." (Benjamin Franklin Butler, *Autobiography and Personal Reminiscences of Major-General Benj. F. Butler*—BUTLER'S BOOK. *A Review of His Legal, Political and Military Career*. (Boston, 1892, pp. 731-33.)

By July 1863, over thirty black regiments were being organized or were already on the field. These units and others previously organized except the 54th and 55th Massachusetts, were designated as United States Colored Troops (USCT). These soldiers were mustered directly into federal service and were fighting for the United States. Following the establishment of USCT regiments, blacks fought and died in every major Civil War action. For a period, they did so by being paid substantially less than white troops. While white privates received $13 per month plus $3.50 in clothing allowance, black troops of any rank were paid only $10 per month. In some units, black soldiers would not accept the lesser pay. Several men from a black Rhode Island artillery unit on duty in Texas were sentenced to hard labor for refusing their pay. When Sergeant William Walker persuaded the men of his South Carolina regiment company to refuse to perform any duty unless they received pay equal to that of white troops, he was brought up on charges of mutiny and executed by firing squad. After vigorous protests by prominent officers of black troops, newspaper editors, and legislators, the

Poster urging blacks to join the Union Army.

1864 Army Appropriation Act was enacted to provide identical pay scales for all soldiers.

The passions of the Civil War resulted in ignoring the then-emerging doctrines of land warfare on issues such as treatment of non-combatants and prisoners of war. The most serious documented breaches of land warfare law were committed by the Confederacy. The barbaric treatment of white Union prisoners of war at Andersonville Prison in Georgia, for example, retains military infamy. Black soldiers who fell into Confederate hands were either re-enslaved or summarily killed. One of the bloodiest such events was the Confederate butchery at Fort Pillow, Tennessee. Congressional Report No. 65, "Fort Pillow Massacre" (April 24, 1864), identified the Confederate leader responsible as General Nathan Bedford Forrest, who would later organize the Ku Klux Klan. According to the report:

> . . . the rebels commenced an indiscriminate slaughter, sparing neither age nor sex, white or black, soldier or civilian. The officers and men seemed to vie with each other in the devilish work; men, women, and even children, wherever found, were deliberately shot down, beaten, and hacked with sabres; some of the children not more than ten years old were forced to stand up and face their murderers while being shot; the sick and wounded were butchered without mercy, the rebels even entering the hospital building and dragging them out to be shot or killing them as they lay there unable to offer the least resistance.

Although somewhat exaggerated in the interest of propaganda, the report clearly established that black troops were murdered while attempting to surrender. The slaughter at Fort Pillow and the murder of captured and wounded black troops at the Battle of Poison Spring, Arkansas would not go unanswered. Black troops assaulted their Confederate enemy with ferocious intensity as they shouted their battle cry, "Remember Fort Pillow!" and "Remember Poison Spring!"

Many black men served in the Union cause, but very few were permitted to do so as officers. Despite strident public opposition and War Department policy unfavorable to the appointment of black officers, nearly one-hundred black men held commissions during the course of the Civil War. Over three-fourths of these commissions were awarded in General Butler's Louisiana regiments. Many blacks gained their appointment as officers in state militias. A few black surgeons and a large number of chaplains also received appointments. After Martin R. Delany, a black physician, had an audience with Abraham Lincoln, the President directed his Secretary of War to meet this "most remarkable black man." Shortly thereafter, on February 26, 1865, Martin R. Delany was commissioned a Major of Infantry, making him the highest ranking black field officer during the war. Before Delany had an opportunity to organize and command an "*armee d'Afrique*," the Civil War ended. Delany was detailed for duty with the freedmen. He retained the rank of major until 1868.

One black officer of the U.S. Colored Troops was commissioned because of his distinguished service with the Navy. Robert Smalls, a slave on board the *Planter*, took the helm of the 300-ton sidewheel Confederate steamer and with his followers delivered the ship to the Union Navy in May, 1862. Fitted with two guns and carrying four others as cargo, the ship was a welcome addition to the Union fleet. Having demonstrated his ability and leadership, the former slave served as pilot of the *Planter* for a time and later piloted the gunboat *Keokuk*. After the war, Robert Smalls was elected to the United States Congress as a representative from the state of South Carolina.

While not accepted into the Union forces, black women also played an important role during this critical era of American history. Many endured great hardship in their effort to keep their families together as their husbands, fathers, and sons marched off to war. While some black women served as volunteer nurses, others took a more aggressive role in support of the Union cause. Both Sojourner Truth and Harriet Tubman used their knowledge of Underground Railroad routes to guide Union forces operating in hostile territory. In one such instance, Miss Tubman led 300 Union cavalrymen on a raid in South Carolina that freed 800 slaves and destroyed cotton valuable to the Confederacy.

The Medal of Honor

America's highest decoration for valor was established during the Civil War when Congress authorized issuance of a Medal of Honor on December 21, 1861. Issuance was initially limited to enlisted men of the Navy and the Marine Corps, but the award was expanded to include the Army on July 12, 1862. On March 3, 1863, commissioned officers also became eligible for the Medal of Honor. During the Civil War, 1,523 Medals of Honor were awarded, twenty-three to black servicemen. The first black recipient was Sergeant William H. Carney, 54th Massachusetts Infantry, for combat valor on July 18, 1863, at Fort Wagner, South Carolina. Fourteen of the medals went to black soldiers who fought in the battle of New Market Heights.

United States Colored Troops had constituted thirteen percent of the Union Army. By the end of the Civil War, over 37,000 black servicemen had died, constituting nearly thirty-five percent of all blacks who served in combat.

A rifle company of black Union soldiers.

◆ THE INDIAN CAMPAIGNS (1866-1890)

Post-Civil War America acquired a new appreciation of the importance of military power. In 1866, the 39th Congress passed legislation to "increase and fix the Military Establishment of the United States." The peacetime army would have five artillery regiments, ten cavalry regiments, and forty-five infantry regiments. This legislation also stipulated "That to the six regiments of cavalry now in service shall be added four regiments, two of which shall be composed of colored men..." Consequently, the nation gained its first all-black Regular Army regiments: The 9th and 10th Cavalry, and the 24th and 25th Infantry—the "Buffalo Soldiers." This nickname was bestowed on the soldiers by Plains Indians who saw a resemblance between their hair and that of the buffalo, an animal the Indians considered sacred. Although the term "Buffalo Soldiers" initially denoted these four post-Civil War regiments, it has been adopted with pride by veterans of all racially-segregated black Army ground units of the 1866-1950 era.

One Hollywood "oversight" involves their depiction of the United States Army of the post-Civil War westward expansion. Approximately twenty percent of Army soldiers on duty in the West were black. According to historian Gary Donaldson, "...even today, few Americans realize that when the cavalry came to the rescue of white settlers in the Old West that the rescuers, those gallant soldiers in blue, might well have been black." (1991, *The History of African-Americans in the Military*). The heroism of black soldiers is attested to the eighteen Medals of Honor they earned during what historians term both "The Indian Campaigns" and "The Plains War."

Black participation in the war against native American Indians was embedded in historical ironies, both in terms of fighting another race subjugated by Anglo-Americans, and in terms of anti-black sentiment within the United States military itself. One of many painful episodes for the original "Buffalo Soldiers" was the case of Second Lieutenant Henry Ossian Flipper. Born in Thomasville, Georgia on March 21, 1856, Flipper was the first black to graduate from the United States Military Academy at West Point, New York. He ranked fiftieth among the seventy-six members of the Class of 1887, and became the only black commissioned officer in the Regular Army. Assigned initially to Fort Sill, Oklahoma Territory, Lieutenant Flipper was eventually

The parents of Marine Private James Anderson, Jr. receive his Medal of Honor, awarded posthumously August 21, 1968.

sent to Fort Davis, Texas. He was assigned the duties routine to a newly-commissioned officer, such as surveying and supervising construction projects. Flipper also acquired some combat experience fighting Apache Indians led by Chief Victoria.

In August 1881, Lieutenant Flipper was arrested and charged with failing to mail $3,700.00 in checks to the Army Chief of Commissary. The young lieutenant was tried by court-martial for embezzlement and conduct unbecoming an officer. He was acquitted of the first charge (the checks were found in his quarters), but convicted of the second. Upon confirmation of his sentence by President Chester Arthur, Flipper was dismissed from the service on June 30, 1882. Returning to civilian life, Flipper used his West Point education as a surveyor and engineer in working for mining companies. He also published his memoirs as well as technical books dealing with both Mexican and Venezuelan laws. Additionally, Flipper served as a translator for the Senate Committee on Foreign Relations, and became a special assistant to the Secretary of the Interior.

Nearly a century after Flipper left West Point, a review of his record indicated that he had been framed by his fellow officers. His records were corrected and he was granted an honorable discharge from the Army. On the 100th anniversary of his graduation, his bust was unveiled and is now displayed in the Cadet Library at the Military Academy.

There were only two other nineteenth century black graduates of West Point: John H. Alexander (1864-1894) in the Class of 1887; and Charles A. Young (1864-1922) in the Class of 1889. It would be forty-seven years before another black cadet graduated from the United States Military Academy.

◆ THE SPANISH-AMERICAN WAR (1898)

America's "Ten Week War" with Spain marked the nation's emergence as a global colonial power. Although the United States had just completed its own "Indian Campaigns," the tension between the two nations arose from Spain's treatment of Cuba's indigenous population, who increasingly resisted autocratic Spanish rule on the island. In 1885, open rebellion by the Cuban people resulted in brutal suppression by the Spanish. The battleship USS Maine was sent to Cuba to protect United States interests there—and, clearly, as a reminder of America's intention to enforce the Monroe Doctrine.

On the evening of February 15, 1898, a gigantic explosion rocked the warship. It sank rapidly in Havana harbor, killing 266 American sailors—twenty-two of them African Americans. The cause of the Maine's sinking was undetermined, but inflamed American passions were represented by the slogan, "Remember the Maine, to hell with Spain."

On March 29th, the United States issued an ultimatum to Spain, demanding (1) release of Cubans from brutal detention camps, (2) declaration of an armistice, and (3) preparations for peace negotiations mediated by President McKinley. The Spanish government did not comply and, on April 19th, the United States Congress proclaimed Cuba free and independent. In its proclamation, Congress authorized the President to use United States troops to remove Spanish forces from Cuba.

In the annals of American military history, the Spanish-American War was of special significance for the black officer. It was the first time that black men served in every Army grade below general officer. This opportunity arose because of a geographically determined national security strategy. Separated from both Europe and Asia by oceans, the United States understood that those waters also provided a mobilization time cushion. Any perceived threat from either direction had to overcome United States naval power before touching the United States. Thus, the Navy became the "first line of defense." The small U.S. Army was really a cadre force.

9th Cavalry

Time would permit recruitment, training and deployment of volunteers—or draftees—who would fight on United States soil led by experienced Regulars. An additional mobilization asset was the various state militias composed of part-time citizen soldiers.

The war with Spain was an expeditionary campaign requiring maritime deployment to foreign soil. Instead of a mobilize-and-defend situation, the United States had to mobilize, transport to, and fight on foreign soil. It was the nation's first large-scale exposure to the complex logistics of overseas operations, experience that would evolve into occupation duty and related counterinsurgency warfare.

The Regular Army of only 28,000 men included the all-black 9th and 10th Cavalry regiments, and the 24th and 25th Infantry regiments. Shortly after arriving in Cuba, the 9th and 10th Cavalry and the 24th and 25th Infantry distinguished themselves in combat. On June 24, 1898, one squadron of the 10th Cavalry, two squadrons of Rough Riders, which were a regiment of U.S. cavalry volunteers recruited by Theodore Roosevelt, and a squadron from the Regular Army's 1st Cavalry, attacked and defeated twice their number of Spanish soldiers. When Rough Riders were pinned down by

Spanish fire while crossing open ground near Las Guasimas, 10th Cavalry troops and soldiers from the 1st Cavalry regiment arrived and silenced the enemy. John J. "Black Jack" Pershing, the 10th Cavalry's regimental quartermaster, credited his men with "relieving the Rough Riders from the volleys that were being poured into them from that portion of the Spanish line."

The 25th Infantry also took part in the action, storming the village of El Caney on the morning of July 1. Armed with a batter of Hotchkiss automatic guns, the 10th Cavalry figured prominently in taking Kettle Hill, and the 24th Infantry with the 71st New York Volunteers stormed San Juan Hill. Black soldiers manned trenches around Santiago de Cuba, which capitulated in mid-July, ending the war in Cuba, but not the danger to the troops stationed in occupation there.

Though hostilities between the United States and Spain were officially ended, American troops in Cuba faced an enemy more deadly than the Spanish forces. More than three of every four deaths among U.S. troops were attributed to disease, particularly typhoid and yellow fever. In the mistaken belief that people of African descent had a natural immunity to tropical disease, troops of the 24th Infantry were assigned work

10th Cavalry

details at a hospital treating victims of typhoid and yellow fever. Roughly half of the black troops assigned to the hospital contracted the illnesses. Many of the black female volunteer nurses who cared for the sick and dying became victims as well.

Black men also served in the United States Volunteer Infantry (USVI), a manpower augmentation of 175,000 troops from the federalized state militia/national guard reserves. The USVI was to include the nation's oldest all black national guard unit, which had its organizational roots in Chicago, Illinois. Formed in the wake of the 1871 Chicago fire, it was originally known as the Hannibal Guards. It became an Illinois militia unit on May 5, 1890 as the 9th Battalion, commanded by Major Benjamin G. Johnson, a black man. When the Spanish American War erupted, other all-black militia regiments were organized; the 3rd Alabama, the 23rd Kansas, the 3rd North Carolina, the 9th Ohio, and the 6th Virginia.

Until converted to artillery battalions in World War II, the 8th Illinois USVI was always commanded by a black officer; Colonel John R. Marshall was the highest ranking black officer of the Spanish American War, and commanded the 8th Illinois until 1914. John R. Marshall was born on March 15, 1859, in Alexandria, Virginia.

After attending public schools in Alexandria and Washington, D.C. he became an apprentice bricklayer. After moving to Chicago, he was appointed Deputy Clerk of Cook County. Marshall joined the Illinois National Guard, organized a battalion and served in it as lieutenant and as major. In June 1892, he was commissioned as a colonel and assumed command of the 8th Illinois USVI Regiment. He led the regiment to Cuba where it joined with the 23rd Kansas and 3rd North Carolina in occupation duty.

The Spanish-American War provided a small increase in the number of black Regular Army officers. Benjamin O. Davis served as a lieutenant in the 8th Illinois USVI. Upon his discharge, he enlisted on June 14, 1899 as a private in the 9th Cavalry. He was promoted to corporal, and then to sergeant major. Davis was commissioned a Regular Army second lieutenant of cavalry on February 2, 1901. Also commissioned as Regular Army officers that year were John R. Lynch and John E. Green. As the twentieth century began, the United States Army had four black commissioned officers (excluding chaplains): Captain Charles Young, and Lieutenants Davis, Green, and Lynch. In 1940, Davis would become the nation's first black general officer.

Although only ten weeks long, the Spanish-American War produced fifty-two Medals of Honor, six to black recipients—five from the 10th Cavalry, which fought as infantry in Cuba. A black sailor won the sixth medal for heroism aboard the USS Iowa in the waters off Santiago, Cuba.

◆ WORLD WAR I (1914-1918)

The nation's entry into World War I raised the question of how to utilize black troops. Of the more than 400,000 black soldiers who served during the war, only about ten percent were assigned to combat duty in two infantry divisions. The 92nd Infantry Division was composed mainly of draftees. Black men from the 8th Infantry of the Illinois National Guard and the 315th Infantry of the New York National Guard formed the 93rd Infantry Division (Provisional). The majority of black World War I soldiers were assigned to stevedore units at ports, or labor units as quartermaster troops.

The most difficult question for the War Department was the demand that blacks be trained as commissioned officers. Initially, the idea was dismissed as ludicrous. It was said to be "common knowledge" that black men inherently lacked leadership qualities.

Only the persistence of the NAACP, the Urban League, and black newspapers like *The Chicago Defender*, eventually changed War Department policy. An all-black Officer Training School was established at Fort Dodge, near Des Moines, Iowa. On October 14, 1917, the school graduated and commissioned 639 black officers. However, the War Department had an iron-clad rule: No black officer could command white officers or enlisted men.

In accordance with this rule, the War Department retired Lieutenant Colonel Charles Young, who some white officers feared would assume command of the 10th Cavalry. Pressured by these officers, the U.S. senators who represented them in Congress, and President Wilson, the War Department developed a strategy to eliminate Young from consideration. Although Young was the highest ranking black officer, a West Point graduate who had trained black troops for combat and led them in action, he was discharged from active duty ostensibly because of ill health. To prove his fitness for active duty, Young rode on horseback from his home in Wilberforce, Ohio to Washington, D.C. While Young received support from the black press and many powerful friends, the War Department relented only five days before the end of World War I. Therefore, he was not given the opportunity to command troops in Europe and contribute to the American victory in the World War. He

was also denied a chance to become the first black general officer in American history. White supremacy was to remain ensconced in the nation's armed services.

One solution to the issue of utilizing black officers and soldiers was characteristic of military racism at this date: several black regiments were "attached" to the allied French Army. Colonel William Hayward, commander of New York's 369th Infantry criticized General John J. Pershing for this decision. Colonel Hayward charged that Pershing "simply put the black orphan in a basket, set it on the doorstep of the French, pulled the bell, and went away" (1936, *From Harlem to the Rhine: The Story of New York's Colored Volunteers* Arthur W. Little).

Despite the imposed "orphan" status, it was the 369th Infantry Regiment (15th New York) that established the best World War I record of any United States Army infantry regiment. The 369th served for 191 consecutive days in the trenches and never lost a foot of ground to the Germans. The so-called "Harlem Hell Fighters" won their laurels attached to the French 4th Army—using French weapons—and wearing United States uniforms.

In 1919, Columbia University President Nicholas Murray Butler gave *Harper's Weekly* his assessment of the 369th Infantry Regiment: "No American soldier saw harder or more constant fighting and none gave better accounts of themselves. When fighting was to be done, this regiment was there." (*The Independent and Harper's Weekly*, XCII, February 26, 1919, p. 286).

Despite the "Jim Crow" atmosphere, black soldiers earned an impressive number of awards for combat bravery defeating German troops. Sergeant Henry Johnson of New York's 369th Infantry Regiment was the first American, black or white, to receive the French Croix de Guerre. France awarded its Croix de Guerre to thirty-four black officers and eighty-nine black enlisted men during the war. In the 92nd Division, fourteen black officers and thirty-four black enlisted men earned the United States Army Distinguished Flying Cross (DFC). Ten officers and thirty-four enlisted men of the 93rd Division were DFC recipients.

Although they were not permitted to serve in the armed forces, Black women also contributed to America's efforts in World War I. They made bandages, worked in hospitals and troop centers, promoted the purchase of Liberty Bonds to finance the war effort, and served in the Red Cross, YWCA and other relief organizations.

Posthumous Medal of Honor Awarded

No Medal of Honor was awarded to a black serviceman during World War I. In 1988, the Department of the

A group of black World War I sailors.

Army researched the National Archives to determine whether racial barriers had prevented award of the nation's highest decoration for valor.

The archives search produced evidence that Corporal Freddie Stowers of Anderson County, South Carolina had been recommended for the award. For "unknown reasons," the recommendation had not been processed. Stowers was a squad leader in Company C, 371st Infantry Regiment, 93rd Division. On September 28, 1918, he led his squad through heavy machine gun fire and destroyed the gun position on Hill 188 in the Champagne Marne Sector, France. Mortally wounded, Stowers continued to lead his men through a second trench line.

On April 24, 1991, President George Bush belatedly presented Stowers's Medal of Honor to his surviving sisters in a White House ceremony.

◆ THE INTERWAR YEARS (1919-1940)

With the end of the war, the nation generally returned to applying the *Plessy v. Ferguson* doctrine—with a vengeance. Some senior white Army officers advocated

barring enlistment or re-enlistment of blacks altogether, an action that would have eventually abolished the four black Regular Army regiments by attrition.

A focal point of the Army's anti-black sentiment was the black commissioned officer. Despite countless well-documented cases of superb combat leadership, most black officers were eliminated from active duty following World War I.

An effective tool against retaining black officers was their alleged poor performance. That was buttressed by criticism of the black Officer Training School (OTS) class at Des Moines, Iowa. One of the severest critics was Major General Charles C. Ballou, commander of the World War I 93rd Infantry Division. Ballou emphasized that while white candidates were required to be college graduates, "only high school educations were required for... the colored... and in many cases these high school educations would have been a disgrace to any grammar school. For the parts of a machine requiring the finest steel, pot metal was provided" (Ballou letter, March 14, 1920).

However, there were combat-experienced white officers who held a decidedly different view of black

369th Infantry Regiment

officer training, such as Major Thomas A. Roberts. "As I understand the question," Roberts wrote in April 1920, "what the progressive Negro desires today is the removal of discrimination against him; that this can be accomplished in a military sense I believe to be largely possible, but not if men of the two races are segregated." Noting his appreciation of the "tremendous force of the prejudice against association between negroes and whites," Roberts declared "my experience has made me believe that the better element among the negroes desires the removal of the restriction rather than the

association itself" (Roberts letter to Asst. Comdt Gen. Staff College, April 5, 1920).

The anti-black campaign was also evident in the Army's civilian components, the National Guard and Officers Reserve. New York's 369th Infantry Regiment was maintained at full strength, although the 8th Illinois lost one battalion.

As for commissioned officers, the Reserve Officers' Training Corps (ROTC) detachments at Howard and Wilberforce Universities provided the bulk of new black second lieutenants. With no allocations for black officers to attend service schools, the lack of opportunity to maintain proficiency caused considerable attrition in the number of black reserve officers. To retain their commissions, other officers took advantage of correspondence and specially organized lecture/seminar courses.

◆ WORLD WAR II (1941-1945)

Less than two months after war began in Europe, the nation's preeminent black organizations, the NAACP and the National Urban League, had mobilized to defeat American racial segregation as well as Axis fascism. The black community clearly foresaw that the United States would eventually ally itself with Britain and France in war against Germany, Italy, and Japan.

Military mobilization began on August 27, 1940 with the federalizing of the National Guard, and activation of the Organized Reserve. When Japan attacked Pearl Harbor on December 7, 1941, there were 120,000 officers and 1,523,000 enlisted men on active duty in the Army and its Air Corps. On September 16, 1940, the nation began its first peacetime draft. By the end of World War II, the Selective Service System had inducted 10,110,104 men; 1,082,539 (10.7 percent) were black.

America's war effort required rapid expansion of both military and industrial power. Victory depended on the constant provision of ammunition, guns, planes, tanks, naval vessels, and merchant ships. The nation would have to unite to survive. A minority number of blacks, including Nation of Islam founder Elijah Muhammad, openly favored a Japanese victory; Muhammad's stance led to a four-year term in the United States Penitentiary at Milan, Michigan.

Essential to the desegregation activism of both the NAACP and the Urban League was the impact of black-owned weekly newspapers such as Robert S. Abbott's *Chicago Defender* and Robert Vann's *Pittsburgh Courier*. The rallying slogan was the "Double V"—victory against fascism abroad and racial discrimination in the United States. The goal was equal opportunity in both the armed services and within the civilian defense industries.

Soon, the NAACP and the Urban League were joined by the black activists of the March on Washington Movement led by A. Philip Randolph of the Brotherhood of Sleeping Car Porters and Maids. Randolph predicted that upwards of 100,000 blacks would march on Washington demanding equal employment opportunities in defense plant employment. On June 25, 1941, a week before the scheduled march, President Franklin D. Roosevelt forestalled the March by issuing Executive Order 8802. The President's order established a Committee on Fair Employment Practice "to provide for the full and equitable participation of all workers in defense industries, without discrimination." Of course, the Executive Order did not apply to the armed services.

The necessity of winning the war opened the economy to millions of black men and women who surged into defense plants, earning the same wages as their white co-workers. The war years thus brought economic upward mobility for many black civilians. Through the postwar benefits of the G.I. Bill of Rights, furthermore, the number of black college graduates and home owners would increase dramatically.

What has been largely ignored is that the United States Army took its first steps toward racial integration early in World War II. The obvious waste of duplicated facilities caused the Army to operate all of its twenty-four Officer Candidate Schools as racially-integrated institutions, where the primary quality sought was proven leadership capacity. The so-called "ninety-day wonders" who survived the standard three-month course were commissioned as second lieutenants in one the twenty-four Army branches ranging from the Army Air Forces Administrative School (Miami, Florida) to the Tank Destroyer School (Camp Hood, Texas). Of course, upon graduation, black officers were only assigned to black units.

The Army Air Force (AAF)

The exception in racially-integrated Army officer procurement during World War II was the Army Air Force Aviation Cadet program that trained pilots, bombardiers, and navigators. Ironically, black non-flying officers graduated from the integrated AAF Officer Candidates School at Miami Beach.

A total of 926 black pilots earned their commissions and wings at the segregated Tuskegee Army Air Field (TAAF) near Chehaw, Alabama. The 673 single-engine TAAF pilot graduates would eventually form the four squadrons of the 332nd Fighter Group.

Led by Lieutenant Colonel Benjamin O. Davis, Jr., a 1936 West Point graduate, the 99th Fighter Squadron was assigned to the 33rd Fighter Group commanded by Colonel William M. Momeyer. The 99th's first operational mission was a June 2, 1943 strafing attack on the Italian island of Pantelleria. On this date, Captain Charles B. Hall scored the squadron's first air victory by shooting down a FW-190 and damaging a ME-109. The 99th then settled into normal operations—or so the men thought.

In September Colonel Davis was recalled to take command of the 332nd Fighter Group. That is when he and the black community discovered that the "Tuskegee Experiment" was about to be labeled a failure. To this

Brigadier General Benjamin Davis reviews troops, Camp Breckinridge, 1943.

effect, Colonel Meyer submitted an appraisal of the 99th Fighter Squadron that was extremely negative:

> "Based on the performance of the 99th Fighter Squadron to date, it is my opinion that they are not of the fighting caliber of any squadron in this group. They have failed to display the aggressiveness and daring for combat that are necessary to a first class fighting organization. It may be expected that we will get less work and less operational time out of the 99th Fighter Squadron than any squadron in this group."

On October 16, 1943, squadron commander Davis appeared before the War Department's Committee on Special [Negro] Troop Policies to answer his group commander's allegations.

In his 1991 autobiography, written after his retirement as a retired Air Force lieutenant general, Davis describes the problem he faced at the Pentagon as a lieutenant colonel: "It would have been hopeless for me to stress the hostility and racism of whites as the motive behind the letter, although that was clearly the case. Instead, I had to adopt a quiet, reasoned approach, presenting the facts about the 99th in a way that would appeal to fairness and win out over ignorance and racism."

Davis presented such a convincing factual case that Army Chief of Staff General George C. Marshall ordered a G-3 [operations] study of the black squadron. The study's title, "Operations of the 99th Fighter Squadron Compared with Other P-40 Squadrons in the Mediterranean Theatre of Operations," precisely describes its contents. In his book, General Davis describes the G-3 study: "It rated the 99th according to readiness, squadron missions, friendly losses versus enemy losses, and sorties dispatched. The opening statement in the report was the clincher: 'An examination' of the record of the 99th Fighter Squadron reveals no significant general difference between this squadron and the balance of the P-40 squadrons in the Mediterranean Theatre of Operations.'"

On October 13, 1942, the Army had activated the 100th, 301st, and 302nd Fighter Squadrons. Combined with the 99th, the four squadrons would become the 332nd Fighter Group. Colonel Robert R. Selway, Jr., a white pilot, was its initial commanding officer. With the 99th vindicated by the G-3 study, Davis assumed command of the Fighter Group at Selfridge Army Air Field,

General Benjamin Davis, Sr. pins the Distinguished Flying Cross on son, Colonel Benjamin Davis, Jr.

Michigan. The 332nd departed for Italy on January 3, 1944 and absorbed the 99th as its fourth squadron.

During the period that the 99th was deployed and the 332nd was organizing, the TAAF program expanded to training two-engine B-25 pilots. While the fighter pilot fought alone, the B-25 "Mitchell" medium bomber required a five to six man crew that included two pilots and a bombardier-navigator. The 253 medium bomber pilots trained at TAAF, as well as 393 black navigators and bombardiers from Hondo and Midland Fields in Texas, formed the nation's second black flying organization when the Army Air Force activated the four squadron 477th Bombardment Group (Medium) in June 1943.

The 477th was plagued from the start by a shortage of enlisted aircrew members, ground technicians, and even airplanes. Fifteen months after activation, the 477th was still short twenty-six pilots, forty-three co-pilots, two bombardier-navigators, and all of its authorized 288 gunners. Moving from base to base for "operational training," the 477th logged 17,875 flying hours in one year without a major accident. Although finally earmarked for duty in the Pacific, the war ended before the 477th was deployed overseas.

As for the 332nd Fighter Group, it became a famous flying escort for heavy bombers. It was the only AAF fighter group that never lost an escorted bomber to enemy planes. The wartime record of the 332nd Fighter Group was 103 enemy aircraft destroyed during 1,578 combat missions. In addition to more than 100 Distinguished Flying Crosses, the 332nd also earned three Distinguished Unit Citations.

The so-called "Tuskegee Experiment" thus proved that black men could fly "state-of-the-art" aircraft, and could also conduct highly successful combat operations meeting AAF standards. The fruit of the Tuskegee Airmen's efforts would be harvested in less than three years—the 1948 racial desegregation of the United States military.

The Ground War

During World War II, the United States Army fielded two major black combat organizations: the 92nd Infantry Division in Europe, and the 93rd Infantry Division in the Pacific. Both of the Divisions suffered from avoidable impediments.

Just as in World War I, the 93rd Division was employed only in a fragmented manner. Major General Raymond G. Lehman's headquarters sailed from San Francisco, California on January 11, 1944; the artillery and infantry battalions and division headquarters assembled on Guadalcanal at the end of February. As Professor Ulysses Lee observed, "This was the last time until the end of the war that all elements of the division were gathered in the same location" (1966, *The Employment of Negro Troops*). The division would spend the rest of the war island-hopping, relieving units that had defeated Japanese troops. The 93rd Division World War II casualties were 12 killed in action; 121 wounded in action; and 5 who died of wounds.

Elements of the 93rd Division, primarily the 24th Infantry Regiment, performed well during the 1944 Bougainville campaign. Generally, the division's performance was considered adequate and acceptable. The usual after-action comments were made concerning the lack of initiative by junior officers, but overall the 93rd Division was described as well-disciplined and having good morale.

The 92nd Infantry Division, in contrast, gained a reputation as a chaotic outfit. During its preparation for deployment overseas, portions of the 92nd Division were sprinkled across the United States. While the division headquarters were at Fort Huachuca, Arizona, subordinate units were stationed at Fort McClellan, Alabama; Camp Robinson, Arkansas; Camp Breckinridge, Kentucky; and Camp Atterbury, Indiana. The division's

World War II casualties figures were vastly different than those of the 93rd Division: 548 killed in action; 2,187 wounded in action; and 68 who died of wounds. From its training in the United States through combat in Europe, the division's main problem seemed to be its commander, Major General Edward M. Almond. Many veterans of the 92nd Division continue to blame General Almond for the division's reputation and casualties.

It appears that "Ned" Almond was a racist. In a 1984 interview, retired Lieutenant General William P. Ennis, Jr. gave a "warts and all" description of Almond. As a World War II brigadier general, Ennis had commanded the corps artillery that supported the 92nd Division. According to Ennis, Almond and many white Southern officers in the division were selected because "in theory, they knew more about handling Negroes than anybody else, though I can't imagine why because [Almond] just despised the ground they walked on" (1992, *The Journal of Military History*).

The contrast of attitude at the division's various posts was amazing. While Almond denigrated the competence of black officers, Officer Candidate School (OCS) commandants generally held opposite views. For example, Brigadier General H. T. Mayberry, who commanded the Tank Destroyer OCS, observed in a 1945 interview that "a considerable number of young, potentially outstanding Negro officers were graduated. It was surprising— to me, at least—how high the Negroes (those who graduated) stood in the classes."

Lieutenant Colonel Robert C. Ross, a field artillery battalion commander in the 92nd Division, reported to Almond on five black officers who completed the basic artillery course. Three were made course instructors, while two were selected "as outstanding students from the entire forty-eight officers, both white and colored, from the first Officers Basic School."

One black officer, Captain Hondon B. Hargrove, was a 1938 Wilberforce University ROTC graduate. After his wartime service in the division's 597th Field Artillery Battalion, he commented that Almond did not believe "any black, no matter what his file showed, or how much training he had, was able in an officer's position . . . . He firmly believed only white officers could get the best out of [Negro troops] . . . [and] just could not countenance black officers leading them."

General Almond established his headquarters at Viareggio, Italy on Oct. 5, 1944. Two days later, the division's 370th Infantry Regiment began its assault on Massa. Professor Lee described the 92nd Division's major weakness: "It was a problem in faith and lack of it—the wavering faith of commanders in the ability and determination of subordinates and enlisted men, and the continuation in the minds of enlisted men of training period convictions that they could not trust their leaders." Thus, the Massa attack degenerated into chaos. In what was to be a major charge against the division, the men began to "melt away" from the fighting. After Massa, there were increasing cases of mutinous behavior toward both black and white officers.

In February 1945, the 92nd became the focus of serious Pentagon scrutiny. The man who would examine the situation was Truman K. Gibson, Jr., a black insurance company lawyer from Chicago, and Civilian Aide to Secretary of War Henry L. Stimpson. In his assessment, Gibson refused to blame the victim, or to generalize about the capabilities of black soldiers based on the performance of General Almond's 92nd Division. In a March 14th news conference in Rome, Gibson maintained that "If the division proves anything, it does not prove that Negroes can't fight. There is no question in my mind about the courage of Negro officers or soldiers and any generalization on the basis of race is entirely unfounded."

On May 14, 1945, a week after Germany surrendered, Lieutenant Colonel Marcus H. Ray wrote a letter to Gibson. A Chicagoan, as was Gibson, Colonel Ray was a National Guard officer of the 8th Illinois when it was mobilized in 1940. He ended the war as commanding officer of the 600th Field Artillery Battalion of the 92nd Division. Colonel Ray closed his letter to Gibson by observing that "those who died in the proper performance of their assigned duties are our men of the decade and all honor should be paid them. They were Americans before all else. Racially, we have been the victims of an unfortunate chain of circumstances backgrounded by the unchanged American attitude as regards the proper 'place' of the Negro . . . . I do not believe the 92nd a complete failure as a combat unit, but when I think of what it might have been, I am heart-sick . . . ."

The 761st Tank Battalion

The most highly acclaimed black ground combat unit of World War II was the 761st Tank Battalion. As an organization, it enjoyed the substantially better circumstances than the 92nd Division. Again, however, the "command climate" would be formative. Before the United States entered World War II, some white United States Army officers favored opening opportunities for black soldiers. They rejected the dogma of their colleagues who declared that modern weaponry was "too technical" for blacks. Fortunately, one such officer became the Commanding General of Army Ground Forces.

92nd Division, Ponsacco, Italy.

In this post, Lieutenant General Lesley James McNair spent most of his time visiting the nationwide array of ground forces training camps. When he visited the 761st at Camp Claiborne, Louisiana, he openly praised and encouraged the Army's first black tankers. When the 761st went ashore in France on October 10, 1944, the men believed that their outfit's existence was due mainly to McNair. (General McNair was killed by United States "friendly fire" on July 25, 1944 in France. The Joint Chiefs of Staff National Defense University is located at Fort Lesley J. McNair, named in his honor, in Washington, DC).

The 761st joined the 26th Division on October 31st and was welcomed by the division commander, Major General Willard S. Paul: "I am damned glad to have you with us. We have been expecting you for a long time, and I am sure you are going to give a good account of yourselves." Two days later, General George S. Patton visited and welcomed the 761st.

The 761st initial combat was on November 8, 1944 at Athaniville, France—the first of 183 continuous days of combat for the battalion. During their advance through six European countries, the 761st proved to be a stellar combat organization. The battalion is credited with killing 6,266 enemy soldiers, and capturing 15,818. Despite its outstanding combat record, the 761st did not receive a well-deserved Presidential Unit Citation until January 24, 1978.

The veterans of the 761st still pursue a World War II mission: posthumous Medal of Honor for Staff Sergeant Ruben Rivers, of Tecumseh, Oklahoma. Sergeant Rivers was severely wounded on November 16, 1944, when his tank ran over two mines near Guebling, France. With his lower thigh torn and his kneebone protruding, Sergeant Rivers refused evacuation. Instead, he remained with his tank and crew for three days of continuous combat. When his company was taken under fire by German heavy weapons, the company commander ordered his tanks to pull back below the crest of a hill. Sergeant Rivers' tank opened fire at the enemy and continued firing until it was hit in the turret by an armor piercing round that killed Sergeant Rivers.

The veterans of the 761st have been acknowledged—unfortunately, not without some controversy—by the Public Broadcasting System. On Nov. 11, 1992, PBS presented an hour-long documentary, "The Liberators," focusing on the exploits of the 761st Tank Battalion. Moreover, the broadcast asserted that the 761st helped liberate the most infamous of all Nazi concentration camps—Buchenwald and Dachau. Unquestionably, the 761st did liberate some concentration camps, but the assertion that the Battalion played a role in the liberation of those two specific camps has been challenged by some 761st veterans. The April 1945 after-action report of the 761st contains no entries concerning either of the two camps. Furthermore, the April 1945 location entries place the 761st miles from either camp. PBS therefore withdrew "The Liberators" from further exhibition pending additional research.

Smaller African American combat units made significant contributions in combat operations in both Europe and the Pacific. Fire from black artillerymen helped dislodge German troops as American forces fought to cross the Rhine River. For its defense of Bastogne, a strategic city in Belgium, the 969th Field Artillery Battalion received a Distinguished Unit Citation for meritorious service performed while attached to a white organization. Company C of the 614th Tank Destroyer Battalion became the first black ground unit to win this honor in World War II for driving off a German force that blocked the 411th Infantry in its advance on Climbach, Germany. Black antiaircraft outfits protected outposts in the Pacific and shot down German aircraft in Europe.

Because of a policy of racial segregation and discrimination, most of the one million African Americans in uniform during World War II were not assigned combat duty. Instead, they were assigned duty in the Service of Supply (SOS). In this capacity, they proved instrumental in the outcome of the war by operating bulldozers and cranes, setting up communications systems, and transporting essential supplies to the front. Over seventy percent of the truck companies in the Army's Motor Transport Service were black. Their role was critical in Europe because the railroads in France were destroyed by retreating German forces. Therefore, Allied forces had to be supplied by truck. The Red Ball Express was formed to meet this need in August, 1944, with an original route between St. Lo and Paris. "On an average day, 899 vehicles on the Red Ball Express traveled 1,504,616 ton-miles on the trip that took an average time of 54 hours." (Department of Defense *Black Americans in Defense of Our Nation*, n.d., p. 100).

The White Ball Route replaced the Red Ball Express in November, 1944. Four of the nine truck companies transporting supplies from Le Havre and Rouen to forward areas were black. Black truck companies also saw duty on the Antwerp-Brussels-Charleroi Route and the Green Diamond Route between Normandy and the Brest peninsula. The 3917th Gasoline Supply Company supplied the Third Army with up to 165,000 gallons of gas a day. Black truckers were also well represented among the twelve amphibian truck companies. Though assigned transport duty, black truckers were subject to hostile fire and were called upon to fight in emergencies. A number received military honors from both the United States and France for courage and meritorious service in combat.

The Women's Auxiliary Army Corps

With the creation of the Women's Auxiliary Army Corps on May 14, 1942, black women could serve in the American military in greater numbers than ever before. Many of the 4,000 black volunteers were assigned duties unlike their white counterparts in the renamed Women's Army Corps. While white women typically typed in offices, most black women were assigned to clean-up details and laundry and mess duty. This was not always the case, however. Overseas, the 6888th Postal Battalion commanded by Major Charity Adams arrived in England in 1945. The unit was later sent to the European mainland where it improved the mail delivery system, a system invaluable to troop morale.

Black women also served in the Army Nurse Corps. Initially, these women were only permitted to care for black patients, but this policy proved impractical. The resentment generated when black women were assigned to care for German prisoners of war ultimately led to a change in policy, enabling black nurses to care for wounded Americans, regardless of race.

The Sea Services

Following a decade of excluding blacks from enlistment, the United States Navy in 1932 decided upon a place for them—their own branch. The branch was known as the Stewards' Service, referred to in the black community as "sea-going bell hops." The 1940 Navy consisted of 170,000 men of whom 4,007 or 2.3 percent were blacks in the Stewards' Service. In addition to blacks, Navy stewards were also recruited from among Filipinos and other Asian-American populations.

The advent of World War II transformed this situation. President Franklin D. Roosevelt had served as assistant secretary of the Navy during World War I, and considered it "his branch" of the armed services. Therefore his January 9, 1942 memo to the Navy had tremendous impact. The President noted to then-Secretary of the Navy Frank Knox: "I think that with all the Navy activities, Bureau of Navy might invent something that colored enlistees could do in addition to the rating of messman."

The Navy did relent on April 7, 1942 by announcing it would accept 14,000 black enlistees in all ratings and branches. The initial training of black sailors was conducted at the Great Lakes Naval Training Station, north of Chicago, Illinois.

It was at Great Lakes that the Navy finally made a breakthrough in regard to black personnel. In January 1944, sixteen black petty officers began a special and intensive course of instruction that was conducted without public announcement. Three months later, the Navy announced the commissioning of twelve black ensigns and one warrant officer. They were then and are now the Navy's "Golden Thirteen" (1933, *The Golden Thirteen: Recollections of the First Black Naval Officers.* Annapolis, Maryland: Naval Institute Press).

Shortly after the "Golden Thirteen" were commissioned, the Navy opened the V-12 officer training programs to black men. Among the V-12 graduates who became Navy officers in World War II were Samuel L. Gravely, Jr. and Carl T. Rowan. Gravely became the Navy's first black admiral; Rowan is a syndicated columnist and broadcaster.

By the end of World War II, 165,000 blacks had served in the Navy; 17,000 in the Marine Corps; 5,000 in the Coast Guard; 12,000 in Construction Battalions (Sea Bees); and 24,000 in the Merchant Marine. These African American soldiers served with distinction. Notable among them is the mess steward Dorie Miller, who on December 7, 1941 manned a machine gun aboard the *USS Arizona* as Japanese aircraft attacked Pearl Harbor. Miller destroyed two of the attackers and, after some delay, was awarded the Navy Cross. He was also promoted to mess attendant first class. Miller died when the escort aircraft carrier *USS Liscome Bay* was sunk on November 24, 1943. Three other black mess attendants received the Navy Cross during World War II: Eli Benjamin (*USS Intrepid*); Leonard Harmon (*USS San Francisco*); and William Pinkney (*USS Enterprise*). Dorie Miller is memorialized by one of the three Navy warships named for black Americans: the frigates *USS Miller* and *USS Jesse L. Brown*, and the missile submarine *USS George Washington Carver*.

Desegregation of the Military

As the Allied victory of World War II approached, the highest levels of the United States government recognized that a new domestic racial era had emerged. The war to defeat Fascism had, indeed, involved the entire United States population.

One impetus for change of military policy toward blacks was an August 5, 1945 letter from Colonel Noel F. Parrish, commander of Tuskegee Army Air Field, to Brigadier General William E. Hall, Headquarters Army Air Forces. (1986. Bernard C. Nalty. *Strength For the Fight* New York: The Free Press, 213-214). Colonel Parrish recommended "that future policy, instead of retreating defensibly further and further, with more and more group concessions, openly progress by slow and reasonable but definite steps toward the employment and treatment of Negroes as individuals which law requires and military efficiency demands."

Although Secretary of War Henry L. Stimson often revealed racist tendencies, his assistant, John R. McCloy, was considerably more liberal. Stimson was succeeded by Robert P. Patterson who adopted McCloy's suggestion for a study of future use of blacks in the military. The study was made by a board of three Army generals: Lieutenant General Alvan C. Gillem, Jr., a former corps commander; Major General Lewis A. Pick, who built the Ledo Road in Burma; and Brigadier General Winslow C. Morse, of the Army Air Force. During a six week period, the so-called Gillem Board took testimony from more than fifty witnesses toward forming the Army's postwar racial policy. Two key individuals who worked with the Gillem Board were the two black Chicagoans who served sequentially as Civilian Aide to the Secretary of War: Truman K. Gibson, Jr. and the recently-discharged Lieutenant Colonel Marcus H. Ray. It is noteworthy that racial desegregation of the military was driven by the considerable political and economic influence of black Chicago.

The Gillem Board's findings leaned toward more "efficient" use of Negro manpower, but did not advocate actual desegregation.

That vagueness reactivated the pre-war coalition of the NAACP, the National Urban League, and the grassroots labor forces led by A. Philip Randolph.

The advent of the Cold War led to the National Security Act of 1947. One of the major elements of the new law was the establishment of the Department of Defense (DOD), with the subordinate Departments of Army, Navy and, Air Force. The other new entity created was the Central Intelligence Agency (CIA).

In the continuing movement toward desegregation of the armed forces, 1947 brought two important black personnel shifts within the Department Of Defense: Lieutenant Colonel Marcus H. Ray returned to active duty as senior advisor on racial matters in Europe and in the Pentagon, Dr. James C. Evans, a Howard University professor and Department of Army official, moved to the new post of Special Assistant to the Secretary of Defense. As the highest-ranking black civilian in the Department Of Defense, Dr. Evans served under ten secretaries of Defense until his retirement in 1970.

The demand for desegregation of the military became a key political issue in black America. As preparations for the 1948 presidential election intensified, President Truman faced a campaign against Republican Thomas E. Dewey, States Rights segregationist Strom Thurmond, and the Communist Party-supported Progressive Party of former Vice-President Henry A. Wallace. In such a fragmented situation, the black vote became crucial.

By May 1948, President Truman had decided to desegregate the armed forces by an Executive Order. Dr. Evans guided the politically sensitive staff coordination effort through the Pentagon. In other Executive branch and Capitol Hill offices, two political concessions were required. First, no deadlines would be imposed. Second, the order would not denounce racial segregation. With a final sign-off by the Attorney General, President Truman issued Executive Order No. 9981, which signalled a policy to end segregation in the military.

◆ THE KOREAN WAR (1950-1953)

On June 25, 1950, North Korean forces surged across the 38th parallel and invaded South Korea. The United States ground forces in Korea were savaged by the North Koreans and driven south. At the start of the Korean War, the Air Force was the only branch of the military that was desegregated.

The first United States victory of the Korean War was won by black soldiers of the 24th Infantry Regiment on July 20, 1950, at Yechon. Captain Charles M. Bussey, a World War II Tuskegee Airman, was the ground commander and earned a Silver Star at Yechon. Two black soldiers were awarded posthumous Medals of Honor during the Korean War: Private First Class William Thompson and Sergeant Cornelius H. Charlton, both of the 24th Infantry Regiment.

Thompson distinguished himself by bravery and determination above and beyond the call of duty in action against the enemy on August 6, 1950, near Haman,

Korea. While his platoon was reorganizing under cover of darkness, enemy forces overwhelmed the unit with a surprise attack. Johnson set up his machine gun in the path of the onslaught and swept the enemy with fire, momentarily pinning them down and thus permitting the remainder of his platoon to withdraw to a more secure position. Although hit repeatedly by grenade fragments and small-arms fire, he resisted his comrades' efforts to induce him to withdraw. Steadfast at his machine-gun, he continued to deliver fire until he was mortally wounded by an enemy grenade.

Charlton, a member of Company C, distinguished himself in action against the enemy on June 2, 1931, near Chipo-Ri, Korea. His platoon was attacking heavily defended hostile positions on commanding ground when the leader was wounded and evacuated. Carlton assumed command, rallied the men, and spearheaded the assault against the hill. Personally eliminating two hostile positions and killing six of the enemy with his rifle-fire and grenades, he continued up the slope until the unit suffered heavy casualties and was stalled. Regrouping the men, he led them forward, only to be again forced back by a shower of grenades. Despite a severe chest wound, Charlton refused medical attention and led a third daring charge that would advance to the crest of the ridge. He then charged a remaining enemy position on a nearby slope alone and, though hit by a grenade, raked the position with fire that eliminated it and routed the defenders. He died of wounds he received during his daring exploits.

The Korean War Evolution

The early defeats American forces experienced in Korea prompted President Truman to replace his close friend, Secretary of Defense Louis A. Johnson. To succeed Johnson, President Truman selected retired General of the Army George C. Marshall, who had been Truman's Secretary of State during 1947-1949.

One of Marshall's first acts as Secretary of Defense was the creation of a new entity: Office of Assistant Secretary of Defense for Manpower and Reserves (OASD MPR). Marshall appointed Mrs. Anna M. Rosenberg, a forty-eight-year old New York City labor and public relations consultant, as head of this Office. In 1944, she had persuaded President Franklin D. Roosevelt to have Congress enact the education provisions of the World War II G.I. Bill of Rights. Dr. James C. Evans' Office of Special Assistant became a part of the OASD (MPR). This brought together two individuals knowledgeable in the rigors of discrimination—a Hungarian Jewish immi-

Black members of the 2nd Infantry Division, Korea, 1950.

grant woman and a black male college professor. Known affectionately in the Pentagon as "Aunt Anna," Mrs. Rosenberg's OASD (MPR) was responsible for industrial and military manpower, including Selective Service System policies. Secretary Rosenberg viewed military desegregation as an impetus for civilian society reform observing that, "In the long run, I don't think a man can live and fight next to one of another race and share experiences where life is at stake, and not have a strong feeling of understanding when he comes home."

The effective implementation of Executive Order No. 9981 turned on how well their hard-won opportunities were used by black military personnel. The one individual who was truly the mentor of the black military professional, especially black officers, was Dr. James C. Evans. During much of his tenure in the Pentagon, Dr. Evans' Executive Officer was Army Colonel John T. Martin, who later was Director of the Selective Service System for the District of Columbia. Commenting in 1993, Colonel Martin reflected that "James C. Evans and his associates accomplished much behind the scenes— and with no fingerprints—to advance the careers of all [black] personnel in the military." One bit of mentoring at which Dr. Evans excelled was "informal" career

counselling. A wise young black officer would heed an Evans "suggestion" to explore a certain military career field, complete a particular service school course, or obtain an advanced degree in a particular discipline. If a young officer hesitated, Dr. Evans might again "suggest" that a particular course of action would benefit the officer "in due course." The counsel came from a man able to accurately forecast future officer education and experience requirements. Many black generals and admirals owe their stars to the wise counsel of James C. Evans.

By the end of the Korean War, racial segregation had been totally removed from the United States armed services. In the years preceding the Vietnam War, blacks increasingly entered the services and opted for full careers. Between 1953 and 1961, there was a slow but steady increase in the number of black career officers in each service.

◆ THE VIETNAM WAR (1964-1973)

During the brief period of cease-fire between the end of the Korean War and the heightening of conflict in

Vietnam, the Kennedy Administration—prompted by Congressman Adam Clayton Powell, Jr., and others—sought to end any remaining discrimination in the Armed Forces. Through Secretary of Defense Robert McNamara, Kennedy stressed to military leaders the need for fostering friendship and equal opportunity for black servicemen, both on and off base.

Extensive American involvement in Vietnam began during the summer of 1964 following an attack on the

By the end of the Korean War, racial segregation had been totally removed from the United States armed services.

Between 1953 and 1961 there was a slow, but steady, increase in the number of black career officers. Pictured Major Jerome Cooper, 9th Marines.

USS Maddox by North Vietnamese naval vessels in the Gulf of Tonkin. Within four months, the United States had 23,000 soldiers fighting in Vietnam. Shortly thereafter, the Army, Navy, and Marine Corps of the United States were all engaged in the action in ever increasing numbers. While the American fighting force in Vietnam was composed of all American racial and ethnic groups, blacks were disporportionately represented and most likely to be placed in high-risk combat units. Although blacks consituted about 10.5 percent of the Army, they accounted for nearly 13 percent of those killed and wounded. By 1965, the conflict in Vietnam had escalated into a full-scale war to support both the South Vietnamese people and U.S. interests in Southeast Asia, a war that was deadlier than the Korean War and longer than any other in American history.

The uncertain objectives of the Vietnam War, the high casualties, and the disporportionate number of black U.S. soldiers in Vietnam caused tremendous controversy in the African American community. In 1965, Malcolm X claimed that the U.S. government was "causing American soldiers to be murdered every day, for no reason at all." Martin Luther King Jr., criticized African American involvement in Vietnam, remarking that "we are taking young black men who have been crippled by our society and sending them 8,000 miles away to guarantee liberties in Southeast Asia which they have not found in southwest Georgia or East Harlem."

With the assassinations of Dr. King and Senator Robert Kennedy in 1968, some black soldiers became increasingly demoralized and disenchanted. Their anger intensified as racial prejudice remained common in Vietnam, on military bases stateside, and onboard the aircraft carriers *Kitty Hawk*, *Constellation*, and *Franklin D. Roosevelt*. One of the most famous black protesters of the Vietnam War was heavyweight champion

Blacks increasingly entered the services and opted for full careers. Pictured Brigadier General Davis and Captain Murray, Vietnam.

Muhammad Ali. A Black Muslim, Ali declared himself a conscientious objector in 1968 on religious grounds. He was convicted of violating the Selective Service Act, stripped of his heavyweight boxing championship, and threatened with an extensive jail term. In 1970, the Supreme Court cleared Ali of wrongdoing.

Still, most young African American men were willing to answer the draft board's call when it came. Private First Class Milton Olive of Chicago was typical of African Americans who risked, and sometimes lost, their lives during the war. Olive was killed by an exploding grenade on which he had fallen to save the lives of his comrades; the government acknowledged his heroism by awarding a posthumous Congressional Medal of Honor.

By mid-1969, nine other African Americans had joined Olive as recipients of the Congressional Medal of Honor: Captain Riley L. Pitts; First Lieutenant Ruppert L. Sargent; Sergeants Rodney M. Davis, Matthew Leonard, and Donald R. Long; Specialists Five Lawrence Joel, Clarence E. Sasser, and Dwight H. Johnson; and Private First Class James Anderson, Jr.

According to the *New York Times* reporter Thomas Johnson, officers in the Military Assistance Command said that the 173rd Airborne Brigade, a crack outfit with a heavy black representation, was "the best performing unit in Vietnam." In such elite combat units, one out of every four combat troops was a black man.

In 1973, the United States withdrew all troops from Vietnam, ending on of the most painful chapters in American history.

◆ MILITARY PARTICIPATION IN THE 1970S AND 1980S

In 1972, a year before the final withdrawal of U.S. troops from Vietnam, the Defense Department issued "The Search for Military Justice." This report recognized that discrimination still existed in the military. In particular, it found that African Americans and Hispanics were involved in more disciplinary incidents and were often punished more severely.

General Colin Powell at the Vietnam Veterans Memorial, Washington, DC.

In the 1970s, blacks represented about 13 percent of discharged servicemen, but received 33 percent of the dishonorable discharges, 21 percent of bad conduct discharges, 16 percent of undesirable discharges, and 20 percent of general discharges. Less than honorable discharges can negatively affect a person for life, threatening one's civilian career, earning ability, and level of veteran's benefits.

Fortunately, high-ranking government and military officials are moving to eliminate racial prejudices and barriers. Today, in many ways, military life is less discriminatory than civilian life. Also, in the 1980s, increasing numbers of women joined the military and work side by side with men in a wide variety of areas. This helps to facilitate the breakdown of gender, as well as racial, obstacles to success in the military.

By the end of the 1980s, blacks represented 28 percent of the total enlisted Army force, while black women numbered nearly 45 percent of enlisted women. However, recruiting blacks as officers was difficult in the 1980s due, in part, to competition with industry, law schools, and other professions that can offer talented black men and women higher salaries than the military.

◆ THE PERSIAN GULF WAR (1991)

African Americans were deeply divided over American involvement in the Gulf War, with almost 50 percent of those polled at the time opposed to it. Several black leaders, including Representative Charles Rangel of New York, were concerned in particular about the high number of blacks fighting to liberate Kuwait from Iraq. Military leader Colin Powell himself initially favored economic sanctions (embargoes) over military actions,

Petty Officer First Class John T. Winstead holds the folded American flag.

until war became the stated policy of President George Bush. From then on, Powell earned credit for drafting and putting into action a brilliant campaign—which began with the largest single air attack in history—that minimized the loss of American lives.

About 104,000 of the 400,000 troops serving in the Persian Gulf were black. According to the Department of Defense, blacks accounted for 30 percent of the Army, 21 percent of the Navy, 17 percent of the Marines, and 14 percent of the Air Force personnel stationed in the Gulf (in 1991 blacks comprised only 12.4 percent of the U.S. population). For Powell, the high participation of blacks, as shown by the Gulf War numbers, is a positive, rather than a negative: "To those who question the proportion of blacks in the armed services, my answer is simple. The military of the United States is the greatest equal opportunity employer around."   Since the end of the Persian Gulf War in 1991, African American military men and women have been well represented in peacekeeping missions in Somalia, Haiti, and Bosnia-Herzegovina.

◆ OUTSTANDING MILITARY FIGURES

Ensign Jesse L. Brown (1926-1950)
Naval Aviator

Jesse Leroy Brown was the first African American to become a naval aviator and the first black naval officer to be killed in action during the Korean War.

Brown was born October 13, 1926 in Hattiesburg, Mississippi. He graduated from Eureka High School in 1944 and studied engineering at Ohio State University from 1944 to 1947. In 1946 Brown joined the Naval Reserve and in 1947 he became an aviation cadet.

Brown's flight training was at Pensacola, Florida and in 1948 he became the first African American to earn the Navy Wings. In 1949 Brown was assigned to the *USS Leyte* and won the Air Medal and the Korean Service Medal for his 20 air combat missions. On December 4, 1950 he was shot down while flying air support for United States Marines at the Battle of the Chosin Reservoir. He was posthumously awarded the Purple Heart and the Distinguished Flying Cross for exceptional courage, airmanship and devotion to duty. Brown was the first African-American naval officer to lose his life in combat.

In 1973 the *USS Jesse L. Brown*, a destroyer escort was named in his honor and launched at the Avondale Shipyard at Westwege, Louisiana.

Sharian Grace Cadoria (1940-)
Military Officer

Born on January 26, 1940, in Marksville, Louisiana, Cadoria became the first black woman in the regular U.S. Army and the second African American female in history to rise to the rank of brigadier general. As a child, she and her two siblings helped pick cotton in the rural fields. After high school, Cadoria attended the state's Southern University, where, in the early 1960s, she was recruited for a four-week Women's Army Corp (WAC) training program conducted at Fort McClellan in Alabama. Thus began a 29-year-long, distinguished military career of "firsts," even after the WAC was dissolved in 1978 at which point she joined the male corp. Before fully devoting herself to the military, Cadoria earned her B.S. in Business Education from Southern and later obtained an M.A. in social work from the University of Oklahoma in 1974.

Among her marks of distinction, Cadoria was the first woman to command a male battalion; the first African American director of manpower and personnel for the Joint Chiefs of Staff—a position that required her to fill openings in all branches of the armed services, including the Army, Air Force, Navy, Marines, and affiliated reserve corps; the first black woman to attend the U.S. Army Command and General Staff College in addition to having attended the U.S. Army War College and having taken the Adjunct General School's advance course; and the first woman to achieve the rank of general through the military police rather than through the nursing corps.

Cadoria retired from the military in 1990, having spent the majority of her life breaking down the barriers presented by gender and racial discrimination. For outstanding contributions, Cadoria was awarded an Air Medal, an Army Commendation Medal, a Bronze Star, a Defense Superior Service Medal, a Distinguished Service Medal, and a Meritorious Service Medal during her career.

Sergeant William H. Carney (1840-1908)
First African American Medal of Honor Recipient

William Carney was born a slave in Norfolk, Virginia, in 1840. Around 1856, Carney's father moved the family to New Bedford, Massachusetts. In 1863 Carney enlisted in the 54th Massachusetts Colored Infantry. On July 18, 1863, Carney and the 54th Massachusetts led an assault on Fort Wagner, South Carolina, during which Carney was severely wounded. On May 23, 1900, Carney was issued a Medal of Honor. He died in 1908.

Lieutenant General Benjamin O. Davis, Jr. (1912-)
First African American General, United States Air Force

Born in Washington, DC, in 1912, Davis was educated in Alabama (his father taught military science at Tuskegee), and later, in Cleveland, where he graduated as president of his class. Davis went on to attend Western Reserve

University and the University of Chicago before accepting an appointment to the United States Military Academy in 1932. In 1936 Davis graduated 35th in his class of 276.

After serving in the infantry for five years, he transferred to the Army Air Corps in 1942 and was among the first six black air cadets to graduate from the Advanced Army Flying School.

As Commander of the 99th Fighter Squadron (and later commander of the all-black 332nd Fighter Group), Davis flew 60 missions in 224 combat hours during World War II, winning several medals, including the Silver Star.

In 1957 Davis was made chief of staff, of the 12th Air Force, United States Air Forces in Europe (USAFE). In 1961 he was made director of Manpower Organization, and in 1965 he became chief of staff for the United Nations Command and United States Forces in Korea. Davis was assigned as deputy commander in chief, US Strike Command in 1968. He retired from active duty in 1970.

Brigadier General Benjamin O. Davis, Sr. (1877-1970)
First African American General, United States Army

Born in Washington, D.C., on July 1, 1877, Benjamin O. Davis, Sr. graduated from Howard University and joined the army in 1898 during the Spanish-American War. At the end of that war, he reenlisted in the 9th Cavalry and was made second lieutenant in 1901. Black promotions were rare in those years, but Davis rose through the officer's ranks until he was made a full colonel in 1930. During that time, in addition to his military commands, he was a professor of military science and tactics at Wilberforce and Tuskegee universities, military attache to Liberia, and instructor of the 372nd Infantry of the Ohio National Guard. After his promotion to brigadier general and his service in World War II, he became an assistant to the inspector general in Washington, D.C. until his retirement in 1948.

Among General Davis' many awards and decorations are the Distinguished Service Medal, the Bronze Star Medal, the Grade of Commander of the Order of the Star of Africa, from the Liberian government, and the French Croix de Guerre with palm. General Davis died on November 26, 1970.

Lieutenant Henry Ossian Flipper (1856?-1940)
First African American Graduate of the United States Military Academy

Henry Ossian Flipper was born a slave in Thomasville, Georgia, on March 21, 1856; his father, a craftsman, bought his family's freedom. Flipper attended Atlanta University and in 1873 was appointed to the United States Military Academy.

Lieutenant General Benjamin O. Davis, Jr.

He graduated from the academy in 1877 and was commissioned as second lieutenant and assigned to the all-black 10th Cavalry. However, in 1881, Flipper became the victim of a controversial court-martial proceeding which cut short his career.

Flipper went on, as a civilian, to become a notable figure on the American frontier—as a mining engineer and consultant and later, as a translator of Spanish land grants. Flipper tried on many occasions to vindicate himself, befriending such prominent Washington officials as Senator A. B. Fall of New Mexico. When Fall became Secretary of the Interior, Flipper became his assistant until the infamous Teapot Dome affair severed their relationship.

Flipper returned to Atlanta at the close of his mining career, living with his brother, an AME bishop, until his death in 1940. His quest to remove the stain of "conduct unbecoming an officer and a gentleman" remained unfulfilled to his dying day.

Vice Admiral Samuel L. Gravely, Jr. (1922-)
First African American Admiral, United States Navy

Samuel L. Gravely Jr. was born in Richmond, Virginia on June 4, 1922. He enrolled at Virginia Union Universi-

Brigadier General Benjamin O. Davis, Sr.

Lieutenant Henry O. Flipper

ty, but quit school to enlist in the U.S. Navy. He received naval training at the Great Lakes facility at Great Lakes, Illinois, the midshipmen school at Columbia University in New York, and Officer Training Camp at the University of California, Los Angeles. During World War II, Gravely served aboard a submarine chaser. After the war ended, he returned to school and received a B.A. in history from Virginia Union University in 1948.

Gravely was called back to active duty in 1949 and decided to make a career of the navy. During the Korean War, he served aboard the cruiser *USS Toledo*. He was steadily promoted through the ranks and, in 1962, he accepted command of the destroyer escort *USS Falgout*. Stationed at Pearl Harbor, Hawaii as part of the Pacific Fleet, he became the first African American to assume command of a navy combat ship. In 1971, while commanding the guided missile frigate *USS Jouett*, Gravely was promoted to admiral, the first African American to achieve that rank. In 1976, he was promoted to vice admiral and placed in command of the United States Navy's 3rd Fleet, a position he held until 1978. Gravely, now retired, has also served as director of the Defense Communications Agency from 1978 until 1980, and the executive director of education and training for the

Armed Forces Communications and Electronics Association.

While in the Navy, Gravely received many medals, including the Legion of Merit with Gold Star, Bronze Star, Meritorious Service Medal, Joint Service Commendation Medal, Navy Commendation Medal, World War II Victory Medal, Naval Reserve Medal for 10 years of service in the U.S. Naval Reserve, American Campaign Medal, Korean Presidential Unit Citation, National Defense Medal with one bronze star, China Service Medal, Korean Service Medal with two bronze stars, United Nations Service Medal, Armed Forces Expeditionary Medal, Vietnam Service Medal with six bronze stars, and the Antarctic Service Medal.

Gravely has also received numerous civilian awards, including the Founding Fathers Military Commands Award presented by the Masons (1975), Military Headliner of the Year Award given by the San Diego Press Club (1975) and Savannah State College's Award of Excellence (1974). In 1972, Gravely received the Distinguished Virginian Award presented by the Governor of Virginia. The Virginia Press Association named him Virginian of the Year in 1979. In 1991, Gravely was named Aide-de-Camp to the Governor of Virginia.

General Daniel James, Jr. (1920-1978)
First African American Four Star General, United States Air Force

Appointed Commander of NORAD on August 29, 1975, Daniel "Chappie" James was the first African American four-star general in United States military history. Before coming to this post, he had been a flying ace in the Korean War, had served as deputy secretary of defense, and was vice commander of military airlift command.

Born on February 11, 1920 in Pensacola, Florida, he attended Tuskegee Institute, where he took part in the Army Air Corps program and was commissioned a second lieutenant in 1943. During the Korean War, James flew 101 combat missions in F-51 and F-80 aircraft. After the war, he performed various staff assignments until 1957, when he graduated from the Air Command and Staff College at Maxwell Air Force Base, Alabama. In 1966, he became deputy commander for operations of the 8th Tactical Fighter Wing stationed in Thailand, before promotion to commander of the 7272nd Flying Training Wing at Wheelus Air Force Base in Libya.

James became a brigadier general in 1970, a lieutenant general in 1973. He has received numerous civilian awards. His military awards include Legion of Merit with one oak leaf cluster, Distinguished Flying Cross, Air Medal with ten clusters, Distinguished Unit Citation, Presidential Unit Citation, and Air Force Outstanding Unit Award. In 1975 James was appointed commander in chief, NORAD/ADCOM, and was promoted to four-star general.

On February 25, 1978, James died of a heart attack at the age of fifty-eight in Colorado Springs.

General Hazel W. Johnson (1927-)
First African American Female General, United States Army

Johnson was born in 1927 in West Chester, Pennsylvania and received nurses training at Harlem Hospital in New York. She enlisted in the United States Army in 1955 and in 1960 Johnson joined the Army's Nursing Corps as a first lieutenant. Johnson then went on to earn a bachelors degree in nursing from Villanova University, a masters degree in nursing education from Columbia University, and a doctorate in education administration from Catholic University in Washington, DC.

In 1979 Johnson was promoted to brigadier general, the first African-American woman to hold that rank and was placed in command of the Army Nurse Corps. In

1983 she retired from the service and began working for the American Nursing Association as director of their government affairs division. In 1986 she jointed the faculty of George Mason University in Virginia as a professor of nursing.

Johnson is a recipient of the Army's Distinguished Service Medal, Legion of Merit, Meritorious Service Medal, and the Army Commendation Medal with oak leaf cluster.

Sergeant Henry Johnson (1897-1929)
369th Infantry Regiment, 93rd Division, United States Army

Henry Johnson was born in 1897 in Winston-Salem, North Carolina. A member of the 15th National Guard of New York, which became the 369th Infantry, Henry Johnson was probably the most famous black soldier to have fought in World War I.

The 369th itself was the first group of black combat troops to arrive in Europe. After a summer of training, the group saw action at Champagne and fought its way to the Rhine River in Germany, receiving the Croix de Guerre from the French government. Johnson and another soldier (Needham Roberts) were the first Americans to receive this French medal for individual heroism in combat; Johnson was cited by the French as a "magnificent example of courage and energy." He was later promoted to sergeant. Johnson died on July 2, 1929.

Dorie Miller (1919-1943)
Mess Attendent Third Class, United States Navy

A messman aboard the *USS Arizona*, Dorie Miller had his first taste of combat at Pearl Harbor on December 7, 1941, when he manned a machine gun and brought down four Japanese planes.

Born on a farm near Waco, Texas on October 12, 1919, Miller was the son of a sharecropper and grew up to become star fullback on the Moore High School football team in his native city. At 19, he enlisted in the United States Navy, and was nearing the end of his first hitch at the time of the Pearl Harbor attack.

For his heroism, Miller was awarded the Navy Cross, which was conferred by Admiral Chester W. Nimitz, the Commander in Chief of the Pacific Fleet.

He remained a messman during the hostilities, serving aboard the aircraft carrier *USS Liscome* Bay and being promoted to Mess Attendant Third Class. He was killed in action in the South Pacific in December of 1943.

General Daniel "Chappie" James, the first African American four star general.

Miller was commended for "distinguished devotion to duty, extreme courage, and disregard of his personal safety during attack."

General Frank E. Petersen (1932-)
First African American General in the United States Marine Corps

Frank E. Petersen, Jr. was born March 2, 1932 in Topeka, Kansas. He attended Washington University, in St. Louis, and George Washington University, in Washington, DC, eventually earning a BS in 1967 and a MS in 1973. In 1951, Petersen entered the Naval Reserve as an aviation cadet.

In 1952, Petersen was commissioned as a second lieutenant in the United States Marine Corps. He was a designated naval aviator and received flight training at the United States Air Station at Pensacola, Florida. He also received flight training at Corpus Christie, Texas and the Marine Corps Air Station at Santa Ana, California.

Daniel James, Jr. seated in the cockpit of his jet fighter plane.

Petersen flew thirty-one air combat missions during the Korean War. In 1953 and 1954, he was assigned to the 1st Marine Aircraft Wing as its liaison officer. From 1954 to 1960, he was assigned to the Marine Corps' Santa Ana, California facility and, in 1968, he commanded the Marine Aircraft Group in Vietnam. In 1979, Petersen was promoted to the rank of brigadier general. From 1985 to 1988, he served as senior ranking pilot of the U.S. Navy & U.S. Marine Corps. He was also the senior pilot of the U.S. armed forces from 1986 to 1988. In 1989, Petersen retired from the service and became a vice president at DuPont.

As an African American Marine Corps officer, Petersen accomplished many firsts. He was the first African American to receive a commission as aviator, the first African American to attend the National War College, the first African American to command a tactical air squadron, and the first African American general in the U.S. Marine Corps.

Petersen is a recipient of over twenty individual medals for combat valor, including the Distinguished Flying Cross, the Air Medal with silver star, the Korean Service Medal, the Korean Presidential Citation, the National Defense Service Medal with bronze star, and the United Nations Service Medal.

Petersen is a member of the Tuskegee Airman and Business Executives for National Security. He is also on the board of directors for the National Bone Marrow Foundation and the Higher Education Assistance Foundation.

General Hazel Johnson

General Colin L. Powell (1937-)
First African American Chairman of the Joint Chiefs of Staff

Colin L. Powell was born in New York City on April 5, 1937 and graduated from Morris High School in 1954. In 1958 he received a B.S. degree in geology from City College of New York; while in college Powell was very active in the ROTC program and attained the rank of cadet colonel.

Powell began his military career by accepting a second lieutenant's commission in the United States Army. In 1962, he served as a military advisor in South Vietnam and eventually became battalion executive officer and division operations officer in Vietnam in 1968. Returning to the United States, Powell earned an MBA degree from George Washington University in 1971. From 1972 to 1973, he served as assistant to the deputy director of the Office of Management and Budget. In 1973, he became a batallion commander in South Korea. Powell graduated from the National War College in 1976 and became commander of the Second Brigade of the 101st Airborne Division at Fort Campbell, Kentucky. In 1979, he became executive assistant to the Secretary of Energy and senior military assistant to the deputy Secretary

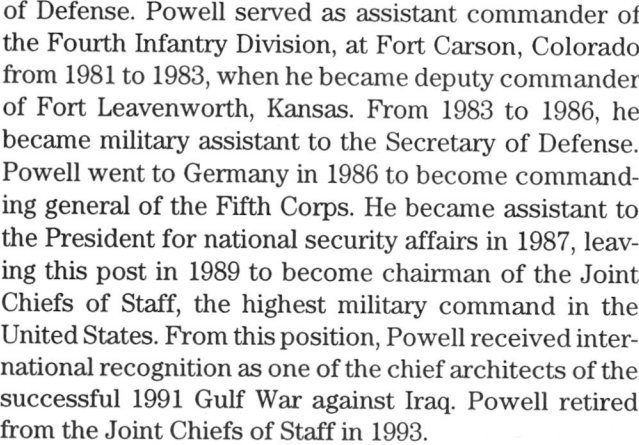

Admiral Nimitz awards Dorie Miller with the Navy Cross.

General Frank E. Petersen

of Defense. Powell served as assistant commander of the Fourth Infantry Division, at Fort Carson, Colorado from 1981 to 1983, when he became deputy commander of Fort Leavenworth, Kansas. From 1983 to 1986, he became military assistant to the Secretary of Defense. Powell went to Germany in 1986 to become commanding general of the Fifth Corps. He became assistant to the President for national security affairs in 1987, leaving this post in 1989 to become chairman of the Joint Chiefs of Staff, the highest military command in the United States. From this position, Powell received international recognition as one of the chief architects of the successful 1991 Gulf War against Iraq. Powell retired from the Joint Chiefs of Staff in 1993.

Powell wrote his memoir *My American Journey* and embarked on a nationwide tour in 1995 to promote the book. During the tour, there was widespread speculation that he would become a candidate for President in 1996. However, on November 9, 1995, Powell held a press conference and announced that he would not enter the race as a presidential candidate.

Powell remains active as a lecturer and guest speaker. In 1996, he was named to the board of trustees at Howard University.

During his tenure in the military, Powell was a recipient of several service medals, including the Purple Heart and the Bronze Star (1963), Legion of Merit Award (1969 and 1971), Distinguished Service Medal, Soldiers Medal, and the Secretary's Award (1988). He has received civilian honors as well. In 1993, former President Ronald Reagan presented Powell with the Ronald Reagan Freedom Award. That same year, he received an honorary doctoral degree from Yeshiva University.

General Roscoe Robinson, Jr. (1928-1993)
First African American Four Star General, United States Army

Roscoe Robinson, Jr. was the first African American four-star Army general. He was born on October 11, 1928, in St. Louis, Missouri and graduated from the United States Military Academy with a bachelor's degree in military engineering. He also earned a master's degree in international affairs from the University of Pittsburgh and received further training at the National War College, the Army Command and General Staff College, and the Army's Infantry School.

After graduating from West Point, Robinson was commissioned a second lieutenant in the United States

General Colin Powell with Brigade Commander Kristin Baker.

Army. He served as a personnel management officer from 1965 to 1967, and in 1968 he was promoted to commanding officer of the 7th Cavalry. He became commanding officer of the 82nd Airborne Division's 2nd Brigade at Fort Bragg, North Carolina in 1972. Robinson was promoted to the rank of general in 1973 and was placed in command of forces in Okinawa. He served in this capacity until 1976, when he became commanding general of the 82nd Airborne Division. In 1978, he was placed in command of the 7th Army. He served in this post until 1980, when he commanded the U.S. Army in Japan. From 1982 to 1985 Robinson served as the United States representative to NATO. He also held the position of executive chief of staff, United States Pacific Command. Robinson retired from active service in 1985.

Robinson received numerous military awards, including the Silver Star with oak leaf cluster, Legion of Merit with oak leaf cluster, Bronze Star, 10 Air Medals, an Army Commendation Medal, Combat Infantryman Badge, Distinguished Flying Cross, Master Parachutist Badge, Defense Distinguished Service Medal, and Army Distinguished Medal with oak leaf cluster.

On July 22, 1993, Robinson died of leukemia.

Roderick K. von Lipsey (1959-)
Fighter Pilot, United States Marine Corps.

Roderick K. von Lipsey was born on January 13, 1959, in Philadelphia, Pennsylvania. He attended the U.S. Naval Academy in Annapolis, Maryland, graduating in 1980. In 1989, he completed a master of arts degree from Catholic University. He has also received further training at the Amphibious Warfare School in Quantico, Virginia.

In 1980, von Lipsey was commissioned as a second lieutenant in the U.S. Marine Corps and learned to fly various types of fighter aircraft. He was stationed at Fort Beaufort, South Carolina, in 1983, promoted to the rank of captain in 1984 and became the officer in charge of aircraft maintenance for the F-4 Phantom. Von Lipsey was then tapped for duty with NATO exercises in Europe and the Mediterranean in 1986. He was sent to the prestigious Navy Fighter Weapons School at Naval Station Miramar in California and completed the grueling six-week program. In 1989, von Lipsey was stationed with the Marine Fighter Attack Squadron at Kaneohe Bay, Hawaii.

On August 2, 1990, Iraq invaded Kuwait. Von Lipsey was sent to Saudi Arabia as part of Operation Desert Shield designed to prevent further Iraqi aggression. While in the Middle East, von Lipsey joined Marine Fighter Attack Squadron 235. On January 20, 1991, the start of Operation Desert Storm against Iraqi forces in Kuwait, von Lipsey led an attack of 35 aircraft from the Third Marine Aircraft Wing. All of the planes under von Lipsey's command returned safely. The attack was one of more than 40 sorties flown by von Lipsey during the Gulf War. For his meritorious service in the Gulf War, he was awarded with the Distinguished Flying Cross.

Following his return from the Middle East, von Lipsey was chosen as one of two aides-de-camp to Joint Chiefs of Staff Chairman Colin Powell. He remained in this assignment until 1993, when he was awarded a White House Fellowship. Eventually, he gained a position as a special assistant to White House Chief of Staff Thomas McLarty III in 1994. Von Lipsey was awarded a second fellowship in 1994 with the Council on Foreign Relations. When this fellowship ended during 1995, he was assigned to Marine Corps Air Squadron El Toro, based in Santa Ana, California.

Appendix

Appendix

◆ AFRICAN AMERICAN RECIPIENTS OF SELECTED AWARDS

ACADEMY AWARD OF MERIT (OSCAR)— ACADEMY OF MOTION PICTURE ARTS AND SCIENCES

Best Performance by an Actor in a Leading Role

1963   Sidney Poitier, in *Lilies of the Field*

Best Performance by an Actor in a Supporting Role

1982   Louis Gossett, Jr., in *An Officer and a Gentleman*

1989   Denzel Washington, in *Glory*

Best Performance by an Actress in a Supporting Role

1939   Hattie McDaniel, in *Gone with the Wind*

1990   Whoopi Goldberg, in *Ghost*

Best Original Score

1984   Prince, for *Purple Rain*

1986   Herbie Hancock, for *'Round Midnight*

AMERICAN ACADEMY AND INSTITUTE OF ARTS AND LETTERS AWARD

Art

1946   Richmond Barthe

1966   Romare Bearden

1971   Norman Lewis

Literature

1946   Gwendolyn Brooks; Langston Hughes

1956   James Baldwin

1961   John A. Williams

1970   James A. McPherson

1971   Charles Gordone

1972   Michael S. Harper

1974   Henry Van Dyke

1978   Lerone Bennett, Jr.; Toni Morrison

1985   John Williams

1987   Ernest J. Gaines

1992   August Wilson

Music

1974   Olly Wilson

1981   George Walker

1988   Hale Smith

1991   Tania J. Leon

EMMY AWARD—ACADEMY OF TELEVISION ARTS AND SCIENCES

Outstanding Supporting Actor in a Comedy, Variety, or Music Series

1985   Robert Guillaume, in "Benson" (ABC)

1979   Robert Guillaume, in "Soap" (ABC)

Outstanding Lead Actor in a Drama Series

1966   Bill Cosby as Alexander Scott, in "I Spy" (NBC)

1967   Bill Cosby as Alexander Scott, in "I Spy" (NBC)

1968 Bill Cosby as Alexander Scott, in "I Spy" (NBC)

1991 James Earl Jones, in "Gabriel's Fire" (ABC)

Outstanding Supporting Actor in a Miniseries or a Special

1991 James Earl Jones, in "Heatwave" (TNT)

Outstanding Lead Actress in a Comedy Series

1981 Isabel Sanford, in "The Jeffersons" (CBS)

Outstanding Supporting Actress in a Drama Series

1984 Alfre Woodard, in "Doris in Wonderland" episode of "Hill Street Blues" (NBC)

1991 Madge Sinclair, in "Gabriel's Fire" (ABC)

Outstanding Supporting Actress in a Miniseries or a Special

1991 Ruby Dee, in "Decoration Day" (NBC)

Outstanding Lead Actress in a Comedy or Drama Special

1974 Cicely Tyson, in "The Autobiography of Miss Jane Pittman" (CBS)

Outstanding Lead Actress in a Miniseries or a Special

1991 Lynn Whitfield, in "The Josephine Baker Story" (HBO)

Outstanding Achievement in Music Composition for a Series

1977 Quincy Jones and Gerald Fried, for "Roots" (ABC)

Outstanding Directing in a Drama Series

1986 Georg Stanford Brown, for "Parting Shots," episode of "Cagney & Lacey" (ABC)

1990 Thomas Carter, for "Equal Justice" episode of "Promises to Keep" (ABC)

1991 Thomas Carter, for "Equal Justice" episode of "In Confidence" (ABC)

1992 Eric Laneuville, for "I'll Fly Away" episode of "All God's Children" (NBC)

Outstanding Achievement in Music Composition

1971 Ray Charles, for "The First Nine Months Are the Hardest" (NBC)

1972 Ray Charles, for "The Funny Side of Marriage" (NBC)

GRAMMY AWARD—NATIONAL ACADEMY OF RECORDING ARTS AND SCIENCES

Record of the Year

1967 *Up, Up and Away*, by 5th Dimension

1969 *Aquarius/Let the Sun Shine In*, by 5th Dimension

1972 *The First Time Ever I Saw Your Face*, by Roberta Flack

1973 *Killing Me Softly with His Song*, by Roberta Flack

1976 *This Masquerade*, by George Benson

1983 *Beat It*, by Michael Jackson

1984 *What's Love Got To Do with It*, by Tina Turner

1985 *We Are the World*, by USA For Africa; produced by Quincy Jones

1988 *Don't Worry, Be Happy*, by Bobby McFerrin

1991 *Unforgettable*, by Natalie Cole with Nat "King" Cole

Album of the Year

1973 *Innervisions*, by Stevie Wonder; produced by Stevie Wonder

1974 *Fulfillingness' First Finale*, by Stevie Wonder; produced by Stevie Wonder

1976 *Songs in the Key of Life*, by Stevie Wonder; produced by Stevie Wonder

1983 *Thriller*, by Michael Jackson; produced by Quincy Jones

1984 *Can't Slow Down*, by Lionel Richie; produced by Lionel Richie and James Anthony Carmichael

1990 *Back on the Block*, by Quincy Jones; produced by Quincy Jones

1991 *Unforgettable*, by Natalie Cole

HEISMAN MEMORIAL TROPHY—DOWNTOWN ATHLETIC CLUB OF NEW YORK CITY, INC.

1961 Ernie Davis, Syracuse University, TB

1965 Michael Garrett, University of Southern California, TB

1968 O. J. Simpson, University of Southern California, TB

1971 Pat Sullilvan, Auburn University, QB

1972 Johnny Rodgers, University of Nebraska, FL

1974 Archie Griffin, University of Ohio State, HB

1975 Archie Griffin, University of Ohio State, HB

1976 Anthony Dorsett, University of Pittsburgh, HB

1977 Earl Campbell, University of Texas, FB

1978 Billy Sims, University of Oklahoma, HB

1979 Charles White, University of Southern California, TB

1980 George Rogers, University of South Carolina, HB

1981 Marcus Allen, University of Southern California, TB

1982 Herschel Walker, University of Georgia, HB

1983 Mike Rozier, University of Nebraska, TB

1985 Bo Jackson, Auburn University, TB

1987 Tim Brown, University of Notre Dame, FL

1988 Barry Sanders, Oklahoma State University, HB

1989 Andre Ware, University of Houston, QB

1991 Desmond Howard, University of Michigan, WR

CLARENCE L. HOLTE LITERARY PRIZE (BIANNUAL)—CO-SPONSORED BY THE PHELPS-STOKES FUND AND THE SCHOMBURG CENTER FOR RESEARCH IN BLACK CULTURE OF THE NEW YORK PUBLIC LIBRARY

1979 Dr. Chancellor Williams, for *The Destruction of Black Civililzation: Great Issues of a Race from 4500 B.C. to 2000 A.D.*

1981 Ivan Van Sertima, for *They Came Before Columbus*

1983 Vincent Harding, for *There Is a River: The Black Struggle for Freedom in America*

1985 No award

1986 John Hope Franklin, for *George Washington Williams: A Biography*

1988 Arnold Rampersad, for *The Life of Langston Hughes, Volume 1 (1902-1941): I, Too, Sing America*

1990 No award

1992 No award

KENNEDY CENTER HONORS—JOHN F. KENNEDY CENTER FOR THE PERFORMING ARTS

1978 Marian Anderson

1979 Ella Fitzgerald

1980 Leontyne Price

1981 William "Count" Basie

1983 Katherine Dunham

1984 Lena Horne

1986 Ray Charles

1987 Sammy Davis, Jr.

1988 Alvin Ailey

1989 Harry Belafonte

1990 Dizzy Gillespie

1991 Fayard and Harold Nicholas

1992 Lionel Hampton

MARTIN LUTHER KING, JR. NONVIOLENT PEACE PRIZE—MARTIN LUTHER KING, JR. CENTER FOR NONVIOLENT SOCIAL CHANGE, INC.

1973 Andrew Young

1974 Cesar Chavez

1975 John Lewis

1976 Randolph Blackwell

1977 Benjamin E. Mays

1978 Kenneth D. Kaunda; Stanley Levison

1979 Jimmy Carter

1980 Rosa Parks

1981 The Hon. Ivan Allen, Jr.

1982 Harry Belafonte

1983 Sir Richard Attenborough; Martin Luther King, Sr.

1984 No award

1985 No award

1986 Bishop Desmond Tutu

1987 Corazon Aquino

1988 No award

1989 No award

1990 Mikhail Gorbachev

1991 No award

1992 No award

1993 Jesse Jackson

MEDAL OF HONOR

Civil War

Army

William H. Barnes, Private, Company C, 38th United States Colored Troops.

Powhatan Beaty, First Sergeant, Company G, 5th United States Colored Troops.

James H. Bronson, First Sergeant, Company D, 5th United States Colored Troops.

William H. Carney, Sergeant, Company C, 54th Massachusetts Infantry, United States Colored Troops.

Decatur Dorsey, Sergeant, Company B, 39th United States Colored Troops.

Christian A. Fleetwood, Sergeant Major, 4th United States Colored Troops.

James Gardiner, Private, Company 1, 36th United States Colored Troops.

James H. Harris, Sergeant, Company B, 38th United States Colored Troops.

Thomas R. Hawkins, Sergeant Major, 6th United States Colored Troops.

Alfred B. Hilton, Sergeant, Company H, 4th United States Colored Troops.

Milton M. Holland, Sergeant, 5th United States Colored Troops.

Alexander Kelly, First Sergeant, Company F, 6th United States Colored Troops.

Robert Pinn, First Sergeant, Company I, 5th United States Colored Troops.

<n.LEdward Radcliff, First Sergeant, Company C, 38th United States Colored Troops.

Charles Veal, Private, Company D, 4th United States Colored Troops.

Navy

Aaron Anderson, Landsman, *USS Wyandank*.

Robert Blake, Powder Boy, *USS Marblehead*.

William H. Brown, Landsman, *USS Brooklyn*.

Wilson Brown, *USS Hartford*.

John Lawson, Landsman, *USS Hartford*.

James Mifflin, Engineer's Cook, *USS Brooklyn*.

Joachim Pease, Seaman, *USS Kearsarge*.

Interim Period

Navy

Daniel Atkins, Ship's Cook, First Class, *USS Cushing*.

John Davis, Seaman, *USS Trenton*.

Alphonse Girandy, Seaman, *USS Tetrel*.

John Johnson, Seaman, *USS Kansas*.

William Johnson, Cooper, *USS Adams*.

Joseph B. Noil, Seaman, *USS Powhatan*.

John Smith, Seaman, *USS Shenandoah*.

Robert Sweeney, Seaman, *USS Kearsage*, *USS Jamestown*.

Western Campaigns

Army

Thomas Boyne, Sergeant, Troop C, 9th United States Cavalry.

Benjamin Brown, Sergeant, Company C, 24th United States Infantry.

John Denny, Sergeant, Troop C, 9th United States Cavalry.

Pompey Factor, Seminole Negro Indian Scouts.

Clinton Greaves, Corporal, Troop C, 9th United States Cavalry.

Henry Johnson, Sergeant, Troop D, 9th United States Cavalry.

George Jordan, Sergeant, Troop K, 9th United States Cavalry.

William McBreyar, Sergeant, Troop K, 10th United States Cavalry.

Isaiah Mays, Corporal, Company B, 24th United States Infantry.

Issac Payne, Private (Trumpeteer) Seminole Negro Indian Scouts.

Thomas Shaw, Sergeant, Troop K, 9th United States Cavalry.

Emanuel Stance, Sergeant, Troop F, 9th United States Cavalry.

Augustus Walley, Private, Troop 1, 9th United States Cavalry.

John Ward, Sergeant, Seminole Negro Indian Scouts.

Moses Williams, First Sergeant, Troop 1, 9th United States Cavalry.

William O. Wilson, Corporal, Troop 1, 9th United States Cavalry.

Brent Woods, Sergeant, Troop B, 9th United States Cavalry.

Spanish-American War

Army

Edward L. Baker, Jr., Sergeant Major, 10th United States Cavalry.

Dennis Bell, Private, Troop H, 10th United States Cavalry.

Fitz Lee, Private, Troop M, 10th United States Cavalry.

William H. Thompkins, Private, Troop G, 10th United States Cavalry.

George H. Wanton, Sergeant, Troop M, 10th United States Cavalry.

Navy

Robert Penn, Fireman, First Class, *USS Iowa*.

World War I

Army

Freddie Stowers, Corporal, Company C, 371st Infantry Regiment, 93rd Infantry Division.

Korean Conflict

Army

Cornelius H. Charlton, Sergeant, 24th Infantry Regiment, 25th Division.

William Thompson, Private, 24th Infantry Regiment, 25th Division.

Vietnam Conflict

Army

Webster Anderson, Sergeant, Battery A, 2nd Battalion, 320th Artillery, 101st Airborne Division.

Eugene Ashley, Jr., Sergeant, Company C, 5th Special Forces Group (Airborne), 1st Special Forces.

William M. Bryant, Sergeant First Class, Company A, 5th Special Forces Group, 1st Special Forces.

Lawrence Joel, Specialist Sixth Class, Headquarters and Headquarters Company, 1st Battalion, 173d Airborne Brigade.

Dwight H. Johnson, Specialist Fifth Class, Company B, 1st Battalion, 69th Armor, 4th Infantry Division.

Garfield M. Langhorn, Private First Class, Troop C, 7th Squadron, 17th Cavalry, 1st Aviation Brigade.

Matthew Leonard, Platoon Sergeant, Company B, 1st Battalion, 16th Infantry, 1st Infantry Division.

Milton L. Olive III, Private First Class, Company B, 2nd Battalion 503d Infantry, 173d Airborne Brigade.

Charles C. Rogers, Lieutenant Colonel, 1st Battalion, 5th Infantry, 1st Infantry Division.

Donald R. Long, Sergeant, Troop C, 1st Squadron, 4th Cavalry, 1st Infantry Division.

Riley L. Pitts, Captain, Company C, 2nd Battalion, 27th Infantry, 25th Infantry Division.

Rupert L. Sargent, First Lieutenant, Company B, 4th Battalion, 9th Infantry, 25th Infantry Division.

Clarence E. Sasser, Specialist 5th Class, Headquarters Company, 3rd Battalion, 60th Infantry, 90th Infantry Division.

Clifford C. Sims, Staff Sergeant, Company D, 2nd Battalion, 501st Infantry, 101st Airborne Division.

John E. Warren, Jr., First Lieutenant, Company C, 2nd Battalion, 22d Infantry, 25th Infantry Division.

Marines

James A. Anderson, Jr. Private First Class, 2nd Platoon, Company F, 2nd Battalion, 3rd Marine Division.

Oscar P. Austin, Private First Class, Company E, 7th Marines, 1st Marine Division.

Rodney M. Davis, Sergeant, Company B, 1st Battalion, 5th Marines, 1st Marine Division.

Robert H. Jenkins, Jr., Private First Class, 3rd Reconnaissance Battalion, 3rd Marine Division.

Ralph H. Johnson, Private First Class, Company A, 1st Recon Battalion, 1st Marine Division.

MISS AMERICA—MISS AMERICA ORGANIZATION

1984 Vanessa Williams (New York); Suzette Charles (New Jersey)

1990 Debbye Turner (Missouri)

MISS BLACK AMERICA—J. MORRIS ANDERSON PRODUCTION COMPANY

1968 Sandy Willliams (Pennsylvania)

1969 G. O. Smith (New York)

1970 Stephanie Clark (District of Columbia)

1971 Joyce Warner (Florida)

1972 Linda Barney (New Jersey)

1973 Arnice Russell (New York)

1974 Von Gretchen Sheppard (California)

1975 Helen Ford (Mississippi)

1976 Twanna Kilgore (District of Columbia)

1977 Claire Ford (Tennessee)

1978 Lydia Jackson (New Jersey)

1979 Veretta Shankle (Mississippi)

1980 Sharon Wright (Illinois)

1981 Pamela Jenks (Massachusetts)

1982 Phyllis Tucker (Florida)

1983 Sonia Robinson (Wisconsin)

1984 Lydia Garrett (South Carolina)

1985 Amina Fakir (Michigan)

1986 Rachel Oliver (Massachusetts)

1987 Leila McBride (Colorado)

1989 Paula Swynn (District of Columbia)

1990 Rosie Jones (Connecticut)

1991 Sharmelle Sullivan (Indiana)

1992 Marilyn DeShields

1993 Pilar Ginger Fort

1994 Karen Wallace

1995 Asheera Ahmad

MISS USA—MADISON SQUARE GARDEN TELEVISION PRODUCTIONS

1990 Carole Gist (Michigan)

1992 Shannon Marketic

1993 Kenya Moore (Michigan)

1994 Frances Louise "Lu" Parker

1995 Chelsi Smith (Texas)

1996 Ali Landry

NATIONAL BASEBALL HALL OF FAME

1969 Roy Campanella

1962 Jackie Robinson

1971 Leroy R. "Satchel" Paige

1972 Josh Gibson; Walter "Buck" Leonard

1973 Roberto W. Clemente; Monford Irvin

1974 James T. "Cool Papa" Bell

1975 William "Judy" Johnson

1976 Oscar M. Charleston

1977 Ernest Banks; Martin Dihigo; John H. Lloyd

1979 Willie Mays

1981 Rube Foster; Robert T. Gibson

1982 Hank Aaron; Frank Robinson

1983 Jaun A. Marichal

1985 Lou Brock

1986 Willie L. "Stretch" McCovey

1987 Ray Dandridge; Billy Williams

1988 Willie Stargell

1990 Joe Morgan

1991 Rod Carew; Ferguson Jenkins

1993 Reggie Jackson

NATIONAL BOOK AWARD—NATIONAL BOOK FOUNDATION

1953 Ralph Ellison, for *Invisible Man*, Fiction

1969 Winthrop D. Jordan, for *White over Black: American Attitudes toward the Negro, 1550-1812*, History and Biography

1983 Gloria Naylor, for *The Women of Brewster Place*, First Novel; Joyce Carol Thomas, for *Marked By Fire*, Children's Literature; Alice Walker, for *The Color Purple*, Fiction

1990 Charles Johnson, for *Middle Passage*, Fiction

1991 Melissa Fay Green, for *Praying for Sheetrock*, Nonfiction

1992 Edward P. Jones, for *Lost in the City*, Fiction

NATIONAL MEDAL OF ARTS—NATIONAL ENDOWMENT FOR THE ARTS

1985 Ralph Ellison (writer); Leontyne Price (singer)

1986 Marian Anderson (singer)

1987 Romare Bearden (artist); Ella Fitzgerald (singer)

1988 Gordon Parks (photographer and film director)

1989 Katherine Dunham (choreographer); Dizzy Gillespie (musician)

1990 Riley "B. B." King (musician)

1991 James Earl Jones (actor); Billy Taylor (musician)

1994 Harry Belafonte (singer)

1995 Gwendolyn Brooks (poet); Ossie Davis (actor); Ruby Dee (actress)

NATIONAL SOCIETY OF ARTS AND LETTERS GOLD MEDAL OF MERIT AWARD

1982 Andre Watts (music)

NATIONAL TRACK AND FIELD HALL OF FAME—THE ATHLETICS CONGRESS OF THE USA

1974 Ralph Boston; Lee Calhoun; Harrison Dillard; Rafer Johnson; Jesse Owens; Wilma Rudolph; Malvin Whitfield

1975 Ralph Metcalfe

1976 Robert Hayes; Hayes Jones

1977 Robert Beamon; Andrew W. Stanfield

1978 Tommie Smith; John Woodruff

1979 Jim Hines; William DeHart Hubbard

1980 Wyomia Tyus

1981 Willye White

1982 Willie Davenport; Eddie Tolan

1983 Lee Evans

1984 Madeline Manning Mims

1986 Henry Barney Ewell

1988 Gregory Bell

1989 Milt Campbell; Edward Temple

1990 Charles Dumas

1994 Cornelius Johnson; Edwin Moses

NEW YORK DRAMA CRITICS' CIRCLE AWARD

Best American Play

1959 *A Raisin in the Sun*, by Lorraine Hansberry

1975 *The Taking of Miss Janie*, by Ed Bullins

1982 *A Soldier's Play*, by Charles Fuller

1996 *Seven Guitars*, by August Wilson

Best New Play

1985 *Ma Rainey's Black Bottom*, by August Wilson

1987 *Fences*, by August Wilson

1988 *Joe Turner's Come and Gone*, by August Wilson

1990 *The Piano Lesson*, by August Wilson

NOBEL PEACE PRIZE—NOBEL FOUNDATION

1950 Ralph J. Bunche

1964 Martin Luther King, Jr.

ANTOINETTE PERRY (TONY) AWARD—LEAGUE OF AMERICAN THEATRES AND PRODUCERS

Actor (Dramatic)

1969 James Earl Jones, for *The Great White Hope*

1975 John Kani, for *Sizwe Banzi*; Winston Ntshona, for *The Island*

1987 James Earl Jones, for *Fences*

Supporting or Featured Actor (Dramatic)

1982 Zakes Mokae, for *Master Harold … and the Boys*

1992 Larry Fishburne, for *Two Trains Running*

Actor (Musical)

1970 Cleavon Litte, for *Purlie*

1973 Ben Vereen, for *Pippin*

1982 Ben Harvey, for *Dreamgirls*

1992 Gregory Hines, for *Jelly's Last Jam*

Supporting or Featured Actor (Musical)

1954 Harry Belafonte, for *John Murray Anderson's Almanac*

1975 Ted Rose, for *The Wiz*

1981 Hinton Battle, for *Sophisticated Ladies*

1982 Cleavant Derricks, for *Dreamgirls*

1983 Charles "Honi" Coles, for *My One and Only*

1984 Hinton Battle, for *The Tap Dance Kid*

1991 Hinton Battle, for *Miss Saigon*

Supporting or Featured Actress (Dramatic)

1977 Trazana Beverley, for *For Colored Girls Who Have Considered Suicide/When the Rainbow Is Enuf*

1987 Mary Alice, for *Fences*

1988 L. Scott Caldwell, for *Joe Turner's Come and Gone*

Actress (Musical)

1962 Diahann Carroll, for *No Strings*

1968 Leslie Uggams, for *Hallelujah, Baby*

1974 Virginia Capers, for *Raisin*

1982 Jennifer Holliday, for *Dreamgirls*

1989 Ruth Brown, for *Black and Blue*

Supporting or Featured Actress (Musical)

1950 Juanita Hall, for *South Pacific*

1968 Lillian Hayman, for *Halleluja, Baby*

1970 Melba Moore, for *Purlie*

1975 Dee Dee Bridgewater, for *The Wiz*

1977 Delores Hall, for *Your Arms's Too Short To Box with God*

1978 Nell Carter, for *Ain't Misbehavin*

1992 Tonya Pinkins, for *Jelly's Last Jam*

Play

1974 *The River Niger*, by Joseph A. Walker

1987 *Fences*, by August Wilson

PRESIDENTIAL MEDAL OF FREEDOM—UNITED STATES EXECUTIVE OFFICE OF THE PRESIDENT

1963 Marian Anderson; Ralph J. Bunche

1964 John L. Lewis; Leontyne Price; A. Philip Randolph

1969 Edward Kennedy "Duke" Ellington; Ralph Ellison; Roy Wilkins; Whitney M. Young, Jr.

1976 Jesse Owens

1977 Dr. Martin Luther King, Jr. (posthumously)

1981 James H. Eubie Blake; Andrew Young

1984 Jack Roosevelt Robinson (posthumously)

1985 William "Count" Basie (posthumously)

1988 Pearl Bailey

1991 General Colin L. Powell

1992 Ella Fitzgerald

1993 Colin L. Powell

1994 Dorothy Height; Barbara Jordan

1995 William T. Coleman, Jr.; John Hope Franklin; A. Leon Higginbotham, Jr.

PRO FOOTBALL HALL OF FAME

1967 Emlen Tunnell

1968 Marion Motley

1969 Fletcher "Joe" Perry

1971 Jim Brown

1972 Ollie Matson

1973 Jim Parker

1974 Richard "Night Train" Lane

1975 Roosevelt Brown; Leonard "Lenny" Moore

1976 Leonard "Len" Ford

1977 Gale Sayers; Bill Willis

1980 Herb Adderley; David "Deacon" Jones

1981 Willie Davis

1983 Bobby Bell; Bobby Mitchell; Paul Warfield

1984 Willie Brown; Charley Taylor

1985 O. J. Simpson

1986 Ken Houston; Willie Lanier

1987 Joe Greene; John Henry Johnson; Gene Upshaw

1988 Alan Page

1989 Mel Blount; Art Shell; Willie Wood

1990 Junious "Buck" Buchanan; Franco Harris

1991 Earl Campbell

1992 Lem Barney; John Mackey

1993 Larry Little; Walter Payton

1994 Tony Dorsett, Leroy Kelly

1995 Lee Roy Selmon

1996 Charlie Joiner, Mel Renfro

PULITZER PRIZE—COLUMBIA UNIVERSITY GRADUATE SCHOOL OF JOURNALISM

Journalism: Commentary

1996 E. R. Shipp

Letters: Drama

1970 *No Place To Be Somebody*, by Charles Gordone

1982 *A Soldier's Play*, by Charles Fuller

1987 *Fences*, by August Wilson

1990 *The Piano Lesson*, by August Wilson

Letters: Fiction

1978 *Elbow Room*, by James Alan McPherson

1983 *The Color Purple*, by Alice Walker

1988 *Beloved*, by Toni Morrison

Letters: Poetry

1950 *Annie Allen*, by Gwendolyn Brooks

1987 *Thomas and Beulah*, by Rita Dove

Letters: Special Awards and Citations

1977 Alexander Palmer Haley, for *Roots*

Music: Special Awards and Citations

1976 Scott Joplin

1996 George Walker

SPINGARN MEDAL—NATIONAL ASSOCIATION FOR THE ADVANCEMENT OF COLORED PEOPLE

1915 Prof. Ernest E. Just—head of the department of physiology at Howard University Medical School.

1916 Major Charles Young—United States Army.

1917 Harry T. Burleigh—composer, pianist, singer.

1918 William Stanley Braithwaite—poet, literary critic, editor.

1919 Archibald H. Grimke—former U.S. Consul in Santo Domingo, president of the American Negro Academy, author, president of the District of Columbia branch of the NAACP.

1920 William Edward Burghardt DuBois—author, editor, organizer of the first Pan African Congress.

1921 Charles S. Gilpin—actor.

1922 Mary B. Talbert—former president of the National Association of Colored Women.

1923 George Washington Carver—head of research and director of the experiment station at Tuskegee Institute.

1924 Roland Hayes—singer.

1925 James Weldon Johnson—former United States Consul in Venezuela and Nicaragua, author, editor, poet; secretary of the NAACP.

1926 Carter G. Woodson—editor, historian; founder of the Association for the Study of Negro Life and History.

1927 Anthony Overton—businessman; president of the Victory Life Insurance Company (the first black organization permitted to do business under the rigid requirements of the State of New York).

1928 Charles W. Chestnutt—author.

1929 Mordecai Wyatt Johnson—the first black president of Howard University.

1930 Henry A. Hunt—principal of Fort Valley High and Industrial School, Fort Valley, Georgia.

1931 Richard Berry Harrison—actor.

1932 Robert Russa Moton—principal of Tuskegee Institute.

1933 Max Yergan—secretary of the YMCA in South Africa.

1934 William Taylor Burwell Williams—dean of Tuskegee Institute.

1935 Mary McLeod Bethune—founder and president of Bethune Cookman College.

1936 John Hope—president of Atlanta University.

1937 Walter White—executive secretary of the NAACP.

1939 Marian Anderson—singer.

1940 Louis T. Wright—surgeon.

1941 Richard Wright—author.

1942 A. Philip Randolph—labor leader, international president of the Brotherhood of Sleeping Car Porters.

1943 William H. Hastie—jurist, educator.

1944 Charles Drew—scientist.

1945 Paul Robeson—singer, actor.

1946 Thurgood Marshall—special counsel of the NAACP

1947 Dr. Percy Julian—research chemist.

1948 Channing H. Tobias—,minister, educator.

1949 Ralph J. Bunche—international civil servant, acting United Nations mediator in Palestine.

1950 Charles Hamilton Houston—chairman of the NAACP Legal Committee.

1951 Mabel Keaton Staupers—leader of the National Association of Colored Graduate Nurses.

1952 Harry T. Moore—state leader of the Florida NAACP.

1953 Paul R. Williams—architect.

1954 Theodore K. Lawless—physician, educator, philanthropist.

1955 Carl Murphy—editor, publisher, civic leader.

1956 Jack Roosevelt Robinson—athlete.

1957 Martin Luther King, Jr.—minister, civil rights leader.

1958 Daisy Bates and the Little Rock Nine—for their pioneer role in upholding the basic ideals of American democracy in the face of continuing harassment and constant threats of bodily injury.

1959 Edward Kennedy (Duke) Ellington—composer, musician, orchestra leader.

1960 Langston Hughes—poet, author, playwright.

1961 Kenneth B. Clark—professor of psychology at the City College of the City University of New York, founder and director of the Northside Center for Child Development, prime mobilizer of the resources of modern psychology in the attack upon racial segregation.

1962 Robert C. Weaver—administrator of the Housing and Home Finance Agency.

1963 Medgar Wiley Evers—NAACP field secretary for Mississippi, World War II veteran.

1964 Roy Wilkins executive director of the NAACP.

1965 Leontyne Price—singer.

1966 John H. Johnson—founder and president of the Johnson Publishing Company.

1967 Edward W. Brooke III—the first African-American to win popular election to the United States Senate.

1968 Sammy Davis, Jr.—performer, civil rights activist.

1969 Clarence M. Mitchell, Jr.—director of the Washington Bureau of the NAACP, civil rights activist.

1970 Jacob Lawrence—artist, teacher, humanitarian.

1971 Leon H. Sullivan—minister.

1972 Gordon Alexander Buchanan Parks—writer, photographer, filmmaker.

1973 Wilson C. Riles—educator.

1974 Damon Keith—jurist.

1975 Hank Aaron—athlete.

1976 Alvin Ailey—dancer, choreographer, artistic director.

1977 Alexander Palmer Haley—author, biographer, lecturer.

1978 Andrew Young—United States Ambassador to the United Nations, diplomat, cabinet member, civil rights activist, minister.

1979 Rosa Parks—community activist.

1980 Rayford W. Logan—educator, historian, author.

1981 Coleman A. Young—mayor of the City of Detroit, public servant, labor leader, civil rights activist.

1982 Benjamin E. Mays—educator, theologian, humanitarian).

1983 Lena Horn—performer, humanitarian.

1984 Tom Bradley—government executive, public servant, humanitarian.

1985 Dr. William H. Cosby—comedian, actor, educator, humanitarian.

1986 Benjamin Lawson Hooks—executive director of The NAACP.

1987 Percy Ellis Sutton—public servant, businessman, community leader.

1988 Frederick Douglass Patterson—doctor of veterinary medicine, educator, humanitarian, founder of the United Negro College Fund.

1989 Jesse Jackson—minister, political leader, civil rights activist.

1990 L. Douglas Wilder—governor of Virginia.

1991 General Colin L. Powell—chairman of the Joint Chiefs of Staff.

1992 Barbara C. Jordan—educator, former congresswoman.

1993 Dorothy I. Height—president of the National Council of Negro Woman

1994 Maya Angelou—poet, author, performing artist

1995 John Hope Franklin—historian

UNITED STATES POET LAUREATE

1993 Rita Dove

WIMBLEDON—ALL ENGLAND LAWN TENNIS AND CROQUET CLUB

Men's Singles

1975 Arthur Ashe

Ladies' Singles

1957 Althea Gibson

1958 Althea Gibson

1990 Zina Garrison, runner-up

Ladies' Doubles

1957 Althea Gibson, with Darlene Hard

1958 Althea Gibson, with Maria Bueno

Bibliography

Bibliography

Compiled by Donald Franklin Joyce

Included in this selected bibliography are titles which were published between 1990 and 1992, reviewed favorably in the reviewing media, and judged to be significant contributions to the study of black history and culture in the United States and in Africa. The titles are arranged under two major divisions: "Africana" and "African Americana." Within these two divisions titles are arranged alphabetically by author under categories indicative of their subject matter.

◆ AFRICANA

Agriculture

Barnett, Tony, and Abbas Abdelkarim. *Sudan: The Gezira Scheme and Agricultural Transition*. London: Frank Cass, 1991.

Freeman, Donald B. *A City of Farmers: Informal Urban Agriculture in the Open Spaces of Nairobi, Kenya*. Montreal: McGill-Queen's University Press, 1991.

Gyllstrom, Bjorn. *State Administrative Rural Change: Agricultural Cooperatives in Rural Kenya*. New York: Routledge, 1991.

Kidane, Mengisteab. *Ethiopia: Failure of Land Reform and Agricultural Crisis*. Westport, CT: Greenwood Press, 1990.

Apartheid

Burman, Sandra, and Pamela Reynolds, eds. *Growing Up In a Divided Society*. With forewords by Archbishop Desmond Tutu and Robert Coles. Evanston, IL: Northwestern University Press, 1992.

Cohen, Robin, Yvonne G. Muthien, and Abebe Zegeye, eds. *Repression and Resistance: Inside Accounts of Apartheid*. London; New York: Hans Zell Publishers, 1990.

Davis, R. Hunt, ed. *Apartheid Unravels*. Gainesville, FL: University of Florida Presses, 1991.

Dumor, E.K. *Ghana, OAU and Southern Africa: An African Response to Apartheid*. Accra: Ghana University Press, 1991.

Ellis, Stephen. *Comrades Against Apartheid: The ANC and the South African Communist Party in Exile*. London: James Currey/Indiana University Press, 1992.

Ellman, Stephen. *In a Time of Trouble: Law and Liberty in South Africa's State of Emergency*. New York: Oxford University Press, 1992.

Giliomee, Herman, and Laurence Schlemmer. *From Apartheid to Nation-Building*. Capetown, S.A.: Oxford University Press, 1990.

Grundy, Kenneth. *South Africa: Domestic Crisis and Global Challenge*. Boulder, CO: Westview Press, 1991.

Heard, Anthony Hazlett. *The Cape of Storms: A Personal History of the Crisis in South Africa*. Fayetteville: University of Arkansas Press, 1990.

Holland, Heidi. *The Struggle: A History of the African National Congress*. New York: Braziller, 1990.

Hull, Richard W. *American Enterprise in South Africa: Historical Dimensions of Engagement and Disengagement*. New York: New York University Press, 1990.

Human Rights Watch. *The Killings of South Africa: The Role of the Security Forces and the Response of the State*. New York: Human Rights Watch, 1991.

Johns, Sheridan, and R. Hunt Davis, eds. *Mandela, Tambo and the African National Congress: The Struggle Against Apartheid, 1948-1990: A Documentary Survey*. New York: Oxford University Press, 1991.

Kalley, Jacqueline A. *South Africa Road to Change, 1987-1990.* Westport, CT: Greenwood Press, 1991.

Lemon, Anthony, ed. *Homes Apart: South Africa's Segregated Cities.* Bloomington: Indiana University Press, 1991.

Maasdorp, Gavin, and Alan Whiteside, eds. *Towards a Post-Apartheid Future: Political and Economic Relations in South Africa.* New York: St. Martin's Press, 1992.

Mallaby, Sebastian. *After Apartheid: The Future of South Africa.* New York: Times Books, 1992.

Moss, Rose. *Shouting at the Crocodile: Popo Molefe, Patrick Lekota, and the Freeing of South Africa.* Boston: Beacon Press, 1990. (Dist. by Farrar, Strauss, Giroux)

Price, Robert M. *The Apartheid State in Crisis: Political Transformation in South Africa, 1975-1990.* New York: Oxford University Press, 1991.

Segal, Ronald. *The Black Diaspora: Five Centuries of the Black Experience Outside Africa.* New York: Farrar, Straus and Giroux, 1995.

Shepherd, George W., ed. *Effective Sanctions on South Africa: The Cutting Edge of Economic Intervention.* Westport, CT: Greenwood Press, 1991.

Sparks, Allister. *The Mind of South Africa.* New York: Knopf, 1990.

Spink, Kathryn. *Black Sash: The Beginning of a Bridge in South Africa.* With a foreword by Archbishop Desmond Tutu.

London: Methuen, 1991.

Art

Courtney-Clarke, Margaret. *African Canvas: The Art of West African Women.* New York: Rizzoli, 1990.

Okediji, Mayo, ed. *Principles of "Traditional" African Art.* Ile Ife: Bard Book, 1992 (Dist. by Avon).

Smithsonian Institution. Libraries. National Museum of African Art Branch. *Catalog of the Library of the National Museum of African Art Branch of the Smithsonian Library.* Boston: G.K. Hall, 1991.

Vogel, Susan. *Africa Explores: Twentieth Century African Art.* New York: The Center for African Art, 1991.

Williams College Museum of Art. *Assuming the Guise: African*

Masks Considered and Reconsidered. Williamstown, MA: Williams College Museum of Art, 1991.

Williamson, Sue. *Resistance Art in South Africa.* New York: St. Martin's Press, 1990.

Autobiography and Biography

Appiah, Joseph. *Joe Appiah: The Autobiography of an African Patriot.* New York: Praeger, 1990.

Bunche, Ralph Johnson. *An African American in South Africa: The Travel Notes of Ralph J. Bunche, 28 September 1937 - 1 January 1938.* Edited by Roger R. Edgar. Athens: Ohio University Press, 1992.

Gastrow, Shelagh, ed., *Who's Who in South African Politics.* 3rd ed., London: Hans Zell Publishers, 1990.

Glickman, Harvey, ed., *Political Leaders of Contemporary Africa South of the Sahara: A Biographical Dictionary.* Westport, CT: Greenwood Press, 1992.

Harris, Eddy L. *Native Stranger: A Black American's Journey into the Heart of Africa.* New York: Simon & Schuster, 1992.

Isert, Paul Erdmann. *Letters on West Africa: Paul Erdmann Isert's Journey to Guinea and the Caribbean Islands in Columbia (1788).* Translated by Selena Axelrod Winsnes. New York: Oxford University Press, 1992.

Lockot, Hans Wilhelm. *The Mission: The Life, Reign and Character of Haile Selassie I.* New York: St. Martin's Press, 1990.

Mashinini, Emma. *Strikes Have Followed Me All My Life: A South African Autobiography.* New York: Routledge, 1991.

Meer, Fatima. *Higher Than Hope: The Authorized Biography of Nelson Mandela.* New York: Harper & Row, 1990.

Mendelsohn, Richard. *Sammy Marks: the Uncrowned King of the Transvaal.* Athens: Ohio University Press, 1991.

Modisan, Blake. *Blame Me on History.* New York: Simon & Schuster, 1990.

Nkrumah, Kwame. *Kwame Nkrumah: The Conakry Years: His Life and Letters.* Compiled by June Milne. New York: Zed Books, 1991. (Dist. by Humanities Press)

Rake, Alan. *Who's Who in Africa: Leaders for the 1990s.* Metuchen, NJ: Scarecrow, 1992.

Rodney, Walter. *Walter Rodney Speaks: The Making of an African Intellectual.* With introduction by Robert Hill. Foreword by Howard Dodson. Trenton, NJ: Africa World Press, 1990.

Vaillant, Janet G. *Black, French and African: A Life of Leopold Sedar Senghor.* Cambridge: Harvard University Press, 1990.

Vige, Randolph, ed. *A Gesture of Belong: Letters from Bessie Head, 1965-1979.* Portsmouth, NH: Heinemann, 1991.

Wiseman, John A. *Political Leaders in Black Africa: A Biographical Dictionary of the Major Politicians Since Independence.* Brookfield, VT: Gower Publishing Co., 1991.

Economics

Blumenfield, Jesmond. *Economic Interdependence in Southern Africa: From Conflict to Cooperation.* New York: Printer/St. Martin's Press, 1991.

Chole, Eschetu, ed. *Food Crisis in Africa: Policy and Management Issues.* New Delhi: Vikas Publishing House, 1990. (Dist. by Advent House)

Claessen, Henri J.M., and Pieter van de Velde, eds. *Early State Economies.* New Brunswick, NJ: Transaction Publishers, 1991.

Cock, Jacklyn, ed. *Going Green: People, Politics and the Environment in South Africa.* New York: Oxford University Press, 1991.

Crockcroft, Laurence. *Africa's Way: A Journey from the Past.* UK: Tauris, 1990. (Dist. by St. Martin's Press)

Crush, Jonathan, Alan Jeeves, and Donald Yudelman *Africa's Labor Empire: A History of Black Migrancy to the Gold Mines.* Boulder, CO: Westview Press/D. Philip, 1991.

Edington, J.A.S. *Rubber in West Africa.* Anaheim, CA: Collings, 1991.

Henige, David, and T.C. McCaskie, eds. *West African Economic and Social History: Studies in Memory of Marion Johnson.* Madison: African Studies Program, University of Wisconsin, 1990.

Hodd, Michael. *The Economies of Africa: Geography, Population, History, Stability, Performance, Forecasts.* Boston: G. K. Hall, 1991.

Mahjoub, Azzam, ed. *Adjustment or Delinking? The African Experience.* London: Zed Press, 1990. (Dist. by Humanities Press)

Martin, Matthew. *The Crumbling Facade of African Debt Negotiations: No Winners.* New York: St. Martin's Press, 1991.

Mingst, Karen A. *Politics and the African Development Bank.* Lexington: University of Kentucky Press, 1990.

Nyango'oro, Julius, and Timothy Shaw, eds. *Beyond Structural Adjustment in Africa: The Political Economy of Sustainable and Democratic Development.* New York: Praeger, 1992.

Okolo, Julius Emeka, and Stephen Wright, eds. *West African Regional Cooperation and Development.* Boulder, CO: Westview Press, 1990.

Peckett, James, and Hans Singer, eds. *Towards Economic Recovery in Sub-Saharan Africa: Essays in Honor of Robert Gardner.* New York: Routledge, 1991.

Pradervand, Pierre. *Listening to Africa: Developing Africa from the Grassroots.* New York: Praeger, 1990.

Pryor, Frederic L. *The Political Economy of Poverty, Equity and Growth: Malawi and Madagascar.* New York: Oxford University for the World Bank, 1990.

Rau, Bill. *From Feast to Famine: Official Cures and Grassroots Remedies to Africa's Food Crisis.* New York: Zed Books, 1991 (Dist. by Humanities Press).

Riddell, Roger C. *Manufacturing Africa: Performance and Prospects of Seven Countries in Sub-Saharan Africa.* Portsmouth, NH: Heinemann, 1990.

Sarhof, Joseph A. *Hydropower Development in West Africa: A Study in Resource Development.* New York: P. Lang, 1990.

Siddle, David, and Ken Swindell. *Rural Change in Tropical Africa: From Colonies to Nation-States.* Cambridge, MA: Basil Blackwell, 1990.

Stewart, Frances, ed. *Alternative Development Strategies in Sub-Saharan Africa.* New York: St. Martin's Press, 1992.

Education

King, Kenneth, ed., *Botswana: Education, Culture and Politics.* Edinburgh: University of Edinburgh Press, 1990.

Mungazi, Dickson A. *Colonial Education for Africana: George Starks in Zimbabwe.* Westport, CT: Praeger, 1991.

Njobe, M.W. *Education for Liberation.* Johannesburg: Skotaville, 1990.

Okeem, E.O., ed. *Education in Africa: Search for Realistic Alternatives.* London: Institute for African Alternatives, 1990.

Okunor, Shiame. *Politics, Misunderstandings, Misconceptions: The History of Colonial Universities.* New York: P. Lang, 1991.

Folklore and Folk Culture

Berry, Jack, comp. and trans. *West African Folktales.* Edited with introduction by Richard Spears. Evanston, IL: Northwestern University Press, 1991.

Gunter, Liz, and Mafika Gwala, eds. and trans., *Mushal: Zula*

Popular Praises. East Lansing: Michigan State University Press, 1991.

McDermott, Gerald. *Zomo the Rabbit: A Trickster Tale from West Africa.* San Diego: Harcourt Brace Jovanovich, 1992.

Mohindra, Kamlesh. *Folk Tales of West Africa.* New Delhi: Sterling Pubs., 1991. (Dist. by APT Books)

Njoku, John E. Eberegbulaum. *The Igbos of Nigeria: Ancient Rites, Changes and Survival.* Lewiston, NY: Edwin Mellen Press, 1990.

Schipper, Mineke. *Source of All Evil: African Proverbs and Sayings on Women.* Chicago: Ivan R. Dee, 1991.

Smith, Alexander McCall. *Children of Wax: African Folk Tales.* New York: Interlink Books, 1991.

Ugorji, Okechukwu K. *The Adventures of Torti: Tales from West Africa.* Trenton, NJ: Africa World Press, 1991.

General Reference

Asante, Molafi Keto *The Book of African Names.* Trenton, NJ: Africa World Press, 1991.

Blackhurst, Hector, comp. *Africa Bibliography 1989.* Manchester, UK: Manchester University Press,

1991. (Dist. by St. Martin's Press, Inc.)

Fredland, Richard. *A Guide to African International Organizations.* New York: Hans Sell Publishers, 1991.

Morrison, Donald George, Robert Cameron Mitchell, and John Naber Paden. *Black Africa: A Comparative Handbook.* 2nd ed., New York: Paragon House/Irvington, 1990.

Moss, Joyce, and George Wilson. *Peoples of the World: Africans South of the Sahara.* Detroit: Gale Research Inc., 1991.

Sarfoh, Joseph A. *Energy in the Development of West Africa: A Selected Annotated Bibliography.* New York: Greenwood Press, 1991.

Thurston, Anne. *Guide to Archives and Manuscripts Relating to Kenya and East Africa in the United Kingdom.* New York: Hans Zell Publishers, 1991.

Zell, Hans M. *The African Studies Companion: A Resources Guide and Directory.* Providence, NJ: Hans Zell Publishers, 1990.

Government and Politics

Bowman, Larry W. *Mauritius: Democracy and Development in the Indian Ocean.* Boulder, CO: Westview Press, 1991.

Charlick, Robert B. *Niger: Personal Rule and Survival in the Sahel.* Boulder, CO: Westview Press, 1991.

Clingman, Stephen, ed. *Regions and Repertoires: Topics in South African Politics and Culture.* Johannesburg: Raven Press, 1991. (Dist. by Ohio University Press.)

Clough, Marshall S. *Fighting Two Sides: Kenyan Chiefs and Politicians, 1918-1940.* Niwot, CO: University Press of Colorado, 1990.

Cowell, Alan. *Killing the Wizards: Wars of Power and Freedom from Zaire to South Africa.* New York: Simon & Schuster, 1992.

Deng, Frances M., and I. William Zartman, eds. *Conflict Resolution in Africa.* Washington: Brookings Institution, 1991.

Forrest, Joshua B. *Guinea-Bissau: Power, Conflict and Renewal in a West African Nation.* Boulder, CO: Westview Press, 1992.

Gambari, I.A. *Political and Comparative Dimensions of Regional Integration: The Case of ECOWAS.* New York: The Humanities Press, 1991.

Hanlon, Joseph. *Mozambique: Who Calls the Shots.* Bloomington: Indiana University Press, 1991.

Hansen, Holger Bernt, ed. *Changing Uganda: The Dilemmas of Structural Adjustment and Revolutionary Change.* Athens: Ohio University Press, 1991.

Henze, Paul B. *The Horn of Africa: From War to Peace.* New York: St. Martin's Press, 1991.

Herbst, Jeffrey. *State Politics in Zimbabwe.* Berkeley: University of California, 1990.

Hughes, Arnold, ed. *The Gambia: Studies in Society and Politics.* Birmingham, UK: University of Birmingham, Centre for African Studies, 1991.

Ingham, Kenneth. *Politics in Modern Africa: The Uneven Tribal Dimension.* New York: Routledge, 1990.

Johnson, Willard R. *West African Governments and Volunteer Development Organizations: Priorities for Partnerships.* Lanham, MD: University Press of America, 1990.

Khalid, Mansour. *The Government They Deserve: The Role of the Elite in Sudan's Political Evolution.* New York: Kegan Paul International, 1990.

Kriger, Norma J. *Zimbabwe's Guerrilla War: Peasant Voices.* New York: Cambridge University Press, 1991.

Machobane, L.B.B.J. *Government and Change in Lesotho, 1800-1966: A Study of Political Institutions.* New York: Macmillan, 1990.

Moss, Glenn, and Ingrid Obery, eds. and comps. *South Africa Contemporary Analysis.* London: Hans Zell Publishers, 1990.

Nyang'oro, Julius E., and Timothy M. Shaw, eds. *Beyond Structural Adjustment in Africa: The Political*

Economy of Sustainable and Democratic Development. New York: Praeger, 1992.

O'Brien, Donal B. Cruise, John Dunn, and Richard Rathbone, eds. *Contemporary West African States.* New York: Cambridge University Press, 1990.

Ogunsanwo, Alaba. *The Transformation of Nigeria: Scenarios and Metaphors.* Lagos: University of Lagos Press, 1991.

Reyna, Stephen P. *Wars Without End: The Political Economy of a Precolonial African State.* Hanover, NH: University Press of New England, 1990.

Riley, Eileen. *Major Political Events in South Africa, 1948-1990.* New York: Facts on File, 1991.

Schlosser, Dirk Berg, and Rainer Siegler. *Political Stability and Development: A Comparative Analysis of Kenya, Tanzania and Uganda.* Boulder, CO: Lynne Rienner, 1990.

Sklar, Richard L., and C. S. Whitaker. *African Politics and Problems in Development.* Boulder, CO: Lynne Rienner, 1991.

Tareke, Gebru. *Ethiopia, Power and Protest: Peasant Revolts in the Twentieth Century.* New York: Cambridge University Press, 1991.

Vines, Alex. *Renamo: Terrorism in Mozambique.* Bloomington: Indiana University Press, 1991.

Wunsch, James S., and Dele Olowu, eds. *The Failure of the Centralized State: Institutions and Self-Governance in Africa.* Boulder, CO: Westview Press, 1990.

Wylie, Diana. *A Little God. The Twilight of Patriarchy in a Southern Africa Chiefdom.* Hanover, NH: University Press of New England, 1990.

Health

Baron, Vida C. *African Power: Secrets of the Ancient Ibo Tribe.* San Diego, Barez Publishing Co., 1992.

Falala, Toyin, ed. *The Political Economy of Health in Africa.* Athens: Ohio University for International Studies/Ohio University Press, 1992.

King, Richard D. *African Origin of Biological Psychiatry.* Germantown, TN: Seymour-Smith, Inc., 1990.

Turner, Edith L.B., et al. *Experiencing Ritual: A New Interpretation of African Healing.* Philadelphia: University of Pennsylvania Press, 1992.

Williams, A. Olufemi. *AIDS: An African Perspective.* Boca Rotan, FL: CRC Press, 1992.

Wolff, James, et. al. *Beyond Clinic Walls, Case Studies in Community-Based Distribution.* West Hartford, CT: Kumarian Press, 1990.

History

Ayittey, George B.N. *Indigenous African Institutions.* Ardsley-on-Hudson, NY: Transnational Publishers, 1991.

Banbera, Tayiru. *A State of Intrigue: The Epic of Bamana Segu According to Tayiru Banbera.* Edited by David Conrad; transcribed and translated with the assistance of Soumaila Diakit'e. Oxford, UK: Oxford University Press, 1990.

Cammack, Diana. *The Rand at War, 1899-1902: The Witwatersrand and the Anglo-Boer War.* Berkeley: University of California Press, 1990.

Collelo, Thomas. *Angola: A Country Study* 3rd ed., Washington, DC: Government Printing Office, 1991.

Collins, Robert O. *Western African History.* New York: W. Wiener, 1990.

Crais, Clifton C. *White Supremacy and Black Resistance in Pre-Industrial South Africa: The Making of the Colonial Order in the Eastern Cape, 1770-1865.* Cambridge, UK: Cambridge University Press, 1992.

Digre, Brian. *Imperialism's New Clothes: The Repartition of Tropical Africa, 1914-1919.* New York: P. Lang, 1990.

Diop, Cheikh Anta. *Civilization or Barbarism: An Authentic Anthropology.* Translated by Yaa-Lengi Meema Ngemi; edited by Harold J. Salemson and Marjolijn de Jager. Brooklyn: Lawrence Hill Books, 1991.

Echenberg, Myron J. *Colonial Conscripts: The Tirailleurs S'en'egalais in French West Africa, 1857-1960.* Portsmouth, NH: Heinemann, 1991.

Friedman, Kajsa Ekholm. *Catastrophe and Creation: The Transformation of an African Culture.* Philadelphia: Hardwood Academic Publishers, 1991.

Gann, L.H., and Pete Duignan. *Hope for Africa.* Stanford, CA: Stanford University Press, 1991.

Gordon, April, ed. *Understanding Contemporary Africa.* Boulder, CO: Lynne Reinner Publishers, 1992.

Hair, P.E.H. *Black Africa in Time Perspective: Four Talks on Wide Historical Themes.* Liverpool, UK: Liverpool University Press, 1990. (Dist. by University of Pennsylvania Press).

Hair, P.E.H. *English Seamen and Traders in Guinea, 1553-1565: The New Evidence of their Wills.* Lewiston, NY: E. Mellen Press, 1992.

Hansen, Emmanuel. *Ghana Under Rawlings: Early Years.* Lagos: Malthouse Press, 1991.

Hassen, Mohammed. *The Oromo of Ethiopia: A History.* New York: Cambridge University Press, 1990.

Hudson, Peter. *Two Rivers: In the Footsteps of Mungo Park.* London: Chapmans Publishers, 1991.

Human Rights Watch. *Evil Days: Thirty Years of War and Famine in Ethiopia.* New York: Human Rights Watch, 1990.

Ki-Zerbo, J., ed.UNESCO General History of Africa, Vol. 1: Methodology and African Prehistory. Berkeley: University of California Press, 1990.

Lamphear, John. *The Scattering Time: Turkans Responses to Colonial Time.* New York: Oxford University Press, 1992.

Law, Robin. *The Slave Coast of West Africa, 1550-1750: The Impact of the Atlantic Slave Trade on African Society.* New York: Oxford University Press, 1991.

Manning, Patrick. *Slavery and African Life: Occidental, Oriental and African Slave Trades.* New York: Cambridge University Press, 1990.

Metaferia, Getchew. *The Ethiopian Revolution of 1974 and the Exodus of Ethiopia's Trained Human Resources.* Lewiston, NY: Edwin Mellen Press, 1991.

Mokhtar, G., ed. *UNESCO General History of Africa, Vol. II: Ancient History of Africa.* Berkeley: University of California Press, 1990.

Mooncraft, Paul L. *African Nemesis: War and Revolution in Southern Africa (1945-2010).* Riverside, NJ: Pergamon Press, 1990.

Morton, Fred. *Children of Ham: Freed Slaves and Fugitive Slaves on the Kenya Coast, 1873-1907.* Boulder, CO: Westview, 1990.

Mostert, Noel. *Frontiers: The Epic of South Africa's Creation and the Tragedy of the Xhosa People.* New York: Knopf, 1992.

Munford, Clarence J. *The Black Ordeal of Slavery and Slave Trading in the French West Indies, 1625-1715.* Lewiston, NY: Edwin Mellen Press, 1991.

Nasson, Bill. *Abraham Esau's War: A Black South African War in the Cape, 1899-1902.* New York: Cambridge University Press, 1991.

Obasanjo, Olusegun, and Hans d'Orville, eds. *The Impact of Europe in 1992 on West Africa.* New York: C. Russak, 1990.

Ochieng, William, ed. *Themes in Kenyan History.* Nairobi: Heinmann Kenya, 1990.

Ogot, B.A., ed. *Africa from the Sixteenth to the Eighteenth Century.* Berkeley: University of California Press, 1992.

Remmer, Douglas, ed. *Africa Thirty Years Ago.* Portsmouth, NH: Heinemann, 1991.

Shillington, Kevin. *History of Africa.* New York: St. Martin's Press, 1990.

Solow, Barbara L., ed. *Slavery and the Rise of the Atlantic System.* Cambridge, UK; New York: Cambridge University Press, 1991.

Stauton, Irene, comp. and ed. *Mothers of the Revolution: The War Experiences of Thirty Zimbabwean Women.* Bloomington: Indiana University Press, 1991.

Stedman, Stephen John. *Peacemaking in the Civil War: International Mediation in Zimbabwe, 1974-1980.* Boulder, CO: Lynne Rienner, 1991.

Temperley, Howard. *White Dreams, Black Africa: The Anti-Slavery Expedition to the River Niger, 1841-42.* New Haven: Yale University Press, 1991.

Thompson, Leonard. *A History of South Africa.* New Haven: Yale University Press, 1990.

Wyse, Akintola J.G., and H.C. Bankhole-Bight. *Politics in Colonial Sierra Leone, 1919-1958.* New York:Cambridge University Press, 1991.

Yarak, Larry W. *Asante and the Dutch, 1744-1873.* New York: Oxford University Press, 1990.

Young, John. *They Fell Like Stones: Battles and Casualties of the Zulu War, 1879.* Novato, CA: Presidio Press, 1991.

International Relations

Kent, John. *The Internationalization of Colonialism: Britain, France and Black Africa.* New York: Oxford University Press, 1992.

Russell, Sharon Stanton, Karen Jacobsen, and William Deane Stanley. *International Migration and Development in Sub-Sahara Africa.* Washington, DC: The World Bank, 1991.

Thompson, Joseph E. *American Policy and African Famine: The Nigeria-Biafra War, 1966-1970.* New York: Greenwood Press, 1970.

Winros, Gareth M. *The Foreign Policy of GDR in Africa.* Cambridge, UK: Cambridge University Press, 1991.

Language and Literature

Abraham, Cecils ed. *The Tragic Life: Bessie Head and Literature in South Africa.* Trenton, NJ: Africa World Press, 1990.

Achebe, Chinua. *Hopes and Impediments: Selected Essays.* New York: Doubleday, 1990.

Bjornson, Richard. *The African Quest for Freedom and Identity: Cameroonian Writing and the National Experience.* Bloomington: Indiana University Press, 1991.

Dram'e, Kandioura. *The Novel as Transformation Myth: A Study of the Novels of Mongo Beti and Ngugi wa Thiongo.* Syracuse, NY: Syracuse University, 1990.

Dunton, Chris. *Make Man Talk True: Nigerian Drama in English Since 1970.* New York: Hans Zell Publishers, 1992.

Elimimian, Isaac Iraber. *Theme and Style in African Poetry.* Lewiston, NY: E. Mellen, 1991.

February, V.A. *Mind Your Colour: The Coloured Stereotype in South African Literature.* London and New York: Kegan Paul International, 1991. (Dist. by Routledge, Chapman & Hall, Inc.).

Gikandi, Simon. *Reading Chinua Achebe: Language and Ideology in Fiction.* Portsmouth, NH: Heinemann, 1991.

Gunner, Liz, ed., and trans. *Musho!: Zulu Popular Praises.* East Lansing: Michigan State University Press, 1991.

Hale, Thomas A. *Scribe, Griot and Novelist: Narrative Interpreters of the Songhay Empire Followed by the Epic of Askia Mohammed Recounted,* Gainesville, FL: University of Florida Press/Center for African Studies, 1990.

Harrow, Kenneth, ed., *Faces of Islam in African Literature.* Portsmouth, NH: Heinemann, 1991.

Harrow, Kenneth, Jonathan Ngate, and Clarissa Zimra, eds. *Crisscrossing Boundaries in African Literatures, 1986.* Washington, DC: Three Continents Press/African Literature

Association, 1991.

Ikonne, Chidi, Emelia Oko, and Peter Onwudinjo, eds. *African Literature and African Historical Experience.* New York: Heinemann, 1991.

Innes, Catherine Lynette. *Chinua Achebe.* New York: Cambridge University Press, 1990.

Innes, Catherine Lynette. *The Devil's Own Mirror: The Irishman and the African Modern Literature.* Washington, DC: Three Continents Press, 1990.

James, Adeola, ed., *In Their Own Voices: African Women Writers Talk.* Portsmouth, NH: Heinemann, 1990.

Jones, Eldred Durosimi, ed. *The Question of Language in African Literature Today: Borrowing and Carrying: A Review.* Trenton, NJ: Africa World Press, 1991.

Julien, Eileen. *African Novels and the Question of Orality.* Bloomington: Indiana University Press, 1992.

Lazarus, Neil. *Resistance in Postcolonial African Fiction.* New Haven, CT: Yale University Press, 1991.

Lindfors, Bernth. *Popular Literature in Africa.* Trenton, NJ: Africa World Press, 1991.

Liyong, Taban Lo. *Another Last Word.* New York: Heinemann, 1990.

Miller, Christopher L. *Theories of Africans: Franco-Phone Literature and Anthropology in Africa.* Chicago: University of Chicago Press, 1990.

Mortimer, Mildred. *Journey Through the French African Novel.* Portsmouth, NH: Heinemann, 1990.

Nethersole, Reingard, ed. *Emerging Literature.* New York: P. Lang, 1990.

Ngara, Emmanuel. *Ideology and Form in African Poetry: Implications for Communication.* Portsmouth, NH: Heinemann, 1990.

Obiechina, Emmanuel N. *Language and Theme: Essays on African Literature.* Washington, DC: Howard University Press, 1990.

Orisawayi, Dele, et. al., eds. *Literature and Black Aesthetics.* New York: Heinemann, 1990.

Owomoyela, Onjekan. *Visions and Revisions: Essays on African Literatures and Criticisms.* New York: P. Lang, 1991.

Research in African Literatures: Critical Theory and African Literature. Bloomington: Indiana University Press, 1990.

Research in African Literature: Dictatorship and Oppression. Bloomington: Indiana University Press, 1990.

Roscoe, Adrian A., and Hangson Msika. *The Quiet Chameleon: Modern Poetry from Central Africa.* New York: Hans Zell Publishers, 1992.

Scheub, Harold. *The African Storyteller: Stories from African Oral Traditions.* Dubuque, IA: Kendell/Hunt, 1991.

Schipper, Mineke. *Beyond the Boundaries: Text and Context in African Literature.* Chicago: Ivan R. Dee, 1990.

Sicherman, Carol. *Ngugi wa Thiong: A Source Book on Kenyan Literature and Resistance.* New York: Hans Zell Publishers, 1990.

Soyinka, Wole. *Myth, Literature, and the African World.* New York: Cambridge University Press, 1990.

Trump, Martin, ed. *Rendering Things Visible: Essays on South African Literary Culture.* Athens: Ohio University Press, 1991.

Wilentz, Gay Alden. *Binding Cultures: Black Women Writers in Africa and the Diaspora.* Bloomington: Indiana University Press, 1992.

Wylie, Hal, Dennis Brutus, and Juris Silenieks, eds. *African Literature, 1988: New Masks.* Washington, DC: Three Continents Press/The African Literature Association, 1990.

Law, Law Enforcement, Civil and Human Rights

Ahire, Philip Terdo. *Imperial Policing: The Emergence and Role of the Police in Nigeria, 1860-1960*. Philadelphia: Open University Press, 1991.

Bazille, Susan, ed. *Putting Women on the Agenda*. Johannesburg, S.A.: Raven Press, 1991. (Dist. by Ohio University Press).

Braham, Peter, ed. *Racism and Antiracism: Inequalities in Opportunities and Policies*. Philadelphia: Sage/Open University Press, 1992.

Hansson, Desiree, and Dirk van Zyl Smit, eds. *Toward Justice? Crime and State Control in South Africa*. New York: Oxford University Press, 1990.

Mann, Kristin, ed. *Law in Colonial Africa*. Portsmouth, NH: Heinemann, 1991.

Shepherd, George W., and Mark O.G. Anikpo, eds. *Emerging Human Rights: The African Political Economy Concept*. Westport, CT: Greenwood Press, 1990.

Media

Faringer, Gunilla L. *Press Freedom in Africa*. Westport, CT: Praeger, 1991.

Harden, Blaine. *Africa: Dispatches from a Fragile Continent*. London: Harper Collins, 1990.

Hawk, Beverly G., ed. *Africa's Media Image*. New York: Praeger, 1992.

Sturges, Paul, and Richard Neill. *The Quiet Struggle: Libraries and Information for Africa*. New York: Mansell, 1990.

Music

Arom, Simha. *African Polyphony and Polyrhythm: Musical Structure and Methodology*. Translated by Martin Thom and Barbara Tucker. New York: Cambridge University Press, 1991.

Bender, Wolfgang. *Sweet Mother: Modern African Music*. Translated by Wolfgang Freis. Chicago: University of Chicago Press, 1991.

Collins, John. *West African Pop Roots*. Philadelphia: Temple University Press, 1992.

Gray, John. *African Music: A Bibliographic Guide to the Traditional Popular Art and Liturgical Music of Sub-Saharan Africa*. Westport, CT: Greenwood Press, 1991.

Lems-Dworkin, Carol. *African Music: A Pan-African Annotated Bibliography*. New York: Hans Zell Publishers, 1991.

Stewart, Gary. *Breakout: Profiles in African Rhythm*. Chicago: University of Chicago Press, 1992.

Waterman, Christopher Alan. *Juju: A Social History and Ethnography of an African Popular Music*. Chicago: University of Chicago Press, 1990.

Pan-Africanism

Agyeman, Opoku. *Nkrumah's Ghana and Esat Africa: Pan-Africanism and African Interstate Relations*. Cranbury, NJ: Fairleigh Dickinson University Press, 1992.

Clarke, John H. *Africans at the Crossroads: Notes for an African World Revolution*. Trenton, NJ: Africa World Press, 1992.

Staniland, Martin. *American Intellectuals and African Nationalists, 1950-1970*. New Haven: Yale University Press, 1991.

Performing Arts

Diawara, Manthia. *African Cinema: Politics and Culture*. Bloomington: Indiana University Press, 1992.

Erlman, Veit. *African Stars: Studies in Black South African Performance*. Chicago: University of Chicago Press, 1991.

Lee, Jacques K. *Sega: The Mauritius Folk Dance*. London: Nautilus Publishing Co., 1990.

Orkin, Martin. *Drama and the South African State*. Manchester, UK: Manchester University Press, 1991. (Dist. by St. Martin's Press)

Religion and Philosophy

Dankwa, Nano O., III. *Christianity and African Traditional Beliefs*. Edited by John W. Branch. New York: Power of the World Publishing Co., 1990.

Felder, Cain Hope, ed. *Stony the Road We Trod: African American Biblical Interpretation*. Minneapolis: Fortress Press, 1991.

Gbadegesin, Segun. *African Philosophy: Traditional Yoruba Philosophy and Contemporary African Realities*. New York: Lang, 1991.

Gifford, Paul. *The New Crusaders: Christianity and the New Right in Southern Africa*. London: Pluto, 1991.

Gray, Richard. *Black Christians and White Missionaries*. New Haven: Yale University Press, 1991.

Oldfield, J.R. *Alexander Crummell (1819-1898) and the Creation of an African-American Church in Africa*. Lewiston, NY: Edwin Mellin Press, 1990.

Olupona, Jacob K. *African Traditional Religions in Contemporary Society.* New York: Paragon, 1991.

Oruka, H. O. *Trends in Contemporary African Philosophy.* Nairobi, Kenya: Shirikon Publishers, 1990.

Peek, Philip M., ed. *African Divination Systems: Ways of Knowing.* Bloomington: Indiana University Press, 1991.

Prozesky, Martin, ed. *Christianity Amidst Apartheid* New York: London, Macmillan, 1990.

Soyinka, Wole. *The Credo of Being and Nothingness.* Ibadan: Spectrum Books, 1990.

Vanderaa, Larry A. *A Survey of Christian Reformed World Missions and Churches in West Africa.* Grand Rapids, MI: Christian Reformed World Missions, 1991.

Sociology and Psychology

Barnes, James Franklin. *Gabon: Beyond the Colonial Legacy.* Boulder, CO: Westview Press, 1992.

Bell, Leland V. *Mental and Social Disorder in Sub-Saharan Africa: The Case of Sierra Leone, 1787-1990.* Westport, CT: Greenwood Press, 1991.

Carr-Hill, Roy A. *Social Conditions in Sub-Saharan Africa.* London; New York: Macmillan, 1991.

Cleaver, Tessa, and Marion Wallace. *Namibia: Women in War.* Foreword by Glenys Kinnock. Atlantic Highlands, NJ: Zed Books, 1990.

Cobley, Alan Gregord. *Class and Consciousness: The Black Petty Bourgeoisie in South Africa, 1924-1950.* Westport, CT: Greenwood Press, 1990.

Coles, Catherine, and Beverly Mack, eds. *Hausa Women in the Twentieth Century.* Madison: University of Wisconsin Press, 1991.

Gordon, Robert J. *The Bushman Myth: The Making of a Nambian Underclass.* Boulder, CO: Westview Press, 1992.

Hill, Martin J.D., ed. *The Harambee Movement in Kenya: Self-Help Development and Education Among the Kamba of Chat District.* Atlantic Highlands, NJ: Athlone Press, 1991.

Kilbride, Philip Leroy. *Changing Family Life in East Africa: Women and Children at Risk,* Philadelphia: Pennsylvania State University Press, 1990.

Mohammad, Duri, ed., *Social Development in Africa: Strategies, Policies and Programmes After the Lagos Plan.* Providence, NJ: H. Zell Publishers, 1991.

Moran, Mary. *Civilized Women: Gender and Prestige in Southeastern Liberia.* Ithaca, NY: Cornell University Press, 1991.

Nsamenang, A. Bame. *Human Development in Cultural Conflict.* Foreword by Michael Lamb. Newbury Park, CA: Sage Publications, 1992.

Ominde, S. H., ed. *Kenya's Population Growth and Development to the Year 2000.* Columbus: Ohio University Press, 1990.

Reynolds, Pamela. *Dance Cat: Child Labour in the Zambezi Valley.* London: Hans Zell Books, 1991.

Riseman, Paul. *First Find Your Child A Good Mother: The Construction of Self in Two African Communities.* New Brunswick, NJ: Rutgers University Press, 1992.

Robertson, Struan. *The Cold Choice: Pictures of a South African Reality.* Grand Rapids, MI: Wm. B. Erdmans Publishing Co., 1992.

◆ AFRICAN AMERICANA

Art, Architecture, and Photography

Bearden, Romare. *Memory and Metaphor: The Art of Romare Bearden, 1940-1987.* New York: Studio Museum of Harlem/Oxford University Press, 1991.

Durham, Michael S. *Powerful Days: The Civil Rights Photography of Charles Moore.* Introduction by Andrew Young. New York: Stewart, Tabori & Chang, 1991.

Easter, Eric, D. Michael Cheers, and Dudley M. Brooks, eds. *Songs of My People: African Americans: A Self-Portrait.* Introduction by Gordon Parks. Essays by Sylvester Monroe. Boston: Little, Brown, 1992.

Gumbo Ya Ya: Anthology of Contemporary African-American Women Artists, New York: Mid-March Arts Press, 1995.

McElroy, Guy C. *Facing History: The Black Image in American Art, 1710-1940.* Edited by Christopher C. French. Washington, DC: Bedford Arts/Corcoran Gallery, 1990.

Powell, Richard J. *Homecoming: The Art and Life of William H. Johnson.* New York: National Museum of American Art/Rizzoli, 1991.

Rozelle, Robert V., et. al. eds. *Black Art: Ancestral Legacy: The African-American Impulse in African-American Art.* New York: Abrams, 1990.

Thomison, Dennis, comp. *The Black Artist in America: An Index to Reproductions.* Metuchen, NJ: Scarecrow Press, 1991.

Travis, Jack, ed. *African-American Architects in Current Practice.* New York: Princeton Architecture Press, 1991.

Autobiography and Biography

Baker, Donald P. *Wilder: Hold Fast to Dreams: A Biography of L. Douglas Wilder.* Cabin John, MD: Seven Locks, 1990.

Baldwin, Lewis V. *There Is a Balm in Gilead: The Cultural Roots of Martin Luther King, Jr.* Minneapolis: Fortress Press, 1991.

Bigelow, Barbara Carlisle, ed. *Contemporary Black Biography.* Detroit: Gale Research Inc., 1992.

Bjarkman, Peter C. *Ernie Banks.* Introduction by Jim Murray. New York: Chelsea House, 1992.

Brown, Drew T., III. *You Gotta Believe!: Education + Hard Work - Drugs = The American Dream.* New York: Morrow, 1991.

Brown, James, and Bruce Tucker. *James Brown: The Godfather of Soul.* New York: Thunder's Mouth Press, 1990.

Buchmann-Moller, Frank. *You Just Fight for Your Life: The Story of Lester Young.* New York: Praeger, 1990.

Campbell, James. *Talking at the Gate: A Life of James Baldwin.* New York: Viking, 1991.

Carson, Clayborne. *Malcolm X; The FBI File.* Introduction by Spike Lee. Edited by David Gallen. New York: Carroll & Graf Publishers, Inc., 1991.

Carson, Clayborne, ed. *The Papers of Martin Luther King, Jr.* Berkeley: University of California Press, 1991.

Chilton, John. *The Song of the Hawk: The Life and Recordings of Coleman Hawkins.* New York: St. Martin's Press, 1990.

Davis, Benjamin O., Jr. *Benjamin O. Davis, Jr., American: An Autobiography.* Washington, DC: Smithsonian Institution, 1991.

Davis, Miles, and Quincy Troupe. *Miles, The Autobiography.* New York: Simon & Schuster, 1990.

Deane, Bill. *Bob Gibson.* Introduction by Jim Murray. New York: Chelsea House, 1992.

Dees, Morris. *A Season for Justice: The Life and Times of Civil Rights Lawyer Morris Dees.* New York: Scribner, 1991.

Faser, Jane. *Walter White.* New York: Chelsea House, 1991.

Goldman, Roger, and David Gallen. *Thurgood Marshall: Justice for All.* New York: Carroll & Graf, 1992.

Hamilton, Charles V. *Adam Clayton Powell, Jr.: The Political Biography of an American Dilemma.* New York: Atheneum, 1991.

Hawkins, Walter L. *African American Biographies: Profiles of 558 Current Men and Women.* Jefferson, NC: McFarland & Co., 1992.

Hayes, Bob. *Run, Bullet, Run.* New York: Harper Collins, 1990.

Kranz, Rachel C. *The Biographical Dictionary of Black Americans.* New York: Facts on File, 1992.

Kremer, Gary R. *James Milton Turner and the Promise of America: The Public Life of a Post-Civil War Black Leader.* Columbia: University of Missouri Press, 1991.

Levi, Darrell E. *Michael Manley: The Making of a Leader.* Athens: University of Georgia Press, 1990.

McFeely, William S. *Frederick Douglass.* New York: Norton, 1990.

Mosby, Dewey F., and Darrel Sewell. *Henry Ossawa Tanner.* New York: Rizzoli, 1991.

Naughton, Jim. *Taking to the Air: The Rise of Michael Jordan.* New York: Warner Books, 1992.

Pallister, Janis L. *Aime Cesaire.* New York: Twayne, 1991.

Perry, Bruce. *Malcolm: The Life of a Man Who Changed Black America.* Barrytown, NY: Station Hill, 1991.

Pfieffer, Paula F. *A. Philip Randolph, Pioneer of the Civil Rights Movement.* Baton Rouge: Louisiana State University Press, 1990.

Phelps, J. Alfred. *Chappie: America's First Black Four-Star General.* Novato, CA: Presidio Press, 1991.

Phelps, Shirelle, ed. *Who's Who Among Black Americans, 1993-94.* 7th ed., William C. Matney, Jr., Consulting Editor.

Detroit: Gale Research Inc., 1993.

Pickens, William. *Bursting Bonds: Enlarged edition (of) The Heir of Slaves: The Autobiography of a "New Negro".* Edited by William L. Andrews. Bloomington: Indiana University Press, 1991.

Rattenbury, Ken. *Duke Ellington, Jazz Composer.* New Haven: Yale University Press, 1991.

Rivlin, Benjamin, ed. *Ralph Bunche, The Man and His Times.* Foreword by Donald F. Henry. New York: Holmes & Meier, 1990.

Rose, Cynthia. *Living in America: The Soul Saga of James Brown.* London: Serpent Tale, 1990 (Dist. by Consortium Book Sales Distribution.)

Rout, Kathleen. *Eldridge Cleaver.* Boston: Twayne/G.K. Hall, 1991.

Schwartzman, Myron. *Romare Bearden: His Life and Art.* New York: Abrams, 1990.

Shapiro, Leonard. *Big Man on Campus: John Thompson and the Georgetown Hoyas*. New York: Holt, 1991.

Shapiro, Miles. *Bill Russell*. Introductory essay by Coretta Scott King. New York: Chelsea House, 1991.

Sifford, Charlie. *Just Let Me Play: The Story of Charlie Sifford: The First Black PGA Golfer*. Latham, NY: British American Publishers, 1992.

Smith, Eric Ledell. *Bert Williams: A Biography of the Pioneer Black Comedian*. Jefferson, NC: McFarland, 1992.

Stewart, James Brewer. *William Lloyd Garrison and the Challenge of Emancipation*. Arlington Heights, IL: Harlan Davidson, 1992.

Strode, Woody, and Sam Young. *Goal Dust: An Autobiography*. Lantham, MD: Madison Books, 1990.

Tucker, Ken. *Ellington: The Early Years*. Champaign: University of Illinois Press, 1991.

Urban, Wayne J. *Black Scholar: Horace Mann Bond, 1904-1972*. Athens: University of Georgia Press, 1992.

Vache, Warren W. *Crazy Fingers: Claude Hopkins' Life in Jazz*. Washington, DC: Smithsonian Institution Press, 1992.

Watts, Jill. *God, Harlem U.S.A.: The Father Divine Story*. Berkeley: University of California Press, 1992.

Weland, Gerald. *Of Vision and Valor: General O. O. Howard, A Biography*. Canton, OH: Daring Publishing Group, 1991.

Wells, Dicky. *The Night People: The Jazz Life of Dicky Wells*. As told to Stanley Dance. rev. ed., Washington, DC: Smithsonian Institution Press, 1991.

Wills, Maury, and Mike Celizic. *On the Run: The Never Dull and Often Shocking Life of Maury Wills*. New York: Carroll & Graf, 1991.

Black Nationalism and Pan-Africanism in the United States

Crosby, Edward W., and Linus A. Hoskins, eds. *Africa for the Africans: Selected Speeches of Marcus Mosiah Garvey; Malcolm X; and Nelson Kolihlahla Mandela*. Kent, OH: The Institute for African American Affairs, Department of Pan-African Studies, Kent State University, 1991.

Crummell, Alexander. *Destiny and Race: Selected Writings, 1840-1898*. Edited with introduction by Wilson J. Moses. Amherst: University of Massachusetts Press, 1992.

Drake, St. Clair. *Black Folks Here and There: An Essay in History and Anthropology*. 2 vols. Los Angeles: University of California, Los Angeles, Center for Afro-American Studies, 1991.

Harris, Robert, et. al. *Carlos Cooks: And Black Nationalism from Garvey to Malcolm*. Dover, MA: Majority Press, 1992.

Jacques, Geoffrey. *The African-American Movement Today*. New York: Watts, 1992.

Lemelle, Sid. *Pan-Africanism for Beginners*. New York: Writers and Readers Publishing, Inc., 1992.

Lewis, Rupert, ed. *Garvey: His Work and Impact*. Trenton, NJ: Africa World Press, 1991.

Martin, Tony, comp. and ed. *African Fundamentalism: A Literary and Cultural Anthropology of Garvey's Harlem Renaissance*. Dover, MA: Majority Press, 1991.

Moses, Wilson J. *Alexander Crummell: A Study of Civilization and Discontent*. Amherst: University of Massachusetts Press, 1992.

Civil Rights, Law, and Civil Protests

Administrative History of the Civil Rights Division of the Department of Justice During the Johnson Administration. 2 vol., New York: Garland Publishing Co., 1991.

Aguirre, Adalberto, Jr., and David V. Baker. *Race, Racism and the Death Penalty in the United States*. Barrien Springs, MI: Vande Vere Publishers, 1992.

Belknap, Michal. *Racial Violence and Law Enforcement in the South*. New York: Garland Publishing Co., 1991.

Belknap, Michal. *Securing the Enactment of Civil Rights Legislation, 1965-1968*. New York: Garland Publishing Co., 1991.

Belknap, Michal. *Urban Race Riots*. New York: Garland Publishing Co., 1991.

Belknap, Michal. *Voting Rights*. New York: Garland Publishing Co., 1991.

Belz, Herman. *Equality Transformed: A Quarter-Century of Affirmative Action*. New Brunswick, NJ: Transaction, 1991.

Blumberg, Rhoda L. *Civil Rights, the Freedom Struggle*. rev. ed., Boston: Twayne G.K. Hall, 1991.

Bolick, Clint. *Unfinished Business: A Civil Rights Strategy for America's Third Century*. San Francisco: Research Institute of Public Policy, 1990.

Cagin, Seth, and Philip Dray. *We Are Not Afraid: The Story of Goodman, Schwerner and Chaney and the Civil Rights Campaign for Mississippi*. New York: Bantam Books, 1991.

Capeci, Dominic, and Martha Wilkerson. *Layered Violence: the Detroit Rioters of 1943.* Jackson: University Press of Mississippi, 1991.

Carson, Clayborne, et. al. eds. *"The Eyes on the Prize" Civil Rights Reader: Documents, Speeches, and Firsthand Accounts from the Black Freedom Struggle, 1954-1990.* New York: Viking, 1991.

Cashman, Sean Dennis. *African-Americans and the Quest for Civil Rights, 1900-1990.* New York: New York University Press, 1991.

Cashmore, Ellis, and Eugene McLaughlin, eds. *Out of Order?: Policing Black People.* New York: Routledge, 1991.

Cone, James H. *Martin and Malcolm and America: A Dream or a Nightmare.* New York: Orbis Books, 1991.

Cook, Anthony. *Law, Race and Social Theory.* Boston: New England School of Law, 1991.

Detefsen, Robert R. *Civil Rights Under Reagan.* San Francisco: ICS Press, 1991.

Encyclopedia of African American Civil Rights: From Emancipation to the Present. Westport, CT: Greenwood Press, 1992.

Epstein, Richard Allen. *Forbidden Grounds: The Case Against Employment Discrimination Laws.* Cambridge: Harvard University Press, 1992.

Ezorsky, Gertrude. *Racism and Justice: The Case for Affirmative Action.* Ithaca, NY: Cornell University Press, 1991.

Fendrich, James Max. *Ideal Citizens: The Legacy of the Civil Rights Movement.* Albany: State University of New York Press, 1993.

Finkelman, Paul, ed. *African Americans and the Law.* New York: Garland Publishing Co., 1991 (*Race, Law and American History, 1700-1900. The African American Experience.*)

Finkelman, Paul, ed. *African-Americans and the Legal Profession in Historical Perspective.* New York: Garland Publishing Co., 1991 (*Race, Law, and American History, 1700-1990. The African American Experience.* vol. 10).

Finkelman, Paul, ed. *African-Americans and the Right to Vote.* Edited by Paul Finkelman. New York: Garland Publishing Co., 1992. (*Race, Law, and American History, 1700-1900. The African-American Experience.* vol. 6).

Finkelman, Paul, ed. *Lynching, Racial Violence, and Law.* New York: Garland Publishing Co., 1992. (*Race, Law, and American History, 1700-1990. The African-American Experience*, vol. 9.)

Finkelman, Paul, ed. *Race and Criminal Justice.* New York: Garland Publishing Co., 1992. (*Race, Law, and American History, 1700-1900. The American Experience*, vol. 8.)

Finkelman, Paul, ed. *Race and Law Before Emancipation.* New York: Garland Publishing Co., 1992. (*Race, Law and American History, 1700-1990. The African American Experience*, vol. 2.)

Finkelman, Paul, ed. *The Era of Integration and Civil Rights, 1930-1990.* New York: Garland Publishing Co., 1992. (*Race, Law, and American History, 1700-1990. The African American Experience* vol. 5).

Fiscus, Ronald Jerry. *The Constitutional Logic of Affirmative Action.* Edited by Stephen Wasby. Durham, NC: Duke University Press, 1992.

Fisher, Sethard. *From Margin to Mainstream: The Social Progress of Black Americans.* 2nd ed., Savage, MD: Rowman & Littlefield, 1992.

Goings, Kenneth W. *The NAACP Comes of Age: The Defeat of Judge Parker.* Bloomington: Indiana University Press, 1990.

Goldwin, Robert A. *Why Blacks, Women and Jews Are Not Mentioned in the Constitution, and Other Unorthodox Views.* Washington, DC: American Enterprise Institute, 1990.

Graetz, Robert S. *Montgomery, A White Preachers Memoir.* Minneapolis: Fortress Press, 1991.

Grafman, Bernard, ed. *Controversies in Minority Voting: The Voting Rights Act in Perspective.* Washington, DC: Brookings Institute, 1992.

Graham, Hugh Davis. *The Civil Rights Era: Race, Gender and National Policy, 1960-1972.* New York: Oxford University Press, 1990.

Hampton, Henry, and Steve Fayer, comps. *Voices of Freedom: An Oral History of the Civil Rights Movement from the 1950s Through the 1980s.* New York: Bantam Books, 1990.

Harding, Vincent. *Hope and History: Why We Must Share the Story of the Movement.* Maryknoll, NY: Orbis Books, 1990.

Harris, Jacqueline. *A History of the NAACP.* New York: Watts, 1992.

Jackson, James E. *The Bold Bad '60s: Pushing the Point for Equality Down South and Out Yonder.* New York: International Publishers, 1992.

James, Hunter. *They Didn't Put That on the Huntley-Brinkley Report!: A Vagabound Reporter Encounters the New South.* Athens: University of Georgia, 1993.

Justice Department Briefs in Crucial Civil Rights Cases. 2 vols., New York: Garland, 1991.

Kapur, Sudarshan. *Raising Up a Prophet: The African-American Encounter with Gandhi*. Boston: Beacon, 1992.

King, Richard. *Civil Rights and the Idea of Freedom*. New York: Oxford University Press, 1992.

Kull, Andrew. *The Color-Blind Constitution*. Cambridge: Harvard University Press, 1992.

Levy, Peter B., ed. *Dictionary History of the Modern Civil Rights Movement*. New York: Greenwood Press, 1992.

Levy, Peter B., ed. *Let Freedom Ring: A Documentary History of the Modern Civil Rights Movement*. New York: Praeger, 1992.

Lyon, Danny. *Memories of the Civil Rights Movement*. Text and photographs by Danny Lyon; foreword by Julian Bond. Chapel Hill: University of North Carolina Press, 1992.

Meier, August, et. al. eds. *Black Protest in the Sixties*. New York: M. Wiener, 1991.

Meier, August. *A White Scholar and the Black Community, 1945-1965: Essays and Reflections*. Afterword by John H. Bracey, Jr. Amherst: University of Massachusetts Press, 1992.

Mills, Nicolaus. *Like a Holy Crusade: Mississippi, 1964— The Turning of the Civil Rights Movement in America*. Chicago: I.R. Dee, 1992.

Nieli, Russell, ed. *Racial Preference and Racial Justice: The New Affirmative Action Controversy*. Washington, DC: Ethics and Public Policy Center, 1991 (Dist. by National Book Network.)

Nieman, Donald G. *Promises to Keep: African Americans and the Constitutional Order, 1776 to the Present*. New York: Oxford University Press, 1991.

O'Reilly, Kenneth. *Racial Matters: The FBI's Secret File on Black America, 1960-1972*. New York: Free Press, 1991.

Powledge, Fred. *Free At Last?: The Civil Rights Movement and the People Who Made It*. Boston: Little, Brown, 1990.

Reed, Merl E. *Seedtime for the Modern Civil Rights Movement: The President's Committee on Fair Employment Practice, 1941-1946*. Baton Rouge: Louisiana State University Press, 1991.

Robinson, Amelia Boynton. *Bridge Across Jordan*. rev. ed., Washington, DC: Schiller Institute, 1991.

Robinson, Armistead L., and Patricia Sullivan, eds. *New Directions in Civil Rights Studies*. Charlottesville: University Press of Virginia, 1991.

Sigelman, Lee, and Susan Welch. *Black Americans' Views of Racial Inequality: The Dream Deferred*. New York: Cambridge University Press, 1991.

Sikora, Frank. *Until Justice Rolls Down: The Birmingham Church Bombing Case* Tuscaloosa: University of Alabama Press, 1991.

Stern, Mark. *Calculating Visions: Kennedy, Johnson and Civil Rights*. New Brunswick, NJ: Rutger University Press, 1992.

Swift, Jeanne, ed. *Dream and Reality: The Modern Black Struggle for Freedom and Equality*. New York: Greenwood Press, 1991.

Thomas, Clarence. *Clarence Thomas: Confronting the Future: Selections from the Senate Confirmation Hearing and Prior Speeches*. Washington, DC: Regnery Gateway, 1992.

Urofsky, Melvin I. *A Conflict of Rights: The Supreme Court and Affirmative Action*. New York: Scribners, 1991.

Watson, Denton L. *Lion in the Lobby: Clarence Mitchell, Jr.'s Struggle for the Passage of Civil Rights Laws*. New York: Morrow, 1990.

Wright, Roberta Hughes. *The Birth of the Montgomery Bus Boycott*. Southfield, MI: Charro Book Co., 1991.

Economics, Entrepreneurship, and Labor

Broadnax, Derek. *The Black Entrepreneurs Guide to Million Dollar Business Opportunities*. Austin, TX: Black Entrepreneurs Press, 1990.

Broadnax, Derek. *The Black Entrepreneurs Guide to Money Sources: How to Get Your Share*. Austin, TX: Black Entrepreneurs Press, 1990.

Butler, John Sibley. *Entrepreneurship and Self-Help Among Black Americans: A Reconsideration of Race and Economics*. Albany: State University of New York Press, 1991.

Dewart, Janet, ed. *The State of Black America, 1991*. New York: National Urban League, 1991.

Duncan, Mike. *Reach Your Goals In Spite of the Old Boy Network: A Guide for African American Employees*. Edgewood, MD:

M.E. Duncan and Co., 1990.

Grant, Nancy L. *TVA and Black Americans: Planning for the Status Quo*. Philadelphia: Temple University Press, 1990.

Green, Shelley, and Paul Pryde. *Black Entrepreneurship in America*. Brunswick, NJ: Transactions Publishers, 1990.

Greenberg, Jonathan D. *Staking a Claim: Jake Simmons and the Making of an African-American Oil Dynasty*. New York: Atheneum, 1991.

Reed, Wornie, ed. *Social, Political and Economic Issues in Black America*. Amherst: University of Massachusetts, William Monroe Trotter Institute, 1990.

Rosen, George H. *Black Money*. Chelsea, MI: Scaraborough House, 1990.

Education

Allen, Walter R., Edgar Epps, and Nesha Z. Haniff, eds. *College in Black and White: African American Students in Predominately White and Historically Black Public Universities*. Albany: State University of New York Press, 1991.

Altbach, Philip G., and Kofi Lomotey, eds. *The Racial Crisis in American Higher Education*. Albany: State University of New York Press, 1991.

Bowman, J. Wilson. *America's Black Colleges*. South Pasadena, CA: Sandcastle Publishing Co., 1992.

Fife, Brian L. *Desegregation in American Schools: Comparative Intervention Strategies*. New York: Praeger, 1992.

Finkelman, Paul, ed. *The Struggle for Equal Education*. New York: Garland Publishing Co., 1992. (*Race, Law, and American History, 1700-1990. African-American Experience*, vol. 7.)

Formisano, Ronald P. *Boston Against Busing: Race, Class, and Ethnicity in the 1960s and 1970s*. Chapel Hill: University of North Carolina Press, 1991.

Harmon, Marylen E. *The Infusion of African and African American Studies into the Curriculum*. Roanoke, VA: Absolute Writings Ltd., 1991.

Irvine, Jacqueline Jordan. *Black Students and School Failure: Policies, Practices, and Prescriptions*. Westport, CT: Greenwood Press, 1990.

Lomotey, Kofi, ed. *Going to School: The African-American Experience*. Albany: State University of New York Press, 1990.

Lusane, Clarence. *The Struggle for Equal Education*. New York: F. Watts, 1992.

Margo, Robert A. *Race and Schooling in the South, 1880-1950*. Chicago: University of Chicago Press, 1991.

National Afro-American Museum and Cultural Center. *From Victory to Freedom: The African American Experience: Curriculum Guide, Secondary School Course of Study*. Wilberforce, OH: National Afro-American Museum and Cultural Center, 1991.

Neufeldt, Harvey G., and Leo McGee, eds. *Education of the African American Adult: An Historical Overview*. Westport, CT: Greenwood, 1990.

Pratt, Robert A. *The Color of Their Skin: Education and Race in Richmond, Virginia, 1954-89*. Charlottesville: University of Virginia Press, 1992.

Sachar, Emily. *Shut Up and Let the Lady Teach: A Teacher's Year in a Public School*. New York: Poseidon Press, 1991.

Thompkins, Susie Powers. *Cotton-Patch Schoolhouse*. Tuscaloosa: University of Alabama Press, 1992.

Willie, Charles V., Anatoine M. Garibaldi, and Wornie L. Reed, eds. *The Education of African Americans*. Westport, CT: Auburn House/Greenwood Publishing Group, 1991.

Folklore and Folk Culture

Abrahams, Roger D. *Singing the Master: The Emergence of African American Culture in the Plantation South*. New York: Pantheon Books, 1992.

Hall, Gwendolyn Midlo. *Africans in Colonial Louisiana: The Development of Afro-Creole Culture*. Baton Rouge: Louisiana State University Press, 1992.

Hazzard-Gordon, Katrina. *Jookin': The Rise of Social Dance Formation in African-American Culture*. Philadelphia: Temple University Press, 1990.

Hill, James L., ed. *Studies in African and African American Culture*. New York: P. Lang, 1990.

Holloway, Joseph E., ed. *Africanisms in American Culture*. Bloomington: Indiana University Press, 1990.

Njeri, Itabari. *Every Good-Bye Ain't Gone: Family Portraits and Personal Escapades*. New York: Times Books, 1990.

Roberts, John W. *From Trickster to Badman: The Black Folk Hero in Slavery and Freedom*. Philadelphia: University of Pennsylvania Press, 1990.

Spalding, Henry D., comp. and ed. *Encyclopedia of Black Folklore and Humor*. Introduction by J. Mason Brewer. Middle Village, NY: Jonathan David Publishers, 1990.

Sundquist, Eric J. *The Hammers of Creation: Folk Culture in Modern African-American Culture*. Athens: University of Georgia Press, 1992.

Twining, Mary A., and Keith E. Baird, eds. *Sea Island Roots: African Presence in Carolina and Georgia*. Trenton, NJ: Africa World Press, 1991.

General Reference

Asante, Molefi K. *The Historical and Cultural Atlas of African Americans*. New York: Macmillan, 1991.

The Black Resource Guide, 1990-1991 Edition. Washington, DC: Black Resource Guide, Inc., 1991.

Bogle, Donald, ed. *Black Arts Annual, 1988/89*. New York: Garland, 1990.

Donovan, Richard X. *Black Scientists of America*. Portland, OR: National Book Co., 1990.

Fitzpatrick, Sandra, and Maria Godwin. *The Guide to Black Washington: Places and Events of Historical and Cultural Significance in the Nation's Capital*. New York: Hippocrene, 1990.

Furtaw, Julia C., ed. *Black American Information Directory*. 2nd ed., Detroit: Gale Research Inc., 1992.

Hancock, Sybil. *Famous Firsts of Black Americans*. Gretna, LA: Pelican Publishing Co., 1991.

Horton, Carrell Peterson, and Jessie Carney Smith, comps. and eds. *Statistical Record of Black America*. 2nd ed., Detroit: Gale Research Inc., 1991.

Smithsonian Institution. *African and African American Resources at the Smithsonian*. Washington, DC: Smithsonian Institution, 1991.

Southern, Eileen, and Josephine Wright, comps. *African American Traditions in Song, Sermon, Tale, and Dance, 1600s-1920: An Annotated Bibliography of Literature, Collections, and Artworks*. Westport, CT: Greenwood Press, 1990.

Thum, Marcella. *Hippocrene U.S.A. Guide to Black America: A Directory of Historic and Cultural Sites Relating to Black America*. New York: Hippocrene Books, 1992.

Health

Bailey, A. Peter. *The Harlem Hospital Story: 100 Years of Struggle Against Illness*. Richmond, VA: Native Sun Publishers, 1991.

Bailey, Eric J. *Urban African American Health Care*. Lantham, MD: University Press of America, 1991.

The Black Women's Health Book: Speaking for Ourselves. Seattle: Seal Press, 1990.

Dixon, Barbara M., with Josleen Wilson, *Good Health for African-American Kids,*, Crown Trade Paperbacks, 1995.

Duh, Samuel V. *Blacks and AIDS: Genetic or Environmental Causes*. Newbury Park, CA: Sage Publications, 1991.

Health of Black Americans from Post Reconstruction to Integration, 1871-1960: An Annotated Bibliography of Contemporary Sources. Westport, CT: Greenwood Press, 1990.

McBride, David. *From TB to AIDS: Epidemics Among Urban Blacks Since 1900*. Albany: State University of New York Press, 1991.

National Black Health Leadership Directory, 1990-91. Washington, DC: NRW Associates, 1991.

Villarosa, Linda, ed. *Body & Soul: The Black Woman's Guide to Physical Health and Mental Well-Being*. HarperCollins, 1994.

History

The African American Experience: A History. Sharon Harley, Stephen Middleton, and Charlotte Stokes, Consultants. Englewood Cliffs, NJ: Prentice-Hall, 1992.

America, Richard, ed. *The Wealth of Races: The Present Value of Benefits from Past Injustices*. Westport, CT: Greenwood Press, 1991.

Anderson, Eric, and Alfred Moss, Jr., eds. *The Facts of Reconstruction: Essays in Honor of John Hope Franklin*. Baton Rouge: Louisiana State University Press, 1991.

Andrews, George Reid. *Blacks and Whites in Sao Paulo Brazil, 1888-1988*. Madison: University of Wisconsin Press, 1992.

Aptheker, Herbert. *Anti-Racism in U.S. History: The First Hundred Years*. New York: Greenwood Press, 1992.

Aptheker, Herbert. *To Be Free: Pioneering Studies in Afro-American History*. Introduction by John Hope Franklin. New York: Citadel Press, 1991.

Bailey, Richard. *Neither Carpetbaggers Nor Scalawags: Black Officeholders During the Reconstruction in Alabama*. Montgomery, AL: R. Bailey Publishers, 1991.

Beeth, Howard, and Cary E. Wintz, eds. *Black Dixie: Afro-Texan History and Culture in Houston*. College Station, TX: Texas A&M University Press, 1992.

Berlin, Irs, and Philip D. Morgan, eds. *The Slaves' Economy: Independent Production by Slaves in the Americas*. London: F. Cass, 1991.

Berlin, Irs, et. al., eds. *Slaves No More: Three Essays on Emancipation and the Civil War*. New York: Cambridge University Press, 1992.

The Black Abolitionist Papers, Vol. 3: The United States, 1830-1846. Chapel Hill: University of North Carolina Press, 1991.

Boney, F.N., Richard L. Hume, and Rafia Zafar. *God Made Man, Man Made the Slave*. Macon, GA: Mercer University Press, 1990.

Bryan, Patrick. *The Jamaican People, 1880-1902: Race and Social Control*. New York: Macmillan, 1991.

Bush, Barbara. *Slave Women in Caribbean Society, 1650-1838*. Bloomington: University of Indiana Press, 1990.

Campbell, Randolph B. *An Empire for Slavery: The Peculiar Institution in Texas, 1821-1865*. Baton Rouge: Louisiana State University Press, 1991.

Cantor, George. *Historic Landmarks of Black America*. Detroit: Gale Research Inc., 1991.

Cohen, William. *At Freedom Edge: Black Mobility at the Southern Quest for Racial Control, 1861-1915*. Baton Rouge: Louisiana State University Press, 1991.

Cornelius, Janet Duitsman. *"When I Can Read My Title Clear": Literacy, Slavery, and Religion in the Antebellum South*. Columbia: University of South Carolina Press, 1991.

Counter, S. Allen. *North Pole Legacy: Black, White and Eskimo*. Amherst: University of Massachusetts Press, 1991.

Crouch, Berry A. *The Freedmen's Bureau and Black Texans*. Austin: University of Texas Press, 1992.

Davis, Lenwood G. *A Travel Guide to Black Historical Sites and Landmarks in North Carolina*. Winston-Salem, NC: Bandit Books, 1991.

Deromantizing Black History: Critical Essays and Reappraisals. Knoxville: University of Tennessee Press, 1991.

Dillon, Merton L. *Slavery Attacked: Southern Slaves and Their Allies, 1619-1865*. Baton Rouge: Louisiana State University Press, 1990.

Downey, Dennis B., and Raymond M. Hyser. *No Crooked Death: Coatsville, Pennsylvania, and the Lynching of Zachariah Walker*. Champaign: University of Illinois Press, 1991.

Drago, Edmund L., ed. *Broke by the War: Letters of a Slave Trader*. Columbia: University of South Carolina Press, 1991.

Dykstra, Robert. *Bright Radical Star: Black Freedom and White Supremacy on the Hawkeye Frontier*. Cambridge: Harvard University Press, 1993.

Fede, Andrew. *People Without Rights: An Interpretation of the Fundamentals of the Law of Slavery in the U.S. South*. New York: Garland Publishing Co., 1992.

Ferguson, Leland G. *Uncommon Ground: Archaeology and Early African America, 1650-1800*. Washington, DC: Smithsonian Institution Press, 1992.

Finkelman, Paul, ed. *The Age of Jim Crow: Segregation from the End of Reconstruction to the Great Depression*. New York: Garland Publishing Co., 1992. (*Race, Law, and American History, 1760-1990. The African American Experience*, vol. 4.)

Finkelman, Paul, ed. *Emancipation and Reconstruction*. New York: Garland Publishing Co., 1992. (*Race, Law and American History, 1700-1990. The African American Experience*. vol. 3.)

Franklin, Vincent P. *Black Self-Determinism: A Cultural History of African-American Resistance*. 2nd ed., Brooklyn, NY: Lawrence Hill Books, 1992.

Frey, Sylvia. *Water from the Rock: Black Resistance in a Revolutionary Age*. Princeton, NJ: Princeton University Press, 1992.

Gatewood, Willard B. *Aristocrats of Color: The Black Elite, 1880-1920*. Bloomington: Indiana University Press, 1990.

Genovese, Eugene D. *The Slaveholders' Dilemma: Freedom and Progress in Southern Conservative Thought, 1820-1860*. Columbia: University of South Carolina Press, 1992.

Greenberg, Cheryl Lynn. *"Or Does It Explode?": Black Harlem in the Great Depression*. New York: Oxford University Press, 1991.

Hamilton, Kenneth Marvin. *Black Towns and Profit, Promotion and Development in the Trans-Appalachian West, 1877-1915*. Champaign: University of Illinois Press, 1991.

Harley, Sharon. *The African American Experience: A History*. Englewood Cliffs, NJ: Globe, 1992.

Harris, Richard S. *Politics & Prejudice: A History of Chester, Pennsylvania Negroes*. Apache Junction, AZ: Relmo Pubs., 1991.

Harrison, Alfredteen, ed. *Black Exodus: The Great Migration from the American South*. Oxford: University Press of Mississippi, 1991.

Henry, Paget, and Paul Buhle, eds. *C.L.R. James' Caribbean*. Durham, NC: Duke University Press, 1992.

Hornsby, Jr., Alton. *Chronology of African-American History: Significant Events and People from 1619 to the Present*. Detroit: Gale Research Inc., 1991.

Horton, James Oliver. *Free People of Color: Inside the African American Community*. Washington, DC: Smithsonian Institution, 1993.

Inikoroi, Joseph E., and Stanley L. Engerman, eds. *The Atlantic Slave Trade: Effects on Economic Societies, and Peoples in Africa, the Americas and Europe*. Durham, NC: Duke University Press, 1992.

Jackson, Terrance. *Putting It All Together: World Conquest, Global Genocide and African Liberation.* Bronx, NY: AKASA, 1991.

Jones, Howard. *The Red Diary: A Chronological History of Black Americans in Houston and Some Neighboring Harris County Communities-122 Years Later.* Austin, TX: Nortex Press, 1992.

Jones, Norrece T. *Born a Child of Freedom, Yet A Slave: Mechanisms of Control and Strategies of Resistance in Antebellum South Carolina.* Middletown, CT: Wesleyan University Press, 1990.

Jordan, Winthrop. *Tumult and Silence at Second Creek: An Inquiry into a Civil War Slave Conspiracy.* Baton Rouge: Louisiana State University Press, 1993.

Katz, William Loren. *Breaking the Chains: African American Slave Resistance.* New York: Atheneum, 1990.

Lane, Roger. *William Dorsey's Philadelphia and Ours: On the Origins and Future Prospects of Urban Black America.* New York: Oxford University Press, 1991.

Lesko, Kathleen M., ed. *Black Georgetown Remembered: A History of Its Black Community from the Founding of "The Town of George" in 1751 to the Present Day.* Washington, DC: Georgetown University Press, 1991.

Malone, Ann Patton. *Sweet Chariot: Slave Family and Household Structure in Nineteenth Century Louisiana.* Chapel Hill: University of North Carolina Press, 1992.

McLaurin, Melton A. *Celia, a Slave.* Athens: University of Georgia Press, 1991.

McMillen, Sally Gregory. *Southern Women: Black and White in the Old South.* Arlington Heights, IL: Harlan Davidson, 1992.

Meillassaux, Claude. *The Anthropology of Slavery: The Womb of Iron and Gold.* Translated by Alide Dasnois. Chicago: University of Chicago Press, 1991.

Meyer, Mary K. *Free Blacks in Hartford, Somerset, and Talbort Counties, Maryland.* Mt. Airy, MD: Pipe Creek Publications, 1991.

Middleton, Stephen. *The Black Laws in the Old Northwest: A Documentary History.* New York: Greenwood Press, 1992.

Munford, Clarence J. *The Black Ordeal of Slavery and Slave Trading in the French West Indies, 1625-1715.* Lewiston, ME: Edwin Mellen, 1991.

Nash, Gary B. *Freedom by Degrees: Emancipation in Pennsylvania and Its Aftermath.* New York: Oxford University Press, 1991.

Nash, Gary B. *Race and Revolution.* Madison, WI: Madison House, 1990.

Oakes, James. *Slavery and Freedom: An Interpretation of the Old South.* New York: Knopf, 1990.

Pearson, Edward. *Slave Work and Culture in Town and Country.* Williamsburg, VA: Institute of Early American History and Culture, 1991.

Perdue, Charles L., ed. *Weevils in the Wheat: Interviews with Virginia Ex-Slaves.* Charlottesville: University Press of Virginia, 1992.

Reidy, Joseph. *From Slavery to Agrarian Capitalism in the Cotton Plantation South: Central Georgia, 1800-1880.* Chapel Hill: University of North Carolina Press, 1992.

Richardson, Bonham C. *The Caribbean in the Wide World, 1492-1922.* New York: Cambridge University Press, 1992.

Richter, William L. *Overreached on All Sides: The Freedmen's Bureau Administrators in Texas, 1865-1868.* College Station: Texas A&M University Press, 1991.

Schwartz, Stuart B. *Slaves, Peasants, and Rebels: Reconsidering Brazilian Slavery.* Champaign: University of Illinois Press, 1992.

Schweninger, Loren. *Black Property Owners in the South, 1790-1915.* Champaign: University of Illinois Press, 1990.

Slaughter, Thomas P. *Bloody Dawn: The Christiana Riot and Racial Violence in Antebellum North.* New York: Oxford University Press, 1991.

Solow, Barbara L., ed. *Slavery and the Rise of the Atlantic System.* New York: Cambridge University Press/ W.E.B. DuBois Institute for Afro-American Research, 1991.

Stanisland, Martin. *American Intellectuals and African Nationalists; 1955-1970.* New Haven, CT: Yale University Press, 1991.

Stevenson, Lisbeth Gant. *African-American History: Heroes in Hardship.* Cambridge, MA: Cambridgeport Press, 1992.

Stone, Albert E. *The Return of Nat Turner: History, Literature, and Cultural Politics in Sixties America.* Athens: University of Georgia, 1992.

Stone, Frank Andrews. *African American Connecticut: African Origins, New England Roots.* Storrs, CT: Isaac N. Thut World Education Center, 1991.

Terry, Ted. *American Black History: Reference Manual.* Tulsa, OK: Myles Publishing Co., 1991.

Thomas, Richard W. *Life for Us: Building Black Community in Detroit, 1915-1945.* Bloomington: Indiana University Press, 1992.

Thornton, John. *Africa and Africans in the Making of the Atlantic World, 1400-1680.* New York: Cambridge University Press, 1992.

White, Shane. *Somewhat More Independent: The End of Slavery in New York City 1770-1870.* Athens: University of Georgia Press, 1991.

Williams, Jacob C. *Lillie: Black Life in Martins Ferry, Ohio During the 1920s and 1930s.* Ann Arbor, MI: Braun-Brumfield, 1991.

Williams, Lee E. *Post-War Riots in America, 1919 and 1946: How the Pressures of War Exacerbated American Urban Tensions to the Breaking Points.* Lewiston, NY: E. Mellen, 1991.

Language, Literature, and Drama

Babb, Valerie Melissa. *Ernest Gaines.* Boston: Twayne/G.K. Hall, 1991.

Bailey, Guy, Natalie Maynor, and Patricia Cukor-Avila, eds. *The Emergence of Black English: Text and Commentary.* Philadelphia: J. Benjamins Publishing Co., 1991.

Baker, Houston A., and Patricia Redmond, eds. *Afro-American Literary Study in the 1990s.* Chicago: University of Chicago Press, 1990.

Baraka, Imamu Amiri. *The Leroi Jones/Amiri Baraka Reader.* Edited William J. Harris. New York: Thunder's Mouth Press, 1991.

Barksdale, Richard K. *Praisesong of Survival: Lectures and Essays, 1957-1989.* Introduction by R. Baxter Miller. Urbana: University of Illinois, 1992.

Bassett, John E. *Harlem in Review: Critical Reactions to Black American Writers, 1917-1939.* Selinsgrove, PA: Susquehanna University Press, 1992.

Benitoz-Rojo, Antonio. *The Repeating Island: The Caribbean and the Postmodern Perspective.* Durham, NC: Duke University Press, 1992.

Blackshire-Belay, Carol Aisha, ed. *Language and Literature in the African American Imagination.* Westport, CT: Greenwood Press, 1992.

Bloom, Harold, ed. *Bigger Thomas.* New York: Chelsea House, 1990.

Brown, Stewart, ed. *The Art of Derek Walcott.* UK: Seren Books, 1992. (Dist. by Dufour Editions, Inc.)

Busby, Mark. *Ralph Ellison.* Boston: Twayne/G.K. Hall, 1991.

Butler, Robert. *Native Son: The Emergence of a New Black Hero.* Boston: Twayne/G.K. Hall, 1991.

Cartey, Wilfred. *Whispers form the Caribbean: I Going Away,*

I Going Home. Los Angeles: University of California, Los Angeles, Center for Afro-American Studies, 1991.

DeJongh, James. *Vicious Modernism: Black Harlem and the Literary Imagination.* New York: Cambridge University Press, 1990.

Dieke, Ikenna. *The Primordial Image: African, Afro-American, and Caribbean Mythopoetic Text.* New York: P. Lang, 1991.

Draper, James P., ed. *Black Literature Criticism: Excerpts from Criticism of the Most Significant Works of Black Authors over the Past 200 Years.* 3 vols., Detroit: Gale Research Inc., 1992.

Edwards, Walter F., and Donald Winford, eds. *Verb Phrase Patterns in Black English and Creole.* Detroit: Wayne State University Press, 1991.

Fabre, Michel. *Richard Wright: Books and Writers.* Oxford: University Press of Mississippi, 1990.

Gates, Henry Louis, Jr. *Loose Canons: Notes on the Culture Wars.* New York: Oxford University Press, 1992.

Hamalian, Leo, and James V. Hatch, eds. *The Roots of African American Drama: An Anthology of Early Plays, 1858-1938.* Detroit: Wayne State University Press, 1991.

Hord, Fred L. *Reconstructing Memory: Black Literary Criticism.* Chicago: Third World Press, 1991.

Johnson, Dianne. *Telling Tales: The Pedagogy and Power of African American Literature for Youth.* New York: Greenwood Press, 1990.

Jones, Gayl. *Liberating Voices: Oral Tradition in African American Literature.* Cambridge, MA: Harvard University Press, 1991.

Joseph, Margaret Paul. *Caliban in Exile: The Outsider in Caribbean Fiction.* New York: Greenwood Press, 1992.

Kinnamon, Kenneth, ed. *New Essays on Native Son.* New York: Cambridge University Press, 1990.

Metzger, Linda, Hal May, Deborah A. Straub, and Susan M. Trotsky, eds. *Black Writers.* Detroit: Gale Research Inc., 1989.

Mikolyzk, Thomas A. comp. *Langston Hughes: A Bio-Bibliography.* Westport, CT: Greenwood Press, 1990.

Miller, R. Baxter. *The Art and Imagination of Langston Hughes.* Lexington: University of Kentucky Press, 1990.

Morrison, Toni. *Playing in the Dark: Whiteness and the Literary Imagination.* Cambridge, MA: Harvard University Press, 1992.

Newby, James Edwards. *Black Authors: A Selected Annotated Bibliography.* New York: Garland, 1990.

Ntire, Daphne Williams, ed., and comp. *Roots and Blossoms; African American Plays for Today.* Troy, MI: Bedford Publishers, 1991.

Peterson, Bernard L. *Early Black American Playwrights and Dramatic Writers: A Biographical Dictionary and Catalog of Plays, Films and Broadcasting Scripts.* Westport, CT: Greenwood Press, 1990.

Rajiv, Sudhi. *Forms of Black Consciousness.* New York: Advent Books, 1992.

Rollock, Barbara. *Black Authors and Illustrators of Children's Books: A Biographical Dictionary.* 2nd ed., New York: Garland, 1992.

Smith, Valerie. *Self-Discovery and Authority in Afro-American Narrative.* Cambridge, MA; Harvard University Press, 1991.

Stepto, Robert B. *From Behind the Veil: A Study of Afro-American Narrative.* 2nd ed., Urbana: University of Illinois Press, 1991.

Thurman, Wallace. *Infants of the Spring.* With foreword by Amritjit Singh. Boston: Northeastern University Press, 1992.

Toomer, Jean. *Essentials.* Edited by Rudolph P. Bird.

Athens: University of Georgia Press, 1991.

Washington, Mary Helen, ed. *Memory of Kin: Stories About Family by Black Writers.* New York: Doubleday, 1991.

Wilson, August. *Two Trains Running.* New York: Dutton, 1992.

Media, Publishing, and Book Collecting

Chester, Thomas Morris. *Thomas Morris Chester, Black Civil War Correspondent: His Dispatches from the Virginia Front.* With Biographical Essay and Notes by R.J.M. Blackett. New York: DeCapo Press, 1991.

Dates, Jannette L., and William Barlow. *Split Image: African Americans in the Mass Media.* Washington, DC: Howard University Press, 1990.

Hill, George. *Black Women in Television: An Illustrated History and Bibliography.* New York: Garland Publishing Co., 1990.

Joyce, Donald Franklin. *Black Book Publishers in the United States: A Historical Dictionary of the Press, 1817-1990.* Westport, CT: Greenwood Press, 1991.

Schuyler, George S. *Black Empire: George S. Schuyler Writing As Samuel I. Brooks.* Edited by Robert A. Hill and R. Kent Rasmussen. Boston: Northeastern University, 1991.

Silk, Catherine, and John Silk. *Racism and Anti-Racism in*

American Popular Culture: Portrayals of African-Americans in Fiction and Film. Manchester, UK: Manchester University Press, 1990. (Dist. by St. Martin's Press)

Sinnette, Elinor Des Verney, W. Paul Coates, and Thomas C. Battle, eds. *Black Bibliophiles and Collectors: Preservers of Black History.* Washington, DC: Howard University Press, 1990.

Military Participation

Collum, Danny Duncan, ed. *African Americans in the Spanish Civil War: "This Ain't Ethiopia, but It'll Do".* New York: G.K.Hall, 1992.

Cox, Clinton. *Undying Glory: The Story of the Massachusetts 54th Regiment.* New York: Scholastic, Inc., 1991.

Donaldson, Gary. *The History of African-Americans in the Military: Double V.* Malabar, FL: Krieger Publishing Co., 1991.

Gooding, James Henry. *On the Alter of Freedom: A Black Soldier's Civil War Letters from the Front.* Edited by Virginia Matzke Adams. Amherst: University of Massachusetts Press, 1991.

Johnson, Charles. *African American Soldiers in the National Guard: Recruitment and Deployment During Peacetime and War.* New York: Greenwood Press, 1992.

Redkey, Edwin S., ed. *A Grand Army of Black Men: Letters from African-American Soldiers in the Union Army.* New York: Cambridge University Press, 1992.

Music

Allen, Ray. *Singing in the Spirit: African-American Sacred Quartets in New York City.* Philadelphia: University of Pennsylvania Press, 1991.

Boggs, Vernon W. *Salsiology: Afro-Cuban Music and the Evolution of Salsa in New York City.* Westport, CT: Greenwood Press, 1992.

Booth, Stanley. *Rhythm Oil: A Journey Through the Music of the American South.* New York: Pantheon, 1991.

Cantor, Louis. *Wheelin' on Beale.* Foreword by B.B. King. New York: Pharos, 1992.

Costello, Mark, and David Foster Wallace. *Signifying Rappers: Rap and Race in the Urban Present.* New York: Ecco Press, 1990.

Donovan, Richard X. *Black Musicians of America.* Portland, OR: National Book Co., 1991.

Finn, Julio. *The Bluesman: The Musical Heritage of Black Men and Women in the Americas.* New York: Interlink Books, 1991.

Floyd, Samuel A., ed. *Black Music in the Harlem Renaissance: A Collection of Essays.* Westport, CT: Greenwood Press, 1990.

Friedwall, Will. *Jazz Singing: America's Great Voices from Bessie Smith to Bebop and Beyond.* New York: Scribner's, 1990.

Harris, Michael W. *The Rise of Gospel Blues: The Music of Thomas Andrew Dorsey in the Urban Church.* New York: Oxford University Press, 1992.

Horne, Aaron, comp. *Keyboard Music of Black Composers: A Bibliography.* Westport, CT: Greenwood Press, 1992.

Horne, Aaron, comp. *String Music of Black Composers: A Bibliography.* Westport, CT: Greenwood Press, 1991.

Horne, Aaron. comp. *Woodwind Music of Black Composers* Westport, CT: Greenwood Press, 1990.

Jackson, John A. *Big Beat Heat: Alan Freed and the Early Years of Rock & Roll.* New York: Schirmer/Macmillan, 1991.

Merrill, Hugh. *The Blues Route.* New York: Morrow, 1990.

Morgan, Thomas L. *From Cakewalk to Concert Hall: An Illustrated History of African American Popular Music from 1895 to 1930.* Washington, DC: Elliott & Clark Publishers, 1992.

Morton, David C. and Charles K. Wolfe. *DeFord Bailey: A Black Star in Early Country Music.* Knoxville: University of Tennessee Press, 1991.

Peretti, Burton W. *The Creation of Jazz: Music, Race and Culture in Urban America.* Urbana: University of Illinois Press, 1992.

Perry, Frank. *Afro-American Vocal Music: A Select Guide to Fifteen Composers.* Berrien Springs, MD: Vande Verde Publishers, 1991.

Porter, Lewis, ed. *A Lester Young Reader.* Washington, DC: Smithsonian Institution Press, 1991.

Price, Sammy. *What Do They Want: A Jazz Autobiography.* Edited by Caroline Richmond. Chronological discography compiled by Bob Weir. Urbana: University of Illinois Press, 1990.

Roach, Hildred. *Black American Music Past and Present: Pan-African Composers.* 2nd ed., Malabar, FL: Kruger, 1992.

Rosenthal, David H. *Hard Bop: Jazz and Black Music, 1955-1965.* New York: Oxford University Press, 1992.

Scott, Frank. *The Down Home Guide to the Blues.* Pennington, NJ: A Capella Books, 1990.

Spencer, Jon Michael, ed. *The Emergency Black and the Emergence of Rap.* Durham: Duke University Press, 1991.

Spencer, Jon Michael, ed. *Sacred Music of the Secular City: From Blues to Rap.* Durham: Duke University Press, 1992.

Story, Rosalyn. *And So I Sing: African American Divas of Opera and Concert.* New York: Warner Books, 1990.

Tate, Greg. *Flyboy in the Buttermilk: Essays on Contemporary America.* New York: Simon and Schuster, 1992.

Turner, Patricia. *Dictionary of Afro-American Performers: 78 RPM and Cylinder Recordings of Opera, Choral Music and Song, ca. 1900-1949.* New York: Garland, 1990.

Walker-Hill, Helen. *Piano-Music by Black Women Composers: A*

Catalogue of Solo and Ensemble Works. New York: Greenwood Press, 1992.

Wright, Josephine, and Samuel A. Floyd, Jr., eds. *New Perspectives on Music: Essays in Honor of Eileen Southern.* Warren, MI: Harmonie Park Press, 1992.

Performing Arts

Adamczke, Alice J. *Black Dance: An Annotated Bibliography.* New York: Garland Publishing Co., 1990.

Ely, Melvin Patrick. *The Adventures of Amos 'n' Andy: A Social History of an American Phenomenon.* New York: Free Press, 1991.

Gray, John, comp. *Black Theatre and Performance: A PanAfrican Bibliography.* Westport, CT: Greenwood Press, 1990.

Gray, John, comp. *Blacks in Film and Television: A Pan-African Bibliography of Films, Filmmakers, and Performers.* Westport, CT: Greenwood Press, 1990.

Hansberry, Lorraine. *A Raisin in the Sun: The Unfilmed Original Screenplay.* Edited by Robert Nemiroff. Foreword by Jewell Gres. Afterword by Spike Lee. New York: Dutton, 1992.

Hughes, Langston, and Zora Neale Hurston. *Mule Bone: A Comedy of Negro Life.* Edited by George H. Bass and Henry L. Gates. New York: Harper Collins, 1991.

Jhally, Sut, and Justin Lewis. *Enlightened Racism: The Cosby Show, Audiences, and the Myth of the American Dream.* Boulder, CO: Westview Press, 1992.

Jones, G. William. *Black Cinema Treasurey: Lost and Found.* Denton, TX: University of North Texas Press, 1991.

Klotman, Phyllis Rauch, ed. *Screenplays of the African American Experience.* Bloomington: Indiana University Press, 1991.

Mapp, Edward. *Directory of Blacks in the Performing Arts.* 2nd ed., Metuchen, NJ: Scarecrow Press, 1990.

Politics

Barker, Lucius J., ed. *Ethnic Politics and Civil Liberties.* New Brunswick, NJ: Transaction Books, 1992.

Clavel, Pierre, and Wim Wiewel, eds. *Harold Washington and the Neighborhoods: Progressive City Government in Chicago, 1983-1987.* New Brunswick, NJ: Rutgers University Press, 1991.

Gomes, Ralph C., and Linda Faye Williams eds. *From Exclusion to Inclusion: The Long Struggle for African American Political Power.* Westport, CT: Greenwood Press, 1992.

Henry, Charles P. *Culture and African American Politics.* Bloomington: Indiana University Press, 1990.

Henry, Charles P. *Jesse Jackson: The Search for Common Ground.* Oakland, CA: Black Scholar Press, 1990.

Jennings, James. *The Politics of Black Empowerment: The Transformation of Black Activism in Urban America.* Detroit: Wayne State University Press, 1992.

Joint Center for Political and Economic Studies. *Black Elected Officials: A National Roster.* Washington, DC: Joint Center for Political and Economic Studies Press, 19–.

Kimball, Penn. *Keep Hope Alive: Super Tuesday and Jesse Jackson's 1988 Campaign for the Presidency.* Washington, DC: Joint Center for Political and Economic Studies, 1992.

Lawson, Steven. *Running for Freedom: Civil Rights and Black Politics in America Since 1941.* Philadelphia: Temple University Press, 1990.

Marable, Manning. *The Crisis of Color and Democracy: Essays on Race, Class and Power.* Monroe, ME: Common Courage Press, 1992.

McCartney, John T. *Black Power Ideologies: An Essay in African American Political Thought.* Philadelphia: Temple University Press, 1992.

Natanson, Nicholas. *The Black Image in the New Deal: The Politics of FSA.* Knoxville: University of Tennessee Press, 1992.

Orfield, Gar, and Carole Ashkinaze. *The Closing Door: Conservative Policy and Black Opportunity.* Chicago: University of Chicago Press, 1991.

Parker, Frank R. *Black Votes Count: Political Empowerment in Mississippi After 1965.* Chapel Hill: University of North Carolina Press, 1990.

Rees, Matthew. *From the Deck to the Sea: Blacks and the Republican Party.* Wakefield, NH: Longwood Press, 1991.

Rivlin, Gar. *Fire on the Prairie: Chicago's Harold Washington and the Politics of Race.* New York: Holt, 1992.

Van DeBurg, William L. *New Day in Babylon: The Black Power Movement and American Culture.* Chicago: University of Chicago Press, 1992.

Race Relations

Brady, Paul L. *A Certain Blindness: A Black Family's Quest for the Promise of America.* Atlanta: ALP Publishers, 1990.

Brooks, Roy L. *Rethinking the American Race Problem.* Berkeley: University of California, 1991.

Collier, Peter, ed. *Second Thoughts About Race in America.* Lanham, MD: Madison Books, 1991.

Crouch, Stanley. *Notes of a Hanging Judge: Essays and Reviews.* New York: Oxford University Press, 1990.

Davis, F. James. *Who Is Black: One Nation's Definition.* University Park: Pennsylvania State University Press, 1991.

DeSantis, John. *For the Color of His Skin: The Murder of Yusuf Hawkins and the Trial of the Bensonhurst.* Introduction by Alan M. Dershowitz. New York: Pharos Books, 1991.

Essed, Philomena. *Understanding Racism: An Interdisciplinary Theory.* Newbury Park, CA: Sage, 1991.

Hacker, Andrew. *Two Nations: Black and White, Separate, Hostile, Unequal.* New York: Scribner's, 1992.

Horowitz, Irving Louis. *Daydreams and Nightmares: Reflections on a Harlem Childhood.* Jackson: University Press of Mississippi, 1990.

Hynes, Charles J., and Bob Drury. *Incident at Howard Beach: The Case for Murder.* New York: Putnam, 1990.

Leiman, Melvin M. *Racism in the U.S.A.: History and Political Economy.* Concord, MA: Paul & Co., 1992.

Lewis, Earl. *In Their own Interests: Race, Class, and Power in Twentieth-Century Nolf, Virginia.* Berkeley: University of California Press, 1991.

McFadden, Robert, et. al. *Outrage: The Story Behind the Tawana Brawley Hoax.* New York: Bantam, 1990.

Pemberton, Gayle. *The Hottest Water in Chicago: One Family, Race, Time and American Culture.* Winchester, MA: Faber & Faber, 1992.

Perlmutter, Philip. *Divided We Fall: A History of Ethnic, Religious, and Racial Prejudice in America.* Ames: Iowa State University Press, 1992.

Rasberry, William. *Looking Backward at Us.* Jackson: University Press of Mississippi, 1991.

Salzman, Jack, ed. *Bridges and Boundaries: African Americans and American Jews.* New York: Braziller, 1992.

Steele, Shelby. *The Contest of Our Character: A New Vision of Race in America.* New York: St. Martin's Press, 1990.

Stepan, Nancy Leys. *The Hour of Eugenics: Race, Gender, and Nation.* Ithaca, NY: Cornell University Press, 1991.

Terkel, Studs. *Race: How Blacks and Whites Think and Feel About the American Obsession.* New York: New Press/Norton, 1992.

Welch, Susan, and Lee Sigelman. *Black America's Views of Racial Equality: The Dream Deferred.*, New York: Cambridge University Press, 1991.

Zegeye, Abebe, ed. *Exploitation and Exclusion: Race and Class in Contemporary U.S. Society.* London: Hans Zell Publishers, 1991.

Zweigenhaft, Richard L., and G. William Domhoff. *Blacks in the White Establishment: A Study of Race and Class in America.* New Haven, CT: Yale University Press, 1991.

Religion and Philosophy

Baer, Hans, and Merrill Singer. *African-American Religion in the Twentieth Century: Varieties of Protest and Accommodation.* Knoxville: University of Tennessee, 1992.

Davis, Lenwood G. *Daddy Grace: An Annotated Bibliography.* New York: Greenwood Press, 1992.

Dvorak, Katherine L. *An African-American Exodus: the Segregation of Southern Churches.* With preface by Jerald C. Brauer. Brooklyn, NY: Carlson Publishing Co., 1991.

Harris, Leonard, ed. *The Philosophy of Alain Locke.* Philadelphia: Temple University Press, 1990.

Haynes, Lemuel. *Black Preacher to White America: the Collected Writings of Lemuel Haynes, 1774-1833.* Edited by Richard Newman. New York: Carlson Publishing Co., 1990.

Hopkins, Dwight N., and George C.L. Cummings, eds. *Cut Loose*

Your Stammering Tongue: Black Theology in the Slave Narratives. Maryknoll, NY: Orbis Books, 1991.

Howard, Victor B. *Conscience and Slavery: the Evangelistic Calvinistic Domestic Missions, 1837-1861.* Kent, OH: Kent State University Press, 1990.

Irvin, Dona L. *The Unsung Heart of Black America: A Middle-Class Church at Midcentury.* Columbia: University of Missouri Press, 1992.

Jacobs, Claude F., and Andrew J. Kaslow. *The Spiritual Churches of New Orleans: Origins, Beliefs and Rituals of an African-American Religion.* Knoxville: University of Tennessee Press, 1991.

Johnson, John L. *Black Biblical Heritage.* Nashville: Winston-Derek Publishers, 1990.

Lincoln, C. Eric, and Lawrence H. Mamiya. *The Black Church in the American Experience.* Durham: Duke University Press, 1990.

Martin, Sandy D. *Black Baptists and African Missions: the Origins of a Movement, 1880-1915.* Macon: Mercer University Press, 1990.

Ochs, Stephen J. *Desegregating the Alter: The Josephites and the Struggle for Black Priests, 1871-1960.* Baton Rouge: Louisiana State University Press, 1990.

Payne, Wardell J., ed. *Directory of African American Religious Bodies: A Compendium by the Howard University School of Divinity.* Prepared under the auspices of the Research Center on Black Religious Bodies, Howard University School of Divinity. Washington, DC: Howard University Press, 1991.

Seymour, Robert E. *Whites Only: A Pastor's Retrospective on Signs of a New South.* Valley Forge, PA: Judson Press, 1991.

Spencer, Jon Michael. *Black Hymnody: A Hymnological History of the African-American Church.* Knoxville: University of Tennessee Press, 1992.

Spencer, Jon Michael. *Protest and Praise: Sacred Music of Black Religion.* Minneapolis: Augsburg Fortress Publishers, 1990.

Walker, Theodore, Jr. *Empower the People: Social Ethics for the African-American Church.* Maryknoll, NY: Orbis Books, 1991.

Walker, Wyatt Tee. *Spirits That Dwell in Deep Woods III: The Prayer and Praise Hymns of the Black Religious Experience.* New York: Martin Luther King Press, 1991.

Wood, Forrest G. *The Arrogance of Faith: Christianity and Race in America from the Colonial Era to the Twentieth Century.* New York: Knopf, 1990.

Sociology and Psychology

Andersen, Margaret L. *Race, Class and Gender: An Anthology*. Belmont, CA: Wadsworth Publishing Co., 1992.

Anderson, Elijah. *Streetwise: Race, Class and Social Change in an Urban Community*. Chicago: University of Chicago Press, 1990.

Baer, Hans, and Yvonne Jones, eds. *African Americans in the South: Issues of Race, Class and Gender*. Athens: University of Georgia Press, 1992.

Benjamin, Lois. *The Black Elite: Facing the Color Line in the Twentieth Century*. Chicago: Nelson-Hall, 1991.

Billingsley, Andrew. *Climbing Jacob's Ladder: The Future of*

the African-American Family New York: Simon and Schuster, 1991.

Blackwell, James Edward. *The Black Community: Diversity and Unity.* 3rd ed., New York: Harper Collins, 1991.

Bowser, Benjamin, ed. *Black Male Adolescents: Parenting and Education in Community Context*. Latham, MD: University Press of America, 1991.

Consortium for Research on Black Adolescence Staff and Patricia Bell-Scott. *Black Adolescence: Current Issues and Annotated Bibliography*. Boston: G.K. Hall, 1990.

Edelman, Marian Wright. *The Measure of Our Success: A Letter to My Children and Yours*. Boston: Beacon Press, 1992.

Hay, Fred J. *African-American Community Studies from North America. A Classified, Annotated Bibliography*. New York: Garland, 1991.

Hopson, Darlene, and Derek Hopson. *Different and Wonderful: Raising Black Children in a Race Conscious Society*. New York: Simon and Schuster, 1992.

Jones, Howard, and Wanda Jones. *Heritage and Hope: The Legacy and Future of the Black Family in America*. Wheaton, IL: Victor Books, 1992.

Kunjufu, Jawanza. *Countering the Conspiracy to Destroy Black Boys*. Chicago: African American Images, 1990.

Leigh, Wilhemina A., ed. *The Housing Status of Black Americans*. New Brunswick, NJ: Transaction Books, 1992.

Lemann, Nicholas. *The Promised Land: The Great Black Migration and How It Changed America*. New York: Knopf, 1991.

Platat, Anthony M. *E. Franklin Frazier Reconsidered*. New Brunswick, NJ: Rutgers University Press, 1991.

Trotter, Joe William, ed. *The Great Migration in Historical Perspective: New Dimensions of Race, Class and Gender*. Bloomington: Indiana University Press, 1991.

Sports

Cooper, Michael L. *Playing America's Game: The Story of Negro League Baseball*. New York: Lodestar Books, 1993.

Page, James A. *Black Olympian Medalists*. Englewood, CO: Libraries Unlimited, 1991.

Women

Alexander, Adele Logan. *Free Women of Color in Rural Georgia, 1789-1879*. Fayetteville: University of Arkansas Press, 1991.

Baker, Houston A. *Working of the Spirit: The Poetics of Afro-American Women's Writings*. Chicago: University of Chicago Press, 1991.

The Black Women Oral History Project. *Guide to the Transcripts*. Edited by Ruth E. Hill. Westport, CT: Meckler, 1991.

Braxton, Joanne M. *Black Women Writing Autobiography: A Tradition Within a Tradition*. Philadelphia: Temple University Press, 1990.

Braxton, Joanne M., and Andree Nicola McLaughlin, eds. *Wild Women in the Whirlwind: Afro-American Culture and the Contemporary Literary Renaissance*. New Brunswick, NJ: Rutgers University Press, 1990.

Brown, Karen McCarthy. *Mama Lola: A Voodoo Priestess in Brooklyn*. Berkeley, University of California Press, 1991.

Brown-Guillory, Elizabeth, ed., and comp. *Wines in the Wilderness: Plays by African American Women from the Harlem Renaissance to the Present*. Westport, CT: Greenwood Press, 1990.

Bundles, A'Lelia Perry. *Madam C. J. Walker*. New York: Chelsea House, 1991.

Busby, Margaret, ed. *Daughters of Africa: An International Anthology of Words and Writings by Women of African Descent; From the Ancient World to Present*. New York: Pantheon, 1992.

Butler-Evans, Elliott. *Race, Gender, and Desire: Narrative Strategies in the Fiction of Toni Cade Bambara, Toni Morrison, and Alice Walker*. Philadelphia: Temple University Press, 1990.

Caraway, Nancie. *Segregated Sisterhood: Racism and the Politics of American Feminism*. Knoxville: University of Tennessee Press, 1991.

Celsi, Teresa N. *Rosa Parks and the Montgomery Bus Boycott.* Brookfield, CT: Millbrook Press, 1991.

Crawford, Vicki L. Crawford, Jacqueline Anne Reese, and Barbara Woods, eds. *Women in the Civil Rights Movement: Trailblazers and Torchbears, 1941-1965.* Brooklyn, NY: Carlson Publishing Co., 1990. (*Black Women in United States History*, vol. 16.)

Davis, Michael D. *Black American Women in Olympic Track and Field: A Complete Illustrated Reference.* Jefferson, NC: McFarland, 1992.

Gates, Henry Louis, Jr. *Reading Black, Reading Feminist.* New York: Meridan, 1991.

Glassman, Steve, and Kathryn Lee Seidel, eds. *Zora in Florida.* Gainesville: University Presses of Florida, 1991.

Guy-Sheftall, Beverly. *Daughters of Sorrow: Attitudes Toward Black Women.* New York: Carlson Publishing Co., 1990. (*Black Women in United States History*, vol. II.)

Guy, Sheftall, Beverly. *Words of Fire: An Anthology of African American Feminist Thought.* New Press, 1995.

Harris, Trudier. *Fiction and Folklore: The Novels of Toni Morrison.* Knoxville: University of Tennessee Press, 1991.

Hine, Darlene Clark, ed. *Black Women in American History, From Colonial Times Through the Nineteenth Century.* Brooklyn, NY: Carlson Publishing Co., 1990.

Hooks, Bell. *Black Looks: Race and Representation.* Boston: South End Press, 1992.

Ihle, Elizabeth L., ed. *Black Women in Higher Education: An Anthology of Essays, Studies and Documents.* New York: Garland Publishing Co., 1992.

Jackson, Carlton. *Hattie: The Life of Hattie McDaniel.* Lantham, MD: Madison Books, 1990.

Jones, Adrienne Lash. *Jane Edna Hunter: A Case Study of Black Leadership.* Brooklyn, NY: Carlson Publishing Co., 1990.

(*Black Women in United States History*, vol. 12)

Jones, Beverly Washington. *Quest for Equality: The Life and Writing of Mary Eliza Church Terrell, 1863-1954.* Brooklyn, NY: Carlson Publishing Co., 1990. (*Black Women in United States History*, vol. 13.)

Kent, George E. *A Life of Gwendolyn Brooks.* Lexington: University of Kentucky Press, 1990.

King, Joyce Elaine, and Carolyn Ann Mitchell. *Black Mothers to Sons: Juxtaposing African American Lit-erature and the Social Practice.* New York: Peter Lang, 1990.

Kubitschek, Missy Dehn. *Claiming the Heritage: African-American Women Novelists and History.* Oxford: University Press of Mississippi, 1991.

Mabalia, Dorethea Drummond, *Toni Morrison's Developing Class*

Consciousness. Cranbury, NJ: Susquehanna University

Press/Associated University Presses, 1991.

Morton, Patricia. *Disfigured Images: The Historical Assault on Afro-American Women.* Westport, CT: Greenwood Press, 1991.

Nathiri, N.Y., ed. *Zora! Zora Neale Hurston: A Woman and Her Community.* Orlando, FL: Sentinel Books, 1991.

Neverdon-Morton, Cynthia. *Afro-American Women of the South and the Advancement of the Race, 1895-1925.* Knoxville: University of Tennessee Press, 1990.

Otfinoski, Steven. *Marian Wright Edelman—Defender of Children's Rights.* New York: Rosen Publishing Group, 1991.

Reckley, Ralph. *Twentieth Century Black Women in Print: Essays.* Acton, MA: Copley Publishers, 1991.

Roses, Lorraine Elena, and Ruth Elizabeth Randolph. *Harlem Renaissance and Beyond: Literary Biographies of 100 Black Women Writers, 1900-1945.* Boston: G.K. Hall, 1990.

Salem, Dorothy. *To Better Our World: Black Women in Organized Reform.* Brooklyn, NY: Carlson Publishing Co., 1990. (*Black Women in United States History*, vol. 14.)

Samuels, Wilfred D., and Clenora Hudson-Weems. *Toni Morrison.* Boston: G.K. Hall, 1990.

Scott, Kesho Yvonne. *The Habit of Surviving: Black Women's Strategies for Life.* New Brunswick, NJ: Rutgers University Press, 1991.

Smith, Jesse Carney, ed. *Notable Black American Women.* Detroit: Gale Research Inc., 1991.

Smith, Rita Webb, and Tony Chapelle. *The Woman Who Took Back Her Streets: One Woman Fights the Drug*

Wars and Rebuilds Her Community. Far Hill, NJ: New Horizon, 1991.

Thompson, Mildred I. *Ida B. Wells-Barnett: An Exploratory Study of An American Black Woman, 1893-1930.* Brooklyn, NY: Carlson Publishing Co., 1990. (*Black Women in United States History,* vol. 15)

Walker, Melissa. *Down From the Mountaintop: Black Women's Novels in the Wake of the Civil Rights Movement, 1966-1989.* New Haven, CT: Yale University Press, 1991.

Walker, Robbie Jean, ed. *The Rhetoric of Struggle: Public Addresses by African American Women.* New York: Garland Publishing Co., 1992.

Werner, Craig. *Black American Women Novelists: An Annotated Bibliography.* Englewood Cliffs, NJ: Salem Press, 1990.

Williams, Constance Willard. *Black Teenage Mothers: Pregnancy and Child Rearing from Their Perspective.* Lexington, MA: Lexington Books, 1991.

Woody, Bette. *Black Women in the Workplace: Impacts of Structural Change in the Economy.* Westport, CT: Greenwood Press, 1992.

Yee, Shirley J. *Black Women Abolitionists: A Study in Activism, 1828-1860.* Knoxville: University of Tennessee Press, 1992.

Picture and Text Credits

Photo and Text Credits

Photographs

Courtesy of ABC Records/Ron Rogers, used with permission: p. 931 (King, B. B., performing). **Courtesy of ABC-TV:** p. 739 (Goode, Mal, photograph). **A. Phillip Randolph Institute,** used with permission: p. 375 (African Americans in front of Voter Registration Headquarters, photograph). **AP/Wide World Photos,** reproduced by permission: pp. 29 (Randolph, Asa Philip, photograph); 33 (Segregation sign "White Waiting Room", photograph); 36 (Parks, Rosa, being fingerprinted, photograph); 39 (Student sit-in , Atlanta, GA, photograph); 49 (1967 Detroit Riots, aerial view, photograph); 51 (King, Martin Luther, Jr., King's funeral, photograph); 57 (J. Bruce Llewellyn); 58 (Chisholm, Shirley, photograph); 61 (Bakke Decision March, photograph); 67 (Hooks, Benjamin L., photograph); 67 (Wilson, Margaret Bush, speaking, photograph); 70 (Black leaders urging sanctions against South Africa, photograph); 75 (Wilder, Lawrence Douglas, photograph); 78 (Powell, Colin, visiting troops during Gulf War, photograph); 82 (Brown, Jesse L., Clinton, Bill, photograph); 95 (*U.S.S. Harmon*, photograph); 96 (Campanella, Roy, photograph); 102 (Alexander, Clifford, photograph); 102 (Harris, Patricia Roberts, photograph); 103 (Dinkins, David, photograph); 103 (Wilder, Lawrence, photograph); 104 (Mosely-Braun, Carol, at Democratic Convention, photograph); 125 (Frederick Douglass); 136 (Ku Klux Klan, cross burning, photograph); 141 (Segregation sign, man placing segregation sign, photograph; 152 (Federal troops escorting four black students, photo-

graph); 160 (Johnson, Lyndon B., photograph); 175 (Tuskegee Institute, view of chapel, photograph); 176 (Central High School, Little Rock, AR, photograph); 183 (Ebenezer Baptist Church, photograph); 188 (Attucks, Crispus, photograph); 193 (Lincoln University, photograph); 196 (Abysinnian Baptist Church, photograph); 197 (Apollo Theater, photograph); 207 (Harper's Ferry National Park, photograph); 302 (Douglass, Frederick, photograph); 316 (Civil Rights Protest in Birmingham, AL, photograph); 317 (Rustin, Bayard, photograph); 318 (Rights Protest in Birmingham, AL, photograph); 321 (King, Martin Luther, Jr., riding on bus, photograph); 322 (Bates, Daisy, photograph); 322 (Carmichael, Stokley, photograph); 325 (Evers, Medgar, photograph); 326 (Hamer, Fannie Lou, photograph); 328 (Coretta Scott King); 330 (King, Martin Luther, Jr., with group of people, photograph); 334 (Sharpton, Al, photograph); 349 (Farrakhan, Louis, photograph); 361 (King, Martin Luther, Jr., facing microphone, photograph); 362 (Chavis, Benjamin Franklin, Jr., photograph); 363 (Carmichael, Stokley, photograph); 364 (Seale, Bobby, photograph); 365 (Robinson, Randall, with Nelson Mandela, photograph); 366 (Chavis, Benjamin Franklin, Jr., photograph); 367 (Farmer, James, photograph); 369 (Hooks, Benjamin L., photograph); 370 (Innis, Roy, photograph); 371 (Jacob, John E., photograph); 372 (Jordan, Vernon E., Jr., photograph); 373 (Lowery, Joseph E., photograph); 376 (Robinson, Randall, photograph); 421 (Thomas, Clarence, photograph); 437 (Busing Protests/Segregation Ends, photograph); 438 (Lunch counter sit-in, photograph); 439 (Lewis, Woodrow T., with Albert L. Dunn, photograph); 425 (Segregation sign at Rail-

Michael, photograph); 978 (Jones, Quincy, photograph); 981 (Knight, Gladys, with Pips, photograph); 983 (Little Richard, clapping and singing, photograph); 984 (Pride, Charley, photograph); 985 (Prince, photograph); 988 (Ross, Diana, with the Supremes, photograph); 989 (Turner, Tina, photograph); 990 (Wilson, Jackie, photograph); 993 (Wonder, Stevie, photograph); 1010 (Barthe, Richmond, photograph); 1014 (Blackburn, Robert, photograph); 1017 (DeCarava, Roy); 1030 (Perkins, Marion, photograph); 1037 (Van der Zee, James, photograph); 1058 (Percy, Julian, holding beaker, photograph); 1062 (Bluford, Guion, photograph); 1065 (Bolden, Charles, Frank, Jr., photograph); 1074 (Lawrence, Robert H., Jr., photograph); 1076 (McNair, Ronald, photograph); 1076 (Morgan, Garrett A., photograph); 1087 (Dickerson, Eric, photograph); 1088 (Frazier, Joe, photograph); 1089 (Hagler, Marvin, photograph); 1090 (Abdul-Jabbar, Kareem, shooting basketball, photograph); 1090 (Jordan, Michael, photograph); 1092 (Joyner, Florence Griffith, in Olympic uniform, photograph); 1093 (Gibson, Althea, photograph); 1094 (Aaron, Hank, photograph); 1095 (Abdul-Jabbar, Kareem, ceremony with Governor, photograph); 1096 (Armstrong, Henry, photograph); 1100 (Chamberlain, Wilt, photograph); 1100 (Elder, Lee, photograph); 1102 (Gibson, Althea, photograph); 1104 (Jackson, Reggie, photograph); 1106 (Jordan, Michael, photograph); 1106 (Joyner, Florence Griffith, photograph); 1111 (Owens, Jesse, photograph); 1114 (Joyner, Florence Griffith, and Wilma Rudolph, photograph); 1115 (Russell, Bill, photograph); 1116 (Simpson, O. J., photograph); 1117 (White, Bill, photograph); 1118 (Stargell, Willie, photograph); 1119 (Joiner, Charlie, photograph); 1119 (Owens, Jesse, broad jumping, photograph); 1136 (Anderson, James, Jr., parents of, photograph); 1152 (Davison, F.-Brig. General, photograph); 1153 (Powell, Colin at Vietnam War Memorial, photograph); 1158 (James, Daniel "Chappie", photograph); 1159 (Johnson, Hazel, photograph); 1161 (Powell, Colin, with Kristen Baker, photograph). **Archive Photos, Inc.,** used with permission: pp. 305 (Truth, Sojourner, photograph); 343 (Delaney, Martin R., photograph); 345 (Malcolm X at black Muslim gathering, photograph); 352 (Muhammad, Elijah, photograph); 353 (Henry McNeal Turner); 489 (Dinkins, David, photograph); 663 (Baptism on the Potomac, photograph); 845 (McQueen, Butterfly); 850 (Roundtree, Richard, photograph); 856 (Washington, Denzel, kneeling in Mosque); 883 (Kay, Ulysses); 893 (Still, William Grant, photograph). **Archive Photos/Frank Driggs Collection,** reproduced by permission: p. 953 (Jordan, Louis, photograph). **Archive Photos/Lass,** used with permission: p. 11 (Blacks weighing cotton, photograph). **Courtesy of Molefi Kete Asante:** p. 630 (Molefi Kete Asante). **Courtesy of Associated Publishers:** p. 757 (Murphy, John Henry, photograph). **Bahama News Bureau:** p. 261 (Nassau Police Band, photograph). **Bettmann,** used

with permission: pp. 5 (African slaves arrive on the shores of America); 44 (Selma to Montgomery march, photograph); 45 (Marshall, Thurgood, with Javits and Kennedy, photograph); 46 (Watts Riot, 1965, photograph); 50 (Johnson, Lyndon B., photograph); 80 (National Guards in front of grafitti covered building, photograph); 100 (Motley, Constance Baker, photograph); 124 (Slave Auction, photograph); 324 (DuBois, W. E. B., photograph); 329 (McKissick, Floyd B., photograph); 417 (Marshall, Thurgood, photograph); 479 (Brown, Ron, photograph); 571 (Beckwourth, Jim); 627 (Busing-Woodville, Mississippi, photograph); 666 (Worshipers of the Pentacostal denomination); 676 (Muhammad, Elijah, speaking into microphone, photograph); 685 (Marino, Eugene, photograph); 883 (Joplin, Scott, photograph); 925 (Handy, W. C., photograph); 1057 (Carver, George Washington, photograph); 1026 (Lawarence, Jacob, photograph); 1079 (Williams, Daniel Hale, photograph); 1108 (Louis, Joe, photograph). **The Bettmann Archive,** reproduced with permission: pp. 38 (Federal troops escorting black students, photograph); 40 (Freedom Riders, photograph); 41 (Shabazz, Betty, photograph); 52 (Resurrection City, Washington, DC, photograph); 66 (Washington, Harold, in office, photograph); 81 (Brown, Ron, photograph); 138 (Washington, Booker T., photograph); 167 (Height, Dorothy, with George Bush, photograph); 298 (Lincoln, Abraham, photograph); 315 (DuBois, W. E. B., photograph); 320 (Abernathy, Ralph, Rev., photograph); 323 (Davis, Angela, press conference, photograph); 333 (King, Martin Luther, Jr., crowd of people at funeral); 344 (Garvey, Marcus, photograph); 365 (Brown, H. Rap, photograph); 369 (Height, Dorothy, photograph); 374 (Newton, Huey P., photograph); 377 (Seale, Bobby, photograph); 429 (Black school room in Missouri, c. 1930, photograph); 450 (Higginbotham, A. Leon, photograph); 466 (Waters, Maxine, speaking at conference, photograph); 474 (Bradley, Thomas, photograph); 475 (Moseley-Braun, Carol, photograph); 478 (Bond, Julian, photograph); 490 (Dixon, Sharon Pratt, photograph); 549 (Female firefighter, photograph); 687 (Powell, Adam Clayton, Sr., at pulpit, photograph); 755 (Johnson, John H., photograph); 817 (Hines, Gregory, with brother Maurice, photograph); 840 (Ingram, Rex, photograph); 858 (Williams, Bert, photograph); 873 (Coleridge, Samuel Taylor, photograph); 903 (Henderson, Fletcher, portrait standing); 904 (Eldridge, Roy, with Ella Fitzgerald, photograph); 926 (Henderson, Fletcher, photograph); 944 (Waller, Thomas "Fats", photograph); 986 (Redding, Otis, photograph); 1029 (Motley, Archibald, photograph); 1030 (Parks, Gordon, photograph); 1035 (Smith, Willi, photograph); 1085 (Gibson, Josh, photograph); 1091 (Ashe, Arthur, photograph); 1160 (Petersen, Frank E., photograph); 1114 (Robinson, Jackie, photograph). **The Bettmann Archive/Newsphotos, Inc.,** used with permission: pp. 20 (Lincoln, Abraham, with Mathew

Brady, photograph); 43 (Malcolm X, at microphone, photograph); 48 (National Guard arrest three men, photograph); 55 (Protest against forced busing, Montgomery, AL, photograph); 64 (Pierce, Samuel R., photograph); 99 (Brooks, Gwendolyn, photograph); 101 (Marshall, Thurgood, photograph); 351 (Malcolm X, with hat and scarf, photograph); 430 (Busing-group of students, photograph); 455 (Marshall, Thurgood, in robes, photograph); 480 (Brown, Ron); 500 (Mitchell, Arthur W., seated, photograph); 542 (Assembly Line Worker, photograph); 886 (Mitchell, Leona, photograph); 935 (Mingus, Charles, photograph); 936 (Morton, Ferdinand "Jelly Roll", photograph). **Bettmann Newsphotos,** used with permission: pp. 443 (Firefighter in Miami, Florida, photograph); 578 (Sims, Naomi, photograph); 1105 (Johnson, Earvin "Magic," photograph). **(c) Bill Sparrow/***Encore Magazine:* p. 378 (Wilkins, Roy, photograph). **Courtesy of Dave Bing:** p. 572 (Dave Bing). *Black Enterprise Magazine,* courtesy of: p. 754 (Graves, Earl G., photograph). **Black Entertainment Television,** p. 745 (Johnson, Robert L., photograph). **Burton Historical Collection/Detroit Public Library,** used with permission: p. 191 (Second Baptist Church, Detroit, MI, photograph). **Clement-Petrocik Company,** p. 268 (Guadeloupe, open air market, photograph). **Courtesy of Columbia Records:** p. 928 (Holiday, Billie, photograph). **Consulate General of Jamaica:** p. 145 (Garvey, Marcus, photograph). **(c) Darlene Hammond/Archive Photos,** used with permission: p. 860 (Winfrey, Oprah, photograph). **Courtesy of Denver Public Library:** p. 203 (Love, Nat, photograph). **Denver Public Library-Wester Collection:** p. 524 (Nicodemus, Kansas). **Ken Estell,** reproduced by permission: pp. 522 (Downtown Detroit, photograph); 523 (Men playing chess, photograph); 528 (Children playing with water hydrant, photograph); 529 (African American children with woman, photograph); 546 (Black family, photograph); 549 (Blue collar workers); 570 (Spight, Benita, photograph); 591 (African American boy with glasses, photograph). **Fairchild Publications:** p. 1009 (Burrows, Stephen). **Fisk University Library:** p. 580. **Courtesy of General Motors Public Relations,** used with permission: p. 1038 (1993 Oldsmobile Achieva SC, photograph). **Geoffrey Clements Photography,** used with permission: p. 1005 (Bearden, Romare "Eastern Barn,"). **Courtesy of Geoffrey Clements Photgraphy/Whitney Museum:** pp. 1004 (Jacob Lawrence's "Depression"); 1025 (Jacob Lawrence's "Tombstones"). **(c) Bruce Giffin,** used with permission: p. 629 (Malcolm X Academy school, photograph). **Courtesy of Hurok Attractions:** p. 869 (Anderson, Marian, photograph). **Courtesy of The John F. Kennedy Library:** p. 639 (Mays, Benjamin E., photograph). **Brian V. Jones:** pp. 585 (African American family); 586 (Extended family); 588 (Father with daughters). **(c) Faustine Jones-Wilson,** used with permission: pp. 584 (Black family-turn of the century-

wedding, photograph. **Courtesy of The Library of Congress:** pp. 6 (Advertisement for a slave auction); 8 (Typical slave life, photograph); 11 (Jefferson, Thomas, photograph); 16 (Typical slave family, photograph); 17 (Scott, Dred, photograph); 34 (Lynching victim, man hanging in tree, photograph); 37 (Faubus, Orval, photograph); 41 (Wallace, George, photograph); 90 (Langston, John Mercer, photograph); 112 (Delegates meet to draft a national Constitution); 114 (Franklin, Benjamin, photograph); 116 (Slave Cell, photograph); 120 (*Liberator Newspaper, The,* photograph); 122 (Escaped slaves being returned, photograph); 125 (Douglass, Frederick, photograph); 130 (Lincoln, Abraham, seated with other men, photograph); 284 (Slaves and slave ships, photograph); 285 (Slave ship diagram); 286 (Slave catching apparatus, photograph); 287 (Attucks, Crispus, photograph); 289 (Slaves standing outside of slave quarters, photograph); 290 (Slave women sitting in pile of cotton, photograph); 292 (Slave catcher poster, photograph); 296 (Escaped slaves on the Underground Railway, photograph); 298 (Freed slaves leaving the South, photograph); 300 (Freed Man's Bureau poster, photograph); 301 (Typical rural residence, people outside of cabin, photograph); 305 (Tubman, Harriet, photograph); 312 (Douglass, Frederick); 314 (Colored Drinking Fountain, photograph); 331 (Martin Luther King, Jr.); 347 (Black Muslims, photograph); 347 (Blyden, Edward Wilmot, photograph.); 358 (DuBois, W. E .B., profile); 360 (Women laundry workers, photograph); 424 (Freed man being sold to pay his fine, photograph); 437 ("Colored Waiting Room," photograph); 508 (Smalls, Robert, photograph); 564 (Slaves picking cotton, photograph); 615 (Black segregated school, photograph); 617 (Black school children c. 1865, photograph); 618 (Freedman's school); 619 (Snow Hill Institute, photograph); 622 (Tuskegee Institute, photograph); 623 (Fisk University); 1067 (Carver, George Washington, photograph); 807 (Minstrel show poster, photograph); 1135 (Rifle company); 1138 (Troop H, 10th Cavalry, photograph). **Courtesy of The Library of Congress, Prints and Photographs Division:** pp. 31 (Klu Klux Klan, front view of march, photograph). **Courtesy of Helen Marcus:** p. 721 (Morrison, Toni, photograph). **Martha Swope Associates/Carol Rosegg:** p. 839 (Hyman, Earle, photograph). **Courtesy of National Archives:** pp. 919 (Europe, James Reese, photograph); 1156 (Flipper, Henry O., photograph). **NAACP,** used with permission: pp. 359 (NAACP office, 1945, photograph); 428 (Gaines, Lloyd, photograph). **National Museum of African Art:** p. 214 (Tuareg peoples, woman pounding grain, photograph); 221 (Kongo peoples, photograph); 227 (Koranic school in Chad, photograph); 245 (Laoye I, John Adetoyese, photograph); 258 (Mbuti people of Ituri Forest, Zaire, photograph); 260 (Man and oxcart, photograph). **National Museum of American Art/Art Resource:** p. 1000 (Edward Mitchell Bannister's

"Newspaper Boy"); 1023 (William H. Johnson's "Going to Chruch"); 1033 (Augusta Savage's "Gamin"). **National Park Service, Department of the Interior:** p. 180 (Douglass, Frederick, two story house, photograph). **National Portrait Gallery/Smithsonian,** used with permission: pp. 293 (Pennsylvania Abolition Society, photograph); 312 (Allen, Richard, photograph). **National Urban League:** p. 378 (Young, Whitney M., Jr., photograph). **NBC-TV,** used with permission: p. 1108 (Lewis, Carl, photograph). **Carl Nesfield,** courtesy of: p. 1096 (Clay, Cassius, photograph). *New York Amsterdam News,* used with permission: pp. 164 (Black Panthers demonstrating outside of courthouse, photograph); 332 (King, Martin Luther, Jr.); 362 (McKissick, Floyd B., photograph). *New York Daily News,* used with permission: p. 674 (Black Rabbi, photograph). **New York Historical Society:** p. 725 (Vassa, Gustavus, photograph). **New York Public Library Picture Collection,** reproduced by permission: pp. 312 (Allen, Richard, photograph); 662 (Allen, Richard, photograph); 941 (Smith, Bessie, photograph). **Andy Roy:** p. 565 (Freedom National Bank). **Courtesy of Ron Scherl:** p. 812 (Jones, James Earl, cast of "Fences," photograph). **Schomburg Center for Black Culture,** reproduced by permission: pp. 204 (Haley's boyhood home); 616 (New York African Free School No. 2, photograph); 696 (Fauset, Jessie, photograph); 837 (Horne, Lena, photograph); 863 (Jones, Matilda Sisieretta). **Stanley B. Burns, M.D. and the Burns Archive,** used with permission: pp. 524 (Rural black family in Savannah, GA, photograph); 664 (A.M.E. Church Reunion, photograph); 923 (Hampton, Lionel, photograph). **Susan Stetler:** pp. 545 (White collar worker); 551 (Woman using computer). **Tony Brown Productions, Inc.:** p. 744 (Brown, Tony, photograph). **Turner Broadcasting System Management:** p. 751. **United Nations:** pp. 212 (Pan-African Movement leaders); 220 (Angolans celebrating independence); 224 (Woman husking corn, photograph); 225 (Central Africa family, photograph); 226 (Rural farmers in Chad, photograph); 230 (Children in Equitorial Guinea, photograph); 231 (Selassie, Haile, photograph); 232 (Ethiopia, market, photograph); 233 (Cattleherders in rural Gambia, photograph); 234 (Jawara, Prime Minister, photograph); 236 (Masai tribesman, Kajiado, Kenya, photograph); 242 (Morocccan dancers, photograph); 245 (Minaret in Agadez, Niger, photograph); 249 (South African youths, photograph); 250 (South African children, photograph); 252 (South African village of Cross Roads, photograph); 253 (Swazi woman, South Africa, photograph); 256 (Togolese woman, photograph); 266 (Santo Domingo, Dominican Republic, photograph); 267 (Stevedores carrying bananas, photograph); 270 (Workers on banana plantation, photograph); 271 (Jamaican children, Hope Gardens, photograph); 273 (Nicaragua, open air market, photograph); 507 (Sampson, Edith, photograph). **UPI/Bettmann,** used with permission: pp. 29 (Scottsboro Boys, photograph); 32 (Marian Anderson); 206 (Washington, Booker T., boyhood home, photograph); 436 (Lunch counter sit-in, photograph); 711 (Haley, Alex, photograph); 845 (McDonald, Hattie); 1072 (Jemison, Mae C., photograph). **Courtesy of the U.S. Air Force:** p. 1155 (Davis, Benjamin O., Jr., photograph). **Courtesy of the U.S. Army:** p. 1143 (Davis, Benjamin O., Sr., photograph); 1144 (Davis, Benjamin O., Sr. pins medal on his son, photograph); 1146 (Soldiers from the 92nd Division, 1944, photograph); 1150 (Korean Conflict, photograph); 1156 (Davis, Benjamin O., Sr., portrait). **Courtesy of the U.S. Marine Corps:** p. 1151 (Cooper, Capt. Jerome, photograph); 1152 (Military officers). **Courtesy of the U.S. National Aeronautics and Space Administration:** pp. 550 (Caw, Lawrence, photograph). **Courtesy of the U.S. Navy:** p. 1153 (Winstead, John T., photograph); 1160 (Miller, Dorie, photograph). **Courtesy of the U.S. Senate Historical Office:** pp. 480 (Bruce, Blanche K., photograph); 506 (Revels, Hiram Rhodes, photograph). **U.S. Signal Corps-National Archives:** p. 23 (Freed slaves waiting for work opportunities, photograph); 1137 (Ninth U.S. Calvalry, 1889, photograph). **Walker Collection of A'Lelia Perry Bundles:** p. 567 (Madame C. J. Walker). **Courtesy of the U.S. War Department General Staff National Archives:** pp. 27 (Black soldiers leaving for war, photograph); 1140 (Black sailors, photograph). **The Washington Post Writers Group,** used with permission: p. 759 (Raspberry, William, photograph). **Alix B. Williamson:** p. 895 (Watts, Andre, photograph). **William Morris Agency:** p. 917 (Davis, Miles). **Edwin L. Wilson, Sr.:** p. 601 (Children playing basketball).

Text

Edward B. Marks Music Company, used by permission: "Lift Every Voice and Sing." **Reprinted by arrangement with The Heirs to the Estate of Martin Luther King, Jr., c/o Joan Daves Agency as agent for the proprietor; copyright 1963 by Martin Luther King, Jr., copyright renewed 1991 by Coretta Scott King:** "I Have a Dream." Copyright 1995 by University of Sankore Press: "Million Man March/Day of Absence Mission Statement."

Index

Index

B

Holmesburg Unclassified School   614
Holmes, Larry   1086, 1102
Holmes v. Atlanta   436
Holsey, Lucius   664
Holt, Ben   881
Holyfield, Evander   1087
Home for Colored Children   614, 688
Homecoming   723, 1102
Home Girls, A Black Feminist Anthology   761
homegirls and handgrenades   723
Home Modernization and Supply Company   567
Home to Harlem   719
homicides   584, 596, 599
homosexuality   588, 589, 602, 680
Honduras   261, 269, 447
Hooker, John Lee   927, 973
hooks, bell   634
Hooks, Matthew Bones   204
Hooks, Robert   812, 813
Hoover, Herbert   622
Hoover, J. Edgar   53, 56, 60
Hope, John   57, 541, 615, 630, 634, 635, 651, 1018
Hope of Liberty, The   714
Horne, Lena   837, 853, 910, 913
Horn, Shirley   908
Horton, George Moses   695, 714
Hoston v. Louisiana   38
Hot Chocolates   808, 910, 913
Hotel Theresa   196
Hot Fives   903
Hot Sevens   903
Hottentots   221, 253
Houphouët-Boigny, Felix   228
House Behind the Cedars, The   705
House, Eddie "Son"   900
House of Blues Foundation   982
housing   33, 34, 39, 43, 45, 48-50, 54, 56, 58, 60, 63,
   68, 69, 71, 76, 82, 98, 100, 163, 165, 166, 182, 187,
   329, 335, 359, 366, 371, 373, 375, 383, 388-391, 393,
   400, 401, 404, 423, 424, 434, 440, 447, 467-469, 473,
   481, 482, 490, 493, 494, 504, 505, 507, 511-513, 516,
   529, 530, 576, 584, 591, 593, 599, 665, 708, 734, 735,
   752, 821, 972, 986, 991, 1018, 1115
Houston, Charles Hamilton   420, 450
Houston, Cissy   974
Houston Defender   781
Houston Forward Times   781
Houston Informer   781
Houston Lawyers v. Texas   77
Houston Sun   781
Houston, Whitney   719, 961, 963, 969, 974
Howard, Oliver Otis   180, 614
Howard University   58, 66, 74, 83, 84, 90-92, 180,
   200, 322, 364, 367, 368, 370, 420, 444, 448, 450-454,
   458, 476, 480, 487, 489, 490, 493, 496, 501, 513, 573,

578, 601, 614, 621, 626, 630, 633-635, 637, 638, 641,
   643, 648, 650, 651, 691, 701, 704, 716, 720, 734, 735,
   741, 744, 750, 752, 758, 785, 818, 826, 850, 872, 880,
   886, 887, 896, 923, 969, 997, 1008, 1014, 1017, 1021,
   1023, 1024, 1028, 1031, 1033, 1035, 1037, 1038,
   1045, 1057-1059, 1061, 1063, 1064, 1066-1068,
   1088, 1149, 1155, 1160
Howard University Gallery of Art   1045
Howard University Law School   91, 200, 420, 458,
   489, 513
Howard University Medical School   90, 1067, 1068
Howard University Press   734, 735
Howard University School of Law   91, 448, 643
How Do You Do   704
Howe, Cato   187
Howells, William Dean   25
Howlin' Wolf   900, 901, 922, 927, 943
How to Be a Top Model   578
Hudson, Cheryl Willis   735, 754
Hudson Valley Black Press   778
Hudson, Wade   735, 754
Hue and Cry   720
Huff's Art Studio   1049
Hughes, Langston   27, 696, 702, 705, 714, 715, 725,
   726, 809, 812, 845, 871, 872, 893, 1016
Hughes, Sarah Ann   662
Hulsinger, George   1002
human rights   119, 144, 145, 155, 215, 255, 263, 269,
   293, 317, 318, 320, 321, 323-328, 331, 333-338, 363,
   375, 379, 389, 392, 394, 399, 405, 407, 446, 448, 451,
   454-456, 473, 474, 476, 479, 482, 483, 485, 490, 491,
   493, 495, 497 499, 503, 508, 513, 589, 636, 665, 678,
   683, 687, 688, 690, 691, 880, 892, 1075, 1077, 1091
Human Rights Campaign Fund (HRCF)   589
Hunter, Alberta   908
Hunter, Eddie   837, 838
Hunter-Gault, Charlayne   573, 744, 762
Hunt, Richard   1021
Hurd v. Hodge   439
Hurston, Zora Neale   653, 696, 698, 715, 725, 726
Hurt, Mississippi John   900
Huston-Tillotson College   643
Hutton, Bobby   376
Hutu   222, 245
Hyde Park Citizen   773
Hyers, Anna Madah   864
Hyers, Emma Louise   864
Hyman, Earle   809, 838, 847
Hyman, Flo   1093

I

I Am A Black Woman   708
Ibibio   282
ibn Abdalla, Mohammed Ahmed   251

N

S